Pocket Oxford Dictionary and Thesaurus

SECOND EDITION

Edited by
Sara Hawker

OXFORD
UNIVERSITY PRESS

Great Clarendon Street, Oxford OX2 6DP

Oxford University Press is a department of the University of Oxford.
It furthers the University's objective of excellence in research, scholarship,
and education by publishing worldwide in

Oxford New York

Auckland Cape Town Dar es Salaam Hong Kong Karachi
Kuala Lumpur Madrid Melbourne Mexico City Nairobi
New Delhi Shanghai Taipei Toronto

With offices in

Argentina Austria Brazil Chile Czech Republic France Greece
Guatemala Hungary Italy Japan Poland Portugal Singapore
South Korea Switzerland Thailand Turkey Ukraine Vietnam

Oxford is a registered trade mark of Oxford University Press
in the UK and in certain other countries

Published in the United States
by Oxford University Press Inc., New York

© Oxford University Press 2004, 2008

Database right Oxford University Press (maker)

First edition 2004
Second edition 2008

British Library Cataloguing in Publication Data

Data available

Library of Congress Cataloging in Publication Data

Data available

Typeset in Frutiger and Parable
by Asiatype, Inc
Printed and bound in Great Britain
by Clays Ltd, St Ives plc

ISBN 978-0-19-953286-5

10 9 8 7 6 5 4 3 2 1

Contents

Note on trademarks and proprietary status

Introduction

This brand-new edition of the *Pocket Oxford Dictionary and Thesaurus* provides you with both definitions and synonyms in convenient, multipurpose entries. Whether you want to check the meaning of a word or find a range of alternative terms with the same meaning, you only need to look at one main entry. This unique, user-friendly feature makes the *Pocket Oxford Dictionary and Thesaurus* an invaluable resource for all your language needs, and especially for solving crossword puzzles and other word games.

The text is based on the seventh edition of the *Oxford Mini Dictionary* and the fourth edition of the *Oxford Mini Thesaurus*, both of which draw on our systematic analysis of the Oxford English Corpus, an enormous database containing billions of words of real English drawn from a wide variety of different sources. The dictionary component provides wide-ranging, up-to-date coverage of a broad range of vocabulary, with definitions written in straightforward language and a clear, accessible style. The synonym sections work just like a thesaurus. Lists of alternative words are arranged in order of their closeness in meaning to the main entry word, with the closest one given first and printed in bold type. Lots of example sentences are provided to make it even easier to find the sense you are looking for.

Extra language information is provided in the form of Word Links, which contain a selection of additional vocabulary linked to various main entries. At the Word Link for **bird**, for example, you will find the terms **ornithology** (the study of birds) and **avian** (relating to birds). Special notes throughout the book give help with difficult spellings and offer guidance about certain words that are often confused with each other (e.g. **affect** and **effect**, or **flaunt** and **flout**).

The Wordfinder section in the centre of the book provides still more vocabulary and information to help with crosswords and puzzle-solving, in the form of handy quick-reference lists on a variety of topics including animal breeds, plant species, and countries of the world.

Guide to the dictionary and thesaurus

This dictionary and thesaurus is intended to be as easy to use and understand as possible. Here is an explanation of the main features that you will find.

1. STRUCTURE OF THE ENTRIES

Part of speech
Headword
Core synonym – the word closest in meaning to the headword

Verb inflections

appal v. (**appalling, appalled**) dismay or horrify.
▷ SYNONYMS: **horrify**; shock, dismay, distress, outrage, scandalize, disgust, revolt, sicken, nauseate, offend, make someone's blood run cold.

Words that can be used as alternatives to the headword

Plural form

army n. (pl. **armies**) **1** an organized military force for fighting on land. **2** a large number.
▷ SYNONYMS: **1 armed force**, military force, land force, military, soldiery, infantry, militia, troops, soldiers.
2 *an army of tourists*: **crowd**, swarm, horde, mob, gang, throng, mass, flock, herd, pack.

Sense number

Example of use, to help distinguish different senses

Word links, providing extra vocabulary linked to the headword

> **WORD LINKS**
> **military** relating to war or armed forces

Pronunciation (given for difficult words)

buoy /boy/ n. a floating object used to mark an area of water.
▷ SYNONYMS: **float**, marker, beacon.
• v. **1** keep afloat. **2** (**be buoyed up**) be cheerful and confident.

Typical use of the headword

Spelling note

> **USAGE** Remember: *u* before *o* in b*uo*y and b*uo*yant.

Register label showing how the following synonym(s) are used

flout v. openly fail to follow a rule etc.
▷ SYNONYMS: **defy**, refuse to obey, disobey, break, violate, fail to comply with, fail to observe, contravene, infringe, breach, commit a breach of, transgress against, ignore, disregard; informal: cock a snook at.
– ANTONYMS: observe.

Word or words meaning the opposite of the headword

Note giving help with the use of the entry word

> **USAGE** Don't confuse **flout** with **flaunt**, which means 'display obviously'.

Geographical label showing where the sense of the headword is used	**cute** adj. **1** charmingly pretty; sweet. **2** US informal clever.	Register label showing how the sense of the headword is used
Geographical label showing where the following synonym(s) are used	▷ SYNONYMS: **endearing**, adorable, lovable, sweet, lovely, appealing, engaging, delightful, dear; informal twee; Brit. informal dinky. ■ **cutely** adv. **cuteness** n.	Words derived from the headword (in alphabetical order)
Different spelling of headword (both allowed)	**bosun** (or bo'sun) var. of BOATSWAIN. **botany** n. the study of plants. ■ **botanical** adj. **botanist** n.	Cross-reference to another entry

2. LABELS

Most of the words and senses in the *Pocket Oxford Dictionary and Thesaurus* are part of standard English, which means they are the kinds of words that can be used in every type of situation, whether at home, with friends, or in a formal environment. Some words, however, are only suitable for certain situations or types of writing and where this is the case a label (or a combination of labels) is used.

Register labels

Register labels refer to a particular level of use in language. They show that a term is informal, formal, old-fashioned, or literary, and so on. These are the register labels used in this dictionary and thesaurus:

informal	normally used only in speech or informal writing or email (e.g. *barmy* or *gawp*)
formal	normally used only in writing, especially in official documents (e.g. *therein*)
dated	no longer used by most people (e.g. *victuals*)
old use	not in ordinary use today, though sometimes used to give an old-fashioned effect (e.g. *comely*)
historical	historical – only used today to refer to things that are no longer part of modern life (e.g. *alms*)
literary	found only or mainly in works of literature (e.g. *swoon*)
technical	normally used only in technical language (e.g. *occlude*)
derogatory	meant to convey a low opinion or to insult someone (e.g. *pleb*)

Geographical labels

English is spoken throughout the world, and while most of the words used in standard British English will be the same as those used in other varieties, there are some words which are only found in one type of English. If a word has the geographical label Brit. in this dictionary and thesaurus, this means that it is used in standard British English but not in American English, although it may be found in other varieties such as Australian English. The labels

US and N. Amer., on the other hand, mean that the word is typically American and is not standard in British English, though it may be found elsewhere.

Subject labels

These are used to show that a word or sense is connected with a particular subject or specialist activity such as Medicine or Computing.

3. PRONUNCIATIONS

The *Pocket Oxford Dictionary and Thesaurus* uses a respelling system is which is very easy to understand. Pronunciations are given for those words which might cause problems, but not for everyday words which are assumed to be familiar (such as **table** or **happy**). The pronunciations are divided into syllables by means of hyphens and the syllable that is printed in bold type is the one that is stressed when the word is spoken.

List of symbols

vowels	examples	vowels	examples	consonants	examples	consonants	examples
a	as in **cat**	oi	as in **join**	b	as in **bat**	p	as in **pen**
ah	as in **calm**	oo	as in **soon**	ch	as in **chin**	r	as in **red**
air	as in **hair**	oor	as in **poor**	d	as in **day**	s	as in **sit**
ar	as in **bar**	or	as in **corn**	f	as in **fat**	sh	as in **shop**
aw	as in **law**	ow	as in **cow**	g	as in **get**	t	as in **top**
ay	as in **say**	oy	as in **boy**	h	as in **hat**	th	as in **thin**
e	as in **bed**	u	as in **cup**	j	as in **jam**	*th*	as in **this**
ee	as in **meet**	uh	as in the first part of **ago**	k	as in **king**	v	as in **van**
eer	as in **beer**			kh	as in **loch**	w	as in **will**
er	as in **her**	uu	as in **book**	l	as in **leg**	y	as in **yes**
ew	as in **few**	y	as in **cry**	m	as in **man**	z	as in **zebra**
i	as in **pin**	yoo	as in **unit**	n	as in **not**	*zh*	as in **vision**
I	as in **eye**	yoor	as in **Europe**	ng	as in **sing, finger**		
o	as in **top**			nk	as in **thank**		
oh	as in **most**						

4. ABBREVIATIONS USED IN THE DICTIONARY AND THESAURUS

adj.	adjective	fem.	feminine	possess.	possessive
abbrev.	abbreviation	Gk. Myth	Greek Mythology	pron.	pronoun
adv.	adverb	hist.	historical	prep.	preposition
Austral.	Australian	Math.	Mathematics	pres. part.	present participle
aux. v.	auxiliary verb	n.	noun	pron.	pronoun
Chem.	Chemistry	N. English	northern English	sing.	singular
comb. form	combining form	offens.	offensive	usu.	usually
conj.	conjunction	past part.	past participle	v.	verb
esp.	especially	pl.	plural	var.	variant
exclam.	exclamation	pl. n.	plural noun	vars.	variants

Abbreviations that are in common use (such as cm, RC, US, and USA) have their own entries.

Aa

a adj. **1** used when mentioning someone or something for the first time; the indefinite article. **2** one single. **3** per: *twice a week.*

@ symb. 'at', used: **1** to show cost or rate per unit. **2** in Internet addresses between the user's name and the domain name: *john.smith@oup.com.*

AA abbrev. **1** Alcoholics Anonymous. **2** Automobile Association.

aardvark n. an African mammal with a long snout.

aback adv. (**taken aback**) surprised and disconcerted.

abacus n. a frame with rows of wires along which beads are slid, used for counting.

abandon v. **1** leave permanently. **2** give up.
▷ SYNONYMS: **1** *he abandoned his wife:* **desert**, leave, turn your back on, cast aside, finish with, jilt, throw over; informal walk/run out on, dump, ditch; literary forsake. **2** *she had abandoned painting:* **give up**, stop, have done with; informal pack in, quit; Brit. jack in. **3** *they abandoned the car:* **leave**, vacate, dump, quit, evacuate, discard, jettison. **4** *the party abandoned those policies:* **renounce**, relinquish, dispense with, discard, give up, drop; informal ditch, scrap, junk; formal forswear.
– ANTONYMS: keep.
• n. lack of inhibition.
▷ SYNONYMS: **uninhibitedness**, recklessness, lack of restraint, lack of inhibition.
– ANTONYMS: self-control.
■ **abandonment** n.

abandoned adj. wild or uncontrolled.

abase v. humiliate or degrade.
■ **abasement** n.

abashed adj. embarrassed or ashamed.

abate v. become less severe or widespread.
▷ SYNONYMS: **subside**, die down/away,

lessen, ease, let up, decrease, diminish, fade, weaken.
– ANTONYMS: intensify.
■ **abatement** n.

abattoir /a-buh-twar/ n. Brit. a slaughterhouse.

abbey n. a building occupied by a community of monks or nuns.

abbot n. (fem. **abbess**) the head of an abbey.

abbreviate v. shorten a word or phrase.
▷ SYNONYMS: **shorten**, reduce, cut, contract, condense, compress, abridge, summarize, precis.
– ANTONYMS: lengthen, expand.

abbreviation n. a shortened form of a word or phrase.
▷ SYNONYMS: **short form**, contraction, acronym, initialism.

abdicate v. **1** give up the throne. **2** fail to carry out a duty.
▷ SYNONYMS: **resign**, retire, stand down, step down, renounce the throne.
■ **abdication** n.

abdomen n. the part of the body containing the digestive organs.
▷ SYNONYMS: **stomach**, belly, gut, middle, viscera; informal tummy, guts.
■ **abdominal** adj.

abduct v. kidnap.
▷ SYNONYMS: **kidnap**, carry off, seize, capture, run away/off with, take hostage; informal snatch.
■ **abduction** n. **abductor** n.

aberrant adj. not normal or acceptable.

aberration n. a departure from what is normal or acceptable.
▷ SYNONYMS: **anomaly**, deviation, abnormality, irregularity, variation, freak, oddity, peculiarity, curiosity, mistake.

abet v. (**abetting, abetted**) encourage or help in wrongdoing.
■ **abettor** n.

abeyance n. (**in abeyance**) in temporary disuse.

a

abhor v. (abhorring, abhorred) detest.
▷ SYNONYMS: **hate**, detest, loathe, despise, shudder at; formal abominate.
– ANTONYMS: love, admire.

abhorrent adj. disgusting; hateful.
▷ SYNONYMS: **hateful**, detestable, loathsome, abominable, repellent, repugnant, repulsive, revolting, vile, odious, disgusting, horrible, horrid, horrifying, awful, heinous.
– ANTONYMS: admirable.
■ abhorrence n.

abide v. 1 (abide by) accept or obey a rule or decision. 2 (cannot abide) dislike greatly.
▷ SYNONYMS: 1 *you must abide by the rules:* **comply with**, obey, observe, follow, keep to, adhere to, stick to, accept, go along with, respect. 2 *I can't abide smoke:* **stand**, bear; Brit. informal stick.

abiding adj. lasting; enduring.
▷ SYNONYMS: **enduring**, lasting, ever-lasting, perpetual, eternal, unending, permanent.

ability n. (pl. abilities) 1 the power to do something. 2 talent.
▷ SYNONYMS: 1 **capacity**, capability, power, potential, faculty, facility, wherewithal, means. 2 **talent**, skill, aptitude, expertise, savoir faire, prowess, accomplishment, competence, proficiency, flair, gift, knack, genius; informal know-how.
– ANTONYMS: inability.

abject adj. 1 wretched. 2 completely without pride.
■ abjectly adv.

abjure v. renounce a belief, claim, etc.

ablaze adj. burning fiercely.

able adj. 1 capable of doing something. 2 talented.
▷ SYNONYMS: **intelligent**, clever, talented, skilful, skilled, expert, accomplished, gifted, proficient, apt, adroit, adept, capable, competent.
– ANTONYMS: incompetent.
■ ably adv.

ablutions pl. n. the act of washing yourself.

abnegation n. the giving up of something wanted.

abnormal adj. not normal.
▷ SYNONYMS: **unusual**, uncommon, atypical, untypical, unexpected, unrepresentative, irregular, anomalous, deviant, aberrant, freak, strange, odd, peculiar, eccentric, bizarre, weird, unnatural, perverted, twisted, warped; informal funny, freaky, kinky.
– ANTONYMS: normal.

■ abnormally adv.

abnormality n. (pl. abnormalities) a feature or event which is not normal, or the state of being abnormal.
▷ SYNONYMS: **deformity**, defect, malformation, oddity, strangeness, irregularity, anomaly, deviation, aberration.

aboard adv. & prep. on board.

abode n. a house or home.

abolish v. put an end to a law or custom.
▷ SYNONYMS: **put an end to**, get rid of, scrap, cancel, end, remove, dissolve, stop, ban; informal do away with, axe, ditch.
■ abolition n.

abominable adj. causing disgust.
▷ SYNONYMS: **loathsome**, detestable, hateful, obnoxious, despicable, contemptible, disgusting, revolting, repellent, repulsive, repugnant, abhorrent, reprehensible, atrocious, execrable, foul, vile, wretched, horrible, awful, dreadful, appalling, nauseating; informal terrible, shocking, God-awful; Brit. informal beastly.
– ANTONYMS: good, admirable.
■ abominably adv.

abominate v. hate; detest.
■ abomination n.

aboriginal adj. existing in a land from its earliest times.
• n. (Aboriginal) a member of one of the original peoples of Australia.

Aborigine /ab-uh-**ri**-ji-nee/ n. an Australian Aboriginal.

abort v. 1 carry out the abortion of a fetus. 2 end before complete, because of a problem.
▷ SYNONYMS: *the crew aborted the take-off:* **halt**, stop, end, call off, abandon, discontinue, terminate; informal pull the plug on.

abortion n. the deliberate ending of a human pregnancy.
▷ SYNONYMS: **termination**, miscarriage.

abortionist n. derogatory a person who carries out abortions.

abortive adj. unsuccessful.
▷ SYNONYMS: **unsuccessful**, failed, vain, ineffective, ineffectual, unproduc-tive, futile, useless, unavailing.
– ANTONYMS: successful.

abound v. be plentiful.
▷ SYNONYMS: **be plentiful**, be abundant, be numerous, be thick on the ground; informal grow on trees, be two/ten a penny.

about prep. & adv. 1 concerning. 2 here and there within a place. 3 nearly.

▷ SYNONYMS: **1 regarding**, concerning, referring to, with regard to, with respect to, relating to, on, dealing with, on the subject of. **2 approximately**, roughly, around, in the region of, circa, of the order of, or so, or thereabouts, more or less; Brit. getting on for; N. Amer. informal in the ballpark of.
□ **about-turn** Brit. a complete change of direction or policy.

above prep. & adv. **1** at a higher level than. **2** more than.
▷ SYNONYMS: **1 over**, higher than, on top of, on, upon. **2 superior to**, senior to, over, in charge of, commanding.
– ANTONYMS: above.
□ **above board** lawful and honest.

abracadabra exclam. said by magicians when performing a trick.

abrasion n. **1** scraping or wearing away. **2** an area of scraped skin.
▷ SYNONYMS: **1 graze**, cut, scrape, scratch, gash, laceration. **2 erosion**, wearing away/down.

abrasive adj. **1** rough and used for polishing or cleaning. **2** harsh or hurtful.
▷ SYNONYMS: **1 rough**, coarse, harsh, scratchy, chafing. **2 curt**, brusque, sharp, harsh, caustic, grating.
– ANTONYMS: gentle.

abreast adv. **1** side by side. **2** (**abreast of**) up to date with.

abridge v. shorten a book, account, etc.
▷ SYNONYMS: **shorten**, cut, abbreviate, edit, condense, compress, truncate, prune, summarize, precis, synopsize; (**abridged**) concise, potted.
▷ ANTONYMS: extend.
■ **abridgement** n.

abroad adv. away from your home country.

abrogate v. cancel or abolish.
■ **abrogation** n.

abrupt adj. **1** sudden. **2** curt.
▷ SYNONYMS: **1 sudden**, rapid, quick, hasty, unexpected, unanticipated, unforeseen, precipitate. **2 curt**, brusque, blunt, short, rude, sharp, terse, brisk, unceremonious.
– ANTONYMS: gradual, gentle.
■ **abruptly** adv. **abruptness** n.

abscess n. a swelling containing pus.

USAGE Remember the s and c: abscess.

abscond v. leave quickly and secretly.
▷ SYNONYMS: **run away**, run off, escape, bolt, flee, make off, take flight, take off, decamp; informal scarper, vamoose, do a bunk, do a runner.

abseil /ab-sayl/ v. Brit. climb down a rock face using a rope fixed at a higher point.

absence n. **1** the state of being absent. **2** (**absence of**) lack of.
▷ SYNONYMS: **1 non-attendance**, absenteeism, truancy, leave, holiday, sabbatical; N. Amer. vacation. **2 lack**, want, non-existence, unavailability, scarcity, shortage, dearth.
– ANTONYMS: presence.

absent adj. not present.
▷ SYNONYMS: **1 away**, off, out, elsewhere, off duty, on holiday, on leave, playing truant; informal AWOL. **2 non-existent**, lacking, missing.
– ANTONYMS: present.
• v. (**absent yourself**) stay away.

absentee n. a person who is absent from something.
■ **absenteeism** n.

absent-minded adj. forgetful.
▷ SYNONYMS: **forgetful**, distracted, scatterbrained, preoccupied, inattentive, vague; informal with a mind/memory like a sieve.

absinthe /ab-sinth/ n. a green liqueur.

absolute adj. **1** complete. **2** not limited.
▷ SYNONYMS: **1** absolute silence | an absolute disgrace: **complete**, total, utter, out-and-out, outright, perfect, pure, thorough, unqualified, unreserved, downright, unmitigated, sheer, unadulterated. **2** absolute power: **unlimited**, unrestricted, unrestrained, infinite, total, supreme, unconditional. **3** an absolute ruler: **autocratic**, dictatorial, all-powerful, omnipotent, supreme.
– ANTONYMS: partial, qualified, limited.
■ **absolutely** adv.

absolution n. formal forgiveness of a person's sins.

absolutism n. the principle of government with unrestricted power.
■ **absolutist** n. & adj.

absolve v. formally clear of guilt, blame, or sin.

absorb v. **1** soak up liquid. **2** understand information. **3** hold the attention of. **4** reduce in effect or strength.
▷ SYNONYMS: **1 soak up**, suck up, draw up/in, take up/in, mop up. **2 engross**, captivate, occupy, preoccupy, engage, rivet, grip, hold, immerse, involve, enthral, spellbind, fascinate.

absorbent adj. able to soak up liquid.
▷ SYNONYMS: **spongy**, sponge-like, porous, permeable.

absorbing adj. very interesting.

▷ SYNONYMS: **fascinating**, interesting, captivating, gripping, engrossing, compelling, compulsive, enthralling, riveting, spellbinding; informal unputdownable.
− ANTONYMS: boring.

absorption n. the process of absorbing.
▷ SYNONYMS: **1 soaking up**, sucking up. **2 involvement**, immersion, raptness, preoccupation, captivation, fascination, enthralment.

abstain v. **1** stop yourself from doing something. **2** choose not to vote.
▷ SYNONYMS: **refrain**, desist, forbear, give up, renounce, avoid, eschew, forgo, go/do without, refuse, decline; informal cut out.
■ **abstainer** n. **abstention** n.

abstemious adj. limiting your intake of food or alcohol.
▷ SYNONYMS: **moderate**, restrained, temperate, self-disciplined, self-restrained, self-denying, sober, austere, ascetic, puritanical, spartan.
− ANTONYMS: self-indulgent.

abstinence n. the avoidance of doing or indulging in something.
▷ SYNONYMS: **self-denial**, self-restraint, teetotalism, temperance, sobriety, abstemiousness.

abstract adj. **1** relating to ideas or qualities; not physical. **2** (of art) not representing things pictorially.
▷ SYNONYMS: **theoretical**, conceptual, intellectual, metaphysical, philosophical, academic.
− ANTONYMS: actual, concrete.
• v. take out or remove.
• n. a summary of a book or article.
▷ SYNONYMS: **summary**, synopsis, precis, résumé, outline, abridgement; N. Amer. wrap-up.
■ **abstraction** n.

abstruse adj. hard to understand.
▷ SYNONYMS: **obscure**, arcane, esoteric, rarefied, recondite, difficult, hard, cryptic, over/above your head, incomprehensible, unfathomable, impenetrable.

absurd adj. completely illogical or ridiculous.
▷ SYNONYMS: **irrational**, illogical, inappropriate, ridiculous, ludicrous, farcical, comical, stupid, idiotic, asinine, hare-brained, foolish, silly, pointless, senseless, preposterous; informal crazy, cockeyed; Brit. informal barmy, daft.
− ANTONYMS: sensible.
■ **absurdity** n. **absurdly** adv.

abundance n. a very large quantity.

▷ SYNONYMS: **profusion**, plethora, host, cornucopia, superabundance, multitude.
− ANTONYMS: scarcity.

abundant adj. **1** plentiful. **2** having plenty of something.
▷ SYNONYMS: **plentiful**, copious, ample, profuse, large, huge, great, bumper, prolific, overflowing, teeming, superabundant; informal galore.
− ANTONYMS: scarce.
■ **abundantly** adv.

abuse v. **1** use badly or wrongly. **2** treat cruelly. **3** insult.
▷ SYNONYMS: **1 misuse**, exploit, take advantage of. **2 mistreat**, maltreat, ill-treat, hurt, harm, beat, molest, interfere with. **3 insult**, be rude to, swear at, shout at, vilify, curse.
• n. **1** cruel treatment or misuse. **2** insulting language.
▷ SYNONYMS: **1 misuse**, exploitation. **2 mistreatment**, maltreatment, ill-treatment, molestation. **3 insults**, expletives, swear words, swearing, name-calling, invective, vilification, curses.

abusive adj. **1** very insulting. **2** cruel and violent.
▷ SYNONYMS: **1 insulting**, rude, offensive, derogatory, defamatory, slanderous, libellous. **2 violent**, brutal, cruel, harsh, oppressive.
− ANTONYMS: polite.
■ **abusively** adv.

abut v. (**abutting**, **abutted**) be next to or touching.

abysmal adj. very bad.
▷ SYNONYMS: **terrible**, dreadful, awful, appalling, frightful, atrocious, disgraceful, deplorable, lamentable; informal rotten, pathetic, pitiful, woeful, useless, lousy, dire, poxy, the pits; Brit. informal chronic, shocking.

abyss n. a very deep hole.
▷ SYNONYMS: **chasm**, crevasse, gulf, pit, void.

AC abbrev. alternating current.
a/c abbrev. account.
acacia /uh-kay-shuh/ n. a tree or shrub with yellow or white flowers.
academic adj. **1** of education or study. **2** not related to a real situation; theoretical.
▷ SYNONYMS: **1 educational**, scholastic. **2 scholarly**, learned, literary, intellectual, erudite, highbrow, bookish, studious. **3 theoretical**, hypothetical, notional, speculative, conjectural, irrelevant, beside the point.
• n. a teacher or scholar in a university or college.

▷ SYNONYMS: **scholar**, intellectual, don, professor, man/woman of letters, thinker; informal **egghead**; Brit. informal **boffin**.
■ **academically** adv.

academician n. a member of an academy.

academy n. (pl. **academies**) **1** a place for training in a special field. **2** a society of artists or scientists.
▷ SYNONYMS: **college**, school, university, institute.

accede /uhk-**seed**/ v. agree to a demand or request.

accelerate v. begin to move more quickly.
▷ SYNONYMS: **1 speed up**, go faster, gain momentum, increase speed, pick up speed, gather speed. **2 hasten**, quicken, speed up, further, advance, expedite; informal **crank up**.
– ANTONYMS: decelerate, delay.
■ **acceleration** n.

accelerator n. a foot pedal which controls a vehicle's speed.

accent n. **1** a way of pronouncing a language. **2** emphasis. **3** a written mark guiding pronunciation.
▷ SYNONYMS: **1 pronunciation**, intonation, enunciation, articulation, inflection. **2 emphasis**, stress, priority, importance, prominence.
• v. **1** (**accented**) spoken with an accent. **2** emphasize.

accentuate v. make more noticeable.
▷ SYNONYMS: **focus attention on**, draw attention to, point up, underline, underscore, accent, highlight, spotlight, foreground, bring to the fore, emphasize, stress.
■ **accentuation** n.

accept v. **1** say yes to. **2** believe to be valid or correct. **3** resign yourself to.
▷ SYNONYMS: **1 receive**, take, get, obtain, acquire, pick up. **2 agree to**, accede to, consent to, acquiesce in, concur with, endorse, comply with, go along with, defer to, put up with, recognize, acknowledge, admit. **3 believe**, trust, credit, be convinced of, have faith in; informal **buy**, swallow. **4** (**accepted**) **recognized**, acknowledged, established, traditional, orthodox, agreed, approved, customary, normal, standard.
– ANTONYMS: reject.
■ **acceptance** n.

acceptable adj. satisfactory.
▷ SYNONYMS: **satisfactory**, adequate, reasonable, fair, good enough, sufficient, tolerable, passable.
■ **acceptability** n. **acceptably** adv.

access n. **1** a way in. **2** the right or opportunity to use something or see someone.
▷ SYNONYMS: **1** *a side access:* **entrance**, entry, approach, path, drive, way in. **2** *they were denied access:* **admission**, admittance, entry.
• v. obtain data from a computer.

accessible adj. able to be reached, used, or understood.
▷ SYNONYMS: **approachable**, attainable, reachable, obtainable, available, understandable, comprehensible, intelligible; informal **get-at-able**.
■ **accessibility** n. **accessibly** adv.

accession n. **1** the gaining of a position or rank. **2** an addition to a library or museum collection.

accessory n. (pl. **accessories**) **1** a thing added as a supplement or decoration. **2** a person who helps in a crime.
▷ SYNONYMS: **1 extra**, add-on, addition, supplement, attachment, fitment. **2 accomplice**, abetter, collaborator, co-conspirator, henchman, associate.

accident n. **1** an unpleasant incident that happens unexpectedly. **2** an incident that happens by chance.
▷ SYNONYMS: **1 mishap**, misadventure, disaster, tragedy, catastrophe, calamity. **2 crash**, collision, smash, bump, derailment; N. Amer. **wreck**; informal **smash-up**, pile-up; Brit. informal **shunt**. **3 chance**, fate, fortune, luck, good luck, fluke, coincidence.

accidental adj. happening by chance.
▷ SYNONYMS: **1 chance**, coincidental, unexpected, incidental, fortuitous, serendipitous. **2 unintentional**, unintended, unplanned, inadvertent, unwitting, unpremeditated.
– ANTONYMS: intentional.
■ **accidentally** adv.

acclaim v. praise enthusiastically.
▷ SYNONYMS: **praise**, applaud, cheer, commend, approve, welcome, hail, celebrate, eulogize; formal **laud**.
– ANTONYMS: criticize.
• n. enthusiastic praise.
▷ SYNONYMS: **praise**, applause, tributes, plaudits, approval, admiration, congratulations, commendation, eulogies.
– ANTONYMS: criticism.
■ **acclamation** n.

acclimatize (or **-ise**) v. get used to new conditions.
▷ SYNONYMS: **adjust**, adapt, get used, familiarize yourself, find your feet, get your bearings; N. Amer. **acclimate**.
■ **acclimatization** n.

accolade n. a thing given as a special

honour or reward.

accommodate v. **1** provide lodging or space for. **2** adapt to.
▷ SYNONYMS: **1** *refugees were accommodated in army camps*: **lodge**, house, put up, billet, board. **2** *the cottages accommodate six people*: **hold**, take, have room for, sleep, seat. **3** *we tried to accommodate her*: **help**, assist, oblige, cater for, fit in with, satisfy, meet the needs of.

> **USAGE** Double *c*, double *m*: accommodate.

accommodating adj. willing to do as asked.
▷ SYNONYMS: **obliging**, cooperative, helpful, amenable, hospitable, flexible.

accommodation n. a place to live.
▷ SYNONYMS: **housing**, home, lodging, living quarters, rooms, billet, shelter, a roof over your head; informal digs, pad; formal residence, dwelling, abode.

accompaniment n. **1** a musical part which accompanies an instrument, voice, etc. **2** something that adds to or improves something else.
▷ SYNONYMS: **1 backing**, support, background, soundtrack. **2 complement**, addition, adjunct, accessory, companion.
■ accompanist n.

accompany v. (**accompanying**, **accompanied**) **1** go with. **2** play musical backing for an instrument or voice.
▷ SYNONYMS: **1 escort**, go with, travel with, keep someone company, chaperone, partner, show, see, usher, conduct. **2 occur with**, go together with, attend, be linked with, go hand in hand with.
■ accompanist n.

accomplice n. a person who helps another commit a crime.
▷ SYNONYMS: **partner in crime**, abetter, accessory, collaborator, co-conspirator, henchman, associate; informal sidekick.

accomplish v. succeed in doing or achieving.
▷ SYNONYMS: **achieve**, succeed in, realize, attain, manage, bring off, carry through, execute, effect, perform, complete.

accomplished adj. highly skilled.
▷ SYNONYMS: **expert**, skilled, skilful, masterly, virtuoso, master, proficient, polished, practised, consummate, talented, gifted, able, capable; informal mean, nifty, crack, ace.

accomplishment n. **1** a skill or special ability. **2** something achieved successfully.
▷ SYNONYMS: **1 achievement**, success, act, deed, exploit, effort, feat, coup. **2 talent**, skill, gift, ability.

accord v. **1** give power or recognition to. **2** be consistent with.
SYNONYMS: **1 give**, grant, present, award, confer on, bestow on. **2 correspond**, agree, tally, match, concur, be in harmony, be in tune.
– ANTONYMS: disagree, differ.
● n. agreement in opinion.
▷ SYNONYMS: **1** *a peace accord*: **pact**, treaty, agreement, settlement, deal, entente, protocol. **2** *the two sides failed to reach accord*: **agreement**, consensus, unanimity, harmony.
– ANTONYMS: disagreement.
□ **of your own accord** willingly.

accordance n. (**in accordance with**) in a way conforming with.

according adv. (**according to**) **1** as stated by. **2** following or agreeing with.

accordingly adv. **1** appropriately. **2** therefore.

accordion n. a musical instrument with bellows and keys or buttons.

accost v. approach and speak to.

account n. **1** a description of an event. **2** a record of money spent and received. **3** a credit arrangement with a bank or firm.
▷ SYNONYMS: **1 description**, report, version, story, statement, explanation, tale, chronicle, narrative, history, record, log. **2 financial record**, ledger, balance sheet, financial statement; (**accounts**) books. **3** *his background is of no account*: **importance**, import, significance, consequence, value.
● v. (**account for**) explain.
□ **on account of** because of.

accountable adj. responsible for actions and expected to explain them.
▷ SYNONYMS: **responsible**, liable, answerable, to blame.
■ accountability n.

accountant n. a person who keeps or inspects financial accounts.
■ accountancy n.

accoutrement /uh-koo-truh-muhnt/ n. an extra item of dress or equipment.

accredited adj. officially authorized.

accretion n. growth or increase by a gradual build-up.

accrue v. (**accruing**, **accrued**) collect or accumulate.

■ **accrual** n.

accumulate v. **1** acquire more and more of. **2** increase.
▷ SYNONYMS: **gather**, collect, amass, stockpile, pile up, build up, store, hoard, lay in/up, increase, accrue, run up.
– ANTONYMS: disperse.

USAGE Two c's and one m: accumulate.

accumulation n. a quantity of something that has accumulated or been acquired.
▷ SYNONYMS: **mass**, build-up, pile, collection, stock, store, stockpile, hoard.

accumulator n. **1** Brit. a rechargeable electric battery. **2** a series of bets with the winnings from each placed on the next.

accuracy n. the state of being accurate.
▷ SYNONYMS: **correctness**, precision, exactness, fidelity, truth, truthfulness, authenticity, realism, verisimilitude.

accurate adj. with no errors.
▷ SYNONYMS: **1 correct**, precise, exact, right, factual, literal, faithful, true, truthful, on the mark, authentic, realistic; Brit. informal spot on, bang on; N. Amer. informal on the money, on the button. **2 well aimed**, on target, unerring, deadly, true.
■ **accurately** adv.

accusation n. a claim that someone has done something illegal or wrong.
▷ SYNONYMS: **allegation**, charge, indictment, impeachment, claim, assertion, imputation.

accusative n. the grammatical case used for the object of a verb.

accuse v. charge with committing an offence or crime.
▷ SYNONYMS: **1 charge**, indict, impeach, prefer charges against, arraign. **2 blame**, hold responsible, condemn, criticize, denounce; informal point the finger at.
■ **accuser** n.

accustom v. make or be used to.
▷ SYNONYMS: **adapt**, adjust, acclimatize, habituate, familiarize, become reconciled, get used to, come to terms with, learn to live with; N. Amer. acclimate.

accustomed adj. customary; usual: *his accustomed route*.
▷ SYNONYMS: **customary**, established, habitual, usual, normal, regular, routine; literary wonted.

ace n. **1** a playing card with a single spot. **2** informal an expert. **3** Tennis a

serve that an opponent cannot return.

acerbic /uh-**ser**-bik/ adj. sharp and direct.
■ **acerbity** n.

acetate /**a**-si-tayt/ n. a synthetic textile fibre.

acetic acid /uh-**see**-tik/ n. the acid that gives vinegar its taste.

acetone /**a**-si-tohn/ n. a colourless liquid used as a solvent.

acetylene /uh-**set**-i-leen/ n. a gas which burns with a bright flame.

ache n. a continuous dull pain.
▷ SYNONYMS: **pain**, twinge, pang, soreness, tenderness, irritation, discomfort, burning, throbbing, cramp.
● v. have an ache.
▷ SYNONYMS: **hurt**, be sore, be painful, be tender, burn, be in pain, throb.

achieve v. succeed in doing by effort or skill.
▷ SYNONYMS: **attain**, reach, realize, bring off, pull off, accomplish, carry through, fulfil, complete, succeed in, manage, effect; informal wrap up, swing.
■ **achievable** adj. **achiever** n.

achievement n. **1** the process of achieving something. **2** something that has been achieved.
▷ SYNONYMS: **1 attainment**, realization, accomplishment, fulfilment, implementation, completion. **2 feat**, exploit, triumph, coup, accomplishment, act, action, deed, effort, work, handiwork.

Achilles heel n. a weak point.

Achilles tendon n. the tendon connecting calf muscles to the heel.

acid n. a substance that turns litmus red, neutralizes alkalis, and dissolves some metals.
● adj. **1** sour. **2** unkind; cutting.
▷ SYNONYMS: **1 sour**, acidic, tart, sharp, vinegary. **2 sharp**, sharp-tongued, catty, sarcastic, scathing, cutting, biting, stinging, caustic; informal bitchy.
– ANTONYMS: sweet.
□ **acid rain** rain made acidic by pollution. **acid test** a decisive test of something.
■ **acidic** adj. **acidity** n. **acidly** adv.

acknowledge v. **1** accept the truth of. **2** confirm receipt of. **3** show recognition of.
▷ SYNONYMS: **1 admit**, accept, grant, agree, own, allow, concede, confess, recognize. **2 answer**, reply to, respond to. **3 greet**, salute, address, nod to, wave to.
– ANTONYMS: deny, ignore.

a

■ acknowledgement n.

acme /ak-mi/ n. the height of achievement or excellence.

acne n. a skin condition causing red pimples.

acolyte /ak-uh-lyt/ n. an assistant or follower.

acorn n. the oval nut of the oak tree.

acoustic adj. **1** of sound. **2** not electrically amplified.
• n. (**acoustics**) the aspects of a room that affect the way sound is carried.

acquaint v. **1** make aware of. **2** (**be acquainted with**) know slightly.
▷ SYNONYMS: **familiarize**, make aware of, inform of, advise of, brief; informal fill in on, clue in on.

acquaintance n. **1** a person you know slightly. **2** knowledge or familiarity.
▷ SYNONYMS: **1** *a business acquaintance*: **contact**, associate, colleague. **2** *my acquaintance with George*: **association**, relationship. **3** *some acquaintance with the language*: **familiarity with**, knowledge of, experience of, awareness of, understanding of, grasp of.

acquiesce v. accept without protest.
■ acquiescence n. acquiescent adj.

acquire v. buy or get.
▷ SYNONYMS: **get**, obtain, come by, receive, collect, gain, buy, earn, win, come into, secure, pick up, procure; informal get your hands on, get hold of, land, bag, score.

acquisition n. **1** something acquired. **2** the act of acquiring.
▷ SYNONYMS: **purchase**, addition, investment, possession, accession; informal buy.

acquisitive adj. eager to acquire things.
■ acquisitiveness n.

acquit v. (**acquitting, acquitted**) **1** declare to be not guilty. **2** (**acquit yourself**) behave in a particular way.
▷ SYNONYMS: **1** **clear**, exonerate, find innocent, absolve, discharge, free, release; informal let off. **2** *the boys acquitted themselves well*: **behave**, conduct yourself, perform, act.
– ANTONYMS: convict.
■ acquittal n.

acre n. a unit of land area equal to 4,840 sq. yds (0.405 hectare).
■ acreage n.

acrid adj. unpleasantly bitter.
▷ SYNONYMS: **pungent**, bitter, sharp, harsh, stinging, burning.

acrimonious adj. angry and bitter.
▷ SYNONYMS: **bitter**, angry, rancorous, harsh, vicious, nasty, bad-tempered,
ill-natured.
■ acrimony n.

acrobat n. a performer of spectacular gymnastic feats.

acrobatic adj. involving spectacular gymnastic feats.
• n. (**acrobatics**) acrobatic feats.

acronym n. a word formed from the first letters of other words, e.g. *Aids*.

across prep. & adv. from one side to the other of.

acrostic n. a poem or puzzle in which certain letters in each line form a word or words.

acrylic adj. (of a fabric, paint, etc.) made from acrylic acid (an organic acid).

act v. **1** do something. **2** have an effect. **3** behave. **4** (**acting**) temporarily doing another's duties. **5** perform in a play or film.
▷ SYNONYMS: **1** **take action**, take steps, take measures, move. **2** **behave**, conduct yourself, react. **3** (**acting**) **temporary**, interim, caretaker, pro tem, provisional, stopgap; N. Amer. informal pinch-hitting. **4** **perform**, play, appear; informal tread the boards.
• n. **1** a thing done. **2** a law made by a parliament. **3** a section of a play or opera. **4** a set performance or performing group.
▷ SYNONYMS: **1** **deed**, action, step, move, gesture, feat, exploit. **2** **law**, decree, statute, bill, edict, ruling, order. **3** **performance**, turn, routine, number, sketch. **4** **pretence**, show, front, facade, masquerade, charade, pose.

actinium n. a radioactive chemical element.

action n. **1** the process of doing something. **2** a thing done. **3** a lawsuit. **4** armed conflict.
▷ SYNONYMS: **1** **deed**, act, undertaking, feat, exploit, behaviour, conduct, activity. **2** **measures**, steps, initiatives, activism, campaigning, pressure. **3** **operation**, working, effect, influence, process, power. **4** **battle**, combat, hostilities, fighting, conflict, active service. **5** **lawsuit**, suit, case, prosecution, litigation, proceedings.

actionable adj. giving cause for legal action.

activate v. cause to act or work.
▷ SYNONYMS: **start**, switch on, turn on, set going, trigger, set off, energize.
■ activation n. activator n.

active adj. **1** energetic; lively. **2** functioning. **3** Grammar (of a verb) having as its subject the person or thing doing the action.

▷ SYNONYMS: **1 busy**, lively, dynamic, vigorous, sprightly, spry, mobile; informal on the go, full of beans. **2 hard-working**, industrious, tireless, energetic, diligent, enthusiastic, keen, committed, devoted, zealous. **3 working**, operative, functioning, operational, in action, in operation, in force; informal up and running.
– ANTONYMS: inactive.
■ **actively** adv.

activist n. a person campaigning for political change.
■ **activism** n.

activity n. (pl. **activities**) **1** the state of being active. **2** an action or pastime.
▷ SYNONYMS: **1 action**, bustle, movement, life, hurly-burly; informal toing and froing, comings and goings. **2 pursuit**, occupation, hobby, pastime, recreation, diversion, venture, undertaking, enterprise, project, scheme.

actor n. (fem. **actress**) a person who acts in a play or film.
▷ SYNONYMS: **performer**, player, thespian, star, starlet; Brit. informal luvvie.

actual adj. existing in fact.
▷ SYNONYMS: **real**, true, genuine, authentic, bona fide, confirmed, definite, hard, concrete; informal real live.
– ANTONYMS: imaginary.
■ **actuality** n.

actually adv. in truth; really.
▷ SYNONYMS: **really**, in fact, in point of fact, as a matter of fact, in reality, in truth, if truth be told, to tell the truth.

actuary n. (pl. **actuaries**) a person who calculates insurance risks.

actuate v. **1** activate. **2** motivate.

acumen n. shrewdness.

acupuncture n. the insertion of needles into the skin as a medical treatment.
■ **acupuncturist** n.

acute adj. **1** serious or severe. **2** sharp-witted. **3** (of an angle) less than 90°.
▷ SYNONYMS: **1 severe**, dire, terrible, grave, serious, desperate, urgent, pressing. **2 excruciating**, sharp, severe, stabbing, agonizing, racking, searing. **3 quick**, astute, shrewd, sharp, keen, penetrating, razor-sharp, quick-witted, agile, nimble, intelligent, canny, discerning, perceptive.
– ANTONYMS: mild, dull.
▫ **acute accent** the accent (´).
■ **acutely** adv. **acuteness** n.

AD abbrev. Anno Domini (used in dates counted from the traditional date of Jesus's birth).

adage /ad-ij/ n. a saying expressing an accepted truth.

adagio /uh-**dah**-ji-oh/ adv. Music in slow time.

adamant adj. refusing to change your mind.
▷ SYNONYMS: **unshakeable**, unwavering, unswerving, immovable, resolute, resolved, determined, firm, dead set.

Adam's apple n. the lump of cartilage at the front of the neck.

adapt v. make or become suitable for a new use or purpose.
▷ SYNONYMS: **1** the policy can be adapted: **modify**, alter, change, adjust, remodel, reorganize, customize, tailor; informal tweak. **2** he adapts well to new surroundings: **adjust**, conform, acclimatize, accommodate, get used, get accustomed, habituate yourself.
■ **adaptation** n.

adaptable adj. able to adapt or be adapted.
■ **adaptability** n.

adaptor (or **adapter**) n. Brit. a device for connecting several electric plugs to one socket.

add v. **1** join to or put with something else. **2** put together numbers to find their total value. **3** say as a further remark.
▷ SYNONYMS: **1 attach**, append, tack on, join on. **2** they added the figures up: **total**, count, reckon up, tally; Brit. tot up.
– ANTONYMS: subtract.

addendum n. (pl. **addenda**) an extra item added to a book.

adder n. a poisonous snake.

addict n. a person addicted to something.
▷ SYNONYMS: **1 abuser**; informal junkie, druggy; N. Amer. informal hophead. **2 enthusiast**, fan, lover, devotee, aficionado; informal buff, freak, nut, fanatic.

addicted adj. **1** dependent on a substance. **2** devoted to an activity.
▷ SYNONYMS: **dependent**, obsessed, fixated, fanatical, passionate, a slave to; informal hooked.

addiction n. the fact or condition of being addicted.
▷ SYNONYMS: **dependency**, dependence, habit, obsession, fixation, passion, love, mania, enslavement.
■ **addictive** adj.

addition n. **1** the act of adding. **2** a thing added.
▷ SYNONYMS: **1 adding**, inclusion,

additional adj. added; extra.
▷ SYNONYMS: **extra**, added, supplementary, further, more, spare, other, new, fresh.
■ **additionally** adv.

additive n. a substance added to improve or preserve something.

addled adj. muddled or confused.

address n. **1** the details of a building's location or a person's home. **2** a speech. **3** a string of characters identifying a destination for email.
▷ SYNONYMS: **1 house**, flat, apartment, home, location, whereabouts; formal residence, abode, dwelling, domicile. **2 speech**, lecture, talk, presentation, dissertation, sermon, oration.
• v. **1** write an address on. **2** speak to. **3** begin to deal with.
▷ SYNONYMS: **1 speak to**, talk to, give a talk to, lecture, hold forth to. **2 attend to**, apply yourself to, tackle, deal with, confront, get to grips with, concentrate on, focus on.
■ **addressee** n.

adduce v. refer to as evidence.

adenoids pl. n. a mass of tissue between the back of the nose and the throat.
■ **adenoidal** adj.

adept adj. very skilled or able.
▷ SYNONYMS: **expert**, proficient, accomplished, skilful, practised, masterly, consummate.
– ANTONYMS: inept.

adequate adj. satisfactory or acceptable.
▷ SYNONYMS: **1** *he has adequate financial resources:* **sufficient**, enough. **2** *an adequate service:* **satisfactory**, acceptable, passable, reasonable, tolerable, fair, average, all right, middling; informal OK.
– ANTONYMS: insufficient, inadequate.
■ **adequacy** n. **adequately** adv.

adhere v. **1** stick firmly. **2** follow or support.
▷ SYNONYMS: **stick**, cling, bond, hold.
■ **adherence** n.

adherent n. a supporter of a particular party, person, or set of ideas.
▷ SYNONYMS: **follower**, supporter, upholder, defender, advocate, disciple, devotee, member.
– ANTONYMS: opponent.

adhesion n. the process of adhering.

incorporation, introduction. **2 add-on**, extra, adjunct, appendage, supplement, rider, addendum, postscript, appendix.
– ANTONYMS: subtraction.

adhesive n. a sticky substance.
• adj. sticky.

ad hoc adj. & adv. created or done for a particular purpose only.

adieu /uh-dyoo/ exclam. goodbye.

ad infinitum adv. endlessly.

adipose adj. (of body tissue) fatty.

adjacent adj. near or next to.
▷ SYNONYMS: **adjoining**, neighbouring, next-door, abutting; formal contiguous.

adjective n. a word which adds information about a noun.
■ **adjectival** adj.

adjoin v. be next to.
▷ SYNONYMS: **1 be adjacent to**, border, abut. **2 (adjoining) connecting**, connected, interconnecting, bordering, attached, adjacent, neighbouring, next-door.

adjourn v. break off a meeting until later.
▷ SYNONYMS: **suspend**, break off, discontinue, interrupt, recess, postpone, put off/back, defer, delay, hold over.
■ **adjournment** n.

adjudge v. declare to be.

adjudicate v. **1** make a formal judgement. **2** judge a competition.
■ **adjudication** n. **adjudicator** n.

adjunct n. an additional part.

adjust v. **1** alter slightly. **2** adapt to a new situation.
▷ SYNONYMS: **1 modify**, alter, regulate, tune, fine-tune, balance, tailor, customize, rearrange, change, reshape; informal tweak. **2** *she adjusted to her new life:* **adapt**, become accustomed, get used, accommodate, acclimatize, habituate yourself, assimilate, come to terms with, fit in with; N. Amer. acclimate.
■ **adjustable** adj. **adjustment** n.

adjutant n. an army officer assisting with administrative work.

ad-lib v. (ad-libbing, ad-libbed) speak without preparing first.
• adv. & adj. spoken without preparation.

administer v. **1** organize or put into effect. **2** give or apply a drug or remedy.
▷ SYNONYMS: **1 manage**, direct, control, operate, regulate, coordinate, conduct, handle, run, organize, govern, steer. **2 dispense**, issue, give out, provide, apply, offer, distribute, deliver, hand out, deal out, dole out.

administrate v. manage the business affairs of.
■ **administrative** adj. **administrator** n.

administration n. **1** the action of organizing or administering something. **2** the government in power.
▷ SYNONYMS: **1 management**, direction, control, conduct, operation, running, coordination, governance, supervision, regulation. **2 government**, regime, executive, cabinet, authority, directorate, council, leadership, management, incumbency, term of office.

admirable adj. deserving respect.
▷ SYNONYMS: **commendable**, praiseworthy, laudable, creditable, exemplary, worthy, deserving, respectable, worthwhile, good, sterling, fine, excellent.
– ANTONYMS: deplorable.
■ **admirably** adv.

admiral n. a naval officer of the highest rank.

admiration n. respect and warm approval.
▷ SYNONYMS: **respect**, approval, appreciation, high regard, esteem, recognition.
– ANTONYMS: scorn.

admire v. **1** greatly respect. **2** look at with pleasure.
▷ SYNONYMS: **1 respect**, think highly of, look up to, have a high opinion of, hold in high regard, rate highly, esteem, prize, approve of. **2 adore**, love, worship, be taken with, be attracted to, idolize, hero-worship; informal carry a torch for, have a thing about.
– ANTONYMS: despise.
■ **admirer** n.

admissible adj. acceptable or valid.
■ **admissibility** n.

admission n. **1** entry to or permission to enter somewhere. **2** a confession.
▷ SYNONYMS: **1 admittance**, entry, entrance, access, entrée, acceptance, initiation. **2 confession**, acknowledgement, acceptance, concession, disclosure, divulgence.

admit v. (**admitting**, **admitted**) **1** confess to be true. **2** allow to enter. **3** accept as valid.
▷ SYNONYMS: **1** *he admitted that he was angry*: **confess**, acknowledge, concede, grant, accept, allow, own, reveal, disclose, divulge. **2** *he admitted the offence*: **confess to**, plead guilty to, own up to. **3 let in**, accept, receive, initiate.
– ANTONYMS: deny.

admittance n. admission to a place.
▷ SYNONYMS: **entry**, admission, entrance,

access, entrée.
– ANTONYMS: exclusion.

admittedly adv. it must be admitted that.

admixture n. a mixture.

admonish v. reprimand firmly.
■ **admonition** n.

ad nauseam adv. to a boringly excessive extent.

ado n. trouble; fuss.

adobe /uh-**doh**-bi/ n. clay used as a building material.

adolescent adj. developing from a child into an adult.
▷ SYNONYMS: **teenage**, young, pubescent, immature, childish, juvenile, infantile, puerile; informal teen.
– ANTONYMS: mature.
● n. an adolescent boy or girl.
▷ SYNONYMS: **teenager**, youth, juvenile; informal teen, teeny-bopper.
■ **adolescence** n.

adopt v. **1** legally bring up another's child as your own. **2** choose a course of action.
▷ SYNONYMS: **take on**, embrace, take up, espouse, assume, follow, choose, endorse, approve.
– ANTONYMS: abandon.
■ **adoption** n.

adoptive adj. related by adoption.

adorable adj. lovable or charming.

adore v. love or like very much.
▷ SYNONYMS: **love**, be devoted to, dote on, cherish, treasure, prize, think the world of, admire, look up to, revere, worship.
– ANTONYMS: hate.
■ **adoration** n.

adorn v. make more attractive; decorate.
▷ SYNONYMS: **decorate**, embellish, array, ornament, bedeck, trim, enhance.
– ANTONYMS: disfigure.
■ **adornment** n.

adrenal /uh-**dree**-n'l/ adj. of the **adrenal glands**, a pair of glands above the kidneys.

adrenalin (or **adrenaline**) n. a hormone produced by the adrenal glands in response to stress.

adrift adj. & adv. **1** drifting. **2** no longer attached.
▷ SYNONYMS: **1 lost**, off course, drifting, rootless, unsettled. **2 loose**, free, detached, unsecured, unfastened.

adroit adj. clever or skilful.

adsorb v. (of a solid) hold a gas or liquid as a thin film on its surface.

adulation n. excessive admiration.
■ **adulatory** adj.

adult n. a fully grown person.
• adj. fully grown.
▷ SYNONYMS: **mature**, grown-up, fully grown, fully developed, of age.
■ **adulthood** n.

adulterate v. make poorer in quality by adding another substance.
■ **adulteration** n.

adulterer n. a person who has committed adultery.

adultery n. sex with someone other than your husband or wife.
■ **adulterous** adj.

advance v. **1** move or put forward. **2** make progress. **3** pay money as a loan or before it is due.
▷ SYNONYMS: **1 move forward**, press on, push on, attack, make progress, make headway, gain ground, forge ahead. **2** *the move advanced his career:* **promote**, further, forward, help, aid, assist, boost. **3** *technology has advanced:* **progress**, develop, evolve, make strides, move forward, move on. **4 lend**, loan, put up, come up with; Brit. informal sub.
– ANTONYMS: retreat.
• n. **1** a forward movement. **3** a loan. **4** (**advances**) romantic or sexual approaches.
▷ SYNONYMS: **1 progress**, forward movement, attack. **2 breakthrough**, development, step forward, quantum leap.
■ **advancement** n.

advanced adj. **1** far on in progress or life. **2** not basic; complex.
▷ SYNONYMS: **1 state-of-the-art**, modern, sophisticated, up to date, up to the minute, cutting-edge, new, the latest, pioneering, innovative, progressive, trendsetting. **2 higher-level**, higher, tertiary.
– ANTONYMS: primitive, elementary.

advantage n. something that puts you in a favourable position.
▷ SYNONYMS: **1 upper hand**, edge, lead, sway, whip hand, superiority, dominance, supremacy. **2 benefit**, value, good/strong point, asset, plus, bonus, boon, blessing, virtue, profit, good.
– ANTONYMS: disadvantage.
□ **take advantage of 1** exploit. **2** make good use of.

advantageous adj. good or useful in a particular situation.
▷ SYNONYMS: **1 beneficial**, of benefit, helpful, of assistance, useful, of value, profitable, in someone's interests. **2 superior**, dominant, powerful, fortunate, lucky, favourable.
– ANTONYMS: disadvantageous.

advent n. **1** an arrival. **2** (**Advent**) the time before Christmas.

adventure n. an exciting and daring experience.
▷ SYNONYMS: **1 exploit**, escapade, undertaking, experience, incident. **2 excitement**, thrills, action, stimulation, risk, danger.
■ **adventurer** n.

adventurous adj. open to or involving new, interesting, or exciting experiences.
▷ SYNONYMS: **1 intrepid**, daring, daredevil, bold, fearless, brave; informal gutsy. **2 risky**, dangerous, perilous, hazardous, exciting.
– ANTONYMS: cautious, safe.

adverb n. a word adding information about an adjective, verb, or other adverb.
■ **adverbial** adj.

adversary n. (pl. **adversaries**) an opponent.
▷ SYNONYMS: **opponent**, rival, enemy, antagonist, challenger, contender, competitor, opposition, competition; literary foe.
– ANTONYMS: ally.
■ **adversarial** adj.

adverse adj. harmful; unfavourable.
▷ SYNONYMS: **1** *adverse weather:* **unfavourable**, inclement, bad, poor, untoward, inauspicious, unpropitious. **2** *adverse side effects:* **harmful**, dangerous, injurious, detrimental, deleterious, inimical. **3** *an adverse response:* **hostile**, unfavourable, antagonistic, unfriendly, negative.
– ANTONYMS: favourable, beneficial.
■ **adversely** adv.

USAGE Don't confuse **adverse** with **averse**, which means 'opposed to'.

adversity n. (pl. **adversities**) difficulty; misfortune.
▷ SYNONYMS: **misfortune**, bad luck, trouble, difficulty, hardship, disaster, suffering, sorrow, misery, woe, trials and tribulations.

advertise v. describe a product, service, etc. in the media to increase sales, or a job vacancy to encourage applications.
▷ SYNONYMS: **publicize**, make public, announce, broadcast, proclaim, trumpet, promote, market; informal push, plug, hype; N. Amer. informal ballyhoo.
■ **advertiser** n.

advertisement (or Brit. informal **advert**) n. a notice or display

advertising something.
▷ SYNONYMS: **announcement**, notice, commercial, promotion, blurb, write-up; informal ad, push, plug.

advice n. recommendations about future action.
▷ SYNONYMS: **guidance**, counselling, counsel, help, direction, recommendations, guidelines, suggestions, hints, tips, pointers.

advisable adj. prudent or sensible.
▷ SYNONYMS: **wise**, sensible, prudent, expedient, politic, in your best interests.
■ **advisability** n.

advise v. **1** recommend a course of action. **2** inform.
▷ SYNONYMS: **1 counsel**, give guidance, guide, offer suggestions, give hints/tips/pointers. **2 recommend**, advocate, suggest, urge. **3 inform**, notify, give notice, apprise, warn.
■ **advisory** adj.

adviser (or **advisor**) n. a person who gives advice.
▷ SYNONYMS: **counsellor**, aide, mentor, guide, consultant, confidant, confidante, guru.

advocate n. **1** a person who recommends a policy. **2** a person arguing a case on another's behalf.
▷ SYNONYMS: **champion**, upholder, supporter, apologist, backer, promoter, proponent, campaigner, lobbyist; N. Amer. booster.
– ANTONYMS: critic.
• v. recommend.
▷ SYNONYMS: **recommend**, champion, uphold, support, back, promote, campaign for, urge, subscribe to, speak for, argue for, lobby for.
– ANTONYMS: oppose.
■ **advocacy** n.

adze n. a tool like an axe, with an arched blade.

aegis /ee-jiss/ n. protection or support.

aeon /ee-on/ (US **eon**) n. a very long period of time.

aerate v. bring air into.

aerial n. a structure for transmitting or receiving radio or television signals.
• adj. **1** existing or taking place in the air. **2** by or from aircraft.

aerobatics pl. n. spectacular feats by aircraft in flight.
■ **aerobatic** adj.

aerobics pl. n. vigorous exercises intended to increase oxygen intake.
■ **aerobic** adj.

aerodrome n. Brit. a small airfield.

aerodynamics n. the science

concerned with the movement of objects through the air.
■ **aerodynamic** adj.

aerofoil n. Brit. a curved structure, such as a wing, designed to give an aircraft lift.

aeronautics n. the study or practice of travel through the air.
■ **aeronautical** adj.

aeroplane n. Brit. a powered flying vehicle with fixed wings.

aerosol n. a substance sealed in a container under pressure and released as a fine spray.

aerospace n. the technology and industry concerned with flight.

aesthete /eess-theet/ (US **esthete**) n. a person who appreciates art and beauty.

aesthetic /ess-thet-ik/ (US **esthetic**) adj. **1** concerned with beauty. **2** pleasant in appearance.
• n. **1** the aesthetic qualities of something. **2** (**aesthetics**) the philosophical study of beauty.
■ **aesthetically** adv.

aetiology /eet-i-ol-uh-ji/ (US **etiology**) n. the cause of a disease or condition.

afar adv. far away.

affable adj. good-natured and friendly.
■ **affability** n. **affably** adv.

affair n. **1** an event or series of events. **2** a person's responsibility or concern. **3** a love affair.
▷ SYNONYMS: **1 event**, incident, episode, case, matter, business. **2 business**, concern, matter, responsibility, problem; Brit. informal lookout. **3** (**affairs**) **transactions**, activities, dealings, undertakings, ventures, business. **4 relationship**, romance, fling, dalliance, liaison, involvement, amour; informal hanky-panky; Brit. informal carry-on.

affect v. **1** make a difference to. **2** pretend to feel, have, etc.
▷ SYNONYMS: **1 influence**, have an effect on, have an impact on, act on, change, alter, modify. **2 move**, touch, hit hard, make an impression on, upset, trouble, distress, disturb, shake. **3 put on**, assume, take on, adopt, feign.

USAGE Don't confuse **affect** and **effect**: **effect** mainly means 'a change which is the result of something', as in *the effects of global warming*.

affectation n. artificial and pretentious behaviour.
▷ SYNONYMS: **pretension**, pretentiousness, affectedness, artificiality,

posturing, airs and graces; Brit. informal side.

affected adj. false and intended to impress.

affection n. fondness or liking.
▷ SYNONYMS: **fondness**, love, liking, soft spot, tenderness, warmth, devotion, caring, attachment, friendship.

affectionate adj. loving.
▷ SYNONYMS: **fond**, loving, adoring, devoted, caring, tender, warm, friendly, demonstrative; informal touchy-feely, lovey-dovey.
– ANTONYMS: cold.
∎ **affectionately** adv.

affidavit n. a written statement sworn on oath to be true.

affiliate v. link a person or group to a larger organization.
▷ SYNONYMS: **associate**, unite, combine, join, join forces, link up, ally, align, amalgamate, merge.
∎ **affiliation** n.

affinity n. (pl. **affinities**) **1** a natural liking or understanding. **2** a close relationship between similar people or things.
▷ SYNONYMS: **empathy**, rapport, sympathy, accord, harmony, similarity, relationship, bond, closeness, understanding; informal chemistry.
– ANTONYMS: aversion.

affirm v. state firmly or publicly.
▷ SYNONYMS: **declare**, state, assert, proclaim, pronounce, attest, swear, maintain, avow.
– ANTONYMS: deny.
∎ **affirmation** n.

affirmative adj. agreeing with or to a statement or request.
▷ SYNONYMS: **positive**, assenting, consenting, approving, favourable.
– ANTONYMS: negative.

affix v. attach or fasten.
• n. a prefix or suffix.

afflict v. cause pain or suffering to.
▷ SYNONYMS: **trouble**, burden, distress, beset, harass, worry, oppress, torment, plague, bedevil.
∎ **affliction** n.

affluent adj. wealthy.
▷ SYNONYMS: **wealthy**, rich, prosperous, well off, well-to-do, of means; informal well heeled, rolling in it, made of money, loaded.
– ANTONYMS: poor.
∎ **affluence** n.

afford v. **1** have enough money or time for. **2** give or provide.
▷ SYNONYMS: **1 pay for**, run to, stretch to, stand, manage, spare. **2 give**, offer,

supply, provide, furnish, yield.
∎ **affordable** adj.

afforestation n. the planting of an area with trees to form a forest.

affray n. a fight or violent behaviour.

affront n. an insult.
• v. insult; offend.

Afghan n. a person from Afghanistan.
• adj. of Afghanistan.

aficionado /uh-fi-shuh-**nah**-doh/ n. (pl. **aficionados**) an enthusiastic fan of an activity.

afield adv. to or at a distance.

afloat adj. & adv. **1** floating. **2** out of debt or difficulty.

afoot adv. & adj. going on.

aforementioned adj. mentioned previously.

afraid adj. frightened.
▷ SYNONYMS: **1 frightened**, scared, terrified, fearful, nervous, petrified, intimidated, cowardly, faint-hearted; informal scared stiff, chicken; N. Amer. informal spooked. **2 reluctant**, hesitant, unwilling, slow, shy.
– ANTONYMS: brave, confident.
□ **I'm afraid** I regret.

afresh adv. in a new or different way.

African adj. of Africa or its people.
• n. an African person.

Afrikaans n. a language of southern Africa.

Afrikaner n. an Afrikaans-speaking white person in South Africa.

aft adv. & adj. at or towards the rear of a ship or aircraft.

after prep. **1** later than. **2** behind. **3** pursuing.
▷ SYNONYMS: **following**, subsequent to, at the end of, in the wake of.
• conj. & adv. in the time following an event.
□ **afterbirth** the placenta discharged from the womb after a birth. **after-effect** an effect that occurs some time after its cause. **aftermath** the results of an unpleasant event. **afternoon** the time between noon and evening. **aftershave** a scented lotion used after shaving. **afterthought** a thing thought of or added later. **afterwards** at a later time.

again adv. once more; another time.
▷ SYNONYMS: **once more**, another time, afresh, anew.

against prep. **1** in opposition to. **2** in or into contact with.
▷ SYNONYMS: **opposed to**, in opposition to, hostile to, antagonistic towards, unsympathetic to, at odds with, in

disagreement with; informal anti.

agar /ay-gah/ n. a substance obtained from seaweed, used as a thickener in foods.

agate /ag-uht/ n. a form of quartz with bands of colour.

age n. **1** the length of life or existence. **2** a period of history. **3** informal a very long time.
▷ SYNONYMS: **1 old age**, maturity, advancing years, elderliness, seniority, senescence. **2 era**, epoch, period, time, generation.
• v. (**ageing** or **aging**, **aged**) grow or cause to appear older.
▷ SYNONYMS: **1 mature**, mellow, ripen, soften, season, weather. **2 grow old**, decline, wither, fade

aged adj. **1** /ayjd/ of a specified age. **2** /ay-jid/ old.

ageism n. prejudice on the grounds of age.
■ **ageist** adj.

ageless adj. not ageing or appearing to age.

agency n. **1** an organization providing a particular service. **2** action or intervention.
▷ SYNONYMS: **business**, organization, company, firm, office, bureau.

agenda n. a list of items to be dealt with, esp. at a meeting.
▷ SYNONYMS: **programme**, schedule, to-do list, timetable, plan.

agent n. **1** a person who provides a particular service. **2** a person or thing producing an effect.
▷ SYNONYMS: **1 representative**, intermediary, middleman, negotiator, go-between, proxy, broker, emissary, envoy, spokesperson, delegate; informal rep. **2 spy**, secret agent, operative, mole; N. Amer. informal **spook**, G-man.

agent provocateur /a-zhon pruh-vo-kuh-**ter**/ n. a person who tempts others to do something illegal.

agglomerate v. collect into a mass.
■ **agglomeration** n.

aggrandize (or **-ise**) v. increase the power or status of.
■ **aggrandizement** n.

aggravate v. **1** make worse. **2** informal annoy.
▷ SYNONYMS: **1 worsen**, make worse, exacerbate, inflame, compound. **2 annoy**, antagonize, irritate, exasperate, nettle, provoke, get on someone's nerves; Brit. **rub up the wrong way**; informal needle, hack off, get someone's goat; Brit. informal **wind up**; N. Amer. informal **tick off**.
– ANTONYMS: alleviate, improve.

■ **aggravation** n.

aggregate n. a whole formed by combining several elements.
▷ SYNONYMS: **total**, sum, grand total, combined score.
• adj. formed or calculated by combining several items.
• v. combine into a whole.
■ **aggregation** n.

aggression n. hostile or violent behaviour or attitudes.
▷ SYNONYMS: **hostility**, belligerence, force, violence, attack.

aggressive adj. showing aggression.
▷ SYNONYMS: **1** aggressive behaviour: **violent**, confrontational, antagonistic, combative, pugnacious.
2 aggressive foreign policy: **warmongering**, warlike, warring, belligerent, bellicose, hawkish, militaristic, expansionist; informal gung-ho. **3** an aggressive sales campaign: **assertive**, forceful, pushy, vigorous, energetic, dynamic, audacious; informal in-your-face, feisty.
– ANTONYMS: peaceable, peaceful.
■ **aggressively** adv.

> USAGE Double g, double s: aggressive.

aggressor n. a person or country that begins hostilities.

aggrieved adj. having a grievance.

aghast adj. filled with horror.

agile adj. able to move quickly and easily.
▷ SYNONYMS: **1 nimble**, lithe, supple, graceful, fit, acrobatic, sprightly, spry. **2 alert**, sharp, acute, shrewd, astute, perceptive, quick.
– ANTONYMS: clumsy.
■ **agility** n.

agitate v. **1** worry; disturb. **2** campaign to arouse public concern. **3** stir briskly.
▷ SYNONYMS: **1 upset**, fluster, ruffle, disconcert, unnerve, disquiet, disturb, distress, unsettle, worry, perturb, trouble; informal rattle, faze. **2 shake**, whisk, beat, stir.
■ **agitation** n. **agitator** n.

AGM abbrev. Brit. annual general meeting.

agnostic n. a person who believes it is not possible to know whether or not God exists.
■ **agnosticism** n.

ago adv. before the present.

agog adj. eager and expectant.

agonize (or **-ise**) v. worry greatly.

agonizing (or **-ising**) adj. very painful or worrying.
SYNONYMS: an agonizing experience:

excruciating, painful, searing, harrowing, torturous.

agony n. (pl. **agonies**) extreme suffering.
▷ SYNONYMS: **suffering**, torture, pain, torment, anguish.

agoraphobia n. abnormal fear of open or public places.
■ **agoraphobic** adj. & n.

agrarian adj. of agriculture.

agree v. (**agreeing**, **agreed**) **1** have the same opinion. **2** be willing to do something suggested.
▷ SYNONYMS: **1** concur, see eye to eye, be in sympathy, be as one, be unanimous. **2** *they agreed to a ceasefire:* **consent**, assent, acquiesce, allow, approve; formal accede. **3** *your account does not agree with his:* **match**, correspond, conform, coincide, fit, tally, be consistent; informal square. **4** *we agreed on a price:* **decide on**, settle, arrive at, negotiate, shake hands on.
– ANTONYMS: disagree.
□ **agree with 1** be consistent with. **2** be good for.

agreeable adj. **1** pleasant. **2** willing to agree.
▷ SYNONYMS: **1** *an agreeable atmosphere:* **pleasant**, pleasing, enjoyable, pleasurable, nice, appealing, relaxing, friendly, congenial. **2** *an agreeable man:* **likeable**, amiable, affable, pleasant, nice, friendly, good-natured, sociable, genial. **3** **willing**, amenable, in agreement.
– ANTONYMS: unpleasant, disagreeable.
■ **agreeably** adv.

agreement n. **1** the sharing of opinion. **2** an arrangement agreed between people.
▷ SYNONYMS: **1** accord, concurrence, consensus, assent, acceptance, consent, acquiescence. **2** **contract**, treaty, pact, concordat, accord, settlement, understanding, bargain. **3** **correspondence**, consistency, compatibility, accord, similarity, resemblance, likeness.
– ANTONYMS: discord, disagreement.

agriculture n. the science or practice of farming.
▷ SYNONYMS: **farming**, cultivation, husbandry, agribusiness, agronomy.
■ **agricultural** adj.

WORD LINKS
agrarian relating to agriculture

---

agronomy n. the science of soil management and crop production.

aground adj. & adv. (of a ship) on the bottom in shallow water.

ague /**ay**-gyoo/ n. old use an illness involving fever and shivering.

ahead adv. further forward.

ahoy exclam. Naut. a call to attract attention.

aid n. help or support.
▷ SYNONYMS: **1** *with the aid of his colleagues:* **assistance**, support, help, backing, cooperation, a helping hand. **2** *humanitarian aid:* **relief**, assistance, support, subsidy, funding, donations, grants; historical alms.
– ANTONYMS: hindrance.
• v. give help or support.
▷ SYNONYMS: **help**, assist, be of service, support, encourage, further, boost, promote, facilitate.
– ANTONYMS: hinder.

aide n. an assistant to a political leader.
▷ SYNONYMS: **assistant**, helper, adviser, supporter, right-hand man/woman, adjutant, deputy, second in command, lieutenant.
□ **aide-de-camp** a military officer who assists a senior officer.

Aids n. acquired immune deficiency syndrome, a disease caused by the HIV virus, which breaks down the sufferer's defences against infection.

aikido /I-**kee**-doh/ n. a Japanese martial art.

ail v. cause suffering to.

aileron n. a hinged flap on an aircraft's wing.

ailing adj. in poor health.
▷ SYNONYMS: **1** ill, sick, unwell, sickly, poorly, weak, in poor/bad health, infirm. **2** *the ailing economy:* **failing**, weak, poor, fragile, unstable.
▷ ANTONYMS: healthy.

ailment n. a minor illness.
▷ SYNONYMS: **illness**, disease, disorder, affliction, malady, complaint, infirmity; informal bug, virus.

aim v. **1** point or direct towards. **2** try to achieve.
▷ SYNONYMS: **1** *he aimed the rifle:* **point**, direct, train, sight, line up. **2** *she aimed at the target:* **take aim**, fix on, zero in on, draw a bead on. **3** *this food is aimed at children:* **target**, intend, direct, design, tailor, market, pitch. **4** **intend**, mean, hope, want, plan, propose.
• n. a purpose or intention.
▷ SYNONYMS: **objective**, object, goal, end, target, design, desire, intention, intent, plan, purpose, ambition, aspiration, wish, dream, hope.

aimless adj. without purpose.
▷ SYNONYMS: **purposeless**, pointless,

directionless, undirected, random.
– ANTONYMS: purposeful.
■ **aimlessly** adv.

ain't contr. informal **1** am not; are not; is not. **2** has not; have not.

air n. **1** the mixture of gases surrounding the earth. **2** an impression. **3** (**airs**) an affected and condescending manner. **4** a tune.
▷ SYNONYMS: **1 breeze**, draught, wind, gust/puff of wind; literary zephyr. **2** *an air of defiance:* **look**, appearance, impression, aspect, manner, tone, feel, atmosphere, mood.
• v. **1** express an opinion publicly. **2** expose to fresh or warm air.
▷ SYNONYMS: **1 express**, voice, make public, articulate, give vent to, state, declare. **2 ventilate**, freshen, refresh, cool.

□ **airbag** a car safety device that fills with air in a collision to protect the driver. **airborne 1** carried by air. **2** (of an aircraft) flying. **air conditioning** a system that cools the air in a building or vehicle. **aircraft** a machine capable of flight. **aircraft carrier** a warship acting as a base for aircraft. **airfield** an area where aircraft can take off and land. **air force** the branch of the armed forces using aircraft. **air gun** a gun using compressed air to fire pellets. **airlift** an act of transporting supplies by aircraft. **airline** a company providing flights for public use. **airliner** a passenger aircraft. **airlock 1** an air bubble stopping the flow in a pipe or pump. **2** an airtight compartment. **airmail** mail carried overseas by air. **airman** a member of an air force. **airplane** US an aeroplane. **airport** an airfield with facilities for passengers and goods. **air raid** an attack by aircraft. **airship** a large aircraft filled with gas that is lighter than air. **airspace** the part of the air above a country. **airstrip** a strip of ground where aircraft can take off and land. **airtight** not allowing air to enter or escape. **airwaves** the radio frequencies used for broadcasting. **airway 1** a passage for air into the lungs. **2** a regular route for aircraft. **airworthy** (of an aircraft) safe to fly.

> **WORD LINKS**
> **aerial** relating to air

airless adj. lacking fresh air or ventilation.
▷ SYNONYMS: **stuffy**, close, muggy, humid, stifling, suffocating, oppressive, unventilated.
– ANTONYMS: airy.

airy adj. (**airier**, **airiest**) **1** well ventilated. **2** casual; dismissive.
▷ SYNONYMS: **spacious**, uncluttered, light, bright, well ventilated, fresh.
– ANTONYMS: airless, stuffy.
■ **airily** adv. **airiness** n.

aisle n. a passage between rows of seats or between shelves in a shop.
▷ SYNONYMS: **passage**, passageway, lane, path, gangway, walkway.

ajar adv. & adj. (of a door) slightly open.

aka abbrev. also known as.

akimbo adv. with hands on the hips and elbows turned outwards.

akin adj. related; similar.
▷ SYNONYMS: **similar**, related, close, near, comparable, equivalent, connected, alike, analogous.
– ANTONYMS: unlike.

alabaster n. a white translucent mineral.

à la carte adj. (of a menu) having separately priced dishes.

alacrity n. eager enthusiasm.

alarm n. **1** fear and anxiety. **2** a warning sound or device. **3** a warning of danger.
▷ SYNONYMS: **1 fear**, anxiety, apprehension, distress, agitation, consternation, fright, panic, trepidation. **2 warning**, danger signal, siren, bell, detector, sensor.
– ANTONYMS: calmness, composure.
• v. frighten or disturb.
▷ SYNONYMS: **frighten**, scare, panic, unnerve, distress, agitate, upset, disconcert, shock, disturb; informal rattle, spook; Brit. informal put the wind up.

alarmist n. a person who exaggerates a danger, causing unnecessary alarm.

alas exclam. an expression of sorrow.

albatross n. a very large seabird.

albeit conj. though.

albino n. (pl. **albinos**) a person or animal without pigment in the skin and hair.

album n. **1** a blank book for photos, stamps, etc. **2** a collection of recordings issued as a single item.

albumen n. egg white.

alchemy n. a medieval form of chemistry, concerned with trying to turn other metals into gold.
■ **alchemist** n.

alcohol n. **1** drinks containing an intoxicating liquid, such as wine, beer, and spirits. **2** this liquid.

alcoholic adj. of alcohol.
▷ SYNONYMS: **intoxicating**, strong, hard, stiff, fermented, brewed, distilled.

• n. a person addicted to drinking alcohol.

▷ SYNONYMS: **drunkard**, dipsomaniac, drunk, problem drinker, alcohol-abuser; informal lush, alky, dipso, soak, wino; Austral./NZ informal hophead.

■ **alcoholism** n.

alcopop n. a ready-mixed fizzy drink containing alcohol.

alcove n. a recess in a wall.

al dente /al den-tay/ adj. & adv. (of food) cooked so as to be still firm when bitten.

alder n. a tree of the birch family, which bears catkins.

alderman n. hist. a member of an English county or borough council.

ale n. beer.

alert adj. quick to notice and respond.

▷ SYNONYMS: **1 vigilant**, watchful, attentive, observant, wide awake, on the lookout, on your guard; informal keeping your eyes open/peeled. **2 quick-witted**, sharp, bright, quick, perceptive, on your toes; informal on the ball, quick on the uptake, all there, with it.

– ANTONYMS: inattentive.

• v. warn of a danger or problem.

▷ SYNONYMS: **warn**, notify, inform, apprise, forewarn, put on your guard; informal tip off.

• n. **1** a watchful state. **2** a warning.

▷ SYNONYMS: **1 vigilance**, watchfulness, attentiveness, alertness. **2 warning**, notification, notice, siren, alarm, signal.

A level n. (in the UK except Scotland) the higher of the two main levels of the GCE exam.

alfalfa n. a plant used as fodder for livestock.

alfresco adv. & adj. in the open air.

algae /al-jee, al-gee/ pl. n. simple plants with no true stems or leaves.

algebra n. a branch of mathematics using letters and symbols to represent quantities.

■ **algebraic** adj.

algorithm n. a step-by-step procedure for calculations.

alias adv. also called.

• n. a false identity.

alibi n. evidence that a person was elsewhere when a crime was committed.

alien adj. **1** foreign. **2** unfamiliar. **3** extraterrestrial.

▷ SYNONYMS: **foreign**, unfamiliar, unknown, peculiar, exotic, strange.

– ANTONYMS: native, familiar.

• n. **1** a foreigner. **2** a being from another world.

▷ SYNONYMS: **1 foreigner**, non-native, immigrant, émigré, stranger. **2 extra-terrestrial**, ET; informal little green man.

alienate v. **1** cause to feel isolated. **2** lose the support or sympathy of.

▷ SYNONYMS: **isolate**, distance, estrange, cut off, turn away, drive apart, set at variance/odds, drive a wedge between.

■ **alienation** n.

alight v. **1** get off a train or bus. **2** (of a bird) land on.

• adj. & adv. on fire.

▷ SYNONYMS: **burning**, ablaze, on fire, in flames, blazing, lit.

align v. **1** bring into the correct position. **2** ally yourself.

▷ SYNONYMS: **1 line up**, range, rank, straighten, even up, arrange, coordinate. **2** *he aligned himself with the workers:* **ally**, affiliate, associate, side, join forces, team up, band together, throw in your lot.

■ **alignment** n.

alike adj. similar.

▷ SYNONYMS: **similar**, much the same, analogous, corresponding, indistinguishable, identical, uniform, interchangeable; informal much of a muchness.

– ANTONYMS: different.

• adv. in a similar way.

alimentary canal n. the passage along which food passes through the body.

alimony n. financial support for a wife or husband after separation or divorce.

alive adj. **1** living; existing. **2** lively. **3** (**alive to**) aware of.

▷ SYNONYMS: **1 active**, in existence, functioning, in operation, operative, on the map. **2 alert**, awake, aware, conscious, mindful, heedful, sensitive.

– ANTONYMS: dead, unaware.

alkali n. a substance that turns litmus blue and neutralizes acids.

■ **alkaline** adj.

all adj. the whole quantity or extent of.

• pron. everything or everyone.

• adv. completely.

□ **all clear** a signal that danger is over. **all out** using all your effort.

allay v. reduce fear or concern.

▷ SYNONYMS: **reduce**, diminish, decrease, lessen, alleviate, assuage, ease, relieve, soothe, soften, calm.

– ANTONYMS: increase, intensify.

allegation n. an unproven accusation.
▷ SYNONYMS: **claim**, assertion, charge, accusation, contention.

allege v. claim without proof.
▷ SYNONYMS: **claim**, assert, accuse, contend, state, declare, maintain.

alleged adj. said, without proof, to have happened or to have done something.
▷ SYNONYMS: **reported**, supposed, so-called, claimed, professed, purported, ostensible, unproven.
■ **allegedly** adv.

allegiance n. loyal support.
▷ SYNONYMS: **loyalty**, faithfulness, fidelity, obedience, adherence, devotion; historical fealty.
– ANTONYMS: disloyalty, treachery.

allegory n. (pl. **allegories**) a story, picture, etc. with a hidden meaning.
■ **allegorical** adj. **allegorically** adv.

allegro /uh-**lay**-groh/ adv. Music briskly.

alleluia var. of HALLELUJAH.

allergen n. a substance causing an allergic reaction.

allergic adj. having or caused by an allergy.

allergy n. (pl. **allergies**) a condition causing an unfavourable bodily reaction to certain substances.

alleviate v. lessen pain or distress.
▷ SYNONYMS: **ease**, relieve, take the edge off, deaden, dull, lessen, reduce, moderate, allay, assuage, soothe, help, soften.
– ANTONYMS: aggravate.
■ **alleviation** n.

alley n. (pl. **alleys**) **1** a narrow street. **2** a long, narrow area for tenpin bowling or skittles.
▷ SYNONYMS: **passage**, passageway, alleyway, backstreet, lane, path, pathway, walk.

alliance n. a relationship formed between countries or groups for a joint purpose.
▷ SYNONYMS: **association**, union, league, confederation, federation, syndicate, consortium, cartel, coalition, partnership, relationship, marriage, cooperation.

allied adj. joined by an alliance.
▷ SYNONYMS: **associated**, united, related, connected, interconnected, linked, cooperating, in league, affiliated, combined, coupled, married.
– ANTONYMS: unrelated, independent.

alligator n. a large reptile similar to a crocodile.

alliteration n. the occurrence of the same letter or sound at the start of adjacent words.

■ **alliterative** adj.

allocate v. allot or assign.
▷ SYNONYMS: **allot**, assign, set aside, earmark, consign, distribute, apportion, share out, dole out, give out.
■ **allocation** n.

allot v. (**allotting**, **allotted**) give or share out.

allotment n. **1** Brit. a small plot of land rented for cultivating vegetables etc. **2** an allotted share.

allotrope n. each of the physical forms in which a chemical element can exist.

allow v. **1** let someone do something. **2** provide; set aside. **3** admit. **4** (**allow for**) take into account.
▷ SYNONYMS: **1 permit**, let, enable, authorize, give leave, license, entitle, consent to, assent to, acquiesce in, agree to, approve; informal give the go-ahead to, give the thumbs up to, OK, give the green light to; formal accede to. **2 set aside**, allocate, allot, earmark, designate, reserve.
– ANTONYMS: prevent, forbid.
■ **allowable** adj.

allowance n. **1** a permitted amount. **2** a sum of money paid regularly.
▷ SYNONYMS: **1 allocation**, allotment, quota, share, ration, grant, limit. **2 payment**, contribution, grant, handout, subsidy, maintenance.
□ **make allowances** be lenient because of mitigating circumstances.

alloy n. a mixture of two or more metals.
• v. mix metals to make an alloy.

all right adj. **1** unhurt. **2** satisfactory.
▷ SYNONYMS: **1 unhurt**, uninjured, unharmed, in one piece, safe and sound, alive and well; informal OK. **2 satisfactory**, acceptable, adequate, passable, reasonable; informal so-so, OK.

allspice n. a spice made from the fruit of a Caribbean tree.

allude v. (**allude to**) mention briefly or indirectly.
▷ SYNONYMS: **refer to**, touch on, suggest, hint, imply, mention, intimate.
■ **allusive** adj.

allure n. attractiveness or charm.

alluring adj. attractive; tempting.

allusion n. an indirect reference.
▷ SYNONYMS: **reference**, mention, suggestion, intimation, hint.

alluvium n. a fertile mix of clay, silt, etc. left by flood water.
■ **alluvial** adj.

ally n. (pl. **allies**) a person or country that cooperates with another.
▷ SYNONYMS: **associate**, colleague,

friend, confederate, partner, supporter.

– ANTONYMS: enemy, opponent.

• v. (**allying, allied**) **1** (**ally yourself with**) support. **2** (**allied to/with**) combined with.

▷ SYNONYMS: **unite**, combine, join up, join forces, band together, team up, collaborate, side, align yourself.

alma mater n. a person's former school, college, or university.

almanac n. **1** a calendar giving important dates and information about the sun, tides, etc. **2** a yearbook on a particular topic.

almighty adj. **1** all-powerful. **2** informal huge.

almond n. an edible oval nut.

almost adv. very nearly.

▷ SYNONYMS: **nearly**, (just about, practically, virtually, all but, as good as, close to, not quite; informal pretty much/well; literary well nigh, nigh on.

alms /ahmz/ pl. n. hist. charitable donations to the poor.

□ **almshouse** a house providing accommodation for the poor.

aloe n. a tropical plant with fleshy leaves.

aloft adv. up in or into the air.

alone adj. & adv. **1** on your own. **2** only.

▷ SYNONYMS: **by yourself**, on your own, unaccompanied, solo, single, isolated, solitary, lonely, deserted, abandoned, friendless; Brit. informal on your tod.

– ANTONYMS: accompanied.

along prep. & adv. **1** moving or extending on. **2** in company with others.

alongside prep. close to the side of.

aloof adj. unfriendly; distant.

▷ SYNONYMS: **distant**, detached, unfriendly, remote, unapproachable, reserved, unforthcoming, uncommunicative; informal standoffish.

– ANTONYMS: friendly.

■ **aloofness** n.

alopecia /a-luh-**pee**-shuh/ n. abnormal hair loss.

aloud adv. in an audible voice.

alpaca n. a long-haired South American llama.

alpha n. the first letter of the Greek alphabet (A, α).

• adj. dominant within a group.

alphabet n. an ordered set of letters representing the sounds of a language.

■ **alphabetical** adj. **alphabetically** adv. **alphabetize** (or **-ise**) v.

alpine adj. of high mountains.

already adv. **1** before this time. **2** sooner than expected.

Alsatian n. Brit. a German shepherd dog.

also adv. in addition.

▷ SYNONYMS: **too**, as well, besides, in addition, additionally, furthermore, further, moreover, into the bargain, on top of that, to boot.

altar n. a table used in religious services.

□ **altarpiece** a painting behind an altar.

alter v. make or become different.

▷ SYNONYMS: **change**, make/become different, adjust, adapt, amend, modify, revise, rework, redo, transform; informal tweak.

alteration n. a change or modification.

▷ SYNONYMS: **change**, adjustment, adaptation, modification, amendment, variation, transformation.

altercation n. a noisy dispute.

alternate v. occur in turn repeatedly.

▷ SYNONYMS: **1 be interspersed**, follow one another, take turns, take it in turns, oscillate, see-saw. **2 rotate**, swap, exchange, interchange.

• adj. **1** every other. **2** (of two things) repeatedly following and replacing each other.

▷ SYNONYMS: **every other**, every second, alternating.

□ **alternating current** an electric current that reverses direction many times a second.

■ **alternately** adv. **alternation** n.

alternative adj. **1** available as another choice. **2** unconventional.

▷ SYNONYMS: **1 different**, other, second, substitute, replacement, standby, emergency, reserve, backup, auxiliary, fallback; N. Amer. alternate. **2 unorthodox**, unconventional, nonconformist, radical, revolutionary, avant-garde; informal offbeat, way-out.

• n. an available option.

▷ SYNONYMS: **option**, choice, substitute, replacement.

■ **alternatively** adv.

alternator n. a dynamo that generates an alternating current.

although conj. in spite of the fact that.

altimeter n. an instrument in an aircraft showing altitude.

altitude n. height above sea level or ground level.

alto n. (pl. altos) the highest adult male or lowest female singing voice.

altogether adv. **1** completely. **2** in

total. **3** on the whole.

▷ SYNONYMS: **1 completely**, totally, entirely, absolutely, wholly, fully, thoroughly, utterly, perfectly, one hundred per cent, in all respects. **2 in all**, all told, in total.

altruism n. unselfishness.
■ **altruist** n. **altruistic** adj.

aluminium n. a lightweight silvery-grey metal.

always adv. **1** at all times. **2** forever.

▷ SYNONYMS: **1** *he's always late:* **every time**, all the time, without fail, consistently, invariably, regularly, habitually, unfailingly. **2** *she's always complaining:* **continually**, continuously, constantly, forever, all the time, day and night; informal 24-7. **3** *the place will always be dear to me:* **forever**, for good, for evermore, for ever and ever, until the end of time, eternally.

– ANTONYMS: never, seldom.

Alzheimer's disease /alts-hy-merz/ n. a disease which affects the functioning of the brain.

AM abbrev. amplitude modulation.

am see BE.

a.m. abbrev. before noon.

amalgam n. **1** a blend. **2** an alloy of mercury with another metal.

amalgamate v. combine or unite.

▷ SYNONYMS: **combine**, merge, unite, join, fuse, blend, meld, mix, incorporate.

– ANTONYMS: separate.

■ **amalgamation** n.

amass v. collect or accumulate.

▷ SYNONYMS: **gather**, collect, assemble, accumulate, stockpile, hoard.

amateur n. a person who does something as a pastime rather than as a profession.

▷ SYNONYMS: **non-professional**, non-specialist, layman, layperson, dilettante, dabbler.

amateurish adj. unskilful.

▷ SYNONYMS: **incompetent**, inept, inexpert, unprofessional, amateur, clumsy, crude, second-rate; Brit. informal bodged.

amatory adj. relating to love.

amaze v. astonish.

▷ SYNONYMS: **astonish**, astound, surprise, stun, stagger, nonplus, shock, startle, stop someone in their tracks, leave someone at a loss for words, leave speechless, dumbfound; informal bowl over, be flabbergasted, be gobsmacked, be thunderstruck.

amazement n. a feeling of great surprise.

▷ SYNONYMS: **astonishment**, surprise, shock, incredulity, speechlessness, awe, wonder.

amazing adj. very surprising.

▷ SYNONYMS: **astonishing**, astounding, surprising, stunning, staggering, breathtaking, awesome, awe-inspiring, sensational, remarkable, spectacular, stupendous, phenomenal, extraordinary, incredible, unbelievable; informal mind-blowing; literary wondrous.

Amazon n. a very tall, strong woman.

ambassador n. a diplomat representing their country abroad.

▷ SYNONYMS: **envoy**, emissary, representative, diplomat, minister, consul, attaché.

amber n. **1** a hard yellowish substance used in jewellery. **2** a yellowish colour.

ambidextrous adj. able to use either hand equally well.

ambience n. a place's atmosphere.

ambient adj. surrounding.

ambiguous adj. having more than one meaning.

▷ SYNONYMS: **vague**, unclear, ambivalent, double-edged, equivocal, inconclusive, enigmatic, cryptic.

– ANTONYMS: clear.

■ **ambiguity** n. **ambiguously** adv.

ambit n. scope or extent.

ambition n. a strong desire to achieve something.

▷ SYNONYMS: **1 drive**, determination, enterprise, initiative, eagerness, motivation; informal get-up-and-go. **2 aspiration**, desire, dream, intention, goal, aim, objective, plan.

ambitious adj. **1** determined to succeed. **2** intended to reach a high standard and so difficult to achieve.

▷ SYNONYMS: **1 aspiring**, determined, motivated, energetic, committed, purposeful, power-hungry; informal go-ahead, go-getting. **2 challenging**, exacting, demanding, formidable, difficult, hard, tough.

■ **ambitiously** adv.

ambivalent adj. having mixed feelings.
■ **ambivalence** n.

amble v. walk at a leisurely pace.

ambrosia n. something delicious.

ambulance n. a vehicle equipped to carry sick or injured people.

ambush n. a surprise attack by people lying in wait.
• v. make a surprise attack.

▷ SYNONYMS: **surprise**, waylay, trap, ensnare, attack, jump on, pounce on; N. Amer. bushwhack.

ameba US = AMOEBA.

ameliorate v. make better.
■ amelioration n.

amen exclam. so be it (used at the end of a prayer).

amenable adj. cooperative.

amend v. make minor changes or improvements to.
▷ SYNONYMS: **revise**, alter, change, modify, adapt, adjust, edit, rewrite, redraft, rephrase, reword.
□ make amends make up for a wrongdoing.
■ amendment n.

amenity n. (pl. **amenities**) a useful or desirable feature of a place.
▷ SYNONYMS: **facility**, service, resource, convenience, comfort.

American adj. of America or the USA.
• n. an American person.
□ American football a kind of football played with an oval ball.

Americanism n. a word or phrase originating in the USA.

amethyst /am-uh-thist/ n. a violet or purple precious stone.

amiable adj. friendly or likeable.
▷ SYNONYMS: **friendly**, affable, amicable, cordial, good-natured, nice, pleasant, agreeable, likeable, genial, good-humoured, companionable.
– ANTONYMS: unfriendly, disagreeable.
■ amiability n. amiably adv.

amicable adj. friendly.
■ amicably adv.

amid (or **amidst**) prep. in the middle of.

amino acid n. any of the organic compounds which form proteins.

amiss adj. not quite right.
□ take amiss be offended by.

amity n. friendly relations between people or countries.

ammeter n. an instrument for measuring electric current.

ammonia n. a strong-smelling gas which can be used to make a cleaning fluid.

ammonite n. a fossilized spiral shell of an extinct sea animal.

ammunition n. a supply of bullets and shells.

amnesia n. loss of memory.
■ amnesiac adj.

amnesty n. (pl. **amnesties**) a pardon for crimes against the state.
▷ SYNONYMS: **pardon**, reprieve, forgive-ness, release, discharge; informal let-off.

amniocentesis n. a test for possible abnormality in a fetus, involving the removal of some amniotic fluid.

amniotic fluid n. the fluid surrounding a fetus before birth.

amoeba /uh-mee-buh/ (US **ameba**) n. (pl. **amoebas** or **amoebae**) a single-celled organism that can change its shape.

amok (or **amuck**) adv. (**run amok**) be out of control.

among (or **amongst**) prep.
1 surrounded by. **2** included in.
3 shared by; between.

amoral adj. not concerned about right or wrong.

amorous adj. showing sexual desire.

amorphous adj. without definite shape.

amount n. **1** the total of something. **2** a quantity.
▷ SYNONYMS: **quantity**, number, total, aggregate, sum, quota, size, mass, weight, volume.
• v. (**amount to**) **1** add up to. **2** be equivalent to.

amp n. informal an amplifier.

ampere /am-pair/ n. a basic unit of electric current.

ampersand n. the sign & (= and).

amphetamine n. a drug used as a stimulant.

amphibian n. an animal such as a frog, able to live both on land and in water.

amphibious adj. living in or suited for both land and water.

amphitheatre n. a round open building with tiers of seats surrounding a central area.

ample adj. **1** quite enough; plentiful. **2** large.
▷ SYNONYMS: **1 enough**, sufficient, adequate, plenty of, more than enough, abundant, copious, profuse, lavish, liberal, generous; informal galore. **2 spacious**, full, capacious, roomy, voluminous, loose-fitting, baggy, sloppy.
– ANTONYMS: insufficient.
■ amply adv.

amplify v. (**amplifying**, **amplified**) **1** make a sound or electrical signal stronger. **2** explain in more detail.
▷ SYNONYMS: **1 make louder**, turn up, increase, raise. **2 expand**, enlarge on, elaborate on, develop, flesh out.
■ amplification n. amplifier n.

amplitude n. great size or extent.

ampoule n. a small sealed capsule containing liquid for injection.

amputate v. cut off a limb.
■ amputation n.

amuck var. of AMOK.

amulet n. something worn as

protection against evil.

amuse v. **1** cause to laugh. **2** make time pass pleasantly for.
▷ SYNONYMS: **1 entertain**, delight, divert, cheer, cheer up, please, charm, tickle; Brit. informal crack up, crease up. **2 occupy**, engage, busy, absorb, engross, entertain.
− ANTONYMS: bore.

amusement n. **1** the state of finding something funny. **2** something that provides entertainment and pleasure.
▷ SYNONYMS: **1 mirth**, merriment, hilarity, glee, delight. **2 entertain-ment**, pleasure, leisure, relaxation, fun, enjoyment, interest. **3 activity**, entertainment, diversion, pastime, recreation, game, sport.

amusing adj. causing laughter or providing entertainment.
▷ SYNONYMS: **funny**, comical, humorous, light-hearted, jocular, witty, droll, entertaining, diverting.

an adj. the form of 'a' used before vowel sounds.

anabolic steroid n. a synthetic hormone used to build up muscle.

anachronism n. something which seems to belong to another time.
■ anachronistic adj.

anaconda n. a large South American snake.

anaemia /uh-nee-mi-uh/ (US **anemia**) n. a shortage of red cells or haemoglobin in the blood.
■ anaemic adj.

anaerobic adj. not using oxygen from the air.

anaesthetic /an-iss-thet-ik/ (US **anesthetic**) n. a drug or gas that stops you feeling pain.

anaesthetist /uh-neess-thuh-tist/ (US **anesthetist**) n. a medical specialist who gives anaesthetics.
■ anaesthetize (or -ise) v.

anagram n. a word or phrase formed by rearranging the letters of another.

anal /ay-n'l/ adj. of the anus.

analgesic n. a pain-relieving drug.

analogous adj. comparable.

analogue adj. using a variable physical effect, e.g. voltage, to represent information, rather than a digital display.
• n. a comparable thing.

analogy n. (pl. **analogies**) **1** a comparison. **2** a partial similarity.
▷ SYNONYMS: **similarity**, parallel, corres-pondence, likeness, resemblance, correlation, relation, comparison.
− ANTONYMS: dissimilarity.

analyse (US **analyze**) v. **1** examine in detail. **2** psychoanalyse.
▷ SYNONYMS: **examine**, inspect, survey, study, scrutinize, investigate, probe, explore, evaluate, break down.
■ analyst n.

analysis n. (pl. **analyses**) **1** a detailed examination or study. **2** psychoanalysis.
▷ SYNONYMS: **examination**, inspection, study, scrutiny, breakdown, investi-gation, exploration, evaluation.

analytical (or **analytic**) adj. of analysis.
▷ SYNONYMS: **systematic**, logical, scien-tific, methodical, precise, meticulous, rigorous, investigative, enquiring.
■ analytically adv.

anarchist n. a person who believes that government should be abolished.
■ anarchism n.

anarchy n. complete disorder due to lack of government or control.
▷ SYNONYMS: **lawlessness**, disorder, chaos, pandemonium, mayhem, riot, revolution.
− ANTONYMS: order.
■ anarchic adj.

anathema /uh-na-thuh-muh/ n. something hated.

anatomize (or **-ise**) v. examine in detail.

anatomy n. (pl. **anatomies**) **1** the scientific study of the structure of the body. **2** a detailed analysis.
▷ SYNONYMS: **structure**, make-up, composition, constitution, form, body, physique.
■ anatomical adj. anatomically adv.

ancestor n. a person from whom someone is descended.
▷ SYNONYMS: **forefather**, forebear, predecessor, antecedent, progenitor, parent, grandparent.
− ANTONYMS: descendant.
■ ancestral adj.

ancestry n. (pl. **ancestries**) a person's ancestors.
▷ SYNONYMS: **ancestors**, forebears, forefathers, progenitors, antecedents, family tree, lineage, genealogy, parentage, blood.

anchor n. a heavy metal object for mooring a ship to the sea bottom.
• v. **1** moor with an anchor. **2** fix firmly.
□ **anchorage** a place where ships may anchor. **anchorman** a presenter of a live TV or radio programme.

anchovy n. (pl. **anchovies**) a small strong-tasting fish.

ancient adj. **1** of the very distant past. **2** very old.

a

▷ SYNONYMS: **1** *ancient civilizations:* **early**, prehistoric, primeval, primordial, primitive, bygone. **2** *an ancient custom:* **old**, age-old, venerable, time-worn, time-honoured, archaic, antique, obsolete. **3** *I feel ancient:* **antiquated**, antediluvian, geriatric; informal out of the ark; Brit. informal past its/your sell-by date, superannuated.
– ANTONYMS: contemporary, recent.

ancillary adj. **1** providing support. **2** extra.

and conj. used to connect words, clauses, or sentences.

andante /an-**dan**-tay/ adv. Music in moderately slow time.

androgynous /an-**dro**-ji-nuhss/ adj. partly male and partly female.

android n. a robot with a human appearance.

anecdotal adj. (of a story) not backed up by facts.

anecdote n. a short, entertaining true story.
▷ SYNONYMS: **story**, tale, narrative, reminiscence; informal yarn.

anemia US = ANAEMIA.

anemometer /an-i-**mom**-i-ter/ n. an instrument for measuring wind speed.

anemone /uh-**nem**-uh-ni/ n. a plant with red, purple, or white flowers.

anesthesia etc. US = ANAESTHESIA etc.

aneurysm /an-yuu-ri-z'm/ n. a swelling of the wall of an artery.

anew adv. **1** in a different way. **2** again.

angel n. **1** a spiritual being acting as a messenger of God. **2** a beautiful or good person.

angelic adj. **1** relating to angels. **2** very innocent, beautiful, or kind.
▷ SYNONYMS: **innocent**, pure, virtuous, saintly, cherubic.

angelica n. the candied stalks of a plant, used in cake decoration.

angelus n. a Roman Catholic prayer said at morning, noon, and sunset.

anger n. a strong feeling of displeasure.
▷ SYNONYMS: **annoyance**, vexation, temper, indignation, rage, fury, wrath, outrage; literary ire.
• v. make angry.
▷ SYNONYMS: **annoy**, irk, vex, enrage, incense, infuriate, rile, provoke, outrage.
– ANTONYMS: pacify, placate.

angina /an-**jy**-nuh/ (or **angina pectoris**) n. pain in the chest caused by an inadequate blood supply to the heart.

angle n. **1** the space between two lines or surfaces that meet. **2** a position from which someone or something is viewed. **3** a point of view.
▷ SYNONYMS: **1 gradient**, slope, slant, inclination. **2 corner**, point, fork, nook, crook, edge. **3 perspective**, point of view, viewpoint, standpoint, position, aspect, slant, direction, approach, tack.
• v. **1** place in a slanting position. **2** present from a certain point of view. **3** fish with a rod and line. **4** try to get by hinting.
▷ SYNONYMS: **tilt**, slant, twist, swivel, lean, tip, turn.
■ **angler** n.

Anglican adj. of the Church of England.
• n. a member of the Church of England.
■ **Anglicanism** n.

anglicize (or **-ise**) v. make English in character.

Anglo- comb. form English or British.

Anglo-Saxon n. **1** a Germanic inhabitant of England between the 5th century and the Norman Conquest. **2** the Old English language.

angora n. soft fabric made from the hair of a long-haired goat or rabbit.

angry adj. (**angrier**, **angriest**) feeling or showing anger.
▷ SYNONYMS: **furious**, irate, vexed, wrathful, irked, enraged, incensed, seething, infuriated, in a temper, fuming, apoplectic, outraged, cross; informal mad, hopping mad, up in arms, foaming at the mouth, steamed up, in a paddy; Brit. informal shirty; N. Amer. informal sore.
– ANTONYMS: pleased.
■ **angrily** adv.

angst n. great anxiety.

angstrom n. a unit of measurement for wavelengths.

anguish n. severe pain or distress.
▷ SYNONYMS: **agony**, pain, torment, torture, suffering, distress, woe, misery, sorrow, heartache.
– ANTONYMS: happiness.
■ **anguished** adj.

angular adj. having angles or sharp corners.

anhydrous adj. containing no water.

aniline /an-i-**leen**/ n. an oily liquid used in making dyes, drugs, and plastics.

animal n. **1** a living being with sense organs, that can move of its own accord. **2** a mammal, as opposed to a

bird, reptile, fish, or insect.
▷ SYNONYMS: **creature**, beast, living thing; (**animals**) wildlife, fauna.

> **WORD LINKS**
> **zoological** relating to animals or zoology
> **zoology** the scientific study of animals

animate v. **1** bring life or energy to. **2** make drawings into an animated film.
▷ SYNONYMS: **enliven**, energize, invigorate, liven up, inspire, fire, rouse, stir, galvanize, stimulate, excite, move, revitalize, revive, rejuvenate.
• adj. alive.
▷ SYNONYMS: **living**, alive, live, sentient, breathing.
– ANTONYMS: inanimate.
■ animator n.

animated adj. **1** lively. **2** (of a film) made using animation.
▷ SYNONYMS: **lively**, spirited, energetic, full of life, excited, enthusiastic, eager, alive, vigorous, vibrant, vivacious, exuberant, ebullient, bouncy, bubbly, perky; informal bright-eyed and bushy-tailed, full of beans, bright and breezy, chirpy, chipper.
– ANTONYMS: lethargic, lifeless.

animation n. **1** liveliness. **2** the technique of filming a sequence of drawings to give the appearance of movement.

animism n. the belief that all natural things have a soul.

animosity n. hatred or strong dislike.
▷ SYNONYMS: **hostility**, antipathy, antagonism, rancour, enmity, resentment, hatred, loathing, ill feeling/will, dislike, bad blood, animus.
– ANTONYMS: goodwill, friendship.

animus n. animosity.

anion n. an ion with a negative charge.

aniseed n. the seed of the **anise plant**, used as a flavouring.

ankle n. the joint connecting the foot with the leg.

anklet n. a chain or band worn round the ankle.

annals pl. n. a historical record of events year by year.

anneal v. toughen metal or glass by heating and slow cooling.

annex v. **1** take possession of another country's territory. **2** add or attach.
• n. (or **annexe**) a building attached or near to a main building.
■ annexation n.

annihilate v. destroy completely.
▷ SYNONYMS: **destroy**, obliterate, wipe out, eradicate, wipe off the face of the earth; informal rub out, snuff out.
– ANTONYMS: create.
■ annihilation n.

anniversary n. (pl. **anniversaries**) the date on which an event took place in a previous year.

annotate v. add explanatory notes to.
■ annotation n.

announce v. make a public statement about.
▷ SYNONYMS: **make public**, make known, report, declare, state, give out, publicize, broadcast, publish, advertise, circulate, proclaim, release, disclose, divulge.
■ announcer n.

announcement n. **1** a public statement. **2** the action of announcing something.
▷ SYNONYMS: **statement**, declaration, proclamation, pronouncement, bulletin, communiqué; N. Amer. advisory.

annoy v. make slightly angry.
▷ SYNONYMS: **irritate**, bother, vex, make cross, exasperate, irk, anger, antagonize, nettle, rankle with; Brit. rub up the wrong way; informal aggravate, peeve, miff, rile, needle, bug, hack off, wind up; Brit. informal nark, get on someone's wick; N. Amer. informal tee off, tick off.
– ANTONYMS: please.

annoyance n. the feeling or state of being annoyed.
▷ SYNONYMS: **irritation**, exasperation, vexation, indignation, anger, displeasure, chagrin.

annoyed adj. slightly angry.
▷ SYNONYMS: **irritated**, cross, angry, vexed, exasperated, irked, piqued, displeased, put out, disgruntled, nettled; informal aggravated, peeved, miffed, riled, hacked off, hot under the collar, narked, shirty; N. Amer. informal teed off, ticked off, sore.

annoying adj. causing annoyance.
▷ SYNONYMS: **irritating**, infuriating, exasperating, maddening, trying, tiresome, troublesome, irksome, vexing, galling; informal aggravating.

annual adj. yearly.
▷ SYNONYMS: **yearly**, once-a-year, year-long, twelve-month.
• n. **1** a plant living for a year or less. **2** a book published once a year.
■ annually adv.

annuity n. (pl. **annuities**) a fixed sum of money paid each year.

annul v. (**annulling**, **annulled**) declare a legal contract to be invalid.

a

▷ SYNONYMS: **declare invalid**, declare null and void, nullify, invalidate, void, repeal, revoke.
■ **annulment** n.

annular adj. ring-shaped.

Annunciation n. the announcement by the angel Gabriel to the Virgin Mary that she was to be the mother of Jesus.

anode n. an electrode with a positive charge.

anodized (or **-ised**) adj. (of metal) coated with a protective layer by electrolysis.

anodyne adj. bland and inoffensive. • n. a painkilling drug.

anoint v. smear or rub with oil as part of a religious ceremony.

anomaly n. (pl. **anomalies**) something differing from what is standard or normal.
▷ SYNONYMS: **oddity**, peculiarity, abnormality, irregularity, inconsistency, aberration, quirk.
■ **anomalous** adj.

anon adv. old use soon.

anonymous adj. having a name that is not publicly known.
▷ SYNONYMS: **unnamed**, nameless, unidentified, unknown, incognito, unsigned.
■ **anonymity** n. **anonymously** adv.

anorak n. a waterproof jacket with a hood.

anorexia (or **anorexia nervosa**) n. a disorder in which a person refuses to eat because they want to be thinner.
■ **anorexic** adj. & n.

another adj. & pron. **1** one more. **2** a different.

answer n. **1** something said or written in reaction to a question or statement. **2** the solution to a problem.
▷ SYNONYMS: **1 reply**, response, rejoinder, reaction, retort, riposte; informal comeback. **2 solution**, remedy, way out, explanation.
– ANTONYMS: question.
• v. **1** give an answer. **2** (**answer for**) be responsible for. **3** meet a need.
▷ SYNONYMS: **reply**, respond, rejoin, retort, riposte.
□ **answering machine** a machine which answers phone calls and records callers' messages.

answerable adj. having to account for something.
▷ SYNONYMS: **accountable**, responsible, liable.

ant n. a small insect that lives with many others in an organized group.

□ **anteater** a mammal that feeds on ants and termites.

antacid adj. (of a medicine) reducing excess acid in the stomach.

antagonism n. open hostility.

antagonist n. an opponent or enemy.

antagonistic adj. showing or feeling active opposition or hostility.
▷ SYNONYMS: **hostile**, opposed, antipathetic, ill-disposed, resistant, in disagreement; informal anti.

antagonize (or **-ise**) v. make someone hostile.
▷ SYNONYMS: **provoke**, intimidate, alienate, anger, annoy, irritate.
– ANTONYMS: pacify.

Antarctic adj. of the region around the South Pole.

ante n. a stake put up by a poker player before receiving cards.

antecedent n. **1** a thing that comes before another. **2** (**antecedents**) a person's ancestors.
• adj. previous.

antechamber n. an anteroom.

antedate v. precede in time.

antediluvian adj. **1** very old-fashioned. **2** of the time before the biblical Flood.

antelope n. a swift deer-like animal.

antenatal adj. Brit. before birth; during pregnancy.

antenna n. (pl. **antennae**) **1** an insect's feeler. **2** (pl. also **antennas**) an aerial.

anterior adj. at or nearer the front.

anteroom n. a small room leading to a main one.

anthem n. **1** a song chosen by a country to express patriotic feelings. **2** a piece of music to be sung in a religious service.
▷ SYNONYMS: **hymn**, song, chorale, chant, psalm, canticle.

anther n. the part of a flower's stamen that contains pollen.

anthology n. (pl. **anthologies**) a collection of poems or other pieces of writing or music.
▷ SYNONYMS: **collection**, selection, compendium, compilation, miscellany, treasury.

anthracite n. hard coal that burns with little flame and smoke.

anthrax n. a serious disease of sheep and cattle, able to be transmitted to humans.

anthropoid adj. of apes that resemble humans, e.g. chimpanzees.

anthropology n. the study of human origins, societies, and cultures.
■ **anthropological** adj. **anthropologist** n.

anthropomorphic adj. treating a god, animal, or object as if they were human.
■ **anthropomorphism** n.

anti- prefix **1** opposed to. **2** preventing or relieving.

antibiotic n. a medicine that kills bacteria.

antibody n. (pl. **antibodies**) a protein produced in the blood in reaction to harmful substances.

anticipate v. **1** be aware of and prepared for a future event. **2** expect or look forward to.
▷ SYNONYMS: **1 expect**, foresee, predict, be prepared for, bargain on, reckon on; N. Amer. informal figure on. **2 look forward to**, await, long for; informal lick your lips.
■ **anticipation** n. **anticipatory** adj.

anticlimax n. a disappointing end to exciting events.
▷ SYNONYMS: **let-down**, disappointment, comedown, non-event, disillusion-ment, bathos; Brit. damp squib; informal washout.

anticlockwise adv. & adj. Brit. in the opposite direction to the rotation of the hands of a clock.

antics pl. n. silly or playful behaviour.
▷ SYNONYMS: **capers**, pranks, larks, high jinks, skylarking, horseplay, clowning; Brit. informal monkey tricks.

anticyclone n. an area of high atmospheric pressure around which air slowly circulates.

antidote n. a medicine taken to counteract a poison.
▷ SYNONYMS: **remedy**, cure, solution, countermeasure, corrective.

antifreeze n. a liquid added to water to prevent it from freezing.

antigen n. a harmful substance which causes the body to produce antibodies.

anti-hero n. a central character in a story, film, etc. who is either ordinary or unpleasant.

antihistamine n. a drug used in treating allergies.

antimacassar n. a cloth used to protect the back of a chair from dirt.

antimony n. a silvery-white metallic element.

antioxidant n. a substance that counteracts oxidation.

antipasto n. (pl. **antipasti**) an Italian hors d'oeuvre.

antipathy n. (pl. **antipathies**) strong dislike.
▷ SYNONYMS: **hostility**, antagonism,

animosity, aversion, animus, distaste, dislike, hatred, abhorrence, loathing.
– ANTONYMS: affinity, liking.
■ **antipathetic** adj.

antiperspirant n. a substance that reduces sweating.

antiphonal adj. sung or recited alternately between two groups.

Antipodes /an-ti-puh-deez/ pl. n. Australia and New Zealand.
■ **Antipodean** adj. & n.

antiquarian adj. relating to the collection of antiques or rare books.

antiquated adj. old-fashioned or outdated.
▷ SYNONYMS: **outdated**, outmoded, outworn, behind the times, old, old-fashioned, anachronistic, antediluvian; informal out of the ark, superannuated, clunky.
– ANTONYMS: modern.

antique n. an old and valuable object.
▷ SYNONYMS: **collector's item**, museum piece, period piece, antiquity.
● adj. valuable because of its age.
▷ SYNONYMS: **antiquarian**, old, collect-able, vintage, classic.
– ANTONYMS: modern.

antiquity n. (pl. **antiquities**) **1** the distant past. **2** an object from the distant past.

anti-Semitism n. prejudice against Jews.
■ **anti-Semitic** adj.

antiseptic adj. preventing the growth of microorganisms that cause disease or infection.
● n. an antiseptic substance.

antisocial adj. **1** acting in a way that is unacceptable to others. **2** avoiding the company of other people.
▷ SYNONYMS: **1** antisocial behaviour: **objectionable**, offensive, unaccept-able, disruptive, rowdy. **2** I'm feeling a bit antisocial: **unsociable**, unfriendly, uncommunicative, reclusive, misanthropic.
– ANTONYMS: acceptable, sociable.

antithesis n. (pl. **antitheses**) a person or thing that is the direct opposite of another.
■ **antithetical** adj.

antitoxin n. a substance that neutralizes a toxin.

antler n. each of a pair of branched horns on a male deer.

antonym n. a word opposite in meaning to another.

anus /ay-nuhss/ n. the opening through which solid waste leaves the body.

anvil n. an iron block on which metal

is hammered and shaped.

anxiety n. (pl. **anxieties**) an anxious feeling or state.
▷ SYNONYMS: **worry**, concern, apprehension, unease, fear, disquiet, doubts, nervousness, nerves, tension, stress, angst; informal butterflies, the jitters, collywobbles.

anxious adj. **1** worried or uneasy. **2** very eager.
▷ SYNONYMS: **1 worried**, concerned, apprehensive, fearful, uneasy, disturbed, fretful, agitated, nervous, on edge, worked up, jumpy, tense, distraught; informal uptight, with butterflies in your stomach, jittery, twitchy; N. Amer. informal antsy. **2** she was anxious for news: **eager**, keen, itching, impatient, desperate.
– ANTONYMS: unconcerned.
■ **anxiously** adv.

any adj. & pron. **1** one or some. **2** whichever or whatever you choose.

anybody pron. anyone.

anyhow adv. **1** anyway. **2** in a careless way.

anyone pron. any person or people.

anything pron. a thing of any kind.

anyway adv. **1** used to emphasize something just said or to change the subject. **2** nevertheless.

anywhere adv. in or to any place.
• pron. any place.

AOB abbrev. any other business.

aorta /ay-or-tuh/ n. the main artery carrying blood from the heart.

apace adv. quickly.

apart adv. **1** separated by a distance. **2** into pieces.
□ **apart from** except for.

apartheid /uh-par-tayt/ n. the former official system of racial segregation in South Africa.

apartment n. **1** a flat. **2** a set of private rooms in a large house.
▷ SYNONYMS: **1 flat**, penthouse; Austral. home unit. **2 suite**, rooms, quarters, accommodation.

apathetic adj. not interested or enthusiastic.
▷ SYNONYMS: **uninterested**, indifferent, unenthusiastic, unconcerned, unmoved, uninvolved, unemotional, unresponsive, lukewarm, half-hearted, lethargic; informal couldn't-care-less.
– ANTONYMS: enthusiastic.

apathy n. lack of interest or enthusiasm.

ape n. an animal like a monkey but without a tail, e.g. a chimpanzee.
• v. imitate.

aperitif n. an alcoholic drink taken before a meal.

aperture n. an opening, esp. one letting in light.
▷ SYNONYMS: **opening**, hole, gap, slit, slot, vent, crevice, chink, crack; technical orifice.

apex n. the top or highest point.

aphasia /uh-**fay**-zi-uh/ n. inability to understand or produce speech due to brain damage.

aphid /**ay**-fid/ n. a small insect feeding on the sap of plants.

aphorism /**af**-uh-ri-z'm/ n. a short clever phrase which makes a true point.

aphrodisiac /af-ruh-**diz**-i-ak/ n. a food, drink, or drug that arouses sexual desire.

apiary n. (pl. **apiaries**) a place where bees are kept.
■ **apiarist** n.

apiece adv. for or by each one.

aplomb /uh-**plom**/ n. calm self-confidence.

apocalypse n. **1** an event involving great destruction. **2** (**the Apocalypse**) the final destruction of the world, as described in the biblical book of Revelation.
■ **apocalyptic** adj.

Apocrypha n. those books of the Old Testament not accepted as part of Hebrew scripture.

apocryphal adj. (of a story) widely circulated but unlikely to be true.

apogee /**ap**-uh-jee/ n. **1** the highest point. **2** the point in the moon's orbit furthest from the earth.

apologetic adj. admitting and showing regret for a wrongdoing.
▷ SYNONYMS: **sorry**, regretful, contrite, remorseful, penitent, repentant, shamefaced, sheepish.
– ANTONYMS: unrepentant.
■ **apologetically** adv.

apologist n. a person who defends something controversial.

apologize (or **-ise**) v. express regret for a wrongdoing.
▷ SYNONYMS: **say sorry**, ask forgiveness, ask for pardon, eat humble pie.

apology n. (pl. **apologies**) **1** an expression of regret for a wrongdoing. **2** (**an apology for**) a very poor example of.

▷ **apoplectic** adj. **1** furious. **2** dated of apoplexy.

apoplexy n. (pl. **apoplexies**) **1** extreme

anger. **2** Med., dated a stroke.

apostasy /uh-poss-tuh-si/ n.
abandonment of a belief or principle.

apostate /ap-uh-stayt/ n. a person
who abandons a belief or principle.

apostle n. **1** (**Apostle**) each of the
twelve chief disciples of Jesus. **2** an
enthusiastic supporter of an idea or
cause.
■ **apostolic** adj.

apostrophe /uh-**poss**-truh-fi/ n. a
punctuation mark (') used to indicate
either possession or the omission of
letters or numbers.

apothecary n. (pl. **apothecaries**) old
use a person who prepared and sold
medicines.

apotheosis /uh-po-thi-**oh**-siss/ n.
(pl. **apotheoses**) the highest level of
something.

appal v. (**appalling**, **appalled**) dismay
or horrify.
▷ SYNONYMS: **horrify**, shock, dismay,
distress, outrage, scandalize, disgust,
revolt, sicken, nauseate, offend, make
someone's blood run cold.

appalling adj. shockingly bad.
▷ SYNONYMS: **1** *an appalling crime:*
horrific, shocking, horrible, terrible,
awful, dreadful, ghastly, hideous,
horrendous, frightful, atrocious,
abominable, outrageous. **2** *your
schoolwork is appalling:* **dreadful**,
terrible, atrocious, deplorable,
hopeless, lamentable; informal rotten,
crummy, woeful, useless, lousy,
abysmal, dire; Brit. informal chronic,
shocking.

apparatus n. equipment for a
particular activity or purpose.
▷ SYNONYMS: **equipment**, gear, tackle,
mechanism, appliance, device, instrument, machine, tool.

apparel n. clothing.

apparent adj. **1** clearly seen or
understood. **2** seeming real, but not
necessarily so.
▷ SYNONYMS: **1** **evident**, plain, obvious,
clear, manifest, visible, discernible, noticeable, perceptible,
unmistakable, patent. **2** **seeming**,
ostensible, outward, superficial.
– ANTONYMS: unclear, real.
■ **apparently** adv.

apparition n. a ghost.

appeal v. **1** make a serious or earnest
request. **2** be attractive or interesting.
3 refer a decision to a higher court.
▷ SYNONYMS: **ask**, request, call, petition,
plead, entreat, beg, implore, beseech.
● n. **1** an act of appealing.
2 attractiveness or interest.

▷ SYNONYMS: **1** **plea**, request, petition,
entreaty, cry, call, cri de cœur.
2 **attraction**, allure, charm, fascination, magnetism, pull.

appealing adj. attractive or
interesting.
▷ SYNONYMS: **attractive**, engaging,
alluring, enchanting, captivating,
bewitching, fascinating, tempting,
enticing, irresistible, charming; Brit.
informal **tasty**.

appear v. **1** become visible. **2** seem.
▷ SYNONYMS: **1** **become visible**, come
into view, materialize, turn up, show
up. **2** *differences were beginning to
appear:* **be revealed**, emerge, surface,
manifest itself, become apparent/
evident, come to light, arrive, arise,
crop up, show up. **3** *they appeared
completely devoted:* **seem**, look, give
the impression of being, come across
as, strike someone as.
– ANTONYMS: vanish.

appearance n. **1** the way that
someone or something looks or
seems. **2** an act of appearing.
▷ SYNONYMS: **1** *her dishevelled appearance:* **look**, air, aspect, mien,
expression. **2** *an appearance of
respectability:* **impression**, air, show,
semblance, illusion, facade, front,
pretence. **3** **occurrence**, manifestation, emergence, arrival, development, materialization.

appease v. pacify someone by
agreeing to their demands.
▷ SYNONYMS: **placate**, conciliate, pacify,
mollify, reconcile, win over; informal
sweeten.
– ANTONYMS: provoke.
■ **appeasement** n.

appellation n. a name or title.

append v. add to the end of a
document.

appendage n. a thing attached to
something larger or more important.

appendectomy n. (pl.
appendectomies) the surgical
removal of the appendix.

appendicitis n. inflammation of the
appendix.

appendix n. (pl. **appendices** or
appendixes) **1** a small tube of tissue
attached to the large intestine. **2** a
section of additional information at
the end of a book.
▷ SYNONYMS: **supplement**, addendum,
postscript, codicil, coda, epilogue,
afterword, tailpiece.

appertain v. relate to.

appetite n. **1** desire for food. **2** a
liking or inclination.

a

▷ SYNONYMS: **1 hunger**, taste, palate, stomach. **2** *my appetite for learning*: desire, liking, hunger, thirst, longing, yearning, passion, enthusiasm, keenness, eagerness; informal yen.

appetizer (or **-iser**) n. something eaten or drunk to stimulate the appetite.

appetizing (or **-ising**) adj. stimulating the appetite.

▷ SYNONYMS: **mouth-watering**, inviting, tempting, tasty, delicious, flavoursome, toothsome, delectable; informal scrumptious, scrummy, yummy, moreish.

applaud v. show approval, esp. by clapping.

▷ SYNONYMS: **1 clap**, give someone a standing ovation, put your hands together; informal give someone a big hand. **2 praise**, congratulate, commend, salute, welcome, celebrate, approve of.

– ANTONYMS: boo, criticize.

■ applause n.

apple n. a round fruit with crisp flesh.

appliance n. a machine for use in the home.

▷ SYNONYMS: **device**, machine, instrument, gadget, tool, contraption, apparatus, mechanism, contrivance, labour-saving device; informal gizmo.

applicable adj. relevant; appropriate.

▷ SYNONYMS: **relevant**, appropriate, pertinent, apposite, material, fitting, suitable, apt.

– ANTONYMS: inappropriate, irrelevant.

■ applicability n.

applicant n. a person who applies for something.

▷ SYNONYMS: **candidate**, interviewee, contender, entrant, claimant, petitioner, job-seeker.

application n. **1** a formal request. **2** the act of applying something. **3** continued effort. **4** a computer program designed for a particular purpose.

▷ SYNONYMS: **1 request**, appeal, petition, approach, claim, demand. **2 implementation**, use, exercise, employment, execution, enactment. **3 hard work**, diligence, industry, effort, commitment, dedication, devotion, perseverance, persistence, concentration.

applicator n. a device for inserting or spreading something.

applied adj. practical rather than theoretical.

appliqué /uh-**plee**-kay/ n. needlework

in which fabric shapes are attached to a fabric background.

apply v. (**applying**, **applied**) **1** request formally. **2** bring into operation. **3** be relevant. **4** spread on a surface. **5** (**apply yourself**) concentrate on a task.

▷ SYNONYMS: **1** *300 people applied for the job*: **put in**, bid, try, audition, seek, solicit, claim, request, ask, petition. **2** *the Act did not apply to Scotland*: **be relevant**, pertain, appertain, relate, concern, affect, involve, cover, touch, deal with, have a bearing on. **3 implement**, put into practice, introduce. **4 put on**, rub in/on, work in, spread, smear on, slap on. **5 exert**, administer, use, exercise, employ, utilize, bring to bear.

appoint v. give a job or role to.

▷ SYNONYMS: **nominate**, name, designate, install, commission, engage, co-opt, select, choose, elect, vote in.

■ appointee n.

appointed adj. **1** prearranged. **2** equipped or furnished.

▷ SYNONYMS: **scheduled**, arranged, prearranged, specified, agreed, designated, set, allotted, fixed.

appointment n. **1** an arrangement to meet. **2** a job.

▷ SYNONYMS: **1 meeting**, engagement, interview, consultation, rendezvous, date, assignation; literary tryst. **2 nomination**, naming, designation, installation, commissioning, engagement, co-option, selection, election. **3 job**, post, position, situation, place, office.

apportion v. share out.

apposite /ap-puh-zit/ adj. very appropriate.

apposition n. Grammar a relationship in which a word or phrase is placed next to another so as to qualify or explain it (e.g. *my friend Sue*).

appraisal n. an act of appraising someone or something.

▷ SYNONYMS: **assessment**, evaluation, estimation, judgement, consideration.

appraise v. assess the quality or value of.

▷ SYNONYMS: **assess**, evaluate, judge, consider, rate; informal size up.

appreciable adj. considerable.

■ appreciably adv.

appreciate v. **1** recognize the value of. **2** understand fully. **3** be grateful for. **4** rise in value.

▷ SYNONYMS: **1 value**, admire, respect, think highly of, think much of, be grateful for, be glad of. **2 recognize**,

realize, know, be aware of, be conscious of, be sensitive to, understand, sympathize with. **3 increase**, gain, grow, rise, go up, soar.
– ANTONYMS: disparage, depreciate.

appreciation n. **1** recognition of the worth of something. **2** gratitude. **3** a favourable written assessment of a person or their work. **4** increase in value.
▷ SYNONYMS: **1 acknowledgement**, recognition, realization, knowledge, awareness, consciousness, understanding. **2 gratitude**, thanks, gratefulness. **3 review**, critique, criticism, analysis, assessment, evaluation, judgement. **4 increase**, gain, growth, rise, inflation, escalation.
– ANTONYMS: ingratitude, depreciation.

appreciative adj. feeling or showing gratitude or pleasure.
▷ SYNONYMS: **1 grateful**, thankful, obliged, indebted. **2** *an appreciative audience:* **admiring**, enthusiastic, approving, complimentary.

apprehend v. **1** arrest a suspect. **2** understand.

apprehension n. **1** worry or anxiety. **2** understanding. **3** an arrest.
▷ SYNONYMS: **1 anxiety**, worry, unease, nervousness, nerves, misgivings, disquiet, concern, trepidation. **2 arrest**, capture, seizure, detention.
– ANTONYMS: confidence.

apprehensive adj. worried or anxious.
▷ SYNONYMS: **anxious**, worried, uneasy, nervous, concerned, fearful.
– ANTONYMS: confident.
■ **apprehensively** adv.

apprentice n. a person learning a trade.
▷ SYNONYMS: **trainee**, learner, probationer, novice, beginner, tyro, starter, pupil, student; informal rookie; N. Amer. informal tenderfoot, greenhorn.
– ANTONYMS: veteran.
■ **apprenticeship** n.

apprise v. inform.

approach v. **1** come near to. **2** make a proposal or request to. **3** start to deal with.
▷ SYNONYMS: **1 move towards**, near, come near, close in on, close with, gain on. **2 speak to**, talk to, sound out, proposition, appeal to. **3 tackle**, address, manage, deal with, set about, get to grips with, go about, start work on.
– ANTONYMS: leave.
• n. **1** a way of dealing with something. **2** the act of approaching.

3 a way leading to a place.
▷ SYNONYMS: **1 method**, procedure, technique, modus operandi, style, way, strategy, tactic, system, means, line of action. **2 proposal**, submission, application, appeal, plea, request, overture, proposition. **3 advance**, arrival, appearance. **4 driveway**, drive, road, path, entry, way.

approachable adj. easy to talk to.
▷ SYNONYMS: **1 friendly**, welcoming, pleasant, agreeable, affable, sympathetic, congenial. **2 accessible**, reachable, attainable; informal get-at-able.
– ANTONYMS: aloof, inaccessible.

approbation n. approval.

appropriate adj. suitable; proper.
▷ SYNONYMS: **suitable**, proper, fitting, seemly, apt, right, convenient, opportune, relevant, apposite.
– ANTONYMS: inappropriate.
• v. **1** take and use without permission. **2** set money aside for a purpose.
▷ SYNONYMS: **seize**, commandeer, requisition, expropriate, usurp, take over, hijack, steal; informal swipe, nab; Brit. informal pinch, nick.
■ **appropriately** adv. **appropriation** n.

approval n. **1** a favourable opinion of someone or something. **2** official acceptance.
▷ SYNONYMS: **1 acceptance**, agreement, consent, assent, permission, rubber stamp, sanction, blessing, endorsement, ratification, authorization; informal the go-ahead, the green light, the OK, the thumbs up. **2 favour**, liking, appreciation, admiration, regard, esteem, respect.
– ANTONYMS: refusal, disapproval.

approve v. **1** regard as good or acceptable. **2** officially accept as satisfactory.
▷ SYNONYMS: **agree to**, accept, consent to, assent to, give your blessing to, bless, ratify, sanction, endorse, authorize, validate, pass, rubber-stamp; informal give the go-ahead to, give the green light to, give the OK to, give the thumbs-up to.
– ANTONYMS: refuse.

approximate adj. almost but not completely accurate.
▷ SYNONYMS: **estimated**, rough, imprecise, inexact, broad, loose; N. Amer. informal ballpark.
– ANTONYMS: precise.
• v. be very similar to.
■ **approximation** n.

approximately adv. roughly; not exactly.

a

▷ SYNONYMS: **roughly**, about, around, circa, round about, more or less, nearly, almost, approaching; Brit. getting on for; N. Amer. informal in the ballpark of.

APR abbrev. annual percentage rate.

après-ski n. social activities after skiing.

apricot n. an orange-yellow fruit like a small peach.

April n. the fourth month.

a priori adj. & adv. using known facts to decide what an unknown outcome will be.

apron n. **1** a garment worn to protect the front of clothes from dirt. **2** an area on an airfield for manoeuvring or parking aircraft. **3** a strip of stage extending in front of the curtain.

apropos /a-pruh-**poh**/ prep. (**apropos of**) with reference to.

apse n. a recess with a domed or arched roof at the end of a church.

apt adj. **1** appropriate. **2** (**apt to**) tending to.

▷ SYNONYMS: **1 suitable**, fitting, appropriate, relevant, apposite, felicitous; Brit. informal spot on. **2 inclined**, given, likely, liable, prone. **3 clever**, quick, bright, sharp, smart, able, gifted, talented.

– ANTONYMS: inappropriate.

■ **aptly** adv.

aptitude n. a natural ability.

▷ SYNONYMS: **talent**, gift, flair, bent, skill, knack, facility, ability, capability, potential, capacity, faculty.

aqualung n. a piece of equipment enabling divers to breathe underwater.

aquamarine n. a bluish-green precious stone.

aquaplane v. (of a vehicle) slide uncontrollably on a wet surface.

aquarium n. (pl. **aquaria** or **aquariums**) a water-filled glass tank for keeping fish in.

aquatic adj. taking place or living on or in water.

aqueduct n. a structure carrying water across country.

aqueous /ay-kwee-uhss/ adj. of or containing water.

aquifer n. a body of rock that holds water or through which water flows.

aquiline adj. **1** (of a nose) narrow and curved. **2** like an eagle.

Arab n. a member of a people of the Middle East and North Africa.

■ **Arabian** n. & adj.

arabesque n. **1** a ballet posture in which one leg is extended backwards and the arms are outstretched. **2** an ornamental design of intertwined lines.

Arabic n. the language of the Arabs.

● adj. of the Arabs.

□ **Arabic numerals** the numerals 0, 1, 2, 3, etc.

arable adj. (of land) suitable for growing crops.

arachnid n. a creature of a class including spiders and scorpions.

arbiter n. **1** a person who settles a dispute. **2** a person whose taste or opinions are influential.

arbitrary adj. not seeming to be based on a reason or plan.

▷ SYNONYMS: **random**, unpredictable, capricious, subjective, whimsical, wanton, motiveless, irrational, groundless, unjustified.

■ **arbitrarily** adv.

arbitration n. the settling of a dispute by an officially appointed person or body.

▷ SYNONYMS: **adjudication**, judgement, mediation, conciliation, intervention.

■ **arbitrate** v.

arbitrator n. a person or body officially appointed to settle a dispute.

▷ SYNONYMS: **adjudicator**, arbiter, judge, referee, umpire, mediator, go-between.

arboreal adj. of or living in trees.

arboretum n. (pl. **arboretums** or **arboreta**) a place where trees are grown for study and display.

arbour (US **arbor**) n. a place or seat in a garden shaded by trees or climbing plants.

arc n. **1** a curve forming part of the circumference of a circle. **2** a curving movement through the air. **3** a glowing electrical discharge between two points.

▷ SYNONYMS: **curve**, arch, bow, curl, crescent, semicircle, half-moon.

arcade n. **1** a covered passage with arches along one or both sides. **2** a covered walk with shops along the sides.

arcane adj. secret and mysterious.

arch n. **1** a curved structure supporting a bridge, roof, or wall. **2** the inner side of the foot.

▷ SYNONYMS: **archway**, vault, span.

● v. form an arch.

▷ SYNONYMS: **curve**, arc, bend, bow, crook, hunch.

● adj. playfully knowing.

□ **archway** a passageway under an arch.

arch- comb. form chief, main: *arch-enemy*.

archaeology (US **archeology**) n. the study of ancient history by examining objects dug up from the ground.
■ **archaeological** adj. **archaeologist** n.

archaic adj. belonging to former or ancient times.

archaism n. an old or old-fashioned word or phrase.

archangel n. an angel of high rank.

archbishop n. a bishop of the highest rank.

archdeacon n. a senior Christian priest.

archer n. a person who shoots with a bow and arrows.
■ **archery** n.

archetype /ar-ki-typ/ n. **1** a typical example. **2** an original model.
■ **archetypal** adj.

archipelago /ar-ki-**pel**-uh-goh/ n. (pl. **archipelagos** or **archipelagoes**) a group of many islands.

architect n. a person who designs buildings.
▷ SYNONYMS: **designer**, planner, originator, author, creator, founder, inventor.

architecture n. **1** the design and construction of buildings. **2** the style of a building.
▷ SYNONYMS: **building**, planning, design, construction.
■ **architectural** adj.

architrave n. the frame round a doorway or window.

archive /ar-kyv/ n. a collection of documents, data, etc. kept for historical purposes.
▷ SYNONYMS: *the family archives:* **records**, papers, documents, files, annals, chronicles, history.

archivist /ar-ki-vist/ n. a person in charge of archives.

Arctic adj. of the regions around the North Pole.

| USAGE Remember the c: Arctic. |

ardent adj. enthusiastic or passionate.
▷ SYNONYMS: **passionate**, fervent, zealous, wholehearted, intense, fierce, enthusiastic, keen, eager, avid, committed, dedicated.
– ANTONYMS: apathetic.
■ **ardently** adv.

ardour (US **ardor**) n. enthusiasm or passion.

arduous adj. difficult and tiring.
▷ SYNONYMS: **tough**, difficult, hard, heavy, laborious, onerous, taxing, strenuous, back-breaking, demanding, challenging, punishing, gruelling; informal **killing**; Brit. informal knackering.
– ANTONYMS: easy.

are see BE.

area n. **1** a part of a place, object, or surface. **2** the extent or measurement of a surface. **3** a subject.
▷ SYNONYMS: **1 district**, zone, region, sector, quarter, locality, neighbourhood; informal **neck of the woods**; Brit. informal **manor**; N. Amer. informal **turf**. **2** *the dining area:* **space**, section, part, place, room. **3** *specific areas of knowledge:* **field**, sphere, realm, domain, sector, province, territory.

arena n. **1** a level area surrounded by seating, for sports and other events. **2** an area of activity.
▷ SYNONYMS: **1 stadium**, amphitheatre, ground, field, ring, rink, pitch, court; N. Amer. **bowl**, park. **2 scene**, sphere, realm, province, domain, forum, territory, world.

aren't contr. are not.

argon n. an inert gas, present in small amounts in the air.

argot /ar-goh/ n. jargon or slang.

arguable adj. **1** able to be supported by reasons. **2** open to disagreement.
■ **arguably** adv.

argue v. **1** exchange conflicting views heatedly. **2** give reasons for an opinion.
▷ SYNONYMS: **1 quarrel**, disagree, dispute, squabble, bicker, have words, cross swords, fight, wrangle; Brit. **row**. **2 claim**, maintain, insist, contend, assert, hold, reason, allege.

argument n. **1** a heated exchange of conflicting views. **2** a set of reasons given in support of an idea.
▷ SYNONYMS: **1 quarrel**, disagreement, difference of opinion, squabble, dispute, altercation, fight, wrangle; Brit. **row**; informal **slanging match**, tiff, set-to; Brit. informal **barney**. **2 reasoning**, justification, explanation, case, defence, vindication, evidence, reasons, grounds.

| USAGE No e in the middle: *argument*, not *argue-*. |

argumentative adj. apt to argue.

aria n. a solo in an opera.

arid adj. dry; parched.
▷ SYNONYMS: **dry**, waterless, parched, scorched, desiccated, desert, barren, infertile.
– ANTONYMS: wet, fertile.
■ **aridity** n.

arise v. (**arising**, **arose**; past part. **arisen**)

a

1 start to exist or be noticed. **2** occur as a result of. **3** get up.
▷ SYNONYMS: **1** *many problems arose:* **come about**, happen, occur, come into being, emerge, crop up, come to light, become apparent, appear, turn up, surface, spring up. **2** *injuries arising from defective products:* **result**, stem, originate, proceed, follow, ensue, be caused by.

aristocracy n. (pl. **aristocracies**) the highest social class, consisting of people with hereditary titles.

aristocrat n. a member of the aristocracy.
▷ SYNONYMS: **nobleman**, **noblewoman**, lord, lady, member of the peerage, peer of the realm, patrician; Brit. informal **toff**, nob.
– ANTONYMS: commoner.

aristocratic adj. relating to the aristocracy.
▷ SYNONYMS: **noble**, titled, upper-class, blue-blooded, high-born, patrician; informal **upper crust**, top drawer; Brit. informal **posh**.

arithmetic n. the use of numbers in calculation.
■ **arithmetical** adj. **arithmetically** adv.

ark n. **1** (in the Bible) the ship built by Noah to escape the Flood. **2** a chest housing the holy scrolls in a synagogue.

arm n. **1** each of the two upper limbs of the body. **2** a side part of a chair. **3** a branch or division of an organization. **4** (**arms**) weapons.
▷ SYNONYMS: (**arms**) **weapons**, weaponry, firearms, guns, ordnance, artillery, armaments, munitions.
• v. **1** supply with weapons. **2** make a bomb ready to explode.
▷ SYNONYMS: **equip**, provide, supply, furnish, issue, fit out.
□ **armchair** an upholstered chair with side supports for a person's arms. **armpit** the hollow under the arm at the shoulder.

armada n. a fleet of warships.

armadillo n. (pl. **armadillos**) a mammal of South America, with a body covered in bony plates.

Armageddon n. **1** (in the Bible) the last battle between good and evil before the Day of Judgement. **2** a huge and destructive conflict.

armament (or **armaments**) n. military weapons.
▷ SYNONYMS: **arms**, weapons, weaponry, firearms, guns, ordnance, artillery, munitions, materiel.

armature n. the rotating coil of a

dynamo or electric motor.

armistice n. a truce.
▷ SYNONYMS: **truce**, ceasefire, peace, suspension of hostilities.

armorial adj. of coats of arms.

armour (US **armor**) n. **1** metal coverings formerly worn to protect the body in battle. **2** the tough metal layer covering a military vehicle or ship.
■ **armoured** adj. **armourer** n.

armoury (US **armory**) n. (pl. **armouries**) a store or supply of weapons.

army n. (pl. **armies**) **1** an organized military force for fighting on land. **2** a large number.
▷ SYNONYMS: **1** **armed force**, military force, land force, military, soldiery, infantry, militia, troops, soldiers. **2** *an army of tourists:* **crowd**, swarm, horde, mob, gang, throng, mass, flock, herd, pack.

> **WORD LINKS**
> **military** relating to war or armed forces

aroma n. a pleasant smell.
▷ SYNONYMS: **smell**, odour, fragrance, scent, perfume, bouquet, nose.

aromatherapy n. the use of aromatic oils for healing.
■ **aromatherapist** n.

aromatic adj. having a pleasant smell.
▷ SYNONYMS: **fragrant**, scented, sweet-scented, perfumed, fragranced.

arose past of ARISE.

around adv. & prep. **1** on every side. **2** in or to many places throughout an area.
• adv. **1** so as to face in the opposite direction. **2** approximately.
▷ SYNONYMS: **approximately**, about, round about, circa, roughly, more or less, nearly, almost, approaching; Brit. getting on for; N. Amer. informal in the ballpark of.

arouse v. **1** bring about a feeling or response. **2** excite someone sexually. **3** awaken.
▷ SYNONYMS: **1** **provoke**, trigger, stir up, engender, cause, whip up, rouse, inflame, agitate, incite, galvanize, electrify, stimulate, inspire, fire up. **2** **wake**, wake up, awaken, bring to/round, rouse.
– ANTONYMS: allay.

arpeggio /ar-pej-ji-oh/ n. (pl. **arpeggios**) the notes of a musical chord played in succession.

arraign /uh-**rayn**/ v. call before a court to answer a criminal charge.
■ **arraignment** n.

arrange v. **1** put into order.
2 organize. **3** adapt music for
different instruments or voices.
▷ SYNONYMS: **1 set out**, put in order, lay
out, align, position, present, display,
exhibit, group, sort, organize, tidy.
2 organize, fix up, plan, schedule,
contrive, determine, agree. **3** *he
arranged the piece for a full orchestra*:
adapt, set, score, orchestrate.

arrangement n. **1** a plan for a future
event. **2** something made up of things
placed in an attractive or ordered
way. **3** an arranged piece of music.
▷ SYNONYMS: **1 preparation**, plan, planning, provision. **2 agreement**, deal,
understanding, bargain, settlement,
pact. **3 positioning**, presentation,
grouping, organization, alignment.

arrant adj. utter; complete.

array n. **1** a display or wide range.
2 an arrangement. **3** literary elaborate
clothing.
▷ SYNONYMS: **range**, collection, selection,
assortment, variety, arrangement,
line-up, display, exhibition.
• v. (usu. **be arrayed**) **1** be arranged
impressively. **2** be clothed.
▷ SYNONYMS: **arrange**, assemble, group,
order, range, place, position, set out,
lay out, spread out, display, exhibit.

arrears pl. n. money owed that should
already have been paid.

arrest v. **1** seize and take into custody.
2 stop or delay.
▷ SYNONYMS: **1 detain**, apprehend, seize,
capture, take into custody; informal
pick up, pull in, collar; Brit. informal
nick. **2 stop**, halt, check, block, curb,
prevent, obstruct, stem, slow, interrupt, delay.
– ANTONYMS: release.
• n. **1** the act of arresting someone. **2** a
sudden stop.
▷ SYNONYMS: **detention**, apprehension,
seizure, capture.

arresting adj. attracting attention.
▷ SYNONYMS: **striking**, eye-catching,
conspicuous, impressive, imposing,
spectacular, dramatic, breathtaking,
stunning, awe-inspiring.
– ANTONYMS: inconspicuous.

arrival n. **1** the process of arriving. **2** a
person or thing that has arrived.
▷ SYNONYMS: **coming**, appearance,
entrance, entry, approach, advent.
– ANTONYMS: departure.

arrive v. **1** reach a destination. **2** (of
a moment) come about. **3** (**arrive at**)
reach a conclusion or decision.
▷ SYNONYMS: **come**, turn up, make it,

appear; informal show up, roll in/up,
blow in.
– ANTONYMS: depart, leave.

arriviste /ar-ri-**veest**/ n. usu. derog. a
person who has recently become rich
or risen in status.

arrogant adj. behaving in an
unpleasantly superior way.
▷ SYNONYMS: **haughty**, conceited,
self-important, cocky, supercilious,
condescending, full of yourself,
overbearing, imperious, proud; informal
high and mighty, too big for your
boots.
– ANTONYMS: modest.
■ **arrogance** n. **arrogantly** adv.

arrogate v. take or claim for yourself
without justification.

arrow n. **1** a stick with a sharp pointed
head, shot from a bow. **2** a sign
shaped like this, showing direction.

arrowroot n. a powdery starch used
as a thickener in cookery.

arsenal n. a store of weapons and
ammunition.

arsenic n. a brittle grey element with
many highly poisonous compounds.

arson n. the criminal act of
deliberately setting fire to property.
■ **arsonist** n.

art n. **1** the expression of creative
skill in a visual form. **2** paintings,
drawings, and sculpture. **3** (**the arts**)
creative activities such as painting,
music, and drama. **4** a skill.
▷ SYNONYMS: **1 fine art**, design, artwork,
aesthetics. **2 skill**, craft, technique,
knack, facility, aptitude, talent, flair,
mastery, expertise.
□ **artwork** illustrations to be included
in a publication.

artefact (US **artifact**) n. a man-made
object.

arteriosclerosis /ar-teer-i-oh-skluh-
roh-siss/ n. thickening of the walls of
the arteries.

artery n. (pl. **arteries**) **1** any of the
tubes carrying blood from the heart
around the body. **2** an important
transport route.
■ **arterial** adj.

artesian well n. a well in which
water comes to the surface through
natural pressure.

artful adj. clever in a cunning way.
■ **artfully** adv.

arthritis n. painful inflammation and
stiffness of the joints.
■ **arthritic** adj. & n.

arthropod n. an animal with a
segmented body, such as an insect,
spider, or crab.

a

artichoke n. a round vegetable with fleshy green leaves.

article n. 1 a particular object. 2 a piece of writing in a newspaper or magazine. 3 a clause in a legal document.
▷ SYNONYMS: 1 **object**, thing, item, piece, artefact, device, implement. 2 **report**, account, story, essay, feature, item, piece, column. 3 **clause**, section, paragraph, point, item.

articulate adj. fluent and clear in speech.
▷ SYNONYMS: **eloquent**, fluent, effective, persuasive, lucid, expressive, silver-tongued, clear, coherent.
– ANTONYMS: inarticulate.
• v. 1 pronounce or express clearly. 2 (**articulated**) having sections connected by a flexible joint or joints.
▷ SYNONYMS: **express**, voice, vocalize, put in words, communicate, state.
■ **articulately** adv. **articulation** n.

artifact US = ARTEFACT.

artifice n. the clever use of tricks so as to deceive.

artificial adj. 1 made as a copy of something natural. 2 not sincere.
▷ SYNONYMS: 1 **synthetic**, fake, imitation, mock, ersatz, man-made, manufactured, plastic, simulated, faux; informal pretend. 2 **insincere**, feigned, false, unnatural, contrived, put-on, forced, laboured, hollow; informal pretend, phoney.
– ANTONYMS: natural, genuine.
□ **artificial insemination** the insertion of semen through a syringe into the vagina or womb. **artificial intelligence** the performance by computers of tasks normally requiring human intelligence.
■ **artificiality** n. **artificially** adv.

artillery n. 1 large guns used in warfare. 2 a branch of an army using artillery.

artisan n. a skilled worker who makes things by hand.

artist n. 1 a person who paints or draws. 2 a person who performs any of the creative arts.
■ **artistry** n.

artiste /ar-teest/ n. a professional singer or dancer.

artistic adj. 1 having creative skill. 2 of art or artists.
▷ SYNONYMS: 1 **creative**, imaginative, inventive, sensitive, perceptive, discerning. 2 **attractive**, aesthetic, beautiful, stylish, ornamental, decorative, graceful, subtle, expressive.
■ **artistically** adv.

artless adj. sincere and straight-forward.
■ **artlessly** adv.

arty adj. (**artier**, **artiest**) informal displaying a pretentious interest in the arts.

as adv. used in comparisons to refer to extent or amount.
• conj. 1 while. 2 in the way that. 3 because. 4 even though.
• prep. 1 in the role of. 2 while; when.

asafoetida /ah-suh-fee-ti-duh/ n. a strong-smelling resin used in Indian cookery.

asap abbrev. as soon as possible.

asbestos n. a fibrous mineral used in fire-resistant materials.

asbestosis n. a serious lung disease caused by inhaling asbestos dust.

ASBO abbrev. Brit. antisocial behaviour order.

ascend v. go up; climb or rise.

ascendant adj. rising in power or status.
■ **ascendancy** n.

ascension n. 1 the act of ascending. 2 (**the Ascension**) the ascent of Jesus into heaven.

ascent n. 1 an act of ascending. 2 an upward slope.
▷ SYNONYMS: 1 *the ascent of the Matterhorn:* **climbing**, scaling, conquest. 2 *the ascent grew steeper:* **slope**, incline, gradient, hill, climb.
– ANTONYMS: descent, drop.

ascertain v. find out.
▷ SYNONYMS: **find out**, discover, get to know, work out, make out, fathom out, learn, deduce, divine, establish, determine; informal figure out.
■ **ascertainable** adj.

ascetic /uh-set-ik/ adj. choosing to live without pleasures or luxuries.
• n. an ascetic person.
■ **asceticism** n.

ASCII abbrev. Computing American Standard Code for Information Interchange.

ascorbic acid n. vitamin C.

ascribe v. (**ascribe to**) consider to be caused by.
■ **ascription** n.

aseptic adj. free from harmful bacteria.

asexual adj. without sex or sexual organs.
■ **asexually** adv.

ash n. 1 the powder remaining after something has been burned. 2 a tree with a silver-grey bark.
□ **ashtray** a small container for

tobacco ash and cigarette ends.

ashamed adj. feeling shame.
▷ SYNONYMS: **1 sorry**, shamefaced, sheepish, guilty, contrite, remorseful, regretful, apologetic, mortified, red-faced, repentant, penitent, rueful, chagrined. **2 reluctant**, loath, unwilling, afraid, embarrassed.
− ANTONYMS: proud.

ashen adj. very pale, esp. from shock.

ashlar n. masonry made of large square-cut stones.

ashore adv. to or on the shore.

ashram n. a Hindu religious retreat or community.

Asian adj. of Asia or its people.
• n. an Asian person.

Asiatic adj. of Asia.

aside adv. to one side.
• n. a remark made so that only certain people will hear.

asinine adj. very silly.

ask v. **1** say in order to get an answer or some information. **2** make a request. **3** invite someone. **4** expect or demand.
▷ SYNONYMS: **1 enquire**, want to know, question, interrogate, quiz. **2** *they asked a few questions*: **put forward**, pose, raise, submit. **3 request**, demand, seek, solicit, apply, petition, call, appeal.
− ANTONYMS: answer.

askance adv. with a suspicious or disapproving look.

askew adv. & adj. not straight or level.

asleep adj. & adv. in or into a state of sleep.
▷ SYNONYMS: **sleeping**, napping, dozing, drowsing; informal snoozing, dead to the world; humorous in the land of Nod.
− ANTONYMS: awake.

asp n. a small viper.

asparagus n. a vegetable consisting of the shoots of a tall plant.

aspect n. **1** a part or feature of a matter. **2** an appearance or quality. **3** the direction in which a building faces.
▷ SYNONYMS: **1 feature**, facet, side, characteristic, particular, detail. **2 point of view**, position, standpoint, viewpoint, perspective, angle, slant. **3** *his face had a sinister aspect*: **appearance**, look, air, mien, demeanour, expression.

aspen n. a poplar tree.

asperity n. harshness of manner.

aspersions pl. n. critical remarks.

asphalt n. a tar-like substance used in surfacing roads or roofs.

asphyxia n. deprivation of oxygen, leading to unconsciousness or death.

asphyxiate v. die or kill by deprivation of oxygen.
■ **asphyxiation** n.

aspic n. a savoury jelly made with meat stock.

aspidistra n. a plant with broad tapering leaves.

aspirant n. a person with ambitions to do or be something.

aspirate v. pronounce with an *h*.

aspiration n. a hope or ambition.
▷ SYNONYMS: **desire**, hope, dream, wish, longing, yearning, aim, ambition, expectation, goal, target.

aspire v. have ambitions.
▷ SYNONYMS: *she aspired to study at Cambridge*: **desire**, aim, hope, long, yearn, set your heart on, dream of, wish for, want, seek, set your sights on.

aspirin n. a medicine that relieves pain and reduces fever.

aspiring adj. hoping to be or do something.
▷ SYNONYMS: **would-be**, hopeful, budding, potential, prospective; informal wannabe.

ass n. **1** a donkey. **2** informal a stupid person.

assail v. attack violently.
■ **assailant** n.

assassin n. a person who assassinates someone.
▷ SYNONYMS: **murderer**, killer, gunman, executioner; informal hit man.

assassinate v. murder a political or religious leader.
▷ SYNONYMS: **murder**, kill, eliminate, liquidate, execute; N. Amer. terminate; informal hit.
■ **assassination** n.

assault n. a violent attack.
▷ SYNONYMS: **1 violence**, battery; Brit. grievous bodily harm, GBH, actual bodily harm, ABH. **2 attack**, strike, onslaught, offensive, charge, push, thrust, raid.
• v. make an assault on.
▷ SYNONYMS: **attack**, hit, strike, beat up; informal lay into, rough up, do over.

assay n. a test of metal for quality.
• v. test a metal.

assemblage n. **1** a collection or gathering. **2** something made of pieces fitted together.

assemble v. **1** come or bring together. **2** construct by fitting parts together.
▷ SYNONYMS: **1 gather**, collect, get together, congregate, convene, meet,

muster, rally, round up, marshal.
2 construct, build, erect, set up, make, manufacture, fabricate, put together, connect.
– ANTONYMS: disperse, dismantle.

assembly n. (pl. **assemblies**) **1** a group of people gathered together. **2** a body of people with law-making powers. **3** the assembling of parts.
▷ SYNONYMS: **1 gathering**, meeting, congregation, convention, council, rally, group, crowd; informal get-together. **2 construction**, manufacture, building, fabrication, erection.

assent n. agreement.
• v. agree.

assert v. **1** state confidently. **2** (**assert yourself**) be confident and forceful. **3** make others recognize your rights.
▷ SYNONYMS: **1 declare**, state, maintain, contend, argue, claim, insist. **2** *you should assert your rights*: **insist on**, stand up for, uphold, defend, press/ push for.

assertion n. **1** a confident, forceful statement. **2** the action of asserting something.
▷ SYNONYMS: **declaration**, contention, statement, claim, opinion, protestation.

assertive adj. confident and forceful.
▷ SYNONYMS: **confident**, self-confident, bold, decisive, forceful, insistent, emphatic, determined, strong-willed, commanding, pushy; informal feisty.
– ANTONYMS: timid.

assess v. evaluate the value, importance, or quality of.
▷ SYNONYMS: **evaluate**, judge, gauge, rate, estimate, appraise, weigh up, calculate, value, work out, determine; informal size up.
■ **assessment** n. **assessor** n.

asset n. **1** a useful or valuable thing or person. **2** (**assets**) property owned by a person or company.
▷ SYNONYMS: **1 benefit**, advantage, blessing, good/strong point, strength, forte, virtue, recommendation, attraction, resource. **2** *the seizure of all their assets*: **property**, resources, estate, holdings, funds, valuables, possessions, effects, belongings.
– ANTONYMS: liability.

assiduous adj. very careful and thorough.
■ **assiduity** n. **assiduously** adv.

assign v. **1** give a task or duty to. **2** provide with a value, date, etc.
▷ SYNONYMS: **1 allocate**, give, set, charge with, entrust with. **2 appoint**,

promote, delegate, nominate, commission, post, co-opt; Military detail. **3 earmark**, designate, set aside, reserve, appropriate, allot, allocate.

assignation n. a secret arrangement to meet.
▷ SYNONYMS: **rendezvous**, date, appointment, meeting; literary tryst.

assignment n. a task assigned to someone.
▷ SYNONYMS: **task**, job, duty, responsibility, mission, errand, undertaking, commission.

assimilate v. **1** take in and understand information. **2** absorb into a larger group.
■ **assimilation** n.

assist v. help or support.
▷ SYNONYMS: **1 help**, aid, lend a hand, support, back up, work with, cooperate with. **2** *the aim was to assist cash flow*: **facilitate**, aid, ease, promote, boost, speed, benefit, encourage, further.
– ANTONYMS: hinder.

assistance n. help or support.
▷ SYNONYMS: **help**, aid, a helping hand, support, backing, reinforcement.
– ANTONYMS: hindrance.

assistant n. a person employed to help someone more senior.
▷ SYNONYMS: **helper**, aide, deputy, second in command, number two, right-hand man/woman, PA, auxiliary, attendant, henchman; informal sidekick, gofer; Brit. informal dogsbody, skivvy.

assizes n. hist. a county court.

associate v. **1** connect in the mind. **2** frequently meet or have dealings with. **3** (**associate yourself with**) be involved with.
▷ SYNONYMS: **1 link**, connect, relate, bracket, identify, equate. **2 mix**, keep company, mingle, socialize, go around, have dealings; informal hobnob, hang out/around.
– ANTONYMS: avoid.
• n. a work partner or colleague.
▷ SYNONYMS: **partner**, colleague, co-worker, workmate, collaborator, comrade, ally; informal crony.

associated adj. connected with something else.
▷ SYNONYMS: **related**, connected, linked, similar, corresponding, attendant, accompanying, incidental.
– ANTONYMS: unrelated.

association n. **1** a group of people organized for a joint purpose. **2** a connection or link.
▷ SYNONYMS: **1 alliance**, consortium, coalition, union, league, guild,

syndicate, federation, confederation, cartel, cooperative, partnership.
2 relationship, relation, inter-relation, connection, interconnection, interdependence, link, bond.

assonance n. the rhyming of vowel sounds.

assorted adj. of various sorts.
▷ SYNONYMS: **various**, miscellaneous, mixed, varied, diverse, different, sundry.
– ANTONYMS: uniform.

assortment n. a varied collection.
▷ SYNONYMS: **variety**, mixture, array, mix, miscellany, selection, medley, melange, ragbag, potpourri.

assuage /uh-swayj/ v. **1** lessen an unpleasant feeling. **2** satisfy a desire.

assume v. **1** accept as true without proof. **2** take responsibility or control. **3** begin to have. **4** pretend to have.
▷ SYNONYMS: **1 presume**, suppose, take it, take for granted, take as read, conclude, infer, think, fancy, imagine, surmise, believe, understand, gather, suspect; N. Amer. figure. **2 accept**, shoulder, bear, undertake, take on/ up. **3 seize**, take, appropriate, wrest, usurp. **4** *he assumed an Irish accent:* **affect**, adopt, put on; (**assumed**) false, fictitious, fake, bogus, invented, made-up; informal pretend, phoney.

assumption n. a thing assumed to be true.
▷ SYNONYMS: **supposition**, presumption, inference, conjecture, belief, surmise, hypothesis, theory, suspicion, guess.

assurance n. **1** an assertion or promise. **2** self-confidence. **3** Brit. life insurance.
▷ SYNONYMS: **1 promise**, word, pledge, vow, oath, undertaking, guarantee, commitment. **2 confidence**, self-confidence, self-assurance, self-possession, aplomb, nerve, poise; informal cool. **3 insurance**, indemnity, protection, security, cover.

assure v. **1** tell confidently. **2** make certain.
▷ SYNONYMS: **1 reassure**, convince, satisfy, persuade. **2 promise**, guarantee, swear, confirm, certify, vow, give your word. **3 ensure**, secure, guarantee, seal, clinch; informal sew up.

assured adj. **1** confident. **2** certain; guaranteed.
▷ SYNONYMS: **1 confident**, self-confident, self-assured, self-possessed, poised, composed, imperturbable, unruffled; informal unflappable, together.
2 guaranteed, certain, sure, secure,

reliable, dependable; informal sure-fire.
– ANTONYMS: nervous, uncertain.
■ **assuredly** adv.

astatine /ass-tuh-teen/ n. a very unstable radioactive chemical element.

asterisk n. a symbol (*) used as a pointer to a note.

| USAGE Remember: aster*isk*, not *-ix*. |

astern adv. behind or towards the rear of a ship or aircraft.

asteroid n. a small rocky planet orbiting the sun.

asthma /ass-muh/ n. a medical condition causing difficulty in breathing.
■ **asthmatic** adj. & n.

astigmatism n. a defect in the eye preventing proper focusing.
■ **astigmatic** adj.

astonish v. surprise greatly.
▷ SYNONYMS: **amaze**, astound, stagger, startle, stun, surprise, confound, dumbfound, nonplus, take aback, leave open-mouthed; informal flabbergast, bowl over; Brit. informal knock for six.
■ **astonishment** n.

astonishing adj. extremely surprising.
▷ SYNONYMS: **amazing**, astounding, staggering, surprising, breathtaking, remarkable, extraordinary, incredible, unbelievable, phenomenal; informal mind-boggling.

astound v. shock or greatly surprise.
▷ SYNONYMS: **amaze**, astonish, stagger, surprise, startle, stun, confound, dumbfound, take aback, leave open-mouthed; informal flabbergast, bowl over; Brit. informal knock for six.

astounding adj. surprisingly impressive or notable.
▷ SYNONYMS: **amazing**, astonishing, staggering, surprising, breathtaking, remarkable, extraordinary, incredible, unbelievable, phenomenal; informal mind-boggling.

astral adj. of the stars.

astray adv. away from the correct course.

astride prep. & adv. with a leg on each side of.

astringent adj. **1** causing body tissue to contract. **2** sharp or severe.
• n. an astringent lotion.
■ **astringency** n.

astrology n. the study of the supposed influence of stars and planets on human affairs.
■ **astrologer** n. **astrological** adj.

astronaut n. a person trained to travel in a spacecraft.

astronomical adj. **1** of astronomy. **2** informal very large.
■ **astronomically** adv.

astronomy n. the science of stars, planets, and the universe.
■ **astronomer** n.

astrophysics n. the study of the physical nature of stars and planets.
■ **astrophysicist** n.

astute adj. good at making accurate judgements.
▷ SYNONYMS: **shrewd**, sharp, acute, quick, clever, intelligent, bright, smart, canny, perceptive, perspicacious; informal quick on the uptake.
– ANTONYMS: stupid.
■ **astutely** adv.

asunder adv. literary apart.

asylum n. **1** protection from danger, esp. for those who leave their country for political reasons. **2** dated an institution for mentally ill people.
▷ SYNONYMS: **refuge**, sanctuary, shelter, protection, immunity, a safe haven.

asymmetrical (or **asymmetric**) adj. lacking symmetry.
■ **asymmetrically** adv. **asymmetry** n.

at prep. used to express: **1** location, arrival, or time. **2** a value, rate, or point on a scale. **3** a state or condition. **4** direction towards.

atavistic adj. inherited from the earliest humans.
■ **atavism** n.

ate past of EAT.

atheism n. the belief that God does not exist.
■ **atheist** n.

atherosclerosis n. damage to the arteries caused by a build-up of fatty deposits.

athlete n. **1** a person who is good at sports. **2** a person who takes part in athletics.
□ **athlete's foot** a form of ringworm affecting the feet.

athletic adj. **1** fit and good at sport. **2** of athletics.
▷ SYNONYMS: **muscular**, fit, strapping, well built, strong, sturdy, powerful, brawny, burly.
• n. (**athletics**) Brit. track and field sports.
■ **athletically** adv. **athleticism** n.

Atlantic adj. of the Atlantic Ocean.

atlas n. a book of maps or charts.

atmosphere n. **1** the gases surrounding the earth or another planet. **2** the quality of the air in a place. **3** an overall tone or mood. **4** a unit of pressure.
▷ SYNONYMS: **1 air**, sky; literary the heavens, the ether. **2** a relaxed atmosphere: **ambience**, spirit, air, mood, feel, feeling, character, tone, aura, quality, environment, climate; informal vibe.
■ **atmospheric** adj.

> **WORD LINKS**
> **meteorology** the study of the atmosphere

atoll n. a ring-shaped coral reef or chain of islands.

atom n. **1** the smallest particle of a chemical element. **2** a very small amount.
□ **atom bomb** a bomb deriving its power from the fission of atomic nuclei.
■ **atomic** adj.

atomize (or **-ise**) v. convert into very fine particles or droplets.
■ **atomizer** n.

atonal /ay-toh-n'l/ adj. not written in any musical key.

atone v. (**atone for**) make amends for.
■ **atonement** n.

atrium n. (pl. **atria** or **atriums**) **1** a central hall rising through several storeys. **2** each of the two upper cavities of the heart. **3** an open central court in an ancient Roman house.

atrocious adj. **1** horrifyingly wicked. **2** very bad.
▷ SYNONYMS: **1 wicked**, cruel, brutal, barbaric, vicious, monstrous, vile, inhuman, fiendish. **2 appalling**, awful, dreadful, terrible, miserable; informal abysmal, dire, rotten, lousy; Brit. informal shocking.
– ANTONYMS: admirable, superb.
■ **atrociously** adv.

atrocity n. (pl. **atrocities**) a very wicked or cruel act.
▷ SYNONYMS: **1** a number of atrocities: **outrage**, horror, violation, abuse, crime. **2** scenes of hardship and atrocity: **wickedness**, cruelty, brutality, barbarity, viciousness, savagery, inhumanity.

atrophy v. (**atrophies**, **atrophying**, **atrophied**) (of part of the body) waste away.
• n. the condition or process of atrophying.

attach v. **1** fasten or join. **2** regard as important.
▷ SYNONYMS: **1 fasten**, fix, affix, join, secure, stick, connect, tie, link, couple, pin, hitch. **2** they attach

importance to research: **ascribe**, assign, attribute, accredit, impute.
– ANTONYMS: detach.

attaché /uh-tash-ay/ n. a person on an ambassador's staff.
☐ **attaché case** a small briefcase for documents.

attached adj. very fond of someone.
▷ SYNONYMS: he became increasingly attached to her: **fond of**, devoted to, keen on; informal mad about, crazy about.

attachment n. **1** an extra part attached to something. **2** a computer file sent with an email.
▷ SYNONYMS: **1 accessory**, fitting, extension, add-on. **2 bond**, closeness, devotion, loyalty, fondness for, love for, affection for, feeling for, sympathy for.

attack v. **1** take violent action against. **2** criticize fiercely. **3** (in sport) try to score goals or points.
▷ SYNONYMS: **1 assault**, beat up, set upon, mug, charge, pounce on, raid, rush, storm, assail; informal lay into, do over, work over, rough up; Brit. informal duff up. **2 criticize**, censure, condemn, denounce, revile, vilify, impugn, disparage; informal knock, slam, lay into; Brit. informal slate, slag off, rubbish.
– ANTONYMS: defend, praise.
• n. **1** an act of attacking. **2** a sudden spell of an illness.
▷ SYNONYMS: **1 assault**, onslaught, offensive, strike, blitz, raid, incursion, sortie, foray, charge, invasion. **2 criticism**, censure, condemnation, vilification, disparagement; Brit. informal slating. **3 fit**, seizure, spasm, convulsion, paroxysm, bout, episode.
– ANTONYMS: defence, praise.

attacker n. a person who attacks someone or something.
▷ SYNONYMS: **assailant**, assaulter, mugger, aggressor, raider, invader.

attain v. succeed in doing.
▷ SYNONYMS: **achieve**, accomplish, reach, obtain, gain, secure, get, win, earn, realize, fulfil; informal clinch, bag, wrap up.
■ **attainable** adj. **attainment** n.

attar n. a scented oil made from rose petals.

attempt v. try.
▷ SYNONYMS: **try**, strive, aim, venture, endeavour, seek, have a go, bid.
• n. an effort.
▷ SYNONYMS: **try**, effort, endeavour, venture, bid, go; informal crack, shot, stab.

attend v. **1** be present at. **2** (attend

to) deal with or pay attention to.
3 accompany.
▷ SYNONYMS: **1 be present at**, sit in on, take part in, appear at, turn up at, visit, go to; informal show up at. **2 deal with**, see to, organize, sort out, handle, take care of, take charge of, take in hand, tackle. **3 pay attention**, listen, be attentive, concentrate.
■ **attendance** n.

attendant n. **1** an employee providing help in a public place. **2** an assistant.
▷ SYNONYMS: **assistant**, aide, companion, escort, steward, equerry, servant, retainer, valet, maid.
• adj. accompanying.
▷ SYNONYMS: **accompanying**, associated, concomitant, related, connected, resulting, consequent.

attention n. **1** special care, notice, or consideration. **2** a straight standing position in military drill.
▷ SYNONYMS: **1 consideration**, contemplation, deliberation, thought, study, observation, mind, investigation, action. **2 awareness**, notice, scrutiny, eye, gaze. **3** medical attention: **care**, ministrations, treatment, therapy, relief, aid, assistance.

attentive adj. **1** paying attention. **2** considerate; helpful.
▷ SYNONYMS: **1** an attentive pupil: **alert**, perceptive, observant, acute, aware, heedful, focused, studious, diligent, conscientious, earnest. **2** the most attentive of husbands: **considerate**, conscientious, thoughtful, helpful, kind, caring, solicitous, understanding, sympathetic.
– ANTONYMS: inattentive.
■ **attentively** adv. **attentiveness** n.

attenuate v. make thin or weaker.
■ **attenuation** n.

attest v. **1** provide proof of. **2** declare to be true.
■ **attestation** n.

attic n. a space or room inside the roof of a building.
▷ SYNONYMS: **loft**, garret.

attire n. clothes.
• v. (**be attired**) be dressed.

attitude n. **1** a way of thinking. **2** a posture of the body. **3** informal self-confident or hostile behaviour.
▷ SYNONYMS: **1 view**, viewpoint, outlook, perspective, stance, standpoint, position, frame of mind, approach, opinion. **2** an attitude of prayer: **posture**, position, pose, stance.

attorney n. (pl. **attorneys**) **1** a person who acts for another in legal matters. **2** esp. US a lawyer.

a

attract v. **1** cause to come somewhere or do something. **2** cause to like or admire. **3** draw closer by an unseen force.
▷ SYNONYMS: **1 appeal to**, fascinate, charm, captivate, interest, tempt, entice, lure, bewitch, beguile, seduce. **2 draw**, pull, magnetize.
– ANTONYMS: repel.

attraction n. **1** the action or power of attracting. **2** an interesting or appealing quality or feature.
▷ SYNONYMS: **1 appeal**, attractiveness, pull, desirability, fascination, allure, charisma, charm. **2** *the town's main attractions:* **entertainment**, activity, diversion, amenity, service.
– ANTONYMS: repulsion.

attractive adj. **1** pleasing in appearance. **2** arousing interest.
▷ SYNONYMS: **1 good-looking**, beautiful, pretty, handsome, lovely, stunning, striking, desirable, gorgeous, prepossessing, fetching; Scottish & N. English bonny; informal drop-dead gorgeous, hunky; Brit. informal fit; N. Amer. informal cute; old use comely. **2 appealing**, inviting, tempting, pleasing, interesting.
– ANTONYMS: unattractive, ugly.
■ **attractively** adv. **attractiveness** n.

attribute v. (**attribute to**) regard as belonging to or caused by.
▷ SYNONYMS: **ascribe**, assign, accredit, credit, put down, chalk up, pin on.
• n. a quality or feature.
▷ SYNONYMS: **quality**, characteristic, trait, feature, element, aspect, property, sign, hallmark, mark.
■ **attributable** adj. **attribution** n.

attributive adj. Grammar (of an adjective) coming before the word that it describes.

attrition n. gradual wearing down.

attune v. (**be attuned**) be receptive to and able to understand.

atypical adj. not typical.
■ **atypically** adv.

aubergine /**oh**-ber-zheen/ n. a purple vegetable.

auburn n. a reddish-brown colour.

auction n. a public sale where articles are sold to the highest bidder.
• v. sell at an auction.

auctioneer n. a person who conducts auctions.

audacious adj. daring.
■ **audaciously** adv. **audacity** n.

audible adj. able to be heard.
▷ SYNONYMS: **perceptible**, discernible, detectable, distinct, clear.
– ANTONYMS: inaudible, faint.

■ **audibly** adv.

audience n. **1** a group of listeners or spectators. **2** a formal meeting with an important person.
▷ SYNONYMS: **1 spectators**, **listeners**, viewers, onlookers, crowd, throng, gallery, congregation, turnout. **2 meeting**, interview, consultation, conference, hearing, reception.

audio n. sound or the reproduction of sound.
□ **audio tape** magnetic tape on which sound can be recorded. **audio-visual** using both sight and sound.

audit n. an official inspection of an organization's accounts.
• v. (**auditing**, **audited**) make an audit of.
■ **auditor** n.

audition n. a test of a performer's ability for a particular part.
• v. test or be tested by an audition.

auditorium n. (pl. **auditoriums** or **auditoria**) the part of a theatre or hall in which the audience sits.

auditory adj. of hearing.

au fait /oh **fay**/ adj. (**au fait with**) having good knowledge of.

auger /**aw**-ger/ n. a tool for boring holes.

augment v. increase.
▷ SYNONYMS: **increase**, add to, supplement, enhance, build up, raise, boost, up, hike up, enlarge, swell, expand, extend.
– ANTONYMS: decrease, reduce.
■ **augmentation** n.

au gratin /oh gra-**tan**/ adj. cooked with a topping of breadcrumbs or grated cheese.

augur /**aw**-ger/ v. be an omen.

augury /**aw**-gyoo-ri/ n. (pl. **auguries**) a sign of what will happen.

August n. the eighth month.

august /aw-**gust**/ adj. inspiring respect.
▷ SYNONYMS: **distinguished**, respected, eminent, venerable, illustrious, prestigious, renowned, celebrated, honoured, acclaimed, esteemed.

auk n. a black and white seabird.

aunt n. the sister of your father or mother or the wife of your uncle.

au pair n. a foreign girl employed to look after children and help with housework.

aura n. the atmosphere surrounding a place or person.
▷ SYNONYMS: **atmosphere**, ambience, air, quality, character, mood, feeling; informal vibe.

aural /aw-ruhl/ adj. of the ear.
■ **aurally** adv.

aureole n. a halo.

au revoir /aw ruh-**vwar**/ exclam. goodbye.

aurora borealis /aw-raw-ruh bo-ri-ay-liss/ n. bands of light seen in the sky near the North Pole; the Northern Lights.

auspices pl. n. (under the auspices of) with the support or protection of.

auspicious adj. suggesting that there is a good chance of success.
▷ SYNONYMS: **favourable**, promising, encouraging, fortunate, opportune, timely, advantageous, good.
– ANTONYMS: inauspicious, unfavourable.
■ **auspiciously** adv.

austere adj. **1** severe or strict. **2** very simple or plain.
▷ SYNONYMS: **1 severe**, stern, strict, harsh, dour, grim, cold, frosty, unfriendly. **2 spartan**, frugal, ascetic, puritanical, abstemious, strict, simple, hard. **3** *an austere building*: **plain**, simple, basic, functional, unadorned, bleak, bare, clinical.
– ANTONYMS: easy-going, ornate.
■ **austerity** n.

Australasian adj. of Australasia, a region made up of Australia, New Zealand, and islands of the SW Pacific.

Australian n. a person from Australia.
• adj. of Australia.

authentic adj. known to be real; genuine.
▷ SYNONYMS: **1 genuine**, real, bona fide, true, legitimate; informal pukka, kosher; Austral./NZ informal dinkum. **2 accurate**, factual, true, truthful, reliable, trustworthy, honest, faithful.
– ANTONYMS: fake, unreliable.
■ **authentically** adv. **authenticity** n.

authenticate v. prove to be authentic.
▷ SYNONYMS: **verify**, validate, prove, substantiate, corroborate, confirm, support, back up.
– ANTONYMS: disprove.
■ **authentication** n.

author n. **1** a writer of a book etc. **2** the inventor of a plan or idea.
▷ SYNONYMS: **1 writer**, novelist, poet, playwright, dramatist, columnist, reporter, wordsmith; informal scribe, scribbler. **2 creator**, originator, founder, father, architect, designer, producer.
■ **authorial** adj. **authorship** n.

authoritarian adj. demanding strict obedience to authority.
▷ SYNONYMS: **strict**, autocratic, dictatorial, despotic, tyrannical, domineering, imperious, illiberal, undemocratic; informal bossy.
– ANTONYMS: democratic, liberal.

authoritative adj. **1** reliably true or accurate. **2** commanding and self-confident.
▷ SYNONYMS: **1 reliable**, dependable, trustworthy, accurate, authentic, valid, definitive, classic. **2 commanding**, masterful, assertive, self-assured, self-confident.
– ANTONYMS: unreliable.
■ **authoritatively** adv.

authority n. (pl. **authorities**) **1** the power to give orders and make others obey. **2** a person or group with official power. **3** official permission. **4** a trusted expert.
▷ SYNONYMS: **1** *a rebellion against those in authority*: **power**, command, control, charge, dominance, jurisdiction, rule; informal clout. **2** *the authority to arrest drug traffickers*: **right**, authorization, power, mandate, prerogative, licence. **3** *they need parliamentary authority*: **permission**, authorization, consent, sanction, assent, agreement, approval, clearance; informal the go-ahead. **4** (the authorities) **officials**, officialdom, government, administration, establishment, police; informal the powers that be. **5 expert**, specialist, professional, master, connoisseur, pundit, guru, doyen/doyenne.

authorize (or -ise) v. give official permission for.
▷ SYNONYMS: **1** *they authorized further action*: **permit**, sanction, allow, approve, consent to, assent to; informal give the go-ahead to, OK. **2** *the troops were authorized to fire*: **empower**, mandate, commission, entitle.
– ANTONYMS: forbid.
■ **authorization** n.

authorized (or -ised) adj. having official permission: *an authorized distributor*.
▷ SYNONYMS: **approved**, sanctioned, accredited, recognized, licensed, certi-fied, official, legal, legitimate.
– ANTONYMS: unauthorized, unofficial.

autism /aw-ti-z'm/ n. a mental condition in which a person has communication difficulties.
■ **autistic** adj. & n.

auto- comb. form self; own.

autobiography n. (pl. **autobiographies**) an account of a person's life written by that person.
■ **autobiographical** adj.

a

autocracy n. (pl. **autocracies**) government in which one person has total power.

autocrat n. a ruler with total power.
■ **autocratic** adj.

autocue n. trademark a device displaying a presenter's script on a television screen, unseen by the audience.

autodidact /aw-toh-dy-dakt/ n. a self-taught person.

autograph n. a celebrity's signature.
• v. write an autograph on.

autoimmune adj. (of disease) caused by antibodies produced to counteract substances naturally present in the body.

automate v. convert a process or facility to operate automatically.
■ **automation** n.

automatic adj. **1** operating without human control. **2** done without conscious thought.
▷ SYNONYMS: **1 mechanized**, powered, mechanical, automated, computer-ized, electronic, robotic. **2 instinctive**, involuntary, unconscious, reflex, knee-jerk, subconscious, spon-taneous, impulsive, unthinking, mechanical; informal gut. **3 inevitable**, unavoidable, inescapable, certain.
− ANTONYMS: manual, conscious, deliberate.
■ **automatically** adv.

automaton n. (pl. **automata** or **automatons**) a robot.

automobile n. US a car.

automotive adj. of motor vehicles.

autonomous adj. self-governing or independent.
▷ SYNONYMS: **self-governing**, independent, sovereign, free.
− ANTONYMS: dependent.

autonomy n. self-government or freedom of action.
▷ SYNONYMS: **self-government**, self-rule, home rule, self-determination, independence, sovereignty, freedom.
− ANTONYMS: dependence.

autopilot n. a device for keeping an aircraft on course automatically.

autopsy n. (pl. **autopsies**) a post-mortem.

autumn n. the season between summer and winter.
■ **autumnal** adj.

auxiliary adj. giving help and support.
▷ SYNONYMS: **additional**, supplementary, extra, reserve, backup, emergency, fallback, second.
• n. (pl. **auxiliaries**) an auxiliary person or thing.

□ **auxiliary verb** a verb used to form tenses of other verbs (e.g. *be*).

avail v. (**avail yourself of**) make use of.
• n. use or benefit.

available adj. able to be used or obtained.
▷ SYNONYMS: **obtainable**, accessible, to/at hand, to be had, on sale, untaken, unsold, free, vacant, unoccupied; informal up for grabs, on tap.
■ **availability** n.

avalanche n. a mass of snow and ice falling down a mountainside.
▷ SYNONYMS: *an avalanche of enquiries:* **barrage**, flood, deluge, torrent, wave, onslaught.

avant-garde /a-von gard/ adj. (in the arts) new and experimental.
▷ SYNONYMS: **experimental**, modern, cutting-edge, progressive, unorthodox, unconventional; informal edgy, offbeat, way-out.
− ANTONYMS: conservative, traditional.

avarice n. greed for wealth.
▷ SYNONYMS: **greed**, acquisitiveness, covetousness, materialism.
− ANTONYMS: generosity.
■ **avaricious** adj.

avenge v. take revenge for.
■ **avenger** n.

avenue n. **1** a broad road. **2** a way of achieving something.

aver v. (**averring, averred**) declare to be the case.

average n. **1** the result obtained by adding several amounts together and then dividing the total by the number of amounts. **2** a usual amount or level.
▷ SYNONYMS: **mean**, median, mode, norm, standard, par.
• adj. **1** being an average. **2** usual or ordinary.
▷ SYNONYMS: **1** *the average temperature:* **mean**, median. **2** *a woman of average height:* **normal**, standard, typical, ordinary, common, regular.
− ANTONYMS: abnormal, unusual.

averse adj. (**averse to**) strongly disliking.
▷ SYNONYMS: **opposed**, hostile, antagon-istic, resistant, disinclined, reluctant, loath; informal anti.
− ANTONYMS: keen.

> **USAGE** Don't confuse **averse** with **adverse**, which means 'harmful or unfavourable'.

aversion n. a strong dislike.
▷ SYNONYMS: **dislike**, hatred, loathing, abhorrence, distaste, antipathy, hostility, reluctance, disinclination.
− ANTONYMS: liking.

avert v. **1** turn your eyes away.
2 prevent an unpleasant event.
▷ SYNONYMS: **1 turn aside**, turn away,
shift, redirect. **2 prevent**, avoid, stave
off, ward off, head off, forestall.

avian adj. of birds.
□ **avian flu** = BIRD FLU.

aviary n. (pl. **aviaries**) a large enclosure
for keeping birds in.

aviation n. the activity of operating
and flying aircraft.
■ **aviator** n.

avid adj. very interested or
enthusiastic.
▷ SYNONYMS: **keen**, eager, enthusiastic,
ardent, passionate, zealous, devoted.
– ANTONYMS: apathetic.
■ **avidly** adv.

avionics n. electronics used in
aviation.

avocado n. (pl. **avocados**) a pear-
shaped tropical fruit.

avocet n. a wading bird with a long
upturned bill.

avoid v. keep away or refrain from.
▷ SYNONYMS: **1 keep away from**, steer
clear of, give a wide berth to. **2 evade**,
dodge, sidestep, escape, run away
from; informal duck, wriggle out of,
get out of. **3** book early to avoid
disappointment: **prevent**, preclude,
stave off, forestall, head off, ward
off. **4** avoid alcohol: **refrain from**,
abstain from, desist from, steer clear
of, eschew.
– ANTONYMS: confront, face.
■ **avoidable** adj. **avoidance** n.

avoirdupois /av-war-dyoo-**pwah**/ n. a
system of weights based on a pound
of 16 ounces.

avow v. declare.
■ **avowal** n.

avuncular adj. kind and friendly
towards a younger person.

await v. wait for.
▷ SYNONYMS: **1 wait for**, expect, look
forward to, anticipate. **2 be in store
for**, lie ahead of, be waiting for, be
round the corner.

awake v. (**awaking**, **awoke**; past part.
awoken) stop sleeping.
▷ SYNONYMS: **wake up**, wake, awaken,
waken, stir, come to, come round;
rouse, call.
• adj. not asleep.
▷ SYNONYMS: **1 sleepless**, wide awake,
restless, insomniac. **2** too few are
awake to the dangers: **aware of**,
conscious of, mindful of, alert to.
– ANTONYMS: asleep, oblivious.

awaken v. **1** stop sleeping. **2** stir up
a feeling.

▷ SYNONYMS: **1** See AWAKE. **2 arouse**,
kindle, bring out, trigger, stir up,
stimulate, revive.

award v. give officially as a prize or
reward.
▷ SYNONYMS: **give**, grant, accord, confer
on, bestow on, present to, decorate
with.
• n. **1** something awarded. **2** the act of
awarding.
▷ SYNONYMS: **1 prize**, trophy, medal,
decoration, reward; informal gong.
2 grant, scholarship, endowment; Brit.
bursary.

aware adj. having knowledge of
something.
▷ SYNONYMS: **1** she is aware of the
dangers: **conscious of**, mindful of,
informed about, acquainted with,
familiar with, alive to, alert to; informal
wise to, in the know, in the picture.
2 environmentally aware: **sensitive**,
enlightened, knowledgeable,
informed; informal clued-up; Brit. informal
switched-on.
– ANTONYMS: ignorant.

awareness n. the fact of being aware
of something.
▷ SYNONYMS: **consciousness**, recognition, realization, perception,
understanding, grasp, appreciation,
knowledge, familiarity.

awash adj. covered or flooded with
water.

away adv. **1** to or at a distance. **2** until
disappearing. **3** constantly.
▷ SYNONYMS: **elsewhere**, abroad, gone,
off, out, absent, on holiday; N. Amer. on
vacation.
• adj. (of a match) played at the
opponents' ground.

awe n. great respect mixed with fear.
▷ SYNONYMS: **wonder**, wonderment,
admiration, reverence, respect, fear,
dread.
• v. fill with awe.

awesome adj. inspiring awe.
▷ SYNONYMS: **breathtaking**, awe-
inspiring, magnificent, amazing,
stunning, staggering, imposing,
formidable, intimidating; informal
mind-boggling, mind-blowing,
brilliant.
– ANTONYMS: unimpressive.

awful adj. **1** very bad or unpleasant.
2 used for emphasis: an awful lot.
▷ SYNONYMS: **1** the place smells awful:
disgusting, terrible, dreadful,
ghastly, horrible, vile, foul, revolting,
repulsive, repugnant, sickening,
nauseating; informal gross; Brit. informal
beastly. **2** an awful book: **dreadful**,

terrible, frightful, atrocious, lamentable; informal crummy, pathetic, rotten, woeful, lousy, appalling, abysmal, dismal, dire; Brit. informal rubbish. **3** *I feel awful:* ill, unwell, sick, nauseous, off colour, poorly; Brit. informal grotty, ropy; Austral./NZ informal crook.
– ANTONYMS: delightful, excellent, well.
■ **awfully** adv.

awhile adv. for a short time.

awkward adj. **1** hard to do or deal with. **2** causing or feeling embarrassment. **3** inconvenient. **4** clumsy.
▷ SYNONYMS: **1 difficult**, tricky, cumbersome, unwieldy; Brit. informal fiddly. **2 unreasonable**, uncooperative, unhelpful, difficult, obstructive, contrary, perverse, obstinate, stubborn; Brit. informal bloody-minded, bolshie; N. Amer. informal balky. **3** *he put her in an awkward position:* **embarrassing**, uncomfortable, unenviable, delicate, tricky, problematic, troublesome, humiliating, compromising; informal sticky. **4** *she felt awkward:* **uncomfortable**, uneasy, tense, nervous, edgy, self-conscious, embarrassed. **5** *an awkward time:* **inconvenient**, inappropriate, inopportune, difficult. **6** *his awkward movements:* **clumsy**, ungainly, uncoordinated, graceless, inelegant, gauche, gawky, stiff, unskilful, inept, blundering; informal ham-fisted, cackhanded; Brit. informal all fingers and thumbs.
– ANTONYMS: easy, amenable, convenient, graceful.

■ **awkwardly** adv.

awl n. a pointed tool for making holes.

awning n. a sheet of canvas on a frame, used for shelter.

awoke past of AWAKE.

awoken past part. of AWAKE.

AWOL /ay-wol/ adj. absent without leave.

awry /uh-ry/ adv. & adj. away from the expected course or position.

axe (US **ax**) n. a chopping tool with a heavy blade.
▷ SYNONYMS: **hatchet**, chopper, cleaver; historical battleaxe.
• v. ruthlessly cancel or dismiss.
▷ SYNONYMS: **1 cancel**, withdraw, drop, scrap, cut, discontinue, end; informal ditch, dump, pull the plug on. **2 dismiss**, make redundant, lay off, get rid of; informal sack, fire.

axiom n. a statement regarded as obviously true.
■ **axiomatic** adj.

axis n. (pl. **axes**) **1** an imaginary line around which an object rotates. **2** a fixed line against which points on a graph are measured.

axle n. a rod on which wheels turn.
▷ SYNONYMS: **shaft**, spindle, rod.

ayatollah n. a religious leader in Iran.

aye exclam. old use or dialect yes.

azalea /uh-zay-li-uh/ n. a shrub with brightly coloured flowers.

Aztec n. a member of an American Indian people ruling Mexico before the Spanish conquest in the 16th century.

azure /az-yuur/ n. a bright blue colour.

Bb

BA abbrev. Bachelor of Arts.

baa v. (**baaing, baaed**) (of a sheep or lamb) bleat.

babble v. talk rapidly in a foolish or confused way.
▷ SYNONYMS: **prattle**, rattle on, gabble, chatter, jabber, twitter, burble, blather; informal yatter, blabber, jaw, gas, shoot your mouth off; Brit. informal witter, rabbit, chunter, natter, waffle.
• n. foolish or confused talk.

babe n. **1** a baby. **2** informal an attractive young woman.

babel n. a confused mixture of voices.

baboon n. a large monkey.

baby n. (pl. **babies**) **1** a very young child or animal. **2** a timid or childish person.
▷ SYNONYMS: **infant**, newborn, child; Scottish & N. English bairn; technical neonate; informal sprog, tot; literary babe.
• adj. small or very young.
▷ SYNONYMS: **miniature**, mini, little, toy, pocket, midget, dwarf; Scottish wee; N. Amer. vest-pocket; informal teeny, teensy, tiddly, bite-sized; Brit. informal titchy.

babyish adj. childish or immature.
▷ SYNONYMS: **childish**, infantile, juvenile, puerile, immature.
– ANTONYMS: mature.

babysit v. (**babysitting, babysat**) look after a child while the parents are out.
■ **babysitter** n.

baccalaureate /ba-kuh-**lor**-i-uht/ n. an exam taken to qualify for higher education.

baccarat /**bak**-kuh-rah/ n. a gambling card game.

bacchanalian /bak-kuh-**nay**-li-uhn/ adj. (of a party) drunken and wild.

bachelor n. **1** an unmarried man. **2** a holder of a first degree from a university.

bacillus /buh-**sil**-luhss/ n. (pl. **bacilli**) a rod-shaped bacterium.

back n. **1** the rear surface of a person's body, or the upper part of an animal's body. **2** the side or part furthest from the front. **3** a defending player in a team game.
▷ SYNONYMS: **1 spine**, backbone, spinal column, vertebral column. **2 rear**, end, rear end, tail end; Nautical stern. **3 reverse**, other side, underside; informal flip side.
– ANTONYMS: front.
• adv. **1** at or towards the rear. **2** in or into a previous time, position, or state. **3** in return.
• v. **1** give support to. **2** move backwards. **3** bet money on. **4** (**back on to**) (of a building) have its back facing.
▷ SYNONYMS: **1 sponsor**, finance, fund, subsidize, underwrite; informal pick up the bill for. **2 support**, endorse, sanction, give your blessing to, smile on, favour, advocate, promote, champion; informal throw your weight behind. **3 reverse**, draw back, step back, pull back, retreat, withdraw. **4 bet on**, gamble on, stake money on.
– ANTONYMS: oppose, advance.
• adj. **1** at or towards the back. **2** of the past.
▷ SYNONYMS: **1 rear**, rearmost, hind, hindmost, posterior. **2 past**, old, previous, earlier.
– ANTONYMS: front, future.
□ **backbencher** a member of parliament who does not hold a government or opposition post. **back down** give in. **back out** withdraw from a commitment. **back-pedal** reverse a previous action or opinion. **back up 1** support. **2** Computing make a spare copy of data or a disk.

> **WORD LINKS**
> **dorsal**, **lumbar** relating to the back
> **supine** lying on your back

backbiting n. spiteful talk about an absent person.

backbone n. the spine.
▷ SYNONYMS: **1 spine**, spinal column,

b

vertebral column, vertebrae. **2 mainstay**, cornerstone, foundation.
3 strength of character, strength of will, firmness, resolution, resolve, grit, determination, fortitude, mettle, spirit.

backchat n. Brit. informal cheeky replies.

backdate v. Brit. make valid from an earlier date.

backdrop (or **backcloth**) n. a painted cloth at the back of a theatre stage.

backer n. a person, institution, etc. that supports someone or something.
▷ SYNONYMS: **1 sponsor**, investor, underwriter, financier, patron, benefactor; informal angel. **2 supporter**, defender, advocate, promoter; N. Amer. booster.

backfire v. **1** produce an undesired effect. **2** (of an engine) make a bang due to fuel igniting wrongly.
▷ SYNONYMS: **rebound**, boomerang, come back, fail; informal blow up in someone's face.

backgammon n. a board game played with counters and a dice.

background n. **1** the back part of a scene or picture. **2** the circumstances that explain or influence something.
▷ SYNONYMS: **1 backdrop**, backcloth, surroundings, setting, scene, framework. **2 social circumstances**, family circumstances, environment, class, culture, tradition. **3 experience**, record, history, past, training, education.
– ANTONYMS: foreground.

backhand n. a stroke played with the back of the hand turned forwards.

backhanded adj. indirect or ambiguous.

backhander n. **1** a backhand stroke. **2** Brit. informal a bribe.

backing n. **1** support. **2** music or singing accompanying a pop singer.
▷ SYNONYMS: **1 support**, endorsement, approval, blessing, assistance, aid, help. **2 sponsorship**, finance, funding, subsidy, patronage.

backlash n. an angry reaction.
▷ SYNONYMS: **adverse reaction**, counterblast, repercussion, comeback, retaliation, reprisal.

backlog n. a build-up of work.

backpack n. a rucksack.
■ **backpacker** n.

backside n. informal the buttocks.

backslide v. revert to previous bad behaviour.

backstage adv. & adj. behind the stage in a theatre.

backstroke n. a swimming stroke

performed on the back.

backtrack v. **1** retrace your steps. **2** reverse your opinion.

backward adj. **1** towards the back. **2** having made less than normal progress.
▷ SYNONYMS: **1 rearward**, towards the rear, behind you, reverse. **2** a backward step: **retrograde**, regressive, for the worse, in the wrong direction, downhill, negative.
– ANTONYMS: forward, advanced.
• adv. (or **backwards**) **1** towards the back or back towards the start. **2** in reverse.
■ **backwardly** adv. **backwardness** n.

backwash n. waves flowing outwards behind a ship.

backwater n. **1** a stretch of stagnant water on a river. **2** a place unaffected by progress.

backwoods pl. n. a remote area.

bacon n. salted or smoked meat from a pig.

bacteria pl. n. (sing. **bacterium**) a group of microscopic organisms, many of which cause disease.
■ **bacterial** adj. **bacteriologist** n. **bacteriology** n.

> USAGE **bacteria** should always be used with a plural verb, e.g. *the bacteria were multiplying*.

bad adj. (**worse, worst**) **1** poor in quality. **2** unpleasant. **3** severe; serious. **4** wicked. **5** harmful. **6** injured, ill, or diseased. **7** (of food) decayed.
▷ SYNONYMS: **1** bad workmanship: **unsatisfactory**, substandard, poor, inferior, second-rate, second-class, inadequate, deficient, imperfect, defective, faulty, shoddy, negligent, disgraceful, awful, terrible, appalling, dreadful, frightful, atrocious, abysmal; informal crummy, rotten, pathetic, useless, woeful, lousy, diabolical; Brit. informal duff, rubbish. **2** the alcohol had a bad effect: **harmful**, damaging, detrimental, injurious, hurtful, destructive, deleterious, inimical. **3** bad news: **unpleasant**, disagreeable, unwelcome, unfavourable, unfortunate, grim, distressing, gloomy. **4** a bad accident: **serious**, severe, grave, critical, acute. **5** a bad time to arrive: **unfavourable**, inauspicious, unpropitious, inopportune, unfortunate, disadvantageous, inappropriate, unsuitable. **6** the bad guys: **wicked**, evil, sinful, criminal, immoral, corrupt, villainous; informal

crooked, bent. **7** *you bad girl!:*
naughty, badly behaved, disobedient,
wayward, wilful, defiant, unruly,
undisciplined. **8** *a bad knee:* **injured**,
wounded, diseased; informal **gammy**;
Brit. informal **knackered**; Austral./NZ informal
crook. 9 *the meat's bad:* **rotten**, off,
decayed, putrid, rancid, curdled, sour,
mouldy.
– ANTONYMS: good, beneficial, virtuous,
favourable.
■ **badness** n.

bade past of **BID²**.

badge n. a small flat object worn to
show membership or rank.
▷ SYNONYMS: **1 brooch**, pin, emblem,
crest, insignia; N. Amer. button. **2** *a
badge of success:* **sign**, symbol,
indication, signal, mark, hallmark,
trademark.

badger n. a large nocturnal mammal
with a black-and-white striped head.
• v. pester.
▷ SYNONYMS: **pester**, harass, hound,
harry, nag, bother, go on at; informal
hassle, bug.

badly adv. (**worse**, **worst**) **1** in an
unacceptable way. **2** severely. **3** very
much.
▷ SYNONYMS: **1 poorly**, unsatisfactorily,
inadequately, incorrectly, faultily,
defectively, shoddily, amateurishly,
carelessly, incompetently, inexpertly.
2 unfavourably, ill, critically,
disapprovingly. **3 naughtily**,
disobediently, wilfully, mischievously. **4 cruelly**, wickedly, unkindly,
harshly, shamefully, unfairly,
unjustly, wrongly. **5 unfavourably**, unsuccessfully, adversely,
unfortunately. **6 severely**, seriously,
gravely, acutely, critically.
– ANTONYMS: well.
□ **badly off** poor.

badminton n. a game with rackets
in which a shuttlecock is hit across a
high net.

bad-tempered adj. easily angered or
annoyed.
▷ SYNONYMS: **irritable**, irascible, tetchy,
testy, grumpy, grouchy, crotchety,
cantankerous, curmudgeonly, ill-
tempered, peevish, cross, fractious,
petulant, pettish, crabby, quarrelsome, dyspeptic; informal **snappish**; Brit.
informal **shirty**, stroppy, ratty; N. Amer.
informal **cranky**, ornery.
– ANTONYMS: good-humoured, affable.

baffle v. puzzle.
▷ SYNONYMS: **puzzle**, perplex, bewilder,
mystify, confuse; informal **flummox**,
stump, beat, fox.

■ **bafflement** n.

bag n. **1** a flexible container with
an opening at the top. **2** (**bags of**)
Brit. informal plenty of. **3** informal an
unpleasant woman.
▷ SYNONYMS: **suitcase**, case, valise,
portmanteau, holdall, grip, rucksack,
haversack, satchel, handbag.
• v. (**bagging, bagged**) **1** put in a bag.
2 informal manage to get.
▷ SYNONYMS: **1 catch**, land, capture,
trap, net, snare. **2 get**, secure, obtain,
acquire, pick up, win, achieve; informal
land, net.

bagatelle n. **1** a board game in which
balls are hit into numbered holes.
2 something unimportant.

bagel /bay-g'l/ n. a ring-shaped bread
roll with a heavy texture.

baggage n. luggage.
▷ SYNONYMS: **luggage**, suitcases, cases,
bags, belongings.

baggy adj. (**baggier, baggiest**)
hanging in loose folds.
▷ SYNONYMS: **loose**, roomy, generously
cut, sloppy, voluminous, full.
– ANTONYMS: tight.

bagpipes pl. n. a musical instrument
with pipes sounded by wind squeezed
from a bag.

baguette /ba-get/ n. a loaf of French
bread.

bail n. **1** the release of an accused
person on condition that a sum of
money is left with the court, which
will be returned as long as the person
attends their trial. **2** money paid for
this reason. **3** each of two crosspieces
resting on the stumps in cricket.
▷ SYNONYMS: **surety**, security, indemnity,
bond, guarantee, pledge.
• v. **1** free an accused person on
payment of bail. **2** (or Brit. **bale**) scoop
water out of.
□ **bail** (or Brit. **bale**) **out 1** make an
emergency parachute jump from an
aircraft. **2** rescue from difficulty.

bailey n. the outer wall of a castle.

bailiff n. a person who delivers writs
and seizes property for non-payment
of fines or debts.

bailiwick n. an area of authority or
interest.

bairn n. Scottish & N. English a child.

bait n. food put on a hook or in a trap
to catch fish or other animals.
▷ SYNONYMS: **enticement**, lure, decoy,
snare, trap, inducement, carrot,
attraction; informal **come-on**.
• v. **1** taunt or tease. **2** put bait on
or in.
▷ SYNONYMS: **taunt**, tease, goad, pick on,

torment, persecute, harass; informal
needle; Brit. informal wind up.

baize n. thick green material used to
cover billiard tables.

bake v. cook or harden by dry heat.

baker n. a person whose trade is
making bread and cakes.
□ **baker's dozen** a group of thirteen.
■ **bakery** n.

baksheesh n. (in eastern countries) a
tip or bribe.

balaclava n. a woollen hat covering
the head and neck.

balalaika n. a Russian musical
instrument like a guitar.

balance n. **1** an even distribution
of weight. **2** a situation in which
elements are in the correct
proportions. **3** a device for weighing.
4 the difference between credits and
debits in an account. **5** an amount still
owed after paying part of a debt.
▷ SYNONYMS: **1 stability**, equilibrium,
steadiness, footing. **2 fairness**,
justice, impartiality, parity, equity,
evenness, uniformity, comparability.
3 remainder, outstanding amount,
rest, residue, difference.
– ANTONYMS: instability, bias.
• v. **1** be or put in a steady position.
2 compare.
▷ SYNONYMS: **1 steady**, stabilize, poise,
level. **2 weigh up**, compare, evaluate,
consider, assess. **3 counterbalance**,
balance out, offset, counteract,
compensate for, make up for.

balcony n. (pl. **balconies**) **1** an
enclosed platform projecting from
the outside of a building. **2** the
highest level of seats in a theatre or
cinema.

bald adj. **1** having no hair on the head.
2 (of a tyre) with the tread worn
away. **3** without details.
▷ SYNONYMS: **1 hairless**, smooth, shaven,
depilated. **2 plain**, simple, direct,
blunt, unadorned, unvarnished,
unembellished, stark; informal upfront.
– ANTONYMS: hairy.
■ **baldly** adv. **baldness** n.

balderdash n. nonsense.

balding adj. going bald.

bale (see also **bail**) n. a large bundle of
cloth, paper, or hay.
• v. make into bales.

baleful adj. menacing.
■ **balefully** adv.

balk US = **BAULK**.

ball n. **1** a rounded object used in
games. **2** a throw or kick of the ball in
a game. **3** a rounded part or thing. **4** a
formal social gathering for dancing.
▷ SYNONYMS: **sphere**, globe, orb, globule,
spheroid.
□ **ball bearing** a ring of small metal
balls reducing friction between
moving parts of a machine, or one
of these balls. **ballcock** a valve
controlling the water level in a
cistern. **ballpoint pen** a pen with a
tiny ball as its writing point. **ballroom**
a large room for formal dancing.

ballad n. **1** a poem or song telling a
story. **2** a slow sentimental song.

ballast n. **1** heavy material carried by
a ship to keep it stable. **2** coarse stone
used as the base of a railway or road.

ballerina n. a female ballet dancer.

ballet n. an artistic dance form
performed to music.
■ **balletic** adj.

ballistics n. the science of missiles
and firearms.
□ **ballistic missile** a missile which
is fired into the air and falls under
gravity on to its target.

balloon n. **1** a small inflatable rubber
bag used as a toy. **2** (or **hot-air
balloon**) a large bag filled with hot
gas to make it rise, with a basket for
carrying passengers.
• v. swell or increase.

ballot n. a way of voting secretly by
means of paper slips placed in a box.
▷ SYNONYMS: **vote**, poll, election, referendum, show of hands, plebiscite.
• v. (**balloting**, **balloted**) ask for a
secret vote from.

ballyhoo n. informal a fuss.

balm n. **1** a scented ointment.
2 something that soothes or heals.

balmy adj. (of the weather) pleasantly
warm.

baloney n. informal nonsense.

balsa n. lightweight wood from a
tropical American tree.

balsam n. a scented resin used in
perfumes and medicines.

baluster n. a short pillar forming part
of a series supporting a rail.

balustrade n. a railing supported by
balusters.

bamboo n. a giant tropical grass with
hollow stems.

bamboozle v. informal cheat or deceive.

ban v. (**banning**, **banned**) forbid
officially.
▷ SYNONYMS: **prohibit**, forbid, veto,
proscribe, outlaw, make illegal, bar,
debar, prevent, exclude, banish.
– ANTONYMS: permit, admit.
• n. an official order forbidding
something.

▷ SYNONYMS: **prohibition**, embargo, veto, boycott, bar, proscription, moratorium, injunction.

banal /buh-**nahl**/ adj. predictable and unoriginal.

▷ SYNONYMS: **unoriginal**, unimaginative, uninspired, trite, hackneyed, clichéd, platitudinous, commonplace, stereotyped, overused, stale, boring, dull, obvious, predictable, tired, pedestrian; informal corny, old hat.

− ANTONYMS: original.

■ **banality** n.

banana n. a curved yellow fruit.

band n. **1** a piece of material used for fastening, strengthening, etc. **2** a stripe or strip. **3** a range of values or frequencies within a series. **4** a group of musicians. **5** a group of people with a shared aim or feature.

▷ SYNONYMS: **1 loop**, wristband, headband, ring, hoop, circlet, belt, sash, girdle, strap, strip, tape, circle. **2 stripe**, strip, line, belt, bar, streak, border, swathe. **3 ensemble**, group, orchestra; informal combo. **4 gang**, group, mob, pack, troop, troupe, company, set, party, crew, body, team; informal bunch.

• v. form a group.

□ **bandstand** a covered outdoor platform for a band playing music. **bandwagon** an activity or cause that has suddenly become popular.

■ **banded** adj.

bandage n. a strip of material for tying round a wound.

▷ SYNONYMS: **dressing**, covering, plaster, compress, gauze, lint.

• v. tie a bandage round.

▷ SYNONYMS: **bind**, dress, cover, strap up.

bandanna (or **bandana**) n. a square of cloth tied round the head or neck.

B. & B. abbrev. bed and breakfast.

bandit n. a member of a gang of armed robbers.

▷ SYNONYMS: **robber**, thief, raider, mugger, pirate, outlaw, hijacker, looter, marauder, gangster; literary brigand; historical rustler, highwayman, footpad.

bandy adj. (of a person's legs) curved outwards at the knees.

• v. (**bandying**, **bandied**) mention frequently or casually.

□ **bandy words** exchange angry remarks.

bane n. a cause of great distress or annoyance.

bang n. **1** a sudden loud, sharp noise. **2** a sharp blow.

▷ SYNONYMS: **1 crash**, crack, thud, thump, bump, boom, blast, clap, report, explosion. **2 blow**, bump, knock, hit, smack, crack, thump; informal bash, whack.

• v. **1** hit or put down noisily. **2** make a bang.

▷ SYNONYMS: **1 hit**, strike, beat, thump, hammer, knock, rap, pound, thud, punch, bump, smack, crack, slap, slam; informal bash, whack, clobber, clout, wallop. **2 crash**, boom, pound, explode, detonate, burst, blow up.

• adv. Brit. informal exactly: *bang on time*.

banger n. Brit. informal **1** a sausage. **2** an old car. **3** a loud explosive firework.

bangle n. a bracelet made of rigid material.

banish v. **1** send into exile. **2** get rid of; drive away.

▷ SYNONYMS: **1 exile**, expel, deport, eject, repatriate, transport, extradite, evict, throw out, exclude, shut out, ban. **2 dispel**, dismiss, disperse, scatter, dissipate, drive away, chase away, shut out.

■ **banishment** n.

banisters (or **bannisters**) pl. n. the upright posts and handrail at the side of a staircase.

banjo n. (pl. **banjos**) a guitar-like musical instrument with a circular body.

bank n. **1** an organization that keeps customers' money and provides other financial services. **2** the land alongside a river. **3** a stock or supply. **4** a long, high slope or mass. **5** a row of similar objects.

▷ SYNONYMS: **1 edge**, shore, side, embankment, levee, margin, verge, brink. **2 store**, reserve, stock, stockpile, supply, pool, fund, cache, hoard, deposit. **3 slope**, rise, incline, gradient, ramp, mound, pile, heap, ridge, hillock, knoll, bar, shoal, mass, drift. **4 array**, row, line, tier, group, series.

• v. **1** put money in a bank. **2** (**bank on**) rely on. **3** form into a mound or mass. **4** (of an aircraft) tilt sideways when turning.

▷ SYNONYMS: **1 deposit**, pay in, save. **2** (**bank on**) **rely on**, depend on, count on, reckon on, be sure of. **3 pile up**, heap up, stack up, amass. **4 tilt**, lean, tip, slant, incline, angle, list, camber, pitch.

□ **bank holiday** Brit. a public holiday. **banknote** a piece of paper money.

■ **banker** n.

bankrupt adj. officially declared not to have enough money to pay debts.

b

▷ SYNONYMS: **insolvent**, ruined; Brit. in administration, in receivership; informal bust, broke, belly up, wiped out.
– ANTONYMS: solvent.
• n. a bankrupt person.
• v. make bankrupt.
■ **bankruptcy** n.

banner n. a strip of cloth with a slogan or design, hung up or carried on poles.
▷ SYNONYMS: **1 placard**, sign, poster, notice. **2 flag**, standard, ensign, colours, pennant, pennon, banderole.

banns pl. n. an announcement in church of a forthcoming marriage.

banquet n. an elaborate formal meal for many people.
▷ SYNONYMS: **feast**, dinner; informal spread, blowout; Brit. informal nosh-up, slap-up meal.

banquette /bang-ket/ n. a padded bench along a wall.

banshee n. (in Irish legend) a female spirit whose wailing warns of a death.

bantam n. a small chicken.
□ **bantamweight** a weight in boxing between flyweight and featherweight.

banter n. friendly teasing.
▷ SYNONYMS: **repartee**, witty conversation, raillery, wordplay, cut and thrust, badinage, persiflage.
• v. tease in a friendly way.
▷ SYNONYMS: **joke**, jest; informal josh, wisecrack.

Bantu n. (pl. **Bantu** or **Bantus**) a member of a large group of indigenous African peoples.

> USAGE **Bantu** is a very offensive word in South African English, esp. when used to refer to individual people.

bap n. Brit. a soft bread roll.

baptism n. a Christian ceremony in which a person is sprinkled with or dipped in water as a sign of purification and entry to the Church.
■ **baptismal** adj.

Baptist n. a member of a Protestant group believing that only adults should be baptized.

baptize (or **-ise**) v. **1** perform baptism on. **2** give a name or nickname to.
▷ SYNONYMS: **1 christen. 2** they were baptized into the church: **admit**, initiate, enrol, recruit. **3 name**, call, dub.

bar n. **1** a long rigid bar of wood, metal, etc. **2** a counter, room, etc. where alcohol is served. **3** a barrier. **4** one of the short units into which a

piece of music is divided. **5** (**the Bar**) barristers or their profession. **6** a unit of atmospheric pressure.
▷ SYNONYMS: **1 rod**, stick, pole, batten, shaft, rail, spar, strut, crosspiece, beam. **2 block**, slab, cake, tablet, wedge, ingot. **3 counter**, table, buffet. **4 inn**, tavern, hostelry; Brit. pub, public house; Brit. informal local, boozer. **5 obstacle**, impediment, hindrance, obstruction, block, hurdle, barrier.
– ANTONYMS: aid.
• v. (**barring**, **barred**) **1** fasten with a bar or bars. **2** forbid or prevent.
▷ SYNONYMS: **1 bolt**, lock, fasten, secure, block, barricade, obstruct. **2 prohibit**, debar, preclude, forbid, ban, exclude, obstruct, prevent, hinder, block, stop.
• prep. except for.
□ **bar code** a row of printed stripes identifying a product and its price, readable by a computer. **barman** (or **barmaid**) a person serving drinks in a pub or bar.

barb n. **1** a backward-pointing part of fish hook etc. **2** a spiteful remark.

barbarian n. an uncivilized or cruel person.
▷ SYNONYMS: **savage**, heathen, brute, beast, philistine, boor, yahoo, oaf, lout, vandal; Brit. informal yob.

barbaric adj. **1** savagely cruel. **2** not civilized.
▷ SYNONYMS: **1 cruel**, brutal, barbarous, brutish, savage, vicious, wicked, ruthless, vile, inhuman. **2 uncultured**, uncivilized, barbarian, philistine, boorish, loutish; Brit. informal yobbish.
– ANTONYMS: civilized.
■ **barbarity** n.

barbarous adj. barbaric.
■ **barbarism** n.

barbecue n. **1** an outdoor meal at which food is grilled over an open fire. **2** a structure or device for grilling food outdoors.
• v. cook on a barbecue.

barbed adj. **1** having a barb or barbs. **2** spiteful.
□ **barbed wire** wire with clusters of sharp points along it.

barber n. a men's hairdresser.

barbiturate n. a sedative drug.

bard n. literary a poet.

bare adj. **1** not clothed. **2** lacking the usual covering or contents. **3** only just enough.
▷ SYNONYMS: **1 naked**, unclothed, undressed, uncovered, stripped, nude; informal without a stitch on, in the altogether; Brit. informal starkers; N. Amer. informal buck naked. **2 empty**,

unfurnished, clear, undecorated, unadorned, bleak, austere. **3 basic**, essential, fundamental, plain, straightforward, simple, unembellished, pure, stark, bald, cold, hard.
• v. uncover or reveal.
□ **bareback** on horseback without a saddle. **barefaced** done openly and without shame.

barely adv. only just.
▷ SYNONYMS: **hardly**, scarcely, only just, narrowly, by the skin of your teeth, by a hair's breadth; informal by a whisker; Brit. informal at a push.

bargain n. **1** a thing bought at a low price. **2** an agreement where each party does something for the other.
▷ SYNONYMS: **1 agreement**, arrangement, understanding, deal, contract, pact. **2 good value**; informal good buy, snip, steal, giveaway.
• v. **1** discuss the terms of an agreement. **2** (**bargain for/on**) expect.
▷ SYNONYMS: **haggle**, negotiate, discuss terms, deal, barter.

barge n. a long flat-bottomed boat used on canals and rivers.
• v. **1** move forcefully. **2** (**barge in**) burst in on rudely.

baritone n. a man's singing voice between tenor and bass.

barium n. a white metallic element.

bark n. **1** the sharp cry of a dog. **2** the outer layer of a tree.
▷ SYNONYMS: **rind**, skin, peel, covering.
• v. **1** give a bark. **2** say suddenly or fiercely. **3** scrape the skin off your shin accidentally.
▷ SYNONYMS: **1 woof**, yap. **2 shout**, snap, bawl, yell, roar, bellow, thunder; informal holler.
– ANTONYMS: whisper.

barley n. a type of cereal plant with bristly heads.
□ **barley sugar** a sweet made of boiled sugar.

bar mitzvah n. a religious ceremony in which a Jewish boy aged 13 takes on the responsibilities of an adult.

barmy adj. (**barmier, barmiest**) Brit. informal mad.

barn n. a large farm building used for storing grain etc.

barnacle n. a shellfish which fixes itself to objects under water.

barney n. (pl. **barneys**) informal a noisy quarrel.

barometer n. an instrument that measures atmospheric pressure, used in weather forecasting.
■ **barometric** adj.

baron n. **1** a man belonging to the lowest rank of the nobility. **2** a powerful businessman.
■ **baronial** adj.

baroness n. **1** a baron's wife or widow. **2** a woman with the rank of baron.

baronet n. a man who holds a title below that of baron.
■ **baronetcy** n.

baroque n. an ornate style of architecture, art, and music of the 17th and 18th centuries.
• adj. ornate in style.

barque /bark/ n. a sailing ship.

barrack v. Brit. shout insults at a performer or speaker.
• pl. n. (**barracks**) buildings for housing soldiers.
▷ SYNONYMS: **garrison**, camp, encampment, depot, billet, quarters, fort, cantonment.

barracuda n. a large, predatory tropical sea fish.

barrage n. **1** a continuous artillery attack. **2** a large number of questions or complaints. **3** an artificial barrier across a river.
▷ SYNONYMS: **1 bombardment**, gunfire, shelling, salvo, volley, fusillade; historical broadside. **2 deluge**, stream, storm, torrent, onslaught, flood, spate, tide, avalanche, hail, blaze. **3 dam**, barrier, weir, dyke, embankment, wall.

barre n. a horizontal bar used for support in ballet exercises.

barrel n. **1** a cylindrical container with flat ends. **2** a tube forming part of a gun, pen, etc.
▷ SYNONYMS: **cask**, keg, butt, vat, tun, drum, hogshead, firkin.
□ **barrel organ** a small organ playing a set tune when a handle is turned.

> **WORD LINKS**
> **cooper** a person who makes barrels

barren adj. **1** (of land) not fertile. **2** unable to bear young. **3** empty or lifeless.
▷ SYNONYMS: **unproductive**, infertile, unfruitful, sterile, arid, desert, waste, lifeless, empty.
– ANTONYMS: fertile.
■ **barrenness** n.

barricade n. a makeshift barrier.
▷ SYNONYMS: **barrier**, roadblock, blockade, obstacle, obstruction.
• v. block or defend with a barricade.
▷ SYNONYMS: **seal up**, close up, block off, shut off/up, defend, protect, fortify, occupy.

barrier n. an obstacle that prevents

movement, access, or progress.
▷ SYNONYMS: **1 fence**, railing, barricade, hurdle, bar, blockade, roadblock. **2** *a barrier to international trade*: **obstacle**, obstruction, hurdle, stumbling block, bar, impediment, hindrance, curb.

barring prep. except for; if not for.

barrister n. Brit. a lawyer qualified to argue a case in court.

barrow n. **1** Brit. a two-wheeled handcart used by street traders. **2** an ancient burial mound.

barter v. exchange goods or services for other goods or services.
▷ SYNONYMS: **1 swap**, trade, exchange, sell. **2 haggle**, bargain, negotiate, deal.
• n. trading by bartering.

basal /bay-s'l/ adj. forming or belonging to a base.

basalt /ba-sawlt/ n. a dark volcanic rock.

base n. **1** the lowest or supporting part of something. **2** the main place where a person works or stays. **3** a centre of operations. **4** a main element to which others are added. **5** a substance able to react with an acid to form a salt and water. **6** the number on which a system of counting is based. **7** Baseball each of the four points that must be reached in turn to score a run.
▷ SYNONYMS: **1 foundation**, bottom, foot, support, stand, pedestal, plinth, rest. **2 basis**, foundation, bedrock, starting point, source, origin, root, core, key component. **3 headquarters**, camp, site, station, settlement, post, centre.
– ANTONYMS: top.
• v. **1** (**base on**) use something as the foundation for. **2** put at a centre of operations.
▷ SYNONYMS: **1 found**, build, construct, form, ground; (**be based on**) derive from, spring from, stem from, depend on. **2 locate**, situate, position, install, station, site.
• adj. bad or immoral.
▷ SYNONYMS: **sordid**, ignoble, low, mean, immoral, unscrupulous, unprincipled, dishonest, dishonourable, shameful, shabby, contemptible, despicable.
– ANTONYMS: noble.
□ **baseball** a team game played with a bat and ball on a circuit of four bases, which a batter must run around to score.

baseless adj. not based on fact; untrue.

basement n. a room or floor below ground level.

bash informal v. hit hard.
• n. **1** a heavy blow. **2** a party.

bashful adj. shy.
▷ SYNONYMS: **shy**, reserved, diffident, inhibited, retiring, reticent, reluctant, shrinking, self-effacing, unassertive, timid, nervous, self-conscious.
– ANTONYMS: bold, confident.
■ **bashfully** adv. **bashfulness** n.

BASIC n. a high-level computer programming language.

basic adj. **1** forming an essential foundation; fundamental. **2** consisting of the minimum needed or offered.
▷ SYNONYMS: **1 fundamental**, essential, vital, primary, principal, cardinal, elementary, intrinsic, central, pivotal, critical, key, focal. **2 plain**, simple, unsophisticated, straightforward, adequate, spartan, stark, severe, austere, limited, meagre, rudimentary, patchy, sketchy, minimal, crude, makeshift; informal bog-standard.
– ANTONYMS: unimportant, luxurious.
• n. (**basics**) essential facts or principles.
▷ SYNONYMS: **fundamentals**, essentials, first principles, foundations, preliminaries, groundwork, essence, basis, core; informal nitty-gritty, brass tacks, nuts and bolts, ABC.

basically adv. in the most fundamental respects.
▷ SYNONYMS: **fundamentally**, essentially, first and foremost, primarily, at heart, at bottom, intrinsically, inherently, principally, chiefly, above all, mostly, mainly, on the whole, by and large.

basil n. a herb used in cookery.

basilica n. a large church with two rows of columns and a curved end.

basilisk n. a mythical reptile whose gaze or breath was deadly.

basin n. **1** a round open container for food or liquid. **2** a circular valley. **3** an area drained by a river. **4** an enclosed area of water for mooring boats.
▷ SYNONYMS: **bowl**, dish, pan, container, receptacle, vessel.

basis n. (pl. **bases**) **1** the foundation of a theory or process. **2** a way in which things are done: *they met on a regular basis.*
▷ SYNONYMS: **1** *the basis of his method*: **foundation**, support, base, reasoning, rationale, defence, reason, grounds, justification. **2** *the basis of discussion*: **starting point**, base, point of departure, beginning, premise, fundamental point/principle, cornerstone, core, heart. **3** *on a part-time basis*:

footing, condition, status, position, arrangement.

bask v. lie in the sun for pleasure.
▷ SYNONYMS: **1 laze**, lie, lounge, relax, sprawl, loll, luxuriate. **2 revel**, wallow, delight, take great pleasure, enjoy, relish, savour.

basket n. a container for carrying things, made from strips of cane or wire.
□ **basketball** a team game in which goals are scored by throwing a ball through a hoop.

Basque n. **1** a member of a people living in the western Pyrenees in France and Spain. **2** the language of the Basques.

bas-relief n. a carving with figures standing out slightly from the background.

bass¹ /bayss/ n. **1** the lowest male singing voice. **2** the deep, low-frequency output of a radio or audio system.
• adj. of the lowest pitch in music.
▷ SYNONYMS: **low**, deep, resonant, sonorous, rumbling, booming, resounding.
– ANTONYMS: high.

bass² /bass/ n. (pl. **bass** or **basses**) an edible fish related to the perch.

bassoon n. a large bass woodwind instrument.

bastard n. **1** old use or derogatory an illegitimate child. **2** informal an unpleasant person.

bastardize (or **-ise**) v. make less good by adding new elements.

baste v. **1** pour fat or juices over meat during cooking. **2** sew together temporarily with loose stitches.

bastion n. **1** a stronghold of a principle or activity. **2** a projecting part of a fortification.

bat n. **1** an implement for hitting the ball in sports. **2** a flying mammal active at night.
• v. (**batting**, **batted**) **1** (in sport) take the role of hitting the ball. **2** hit with the flat of the hand.
□ **batsman** a player who bats in cricket.

batch n. a quantity of goods produced or dispatched at one time.
▷ SYNONYMS: **group**, quantity, lot, bunch, cluster, raft, set, collection, bundle, pack, consignment, shipment.

bated adj. (**with bated breath**) in great suspense.

USAGE The spelling is bated, not baited.

bath n. **1** a large tub filled with water for washing the body. **2** an act of washing in a bath. **3** (also **baths**) Brit. a public swimming pool.
• v. Brit. wash in a bath.
□ **bathroom** a room with a bath, washbasin, toilet, etc.

bathe v. **1** soak or wipe gently with liquid. **2** Brit. take a swim.
▷ SYNONYMS: **1 swim**, take a dip. **2 clean**, wash, rinse, wet, soak, steep. **3 envelop**, cover, flood, fill, wash, pervade, suffuse.
• n. Brit. a swim.
■ **bather** n.

bathos /bay-thoss/ n. (in literature) a change from a serious mood to something trivial or ridiculous.

batik /ba-teek/ n. a method of producing designs on cloth by waxing the parts not to be dyed.

batman n. dated (in the armed forces) an officer's personal attendant.

baton n. **1** a thin stick used to conduct an orchestra or choir. **2** a short stick passed from runner to runner in a relay race.
▷ SYNONYMS: **stick**, rod, staff, wand, truncheon, club, mace.

battalion n. an army unit forming part of a brigade.

batten n. a long wooden or metal strip for strengthening or securing something.

batter n. **1** a mixture of flour, eggs, and milk or water, used in cooking. **2** a player who bats in baseball.
• v. hit hard and repeatedly.
▷ SYNONYMS: **beat up**, pummel, pound, rain blows on, buffet, belabour, thrash; informal knock about/around, lay into, do over.
□ **battering ram** a heavy object swung or rammed against a door to break it down.

battery n. (pl. **batteries**) **1** a device containing an electrical cell or cells, used as a source of power. **2** Brit. a set of small cages for the intensive rearing of poultry. **3** Law the crime of physically attacking another person. **4** a group of heavy guns.

battle n. **1** a fight between organized armed forces. **2** a long and difficult struggle.
▷ SYNONYMS: **1** he was killed in the battle: **fight**, engagement, armed conflict, clash, struggle, skirmish, fray, war, campaign, crusade, warfare, combat, action, hostilities; informal scrap, dogfight, shoot-out. **2** a legal battle: **conflict**, clash, struggle, disagreement, argument, dispute, tussle.

b

b

• v. fight or struggle with determination.

▷ SYNONYMS: **fight**, combat, contend with, resist, withstand, stand up to, confront, war, feud, struggle, strive, work.

□ **battleaxe 1** a large axe used in ancient warfare. **2** informal an aggressive woman. **battlefield** the scene of a battle. **battlement** a parapet with gaps for firing through. **battleship** a large, heavily armoured warship.

batty adj. (**battier**, **battiest**) informal mad.

bauble n. a small, showy trinket or decoration.

baulk (US **balk**) v. **1** (**baulk at**) hesitate to accept. **2** thwart or hinder.

bauxite n. a clay-like rock from which aluminium is obtained.

bawdy adj. (**bawdier**, **bawdiest**) referring to sex in an amusing way.

▷ SYNONYMS: **ribald**, indecent, risqué, racy, earthy, rude, suggestive, titillating, naughty, improper, indelicate, vulgar, crude, smutty; informal raunchy.

■ **bawdiness** n.

bawl v. **1** shout. **2** weep noisily.

▷ SYNONYMS: **1 shout**, yell, roar, bellow, screech, scream, shriek, bark, thunder; informal yammer, holler. **2 cry**, sob, weep, wail, whine, howl; Scottish informal greet.

− ANTONYMS: whisper.

bay n. **1** a broad curved inlet of the sea. **2** a shrub whose leaves are used in cookery. **3** a window area that projects outwards from a wall. **4** an area with a particular purpose: *a loading bay*.

▷ SYNONYMS: **1 cove**, inlet, gulf, sound, bight, basin, fjord. **2 alcove**, recess, niche, nook, opening, inglenook.

• v. (of a dog) howl loudly.

• adj. (of a horse) reddish-brown.

□ **bay window** a window projecting out from a wall.

bayonet n. a long blade fixed to a rifle.

• v. (**bayoneting**, **bayoneted**) stab with a bayonet.

bazaar n. **1** a market in a Middle Eastern country. **2** a sale of goods to raise funds.

▷ SYNONYMS: **1 market**, marketplace, souk, mart. **2 fete**, fair, fund-raiser; Brit. jumble sale, bring-and-buy sale, car boot sale; N. Amer. rummage sale, tag sale.

bazooka n. a short-range rocket launcher used against tanks.

BBC abbrev. British Broadcasting Corporation.

BC abbrev. before Christ (used to indicate that a date is before the Christian era).

be v. (sing. present **am**; **are**; **is**; pl. present **are**; 1st & 3rd sing. past **was**; 2nd sing. past & pl. past **were**; pres. part. **being**; past part. **been**) **1** exist; be present. **2** happen. **3** have a specified state, nature, or role.

▷ SYNONYMS: **1 exist**, live, be alive, breathe, be extant. **2 occur**, happen, take place, come about, arise, fall; literary come to pass, befall, betide. **3 be situated**, be located, be found, be present, be set, be positioned, be placed, be installed, sit, lie.

• aux. v. used to form tenses of other verbs.

beach n. an area of sand or pebbles at the edge of the sea.

▷ SYNONYMS: **sands**, seaside, seashore, coast; literary strand, littoral.

• v. bring on to a beach from the water.

▷ SYNONYMS: **land**, ground, strand, run ashore.

□ **beachcomber** a person who searches beaches for things of value. **beachhead** a fortified position on a beach taken by landing forces.

beacon n. **1** a fire lit on a hill as a signal. **2** a light acting as a signal for ships or aircraft.

▷ SYNONYMS: **signal**, light, fire, danger signal, bonfire, lighthouse.

bead n. **1** a small piece of glass, stone, etc., threaded in a string with others. **2** a small drop of liquid.

▷ SYNONYMS: **1 ball**, pellet, pill, globule, sphere, spheroid, orb, round; (**beads**) necklace, rosary, chaplet. **2** *beads of sweat*: **droplet**, drop, drip, blob, pearl, dot.

■ **beaded** adj.

beadle n. hist. a parish officer who dealt with minor offenders.

beady adj. (of eyes) small, round, and observant.

beagle n. a small breed of hound.

beak n. **1** a bird's horny projecting jaws. **2** informal a magistrate.

beaker n. Brit. **1** a tall plastic cup. **2** a glass container used in laboratories.

▷ SYNONYMS: **cup**, tumbler, glass, mug, drinking vessel.

beam n. **1** a long piece of timber or metal used as a support in building. **2** a ray of light or particles. **3** a radiant smile. **4** the width of a ship.

▷ SYNONYMS: **1 plank**, timber, joist, rafter, lintel, spar, girder, support. **2 ray**, shaft, stream, streak, pencil,

flash, gleam, glint. **3** grin, smile.
– ANTONYMS: frown.
• v. **1** transmit a radio signal. **2** shine
brightly. **3** smile radiantly.
▷ SYNONYMS: **1** broadcast, transmit,
relay, disseminate, direct, send, aim.
2 shine, radiate, glare, gleam. **3** grin,
smile.
– ANTONYMS: frown.

bean n. **1** an edible seed growing in
long pods on certain plants. **2** the
seed of a coffee or cocoa plant.

bear¹ v. (**bearing**, **bore**; past part. **borne**)
1 carry. **2** support a weight. **3** (**bear
yourself**) behave in a particular way.
4 tolerate. **5** give birth to a child.
6 produce fruit or flowers. **7** take a
specified direction.
▷ SYNONYMS: **1** carry, bring, transport,
move, convey, take, fetch; informal tote.
2 display, be marked with, show,
carry, exhibit. **3** withstand, support,
sustain, stand, take, carry, hold up,
cope with, handle. **4** *he still bears a
grudge against them*: harbour, foster,
entertain, cherish, nurse. **5** *I can't
bear sport*: endure, tolerate, put up
with, stand, abide, countenance,
stomach; informal hack, swallow; Brit.
informal stick, wear; formal brook. **6** give
birth to, bring forth, deliver, have,
produce, spawn. **7** produce, yield,
give, provide, supply.
□ **bear down on** approach in a
purposeful way. **bear out** support or
confirm. **bear up** remain cheerful in
adversity. **bear with** be patient with.
■ bearable adj. bearer n.

bear² n. a large mammal with thick
fur.
□ **bearskin** a tall furry cap worn by
certain troops.

> WORD LINKS
> **ursine** relating to bears

beard n. a growth of hair on a man's
chin.
• v. boldly confront an important
person.
■ bearded adj.

bearing n. **1** a way of standing,
moving, or behaving. **2** relevance. **3** a
device allowing two parts to rotate
or move in contact with each other.
4 direction or position in relation
to a fixed point. **5** (**your bearings**)
awareness of where you are.
▷ SYNONYMS: **1** posture, stance, carriage,
gait, demeanour, manner, mien, air,
aspect, attitude, style; Brit. deportment. **2** *this has no bearing on the
matter*: relevance, pertinence,
connection, relation, relationship,

import, significance, application.
3 direction, orientation, course,
trajectory, heading, tack, path. **4** *I
lost my bearings*: orientation, sense
of direction, whereabouts, location,
position.

beast n. **1** a large animal. **2** a very
cruel or wicked person.
▷ SYNONYMS: **1** creature, animal; N. Amer.
informal critter. **2** monster, brute,
savage, barbarian, animal, swine,
ogre, fiend, sadist, demon, devil.

beastly adj. Brit. informal very
unpleasant.
■ beastliness n.

beat v. (**beating**, **beat**; past part. **beaten**)
1 hit repeatedly. **2** defeat or outdo.
3 move or throb rhythmically. **4** stir
cooking ingredients vigorously.
▷ SYNONYMS: **1** hit, strike, batter, thump,
bang, hammer, punch, knock, thrash,
pound, pummel, slap, rain blows on,
assault; informal wallop, belt, bash,
whack, clout, clobber. **2** defeat,
conquer, vanquish, trounce, rout,
overpower, overcome; informal lick,
thrash, whip. **3** *he's beaten the world
record*: exceed, surpass, better,
improve on, eclipse, transcend, top,
trump, cap. **4** throb, pulse, pulsate,
pump, palpitate, pound, thump, thud,
hammer, drum. **5** flap, flutter, thrash,
wave, vibrate. **6** whisk, mix, blend,
whip.
• n. **1** an act of beating. **2** a main
accent in music or poetry. **3** an area
patrolled by a police officer.
▷ SYNONYMS: **1** rhythm, pulse, metre,
time, measure, cadence, stress,
accent. **2** pulse, pulsation, vibration,
throb, palpitation, reverberation,
pounding, thump, thud, hammering,
drumming. **3** circuit, round, route,
path.
□ **beat up** attack violently.

beatific /bee-uh-tif-ik/ adj. very
happy.
■ beatifically adv.

beatify /bi-at-i-fy/ v. (**beatifying**,
beatified) (in the RC Church) declare
a dead person to be in a state of bliss,
the first step towards canonization.

beatitude /bi-at-i-tyood/ n. a state of
blessedness.

beautician n. a person whose job is to
give beauty treatments.

beautiful adj. **1** very pleasing to the
senses. **2** excellent.
▷ SYNONYMS: attractive, pretty,
handsome, good-looking, fetching,
lovely, charming, graceful, elegant,

appealing, winsome, ravishing, gorgeous, stunning, glamorous; Scottish & N. English **bonny**; informal **tasty, knockout, drop-dead gorgeous**; Brit. informal **smashing**; N. Amer. informal **cute, foxy**; Austral./NZ informal **beaut, spunky**; old use **comely**.
– ANTONYMS: ugly.
■ **beautifully** adv.

beautify v. (**beautifying, beautified**) make beautiful.
▷ SYNONYMS: **adorn**, embellish, enhance, decorate, ornament, prettify, glamorize; informal **do up, tart up**.

beauty n. (pl. **beauties**) **1** the quality of being very pleasing to the senses. **2** a beautiful woman. **3** an excellent example.
▷ SYNONYMS: **1 attractiveness**, prettiness, good looks, loveliness, appeal, winsomeness, charm, grace, elegance, exquisiteness, glamour; literary **pulchritude. 2 belle**, vision, goddess, picture, Venus; informal **babe, looker, lovely, stunner, knockout, bombshell, cracker.**
– ANTONYMS: ugliness.

beaver n. a large rodent that lives partly in water.
• v. (**beaver away**) informal work hard.

becalmed adj. (of a sailing ship) unable to move through lack of wind.

because conj. for the reason that.
▷ SYNONYMS: **since**, as, seeing that, in view of the fact that, in that, owing to the fact that.

beck n. (**at someone's beck and call**) doing whatever someone asks.

beckon v. make a summoning gesture.
▷ SYNONYMS: **1 gesture**, signal, wave, gesticulate, motion. **2 entice**, invite, tempt, lure, charm, attract, draw, call.

become v. (**becoming, became**; past part. **become**) **1** begin to be. **2** turn into. **3** (**become of**) happen to. **4** suit or be appropriate to.
▷ SYNONYMS: **1** *she became rich*: **grow**, get, turn, come to be, get to be. **2** *he became a tyrant*: **turn into**, change into, be transformed into, develop into, evolve into. **3** *he became Foreign Secretary*: **be appointed**, be nominated, be elected. **4** suit, flatter, look good on, set off; informal **do something for.**

becoming adj. **1** making someone look attractive. **2** appropriate or suitable.
▷ SYNONYMS: **flattering**, fetching, attractive, pretty, elegant, well chosen, stylish, fashionable, tasteful.

becquerel n. a unit of radioactivity.

bed n. **1** a piece of furniture for sleeping on. **2** an area of ground where flowers are grown. **3** a flat base or foundation.
▷ SYNONYMS: **1 couch**, berth, billet, cot; informal **the sack. 2** *a flower bed*: **patch**, plot, border, strip. **3 base**, foundation, footing, support, basis.
• v. (**bedding, bedded**) (**bed down**) sleep in an improvised place.
□ **bedclothes** sheets, blankets, etc. **bedpan** a container used as a toilet by a bedridden person. **bedridden** confined to bed due to illness or old age. **bedrock 1** a layer of solid rock under soil. **2** the central principles on which something is based. **bedroom** a room for sleeping in. **bedsit** (or **bedsitter**) Brit. a rented room combining a bedroom and living room. **bedsore** a sore caused by lying in bed in one position for a long time. **bedspread** a decorative bed covering. **bedstead** the framework of a bed.

bedding n. bedclothes.

bedevil v. (**bedevilling, bedevilled**; US **bedeviling, bedeviled**) cause continual trouble to.

bedlam n. a noisy, confused scene.

Bedouin /bed-oo-in/ n. (pl. **Bedouin**) an Arab living as a nomad in the desert.

bedraggled adj. untidy.
▷ SYNONYMS: **dishevelled**, disordered, untidy, unkempt, tousled; N. Amer. informal **mussed.**
– ANTONYMS: neat.

bee n. a winged insect which makes wax and honey.
□ **beehive** a structure in which bees are kept. **beeswax** wax produced by bees to make honeycombs, used in polishes etc. **make a beeline for** hurry straight to.

WORD LINKS
apian relating to bees
apiary a place where bees are kept

beech n. a large tree with grey bark.

beef n. meat from a cow, bull, or ox.
• v. (**beef up**) informal make stronger or larger.
□ **beefburger** a fried or grilled cake of minced beef. **beefeater** a warder in the Tower of London.

beefy adj. informal muscular or strong.

been past part. of BE.

beep n. a short, high-pitched sound made by electronic equipment or a car's horn.
• v. make a beep.

■ **beeper** n.

beer n. an alcoholic drink made from malt and hops.

beet n. a plant with a fleshy root, grown as food and for making into sugar.

beetle n. an insect with hard, shiny covers over its wings.

beetroot n. Brit. the edible dark red root of a kind of beet.

befall v. (**befalling**, **befell**; past part. **befallen**) happen to.

befit v. (**befitting**, **befitted**) be appropriate for.

before prep., conj., & adv. **1** during the time preceding. **2** in front of. **3** rather than.
▷ SYNONYMS: **1 prior to**, previous to, earlier than, preparatory to, in advance of, ahead of, pre-. **2 previously**, until now/then, up to now/then, earlier, formerly, hitherto, in the past. **3 in preference to**, rather than, sooner than.
– ANTONYMS: after.

beforehand adv. in advance.
▷ SYNONYMS: **in advance**, in readiness, ahead of time, before, earlier, previously, already, sooner.
– ANTONYMS: afterwards.

befriend v. become a friend to.

befuddled adj. muddled or confused.

beg v. (**begging**, **begged**) **1** ask humbly for something. **2** ask for food or money as charity.
▷ SYNONYMS: **1 ask for money**, seek charity; informal sponge, cadge, scrounge, bum. **2** *we begged for mercy*: **plead for**, request, ask for, appeal for, call for, sue for, solicit, seek. **3** *he begged her not to go*: **implore**, entreat, plead with, appeal to, pray to, call on, petition; literary beseech.

beget v. (**begetting**, **begot**; past part. **begotten**) literary **1** cause. **2** father a child.

beggar n. a person who lives by begging for food or money.
▷ SYNONYMS: **tramp**, vagrant, vagabond, mendicant; N. Amer. hobo; informal scrounger, sponger, cadger, freeloader; Brit. informal dosser; N. Amer. informal bum; Austral./NZ informal bagman.
■ **beggarly** adj.

begin v. (**beginning**, **began**; past part. **begun**) **1** carry out or experience the first part of an action or activity. **2** come into being. **3** have as its starting point.
▷ SYNONYMS: **1 start**, commence, set about, go about, embark on, launch into, get down to, take up, initiate, set in motion, get going, get off the ground, lead off, institute, inaugurate, open; informal get cracking on, kick off. **2 appear**, arise, become apparent, spring up, crop up, turn up, come into existence, originate, start, commence, develop.
– ANTONYMS: finish, end.

beginner n. a person just starting to learn or take part in something.
▷ SYNONYMS: **novice**, learner, starter, raw recruit, newcomer, tyro, fresher, probationer, apprentice, trainee; N. Amer. informal rookie, tenderfoot, greenhorn.
– ANTONYMS: expert, veteran.

beginning n. **1** the time or place at which something begins. **2** the first or earliest part.
▷ SYNONYMS: **1 start**, commencement, creation, birth, inception, conception, origination, origin, genesis, germ, emergence, rise, dawn, launch, onset, outset, day one; informal kick-off. **2 opening**, start, commencement, first part, introduction, preamble.
– ANTONYMS: end, conclusion.

begonia n. a plant with brightly coloured flowers.

begrudge v. **1** feel envious that someone possesses something. **2** give reluctantly.
▷ SYNONYMS: **envy**, resent, grudge, be jealous of, be envious of, mind, object to.

beguile v. charm or trick.

behalf n. (**on behalf of**) **1** in the interests of. **2** as a representative of.

behave v. **1** act in a certain way. **2** (also **behave yourself**) act in a polite or acceptable way.
▷ SYNONYMS: **1** *she behaved badly*: **act**, conduct yourself, acquit yourself. **2** *the children behaved themselves*: **act correctly**, be good, be well behaved, mind your manners; informal mind your Ps and Qs.
– ANTONYMS: misbehave.

behaviour (US **behavior**) n. a way of behaving.
▷ SYNONYMS: **conduct**, actions, manners, ways, deportment, bearing, etiquette.
■ **behavioural** adj.

behead v. execute someone by cutting off their head.

behemoth /bi-hee-moth/ n. something very large, esp. an organization.

behest n. (**at the behest of**) at the request or order of.

behind prep. & adv. **1** at or to the back

of. **2** less advanced than others. **3** in support of. **4** responsible for an event or plan. **5** late in doing something.

▷ SYNONYMS: **1 at the back of**, at the rear of, beyond, on the far side of; N. Amer. in back of. **2 after**, following, at the back/rear of, hard on the heels of, in the wake of. **3 supporting**, backing, for, on the side of, in agreement with; informal rooting for. **4 responsible for**, at the bottom of, the cause of, the perpetrator of, to blame for, guilty of. ● n. informal the buttocks.

behold v. (**beholding, beheld**) old use see or observe.

beholden adj. owing something in return for a favour.

behove v. (**it behoves someone to do**) it is right or necessary for someone to do.

beige n. a pale fawn colour.

being n. **1** existence. **2** the nature of a person. **3** a living creature.

▷ SYNONYMS: **1 existence**, living, life, reality, lifeblood, vital force. **2 soul**, spirit, nature, essence, psyche, heart, bosom, breast. **3 creature**, life form, organism, living thing, individual, person, human.

belabour (US **belabor**) v. attack.

belated adj. coming late or too late.

▷ SYNONYMS: **late**, overdue, behindhand, delayed, tardy, unpunctual.

– ANTONYMS: early.

■ **belatedly** adv.

belay v. secure a rope by winding it round something.

belch v. **1** noisily expel wind from the stomach through the mouth. **2** give out smoke or flames with great force. ● n. an act of belching.

beleaguered adj. **1** in difficulties. **2** under siege.

▷ SYNONYMS: **1 besieged**, blockaded, surrounded, encircled, hemmed in, under attack. **2 troubled**, harassed, hard-pressed, in difficulties, under pressure, in a tight corner; informal up against it.

belfry n. (pl. **belfries**) the place in a bell tower in which bells are housed.

belie v. (**belying, belied**) **1** fail to give a true idea of. **2** show to be untrue.

belief n. **1** a feeling that something exists or is true. **2** a firmly held opinion. **3** trust or confidence. **4** religious faith.

▷ SYNONYMS: **1 opinion**, view, conviction, judgement, thinking, idea, theory, thought, feeling. **2 faith**, trust, reliance, confidence, credence. **3 ideology**, principle, ethic, tenet,

doctrine, teaching, dogma, creed, credo.

– ANTONYMS: disbelief, doubt.

believe v. **1** accept that something is true or that someone is telling the truth. **2** (**believe in**) have faith in the truth or existence of. **3** think or suppose. **4** have religious faith.

▷ SYNONYMS: **1** *I don't believe you:* **trust**, have confidence in, consider honest, consider truthful. **2** *do you believe that story?:* **accept**, be convinced by, give credence to, credit, trust, put confidence in; informal swallow, buy, go for. **3 think**, be of the opinion that, imagine, assume, presume, take it, understand, gather; informal reckon, figure.

– ANTONYMS: doubt.

believer n. a person who believes in something, or a person with religious faith.

▷ SYNONYMS: **disciple**, follower, supporter, adherent, devotee, upholder, worshipper.

– ANTONYMS: sceptic.

belittle v. dismiss as unimportant.

▷ SYNONYMS: **disparage**, denigrate, run down, deprecate, play down, trivialize, minimize; informal do down, pooh-pooh.

bell n. **1** a metal cup that sounds a clear musical note when struck. **2** a device that buzzes or rings to give a signal.

belladonna n. a drug made from deadly nightshade.

belle n. a beautiful woman.

bellicose adj. eager to fight.

belligerent adj. **1** aggressive. **2** engaged in a war.

▷ SYNONYMS: **1 hostile**, aggressive, threatening, antagonistic, pugnacious, bellicose, truculent, confrontational, contentious, militant, combative, argumentative; informal spoiling for a fight; Brit. informal stroppy, bolshie; N. Amer. informal scrappy. **2** *the belligerent states:* **warring**, combatant, fighting, battling.

– ANTONYMS: peaceable.

■ **belligerence** n. **belligerently** adv.

bellow v. **1** give a deep roar of pain or anger. **2** shout very loudly.

▷ SYNONYMS: **roar**, shout, bawl, thunder, boom, bark, yell, shriek, howl, scream; informal holler.

– ANTONYMS: whisper.

● n. a deep shout or noise.

bellows pl. n. a device used for blowing air into a fire.

belly n. (pl. **bellies**) **1** the abdomen. **2** a person's stomach.
▷ SYNONYMS: **stomach**, abdomen, paunch, middle, midriff, girth; informal tummy, gut, insides.
■ **bellyful** n.

belong v. **1** (**belong to**) be the property of. **2** (**belong to**) be a member of. **3** be in the right place or category. **4** feel at ease in a particular situation.
▷ SYNONYMS: **1 be owned by**, be held by, be in the hands of. **2 be a member of**, be affiliated to, be allied to, be associated with, be part of.

belongings pl. n. personal possessions.
▷ SYNONYMS: **possessions**, effects, worldly goods, chattels, property; informal gear, tackle, kit, things, stuff, bits and pieces; Brit. informal clobber.

beloved adj. dearly loved.
▷ SYNONYMS: **darling**, dear, precious, adored, cherished, treasured, prized, valued, idolized.

below prep. & adv. at a lower level than.
▷ SYNONYMS: **1 beneath**, under, underneath, lower than. **2 inferior to**, subordinate to, under, beneath.
– ANTONYMS: above, over.

belt n. **1** a strip of material worn round the waist. **2** a continuous band in machinery that connects two wheels. **3** a strip or encircling area.
▷ SYNONYMS: **1 sash**, girdle, band, strap, cummerbund. **2 region**, strip, stretch, zone, area, district, sector, territory.
• v. **1** fasten with a belt. **2** informal hit very hard. **3** (**belt up**) Brit. informal be quiet.
□ **below the belt** unfair.

belying pres. part. of BELIE.

bemoan v. complain about.

bemused adj. confused; bewildered.
▷ SYNONYMS: **bewildered**, confused, puzzled, perplexed, baffled, mystified, nonplussed, dumbfounded, at sea, at a loss; informal flummoxed, bamboozled, fazed.
■ **bemusement** n.

bench n. **1** a long seat for more than one person. **2** a long work table. **3** (**the bench**) the office of judge or magistrate.
▷ SYNONYMS: **1 seat**, form, pew, stall, settle. **2 workbench**, worktop, counter.

benchmark n. a standard against which things may be compared.
▷ SYNONYMS: **standard**, point of reference, guide, guideline, norm, touch-stone, yardstick, barometer, model, gauge, criterion.

bend v. (**bending, bent**) **1** make or become curved. **2** lean or curve the body downwards. **3** change a rule to suit yourself.
▷ SYNONYMS: **1 curve**, crook, flex, angle, hook, bow, arch, buckle, warp, contort, distort, deform, twist. **2 turn**, curve, incline, swing, veer, fork, change course, curl, loop. **3 stoop**, bow, crouch, hunch, lean down/over.
– ANTONYMS: straighten.
• n. a curve or turn.
▷ SYNONYMS: **curve**, turn, corner, kink, angle, arc, twist.
■ **bendy** adj.

beneath prep. & adv. **1** extending or directly underneath. **2** of lower status or worth than.
▷ SYNONYMS: **1 under**, underneath, below, at the foot of, at the bottom of, lower than. **2 inferior to**, below, lower than, subordinate to. **3 unworthy of**, unbecoming to, unbefitting to.
– ANTONYMS: above.

benediction n. the speaking of a blessing.

benefactor n. a person who gives money or other help.
▷ SYNONYMS: **patron**, supporter, backer, sponsor, donor, contributor, subscriber; informal angel.
■ **benefaction** n.

benefice n. an arrangement by which a Christian priest is paid and given accommodation in return for their duties.

beneficent adj. doing or resulting in good.
■ **beneficence** n.

beneficial adj. favourable or advantageous.
▷ SYNONYMS: **advantageous**, favourable, helpful, useful, of assistance, valuable, salutary, worthwhile, fruitful, productive, profitable, rewarding, gainful.
– ANTONYMS: disadvantageous.
■ **beneficially** adv.

beneficiary n. (pl. **beneficiaries**) a person who benefits from something.
▷ SYNONYMS: **recipient**, payee, heir, heiress, inheritor.

benefit n. **1** advantage or profit. **2** a payment made by the state to someone in need.
▷ SYNONYMS: **1 good**, sake, welfare, well-being, advantage, comfort, ease, convenience, help, aid, assistance, service. **2 advantage**, profit, plus

b

point, boon, blessing, reward; informal perk. **3 social security payment**, welfare, charity; informal the dole.
− ANTONYMS: detriment, disadvantage.
• v. (**benefiting**, **benefited** or **benefitting**, **benefitted**) **1** receive an advantage; profit. **2** bring advantage to.
▷ SYNONYMS: **1 profit**, gain, reap reward, make the most of, exploit, turn to your advantage, put to good use. **2 help**, be advantageous to, be beneficial to, profit, be of service to, serve, be useful to, be helpful to, aid, assist.
− ANTONYMS: harm.

benevolent adj. well meaning and kindly.
▷ SYNONYMS: **kind**, kindly, kind-hearted, good-natured, compassionate, caring, altruistic, humanitarian, philanthropic, beneficent, well meaning, benign.
− ANTONYMS: unkind.
■ **benevolence** n.

benighted adj. lacking understanding of cultural, intellectual, or moral matters.

benign adj. **1** kindly. **2** (of a tumour) not malignant.
▷ SYNONYMS: **1 kindly**, kind, warm-hearted, good-natured, friendly, genial, tender-hearted, gentle, sympathetic, compassionate, caring, well disposed, benevolent. **2 mild**, temperate, gentle, balmy, soft, pleasant, favourable, healthy. **3 harmless**, non-malignant, non-cancerous.
− ANTONYMS: unkind, malignant.

bent past & past part. OF BEND.
• adj. **1** Brit. informal dishonest; corrupt. **2** (**bent on**) determined to do.
▷ SYNONYMS: **1 twisted**, crooked, warped, contorted, deformed, misshapen, out of shape, bowed, arched, curved, angled, hooked; N. Amer. informal pretzeled. **2 corrupt**, dishonest, fraudulent, criminal, untrustworthy.
− ANTONYMS: straight.
• n. a natural talent.
▷ SYNONYMS: **inclination**, leaning, tendency, talent, gift, flair, aptitude, facility, skill.

benzene n. a liquid hydrocarbon found in coal tar and petroleum.

bequeath v. leave property to someone by a will.
▷ SYNONYMS: **leave**, will, hand down, pass on, entrust, make over, grant, transfer, give, bestow on, confer on.

bequest n. a legacy.
▷ SYNONYMS: **legacy**, estate, inheritance,

endowment, settlement.

berate v. scold angrily.

bereaved v. (**be bereaved**) be deprived of a relation or friend through their death.
■ **bereavement** n.

bereft adj. **1** (**bereft of**) without. **2** lonely and abandoned.

beret /be-ray/ n. a flat round cap with no peak.

bergamot /ber-guh-mot/ n. an oily substance found in some oranges, used as a flavouring.

beriberi n. a disease caused by a lack of vitamin B_1.

berk n. Brit. informal a stupid person.

berry n. (pl. **berries**) a small round juicy fruit without a stone.

berserk adj. out of control with anger etc.
▷ SYNONYMS: **mad**, crazy, insane, out of your mind, hysterical, frenzied, crazed, demented, maniacal, manic, frantic, raving, wild, out of control, amok, on the rampage; informal off your head, off the deep end, ape, bananas, bonkers; Brit. informal spare; N. Amer. informal postal.

berth n. **1** a place for a ship to moor. **2** a bunk on a ship or train.
▷ SYNONYMS: **1 bunk**, bed, cot, couch, hammock. **2 mooring**, dock, pier, jetty, quay.
• v. moor in a berth.
▷ SYNONYMS: **dock**, moor, land, tie up, make fast.

beryl n. a transparent pale green, blue, or yellow gem.

beryllium n. a lightweight grey metallic element.

beseech v. (**beseeching**, **besought** or **beseeched**) ask in a pleading way.
▷ SYNONYMS: **implore**, beg, entreat, plead with, appeal to, call on, importune, pray to, ask, petition.

beset v. (**besetting**, **beset**) trouble or worry continuously.

beside prep. **1** at the side of. **2** compared with. **3** (or **besides**) as well as.
▷ SYNONYMS: **alongside**, by/at the side of, next to, parallel to, abreast of, adjacent to, next door to, neighbouring.
• adv. (**besides**) as well.
▷ SYNONYMS: **in addition to**, as well as, over and above, on top of, apart from, other than, aside from, not counting, excluding, leaving aside; N. Amer. informal outside of.
□ **beside yourself** frantic with worry.

besiege v. **1** surround with armed

forces. **2** overwhelm with requests etc.
▷ SYNONYMS: **1** lay siege to, beleaguer, blockade. **2** surround, mob, harass, pester, badger. **3** overwhelm, bombard, inundate, deluge, flood, swamp, snow under.

besmirch v. damage someone's reputation.

besom /bee-zuhm/ n. a broom made of twigs tied round a stick.

besotted adj. infatuated.

besought past & past part. of BESEECH.

bespeak v. (bespeaking, bespoke; past part. bespoken) be evidence of.

bespoke adj. Brit. made to a customer's requirements.

best adj. **1** of the highest quality. **2** most suitable or sensible.
▷ SYNONYMS: **finest**, premier, greatest, top, foremost, leading, pre-eminent, supreme, superlative, unrivalled, second to none, without equal, unsurpassed, unparalleled, unbeatable, optimum, ultimate, incomparable, record-breaking; informal star, number-one, a cut above the rest, top-drawer.
• adv. **1** to the highest degree or standard. **2** most suitably or sensibly.
• n. (**the best**) that which is of the highest quality.
▷ SYNONYMS: *only the best will do:* **finest**, choicest, top, cream, choice, prime, elite, crème de la crème, flower, jewel in the crown.
– ANTONYMS: worst.
☐ **best man** a man chosen by a bridegroom to assist him at his wedding.

bestial adj. savagely cruel.
■ **bestiality** n.

bestir v. (bestirring, bestirred) (**bestir yourself**) rouse yourself to action.

bestow v. award an honour, gift, etc.
▷ SYNONYMS: **confer on**, grant, accord, afford, endow with, present, award, give, donate, entrust with, vouchsafe.

bestride v. (bestriding, bestrode; past part. **bestridden**) stand astride over.

bet v. (betting, bet or betted) **1** risk money against someone else's on the outcome of an unpredictable event. **2** informal feel sure.
▷ SYNONYMS: **1** wager, gamble, stake, risk, venture, hazard, chance; Brit. informal punt, have a flutter. **2** be certain, be sure, be convinced, be confident, expect, predict, guess.
• n. an act of betting or the money betted.
▷ SYNONYMS: **1** wager, gamble, stake,

ante; Brit. informal punt, flutter. **2** *your best bet is to go early:* **option**, choice, alternative, course of action, plan.

beta blocker /bee-tuh/ n. a drug used to treat high blood pressure and angina.

betake v. (betaking, betook; past part. **betaken**) (**betake yourself to**) go to.

bête noire /bet nwar/ n. (pl. **bêtes noires**) a person or thing that you particularly dislike.

betide v. literary happen or happen to.

betimes adv. literary early.

betoken v. be a sign of.

betray v. **1** act treacherously towards your country by helping an enemy. **2** be disloyal to. **3** reveal unintentionally.
▷ SYNONYMS: **1** be disloyal to, be unfaithful to, break faith with, play someone false, inform on/against, give away, denounce, sell out, stab in the back; informal split on, rat on, stitch up, do the dirty on, sell down the river; Brit. informal grass on, shop, sneak on; N. Amer. informal rat out, drop the dime on, finger; Austral./NZ informal dob in. **2** reveal, disclose, divulge, tell, give away, leak.
■ **betrayer** n.

betrayal n. disloyalty or treachery.
▷ SYNONYMS: **disloyalty**, treachery, bad faith, breach of faith, breach of trust, faithlessness, duplicity, deception, double-dealing, stab in the back, double-cross, sell-out.
– ANTONYMS: loyalty.

betrothed adj. engaged to be married.
■ **betrothal** n.

better adj. **1** more satisfactory or suitable. **2** recovered from illness or injury.
▷ SYNONYMS: **1** superior, finer, of higher quality, preferable; informal a cut above, streets ahead, head and shoulders above, ahead of the pack/field. **2** healthier, fitter, stronger, cured, healed, recovered, recovering, on the road to recovery, on the mend.
– ANTONYMS: worse, inferior.
• adv. **1** in a better way. **2** to a greater degree.
• n. (**your betters**) people who are more important than you.
• v. **1** improve on. **2** (**better yourself**) improve your social status.
▷ SYNONYMS: **1** surpass, improve on, beat, exceed, top, cap, trump, eclipse. **2** improve, ameliorate, raise, advance, further, lift, upgrade, enhance.
– ANTONYMS: worsen.

b

□ **better off** in a more favourable position. **get the better of** defeat.

between prep. & adv. **1** at, across, or in the space or period separating two things. **2** indicating a connection or relationship. **3** shared by; together with.

betwixt prep. & adv. old use between.

bevel n. an edge cut at an angle.
• v. (**bevelling**, **bevelled**; US **beveling**, **beveled**) cut a bevel on.

beverage n. a drink.

bevy n. (pl. **bevies**) a large group.

bewail v. express great regret or sorrow over.

beware v. be aware of danger.
▷ SYNONYMS: **watch out**, look out, mind out, be alert, be on your guard, keep your eyes open/peeled, keep an eye out, take care, be careful, be cautious, watch your step, guard against.

bewilder v. puzzle or confuse.
▷ SYNONYMS: **baffle**, mystify, bemuse, perplex, puzzle, confuse, nonplus; informal flummox, bamboozle, faze, mindboggle, beat; N. Amer. informal discombobulate.
■ **bewilderment** n.

bewitch v. **1** cast a spell over. **2** attract and delight.
▷ SYNONYMS: **captivate**, enchant, entrance, enrapture, charm, beguile, delight, fascinate, enthral, cast a spell on.

beyond prep. & adv. **1** at or to the further side of. **2** outside the range or limits of. **3** happening or continuing after.
▷ SYNONYMS: **1 on the far side of**, behind, past, after. **2 greater than**, more than, exceeding, in excess of, above, upwards of.

bezel n. a groove holding the glass cover of a watch in place.

bhaji /bah-ji/ n. an Indian dish of vegetables fried in batter.

bi- comb. form **1** two. **2** twice.

biannual adj. occurring twice a year.

bias n. **1** a feeling for or against someone or something that is not based on fair judgement. **2** a direction diagonal to the grain of a fabric.
▷ SYNONYMS: **prejudice**, partiality, favouritism, partisanship, unfairness, one-sidedness, discrimination, leaning, tendency, inclination.
– ANTONYMS: impartiality.
• v. (**biasing**, **biased**) cause to be prejudiced for or against.
▷ SYNONYMS: **prejudice**, influence, colour, sway, predispose, distort, skew, slant.

biased adj. having a bias; prejudiced.
▷ SYNONYMS: **prejudiced**, partial, partisan, one-sided, bigoted, discriminatory, distorted, warped, twisted, skewed.
– ANTONYMS: impartial.

bib n. **1** a piece of material fastened under a child's chin to protect its clothes. **2** the upper front part of an apron or pair of dungarees.

Bible n. **1** the Christian or Jewish scriptures. **2** (**bible**) informal an authoritative book.
■ **biblical** adj.

bibliography n. (pl. **bibliographies**) **1** a list of the books referred to in a written work. **2** a list of books on a particular subject.
■ **bibliographer** n. **bibliographic** adj.

bibliophile n. a person who collects books.

bicarbonate of soda n. a soluble powder used in baking.

bicentenary n. (pl. **bicentenaries**) a 200th anniversary.
■ **bicentennial** n. & adj.

biceps n. (pl. **biceps**) a large muscle in the upper arm.

bicker v. argue about trivial things.

bicycle n. a two-wheeled vehicle propelled by pedals.
• v. ride a bicycle.

bid^1 v. (**bidding**, **bid**) **1** offer a price for. **2** try to get or do.
▷ SYNONYMS: **offer**, put up, tender, proffer, propose.
• n. an act of bidding.
▷ SYNONYMS: **1 offer**, tender, proposal. **2 attempt**, effort, endeavour, try; informal crack, go, shot, stab.
■ **bidder** n. **bidding** n.

bid^2 v. (**bidding**, **bid** or **bade**; past part. **bid**) **1** say hello or goodbye to. **2** old use command.

biddable adj. obedient.

bide v. (**bide your time**) wait patiently for an opportunity.

bidet /bee-day/ n. a low basin for washing the genitals.

biennial adj. **1** taking place every other year. **2** (of a plant) living for two years.

bier /beer/ n. a platform on which a coffin is placed before burial.

bifocal adj. (of a lens) made in two sections, one for distant and one for close vision.
• n. (**bifocals**) glasses with bifocal lenses.

big adj. (**bigger**, **biggest**) **1** large in size, amount, or extent. **2** very

important or serious. **3** (of a sibling) older.
▶ SYNONYMS: **1 large**, sizeable, substantial, considerable, great, huge, immense, enormous, extensive, colossal, massive, mammoth, vast, gigantic, giant, spacious; informal jumbo, whopping, thumping, bumper, mega; Brit. informal whacking, ginormous; formal commodious. **2 well built**, sturdy, brawny, burly, broad-shouldered, muscular, bulky, hulking, strapping, hefty, tall, huge, fat, stout; informal hunky, beefy. **3 elder**, older, grown-up, adult, mature, grown. **4 important**, significant, major, momentous, weighty, far-reaching, key, vital, crucial. **5** *that was big of you:* **generous**, kind, kindly, caring, compassionate, loving.
– ANTONYMS: small, minor.

bigamy n. the crime of marrying someone while already married to another person.
■ **bigamist** n. **bigamous** adj.

bigot n. a prejudiced and intolerant person.
■ **bigotry** n.

bigoted adj. prejudiced; intolerant.
▶ SYNONYMS: **prejudiced**, biased, partial, one-sided, sectarian, discriminatory, opinionated, dogmatic, intolerant, narrow-minded, blinkered, illiberal.
– ANTONYMS: open-minded.

bijou /bee-*zh*oo/ adj. (of a place) small and elegant.

bike n. a bicycle or motorcycle.
• v. ride a bike.
■ **biker** n.

bikini n. (pl. **bikinis**) a woman's two-piece swimsuit.

bilateral adj. **1** involving two parties. **2** having two sides.
■ **bilaterally** adv.

bilberry n. a small blue edible berry.

bile n. **1** a fluid produced by the liver. **2** anger.

bilge n. **1** the bottom of a ship's hull. **2** informal nonsense.

bilingual adj. speaking or expressed in two languages.

bilious adj. feeling sick.

bill n. **1** a written statement of charges for goods or services. **2** a draft of a proposed law. **3** a programme of entertainment at a theatre or cinema. **4** an advertising poster. **5** US a banknote. **6** a bird's beak.
▶ SYNONYMS: **1 invoice**, account, statement, list of charges; humorous the damage; N. Amer. check; informal tab. **2 draft law**, proposal, measure.

3 programme, line-up; N. Amer. playbill. **4 banknote**, note; US informal greenback. **5 poster**, advertisement, notice, announcement, flyer, leaflet, handbill; informal ad; Brit. informal advert.
• v. **1** list in a programme. **2** send a statement of charges to.
▶ SYNONYMS: **1 invoice**, charge, debit. **2 advertise**, announce, schedule, programme, timetable; N. Amer. slate. **3** *he was billed as the new Sean Connery:* **describe**, call, style, label, dub, promote, talk up; informal hype.
□ **billboard** a hoarding for advertising posters. **billhook** a pruning tool with a curved blade.

billabong n. Austral. a branch of a river forming a stagnant pool.

billet n. a private house where soldiers live temporarily.
• v. (**be billeted**) (of a soldier) stay in a private house.

billet-doux /bil-li-doo/ n. (pl. **billets-doux**) a love letter.

billiards n. a game played on a table with pockets at the sides and corners, into which balls are struck with a cue.

billion n. **1** a thousand million. **2** (**billions**) informal very many.
■ **billionth** adj.

billionaire n. a person owning money and property worth at least a billion pounds or dollars.

billow v. **1** (of smoke, cloud, etc.) roll outward. **2** fill with air and swell out.
▶ SYNONYMS: **1 swirl**, spiral, roll, undulate, eddy, pour, flow. **2 puff out**, balloon out, swell, fill out.
• n. a large rolling mass of cloud, smoke, etc.

bimbo n. (pl. **bimbos**) informal an attractive but unintelligent woman.

bin n. **1** Brit. a container for rubbish. **2** a large storage container.
• v. (**binning**, **binned**) throw away.

binary adj. **1** composed of or involving two things. **2** of a system of numbers with two as its base, using the digits 0 and 1.

bind v. (**binding**, **bound**) **1** firmly tie, wrap, or fasten. **2** hold together in a united group or mass. **3** place under a legal obligation. **4** (**bind over**) (of a court of law) require someone to do something. **5** enclose the pages of a book in a cover. **6** trim the edge of material with a fabric strip.
▶ SYNONYMS: **1 tie up**, fasten together, secure, make fast, attach, rope, lash, tether. **2 bandage**, dress, cover, wrap, strap up, tape up. **3 trim**, hem, edge,

border, fringe.
– ANTONYMS: untie.
 • n. informal a difficult situation.

binding n. **1** a covering holding the pages of a book together. **2** fabric in a strip, used for trimming material.
 • adj. (of an agreement) involving a legal obligation.
▷ SYNONYMS: **irrevocable**, unalterable, inescapable, unbreakable, contractual, compulsory, obligatory, mandatory, incumbent.

binge informal n. a bout of uncontrolled eating or drinking.
 • v. eat or drink uncontrollably.

bingo n. a game in which players mark off on a card numbers called at random.

binocular adj. using both eyes.
 • n. (binoculars) an instrument with a separate lens for each eye, for viewing distant objects.

binomial n. an algebraic expression consisting of two terms linked by a plus or minus sign.

biochemistry n. the study of the chemical processes that occur within living things.
 ■ biochemical adj. biochemist n.

biodegradable adj. able to be decomposed by bacteria or other living organisms.

biodiversity n. the variety of living things in an environment.

biography n. (pl. biographies) an account of a person's life written by someone else.
 ■ biographer n. biographical adj.

biology n. the scientific study of living organisms.
 ■ biological adj. biologist n.

bionic adj. (of an artificial body part) electronically powered.

biopsy n. (pl. biopsies) an examination of tissue taken from the body.

biorhythm n. a recurring cycle in the functioning of an organism.

biosecurity n. the measures taken to protect the population, environment, etc. from contamination with harmful biological or biochemical substances.

biotechnology n. the use of microorganisms in industry and medicine.

bioterrorism n. the use of harmful biological or biochemical substances as weapons of terrorism.

bipartisan adj. involving two political parties.

bipartite adj. involving two separate groups.

biped /by-ped/ n. an animal that walks on two feet.

biplane n. an aircraft with two pairs of wings, one above the other.

birch n. a slender tree with thin, peeling bark.

bird n. **1** an egg-laying animal with feathers and wings, usu. able to fly. **2** Brit. informal a young woman or girlfriend.
▷ SYNONYMS: fowl, chick, fledgling, nestling.

> **WORD LINKS**
> **avian** relating to birds
> **ornithology** the study of birds

bird flu n. a severe type of influenza that affects birds and can also be fatal to humans.

birdie n. (pl. birdies) Golf a score of one stroke under par at a hole.

biro n. (pl. biros) Brit. trademark a ballpoint pen.

birth n. **1** the emergence of a baby or other young from its mother's body. **2** the beginning of something. **3** a person's ancestry.
▷ SYNONYMS: **1** childbirth, delivery, nativity; technical parturition. **2** beginning, emergence, genesis, dawn, dawning, rise, start. **3** ancestry, lineage, blood, descent, parentage, family, extraction, origin, stock.
– ANTONYMS: death, end.
 □ birth control the use of contraceptives. birthday the anniversary of the day on which a person was born. birthmark an unusual mark on the body which is there from birth. birthright a right or privilege possessed from birth.

> **WORD LINKS**
> **antenatal** before birth
> **post-natal** after birth
> **obstetrics** the branch of medicine concerned with birth

biscuit n. Brit. a small, flat, crisp cake.

bisect v. divide into two parts.

bisexual adj. sexually attracted to both men and women.
 • n. a bisexual person.
 ■ bisexuality n.

bishop n. **1** a senior member of the Christian clergy. **2** a chess piece that can move diagonally.

bishopric n. the position or diocese of a bishop.

bismuth n. a reddish-grey metallic element.

bison n. (pl. bison) a shaggy-haired

wild ox.

bistro n. (pl. **bistros**) a small, inexpensive restaurant.

bit n. **1** a small piece or quantity. **2** a short time or distance. **3** the mouthpiece of a horse's bridle. **4** a tool for boring or drilling. **5** Computing the smallest unit of information, expressed as either 0 or 1.
▷ SYNONYMS: **piece**, portion, section, part, chunk, lump, hunk, fragment, scrap, shred, crumb, grain, speck, spot, drop, pinch, dash, morsel, mouthful, bite, sample, iota, jot, whit, atom, particle, trace, touch, suggestion, hint, tinge; informal smidgen, tad. □ **a bit** rather; slightly.

bitch n. **1** a female dog. **2** informal a spiteful or unpleasant woman.
• v. informal make spiteful comments.
■ **bitchiness** n. **bitchy** adj.

bite v. (**biting, bit**; past part. **bitten**) **1** cut into with the teeth. **2** (of a tool, tyre, etc.) grip a surface. **3** take effect, with unpleasant consequences.
▷ SYNONYMS: **1 chew**, sink your teeth into, munch, crunch, champ. **2 grip**, hold, get a purchase. **3 take effect**, work, act, have results.
• n. **1** an act of biting or a piece bitten off. **2** informal a quick snack.
▷ SYNONYMS: **1 chew**, munch, nibble, gnaw, nip, snap. **2 mouthful**, piece, bit, morsel, snack. **3 piquancy**, pungency, spiciness, tang, zest; informal kick, punch, zing.

biting adj. **1** (of wind) very cold. **2** sharply critical.
▷ SYNONYMS: **1 freezing**, icy, arctic, bitter, piercing, penetrating, raw. **2 vicious**, harsh, cruel, savage, cutting, sharp, bitter, scathing, caustic, acerbic, acid, acrimonious, spiteful, venomous, vitriolic; informal bitchy, catty.
− ANTONYMS: mild.

bitter adj. **1** having a sharp taste; not sweet. **2** resentful. **3** (of a conflict) intense and full of hatred. **4** intensely cold.
▷ SYNONYMS: **1 sharp**, acid, acrid, tart, sour, vinegary. **2** a bitter woman: **resentful**, embittered, aggrieved, spiteful, jaundiced, sullen, sour. **3 acrimonious**, hostile, angry, rancorous, spiteful, vicious, vitriolic, savage, ferocious, nasty. **4 freezing**, icy, arctic, biting, piercing, penetrating, raw.
− ANTONYMS: sweet, mild.
• n. Brit. bitter-tasting beer.
■ **bitterly** adv. **bitterness** n.

bittern n. a marshland bird with a booming call.

bitumen n. a black sticky substance obtained from petroleum.
■ **bituminous** adj.

bivalve n. a mollusc with a shell divided into two parts, e.g. a mussel.

bivouac n. a temporary camp without tents.
• v. (**bivouacking, bivouacked**) stay in a bivouac.

bizarre adj. very strange or unusual.
▷ SYNONYMS: **strange**, peculiar, odd, funny, fantastic, extraordinary, curious, outlandish, eccentric, unconventional, unorthodox, weird, outré, surreal; informal wacky, oddball, way out, freaky; N. Amer. informal wacko.
− ANTONYMS: normal.

blab v. (**blabbing, blabbed**) informal reveal a secret.

black adj. **1** of the very darkest colour. **2** relating to people with dark-coloured skin. **3** (of coffee or tea) without milk. **4** marked by disaster or despair. **5** (of humour) presenting distressing situations in comic terms. **6** hostile.
▷ SYNONYMS: **1 dark**, pitch-black, coal-black, jet-black, ebony, inky, sable. **2** a black day: **tragic**, dark, disastrous, calamitous, catastrophic, cataclysmic, fateful. **3** a black mood: **miserable**, unhappy, sad, wretched, heartbroken, grief-stricken, sorrowful, anguished, desolate, despairing, disconsolate, downcast, dejected, gloomy; informal blue. **4 macabre**, cynical, unhealthy, ghoulish, weird, morbid, gruesome; informal sick.
− ANTONYMS: white, bright.
• n. **1** black colour. **2** a black person.
• v. **1** make black. **2** (**black out**) faint. □ **black eye** an area of bruising round the eye. **black economy** unofficial and untaxed business activity. **black hole** a region in space with a gravitational field so strong that no matter or radiation can escape. **black magic** magic involving the summoning of evil spirits. **black market** illegal trading in officially controlled goods. **black pudding** a sausage containing dried pig's blood. **black sheep** a person seen as a disgrace to their family.
■ **blackness** n.

blackball v. prevent from joining a club.

blackberry n. the dark edible fruit of a prickly shrub.

blackbird n. a bird with black feathers

and a yellow beak.

blackboard n. a dark board for writing on with chalk.

blackcurrant n. a small round edible black berry.

blacken v. **1** become or make black. **2** damage someone's reputation.

blackguard /blag-gerd/ n. dated a dishonest or unprincipled man.

blackhead n. a lump of oily matter blocking a pore in the skin.

blackleg n. Brit. derogatory a person who continues working when fellow workers are on strike.

blacklist n. a list of people seen as unacceptable or untrustworthy.
• v. put on a blacklist.
▷ SYNONYMS: boycott, ostracize, avoid, embargo, ignore, refuse to employ.

blackmail n. the demanding of money from someone in return for not revealing information that could disgrace them.
▷ SYNONYMS: **extortion**, demanding money with menaces, threats, intimidation.
• v. use blackmail on.
▷ SYNONYMS: **1 extort money from**, threaten, hold to ransom, intimidate. **2 coerce**, pressure, force, dragoon; informal lean on, twist someone's arm.
■ **blackmailer** n.

blackout n. **1** a sudden failure of electric lights. **2** a short loss of consciousness. **3** an official restriction on the publishing of news. **4** a period when all lights must be turned out during an enemy air raid.

blacksmith n. a person who makes and repairs iron objects.

bladder n. a bag-like organ in the abdomen which stores urine for excretion.

blade n. **1** the flat cutting edge of a knife or other tool or weapon. **2** the broad flat part of an oar, leaf, etc. **3** a long narrow leaf of grass.

blame v. hold responsible for a fault or wrong.
▷ SYNONYMS: **1 hold responsible**, hold accountable, condemn, accuse, find/ consider guilty. **2** *they blame youth crime on unemployment:* **attribute to**, ascribe to, impute to, lay at the door of, put down to; informal pin.
– ANTONYMS: absolve.
• n. responsibility for a fault or wrong.
▷ SYNONYMS: **responsibility**, guilt, accountability, liability, culpability, fault.
■ **blameworthy** adj.

blameless adj. free from blame or responsibility.
▷ SYNONYMS: **innocent**, guiltless, above reproach, irreproachable, unimpeachable, in the clear, exemplary, impeccable, unblemished; informal squeaky clean.
– ANTONYMS: guilty.

blanch v. **1** become white or pale. **2** immerse vegetables briefly in boiling water.

blancmange /bluh-monzh/ n. Brit. a jelly-like dessert made with milk.

bland adj. lacking interesting qualities or features.
▷ SYNONYMS: **1 uninteresting**, dull, boring, tedious, monotonous, ordinary, run-of-the-mill, drab, dreary, unexciting, lacklustre, flat, stale, trite. **2 tasteless**, flavourless, plain, insipid, weak, watery, thin, wishy-washy.
– ANTONYMS: interesting, tangy.

blandishments pl. n. flattery intended to persuade.

blank adj. **1** not marked or decorated. **2** not understanding or reacting.
▷ SYNONYMS: **1 empty**, unmarked, unused, clear, free, bare, clean, plain. **2 expressionless**, deadpan, wooden, stony, impassive, inscrutable, glazed, fixed, lifeless.
– ANTONYMS: expressive.
• n. **1** an empty space. **2** a cartridge containing gunpowder but no bullet.
▷ SYNONYMS: **space**, gap, void.
• v. (**blank out**) hide or block out.
□ **blank verse** poetry that does not rhyme.

blanket n. **1** a warm covering made of woollen material. **2** a thick mass or layer.
▷ SYNONYMS: *a blanket of cloud:* **covering**, layer, coating, carpet, cloak, mantle, veil, pall, shroud.
• v. (**blanketing, blanketed**) cover with a thick layer.
▷ SYNONYMS: **cover**, coat, carpet, cloak, shroud, swathe, envelop.

blare v. make a loud, harsh sound.
• n. a blaring sound.

blarney n. charming or flattering talk.

blasé /blah-zay/ adj. unimpressed with something through overfamiliarity.
▷ SYNONYMS: **indifferent**, unconcerned, casual, nonchalant, offhand, uninterested, unimpressed, unmoved, uncaring; informal laid-back.

blaspheme v. speak disrespectfully about God or sacred things.

blasphemous adj. showing disrespect towards God or sacred things.

▷ SYNONYMS: **sacrilegious**, profane, irreligious, irreverent, impious, ungodly, godless.
– ANTONYMS: reverent.

blasphemy n. disrespectful talk about God or sacred things.
▷ SYNONYMS: **profanity**, sacrilege, irreverence, taking the Lord's name in vain, impiety, desecration.
– ANTONYMS: reverence.

blast n. **1** an explosion, or the rush of air spreading out from it. **2** a strong gust of wind. **3** a loud note of a horn or whistle.
▷ SYNONYMS: **1 explosion**, detonation, discharge, burst. **2 gust**, rush, gale, squall, flurry. **3** *the shrill blast of the trumpets*: **blare**, wail, roar, screech, shriek, hoot, honk, beep.
• v. **1** blow up with explosives. **2** (**blast off**) (of a rocket etc.) take off. **3** produce loud music or noise.
▷ SYNONYMS: **1 blow up**, bomb, dynamite, explode, fire, shoot, blaze, let fly, discharge. **2 blare**, boom, roar, thunder, bellow, shriek, screech.

blatant adj. open and unashamed.
▷ SYNONYMS: **flagrant**, glaring, obvious, undisguised, open, overt, outright, naked, shameless, barefaced, unashamed, brazen.
– ANTONYMS: discreet, inconspicuous.
■ **blatantly** adv.

USAGE The ending is -*ant*, not -*ent*: blat*ant*.

blather v. chatter foolishly.

blaze n. **1** a large or fierce fire. **2** a bright light or display of colour. **3** an outburst. **4** a white stripe on an animal's face.
▷ SYNONYMS: **1 fire**, flames, conflagration, inferno, holocaust. **2** *a blaze of light*: **glare**, flash, burst, flare, streak, radiance, brilliance, beam, glitter.
• v. burn or shine fiercely or brightly.
▷ SYNONYMS: **1 burn**, be alight, be on fire, be in flames. **2 shine**, flash, flare, glare, gleam, glitter, glisten. **3 fire**, shoot, blast, let fly.
□ **blaze a trail 1** mark out a path. **2** pioneer something.

blazer n. a jacket worn by schoolchildren or sports players as part of a uniform.

blazon v. display or describe prominently.

bleach v. lighten by chemicals or sunlight.
▷ SYNONYMS: **turn white**, whiten, turn pale, blanch, lighten, fade.
– ANTONYMS: darken.
• n. a chemical used to bleach or sterilize things.

bleak adj. **1** barren and exposed. **2** dreary and unwelcoming. **3** (of a situation) not hopeful.
▷ SYNONYMS: **1 bare**, exposed, desolate, stark, desert, lunar, open, empty, windswept. **2 unpromising**, unfavourable, dim, gloomy, black, grim, discouraging, disheartening, depressing, dismal.
– ANTONYMS: lush, promising.
■ **bleakly** adv. **bleakness** n.

bleary adj. (**blearier**, **bleariest**) (of the eyes) dull and unfocused.
▷ SYNONYMS: **blurry**, unfocused, fogged, clouded, misty, watery, rheumy.
– ANTONYMS: clear.
■ **blearily** adv.

bleat v. **1** (of a sheep or goat) make a weak, wavering cry. **2** speak or complain feebly.
• n. a bleating sound.

bleed v. (**bleeding**, **bled**) **1** lose blood from the body. **2** draw blood or fluid from. **3** informal drain of money or resources.

bleep n. a short high-pitched sound made by an electronic device.
• v. make a bleep.
■ **bleeper** n.

blemish n. a small mark or flaw.
▷ SYNONYMS: **imperfection**, flaw, defect, fault, discoloration, stain, scar, mark, spot.
• v. spoil the appearance of.
▷ SYNONYMS: **mar**, spoil, impair, disfigure, deface, mark, stain, scar, blight, tarnish.
– ANTONYMS: enhance.

blench v. flinch suddenly.

blend v. **1** mix and combine. **2** (**blend in**) merge so as to be unnoticeable.
▷ SYNONYMS: **1 mix**, mingle, combine, merge, fuse, amalgamate, stir, whisk, fold in. **2 harmonize**, go well, fit in, coordinate, match, complement, suit.
• n. a mixture.
▷ SYNONYMS: **mixture**, mix, melange, combination, synthesis, compound, amalgam, fusion, alloy.

blender n. an electric device for liquidizing food.

bless v. **1** make holy. **2** ask God to protect. **3** (**be blessed with**) be fortunate in having.
▷ SYNONYMS: **1 consecrate**, sanctify, dedicate to God, make holy; formal hallow. **2 endow**, bestow, furnish, give, favour, confer on. **3 sanction**, consent to, endorse, agree to, approve, back,

b

b

support; informal give the green light to, OK.

– ANTONYMS: curse, oppose.

blessed adj. **1** holy. **2** bringing welcome pleasure or relief.

▷ SYNONYMS: **holy**, sacred, hallowed, consecrated, sanctified, ordained, canonized, beatified.

– ANTONYMS: cursed.

■ **blessedly** adv.

blessing n. **1** God's protection, or a prayer asking for this. **2** something for which you are very grateful. **3** a person's approval or support.

▷ SYNONYMS: **1 benediction**, dedication, consecration, grace, invocation, intercession. **2 advantage**, godsend, boon, benefit, help, bonus, plus, stroke of luck, windfall. **3 sanction**, endorsement, approval, consent, assent, agreement, backing, support.

– ANTONYMS: condemnation.

blew past of BLOW.

blight n. **1** a plant disease. **2** a cause of harm.

▷ SYNONYMS: **1** *potato blight:* **disease**, canker, infestation, fungus, mildew, mould. **2** *the blight of aircraft noise:* **curse**, scourge, affliction, plague, menace, misfortune, bane, trouble, nuisance, pest.

•v. spoil or harm.

▷ SYNONYMS: **ruin**, wreck, spoil, mar, frustrate, disrupt, undo, scotch, destroy, shatter, devastate, demolish; informal mess up, foul up, put paid to, put the kibosh on, stymie; Brit. informal scupper.

blind adj. **1** unable to see. **2** lacking awareness or judgement. **3** concealed, closed, or blocked off.

▷ SYNONYMS: **1 sightless**, unsighted, visually impaired, unseeing. **2 uncritical**, unreasoned, unthinking, unquestioning, mindless, undiscerning, indiscriminate. **3** *blind to the realities of the situation:* **unaware of**, oblivious to, ignorant of, unmindful of, heedless of, insensible to, indifferent to.

•v. **1** make blind. **2** prevent from thinking clearly.

•n. a screen for a window.

▷ SYNONYMS: **screen**, shade, sunshade, curtain, awning, canopy, louvre, jalousie, shutter.

▢ **blindfold** a piece of cloth used to cover a person's eyes.

■ **blindly** adv. **blindness** n.

blink v. **1** shut and open the eyes quickly. **2** shine unsteadily.

•n. an act of blinking.

blinkered adj. having a limited point of view.

blinkers pl. n. a pair of flaps attached to a bridle to prevent a horse from seeing sideways.

blip n. **1** a short high-pitched sound. **2** a flashing point of light on a radar screen. **3** a temporary change in an otherwise steady situation.

bliss n. perfect happiness.

▷ SYNONYMS: **joy**, happiness, pleasure, delight, ecstasy, elation, rapture, euphoria, seventh heaven.

– ANTONYMS: misery.

■ **blissful** adj. **blissfully** adv.

blister n. **1** a small bubble on the skin filled with watery liquid. **2** a similar bubble on a surface.

•v. form blisters.

blithe adj. casually indifferent.

■ **blithely** adv.

blitz n. **1** a sudden military attack. **2** informal a sudden and concentrated effort.

▷ SYNONYMS: **bombing**, air raid, air strike, bombardment, barrage, attack, assault.

•v. make a sudden attack on.

blizzard n. a severe snowstorm.

bloat v. cause to swell with fluid or gas.

bloated adj. swollen with fluid or gas.

▷ SYNONYMS: **swollen**, distended, bulging, puffed out, inflated, dilated.

bloater n. a salted smoked herring.

blob n. **1** a drop of a thick liquid. **2** a roundish mass.

▷ SYNONYMS: **drop**, droplet, globule, bead, bubble, spot, dab, blotch, blot, dot, smudge; informal splodge.

bloc n. a group of allied countries with similar political systems.

▷ SYNONYMS: **group**, alliance, coalition, federation, confederation, league, union, axis, association.

block n. **1** a solid piece of material with flat surfaces on each side. **2** Brit. a large building divided into flats or offices. **3** a group of buildings bounded by four streets. **4** an obstacle.

▷ SYNONYMS: **1 chunk**, hunk, lump, wedge, cube, brick, ingot, slab, piece. **2 building**, complex, structure, development. **3 obstacle**, bar, barrier, impediment, hindrance, check, hurdle.

•v. prevent movement, flow, or progress in.

▷ SYNONYMS: **1 clog**, stop up, choke, plug, bung up, obstruct, gum up, dam up, congest, jam. **2 hinder**, hamper, obstruct, impede, inhibit, halt, stop, bar, check, prevent, fend off, hold

off, repel.
– ANTONYMS: clear, aid.
□ **blockbuster** informal a very successful film or book. **block capitals** plain capital letters.

blockade n. an act of sealing off a place to prevent goods or people from entering or leaving.
• v. set up a blockade of.

blockage n. an obstruction.
▷ SYNONYMS: **obstruction**, stoppage, block, jam, congestion, bottleneck.

blog n. a weblog.
• v. (**blogging**, **blogged**) keep a weblog.
■ **blogger** n.

bloke n. Brit. informal a man.

blonde adj. (or **blond**) **1** (of hair) fair. **2** having fair hair.
▷ SYNONYMS: **fair**, light, yellow, flaxen, golden.
– ANTONYMS: dark.
• n. a woman with blonde hair.

blood n. **1** the red liquid circulating in the arteries and veins. **2** family background.
▷ SYNONYMS: **1 lifeblood**, gore, vital fluid. **2 ancestry**, lineage, descent, parentage, family, birth, extraction, origin, stock.
• v. initiate in an activity.
□ **bloodbath** a massacre. **blood-curdling** horrifying. **bloodhound** a large dog used in tracking scents. **bloodless** without violence or killing. **bloodshot** (of eyes) red from dilated blood vessels. **blood sport** a sport involving the killing of animals. **bloodstream** the blood circulating in the body.

WORD LINKS
haematology the branch of medicine concerned with blood

---

bloodshed n. the killing or wounding of people.
▷ SYNONYMS: **slaughter**, massacre, killing, wounding, carnage, butchery, bloodletting, bloodbath.

bloodthirsty adj. taking pleasure in killing or violence.
▷ SYNONYMS: **murderous**, homicidal, violent, vicious, barbarous, barbaric, savage, brutal, cut-throat.

bloody adj. (**bloodier**, **bloodiest**) **1** covered in blood. **2** involving much violence or cruelty.
▷ SYNONYMS: **1 bloodstained**, blood-soaked, gory, bleeding. **2 vicious**, ferocious, savage, fierce, brutal, cruel, murderous, gory.
• v. (**bloodying**, **bloodied**) cover or

stain with blood.
□ **bloody-minded** Brit. informal deliberately uncooperative.

bloom v. **1** produce flowers. **2** be very healthy.
▷ SYNONYMS: **1 flower**, blossom, open, mature. **2 flourish**, thrive, prosper, progress, burgeon; informal be in the pink.
– ANTONYMS: wither, decline.
• n. **1** a flower. **2** the state or period of blooming. **3** a healthy glow in the complexion.

bloomers pl. n. **1** women's long baggy knickers. **2** hist. women's loose-fitting trousers.

blossom n. a flower or a mass of flowers on a tree.
▷ SYNONYMS: **flower**, bloom, bud.
• v. **1** produce blossom. **2** develop and flourish.
▷ SYNONYMS: **1 bloom**, flower, open, mature. **2 develop**, grow, mature, progress, evolve, burgeon, flourish, thrive, prosper, bloom.
– ANTONYMS: wither, decline.

blot n. **1** a spot of ink. **2** a thing that spoils something good.
▷ SYNONYMS: **1 patch**, dab, smudge, blotch, mark, dot, spot; Brit. informal splodge. **2 blemish**, taint, stain, blight, flaw, fault. **3** a blot on the landscape: **eyesore**, monstrosity, carbuncle, mess; informal sight.
• v. (**blotting**, **blotted**) **1** dry with an absorbent material. **2** mark or spoil. **3** (**blot out**) hide or cover.

blotch n. a large irregular mark.
■ **blotchy** adj.

blouse n. a woman's top with buttons down the front.

blouson /bloo-zon/ n. a short loose-fitting jacket.

blow v. (**blowing**, **blew**; past part. **blown**) **1** (of wind) move. **2** send out air through pursed lips. **3** play a wind instrument. **4** break open with explosives. **5** burst or burn out through pressure or overheating. **6** informal spend money recklessly. **7** informal waste an opportunity.
▷ SYNONYMS: **1 gust**, puff, flurry, blast, roar, bluster, rush, storm. **2 sweep**, carry, toss, drive, push, force, drift, flutter, waft, float, glide, whirl. **3** he blew the trumpet: **sound**, blast, toot, play, pipe, trumpet.
• n. **1** an act of blowing. **2** a stroke with the hand or a weapon. **3** a shock or disappointment.
▷ SYNONYMS: **1 stroke**, knock, bang, hit, punch, thump, smack, crack, rap;

informal **whack**, **bash**, **clout**, **wallop**.
2 upset, disaster, setback, misfortune,
disappointment, calamity, catastrophe, thunderbolt, bombshell,
shock, surprise, jolt.
□ **blowfly** a large fly which lays its
eggs in meat. **blowout** the release of
air or gas from a tyre, oil well, etc.
blowtorch (or **blowlamp**) a portable
device producing a hot flame, for
burning off paint. **blow up 1** explode.
2 enlarge an image.
■ **blowy** adj.

blowsy (or **blowzy**) adj. (of a woman)
plump and untidy.

blub v. (**blubbing**, **blubbed**) informal sob
noisily.

blubber n. the fat of whales and seals.
● v. informal sob noisily.

bludgeon n. a heavy stick used as a
weapon.
● v. **1** hit with a bludgeon. **2** bully into
doing something.

blue adj. **1** of the colour of the sky on a
sunny day. **2** informal sad or depressed.
3 informal indecent or pornographic.
▷ SYNONYMS: azure, cobalt, sapphire,
navy, indigo, sky-blue, ultramarine,
aquamarine, turquoise, cyan.
● n. **1** blue colour or material.
2 (**blues**) slow sad music of black
American origin. **3** (**the blues**)
sadness or depression.
□ **bluebell** a plant with blue bell-
shaped flowers. **bluebottle** a large
bluish fly. **blue-collar** of manual work.
bluestocking a serious intellectual
woman. **out of the blue** informal
unexpectedly.
■ **blueness** n. **bluish** adj.

blueprint n. **1** a technical drawing or
plan. **2** a model or prototype.
▷ SYNONYMS: **plan**, design, diagram,
drawing, sketch, layout, model,
template, pattern, example, guide,
prototype, pilot.

bluff v. try to make someone believe
that you know or will do something.
▷ SYNONYMS: **pretend**, sham, fake, feign,
lie, deceive, delude, mislead, trick,
fool, hoodwink, dupe, hoax; informal
con, kid, have on.
● n. **1** an act of bluffing. **2** a steep cliff.
▷ SYNONYMS: **trick**, deception, fraud,
ruse, pretence, sham, fake, hoax,
charade; informal put-on.
● adj. frank and direct.
▷ SYNONYMS: **plain-spoken**, straightforward, blunt, direct, no-nonsense,
frank, open, candid, forthright,
unequivocal; informal upfront.
– ANTONYMS: guarded.

blunder n. a clumsy mistake.
▷ SYNONYMS: **mistake**, error, gaffe, slip,
oversight, faux pas; informal slip-up,
boo-boo; Brit. informal clanger, boob,
howler; N. Amer. informal blooper.
● v. **1** make a blunder. **2** move
clumsily.
▷ SYNONYMS: **1 make a mistake**, err,
miscalculate, bungle, trip up; informal
slip up, screw up, blow it, goof;
Brit. informal boob. **2 stumble**, lurch,
stagger, flounder, grope.

blunderbuss n. hist. a gun with a
short, wide barrel.

blunt adj. **1** lacking a sharp edge or
point. **2** frank and direct.
▷ SYNONYMS: **1** *a blunt knife:* dull,
worn. **2** *a broad leaf with a blunt tip:*
rounded, flat, stubby. **3 straightforward**, frank, plain-spoken, candid,
direct, bluff, forthright, unequivocal,
brusque, abrupt, curt, bald, brutal,
harsh, stark; informal upfront.
– ANTONYMS: sharp, subtle.
● v. make or become blunt.
▷ SYNONYMS: **dull**, deaden, dampen,
numb, take the edge off, weaken,
allay, diminish, lessen.
– ANTONYMS: intensify.
■ **bluntly** adv.

blur v. (**blurring**, **blurred**) make or
become less distinct.
▷ SYNONYMS: **1 cloud**, fog, obscure, dim,
soften, dull. **2 (blurred) indistinct**,
fuzzy, hazy, misty, foggy, clouded,
cloudy, faint, dim, unclear, vague,
indefinite, unfocused.
● n. something perceived indistinctly.
■ **blurry** adj.

blurb n. a short description written to
promote a book, film, etc.

blurt v. say suddenly and without
thinking.

blush v. become red-faced through
shyness or embarrassment.
▷ SYNONYMS: **redden**, go pink, go red,
flush, colour, burn up.
● n. an act of blushing.
▷ SYNONYMS: **flush**, rosiness, redness,
pinkness, bloom, high colour, glow.

blusher n. a cosmetic used to give a
rosy tinge to the cheeks.

bluster v. **1** talk loudly or aggressively
but with little effect. **2** blow in gusts.
● n. loud and empty talk.

blustery adj. marked by strong winds.
▷ SYNONYMS: **stormy**, gusty, blowy,
windy, squally, wild.
– ANTONYMS: calm.

boa n. **1** a large snake which crushes
its prey. **2** a thin scarf made of
feathers or fur.

boar n. (pl. **boar** or **boars**) **1** a wild pig with tusks. **2** a male pig.

board n. **1** a long, thin, flat piece of sawn wood. **2** a rectangular piece of stiff material used as a surface. **3** the decision-making body of an organization. **4** the provision of regular meals in return for payment.
▷ SYNONYMS: **1 plank**, beam, panel, slat, batten, timber. **2 committee**, council, panel, directorate, commission.
• v. **1** get on a ship, aircraft, etc. **2** receive meals and accommodation in return for payment. **3** cover or seal with pieces of wood.
▷ SYNONYMS: **1 get on**, go aboard, enter, mount, ascend, embark, catch. **2 lodge**, live, reside, stay, be housed; N. Amer. **room**; informal put up.
□ **boarding house** a private house providing meals and accommodation for paying guests. **boarding school** a school in which the pupils live during term time. **boardroom** a room in which a board of directors meets. **on board** on or in a ship, aircraft, etc. ■ **boarder** n.

boast v. **1** talk about yourself with excessive pride. **2** possess an impressive feature.
▷ SYNONYMS: **1 brag**, crow, swagger, swank, show off, blow your own trumpet, sing your own praises; informal talk big, lay it on thick; Austral./ NZ informal skite. **2** *the hotel boasts a fine restaurant:* have, possess, own, enjoy, pride yourself/itself on, offer.
• n. an act of boasting.
▷ SYNONYMS: **brag**, exaggeration, over-statement; informal swank; Austral./NZ informal skite.

boastful adj. showing excessive pride in yourself.
▷ SYNONYMS: **bragging**, swaggering, bumptious, swollen-headed, puffed up, full of yourself, cocky, conceited, arrogant; informal big-headed.
– ANTONYMS: modest.
■ **boastfully** adv.

boat n. a vehicle for travelling on water.
■ **boating** n.

boater n. a flat-topped straw hat.

boatswain /boh-s'n/ n. a ship's officer in charge of equipment and crew.

bob v. (**bobbing**, **bobbed**) move quickly up and down.
▷ SYNONYMS: **move up and down**, bounce, toss, skip, dance, wobble, jiggle, joggle, jolt, jerk.
• n. **1** a bobbing movement. **2** a short hairstyle that hangs evenly all round.

□ **bobsleigh** a sledge used for racing down an ice-covered run.

bobbin n. a reel for holding thread.

bobble n. a small ball made of strands of wool.

bode v. (**bode well/ill**) be a sign of a good or bad outcome.

bodge v. Brit. informal make or repair badly.

bodice n. **1** the part of a dress above the waist. **2** a woman's sleeveless undergarment.

bodily adj. of the body.
▷ SYNONYMS: **physical**, corporeal, corporal, mortal, material, tangible, concrete, real, actual, incarnate.
– ANTONYMS: spiritual, mental.
• adv. by taking hold of a person with force.
▷ SYNONYMS: **forcefully**, forcibly, violently, completely, entirely.

bodkin n. a thick, blunt needle.

body n. (pl. **bodies**) **1** the physical structure of a person or animal. **2** the main part. **3** a mass or collection. **4** a group organized for a particular purpose.
▷ SYNONYMS: **1 figure**, frame, form, physique, anatomy, torso, trunk. **2 corpse**, carcass, skeleton, remains; Medicine cadaver; informal stiff. **3 main part**, core, heart, hub. **4 association**, organization, assembly, delegation, committee, executive, company, society, corporation, group.
□ **bodyguard** a person paid to protect an important person. **bodywork** the metal outer shell of a vehicle.

> **WORD LINKS**
> **corporal, corporeal** relating to the body

Boer n. a member of the Dutch people who settled in southern Africa.

boffin n. Brit. informal a scientist.

bog n. **1** an area of soft, wet ground. **2** informal a toilet.
▷ SYNONYMS: **marsh**, swamp, mire, quag-mire, morass, slough, fen, wetland.
• v. (**be/get bogged down**) be prevented from progressing.
■ **boggy** adj.

bogey n. (pl. **bogeys**) **1** Golf a score of one stroke over par at a hole. **2** (or **bogy**) a cause of fear or alarm.

boggle v. informal be astonished or baffled.

bogus adj. not genuine or true.
▷ SYNONYMS: **fake**, spurious, false, fraudulent, sham, counterfeit, forged, feigned; informal phoney, pretend.
– ANTONYMS: genuine.

b

Bohemian adj. artistic and unconventional.

boil v. **1** (of a liquid) reach a temperature at which it bubbles and turns to vapour. **2** cook in boiling water.

▷ SYNONYMS: **simmer**, bubble, stew, seethe, froth, foam.

● n. **1** the process of boiling. **2** an inflamed pus-filled swelling.

▷ SYNONYMS: **swelling**, spot, pimple, blister, gathering, pustule, carbuncle, abscess.

boiler n. a device for heating water.

boisterous adj. noisy, lively, and high-spirited.

▷ SYNONYMS: **lively**, animated, exuberant, spirited, noisy, loud, rowdy, unruly, wild, uproarious, unrestrained, uninhibited, uncontrolled, rough, disorderly, riotous; informal rumbustious.

– ANTONYMS: restrained.

bold adj. **1** confident and brave. **2** (of a colour or design) strong or vivid. **3** (of printing) in thick, dark type.

▷ SYNONYMS: **1 daring**, intrepid, brave, courageous, valiant, valorous, fearless, dauntless, audacious, dare-devil, adventurous, heroic, plucky; informal gutsy, spunky. **2 striking**, vivid, bright, strong, eye-catching, prominent, gaudy, lurid, garish.

– ANTONYMS: timid, faint.

■ **boldly** adv. **boldness** n.

bole n. a tree trunk.

bolero n. (pl. **boleros**) **1** /buh-**lair**-oh/ a Spanish dance. **2** /**bol**-uh-roh/ a woman's short open jacket.

boll n. the rounded seed capsule of plants such as cotton.

bollard n. a short thick post.

bolshie (or **bolshy**) adj. Brit. informal hostile and uncooperative.

bolster n. a long, firm pillow.

● v. support or strengthen.

▷ SYNONYMS: **strengthen**, reinforce, boost, fortify, support, prop up, buoy up, shore up, buttress, maintain, help, augment, increase.

bolt n. **1** a metal pin that screws into a nut, used to fasten things. **2** a sliding bar used to fasten a door or window. **3** a flash of lightning. **4** a roll of fabric.

▷ SYNONYMS: **1** the bolt on the door: **bar**, lock, catch, latch, fastening. **2** nuts and bolts: **pin**, rivet, peg, screw.

● v. **1** fasten with a bolt. **2** run away. **3** eat food quickly.

▷ SYNONYMS: **1** he bolted the door: **lock**, bar, latch, fasten, secure. **2** the lid was

bolted down: **pin**, rivet, peg, screw, fasten, fix. **3 dash**, dart, run, sprint, hurtle, rush, fly, shoot; informal tear, scoot, leg it. **4 gobble**, gulp, wolf, guzzle, devour; informal demolish, polish off, shovel down; N. Amer. informal scarf, snarf.

□ **bolt-hole** a place where a person can escape to and hide.

bomb n. **1** a device intended to explode and cause damage. **2** (**the bomb**) nuclear weapons. **3** (**a bomb**) Brit. informal a large sum of money.

▷ SYNONYMS: **explosive**, incendiary device, missile, projectile.

● v. **1** attack with bombs. **2** Brit. informal move very quickly. **3** informal fail badly.

▷ SYNONYMS: **blow up**, blast, shell, blitz, strafe, pound, bombard, attack, assault, destroy, demolish.

□ **bombshell** a great surprise or shock.

bombard v. **1** attack with bombs or other missiles. **2** direct a flow of questions or information at.

▷ SYNONYMS: **1 shell**, pound, blitz, strafe, bomb, batter, blast, pelt. **2 swamp**, inundate, flood, deluge, snow under, overwhelm.

bombardier n. a rank of non-commissioned artillery officer.

bombardment n. an act of bombarding a place or person.

▷ SYNONYMS: **assault**, attack, bombing, shelling, strafing, blitz, air raid, cannonade, fusillade, barrage, broadside.

bombast n. pompous language with little meaning.

■ **bombastic** adj.

bomber n. **1** an aircraft that drops bombs. **2** a person who plants bombs.

bona fide /boh-nuh **fy**-di/ adj. genuine.

bonanza n. a situation creating wealth or success.

▷ SYNONYMS: **windfall**, godsend, blessing, bonus, stroke of luck; informal jackpot.

bond n. **1** a force or feeling that links people. **2** a thing used for fastening. **3** (**bonds**) ropes or chains used to restrain someone. **4** an agreement with legal force. **5** a certificate issued by a government or a public company promising to repay money lent to it at a fixed rate of interest.

▷ SYNONYMS: **1 friendship**, relationship, fellowship, partnership, association, affiliation, alliance, attachment, tie, connection, link. **2 promise**, pledge, vow, oath, word, word of honour,

guarantee, assurance, agreement, contract, pact, deal.
•v. **1** join securely. **2** form a relationship based on shared feelings etc.
▷ SYNONYMS: **join**, fasten, fix, affix, attach, secure, bind, stick, fuse.

bondage n. the state of being a slave or prisoner.

bone n. any of the pieces of hard material making up the skeleton in vertebrates.
•v. **1** remove the bones from meat or fish. **2** (**bone up on**) informal study a subject intensively.

bonfire n. a large open-air fire.

bongo n. (pl. **bongos**) each of a pair of small drums held between the knees.

bonhomie /bon-uh-mee/ n. good-natured friendliness.

bonnet n. **1** a hat with strings that tie under the chin. **2** Brit. the hinged cover over the engine of a vehicle.

bonny adj. (**bonnier, bonniest**) Scottish & N. English attractive and healthy-looking.

bonsai /bon-sy/ n. the art of growing miniature ornamental trees.

bonus n. **1** a sum of money added to wages for good performance. **2** an unexpected extra benefit.
▷ SYNONYMS: **1 advantage**, plus, benefit, extra, boon, blessing, godsend, stroke of luck, attraction. **2 gratuity**, handout, gift, present, reward, prize, incentive; informal perk, sweetener.
– ANTONYMS: disadvantage.

bon voyage /bon voy-**yahzh**/ exclam. have a good journey.

bony adj. (**bonier, boniest**)
1 containing or resembling bones.
2 very thin, with the bones showing.
▷ SYNONYMS: **skinny**, thin, lean, gaunt, scrawny, spare, skin and bone, skeletal, emaciated, underweight.
– ANTONYMS: plump.

boo exclam. **1** said suddenly to surprise someone. **2** said to show disapproval.
•v. (**booing, booed**) shout 'boo'.

boob Brit. informal n. an embarrassing mistake.
•v. make such a mistake.

booby n. (pl. **boobies**) informal a stupid person.
□ **booby prize** a prize given to the person who comes last in a contest. **booby trap** an object containing a hidden explosive device.

boogie v. (**boogieing, boogied**) informal dance to pop music.

book n. **1** a written or printed work consisting of pages bound in a cover. **2** a main division of a literary work.

3 (**books**) a set of records or accounts.
▷ SYNONYMS: **1 volume**, tome, publication, title, novel, treatise, manual. **2 notepad**, notebook, pad, exercise book, logbook, ledger, journal, diary; Brit. jotter, pocketbook; N. Amer. scratch pad.
•v. **1** reserve accommodation, a ticket, etc. **2** engage a performer for an event. **3** officially note the name of someone who has broken a law or rule.
▷ SYNONYMS: **reserve**, prearrange, order; informal bag.
□ **bookcase** a cabinet containing shelves for books. **bookkeeping** the keeping of records of financial transactions. **bookmaker** a person who takes bets and pays out winnings. **bookmark 1** a strip of card or leather to mark a place in a book. **2** a record of the address of a computer file, website, etc. enabling quick access by the user. **bookworm** informal a person who loves reading.
■ **booker** n. **booking** n.

> **WORD LINKS**
> **bibliography** a list of books

bookie n. informal a bookmaker.

booklet n. a small thin book.
▷ SYNONYMS: **pamphlet**, brochure, leaflet, tract; N. Amer. folder, mailer.

boom n. **1** a loud, deep sound. **2** a period of rapid economic growth. **3** a pivoted beam at the foot of a sail. **4** a movable arm carrying a microphone or film camera. **5** a beam forming a barrier across a harbour mouth.
▷ SYNONYMS: **1 roar**, rumble, thunder, crashing, drumming, pounding, echoing, resonance, reverberation. **2 increase**, growth, advance, boost, escalation, improvement, upsurge, upturn.
– ANTONYMS: slump.
•v. **1** make a loud, deep sound.
2 experience rapid economic growth.
▷ SYNONYMS: **1 roar**, rumble, thunder, crash, roll, clap, explode, bang, resound, blare, echo, resonate, reverberate. **2 shout**, yell, bellow, roar, thunder, bawl; informal holler. **3 flourish**, thrive, prosper, burgeon, progress, improve, pick up, expand.

boomerang n. a curved flat piece of wood that can be thrown so as to return to the thrower.

boon n. a very useful thing.

boor n. a rough, bad-mannered person.

boorish adj. uncouth; bad-mannered.
▷ SYNONYMS: **coarse**, uncouth, rude,

ill-mannered, vulgar, uncivilized, unrefined, oafish, ignorant, uncultured, philistine, rough, thuggish, loutish, Neanderthal; Brit. informal yobbish; Austral. informal ocker.
– ANTONYMS: refined.

boost v. help or encourage.
▷ SYNONYMS: **increase**, raise, escalate, improve, strengthen, inflate, push up, promote, advance, foster, stimulate, encourage, facilitate, help, assist, aid; informal hike, bump up.
– ANTONYMS: decrease.
• n. **1** a source of help or encouragement. **2** an increase.
▷ SYNONYMS: **1** *a boost to your morale:* **uplift**, lift, spur, encouragement, help, inspiration, stimulus, fillip; informal shot in the arm. **2** *a boost in sales:* **increase**, expansion, upturn, upsurge, rise, escalation, improvement, advance, growth, boom.
– ANTONYMS: decrease.

booster n. **1** a dose of a vaccine that increases or renews the effect of an earlier one. **2** the part of a rocket or spacecraft giving acceleration after lift-off.

boot n. **1** an item of footwear covering the foot and ankle or lower leg. **2** Brit. a space at the back of a car for luggage. **3** (**the boot**) informal dismissal from a job.
• v. **1** kick hard. **2** start a computer and make it ready to operate.
▷ SYNONYMS: **kick**, punt, tap, propel, drive, knock.

bootee n. a baby's woollen shoe.

booth n. **1** an enclosed compartment allowing privacy when telephoning etc. **2** a stall or stand for selling goods etc. at a fair or market.
▷ SYNONYMS: **1** stall, stand, kiosk. **2** *a phone booth:* **cubicle**, kiosk, box, compartment, enclosure, cabin.

bootleg adj. made or distributed illegally.
■ **bootlegger** n. **bootlegging** n.

booty n. valuable stolen goods.
▷ SYNONYMS: **loot**, plunder, haul, spoils, ill-gotten gains, pickings; informal swag.

booze informal n. alcoholic drink.
• v. drink alcohol.
■ **boozer** n. **boozy** adj.

bop v. (**bopping**, **bopped**) informal dance to pop music.

borax n. a white mineral used in making glass.

border n. **1** a boundary between two countries etc. **2** a decorative band around the edge of something. **3** a flower bed along the edge of a lawn.
▷ SYNONYMS: **1** edge, margin, perimeter, circumference, periphery, rim, fringe, verge, sides. **2** frontier, boundary, borderline, perimeter.
• v. **1** form a border around or along. **2** (**border on**) come close to.
▷ SYNONYMS: **1** surround, enclose, encircle, edge, fringe, bound, flank. **2** edge, fringe, hem, trim, pipe, finish. **3** adjoin, abut, be next to, be adjacent to, touch.
□ **borderline** between two states or categories.

bore¹ v. **1** make someone feel weary and unenthusiastic by being dull. **2** make a hole with a drill or other tool.
▷ SYNONYMS: **1** weary, tire, fatigue; pall on. **2** drill, pierce, perforate, puncture, punch, tunnel, burrow, mine, dig, gouge, sink.
• n. **1** a dull person or activity. **2** the hollow part inside a gun barrel.
▷ SYNONYMS: **bother**, nuisance, annoyance, trial, thorn in your flesh/side; informal drag, yawn, pain in the neck, headache, hassle.

bore² past of BEAR¹.

boredom n. the state of being bored.
▷ SYNONYMS: **tedium**, ennui, apathy, weariness, dullness, monotony, repetitiveness, flatness, dreariness.
– ANTONYMS: interest, excitement.

boric acid n. a substance made from boron, used as an antiseptic.

boring adj. not interesting; dull.
▷ SYNONYMS: **tedious**, dull, dreary, monotonous, repetitive, uneventful, unimaginative, characterless, featureless, colourless, lifeless, uninteresting, unexciting, lacklustre, humdrum, mind-numbing, soul-destroying, wearisome, tiresome; informal deadly; Brit. informal samey; N. Amer. informal dullsville.
– ANTONYMS: interesting, exciting.

born adj. **1** existing as a result of birth. **2** having a particular natural ability.
□ **born-again** newly converted to Christianity or a particular cause.

borne past part. of BEAR¹.

boron n. a chemical element used in making steel.

borough n. Brit. a town with a corporation and privileges granted by a royal charter.

borrow v. take and use something belonging to someone else and return it later.
▷ SYNONYMS: **1** loan, lease, hire; informal cadge, scrounge, bum, touch someone

for; N. Amer. informal **mooch**; Austral./NZ informal **bludge**. **2 adopt**, take on, acquire, embrace, copy, imitate.
– ANTONYMS: lend.
■ **borrower** n.

borstal n. Brit. hist. a prison for young offenders.

bosom n. a woman's breasts or chest.
• adj. (of a friend) very close.

boss n. **1** a person in charge of an employee or organization. **2** a knob at the centre of a shield etc.
▷ SYNONYMS: **head**, chief, principal, director, president, chief executive, chair, manager, supervisor, foreman, overseer, controller, employer, owner, proprietor; Brit. informal **gaffer**, **governor**; N. Amer. informal **head honcho**.
• v. informal give orders in a domineering way.
▷ SYNONYMS: **order around**, dictate to, bully, push around/about, call the shots, lay down the law; informal bulldoze, walk all over, railroad.
□ **boss-eyed** Brit. cross-eyed.

bossy adj. (**bossier, bossiest**) informal tending to give orders.
▷ SYNONYMS: **domineering**, pushy, overbearing, imperious, officious, high-handed, authoritarian, dictatorial, autocratic; informal high and mighty.
– ANTONYMS: submissive.
■ **bossily** adv. **bossiness** n.

bosun (or bo'sun) var. of **BOATSWAIN**.

botany n. the study of plants.
■ **botanical** adj. **botanist** n.

botch v. informal do badly or carelessly.

both adj. & pron. two people or things regarded together.

bother v. **1** take the trouble to do something. **2** worry, disturb, or upset.
▷ SYNONYMS: **1** something was bothering him: **worry**, trouble, concern, perturb, disturb, disquiet; informal rattle. **2** don't bother about me: **mind**, care, worry, concern yourself, trouble yourself. **3** no one bothered her: **disturb**, trouble, inconvenience, pester, badger, harass, plague; informal hassle, bug; N. English informal mither; N. Amer. informal ride.
• n. **1** trouble and fuss. **2** (**a bother**) a cause of trouble or fuss.
▷ SYNONYMS: **1 trouble**, effort, exertion, inconvenience, fuss, pains; informal hassle. **2 nuisance**, pest, palaver, rigmarole, job, trial, bind, bore, drag, inconvenience, trouble; informal hassle, headache, pain. **3** a spot of bother in the public bar: **disorder**, fighting, trouble, disturbance, commotion,

uproar; informal hoo-ha, aggro, argy-bargy, kerfuffle.
■ **bothersome** adj.

bottle n. a container with a narrow neck, for storing liquids.
▷ SYNONYMS: **flask**, carafe, decanter, pitcher, flagon, magnum, demijohn, phial.
• v. **1** put in bottles. **2** (**bottle up**) hide your feelings.
□ **bottleneck** a narrow part of a road where congestion occurs.

bottom n. **1** the lowest or furthest point, part, or position. **2** the buttocks.
▷ SYNONYMS: **1 foot**, lowest part, base, foundation. **2 underside**, underneath, undersurface, underbelly. **3 floor**, bed, depths. **4 farthest point**, extremity, far end. **5 buttocks**, rear, rump, seat, derrière; informal behind, backside; Brit. informal bum, jacksie; N. Amer. informal butt, fanny; humorous posterior.
– ANTONYMS: top, surface.
• adj. in the lowest or furthest position.
▷ SYNONYMS: **lowest**, last, bottommost.
– ANTONYMS: top.
□ **the bottom line** informal the most important factor.
■ **bottomless** adj.

botulism n. a dangerous form of food poisoning.

boudoir /boo-dwar/ n. a woman's bedroom or small private room.

bouffant /boo-fon/ adj. (of hair) standing out from the head in a rounded shape.

bougainvillea /boo-guhn-**vil**-li-uh/ n. a tropical plant with brightly coloured bracts.

bough n. a large branch.

bought past & past part. of **BUY**.

boulder n. a large rock.

boulevard n. a wide street.

bounce v. **1** move quickly up from a surface after hitting it. **2** move up and down repeatedly. **3** informal (of a cheque) be returned by a bank when there is not enough money in an account to meet it.
▷ SYNONYMS: **1 rebound**, spring back, ricochet; N. Amer. carom. **2 bound**, leap, jump, spring, bob, hop, skip, gambol, trip, prance.
• n. **1** an act of bouncing. **2** lively self-confidence.
▷ SYNONYMS: **1 springiness**, resilience, elasticity, give. **2 vitality**, vigour, energy, vivacity, liveliness, animation, sparkle, verve, spirit; informal get-up-and-go, pep, zing.

b

■ **bouncy** adj.

bouncer n. a person employed by a nightclub to control or keep out troublemakers.

bound¹ v. **1** move with leaping strides. **2** form the boundary of. **3** restrict.
▷ SYNONYMS: **1 leap**, jump, spring, vault, bounce, hop, skip, dance, prance, gambol, gallop. **2 enclose**, surround, encircle, circle, border, close in/off, hem in. **3 limit**, restrict, confine, circumscribe, demarcate, delimit.
• n. **1** a leaping movement. **2** a boundary or limit.
• adj. **1** going towards somewhere. **2** certain to: *he's bound to win.*
▷ SYNONYMS: **certain**, sure, very likely, destined.
□ **out of bounds** beyond permitted limits.

bound² past & past part. of BIND.

boundary n. (pl. **boundaries**) a line marking the limits of an area.
▷ SYNONYMS: **1 border**, frontier, borderline, partition, dividing line. **2** *the boundary of his estate:* **limits**, confines, bounds, margins, edges, fringes, border, periphery, perimeter.

boundless adj. unlimited.
▷ SYNONYMS: **limitless**, untold, immeasurable, abundant, inexhaustible, endless, infinite, unfailing, ceaseless, everlasting.
– ANTONYMS: limited.

bounteous adj. old use bountiful.

bountiful adj. **1** plentiful. **2** giving generously.

bounty n. (pl. **bounties**) **1** literary generosity, or something given in large amounts. **2** a reward for killing or capturing someone.

bouquet n. **1** a bunch of flowers. **2** the scent of a wine or perfume.
▷ SYNONYMS: **1 posy**, nosegay, spray, corsage, buttonhole, garland, wreath, arrangement. **2 aroma**, nose, smell, fragrance, perfume, scent, odour.

bourbon /ber-buhn/ n. an American whisky made from maize and rye.

bourgeois /boor-zhwah/ adj. of the middle class, esp. in being conventional.
▷ SYNONYMS: **middle-class**, conservative, conformist, conventional, propertied, provincial, suburban, small-town.
– ANTONYMS: proletarian.

bourgeoisie /boor-zhwah-zee/ n. the middle class.

bout n. **1** a period of illness or intense activity. **2** a wrestling or boxing match.
▷ SYNONYMS: **1 spell**, period, stretch,

stint, session, burst, flurry, spurt. **2 attack**, fit, spasm. **3 contest**, fight, match, round, competition, meeting, encounter.

boutique n. a small shop selling fashionable clothes.

bovine adj. **1** of cattle. **2** sluggish or stupid.

bow¹ n. **1** a knot tied with two loops and two loose ends. **2** a weapon for shooting arrows. **3** a rod with horsehair stretched along its length, for playing a violin etc.
□ **bow-legged** having legs that curve outwards at the knee.

bow² v. **1** bend the head or upper body as a sign of respect. **2** bend under a heavy weight. **3** give in to pressure.
▷ SYNONYMS: **1 incline your head**, bend, stoop, bob, curtsy, kneel, genuflect. **2** *the mast bowed in the wind:* **bend**, buckle, curve, flex. **3** *the government bowed to pressure:* **give in**, submit, yield, surrender, succumb, capitulate.
• n. **1** an act of bowing. **2** (or **bows**) the front of a ship.
▷ SYNONYMS: **1 nod**, bob, obeisance, curtsy, genuflection, salaam. **2 prow**, front, stem, nose, head.

bowdlerize (or **-ise**) v. remove indecent or offensive material from a text.

bowel n. **1** the intestine. **2** (**bowels**) the innermost parts of something.
▷ SYNONYMS: **1 intestines**, entrails, viscera, innards, digestive system; Medicine gut; informal guts, insides. **2 interior**, inside, core, belly, depths, recesses.

bower n. a shady place under trees.

bowl n. **1** a round, deep dish or basin. **2** a rounded, hollow part of an object. **3** (**bowls**) a game in which heavy wooden balls are rolled as close as possible to a small white ball. **4** a ball used in the game of bowls.
▷ SYNONYMS: **dish**, basin, pot, crock, vessel, receptacle.
• v. **1** roll a round object along the ground. **2** Cricket throw the ball towards the wicket. **3** Brit. move rapidly and smoothly. **4** (**bowl over**) knock down. **5** (**bowl over**) informal impress or astonish.
▷ SYNONYMS: **throw**, pitch, hurl, toss, lob, fling, roll, launch, propel; informal chuck, sling, bung.

bowler n. **1** Cricket a member of the fielding side who bowls. **2** a player at bowls. **3** a hard black felt hat with a rounded top.

box n. **1** a straight-sided container

with a lid. **2** an enclosed area reserved for a group of people in a theatre, sports ground, etc. **3** (**the box**) informal television. **4** a shrub with small glossy leaves.
▷ SYNONYMS: **1 carton**, pack, packet, case, crate, chest, coffer, casket. **2** *a telephone box*: **booth**, kiosk, cubicle, compartment, cabin, hut.
 • v. **1** put in a box. **2** fight with the fists as a sport.
▷ SYNONYMS: **fight**, spar, battle, brawl; informal scrap.
 □ **box office** the place at a theatre or cinema where tickets are sold.
 ■ **boxing** n.

boxer n. **1** a person who boxes as a sport. **2** a dog with a brown coat and pug-like face.
▷ SYNONYMS: **fighter**, pugilist, prize-fighter; informal bruiser, scrapper.
 □ **boxer shorts** men's underpants resembling shorts.

boy n. a male child.
▷ SYNONYMS: **lad**, youth, young man, stripling; Scottish & N. English laddie.
 ■ **boyhood** n. **boyish** adj.

boycott v. refuse to have dealings with or trade with.
▷ SYNONYMS: **shun**, snub, spurn, avoid, ostracize, blacklist, blackball, reject, veto, send to Coventry.
 • n. an act of boycotting.
▷ SYNONYMS: **ban**, veto, embargo, prohibition, moratorium, sanction, restriction, avoidance, rejection.

boyfriend n. a person's regular male romantic or sexual partner.
▷ SYNONYMS: **lover**, sweetheart, beloved, darling, partner, man; N. Amer. informal squeeze; dated beau; literary swain.

bra n. a woman's undergarment worn to support the breasts.

brace n. **1** a strengthening or supporting part. **2** (**braces**) Brit. a pair of straps that pass over the shoulders and fasten to trousers to hold them up. **3** a wire device used to straighten the teeth. **4** (pl. **brace**) a pair.
▷ SYNONYMS: **prop**, strut, stay, support, bracket.
 • v. **1** make stronger or firmer with a brace. **2** (**brace yourself**) prepare for something difficult.
▷ SYNONYMS: **1 support**, shore up, prop up, hold up, buttress, reinforce. **2 steady**, secure, stabilize, poise, fix. **3** *brace yourself for disappointment*: **prepare**, get ready, gear up, nerve, steel, fortify; informal psych yourself up.

bracelet n. an ornamental band or

chain worn on the arm.

bracing adj. fresh and invigorating.
▷ SYNONYMS: **invigorating**, refreshing, stimulating, energizing, exhilarating, restorative, rejuvenating.

bracken n. a tall fern.

bracket n. **1** each of a pair of marks ( ) [ ] { } < > used to enclose words or figures. **2** a category. **3** a right-angled support projecting from a wall.
▷ SYNONYMS: **1 support**, prop, stay, batten, rest, mounting, rack, frame. **2 group**, category, grade, classification, division.
 • v. (**bracketing**, **bracketed**) **1** enclose in brackets. **2** put in the same category.

brackish adj. (of water) slightly salty.

bract n. a leaf with a flower in the angle where it meets the stem.

brag v. (**bragging**, **bragged**) boast.
▷ SYNONYMS: **boast**, crow, swagger, swank, show off, blow your own trumpet, sing your own praises; informal talk big.

braggart n. a boastful person.

braid n. **1** threads woven into a decorative band. **2** a plait of hair.
 • v. **1** plait hair. **2** trim with thread.

Braille n. a written language for blind people, using raised dots.

brain n. **1** an organ of soft tissue in the skull, the centre of the nervous system. **2** intellectual ability.
▷ SYNONYMS: **intelligence**, intellect, brainpower, cleverness, wit, reasoning, wisdom, judgement, understanding, sense; informal nous, grey matter; N. Amer. informal smarts.
 □ **brainchild** a person's idea or invention. **brainstorm 1** Brit. a moment in which you are unable to think clearly. **2** a group discussion to produce ideas. **brainwash** pressure someone into accepting an idea or belief. **brainwave** a sudden clever idea.

> **WORD LINKS**
> **cerebral** relating to the brain

brainy adj. (**brainier**, **brainiest**) informal clever.

braise v. fry food lightly and then stew it slowly in a closed container.

brake n. a device for slowing or stopping a moving vehicle.
▷ SYNONYMS: **curb**, check, restraint, constraint, control, limit.
 • v. slow or stop a vehicle with a brake.
▷ SYNONYMS: **slow down**, decelerate, reduce speed.
 – ANTONYMS: accelerate.

bramble n. a blackberry bush or similar shrub.

bran n. pieces of grain husk separated from flour after milling.

branch n. **1** a part of a tree growing out from the trunk. **2** a river, road, or railway extending out from a main one. **3** a division of a larger group.
▷ SYNONYMS: **1 bough**, limb, arm, offshoot, twig. **2 division**, subdivision, section, subsection, department, unit, sector, wing, office, bureau, agency, subsidiary.
• v. **1** divide into one or more branches. **2** (**branch out**) embark on new activities.
▷ SYNONYMS: **1 fork**, divide, split, bifurcate. **2** *narrow paths branched off the road:* **diverge**, split off, fan out, radiate.

brand n. **1** a type of product made by a company under a particular name. **2** (or **brand name**) a name given to a product by its maker. **3** a mark burned on livestock with hot metal.
▷ SYNONYMS: **1 make**, line, label, marque, trade name, trademark, proprietary name. **2 type**, kind, sort, variety, class, category, genre, style, ilk; N. Amer. stripe.
• v. **1** describe as being bad in a particular way. **2** give a brand name to. **3** mark with hot metal.
▷ SYNONYMS: **1 mark**, stamp, burn, sear. **2 stigmatize**, characterize, label, mark out, denounce, discredit, vilify.
□ **brand new** completely new.

brandish v. wave something as a threat or in anger or excitement.
▷ SYNONYMS: **flourish**, wave, shake, wield, swing, swish.

brandy n. (pl. **brandies**) a strong alcoholic spirit made from wine or fermented fruit juice.

brash adj. aggressively self-confident.
▷ SYNONYMS: **1 self-assertive**, pushy, cocky, self-confident, arrogant, bold, audacious, brazen. **2 garish**, gaudy, loud, flamboyant, showy, tasteless; informal flashy, tacky.
– ANTONYMS: meek.
■ **brashness** n.

brass n. **1** a yellow alloy of copper and zinc. **2** Brit. a brass memorial plaque. **3** brass wind instruments forming a section of an orchestra.

brasserie /brass-uh-ri/ n. (pl. **brasseries**) an inexpensive French or French-style restaurant.

brassica n. a plant of the cabbage family.

brassiere /braz-i-er/ n. a bra.

brassy adj. (**brassier**, **brassiest**) **1** like brass. **2** tastelessly showy.

brat n. informal a badly behaved child.

bravado n. confidence that is intended to impress.

brave adj. having or showing courage.
▷ SYNONYMS: **courageous**, intrepid, bold, plucky, heroic, fearless, daring, audacious, dauntless, valiant, valorous, doughty, indomitable, stout-hearted; informal game, gutsy.
– ANTONYMS: cowardly.
• v. face unpleasant conditions with courage.
▷ SYNONYMS: **endure**, put up with, bear, withstand, weather, suffer, face, confront, defy.
• n. dated an American Indian warrior.
■ **bravely** adv.

bravery n. courageous behaviour.
▷ SYNONYMS: **courage**, boldness, heroism, intrepidity, nerve, daring, fearlessness, audacity, pluck, valour; informal guts; Brit. informal bottle.

bravo exclam. well done!

bravura n. great skill and enthusiasm.

brawl n. a noisy fight or quarrel.
▷ SYNONYMS: **fight**, skirmish, scuffle, tussle, fray, melee, fracas, fisti-cuffs; informal scrap, set-to; Brit. informal punch-up.
• v. take part in a brawl.

brawn n. physical strength.

brawny adj. physically strong.
▷ SYNONYMS: **strong**, muscular, muscly, well built, powerful, strapping, burly, sturdy; informal beefy, hulking.
– ANTONYMS: puny, weak.

bray v. (of a donkey) make a loud, harsh cry.
• n. the cry of a donkey.

brazen adj. bold and shameless.
▷ SYNONYMS: **bold**, shameless, unashamed, unrepentant, unabashed, defiant, impudent, impertinent, cheeky, barefaced, blatant, flagrant.
• v. (**brazen it out**) endure an awkward situation without seeming ashamed.
■ **brazenly** adv.

brazier n. a portable heater holding lighted coals.

Brazil nut n. a large three-sided nut from a South American tree.

breach v. **1** make a hole in. **2** break a rule or agreement.
▷ SYNONYMS: **1 break**, burst, rupture. **2 contravene**, break, violate, infringe, defy, disobey, flout.
• n. **1** a gap made in a wall or barrier. **2** an act of breaking a

rule or agreement. **3** a quarrel or disagreement.

▷ SYNONYMS: **1 break**, rupture, split, crack, fracture, opening, gap, hole, fissure. **2 contravention**, violation, infringement, infraction, transgression. **3 rift**, severance, estrangement, parting, parting of the ways, split, falling-out, schism.

bread n. **1** food made of flour, water, and yeast mixed together and baked. **2** informal money.
□ **breadwinner** a person who earns money to support their family. **on the breadline** Brit. very poor.

breadth n. **1** the distance from side to side of something. **2** wide range.

▷ SYNONYMS: **1 width**, broadness, thickness, span, diameter. **2 range**, extent, scope, depth, reach, compass, scale.

break v. (**breaking**, **broke**; past part. **broken**) **1** separate into pieces as a result of a blow or strain. **2** stop functioning or working. **3** interrupt a sequence or course. **4** fail to obey a rule or agreement. **5** beat a record. **6** soften a fall. **7** suddenly make or become public. **8** (of a boy's voice) deepen at puberty. **9** (of the weather) change suddenly.

▷ SYNONYMS: **1 shatter**, smash, crack, snap, fracture, fragment, splinter, split, burst; informal bust. **2 stop working**, break down, give out, go wrong, malfunction, crash; informal go kaput, conk out; Brit. informal pack up. **3 violate**, contravene, infringe, breach, defy, flout, disobey. **4** *the film broke box-office records:* **beat**, surpass, exceed, better, cap, top, outdo, outstrip. **5** *he tried to break the news gently:* **reveal**, disclose, divulge, impart, tell, announce, release.

– ANTONYMS: repair, obey.

• n. **1** a pause, gap, or short rest. **2** an instance of breaking, or the point where something is broken. **3** a sudden rush or dash. **4** informal a chance.

▷ SYNONYMS: **1 interval**, interruption, gap, disruption, stoppage, cessation, halt, stop. **2 rest**, respite, recess, pause, intermission; informal breather, time out. **3 gap**, opening, space, hole, breach, chink, crack, fracture, fissure, tear, split.

□ **break down 1** stop functioning. **2** lose control of your emotions. **break in 1** force entry to a building. **2** make a horse used to being ridden. **breakneck** dangerously fast. **break out 1** start suddenly. **2** escape. **break**

up (of a gathering or relationship) end. **breakwater** a barrier built out into the sea to protect a coast etc. from waves.
■ **breakable** adj.

breakage n. the action of breaking something.

breakdown n. **1** a failure or collapse. **2** a careful analysis.

▷ SYNONYMS: **1 failure**, collapse, disintegration, foundering. **2 malfunction**, failure, crash. **3 analysis**, itemization, classification, examination, investigation, explanation.

breaker n. a heavy wave that breaks on the shore.

breakfast n. the first meal of the day.

breakthrough n. a sudden important development or success.

▷ SYNONYMS: **advance**, development, step forward, success, improvement, discovery, innovation, revolution, quantum leap.

– ANTONYMS: setback.

bream n. (pl. **bream**) a freshwater fish.

breast n. **1** either of the two organs on a woman's chest which produce milk after pregnancy. **2** a person's or animal's chest.

▷ SYNONYMS: **chest**, bosom, bust; informal boobs, knockers.

□ **breastbone** the bone down the centre of the chest. **breaststroke** a swimming stroke in which the arms are pushed forwards and swept back while the legs are kicked out.

breath n. **1** air taken into or sent out of the lungs. **2** an act of breathing in or out. **3** a slight movement of air.

▷ SYNONYMS: **inhalation**, exhalation, gulp of air, puff, gasp; Medicine respiration.
■ **breathless** adj.

breathalyser (US trademark **Breathalyzer**) n. a device for measuring the amount of alcohol in a driver's breath.
■ **breathalyse** (US **-yze**) v.

breathe v. **1** take air into the lungs and send it out again. **2** say quietly.

▷ SYNONYMS: **1 inhale**, exhale, respire, draw breath, puff, pant, blow, gasp, wheeze; Medicine inspire, expire. **2 whisper**, murmur, purr, sigh.

WORD LINKS
respiratory relating to breathing
---

breather n. informal a brief pause for rest.

breathtaking adj. astonishing or awe-inspiring.

▷ SYNONYMS: **spectacular**, magnificent,

awe-inspiring, awesome, astonishing, amazing, stunning, thrilling; informal sensational, out of this world.

bred past & past part. of BREED.

breech n. the back part of a rifle or gun barrel.
□ **breech birth** a birth in which the baby's buttocks or feet are delivered first.

breeches pl. n. short trousers fastened just below the knee.

breed v. (breeding, bred) **1** (of animals) mate and produce offspring. **2** keep animals for the young that they produce. **3** produce or cause.
▷ SYNONYMS: **1 reproduce**, produce offspring, procreate, multiply, mate. **2 bring up**, rear, raise, nurture. **3 cause**, produce, bring about, give rise to, occasion, arouse, stir up, generate, foster.
• n. **1** a particular type within a species of animals. **2** a type.
▷ SYNONYMS: **1** *a breed of cow:* **variety**, stock, strain, race, species. **2** *a new breed of journalist:* **type**, kind, sort, variety, class, genre, generation.
■ **breeder** n.

breeding n. upper-class good manners.
▷ SYNONYMS: **good manners**, gentility, refinement, cultivation, polish, urbanity; informal class.

breeze n. a gentle wind.
▷ SYNONYMS: **gentle wind**, puff of air, gust, draught; literary zephyr.
□ **breeze block** Brit. a lightweight building block.

breezy adj. (breezier, breeziest) **1** windy. **2** cheerfully casual or brisk.
▷ SYNONYMS: **1 windy**, fresh, blowy, blustery, gusty. **2 jaunty**, cheerful, cheery, brisk, carefree, easy, casual, relaxed, informal, light-hearted, upbeat.

brethren pl. n. fellow Christians or members of a group.

breve /breev/ n. Music a note twice as long as a semibreve.

brevity n. **1** concise and exact use of words. **2** shortness of time.
▷ SYNONYMS: **conciseness**, concision, succinctness, pithiness, incisiveness, shortness, compactness.

brew v. **1** make beer. **2** make a drink of tea or coffee. **3** begin to develop.
▷ SYNONYMS: **1 ferment**, make, prepare, infuse; Brit. informal mash. **2 develop**, loom, be imminent, be on the horizon, be in the offing, be just around the corner.
• n. something brewed.

▷ SYNONYMS: **1** *home brew:* **beer**, ale. **2** *a hot reviving brew:* **drink**, beverage, infusion. **3 mixture**, mix, blend, combination, amalgam, cocktail.
■ **brewer** n.

brewery n. (pl. breweries) a place where beer is made.

briar (or **brier**) n. a prickly shrub, esp. a wild rose.

bribe v. dishonestly pay someone to help you.
▷ SYNONYMS: **buy off**, pay off, suborn; informal grease someone's palm, keep someone sweet, square; Brit. informal nobble.
• n. something offered in an attempt to bribe.
▷ SYNONYMS: **inducement**; informal bung, backhander, pay-off, kickback, sweetener.

bribery n. the giving or taking of bribes.
▷ SYNONYMS: **corruption**; N. Amer. payola; informal palm-greasing, graft, hush money.

> **WORD LINKS**
> **venal** susceptible to bribery

bric-a-brac n. various objects of little value.

brick n. a small rectangular block of fired clay, used in building.
• v. block or enclose with a wall of bricks.
□ **brickbat** a critical remark. **brick-layer** a person who builds structures with bricks.

bridal adj. of a bride or a newly married couple.

bride n. a woman at the time of her wedding.
□ **bridegroom** a man at the time of his wedding. **bridesmaid** a girl or woman who accompanies a bride at her wedding.

bridge n. **1** a structure providing a way across a river, road, etc. **2** the platform on a ship from which the captain directs its course. **3** the upper bony part of the nose. **4** the part on a stringed instrument over which the strings are stretched. **5** a card game played between two pairs of players.
▷ SYNONYMS: **1 viaduct**, flyover, over-pass, aqueduct. **2 link**, connection, bond, tie.
• v. be or make a bridge over.
▷ SYNONYMS: **span**, cross, extend across, traverse, arch over, straddle.
□ **bridgehead** a strong position gained by an army inside enemy territory.

WORD LINKS
pontine relating to bridges

bridle n. the harness used to control a horse.
• v. **1** put a bridle on. **2** show resentment or anger.
□ **bridleway** (or **bridle path**) Brit. a path for horse riders or walkers.

brief adj. **1** lasting a short time. **2** using few words. **3** (of clothes) not covering much of the body.
▷ SYNONYMS: **1** short, flying, fleeting, hasty, hurried, quick, cursory, perfunctory, temporary, short-lived, momentary, ephemeral, transient, transitory. **2** concise, succinct, short, pithy, compact, thumbnail, potted, condensed, to the point, terse, summary.
– ANTONYMS: long.
• n. Brit. **1** a set of instructions about a task. **2** a summary of the facts in a case given to a barrister to argue in court. **3** (**briefs**) short underpants.
▷ SYNONYMS: **1** my brief is to reorganize the project: **instructions**, directions, directive, remit, mandate. **2** a barrister's brief: **case**, summary, argument, contention, dossier.
• v. instruct someone about a task.
▷ SYNONYMS: **inform**, tell, update, notify, advise, prepare, prime, instruct; informal fill in, put in the picture.
□ **briefcase** a flat case for carrying documents.
■ **briefly** adv.

briefing n. a meeting for giving information or instructions.

brier var. of BRIAR.

brig n. a sailing ship with two masts.

brigade n. **1** a large army unit forming part of a division. **2** a particular group: the anti-smoking brigade.
▷ SYNONYMS: **squad**, team, group, band, party, crew, force, outfit.

brigadier n. the army rank above colonel.

brigand n. a member of a gang of bandits.

bright adj. **1** giving out or filled with light. **2** (of colour) vivid. **3** intelligent. **4** cheerfully lively. **5** (of prospects) good.
▷ SYNONYMS: **1** shining, brilliant, dazzling, glaring, sparkling, flashing, glittering, gleaming, glistening, shimmering, radiant, glowing, luminous, shiny, glossy, lustrous. **2** sunny, cloudless, clear, fair, fine. **3** bright colours: vivid, brilliant,

intense, strong, vibrant, bold, gaudy, lurid, garish. **4** clever, intelligent, quick-witted, smart, canny, astute, perceptive, ingenious; informal brainy.
– ANTONYMS: dull, cloudy, dark, stupid.
■ **brightly** adv. **brightness** n.

brighten v. **1** make or become brighter. **2** make or become more cheerful.
▷ SYNONYMS: **1** illuminate, light up, lighten. **2** cheer up, perk up, liven up, rally, take heart; informal buck up.

brilliance n. **1** intense brightness. **2** exceptional talent or intelligence.
▷ SYNONYMS: **1** brightness, vividness, intensity, sparkle, glitter, blaze, luminosity, radiance. **2** genius, intelligence, talent, ability, prowess, skill, expertise, aptitude, flair, wisdom, intellect.
– ANTONYMS: dullness, stupidity.

brilliant adj. **1** very bright or vivid. **2** very clever or talented. **3** Brit. informal excellent.
▷ SYNONYMS: **1** bright, shining, sparkling, blazing, dazzling, vivid, intense, glaring, luminous, radiant. **2** clever, bright, intelligent, smart, able, talented, gifted, skilful, astute; informal brainy. **3** her brilliant career: superb, glorious, illustrious, successful, impressive, remarkable, exceptional, excellent, outstanding, distinguished.
– ANTONYMS: dim, dull, stupid, undistinguished.
■ **brilliantly** adv.

brim n. **1** the projecting edge of a hat. **2** the lip of a cup, bowl, etc.
▷ SYNONYMS: **1** peak, visor, shield. **2** rim, lip, brink, edge.
• v. (**brimming, brimmed**) be full to the point of overflowing.
▷ SYNONYMS: be full, overflow, run over, well over.

brimstone n. old use sulphur.

brindle (or **brindled**) adj. (of an animal) brownish with streaks of grey or black.

brine n. water containing dissolved salt.
■ **briny** adj.

bring v. (**bringing, brought**) **1** carry or take to a place. **2** cause to be in a particular position or state. **3** begin legal action.
▷ SYNONYMS: **1** fetch, carry, bear, take, convey, transport, shift. **2** escort, conduct, guide, lead, usher. **3** cause, produce, create, bring about, generate, precipitate, occasion, provoke, lead to, give rise to, result in.

□ **bring about** cause to happen. **bring off** achieve. **bring on** cause to occur. **bring out 1** produce and launch. **2** emphasize a feature. **bring up 1** rear a child. **2** raise for discussion.

brink n. **1** the edge of land before a steep slope or an area of water. **2** the point just before a new situation.

▷ SYNONYMS: **1 edge**, verge, margin, rim, lip, border, boundary. **2** *on the brink of war:* **verge**, threshold, point, edge.

□ **brinkmanship** the pursuing of a dangerous course of action to the limits of safety before stopping.

brisk adj. **1** active and energetic. **2** practical and efficient.

▷ SYNONYMS: **1 quick**, rapid, fast, swift, speedy, hurried, energetic, lively; informal **nippy. 2 no-nonsense**, businesslike, decisive, brusque, abrupt, short, sharp, curt, blunt, terse; informal **snappy.**

– ANTONYMS: leisurely.

■ **briskly** adv.

brisket n. meat from the breast of a cow.

bristle n. a short, stiff hair.

▷ SYNONYMS: **1 hair**, whisker; (**bristles**) stubble, five o'clock shadow. **2 spine**, prickle, quill, barb.

• v. **1** (of hair or fur) stand upright away from the skin. **2** react angrily. **3** (**bristle with**) be covered with.

▷ SYNONYMS: **1 rise**, stand up, stand on end. **2 take offence**, bridle, take umbrage, be offended. **3 be crowded**, be full, be packed, be jammed, be covered, overflow; informal be thick, be chock-full.

■ **bristly** adj.

British adj. of Great Britain.

Briton n. a British person.

brittle adj. hard but easily broken.

▷ SYNONYMS: **breakable**, fragile, crisp, crumbly, delicate.

– ANTONYMS: flexible.

broach v. **1** raise a subject for discussion. **2** pierce a container.

▷ SYNONYMS: **bring up**, raise, introduce, mention, touch on, air.

broad adj. **1** larger than usual from side to side; wide. **2** large in area or range. **3** without detail. **4** (of an accent) very strong.

▷ SYNONYMS: **1 wide**, extensive, vast, immense, great, spacious, expansive, sizeable, sweeping. **2 comprehensive**, inclusive, extensive, wide, all-embracing, unlimited. **3** *a broad outline:* **general**, non-specific, rough, approximate, basic, loose, vague.

– ANTONYMS: narrow, limited.

□ **broadband** a telecommunications technique which uses a wide range of frequencies, enabling messages to be sent simultaneously. **broad bean** a large flat green bean. **broadsheet** a large-sized newspaper. **broadside 1** a fierce critical attack. **2** hist. a firing of all the guns from one side of a ship.

■ **broadly** adv.

broadcast v. (**broadcasting**, **broadcast**) **1** transmit by radio or television. **2** make generally known.

▷ SYNONYMS: **1 transmit**, relay, air, beam, show, televise, screen. **2 report**, announce, publicize, advertise, make public, proclaim, spread, circulate, promulgate.

• n. a radio or television programme.

▷ SYNONYMS: **transmission**, programme, show, telecast, production.

■ **broadcaster** n.

broaden v. make or become broader.

▷ SYNONYMS: **1** *her smile broadened:* **widen**, expand, stretch out, spread. **2** *the government tried to broaden its political base:* **expand**, enlarge, extend, widen, swell, increase, add to, develop.

– ANTONYMS: narrow, restrict.

broad-minded adj. not easily shocked.

▷ SYNONYMS: **liberal**, tolerant, freethinking, indulgent, progressive, permissive, unshockable, unprejudiced, unbiased.

– ANTONYMS: intolerant.

brocade n. a rich fabric woven with a raised pattern.

broccoli n. a vegetable with heads of small green or purplish flower buds.

> USAGE Two c's, one l: broccoli.

brochure n. a booklet containing information about a product or service.

▷ SYNONYMS: **booklet**, prospectus, catalogue, pamphlet, leaflet, circular, mailshot; N. Amer. folder.

broderie anglaise /broh-duh-ri ong-glayz/ n. open embroidery on white cotton or linen.

brogue n. **1** a strong shoe with perforated patterns in the leather. **2** a strong regional accent.

broil v. US grill meat or fish.

broke past of BREAK.

• adj. informal having no money.

broken past part. of BREAK.

• adj. (of a language) spoken hesitantly, with many mistakes.

▷ SYNONYMS: **1 smashed**, shattered, fragmented, splintered, crushed, snapped, in bits, in pieces, cracked, split, fractured; informal in smithereens. **2 faulty**, damaged, defective, not working, malfunctioning, out of order, broken down, down; informal kaput, bust; Brit. informal knackered. **3** broken English: **halting**, hesitating, disjointed, faltering, imperfect.

broken-hearted adj. overwhelmed with grief.
▷ SYNONYMS: **heartbroken**, grief-stricken, desolate, devastated, inconsolable, miserable, wretched, forlorn, heavy-hearted, woeful.

broker n. a person who buys and sells on behalf of others.
▷ SYNONYMS: **dealer**, agent, middleman, intermediary, mediator, factor, stockbroker.
• v. arrange a deal or plan.
▷ SYNONYMS: **arrange**, organize, orchestrate, work out, settle, clinch, negotiate, mediate.
■ **brokerage** n.

brolly n. (pl. **brollies**) informal an umbrella.

bromide n. a compound of bromine, used in medicine.

bromine n. a dark red liquid chemical element.

bronchial adj. of the tubes leading to the lungs.

bronchitis /brong-ky-tiss/ n. inflammation of the bronchial tubes.

bronco n. (pl. **broncos**) a wild or half-tamed horse of the western US.

brontosaurus n. a huge plant-eating dinosaur.

bronze n. **1** a yellowish-brown alloy of copper and tin. **2** a yellowish-brown colour. **3** an object made of bronze.
• v. make suntanned.

brooch n. an ornament fastened to clothing with a hinged pin.

brood n. a family of young animals born or hatched at one time.
▷ SYNONYMS: **offspring**, young, family, litter, clutch, progeny.
• v. **1** think deeply about an unpleasant subject. **2** (of a bird) sit on eggs to hatch them.
▷ SYNONYMS: **think**, ponder, contemplate, meditate, ruminate, muse, worry, dwell on, fret, agonize.

broody adj. **1** (of a hen) wishing to hatch eggs. **2** informal (of a woman) wanting to have a baby. **3** thoughtful and unhappy.

brook n. a small stream.
▷ SYNONYMS: **stream**, rill; N. English beck; Scottish & N. English burn; N. Amer. & Austral./ NZ creek.

• v. tolerate or allow.

broom n. **1** a long-handled brush for sweeping. **2** a shrub with yellow flowers.
□ **broomstick** the handle of a broom, on which witches are said to fly.

Bros abbrev. brothers.

broth n. thin soup or stock.

brothel n. a house where men visit prostitutes.

brother n. **1** a man or boy in relation to other children of his parents. **2** a male colleague or friend. **3** (pl. also **brethren**) a male fellow Christian or member of a religious order.
□ **brotherhood 1** the relationship between brothers. **2** comradeship. **3** a group linked by a shared interest.
brother-in-law (pl. **brothers-in-law**) the brother of a person's wife or husband, or the husband of a person's sister.

brotherly adj. relating to or like a brother.
▷ SYNONYMS: **fraternal**, friendly, comradely, affectionate, kind, devoted, loyal.

brought past & past part. of BRING.

brow n. **1** the forehead. **2** an eyebrow. **3** the highest point of a hill.
▷ SYNONYMS: **1 forehead**, temple.
2 summit, peak, top, crest, crown, head, pinnacle, apex.

browbeat v. intimidate.
▷ SYNONYMS: **bully**, intimidate, force, coerce, compel, dragoon, bludgeon, pressure, pressurize, tyrannize, terrorize; informal bulldoze, railroad.

brown adj. **1** of the colour of rich soil. **2** suntanned.
▷ SYNONYMS: **1** hazel, chestnut, chocolate, coffee, sepia, mahogany, tan, cafe au lait, caramel. **2 tanned**, suntanned, bronzed, swarthy.
• n. brown colour.
• v. make or become brown.
▷ SYNONYMS: **grill**, toast, singe, sear, barbecue, sauté.
□ **browned off** Brit. informal annoyed or dissatisfied.
■ **brownish** adj.

browse v. **1** read or look at something in a leisurely way. **2** look at information on a computer. **3** (of an animal) feed on leaves, twigs, etc.
▷ SYNONYMS: **look through**, scan, skim, glance, peruse, thumb, leaf, flick, dip into.

browser n. **1** a person or animal that browses. **2** a computer program for navigating the Internet.

b

bruise n. an area of discoloured skin on the body, caused by a blow.
▷ SYNONYMS: **contusion**, bump, swelling, lump, mark, injury, welt.
• v. cause a bruise on.

bruiser n. informal a tough, aggressive person.

brunch n. a meal combining breakfast and lunch.

brunette n. a woman or girl with dark brown hair.

brunt n. the chief impact of something bad.

brush n. **1** an implement with a handle and a block of bristles or wire. **2** an act of brushing. **3** a brief encounter with something bad. **4** a fox's tail. **5** undergrowth and shrubs.
▷ SYNONYMS: **1 broom**, besom. **2** a brush with the law: **encounter**, clash, confrontation, conflict, altercation; informal run-in, to-do. **3 undergrowth**, scrub, brushwood, shrubs, bushes; N. Amer. chaparral.
• v. **1** clean, smooth, or apply with a brush. **2** touch lightly. **3** (**brush off**) dismiss curtly. **4** (**brush up**) work to regain a former skill.
▷ SYNONYMS: **1 sweep**, clean, buff, polish, scrub. **2 groom**, comb, neaten, tidy, smooth, arrange. **3** his lips brushed her cheek: **touch**, stroke, caress, skim, sweep, graze, kiss.

brusque /bruusk/ adj. abrupt or offhand.
▷ SYNONYMS: **curt**, abrupt, blunt, short, sharp, brisk, peremptory, gruff, discourteous, impolite, rude.
– ANTONYMS: polite.
■ **brusquely** adv.

Brussels sprout n. a green vegetable like a very small cabbage.

brutal adj. savagely violent.
▷ SYNONYMS: **savage**, violent, cruel, vicious, ferocious, barbaric, wicked, murderous, bloodthirsty, cold-blooded, callous, ruthless, heartless, merciless, sadistic, inhuman.
– ANTONYMS: gentle.
■ **brutality** n. **brutally** adv.

brutalize (or **-ise**) v. **1** make brutal by frequent exposure to violence. **2** treat in a cruel way.

brute n. a violent or cruel person or a large, uncontrollable animal.
• adj. involving physical strength rather than reason: brute force.
■ **brutish** adj.

BSc abbrev. Bachelor of Science.

BSE abbrev. bovine spongiform encephalopathy, a fatal brain disease in cattle.

BST abbrev. British Summer Time.

bubble n. **1** a thin sphere of liquid enclosing a gas. **2** a gas-filled sphere in a liquid, glass, etc.
• v. **1** (of a liquid) contain rising bubbles. **2** (**bubble with**) be filled with.

bubbly adj. (**bubblier**, **bubbliest**) **1** containing bubbles. **2** cheerful and high-spirited.
▷ SYNONYMS: **1 fizzy**, sparkling, effervescent, aerated, carbonated, frothy, foamy. **2 vivacious**, animated, high-spirited, ebullient, lively, bouncy, merry, happy, cheerful, sunny; informal chirpy.

bubonic plague n. a form of plague passed on by rat fleas.

buccaneer n. **1** hist. a pirate. **2** a recklessly adventurous person.

buck n. **1** the male of some animals, e.g. deer and rabbits. **2** US & Austral. a dollar. **3** old use a fashionable young man.
• v. **1** (of a horse) jump with the back arched. **2** resist or go against. **3** (**buck up**) informal make or become more cheerful.
□ **buck teeth** teeth that stick out. **pass the buck** informal shift responsibility to someone else.

bucket n. an open container with a handle, for carrying liquids.
• v. (**bucketing**, **bucketed**) Brit. informal rain heavily.

buckle n. a flat frame with a hinged pin, used as a fastener.
▷ SYNONYMS: **clasp**, clip, catch, hasp, fastener.
• v. **1** fasten with a buckle. **2** crumple under pressure. **3** (**buckle down**) tackle a task with determination.
▷ SYNONYMS: **1 fasten**, do up, hook, secure, clasp, clip. **2 bend**, warp, twist, distort, contort, deform, crumple, collapse, give way.

bucolic /byoo-kol-ik/ adj. of country life.

bud n. a growth on a plant which develops into a leaf or flower.
• v. (**budding**, **budded**) form a bud or buds.

Buddhism n. a religion based on the teachings of Buddha.
■ **Buddhist** n. & adj.

budding adj. beginning and showing signs of promise.
▷ SYNONYMS: **promising**, up-and-coming, rising, in the making, aspiring, future, fledgling, developing.

buddleia n. a shrub with lilac or white flowers.

buddy n. (pl. **buddies**) US informal a friend.

budge v. move slightly.
▷ SYNONYMS: **1 move**, shift, stir, go. **2 persuade**, convince, influence, sway, bend.

budgerigar n. a small Australian parakeet.

budget n. **1** an estimate of income and spending for a set period. **2** the amount of money available for a purpose.
▷ SYNONYMS: **1 financial plan**, forecast. **2** *the defence budget:* **allowance**, allocation, quota, funds, resources, capital.
• v. (**budgeting, budgeted**) plan to spend a particular amount.
▷ SYNONYMS: **allocate**, allot, allow, earmark, designate, set aside.
■ **budgetary** adj.

budgie n. (pl. **budgies**) a budgerigar.

buff n. **1** a yellowish-beige colour. **2** informal an expert on a particular subject.
▷ SYNONYMS: **enthusiast**, fan, devotee, lover, admirer, expert, aficionado, authority; informal freak, nut, addict.
• v. polish.
▷ SYNONYMS: **polish**, burnish, shine, smooth, rub.

buffalo n. (pl. **buffalo** or **buffaloes**) **1** a wild ox. **2** the North American bison.

buffer n. **1** (**buffers**) Brit. shock-absorbing devices on a railway track or railway vehicle. **2** a person or thing that lessens the impact of harmful effects.
▷ SYNONYMS: **cushion**, bulwark, shield, barrier, guard, safeguard.

buffet¹ /boo-fay, buf-fay/ n. **1** a meal in which guests serve themselves. **2** a counter at which snacks are sold.
▷ SYNONYMS: **1 cold table**, self-service meal, smorgasbord. **2 cafe**, cafeteria, snack bar, canteen, restaurant.

buffet² /buf-fit/ v. (**buffeting, buffeted**) (esp. of wind or waves) hit repeatedly.
▷ SYNONYMS: **batter**, pound, lash, strike, hit, beat.

buffoon n. a ridiculous but amusing person.
■ **buffoonery** n.

bug n. **1** informal a germ, or an illness caused by one. **2** a small insect. **3** a microphone used for secret recording. **4** an error in a computer program or system.
▷ SYNONYMS: **1 illness**, disease, sickness, disorder, upset, ailment, infection, virus; Brit. informal lurgy. **2 insect**, mini-

beast; informal creepy-crawly, beastie. **3 listening device**, hidden microphone, wire, wiretap, tap. **4 fault**, error, defect, flaw, virus; informal glitch, gremlin.
• v. (**bugging, bugged**) **1** hide a microphone in. **2** informal annoy.
▷ SYNONYMS: **eavesdrop on**, spy on, tap, monitor.
□ **bugbear** a cause of worry or irritation.

buggery n. anal sex.

buggy n. (pl. **buggies**) **1** a folding pushchair. **2** a small open-topped motor vehicle.

bugle n. a brass instrument like a small trumpet.
■ **bugler** n.

build v. (**building, built**) **1** construct by putting parts together. **2** (**build up**) increase over time.
▷ SYNONYMS: **1 construct**, erect, put up, assemble, make, create, fashion, model, shape. **2** (**build up**) **increase**, grow, develop, mount up, intensify, strengthen, augment, swell, expand, accumulate, amass, collect.
– ANTONYMS: demolish, dismantle.
• n. bodily proportions.
▷ SYNONYMS: **physique**, frame, body, figure, form, shape, stature, proportions; informal vital statistics.
■ **builder** n.

building n. a structure with a roof and walls.
▷ SYNONYMS: **structure**, construction, edifice, pile, property, premises, establishment.
□ **building society** Brit. an organization that pays interest on members' investments and lends money for mortgages.

> **WORD LINKS**
> **architectural** relating to building

built-in adj. included as part of a larger structure.

built-up adj. covered by many buildings.

bulb n. **1** the rounded base of the stem of some plants. **2** a glass ball giving light in an electric lamp.

bulbous adj. round or bulging.
▷ SYNONYMS: **bulging**, round, fat, rotund, swollen, distended, bloated.

bulge n. a rounded swelling.
▷ SYNONYMS: **swelling**, bump, lump, hump, protrusion, protuberance.
• v. swell or stick out.
▷ SYNONYMS: **swell**, stick out, project, protrude, stand out, puff out, balloon out, fill out, distend.

bulimia /buu-lim-i-uh/ n. a disorder marked by bouts of overeating, followed by fasting or vomiting.
■ **bulimic** adj. & n.

bulk n. **1** the mass or size of something large. **2** the greater part. **3** a large mass or shape.
▷ SYNONYMS: **1 size**, volume, dimensions, proportions, mass, scale. **2 majority**, mass, generality, main part, lion's share, preponderance.
□ **bulkhead** a partition in a ship or aircraft. **in bulk** (of goods) in large quantities.

bulky adj. (**bulkier**, **bulkiest**) large and unwieldy.
▷ SYNONYMS: **unwieldy**, cumbersome, unmanageable, awkward, ponderous, outsize, oversized; informal hulking.

bull n. **1** an adult male of the cattle family. **2** a male whale, elephant, etc. **3** a bullseye. **4** an official order issued by the pope.
□ **bulldog** a powerful dog with a flat wrinkled face. **bulldozer** a tractor with a device for clearing ground. **bullfighting** the sport of baiting and killing a bull. **bullseye** the centre of the target in archery and darts.

bullet n. a small missile fired from a gun.
▷ SYNONYMS: **ball**, shot, pellet; informal slug.

bulletin n. a short official statement or summary of news.
▷ SYNONYMS: **1 report**, dispatch, story, newsflash, statement, announcement, message, communication, communiqué. **2 newsletter**, news-sheet, proceedings, newspaper, magazine, gazette, review.

bullion n. gold or silver in bulk or bars.

bullish adj. aggressively confident.

bullock n. a castrated bull.

bully n. (pl. **bullies**) a person who intimidates weaker people.
▷ SYNONYMS: **persecutor**, oppressor, tyrant, tormentor, intimidator, bully boy, thug.
• v. (**bullying**, **bullied**) intimidate.
▷ SYNONYMS: **1** the others bully him: **persecute**, oppress, tyrannize, browbeat, intimidate, dominate, terrorize; informal push around/about. **2** she was bullied into helping: **coerce**, pressure, press, push, prod, browbeat, dragoon, strong-arm; informal bulldoze, railroad, lean on.

bulrush n. a tall waterside plant with a long brown head.

bulwark n. **1** a defensive wall. **2** a ship's side above deck level.

bum n. informal **1** Brit. a person's bottom. **2** US a lazy or worthless person.

bumble v. act or speak in an awkward or confused way.

bumblebee n. a large hairy bee.

bumf (or **bumph**) n. Brit. informal printed information.

bump n. **1** a light blow or collision. **2** a projection on a level surface.
▷ SYNONYMS: **1 jolt**, crash, smash, smack, crack, bang, thud, thump, clang, knock, clunk, boom; informal whack, wallop. **2 swelling**, bulge, injury, contusion, hump, knob.
• v. **1** knock or run into. **2** travel with a jolting movement. **3** (**bump into**) meet by chance.
▷ SYNONYMS: **1 hit**, crash into, smash into, slam into, bang, knock, run into, plough into, ram, collide with, strike; N. Amer. impact. **2 bounce**, jolt, jerk, rattle, shake.

bumper n. a bar across the front or back of a vehicle to reduce damage in a collision.
• adj. exceptionally large or successful.
▷ SYNONYMS: **exceptional**, large, abundant, rich, bountiful, good, plentiful, record, successful; informal whopping.
– ANTONYMS: meagre.

bumpkin n. an unsophisticated country person.

bumptious adj. irritatingly self-important.

bumpy adj. (**bumpier**, **bumpiest**) full of bumps.
▷ SYNONYMS: **1 uneven**, rough, rutted, pitted, potholed, lumpy, rocky. **2 bouncy**, rough, uncomfortable, jolting, lurching, jerky, jarring, bone-shaking.
– ANTONYMS: smooth.

bun n. **1** a small cake or bread roll. **2** a tight coil of hair at the back of the head.

bunch n. **1** a number of things held or grouped together. **2** informal a group of people.
▷ SYNONYMS: **1 bouquet**, posy, nosegay, spray, wreath, garland. **2 cluster**, clump, knot, group, bundle.
• v. collect into a bunch.
▷ SYNONYMS: **cluster**, huddle, gather, congregate, collect, amass, group, crowd.

bundle n. a group of things tied or wrapped up together.
▷ SYNONYMS: **collection**, roll, clump, wad, parcel, sheaf, bale, pile, stack, heap, mass, bunch; informal load, wodge.

• v. **1** tie or roll up in a bundle.
2 informal push or carry forcibly.
▷ SYNONYMS: **1 tie**, parcel, wrap, swathe, roll, fold, bind, pack. **2** *he was bundled into a van:* **push**, shove, thrust, throw, propel, jostle, manhandle.

bung n. a stopper for a container.
• v. **1** (**bung up**) block up. **2** Brit. informal put or throw casually.

bungalow n. a one-storeyed house.

bungee jumping n. the sport of leaping from a high place, attached by an elastic cord around the ankles.

bungle v. perform a task badly or incompetently.
▷ SYNONYMS: **mishandle**, mismanage, mess up, spoil, ruin; informal blow, botch, fluff, make a hash of, screw up; Brit. informal make a pig's ear of; N. Amer. informal goof up.
• n. a mistake or failure.
■ **bungler** n.

bunion n. a painful swelling on the big toe.

bunk n. a narrow bed on a ship etc.
□ **do a bunk** informal run away.

bunker n. **1** a container for storing fuel. **2** an underground shelter for use in wartime. **3** a hollow filled with sand on a golf course.

bunkum n. informal nonsense.

bunny n. (pl. **bunnies**) informal a rabbit.

Bunsen burner n. a small gas burner used in laboratories.

bunting n. **1** a small songbird.
2 decorative flags.

buoy /boy/ n. a floating object used to mark an area of water.
▷ SYNONYMS: **float**, marker, beacon.
• v. **1** keep afloat. **2** (**be buoyed up**) be cheerful and confident.

> USAGE Remember: *u* before *o* in b*uoy* and b*uoy*ant.

buoyant adj. **1** able to float.
2 cheerful.
▷ SYNONYMS: **1 floating**, floatable.
2 cheerful, cheery, happy, light-hearted, carefree, joyful, bubbly, bouncy, sunny, upbeat.
– ANTONYMS: gloomy.
■ **buoyancy** n.

burble v. **1** make a continuous murmuring noise. **2** speak at length in a confused way.

burden n. **1** a heavy load. **2** a cause of hardship or distress.
▷ SYNONYMS: **responsibility**, onus, obligation, duty, liability, trouble, care, problem, difficulty, worry, strain.
• v. **1** load heavily. **2** cause hardship or distress to.

▷ SYNONYMS: **oppress**, trouble, worry, weigh down, overload, encumber, saddle, tax, afflict.
■ **burdensome** adj.

bureau /byoor-oh/ n. (pl. **bureaux** or **bureaus**) **1** Brit. a writing desk with a sloping top. **2** US a chest of drawers. **3** an office or organization providing a service. **4** a government department.
▷ SYNONYMS: **1 desk**, writing table, secretaire. **2 department**, agency, office, division, branch, section, station, unit.

bureaucracy /byuu-rok-ruh-si/ n. (pl. **bureaucracies**) **1** excessively complicated administrative procedure. **2** a system of government in which most decisions are taken by unelected officials.
▷ SYNONYMS: **1 red tape**, rules and regulations, protocol, officialdom, paperwork. **2 civil service**, government, administration, establishment, system, powers that be, authorities.

bureaucrat n. a government official, esp. one who follows guidelines rigidly.
▷ SYNONYMS: **official**, administrator, civil servant, minister, functionary, mandarin; derogatory apparatchik.
■ **bureaucratic** adj.

burgeon /ber-juhn/ v. grow or increase rapidly.
▷ SYNONYMS: **grow**, increase, rocket, mushroom, expand, escalate, swell, boom, flourish, thrive, prosper.

burger n. a hamburger.

burgher /ber-guh/ n. old use a citizen of a town or city.

burglar n. a person who breaks into a building to steal its contents.
▷ SYNONYMS: **housebreaker**, thief, intruder, robber, raider, looter.
■ **burgle** v.

burglary n. (pl. **burglaries**) the crime of breaking into a building and stealing its contents.
▷ SYNONYMS: **housebreaking**, breaking and entering, break-in, theft, raid, robbery, larceny, looting; N. Amer. informal smash-and-grab; N. Amer. informal heist.

burgundy n. (pl. **burgundies**) **1** a red wine. **2** a deep red colour.

burial n. the burying of a dead body.
▷ SYNONYMS: **funeral**, interment, committal, inhumation, entombment, obsequies, exequies.
– ANTONYMS: exhumation.

burlesque n. a comically exaggerated imitation.

burly adj. (**burlier**, **burliest**) (of a man)

large and strong.

▷ SYNONYMS: **strapping**, well built, strong, muscular, muscly, hefty, sturdy, brawny; informal hunky, beefy.

– ANTONYMS: puny.

burn v. (**burning, burned** or **burnt**)
1 (of a fire) flame or glow while using up a fuel. **2** harm or destroy by fire. **3** feel a strong desire or emotion. **4** (**burn out**) become exhausted through overwork.

▷ SYNONYMS: **1 be on fire**, be alight, blaze, go up in smoke, be in flames, smoulder, glow. **2 set fire to**, set alight, set light to, kindle, ignite, touch off, incinerate, cremate; informal torch. **3 scorch**, singe, sear, char, blacken, brand.

• n. **1** an injury caused by burning. **2** Scottish a stream.

burner n. a part of a cooker, lamp, etc. that gives out a flame.

burning adj. **1** intense. **2** important and urgent.

▷ SYNONYMS: **1 on fire**, blazing, flaming, fiery, glowing, red-hot, smouldering. **2** *a burning desire to win:* **intense**, passionate, deep-seated, profound, strong, ardent, fervent, urgent, fierce, consuming. **3** *burning issues:* **important**, crucial, critical, vital, essential, pivotal, urgent, pressing, compelling.

burnish v. polish by rubbing.

burp v. & n. informal (make) a belch.

burr n. **1** a strong pronunciation of the letter *r*. **2** a prickly seed case that clings to clothing and fur.

burrow n. a hole dug by a small animal to live in.

▷ SYNONYMS: **warren**, tunnel, hole, dugout, lair, set, den, earth.

• v. **1** dig a burrow. **2** hide underneath or search inside something.

▷ SYNONYMS: **tunnel**, dig, excavate, mine, bore, channel.

bursar n. a person who manages the financial affairs of a college or school.

bursary n. (pl. **bursaries**) Brit. a grant for study.

burst v. (**bursting, burst**) **1** break suddenly and violently apart. **2** be very full. **3** move or be opened suddenly and forcibly. **4** suddenly do something as a result of strong emotion.

▷ SYNONYMS: **1** *one balloon burst:* **split**, rupture, break, tear. **2** *a shell burst:* **explode**, blow up, detonate, go off. **3** *smoke burst through the hole:* **gush**, erupt, surge, rush, stream, flow, pour, spurt, jet. **4** *he burst into the room:*

charge, plunge, barge, plough, hurtle, career, rush, dash, tear.

• n. **1** an instance of bursting. **2** a sudden brief outbreak.

▷ SYNONYMS: **1 rupture**, puncture, breach, split, blowout. **2 explosion**, detonation, blast, eruption, bang. **3** *a burst of gunfire:* **volley**, salvo, barrage, hail, rain. **4** *a burst of activity:* **outbreak**, eruption, flare-up, blaze, attack, fit, rush, storm, surge, spurt.

bury v. (**burying, buried**) **1** put underground. **2** place a dead body in the earth or a tomb. **3** conceal or cover. **4** (**bury yourself**) involve yourself deeply in something.

▷ SYNONYMS: **1 inter**, lay to rest, entomb. **2 hide**, conceal, cover, enfold, sink. **3** *the bullet buried itself in the wood:* **embed**, sink, implant, submerge, lodge.

– ANTONYMS: exhume.

bus n. (pl. **buses**) a large vehicle carrying customers along a fixed route.

• v. (**busing, bused** or **bussing, bussed**) transport or travel in a bus.

busby n. (pl. **busbies**) a tall fur hat worn by certain troops.

bush n. **1** a shrub. **2** (**the bush**) wild or uncultivated country.

▷ SYNONYMS: **1 shrub**, thicket; (**bushes**) undergrowth, shrubbery. **2** *the bush:* **wilds**, wilderness, backwoods; N. Amer. backcountry; Austral./NZ outback, back-blocks; N. Amer. informal boondocks.

□ **bushbaby** a small African mammal with large eyes.

bushel n. **1** Brit. a measure of capacity equal to 8 gallons (36.4 litres). **2** US a measure of capacity equal to 64 US pints (35.2 litres).

bushy adj. (**bushier, bushiest**) **1** growing thickly. **2** covered with bushes.

▷ SYNONYMS: **thick**, shaggy, curly, fuzzy, bristly, fluffy, woolly.

business n. **1** a person's regular occupation. **2** commercial activity. **3** a commercial organization. **4** work to be done or matters to be attended to. **5** a person's concern.

▷ SYNONYMS: **1 work**, occupation, profession, career, employment, job, position. **2 trade**, commerce, dealing, traffic, transactions, negotiations. **3 firm**, company, concern, enterprise, venture, organization, operation, undertaking; informal outfit. **4** *it's none of your business:* **concern**, affair, responsibility, duty. **5** *an odd business:* **affair**, matter, case, circumstance, situation, event, incident.

businesslike adj. efficient and practical.
▷ SYNONYMS: **professional**, efficient, organized, slick, methodical, systematic, orderly, structured, disciplined, practical, pragmatic.

businessman (or **businesswoman**) n. (pl. **businessmen** or **businesswomen**) a person who works in commerce.
▷ SYNONYMS: **executive**, entrepreneur, industrialist, merchant, dealer, trader, manufacturer, tycoon, employer, seller, retailer, supplier.

busk v. play music in the street for voluntary donations.
■ **busker** n.

bust n. **1** a woman's breasts. **2** a sculpture of a person's head, shoulders, and chest.
▷ SYNONYMS: **1 bosom**, breasts, chest; informal boobs, knockers. **2 sculpture**, carving, effigy, statue, head and shoulders.
• v. (**busting**, **busted** or **bust**) informal burst or break.
□ **bust-up** informal a quarrel or fight. **go bust** informal become bankrupt.

bustle v. **1** move energetically or noisily. **2** (**bustling**) full of activity.
▷ SYNONYMS: **1 rush**, dash, hurry, scurry, scuttle, scamper, scramble; informal scoot, beetle, buzz. **2** (**bustling**) **busy**, crowded, swarming, teeming, humming, buzzing, hectic, lively.
• n. **1** excited activity. **2** hist. a pad or frame worn under a skirt to puff it out.
▷ SYNONYMS: **activity**, action, liveliness, excitement, tumult, commotion, hubbub, hurly-burly, whirl; informal toing and froing.

busy adj. (**busier**, **busiest**) **1** having a great deal to do. **2** occupied with an activity. **3** full of activity.
▷ SYNONYMS: **1** *I'm very busy:* **hard at work**, involved, rushed off your feet, hard-pressed, pushed; informal on the go, hard at it; Brit. informal on the hop. **2** *I'm sorry, she's busy:* **unavailable**, engaged, occupied, absorbed, engrossed, immersed, preoccupied, working; informal tied up. **3** *a busy day:* **hectic**, active, lively, full, eventful, energetic, tiring.
– ANTONYMS: idle, free, quiet.
• v. (**busying**, **busied**) (**busy yourself**) keep occupied.
▷ SYNONYMS: **occupy**, involve, engage, concern, absorb, engross, immerse, distract.
□ **busybody** an interfering person.

■ **busily** adv.

but conj. **1** nevertheless. **2** on the contrary; whereas.
▷ SYNONYMS: **however**, nevertheless, nonetheless, even so, yet, still.
• prep. except; apart from.
▷ SYNONYMS: **except**, apart from, other than, besides, aside from, with the exception of, bar.
• adv. only.

butane n. a flammable gas used in liquid form as a fuel.

butch adj. informal aggressively masculine.

butcher n. **1** a person who cuts up and sells meat. **2** a person who kills brutally.
• v. **1** slaughter or cut up an animal for food. **2** kill brutally.
■ **butchery** n.

butler n. the chief male servant of a house.

butt v. **1** hit with the head or horns. **2** (**butt in**) interrupt.
▷ SYNONYMS: **1 ram**, headbutt, bump, poke, prod, push, shove, thrust. **2** (**butt in**) **interrupt**, cut in, interfere, put your oar in; informal chip in, poke your nose in.
• n. **1** the thicker end of a weapon or tool. **2** a cigarette stub. **3** a cask for holding liquid. **4** an object of criticism or ridicule.
▷ SYNONYMS: **1 stock**, end, handle, hilt, haft. **2 stub**, end, stump; informal fag end, dog end. **3 target**, victim, object, dupe, laughing stock.

butter n. a yellow fatty substance made by churning cream.
• v. **1** spread with butter. **2** (**butter up**) informal flatter.
□ **butter bean** Brit. a large flat edible bean. **buttercup** a plant with yellow cup-shaped flowers. **buttermilk** the liquid left after butter has been churned. **butterscotch** a sweet made with butter and brown sugar.

butterfly n. **1** an insect with two pairs of large wings. **2** a swimming stroke in which both arms are raised out of the water together.

buttock n. either of the two round fleshy parts of the body that form the bottom.
▷ SYNONYMS: (**buttocks**) **bottom**, rear, rump, seat, derrière, cheeks; informal behind, backside; Brit. informal bum; N. Amer. informal butt, fanny; humorous posterior.

button n. **1** a disc sewn on to a garment to fasten it. **2** a knob pressed to operate equipment.

b

• v. fasten with buttons.

buttonhole n. **1** a slit in a garment through which a button is pushed to fasten it. **2** Brit. a flower worn in a lapel buttonhole.
• v. informal stop and detain in conversation.

buttress n. a projecting support built against a wall.
• v. support or strengthen.
▷ SYNONYMS: **strengthen**, shore up, reinforce, fortify, support, bolster, underpin, cement, uphold, defend, back up.

buxom adj. (of a woman) plump and large-breasted.

buy v. (**buying**, **bought**) **1** get in return for payment. **2** informal accept the truth of.
▷ SYNONYMS: **purchase**, acquire, obtain, get, pick up, snap up, invest in; informal get hold of, score.
– ANTONYMS: sell.
• n. a purchase.
▷ SYNONYMS: **purchase**, deal, bargain, investment, acquisition.

buyer n. a person who buys something.
▷ SYNONYMS: **purchaser**, customer, consumer, shopper, investor; (**buyers**) clientele, market.

buzz n. **1** a low continuous sound. **2** an atmosphere of excitement and activity. **3** informal a thrill.
▷ SYNONYMS: **hum**, murmur, drone, whirr.
• v. **1** make a low continuous sound. **2** be full of excitement or activity. **3** (**buzz off**) informal go away.
◻ **buzzword** informal a specialist word that has become fashionable.

buzzard n. a large bird of prey.

buzzer n. an electrical device that buzzes as a signal.

by prep. **1** through the action of. **2** indicating the end of a period. **3** beside. **4** past and beyond. **5** during.
• adv. so as to go past.
◻ **by and by** before long. **by and large** on the whole.

bye exclam. informal goodbye.
• n. **1** the moving of a competitor straight to the next round in the absence of an opponent. **2** Cricket a run scored from a ball not hit by the batsman.

by-election n. Brit. an election held during a government's term of office to fill a vacant seat.

bygone adj. belonging to the past.

by-law (or **bye-law**) n. Brit. a rule made by a local authority.

byline n. a line in a newspaper naming the writer of an article.

bypass n. **1** a road passing round a town. **2** an operation to help the circulation of blood by directing it through a new passage.
▷ SYNONYMS: **ring road**, detour, diversion, alternative route; Brit. relief road.
• v. go past or round.

by-product n. a product produced in the making of something else.

byre n. Brit. a cowshed.

bystander n. a person who is at an event but does not take part.
▷ SYNONYMS: **onlooker**, passer-by, observer, spectator, eyewitness.

byte n. a unit of information stored in a computer, equal to eight bits.

byway n. a minor road.

byword n. **1** a notable example. **2** a saying.

Cc

C (or **c**) n. the Roman numeral for 100.
• abbrev. **1** Celsius or centigrade.
2 cents. **3** (**c.**) century or centuries.
4 (**c** or **ca.**) circa. **5** (©) copyright.
cab n. **1** a taxi. **2** the driver's
compartment in a truck, bus, or train.
▷ SYNONYMS: **taxi**, taxi cab; Brit. minicab,
hackney carriage; N. Amer. hack.
cabal /kuh-**bal**/ n. a secret political
group.
cabaret /**kab**-uh-ray/ n. entertainment
held in a nightclub.
cabbage n. a round vegetable with
green or purple leaves.
cabby n. (pl. **cabbies**) informal a taxi
driver.
caber n. a tree trunk thrown in a
Scottish Highland sport.
cabin n. **1** a compartment on a ship or
in an aircraft. **2** a small hut.
▷ SYNONYMS: **1 berth**, stateroom,
compartment. **2 hut**, log cabin,
shanty, shack, chalet; Scottish bothy;
N. Amer. cabana.
cabinet n. **1** a cupboard with drawers
or shelves. **2** (**Cabinet**) a committee
of senior government ministers.
▷ SYNONYMS: **cupboard**, bureau, chest of
drawers.
□ **cabinetmaker** a skilled joiner who
makes furniture.
cable n. a thick rope of wire or fibre,
esp. for carrying electricity or
telecommunication signals.
▷ SYNONYMS: **1** *a thick cable moored the
ship:* rope, cord, line, guy; Nautical
hawser. **2** *electric cables:* **wire**, lead,
cord, power line; Brit. flex.
□ **cable car** a small carriage hung
from a moving cable for travelling
up and down a mountain. **cable
television** a system transmitting
programmes by cable.
cabriolet /**kab**-ri-oh-lay/ n. a car with
a roof that folds down.
cacao /kuh-**kah**-oh/ n. the seeds from
which cocoa and chocolate are made.
cache n. a hidden store of things.

▷ SYNONYMS: **hoard**, store, stockpile,
stock, supply, reserve, arsenal; informal
stash.
cachet /ka-**shay**/ n. the state of being
respected or admired; prestige.
cackle n. a noisy clucking cry or laugh.
• v. make a cackle.
cacophony /kuh-**koff**-uh-ni/ n. (pl.
cacophonies) a harsh mixture of
sounds.
■ **cacophonous** adj.
cactus n. (pl. **cacti** or **cactuses**) a plant
with thick fleshy stems bearing
spines but no leaves.
cad n. dated a dishonourable man.
■ **caddish** adj.
cadaver n. a corpse.
cadaverous adj. very pale and thin.
caddie (or **caddy**) n. (pl. **caddies**) a
person who carries a golfer's clubs.
• v. (**caddying**, **caddied**) work as a
caddie.
caddy n. (pl. **caddies**) a small tin or
box.
cadence n. **1** the rise and fall of
a person's voice. **2** the close of a
musical phrase.
▷ SYNONYMS: **rhythm**, tempo, metre,
beat, pulse, intonation, modulation,
lilt.
cadenza n. a difficult solo passage in a
musical work.
cadet n. a young trainee in the armed
services or police.
cadge v. informal ask for or get
something without paying or working
for it.
cadmium n. a silvery-white metallic
element.
cadre /**kah**-der/ n. a small group
of people trained for a particular
purpose or at the centre of a political
organization.
caecum /**see**-kuhm/ (US **cecum**) n. (pl.
caeca) a pouch at the junction of the
small and large intestines.
Caesarean /si-**zair**-i-uhn/ (US
Cesarean) n. an operation for

delivering a child by cutting through the wall of the mother's abdomen.

caesium /see-zi-uhm/ (US **cesium**) n. a soft silvery metallic element.

cafe /ka-fay/ n. a small restaurant selling light meals and drinks.
▷ SYNONYMS: **snack bar**, cafeteria, coffee bar/shop, tea room/shop, bistro, brasserie; N. Amer. diner, luncheon.

cafeteria n. a self-service restaurant.
▷ SYNONYMS: **self-service restaurant**, canteen, cafe, buffet, refectory, mess hall.

cafetière /ka-fuh-tyair/ n. a coffee pot with a plunger to push the grounds to the bottom.

caffeine n. a stimulant found in tea and coffee.

caftan var. of KAFTAN.

cage n. a structure of bars or wires for confining animals.
▷ SYNONYMS: **enclosure**, pen, pound, coop, hutch, birdcage, aviary.
• v. enclose in a cage.
▷ SYNONYMS: **confine**, shut in/up, pen, coop up, enclose.

cagey (or **cagy**) adj. informal cautiously reluctant to speak.
▷ SYNONYMS: **secretive**, guarded, tight-lipped, reticent, evasive; informal playing your cards close to your chest.
■ **cagily** adv.

cagoule n. Brit. a light hooded waterproof jacket.

cahoots pl. n. (**in cahoots**) informal making secret plans together.

caiman (or **cayman**) n. an American reptile like an alligator.

cairn n. a mound of stones built as a memorial or landmark.

cajole v. persuade by using flattery.
▷ SYNONYMS: **persuade**, wheedle, coax, talk into, prevail on; informal sweet-talk, soft-soap.

Cajun /kay-juhn/ adj. of the French-speaking community of Louisiana.

cake n. **1** an item of soft sweet food made from baking a mixture of flour, fat, eggs, and sugar. **2** a flat compact mass of something.
▷ SYNONYMS: **1 bun**, pastry, gateau, slice. **2 bar**, tablet, block, slab, lump, wedge.
• v. (of a thick substance) cover and form a crust on.
▷ SYNONYMS: *boots caked with mud:* **coat**, encrust, plaster, cover.

calamine n. a pink powder used to make a soothing lotion.

calamity n. (pl. **calamities**) a sudden disastrous event.

▷ SYNONYMS: **disaster**, catastrophe, tragedy, cataclysm, accident, misfortune, misadventure.
■ **calamitous** adj.

calcify v. (**calcifying, calcified**) harden by a deposit of calcium salts.

calcium n. a soft grey metallic element.

calculate v. **1** work out using mathematics. **2** intend to have a particular effect.
▷ SYNONYMS: **1 compute**, work out, reckon, figure, add up/together, count up, tally, total; Brit. tot up. **2 intend**, mean, design.
■ **calculation** n.

calculated adj. done with awareness of the likely effect.
▷ SYNONYMS: **deliberate**, premeditated, planned, pre-planned, preconceived, intentional, intended.
– ANTONYMS: unintentional.

calculating adj. craftily planning things to your own advantage.
▷ SYNONYMS: **cunning**, crafty, wily, sly, scheming, devious, disingenuous.

calculator n. an electronic device for mathematical calculations.

calculus n. the branch of mathematics dealing with rates of variation.

caldron US = CAULDRON.

Caledonian adj. of Scotland.

calendar n. a chart showing the days, weeks, and months of a year.
▷ SYNONYMS: **schedule**, diary, programme, timetable, agenda.

calf n. (pl. **calves**) **1** a young cow, bull, elephant, etc. **2** the back of a person's leg below the knee.

calibrate v. check the accuracy of an instrument by comparing the readings with those of a standard.
■ **calibration** n.

calibre (US **caliber**) n. **1** quality or ability. **2** the diameter of a bullet, shell, or the inside of a gun barrel.
▷ SYNONYMS: **1 quality**, standard, level, merit, distinction, stature, excellence, ability, expertise, talent, capability. **2 bore**, diameter, gauge.

calico n. plain cotton cloth.

californium n. a radioactive metallic element.

caliper (or **calliper**) n. **1** (or **calipers**) a measuring instrument with two hinged legs. **2** a metal support for a person's leg.

caliph /kay-lif/ n. hist. the chief Muslim ruler.

calk US = CAULK.

call v. **1** shout to attract attention.

2 ask to come somewhere.
3 telephone. **4** name or describe as.
5 pay a brief visit. **6** announce an event.
▷ SYNONYMS: **1 cry**, cry out, shout, yell, sing out, exclaim, shriek, scream, roar; informal holler. **2 wake**, wake up, awaken, rouse; Brit. informal knock up. **3 summon**, convene, assemble, send for, order. **4 phone**, telephone; Brit. ring, give someone a ring; informal give someone a buzz; Brit. informal give someone a bell. **5 name**, christen, baptize, designate, style, term, dub. **6 describe as**, regard as, look on as, think of as, consider to be.
• n. **1** an act of calling. **2** a brief visit. **3** a bird or animal's cry. **4** (**call for**) demand or need for.
▷ SYNONYMS: **1 cry**, shout, yell, exclamation, shriek, scream, roar; informal holler. **3** *there's no call for that kind of language:* **need**, necessity, reason, justification, excuse. **4** *there's no call for expensive wine here:* **demand**, desire, market.
□ **call centre** an office which handles large numbers of phone calls for an organization. **call for** require. **call off** cancel. **call on** turn to for help.
■ **caller** n.

calligraphy n. decorative handwriting.
■ **calligrapher** n.

calling n. **1** a profession or occupation. **2** a vocation.
▷ SYNONYMS: **profession**, occupation, job, vocation, career, métier, work, line of work, employment, trade, craft.

callisthenics (US **calisthenics**) pl. n. gymnastic exercises.

callous adj. insensitive and cruel.
▷ SYNONYMS: **heartless**, unfeeling, uncaring, cold, cold-hearted, hard, hardbitten, as hard as nails, hard-hearted, insensitive, unsympathetic.
– ANTONYMS: kind, compassionate.
• n. (or **callus**) a patch of hardened skin.
■ **calloused** adj. **callousness** n.

callow adj. inexperienced and immature.

calm adj. **1** not nervous, angry, or excited. **2** peaceful and undisturbed.
▷ SYNONYMS: **1 relaxed**, composed, self-possessed, poised, serene, tranquil, unruffled, unperturbed, unflustered, untroubled, unexcitable, level-headed, unemotional, phlegmatic, imperturbable; informal **unflappable**,

laid-back. **2 windless**, still, quiet, tranquil, smooth.
– ANTONYMS: excited, nervous, stormy.
• n. a calm state or period.
▷ SYNONYMS: **1** *his usual calm deserted him:* **composure**, coolness, calmness, self-possession, sangfroid, serenity, tranquillity; informal cool, unflappability. **2** *calm prevailed:* **tranquillity**, stillness, quiet, peace.
• v. make or become calm.
■ **calmly** adv. **calmness** n.

calorie n. (pl. **calories**) **1** a unit for measuring how much energy food will produce. **2** a unit of heat.

calorific adj. of heat or calories.

calumny n. (pl. **calumnies**) slander.

calve v. give birth to a calf.

calves pl. of CALF.

Calvinism n. the form of Protestantism following the teachings of John Calvin.
■ **Calvinist** n.

calypso n. (pl. **calypsos**) a West Indian song on a topical theme.

calyx n. (pl. **calyces** or **calyxes**) the ring of leaves (sepals) covering a flower bud.

cam n. a projecting part on a wheel or shaft changing rotary into to-and-fro motion.
□ **camshaft** a shaft with one or more cams attached.

camaraderie n. trust and friendship.

camber n. a slight upward curve on a horizontal surface, esp. a road.

cambric n. a light linen or cotton fabric.

camcorder n. a combined video camera and video recorder.

came past of COME.

camel n. a large mammal of desert countries, with either one or two humps on the back.

camellia n. a shrub with showy flowers.

cameo n. (pl. **cameos**) **1** a piece of jewellery with a head carved in relief on a differently coloured background. **2** a small role played by a well-known actor.

camera n. a device for taking photos or recording moving images.
□ **in camera** Law with the press and public excluded.

camiknickers pl. n. a woman's one-piece undergarment combining a camisole and knickers.

camisole n. a woman's loose-fitting undergarment for the upper body.

camomile (or **chamomile**) /kam-uh-myl/ n. a plant with white and yellow flowers.

camouflage n. **1** clothing etc. used to make soldiers and military equipment blend in with the surroundings. **2** an animal's natural appearance which allows it to blend in with its surroundings.
▷ SYNONYMS: **disguise**, mask, screen, cover, cloak, front, facade, blind, concealment, subterfuge.
• v. hide by means of camouflage.
▷ SYNONYMS: **disguise**, hide, conceal, mask, screen, cover.

camp n. **1** a place where soldiers, refugees, etc. live temporarily in tents or huts. **2** a complex of buildings for holidaymakers. **3** the supporters of a particular party or viewpoint.
▷ SYNONYMS: **1 campsite**, encampment, bivouac, base, settlement. **2 faction**, wing, group, lobby, caucus, bloc.
• v. live in tent while on holiday.
• adj. informal exaggeratedly effeminate or theatrical.
□ **camp bed** Brit. a folding portable bed.
■ **camper** n.

campaign n. **1** a series of military operations in a particular area. **2** an organized course of action to achieve a goal.
▷ SYNONYMS: **1** Napoleon's Russian campaign: **operation**, manoeuvres, offensive, attack, war, battle, crusade. **2** the campaign to reduce vehicle emissions: **effort**, drive, push, struggle, movement, crusade, operation, strategy.
• v. work towards a goal.
▷ SYNONYMS: **fight**, battle, push, press, strive, struggle, lobby, agitate.
■ **campaigner** n.

campanology n. the art of bell-ringing.

camphor n. a strong-smelling substance used esp. in insect repellents.

campus n. (pl. **campuses**) the grounds and buildings of a university or college.

can[1] aux. v. (past **could**) be able or allowed to.

can[2] n. a cylindrical metal container.
• v. (**canning**, **canned**) preserve in a can.

Canadian n. a person from Canada.
• adj. of Canada.

canal n. **1** an artificial waterway. **2** a tubular passage in a plant or animal.

canapé /kan-uh-pay/ n. a small piece of bread or pastry with a savoury topping.

canard n. an unfounded rumour.

canary n. (pl. **canaries**) a bright yellow finch with a tuneful song.

cancan n. a lively high-kicking stage dance.

cancel v. (**cancelling**, **cancelled**; US **canceling**, **canceled**) **1** decide that a planned event will not happen. **2** end an agreement. **3** (**cancel out**) have an equal but opposite effect on. **4** mark a ticket to show that it has been used.
▷ SYNONYMS: **1 call off**, abandon, scrap, drop, axe; informal redline. **2 annul**, invalidate, declare null and void, void, revoke, rescind, retract, withdraw.
■ **cancellation** n.

cancer n. **1** a disease caused by uncontrolled growth of abnormal cells. **2** a harmful tumour resulting from this.
▷ SYNONYMS: **tumour**, malignant growth, malignancy; technical carcinoma, sarcoma.
■ **cancerous** adj.

> **WORD LINKS**
> **carcinogenic** causing cancer
> **oncology** the branch of medicine concerned with cancer

candela n. the basic unit of luminous intensity.

candelabrum (or **candelabra**) n. (pl. **candelabra**) a large branched candlestick.

candid adj. truthful and straightforward.
▷ SYNONYMS: **frank**, forthright, direct, blunt, outspoken, plain-spoken, open, honest, truthful, sincere; informal upfront; N. Amer. informal on the up and up.
– ANTONYMS: guarded.
■ **candidly** adv.

candidate n. a person applying for a job, nominated for election, or taking an exam.
▷ SYNONYMS: **applicant**, contender, competitor, entrant, claimant, nominee, interviewee, examinee, possible; Brit. informal runner.
■ **candidacy** n.

candied adj. (of fruit) preserved in sugar.

candle n. a stick of wax with a central wick which is burnt to give light.
□ **candlestick** a holder for a candle.

candour (US **candor**) n. frankness.

candy n. (pl. **candies**) US sweets.

◻ **candyfloss** Brit. a mass of spun sugar on a stick.

cane n. **1** the hollow stem of tall reeds, grasses, etc. **2** a stick used as a support or to beat someone.
• v. beat with a cane.

canine /kay-nyn/ adj. of dogs.
• n. a pointed tooth next to the incisors.

canister n. a cylindrical container.

canker n. **1** a fungal disease of plants. **2** a disease in animals causing open sores.

cannabis n. a drug obtained from the hemp plant.

cannelloni pl. n. rolls of pasta with a savoury filling.

cannibal n. a person who eats human flesh.
■ cannibalism n.

cannibalize (or **-ise**) v. use a machine as a source of spare parts for others.

cannon n. (pl. **cannon** or **cannons**) a large heavy gun.
• v. bump heavily into.

cannonade n. continuous heavy gunfire.

cannot contr. can not.

canny adj. (**cannier**, **canniest**) shrewd.
▷ SYNONYMS: **shrewd**, astute, smart, sharp, discerning, discriminating, perceptive, clever, judicious, wise.
– ANTONYMS: foolish.
■ cannily adv.

canoe n. a narrow boat with pointed ends, propelled with a paddle.
• v. (**canoeing**, **canoed**) travel in a canoe.
■ canoeist n.

canon n. **1** a general rule or principle. **2** the authentic set of works of an author or artist. **3** a member of the clergy of a cathedral.
■ canonical adj.

canonize (or **-ise**) v. officially declare a dead person to be a saint.
■ canonization n.

canoodle v. informal kiss and cuddle.

canopy n. (pl. **canopies**) a cloth covering held up over a throne or bed.
▷ SYNONYMS: **awning**, shade, sunshade, covering.
■ canopied adj.

cant n. **1** insincere talk. **2** the language of a particular group.

can't contr. cannot.

cantaloupe n. a small melon with orange flesh.

cantankerous adj. bad-tempered and uncooperative.

cantata n. a musical work for accompanied solo voices and chorus.

canteen n. **1** a restaurant in a workplace, school, etc. **2** Brit. a case of cutlery.

canter n. a horse's pace between a trot and a gallop.
• v. move at a canter.

cantilever n. a girder fixed at only one end, used in bridge construction.

canto n. (pl. **cantos**) a section of a long poem.

canton n. a political division of a country, esp. Switzerland.

canvas n. (pl. **canvases** or **canvasses**) **1** a strong coarse cloth. **2** an oil painting on canvas.

canvass v. **1** visit someone to seek their vote in an election. **2** question someone to find out their opinion.
▷ SYNONYMS: **1** campaign, electioneer. **2** poll, question, survey, interview, consult.
■ canvasser n.

canyon n. a deep gorge.
▷ SYNONYMS: **ravine**, gorge, gully, chasm, abyss, gulf; N. Amer. gulch, coulee.

cap n. **1** a soft hat with a peak. **2** a lid or cover. **3** an upper limit on spending or borrowing. **4** a case of explosive powder for a toy gun.
▷ SYNONYMS: **1** lid, top, stopper, cork, bung; N. Amer. stopple. **2** limit, ceiling, curb, check.
• v. (**capping**, **capped**) **1** put a cover on. **2** provide a fitting end to. **3** put a limit on. **4** (**be capped**) Brit. be chosen as a member of a national sports team.
▷ SYNONYMS: **1** top, crown, cover, coat, tip. **2** limit, restrict, curb, control, peg.

capability n. (pl. **capabilities**) the power or ability to do something.
▷ SYNONYMS: **ability**, capacity, power, potential, competence, aptitude, faculty, skill, talent, flair; informal know-how.
– ANTONYMS: incapability.

capable adj. **1** having the ability to do something. **2** competent and efficient.
▷ SYNONYMS: **able**, competent, effective, proficient, accomplished, experienced, skilful, talented, gifted; informal useful.
– ANTONYMS: incapable, incompetent.
■ capably adv.

capacious adj. roomy.

capacitance n. the ability to store electric charge.

capacitor n. a device used to store electric charge.

capacity n. (pl. **capacities**) **1** the maximum amount that something

can contain or produce. **2** the ability to do something. **3** a role or position: *employed in a voluntary capacity.*
▷ SYNONYMS: **1 volume**, size, dimensions, measurements, proportions. **2 ability**, capability, power, potential, competence, aptitude, faculty, skill, talent, flair. **3 role**, function, position, post, job, office.

caparison v. (**be caparisoned**) be dressed in rich decorative coverings.

cape n. **1** a short cloak. **2** a coastal promontory.
▷ SYNONYMS: **1 cloak**, mantle, shawl, poncho, pashmina. **2 headland**, promontory, point, head, horn, mull, peninsula.

caper¹ v. skip about in a lively way.
• n. informal a light-hearted or dishonest activity.

caper² n. an edible pickled flower bud.

capillarity (or **capillary action**) n. the force which acts on a liquid in a narrow tube to push it up or down.

capillary n. (pl. **capillaries**) a very small blood vessel or tube.

capital n. **1** the chief city of a country or region. **2** wealth that is owned, invested, lent, or borrowed. **3** a capital letter. **4** the top part of a pillar.
▷ SYNONYMS: **money**, finances, funds, cash, wherewithal, means, assets, wealth, resources.
• adj. **1** (of a letter) large and used to begin sentences and names. **2** involving the death penalty. **3** informal, dated excellent.

capitalism n. a system in which a country's trade and industry are controlled by private owners.
▷ SYNONYMS: **private enterprise**, free enterprise, the free market, private ownership.
– ANTONYMS: communism.
■ **capitalist** n. & adj.

capitalize (or **-ise**) v. **1** (**capitalize on**) take advantage of. **2** convert into or provide with financial capital. **3** write as or with a capital letter.
▷ SYNONYMS: **take advantage of**, profit from, make the most of, exploit, develop; informal cash in on.
■ **capitalization** n.

capitation n. a fee or tax of an equal amount per person.

capitulate v. give in to an opponent or demand.
▷ SYNONYMS: **surrender**, give in, yield, concede defeat, give up, submit, lay down your arms, throw in the towel/sponge.
– ANTONYMS: resist.

■ **capitulation** n.

capon /**kay**-pon/ n. a castrated domestic cock fattened up for eating.

cappuccino /kap-puh-**chee**-noh/ n. (pl. **cappuccinos**) coffee made with frothed milk.

caprice /kuh-**preess**/ n. a sudden change of mood.

capricious adj. prone to sudden changes of mood.
▷ SYNONYMS: **fickle**, volatile, unpredictable, temperamental, mercurial, impulsive, changeable, unreliable, erratic, wayward, whimsical, flighty.
– ANTONYMS: consistent.
■ **capriciously** adv.

capsicum n. a sweet pepper.

capsize v. (of a boat) overturn.
▷ SYNONYMS: **overturn**, turn over, turn upside down, upend, flip/tip over, keel over, turn turtle.

capstan n. a broad revolving post used to wind a cable.

capsule n. **1** a small soluble gelatin case containing medicine. **2** a small case or container.
▷ SYNONYMS: **1 pill**, tablet, lozenge, pastille; informal tab. **2 module**, craft, probe.

captain n. **1** the person in command of a ship or civil aircraft. **2** the naval rank above commander. **3** the army rank above lieutenant. **4** the leader of a team.
▷ SYNONYMS: **1** *the ship's captain:* **commander**, master; informal skipper. **2** *the team captain:* **leader**, head, chief; informal boss, skipper.
• v. be the captain of.
■ **captaincy** n.

caption n. **1** a title or explanation printed with a picture etc. **2** a piece of text appearing with a film or television broadcast.
▷ SYNONYMS: **title**, heading, legend, description.

captious adj. prone to petty fault-finding.

captivate v. attract and hold the interest of.
▷ SYNONYMS: **enthral**, charm, enchant, bewitch, fascinate, beguile, entrance, delight, attract, allure.
– ANTONYMS: bore.

captive n. a person who is held prisoner.
▷ SYNONYMS: **prisoner**, convict, detainee, hostage, prisoner of war, internee.
• adj. unable to leave or choose: *a captive audience.*
▷ SYNONYMS: **confined**, caged, incarcerated, locked up, jailed,

imprisoned, interned, detained.
– ANTONYMS: free.
captivity n. the state of being captive.
▷ SYNONYMS: **imprisonment**, incarceration, confinement, detention, internment.
– ANTONYMS: freedom.
captor n. a person who captures another.
capture v. **1** take or get by force. **2** take prisoner. **3** record accurately in words or pictures. **4** cause data to be stored in a computer.
▷ SYNONYMS: **1 catch**, apprehend, seize, arrest, take prisoner, take into custody, detain. **2 occupy**, invade, conquer, seize, take.
– ANTONYMS: release, liberate.
• n. the act of capturing.
▷ SYNONYMS: **arrest**, apprehension, detention, seizure.
car n. **1** a motor vehicle for a small number of people. **2** a railway carriage.
▷ SYNONYMS: **1 motor**, motor car, automobile; informal **wheels**; N. Amer. informal auto. **2 carriage**, coach; Brit. saloon.
□ **carport** an open-sided shelter for a car.
carafe /kuh-**raf**/ n. a glass flask for serving wine or water.
caramel n. **1** sugar or syrup heated until brown. **2** a toffee made with sugar and butter.
■ **caramelize** (or **-ise**) v.
carapace n. the hard upper shell of a tortoise, lobster, etc.
carat n. **1** a measure of the purity of gold. **2** a unit of weight for precious stones.
caravan n. **1** a vehicle equipped for living in, able to be towed by a vehicle or a horse. **2** a group of people with vehicles or animals who are travelling together.
■ **caravanning** n.
caraway n. a spice made from the seeds of a plant.
carbine n. an automatic rifle.
carbohydrate n. an energy-producing substance (e.g. sugar and starch) found in food.
carbolic (or **carbolic acid**) n. a disinfectant.
carbon n. **1** a chemical element with two main pure forms (diamond and graphite), found in all organic compounds. **2** carbon dioxide or other gaseous carbon compounds released into the atmosphere. □ **carbon copy 1** a copy made with carbon paper. **2** a person or thing

identical to another. **carbon dating** a way of finding out the age of an object by measuring how much radioactive carbon is in it. **carbon dioxide** a gas produced by burning carbon and also by breathing. **carbon footprint** the amount of carbon dioxide produced as a result of the activities of a particular person, group, etc. **carbon monoxide** a poisonous flammable gas. **carbon-neutral** releasing no carbon dioxide into the atmosphere, or balancing carbon dioxide emissions by offsetting them, e.g. by planting trees. **carbon offsetting** the process of balancing carbon dioxide emissions with something that reduces carbon dioxide in the atmosphere by an equivalent amount. **carbon paper** thin paper coated with carbon, used to make a copy of a document.
carbonate n. a compound containing carbon and oxygen together with a metal.
carbonated adj. (of a drink) fizzy because it contains dissolved carbon dioxide.
carborundum n. a very hard black substance used for grinding and polishing.
carboy n. a large round bottle with a narrow neck, used for holding acids.
carbuncle n. **1** a severe abscess. **2** a garnet cut in a round shape.
carburettor (US **carburetor**) n. a device in an engine that mixes air with the fuel.
carcass (or **carcase**) n. **1** the dead body of an animal. **2** the structural framework or remains of something.
▷ SYNONYMS: **corpse**, dead body, remains; Medicine cadaver; informal stiff.
carcinogen /kar-**sin**-uh-juhn/ n. a substance that can cause cancer.
■ **carcinogenic** adj.
carcinoma /kar-si-**noh**-muh/ n. (pl. **carcinomas**) a cancerous tumour.
card n. **1** thick, stiff paper or thin cardboard. **2** a piece of card printed with information, greetings, etc. **3** a rectangle of plastic containing information readable by a computer: *a credit card.* **4** a playing card. **5** (**cards**) a game played with playing cards.
• v. comb wool with a toothed instrument.
□ **cardboard** stiff paper made from paper pulp. **card sharp** a person who cheats at cards.
cardamom n. a spice used in cooking.

C

cardiac adj. of the heart.

cardigan n. a knitted jumper with buttons down the front.

cardinal n. a leading Roman Catholic clergyman.
- adj. most important; chief.
□ **cardinal number** a number expressing quantity (1, 2, 3, etc.), rather than order.

cardiograph n. an instrument recording heart movements.

cardiology n. the branch of medicine concerned with the heart.
■ **cardiologist** n.

care n. 1 special attention to avoid damage, risk, or error. 2 the provision of welfare and protection. 3 a cause for anxiety, or a worried feeling.
▷ SYNONYMS: 1 **caution**, thought, regard, consideration, sensitivity, discretion. 2 **safe keeping**, supervision, custody, charge, protection, responsibility, guardianship. 3 **worry**, anxiety, trouble, concern, stress, pressure, strain.
– ANTONYMS: neglect, carelessness.
- v. 1 feel concern or interest. 2 feel affection or liking. 3 (**care for/to do**) like to have or be willing to do. 4 (**care for**) look after.
▷ SYNONYMS: **be concerned**, worry, trouble/concern yourself, bother, mind, be interested; informal give a damn/hoot.

careen v. (of a ship) tilt to one side.

career n. an occupation undertaken for a long period of a person's life.
▷ SYNONYMS: **profession**, occupation, vocation, calling, life's work, employment.
- v. move swiftly in an uncontrolled way.
▷ SYNONYMS: **hurtle**, rush, shoot, race, speed, charge, hare, fly; informal belt, tear; Brit. informal bucket.

careerist n. a person intent on progressing in their career.

carefree adj. free from anxiety or responsibility.
▷ SYNONYMS: **unworried**, untroubled, blithe, nonchalant, happy-go-lucky, free and easy, easy-going, relaxed; informal laid-back.
– ANTONYMS: troubled.

careful adj. 1 taking care to avoid harm or trouble. 2 showing thought and attention.
▷ SYNONYMS: 1 *be careful on the stairs:* **cautious**, alert, attentive, watchful, vigilant, wary, on your guard, circumspect. 2 *careful with money:* **prudent**, thrifty, economical, sparing, frugal.

3 *careful consideration of the facts:* **attentive**, conscientious, painstaking, meticulous, diligent, assiduous, scrupulous, methodical.
– ANTONYMS: careless.
■ **carefully** adv.

careless adj. not giving enough attention to avoiding harm or mistakes.
▷ SYNONYMS: 1 *careless motorists:* **inattentive**, negligent, heedless, irresponsible, impetuous, reckless. 2 *careless work:* **shoddy**, slapdash, slipshod, scrappy, slovenly, sloppy, negligent, lax, slack, disorganized, hasty, hurried. 3 *a careless remark:* **thoughtless**, insensitive, indiscreet, unguarded, incautious, inadvertent.
– ANTONYMS: careful.
■ **carelessly** adv. **carelessness** n.

carer n. a person who cares for a sick, elderly, or disabled person.

caress v. touch or stroke gently or lovingly.
▷ SYNONYMS: **stroke**, touch, fondle, brush, feel, skim.
- n. a gentle or loving touch.

caretaker n. a person employed to look after a public building.
▷ SYNONYMS: **janitor**, attendant, porter, custodian, concierge; N. Amer. superintendent.

careworn adj. showing signs of prolonged worry.

cargo n. (pl. **cargoes** or **cargos**) goods carried on a ship, aircraft, or truck.
▷ SYNONYMS: **freight**, load, haul, consignment, delivery, shipment, goods, merchandise.

Caribbean adj. of the Caribbean Sea and its islands.

| USAGE One *r*, two *b*s: Caribbean. |

caribou n. (pl. **caribou**) US a reindeer.

caricature n. a portrayal in which a person's characteristics are comically exaggerated.
▷ SYNONYMS: **cartoon**, parody, satire, lampoon, burlesque; informal send-up, take-off.
- v. make a caricature of.
▷ SYNONYMS: **parody**, satirize, lampoon, make fun of, mock, ridicule; informal send up, take off.
■ **caricaturist** n.

caries /kair-eez/ n. decay of a tooth or bone.

carillon /ka-ril-lyuhn/ n. a set of bells sounded by an automatic mechanism.

carmine n. vivid crimson.

carnage n. the killing of a large number of people.

▷ SYNONYMS: **slaughter**, massacre, murder, butchery, bloodbath, bloodletting, holocaust.

carnal adj. of sexual urges and activities.
■ **carnally** adv.

carnation n. a garden plant with pink, red, or white flowers.

carnelian (or **cornelian**) n. a dull red or pink semi-precious stone.

carnival n. a public festival involving a procession and music.
▷ SYNONYMS: **festival**, fiesta, fete, fair, gala, Mardi Gras.

carnivore n. an animal that eats meat.
■ **carnivorous** adj.

carob n. a chocolate substitute made from the pod of an Arabian tree.

carol n. a Christmas hymn or song.
• v. (**carolling, carolled**; US **caroling, caroled**) **1** sing carols. **2** sing or say happily.

carotene n. an orange or red substance found in carrots, tomatoes, etc.

carotid artery /kuh-**rot**-id/ n. either of the two main arteries carrying blood to the head.

carouse /kuh-**rowz**/ v. drink alcohol and enjoy yourself.

carousel n. **1** a merry-go-round at a fair. **2** a conveyor system for baggage at an airport.

carp n. (pl. **carp**) an edible freshwater fish.
• v. complain continually.
▷ SYNONYMS: **complain**, find fault, quibble, grumble, grouse, whine; informal nit-pick, gripe, moan, bitch, whinge.

carpel n. the female reproductive organ of a flower.

carpenter n. a person who makes wooden objects and structures.
▷ SYNONYMS: **woodworker**, joiner, cabinetmaker; Brit. informal chippy.
■ **carpentry** n.

carpet n. **1** a floor covering of thick woven fabric. **2** a thick, soft layer.
• v. (**carpeting, carpeted**) **1** cover with a carpet. **2** informal reprimand severely.
□ **carpet-bomb** bomb an area intensively.

carpus n. (pl. **carpi**) the group of small bones in the wrist.
■ **carpal** adj.

carriage n. **1** a horse-drawn passenger vehicle. **2** a passenger vehicle in a train. **3** the carrying of goods from one place to another. **4** a person's way of standing or moving.

▷ SYNONYMS: **1** a railway carriage: **coach**, car; Brit. saloon. **2** a horse and carriage: **wagon**, coach. **3** **posture**, bearing, gait; Brit. deportment.
□ **carriage clock** a portable clock with a handle on top. **carriageway** the part of a road intended for vehicles.

carrier n. **1** a person or thing carrying something. **2** a company that transports goods or people.
□ **carrier bag** a plastic or paper shopping bag.

carrion n. the decaying flesh of dead animals.

carrot n. **1** a tapering orange root vegetable. **2** an incentive.

carry v. (**carrying, carried**) **1** move or take somewhere. **2** support the weight of. **3** assume responsibility. **4** have as a feature or result. **5** (of a sound or voice) be heard from a distance. **6** approve a proposal by a majority of votes. **7** (**carry yourself**) stand and move in a specified way.
▷ SYNONYMS: **1** convey, transfer, transport, move, take, bring, bear, fetch; informal cart, hump, lug. **2** transmit, conduct, relay, communicate, convey, beam, send. **3** approve, pass, accept, endorse, ratify. **4** be audible, travel, reach, be heard.
□ **be/get carried away** lose self-control. **carry off 1** succeed in doing. **2** take away by force. **carry on** continue. **carry out** perform a task.

cart n. an open, wheeled vehicle for carrying loads.
• v. **1** transport in a cart. **2** informal carry with difficulty.
□ **carthorse** a large, strong horse. **cartwheel** a sideways handspring with the arms and legs extended.

carte blanche /kart blahnsh/ n. complete freedom to act as you wish.

cartel n. a group of manufacturers or suppliers formed to keep prices high.

cartilage n. firm, flexible tissue forming part of the skeleton of vertebrates.

cartography n. map-drawing.
■ **cartographer** n.

carton n. a cardboard container.
▷ SYNONYMS: **box**, package, cardboard box, case, container, pack, packet.

cartoon n. **1** a humorous drawing. **2** an animated film made from a sequence of drawings.
▷ SYNONYMS: **1** animation, animated film, comic strip, graphic novel. **2** caricature, parody, lampoon, satire; informal take-off, send-up.
■ **cartoonist** n.

cartridge n. **1** a container holding film, ink, etc., for inserting into a mechanism. **2** a casing containing a charge and a bullet for a gun.
▷ synonyms: **cassette**, magazine, canister, case, container.
▫ **cartridge paper** thick drawing paper.

carve v. **1** cut into a hard material to form an object or design. **2** cut cooked meat into slices.
▷ synonyms: **1 sculpt**, cut, hew, whittle, chisel, shape, fashion. **2 engrave**, incise, score, cut. **3 slice**, cut up, chop.
■ **carving** n.

carvery n. (pl. **carveries**) a restaurant where cooked joints are carved as required.

Casanova n. a man known for seducing many women.

casbah n. var. of KASBAH.

cascade n. **1** a waterfall. **2** a mass of something falling or hanging down.
▷ synonyms: **waterfall**, cataract, falls, rapids, white water, flood, torrent.
• v. fall or flow in large quantities.
▷ synonyms: **pour**, gush, surge, spill, stream, flow, issue, spurt, jet.

case n. **1** an instance of a particular situation. **2** a lawsuit. **3** a set of arguments supporting one side of a debate or lawsuit. **4** a container. **5** a suitcase. **6** a form of a noun, adjective, or pronoun expressing its role in a sentence.
▷ synonyms: **1** *a classic case of overreaction:* **instance**, example, occurrence, occasion, demonstration, illustration. **2** *is that the case?:* **situation**, position, state of affairs, circumstances, conditions, facts; Brit. state of play; informal ball game. **3** *he lost his case:* **lawsuit**, legal action, trial, litigation. **4** *the case against animal testing:* **argument**, defence, justification, vindication, thesis. **5 container**, box, canister, holder, casing, cover, sheath, envelope, sleeve, jacket, shell. **6 suitcase**, travel bag, valise; (**cases**) luggage, baggage.
• v. enclose in a case.

casement n. a window hinged at the side.

cash n. money in coins or notes.
▷ synonyms: **1 money**, currency, bank notes, coins, change; N. Amer. bills; informal dough, loot; Brit. informal dosh, brass; N. Amer. informal dinero. **2 finance**, money, resources, funds, assets, means, wherewithal.
• v. **1** give or obtain notes or coins for a cheque. **2** (**cash in on**) informal take advantage of. **3** (**cash in**) convert an insurance policy or savings account into money.
▫ **cashpoint** trademark a machine dispensing cash when a special card is inserted.

cashew n. an edible kidney-shaped nut.

cashier n. a person who pays out and receives money in a shop, bank, etc.
▷ synonyms: **clerk**, teller, banker, treasurer, bursar, purser.
• v. dismiss from the armed forces.

cashmere n. very fine soft wool.

casing n. a protective cover.

casino n. (pl. **casinos**) a public building or room for gambling.

cask n. a large barrel for storing alcoholic drinks.
▷ synonyms: **barrel**, keg, butt, tun, vat, drum, hogshead; historical firkin.

casket n. **1** a small ornamental box for valuables. **2** esp. US a coffin.

cassava n. the starchy root of a tropical American tree, used as food.

casserole n. **1** a covered dish for cooking food slowly. **2** a kind of stew cooked slowly.
• v. cook in a casserole.

cassette n. a sealed case containing audio tape, videotape, etc.

cassock n. a long garment worn by some Christian clergy and members of church choirs.

cassowary n. (pl. **cassowaries**) a large flightless bird, native to New Guinea.

cast v. **1** throw forcefully. **2** direct the eyes or thoughts towards something. **3** cause light or shadow to appear on something. **4** register a vote. **5** give a part to an actor or allocate parts in a play or film. **6** leave aside or discard. **7** shape molten metal in a mould. **8** make a magic spell.
▷ synonyms: **1 throw**, toss, fling, pitch, hurl, lob; informal chuck, sling, bung. **2 direct**, shoot, throw, fling, send. **3 register**, record, enter, file. **4 emit**, give off, throw, send out, radiate. **5 mould**, fashion, form, shape, forge.
• n. **1** the actors in a play or film. **2** an object made by casting molten metal. **3** (or **plaster cast**) a bandage stiffened with plaster of Paris to support and protect a broken limb. **4** appearance or character.
▷ synonyms: **1 mould**, die, matrix, shape, casting, model. **2 actors**, performers, players, company, troupe, dramatis personae, characters.
▫ **casting vote** an extra vote used by a chairperson to decide an issue when

votes on each side are equal. **cast iron** a hard alloy of iron and carbon cast in a mould. **cast-iron** firm and unchangeable. **cast-off** a discarded garment.

castanets pl. n. two small curved pieces of wood, clicked together in the hand to accompany Spanish dancing.

castaway n. a shipwrecked person.

caste n. each of the Hindu social classes.
▷ SYNONYMS: **class**, rank, level, order, stratum, echelon, status.

castellated adj. having battlements.

castigate v. reprimand severely.
■ **castigation** n.

castle n. a large medieval fortified building.
▷ SYNONYMS: **fortress**, fort, stronghold, fortification, keep, citadel, palace, chateau, tower.

castor (or **caster**) n. **1** a small swivelling wheel fixed to the legs or base of a piece of furniture. **2** a small container with a perforated top for sprinkling salt, sugar, etc.
□ **castor oil** oil from the seeds of an African shrub, used as a laxative. **castor sugar** white sugar in fine granules.

castrate v. remove the testicles of.
■ **castration** n.

casual adj. **1** relaxed and unconcerned. **2** lacking care or thought. **3** not regular; occasional: *casual work.* **4** happening by chance. **5** informal.
▷ SYNONYMS: **1** *a casual attitude:* **unconcerned**, uncaring, indifferent, lackadaisical, nonchalant, offhand, flippant, easy-going, free and easy, blithe, carefree, devil-may-care; informal laid-back. **2** *a casual remark:* **offhand**, spontaneous, unthinking, unconsidered, impromptu, throw-away, unguarded; informal off-the-cuff. **3** *a casual glance:* **cursory**, perfunctory, superficial, passing, fleeting. **4** *casual work:* **temporary**, freelance, irregular, occasional. **5** *a casual meeting:* **chance**, accidental, unplanned, unintended, unexpected, unforeseen. **6** *a casual atmosphere:* **relaxed**, friendly, informal, easy-going, free and easy; informal laid-back.
– ANTONYMS: serious, deliberate, formal.
■ **casually** adv.

casualty n. (pl. **casualties**) a person killed or injured in a conflict or accident.
▷ SYNONYMS: **victim**, sufferer, fatality, death, loss, wounded person, injured person.

casuistry n. the use of clever but false reasoning.
■ **casuist** n.

cat n. **1** a small furry mammal kept as a pet. **2** a wild animal related to this.
▷ SYNONYMS: **feline**, tomcat, tom, kitten; informal pussy, puss, kitty; Brit. informal moggie, mog.
□ **catcall** a whistle of disapproval. **catgut** material used for the strings of musical instruments, made of the dried intestines of sheep or horses. **catkin** a spike of small flowers hanging from a willow etc. **catnap** a short nap. **catseye** Brit. trademark each of a series of reflective studs marking the lanes of a road. **cat's paw** a person used by another to perform an unpleasant task. **catsuit** a woman's close-fitting one-piece garment. **catwalk** a narrow platform along which models walk to display clothes.

> **WORD LINKS**
> **feline** relating to cats

cataclysm n. a violent upheaval or disaster.
■ **cataclysmic** adj.

catacomb /kat-uh-koom/ n. an underground cemetery with recesses for tombs.

catafalque n. a decorated wooden support for a coffin.

catalepsy n. a medical condition involving loss of consciousness and the body becoming rigid.
■ **cataleptic** adj. & n.

catalogue (US **catalog**) n. **1** a list of items arranged in order. **2** a publication containing details of items for sale.
▷ SYNONYMS: **directory**, register, index, list, listing, record, schedule, archive, inventory.
• v. (**cataloguing**, **catalogued**; US **cataloging**, **cataloged**) list in a catalogue.
▷ SYNONYMS: **classify**, categorize, index, list, archive, record, itemize.

catalyse v. cause or speed up a reaction by acting as a catalyst.
■ **catalysis** n.

catalyst n. **1** a person or thing that causes something to happen. **2** a substance that speeds up a chemical reaction while remaining unchanged itself.

catalytic converter n. a device in a vehicle's exhaust system for converting pollutant gases into less harmful ones.

catamaran n. a boat with twin parallel hulls.

catapult n. a forked stick with an elastic band attached, for shooting small stones.

• v. throw forcefully.

cataract n. **1** a cloudy area on the lens of the eye, causing blurred vision. **2** a large waterfall.

catarrh /kuh-**tar**/ n. excessive mucus in the nose or throat.

catastrophe /kuh-**tass**-truh-fi/ n. a sudden great disaster.

▷ SYNONYMS: **disaster**, calamity, cataclysm, ruin, tragedy, fiasco, debacle. ■ **catastrophic** adj. **catastrophically** adv.

catatonia /kat-uh-toh-ni-uh/ n. a medical condition involving periods of unconsciousness or overactivity. ■ **catatonic** adj.

catch v. (**catching**, **caught**) **1** seize and hold something moving. **2** capture. **3** be in time to board a vehicle or see a person etc. **4** surprise someone in the act of doing something. **5** hear or understand. **6** become infected with.

▷ SYNONYMS: **1 seize**, grab, snatch, grasp, grip, clutch, intercept, trap, receive, get. **2 capture**, apprehend, seize, arrest, take prisoner, trap, snare, net; informal nab, collar; Brit. informal nick. **3 become trapped**, become entangled, snag, jam, wedge, lodge, get stuck. **4 discover**, find, come across, stumble on, chance on, surprise. **5 contract**, go/come down with, be taken ill with, develop, pick up, succumb to.

– ANTONYMS: drop, release.

• n. **1** an act of catching. **2** a device for fastening a window etc. **3** a hidden problem. **4** an amount of fish caught.

▷ SYNONYMS: **1 haul**, net, bag, yield. **2 latch**, lock, fastener, clasp, hasp. **3 snag**, disadvantage, drawback, stumbling block, hitch, complication, problem, trap, trick.

□ **catch on** informal **1** become popular. **2** understand. **catch out** discover that someone has done something wrong. **catchphrase** a well-known phrase. **catch-22** a difficult situation from which there is no escape because it involves conflicting conditions. **catch up 1** succeed in reaching a person ahead. **2** do tasks that should have been done earlier. **catchword** a word or phrase frequently used to sum something up.

catching adj. infectious.

▷ SYNONYMS: **infectious**, contagious, communicable; dated infective.

catchment area n. **1** the area from which a hospital's patients or a school's pupils are drawn. **2** the area from which rainfall flows into a river or lake.

catchy adj. (**catchier**, **catchiest**) (of a tune) appealing and easy to remember.

▷ SYNONYMS: **memorable**, unforgettable, haunting, appealing, popular.

– ANTONYMS: forgettable.

catechism /kat-i-ki-z'm/ n. a summary of the principles of Christian religion in the form of questions and answers.

catechize (or **-ise**) v. teach by using a catechism.

categorical (or **categoric**) adj. completely clear and direct.

▷ SYNONYMS: **unqualified**, unconditional, unequivocal, absolute, explicit, unambiguous, definite, direct, emphatic, positive, out-and-out. ■ **categorically** adv.

categorize (or **-ise**) v. place in a category. ■ **categorization** n.

category n. (pl. **categories**) a class of people or things with shared characteristics.

▷ SYNONYMS: **class**, classification, group, grouping, bracket, heading, set, type, sort, kind, grade, order, rank.

cater v. **1** (**cater for**) Brit. provide food and drink. **2** (**cater for/to**) provide with what is needed or required.

▷ SYNONYMS: **1** a resort catering for older holidaymakers: **serve**, provide for, meet the needs/wants of, accommodate. **2** we cater for all tastes: **take into account**, take into consideration, allow for, consider, bear in mind, make provision for. ■ **caterer** n.

caterpillar n. **1** the larva of a butterfly or moth. **2** (or **caterpillar track** or **tread**) trademark a steel band passing round the wheels of a vehicle for travel on rough ground.

caterwaul /kat-er-wawl/ v. wail or howl.

catharsis n. the release of pent-up emotions. ■ **cathartic** adj.

cathedral n. the principal church of a diocese.

Catherine wheel n. Brit. a rotating firework.

catheter n. a tube inserted into the bladder etc. to remove fluid.

cathode n. an electrode with a negative charge.

□ **cathode ray tube** a vacuum tube

in which beams of electrons produce a luminous image on a fluorescent screen.

catholic adj. **1** including a wide range of things. **2** (**Catholic**) Roman Catholic.
• n. (**Catholic**) a Roman Catholic.
■ **Catholicism** n.

cation /kat-I-uhn/ n. an ion with a positive charge.

cattery n. (pl. **catteries**) a place where cats are kept while their owners are away.

cattle pl. n. cows, bulls, and oxen.
▷ SYNONYMS: **cows**, oxen, livestock, herd.

> **WORD LINKS**
> **bovine** relating to cattle

catty adj. spiteful.

Caucasian /kaw-kay-zh'n/ adj. **1** of peoples from Europe, western Asia, and parts of India and North Africa. **2** white-skinned.

caucus n. (pl. **caucuses**) **1** a meeting of a political party's policy-making committee. **2** a group with shared concerns within a larger organization.

caught past & past part. of CATCH.

caul n. a membrane enclosing a fetus in the womb.

cauldron (US **caldron**) n. a large metal cooking pot.

cauliflower n. a vegetable with a large white flower head.

caulk (US **calk**) n. a waterproof substance for filling cracks and joins.

causal adj. of or being a cause.
■ **causally** adv. **causality** n.

causation n. the causing of an effect.
■ **causative** adj.

cause n. **1** a person or thing that produces an effect. **2** a reason for doing something. **3** a principle or movement to support.
▷ SYNONYMS: **1** *the cause of the fire:* **source**, root, origin, beginnings, starting point, originator, author, creator, agent. **2** *there is no cause for alarm:* **reason**, grounds, justification, call, need, necessity, occasion, excuse. **3** *raising money for good causes:* **principle**, ideal, belief, conviction, object, aim, objective, purpose, charity.
• v. make happen.
▷ SYNONYMS: **bring about**, give rise to, lead to, result in, create, produce, generate, engender, spawn, bring on, precipitate, prompt, provoke, trigger, make happen, induce, inspire, promote, foster.
□ **cause célèbre** (pl. **causes célèbres**) a matter causing great public interest.

causeway n. a raised road across low or wet ground.

caustic adj. **1** able to burn by chemical action. **2** sarcastic.
▷ SYNONYMS: **1 corrosive**, acid, burning. **2 sarcastic**, cutting, biting, mordant, sharp, scathing, sardonic, scornful, trenchant, acerbic, vitriolic.
□ **caustic soda** sodium hydroxide.

cauterize (or **-ise**) v. burn the area around a wound to stop bleeding or prevent infection.

caution n. **1** care taken to avoid danger or mistakes. **2** Brit. a formal warning given for a minor offence.
▷ SYNONYMS: **1 care**, attention, alertness, circumspection, discretion, prudence. **2 warning**, admonishment, injunction, reprimand, rebuke; informal telling-off, dressing-down; Brit. informal ticking-off.
• v. **1** warn. **2** give a caution to.
▷ SYNONYMS: **1** *advisers cautioned against tax increases:* **advise**, warn, counsel, urge. **2** *he was cautioned by the police:* **warn**, admonish, reprimand; informal tell off; Brit. informal tick off.

cautionary adj. acting as a warning.

cautious adj. careful to avoid danger or mistakes.
▷ SYNONYMS: **careful**, attentive, alert, judicious, circumspect, prudent, tentative, guarded.
– ANTONYMS: reckless.
■ **cautiously** adv.

cavalcade n. a procession.

cavalier adj. showing a lack of proper concern.
• n. (**Cavalier**) a supporter of Charles I in the English Civil War.

cavalry n. (pl. **cavalries**) soldiers who formerly fought on horseback.

cave n. a natural hollow in a hill or cliff, or underground.
▷ SYNONYMS: **cavern**, grotto, pothole, chamber, gallery, hollow.
• v. **1** (**cave in**) collapse. **2** (**cave in**) give in to demands. **3** (**caving**) exploring caves as a sport.

> **WORD LINKS**
> **speleology** (Brit. **potholing**; N. Amer. **spelunking**) the exploration of caves

caveat /ka-vi-at/ n. a warning.

cavern n. a large cave.

cavernous adj. huge or gloomy.

caviar n. the pickled roe of the sturgeon.

cavil v. (**cavilling, cavilled**; US **caviling, caviled**) raise petty objections.
• n. a petty objection.

cavity n. (pl. **cavities**) **1** a hollow space

within a solid object. **2** a decayed part of a tooth.
▷ SYNONYMS: **space**, chamber, hollow, hole, pocket, gap, crater, pit.

cavort v. jump around excitedly.

caw v. (of a rook or crow) make a harsh cry.

cayenne n. a hot red powder made from dried chillies.

cayman var. of CAIMAN.

CB abbrev. **1** Citizens' Band. **2** Companion of the Order of the Bath.

CBE abbrev. Commander of the Order of the British Empire.

cc (or **c.c.**) abbrev. **1** carbon copy. **2** cubic centimetres.

CCTV abbrev. closed-circuit television.

CD abbrev. compact disc.

CD-ROM n. a compact disc used in a computer as a read-only device for data.

cease v. come or bring to an end.
▷ SYNONYMS: **stop**, come/bring to an end, come/bring to a halt, end, halt, conclude, terminate, finish, wind up, discontinue, suspend, break off.
– ANTONYMS: start, continue.
□ **ceasefire** a temporary truce.

ceaseless adj. never stopping.
▷ SYNONYMS: **continual**, constant, continuous, incessant, unending, endless, never-ending, interminable, non-stop, unremitting, relentless, unrelenting, sustained, persistent, eternal, perpetual.
– ANTONYMS: intermittent.

cecum US = CAECUM.

cedar n. a coniferous tree with aromatic wood.

cede v. give up power or territory.

cedilla n. a mark (˛) written under the letter c to show that it is pronounced like an s.

ceilidh /kay-li/ n. a social event with Scottish or Irish folk music and dancing.

ceiling n. **1** the top surface of a room. **2** an upper limit.

celandine n. a small yellow-flowered plant.

celebrant n. a person who performs a religious ceremony.

celebrate v. **1** mark an important occasion by doing something special. **2** perform a religious ceremony.
▷ SYNONYMS: **1 commemorate**, observe, mark, keep, honour, remember. **2 enjoy yourself**, make merry, have fun; N. Amer. step out; informal party, whoop it up, have a ball. **3** *a priest*

celebrated mass: **perform**, observe, officiate at.
■ **celebratory** adj.

celebrated adj. famous.
▷ SYNONYMS: **acclaimed**, admired, highly rated, esteemed, exalted, vaunted, eminent, great, distinguished, prestigious, illustrious, notable.
– ANTONYMS: unsung.

celebration n. **1** the action of celebrating. **2** a social occasion held to celebrate something.
▷ SYNONYMS: **1 party**, function, gathering, festivities, festival, fete, carnival, jamboree; informal do, bash. **3 commemoration**, observance, solemnization. **2 merrymaking**, jollification, revelry, revels, festivities; informal partying.

celebrity n. (pl. **celebrities**) **1** a famous person. **2** fame.
▷ SYNONYMS: **1 famous person**, VIP, personality, big name, household name, star, superstar; informal celeb, megastar. **2 fame**, prominence, renown, stardom, popularity, distinction, prestige, stature, repute, reputation.
– ANTONYMS: obscurity.

celeriac n. a vegetable with a large edible root.

celerity n. literary speed.

celery n. a vegetable with crisp stalks.

celestial adj. of heaven or the sky.
▷ SYNONYMS: **heavenly**, holy, saintly, divine, godly, godlike, ethereal, angelic.

celiac n. US = COELIAC.

celibate adj. not marrying or having sex.
▷ SYNONYMS: **unmarried**, single, chaste, pure, virginal.
■ **celibacy** n.

cell n. **1** a small room for a prisoner, monk, or nun. **2** the smallest unit of a living organism. **3** a small political group. **4** a device for producing electricity by chemical action or light.
▷ SYNONYMS: **1 room**, cubicle, chamber, dungeon, compartment, lock-up. **2 unit**, squad, detachment, group.

cellar n. **1** an underground storage room. **2** a stock of wine.
▷ SYNONYMS: **basement**, vault, crypt.

cello /chel-loh/ n. (pl. **cellos**) a large bass instrument of the violin family.
■ **cellist** n.

cellophane n. trademark a thin transparent wrapping material.

cellphone n. a mobile phone.

cellular adj. **1** of or made up of cells. **2** (of a mobile phone system) using a number of short-range radio stations.

cellulite n. fat that builds up under the skin, causing a dimpled effect.

celluloid n. transparent plastic formerly used for cinema film.

cellulose n. a substance in plant tissues, used to make plastics and textiles.

Celsius n. a scale of temperature on which water freezes at 0° and boils at 100°.

Celt /kelt/ n. a member of an ancient European people or their descendants. ■ **Celtic** adj.

cement n. a powdery substance made from lime and clay, used to make mortar and concrete.
▷ SYNONYMS: **adhesive**, glue, fixative, gum, paste.
• v. **1** fix with cement. **2** strengthen.

cemetery n. (pl. **cemeteries**) a large burial ground.
▷ SYNONYMS: **graveyard**, churchyard, burial ground, necropolis, garden of remembrance, mass grave; Scottish kirkyard.

cenotaph n. a memorial to members of the armed forces killed in a war.

censer n. a container for burning incense.

censor n. an official who examines books, films, etc. and bans anything considered offensive or a threat to security.
• v. ban unacceptable parts of a book, film, etc.
▷ SYNONYMS: **cut**, edit, expurgate, sanitize, clean up, ban, delete.
■ **censorship** n.

USAGE Don't confuse **censor** with **censure**.

censorious adj. very critical.
▷ SYNONYMS: **critical**, overcritical, hypercritical, disapproving, condemnatory, judgemental, moralistic, faultfinding, reproachful.

censure v. criticize strongly.
▷ SYNONYMS: **condemn**, criticize, attack, reprimand, rebuke, admonish, upbraid, reproach.
– ANTONYMS: defend, praise.
• n. strong disapproval or criticism.
▷ SYNONYMS: **condemnation**, criticism, attack, reprimand, rebuke, admonishment, reproof, disapproval, reproach.
– ANTONYMS: approval, praise.

census n. (pl. **censuses**) an official count of a population.

cent n. a 100th of a dollar, euro, or other decimal currency unit.

centaur n. a mythical creature with a man's upper body and a horse's lower body and legs.

centenarian n. a person who is 100 or more years old.

centenary n. (pl. **centenaries**) Brit. the 100th anniversary of an event.

centennial n. a centenary.

center US = CENTRE.

centigrade adj. measured by the Celsius scale of temperature.

centilitre (US **centiliter**) n. a 100th of a litre.

centimetre (US **centimeter**) n. a 100th of a metre.

centipede n. an insect-like creature with many legs.

central adj. **1** in or near the centre. **2** very important.
▷ SYNONYMS: **1** *a central position*: **middle**, centre, halfway, midway, mid. **2** *central London*: **inner**, innermost, middle, mid. **3** **main**, chief, principal, primary, foremost, key, crucial, vital, essential, basic, fundamental, core; informal **number-one**.
– ANTONYMS: side, outer.
□ **central heating** heating conducted from a boiler through pipes and radiators. **central nervous system** the brain and spinal cord in vertebrates.
■ **centrality** n. **centrally** adv.

centralize (or **-ise**) v. bring under the control of a central authority.
▷ SYNONYMS: **concentrate**, consolidate, amalgamate, condense, unify, focus.
– ANTONYMS: devolve.
■ **centralism** n. **centralization** n.

centre (US **center**) n. **1** a point in the middle of something. **2** a place devoted to a particular activity. **3** a point from which something spreads or to which something is directed.
▷ SYNONYMS: **middle**, nucleus, heart, core, hub.
– ANTONYMS: edge.
• v. (**centring**, **centred**; US **centering**, **centered**) **1** place in the centre. **2** (**centre on/around**) have as a major concern.
▷ SYNONYMS: *the story centres on a doctor*: **focus**, concentrate, pivot, revolve, be based.
□ **centrefold** the two middle pages of a magazine.

centrifugal force n. a force which appears to cause something moving round a centre to fly outwards.

centrifuge n. a machine with a rapidly rotating container, used to separate substances.

centurion n. a commander in the ancient Roman army.

C

century n. (pl. **centuries**) **1** a period of 100 years. **2** a batsman's score of 100 runs in cricket.

cephalopod n. a mollusc of a group including octopuses and squids.

ceramic adj. made of clay hardened by heat.
• n. (**ceramics**) the art of making ceramic objects.

cereal n. **1** a grass producing an edible grain, e.g. wheat. **2** a breakfast food made from this.

cerebellum n. (pl. **cerebellums** or **cerebella**) the part of the brain at the back of the skull.

cerebral adj. **1** of the cerebrum. **2** intellectual.
□ **cerebral palsy** a medical condition involving difficulty in controlling the muscles.

cerebrum n. (pl. **cerebra**) the main part of the brain.

ceremonial adj. of ceremonies.
▷ SYNONYMS: **formal**, official, state, public, ritual, ritualistic, stately, solemn.
– ANTONYMS: informal.
■ **ceremonially** adv.

ceremonious adj. done in a grand and formal way.
■ **ceremoniously** adv.

ceremony n. (pl. **ceremonies**) **1** a formal occasion celebrating an event. **2** the set procedures followed at certain formal occasions.
▷ SYNONYMS: **1 rite**, ritual, observance, service, event, function. **2 pomp**, protocol, formality, formalities, niceties, decorum, etiquette, pageantry, ceremonial.
□ **stand on ceremony** insist on formal behaviour.

cerise /suh-reess/ n. a pinkish red colour.

certain adj. **1** able to be relied on to happen or be the case. **2** feeling sure. **3** specific but not directly stated.
▷ SYNONYMS: **1** *I'm certain he's guilty*: **sure**, confident, positive, convinced, in no doubt, satisfied. **2** *it is certain that more changes are in the offing*: **unquestionable**, sure, definite, beyond question, indubitable, undeniable, indisputable. **3** *they are certain to win*: **sure**, bound, destined. **4** *certain defeat*: **inevitable**, assured, unavoidable, inescapable, inexorable. **5** *there is no certain cure*: **reliable**, dependable, foolproof, guaranteed, sure, infallible; informal sure-fire.
– ANTONYMS: doubtful, unlikely, possible.

certainly adv. **1** definitely. **2** yes.
▷ SYNONYMS: **definitely**, surely, assuredly, unquestionably, beyond/without question, undoubtedly, without doubt, indubitably, undeniably, irrefutably, indisputably.

certainty n. (pl. **certainties**) **1** the state of being certain. **2** something that is certain.
▷ SYNONYMS: **1 confidence**, sureness, conviction, assurance. **2 inevitability**, foregone conclusion; informal sure thing; Brit. informal dead cert.
– ANTONYMS: doubt, possibility.

certifiable adj. able or needing to be officially declared insane.

certificate n. an official document recording a fact or event.
▷ SYNONYMS: **guarantee**, document, authorization, authentication, accreditation, credentials, testimonial.
■ **certification** n.

certify v. (**certifying**, **certified**) **1** declare in a certificate. **2** officially declare insane.
▷ SYNONYMS: **1 verify**, guarantee, attest, validate, confirm, endorse. **2 accredit**, recognize, license, authorize, approve.

certitude n. a feeling of certainty.

cerulean /si-roo-li-uhn/ adj. deep blue.

cervical /ser-vi-k'l, ser-vy-k'l/ adj. of the cervix.
□ **cervical smear** a specimen of cells taken from the neck of the womb and examined for signs of cancer.

cervix n. (pl. **cervices**) the narrow passage forming the lower end of the womb.

Cesarean US = CAESAREAN.

cesium US = CAESIUM.

cessation n. an act of stopping.
▷ SYNONYMS: **end**, termination, halt, finish, stoppage, conclusion, winding up, pause, suspension.
– ANTONYMS: start, resumption.

cession n. the giving up of rights or territory by a state.

cesspool (or **cesspit**) n. an underground tank or covered pit for liquid waste and sewage.

cetacean /si-tay-sh'n/ n. a sea mammal of a group including whales and dolphins.

cf. abbrev. compare.

CFC abbrev. chlorofluorocarbon, a gas used in fridges and aerosols and harmful to the ozone layer.

CGI abbrev. computer-generated imagery.

chador n. a piece of cloth worn by Muslim women around the head and upper body.

chafe v. **1** make sore or wear away by rubbing. **2** warm by rubbing. **3** become impatient because of restrictions.

chafer n. a large flying beetle.

chaff n. husks of grain separated from the seed.
• v. tease.

chaffinch n. a pink-breasted finch.

chagrin n. annoyance or shame at having failed.

chain n. **1** a series of connected metal links. **2** a connected series, set, or sequence.
▷ SYNONYMS: **1 fetters**, shackles, irons, manacles, handcuffs; informal cuffs, bracelets. **2 series**, succession, string, sequence, train, course.
• v. fasten or restrain with a chain.
▷ SYNONYMS: **secure**, fasten, tie, tether, hitch, restrain, shackle, fetter, manacle, handcuff.
□ **chain reaction** a series of events, each caused by the previous one. **chainsaw** a power-driven saw with teeth set on a moving chain.

chair n. **1** a seat for one person, with a back and four legs. **2** the person in charge of a meeting or an organization.
• v. be in charge of a meeting.
□ **chairlift** a series of chairs on a moving cable, for carrying passengers up and down a mountain. **chairman** (or **chairwoman**) a person in charge of a meeting or organization. **chairperson** a person in charge of a meeting.

chaise longue /shayz **long**/ n. (pl. **chaises longues**) a sofa with a backrest at only one end.

chalcedony n. a type of quartz.

chalet /**sha**-lay/ n. **1** a wooden house with overhanging eaves, found in the Alps. **2** a small cabin used by holidaymakers.

chalice n. a goblet.

chalk n. **1** a white soft limestone. **2** a similar substance made into sticks, used for drawing or writing.
■ **chalky** adj.

challenge n. **1** a demanding task or situation. **2** an invitation to take part in a contest or to prove something.
▷ SYNONYMS: **1 problem**, difficult task, test, trial. **2 dare**, provocation, offer.
• v. **1** dispute or query something. **2** call on someone to fight or do something difficult.

▷ SYNONYMS: **1 question**, dispute, take issue with, call into question, protest against, oppose. **2 dare**, defy, invite, throw down the gauntlet to. **3 test**, tax, strain, make demands on, stretch.
■ **challenger** n.

challenging adj. presenting a test of your abilities.
▷ SYNONYMS: **demanding**, testing, taxing, exacting, hard, difficult, stimulating.
– ANTONYMS: easy.

chamber n. **1** a large room for formal or public events. **2** an enclosed space or cavity. **3** each of the houses of a parliament. **4** (**chambers**) rooms used by a barrister. **5** old use a bedroom.
□ **chambermaid** a woman who cleans rooms in a hotel. **chamber music** classical music played by a small group of musicians. **chamber pot** a bowl kept in a bedroom and used as a toilet.

chamberlain n. hist. an officer who managed the household of a monarch or noble.

chameleon /kuh-**mee**-li-uhn/ n. a small lizard that changes colour according to its surroundings.

chamfer /**cham**-fer/ v. (**chamfering**, **chamfered**) cut an angled edge on.

chamois n. (pl. **chamois**) **1** /**sham**-wah/ a mountain antelope of southern Europe. **2** /**sham**-mi/ a piece of soft leather for cleaning windows etc.

chamomile var. of CAMOMILE.

champ v. munch noisily.
□ **champ at the bit** be very impatient.

champagne n. a white sparkling French wine.

champion n. **1** the winner of a contest. **2** a person who argues or fights for a cause.
▷ SYNONYMS: **1 winner**, title-holder, gold medallist, prizewinner; informal champ, number one. **2 advocate**, proponent, promoter, supporter, defender, upholder, backer; N. Amer. booster.
• v. strongly support.
▷ SYNONYMS: **advocate**, promote, defend, uphold, espouse, stand up for, campaign for, lobby for, fight for.
– ANTONYMS: oppose.
■ **championship** n.

chance n. **1** a possibility of something happening. **2** an opportunity. **3** occurrence without any obvious plan or cause.
▷ SYNONYMS: **1 possibility**, prospect, probability, likelihood, risk, threat, danger. **2 opportunity**, opening, occasion, window; N. Amer. & Austral./NZ show; Brit. informal look-in. **3** *he took an*

awful chance: **risk**, gamble, leap in the dark. **4 coincidence**, accident, fate, destiny, providence, happenstance, good fortune, luck, fluke.

– ANTONYMS: certainty.

• v. **1** happen or do something by chance. **2** informal do something risky.

□ **on the off chance** just in case.

chancel n. the part of a church near the altar.

chancellor n. **1** a senior state or legal official. **2** the head of the government in some European countries. **3** (or **Chancellor of the Exchequer**) (in the UK) the chief finance minister.

■ **chancellorship** n.

Chancery n. (in the UK) a division of the High Court of Justice.

chancy adj. informal risky.

chandelier n. a large hanging light with branches for several light bulbs or candles.

chandler n. a dealer in supplies for ships.

change v. **1** make or become different. **2** exchange for another. **3** move from one to another. **4** exchange a sum of money for the same sum in a different currency or smaller units.

▷ SYNONYMS: **1 alter**, make/become different, adjust, adapt, amend, modify, revise, vary, transform, metamorphose, evolve. **2 exchange**, substitute, swap, switch, replace, alternate.

• n. **1** an act of changing. **2** money returned as the balance of a sum paid. **3** coins as opposed to banknotes.

▷ SYNONYMS: **1 alteration**, modification, variation, revision, amendment, adjustment, adaptation, metamorphosis, transformation, evolution. **2 replacement**, exchange, substitution, swap, switch.

□ **changeling** a child believed to have been exchanged by fairies for the parents' real child. **changeover** a change from one system etc. to another.

■ **changeless** adj.

changeable adj. likely to change, or able to be changed.

▷ SYNONYMS: **variable**, varying, changing, fluctuating, irregular, erratic, inconsistent, unstable, unsettled, inconstant, fickle, capricious, temperamental, volatile, mercurial, unpredictable.

– ANTONYMS: constant.

channel n. **1** a band of frequencies used in radio and television transmission. **2** a means of

communication. **3** a passage along which liquid flows. **4** a stretch of water joining two seas.

▷ SYNONYMS: **1 means**, medium, instrument, mechanism, agency, vehicle, route, avenue. **2 duct**, gutter, conduit, trough, sluice, drain. **3 strait**, sound, narrows, passage.

• v. (**channelling, channelled**; US **channeling, channeled**) direct towards a purpose or by a particular route.

▷ SYNONYMS: **convey**, transmit, conduct, direct, relay, pass on, transfer.

chant n. a repeated rhythmic phrase, shouted or sung.

▷ SYNONYMS: **shout**, cry, call, slogan, chorus, refrain.

• v. say, shout, or sing rhythmically.

▷ SYNONYMS: **shout**, chorus, repeat, call.

chaos n. complete disorder and confusion.

▷ SYNONYMS: **disorder**, disorganization, confusion, mayhem, bedlam, pandemonium, havoc, turmoil, anarchy, lawlessness; Brit. a shambles.

– ANTONYMS: order.

chaotic adj. in a state of complete confusion and disorder.

▷ SYNONYMS: **disorderly**, disorganized, in confusion, in turmoil, in disarray, topsy-turvy, anarchic, lawless; Brit. informal shambolic.

■ **chaotically** adv.

chap n. informal a man.

▷ SYNONYMS: **man**, boy, individual, character; informal fellow, guy, geezer; Brit. informal bloke, lad; N. Amer. informal dude, hombre.

chapatti n. (pl. **chapattis**) (in Indian cookery) a flat round piece of unleavened bread.

chapel n. **1** a small building or room for Christian worship. **2** a part of a large church with its own altar.

chaperone n. **1** a person who accompanies and looks after another person or people. **2** dated an older woman in charge of an unmarried girl at social occasions.

• v. go with and look after.

chaplain n. a member of the clergy attached to a chapel in a private house or an institution, or to a military unit.

■ **chaplaincy** n.

chapped adj. (of the skin) cracked and sore.

chapter n. **1** a main division of a book. **2** the governing body of a cathedral or other religious community.

▷ SYNONYMS: **1 section**, part, division,

topic, stage, episode. **2 period**, phase, page, stage, epoch, era.

char v. (**charring, charred**) blacken by burning.
• n. informal **1** a woman employed to clean a house. **2** tea.

charabanc /**sha**-ruh-bang/ n. an early form of bus.

character n. **1** the distinctive qualities of a person or thing. **2** strong personal qualities. **3** a person's good reputation. **4** a person in a novel, play, or film. **5** informal an eccentric or amusing person. **6** a printed or written letter or symbol.
▷ SYNONYMS: **1 personality**, nature, quality, disposition, temperament, mentality, make-up, spirit, identity, tone, feel. **2 integrity**, honour, moral strength/fibre, strength, backbone, resolve, grit, will power; informal guts; Brit. informal bottle. **3 reputation**, name, standing, position, status. **4 eccentric**, oddity, crank, original, individualist, madcap, nonconformist; informal oddball. **5 person**, man, woman, soul, creature, individual, customer; informal cookie; Brit. informal , guy. **6 letter**, figure, symbol, mark, device, sign, hieroglyph.
■ **characterless** adj.

characteristic n. a quality typical of a person or thing.
▷ SYNONYMS: **attribute**, feature, quality, property, trait, aspect, idiosyncrasy, peculiarity, quirk.
• adj. typical of a particular person or thing.
▷ SYNONYMS: **typical**, usual, normal, distinctive, representative, particular, special, peculiar, idiosyncratic.
– ANTONYMS: abnormal.
■ **characteristically** adv.

characterize (or **-ise**) v. **1** describe the character of. **2** be typical of.
▷ SYNONYMS: **1 distinguish**, mark, typify, set apart. **2 portray**, depict, present, represent, describe, categorize, class, brand.
■ **characterization** n.

charade /shuh-**rahd**/ n. **1** an absurd pretence. **2** (**charades**) a game of guessing a word or phrase from acted clues.
▷ SYNONYMS: **pretence**, act, masquerade, show, facade, pantomime, farce, travesty, mockery, parody.

charcoal n. a black form of carbon made by burning wood slowly.

charge v. **1** ask an amount as a price. **2** formally accuse someone of something. **3** rush forward, esp. in

attack. **4** entrust with a task. **5** store electrical energy in a battery. **6** fill with.
▷ SYNONYMS: **1 ask**, demand, bill, invoice. **2 accuse**, indict, arraign, prosecute, try, put on trial; N. Amer. impeach. **3 rush**, storm, stampede, push, plough, launch yourself, go headlong; informal steam; N. Amer. informal barrel. **4 attack**, storm, assault, assail, descend on; informal lay into, tear into. **5 entrust**, burden, encumber, saddle, tax.
• n. **1** a price asked. **2** a formal accusation against someone.
3 responsibility for care or control. **4** a person or thing entrusted to someone's care. **5** a rush forward. **6** electricity existing naturally in a substance. **7** energy stored in a battery. **8** a quantity of explosive.
▷ SYNONYMS: **1 fee**, payment, price, rate, tariff, fare, levy. **2 accusation**, allegation, indictment, arraignment; N. Amer. impeachment. *The child was in her charge:* care, protection, safe keeping, control, custody, hands. **4 attack**, assault, offensive, onslaught, drive, push.
□ **charge card** a credit card issued by a shop.
■ **chargeable** adj.

chargé d'affaires /shar-zhay da-**fair**/ n. (pl. **chargés d'affaires**) an ambassador's deputy.

charger n. **1** a device for charging a battery. **2** a cavalry horse.

chariot n. a two-wheeled horse-drawn vehicle, used in ancient warfare and racing.
■ **charioteer** n.

charisma /kuh-**riz**-muh/ n. the power to inspire admiration or enthusiasm in other people.
▷ SYNONYMS: **charm**, presence, personality, strength of character, magnetism, appeal, allure.

charismatic adj. inspiring admiration or enthusiasm in other people.
▷ SYNONYMS: **charming**, magnetic, compelling, inspiring, captivating, mesmerizing, appealing, alluring, glamorous.

charitable adj. **1** of charity or charities. **2** tolerant in judging others.
▷ SYNONYMS: **1 philanthropic**, generous, open-handed, giving, munificent, benevolent, altruistic, unselfish, public-spirited, humanitarian, non-profit-making. **2 magnanimous**, generous, liberal, tolerant, sympathetic, understanding, lenient,

indulgent, forgiving.

– ANTONYMS: commercial, mean.

■ **charitably** adv.

charity n. (pl. **charities**) **1** an organization set up to help people in need. **2** the giving of money or help to people in need. **3** tolerance in judging others.

▷ SYNONYMS: **1 voluntary organization**, charitable institution, fund, trust, foundation. **2 aid**, financial assistance, welfare, relief, donations, handouts, gifts, largesse; historical alms. **3 philanthropy**, humanitarianism, altruism, public-spiritedness, social conscience, benevolence. **4 goodwill**, compassion, consideration, concern, kindness, sympathy, indulgence, tolerance, leniency.

charlatan n. a person falsely claiming to have a skill.

charm n. **1** the power to delight or fascinate others. **2** a small ornament worn on a bracelet. **3** an object or saying believed to have magic power.

▷ SYNONYMS: **1 appeal**, attraction, fascination, beauty, loveliness, allure, seductiveness, magnetism, charisma; informal pulling power. **2 spell**, incantation, formula; N. Amer. mojo, hex. **3 talisman**, trinket, amulet, mascot, fetish.

• v. **1** delight greatly. **2** influence someone by using your charm. **3** (**charmed**) unusually lucky as if protected by magic.

▷ SYNONYMS: **1 delight**, please, win over, attract, captivate, lure, fascinate, enchant, beguile. **2 coax**, cajole, wheedle; informal sweet-talk, soft-soap.

■ **charmer** n.

charming adj. very pleasant, attractive, or likeable.

▷ SYNONYMS: **delightful**, pleasing, endearing, lovely, adorable, appealing, attractive, good-looking, alluring, winning, fetching, captivating, enchanting, entrancing.

charnel house n. hist. a building in which corpses or bones were kept.

chart n. **1** a table, graph, or diagram. **2** a map for navigation. **3** (**the charts**) a weekly listing of the current bestselling pop records.

▷ SYNONYMS: **graph**, table, diagram, plan, map; Computing graphic.

• v. plot or record on a chart.

▷ SYNONYMS: **1 plot**, tabulate, graph, record, register, represent. **2 follow**, trace, outline, describe, detail, record, document.

charter n. **1** an official document

granting or setting out rights. **2** a document setting out an organization's functions. **3** the hiring of an aircraft, ship, or vehicle.

▷ SYNONYMS: **1** a Royal charter: **authority**, authorization, sanction, dispensation, permit, licence, warrant. **2** the UN Charter: **constitution**, code, principles.

• v. **1** hire an aircraft, ship, or vehicle. **2** grant a charter to.

▷ SYNONYMS: **hire**, lease, rent, book.

□ **charter flight** a flight by an aircraft chartered for a specific journey.

chartered adj. (of an accountant, engineer, etc.) qualified as a member of a professional body that has a royal charter.

chary adj. cautiously reluctant.

chase v. **1** pursue so as to catch. **2** try to get.

▷ SYNONYMS: **1 pursue**, run after, follow, hunt, track, trail; informal tail. **2** she chased away the dogs: **drive**, send, scare; informal send packing. **3** she chased away all thoughts of him: **dispel**, banish, dismiss, drive away, shut out, put out of your mind.

• n. **1** an act of chasing. **2** (**the chase**) hunting as a sport.

▷ SYNONYMS: **pursuit**, hunt, trail.

chaser n. informal a strong alcoholic drink taken after a weaker one.

chasm n. a deep crack in the earth.

chassis /shas-si/ n. (pl. **chassis** /shas-siz/) the base frame of a vehicle.

chaste adj. **1** not having sex at all or not having sex outside marriage. **2** simple and undecorated.

■ **chastity** n.

chasten v. cause to feel subdued or ashamed.

chastise v. reprimand severely.

■ **chastisement** n.

chat v. (**chatting**, **chatted**) talk in an informal way.

▷ SYNONYMS: **talk**, gossip; informal gas, jaw, chew the rag/fat, natter, have a chinwag; N. Amer. informal shoot the breeze/bull.

• n. an informal conversation.

▷ SYNONYMS: **talk**, conversation, gossip; informal jaw, gas, confab, natter, chinwag.

□ **chat room** an area on the Internet where users can email each other.

■ **chatty** adj.

chateau /sha-toh/ n. (pl. **chateaux** or **chateaus**) a large French country house or castle.

chatelaine /sha-tuh-layn/ n. dated a woman in charge of a large house.

chattel n. a personal possession.

chatter v. 1 talk informally about unimportant matters. 2 (of teeth) click together.

▷ SYNONYMS: **prattle**, chat, gossip, jabber, babble; informal **yatter**; Brit. informal natter, chunter, rabbit on.

• n. 1 informal talk. 2 a series of short high-pitched sounds.

▷ SYNONYMS: **prattle**, chat, gossip, patter, jabber, babble; informal chit-chat, yattering; Brit. informal nattering, chuntering, rabbiting on.

□ **chatterbox** informal a person who chatters.

chauffeur n. a person employed to drive a car.

chauvinism n. 1 extreme or unreasonable support for your own country. 2 the belief held by some men that men are superior to women. ■ **chauvinist** n. & adj. **chauvinistic** adj.

cheap adj. 1 low in price. 2 charging low prices. 3 low in price and quality. 4 worthless because achieved in a regrettable way.

▷ SYNONYMS: 1 **inexpensive**, low-priced, low-cost, economical, competitive, affordable, reasonable, budget, economy, bargain, cut-price, reduced, discounted; informal dirt cheap. 2 **poor-quality**, second-rate, substandard, inferior, vulgar, shoddy, trashy, tawdry; informal tacky; Brit. informal naff. 3 **despicable**, contemptible, immoral, unscrupulous, unprincipled, cynical.

– ANTONYMS: expensive.

□ **cheapskate** informal a miserly person. ■ **cheapen** v. **cheaply** adv. **cheapness** n.

cheat v. 1 act dishonestly or unfairly to gain an advantage. 2 deprive of something by unfair or dishonest means.

▷ SYNONYMS: **swindle**, defraud, deceive, trick, dupe, hoodwink, double-cross, gull; informal rip off, diddle, con, pull a fast one on; N. Amer. informal sucker.

• n. a person who cheats.

▷ SYNONYMS: **swindler**, fraudster, confidence trickster, double-dealer, double-crosser, fraud, fake, charlatan; informal con artist.

check v. 1 examine the accuracy or quality of. 2 make sure that something is the case. 3 stop or slow the progress of. 4 Chess move a piece to a square where it directly attacks the opposing king.

▷ SYNONYMS: 1 **examine**, inspect, look at/over, scrutinize, study, investigate, probe, look into, enquire into; informal check out, give something a once-over. 2 **make sure**, confirm, verify. 3 **halt**, stop, arrest, bar, obstruct, foil, thwart, curb, block.

• n. 1 an act of checking. 2 a control or restraint. 3 a pattern of small squares. 4 US a restaurant bill. 5 US = CHEQUE.

▷ SYNONYMS: 1 **examination**, inspection, scrutiny, perusal, study, investigation, test, check-up; informal once-over. 2 **control**, restraint, constraint, curb, limitation.

• adj. (or **checked**) having a pattern of small squares.

□ **check in** register at a hotel or airport. **checkmate** Chess a position from which a king cannot escape. **checkout** a point at which goods are paid for in a shop. **check out** pay a hotel bill before leaving. **checkpoint** a barrier where security checks are carried out on travellers. **check-up** a medical examination.

checkers US = CHEQUERS.

Cheddar n. a firm smooth cheese.

cheek n. 1 either side of the face below the eye. 2 rude or disrespectful remarks or behaviour.

▷ SYNONYMS: **impudence**, impertinence, insolence, rudeness, disrespect; informal brass neck, lip, mouth, chutzpah; Brit. informal backchat; N. Amer. informal sass, back talk.

• v. informal speak rudely to.

cheeky adj. (**cheekier**, **cheekiest**) cheerfully disrespectful.

▷ SYNONYMS: **impudent**, impertinent, insolent, rude, disrespectful; informal brass-necked, lippy, mouthy, fresh; N. Amer. informal sassy, nervy.

– ANTONYMS: respectful, polite.

■ **cheekily** adv. **cheekiness** n.

cheep n. a shrill cry made by a young bird.

• v. make a cheep.

cheer v. 1 shout for joy or to praise or encourage. 2 (**cheer up**) make or become less miserable.

▷ SYNONYMS: 1 **applaud**, hail, salute, shout for, clap, put your hands together for, bring the house down; informal holler for, give someone a big hand; N. Amer. informal ballyhoo. 2 **please**, raise/lift someone's spirits, brighten, buoy up, hearten, gladden, perk up, encourage; informal buck up.

– ANTONYMS: boo, depress.

• n. 1 a shout of joy, encouragement, or praise. 2 cheerfulness; optimism.

▷ SYNONYMS: **hurrah**, hurray, whoop, bravo, shout; (**cheers**) acclaim, applause, ovation.

– ANTONYMS: boo.

cheerful adj. **1** happy and optimistic. **2** bright and pleasant.
▷ SYNONYMS: **1 happy**, jolly, merry, bright, sunny, joyful, in good/high spirits, buoyant, cheery, animated, smiling, good-humoured; informal chipper, chirpy, full of beans. **2 pleasant**, attractive, agreeable, bright, sunny, friendly, welcoming.
– ANTONYMS: sad, gloomy.
■ **cheerfully** adv. **cheerfulness** n.

cheerless adj. gloomy; depressing.
▷ SYNONYMS: **1 gloomy**, dreary, dull, dismal, bleak, drab, sombre, dark, dim, dingy, funereal, austere, stark, unwelcoming, uninviting, depressing.

cheers exclam. informal **1** expressing good wishes before drinking. **2** thank you. **3** goodbye.

cheery adj. (**cheerier**, **cheeriest**) happy and optimistic.
■ **cheerily** adv. **cheeriness** n.

cheese n. a food made from the pressed curds of milk.
□ **cheesecake** a rich sweet tart made with cream and soft cheese. **cheesecloth** thin, loosely woven cotton cloth. **cheese-paring** meanness with money.
■ **cheesy** adj.

cheetah n. a large swift spotted cat of Africa and Asia.

chef n. a professional cook.

chef d'oeuvre /shay-**dervr**/ n. (pl. **chefs d'oeuvre**) a masterpiece.

chemical adj. of chemistry or chemicals.
• n. an artificially prepared or purified substance.
■ **chemically** adv.

chemise /shuh-**meez**/ n. a woman's loose-fitting dress or petticoat.

chemist n. **1** a person authorized to dispense medicines prescribed by a doctor. **2** a shop where medicines, toiletries, etc. are sold. **3** a scientist who studies chemistry.
▷ SYNONYMS: **pharmacist**, dispenser; N. Amer. **druggist**; old use apothecary.

chemistry n. **1** the scientific study of the nature of substances and how they react with each other. **2** attraction or interaction between two people.

chemotherapy /kee-moh-**the**-ruh-pi/ n. the treatment of cancer with drugs.

chenille /shuh-**neel**/ n. a fabric with a velvety pile.

cheque (US **check**) n. a written order to a bank to pay a stated sum from an account.

□ **cheque card** a card issued by a bank guaranteeing payment of cheques.

chequered adj. **1** marked with chequers. **2** marked by periods of varied fortune.

chequers (US **checkers**) n. **1** a pattern of alternately coloured squares. **2** (**checkers**) US the game of draughts.

cherish v. **1** protect and care for lovingly. **2** remember, esp. with pleasure.
▷ SYNONYMS: **1 adore**, love, dote on, be devoted to, revere, think the world of, care for, look after, keep safe. **2 treasure**, prize, hold dear. **3 harbour**, entertain, nurse, cling to, foster.
– ANTONYMS: hate.

cheroot n. a cigar with both ends open.

cherry n. (pl. **cherries**) **1** a small, round red fruit with a stone. **2** a bright deep red colour.

cherub n. **1** (pl. **cherubim** or **cherubs**) a type of angel, shown in art as a chubby child with wings. **2** (pl. **cherubs**) a beautiful or innocent-looking child.
■ **cherubic** adj.

chervil n. a herb with an aniseed flavour.

chess n. a board game for two players, the aim being to put the opponent's king into checkmate.

chest n. **1** the front of a person's body between the neck and the stomach. **2** a large strong box.
▷ SYNONYMS: **1 breast**, upper body, torso, trunk, front. **2 box**, case, casket, crate, trunk, coffer, strongbox.
□ **chest of drawers** a piece of furniture consisting of a set of drawers.

WORD LINKS
pectoral, **thoracic** relating to the chest

chestnut n. **1** an edible brown nut. **2** the tree producing chestnuts. **3** a deep reddish-brown colour. **4** a reddish-brown horse. **5** (**old chestnut**) a joke or story that has been repeated too often.

chevron n. a V-shaped symbol.

chew v. bite and work food between the teeth.
▷ SYNONYMS: **munch**, champ, chomp, crunch, gnaw, bite, masticate.
■ **chewy** adj.

chiaroscuro /ki-ah-ruh-**skoor**-oh/ n. the treatment of light and shade in drawing and painting.

chic /sheek/ **adj.** elegant and fashionable.
▷ SYNONYMS: **stylish**, smart, elegant, sophisticated, fashionable; informal trendy; Brit. informal swish; N. Amer. informal kicky, tony.
– ANTONYMS: unfashionable.
• n. stylishness and elegance.

chicane /shi-**kayn**/ n. a sharp double bend on a motor-racing track.

chicanery n. trickery.

chick n. a newly hatched young bird.

chicken n. **1** a domestic fowl kept for its eggs or meat. **2** informal a coward.
• v. (**chicken out**) informal be too scared to do something.
• adj. informal cowardly.
□ **chicken feed** informal a very small sum of money. **chickenpox** a disease causing itchy red pimples.

chickpea n. a yellowish seed eaten as a vegetable.

chicory n. a plant with edible leaves and a root which can be used instead of coffee.

chide v. scold or rebuke.

chief n. **1** a leader or ruler. **2** the head of an organization.
▷ SYNONYMS: **1** *a Highland chief:* **leader**, chieftain, head, ruler, master, commander. **2** *the chief of the central bank:* **head**, chief executive, chief executive officer, CEO, president, chairman, chairwoman, principal, governor, director, manager; informal boss, head honcho; Brit. informal gaffer, guv'nor.
• adj. **1** most important. **2** highest in rank.
▷ SYNONYMS: **1 main**, principal, primary, prime, first, cardinal, central, key, crucial, essential; informal number-one. **2 head**, leading, principal, premier, highest, supreme, arch.
– ANTONYMS: minor, subordinate.

chiefly adv. mainly; mostly.
▷ SYNONYMS: **mainly**, in the main, primarily, principally, predominantly, mostly, for the most part, usually, typically, commonly, generally, on the whole, largely.

chieftain n. the leader of a people or clan.

chiffon n. a light, see-through fabric.

chignon /**sheen**-yon/ n. a coil of hair arranged on the back of a woman's head.

chihuahua /chi-**wah**-wuh/ n. a very small smooth-haired dog.

chilblain n. a painful swelling on a hand or foot caused by cold weather.

child n. (pl. **children**) **1** a young human being. **2** a son or daughter.
▷ SYNONYMS: **youngster**, baby, infant, toddler, minor, juvenile, junior, descendant; Scottish & N. English bairn; informal kid, kiddie, nipper, tiny, tot; derogatory brat.
□ **childbirth** the act of giving birth to a child.
■ **childhood** n. **childless** adj.

> **WORD LINKS**
> **paediatrics** the branch of medicine concerned with children

childish adj. **1** silly and immature. **2** like a child.
▷ SYNONYMS: **immature**, babyish, infantile, juvenile, puerile, silly.
– ANTONYMS: mature.

childlike adj. innocent or simple.
▷ SYNONYMS: **youthful**, innocent, unsophisticated, naive, trusting, artless, unaffected, uninhibited, natural, spontaneous.
– ANTONYMS: adult.

chill n. **1** an unpleasant feeling of coldness. **2** a feverish cold.
▷ SYNONYMS: **coldness**, chilliness, coolness, nip; shiver, frisson.
– ANTONYMS: warmth.
• v. **1** make cold. **2** frighten. **3** informal relax.
▷ SYNONYMS: **scare**, frighten, petrify, terrify, alarm, make someone's blood run cold; Brit. informal put the wind up.
– ANTONYMS: warm.
• adj. chilly.
▷ SYNONYMS: **cold**, chilly, cool, fresh, wintry, frosty, icy, arctic, bitter, freezing; informal nippy; Brit. informal parky.

chilli (US **chili**) n. (pl. **chillies**) a small hot-tasting pepper.

chilly adj. (**chillier**, **chilliest**) **1** unpleasantly cold. **2** unfriendly.
▷ SYNONYMS: **1 cold**, cool, crisp, fresh, wintry, frosty, icy; informal nippy; Brit. informal parky. **2 unfriendly**, unwelcoming, cold, cool, frosty; informal stand-offish.
– ANTONYMS: warm.

chime n. **1** a tuneful ringing sound. **2** a bell or a metal bar used in a set to ring when struck.
• v. **1** make a tuneful ringing sound. **2** (**chime in**) interrupt with a remark.

chimera /ky-**meer**-uh/ n. **1** an unrealistic idea or hope. **2** Gk Myth. a female monster with a lion's head, a goat's body, and a serpent's tail.

chimney n. (pl. **chimneys**) a vertical pipe taking smoke and gases up from a fire or furnace.

□ **chimney breast** a projecting part of an inside wall surrounding a chimney. **chimney pot** a pipe at the top of a chimney.

chimp n. informal a chimpanzee.

chimpanzee n. an African ape.

chin n. the part of the face below the mouth.

china n. **1** a fine white ceramic material. **2** objects made of china.
▷ SYNONYMS: **crockery**, dishes, plates, cups and saucers, tableware, porcelain, dinnerware, dinner service, tea service.

chinchilla n. a small squirrel-like South American rodent.

chine n. a joint of meat containing part of an animal's spine.

Chinese n. (pl. **Chinese**) **1** the language of China. **2** a person from China.
• adj. of China.

chink n. **1** a narrow opening. **2** a thin beam of light. **3** a high-pitched ringing sound.
▷ SYNONYMS: **gap**, crack, space, hole, aperture, fissure, cranny, cleft, split, slit.
• v. make a high-pitched ringing sound.

chinos /chee-nohz/ pl. n. casual trousers made from a smooth cotton fabric.

chintz n. a shiny cotton fabric used for furnishings.

chip n. **1** a small piece cut or broken off from something hard. **2** Brit. a strip of deep-fried potato. **3** a microchip. **4** a counter used in gambling.
▷ SYNONYMS: **1 fragment**, sliver, splinter, shaving, shard, flake. **2 nick**, crack, scratch. **3 counter**, token; N. Amer. check.
• v. (**chipping**, **chipped**) **1** cut or break a chip from something hard. **2** (**chip in**) informal make a contribution.
▷ SYNONYMS: **1 nick**, crack, scratch. **2** chip off the old plaster: **cut**, hack, chisel, carve, hew, whittle.
□ **a chip on your shoulder** informal a long-held grievance. **chipboard** board made of compressed wood chips.

chipmunk n. a striped burrowing squirrel.

chipolata n. Brit. a small sausage.

chippings pl. n. fragments of stone or wood.

chiropody /ki-rop-uh-di/ n. medical treatment of the feet.
■ **chiropodist** n.

chiropractic /ky-roh-**prak**-tik/ n. a system of complementary medicine based on manipulation of the joints.
■ **chiropractor** n.

chirp v. (of a small bird) make a short, high-pitched sound.
• n. a chirping sound.

chirpy adj. informal cheerful and lively.

chisel n. a tool with a long blade for shaping wood or stone.
• v. (**chiselling**, **chiselled**; US **chiseling**, **chiseled**) cut or shape with a chisel.

chit n. **1** a disrespectful young woman. **2** an official note recording money owed.

chivalrous adj. (of a man) polite and gallant towards women.
▷ SYNONYMS: **gallant**, gentlemanly, honourable, respectful, considerate, courteous, polite, gracious, well mannered.
– ANTONYMS: rude.
■ **chivalrously** adv.

chivalry n. **1** an honourable code of behaviour which medieval knights were expected to follow. **2** polite behaviour by a man towards women.

chives pl. n. a herb with thin onion-flavoured leaves.

chivvy v. (**chivvying**, **chivvied**) nag or pester.

chloride n. a compound of chlorine with another substance.

chlorinate v. treat water with chlorine.

chlorine n. a green gaseous chemical element.

chloroform n. a liquid used as a solvent and formerly as an anaesthetic.

chlorophyll n. a green pigment in plants which allows them to convert sunlight into energy.

chock n. a wedge or block placed against a wheel to prevent it from moving.
□ **chock-a-block** informal crammed full.

chocolate n. **1** a dark brown food made from roasted cacao seeds, eaten as a sweet, or made into a drink. **2** a sweet covered with chocolate.

choice n. **1** an act of choosing. **2** the right or ability to choose. **3** a range from which to choose. **4** something chosen.
▷ SYNONYMS: **1** freedom of choice: **selection**, choosing, picking, pick, preference, decision, say, vote. **2** you have no other choice: **option**, alternative, course of action. **3** an extensive choice: **range**, variety, selection, assortment.
• adj. of very good quality.
▷ SYNONYMS: **superior**, first-class, first-rate, prime, premier, grade A, best, finest, select, quality, top, top-quality, high-grade, prize; informal A1,

top-notch.
– ANTONYMS: inferior.

choir n. **1** an organized group of singers. **2** the part of a church used by a choir.

choke v. **1** prevent someone from breathing by blocking their throat. **2** have trouble breathing. **3** fill or clog up.
▷ SYNONYMS: **1 suffocate**, asphyxiate, smother, stifle, strangle, throttle; informal strangulate. **2 gag**, retch, cough, fight for breath. **3 clog up**, bung up, stop up, block, obstruct.
• n. a valve controlling the flow of air into a petrol engine.

choker n. a close-fitting necklace.

cholera n. an infectious disease causing severe vomiting and diarrhoea.

choleric adj. irritable.

cholesterol n. a substance in most body tissues, believed to cause disease of the arteries if present in excessive levels in the blood.

chomp v. munch noisily.

choose v. (**choosing**, **chose**; past part. **chosen**) pick out as being the best of the available alternatives.
▷ SYNONYMS: **1 select**, pick, opt for, plump for, settle on, prefer, decide on, fix on, elect, adopt. **2** *I'll stay as long as I choose to*: **wish**, want, desire, please, like.

choosy adj. (**choosier**, **choosiest**) informal very careful in making a choice.
▷ SYNONYMS: **fussy**, finicky, fastidious, over-particular, hard to please; informal picky, pernickety; N. Amer. informal persnickety.

chop v. (**chopping**, **chopped**) **1** cut into pieces with a knife or axe. **2** hit with a short, downward stroke. **3** end something or reduce it by a large amount.
▷ SYNONYMS: **cut up**, cube, dice, hew, split, fell; N. Amer. hash.
• n. **1** a thick slice of meat, usu. including a rib. **2** a downward cutting blow.

chopper n. **1** a short large-bladed axe. **2** informal a helicopter.

choppy adj. (of the sea) having many small waves.
▷ SYNONYMS: **rough**, turbulent, heavy, heaving, stormy, tempestuous, squally.
– ANTONYMS: calm.

chopstick n. each of a pair of thin sticks used as eating utensils in China and Japan.

chop suey n. a Chinese-style dish of meat fried with vegetables.

choral adj. sung by a choir.

chorale n. a simple, stately hymn tune.

chord n. a group of three or more notes sounded together.

chore n. a routine or boring task.
▷ SYNONYMS: **task**, job, duty, errand, burden; informal hassle.

choreograph /ko-ri-uh-grahf/ v. compose the sequence of steps and moves for a dance.
■ **choreographer** n. **choreography** n.

chorister n. a member of a choir.

chortle v. laugh loudly.

chorus n. (pl. **choruses**) **1** the refrain of a song. **2** a group of singers or dancers in a musical or opera. **3** something said at the same time by many people.
• v. (of a group) say the same thing at the same time.

chose past of CHOOSE.

chosen past part. of CHOOSE.

choux pastry /shoo/ n. light pastry, used for eclairs.

chow n. **1** informal food. **2** a Chinese breed of dog with a tail curled over its back.

chowder n. thick soup containing fish, seafood, etc.

chow mein /mayn/ n. a Chinese-style dish of fried noodles with shredded meat etc.

Christ n. the title given to Jesus.

christen v. name a baby at baptism.
▷ SYNONYMS: **1** *she was christened Sara*: **baptize**, name, call. **2** *a group christened 'The Magic Circle'*: **call**, name, dub, style, term, label, nickname.

Christendom n. literary the worldwide body of Christians.

Christian adj. of or believing in Christianity.
• n. a believer in Christianity.
□ **Christian name** a forename.

Christianity n. the religion based on the teaching and works of Jesus.

Christmas n. the annual Christian festival celebrating Jesus's birth, held on 25 December.

chromatic adj. **1** (of a musical scale) rising or falling by semitones. **2** of or produced by colour.

chromatography n. a technique for separating a mixture by passing it through a material in which the components move at different rates.
■ **chromatographic** adj.

chrome n. a hard shiny coating made

from chromium.

chromium n. a hard white metallic element.

chromosome n. a thread-like structure in a cell nucleus, carrying the genes.

chronic adj. **1** (of an illness etc.) lasting a long time. **2** having a chronic illness or habit. **3** Brit. informal very bad.
▷ SYNONYMS: **1** *a chronic illness:* **persistent**, long-standing, long-term, incurable. **2** *chronic economic problems:* **constant**, continuing, persistent, long-lasting, severe, serious, acute, grave, dire. **3** *a chronic liar:* **inveterate**, hardened, dyed-in-the-wool, incorrigible, compulsive; informal pathological.
− ANTONYMS: acute, temporary.
■ **chronically** adv.

chronicle n. a record of historical events.
▷ SYNONYMS: **record**, account, history, annals, archives, log, diary, journal.
• v. record a series of events.
▷ SYNONYMS: **record**, write down, set down, document, report.
■ **chronicler** n.

chronological adj. following the order in which things occurred.
■ **chronologically** adv.

chronology n. the arrangement of events in order of occurrence.

chronometer n. an instrument measuring time.

chrysalis n. (pl. **chrysalises**) **1** an insect pupa, esp. of a butterfly or moth. **2** the hard case enclosing a pupa.

chrysanthemum n. a garden plant with bright flowers.

chubby adj. (**chubbier**, **chubbiest**) plump and rounded.
▷ SYNONYMS: **plump**, tubby, flabby, rotund, portly, chunky; Brit. informal podgy; N. Amer. informal zaftig, corn-fed.
− ANTONYMS: skinny.

chuck v. **1** informal throw carelessly. **2** touch playfully under the chin.
▷ SYNONYMS: **1** **throw**, toss, fling, hurl, pitch, cast, lob; informal sling, bung. **2** **throw away**, throw out, discard, dispose of, get rid of, dump, bin, jettison; informal ditch, junk; N. Amer. informal trash. **3** **give up**, leave, resign from; informal quit, pack in; Brit. informal jack in. **4** **jilt**, finish with, break off with, leave; informal dump, ditch, give someone the elbow; Brit. informal give someone the push.
• n. **1** a device holding something in a lathe or a tool in a drill. **2** a cut of beef from the neck to the ribs.

chuckle v. laugh quietly.
▷ SYNONYMS: **laugh**, chortle, giggle, titter, snigger.
• n. a quiet laugh.

chuff v. (of a steam engine) move with a regular puffing sound.

chuffed adj. Brit. informal pleased.

chug v. (**chugging**, **chugged**) (of a vehicle) move slowly with muffled regular sounds.

chum n. informal a close friend.
▷ SYNONYMS: **friend**, companion, play-mate, classmate, schoolmate, work-mate; informal pal, crony; Brit. informal mate; N. Amer. informal buddy.
− ANTONYMS: enemy.
■ **chummy** adj.

chump n. informal a foolish person.

chunk n. **1** a thick, solid piece. **2** a large amount.
▷ SYNONYMS: **lump**, hunk, wedge, block, slab, square, nugget, brick, cube; informal wodge; N. Amer. informal gob.
■ **chunky** adj.

church n. **1** a building for public Christian worship. **2** (**Church**) a particular Christian organization. **3** (**the Church**) Christians as a whole. □ **churchwarden** either of two people elected by an Anglican congregation to oversee church property. **churchyard** an enclosed area surrounding a church.

churlish adj. rude or bad-tempered.
▷ SYNONYMS: **rude**, ill-mannered, discourteous, ungracious, impolite, inconsiderate, surly, sullen.
− ANTONYMS: polite.
■ **churlishly** adv.

churn v. **1** (of liquid) move about vigorously. **2** (**churn out**) produce quickly and in large quantities. **3** shake milk or cream in a machine to make butter.
▷ SYNONYMS: **disturb**, stir up, agitate, beat.
• n. **1** a machine for making butter by shaking milk or cream. **2** a large metal milk can.

chute n. a sloping channel for moving things to a lower level.

chutney n. (pl. **chutneys**) a spicy pickle made of fruit or vegetables with vinegar and sugar.

CIA abbrev. (in the US) Central Intelligence Agency.

ciabatta /chuh-bah-tuh/ n. a flat Italian bread made with olive oil.

cicada /si-kah-duh/ n. a chirping insect like a grasshopper.

cicatrix n. (pl. **cicatrices**) a scar.

CID abbrev. (in the UK) Criminal Investigation Department.

cider n. an alcoholic drink made from fermented apple juice.

cigar n. a cylinder of tobacco in tobacco leaves for smoking.

cigarette n. a cylinder of finely cut tobacco in paper for smoking.

cinch n. informal a very easy task.

cinder n. a piece of partly burnt coal or wood.

cine adj. of film-making.

cinema n. Brit. **1** a theatre where films are shown. **2** the production of films as an art or industry.
▷ SYNONYMS: **1 the movies**, the pictures, multiplex; informal the flicks. **2** British *cinema:* **films**, film, movies, motion pictures.
■ **cinematic** adj.

cinematography n. the art of camerawork in film-making.
■ **cinematographer** n.

cinnamon n. a spice made from the bark of an Asian tree.

cipher (or **cypher**) n. **1** a code. **2** an unimportant person or thing.

circa prep. approximately.
▷ SYNONYMS: **approximately**, about, round about, around, in the region of, roughly, or so, or thereabouts, more or less; N. Amer. informal in the ballpark of.
– ANTONYMS: exactly.

circle n. **1** a round flat shape whose edge is at the same distance from the centre all the way round. **2** a group with shared interests, friends, etc. **3** Brit. a curved upper tier of seats in a theatre.
▷ SYNONYMS: **1 ring**, band, hoop, circlet, halo, disc. **2 group**, set, crowd, band, company, clique, coterie, club, society; informal gang, bunch.
● v. **1** move or be placed all the way around. **2** draw a line round.
▷ SYNONYMS: **1** *seagulls circled above:* **wheel**, revolve, rotate, whirl, spiral. **2** *satellites circling the earth:* **go round**, travel round, circumnavigate, orbit. **3** *the abbey was circled by a wall:* **surround**, encircle, ring, enclose.

circlet n. a circular band worn on the head.

circuit n. **1** a roughly circular route. **2** Brit. a motor-racing track. **3** a system of components forming a complete path for an electric current. **4** a series of sporting events.
▷ SYNONYMS: **1** *two circuits of the track:* **lap**, turn, round, circle. **2** *a racing circuit:* **track**, racetrack, course, route, stadium.

circuitous /ser-kyoo-i-tuhss/ adj. (of a route) long and indirect.
▷ SYNONYMS: **roundabout**, indirect, winding, meandering, twisting, tortuous.
– ANTONYMS: direct.

circuitry n. electric circuits.

circular adj. **1** having the shape of a circle. **2** (of an argument) false because it uses as evidence the point to be proved.
▷ SYNONYMS: **round**, ring-shaped.
● n. a letter or leaflet sent to a large number of people.
▷ SYNONYMS: **leaflet**, pamphlet, handbill, flyer, advertisement, notice.

circulate v. **1** move continuously through a closed system or area. **2** pass from place to place or person to person.
▷ SYNONYMS: **1 spread**, communicate, disseminate, make known, make public, broadcast, publicize, distribute. **2 socialize**, mingle, mix, wander, stroll.

circulation n. **1** movement around something, esp. the continuous movement of blood round the body. **2** the number of copies sold of a newspaper or magazine. **3** the public availability of something.

circumcise v. cut off the foreskin or clitoris of.
■ **circumcision** n.

circumference n. **1** the boundary of a circle. **2** the distance around something.

circumflex n. the accent (^).

circumlocution n. the use of many words where fewer would do.

circumnavigate v. sail all the way around.
■ **circumnavigation** n.

circumscribe v. restrict; limit.

circumspect adj. cautious; sensible.
▷ SYNONYMS: **cautious**, wary, careful, chary, guarded, on your guard; informal cagey.
– ANTONYMS: unguarded.

circumstance n. **1** a fact or condition connected with an event or action. **2** events that are beyond your control.
▷ SYNONYMS: *the economic circumstances seemed favourable:* **situation**, conditions, state of affairs, position, the lie of the land, turn of events, factors, facts, background, environment, context.

circumstantial adj. (of evidence) suggesting but not proving something.

circumvent v. evade a difficulty.

circus n. (pl. **circuses**) a travelling show with acrobats, trained animals, and clowns.

cirque n. a steep-sided hollow on a mountain.

cirrhosis /si-roh-siss/ n. a liver disease.

cirrus /si-ruhss/ n. (pl. **cirri**) a high wispy cloud.

cistern n. a water storage tank connected to a toilet.

citadel n. a fortress overlooking a city.

citation n. 1 a quotation from a book or author. 2 an official mention of a notable act.

cite v. quote a book or author as evidence for an argument.

▷ SYNONYMS: **quote**, mention, refer to, allude to, instance, specify, name.

citizen n. 1 a person legally recognized as a member of a country. 2 an inhabitant of a town or city.

▷ SYNONYMS: 1 *a British citizen:* **subject**, national, passport holder. 2 *the citizens of Edinburgh:* **inhabitant**, resident, native, townsman, townswoman, taxpayer; formal denizen.

■ **citizenship** n.

citrus n. (pl. **citruses**) a fruit of a group including lemons, oranges, etc.

■ **citric** adj.

city n. (pl. **cities**) 1 a large town, esp. (Brit.) one created by charter and containing a cathedral. 2 (**the City**) the part of London that is a centre of finance and business.

▷ SYNONYMS: **town**, municipality, metropolis, conurbation, urban area; Scottish burgh; informal big smoke; N. Amer. informal burg.

> **WORD LINKS**
> **civic**, **metropolitan**, **urban** relating to cities

civet /siv-it/ n. 1 a cat native to Africa and Asia. 2 a strong perfume obtained from its glands.

civic adj. of a city or town.

▷ SYNONYMS: **municipal**, city, town, urban, metropolitan, public, community.

civil adj. 1 of civilians. 2 polite. 3 (of a court) dealing with personal legal matters.

▷ SYNONYMS: 1 **secular**, non-religious, lay. 2 **non-military**, civilian. 3 **polite**, courteous, well mannered, gentlemanly, chivalrous, ladylike.

– ANTONYMS: religious, military, rude.

□ **civil engineer** an engineer who designs roads, bridges, etc. **civil**

partnership (or **civil union**) a legally recognized union of a same-sex couple, with rights similar to those of marriage. **civil servant** a member of the civil service. **civil service** the departments that carry out the work of the government. **civil war** a war between people of the same country.

■ **civilly** adv.

civilian n. a person not in the armed services or the police force.

civility n. (pl. **civilities**) politeness.

civilization (or **-isation**) n. 1 an advanced stage of social development. 2 the process of achieving this. 3 a civilized nation or area.

▷ SYNONYMS: 1 **human development**, advancement, progress, enlightenment, culture, refinement, sophistication. 2 **culture**, society, nation, people.

civilize (or **-ise**) v. bring to an advanced stage of social development.

▷ SYNONYMS: **enlighten**, improve, educate, instruct, refine, cultivate, socialize.

civilized (or **-ised**) adj. 1 at an advanced stage of social development. 2 polite and good-mannered.

▷ SYNONYMS: 1 **advanced**, developed, sophisticated, enlightened, educated, cultured, cultivated. 2 **polite**, courteous, well mannered, civil, refined, polished.

– ANTONYMS: unsophisticated, rude.

CJD abbrev. Creutzfeldt–Jakob disease, a fatal brain disease.

cl abbrev. centilitre.

clack v. make a sharp sound like that of one hard object hitting another.

• n. a clacking sound.

clad adj. clothed.

cladding n. a covering or coating on a structure or material.

claim v. 1 state as being the case, without giving proof. 2 request as your right. 3 cause loss of life.

▷ SYNONYMS: 1 **assert**, declare, profess, protest, maintain, insist, contend, allege. 2 **request**, ask for, apply for, demand.

• n. 1 a statement that something is true. 2 a request for something to which you have a right.

▷ SYNONYMS: 1 **assertion**, declaration, profession, protestation, insistence, contention, allegation. 2 **application**, request, demand.

■ **claimant** n.

clairvoyant n. a person claiming the

power to see into the future.
■ **clairvoyance** n.

clam n. a shellfish with a hinged shell.
• v. (**clam up**) informal refuse to talk.

clamber v. climb with difficulty.

clammy adj. damp and sticky.

clamour (US **clamor**) n. **1** a loud confused noise. **2** a strong protest or demand.
▷ SYNONYMS: **noise**, din, racket, rumpus, uproar, shouting, commotion, hubbub; Brit. row; informal hullabaloo.
• v. make a clamour.
■ **clamorous** adj.

clamp n. a device for holding something tightly.
• v. **1** fasten or hold tightly. **2** fit a clamp to the wheel of a car to immobilize it. **3** (**clamp down**) take strict action to prevent something.
▷ SYNONYMS: **fasten**, secure, fix, attach, clench, grip, hold, press, clasp, screw, bolt.

clan n. a group of related families.
▷ SYNONYMS: **family**, house, dynasty, tribe.

clandestine adj. done secretly.
▷ SYNONYMS: **secret**, covert, furtive, surreptitious, stealthy, cloak-and-dagger, underhand; informal hush-hush.

clang n. a loud metallic sound.
• v. make a clang.

clanger n. informal a mistake.

clangour (US **clangor**) n. a continuous clanging sound.

clank n. a sharp sound like that of pieces of metal hitting each other.
• v. make a clank.

clap v. (**clapping**, **clapped**) **1** strike the palms of the hands together repeatedly, esp. to applaud. **2** slap on the back.
▷ SYNONYMS: **applaud**, give someone a round of applause, put your hands together; informal give someone a big hand; N. Amer. informal give it up.
• n. **1** an act of clapping. **2** a sharp sound of thunder.
▷ SYNONYMS: **1** round of applause, hand-clap; informal hand. **2** crack, peal, crash, bang, boom.
□ **clapped-out** Brit. informal worn out.
claptrap nonsense.

clapper n. the striking part of a bell.
□ **clapperboard** hinged boards struck together at the start of filming to synchronize picture and sound machinery.

claret n. a dry red wine.

clarify v. (**clarifying**, **clarified**) **1** make easier to understand. **2** melt butter to separate out the impurities.

▷ SYNONYMS: **make clear**, shed/throw light on, illuminate, elucidate, explain, interpret, spell out, clear up.
– ANTONYMS: confuse.
■ **clarification** n.

clarinet n. a woodwind instrument.
■ **clarinettist** n.

clarion call n. a clear demand for action.

clarity n. clearness.
▷ SYNONYMS: **1** the clarity of his explanation: **lucidity**, precision, coherence, transparency, simplicity. **2** the clarity of the image: **sharpness**, clearness, crispness, definition. **3** the clarity of the water: **transparency**, clearness, limpidity, translucence.

clash v. **1** come into violent conflict. **2** disagree. **3** look or sound unpleasant together. **4** (of events) occur inconveniently at the same time.
▷ SYNONYMS: **1** fight, battle, confront, skirmish, contend, come to blows. **2** disagree, differ, wrangle, dispute, cross swords, lock horns, be at loggerheads. **3** conflict, coincide, overlap. **4** bang, strike, clang, crash.
• n. an act of clashing.
▷ SYNONYMS: **1** fight, battle, confrontation, skirmish, engagement, encounter, conflict. **2** argument, altercation, confrontation, quarrel, disagreement, dispute; informal run-in, slanging match. **3** crash, clang, bang, clatter, clangour.

clasp v. **1** grasp tightly with your hand. **2** place your arms tightly around. **3** fasten with a clasp.
▷ SYNONYMS: **grasp**, grip, clutch, hold, squeeze, seize, grab, embrace, hug.
• n. **1** a device with interlocking parts used for fastening. **2** an act of clasping.
▷ SYNONYMS: **1** fastener, catch, clip, pin, buckle. **2** grasp, grip, squeeze, embrace, hug.

class n. **1** a group of things having a common characteristic. **2** a group having the same social status. **3** a group of students taught together. **4** a lesson. **5** informal impressive stylishness.
▷ SYNONYMS: **1** kind, sort, type, variety, genre, category, grade, rating, classification. **2** group, grouping, rank, stratum, level, echelon, status, caste.
• v. put in a category.
▷ SYNONYMS: **classify**, categorize, group, grade, order, rate, bracket, designate, label, rank.
□ **classroom** a room in which a class

of students is taught.

■ **classless** adj.

classic adj. **1** of recognized high quality. **2** typical.

▷ SYNONYMS: **1 definitive**, authoritative, outstanding, first-rate, first-class, best, finest, excellent, superior, masterly. **2 typical**, archetypal, quintessential, model, representative, perfect, prime, textbook. **3 timeless**, traditional, simple, elegant, understated.

● n. **1** a work of art recognized as being of high quality. **2** (**Classics**) the study of ancient Greek and Latin culture, literature, etc.

▷ SYNONYMS: **definitive example**, model, epitome, paradigm, exemplar, masterpiece, master work.

■ **classicism** n. **classicist** n.

classical adj. **1** of ancient Greek or Latin culture etc. **2** (of music) written in the formal European tradition.

■ **classically** adv.

classified adj. **1** (of newspaper or magazine advertisements) organized in categories. **2** (of information or documents) officially secret.

classify v. (**classifying**, **classified**) **1** arrange a group in classes. **2** put in a category.

▷ SYNONYMS: **categorize**, group, grade, rank, order, organize, sort, type, codify, bracket.

■ **classifiable** adj. **classification** n. **classifier** n.

classy adj. (**classier**, **classiest**) informal stylish and sophisticated.

▷ SYNONYMS: **stylish**, high-class, superior, exclusive, chic, elegant, smart, sophisticated; Brit. upmarket; N. Amer. high-toned; informal posh, ritzy, plush, swanky; Brit. informal swish.

clatter n. a loud rattling sound like that of hard objects hitting each other.

● v. make a clatter.

clause n. **1** a distinct part of a sentence, with its own verb. **2** a part of a treaty, law, or contract.

▷ SYNONYMS: **section**, paragraph, article, passage, subsection, chapter, condition, proviso, rider.

claustrophobia n. extreme fear of being in an enclosed place.

■ **claustrophobic** adj.

clavichord n. an early keyboard instrument.

clavicle n. the collarbone.

claw n. **1** a horny nail on an animal's or bird's foot. **2** the pincer of a shellfish.

▷ SYNONYMS: **talon**, nail, pincer.

● v. scratch or tear at with claws or hands.

▷ SYNONYMS: **scratch**, lacerate, tear, rip, scrape, dig into.

clay n. sticky earth used for making bricks and pottery.

□ **clay pigeon** a disc of baked clay thrown up as a target for shooting.

clean adj. **1** free from dirt or harmful substances. **2** not obscene or immoral.

▷ SYNONYMS: **1 washed**, scrubbed, cleansed, cleaned, laundered, spotless, unstained, unsullied, unblemished, immaculate, pristine, disinfected, sterilized, sterile, aseptic, decontaminated. **2 blank**, empty, clear, plain, unused, new, pristine, fresh, unmarked. **3 pure**, clear, fresh, unpolluted, uncontaminated.

– ANTONYMS: dirty, polluted.

● v. make clean.

▷ SYNONYMS: **wash**, cleanse, wipe, sponge, scrub, mop, rinse, scour, swab, shampoo, launder, dry-clean.

– ANTONYMS: dirty.

■ **cleaner** n. **cleanliness** /klen-li-nuhss/ n. **cleanly** adv.

cleanse v. make thoroughly clean or pure.

▷ SYNONYMS: **1 clean**, wash, bathe, rinse, disinfect. **2** *cleansing the environment of traces of lead:* **rid**, clear, free, purify, purge.

clear adj. **1** easy to see, hear, or understand. **2** leaving or feeling no doubt. **3** transparent. **4** free of obstructions or anything unwanted.

▷ SYNONYMS: **1 understandable**, comprehensible, intelligible, plain, uncomplicated, explicit, lucid, coherent, simple, straightforward, unambiguous, clear-cut, legible, audible. **2 obvious**, evident, plain, sure, definite, unmistakable, manifest, indisputable, unambiguous, patent, incontrovertible, visible, conspicuous, overt, blatant, glaring. **3 transparent**, limpid, translucent, crystal clear, pellucid. **4 bright**, cloudless, unclouded, blue, sunny, starry. **5 unobstructed**, passable, open, unrestricted, unhindered.

– ANTONYMS: incoherent, vague, cloudy.

● v. **1** make or become clear. **2** get past or over. **3** prove innocent. **4** give official approval to.

▷ SYNONYMS: **1 disappear**, go away, stop, die away, fade, wear off, lift, settle, evaporate, dissipate, decrease, lessen, shift. **2 unblock**, unstop, clean out. **3 evacuate**, vacate, empty, leave. **4 remove**, strip, take away, carry

away, tidy away/up. **5 go over**, pass over, sail over, jump over, vault over, leap over. **6 acquit**, declare innocent, find not guilty, absolve, exonerate; informal let off.
□ **clear off** informal go away. **clear out** empty. **clear up 1** (of an illness) become cured. **2** solve or explain.

clearway Brit. a main road on which vehicles are not allowed to stop.

clearance n. **1** the act of clearing. **2** official authorization. **3** space allowed for one thing to pass another.
▷ SYNONYMS: **1 removal**, clearing, demolition. **2 authorization**, permission, consent, approval, leave, sanction, licence, dispensation; informal the go-ahead. **3 space**, room, headroom, margin, leeway.

clear-cut adj. easy to see or understand.
▷ SYNONYMS: **definite**, distinct, precise, specific, explicit, unambiguous, unequivocal, black and white.
− ANTONYMS: vague.

clearing n. an open space in a forest.

cleat n. **1** a projection for attaching a rope. **2** a projection on the sole of a shoe.

cleavage n. **1** the space between a woman's breasts. **2** a marked difference or division.

cleave v. (**cleaving**, **clove** or **cleft** or **cleaved**; past part. **cloven** or **cleft** or **cleaved**) **1** divide or split in two. **2** (**cleave to**) stick to.

cleaver n. a tool for chopping meat.

clef n. Music a symbol on a stave showing the pitch of the notes.

cleft adj. split.
• n. a split or crack.
▷ SYNONYMS: **split**, crack, fissure, crevice.
□ **cleft lip** (or **palate**) a split in the upper lip (or roof of the mouth), present from birth.

clematis n. a climbing plant with showy flowers.

clemency n. kind or merciful treatment.

clement adj. (of weather) mild.

clementine n. a variety of tangerine.

clench v. close your fist or hold your teeth or muscles together tightly.
▷ SYNONYMS: **grip**, grasp, grab, clutch, clasp, clamp, hold tightly, seize, squeeze.

clerestory /kleer-stor-i/ n. (pl. **clerestories**) an upper row of windows in a large church.

clergy n. the priests and ministers of a religion, esp. those of the Christian Church.

clergyman, (or **clergywoman**) n. (pl. **clergymen** or **clergywomen**) a Christian priest or minister.
▷ SYNONYMS: **priest**, cleric, minister, preacher, chaplain, man of the cloth, padre, father, pastor, vicar, rector, parson, curate; Scottish kirkman.

cleric n. a priest or religious leader.

clerical adj. **1** of office work. **2** of the clergy.
▷ SYNONYMS: **1 office**, desk, administrative, secretarial, white-collar. **2 ecclesiastical**, church, priestly, religious, spiritual, holy.

clerk n. an office worker who carries out administrative work, keeps accounts, etc.

clever adj. **1** quick to understand and learn. **2** skilled at doing something.
▷ SYNONYMS: **1 intelligent**, bright, smart, astute, quick-witted, shrewd, talented, gifted, capable, able, competent; informal brainy. **2** a clever scheme: **ingenious**, canny, cunning, crafty, artful, slick, neat. **3** she was clever with her hands: **skilful**, dexterous, adroit, adept, deft, nimble, handy, skilled, talented, gifted.
− ANTONYMS: stupid.

cliché /klee-shay/ n. an overused phrase or idea.
▷ SYNONYMS: **platitude**, hackneyed phrase, commonplace, banality, truism, stock phrase; informal old chestnut.
■ **clichéd** adj.

click n. **1** a short, sharp sound. **2** an act of pressing a button on a computer mouse.
• v. **1** make a click. **2** press a computer mouse button. **3** informal become friendly. **4** informal become suddenly clear.
▷ SYNONYMS: **1 clack**, snick, snap, clink. **2 take to each other**, get along, be compatible, be like-minded, see eye to eye, be on the same wavelength; informal hit it off. **3 fall into place**, make sense, dawn on someone, register, get through, sink in.

client n. a person using the services of a professional person or organization.
▷ SYNONYMS: **customer**, buyer, purchaser, shopper, patient, patron; Brit. informal punter.

clientele /klee-on-**tel**/ n. clients or customers.

cliff n. a steep rock face on the coast.
▷ SYNONYMS: **precipice**, rock face, crag, bluff, ridge, escarpment, scar, scarp.
□ **cliffhanger** a story or event that is exciting because its outcome is

uncertain.

climate n. 1 the general weather conditions in an area over a long period. 2 a trend or general attitude.
▷ SYNONYMS: *the political climate of the 1970s:* **atmosphere**, mood, trend, spirit, ethos, attitude, feeling, ambience, environment.
■ **climatic** adj.

climax n. 1 the most intense, exciting, or important point. 2 an orgasm.
▷ SYNONYMS: **peak**, pinnacle, height, high point, top, zenith, culmination.
– ANTONYMS: anticlimax, nadir.
• v. reach a climax.
■ **climactic** adj.

climb v. go or come up to a higher position.
▷ SYNONYMS: 1 **ascend**, mount, scale, scramble up, clamber up, shin up, conquer. 2 **rise**, ascend, go up, gain height, soar, rocket. 3 *the road climbs steeply:* **slope upwards**, rise, go uphill, incline.
– ANTONYMS: descend.
• n. 1 an act of climbing. 2 a route up a mountain etc.
■ **climber** n.

clime n. literary a region in terms of its climate.

clinch v. settle conclusively.
▷ SYNONYMS: 1 *he clinched the deal:* **secure**, settle, conclude, close, confirm, seal, finalize, wrap up; informal sew up. 2 *these findings clinched the matter:* **settle**, decide, determine, resolve.
• n. 1 a tight hold in a fight. 2 an embrace.

cling v. (**clinging**, **clung**) (**cling to/on to**) 1 hold on tightly to. 2 stick to or depend on.
▷ SYNONYMS: **stick**, adhere, hold.
■ **clingy** adj.

clinic n. a place where medical treatment or advice is given.

clinical adj. 1 of the treatment of patients. 2 efficient and unemotional.
▷ SYNONYMS: 1 **detached**, impersonal, dispassionate, indifferent, uninvolved, distant, remote, aloof, cold. 2 **plain**, stark, austere, spartan, bleak, bare, functional, basic, institutional.
– ANTONYMS: emotional.
■ **clinically** adv.

clink n. a sharp ringing sound.
• v. make a clink.

clinker n. the stony remains of burnt coal.

clip n. 1 a device for holding objects together or in place. 2 an act of

cutting. 3 an excerpt of a film or broadcast. 4 informal a sharp blow.
▷ SYNONYMS: 1 **fastener**, clasp, hasp, catch, hook, buckle, lock. 2 **extract**, excerpt, snippet, fragment, trailer.
• v. (**clipping**, **clipped**) 1 fasten with a clip. 2 cut with shears or scissors. 3 hit sharply.
▷ SYNONYMS: 1 **fasten**, attach, fix, join, pin, staple, tack. 2 **trim**, prune, cut, snip, crop, shear, lop. 3 **hit**, strike, graze, glance off, scrape.

clipper n. 1 (**clippers**) a tool for clipping. 2 hist. a fast sailing ship.

clipping n. 1 a piece clipped off. 2 a newspaper cutting.

clique /cleek/ n. a small group who tend to exclude non-members.
▷ SYNONYMS: **coterie**, set, circle, ring, in-crowd, group, gang, fraternity.

clitoris n. the small sensitive organ just in front of the vagina.

cloak n. a loose sleeveless outer garment.
▷ SYNONYMS: 1 **cape**, robe, wrap, mantle. 2 *a cloak of secrecy:* **cover**, veil, mantle, shroud, screen, blanket.
• v. cover or hide.
▷ SYNONYMS: **conceal**, hide, cover, veil, shroud, mask, obscure, cloud, envelop, swathe, surround.
□ **cloakroom** 1 a room where coats and bags may be left. 2 Brit. a room containing a toilet.

clobber informal n. Brit. clothing and personal belongings.
• v. hit hard.

cloche /klosh/ n. a cover for protecting tender plants.

clock n. an instrument that shows the time.
• v. (**clock in/out** or **on/off**) register your arrival at or departure from work.
□ **clockwise** moving in the direction of the hands of a clock. **clockwork** a mechanism with a spring and toothed gearwheels, used to drive a clock etc.

clod n. a lump of earth.

clog n. a shoe with a thick wooden sole.
• v. (**clogging**, **clogged**) block up.
▷ SYNONYMS: **block**, obstruct, congest, jam, choke, bung up, plug, stop up.

cloister n. a covered passage round a courtyard in a convent, monastery, etc.

cloistered adj. 1 having a cloister. 2 protected from the problems of daily life.

clone n. an animal or plant created from the cells of another, to which it is genetically identical.
• v. 1 create as a clone. 2 make an

identical copy of.

close adj. **1** near in space or time.
2 very similar. **3** very affectionate
or friendly. **4** careful and thorough.
5 humid or airless.
▷ SYNONYMS: **1 near**, nearby, adjacent,
neighbouring, adjoining, abutting,
at hand. **2 neck and neck**, even, nip
and tuck. **3** *a close resemblance*: **noticeable**, marked, distinct, pronounced,
strong. **4** *close friends*: **intimate**,
dear, bosom, close-knit, inseparable,
devoted, faithful, special, firm.
5 careful, detailed, thorough, minute,
searching, painstaking, meticulous,
rigorous. **6 humid**, muggy, stuffy,
airless, heavy, sticky, sultry, stifling.
– ANTONYMS: far, distant.
• v. **1** move so as to cover an opening.
2 bring two parts of something
together. **3** bring or come to an end.
4 (**close on/in on**) gradually surround
or get nearer to.
▷ SYNONYMS: **1** *she closed the door*:
shut, pull to, push to, slam. **2** *close
the hole*: **block**, stop up, plug, seal,
bung up, clog up, choke, obstruct.
3 end, conclude, finish, terminate,
wind up. **4 shut down**, close down,
cease production, cease trading, be
wound up, go out of business; informal
fold, go to the wall, go bust. **5 clinch**,
settle, secure, seal, confirm, pull off,
conclude, finalize; informal wrap up.
– ANTONYMS: open, start.
• adv. so as to be very near.
• n. **1** the end of a period or an
activity. **2** Brit. a street closed at one
end. **3** the grounds of a cathedral.
▷ SYNONYMS: **end**, finish, conclusion.
– ANTONYMS: beginning.
□ **closed-circuit television** a television
system in which signals are sent by
cable to a restricted set of monitors.
close-up a photo or film sequence
taken at close range.
■ **closely** adv. **closeness** n.
closet n. a cupboard or wardrobe.
▷ SYNONYMS: **cupboard**, wardrobe,
cabinet, locker.
• adj. secret.
▷ SYNONYMS: **secret**, covert, private,
surreptitious, clandestine.
• v. (**closeting**, **closeted**) shut yourself
in a private place, esp. to talk to
someone.
▷ SYNONYMS: **shut away**, sequester,
seclude, cloister, confine, isolate.
closure n. **1** the act of closing. **2** a
feeling that an upsetting experience
has been resolved.
clot n. **1** a thick mass of a semi-liquid

substance, esp. blood. **2** Brit. informal a
foolish person.
▷ SYNONYMS: **lump**, clump, mass, thrombosis; informal glob; Brit. informal gob.
• v. (**clotting**, **clotted**) form into clots.
▷ SYNONYMS: **coagulate**, set, congeal,
thicken, solidify.
□ **clotted cream** very thick cream.
cloth n. (pl. **cloths**) **1** fabric made from
a soft fibre such as cotton. **2** a piece of
cloth for a particular purpose. **3** (**the
cloth**) Christian clergy.
▷ SYNONYMS: **1 fabric**, material, textiles,
stuff. **2 rag**, wipe, duster, flannel;
Austral. washer.
clothe v. **1** provide with clothes. **2** (**be
clothed in**) be dressed in.
▷ SYNONYMS: **dress**, attire, robe, garb,
costume, swathe, deck out, turn out,
fit out, rig out; informal get up.
clothes pl. n. things worn to cover
the body.
▷ SYNONYMS: **clothing**, garments, attire,
garb, dress, wear, costume, wardrobe;
informal gear, togs; Brit. informal clobber;
N. Amer. informal threads; formal apparel.

> **WORD LINKS**
> **sartorial** relating to clothes
> **clothier**, **couturier**, **tailor** a person
> who sells or makes clothes

clothing n. clothes.
cloud n. **1** a mass of condensed watery
vapour floating in the sky. **2** a mass of
smoke, dust, etc. **3** a state or cause of
gloom or anxiety.
▷ SYNONYMS: *a cloud of exhaust smoke*:
mass, billow, mantle, blanket, pall.
• v. **1** become full of clouds. **2** make
less clear. **3** become sad or gloomy.
▷ SYNONYMS: *she allows emotion to cloud
the issue*: **confuse**, muddle, obscure.
□ **cloudburst** a sudden fall of heavy
rain.
cloudy adj. (**cloudier**, **cloudiest**)
1 having many clouds. **2** (of liquid)
not clear or transparent.
▷ SYNONYMS: **1 overcast**, dark, grey,
black, leaden, murky, gloomy, sunless,
starless. **2 murky**, muddy, milky,
dirty, turbid.
clout informal n. **1** a heavy blow.
2 influence.
• v. hit hard.
clove¹ n. **1** the dried bud of a tropical
tree, used as a spice. **2** any of the
segments making up a bulb of garlic.
clove² past of CLEAVE.
□ **clove hitch** a knot used to fasten a
rope round a pole etc.
cloven past part. of CLEAVE.
□ **cloven hoof** the divided hoof of

animals such as cattle, sheep, etc.

clover n. a flowering plant having leaves with three lobes.
□ **in clover** in ease and luxury.

clown n. an entertainer who does comical tricks.
▷ SYNONYMS: **1 joker**, comedian, comic, wag, wit, jester. **2 fool**, idiot, buffoon, dolt, ignoramus; informal moron, ass, numbskull, halfwit, fathead; Brit. informal prat, berk, twit, twerp.
• v. behave in a silly or playful way.
■ **clownish** adj.

cloying adj. excessively sweet or sentimental.

club n. **1** a group who meet for a particular activity. **2** an organization providing benefits for members. **3** a nightclub with dance music. **4** a heavy stick used as a weapon. **5** a stick with a thick head, used to hit the ball in golf. **6** (**clubs**) a suit of playing cards, represented by a black clover leaf.
▷ SYNONYMS: **1 society**, association, group, circle, league, guild, union, team, squad, side. **2 stick**, cudgel, truncheon, bludgeon, baton, mace, bat; N. Amer. blackjack, nightstick; Brit. informal cosh.
• v. (**clubbing**, **clubbed**) **1** (**club together**) combine with others to do something. **2** go to nightclubs. **3** beat with a club.
▷ SYNONYMS: **hit**, beat, strike, cudgel, bludgeon, batter; informal clout, clobber.
■ **clubber** n.

cluck v. (of a hen) make a short, low sound.
• n. a clucking sound.

clue n. a fact that helps solve a mystery or problem.
▷ SYNONYMS: **hint**, indication, sign, signal, pointer, lead, tip, evidence.

clueless adj. unable to understand or do something.

clump n. **1** a cluster of trees or plants. **2** a mass or lump.
▷ SYNONYMS: **1 cluster**, thicket, group, bunch. **2 lump**, clod, mass, chunk.
• v. **1** form into a clump. **2** tread heavily.
■ **clumpy** adj.

clumsy adj. (**clumsier**, **clumsiest**)
1 awkward in movement or performance. **2** difficult to use.
▷ SYNONYMS: **1 awkward**, uncoordinated, ungainly, graceless, lumbering, inelegant, inept, unskilful, accident-prone, all fingers and thumbs; informal cack-handed, ham-fisted,

butterfingered; N. Amer. informal klutzy. **2 unwieldy**, cumbersome, bulky, awkward.
– ANTONYMS: graceful.
■ **clumsily** adv. **clumsiness** n.

clung past & past part. of **CLING**.

cluster n. a small close group of similar things.
▷ SYNONYMS: **bunch**, clump, mass, knot, group, clutch, huddle, crowd.
• v. form a cluster.
▷ SYNONYMS: **congregate**, gather, collect, group, assemble, huddle, crowd.

clutch v. hold tightly.
▷ SYNONYMS: **grip**, grasp, clasp, cling to, hang on to, clench, hold, grab, snatch.
• n. **1** a tight hold. **2** a mechanism in a vehicle for connecting the engine with the axle and wheels. **3** a group of eggs laid at one time. **4** a brood of chicks.

clutter v. fill with an untidy assortment of things.
▷ SYNONYMS: **litter**, mess up, be strewn, be scattered, cover, bury.
• n. things lying about untidily.
▷ SYNONYMS: **disorder**, chaos, mess, disarray, untidiness, confusion, litter, rubbish, junk.

cm abbrev. centimetres.

Co. abbrev. **1** company. **2** county.

c/o abbrev. care of.

co- prefix joint; jointly.

coach n. **1** Brit. a long-distance bus. **2** a sports instructor or trainer. **3** a private tutor. **4** a railway carriage. **5** a horse-drawn carriage.
▷ SYNONYMS: **1 bus**; dated omnibus, chara-banc. **2 instructor**, trainer, teacher, tutor, mentor, guru. **3** a railway coach: **carriage**, wagon; N. Amer. car.
• v. train or teach as a coach.
▷ SYNONYMS: **instruct**, teach, tutor, school, educate, drill, train.

coagulate /koh-ag-yoo-layt/ v. (of a liquid) become semi-solid or solid.
▷ SYNONYMS: **congeal**, clot, thicken, solidify, harden, set, dry.
■ **coagulant** n. **coagulation** n.

coal n. a black rock burnt as fuel.
□ **coalfield** a large area rich in underground coal. **coal tar** a thick black liquid made from coal.

coalesce v. form into a mass or whole.

coalition n. a temporary alliance, esp. one enabling political parties to form a government.
▷ SYNONYMS: **alliance**, union, partner-ship, bloc, federation, league, associ-ation, confederation, consortium, syndicate, amalgamation, merger.

coarse adj. **1** rough in texture.

2 consisting of large particles. **3** rude or vulgar.
▷ SYNONYMS: **1 rough**, scratchy, prickly, wiry, harsh. **2** *coarse manners:* **uncouth**, oafish, loutish, boorish, rude, impolite, ill-mannered, vulgar, common, rough. **3** *a coarse remark:* **vulgar**, crude, rude, off colour, lewd, smutty, indelicate.
– ANTONYMS: soft, refined, polite.
□ **coarse fish** Brit. any freshwater fish other than salmon and trout.
■ **coarsen** v.

coast n. land next to or near the sea.
▷ SYNONYMS: **shore**, coastline, seashore, seaboard, shoreline, seaside; literary strand.
• v. move easily without using power.
▷ SYNONYMS: **freewheel**, cruise, taxi, drift, glide, sail.
□ **coastguard** an organization or person that keeps watch over coastal waters. **coastline** the land along a coast.
■ **coastal** adj.

> **WORD LINKS**
> **littoral** relating to a coast or seashore

coaster n. a small mat for a glass.
coat n. **1** a long outer garment with sleeves. **2** an animal's covering of fur or hair. **3** a covering layer.
▷ SYNONYMS: **1 fur**, hair, wool, fleece, hide, pelt, skin. **2 layer**, covering, coating, skin, film, deposit.
• v. cover with a layer.
▷ SYNONYMS: **cover**, surface, plate, spread, daub, smear, plaster, cake.
□ **coat of arms** a design on a shield as the emblem of a family or institution.
coating n. a covering layer.
coax v. **1** persuade gently. **2** manipulate carefully.
▷ SYNONYMS: **persuade**, wheedle, cajole, get round, inveigle, manoeuvre; informal sweet-talk, soft-soap, twist someone's arm.
coaxial /koh-ak-si-uhl/ adj. (of a cable) having two wires, one wrapped around the other but separated by insulation.
cob n. **1** the central part of an ear of maize. **2** Brit. a round loaf. **3** a hazelnut.
cobalt n. a silvery-white metallic element.
cobble n. a small round stone used to surface roads.
• v. (**cobble together**) roughly assemble from available parts.
■ **cobbled** adj.
cobbler n. a person whose job is

mending shoes.
cobra n. a poisonous snake native to Africa and Asia.
cobweb n. a spider's web.
cocaine n. a drug used as an illegal stimulant.
coccyx /kok-siks/ n. the bone at the base of the spine.
cochineal /koch-i-neel/ n. red food colouring.
cock n. **1** a male chicken or game bird. **2** a firing lever in a gun.
• v. **1** tilt or bend. **2** set a gun ready for firing. **3** (**cock up**) Brit. informal do badly; ruin.
□ **cock-a-hoop** very pleased.
cockade n. a rosette worn on a hat as a badge.
cockatoo n. a crested parrot.
cockerel n. a young domestic cock.
cockeyed adj. informal **1** crooked. **2** impractical.
cockle n. an edible shellfish.
cockney n. (pl. **cockneys**) **1** a person from the East End of London. **2** the dialect or accent used in this area.
cockpit n. **1** a compartment for the pilot in an aircraft. **2** the driver's compartment in a racing car.
cockroach n. a beetle-like insect.
cocksure adj. arrogantly confident.
cocktail n. **1** a mixed alcoholic drink. **2** a mixture.
cocky adj. (**cockier**, **cockiest**) too self-confident.
▷ SYNONYMS: **arrogant**, conceited, overconfident, swollen-headed, self-important, full of yourself, egotistical, presumptuous, boastful; informal too big for your boots.
– ANTONYMS: modest.
■ **cockily** adv. **cockiness** n.
cocoa n. a drink made from powdered cacao seeds, mixed with hot milk.
coconut n. the large brown seed of a tropical palm, with edible white flesh.
cocoon n. a silky case protecting a chrysalis.
• v. surround or cover in a protective way.
cod n. (pl. **cod**) a large edible sea fish.
coda n. the final part of a musical composition.
coddle v. treat in an overprotective way.
code n. **1** a system of words, figures, or symbols used to represent others, esp. for secrecy. **2** a sequence of numbers dialled to connect a phone line with another exchange. **3** a set of laws or rules. **4** instructions for a computer

program.
▷ SYNONYMS: **1 cipher. 2 convention**, etiquette, protocol, ethic. **3 laws**, rules, regulations, constitution, system.
• v. convert into a code.
codeine n. a painkilling drug.
codex n. (pl. **codices** /koh-di-seez/ or **codexes**) an ancient manuscript in book form.
codicil n. an addition or alteration to a will.
codify v. (**codifying, codified**) organize laws or rules into a system.
co-education n. the education of pupils of both sexes together.
■ **co-educational** adj.
coefficient n. a quantity which is placed before another which it multiplies (e.g. 4 in $4x2$).
coelacanth /seel-uh-kanth/ n. a large sea fish.
coeliac disease /seel-i-ak/ (US **celiac**) n. a disease in which the small intestine fails to digest and absorb food.
coerce v. force into doing something.
▷ SYNONYMS: **pressure**, press, push, constrain, force, compel, oblige, browbeat, bully, threaten, intimidate, dragoon, twist someone's arm; informal railroad, steamroller, lean on.
■ **coercion** n. **coercive** adj.
coeval adj. contemporary.
coexist v. exist together, esp. harmoniously.
■ **coexistence** n.
C. of E. abbrev. Church of England.
coffee n. a hot drink made from the seeds of a tropical shrub.
coffer n. **1** a small chest for holding valuables. **2** (**coffers**) financial resources.
coffin n. a box in which a dead body is buried or cremated.
cog n. a wheel or bar with projections on its edge, which engage with projections on another wheel or bar.
cogent adj. logical and convincing.
▷ SYNONYMS: **convincing**, persuasive, compelling, strong, forceful, powerful, potent, effective, sound, telling, coherent, clear, lucid, logical, well argued.
■ **cogency** n. **cogently** adv.
cogitate v. think deeply.
■ **cogitation** n.
cognac /kon-yak/ n. French brandy.
cognition n. the gaining of knowledge through thought and the senses.

■ **cognitive** adj.
cognizance (or **-isance**) n. knowledge or awareness.
■ **cognizant** adj.
cognoscenti /kon-yuh-**shen**-ti/ pl. n. people well informed about a particular subject.
cohabit v. live together and have a sexual relationship without being married.
■ **cohabitation** n.
cohere v. hold firmly together; form a whole.
coherent adj. **1** logical and consistent. **2** articulate.
▷ SYNONYMS: **logical**, reasoned, rational, sound, cogent, consistent, clear, lucid, articulate, intelligible.
− ANTONYMS: muddled.
■ **coherence** n. **coherently** adv.
cohesion n. the state of being coherent.
■ **cohesive** adj.
cohort n. **1** a large group of people. **2** a tenth part of an ancient Roman legion.
coiffure /kwah-**fyoor**/ n. a hairstyle.
coil n. **1** a length of something wound in a spiral. **2** a contraceptive device placed in the womb.
• v. form or arrange into a coil.
▷ SYNONYMS: **wind**, loop, twist, curl, spiral, twine, wrap.
coin n. a flat metal disc used as money.
• v. **1** invent a new word. **2** make coins.
▷ SYNONYMS: **invent**, create, make up, conceive, originate, think up, dream up.

> **WORD LINKS**
> **numismatic** relating to coins

coinage n. **1** coins of a particular type. **2** a currency. **3** a newly invented word.
coincide v. **1** happen at the same time or place. **2** be the same or similar.
▷ SYNONYMS: **1** occur **simultaneously**, happen together, co-occur, coexist. **2** tally, correspond, agree, accord, match up, be compatible, dovetail, mesh; informal square.
− ANTONYMS: differ.
coincidence n. **1** a remarkable instance of things happening together by chance. **2** the fact of things being the same or similar.
▷ SYNONYMS: **accident**, chance, providence, happenstance, fate, luck, fortune, fluke.
coincidental adj. resulting from a coincidence.
▷ SYNONYMS: **accidental**, chance, fluky,

random, fortuitous, unintentional, unplanned.

■ **coincidentally** adv.

coir /**koy**-uh/ n. coconut fibre.

coitus n. sexual intercourse.

■ **coital** adj.

coke n. **1** a solid fuel made by heating coal in the absence of air. **2** informal cocaine.

col n. the lowest point between two peaks of a mountain ridge.

colander n. a bowl with holes in it, used for draining food.

cold adj. **1** at a low temperature. **2** not feeling or showing emotion. **3** without preparation.

▷ SYNONYMS: **1** chilly, chill, cool, freezing, icy, wintry, frosty, raw, bitter; informal nippy; Brit. informal parky. **2** unfriendly, inhospitable, unwelcoming, cool, frigid, frosty, distant, formal, stiff.

– ANTONYMS: hot, warm.

• n. **1** cold weather or surroundings. **2** an infection causing a streaming nose and sneezing.

□ **cold-blooded 1** (of reptiles and fish) having a body temperature varying with that of the environment. **2** heartless and cruel. **cold sore** an inflamed blister near the mouth. **cold turkey** informal the unpleasant effects caused by the abrupt withdrawal of an addictive drug. **cold war** the state of hostility between the Soviet Union and its allies and Western nations after the Second World War.

■ **coldly** adv. **coldness** n.

coleslaw n. a salad of shredded raw cabbage and carrots in mayonnaise.

coley n. an edible sea fish.

colic n. severe abdominal pain.

■ **colicky** adj.

collaborate v. work together on an activity.

▷ SYNONYMS: **1** cooperate, join forces, work together, combine, pool resources, club together. **2** fraternize, conspire, collude, cooperate, consort.

■ **collaboration** n. **collaborative** adj.

collaborator n. a person who collaborates.

▷ SYNONYMS: **1** co-worker, partner, associate, colleague, confederate, assistant. **2** sympathizer, traitor, quisling, fifth columnist.

collage /**kol**-lah*zh*/ n. a form of art in which various materials are arranged and stuck to a backing.

collagen n. a protein forming the main component of connective tissue.

collapse v. **1** fall down suddenly. **2** fail

and come to a sudden end.

▷ SYNONYMS: **1** cave in, fall in, subside, fall down, give way, crumple, crumble, disintegrate. **2** faint, pass out, black out, lose consciousness. **3** go to pieces, break down, be overcome; informal crack up. **4** fail, break down, fall through, fold, founder; informal flop, fizzle out.

• n. an instance of collapsing.

▷ SYNONYMS: **1** cave-in, disintegration. **2** breakdown, failure.

collapsible adj. able to be folded down.

collar n. **1** a band of material round the neck of a garment. **2** a band put round the neck of a dog or cat.

• v. informal seize or arrest.

collate v. collect and combine documents or information.

■ **collation** n.

collateral n. something promised if you cannot repay a loan.

• adj. additional but less important.

colleague n. a person that you work with.

▷ SYNONYMS: co-worker, fellow worker, workmate, teammate, associate, partner, collaborator, ally, confederate.

collect v. **1** bring or come together. **2** call for and take away. **3** buy or find items of a particular kind as a hobby. **4** (collected) calm.

▷ SYNONYMS: **1** gather, accumulate, assemble, amass, stockpile, pile up, heap up, store, hoard, save. **2** a crowd soon collected: gather, assemble, meet, muster, congregate, convene, converge. **3** fetch, pick up, go/come and get, call for, meet. **4** (collected) calm, cool, self-possessed, self-controlled, composed, poised, serene, tranquil, relaxed; informal laid-back.

– ANTONYMS: distribute, disperse.

■ **collectable** (or **collectible**) adj. & n. **collector** n.

collection n. **1** the action of collecting. **2** a number of things that have been collected.

▷ SYNONYMS: **1** hoard, pile, heap, stock, store, stockpile, accumulation, reserve, supply, bank, pool, fund; informal stash. **2** group, crowd, body, gathering, knot, cluster. **3** anthology, selection, compendium, compilation, miscellany, treasury.

collective adj. **1** done by or relating to all the members of a group. **2** taken as a whole.

▷ SYNONYMS: common, shared, joint, combined, mutual, communal,

pooled, united, allied, cooperative, collaborative.
– ANTONYMS: individual.
□ **collective noun** a noun that refers to a group of people or things (e.g. *staff*, *herd*).

college n. an establishment providing higher education or specialized training.
■ **collegiate** adj.

collide v. hit accidentally when moving.
▷ SYNONYMS: **crash**, hit, strike, run into, bump into.

collie n. a breed of sheepdog with long hair.

colliery n. (pl. **collieries**) a coal mine.

collision n. an instance of colliding.
▷ SYNONYMS: **crash**, accident, smash; N. Amer. **wreck**; informal pile-up; Brit. informal **shunt**, prang.

colloquial adj. (of language) used in ordinary conversation.
▷ SYNONYMS: **informal**, conversational, everyday, familiar, popular, casual, idiomatic, slangy, vernacular.
– ANTONYMS: formal.
■ **colloquialism** n. **colloquially** adv.

collude v. cooperate secretly for a dishonest or underhand purpose.
■ **collusion** n.

cologne /kuh-**lohn**/ n. a light perfume.

colon n. **1** a punctuation mark (:). **2** the main part of the large intestine.
■ **colonic** adj.

colonel /**ker**-nuhl/ n. the army rank above lieutenant colonel.

colonial adj. of a colony or colonialism.

colonialism n. the practice of gaining control over other countries and occupying them with settlers.
■ **colonialist** n. & adj.

colonize (or **-ise**) v. **1** establish a colony in. **2** take over for your own use.
▷ SYNONYMS: **settle in**, people, populate, occupy, take over, invade.
■ **colonist** n. **colonization** n.

colonnade n. a row of columns supporting a roof.

colony n. (pl. **colonies**) **1** a country under the control of another and occupied by settlers from there. **2** a group of one nationality or race living in a foreign place. **3** a community of animals or plants of one kind.
▷ SYNONYMS: **territory**, dependency, protectorate, satellite, settlement, outpost, province.

color etc. US = **COLOUR** etc.

coloration (or **colouration**) n. natural colouring.

coloratura n. elaborate ornamentation of a vocal melody, e.g. in opera.

colossal adj. very large.
▷ SYNONYMS: **huge**, massive, enormous, gigantic, giant, mammoth, vast, immense, monumental, mountainous; informal monster, whopping, humongous; Brit. informal ginormous.
– ANTONYMS: tiny.
■ **colossally** adv.

colossus n. (pl. **colossi**) a very large or important person or thing.

colostomy n. (pl. **colostomies**) an operation in which the colon is shortened and the cut end diverted to an opening in the abdominal wall.

colour (US **color**) n. **1** the appearance that an object has, resulting from the way it reflects or gives out light. **2** one of the parts into which light can be separated. **3** the natural shade of the skin.
▷ SYNONYMS: **1 hue**, shade, tint, tone, coloration. **2 paint**, pigment, colourant, dye, stain.
• v. **1** give a colour to. **2** blush. **3** influence or affect.
▷ SYNONYMS: **1 tint**, dye, stain, tinge. **2 influence**, affect, taint, warp, skew, distort.
□ **colour-blind** unable to distinguish between certain colours.

> **WORD LINKS**
> **chromatic** relating to colour

colourant (US **colorant**) n. a dye.

coloured (US **colored**) adj. **1** having a colour or colours. **2** offens. not having white skin.

colourful (US **colorful**) adj. **1** full of colours. **2** lively and exciting.
▷ SYNONYMS: **1 bright**, vivid, vibrant, brilliant, radiant, gaudy, garish, multicoloured, psychedelic; informal jazzy. **2** *a colourful account*: **vivid**, graphic, lively, animated, dramatic, fascinating, interesting, stimulating, scintillating, evocative.
– ANTONYMS: drab, dull.
■ **colourfully** adv.

colouring (US **coloring**) n. **1** visual appearance in terms of colour. **2** a substance used to colour something.

colourless (US **colorless**) adj. **1** without colour. **2** dull.

colt n. a young male horse.

column n. **1** an upright pillar. **2** a long line of people or vehicles. **3** a vertical division of a page. **4** a regular article in a newspaper or magazine.

▷ SYNONYMS: **1 pillar**, post, support, upright, pier, pile. **2 article**, piece, feature. **3 line**, file, queue, procession, convoy; informal crocodile.

columnist n. a journalist who writes a column in a newspaper or magazine.

coma n. deep and prolonged unconsciousness.

comatose adj. in a coma.

comb n. **1** an object with a row of narrow teeth for tidying the hair. **2** a chicken's fleshy crest.
• v. **1** tidy the hair with a comb. **2** search thoroughly.

▷ SYNONYMS: **1 groom**, brush, untangle, smooth, straighten, neaten, tidy, arrange. **2 search**, scour, explore, sweep.

combat n. fighting, esp. between armed forces.

▷ SYNONYMS: **battle**, fighting, action, hostilities, conflict, war, warfare.
• v. (**combating, combated**) take action against.

▷ SYNONYMS: **fight**, battle, tackle, attack, counter, resist.
■ **combatant** n.

combative adj. ready or eager to fight or argue.

▷ SYNONYMS: **aggressive**, pugnacious, antagonistic, quarrelsome, argumentative, hostile, truculent, belligerent; informal spoiling for a fight.
− ANTONYMS: conciliatory.

combe (or **coomb**) /koom/ n. Brit. a short valley.

combination n. **1** something made up of distinct elements. **2** the act of combining things.

▷ SYNONYMS: **mixture**, mix, blend, fusion, amalgamation, amalgam, merger, marriage, synthesis.
□ **combination lock** a lock opened using a specific sequence of letters or numbers.

combine v. join or mix together.

▷ SYNONYMS: **1 mix**, blend, fuse, amalgamate, integrate, merge, marry. **2 unite**, collaborate, join forces, get together, team up.
• n. a group acting together for a commercial purpose.
□ **combine harvester** a farming machine that reaps and threshes in one operation.

combustible adj. able to catch fire.

combustion n. **1** burning. **2** rapid chemical combination with oxygen, involving the production of heat.

come v. (**coming, came**; past part. **come**) **1** move towards or into a place.

2 arrive at. **3** happen. **4** achieve a specified position.

▷ SYNONYMS: **1** come and listen: **approach**, advance, draw close/closer, draw near/nearer. **2** they came last night: **arrive**, get here/there, make it, appear, turn up, materialize; informal show up, roll up. **3** they came to a stream: **reach**, arrive at, get to, come across, run across, happen on, chance on, come upon, stumble on, end up at; informal wind up at. **4** she comes from Belgium: **be from**, be a native of, hail from, live in, reside in. **5 happen**, occur, take place, come about, fall, crop up.
− ANTONYMS: go, leave.
□ **come about** happen. **come across 1** give a particular impression. **2** find by chance. **comeback 1** a return to fame or popularity. **2** a quick reply. **come by** manage to get. **comedown** informal a loss of status. **come into** inherit. **come off** succeed. **come out** (of a fact) become known. **come round 1** Brit. recover consciousness. **2** be persuaded. **come to** recover consciousness. **come up** occur. **comeuppance** informal deserved punishment.

comedian n. (fem. **comedienne**) an entertainer whose act is intended to make people laugh.

▷ SYNONYMS: **1 comic**, comedienne, funny man/woman, humorist, stand-up; N. Amer. tummler. **2 joker**, wit, wag, comic, clown; informal laugh, hoot.

comedy n. (pl. **comedies**) an amusing film, play, or other entertainment.

▷ SYNONYMS: **humour**, fun, hilarity, funny side, laughs, jokes.
− ANTONYMS: tragedy.

comely adj. old use attractive.

comestibles pl. n. food.

comet n. a mass of ice and dust with a long tail, moving around the solar system.

comfort n. **1** a state of ease and relaxation. **2** consolation for grief or anxiety. **3** (**comforts**) things giving comfort.

▷ SYNONYMS: **1 ease**, repose, relaxation, well-being, prosperity, luxury. **2 consolation**, condolence, sympathy, commiseration, support, reassurance, cheer.
− ANTONYMS: discomfort.
• v. make less unhappy.

▷ SYNONYMS: **console**, support, reassure, soothe, calm, cheer, hearten.
− ANTONYMS: distress, depress.
■ **comforter** n.

comfortable adj. **1** giving or enjoying comfort. **2** free from financial worry.
▷ SYNONYMS: **1 affluent**, prosperous, well-to-do, pleasant, luxurious, opulent. **2 cosy**, snug, warm, pleasant, agreeable, homely; informal comfy. **3 loose**, loose-fitting, roomy, casual; informal comfy.
■ **comfortably** adv.

comfy adj. (**comfier**, **comfiest**) informal comfortable.

comic adj. **1** causing laughter. **2** of comedy.
▷ SYNONYMS: **humorous**, funny, amusing, hilarious, comical, zany, witty, droll.
– ANTONYMS: serious.
• n. **1** a comedian. **2** a children's magazine with comic strips.
▷ SYNONYMS: **comedian**, comedienne, funny man/woman, humorist, wit, joker.
□ **comic strip** a sequence of drawings telling an amusing story.

comical adj. amusing, especially in a ludicrous way.
▷ SYNONYMS: **1 funny**, humorous, droll, witty, comic, amusing, entertaining; informal wacky. **2 absurd**, silly, ridiculous, laughable, ludicrous, preposterous, foolish; informal crazy.
– ANTONYMS: serious.
■ **comically** adv.

comma n. a punctuation mark (,).

command v. **1** give an order. **2** be in charge of a military unit. **3** be in a position to receive.
▷ SYNONYMS: **1 order**, tell, direct, instruct, call on, require, charge, enjoin, ordain; old use bid. **2 be in charge of**, be in command of, head, lead, control, direct, manage, supervise, oversee; informal head up.
• n. **1** an order. **2** authority. **3** a group of officers in control of a unit or operation. **4** the ability to use or control something.
▷ SYNONYMS: **1 order**, instruction, direction, directive, injunction, decree, edict, dictate, mandate, commandment, fiat. **2** *he had 160 men under his command*: **authority**, control, charge, power, direction, dominion, guidance, leadership, rule, government, management, supervision, jurisdiction. **3 knowledge**, mastery, grasp, comprehension, understanding.

commandant /kom-muhn-dant/ n. an officer in charge of a force or institution.

commandeer v. officially take possession of.

commander n. **1** a person in command. **2** the navy rank below captain.
▷ SYNONYMS: **leader**, head, chief, overseer, director, controller; informal boss, skipper, head honcho; Brit. informal gaffer, guv'nor.

commanding adj. **1** indicating or expressing authority. **2** having or giving superior strength.
▷ SYNONYMS: **dominant**, controlling, superior, powerful, advantageous, favourable.

commandment n. a divine rule.

commando n. (pl. **commandos**) a soldier trained for carrying out raids.

commemorate v. honour the memory of.
▷ SYNONYMS: **celebrate**, remember, recognize, acknowledge, observe, mark, pay tribute to, pay homage to, honour, salute.
■ **commemoration** n. **commemorative** adj.

commence v. begin.
▷ SYNONYMS: **begin**, inaugurate, start, initiate, launch into, open, get the ball rolling, get going, get under way, get off the ground, set about, embark on; informal kick off.
– ANTONYMS: conclude.
■ **commencement** n.

commend v. **1** praise publicly. **2** recommend.
▷ SYNONYMS: **1 praise**, compliment, congratulate, applaud, salute, honour, sing the praises of, pay tribute to. **2 recommend**, endorse, vouch for, speak for, support, back.
– ANTONYMS: criticize.
■ **commendation** n.

commendable adj. deserving praise.
▷ SYNONYMS: **admirable**, praiseworthy, creditable, laudable, meritorious, exemplary, honourable, respectable.
– ANTONYMS: reprehensible.
■ **commendably** adv.

commensurable adj. measurable by the same standard.

commensurate adj. corresponding or in proportion.

comment n. a remark expressing an opinion or reaction.
▷ SYNONYMS: **1 remark**, observation, statement, pronouncement, judgement, reflection, opinion, view. **2 discussion**, debate, interest. **3 note**, annotation, commentary, footnote, gloss, explanation.
• v. express an opinion or reaction.
▷ SYNONYMS: **remark**, observe, say, state,

note, point out, mention, interject; formal opine.

commentary n. (pl. **commentaries**) **1** a broadcast report of an event as it happens. **2** a discussion of a situation. **3** a set of notes on a text.
▷ SYNONYMS: **1 narration**, description, report, review, voice-over. **2 explanation**, elucidation, interpretation, analysis, assessment, review, criticism, notes, comments.

commentate v. provide a commentary on an event.

commentator n. **1** a person who comments on events. **2** a person who provides commentary on a live event.
▷ SYNONYMS: **1 pundit**, critic, columnist, leader-writer, opinion-former, monitor, observer. **2 reporter**, newscaster, sportscaster.

commerce n. the activity of buying and selling.
▷ SYNONYMS: **trade**, trading, business, dealing, buying and selling, traffic, trafficking.

commercial adj. **1** concerned with commerce. **2** intended to make a profit.
▷ SYNONYMS: **1 trade**, trading, business, mercantile, sales. **2 profit-making**, materialistic, mercenary.
• n. a television or radio advertisement.
■ **commercially** adv.

commercialize (or **-ise**) v. manage in a way intended to make a profit.
■ **commercialization** n.

commiserate v. express sympathy or pity.
■ **commiseration** n.

commission n. **1** an instruction, command, or duty. **2** a formal request for something to be designed or made. **3** a group given official authority to do something. **4** payment to an agent for selling something. **5** the position of officer in the armed forces.
▷ SYNONYMS: **1 percentage**, share, premium, fee, bonus, royalty; informal cut, rake-off, slice; Brit. informal whack. **2 contract**, engagement, assignment, booking, job. **3 committee**, board, council, panel, body.
• v. **1** order the production of. **2** bring into working order. **3** (**commissioned**) having the rank of military officer.
▷ SYNONYMS: **1 engage**, contract, book, employ, hire, recruit, take on, retain, appoint. **2 order**, place an order for, pay for.

□ **out of commission** not in working order.

commissionaire n. Brit. a uniformed door attendant at a hotel, theatre, etc.

commissioner n. **1** a member of a commission. **2** a representative of the highest authority in an area.

commit v. (**committing**, **committed**) **1** do something wrong or illegal. **2** allocate to a particular use. **3** (**commit yourself**) promise to do something. **4** put in a safe place. **5** send to prison or a psychiatric hospital.
▷ SYNONYMS: **1 carry out**, do, perpetrate, engage in, execute, accomplish, be responsible for; informal pull off. **2 entrust**, consign, assign, deliver, hand over. **3 consign**, send, confine.

commitment n. **1** dedication to a cause, activity, etc. **2** a promise. **3** an obligation.
▷ SYNONYMS: **1 responsibility**, obligation, duty, liability, engagement, tie. **2 dedication**, devotion, allegiance, loyalty. **3 promise**, vow, pledge, undertaking.

USAGE Two *ms*, but only one *t* in the middle: *commitment*.

committal n. the sending of someone to prison or a psychiatric hospital, or for trial.

committed adj. dedicated to a cause, job, etc.
▷ SYNONYMS: **devoted**, dedicated, staunch, loyal, faithful, devout, firm, steadfast, unwavering, passionate, ardent, sworn.
– ANTONYMS: apathetic.

committee n. a group of people appointed for a particular function by a larger group.

USAGE Double *m*, double *t*: *committee*.

commode n. a seat with a concealed chamber pot.

commodious adj. roomy and comfortable.

commodity n. (pl. **commodities**) **1** an article that can be bought and sold. **2** something valuable.

commodore n. **1** the naval rank above captain. **2** the president of a yacht club.

common adj. **1** occurring, found, or done often; not rare. **2** ordinary. **3** shared. **4** Brit. not well mannered or tasteful.
▷ SYNONYMS: **1** a common occurrence: **frequent**, regular, everyday, normal, usual, ordinary, familiar,

standard, commonplace, average, unexceptional, typical. **2** *a common belief*: **widespread**, general, universal, popular, mainstream, prevalent, rife, established, conventional, accepted. **3 collective**, communal, shared, community, public, popular, general. **4 uncouth**, vulgar, coarse, rough, uncivilized, unsophisticated, unrefined, inferior, plebeian; informal plebby.

– ANTONYMS: unusual, rare.

• n. a piece of open land for public use. □ **common denominator** a number that can be divided exactly by all the numbers below the line in a set of fractions. **common law** English law developed from custom and judges' decisions. **the Common Market** the European Union. **common room** a room in a school or college for students or staff to use outside teaching hours. **commonwealth 1** (**the Commonwealth**) an association of the UK and independent states formerly under British rule. **2** an independent state.

■ **commonly** adv.

commoner n. an ordinary person as opposed to an aristocrat.

commonplace adj. ordinary.

• n. a cliché.

common sense n. good sense in practical matters.

▷ SYNONYMS: **good sense**, native wit, level-headedness, prudence, wisdom; informal horse sense, nous; N. Amer. informal smarts.

– ANTONYMS: stupidity.

commotion n. noisy confusion or disturbance.

▷ SYNONYMS: **disturbance**, uproar, disorder, confusion, rumpus, fuss, furore, hue and cry, stir, storm, chaos, havoc, pandemonium.

communal adj. shared or done by a group.

▷ SYNONYMS: **1** *a communal kitchen*: **shared**, joint, common, public, general. **2** *they farm on a communal basis*: **collective**, cooperative, community.

– ANTONYMS: private, individual.

■ **communally** adv.

commune n. a group of people living together and sharing possessions and responsibilities.

• v. communicate mentally or spiritually.

communicable adj. (of a disease) able to be passed on to others.

communicant n. a person who receives Holy Communion.

communicate v. **1** share or exchange information. **2** pass on or convey an emotion, disease, etc.

▷ SYNONYMS: **1 liaise**, be in touch, be in contact, have dealings, talk, speak, interface. **2 convey**, tell, relay, transmit, impart, pass on, report, recount, relate. **3 transmit**, spread, transfer, pass on.

■ **communicator** n.

communication n. **1** the act of communicating. **2** a letter or message. **3** (**communications**) means of travelling or sending information.

▷ SYNONYMS: **1 contact**, dealings, relations, connection, correspondence, dialogue, conversation. **2 message**, statement, announcement, report, dispatch, bulletin, disclosure, communiqué, letter, correspondence.

communicative adj. willing to talk or give information.

▷ SYNONYMS: **forthcoming**, expansive, expressive, unreserved, vocal, outgoing, frank, open, candid, talkative, chatty.

communion n. **1** the sharing of thoughts and feelings. **2** (or **Holy Communion**) the Christian service at which bread and wine are made holy and shared.

communiqué /kuh-**myoo**-ni-kay/ n. an official announcement.

communism n. **1** a political system in which all property is owned by the community. **2** a system of this kind based on Marxism.

■ **communist** n. & adj.

community n. (pl. **communities**) **1** a group of people living together in one place or sharing a religion, race, etc. **2** (**the community**) the people of an area as a group.

▷ SYNONYMS: **society**, population, populace, people, public, residents, inhabitants, citizens.

commute v. **1** travel regularly between your home and place of work. **2** reduce a judicial sentence to a less severe one.

■ **commuter** n.

compact adj. **1** closely and neatly packed together. **2** having all the necessary parts fitted into a small space.

▷ SYNONYMS: **1 dense**, tightly packed, compressed, thick, tight, firm, solid. **2 neat**, small, handy, portable. **3 concise**, succinct, condensed, brief, pithy, to the point, short and sweet;

informal **snappy**.
- ANTONYMS: loose, bulky, lengthy.
- v. compress.
▷ SYNONYMS: **compress**, condense, pack down, tamp down, flatten.
- n. **1** a small flat case for face powder. **2** a formal agreement.
▷ SYNONYMS: **treaty**, pact, accord, agreement, contract, bargain, deal, settlement.
□ **compact disc** a small disc on which digital information is stored.

companion n. **1** a person that you spend time or travel with. **2** a thing intended to complement another.
▷ SYNONYMS: **comrade**, fellow, partner, associate, escort, compatriot, confederate, friend; informal pal, chum, crony; Brit. informal **mate**; N. Amer. informal buddy.
□ **companionway** a staircase from a ship's deck down to a lower deck.
■ **companionship** n.

companionable adj. friendly.

company n. (pl. **companies**) **1** a commercial business. **2** the fact of being with others. **3** a division of an infantry battalion. **4** a group of actors, singers, or dancers.
▷ SYNONYMS: **1 firm**, business, corporation, establishment, agency, office, house, institution, concern, enterprise, consortium, syndicate; informal outfit. **2 companionship**, fellowship, society, presence. **3 unit**, section, detachment, corps, squad, platoon.

> **WORD LINKS**
> **corporate** relating to a commercial business

comparable adj. able to be compared; similar.
▷ SYNONYMS: **1 similar**, close, near, approximate, equivalent, proportionate. **2** *nobody is comparable with him*: **equal to**, as good as, in the same league as, on a level with, a match for.
- ANTONYMS: incomparable.
■ **comparably** adv.

comparative adj. **1** involving or measured by comparison. **2** (of an adjective or adverb) expressing a higher degree of a quality (e.g. *braver*).
■ **comparatively** adv.

> **USAGE** compar*ative*, not *-itive*.

compare v. **1** assess the similarity between. **2** be similar to.
▷ SYNONYMS: **1 contrast**, balance, set against, weigh up. **2 liken**, equate, class with, bracket with. **3 be as good**

as, be comparable to, bear comparison with, be the equal of, match up to, be on a par with, be in the same league as, come close to, rival.

comparison n. **1** an instance of comparing things or people. **2** the quality of being similar.
▷ SYNONYMS: **resemblance**, likeness, similarity, correspondence.

compartment n. a separate section of a structure or container.
▷ SYNONYMS: **bay**, locker, recess, alcove, cell, cubicle, pod, pigeonhole, cubbyhole.

compass n. **1** a device showing the direction of magnetic north. **2** a hinged instrument for drawing circles. **3** range or scope.
▷ SYNONYMS: **scope**, range, extent, reach, span, breadth, ambit, limits, parameters, bounds.

compassion n. pity and concern.
▷ SYNONYMS: **sympathy**, empathy, understanding, fellow feeling, pity, care, concern, sensitivity, kindness.
- ANTONYMS: indifference, cruelty.

compassionate adj. showing pity and concern for others.
▷ SYNONYMS: **sympathetic**, understanding, pitying, caring, sensitive, warm, loving, kind.
- ANTONYMS: unsympathetic, uncaring.

compatible adj. **1** able to exist or be used together. **2** (of two people) well suited to each other. **3** consistent.
▷ SYNONYMS: **well matched**, well suited, like-minded, in tune, in harmony, in keeping, consistent, consonant; informal on the same wavelength.
■ **compatibility** n.

compatriot n. a fellow citizen of a country.

compel v. (**compelling**, **compelled**) force to do something.
▷ SYNONYMS: **force**, pressure, coerce, dragoon, press, push, oblige, require, make; informal lean on, railroad, put the screws on.

compelling adj. attracting much attention or admiration.
▷ SYNONYMS: **1 enthralling**, captivating, gripping, riveting, spellbinding, mesmerizing, absorbing.
2 convincing, persuasive, cogent, irresistible, powerful, strong.
- ANTONYMS: boring, weak.

compendious adj. giving much information in a concise way.

compendium n. (pl. **compendiums** or **compendia**) **1** a collection of facts on a subject. **2** a collection of similar items.

compensate v. **1** give a payment to reduce the bad effect of loss, injury, etc. **2** (**compensate for**) reduce something bad by having an opposite effect.
▷ SYNONYMS: **1 recompense**, repay, pay back, reimburse, remunerate, indemnify. **2** (**compensate for**) **balance out**, counterbalance, counteract, offset, make up for, cancel out.

compensation n. **1** something given to compensate for loss, suffering, or injury. **2** something that makes up for an undesirable situation.
▷ SYNONYMS: **recompense**, repayment, reimbursement, remuneration, redress, amends, damages; N. Amer. informal **comp**.

compère /kom-pair/ Brit. n. a person who introduces the acts in a variety show.
• v. act as a compère for.

compete v. try to gain or win something by defeating others.
▷ SYNONYMS: **1 take part**, participate, be a contestant, play, enter, go in for. **2** they had to compete with other firms: **contend**, vie, battle, jockey, go head to head, pit yourself against, challenge, take on.

competence n. the ability to do something well.
▷ SYNONYMS: **ability**, capability, proficiency, accomplishment, expertise, skill, prowess; informal know-how.

competent adj. **1** having the necessary skill or knowledge. **2** satisfactory.
▷ SYNONYMS: **1 able**, capable, proficient, adept, accomplished, skilful, skilled, expert. **2 satisfactory**, adequate, reasonable, acceptable, suitable, fit.
■ **competently** adv.

competition n. **1** the act of competing. **2** an event in which people compete. **3** the people that you are competing with.
▷ SYNONYMS: **1 contest**, tournament, championship, match, game, heat. **2 rivalry**, competitiveness, conflict; informal keeping up with the Joneses. **3 opposition**, rivals, other side, field, enemy.

competitive adj. **1** involving competition. **2** keen to be more successful than others.
▷ SYNONYMS: **1** a competitive player: **ambitious**, zealous, keen, combative, aggressive; informal go-ahead. **2** a highly competitive industry: **ruthless**, aggressive, fierce, cut-throat; informal

dog-eat-dog. **3** competitive prices: **reasonable**, moderate, keen, low, cheap, budget, bargain, rock-bottom, bargain-basement.
■ **competitively** adv. **competitiveness** n.

competitor n. a person or organization that competes.
▷ SYNONYMS: **1 contestant**, contender, challenger, participant, entrant, player. **2 rival**, challenger, opponent, competition, opposition.

compile v. produce a book, record, etc. by assembling material from other sources.
▷ SYNONYMS: **assemble**, put together, make up, collate, compose, organize, arrange, gather, collect.
■ **compilation** n. **compiler** n.

complacent adj. smugly self-satisfied.
▷ SYNONYMS: **smug**, self-satisfied, self-congratulatory, resting on your laurels, pleased with yourself.
■ **complacency** n. **complacently** adv.

complain v. **1** express dissatisfaction. **2** (**complain of**) state that you are suffering from a symptom.
▷ SYNONYMS: **protest**, grumble, whine, bleat, carp, cavil, grouse, make a fuss, object, find fault; informal whinge, gripe, moan, bitch.

complainant n. Law a plaintiff.

complaint n. **1** an act of complaining. **2** a minor illness.
▷ SYNONYMS: **1 protest**, objection, grievance, grouse, grumble, criticism; informal gripe, whinge. **2 disorder**, disease, illness, sickness, ailment, infection, condition, problem, upset, trouble.

complaisant adj. willing to please others.

complement n. **1** a thing that completes or improves something. **2** the full number required.
▷ SYNONYMS: **1 accompaniment**, companion, addition, supplement, accessory, finishing touch. **2 amount**, contingent, capacity, allowance, quota.
• v. add to in a way that improves.
▷ SYNONYMS: **accompany**, go with, round off, set off, suit, harmonize with, enhance, complete.

USAGE Don't confuse **complement** and **compliment**, which means 'politely congratulate or praise'.

complementary adj. combining so as to form a whole or to improve each other.
▷ SYNONYMS: **harmonious**, compatible, corresponding, matching, reciprocal.

◻ **complementary medicine** medical therapy that is not part of scientific medicine but may be used alongside it.

complete adj. **1** having all necessary parts. **2** finished. **3** to the greatest degree.
▷ SYNONYMS: **1 entire**, whole, full, total, uncut, unabridged, unexpurgated. **2 finished**, ended, concluded, completed; informal wrapped up, sewn up. **3 absolute**, utter, out-and-out, total, downright, prize, perfect, unqualified, unmitigated, sheer; N. Amer. full-bore.
– ANTONYMS: partial, unfinished.
• v. **1** make complete. **2** fill in a form.
▷ SYNONYMS: **1 finish**, end, conclude, finalize, wind up, clinch; informal wrap up. **2 finish off**, round off, top off, crown, cap, add the finishing touch.
■ **completion** n.

completely adv. totally; in every respect.
▷ SYNONYMS: **totally**, entirely, wholly, thoroughly, fully, utterly, absolutely, perfectly, downright.

complex adj. **1** consisting of many parts. **2** hard to understand.
▷ SYNONYMS: **1 compound**, composite, multiplex. **2 complicated**, involved, intricate, convoluted, elaborate, difficult; Brit. informal fiddly.
– ANTONYMS: simple.
• n. **1** a group of buildings. **2** an interlinked system. **3** a set of repressed feelings affecting behaviour.
▷ SYNONYMS: **1 network**, system, nexus, web. **2 obsession**, fixation, preoccupation, neurosis; informal hang-up, thing.
■ **complexity** n.

complexion n. **1** the condition of the skin of a person's face. **2** the general character of something.
▷ SYNONYMS: **1 skin**, skin colour/tone, colouring. **2 kind**, nature, character, colour, persuasion, outlook.

compliant adj. **1** meeting rules or standards. **2** excessively obedient.
■ **compliance** n.

complicate v. make more intricate or confusing.
▷ SYNONYMS: **obscure**, obfuscate, mix up, confuse, muddle.
– ANTONYMS: simplify.

complicated adj. involving many connected parts or confusing aspects.
▷ SYNONYMS: **complex**, involved, intricate, convoluted, elaborate, difficult, knotty, tortuous, labyrinthine, Byzan-

tine; Brit. informal fiddly.
– ANTONYMS: simple, straightforward.

complication n. **1** a difficulty. **2** a new medical condition which makes treatment of an existing one more complicated.
▷ SYNONYMS: **difficulty**, problem, obstacle, hurdle, stumbling block, snag, catch, hitch; Brit. spanner in the works; informal headache.

complicity n. involvement in wrongdoing.
■ **complicit** adj.

compliment n. an expression of praise or admiration.
▷ SYNONYMS: **tribute**, accolade, commendation, pat on the back; (**compliments**) praise, acclaim, admiration, flattery, congratulations.
– ANTONYMS: criticism, insult.
• v. politely congratulate or praise.
▷ SYNONYMS: **praise**, pay tribute to, flatter, commend, acclaim, applaud, salute, congratulate.
– ANTONYMS: criticize.

USAGE Don't confuse **compliment** with **complement**, which means 'add to in a way that improves'.

complimentary adj. **1** praising or approving. **2** free of charge.
▷ SYNONYMS: **1 flattering**, appreciative, congratulatory, admiring, approving, favourable, glowing. **2 free**, gratis; informal on the house.
– ANTONYMS: critical.

comply v. (**complying, complied**) **1** do what is requested or ordered. **2** meet specified standards.
▷ SYNONYMS: **obey**, observe, abide by, adhere to, conform to, follow, respect, go along with.
– ANTONYMS: disobey.

component n. a part of a whole.
▷ SYNONYMS: **part**, piece, bit, element, constituent, ingredient, unit, module.

comport v. (**comport yourself**) behave in a particular way.

compose v. **1** make up a whole. **2** create music or poetry. **3** arrange in an orderly or artistic way. **4** (**composed**) calm and controlled.
▷ SYNONYMS: **1 make up**, constitute, form, comprise. **2 write**, devise, make up, think up, produce, invent, pen, author. **3 organize**, arrange, construct, set out. **4** (**composed**) **calm**, collected, cool, self-possessed, poised, serene, relaxed, at ease, unruffled, unperturbed; informal unflappable, together, laid-back.
■ **composer** n.

composite adj. made up of various parts.

composition n. **1** the way in which something is made up. **2** a work of music, literature, or art. **3** a thing composed of various elements.
▷ SYNONYMS: **1 make-up**, constitution, configuration, structure, formation, anatomy, organization. **2 work**, creation, opus, piece. **3 essay**, paper, study, piece of writing; N. Amer. theme. **4 arrangement**, layout, proportions, balance, symmetry.

compositor n. a typesetter.

compost n. decayed organic material used as a fertilizer.

composure n. calmness.
▷ SYNONYMS: **self-control**, self-possession, calm, equanimity, equilibrium, serenity, tranquillity, poise, presence of mind, sangfroid, placidness, impassivity; informal cool.

compote n. fruit cooked in syrup.

compound n. **1** a thing made up of two or more elements. **2** a large open area enclosed by a fence.
▷ SYNONYMS: **amalgam**, blend, mixture, mix, alloy.
• adj. made up of several parts.
▷ SYNONYMS: **composite**, complex, multiple.
– ANTONYMS: simple.
• v. **1** make up a whole. **2** make worse.
▷ SYNONYMS: **1 mix**, combine, blend. **2 aggravate**, exacerbate, worsen, add to, augment, intensify, heighten, increase.

comprehend v. understand.
▷ SYNONYMS: **understand**, grasp, see, take in, follow, make sense of, fathom; informal work out, figure out, get.

comprehensible adj. able to be understood.
▷ SYNONYMS: **intelligible**, understandable, lucid, coherent, accessible, self-explanatory, clear, plain, straightforward.

comprehension n. the ability to understand.
▷ SYNONYMS: **understanding**, grasp, mastery, conception, knowledge, awareness.
– ANTONYMS: ignorance.

comprehensive adj. including all or nearly all.
▷ SYNONYMS: **inclusive**, all-inclusive, complete, full, thorough, extensive, all-embracing, blanket, exhaustive, detailed, sweeping, wholesale, broad, wide-ranging.
– ANTONYMS: limited.
• n. Brit. a secondary school in which pupils of all abilities are educated together.
■ **comprehensively** adv.

compress v. **1** force into a smaller space. **2** squeeze together.
▷ SYNONYMS: **1 squeeze**, press, squash, crush, compact. **2 shorten**, abridge, condense, abbreviate, contract, telescope, summarize, precis.
– ANTONYMS: expand, pad out.
• n. a pad to reduce inflammation or stop bleeding.
■ **compression** n. **compressor** n.

comprise v. **1** be made up of. **2** make up a whole.
▷ SYNONYMS: **1** the country comprises twenty states: **consist of**, be made up of, be composed of, contain. **2** this breed comprises half the herd: **make up**, constitute, form, account for.

compromise n. an agreement reached by each side making concessions.
▷ SYNONYMS: **agreement**, understanding, settlement, terms, deal, trade-off, bargain, middle ground.
• v. **1** make concessions so as to settle a dispute. **2** cause embarrassment or risk by unthinking behaviour.
▷ SYNONYMS: **1 meet each other halfway**, come to an understanding, make a deal, make concessions, find a happy medium, strike a balance. **2 undermine**, weaken, damage, harm, jeopardize, prejudice.

compulsion n. **1** pressure to do something. **2** an irresistible urge.
▷ SYNONYMS: **1** he is under no compulsion to go: **obligation**, pressure, coercion. **2 urge**, impulse, need, desire, drive, obsession, fixation, addiction.

compulsive adj. **1** resulting from or acting on an irresistible urge. **2** irresistibly exciting.
▷ SYNONYMS: **1** a compulsive desire: **irresistible**, uncontrollable, compelling, overwhelming. **2** compulsive eating: **obsessive**, obsessional, addictive, uncontrollable. **3 inveterate**, chronic, incorrigible, incurable, hopeless, persistent, habitual; informal pathological. **4 fascinating**, compelling, gripping, riveting, engrossing, enthralling, captivating.

compulsory adj. required by law or a rule.
▷ SYNONYMS: **obligatory**, mandatory, required, requisite, necessary, binding, enforced, prescribed.
– ANTONYMS: optional.

compunction a feeling of guilt or shame.

compute v. calculate a figure or amount.
▷ SYNONYMS: **calculate**, work out, reckon, determine, evaluate, add up, total.
■ **computation** n. **computational** adj.

computer n. an electronic device for storing and processing information.

computerize (or **-ise**) v. convert to a system controlled by or stored on computer.

comrade n. a fellow member or soldier.
▷ SYNONYMS: **companion**, friend, colleague, associate, partner, ally; Brit. informal **mate**; N. Amer. informal **buddy**.
■ **comradeship** n.

con informal v. (**conning**, **conned**) deceive or trick.
• n. a deception.
□ **pros and cons** see PRO.

concatenation n. a connected series.

concave adj. having an outline or surface that curves inwards.

conceal v. prevent from being seen or known.
▷ SYNONYMS: **1** *clouds concealed the sun:* **hide**, screen, cover, obscure, block out, blot out, mask. **2** *he concealed his true feelings:* **keep secret**, hide, disguise, mask, veil, bottle up; informal keep a lid on.
– ANTONYMS: reveal, confess.
■ **concealment** n.

concede v. **1** admit to be true. **2** give up an advantage or right. **3** admit defeat in a contest.
▷ SYNONYMS: **1 admit**, acknowledge, accept, allow, grant, recognize, own, confess, agree. **2 surrender**, yield, give up, relinquish, hand over.
– ANTONYMS: deny.

conceit n. **1** excessive pride in yourself. **2** a complicated metaphor.
▷ SYNONYMS: **vanity**, pride, arrogance, egotism, self-importance, narcissism, self-admiration.
– ANTONYMS: humility.

conceited adj. excessively proud of yourself.
▷ SYNONYMS: **vain**, proud, arrogant, egotistic, self-important, narcissistic, full of yourself, swollen-headed, boastful, cocky, self-satisfied, smug; informal big-headed, stuck-up.

conceivable adj. able to be imagined or understood.
▷ SYNONYMS: **imaginable**, possible, plausible, credible, believable, feasible.
■ **conceivably** adv.

conceive v. **1** become pregnant. **2** imagine.

▷ SYNONYMS: **1 think up**, think of, dream up, devise, formulate, design, create, develop; informal cook up. **2 imagine**, envisage, visualize, picture.

concentrate v. **1** focus all your attention. **2** gather together in one place. **3** (**concentrated**) (of a solution) strong.
▷ SYNONYMS: **1 focus on**, pay attention to, give your attention to, put your mind to, keep your mind on, be absorbed in, be engrossed in, be immersed in. **2 collect**, gather, congregate, converge, mass, rally.
• n. a concentrated substance.

concentration n. **1** the ability to concentrate. **2** a great deal of things gathered in one place. **3** the amount of a substance in a solution or mixture.
▷ SYNONYMS: **close attention**, attentiveness, application, single-mindedness, absorption.
– ANTONYMS: inattention.
□ **concentration camp** a camp for holding political prisoners.

concentric adj. (of circles) having the same centre.

concept n. an abstract idea.
▷ SYNONYMS: **idea**, notion, conception, abstraction, theory, hypothesis.
■ **conceptual** adj. **conceptualize** (or **-ise**) v.

conception n. **1** the act of conceiving. **2** a concept.
▷ SYNONYMS: **1 pregnancy**, fertilization, impregnation, insemination. **2 inception**, genesis, origination, creation, invention, beginning, origin. **3 plan**, idea, notion, scheme, project, proposal, intention, aim.

concern v. **1** be about. **2** affect or involve. **3** make anxious.
▷ SYNONYMS: **1 be about**, deal with, cover, relate to, pertain to. **2 affect**, involve, be relevant to, apply to, have a bearing on, impact on. **3 worry**, disturb, trouble, bother, perturb, unsettle.
• n. **1** anxiety. **2** a matter of interest or importance. **3** a business.
▷ SYNONYMS: **1 anxiety**, worry, disquiet, apprehensiveness, unease, misgiving. **2 care**, consideration, solicitude, sympathy. **3 responsibility**, business, affair, duty, job; informal bailiwick; Brit. informal lookout. **4** *issues of concern to women:* **interest**, importance, relevance, significance. **5 firm**, business, company, enterprise, operation, corporation; informal outfit.
– ANTONYMS: indifference.

concerned adj. anxious.
▷ SYNONYMS: **1 worried**, anxious, upset, troubled, uneasy, bothered. **2 interested**, involved, affected, implicated.
– ANTONYMS: unconcerned.

concerning prep. about.
▷ SYNONYMS: **about**, regarding, relating to, with reference to, referring to, with regard to, as regards, touching, in connection with, re, apropos.

concert n. a public musical performance.

concerted adj. done jointly or in a determined way.
▷ SYNONYMS: **1** *a concerted effort:* **strenuous**, vigorous, intensive, all-out, intense, concentrated. **2** *concerted action:* **joint**, united, collaborative, collective, combined, cooperative.

concertina n. a small musical instrument with bellows and buttons.
• v. (**concertinaing**, **concertinaed**) compress in folds like those of a concertina.

concerto /kuhn-**cher**-toh/ n. (pl. **concertos** or **concerti**) a musical composition for an orchestra and a solo instrument.

concession n. **1** a thing given up to settle a dispute. **2** a reduction in price. **3** a right to use land for a specific purpose.
▷ SYNONYMS: **1 compromise**, accommodation, trade-off, sop. **2 reduction**, cut, discount, deduction, rebate; informal break. **3 right**, privilege, licence, permit, franchise, warrant.

conch n. a shellfish with a spiral shell.

conciliate v. try to bring the sides in a dispute together.
■ **conciliation** n. **conciliatory** adj.

concise adj. giving information clearly and in few words.
▷ SYNONYMS: **succinct**, pithy, brief, abridged, condensed, abbreviated, compact, potted.
– ANTONYMS: lengthy.
■ **concisely** adv. **concision** n.

conclave n. a private meeting.

conclude v. **1** end. **2** reach an opinion by reasoning. **3** formally settle an agreement.
▷ SYNONYMS: **1 finish**, end, come/bring to an end, draw to a close, close, wind up, terminate, stop, cease; informal wrap up. **2 settle**, clinch, finalize, tie up; informal sew up. **3 deduce**, infer, gather, judge, decide, surmise; N. Amer. figure.
– ANTONYMS: begin.

conclusion n. **1** an ending. **2** an opinion reached by reasoning.
▷ SYNONYMS: **1 end**, ending, finish, close. **2 settlement**, clinching, completion, arrangement. **3 deduction**, inference, interpretation, judgement, verdict.
– ANTONYMS: beginning.

conclusive adj. decisive or convincing.
▷ SYNONYMS: **incontrovertible**, undeniable, indisputable, irrefutable, unquestionable, convincing, certain, decisive, definitive, definite, positive, categorical, unequivocal.
– ANTONYMS: unconvincing, inconclusive.
■ **conclusively** adv.

concoct v. **1** prepare a dish from ingredients. **2** invent a story or plan.
▷ SYNONYMS: **make up**, dream up, fabricate, invent, devise, formulate, hatch, brew; informal cook up.
■ **concoction** n.

concomitant adj. accompanying or associated with something.

concord n. agreement; harmony.

concordance n. an index of the important words in a written work.

concourse n. a large open area in a public building.

concrete n. a building material made from gravel, sand, cement, and water.
• adj. **1** existing in a physical form; not abstract. **2** definite.
▷ SYNONYMS: **1 solid**, material, real, physical, tangible. **2 definite**, specific, firm, positive, conclusive, definitive.
– ANTONYMS: abstract, imaginary.
• v. cover with concrete.

concubine n. (in some societies) a woman who lives with a man but has lower status than his wife or wives.

concur v. (**concurring**, **concurred**) agree.
▷ SYNONYMS: **agree**, be in agreement, accord, be in sympathy, see eye to eye, be of the same mind, be of the same opinion.
– ANTONYMS: disagree.

concurrent adj. existing or happening at the same time.
■ **concurrence** n. **concurrently** adv.

concussion n. temporary unconsciousness or confusion caused by a blow on the head.
■ **concussed** adj.

condemn v. **1** express strong disapproval of. **2** sentence to a punishment. **3** force to endure. **4** declare unfit for use.
▷ SYNONYMS: **1 censure**, criticize, denounce, deplore, decry; informal slam; Brit. informal slate, slag off. **2** *his illness condemned him to a lonely*

childhood: **doom**, destine, damn, sentence.
− ANTONYMS: praise.
■ **condemnation** n.

condensation n. water from humid air collecting as droplets on a cold surface.

condense v. **1** make more concentrated. **2** change from a gas or vapour to a liquid. **3** express in fewer words.
▷ SYNONYMS: **abridge**, compress, summarize, shorten, cut, abbreviate, edit.
− ANTONYMS: expand.

condescend v. **1** behave as if you are better than others. **2** do something you regard as being beneath your dignity.
▷ SYNONYMS: **1 patronize**, talk down to, look down your nose at, look down on. **2** *he condescended to see us:* **deign**, stoop, lower yourself, demean yourself, consent.
■ **condescension** n.

condescending adj. feeling or showing that you think you are better than other people.
▷ SYNONYMS: **patronizing**, supercilious, superior, disdainful, lofty, haughty; informal snooty, stuck-up; Brit. informal toffee-nosed.

condiment n. a seasoning for food.

condition n. **1** state as regards appearance, fitness, etc.
2 (**conditions**) circumstances. **3** a situation that must exist before something else is possible.
▷ SYNONYMS: **1 state**, shape, order, fitness, health, form; Brit. informal nick, fettle. **2 circumstances**, surroundings, environment, situation, state of affairs, position.
3 disorder, problem, complaint, illness, disease, ailment, malady.
4 stipulation, constraint, prerequisite, precondition, requirement, term, proviso.
• v. **1** influence. **2** bring into a desired condition. **3** train or accustom.
▷ SYNONYMS: **train**, teach, educate, guide, accustom, adapt, habituate, mould.

conditional adj. depending on one or more conditions being met.
▷ SYNONYMS: **qualified**, dependent, contingent, with reservations, limited, provisional, provisory.
■ **conditionally** adv.

conditioner n. a substance for improving the condition of hair or fabric.

condolence n. an expression of sympathy.

condom n. a rubber sheath worn on the penis during sex to prevent conception or infection.

condominium n. US a building containing a number of individually owned flats.

condone v. accept or forgive an offence or wrong.
▷ SYNONYMS: **disregard**, accept, allow, let pass, turn a blind eye to, overlook, forget, forgive, pardon, excuse.
− ANTONYMS: condemn.

condor n. a large South American vulture.

conducive adj. (**conducive to**) contributing or helping towards.
▷ SYNONYMS: **favourable**, beneficial, advantageous, opportune, encouraging, promising, convenient, good, helpful, instrumental.
− ANTONYMS: unfavourable.

conduct n. **1** behaviour.
2 management or direction.
▷ SYNONYMS: **1 behaviour**, actions, deeds, doings, exploits. **2 management**, running, direction, control, supervision, regulation, administration, organization, coordination, handling.
• v. **1** organize and carry out. **2** direct the performance of an orchestra etc.
3 guide or lead. **4** transmit heat or electricity.
▷ SYNONYMS: **1 manage**, direct, run, administer, organize, coordinate, orchestrate, handle, carry out/on.
2 escort, guide, lead, usher, steer.
3 transmit, convey, carry, channel.

conduction n. the transmission of heat or electricity directly through a substance.
■ **conductive** adj. **conductivity** n.

conductor n. **1** a person who conducts an orchestra or choir. **2** a material or device that conducts heat or electricity. **3** a person who collects fares on a bus.

conduit n. **1** a channel for liquid. **2** a tube protecting electric wiring.

cone n. **1** an object which tapers from a circular base to a point. **2** the dry fruit of a conifer.

coney n. (pl. **coneys**) a rabbit.

confection n. **1** an elaborate sweet dish. **2** an elaborately constructed thing.

confectionery n. sweets and chocolates.
■ **confectioner** n.

confederacy n. (pl. **confederacies**) an

alliance of states.

confederate adj. joined by an agreement or treaty.
• n. an accomplice.

confederation n. an alliance of states or groups.

confer v. (**conferring**, **conferred**) **1** grant a title, degree, etc. **2** have discussions.
▷ SYNONYMS: **1 bestow**, present, grant, award, honour with. **2 consult**, talk, speak, converse, have a chat, deliberate, compare notes.

conference n. a formal meeting for discussion.
▷ SYNONYMS: **meeting**, congress, convention, seminar, discussion, council, forum, summit.

confess v. **1** admit to a crime etc. **2** acknowledge reluctantly. **3** formally declare your sins to a priest.
▷ SYNONYMS: **1 admit**, acknowledge, reveal, disclose, divulge, own up, plead guilty, accept the blame; informal come clean. **2** *I confess I don't know:* **acknowledge**, admit, concede, grant, allow, own.
– ANTONYMS: deny.
■ confession n.

confessional n. an enclosed stall in a church for hearing confessions.

confessor n. a priest who hears confessions.

confetti n. bits of coloured paper thrown over a bride and groom.

confidant n. (fem. **confidante**) a person that you confide in.

confide v. tell someone about a secret or private matter.
▷ SYNONYMS: **reveal**, disclose, divulge, impart, declare, vouchsafe, tell, confess.

confidence n. **1** faith, certainty, or trust. **2** the belief that you are able to do things well.
▷ SYNONYMS: **1 trust**, belief, faith, credence. **2 self-assurance**, self-confidence, self-possession, assertiveness, self-belief, conviction.
– ANTONYMS: distrust, doubt.
□ **confidence trick** an act of cheating someone by gaining their trust.

confident adj. feeling confidence.
▷ SYNONYMS: **1 sure**, certain, positive, convinced, in no doubt, satisfied. **2 self-assured**, assured, self-confident, positive, assertive, self-possessed.
■ confidently adv.

confidential adj. to be kept secret.
▷ SYNONYMS: **private**, personal, intimate, quiet, secret, sensitive, classified, restricted; informal hush-hush.
■ confidentiality n. confidentially adv.

configuration n. a particular arrangement of parts.
■ configure v.

confine v. **1** (**confine to**) keep within certain limits. **2** (**be confined to**) be unable to leave somewhere due to illness etc.
▷ SYNONYMS: **1 enclose**, incarcerate, imprison, intern, hold captive, cage, lock up, coop up. **2 restrict**, limit.
• n. (**confines**) boundaries.

confinement n. **1** the state of being confined. **2** dated the time of childbirth.

confirm v. **1** establish the truth of. **2** make definite. **3** (**confirmed**) firmly established in a habit etc. **4** (**be confirmed**) undergo the rite of confirmation.
▷ SYNONYMS: **1 corroborate**, verify, prove, substantiate, justify, vindicate, bear out. **2 affirm**, reaffirm, assert, assure someone, repeat. **3 ratify**, approve, endorse, validate, sanction, authorize.
– ANTONYMS: contradict, deny.

confirmation n. **1** the act of confirming. **2** the rite at which a baptized person is admitted as a full member of the Christian Church.

confiscate v. officially seize property.
▷ SYNONYMS: **impound**, seize, commandeer, requisition, appropriate, expropriate, take, sequestrate.
■ confiscation n.

conflagration n. a large fire.

conflate v. combine into one.

conflict n. **1** a serious disagreement. **2** an armed struggle. **3** a difference of opinions etc.
▷ SYNONYMS: **1 dispute**, quarrel, squabble, disagreement, clash, feud, discord, friction, strife, antagonism, hostility. **2 war**, campaign, fighting, engagement, struggle, hostilities, warfare, combat. **3** *a conflict between work and home life:* **clash**, incompatibility, friction, mismatch, variance, contradiction.
– ANTONYMS: agreement, peace, harmony.
• v. be different or in opposition.
▷ SYNONYMS: **clash**, be incompatible, be at odds, differ, diverge, disagree.

conflicting adj. incompatible or contradictory.
▷ SYNONYMS: **contradictory**, incompatible, inconsistent, irreconcilable, contrary, opposite, opposing, different.

confluence n. the junction of two rivers.

conform v. comply with rules, standards, or conventions.
▷ SYNONYMS: **1** *visitors have to conform to our rules:* **comply with**, abide by, obey, observe, follow, keep to, stick to, adhere to, uphold, heed, accept, go along with. **2 fit in**, behave, toe the line, obey the rules; informal play by the rules.
– ANTONYMS: flout, rebel.
■ conformity n.

conformist n. a person who behaves in a conventional way.

confound v. **1** surprise or bewilder. **2** prove wrong.
▷ SYNONYMS: **baffle**, bewilder, mystify, bemuse, perplex, puzzle, confuse, dumbfound, throw; informal flabbergast, flummox.

confront v. **1** meet an opponent face to face. **2** deal with or force to face a problem.
▷ SYNONYMS: **1 challenge**, square up to, face, come face to face with, meet, accost, stand up to, tackle. **2 face**, bedevil, beset, plague, bother, trouble, threaten. **3** *they must confront these issues:* **tackle**, address, face up to, get to grips with, grapple with, deal with, sort out.
– ANTONYMS: evade.

confrontation n. a situation of angry disagreement or opposition.
▷ SYNONYMS: **conflict**, clash, fight, battle, encounter, head-to-head; informal set-to, run-in, dust-up, showdown.

confuse v. **1** make bewildered. **2** make less easy to understand. **3** mistake one for another.
▷ SYNONYMS: **1 bewilder**, baffle, mystify, bemuse, perplex, puzzle, nonplus; informal flummox, faze. **2** *the authors have confused the issue:* **complicate**, muddle, blur, obscure, cloud. **3** *some confuse strokes with heart attacks:* **mix up**, muddle up, mistake for.
– ANTONYMS: enlighten, simplify.

confused adj. **1** unable to think clearly or understand. **2** lacking order and so difficult to understand or make sense of.
▷ SYNONYMS: **1 puzzled**, bemused, bewildered, perplexed, baffled, mystified, disorientated, muddled, befuddled; informal flummoxed. **2 disorderly**, disorganized, untidy, jumbled, mixed up, chaotic, topsy-turvy, tangled; informal higgledy-piggledy; Brit. informal shambolic.
– ANTONYMS: clear, lucid.

confusion n. **1** uncertainty or lack of understanding. **2** a situation of panic or disorder.
▷ SYNONYMS: **1 bewilderment**, bafflement, perplexity, puzzlement, bemusement, mystification, befuddlement, disorientation, uncertainty. **2 disorder**, disarray, muddle, mess, chaos, mayhem, pandemonium, turmoil; informal shambles.
– ANTONYMS: clarity, order.

confute v. prove wrong.

conga n. a dance performed in single file.

congeal v. become semi-solid.
▷ SYNONYMS: **coagulate**, clot, thicken, cake, set, gel.

congenial adj. suited or pleasing to your tastes.
▷ SYNONYMS: **agreeable**, pleasant, friendly, amicable, amiable, nice.
– ANTONYMS: unfriendly, unpleasant.

congenital adj. present from birth.

conger eel n. a large sea eel.

congested adj. **1** very crowded. **2** abnormally full of blood. **3** blocked with mucus.
▷ SYNONYMS: **blocked**, clogged, choked, jammed, obstructed, crowded, overcrowded, overflowing, packed; informal snarled up, gridlocked.
– ANTONYMS: clear.
■ congestion n.

conglomerate n. **1** a corporation formed by a merger of separate firms. **2** something consisting of a number of distinct things.
■ conglomeration n.

congratulate v. express good wishes or praise at the happiness or success of.
▷ SYNONYMS: **compliment**, wish someone happiness, pay tribute to, pat on the back, take your hat off to, praise, applaud, salute, honour.
– ANTONYMS: criticize.
■ congratulatory adj.

congratulation n.
1 (congratulations) praise or good wishes on a special occasion. **2** the action of congratulating.
▷ SYNONYMS: **best wishes**, compliments, felicitations.

congregate v. gather in a crowd.
▷ SYNONYMS: **assemble**, gather, collect, come together, convene, rally, muster, meet, cluster, group.
– ANTONYMS: disperse.

congregation n. people gathered for religious worship.

congress n. **1** a formal meeting between delegates. **2** (Congress) a

congruent adj. **1** in agreement or harmony. **2** (of geometrical figures) identical in form.
■ **congruence** n.

conical adj. cone-shaped.

conifer n. an evergreen tree bearing cones.
■ **coniferous** adj.

conjecture n. & v. (make) a guess.

conjoin v. join.

conjugal adj. of marriage.

conjugate v. give the different forms of a verb.
■ **conjugation** n.

conjunction n. **1** a word used to connect words or clauses (e.g. *and*, *if*). **2** an instance of two or more events occurring together.

conjunctivitis n. inflammation of the membrane connecting the eyeball and eyelid.

conjure v. **1** cause to appear as if by magic. **2** call to the mind.
▷ SYNONYMS: **1 produce**, magic, summon. **2** *the picture that his words conjured up:* **bring to mind**, call to mind, evoke, summon up, suggest.

conjuror (or **conjurer**) n. a performer of seemingly magical tricks.

conk informal v. (**conk out**) (of a machine) break down.
●n. a nose.

conker n. Brit. the fruit of the horse chestnut tree.

connect v. **1** join or bring together. **2** (**be connected**) be related in some way.
▷ SYNONYMS: **1 attach**, join, fasten, fix, link, hook, secure, hitch, stick. **2 associate**, link, couple, identify, relate to.
– ANTONYMS: detach.
■ **connective** adj. **connector** n.

connection n. **1** a link or relationship. **2** (**connections**) influential friends or relatives. **3** a train, bus, etc. that arrives in time for passengers to catch another.
▷ SYNONYMS: **1 link**, relationship, relation, interconnection, inter-dependence, association, bond, tie, tie-in, correspondence. **2** *he has the right connections:* **contact**, friend, acquaintance, ally, colleague, associate, relation.

connive v. **1** (**connive at/in**) secretly allow something wrong. **2** conspire to do something.
▷ SYNONYMS: **1 ignore**, overlook, disregard, pass over, take no notice of, turn a blind eye to. **2 conspire**, collude, collaborate, plot, scheme.
■ **connivance** n.

conniving adj. devious or underhand.
▷ SYNONYMS: **scheming**, cunning, calculating, devious, wily, sly, artful, manipulative, Machiavellian, deceitful.

connoisseur /kon-nuh-**ser**/ n. an expert judge in matters of taste.

connotation n. an idea or feeling suggested by a word in addition to its main meaning.
▷ SYNONYMS: **overtone**, undertone, undercurrent, implication, nuance, hint, echo, association.

connote v. (of a word) suggest in addition to its main meaning.

conquer v. **1** take control of by military force. **2** overcome a problem.
▷ SYNONYMS: **1 defeat**, beat, vanquish, triumph over, overcome, overwhelm, overpower, overthrow, subdue, subju-gate. **2** *Peru was conquered by Spain:* **seize**, take, appropriate, capture, occupy, invade, annex, overrun. **3 overcome**, get the better of, control, master, deal with, cope with, rise above; informal lick.
■ **conqueror** n.

conquest n. **1** the action of conquering. **2** a conquered territory.
▷ SYNONYMS: **1 defeat**, overthrow, subju-gation. **2 seizure**, takeover, capture, occupation, invasion, annexation.

conscience n. a person's sense of right and wrong.
▷ SYNONYMS: **moral sense**, morals, sense of right and wrong, standards, values, principles, ethics, beliefs, scruples, qualms.

conscientious adj. careful and thorough in carrying out your work or duty.
▷ SYNONYMS: **diligent**, industrious, punctilious, painstaking, dedicated, careful, meticulous, thorough, attentive, hard-working, rigorous, scrupulous.
– ANTONYMS: casual.
□ **conscientious objector** a person who refuses to serve in the armed forces for moral reasons.

conscious adj. **1** awake and responsive. **2** aware. **3** intentional.
▷ SYNONYMS: **1 aware**, awake, respon-sive; informal with us. **2 deliberate**, purposeful, knowing, considered, calculated, wilful, premeditated.
– ANTONYMS: unaware, unconscious.
■ **consciously** adv. **consciousness** n.

conscript v. summon for compulsory military service.
• n. a conscripted person.
■ **conscription** n.

consecrate v. make or declare sacred.
■ **consecration** n.

consecutive adj. following in unbroken sequence.
▷ SYNONYMS: **successive**, succeeding, in succession, running, in a row, straight; informal on the trot.
■ **consecutively** adv.

consensual adj. involving consent.

consensus n. general agreement.
▷ SYNONYMS: **1 agreement**, unanimity, harmony, accord, unity, solidarity. **2** the consensus was that they should act: **general opinion**, common view.
– ANTONYMS: disagreement.

USAGE consensus, not -cen-.

consent n. permission or agreement.
▷ SYNONYMS: **agreement**, assent, acceptance, approval, permission, authorization, sanction; informal go-ahead, green light, OK.
– ANTONYMS: dissent.
• v. **1** give permission. **2** agree to do.
▷ SYNONYMS: **agree**, assent, submit, allow, sanction, approve, go along with.
– ANTONYMS: forbid, refuse.

consequence n. **1** a result or effect. **2** importance.
▷ SYNONYMS: **1 result**, upshot, outcome, effect, repercussion, ramification, product, end result. **2** the past is of no consequence: **importance**, import, significance, account, value, concern.
– ANTONYMS: cause.

consequent adj. resulting.
▷ SYNONYMS: **resulting**, resultant, ensuing, consequential, following, subsequent.
■ **consequential** adj.

consequently adv. as a result.
▷ SYNONYMS: **as a result**, as a consequence, so, thus, therefore, accordingly, hence, for this/that reason, because of this/that; formal ergo.

conservancy n. (pl. **conservancies**) an organization helping to preserve natural resources.

conservation n. **1** preservation of the natural environment. **2** preservation and repair of historical sites etc.
▷ SYNONYMS: **preservation**, protection, safe keeping, husbandry, upkeep, maintenance, repair, restoration.
■ **conservationist** n.

conservative adj. **1** opposed to change. **2** (in politics) favouring free enterprise and private ownership. **3** (**Conservative**) of the British Conservative Party. **4** (of an estimate) deliberately low.
▷ SYNONYMS: **1 right-wing**, reactionary, traditionalist, old-fashioned, dyed-in-the-wool, hidebound, unadventurous, set in your ways; informal stick-in-the-mud. **2 conventional**, sober, modest, sensible, restrained; informal square.
– ANTONYMS: socialist, radical.
• n. **1** a conservative person. **2** (**Conservative**) a member of the Conservative Party.
■ **conservatism** n. **conservatively** adv.

conservatory n. (pl. **conservatories**) Brit. a room with a glass roof and walls, attached to a house.

conserve v. protect from harm or overuse.
▷ SYNONYMS: **preserve**, protect, save, safeguard, keep, look after, sustain, husband.
– ANTONYMS: squander.
• n. jam.

consider v. **1** think carefully about. **2** believe or think. **3** take into account.
▷ SYNONYMS: **1 think about**, contemplate, reflect on, mull over, ponder, deliberate on, chew over, meditate on, ruminate on, evaluate, weigh up, appraise, take account of, bear in mind; informal size up. **2 deem**, think, believe, judge, rate, count, find, regard as, hold to be, reckon to be, view as, see as.

considerable adj. great in amount or importance.
▷ SYNONYMS: **sizeable**, substantial, appreciable, noticeable, marked, significant, great, large; informal tidy.
– ANTONYMS: paltry.

considerably adv. to a large extent.
▷ SYNONYMS: **greatly**, very much, a great deal, a lot, lots, significantly, substantially, appreciably, markedly, noticeably; informal plenty.

considerate adj. careful not to harm or inconvenience others.
▷ SYNONYMS: **attentive**, thoughtful, solicitous, kind, unselfish, caring, polite, sensitive.
■ **considerately** adv.

consideration n. **1** careful thought. **2** a fact taken into account when making a decision. **3** thoughtfulness. **4** a payment or reward.
▷ SYNONYMS: **1 thought**, deliberation, reflection, contemplation, examination, inspection, scrutiny, analysis,

discussion, attention. **2 factor**,
issue, matter, concern, aspect,
feature. **3 attentiveness**, concern,
care, thoughtfulness, solicitude,
understanding, respect, sensitivity.

considering prep. taking into
account.
▷ SYNONYMS: **bearing in mind**, taking
into consideration, taking into
account, in view of, in the light of.

consign v. **1** put aside or in an
unpleasant situation. **2** deliver.

consignment n. a batch of goods
sent.

consist v. (**consist of**) be composed of.
▷ SYNONYMS: **be composed of**, be made
up of, be formed of, comprise,
include, contain.

consistency n. (pl. **consistencies**)
1 being consistent. **2** the thickness of
a liquid.

consistent adj. **1** regular; unchanging.
2 in agreement.
▷ SYNONYMS: **1 constant**, regular,
uniform, steady, stable, even,
unchanging. **2** *her injuries were
consistent with a knife attack*: **compatible**, in tune, in line, corresponding
to, conforming to, consonant with.
– ANTONYMS: inconsistent, incompatible.
■ **consistently** adv.

consolation n. **1** comfort received
after a loss or disappointment. **2** a
source of such comfort.
▷ SYNONYMS: **comfort**, solace, sympathy,
pity, commiseration, relief, encouragement, reassurance.

console v. comfort in a time of grief
etc.
▷ SYNONYMS: **comfort**, sympathize with,
commiserate with, help, support,
cheer, hearten, encourage, reassure,
soothe.
– ANTONYMS: upset.
● n. **1** a panel containing a set of
controls. **2** a machine for playing
computerized video games.

consolidate v. **1** make stronger or
more secure. **2** combine.
▷ SYNONYMS: **1 strengthen**, secure,
stabilize, reinforce, fortify.
2 combine, unite, merge, integrate,
amalgamate, fuse, synthesize.
■ **consolidation** n.

consommé /kuhn-som-may/ n. a
clear soup.

consonant n. a letter of the alphabet
representing a sound in which
the breath is completely or partly
obstructed.
● adj. (**consonant with**) in agreement
with.

consort n. a wife or husband.
● v. (**consort with**) associate with.

consortium n. (pl. **consortia** or
consortiums) an association of several
companies.

conspicuous adj. **1** clearly visible.
2 attracting notice.
▷ SYNONYMS: **obvious**, evident, apparent,
visible, noticeable, clear, plain,
marked, patent, blatant.
– ANTONYMS: inconspicuous.
■ **conspicuously** adv.

conspiracy n. (pl. **conspiracies**)
a secret plan by a group to do
something unlawful.
▷ SYNONYMS: **plot**, scheme, intrigue,
plan, collusion.

conspire v. **1** jointly make secret
plans to commit a wrongful act. **2** (of
events) seem to be acting together to
cause something bad.
▷ SYNONYMS: **1 plot**, scheme, intrigue,
manoeuvre, plan. **2 combine**, unite,
join forces, work together.
■ **conspirator** n. **conspiratorial** adj.

constable n. Brit. a police officer of the
lowest rank.

constabulary n. (pl. **constabularies**) a
police force.

constant adj. **1** occurring
continuously. **2** unchanging.
3 faithful.
▷ SYNONYMS: **1** *constant noise*:
continuous, persistent, sustained,
ceaseless, unceasing, perpetual,
incessant, never-ending, eternal,
endless, non-stop. **2** *a constant
speed*: **consistent**, regular, steady,
uniform, even, invariable, unvarying,
unchanging. **3 faithful**, loyal,
devoted, true, fast, firm, unswerving.
– ANTONYMS: intermittent, variable,
fickle.
● n. a number or quantity that does
not change its value.
■ **constancy** n. **constantly** adv.

constellation n. a group of stars.

consternation n. anxiety or dismay.
▷ SYNONYMS: **dismay**, distress, disquiet,
discomposure, surprise, alarm, fear,
fright, shock.

constipation n. difficulty in
emptying the bowels.
■ **constipated** adj.

constituency n. (pl. **constituencies**)
an area or group of voters that elects
a representative to a law-making
body.

constituent adj. being a part of a
whole.
● n. **1** a voter in a constituency. **2** a
constituent part.

constitute v. **1** be a part of a whole. **2** be or be equivalent to.
▷ SYNONYMS: **1 comprise**, make up, form, account for. **2 amount to**, be tantamount to, be equivalent to, represent. **3 establish**, inaugurate, found, create, set up.

constitution n. **1** the principles by which a state is governed. **2** composition or formation. **3** a person's physical or mental state.
▷ SYNONYMS: **1 composition**, make-up, structure, construction, arrangement, configuration, formation, anatomy. **2 health**, condition, strength, stamina, build, physique.

constitutional adj. of or in accordance with a constitution.
• n. dated a walk taken for exercise.

constrain v. **1** force. **2** restrict.

constraint n. **1** a restriction. **2** strict control of your behaviour.
▷ SYNONYMS: **1 restriction**, limitation, curb, check, restraint, control. **2 inhibition**, uneasiness, embarrassment, self-consciousness, awkwardness.
– ANTONYMS: freedom, ease.

constrict v. **1** make or become narrower or tighter. **2** restrict.
▷ SYNONYMS: **narrow**, tighten, compress, contract, squeeze, strangle.
– ANTONYMS: expand, dilate.
■ **constriction** n. **constrictor** n.

construct v. build or put together.
▷ SYNONYMS: **1 build**, erect, put up, set up, assemble, fabricate. **2 formulate**, create, form, put together, devise, compose, work out, frame.
– ANTONYMS: demolish.
• n. an idea or theory containing various elements.
■ **constructor** n.

construction n. **1** the process of constructing. **2** a building or other structure. **3** an interpretation.
▷ SYNONYMS: **1 structure**, building, edifice, work. **2 interpretation**, explanation, analysis, reading, meaning; informal take.

constructive adj. useful or helpful.
▷ SYNONYMS: **useful**, helpful, productive, positive, practical, valuable, profitable, worthwhile.
■ **constructively** adv.

construe v. interpret in a specific way.

consul n. an official representative of a state in a foreign city.
■ **consular** adj.

consulate n. the place where a consul works.

consult v. seek information or advice from.
▷ SYNONYMS: **1 seek advice from**, ask, call on, turn to; informal pick someone's brains. **2 confer**, talk things over, communicate, deliberate, compare notes. **3 refer to**, look at, check.
■ **consultative** adj.

consultant n. a specialist consulted for professional advice.
▷ SYNONYMS: **adviser**, expert, specialist, authority.
■ **consultancy** n.

consultation n. the process or an act of consulting someone or something.
▷ SYNONYMS: **discussion**, talk, dialogue, debate, negotiation, deliberation; meeting, interview, hearing.

consume v. **1** eat or drink. **2** use up. **3** (of a fire) destroy. **4** fill the mind of.
▷ SYNONYMS: **1 eat**, devour, swallow, gobble up, wolf down, guzzle, drink. **2 use**, expend, deplete, exhaust, spend. **3 destroy**, demolish, lay waste, raze, devastate, gut, ruin, wreck. **4 eat up**, devour, grip, overwhelm, absorb, obsess, preoccupy.

consumer n. a person who buys or uses goods or services.
▷ SYNONYMS: **buyer**, purchaser, customer, shopper, user.

consummate v. /kon-syuu-mayt/ make a marriage or relationship complete by having sex.
• adj. /kuhn-**sum**-muht/ highly skilled.
■ **consummation** n.

consumption n. **1** the process of consuming. **2** dated tuberculosis.
■ **consumptive** adj. & n. (dated).

contact n. **1** physical touching. **2** communication. **3** a person who may be asked for information or help. **4** an electrical connection.
▷ SYNONYMS: **1 communication**, correspondence, connection, relations, dealings, touch. **2 connection**, link, acquaintance, associate, friend.
• v. get in touch with.
▷ SYNONYMS: **get in touch with**, communicate with, approach, notify, speak to, write to, come forward; informal get hold of.
□ **contact lens** a plastic lens placed on the surface of the eye to correct visual defects.

contagion n. the spreading of a disease by close contact.

contagious adj. **1** (of a disease) spread by contact between people. **2** having a contagious disease.
▷ SYNONYMS: **infectious**, communicable, catching, transmittable, transmissible.

contain v. **1** have or hold within.

2 control or restrain.
▷ SYNONYMS: **1 hold**, carry, enclose, accommodate, have room for. **2 include**, comprise, incorporate, involve, consist of, be made up of, be composed of. **3 restrain**, control, curb, rein in, suppress, stifle, swallow, bottle up, keep in check.

container n. **1** an object for holding something. **2** a large metal box for transporting goods.
▷ SYNONYMS: **receptacle**, vessel, holder, repository.

containment n. the limitation of something harmful.

contaminate v. pollute.
▷ SYNONYMS: **pollute**, taint, poison, stain, adulterate, defile, debase, corrupt.
– ANTONYMS: purify.
■ **contamination** n.

contemplate v. **1** look at thoughtfully. **2** think about.
▷ SYNONYMS: **1 look at**, gaze at, stare at, view, regard, examine, inspect, observe, survey, study, eye. **2 think about**, ponder, reflect on, consider, mull over, muse on, dwell on, deliberate over, meditate on, ruminate on, chew over. **3 envisage**, consider, think about, have in mind, intend, plan, propose.
■ **contemplation** n.

contemplative adj. showing or involving deep thought.
▷ SYNONYMS: **thoughtful**, pensive, reflective, meditative, ruminative, introspective, brooding, deep/lost in thought.

contemporaneous adj. existing or occurring at the same time.

contemporary adj. **1** living or occurring at the same time. **2** of or happening in the present.
▷ SYNONYMS: **1** *contemporary sources:* **of the time**, contemporaneous, concurrent, coexisting, coeval. **2** *contemporary society:* **modern**, present-day, present, current. **3** *a very contemporary design:* **modern**, up to date, up to the minute, fashionable, recent; informal trendy.
– ANTONYMS: former, old-fashioned.
• n. (pl. **contemporaries**) a person of the same age or living at the same time as another.

contempt n. **1** the feeling that someone or something is worthless. **2** disobedience or disrespect to a court of law.
▷ SYNONYMS: **scorn**, disdain, derision, disgust, disrespect.
– ANTONYMS: respect.

contemptible adj. deserving contempt.
▷ SYNONYMS: **despicable**, detestable, beneath contempt, reprehensible, deplorable, unspeakable, disgraceful, shameful, ignominious, abject, low, mean, cowardly, discreditable, worthless, shabby, cheap.
– ANTONYMS: admirable.

contemptuous adj. showing or feeling contempt.
▷ SYNONYMS: **scornful**, disdainful, derisive, mocking, sneering, scoffing, condescending, supercilious, superior, dismissive.
– ANTONYMS: respectful.
■ **contemptuously** adv.

contend v. **1** struggle to deal with a difficulty. **2** struggle to achieve. **3** assert.
▷ SYNONYMS: **1 compete**, vie, battle, tussle, struggle, jostle, strive. **2 assert**, maintain, hold, claim, argue, insist, allege.
■ **contender** n.

content adj. happy or satisfied.
▷ SYNONYMS: **satisfied**, contented, pleased, gratified, fulfilled, happy, glad, cheerful, at ease, at peace, relaxed, comfortable, untroubled.
– ANTONYMS: discontent, dissatisfied.
• n. **1** (also **contents**) what is contained in something. **2** the material in a piece of writing rather than its form or style. **3** happiness or satisfaction.
▷ SYNONYMS: **1 amount**, proportion, level, constituents, ingredients, components. **2 subject matter**, theme, argument, thesis, message, substance, material, ideas.
• v. satisfy or please.
▷ SYNONYMS: **satisfy**, comfort, gratify, gladden, please, soothe, placate, appease, mollify.
■ **contented** adj.

contention n. **1** disagreement. **2** an assertion.

contentious adj. causing disagreement or controversy.
▷ SYNONYMS: **controversial**, debatable, disputed, open to debate, moot, vexed.

contentment n. happiness and satisfaction.
▷ SYNONYMS: **contentedness**, content, satisfaction, fulfilment, happiness, pleasure, cheerfulness, ease, comfort, well-being, peace.

contest n. a competitive event.
▷ SYNONYMS: **1 competition**, match, tournament, rally, race, game, bout.

2 fight, battle, tussle, struggle, competition, race.
• v. **1** participate in a competition or election. **2** challenge or dispute.
▷ SYNONYMS: **1 compete**, contend, participate, take part, vie, fight. **2 oppose**, challenge, take issue with, question, dispute, call into question, object to.

contestant n. a person taking part in a contest.
▷ SYNONYMS: **competitor**, participant, player, contender, candidate, entrant.

context n. **1** the circumstances surrounding an event etc. **2** the parts that precede and follow a word or passage and clarify its meaning.
▷ SYNONYMS: **circumstances**, conditions, frame of reference, factors, state of affairs, situation, background, scene, setting.
■ **contextual** adj.

contiguous adj. adjacent or touching.
■ **contiguity** n.

continent[1] n. **1** any of the world's main land masses. **2** (**the Continent**) the mainland of Europe.
■ **continental** adj.

continent[2] adj. **1** able to control the bowels and bladder. **2** self-restrained.
■ **continence** n.

contingency n. (pl. **contingencies**) a possible future event.
▷ SYNONYMS: **eventuality**, possibility, chance event, incident, occurrence, accident, emergency.

contingent n. a distinct group of people within a larger group.
• adj. (**contingent on**) dependent on.

continual adj. happening repeatedly or often.
▷ SYNONYMS: **1** continual breakdowns: **frequent**, regular, repeated, constant, recurrent, recurring, habitual. **2** continual pain: **constant**, continuous, unremitting, unrelenting, non-stop, sustained, chronic, uninterrupted, incessant, ceaseless, unceasing, never-ending, unbroken, perpetual.
– ANTONYMS: occasional, temporary.
■ **continually** adv.

continue v. **1** keep doing. **2** keep existing or happening. **3** carry on in the same direction. **4** start again.
▷ SYNONYMS: **1 carry on**, go on, keep on, persist, persevere, proceed, pursue, keep at; informal stick at. **2** we hope to continue this relationship: **maintain**, keep up, sustain, keep going, keep alive, preserve, perpetuate. **3** his willingness to continue in office: **remain**, stay, carry on, keep going.

4 we continued our conversation: **resume**, pick up, take up, carry on with, return to, revisit.
– ANTONYMS: stop.
■ **continuation** n. **continuity** n.

continuous adj. without interruptions or gaps.
▷ SYNONYMS: **continual**, persistent, sustained, ceaseless, unceasing, unremitting, unrelenting, perpetual, incessant, never-ending, eternal, endless, non-stop, unbroken, uninterrupted.
– ANTONYMS: intermittent.
■ **continuously** adv.

continuum n. (pl. **continua**) a continuous sequence in which the elements change gradually.

contort v. twist or bend out of normal shape.
▷ SYNONYMS: **twist**, bend out of shape, distort, misshape, warp, buckle, deform.
■ **contortion** n.

contortionist n. an entertainer who contorts their body.

contour n. **1** an outline. **2** a line on a map joining points of equal height.

contra- prefix against; opposite.

contraband n. smuggled goods.

contraception n. the use of contraceptives.

contraceptive n. a device or drug that prevents pregnancy.
• adj. preventing pregnancy.

contract n. a legally binding agreement.
▷ SYNONYMS: **agreement**, arrangement, commitment, settlement, understanding, compact, covenant, deal, bargain.
• v. **1** make or become smaller or shorter. **2** make or arrange by a contract. **3** catch a disease.
▷ SYNONYMS: **1 shrink**, diminish, reduce, decrease, dwindle, decline. **2 tighten**, tense, flex, constrict, draw in. **3 engage**, take on, hire, commission, employ. **4 catch**, pick up, come/go down with, develop.
– ANTONYMS: expand, relax, lengthen.
■ **contractual** adj. **contractor** n.

contractile adj. able to contract or produce contraction.

contraction n. **1** the process of contracting. **2** a shortening of the muscles of the womb during childbirth. **3** a shortened form of a word or words.
▷ SYNONYMS: **1 shrinking**, shrinkage, decline, decrease, diminution, dwindling. **2 tightening**, tensing,

flexing. **3 abbreviation**, short form, shortening.

contradict v. deny the truth of a statement by saying the opposite.
▷ SYNONYMS: **1 deny**, refute, rebut, dispute, challenge, counter. **2 argue with**, go against, challenge, oppose.
– ANTONYMS: confirm, agree with.

contradiction n. **1** a combination of statements, ideas, etc. which are opposed to one another. **2** the action of contradicting something.
▷ SYNONYMS: **1 conflict**, clash, disagreement, inconsistency, mismatch. **2 denial**, refutation, rebuttal, countering.
– ANTONYMS: agreement, confirmation.

contradictory adj. opposed or inconsistent, or containing inconsistent elements.
▷ SYNONYMS: **inconsistent**, incompatible, irreconcilable, opposed, opposite, contrary, conflicting, at variance.

contraflow n. Brit. a flow of traffic in a direction opposite to and alongside the usual flow.

contralto n. (pl. **contraltos**) the lowest female singing voice.

contraption n. a strange machine or device.
▷ SYNONYMS: **device**, gadget, apparatus, machine, appliance, mechanism, invention, contrivance; informal gizmo, widget; Brit. informal gubbins.

contrapuntal adj. of or in counterpoint.

contrary adj. **1** opposite in nature, direction, or meaning. **2** /kuhn-**trair**-i/ inclined to do the opposite of what is desired.
▷ SYNONYMS: **1 opposite**, opposing, contradictory, clashing, conflicting, antithetical, incompatible, irreconcilable. **2 perverse**, awkward, difficult, uncooperative, obstinate, pig-headed, intractable; Brit. informal bloody-minded, stroppy; N. Amer. informal balky.
– ANTONYMS: compatible, accommodating.
• n. (**the contrary**) the opposite.
▷ SYNONYMS: **opposite**, reverse, converse, antithesis.

contrast n. the state of being noticeably different when compared.
▷ SYNONYMS: **1 difference**, dissimilarity, disparity, divergence, variance, distinction, comparison. **2 opposite**, antithesis, foil, complement.
– ANTONYMS: similarity.
• v. **1** differ noticeably. **2** compare so as to note differences.
▷ SYNONYMS: **1 differ**, be at variance,

be contrary, conflict, be at odds, disagree, clash. **2 compare**, juxtapose, measure, distinguish, differentiate.
– ANTONYMS: resemble, liken.

contravene v. break a law, treaty, etc.
■ **contravention** n.

contretemps /kon-truh-ton/ n. (pl. **contretemps**) a minor disagreement.

contribute v. **1** give so as to help achieve or provide something. **2** help to cause.
▷ SYNONYMS: **give**, donate, put up, grant, provide, supply, present, offer; informal chip in; Brit. informal stump up.
■ **contribution** n. **contributory** adj.

contribution n. **1** a gift, payment, or donation. **2** an action or service that helps to bring something about.
▷ SYNONYMS: **gift**, donation, offering, present, handout, grant, subsidy.

contributor n. a person who contributes something.
▷ SYNONYMS: **donor**, benefactor, supporter, backer, patron, sponsor.

contrite adj. sorry for having done wrong.
▷ SYNONYMS: **remorseful**, repentant, penitent, regretful, sorry, apologetic, rueful, sheepish, hangdog, ashamed, shamefaced.
■ **contrition** n.

contrivance n. **1** a clever device or scheme. **2** the act of contriving.

contrive v. **1** plan or achieve skilfully. **2** manage to do.
▷ SYNONYMS: **1 create**, engineer, manufacture, devise, concoct, construct, fabricate, hatch. **2 manage**, find a way, engineer a way, arrange.
– ANTONYMS: fail.

contrived adj. artificial; seeming false.
▷ SYNONYMS: **forced**, strained, laboured, overdone, unnatural, artificial, false, affected.
– ANTONYMS: natural.

control n. **1** the power to influence or limit something. **2** a means of limiting or regulating something. **3** a standard for checking the results of an experiment.
▷ SYNONYMS: **1 power**, authority, command, dominance, sway, management, direction, leadership, rule, government, sovereignty, supremacy. **2 limit**, limitation, restriction, restraint, check, curb, regulation. **3 self-control**, self-restraint, composure, calm; informal cool.
• v. (**controlling**, **controlled**) **1** have power over. **2** limit or regulate.
▷ SYNONYMS: **1 run**, manage, direct,

preside over, supervise, command, rule, govern, lead, dominate. **2** *she struggled to control her temper:* **restrain**, keep in check, curb, hold back, suppress, repress. **3** *public spending was controlled:* **limit**, restrict, curb, cap.
■ **controllable** adj. **controller** n.

controversial adj. causing controversy.
▷ SYNONYMS: **disputed**, contentious, moot, debatable, arguable, vexed.
■ **controversially** adv.

controversy n. (pl. **controversies**) public debate about a matter which arouses conflicting opinions.
▷ SYNONYMS: **dispute**, disagreement, argument, debate, contention, quarrel, war of words, storm; Brit. row.

contusion n. a bruise.

conundrum n. a puzzle or problem.

conurbation n. a large urban area where several towns have merged together.

convalesce v. regain health after illness.
▷ SYNONYMS: **recuperate**, get better, recover, get well, get back on your feet.
■ **convalescence** n. **convalescent** adj. & n.

convection n. transference of heat within a fluid caused by the tendency of warmer material to rise.
■ **convector** n.

convene v. come or bring together for a meeting.
▷ SYNONYMS: **1** *he convened a meeting:* **summon**, call, order. **2** *the committee convened:* **assemble**, gather, meet, come together; formal foregather.
■ **convener** (or **convenor**) n.

convenience n. **1** freedom from effort or difficulty. **2** a useful thing. **3** Brit. a public toilet.
▷ SYNONYMS: **1 advantage**, benefit, expedience, suitability. **2 ease of use**, usefulness, utility, accessibility, availability.
– ANTONYMS: inconvenience.

convenient adj. **1** fitting in with needs or plans. **2** involving little trouble or effort.
▷ SYNONYMS: **1 suitable**, favourable, advantageous, appropriate, opportune, timely, expedient. **2 nearby**, handy, well situated, practical, useful, accessible.
■ **conveniently** adv.

convent n. a building occupied by a community of nuns.

convention n. **1** a way in which

something is usually done. **2** socially acceptable behaviour. **3** an agreement between countries. **4** a conference.
▷ SYNONYMS: **1 custom**, usage, practice, tradition, etiquette, protocol; formal praxis. **2 agreement**, accord, protocol, pact, treaty. **3 conference**, meeting, congress, assembly, gathering.

conventional adj. **1** based on or in accordance with what is generally done. **2** following social conventions.
▷ SYNONYMS: **1 orthodox**, traditional, established, accepted, customary, received, prevailing, normal, standard, regular, ordinary, usual, typical, unoriginal, formulaic, predictable, run-of-the-mill, routine, pedestrian. **2 conservative**, traditional, conformist, old-fashioned, unadventurous; informal square, stick-in-the-mud.
– ANTONYMS: unconventional, original.
■ **conventionally** adv.

converge v. come to or towards the same point.
▷ SYNONYMS: **meet**, intersect, cross, connect, link up, join, merge.
– ANTONYMS: diverge.
■ **convergence** n. **convergent** adj.

conversant adj. (**conversant with**) having knowledge of.

conversation n. an informal talk between people.
▷ SYNONYMS: **discussion**, talk, chat, gossip, tête-à-tête, exchange, dialogue; Brit. informal chinwag, natter.
■ **conversational** adj.

converse v. hold a conversation.
● n. the opposite.
● adj. opposite.
■ **conversely** adv.

conversion n. **1** the action of converting. **2** a building that has been converted to a new purpose.
▷ SYNONYMS: **change**, transformation, metamorphosis, alteration, adaptation, modification, redevelopment, remodelling.

convert v. **1** change in form, character, or function. **2** change money or units into others of a different kind. **3** change your religious faith.
▷ SYNONYMS: **1 change**, transform, alter, adapt, turn, modify, redevelop, remodel, rebuild, reorganize, metamorphose. **2 win over**, convince, persuade, redeem, save, reform, re-educate, proselytize, evangelize.
● n. a person who has changed their religious faith.

convertible adj. able to be converted.

• n. a car with a folding or detachable roof.

convex adj. having an outline or surface that curves outwards.

convey v. 1 transport or carry. 2 communicate an idea or feeling.
▷ SYNONYMS: 1 **transport**, carry, bring, take, fetch, move. 2 **communicate**, pass on, impart, relate, relay, transmit, send. 3 **express**, get across/over, put across/over, communicate, indicate.

conveyance n. 1 the act of conveying. 2 a means of transport. 3 the legal transfer of ownership of property.
■ **conveyancing** n.

conveyor belt n. a continuous moving band for transporting objects.

convict v. officially declare guilty of a criminal offence.
▷ SYNONYMS: **find guilty**, sentence.
– ANTONYMS: acquit.
• n. a convicted person serving a prison sentence.
▷ SYNONYMS: **prisoner**, inmate, criminal, offender, felon; informal jailbird, con, old lag.

conviction n. 1 an instance of being convicted of a criminal offence. 2 a firm belief. 3 strong belief in something.
▷ SYNONYMS: 1 **beliefs**, opinions, views, persuasion, ideals, position, stance, values. 2 **assurance**, confidence, certainty.
– ANTONYMS: diffidence.

convince v. 1 cause to feel certain that something is true. 2 persuade to do.
▷ SYNONYMS: 1 *he convinced me I was wrong*: **assure**, persuade, satisfy, prove to. 2 *I convinced her to marry me*: **persuade**, induce, prevail on, talk into, talk round, win over, coax, cajole.

convincing adj. 1 able to convince. 2 (of a victory) decisive.
▷ SYNONYMS: 1 **persuasive**, powerful, strong, forceful, compelling, cogent, plausible, irresistible, telling. 2 *a convincing win*: **resounding**, emphatic, decisive, conclusive.
– ANTONYMS: unconvincing.

convivial adj. friendly and lively.
▷ SYNONYMS: **friendly**, genial, affable, amiable, congenial, agreeable, cordial, warm, sociable, outgoing, gregarious, cheerful.

convocation n. a large assembly of people.

convoluted adj. 1 very complex. 2 intricately folded or twisted.

■ **convolution** n.

convolvulus n. a twining plant with trumpet-shaped flowers.

convoy n. a group of ships or vehicles travelling together under armed protection.
▷ SYNONYMS: **group**, fleet, cavalcade, motorcade, cortège, caravan, line.

convulse v. 1 suffer convulsions. 2 (**be convulsed**) laugh uncontrollably.
■ **convulsive** adj.

convulsion n. 1 a sudden uncontrolled movement of the body. 2 (**convulsions**) uncontrollable laughter.

coo v. (of a pigeon or dove) make a soft murmuring sound.
• n. a cooing sound.

cook v. 1 prepare food by heating ingredients. 2 (**cook up**) informal invent a story.
▷ SYNONYMS: **prepare**, make, put together; informal fix, rustle up; Brit. informal knock up.
• n. a person who cooks.

> **WORD LINKS**
> **culinary** relating to cooking

cooker n. Brit. an appliance for cooking food.

cookery n. the practice or skill of cooking.

cookie n. (pl. **cookies**) US a sweet biscuit.

cool adj. 1 fairly cold. 2 unfriendly or unenthusiastic. 3 calm. 4 informal fashionably attractive or impressive.
▷ SYNONYMS: 1 **chilly**, chill, bracing, cold, brisk, crisp, fresh; informal nippy; Brit. informal parky. 2 **unenthusiastic**, lukewarm, tepid, indifferent, uninterested, apathetic. 3 **unfriendly**, distant, remote, aloof, cold, chilly, frosty, unwelcoming; informal stand-offish. 4 **calm**, collected, composed, self-possessed, poised, serene, relaxed, at ease, unruffled, unperturbed; informal unflappable, together, laid-back.
– ANTONYMS: warm, enthusiastic, friendly.
• v. make or become cool.
▷ SYNONYMS: **chill**, refrigerate, freeze.
– ANTONYMS: warm.
• n. low temperature.
▷ SYNONYMS: 1 **chill**, chilliness, coldness, coolness. 2 **self-control**, control, composure, self-possession, calmness, aplomb, poise.
– ANTONYMS: warmth.
□ **keep** (or **lose**) **your cool** informal stay

(or fail to stay) calm.
■ **coolly** adv. **coolness** n.

coolant n. a fluid used for cooling machinery.

coolie n. (pl. **coolies**) dated an unskilled labourer in some Asian countries.

coomb var. of COMBE.

coop n. a cage for poultry.
• v. (**coop up**) confine in a small space.

cooper n. a person who makes or repairs casks and barrels.

cooperate v. **1** work together to achieve something. **2** comply with a request.

▷ SYNONYMS: **1 collaborate**, work together, pull together, join forces, team up, unite, combine, pool resources. **2 assist**, help, lend a hand, be of service, do your bit; informal play ball.

cooperation n. the action of cooperating.

▷ SYNONYMS: **collaboration**, joint action, combined effort, teamwork, give and take, compromise.

cooperative adj. **1** involving cooperation. **2** willing to help. **3** (of a business) owned and run jointly by its members.

▷ SYNONYMS: **1 collaborative**, collective, combined, joint, shared, united, concerted. **2 helpful**, eager to help, obliging, accommodating, willing.
• n. a cooperative business.
■ **cooperatively** adv.

co-opt v. appoint to a committee by the invitation of existing members.

coordinate v. **1** organize the different elements of an activity so that it works efficiently. **2** match or harmonize well.

▷ SYNONYMS: **organize**, arrange, order, synchronize, bring together, orchestrate.
• n. **1** each of the numbers used to indicate the position of a point. **2** (**coordinates**) matching items of clothing.
■ **coordination** n. **coordinator** n.

coot n. a black waterbird.

cop informal n. a police officer.
• v. (**copping, copped**) **1** catch or arrest. **2** (**cop out**) avoid doing something that you ought to do.

cope v. deal effectively with something difficult.

▷ SYNONYMS: **1 manage**, survive, look after yourself, fend for yourself, shift for yourself, get by/through, hold your own. **2** *his inability to cope with the situation*: **deal with**, handle, manage, address, face up to, confront,

tackle, get to grips with.

copier n. a copying machine.

coping n. the top layer of a brick or stone wall.

copious adj. abundant; plentiful.

▷ SYNONYMS: **abundant**, plentiful, ample, profuse, extensive, generous, lavish, liberal, overflowing, in abundance, numerous, many; informal galore; literary plenteous.

– ANTONYMS: sparse.
■ **copiously** adv.

copper n. **1** a red-brown metallic element. **2** (**coppers**) Brit. coins made of copper or bronze. **3** a reddish-brown colour. **4** Brit. informal a police officer.
□ **copper-bottomed** Brit. thoroughly reliable. **copperplate** neat slanting handwriting.

coppice n. a small wood in which the trees are regularly cut back to ground level.

copse n. a small group of trees.

copulate v. have sex.
■ **copulation** n.

copy n. (pl. **copies**) **1** a thing made to look like another. **2** a single example of a book, record, etc. **3** matter to be printed in a newspaper etc.

▷ SYNONYMS: **1 duplicate**, facsimile, photocopy; trademark Xerox. **2 replica**, reproduction, imitation, likeness, forgery, fake, counterfeit.
• v. (**copying, copied**) **1** make a copy of. **2** imitate.

▷ SYNONYMS: **1 duplicate**, photocopy, xerox, photostat, reproduce. **2 repro-duce**, replicate, forge, fake, counter-feit. **3 imitate**, reproduce, emulate, mimic; informal rip off.
□ **copyright** the exclusive right to publish or record a work. **copywriter** a person who writes advertisements or publicity material.

coquette n. a woman who flirts.
■ **coquetry** n. **coquettish** adj.

coracle n. a small wicker boat.

coral n. **1** a hard substance consisting of the skeletons of certain sea animals. **2** a pinkish-red colour.

cor anglais /kor ong-glay/ n. (pl. **cors anglais**) a woodwind instrument of the oboe family.

corbel n. a stone or wooden support projecting from a wall.

cord n. **1** thin string or rope made from several twisted strands. **2** an electric flex. **3** corduroy.

▷ SYNONYMS: **string**, thread, line, rope, cable, wire, twine, yarn.
□ **cordless** (of an electrical appliance)

working without connection to a mains supply.

cordial adj. **1** warm and friendly. **2** deeply felt.
• n. Brit. a fruit-flavoured drink.
■ **cordiality** n. **cordially** adv.

cordite n. a smokeless explosive.

cordon n. a line or circle of police, soldiers, etc. forming a barrier.
▷ SYNONYMS: **barrier**, line, chain, ring, circle.
• v. (**cordon off**) close off by means of a cordon.

cordon bleu /kor-don **bler**/ adj. Cookery of the highest class.

corduroy n. thick cotton fabric with velvety ribs.

core n. **1** the tough central part of some fruits. **2** the central or most important part.
▷ SYNONYMS: **1** the earth's core: **centre**, interior, middle, nucleus. **2** the core of the argument: **heart**, nucleus, nub, kernel, meat, essence, crux, pith, substance; informal nitty-gritty.
• v. remove the core from a fruit.

co-respondent n. the person named in a divorce case as having committed adultery with the respondent.

corgi n. (pl. **corgis**) a short-legged breed of dog.

coriander n. a herb used in cookery.

cork n. **1** a light substance obtained from the bark of a tree. **2** a bottle stopper made of cork.
• v. **1** seal with a cork. **2** (**corked**) (of wine) spoilt by a decayed cork.
□ **corkage** a charge made by a restaurant for serving wine brought in by a customer. **corkscrew** a device for pulling corks from bottles.

corm n. an underground storage organ of some plants.

cormorant n. a large black seabird.

corn n. **1** wheat, oats, or maize; grain. **2** a small painful area of thickened skin on the foot.
□ **cornflour** Brit. fine flour made from maize. **cornflower** a blue-flowered plant.

cornea n. the transparent layer forming the front of the eye.

cornelian var. of CARNELIAN.

corner n. **1** a place or angle where sides or edges meet. **2** a free kick or hit taken from a corner of the field in football or hockey.
▷ SYNONYMS: **1** bend, curve, turn, junction; Brit. hairpin bend. **2** district, region, area, quarter; informal neck of the woods.
• v. **1** force into a situation from

which it is hard to escape. **2** go round a bend in a road. **3** control a market by dominating the supply of a commodity.
▷ SYNONYMS: **1** surround, trap, hem in, pen in, cut off. **2** gain control of, take over, dominate, monopolize, capture; informal sew up.
□ **cornerstone** a vital part; a foundation.

cornet n. **1** a brass instrument like a small trumpet. **2** Brit. a cone-shaped wafer holding ice cream.

cornice n. a decorative moulding round the wall of a room below the ceiling.

cornucopia n. an abundant supply of good things.

corny adj. (**cornier, corniest**) informal sentimental or unoriginal.

corolla n. the petals of a flower.

corollary n. (pl. **corollaries**) **1** a direct consequence. **2** a proposition that follows logically from another.

corona n. (pl. **coronae**) the gases surrounding the sun or another star.

coronary adj. of the arteries which supply the heart.
• n. (pl. **coronaries**) a blockage of the flow of blood to the heart.

coronation n. the ceremony of crowning a monarch.

coroner n. an official who holds inquests into violent, sudden, or suspicious deaths.

coronet n. a small crown.

corpora pl. of CORPUS.

corporal n. the army rank below sergeant.
• adj. of the human body.
□ **corporal punishment** physical punishment, e.g. caning.

corporate adj. **1** of a business corporation. **2** of or shared by all members of a group.

corporation n. **1** a large company or a group of companies as a unit. **2** Brit. a group of people elected to govern a town.
▷ SYNONYMS: **company**, firm, business, concern, operation, conglomerate, group, chain, multinational.

corporeal adj. of the body; physical.

corps /kor/ n. (pl. **corps**) **1** a military unit. **2** a group of people involved in a particular activity.

corpse n. a dead body.
▷ SYNONYMS: **dead body**, carcass, remains; informal stiff; Medicine cadaver.

corpulent adj. fat.

corpus n. (pl. **corpora** or **corpuses**) a

collection of written works.

corpuscle n. a blood cell.

corral n. US a pen for livestock.
• v. (**corralling**, **corralled**) put or keep in a corral.

correct adj. **1** free from error; true. **2** following accepted social standards.
▷ SYNONYMS: **1** right, accurate, exact, true, perfect; informal spot on. **2** proper, decent, right, respectable, decorous, seemly, suitable, appropriate, accepted.
– ANTONYMS: wrong, improper.
• v. **1** put right. **2** mark errors in a text.
▷ SYNONYMS: rectify, right, put right, set right, amend, remedy, repair, reform, cure.
■ **correction** n. **correctly** adv. **correctness** n.

corrective adj. designed to correct something undesirable.

correlate v. have or bring into a dependent relationship.
■ **correlation** n.

correspond v. **1** be similar or equivalent. **2** exchange letters.
▷ SYNONYMS: **1** be consistent, correlate, agree, accord, coincide, tally, tie in, match; informal square. **2** *a rank corresponding to a British sergeant:* be equivalent, be analogous, be comparable, equate. **3** exchange letters, write, communicate.

correspondence n. **1** letters sent or received. **2** a close link or similarity.
▷ SYNONYMS: **1** parallel, correlation, agreement, consistency, conformity, similarity, resemblance, comparability. **2** letters, messages, mail, post, communication.

correspondent n. **1** a journalist reporting on a particular subject. **2** a person who writes letters.
▷ SYNONYMS: reporter, journalist, columnist, writer, contributor, commentator.

corresponding adj. comparable or equivalent.
▷ SYNONYMS: equivalent, related, parallel, matching, comparable, analogous, commensurate.

corridor n. **1** a passage in a building or train, with doors leading into rooms or compartments. **2** a strip of land linking two other areas.

corroborate v. confirm or support.
■ **corroboration** n.

corrode v. (of metal etc.) wear or be worn away slowly by chemical action.
■ **corrosion** n. **corrosive** adj.

corrugated adj. shaped into alternate ridges and grooves.

■ **corrugation** n.

corrupt adj. **1** willing to act dishonestly in return for money etc. **2** evil or immoral. **3** (esp. of computer data) full of errors.
▷ SYNONYMS: **1** dishonest, unscrupulous, criminal, fraudulent, illegal, unlawful; informal crooked; Brit. informal bent. **2** immoral, depraved, degenerate, debauched, vice-ridden, perverted, dissolute.
– ANTONYMS: honest, ethical, pure.
• v. make corrupt.
▷ SYNONYMS: deprave, pervert, lead astray, debauch, defile, pollute, sully.

corruption n. **1** dishonest or illegal behaviour. **2** the action of corrupting.
▷ SYNONYMS: **1** dishonesty, fraud, unscrupulousness, double-dealing, misconduct, bribery, venality; N. Amer. payola; informal graft, sleaze. **2** immorality, depravity, vice, degeneracy, perversion, debauchery, wickedness, evil, sin.
– ANTONYMS: honesty, morality.

corsair n. old use a pirate.

corset n. a tight-fitting undergarment worn to shape or support the body.

cortège /kor-tezh/ n. a funeral procession.

cortex n. (pl. **cortices**) the outer layer of a bodily organ, esp. of the brain.

cortisone n. a hormone used to treat inflammation and allergy.

corvette n. a small warship.

cos abbrev. cosine.

cosh n. a heavy stick or bar used as a weapon.
• v. hit with a cosh.

cosine n. (in a right-angled triangle) the ratio of the side adjacent to an acute angle to the hypotenuse.

cosmetic adj. **1** intended to improve the appearance. **2** superficial.
▷ SYNONYMS: **superficial**, surface, skin-deep, outward, external.
– ANTONYMS: fundamental.
• n. a cosmetic substance for the face and body.

cosmic adj. of the universe.

cosmology n. the science of the origin and development of the universe.
■ **cosmological** adj. **cosmologist** n.

cosmonaut n. a Russian astronaut.

cosmopolitan adj. **1** made up of people from many different countries. **2** familiar with many different countries.
▷ SYNONYMS: **1** multicultural, multiracial, international, worldwide, global. **2** sophisticated, cultivated,

cultured, worldly, suave, urbane.

cosmos n. the universe.

Cossack n. a member of a people of Russia and Ukraine noted for their horsemanship.

cosset v. (**cosseting, cosseted**) look after with excessive kindness.

cost v. (**costing, cost**) **1** be obtainable for a specific price. **2** involve the loss of. **3** (**costing, costed**) estimate the cost of.

▷ SYNONYMS: **1 be priced at**, sell for, be valued at, fetch, come to, amount to; informal set someone back, go for. **2 price**, value, put a figure on.
• n. what something costs.

▷ SYNONYMS: **1 price**, fee, tariff, fare, toll, levy, charge, payment, value, rate, outlay; humorous damage. **2** *we need to cover our costs:* **expenses**, outgoings, overheads, expenditure, spend, outlay.

co-star n. a performer appearing with another of equal importance.

costermonger n. dated a person who sells fruit and vegetables in the street.

costly adj. (**costlier, costliest**) **1** expensive. **2** causing suffering or loss.

▷ SYNONYMS: **1 expensive**, dear, high-cost, overpriced; informal steep, pricey. **2 catastrophic**, disastrous, calamitous, ruinous, damaging, harmful, deleterious.
– ANTONYMS: cheap.

costume n. **1** a set of clothes typical of a country or historical period. **2** clothes worn by an actor or performer.

▷ SYNONYMS: **clothes**, garments, outfit, ensemble, dress, clothing, attire, garb, uniform, livery; formal apparel.

cosy (US **cozy**) adj. (**cosier, cosiest**) **1** comfortable, warm, and secure. **2** not difficult or demanding.

▷ SYNONYMS: **1 snug**, comfortable, warm, homely, welcoming, safe, sheltered, secure; informal comfy. **2 intimate**, relaxed, informal, friendly.
• n. (pl. **cosies**) a cover to keep a teapot hot.
■ **cosily** adv. **cosiness** n.

cot n. a child's bed with high barred sides.
□ **cot death** the unexplained death of a baby in its sleep.

coterie /koh-tuh-ri/ n. a small exclusive group.

cottage n. a small house in the country.

▷ SYNONYMS: **lodge**, chalet, cabin, shack, shanty; (in Russia) **dacha**; Scottish **bothy**; Austral. informal **weekender**.
□ **cottage cheese** soft, lumpy white cheese. **cottage industry** a business or manufacturing activity carried on in the home.

cotton n. **1** soft white fibres round the seeds of a tropical plant. **2** cloth or thread made from these fibres.
• v. (**cotton on**) informal understand.
□ **cotton wool** fluffy cotton material for wiping the skin.

cotyledon /ko-ti-lee-duhn/ n. the first leaf growing from a seed.

couch n. a sofa.
• v. express in a particular way.
□ **couch potato** informal a person who watches a lot of television.

couchette /koo-shet/ n. a railway carriage with seats convertible into beds.

cougar /koo-ger/ US a puma.

cough v. **1** send out air from the lungs with a sudden sharp sound. **2** (**cough up**) informal give money reluctantly.

▷ SYNONYMS: **hack**, hawk, bark, clear your throat.
• n. **1** an act of coughing. **2** an illness causing coughing.

▷ SYNONYMS: **bark**, hack; informal frog in your throat.

could past of CAN¹.

couldn't contr. could not.

coulomb n. a unit of electric charge.

council n. **1** a group meeting regularly for debate and administration. **2** a group elected to govern a town or region.

▷ SYNONYMS: **1** *the town council:* **authority**, government, administration, executive, chamber, assembly; Brit. corporation. **2** *the Schools Council:* **committee**, board, commission, assembly, panel, synod.
□ **council tax** a UK tax charged on households by local authorities.
■ **councillor** n.

counsel n. **1** advice. **2** (pl. **counsel**) a barrister.

▷ SYNONYMS: **1 advice**, guidance, counselling, recommendations, suggestions, direction. **2 barrister**, lawyer; Scottish advocate; N. Amer. attorney, counselor-at-law.
• v. (**counselling, counselled**; US **counseling, counseled**) **1** advise. **2** professionally advise someone with personal or psychological problems.

▷ SYNONYMS: **advise**, recommend, advocate, encourage, warn, caution, guide.
■ **counsellor** n.

count v. **1** find the total number of.

2 say numbers in order. **3** include.
4 regard as being. **5** be important.
6 (**count on**) rely on.
▷ SYNONYMS: **1 add up**, reckon up,
total, tally, calculate, compute; Brit.
tot up. **2 include**, take into account/
consideration, take account of, allow
for. **3 consider**, think, feel, regard,
look on as, view as, hold to be, judge,
deem. **4 matter**, be important, be of
consequence, be significant, signify,
carry weight, rate.
• n. **1** an act of counting. **2** a total.
3 a point to consider. **4** a charge
against an accused person. **5** a foreign
nobleman.
□ **countdown 1** the counting of
seconds backwards to zero to launch
a rocket. **2** the final moments before a
significant event.

countenance n. a person's face or
expression.
• v. allow.

counter n. **1** a long flat surface over
which goods are sold or across which
business is conducted. **2** a small disc
used in board games.
• v. speak or act against.
▷ SYNONYMS: **1 respond to**, parry, hit
back at, answer. **2 oppose**, dispute,
argue against/with, contradict, challenge, contest.
– ANTONYMS: support.
• adv. (**counter to**) in the opposite
direction or in opposition to.

counter- prefix **1** opposing or done in
return. **2** corresponding.

counteract v. reduce or prevent the
effects of.
▷ SYNONYMS: **offset**, counterbalance,
balance out, cancel out, work against,
countervail, neutralize, nullify,
prevent.

counter-attack n. an attack made in
response to an attack.
• v. make a counter-attack.

counterbalance n. a weight or
influence that balances or neutralizes
another.
• v. have an equal but opposite effect
on.

counterfeit adj. not genuine; forged.
▷ SYNONYMS: **fake**, pirate, bogus, forged,
imitation; informal phoney.
– ANTONYMS: genuine.
• n. a forgery.
▷ SYNONYMS: **fake**, forgery, copy, reproduction, imitation, fraud, sham;
informal phoney.
– ANTONYMS: original.
• v. imitate fraudulently.
▷ SYNONYMS: **fake**, forge, copy, repro-

duce, imitate, falsify.

counterfoil n. the part of a cheque,
ticket, etc. kept as a record by the
person issuing it.

countermand v. cancel an order.

counterpane n. a bedspread.

counterpart n. a person or thing that
corresponds to another.
▷ SYNONYMS: **equivalent**, opposite
number, peer, equal, parallel, complement, analogue, match, twin, mate,
fellow.

counterpoint n. **1** the technique
of combining musical melodies. **2** a
contrasting idea or thing.

counterproductive adj. having the
opposite of the desired effect.

countersign v. sign a document
already signed by another person.

countersink v. (**countersinking**,
countersunk) insert a screw or bolt
so that the head is level with the
surface.

countertenor n. the highest male
adult singing voice.

counterterrorism n. political
or military activities designed to
prevent terrorism.

countess n. **1** the wife or widow of
a count or earl. **2** a woman with the
rank of count or earl.

countless adj. too many to be
counted.
▷ SYNONYMS: **innumerable**, numerous,
untold, legion, numberless, limitless,
incalculable; informal umpteen; N. Amer.
informal gazillions of.
– ANTONYMS: few.

countrified adj. characteristic of the
country or country life.

country n. (pl. **countries**) **1** a nation
with its own government. **2** areas
outside large towns and cities.
▷ SYNONYMS: **1 nation**, state, kingdom,
realm, land, territory, province.
2 people, public, population,
populace, citizens, nation; Brit.
informal Joe Public. **3 terrain**, land,
territory, landscape, countryside,
scenery, surroundings, environment.
4 countryside, provinces, rural areas,
backwoods, hinterland; Austral./NZ
outback, bush, back country; informal
sticks.
□ **countryman** (or **countrywoman**) **1** a
person from your country. **2** a person
living in the country. **country music**
(or **country and western**) popular
music from the rural southern US.
countryside the land of a rural area.

county n. (pl. **counties**) each of the
main administrative areas into which

some countries are divided.

▷ SYNONYMS: **shire**, province, territory, region, district, area.

coup /koo/ n. (pl. **coups** /kooz/) **1** (or **coup d'état** /koo day-**tah**/) a sudden violent seizure of power from a government. **2** a successful move.

▷ SYNONYMS: **1 takeover**, coup d'état, overthrow, palace revolution, rebellion, uprising. **2 success**, triumph, feat, masterstroke, accomplishment, achievement, scoop.

coup de grâce /koo duh **grahss**/ n. (pl. **coups de grâce**) a final blow or shot given to kill a wounded person or animal.

coupe /koo-pay, koop/ n. a two-door car with a fixed roof and a sloping back.

couple n. **1** two people or things of the same sort. **2** two people who are married or romantically involved. **3** informal a small number.

▷ SYNONYMS: **1 pair**, duo, twosome, two, brace. **2 husband and wife**, twosome, partners, lovers; informal item.

• v. **1** connect or combine. **2** have sex.

▷ SYNONYMS: **1 combine**, accompany, ally, mix, incorporate, add to. **2 connect**, attach, join, fasten, fix, link, secure, hook.

– ANTONYMS: detach.

couplet n. two successive rhyming lines of verse.

coupling n. a connecting device.

coupon n. **1** a voucher entitling the holder to something. **2** a detachable order form.

▷ SYNONYMS: **voucher**, token, ticket, slip.

courage n. the ability to control fear when facing danger or pain.

▷ SYNONYMS: **bravery**, pluck, valour, fearlessness, nerve, daring, audacity, boldness, grit, heroism, gallantry; informal **guts**; Brit. informal bottle.

– ANTONYMS: cowardice.

courageous adj. not deterred by danger or pain; brave.

▷ SYNONYMS: **brave**, plucky, fearless, intrepid, valiant, heroic, undaunted, dauntless; informal gutsy, have-a-go.

– ANTONYMS: cowardly.

■ **courageously** adv.

courgette /koor-**zhet**/ n. Brit. a small vegetable marrow.

courier /kuu-ri-er/ n. **1** a person employed to deliver things quickly. **2** a person employed to assist a group of tourists.

course n. **1** a direction taken or intended. **2** the way something progresses. **3** (or **course of action**)

a procedure adopted. **4** one of the stages of a meal. **5** a series of lessons. **6** a series of treatments. **7** an area for racing, golf, etc.

▷ SYNONYMS: **1 route**, way, track, path, line, trail, trajectory, bearing, heading. **2 procedure**, plan, practice, approach, technique, policy, strategy, tactic. **3 racecourse**, racetrack, track. **4 course of study**, curriculum, syllabus, classes, lectures, studies. **5 programme**, series, sequence, system, schedule, regime.

• v. **1** flow. **2** (**coursing**) hunting hares with greyhounds.

▷ SYNONYMS: **flow**, pour, stream, run, rush, gush, cascade, flood, roll.

☐ **of course 1** as expected. **2** yes.

court n. **1** the judge, jury, and law officers who hear legal cases. **2** the place where a law court meets. **3** an area for playing tennis, squash, etc. **4** a courtyard. **5** the home, advisers, and staff of a sovereign.

▷ SYNONYMS: **1 court of law**, law court, bench, bar, tribunal, assizes. **2 household**, retinue, entourage, train, courtiers, attendants.

• v. **1** try to win the support of. **2** risk danger etc. **3** dated try to win the love of.

▷ SYNONYMS: **1 cultivate**, flatter, curry favour with, wine and dine; informal butter up. **2** *he's never courted publicity:* seek, pursue, go after, strive for, solicit. **3 risk**, invite, attract, bring on yourself. **4 woo**, go out with, date.

☐ **court martial** (pl. **courts martial**) a court trying offences against military law. **courtship** the act or period of courting someone. **court shoe** a woman's shoe with a low-cut upper and no fastening. **courtyard** an open area enclosed by walls or buildings.

> **WORD LINKS**
> **forensic** relating to courts of law

courteous /ker-ti-uhss/ adj. polite.

▷ SYNONYMS: **polite**, well mannered, civil, respectful, well behaved, gracious, obliging, considerate.

– ANTONYMS: rude.

■ **courteously** adv.

courtesan /kor-ti-zan/ n. a prostitute with upper-class clients.

courtesy n. (pl. **courtesies**) **1** polite behaviour. **2** a polite action.

▷ SYNONYMS: **politeness**, good manners, civility, respect, grace, consideration, thought.

courtier n. a sovereign's companion

or adviser.

courtly adj. dignified and polite.

couscous /kuuss-kuuss/ n. a North African dish of steamed semolina.

cousin n. (or **first cousin**) a child of your uncle or aunt.
□ **second cousin** a child of your parent's first cousin.

couture /koo-tyoor/ n. the design and making of fashionable clothes.
■ **couturier** n.

cove n. a small bay.
▷ SYNONYMS: **bay**, inlet, fjord.

coven /kuv-uhn/ n. a group of witches who meet regularly.

covenant n. a formal agreement, esp. one to make regular payments to a charity.

cover v. 1 put something over or in front of to protect or hide. 2 spread or extend over. 3 deal with or report on. 4 travel a specified distance. 5 be enough to pay for. 6 protect by insurance. 7 (**cover up**) try to hide a mistake or crime. 8 (**cover for**) temporarily take over their job.
▷ SYNONYMS: 1 **protect**, shield, shelter, hide, conceal, mask, screen, veil, obscure, spread over, extend over, overlay. 2 **cake**, coat, encrust, plaster, smother, blanket, carpet, shroud. 3 **deal with**, consider, take in, include, involve, incorporate, embrace.
– ANTONYMS: reveal.
•n. 1 something that covers or protects. 2 protection by insurance.
▷ SYNONYMS: 1 *a protective cover:* **covering**, sleeve, wrapping, wrapper, envelope, sheath, housing, jacket, casing, cowling, canopy. 2 *a manhole cover:* **lid**, top, cap. 3 *a book cover:* **binding**, jacket, dust jacket, dust cover, wrapper. 4 **coating**, coat, covering, layer, carpet, blanket, film, sheet, veneer, crust, skin, cloak, mantle, veil, pall, shroud. 5 **shelter**, protection, refuge, sanctuary.
□ **coverage 1** the treatment of a subject by the media. **2** the extent to which something is covered. **covering letter** an explanatory letter enclosed with goods. **coverlet** a bedspread. **cover-up** an attempt to hide a mistake or crime.

covert adj. done secretly.
▷ SYNONYMS: **secret**, furtive, clandestine, surreptitious, stealthy, cloak-and-dagger, backstairs, hidden, concealed, private, undercover, underground; informal hush-hush.
– ANTONYMS: overt.

•n. a thicket in which game can hide.
■ **covertly** adv.

covet v. (**coveting**, **coveted**) long to possess something belonging to someone else.
▷ SYNONYMS: **desire**, yearn for, crave, have your heart set on, long for, hanker after/for, hunger after/for, thirst for.
■ **covetous** adj.

covey /kuv-i/ n. (pl. **coveys**) a small flock of game birds.

cow n. 1 a mature female animal of cattle and of the elephant or whale. 2 informal, derogatory a woman.
•v. intimidate.
□ **cowboy 1** a man on horseback who herds cattle in the western US. 2 informal a dishonest or unqualified tradesman.

coward n. a person who lacks courage.
▷ SYNONYMS: informal **wimp**, chicken, scaredy-cat, sissy; Brit. informal big girl's blouse; N. Amer. informal pantywaist.
■ **cowardice** n.

cowardly adj. lacking courage.
▷ SYNONYMS: **faint-hearted**, lily-livered, spineless, craven, timid, timorous, fearful; informal yellow, wimpy, chicken, gutless, yellow-bellied.
– ANTONYMS: brave.

cower v. crouch or shrink back in fear.
▷ SYNONYMS: **cringe**, shrink, flinch, crouch, blench.

cowl n. 1 a loose hood on a monk's robe. 2 a covering for a chimney.

cowling n. a removable cover for an engine.

cowrie n. a shellfish with a glossy shell.

cowslip n. a wild plant with small yellow flowers.

cox n. a person who steers a rowing boat.

coxcomb n. old use a vain man.

coxswain /kok-suhn/ n. = cox.

coy adj. 1 pretending to be shy or modest. 2 reluctant to give details about something.
▷ SYNONYMS: **demure**, shy, modest, bashful, diffident, self-effacing, shrinking.
– ANTONYMS: brazen.
■ **coyly** adv.

coyote /koy-oh-ti/ n. a North American wolf-like wild dog.

coypu n. a large beaver-like South American rodent.

cozy US = cosy.

crab n. a ten-legged shellfish.

crab apple n. a small, sour apple.

crabbed adj. **1** (of writing) hard to read. **2** (or **crabby**) bad-tempered.

crack n. **1** a line where something has broken but not separated. **2** a sudden sharp noise. **3** a sharp blow. **4** informal a joke. **5** informal an attempt. **6** a strong form of cocaine.

▷ SYNONYMS: **1** *a crack in the glass*: **split**, break, chip, fracture, rupture. **2** *a crack between two rocks*: **space**, gap, crevice, fissure, cleft, cranny, chink. **3** **bang**, report, explosion, detonation, clap, crash. **4** *a crack on the head*: **blow**, bang, hit, knock, rap, bump, smack, slap; informal bash, whack, clout.
• v. **1** break without separating. **2** give way under pressure. **3** make a sudden sharp sound. **4** hit hard. **5** (of a voice) suddenly change in pitch. **6** informal solve.

▷ SYNONYMS: **1** **break**, split, fracture, rupture, snap. **2** **break down**, give way, cave in, go to pieces, give in, yield, succumb. **3** **hit**, strike, smack, slap, beat, thump, knock, rap; informal bash, whack, clobber, clout, clip. **4** **decipher**, interpret, decode, break, solve.
• adj. very good or skilful.
☐ **crackdown** a series of severe measures against something. **crack down on** informal take severe measures against. **crackpot** informal eccentric or impractical. **crack up** informal suffer an emotional breakdown.

cracker n. **1** a paper tube making a sharp noise when pulled apart. **2** an explosive firework. **3** a thin, dry biscuit.

crackers adj. informal mad.

crackle v. make a series of slight cracking noises.
• n. a crackling sound.
■ **crackly** adj.

crackling n. the crisp fatty skin of roast pork.

cradle n. **1** a baby's bed on rockers. **2** a place where something originates. **3** a supporting framework.

▷ SYNONYMS: **1** **crib**, Moses basket, cot, carrycot. **2** **birthplace**, fount, fountainhead, source, spring, origin.
• v. hold or support gently.

▷ SYNONYMS: **hold**, support, cushion, pillow, nurse, rest.

craft n. **1** an activity involving skill in making things by hand. **2** skill. **3** (pl. **craft**) a ship or boat.

▷ SYNONYMS: **1** **activity**, occupation, trade, profession, work, line of work, job. **2** **cunning**, craftiness, guile, wiliness, artfulness, deviousness, slyness,

trickery, duplicity, dishonesty, deceit, deceitfulness, deception, intrigue, subterfuge, wiles, ploys, ruses, schemes, tricks. **3** **vessel**, ship, boat, aircraft, spacecraft.
• v. make skilfully.

craftsman n. a worker skilled in a craft.

▷ SYNONYMS: **artisan**, artist, skilled worker, technician, expert, master.
■ **craftsmanship** n.

crafty adj. (**craftier, craftiest**) clever at deceiving people; cunning.

▷ SYNONYMS: **cunning**, wily, sly, artful, devious, tricky, scheming, calculating, shrewd, canny, dishonest, deceitful.
– ANTONYMS: honest.
■ **craftily** adv. **craftiness** n.

crag n. a steep or rugged rock face.
■ **craggy** adj.

cram v. (**cramming, crammed**)
1 force into too small a space. **2** fill to overflowing. **3** study hard for an exam.

▷ SYNONYMS: **1** *wardrobes crammed with clothes*: **fill**, stuff, pack, jam, fill to overflowing, overload, crowd, throng. **2** *he crammed his clothes into a case*: **push**, thrust, shove, force, ram, jam, stuff, pack, pile, squash, squeeze, compress. **3** **revise**, study; informal swot, mug up, bone up.

cramp n. painful involuntary tightening of a muscle.

▷ SYNONYMS: **spasm**, pain, shooting pain, twinge, pang, convulsion.
• v. restrict.

▷ SYNONYMS: **hinder**, impede, inhibit, hamper, constrain, hamstring, interfere with, restrict, limit, slow.

cramped adj. very small or crowded.

▷ SYNONYMS: **poky**, uncomfortable, confined, restricted, constricted, small, tiny, narrow, crowded, congested.
– ANTONYMS: spacious.

crampon n. a spiked plate fixed to a boot for climbing on ice.

cranberry n. a small sour red berry.

crane n. **1** a tall machine for lifting and moving heavy objects. **2** a long-legged wading bird.
• v. stretch out your neck to see something.

cranium n. (pl. **craniums** or **crania**) the skull.

crank n. **1** a right-angled part of an axle or shaft for converting linear to circular motion. **2** an eccentric person.
• v. turn a crankshaft or handle.
☐ **crankshaft** a shaft driven by a crank.

cranky adj. informal eccentric or strange.

cranny n. (pl. **crannies**) a crevice.

craps n. a gambling game played with two dice.

crash v. **1** (of a vehicle) collide violently with something. **2** (of an aircraft) fall from the sky and hit the land or sea. **3** move loudly and forcefully. **4** Computing fail suddenly.
▷ SYNONYMS: **1** *the car crashed into a tree:* **smash into**, collide with, be in collision with, hit, strike, ram, cannon into, plough into, meet head-on; N. Amer. **impact**. **2** *he crashed his car:* **smash**, wreck; Brit. write off; Brit. informal prang; N. Amer. informal total. **3 fall**, drop, plummet, plunge, sink, dive, tumble. **4 fail**, fold, collapse, go under, go bankrupt; informal go bust, go to the wall.
• n. **1** an instance of crashing. **2** a sudden loud noise.
▷ SYNONYMS: **1 accident**, collision, smash; N. Amer. wreck; informal pile-up; Brit. informal shunt, prang. **2 bang**, smash, smack, crack, bump, thud, explosion. **3 failure**, collapse, liquidation, bankruptcy.
• adj. rapid and concentrated.
□ **crash helmet** a helmet worn to protect the head. **crash-land** (of an aircraft) land roughly in an emergency.

crass adj. very thoughtless and stupid.

crate n. **1** a wooden box for transporting goods. **2** a container divided into sections for holding bottles.
▷ SYNONYMS: **packing case**, chest, tea chest, box, container.
• v. pack in a crate.

crater n. a large hollow in the ground or forming the mouth of a volcano.
▷ SYNONYMS: **hollow**, bowl, basin, hole, cavity, depression, dip; Geology caldera.

cravat n. a man's scarf worn tucked inside a shirt.

crave v. **1** feel a strong desire for. **2** old use ask for.
▷ SYNONYMS: **long for**, yearn for, hanker after, desire, want, hunger for, thirst for, pine for; informal be dying for.

craven adj. cowardly.

craving n. a strong desire for something.
▷ SYNONYMS: **longing**, yearning, desire, hankering, hunger, thirst, appetite, greed, lust.

crawl v. **1** move forward on the hands and knees or with the body on the ground. **2** move along very slowly. **3** (**be crawling with**) be crowded with. **4** informal be very submissive or friendly so as to gain favour.
▷ SYNONYMS: **1 creep**, worm your way, go on all fours, wriggle, slither, squirm. **2 grovel**, kowtow, pander, toady, bow and scrape, fawn; informal suck up, lick someone's boots.
• n. **1** a crawling movement or pace. **2** an overarm swimming stroke.
■ **crawler** n.

crayfish n. a shellfish like a small lobster.

crayon n. a stick of coloured chalk or wax, used for drawing.
• v. draw with a crayon or crayons.

craze n. a widespread but short-lived enthusiasm for something.
▷ SYNONYMS: **fad**, fashion, trend, vogue, enthusiasm, mania, passion, rage; informal thing.

crazy adj. (**crazier**, **craziest**) **1** mad. **2** very foolish. **3** informal very enthusiastic or fond.
▷ SYNONYMS: **1 mad**, insane, out of your mind, deranged, demented, crazed, lunatic, unbalanced, unhinged; informal mental, off your head, round the bend; Brit. informal barmy, crackers, barking, potty, round the twist. **2** *a crazy idea:* **stupid**, foolish, idiotic, silly, absurd, ridiculous, ludicrous, preposterous, asinine; informal cockeyed, half-baked; Brit. informal barmy, daft. **3** *he's crazy about her:* **passionate**, very keen, enamoured, infatuated, smitten, enthusiastic, fanatical; informal wild, mad, nuts; Brit. informal potty.
− ANTONYMS: sane, sensible.
□ **crazy paving** paving made of irregular flat stones.
■ **crazily** adv. **craziness** n.

creak v. make a harsh, high sound.
• n. a creaking sound.
■ **creaky** adj.

cream n. **1** the thick fatty part of milk. **2** a thick liquid substance. **3** the very best of a group. **4** a pale yellowish-white colour.
▷ SYNONYMS: **1 lotion**, ointment, moisturizer, cosmetic, salve, rub. **2 best**, finest, pick, flower, crème de la crème, elite.
− ANTONYMS: dregs.
• v. **1** mash a cooked vegetable with milk or cream. **2** (**cream off**) take away the best of.

creamy adj. resembling or containing cream.
▷ SYNONYMS: **smooth**, thick, velvety, rich, buttery.

crease n. **1** a line or ridge made on

paper or cloth by folding or pressing.
2 a line on a cricket pitch marking the position of the bowler etc.
▷ SYNONYMS: **fold**, line, crinkle, ridge, furrow, groove, corrugation, wrinkle, crow's foot.
• v. make or develop creases in.
▷ SYNONYMS: **crumple**, wrinkle, crinkle, line, scrunch up, rumple, ruck up, pucker.

create v. **1** bring into existence.
2 cause to happen.
▷ SYNONYMS: **1 produce**, generate, bring into being, make, fashion, build, construct. **2 bring about**, give rise to, lead to, result in, cause, breed, generate, engender, produce. **3 establish**, found, initiate, institute, constitute, inaugurate, launch, set up, form.
– ANTONYMS: destroy, abolish.

creation n. **1** the action of creating something. **2** a thing that has been created or invented. **3** (**Creation**) literary the universe.
▷ SYNONYMS: **1 establishment**, formation, foundation, initiation, institution, inauguration, constitution, setting up. **2 work**, work of art, production, opus, oeuvre, achievement, concoction, invention; informal brainchild. **3 the world**, the universe, the cosmos, nature.
– ANTONYMS: abolition, destruction.

creative adj. involving the use of imagination to create something.
▷ SYNONYMS: **inventive**, imaginative, innovative, experimental, original, artistic, inspired, visionary.
– ANTONYMS: unimaginative.
■ **creatively** adv. **creativity** n.

creator n. a person or thing that creates something.
▷ SYNONYMS: **maker**, producer, author, designer, deviser, originator, inventor, architect, mastermind.

creature n. a living being.
▷ SYNONYMS: **animal**, beast, brute, living thing, living being; N. Amer. informal critter.

crèche /kresh/ n. a day nursery.

credence n. belief that something is true.

credentials pl. n. **1** qualifications or qualities indicating a person's suitability for something.
2 documents proving qualifications etc.
▷ SYNONYMS: **1 suitability**, eligibility, attributes, qualifications, record, experience, background.
2 documents, identity papers, ID,

passport, testimonial, reference, certification.

credible adj. able to be believed.
▷ SYNONYMS: **believable**, plausible, conceivable, persuasive, convincing, trustworthy, tenable, probable, possible, feasible, reasonable.
■ **credibility** n. **credibly** adv.

credit n. **1** a system allowing customers to pay at a later date for goods or services supplied. **2** public recognition or praise. **3** a source of pride. **4** (**credits**) a list of the contributors to a film or television programme, displayed at the end.
5 an entry in an account recording a sum received.
▷ SYNONYMS: **praise**, commendation, acclaim, acknowledgement, recognition, kudos, glory, respect, appreciation.
• v. (**crediting, credited**) **1** (**credit with**) attribute something to.
2 believe. **3** add money to an account.
▷ SYNONYMS: **1** you wouldn't credit it!: believe, accept, give credence to, trust, have faith in. **2 ascribe to**, attribute to, put down to.
□ **credit card** a plastic card allowing the holder to make purchases on credit.

creditable adj. deserving praise.
■ **creditably** adv.

creditor n. a person or company to whom money is owed.

credulous adj. too ready to believe things.
▷ SYNONYMS: **gullible**, naive, easily taken in, impressionable, unsuspecting, unsuspicious, innocent, inexperienced, unsophisticated, wide-eyed.
– ANTONYMS: suspicious.
■ **credulity** n.

creed n. **1** a system of religious belief.
2 a set of beliefs or principles.
▷ SYNONYMS: **1** people of many creeds: **faith**, religion, belief, religious persuasion. **2** his political creed: **beliefs**, principles, articles of faith, tenets, ideology, credo, doctrines, teachings.

creek n. **1** an inlet in a shoreline. **2** US a stream.
▷ SYNONYMS: **inlet**, bay, estuary, fjord; Scottish firth.

creep v. (**creeping, crept**) **1** move slowly and cautiously. **2** progress or develop gradually.
▷ SYNONYMS: **tiptoe**, steal, sneak, slink, edge, inch, skulk, prowl.
• n. **1** informal an unpleasant person.
2 slow and gradual movement.

creeper n. a plant that grows along the ground or another surface.

creepy adj. (**creepier**, **creepiest**) informal frightening or disturbing.
▷ SYNONYMS: **frightening**, eerie, disturbing, sinister, weird, menacing, threatening; informal spooky, scary.

cremate v. burn a corpse to ashes.
■ **cremation** n.

crematorium n. (pl. **crematoria** or **crematoriums**) a building where the dead are cremated.

crenellated adj. having battlements.
■ **crenellations** pl. n.

Creole /kree-ohl/ n. **1** (in the Caribbean) a person of mixed European and black descent. **2** a descendant of French settlers in the southern US. **3** a combination of a European language and an African one.

creosote n. a dark brown oil used as a wood preservative.

crêpe n. **1** /krayp/ a fabric or a type of rubber with a wrinkled surface. **2** /krep/ a thin pancake.

crept past & past part. of CREEP.

crepuscular adj. resembling twilight.

crescendo n. (pl. **crescendos** or **crescendi**) a gradual increase in loudness.

crescent n. a narrow curved shape tapering to a point at each end.

cress n. a salad vegetable with small leaves.

crest n. **1** the top of a hill or wave. **2** a tuft of feathers or a growth of skin on a bird's or animal's head. **3** a plume of feathers on a helmet. **4** a design above a shield on a coat of arms.
▷ SYNONYMS: **1 summit**, peak, top, ridge, pinnacle, brow, crown, apex. **2 tuft**, comb, plume, crown. **3 insignia**, emblem, coat of arms, arms, badge, device, regalia.
■ **crested** adj.

crestfallen adj. sad and disappointed.
▷ SYNONYMS: **downhearted**, downcast, despondent, disappointed, disconsolate, disheartened, discouraged, dispirited, dejected, sad, dismayed, unhappy, forlorn.

cretin n. informal a stupid person.
■ **cretinous** adj.

crevasse n. a deep open crack in a glacier.

crevice n. a narrow opening in a rock or wall.
▷ SYNONYMS: **crack**, fissure, interstice, cleft, chink, cranny, slit, split.

crew¹ n. **1** the people working on a

ship, aircraft, etc. **2** a group working together.
▷ SYNONYMS: **1** the ship's crew: **company**, complement, sailors, hands. **2** a film crew: **team**, squad, company, unit, party, gang.
• v. act as a member of a crew.
□ **crew cut** a very short haircut. **crew neck** a close-fitting round neckline.

crew² past of CROW.

crib n. **1** a child's cot. **2** informal a list of facts, often used to cheat in a test. **3** a rack for animal fodder.
• v. (**cribbing**, **cribbed**) informal copy dishonestly.

cribbage n. a card game.

crick n. a painful stiff feeling in the neck or back.
• v. cause a crick in.

cricket n. **1** an open-air team game played with a bat, ball, and wickets. **2** an insect like a grasshopper.
■ **cricketer** n.

cried past & past part. of CRY.

crime n. **1** an act that is illegal and can be punished by law. **2** illegal actions.
▷ SYNONYMS: **1 offence**, unlawful act, illegal act, felony, violation, misdemeanour. **2 lawbreaking**, delinquency, wrongdoing, criminality, misconduct, illegality, villainy, vice.

criminal n. a person who has committed a crime.
▷ SYNONYMS: **lawbreaker**, felon, offender, malefactor, villain, delinquent, culprit, miscreant, wrongdoer; informal crook.
• adj. of crime or a crime.
▷ SYNONYMS: **1 unlawful**, illegal, illicit, lawless, delinquent, corrupt, felonious, nefarious; informal crooked; Brit. informal bent. **2 deplorable**, shameful, reprehensible, disgraceful, inexcusable, outrageous, scandalous.
− ANTONYMS: lawful.
■ **criminality** n. **criminally** adv.

criminology n. the study of crime.
■ **criminologist** n.

crimp v. press into ridges.

crimson n. a deep red colour.

cringe v. **1** cower in fear. **2** feel embarrassment or disgust.
▷ SYNONYMS: **1 cower**, shrink, recoil, shy away, flinch, quail, blench, tremble, quiver, quake. **2 wince**, shudder, squirm, feel embarrassed/mortified.

crinkle v. form small creases.
• n. a small crease.
■ **crinkly** adj.

crinoline n. a petticoat stiffened with hoops, formerly worn to make a long skirt stand out.

cripple n. old use or offens. a person unable to walk properly through disability or injury.
• v. **1** make unable to walk properly. **2** severely damage.
▷ SYNONYMS: *the industry has been crippled by the war*: **damage**, weaken, paralyse, immobilize, bring to a standstill, put out of action, put out of business.

crisis n. (pl. **crises**) a time of severe difficulty or danger.
▷ SYNONYMS: **1 emergency**, disaster, catastrophe, calamity, meltdown, predicament, plight, dire straits. **2 critical point**, turning point, crossroads, head, point of no return, moment of truth; informal crunch.

crisp adj. **1** firm, dry, and brittle. **2** cold and bracing. **3** brisk and decisive.
▷ SYNONYMS: **1 crunchy**, crispy, brittle, breakable, dry. **2 invigorating**, brisk, cool, fresh, refreshing, exhilarating.
– ANTONYMS: soft.
• n. a thin slice of fried potato.
□ **crispbread** a thin, crisp biscuit made from rye or wheat.
■ **crisply** adv. **crispness** n. **crispy** adj.

criss-cross adj. with a pattern of crossing lines.
• v. form a criss-cross pattern on.

criterion n. (pl. **criteria**) a standard by which something may be judged.
▷ SYNONYMS: **standard**, measure, gauge, test, benchmark, yardstick, touchstone, barometer.

USAGE The singular form is **criterion** and the plural form is **criteria**. Don't use **criteria** as a singular, as in *a further criteria needs to be considered*.

critic n. **1** a person who points out faults. **2** a person who assesses literary or artistic works.
▷ SYNONYMS: **1 detractor**, attacker, fault-finder. **2 reviewer**, commentator, analyst, judge, pundit, expert.

critical adj. **1** expressing disapproving comments. **2** assessing a literary or artistic work. **3** having a decisive importance. **4** at a point of danger or crisis.
▷ SYNONYMS: **1 disapproving**, disparaging, scathing, fault-finding, judgemental, negative, unfavourable, censorious; informal nit-picking, picky. **2 serious**, grave, precarious, touch-and-go, in the balance, desperate, dire, acute, life-and-death. **3 crucial**, vital, essential, all-important, para-

mount, fundamental, key, pivotal.
– ANTONYMS: complimentary.
■ **critically** adv.

criticism n. **1** expression of disapproval. **2** the assessment of literary or artistic works.
▷ SYNONYMS: **1 fault-finding**, censure, condemnation, disapproval, disparagement; informal flak, a bad press, panning; Brit. informal stick. **2 evaluation**, assessment, appraisal, appreciation, analysis, critique, judgement, commentary.
– ANTONYMS: praise.

criticize (or **-ise**) v. **1** express disapproval of. **2** assess a literary or artistic work.
▷ SYNONYMS: **find fault with**, censure, condemn, attack, disparage, denigrate, run down; informal knock, pan, pull to pieces; Brit. informal slag off, slate, rubbish; N. Amer. informal trash.
– ANTONYMS: praise.

critique n. a critical assessment.

croak n. a deep hoarse sound, like that made by a frog.
• v. make a croak.
■ **croaky** adj.

crochet /kroh-shay/ n. a handicraft in which yarn is made into a fabric by means of a hooked needle.
• v. make in this way.

crock n. **1** an earthenware pot. **2** informal a feeble old person.

crockery n. china or earthenware plates, cups, etc.

crocodile n. **1** a large tropical reptile living partly in water. **2** Brit. informal a line of schoolchildren walking in pairs.
□ **crocodile tears** false sorrow.

crocus n. (pl. **crocuses**) a small spring-flowering plant.

croft n. a small rented farm in Scotland.
■ **crofter** n.

croissant /krwass-on/ n. a crescent-shaped flaky bread roll.

crone n. an ugly old woman.

crony n. (pl. **cronies**) informal a close friend or companion.

crook n. **1** informal a criminal. **2** a hooked staff. **3** the inner bend at the elbow.
• v. bend a finger.

crooked adj. **1** not straight. **2** informal dishonest.
▷ SYNONYMS: **1 winding**, twisting, zigzag, meandering, tortuous, serpentine. **2 bent**, twisted, misshapen, deformed, malformed, contorted, warped, bowed, distorted. **3 lopsided**,

askew, awry, off-centre, out of true, at an angle, slanting, squint; Scottish **agley**; Brit. informal **skew-whiff**, wonky. **4 dishonest**, criminal, illegal, unlawful, nefarious, fraudulent, corrupt; informal **shady**; Brit. informal **bent**.
– ANTONYMS: straight.
■ **crookedly** adv.

croon v. hum, sing, or speak in a soft, low voice.
■ **crooner** n.

crop n. **1** a plant grown for food or other use. **2** a harvest from this. **3** a very short hairstyle. **4** a riding crop. **5** a pouch in a bird's throat where food is prepared for digestion.
▷ SYNONYMS: **harvest**, yield, fruits, produce, vintage.
● v. (**cropping**, **cropped**) **1** cut or bite off very short. **2** (**crop up**) occur unexpectedly. **3** produce a crop.
▷ SYNONYMS: **1 cut**, clip, trim, shear, shave, lop off, chop off, hack off, dock. **2 graze on**, browse on, feed on, nibble, eat.

cropper n. (**come a cropper**) informal fall or fail heavily.

croquet /kroh-kay/ n. a game in which balls are hit through hoops with a mallet.

croquette /kroh-ket/ n. a small roll or cake of vegetables etc. fried in breadcrumbs.

crosier var. of CROZIER.

cross n. **1** a mark, object, or shape formed by two intersecting lines or pieces (+ or ×). **2** a mixture of two things. **3** a hybrid animal or plant. **4** a pass of the ball across the field in football. **5** a thing that has to be endured.
▷ SYNONYMS: **1** *a cross between a yak and a cow*: **mixture**, blend, combination, amalgam, hybrid, cross-breed, mongrel. **2** *we all have our crosses to bear*: **burden**, trouble, worry, trial, tribulation, affliction, curse, misfortune, woe; informal **hassle**, headache.
● v. **1** go or extend across. **2** pass in an opposite or different direction. **3** place crosswise. **4** oppose the wishes of. **5** draw a line or lines across. **6** Brit. mark a cheque so that it must be paid into a named account. **7** pass the ball across the field in football. **8** cause to interbreed.
▷ SYNONYMS: **1 travel across**, traverse, negotiate, navigate, cover. **2 intersect**, meet, join, connect. **3 oppose**, resist, defy, obstruct, contradict, argue with, stand up to. **4 hybridize**,

cross-breed, interbreed, cross-fertilize, cross-pollinate.
● adj. annoyed.
▷ SYNONYMS: **angry**, annoyed, irate, vexed, irritated, in a bad mood, put out, exasperated; informal **hot under the collar**, peeved; Brit. informal **shirty**, **ratty**; N. Amer. informal **sore**, ticked off.
– ANTONYMS: pleased.
□ **at cross purposes** misunderstanding one another.

crossbow a mechanical bow with a wooden support. **cross-breed** produce an animal by interbreeding. **cross-check** verify figures etc. by an alternative method. **cross-dressing** the wearing of clothing typical of the opposite sex. **cross-examine** question a witness called by the other party in a court of law. **cross-eyed** having one or both eyes turned inwards. **crossfire** gunfire crossing another line of fire. **cross reference** a reference to another part in the same book. **crossroads** a place where roads cross each other. **cross section 1** a surface exposed by cutting across something. **2** a representative sample. **crosswise** (or **crossways**) **1** in the form of a cross. **2** diagonally. **crossword** a puzzle consisting of a grid of squares into which intersecting words are written according to clues.
■ **crossly** adv. **crossness** n.

crossing n. **1** a place where roads or railway lines cross. **2** a place to cross a road or railway line.
▷ SYNONYMS: **1 junction**, crossroads, intersection, interchange, level crossing. **2 journey**, passage, voyage.

crotch n. the part of the body between the legs.

crotchet n. a musical note having the value of half a minim.

crotchety adj. irritable.

crouch v. bend the knees and bring the upper body forward and down.
▷ SYNONYMS: **squat**, bend down, hunker down, hunch over, stoop, duck, cower.
● n. a crouching position.

croup n. **1** inflammation of the throat in children, causing coughing and breathing difficulties. **2** the rump of a horse.

croupier /kroo-pi-ay/ n. the person in charge of a gambling table at a casino.

crouton /kroo-ton/ n. a small piece of fried or toasted bread used as a garnish.

crow n. **1** a large black bird. **2** the cry of a cock.
● v. (**crowing**, **crowed** or **crew**) **1** (of

a cock) make its loud shrill cry.
2 express gloating triumph.

▷ SYNONYMS: **boast**, brag, blow your own trumpet, swagger, swank, gloat.

crowbar n. an iron bar with a flattened end, used as a lever.

crowd n. a large group of people gathered together.

▷ SYNONYMS: **1 horde**, throng, mass, multitude, host, army, herd, swarm, troop, mob, rabble; informal gaggle. **2** *they're a nice crowd:* **group**, set, circle, clique; informal gang, bunch, crew, lot. **3** *a capacity crowd:* **audience**, spectators, listeners, viewers, house, turnout, attendance, gate, congregation.

• v. **1** fill a space almost completely. **2** move or gather in a crowd.

▷ SYNONYMS: **cluster**, flock, swarm, mill, throng, gather, assemble, congregate, converge, surge, push, jostle, elbow your way, squeeze, pile, cram.

crowded adj. filled almost completely by a large number of people.

▷ SYNONYMS: **packed**, full, filled to capacity, full to bursting, congested, overflowing, teeming, swarming, thronged, populous, overpopulated, busy; informal jam-packed, stuffed, chock-a-block, chock-full, bursting at the seams, full to the gunwales, wall-to-wall, mobbed; Austral./NZ informal chocker.

– ANTONYMS: deserted.

crown n. **1** a monarch's ceremonial headdress. **2** (**the Crown**) the monarchy or reigning monarch. **3** the top or highest part. **4** an artificial covering for a tooth.

▷ SYNONYMS: **1 coronet**, diadem, tiara, circlet. **2 monarch**, sovereign, king, queen, emperor, empress, monarchy, royalty. **3 top**, crest, summit, peak, pinnacle, tip, brow, apex.

• v. **1** formally place a crown on the head of a new monarch. **2** rest on or form the top of. **3** be the climax of.

▷ SYNONYMS: *the post at Harvard crowned his career:* **round off**, cap, be the climax of, be the culmination of, top off, complete, perfect.

☐ **Crown prince** (or **Crown princess**) the heir to a throne.

crozier (or **crosier**) n. a bishop's hooked staff.

crucial adj. very important to the success or failure of something.

▷ SYNONYMS: **1 pivotal**, critical, key, decisive, life-and-death. **2 all-important**, of the utmost importance, of the essence, critical, paramount,

essential, vital.

– ANTONYMS: insignificant, unimportant.

■ **crucially** adv.

crucible n. a container in which metals are melted.

crucifix n. a model of a cross with a figure of Jesus on it.

crucifixion n. **1** an act of crucifying someone. **2** (**the Crucifixion**) the killing of Jesus in this way.

cruciform adj. cross-shaped.

crucify v. (**crucifying**, **crucified**) **1** put to death by nailing or binding to a cross. **2** informal criticize severely.

crude adj. **1** in a natural or unprocessed state. **2** rough or simple. **3** coarse or vulgar.

▷ SYNONYMS: **1 unrefined**, unpurified, unprocessed, untreated, coarse, raw, natural. **2 primitive**, simple, basic, homespun, rudimentary, rough and ready, makeshift, improvised, unsophisticated. **3 vulgar**, rude, dirty, naughty, smutty, indecent, obscene, coarse; informal blue.

– ANTONYMS: refined.

■ **crudely** adv. **crudity** n.

crudités /kroo-di-tay/ pl. n. mixed raw vegetables to dip in a sauce.

cruel adj. (**crueller**, **cruellest** or **crueler**, **cruelest**) **1** taking pleasure in others' suffering. **2** causing pain or suffering.

▷ SYNONYMS: **1** *a cruel man:* **brutal**, savage, inhuman, barbaric, vicious, sadistic, monstrous, callous, ruthless, merciless, heartless, pitiless, implacable, unkind, inhumane. **2** *her death was a cruel blow:* **harsh**, severe, bitter, heartbreaking, heart-rending, painful, agonizing, traumatic.

– ANTONYMS: compassionate.

■ **cruelly** adv. **cruelty** n.

cruet n. a set of containers for salt, pepper, etc. for use at the table.

cruise v. **1** travel around slowly, esp. by ship. **2** travel at a moderate economical speed.

▷ SYNONYMS: **1 sail**, voyage. **2 drive slowly**, drift; informal mosey, tootle; Brit. informal pootle.

• n. a voyage on a ship taken as a holiday.

cruiser n. **1** a fast warship. **2** a motorboat with a cabin.

crumb n. **1** a small fragment of bread etc. **2** a tiny amount.

▷ SYNONYMS: **fragment**, bit, morsel, particle, speck, scrap, shred, atom, trace, mite, jot, ounce; informal smidgen, tad.

crumble v. break or fall apart into small fragments.

▷ SYNONYMS: **1 disintegrate**, fall apart, fall to pieces, collapse, decompose, break up, decay, deteriorate, degenerate. **2 break up**, crush, fragment, pulverize.

• n. Brit. a baked pudding made with fruit and a crumbly topping.

■ **crumbly** adj.

crummy adj. informal bad or unpleasant.

crumpet n. **1** a flat soft cake eaten toasted. **2** Brit. informal sexually attractive women.

crumple v. **1** crush so as to become creased. **2** collapse.

▷ SYNONYMS: **1 crush**, scrunch up, screw up, squash, squeeze. **2 crease**, wrinkle, crinkle, rumple. **3 collapse**, give way, cave in, go to pieces, break down, crumble.

crunch v. **1** crush noisily with the teeth. **2** move with a noisy grinding sound.

▷ SYNONYMS: **munch**, chomp, champ, bite into, crush, grind.

• n. **1** a crunching sound. **2** (**the crunch**) informal the crucial point.

■ **crunchy** adj.

crusade n. **1** (**the Crusades**) a series of medieval Christian military expeditions to recover the Holy Land from the Muslims. **2** a campaign for a cause.

▷ SYNONYMS: **campaign**, drive, push, movement, effort, struggle, battle, war, offensive.

• v. take part in a crusade.

▷ SYNONYMS: **campaign**, fight, battle, do battle, strive, struggle, agitate, lobby.

■ **crusader** n.

crush v. **1** press so as to squash, crease, or break up. **2** defeat completely.

▷ SYNONYMS: **1 squash**, squeeze, press, pulp, mash, mangle, pulverize. **2 crease**, crumple, rumple, wrinkle, scrunch up. **3 suppress**, put down, quell, stamp out, repress, subdue, extinguish. **4 demoralize**, deflate, flatten, squash, devastate, shatter, mortify, humiliate.

• n. **1** a crowded mass of people. **2** informal an infatuation.

▷ SYNONYMS: **crowd**, throng, horde, swarm, press, mob.

crust n. a hard outer layer, esp. of bread.

▷ SYNONYMS: **covering**, layer, coating, surface, topping, sheet, film, skin, shell, scab.

crustacean /kruss-**tay**-sh'n/ n. a hard-shelled animal such as a crab, usu. living in water.

crusty adj. (**crustier**, **crustiest**) **1** having a crust. **2** irritable.

crutch n. **1** a stick with a crosspiece used as a support by a lame person. **2** the crotch.

crux n. the most important point under discussion.

cry v. (**crying**, **cried**) **1** shed tears. **2** shout or scream loudly. **3** (**cry off**) informal fail to keep to an arrangement.

▷ SYNONYMS: **1 weep**, shed tears, sob, wail, snivel, whimper; Scottish **greet**; informal **blub**, blubber; Brit. informal **grizzle**. **2 call**, shout, exclaim, sing out, yell, bawl, bellow, roar; informal **holler**.

– ANTONYMS: laugh.

• n. (pl. **cries**) **1** a period of crying. **2** a shout or scream. **3** an animal's call.

▷ SYNONYMS: **call**, shout, exclamation, yell, bawl, bellow, roar; informal **holler**.

cryogenics n. the study of very low temperatures.

■ **cryogenic** adj.

crypt n. an underground room or vault in a church.

▷ SYNONYMS: **tomb**, vault, burial chamber, sepulchre, catacomb.

cryptic adj. mysterious or obscure in meaning.

▷ SYNONYMS: **enigmatic**, mysterious, mystifying, puzzling, obscure, abstruse, arcane, unintelligible.

– ANTONYMS: clear.

■ **cryptically** adv.

cryptogram n. a document written in code.

cryptography n. the art of writing or solving codes.

crystal n. **1** a transparent mineral, esp. quartz. **2** a piece of a solid substance with symmetrical flat sides. **3** very clear glass.

crystalline adj. **1** of or like a crystal. **2** very clear.

crystallize (or **-ise**) v. **1** form crystals. **2** make or become definite and clear. **3** (**crystallized**) (of fruit) preserved in sugar.

■ **crystallization** n.

CS gas n. tear gas used in the control of riots.

cu. abbrev. cubic.

cub n. the young of a fox, bear, lion, etc.

cubbyhole n. a small space or room.

cube n. **1** a three-dimensional shape with six equal square faces. **2** the product of a number multiplied by itself twice.

• v. **1** cut into cubes. **2** find the cube of a number.

□ **cube root** the number which

produces a given number when cubed.

■ **cubic** adj.

cubicle n. a small area partitioned off in a large room.

cubism n. a style of painting in which objects are shown as geometric shapes.

■ **cubist** n. & adj.

cuckold n. a man whose wife has been unfaithful.

cuckoo n. a bird that lays its eggs in the nests of other birds.

cucumber n. a long, green fruit eaten in salads.

cud n. food that cattle etc. bring back from the first stomach to the mouth for further chewing.

cuddle v. **1** hug lovingly. **2** lie or sit close.

▷ SYNONYMS: **1** hug, embrace, clasp, hold in your arms, caress, pet, fondle; informal canoodle, smooch. **2** snuggle, nestle, curl, nuzzle.

• n. an affectionate hug.

cuddly adj. pleasantly soft or plump.

cudgel n. a short thick stick used as a weapon.

▷ SYNONYMS: **club**, truncheon, bludgeon, baton, shillelagh, mace; N. Amer. black-jack, nightstick; Brit. informal cosh.

• v. (**cudgelling, cudgelled**; US **cudgeling, cudgeled**) beat with a cudgel.

▷ SYNONYMS: **club**, bludgeon, beat, batter, bash; Brit. informal cosh.

cue n. **1** a signal for action, esp. to an actor to enter or to begin their speech. **2** a long rod for hitting the ball in snooker etc.

▷ SYNONYMS: **signal**, sign, indication, prompt, reminder.

• v. (**cueing** or **cuing, cued**) **1** give a signal to. **2** use a cue to hit a ball.

cuff n. **1** the end part of a sleeve. **2** a blow with an open hand.

• v. hit with an open hand.

□ **cufflink** a device for fastening together the sides of a shirt cuff. **off the cuff** informal without preparation.

cuisine /kwi-zeen/ n. a style of cooking.

cul-de-sac n. (pl. **cul-de-sacs**) a street closed at one end.

culinary adj. of cooking.

cull v. **1** kill certain animals to reduce numbers. **2** select from a wide range.

culminate v. reach a climax or point of highest development.

▷ SYNONYMS: **come to a climax**, come to a head, climax, end, finish, conclude, build up to, lead up to.

culmination n. a climax or point of highest development.

▷ SYNONYMS: **climax**, peak, pinnacle, high point, height, summit, zenith, apotheosis, apex, apogee.

culottes pl. n. women's wide-legged knee-length trousers.

culpable adj. deserving blame.

▷ SYNONYMS: **to blame**, guilty, at fault, in the wrong, answerable, accountable, responsible.

– ANTONYMS: innocent.

■ **culpability** n.

culprit n. a person responsible for an offence.

▷ SYNONYMS: **guilty party**, offender, wrongdoer, miscreant, criminal, lawbreaker, felon, delinquent; informal baddy, crook.

cult n. **1** a small, unconventional religious group. **2** a system of religious beliefs or practices. **3** something popular among a group.

▷ SYNONYMS: **1** sect, group, movement. **2** obsession, fixation, idolization, devotion, worship, veneration.

cultivate v. **1** prepare and use land for crops. **2** grow plants or crops. **3** try to develop a quality. **4** try to win the friendship or support of. **5** (**cultivated**) well educated and having good taste.

▷ SYNONYMS: **1** farm, work, till, plough, dig. **2** grow, raise, rear, tend, plant, sow. **3** woo, court, curry favour with, ingratiate yourself with; informal get in someone's good books. **4** improve, better, refine, educate, develop, enrich.

■ **cultivation** n. **cultivator** n.

cultural adj. **1** relating to the culture of a society. **2** relating to the arts and to intellectual achievement.

▷ SYNONYMS: **1** social, sociological, anthropological. **2** aesthetic, artistic, intellectual, educational, civilizing.

■ **culturally** adv.

culture n. **1** the arts, customs, etc. of a nation or group. **2** the arts and intellectual achievements as a whole. **3** cells or bacteria grown for scientific study.

▷ SYNONYMS: **1** civilization, society, way of life, lifestyle, customs, traditions, heritage, values. **2** *a lover of culture:* **the arts**, high art. **3** *a man of culture:* **education**, cultivation, enlighten-ment, discernment, discrimination, taste, refinement, sophistication.

• v. grow cells etc. for study.

cultured adj. well educated and having good taste.

▷ SYNONYMS: **cultivated**, artistic, enlightened, civilized, educated, well read, learned, discerning, discriminating, refined, sophisticated; informal arty.
− ANTONYMS: ignorant.

culvert n. a drain under a road.

cum prep. combined with: *a study-cum-bedroom.*

cumbersome adj. heavy and awkward to carry or use.

cumin n. a spice made from the seeds of a plant.

cummerbund n. a sash worn around the waist.

cumulative adj. increasing by successive additions.
■ **cumulatively** adv.

cumulus /kyoo-myuu-luhss/ n. (pl. **cumuli**) cloud forming rounded masses on a flat base.

cuneiform /kyoo-ni-form/ n. an ancient writing system using wedge-shaped characters.

cunning adj. **1** skilled at deception. **2** skilful or clever.
▷ SYNONYMS: **1 crafty**, wily, artful, devious, Machiavellian, sly, scheming, canny, dishonest, deceitful. **2 clever**, shrewd, astute, canny, ingenious, imaginative, enterprising, inventive, resourceful, creative, original, inspired, brilliant.
− ANTONYMS: honest, stupid.
• n. craftiness.
▷ SYNONYMS: **1 guile**, craftiness, deviousness, trickery, duplicity. **2 ingenuity**, imagination, inventiveness, enterprise, resourcefulness.
■ **cunningly** adv.

cup n. **1** a small curved drinking container with a handle. **2** a cup-shaped trophy with a stem.
• v. (**cupping**, **cupped**) form the hands into a curved shape.

cupboard n. a piece of furniture or small recess with a door, used for storage.

cupidity n. greed for money etc.

cupola n. a small dome.

cur n. a mongrel dog.

curare /kyuu-**rah**-ri/ n. a paralysing poison obtained from plants.

curate n. a member of the clergy who assists a parish priest.
■ **curacy** n.

curator n. a keeper of a museum or other collection.
▷ SYNONYMS: **custodian**, keeper, conservator, guardian, caretaker.

curb v. control or limit.

▷ SYNONYMS: **restrain**, hold back, keep in check, control, rein in, contain; informal keep a lid on.
• n. **1** a control or limit. **2** US = **KERB**.
▷ SYNONYMS: **restraint**, restriction, check, brake, control, limit.

curd (or **curds**) n. a soft, white substance formed when milk coagulates.

curdle v. (of a liquid) form lumps.

cure v. **1** make well again. **2** get rid of a disease, problem, etc. **3** preserve by salting, drying, or smoking.
▷ SYNONYMS: **1 heal**, restore to health, make well/better. **2 rectify**, remedy, put/set right, right, fix, mend, repair, solve, sort out, eliminate, end. **3 preserve**, smoke, salt, dry, pickle.
• n. **1** a remedy. **2** the healing of someone who is ill.
▷ SYNONYMS: **remedy**, medicine, medication, antidote, treatment, therapy.
■ **curable** adj. **curative** adj.

curfew n. **1** a regulation requiring people to remain indoors between specified hours. **2** the time when this begins.

curie n. a unit of radioactivity.

curio n. (pl. **curios**) an unusual and interesting object.

curiosity n. (pl. **curiosities**) **1** a strong desire to know something. **2** a curio.
▷ SYNONYMS: **1 interest**, inquisitiveness, attention, spirit of enquiry; informal nosiness. **2 oddity**, curio, novelty, rarity.

curious adj. **1** eager to know something. **2** strange; unusual.
▷ SYNONYMS: **1 intrigued**, interested, eager, inquisitive. **2 strange**, odd, peculiar, funny, unusual, queer, bizarre, weird, eccentric, extraordinary, abnormal, anomalous.
− ANTONYMS: uninterested, normal.
■ **curiously** adv.

curl v. form a curved or spiral shape.
▷ SYNONYMS: **spiral**, coil, wreathe, twirl, swirl, wind, curve, twist and turn, snake, corkscrew, twine, entwine, wrap.
• n. something in the shape of a spiral or coil.
▷ SYNONYMS: **1 ringlet**, corkscrew, kink, lock. **2** *a curl of smoke:* **spiral**, coil, twirl, swirl, twist, corkscrew.

curler n. a roller around which hair is wound to curl it.

curlew n. a wading bird with a long curved bill.

curlicue n. a decorative curl or twist.

curling n. a game like bowls played on ice.

C

curly adj. (**curlier**, **curliest**) having curls.
▷ SYNONYMS: **wavy**, curling, curled, frizzy, kinky, corkscrew.
– ANTONYMS: straight.

curmudgeon n. a bad-tempered person.

currant n. **1** a dried grape. **2** a shrub producing edible berries.

currency n. (pl. **currencies**) **1** a system of money used in a country. **2** the state or period of being current.
▷ SYNONYMS: **1 money**, legal tender, cash, banknotes, notes, coins; N. Amer. bills. **2 popularity**, circulation, exposure, acceptance, prevalence.

current adj. **1** happening or being used now. **2** in general use.
▷ SYNONYMS: **1 contemporary**, present-day, modern, topical, live, burning. **2 prevalent**, common, accepted, in circulation, popular, widespread. **3 valid**, usable, up to date. **4 incumbent**, present, in office, in power, reigning.
– ANTONYMS: past, former.
• n. **1** a body of water or air moving in a particular direction. **2** a flow of electricity.
▷ SYNONYMS: **1 flow**, stream, draught, jet, tide. **2 course**, progress, progression, flow, tide, movement.
□ **current account** Brit. a bank account from which money may be withdrawn at any time.
■ **currently** adv.

curriculum n. (pl. **curricula** or **curriculums**) a course of study.
□ **curriculum vitae** an outline of a person's qualifications and previous jobs.
■ **curricular** adj.

curry n. (pl. **curries**) a dish cooked in a hot, spicy sauce.
• v. (**currying**, **curried**) **1** (**curried**) made as a curry. **2** (**curry favour**) try to win favour by flattery.
□ **curry comb** a rubber device for grooming horses.

curse n. **1** an appeal to a supernatural power to harm a person or thing. **2** a cause of harm or misery. **3** a swear word.
▷ SYNONYMS: **1 jinx**, malediction; N. Amer. hex; formal imprecation, anathema. **2 affliction**, burden, misery, ordeal, evil, scourge. **3 swear word**, expletive, oath, profanity, four-letter word, dirty word, obscenity; informal cuss word.
• v. **1** use a curse against. **2** (**be cursed**

with) be afflicted with. **3** use swear words.
▷ SYNONYMS: **swear**, take the Lord's name in vain, blaspheme; informal cuss, turn the air blue, eff and blind.

cursive adj. (of writing) written with the characters joined.

cursor n. a movable indicator on a computer screen.

cursory adj. hasty and so not thorough.
▷ SYNONYMS: **brief**, hasty, hurried, quick, rapid, passing, perfunctory, desultory, casual.
– ANTONYMS: thorough.
■ **cursorily** adv.

curt adj. rudely brief.
▷ SYNONYMS: **terse**, brusque, abrupt, clipped, blunt, short, sharp, rude, ungracious; informal snappy.
– ANTONYMS: expansive.
■ **curtly** adv.

curtail v. reduce or restrict.
▷ SYNONYMS: **reduce**, shorten, cut, cut down, decrease, trim, restrict, limit, curb, rein in/back, cut short, truncate; informal slash.
– ANTONYMS: increase, extend.
■ **curtailment** n.

curtain n. a piece of material hung as a screen, esp. at a window.

curtsy (or **curtsey**) n. (pl. **curtsies** or **curtseys**) a woman's respectful greeting, made by bending the knees.
• v. (**curtsying**, **curtsied**) perform a curtsy.

curvaceous adj. having an attractively curved shape.

curvature n. the fact of being curved.

curve n. a line which gradually turns from a straight course.
▷ SYNONYMS: **bend**, turn, loop, arc, arch, bow, crescent, curvature.
• v. form a curve.
▷ SYNONYMS: **bend**, turn, loop, wind, meander, snake, arc, arch.
■ **curvy** adj.

> **WORD LINKS**
> **sinuous** having many curves

curvilinear adj. contained by or consisting of curved lines.

cushion n. **1** a stuffed bag for sitting or leaning on. **2** a means of protection against impact etc.
▷ SYNONYMS: *a cushion against inflation:* **protection**, buffer, shield, defence, bulwark.
• v. **1** soften the effect of an impact on. **2** reduce the bad effects of.
▷ SYNONYMS: **1** *cushioned from the outside world:* **protect**, shield, shelter,

cocoon. **2** *cushion the blow:* **soften**,
lessen, diminish, mitigate, alleviate,
take the edge off, dull, deaden.

cushy adj. (**cushier**, **cushiest**) informal
easy and undemanding.

cusp n. **1** a pointed end where two
curves meet. **2** a point of change
between different states.

cussed /kuss-id/ adj. informal awkward
or annoying.

custard n. a sweet sauce made with
milk and eggs or flavoured cornflour.

custodian n. a guardian or keeper.

custody n. **1** protective care.
2 imprisonment.
▷ SYNONYMS: **care**, guardianship, charge,
supervision, safe keeping, responsibility, protection.
  ■ **custodial** adj.

custom n. **1** a traditional way of
behaving or doing something.
2 regular dealings by customers.
3 (**customs**) duties charged on
imported goods.
▷ SYNONYMS: **1** *local customs:* **tradition**,
practice, usage, way, convention,
formality, ritual, mores. **2** *it was his
custom to sleep in a chair:* **habit**, practice, routine, way; formal wont.

customary adj. usual.
▷ SYNONYMS: **usual**, traditional,
normal, conventional, habitual,
familiar, accepted, accustomed,
routine, established, time-honoured,
prevailing.
– ANTONYMS: unusual.
  ■ **customarily** adv.

customer n. a person buying goods or
services from a shop etc.
▷ SYNONYMS: **consumer**, buyer,
purchaser, patron, client, shopper;
Brit. informal **punter**.

customize (or **-ise**) v. modify to suit a
person or task.

cut v. (**cutting**, **cut**) **1** open or wound
with a sharp implement. **2** make,
divide, or remove in this way.
3 reduce. **4** go across or through.
5 move to another shot in a film.
6 divide a pack of cards.
▷ SYNONYMS: **1** **gash**, slash, lacerate,
slit, wound, scratch, graze, nick.
2 **slice**, chop, dice, cube, carve; N. Amer.
hash. **3** **carve**, engrave, incise, etch,
score, chisel, whittle. **4** **reduce**, cut
back/down on, decrease, lessen,
mark down, discount, lower; informal
slash. **5** **shorten**, abridge, condense,
abbreviate, truncate, edit, censor.
6 **delete**, remove, take out, excise.
• n. **1** an act of cutting. **2** an incision
or wound. **3** a reduction. **4** a style in

which a garment or the hair is cut. **5** a
piece of meat cut off. **6** informal a share.
▷ SYNONYMS: **1** **gash**, slash, laceration,
incision, wound, scratch, graze,
nick. **2** **reduction**, cutback, decrease,
economy, saving, lessening; N. Amer.
rollback. **3** **style**, design, line, fit.
4 **piece**, joint, fillet, section. **5** **share**,
portion, quota, percentage; informal
slice.
  □ **cut off** isolated. **cut-throat** ruthless
and fierce.

cute adj. **1** charmingly pretty; sweet.
2 US informal clever.
▷ SYNONYMS: **endearing**, adorable,
lovable, sweet, lovely, appealing,
engaging, delightful, dear; informal
twee; Brit. informal **dinky**.
  ■ **cutely** adv. **cuteness** n.

cuticle n. the skin at the base of a nail.

cutlass n. a short curved sword.

cutlery n. knives, forks, and spoons.

cutlet n. **1** a lamb or veal chop from
behind the neck. **2** a flat cake of
minced meat, nuts, etc., covered in
breadcrumbs and fried.

cutter n. **1** a person or thing that cuts.
2 a fast patrol boat or sailing boat.

cutting n. **1** an article cut from a
newspaper. **2** a piece cut from a plant
to grow a new one. **3** a passage cut
through high ground for a railway
etc.
▷ SYNONYMS: **clipping**, article, piece,
column, paragraph.
  • adj. hurtful.
▷ SYNONYMS: **hurtful**, wounding, barbed,
sharp, scathing, caustic, sarcastic,
snide, spiteful, malicious, vicious,
cruel; informal **bitchy**.
  □ **the cutting edge** the most advanced
stage.

cuttlefish n. a sea animal like a squid.

CV abbrev. curriculum vitae.

cwt abbrev. hundredweight.

cyan /sy-uhn/ n. a greenish-blue
colour.

cyanide n. a highly poisonous
compound.

cyber- comb. form of information
technology, the Internet, etc.

cybernetics n. the science of systems
of communication and control in
machines and living things.

cyberspace n. the hypothetical
environment in which
communication over computer
networks occurs.

cyclamen n. a plant with pink, red, or
white flowers.

cycle n. **1** a recurring series of events.

2 a bicycle. **3** a series of musical or literary works composed around a theme.

▷ SYNONYMS: **1** *the cycle of birth, death, and rebirth:* **circle**, round, pattern, rhythm, loop. **2** *a cycle of three plays:* **series**, sequence, set, succession, run.
• v. ride a bicycle.
■ **cyclist** n.

cyclic (or **cyclical**) adj. occurring in cycles.

cyclone n. **1** a violent wind rotating round a central area. **2** a violent tropical storm.
■ **cyclonic** adj.

cyclotron n. a machine for accelerating charged atomic or subatomic particles in a spiral path.

cygnet n. a young swan.

cylinder n. an object with straight parallel sides and circular ends.
■ **cylindrical** adj.

cymbal n. a musical instrument consisting of a round brass plate struck against another or hit with a stick.

cynic n. **1** a person who believes that people's motives are always selfish. **2** a person who raises doubts about something.

▷ SYNONYMS: **sceptic**, doubter, doubting Thomas, pessimist, prophet of doom.
– ANTONYMS: idealist, optimist.
■ **cynicism** n.

cynical adj. **1** believing that people always act from selfish motives. **2** sceptical or doubtful.

▷ SYNONYMS: **sceptical**, doubtful, distrustful, suspicious, disbelieving, pessimistic, negative, world-weary, disillusion ed, disenchanted, jaundiced.
– ANTONYMS: idealistic, optimistic.
■ **cynically** adv.

cynosure /**sin**-uh-zyoor/ n. a centre of attention.

cypher var. of CIPHER.

cypress n. an evergreen tree.

cyst n. an abnormal sac or cavity in the body, containing fluid.

cystic adj. **1** of cysts. **2** of the bladder or the gall bladder.
□ **cystic fibrosis** a hereditary disorder which often results in respiratory infection.

cystitis n. inflammation of the bladder.

cytology n. the study of the structure and function of cells.
■ **cytological** adj.

czar var. of TSAR.

Dd

D n. the Roman numeral for 500.

dab v. (**dabbing**, **dabbed**) **1** press lightly with something absorbent. **2** apply with light, quick strokes.
▷ SYNONYMS: **pat**, press, touch, blot, swab, daub, wipe.
• n. a small amount lightly applied.
▷ SYNONYMS: **drop**, spot, smear, splash, bit.
□ **dab hand** Brit. informal an expert in a particular activity.

dabble v. **1** splash around gently in water. **2** take part in an activity in a casual way.
▷ SYNONYMS: **toy with**, dip into, flirt with, tinker with, play with.

dace n. (pl. **dace**) a small freshwater fish.

dacha /da-chuh/ n. a Russian country cottage.

dachshund n. a dog with a long body and very short legs.

dad (or **daddy**) n. informal a person's father.

daddy-long-legs n. Brit. informal a long-legged flying insect.

dado /day-doh/ n. (pl. **dados**) the lower part of a wall decorated differently from the upper part.

daffodil n. a plant having yellow flowers with a trumpet-shaped centre.

daft adj. informal silly; foolish.
▷ SYNONYMS: **absurd**, preposterous, ridiculous, ludicrous, idiotic, stupid, foolish, asinine, senseless, inane; informal crazy, cockeyed, half-baked; Brit. informal barmy.
– ANTONYMS: sensible.

dagger n. a short pointed knife, used as a weapon.

daguerreotype /duh-**ger**-ruh-typ/ n. an early kind of photograph.

dahlia /day-li-uh/ n. a garden plant with brightly coloured flowers.

daily adj. & adv. every day or every weekday.
▷ SYNONYMS: *their daily routine*:

everyday, day-to-day; formal quotidian.
• n. (pl. **dailies**) informal a daily newspaper.

dainty adj. (**daintier**, **daintiest**) delicately small and pretty.
▷ SYNONYMS: **1 delicate**, fine, elegant, exquisite, graceful. **2 fastidious**, fussy, particular, finicky; informal choosy, picky; Brit. informal faddy.
– ANTONYMS: unwieldy.
■ **daintily** adv. **daintiness** n.

daiquiri /da-ki-ri/ n. (pl. **daiquiris**) a cocktail containing rum and lime juice.

dairy n. (pl. **dairies**) a building where milk and milk products are produced.

dais /day-iss/ n. a low platform for a lectern or throne.

daisy n. (pl. **daisies**) a small flower with many white petals.

dale n. a valley.

dally v. (**dallying**, **dallied**) **1** waste time. **2** (**dally with**) have a casual relationship with.
■ **dalliance** n.

Dalmatian n. a large white dog with dark spots.

dam n. **1** a barrier built across a river to hold back water. **2** the female parent of an animal.
▷ SYNONYMS: **barrage**, barrier, wall, embankment, barricade, obstruction.
• v. (**damming**, **dammed**) build a dam across.

damage n. **1** physical harm reducing the value or usefulness of something. **2** harmful effects. **3** (**damages**) money paid to compensate for a loss or injury.
▷ SYNONYMS: **1 harm**, destruction, vandalism, injury, ruin, devastation. **2** *she won £4,000 damages*: **compensation**, recompense, restitution, redress, reparation; N. Amer. informal comp.
• v. cause harm to.
▷ SYNONYMS: **harm**, injure, deface, spoil, impair, vandalize, ruin, destroy,

wreck; N. Amer. informal trash.
– ANTONYMS: repair.

damaging adj. causing harm.
▷ SYNONYMS: **harmful**, detrimental, injurious, hurtful, destructive, ruinous, deleterious.
– ANTONYMS: beneficial.

damask n. a fabric with a pattern woven into it.

dame n. **1** (**Dame**) the title of a woman awarded a knighthood. **2** US informal a woman.

damn v. **1** (**be damned**) be condemned by God to eternal punishment in hell. **2** strongly criticize.
▷ SYNONYMS: **condemn**, censure, criticize, attack, denounce.
– ANTONYMS: praise.
 • exclam. informal expressing anger.
 • adj. (or **damned**) informal used to emphasize anger.
 ■ damnation n. & exclam.

damnable adj. very bad or unpleasant.

damp adj. slightly wet.
▷ SYNONYMS: **moist**, humid, muggy, clammy, sweaty, dank, wet, rainy, drizzly, showery, misty, foggy, dewy.
– ANTONYMS: dry.
 • n. moisture.
▷ SYNONYMS: **moisture**, liquid, wet, wetness, dampness, humidity.
 • v. **1** make damp. **2** (**damp down**) control a feeling or situation.
 ■ dampness n.

dampen v. **1** make damp. **2** make less strong or intense.
▷ SYNONYMS: **1 moisten**, damp, wet, soak. **2 lessen**, decrease, diminish, reduce, moderate, cool, suppress, stifle, inhibit.
– ANTONYMS: dry, heighten.
 ■ dampener n.

damper n. **1** a pad for silencing a piano string. **2** a metal plate regulating the air flow in a chimney.

damsel n. old use a young woman.

damson n. a small purple plum-like fruit.

dance v. **1** move rhythmically to music. **2** move in a quick and lively way.
▷ SYNONYMS: **1 jive**, sway, twirl, whirl, pirouette, gyrate; informal boogie, bop, trip the light fantastic; N. Amer. informal get down. **2** *the girls danced round me*: caper, cavort, frolic, skip, prance, gambol, leap, hop, jig, bounce.
 • n. **1** a series of steps and movements performed to music. **2** a social gathering at which people dance.
▷ SYNONYMS: **ball**; N. Amer. prom,

hoedown; informal disco, rave, hop, bop.
 ■ dancer n.

> **WORD LINKS**
> **choreography** the sequence of steps in a ballet or other dance

dandelion n. a weed with large yellow flowers.

dandle v. gently bounce a young child on your knees.

dandruff n. flakes of dead skin from the scalp.

dandy n. (pl. **dandies**) a man who is too concerned with looking stylish and fashionable.
 ■ dandified adj.

Dane n. a person from Denmark.
 ■ Danish adj. & n.

danger n. **1** the possibility of suffering harm or of experiencing something unpleasant. **2** a cause of harm.
▷ SYNONYMS: **1 peril**, risk, jeopardy, hazard, endangerment, menace. **2 possibility**, chance, risk, probability, likelihood, threat.
– ANTONYMS: safety.

dangerous adj. likely to cause harm or problems.
▷ SYNONYMS: **1 menacing**, threatening, treacherous. **2 hazardous**, perilous, risky, unsafe, unpredictable, precarious, insecure; informal dicey, hairy; Brit. informal dodgy.
– ANTONYMS: harmless, safe.
 ■ dangerously adv.

dangle v. **1** hang so as to swing freely. **2** offer an incentive.
▷ SYNONYMS: **hang**, swing, droop, wave, trail, stream.
 ■ dangly adj.

dank adj. damp and cold.
▷ SYNONYMS: **damp**, musty, chilly, clammy.
– ANTONYMS: dry.

dapper adj. (of a man) neat and smart in appearance.
▷ SYNONYMS: **smart**, spruce, trim, debonair, neat, well dressed, elegant; informal snappy, natty; N. Amer. informal spiffy, fly.
– ANTONYMS: scruffy.

dapple v. mark with small patches of colour, light, etc.
 □ **dapple grey** (of a horse) grey with darker ring-shaped markings.

dare v. **1** have the courage to do. **2** challenge to do.
▷ SYNONYMS: **1 be brave enough**, have the courage, venture, have the nerve, risk, take the liberty of; N. Amer. take a flyer; informal stick your neck

out. **2 challenge**, defy, invite, bid, provoke, goad.
• n. a challenge to do something brave or risky.
▷ SYNONYMS: **challenge**, invitation, wager, bet.
□ **daredevil** a recklessly daring person.

daring adj. **1** willing to do dangerous things. **2** involving danger.
▷ SYNONYMS: **bold**, audacious, intrepid, fearless, brave, heroic, dashing; informal gutsy.
– ANTONYMS: cowardly, timid.
• n. adventurous courage.
▷ SYNONYMS: **boldness**, audacity, temerity, fearlessness, bravery, courage, pluck; informal nerve, guts; Brit. informal **bottle**; N. Amer. informal **moxie**.
– ANTONYMS: cowardice.
■ **daringly** adv.

dark adj. **1** with little or no light. **2** of a deep colour. **3** (of skin, hair, or eyes) brown or black. **4** depressing or gloomy. **5** evil or sinister. **6** mysterious.
▷ SYNONYMS: **1** a dark room: **dingy**, gloomy, shadowy, murky, poorly lit, inky, black, grey, louring. **2** dark hair: **brunette**, dark brown, sable, jet-black, ebony. **3** dark skin: **swarthy**, dusky, olive, black, ebony. **4** dark thoughts: **gloomy**, dismal, negative, downbeat, bleak, grim, fatalistic, black. **5** a dark look: **angry**, forbidding, threatening, ominous, moody, brooding, sullen, scowling, glowering. **6** dark deeds: **evil**, wicked, sinful, bad, iniquitous, ungodly, vile, foul, monstrous; informal dirty, shady, crooked.
– ANTONYMS: bright, light, fair, pale.
• n. **1** (**the dark**) the absence of light. **2** night.
▷ SYNONYMS: **night**, night-time, darkness, nightfall, blackout.
□ **dark horse** a person about whom little is known. **darkroom** a darkened room for developing photos.
■ **darken** v. **darkly** adv. **darkness** n.

darling n. **1** an affectionate form of address. **2** a lovable or popular person.
▷ SYNONYMS: **1 dear**, dearest, love, sweetheart, beloved; informal honey, angel, pet, sweetie, baby, poppet. **2 favourite**, idol, hero, heroine; Brit. informal blue-eyed boy/girl.
• adj. **1** much loved. **2** charming.
▷ SYNONYMS: **1 dear**, dearest, precious, beloved. **2 adorable**, charming, cute, sweet, enchanting, dear, delightful; Scottish & N. English bonny.

darn v. mend knitted material by weaving yarn across it.
• adj. (or **darned**) informal damn.

dart n. **1** a small pointed missile. **2** (**darts**) an indoor game in which darts are thrown at a dartboard. **3** a sudden run. **4** a tapered tuck in a garment.
• v. run suddenly.
▷ SYNONYMS: **1 dash**, rush, tear, shoot, sprint, bound, scurry, scamper; informal scoot, whip. **2 direct**, cast, throw, shoot, send, flash.
□ **dartboard** a circular target used in the game of darts.

dash v. **1** run or travel in a great hurry. **2** hit or throw with great force. **3** destroy.
▷ SYNONYMS: **1 rush**, race, run, sprint, career, charge, shoot, hurtle, hare, fly, speed, zoom; informal tear, belt; Brit. informal bomb; N. Amer. informal barrel. **2 hurl**, smash, fling, slam, throw, toss, cast; informal chuck, sling. **3 shatter**, destroy, wreck, ruin, demolish, scotch, frustrate, thwart; informal put paid to; Brit. informal scupper.
– ANTONYMS: dawdle.
• n. **1** an act of dashing. **2** a small amount added. **3** style and confidence. **4** a horizontal stroke (-) in writing.
▷ SYNONYMS: **1 rush**, race, run, sprint, bolt, dart, leap, charge, bound. **2 pinch**, touch, sprinkle, taste, spot, drop, dab, splash; informal smidgen, tad.
□ **dashboard** the instrument panel in a vehicle.

dashing adj. (of a man) attractive, stylish, and confident.
▷ SYNONYMS: **debonair**, stylish, dapper, devil-may-care, raffish, flamboyant, swashbuckling.

dastardly adj. dated wicked and cruel.

data n. **1** facts or statistics used for reference or analysis. **2** information processed by a computer.
▷ SYNONYMS: **facts**, figures, statistics, details, particulars, information.
□ **database** a set of data held in a computer.

USAGE Although **data** is the plural of Latin **datum**, in everyday English use it is usually treated as a singular noun, taking a singular verb, as in the data was analysed.

date n. **1** the day of the month or year as specified by a number. **2** the day or year of an event's occurrence. **3** a social or romantic appointment. **4** a sweet, dark brown, oval fruit.

▷ SYNONYMS: **1 day**, occasion, time, year, age, period, era, epoch. **2 appointment**, meeting, engagement, rendezvous, commitment, assignation; literary tryst. **3 partner**, escort, girlfriend, boyfriend.

• v. **1** establish the date of. **2** mark with a date. **3** (**date back to**) originate from. **4** seem old-fashioned. **5** informal go on regular dates with.

▷ SYNONYMS: **1 age**, grow old, become dated, show its age, be of its time. **2 go out with**, take out, go with, see; informal go steady with; dated court, woo.

□ **to date** until now.
■ **datable** (or **dateable**) adj.

> **WORD LINKS**
> **chronological** relating to dates

dated adj. old-fashioned.
▷ SYNONYMS: **old-fashioned**, outdated, outmoded, unfashionable, passé, behind the times, archaic, obsolete, antiquated; informal old hat, out of the ark.
− ANTONYMS: modern.

dative n. (in certain languages) the case of nouns and pronouns indicating the indirect object.

datum n. (pl. **data**) a piece of information.

daub v. smear with a thick substance.
• n. **1** a smear. **2** an unskilful painting.

daughter n. a girl or woman in relation to her parents.
□ **daughter-in-law** (pl. **daughters-in-law**) the wife of a person's son.

daunt v. intimidate or discourage.
▷ SYNONYMS: **discourage**, deter, demoralize, put off, dishearten, intimidate, overawe, awe.

daunting adj. likely to be difficult to do or deal with.
▷ SYNONYMS: **intimidating**, forbidding, challenging, formidable, unnerving, discouraging, disheartening, demoralizing, dismaying, frightening, alarming.

dauntless adj. fearless and determined.

dauphin /doh-fan/ n. hist. the eldest son of the King of France.

davit n. a small crane on a ship.

dawdle v. move slowly.
▷ SYNONYMS: **linger**, take your time, be slow, waste time, dally, amble, stroll, trail, move at a snail's pace; informal dilly-dally.
− ANTONYMS: hurry.

dawn n. **1** the first appearance of light in the morning. **2** the beginning of something.

▷ SYNONYMS: **1 daybreak**, sunrise, first light, daylight, cockcrow, first thing; N. Amer. sunup. **2 beginning**, start, birth, inception, genesis, emergence, advent, appearance, arrival, rise, origin.
− ANTONYMS: dusk.

• v. **1** (of a day) begin. **2** come into existence. **3** (**dawn on**) become evident to.

▷ SYNONYMS: **1** *Thursday dawned crisp and sunny:* **begin**, break, arrive, emerge. **2** *a bright new future has dawned:* **begin**, start, commence, be born, appear, arrive, emerge, arise, rise, unfold, develop. **3** *the reality dawned on him:* **become evident**, register, cross someone's mind, suggest itself, occur to, come to, strike, hit.

day n. **1** a period of 24 hours. **2** the time between sunrise and sunset. **3** a particular period, esp. of the past.

▷ SYNONYMS: **1 daytime**, daylight hours, waking hours. **2 period**, time, date, age, era, generation.
− ANTONYMS: night.

□ **daybreak** dawn. **daydream** a series of pleasant distracting thoughts. **daylight 1** the natural light of the day. **2** dawn.

> **WORD LINKS**
> **diurnal** relating to the day

daze v. stun or bewilder.
▷ SYNONYMS: **1 dumbfound**, stupefy, stun, shock, stagger, bewilder, take aback, nonplus; informal flabbergast; Brit. informal knock for six.

• n. a dazed state.
▷ SYNONYMS: **stupor**, trance, haze, spin, whirl, muddle, jumble.

dazzle v. **1** (of a bright light) blind temporarily. **2** amaze with an impressive quality.
▷ SYNONYMS: **1 blind**, confuse, disorient. **2 overwhelm**, overcome, impress, move, stir, touch, awe, overawe; informal bowl over, blow away, knock out.

• n. blinding brightness.

dB abbrev. decibels.

DC abbrev. direct current.

DDT abbrev. an insecticide.

deacon n. **1** a Christian minister ranking below a priest. **2** (in some Protestant Churches) a lay officer assisting a minister.
■ **deaconess** n.

dead adj. **1** no longer alive. **2** (of a body part) numb. **3** without activity or excitement. **4** not functioning or current. **5** complete: *dead silence.*

▷ SYNONYMS: **1 passed on**, passed away, departed, late, lost, perished, fallen, killed, lifeless, extinct; informal six feet under, pushing up daisies; formal deceased. **2 boring**, uninteresting, unexciting, uninspiring, dull, flat, quiet, sleepy, slow, lifeless; informal one-horse; N. Amer. informal dullsville. **3 not working**, out of order, inoperative, inactive, broken, defective; informal kaput, conked out, on the blink, bust; Brit. informal knackered. **4 obsolete**, extinct, defunct, disused, abandoned, superseded, vanished, archaic, ancient.
– ANTONYMS: alive, living, lively.
• adv. **1** completely, exactly, or directly. **2** Brit. informal very.
▷ SYNONYMS: **1 completely**, absolutely, totally, utterly, deadly, perfectly, entirely, quite, thoroughly. **2 directly**, exactly, precisely, immediately, right, straight, due.
□ **dead end** a road or passage that is closed at one end. **dead heat** a result in a race in which competitors finish at exactly the same time. **deadline** the latest time or date for completing something. **deadlocked** in a deadlock. **deadpan** expressionless.

deaden v. **1** make quieter or less intense. **2** make numb.
▷ SYNONYMS: **1 muffle**, mute, smother, stifle, damp down, soften, cushion. **2 numb**, dull, blunt, alleviate, mitigate, diminish, reduce, lessen, ease, soothe, relieve, assuage.
– ANTONYMS: intensify, amplify.

deadlock n. Brit. a situation in which no progress can be made.
▷ SYNONYMS: **stalemate**, impasse, checkmate, stand-off, standstill, gridlock.

deadly adj. (**deadlier**, **deadliest**) **1** causing death. **2** complete; total.
▷ SYNONYMS: **1 fatal**, lethal, mortal, life-threatening, noxious, toxic, poisonous. **2** *deadly enemies:* **mortal**, irreconcilable, implacable, bitter, sworn. **3** *his aim is deadly:* **unerring**, unfailing, perfect, true, accurate; Brit. informal spot on.
– ANTONYMS: harmless.
• adv. very: *deadly serious.*
□ **deadly nightshade** a plant with poisonous black berries.

deaf adj. **1** unable to hear. **2** (**deaf to**) unwilling to listen to.
■ **deafen** v. **deafness** n.

deafening adj. extremely loud.
▷ SYNONYMS: **ear-splitting**, thunderous,

almighty, booming, piercing.
– ANTONYMS: low, soft.

deal v. (**dealing**, **dealt**) **1** (**deal out**) distribute. **2** trade in a product. **3** buy and sell illegal drugs. **4** give out cards to players of a game.
▷ SYNONYMS: **1 distribute**, give out, share out, divide out, hand out, pass out, pass round, dispense, allocate. **2 trade in**, buy and sell, purvey, supply, market, traffic in.
• n. **1** an agreement. **2** a way of being treated: *a fair deal.*
▷ SYNONYMS: **agreement**, understanding, pact, bargain, covenant, contract, treaty, arrangement, compromise, settlement, terms.
□ **a big deal** informal an important thing. **deal a blow to** hit or be harmful to. **deal with 1** take action to put right. **2** cope with. **3** have as a subject. **a good** (or **great**) **deal** a large amount.

dealer n. **1** a person who buys and sells goods. **2** a person who sells illegal drugs. **3** a player who deals cards in a card game.
▷ SYNONYMS: **trader**, merchant, seller, vendor, purveyor, distributor, supplier, shopkeeper, retailer, wholesaler, tradesman, tradesperson, pedlar; Brit. stockist.

dean n. **1** the head of the governing body of a cathedral. **2** the head of a university department etc.

dear adj. **1** much loved. **2** expensive.
▷ SYNONYMS: **1 beloved**, precious, treasured, valued, prized, cherished, special. **2 expensive**, costly, high-priced, overpriced, exorbitant, extortionate; Brit. over the odds; informal pricey.
• n. a lovable person.
▷ SYNONYMS: **darling**, dearest, love, beloved, sweetheart, precious; informal sweetie, sugar, honey, baby, pet, poppet.
• adv. at a high cost.
• exclam. used in expressions of surprise or dismay.
■ **dearly** adv.

dearth /derth/ n. a scarcity or lack.
▷ SYNONYMS: **lack**, scarcity, shortage, shortfall, deficiency, insufficiency, inadequacy, absence.
– ANTONYMS: surfeit.

death n. **1** the act or fact of dying. **2** the state of being dead. **3** the end of something.
▷ SYNONYMS: **1 dying**, demise, end, passing, loss of life; formal decease. **2 end**, finish, termination, extinction,

d

extinguishing, collapse, destruction.
– ANTONYMS: life, birth.
□ **deathtrap** a dangerous building, vehicle, etc. **death-watch beetle** a beetle whose larvae bore into wood.

> WORD LINKS
> **fatal**, **lethal**, **mortal** causing death

deathly adj. suggesting death.
▷ SYNONYMS: **deathlike**, ghostly, ghastly, ashen, white, pale, pallid.

debacle /day-bah-k'l/ n. a complete failure or disaster.
▷ SYNONYMS: **fiasco**, failure, catastrophe, disaster.

debar v. (**debarring**, **debarred**) ban from doing something.

debase v. lower in quality or value.
▷ SYNONYMS: **degrade**, devalue, demean, cheapen, prostitute, discredit, drag down, tarnish, blacken, disgrace, dishonour, shame.
– ANTONYMS: enhance.
■ **debasement** n.

debatable adj. open to discussion.
▷ SYNONYMS: **arguable**, questionable, open to question, disputable, controversial, contentious, doubtful, dubious, uncertain, borderline, moot.

debate n. 1 a formal discussion. 2 an argument.
▷ SYNONYMS: **discussion**, argument, dispute, talks.
• v. 1 discuss. 2 consider.
▷ SYNONYMS: 1 **discuss**, talk over/through, talk about, thrash out, argue, dispute. 2 **consider**, think over/about, chew over, mull over, weigh up, ponder, deliberate.

debauchery n. excessive behaviour involving sex, alcohol, or drugs.
▷ SYNONYMS: **dissipation**, dissoluteness, decadence, immorality, degeneracy, depravity, profligacy, intemperance, lewdness, licentiousness.
■ **debauched** adj.

debenture n. a certificate issued by a company acknowledging that it has borrowed money on which interest is being paid.

debilitate v. severely weaken.
■ **debilitation** n.

debility n. (pl. **debilities**) physical weakness.

debit n. 1 an entry in an account recording a sum owed. 2 a payment made or owed.
• v. (**debiting**, **debited**) (of a bank) take money from a customer's account.

debonair adj. (of a man) confident, stylish, and charming.

debrief v. question in detail about a completed mission.

debris /deb-ree/ n. scattered rubbish or broken pieces.
▷ SYNONYMS: **ruins**, remains, rubble, wreckage, detritus, refuse, rubbish, waste, scrap, flotsam and jetsam.

debt n. 1 a sum of money owed. 2 the state of owing something. 3 gratitude for a favour.
▷ SYNONYMS: 1 **bill**, account, dues, arrears, charges. 2 **indebtedness**, obligation, gratitude, appreciation.

debtor n. a person who owes money.

debunk v. reveal a belief to be false.

debut /day-byoo/ n. a person's first appearance in a role.
• v. make a debut.

debutante /deb-yuh-tahnt/ n. a young upper-class woman making her first formal appearance in society.

decade n. a period of ten years.

decadent adj. immoral and interested only in pleasure.
■ **decadence** n.

decaffeinated adj. with the caffeine removed or reduced.

decagon n. a plane figure with ten straight sides and angles.

decamp v. leave suddenly or secretly.

decant v. pour liquid from one container into another to remove sediment.

decanter n. a container into which wine etc. is decanted.

decapitate v. behead.
■ **decapitation** n.

decathlon n. an athletic contest involving ten events.

decay v. 1 rot. 2 become worse or weaker.
▷ SYNONYMS: 1 **decompose**, rot, putrefy, go bad, go off, spoil, fester, perish. 2 **deteriorate**, degenerate, decline, go downhill, slump, slide, go to rack and ruin, go to seed; informal go to the dogs.
• n. the state or process of decaying.
▷ SYNONYMS: 1 **decomposition**, putrefaction, rot. 2 **deterioration**, degeneration, decline, weakening, crumbling, disintegration, collapse.

decease n. death.

deceased adj. recently dead.

deceit n. behaviour intended to mislead or deceive.
▷ SYNONYMS: **deception**, deceitfulness, duplicity, double-dealing, lies, fraud, cheating, trickery.
– ANTONYMS: honesty.

deceitful adj. deliberately misleading or deceiving other people.

▷ SYNONYMS: **dishonest**, untruthful, insincere, false, disingenuous, untrustworthy, unscrupulous, unprincipled, two-faced, duplicitous, fraudulent, double-dealing; informal sneaky, tricky, crooked; Brit. informal bent.
− ANTONYMS: honest.
■ **deceitfully** adv.

deceive v. **1** cause to believe something false. **2** give a misleading impression.
▷ SYNONYMS: **trick**, cheat, defraud, swindle, hoodwink, hoax, dupe, take in, mislead, delude, fool; informal con, pull the wool over someone's eyes; N. Amer. informal sucker, goldbrick.
■ **deceiver** n.

decelerate v. slow down.
■ **deceleration** n.

December n. the twelfth month.

decency n. decent behaviour.
▷ SYNONYMS: **1 propriety**, decorum, good taste, respectability, morality, virtue, modesty. **2 courtesy**, politeness, good manners, civility, consideration, thoughtfulness.

decent adj. **1** following accepted moral standards. **2** of an acceptable quality. **3** Brit. informal kind or generous.
▷ SYNONYMS: **1 proper**, correct, right, appropriate, suitable, respectable, decorous, modest, seemly, accepted; informal pukka. **2 satisfactory**, reasonable, fair, acceptable, adequate, sufficient, all right, tolerable, passable, suitable; informal OK. **3 kind**, generous, thoughtful, considerate, obliging, courteous, polite, well mannered, neighbourly, hospitable, pleasant, agreeable, amiable.
− ANTONYMS: improper, indecent, unsatisfactory.
■ **decently** adv.

decentralize (or **-ise**) v. transfer from central to local control.

deception n. **1** the act of deceiving. **2** a thing that deceives.
▷ SYNONYMS: **1 deceit**, duplicity, double-dealing, fraud, cheating, trickery, guile, bluff, lying, pretence, treachery. **2 trick**, sham, fraud, pretence, hoax, ruse, scheme, dodge, cheat, swindle; informal con, set-up, scam.

deceptive adj. misleading.
▷ SYNONYMS: **misleading**, confusing, illusory, distorted, ambiguous.
■ **deceptively** adv.

decibel n. a unit for measuring the intensity of sound.

decide v. **1** think about and choose.

2 settle a matter or contest.
▷ SYNONYMS: **1 resolve**, determine, make up your mind, choose, opt, plan, aim, intend, have in mind, set your sights on. **2 settle**, resolve, determine, work out, answer; informal sort out. **3 adjudicate**, arbitrate, judge, pronounce on, give a verdict on, rule on.

decided adj. definite; clear.
▷ SYNONYMS: **distinct**, clear, marked, obvious, noticeable, unmistakable, manifest, definite, unequivocal.
■ **decidedly** adv.

deciduous adj. (of a tree) shedding its leaves annually.

decimal adj. of a system of numbers based on the number ten.
• n. a fraction in the decimal system, with figures either side of a full point.
□ **decimal place** the position of a digit to the right of a decimal point.
decimal point a full point placed after the figure representing units in a decimal.

decimate v. kill or destroy a large proportion of.
■ **decimation** n.

decipher v. **1** succeed in understanding. **2** convert from code into normal language.

decision n. **1** a choice made after consideration. **2** the ability to decide quickly.
▷ SYNONYMS: **1 resolution**, conclusion, settlement, choice, option, selection. **2 verdict**, finding, ruling, judgement, adjudication, sentence.

decisive adj. **1** very important for the outcome of a situation. **2** able to decide quickly.
▷ SYNONYMS: **1 resolute**, firm, strong-minded, strong-willed, determined, purposeful. **2 deciding**, conclusive, determining, key, pivotal, critical, crucial.
■ **decisively** adv. **decisiveness** n.

deck n. **1** a floor of a ship or bus. **2** a pack of cards. **3** a player or recorder for discs or tapes.
• v. decorate.
□ **deckchair** a folding canvas chair.

declaim v. speak or recite in a dramatic way.
■ **declamation** n. **declamatory** adj.

declaration n. a formal statement or announcement.
▷ SYNONYMS: **1 announcement**, statement, communication, pronouncement, proclamation; N. Amer. advisory. **2 assertion**, profession, affirmation, testimony, avowal, protestation.

d

declare v. **1** announce openly or formally. **2** state that you have income or goods on which tax or duty is payable.
▷ SYNONYMS: **1 announce**, proclaim, state, reveal, air, voice, articulate, express, vent, set forth, publicize, broadcast. **2 assert**, profess, affirm, maintain, contend, claim, argue, insist, avow.

declassify v. (**declassifying**, **declassified**) officially declare to be no longer secret.

declension n. the changes in the form of a noun, pronoun, or adjective that identify its grammatical case, number, and gender.

decline v. **1** become smaller, weaker, or worse. **2** politely refuse.
▷ SYNONYMS: **1 turn down**, reject, brush aside, refuse, rebuff, spurn, repulse, dismiss, pass up, say no; informal give something a miss. **2 decrease**, reduce, lessen, diminish, dwindle, contract, shrink, fall off, tail off, drop, fall, go down. **3 deteriorate**, degenerate, decay, crumble, collapse, slump, slip, slide, go downhill, worsen; informal go to the dogs.
– ANTONYMS: accept, increase, improve.
• n. a gradual loss of strength, numbers, or value.
▷ SYNONYMS: **1 reduction**, decrease, downturn, downswing, diminution, ebb, drop, slump, plunge. **2 deterior-ation**, degeneration, degradation, shrinkage, erosion.
– ANTONYMS: rise, improvement.

declivity n. (pl. **declivities**) a downward slope.

decoction n. a concentrated liquid produced by heating or boiling.

decode v. **1** convert a coded message into understandable language. **2** convert audio or video signals from analogue to digital.
■ **decoder** n.

décolletage /day-kol-i-**tahzh**/ n. a low neckline on a woman's dress or top.

decompose v. decay.
▷ SYNONYMS: **decay**, rot, putrefy, go bad, go off, spoil, perish, deteriorate, degrade, break down.
■ **decomposition** n.

decompress v. **1** reduce air pressure in or on. **2** expand compressed computer data to its normal size.
■ **decompression** n.

decongestant n. a medicine that relieves a blocked nose.

deconstruct v. reduce something to

its basic elements so as to interpret it differently.
■ **deconstruction** n.

decontaminate v. remove dangerous substances from.
■ **decontamination** n.

decor /**day**-kor/ n. the furnishing and decoration of a room.
▷ SYNONYMS: **decoration**, furnishing, colour scheme.

decorate v. **1** add ornamentation to make more attractive. **2** apply paint or wallpaper to. **3** give an award or medal to.
▷ SYNONYMS: **1 ornament**, adorn, trim, embellish, garnish, furnish, enhance. **2 paint**, wallpaper, paper, refurbish, renovate, redecorate; informal do up, give something a facelift, give something a makeover. **3 give a medal to**, honour, cite, reward.
■ **decorator** n.

decoration n, **1** the act of decorating or the way something is decorated. **2** a decorative thing. **3** a medal or award.
▷ SYNONYMS: **1 ornamentation**, adorn-ment, trimming, embellishment, beautification. **2 ornament**, bauble, trinket, knick-knack. **3 medal**, award, prize; Brit. informal gong.

decorative adj. making something look attractive.
▷ SYNONYMS: **ornamental**, fancy, ornate, attractive, pretty, showy.
– ANTONYMS: functional.
■ **decoratively** adv.

decorous adj. polite and restrained.
■ **decorously** adv.

decorum /di-**kor**-uhm/ n. polite and socially acceptable behaviour.
▷ SYNONYMS: **1 propriety**, seemliness, decency, good taste, correctness, politeness, good manners. **2 etiquette**, protocol, good form, custom, convention.
– ANTONYMS: impropriety.

decoy n. **1** a real or imitation animal used to lure game. **2** a person or thing used to mislead or trap.
• v. lure by a decoy.

decrease v. make or become smaller or fewer.
▷ SYNONYMS: **lessen**, reduce, drop, diminish, decline, dwindle, fall off, plummet, plunge.
– ANTONYMS: increase.
• n. **1** the amount by which something decreases. **2** the act of decreasing.
▷ SYNONYMS: **reduction**, drop, decline, downturn, cut, cutback, diminution.
– ANTONYMS: increase.

decree n. an official order with the force of law.
▷ SYNONYMS: **1** *a presidential decree:* **order**, command, commandment, edict, proclamation, law, statute, act. **2** *a court decree:* **judgement**, verdict, adjudication, finding, ruling, decision.
• v. order officially.
▷ SYNONYMS: **order**, direct, command, rule, dictate, pronounce, proclaim, ordain.

decrepit adj. worn out or weakened because of age or neglect.
▷ SYNONYMS: **dilapidated**, rickety, run down, tumbledown, ramshackle, derelict, ruined, in disrepair, gone to rack and ruin, on its last legs, decayed, crumbling.
■ **decrepitude** n.

decriminalize (or **-ise**) v. cease to treat as illegal.

decry v. (**decrying**, **decried**) publicly declare to be wrong.

dedicate v. **1** give time or effort to. **2** address a book to a person as a tribute.
▷ SYNONYMS: **1 commit**, devote, pledge, give, sacrifice, set aside. **2 inscribe**, address, offer.

dedicated adj. **1** devoted to a task or purpose. **2** used or intended for one purpose only.
▷ SYNONYMS: **1 committed**, devoted, enthusiastic, keen, staunch, firm, steadfast, loyal, faithful. **2 specialized**, custom-built, customized, purpose-built, exclusive.
– ANTONYMS: half-hearted.

dedication n. **1** devotion to a purpose or task. **2** the words with which a book is dedicated.
▷ SYNONYMS: **1 commitment**, devotion, loyalty, allegiance, application, resolve, conscientiousness, perseverance, persistence. **2 inscription**, message.
– ANTONYMS: apathy.

deduce v. reach a conclusion on the basis of available information.
▷ SYNONYMS: **conclude**, reason, work out, infer, understand, assume, presume, surmise, reckon; informal figure out, put two and two together; Brit. informal suss out.
■ **deducible** adj.

deduct v. subtract.
▷ SYNONYMS: **subtract**, take away, take off, debit, dock, stop; informal knock off.
– ANTONYMS: add.
■ **deductible** adj.

deduction n. **1** the act of deducting.

2 an amount deducted. **3** the act of deducing.
▷ SYNONYMS: **1 subtraction**, removal, debit. **2 stoppage**, tax, expenses, rebate, discount, concession. **3 conclusion**, inference, supposition, hypothesis, assumption, presumption, suspicion.
■ **deductive** adj.

deed n. **1** an action performed deliberately. **2** a legal document.
▷ SYNONYMS: **1 act**, action, feat, exploit, achievement, accomplishment, endeavour. **2 document**, contract, instrument.

deem v. consider to be.

deep adj. **1** extending or situated far down in or from the top or surface. **2** low-pitched. **3** (of colour) dark. **4** very intense or extreme. **5** difficult to understand.
▷ SYNONYMS: **1 cavernous**, yawning, gaping, huge, extensive, bottomless, fathomless. **2 low-pitched**, low, bass, rich, resonant, booming, sonorous. **3 dark**, intense, rich, strong, vivid. **4 intense**, keen, acute, heartfelt, strong, wholehearted, deep-seated, sincere, profound, genuine, earnest, enthusiastic, great, extreme. **5** *he was deep in concentration:* **rapt**, absorbed, engrossed, preoccupied, intent, immersed, lost, gripped. **6 obscure**, complex, mysterious, unfathomable, opaque, abstruse, esoteric, enigmatic.
– ANTONYMS: shallow, superficial, high.
■ **deepen** v. **deeply** adv.

deer n. (pl. **deer**) a hoofed animal, the male of which usu. has antlers.
□ **deerstalker** a cap with peaks in front and behind and ear flaps.

deface v. spoil the appearance of.
▷ SYNONYMS: **vandalize**, disfigure, spoil, ruin, damage; N. Amer. informal trash.

de facto /day **fak**-toh/ adj. existing, whether legally accepted or not.

defame v. damage the good reputation of.
■ **defamation** n. **defamatory** adj.

default n. **1** failure to do something required by law. **2** an option adopted by a computer program when no alternative is specified.
• v. fail to fulfil a legal obligation.
□ **by default** because of a lack of opposition or positive action.
■ **defaulter** n.

defeat v. **1** win a victory over. **2** cause to fail.
▷ SYNONYMS: **1 beat**, conquer, win against, triumph over, get the better of, vanquish, rout, trounce, overcome,

d

overpower; informal lick, thrash.
2 thwart, frustrate, foil, ruin, scotch, derail; informal put paid to, stymie; Brit. informal scupper.
• n. an act of defeating or the state of being defeated.
▷ SYNONYMS: **loss**, conquest, rout; informal thrashing, hiding, drubbing, licking.
– ANTONYMS: victory.

defeatist n. a person who accepts failure too readily.
■ **defeatism** n.

defecate v. discharge waste matter from the bowels.
■ **defecation** n.

defect n. an imperfection.
▷ SYNONYMS: **fault**, flaw, imperfection, deficiency, deformity, blemish, mistake, error.
• v. abandon your country or cause for an opposing one.
■ **defection** n. **defector** n.

defective adj. imperfect or faulty.
▷ SYNONYMS: **faulty**, flawed, imperfect, unsound, inoperative, malfunctioning, out of order, broken; informal on the blink; Brit. informal duff.
– ANTONYMS: perfect.

defence (US **defense**) n. **1** the act of defending. **2** protective military measures or resources. **3** attempted justification. **4** the case presented by the person being accused or sued in a lawsuit.
▷ SYNONYMS: **1 protection**, guarding, security, fortification, resistance. **2 armaments**, weapons, weaponry, arms, the military, the armed forces. **3 justification**, vindication, explanation, mitigation, excuse, alibi, denial, rebuttal, plea, pleading, argument, case.
– ANTONYMS: attack, prosecution.

defenceless (US **defenseless**) adj. without protection.
▷ SYNONYMS: **vulnerable**, helpless, powerless, weak, undefended, unprotected, unguarded, unarmed, exposed, open to attack.

defend v. **1** protect from attack. **2** attempt to justify. **3** act as a lawyer for the defendant.
▷ SYNONYMS: **1 protect**, guard, safeguard, secure, shield, fortify, watch over. **2 justify**, vindicate, explain, argue for, support, uphold, back, stand by, make a case for, stick up for.
– ANTONYMS: attack, criticize.

defendant n. a person sued or accused in a court of law.

defender n. a person who defends someone or something.

▷ SYNONYMS: **1 protector**, guardian, guard, custodian, watchdog. **2 supporter**, upholder, backer, champion, advocate, apologist.

defensible adj. able to be defended.

defensive adj. **1** intended for defence. **2** anxious to challenge criticism.
▷ SYNONYMS: **1 defending**, protective. **2 self-justifying**, oversensitive, prickly, paranoid, neurotic; informal twitchy.
■ **defensively** adv.

defer v. (**deferring**, **deferred**) **1** put off to a later time. **2** (**defer to**) give in to.
▷ SYNONYMS: **postpone**, put off, delay, hold over/off, put back, shelve, suspend; N. Amer. table; informal put on ice, put on the back burner.
■ **deferment** n. **deferral** n.

deference n. polite respect.
■ **deferential** adj. **deferentially** adv.

defiance n. open disobedience.
▷ SYNONYMS: **resistance**, opposition, non-compliance, disobedience, insubordination, rebellion, disregard, contempt, insolence.
– ANTONYMS: obedience.

defiant adj. openly disobedient.
▷ SYNONYMS: **disobedient**, resistant, obstinate, uncooperative, non-compliant, recalcitrant, insubordinate; Brit. informal stroppy, bolshie.
– ANTONYMS: cooperative, obedient.
■ **defiantly** adv.

deficiency n. (pl. **deficiencies**) **1** a lack or shortage. **2** a fault or shortcoming.
▷ SYNONYMS: **1 lack**, insufficiency, shortage, inadequacy, deficit, shortfall, scarcity, dearth. **2 defect**, fault, flaw, failing, weakness, shortcoming, limitation.
– ANTONYMS: surplus, strength.

deficient adj. **1** not having enough of a specified thing. **2** inadequate.

deficit n. **1** the amount by which something falls short. **2** an excess of money spent over money earned.
▷ SYNONYMS: **shortfall**, deficiency, shortage, debt, arrears, loss.
– ANTONYMS: surplus.

defile v. **1** make dirty. **2** desecrate.
• n. a narrow gorge or mountain pass.

define v. **1** describe the exact nature of. **2** give the meaning of a word. **3** mark out the limits of.
▷ SYNONYMS: **1 explain**, describe, spell out, expound, interpret. **2 determine**, establish, fix, specify, designate, decide, stipulate, set out.

definite adj. **1** clearly stated or decided. **2** certain. **3** known to be true

or real. **4** having exact physical limits.
▷ SYNONYMS: **specific**, explicit, express,
precise, exact, clear, clear-cut,
unambiguous, certain, sure,
positive, conclusive, decisive,
firm, unequivocal, unmistakable,
proven, decided, marked, distinct,
identifiable.
– ANTONYMS: vague, ambiguous.
◻ **definite article** the word *the*.

USAGE *-ite*, not *-ate*: defin*ite*.

definitely adv. without doubt;
certainly.
▷ SYNONYMS: **certainly**, surely, for sure,
unquestionably, without doubt,
undoubtedly, undeniably, clearly,
positively, absolutely, unmistakably,
unequivocally.

definition n. **1** a statement of the
meaning of a word or the nature of
something. **2** sharpness of outline.
▷ SYNONYMS: **1 meaning**, sense, interpretation, explanation, description.
2 clarity, sharpness, focus, crispness,
resolution.

definitive adj. **1** settling something
finally with authority. **2** the most
accurate of its kind.
▷ SYNONYMS: **1 conclusive**, final,
unqualified, absolute, categorical,
positive, definite. **2 authoritative**,
best, ultimate, classic, standard,
recognized, accepted, exhaustive.
■ **definitively** adv.

deflate v. **1** let air or gas out of a tyre
etc. **2** make less confident. **3** reduce
price levels in an economy.
■ **deflation** n. **deflationary** adj.

deflect v. turn aside.
▷ SYNONYMS: **divert**, turn away, draw
away, distract, fend off, parry, stave
off.
■ **deflection** n.

deflower v. literary have sex with a
woman who is a virgin.

defoliate v. remove the leaves from.
■ **defoliation** n.

deforest v. clear of trees.
■ **deforestation** n.

deform v. change or spoil the shape
of.

deformed adj. having a distorted
shape or form.
▷ SYNONYMS: **misshapen**, distorted,
malformed, contorted, out of shape,
twisted, crooked, warped, buckled,
gnarled, disfigured, mutilated,
mangled.

deformity n. (pl. **deformities**) **1** a
deformed part. **2** the state of being
deformed.

defraud v. obtain money from by
deception.
▷ SYNONYMS: **swindle**, cheat, rob,
deceive, dupe, hoodwink, double-
cross, trick; informal con, do, sting,
diddle, rip off, shaft, pull a fast one
on, put one over on, sell a pup to;
N. Amer. informal sucker, snooker, stiff;
Austral. informal pull a swifty on.

defray v. provide money to pay a cost.

defrock v. officially remove a
Christian priest from his job.

defrost v. **1** remove ice from. **2** thaw
frozen food.

deft adj. quick and skilful.
▷ SYNONYMS: **skilful**, adept, adroit,
dexterous, agile, nimble, handy,
able, capable, skilled, proficient,
accomplished, expert, polished, slick,
professional.
– ANTONYMS: clumsy.
■ **deftly** adv.

defunct adj. no longer existing or
functioning.

defuse v. **1** make a situation less tense
or difficult. **2** remove the fuse from
an explosive device.

USAGE Don't confuse **defuse** with
diffuse, meaning 'spread over a wide
area'.

defy v. (**defying**, **defied**) **1** openly
resist or refuse to obey. **2** challenge
to do.
▷ SYNONYMS: **disobey**, flout, disregard,
ignore, break, violate, contravene,
breach, challenge, fly in the face of,
confront.
– ANTONYMS: obey.

degenerate v. become worse or
weaker.
▷ SYNONYMS: **deteriorate**, decline,
worsen, slip, slide, go downhill; informal
go to the dogs.
– ANTONYMS: improve.
• adj. immoral.
▷ SYNONYMS: **corrupt**, perverted,
decadent, dissolute, dissipated,
debauched, immoral, unprincipled,
disreputable.
• n. an immoral person.
■ **degeneracy** n. **degeneration** n.

degrade v. **1** cause to lose self-
respect. **2** make worse. **3** cause to
break down chemically.
▷ SYNONYMS: **demean**, debase,
humiliate, humble, belittle, mortify,
dehumanize, brutalize.
– ANTONYMS: dignify.
■ **degradation** n.

degree n. **1** the extent to which
something happens or is present. **2** a

unit for measuring angles. **3** a stage in a scale, e.g. of temperature. **4** a qualification awarded by a university.
▷ SYNONYMS: **level**, standard, grade, stage, mark, amount, extent, measure, intensity, strength, proportion.

dehumanize (or **-ise**) v. deprive of good human qualities.

dehydrate v. **1** cause to lose a large amount of moisture. **2** remove water from food to preserve it.
■ **dehydration** n.

deify /day-i-fy/ v. (**deifying**, **deified**) worship as a god.
■ **deification** n.

deign /dayn/ v. (**deign to do**) condescend to do.
▷ SYNONYMS: **condescend**, stoop, lower yourself, demean yourself, humble yourself, consent.

deity /day-i-ti/ n. (pl. **deities**) a god or goddess.

déjà vu /day-zhah **voo**/ n. a feeling of having already experienced the present situation.

dejected adj. sad and in low spirits.
▷ SYNONYMS: **downcast**, downhearted, despondent, disconsolate, dispirited, crestfallen, disheartened, depressed; informal down in the mouth, down in the dumps.
− ANTONYMS: cheerful.
■ **dejection** n.

delay v. **1** make late or slow. **2** postpone.
▷ SYNONYMS: **1 detain**, hold up, make late, slow up/down, bog down, hinder, hamper, impede, obstruct. **2 linger**, drag your feet, hold back, dawdle, waste time, stall, hesitate, dither, shilly-shally; informal dilly-dally. **3 postpone**, put off, defer, hold over, adjourn, reschedule.
− ANTONYMS: hurry, advance.
• n. **1** the time that someone or something is delayed. **2** the act of delaying.
▷ SYNONYMS: **1 hold-up**, wait, interruption, stoppage. **2** the delay of his trial: **postponement**, deferral, adjournment.

delectable adj. delightful or delicious.
■ **delectably** adv.

delectation n. pleasure and delight.

delegate n. **1** a person sent to represent others. **2** a member of a committee.
▷ SYNONYMS: **representative**, envoy, emissary, commissioner, agent, deputy.
• v. give a task or responsibility to a subordinate.
▷ SYNONYMS: **assign**, entrust, pass on, hand on/over, turn over, devolve.

delegation n. **1** a group of delegates. **2** the act of delegating.
▷ SYNONYMS: **deputation**, mission, commission, contingent, legation.

delete v. cross out or remove something written or stored in a computer's memory.
▷ SYNONYMS: **remove**, cut, take out, edit out, excise, cancel, cross out, strike out, obliterate, rub out, erase.
− ANTONYMS: add.
■ **deletion** n.

deleterious adj. harmful.

deliberate adj. **1** done on purpose. **2** careful and unhurried.
▷ SYNONYMS: **1 intentional**, calculated, conscious, intended, planned, wilful, premeditated. **2 careful**, cautious, measured, regular, even, steady. **3 methodical**, systematic, careful, painstaking, meticulous, thorough.
− ANTONYMS: accidental, hasty.
• v. consider carefully and at length.
▷ SYNONYMS: **think**, think about/over, ponder, consider, contemplate, reflect on, muse on, meditate on, ruminate on, mull over.

deliberately adv. in a deliberate way.
▷ SYNONYMS: **1 intentionally**, on purpose, purposely, by design, knowingly, wittingly, consciously, wilfully. **2 carefully**, cautiously, slowly, steadily, evenly.

deliberation n. **1** long and careful consideration. **2** carefulness and lack of haste.
▷ SYNONYMS: **thought**, consideration, reflection, contemplation, rumination.

delicacy n. (pl. **delicacies**) **1** the quality of being delicate. **2** a tasty, expensive food.
▷ SYNONYMS: **1 fineness**, delicateness, fragility, thinness, lightness, flimsiness. **2 difficulty**, trickiness, sensitivity, ticklishness, awkwardness. **3 care**, sensitivity, tact, discretion, diplomacy, subtlety. **4 treat**, luxury, titbit, speciality.

delicate adj. **1** very fine in quality or structure. **2** easily broken or damaged. **3** prone to illness. **4** requiring tact and discretion.
▷ SYNONYMS: **1** delicate embroidery: **fine**, intricate, dainty, exquisite, graceful. **2** a delicate shade of blue: **subtle**, soft, pale, muted, pastel, light. **3** delicate china cups: **fragile**, dainty. **4** his wife is very delicate: **sickly**, unhealthy,

frail, feeble, weak. **5** *a delicate issue:* **difficult**, tricky, sensitive, ticklish, awkward, touchy, embarrassing; informal sticky, dicey. **6** *the matter needs delicate handling:* **careful**, sensitive, tactful, diplomatic, discreet, kid-glove, subtle.
– ANTONYMS: coarse, strong, robust.
■ **delicately** adv.

delicatessen n. a shop selling unusual or foreign prepared foods.

delicious adj. **1** very pleasant to eat or drink. **2** delightful.
▷ SYNONYMS: **delectable**, mouth-watering, appetizing, tasty, flavour-some; informal scrumptious, moreish; N. Amer. informal finger-licking.
– ANTONYMS: unpalatable.
■ **deliciously** adv.

delight v. **1** please greatly. **2** (**delight in**) take great pleasure in.
▷ SYNONYMS: **charm**, enchant, captivate, entrance, thrill, entertain, amuse, divert; informal send, tickle pink, bowl over.
– ANTONYMS: dismay, disgust.
• n. great pleasure, or a cause of this.
▷ SYNONYMS: **pleasure**, happiness, joy, glee, excitement, amusement, bliss, ecstasy.
– ANTONYMS: displeasure.

delighted adj. feeling or showing great pleasure.
▷ SYNONYMS: **pleased**, glad, happy, thrilled, overjoyed, ecstatic, elated, on cloud nine, walking on air, in seventh heaven, jumping for joy, gleeful, cock-a-hoop; informal over the moon, tickled pink, as pleased as Punch, on top of the world, as happy as Larry; Brit. informal chuffed; N. English informal made up; Austral. informal wrapped.

delightful adj. very pleasing.
▷ SYNONYMS: **1** *a delightful evening:* **lovely**, enjoyable, amusing, entertaining, pleasant, pleasur-able. **2** *a delightful girl:* **charming**, enchanting, captivating, bewitching, appealing, sweet, endearing, cute, adorable, delectable.
■ **delightfully** adv.

delineate v. describe or indicate precisely.
■ **delineation** n.

delinquent adj. tending to commit crime.
• n. a delinquent person.
■ **delinquency** n.

delirious adj. **1** suffering from delirium. **2** very excited or happy.
■ **deliriously** adv.

delirium n. a disturbed state of mind occurring esp. during a fever.

deliver v. **1** bring and hand over to the intended person. **2** provide something promised. **3** give a speech. **4** aim a blow. **5** save or set free. **6** assist in a baby's birth.
▷ SYNONYMS: **1 bring**, take, convey, carry, transport, send, distribute, dispatch, ship. **2 state**, utter, give, read, broadcast, pronounce, announce, declare, proclaim, hand down, return. **3 administer**, deal, inflict, give; informal land.

deliverance n. the process of being saved or set free.

delivery n. (pl. **deliveries**) **1** the act of delivering. **2** something delivered. **3** the manner of giving a speech.
▷ SYNONYMS: **1 conveyance**, carriage, transportation, transport, distri-bution, dispatch, shipping. **2 consign-ment**, load, shipment. **3 speech**, pronunciation, enunciation, articu-lation, elocution.

dell n. a small valley.

delphinium n. a tall garden plant with blue flowers.

delta n. an area where the mouth of a river has split into several channels.

delude v. deceive or mislead.

deluge n. **1** a severe flood or heavy fall of rain. **2** a large number of things arriving at the same time.
• v. **1** overwhelm with many things. **2** flood.

delusion n. a mistaken belief or impression.
▷ SYNONYMS: **misapprehension**, misconception, false impression, misunderstanding, mistake, error, misconstruction, illusion, fantasy, fancy.
■ **delusional** adj.

deluxe adj. of a high quality.

delve v. **1** search within. **2** (**delve into**) research thoroughly.
▷ SYNONYMS: **1 rummage**, search, hunt, scrabble about, root about, ferret, fish about, dig, rifle through. **2 investi-gate**, enquire, probe, explore, research, look into, go into.

demagogue n. a political leader appealing to popular desires and prejudices.
■ **demagogic** adj.

demand n. **1** a firm request. **2** (**demands**) urgent or difficult requirements. **3** consumers' desire for a product or service.
▷ SYNONYMS: **1** *I gave in to her demands:* **request**, call, command, order,

d

dictate. **2** *the demands of a young family:* **requirement**, need, claim, commitment, imposition. **3 market**, call, appetite, desire.
• v. **1** ask for firmly. **2** need a quality etc.
▷ SYNONYMS: **1 call for**, ask for, request, push for, press for, seek, claim, insist on. **2 order**, command, enjoin, require. **3 ask**, enquire, question, query. **4 require**, need, necessitate, call for, involve, entail. **5 insist on**, stipulate, expect, look for.

demanding adj. requiring much skill or effort.
▷ SYNONYMS: **1 difficult**, challenging, taxing, exacting, tough, hard, onerous, formidable, arduous, gruelling, back-breaking, punishing. **2 nagging**, trying, tiresome, hard to please, high-maintenance.
− ANTONYMS: easy.

demarcation n. **1** the fixing of boundaries. **2** a dividing line.

demean v. lower the dignity of.

demeaning adj. humiliating.
▷ SYNONYMS: **degrading**, humiliating, shameful, undignified, menial; informal infra dig.

demeanour (US **demeanor**) n. outward behaviour or bearing.
▷ SYNONYMS: **manner**, air, attitude, appearance, look, mien, bearing, carriage, behaviour, conduct.

demented adj. **1** having dementia. **2** informal wild or irrational.

dementia n. a serious mental disorder.

demerara sugar n. light brown sugar.

demi- prefix half.

demilitarize (or **-ise**) v. remove military forces from.
■ **demilitarization** n.

demise n. **1** death. **2** the end or failure of something.
▷ SYNONYMS: **1 death**, dying, passing, end. **2 end**, break-up, disintegration, fall, downfall, collapse, overthrow.
− ANTONYMS: birth.

demo informal n. (pl. **demos**) a demonstration.
• v. (**demos**, **demoing**, **demoed**) demonstrate something.

demob v. (**demobbing**, **demobbed**) Brit. informal demobilize.

demobilize (or **-ise**) v. release from military service.
■ **demobilization** n.

democracy n. (pl. **democracies**) **1** a form of government in which the people vote for representatives to

govern on their behalf. **2** a state governed in this way.

democrat n. **1** a supporter of democracy. **2** (**Democrat**) (in the US) a member of the Democratic Party.

democratic adj. **1** relating to or supporting democracy. **2** (**Democratic**) (in the US) of the Democratic Party.
▷ SYNONYMS: **elected**, representative, parliamentary, popular, egalitarian, self-governing.
■ **democratically** adv.

demography n. the statistical study of human populations.
■ **demographic** adj.

demolish v. pull or knock down a building.
▷ SYNONYMS: **1 knock down**, pull down, tear down, destroy, flatten, raze to the ground, dismantle, level, bull-doze, blow up. **2 destroy**, ruin, wreck, overturn, explode, drive a coach and horses through; informal shoot full of holes.
− ANTONYMS: build.
■ **demolition** n.

demon n. an evil spirit or devil.
• adj. forceful or skilful.
■ **demoniac** adj. **demonic** adj. **demonically** adv.

demonize (or **-ise**) v. portray as wicked or threatening.

demonstrable adj. clearly apparent or able to be proved.
■ **demonstrably** adv.

demonstrate v. **1** clearly show to exist or be true. **2** show and explain how something works. **3** take part in a public demonstration.
▷ SYNONYMS: **1 indicate**, prove, show, establish, confirm, verify. **2 reveal**, manifest, indicate, illustrate, signify, signal, denote, show, display, exhibit. **3 protest**, march, parade, picket, strike.
■ **demonstrator** n.

demonstration n. **1** an act of demonstrating. **2** a public meeting or march to express an opinion on an issue.
▷ SYNONYMS: **1 exhibition**, presentation, display. **2 manifestation**, indication, sign, mark, proof, testimony. **3 protest**, march, rally, mass lobby, sit-in; informal demo.

demonstrative adj. **1** showing your feelings openly. **2** demonstrating something.
▷ SYNONYMS: **expressive**, open, forth-coming, communicative, unreserved, emotional, effusive, affectionate,

loving, warm, friendly, approachable; informal touchy-feely.
− ANTONYMS: reserved.
■ **demonstratively** adv.

demoralize (or **-ise**) v. dishearten.
▷ SYNONYMS: **dishearten**, discourage, dispirit, depress, cast down, dismay, daunt, crush.

demote v. move to a less senior position.
■ **demotion** n.

demur v. (**demurring, demurred**) show reluctance.
□ **without demur** without hesitating or objecting.

demure adj. modest and shy.
▷ SYNONYMS: **modest**, reserved, shy, unassuming, decorous, decent, proper.
− ANTONYMS: brazen.
■ **demurely** adv.

demystify v. (**demystifying, demystified**) make easier to understand.

den n. **1** a wild animal's lair. **2** informal a person's private room.
▷ SYNONYMS: **1 lair**, burrow, hole, shelter, hiding place, hideout. **2 study**, studio, workshop, retreat, sanctuary, hideaway; informal hidey-hole.

denationalize (or **-ise**) v. privatize a nationalized industry.

deniable adj. able to be denied.

denial n. **1** a statement denying something. **2** refusal to accept something unpleasant.
▷ SYNONYMS: **1 contradiction**, rebuttal, repudiation, refutation, disclaimer. **2 refusal**, withholding.

denier /**den**-yer/ n. a unit for measuring the fineness of yarn.

denigrate v. criticize unfairly.
■ **denigration** n.

denim n. **1** a hard-wearing cotton twill fabric. **2** (**denims**) denim jeans.

denizen n. an inhabitant.

denomination n. **1** a recognized branch of a Church or religion. **2** the face value of a banknote, coin, etc.
▷ SYNONYMS: **1 religious group**, sect, cult, movement, persuasion, order, creed, school, church. **2 value**, unit, size.
■ **denominational** adj.

denominator n. the number below the line in a fraction.

denote v. **1** be a sign of. **2** (of a word) have as a main meaning.
▷ SYNONYMS: **indicate**, be a mark of, signify, signal, designate, symbolize, represent.

■ **denotation** n.

denouement /**day-noo-mon**/ n. the final outcome of a play, film, etc.

denounce v. publicly declare to be wrong or evil.
▷ SYNONYMS: **1 condemn**, attack, censure, decry, stigmatize, deprecate, disparage, revile, damn. **2 expose**, betray, inform on, incriminate, implicate, cite, accuse.

dense adj. **1** closely packed together. **2** thick in texture. **3** informal stupid.
▷ SYNONYMS: **1** *a dense forest*: **thick**, crowded, compact, solid, tight, overgrown, impenetrable, impassable. **2** *dense smoke*: **thick**, heavy, opaque, murky. **3 stupid**, brainless, foolish, slow, simple-minded, empty-headed, obtuse; informal thick, dim, dopey.
− ANTONYMS: sparse, thin.
■ **densely** adv.

density n. (pl. **densities**) the degree to which something is dense.

dent n. a slight hollow made by a blow or pressure.
▷ SYNONYMS: **knock**, indentation, dint, depression, hollow, crater, pit; N. Amer. informal ding.
• v. **1** mark with a dent. **2** have a bad effect on.
▷ SYNONYMS: **knock**, dint, mark; N. Amer. informal ding.

dental adj. of the teeth or dentistry.

dentine n. the hard tissue forming the main part of a tooth.

dentist n. a person qualified to treat conditions affecting the teeth and gums.
■ **dentistry** n.

denture n. a removable plate or frame holding a false tooth or teeth.

denude v. make bare or empty.

denunciation n. the act of denouncing.

deny v. (**denying, denied**) **1** state that something is not true. **2** refuse to admit. **3** prevent from having something wanted.
▷ SYNONYMS: **1 contradict**, rebut, repudiate, refute, challenge, contest. **2 refuse**, turn down, reject, rebuff, decline, veto, dismiss; informal give the thumbs down to.
− ANTONYMS: confirm, allow, accept.

deodorant n. a substance which prevents unpleasant bodily odours.

deodorize (or **-ise**) v. prevent an unpleasant smell in.

depart v. **1** leave. **2** (**depart from**) do something different from what is usual.
▷ SYNONYMS: **1 leave**, go away, withdraw,

d

absent yourself, quit, exit, decamp, retreat, retire, make off; informal make tracks, take off, split; Brit. informal sling your hook. **2 deviate**, diverge, digress, stray, veer, differ, vary.
– ANTONYMS: arrive.
departed adj. dead.
department n. a section of a large organization.
▷ SYNONYMS: **division**, section, sector, unit, branch, wing, office, bureau, agency, ministry.
□ **department store** a large shop selling many types of goods.
■ **departmental** adj. **departmentally** adv.
departure n. **1** the act of leaving. **2** a change from usual procedure.
▷ SYNONYMS: **1 leaving**, going, leave-taking, withdrawal, exit. **2 deviation**, divergence, digression, shift, variation. **3 change**, innovation, novelty.
depend v. (**depend on**) **1** be determined by. **2** rely on.
▷ SYNONYMS: **1** *her career depends on this:* be dependent on, hinge on, hang on, rest on, rely on. **2** *my family depends on me:* rely on, lean on, count on, bank on, trust, pin your hopes on.
dependable adj. reliable.
▷ SYNONYMS: **reliable**, trustworthy, trusty, faithful, loyal, stable, sensible, responsible.
■ **dependability** n.
dependant (or **dependent**) n. a person who relies on another for financial support.
dependency n. (pl. **dependencies**) **1** a country or province controlled by another. **2** the state of being dependent.
dependent adj. **1** relying on for support or survival. **2** (**dependent on**) determined by.
▷ SYNONYMS: **1 addicted**, reliant; informal hooked. **2 reliant**, needy, helpless, infirm, invalid, incapable, debilitated.
– ANTONYMS: independent.
• n. var. of **DEPENDANT**.
■ **dependence** n.
depict v. represent in a picture or in words.
▷ SYNONYMS: **1 portray**, show, represent, picture, illustrate, reproduce, render. **2 describe**, detail, relate, present, set forth, set out, outline.
■ **depiction** n.
depilatory adj. used to remove unwanted hair.
deplete v. reduce the number or quantity of.
▷ SYNONYMS: **reduce**, decrease, diminish, exhaust, use up, consume, expend,

drain, empty.
– ANTONYMS: augment.
■ **depletion** n.
deplorable adj. shockingly bad.
■ **deplorably** adv.
deplore v. strongly disapprove of.
▷ SYNONYMS: **1 abhor**, find unacceptable, frown on, disapprove of, take a dim view of, take exception to, condemn, denounce. **2 regret**, lament, mourn, bemoan, bewail, complain about, grieve over, sigh over.
– ANTONYMS: applaud.
deploy v. **1** bring or move into position for military action. **2** use effectively.
▷ SYNONYMS: **1 position**, station, post, place, install, locate, base. **2 use**, utilize, employ, take advantage of, exploit, call on.
■ **deployment** n.
depopulate v. reduce the population of.
■ **depopulation** n.
deport v. expel a foreigner from a country.
▷ SYNONYMS: **expel**, banish, extradite, repatriate.
– ANTONYMS: admit.
■ **deportation** n.
deportment n. the way a person stands and walks.
depose v. remove from power.
▷ SYNONYMS: **overthrow**, unseat, dethrone, topple, remove, supplant, displace, oust.
deposit n. **1** a sum of money paid into an account. **2** a first instalment in buying something. **3** a returnable sum paid to cover possible loss of or damage to something rented. **4** a layer of a substance that has accumulated.
▷ SYNONYMS: **1 down payment**, advance payment, prepayment, instalment, retainer, security. **2 layer**, covering, coating, accumulation, sediment; seam, vein, lode, stratum.
• v. (**depositing**, **deposited**) **1** put down. **2** store for safe keeping. **3** pay as a deposit. **4** lay down a layer of a substance.
▷ SYNONYMS: **1 put down**, place, set down, unload, rest, drop; informal dump, park, plonk; N. Amer. informal plunk. **2 lodge**, bank, house, store, stow. **3 leave**, precipitate, dump, wash up, cast up.
□ **deposit account** a bank account paying interest.
■ **deposition** n. **depositor** n.
depository n. (pl. **depositories**) a

place where things are stored.

depot /dep-oh/ n. **1** a place for storing goods. **2** a place where vehicles are housed.

▷ SYNONYMS: **1 terminal**, terminus, station, garage, headquarters, base. **2 storehouse**, warehouse, store, repository, depository, cache, arsenal, armoury, dump.

deprave v. corrupt morally.
■ depravity n.

deprecate v. express disapproval of.
■ deprecation n. deprecatory adj.

depreciate v. **1** reduce in value over time. **2** dismiss as unimportant.
■ depreciation n.

depredation n. a harmful or damaging act.

depress v. **1** make very unhappy. **2** make less active. **3** push down.

▷ SYNONYMS: **1 sadden**, dispirit, cast down, get down, dishearten, demoralize, crush, weigh down on. **2 slow down**, weaken, impair, inhibit, restrict. **3 reduce**, lower, cut, cheapen, discount, deflate, diminish, depreciate, devalue. **4 press**, push, hold down.

– ANTONYMS: cheer, boost, raise.
■ depressant n. & adj.

depressed adj. **1** very unhappy. **2** suffering the effects of an economic slump.

▷ SYNONYMS: **1 sad**, unhappy, miserable, gloomy, dejected, downhearted, downcast, down, despondent, dispirited, low, morose, dismal, desolate; informal blue, down in the dumps, down in the mouth. **2 weak**, inactive, flat, slow, slack, sluggish, stagnant. **3 poverty-stricken**, poor, disadvantaged, deprived, needy, distressed, run down.

– ANTONYMS: cheerful.

depressing adj. causing unhappiness or gloom.

▷ SYNONYMS: **gloomy**, sad, unhappy, sombre, bleak, black, melancholy, dreary, funereal, grim, cheerless.

depression n. **1** a mental state involving great unhappiness and hopelessness. **2** a long economic slump. **3** a sunken place or hollow. **4** an area of low pressure which may bring rain.

▷ SYNONYMS: **1 unhappiness**, sadness, melancholia, melancholy, misery, sorrow, gloom, despondency, low spirits. **2 recession**, slump, decline, downturn. **3 hollow**, indentation, dent, cavity, dip, pit, crater, basin, bowl.
■ depressive adj.

deprivation n. **1** hardship resulting from the lack of basic necessities. **2** the lack or removal of something necessary.

▷ SYNONYMS: **1 poverty**, impoverishment, privation, hardship, destitution, need, want. **2 dispossession**, withholding, withdrawal, removal, seizure.

deprive v. prevent from having or using something.

▷ SYNONYMS: **dispossess**, strip, divest, relieve, rob, cheat out of.

deprived adj. lacking the basic necessities of life.

▷ SYNONYMS: **disadvantaged**, underprivileged, poverty-stricken, impoverished, poor, destitute, needy.

– ANTONYMS: privileged.

depth n. **1** the distance from the top or surface down, or from front to back. **2** detailed thought or study. **3** intense quality. **4** (**the depths**) the deepest, lowest, or inmost part.

▷ SYNONYMS: **1 deepness**, drop, height. **2 extent**, range, scope, breadth, width. **3 profundity**, wisdom, understanding, intelligence, discernment, penetration, insight, awareness. **4 intensity**, richness, vividness, strength, brilliance.

□ **depth charge** a device designed to explode under water.

deputation n. a group of people sent to represent others.

depute v. delegate authority or a task to someone.

deputize (or **-ise**) v. act as a deputy for someone.

▷ SYNONYMS: **stand in**, sit in, fill in, cover, substitute, replace, take someone's place, take over, hold the fort, step into the breach.

deputy n. (pl. **deputies**) a person appointed to act on behalf of another.

▷ SYNONYMS: **second in command**, number two, assistant, aide, proxy, stand-in, replacement, substitute, representative, reserve.

derail v. **1** make a train leave the tracks. **2** obstruct a process.
■ derailment n.

deranged adj. insane.
■ derangement n.

deregulate v. remove regulations from.
■ deregulation n.

derelict adj. left to fall into ruin.

▷ SYNONYMS: **dilapidated**, ramshackle, run down, tumbledown, in ruins, falling down, disused, abandoned, deserted.

dereliction n. **1** the state of being derelict. **2** (**dereliction of duty**) failure to do your duty.

deride v. ridicule.

de rigueur /duh ri-ger/ adj. necessary for social acceptance.

derision n. scornful ridicule.

▷ SYNONYMS: **mockery**, ridicule, jeers, sneers, taunts, disdain, disparagement, denigration, insults.

■ **derisive** adj. **derisively** adv.

derisory adj. ridiculously small or inadequate.

derivative adj. imitating another artist, writer, etc.; not original.
• n. something derived from another source.

derive v. (**derive from**) **1** obtain from. **2** arise or originate from.

■ **derivation** n.

dermatitis n. inflammation of the skin.

dermatology n. the branch of medicine concerned with skin disorders.

■ **dermatologist** n.

derogatory adj. critical or disrespectful.

▷ SYNONYMS: **disparaging**, disrespectful, demeaning, critical, pejorative, negative, unfavourable, uncomplimentary, unflattering, insulting, defamatory, slanderous, libellous.

– ANTONYMS: complimentary.

derrick n. **1** a crane with a pivoted arm. **2** the framework over an oil well.

dervish n. a member of a Muslim religious group, some orders of which are known for their wild rituals.

desalinate v. remove salt from seawater.

■ **desalination** n.

descant n. a melody sung or played above a basic melody.

descend v. **1** move, slope, or lead down. **2** (**descend to**) do something shameful. **3** make an attack or unexpected visit. **4** (**be descended from**) have as an ancestor.

▷ SYNONYMS: **1 go down**, come down, drop, fall, sink, dive, plummet, plunge, nosedive. **2 slope**, dip, slant, go down, fall away. **3 alight**, disembark, get down, get off, dismount.

– ANTONYMS: climb, board.

descendant n. a person descended from another.

descent n. **1** an act of descending. **2** a downward slope. **3** a person's origin or nationality.

▷ SYNONYMS: **1 dive**, drop, fall, plunge, nosedive. **2 slope**, incline, dip, drop, gradient. **3 decline**, slide, fall, degeneration, deterioration. **4 ancestry**, parentage, ancestors, family, extraction, origin, derivation, birth, lineage, stock, blood, roots, origins.

describe v. **1** give a detailed account of. **2** mark out or draw a shape.

▷ SYNONYMS: **1 report**, recount, relate, narrate, tell of, set out, detail, give a rundown of. **2 portray**, depict, paint, define, characterize, call, label, class, brand. **3 mark out**, delineate, outline, trace, draw.

description n. **1** a spoken or written account. **2** the act of describing. **3** a sort or kind.

▷ SYNONYMS: **1 account**, report, narrative, story, portrayal, portrait, sketch, details. **2 designation**, labelling, naming, dubbing, characterization, definition, classification, branding. **3 sort**, variety, kind, type.

■ **descriptive** adj. **descriptively** adv.

descry v. (**descrying, descried**) literary catch sight of.

desecrate v. treat something sacred with violent disrespect.

■ **desecration** n.

desegregate v. end racial segregation in.

■ **desegregation** n.

deselect v. Brit. reject an existing MP as a candidate in a forthcoming election.

■ **deselection** n.

desert v. **1** leave someone without help or support. **2** leave a place, making it empty. **3** illegally leave the armed forces.

▷ SYNONYMS: **1 abandon**, leave, jilt, leave high and dry, leave in the lurch, leave behind, strand, maroon; informal walk/run out on, dump, ditch; literary forsake. **2 abscond**, defect, run away, decamp, flee, turn tail, take French leave; Military go AWOL.
• n. a waterless, empty area of land with few plants.

▷ SYNONYMS: **wasteland**, wastes, wilderness, dust bowl.

■ **deserter** n. **desertion** n.

deserted adj. having been left or abandoned.

▷ SYNONYMS: **1 abandoned**, jilted, cast aside, stranded, marooned; literary forsaken. **2 empty**, uninhabited, unoccupied, abandoned, evacuated, desolate, lonely.

deserts /di-zerts/ pl. n. the reward or

punishment that someone deserves.

deserve v. be worthy of a reward or punishment.

▷ SYNONYMS: **1 merit**, earn, warrant, rate, justify, be worthy of, be entitled to. **2** (deserved) *a deserved reputation:* **well earned**, merited, warranted, justified, rightful, due, fitting, just, proper.

■ **deservedly** adv.

deserving adj. worthy of favourable treatment or help.

▷ SYNONYMS: **worthy**, commendable, praiseworthy, admirable, estimable, creditable.

déshabillé /day-za-bee-yay/ n. the state of being partly clothed.

desiccate v. remove the moisture from.

■ **desiccation** n.

desideratum n. (pl. **desiderata**) something needed or wanted.

design n. **1** a plan or drawing showing how something is to be made. **2** a decorative pattern. **3** purpose or deliberate planning.

▷ SYNONYMS: **1 plan**, blueprint, drawing, sketch, outline, map, plot, diagram, draft. **2 pattern**, motif, device, style, theme, layout.

• v. **1** produce a design for. **2** intend for a purpose.

▷ SYNONYMS: **1 invent**, create, think up, come up with, devise, formulate, conceive; informal dream up. **2 intend**, aim, mean.

■ **designer** n.

designate v. **1** officially give a status or name to. **2** appoint to a job.

▷ SYNONYMS: **1 appoint**, nominate, delegate, select, choose, pick, elect, name, identify, assign. **2 classify**, class, label, tag, name, call, term, dub.

• adj. appointed to a post but not yet having taken it up.

■ **designation** n.

designing adj. cunning and deceitful.

desirable adj. **1** wished for as being attractive, useful, or necessary. **2** sexually attractive.

▷ SYNONYMS: **1 attractive**, sought-after, in demand, popular, enviable; informal to die for, must-have. **2 advantageous**, advisable, wise, sensible, recommended, beneficial, preferable. **3 sexually attractive**, seductive, alluring, irresistible, appealing, beautiful, pretty; informal sexy.

– ANTONYMS: unattractive.

■ **desirability** n.

desire n. **1** a strong feeling of wanting something. **2** strong sexual appetite.

▷ SYNONYMS: **1 wish**, want, aspiration, yearning, longing, craving, hankering, hunger; informal yen, itch. **2 lust**, passion, sensuality, sexuality, libido, lasciviousness.

• v. **1** strongly wish for or want. **2** want sexually.

▷ SYNONYMS: **want**, wish for, long for, yearn for, crave, hanker after, be desperate for, be bent on, covet, aspire to.

desirous adj. strongly wishing for.

desist v. stop doing.

desk n. **1** a piece of furniture for working on. **2** a counter in a hotel, airport, etc. **3** a section of a news organization.

□ **desktop 1** a computer suitable for use at a desk. **2** the working area of a computer screen.

desolate adj. **1** bleak and empty. **2** very unhappy.

▷ SYNONYMS: **1 bleak**, stark, bare, dismal, grim, wild, inhospitable, deserted, uninhabited, empty, abandoned, godforsaken, isolated, remote. **2 miserable**, unhappy, despondent, depressed, disconsolate, devastated, despairing, inconsolable, wretched, broken-hearted.

• v. make very unhappy.

■ **desolation** n.

despair n. complete lack of hope.

▷ SYNONYMS: **desperation**, anguish, unhappiness, despondency, depression, misery, wretchedness, hopelessness.

– ANTONYMS: hope, joy.

• v. lose or be without hope.

▷ SYNONYMS: **lose hope**, give up, lose heart, be discouraged, be despondent, be demoralized.

despatch var. of **DISPATCH**.

desperado n. (pl. **desperadoes** or **desperados**) a reckless and dangerous criminal.

desperate adj. **1** feeling or involving despair. **2** done when all else has failed. **3** very serious.

▷ SYNONYMS: **1 despairing**, hopeless, anguished, distressed, wretched, desolate, forlorn, distraught, at your wits' end, at the end of your tether. **2 last-ditch**, last-gasp, eleventh-hour, do-or-die, final, frantic, frenzied, wild. **3 grave**, serious, critical, acute, urgent, pressing, drastic, extreme.

■ **desperately** adv.

| USAGE des*pe*rate, not -*parate*. |

desperation n. a state of despair.

▷ SYNONYMS: **hopelessness**, despair,

distress, anguish, agony, torment, misery, wretchedness.

despicable adj. deserving hatred and contempt.
■ **despicably** adv.

despise v. feel hatred or disgust for.
▷ SYNONYMS: **detest**, hate, loathe, abhor, deplore, scorn, disdain, deride, sneer at, revile, spurn, shun.
– ANTONYMS: adore, respect.

despite prep. in spite of.
▷ SYNONYMS: **in spite of**, notwith-standing, regardless of, in the face of, in the teeth of, undeterred by, for all, even with.

despoil v. literary steal valuable possessions from.

despondent adj. sad and dispirited.
■ **despondency** n. **despondently** adv.

despot n. a ruler with total power, esp. a cruel one.
■ **despotic** adj. **despotism** n.

dessert n. the sweet course eaten at the end of a meal.
□ **dessertspoon** a spoon between a tablespoon and a teaspoon in size.

destabilize (or **-ise**) v. make unstable.

destination n. the place to which someone or something is going.

destined adj. **1** intended for a particular purpose. **2** bound for a particular destination.
▷ SYNONYMS: **1 fated**, ordained, predestined, doomed, meant, intended. **2** *computers destined for Pakistan:* **heading**, bound, en route, scheduled, headed.

destiny n. (pl. **destinies**) **1** the events that will happen to a person. **2** the power believed to control future events; fate.
▷ SYNONYMS: **1 future**, fate, fortune, doom, lot. **2 providence**, fate, God, the stars, luck, fortune, chance, karma, kismet.

destitute adj. very poor.
▷ SYNONYMS: **penniless**, poor, impoverished, poverty-stricken, impecunious, indigent, down and out, Brit. on the breadline; informal broke, on your uppers; Brit. informal stony broke, skint; formal penurious.
– ANTONYMS: rich.
■ **destitution** n.

destroy v. **1** end the existence of something by badly damaging it. **2** kill an animal in a painless way.
▷ SYNONYMS: **1 demolish**, knock down, level, raze to the ground, blow up, annihilate, obliterate. **2 spoil**, ruin, wreck, blight, devastate, shatter, wreak havoc on. **3 kill**, put down, put

to sleep, slaughter, cull.
– ANTONYMS: build.

destroyer n. **1** a person or thing that destroys. **2** a small, fast warship.

destruction n. the destroying of something.
▷ SYNONYMS: **devastation**, carnage, ruin, chaos, wreckage, demolition, annihi-lation, obliteration, devastation.
– ANTONYMS: preservation.
■ **destructive** adj.

desuetude /dess-wi-tyood/ n. disuse.

desultory /dess-uhl-tuh-ri/ adj. lacking enthusiasm or purpose.
■ **desultorily** adv.

detach v. **1** disconnect and remove. **2** (**detach yourself from**) distance yourself from.
▷ SYNONYMS: **disconnect**, separate, unfasten, disengage, uncouple, isolate, remove, loose, unhitch, unhook, free, pull off, cut off, break off, split off, sever.
– ANTONYMS: attach, join.
■ **detachable** adj.

USAGE Only one *t*: *detach*, not *-tatch*.

detached adj. **1** separate or disconnected. **2** not involved; objective.
▷ SYNONYMS: **1 disconnected**, separated, separate, unfastened, disengaged, uncoupled, isolated, loosened, unhitched, unhooked, free, severed, cut off. **2 dispassionate**, disinter-ested, objective, outside, neutral, unbiased, impartial.

detachment n. **1** the state of being uninvolved. **2** a group of troops etc. sent on a separate mission.
▷ SYNONYMS: **1 objectivity**, dispassion, disinterest, neutrality, impartiality. **2 unit**, squad, detail, troop, contin-gent, task force, party, platoon.

detail n. **1** a small individual item or fact. **2** small items or facts as a group. **3** a small detachment of troops or police officers.
▷ SYNONYMS: **1 feature**, respect, particular, characteristic, specific, aspect, fact, point, element, item. **2 triviality**, technicality, nicety, fine point. **3 unit**, detachment, squad, troop, contingent, outfit, task force, party, platoon.
• v. **1** describe fully. **2** order to undertake a task.
▷ SYNONYMS: **describe**, relate, catalogue, list, spell out, itemize, identify, specify.

detailed adj. giving many details.
▷ SYNONYMS: **comprehensive**, full,

complete, thorough, exhaustive, inclusive, elaborate, minute, precise, itemized, blow-by-blow.
– ANTONYMS: general.

detain v. 1 keep from going somewhere. 2 keep in custody.
▷ SYNONYMS: 1 **hold**, take into custody, confine, imprison, intern, arrest, apprehend, seize; informal pick up; Brit. informal nick. 2 **delay**, hold up, make late, keep, slow up/down, hinder.
– ANTONYMS: release.
■ **detainment** n.

detainee n. a person who is kept in custody.

detect v. 1 discover the presence of. 2 investigate a crime.
▷ SYNONYMS: 1 **notice**, perceive, discern, become aware of, note, make out, spot, recognize, identify, catch, sense. 2 **discover**, uncover, turn up, unearth, dig up, root out, expose. 3 **catch**, hunt down, track down, find out, expose, reveal, unmask, smoke out.
■ **detection** n. **detector** n.

detective n. a person whose job is to investigate crimes.
▷ SYNONYMS: **investigator**, police officer; informal private eye, sleuth; N. Amer. informal gumshoe.

détente /day-**tahnt**/ n. the easing of hostility between countries.

detention n. 1 the state of being detained in custody. 2 the punishment of being kept behind at school.
▷ SYNONYMS: **custody**, imprisonment, incarceration, internment, captivity, remand, arrest, quarantine.
– ANTONYMS: release.

deter v. (deterring, deterred) discourage from action.
▷ SYNONYMS: 1 **discourage**, dissuade, put off, scare off, dishearten, demoralize, daunt, intimidate. 2 **prevent**, stop, avert, stave off, ward off.
– ANTONYMS: encourage.

detergent n. a chemical substance used for cleaning.

deteriorate v. become gradually worse.
▷ SYNONYMS: **worsen**, decline, degenerate, fail, go downhill, wane.
– ANTONYMS: improve.
■ **deterioration** n.

determinant n. a determining factor.

determination n. 1 persistence in the face of difficulty. 2 the act of establishing something exactly.
▷ SYNONYMS: **resolution**, resolve, will power, strength of character, dedication, single-mindedness, perseverance, persistence, tenacity, staying

power, doggedness; informal guts.

determine v. 1 cause to occur in a particular way or be of a specific type. 2 firmly decide. 3 establish by research or calculation.
▷ SYNONYMS: 1 **control**, decide, regulate, direct, dictate, govern. 2 **resolve**, decide, make up your mind, choose, elect, opt. 3 **specify**, set, fix, decide on, settle, establish, ordain, prescribe, decree. 4 **ascertain**, find out, discover, learn, establish, calculate, work out; informal figure out.

determined adj. persisting even in the face of difficulty.
▷ SYNONYMS: **resolute**, purposeful, adamant, single-minded, unswerving, unwavering, persevering, persistent, tenacious, dedicated, dogged.
– ANTONYMS: irresolute.

deterrent n. a thing that deters or is intended to deter.
▷ SYNONYMS: **disincentive**, discouragement, damper, curb, check, restraint, inhibition.
– ANTONYMS: incentive.
■ **deterrence** n.

detest v. dislike intensely.
▷ SYNONYMS: **hate**, abhor, loathe, be unable to bear, despise, abominate.
– ANTONYMS: love.
■ **detestable** adj. **detestation** n.

dethrone v. remove a monarch from power.

detonate v. explode or cause to explode.
■ **detonation** n. **detonator** n.

detour n. a long or roundabout route.

detoxify v. (detoxifying, detoxified) remove harmful substances from.

detract v. (detract from) cause to seem less valuable or impressive.

detractor n. a critic of someone or something.

detriment n. harm or damage.

detrimental adj. causing harm or damage.
▷ SYNONYMS: **harmful**, damaging, injurious, hurtful, inimical, deleterious, destructive, pernicious, undesirable, unfavourable.
– ANTONYMS: beneficial.
■ **detrimentally** adv..

detritus /di-**try**-tuhss/ n. debris or waste material.

deuce n. the score of 40 all in a game in tennis.

Deutschmark /**doych**-mark/ n. the former basic unit of money in Germany.

devalue v. reduce the value or worth of.
■ **devaluation** n.

devastate v. destroy or ruin.
▷ SYNONYMS: **destroy**, ruin, wreck, lay waste, ravage, demolish, raze to the ground, level, flatten.
■ **devastation** n.

devastated adj. overwhelmed with shock or grief.
▷ SYNONYMS: **shattered**, shocked, stunned, dazed, dumbfounded, traumatized, distressed; Brit. informal knocked for six.

devastating adj. **1** very destructive. **2** very distressing. **3** informal very impressive or attractive.

develop v. (**developing**, **developed**) **1** become or make larger or more advanced. **2** start to exist, experience, or possess. **3** convert land to a new purpose. **4** treat a film with chemicals to make a visible image.
▷ SYNONYMS: **1 grow**, expand, spread, advance, progress, evolve, mature. **2** individuals can develop their personal skills: **expand**, augment, broaden, supplement, reinforce, enhance, refine, improve, perfect. **3** widespread social unrest developed: **start**, begin, emerge, erupt, break out, arise.
■ **developer** n.

development n. **1** the action of developing. **2** a new product, idea, or phase. **3** an area with new buildings on it.
▷ SYNONYMS: **1 evolution**, growth, expansion, enlargement, spread, progress. **2 event**, change, circumstance, incident, occurrence. **3 estate**, complex, site.

deviant adj. different from what is considered normal.
• n. a deviant person.
■ **deviance** n.

deviate v. depart from an established course or normal standards.
▷ SYNONYMS: **diverge**, digress, drift, stray, veer, swerve, get sidetracked, branch off, differ, vary.
■ **deviation** n.

device n. **1** a piece of equipment with a particular purpose. **2** a plan or method.
▷ SYNONYMS: **1 implement**, gadget, utensil, tool, appliance, apparatus, instrument, machine, mechanism, contrivance, contraption; informal gizmo. **2 ploy**, tactic, move, stratagem, scheme, manoeuvre, plot, trick, ruse.

devil n. **1** (**the Devil**) (in Christian and Jewish belief) the most powerful evil spirit. **2** an evil spirit. **3** a very cruel person. **4** a mischievous person.

5 informal a specified type of person: the poor devil.
▷ SYNONYMS: **1 Satan**, Beelzebub, Lucifer, the Prince of Darkness; informal Old Nick. **2 evil spirit**, demon, fiend. **3 brute**, beast, monster, fiend, villain, sadist, barbarian, ogre.
□ **devil-may-care** cheerful and reckless. **devil's advocate** a person who expresses an opinion so as to provoke debate.
■ **devilish** adj.

> **WORD LINKS**
> **diabolic, diabolical, satanic**
> relating to the Devil

devilment n. mischief.

devilry n. **1** wickedness. **2** mischief.

devious adj. **1** cunning and underhand. **2** (of a route) indirect.
▷ SYNONYMS: **1 underhand**, dishonest, crafty, cunning, conniving, scheming, sneaky, furtive; informal crooked, shady; Brit. informal dodgy. **2 circuitous**, roundabout, indirect, meandering, tortuous.
– ANTONYMS: honest, direct.
■ **deviously** adv. **deviousness** n.

devise v. plan or invent.
▷ SYNONYMS: **conceive**, think up, dream up, work out, formulate, concoct, hatch, contrive, design, invent, coin; informal cook up.

devoid adj. (**devoid of**) completely lacking in.
▷ SYNONYMS: **empty of**, free of, bereft of, lacking, deficient in, without, wanting in; informal minus.

devolution n. the transfer of power by central government to local or regional governments.

devolve v. **1** transfer power to a lower level. **2** (**devolve on/to**) (of responsibility) pass to.

devote v. (**devote to**) give time or resources to.
▷ SYNONYMS: **dedicate**, allocate, assign, allot, commit, give, consign, pledge, set aside, earmark, reserve.

devoted adj. very loving or loyal.
▷ SYNONYMS: **dedicated**, committed, devout, loyal, faithful, true, staunch, steadfast, fond, loving.

devotee n. **1** an enthusiast. **2** a follower of a particular religion or god.
▷ SYNONYMS: **enthusiast**, fan, lover, aficionado, admirer, supporter, disciple; informal buff, freak, nut, fanatic.

devotion n. **1** great love or loyalty. **2** religious worship. **3** (**devotions**) prayers.

▷ SYNONYMS: **1 loyalty**, fidelity, commitment, allegiance, dedication, fondness, love, care. **2 piety**, spirituality, godliness, holiness, sanctity.
■ **devotional** adj.

devour v. **1** eat greedily. **2** (of a force) destroy completely. **3** read quickly and eagerly.
▷ SYNONYMS: **1 gobble**, guzzle, gulp down, bolt, wolf; informal polish off; Brit. informal scoff. **2 consume**, engulf, envelop.

devout adj. **1** deeply religious. **2** earnestly sincere.
▷ SYNONYMS: **dedicated**, devoted, committed, loyal, sincere, fervent, pious, reverent, God-fearing, dutiful, churchgoing.
■ **devoutly** adv.

dew n. drops of condensed moisture forming on cool surfaces at night.
■ **dewy** adj.

dewlap n. a fold of loose skin hanging from an animal's throat.

dexterity n. skill in performing tasks.
■ **dexterous** (or **dextrous**) adj.

dextrose n. a form of glucose.

dhal (or **dal**) n. (in Indian cookery) cooked split pulses.

diabetes n. an illness in which a lack of insulin results in a failure to absorb sugar and starch properly.
■ **diabetic** adj. & n.

diabolical adj. **1** (or **diabolic**) of or like the Devil. **2** informal very bad.
■ **diabolically** adv.

diadem n. a jewelled crown.

diagnose v. identify the nature of an illness or problem by examining the symptoms.
▷ SYNONYMS: **identify**, determine, distinguish, recognize, interpret, detect, pinpoint.

diagnosis n. (pl. **diagnoses**) the identification of an illness or problem by examining the symptoms.
▷ SYNONYMS: **1 identification**, detection, recognition, determination, discovery, pinpointing. **2 opinion**, judgement, verdict, conclusion.
■ **diagnostic** adj.

diagonal adj. **1** (of a line) joining opposite corners of a rectangle or square. **2** slanting.
▷ SYNONYMS: **crosswise**, crossways, slanting, slanted, oblique, angled, cornerways, cornerwise.
• n. a diagonal line.
■ **diagonally** adv.

diagram n. a simplified drawing showing the appearance or structure of something.

▷ SYNONYMS: **drawing**, representation, plan, outline, figure, chart, graph.
■ **diagrammatic** adj.

dial n. **1** a disc marked to show the time or to indicate a measurement. **2** a disc with numbered holes on a phone, turned to make a call. **3** a disc turned to select a setting on a radio, cooker, etc.
• v. (**dialling, dialled**; US **dialing, dialed**) call a phone number.

dialect n. a local form of a language.
■ **dialectal** adj.

dialectic (or **dialectics**) n. the investigation of the truth of opposing opinions by logical discussion.
■ **dialectical** adj.

dialogue (US **dialog**) n. **1** conversation as a feature of a book, play, etc. **2** a discussion.
▷ SYNONYMS: **conversation**, talk, discussion, chat, tête-à-tête, exchange, debate, conference, consultation; informal confab.

dialysis n. (pl. **dialyses**) the use of a machine to purify the blood of a person whose kidneys do not work properly.

diamanté /dy-uh-**mon**-tay/ adj. decorated with artificial diamonds.

diameter n. a straight line passing from side to side through the centre of a circle or sphere.

diametrical adj. **1** (of opposites) complete. **2** of a diameter.
■ **diametrically** adv.

diamond n. **1** a very hard, clear precious stone. **2** a figure with four sides of equal length forming two opposite acute angles and two opposite obtuse angles. **3** (**diamonds**) one of the four suits in a pack of cards.
☐ **diamond wedding** Brit. the 60th anniversary of a wedding.

diaper n. US a baby's nappy.

diaphanous /dy-**af**-fuh-nuhss/ adj. delicate and semi-transparent.

diaphragm /dy-uh-fram/ n. **1** a layer of muscle between the lungs and the stomach. **2** a thin contraceptive cap fitting over the cervix.

diarrhoea /dy-uh-**ree**-uh/ (US **diarrhea**) n. a condition involving frequent liquid bowel movements.

diary n. (pl. **diaries**) a book for keeping a daily record of events, or for noting appointments.
▷ SYNONYMS: **1 appointment book**, engagement book, personal organizer; trademark Filofax. **2 journal**, memoir, chronicle, log, logbook,

d

history, annal, record, weblog, blog;
N. Amer. daybook.
■ **diarist** n.

diaspora /dy-ass-puh-ruh/ n. the
dispersion of a people from their
homeland, esp. that of the Jews from
Israel.

diatribe n. a vehement verbal attack.

dice n. (pl. **dice**; sing. also **die**) a small
cube with faces bearing from one to
six spots, used in games of chance.
• v. **1** cut food into small cubes. **2** (**dice
with**) take great risks with.

dicey adj. (**dicier, diciest**) informal
difficult or risky.

dichotomy /dy-kot-uh-mi/ n. (pl.
dichotomies) a division or contrast
between two things.
■ **dichotomous** adj.

dicky adj. Brit. informal not strong,
healthy, or working reliably.

dictate v. **1** state or order with
authority. **2** control or determine.
3 speak words to be typed or written
down.
▷ SYNONYMS: **1** prescribe, lay down,
impose, set down, order, command,
decree, ordain, direct. **2** determine,
control, govern, decide, influence,
affect.
• n. an order or command.
■ **dictation** n.

dictator n. a ruler with total power
over a country.
▷ SYNONYMS: autocrat, despot, tyrant,
absolute ruler.
– ANTONYMS: democrat.
■ **dictatorship** n.

dictatorial adj. **1** relating to
a dictator. **2** insisting on total
obedience.
▷ SYNONYMS: domineering, autocratic, authoritarian, oppressive,
imperious, overweening, overbearing,
peremptory; informal bossy,
high-handed.

diction n. **1** a person's way of
pronouncing words. **2** the choice and
use of words in literature.

dictionary n. (pl. **dictionaries**) a book
that lists the words of a language
and gives their meaning, or their
equivalent in a different language.
▷ SYNONYMS: lexicon, glossary,
vocabulary.

> **WORD LINKS**
> **lexicography** the writing of
> dictionaries

dictum n. (pl. **dicta** or **dictums**) **1** a
formal announcement. **2** a saying.

did past of **DO**.

didactic adj. intended to teach or give
moral guidance.

diddle v. informal cheat or swindle.

didgeridoo n. an Australian
Aboriginal wind instrument in the
form of a long wooden tube.

didn't contr. did not.

die v. (**dying, died**) **1** stop living. **2** (**die
out**) become extinct. **3** become less
loud or strong. **4** (**be dying for/to do**)
informal be very eager for or to do.
▷ SYNONYMS: **1** pass away, pass on,
perish; informal give up the ghost, kick
the bucket, croak, bite the dust; Brit.
informal snuff it, peg out, pop your
clogs; N. Amer. informal buy the farm.
2 lessen, subside, drop, ease off, let
up, moderate, abate, fade, peter out,
wane, ebb. **3** *the engine died:* fail,
cut out, give out, break down, stop;
informal conk out, go kaput; Brit. informal
pack up.
– ANTONYMS: live.
• n. **1** (pl. **dies**) a device for cutting or
moulding metal or for stamping a
design. **2** sing. of **DICE**.
□ **diehard** a person who stubbornly
supports something in spite of
change or opposition.

diesel n. **1** an internal-combustion
engine in which the heat of
compressed air is used to ignite the
fuel. **2** a form of petroleum used to
fuel diesel engines.

diet n. **1** the food that a person or
animal usually eats. **2** a limited
range or amount of food, adopted to
lose weight or for medical reasons.
3 a law-making assembly in certain
countries.
▷ SYNONYMS: **1** *a healthy diet:* food,
nutrition, eating habits. **2** *she's on
a diet:* dietary regime, regimen,
restricted diet, fast.
• v. (**dieting, dieted**) keep to a special
diet to lose weight.
▷ SYNONYMS: be on a diet, slim, lose
weight, watch your weight; N. Amer.
reduce; N. Amer. informal slenderize.
• adj. with reduced fat or sugar
content.
■ **dieter** n. **dietary** adj.

dietetics n. the study of diet and its
effects on health.
■ **dietetic** adj.

dietitian (or **dietician**) n. an expert on
diet and nutrition.

differ v. **1** be unlike. **2** disagree.
▷ SYNONYMS: **1** *the second set of data
differed from the first:* contrast with,
be different to, vary from, deviate

from, conflict with, run counter to, be at odds with, contradict. **2 disagree**, conflict, be at variance/odds, be in dispute, not see eye to eye.
– ANTONYMS: resemble, agree.
difference n. **1** a way in which people or things are not the same. **2** a disagreement or dispute. **3** the remainder left after one value is subtracted from another.
▷ SYNONYMS: **1 dissimilarity**, contrast, distinction, differentiation, variance, variation, divergence, disparity, contradiction. **2 disagreement**, difference of opinion, dispute, argument, quarrel; Brit. row. **3** *I'll pay the difference:* **balance**, remainder, rest.
– ANTONYMS: similarity.
different adj. **1** not the same as another or each other. **2** separate. **3** new and unusual.
▷ SYNONYMS: **1 dissimilar**, unlike, contrasting, differing, varying, disparate, poles apart, incompatible, mismatched; informal like chalk and cheese. **2 changed**, altered, transformed, new, unfamiliar, unknown, strange. **3 distinct**, separate, individual, independent. **4 unusual**, out of the ordinary, unfamiliar, novel, new, fresh, original, unconventional, exotic.
– ANTONYMS: similar, ordinary.
■ **differently** adv.
differential adj. involving a difference.
• n. **1** Brit. an agreed difference in wage rates. **2** a gear allowing a vehicle's wheels to revolve at different speeds when cornering.
differentiate v. **1** recognize as different. **2** cause to appear different.
■ **differentiation** n.
difficult adj. **1** needing much effort or skill to do, deal with, or understand. **2** hard to please.
▷ SYNONYMS: **1** *a difficult job:* **laborious**, strenuous, arduous, hard, tough, demanding, punishing, gruelling, back-breaking, exhausting, tiring; informal hellish, killing, no picnic. **2** *a difficult problem:* **hard**, complicated, complex, puzzling, perplexing, baffling, problematic, thorny, ticklish. **3** *a difficult child:* **troublesome**, tiresome, trying, exasperating, awkward, demanding, contrary, recalcitrant, uncooperative, fussy.
– ANTONYMS: easy, simple, cooperative.
difficulty n. (pl. **difficulties**) **1** the state of being difficult. **2** a difficult situation; a problem.

▷ SYNONYMS: **1 strain**, stress, trouble, problems, struggle; informal hassle. **2 problem**, complication, snag, hitch, obstacle, hurdle, stumbling block, pitfall; Brit. spanner in the works; informal headache. **3** *he got into difficulties:* **trouble**, predicament, plight, hard times; informal fix, scrape, jam.
– ANTONYMS: ease.
diffident adj. lacking self-confidence.
▷ SYNONYMS: **shy**, bashful, modest, self-effacing, unassuming, meek, unconfident, insecure, unassertive, timid, shrinking, reticent.
– ANTONYMS: confident.
■ **diffidence** n. **diffidently** adv.
diffract v. cause a beam of light to be spread out as a result of passing through a narrow opening or across an edge.
■ **diffraction** n.
diffuse v. **1** spread over a wide area. **2** (of a gas or liquid) become mingled with a substance.
• adj. **1** spread out over a large area. **2** not clear or concise.
■ **diffusely** adv. **diffuser** n. **diffusion** n.

> USAGE Don't confuse **diffuse** with **defuse**, which means 'make a situation less tense'.

dig v. (**digging, dug**) **1** break up and turn over or move earth. **2** remove or make by digging. **3** push or poke sharply. **4** (**dig into/through**) search in. **5** (**dig out/up**) discover facts.
▷ SYNONYMS: **1** *she began to dig the soil:* **turn over**, work, break up. **2** *he dug a hole:* **excavate**, dig out, quarry, hollow out, scoop out, bore, burrow, mine. **3 poke**, prod, jab, stab, shove, ram, push, thrust, drive, stick. **4 delve**, probe, search, enquire, look, investigate, research.
• n. **1** an act of digging. **2** an archaeological excavation. **3** a sharp push or poke. **4** informal a critical remark. **5** (**digs**) informal lodgings.
▷ SYNONYMS: **1 poke**, prod, jab, stab, shove, push. **2 snide remark**, cutting remark, jibe, taunt, sneer, insult; informal wisecrack, put-down.
■ **digger** n.
digest v. **1** break down food in the body so that it can be easily absorbed. **2** reflect on and absorb information.
▷ SYNONYMS: **assimilate**, absorb, take in, understand, comprehend, grasp.
• n. a summary or collection of information.
▷ SYNONYMS: **summary**, synopsis, abstract, precis, résumé, summation.

■ **digestible** adj. **digestion** n. **digestive** adj.

digit n. **1** any of the numerals from 0 to 9. **2** a finger, thumb, or toe.

digital adj. **1** of information represented as a series of binary digits, as in a computer. **2** involving computer technology. **3** (of a clock) showing the time by displaying numbers electronically. **4** (of a camera) producing images that can be stored in a computer and displayed on screen.
■ **digitally** adv.

digitalis /di-ji-tay-liss/ n. a heart stimulant made from foxgloves.

digitize (or **-ise**) v. convert pictures or sound into a digital form.

dignified adj. showing dignity.
▷ SYNONYMS: **stately**, noble, majestic, distinguished, regal, imposing, impressive, grand, solemn, formal, ceremonious, decorous, sedate.

dignify v. (**dignifying**, **dignified**) make impressive or worthy of respect.

dignitary n. (pl. **dignitaries**) a high-ranking or important person.

dignity n. (pl. **dignities**) **1** the state of being worthy of respect. **2** a calm or serious manner. **3** pride in yourself.
▷ SYNONYMS: **1 stateliness**, nobility, majesty, impressiveness, grandeur, magnificence, ceremoniousness, formality, decorum, propriety, respectability, worthiness, integrity, solemnity, gravitas. **2 self-respect**, pride, self-esteem, self-worth.

digress v. depart from the main subject temporarily.
■ **digression** n.

dike var. of DYKE.

diktat n. a decree imposed by someone in power.

dilapidated adj. in a state of disrepair or ruin.
▷ SYNONYMS: **run down**, tumbledown, ramshackle, in disrepair, shabby, battered, rickety, crumbling, in ruins, ruined, decaying, decrepit, neglected, uncared-for, gone to rack and ruin.
■ **dilapidation** n.

USAGE dil-, not del-: dilapidated.

dilate v. make or become wider or more open.
■ **dilation** n.

dilatory /di-luh-tri/ adj. **1** slow to act. **2** causing delay.

dilemma n. a situation in which a difficult choice has to be made.
▷ SYNONYMS: **quandary**, predicament, catch-22, vicious circle, plight,

conflict; informal fix, tight spot/corner; (**in a dilemma**) between the devil and the deep blue sea, between a rock and a hard place.

dilettante /di-li-tan-tay/ n. (pl. **dilettanti** or **dilettantes**) a person who dabbles in a subject for enjoyment.

diligent adj. careful and conscientious.
▷ SYNONYMS: **industrious**, hard-working, assiduous, conscientious, particular, punctilious, meticulous, painstaking, rigorous, careful, thorough, sedulous.
– ANTONYMS: lazy.
■ **diligence** n. **diligently** adv.

dill n. a herb.

dilly-dally v. (**dilly-dallying**, **dilly-dallied**) informal dawdle or be indecisive.

dilute v. **1** make a liquid thinner or weaker by adding water etc. **2** reduce the forcefulness of.
▷ SYNONYMS: **1** dilute the bleach with water: **make weaker**, water down, thin, doctor, adulterate; informal cut. **2** the original plans have been diluted: **tone down**, moderate, weaken, water down, compromise.
• adj. (of a liquid) diluted.
■ **dilution** n.

dim adj. (**dimmer, dimmest**) **1** not bright or well lit. **2** indistinct. **3** informal stupid.
▷ SYNONYMS: **1** the dim light: **faint**, weak, feeble, soft, pale, dull, subdued, muted. **2** long dim corridors: **dark**, badly lit, dingy, dismal, gloomy, murky. **3** a dim figure: **indistinct**, ill-defined, vague, shadowy, nebulous, blurred, fuzzy. **4** dim memories: **vague**, imprecise, imperfect, unclear, indistinct, sketchy, hazy. **5** see STUPID.
– ANTONYMS: bright, distinct, clear.
• v. (**dimming, dimmed**) make or become dim.
▷ SYNONYMS: **1 turn down**, lower, soften, subdue. **2 fade**, dwindle, dull.
– ANTONYMS: brighten.
■ **dimly** adv. **dimness** n.

dime n. US a 10-cent coin.

dimension n. **1** a measurable extent, such as length, breadth, or height. **2** an aspect or feature.
▷ SYNONYMS: **1 size**, measurements, proportions, extent, length, width, breadth, depth. **2 aspect**, feature, element, angle, facet, side.
■ **dimensional** adj.

diminish v. make or become smaller, weaker, or less.
▷ SYNONYMS: **1 subside**, lessen, decline, reduce, decrease, dwindle, fade,

slacken off, let up. **2** *new laws diminished the courts' authority:* **reduce**, decrease, lessen, curtail, cut, limit, curb.
– ANTONYMS: increase.

diminuendo adv. & adj. Music with a decrease in loudness.

diminution n. a reduction.

diminutive adj. very small.
• n. a shortened informal form of a name.

dimmer n. a device for varying the brightness of an electric light.

dimple n. a small depression, esp. in the cheeks when someone smiles.
• v. form or show dimples.

din n. a prolonged loud and unpleasant noise.
▷ SYNONYMS: **noise**, racket, rumpus, cacophony, hubbub, uproar, commotion, clangour, clatter, clamour; Brit. row; informal hullabaloo.
– ANTONYMS: silence.
• v. (**dinning, dinned**) (**din into**) teach someone something by constant repetition.

dinar /dee-nar/ n. the basic unit of money of Serbia and some Middle Eastern and North African countries.

dine v. eat dinner.
▷ SYNONYMS: **eat**, have dinner, have lunch.

diner n. **1** a person who dines. **2** US a small roadside restaurant.

dinghy n. (pl. **dinghies**) **1** a small open sailing boat. **2** a small inflatable rubber boat.

dingle n. literary a wooded valley.

dingo n. (pl. **dingoes** or **dingos**) a wild Australian dog.

dingy /din-ji/ adj. (**dingier, dingiest**) gloomy and drab.
▷ SYNONYMS: **gloomy**, dark, dull, dim, dismal, dreary, drab, sombre, grim, cheerless, dirty, grimy, shabby, seedy, run down.
– ANTONYMS: bright.
■ dinginess n.

dinky adj. (**dinkier, dinkiest**) Brit. informal attractively small and neat.

dinner n. **1** the main meal of the day. **2** a formal evening meal.
▷ SYNONYMS: **main meal**, lunch, evening meal, supper, feast, banquet; Brit. tea.
□ **dinner jacket** a man's jacket worn for formal evening occasions.

dinosaur n. an extinct prehistoric reptile, often of enormous size.

dint n. (**by dint of**) by means of.

diocese /dy-uh-siss/ n. a district for

which a bishop is responsible.
■ diocesan adj.

diode n. a semiconductor device with two terminals, allowing the flow of current in one direction only.

dioxide n. an oxide with two atoms of oxygen to one of a metal or other element.

dioxin /dy-ok-sin/ n. a highly poisonous organic compound.

dip v. (**dipping, dipped**) **1** (**dip in/into**) put or lower briefly in or into. **2** move or slope downwards. **3** (of a level or amount) temporarily drop.
▷ SYNONYMS: **1 immerse**, submerge, plunge, dunk, bathe, sink. **2 sink**, drop, fall, descend, go down. **3 decrease**, fall, drop, fall off, decline, diminish, dwindle, slump, plummet, plunge.
– ANTONYMS: rise, increase.
• n. **1** an act of dipping. **2** a thick sauce in which pieces of food are dipped before eating. **3** a brief swim. **4** a brief downward slope.
▷ SYNONYMS: **1 slope**, incline, decline, descent, hollow, depression, basin. **2 decrease**, fall, drop, downturn, decline, falling-off, slump, reduction.

diphtheria n. a serious infectious disease causing inflammation of the throat.

diphthong n. a compound vowel sound (as in *coin*).

diploma n. a certificate awarded on completing a course of study.

diplomacy n. **1** the profession or skill of managing international relations. **2** skill and tact in dealing with people.
▷ SYNONYMS: **1 statesmanship**, state-craft; negotiations, discussions, talks. **2 tact**, tactfulness, sensitivity, discretion.

diplomat n. an official representing a country abroad.
▷ SYNONYMS: **ambassador**, attaché, consul, chargé d'affaires, envoy, emissary.

diplomatic adj. **1** of diplomacy. **2** tactful.
▷ SYNONYMS: **tactful**, sensitive, subtle, delicate, polite, discreet, judicious, politic.
– ANTONYMS: tactless.
■ diplomatically adv.

dipper n. a small diving bird.

dipsomania n. alcoholism.
■ dipsomaniac n.

diptych /dip-tik/ n. a painting on two hinged panels, forming an altarpiece.

dire adj. **1** very serious or urgent. **2** informal very bad.

ᐅ SYNONYMS: **terrible**, dreadful, appalling, frightful, awful, grim, sore, alarming, acute, grave, serious, urgent, pressing, wretched, desperate, parlous.

direct adj. **1** going straight from one place to another. **2** with nothing or no one in between. **3** frank. **4** clear and explicit.
ᐅ SYNONYMS: **1 straight**, short, quick. **2 non-stop**, through, unbroken, uninterrupted. **3 frank**, candid, straightforward, open, blunt, plain-spoken, outspoken, forthright, no-nonsense, matter-of-fact; informal upfront.
• adv. in a direct way or by a direct route.
• v. **1** aim towards. **2** tell or show someone the way. **3** control the operations of. **4** supervise and control a film, play, etc. **5** give an order to.
ᐅ SYNONYMS: **1 aim**, target, address to, intend for, mean for, design for. **2 manage**, govern, run, administer, control, conduct, handle, be in charge of, preside over, lead, head, rule. **3 instruct**, tell, command, order, require; old use bid.
☐ **direct current** electric current flowing in one direction only. **direct debit** Brit. an arrangement with a bank to transfer money regularly from an account to a third party. **direct object** the person or thing directly affected by the action of a transitive verb. **direct speech** the actual words of a speaker quoted in writing.

direction n. **1** a course along which someone or something moves. **2** a point to or from which someone or something faces. **3** control or management. **4** (**directions**) instructions.
ᐅ SYNONYMS: **1 way**, route, course, line, bearing, orientation. **2 running**, management, administration, conduct, handling, supervision, super-intendence, command, rule, leader-ship. **3 instruction**, order, command, rule, regulation, requirement.
■ **directional** adj.

directive n. an official instruction.
ᐅ SYNONYMS: **instruction**, direction, command, order, injunction, decree, dictum, edict.

directly adv. **1** in a direct way. **2** exactly in a specified position. **3** immediately.
ᐅ SYNONYMS: **1** they flew directly to New York: **straight**, as the crow flies. **2** the houses directly opposite: **exactly**, right, immediately, diametrically; informal **bang**. **3** directly after breakfast: **immediately**, right, straight, without delay, promptly. **4 frankly**, candidly, openly, bluntly, forthrightly, without beating about the bush.
• conj. Brit. as soon as.

director n. **1** a person in charge of an organization or activity. **2** a member of the board managing a business. **3** a person who directs a film, play, etc.
ᐅ SYNONYMS: **manager**, head, chief, principal, leader, governor, president, chair, chief executive; informal **boss**, gaffer.
■ **directorial** adj.

directorate n. **1** the board of directors of a company. **2** a section of a government department in charge of a particular activity.

directory n. (pl. **directories**) **1** a book listing names, addresses, and phone numbers. **2** a computer file listing other files.

dirge n. a mournful song or piece of music.

dirigible n. an airship.

dirk n. a short dagger.

dirndl n. a full, wide skirt.

dirt n. **1** a substance causing something not to be clean. **2** soil. **3** informal scandalous or damaging information.
ᐅ SYNONYMS: **1 grime**, filth, muck, dust, mud, pollution; Brit. informal gunge. **2** a dirt road: **earth**, soil, clay, loam.

dirty adj. (**dirtier, dirtiest**) **1** covered or marked with mud, dust, etc. **2** obscene. **3** dishonest or unfair.
ᐅ SYNONYMS: **1 soiled**, grimy, grubby, filthy, mucky, stained, unwashed, greasy, muddy, dusty, polluted, contaminated, foul, unhygienic; Brit. informal manky, grotty. **2 obscene**, indecent, rude, naughty, vulgar, smutty, coarse, crude, filthy, off colour, pornographic, explicit, X-rated; informal blue; euphemistic adult. **3** a dirty look: **malevolent**, hostile, black, angry, disapproving.
– ANTONYMS: clean.
• v. (**dirtying, dirtied**) make dirty.
ᐅ SYNONYMS: **soil**, stain, muddy, blacken, mess up, mark, spatter, smudge, smear, splatter, sully, pollute, foul.
■ **dirtiness** n.

disability n. (pl. **disabilities**) **1** a physical or mental condition that limits a person's movements, senses, or activities. **2** a disadvantage.

disable v. **1** limit someone in their movements, senses, or activities.

2 put out of action.
■ **disablement** n.

disabled adj. having a physical or mental disability.

disabuse v. persuade someone that a belief is mistaken.

disadvantage n. something causing a problem or reducing the chances of success.
▷ SYNONYMS: **1 drawback**, snag, downside, fly in the ointment, catch, nuisance, handicap, trouble, informal minus. **2 detriment**, prejudice, harm, loss, hurt.
– ANTONYMS: advantage.
• v. **1** put in an unfavourable position. **2** (**disadvantaged**) having less money and fewer opportunities than most people.
■ **disadvantageous** adj.

disaffected adj. discontented and no longer loyal.
■ **disaffection** n.

disagree v. **1** have a different opinion. **2** be inconsistent. **3** (**disagree with**) make slightly unwell.
▷ SYNONYMS: **1 be of a different opinion**, not see eye to eye, take issue, challenge, contradict, differ, dissent, be in dispute, clash. **2 differ**, be dissimilar, be different, be at variance/odds, vary, contradict each other, conflict. **3** the food disagreed with her: **make ill**, make unwell, upset, nauseate.
– ANTONYMS: agree.

disagreeable adj. **1** unpleasant. **2** bad-tempered.
▷ SYNONYMS: **unpleasant**, distasteful, off-putting, unpalatable, nasty, objectionable, disgusting, horrible, offensive, repulsive, obnoxious, odious, repellent, revolting, vile, foul.
– ANTONYMS: pleasant.

disagreement n. the action or fact of disagreeing.
▷ SYNONYMS: **dissent**, difference of opinion, controversy, discord, division, dispute, quarrel.
– ANTONYMS: agreement.

disallow v. declare to be invalid.

disappear v. cease to be visible or to exist.
▷ SYNONYMS: **1 vanish**, be lost to view/sight, recede, fade away, melt away, clear. **2 die out**, cease to exist, end, go, pass away, pass into oblivion, vanish, perish.
– ANTONYMS: materialize, appear.
■ **disappearance** n.

disappoint v. fail to fulfil the hopes of.
▷ SYNONYMS: **let down**, fail, dissatisfy,
upset, dismay, sadden, disenchant, disillusion, shatter someone's illusions.

disappointed adj. sad or displeased because hopes have not been fulfilled.
▷ SYNONYMS: **upset**, saddened, let down, displeased, dissatisfied, disheartened, downhearted, discouraged, crestfallen, disenchanted, disillusioned; informal **choked**, cut up; Brit. informal gutted, as sick as a parrot.
– ANTONYMS: delighted.

disappointment n. **1** sadness or displeasure felt when your hopes are not fulfilled. **2** a cause of such feelings.
▷ SYNONYMS: **1 sadness**, sorrow, regret, dismay, displeasure, dissatisfaction, disenchantment, disillusionment. **2 let-down**, non-event, anticlimax; Brit. damp squib; informal washout.
– ANTONYMS: delight.

disapprobation n. strong disapproval.

disapproval n. the feeling that something is wrong or bad.
▷ SYNONYMS: **disfavour**, objection, dislike, dissatisfaction, distaste, displeasure, criticism, censure, condemnation, denunciation.
– ANTONYMS: approval.

disapprove v. consider to be wrong or bad.
▷ SYNONYMS: she disapproved of gambling: **object to**, take exception to, dislike, take a dim view of, look askance at, frown on, be against, deplore, censure, condemn, denounce.
– ANTONYMS: approve.

disarm v. **1** take weapons away from. **2** (of a country or force) reduce or withdraw its armed forces or weapons. **3** win over a hostile person.
▷ SYNONYMS: **1 lay down your arms**, demobilize, disband, demilitarize. **2 defuse**, disable, deactivate, make safe. **3 win over**, charm, persuade, soothe, mollify, appease, placate.
– ANTONYMS: arm, antagonize.

disarmament n. the reduction or withdrawal of armed forces or weapons.
▷ SYNONYMS: **demilitarization**, demobilization, disbandment, decommissioning, arms reduction, arms limitation.

disarming adj. making people feel less hostile or suspicious.
▷ SYNONYMS: **winning**, charming, irresistible, persuasive, soothing, conciliatory, mollifying.

disarrange v. make untidy.

disarray n. disorder or confusion.

▷ SYNONYMS: **disorder**, confusion, chaos, untidiness, disorganization, a mess, a muddle, a shambles.

– ANTONYMS: tidiness.

disassociate var. of DISSOCIATE.

disaster n. **1** a sudden event causing great damage or loss of life. **2** a sudden misfortune.

▷ SYNONYMS: **1** catastrophe, calamity, cataclysm, tragedy, act of God, accident. **2** misfortune, mishap, misadventure, setback, reversal, stroke of bad luck, blow. **3** failure, fiasco, catastrophe; informal flop, washout, dead loss.

– ANTONYMS: success.

disastrous adj. **1** causing great damage. **2** informal very unsuccessful.

▷ SYNONYMS: **catastrophic**, calamitous, cataclysmic, tragic, devastating, ruinous, terrible, awful.

■ **disastrously** adv.

disavow v. deny any responsibility or support for.

■ **disavowal** n.

disband v. (of an organized group) break up.

disbar v. (**disbarring**, **disbarred**) expel a barrister from the Bar.

disbelief n. inability to believe that something is true or real.

▷ SYNONYMS: **incredulity**, incredulousness, scepticism, doubt, cynicism, suspicion, distrust, mistrust.

disbelieve v. be unable to believe.

disburse v. pay out money from a fund.

■ **disbursement** n.

disc (US **disk**) n. **1** a flat, thin, round object. **2** (**disk**) a device on which computer data is stored. **3** a layer of cartilage separating vertebrae in the spine. **4** a compact disc or record. □ **disc jockey** a DJ.

discard v. get rid of something useless or unwanted.

▷ SYNONYMS: **dispose of**, throw away/ out, get rid of, toss out, jettison, dispense with, scrap, reject, drop; informal ditch, bin, junk; Brit. informal get shot of; N. Amer. informal trash.

– ANTONYMS: keep.

discern v. **1** recognize or be aware of. **2** see or hear with difficulty.

■ **discernible** adj.

discerning adj. having or showing good judgement.

■ **discernment** n.

discharge v. **1** dismiss or allow to leave. **2** send out a liquid, gas, etc.

3 fire a gun or missile. **4** fulfil a responsibility.

▷ SYNONYMS: **1** dismiss, eject, expel, throw out, make redundant, release, let go; Military cashier; informal sack, fire. **2** free, set free, release, let out, liberate. **3** emit, give off, let out, send out, exude, leak, secrete, excrete, release. **4** fire, shoot, let off, set off, loose off, trigger, launch. **5** unload, offload, put off, remove. **6** carry out, perform, execute, conduct, fulfil, complete.

– ANTONYMS: recruit, imprison.

•n. **1** the act of discharging. **2** a substance discharged.

▷ SYNONYMS: **1** dismissal, release, removal, ejection, expulsion; Military cashiering; informal the sack, the boot. **2** leak, leakage, emission, secretion, excretion, suppuration, pus. **3** carrying out, performance, execution, conduct, fulfilment, accomplishment, completion.

disciple n. **1** one of the original followers of Jesus. **2** a follower of a teacher, leader, etc.

▷ SYNONYMS: **follower**, adherent, believer, admirer, devotee, acolyte, apostle, supporter, advocate.

disciplinarian n. a person who enforces strict discipline.

disciplinary adj. of discipline.

discipline n. **1** the training of people to obey rules or a code of behaviour. **2** controlled behaviour resulting from this. **3** a branch of academic study.

▷ SYNONYMS: **1** control, regulation, direction, order, authority, strictness. **2** good behaviour, order, control, obedience. **3** field, branch of knowledge, subject, area, speciality.

•v. **1** train to be obedient or self-controlled. **2** punish for an offence.

▷ SYNONYMS: **1** train, drill, teach, school, coach. **2** punish, penalize, bring to book, reprimand, rebuke.

disclaim v. deny responsibility for or knowledge of.

disclaimer n. a statement disclaiming responsibility.

disclose v. reveal.

▷ SYNONYMS: **reveal**, make known, divulge, tell, impart, communicate, pass on, release, make public, broadcast, publish.

– ANTONYMS: conceal.

■ **disclosure** n.

disco n. (pl. **discos**) a club or party at which people dance to pop music.

discolour (US **discolor**) v. make or become stained or otherwise changed

in colour.
▷ SYNONYMS: **stain**, mark, soil, dirty, streak, smear, tarnish, spoil.
■ **discoloration** n.

discomfit v. (**discomfiting, discomfited**) make uneasy or embarrassed.
■ **discomfiture** n.

discomfort n. **1** slight pain. **2** slight anxiety or embarrassment.
▷ SYNONYMS: **1 pain**, aches and pains, soreness, aching, twinge, pang, throb, cramp. **2 inconvenience**, difficulty, problem, trial, tribulation, hardship. **3 embarrassment**, discomfiture, unease, awkwardness, discomposure, confusion, nervousness, distress, anxiety.

disconcert v. unsettle; upset.

disconnect v. **1** break the connection of or between. **2** detach an electrical device from a power supply.
▷ SYNONYMS: **1 detach**, disengage, uncouple, unhook, unhitch, undo, unfasten, unyoke. **2 separate**, cut off, divorce, sever, isolate, dissociate, remove. **3 deactivate**, shut off, turn off, switch off, unplug.
– ANTONYMS: attach, connect.
■ **disconnection** n.

disconsolate adj. very unhappy.

discontent n. unhappiness or dissatisfaction.
▷ SYNONYMS: **dissatisfaction**, disaffection, grievances, unhappiness, displeasure, resentment, envy, restlessness, unrest, unease.
– ANTONYMS: contentment, satisfaction.
■ **discontentment** n.

discontented adj. feeling dissatisfied.
▷ SYNONYMS: **dissatisfied**, disgruntled, disaffected, unhappy, aggrieved, displeased, resentful, envious, restless, frustrated; informal fed up.
– ANTONYMS: contented, satisfied.

discontinue v. stop doing, providing, or making.
■ **discontinuation** n.

discontinuous adj. having intervals or gaps.
■ **discontinuity** n.

discord n. **1** lack of agreement or harmony. **2** lack of harmony between musical notes sounding together.

discordant adj. **1** (of a sound) harsh and unpleasant. **2** not in agreement.
▷ SYNONYMS: **tuneless**, inharmonious, off-key, dissonant, harsh, jarring, grating, jangly, jangling, strident, shrill, cacophonous.
– ANTONYMS: harmonious.

discotheque n. a disco.

discount n. a deduction from the usual price.
▷ SYNONYMS: **reduction**, deduction, mark-down, price cut, concession, rebate.
• v. **1** reduce the price of. **2** disregard because unlikely.
▷ SYNONYMS: **1 disregard**, pay no attention to, take no notice of, dismiss, ignore, overlook; informal pooh-pooh. **2 reduce**, mark down, cut, lower; informal knock down.

discourage v. **1** cause to lose enthusiasm or confidence. **2** try to persuade not to do something.
▷ SYNONYMS: **1 dissuade**, deter, put off, talk out of. **2 dishearten**, dispirit, demoralize, disappoint, put off, unnerve, daunt, intimidate. **3 prevent**, deter, stop, avert, inhibit, curb.
– ANTONYMS: encourage.
■ **discouragement** n.

discourse n. **1** written or spoken communication or debate. **2** a formal discussion of a topic.
• v. speak or write authoritatively about a topic.

discourteous adj. rude and inconsiderate.
■ **discourteously** adv. **discourtesy** n.

discover v. **1** find. **2** gain knowledge or become aware of. **3** be the first to find or observe.
▷ SYNONYMS: **1 find**, locate, come across/upon, stumble on, chance on, uncover, unearth, turn up. **2 find out**, learn, realize, ascertain, work out, recognize; informal figure out; Brit. informal twig.

discovery n. (pl. **discoveries**) **1** the act of discovering. **2** a person or thing discovered.
▷ SYNONYMS: **1 finding**, location, uncovering, unearthing. **2 realization**, recognition, revelation, disclosure. **3 breakthrough**, finding, find, innovation.

discredit v. (**discrediting, discredited**) **1** harm the good reputation of. **2** cause to seem false or unreliable.
▷ SYNONYMS: **1 bring into disrepute**, disgrace, dishonour, blacken the name of, put/show in a bad light, compromise, smear, tarnish; N. Amer. slur. **2 disprove**, invalidate, explode, refute; informal debunk.
– ANTONYMS: honour, prove.
• n. loss or lack of reputation.
▷ SYNONYMS: **dishonour**, disgrace, shame, humiliation, ignominy.

discreditable adj. bringing discredit;

shameful.

discreet adj. careful to keep something secret or to avoid causing embarrassment.
▷ SYNONYMS: **tactful**, circumspect, diplomatic, judicious, sensitive, careful, cautious, strategic.
■ **discreetly** adv.

USAGE Don't confuse **discreet** with **discrete**.

discrepancy n. (pl. **discrepancies**) a difference between things expected to be the same.
▷ SYNONYMS: **difference**, disparity, variation, deviation, divergence, disagreement, inconsistency, mismatch, conflict.
– ANTONYMS: correspondence.

discrete adj. separate and distinct.

discretion n. **1** the quality of being discreet. **2** freedom to decide.
▷ SYNONYMS: **1 tact**, diplomacy, delicacy, sensitivity, good sense, prudence, circumspection. **2** *at the discretion of the council:* choice, option, preference, disposition, pleasure, will, inclination.

discretionary adj. done or used according to a person's judgement.

discriminate v. **1** recognize a difference. **2** treat differently and unfairly on grounds of race, sex, etc.
▷ SYNONYMS: **1 differentiate**, distinguish, draw a distinction, tell the difference, tell apart, separate. **2** *policies that discriminate against women:* be biased, be prejudiced, treat differently, treat unfairly, put at a disadvantage, victimize, pick on.
■ **discriminatory** adj.

discriminating adj. having good taste or judgement.
▷ SYNONYMS: **discerning**, perceptive, judicious, selective, tasteful, refined, sensitive, cultivated, cultured.
– ANTONYMS: indiscriminate.

discrimination n. **1** unfair treatment on the grounds of race, sex, or age. **2** recognition of the difference between one thing and another. **3** good judgement or taste.
▷ SYNONYMS: **1 prejudice**, bias, bigotry, intolerance, favouritism, partisanship. **2 discernment**, judgement, perceptiveness, good taste, refinement, sensitivity, cultivation.
– ANTONYMS: impartiality.

discursive adj. moving from subject to subject.

discus n. (pl. **discuses**) a heavy disc thrown in athletic contests.

discuss v. **1** talk about so as to reach a decision. **2** talk or write about in detail.
▷ SYNONYMS: **1 talk over**, talk about, talk through, debate, confer about. **2 examine**, explore, study, analyse, go into, deal with, consider, tackle.

discussion n. **1** conversation or debate. **2** a detailed written treatment of a topic.
▷ SYNONYMS: **1 conversation**, talk, chat, dialogue, conference, debate, exchange of views, consultation, deliberation; informal confab. **2 examination**, exploration, study, analysis, treatment, consideration.

disdain n. a feeling of scornful superiority.
▷ SYNONYMS: **contempt**, scorn, derision, disrespect, condescension, superciliousness, hauteur, haughtiness.
– ANTONYMS: respect.
• v. treat with disdain.
▷ SYNONYMS: **scorn**, deride, regard with contempt, sneer at, look down your nose at, look down on, despise.
■ **disdainful** adj. **disdainfully** adv.

disease n. an illness.
▷ SYNONYMS: **illness**, sickness, ill health, infection, ailment, malady, disorder, condition, problem; informal bug, virus; Brit. informal lurgy.
■ **diseased** adj.

WORD LINKS
pathological relating to disease

disembark v. leave a ship, aircraft, or train.
■ **disembarkation** n.

disembodied adj. (of a sound) coming from a person who cannot be seen.

disembowel v. (**disembowelling**, **disembowelled**; US **disemboweling**, **disemboweled**) cut out the internal organs of.

disempower v. make less powerful or confident.

disenchant v. disillusion.
■ **disenchantment** n.

disenfranchise v. deprive of the right to vote.

disengage v. release or detach.
■ **disengagement** n.

disentangle v. free from being tangled.

disestablish v. deprive a national Church of its official status.

disfavour (US **disfavor**) n. disapproval or dislike.

disfigure v. spoil the appearance of.
■ **disfigurement** n.

disgorge v. cause to pour out.

disgrace n. **1** the loss of the respect of others. **2** a shamefully bad person or thing.
▷ SYNONYMS: **1 dishonour**, shame, discredit, ignominy, disrepute, infamy, scandal, stigma, humiliation, loss of face. **2 scandal**, discredit, reproach, stain, blemish, blot, black mark, outrage, affront.
– ANTONYMS: honour, credit.
• v. bring disgrace on.
▷ SYNONYMS: **shame**, bring shame on, dishonour, discredit, stigmatize, taint, sully, tarnish, stain, blacken.
– ANTONYMS: honour.
■ **disgracefully** adv..

disgraceful adj. shockingly unacceptable.
▷ SYNONYMS: **shameful**, scandalous, contemptible, dishonourable, discreditable, disreputable, reprehensible, blameworthy, unworthy, ignoble.
– ANTONYMS: admirable.
■ **disgracefully** adv.

disgruntled adj. angry or dissatisfied.
▷ SYNONYMS: **dissatisfied**, discontented, fed up, put out, aggrieved, resentful, displeased, unhappy, disappointed, annoyed; informal hacked off, browned off; Brit. informal cheesed off, narked; N. Amer. informal sore, ticked off.
– ANTONYMS: contented.
■ **disgruntlement** n.

disguise v. **1** change in appearance or nature to prevent recognition. **2** hide a feeling.
▷ SYNONYMS: **camouflage**, conceal, hide, cover up, mask, screen, veil, paper over.
– ANTONYMS: expose.
• n. **1** a means of disguising yourself. **2** the state of being disguised.

disgust n. revulsion or strong disapproval.
▷ SYNONYMS: **revulsion**, repugnance, aversion, distaste, abhorrence, loathing, hatred.
– ANTONYMS: delight.
• v. cause disgust in.
▷ SYNONYMS: **revolt**, repel, repulse, sicken, nauseate, horrify, appal, shock, turn someone's stomach, scandalize, outrage, offend, affront; N. Amer. informal gross out.
– ANTONYMS: delight.

disgusting adj. causing revulsion or strong disapproval.
▷ SYNONYMS: **1** the food was disgusting: revolting, repulsive, sickening, nauseating, stomach-turning, off-putting; N. Amer. vomitous; informal gross, sick-making. **2** their attitude is disgusting: outrageous, objectionable, abhorrent, repellent, loathsome, offensive, appalling, shocking, horrifying, scandalous, monstrous, detestable; informal sick.
– ANTONYMS: delightful.

dish n. **1** a shallow container for cooking or serving food. **2** a particular kind of prepared food. **3** a shallow concave object.
▷ SYNONYMS: **1 bowl**, plate, platter, salver, pot. **2 recipe**, meal, course, fare.
• v. **1** (**dish out/up**) put food on to plates before a meal. **2** (**dish out**) distribute or provide.
□ **dishwasher** a machine for washing dishes.

disharmony n. lack of harmony.

dishearten v. cause to lose determination or confidence.

dishevelled (US **disheveled**) adj. untidy in appearance.
▷ SYNONYMS: **untidy**, unkempt, scruffy, messy, disarranged, rumpled, bedraggled, tousled, tangled, wind-swept; N. Amer. informal mussed up.
– ANTONYMS: tidy.

dishonest adj. not honest, sincere, or trustworthy.
▷ SYNONYMS: **fraudulent**, cheating, underhand, devious, treacherous, unfair, dirty, criminal, illegal, unlawful, false, untruthful, deceitful, lying, corrupt, dishonourable, untrustworthy, unscrupulous; informal crooked, shady, sharp; Brit. informal bent; Austral./NZ informal shonky.
– ANTONYMS: honest.
■ **dishonestly** adv. **dishonesty** n.

dishonour (US **dishonor**) n. a state of shame or disgrace.
• v. **1** bring dishonour to. **2** fail to keep an agreement.

dishonourable (US **dishonorable**) adj. bringing shame or disgrace.
▷ SYNONYMS: **disgraceful**, shameful, discreditable, ignoble, reprehensible, shabby, shoddy, despicable, contemptible, base, low.

dishy adj. (**dishier**, **dishiest**) informal sexually attractive.

disillusion v. cause to realize that a belief is mistaken or unrealistic.
• n. disappointment from realizing that a belief is mistaken or unrealistic.
■ **disillusionment** n.

disincentive n. a factor discouraging a particular action.

disinclination n. unwillingness.

disinclined adj. reluctant; unwilling.

disinfect v. use disinfectant to destroy bacteria.
■ **disinfection** n.

disinfectant n. a chemical liquid that destroys bacteria.

disinformation n. information intended to mislead.

disingenuous adj. not sincere.
■ **disingenuously** adv.

disinherit v. prevent from inheriting.

disintegrate v. break up into small parts.
▷ SYNONYMS: **break up**, crumble, break apart, fall apart, fall to pieces, collapse, fragment, shatter, splinter.
■ **disintegration** n.

disinter v. (**disinterring**, **disinterred**) dig up something buried.

disinterest n. **1** impartiality. **2** lack of interest.

disinterested adj. not influenced by personal feelings; impartial.
▷ SYNONYMS: **unbiased**, unprejudiced, impartial, neutral, detached, objective, dispassionate, non-partisan.

> USAGE Don't confuse **disinterested** with **uninterested**, which means 'not interested'.

disjointed adj. lacking logical or coherent connection.

disjunction n. a difference between things expected to be similar.

disk US & Computing = **DISC**.

diskette n. a floppy disk.

dislike v. find unpleasant.
▷ SYNONYMS: **regard with distaste**, have an aversion to, disapprove of, object to, take exception to, have no taste for, hate, despise.
– ANTONYMS: like.
• n. the feeling that someone or something is unpleasant.
▷ SYNONYMS: **distaste**, aversion, disfavour, antipathy, disgust, abhorrence, hatred.
– ANTONYMS: liking.

dislocate v. **1** displace a bone from its proper position. **2** disrupt.
■ **dislocation** n.

dislodge v. remove from the usual position.

disloyal adj. not loyal or faithful.
▷ SYNONYMS: **unfaithful**, faithless, false, untrue, inconstant, two-faced, double-dealing, double-crossing, deceitful, treacherous, subversive, seditious, unpatriotic; informal back-stabbing, two-timing; literary perfidious.
■ **disloyalty** n.

dismal adj. **1** gloomy or depressing. **2** informal very bad.
▷ SYNONYMS: **1** a dismal look: **gloomy**, glum, melancholy, morose, doleful, woebegone, forlorn, dejected, downcast. **2** a dismal hall: **dim**, dingy, dark, gloomy, dreary, drab, dull.
– ANTONYMS: cheerful, bright.
■ **dismally** adv.

dismantle v. take to pieces.
▷ SYNONYMS: **take apart**, take to pieces, pull to pieces, disassemble, break up, strip.
– ANTONYMS: build.

dismay n. distress resulting from an unpleasant surprise.
▷ SYNONYMS: **alarm**, distress, concern, surprise, consternation, disquiet.
– ANTONYMS: pleasure, relief.
• v. cause to feel dismay.
▷ SYNONYMS: **concern**, distress, disturb, worry, alarm, disconcert, take aback, unnerve, unsettle.
– ANTONYMS: encourage.

dismember v. tear or cut the limbs from.
■ **dismemberment** n.

dismiss v. **1** order or allow to leave. **2** order an employee to leave a job. **3** treat as unworthy of consideration.
▷ SYNONYMS: **1** give someone their notice, discharge, lay off, make redundant; informal sack, fire. **2** send away, let go, release, disband, discharge. **3** banish, set aside, put out of your mind, brush aside, reject, repudiate, spurn; informal pooh-pooh.
■ **dismissal** n.

dismissive adj. treating something as unworthy of consideration.
■ **dismissively** adv.

dismount v. get off a bicycle or horse.

disobedient adj. not obedient.
▷ SYNONYMS: **naughty**, insubordinate, defiant, unruly, wayward, badly behaved, delinquent, rebellious, mutinous, troublesome, wilful.
– ANTONYMS: obedient.
■ **disobedience** n.

disobey v. fail or refuse to obey.
▷ SYNONYMS: **defy**, go against, flout, contravene, infringe, transgress, violate, disregard, ignore, pay no heed to.

disorder n. **1** untidiness or disorganization. **2** the disruption of peaceful and law-abiding behaviour. **3** an illness.
▷ SYNONYMS: **1** untidiness, mess, disarray, chaos, confusion, clutter,

jumble, a muddle, a shambles.
2 unrest, disturbance, turmoil,
mayhem, violence, fighting, fracas,
rioting, lawlessness, anarchy, breach
of the peace. **3 disease**, infection,
complaint, condition, affliction,
malady, sickness, illness, ailment.
– ANTONYMS: order, tidiness, peace.
■ **disordered** adj.

disorderly adj. **1** disorganized or
untidy. **2** involving a breakdown of
peaceful and law-abiding behaviour.
▷ SYNONYMS: **1 untidy**, disorganized,
topsy-turvy, at sixes and sevens,
messy, jumbled, cluttered, in disarray,
chaotic; informal higgledy-piggledy; Brit.
informal shambolic. **2 unruly**, riotous,
disruptive, troublesome, disobedient,
lawless.
– ANTONYMS: orderly, tidy, peaceful.

disorganized (or **-ised**) adj. not
properly planned or arranged.
▷ SYNONYMS: **unmethodical**, unsystematic, undisciplined, unstructured,
haphazard, chaotic, muddled, hit-or-
miss, sloppy, slapdash, slipshod; Brit.
informal shambolic.
– ANTONYMS: organized.
■ **disorganization** n.

disorientate (or **disorient**) v. cause
someone to lose their bearings.
■ **disorientation** n.

disown v. refuse to have anything
further to do with.
▷ SYNONYMS: **reject**, cast off/aside,
abandon, renounce, repudiate, deny,
turn your back on, wash your hands
of, disinherit.

disparage v. speak critically of.
■ **disparagement** n.

disparate adj. very different in kind.
■ **disparity** n.

dispassionate adj. unemotional and
impartial.
■ **dispassionately** adv.

dispatch (or **despatch**) v. **1** send to a
destination, esp. for a purpose. **2** deal
with a task quickly. **3** kill.
▷ SYNONYMS: **1 send**, post, mail, forward.
2 deal with, finish, conclude,
settle, discharge, perform. **3 kill**,
put to death, massacre, wipe out,
exterminate, eliminate, murder,
assassinate, execute.
• n. **1** the act of dispatching. **2** an
official report on military affairs.
3 a report by a journalist abroad.
4 promptness and efficiency.
▷ SYNONYMS: **message**, report, communication, communiqué, bulletin, statement, letter, news, intelligence.

dispel v. (**dispelling**, **dispelled**) make a

doubt or feeling disappear.
▷ SYNONYMS: **banish**, drive away/
off, chase away, scatter, eliminate,
dismiss, allay, ease, quell.

dispensable adj. not essential.

dispensary n. (pl. **dispensaries**) a
room where medicines are dispensed.

dispensation n. **1** permission to be
exempt from a rule. **2** a religious or
political system.

dispense v. **1** distribute to a number
of people. **2** prepare and supply
medicine. **3** (**dispense with**) get rid of
or manage without.
▷ SYNONYMS: **1 distribute**, pass round,
hand out, dole out, dish out, share
out. **2 administer**, deliver, issue, deal
out, mete out. **3** dispensing medicines:
prepare, make up, supply, provide.
■ **dispenser** n.

disperse v. **1** go or send in different
directions. **2** spread over a wide area.
▷ SYNONYMS: **1 break up**, split up,
disband, scatter, leave, go their
separate ways, drive away/off, chase
away. **2 dissipate**, dissolve, melt
away, fade away, clear, lift. **3 scatter**,
distribute, spread, disseminate.
– ANTONYMS: assemble, gather.
■ **dispersal** n. **dispersion** n.

dispirited adj. disheartened or
depressed.
■ **dispiriting** adj.

displace v. **1** move from the proper or
usual position. **2** take over the role of.
3 force someone to leave their home.
▷ SYNONYMS: **1 dislodge**, dislocate, move
out of place/position, shift. **2 replace**,
take the place of, supplant, supersede, oust, remove, depose.
■ **displacement** n.

display v. **1** present for viewing,
esp. in an attractive way. **2** show
something.
▷ SYNONYMS: **1 exhibit**, show, arrange,
array, present, lay out, set out.
2 show off, parade, highlight, reveal,
showcase. **3 manifest**, be evidence of,
reveal, demonstrate, show.
– ANTONYMS: conceal.
• n. **1** a public performance or show.
2 a thing or things displayed.
▷ SYNONYMS: **1 exhibition**, exposition,
array, arrangement, presentation,
demonstration, spectacle, show,
parade. **2 manifestation**, expression,
show, proof, demonstration, evidence.

displease v. annoy or upset.
▷ SYNONYMS: **annoy**, irritate, anger,
incense, irk, vex, nettle, put out,
upset, exasperate.

displeasure n. annoyance.

disport v. (**disport yourself**) old use enjoy yourself freely.

disposable adj. **1** intended to be thrown away after use. **2** (of income) available for use as required.

disposal n. the act of disposing. □ **at someone's disposal** available for someone to use as and when they wish.

dispose v. **1** (**dispose of**) get rid of. **2** (**be disposed to**) be inclined to do or think. **3** (**disposed**) having a specified attitude. **4** arrange in a particular position.
▷ SYNONYMS: **throw away**, throw out, get rid of, discard, jettison, scrap; informal dump, junk, ditch, chuck out/away.

disposition n. **1** a person's character. **2** a tendency. **3** the arrangement of something.
▷ SYNONYMS: **1 temperament**, nature, character, constitution, make-up, mentality. **2 arrangement**, positioning, placement, configuration, set-up, line-up, layout.

dispossess v. take land or property from.
■ **dispossession** n.

disproportionate adj. relatively too large or too small.
■ **disproportionately** adv.

disprove v. prove to be false.
▷ SYNONYMS: **refute**, prove false, rebut, debunk, give the lie to, demolish; informal shoot full of holes, blow out of the water.

disputation n. debate or argument.

disputatious adj. fond of arguing.

dispute v. **1** argue about. **2** question the truth of. **3** compete for.
▷ SYNONYMS: **1 debate**, discuss, exchange views, quarrel, argue, disagree, clash, fall out, wrangle, bicker, squabble. **2 challenge**, contest, question, call into question, quibble over, contradict, argue about, disagree with, take issue with.
– ANTONYMS: accept.
• n. an argument or disagreement.
▷ SYNONYMS: **1 debate**, discussion, argument, controversy, disagreement, dissent, conflict. **2 quarrel**, argument, altercation, squabble, falling-out, disagreement, difference of opinion, clash; Brit. row.
– ANTONYMS: agreement.
■ **disputable** adj.

disqualify v. (**disqualifying**, **disqualified**) prevent from performing an activity or taking a job because of unsuitability or a breach of rules.

▷ SYNONYMS: **rule out**, bar, exclude, prohibit, debar, preclude.
■ **disqualification** n.

disquiet n. anxiety or unease.
• v. make anxious or uneasy.

disquisition n. a long or complex discussion of a subject.

disregard v. pay no attention to.
▷ SYNONYMS: **ignore**, take no notice of, pay no attention to, discount, overlook, turn a blind eye to, shut your eyes to, gloss over, brush off/aside, shrug off.
– ANTONYMS: heed.
• n. lack of attention.
▷ SYNONYMS: **indifference**, non-observance, inattention, heedlessness, neglect, contempt.
– ANTONYMS: attention.

disrepair n. a poor condition due to neglect.

disreputable adj. not respectable.

disrepute n. the state of having a bad reputation.

disrespect n. lack of respect.
■ **disrespectful** adj. **disrespectfully** adv.

disrobe v. undress.

disrupt v. interrupt the normal operation of an activity or process.
▷ SYNONYMS: **interrupt**, disturb, interfere with, play havoc with, upset, unsettle, obstruct, impede, hold up, delay.
■ **disruption** n.

disruptive adj. causing disruption.
▷ SYNONYMS: disruptive students: **troublesome**, unruly, badly behaved, rowdy, disorderly, undisciplined, unmanageable, uncontrollable, uncooperative.

dissatisfied adj. not content or happy.
▷ SYNONYMS: **discontented**, disappointed, disaffected, displeased, disgruntled, aggrieved, unhappy.
– ANTONYMS: satisfied, contented.
■ **dissatisfaction** n.

dissect v. cut up a body or plant so as to study its internal parts.
■ **dissection** n.

dissemble v. hide or disguise your feelings.

disseminate v. spread widely.
■ **dissemination** n.

dissension n. disagreement within a group.

dissent v. disagree with a widely held or official view.
▷ SYNONYMS: **disagree**, differ, demur, be at variance/odds, take issue, protest, object.
– ANTONYMS: agree, conform.
• n. disagreement.
▷ SYNONYMS: **disagreement**, difference

of opinion, argument, dispute, resistance, objection, protest, opposition.
– ANTONYMS: agreement, conformity.
■ **dissenter** n.

dissertation n. a long essay.

disservice n. a harmful action.

dissident n. a person who opposes official policy.
▷ SYNONYMS: **dissenter**, objector, protester, rebel, revolutionary, subversive, agitator, refusenik.
• adj. opposing official policy.
▷ SYNONYMS: **dissenting**, opposing, rebellious, revolutionary, subversive, nonconformist, heterodox.
– ANTONYMS: conformist.
■ **dissidence** n.

dissimilar adj. not similar; different.
▷ SYNONYMS: **different**, differing, unalike, variant, diverse, divergent, heterogeneous, disparate, unrelated, distinct, contrasting.
■ **dissimilarity** n.

dissimulate v. hide or disguise your feelings.
■ **dissimulation** n.

dissipate v. **1** disperse. **2** waste money etc. **3** (**dissipated**) indulging too much in physical pleasures.
■ **dissipation** n.

dissociate v. **1** disconnect or separate. **2** (**dissociate yourself from**) declare that you are not connected with.
▷ SYNONYMS: **separate**, detach, disconnect, sever, cut off, divorce, isolate, alienate.
– ANTONYMS: associate.
■ **dissociation** n.

dissolute adj. indulging too much in physical pleasures.

dissolve v. **1** disperse in a liquid so as to form a solution. **2** close down or end an assembly or agreement. **3** give way to strong emotion.
▷ SYNONYMS: **1 break down**, liquefy, melt, deliquesce, disintegrate. **2 disband**, disperse, bring to an end, end, terminate, discontinue, break up, close down, wind up/down, suspend, adjourn. **3 annul**, nullify, void, invalidate, revoke.
■ **dissolution** n.

dissonant adj. lacking harmony.
■ **dissonance** n.

dissuade v. persuade not to do.
▷ SYNONYMS: **discourage**, deter, prevent, stop, talk out of, persuade against, advise against, argue out of.
– ANTONYMS: encourage.
■ **dissuasion** n.

distaff n. a stick on to which wool or flax is wound for spinning.

□ **distaff side** the female side of a family.

distance n. **1** the length of the space between two points. **2** the state of being distant. **3** a far-off point or place. **4** the full length of a race.
▷ SYNONYMS: **1 interval**, space, span, gap, extent, length, range, reach. **2 aloofness**, remoteness, detachment, unfriendliness, reserve, reticence, formality; informal stand-offishness.
– ANTONYMS: proximity.
• v. (**distance yourself**) become less friendly or supportive.

distant adj. **1** far away. **2** at a specified distance. **3** far apart in resemblance or relationship. **4** aloof.
▷ SYNONYMS: **1 faraway**, far-off, far-flung, remote, out of the way, outlying. **2 bygone**, remote, ancient, prehistoric. **3 vague**, faint, dim, indistinct, sketchy, hazy. **4 aloof**, reserved, remote, detached, unapproachable, unfriendly; informal stand-offish. **5 distracted**, absent, faraway, detached, vague.
– ANTONYMS: near, close, recent.
■ **distantly** adv.

distaste n. dislike.

distasteful adj. unpleasant or offensive.
▷ SYNONYMS: **unpleasant**, disagreeable, displeasing, undesirable, objectionable, offensive, unsavoury, unpalatable.
– ANTONYMS: agreeable.

distemper n. **1** a kind of paint for walls. **2** a disease of dogs.

distend v. swell because of internal pressure.
■ **distension** n.

distil (US **distill**) v. (**distilling**, **distilled**) **1** purify a liquid by heating it so that it vaporizes and then condensing the vapour. **2** make whisky etc. in this way. **3** extract the most important aspects of.
■ **distillation** n.

distiller n. a person or company that manufactures spirits.
■ **distillery** n.

distinct adj. **1** noticeably different. **2** clearly perceptible. **3** definite; unmistakable.
▷ SYNONYMS: **1** two distinct categories: **discrete**, separate, different, unconnected, distinctive, contrasting. **2** the tail has distinct black tips: **clear**, well defined, unmistakable, easily distinguishable, recognizable, visible, obvious, pronounced, prominent, striking. **3** a distinct lack

of enthusiasm: **definite**, unmistakable, decided, marked, manifest, patent.
− ANTONYMS: similar, indistinct.
■ **distinctly** adv. **distinctness** n.

distinction n. **1** a difference or contrast. **2** outstanding excellence. **3** a special honour or award.
▷ SYNONYMS: **1 difference**, contrast, variation, division, differentiation, discrepancy. **2 merit**, worth, greatness, excellence, quality, repute, renown, honour, credit.
− ANTONYMS: similarity.

distinctive adj. characteristic of a person or thing and distinguishing them from others.
▷ SYNONYMS: **distinguishing**, characteristic, typical, individual, particular, peculiar, unique, exclusive, special.
− ANTONYMS: common.
■ **distinctively** adv. **distinctiveness** n.

distinguish v. **1** recognize or treat as different. **2** manage to see or hear. **3** be a characteristic of. **4** (**distinguish yourself**) do something very well.
▷ SYNONYMS: **1 differentiate**, tell apart, discriminate between, tell the difference between. **2 discern**, see, perceive, make out, detect, recognize, identify. **3 separate**, set apart, make distinctive, make different, single out, mark off.
■ **distinguishable** adj.

distinguished adj. **1** successful and highly respected. **2** dignified in appearance.
▷ SYNONYMS: **eminent**, famous, renowned, prominent, well known, great, esteemed, respected, notable, illustrious, acclaimed, celebrated.
− ANTONYMS: unknown, obscure.

distort v. **1** pull or twist out of shape. **2** misrepresent.
▷ SYNONYMS: **1** *metal and glass had been distorted by the heat:* **twist**, warp, contort, buckle, make misshapen, disfigure, bend out of shape. **2** *he has distorted the facts:* **misrepresent**, pervert, twist, falsify, misstate, garble.
■ **distortion** n.

distract v. draw away the attention of.
▷ SYNONYMS: **divert**, sidetrack, draw away, lead astray, disturb, put off.

distracted adj. unable to concentrate; not paying attention.
▷ SYNONYMS: **preoccupied**, inattentive, vague, abstracted, absent-minded, faraway, in a world of your own; *informal* miles away.
− ANTONYMS: attentive.

distraction n. **1** a thing that

distracts someone's attention. **2** an entertainment. **3** mental agitation.
▷ SYNONYMS: **1 diversion**, interruption, disturbance, interference. **2 amusement**, entertainment, diversion, recreation, pastime, leisure pursuit.

distraught adj. very worried and upset.
▷ SYNONYMS: **distressed**, frantic, fraught, overcome, overwrought, beside yourself, out of your mind, desperate, hysterical, worked up, at your wits' end; *informal* in a state.
− ANTONYMS: calm.

distress n. extreme anxiety, pain, or hardship.
▷ SYNONYMS: **1 anguish**, suffering, pain, agony, torment, heartache, heartbreak, sorrow, sadness, unhappiness. **2** *a ship in distress:* **danger**, peril, difficulty, trouble, jeopardy, risk.
− ANTONYMS: happiness.
● v. cause distress to.
▷ SYNONYMS: **upset**, pain, trouble, worry, perturb, disturb, disquiet, agitate, torment.
− ANTONYMS: comfort.

distribute v. **1** hand or share out. **2** (**be distributed**) be spread over an area. **3** supply goods to retailers.
▷ SYNONYMS: **1 give out**, deal out, dole out, dish out, hand out/round, share out, divide out/up, parcel out, apportion, allocate, allot, supply. **2** *the newsletter is distributed free:* **circulate**, issue, deliver.
− ANTONYMS: collect.
■ **distributive** adj.

distribution n. **1** the action of distributing. **2** the way in which something is distributed.
▷ SYNONYMS: **1 giving out**, handing out, issuing, allocation, sharing out, dividing up/out, supply. **2 spread**, dissemination, dispersal.

distributor n. **1** an agent who supplies goods to retailers. **2** a device in a petrol engine for passing electric current to the spark plugs.

district n. a particular area of a town or region.
▷ SYNONYMS: **area**, region, quarter, sector, zone, territory, locality, neighbourhood, community.

distrust n. lack of trust.
▷ SYNONYMS: **mistrust**, suspicion, wariness, scepticism, doubt, cynicism, misgivings, qualms.
− ANTONYMS: trust.
● v. have little trust in.
▷ SYNONYMS: **mistrust**, be suspicious of, be wary of, be chary of, regard

with suspicion, suspect, be sceptical of, doubt, be unsure of/about, have misgivings about.
– ANTONYMS: trust.
■ **distrustful** adj.

disturb v. **1** interrupt the activity, rest, etc. of. **2** move from the normal place. **3** make anxious. **4** (**disturbed**) having emotional or mental problems.
▷ SYNONYMS: **1 interrupt**, intrude on, butt in on, barge in on, distract, disrupt, bother, trouble, pester, harass. **2 move**, rearrange, mix up, interfere with, mess up. **3 perturb**, trouble, concern, worry, upset, fluster, disconcert, dismay, alarm, distress, unsettle. **4** (**disturbed**) **troubled**, distressed, upset, distraught, unbalanced, unstable, disordered, dysfunctional, maladjusted, neurotic; informal screwed up.
– ANTONYMS: calm, reassure.

disturbance n. **1** the interruption of a normal or settled condition. **2** a breakdown of peaceful behaviour.
▷ SYNONYMS: **1 disruption**, distraction, interference, inconvenience, upset, annoyance, irritation, intrusion. **2 riot**, fracas, brawl, street fight, free-for-all, commotion, disorder.
– ANTONYMS: order.

disunited adj. not united.
■ **disunity** n.

disuse n. the state of not being used.
■ **disused** adj.

ditch n. a narrow trench for drainage.
▷ SYNONYMS: **trench**, trough, channel, dyke, drain, gutter, gully, watercourse.
• v. informal get rid of.

dither v. be indecisive.

ditto n. (in lists) the same thing again.

ditty n. (pl. **ditties**) a short, simple song.

diuretic n. a drug that causes more urine to be excreted.

diurnal adj. of or in the daytime.

diva /dee-vuh/ n. a famous female singer.

Divali var. of DIWALI.

divan n. **1** a bed consisting simply of a base and mattress. **2** a sofa without a back or arms.

dive v. **1** plunge head first into water. **2** swim under water. **3** move quickly downwards or under cover.
▷ SYNONYMS: **1 plunge**, plummet, nose-dive, jump, fall, drop, pitch. **2 leap**, jump, lunge, throw/fling yourself, go headlong.
• n. **1** an act of diving. **2** informal a disreputable nightclub or bar.

▷ SYNONYMS: **1 plunge**, nosedive, jump, fall, drop, swoop. **2 lunge**, spring, jump, leap.
■ **diver** n.

diverge v. separate and go in a different direction.
▷ SYNONYMS: **1 separate**, part, fork, divide, split, bifurcate. **2 differ**, be different, be dissimilar, disagree, be at variance/odds, conflict, clash.
– ANTONYMS: converge, agree.
■ **divergence** n. **divergent** adj.

diverse adj. widely varied.
▷ SYNONYMS: **various**, sundry, varied, varying, miscellaneous, assorted, mixed, diversified, divergent, different, differing, distinct, unlike, dissimilar.
– ANTONYMS: similar.

diversify v. (**diversifying, diversified**) **1** make or become more varied. **2** (of a company) expand its range of products or markets.
■ **diversification** n.

diversion n. **1** the act of diverting. **2** Brit. an alternative route avoiding a closed road. **3** something intended to distract attention. **4** a recreational activity.
▷ SYNONYMS: **1 detour**, deviation, alternative route, re-routing, redirection. **2 distraction**, disturbance, smoke-screen; informal red herring. **3 entertainment**, amusement, pastime, delight, fun, recreation, pleasure.

diversity n. (pl. **diversities**) **1** the state of being varied. **2** a range of different things.
▷ SYNONYMS: **variety**, miscellany, assortment, mixture, mix, range, array, multiplicity, variation, difference.
– ANTONYMS: uniformity.

divert v. **1** change the direction or course of. **2** distract. **3** amuse or entertain.
▷ SYNONYMS: **1 re-route**, redirect, change the course of, deflect, channel. **2 distract**, sidetrack, disturb, draw away, put off. **3 amuse**, entertain, distract, delight, enchant, interest, fascinate, absorb, engross, rivet, grip.

divest v. (**divest of**) deprive of.

divide v. **1** separate into parts. **2** share out. **3** cause to disagree. **4** find how many times one number contains another.
▷ SYNONYMS: **1** he divided his kingdom into four: **split**, cut up, carve up, dissect, bisect, halve, quarter. **2** a curtain divided her cabin from the galley: **separate**, segregate, partition, screen off, section off. **3 diverge**,

d

separate, part, branch off, fork.
4 share out, ration out, parcel out, deal out, dole out, dish out, distribute. **5 disunite**, drive apart, drive a wedge between, break up, split up, separate, isolate, alienate.
– ANTONYMS: unify, converge, unite.
• **n.** a wide difference between two groups.

dividend n. **1** a sum of money paid to a company's shareholders out of its profits. **2** (**dividends**) benefits.

divider n. **1** a screen dividing a room. **2** (**dividers**) a measuring compass.

divination n. the use of supernatural means to find out about the future.

divine adj. **1** of God or a god. **2** informal excellent.
▷ SYNONYMS: **godly**, angelic, heavenly, celestial, holy, sacred.
– ANTONYMS: mortal.
• **v.** discover by intuition.
▷ SYNONYMS: **guess**, surmise, deduce, infer, discern, discover, perceive; informal **figure out**; Brit. informal **suss**.
■ **divinely** adv. **diviner** n.

divinity n. (pl. **divinities**) **1** the state of being divine. **2** a god or goddess.

divisible adj. capable of being divided.

division n. **1** the act of dividing. **2** each of the parts into which something is divided. **3** a partition.
▷ SYNONYMS: **1** *the division of the island:* **dividing**, breaking up, break-up, carving up, splitting, dissection, partitioning, separation, segregation. **2 dividing line**, divide, boundary, border, demarcation line, gap, gulf. **3 section**, subsection, subdivision, category, class, group, grouping, set. **4 department**, branch, arm, wing.
– ANTONYMS: unification.
■ **divisional** adj.

divisive adj. causing disagreement.

divisor n. a number by which another is to be divided.

divorce n. the legal ending of a marriage.
▷ SYNONYMS: **1 dissolution**, annulment, decree nisi, separation. **2** *the divorce between the church and people:* **separation**, division, split, gulf, disunity, alienation, schism.
– ANTONYMS: marriage.
• **v. 1** legally end your marriage with. **2** (**divorce from**) separate from.
▷ SYNONYMS: **1 split up**, get a divorce, separate. **2** *religion cannot be divorced from morality:* **separate**, divide, detach, isolate, alienate, set apart, cut off.

divorcee n. a divorced person.

divot n. a piece of turf cut out of the ground.

divulge v. reveal information.
▷ SYNONYMS: **disclose**, reveal, tell, communicate, pass on, publish, give away, let slip.
– ANTONYMS: conceal.

Diwali n. a Hindu festival with lights, held in October and November.

DIY n. Brit. the activity of doing your own home decoration and repairs.

dizzy adj. (**dizzier**, **dizziest**) having a sensation of spinning around.
▷ SYNONYMS: **giddy**, light-headed, faint, unsteady, shaky, muzzy, wobbly; informal **woozy**.
■ **dizzily** adv. **dizziness** n.

DJ n. **1** a person who introduces and plays recorded pop music on the radio or at a club. **2** a dinner jacket.

djellaba /jel-luh-buh/ n. an Arab cloak.

DNA n. deoxyribonucleic acid, a substance carrying genetic information.

do v. (**does**, **doing**, **did**; past part. **done**) **1** carry out an action or task. **2** act or perform. **3** work on. **4** make or provide. **5** be suitable or acceptable.
▷ SYNONYMS: **1** *she did most of the work:* **carry out**, undertake, discharge, execute, perform, accomplish, achieve, bring about, engineer; informal **pull off**. **2** *they can do as they please:* **act**, behave, conduct yourself. **3** *we're doing a new design:* **make**, create, produce, work on, design, manufacture. **4 suffice**, be adequate, be satisfactory, fill/fit the bill, serve.
• **aux. v.** used in questions, for emphasis, or to avoid repeating a verb just used.
• **n.** (pl. **dos** or **do's**) Brit. a party.
□ **do away with** informal put an end to. **do-gooder** a well-meaning but interfering person. **do in** informal **1** kill. **2** tire out. **dos and don'ts** rules of behaviour. **do up 1** fasten or wrap. **2** informal renovate.

Dobermann (or **Dobermann pinscher**) n. a large breed of dog with powerful jaws.

docile adj. quiet and easy to control.
▷ SYNONYMS: **compliant**, obedient, pliant, submissive, deferential, unassertive, cooperative, amenable, accommodating, biddable.
– ANTONYMS: disobedient, wilful.
■ **docilely** adv. **docility** n.

dock n. **1** an enclosed area of water for the loading, unloading, and repair of ships. **2** the enclosure in a court for a person on trial. **3** a weed with broad leaves.

▷ SYNONYMS: **harbour**, marina, port, wharf, quay, pier, jetty, landing stage.
• v. **1** come or bring into a dock. **2** (of a spacecraft) join with another craft in space. **3** deduct money from a person's wages. **4** cut short an animal's tail.

▷ SYNONYMS: **1 moor**, berth, put in, tie up, anchor. **2 deduct**, subtract, remove, debit, take off/away; informal knock off.

□ **dockyard** an area where ships are repaired and built.

docker n. a person who loads and unloads ships.

docket n. Brit. a document accompanying goods, listing the contents etc.

doctor n. **1** a person qualified to practise medicine. **2** a person holding a doctorate.

▷ SYNONYMS: **physician**, medical practitioner, general practitioner, GP, clinician, consultant; informal doc, medic; Brit. informal **quack**.
• v. **1** change information so as to deceive. **2** add a harmful ingredient to.

▷ SYNONYMS: **1 falsify**, tamper with, interfere with, alter, change, forge, fake; Brit. informal fiddle. **2 adulterate**, tamper with, lace; informal spike.

doctorate n. the highest degree awarded by a university.
■ **doctoral** adj.

doctrinaire adj. very strict in applying beliefs.

doctrine n. a set of beliefs or principles held by a religious, political, or other group.

▷ SYNONYMS: **creed**, credo, dogma, belief, teaching, ideology, tenet, maxim, canon, principle.
■ **doctrinal** adj.

document n. a piece of written, printed, or electronic matter providing information or evidence.

▷ SYNONYMS: **paper**, certificate, deed, form, contract, agreement, report, record.
• v. record in written or other form.

▷ SYNONYMS: **record**, register, report, log, chronicle, authenticate, verify.
■ **documentation** n.

documentary n. (pl. **documentaries**) a film or television or radio programme giving a factual report.
• adj. consisting of documents.

dodder v. be slow and unsteady.
■ **doddery** adj.

dodecagon n. a plane figure with twelve sides.

dodge v. **1** avoid by a sudden quick movement. **2** avoid in a cunning way.

▷ SYNONYMS: **1** *he dodged the police*: **elude**, evade, avoid, escape, run away from, lose, shake off; informal give someone the slip. **2** *the minister tried to dodge the debate*: **avoid**, evade, get out of, back out of, sidestep; informal duck, wriggle out of.
• n. an act of dodging.

▷ SYNONYMS: *a clever dodge* | *a tax dodge*: **ruse**, scheme, tactic, stratagem, ploy, subterfuge, trick, hoax, cheat, deception, fraud; informal scam; Brit. informal wheeze.
■ **dodger** n.

dodgem n. a small electric car driven at a funfair with the aim of bumping other such cars.

dodgy adj. Brit. informal **1** dishonest. **2** risky. **3** not good or reliable.

dodo n. (pl. **dodos** or **dodoes**) a large extinct bird.

doe n. a female deer, hare, or rabbit.

does 3rd person sing. present of **DO**.

doesn't contr. does not.

doff v. remove your hat when greeting someone.

dog n. **1** a domesticated meat-eating mammal. **2** the male of this, or of a fox or wolf.

▷ SYNONYMS: **hound**, canine, man's best friend, mongrel; informal pooch, mutt.
• v. (**dogging**, **dogged**) follow or affect persistently.

▷ SYNONYMS: **plague**, beset, bedevil, blight, trouble.
□ **dog collar** informal a white upright collar worn by Christian clergy. **dog-eared** having turned-down corners. **dogfish** a small shark. **dog rose** a wild rose. **dogsbody** Brit. informal a person given menial tasks. **in the doghouse** informal in disgrace.
■ **doggy** adj.

> **WORD LINKS**
> **canine** relating to dogs

doge n. hist. the chief magistrate of Venice or Genoa.

dogged /dog-gid/ adj. persistent.

▷ SYNONYMS: **tenacious**, determined, resolute, stubborn, obstinate, purposeful, persistent, persevering, single-minded, tireless.
– ANTONYMS: half-hearted.
■ **doggedly** adv.

doggerel n. badly written verse.

doggo adv. (**lie doggo**) informal remain still and quiet to avoid being found.

dogma n. a set of principles intended to be accepted without question.

dogmatic adj. firmly putting forward your opinions and unwilling to accept those of others.

▷ SYNONYMS: **opinionated**, assertive, insistent, emphatic, adamant, doctrinaire, authoritarian, imperious, dictatorial, uncompromising.

■ **dogmatically** adv. **dogmatism** n.

doily n. (pl. **doilies**) a small ornamental lace or paper mat.

doldrums pl. n. (**the doldrums**) a state of inactivity or depression.

dole n. Brit. informal unemployment benefit.

● v. (**dole out**) distribute.

▷ SYNONYMS: **deal out**, share out, divide up, allocate, distribute, dispense, hand out, give out, dish out.

doleful adj. mournful.

■ **dolefully** adv.

doll n. a child's toy in the form of a small human figure.

● v. (**be dolled up**) informal be dressed in smart or fancy clothes.

dollar n. the basic unit of money of the US and various other countries.

dollop n. informal a mass of something soft.

dolmen n. a prehistoric tomb with a large flat stone laid on upright ones.

dolour (US **dolor**) n. literary great sorrow.

■ **dolorous** adj.

dolphin n. a small whale with a beak-like snout.

dolt n. a stupid person.

domain n. **1** an area controlled by a ruler or government. **2** an area of activity. **3** a part of the Internet with addresses sharing a common suffix.

▷ SYNONYMS: **1 realm**, kingdom, empire, dominion, province, territory, land. **2 field**, area, sphere, discipline, province, world.

dome n. a rounded roof with a circular base.

■ **domed** adj.

domestic adj. **1** of a home or family. **2** (of an animal) tame and kept by humans. **3** of or inside a country; not foreign.

▷ SYNONYMS: **1 family**, home, household. **2 domesticated**, homely, home-loving. **3 tame**, pet, domesticated; Brit. house-trained. **4 national**, state, home, internal.

● n. a person employed to do household tasks.

■ **domestically** adv.

domesticate v. tame an animal and keep it as a pet or for farm produce.

■ **domestication** n.

domesticity n. home life.

domicile n. the country in which a person lives permanently.

● v. (**be domiciled**) be living in a particular place.

dominant adj. most important or influential.

▷ SYNONYMS: **1 ruling**, governing, controlling, presiding, commanding. **2 assertive**, authoritative, forceful, domineering, commanding, controlling, pushy. **3 main**, principal, prime, chief, primary, central, key, crucial, core.

– ANTONYMS: subservient, subsidiary.

■ **dominance** n.

dominate v. **1** have a very strong influence over. **2** be the most important or noticeable person or thing in.

▷ SYNONYMS: **1 control**, influence, command, be in charge of, rule, govern, direct, have the whip hand over. **2** *he dominated all other players from his own country:* **outclass**, overshadow, eclipse, put in the shade, upstage, tower above/over; informal stand head and shoulders above.

domination n. the action of dominating, or the state of being dominated.

▷ SYNONYMS: **control**, power, command, authority, dominion, rule, supremacy, superiority, ascendancy, sway, mastery.

domineering adj. arrogant and overbearing.

▷ SYNONYMS: **overbearing**, authoritarian, imperious, high-handed, peremptory, autocratic, dictatorial, despotic, strict, harsh; informal bossy.

dominion n. **1** supreme power or control. **2** a ruler's territory.

domino n. (pl. **dominoes**) any of the small oblong pieces marked with 0–6 pips in each half, used in the game of **dominoes**.

don n. a university teacher.

● v. (**donning, donned**) put on an item of clothing.

▷ SYNONYMS: **put on**, get dressed in, dress yourself in, get into, slip into/on, change into.

donate v. **1** give to a good cause. **2** give blood or an organ for use in treating another person.

▷ SYNONYMS: **give**, contribute, gift, subscribe, grant, present, endow; informal chip in, stump up.

donation n. something that is donated to a good cause.
▷ SYNONYMS: **gift**, contribution, subscription, present, handout, grant, offering.

done past part. of DO.

donkey n. (pl. **donkeys**) a long-eared mammal of the horse family.
□ **donkey jacket** Brit. a heavy jacket with waterproof material across the shoulders. **donkey's years** informal a very long time.

donor n. a person who donates something.
▷ SYNONYMS: **giver**, contributor, benefactor, benefactress, subscriber, supporter, backer, patron, sponsor.
– ANTONYMS: beneficiary.

don't contr. do not.

donut US = DOUGHNUT.

doodle v. draw absent-mindedly.
• n. a doodled drawing.

doom n. death or another terrible fate.
▷ SYNONYMS: **destruction**, downfall, ruin, extinction, annihilation, death, nemesis.
• v. (**be doomed**) be fated to fail or be destroyed.
▷ SYNONYMS: (**doomed**) **ill-fated**, ill-starred, cursed, jinxed, damned; literary star-crossed.
□ **doomsday** the last day of the world's existence.

door n. a movable barrier at the entrance to a building, room, etc.
□ **doorway** an entrance with a door.

dope informal n. **1** an illegal drug. **2** a stupid person.
• v. give a drug to.

dopey (or **dopy**) adj. informal **1** half-asleep. **2** stupid.

doppelgänger /dop-puhl-gang-er/ n. a ghost or double of a living person.

dormant adj. temporarily inactive with physical functions slowed down.

dormer n. an upright window set into a sloping roof.

dormitory n. (pl. **dormitories**) a bedroom for a number of people in a school etc.

dormouse n. (pl. **dormice**) a small mouse-like rodent with a bushy tail.

dorsal adj. of or on the back.

dosage n. the size of a dose.

dose n. **1** a quantity of a medicine taken at one time. **2** an amount of radiation received at one time.
▷ SYNONYMS: **measure**, portion, draught, dosage.
• v. give a dose of medicine to.

doss v. Brit. informal **1** sleep in rough or makeshift conditions. **2** spend time idly.
■ **dosser** n.

dossier n. a collection of documents about a person or subject.

dot n. a small round mark.
▷ SYNONYMS: **spot**, speck, fleck, speckle, full stop, decimal point.
• v. (**dotting, dotted**) **1** mark with a dot or dots. **2** scatter over an area.
▷ SYNONYMS: **1 spot**, fleck, mark, spatter. **2 scatter**, pepper, sprinkle, strew, spread.
□ **dot-com** a company doing business on the Internet. **on the dot** informal exactly on time.

dotage n. the period of life when a person is old and weak.

dote v. (**dote on**) be excessively fond of.
▷ SYNONYMS: **adore**, love dearly, be devoted to, idolize, treasure, cherish, worship.
■ **doting** adj.

dotty adj. Brit. informal slightly mad or eccentric.

double adj. **1** consisting of two equal or similar parts or things. **2** of twice the usual size. **3** for use by two people.
▷ SYNONYMS: **dual**, duplex, twin, binary, duplicate, coupled, matching, twofold, in pairs.
– ANTONYMS: single.
• adv. twice as much.
• n. **1** a double quantity or thing. **2** a person who looks exactly like another. **3** (**doubles**) a game with two players on each side.
▷ SYNONYMS: **lookalike**, twin, clone, duplicate, exact likeness, replica, copy, facsimile, doppelgänger; informal spitting image, dead ringer.
• v. **1** make or become double. **2** fold or bend over on itself. **3** have two uses or roles. **4** (**double back**) go back in the direction you came from.
□ **at the double** very fast. **double bass** the largest and lowest-pitched instrument of the violin family. **double-breasted** (of a coat) having an overlap at the front and two rows of buttons. **double chin** a roll of flesh below a person's chin. **double cream** Brit. thick cream with a high fat content. **double-cross** betray. **double dealing** deceitful behaviour. **double-decker** a bus with two levels. **double Dutch** Brit. incomprehensible speech. **double entendre** /doo-b'l on-**ton**-druh/ a word or phrase with

d

d

two meanings, one of which is rude. **double glazing** two sheets of glass in a window, designed to reduce heat loss. **double take** a second reaction to something unexpected, just after your first one.
■ **doubly** adv.

doublet n. hist. a man's short close-fitting jacket.

doubloon n. hist. a Spanish gold coin.

doubt n. a feeling of uncertainty.
▷ SYNONYMS: **1 uncertainty**, indecision, hesitation, irresolution, hesitancy, vacillation, lack of conviction. **2 scepticism**, distrust, mistrust, suspicion, cynicism, wariness, reservations, misgivings, suspicions.
– ANTONYMS: certainty, trust.
• v. **1** feel uncertain about. **2** disbelieve or mistrust.
▷ SYNONYMS: **disbelieve**, distrust, mistrust, suspect, be suspicious of, have misgivings about.
■ **doubter** n.

doubtful adj. **1** uncertain. **2** not probable.
▷ SYNONYMS: **1 hesitant**, in doubt, unsure, uncertain, in two minds, in a quandary, in a dilemma. **2 in doubt**, uncertain, open to question, unsure, debatable, up in the air, inconclusive, unconfirmed. **3 unlikely**, improbable. **4 distrustful**, mistrustful, sceptical, suspicious, having reservations, wary, chary, leery. **5 questionable**, dubious, suspect, suspicious.
– ANTONYMS: confident, certain.
■ **doubtfully** adv.

doubtless adv. very probably.
▷ SYNONYMS: **undoubtedly**, no doubt, unquestionably, indisputably, undeniably, certainly, surely, of course.

douche /doosh/ n. a jet of water applied to part of the body.

dough n. a thick mixture of flour and liquid, for baking into bread or pastry.
□ **doughnut** (US **donut**) a small fried cake or ring of sweetened dough.
■ **doughy** adj.

doughty /dow-ti/ adj. brave and resolute.

dour adj. stern or gloomy.

douse v. **1** drench with liquid. **2** extinguish a fire.
▷ SYNONYMS: **1 drench**, soak, saturate, wet. **2 extinguish**, put out, quench, smother.

dove n. **1** a bird with a cooing call. **2** a person favouring a policy of peace and negotiation.

□ **dovecote** a shelter for domesticated pigeons.

dovetail v. fit together neatly.
• n. a wedge-shaped joint interlocking two pieces of wood.

dowager n. a widow holding a title that belonged to her late husband.

dowdy adj. not smart or fashionable.
▷ SYNONYMS: **unfashionable**, frumpy, old-fashioned, shabby, frowzy; Brit. informal mumsy.
– ANTONYMS: fashionable.

dowel n. a headless peg for holding together components.

down adv. **1** to, in, or at a lower place or level. **2** to a smaller amount or size. **3** in or into a weaker or worse position or condition. **4** from an earlier to a later point.
• prep. **1** from a higher to a lower point of. **2** at a point further along.
• adj. **1** directed or moving downwards. **2** unhappy. **3** (of a computer system) out of action.
• v. informal drink quickly.
• n. **1** soft fine feathers or hairs. **2** a gently rolling hill.
□ **down and out** homeless and without money. **downbeat 1** gloomy. **2** relaxed and low-key. **downcast 1** (of eyes) looking downwards. **2** dejected. **downhearted** sad or discouraged. **downhill 1** towards the foot of a slope. **2** into a worsening situation. **downmarket** cheap and of poor quality. **downpour** a heavy fall of rain. **downsize** reduce the number of employees in a company. **downstairs** on or to a lower floor. **downstream** in the direction in which a stream or river flows. **down-to-earth** practical and realistic. **downtown** esp. US in, to, or towards the central area of a city. **downtrodden** oppressed. **down under** informal Australia and New Zealand.
■ **downward** adj. & adv. **downwards** adv.

downfall n. a loss of power or status.
▷ SYNONYMS: **ruin**, undoing, defeat, overthrow, destruction, annihilation, end, collapse, fall, crash, failure.
– ANTONYMS: rise.

downgrade v. move to a lower rank or level.
▷ SYNONYMS: **demote**, reduce, relegate.
– ANTONYMS: promote.

download v. copy data from one computer system to another.
• n. a downloaded computer file.

downright adj. utter; complete: a downright lie.
▷ SYNONYMS: **complete**, total, absolute, utter, thorough, out-and-out,

outright, sheer, arrant, pure.
• adv. extremely: *he was downright rude.*

Down's syndrome n. a congenital disorder causing physical abnormalities and below-average intellectual ability.

downy adj. covered with fine soft hair or feathers.

dowry n. (pl. **dowries**) property or money brought by a bride to her husband at their marriage.

dowse /dowz/ v. search for underground water or minerals with a stick which supposedly moves when these are present.

doxology n. (pl. **doxologies**) a prayer praising God.

doyen n. (fem. **doyenne**) the most respected or prominent person in a particular field.

doze v. sleep lightly.
• n. a short, light sleep.
■ **dozy** adj.

dozen n. 1 (pl. **dozen**) a group of twelve. 2 (**dozens**) a lot.

Dr abbrev. (as a title) Doctor.

drab adj. (**drabber**, **drabbest**) dull and uninteresting.
▷ SYNONYMS: 1 **colourless**, grey, dull, washed out, dingy, dreary, dismal, cheerless, gloomy, sombre. 2 **uninteresting**, dull, boring, tedious, monotonous, dry, dreary.
– ANTONYMS: bright, interesting.

drachma n. the former basic unit of money in Greece.

draconian adj. very harsh or strict.

draft n. 1 a preliminary version of a piece of writing. 2 a written order to a bank to pay a specified sum. 3 US military conscription. 4 US = **DRAUGHT**.
▷ SYNONYMS: 1 **version**, sketch, attempt, effort, outline, plan. 2 **cheque**, order, money order, bill of exchange.
• v. 1 prepare a draft of. 2 select someone for a purpose.

drafty US = **DRAUGHTY**.

drag v. (**dragging**, **dragged**) 1 pull along with effort. 2 trail along the ground. 3 (of time) pass slowly. 4 (**drag out**) prolong unnecessarily. 5 search the bottom of a lake etc. with hooks or nets. 6 move an image across a computer screen using a mouse.
▷ SYNONYMS: **haul**, pull, tug, heave, lug, draw, trail.
• n. 1 informal a boring or annoying person or thing. 2 informal women's clothes worn by a man. 3 informal an inhalation of smoke from a cigarette. 4 the force exerted by air or water to

slow down a moving object.
▷ SYNONYMS: 1 **bore**, nuisance, bother, trouble, pest, annoyance, trial; informal pain, bind, headache, hassle. 2 **pull**, resistance, tug.
□ **dragnet** a net drawn through water to trap fish.

dragon n. a mythical monster that can breathe out fire.
□ **dragonfly** a long-bodied insect with two pairs of wings.

dragoon v. force into doing something.
• n. a member of certain British regiments.

drain v. 1 make empty or dry by removing liquid. 2 (of liquid) run off or out. 3 exhaust the strength or resources of. 4 drink the entire contents of.
▷ SYNONYMS: 1 *a valve for draining the tank:* **empty**, void, clear, evacuate, unload. 2 *drain off any surplus liquid:* **draw off**, extract, siphon off, pour out, pour off, bleed, tap, filter, discharge. 3 *the water drained away:* **flow**, pour, trickle, stream, run, rush, gush, flood, surge, leak, ooze, seep, dribble. 4 **use up**, exhaust, deplete, consume, expend, get through, sap, milk, bleed. 5 **drink**, gulp, guzzle, quaff, swallow, finish off, toss off; informal sink, down, swig, swill, knock back.
– ANTONYMS: fill.
• n. 1 a channel or pipe carrying off surplus liquid. 2 a thing that uses up a resource or strength.
▷ SYNONYMS: 1 **sewer**, channel, ditch, culvert, duct, pipe, gutter. 2 **strain**, pressure, burden, load, demand.
■ **drainage** n.

drake n. a male duck.

dram n. a small drink of spirits.

drama n. 1 a play. 2 plays as a literary form. 3 an exciting series of events.
▷ SYNONYMS: 1 **play**, show, piece, theatrical work, stage show, dramatization. 2 **acting**, the theatre, the stage, dramatic art, stagecraft, dramaturgy. 3 **incident**, scene, spectacle, crisis, disturbance, row, commotion, excitement, thrill, sensation, dramatics, theatrics, histrionics.

dramatic adj. 1 of drama. 2 sudden and striking. 3 exciting or impressive.
▷ SYNONYMS: 1 **theatrical**, thespian, dramaturgical. 2 **considerable**, substantial, significant, remarkable, extraordinary, exceptional, phenomenal. 3 **exciting**, stirring, action-packed, sensational, spectacular,

d

startling, unexpected, tense, gripping, riveting, thrilling, hair-raising, lively. **4 striking**, impressive, imposing, spectacular, breathtaking, dazzling, sensational, awesome, awe-inspiring, remarkable. **5 exaggerated**, theatrical, ostentatious, actressy, stagy, showy, melodramatic.
– ANTONYMS: unremarkable, boring.
■ **dramatically** adv.

dramatist n. a person who writes plays.

dramatize (or **-ise**) v. **1** present a novel etc. as a play. **2** cause to seem more exciting or serious.
▷ SYNONYMS: **1 adapt**, rework.
2 exaggerate, overdo, overstate, magnify, amplify, inflate, sensationalize, embroider, colour, aggrandize, embellish, elaborate; informal blow up out of all proportion.
■ **dramatization** n.

drank past of DRINK.

drape v. arrange loosely on or round something.
▷ SYNONYMS: **wrap**, cover, envelop, shroud, wind, swathe, festoon, hang.
• pl. n. (**drapes**) US long curtains.

drapery n. (pl. **draperies**) fabric hanging in loose folds.

drastic adj. having a strong or far-reaching effect.
▷ SYNONYMS: **extreme**, serious, desperate, radical, far-reaching, momentous, substantial.
– ANTONYMS: moderate.
■ **drastically** adv.

draught (US **draft**) n. **1** a current of cool air indoors. **2** an act of drinking or breathing in. **3** old use a medicinal drink. **4** (**draughts**) Brit. a game played on a chequered board.
▷ SYNONYMS: **1 current of air**, wind, breeze, gust, puff, waft. **2 gulp**, drink, swallow, mouthful; informal swig.
• adj. **1** (of beer) served from a cask. **2** (of an animal) used for pulling loads.
□ **draughtsman** a person who makes detailed technical plans or drawings.
■ **draughty** adj.

draw v. (**drawing**, **drew**; past part. **drawn**) **1** produce a picture or diagram by making lines and marks on paper. **2** pull a vehicle. **3** move in a specified direction. **4** pull curtains shut or open. **5** arrive at a point in time. **6** take out. **7** attract to a place. **8** reach a conclusion. **9** finish a contest or game with an even score. **10** take in a breath.
▷ SYNONYMS: **1 sketch**, outline, rough

out, illustrate, render, represent, trace, portray, depict. **2 pull**, haul, drag, tug, heave, lug, tow; informal yank. **3 move**, go, come, proceed, progress, pass, drive, inch, roll, glide, cruise, sweep. **4 pull out**, take out, produce, fish out, extract, withdraw, unsheathe. **5 attract**, win, capture, catch, engage, lure, entice, bring in.
• n. **1** a game that ends with the scores even. **2** a random selection of names or numbers for prizes etc. **3** a very attractive or interesting person or thing.
▷ SYNONYMS: **1 tie**, dead heat, stalemate. **2 raffle**, lottery, sweepstake, sweep, tombola, ballot. **3 attraction**, lure, allure, pull, appeal, temptation, charm, fascination.
□ **drawbridge** a bridge hinged at one end so that it can be raised. **draw on** use as a resource. **draw out 1** make something last longer. **2** encourage to talk. **drawstring** a string that can be pulled to close an opening. **draw up 1** come to a halt. **2** prepare a plan or document.

drawback n. a disadvantage.
▷ SYNONYMS: **disadvantage**, snag, downside, catch, pitfall, stumbling block, hitch, fly in the ointment, weakness, flaw, imperfection; informal minus.
– ANTONYMS: advantage, benefit.

drawer n. **1** a storage compartment that slides horizontally in and out of a desk or chest. **2** (**drawers**) dated knickers or underpants.

drawing n. a picture made with a pencil or pen.
▷ SYNONYMS: **sketch**, picture, illustration, representation, portrayal, depiction, diagram, outline.
□ **drawing pin** a pin for fastening paper to a surface. **drawing room** a formal sitting room.

> **WORD LINKS**
> **graphic** relating to drawing

drawl v. speak slowly with prolonged vowels.
• n. a drawling accent.

drawn past part. of DRAW.
• adj. looking strained from illness or exhaustion.

dray n. a low cart without sides.

dread v. fear greatly.
▷ SYNONYMS: **fear**, be afraid of, worry about, be anxious about, shudder at the thought of.
• n. great fear or anxiety.
▷ SYNONYMS: **fear**, apprehension, trepidation, anxiety, panic, alarm, terror,

disquiet, unease.

dreadful adj. very bad or serious.
▷ SYNONYMS: **1** *a dreadful accident:*
terrible, frightful, horrible, grim,
awful, horrifying, shocking,
distressing, appalling, harrowing,
ghastly, gruesome, fearful, horrendous, tragic. **2** *a dreadful meal:* **very
bad**, frightful, shocking, awful,
abysmal, dire, atrocious, disgraceful,
deplorable; informal woeful, rotten,
lousy, ropy; Brit. informal duff, rubbish.
3 *a dreadful flirt:* **outrageous**,
shocking, real, awful, terrible,
inordinate, incorrigible.
– ANTONYMS: wonderful, excellent.
■ **dreadfully** adv.

dreadlocks pl. n. a Rastafarian
hairstyle with the hair twisted into
tight ringlets.

dream n. **1** a series of images and
feelings occurring in the mind during
sleep. **2** an ambition or wish.
▷ SYNONYMS: **1** daydream, reverie,
trance, daze, stupor. **2** ambition, aspiration, hope, goal, aim, objective, intention, desire, wish, daydream, fantasy.
3 delight, joy, marvel, wonder, gem,
treasure.
– ANTONYMS: nightmare.
● v. (**dreaming, dreamed** or **dreamt**)
1 have dreams while asleep. **2** think
of as possible. **3** (**dream up**) invent.
▷ SYNONYMS: **1** fantasize, daydream,
wish, hope, long, yearn, hanker.
2 daydream, be in a trance, be lost
in thought, be preoccupied, be
abstracted, stare into space, be in
cloud cuckoo land.
■ **dreamer** n. **dreamless** adj.

dreamy adj. **1** tending to daydream.
2 seeming pleasantly unreal.

dreary adj. (**drearier, dreariest**) dull,
bleak, and depressing.
▷ SYNONYMS: **dull**, uninteresting,
tedious, boring, unexciting,
unstimulating, uninspiring, soul-
destroying, monotonous, uneventful.
– ANTONYMS: exciting.
■ **drearily** adv. **dreariness** n.

dredge v. scoop up mud and objects
from the bed of a river etc.
■ **dredger** n.

dregs pl. n. **1** the last drops of liquid
and any sediment left in a container.
2 the most worthless parts.

drench v. wet thoroughly.
▷ SYNONYMS: **soak**, saturate, wet
through, douse, steep, flood, drown.

dress v. **1** put on clothes. **2** (**dress up**)
dress in smart clothes or in a special
costume. **3** decorate in an attractive

way. **4** clean and cover a wound.
▷ SYNONYMS: **1** clothe, attire, deck out,
garb, robe; informal get up. **2** decorate,
trim, adorn, arrange, prepare.
3 bandage, cover, bind, wrap.
– ANTONYMS: undress.
● n. **1** a woman's garment that covers
the body and extends down over the
legs. **2** clothing.
▷ SYNONYMS: **1** *a long blue dress:* **frock**,
gown, robe, shift. **2** *full evening dress:*
clothes, clothing, garments, garb,
attire, costume, outfit; informal get-up,
gear; Brit. informal clobber; formal apparel.
□ **dress circle** the first level of seats
in a theatre. **dress rehearsal** a final
rehearsal, in full costume, before a
real performance.

WORD LINKS
sartorial relating to a person's style
of dress

dressage /dress-ah*z*h/ n. controlled
movements performed by a horse at
the rider's command.

dresser n. **1** a sideboard with shelves
above for crockery. **2** a person who
dresses in a particular way.

dressing n. **1** a sauce for a salad. **2** a
protective covering for a wound.
□ **dressing-down** informal a severe
reprimand. **dressing gown** a long
robe worn after getting out of bed or
bathing. **dressing table** a table with a
mirror, used while applying make-up.

dressy adj. (of clothes) smart or
formal.

drew past of DRAW.

drey n. a squirrel's nest.

dribble v. **1** (of a liquid) fall slowly in
drops or a thin stream. **2** let saliva run
from the mouth. **3** (in sport) take the
ball forward with slight touches.
▷ SYNONYMS: **1** drool, slaver, slobber.
2 trickle, drip, roll, run, drizzle, ooze,
seep, leak.
● n. a thin stream of liquid.

dried past & past part. of DRY.

drier var. of DRYER.

drift v. **1** be carried slowly by a
current of air or water. **2** go slowly or
aimlessly.
▷ SYNONYMS: **1** be carried, be borne,
float, bob, glide, coast, waft.
2 wander, meander, stray, stroll,
dawdle, float, roam. **3** stray, digress,
wander, deviate, get sidetracked.
4 pile up, bank up, heap up, accumulate, gather, amass.
● n. **1** a drifting movement. **2** the
general meaning of someone's
remarks. **3** a mass of snow piled up by

the wind.

▷ SYNONYMS: **1 movement**, shift, flow, transfer, gravitation. **2 gist**, meaning, sense, significance, thrust, import, tenor, intention, direction. **3 pile**, heap, bank, mound, mass, accumulation.

□ **driftwood** pieces of wood floating on the sea or washed ashore.

drifter n. a person who moves aimlessly from place to place.

drill n. **1** a tool or machine for boring holes. **2** training in military exercises. **3** (**the drill**) informal the correct procedure. **4** a strong twilled cotton fabric.

▷ SYNONYMS: **1 training**, instruction, coaching, teaching, exercises; informal square-bashing. **2 procedure**, routine, practice, programme, schedule, method, system.

• v. **1** bore a hole with a drill. **2** give training or instruction to.

▷ SYNONYMS: **1 bore**, pierce, puncture, perforate. **2 train**, instruct, coach, teach, discipline, exercise.

drily (or **dryly**) adv. in a humorously ironic way.

drink v. (**drinking**, **drank**; past part. **drunk**) **1** swallow liquid. **2** consume alcohol.

▷ SYNONYMS: **1 swallow**, gulp, quaff, guzzle, imbibe, sip, drain; informal swig, down, knock back. **2 drink alcohol**, tipple, indulge, carouse; informal hit the bottle, booze; Brit. informal bevvy.

• n. **1** a liquid for drinking. **2** alcohol.

▷ SYNONYMS: **1 beverage**, liquid refreshment; Brit. informal bevvy. **2 alcohol**, intoxicating liquor, spirits; informal booze, the hard stuff, the bottle, grog. **3 swallow**, gulp, mouthful, draught, sip; informal swig, slug.

■ **drinker** n.

drip v. (**dripping**, **dripped**) fall or let fall in small drops.

▷ SYNONYMS: **drop**, dribble, leak, trickle, run, splash, sprinkle.

• n. **1** a small drop of a liquid. **2** a device for slowly passing a substance into a patient's body through a vein. **3** informal a weak person.

▷ SYNONYMS: **drop**, dribble, spot, trickle, splash, bead.

□ **drip-dry** (of a garment) able to dry without creases if hung up when wet.

dripping n. Brit. fat melted from roasting meat.

drive v. (**driving**, **drove**; past part. **driven**) **1** operate a vehicle. **2** carry in a vehicle. **3** carry or urge along. **4** compel to do something. **5** provide

the energy to keep a machine in motion.

▷ SYNONYMS: **1 operate**, handle, manage, pilot, steer, work. **2 go by car**, motor. **3 run**, chauffeur, give someone a lift, take, ferry, transport, convey. **4 power**, propel, move, push. **5 hammer**, screw, ram, sink, plunge, thrust, knock. **6 force**, compel, prompt, precipitate, oblige, coerce, pressure, spur, prod.

• n. **1** a car journey. **2** a short private road leading to a house. **3** a natural urge. **4** an organized effort to achieve something. **5** determination.

▷ SYNONYMS: **1 excursion**, outing, trip, jaunt, tour, ride, run, journey; informal spin. **2 motivation**, ambition, single-mindedness, determination, will power, dedication, dogged-ness, tenacity, enthusiasm, zeal, commitment, energy, vigour; informal get-up-and-go. **3 campaign**, crusade, movement, effort, push, initiative.

■ **driver** n.

drivel n. nonsense.

drizzle n. light rain falling in fine drops.

• v. rain lightly.

■ **drizzly** adj.

droll adj. strange and amusing.

dromedary n. (pl. **dromedaries**) an Arabian camel, with one hump.

drone v. **1** make a low humming sound. **2** (**drone on**) speak tediously and at length.

• n. **1** a low humming sound. **2** a male bee.

drool v. **1** let saliva dribble. **2** (**drool over**) informal show great pleasure or desire for.

droop v. bend or hang down limply.

▷ SYNONYMS: **hang down**, wilt, dangle, sag, flop, sink, slump, drop.

■ **droopy** adj.

drop v. (**dropping**, **dropped**) **1** fall or let fall. **2** make or become lower or less. **3** give up a course of action. **4** set down a passenger or load.

▷ SYNONYMS: **1 let fall**, let go of, release. **2 fall**, descend, plunge, plummet, dive, sink, dip, tumble. **3 decrease**, lessen, reduce, fall, decline, dwindle, sink, slump. **4 abandon**, give up, discontinue, finish with, renounce, reject, forgo, relinquish, dispense with, leave out; informal dump, pack in, quit.

− ANTONYMS: rise, increase.

• n. **1** a small rounded mass of liquid. **2** a small drink. **3** an act of dropping. **4** an abrupt fall or slope.

▷ SYNONYMS: **1 droplet**, blob, globule, bead. **2 small amount**, little, bit, dash, spot, dribble, sprinkle, trickle, splash, mouthful; informal smidgen, tad. **3 decrease**, reduction, decline, fall-off, downturn, slump. **4 cliff**, precipice, slope, descent, incline.
□ **drop off** fall asleep. **dropout** a person who lives an alternative lifestyle or has given up a course of study. **drop out** stop participating.

droplet n. a very small drop of a liquid.

dropper n. a glass tube for measuring out liquid.

droppings pl. n. animal dung.

dross n. rubbish.

drought /drowt/ n. a very long period of little or no rainfall.

drove past of DRIVE.
• n. **1** a large number of people. **2** a flock of animals being herded along.

drown v. **1** die or kill through submersion in water. **2** make inaudible by being much louder.

drowse v. be half asleep; doze.

drowsy adj. sleepy.
■ **drowsily** adv. **drowsiness** n.

drubbing n. informal a thorough defeat.

drudge n. a person made to do hard or dull work.
■ **drudgery** n.

drug n. **1** a substance used as a medicine. **2** an illegal substance taken for its stimulating or other effects.
▷ SYNONYMS: **1 medicine**, medication, remedy, cure, antidote. **2 narcotic**, stimulant, hallucinogen; informal dope, gear.
• v. (**drugging**, **drugged**) give or add a drug to.
▷ SYNONYMS: **1 anaesthetize**, knock out; informal dope. **2 tamper with**, lace, poison; informal dope, spike, doctor.
□ **drugstore** US a pharmacy also selling toiletries etc.

> **WORD LINKS**
> **pharmacology** the branch of medicine concerned with drugs
> **pharmacy** (Brit. **chemist**; N. Amer. **drugstore**) a shop selling drugs

Druid n. a priest in the ancient Celtic religion.

drum n. **1** a percussion instrument with a skin stretched across a frame, sounded by being struck. **2** a cylindrical container or part.
▷ SYNONYMS: **canister**, barrel, cylinder, tank, bin, can.
• v. (**drumming**, **drummed**) **1** play

on a drum. **2** make a continuous rhythmic noise. **3** (**drum into**) teach by constant repetition. **4** (**drum up**) try to get support or business.
▷ SYNONYMS: **1 tap**, beat, rap, thud, thump, tattoo, thrum. **2 instil**, drive, din, hammer, drill, implant, ingrain, inculcate.
□ **drumstick 1** a stick used for beating a drum. **2** the lower part of a cooked chicken's leg.
■ **drummer** n.

drunk past part. OF DRINK.
• adj. strongly affected by alcohol.
▷ SYNONYMS: **intoxicated**, inebriated, drunken, tipsy, under the influence; informal tight, merry, plastered, sloshed, pickled, tanked up, hammered, wrecked, three sheets to the wind, squiffy, sozzled, blotto; Brit. informal legless, paralytic, Brahms and Liszt, tiddly; N. Amer. informal loaded.
– ANTONYMS: sober.
• n. (or **drunkard**) a person who is drunk or often drunk.
▷ SYNONYMS: **drunkard**, alcoholic, dipsomaniac, inebriate; informal boozer, soak, wino, alky.
■ **drunken** adj. **drunkenly** adv. **drunkenness** n.

dry adj. (**drier**, **driest**) **1** free from moisture or liquid. **2** serious and boring. **3** (of humour) subtle and usu. ironic. **4** (of wine) not sweet.
▷ SYNONYMS: **1 arid**, parched, waterless, dehydrated, desiccated, withered, shrivelled, wizened. **2 dull**, uninteresting, boring, unexciting, tedious, dreary, monotonous, unimaginative, sterile; informal deadly. **3 wry**, subtle, laconic, ironic, sardonic, sarcastic, cynical.
– ANTONYMS: wet, moist.
• v. (**drying**, **dried**) **1** make or become dry. **2** preserve by evaporating the moisture from. **3** (**dry up**) (of a supply) decrease and stop.
▷ SYNONYMS: **1 parch**, scorch, bake, sear, dehydrate, desiccate, wither, shrivel. **2 wipe**, towel, rub dry, drain.
– ANTONYMS: wet, moisten.
□ **dry-clean** clean a garment with a chemical. **dry ice** white mist produced artificially as a theatrical effect. **dry rot** a fungus causing wood decay. **dry run** a rehearsal.
■ **dryness** n.

dryer (or **drier**) n. a machine or device for drying something.

dryly var. of DRILY.

dual adj. consisting of two parts.
▷ SYNONYMS: **double**, twofold, duplex,

d

binary, twin, matching, paired, coupled.

– ANTONYMS: single.

□ **dual carriageway** Brit. a road with two or more lanes in each direction. ■ **duality** n.

dub v. (**dubbing**, **dubbed**) **1** give an unofficial name to. **2** knight someone. **3** provide a film with a soundtrack in a different language from the original.

▷ SYNONYMS: **name**, call, nickname, label, christen, term, tag.

dubbin n. Brit. a grease for softening and waterproofing leather.

dubiety n. doubt or uncertainty.

dubious adj. **1** doubtful or hesitant. **2** probably not honest. **3** of uncertain value.

▷ SYNONYMS: **1 doubtful**, uncertain, unsure, hesitant, sceptical, suspicious; informal iffy. **2 suspicious**, suspect, untrustworthy, unreliable, questionable; informal shady; Brit. informal dodgy.

– ANTONYMS: certain, trustworthy. ■ **dubiously** adv.

ducal adj. of a duke.

ducat /duk-uht/ n. a former European gold coin.

duchess n. **1** a duke's wife or widow. **2** a woman holding a rank equivalent to duke.

duchy n. (pl. **duchies**) the territory of a duke or duchess.

duck n. (pl. **duck** or **ducks**) **1** a waterbird with a broad bill and webbed feet. **2** a female duck. **3** a batsman's score of nought in cricket. • v. **1** lower yourself quickly to avoid being hit or seen. **2** push someone under water. **3** informal avoid a duty.

▷ SYNONYMS: **1 bob down**, bend down, stoop, crouch, squat, hunch down, hunker down. **2 shirk**, dodge, evade, avoid, elude, escape, sidestep.

□ **duckboards** wooden slats forming a path over mud. **duckling** a young duck.

duct n. **1** a tube or passageway for air, cables, etc. **2** a tube in the body through which fluid passes.

▷ SYNONYMS: **tube**, channel, canal, vessel, conduit, pipe, outlet, inlet, flue, shaft, vent.

ductile adj. (of a metal) able to be drawn out into a thin wire. ■ **ductility** n.

dud n. informal a thing that fails to work properly.

dude n. US informal a man.

dudgeon n. (**in high dudgeon**) angry or resentful.

due adj. **1** expected at a certain time. **2** needing to be paid or given; owing. **3** owed or deserving something. **4** proper or required.

▷ SYNONYMS: **1** their fees were due: **owing**, owed, payable, outstanding, overdue, unpaid, unsettled. **2** the chancellor's statement is due today: **expected**, anticipated, scheduled, awaited, required. **3 deserved**, merited, warranted, justified, owing, appropriate, fitting, right, rightful, proper. **4 proper**, correct, suitable, appropriate, adequate, sufficient. • n. **1** (**someone's due/dues**) what someone deserves or is owed. **2** (**dues**) fees.

▷ SYNONYMS: **fee**, subscription, charge, payment, contribution, levy. • adv. directly: due south.

▷ SYNONYMS: **directly**, straight, exactly, precisely, dead.

□ **due to 1** caused by. **2** because of.

duel n. **1** hist. a fight between two people to settle a point of honour. **2** a contest between two parties.

▷ SYNONYMS: **1 single combat**, fight, confrontation, head-to-head; informal shoot-out. **2 contest**, match, game, meet, encounter, clash. • v. (**duelling**, **duelled**; US **dueling**, **dueled**) fight a duel.

duet n. a musical composition for two performers.

duff Brit. informal adj. worthless or false. • v. (**duff up**) beat up.

duffel coat n. a thick hooded overcoat.

duffer n. informal an incompetent or stupid person.

dug past & past part. of DIG. • n. an udder or teat.

dugong n. an Asian sea mammal.

dugout n. a low or underground shelter.

duke n. **1** the highest rank of nobleman in Britain and certain other countries. **2** hist. a male ruler of a small independent state. ■ **dukedom** n.

dulcet adj. (of a sound) sweet and soothing.

dulcimer n. a musical instrument with strings struck with hand-held hammers.

dull adj. **1** lacking interest. **2** lacking brightness. **3** slow to understand.

▷ SYNONYMS: **1 uninteresting**, boring, tedious, monotonous, unimaginative, uneventful, featureless, colourless, lifeless, unexciting, uninspiring, flat,

bland, stodgy, dreary; informal **deadly**;
N. Amer. informal **dullsville**. **2 overcast**,
cloudy, gloomy, dark, dismal, dreary,
sombre, grey, murky, sunless. **3 drab**,
dreary, sombre, dark, subdued,
muted. **4 muffled**, muted, quiet, soft,
faint, indistinct, stifled. **5 unintelligent**, stupid, slow, brainless, mindless, foolish, idiotic; informal dense,
dim, half-witted, thick.
– ANTONYMS: interesting, bright.
  • v. make or become dull.
▷ SYNONYMS: **lessen**, decrease, diminish,
reduce, dampen, blunt, deaden, ease.
– ANTONYMS: intensify.
  ■ **dullness** n. **dully** adv.

dullard n. a stupid person.

duly adv. as is required or expected.

dumb adj. **1** offens. unable to speak.
2 silent. **3** US informal stupid.
▷ SYNONYMS: **1 mute**, speechless, tongue-
tied, silent, at a loss for words.
2 stupid, unintelligent, ignorant,
dense, brainless, foolish, slow; informal
thick, dim; Brit. informal.
– ANTONYMS: talkative, clever.
  • v. (**dumb down**) informal make easier
to understand.
  □ **dumb-bell** a short bar with
weighted ends, used for exercise.
dumbfound astonish greatly.

dumdum n. a soft-nosed bullet that
expands on impact.

dummy n. (pl. **dummies**) **1** a model
of a human being. **2** a model of
something used as a substitute. **3** Brit.
a plastic teat for a baby to suck on.
4 informal a stupid person.
▷ SYNONYMS: **mannequin**, model, figure.
  □ **dummy run** a practice or trial.

dump n. **1** a site where rubbish or
waste is left. **2** informal an unpleasant
or dull place. **3** a temporary store of
weapons or provisions.
▷ SYNONYMS: **1 tip**, rubbish dump,
dumping ground. **2 hovel**, slum;
informal hole, pigsty.
  • v. **1** get rid of. **2** put down carelessly.
▷ SYNONYMS: **1 put down**, set down,
deposit, place, shove, unload, drop,
throw down; informal stick, park, plonk;
Brit. informal bung. **2 dispose of**, get
rid of, throw away/out, discard, bin,
jettison; informal ditch, junk.
  □ **down in the dumps** informal unhappy.

dumpling n. a ball of dough cooked
in a stew.

dumpy adj. short and stout.

dun n. a greyish-brown colour.

dunce n. a person slow at learning.

dune n. a mound of drifted sand.
▷ SYNONYMS: **bank**, mound, hillock,

hummock, knoll, ridge, heap, drift.

dung n. animal excrement.

dungarees pl. n. a garment consisting
of trousers held up by shoulder
straps.

dungeon n. an underground prison
cell.

dunk v. dip food into a drink or soup
before eating it.

duo n. (pl. **duos**) **1** a pair of people or
things. **2** a duet.

duodenum /dyoo-uh-**dee**-nuhm/ n.
(pl. **duodenums**) the part of the small
intestine next to the stomach.
  ■ **duodenal** adj.

dupe v. deceive or trick.
  • n. a duped person.

duple adj. (of rhythm) having two
main beats to the bar.

duplex n. US a building divided into
two flats.

duplicate adj. **1** exactly like
something else. **2** having two
corresponding parts.
▷ SYNONYMS: **matching**, identical, twin,
corresponding, equivalent.
  • n. an exact copy.
▷ SYNONYMS: **copy**, photocopy, facsimile,
reprint, replica, reproduction, clone;
trademark Xerox, photostat.
  • v. **1** make or be an exact copy
of. **2** multiply by two. **3** do again
unnecessarily.
▷ SYNONYMS: **1 copy**, photocopy, photostat, xerox, reproduce, reprint, run
off. **2 repeat**, redo, replicate.
  ■ **duplication** n. **duplicator** n.

duplicity n. deceitful behaviour.
  ■ **duplicitous** adj.

durable adj. **1** hard-wearing. **2** (of
goods) able to be kept.
▷ SYNONYMS: **1 hard-wearing**, wear-
resistant, heavy-duty, tough,
long-lasting, strong, sturdy, robust,
utilitarian. **2 lasting**, long-lasting,
long-term, enduring, persistent,
abiding, permanent, undying,
everlasting.
– ANTONYMS: delicate, short-lived.
  ■ **durability** n.

duration n. the time during which
something continues.
▷ SYNONYMS: **length**, time, period, term,
span, extent, stretch.

duress n. threats or violence used to
force a person to do something.

during prep. **1** throughout. **2** at a point
in the course of.

dusk n. the darker stage of twilight.
▷ SYNONYMS: **twilight**, nightfall, sunset,
sundown, evening, close of day,

semi-darkness, gloom; literary gloaming.
– ANTONYMS: dawn.
dusky adj. darkish in colour.
dust n. fine, dry particles of earth or other matter.
• v. **1** remove dust from the surface of. **2** cover lightly with a powdered substance.
▷ SYNONYMS: **1 wipe**, clean, brush, sweep. **2** *dust the cake with icing sugar:* **sprinkle**, scatter, powder, dredge, sift, cover.
□ **dustbin** Brit. a large container for household rubbish. **dustman** Brit. a man employed to empty dustbins. **dustpan** a container into which dust and waste can be swept.
■ **dusty** adj.
duster n. a cloth for dusting furniture.
Dutch adj. of the Netherlands.
• n. the language of the Netherlands.
□ **Dutch courage** confidence gained from drinking alcohol. **go Dutch** share the cost of a meal equally.
dutiable adj. on which duty must be paid.
dutiful adj. obedient and conscientious.
▷ SYNONYMS: **conscientious**, responsible, dedicated, devoted, attentive, obedient, deferential.
– ANTONYMS: remiss.
■ **dutifully** adv.
duty n. (pl. **duties**) **1** a moral or legal obligation. **2** a task required as part of your job. **3** a tax on the import, export, or sale of goods.
▷ SYNONYMS: **1** *a sense of duty:* **responsibility**, obligation, commitment, allegiance, loyalty. **2** *it was his duty to attend the king:* **job**, task, assignment, mission, function, role. **3 tax**, levy, tariff, excise, toll, rate.
□ **on** (or **off**) **duty** doing (or not doing) your regular work.
duvet /doo-vay/ n. a thick quilt used instead of a top sheet and blankets.
DVD abbrev. digital versatile disc.
dwarf n. (pl. **dwarfs** or **dwarves**) **1** a mythical short human-like being. **2** an unusually small person.
• v. cause to seem comparatively small.
▷ SYNONYMS: **1 dominate**, tower over, loom over, overshadow. **2 overshadow**, outshine, surpass, exceed, outclass, outstrip, outdo, top.
dwell v. (**dwelling**, **dwelt** or **dwelled**) **1** live in or at a place. **2** (**dwell on**)

think at length about.
▷ SYNONYMS: **reside**, live, be housed, lodge, stay; informal **put up**; formal **abide**.
■ **dweller** n.
dwelling n. a place where someone lives.
dwindle v. gradually become smaller or weaker.
▷ SYNONYMS: **diminish**, decrease, reduce, lessen, shrink, wane.
– ANTONYMS: increase.
dye n. a substance used to colour something.
▷ SYNONYMS: **colouring**, dyestuff, pigment, tint, stain, wash.
• v. colour with dye.
dying pres. part. of DIE. adj. **1** on the point of death. **2** gradually ending or ceasing to exist.
▷ SYNONYMS: **1 terminally ill**, at death's door, on your deathbed, fading fast, not long for this world, moribund, in extremis. **2 declining**, vanishing, fading, waning; informal **on the way out**.
dyke (or **dike**) n. **1** a barrier built to prevent flooding from the sea. **2** a drainage ditch.
dynamic adj. **1** constantly changing or active. **2** full of energy and new ideas. **3** Physics of forces producing motion.
▷ SYNONYMS: **energetic**, spirited, active, lively, vigorous, forceful, highpowered, aggressive, enterprising; informal **go-getting**, go-ahead.
■ **dynamically** adv.
dynamics n. **1** the study of the forces involved in movement. **2** forces which stimulate change.
dynamism n. the quality of being dynamic.
dynamite n. a kind of high explosive.
dynamo n. (pl. **dynamos**) a machine for converting mechanical energy into electrical energy.
dynasty n. (pl. **dynasties**) a series of related rulers or powerful people.
▷ SYNONYMS: **family**, house, line, lineage, regime, empire.
■ **dynastic** adj.
dysentery n. a disease causing severe diarrhoea.
dysfunctional adj. **1** not operating properly. **2** unable to deal with normal social relations.
■ **dysfunction** n.
dyslexia n. a disorder involving difficulty in reading.
■ **dyslexic** adj. & n.
dyspepsia n. indigestion.
■ **dyspeptic** adj.

Ee

E abbrev. **1** East or Eastern. **2** (€) euro or euros. **3** informal the drug Ecstasy.
□ **E-number** Brit. a code number given to food additives.

each adj. & pron. every one of two or more, regarded separately.
• adv. to, for, or by every one of a group.
▷ SYNONYMS: **apiece**, per person, per head, per capita.

eager adj. strongly wanting to do or have.
▷ SYNONYMS: **1 keen**, enthusiastic, avid, ardent, zealous, highly motivated, committed, earnest. **2** we were eager for news: **anxious**, impatient, agog, longing, yearning, wishing, hoping; informal itching, dying, raring.
– ANTONYMS: apathetic.
■ **eagerly** adv. **eagerness** n.

eagle n. a large bird of prey.
□ **eagle-eyed** very observant.

ear n. **1** the organ of hearing. **2** an ability to recognize and appreciate music or language. **3** the seed-bearing head of a cereal plant.
▷ SYNONYMS: he has an ear for a good song: **appreciation**, feel, instinct, intuition, sense.
□ **eardrum** a membrane in the ear which vibrates in response to sound waves. **earphones** devices worn on the ears to listen to radio, recorded sound, etc. **earring** a piece of jewellery worn on the ear. **earwig** a small insect with pincers at its rear end. **within** (or **out of**) **earshot** near enough (or too distant) to be heard.

> **WORD LINKS**
> **aural** relating to the ear

earl n. a British nobleman ranking above a viscount.
■ **earldom** n.

early adj. (**earlier**, **earliest**) & adv. **1** before the usual or expected time. **2** near the beginning of a period or sequence.
▷ SYNONYMS: **1** his early death: **untimely**, premature, unseasonable. **2** an early response: **prompt**, timely, quick, speedy. **3** early man: **primitive**, ancient, prehistoric, primeval. **4** they arrived early: **in advance**, in good time, ahead of schedule, with time to spare; prematurely, too soon.
– ANTONYMS: late, overdue.

earmark v. choose for a particular purpose.
▷ SYNONYMS: **set aside**, keep back, reserve, designate, assign, allocate.

earn v. **1** be given money or reward in return for work or merit. **2** (of money invested) gain as interest.
▷ SYNONYMS: **1 be paid**, take home, gross, receive, get, make, collect, bring in; informal pocket, bank. **2 deserve**, merit, warrant, justify, be worthy of, gain, win, secure, obtain.
– ANTONYMS: lose.
■ **earner** n.

earnest adj. very serious.
▷ SYNONYMS: **1 serious**, solemn, grave, sober, humourless, staid, intense. **2 devout**, heartfelt, wholehearted, sincere, impassioned, fervent, intense.
– ANTONYMS: frivolous, half-hearted.
□ **in earnest 1** more intensely than before. **2** in a serious or sincere way.
■ **earnestly** adv.

earnings pl. n. money or income earned.
▷ SYNONYMS: **income**, pay, wages, salary, stipend, remuneration, fees, revenue, yield, profit, takings, proceeds.

earth n. **1** (or **Earth**) the planet we live on. **2** soil. **3** Brit. electrical connection to the ground. **4** a fox's den.
▷ SYNONYMS: **1 world**, globe, planet. **2 land**, ground, terra firma, floor. **3 soil**, clay, dust, dirt, loam, ground, turf.
• v. Brit. connect an electrical device to earth.
□ **earthwork** a large defensive bank of soil. **earthworm** a worm that burrows in the soil.

WORD LINKS
terrestrial relating to the earth
geography, **geology** the study of the earth

earthen adj. made of earth or fired clay. □ **earthenware** pottery made of fired clay.

earthly adj. **1** of the earth or human life. **2** informal used for emphasis: *no earthly reason*.
▷ SYNONYMS: **worldly**, temporal, mortal, human, material, carnal, fleshly, bodily, physical, corporeal, sensual.
– ANTONYMS: spiritual, heavenly.

earthquake n. a sudden violent movement in the earth's crust.
▷ SYNONYMS: **tremor**, shock, convulsion; informal quake.

WORD LINKS
seismic relating to earthquakes
seismology the study of earthquakes

earthy adj. **1** like soil. **2** treating sex or bodily functions in a direct way.
▷ SYNONYMS: **1 down-to-earth**, unsophisticated, unrefined, simple, plain, unpretentious, natural. **2 bawdy**, ribald, racy, rude, crude, coarse, indelicate, indecent; informal raunchy; Brit. informal fruity. ■ **earthiness** n.

ease n. **1** lack of difficulty or effort. **2** freedom from problems.
▷ SYNONYMS: **1 effortlessness**, no trouble, simplicity. **2 naturalness**, casualness, informality, composure, nonchalance, insouciance. **3 affluence**, wealth, prosperity, luxury, plenty, comfort, enjoyment, well-being.
– ANTONYMS: difficulty.
• v. **1** make or become less severe or intense. **2** move carefully or gradually.
▷ SYNONYMS: **1 relieve**, alleviate, soothe, moderate, dull, deaden, numb. **2** *the rain eased off:* **let up**, abate, subside, die down, slacken off, diminish, lessen. **3 calm**, quieten, pacify, soothe, comfort, console. **4 slide**, slip, squeeze, guide, manoeuvre, inch, edge.
– ANTONYMS: aggravate, intensify.

easel n. a frame on legs for holding an artist's work.

easily adv. **1** without difficulty. **2** definitely.
▷ SYNONYMS: **effortlessly**, comfortably, simply, without difficulty, readily, without a hitch.

east n. **1** the direction in which the sun rises. **2** the eastern part of a place.

• adj. & adv. **1** towards or facing the east. **2** (of a wind) from the east.
■ **easterly** adj. & adv. **eastward** adj. & adv. **eastwards** adv.

Easter n. the Christian festival celebrating the resurrection of Jesus.

eastern adj. situated in or facing the east.

easterner n. a person from the east of a region.

easy adj. (**easier**, **easiest**) **1** achieved without great effort. **2** free from worry or problems.
▷ SYNONYMS: **1 uncomplicated**, undemanding, effortless, painless, trouble-free, simple, straight-forward, elementary, plain sailing; informal a piece of cake, child's play, a cinch. **2 natural**, casual, informal, unceremonious, unreserved, unaffected, easy-going, amiable, affable, genial, good-humoured, care-free, nonchalant, unconcerned; informal laid-back. **3 quiet**, tranquil, serene, peaceful, untroubled, contented, relaxed, comfortable, secure, safe; informal cushy. **4** *an easy pace:* **leisurely**, unhurried, comfortable, undemanding, easy-going, gentle, sedate, moderate, steady.
– ANTONYMS: difficult, demanding.
□ **easy chair** a comfortable chair.

easy-going adj. relaxed and open-minded.
▷ SYNONYMS: **relaxed**, even-tempered, placid, happy-go-lucky, carefree, imperturbable, undemanding, patient, tolerant, lenient, broad-minded, open-minded, under-standing; informal laid-back, unflappable.
– ANTONYMS: intolerant.

eat v. (**eating**, **ate**; past part. **eaten**) **1** chew and swallow food. **2** (**eat away**) erode or destroy. **3** (**eat up**) use up resources.
▷ SYNONYMS: **1 consume**, devour, swallow, partake of, munch, chomp; informal tuck into, put away. **2 have a meal**, feed, snack, dine; informal graze. ■ **eatable** adj. **eater** n.

eatery n. (pl. **eateries**) informal a restaurant or cafe.

eau de cologne /oh duh kuh-**lohn**/ = COLOGNE.

eaves pl. n. the overhanging edge of a roof.

eavesdrop v. (**eavesdropping**, **eavesdropped**) secretly listen to a conversation.
▷ SYNONYMS: **listen in**, spy, overhear; informal snoop, earwig.

■ **eavesdropper** n.

ebb n. the movement of the tide away from the land. **2** gradually lessen.
• v. **1** (of the tide) move away from the land. **2** gradually lessen.
▷ SYNONYMS: **1 recede**, go out, retreat. **2 diminish**, dwindle, wane, fade away, peter out, decline, flag.
− ANTONYMS: flow, increase.
□ **at a low ebb** in a weakened or depressed state.

ebony n. **1** heavy dark wood from a tropical tree. **2** a deep black colour.

ebullient adj. cheerful and full of energy.
▷ SYNONYMS: **exuberant**, buoyant, cheerful, cheery, merry, jolly, sunny, jaunty, animated, sparkling, vivacious, irrepressible; informal bubbly, bouncy, upbeat, chirpy, full of beans.
− ANTONYMS: depressed.
■ **ebullience** n.

EC abbrev. European Community.

eccentric adj. **1** unconventional and rather strange. **2** not concentric.
▷ SYNONYMS: **unconventional**, abnormal, anomalous, odd, strange, peculiar, weird, bizarre, outlandish, idiosyncratic, quirky; informal oddball, kooky, cranky.
− ANTONYMS: conventional.
• n. an eccentric person.
▷ SYNONYMS: **oddity**, free spirit, misfit; informal oddball, weirdo.
■ **eccentrically** adv. **eccentricity** n.

ecclesiastical adj. of the Christian Church or its clergy.

echelon /esh-uh-lon/ n. a level in an organization, profession, etc.

echo n. (pl. **echoes**) **1** a repetition of sound caused by the reflection of sound waves. **2** a reflected radio or radar beam.
▷ SYNONYMS: **reverberation**, reflection, ringing, repetition, repeat.
• v. **1** (of a sound) reverberate or be repeated as an echo. **2** be similar to. **3** repeat someone's words.
▷ SYNONYMS: **1 reverberate**, resonate, resound, reflect, ring, vibrate. **2 repeat**, restate, reiterate, imitate, parrot, mimic, reproduce, recite.

eclair /i-klair/ n. a long cake of choux pastry filled with cream.

éclat /ay-klah/ n. an impressive or successful effect.

eclectic adj. using ideas from a wide range of sources.

eclipse n. **1** an occasion when one planet, the moon, etc. blocks out the light from another. **2** a sudden loss of significance or power.
• v. **1** (of a planet etc.) block the light from or to another. **2** make less significant or powerful.
▷ SYNONYMS: **outshine**, overshadow, surpass, exceed, outclass, outstrip, outdo, transcend.

eco-friendly adj. not harmful to the environment.

E. coli /ee koh-ly/ n. a bacterium which can cause severe food poisoning.

ecology n. the study of the relationships of living things to one another and to their surroundings.
■ **ecological** adj. **ecologist** n.

economic adj. **1** of economics or the economy of a country. **2** profitable.
▷ SYNONYMS: **1 financial**, monetary, budgetary, commercial, fiscal. **2 profitable**, moneymaking, lucrative, remunerative, fruitful, productive.
− ANTONYMS: unprofitable.

economical adj. **1** giving good value in relation to outlay. **2** careful in the use of money or resources.
▷ SYNONYMS: **1 cheap**, inexpensive, low-cost, budget, economy, cut-price, bargain. **2 thrifty**, provident, prudent, sensible, frugal.
− ANTONYMS: expensive, spendthrift.
■ **economically** adv.

economics n. the study of the production, consumption, and transfer of wealth.
■ **economist** n.

economize (or **-ise**) v. spend less.
▷ SYNONYMS: **save money**, cut costs, cut back, make cutbacks, retrench, scrimp.

economy n. (pl. **economies**) **1** the state of a country in terms of the production and consumption of goods and services and the supply of money. **2** careful management of resources.
▷ SYNONYMS: **1 wealth**, financial resources, financial management. **2 thrift**, thriftiness, prudence, careful budgeting, economizing, saving, restraint, frugality.
− ANTONYMS: extravagance.

ecosystem n. a biological community of interacting living things and their environment.

ecru n. a light beige colour.

ecstasy n. (pl. **ecstasies**) **1** intense happiness. **2** (**Ecstasy**) an illegal drug.
▷ SYNONYMS: **rapture**, bliss, joy, elation, euphoria, rhapsodies.
− ANTONYMS: misery.

USAGE No *x*: -*cs*- at the beginning and *s* at the end: ecstasy.

e

ecstatic adj. very happy.
▷ SYNONYMS: **euphoric**, elated, rapturous, joyful, overjoyed, blissful, enraptured; informal over the moon, on top of the world.
■ **ecstatically** adv.

ectopic pregnancy n. a pregnancy in which the fetus develops outside the womb.

ecumenical adj. representing or promoting unity among the different Christian Churches.

eczema /eks-muh/ n. a condition causing dry, itchy patches on the skin.

eddy n. (pl. **eddies**) a circular movement of water.
▷ SYNONYMS: **swirl**, whirlpool, vortex.
• v. (**eddying**, **eddied**) move in eddies.
▷ SYNONYMS: **swirl**, whirl, spiral, wind, twist.

edelweiss /ay-duhl-vyss/ n. an alpine plant.

edema US = OEDEMA.

edge n. **1** the outside limit of an object or area. **2** the sharpened side of a blade. **3** a slight advantage. **4** an intense or exciting quality.
▷ SYNONYMS: **1 border**, boundary, extremity, fringe, margin, side, lip, rim, brim, brink, verge, perimeter. **2 sharpness**, severity, bite, sting, sarcasm, malice, spite, venom. **3 advantage**, lead, head start, the whip hand, the upper hand, dominance.
− ANTONYMS: middle.
• v. **1** provide with an edge. **2** move gradually and carefully.
▷ SYNONYMS: **1 border**, fringe, skirt, surround, enclose, encircle, bound. **2 trim**, decorate, finish, border, fringe. **3 creep**, inch, work your way, ease yourself, sidle, steal.
□ **edgeways** (or **edgewise**) with the edge uppermost or towards the viewer. **on edge** tense or irritable.

edging n. a decorative border.

edgy adj. (**edgier**, **edgiest**) tense or irritable.
▷ SYNONYMS: **tense**, nervous, on edge, anxious, apprehensive, uneasy, unsettled, twitchy, jumpy, nervy, keyed up, restive; informal uptight, wired.
− ANTONYMS: calm.
■ **edgily** adv. **edginess** n.

edible adj. fit to be eaten.

edict n. an official order.

edifice n. a large and impressive building.

edify v. (**edifying**, **edified**) improve the mind or character of.
■ **edification** n.

edit v. (**editing**, **edited**)**1** prepare written material for publication. **2** prepare material for a film or broadcast.
▷ SYNONYMS: **correct**, check, copy-edit, improve, polish, modify, adapt, revise, rewrite, reword, shorten, condense, cut, abridge.

edition n. **1** a version of a published written work. **2** all the copies of a book etc. issued at one time.
▷ SYNONYMS: **issue**, number, volume, printing, impression, publication, programme, version.

editor n. **1** a person in charge of a newspaper or magazine. **2** a person who edits material for publication or broadcast.

editorial adj. of the editing of material.
• n. a newspaper article giving an opinion on a topical issue.

educate v. give intellectual or moral instruction to.
▷ SYNONYMS: **teach**, school, tutor, instruct, coach, train, inform, enlighten.

educated adj. showing or having had a good education.
▷ SYNONYMS: **informed**, literate, schooled, tutored, well read, learned, knowledgeable, enlightened, intellectual, academic, erudite, scholarly, cultivated, cultured.
− ANTONYMS: uneducated.

education n. **1** the process of teaching, training, or learning. **2** the theory of teaching.
▷ SYNONYMS: **1 teaching**, schooling, tuition, tutoring, instruction, coaching, training, guidance. **2 learning**, knowledge, literacy, scholarship, enlightenment.
■ **educationally** adv..

educational adj. relating to education.
▷ SYNONYMS: **1 academic**, scholastic, pedagogic. **2** an educational experience: **instructive**, instructional, educative, informative, illuminating, enlightening; formal edifying.
■ **educationally** adv.

Edwardian adj. of the reign of King Edward VII (1901–10).

EEC abbrev. European Economic Community.

eel n. a snake-like fish.

eerie adj. (**eerier**, **eeriest**) strange and frightening.
▷ SYNONYMS: **uncanny**, sinister, ghostly, unnatural, unearthly, supernatural, other-worldly, strange, abnormal,

weird, freakish; informal creepy, scary, spooky.
■ **eerily** adv.

efface v. **1** rub off or cause to disappear. **2** (**efface yourself**) make yourself appear inconspicuous.

effect n. **1** a change produced by an action or other cause; a result. **2** the state of being operative or effective. **3** (**effects**) personal belongings. **4** (**effects**) the lighting, sound, or scenery used in a play or film.
▷ SYNONYMS: **1** *the effect of these changes*: **result**, consequence, upshot, outcome, repercussions, end result, aftermath. **2** *the effect of the drug*: **impact**, action, effectiveness, power, potency, strength, success. **3** *the dead man's effects*: **belongings**, possessions, worldly goods, chattels, property; informal things, stuff; Brit. informal clobber.
− ANTONYMS: cause.
● v. bring about a result.
▷ SYNONYMS: **achieve**, accomplish, carry out, manage, bring off, execute, conduct, engineer, perform, do, cause, bring about, produce.

> **USAGE** Don't confuse **affect** and **effect**: **affect** is a verb which chiefly means 'make a difference to'.

effective adj. **1** producing an intended result. **2** operative. **3** existing in fact, though not formally acknowledged as such.
▷ SYNONYMS: **1 successful**, effectual, potent, powerful, helpful, beneficial, advantageous, valuable, useful. **2 convincing**, compelling, strong, forceful, persuasive, plausible, credible, logical, reasonable, cogent. **3 operative**, in force, in effect, valid, official, legal, binding. **4 virtual**, practical, essential, actual.
− ANTONYMS: ineffective.
■ **effectively** adv. **effectiveness** n.

effectual adj. effective.
■ **effectually** adv.

effeminate adj. (of a man) having characteristics regarded as typical of a woman.
■ **effeminacy** n.

effervescent adj. **1** fizzy. **2** lively and enthusiastic.
▷ SYNONYMS: **fizzy**, sparkling, carbonated, aerated, gassy, bubbly.
− ANTONYMS: still.
■ **effervesce** v. **effervescence** n.

effete adj. **1** weak; feeble. **2** (of a man) effeminate.

efficacious adj. effective.
■ **efficacy** n.

efficient adj. working productively with no waste of money or effort.
▷ SYNONYMS: **1 economic**, productive, effective, cost-effective, streamlined, organized, methodical, systematic, orderly. **2 competent**, capable, able, proficient, skilful, skilled, effective, productive, organized, businesslike.
− ANTONYMS: inefficient, incompetent.
■ **efficiency** n. **efficiently** adv.

effigy n. (pl. **effigies**) a model of a person.

efflorescence n. a high stage of development.

effluent n. liquid waste or sewage.

effluvium n. (pl. **effluvia**) an unpleasant or harmful smell or discharge.

effort n. **1** a determined attempt. **2** the physical or mental energy needed to do something.
▷ SYNONYMS: **1 attempt**, try, endeavour; informal shot, stab, bash. **2 achievement**, accomplishment, feat, undertaking, enterprise, work, result, outcome. **3 exertion**, energy, work, application; informal elbow grease; Brit. informal graft.
■ **effortless** adj.

effrontery n. insolence or disrespect.

effusion n. an outpouring, esp. of feeling.

effusive adj. expressing pleasure or approval in an unrestrained way.
■ **effusively** n.

e.g. abbrev. for example.

egalitarian adj. believing in the principle of equal rights for all.
● n. an egalitarian person.
■ **egalitarianism** n.

egg n. **1** an oval or round object laid by a female bird, reptile, etc., and containing a cell which can develop into a new organism. **2** an ovum.
▷ SYNONYMS: **ovum**, gamete; (**eggs**) roe, spawn.
● v. (**egg on**) urge to do something foolish.
□ **egghead** informal a very studious person. **eggplant** US an aubergine.
■ **eggy** adj.

> **WORD LINKS**
> **ovoid** egg-shaped

ego n. (pl. **egos**) **1** a person's sense of their own value. **2** the part of the mind responsible for a person's sense of identity.

egocentric adj. self-centred.

egotism (or **egoism**) n. the quality of being very conceited or self-centred.
■ **egotist** n.

egotistic, (or **egoistic**) adj. very conceited or self-centred.
▷ SYNONYMS: **self-centred**, selfish, egocentric, self-interested, self-seeking, self-absorbed, self-obsessed, narcissistic, vain, conceited, self-important, boastful.
■ **egotistical** adj..

egregious /i-gree-juhss/ adj. very bad.

egress n. 1 the act of going out. 2 a way out.

Egyptian n. a person from Egypt.
• adj. of Egypt.

Egyptology n. the study of ancient Egypt.
■ **Egyptologist** n.

Eid /eed/ (or **Id**) n. 1 the Muslim festival marking the end of the fast of Ramadan. 2 the Muslim festival marking the end of the annual pilgrimage to Mecca.

eider n. a large northern sea duck.
□ **eiderdown** Brit. a quilt filled with down or other soft material.

eight adj. & n. one more than seven; 8.
■ **eighth** adj. & n.

eighteen adj. & n. one more than seventeen; 18.
■ **eighteenth** adj. & n.

eighty adj. & n. (pl. **eighties**) ten less than ninety; 80.
■ **eightieth** adj. & n.

einsteinium n. an unstable radioactive element.

eisteddfod /I-steth-vod/ n. a Welsh festival with music and poetry competitions.

either conj. & adv. 1 as the first of two alternatives specified. 2 indicating a link with a previous statement.
• adj. & pron. 1 one or the other of two. 2 each of two.

ejaculate v. 1 eject semen from the penis. 2 dated say suddenly.
■ **ejaculation** n.

eject v. force or throw out.
▷ SYNONYMS: 1 **emit**, spew out, discharge, disgorge, give off, send out, belch, vent. 2 **expel**, throw out, remove, oust, evict, banish; informal kick out, turf out, boot out.
■ **ejection** n. **ejector** n.

eke v. (**eke out**) 1 use sparingly. 2 make a living with difficulty.

elaborate adj. with many carefully arranged parts.
▷ SYNONYMS: 1 **complicated**, complex, intricate, involved, detailed. 2 **ornate**, decorated, embellished, adorned, ornamented, fancy, fussy, busy.
– ANTONYMS: simple, plain.

• v. 1 develop in detail. 2 add detail to something said.
▷ SYNONYMS: **expand on**, enlarge on, add to, flesh out, develop, fill out, amplify.
■ **elaborately** adv. **elaboration** n.

élan n. energy and flair.

elapse v. (of time) pass.

elastic adj. 1 able to return to normal size or shape after being stretched or squeezed. 2 flexible.
▷ SYNONYMS: 1 **stretchy**, elasticated, springy, flexible, pliable, supple. 2 **adaptable**, flexible, adjustable, accommodating, variable, fluid, versatile.
– ANTONYMS: rigid.
• n. elastic cord or fabric.
■ **elasticated** adj. **elasticity** n.

elated adj. very happy and excited.
▷ SYNONYMS: **thrilled**, delighted, over-joyed, ecstatic, euphoric, jubilant, rapturous, in raptures, walking on air, on cloud nine, in seventh heaven; informal on top of the world, over the moon, tickled pink.
– ANTONYMS: miserable.
■ **elation** n.

elbow n. the joint between the forearm and the upper arm.
• v. hit or push with the elbow.
□ **elbow grease** informal vigorous cleaning. **elbow room** informal enough space to move in.

elder adj. of a greater age.
▷ SYNONYMS: **older**, senior.
• n. 1 a person older than you. 2 a senior figure in a community. 3 a shrub with white flowers and small dark berries (**elderberries**).
▷ SYNONYMS: **leader**, patriarch, father.

elderly n. old.
▷ SYNONYMS: **aged**, old, ageing, long in the tooth, grey-haired, in your dotage; informal getting on, over the hill.
– ANTONYMS: youthful.

eldest adj. oldest.

elect v. 1 choose for a public position by voting. 2 choose to do.
▷ SYNONYMS: 1 **vote in**, vote for, return, cast your vote for, choose, pick, select. 2 **choose**, decide, opt, prefer, vote.
• adj. elected but not yet in office.

election n. 1 a procedure whereby a person is elected. 2 the act of electing.
▷ SYNONYMS: **ballot**, vote, poll; refer-endum, plebiscite; Brit. by-election; US primary.

> **WORD LINKS**
> **psephology** the study of elections

electioneering n. campaigning to be

elected to a political position.

elective adj. **1** of or chosen by election. **2** chosen by the person concerned.

elector n. a person entitled to vote in an election.
■ **electoral** adj.

electorate n. the people entitled to vote in an election.

electric adj. **1** of, using, or producing electricity. **2** very exciting.
▷ SYNONYMS: *the atmosphere was electric:* exciting, charged, electrifying, thrilling, dramatic, dynamic, stimulating, galvanizing.
• n. (**electrics**) Brit. the electric wiring in a house or vehicle.
□ **electric chair** a chair for executing convicted criminals by electrocution.

electrical adj. of, using, or producing electricity.
■ **electrically** adv.

electrician n. a person who installs and repairs electrical equipment.

electricity n. **1** a form of energy resulting from charged particles. **2** the supply of electric current to a building.

electrify v. (**electrifying, electrified**) **1** charge with electricity. **2** convert to use electrical power.
■ **electrification** n.

electrifying adj. very exciting.
▷ SYNONYMS: **exciting**, thrilling, stimulating, rousing, inspiring, stirring, exhilarating, intoxicating, gripping, compelling.

electroconvulsive adj. (of the treatment of mental illness) using electric shocks applied to the brain.

electrocute v. injure or kill by electric shock.
■ **electrocution** n.

electrode n. a conductor through which electricity enters or leaves something.

electrolysis n. **1** the separation of a liquid into its chemical parts by passing an electric current through it. **2** the removal of hair roots by means of an electric current.

electrolyte n. a liquid or gel that an electric current can pass through.

electromagnet n. a metal core made into a magnet by passing electric current through a surrounding coil.

electromagnetic adj. of electric currents and magnetic fields.
■ **electromagnetism** n.

electromotive adj. producing an electric current.

electron n. a subatomic particle with a negative charge, found in all atoms.
□ **electron microscope** a powerful microscope using electron beams instead of light.

electronic adj. **1** having parts such as microchips and transistors that control and direct electric currents. **2** of electrons or electronics. **3** carried out by computer.
■ **electronically** adv.

electronics n. **1** the study of electrons or electronic devices. **2** electronic circuits or devices.

electroplate v. coat a metal object with another metal using electrolysis.

elegant adj. **1** graceful and stylish. **2** pleasingly clever but simple.
▷ SYNONYMS: **1 stylish**, graceful, tasteful, sophisticated, classic, chic, smart, poised, dignified, cultivated, polished, cultured, refined. **2** *an elegant solution:* **neat**, simple, apt.
– ANTONYMS: inelegant.
■ **elegance** n. **elegantly** adv.

elegy n. (pl. **elegies**) a sad poem, esp. a lament for a dead person.
■ **elegiac** adj.

element n. **1** a basic part. **2** a substance that cannot be chemically changed or broken down into other substances. **3** earth, water, air, and fire, formerly believed to make up all matter. **4** a trace. **5** (**the elements**) the weather, esp. when bad. **6** a part that gives out heat in an electric device.
▷ SYNONYMS: **1 component**, constituent, part, section, portion, piece, segment, aspect, factor, feature, facet, ingredient, strand, detail, member. **2 trace**, touch, hint, smattering, soupçon. **3** (**elements**) **weather**, climate, weather conditions.
□ **in your element** in a situation in which you are happy or relaxed.
■ **elemental** adj.

elementary adj. of the most basic aspects of a subject.
▷ SYNONYMS: **1** *an elementary astronomy course:* **basic**, rudimentary, preparatory, introductory. **2** *a lot of the work is elementary:* **easy**, simple, straightforward, uncomplicated, undemanding, painless, child's play, plain sailing; informal a piece of cake.
– ANTONYMS: advanced, difficult.

elephant n. a very large mammal with a trunk and tusks.

elephantine adj. huge or clumsy.

elevate v. raise to a higher position or level.
▷ SYNONYMS: **1 raise**, lift, hoist, hike up,

haul up. **2 promote**, upgrade, move up, raise; informal kick upstairs.
– ANTONYMS: lower, demote.

elevated adj. **1** higher than the surrounding area. **2** of high rank or status. **3** of a high intellectual or moral level.
▷ SYNONYMS: **1 raised**, overhead, in the air, high up. **2 high**, high-ranking, lofty, exalted, grand, noble. **3 lofty**, grand, fine, sublime, inflated, pompous, bombastic.

elevation n. **1** the act of elevating. **2** height above a given level. **3** one side of a building.

elevator n. US a lift in a building.

eleven adj. & n. one more than ten; 11.
■ **eleventh** adj. & n.

elevenses pl. n. Brit. informal a mid-morning snack.

elf n. (pl. **elves**) an imaginary small being with magic powers.

elfin adj. (of a person) small and delicate.

elicit v. (**eliciting**, **elicited**) draw out a response.
▷ SYNONYMS: **obtain**, draw out, extract, bring out, evoke, induce, prompt, generate, trigger, provoke.

elide v. omit a sound or syllable when speaking.
■ **elision** n.

eligible adj. **1** satisfying the conditions to do or receive something. **2** desirable as a wife or husband.
▷ SYNONYMS: **1 entitled**, permitted, allowed, qualified, able. **2 desirable**, suitable, available, single, unmarried, unattached.
■ **eligibility** n.

eliminate v. get rid of.
▷ SYNONYMS: **1 remove**, get rid of, put an end to, do away with, end, stop, eradicate, destroy, stamp out. **2 knock out**, exclude, rule out, disqualify.
■ **elimination** n.

elite n. a group regarded as the best in a particular sphere or organization.
▷ SYNONYMS: **best**, pick, cream, crème de la crème, flower, high society, beautiful people, aristocracy, ruling class.
– ANTONYMS: dregs.

elitism n. **1** the belief that a society should be run by an elite. **2** the superior attitude associated with an elite.
■ **elitist** adj. & n.

elixir n. a magical potion.

Elizabethan adj. of the reign of Queen Elizabeth I (1558–1603).

elk n. a large deer.

ellipse n. a regular oval.

ellipsis n. (pl. **ellipses**) **1** the omission of words in speech or writing. **2** a set of dots indicating this.

elliptical adj. **1** with a word or words omitted. **2** oval.

elm n. a tall deciduous tree with rough leaves.

elocution n. the skill of speaking clearly.

elongate v. make or become longer.

elope v. run away secretly to get married.
■ **elopement** n.

eloquence n. fluent or persuasive speaking or writing.

eloquent adj. fluent or persuasive.
▷ SYNONYMS: **articulate**, fluent, expressive, persuasive, well expressed, effective, lucid, vivid.
– ANTONYMS: inarticulate.
■ **eloquently** adv.

else adv. **1** in addition. **2** different; instead.
▢ **elsewhere** in or to another place. **or else** otherwise; if not.

elucidate v. explain.
■ **elucidation** n.

elude v. **1** cleverly escape from or avoid. **2** fail to be understood or achieved by.
▷ SYNONYMS: **evade**, avoid, get away from, dodge, escape from, lose, shake off, give the slip to, slip away from, throw off the scent.

elusive adj. hard to find or achieve.
▷ SYNONYMS: **1 difficult to find**, evasive, slippery. **2 indefinable**, intangible, impalpable, fugitive, fleeting, transitory, ambiguous.

elver n. a young eel.

elves pl. of ELF.

emaciated adj. abnormally thin and weak.
▷ SYNONYMS: **thin**, skeletal, bony, gaunt, wasted, thin as a rake, scrawny, skinny, scraggy, skin and bone, starved, cadaverous, shrivelled, shrunken, withered.
– ANTONYMS: fat.
■ **emaciation** n.

email (or **e-mail**) n. **1** the sending of electronic messages from one computer user to another. **2** a message sent by email.
• v. send a message by email.

emanate v. (**emanate from**) come or spread out from.
■ **emanation** n.

emancipate v. free from legal, social, or political restrictions.

■ **emancipation** n.

emasculate v. **1** make weaker or less effective. **2** deprive a man of his male role or identity.
■ **emasculation** n.

embalm v. treat a corpse to preserve it from decay.

embankment n. a wall or bank built to prevent flooding or to carry a road or railway.

embargo n. (pl. **embargoes**) an official ban, esp. on trade with a particular country.
▷ SYNONYMS: **ban**, bar, prohibition, stoppage, veto, moratorium, restriction, block, boycott.
• v. (**embargoing**, **embargoed**) ban officially.
▷ SYNONYMS: **ban**, bar, prohibit, stop, outlaw, blacklist, restrict, block, boycott.
– ANTONYMS: allow.

embark v. **1** board a ship or aircraft. **2** (**embark on**) begin a new course of action.
■ **embarkation** n.

embarrass v. cause to feel self-conscious or ashamed.
▷ SYNONYMS: **humiliate**, shame, put someone to shame, abash, mortify, fluster, discomfit; informal show up.

USAGE Two r's, two s's: emba*rrass*.

embarrassed adj. feeling self-conscious or ashamed.
▷ SYNONYMS: **humiliated**, mortified, red-faced, blushing, abashed, shamed, ashamed, shamefaced, self-conscious, uncomfortable, discomfited, disconcerted, flustered; informal with egg on your face.

embarrassing adj. causing embarrassment.
▷ SYNONYMS: **humiliating**, shameful, mortifying, ignominious, awkward, uncomfortable, compromising; informal cringeworthy, cringe-making, toe-curling.

embarrassment n. a feeling of self-consciousness or shame.
▷ SYNONYMS: **humiliation**, mortification, shame, shamefacedness, awkward-ness, self-consciousness, discomfort, discomfiture.

embassy n. (pl. **embassies**) the official residence or offices of an ambassador.

embattled adj. **1** facing many problems. **2** surrounded by enemy forces.

embed (or **imbed**) v. (**embedding**, **embedded**) fix firmly in a surrounding mass.

embellish v. **1** decorate. **2** add extra details to a story.
▷ SYNONYMS: **decorate**, adorn, ornament, beautify, enhance, trim, garnish, gild, deck, bedeck, festoon, emblazon.
■ **embellishment** n.

ember n. a piece of burning wood or coal in a dying fire.

embezzle v. steal money placed in your trust.
▷ SYNONYMS: **misappropriate**, steal, thieve, pilfer, purloin, appropriate, siphon off, pocket; informal filch; Brit. informal pinch, nick.
■ **embezzlement** n. **embezzler** n.

embittered adj. bitter or resentful.

emblazon v. conspicuously display a design on something.

emblem n. a design or symbol as a badge of a nation, group, etc.
▷ SYNONYMS: **symbol**, representation, token, image, figure, mark, sign, crest, badge, device, insignia, coat of arms, shield, logo, trademark.

emblematic adj. representing a quality or idea.

embody v. (**embodying**, **embodied**) **1** give a tangible or visible form to. **2** include.
▷ SYNONYMS: **1 personify**, manifest, symbolize, represent, express, epitomize, stand for, typify, exemplify. **2 incorporate**, include, contain.
■ **embodiment** n.

embolden v. make braver.

embolism n. obstruction of an artery by a clot or an air bubble.

emboss v. make a raised design on.

embrace v. **1** hold closely in your arms. **2** include or contain. **3** willingly accept or support a change etc.
▷ SYNONYMS: **1 hug**, take/hold in your arms, hold, cuddle, clasp to your bosom, squeeze, clutch, enfold. **2 welcome**, welcome with open arms, accept, take on board, take up, take to your heart, adopt, espouse. **3 include**, take in, comprise, contain, incorporate, encompass, cover, subsume.
• n. an act of embracing.
▷ SYNONYMS: **hug**, cuddle, squeeze, clinch, caress.

embrocation n. a liquid rubbed on the body to relieve aches.

embroider v. **1** sew decorative needlework patterns on. **2** embellish a story.
■ **embroidery** n.

embroil v. involve in a conflict or difficult situation.

embryo n. (pl. **embryos**) an unborn or

unhatched baby or animal in the early stages of development.

embryonic adj. **1** of an embryo. **2** in a very early stage of development.

emend v. correct and revise written material.
■ **emendation** n.

emerald n. **1** a green precious stone. **2** a bright green colour.

emerge v. **1** come out into view. **2** (of facts) become known. **3** survive a difficult period.
▷ SYNONYMS: **1 appear**, come out, come into view, become visible, surface, materialize, issue, come forth. **2 become known**, become apparent, be revealed, come to light, come out, turn up, transpire, unfold, turn out, prove to be the case.
■ **emergence** n. **emergent** adj.

emergency n. (pl. **emergencies**) a serious and unexpected situation requiring immediate action.
▷ SYNONYMS: **crisis**, disaster, catastrophe, calamity, plight; informal panic stations.
• adj. arising from or used in an emergency.

emeritus adj. retired but retaining a title as an honour.

emery board n. a strip of wood or card coated with a rough substance and used as a nail file.

emetic adj. causing vomiting.

emigrate v. leave your own country and settle permanently in another.
▷ SYNONYMS: **move abroad**, move overseas, leave your country, migrate, relocate, resettle.
– ANTONYMS: immigrate.
■ **emigrant** n. **emigration** n.

émigré /em-i-gray/ n. a person who has emigrated.

eminence n. **1** the quality of being distinguished and respected. **2** an important person.

eminent adj. **1** distinguished. **2** obvious.
▷ SYNONYMS: **illustrious**, distinguished, renowned, esteemed, pre-eminent, notable, noted, noteworthy, great, prestigious, important, outstanding, celebrated, prominent, well known, acclaimed, exalted.
– ANTONYMS: unknown.
■ **eminently** adv.

emir n. a Muslim ruler.

emirate n. the territory of an emir.

emissary n. (pl. **emissaries**) a person sent on a special diplomatic mission.

emission n. the action of emitting something, or a substance which is emitted.
▷ SYNONYMS: **discharge**, release, outpouring, outflow, outrush, leak.

emit v. (**emitting**, **emitted**) **1** give out heat, gas, etc. **2** make a sound.
▷ SYNONYMS: **1 discharge**, release, give out/off, pour out, radiate, leak, ooze, disgorge, eject, belch, spew out, exude. **2 utter**, voice, let out, produce, give vent to, come out with.

emollient adj. **1** softening or soothing the skin. **2** attempting to avoid conflict.

emolument n. a salary or fee.

emotion n. **1** a strong feeling, e.g. anger. **2** instinctive feeling as contrasted with reasoning.
▷ SYNONYMS: **1 feeling**, sentiment, reaction, response, instinct, intuition. **2 passion**, strength of feeling, heart.

emotional adj. **1** of the emotions. **2** arousing or showing emotion.
▷ SYNONYMS: **1 passionate**, hot-blooded, ardent, fervent, warm, responsive, excitable, temperamental, demonstrative, sensitive. **2 poignant**, moving, touching, affecting, powerful, stirring, emotive, impassioned, dramatic; informal tear-jerking.
– ANTONYMS: cold, clinical.
■ **emotionally** adv.

emotive adj. arousing strong feeling.

empathize (or **-ise**) v. understand and share the feelings of another.

empathy n. the ability to empathize.

emperor n. the male ruler of an empire.

emphasis n. (pl. **emphases**) **1** special importance or value given to something. **2** stress on a word in speaking.
▷ SYNONYMS: **1 prominence**, importance, significance, value, stress, weight, accent, attention, priority. **2** *the emphasis is on the word 'little'*: **stress**, accent, weight, beat.

emphasize (or **-ise**) v. give special importance to.
▷ SYNONYMS: **stress**, underline, highlight, focus attention on, point up, lay stress on, draw attention to, spotlight, foreground.
– ANTONYMS: understate.

emphatic adj. showing or giving emphasis.
▷ SYNONYMS: **forceful**, firm, vehement, wholehearted, energetic, vigorous, direct, insistent, certain, definite, out-and-out, decided, categorical, unqualified, unconditional, unequivocal, unambiguous, absolute, explicit, downright, outright, clear.
■ **emphatically** adv.

emphysema n. a condition that affects the lungs, causing breathlessness.

empire n. **1** a large group of countries under a single ruler or authority. **2** a large business organization controlled by one person or group.
▷ SYNONYMS: **1 kingdom**, realm, domain, territory, commonwealth, power. **2 business**, firm, company, corporation, multinational, conglomerate, group, consortium, operation.

> **WORD LINKS**
> **imperial** relating to an empire

empirical adj. based on observation or experience rather than theory.
■ **empirically** adv. **empiricism** n. **empiricist** n.

emplacement n. a platform for a gun or battery of guns.

employ v. **1** give work to someone and pay them for it. **2** make use of. **3** keep occupied.
▷ SYNONYMS: **1 hire**, engage, recruit, take on, sign up, appoint, retain. **2 use**, utilize, make use of, apply, exercise, practise, put into practice, exert, bring into play, bring to bear, draw on, resort to, turn to, have recourse to. **3 occupy**, engage, involve, keep busy, tie up.
– ANTONYMS: dismiss.
■ **employer** n.

employee n. a person employed for wages or a salary.
▷ SYNONYMS: **worker**, member of staff, blue-collar worker, white-collar worker, workman, labourer, hand; (**employees**) personnel, staff, workforce.

employment n. the action of employing someone, or the state of being employed.
▷ SYNONYMS: **work**, labour, service, job, post, position, situation, occupation, profession, trade, business, line of work.

emporium n. (pl. **emporia** or **emporiums**) a large shop selling a variety of goods.

empower v. **1** authorize. **2** give strength and confidence to.
▷ SYNONYMS: **1 authorize**, entitle, permit, allow, license, enable. **2 emancipate**, unshackle, set free, liberate, enfranchise.
– ANTONYMS: forbid.
■ **empowerment** n.

empress n. **1** a female ruler of an empire. **2** an emperor's wife or widow.

empty adj. (**emptier, emptiest**) **1** containing nothing; not filled or occupied. **2** having no real meaning.
▷ SYNONYMS: **1 vacant**, unoccupied, uninhabited, bare, clear, free. **2 meaningless**, hollow, idle, vain, futile, worthless, useless, ineffectual. **3 futile**, pointless, purposeless, worthless, meaningless, fruitless, valueless, of no value, senseless.
– ANTONYMS: full, occupied.
• v. (**emptying, emptied**) make or become empty.
▷ SYNONYMS: **1 unload**, unpack, clear, evacuate, drain. **2 remove**, take out, extract, tip out, pour out.
– ANTONYMS: fill, replace.
• n. (pl. **empties**) informal an empty bottle or glass.
■ **emptiness** n.

emu n. a flightless Australian bird similar to an ostrich.

emulate v. try to equal or be better than.
▷ SYNONYMS: **imitate**, copy, mirror, echo, follow, model yourself on, take a leaf out of someone's book.
■ **emulation** n. **emulator** n.

emulsify v. (**emulsifying, emulsified**) combine liquids into an emulsion.
■ **emulsifier** n.

emulsion n. **1** a mixture of two liquids in which particles of one are evenly distributed in the other. **2** a type of paint for walls. **3** a light-sensitive coating for photographic film.

enable v. provide with the ability or means to do something.
▷ SYNONYMS: **allow**, permit, let, equip, empower, make able, fit, authorize, entitle, qualify.
– ANTONYMS: prevent.

enact v. **1** make a bill or other proposal law. **2** act out a role or play.
▷ SYNONYMS: **1 make law**, pass, approve, ratify, validate, sanction, authorize. **2 act out**, perform, appear in, stage, mount, put on, present.
– ANTONYMS: repeal.
■ **enactment** n.

enamel n. **1** a glossy coloured coating for metal or pottery. **2** the hard outer covering of a tooth. **3** a paint that dries to give a hard shiny coat.
• v. (**enamelling, enamelled**; US **enameling, enameled**) coat or decorate with enamel.

enamoured (US **enamored**) adj. (**enamoured of/with**) full of love or admiration for.

encamp v. settle in a camp.

encampment n. a place where a camp is set up.

e

encapsulate v. express clearly and briefly.

encase v. enclose or cover in a case.

encephalitis n. inflammation of the brain.

enchant v. **1** delight. **2** put under a spell.
■ **enchanter** n. **enchantment** n. **enchantress** n.

enchanting adj. delightful; charming.
▷ SYNONYMS: **captivating**, charming, delightful, adorable, lovely, attractive, appealing, engaging, fetching, irresistible, fascinating.

encircle v. form a circle round.

enclave n. a small territory surrounded by a foreign country.

enclose v. **1** surround on all sides. **2** place in an envelope with a letter.
▷ SYNONYMS: **1 surround**, circle, ring, encircle, bound, close in, wall in. **2 include**, insert, put in, send.

> WORD LINKS
> **claustrophobia** fear of enclosed spaces

enclosure n. **1** an enclosed area. **2** a document etc. placed in an envelope with a letter.
▷ SYNONYMS: **compound**, pen, fold, stockade, ring, paddock, yard, run, coop; N. Amer. corral.

encode v. convert into a coded form.
■ **encoder** n.

encomium n. (pl. **encomiums** or **encomia**) a formal expression of praise.

encompass v. **1** include. **2** surround.
▷ SYNONYMS: **include**, cover, embrace, incorporate, take in, contain, comprise, involve, deal with.

encore /ong-kor/ n. an extra item at the end of a concert, as called for by the audience.
• exclam. again!

encounter v. unexpectedly meet or be faced with.
▷ SYNONYMS: **1 experience**, run into, meet, come up against, face, be faced with, confront, suffer. **2 meet**, run into, come across/upon, stumble across/on, chance on, happen on; informal bump into.
• n. **1** an unexpected meeting. **2** a confrontation.
▷ SYNONYMS: **1 meeting**, chance meeting. **2 battle**, fight, skirmish, clash, scuffle, confrontation, struggle; informal run-in, set-to, scrap.

encourage v. give confidence, hope, or support to.
▷ SYNONYMS: **1 hearten**, cheer, buoy up,

uplift, inspire, motivate, spur on, stir, fire up, stimulate, embolden; informal buck up. **2** *she encouraged him to go:* persuade, coax, urge, press, push, prod, egg on. **3 support**, back, promote, further, foster, nurture, cultivate, strengthen.
– ANTONYMS: discourage.

encouragement n. the action of encouraging.
▷ SYNONYMS: **1 support**, inspiration, motivation, stimulation, morale-boosting; informal a shot in the arm. **2 persuasion**, coaxing, urging, prompting, inducement, incentive, carrot. **3 backing**, sponsorship, support, promotion, furtherance, fostering, nurture, cultivation.

encouraging adj. inspiring confidence or hope.
▷ SYNONYMS: **1 promising**, hopeful, auspicious, favourable, heartening, reassuring, cheering, comforting, welcome, pleasing, gratifying. **2 supportive**, understanding, helpful, positive, enthusiastic.

encroach v. (**encroach on**) gradually intrude on territory, rights, etc.
■ **encroachment** n.

encrust v. cover with a hard crust.
■ **encrustation** n.

encrypt v. convert into code.
■ **encryption** n.

encumber v. be a burden to.
■ **encumbrance** n.

encyclical n. a letter sent by the pope to all Roman Catholic bishops.

encyclopedia (or **encyclopaedia**) n. a book or set of books giving information on many subjects.
■ **encyclopedic** adj.

end n. **1** the final part. **2** the furthest part. **3** the stopping of a state or situation. **4** a person's death or downfall. **5** a goal or desired result.
▷ SYNONYMS: **1 conclusion**, termination, ending, finish, close, resolution, climax, finale, culmination, denouement. **2 extremity**, limit, edge, border, boundary, periphery, point, tip, head, top, bottom. **3 aim**, goal, purpose, objective, object, target, intention, aspiration, wish, desire, ambition.
– ANTONYMS: beginning, means.
• v. **1** come or bring to an end. **2** (**end up**) eventually reach a particular state or place.
▷ SYNONYMS: **1 finish**, conclude, terminate, close, stop, cease, culminate, climax. **2 break off**, call off, bring to an end, put an end to,

stop, finish, terminate, discontinue, cancel.
– ANTONYMS: begin.
□ **make ends meet** earn just enough money to live on.
endanger v. **1** put in danger. **2** (**endangered**) in danger of becoming extinct.
▷ SYNONYMS: **jeopardize**, risk, put at risk, put in danger, be a danger to, threaten, compromise, imperil.
– ANTONYMS: safeguard.
endear v. cause to be loved or liked.
endearing adj. inspiring affection.
▷ SYNONYMS: **charming**, appealing, attractive, engaging, winning, captivating, enchanting, cute, sweet, delightful, lovely.
endearment n. a word or phrase expressing affection.
endeavour (US **endeavor**) v. try hard to achieve.
▷ SYNONYMS: **try**, attempt, seek, strive, struggle, labour, toil, work.
•n. **1** a serious attempt to achieve something. **2** hard work.
▷ SYNONYMS: **1 attempt**, try, bid, effort. **2 undertaking**, enterprise, venture, exercise, activity, exploit, deed, act, action, move.
endemic adj. (of a disease) regularly found in a particular group or area.
ending n. an end or final part.
▷ SYNONYMS: **end**, finish, close, conclusion, resolution, summing-up, denouement, finale.
– ANTONYMS: beginning.
endive n. a salad vegetable with bitter leaves.
endless adj. having or seeming to have no end or limit.
▷ SYNONYMS: **1 unlimited**, limitless, infinite, inexhaustible, boundless, unbounded, ceaseless, unending, everlasting, constant, continuous, interminable, unfailing, perpetual, eternal, never-ending. **2 countless**, innumerable, numerous, a multitude of; informal umpteen, no end of; literary myriad.
– ANTONYMS: limited, few.
■ **endlessly** adv.
endocrine adj. (of a gland) producing and discharging hormones etc. directly into the blood.
endorphin n. a painkilling chemical compound produced in the brain.
endorse v. **1** declare approval of. **2** sign a cheque on the back. **3** Brit. record an offence on a driving licence.
▷ SYNONYMS: **support**, back, agree with, approve of, favour, subscribe

to, recommend, champion, uphold, sanction.
– ANTONYMS: oppose.
■ **endorsement** n.
endow v. **1** provide with property or a permanent income. **2** (**be endowed with**) possess a quality or asset.
▷ SYNONYMS: **1 finance**, fund, pay for, subsidize, sponsor. **2** he was endowed with great strength: **provide**, supply, furnish, equip, favour, bless, grace.
endowment n. **1** property or money given to an institution or person to provide them with a regular income. **2** a natural quality or ability.
▷ SYNONYMS: **gift**, present, grant, funding, award, donation, contribution, subsidy, sponsorship, bequest, legacy.
endurance n. the ability to endure something.
▷ SYNONYMS: **toleration**, tolerance, forbearance, patience, resignation, stoicism; resistance, durability, permanence, longevity, strength, toughness, stamina, staying power, fortitude.
endure v. **1** experience and cope with prolonged pain or difficulty. **2** last for a long time.
▷ SYNONYMS: **1 undergo**, go through, live through, experience, cope with, deal with, face, suffer, tolerate, put up with, brave, bear, withstand. **2 last**, live, live on, go on, survive, abide, continue, persist, remain.
■ **endurable** adj.
enema n. a medical procedure in which fluid is injected into the rectum to empty it.
enemy n. (pl. **enemies**) a person or group opposed or hostile to another.
▷ SYNONYMS: **opponent**, adversary, rival, antagonist, combatant, challenger, competitor, opposition, competition, the other side; literary foe.
– ANTONYMS: friend, ally.
energetic adj. showing or involving great energy.
▷ SYNONYMS: **1** an energetic woman: **active**, lively, dynamic, spirited, animated, bouncy, bubbly, sprightly, tireless, indefatigable, enthusiastic; informal full of beans. **2** energetic exercises: **vigorous**, strenuous, brisk, hard, arduous, demanding, taxing, tough, rigorous. **3** an energetic advertising campaign: **forceful**, vigorous, aggressive, hard-hitting, high-powered, all-out, determined, bold, intensive; informal in-your-face.
– ANTONYMS: lethargic.
■ **energetically** adv.

e

energize (or **-ise**) v. give energy and enthusiasm to.

energy n. (pl. **energies**) **1** the strength and vitality required to keep active. **2** power derived from physical or chemical resources to provide light, heat, etc.
▷ SYNONYMS: **vitality**, vigour, strength, stamina, animation, spirit, verve, enthusiasm, zest, exuberance, dynamism, drive; informal punch, bounce, oomph, go, get-up-and-go.

enervate v. cause to feel drained of energy.
■ **enervation** n.

enfant terrible /on-fon te-**ree**-bluh/ n. (pl. **enfants terribles**) a person who behaves in a controversial or unconventional way.

enfeeble v. weaken.

enfold v. envelop or surround.

enforce v. **1** ensure a law etc. is obeyed. **2** force to happen.
▷ SYNONYMS: **1 impose**, apply, administer, carry out, implement, bring to bear, put into effect. **2 force**, compel, coerce, exact.
■ **enforceable** adj. **enforcement** n.

enfranchise v. give the right to vote to.
■ **enfranchisement** n.

engage v. **1** involve someone's interest or attention. **2** (**engage in/with**) become involved in. **3** employ someone. **4** move part of a machine into an operating position. **5** begin to fight with.
▷ SYNONYMS: **1 capture**, catch, arrest, grab, draw, attract, gain, hold, grip, absorb, occupy. **2 employ**, hire, recruit, take on, enrol, appoint. **3** *the chance to engage in a wide range of pursuits:* **participate in**, join in, take part in, partake in/of, enter into, embark on. **4 attack**, fall on, take on, clash with, encounter, meet, fight, do battle with.
– ANTONYMS: lose, dismiss.

engaged adj. **1** occupied. **2** in use. **3** having formally agreed to marry.

engagement n. **1** a formal agreement to get married. **2** an appointment. **3** involvement. **4** a battle.
▷ SYNONYMS: **1 appointment**, meeting, arrangement, commitment, date, assignation, rendezvous. **2 participation**, involvement. **3 battle**, fight, clash, confrontation, encounter, conflict, skirmish, action, hostilities.

engaging adj. charming.
▷ SYNONYMS: **charming**, attractive, appealing, pleasing, pleasant, agreeable, likeable, lovable, sweet, winning, fetching; Scottish & N. English bonny.
– ANTONYMS: unappealing.

engender v. give rise to.
▷ SYNONYMS: **cause**, give rise to, bring about, occasion, lead to, result in, produce, create, generate, arouse, rouse, inspire, provoke, kindle, trigger, spark, stir up, whip up.

engine n. **1** a machine that converts power into motion. **2** a railway locomotive.
▷ SYNONYMS: **motor**, generator, machine, turbine.

engineer n. **1** a person qualified in engineering. **2** a person who controls an engine on an aircraft or ship.
▷ SYNONYMS: **1** *a structural engineer:* **designer**, planner, builder. **2** *a repair engineer:* **mechanic**, repairer, technician, maintenance man, operator, driver.
• v. **1** design and build. **2** arrange for something to occur.
▷ SYNONYMS: **bring about**, arrange, pull off, bring off, contrive, manoeuvre, negotiate, organize, orchestrate, plan, mastermind.

engineering n. the study of the design, building, and use of engines, machines, and structures.

English n. the language of England, used in many varieties throughout the world.
• adj. of England.

engorged adj. swollen.

engrave v. **1** carve a design on a hard surface. **2** (**be engraved on** or **in**) be fixed in the mind.
▷ SYNONYMS: **carve**, cut, etch, inscribe, chisel, score.
■ **engraver** n. **engraving** n.

engross v. absorb all the attention of.
▷ SYNONYMS: (**engrossed**) **absorbed**, involved, interested, occupied, preoccupied, immersed, caught up, riveted, gripped, rapt, fascinated, intent, captivated, enthralled.

engulf v. surround or cover completely.
▷ SYNONYMS: **swamp**, inundate, flood, deluge, immerse, swallow up, submerge, bury, envelop, overwhelm.

enhance v. increase the quality, value, or extent of.
▷ SYNONYMS: **improve**, add to, strengthen, boost, increase, intensify, heighten, magnify, amplify, inflate, build up, supplement, augment.
– ANTONYMS: diminish.
■ **enhancement** n.

enigma n. a mysterious person or thing.
■ **enigmatic** adj. **enigmatically** adv.

enjoin v. instruct or urge to do.

enjoy v. **1** take pleasure in. **2** (**enjoy yourself**) have a pleasant time. **3** possess and benefit from.
▷ SYNONYMS: **1 like**, be fond of, be keen on, delight in, relish, revel in, adore, lap up, savour, luxuriate in, bask in; informal get a thrill out of. **2 benefit from**, be blessed with, be favoured with, be endowed with, possess, own, boast.
– ANTONYMS: dislike, lack.

enjoyable adj. giving pleasure.
▷ SYNONYMS: **entertaining**, amusing, delightful, pleasant, congenial, convivial, agreeable, pleasurable, satisfying.
– ANTONYMS: disagreeable.

enjoyment n. the state of enjoying something.
▷ SYNONYMS: **pleasure**, fun, entertainment, amusement, recreation, relaxation, happiness, merriment, joy, satisfaction, liking.

enlarge v. **1** make or become larger. **2** (**enlarge on**) say more about.
▷ SYNONYMS: **1 extend**, expand, grow, add to, amplify, augment, magnify, build up, stretch, widen, broaden, lengthen, elongate, deepen, thicken. **2 swell**, distend, bloat, bulge, dilate, blow up, puff up.
– ANTONYMS: reduce, shrink.
■ **enlargement** n.

enlighten v. give greater knowledge and understanding to.
▷ SYNONYMS: **inform**, tell, make aware, open someone's eyes; informal put someone in the picture.

enlightened adj. rational, tolerant, and well informed.
▷ SYNONYMS: **informed**, aware, sophisticated, liberal, open-minded, tolerant, broad-minded, educated, well informed, knowledgeable, well read, civilized, refined, cultured.
– ANTONYMS: benighted.

enlightenment n. the gaining of knowledge and understanding.
▷ SYNONYMS: **insight**, understanding, awareness, education, learning, knowledge, illumination, awakening, instruction, teaching, open-mindedness, broad-mindedness, culture, refinement, cultivation, civilization.

enlist v. **1** join the armed services. **2** ask for someone's help in doing something.
▷ SYNONYMS: **1 join up**, enrol, sign up for, volunteer, register. **2 recruit**, call up, enrol, sign up, conscript, mobilize; US draft. **3 obtain**, engage, secure, win, get.
– ANTONYMS: discharge, demobilize.
■ **enlistment** n.

enliven v. make more interesting or lively.

en masse /on mass/ adv. all together.

enmesh v. involve in complicated circumstances.

enmity n. (pl. **enmities**) hostility.

ennoble v. give greater dignity to.

ennui /on-wee/ n. boredom and lethargy.

enormity n. (pl. **enormities**) **1** (**the enormity of**) the extreme seriousness of something bad. **2** great size or scale.
▷ SYNONYMS: **1 wickedness**, vileness, heinousness, baseness, depravity, outrageousness. **2 immensity**, hugeness, size, extent, magnitude.

enormous adj. very large.
▷ SYNONYMS: **huge**, vast, immense, gigantic, giant, massive, colossal, mammoth, tremendous, extensive, mighty, monumental, mountainous; informal mega, monster, whopping; Brit. informal ginormous.
– ANTONYMS: tiny.

enough adj., pron., & adv. as much or as many as is necessary or desirable.
▷ SYNONYMS: *there's enough food:* **sufficient**, plenty of, adequate, ample, abundant, the necessary.
– ANTONYMS: insufficient.

enquire v. **1** ask for information. **2** investigate.
▷ SYNONYMS: **1 ask**, query, question. **2 investigate**, probe, look into, make enquiries, research, examine, explore, delve into; informal check out.

enquiry n. (pl. **enquiries**) **1** an act of enquiring. **2** an official investigation.
▷ SYNONYMS: **1 question**, query. **2 investigation**, probe, examination, exploration, inquest, hearing.

enrage v. make very angry.
▷ SYNONYMS: **anger**, infuriate, incense, madden, inflame, antagonize, provoke; informal drive mad/crazy, make someone see red, make someone's blood boil; (**enraged**) furious, infuriated, irate, incensed, raging, incandescent, fuming, seething, beside yourself; informal mad, livid, foaming at the mouth.
– ANTONYMS: placate.

enrapture v. delight greatly.

enrich v. **1** improve the quality or value of. **2** make wealthier.

▷ SYNONYMS: **enhance**, improve, better, add to, augment, supplement, complement, refine.
■ **enrichment** n.

enrol (US **enroll**) v. (**enrolling**, **enrolled**) officially register as a member or student.

▷ SYNONYMS: **1 register**, sign on/up, put your name down, apply, volunteer, enter, join. **2 accept**, admit, take on, sign on/up, recruit, engage.
■ **enrolment** n.

en route /on **root**/ adv. on the way.

ensconce v. establish comfortably or securely.

ensemble /on-**som**-b'l/ n. **1** a group of performers. **2** a group of items viewed as a whole.

▷ SYNONYMS: **1 group**, band, company, troupe, cast, chorus, corps; informal combo. **2 whole**, unit, body, set, collection, combination, composite, package. **3 outfit**, costume, suit; informal get-up.

enshrine v. preserve in a form that ensures protection and respect.

ensign n. a ship's flag.

enslave v. cause to lose freedom of choice or action.
■ **enslavement** n.

ensnare v. trap or gain control over.

ensue v. happen afterwards or as a result.

▷ SYNONYMS: **result**, follow, develop, succeed, emerge, arise, proceed, stem.

en suite /on **sweet**/ adj. Brit. (of a bathroom) leading directly off a bedroom.

ensure v. make certain that something will occur or be so.

▷ SYNONYMS: **1 make sure**, make certain, see to it, check, confirm, establish, verify. **2 secure**, guarantee, assure, certify.

entail v. involve as a necessary part or result.

▷ SYNONYMS: **involve**, necessitate, require, need, demand, call for, mean, imply, cause, give rise to, occasion.

entangle v. **1** make tangled. **2** involve in complicated circumstances.
■ **entanglement** n.

entente /on-**tont**/ n. a friendly understanding between states.

enter v. **1** come or go into. **2** begin to be involved in or do. **3** register as a participant in. **4** record information in a book, computer, etc.

▷ SYNONYMS: **1 go into**, come into, get into, set foot in, gain access to. **2 penetrate**, pierce, puncture, perforate. **3 join**, enrol in/for, enlist in, volunteer for, sign up for, register for; go in for, participate in, compete in, take part in. **4 record**, write, put down, take down, note, jot down, register, log; key in, type in.
– ANTONYMS: leave.

enteritis n. inflammation of the intestines.

enterprise n. **1** a business or company. **2** a large project. **3** the ability to initiate new projects.

▷ SYNONYMS: **1 undertaking**, endeavour, venture, exercise, activity, operation, task, business, project, scheme. **2 initiative**, resourcefulness, imagination, ingenuity, inventiveness, originality, creativity. **3 business**, company, firm, venture, organization, operation, concern, establishment; informal outfit.

enterprising adj. showing initiative and resourcefulness.

▷ SYNONYMS: **resourceful**, entre-preneurial, imaginative, ingenious, inventive, creative, adventurous, bold; informal go-ahead.

entertain v. **1** provide with amusement or enjoyment. **2** offer hospitality to. **3** consider.

▷ SYNONYMS: **1 amuse**, please, charm, cheer, interest, engage, occupy. **2 receive**, play host/hostess to, throw a party for, wine and dine, feed, fete. **3 consider**, contemplate, think of, hear of, countenance.
– ANTONYMS: bore, reject.
■ **entertainer** n.

entertainment n. **1** the action of entertaining. **2** an event, activity, etc. designed to entertain people.

▷ SYNONYMS: **amusement**, pleasure, leisure, recreation, relaxation, fun, enjoyment, diversion, interest.

enthral (US **enthrall**) v. (**enthralling**, **enthralled**) fascinate and hold the attention of.

▷ SYNONYMS: **fascinate**, entrance, enchant, bewitch, captivate, delight, absorb.

enthralling adj. extremely interesting.

▷ SYNONYMS: **fascinating**, entrancing, enchanting, bewitching, captivating, delightful, absorbing, engrossing, compelling, riveting, gripping, exciting; informal unputdownable.
– ANTONYMS: boring.

enthrone v. ceremonially install a new monarch on a throne.
■ **enthronement** n.

enthuse v. fill with or express great

enthusiasm.

enthusiasm n. great enjoyment and interest.

▷ SYNONYMS: **keenness**, eagerness, passion, fervour, zeal, zest, gusto, energy, vigour, fire, spirit, interest, commitment, devotion; informal get-up-and-go.

– ANTONYMS: apathy.

enthusiast n. a person who is full of enthusiasm for something.

▷ SYNONYMS: **fan**, devotee, supporter, follower, aficionado, lover, admirer; informal buff.

enthusiastic adj. having or showing great enthusiasm.

▷ SYNONYMS: **keen**, eager, avid, ardent, fervent, passionate, zealous, excited, wholehearted, committed, devoted, fanatical, earnest.

– ANTONYMS: apathetic.

■ **enthusiastically** adv.

entice v. attract by offering something desirable.

▷ SYNONYMS: **tempt**, lure, attract, appeal to, invite, persuade, beguile, coax, woo, lead on, seduce; informal sweet-talk.

■ **enticement** n.

entire adj. with no part left out.

▷ SYNONYMS: **whole**, complete, total, full.

entirely adv. wholly; completely.

▷ SYNONYMS: **absolutely**, completely, totally, wholly, utterly, quite, altogether, thoroughly.

entirety n. (the entirety) the whole.

entitle v. 1 give a right to. 2 give a title to a book etc.

▷ SYNONYMS: 1 **qualify**, make eligible, authorize, allow, permit, enable, empower. 2 **name**, title, call, label, designate, dub.

■ **entitlement** n.

entity n. (pl. entities) a thing existing independently from other things.

▷ SYNONYMS: **being**, creature, individual, organism, life form, body, object, article, thing.

entomb v. 1 place in a tomb. 2 bury or completely cover.

entomology n. the study of insects.

■ **entomological** adj. **entomologist** n.

entourage /on-toor-ahzh/ n. the people accompanying an important person.

entrails pl. n. intestines.

entrance[1] n. 1 a door, gate, etc. for entering. 2 an act of entering. 3 the right or opportunity to enter.

▷ SYNONYMS: 1 **entry**, way in, access, approach, door, portal, gate, foyer,

lobby, porch; opening, mouth; N. Amer. entryway. 2 **appearance**, arrival, entry, coming. 3 **admission**, admittance, right of entry, entrée, access.

– ANTONYMS: exit, departure.

entrance[2] v. fill with wonder and delight.

▷ SYNONYMS: **enchant**, bewitch, beguile, captivate, mesmerize, hypnotize, spellbind, transfix, enthral, engross, absorb, fascinate, stun, electrify, charm, delight; informal bowl over, knock out.

entrant n. a person who joins or takes part in something.

▷ SYNONYMS: **competitor**, contestant, contender, participant, candidate, applicant.

entrap v. (entrapping, entrapped) 1 catch in a trap. 2 trick into committing a crime.

■ **entrapment** n.

entreat v. ask earnestly or anxiously.

▷ SYNONYMS: **implore**, beg, plead with, pray, ask, request, bid, enjoin, appeal to, call on; literary beseech.

■ **entreaty** n.

entrée /on-tray/ n. 1 the main course of a meal. 2 the right to enter a place or social group.

entrench v. establish firmly.

▷ SYNONYMS: (**entrenched**) **ingrained**, established, fixed, firm, deep-seated, deep-rooted, unshakeable, ineradicable.

■ **entrenchment** n.

entrepreneur /on-truh-pruh-ner/ n. a person who is successful in setting up businesses.

■ **entrepreneurial** adj.

entropy n. a quantity expressing how much of a system's thermal energy is unavailable for conversion into mechanical work.

entrust v. make responsible for doing or caring for.

▷ SYNONYMS: **charge**, give, vouchsafe, assign, confer on, bestow on, vest in; delegate.

entry n. (pl. entries) 1 an act of entering. 2 an entrance. 3 an item in a list etc.

▷ SYNONYMS: 1 **appearance**, arrival, entrance, coming. 2 **entrance**, way in, access, approach, door, portal, gate, entrance hall, foyer, lobby; N. Amer. entryway. 3 **admission**, admittance, entrance, access. 4 **item**, record, note, memo, memorandum. 5 **submission**, application, entry form.

– ANTONYMS: departure, exit.

entwine v. wind or twist together.

enumerate v. mention items one by one.
■ **enumeration** n.

enunciate v. pronounce or state clearly.
■ **enunciation** n.

envelop v. (**enveloping**, **enveloped**) wrap up or surround completely.
▷ SYNONYMS: **surround**, cover, enfold, engulf, encircle, cocoon, sheathe, swathe, enclose, cloak, veil, shroud.

envelope n. a flat paper container for a letter etc., with a sealable flap.

enviable adj. desirable and so arousing envy.
■ **enviably** adv.

envious adj. feeling or showing envy.
▷ SYNONYMS: **jealous**, covetous, desirous, grudging, begrudging, resentful; informal green with envy.
■ **enviously** adv.

environment n. **1** the surroundings in which a person, animal, or plant lives. **2** the natural world.
▷ SYNONYMS: **1 situation**, setting, milieu, background, backdrop, context, conditions, ambience, atmosphere. **2 the natural world**, nature, the earth, the ecosystem, the biosphere, Mother Nature, wildlife, flora and fauna, the countryside.
■ **environmental** adj. **environmentally** adv.

USAGE Don't forget the *n*: environment.

WORD LINKS
ecology the study of the environment

environmentalist n. a person seeking to protect the environment.
▷ SYNONYMS: **conservationist**, ecologist, nature-lover, green; informal eco-warrior, tree-hugger.
■ **environmentalism** n.

environs pl. n. the surrounding area.

envisage v. **1** see as a possibility. **2** imagine.
▷ SYNONYMS: **1 foresee**, predict, forecast, anticipate, expect, think likely. **2 imagine**, contemplate, picture, conceive of, think of.

envoy n. a messenger or representative.
▷ SYNONYMS: **ambassador**, emissary, diplomat, representative, delegate, spokesperson, agent, intermediary, mediator; informal go-between.

envy n. (pl. **envies**) discontented longing aroused by another person's possessions etc.
▷ SYNONYMS: **jealousy**, covetousness, resentment, bitterness.

• v. (**envying**, **envied**) feel envy of.
▷ SYNONYMS: **1 be envious of**, be jealous of, be resentful of. **2 covet**, desire, aspire to, wish for, want, long for, yearn for, hanker after, crave.

enzyme n. a substance produced by a living organism and assisting in chemical processes.

eon US = AEON.

epaulette n. an ornamental shoulder piece on a uniform.

ephemera pl. n. items of short-lived interest or use.

ephemeral adj. lasting only for a short time.
▷ SYNONYMS: **transitory**, transient, fleeting, passing, short-lived, momentary, brief, short, temporary, impermanent, short-term.
– ANTONYMS: permanent.

epic n. a long poem, book, or film about heroic people or covering a long period of time.
• adj. heroic or on a grand scale.

epicene adj. characteristic of both sexes or neither sex.

epicentre (US **epicenter**) n. the point on the earth's surface directly above the origin of an earthquake.

epicure n. a person who enjoys good food and drink.
■ **epicurean** n. & adj.

epidemic n. a widespread occurrence of an infectious disease in a community.
▷ SYNONYMS: **1 outbreak**, plague, pandemic. **2 spate**, rash, wave, eruption, plague, outbreak, craze, upsurge.

epidemiology n. the study of the spread and control of diseases.
■ **epidemiologist** n.

epidermis n. the outer layer of the skin.

epidural n. an anaesthetic injected into the space around the spinal cord, esp. during childbirth.

epiglottis n. a flap of cartilage that covers the larynx during swallowing.

epigram n. a short witty saying.
■ **epigrammatic** adj.

epilepsy n. a disorder of the nervous system causing convulsions and loss of consciousness.
■ **epileptic** adj. & n.

epilogue n. a short concluding section of a book or play.

Epiphany n. the Christian festival (6 January) commemorating Jesus's appearance to the Magi.

episcopal adj. of or governed by

bishops.

episcopalian n. a supporter of government of a Church by bishops.

episode n. **1** an event occurring as part of a sequence. **2** each part of a serialized story or programme.
▷ SYNONYMS: **1 incident**, event, occurrence, chapter, experience, occasion, interlude, adventure, exploit. **2 instalment**, chapter, passage, part, portion, section, programme, show. **3 period**, spell, bout, attack, phase; informal dose.
■ **episodic** adj.

epistemology n. the branch of philosophy that deals with knowledge.
■ **epistemological** adj.

epistle n. a letter.
■ **epistolary** adj.

epitaph n. words written in memory of a person who has died.

epithet n. a descriptive word or phrase.

epitome /i-pit-uh-mi/ n. a perfect example.
▷ SYNONYMS: **personification**, embodiment, incarnation, essence, quintessence, archetype, paradigm, exemplar, model.

epitomize (or **-ise**) v. be a perfect example of.

epoch n. a long and distinct historical period.
▷ SYNONYMS: **era**, age, period, time, aeon.

eponymous adj. (of a person) giving their name to something.

equable adj. **1** even-tempered. **2** not varying greatly.

equal adj. **1** the same in quantity, size, value, or status. **2** evenly balanced. **3** (**equal to**) able to deal with.
▷ SYNONYMS: **1 identical**, uniform, alike, like, the same, matching, equivalent, corresponding. **2 impartial**, non-partisan, fair, just, equitable, unprejudiced, non-discriminatory. **3 evenly matched**, even, balanced, level, nip and tuck, neck and neck; informal level pegging.
– ANTONYMS: different, unequal.
• n. a person or thing that is equal to another.
▷ SYNONYMS: **equivalent**, peer, fellow, like, counterpart, match, parallel.
• v. (**equalling**, **equalled**; US **equaling**, **equaled**) **1** be equal to. **2** match or rival.
▷ SYNONYMS: **1 be equal to**, be equivalent to, be the same as, come to, amount to, make, total, add up to. **2 match**, reach, parallel, be level with.
■ **equally** adv.

equality n. the state of being equal.
▷ SYNONYMS: **fairness**, equal rights, equal opportunities, impartiality, even-handedness, justice.

equalize (or **-ise**) v. **1** make or become equal. **2** level the score in a match by scoring a goal.
■ **equalization** n. **equalizer** n.

equanimity n. evenness of temper.
▷ SYNONYMS: **composure**, calm, level-headedness, self-possession, presence of mind, serenity, tranquillity, imperturbability, equilibrium, poise, aplomb, sangfroid, nerve; informal cool.
– ANTONYMS: anxiety.

equate v. consider one thing as equal to another.
▷ SYNONYMS: **1** he equates criticism with treachery: **identify**, compare, bracket, class, associate, connect, link, relate. **2 equalize**, balance, even out/up, level, square, tally, match.

equation n. a statement that the values of two mathematical expressions are equal.

equator n. an imaginary line around the earth at equal distances from the North and South Poles.
■ **equatorial** adj.

equerry n. (pl. **equerries**) a male officer of a royal household acting as an attendant to a member of the royal family.

equestrian adj. of horse riding.
■ **equestrianism** n.

equidistant adj. at equal distances.

equilateral adj. having all sides the same length.

equilibrium n. (pl. **equilibria**) a balanced state.
▷ SYNONYMS: **balance**, stability, poise, symmetry, harmony.
– ANTONYMS: imbalance.

equine adj. of or like a horse.

equinox n. the time or date (twice each year) when day and night are of equal length.
■ **equinoctial** adj.

equip v. (**equipping**, **equipped**) supply with what is needed.
▷ SYNONYMS: **1** the boat was equipped with a flare gun: **provide**, furnish, supply, issue, kit out, stock, provision, arm. **2** the course will equip them for the workplace: **prepare**, qualify, ready, suit, train.

equipment n. the items needed for a particular purpose.
▷ SYNONYMS: **apparatus**, paraphernalia, tools, utensils, implements, hardware, gadgetry, things; informal stuff, gear.

equitable adj. treating everyone equally; fair.
■ **equitably** adv.
equitation n. horse riding.
equity n. **1** fairness and impartiality. **2** (equities) stocks and shares not paying a fixed amount of interest. **3** the value of a mortgaged property after all charges and debts have been paid.
equivalent adj. equal in value, amount, meaning, etc.
▷ SYNONYMS: **comparable**, corresponding, commensurate, similar, parallel, analogous.
• n. a person or thing equivalent to another.
▷ SYNONYMS: **counterpart**, parallel, alternative, analogue, twin, opposite number.
■ **equivalence** n.
equivocal adj. unclear in meaning.
▷ SYNONYMS: **ambiguous**, indefinite, non-committal, vague, imprecise, inexact, inexplicit, hazy, unclear, ambivalent, uncertain, unsure.
− ANTONYMS: definite.
■ **equivocally** adv.
equivocate v. deliberately use language that can be interpreted in different ways.
■ **equivocation** n.
era n. a long and distinct historical period.
▷ SYNONYMS: **age**, epoch, period, time, date, day, generation.
eradicate v. remove or destroy completely.
▷ SYNONYMS: **eliminate**, get rid of, remove, obliterate, extinguish, exterminate, destroy, annihilate, kill, wipe out.
■ **eradication** n.
erase v. rub out or remove all traces of.
▷ SYNONYMS: **delete**, rub out, wipe off, blank out, expunge, excise, remove, obliterate.
■ **erasable** adj. **eraser** n. **erasure** n.
ere /air/ prep. & conj. old use before (in time).
erect adj. **1** rigidly upright. **2** (of a body part) enlarged and rigid.
▷ SYNONYMS: **upright**, straight, vertical, perpendicular, standing on end, bristling, stiff.
• v. build.
▷ SYNONYMS: **build**, construct, put up, assemble, put together, fabricate, raise.
− ANTONYMS: demolish, dismantle.
■ **erection** n.

erectile adj. able to become erect.
erg n. a unit of work or energy.
ergo adv. therefore.
ergonomics n. the study of people's efficiency in their working environment.
■ **ergonomic** adj.
ermine n. **1** a stoat. **2** the stoat's white winter fur.
erode v. gradually wear away.
▷ SYNONYMS: **wear away**, abrade, grind down, crumble, weather, undermine, weaken, deteriorate, destroy.
erogenous adj. sensitive to sexual stimulation.
erosion n. the process of eroding or the result of being eroded.
▷ SYNONYMS: **wearing away**, abrasion, attrition, weathering, deterioration, disintegration, destruction.
erotic adj. of sexual desire or excitement.
▷ SYNONYMS: **sexually arousing**, sexually stimulating, titillating, suggestive, pornographic, sexually explicit; informal blue, X-rated; euphemistic adult.
■ **erotically** adv.
erotica n. erotic literature or art.
eroticism n. the quality of being erotic.
err v. **1** make a mistake. **2** do wrong.
errand n. a short journey to deliver or collect something.
▷ SYNONYMS: **task**, job, chore, assignment, mission.
errant adj. doing something wrong.
erratic adj. happening or acting in an irregular way.
▷ SYNONYMS: **unpredictable**, inconsistent, changeable, variable, inconstant, irregular, fitful, unstable, varying, fluctuating, unreliable.
− ANTONYMS: consistent.
■ **erratically** adv.
erratum n. (pl. errata) an error in a printed work.
erroneous adj. incorrect.
error n. **1** a mistake. **2** the state of being wrong.
▷ SYNONYMS: **mistake**, inaccuracy, miscalculation, blunder, slip, oversight, misconception, delusion, misprint; Brit. informal boob.
ersatz adj. used as a poor-quality substitute.
erstwhile adj. former.
erudite adj. knowledgeable or learned.
■ **erudition** n.
erupt v. **1** (of a volcano) throw out lava etc. **2** express emotion in a

sudden and noisy way.
▷ SYNONYMS: *fighting erupted on the border:* **break out,** flare up, blow up, explode, burst out.

eruption n. the action or an instance or erupting.
▷ SYNONYMS: *an eruption of violence:* **outbreak,** flare-up, upsurge, outburst, explosion, wave, spate.

escalate v. increase in intensity or extent.
▷ SYNONYMS: **1 increase rapidly,** soar, rocket, shoot up, spiral; *informal* go through the roof. **2 grow,** develop, mushroom, increase, heighten, intensify, accelerate.
– ANTONYMS: plunge, subside.
■ **escalation** n.

escalator n. a moving staircase.

escalope n. a thin slice of meat coated in breadcrumbs and fried.

escapade n. a daring and adventurous act.

escape v. **1** get free from. **2** succeed in avoiding. **3** fail to be noticed or remembered by. **4** (of gas or liquid) leak from a container.
▷ SYNONYMS: **1 run away,** run off, get away, break out, break free, bolt, make your getaway, slip away, abscond; *informal* vamoose, skedaddle, fly the coop; *Brit. informal* do a runner, do a bunk. **2** *he escaped his pursuers:* **get away from,** elude, avoid, dodge, shake off; *informal* give someone the slip. **3** *they cannot escape their duties:* **avoid,** evade, elude, cheat, sidestep, circumvent, steer clear of, shirk. **4** leak, spill, seep, flow, pour.
● n. an act or means of escaping.
▷ SYNONYMS: **getaway,** breakout, flight.
■ **escapee** n. **escaper** n.

escapement n. a mechanism regulating the movement of a clock or watch.

escapism n. indulging in enjoyable activities so as to ignore unpleasant realities.
■ **escapist** n. & adj.

escapologist n. an entertainer whose act involves breaking free from ropes, handcuffs, etc.
■ **escapology** n.

escarpment n. a steep slope at the edge of an area of high ground.

eschew v. deliberately avoid doing.

escort n. **1** a person, vehicle, or group accompanying another to protect or honour them. **2** a person accompanying a member of the opposite sex to a social event.
▷ SYNONYMS: **guard,** bodyguard, protector, minder, attendant, chaperone, entourage, retinue, protection, convoy.
● v. accompany as an escort.
▷ SYNONYMS: **1 conduct,** accompany, guide, usher, shepherd, take, lead. **2 partner,** accompany, chaperone.

escritoire /ess-kri-**twar**/ n. a writing desk with drawers.

escudo n. (pl. **escudos**) the former basic unit of money of Portugal.

escutcheon n. a shield bearing a coat of arms.

Eskimo n. (pl. **Eskimo** or **Eskimos**) a member of a people inhabiting northern Canada, Alaska, Greenland, and eastern Siberia.

> USAGE Many of the peoples traditionally called **Eskimos** now prefer to call themselves **Inuit**; **Inuit** is the official term in Canada.

esophagus US = OESOPHAGUS.

esoteric adj. intended for or understood by only a few people with specialized knowledge.
▷ SYNONYMS: **abstruse,** obscure, arcane, rarefied, recondite, abstract, enigmatic, cryptic, complex, complicated, incomprehensible, impenetrable, mysterious.

ESP abbrev. extrasensory perception.

espadrille n. a canvas shoe with a plaited fibre sole.

espalier n. a tree trained to grow against a wall.

especial adj. special; particular.

especially adv. **1** in particular. **2** to a great extent.
▷ SYNONYMS: **1 mainly,** mostly, chiefly, particularly, principally, largely, primarily. **2** *a committee formed especially for the purpose:* **expressly,** specially, specifically, exclusively, just, particularly, explicitly. **3** *he is especially talented:* **exceptionally,** particularly, unusually, extraordinarily, uncommonly, uniquely, remarkably, outstandingly.

Esperanto n. an artificial international language.

espionage n. spying.

esplanade n. a promenade.

espouse v. support or adopt a cause or way of life.
■ **espousal** n.

espresso n. (pl. **espressos**) strong black coffee made by forcing steam through ground coffee.

esprit de corps n. pride and loyalty uniting a group.

espy v. (**espying, espied**) catch sight of.

Esq. abbrev. Brit. Esquire, a polite title placed after a man's surname.

essay n. 1 a piece of writing on a particular subject. 2 an attempt.

▷ SYNONYMS: **article**, composition, paper, dissertation, thesis, discourse, study, assignment, treatise, piece, feature; N. Amer. theme.

• v. attempt.

■ **essayist** n.

essence n. 1 the quality which makes something what it is. 2 a concentrated extract obtained from a plant etc.

▷ SYNONYMS: **1 nature**, heart, core, substance, basis, principle, quint-essence, soul, spirit, reality; informal nitty-gritty. **2 extract**, concentrate, elixir, juice, oil.

essential adj. 1 absolutely necessary. 2 central to something's nature.

▷ SYNONYMS: **1 crucial**, key, vital, indispensable, all-important, critical, imperative. **2 basic**, inherent, funda-mental, quintessential, intrinsic, underlying, characteristic, innate, primary.

– ANTONYMS: unimportant, incidental.

• n. (**essentials**) **1** essential things. **2** the basic elements.

▷ SYNONYMS: **1 necessity**, prerequisite; informal must. **2** (**essentials**) fundamentals, basics, rudiments, first principles, foundations, essence, basis, core, kernel, crux; informal nitty-gritty, nuts and bolts.

□ **essential oil** a natural oil extracted from a plant.

■ **essentially** adv.

establish v. 1 set up on a firm or permanent basis. 2 make accepted by others. 3 find out facts.

▷ SYNONYMS: **1 set up**, start, initiate, institute, found, create, inaugurate. **2 prove**, demonstrate, show, indicate, determine, confirm.

established adj. having existed for a long time and so generally accepted.

▷ SYNONYMS: **accepted**, traditional, orthodox, set, fixed, official, usual, customary, common, normal, general, prevailing, accustomed, familiar, expected, conventional, standard.

establishment n. 1 the act of establishing. 2 an organization. 3 (**the Establishment**) the group in society who control policy and resist change.

▷ SYNONYMS: **1 foundation**, institution, formation, inception, creation, instal-lation, inauguration. **2 business**, firm, company, concern, enterprise, venture, organization, operation; informal outfit. **3 institution**, place,

premises, institute. **4** criticism of the Establishment: **the authorities**, the powers that be, the system, the ruling class.

estate n. 1 a large house with extensive grounds. 2 Brit. a residential or industrial area planned as a unit. 3 the money and property owned by a person at the time of their death.

▷ SYNONYMS: **1 property**, grounds, gardens, park, parkland, land, territory. **2** an industrial estate: **area**, development, complex. **3 plantation**, farm, holding, forest, vineyard; N. Amer. ranch. **4 assets**, capital, wealth, riches, holdings, fortune, property, effects, possessions, belongings.

□ **estate agent** a person who sells and rents out houses etc. for clients.

estate car Brit. a car with a large storage area behind the seats and a rear door.

esteem n. respect and admiration.

▷ SYNONYMS: **respect**, admiration, acclaim, appreciation, recognition, honour, reverence, estimation, regard.

• v. respect and admire.

▷ SYNONYMS: **respect**, admire, value, regard highly, appreciate, like, prize, treasure, revere.

esthete etc. US = AESTHETE etc.

estimable adj. worthy of great respect.

estimate v. roughly calculate the amount, value, etc. of.

▷ SYNONYMS: **1 calculate**, approximate, guess, evaluate, judge, assess, weigh up. **2 consider**, believe, reckon, deem, judge, rate.

• n. **1** a rough calculation. **2** a written statement of the likely price for work to be carried out.

▷ SYNONYMS: **calculation**, approxi-mation, estimation, guess, assess-ment, evaluation, costing, quotation, valuation; informal guesstimate.

■ **estimation** n.

estranged adj. **1** no longer close to or friendly with someone. **2** (of a person's husband or wife) no longer living with them.

■ **estrangement** n.

estrogen US = OESTROGEN.

estuary n. (pl. **estuaries**) the mouth of a large river where it becomes affected by tides.

■ **estuarine** adj.

et al. abbrev. and others.

etc. abbrev. et cetera.

et cetera adv. and other similar things.

etch v. **1** produce a picture by engraving a metal plate with acid. **2** fix clearly in the mind.
▷ SYNONYMS: **engrave**, carve, inscribe, incise, score, mark, scratch.
■ **etching** n.

eternal adj. lasting forever.
▷ SYNONYMS: **everlasting**, never-ending, endless, perpetual, undying, immortal, abiding, permanent, enduring, constant, continual, continuous, sustained, uninterrupted, unbroken, non-stop, round-the-clock.
■ **eternally** adv.

eternity n. (pl. **eternities**) **1** unending time. **2** informal a very long period of time.
▷ SYNONYMS: **1 ever**, all time, perpetuity. **2 a long time**, an age, ages, a lifetime, hours, years, forever.

ether n. **1** a liquid used as an anaesthetic and solvent. **2** the upper regions of the air.

ethereal adj. **1** very delicate and light. **2** heavenly or spiritual.

ethic n. **1** a moral principle. **2** (**ethics**) the study of moral principles.
▷ SYNONYMS: **morals**, morality, values, principles, ideals, standards.

ethical adj. **1** of moral principles. **2** morally correct.
▷ SYNONYMS: **moral**, morally correct, right-minded, principled, good, just, honourable, fair.
■ **ethically** adv.

ethnic adj. of a group of people sharing a common origin, culture, or language.
▷ SYNONYMS: **racial**, race-related, national, cultural, folk, tribal, ethnological.
□ **ethnic cleansing** the expelling or killing of members of one ethnic or religious group in an area by those of another.
■ **ethnically** adv. **ethnicity** n.

ethnology n. the study of the characteristics of different peoples.
■ **ethnologist** n.

ethos n. the characteristic spirit of a culture, era, or community.

ethylene n. a flammable hydrocarbon gas.

etiolated adj. (of a plant) pale and weak due to a lack of light.

etiquette n. the rules of polite behaviour in a society.

etymology n. (pl. **etymologies**) an account of a word's origins and development.
■ **etymological** adj.

EU abbrev. European Union.

eucalyptus n. an evergreen Australasian tree important for its oil.

Eucharist n. **1** the Christian ceremony commemorating the Last Supper, in which consecrated bread and wine are consumed. **2** this bread and wine.

eugenics n. the science of improving a population by controlled breeding.

eulogy n. (pl. **eulogies**) a speech or piece of writing praising someone.
■ **eulogize** (or **-ise**) v.

eunuch n. a castrated man.

euphemism n. a less direct word used instead of an offensive one.
■ **euphemistic** adj. **euphemistically** adv.

euphonious /yoo-foh-ni-uhss/ adj. sounding pleasant.
■ **euphony** n.

euphoria n. great happiness.
▷ SYNONYMS: **elation**, happiness, joy, delight, glee, excitement, exhilaration, jubilation, exultation, ecstasy, bliss, rapture.
– ANTONYMS: misery.
■ **euphoric** adj.

Eurasian adj. **1** of mixed European and Asian parentage. **2** of Europe and Asia.

eureka exclam. a cry of joy on discovering something.

eurhythmics pl. n. physical exercises to music.

euro n. the basic unit of money in twelve states of the European Union.

European n. a person from Europe.
• adj. of Europe or the European Union.
□ **European Union** an economic and political association of certain European countries.

Eustachian tube /yoo-stay-sh'n/ n. a passage between the ear and the throat.

euthanasia n. the painless killing of a person with an incurable illness.

evacuate v. **1** send from a place of danger to somewhere safer. **2** empty the bowels.
▷ SYNONYMS: **1 remove**, move out, take away. **2 leave**, vacate, abandon, move out of, quit, withdraw from, retreat from, flee. **3** police evacuated the area: **clear**, empty.
■ **evacuation** n. **evacuee** n.

evade v. avoid doing, dealing with, etc.
▷ SYNONYMS: **1 elude**, avoid, dodge, escape, steer clear of, sidestep, lose, leave behind, shake off; informal give someone the slip. **2 avoid**, dodge, sidestep, bypass, skirt round, fudge; informal duck, cop out of.
– ANTONYMS: confront.

e

evaluate v. assess the amount or value of.
▷ SYNONYMS: **assess**, judge, gauge, rate, estimate, appraise, weigh up; informal size up.
■ evaluation n. evaluator n.
evanescent adj. quickly fading.
■ evanescence n.
evangelical adj. **1** of a tradition within Protestant Christianity which emphasizes biblical authority and salvation through personal faith in Jesus. **2** of the teaching of the gospel. **3** passionately supporting something.
■ evangelicalism n.
evangelist n. **1** a person who tries to convert others to Christianity. **2** the writer of one of the four Gospels.
■ evangelism n. evangelistic adj.
evaporate v. **1** turn from liquid into vapour. **2** disappear.
▷ SYNONYMS: **1 vaporize**, dry up. **2 end**, fizzle out, peter out, wear off, vanish, fade, disappear, melt away.
– ANTONYMS: condense, materialize.
■ evaporation n.
evasion n. the act of evading.
evasive adj. intended to avoid something.
▷ SYNONYMS: **equivocal**, prevaricating, elusive, ambiguous, non-committal, vague, unclear, oblique.
■ evasively adv. evasiveness n.
eve n. the day or period immediately before an event.
even adj. **1** level. **2** equal in number, amount, or value. **3** regular or balanced. **4** (of a number) exactly divisible by two.
▷ SYNONYMS: **1 flat**, smooth, uniform, level, plane. **2 uniform**, constant, steady, stable, consistent, unvarying, unchanging, regular. **3 all square**, drawn, tied, level, neck and neck, nip and tuck; Brit. level pegging; informal even-stevens.
– ANTONYMS: uneven, bumpy, irregular.
● v. make or become even.
● adv. used for emphasis: *even less*.
■ evenly adv. evenness n.
evening n. the period of time at the end of the day.
▷ SYNONYMS: **dusk**, twilight, nightfall, sunset, sundown, night.
evensong n. (in the Anglican Church) an evening service.
event n. **1** a thing that happens. **2** a public or social occasion. **3** a contest forming part of a sports competition.
▷ SYNONYMS: **1 occurrence**, happening, incident, affair, occasion, phenomenon, function, gathering; informal do.

2 competition, contest, tournament, match, fixture, race, game, sport, discipline.
eventful adj. marked by exciting events.
▷ SYNONYMS: **busy**, action-packed, full, lively, active, hectic.
– ANTONYMS: dull, uneventful.
eventual adj. occurring at the end of a process or period.
▷ SYNONYMS: **final**, ultimate, resulting, ensuing, consequent, subsequent.
eventuality n. (pl. **eventualities**) a possible event.
eventually adv. in the end.
▷ SYNONYMS: **in the end**, in due course, by and by, in time, after a time, finally, at last, ultimately, in the long run, at the end of the day, one day, some day, sometime, sooner or later.
ever adv. **1** at any time. **2** always.
▷ SYNONYMS: **1 at any time**, at any point, on any occasion, under any circumstances, on any account, until now. **2 always**, forever, eternally, continually, constantly, endlessly, perpetually, incessantly.
□ **evergreen** a plant having green leaves throughout the year.
everlasting adj. lasting forever or a very long time.
▷ SYNONYMS: **eternal**, endless, never-ending, perpetual, undying, abiding, enduring, infinite.
– ANTONYMS: transient, occasional.
evermore adv. forever.
every adj. **1** each without exception. **2** happening at specified intervals: *every three months*. **3** all possible: *every effort was made*.
everybody (or **everyone**) pron. every person.
▷ SYNONYMS: **everyone**, every person, each person, all, one and all, all and sundry, the whole world, the public.
– ANTONYMS: nobody, no one.
everyday adj. **1** daily. **2** ordinary.
▷ SYNONYMS: **1 daily**, day-to-day, ongoing; formal quotidian. **2 commonplace**, ordinary, common, usual, regular, familiar, conventional, routine, run-of-the-mill, standard, stock, household, domestic; Brit. common or garden.
– ANTONYMS: unusual.
everything pron. all things.
everywhere adv. in or to all places.
▷ SYNONYMS: **all over**, all around, far and wide, near and far, high and low, {here, there, and everywhere}, the world over, worldwide; informal all over the place; Brit. informal all over the shop;

N. Amer. informal **all over the map.**
– ANTONYMS: nowhere.

evict v. legally force to leave a property.
▷ SYNONYMS: **expel**, eject, remove, dislodge, turn out, throw out, drive out, dispossess; informal chuck out, kick out, boot out, throw someone out on their ear; Brit. informal turf out.
■ **eviction** n.

evidence n. **1** information indicating whether something is true or valid. **2** information presented in a law court to support a case.
▷ SYNONYMS: **1 proof**, confirmation, verification, substantiation, corroboration. **2 testimony**, witness statement, declaration, submission; Law deposition, affidavit. **3 signs**, indications, marks, traces, suggestions, hints.
• v. be evidence of.
□ **in evidence** noticeable.

evident adj. clear or obvious.
▷ SYNONYMS: **obvious**, apparent, noticeable, conspicuous, visible, discernible, clear, plain, manifest, patent, unmistakable; informal as clear as day.
■ **evidently** adv.

evil adj. **1** very immoral and wicked. **2** very unpleasant.
▷ SYNONYMS: **1** an evil deed: **wicked**, bad, wrong, immoral, sinful, vile, iniquitous, villainous, vicious, malicious, malevolent, demonic, diabolical, fiendish, dark, monstrous. **2** an evil spirit: **harmful**, bad, malign. **3 unpleasant**, disagreeable, nasty, horrible, foul, filthy, vile.
– ANTONYMS: good, virtuous.
• n. **1** extreme wickedness. **2** something harmful or undesirable.
▷ SYNONYMS: **1** the evil in our midst: **wickedness**, badness, wrongdoing, sin, sinfulness, immorality, vice, iniquity, corruption, villainy. **2** nothing but evil will result: **harm**, pain, misery, sorrow, suffering, trouble, disaster, misfortune, woe.
– ANTONYMS: good.
■ **evilly** adv.

evince v. show or indicate.

eviscerate v. disembowel.

evoke v. **1** bring a feeling or image to the mind. **2** obtain a response.
▷ SYNONYMS: **bring to mind**, put someone in mind of, conjure up, summon up, invoke, elicit, induce, kindle, awaken, arouse.
■ **evocation** n. **evocative** adj.

evolution n. **1** the process by which different kinds of living organism

develop from earlier forms. **2** gradual development.
▷ SYNONYMS: **1 development**, progress, rise, expansion, growth. **2 natural selection**, Darwinism, adaptation, development.
■ **evolutionary** adj.

evolve v. **1** develop gradually. **2** (of an organism) develop by evolution.
▷ SYNONYMS: **develop**, progress, advance, grow, expand, spread.

ewe n. a female sheep.

ewer n. a large jug.

ex n. informal a former spouse or partner.

exacerbate v. make something bad worse.
▷ SYNONYMS: **aggravate**, worsen, inflame, compound, intensify, increase, heighten, magnify, add to.
– ANTONYMS: reduce.
■ **exacerbation** n.

exact adj. **1** correct in all details. **2** precise.
▷ SYNONYMS: **1** an exact description: **precise**, accurate, correct, faithful, close, true, literal, strict, perfect. **2** an exact record keeper: **careful**, meticulous, painstaking, punctilious, conscientious, scrupulous.
– ANTONYMS: inaccurate, careless.
• v. **1** demand and obtain. **2** inflict revenge.
▷ SYNONYMS: **1 demand**, require, impose, extract, compel, force, wring. **2 inflict**, impose, administer, mete out, wreak.
■ **exactness** n.

exacting adj. demanding much effort or skill.
▷ SYNONYMS: **demanding**, stringent, testing, challenging, arduous, laborious, hard, taxing, gruelling, punishing, tough.
– ANTONYMS: easy, easy-going.

exactitude n. exactness.

exactly adv. **1** in an exact way. **2** used to express agreement.
▷ SYNONYMS: **1 precisely**, entirely, absolutely, completely, totally, just, quite, in every respect. **2 accurately**, precisely, unerringly, faultlessly, perfectly, faithfully.

exaggerate v. make something seem larger, better, etc. than in reality.
▷ SYNONYMS: **overstate**, overemphasize, overestimate, inflate, embellish, embroider, elaborate, overplay, dramatize; Brit. informal blow out of all proportion.
– ANTONYMS: understate.
■ **exaggeration** n.

exalt v. **1** praise highly. **2** raise to a

higher rank.

exaltation n. extreme happiness.

exam n. an examination.

examination n. **1** a detailed inspection. **2** a formal test of knowledge or ability.

▷ SYNONYMS: **1** *items spread out for examination:* **scrutiny**, inspection, perusal, study, investigation, consideration, analysis. **2** *a medical examination:* **inspection**, check-up, assessment, appraisal, test, scan. **3** *a school examination:* **test**, exam, assessment; N. Amer. quiz.

examine v. **1** inspect closely. **2** test the knowledge or ability of.

▷ SYNONYMS: **1** **inspect**, scrutinize, investigate, look at, study, appraise, analyse, review, survey; informal check out. **2** **test**, quiz, question, assess, appraise.

■ **examinee** n. **examiner** n.

example n. **1** a thing typical of its kind or illustrating a general rule. **2** a person or thing worthy of being copied.

▷ SYNONYMS: **1** **specimen**, sample, instance, case, illustration. **2** **precedent**, lead, model, pattern, ideal, standard. **3** **warning**, lesson, deterrent, disincentive.

□ **make an example of** punish as a warning to others.

exasperate v. greatly irritate.

▷ SYNONYMS: **infuriate**, anger, annoy, irritate, madden, provoke, irk, vex, gall, get on someone's nerves; Brit. rub up the wrong way; informal aggravate, rile, bug, hack off; Brit. informal nark, get on someone's wick; N. Amer. informal tee off, tick off.

■ **exasperation** n.

excavate v. **1** make a hole by digging. **2** remove earth from an area to find buried remains.

▷ SYNONYMS: **unearth**, dig up, uncover, reveal, disinter, exhume, dig out, quarry, mine.

■ **excavation** n. **excavator** n.

exceed v. **1** be greater than. **2** go beyond the limit of.

▷ SYNONYMS: **be more than**, be greater than, be over, go beyond, top, surpass.

exceedingly adv. extremely.

excel v. (**excelling**, **excelled**) **1** be very good at. **2** (**excel yourself**) perform exceptionally well.

▷ SYNONYMS: **shine**, be excellent, be outstanding, be skilful, be talented, stand out, be second to none.

excellence n. the quality of being excellent.

▷ SYNONYMS: **distinction**, quality, superiority, supremacy, brilliance, greatness, calibre, eminence.

Excellency n. a form of address for certain high officials of state.

excellent adj. very good.

▷ SYNONYMS: **very good**, outstanding, superb, supreme, exceptional, marvellous, wonderful, splendid; informal terrific, fantastic.

– ANTONYMS: inferior.

■ **excellently** adv.

except prep. not including.

▷ SYNONYMS: **excluding**, not including, excepting, except for, omitting, not counting, but, besides, apart from, aside from, barring, bar, other than; informal outside of.

• v. exclude.

> USAGE Don't forget the c in **except** and related words.

excepting prep. except for.

exception n. a person or thing that is excluded or does not follow a rule.

▷ SYNONYMS: **anomaly**, irregularity, deviation, special case, peculiarity, abnormality, oddity.

□ **take exception to** object to.

exceptionable adj. causing disapproval or offence.

exceptional adj. **1** not typical; unusual. **2** unusually good.

▷ SYNONYMS: **1** *the drought was exceptional:* **unusual**, abnormal, atypical, out of the ordinary, rare, unprecedented, unexpected, surprising. **2** *her exceptional ability:* **outstanding**, extraordinary, remarkable, special, phenomenal, prodigious.

– ANTONYMS: normal, average.

■ **exceptionally** adv.

excerpt n. a short extract from a film, book, etc.

▷ SYNONYMS: **extract**, part, section, piece, portion, snippet, clip, citation, quotation, quote, line, passage, fragment.

excess n. **1** an amount more than necessary, allowed, or desirable. **2** (**excesses**) outrageous behaviour.

▷ SYNONYMS: **1** **surplus**, surfeit, over-abundance, superabundance, superfluity, glut. **2** **remainder**, leftovers, extra, rest, residue. **3** **over-indulgence**, intemperance, immoderation, profligacy, extravagance, self-indulgence.

– ANTONYMS: lack, restraint.

• adj. exceeding a limit.

▷ SYNONYMS: *excess oil:* **surplus**, superfluous, redundant, unwanted, unneeded, excessive, extra.

excessive adj. too much.
▷ SYNONYMS: **1 immoderate**, intemperate, overindulgent, unrestrained, uncontrolled, extravagant. **2 exorbitant**, extortionate, unreasonable, outrageous, uncalled for, inordinate, unwarranted, disproportionate; informal over the top.
■ **excessively** adv.

exchange v. give something and receive another thing.
▷ SYNONYMS: **trade**, swap, switch, change.
● n. **1** an act of exchanging. **2** a short conversation. **3** the changing of money for its equivalent in another currency. **4** a building used for trading. **5** a centre where phone lines are connected.
▷ SYNONYMS: **1 interchange**, trade, trading, swapping, traffic, trafficking. **2 conversation**, dialogue, chat, talk, discussion.
■ **exchangeable** adj.

exchequer n. a national treasury.

excise n. a tax on certain goods.
● v. cut out.
■ **excision** n.

excitable adj. easily excited.
▷ SYNONYMS: **temperamental**, volatile, mercurial, emotional, sensitive, highly strung, tempestuous, hot-headed, fiery.
– ANTONYMS: placid.
■ **excitability** n. **excitably** adv.

excite v. **1** make very enthusiastic and eager. **2** arouse sexually. **3** give rise to.
▷ SYNONYMS: **1 thrill**, exhilarate, animate, enliven, rouse, stir, stimulate, galvanize. **2 provoke**, stir up, rouse, arouse, kindle, trigger, spark off, incite, cause.
– ANTONYMS: bore.
■ **excitation** n.

excitement n. **1** great enthusiasm and eagerness. **2** a cause of this.
▷ SYNONYMS: **1** *the excitement of seeing a leopard in the wild:* **thrill**, pleasure, delight, joy; informal kick, buzz. **2** *the excitement in her eyes:* **exhilaration**, elation, animation, enthusiasm, eagerness, anticipation.

exciting adj. causing great interest and eagerness.
▷ SYNONYMS: **thrilling**, exhilarating, stirring, rousing, stimulating, intoxicating, electrifying, invigorating, gripping, compelling, powerful, dramatic.

exclaim v. cry out suddenly.
▷ SYNONYMS: **cry out**, declare, proclaim, blurt out, call out, shout, yell.

exclamation n. a sudden cry or remark.

□ **exclamation mark** a punctuation mark (!) indicating an exclamation.
■ **exclamatory** adj.

exclude v. **1** prevent from being a part of something. **2** choose not to include for consideration.
▷ SYNONYMS: **1 keep out**, deny access to, shut out, bar, ban, prohibit. **2 rule out**, preclude. **3 be exclusive of**, not include.
– ANTONYMS: admit, include.
■ **exclusion** n.

exclusive adj. **1** restricted to the person, group, or area concerned. **2** high-class and expensive. **3** excluding something.
▷ SYNONYMS: **1 select**, chic, high-class, elite, fashionable, stylish, elegant, premier; Brit. upmarket; informal posh, classy; Brit. informal swish. **2 sole**, unshared, unique, individual, personal, private. **3** *prices exclusive of VAT:* **not including**, excluding, leaving out, omitting, excepting.
– ANTONYMS: inclusive.
● n. a story published in only one newspaper etc.
■ **exclusively** adv. **exclusivity** n.

excommunicate v. officially bar from the sacraments and services of a Church.
■ **excommunication** n.

excoriate v. **1** criticize severely. **2** remove part of the skin.
■ **excoriation** n.

excrement n. waste matter discharged from the bowels.

excrescence n. an abnormal growth on an animal or plant.

excreta n. waste discharged from the body.

excrete v. discharge waste material from the body.
■ **excretion** n. **excretory** adj.

excruciating adj. **1** very painful. **2** very embarrassing or tedious.
▷ SYNONYMS: **agonizing**, severe, acute, intense, violent, racking, searing, piercing, stabbing, unbearable, unendurable; informal splitting, killing.

excursion n. a short journey taken for pleasure.
▷ SYNONYMS: **outing**, trip, jaunt, expedition, journey, tour, day out, drive, run; informal spin.

excuse v. **1** justify or defend a fault or offence. **2** release from a duty. **3** forgive.
▷ SYNONYMS: **1 forgive**, pardon. **2 justify**, defend, condone, forgive, overlook, disregard, ignore, tolerate, explain, mitigate. **3 let off**, release, relieve,

exempt, absolve, free.
- ANTONYMS: punish, condemn.
  • n. a reason put forward to justify a fault or offence.
▷ SYNONYMS: **1 justification**, defence, reason, explanation, mitigating circumstances, mitigation. **2 pretext**, pretence; Brit. get-out; informal story, alibi.
■ **excusable** adj.

ex-directory adj. Brit. not listed in a phone directory at your own request.

execrable adj. very bad or unpleasant.

execrate v. loathe.
■ **execration** n.

execute v. **1** carry out a plan, order, etc. **2** perform an action. **3** kill a condemned person as a legal punishment.
▷ SYNONYMS: **1 carry out**, accomplish, bring off/about, implement, achieve, complete, engineer; informal pull off. **2 put to death**, kill, hang, behead, electrocute, shoot.
■ **executioner** n.

execution n. **1** the carrying out of something. **2** the killing of a person who has been condemned to death.
▷ SYNONYMS: **1 implementation**, carrying out, performance, accomplishment, bringing off/about, attainment, realization. **2 killing**, capital punishment, the death penalty.

executive n. **1** a senior manager or managerial group in an organization. **2** (**the executive**) the branch of a government responsible for putting plans or laws into effect.
▷ SYNONYMS: **1 director**, manager, senior official, administrator; informal boss, exec, suit. **2 administration**, management, directorate, government, authority.
  • adj. having the power to put plans, actions, or laws into effect.
▷ SYNONYMS: **administrative**, managerial, decision-making, law-making, governing, controlling.

executor n. a person appointed to carry out the terms of a will.

exemplar n. a typical example or model.

exemplary adj. **1** giving a good example to others. **2** serving as a warning.
▷ SYNONYMS: **perfect**, ideal, model, faultless, flawless, impeccable, irreproachable.
- ANTONYMS: deplorable.

exemplify v. (**exemplifying**, **exemplified**) be or give a typical example of.
▷ SYNONYMS: **typify**, epitomize, be an example of, be representative of, symbolize, illustrate, demonstrate.
■ **exemplification** n.

exempt adj. free from a requirement or duty imposed on others.
▷ SYNONYMS: **free**, not liable, not subject, immune, excepted, excused, absolved.
  • v. make exempt.
▷ SYNONYMS: **excuse**, free, release, exclude, grant immunity, spare, absolve; informal let off.

exemption n. the state of being exempt from something.
▷ SYNONYMS: **immunity**, exception, dispensation, indemnity, exclusion, freedom, release, relief, absolution.

exercise n. **1** physical activity carried out to improve health and fitness. **2** a task set to practise or test a skill. **3** the use of a power, right, etc.
▷ SYNONYMS: **1 physical activity**, a workout, working out, training. **2 task**, piece of work, problem, assignment, practice. **3 manoeuvre**, operation, deployment.
  • v. **1** use a power, right, etc. **2** do physical exercise. **3** worry or puzzle.
▷ SYNONYMS: **1 use**, employ, make use of, utilize, practise, apply. **2 work out**, do exercises, train. **3 concern**, occupy, worry, trouble, bother, disturb, prey on someone's mind, puzzle.

exert v. **1** apply a force, influence, or quality. **2** (**exert yourself**) make an effort.
▷ SYNONYMS: **bring to bear**, apply, use, utilize, deploy.
■ **exertion** n.

exfoliate v. rub the skin with a rough substance to remove dead cells.
■ **exfoliation** n.

ex gratia /eks gray-shuh/ adv. & adj. (of payment) given as a gift or favour rather than a legal requirement.

exhale v. **1** breathe out. **2** give off vapour or fumes.
■ **exhalation** n.

exhaust v. **1** tire out. **2** use up resources completely.
▷ SYNONYMS: **1 tire out**, wear out, over-tire, fatigue, weary, drain; informal take it out of someone, shatter; Brit. informal knacker; N. Amer. informal poop, tucker out. **2 use up**, get through, consume, finish, deplete, spend, empty, drain; informal blow.
- ANTONYMS: invigorate, replenish.
  • n. **1** waste gases discharged from an engine. **2** the device through which waste gases are discharged.

■ **exhaustible** adj.

exhausting adj. making you feel very tired.

▷ SYNONYMS: **tiring**, wearying, taxing, wearing, draining, arduous, strenuous, onerous, demanding, gruelling; informal killing; Brit. informal knackering.

exhaustion n. extreme tiredness.

▷ SYNONYMS: **tiredness**, fatigue, weariness, debility, enervation.

exhaustive adj. covering all aspects fully.

■ **exhaustively** adv.

exhibit v. **1** put on public display. **2** display a quality.

▷ SYNONYMS: **1 put on display**, show, display, unveil, present. **2 show**, reveal, display, manifest, indicate, demonstrate, express, evince, evidence.

• n. an object on public display.

▷ SYNONYMS: **item**, piece, artefact, display, collection.

■ **exhibitor** n.

exhibition n. **1** a public display in an art gallery, museum, etc. **2** a display of a skill or quality.

▷ SYNONYMS: **1 exposition**, display, show, showing, presentation. **2 display**, show, demonstration, manifestation, expression.

exhibitionism n. behaviour intended to attract attention.

■ **exhibitionist** n.

exhilarate v. make very happy or lively.

■ **exhilaration** n.

┌─────────────────────────────────────┐
│ USAGE -arate not -erate: exhilarate. │
└─────────────────────────────────────┘

exhilarating adj. very exciting and enjoyable.

▷ SYNONYMS: **thrilling**, exciting, invigorating, stimulating, intoxicating, electrifying.

exhort v. strongly urge to do something.

▷ SYNONYMS: **urge**, encourage, call on, enjoin, charge, press, bid, appeal to, entreat, implore; literary beseech.

■ **exhortation** n.

exhume v. dig up a buried corpse.

exigency n. (pl. **exigencies**) an urgent need or demand.

■ **exigent** adj.

exiguous adj. very small.

exile n. **1** the state of being barred from your native country. **2** a person who lives in exile.

▷ SYNONYMS: **1 banishment**, expulsion, deportation, eviction, isolation. **2 expatriate**, émigré, deportee, displaced person, refugee.

• v. send into exile.

exist v. **1** be real or present. **2** live.

▷ SYNONYMS: **1 prevail**, occur, be found, be in existence, be the case; formal obtain. **2 live**, be alive, be present. **3 survive**, subsist, live, support yourself, manage, make do, get by, scrape by, make ends meet, eke out a living.

■ **existent** adj.

existence n. **1** the fact of state or existing. **2** a way of life.

▷ SYNONYMS: **1 survival**, continuation. **2 way of life**, life, lifestyle, situation.

existential adj. of existence or existentialism.

existentialism n. a philosophical theory emphasizing individuals' freedom to choose their own actions.

■ **existentialist** n. & adj.

exit n. **1** a way out. **2** an act of leaving.

▷ SYNONYMS: **1 way out**, door, escape route, egress. **2 turning**, turn-off, junction. **3 departure**, leaving, withdrawal, going, retreat, flight, exodus, escape.

– ANTONYMS: entrance, arrival.

• v. (**exiting**, **exited**) go out of or leave a place.

▷ SYNONYMS: **leave**, go out, depart, withdraw, retreat.

– ANTONYMS: enter.

exodus n. a mass departure of people.

ex officio adv. & adj. as a result of a person's position or status.

exonerate v. declare free from blame.

▷ SYNONYMS: **absolve**, clear, acquit, find innocent, discharge; formal exculpate.

– ANTONYMS: convict.

■ **exoneration** n.

exorbitant adj. (of a price) unreasonably high.

▷ SYNONYMS: **extortionate**, excessive, prohibitive, outrageous, unreasonable, inflated; Brit. over the odds; informal steep, stiff, a rip-off; Brit. informal daylight robbery.

– ANTONYMS: cheap.

■ **exorbitantly** adv.

exorcize (or **-ise**) v. drive out an evil spirit from a person or place.

■ **exorcism** n. **exorcist** n.

exotic adj. **1** coming from or characteristic of a distant foreign country. **2** strikingly colourful or unusual.

▷ SYNONYMS: **1** exotic birds: **foreign**, non-native, alien, tropical. **2** exotic places: **foreign**, faraway, far-off, far-flung, distant. **3 striking**, colourful, eye-catching, unusual, unconventional, extravagant, outlandish.

e

■ **exotically** adv. **exoticism** n.

expand v. **1** make or become larger.
2 (**expand on**) give a fuller account of.
▷ SYNONYMS: **1** *metals expand when
heated:* **enlarge**, swell, lengthen,
stretch, spread, thicken, fill out. **2** *the
company is expanding:* **grow**, enlarge,
increase in size, extend, augment,
broaden, widen, develop, diversify,
build up, branch out, spread.
– ANTONYMS: contract.
■ **expandable** adj.

expanse n. a wide continuous area.
▷ SYNONYMS: **area**, stretch, sweep, tract,
swathe, belt, region, sea, carpet,
blanket, sheet.

expansion n. the process of
expanding.
▷ SYNONYMS: **growth**, enlargement,
extension, development, diversification, spread.
– ANTONYMS: contraction.

expansive adj. **1** covering a wide area.
2 friendly and communicative.
■ **expansively** adv.

expatiate /ik-spay-shi-ayt/ v.
(**expatiate on**) speak or write in
detail about.

expatriate n. a person who lives
outside their native country.

expect v. **1** regard as likely to
happen. **2** regard as likely to do or be
something. **3** require or demand as a
person's duty.
▷ SYNONYMS: **1 anticipate**, envisage,
await, look for, hope for, look forward
to, contemplate, bargain for/on,
predict, forecast. **2 suppose**, presume,
imagine, assume, surmise; informal
guess, reckon; N. Amer. informal figure.
3 require, ask for, call for, want,
insist on, demand.

expectant adj. **1** filled with
anticipation. **2** pregnant.
■ **expectancy** n. **expectantly** adv.

expectation n. the belief that
something will happen, or a thing
that is expected to happen.
▷ SYNONYMS: **1 anticipation**, expectancy, eagerness, excitement,
suspense. **2 supposition**, assumption,
presumption, conjecture, calculation,
prediction, hope.

expectorant n. a cough medicine
which helps to bring up phlegm.

expectorate v. cough or spit out
phlegm.

expedient adj. helping to achieve
something, though possibly unfair or
immoral.
▷ SYNONYMS: **convenient**, advantageous,
useful, beneficial, helpful, practical,
pragmatic, politic, prudent, judicious.
● n. a means of achieving something.
▷ SYNONYMS: **measure**, means, method,
stratagem, scheme, plan, move, tactic,
manoeuvre, device, contrivance, ploy,
ruse.
■ **expediency** n.

expedite v. hasten the progress of.

expedition n. a journey made for a
particular purpose.
▷ SYNONYMS: **journey**, voyage, tour,
safari, trek, mission, quest, hike, trip.
■ **expeditionary** adj.

expeditious adj. quick and efficient.
■ **expeditiously** adv.

expel v. (**expelling, expelled**) **1** force
to leave a school, organization, or
place. **2** force out.
▷ SYNONYMS: **throw out**, bar, ban, debar,
drum out, banish, exile, deport, evict;
informal chuck out.
– ANTONYMS: admit.

expend v. spend or use up a resource.

expendable adj. able to be sacrificed
or abandoned to achieve an objective.

expenditure n. **1** the spending of
money etc. **2** the amount of money
spent.

expense n. **1** the cost of something.
2 (**expenses**) money spent in the
course of doing a job etc. **3** something
on which money must be spent.
▷ SYNONYMS: **cost**, expenditure, spending,
outlay, outgoings, payment, price,
charge, fees, overheads, tariff, bill.
– ANTONYMS: income, profit.

expensive adj. costing a lot of money.
▷ SYNONYMS: **costly**, dear, high-priced,
overpriced, exorbitant, extortionate;
informal steep, stiff, pricey.
– ANTONYMS: cheap, inexpensive.

experience n. **1** practical involvement
in an activity, event, etc. **2** knowledge
or skill gained over time. **3** an event
which affects someone.
▷ SYNONYMS: **1 skill**, practical knowledge, understanding, familiarity,
involvement, participation, contact,
acquaintance, exposure, background,
track record, history; informal know-
how. **2 incident**, occurrence, event,
happening, episode, adventure.
● v. **1** undergo or be affected by. **2** feel
an emotion.
▷ SYNONYMS: **undergo**, go through,
encounter, face, meet, come across,
come up against, come into contact
with.

experienced adj. having knowledge
or skill gained over time.
▷ SYNONYMS: **knowledgeable**, skilful,
skilled, expert, proficient, trained,

competent, capable, seasoned, practised, mature, veteran.

experiment n. **1** a scientific procedure to find out or prove something. **2** a new course of action with an uncertain outcome.
▷ SYNONYMS: **test**, investigation, trial, examination, observation, research, assessment, evaluation, appraisal, analysis, study.
• v. **1** perform a scientific experiment. **2** try out new things.
▷ SYNONYMS: **carry out experiments**, test, trial, try out, assess, appraise, evaluate.
■ **experimentation** n.

experimental adj. **1** based on new ideas and not yet fully tested or finalized. **2** relating to scientific experiments.
▷ SYNONYMS: **1 exploratory**, investigational, trial, test, pilot, speculative, tentative, preliminary. **2 new**, innovative, creative, radical, avant-garde, alternative, unorthodox, unconventional, cutting-edge.
■ **experimentally** adv.

expert n. a person having great knowledge or skill in a particular field.
▷ SYNONYMS: **specialist**, authority, professional, pundit, maestro, virtuoso, master, wizard, connoisseur, aficionado; informal ace, pro, hotshot; Brit. informal **dab hand**; N. Amer. informal maven.
– ANTONYMS: amateur.
• adj. having or involving great knowledge or skill.
▷ SYNONYMS: **skilful**, skilled, adept, accomplished, experienced, practised, knowledgeable, talented, masterly, virtuoso; informal ace, crack, mean.
– ANTONYMS: incompetent.
■ **expertly** adv.

expertise n. great skill or knowledge in a particular field.
▷ SYNONYMS: **skill**, prowess, proficiency, competence, knowledge, ability, aptitude, capability; informal know-how.

expiate v. make amends for.
■ **expiation** n.

expire v. **1** cease to be valid. **2** die. **3** breathe out air.
▷ SYNONYMS: **1 run out**, become invalid, become void, lapse, end, finish, stop, terminate. **2 die**, pass away, breathe your last; informal kick the bucket, croak; Brit. informal snuff it, peg out; N. Amer. informal buy the farm.

expiry n. the end of the period for which something is valid.

explain v. **1** make clear by giving a detailed description. **2** give a reason for.
▷ SYNONYMS: **1 describe**, make clear, spell out, put into words, define, elucidate, expound, clarify, throw light on. **2 account for**, justify, excuse.
■ **explanatory** adj.

explanation n. **1** a statement or description that makes something clear. **2** a reason or justification.
▷ SYNONYMS: **1 clarification**, description, statement, interpretation, definition, commentary. **2 account**, reason, justification, answer, excuse, defence, vindication.

expletive n. a swear word.

explicable adj. able to be explained.

explicit adj. clear, detailed, and unambiguous.
▷ SYNONYMS: **1 clear**, plain, straightforward, crystal clear, precise, exact, specific, unequivocal, unambiguous, detailed. **2 graphic**, candid, full-frontal, uncensored.
– ANTONYMS: vague.
■ **explicitly** adv.

explode v. **1** burst or shatter violently. **2** suddenly express emotion. **3** increase suddenly. **4** show a belief to be false.
▷ SYNONYMS: **1 blow up**, detonate, go off, burst, erupt. **2 lose your temper**, blow up; informal fly off the handle, hit the roof, blow your top; Brit. informal go spare; N. Amer. informal blow your lid/stack. **3 increase rapidly**, mushroom, snowball, escalate, burgeon, rocket. **4 disprove**, refute, rebut, repudiate, debunk, give the lie to; informal shoot full of holes, blow out of the water.

exploit v. **1** make use of someone unfairly. **2** make full use of a resource.
▷ SYNONYMS: **1 take advantage of**, abuse, impose on, treat unfairly, misuse, ill-treat; informal walk all over. **2 utilize**, make use of, turn to good use, make the most of, capitalize on, benefit from; informal cash in on.
• n. a daring act.
▷ SYNONYMS: **feat**, deed, act, adventure, stunt, escapade, achievement.
■ **exploitative** adj. **exploitation** n.

explore v. **1** travel through an unfamiliar area so as to learn about it. **2** examine or discuss in detail.
▷ SYNONYMS: **1 travel through**, tour, survey, scout, reconnoitre. **2 investigate**, look into, consider, examine, research, survey, scrutinize, study, review; informal check out.

■ **exploration** n. **exploratory** adj.
explorer n.

explosion n. **1** an act of exploding. **2** a
sudden increase.
▷ SYNONYMS: **1 detonation**, eruption,
bang, blast, boom. **2 outburst**,
flare-up, outbreak, eruption, storm,
rush, surge, fit, paroxysm. **3 sudden
increase**, mushrooming, snowballing,
escalation, multiplication,
burgeoning, rocketing.

explosive adj. able or likely to
explode.
▷ SYNONYMS: **1 volatile**, inflammable,
flammable, combustible, incendiary.
2 fiery, stormy, violent, volatile,
passionate, tempestuous, turbulent,
touchy, irascible. **3** *an explosive
situation:* **tense**, highly charged,
overwrought, dangerous, perilous,
hazardous, sensitive, delicate,
unstable, volatile.
• n. an explosive substance.
▷ SYNONYMS: **bomb**, charge, incendiary
device.

exponent n. **1** a promoter of an idea.
2 a person who does a particular
thing skilfully. **3** a raised figure
beside a number indicating how
many times the number is to be
multiplied by itself.

exponential adj. **1** (of an increase)
becoming more and more rapid. **2** of a
mathematical exponent.
■ **exponentially** adv.

export v. send goods etc. to another
country for sale.
• n. **1** an exported item. **2** the act of
exporting.
■ **exportation** n. **exporter** n.

expose v. **1** uncover and make
visible. **2** show the true nature
of. **3** (**exposed**) unprotected from
the weather. **4** (**expose to**) make
vulnerable to. **5** subject photographic
film to light.
▷ SYNONYMS: **1 reveal**, uncover, lay bare,
unveil, unmask, detect, lift the lid
on; informal blow the whistle on. **2** *he
was exposed to radiation:* **lay open**,
subject, put at risk of, put in jeopardy
of. **3** *they were exposed to new ideas:*
introduce to, bring into contact with,
make aware of, familiarize with,
acquaint with.
– ANTONYMS: cover, protect.

exposé /ik-spoh-zay/ n. a report
in the media revealing shocking
information.

exposition n. **1** a full account and
explanation of a theory. **2** a large
exhibition.

expostulate v. disagree strongly.
■ **expostulation** n.

exposure n. **1** the state of being
exposed. **2** the act of exposing.
3 the quantity of light reaching a
photographic film.
▷ SYNONYMS: **1 frostbite**, cold, hypothermia. **2 uncovering**, revelation,
disclosure, unveiling, unmasking,
discovery, detection. **3 publicity**,
advertising, public attention, media
interest; informal hype.

expound v. explain a theory in detail.

express v. **1** convey a feeling etc. by
words or gestures. **2** squeeze out
liquid or air.
▷ SYNONYMS: **communicate**, convey,
indicate, show, demonstrate, reveal,
put across/over, get across/over,
articulate, put into words, voice, give
voice to, state, air, give vent to.
• adj. **1** operating or delivered very
quickly. **2** stated clearly.
▷ SYNONYMS: **1 rapid**, swift, fast, high-
speed, non-stop, direct. **2 explicit**,
clear, direct, plain, distinct,
unambiguous, categorical.
– ANTONYMS: vague.
• adv. by express delivery.
• n. a fast train that stops at few
stations.
□ **expressway** US an urban motorway.
■ **expressly** adv.

expression n. **1** the act of expressing.
2 a look on someone's face. **3** a word
or phrase.
▷ SYNONYMS: **1 utterance**, uttering,
voicing, declaration, articulation.
2 indication, demonstration, show,
exhibition, token, illustration. **3 look**,
appearance, air, manner, countenance, mien. **4 idiom**, phrase, turn of
phrase, term, proverb, saying, adage,
maxim. **5 emotion**, feeling, spirit,
passion, intensity, style.

expressionism n. a style of art
seeking to express feelings rather
than represent objects realistically.
■ **expressionist** n. & adj.

expressive adj. effectively conveying
a thought or feeling.
▷ SYNONYMS: **1 eloquent**, meaningful,
demonstrative, suggestive.
2 emotional, passionate, poignant,
moving, stirring, emotionally
charged, lyrical.
– ANTONYMS: undemonstrative.
■ **expressively** adv.

expropriate v. take property for
public use.
■ **expropriation** n.

expulsion n. the act of expelling.

▷ SYNONYMS: **1 removal**, debarment, dismissal, exclusion, ejection, banishment, eviction. **2 discharge**, ejection, excretion, voiding, evacuation, elimination, passing.
– ANTONYMS: admission.

expunge v. remove completely.

expurgate v. remove unsuitable matter from a text.
■ **expurgation** n.

exquisite adj. **1** very beautiful and delicate. **2** highly refined. **3** intensely felt.
▷ SYNONYMS: **1 beautiful**, lovely, elegant, fine, delicate, fragile, dainty, subtle. **2** *exquisite taste:* **discriminating**, discerning, sensitive, fastidious, refined.
■ **exquisitely** adv.

extant adj. still existing.

extemporize (or **-ise**) v. improvise.

extend v. **1** make larger or longer. **2** reach over or continue for. **3** stretch out part of the body. **4** offer.
▷ SYNONYMS: **1 expand**, enlarge, increase, lengthen, widen, broaden. **2 continue**, carry on, stretch, reach. **3 widen**, expand, broaden, augment, supplement, increase, add to, enhance, develop. **4 prolong**, lengthen, increase, stretch out, protract, spin out, string out. **5 hold out**, reach out, hold forth, stretch out, outstretch, offer, give, proffer.
– ANTONYMS: reduce, shorten.
■ **extendable** (or **extendible**) adj.

extension n. **1** the act of extending. **2** a part added to enlarge or lengthen something. **3** an additional period of time. **4** an extra phone on the same line as the main one.
▷ SYNONYMS: **1 addition**, add-on, adjunct, annex, wing. **2 expansion**, increase, enlargement, widening, broadening, deepening, augmentation, enhancement, development, growth. **3 prolongation**, lengthening, increase.

extensive adj. large in area, amount, or scope.
▷ SYNONYMS: **1 large**, sizeable, substantial, considerable, ample, great, vast. **2 comprehensive**, thorough, exhaustive, broad, wide, wide-ranging, catholic.
■ **extensively** adv.

extent n. **1** the area covered by something. **2** size or scale. **3** the degree to which something is true.
▷ SYNONYMS: **1 area**, size, expanse, length, proportions, dimensions. **2 degree**, scale, level, magnitude, scope, size, reach, range.

extenuating adj. making an offence less serious by partially excusing it.

exterior adj. of the outside.
▷ SYNONYMS: **outer**, outside, outermost, outward, external.
– ANTONYMS: interior.
• n. an outer surface or structure.
▷ SYNONYMS: **outside**, external surface, outward appearance, facade.
– ANTONYMS: interior.

exterminate v. destroy completely.
■ **extermination** n. **exterminator** n.

external adj. of or on the outside.
▷ SYNONYMS: **outer**, outside, outermost, outward, exterior.
– ANTONYMS: internal.
■ **externally** adv.

externalize (or **-ise**) v. express a thought etc. in words or actions.

extinct adj. **1** (of a species etc.) having no living members. **2** (of a volcano) not having erupted in recorded history.
▷ SYNONYMS: **1 vanished**, lost, gone, died out, wiped out, destroyed. **2 inactive**.
– ANTONYMS: living, dormant.

extinction n. the state of being or process of becoming extinct.
▷ SYNONYMS: **dying out**, disappearance, vanishing, extermination, destruction, elimination, eradication, annihilation.

extinguish v. **1** put out a fire or light. **2** put an end to.
▷ SYNONYMS: **douse**, quench, put out, stamp out, smother, snuff out.
– ANTONYMS: light.
■ **extinguisher** n.

extirpate v. destroy completely.
■ **extirpation** n.

extol v. (**extolling**, **extolled**) praise enthusiastically.
▷ SYNONYMS: **praise**, wax lyrical about, sing the praises of, acclaim, applaud, celebrate, eulogize, rave about, enthuse over; formal laud.
– ANTONYMS: criticize.

extort v. obtain by force or threats.
▷ SYNONYMS: **extract**, exact, wring, wrest, screw, squeeze.
■ **extortion** n.

extortionate adj. (of a price) much too high.
▷ SYNONYMS: **exorbitant**, excessive, outrageous, unreasonable, inordinate, inflated; Brit. informal daylight robbery.

extra adj. added to an existing or usual amount.
▷ SYNONYMS: **additional**, more, added, supplementary, further, auxiliary, ancillary, subsidiary, secondary.

e

• **adv. 1** to a greater extent than usual. **2** in addition.
▷ SYNONYMS: **exceptionally**, particularly, specially, especially, extremely.
• **n. 1** an additional item. **2** a person employed as one of a crowd in a film.
▷ SYNONYMS: **addition**, supplement, bonus, adjunct, addendum, add-on.

extra- prefix **1** outside. **2** beyond the scope of.

extract v. **1** remove with care or effort. **2** obtain from someone unwilling. **3** separate out a substance by a special method.
▷ SYNONYMS: **1 take out**, draw out, pull out, remove, withdraw, release, extricate. **2 wrest**, exact, wring, screw, squeeze, obtain by force, extort. **3 squeeze out**, press out, obtain.
– ANTONYMS: insert.
• **n. 1** a short passage taken from a book, film, etc. **2** the concentrated active ingredient of a substance.
▷ SYNONYMS: **1 excerpt**, passage, citation, quotation. **2 distillation**, distillate, concentrate, essence, juice.
■ **extractor** n.

extraction n. **1** the act of extracting. **2** ancestry or ethnic origin.

extra-curricular adj. done in addition to the normal curriculum.

extradite v. hand over an accused person for trial in the country where the crime was committed.
■ **extradition** n.

extramarital adj. occurring outside marriage.

extramural adj. Brit. for students who are not full-time members of an educational establishment.

extraneous adj. unrelated to the subject.

extraordinary adj. **1** very unusual or remarkable. **2** (of a meeting) held for a special reason.
▷ SYNONYMS: **1** an extraordinary coincidence: **remarkable**, exceptional, amazing, astonishing, astounding, sensational, stunning, incredible, unbelievable, phenomenal; informal fantastic. **2** extraordinary speed: **very great**, tremendous, enormous, immense, prodigious, stupendous, monumental.
– ANTONYMS: unremarkable.
■ **extraordinarily** adv.

extrapolate /ik-strap-uh-layt/ v. use a fact or conclusion valid for one situation and apply it to a different one.
■ **extrapolation** n.

extrasensory perception n. the

supposed ability to perceive things by means other than the known senses.

extraterrestrial adj. of things coming from beyond the earth or its atmosphere.

extravagant adj. **1** spending or using more than is necessary or can be afforded. **2** exceeding reasonable limits.
▷ SYNONYMS: **1 spendthrift**, profligate, wasteful, prodigal, lavish. **2 excessive**, immoderate, exaggerated, gushing, unrestrained, effusive, fulsome. **3 ornate**, elaborate, fancy, over-elaborate, ostentatious, exaggerated; informal flashy.
– ANTONYMS: thrifty, moderate.
■ **extravagance** n. **extravagantly** adv.

extravaganza n. a lavish and spectacular entertainment.

extreme adj. **1** very great. **2** highly unusual. **3** very severe or serious. **4** not moderate. **5** furthest from the centre or a given point.
▷ SYNONYMS: **1** extreme danger: **utmost**, great, greatest, maximum, great, acute, enormous, severe, serious. **2** extreme measures: **drastic**, serious, desperate, dire, radical, far-reaching, draconian; Brit. swingeing. **3 radical**, extremist, immoderate, fanatical, revolutionary, subversive, militant. **4 furthest**, farthest, utmost, remotest, ultra-.
– ANTONYMS: slight, moderate.
• **n. 1** either of two things that are as different from each other as possible. **2** the most extreme degree.
▷ SYNONYMS: **opposite**, antithesis, polar opposite; limit, extremity.

extremely adv. to or in the highest degree.
▷ SYNONYMS: **very**, exceptionally, especially, extraordinarily, tremendously, immensely, supremely, highly, mightily; informal awfully, terribly, seriously; Brit. informal jolly; N. Amer. informal mighty.
– ANTONYMS: slightly.

extremist n. a person holding extreme views.
▷ SYNONYMS: **fanatic**, radical, zealot, fundamentalist, hardliner, militant, activist.
– ANTONYMS: moderate.
■ **extremism** n.

extremity n. (pl. **extremities**) **1** the furthest point or limit. **2** (**extremities**) the hands and feet. **3** extreme hardship.

extricate v. free from a difficulty.
■ **extrication** n.

extrinsic adj. not part of something's basic nature; coming from outside.

extrovert n. a lively, sociable person.
• adj. of an extrovert.
▷ SYNONYMS: **outgoing**, sociable, gregarious, lively, ebullient, exuberant, uninhibited, unreserved.
– ANTONYMS: introvert.

extrude v. thrust or force out.
■ extrusion n.

exuberant adj. lively and cheerful.
▷ SYNONYMS: **ebullient**, buoyant, cheerful, high-spirited, cheery, lively, vivacious, enthusiastic, irrepressible, energetic, animated, full of life, sparkling; informal bubbly, bouncy, full of beans.
■ exuberance n.

exude v. **1** discharge slowly and steadily. **2** display a quality clearly.

exult v. show or feel triumphant joy.
■ exultant adj. exultation n.

eye n. **1** the organ of sight. **2** something compared to an eye in shape, position, etc.
• v. (**eyeing, eyed**) look at closely or with interest.
▷ SYNONYMS: **look at**, observe, view, gaze at, stare at, regard, contemplate, survey, scrutinize, consider, glance at, watch; informal check out, size up; N. Amer. informal eyeball.
□ **eyeball** the round part of the eye within the eyelids. **eyebrow** the strip of hair on the ridge above the eye socket. **eyelash** each of the hairs on the edges of the eyelids. **eyelet** a small round hole through which a lace can be threaded. **eyelid** either of the two folds of skin which cover the eye when closed. **eyeshadow** a cosmetic applied to the skin around the eyes. **eyesight** the ability to see. **eyesore** a very ugly thing. **eyewitness** a person who has seen something happen. **see eye to eye** be in full agreement.

> WORD LINKS
> **ocular, ophthalmic, optic** relating to the eye
> **ophthalmology** the branch of medicine dealing with the eye

eyrie /eer-i/ n. an eagle's nest.

Ff

F abbrev. Fahrenheit.

FA abbrev. Football Association.

fable n. a story with a moral or based on myth.
▷ SYNONYMS: **parable**, allegory, myth, legend, story, tale.

fabled adj. **1** famous. **2** mythical.

fabric n. **1** cloth. **2** the basic structure of a building, system, etc.
▷ SYNONYMS: **1** cloth, material, textile, stuff. **2** structure, construction, make-up, organization, framework, essence.

fabricate v. **1** invent false information. **2** make a product.
▷ SYNONYMS: **falsify**, fake, counterfeit, invent, make up.
■ **fabrication** n.

fabulous adj. **1** very great. **2** informal excellent. **3** mythical.
▷ SYNONYMS: **1** stupendous, prodigious, phenomenal, exceptional, fantastic, breathtaking, staggering, unthinkable, unimaginable, incredible, undreamed of. **2** a fabulous time: see EXCELLENT.
■ **fabulously** adv.

facade n. **1** the front of a building. **2** a misleading outward appearance.
▷ SYNONYMS: **1** front, frontage, face, elevation, exterior, outside. **2** show, front, appearance, pretence, simulation, affectation, act, charade, mask, veneer.

face n. **1** the front of the head. **2** a facial expression. **3** a surface. **4** an aspect.
▷ SYNONYMS: **1** countenance, physiognomy, features, profile; literary visage, lineaments. **2** expression, look, appearance, mien, air. **3** he made a face: grimace, scowl, wince, frown, pout. **4** side, aspect, surface, plane, facet, elevation.
• v. **1** have the face or front towards. **2** confront. **3** put a facing on.
▷ SYNONYMS: **1** look out on, front on to, look towards, look over/across, overlook, be opposite. **2** brave, face up to,

encounter, meet, confront. **3** accept, get used to, adjust to, learn to live with, cope with, deal with, come to terms with, become resigned to. **4** cover, clad, veneer, surface, dress, laminate, coat, line.
□ **facecloth** a small cloth for washing the face. **faceless** remote and impersonal. **facelift** an operation to tighten the skin of the face. **lose** (or **save**) **face** suffer (or avoid) humiliation.

facet n. **1** one of the sides of a cut gem. **2** an aspect.
▷ SYNONYMS: **aspect**, feature, factor, side, dimension, strand, component, element.

facetious adj. treating serious issues with inappropriate humour.
▷ SYNONYMS: **flippant**, flip, glib, frivolous, tongue-in-cheek, joking, jokey, jocular, playful.
− ANTONYMS: serious.
■ **facetiously** adv. **facetiousness** n.

facia var. of FASCIA.

facial adj. of the face.
• n. a beauty treatment for the face.

facile adj. lacking careful thought.

facilitate v. make easy or easier.
▷ SYNONYMS: **make easier**, ease, smooth the way for, enable, assist, help, aid, promote, hasten, speed up.
− ANTONYMS: impede.
■ **facilitation** n. **facilitator** n.

facility n. (pl. **facilities**) **1** a building, service, etc. provided for a purpose. **2** a natural ability or skill.
▷ SYNONYMS: **1** a wealth of local facilities: **amenity**, resource, service, benefit, convenience, equipment. **2** a medical facility: **establishment**, centre, station, location, premises, site, post, base. **3** ease, effortlessness, skill, adroitness, smoothness, fluency, slickness.

facing n. **1** a piece of material sewn to an inside edge of a garment to strengthen it. **2** an outer layer on a wall.

facsimile n. an exact copy of a document.

fact n. a thing known to be true.
▷ SYNONYMS: **1** *a fact we cannot ignore:* **reality**, actuality, certainty, truth, verity, gospel. **2** *every fact was double-checked:* **detail**, particular, finding, point, factor, feature, characteristic, aspect; (**facts**) information, data.
– ANTONYMS: lie, fiction.
□ **the facts of life** information about sexual matters. **in fact** in reality.

faction n. a small group within a larger one that disagrees with some of its beliefs.
▷ SYNONYMS: **1 clique**, coterie, caucus, bloc, camp, group, grouping, splinter group. **2 infighting**, dissent, dispute, discord, strife, conflict, friction, argument, disagreement, disunity, schism.
■ **factional** adj. **factious** adj.

factitious adj. not genuine.

factor n. **1** a circumstance contributing to a result. **2** a level on a scale of measurement: *a high sun protection factor.* **3** a number that divides into another number exactly.
▷ SYNONYMS: **element**, part, component, ingredient, strand, constituent, feature, facet, aspect, characteristic, consideration, influence, circumstance.
• v. (**factor in**) consider when making a decision.

factory n. (pl. **factories**) a building where goods are made or assembled in large numbers.
▷ SYNONYMS: **works**, plant, yard, mill, facility, workshop, shop.

factotum n. an employee who does a wide variety of tasks.

factual adj. based on or containing facts.
▷ SYNONYMS: **truthful**, true, accurate, authentic, historical, genuine, true-to-life, correct, exact.
– ANTONYMS: fictitious.
■ **factually** adv.

faculty n. (pl. **faculties**) **1** a mental or physical power. **2** a department or group of related departments in a university.
▷ SYNONYMS: **1 power**, capability, capacity, facility; (**faculties**) senses, wits, reason, intelligence. **2 department**, school.

fad n. **1** a craze. **2** a fussy like or dislike.
▷ SYNONYMS: **craze**, vogue, trend, fashion, mode, mania, rage.
■ **faddy** adj.

fade v. **1** gradually disappear. **2** lose colour.

▷ SYNONYMS: **grow dim**, grow faint, dwindle, die away, wane, disappear, vanish, decline, melt away.

faeces /fee-seez/ (US **feces**) pl. n. excrement.
■ **faecal** adj.

fag n. Brit. informal **1** a cigarette. **2** a tiring or boring task.

faggot n. **1** Brit. a ball of seasoned chopped liver, baked or fried. **2** a bundle of sticks tied together.

Fahrenheit n. a scale of temperature on which water freezes at 32° and boils at 212°.

faience /fy-ahns/ n. painted glazed earthenware.

fail v. **1** be unsuccessful in a task or exam. **2** neglect to do. **3** stop working properly. **4** become weaker. **5** let down.
▷ SYNONYMS: **1 be unsuccessful**, fall through, fall flat, collapse, founder, backfire, miscarry, come unstuck; informal flop, bomb. **2 break down**, stop working, cut out, crash, malfunction, go wrong; informal conk out; Brit. informal pack up. **3 collapse**, crash, go under, go bankrupt, cease trading, be wound up; informal fold, go bust. **4 deteriorate**, degenerate, decline, fade. **5 let down**, disappoint, desert, abandon, betray, be disloyal to.
– ANTONYMS: succeed, pass, improve.
• n. a mark too low to pass an exam.

failing n. a character weakness.
▷ SYNONYMS: **fault**, shortcoming, weakness, imperfection, deficiency, defect, flaw, frailty.
– ANTONYMS: strength.
• prep. if not.

failure n. **1** lack of success. **2** an unsuccessful person or thing. **3** an act of failing.
▷ SYNONYMS: **1 lack of success**, defeat, collapse, foundering. **2 fiasco**, debacle, catastrophe, disaster; informal flop, washout, dead loss. **3 loser**, underachiever, ne'er-do-well, disappointment; informal no-hoper, dud. **4 negligence**, dereliction, omission, oversight. **5 breakdown**, malfunction, crash. **6 collapse**, crash, bankruptcy, insolvency, liquidation, closure.
– ANTONYMS: success.

fain adv. old use gladly.

faint adj. **1** not clearly perceived. **2** slight. **3** about to faint.
▷ SYNONYMS: **1 indistinct**, vague, unclear, indefinite, ill-defined, imperceptible, pale, light, faded. **2 quiet**, muted, muffled, stifled,

feeble, weak, low, soft, gentle.
3 slight, slender, slim, small, tiny,
remote, vague. **4 dizzy**, giddy, light-
headed, unsteady; informal **woozy**.
– ANTONYMS: clear, loud, strong.
• **v.** lose consciousness briefly.
▷ SYNONYMS: **pass out**, black out, keel
over; literary **swoon**.
• **n.** a brief loss of consciousness.
▷ SYNONYMS: **blackout**, fainting fit,
coma; literary **swoon**.
□ **faint-hearted** timid.
■ **faintly** adv.

fair adj. **1** treating people equally.
2 just or appropriate. **3** quite large.
4 quite good. **5** light in colour. **6** (of
weather) fine and dry.
▷ SYNONYMS: **1 just**, equitable, honest,
impartial, unbiased, unprejudiced,
neutral, even-handed. **2 reasonable**,
passable, tolerable, satisfactory,
acceptable, respectable, decent, all
right, good enough, pretty good.
3 blonde, blond, yellow, golden,
flaxen, light. **4 pale**, light, pink,
white, creamy. **5 fine**, dry, bright,
clear, sunny, cloudless.
– ANTONYMS: unfair, dark, poor.
• **adv.** in a fair way.
• **n. 1** a funfair. **2** an event held to sell
or promote goods.
▷ SYNONYMS: **1 fete**, gala, festival,
carnival. **2 market**, bazaar, exchange,
sale. **3 exhibition**, display, show,
exposition.
□ **fairground** an outdoor area where
a funfair is held. **fairway** a part of a
golf course between a tee and a green.
■ **fairness** n.

fairing n. a streamlining structure
added to a vehicle, boat, etc.

fairly adv. **1** justly. **2** quite.
▷ SYNONYMS: **1 justly**, equitably,
impartially, without bias, without
prejudice, even-handedly, equally.
2 reasonably, passably, tolerably,
adequately, moderately, quite,
relatively, comparatively; informal
pretty. **3 positively**, really, simply,
absolutely.

fairy n. (pl. **fairies**) a small imaginary
being with magical powers.
▷ SYNONYMS: **sprite**, pixie, elf, imp,
brownie, puck, leprechaun.
□ **fairy godmother** a person who
helps someone in difficulty. **fairy
lights** small decorative electric lights.

fait accompli /fayt uh-**kom**-pli/ n. a
thing that has been done and cannot
be altered.

faith n. **1** complete trust or confidence.
2 strong religious belief. **3** a system

of religious belief.
▷ SYNONYMS: **1 trust**, belief, confidence,
conviction, reliance. **2 religion**,
belief, creed, church, persuasion,
ideology, doctrine.
– ANTONYMS: mistrust.

faithful adj. **1** loyal. **2** true to the facts
or the original.
▷ SYNONYMS: **1 loyal**, constant, true,
devoted, staunch, steadfast, dedicated,
committed, trusty, dependable,
reliable. **2 accurate**, precise, exact,
true, strict, realistic, authentic.
– ANTONYMS: unfaithful, disloyal,
treacherous.
■ **faithfully** adv. **faithfulness** n.

faithless adj. disloyal.

fake adj. not genuine.
▷ SYNONYMS: **1 counterfeit**, forged,
fraudulent, sham, pirated, false,
bogus; informal **phoney**, dud.
2 imitation, artificial, synthetic,
simulated, reproduction, replica,
ersatz, man-made, dummy, false,
mock; informal **pretend**. **3 feigned**,
faked, put-on, assumed, invented,
affected.
– ANTONYMS: genuine, real, authentic.
• **n.** a fake person or thing.
▷ SYNONYMS: **1 forgery**, counterfeit,
copy, sham, fraud, hoax, imitation;
informal **phoney**, rip-off. **2 charlatan**,
quack, sham, fraud, impostor.
• **v. 1** make a copy in order to deceive.
2 pretend to have.
▷ SYNONYMS: **1 forge**, counterfeit,
falsify, copy, pirate. **2 feign**, pretend,
simulate, put on, affect.

fakir n. a Muslim or Hindu holy man
who lives by asking for money or food.

falcon n. a fast-flying bird of prey.

falconry n. the keeping and training
of birds of prey.
■ **falconer** n.

fall v. (**falling**, **fell**; past part. **fallen**)
1 move downwards quickly and
without control. **2** collapse to the
ground. **3** hang or slope down.
4 become less or lower. **5** become.
6 be captured or defeated.
▷ SYNONYMS: **1 drop**, descend, plummet,
plunge, sink, dive, tumble, cascade.
2 topple over, tumble over, fall down/
over, collapse. **3 subside**, recede,
drop, retreat, fall away, go down, sink.
4 decrease, decline, diminish, fall off,
drop off, lessen, dwindle, plummet,
plunge, slump, sink. **5 surrender**,
yield, submit, give in, capitulate,
succumb, be taken, be overwhelmed.
– ANTONYMS: rise.
• **n. 1** an act of falling. **2** a thing which

has fallen. **3** (**falls**) a waterfall. **4** a drop in size or number. **5** US autumn.
▷ SYNONYMS: **1 tumble**, trip, spill, topple. **2 decline**, fall-off, drop, decrease, cut, dip, reduction, slump; informal crash. **3 downfall**, collapse, failure, decline, destruction, overthrow, demise. **4 surrender**, capitulation, yielding, submission, defeat.
– ANTONYMS: rise.
□ **fall for** informal **1** begin to love. **2** be tricked by. **fallout** airborne radioactive debris. **fall out** quarrel. **fall through** fail.

fallacy n. (pl. **fallacies**) **1** a mistaken belief. **2** unsound reasoning.
■ **fallacious** adj.

fallible adj. capable of making mistakes.
■ **fallibility** n.

Fallopian tube n. either of two tubes connecting the ovaries to the uterus.

fallow adj. (of farmland) not planted with crops.

false adj. **1** not true or correct. **2** fake; artificial. **3** mistaken.
▷ SYNONYMS: **1 incorrect**, untrue, wrong, inaccurate, untruthful, fictitious, fabricated, invented, made up, trumped up, counterfeit, forged, fraudulent. **2 disloyal**, faithless, unfaithful, untrue, inconstant, treacherous, double-crossing, deceitful, dishonest, duplicitous. **3 fake**, artificial, imitation, synthetic, simulated, reproduction, replica, ersatz, manmade, dummy, mock; informal pretend.
– ANTONYMS: correct, faithful, genuine.
■ **falsely** adv. **falsity** n.

falsehood n. **1** the state of being untrue. **2** a lie.

falsetto n. (pl. **falsettos**) a high-pitched voice used by male singers.

falsify v. (**falsifying**, **falsified**) alter so as to mislead.
▷ SYNONYMS: **forge**, fake, counterfeit, fabricate, alter, change, doctor, tamper with, manipulate, misrepresent, misreport, distort.
■ **falsification** n.

falter v. **1** lose strength or momentum. **2** move or speak hesitantly.
▷ SYNONYMS: **hesitate**, delay, drag your feet, stall, waver, vacillate, be indecisive, be irresolute; Brit. hum and haw; informal sit on the fence.

fame n. the state of being famous.
▷ SYNONYMS: **renown**, celebrity, stardom, popularity, prominence, distinction, esteem, eminence, repute.
– ANTONYMS: obscurity.
■ **famed** adj.

familial adj. of a family.

familiar adj. **1** well known. **2** often encountered. **3** (**familiar with**) having knowledge of. **4** friendly.
▷ SYNONYMS: **1 well known**, recognized, accustomed, everyday, day-to-day, habitual, customary, routine. **2** are you familiar with the subject?: **acquainted**, conversant, versed, knowledgeable, well informed, au fait; informal well up on.
• n. a spirit believed to accompany a witch.
■ **familiarity** n. **familiarly** adv.

familiarize (or **-ise**) v. give knowledge or understanding to.
■ **familiarization** n.

family n. (pl. **families**) **1** a group consisting of parents and their children. **2** a group related by blood or marriage. **3** a person's children. **4** a group of related things.
▷ SYNONYMS: **1 relatives**, relations, kin, next of kin, kith and kin, clan, tribe; informal folks. **2 species**, order, class, genus, phylum.

famine n. a time of severe food shortages.
▷ SYNONYMS: **1 food shortage**, hunger, starvation, malnutrition. **2 shortage**, scarcity, lack, dearth, deficiency, insufficiency, shortfall.
– ANTONYMS: plenty.

famished adj. informal very hungry.
▷ SYNONYMS: **ravenous**, hungry, starving, starved, empty, unfed; informal peckish.
– ANTONYMS: replete.

famous adj. **1** known about by many people. **2** informal excellent.
▷ SYNONYMS: **well known**, prominent, famed, popular, renowned, noted, eminent, distinguished, celebrated, illustrious, legendary.
– ANTONYMS: unknown.
■ **famously** adv.

fan n. **1** a device creating a cooling current of air. **2** an enthusiastic admirer or supporter.
▷ SYNONYMS: **enthusiast**, devotee, admirer, lover, aficionado, supporter, follower, disciple, adherent; informal buff.
• v. (**fanning**, **fanned**) **1** drive a current of air towards. **2** strengthen a feeling etc. **3** (**fan out**) spread out from a central point.
□ **fan belt** a belt driving the fan that cools a vehicle's engine.

fanatic n. **1** a person who holds extreme political or religious opinions. **2** informal a person who is very enthusiastic about a hobby etc.

f

▷ SYNONYMS: **extremist**, militant, dogmatist, bigot, zealot, radical, diehard.
■ **fanaticism** n.

fanatical adj. **1** holding extreme political or religious opinions. **2** obsessively concerned with something.
▷ SYNONYMS: **1 zealous**, extremist, extreme, militant, gung-ho, dogmatic, radical, diehard, intolerant, single-minded, blinkered, inflexible, uncompromising. **2 enthusiastic**, eager, keen, fervent, passionate, obsessive, obsessed, fixated.
■ **fanatically** adv.

fancier n. a person who keeps or breeds a particular type of animal.

fanciful adj. **1** imaginary. **2** very unusual or creative.
■ **fancifully** adv.

fancy v. (**fancying**, **fancied**) **1** Brit. informal want or want to do. **2** Brit. informal find sexually attractive. **3** think.
▷ SYNONYMS: **1 wish for**, want, desire, long for, yearn for, crave, thirst for, hanker after, dream of, covet. **2 be attracted to**, find attractive, be infatuated with, be taken with; informal have a crush on, carry a torch for. **3 imagine**, believe, think, be under the impression; informal reckon.
• adj. (**fancier**, **fanciest**) elaborate or highly decorated.
▷ SYNONYMS: **elaborate**, ornate, ornamental, decorative, embellished, intricate, ostentatious, showy, flamboyant, lavish, expensive; informal flashy, snazzy, posh, classy; Brit. informal swish.
– ANTONYMS: plain.
• n. (pl. **fancies**) **1** a brief feeling of attraction. **2** imagination. **3** an unfounded belief.
▷ SYNONYMS: **1 whim**, foible, urge, whimsy, fascination, fad, craze, enthusiasm, passion, caprice. **2 fantasy**, dreaming, imagination, creativity.
□ **fancy dress** a costume representing a famous person, animal, etc., worn for a party.

fandango n. (pl. **fandangoes** or **fandangos**) a lively Spanish dance.

fanfare n. a short tune played on trumpets to announce someone.

fang n. **1** a long sharp tooth. **2** a snake's tooth which injects poison.

fantasia n. a musical composition based on several tunes.

fantasize (or **-ise**) v. imagine something desirable.
■ **fantasist** n.

fantastic adj. **1** hard to believe. **2** strange or exotic. **3** informal excellent.
▷ SYNONYMS: **1 fanciful**, extravagant, extraordinary, irrational, wild, absurd, far-fetched, unthinkable, implausible, improbable, unlikely; informal crazy. **2 strange**, weird, bizarre, outlandish, grotesque, surreal, exotic. **3 marvellous**, wonderful, sensational, outstanding, superb, excellent; informal terrific, fabulous; Brit. informal brilliant; Austral./NZ informal bonzer.
– ANTONYMS: ordinary.
■ **fantastically** adv.

fantasy n. (pl. **fantasies**) **1** a pleasant imagined situation. **2** the imagining of things that do not exist. **3** fiction involving magic and adventure.
▷ SYNONYMS: **1 imagination**, fancy, invention, make-believe, creativity, vision, daydreaming, reverie. **2 dream**, daydream, pipe dream, fanciful notion, wish, fond hope, delusion; informal pie in the sky.
– ANTONYMS: realism.

far adv. **1** at, to, or by a great distance. **2** by a great deal.
▷ SYNONYMS: **1 a long way**, a great distance, a good way, afar. **2 much**, considerably, markedly, greatly, significantly, substantially, appreciably, by a long way, by a mile, easily.
• adj. **1** distant. **2** extreme.
▷ SYNONYMS: **1 distant**, faraway, far-off, remote, out of the way, far-flung, outlying. **2 further**, opposite.
– ANTONYMS: near.
□ **the Far East** China, Japan, and other countries of east Asia. **far-fetched** exaggerated or unlikely.

farad n. the basic unit of electrical capacitance.

farce n. **1** a comedy involving ridiculous situations. **2** an absurd event.
▷ SYNONYMS: **mockery**, travesty, parody, sham, pretence, charade, joke; informal shambles.
– ANTONYMS: tragedy.
■ **farcical** adj. **farcically** adv.

fare n. **1** a charge for travel on public transport. **2** a range of food.
▷ SYNONYMS: **1 price**, cost, charge, fee, toll, tariff. **2 food**, meals, cooking, cuisine.
• v. perform in a specified way.
▷ SYNONYMS: **get on**, get along, cope, manage, do, survive; informal make out.

farewell exclam. old use goodbye.
▷ SYNONYMS: **goodbye**, so long, adieu, au revoir, ciao; informal bye; Brit. informal cheerio.
• n. an act of leaving.

▷ SYNONYMS: **goodbye**, adieu, leave-taking, parting, departure, send-off.

farm n. an area of land and buildings used for growing crops and rearing animals.

▷ SYNONYMS: **smallholding**, farmstead, plantation, estate, farmland; Brit. grange, croft; Scottish steading; N. Amer. ranch; Austral./NZ station.

• v. **1** grow crops or keep animals as a living. **2** (**farm out**) give work to others to do.

▷ SYNONYMS: **breed**, rear, keep, raise, tend.

■ **farmer** n.

> WORD LINKS
> **agriculture**, **husbandry** the science or practice of farming

farrago /fuh-**rah**-goh/ n. (pl. **farragos** or **farragoes**) a confused mixture.

farrier n. a person who shoes horses.

farrow n. a litter of pigs.

• v. give birth to piglets.

farther, **farthest** vars. of FURTHER, FURTHEST.

farthing n. a former UK coin, worth a quarter of an old penny.

fascia (or Brit. **facia**) /**fay**-shuh/ n. **1** Brit. a signboard on a shopfront. **2** a vehicle's dashboard. **3** a detachable cover for a mobile phone.

fascinate v. interest or charm greatly.

fascinating adj. very interesting.

▷ SYNONYMS: **interesting**, captivating, engrossing, absorbing, enchanting, enthralling, spellbinding, riveting, engaging, compelling, compulsive, gripping, charming, attractive, intriguing, diverting, entertaining.

– ANTONYMS: boring.

fascination n. the state of being fascinated, or the power to fascinate.

▷ SYNONYMS: **interest**, preoccupation, passion, obsession, compulsion; allure, lure, charm, attraction, appeal, pull, draw.

fascism /**fash**-i-z'm/ n. a right-wing system of government with extreme nationalistic beliefs.

■ **fascist** n. & adj.

fashion n. **1** a popular trend, esp. in dress. **2** the production and marketing of new styles of clothing. **3** a way of doing something.

▷ SYNONYMS: **1 vogue**, trend, craze, rage, mania, fad, style, look, convention, mode; informal thing. **2 clothes**, clothing design, couture; informal the rag trade. **3 manner**, way, method, style, approach, mode.

• v. make or shape.

▷ SYNONYMS: **construct**, build, make, manufacture, cast, shape, form, mould, sculpt, forge, hew, carve.

fashionable adj. in or adopting a currently popular style.

▷ SYNONYMS: **in vogue**, in fashion, popular, up to date, up to the minute, modern, all the rage, trendsetting, stylish, chic, modish; informal trendy, classy, cool; N. Amer. informal tony.

■ **fashionably** adv.

fast adj. **1** moving or able to move very quickly. **2** happening at high speed. **3** (of a clock etc.) ahead of the correct time. **4** firmly fixed.

▷ SYNONYMS: **1 speedy**, quick, swift, rapid, high-speed, accelerated, express, blistering, breakneck, hasty, hurried; informal nippy, scorching, supersonic; Brit. informal cracking. **2 secure**, fastened, tight, firm, closed, shut, immovable. **3 loyal**, devoted, faithful, firm, steadfast, staunch, true, boon, bosom, inseparable.

– ANTONYMS: slow, loose.

• adv. **1** quickly. **2** firmly or securely.

▷ SYNONYMS: **1 quickly**, rapidly, swiftly, speedily, briskly, at full tilt, hastily, hurriedly, in a hurry; informal double quick, nippily; N. Amer. informal lickety-split. **2 securely**, firmly, tight. **3** he's fast asleep: **deeply**, sound, completely.

• v. go without food.

• n. a period of fasting.

fasten v. **1** close or do up securely. **2** fix or hold in place.

▷ SYNONYMS: **1 bolt**, lock, secure, make fast, chain, seal. **2 attach**, fix, affix, clip, pin, tack, stick, join. **3 tie**, tether, hitch, truss, fetter, lash, anchor, strap, rope.

– ANTONYMS: unlock, unfasten.

■ **fastener** n.

fastidious adj. **1** attentive to detail. **2** very concerned about cleanliness.

■ **fastidiously** adv. **fastidiousness** n.

fastness n. a secure place well protected by natural features.

fat n. **1** an oily substance found in animals. **2** this, or a similar substance made from plants, used in cooking.

▷ SYNONYMS: **1 blubber**, adipose tissue, cellulite. **2 oil**, grease, lard, suet, butter, margarine.

• adj. (**fatter**, **fattest**) **1** having too much fat. **2** informal large.

▷ SYNONYMS: **1 obese**, overweight, plump, stout, chubby, portly, flabby, paunchy, pot-bellied, corpulent; informal tubby; Brit. informal podgy. **2 fatty**, greasy, oily.

– ANTONYMS: thin, slim, lean.

■ **fatness** n. **fatten** v. **fatty** adj.

fatal adj. causing death or disaster.
▷ SYNONYMS: **1 deadly**, lethal, mortal, death-dealing, terminal, incurable, untreatable, inoperable. **2 disastrous**, devastating, ruinous, catastrophic, calamitous, dire.
– ANTONYMS: harmless, beneficial.
■ **fatally** adv.

fatalism n. the belief that all events are decided in advance by a supernatural power.
■ **fatalist** n. **fatalistic** adj.

fatality n. (pl. **fatalities**) a death caused by an accident or disease, or occurring in war.

fate n. **1** a power believed to control all events. **2** the unavoidable events or outcome of a person's life.
▷ SYNONYMS: **1 destiny**, providence, the stars, chance, luck, serendipity, fortune, karma, kismet. **2 future**, destiny, outcome, end, lot. **3 death**, demise, end, sentence.
• v. (**be fated**) be destined to happen in a particular way.
▷ SYNONYMS: **predestine**, preordain, destine, mean, doom.

fateful adj. having important, often unpleasant, consequences.

father n. **1** a male parent. **2** a founder or originator. **3** a title of certain priests.
▷ SYNONYMS: **1 patriarch**, paterfamilias; informal dad, daddy, pop, pa, old man; Brit. informal, dated pater. **2 originator**, initiator, founder, inventor, creator, author, architect.
• v. be the father of; sire.
□ **father-in-law** (pl. **fathers-in-law**) the father of a person's husband or wife.
fatherland a person's native country.
■ **fatherhood** n. **fatherly** adj.

> **WORD LINKS**
> **paternal** relating to a father
> **patricide** the killing of a father by his child

fathom n. a measure of the depth of water, equal to 1.8 m.
• v. understand.

fatigue n. **1** tiredness. **2** brittleness in metal etc. caused by repeated stress. **3** (**fatigues**) loose-fitting military clothing.
▷ SYNONYMS: **tiredness**, weariness, exhaustion.
– ANTONYMS: energy.
• v. make very tired.
▷ SYNONYMS: **tire out**, exhaust, wear out, drain, weary, overtire; informal knock out, take it out of; Brit. informal knacker.

fatuous adj. silly and pointless.
■ **fatuously** adv.

fatwa n. an authoritative ruling on a point of Islamic law.

faucet n. US a tap.

fault n. **1** a defect or mistake. **2** responsibility for a mistake etc. **3** a break in the layers of rock of the earth's crust.
▷ SYNONYMS: **1** he has his faults: **defect**, failing, imperfection, blemish, flaw, shortcoming, weakness, weak point, vice. **2** engineers have located the fault: **defect**, flaw, bug, error, mistake, inaccuracy, oversight; informal glitch. **3 responsibility**, liability, culpability, guilt.
– ANTONYMS: strength.
• v. criticize for being unsatisfactory.
▷ SYNONYMS: **find fault with**, criticize, attack, condemn; informal knock; Brit. informal slag off.

faultless adj. having no mistakes or mistakes.
▷ SYNONYMS: **perfect**, flawless, without fault, error-free, impeccable, accurate, precise, exact, correct, exemplary.
– ANTONYMS: flawed.

faulty adj. (**faultier**, **faultiest**) **1** not working or made correctly. **2** containing mistakes.
▷ SYNONYMS: **1 malfunctioning**, broken, damaged, defective, out of order; informal on the blink, acting up; Brit. informal playing up. **2 flawed**, unsound, inaccurate, incorrect, erroneous, wrong.
– ANTONYMS: working, sound.

faun n. a Roman god with a man's body and a goat's horns, tail, and legs.

fauna n. the animals of a particular region or period.

faux pas /foh pah/ n. (pl. **faux pas**) an embarrassing social blunder.

favour (US **favor**) n. **1** approval or liking. **2** a kind or helpful act. **3** favouritism.
▷ SYNONYMS: **1 good turn**, service, good deed, act of kindness, courtesy. **2 approval**, approbation, goodwill, kindness, benevolence.
– ANTONYMS: disservice, disapproval.
• v. **1** regard or treat with favour. **2** work to the advantage of.
▷ SYNONYMS: **1 advocate**, recommend, approve of, be in favour of, support, back, champion, campaign for, press for, lobby for, promote; informal push for. **2 prefer**, go for, choose, opt for, select, pick, plump for, like better, be biased towards. **3 benefit**, be to

the advantage of, help, assist, aid, advance, be of service to.
– ANTONYMS: oppose.

favourable (US **favorable**) adj.
1 expressing approval or agreement. **2** advantageous or helpful.
▷ SYNONYMS: **1 approving**, positive, complimentary, full of praise, flattering, glowing, enthusiastic, kind, good; informal rave. **2 advantageous**, beneficial, in your favour, good, right, suitable, appropriate, auspicious, promising, encouraging. **3 positive**, affirmative, assenting, approving, encouraging, reassuring.
– ANTONYMS: critical, unfavourable.
■ **favourably** adv.

favourite (US **favorite**) adj. preferred to all others.
▷ SYNONYMS: **favoured**, preferred, chosen, choice, best-loved, dearest, pet.
• n. **1** a favourite person or thing. **2** the competitor expected to win.
▷ SYNONYMS: **first choice**, pick, preference, pet, darling, the apple of your eye; informal golden boy, teacher's pet; Brit. informal blue-eyed boy/girl; N. Amer. informal fair-haired boy/girl.

favouritism (US **favoritism**) n. unfairly generous treatment of one person or group.

fawn n. **1** a young deer in its first year. **2** a light brown colour.
• v. try to please by flattery and being very attentive.

fax n. **1** a copy of a document which has been scanned and sent electronically. **2** a machine for sending and receiving faxes.
• v. send by fax.

faze v. informal unsettle.

FBI abbrev. (in the US) Federal Bureau of Investigation.

FC abbrev. Football Club.

fealty n. hist. loyalty sworn to a feudal lord.

fear n. an unpleasant emotion caused by the threat of danger, pain, etc.
▷ SYNONYMS: **1 terror**, fright, fearfulness, horror, alarm, panic, trepidation, dread, anxiety, angst, apprehension, nervousness. **2 phobia**, aversion, antipathy, dread, nightmare, horror, terror; informal hang-up.
• v. **1** be afraid of. **2** (**fear for**) be anxious about.
▷ SYNONYMS: **1 be afraid of**, be fearful of, be scared of, be apprehensive of, dread, live in fear of, be terrified of. **2 suspect**, be afraid, have a sneaking suspicion, be inclined to think, have

a hunch.

fearful adj. **1** showing or causing fear. **2** informal very great.
▷ SYNONYMS: **1 afraid**, scared, frightened, scared stiff, scared to death, terrified, petrified, nervous, apprehensive, uneasy, anxious, timid; informal jittery. **2 terrible**, dreadful, awful, appalling, frightful, ghastly, horrific, horrible, shocking, gruesome.
– ANTONYMS: unafraid.
■ **fearfully** adv.

fearless adj. feeling no fear; brave.
▷ SYNONYMS: **brave**, courageous, bold, audacious, intrepid, valiant, plucky, heroic, daring, unafraid; informal gutsy.
– ANTONYMS: timid, cowardly.
■ **fearlessly** adv.

fearsome adj. frightening.

feasible adj. **1** able to be done. **2** likely.
▷ SYNONYMS: **practicable**, practical, workable, achievable, attainable, realizable, viable, realistic, possible; informal doable.
– ANTONYMS: unfeasible, impracticable.
■ **feasibility** n. **feasibly** adv.

feast n. **1** a large meal marking a special occasion. **2** an annual religious celebration.
▷ SYNONYMS: **banquet**, dinner; informal spread, blowout; Brit. informal beanfeast, slap-up meal.
• v. **1** have a feast. **2** eat heartily.
▷ SYNONYMS: **gorge**, dine, binge; (**feast on**) devour, consume, partake of, eat your fill of; informal scoff, pig out on, binge on.

feat n. an act requiring great courage, skill, or strength.
▷ SYNONYMS: **achievement**, accomplishment, coup, triumph, undertaking, enterprise, venture, exploit, operation, exercise, endeavour, effort.

feather n. any of the structures covering a bird's body, consisting of a shaft fringed with fine strands.
▷ SYNONYMS: **plume**, quill; (**feathers**) plumage, down.
□ **featherweight** a weight in boxing between bantamweight and lightweight. **feather your nest** make money, esp. at someone's expense.
■ **feathered** adj. **feathery** adj.

feature n. **1** a distinctive element or aspect. **2** a part of the face. **3** a special newspaper or magazine article. **4** the main film showing at a cinema.
▷ SYNONYMS: **1 characteristic**, attribute, quality, property, trait, hallmark, aspect, facet, factor, ingredient, component, element. **2** *her delicate*

features: **face**, countenance, physiognomy; informal **mug**; Brit. informal **mush**, **phizog**; literary **lineaments**, **visage**.
3 centrepiece, special attraction, highlight, focal point, focus, conversation piece. **4 article**, piece, item, report, story, column.
• v. **1** have as a feature. **2** have an important part in.
▷ SYNONYMS: **1 present**, promote, make a feature of, spotlight, highlight, showcase, foreground. **2 star**, appear, participate.

febrile adj. **1** feverish. **2** overactive and excitable.

February n. the second month.

> USAGE *-ruary*, not *-uary*: February.

feces US = FAECES.

feckless adj. irresponsible and weak in character.

fecund adj. fertile.
■ **fecundity** n.

fed past & past part. of FEED.
□ **fed up** informal annoyed or bored.

federal adj. of a system in which several states unite under a central authority but are independent in internal affairs.
■ **federalism** n. **federalist** n. & adj. **federally** adv.

federate v. unite as a federation.

federation n. **1** a group of states united on a federal basis. **2** a group organized like a federation.
▷ SYNONYMS: **confederation**, confederacy, association, league, alliance, coalition, union, syndicate, guild, consortium.

fedora n. a soft hat with a curled brim.

fee n. a sum payable for professional services or to be allowed to do something.
▷ SYNONYMS: **payment**, wage, salary, price, charge, bill, tariff, rate; (**fees**) remuneration, dues, earnings, pay; formal emolument.

feeble adj. **1** weak. **2** not convincing.
▷ SYNONYMS: **1 weak**, weakened, debilitated, enfeebled, frail, decrepit, infirm, delicate, sickly, ailing, unwell, poorly. **2 ineffective**, unconvincing, implausible, unsatisfactory, poor, weak, flimsy, lame. **3 cowardly**, faint-hearted, spineless, timid, timorous, fearful, unassertive, weak, ineffectual; informal sissy, chicken; Brit. informal wet. **4 faint**, dim, weak, pale, soft, subdued, muted.
– ANTONYMS: strong.
■ **feebleness** n. **feebly** adv.

feed v. (**feeding**, **fed**) **1** give food to. **2** eat. **3** supply with material, power, etc. **4** pass gradually through a confined space.
▷ SYNONYMS: **1 cater for**, provide for, cook for, dine, nourish. **2 eat**, graze, browse, crop. **3 supply**, provide, give, deliver.
• n. **1** an act of feeding. **2** food for domestic animals.
▷ SYNONYMS: **fodder**, food, provender.
□ **feedback 1** comments about a product or a person's performance. **2** the return of part of the output of an amplifier to its input, causing a whistling sound.

feeder n. **1** a thing that feeds or supplies something. **2** a minor route linking outlying districts with the main route.

feel v. (**feeling**, **felt**) **1** be aware of or examine by touch. **2** give a sensation when touched. **3** experience an emotion or sensation. **4** have a belief or opinion.
▷ SYNONYMS: **1 touch**, stroke, caress, fondle, finger, paw, handle. **2** *she felt a breeze on her back:* **perceive**, sense, detect, discern, notice, be aware of, be conscious of. **3** *he will not feel any pain:* **experience**, undergo, go through, bear, endure, suffer. **4 grope**, fumble, scrabble. **5 believe**, think, consider it right, be of the opinion, hold, maintain, judge; informal reckon, figure.
• n. **1** an act of touching. **2** the sense of touch. **3** an impression. **4** (**a feel for**) a sensitive appreciation of.
▷ SYNONYMS: **1 texture**, finish, touch, consistency. **2 atmosphere**, ambience, aura, mood, feeling, air, impression, spirit; informal vibes. **3 aptitude**, knack, flair, bent, talent, gift, ability.

feeler n. **1** a long slender organ of touch in some animals. **2** a suggestion made to gauge opinion.

feeling n. **1** an emotional state or reaction. **2** (**feelings**) the emotional side of a person's character. **3** the ability to feel. **4** the sensation of touching or being touched. **5** a belief or opinion.
▷ SYNONYMS: **1 sensation**, sense, perception, awareness, consciousness. **2** *he hurt her feelings:* **sensibilities**, sensitivities, self-esteem, pride. **3 sneaking suspicion**, notion, inkling, hunch, impression, intuition, instinct, fancy, idea. **4 mood**, opinion, attitude, sentiment, emotion, belief, views, consensus. **5 love**, affection, fond-

ness, tenderness, warmth, emotion, passion, desire. **6** atmosphere, ambience, aura, air, mood, impression, spirit; informal vibes. **7** aptitude, knack, flair, bent, talent, feel, gift, ability.

feet pl. of FOOT.

feign v. pretend.

feint n. a pretended attack in boxing or fencing.
• v. make a feint.
• adj. (of paper) printed with faint ruled lines.

feisty /fy-sti/ adj. spirited and lively.

feldspar (or **felspar**) n. a white or red mineral.

felicitations pl. n. congratulations.

felicitous adj. well chosen or appropriate.
▷ SYNONYMS: **apt**, well chosen, fitting, suitable, appropriate, apposite, pertinent, germane, relevant.
– ANTONYMS: inappropriate.

felicity n. (pl. **felicities**) **1** great happiness. **2** an apt and pleasing feature.

feline adj. of a cat or cats.
• n. an animal of the cat family.

fell[1] past of FALL.

fell[2] v. cut or knock down.
▷ SYNONYMS: **1 cut down**, chop down, hack down, saw down, clear. **2 knock down**, knock to the ground, floor, strike down, knock out; informal deck, flatten, lay out.
• n. a hill or high moor in northern England.

fellow n. **1** a man or boy. **2** a person in the same situation as another. **3** a thing like another. **4** a member of a learned society or (Brit.) of the governing body of a college.
▷ SYNONYMS: **1 man**, boy, person, individual, character; informal guy, lad; Brit. informal chap, bloke; N. Amer. informal dude. **2 companion**, friend, comrade, partner, associate, co-worker, colleague; informal pal, buddy; Brit. informal mate.

fellowship n. **1** friendliness and companionship. **2** a group with a shared interest. **3** the position of a fellow of a college or society.
▷ SYNONYMS: **1 companionship**, comradeship, camaraderie, friendship, sociability, solidarity. **2 association**, organization, society, club, league, union, guild, alliance, fraternity, brotherhood.

felon n. a person who has committed a serious crime.
■ felonious adj.

felony n. (pl. **felonies**) (in the US

and formerly also in English Law) a serious crime.

felspar var. of FELDSPAR.

felt[1] n. cloth made by rolling and pressing damp wool.

felt[2] past & past part. of FEEL.

female adj. **1** of the sex that can bear offspring or produce eggs. **2** (of a plant or flower) having a pistil but no stamens. **3** (of a fitting) made hollow to allow insertion of another part.
• n. a female person, animal, or plant.

feminine adj. **1** having qualities associated with women. **2** female.
▷ SYNONYMS: **womanly**, ladylike, soft, gentle, tender, delicate, pretty.
– ANTONYMS: masculine.
■ femininity n.

feminism n. a movement supporting equal rights for women.
■ feminist n. & adj.

femme fatale /fam fuh-**tahl**/ n. (pl. **femmes fatales**) an attractive and seductive woman.

femur n. (pl. **femurs** or **femora**) the thigh bone.
■ femoral adj.

fen n. a low-lying marshy or flooded area of land.

fence n. **1** a barrier made of wire or wood enclosing an area. **2** informal a dealer in stolen goods.
▷ SYNONYMS: **barrier**, paling, railing, enclosure, barricade, stockade.
• v. **1** surround with a fence. **2** practise the sport of fencing.
▷ SYNONYMS: **1 enclose**, surround, encircle. **2 confine**, pen in, coop up, shut in/up; N. Amer. corral.
■ fencer n.

fencing n. **1** the sport of fighting with blunted swords. **2** fences or material for fences.

fend v. **1** (**fend for yourself**) provide for yourself. **2** (**fend off**) defend yourself from.
▷ SYNONYMS: *they were unable to fend off the invasion:* ward off, head off, stave off, hold off, repel, repulse, resist, fight off.

fender n. **1** a low frame around a fireplace. **2** an object hung over a ship's side to cushion it against impact. **3** US the mudguard or wing of a vehicle.

feng shui /feng **shoo**-i, fung **shway**/ n. an ancient Chinese system of designing buildings and arranging objects to ensure a favourable flow of energy.

fennel n. an aniseed-flavoured vegetable and herb.

f

fenugreek n. a spice made from the seeds of a plant.

feral adj. wild.

ferment v. **1** undergo fermentation. **2** stir up unrest.
• n. unrest or excitement.

fermentation n. the chemical breakdown of a substance by bacteria, yeast, etc.

fern n. a flowerless plant with feathery fronds.

ferocious adj. very fierce or violent.
▷ SYNONYMS: **1** *ferocious animals:* **fierce**, savage, wild, predatory, ravening, aggressive, dangerous. **2** *a ferocious attack:* **brutal**, vicious, violent, bloody, barbaric, savage, frenzied.
– ANTONYMS: gentle, mild.
■ **ferociously** adv. **ferocity** n.

ferret n. a domesticated polecat.
• v. (**ferreting**, **ferreted**) search for in a place or container.

ferric (or **ferrous**) adj. of or containing iron.

Ferris wheel n. a funfair ride consisting of a large upright revolving wheel.

ferrule n. a metal cap which protects the end of a stick etc.

ferry n. (pl. **ferries**) a boat for transporting passengers and goods.
• v. (**ferrying**, **ferried**) carry by ferry or other transport.
▷ SYNONYMS: **transport**, convey, carry, run, ship, shuttle.

fertile adj. producing abundant vegetation or crops. **2** able to conceive young or produce seed. **3** productive or inventive.
▷ SYNONYMS: **1 productive**, fruitful, fecund, rich, lush. **2 creative**, inventive, innovative, visionary, original, ingenious, prolific.
– ANTONYMS: barren.
■ **fertility** n.

fertilize (or **-ise**) v. **1** introduce sperm or pollen into an egg or plant. **2** add a substance to soil to make it more fertile.
■ **fertilization** n. **fertilizer** n.

fervent adj. very passionate.
▷ SYNONYMS: **impassioned**, passionate, intense, vehement, ardent, sincere, heartfelt, enthusiastic, zealous, fanatical, wholehearted, avid, eager, keen, committed, dedicated, devout.
– ANTONYMS: apathetic.
■ **fervently** adv.

fervid adj. fervent.

fervour (US **fervor**) n. passionate feeling.
▷ SYNONYMS: **passion**, ardour, intensity, zeal, vehemence, emotion, warmth, avidity, eagerness, keenness, enthusiasm, excitement, animation, vigour, energy, fire, spirit.
– ANTONYMS: apathy.

fester v. **1** become septic. **2** (of ill feeling) become worse.

festival n. **1** a day or period of celebration. **2** a series of concerts, films, etc.
▷ SYNONYMS: **celebration**, festivity, fete, fair, gala, carnival, fiesta, jamboree, feast day, holiday, holy day.

festive adj. of a festival.
▷ SYNONYMS: **jolly**, merry, joyous, joyful, happy, jovial, light-hearted, cheerful, jubilant, celebratory.

festivity n. **1** joyful celebration. **2** (**festivities**) activities or events celebrating a special occasion.

festoon v. decorate with chains of flowers etc.
▷ SYNONYMS: **decorate**, adorn, ornament, trim, deck out, hang, loop, drape, swathe, garland, wreathe, bedeck; informal do up/out, get up.
• n. a decorative chain of flowers etc.

feta n. a salty Greek cheese.

fetch v. **1** go for and bring back. **2** sell for a particular price.
▷ SYNONYMS: **1 go and get**, go for, call for, summon, pick up, collect, bring, carry, convey, transport. **2 sell for**, bring in, raise, realize, yield, make, command; informal go for.

fetching adj. attractive.
▷ SYNONYMS: **attractive**, appealing, sweet, pretty, lovely, delightful, charming, captivating, enchanting; Scottish & N. English **bonny**; Brit. informal **fit**.

fete /fayt/ n. Brit. an outdoor event to raise funds for a particular cause.
• v. honour or entertain lavishly.

fetid (or **foetid**) adj. smelling very unpleasant.

fetish n. **1** an object worshipped for its supposed magical powers. **2** sexual desire in which pleasure is gained from a particular object.
■ **fetishism** n. **fetishist** n.

fetlock n. the joint of a horse's leg between the knee and the hoof.

fetter v. **1** limit the freedom of. **2** restrain with chains or shackles.
• n. **1** (**fetters**) restrictions. **2** a shackle.

fettle n. condition: *in fine fettle.*

fettuccine /fet-tuh-**chee**-ni/ pl. n. pasta made in ribbons.

fetus (or Brit. **foetus**) n. (pl. **fetuses**) an unborn mammal.
■ **fetal** adj.

feud n. a long, bitter dispute.
▷ SYNONYMS: **vendetta**, conflict, quarrel, dispute, row, rivalry, hostility, strife.
• v. take part in a feud.

feudalism n. the social system in medieval Europe, in which people worked and fought for a lord in return for land.
■ **feudal** adj.

fever n. **1** an abnormally high body temperature. **2** nervous excitement.
▷ SYNONYMS: **1 feverishness**, high temperature; Medicine pyrexia. **2 excitement**, agitation, frenzy, passion, mania.
■ **fevered** adj.

feverish adj. **1** having a fever. **2** showing strong feelings of nervous excitement or energy.
▷ SYNONYMS: **1 febrile**, fevered, hot, burning. **2 frenzied**, frenetic, hectic, agitated, excited, restless, nervous, worked up, overwrought, frantic, furious, hysterical, wild, uncontrolled, unrestrained.

few adj., pron., & n. **1** (**a few**) a small number of. **2** not many.
▷ SYNONYMS: **1** *police have only revealed a few details:* **not many**, hardly any, scarcely any, a handful of, a couple of, one or two. **2** *comforts here are few:* **scarce**, scant, meagre, sparse, in short supply, thin on the ground, few and far between.
− ANTONYMS: many, plentiful.

> USAGE There's a difference between **fewer** and **less**. Use **fewer** with plural nouns, as in *eat fewer cakes;* use **less** with nouns referring to things that can't be counted, as in *there is less blossom on this tree.*

fey adj. **1** unworldly and vague. **2** able to see into the future.

fez n. (pl. **fezzes**) a flat-topped conical red hat worn by some Muslim men.

ff. abbrev. following pages.

fiancé n. (fem. **fiancée**) a person to whom you are engaged to be married.

fiasco n. (pl. **fiascos**) a ridiculous or humiliating failure.
▷ SYNONYMS: **failure**, disaster, catastrophe, debacle, farce, mess; informal flop, washout, shambles; Brit. informal cock-up.
− ANTONYMS: success.

fiat n. an official order.

fib n. a trivial lie.
• v. (**fibbing, fibbed**) tell a fib.
■ **fibber** n.

fibre (US **fiber**) n. **1** each of the strands forming plant or animal tissue, cloth,

or minerals. **2** a substance formed of fibres. **3** roughage in food. **4** strength of character.
▷ SYNONYMS: **thread**, strand, filament, wisp, yarn.
□ **fibreglass** a reinforced plastic material containing glass fibres. **fibre optics** the use of glass fibres to send information in the form of light.
■ **fibrous** adj.

fibroid adj. consisting of fibrous tissue.
• n. a benign fibroid tumour in the womb.

fibula n. (pl. **fibulae** or **fibulas**) the outer of the two bones between the knee and the ankle.

fickle adj. changeable in your loyalties.
▷ SYNONYMS: **capricious**, flighty, giddy, changeable, volatile, mercurial, erratic, unpredictable, unreliable, unsteady.
− ANTONYMS: constant.

fiction n. **1** literature describing imaginary events and people. **2** an invented story.
▷ SYNONYMS: **1 novels**, stories, literature, creative writing. **2 fabrication**, invention, lie, fib, tall story, untruth, falsehood, fantasy, nonsense.
− ANTONYMS: fact.
■ **fictional** adj.

fictitious adj. imaginary or invented.
▷ SYNONYMS: **false**, fake, fabricated, bogus, spurious, assumed, affected, adopted, invented, made up; informal pretend, phoney.
− ANTONYMS: genuine.

fiddle informal n. **1** a violin. **2** an act of fraud.
▷ SYNONYMS: **fraud**, swindle, confidence trick; informal racket, scam.
• v. **1** handle restlessly or nervously. **2** falsify expenses etc.
▷ SYNONYMS: **1 fidget**, play, toy, finger, handle. **2** *someone's fiddled the accounts:* **falsify**, manipulate, massage, rig, distort, misrepresent, doctor, tamper with, interfere with; adjust, tinker with, informal fix, cook the books.
■ **fiddler** n.

fiddly adj. Brit. informal complicated and awkward.

fidelity n. **1** faithfulness. **2** accuracy in a copy or reproduction.
▷ SYNONYMS: **1 faithfulness**, loyalty, constancy, allegiance, commitment, devotion. **2 accuracy**, exactness, precision, correctness, strictness, closeness, authenticity.
− ANTONYMS: disloyalty, infidelity.

f

fidget v. (**fidgeting**, **fidgeted**) make small movements through nervousness or impatience.
▷ SYNONYMS: **1 wriggle**, squirm, twitch, jiggle, shuffle, be agitated; informal be jittery. **play**, fuss, toy, twiddle; informal fiddle.
• n. a person who fidgets.

fidgety adj. restless or impatient.
▷ SYNONYMS: **restless**, restive, on edge, uneasy, nervous, nervy, keyed up, anxious, agitated; informal jittery, twitchy.

fiduciary Law adj. held or given in trust.
• n. (**fiduciaries**) a trustee.

fief /feef/ n. **1** a person's area of operation or control. **2** hist. a piece of land held under the feudal system.
■ **fiefdom** n.

field n. **1** an enclosed area of land for crops or grazing animals. **2** a piece of land used for a sport. **3** a subject of study or area of activity. **4** an area within which a force has an effect: *a magnetic field*. **5** the participants in a race etc.
▷ SYNONYMS: **1 meadow**, pasture, paddock, grassland; literary lea, mead, greensward. **2 pitch**, ground; Brit. informal park. **3 area**, sphere, discipline, province, department, domain, territory, branch, subject. **4 scope**, range, sweep, reach, extent. **5 competitors**, entrants, competition, applicants, candidates, runners.
• v. **1** select to play in a game or to stand in an election. **2** try to deal with. **3** Cricket & Baseball try to catch or stop the ball after it has been hit.
▷ SYNONYMS: **1 catch**, stop, retrieve, return, throw back. **2 deal with**, handle, cope with, answer, reply to, respond to.
□ **field day** a good opportunity to do something. **field events** athletic sports other than races. **field marshal** the highest rank of army officer. **fieldwork** practical research done outside a laboratory or office.
■ **fielder** n.

fiend n. **1** an evil spirit. **2** a very cruel person. **3** informal an enthusiast: *an exercise fiend*.

fiendish adj. **1** very cruel. **2** informal very difficult.
▷ SYNONYMS: **1 wicked**, cruel, vicious, evil, malevolent, villainous, brutal, savage, barbaric, barbarous, inhuman, murderous, ruthless, merciless. **2 cunning**, clever, ingenious, crafty, canny, wily, devious. **3 difficult**,

complex, challenging, complicated, intricate.
■ **fiendishly** adv.

fierce adj. **1** violent or aggressive. **2** powerful.
▷ SYNONYMS: **1 ferocious**, savage, vicious, aggressive. **2 aggressive**, cutthroat, keen, intense, strong, relentless, dog-eat-dog. **3 intense**, powerful, vehement, passionate, impassioned, fervent, ardent. **4 powerful**, strong, violent, forceful, stormy, howling, raging, tempestuous.
– ANTONYMS: gentle, mild.
■ **fiercely** adv. **fierceness** n.

fiery adj. (**fierier**, **fieriest**) **1** consisting of or like fire. **2** quick-tempered or passionate.
▷ SYNONYMS: **1 burning**, blazing, on fire, flaming, ablaze. **2 bright**, brilliant, vivid, intense, rich. **3 passionate**, impassioned, excitable, spirited, quick-tempered, volatile, explosive, impetuous.

fiesta n. (in Spanish-speaking countries) a religious festival.

fife n. a small high-pitched flute.

fifteen adj. & n. one more than fourteen; 15.
■ **fifteenth** adj. & n.

fifth adj. & n. next after fourth.

fifty adj. & n. (pl. **fifties**) ten less than sixty; 50.
□ **fifty-fifty** with equal shares or chances.
■ **fiftieth** adj. & n.

fig n. a soft, sweet fruit with many seeds.

fight v. (**fighting**, **fought**) **1** take part in a violent physical struggle. **2** take part in a war or contest. **3** try hard to stop, overcome, or achieve.
▷ SYNONYMS: **1 brawl**, exchange blows, scuffle, grapple, wrestle, tussle, spar; informal scrap; Brit. informal have a punch-up; N. Amer. informal rough-house. **2 do battle**, serve your country, go to war, take up arms, engage, meet, clash, skirmish. **3 wage**, engage in, conduct, prosecute, undertake. **4 quarrel**, argue, bicker, squabble, fall out, feud, wrangle; Brit. row; informal scrap. **5 campaign**, strive, battle, struggle, crusade, agitate, lobby, push, press. **6 oppose**, contest, confront, challenge, appeal against, take a stand against, dispute, resist. **7 repress**, restrain, suppress, stifle, smother, hold back, fight back, keep in check, curb, choke back; informal keep the lid on, cork up.
• n. an act of fighting.

▷ SYNONYMS: **1 brawl**, scuffle, disturbance, fisticuffs, fracas, melee, skirmish, clash, tussle; informal scrap, dust-up; Brit. informal punch-up; N. Amer. informal rough house; dated affray. **2 boxing match**, bout, match, contest. **3 battle**, engagement, conflict, struggle, war, campaign, crusade, action, hostilities. **4 argument**, quarrel, squabble, wrangle, disagreement, falling-out, dispute, feud; Brit. row; informal tiff, spat, scrap; Brit. informal barney, ding-dong. **5 struggle**, battle, campaign, push, effort. **6** *she had no fight left in her:* **will**, resistance, spirit, pluck, grit, strength, backbone, determination, resolution, resolve.

fighter n. **1** a person who fights. **2** a military aircraft designed for attack.
▷ SYNONYMS: **1 soldier**, fighting man/woman, warrior, combatant, serviceman, servicewoman; (**fighters**) troops, personnel, militia. **2 boxer**, pugilist, prizefighter, wrestler.

figment n. a thing that exists only in the imagination.

figurative adj. not using words literally.
▷ SYNONYMS: **metaphorical**, non-literal, symbolic, allegorical, representative, emblematic.
– ANTONYMS: literal.
  ■ **figuratively** adv.

figure n. **1** a number or numerical symbol. **2** a person's body shape. **3** a well-known person. **4** a geometric shape. **5** a diagram or drawing.
▷ SYNONYMS: **1 statistic**, number, quantity, amount, level, total, sum; (**figures**) data, statistics. **2 digit**, numeral, character, symbol. **3 price**, cost, amount, value, valuation. **4 shape**, outline, form, silhouette, proportions, physique, build, frame. **5 person**, personage, individual, character, personality, celebrity. **6 shape**, pattern, design, motif. **7 diagram**, illustration, drawing, picture, plate.
• v. **1** play an important part. **2** US informal think; suppose.
▷ SYNONYMS: *he figures in many myths:* feature, appear, be featured, be mentioned, be referred to.
□ **figurehead** **1** a leader without real power. **2** a carved statue at the front of a sailing ship. **figure of speech** a word or phrase used in a non-literal sense. **figure out** informal understand.

figurine n. a statuette.

filament n. **1** a slender thread. **2** a fine wire giving off light in an electric light bulb.

filbert n. a hazelnut.

filch v. informal steal.

file n. **1** a folder or box for keeping loose papers. **2** a set of computer data stored under a single name. **3** a line of people or things one behind another. **4** a tool with a rough surface for smoothing.
▷ SYNONYMS: **1 folder**, portfolio, binder. **2 dossier**, document, record, report, data, information, documentation, archives. **3 line**, column, row, queue, string, chain, procession; Brit. informal crocodile.
• v. **1** place in a file. **2** present so as to be officially dealt with. **3** walk one behind the other. **4** smooth with a file.
▷ SYNONYMS: **1 categorize**, classify, organize, put in order, order, arrange, catalogue, store, archive. **2 bring**, press, lodge. **3** march, parade, troop. **4 smooth**, buff, rub down, polish, shape, scrape, abrade, rasp, manicure.

filial adj. of a son or daughter.

filibuster n. prolonged speaking which obstructs progress in a law-making assembly.

filigree n. ornamental work of fine gold or silver wire.

filings pl. n. small particles rubbed off by a file.

fill v. **1** make or become full. **2** block up a hole etc. **3** appoint a person to a vacant post. **4** occupy time.
▷ SYNONYMS: **1 fill up**, top up, charge. **2 crowd into**, throng, pack into, occupy, squeeze into, cram into. **3 stock**, pack, load, supply, replenish. **4 block up**, stop up, plug, seal, caulk. **5** *her perfume filled the room:* **pervade**, permeate, suffuse, penetrate, infuse. **6 occupy**, hold, take up.
– ANTONYMS: empty, clear, leave.
• n. (**your fill**) as much as you want or can bear.
□ **fill in 1** complete a form. **2** give information to. **3** act as a substitute. **fill out** put on weight.

filler n. something used to fill a gap or to increase bulk.

fillet n. a boneless piece of meat or fish.
• v. (**filleting**, **filleted**) remove the bones from a fish.

filling n. a substance used to fill something.
▷ SYNONYMS: **stuffing**, padding, wadding, filler, contents.
• adj. (of food) making you feel full.
▷ SYNONYMS: **substantial**, hearty, ample, satisfying, square, heavy, stodgy.

□ **filling station** a petrol station.
fillip n. a stimulus or boost.
filly n. (pl. **fillies**) a young female horse.
film n. **1** a thin flexible strip of light-sensitive material for photos or motion pictures. **2** a story or event recorded by a camera and shown in a cinema or on television. **3** a thin layer covering a surface.
▷ SYNONYMS: **1 layer**, coat, coating, covering, cover, skin, patina, tissue. **2 movie**, picture, feature film, motion picture, video, DVD. **3 cinema**, movies, the pictures, films, the silver screen, the big screen.
• v. make a film of.
▷ SYNONYMS: **1 photograph**, record on film, shoot, capture on film, video. **2 cloud**, mist, haze, blur.
filmy adj. (of fabric) thin and almost transparent.
filo n. Greek pastry in the form of very thin sheets.
filter n. **1** a device or substance for holding back solid particles in a liquid or gas passing through it. **2** a screen which absorbs some of the light passing through it.
▷ SYNONYMS: **strainer**, sifter, sieve, gauze, mesh, net.
• v. **1** pass through a filter. **2** move gradually in or out.
▷ SYNONYMS: **1 sieve**, strain, sift, clarify, purify, refine, treat. **2 seep**, percolate, leak, trickle, ooze, leach.
filth n. **1** disgusting dirt. **2** obscene language or material.
▷ SYNONYMS: **dirt**, muck, grime, mud, sludge, slime, excrement, excreta, ordure, sewage, pollution.
filthy adj. (**filthier**, **filthiest**) **1** disgustingly dirty. **2** obscene. **3** informal very unpleasant.
▷ SYNONYMS: **1 dirty**, mucky, grimy, foul, squalid, sordid, soiled, stained, polluted, contaminated, unwashed. **2 obscene**, rude, vulgar, dirty, smutty, improper, coarse, bawdy, lewd; informal blue.
– ANTONYMS: clean, pleasant.
filtrate n. a filtered liquid.
■ **filtration** n.
fin n. **1** a flattened part projecting from the body of a fish, dolphin, etc., used for swimming and balancing. **2** a projection on an aircraft, rocket, etc. to improve stability.
final adj. **1** coming at the end; last. **2** allowing no dispute.
▷ SYNONYMS: **1 last**, closing, concluding, finishing, end, ultimate, eventual. **2 irrevocable**, unalterable, absolute,

conclusive, irrefutable, incontrovertible, indisputable, unchallengeable, binding.
– ANTONYMS: first, provisional.
• n. **1** the last game in a tournament, deciding the overall winner. **2** (**finals**) Brit. exams at the end of a degree course.
■ **finality** n.
finale /fi-nah-li/ n. the last part of a piece of music or entertainment.
▷ SYNONYMS: **climax**, culmination, end, ending, finish, close, conclusion, termination, denouement.
– ANTONYMS: opening.
finalist n. a competitor in a final.
finalize (or **-ise**) v. complete a plan or agreement.
finally adv. **1** in the end; eventually. **2** as the final point in a series.
▷ SYNONYMS: **1 eventually**, ultimately, in the end, at last, in the long run, in the fullness of time. **2 lastly**, last, in conclusion.
finance n. **1** the management of money. **2** money to support an enterprise. **3** (**finances**) the money held by an organization etc.
▷ SYNONYMS: **1 financial affairs**, money matters, economics, commerce, business, investment. **2 funds**, money, capital, cash, resources, assets, reserves, funding.
• v. fund.
▷ SYNONYMS: **fund**, pay for, back, capitalize, endow, subsidize, invest in, sponsor; N. Amer. informal bankroll.
financial adj. to do with money or finance.
▷ SYNONYMS: **monetary**, money, economic, pecuniary, fiscal, banking, commercial, business, investment.
■ **financially** adv.
financier n. a person who manages the finances of large organizations.
finch n. a small bird with a short bill.
find v. (**finding**, **found**) **1** discover. **2** learn. **3** declare a verdict. **4** reach a state or point.
▷ SYNONYMS: **1 locate**, spot, pinpoint, unearth, obtain, search out, track down, root out, come across/upon, run across/into, chance on, happen on, stumble on, encounter; informal bump into. **2 discover**, invent, come up with, hit on. **3 realize**, become aware, discover, observe, notice, note, learn. **4 consider**, think, feel to be, look on as, view as, see as, judge, deem, regard as. **5 judge**, deem, rule, declare, pronounce.
– ANTONYMS: lose.

•n. a valuable or interesting discovery.

▷ SYNONYMS: **1 discovery**, acquisition. **2 bargain**, godsend, boon, catch, asset; informal good buy. □ **find out** discover information. ■ **finder** n.

finding n. a conclusion reached after an inquiry etc.

fine adj. **1** of very high quality. **2** satisfactory. **3** in good health. **4** (of the weather) bright and free from rain. **5** thin. **6** consisting of small particles. **7** delicate or complex. **8** subtle.

▷ SYNONYMS: **1** *fine wines:* **good**, choice, select, excellent, first-class, first-rate, great, exceptional, outstanding, splendid, magnificent, exquisite, superb, wonderful, superlative, prime, quality, special, superior, of distinction, premium, classic, vintage; informal A1, top-notch. **2** *a fine fellow:* **worthy**, admirable, praiseworthy, laudable, upright, upstanding, respectable. **3** all right, acceptable, suitable, good enough, passable, satisfactory, adequate, reasonable, tolerable; informal OK. **4** healthy, well, good, all right, fit, blooming, thriving, in good shape/condition; informal OK, in fine fettle, in the pink. **5** fair, dry, bright, clear, sunny, cloudless, balmy. **6** keen, quick, alert, sharp, razor-sharp, acute, bright, brilliant, astute, clever, intelligent. **7** elegant, stylish, expensive, smart, chic, fashionable, fancy, sumptuous, lavish, opulent; informal flashy. **8** flyaway, wispy, delicate, thin, light. **9** sheer, light, lightweight, thin, flimsy, diaphanous, fine, seethrough. **10** subtle, ultra-fine, nice, hair-splitting.

•n. a sum of money to be paid as a punishment.

▷ SYNONYMS: **penalty**, forfeit, damages, fee, excess charge.

•v. make someone pay a fine. □ **with a fine-tooth comb** (or **fine-toothed comb**) with a very thorough search or examination. ■ **finely** adv. **fineness** n.

finery n. showy clothes.

finesse n. delicate skill, esp. in handling situations.

finger n. **1** each of the four jointed parts attached to either hand (five, if the thumb is included). **2** a small measure of alcohol in a glass.

▷ SYNONYMS: **digit**.

•v. touch or feel with the fingers.

▷ SYNONYMS: **touch**, feel, handle, stroke, rub, caress, fondle, toy with, play with, fiddle with. □ **fingerboard** a flat strip on the neck of a stringed instrument, against which the strings are pressed to vary the pitch. **fingerprint** a mark made by the pad of a person's finger, used for identification.

finial n. an ornament at the end of a gable etc.

finicky adj. **1** fussy. **2** detailed and fiddly.

finish v. **1** bring or come to an end. **2** eat or drink the whole or the remainder of. **3** reach the end of a race etc. **4** (**finish off**) kill or completely defeat. **5** complete or put the final touches to.

▷ SYNONYMS: **1 complete**, end, conclude, close, terminate, wind up, round off, achieve, accomplish, fulfil; informal wrap up, sew up. **2 come to an end**, end, stop, come to a close, cease. **3 consume**, eat, devour, drink, finish off, polish off, use up, exhaust, empty, drain, get through; informal down. – ANTONYMS: start.

•n. **1** an end or final stage. **2** the way in which a manufactured article is finished.

▷ SYNONYMS: **1 end**, ending, completion, conclusion, close, termination, finale, denouement. **2 surface**, texture, coating, covering, lacquer, glaze, veneer, gloss, patina, sheen, lustre. – ANTONYMS: start.

finite /fy-nyt/ adj. limited.

▷ SYNONYMS: **limited**, restricted, determinate, fixed.

Finn n. a person from Finland. ■ **Finnish** n. & adj.

fiord var. of FJORD.

fir n. an evergreen coniferous tree.

fire n. **1** the light, heat, etc. produced when something burns. **2** an instance of destructive burning. **3** wood or coal that is burning. **4** a gas or electric heater. **5** passion. **6** the firing of guns.

▷ SYNONYMS: **1 blaze**, conflagration, inferno, flames, burning, combustion. **2 dynamism**, energy, vigour, animation, vitality, exuberance, zest, elan, passion, zeal, spirit, verve, vivacity, enthusiasm; informal go, get-up-and-go, oomph. **3 gunfire**, firing, shooting, bombardment, shelling, volley, salvo, hail.

•v. **1** send a bullet, missile, etc. from a gun or other weapon. **2** informal dismiss from a job. **3** stimulate. **4** supply fuel to. **5** bake pottery in a kiln.

▷ SYNONYMS: **1 launch**, shoot, discharge,

let fly with. **2 shoot**, discharge, let off, set off. **3 dismiss**, discharge, give someone their notice, lay off, let go; informal sack. **4 stimulate**, stir up, excite, awaken, rouse, inflame, animate, inspire, motivate.
□ **firearm** a rifle, pistol, or shotgun. **firebrand** a passionate supporter of a cause. **firebreak** a strip of open space to stop a fire from spreading. **fire brigade** Brit. a team of people employed to put out fires. **fire engine** a vehicle carrying firefighters and their equipment. **fire escape** a staircase or ladder used to escape from a burning building. **firefighter** a person whose job is to put out fires. **firefly** a kind of beetle which glows in the dark. **fireman** a male firefighter. **fireplace** a recess at the base of a chimney for a domestic fire. **fireside** the area round a fireplace. **firewall** a part of a computer system that blocks unauthorized access. **firework** a device containing chemicals that explode to produce spectacular effects. **firing squad** a group of soldiers ordered to shoot a condemned person.

> **WORD LINKS**
> **arson** the crime of setting fire to property
> **pyromania** an obsessive desire to set fire to things

firm adj. **1** not giving way under pressure. **2** solidly in place. **3** (of a grip etc.) steady and strong. **4** showing determination and strength of character. **5** fixed or definite.
▷ SYNONYMS: **1 hard**, solid, unyielding, resistant, compacted, compressed, dense, stiff, rigid, set. **2 secure**, stable, steady, strong, fixed, fast, tight, immovable, rooted, stationary, motionless. **3 resolute**, determined, decided, resolved, steadfast, adamant, emphatic, insistent, single-minded, wholehearted, unfaltering, unwavering, unflinching, unswerving, unbending, committed. **4 close**, good, boon, intimate, insepar-able, dear, special, constant, devoted, loving, faithful, long-standing, steady, steadfast. **5 definite**, fixed, settled, decided, cut-and-dried, established, confirmed, agreed.
– ANTONYMS: soft, unstable.
• v. make firm.
• n. a business organization.
▷ SYNONYMS: **business**, company, concern, enterprise, organization,

corporation, conglomerate, office, bureau, agency, consortium; informal outfit, operation.
■ **firmly** adv. **firmness** n.
firmament n. the heavens; the sky.
first adj. & n. **1** coming before all others in time, order, or importance. **2** before doing something else.
▷ SYNONYMS: **1 earliest**, initial, opening, introductory. **2** the first principles of political philosophy: **fundamental**, basic, rudimentary, primary, key, cardinal, central, chief, vital, essen-tial. **3** safety is our first priority: **foremost**, principal, highest, greatest, paramount, top, main, overriding, central, core; informal number-one. **4 top**, best, prime, premier, winning, champion.
– ANTONYMS: last.
□ **at first** at the beginning. **first aid** emergency medical help given before full treatment. **first class** excellent. **first-degree** (of burns) causing only reddening of the skin. **first-hand** directly from the original source. **first name** a personal name. **first-rate** excellent.
■ **firstly** adv.
firth n. a narrow inlet of the sea, esp. in Scotland.
fiscal adj. of government revenue.
fish n. (pl. **fish** or **fishes**) **1** a cold-blooded animal with gills and fins, living in water. **2** the flesh of fish as food.
• v. **1** try to catch fish. **2** take out of water or a container. **3** (**fish for**) try to get by subtle means.
▷ SYNONYMS: **1 go fishing**, angle, trawl. **2 search**, delve, look, hunt, grope, fumble, ferret, rummage.
□ **fisherman** a person who catches fish for a living or for sport. **fishmonger** a person selling fish for food. **fishnet** an open mesh fabric.

> **WORD LINKS**
> **piscine** relating to fish
> **ichthyology** the study of fish

fishery n. (pl. **fisheries**) a place where fish are reared for food, or caught in numbers.
fishy adj. **1** of or like fish. **2** informal arousing suspicion.
fissile adj. **1** able to undergo nuclear fission. **2** (of rock) easily split.
fission n. the act of splitting, esp. of an atomic nucleus with the release of much energy.
fissure n. a long, narrow crack.
fist n. a tightly closed hand.

□ **fisticuffs** fighting with the fists.
■ **fistful** n.

fit adj. (**fitter, fittest**) **1** of a suitable quality, standard, or type. **2** in good health.
▷ SYNONYMS: **1 suitable**, appropriate, suited, apposite, fitting, good enough, apt, competent, able, capable, ready, prepared, equipped. **2 healthy**, well, in good health, in good shape, in trim, in good condition, fighting fit, athletic, muscular, strapping, strong, robust, hale and hearty.
– ANTONYMS: unsuitable, incapable, unfit.
  • v. (**fitting, fitted**) **1** be the right shape and size for. **2** be able to occupy a particular position or space. **3** fix into place. **4** provide with. **5** try clothing on and alter it.
▷ SYNONYMS: **1 lay**, install, put in, position, place, fix, arrange, connect, piece together, attach, join, link. **2 equip**, provide, supply, fit out, furnish. **3 be appropriate to**, suit, match, correspond to, tally with, go with, accord with.
  • n. **1** the way something fits. **2** a sudden attack of violent, uncontrolled movements. **3** a sudden outburst of feeling, coughing, etc.
▷ SYNONYMS: **1 convulsion**, spasm, paroxysm, seizure, attack. **2 outbreak**, outburst, attack, bout, spell. **3 tantrum**, frenzy; informal paddy.
■ **fitness** n.

fitful adj. not steady or continuous.
■ **fitfully** adv.

fitment n. Brit. a fixed item of furniture.

fitter n. **1** a person who assembles or installs machinery. **2** a person who fits clothes.

fitting n. **1** a small part attached to furniture or equipment. **2** (**fittings**) items fixed in a building but removable when the owner moves. **3** an occasion of a garment being fitted.
▷ SYNONYMS: **1 attachment**, part, piece, component, accessory, apparatus. **2 furnishings**, furniture, fixtures, fitments, equipment.
  • adj. appropriate.
▷ SYNONYMS: **apt**, appropriate, suitable, apposite, fit, proper, right, seemly, correct.
– ANTONYMS: unsuitable.
■ **fittingly** adv.

five adj. & n. one more than four; 5.

fiver n. Brit. informal a five-pound note.

fix v. **1** attach or position securely. **2** repair. **3** decide or settle on. **4** make arrangements for. **5** make permanent. **6** (**fix on**) direct the eyes etc. steadily toward. **7** informal influence a result etc. dishonestly.
▷ SYNONYMS: **1 fasten**, attach, affix, secure, connect, couple, link, install, stick, glue, pin, nail, screw, bolt, clamp, clip. **2 repair**, mend, put right, get working, restore. **3 decide on**, select, choose, settle, set, arrange, establish, allot, designate, name, appoint, specify. **4 arrange**, organize, prepare, contrive, manage, engineer; informal swing, wangle. **5 focus**, direct, level, point, train. **6 rig**, tamper with, skew, influence; informal fiddle.
  • n. **1** an act of fixing. **2** informal a difficult situation. **3** informal a dose of an addictive drug.
▷ SYNONYMS: **1 predicament**, plight, difficulty, awkward situation, corner, tight spot, mess; informal pickle, jam, hole, scrape, bind.
  □ **fix up 1** organize. **2** informal provide with.
■ **fixer** n.

fixate v. (**fixate on** or **be fixated on**) be obsessed with.

fixation n. an obsession.
▷ SYNONYMS: **obsession**, preoccupation, mania, addiction, compulsion; informal thing, bug, bee in your bonnet.

fixative n. a substance used to fix or protect something.

fixed adj. **1** attached or fastened securely. **2** not changing or able to be changed.
▷ SYNONYMS: **predetermined**, set, established, arranged, specified, decided, agreed, determined, confirmed, prescribed, definite, defined, explicit, precise.

fixity n. the state of being permanent.

fixture n. **1** a piece of equipment etc. which is fixed in position. **2** (**fixtures**) articles attached to a house that remain when the owner moves. **3** Brit. a sports event on a particular date.

fizz v. produce bubbles of gas with a hissing sound.
▷ SYNONYMS: **bubble**, sparkle, effervesce, froth.
  • n. **1** the quality of being fizzy. **2** informal a fizzy drink.
▷ SYNONYMS: **1 bubbles**, sparkle, fizziness, effervescence, gassiness, froth. **2 crackle**, buzz, hiss, white noise.

fizzle v. **1** make a weak hissing sound. **2** (**fizzle out**) end feebly.

fizzy adj. (**fizzier, fizziest**) (of a drink)

containing bubbles of gas.
▷ SYNONYMS: **sparkling**, effervescent, carbonated, gassy, bubbly, frothy.
– ANTONYMS: still, flat.

fjord (or **fiord**) /fyord, fee-ord/ n. a long, narrow inlet of the sea between high cliffs, esp. in Norway.

fl. abbrev. **1** floruit, used to indicate when a historical figure lived or was most active. **2** fluid.

flab n. informal excess fat on the body.

flabbergasted adj. informal very surprised.

flabby adj. (**flabbier, flabbiest**) fat and floppy.
■ **flabbiness** n.

flaccid /flass-id/ adj. soft and limp.

flag n. **1** a piece of cloth attached to a pole or rope as a symbol or signal. **2** a flagstone.
▷ SYNONYMS: **banner**, standard, ensign, pennant, streamer, colours.
• v. (**flagging, flagged**) **1** mark for attention. **2** (**flag down**) signal to a driver to stop. **3** become tired or less enthusiastic.
▷ SYNONYMS: **1 indicate**, identify, point out, mark, label, tag, highlight. **2 tire**, grow tired, wilt, weaken, grow weak, droop. **3 fade**, decline, wane, ebb, diminish, decrease, lessen, dwindle.
□ **flagship 1** an admiral's ship. **2** the most important product of an organization. **flagstone** a large paving stone.

flagellate v. whip.
■ **flagellation** n.

flagon n. a large bottle or jug for wine, cider, etc.

flagrant adj. very obvious and unashamed.
▷ SYNONYMS: **blatant**, glaring, obvious, conspicuous, barefaced, shameless, brazen, undisguised.
■ **flagrantly** adv.

flail v. move around wildly.
• n. a tool or machine used for threshing grain.

flair n. **1** a natural ability or talent. **2** stylishness.
▷ SYNONYMS: **1 aptitude**, talent, gift, instinct, ability, facility, knack, skill. **2 style**, elegance, panache, dash, elan, poise, taste; informal class.

flak n. **1** anti-aircraft fire. **2** strong criticism.

flake n. a small, flat, thin piece of something.
▷ SYNONYMS: **sliver**, wafer, shaving, paring, chip, fragment, scrap, shred.
• v. **1** come off in flakes. **2** separate into flakes. **3** (**flake out**) informal fall

asleep or drop from exhaustion.
■ **flakiness** n. **flaky** adj.

flambé /flom-bay/ v. (**flambéing, flambéed**) cover food with spirits and set it alight briefly.

flamboyant adj. **1** very confident and lively. **2** brightly coloured or decorated.
▷ SYNONYMS: **1 ostentatious**, exuberant, confident, lively, animated, vibrant, vivacious. **2 colourful**, bright, vibrant, vivid, dazzling, bold, showy, gaudy, garish, loud; informal jazzy, flashy.
– ANTONYMS: restrained.
■ **flamboyance** n. **flamboyantly** adv.

flame n. a glowing stream of burning gas produced by something on fire.
▷ SYNONYMS: **1 fire**, blaze, conflagration, inferno. **2 sweetheart**, boyfriend, girlfriend, lover, partner.
• v. **1** give off flames. **2** (of the face) go red. **3** informal send insulting email to.
□ **old flame** informal a former lover.

flamenco n. a Spanish style of singing and dancing.

flamingo n. (pl. **flamingos** or **flamingoes**) a pink wading bird with long legs.

flammable adj. easily set on fire.

flan n. an open pastry or sponge case with a filling.

flange n. a projecting flat rim.
■ **flanged** adj.

flank n. **1** a side, esp. of the body between the ribs and hip. **2** the left or right side of a group.
▷ SYNONYMS: **1 side**, haunch, quarter, thigh. **2 side**, wing, sector, face, aspect.
• v. be on either side of.
▷ SYNONYMS: **edge**, bound, line, border, fringe.

flannel n. **1** a soft fabric with a raised surface. **2** (**flannels**) trousers made of flannel. **3** Brit. a facecloth. **4** Brit. informal evasive and meaningless talk.

flannelette n. a cotton fabric like flannel.

flap v. (**flapping, flapped**) **1** move up and down or from side to side. **2** Brit. informal be agitated.
▷ SYNONYMS: **1** *ducks flapped their wings:* beat, flutter, agitate, vibrate, wag, thrash, flail. **2** *the flag flapped in the breeze:* flutter, wave, fly, blow, swing, ripple, stir.
• n. **1** a piece of something attached on one side only to cover an opening. **2** a single flapping movement. **3** informal a panic.
▷ SYNONYMS: **1 beat**, stroke, flutter,

movement. **2 panic**, fluster; informal state, stew, tizzy; N. Amer. informal **twit**.

flapjack n. a thick biscuit made with oats.

flare n. **1** a burst of flame or light. **2** a device producing a very bright flame as a signal or marker. **3** a gradual widening towards the hem of a garment. **4** (**flares**) trousers which widen from the knees down.

▷ SYNONYMS: **1 blaze**, flame, flash, burst, flicker. **2 signal**, beacon, rocket, light, torch.

• v. **1** blaze suddenly. **2** suddenly become intense or violent. **3** gradually widen at one end.

▷ SYNONYMS: **1 blaze**, flash, flare up, flame, burn, flicker. **2 spread**, splay, broaden, widen, dilate.

flash v. **1** shine with a bright but brief or irregular light. **2** move or send swiftly. **3** display briefly, repeatedly, or obviously.

▷ SYNONYMS: **1 shine**, flare, blaze, gleam, glint, sparkle, burn, blink, wink, flicker, shimmer, twinkle, glimmer, glisten. **2 zoom**, streak, tear, shoot, dash, dart, fly, whistle, hurtle, rush, bolt, race, speed, career; informal belt, zap; Brit. informal **bomb**; N. Amer. informal **barrel**. **3 show off**, flaunt, flourish, display, parade.

• n. **1** a sudden brief burst of bright light. **2** a camera attachment producing a flash of light. **3** a sudden or brief occurrence. **4** Brit. a coloured patch on a uniform.

▷ SYNONYMS: **flare**, blaze, burst, gleam, glint, sparkle, flicker, shimmer, twinkle, glimmer.

• adj. informal stylish or expensive in a showy way.

□ **flashback** a scene in a film or novel set in a time earlier than the main story. **flash flood** a sudden local flood. **flash in the pan** a sudden but brief success. **flashlight** an electric torch. **flashpoint** a point at which anger or violence flares up.

flashing n. a strip of metal sealing the joins of a roof.

flashy adj. (**flashier**, **flashiest**) attractive in a showy or cheap way.

▷ SYNONYMS: **ostentatious**, flamboyant, showy, conspicuous, extravagant, expensive, vulgar, tasteless, brash, garish, loud, gaudy; informal snazzy, fancy, swanky, flash, glitzy.

– ANTONYMS: understated.

■ **flashily** adv.

flask n. **1** a bottle with a narrow neck. **2** a vacuum flask.

flat adj. (**flatter**, **flattest**) **1** level and even. **2** not sloping. **3** not lively or interesting. **4** no longer fizzy. **5** Brit. (of a battery) having used up its charge. **6** (of a price) fixed. **7** definite and firm. **8** (of musical sound) below true pitch. **9** (of a note) lower by a semitone than a specified note.

▷ SYNONYMS: **1 level**, horizontal, smooth, even, plane. **2 calm**, still, glassy, smooth, placid, like a mill-pond. **3 monotonous**, boring, dull, tedious, uninteresting, unexciting. **4** *the market is flat*: **inactive**, slow, sluggish, slack, quiet, depressed. **5** *a flat fee*: **fixed**, set, invariable, regular, constant. **6** *a flat refusal*: **outright**, direct, absolute, definite, positive, straight, plain, explicit, categorical.

– ANTONYMS: sloping, rough, uneven.

• adv. **1** so as to be flat. **2** informal definitely; absolutely.

▷ SYNONYMS: **stretched out**, outstretched, spreadeagled, sprawling, prone, prostrate, supine, recumbent.

• n. **1** Brit. a set of rooms forming an individual home within a larger building. **2** a flat part or area. **3** a musical note that is a semitone lower than a specified note, or a sign indicating this.

▷ SYNONYMS: **apartment**, suite, pent-house, rooms.

□ **flatfish** a sea fish with a flattened body and both eyes on the upper side. **flatmate** Brit. a person with whom you share a flat. **flat out** as fast or as hard as possible.

■ **flatly** adv. **flatness** n.

flatten v. make or become flat or flatter.

▷ SYNONYMS: **1 level**, even out, smooth out. **2 squash**, compress, press down, crush, compact, trample. **3 demolish**, raze to the ground, tear down, knock down, destroy, wreck, devastate.

– ANTONYMS: crumple.

flatter v. **1** compliment insincerely. **2** (**be flattered**) feel honoured. **3** make someone appear attractive.

▷ SYNONYMS: **1 compliment**, praise, fawn on, humour; informal sweet-talk, soft-soap, butter up, play up to. **2** *I was flattered to be asked*: **honour**, gratify, please, delight; informal tickle pink. **3 suit**, become, look good on, go well with; informal do something for.

– ANTONYMS: insult, offend.

■ **flatterer** n.

flattering adj. **1** full of praise and compliments. **2** pleasing and gratifying. **3** making someone look attractive.

▷ SYNONYMS: **complimentary**, praising, favourable, admiring, appreciative, fulsome, honeyed, obsequious, ingratiating, sycophantic.

flattery n. excessive or insincere praise.

▷ SYNONYMS: **praise**, adulation, compliments, blandishments, honeyed words, blarney; informal sweet talk, soft soap.

flatulent adj. having too much gas in the intestines or stomach.

■ **flatulence** n.

flaunt v. display obviously.

▷ SYNONYMS: **show off**, display, make a great show of, put on show/display, parade, draw attention to, brag about, crow about, vaunt; informal flash.

> **USAGE** Don't confuse **flaunt** with **flout**, which means 'openly fail to follow a rule'.

flautist n. a flute player.

flavour (US flavor) n. **1** the distinctive taste of a food or drink. **2** a particular quality.

▷ SYNONYMS: **1 taste**, savour, tang, smack. **2 flavouring**, seasoning, taste, tang, relish, bite, piquancy, spice. **3 character**, quality, feel, feeling, ambience, atmosphere, air, mood, tone, spirit. **4 impression**, suggestion, hint, taste.

• v. give flavour to.

▷ SYNONYMS: **season**, spice, add piquancy to, ginger up, enrich, infuse.

■ **flavourless** adj.

flavouring (US flavoring) n. a substance used to flavour food or drink.

flaw n. **1** a mark or fault that spoils something. **2** a weakness or mistake.

▷ SYNONYMS: **defect**, blemish, fault, imperfection, deficiency, weakness, weak spot/point, failing; Computing bug; informal glitch.

– ANTONYMS: strength.

flawed adj. damaged or spoiled.

▷ SYNONYMS: **1 faulty**, defective, imperfect, blemished, damaged, broken; Brit. informal duff. **2 unsound**, distorted, inaccurate, incorrect, erroneous, fallacious, wrong.

– ANTONYMS: flawless.

flawless adj. with no imperfections or mistakes.

▷ SYNONYMS: **perfect**, unblemished, unmarked, unimpaired, whole, intact, sound, unbroken, undamaged, mint, pristine, impeccable, immaculate,

accurate, correct, faultless, error-free, exemplary, model, ideal, copybook.

– ANTONYMS: flawed.

flax n. a blue-flowered plant grown esp. for making cloth.

flaxen adj. (of hair) pale yellow.

flay v. **1** strip the skin from. **2** criticize harshly.

flea n. a small jumping bloodsucking insect.

□ **flea market** a street market selling second-hand goods. **fleapit** Brit. informal a run-down cinema.

fleck n. a very small patch or particle.

• v. mark with flecks.

fledged adj. (of a young bird) having wing feathers large enough for flight.

fledgling (or fledgeling) n. a young bird that has just learned to fly.

flee v. (fleeing, fled) run away.

▷ SYNONYMS: **run away**, run off, run for it, make off, take off, take to your heels, make a break for it, bolt, beat a retreat, make a quick exit, escape; informal beat it, clear off/out, skedaddle, scram; Brit. informal scarper.

fleece n. **1** the wool coat of a sheep. **2** a soft, warm fabric with a pile, or a jacket made from this.

• v. informal swindle.

■ **fleecy** adj.

fleet n. **1** a group of ships, vehicles, or aircraft travelling together or having the same owner. **2** a navy.

▷ SYNONYMS: **navy**, armada, flotilla, squadron, convoy.

• adj. fast and nimble.

fleeting adj. passing quickly; brief.

▷ SYNONYMS: **brief**, short-lived, quick, momentary, cursory, transient, ephemeral, passing, transitory.

– ANTONYMS: lasting.

■ **fleetingly** adv.

flesh n. **1** the soft substance in the body consisting of muscle and fat. **2** the soft part of a fruit or vegetable. **3** (the flesh) the physical aspects of the body.

▷ SYNONYMS: **1 tissue**, skin, muscle, fat, meat, body. **2 pulp**, marrow, meat. **3** the pleasures of the flesh: **the body**, human nature, physicality, sensuality, sexuality.

• v. (flesh out) make more detailed.

□ **in the flesh** in person.

■ **fleshly** adj.

fleshy adj. (fleshier, fleshiest) **1** plump. **2** soft and thick.

fleur-de-lis (or fleur-de-lys) /fler-duh-**lee**/ n. (pl. fleurs-de-lis) a design of a lily with three petals.

flew past of FLY.

flex v. **1** bend a limb or joint. **2** tighten a muscle.
• n. Brit. an insulated cable for carrying electric current.
■ **flexion** n.

flexible adj. **1** able to bend easily. **2** easily changed; adaptable.
▷ SYNONYMS: **1 bendy**, pliable, supple, pliant, plastic, elastic, stretchy, springy, resilient, bouncy. **2 adaptable**, adjustable, variable, versatile, open-ended, open. **3 accommodating**, amenable, willing to compromise, cooperative, tolerant.
– ANTONYMS: rigid, inflexible.
■ **flexibility** n. **flexibly** adv.

flexitime n. a system allowing flexible working hours.

flibbertigibbet n. a frivolous person.

flick v. move, hit, or remove with a quick light movement.
▷ SYNONYMS: **1 click**, snap, flip, jerk, throw. **2 swish**, twitch, wave, wag, waggle, shake, whisk.
• n. **1** a sudden quick movement. **2 (the flicks)** informal the cinema.

flicker v. **1** shine or burn unsteadily. **2** appear briefly. **3** make small, quick movements.
▷ SYNONYMS: **1 glimmer**, flare, dance, gutter, twinkle, sparkle, wink, flash. **2 flutter**, quiver, tremble, shiver, shudder, jerk, twitch.
• n. **1** a flickering movement or light. **2** a brief occurrence.

flier var. of FLYER.

flight n. **1** the act of flying. **2** a journey through air or space. **3** the path of something through the air. **4** the act of running away. **5** a group of flying birds or aircraft. **6** a series of steps. **7** the tail of an arrow or dart.
▷ SYNONYMS: **1 aviation**, flying, air transport, aeronautics. **2 flock**, swarm, cloud, throng. **3 escape**, getaway, hasty departure, exit, exodus, breakout, bolt, disappearance; Brit. informal flit.
□ **flight deck 1** the cockpit of a large aircraft. **2** the deck of an aircraft carrier. **flightless** unable to fly.

flighty adj. unreliable and frivolous.

flimsy adj. (flimsier, flimsiest) **1** fragile. **2** light and thin. **3** unconvincing.
▷ SYNONYMS: **1 insubstantial**, fragile, frail, rickety, ramshackle, makeshift, jerry-built, shoddy. **2 thin**, light, fine, filmy, floaty, diaphanous, sheer, delicate, gossamer, gauzy. **3 weak**, feeble, poor, inadequate, insufficient, thin, unsubstantial, unconvincing,

implausible.
– ANTONYMS: sturdy.
■ **flimsily** adv. **flimsiness** n.

flinch v. **1** make a quick, nervous movement from fear or pain. **2 (flinch from)** avoid through fear or anxiety.
▷ SYNONYMS: **1 wince**, start, shudder, quiver, jerk. **2** *he never flinched from his duty:* **shrink from**, recoil from, shy away from, dodge, evade, avoid, duck, baulk at.

fling v. (flinging, flung) throw or move forcefully.
▷ SYNONYMS: **throw**, hurl, toss, sling, launch, pitch, lob; informal chuck, heave.
• n. **1** a short period of enjoyment. **2** a short sexual relationship.
▷ SYNONYMS: **1 good time**, party, spree, fun and games; informal binge, bash, night on the town. **2 affair**, love affair, relationship, romance, liaison, entanglement, involvement.

flint n. **1** a hard grey rock. **2** a piece of flint or a metal alloy, used to produce a spark.
□ **flintlock** an old type of gun.
■ **flinty** adj.

flip v. (flipping, flipped) **1** turn over, throw, or move with a sudden, quick movement. **2** informal lose self-control.
▷ SYNONYMS: **overturn**, turn over, tip over, roll over, upturn, capsize, upend, invert, knock over, keel over, topple over, turn turtle.
• n. a flipping movement.
• adj. flippant.
□ **flip-flop** a sandal with a thong passing between the big and second toes.

flippant adj. not showing proper seriousness or respect.
▷ SYNONYMS: **frivolous**, facetious, tongue-in-cheek, disrespectful, irreverent, cheeky; informal flip, saucy; N. Amer. informal sassy.
– ANTONYMS: serious.
■ **flippancy** n. **flippantly** adv.

flipper n. **1** a sea animal's broad, flat limb used in swimming. **2** each of two flat rubber attachments worn on the feet for underwater swimming.

flirt v. **1** behave as if trying to attract someone sexually but without serious intentions. **2 (flirt with)** show a casual interest in.
• n. a person who flirts.
▷ SYNONYMS: **tease**, coquette, heartbreaker.
■ **flirtation** n. **flirtatious** adj.

flit v. (flitting, flitted) move quickly and lightly.

flitter v. move quickly here and there.

float v. **1** rest or move on the surface of a liquid. **2** move or be held up in the air. **3** put forward a suggestion. **4** offer the shares of a company for sale.
▷ SYNONYMS: **1 drift**, glide, sail, slip, slide, waft. **2 hover**, levitate, be suspended, hang, defy gravity.
– ANTONYMS: sink.
• n. **1** a thing designed to float on water. **2** a vehicle carrying a display in a procession. **3** Brit. a sum of money for minor expenses or giving change.
■ **floaty** adj.

floatation var. of FLOTATION.

flocculent adj. like tufts of wool.

flock n. **1** a number of birds or animals together. **2** a large number or crowd. **3** a Christian congregation. **4** wool or cotton refuse used as stuffing.
▷ SYNONYMS: **1 herd**, drove. **2 flight**, swarm, cloud, gaggle, skein.
• v. gather or move in a flock.
▷ SYNONYMS: **gather**, collect, congregate, assemble, converge, mass, crowd, throng, cluster, swarm, stream, troop.
□ **flock wallpaper** wallpaper with a raised pattern made from powdered cloth.

floe n. a sheet of floating ice.

flog v. (**flogging**, **flogged**) **1** beat with a whip or stick. **2** Brit. informal sell.
▷ SYNONYMS: **whip**, thrash, lash, scourge, birch, cane, beat.

flood n. **1** an overflow of a large amount of water over dry land. **2** an overwhelming quantity or amount. **3** the rising of the tide.
▷ SYNONYMS: **1 inundation**, deluge, torrent, overflow, flash flood; Brit. spate. **2 gush**, outpouring, torrent, rush, stream, surge, cascade.
3 succession, series, string, barrage, volley, battery, avalanche, torrent, stream, storm.
• v. **1** cover with flood water. **2** (of a river) overflow its banks. **3** arrive in very large numbers.
▷ SYNONYMS: **1** the town was flooded: inundate, swamp, deluge, immerse, submerge, drown, engulf. **2** the river could flood: overflow, burst its banks, brim over, run over. **3 glut**, swamp, saturate, oversupply. **4 pour**, stream, flow, surge, swarm, pile, crowd.

floodlight n. a large lamp with a broad, powerful beam.
• v. (**floodlighting**, **floodlit**) light up with floodlights.

floor n. **1** the lower surface of a room. **2** a storey of a building. **3** (**the floor**) the right to speak in a debate.
▷ SYNONYMS: **1 ground**, flooring. **2 storey**, level, deck, tier, stage.
• v. **1** provide with a floor. **2** informal knock down.
▷ SYNONYMS: **1 knock down**, knock over, fell; informal deck, lay out. **2 baffle**, defeat, confound, perplex, puzzle, disconcert; informal throw, beat, stump.
□ **floor show** an entertainment in a nightclub or restaurant.

flooring n. material for a floor.

floozy (or **floozie**) n. (pl. **floozies**) informal a woman who has many sexual partners.

flop v. (**flopping**, **flopped**) **1** hang loosely. **2** sit or lie down heavily. **3** informal fail totally.
▷ SYNONYMS: **1 hang**, dangle, droop, sag, loll. **2 collapse**, slump, crumple, sink, drop. **3 be unsuccessful**, fail, fall flat, founder; informal bomb; N. Amer. informal tank.
• n. **1** a flopping movement. **2** informal a total failure.
▷ SYNONYMS: **failure**, disaster, fiasco, debacle, catastrophe; Brit. damp squib; informal washout, also-ran.
– ANTONYMS: success.

floppy adj. not firm or rigid.
▷ SYNONYMS: **limp**, flaccid, slack, flabby, relaxed, drooping, droopy, loose, flowing.
– ANTONYMS: erect, stiff.
□ **floppy disk** a flexible disk for storing computer data.

flora n. (pl. **floras** or **florae**) the plants of an area or period.

floral adj. of flowers.

floret n. **1** each of the small flowers of a composite flower. **2** each of the flowering stems of a head of cauliflower or broccoli.

florid adj. **1** red or flushed. **2** over-elaborate.

florin n. a former British coin worth two shillings.

florist n. a person who sells flowers.
■ **floristry** n.

floss n. **1** soft thread used to clean between the teeth. **2** silk embroidery thread.
• v. clean the teeth with floss.

flotation (or **floatation**) n. the act of floating, esp. of a company's shares.

flotilla n. a small fleet.

flotsam n. wreckage floating on the sea.
□ **flotsam and jetsam** useless or discarded objects.

flounce v. move in an angry or impatient way.

• n. **1** a flouncing movement. **2** a wide frill.

flounder v. **1** have difficulty doing something. **2** stagger clumsily in mud or water.

▷ SYNONYMS: **1** *floundering in the water:* **struggle**, thrash, flail, twist and turn, splash, stagger, stumble, reel, lurch, blunder. **2** *she floundered, not knowing what to say:* **struggle**, be out of your depth, be confused; informal scratch your head, be flummoxed, be fazed, be floored.

• n. a small edible flatfish.

flour n. a powder produced by grinding grain, used to make bread etc.

■ **floury** adj.

flourish v. **1** grow vigorously. **2** be successful. **3** wave about in a noticeable way.

▷ SYNONYMS: **1** *ferns flourish in the shade:* **grow**, thrive, prosper, do well, burgeon, increase, multiply, proliferate, run riot. **2** *the arts flourished:* **thrive**, prosper, bloom, be in good health, be vigorous, be in its heyday, make progress, advance, expand; informal go places. **3 brandish**, wave, shake, wield, swing, display, show off.

– ANTONYMS: wither, decline.

• n. **1** a bold or exaggerated gesture. **2** an ornamental curve in handwriting. **3** a fanfare.

flout v. openly fail to follow a rule etc.

▷ SYNONYMS: **defy**, refuse to obey, disobey, break, violate, fail to comply with, fail to observe, contravene, infringe, breach, commit a breach of, transgress against, ignore, disregard; informal cock a snook at.

– ANTONYMS: observe.

USAGE Don't confuse **flout** with **flaunt**, which means 'display obviously'.

flow v. **1** move steadily and continuously in a stream. **2** move or proceed smoothly. **3** hang loosely.

▷ SYNONYMS: **1 pour**, run, course, circulate, stream, swirl, surge, sweep, gush, cascade, roll, rush, trickle, seep, ooze, dribble. **2 result**, proceed, arise, follow, ensue, stem, originate, emanate, spring.

• n. **1** a steady, continuous stream. **2** the act of flowing.

▷ SYNONYMS: **movement**, motion, current, circulation, stream, swirl, surge, gush, rush, spate, tide, trickle, ooze.

□ **flow chart** a diagram showing the sequence of stages in a process.

flower n. **1** the part of a plant from which the seed or fruit develops, usu. brightly coloured. **2** the best of a group.

▷ SYNONYMS: **bloom**, blossom.

• v. **1** produce flowers. **2** develop fully and well.

WORD LINKS
floral relating to flowers
florist a person who sells flowers

flowery adj. **1** full of flowers. **2** (of speech or writing) elaborate.

flown past part. of **FLY**.

flu n. influenza.

fluctuate v. vary irregularly.

▷ SYNONYMS: **vary**, change, shift, alter, waver, swing, oscillate, alternate, rise and fall.

■ **fluctuation** n.

flue n. a pipe that takes smoke and gases away from a chimney, heater, etc.

fluent adj. **1** speaking or writing in a clear and natural way. **2** smoothly graceful.

▷ SYNONYMS: **articulate**, eloquent, silver-tongued, communicative, natural, effortless.

– ANTONYMS: inarticulate.

■ **fluency** n. **fluently** adv.

fluff n. a soft mass of fibres or down.

• v. **1** make fuller and softer by shaking or patting. **2** informal fail to do properly.

■ **fluffiness** n. **fluffy** adj.

fluid n. a liquid or gas.

▷ SYNONYMS: **liquid**, solution, liquor, gas, vapour.

• adj. **1** able to flow easily. **2** not stable. **3** graceful.

▷ SYNONYMS: **1 free-flowing**, runny, liquid, liquefied, melted, molten, gaseous. **2 smooth**, fluent, flowing, effortless, easy, continuous, graceful, elegant.

– ANTONYMS: solid.

□ **fluid ounce** Brit. one twentieth of a pint (approx. 0.028 litre).

■ **fluidity** n.

fluke n. **1** a lucky chance occurrence. **2** a parasitic worm.

flume n. **1** an artificial water channel. **2** a water slide.

flummery n. empty talk or compliments.

flummox v. informal baffle.

flung past & past part. of **FLING**.

flunk v. informal fail an exam.

flunkey (or **flunky**) n. (pl. **flunkeys** or **flunkies**) **1** a uniformed male servant. **2** a person who does menial work.

fluorescent adj. **1** giving off bright light when exposed to radiation such as ultraviolet light. **2** vividly colourful.
■ **fluoresce** v. **fluorescence** n.

fluoridate v. add fluoride to.
■ **fluoridation** n.

fluoride n. a compound of fluorine added to water supplies or toothpaste to reduce tooth decay.

fluorine n. a poisonous yellow gas.

fluorite (or **fluorspar**) n. a colourless mineral.

flurry n. (pl. **flurries**) **1** a swirling mass of snow, leaves, etc. **2** a sudden spell of activity or excitement.
▷ SYNONYMS: **1 swirl**, whirl, eddy, shower, gust. **2 burst**, outbreak, spurt, fit, spell, bout, rash, eruption.

flush v. **1** become red; blush. **2** clean or remove by passing large quantities of water through. **3** force into the open.
▷ SYNONYMS: **1 blush**, redden, go pink, go red, go crimson, go scarlet, colour. **2 rinse**, wash, sluice, swill, cleanse, clean; Brit. informal sloosh. **3 chase**, force, drive, dislodge, expel.
● n. **1** a blush. **2** a rush of emotion. **3** an act of flushing. **4** (in poker) a hand of cards all of the same suit.
▷ SYNONYMS: **blush**, colour, rosiness, pinkness, ruddiness, bloom.
− ANTONYMS: pallor.
● adj. **1** level with another surface. **2** informal having plenty of money.

fluster v. agitate or confuse.

flute n. **1** a wind instrument consisting of a tube held sideways with holes along it. **2** a tall, narrow wine glass.

fluted adj. decorated with a series of grooves.

flutter v. **1** fly unsteadily by flapping the wings quickly and lightly. **2** move with a light trembling motion. **3** (of the heart) beat irregularly.
▷ SYNONYMS: **1** butterflies fluttered around: **flit**, hover, dance. **2** a robin fluttered its wings: **flap**, beat, quiver, agitate, vibrate, ruffle. **3** she fluttered her eyelashes: **flicker**, bat. **4** flags fluttered: **flap**, wave, ripple, undulate, quiver, fly.
● n. **1** a state of nervous excitement. **2** a fluttering movement. **3** Brit. informal a small bet.

fluvial adj. of rivers.

flux n. **1** continuous change. **2** a bodily discharge. **3** a substance mixed with a solid to lower the melting point.

fly[1] v. (**flies, flying, flew**; past part. **flown**) **1** (of a winged creature or aircraft) move through the air.
2 control the flight of or transport in an aircraft. **3** move quickly through the air. **4** go or move quickly. **5** flutter in the wind. **6** (of a flag) be displayed on a flagpole. **7** (**fly into**) suddenly become angry. **8** (**fly at**) attack. **9** old use run away.
▷ SYNONYMS: **1 wing**, glide, soar, wheel, take wing, take to the air, hover, swoop. **2 pilot**, operate, control, manoeuvre, steer. **3 dash**, race, rush, bolt, zoom, dart, speed, hurry, career, hurtle; informal tear. **4** the ship flew a French flag: **display**, show, exhibit, hoist, raise, wave.
● n. (pl. **flies**) **1** (Brit. also **flies**) an opening at the crotch of a pair of trousers, closed with a zip or buttons. **2** a flap of material covering the opening of a tent.
□ **flying buttress** a buttress slanting upwards from a separate support.
flying fish a tropical fish with wing-like fins for gliding above the water.
flying saucer a disc-shaped flying craft supposedly piloted by aliens.
flying squad a division of a police force capable of reaching an incident quickly. **fly-tipping** the illegal dumping of waste.

fly[2] n. (pl. **flies**) a two-winged flying insect.
□ **flyblown** contaminated by contact with flies. **fly in the ointment** a minor irritation that spoils something. **fly on the wall** an unnoticed observer.
flyweight a weight in boxing below bantamweight.

flyer (or **flier**) n. **1** a person or thing that flies. **2** a small advertising leaflet.

FM abbrev. frequency modulation.

foal n. a young horse or related animal.
● v. give birth to a foal.

foam n. **1** a mass of small bubbles. **2** a substance containing many small bubbles. **3** lightweight spongy rubber or plastic.
▷ SYNONYMS: **froth**, spume, surf, spray, fizz, effervescence, bubbles, head, lather, suds.
● v. form or produce foam.
▷ SYNONYMS: **froth**, fizz, effervesce, bubble, lather, ferment, boil, seethe.
■ **foamy** adj.

fob n. **1** a chain attached to a watch. **2** a tab on a key ring.
● v. (**fobbing, fobbed**) (**fob off**) try to deceive into accepting excuses or something inferior.

focaccia /fuh-kach-uh/ n. a flat Italian

bread made with olive oil.

focal adj. of a focus.

fo'c's'le var. of FORECASTLE.

focus n. (pl. **focuses** or **foci**) **1** the centre of interest or activity. **2** clear visual definition. **3** the point at which an object must be situated for a lens or mirror to produce a clear image of it. **4** a point where rays or sound waves etc. meet.

▷ SYNONYMS: **1 centre**, focal point, central point, centre of attention, hub, pivot, nucleus, heart, cornerstone, linchpin. **2 subject**, theme, concern, subject matter, topic, point, essence, gist.

• v. (**focusing**, **focused** or **focussing**, **focussed**) **1** bring into focus. **2** adjust the focus of. **3** (**focus on**) concentrate on.

▷ SYNONYMS: **bring into focus**, aim, point, turn.

□ **focus group** a group assembled to assess a new product, policy, etc. ■ **focuser** n.

fodder n. food for animals.

foe n. an enemy.

foetid var. of FETID.

foetus var. of FETUS.

fog n. a thick mist.

▷ SYNONYMS: **mist**, smog, murk, haze; informal pea-souper.

• v. (**fogging**, **fogged**) **1** become covered with mist. **2** confuse.

□ **foghorn** a device making a loud, deep sound as a warning to ships in fog.

■ **foggy** adj.

fogey (or **fogy**) n. (pl. **fogeys** or **fogies**) an old-fashioned person.

foible n. an odd habit or minor eccentricity.

foil v. prevent from succeeding or doing something.

▷ SYNONYMS: **thwart**, frustrate, stop, defeat, block, prevent, obstruct, hinder, snooker, scotch; informal put paid to; Brit. informal scupper.

– ANTONYMS: assist.

• n. **1** a thin flexible sheet of metal. **2** a person or thing emphasizing another's qualities by contrast. **3** a light, blunt-edged fencing sword.

▷ SYNONYMS: **contrast**, complement, antithesis.

foist v. (**foist on**) impose an unwelcome person or thing on.

fold v. **1** bend something over on itself so that one part of it covers another. **2** be able to be folded into a flatter shape. **3** clasp in your arms. **4** informal go out of business. **5** mix an ingredient gently into another.

▷ SYNONYMS: **1 double**, crease, turn, bend, tuck, pleat. **2 fail**, collapse, founder, go bankrupt, cease trading, be wound up, be shut down; informal crash, go bust, go under, go to the wall, go belly up.

• n. **1** a folded part. **2** a line produced by folding. **3** a pen for sheep.

▷ SYNONYMS: **crease**, knife-edge, wrinkle, crinkle, pucker, furrow, pleat.

folder n. a folding cover or wallet for loose papers.

foliage n. leaves.

folic acid n. a vitamin found esp. in green vegetables, liver, and kidney.

folio n. (pl. **folios**) **1** a sheet of paper folded once to form four pages of a book. **2** a book made up of folios.

folk pl. n. **1** (or **folks**) informal people in general. **2** (**your folks**) informal your family. **3** (or **folk music**) music in the traditional style of a country or community.

▷ SYNONYMS: **1 people**, individuals, {men, women, and children}, citizenry, inhabitants, residents, populace, population. **2 relatives**, relations, family, people; informal peeps.

□ **folklore** the traditional beliefs and stories of a community.

folksy adj. traditional and homely. ■ **folksiness** n.

follicle n. a small cavity containing a hair root.

■ **follicular** adj.

follow v. **1** go or come after. **2** go along a route. **3** be or happen as a result or consequence. **4** act according to an instruction or example. **5** accept as a leader, guide, etc. **6** understand or pay attention to. **7** (**follow up**) investigate further.

▷ SYNONYMS: **1 come behind**, come after, go behind, go after, walk behind, escort, accompany. **2 shadow**, trail, stalk, track; informal tail. **3 obey**, comply with, conform to, adhere to, stick to, keep to, act in accordance with, abide by, observe. **4 understand**, comprehend, take in, grasp, fathom, see; informal make head or tail of, figure out; Brit. informal suss out.

– ANTONYMS: lead, flout.

□ **follow suit** do the same as someone else.

follower n. **1** a supporter, fan, or disciple. **2** a person who follows.

▷ SYNONYMS: **1 disciple**, apostle, champion, believer, worshipper. **2 fan**, enthusiast, admirer, devotee, lover,

supporter, adherent.
– ANTONYMS: leader, opponent.

following prep. coming after or as a result of.
• n. a group of supporters.
▷ SYNONYMS: **admirers**, supporters, backers, fans, adherents, devotees, public, audience.
– ANTONYMS: opposition.
• adj. next in time or order.
▷ SYNONYMS: **next**, ensuing, succeeding, subsequent, successive.
– ANTONYMS: preceding.

folly n. (pl. **follies**) **1** foolishness. **2** a foolish act. **3** an ornamental building with no practical purpose.
▷ SYNONYMS: **foolishness**, foolhardiness, stupidity, idiocy, lunacy, madness, rashness, recklessness, irresponsibility.
– ANTONYMS: wisdom.

foment v. stir up conflict.

fond adj. **1** (**fond of**) having an affection or liking for. **2** affectionate. **3** (of a hope) unlikely to be fulfilled.
▷ SYNONYMS: **1** *she was fond of dancing:* **keen on**, partial to, enthusiastic about, attached to; informal into. **2 adoring**, devoted, doting, loving, caring, affectionate, indulgent. **3 unrealistic**, naive, foolish, over-optimistic, absurd, vain.
– ANTONYMS: indifferent, uncaring.
■ **fondly** adv. **fondness** n.

fondant n. a paste of sugar and water, used to make sweets and as icing.

fondle v. stroke lovingly.
▷ SYNONYMS: **caress**, stroke, pat, pet, finger, tickle, play with.

fondue n. a dish of melted cheese etc. into which pieces of food are dipped.

font n. **1** a large stone bowl in a church holding water for baptism. **2** (Brit. also **fount**) a set of type of a particular size and design.

fontanelle n. a soft area between the bones of the skull in a baby or fetus.

food n. any substance that people or animals eat or that plants absorb to stay alive.
▷ SYNONYMS: **nourishment**, sustenance, nutriment, fare, cooking, cuisine, foodstuffs, refreshments, meals, provisions, rations; informal eats, grub, nosh; literary viands; dated victuals.
□ **foodstuff** a substance used as food.

> **WORD LINKS**
> **alimentary** relating to food

fool n. **1** a foolish person. **2** Brit. a cold dessert made of puréed fruit and cream.

▷ SYNONYMS: **1 idiot**, ass, halfwit, blockhead, dunce, simpleton; informal nincompoop, clod, dimwit, dummy, fathead, numbskull; Brit. informal nitwit, twit, clot, berk, prat, pillock, wally, dork, twerp, charlie; N. Amer. informal schmuck; Austral./NZ informal drongo. **2** *she made a fool of me:* **laughing stock**, dupe; informal stooge, sucker, mug, fall guy; N. Amer. informal sap.
– ANTONYMS: genius.
• v. **1** trick or deceive. **2** (**fool about/around**) act in a joking or silly way.
▷ SYNONYMS: **1 deceive**, trick, hoax, dupe, take in, mislead, delude, hoodwink, bluff, gull; informal bamboozle, take for a ride, have on; N. Amer. informal sucker; Austral. informal pull a swifty on. **2 pretend**, make believe, put on an act, act, sham, fake, joke, jest; informal kid; Brit. informal have on.
■ **foolery** n.

foolhardy adj. recklessly bold.
■ **foolhardiness** n.

foolish adj. silly or unwise.
▷ SYNONYMS: **stupid**, idiotic, senseless, mindless, unintelligent, thoughtless, imprudent, unwise, ill-advised, rash, reckless, foolhardy; informal dumb, dim, dim-witted, half-witted, moronic, thick, hare-brained; Brit. informal barmy, daft, potty.
– ANTONYMS: sensible, wise.
■ **foolishly** adv. **foolishness** n.

foolproof adj. unable to go wrong or be wrongly used.
▷ SYNONYMS: **infallible**, dependable, reliable, trustworthy, certain, sure, guaranteed, safe, sound, tried and tested, watertight, airtight, flawless, perfect; informal sure-fire.

foolscap n. Brit. a large size of paper.

foot n. (pl. **feet**) **1** the part of the leg below the ankle. **2** the bottom of something vertical. **3** the end of a bed. **4** a unit of length equal to 12 inches (30.48 cm). **5** a basic unit of metre in poetry.
▷ SYNONYMS: **1 paw**, hoof, trotter, pad. **2 bottom**, base, lowest part, end, foundation.
• v. informal pay a bill.
□ **foot-and-mouth disease** a disease of cattle and sheep, caused by a virus. **footbridge** a bridge for pedestrians. **footfall** the sound of footsteps. **foothill** a low hill at the base of a mountain. **foothold 1** a place where you can put a foot down securely when climbing. **2** a secure position as a basis for progress. **footlights**

a row of spotlights along the front of a stage. **footloose** free to do as you please. **footman** a uniformed manservant. **footnote** a note printed at the bottom of a page. **footpath** a path for walkers. **footprint** the mark left by a foot or shoe on the ground. **footsore** having sore feet from much walking. **footstep** a step taken in walking. **footstool** a low stool for resting the feet on when sitting. **footwear** shoes, boots, etc. **footwork** the manner of moving the feet in dancing and sport.

> **WORD LINKS**
> **chiropody**, **podiatry** medical treatment of the feet

footage n. part of a cinema or television film.

football n. **1** a team game involving kicking a ball, esp. (in the UK) soccer or (in the US) American football. **2** a large ball used in football.
■ **footballer** n.

footing n. **1** a secure grip with the feet. **2** the basis on which something is established or operates.
▷ SYNONYMS: **1** *a solid financial footing:* **basis**, base, foundation. **2** *on an equal footing:* **standing**, status, position, condition, arrangement, basis, relationship, terms.

footling adj. trivial.

fop n. a man who is too concerned about his clothes and appearance.
■ **foppish** adj.

for prep. **1** relating to. **2** in favour or on behalf of. **3** because of. **4** so as to get, have, or do. **5** in place of. **6** in the direction of. **7** over a period or distance.
• conj. literary because.

forage v. search for food etc.
• n. fodder.

foray n. **1** a sudden attack. **2** a brief attempt to become involved in a new activity.

forbear v. (**forbearing**, **forbore**; past part. **forborne**) stop yourself from doing.

forbearing adj. patient or tolerant.
■ **forbearance** n.

forbid v. (**forbidding**, **forbade**; past part. **forbidden**) **1** refuse to allow. **2** order not to do.
▷ SYNONYMS: **prohibit**, ban, outlaw, make illegal, veto, proscribe, embargo, bar, debar, rule out.
– ANTONYMS: permit.

forbidden adj. not permitted.
▷ SYNONYMS: **prohibited**, banned,

verboten, taboo, illegal, illicit, against the law.

forbidding adj. appearing unfriendly or threatening.
▷ SYNONYMS: **threatening**, ominous, menacing, sinister, daunting, off-putting.

force n. **1** physical strength or energy. **2** violence or pressure used to achieve something. **3** influence or power. **4** an organized group of soldiers, police, etc. **5** Physics a measurable influence causing movement.
▷ SYNONYMS: **1** **strength**, power, energy, might, effort. **2** **coercion**, compulsion, constraint, duress, pressure, oppression, harassment, intimidation, violence; informal arm-twisting. **3** **power**, potency, weight, effectiveness, persuasiveness, validity, strength, significance, influence, authority; informal punch. **4** **body**, group, outfit, party, team, detachment, unit, squad.
• v. **1** make someone do something against their will. **2** use strength to move. **3** achieve by effort.
▷ SYNONYMS: **1** **compel**, coerce, make, constrain, oblige, impel, drive, pressure, pressurize, press-gang, bully; informal lean on, twist someone's arm. **2** propel, push, thrust, shove, drive, press, pump.
□ **forcemeat** chopped meat used as a stuffing. **in force 1** in great strength or numbers. **2** in effect.

forced adj. **1** obtained or imposed by force or physical strength. **2** produced with effort: *a forced smile.*
▷ SYNONYMS: **strained**, unnatural, artificial, false, feigned, simulated, contrived, laboured, affected, hollow; informal phoney, pretend, put on.
– ANTONYMS: voluntary, natural.

forceful adj. powerful and confident.
▷ SYNONYMS: **1** **dynamic**, energetic, assertive, authoritative, vigorous, powerful, strong, pushy; informal in-your-face, go-ahead, feisty. **2** **convincing**, cogent, compelling, strong, powerful, persuasive, coherent.
– ANTONYMS: weak.
■ **forcefully** adv. **forcefulness** n.

forceps pl. n. pincers used in surgery.

forcible adj. done by force.
■ **forcibly** adv.

ford n. a shallow place in a river where it can be crossed.
• v. cross at a ford.

fore adj. in or at the front.
□ **to the fore** in or to a prominent position.

forearm n. the arm from the elbow to the wrist.
• v. (**be forearmed**) be prepared in advance for danger.

forebear n. an ancestor.

foreboding n. a feeling that something bad will happen.

forecast v. predict a future event.
▷ SYNONYMS: **predict**, prophesy, foretell, foresee.
• n. a prediction.
▷ SYNONYMS: **prediction**, prophecy, prognostication, prognosis.
■ **forecaster** n.

forecastle (or **fo'c's'le**) /fohk-s'l/ n. the front part of a ship below the deck.

foreclose v. take possession of a property because the occupant has failed to keep up the mortgage payments.
■ **foreclosure** n.

forecourt n. an open area in front of a building.

forefather n. an ancestor.

forefinger n. the finger next to the thumb.

forefoot n. (pl. **forefeet**) an animal's front foot.

forefront n. the leading position.

foregather v. assemble.

forego var. of FORGO.

foregoing adj. preceding.

foregone conclusion n. a predictable result.

foreground n. the part of a view or picture nearest to the observer.

forehand n. (in tennis etc.) a stroke played with the palm of the hand facing forwards.

forehead n. the part of the face above the eyebrows.

foreign adj. **1** of a country or language other than your own. **2** coming from outside. **3** (**foreign to**) not known to or typical of.
▷ SYNONYMS: **alien**, overseas, non-native, imported, distant, external, far-off, exotic, strange.
– ANTONYMS: domestic, native.

USAGE -eign, not -iegn: for*eign*.

foreigner n. **1** a person from a foreign country. **2** informal an outsider.
▷ SYNONYMS: **alien**, stranger, outsider, immigrant, settler, newcomer, incomer.
– ANTONYMS: native, national.

WORD LINKS
xenophobia an irrational dislike or fear of foreigners

foreknowledge n. awareness of something before it happens.

foreleg n. an animal's front leg.

forelock n. a lock of hair just above the forehead.

foreman (or **forewoman**) n. **1** a worker who supervises others. **2** a person who is head of a jury and speaks on its behalf.

foremost adj. highest in importance or position.
▷ SYNONYMS: **leading**, principal, premier, prime, top, greatest, best, supreme, pre-eminent, outstanding, most important, most notable; N. Amer. ranking; informal number-one.
– ANTONYMS: minor.
• adv. in the first place.

forename n. a first name.

forensic adj. **1** of the use of scientific methods to investigate crime. **2** of a court of law.

foreplay n. sexual activity preceding intercourse.

forerunner n. a person or thing coming before and influencing someone or something else.

foresee v. (**foreseeing, foresaw**; past part. **foreseen**) be aware of beforehand.
▷ SYNONYMS: **anticipate**, expect, envisage, predict, forecast, foretell, prophesy.
■ **foreseeable** adj.

foreshadow v. be a sign or warning of.

foreshore n. the part of a shore between the highest and lowest levels reached by the sea.

foreshorten v. **1** portray an object as closer than it really is. **2** end something prematurely.

foresight n. the ability to predict future events.
▷ SYNONYMS: **forethought**, planning, far-sightedness, vision, anticipation, prudence, care, caution; N. Amer. forehandedness.
– ANTONYMS: hindsight.

foreskin n. the roll of skin covering the end of the penis.

forest n. a large area covered thickly with trees.
■ **forested** adj.

forestall v. prevent or delay by taking action first.

forestry n. the science or practice of planting and managing forests.
■ **forester** n.

foretaste n. a sample of something that lies ahead.

foretell v. (foretelling, foretold) predict.
▷ SYNONYMS: **predict**, forecast, prophesy, foresee, anticipate, envisage, warn of.

forethought n. careful planning for the future.

forever adv. **1** for all future time. **2** continually.
▷ SYNONYMS: **1 for always**, evermore, for ever and ever, for good, for all time, until the end of time, eternally; N. Amer. forevermore; informal until the cows come home. **2 always**, continually, constantly, perpetually, incessantly, endlessly, persistently, repeatedly, regularly; informal 24-7.

forewarn v. warn in advance.

foreword n. an introduction in a book.

forfeit v. lose property or a right as a penalty for wrongdoing.
▷ SYNONYMS: **lose**, be deprived of, surrender, relinquish, sacrifice, give up, renounce, forgo.
• n. a penalty for wrongdoing.
▷ SYNONYMS: **penalty**, sanction, punishment, penance, fine, confiscation, loss, forfeiture, surrender.
■ **forfeiture** n.

forge v. **1** make or shape a metal object by heating and hammering. **2** make a fraudulent copy of. **3** move forward gradually or steadily.
▷ SYNONYMS: **1 hammer out**, beat out, fashion. **2 build**, construct, form, create, establish, set up. **3 fake**, falsify, counterfeit, copy, imitate.
• n. **1** a blacksmith's workshop. **2** a furnace for heating metal.
■ **forger** n.

forged adj. not genuine: a forged £20 note.
▷ SYNONYMS: **fake**, false, counterfeit, fraudulent, imitation, copied, pirate, bogus; informal phoney, dud.
– ANTONYMS: genuine.

forgery n. (pl. **forgeries**) the action of forging a banknote, work of art, etc., or an item that has been forged.
▷ SYNONYMS: **fake**, counterfeit, fraud, imitation, replica, copy, pirate copy; informal phoney.

forget v. (forgetting, forgot; past part. **forgotten**) **1** fail or be unable to remember. **2** no longer think of. **3** (**forget yourself**) behave inappropriately.
▷ SYNONYMS: I forgot to close the door: **neglect**, fail, omit.
– ANTONYMS: remember.
□ **forget-me-not** a plant with small blue flowers.

■ **forgettable** adj.

forgetful adj. tending not to remember.
▷ SYNONYMS: **1 absent-minded**, amnesiac, vague, scatterbrained, disorganized, dreamy, abstracted, with a mind/memory like a sieve; informal scatty. **2** forgetful of the time: **heedless**, careless, inattentive to, negligent about, oblivious to, unconcerned about, indifferent to.
■ **forgetfully** adv. **forgetfulness** n.

forgive v. (forgiving, forgave; past part. **forgiven**) stop feeling angry or resentful towards or about.
▷ SYNONYMS: **1 pardon**, exonerate, absolve. **2 excuse**, overlook, disregard, ignore, make allowances for, turn a blind eye to, condone, indulge, tolerate.
– ANTONYMS: blame, resent.
■ **forgivable** adj.

forgiveness n. the action of forgiving or the state of being forgiven.
▷ SYNONYMS: **pardon**, absolution, exoneration, indulgence, clemency, mercy, reprieve, amnesty; informal let-off.
– ANTONYMS: punishment.

forgiving adj. willing to forgive.
▷ SYNONYMS: **merciful**, lenient, compassionate, magnanimous, humane, soft-hearted, forbearing, tolerant, indulgent, understanding.
– ANTONYMS: merciless, vindictive.

forgo (or **forego**) v. (forgoing, forwent; past part. **forgone**) go without something you want.
▷ SYNONYMS: **do without**, go without, give up, waive, renounce, surrender, relinquish, part with, drop, sacrifice, abstain from, refrain from, eschew, cut out; informal swear off; formal forswear, abjure.

fork n. **1** a small pronged implement for lifting or holding food. **2** a large pronged tool for digging or lifting. **3** a point where a road etc. divides into two parts. **4** either of two such parts.
• v. **1** divide into two parts. **2** take one route or the other at a fork. **3** dig or lift with a fork. **4** (**fork out**) informal pay money.
▷ SYNONYMS: **split**, branch, divide, separate, part, diverge, bifurcate.
□ **forklift truck** a vehicle with a forked device for lifting and carrying loads.
■ **forked** adj.

forlorn adj. **1** sad and alone. **2** unlikely to succeed or be achieved.
▷ SYNONYMS: **1 unhappy**, sad, miserable, sorrowful, dejected, despondent, disconsolate, wretched, down,

downcast, dispirited, downhearted, crestfallen, depressed, melancholy, gloomy, glum, mournful, despairing, doleful, woebegone; informal blue, down in the mouth, down in the dumps, fed up. **2 hopeless**, useless, futile, pointless, purposeless, vain, unavailing.
– ANTONYMS: happy.
■ **forlornly** adv.

form n. **1** shape or arrangement. **2** a way in which a thing exists. **3** a type. **4** a document with blank spaces for information. **5** the current standard of a sports player or team. **6** a person's mood or state of health. **7** Brit. a school class or year. **8** the way something is usually done.
▷ SYNONYMS: **1 shape**, configuration, formation, structure, construction, arrangement, appearance, exterior, outline, format, layout, design. **2 body**, shape, figure, frame, physique, anatomy; informal vital statistics. **3 manifestation**, appearance, embodiment, incarnation, semblance, shape, guise. **4 kind**, sort, type, class, category, variety, genre, brand, style. **5 questionnaire**, document, coupon, slip. **6 class**, year; N. Amer. grade. **7 condition**, fettle, shape, health; Brit. informal nick.
• v. **1** create. **2** constitute. **3** establish or develop.
▷ SYNONYMS: **1 make**, construct, build, manufacture, fabricate, assemble, put together, create, fashion, shape. **2 comprise**, make, make up, constitute, compose, add up to. **3 formulate**, develop, devise, conceive, work out, think up, lay, draw up, put together, produce, fashion, concoct, forge, hatch; informal dream up. **4 set up**, establish, found, launch, create, institute, start, inaugurate. **5 arrange**, draw up, line up, assemble, organize, sort, order.
– ANTONYMS: dissolve, disappear.
■ **formless** adj.

formal adj. **1** suitable for official or important occasions. **2** officially recognized. **3** having a recognized form, rules, etc.
▷ SYNONYMS: **1 ceremonial**, ritualistic, ritual, official, conventional, traditional, stately, solemn, ceremonious. **2 aloof**, reserved, remote, detached, unapproachable, stiff, stuffy, correct, proper; informal stand-offish. **3 official**, legal, authorized, approved, certified, endorsed, sanctioned, licensed, recognized.
– ANTONYMS: informal, casual, unofficial.

■ **formalize** (or **-ise**) v. **formally** adv.

formaldehyde /for-mal-di-hyd/ n. a gas used in solution as a preservative and disinfectant.

formalin n. a solution of formaldehyde in water.

formalism n. excessive concern with rules and outward form.

formality n. (pl. **formalities**) **1** a thing done to follow customs or rules. **2** correct and formal behaviour.
▷ SYNONYMS: **1 ceremony**, ritual, protocol, decorum, solemnity. **2 aloofness**, reserve, remoteness, detachment, unapproachability, stiffness, stuffiness, correctness; informal stand-offishness.
– ANTONYMS: informality.

format n. **1** the way something is arranged. **2** the shape and size of a book etc. **3** a structure for the processing, storage, etc. of computer data.
▷ SYNONYMS: **design**, style, appearance, look, form, shape, size, arrangement, plan, structure, scheme, composition, configuration.
• v. (**formatting**, **formatted**) put into a format.

formation n. **1** the act of forming. **2** a structure or arrangement.
▷ SYNONYMS: **1** the formation of the island: **emergence**, genesis, development, evolution, shaping, origin. **2** the formation of a new government: **establishment**, setting up, institution, foundation, creation, inauguration. **3 configuration**, arrangement, grouping, pattern, array, alignment, order.
– ANTONYMS: destruction, dissolution.

formative adj. influencing development.

former adj. **1** having been previously. **2** in the past. **3** referring to the first of two things mentioned.
▷ SYNONYMS: **1 one-time**, erstwhile, sometime, ex-, previous, preceding, earlier, prior, last; formal quondam. **2 earlier**, old, past, bygone, olden, long ago, gone by, long past, of old. **3 first-mentioned**, first.
– ANTONYMS: future, current, latter.

formerly adv. in the past.
▷ SYNONYMS: **previously**, earlier, before, until now/then, once, once upon a time, at one time, in the past.

formic acid n. an acid in the fluid discharged by some ants.

formidable adj. causing fear or respect.
▷ SYNONYMS: **1 intimidating**, daunting,

indomitable, forbidding, alarming, frightening, awesome, fearsome; humorous redoubtable. **2 accomplished**, masterly, virtuoso, expert, impressive, powerful, terrific, superb; informal tremendous, nifty, crack, ace, wizard, magic, mean, wicked, deadly.
■ **formidably** adv.

formula n. (pl. **formulae** or **formulas**) **1** a set of symbols showing chemical constituents or expressing a mathematical relationship. **2** a fixed form of words used in particular situations. **3** a list of ingredients. **4** a classification of racing car.
▷ SYNONYMS: **1 form of words**, set expression, rubric, phrase, saying. **2 recipe**, prescription, blueprint, plan, policy, method, procedure.

formulaic adj. **1** containing a set form of words. **2** following a rule or style too closely.

formulate v. **1** create methodically. **2** express precisely.
▷ SYNONYMS: **1 devise**, conceive, work out, think up, lay, draw up, form, concoct, contrive, forge, hatch, prepare, develop. **2 express**, phrase, word, define, specify, put into words, frame, couch, put, articulate, say.
■ **formulation** n.

fornicate v. have sex outside marriage.
■ **fornication** n. **fornicator** n.

forsake v. (**forsaking, forsook**; past part. **forsaken**) **1** abandon. **2** give up.

forsooth adv. old use indeed.

forswear v. (**forswearing, forswore**; past part. **forsworn**) agree to give up or do without.

forsythia /for-sy-thi-uh/ n. a shrub with bright yellow flowers.

fort n. a fortified building.
▷ SYNONYMS: **fortress**, castle, citadel, bunker, stronghold, fortification, bastion.

forte /for-tay/ n. a thing for which someone has a particular talent.
▷ SYNONYMS: **strength**, strong point, speciality, strong suit, talent, skill, gift; informal thing.
• adv. Music loudly.

forth adv. **1** forwards or into view. **2** onwards in time.

forthcoming adj. **1** about to happen or appear. **2** willing to reveal information.
▷ SYNONYMS: **1 coming**, upcoming, approaching, imminent, impending, future. **2 communicative**, talkative, chatty, informative, expansive, expressive, frank, open, candid.
– ANTONYMS: past, current, reticent.

forthright adj. direct and outspoken.
▷ SYNONYMS: **frank**, direct, straightforward, honest, candid, open, sincere, outspoken, straight, blunt, plain-spoken, no-nonsense, bluff, matter-of-fact, to the point; informal upfront.
– ANTONYMS: secretive, evasive.

forthwith adv. without delay.

fortify v. (**fortifying, fortified**) **1** strengthen against attack. **2** invigorate or encourage. **3** increase the alcoholic content or nutritional value of.
▷ SYNONYMS: **1 strengthen**, secure, barricade, protect, buttress, shore up. **2 invigorate**, strengthen, energize, enliven, animate, vitalize, buoy up; informal pep up, buck up.
■ **fortification** n.

fortissimo adv. Music very loudly.

fortitude n. courage when facing pain or trouble.
▷ SYNONYMS: **courage**, bravery, endurance, resilience, mettle, strength of character, backbone, grit; informal guts; Brit. informal bottle.

fortnight n. Brit. a period of two weeks.
■ **fortnightly** adj. & adv.

fortress n. a fortified building or town.
▷ SYNONYMS: **fort**, castle, citadel, bunker, stronghold, fortification.

fortuitous adj. **1** happening by chance. **2** lucky.
■ **fortuitously** adv.

fortunate adj. lucky.
▷ SYNONYMS: **1 lucky**, favoured, blessed, leading a charmed life, in luck; Brit. informal born with a silver spoon in your mouth, jammy. **2 favourable**, advantageous, timely, opportune.
– ANTONYMS: unfortunate, unlucky, unfavourable.
■ **fortunately** adv.

fortune n. **1** chance as a force affecting people's lives. **2** luck. **3** (**fortunes**) the success or failure of a person or undertaking. **4** a large amount of money.
▷ SYNONYMS: **1 chance**, accident, coincidence, serendipity, destiny, providence; N. Amer. happenstance. **2 luck**, fate, destiny, predestination, the stars, karma, kismet, lot. **3** an upswing in their fortunes: **circumstances**, state of affairs, condition, position, situation. **4 wealth**, money, riches, assets, resources, means, possessions, property, estate.
□ **fortune-teller** a person who predicts

f

future events in people's lives.

forty adj. & n. (pl. **forties**) ten less than fifty; 40.
□ **forty winks** informal a short sleep.
■ **fortieth** adj. & n.

forum n. a meeting or opportunity for an exchange of views.
▷ SYNONYMS: **meeting**, assembly, gathering, rally, conference, seminar, convention, symposium.

forward adv. & adj. **1** in the direction that you are facing or moving. **2** towards a successful end. **3** ahead in time. **4** in or near the front.
▷ SYNONYMS: **ahead**, forwards, onwards, onward, on, further.
– ANTONYMS: backwards, back.
• adj. too familiar or confident.
▷ SYNONYMS: **bold**, brazen, cheeky, shameless, familiar, overfamiliar, presumptuous; informal fresh.
• n. an attacking player in a sport.
• v. send a letter etc. on to a further destination.
▷ SYNONYMS: **1 send on**, post on, redirect, readdress, pass on. **2 send**, dispatch, transmit, carry, convey, deliver, ship.
■ **forwards** adv.

forwent past of FORGO.

fossil n. the remains of a prehistoric plant or animal that have become hardened into rock.
□ **fossil fuel** a fuel such as coal, formed from the remains of animals and plants.
■ **fossilize** (or **-ise**) v.

foster v. **1** encourage the development of. **2** bring up a child that is not your own.
▷ SYNONYMS: **1 encourage**, promote, further, nurture, help, aid, assist, support, back. **2 bring up**, rear, raise, care for, take care of, look after, provide for.

fought past & past part. of FIGHT.

foul adj. **1** having a disgusting smell or taste. **2** very bad. **3** against the rules of a sport. **4** polluted.
▷ SYNONYMS: **1 disgusting**, revolting, repulsive, repugnant, abhorrent, loathsome, offensive, sickening, nauseating; informal ghastly, gruesome, gross. **2 contaminated**, polluted, infected, tainted, impure, filthy, dirty, unclean. **3 vulgar**, crude, coarse, filthy, dirty, obscene, indecent, naughty, offensive; informal blue.
– ANTONYMS: pleasant.
• n. an action that breaks the rules of a sport.
• v. **1** make foul or dirty. **2** (in sport)

commit a foul against. **3** (**foul up**) make a mistake with. **4** entangle or jam.
▷ SYNONYMS: **1 dirty**, pollute, contaminate, poison, taint, sully. **2 tangle up**, entangle, snarl, catch, entwine.
■ **foully** adv.

found[1] past & past part. of FIND.

found[2] v. **1** establish an institution. **2** (**be founded on**) be based on. **3** melt and mould metal to make an object.
▷ SYNONYMS: **establish**, set up, start, begin, get going, institute, inaugurate, launch.

foundation n. **1** the lowest weight-bearing part of a building. **2** an underlying basis. **3** the act of founding an institution. **4** an institution. **5** a cream applied as a base for other make-up.
▷ SYNONYMS: **1 footing**, foot, base, substructure, underpinning. **2 justification**, grounds, evidence, basis. **3 institution**, establishment, charitable body, agency.

founder n. a person who founds an institution etc.
▷ SYNONYMS: **originator**, creator, father, architect, developer, pioneer, author, inventor, mastermind.
• v. **1** (of a plan etc.) fail. **2** (of a ship) sink.
▷ SYNONYMS: **1 fail**, be unsuccessful, fall flat, fall through, collapse, backfire, meet with disaster; informal flop, bomb. **2 sink**, go to the bottom, go down, be lost at sea.
– ANTONYMS: succeed.

foundling n. an infant abandoned by its parents.

foundry n. (pl. **foundries**) a workshop or factory for casting metal.

fount n. **1** a source. **2** literary a spring or fountain. **3** var. of FONT (sense 2).

fountain n. **1** a decorative structure pumping out a jet of water. **2** a source.
▷ SYNONYMS: **1 jet**, spray, spout, spurt, cascade, water feature. **2 source**, fount, well, reservoir, fund, mine.
□ **fountainhead** a source. **fountain pen** a pen with a container supplying ink to the nib.

four adj. & n. one more than three; 4.
□ **four-poster** a bed with four posts supporting a canopy. **foursome** a group of four people. **four-wheel drive** a vehicle with a system providing power directly to all four wheels.
■ **fourfold** adj. & adv.

fourteen adj. & n. one more than thirteen; 14.
■ **fourteenth** adj. & n.

fourth adj. & n. **1** next after third. **2** a quarter.
■ **fourthly** adv.

fowl n. **1** a bird kept for its eggs or meat, e.g. a hen. **2** birds as a group.

fox n. an animal with a bushy tail and a reddish coat.
• v. informal baffle or deceive.
□ **foxglove** a tall plant with bell-shaped flowers. **foxhole** a hole in the ground used by troops as a shelter. **foxhound** a hound trained to hunt foxes in packs. **foxtrot** a ballroom dance with slow and quick steps.
■ **foxy** adj.

foyer /foy-ay/ n. a large entrance hall in a hotel or theatre.
▷ SYNONYMS: **entrance hall**, hallway, entry, porch, reception area, atrium, concourse, lobby, anteroom; N. Amer. entryway.

fracas /fra-kah/ n. (pl. **fracas**) a noisy disturbance or quarrel.
▷ SYNONYMS: **disturbance**, brawl, melee, rumpus, skirmish, struggle, scuffle, scrum, clash, fisticuffs, altercation; informal scrap, dust-up, set-to, shindy, shindig; Brit. informal punch-up, bust-up, ruck; N. Amer. informal rough house; Law, dated affray.

fraction n. **1** a number that is not a whole number. **2** a very small part or amount.
▷ SYNONYMS: **1** *a fraction of the population*: **tiny part**, fragment, snippet, snatch. **2** *he moved a fraction closer*: **bit**, little, touch, soupçon, trifle, mite, shade, jot; informal smidgen, tad.
– ANTONYMS: whole.
■ **fractional** adj. **fractionally** adv.

fractious adj. **1** bad-tempered. **2** difficult to control.
▷ SYNONYMS: **grumpy**, bad-tempered, irascible, irritable, crotchety, grouchy, cantankerous, tetchy, testy, ill-tempered, peevish, cross, pettish, waspish, crabby, crusty; Brit. informal shirty, stroppy, narky, ratty; N. Amer. informal cranky, ornery.

fracture n. **1** a crack or break. **2** the cracking or breaking of something.
▷ SYNONYMS: **break**, crack, split, rupture, fissure.
• v. break or break up.
▷ SYNONYMS: **break**, crack, split, rupture, snap, shatter, fragment, splinter.

fragile adj. **1** easily broken or damaged. **2** delicate or vulnerable.
▷ SYNONYMS: **1 breakable**, delicate,

brittle, flimsy, dainty, fine. **2 tenuous**, shaky, insecure, vulnerable, flimsy. **3 weak**, delicate, frail, debilitated, ill, unwell, poorly, sickly.
– ANTONYMS: sturdy, robust.
■ **fragility** n.

fragment n. **1** a small part broken off. **2** an incomplete part.
▷ SYNONYMS: **1 piece**, bit, particle, speck, chip, shard, sliver, splinter, flake. **2 snatch**, snippet, scrap, bit.
• v. break into fragments.
▷ SYNONYMS: **break up**, crack open, shatter, splinter, fracture, disinte-grate, fall to pieces, fall apart.
■ **fragmentary** adj. **fragmentation** n.

fragrance n. **1** a pleasant, sweet smell. **2** a perfume or aftershave.
▷ SYNONYMS: **1 sweet smell**, scent, perfume, bouquet, aroma, nose. **2 perfume**, scent, eau de toilette.

fragrant adj. having a pleasant, sweet smell.
▷ SYNONYMS: **sweet-scented**, sweet-smelling, scented, perfumed, aromatic.
– ANTONYMS: smelly.

frail adj. **1** weak. **2** fragile.
▷ SYNONYMS: **1** *a frail old lady*: **weak**, deli-cate, feeble, infirm, ill, unwell, sickly, poorly. **2** *a frail structure*: **fragile**, easily damaged, delicate, flimsy, insubstantial, unsteady, unstable, rickety.
– ANTONYMS: strong, robust.
■ **frailty** n.

frame n. **1** a rigid structure surrounding a picture etc. or supporting something. **2** a person's body. **3** a conceptual structure. **4** a single picture in a series forming a cinema or video film. **5** a single game of snooker.
▷ SYNONYMS: **1 framework**, structure, substructure, skeleton, casing, chassis, shell. **2 body**, figure, form, shape, physique, anatomy, build.
• v. **1** put or form a frame around. **2** develop a plan etc. **3** informal produce false evidence against.
▷ SYNONYMS: **1 mount**. **2 formulate**, draw up, draft, shape, compose, put together, form, devise.
□ **frame of mind** a particular mood.

framework n. a supporting structure.
▷ SYNONYMS: **1 frame**, structure, skel-eton, chassis, support, scaffolding, shell. **2 structure**, shape, fabric, order, scheme, system, organization, anatomy; informal make-up.

franc n. the basic unit of money of Switzerland (formerly also of France and Belgium).

franchise n. **1** authorization to use or sell a company's products. **2** the right to vote in public elections.
• v. grant a franchise to.

francium n. a radioactive metallic element.

frank adj. **1** honest and direct. **2** open or undisguised.
▷ SYNONYMS: **1 candid**, direct, forthright, plain, plain-spoken, straightforward, straight, to the point, matter-of-fact, open, honest, not beating about the bush; informal upfront. **2 undisguised**, open, unconcealed, naked, unmistakable, clear, obvious, transparent, patent, evident.
− ANTONYMS: evasive.
• v. mark a letter etc. to indicate that postage has been paid.
■ **frankly** adv. **frankness** n.

frankfurter n. a smoked sausage.

frankincense n. a scented gum burnt as incense.

frantic adj. **1** wildly agitated. **2** hurried and confused.
▷ SYNONYMS: **panic-stricken**, panicky, beside yourself, at your wits' end, distraught, overwrought, worked up, frenzied, frenetic, fraught, feverish, desperate; informal in a state, tearing your hair out; Brit. informal having kittens, in a flat spin.
− ANTONYMS: calm.
■ **frantically** adv.

fraternal adj. like a brother.

fraternity n. (pl. **fraternities**) **1** a group with a common interest. **2** friendship and support in a group.
▷ SYNONYMS: **1 brotherhood**, fellowship, kinship, friendship, mutual support, solidarity, community. **2 profession**, community, trade, set, circle. **3 society**, club, association, group.

fraternize (or **-ise**) v. be on friendly terms.
■ **fraternization** n.

fratricide n. the killing of your brother or sister.
■ **fratricidal** adj.

fraud n. **1** the crime of deceiving someone to get money or goods. **2** a person who deceives others by falsely claiming to be something.
▷ SYNONYMS: **1 deception**, sharp practice, cheating, swindling, trickery, embezzlement, deceit, double-dealing, chicanery. **2 swindle**, racket, deception, trick, cheat, hoax; informal scam, con, rip-off, sting, fiddle; N. Amer. informal hustle. **3 impostor**, fake, sham, charlatan, swindler, fraudster,

confidence trickster; informal phoney.

fraudster n. a person who commits fraud.
▷ SYNONYMS: **swindler**, fraud, confidence trickster, cheat, rogue, charlatan, impostor, hoaxer; informal con man, shark, hustler, phoney, crook.

fraudulent adj. involving fraud.
▷ SYNONYMS: **dishonest**, cheating, swindling, corrupt, criminal, deceitful, double-dealing, duplicitous; informal crooked, shady, dirty; Brit. informal bent, dodgy; Austral./NZ informal shonky.
− ANTONYMS: honest.
■ **fraudulence** n.

fraught adj. **1** (**fraught with**) filled with something undesirable. **2** anxious or stressful.
▷ SYNONYMS: **1** a world fraught with danger: **full of**, filled with, rife with. **2 anxious**, worried, stressed, upset, distraught, overwrought, worked up, agitated, distressed, desperate, frantic, panic-stricken, panicky, beside yourself, at your wits' end, at the end of your tether.

Fräulein /froy-lyn/ n. a title for a young German woman.

fray v. **1** (of a fabric or rope) unravel or become worn at the edge. **2** (of a person's nerves or temper) show the effects of strain.
• n. a battle, fight, or other conflict.

frazzle n. informal an exhausted state.
■ **frazzled** adj.

freak n. **1** informal a person obsessed with a particular interest. **2** an abnormal person, animal, or plant.
▷ SYNONYMS: **1 enthusiast**, fan, devotee, lover, aficionado; informal nut, fanatic, addict, maniac. **2 aberration**, abnormality, oddity, monster, monstrosity, mutant, chimera. **3 eccentric**, misfit, oddity, crank; informal oddball, weirdo, nut; Brit. informal nutter; N. Amer. informal kook.
• adj. very unusual and unexpected.
▷ SYNONYMS: **unusual**, anomalous, aberrant, atypical, unrepresentative, irregular, exceptional, isolated.
• v. (**freak out**) informal react in a wild, excited, or shocked way.
■ **freakish** adj. **freaky** adj.

freckle n. a small light brown spot on the skin.
■ **freckled** adj. **freckly** adj.

free adj. (**freer**, **freest**) **1** costing nothing. **2** not under the control of anyone else. **3** not confined, obstructed, or fixed. **4** not busy or being used. **5** (**free of/from**) not containing or affected by. **6** (**free**

with) giving without restraint.
▷ SYNONYMS: **1 free of charge**, without charge, for nothing, complimentary, gratis; informal for free, on the house. **2 independent**, self-governing, self-determining, sovereign, autonomous, democratic. **3 unoccupied**, not busy, available, off duty, off work, on holiday, on leave, at leisure, with time to spare. **4 vacant**, empty, available, unoccupied, not in use. **5** *free of any pressures:* **without**, unencumbered by, unaffected by, clear of, rid of, exempt from, not liable to, safe from, immune to, excused. **6 unobstructed**, unimpeded, unrestricted, unhampered, clear, open. **7** *she was free with her money:* **generous**, liberal, open-handed, unstinting.
− ANTONYMS: busy, occupied, confined.
• **adv.** at no cost.
• **v.** set free.
▷ SYNONYMS: **release**, set free, let go, liberate, set loose, untie; extricate, rescue.
− ANTONYMS: confine, trap.
□ **free fall** downward movement under the force of gravity. **freehand** drawn by hand without a ruler etc. **freehold** permanent ownership of land or property with the freedom to sell it when you wish. **free house** Brit. a pub not controlled by a brewery. **freelance 1** self-employed and working for different companies. **2** (or **freelancer**) a freelance worker. **freeloader** informal a person who takes advantage of other people's generosity. **the free market** a system in which prices are determined by unrestricted competition between private companies. **free radical** a highly reactive molecule with one odd electron not paired up in a chemical bond. **free-range** (of farming) in which animals are kept in conditions where they may move around freely. **freestyle** having few restrictions on the technique to be used. **freeway** US a dual carriageway. **freewheel** ride a bicycle without pedalling. **free will** the power to act according to your own wishes.
■ **freely** adv.
freebie n. informal a thing given free of charge.
freedom n. **1** the right to act or speak freely. **2** the state of being free. **3** a special honour or right granted by a city.
▷ SYNONYMS: **1 independence**, self-government, self-determination, self-rule, home rule, sovereignty,

autonomy, democracy, liberty, liberation. **2** *freedom from political accountability:* **exemption**, immunity, dispensation, impunity. **3 right**, entitlement, privilege, prerogative, discretion, latitude, elbow room, licence, free rein, a free hand, carte blanche.
− ANTONYMS: captivity, obligation.
Freemason n. a member of an organization established for mutual help, which holds secret ceremonies.
■ **Freemasonry** n.
freesia n. a plant with scented flowers.
freeze v. (**freezing**, **froze**; past part. **frozen**) **1** change from a liquid to a solid as a result of extreme cold. **2** become blocked or rigid with ice. **3** be very cold. **4** preserve by storing at a very low temperature. **5** become motionless. **6** keep or stop at a fixed level or in a fixed state.
▷ SYNONYMS: **1 ice over**, ice up, solidify. **2 stand still**, stop dead in your tracks, go rigid, become motionless. **3 fix**, hold, peg, set, limit, restrict, cap.
− ANTONYMS: thaw.
• n. **1** an act of freezing. **2** a period of very cold weather.
□ **freeze-dry** preserve by freezing and removing the ice in a vacuum.
freezer n. a refrigerated cabinet for preserving food at very low temperatures.
freezing adj. **1** below 0°C. **2** very cold.
▷ SYNONYMS: **1 icy**, bitter, chill, frosty, glacial, arctic, wintry, sub-zero, raw, biting. **2 frozen**, numb with cold, chilled to the bone/marrow.
− ANTONYMS: balmy, hot.
freight n. goods transported in bulk.
▷ SYNONYMS: **goods**, cargo, merchandise.
• v. transport goods.
freighter n. a large ship or aircraft designed to carry freight.
French adj. of France.
• n. the language of France.
□ **French fries** chips. **French horn** a brass instrument with a coiled tube. **French polish** a kind of wood polish producing a high gloss. **French windows** a pair of glazed doors in an outside wall.
frenetic adj. fast, energetic, and disorganized.
■ **frenetically** adv.
frenzied adj. wild or uncontrolled.
▷ SYNONYMS: **wild**, frenetic, frantic, hectic, feverish, fevered, mad, crazed, manic, furious, uncontrolled.
− ANTONYMS: calm.
frenzy n. (pl. **frenzies**) uncontrolled

excitement or wild behaviour.

▷ SYNONYMS: **hysteria**, madness, mania, delirium, wild excitement, fever, lather, passion, panic, fury, rage.

frequency n. (pl. **frequencies**) **1** the rate at which something occurs. **2** the state of being frequent. **3** the number of cycles per second of a sound, light, or radio wave. **4** the particular waveband at which radio signals are transmitted.

frequent adj. **1** occurring or done many times at short intervals. **2** doing something often.

▷ SYNONYMS: **recurrent**, recurring, repeated, periodic, continual, habitual, regular, successive, numerous, several.

– ANTONYMS: occasional.

• v. visit a place often.

▷ SYNONYMS: **visit**, patronize, spend time in, visit regularly, haunt; informal hang out at.

– ANTONYMS: avoid.

frequently adv. often; many times.

▷ SYNONYMS: **often**, all the time, habitually, regularly, customarily, routinely, again and again, repeatedly, recurrently, continually; N. Amer. oftentimes.

fresco n. (pl. **frescoes** or **frescos**) a painting done on wet plaster on a wall or ceiling.

fresh adj. **1** new or different. **2** (of food) recently made or obtained. **3** recently created. **4** (of water) not salty. **5** (of the wind) cool and fairly strong. **6** pleasantly clean and cool. **7** lively. **8** informal overfamiliar.

▷ SYNONYMS: **1 new**, modern, original, novel, different, innovative. **2 recently made**, just picked, crisp, raw, natural, unprocessed. **3 bracing**, brisk, strong, invigorating, refreshing, chilly, cool; informal nippy; Brit. informal parky. **4 refreshed**, rested, restored, energetic, vigorous, invigorated, lively, sprightly, bright, alert, bouncing, perky; informal full of beans, bright-eyed and bushy-tailed. **5 impudent**, impertinent, insolent, presumptuous, forward, cheeky, disrespectful, rude; informal mouthy, saucy, lippy; N. Amer. informal sassy.

– ANTONYMS: old, stale.

□ **freshman** (or Brit. **fresher**) a first-year college or university student. **freshwater** of or found in fresh water. ■ **freshen** v. **freshener** n. **freshly** adv. **freshness** n.

fret v. (**fretting, fretted**) be anxious or restless.

▷ SYNONYMS: **worry**, be anxious, distress yourself, upset yourself, concern yourself, agonize, lose sleep.

• n. each of the ridges on the fingerboard of a guitar etc.

fretful adj. anxious or irritated.

■ **fretfully** adv.

fretsaw n. a narrow saw used for fretwork.

fretwork n. decorative patterns cut in wood.

friable adj. easily crumbled.

friar n. a member of certain religious orders of men.

friary n. (pl. **friaries**) a building occupied by friars.

fricassée /fri-kuh-say/ n. a dish of pieces of meat in a white sauce.

friction n. **1** the resistance encountered by one surface when moving over another. **2** the action of one surface rubbing against another. **3** conflict or disagreement.

▷ SYNONYMS: **1 rubbing**, chafing, grating, rasping, scraping, resistance, drag, abrasion. **2 discord**, disagreement, dissension, dispute, conflict, hostility, animosity, antipathy, antagonism, resentment, acrimony, bitterness, bad feeling.

– ANTONYMS: harmony.

Friday n. the day before Saturday.

fridge n. an appliance for keeping food and drink cold.

fried past & past part. of FRY.

friend n. **1** a person that you like and know well. **2** a supporter of a cause or organization.

▷ SYNONYMS: **companion**, comrade, confidant, confidante, familiar, intimate, soulmate, playmate, playfellow, ally, associate; informal pal, chum; Brit. informal mate; N. Amer. informal buddy, amigo, compadre.

– ANTONYMS: enemy.

USAGE -ie-, not -ei-: friend.

friendly adj. (**friendlier, friendliest**) **1** kind and pleasant to others. **2** not harmful to a specified thing.

▷ SYNONYMS: **1** *a friendly woman:* **amiable**, companionable, sociable, gregarious, comradely, neighbourly, hospitable, easy to get on with, affable, genial, cordial, warm, affectionate, convivial; informal chummy, pally; Brit. informal matey. **2** *friendly conversation:* **amicable**, cordial, pleasant, easy, relaxed, casual, informal, close, intimate, familiar.

– ANTONYMS: hostile.

• n. (pl. **friendlies**) a game not forming

part of a serious competition.
■ **friendliness** n.

friendship n. the relationship between friends.
▷ SYNONYMS: **1** *lasting friendships:* **relationship**, attachment, association, bond, tie, link, union. **2** *ties of love and friendship:* **friendliness**, affection, camaraderie, comradeship, companionship, fellowship, closeness, affinity, unity, intimacy.
− ANTONYMS: hostility.

frieze n. a band of decoration around a wall.

frigate n. a kind of fast warship.

fright n. **1** a sudden strong feeling of fear. **2** a shock.
▷ SYNONYMS: **1** **fear**, terror, horror, alarm, panic, dread, trepidation, dismay, nervousness. **2** **scare**, shock, surprise, turn, jolt, start.

frighten v. make afraid.
▷ SYNONYMS: **scare**, startle, alarm, terrify, petrify, shock, chill, panic, unnerve, intimidate; informal spook; Brit. informal put the wind up.

frightening adj. causing fear.
▷ SYNONYMS: **terrifying**, horrifying, alarming, startling, chilling, spine-chilling, hair-raising, blood-curdling, disturbing, unnerving, intimidating, daunting, eerie, sinister, fearsome, nightmarish, menacing; informal scary, spooky, creepy.

frightful adj. **1** very unpleasant, serious, or shocking. **2** informal very bad.
▷ SYNONYMS: **horrible**, horrific, ghastly, horrendous, awful, dreadful, terrible, nasty; informal horrid.
■ **frightfully** adv.

frigid adj. **1** very cold. **2** (of a woman) unable to be sexually aroused.
■ **frigidity** n.

frill n. **1** a strip of gathered or pleated material used as a decorative edging. **2** (frills) unnecessary extra features.
■ **frilled** adj. **frilly** adj.

fringe n. **1** a decorative edging of threads on clothing etc. **2** Brit. the front part of someone's hair that hangs over the forehead. **3** the outer part of something.
▷ SYNONYMS: **1** **edge**, border, margin, extremity, perimeter, periphery, rim, limits, outskirts. **2** **edging**, border, trimming, frill, flounce, ruffle.
− ANTONYMS: middle.
• adj. not part of the mainstream.
▷ SYNONYMS: **alternative**, avant-garde, experimental, innovative, left-field, radical.
− ANTONYMS: mainstream.

• v. give or form a fringe to.
□ **fringe benefit** a benefit received in addition to regular wages.

frippery n. (pl. **fripperies**) a showy or unnecessary ornament.

frisbee n. trademark a plastic disc for skimming through the air as an outdoor game.

frisk v. **1** pass the hands over to search for hidden weapons or drugs. **2** skip or move playfully.

frisky adj. (**friskier**, **friskiest**) playful and lively.
▷ SYNONYMS: **lively**, bouncy, bubbly, perky, active, energetic, animated, playful, coltish, skittish, spirited, high-spirited, in high spirits, exuberant; informal full of beans.

frisson /free-son/ n. a sudden shiver of excitement.

fritter v. waste time or money on trivial things.
• n. a piece of food coated in batter and deep-fried.

frivolous adj. **1** not having any serious purpose or value. **2** not treating things seriously.
▷ SYNONYMS: **flippant**, glib, facetious, joking, jokey, light-hearted, fatuous, inane; informal flip.
− ANTONYMS: serious.
■ **frivolity** n. **frivolously** adv.

frizz v. (of hair) form into a mass of tight curls.
• n. a mass of tight curls.
■ **frizzy** adj.

frock n. a dress.
□ **frock coat** a man's long, double-breasted coat.

frog n. a tailless amphibian with long hind legs for leaping.
□ **frogman** a diver with a rubber suit, flippers, and breathing equipment. **frogmarch** force someone to walk while pinning their arms from behind. **frogspawn** a mass of frogs' eggs surrounded by transparent jelly.

frolic v. (**frolicking**, **frolicked**) play or move about in a cheerful, lively way.
• n. a playful action.

from prep. **1** indicating the starting point, source, or cause. **2** indicating separation, removal, or prevention.

fromage frais /from-ahzh fray/ n. a smooth soft cheese.

frond n. the leaf or leaf-like part of a palm, fern, etc.

front n. **1** the part of an object that faces forward or that is normally seen first. **2** the position directly ahead. **3** the furthest position reached by an army. **4** the forward edge of an advancing mass of air. **5** a particular situation. **6** a false appearance or way of behaving. **7** a cover for secret activities.

▷ SYNONYMS: **1 fore**, foremost part, forepart, nose, head, bow, prow, foreground. **2 frontage**, face, facing, facade. **3 head**, beginning, start, top, lead. **4 appearance**, air, face, manner, exterior, veneer, outward show, act, pretence. **5 cover**, blind, disguise, facade, mask, cloak, screen, smoke-screen, camouflage.

– ANTONYMS: back.

• **adj.** of or at the front.

▷ SYNONYMS: **leading**, lead, first, foremost.

– ANTONYMS: back, last.

• **v. 1** have the front towards. **2** place or be at the front of. **3** provide with a specified front. **4** be the leader or presenter of.

☐ **frontage 1** the front of a building. **2** a strip of land next to a street or waterway. **frontbencher** a member of the cabinet or shadow cabinet, who sits in the front seats in the House of Commons. **front line** the part of an army closest to the enemy. **front runner** the leader in a competition.

■ **frontal** adj. **frontally** adv.

frontier n. **1** a border separating two countries. **2** the extreme limit of settled land.

▷ SYNONYMS: **border**, boundary, border-line, dividing line, perimeter, limit, edge.

frontispiece n. an illustration facing the title page of a book.

frost n. **1** small white ice crystals on surfaces. **2** cold weather when frost forms.

• **v.** cover with frost.

frostbite n. injury to body tissues caused by exposure to extreme cold.

■ **frostbitten** adj.

frosted adj. (of glass) having a semi-transparent textured surface.

frosting n. US icing.

frosty adj. (**frostier, frostiest**) **1** very cold with frost forming on surfaces. **2** cold and unfriendly.

▷ SYNONYMS: **1 cold**, freezing, frozen, icy, bitter, chill, wintry, arctic; informal nippy; Brit. informal parky. **2 unfriendly**, cold, frigid, icy, glacial, inhospitable, unwelcoming, forbidding, hostile, stony.

– ANTONYMS: warm, friendly.

■ **frostily** adv. **frostiness** n.

froth n. a mass of small bubbles.

▷ SYNONYMS: **foam**, head, bubbles, frothi-ness, fizz, effervescence, lather, suds.

• **v.** form or contain froth.

▷ SYNONYMS: **bubble**, fizz, effervesce, foam, lather, churn, seethe.

■ **frothy** adj.

frown v. **1** wrinkle the forehead in disapproval or thought. **2** (**frown on**) disapprove of.

▷ SYNONYMS: **scowl**, glower, glare, lour, make a face, look daggers, knit your brows; informal give someone a dirty look.

– ANTONYMS: smile.

• **n.** a frowning expression.

frowsty adj. Brit. warm and stuffy.

frowzy (or **frowsy**) adj. scruffy and dingy.

froze past of FREEZE.

frozen past part. of FREEZE.

fructose n. a sugar found in honey and fruit.

frugal adj. **1** sparing with money or food. **2** (of a meal) plain and cheap.

▷ SYNONYMS: **1 thrifty**, economical, careful, cautious, prudent, provident, sparing, abstemious, austere, self-denying, ascetic, spartan. **2 meagre**, scanty, scant, paltry, skimpy, plain, simple, spartan, inexpensive, cheap, economical.

– ANTONYMS: extravagant, lavish.

■ **frugality** n. **frugally** adv.

fruit n. **1** an edible fleshy part of a plant that contains seed. **2** the seed-bearing part of any plant. **3** the result of work or activity.

• **v.** produce fruit.

☐ **bear fruit** have good results. **fruit machine** Brit. a coin-operated gambling machine.

fruiterer n. a person who sells fruit.

fruitful adj. producing a lot of fruit or good results.

▷ SYNONYMS: **productive**, constructive, useful, worthwhile, helpful, bene-ficial, valuable, rewarding, profitable, advantageous.

– ANTONYMS: barren, futile.

■ **fruitfully** adv. **fruitfulness** n.

fruition n. the fulfilment of a plan or project.

▷ SYNONYMS: **fulfilment**, realization, actualization, materialization, achievement, attainment, accomplish-ment, success, completion, consum-mation, conclusion, close, finish, perfection, maturity.

fruitless adj. failing to achieve the desired results.

▷ SYNONYMS: **futile**, vain, in vain, to no avail, to no effect, idle, pointless, useless, worthless, hollow, ineffec-

tual, ineffective, unproductive, unrewarding, profitless, unsuccessful, unavailing, abortive.
– ANTONYMS: fruitful, productive.
■ **fruitlessly** adv.

fruity adj. (**fruitier, fruitiest**) **1** like or containing fruit. **2** (of a voice) deep and rich.
■ **fruitiness** n.

frump n. a dowdy woman.
■ **frumpy** adj.

frustrate v. **1** prevent from progressing or succeeding. **2** cause to feel dissatisfied.
▷ SYNONYMS: **1 thwart**, defeat, foil, block, stop, counter, spoil, check, forestall, scotch, derail, snooker; informal **stymie**; Brit. informal **scupper**. **2 exasperate**, infuriate, discourage, dishearten, disappoint.
– ANTONYMS: further, satisfy.
■ **frustration** n.

fry¹ v. (**frying, fried**) cook in hot fat or oil.
● n. (**fries**) chips.
□ **frying pan** a shallow pan used for frying.
■ **fryer** n.

fry² pl. n. young fish.

ft abbrev. foot or feet.

fuchsia /fyoo-shuh/ n. a plant with drooping pink flowers.

fuddled adj. unable to think clearly.

fuddy-duddy n. (pl. **fuddy-duddies**) informal an old-fashioned and pompous person.

fudge n. **1** a soft sweet made of sugar, butter, and milk. **2** an attempt to present an issue in a vague way.
● v. present in a vague way.
▷ SYNONYMS: **evade**, avoid, dodge, skirt, duck, gloss over, cloud, hedge, beat about the bush, equivocate.

fuel n. **1** material burnt to produce heat or power. **2** something that stirs up emotion.
● v. (**fuelling, fuelled**; US **fueling, fueled**) **1** supply with fuel. **2** stir up strong feeling.
▷ SYNONYMS: **1 power**, fire, drive, run. **2 fan**, feed, stoke up, inflame, intensify, stimulate, encourage, provoke, incite, sustain.

fug n. Brit. informal a warm, stuffy atmosphere.
■ **fuggy** adj.

fugitive n. a person who has escaped from captivity or is in hiding.
▷ SYNONYMS: **escapee**, runaway, deserter, absconder, refugee.

fugue /fyoog/ n. a musical composition in which a short melody

is successively repeated by different voices or instruments.

fulcrum n. the point of support on which a lever turns.

fulfil (US **fulfill**) v. (**fulfilling, fulfilled**) **1** achieve something desired or promised. **2** meet a requirement. **3** (**fulfil yourself**) fully develop your abilities.
▷ SYNONYMS: **1 achieve**, attain, realize, make happen, succeed in, bring to completion, bring to fruition; carry out, perform, accomplish, execute, do, discharge, conduct. **2 meet**, satisfy, comply with, conform to, fill, answer.
■ **fulfilment** n.

full adj. **1** holding as much or as many as possible. **2** (**full of**) having a lot of. **3** complete. **4** rounded. **5** (of flavour etc.) strong or rich.
▷ SYNONYMS: **1 filled**, brimming, brimful, packed, loaded, crammed, crowded, bursting, overflowing, congested; informal **jam-packed**, wall-to-wall, chock-a-block, chock-full, awash. **2 replete**, full up, satisfied, sated, satiated; informal **stuffed**. **3** she'd led a full life: **eventful**, interesting, exciting, lively, action-packed, busy, active. **4** full details: **comprehensive**, thorough, exhaustive, all-inclusive, all-encompassing, all-embracing, in-depth, complete, entire, whole, unabridged. **5** a full figure: **plump**, rounded, buxom, shapely, ample, curvaceous, voluptuous; informal **curvy**; N. Amer. informal **zaftig**. **6** a full skirt: **loose-fitting**, loose, baggy, voluminous, roomy, capacious, billowing.
– ANTONYMS: empty.
● adv. **1** directly. **2** very.
□ **full back** (in football) a defender who plays at the side. **full-blooded** wholehearted and enthusiastic. **full-blown** fully developed. **full moon** the moon when its whole disc is illuminated. **full-scale** (of a model etc.) of the same size as the thing represented. **full stop** a punctuation mark (.) used at the end of a sentence or an abbreviation. **full time 1** the end of a sports match. **2** (**full-time**) working for the whole of the available time.
■ **fullness** n.

fully adv. **1** completely. **2** no less or fewer than.
▷ SYNONYMS: **completely**, entirely, wholly, totally, perfectly, quite, altogether, thoroughly, in all respects, to the hilt.
– ANTONYMS: partly.

fulminate v. protest strongly.
■ **fulmination** n.

fulsome adj. 1 excessively flattering.
2 large in size or quantity.

fumble v. 1 use the hands clumsily.
2 deal with clumsily.
▷ SYNONYMS: **grope**, fish, scrabble, feel.
• n. an act of fumbling.

fume n. a strong-smelling gas or
vapour.
▷ SYNONYMS: **smoke**, vapour, gas,
exhaust, pollution.
• v. 1 send out fumes. 2 feel great
anger.
▷ SYNONYMS: **be furious**, seethe, be livid,
be incensed, boil, be beside yourself,
spit; informal foam at the mouth, see
red.

fumigate v. disinfect with chemical
fumes.
▷ SYNONYMS: **disinfect**, purify, sterilize,
sanitize, decontaminate, cleanse,
clean out.
■ **fumigation** n.

fun n. light-hearted pleasure, or
something that provides it.
▷ SYNONYMS: **1 enjoyment**, entertainment, amusement, pleasure, jollification, merrymaking, recreation,
leisure, relaxation. **2 merriment**,
cheerfulness, jollity, joviality, high
spirits, mirth, laughter, hilarity,
light-heartedness, levity. **3** *he became
a figure of fun*: ridicule, derision,
mockery, scorn, contempt.
– ANTONYMS: boredom.
◻ **funfair** Brit. a gathering of rides,
sideshows, etc. for entertainment.
make fun of mock.

function n. 1 a purpose or natural
activity of a person or thing. 2 a
large or formal social event. 3 Math. a
quantity whose value depends on the
varying values of others.
▷ SYNONYMS: **1 purpose**, task, use, role.
2 responsibility, duty, role, province, activity, assignment, task, job,
mission. **3 social event**, party, social
occasion, affair, gathering, reception,
soirée; N. Amer. levee; informal do, bash.
• v. 1 work or operate. 2 (**function as**)
fulfil the purpose of.
▷ SYNONYMS: **1 work**, go, run, be in
working/running order, operate.
2 act, serve, operate, perform, do
duty.

functional adj. 1 of a function.
2 practical and useful. 3 working or
operating.
▷ SYNONYMS: **1 practical**, useful,
utilitarian, workaday, serviceable,
no-frills. **2 working**, in working

order, functioning, in service, in use,
going, running, operative; informal up
and running.
■ **functionality** n. **functionally** adv.

functionary n. (pl. **functionaries**) an
official.

fund n. 1 a sum of money for a
special purpose. 2 (**funds**) financial
resources. 3 a large stock.
▷ SYNONYMS: **1 collection**, kitty,
reserve, pool, purse, savings, coffers.
2 money, cash, wealth, means, assets,
resources, savings, capital, reserves,
the wherewithal; informal dosh; Brit.
informal lolly.
• v. provide with money.
▷ SYNONYMS: **finance**, pay for, back,
capitalize, subsidize, endow, invest
in, sponsor; N. Amer. informal bankroll.

fundamental adj. of basic
importance.
▷ SYNONYMS: **basic**, underlying, core,
rudimentary, root, primary, prime,
cardinal, principal, chief, key, central,
vital, essential.
– ANTONYMS: secondary, incidental.
• n. a basic rule or principle.

fundamentalism n. strict following
of the basic teachings of a religion.
■ **fundamentalist** n. & adj.

fundamentally adv. in the most
important respects.
▷ SYNONYMS: **essentially**, in essence,
basically, at heart, at bottom, deep
down, profoundly, primarily, above
all.

funeral n. a ceremony in which a dead
person is buried or cremated.
▷ SYNONYMS: **burial**, interment, entombment, committal, laying to rest,
cremation.
◻ **funeral director** an undertaker.

funerary adj. of or used for a funeral.

funereal adj. solemn or mournful.

fungicide n. a chemical that destroys
fungus.
■ **fungicidal** adj.

fungus n. (pl. **fungi**) an organism
without leaves or flowers that grows
on other plants or on decaying matter
(e.g. a mushroom).
■ **fungal** adj.

funicular adj. (of a railway) operating
by cable up and down a steep slope.

funk n. a style of dance music with a
strong rhythm.

funky adj. (**funkier, funkiest**) informal
1 having a strong dance rhythm.
2 stylish and modern.

funnel n. 1 a tube with a wide top for
pouring liquid or powder into small
openings. 2 a chimney on a ship or

steam engine.
• v. (funnelling, funnelled; US funneling, funneled) move through a funnel or narrow space.

funny adj. (funnier, funniest)
1 causing amusement. **2** strange.
▷ SYNONYMS: **1 amusing**, humorous, witty, comic, comical, hilarious, hysterical, riotous, uproarious, farcical; informal rib-tickling, priceless. **2 strange**, peculiar, odd, weird, bizarre, curious, freakish, quirky, unusual. **3 suspicious**, suspect, dubious, untrustworthy, questionable; informal fishy; Brit. informal dodgy.
– ANTONYMS: serious.
□ **funny bone** informal the part of the elbow over which a very sensitive nerve passes.
■ **funnily** adv.

fur n. **1** the short, soft hair of some animals. **2** the skin of an animal with fur on it. **3** Brit. a deposit formed by hard water on the inside of a kettle etc.
■ **furred** adj. **furriness** n. **furry** adj.

furious adj. **1** very angry. **2** intense or energetic.
▷ SYNONYMS: **1 very angry**, enraged, infuriated, irate, incensed, fuming, ranting, raving, seething, beside yourself, outraged; informal hopping mad, wild, livid. **2 fierce**, heated, passionate, fiery, tumultuous, turbulent, tempestuous, violent, stormy, acrimonious.
– ANTONYMS: pleased, calm.
■ **furiously** adv.

furl v. roll up neatly and securely.

furlong n. an eighth of a mile.

furlough /fer-loh/ n. a time when you have permission to leave your work.

furnace n. an enclosed chamber for heating material to very high temperatures.

furnish v. **1** provide with furniture. **2** supply or provide.
▷ SYNONYMS: **1 fit out**, appoint, equip; Brit. informal do out. **2** *they furnished us with waterproofs*: **supply**, provide, equip, issue, kit out; informal fix up.

furnishings pl. n. furniture and fittings.

furniture n. the movable objects used to make a room or building suitable for living or working in.

furore /fyoo-ror-i/ (US **furor**) n. an outbreak of public anger or excitement.
▷ SYNONYMS: **commotion**, uproar, outcry, fuss, upset, brouhaha, stir; informal to-do, hoo-ha, hullabaloo.

furrier n. a person who deals in furs.

furrow n. **1** a long, narrow trench cut in the ground. **2** a deep wrinkle on the face.
• v. make a furrow in.

further adv. (or **farther**) **1** at, to, or over a greater distance. **2** at or to a more advanced stage. **3** in addition.
• adj. **1** (or **farther**) more distant in space. **2** additional.
▷ SYNONYMS: **additional**, more, extra, supplementary, new, fresh.
• v. help the progress of.
▷ SYNONYMS: **promote**, advance, forward, develop, facilitate, aid, assist, help, boost, encourage.
– ANTONYMS: impede.
□ **further education** Brit. education below degree level for people above school age.

furtherance n. the advancement of a plan or interest.

furthermore adv. in addition.
▷ SYNONYMS: **moreover**, further, what's more, also, additionally, in addition, besides, as well, too, on top of that, into the bargain.

furthest (or **farthest**) adj. & adv. at or to the greatest distance.
▷ SYNONYMS: **most distant**, remotest, farthest, furthermost, farthermost, outer, outermost, extreme.
– ANTONYMS: nearest.

furtive adj. secretively trying to avoid notice.
▷ SYNONYMS: **surreptitious**, secretive, secret, clandestine, hidden, covert, conspiratorial, cloak-and-dagger, sneaky; informal shifty.
– ANTONYMS: open.
■ **furtively** adv.

fury n. (pl. **furies**) **1** extreme anger. **2** violent intensity.
▷ SYNONYMS: **1 rage**, anger, wrath, outrage; literary ire. **2 ferocity**, violence, turbulence, tempestuousness, savagery, severity, intensity, vehemence, force.

furze n. gorse.

fuse v. **1** combine to form a whole. **2** melt something so as to join it with something else. **3** Brit. (of an electrical appliance) stop working when a fuse melts. **4** fit with a fuse.
• n. **1** a strip of wire that melts and breaks an electric circuit if the current reaches an unsafe level. **2** a length of material lit to explode a bomb or firework. **3** a device in a bomb controlling the timing of the explosion.
■ **fusible** adj.

f

fuselage /fyoo-zuh-lah*zh*/ **n.** the main body of an aircraft.

Fusilier /fyoo-zi-**leer**/ **n.** a soldier of certain regiments.

fusillade /fyoo-zi-**layd**/ **n.** a series of shots fired at the same time or one after the other.

fusion n. the act of fusing, esp. of atomic nuclei with the release of much energy.

fuss n. 1 unnecessary excitement or activity. **2** a vigorous protest.
▷ SYNONYMS: **1 commotion**, excitement, stir, confusion, disturbance, brouhaha, uproar, furore, storm in a teacup, panic; informal hoo-ha, to-do, song and dance, performance. **2 protest**, complaint, objection, argument; Brit. row. **3 trouble**, bother, inconvenience, effort, exertion, labour; informal hassle.
• **v.** show unnecessary concern.
▷ SYNONYMS: **worry**, fret, be agitated, be worked up, make a mountain out of a molehill, panic; informal flap.

fussy adj. (**fussier, fussiest**) **1** hard to please. **2** full of unnecessary detail.
▷ SYNONYMS: **1 particular**, finicky, fastidious, hard to please, faddish; informal pernickety, choosy, picky; Brit. informal faddy; N. Amer. informal persnickety. **2 over-elaborate**, ornate, fancy, busy, cluttered.
■ **fussily** adv. **fussiness** n.

fustian n. a thick twilled cotton.

fusty adj. 1 smelling stale or damp. **2** old-fashioned.

futile adj. pointless.
▷ SYNONYMS: **fruitless**, vain, pointless, useless, ineffectual, forlorn, hopeless.
– ANTONYMS: useful.
■ **futility** n.

futon /**foo**-ton/ **n.** a padded mattress that can be rolled up.

future n. 1 time still to come. **2** what may happen in time still to come. **3** a prospect of success.
▷ SYNONYMS: **1** *plans for the future:* **time to come**, what lies ahead, the hereafter. **2** *her future lay in acting:* **destiny**, fate, fortune, prospects, chances.
– ANTONYMS: past.
• **adj.** existing or occurring in the future.
▷ SYNONYMS: **1 later**, to come, following, forthcoming, ensuing, succeeding, subsequent, coming, impending, approaching. **2** *her future husband:* **to be**, destined, intended, planned, prospective.
– ANTONYMS: previous, past.

futuristic adj. with very modern technology or design.

fuzz n. a frizzy mass of hair or fibre.

fuzzy adj. (**fuzzier, fuzziest**) **1** frizzy. **2** blurred; not clear.
▷ SYNONYMS: **1 frizzy**, fluffy, woolly, downy. **2 blurred**, indistinct, unclear, out of focus, misty. **3 unclear**, imprecise, unfocused, nebulous, vague, hazy, loose, woolly.
– ANTONYMS: smooth, sharp, clear.
■ **fuzzily** adv. **fuzziness** n.

Gg

G (or **g**) abbrev. **1** giga-. **2** grams. **3** gravity.

gab v. (**gabbing**, **gabbed**) informal talk at length.
□ **the gift of the gab** the ability to speak fluently and persuasively.

gabble v. talk quickly and indistinctly.

gaberdine (or **gabardine**) n. a smooth, hard-wearing cloth for making raincoats.

gable n. the triangular upper part of a wall at the end of a ridged roof.
■ **gabled** adj.

gad v. (**gadding**, **gadded**) (**gad about/around**) informal go from place to place enjoying yourself.
■ **gadabout** n.

gadfly n. a fly that bites livestock.

gadget n. a small mechanical device.
▷ SYNONYMS: **device**, appliance, apparatus, instrument, implement, tool, utensil, contrivance, contraption, machine, mechanism, invention; informal gizmo.
■ **gadgetry** n.

Gaelic /gay-lik, ga-lik/ n. a language spoken in parts of Ireland and western Scotland.

gaff n. a hooked stick for landing large fish.

gaffe n. an embarrassing blunder.
▷ SYNONYMS: **blunder**, mistake, error, slip, faux pas, indiscretion, solecism; informal slip-up, howler, boo-boo; Brit. informal boob, clanger; N. Amer. informal blooper.

gaffer n. informal **1** Brit. a boss. **2** an old man.

gag n. **1** a piece of cloth put over a person's mouth to silence them. **2** a joke.
▷ SYNONYMS: **joke**, quip, jest, witticism; informal crack, wisecrack, one-liner.
• v. (**gagging**, **gagged**) **1** put a gag on. **2** choke or retch.
▷ SYNONYMS: **1 silence**, muzzle, suppress, stifle, censor, curb, restrain. **2 retch**, heave.

gaga adj. informal senile.

gage US = GAUGE.

gaggle n. **1** a flock of geese. **2** informal a disorderly group.

gaiety n. the state of being light-hearted and cheerful.

gaily adv. **1** cheerfully. **2** thoughtlessly. **3** colourfully.

gain v. **1** obtain or secure. **2** reach. **3** (**gain on**) come closer to someone or something pursued. **4** increase in weight, speed, etc. **5** (of a clock) become fast.
▷ SYNONYMS: **1 obtain**, get, secure, acquire, come by, procure, attain, achieve, earn, win, capture; informal land. **2** they stood to gain from the deal: **profit**, make money, benefit, do well out of. **3** they're gaining on us: **catch up with**, catch, reduce someone's lead, narrow the gap. **4** she gained weight: **put on**, increase in, build up.
– ANTONYMS: lose.
• n. **1** a thing gained. **2** an increase in wealth or value.
▷ SYNONYMS: **1 profit**, earnings, income, yield, return, reward, advantage, benefit; informal take. **2 increase**, addition, rise, increment, advance.
– ANTONYMS: loss.

gainful adj. paid; profitable.
▷ SYNONYMS: **profitable**, paid, well paid, remunerative, lucrative, moneymaking, rewarding, fruitful, worthwhile, useful, productive, constructive, beneficial, advantageous, valuable.
■ **gainfully** adv.

gainsay v. (**gainsaying**, **gainsaid**) deny or contradict.

gait n. a way of walking.
▷ SYNONYMS: **walk**, step, stride, pace, tread, way of walking, bearing, carriage; Brit. deportment.

gaiter n. a covering for the ankle and lower leg.

gala n. **1** a social occasion with

entertainment. **2** Brit. a swimming competition.

▷ SYNONYMS: **festival**, fair, fete, carnival, pageant, jubilee, jamboree, celebration.

galaxy n. (pl. **galaxies**) **1** a system of millions or billions of stars. **2** (**the Galaxy**) the galaxy including the sun and the earth.

■ **galactic** adj.

gale n. **1** a very strong wind. **2** an outburst of laughter.

▷ SYNONYMS: **1 high wind**, blast, squall, storm, tempest, hurricane, tornado, cyclone, whirlwind, typhoon. **2** peal, howl, hoot, shriek, roar, fit, paroxysm.

gall /gawl/ n. **1** bold and disrespectful behaviour. **2** annoyance or resentment. **3** a sore made by rubbing. **4** an abnormal growth on plants and trees.

• v. annoy or irritate.

□ **gall bladder** an organ beneath the liver, storing bile. **gallstone** a small hard mass forming in the gall bladder.

gallant adj. **1** brave. **2** charming and attentive.

▷ SYNONYMS: **1 brave**, courageous, valiant, bold, plucky, daring, fearless, intrepid, heroic, stout-hearted; informal gutsy, spunky. **2 chivalrous**, gentlemanly, courteous, polite, attentive, respectful, gracious, considerate, thoughtful.

– ANTONYMS: cowardly, discourteous.

■ **gallantry** n.

galleon n. hist. a large sailing ship.

gallery n. (pl. **galleries**) **1** a building for displaying works of art. **2** an upstairs sitting area in a hall, theatre, etc. **3** a long room or passage.

galley n. (pl. **galleys**) **1** a small kitchen in a ship or aircraft. **2** hist. a sailing ship with several banks of oars.

Gallic adj. of France or the French.

gallium n. a soft metallic element.

gallivant v. informal go from place to place enjoying yourself.

gallon n. a measure for liquids, equal to eight pints (4.55 litres).

gallop n. **1** a horse's fastest pace. **2** a ride on a horse at a gallop.

• v. (**galloping**, **galloped**) **1** go at the pace of a gallop. **2** go fast.

gallows pl. n. a structure with a noose for hanging criminals.

galore adj. in abundance: *there were prizes galore.*

galoshes pl. n. rubber overshoes.

galvanize (or **-ise**) v. **1** shock or excite into action. **2** (**galvanized**) (of iron or steel) coated with zinc.

gambit n. an action or remark intended to gain an advantage.

gamble v. **1** play games of chance for money. **2** bet money. **3** risk in the hope of gaining something.

▷ SYNONYMS: **1 bet**, place a bet, wager, hazard; Brit. informal punt, have a flutter. **2 take a chance**, take a risk; N. Amer. take a flyer; informal stick your neck out; Brit. informal chance your arm.

• n. a risky action.

▷ SYNONYMS: *I took a gamble:* **risk**, chance, leap in the dark, speculation, lottery, pot luck.

■ **gambler** n.

gambol v. (**gambolling**, **gambolled**; US **gamboling**, **gamboled**) run or jump about playfully.

game n. **1** an activity done for amusement or sport. **2** a period of play, ending in a final result. **3** wild mammals or birds hunted for sport or food.

▷ SYNONYMS: **1 pastime**, diversion, entertainment, amusement, distraction, recreation, sport, activity. **2 match**, contest, fixture, meeting, tie, clash.

• adj. eager and willing.

▷ SYNONYMS: **willing**, prepared, ready, disposed, interested, eager, keen, enthusiastic.

• v. gamble for money.

□ **gamekeeper** a person employed to breed and protect game. **gamesmanship** the tactic of winning games by making an opponent feel less confident.

■ **gamely** adv.

gamete n. a reproductive cell.

gamine adj. (of a girl) having a mischievous, boyish charm.

gamma rays pl. n. electromagnetic radiation of shorter wavelength than X-rays.

gammon n. Brit. cured ham.

gammy adj. Brit. informal painful or injured.

gamut n. the whole range or scope.

gamy (or **gamey**) adj. (of meat) having the strong flavour or smell of game when it is high.

gander n. **1** a male goose. **2** informal a look.

gang n. an organized group, esp. of criminals or manual workers.

▷ SYNONYMS: **band**, group, crowd, pack, horde, throng, mob, herd, swarm, troop; informal bunch, gaggle, load.

• v. (**gang up**) join together against someone.

gangling (or **gangly**) adj. tall, thin, and awkward.

ganglion n. (pl. **ganglia** or **ganglions**)
1 a mass of nerve cells. **2** a swelling
on a tendon.

gangplank n. a movable plank used
to board or leave a ship.

gangrene n. the death of body tissue.
■ **gangrenous** adj.

gangster n. a member of a gang of
violent criminals.
▷ SYNONYMS: **hoodlum**, racketeer, thug,
villain, criminal, Mafioso; informal
mobster, crook, tough; N. Amer. informal
hood.

gangway n. **1** Brit. a passage between
rows of seats. **2** a movable bridge
linking a ship to the shore.

gannet n. **1** a large seabird. **2** Brit.
informal a greedy person.

gantry n. (pl. **gantries**) an overhead
structure supporting heavy
equipment.

gaol var. of JAIL.

gap n. **1** a break or hole. **2** a space or
interval.
▷ SYNONYMS: **1 opening**, aperture, space,
breach, chink, slit, crack, crevice,
cleft, cavity, hole, interstice. **2 pause**,
intermission, interval, interlude,
break, breathing space, breather,
respite, hiatus, lull; N. Amer. recess.
3 omission, blank, lacuna. **4** the gap
between rich and poor: **chasm**, gulf,
separation, contrast, difference,
disparity, divergence, imbalance.
□ **gap year** a break taken by a student
between school and university or
college education.
■ **gappy** adj.

gape v. **1** be or become wide open.
2 stare with the mouth open wide in
amazement.
▷ SYNONYMS: **1 open**, part, split. **2 stare**,
goggle, gaze, ogle; informal rubberneck;
Brit. informal gawp.

gaping adj. wide open: a gaping hole.
▷ SYNONYMS: **wide**, yawning, vast,
cavernous.

garage n. **1** a building for storing a
vehicle. **2** a place which sells fuel or
which repairs and sells vehicles.

garb n. clothing.
• v. (**be garbed**) be clothed.

garbage n. rubbish.
▷ SYNONYMS: **1 waste**, refuse, rubbish,
detritus, litter, junk, scrap, scraps,
leftovers, remains; N. Amer. trash.
2 nonsense, rubbish, balderdash, claptrap, twaddle, dross; informal hogwash,
baloney, tripe, bilge, bull, bunk,
poppycock, rot, piffle; Brit. informal tosh,
codswallop.

garble v. confuse or distort a message
etc.
▷ SYNONYMS: **mix up**, muddle, jumble,
confuse, obscure, distort.

garden n. **1** an area next to a house,
with a lawn or flowers. **2** (**gardens**) a
public park.
▷ SYNONYMS: park, estate, grounds.
• v. work in a garden.
■ **gardener** n.

> **WORD LINKS**
> **horticultural** relating to gardens

gargantuan adj. enormous.

gargle v. wash the throat with a liquid
that is kept there by slowly breathing
out through it.

gargoyle n. a grotesque face or figure
carved on the gutter of a building.

garish /gair-ish/ adj. unpleasantly
bright and showy.
▷ SYNONYMS: **gaudy**, lurid, loud, harsh,
showy, glittering, brash, tasteless,
vulgar; informal flashy.
– ANTONYMS: drab, tasteful.
■ **garishly** adv.

garland n. a wreath of flowers and
leaves.
• v. decorate with a garland.

garlic n. the bulb of a plant of the
onion family, used in cookery.
■ **garlicky** adj.

garment n. an item of clothing.
▷ SYNONYMS: (**garments**) **clothes**,
clothing, dress, garb, wardrobe,
costume, attire; informal gear, togs; Brit.
informal clobber; N. Amer. informal threads;
formal apparel.

garner v. gather or collect.

garnet n. a red semi-precious stone.

garnish v. decorate food.
▷ SYNONYMS: **decorate**, adorn, ornament,
trim, dress, embellish.
• n. a decoration for food.
▷ SYNONYMS: **decoration**, adornment,
ornament, embellishment, enhancement, finishing touch.

garret n. an attic.

garrison n. a group of troops in a
fortress or town.
▷ SYNONYMS: **1 troops**, forces, militia,
soldiers, force, detachment, unit.
2 base, camp, station, barracks, fort,
command post.
• v. provide with a garrison.
▷ SYNONYMS: **station**, post, deploy, base,
site, place, billet.

garrotte (US **garrote**) v. strangle with
a wire or cord.
• n. a wire or cord used for garrotting.

garrulous adj. very talkative.
▷ SYNONYMS: **talkative**, loquacious,

voluble, verbose, chatty, gossipy, effusive, expansive, forthcoming, conversational, communicative; informal mouthy, having the gift of the gab.
– ANTONYMS: taciturn.

garter n. a band worn around the leg to keep up a stocking or sock.

gas n. (pl. **gases** or US **gasses**) **1** an air-like substance which expands to fill any available space. **2** gas used as a fuel. **3** US informal petrol.
• v. (**gassing**, **gassed**) **1** harm or kill with gas. **2** informal chatter.
□ **gas chamber** a room filled with poisonous gas to kill people. **gas mask** a mask used as protection against poisonous gas.
■ **gassy** adj.

gaseous adj. of or like a gas.

gash n. a long deep cut.
▷ SYNONYMS: cut, laceration, slash, slit, split, wound, injury.
• v. make a gash in.
▷ SYNONYMS: cut, lacerate, slash, slit, split, wound, injure.

gasket n. a sheet or ring of rubber sealing a joint in an engine etc.

gasoline n. US petrol.

gasp v. draw in breath suddenly or with difficulty.
▷ SYNONYMS: **1 catch your breath**, gulp, draw in your breath. **2 pant**, puff, puff and blow, wheeze, breathe hard/ heavily, choke, fight for breath.
• n. a sudden quick breath.
▷ SYNONYMS: gulp, pant, puff.

gastric adj. of the stomach.

gastro-enteritis n. inflammation of the stomach and intestines.

gastronomy n. the art of cooking and eating good food.
■ **gastronomic** adj.

gastropod n. a mollusc such as a snail or slug.

gate n. **1** a hinged barrier across an opening in a wall, fence, etc. **2** an exit from an airport building to an aircraft. **3** the number of people paying to attend a sports event.
▷ SYNONYMS: **barrier**, turnstile, gateway, doorway, entrance, exit, door, portal; N. Amer. entryway.
□ **gatecrash** go to a party without an invitation. **gateway 1** an opening closed by a gate. **2** a means of access.

gateau n. (pl. **gateaus** or **gateaux**) a cake with layers of cream or fruit.

gather v. **1** come or bring together. **2** increase in speed, force, etc. **3** understand to be the case. **4** collect plants or fruit for food. **5** pull fabric

into folds by drawing thread through it.
▷ SYNONYMS: **1 congregate**, assemble, meet, collect, get together, convene, muster, rally, converge. **2 summon**, call together, bring together, assemble, convene, rally, round up, muster, marshal. **3 harvest**, reap, crop, pick, pluck, collect. **4 understand**, believe, be led to believe, conclude, infer, assume, take it, surmise, hear, learn, discover. **5 pleat**, pucker, tuck, fold, ruffle.
– ANTONYMS: disperse.
• n. (**gathers**) a gathered part of a garment.

gathering n. an assembled group.
▷ SYNONYMS: **assembly**, meeting, convention, rally, council, congress, congregation, audience, crowd, group, throng, mass; informal get-together.

gauche /gohsh/ adj. socially awkward.
▷ SYNONYMS: **awkward**, gawky, inelegant, graceless, ungraceful, clumsy, ungainly, maladroit, inept, unsophisticated.
– ANTONYMS: elegant, sophisticated.

gaucho /gow-choh/ n. (pl. **gauchos**) a South American cowboy.

gaudy adj. (**gaudier**, **gaudiest**) tastelessly bright or showy.
▷ SYNONYMS: **garish**, lurid, loud, glaring, harsh, showy, glittering, ostentatious, tasteless; informal flashy, tacky.
– ANTONYMS: drab, tasteful.
■ **gaudily** adv. **gaudiness** n.

gauge (US **gage**) n. **1** an instrument for measuring the amount or level of something. **2** a measure of thickness, size, etc. **3** the distance between the rails of a railway track.
▷ SYNONYMS: **meter**, measure, indicator, dial, scale, display.
• v. estimate, measure, or judge.
▷ SYNONYMS: **1 measure**, calculate, compute, work out, determine, ascertain, count, weigh, quantify, put a figure on. **2 assess**, evaluate, determine, estimate, form an opinion of, appraise, weigh up, judge, guess; informal size up.

USAGE gau-, not gua-: gauge

gaunt adj. lean and haggard.
▷ SYNONYMS: **haggard**, drawn, thin, lean, skinny, spindly, spare, bony, angular, raw-boned, pinched, hollow-cheeked, scrawny, scraggy, as thin as a rake, cadaverous, skeletal, emaciated, skin and bone, wasted, withered; informal like a bag of bones.
– ANTONYMS: plump.

g

gauntlet n. a glove with a long wide cuff.
▫ **run the gauntlet** go through an intimidating crowd or experience. **throw down the gauntlet** set a challenge.

gauze n. **1** a thin transparent fabric. **2** a fine wire mesh.
■ **gauzy** adj.

gave past of GIVE.

gavel n. a small hammer used by an auctioneer or judge to call for attention or order.

gavotte n. a French dance of the 18th century.

gawky adj. awkward and ungainly.

gawp v. Brit. informal stare in a stupid or rude way.

gay adj. **1** homosexual. **2** dated light-hearted and carefree. **3** dated brightly coloured.
● n. a homosexual person.

gaze v. look steadily.
▷ SYNONYMS: **stare**, gape, look fixedly, goggle, eye, scrutinize, ogle; informal rubberneck; Brit. informal gawp; N. Amer. informal eyeball.
● n. a steady look.
▷ SYNONYMS: **stare**, gape, fixed look, regard, scrutiny.

gazebo /guh-zee-boh/ n. (pl. **gazebos**) a garden shelter with open sides.

gazelle n. a small antelope.

gazette n. a journal or newspaper.

gazetteer n. a list of place names.

gazump v. Brit. informal offer or accept a higher price for a house after a lower price has already been accepted.

GB abbrev. **1** Great Britain. **2** (or **Gb**) gigabytes.

GBH abbrev. Brit. grievous bodily harm.

GCE abbrev. General Certificate of Education.

GCSE abbrev. General Certificate of Secondary Education.

GDP abbrev. gross domestic product.

gear n. **1** (**gears**) a set of toothed wheels that connects the engine to the wheels of a vehicle and controls its speed. **2** a particular setting of gears. **3** informal equipment or clothing.
▷ SYNONYMS: **1 equipment**, apparatus, paraphernalia, tools, utensils, implements, instruments, rig, tackle; informal kit; Brit. informal clobber, gubbins. **2 clothes**, clothing, garments, outfits, attire, garb, wardrobe; informal togs; Brit. informal clobber, kit; N. Amer. informal threads; formal apparel.
● v. **1** adapt for a purpose. **2** adjust the gears in a vehicle. **3** (**gear up**)

prepare.
▫ **gearbox** a set of gears with its casing. **in** (or **out of**) **gear** with a gear (or no gear) engaged.

gecko n. (pl. **geckos** or **geckoes**) a tropical lizard.

geek n. informal **1** an awkward or unfashionable person. **2** an obsessive enthusiast.
■ **geeky** adj.

geese pl. of GOOSE.

Geiger counter /gy-ger/ n. a device for measuring radioactivity.

geisha /gay-shuh/ n. (pl. **geisha** or **geishas**) a Japanese hostess trained to entertain men.

gel /jel/ n. a jelly-like substance.
● v. (**gelling**, **gelled**) **1** (of jelly etc.) set or become firmer. **2** take definite form. **3** style the hair with gel.

gelatin (or **gelatine**) n. a clear substance used to make jelly, glue, etc.
■ **gelatinous** adj.

geld v. castrate.

gelding n. a castrated horse.

gelignite n. a high explosive made from nitroglycerine.

gem n. **1** a precious stone. **2** an outstanding person or thing.
▷ SYNONYMS: **1 jewel**, precious stone, semi-precious stone; informal rock, sparkler. **2 masterpiece**, classic, treasure, prize, find; informal one in a million, the bee's knees.

gender n. **1** the state of being male or female (with reference to social or cultural differences). **2** each of the classes into which nouns are placed in some languages, usu. masculine, feminine, and neuter.

gene n. a distinct sequence of DNA by which offspring inherit parental characteristics.

genealogy n. (pl. **genealogies**) **1** a line of descent from an ancestor. **2** the study of lines of descent.
▷ SYNONYMS: **lineage**, line, family tree, bloodline, pedigree, ancestry, heritage, parentage, family, stock, blood, roots.
■ **genealogical** adj. **genealogist** n.

genera pl. of GENUS.

general adj. **1** affecting or concerning all or most people or things. **2** involving only the main features; not detailed.
▷ SYNONYMS: **1** the general opinion: **widespread**, common, extensive, universal, wide, popular, public, mainstream. **2** it's not our general practice to comment on such issues:

g

usual, customary, habitual, traditional, normal, conventional, typical, standard, regular, accepted, prevailing, routine, established, everyday. **3** *a general description:* broad, rough, loose, approximate, unspecific, vague, imprecise, inexact.
– ANTONYMS: restricted, unusual, detailed.
• n. the army rank above lieutenant general.
□ **general anaesthetic** an anaesthetic causing a loss of consciousness. **general election** an election of parliamentary representatives from the whole country. **general practitioner** a doctor treating patients in a local community. **in general** mainly; as a whole.

generality n. (pl. **generalities**) **1** a general statement. **2** the state of being general.

generalize (or **-ise**) v. **1** make a general statement. **2** make generally available or applicable.
■ **generalization** n.

generally adv. **1** in most cases, or by most people. **2** without discussing the details of something.
▷ SYNONYMS: **1 normally**, in general, as a rule, by and large, mainly, mostly, for the most part, predominantly, on the whole, usually. **2 widely**, commonly, extensively, universally, popularly.

generate v. create or produce.
▷ SYNONYMS: **create**, make, produce, engender, spawn, precipitate, prompt, provoke, trigger, spark off, stir up, induce.
■ **generative** adj.

generation n. **1** all of the people born and living at about the same time. **2** the average period in which a person grows up and has children. **3** a single stage in a family's descent. **4** production or creation.
▷ SYNONYMS: **1 age**, age group, peer group. **2 crop**, batch, wave, range.
■ **generational** adj.

generator n. a machine for generating electricity.

generic adj. **1** of a whole class or group. **2** (of goods) having no brand name.
■ **generically** adv.

generosity n. the fact or quality of being generous.
▷ SYNONYMS: **liberality**, lavishness, magnanimity, bounty, munificence, open-handedness, largesse, unselfishness, altruism, charity.
– ANTONYMS: meanness, selfishness.

generous adj. **1** giving freely. **2** kind. **3** large or plentiful.
▷ SYNONYMS: **1 liberal**, lavish, magnanimous, giving, open-handed, bountiful, unselfish, ungrudging, free, unstinting, munificent; literary bounteous. **2 plentiful**, copious, ample, liberal, large, abundant, rich.
– ANTONYMS: mean, selfish, meagre.
■ **generously** adv.

genesis n. the origin of something.
▷ SYNONYMS: **origin**, source, root, beginning, start.

genetic adj. of genes or genetics.
• n. (**genetics**) the study of heredity and inherited characteristics.
□ **genetically modified** containing genetic material artificially altered to produce a desired characteristic. **genetic engineering** the alteration of an animal's or plant's characteristics by manipulating its DNA. **genetic fingerprinting** the analysis of DNA to identify individuals.
■ **genetically** adv. **geneticist** n.

genial adj. friendly and cheerful.
▷ SYNONYMS: **friendly**, affable, cordial, amiable, warm, easy-going, approachable, sympathetic, good-natured, good-humoured, cheerful, hospitable, companionable, sociable, convivial, outgoing, gregarious; informal chummy, pally; Brit. informal matey.
– ANTONYMS: unfriendly.
■ **geniality** n. **genially** adv.

genie n. a spirit in Arabian folklore.

genital adj. of reproductive organs.
• pl. n. (**genitals** or **genitalia**) the external reproductive organs.

genitive n. the grammatical case showing possession.

genius n. (pl. **geniuses**) **1** exceptional natural ability. **2** a very intelligent or able person.
▷ SYNONYMS: **1 brilliance**, intelligence, intellect, ability, cleverness, brains. **2 talent**, gift, flair, aptitude, facility, knack, ability, expertise, capacity, faculty. **3 brilliant person**, mastermind, Einstein, intellectual, brain, prodigy; informal egghead, bright spark; Brit. informal brainbox, clever clogs; N. Amer. informal brainiac.

genocide n. the deliberate killing of many people from a particular ethnic group or nation.

genre /zhon-ruh/ n. a style of art or literature.
▷ SYNONYMS: **category**, class, classification, group, set, type, sort, kind, variety.

genteel adj. affectedly polite and

refined.

▷ SYNONYMS: **refined**, respectable, well mannered, courteous, polite, proper, correct, seemly, well bred, ladylike, gentlemanly, dignified, gracious.

– ANTONYMS: uncouth.

gentian /jen-sh'n/ n. a plant with deep blue flowers.

Gentile n. a person who is not Jewish.

gentility n. polite and refined behaviour.

gentle adj. **1** kind and mild. **2** not harsh or severe.

▷ SYNONYMS: **1** kind, tender, sympathetic, considerate, understanding, compassionate, humane, mild, placid, serene. **2** light, soft, quiet, low. **3** gradual, slight, easy, slow, imperceptible.

– ANTONYMS: brutal, strong, loud, steep.

■ **gentleness** n. **gently** adv.

gentleman n. **1** a courteous or honourable man. **2** a man of good social position.

■ **gentlemanly** adj.

gentrify v. (**gentrifying**, **gentrified**) renovate a district so that it conforms to middle-class taste.

gentry n. people of the class next below the nobility.

genuflect v. lower the body as a sign of respect by bending one knee.

■ **genuflection** n.

genuine adj. truly what it is said to be.

▷ SYNONYMS: **1 authentic**, real, actual, original, bona fide, true; informal pukka, the real McCoy, the real thing, kosher; Austral./NZ informal dinkum. **2** sincere, honest, truthful, straightforward, direct, frank, candid, open, natural; informal straight, upfront.

– ANTONYMS: bogus, insincere.

■ **genuinely** adv.

genus n. (pl. **genera**) a category in the classification of animals and plants.

geodesic /jee-oh-**dess**-ik/ adj. of a method of construction based on the shortest possible lines between points on a curved surface.

geography n. **1** the study of the earth's physical features and of human activity as it relates to these. **2** the arrangement of the features of a place.

■ **geographer** n. **geographical** (or **geographic**) adj. **geographically** adv.

geology n. **1** the study of the earth's physical structure and substance. **2** the geological features of a district.

■ **geological** adj. **geologically** adv. **geologist** n.

geometric adj. **1** of geometry. **2** (of

a design) featuring regular lines and shapes.

■ **geometrical** adj. **geometrically** adv.

geometry n. the branch of mathematics dealing with points, lines, surfaces, and solids.

Georgian adj. of the time of Kings George I–IV (1714–1830).

geothermal adj. of or produced by the internal heat of the earth.

geranium n. a flowering garden plant.

gerbil n. a small domesticated rodent.

geriatric adj. of old people.

• n. **1** an old person. **2** (**geriatrics**) the branch of medicine dealing with the care of old people.

germ n. **1** a microorganism causing disease. **2** a part of an organism capable of developing into a new one. **3** an early stage of development.

▷ SYNONYMS: **1 microbe**, microorganism, bacillus, bacterium, virus; informal bug. **2** the germ of an idea: **start**, beginnings, seed, embryo, bud, root, origin, source.

German n. **1** a person from Germany. **2** the language of Germany, Austria, and parts of Switzerland.

• adj. of Germany.

□ **German measles** rubella. **German shepherd** a large breed of dog often used as guard dogs.

germane adj. relevant.

Germanic adj. **1** of the language family including English, German, Dutch, and the Scandinavian languages. **2** of Germans or Germany.

germanium n. a grey crystalline element.

germinate v. (of a seed) begin to grow.

■ **germination** n.

gerontology n. the study of old age and old people.

gerrymander v. alter the boundaries of an electoral constituency so as to favour one party.

gerund n. a noun formed from a verb, in English ending in -ing.

Gestapo n. the German secret police under Nazi rule.

gestation n. **1** the growth of a baby in the womb. **2** the development of an idea over time.

gesticulate v. gesture in place of or to emphasize speech.

■ **gesticulation** n.

gesture n. **1** a movement of part of the body to convey a meaning. **2** an action done to convey feelings or intentions.

g

▷ SYNONYMS: **1 signal**, sign, motion, indication, gesticulation. **2 action**, act, deed, move.
• v. make a gesture.

▷ SYNONYMS: **signal**, motion, gesticulate, wave, indicate, give a sign.

get v. (**getting, got**) **1** come to have or hold; receive. **2** succeed in achieving. **3** experience or suffer. **4** fetch. **5** reach a specified state or place. **6** begin to be or do. **7** travel by a form of transport. **8** catch or thwart.

▷ SYNONYMS: **1 obtain**, acquire, come by, receive, gain, earn, win, be given; informal get hold of, score. **2 become**, grow, turn, go. **3 fetch**, collect, go/come for, call for, pick up, bring, deliver, convey. **4 capture**, catch, arrest, apprehend, seize; informal collar, grab, pick up; Brit. informal nick. **5 contract**, develop, go down with, catch, fall ill with. **6 hear**, catch, make out, follow, take in. **7 understand**, comprehend, grasp, see, fathom, follow. **8 arrive**, reach, make it, turn up, appear, present yourself, come along; informal show up. **9 persuade**, induce, prevail on, influence, talk into. **10 prepare**, get ready, cook, make; informal fix, rustle up; Brit. informal knock up.

– ANTONYMS: give.
□ **get across** manage to communicate. **getaway** an escape. **get by** manage to survive or do something. **get off** informal escape punishment. **get on 1** make progress. **2** be friendly. **3** informal grow old. **get over** recover from. **get round** persuade. **get-together** a social gathering. **get-up** informal an outfit.

geyser n. a hot spring intermittently sending a jet of water and steam into the air.

ghastly adj. **1** very frightening or horrible. **2** informal very unpleasant. **3** very pale.

▷ SYNONYMS: **1 terrible**, frightful, horrible, grim, awful, horrifying, shocking, appalling, gruesome, horrendous, monstrous. **2 unpleasant**, objectionable, disagreeable, distasteful, awful, terrible, dreadful, frightful, detestable, vile; informal horrible, horrid.

– ANTONYMS: pleasant.
■ ghastliness n.

ghee n. clarified butter used in Indian cooking.

gherkin n. a small pickled cucumber.

ghetto n. (pl. **ghettos** or **ghettoes**) a part of a city occupied by people of a particular race, nationality, etc.

ghost n. **1** an apparition of a dead person. **2** a faint trace.

▷ SYNONYMS: **spectre**, phantom, wraith, spirit, presence, apparition; informal spook.
□ **ghost town** a town with no inhabitants. **ghost writer** a person who writes a book for someone else who is named as the author.

ghostly adj. (**ghostlier, ghostliest**) relating to or like a ghost.

▷ SYNONYMS: **supernatural**, unearthly, spectral, phantom, unnatural, eerie, weird, uncanny; informal spooky.

ghoul n. **1** an evil spirit. **2** a person excessively interested in death or disaster.
■ ghoulish adj.

GI n. (pl. **GIs**) a private soldier in the US army.

giant n. **1** an imaginary being of superhuman size. **2** an unusually large person, animal, or plant.

▷ SYNONYMS: **colossus**, mammoth, monster, leviathan, ogre.

– ANTONYMS: dwarf.
• adj. very large.

▷ SYNONYMS: **huge**, colossal, massive, enormous, gigantic, mammoth, vast, immense, monumental, mountainous, titanic, towering, gargantuan; informal mega, monster, whopping; Brit. informal ginormous.

– ANTONYMS: miniature.

gibber v. speak rapidly and unintelligibly.

gibberish n. unintelligible speech or writing.

gibbet n. hist. a gallows.

gibbon n. a long-armed SE Asian ape.

gibe var. of JIBE.

giblets pl. n. the liver, heart, etc. of a chicken or other bird.

giddy adj. (**giddier, giddiest**) **1** having a feeling of whirling and being about to fall. **2** not interested in serious things.

▷ SYNONYMS: **1 dizzy**, light-headed, faint, unsteady, wobbly, reeling; informal woozy. **2 flighty**, silly, frivolous, skittish, irresponsible, scatty; informal dizzy.
■ giddily adv. giddiness n.

gift n. **1** a thing given without payment. **2** a natural talent.

▷ SYNONYMS: **1 present**, handout, donation, offering, bonus, award, endowment; informal prezzie. **2 talent**, flair, aptitude, facility, knack, bent, ability, skill, capacity, faculty.
• v. give as a gift.

gifted adj. having exceptional talent.
▷ SYNONYMS: **talented**, skilled, accomplished, expert, able, proficient, intelligent, clever, bright, brilliant, precocious; informal crack, ace.
− ANTONYMS: inept.

gig n. **1** informal a live performance by a musician. **2** esp. hist. a light two-wheeled horse-drawn carriage.

gigabyte n. Computing a unit of information equal to one thousand million bytes.

gigantic adj. very large.
▷ SYNONYMS: **huge**, enormous, vast, giant, massive, colossal, mammoth, immense, monumental, mountainous, gargantuan; informal mega, monster, whopping, humongous; Brit. informal ginormous.
− ANTONYMS: tiny.

giggle v. laugh in a nervous or silly way.
▷ SYNONYMS: **titter**, snigger, chuckle, chortle, laugh.
• n. a nervous or silly laugh.
■ **giggly** adj.

gigolo /jig-uh-loh/ n. (pl. **gigolos**) a man paid by a woman to be her escort or lover.

gild v. cover thinly with gold.
■ **gilding** n.

gilet /zhi-lay/ n. a light sleeveless padded jacket.

gill /jil/ n. a quarter of a pint.

gills /gilz/ pl. n. **1** the organ with which a fish breathes. **2** the plates on the underside of a mushroom.

gilt adj. covered thinly with gold.
• n. a thin layer of gold on a surface.
□ **gilt-edged** (of an investment) very safe.

gimcrack /jim-krak/ adj. showy but poorly made.

gimlet /gim-lit/ n. a small tool with a screw-tip for boring holes.

gimmick n. something intended to attract attention.
■ **gimmicky** adj.

gin n. an alcoholic spirit flavoured with juniper berries.

ginger n. **1** a hot spice made from the root of a SE Asian plant. **2** a light reddish-yellow colour.
□ **gingerbread** cake flavoured with ginger.
■ **gingery** adj.

gingerly adv. cautiously.

gingham /ging-uhm/ n. cotton cloth with a checked pattern.

gingivitis /jin-ji-vy-tiss/ n. inflammation of the gums.

ginseng n. the root of an east Asian and North American plant, used in some medicines.

Gipsy var. of GYPSY.

giraffe n. a large African animal with a very long neck and legs.

gird v. literary encircle with a belt or band.

girder n. a large metal beam.

girdle n. **1** a belt. **2** a corset.
• v. encircle.

girl n. **1** a female child. **2** a young woman.
▷ SYNONYMS: **young woman**, young lady, miss; Scottish & N. English lass, lassie; Irish colleen; informal chick; Austral./NZ informal sheila; old use maid, maiden.
■ **girlhood** n. **girlish** adj. **girlie** adj. & n.

girlfriend n. **1** a person's regular female romantic or sexual partner. **2** a woman's female friend.
▷ SYNONYMS: **sweetheart**, lover, partner, significant other, girl, woman; informal steady; Brit. informal bird; N. Amer. informal squeeze.

giro n. (pl. **giros**) a system of electronic credit transfer involving banks, post offices, etc.

girth n. **1** the measurement around the middle of something. **2** a band attached to a saddle and fastened around a horse's belly.

gist /jist/ n. the general meaning of a speech or text.

give v. (**giving**, **gave**; past part. **given**) **1** cause to have, get, or experience. **2** do an action or make a sound. **3** state information. **4** bend under pressure.
▷ SYNONYMS: **1 donate**, contribute, present with, award, grant, bestow, hand over, bequeath, leave, make over. **2 convey**, pass on, impart, communicate, transmit, send, deliver, relay. **3 sacrifice**, give up, relinquish, devote, dedicate. **4 organize**, arrange, lay on, throw, host, hold, have. **5 perform**, execute, make, do. **6 utter**, let out, emit, produce, make.
− ANTONYMS: receive, take.
• n. the ability to bend under pressure.
□ **give and take** willingness to compromise on both sides. **give away** reveal something secret. **giveaway** informal **1** something that reveals the truth. **2** a free gift. **give in** admit defeat. **give off/out** send out a smell, heat, etc. **give out** stop operating. **give rise to** make happen. **give up** **1** stop making an effort. **2** stop doing regularly. **3** hand over. **give way** **1** collapse. **2** allow other traffic to

go first.

given adj. **1** specified or stated.
2 (**given to**) inclined to.
• **prep.** taking into account.
• **n.** an established fact.
□ **given name** a first name.

gizmo n. (pl. **gizmos**) informal a gadget.

gizzard n. a muscular part of a bird's
stomach for grinding food.

glacé /gla-say/ adj. preserved in sugar.

glacial adj. **1** of ice and glaciers. **2** very
cold.

glaciation n. the formation of
glaciers.

glacier n. a slowly moving mass of ice.

glad adj. (**gladder**, **gladdest**) **1** pleased;
delighted. **2** causing happiness.
▷ SYNONYMS: **1 pleased**, happy, gratified,
delighted, thrilled, overjoyed; informal
over the moon; Brit. informal chuffed; N.
English informal made up. **2** *I'd be glad to
help:* **willing**, eager, happy, pleased,
delighted, ready, prepared.
− ANTONYMS: dismayed, reluctant.
■ **gladden** v. **gladly** adv. **gladness** n.

glade n. an open space in a forest.

gladiator n. a man trained to fight at
public shows in ancient Rome.
■ **gladiatorial** adj.

gladiolus n. (pl. **gladioli**) a tall plant
with brightly coloured flowers.

glamorize (or **-ise**) v. make
something undesirable seem
attractive.

glamorous adj. excitingly attractive
and appealing.
▷ SYNONYMS: **1** *a glamorous woman:*
beautiful, elegant, chic, stylish,
fashionable. **2** *a glamorous lifestyle:*
exciting, glittering, glossy, colourful,
exotic; informal glitzy, jet-setting.
− ANTONYMS: dowdy, dull.

> USAGE **glamorous** drops the *u* of
> **glamour**.

glamour (US **glamor**) n. an attractive
and exciting quality.
▷ SYNONYMS: **1** *she had undeniable
glamour:* **beauty**, allure, elegance,
chic, style, charisma, charm,
magnetism. **2** *the glamour of TV:*
allure, attraction, fascination, charm,
magic, romance, excitement, thrill;
informal glitz, glam.

glance v. **1** look briefly. **2** hit and
bounce off at an angle.
▷ SYNONYMS: **1 look briefly**, look quickly,
peek, peep, glimpse, catch a glimpse.
2 *I glanced through the report:* **read
quickly**, scan, skim, leaf, flick, flip,
thumb, browse.
• **n.** a brief look.

gland n. an organ of the body which
produces a particular chemical
substance.
■ **glandular** adj.

glare v. **1** stare angrily. **2** shine with a
dazzling light.
▷ SYNONYMS: **scowl**, glower, look
daggers, frown, lour; informal give
someone a dirty look.
• **n.** **1** an angry stare. **2** dazzling light.
▷ SYNONYMS: **blaze**, dazzle, shine, beam,
brilliance.

glaring adj. very obvious: *a glaring
inconsistency.*
▷ SYNONYMS: **obvious**, conspicuous,
unmistakable, inescapable,
unmissable, striking, flagrant,
blatant.

glass n. **1** a hard transparent
substance. **2** a glass drinking
container. **3** (**glasses**) a pair of lenses
in a frame that rests on the nose and
ears, used to correct eyesight. **4** a
mirror.
□ **glass ceiling** an imaginary barrier to
progress in a profession. **glasshouse**
Brit. a greenhouse.
■ **glassy** adj.

glaucoma /glaw-koh-muh/ n. a
condition causing gradual loss of
sight.

glaze v. **1** fit or cover with glass.
2 cover with a glaze. **3** (of the eyes)
lose brightness and animation.
▷ SYNONYMS: **cover**, coat, varnish,
lacquer, polish.
• **n.** a shiny surface or coating.
▷ SYNONYMS: **coating**, topping, varnish,
lacquer, polish.

glazier n. a person whose job is to fit
glass into windows.

gleam v. shine brightly with reflected
light.
▷ SYNONYMS: **shine**, glint, glitter,
shimmer, glimmer, sparkle, twinkle,
flicker, wink, glisten, flash.
• **n.** **1** a faint or brief light. **2** a brief or
faint sign of a quality.
▷ SYNONYMS: **flash**, glimmer, glint,
shimmer, twinkle, sparkle, flicker,
beam, ray, shaft.

glean v. **1** collect from various sources.
2 hist. gather leftover grain after a
harvest.
■ **gleanings** pl. n.

glee n. great delight.
■ **gleeful** adj. **gleefully** adv.

glen n. a narrow valley.

glib adj. articulate but insincere or
shallow.
■ **glibly** adv.

glide v. **1** move with a smooth, quiet

motion. **2** fly without power or in a glider.

▷ SYNONYMS: **1** *a gondola glided past:* **slide**, slip, sail, float, drift, flow. **2** *seagulls gliding over the waves:* **soar**, wheel, plane, fly.
• n. an act of gliding.

glider n. a light aircraft with no engine.

glimmer v. shine faintly with a wavering light.
• n. **1** a faint or wavering light. **2** a faint sign of a quality.

glimpse n. a brief or partial view.
▷ SYNONYMS: **glance**, brief/quick look, sight, sighting, peek, peep.
• v. see briefly or partially.
▷ SYNONYMS: **catch sight of**, sight, spot, notice, discern, spy, pick out, make out.

glint v. give out small flashes of light.
• n. a small flash of light.

glisten v. (of something wet) shine or sparkle.

glitch n. informal a sudden problem or fault.

glitter v. **1** sparkle. **2** (**glittering**) impressively successful.
▷ SYNONYMS: **sparkle**, twinkle, glint, shimmer, glimmer, wink, flash, shine.
• n. **1** sparkling light. **2** tiny pieces of sparkling material for decoration.
▷ SYNONYMS: **sparkle**, twinkle, glint, shimmer, glimmer, flicker, flash.
■ **glittery** adj.

glitz n. informal superficial glamour.
■ **glitzy** adj.

gloaming n. literary twilight.

gloat v. be smug or pleased about your own success or another's failure.

global adj. **1** worldwide. **2** of or affecting an entire group.
▷ SYNONYMS: **1 worldwide**, international, world, intercontinental, universal. **2 comprehensive**, overall, general, all-inclusive, all-encompassing, universal, broad.
□ **global warming** the gradual increase in the temperature of the earth's atmosphere due to increased levels of carbon dioxide etc.
■ **globally** adv.

globalization (or **-isation**) n. the process by which businesses start to operate globally.
■ **globalize** v.

globe n. **1** a spherical object. **2** a spherical model of the earth with a map on the surface.

globetrotter n. informal a person who travels widely.
■ **globetrotting** n. & adj.

globule n. a small round drop.
■ **globular** adj.

glockenspiel /glok-uhn-shpeel/ n. a musical instrument consisting of metal bars struck with hammers.

gloom n. **1** partial or total darkness. **2** depression or despair.
▷ SYNONYMS: **1 darkness**, dark, murk, shadows, shade. **2 despondency**, depression, dejection, melancholy, unhappiness, sadness, misery, woe, despair.
– ANTONYMS: light, happiness.

gloomy adj. (**gloomier**, **gloomiest**) **1** dark or poorly lit. **2** causing or feeling depression or despair.
▷ SYNONYMS: **1 dark**, shadowy, murky, sunless, dim, dingy. **2 despondent**, depressed, downcast, downhearted, dejected, dispirited, disheartened, demoralized, crestfallen, glum, melancholy; informal down in the mouth, down in the dumps. **3 pessimistic**, depressing, downbeat, disheartening, disappointing, unfavourable, bleak, black.
– ANTONYMS: bright, cheerful.
■ **gloomily** adv.

glorify v. (**glorifying**, **glorified**) **1** represent as admirable or important, esp. without justification. **2** praise and worship God.
■ **glorification** n.

glorious adj. **1** having or bringing glory. **2** beautiful or splendid.
▷ SYNONYMS: **wonderful**, marvellous, magnificent, superb, sublime, spectacular, lovely, fine, delightful; informal stunning, fantastic, terrific, tremendous, sensational, heavenly, divine, gorgeous, fabulous, awesome.
– ANTONYMS: undistinguished.
■ **gloriously** adv.

glory n. (pl. **glories**) **1** fame and honour. **2** beauty or splendour. **3** a beautiful or splendid thing. **4** praise and worship of God.
▷ SYNONYMS: **1 honour**, distinction, prestige, fame, renown, kudos, eminence, acclaim, celebrity, praise, recognition. **2 magnificence**, splendour, grandeur, majesty, greatness, nobility, opulence, beauty, elegance.
– ANTONYMS: shame.
• v. (**glorying**, **gloried**) (**glory in**) take great pride or pleasure in.
▷ SYNONYMS: *we gloried in our independence:* **delight**, triumph, revel, rejoice, exult, relish, savour, be proud of; informal get a kick out of.

gloss n. **1** the shine on a smooth surface. **2** a type of paint that dries to a shiny finish. **3** a translation or explanation.

▷ SYNONYMS: **shine**, sheen, lustre, gleam, patina, polish, brilliance, shimmer.

• v. **1** (**gloss over**) give only brief or misleading details about. **2** translate or explain a word etc.

glossary n. (pl. **glossaries**) a list of words and their meanings.

glossy adj. (**glossier**, **glossiest**) **1** shiny and smooth. **2** appearing attractive and stylish.

▷ SYNONYMS: **shiny**, gleaming, lustrous, brilliant, glistening, glassy, polished, lacquered, glazed.

– ANTONYMS: dull.

glottis n. the part of the larynx made up of the vocal cords and the opening between them.

■ **glottal** adj.

glove n. a covering for the hand with separate parts for each finger.

glow v. **1** give out steady light. **2** have a warm or flushed look. **3** look very happy.

▷ SYNONYMS: **shine**, gleam, glimmer, flicker, flare.

• n. a glowing state.

▷ SYNONYMS: **radiance**, light, gleam, glimmer, incandescence.

□ **glow-worm** a kind of beetle that gives out light.

glower /**glow**-er/ v. scowl.

• n. a scowling expression.

glowing adj. expressing great praise: *a glowing report.*

▷ SYNONYMS: **complimentary**, favourable, enthusiastic, admiring, rapturous, fulsome; informal rave.

glucose n. a simple sugar which is an important energy source.

glue n. a sticky substance used for joining things.

▷ SYNONYMS: **adhesive**, gum, paste, cement; N. Amer. mucilage; N. Amer. informal stickum.

• v. (**gluing** or **glueing**, **glued**) join with glue.

▷ SYNONYMS: **stick**, gum, paste, fix, seal, cement.

glum adj. (**glummer**, **glummest**) sad or miserable.

▷ SYNONYMS: **gloomy**, downcast, dejected, despondent, crestfallen, disheartened, depressed, doleful, miserable, woebegone; informal fed up, down in the dumps, down in the mouth.

– ANTONYMS: cheerful.

■ **glumly** adv.

glut n. an excessive supply.

• v. (**glutting**, **glutted**) supply to excess.

gluten n. a substance containing protein, found in cereal grains.

glutinous adj. like glue; sticky.

glutton n. **1** a greedy person. **2** a person who is eager for something challenging.

■ **gluttonous** adj. **gluttony** n.

glycerine (US **glycerin**) n. a thick liquid used in cosmetics etc.

glycerol n. glycerine.

GM abbrev. genetically modified.

gm abbrev. grams.

GMT abbrev. Greenwich Mean Time.

gnarled adj. knobbly or twisted.

gnash v. grind your teeth together.

gnat n. a small biting fly.

gnaw v. **1** bite at persistently. **2** cause persistent anxiety or pain.

gnome n. an imaginary being like a tiny man.

gnomic adj. clever but difficult to understand.

gnostic adj. of or having mystical knowledge.

GNP abbrev. gross national product.

gnu /noo/ n. a large heavy antelope.

GNVQ abbrev. General National Vocational Qualification.

go v. (**goes**, **going**, **went**; past part. **gone**) **1** move to or from a place. **2** pass into or be in a particular state. **3** extend. **4** end, disappear, or be used up. **5** (of time) pass. **6** take part in an activity. **7** have a particular outcome. **8** function. **9** match. **10** fit into or be regularly kept in. **11** make a specified sound.

▷ SYNONYMS: **1** *he's gone into town:* travel, move, proceed, make your way, journey, advance, progress, pass. **2** *I'm afraid she's already gone:* leave, depart, take yourself off, go away, withdraw, absent yourself, exit, set off, start out, get under way, be on your way; Brit. make a move; informal make tracks. **3** *the road goes to London:* lead, stretch, reach, extend. **4** *he went crazy:* become, get, turn, grow. **5** be used up, be spent, be exhausted, be consumed. **6** turn out, work out, develop, progress, result, end up; informal pan out. **7** function, work, run, operate. **8** match, harmonize, blend, be complementary, coordinate, be compatible.

• n. (pl. **goes**) informal **1** an attempt. **2** a turn to do something. **3** energy.

▷ SYNONYMS: **1** *here, have a go:* try, attempt, effort, bid; informal shot, stab, crack. **2** turn, opportunity, chance,

stint, spell, time.
□ **go-ahead** informal permission to proceed. **go back on** fail to keep a promise. **go-between** an intermediary or negotiator. **go-cart** (or **go-kart**) a small lightweight racing car. **go for 1** choose. **2** attack. **go-getter** informal an energetic and enterprising person. **go into** investigate. **go off 1** explode. **2** Brit. (of food) become stale or bad. **3** Brit. informal begin to dislike. **go out 1** stop shining or burning. **2** have a regular romantic relationship. **go round** be enough for everyone.

goad v. provoke to action.
• n. **1** a stimulus to action. **2** a pointed stick for driving cattle.

goal n. **1** (in football, rugby, etc.) a framework into or over which the ball has to be sent to score. **2** an act of scoring. **3** an aim or desired result.
▷ SYNONYMS: **objective**, aim, end, target, intention, plan, purpose, ambition, aspiration.
□ **goalkeeper** (in football, hockey, etc.) a player whose role is to keep the ball out of the goal. **goalpost** either of the two upright posts of a goal.

goalie n. informal a goalkeeper.

goat n. an animal with horns, often kept for milk.

goatee n. a small pointed beard.

gob n. Brit. informal a person's mouth.

gobble v. **1** eat hurriedly and noisily. **2** (of a turkey) make a swallowing sound in the throat.
▷ SYNONYMS: **guzzle**, bolt, gulp, devour, wolf; informal tuck into, put away, demolish; Brit. informal scoff; N. Amer. informal scarf.

gobbledegook n. informal complicated and unintelligible language.

goblet n. a drinking glass with a foot and a stem.

goblin n. a mischievous ugly elf.

goby n. (pl. **gobies**) a small sea fish.

God n. **1** (in Christianity and some other religions) the creator and supreme ruler of the universe. **2** (**god**) a superhuman being or spirit.
▷ SYNONYMS: **deity**, goddess, divine being, divinity, immortal.
□ **God-fearing** earnestly religious.

> **WORD LINKS**
> **divine** relating to God or a god
> **theology** the study of God

godchild n. a person in relation to a godparent.

god-daughter n. a female godchild.

goddess n. a female god.

godfather n. **1** a male godparent. **2** the male leader of an illegal organization.

godforsaken adj. (of a place) remote or unattractive.

godhead n. **1** (**the Godhead**) God. **2** divine nature.

godly adj. very religious.

godmother n. a female godparent.

godparent n. a person who promises to be responsible for a child's religious education.

godsend n. a very helpful or welcome thing.

godson n. a male godchild.

goes 3rd person sing. present of **go**.

goggle v. stare with wide open eyes.
• n. (**goggles**) close-fitting protective glasses.

going n. the condition of the ground as suitable for horse racing or walking.
• adj. **1** existing or available. **2** (of a price) current.
□ **going concern** a thriving business.

goitre /goy-ter/ n. a swollen neck resulting from an enlarged thyroid gland.

gold n. **1** a yellow precious metal. **2** a deep yellow colour. **3** articles made of gold.
□ **gold-digger** informal a woman who forms relationships with men purely for financial gain. **goldfish** a small orange carp often kept in ponds and tanks. **gold leaf** gold beaten into a very thin sheet. **gold rush** a rush of people to a place where gold has been discovered. **goldsmith** a person who makes gold articles.

golden adj. **1** made of or like gold. **2** very happy and prosperous. **3** excellent.
▷ SYNONYMS: **blonde**, yellow, fair, flaxen.
– ANTONYMS: dark.
□ **golden handshake** informal a payment given on redundancy or early retirement. **golden jubilee** the 50th anniversary of an important event. **golden wedding** Brit. the 50th anniversary of a wedding.

golf n. an outdoor game in which a small ball is struck with a club into a series of small holes.
■ **golfer** n.

golliwog n. a soft doll with a black face and fuzzy hair.

gonad n. a bodily organ producing gametes; a testis or ovary.

gondola n. a boat with high-pointed

ends and a single oar, used on canals in Venice.

gondolier n. a person who propels a gondola.

gone past part. of **GO**.

gong n. **1** a metal disc that makes a resonant sound when struck. **2** Brit. informal a medal or award.

gonorrhoea /gon-uh-ree-uh/ (US **gonorrhea**) n. a sexually transmitted disease.

goo n. informal a sticky or slimy substance.

■ **gooey** adj.

good adj. (**better**, **best**) **1** having the right qualities; of a high standard. **2** morally right, polite, or obedient. **3** enjoyable or satisfying. **4** appropriate. **5** (**good for**) of benefit to. **6** thorough.
▷ SYNONYMS: **1 fine**, superior, excellent, superb, outstanding, magnificent, exceptional, marvellous, wonderful, first-rate, first-class, quality; informal great, ace, terrific, fantastic, fabulous, class, awesome, wicked; Brit. informal brilliant. **2 capable**, able, proficient, adept, adroit, accomplished, skilful, talented, masterly, expert; informal mean, wicked, nifty; N. Amer. informal crackerjack. **3 virtuous**, righteous, upright, upstanding, moral, ethical, principled, law-abiding, blameless, honourable, decent, respectable, trust-worthy; informal squeaky clean. **4 well behaved**, obedient, dutiful, polite, courteous, respectful. **5** *a very good friend:* **close**, intimate, dear, bosom, special, best, firm, loyal. **6 enjoyable**, pleasant, agreeable, pleasurable, delightful, lovely, amusing. **7** *it was good of you to come:* **kind**, generous, charitable, gracious, noble, altruistic, unselfish. **8 convenient**, suitable, appropriate, fitting, fit, opportune, timely, favourable. **9** *milk is good for you:* **wholesome**, healthy, nourishing, nutritious, beneficial. **10** *good weather:* **fine**, fair, dry, bright, clear, sunny, cloudless, calm, warm, mild. **11** *good reason:* **valid**, genuine, authentic, legitimate, sound, bona fide, convincing, compelling.
– ANTONYMS: bad, wicked, naughty.
• n. **1** morally correct behaviour. **2** something beneficial. **3** (**goods**) products, freight, or possessions.
▷ SYNONYMS: **1 virtue**, righteous-ness, morality, integrity, honesty, truth, honour. **2** *it's for your own good:* **benefit**, advantage, profit, gain, interest, welfare, well-being.

3 (**goods**) **merchandise**, wares, stock, commodities, produce, products, articles.
– ANTONYMS: wickedness, disadvantage.
□ **for good** forever. **good faith** honest or sincere intentions. **good-for-nothing** worthless. **Good Friday** the Friday before Easter Sunday, commemorating the Crucifixion of Jesus. **make good** compensate for loss or damage.

goodbye exclam. used to express good wishes when parting or ending a conversation.
▷ SYNONYMS: **farewell**, adieu, au revoir, ciao, adios; informal bye; Brit. informal cheerio.

good-looking adj. physically attractive.
▷ SYNONYMS: **attractive**, beautiful, pretty, handsome, lovely, stun-ning, striking, arresting, gorgeous, prepossessing, fetching; Scottish & N. English bonny; informal tasty, easy on the eye; Brit. informal fit; N. Amer. informal cute, foxy; old use comely.
– ANTONYMS: ugly.

goodly adj. dated considerable in size or quantity.

goodness n. the quality of being good.
▷ SYNONYMS: **1 virtue**, good, righteous-ness, morality, integrity, rectitude, honesty, honour, decency, respect-ability, nobility, worth, merit. **2 kindness**, humanity, benevolence, tenderness, warmth, affection, love, goodwill, sympathy, compassion, care, concern, understanding, generosity, charity.

goodwill n. friendly feeling or a helpful attitude.
▷ SYNONYMS: **kindness**, compassion, benevolence, consideration, charity, decency, neighbourliness.
– ANTONYMS: hostility.

goody n. (or **goodie**) (pl. **goodies**) informal **1** Brit. a good person in a story etc. **2** (**goodies**) pleasant things to eat.
□ **goody-goody** a person who behaves well to impress others.

goofy adj. informal **1** having front teeth that stick out. **2** US silly.

goose n. (pl. **geese**) **1** a large waterbird with webbed feet. **2** a female goose.
□ **gooseflesh** (or **goose pimples**) small raised bumps on the skin caused by cold or fear. **goose step** a marching step with the legs kept straight.

gooseberry n. **1** an edible berry

with a hairy skin. **2** Brit. informal a third person in the company of two lovers.

gopher n. a burrowing American rodent.

gore n. **1** blood from a wound. **2** a triangular part of a garment, sail, etc. • v. pierce with a horn or tusk.

gorge n. a narrow valley or ravine.
▷ SYNONYMS: ravine, canyon, gully, defile, couloir, chasm, gulf; S. English chine; N. English gill; N. Amer. gulch, coulee.
• v. eat greedily.

gorgeous adj. **1** beautiful. **2** informal very pleasant.
▷ SYNONYMS: **1 good-looking**, attractive, beautiful, pretty, handsome, lovely, stunning; Scottish & N. English bonny; informal fanciable, tasty, hot; Brit. informal fit; N. Amer. informal cute, foxy; old use comely. **2 spectacular**, splendid, superb, wonderful, grand, impressive, awe-inspiring, awesome, stunning, breathtaking; informal sensational, fabulous, fantastic. **3 resplendent**, magnificent, sumptuous, luxurious, elegant, dazzling, brilliant.
– ANTONYMS: ugly, drab.

gorgon n. **1** Gk Myth. each of three sisters able to turn people to stone. **2** an intimidating woman.

gorilla n. a large powerful African ape.

gormless adj. Brit. informal stupid.

gorse n. a yellow-flowered prickly shrub.

gory adj. **1** involving bloodshed. **2** covered in blood.

goshawk /goss-hawk/ n. a short-winged hawk.

gosling n. a young goose.

gospel n. **1** the teachings of Jesus. **2** (**Gospel**) any of the first four books of the New Testament. **3** something absolutely true. **4** a style of black American religious singing.

gossamer n. a fine piece of cobweb. • adj. very fine or flimsy.

gossip n. **1** casual talk about other people. **2** a person who likes gossiping.
▷ SYNONYMS: **1 news**, rumours, scandal, hearsay, tittle-tattle; informal dirt, buzz; N. Amer. informal scuttlebutt. **2 chat**, talk, conversation, chatter, heart-to-heart, tête-à-tête; informal jaw, gas; Brit. informal natter, chinwag; N. Amer. informal gabfest. **3 gossipmonger**, busybody, scandalmonger, rumour-monger, muckraker.
• v. (**gossiping**, **gossiped**) engage in gossip.
▷ SYNONYMS: **1 talk**, whisper, tell tales,

spread rumours; informal dish the dirt. **2** people sat around gossiping: **chat**, talk, converse; informal gas, chew the fat, chew the rag, jaw; Brit. informal natter, chinwag; N. Amer. informal shoot the breeze.

got past & past part. of GET.

Gothic adj. **1** of the style of architecture common in western Europe in the 12th–16th centuries. **2** very gloomy or horrifying.

gouache /goo-ash/ n. **1** a method of painting using watercolours thickened with glue. **2** paint of this kind.

gouge v. cut out roughly. • n. a chisel with a concave blade.

goulash n. a rich Hungarian stew of meat and vegetables.

gourd n. a hard-skinned fruit of a climbing plant, esp. used as a container.

gourmand n. a person who enjoys eating.

gourmet /gor-may/ n. a person knowledgeable about good food.
▷ SYNONYMS: **gastronome**, epicure, epicurean, connoisseur; informal foodie.

gout n. a disease causing swollen painful joints.

govern v. **1** conduct the policy and affairs of a state, organization, etc. **2** control or influence.
▷ SYNONYMS: **1 rule**, preside over, control, be in charge of, command, run, head, manage, oversee, supervise. **2 determine**, decide, control, constrain, regulate, direct, rule, dictate, shape, affect.
■ governance n.

governess n. a woman employed to teach children in a private household.

government n. **1** the group of people who govern a state. **2** the system by which a state is governed.
▷ SYNONYMS: **administration**, executive, regime, authority, council, powers that be, cabinet, ministry.
■ governmental adj.

governor n. **1** an official appointed to govern a town or region. **2** the head of a public institution. **3** a member of a group of people who govern a school etc.
▷ SYNONYMS: **leader**, ruler, chief, head, administrator, principal, director, chairman, chairwoman, chair, superintendent, commissioner, controller; informal boss.

gown n. **1** a long dress. **2** a protective garment. **3** a loose cloak worn by lawyers, academics, etc.

g

▷ SYNONYMS: **dress**, frock, robe, habit, costume.

GP abbrev. general practitioner.

grab v. (**grabbed**, **grabbing**) seize suddenly and roughly.
▷ SYNONYMS: **seize**, grasp, snatch, take hold of, grip, clasp, clutch, catch.
• n. a sudden attempt to seize.

grace n. **1** elegance of movement. **2** polite respect. **3** (**graces**) attractive qualities. **4** a period allowed to do something. **5** a short prayer of thanks for a meal. **6** the unearned favour of God.
▷ SYNONYMS: **1 elegance**, poise, finesse, polish, fluency, smoothness, supple-ness. **2** *he had the grace to apologize:* **courtesy**, decency, good manners, politeness, respect. **3** *he fell from grace:* **favour**, approval, approbation, acceptance, esteem, regard, respect.
– ANTONYMS: awkwardness.
• v. **1** honour by your presence. **2** make more attractive.
▷ SYNONYMS: **adorn**, embellish, decorate, ornament, enhance.
■ **graceless** adj.

graceful adj. having or showing grace or elegance.
▷ SYNONYMS: **elegant**, fluid, fluent, easy, polished, supple.
■ **gracefully** adv.

gracious adj. polite, kind, and pleasant.
▷ SYNONYMS: **courteous**, polite, civil, well mannered, tactful, diplomatic, kind, considerate, thoughtful, obli-ging, accommodating, hospitable.
■ **graciously** adv.

gradation n. **1** a scale of successive stages. **2** a stage in such a scale.

grade n. **1** a level of rank or quality. **2** a mark indicating the quality of a student's work. **3** US a class in school.
▷ SYNONYMS: **1** *hotels within the same grade:* **category**, class, classification, ranking, quality, grouping, group, bracket. **2** *his job is of the lowest grade:* **rank**, level, standing, position, class, status, order, echelon. **3** **mark**, score, assessment, evaluation, appraisal. **4** **year**, form, class.
• v. arrange in or allocate to grades.
▷ SYNONYMS: **classify**, class, categorize, bracket, sort, group, arrange, pigeon-hole, rank, evaluate, rate, value.
□ **make the grade** informal succeed.

gradient n. **1** a slope. **2** the degree to which ground slopes.
▷ SYNONYMS: **slope**, incline, hill, rise, ramp, bank; N. Amer. grade.

gradual adj. **1** taking place in stages

over time. **2** (of a slope) not steep.
▷ SYNONYMS: **1 slow**, steady, measured, unhurried, cautious, piecemeal, step-by-step, bit-by-bit, progressive, continuous. **2 gentle**, moderate, slight, easy.
– ANTONYMS: abrupt, steep.

gradually adv. in a gradual way.
▷ SYNONYMS: **slowly**, steadily, slowly but surely, cautiously, gently, gingerly, piecemeal, bit by bit, inch by inch, by degrees, progressively, systematically.

graduate n. a person awarded a first academic degree.
• v. **1** successfully complete a degree or course. **2** arrange or mark according to a scale.
■ **graduation** n.

graffiti n. writings or drawings on a surface in a public place.

USAGE double *f*, one *t*: graffiti.

graft n. **1** a shoot from one plant inserted into another to form a new growth. **2** a piece of living body tissue transplanted surgically. **3** Brit. informal hard work.
▷ SYNONYMS: **transplant**, implant.
• v. **1** insert or transplant as a graft. **2** Brit. informal work hard.
▷ SYNONYMS: **1 splice**, join, insert, fix. **2 transplant**, implant.

Grail n. (in medieval legend) the cup or bowl used by Jesus at the Last Supper.

grain n. **1** cultivated cereal used as food. **2** a single seed of a cereal. **3** a small, hard particle. **4** a unit of weight. **5** the arrangement of fibres in wood etc.
▷ SYNONYMS: **1 kernel**, seed. **2 granule**, particle, speck, bit, scrap, crumb, fragment, morsel. **3 trace**, hint, tinge, suggestion, shadow, soupçon, ounce, iota, jot, scrap, shred; informal smidgen. **4 texture**, weave, pattern, nap.
□ **against the grain** conflicting with your instinct.
■ **grainy** adj.

gram (or Brit. **gramme**) n. one thousandth of a kilogram.

grammar n. **1** the whole system and structure of a language. **2** knowledge and use of the rules of grammar. **3** a book on grammar.

USAGE *-ar*, not *-er*: grammar.

grammatical adj. following the rules of grammar.
■ **grammatically** adv.

gramophone n. dated a record player.

grampus n. (pl. **grampuses**) a dolphin-like sea animal.

gran n. Brit. informal a person's grandmother.

granary n. (pl. **granaries**) a storehouse for grain.

grand adj. **1** large and impressive. **2** ambitious in scale. **3** highest in importance or rank. **4** informal excellent.

▷ SYNONYMS: **1 magnificent**, imposing, impressive, awe-inspiring, splendid, resplendent, majestic, monumental, palatial, stately; Brit. upmarket; N. Amer. upscale; informal fancy, posh; Brit. informal swish. **2 ambitious**, bold, epic, big, extravagant. **3 august**, distinguished, illustrious, eminent, venerable, dignified, proud. **4 excellent**, marvellous, splendid, first-class, first-rate, wonderful, outstanding; informal superb, terrific, great, super; Brit. informal brilliant.

− ANTONYMS: humble, poor.

• n. informal a thousand dollars or pounds.

□ **grand piano** a large piano with a horizontal body and strings. **grand slam** the winning of all the major championships in a sport in the same year. **grandstand** the main stand at a sports ground.

■ **grandly** adv.

grandad n. informal a person's grandfather.

grandchild n. a child of a person's son or daughter.

granddaughter n. the daughter of a person's son or daughter.

grandeur n. **1** splendour and impressiveness. **2** high rank or social status.

▷ SYNONYMS: **splendour**, magnificence, glory, resplendence, majesty, greatness, stateliness, pomp, ceremony.

grandfather n. the father of a person's father or mother.

□ **grandfather clock** a clock in a tall wooden case.

grandiloquent adj. using long words in a pompous way.

grandiose adj. large and ambitious and intended to impress.

grandma n. informal a person's grandmother.

grandmother n. the mother of a person's father or mother.

grandpa n. informal a person's grandfather.

grandparent n. a grandmother or grandfather.

grandson n. the son of a person's son or daughter.

grange n. Brit. a country house with farm buildings attached.

granite n. a very hard grey rock.

granny (or **grannie**) n. (pl. **grannies**) informal a person's grandmother.

□ **granny flat** a self-contained part of a house suitable for an elderly relative.

grant v. **1** agree to give or allow. **2** give formally or legally. **3** admit to be true.

▷ SYNONYMS: **1** *he granted them leave of absence:* **allow**, permit, agree to, accord, afford, vouchsafe. **2** *he granted them £20,000:* **give**, award, bestow on, confer on, present with, endow with. **3 admit**, accept, concede, allow, appreciate, recognize, acknowledge, confess.

− ANTONYMS: refuse, deny.

• n. a sum of money given from public funds for a particular purpose.

▷ SYNONYMS: **award**, bursary, endowment, scholarship, allowance, subsidy, contribution, handout, donation, gift.

□ **take for granted 1** fail to appreciate. **2** assume to be true.

granulated adj. in the form of granules.

granule n. a small particle or grain.

■ **granular** adj.

grape n. a green or purple berry, used for making wine.

□ **the grapevine** the spreading of information through talk or rumour.

grapefruit n. a large round yellow citrus fruit.

graph n. a diagram showing the relation between variable quantities.

graphic adj. **1** of visual art, esp. drawing and the design of printed material. **2** giving vivid details.

▷ SYNONYMS: **1 visual**, pictorial, illustrative, diagrammatic. **2 vivid**, explicit, detailed, realistic, descriptive, powerful, colourful, lurid, shocking.

− ANTONYMS: vague.

• n. **1** a pictorial image or symbol on a computer screen. **2** (**graphics**) the use of designs or pictures to illustrate books etc.

□ **graphic equalizer** a device for controlling the strength and quality of selected frequency bands.

■ **graphically** adv.

graphite n. a form of carbon.

graphology n. the study of handwriting as a guide to character.

■ **graphologist** n.

grapnel (or **grappling hook**) n. a device with iron claws, for dragging or grasping.

grapple v. **1** wrestle. **2** (**grapple with**)

struggle to deal with.
▷ SYNONYMS: **1 wrestle**, struggle, tussle, scuffle, battle. **2 deal**, cope, get to grips, tackle, confront, face.

grasp v. **1** seize and hold firmly. **2** understand fully.
▷ SYNONYMS: **1 grip**, clutch, clasp, clench, squeeze, catch, seize, grab, snatch. **2 understand**, comprehend, take in, see, apprehend, assimilate, absorb; informal get, take on board; Brit. informal twig.
• n. **1** a firm grip. **2** understanding.
▷ SYNONYMS: **1 grip**, hold, squeeze. **2 reach**, scope, power, range, sights. **3 understanding**, comprehension, awareness, grip, knowledge, mastery, command.

grasping adj. greedy for money or material things.
▷ SYNONYMS: **greedy**, acquisitive, avaricious, rapacious, mercenary, materialistic; informal tight-fisted, tight, money-grubbing.

grass n. **1** a short plant with long narrow leaves. **2** ground covered with grass. **3** informal cannabis. **4** Brit. informal an informer.
• v. **1** cover with grass. **2** Brit. informal act as an informer.
▢ **grasshopper** a jumping insect that makes a chirping sound. **grass roots** the ordinary people in an organization or society.
■ **grassy** adj.

grate v. **1** shred food by rubbing it on a grater. **2** make an unpleasant scraping sound. **3** have an irritating effect.
▷ SYNONYMS: **1 shred**, pulverize, mince, grind, crush, crumble. **2 grind**, rub, rasp, scrape, jar, creak.
• n. a metal frame keeping fuel in a fireplace.

grateful adj. thankful and appreciative.
▷ SYNONYMS: **thankful**, appreciative, indebted, obliged, in someone's debt, beholden.
■ **gratefully** adv.

⟨ **USAGE** grateful, not greatful. ⟩

grater n. a device having a surface covered with sharp-edged holes, used for grating food.

gratify v. (**gratifying**, **gratified**) **1** give pleasure or satisfaction. **2** satisfy a wish.
■ **gratification** n.

grating n. a grid of metal bars over an opening.

gratis adv. & adj. free of charge.

gratitude n. the feeling of being grateful.
▷ SYNONYMS: **thanks**, gratefulness, thankfulness, appreciation, indebtedness, recognition, acknowledgement.

gratuitous adj. without reason or purpose.
■ **gratuitously** adv.

gratuity n. (pl. **gratuities**) a tip given to a waiter etc.

grave n. a hole dug to bury a corpse.
▷ SYNONYMS: **tomb**, burial place, last resting place, vault, mausoleum, sepulchre.
• adj. **1** giving cause for alarm or concern. **2** solemn.
▷ SYNONYMS: **1 serious**, important, weighty, profound, significant, momentous, critical, urgent, pressing, dire, terrible, dreadful. **2 solemn**, serious, sober, unsmiling, grim, sombre, dour.
– ANTONYMS: trivial, light-hearted.
■ **gravely** adv.

grave accent /grahv/ n. the accent (`).

gravel n. small stones used for paths etc.

gravelly adj. **1** made of gravel. **2** rough-sounding.

gravestone n. a stone slab marking a grave.

graveyard n. a burial ground.
▷ SYNONYMS: **cemetery**, churchyard, burial ground, necropolis, garden of remembrance; Scottish kirkyard.

gravitas n. a serious and dignified manner.

gravitate v. be drawn towards.

gravitation n. movement towards a centre of gravity.
■ **gravitational** adj.

gravity n. **1** the force that attracts a body towards the centre of the earth. **2** seriousness. **3** solemnity.
▷ SYNONYMS: **1 seriousness**, importance, significance, weight, consequence, magnitude, acuteness, urgency, dreadfulness. **2 solemnity**, seriousness, sobriety, severity, grimness, sombreness, dourness.

gravy n. (pl. **gravies**) a sauce made from the fat and juices from cooked meat.

gray US = GREY.

graze v. **1** eat grass in a field. **2** injure by scraping the skin. **3** touch lightly in passing.
▷ SYNONYMS: **1 scrape**, skin, scratch, chafe, scuff, rasp. **2 touch**, brush, shave, skim, kiss, scrape, clip, glance off.

g

• n. a grazed area on the skin.
▷ SYNONYMS: **scratch**, scrape, abrasion.
grease n. a fatty or oily substance.
• v. smear or lubricate with grease.
□ **greasepaint** make-up used by
actors.
greasy adj. (**greasier, greasiest**)
1 covered with or like grease. **2** polite
or friendly in a way that seems
excessive and insincere.
▷ SYNONYMS: **oily**, fatty, buttery,
oleaginous, slippery, slick, slimy,
slithery, lubricated; informal slippy.
great adj. **1** considerably above
average in size, intensity, ability,
quality, or importance. **2** informal
excellent. **3** (**great-**) (of a family
relationship) one generation removed
in ancestry or descent.
▷ SYNONYMS: **1** _he has great talent:_
considerable, substantial, significant,
exceptional, extraordinary. **2** _a great
castle:_ **large**, big, extensive, vast,
immense, huge, enormous, massive;
magnificent, imposing, impressive,
awe-inspiring, grand, splendid,
majestic; expansive, broad, wide;
informal humongous; Brit. informal ginormous. **3** _a great author:_ **prominent**,
eminent, distinguished, illustrious,
celebrated, acclaimed, admired,
esteemed, renowned, notable,
famous, well known, leading, top,
major. **4** _a great sportsman:_ **expert**,
skilful, skilled, adept, accomplished,
talented, fine, masterly, master,
brilliant, virtuoso, marvellous,
outstanding, first-class, superb; informal
crack, class. **5** _a great cricket fan:_ **keen**,
eager, enthusiastic, devoted, ardent,
fanatical, passionate, dedicated,
committed. **6** _we had a great time:_
enjoyable, delightful, lovely, excellent, marvellous, wonderful, fine,
splendid; informal terrific, fantastic,
fabulous, super, cool; Brit. informal
brilliant.
– ANTONYMS: little, small, minor.
□ **greatcoat** a heavy overcoat. **Great
Dane** a dog of a very large short-
haired breed.
■ **greatness** n.
greatly adv. very much.
▷ SYNONYMS: **very much**, extremely,
considerably, substantially, significantly, markedly, seriously, materially, enormously, vastly, immensely,
tremendously, mightily.
grebe n. a diving bird.
Grecian adj. of ancient Greece.
greed n. **1** a strong and selfish desire
for wealth or power. **2** a desire to eat

more food than is necessary.
▷ SYNONYMS: **1 avarice**, acquisitiveness, covetousness, materialism,
mercenariness; informal money-
grubbing. **2 gluttony**, hunger,
voracity, self-indulgence; informal
piggishness. **3 desire**, appetite,
hunger, thirst, craving, longing,
yearning, hankering; informal itch.
– ANTONYMS: generosity, temperance.
greedy adj. (**greedier, greediest**)
having or showing greed.
▷ SYNONYMS: **1 gluttonous**, ravenous,
voracious; informal piggish, piggy.
2 avaricious, acquisitive, covetous,
grasping, materialistic, mercenary;
informal money-grubbing.
■ **greedily** adv.
Greek n. **1** a person from Greece.
2 the ancient or modern language of
Greece.
• adj. of Greece.
green adj. **1** of a colour like that of
grass. **2** covered with grass. **3** (**Green**)
concerned with protecting the
environment. **4** inexperienced or
naive.
▷ SYNONYMS: **1 emerald green**, lime
green, bottle green, Lincoln green,
olive green, jade. **2 verdant**, grassy,
leafy. **3 environmental**, ecological,
conservationist, eco-, eco-friendly.
4 inexperienced, callow, raw,
unseasoned, untried, naive, innocent,
unworldly; informal wet behind the
ears.
• n. **1** green colour. **2** a piece of
grassy public land. **3** (**greens**) green
vegetables. **4** (**Green**) a supporter of a
Green political party.
□ **green belt** an area of open land
round a city, on which building is
restricted. **green card** (in the US)
a permit allowing a foreigner to
live and work permanently in the
US. **green fingers** Brit. informal skill
in growing plants. **greenfly** a green
aphid. **greengage** a sweet greenish
plum-like fruit. **greengrocer** Brit. a
person selling fruit and vegetables.
green light permission to go ahead
with a project. **Green Paper** a
preliminary report of government
proposals.
■ **greenish** adj. **greenness** n.
greenery n. green leaves or plants.
greenhouse n. a glass building for
protecting plants from cold weather.
□ **greenhouse effect** the tendency
of atmospheric temperature to rise
because certain gases absorb infrared
radiation from the earth. **greenhouse**

g

gas a gas that contributes to the greenhouse effect.

greet v. **1** meet with friendliness or expressions of welcome. **2** react to in a particular way.
▷ SYNONYMS: **1 say hello to**, address, salute, hail, welcome, meet, receive. **2** *the decision was greeted with outrage*: **receive**, respond to, react to, take.

greeting n. **1** a word or sign of welcome. **2** (**greetings**) a formal expression of good wishes.
▷ SYNONYMS: **1 hello**, salutation, welcome, reception. **2 best wishes**, good wishes, congratulations, compliments, regards, respects.
– ANTONYMS: farewell.

gregarious adj. **1** fond of company. **2** living in flocks or colonies.

gremlin n. a mischievous sprite regarded as responsible for mechanical faults.

grenade n. a small bomb thrown by hand.

grenadier n. hist. a soldier armed with grenades.

grew past of GROW.

grey (US **gray**) adj. **1** of a colour like that of ash. **2** (of weather) cloudy and dull.
▷ SYNONYMS: **1** silvery, gunmetal, slate, charcoal, smoky. **2** cloudy, overcast, dull, dark, sunless, murky, gloomy, cheerless. **3** pale, wan, ashen, pasty, pallid, colourless, waxen. **4** characterless, colourless, nondescript, flat, bland, dull, boring, tedious, monotonous. **5** *a grey area*: **ambiguous**, doubtful, unclear, uncertain, indefinite, debatable.
• n. a grey colour.
• v. (of hair) turn grey.
□ **grey area** a situation that does not fit easily into existing categories.
greyhound a swift, slender breed of dog used in racing. **grey matter** informal intelligence.
■ **greyish** adj. **greyness** n.

grid n. **1** a framework of parallel or crossed bars. **2** a network of crossed lines forming a series of squares. **3** a network of cables or pipes.
□ **gridiron 1** a metal grid for grilling food. **2** a field for American football. **gridlock** a traffic jam affecting linked streets.

griddle n. an iron plate for cooking food.

grief n. deep sorrow.
▷ SYNONYMS: **sorrow**, misery, sadness, anguish, pain, distress, heartache,

heartbreak, agony, woe, desolation.
– ANTONYMS: joy.

grievance n. a cause for complaint.
▷ SYNONYMS: **complaint**, objection, grumble, grouse, ill feeling, bad feeling, resentment; informal gripe.

grieve v. suffer or cause grief.
▷ SYNONYMS: **1 mourn**, sorrow, cry, sob, weep. **2 sadden**, upset, distress, pain, hurt, wound, break someone's heart.
– ANTONYMS: rejoice.

grievous adj. very severe or serious.
□ **grievous bodily harm** Brit. the offence of deliberately inflicting serious physical injury.
■ **grievously** adv.

griffin (or **gryphon**) n. a mythical creature with an eagle's head and wings and a lion's body.

griffon n. a small dog like a terrier.

grill n. Brit. **1** a device on a cooker for directing heat downwards. **2** food cooked using a grill.
• v. **1** cook with a grill. **2** informal interrogate.

grille n. a grating.

grim adj. (**grimmer**, **grimmest**) **1** very serious or gloomy. **2** depressing or unappealing.
▷ SYNONYMS: **1 stern**, forbidding, uninviting, unsmiling, dour, formidable. **2 dreadful**, ghastly, horrible, terrible, awful, appalling, frightful, shocking, grisly, gruesome, depressing, distressing, upsetting. **3 bleak**, dismal, dingy, wretched, miserable, depressing, cheerless, joyless, gloomy, uninviting.
– ANTONYMS: amiable, pleasant.
■ **grimly** adv. **grimness** n.

grimace n. a twisted facial expression, showing disgust, pain, or amusement.
• v. make a grimace.

grime n. ingrained dirt.
■ **grimy** adj.

grin v. (**grinning**, **grinned**) smile broadly.
▷ SYNONYMS: **smile**, beam, smirk.
• n. a broad smile.

grind v. (**grinding**, **ground**) **1** crush into small particles or powder. **2** sharpen or smooth by friction. **3** rub together gratingly. **4** (**grind down**) treat harshly.
▷ SYNONYMS: **1 crush**, pound, pulverize, mill, crumble. **2 sharpen**, whet, hone, mill, machine, polish, smooth. **3 rub**, grate, grind, scrape.
• n. hard dull work.
▷ SYNONYMS: **drudgery**, toil, labour, donkey work, exertion, chores; informal slog.

g

□ **grindstone** a revolving disc for sharpening or polishing.

grip v. (**gripping, gripped**) **1** hold firmly. **2** hold the attention of.
▷ SYNONYMS: **1 grasp**, clutch, clasp, take hold of, clench, cling to, grab, seize, squeeze. **2 engross**, enthral, absorb, rivet, spellbind, fascinate, mesmerize.
• n. **1** a firm hold. **2** understanding. **3** a part by which something is held.
▷ SYNONYMS: **1 grasp**, hold. **2 traction**, purchase, friction, adhesion. **3 control**, power, hold, stranglehold, clutches, influence.

gripe v. informal grumble.
• n. **1** informal a trivial complaint. **2** pain in the stomach.

gripping adj. holding someone's attention or interest.
▷ SYNONYMS: **fascinating**, enthralling, absorbing, riveting, captivating, spellbinding, engrossing, compelling, thrilling, exciting, action-packed, dramatic.
– ANTONYMS: boring.

grisly adj. (**grislier, grisliest**) causing horror or disgust.

grist n. grain to be ground.
□ **grist to the mill** useful experience or knowledge.

gristle n. tough inedible tissue in meat.
■ **gristly** adj.

grit n. **1** particles of stone or sand. **2** courage and determination.
• v. (**gritting, gritted**) spread grit on an icy road.
□ **grit your teeth** resolve to do something difficult.
■ **grittiness** n. **gritty** adj.

grizzle v. Brit. informal cry fretfully.

grizzled adj. grey-haired.

grizzly bear n. a large American brown bear.

groan v. make a deep sound of pain or despair.
▷ SYNONYMS: **1 moan**, cry. **2 complain**, grumble, moan, mutter; informal grouse, bellyache, bitch, whinge. **3 creak**, grate, rasp.
• n. a groaning sound.
▷ SYNONYMS: **1 moan**, cry. **2 complaint**, grumble, grievance, moan, muttering; informal grouse, gripe, whinge. **3 creaking**, creak, grating, grinding.

grocer n. a person selling food and household goods.

grocery n. (pl. **groceries**) **1** a grocer's shop. **2** (**groceries**) items of food sold in a shop.

grog n. spirits mixed with water.

groggy adj. dazed and unsteady.
■ **groggily** adv.

groin n. **1** the area between the abdomen and the thigh. **2** a curved edge formed by two intersecting roof arches. **3** US = **GROYNE**.

grommet n. **1** a protective metal ring or eyelet. **2** Brit. a tube implanted in the eardrum to drain the ear.

groom v. **1** brush and clean the coat of an animal. **2** prepare or train for a particular activity.
▷ SYNONYMS: **1 curry**, brush, clean, rub down. **2 brush**, comb, arrange, do; informal fix. **3 prepare**, prime, condition, coach, train, drill, teach, school.
• n. **1** a person employed to take care of horses. **2** a bridegroom.

groove n. **1** a long, narrow channel. **2** a spiral track in a record. **3** a fixed routine.
▷ SYNONYMS: **furrow**, channel, trench, trough, rut, gutter, canal, hollow, indentation.
■ **grooved** adj.

grope v. try to find or reach by feeling with the hands.
▷ SYNONYMS: **fumble**, scrabble, fish, ferret, rummage, feel, search, hunt.

gross adj. **1** unattractively large. **2** very obvious and unacceptable. **3** informal very unpleasant. **4** vulgar. **5** (of income etc.) before tax has been deducted. **6** (of weight) including contents or other variable items.
▷ SYNONYMS: **1 disgusting**, repulsive, revolting, foul, nasty, obnoxious, sickening, nauseating, stomach-churning. **2 thorough**, complete, utter, out and out, shameful, serious, unacceptable, flagrant, blatant, obvious, barefaced, shameless, brazen. **3 total**, full, overall, combined, before deductions, before tax.
– ANTONYMS: pleasant, net.
• v. produce or earn as gross profit.
▷ SYNONYMS: **earn**, make, bring in, take, get, receive; informal rake in.
• n. (pl. **gross**) twelve dozen.
■ **grossly** adv.

grotesque /groh-**tesk**/ adj. ugly or distorted.
▷ SYNONYMS: **1 misshapen**, deformed, distorted, twisted, monstrous, hideous, freakish, unnatural, abnormal, strange; informal weird. **2 outrageous**, monstrous, shocking, appalling, preposterous, ridiculous, ludicrous, unbelievable, incredible.
• n. a grotesque figure or image.
■ **grotesquely** adv.

g

grotto n. (pl. **grottoes** or **grottos**) a small cave.

grouch n. informal **1** a grumpy person. **2** a complaint.
■ **grouchy** adj.

ground¹ n. **1** the solid surface of the earth. **2** land of a specified kind. **3** an area of land or sea with a specified use. **4** (**grounds**) enclosed land surrounding a large house. **5** (**grounds**) good reasons for doing something. **6** (**grounds**) coffee dregs.
▷ SYNONYMS: **1 floor**, earth, terra firma; informal deck. **2 earth**, soil, turf, land, terrain. **3 stadium**, pitch, field, arena, track; Brit. informal park. **4** *the mansion's grounds:* **estate**, gardens, park, land, property, surroundings, territory. **5** *grounds for dismissal:* **reason**, cause, basis, foundation, justification, rationale, argument, occasion, excuse, pretext.
● v. **1** ban from flying. **2** (**be grounded in/on**) have as a basis.
▷ SYNONYMS: **1 base**, found, establish, root, build. **2** *she was well grounded in the classics:* **teach**, instruct, coach, tutor, educate, school, train, drill.
□ **groundbreaking** pioneering.
groundnut a peanut. **ground rent** Brit. rent paid by a building's owner to the owner of the land on which it stands. **ground rules** basic rules controlling something. **groundsheet** a waterproof sheet used as the floor of a tent. **groundsman** Brit. a person employed to look after a sports ground. **groundswell** a build-up of public opinion. **groundwork** preliminary work.

ground² past & past part. of GRIND.

grounding n. basic training or instruction.

groundless adj. not based on any good reason.

group n. **1** a number of people or things gathered or classed together. **2** a band of pop musicians or singers.
▷ SYNONYMS: **1 category**, class, classification, grouping, cluster, set, batch, type, sort, kind, variety, family. **2 crowd**, party, body, band, company, gathering, congregation, assembly, collection, cluster, clump, knot, flock, pack, troop, gang; informal bunch. **3 band**, ensemble, act; informal line-up, combo, outfit.
● v. place in or form a group or groups.
▷ SYNONYMS: **1 categorize**, classify, class, catalogue, sort, bracket, pigeonhole. **2 assemble**, collect, organize, place, arrange, range, line up, lay out.

grouse n. **1** (pl. **grouse**) a game bird. **2** a complaint.
● v. grumble.

grout n. a paste for filling gaps between tiles.
● v. fill gaps with grout.

grove n. a group of trees.

grovel v. (**grovelling**, **grovelled**; US **groveling**, **groveled**) **1** crouch or crawl on the ground. **2** act humbly to obtain forgiveness or favour.
▷ SYNONYMS: **1 prostrate yourself**, lie, kneel, cringe. **2 be obsequious**, fawn on, kowtow, bow and scrape, toady, dance attendance on, ingratiate yourself with; informal crawl, creep, suck up to, lick someone's boots.

grow v. (**growing**, **grew**; past part. **grown**) **1** (of a living thing) develop and get bigger. **2** increase over time. **3** cultivate a crop. **4** become gradually: *we grew braver.*
▷ SYNONYMS: **1 enlarge**, get bigger, get taller, expand, increase in size, extend, spread, swell, multiply, snowball, mushroom, balloon, build up, mount up, pile up. **2 sprout**, germinate, spring up, develop, bud, bloom, flourish, thrive, run riot. **3 cultivate**, produce, propagate, raise, rear, farm. **4** *he's growing old:* **become**, get, turn, begin to be.
– ANTONYMS: shrink, decline.
□ **grow on** gradually start to appeal to. **grow up** become an adult.
■ **grower** n.

growl v. (of a dog) make a low hostile sound in the throat.
● n. a growling sound.

grown-up adj. adult.
▷ SYNONYMS: *she has two grown-up daughters:* **adult**, mature, of age, fully grown, independent.
● n. informal an adult.

growth n. **1** the process of growing. **2** something that has grown or is growing. **3** a tumour.
▷ SYNONYMS: **1 enlargement**, increase in size, expansion, extension, swelling, multiplication, mushrooming, snowballing, rise, escalation, build-up, development. **2 tumour**, malignancy, cancer, lump, swelling.

groyne (US **groin**) n. a low wall built out into the sea to prevent erosion.

grub n. **1** the larva of an insect. **2** informal food.
● v. (**grubbing**, **grubbed**) dig shallowly in soil.

grubby adj. (**grubbier**, **grubbiest**) dirty.
▷ SYNONYMS: **dirty**, grimy, filthy, mucky,

g

unwashed, stained, soiled; informal cruddy, yucky; Brit. informal manky.
– ANTONYMS: clean.
■ grubbiness n.

grudge n. a long-lasting feeling of resentment or dislike.
▷ SYNONYMS: **grievance**, resentment, bitterness, rancour, ill will, animosity, antipathy, antagonism; informal a chip on your shoulder.
• v. **1** be unwilling to give or allow. **2** resent.
■ grudgingly adv.

gruel n. thin porridge.

gruelling (US **grueling**) adj. very tiring.
▷ SYNONYMS: **exhausting**, tiring, taxing, draining, demanding, exacting, difficult, arduous, strenuous, back-breaking, punishing, crippling; informal murderous; Brit. informal knackering.

gruesome adj. causing disgust or horror.
▷ SYNONYMS: **grisly**, ghastly, frightful, horrid, horrifying, hideous, horrible, grim, awful, dreadful, terrible, horrific; informal sick, sick-making, gross.
– ANTONYMS: pleasant.

gruff adj. **1** (of a voice) rough and low. **2** abrupt in manner.
■ gruffly adv.

grumble v. **1** complain in a bad-tempered way. **2** rumble.
▷ SYNONYMS: **complain**, grouse, whine, mutter, carp, make a fuss; informal moan, bellyache, bitch, whinge; N. English informal mither.
• n. a complaint.
▷ SYNONYMS: **complaint**, grouse, grievance, protest; informal grouch, moan, whinge, beef, gripe.

grumpy adj. bad-tempered and sulky.
▷ SYNONYMS: **bad-tempered**, crabby, tetchy, touchy, irascible, cantankerous, curmudgeonly, surly, fractious; informal grouchy; Brit. informal ratty; N. Amer. informal cranky, ornery.
– ANTONYMS: good-humoured.
■ grumpily adv.

grunge n. a style of rock music with a raucous guitar sound.
■ grungy adj.

grunt v. make a low, short sound.
• n. a grunting sound.

gryphon var. of GRIFFIN.

G-string n. skimpy knickers consisting of a narrow strip of cloth attached to a waistband.

guano /gwah-noh/ n. the excrement of seabirds, used as fertilizer.

guarantee n. **1** a formal promise to

do something. **2** a promise that a product will remain in working order for a stated period. **3** an undertaking to pay or do something on behalf of someone if they fail to do it.
▷ SYNONYMS: **1 promise**, assurance, word, word of honour, pledge, vow, oath, commitment. **2 warranty**. **3 collateral**, security, surety, bond.
• v. give a guarantee for.
▷ SYNONYMS: **1 promise**, swear, pledge, vow, give your word, give an assurance, give an undertaking. **2 underwrite**, stand surety.

guarantor n. a person that gives a guarantee.

guard v. **1** watch over so as to protect or control. **2** take precautions.
▷ SYNONYMS: **protect**, defend, shield, secure, cover, mind, stand guard over, watch, keep an eye on.
• n. **1** a person or group guarding or keeping watch. **2** a protective device. **3** a state of vigilance. **4** Brit. an official in charge of a train.
▷ SYNONYMS: **1 sentry**, sentinel, night-watchman, protector, defender, guardian, lookout, watch. **2 warder**, warden, keeper, jailer; informal screw. **3 cover**, shield, screen, fender, bumper, buffer.

guarded adj. cautious.
▷ SYNONYMS: **cautious**, careful, circumspect, wary, chary, reluctant, non-committal; informal cagey.

guardian n. **1** a defender or protector. **2** a person legally responsible for someone unable to manage their own affairs.
▷ SYNONYMS: **protector**, defender, preserver, custodian, warden, guard, keeper, curator, caretaker, steward, trustee.
■ guardianship n.

WORD LINKS
tutelary relating to a guardian

---

guava /gwah-vuh/ n. a tropical fruit.

gudgeon n. **1** a small freshwater fish. **2** a pivot or socket.

guerrilla (or **guerilla**) n. a member of a small independent group fighting against the government or regular forces.
▷ SYNONYMS: **rebel**, irregular, partisan, freedom fighter, revolutionary, terrorist.

guess v. estimate or suppose without enough information to be sure.
▷ SYNONYMS: **1 estimate**, reckon, judge, speculate, conjecture, hypothesize, surmise. **2 suppose**, think, imagine,

expect, suspect, dare say; informal reckon.

• **n.** an estimate.

▷ SYNONYMS: **hypothesis**, theory, conjecture, surmise, estimate, belief, opinion, supposition, speculation, suspicion, impression, feeling.

□ **guesswork** guessing.

guest n. **1** a person invited to someone's house or to a social occasion. **2** an invited speaker or performer. **3** a person staying at a hotel.

▷ SYNONYMS: **1 visitor**, caller, company. **2 client**, customer, resident, boarder, lodger, patron, diner, holidaymaker, tourist.

– ANTONYMS: host.

□ **guest house** a kind of small hotel.

guffaw n. a loud laugh.

• **v.** laugh loudly.

guidance n. advice or information to solve a problem.

▷ SYNONYMS: **1 advice**, counsel, instruction, suggestions, tips, hints, pointers, guidelines. **2 direction**, control, leadership, management, supervision.

guide n. **1** a person who advises or shows the way to others. **2** an aid to deciding something. **3** a book of information. **4** a structure or mark to direct the movement or position of something.

▷ SYNONYMS: **1 escort**, attendant, courier, leader, usher. **2 outline**, template, example, exemplar, model, pattern, guideline, yardstick, precedent. **3 guidebook**, travel guide, vade mecum, companion, handbook, manual, directory, A to Z, instructions, directions; informal bible.

• **v. 1** act as a guide to. **2** (**guided**) directed by remote control or internal equipment.

▷ SYNONYMS: **1 lead**, conduct, show, usher, shepherd, direct, steer, pilot, escort. **2 direct**, steer, manage, conduct, run, be in charge of, govern, preside over, supervise, oversee. **3 advise**, counsel, direct.

□ **guidebook** a book of information about a place. **guideline** a general rule or principle.

guild n. **1** a medieval association of craftsmen or merchants. **2** an association of people for a common purpose.

▷ SYNONYMS: **association**, society, union, league, organization, company, fellowship, club, order, lodge.

guilder n. the former basic unit of

money of the Netherlands.

guile n. clever but deceitful behaviour.

■ **guileless** adj.

guillemot /gil-li-mot/ n. a seabird with a narrow pointed bill.

guillotine n. **1** a machine for beheading people. **2** a machine for cutting paper or metal.

• **v.** execute by guillotine.

guilt n. **1** the fact of having committed an offence. **2** a feeling of having done something wrong.

▷ SYNONYMS: **1 culpability**, blameworthiness, responsibility. **2 remorse**, shame, regret, contrition, self-reproach, a guilty conscience.

– ANTONYMS: innocence.

■ **guiltless** adj.

guilty adj. (**guiltier**, **guiltiest**) **1** responsible for a wrongdoing. **2** having or showing guilt.

▷ SYNONYMS: **1 culpable**, to blame, at fault, in the wrong, responsible. **2 ashamed**, guilt-ridden, conscience-stricken, remorseful, sorry, contrite, repentant, penitent, regretful, rueful, shamefaced.

– ANTONYMS: innocent.

■ **guiltily** adv.

guinea n. a former British coin worth 21 shillings.

guinea pig n. **1** a small domesticated rodent. **2** a person or thing used as a subject for experiment.

guise n. an external form, appearance, or manner.

guitar n. a stringed musical instrument.

■ **guitarist** n.

gulch n. US a narrow ravine.

gulf n. **1** a large area of sea partly surrounded by land. **2** a deep ravine. **3** a wide difference in opinion or circumstances.

▷ SYNONYMS: **1 bay**, inlet, cove, bight, fjord, estuary, sound; Scottish firth. **2 gap**, divide, separation, difference, contrast.

gull n. a long-winged seabird.

gullet n. the passage by which food passes from the mouth to the stomach.

gullible adj. easily deceived.

▷ SYNONYMS: **credulous**, naive, easily deceived, impressionable, unsuspecting, ingenuous, innocent, inexperienced, green; informal wet behind the ears.

– ANTONYMS: suspicious.

■ **gullibility** n.

gully n. (pl. **gullies** or **gulleys**) a channel or ravine formed by running water.

g

gulp v. **1** swallow food or drink quickly or in large mouthfuls. **2** swallow noisily from strong emotion.
▷ SYNONYMS: **1 swallow**, quaff, swill down; informal swig, down, knock back. **2 gobble**, guzzle, devour, bolt, wolf; informal shovel down; Brit. informal scoff. **3** *she gulped back her tears:* **choke back**, fight/hold back, suppress, stifle, smother.
• n. **1** an act of gulping. **2** a large mouthful of liquid hastily drunk.
▷ SYNONYMS: **mouthful**, swallow, draught; informal swig.

gum n. **1** the firm area of flesh around the roots of the teeth. **2** a sticky substance produced by some trees. **3** glue. **4** chewing gum.
▷ SYNONYMS: **glue**, adhesive, paste, cement; N. Amer. mucilage; N. Amer. informal stickum.
• v. (**gumming**, **gummed**) cover or fasten with glue.
▷ SYNONYMS: **stick**, glue, paste, cement, attach.
☐ **gumboot** Brit. dated a wellington boot. **gumdrop** a firm, jelly-like sweet.
■ **gummy** adj.

gumption n. informal resourcefulness.

gun n. **1** a weapon that fires shells or bullets from a metal tube. **2** a device using pressure to discharge a substance or object.
▷ SYNONYMS: **firearm**, handgun, weapon; informal shooter; N. Amer. informal piece, shooting iron.
• v. (**gunning**, **gunned**) (**gun down**) shoot with a gun.
☐ **gunfire** repeated firing of a gun or guns. **gunman** a man who uses a gun to commit a crime. **gunpowder** an explosive mixture of saltpetre, sulphur, and charcoal. **gunship** a heavily armed helicopter. **gunsmith** a maker and seller of small firearms. **jump the gun** informal act before the proper time.

gunge n. informal sticky and messy matter.

gung-ho adj. too eager to take part in fighting.

gunnel var. of GUNWALE.

gunner n. **1** a person who operates a gun. **2** a British artillery soldier.

gunnery n. the manufacture or firing of heavy guns.

gunrunner n. a smuggler of firearms.
■ **gunrunning** n.

gunwale (or **gunnel**) /gun-n'l/ n. the upper edge of a boat's side.

guppy n. (pl. **guppies**) a small tropical freshwater fish.

gurdwara n. a Sikh temple.

gurgle v. make a low bubbling sound.
• n. a low bubbling sound.

Gurkha n. a member of a Nepalese regiment in the British army.

guru n. **1** a Hindu spiritual teacher. **2** an influential teacher or expert.
▷ SYNONYMS: **1 spiritual teacher**, tutor, sage, mentor, spiritual leader, master. **2 expert**, authority, pundit, leading light, master, specialist.
– ANTONYMS: disciple.

gush v. **1** flow in a strong, fast stream. **2** express approval very enthusiastically.
▷ SYNONYMS: **1 surge**, stream, spout, spurt, jet, rush, pour, spill, cascade, flood; Brit. informal sloosh. **2 enthuse**, wax lyrical, be effusive, go into raptures, rhapsodize, be fulsome in your praise; informal rave.
• n. a strong, fast stream.
▷ SYNONYMS: **stream**, spout, spurt, jet, surge, rush, outpouring, outflow, cascade, flood, torrent.

gusset n. a piece of material sewn into a garment to strengthen or enlarge a part of it.

gust n. a brief, strong rush of wind.
▷ SYNONYMS: **flurry**, blast, puff, blow, rush, squall.
• v. blow in gusts.
■ **gusty** adj.

gusto n. enjoyment or energy.

gut n. **1** the stomach. **2** the intestine. **3** (**guts**) informal courage and determination.
▷ SYNONYMS: **1 stomach**, belly, abdomen, paunch, intestines, viscera; informal tummy, insides, innards. **2** *he has a lot of guts:* **courage**, bravery, backbone, nerve, pluck, spirit, daring, grit, fearlessness, determination; Brit. informal bottle; N. Amer. informal moxie.
• v. (**gutting**, **gutted**) **1** take out the internal organs of a fish. **2** remove or destroy the internal parts of.
▷ SYNONYMS: **1 clean**, disembowel, draw; formal eviscerate. **2 strip**, empty, devastate, lay waste, ravage, ruin, wreck.
• adj. informal instinctive.
▷ SYNONYMS: **instinctive**, intuitive, deep-seated, involuntary, spontaneous, unthinking, knee-jerk.
■ **gutless** adj.

> **WORD LINKS**
> **visceral** relating to the gut

gutsy adj. (**gutsier**, **gutsiest**) informal brave and determined.

gutter n. **1** a shallow trough round

a roof, or a channel beside a road, for carrying away rainwater. **2** (**the gutter**) a very poor environment.
▷ SYNONYMS: **drain**, trough, trench, ditch, sluice, sewer, channel, conduit, pipe.
• v. (of a flame) flicker.
□ **guttersnipe** a scruffy, badly behaved child.

guttural adj. (of a speech sound) produced in the throat.

guy n. **1** informal a man. **2** Brit. a stuffed figure burnt on a bonfire on 5 November. **3** a rope fixed to the ground to secure a tent.
▷ SYNONYMS: **man**, fellow; informal lad; Brit. informal chap, bloke, geezer; N. Amer. informal dude, hombre.
• v. ridicule.

guzzle v. eat or drink greedily.
▷ SYNONYMS: **1 gobble**, bolt, wolf, devour; informal tuck into, shovel down, hoover up; Brit. informal scoff; N. Amer. informal snarf, scarf. **2 gulp down**, quaff, swill; informal knock back, swig, slug, neck.

gybe (US **jibe**) v. Sailing change course by swinging the sail across a following wind.

gym n. **1** a gymnasium. **2** a place with facilities for improving physical fitness. **3** gymnastics.

gymkhana n. a horse-riding competition.

gymnasium n. (pl. **gymnasiums** or **gymnasia**) a room equipped for gymnastics and other physical exercise.

gymnast n. a person trained in gymnastics.

gymnastics n. exercises involving physical agility and flexibility.
■ **gymnastic** adj.

gynaecology /gy-ni-**kol**-uh-ji/ (US **gynecology**) n. the branch of medicine concerned with conditions and diseases specific to women.
■ **gynaecological** adj. **gynaecologist** n.

gypsum n. a chalk-like mineral used for plaster of Paris and in building.

Gypsy (or **Gipsy**) n. (pl. **Gypsies**) a member of a travelling people.

gyrate v. move in a circle or spiral.
▷ SYNONYMS: **rotate**, revolve, wheel, turn, whirl, circle, pirouette, twirl, swirl, spin, swivel.
■ **gyration** n. **gyratory** adj.

gyroscope n. a device consisting of a disc rotating on an axis, used to maintain stability or a fixed direction.

Hh

ha abbrev. hectares.

habeas corpus n. an order requiring an arrested person to be brought to court.

haberdashery n. Brit. sewing materials.
■ haberdasher n.

habit n. **1** a thing that a person does often. **2** informal an addiction. **3** a long, loose garment worn by a monk or nun.
▷ SYNONYMS: **1 custom**, practice, routine, way; formal wont. **2 addiction**, dependence, craving, fixation.

habitable adj. suitable to live in.

habitat n. the natural environment of an animal or plant.

habitation n. a house or home.

habitual adj. **1** done often. **2** usual.
▷ SYNONYMS: **1 constant**, persistent, continual, continuous, perpetual, non-stop, endless, never-ending; informal eternal. **2 inveterate**, confirmed, compulsive, incorrigible, hardened, ingrained, chronic, regular. **3 customary**, accustomed, regular, usual, normal, characteristic; literary wonted.
– ANTONYMS: occasional.
■ habitually adv.

habituate v. make or become used to.

habitué /huh-**bit**-yuu-ay/ n. a frequent visitor to a place.

hacienda n. (in Spanish-speaking countries) a large estate with a house.

hack v. **1** cut with rough or heavy blows. **2** use a computer to gain unauthorized access to another computer system.
▷ SYNONYMS: **cut**, chop, hew, lop, saw, slash.
• n. **1** a journalist producing dull, unoriginal work. **2** a horse for ordinary riding.
□ hacksaw a saw with a narrow blade set in a frame.
■ hacker n.

hackles pl. n. hairs along an animal's back, raised in anger.

hackneyed adj. unoriginal and dull.
▷ SYNONYMS: **overused**, overdone, overworked, worn out, time-worn, stale, tired, threadbare, trite, banal, clichéd.
– ANTONYMS: original.

had past & past part. of HAVE.

haddock n. (pl. **haddock**) an edible sea fish.

hadn't contr. had not.

haematology /hee-muh-**tol**-uh-ji/ (US **hematology**) n. the branch of medicine concerned with the blood.
■ haematologist n.

haemoglobin /hee-muh-**gloh**-bin/ (US **hemoglobin**) n. a red protein transporting oxygen in the blood.

haemophilia /hee-muh-**fi**-li-uh/ (US **hemophilia**) n. a condition in which failure of the blood to clot properly causes heavy bleeding.
■ haemophiliac n.

haemorrhage /**hem**-uh-rij/ (US **hemorrhage**) n. heavy bleeding.
• v. bleed heavily.

haemorrhoid /**hem**-uh-royd/ (US **hemorrhoid**) n. a swollen vein at or near the anus.

hafnium n. a hard metallic element.

haft n. the handle of a knife, axe, etc.

hag n. an ugly old woman.

haggard adj. looking exhausted and unwell.
▷ SYNONYMS: **drawn**, tired, exhausted, drained, careworn, gaunt, pinched, hollow-cheeked, hollow-eyed.

haggis n. a Scottish dish made from offal mixed with suet and oatmeal.

haggle v. bargain over a price.
▷ SYNONYMS: **barter**, bargain, negotiate, wrangle.

haiku /**hy**-koo/ n. (pl. **haiku** or **haikus**) a Japanese poem of 17 syllables.

hail n. **1** pellets of frozen rain falling in showers. **2** a large number of things hurled through the air.
▷ SYNONYMS: **barrage**, volley, shower, stream, salvo.

h

•v. **1** hail falls. **2** call out to. **3** describe enthusiastically. **4** (**hail from**) come from or live in.
▷ SYNONYMS: **1 call out to**, shout to, address, greet, salute; flag down. **2 acclaim**, praise, applaud.
□ **hailstone** a pellet of hail.

hair n. **1** any of the fine thread-like strands growing from the skin. **2** strands of hair.
▷ SYNONYMS: **1 head of hair**, shock of hair, mane, mop, locks, tresses, curls. **2 hairstyle**, haircut; informal hairdo. **3 fur**, wool, coat, fleece, pelt, mane.
□ **hairgrip** informal a hairstyle. **hairgrip** Brit. a flat hairpin. **hairline 1** the edge of a person's hair. **2** (of a crack) very thin. **hairpin** a U-shaped pin for fastening the hair. **hairpin bend** a sharp U-shaped bend. **hair-raising** very frightening. **hairslide** Brit. a clip for keeping hair in place. **hairstyle** a way in which the hair is cut or arranged.

> **WORD LINKS**
> **trichology** the study of the hair and scalp and their diseases

hairdresser n. a person who cuts and styles hair.
▷ SYNONYMS: **hairstylist**, coiffeur, coiffeuse, barber; informal crimper.

hairy adj. (**hairier**, **hairiest**) **1** covered with hair. **2** informal frightening or dangerous.
▷ SYNONYMS: **1 shaggy**, bushy, long-haired, woolly, furry, fleecy. **2 bearded**, unshaven, stubbly, bristly; formal hirsute. **3 risky**, dangerous, perilous, hazardous, tricky; informal dicey; Brit. informal dodgy.
■ **hairiness** n.

hajj n. a pilgrimage made by Muslims to Mecca.

haka n. a ceremonial Maori war dance.

hake n. (pl. **hake**) an edible sea fish.

halal adj. (of meat) prepared according to Muslim law.

halberd n. hist. a combined spear and battleaxe.

halcyon /hal-si-uhn/ adj. (of a past time) happy and peaceful.

hale adj. strong and healthy.

half n. (pl. **halves**) **1** either of two equal parts into which something is divided. **2** Brit. informal half a pint of beer.
•adj. & pron. an amount equal to a half.
•adv. **1** to the extent of half. **2** partly.
□ **at half mast** (of a flag) flown halfway down its mast as a sign of mourning. **half-and-half** in equal parts. **halfback** a player between the

forwards and full backs. **half board** Brit. bed, breakfast, and one main meal at a hotel etc. **half-brother** (or **sister**) a brother (or sister) with whom you have one parent in common. **half-caste** offens. a person of mixed race. **half-life** the time taken for radioactivity to fall to half its original value. **half-term** Brit. a short holiday halfway through a school term. **half-timbered** having walls with a timber frame and a brick or plaster filling. **half-time** an interval between two halves of a sports match. **half-witted** informal stupid.

half-hearted adj. not very enthusiastic.
▷ SYNONYMS: **unenthusiastic**, cool, luke-warm, tepid, apathetic, indifferent.
– ANTONYMS: enthusiastic.

halfpenny /hayp-ni/ n. (pl. **halfpennies; halfpence**) a former British coin worth half a penny.

halfway adj. & adv. at or to a point equal in distance between two others.
▷ SYNONYMS: *the halfway point:* **midway**, middle, mid, central, centre, inter-mediate.

halibut n. (pl. **halibut**) a large edible flatfish.

halitosis n. unpleasant-smelling breath.

hall n. **1** the room or space inside the front entrance of a house. **2** a large room or building for meetings, concerts, etc. **3** Brit. a large country house.
▷ SYNONYMS: **1 entrance hall**, hallway, entry, entrance, lobby, foyer, vesti-bule, atrium. **2 assembly room**, meeting room, chamber, auditorium, theatre, house.

hallelujah (or **alleluia**) exclam. God be praised.

hallmark n. **1** an official mark stamped on gold, silver, or platinum articles to certify their purity. **2** a distinctive feature.
•v. stamp with a hallmark.

hallo var. of HELLO.

hallowed adj. made holy.

Halloween (or **Hallowe'en**) n. 31 October, the eve of All Saints' Day.

hallucinate v. see something which is not actually present.
■ **hallucinatory** adj.

hallucination n. the experience of seeing something which is not actually present.
▷ SYNONYMS: **delusion**, illusion, figment of the imagination, mirage, chimera, fantasy.

hallucinogen n. a drug causing hallucinations.
■ **hallucinogenic** adj.

halo n. (pl. **haloes** or **halos**) (in a painting) a circle of light round the head of a holy person.

halogen n. any of a group of elements including fluorine, chlorine, and iodine.

halt v. stop suddenly.
▷ SYNONYMS: **1** *halt at the barrier*: **stop**, come to a halt, come to a stop, come to a standstill, pull up, draw up. **2** *a strike halted production*: **stop**, bring to a stop, put a stop to, suspend, arrest, check, curb, stem, staunch, block, stall. ● n. **1** a stopping of movement or activity. **2** Brit. a minor stopping place on a railway.
▷ SYNONYMS: **1 stop**, standstill. **2 stoppage**, break, pause, interval, interruption.
– ANTONYMS: start.

halter n. a strap round an animal's head, used for leading it.
□ **halter neck** a style of woman's top fastened behind the neck, leaving the upper back and arms bare.

halting adj. slow and hesitant.
▷ SYNONYMS: **hesitant**, faltering, hesitating, stumbling, stammering, stuttering, broken, imperfect.
– ANTONYMS: fluent.

halve v. **1** divide into halves. **2** reduce by half.

halves pl. of HALF.

halyard n. a rope for raising and lowering a sail or flag.

ham n. **1** salted or smoked meat from a pig's thigh. **2** (**hams**) the thighs and buttocks. **3** a poor actor. **4** informal an amateur radio operator.
● v. (**hamming, hammed**) informal overact.
□ **ham-fisted** informal clumsy.

hamburger n. a flat cake of minced beef.

hamlet n. a small village.

hammer n. **1** a tool with a head for driving in nails etc. **2** a metal ball attached to a wire, thrown in an athletic contest.
● v. **1** hit repeatedly. **2** (**hammer out**) work out the details of.
▷ SYNONYMS: **beat**, batter, bang, pummel, pound, knock, thump.

hammock n. a hanging bed of canvas or rope mesh.

hamper n. a basket with a lid, used to carry picnic items.
● v. prevent or hinder the movement or progress of.

▷ SYNONYMS: **hinder**, obstruct, impede, inhibit, delay, slow down, hold up, interfere with, handicap, hamstring.
– ANTONYMS: help.

hamster n. a small domesticated rodent.

hamstring n. a tendon at the back of the knee.
● v. (**hamstringing, hamstrung**)
1 cripple by cutting the hamstrings.
2 severely restrict.

hand n. **1** the part of the arm below the wrist. **2** a pointer on a clock etc. **3** (**hands**) power or control. **4** help. **5** a manual worker. **6** a round of applause. **7** the cards dealt to a player in a game. **8** a unit of measurement of a horse's height.
▷ SYNONYMS: **1 fist**, palm; informal paw, mitt. **2 handwriting**, writing, script. **3 worker**, employee, workman, labourer, operative, craftsman.
● v. give or pass to.
□ **at hand** near. **handbag** Brit. a small bag for personal items. **handball 1** a game in which the ball is hit with the hand in a walled court. **2** (in football) unlawful touching of the ball with the hand or arm. **handbill** a printed advertisement distributed by hand. **handout 1** a gift of money etc. to a needy person. **2** a piece of printed information given free of charge. **handshake** an act of shaking a person's hand. **handstand** an act of balancing upside down on the hands. **handwriting 1** writing by hand with a pen or pencil. **2** a style of this. **on hand** available. **out of hand** out of control. **to hand** within reach.

> **WORD LINKS**
> **manual** relating to the hands

handbook n. a book giving basic information.
▷ SYNONYMS: **manual**, ABC, A to Z, companion, guide, guidebook, vade mecum.

handcuff n. (**handcuffs**) a pair of lockable linked metal rings for securing a prisoner's wrists.
▷ SYNONYMS: **manacles**, shackles, irons; informal cuffs, bracelets.
● v. put handcuffs on.

handful n. **1** a quantity that fills the hand. **2** a small number or amount. **3** informal a person who is difficult to control.
▷ SYNONYMS: **few**, small number, small amount, small quantity, sprinkling, smattering, one or two, some, not many.
– ANTONYMS: lot.

h

handicap n. **1** an obstacle to progress. **2** dated a physical or mental disability. **3** a disadvantage given to a superior competitor in a sport to make the chances more equal. **4** the number of strokes by which a golfer normally exceeds par for a course.
▷ SYNONYMS: **1 disability**, difficulty. **2 impediment**, hindrance, obstacle, barrier, constraint, disadvantage, stumbling block.
– ANTONYMS: benefit, advantage.
• v. (**handicapping, handicapped**) act as a handicap to.
▷ SYNONYMS: **hamper**, impede, hinder, impair, hamstring, restrict, constrain.
– ANTONYMS: help.

handicraft n. a decorative object made by hand.

handiwork n. (**your handiwork**) something that you have made or done.

handkerchief n. (pl. **handkerchiefs** or **handkerchieves**) a square of material for wiping the nose.

handle v. **1** feel or move with the hands. **2** control. **3** deal with.
▷ SYNONYMS: **1 hold**, pick up, grasp, grip, lift, finger. **2 control**, drive, steer, operate, manoeuvre. **3 deal with**, manage, tackle, take care of, look after, take charge of, attend to, see to, sort out. **4 trade in**, deal in, buy, sell, supply, peddle, traffic in.
• n. a part by which a thing is held, carried, or controlled.
▷ SYNONYMS: **grip**, haft, hilt, stock, shaft.
□ **handlebar** the steering bar of a bicycle or motorbike.

handler n. a person in charge of a trained animal.

handsome adj. **1** good-looking. **2** striking and impressive. **3** (of an amount) large.
▷ SYNONYMS: **1 good-looking**, attractive, striking; informal hunky, dishy, tasty, fanciable; Brit. informal fit; N. Amer. informal cute. **2 substantial**, considerable, sizeable, princely, generous, lavish, ample, bumper; informal tidy, whopping; Brit. informal ginormous.
– ANTONYMS: ugly.
■ **handsomely** adv.

handy adj. (**handier, handiest**) **1** useful. **2** conveniently near.
▷ SYNONYMS: **1 useful**, convenient, practical, neat, easy to use, user-friendly, helpful, functional. **2 ready**, to hand, within reach, accessible, readily available, nearby, at the ready. **3 skilful**, skilled, dexterous, deft, adept, proficient.

□ **handyman** a person who does general building repairs.
■ **handily** adv.

hang v. (**hanging, hung** except in sense 2) **1** suspend or be suspended from above. **2** (past & past part. **hanged**) kill by suspending from a rope tied round the neck. **3** (of a garment) drape in a particular way.
▷ SYNONYMS: **1** lights hung from the trees: **be suspended**, dangle, swing, sway, hover, float. **2** hang the picture at eye level: **suspend**, put up, pin up, display. **3 decorate**, adorn, drape, festoon, deck out. **4 send to the gallows**, execute, lynch; informal string up.
□ **hang-glider** a simple aircraft consisting of a framework from which a person is suspended in a harness. **hangman** a person who executes people by hanging. **hangnail** torn skin at the base of a fingernail. **hang out** informal spend time relaxing.

hangar n. a building for aircraft.

hangdog adj. shamefaced.

hanger n. a curved frame with a hook at the top, for hanging clothes on.

hanging n. a decorative piece of fabric hung on a wall.

hangover n. a headache and other after-effects from drinking too much alcohol.

hang-up n. informal an emotional problem.
▷ SYNONYMS: **neurosis**, phobia, preoccupation, fixation, obsession, inhibition, mental block; informal complex, thing, issue, bee in your bonnet.

hank n. a coil or length of wool etc.

hanker v. feel a desire for or to do.
▷ SYNONYMS: **yearn**, long, wish, hunger, thirst, lust, ache; informal itch.

hanky (or **hankie**) n. (pl. **hankies**) informal a handkerchief.

Hanukkah n. a Jewish festival of lights held in December.

haphazard adj. lacking order; random.
▷ SYNONYMS: **random**, disorderly, indiscriminate, chaotic, hit-and-miss, aimless, chance; informal higgledy-piggledy.
– ANTONYMS: methodical.
■ **haphazardly** adv.

hapless adj. unlucky.
▷ SYNONYMS: **unfortunate**, unlucky, unhappy, wretched, miserable.
– ANTONYMS: lucky.

happen v. **1** take place; occur. **2** (**happen on**) find by chance. **3** (**happen to**) be experienced by.

h

4 (happen to) become of.
▷ SYNONYMS: **1 occur**, take place, come about, arise, develop, result, transpire; N. Amer. informal go down; literary come to pass. **2** *I wonder what happened to her:* **become of;** literary befall, betide.

happening n. an event or occurrence.
▷ SYNONYMS: **occurrence**, event, incident, episode, affair.

happiness n. the state of being happy.
▷ SYNONYMS: **pleasure**, contentment, well-being, satisfaction, cheerfulness, good spirits, merriment, joy, joyfulness, delight, elation, jubilation.
− ANTONYMS: sadness, misery.

happy adj. (**happier**, **happiest**)
1 feeling or showing pleasure.
2 fortunate.
▷ SYNONYMS: **1 cheerful**, cheery, merry, joyful, jovial, jolly, carefree, in good spirits, in a good mood, pleased, contented, content, satisfied, gratified, delighted, sunny, radiant, elated, jubilant; literary blithe. **2 fortunate**, lucky, timely, convenient. *I'm happy to help:* **glad**, pleased, delighted, more than willing.
− ANTONYMS: sad, unhappy, unfortunate.
□ **happy-go-lucky** cheerfully unconcerned.
■ **happily** adv.

hara-kiri n. (formerly, in Japan) ritual suicide by cutting open the stomach with a sword.

harangue v. criticize aggressively.

harass v. **1** subject to constant pressure or interference. **2** attack an enemy repeatedly.
▷ SYNONYMS: **persecute**, intimidate, hound, victimize; pester, bother; informal hassle, bug; N. Amer. informal ride.
■ **harassment** n.

USAGE Only one r: harass.

harassed adj. tired or tense as a result of too many demands on your time.
▷ SYNONYMS: **stressed**, hard-pressed, overstretched, tense, careworn, worried, troubled; informal hassled.
− ANTONYMS: carefree.

harbinger /har-bin-jer/ n. a sign or herald of something.

harbour (US harbor) n. a place on the coast for ships to moor.
▷ SYNONYMS: **port**, dock, haven, marina, mooring, wharf, anchorage, waterfront.
• v. **1** keep a thought etc. secretly in the mind. **2** shelter.
▷ SYNONYMS: **1 shelter**, conceal, hide, shield, protect, give asylum to.

2 bear, hold, nurse, foster.

hard adj. **1** solid, firm, and rigid.
2 requiring effort. **3** not showing weakness. **4** done with force. **5** harsh or unpleasant. **6** (of information) precise and true. **7** (of drink) strongly alcoholic. **8** (of a drug) very addictive. **9** (of water) containing mineral salts.
▷ SYNONYMS: **1 firm**, solid, rigid, stiff, unbreakable, unyielding, compacted, compressed, tough, strong. **2 arduous**, strenuous, tiring, exhausting, back-breaking, gruelling, heavy, laborious, demanding, uphill; Brit. informal knackering. **3** *a hard worker:* **industrious**, diligent, assiduous, conscientious, energetic, keen, enthusiastic, indefatigable.
4 difficult, puzzling, complicated, complex, intricate, knotty, thorny, problematic. **5 forceful**, heavy, strong, sharp, violent, powerful.
6 harsh, unpleasant, grim, austere, difficult, bad, bleak, tough.
− ANTONYMS: soft, easy, gentle.
• adv. **1** with force or effort. **2** so as to be firm.
▷ SYNONYMS: **1 forcefully**, energetically, roughly, heavily, sharply, violently.
2 diligently, industriously, assiduously, conscientiously, doggedly.
□ **hardback** a book bound in stiff covers. **hardbitten** tough and cynical.
hardboard board made of compressed wood pulp. **hard-boiled 1** (of an egg) boiled until solid. **2** tough and cynical. **hard copy** a printed version of computer data. **hard core 1** the most committed members of a group.
2 very explicit pornography. **hard disk** (or **hard drive**) a rigid magnetic disk with a large data storage capacity.
hard-headed tough and realistic.
hard shoulder Brit. a strip of road alongside a motorway for emergency use. **hard up** informal short of money.
hardware 1 the physical components of a computer. **2** tools and household implements. **hardwood** wood from broadleaved trees.
■ **hardness** n.

harden v. make or become hard or harder.
▷ SYNONYMS: **1 solidify**, set, thicken, cake, congeal. **2 toughen**, desensitize, inure, numb.
− ANTONYMS: soften.

hardened adj. fixed in a bad habit or way of life; *hardened criminals.*
▷ SYNONYMS: **inveterate**, seasoned, habitual, chronic, compulsive, confirmed, incorrigible.

h

hardly adv. **1** scarcely. **2** only with difficulty.
▷ SYNONYMS: **scarcely**, barely, only just, just.
hardship n. poverty.
▷ SYNONYMS: **difficulty**, privation, destitution, poverty, austerity, need, distress, suffering, adversity.
− ANTONYMS: prosperity, ease.
hardy adj. (**hardier, hardiest**) capable of surviving difficult conditions.
▷ SYNONYMS: **robust**, healthy, fit, strong, sturdy, tough, rugged.
− ANTONYMS: delicate.
■ **hardiness** n.
hare n. an animal like a large rabbit.
• v. run very fast.
□ **hare-brained** foolish and unlikely to succeed.
harebell n. a plant with blue bell-shaped flowers.
harelip n. offens. a cleft lip.
harem /hah-reem/ n. **1** the women's quarters of a Muslim household. **2** the women in a harem.
haricot /ha-ri-koh/ n. a round white bean.
hark v. **1** literary listen. **2** (**hark back to**) recall an earlier period.
harlequin n. a character in traditional pantomime with a diamond-patterned costume.
• adj. in varied colours.
harlot n. old use a prostitute.
harm n. **1** deliberate injury. **2** damage.
▷ SYNONYMS: **injury**, damage, mischief, detriment, disservice.
− ANTONYMS: good.
• v. cause harm to.
▷ SYNONYMS: **1 hurt**, injure, wound, lay a finger on, mistreat, ill-treat, maltreat. **2 damage**, spoil, affect, undermine, ruin.
− ANTONYMS: heal, help.
harmful adj. causing or likely to cause harm.
▷ SYNONYMS: **damaging**, injurious, detrimental, inimical, dangerous, unhealthy, unwholesome, hurtful, destructive, hazardous; formal deleterious.
− ANTONYMS: beneficial.
■ **harmfully** adv.
harmless adj. not able or likely to cause harm.
▷ SYNONYMS: **safe**, innocuous, gentle, mild, non-toxic.
− ANTONYMS: harmful.
harmonica n. a mouth organ.
harmonious adj. **1** tuneful. **2** pleasingly arranged. **3** free from conflict.

▷ SYNONYMS: **1 melodious**, tuneful, musical, sweet-sounding, mellifluous, dulcet, euphonious. **2 friendly**, amicable, cordial, amiable, congenial, peaceful, in harmony, in tune. **3 balanced**, coordinated, pleasing, tasteful.
− ANTONYMS: discordant, hostile.
■ **harmoniously** adv.
harmonium n. a musical instrument like a small organ.
harmonize (or **-ise**) v. **1** add notes to a melody to produce harmony. **2** make or be harmonious.
▷ SYNONYMS: **1 coordinate**, go together, match, blend, mix, balance, tone in, be compatible, be harmonious, suit each other, set each other off. **2 standardize**, coordinate, integrate, synchronize, make consistent, bring into line, systematize.
− ANTONYMS: clash.
■ **harmonization** n.
harmony n. (pl. **harmonies**) **1** the combination of musical notes to produce chords with a pleasing effect. **2** the quality of forming a pleasing combination. **3** agreement.
▷ SYNONYMS: **1 tunefulness**, euphony, melodiousness, unison. **2 accord**, agreement, peace, friendship, fellowship, cooperation, understanding, rapport, unity.
− ANTONYMS: dissonance, disagreement.
■ **harmonic** adj.
harness n. **1** a set of straps by which a horse is controlled. **2** a set of straps for attaching a person's body to something.
• v. **1** control and use a resource. **2** fit with a harness.
harp n. a musical instrument with strings in a frame.
• v. (**harp on**) talk persistently about.
■ **harpist** n.
harpoon n. a spear-like missile for catching whales etc.
• v. spear with a harpoon.
harpsichord n. a keyboard instrument.
harpy n. (pl. **harpies**) an unpleasant woman.
harridan n. a bossy or aggressive old woman.
harrier n. **1** a hound used for hunting hares. **2** a bird of prey.
harrow n. a heavy frame with spikes for breaking up soil.
• v. draw a harrow over.
harrowing adj. very distressing.
▷ SYNONYMS: **distressing**, traumatic, upsetting, shocking, disturbing,

painful, agonizing.

harry v. (**harrying**, **harried**) harass.
▷ SYNONYMS: **harass**, hound, torment, pester, worry, badger, nag, plague; informal hassle, bug.

harsh adj. **1** unpleasantly bright, strong, rough, etc. **2** cruel or severe.
▷ SYNONYMS: **1 grating**, rasping, strident, raucous, discordant, jarring, dissonant. **2 garish**, loud, glaring, gaudy, lurid. **3 cruel**, savage, barbarous, merciless, inhumane, ruthless, brutal, hard-hearted, unfeeling, unrelenting. **4 severe**, stringent, firm, stiff, stern, rigorous, uncompromising, draconian. **5 rude**, discourteous, unfriendly, sharp, bitter, unkind, critical, disparaging. **6 austere**, grim, spartan, hard, inhospitable. **7 cold**, freezing, icy, bitter, hard, severe, bleak.
– ANTONYMS: kind, mild, gentle.
■ **harshly** adv. **harshness** n.

hart n. an adult male deer.

harvest n. **1** the process or period of gathering in crops. **2** the season's yield or crop.
▷ SYNONYMS: **crop**, yield, vintage, produce.
• v. gather as a harvest.
▷ SYNONYMS: **gather**, bring in, reap, pick, collect.
■ **harvester** n.

has 3rd person sing. present of HAVE.
□ **has-been** informal a person who is no longer important.

hash n. a dish of chopped reheated meat.
□ **make a hash of** informal do badly.

hashish n. cannabis.

hasn't contr. has not.

hasp n. a hinged metal plate fitted over a metal loop as part of a fastening.

hassle informal n. annoying inconvenience.
▷ SYNONYMS: **inconvenience**, bother, nuisance, trouble, annoyance, irritation, fuss; informal aggravation, headache, pain in the neck.
• v. harass or bother.
▷ SYNONYMS: **harass**, pester, be on at, badger, hound, bother, nag, torment; informal bug; N. English informal mither.

hassock n. a cushion for kneeling on in church.

haste n. speed or urgency.
▷ SYNONYMS: **speed**, hurriedness, swiftness, rapidity, quickness, briskness, alacrity; old use celerity.
– ANTONYMS: delay.

hasten v. **1** hurry. **2** cause to happen sooner.

▷ SYNONYMS: **1 hurry**, rush, dash, race, fly, speed; informal zip, hare, scoot, hotfoot it; N. Amer. informal hightail. **2 speed up**, bring on, precipitate, advance.
– ANTONYMS: dawdle, delay.

hasty adj. (**hastier**, **hastiest**) hurried; rushed.
▷ SYNONYMS: **hurried**, rash, impetuous, impulsive, reckless, precipitate, spur-of-the-moment.
– ANTONYMS: considered.
■ **hastily** adv.

hat n. a shaped covering for the head.
□ **hat-trick** three successes of the same kind.

hatch n. a small opening in a floor, wall, or roof allowing access.
• v. **1** come out from an egg. **2** devise a plot. **3** shade with close parallel lines.
□ **hatchback** a car with a back door that opens upwards.

hatchet n. a small axe.
□ **bury the hatchet** end a quarrel.

hate v. feel intense dislike for.
▷ SYNONYMS: **1 loathe**, detest, despise, dislike, abhor, shrink from, be unable to bear/stand; formal abominate. **2 be sorry**, be reluctant, be loath.
• n. intense dislike.
▷ SYNONYMS: **hatred**, loathing, abhorrence, abomination, aversion, disgust.
– ANTONYMS: love.

hateful adj. arousing hate.

hatred n. extreme hate.

haughty adj. (**haughtier**, **haughtiest**) arrogant and superior towards others.
■ **haughtily** adv. **haughtiness** n.

haul v. pull or drag with effort.
▷ SYNONYMS: **drag**, pull, heave, lug, hump.
• n. a quantity of something obtained, esp. illegally.
▷ SYNONYMS: **booty**, loot, plunder, spoils, stolen goods; informal swag.

haulage n. Brit. the commercial transport of goods.

haulier n. Brit. a person or company transporting goods by road.

haunch n. **1** the buttock and thigh. **2** a leg and loin of meat.

haunt v. **1** (of a ghost) appear regularly in a place. **2** visit frequently. **3** linger disturbingly in the mind.
▷ SYNONYMS: *the sight haunted me for years*: **torment**, disturb, trouble, worry, plague, prey on.
• n. a place often visited by a particular person.
▷ SYNONYMS: **meeting place**, stamping ground, spot, venue; N. Amer. stomping ground; informal hang-out.

haunting adj. beautiful or sad in a way that is hard to forget.

▷ SYNONYMS: **evocative**, affecting, stirring, powerful, poignant, memorable.

haute couture /oht kuu-tyoor/ n. high fashion.

haute cuisine /oht kwi-zeen/ n. high-quality cookery.

hauteur /oh-ter/ n. superiority of manner.

have v. (**has**, **having**, **had**) **1** possess. **2** experience. **3** (**have to**) be obliged to. **4** suffer from. **5** cause to be or be done. **6** place, hold, or keep.

▷ SYNONYMS: **1 own**, be in possession of, be blessed with, boast, enjoy. **2 comprise**, consist of, contain, include, incorporate, be composed of, be made up of. **3 eat**, drink, take. **4 organize**, hold, give, throw, put on, lay on. **5** *I have to get up at six:* **must**, be obliged to, be required to, be compelled to, be forced to, be bound to.

• aux. v. used with a past participle to form past tenses.

haven n. a place of safety.

▷ SYNONYMS: **refuge**, retreat, shelter, sanctuary, oasis.

haven't contr. have not.

haversack n. a strong bag carried on the back or over the shoulder.

havoc n. great destruction or disorder.

▷ SYNONYMS: **chaos**, mayhem, bedlam, pandemonium, a shambles.

hawk n. **1** a bird of prey. **2** a person favouring aggressive policies in foreign affairs.

• v. **1** offer goods for sale in the street. **2** clear the throat noisily.

■ **hawker** n. **hawkish** adj.

hawser n. a thick rope or cable for mooring or towing a ship.

hawthorn n. a thorny shrub or tree with small red berries.

hay n. grass cut and dried for use as fodder.

□ **hay fever** an allergy to pollen or dust. **haystack** (or **hayrick**) a large packed pile of hay.

haywire adj. informal out of control.

hazard n. a danger.

▷ SYNONYMS: **danger**, risk, peril, menace, jeopardy, threat.

• v. **1** dare to say. **2** put at risk.

hazardous adj. dangerous.

▷ SYNONYMS: **risky**, dangerous, unsafe, perilous, fraught with danger, high-risk; informal dicey; Brit. informal dodgy.

− ANTONYMS: safe.

haze n. a thin mist.

▷ SYNONYMS: **mist**, fog, cloud, vapour.

hazel n. **1** a tree bearing small round nuts (**hazelnuts**). **2** a rich reddish-brown colour.

hazy adj. (**hazier**, **haziest**) **1** covered by a haze. **2** vague or unclear.

▷ SYNONYMS: **1 misty**, foggy, smoggy, murky. **2 vague**, dim, nebulous, blurred, fuzzy.

■ **hazily** adv.

H-bomb n. a hydrogen bomb.

he pron. **1** the male previously mentioned. **2** a person or animal of unspecified sex.

> **USAGE** The use of **he** to refer to any person, male or female, is considered outdated and sexist by many. Using **he or she** can be clumsy, so **they** is often used instead, as in *everyone needs to feel that they matter.*

head n. **1** the part of the body containing the brain, mouth, and sense organs. **2** a person in charge. **3** the front or top part. **4** a person or animal considered as a unit. **5** a compact mass of leaves or flowers at the top of a stem. **6** (**heads**) the side of a coin bearing the image of a head. **7** pressure of water or steam in an enclosed space.

▷ SYNONYMS: **1 skull**, cranium; informal nut. **2 brain**, brainpower, intellect, intelligence, grey matter; Brit. informal loaf; N. Amer. informal smarts. **3** *a head for business:* aptitude, talent, gift, capacity. **4 leader**, chief, controller, governor, superintendent, commander, captain, director, manager, principal, president; informal boss; Brit. informal gaffer, guv'nor. **5 front**, beginning, start, top.

• adj. chief.

▷ SYNONYMS: **chief**, principal, leading, main, first, top, highest.

• v. **1** be the head of. **2** give a heading to. **3** move in a specified direction. **4** (**head off**) obstruct and turn aside. **5** Football hit the ball with the head.

▷ SYNONYMS: **command**, control, lead, manage, direct, supervise, superintend, oversee, preside over.

□ **come to a head** reach a crisis. **headache 1** a continuous pain in the head. **2** informal a worry. **headdress** a decorative covering for the head. **headgear** hats, helmets, etc. **headhunt** approach someone employed elsewhere to fill a vacant post. **headland** a promontory. **headlight** a powerful light at the front of a vehicle. **headline** a heading in a newspaper. **headlines** a summary

of broadcast news. **headmaster** (or **headmistress**) a male (or female) head teacher. **head-on 1** involving the front of a vehicle. **2** directly confronting. **headphones** a pair of earphones. **head start** an initial advantage. **headstone** a stone slab at the head of a grave. **headstrong** wilful and determined. **headway** progress. **headwind** a wind blowing from directly in front.
■ **headless** adj.

header n. Football an act of heading the ball.

heading n. **1** a title at the top of a page or section of a book etc. **2** a direction or bearing.
▷ SYNONYMS: **title**, caption, legend, rubric, headline.

headlong adv. & adv. **1** with the head first. **2** in a rush.
▷ SYNONYMS: **1** *don't rush headlong into marriage:* **without thinking**, precipitously, impetuously, rashly, recklessly, hastily. **2** *a headlong dash:* **breakneck**, whirlwind, reckless, precipitous.

headquarters pl. n. the place from which an organization or military operation is directed.
▷ SYNONYMS: **head office**, HQ, base, nerve centre, mission control.

heady adj. (**headier**, **headiest**) **1** exciting or exhilarating. **2** intoxicating.
▷ SYNONYMS: **1 exhilarating**, exciting, stimulating, thrilling, intoxicating. **2 potent**, intoxicating, strong.

heal v. make or become healthy again.
▷ SYNONYMS: **1 cure**, make better, restore to health, treat. **2 get better**, be cured, recover, recuperate, mend, be on the mend. **3 put right**, repair, resolve, reconcile, settle; informal patch up.
■ **healer** n.

health n. **1** the state of being free from illness. **2** mental or physical condition.
▷ SYNONYMS: **1 well-being**, fitness, good condition, strength, robustness, vigour. **2** *her poor health forced her to retire:* **condition**, state of health, physical shape, constitution.
– ANTONYMS: illness.
□ **health farm** a place where people try to improve their health by dieting, exercise, etc. **health visitor** Brit. a nurse who visits patients etc. at home.

> **WORD LINKS**
> **salubrious** good for the health

healthy adj. (**healthier**, **healthiest**) **1** having or helping towards good health. **2** sensible or desirable. **3** very satisfactory in size or amount.
▷ SYNONYMS: **1 well**, fit, in good shape, in fine fettle, in tip-top condition, strong, fighting fit; informal in the pink. **2 wholesome**, good for you, health-giving, nutritious, nourishing, invigorating, sanitary, hygienic.
■ **healthily** adv.

heap n. **1** a pile of a substance or of a number of objects. **2** informal a large amount or number.
▷ SYNONYMS: **pile**, stack, mound, mountain.
• v. **1** put in or form a heap. **2** load heavily with.

hear v. (**hearing**, **heard**) **1** perceive a sound with the ears. **2** be told or aware of. **3** (**hear from**) be contacted by. **4** listen to. **5** judge a legal case.
▷ SYNONYMS: **1 make out**, catch, get, perceive, overhear. **2 learn**, find out, discover, gather, glean. **3 try**, judge, adjudicate on.
□ **hearsay** information received which may be unreliable.
■ **hearer** n.

hearing n. **1** the ability to hear. **2** an opportunity to state your case: *a fair hearing.* **3** a formal act of listening to evidence.
▷ SYNONYMS: **1 earshot**, hearing distance. **2 trial**, court case, enquiry, inquest, tribunal.
□ **hearing aid** a small amplifying device worn by a partially deaf person.

> **WORD LINKS**
> **auditory**, **aural** relating to hearing

hearse /herss/ n. a vehicle for carrying the coffin at a funeral.

heart n. **1** the organ that pumps blood around the body. **2** the central or innermost part. **3** capacity for love or compassion. **4** courage or enthusiasm. **5** (**hearts**) one of the four suits in a pack of playing cards.
▷ SYNONYMS: **1 centre**, middle, hub, core. **2 essence**, crux, core, nub, root, meat, substance, kernel; informal nitty-gritty. **3 compassion**, sympathy, humanity, fellow feeling, empathy, understanding, soul; emotions, feelings, sentiments. **4 enthusiasm**, spirit, determination, resolve, nerve, courage; Brit. informal bottle.
□ **break someone's heart** make someone very sad. **by heart** from memory. **heart attack** (or **heart failure**) a sudden failure of the heart

h

to function normally. **heartbeat** a pulsation of the heart. **heartburn** indigestion felt as a burning sensation in the chest. **heart-rending** very distressing. **heart-searching** examination of your feelings and motives. **heart-throb** informal a very attractive famous man. **heart-to-heart** (of a conversation) intimate. **heart-warming** emotionally uplifting.

> **WORD LINKS**
> **cardiac** relating to the heart
> **coronary** relating to the arteries of the heart
> **cardiology** the branch of medicine concerning the heart

h

heartache n. worry or grief.
▷ SYNONYMS: **anguish**, suffering, distress, unhappiness, grief, misery, sorrow, sadness, heartbreak, pain, hurt, worry, anxiety, trauma.
– ANTONYMS: happiness.
heartbreak n. extreme distress.
■ **heartbroken** adj.
heartbreaking adj. very upsetting.
▷ SYNONYMS: **distressing**, upsetting, disturbing, heart-rending, tragic, painful, sad, agonizing, harrowing, traumatic.
– ANTONYMS: comforting.
hearten v. make more cheerful or confident.
heartfelt adj. sincere; deeply felt.
▷ SYNONYMS: **sincere**, genuine, from the heart, earnest, profound, deep, whole-hearted, honest.
– ANTONYMS: insincere.
hearth n. the floor of a fireplace.
heartless adj. unfeeling.
▷ SYNONYMS: **unfeeling**, unsympathetic, unkind, uncaring, hard-hearted, cold, callous, cruel, merciless, pitiless, inhuman.
– ANTONYMS: compassionate.
■ **heartlessly** adv.
hearty adj. (**heartier**, **heartiest**)
1 enthusiastic and friendly. **2** strong and healthy. **3** heartfelt. **4** (of a meal) large.
▷ SYNONYMS: **1 enthusiastic**, exuberant, jovial, ebullient, cheerful, lively, loud, animated, vivacious, energetic, spirited. **2 robust**, healthy, hardy, fit, vigorous, sturdy, strong. **3 whole-hearted**, heartfelt, sincere, genuine, real. **4 substantial**, large, ample, satisfying, filling, generous.
■ **heartily** adv.
heat n. **1** the quality of being hot. **2** hot conditions. **3** strength of feeling. **4** a preliminary round in a

race or contest.
▷ SYNONYMS: **1 warmth**, high temperature; humidity. **2 passion**, intensity, vehemence, fervour, excitement, agitation, anger.
– ANTONYMS: coolness, apathy.
• v. **1** make or become hot. **2** (**heat up**) become more intense.
□ **heatstroke** a condition caused by excessive exposure to sun. **heatwave** a period of unusually hot weather. **on heat** (of a female mammal) ready to mate.

> **WORD LINKS**
> **thermal** relating to heat

heated adj. impassioned or excited: *a heated argument.*
▷ SYNONYMS: **1 vehement**, passionate, impassioned, animated, lively, acrimonious, angry, bitter, furious, fierce. **2 excited**, animated, worked up, wound up, keyed up; informal het up.
■ **heatedly** adv.
heater n. a device supplying heat.
heath n. an area of open uncultivated land covered with heather etc.
heathen n. a person who does not belong to a widely held religion.
heather n. a shrub with small purple flowers.
heating n. equipment used to provide heat.
heave v. (**heaving, heaved** or Naut. **hove**) **1** lift or move with great effort. **2** produce a sigh noisily. **3** rise and fall. **4** try to vomit.
▷ SYNONYMS: **1 haul**, pull, drag, tug; informal yank. **2 throw**, fling, cast, hurl, lob, pitch; informal chuck, sling. **3 let out**, breathe, give, emit, utter. **4 rise and fall**, roll, swell, surge, churn, seethe. **5 retch**, vomit, cough up; Brit. be sick; N. Amer. get sick; informal throw up, puke, chunder, chuck up, hurl, spew; N. Amer. informal barf.
heaven n. **1** (in various religions) the place where God or the gods live. **2** (**the heavens**) literary the sky. **3** a place or state of great happiness.
▷ SYNONYMS: **1 paradise**, the hereafter, the next world, the afterworld, nirvana, Zion, Elysium. **2 bliss**, happiness, delight, joy, paradise.
– ANTONYMS: hell.

> **WORD LINKS**
> **celestial** relating to heaven

heavenly adj. **1** of heaven or the sky. **2** informal wonderful.
▷ SYNONYMS: **1 divine**, angelic, holy, celestial. **2 celestial**, cosmic, stellar,

sidereal. **3 delightful**, wonderful, glorious, sublime, exquisite, beautiful, lovely, gorgeous, enchanting; *informal* divine, super, fantastic, fabulous.
□ **heavenly body** a planet, star, etc.

heavy adj. (**heavier**, **heaviest**) **1** of great weight. **2** thick or dense. **3** of more than the usual size, amount, or force. **4** doing something to excess. **5** done with or needing force or effort. **6** *informal* serious or difficult.
▷ SYNONYMS: **1** *heavy suitcases:* **weighty**, hefty, substantial, ponderous, solid, dense, cumbersome, unwieldy. **2** *a heavy blow:* **forceful**, hard, strong, violent, powerful, mighty, sharp, severe. **3** *heavy work:* **strenuous**, hard, physical, difficult, arduous, demanding, back-breaking, gruelling. **4** *heavy fighting:* **intense**, fierce, relentless, severe, serious. **5** *a heavy meal:* **substantial**, filling, stodgy, rich, big.
– ANTONYMS: light.
□ **heavy-handed** clumsy or insensitive. **heavy industry** industry producing heavy machinery and materials. **heavy metal** a type of loud rock music. **heavyweight** **1** the heaviest weight in boxing etc. **2** *informal* an influential person.
■ **heavily** adv. **heaviness** n.

Hebrew n. **1** a member of an ancient people living in what is now Israel and Palestine. **2** the language of the Hebrews.
■ **Hebraic** adj.

heckle v. interrupt a public speaker with comments or abuse.
■ **heckler** n.

hectare n. a unit of area, 10,000 sq. m (2.471 acres).

hectic adj. full of frantic activity.
▷ SYNONYMS: **frantic**, frenetic, frenzied, feverish, manic, busy, active, fast and furious.
– ANTONYMS: leisurely.
■ **hectically** adv.

hector v. talk to in a bullying way.

hedge n. a barrier of closely growing bushes.
• v. **1** surround with a hedge. **2** avoid making a definite statement or decision.
□ **hedgehog** a small mammal with a spiny coat. **hedgerow** bushes and trees bordering a field.

hedonism n. behaviour based on the belief that pleasure is the most thing important in life.
■ **hedonist** n. **hedonistic** adj.

heed v. pay attention to.
▷ SYNONYMS: **pay attention to**, take notice of, take note of, listen to, consider, take to heart, obey, adhere to, abide by, observe.
– ANTONYMS: disregard.
□ **pay** (or **take**) **heed** pay careful attention.
■ **heedless** adj. **heedlessly** adv.

heel n. **1** the back part of the foot below the ankle. **2** the part of a shoe supporting the heel.
• v. **1** renew the heel on a shoe. **2** (of a ship) tilt to one side.

hefty adj. (**heftier**, **heftiest**) large, heavy, and powerful.
▷ SYNONYMS: **1** burly, sturdy, strapping, bulky, strong, muscular, big, solid, well built; *informal* hulking, beefy. **2** powerful, violent, hard, forceful, mighty. **3** substantial, sizeable, considerable, stiff, large, heavy; *informal* whopping.
– ANTONYMS: light.

hegemony /hi-jem-uh-ni, hi-gem-uh-ni/ n. dominance of one group or state over another.

Hegira /hej-iruh/ n. Muhammad's departure from Mecca to Medina (AD 622).

heifer /hef-fer/ n. a young cow.

height n. **1** measurement from head to foot or from base to top. **2** distance above ground or sea level. **3** the quality of being tall or high. **4** a high place. **5** the most intense part. **6** an extreme example.
▷ SYNONYMS: **1** tallness, stature, elevation, altitude. **2** *mountain heights:* **summit**, top, peak, crest, crown, tip, cap, pinnacle. **3** *the height of their fame:* **highest point**, peak, zenith, pinnacle, acme, climax.
– ANTONYMS: width, nadir.

> **WORD LINKS**
> **acrophobia** fear of heights

heighten v. make or become higher or more intense.
▷ SYNONYMS: **intensify**, increase, enhance, add to, augment, boost, strengthen, deepen, magnify, reinforce.
– ANTONYMS: reduce.

heinous /hay-nuhss, hee-nuhss/ adj. very wicked.
▷ SYNONYMS: **odious**, wicked, evil, atrocious, monstrous, abominable, detestable, despicable, horrific, terrible, awful, abhorrent, loathsome, hideous, unspeakable, execrable.
– ANTONYMS: admirable.

h

heir /air/ n. (fem. **heiress**) a person entitled to inherit property or a rank.
▷ SYNONYMS: **successor**, next in line, inheritor, beneficiary, legatee.
□ **heirloom** a valuable object that has belonged to a family for several generations.

held past & past part. OF HOLD.

helical adj. like a helix.

helicopter n. an aircraft with horizontally revolving overhead blades.

heliport n. an airport for helicopters.

helium n. a light colourless gas that does not burn.

helix n. (pl. **helices**) a spiral.

hell n. **1** (in various religions) a place of punishment for the wicked after death. **2** a state or place of great suffering.
▷ SYNONYMS: **1 the underworld**, the netherworld, eternal damnation, perdition, hellfire, fire and brimstone, the Inferno, Hades. **2 misery**, torture, agony, purgatory, torment, a nightmare.
– ANTONYMS: heaven, bliss.
□ **hell-bent** recklessly determined. **hell for leather** as fast as possible. **hellhole** a very unpleasant place.
■ **hellish** adj.

> **WORD LINKS**
> **infernal** relating to hell

Hellenic adj. Greek.

hello (or **hallo**, **hullo**) exclam. used as a greeting or to attract attention.

helm n. a tiller or wheel for steering a ship or boat.
□ **helmsman** a person who steers a boat.

helmet n. a hard or padded protective hat.

help v. **1** make something easier for someone to do. **2** improve a situation. **3** serve food or drink to. **4** (**help yourself**) take without asking first. **5** (**cannot help**) be unable to stop yourself doing.
▷ SYNONYMS: **1 assist**, aid, abet, lend a hand, give assistance, come to the aid of, be of service, do someone a favour, do someone a good turn, support, rally round, pitch in, contribute. **2** *this injection should help the pain:* **relieve**, soothe, ease, alleviate, improve, lessen. **3** *he could not help laughing:* **resist**, avoid, refrain from, keep from, stop.
– ANTONYMS: hinder, impede.
• n. a person or thing that helps.
▷ SYNONYMS: **1 assistance**, aid, support,

succour. **2 relief**, alleviation, improvement, healing.
– ANTONYMS: hindrance.
□ **helpline** a phone service providing help with problems.

helper n. a person who helps.
▷ SYNONYMS: **assistant**, aide, deputy, auxiliary, supporter, second, mate, right-hand man/woman, attendant.

helpful adj. **1** ready to give help. **2** useful.
▷ SYNONYMS: **1 obliging**, of assistance, supportive, accommodating, cooperative, neighbourly, eager to please. **2 useful**, beneficial, valuable, constructive, informative, instructive. **3 handy**, useful, convenient, practical, easy-to-use, serviceable; informal neat, nifty.
– ANTONYMS: useless.
■ **helpfully** adv. **helpfulness** n.

helping n. a portion of food served.
▷ SYNONYMS: **portion**, serving, piece, slice, share, plateful; informal dollop.

helpless adj. **1** unable to manage without help. **2** uncontrollable.
▷ SYNONYMS: **dependent**, incapable, powerless, paralysed, defenceless, vulnerable, exposed, unprotected.
– ANTONYMS: independent.
■ **helplessly** adv. **helplessness** n.

helter-skelter adj. & adv. in disorderly haste.
• n. Brit. a spiral slide round a tower at a fair.

hem n. the edge of a piece of cloth or clothing turned under and sewn.
• v. (**hemming**, **hemmed**) **1** turn under and sew the edge of. **2** (**hem in**) surround and restrict.

hematology etc. US = HAEMATOLOGY etc.

hemisphere n. **1** a half of a sphere. **2** a half of the earth.
■ **hemispherical** adj.

hemlock n. a poisonous plant.

hemp n. a plant with fibres used to make rope, cloth, etc., and from which cannabis is made.

hen n. a female bird, esp. of a domestic fowl.
□ **hen night** (or **hen party**) Brit. an all-female celebration held for a woman about to get married. **henpecked** (of a man) nagged by his wife.

hence adv. **1** for this reason. **2** from now.
▷ SYNONYMS: **consequently**, as a consequence, for this reason, therefore, so, accordingly, as a result, that being so.
□ **henceforth** (or **henceforward**) from

this or that time on.

henchman n. derogatory a follower or assistant.

henna n. a reddish-brown dye.
■ **hennaed** adj.

henry n. (pl. **henries** or **henrys**) the basic unit of inductance.

hepatic adj. of the liver.

hepatitis n. a serious disease of the liver.

heptagon n. a plane figure with seven sides.
■ **heptagonal** adj.

heptathlon n. an athletic contest involving seven events.
■ **heptathlete** n.

her pron. used as the object of a verb or preposition to refer to a female previously mentioned.
• adj. belonging to her.

herald n. **1** hist. a person who carried official messages and made announcements. **2** a sign of something to come.
• v. be a sign of.

heraldry n. the system by which coats of arms are drawn up and regulated.
■ **heraldic** adj.

herb n. a plant used for flavouring or in medicine.
■ **herbal** adj.

herbaceous /her-**bay**-shuhss/ adj. (of plants) soft-stemmed.
□ **herbaceous border** a garden border containing plants which flower every year.

herbage n. herbaceous plants.

herbalism n. the use of plants in medicine.
■ **herbalist** n.

herbicide n. a substance used to destroy plants.

herbivore n. an animal that feeds on plants.
■ **herbivorous** adj.

Herculean adj. requiring great strength or effort.

herd n. **1** a large group of animals living or kept together. **2** a large crowd of people.
▷ SYNONYMS: **drove**, flock, pack, fold, swarm, mass, crowd, horde.
• v. **1** move in a group. **2** look after livestock.
□ **herdsman** the owner or keeper of a herd of animals.

here adv. in, at, or to this place, position, or point.

hereabouts adv. near this place.

hereafter adv. from now on.
• n. (**the hereafter**) life after death.

hereby adv. by this means.

hereditary adj. of or by inheritance.
▷ SYNONYMS: **1 inherited**, bequeathed, handed down, passed down, family, ancestral. **2 genetic**, inborn, inherited, inbred, innate, in the family, in the blood, in the genes.

heredity n. **1** the passing on of characteristics from one generation to another. **2** the inheriting of a title etc.

herein adv. in this document etc.

heresy n. (pl. **heresies**) a belief or opinion contrary to traditional religious doctrine.

heretic n. a person believing in a heresy.
■ **heretical** adj.

hereto adv. to this.

herewith adv. with this.

heritage n. valued things such as historic buildings, passed down from previous generations.
▷ SYNONYMS: **1 tradition**, history, past, background, culture, customs. **2 ancestry**, lineage, descent, extraction, parentage, roots, heredity, birth.

hermaphrodite n. a person, animal, or plant having both male and female sex organs or characteristics.

hermetic adj. airtight.
■ **hermetically** adv.

hermit n. a person living in solitude, esp. for religious reasons.
▷ SYNONYMS: **recluse**, loner, ascetic; historical anchorite, anchoress; old use eremite.

hermitage n. the home of a hermit.

hernia n. a condition in which part of an organ protrudes through the wall of the cavity containing it.

hero n. (pl. **heroes**) **1** a person admired for their courage or actions. **2** the chief male character in a story.
▷ SYNONYMS: **protagonist**, starring role, lead, leading man; informal good guy.
– ANTONYMS: villain.

heroic adj. very brave.
▷ SYNONYMS: **brave**, courageous, valiant, intrepid, bold, fearless, daring, plucky; informal gutsy, spunky.
– ANTONYMS: cowardly.
• n. (**heroics**) brave behaviour.
■ **heroically** adv.

heroin n. a highly addictive illegal drug.

heroine n. **1** a woman admired for her courage or achievements. **2** the chief female character in a story.
▷ SYNONYMS: **protagonist**, starring role,

h

lead, leading lady; prima donna, diva.

heroism n. great bravery.
▷ SYNONYMS: **bravery**, courage, valour, daring, fearlessness, pluck; informal guts, spunk; Brit. informal bottle; N. Amer. informal moxie.
– ANTONYMS: cowardice.

heron n. a long-legged wading bird.

herpes /her-peez/ n. a viral disease causing blisters.

herring n. (pl. **herring** or **herrings**) an edible fish.
□ **herringbone** a pattern of columns of short slanting parallel lines.

hers possess. pron. belonging to her.

| USAGE No apostrophe: hers. |

herself pron. **1** used when a female who performs an action is also affected by it. **2** she or her personally.

hertz n. (pl. **hertz**) the basic unit of frequency.

hesitant adj. reluctant or uncertain.
▷ SYNONYMS: **1 uncertain**, undecided, unsure, doubtful, dubious, ambivalent, in two minds, wavering, vacillating, irresolute, indecisive; Brit. havering, humming and hawing; informal iffy. **2 timid**, diffident, shy, bashful, insecure, nervous.
– ANTONYMS: certain, decisive, confident.
■ **hesitancy** n. **hesitantly** adv.

hesitate v. **1** pause indecisively. **2** be reluctant to do.
▷ SYNONYMS: **1 pause**, delay, wait, stall, be uncertain, be unsure, be doubtful, be indecisive, vacillate, waver; Brit. haver, hum and haw; informal dilly-dally. **2** *don't hesitate to ask:* **be reluctant**, be unwilling, be disinclined, scruple, have misgivings about, have qualms about, think twice about.
■ **hesitation** n.

hessian n. a strong, coarse fabric.

heterodox adj. not following traditional standards or beliefs.
■ **heterodoxy** n.

heterogeneous adj. varied.
■ **heterogeneity** n.

heterosexual adj. sexually attracted to people of the opposite sex.
• n. a heterosexual person.
■ **heterosexuality** n.

heuristic adj. allowing someone to learn something for themselves.

hew v. (**hewing**, **hewed**, past part. **hewn** or **hewed**) chop or cut with an axe etc.

hex n. US a magic spell.

hexagon n. a plane figure with six sides.

■ **hexagonal** adj.

hexameter n. a line of verse made up of six metrical feet.

heyday n. the period when someone is most successful or active.

HGV abbrev. Brit. heavy goods vehicle.

hiatus /hy-ay-tuhss/ n. (pl. **hiatuses**) a pause or gap in a sequence.

hibernate v. spend the winter in a sleep-like state.
■ **hibernation** n.

Hibernian adj. Irish.
• n. an Irish person.

hibiscus n. a plant with large brightly coloured flowers.

hiccup (or **hiccough**) n. **1** a gulping sound in the throat. **2** a minor setback.
• v. (**hiccuping**, **hiccuped**) make the sound of a hiccup.

hide v. (**hiding**, **hid**; past part. **hidden**) **1** put or keep out of sight. **2** conceal yourself. **3** keep secret.
▷ SYNONYMS: **1 conceal**, secrete, put out of sight, cache; informal stash. **2 obscure**, block out, blot out, obstruct, cloud, shroud, veil, eclipse, camouflage. **3 conceal yourself**, secrete yourself, take cover, lie low, go to ground; informal hole up. **4 keep secret**, conceal, cover up, keep quiet about, hush up, suppress, disguise, mask; informal keep a lid on.
– ANTONYMS: reveal.
• n. **1** Brit. a concealed shelter for observing wildlife. **2** the skin of an animal.

hideaway (or **hideout**) n. a hiding place.
▷ SYNONYMS: **retreat**, refuge, hiding place, safe house, den, bolt-hole; informal hidey-hole.

hidebound adj. unwilling to accept new ideas.

hideous adj. very ugly.
▷ SYNONYMS: **1 ugly**, repulsive, repellent, unsightly, revolting, grotesque. **2 horrific**, terrible, appalling, awful, dreadful, frightful, horrible, horrendous, horrifying, shocking, sickening, gruesome, ghastly.
– ANTONYMS: beautiful, pleasant.
■ **hideously** adv. **hideousness** n.

hiding n. a severe beating.
▷ SYNONYMS: **beating**, thrashing, whipping, drubbing; informal licking, belting, pasting, walloping.

hierarchy n. (pl. **hierarchies**) a system ranking people or things one above the other according to status or importance.
▷ SYNONYMS: **ranking**, order, pecking order, grading, ladder, scale.

■ **hierarchical** adj.

hieroglyphics pl. n. a form of writing consisting of pictorial symbols.
■ **hieroglyphic** adj.

hi-fi adj. of high fidelity.
● n. (pl. **hi-fis**) a set of high-fidelity equipment.

higgledy-piggledy adv. & adj. in disorder.

high adj. **1** extending far upwards. **2** of a specified height. **3** far above ground or sea level. **4** large in amount, value, size, etc. **5** at the peak. **6** great in status. **7** (of a sound) not deep or low. **8** informal under the influence of drugs or alcohol. **9** (of food) beginning to go bad.
▷ SYNONYMS: **1 tall**, lofty, towering, giant, big, multi-storey, high-rise, elevated. **2 high-ranking**, leading, top, prominent, senior, influential, powerful, important, exalted; N. Amer. ranking. **3 inflated**, excessive, unreasonable, expensive, exorbitant, extortionate, informal steep, stiff. **4 high-pitched**, shrill, piercing, squeaky, penetrating, soprano, treble, falsetto.
– ANTONYMS: low, deep.
● n. **1** a high level. **2** an area of high atmospheric pressure. **3** informal a state of high spirits.
● adv. at or to a high or specified level.
– ANTONYMS: low.
□ **highbrow** intellectual or refined. **higher education** education at university etc. **high fidelity** the reproduction of sound with little distortion. **high-handed** using authority arrogantly. **highland** (or **highlands**) an area of high or mountainous land. **high-rise** (of a building) with many storeys. **high school** a secondary school. **high seas** the areas of the sea not under the control of any one country. **high season** Brit. the most popular time for a holiday. **high-spirited** lively and cheerful. **high street** Brit. the main shopping street of a town. **high tea** Brit. a meal eaten in the late afternoon or early evening. **high-tech** involving advanced technology. **high tide** (or **high water**) the tide when it is at its highest level. **high time** at or past the time when something should have happened.

highlight n. **1** an outstanding part of an event etc. **2** a bright area in a picture. **3** (**highlights**) dyed light streaks in the hair.
▷ SYNONYMS: **high point**, climax, peak, pinnacle, height, zenith, summit, focus, feature.
● v. **1** draw attention to. **2** create highlights in hair.
▷ SYNONYMS: **spotlight**, call attention to, focus on, underline, show up, bring out, accentuate, accent, stress, emphasize.
– ANTONYMS: play down.

highly adv. **1** to a high degree. **2** favourably.
□ **highly strung** Brit. nervous and easily upset.

Highness n. (**His, Your,** etc. **Highness**) a title given to a royal person.

highway n. **1** a main road. **2** a public road.
□ **highwayman** hist. a man who held up and robbed travellers.

hijack v. illegally seize control of an aircraft etc. while it is travelling.
▷ SYNONYMS: **commandeer**, seize, take over, appropriate, expropriate.
● n. an act of hijacking.
■ **hijacker** n.

hike n. **1** a long walk. **2** a sharp increase.
▷ SYNONYMS: **1 walk**, trek, tramp, trudge, slog, march, ramble. **2 increase**, rise.
● v. **1** go on a hike. **2** increase sharply.
▷ SYNONYMS: **1 walk**, trek, tramp, trudge, slog, march, ramble, backpack. **2 increase**, raise, up, put up, push up; informal jack up, bump up.
■ **hiker** n.

hilarious adj. very funny.
▷ SYNONYMS: **very funny**, hysterical, uproarious, rib-tickling; informal side-splitting, priceless, a scream, a hoot.
■ **hilariously** adv. **hilarity** n.

hill n. a raised area of land, lower than a mountain.
▷ SYNONYMS: **high ground**, hillock, hill-side, rise, mound, knoll, hummock, fell, mountain; Scottish brae.
■ **hilly** adj.

hillbilly n. (pl. **hillbillies**) US informal an unsophisticated country person.

hillock n. a small hill.

hilt n. the handle of a sword or dagger.
□ **to the hilt** completely.

him pron. used as the object of a verb or preposition to refer to a male previously mentioned.

himself pron. **1** used when a male who performs an action is also affected by it. **2** he or him personally.

hind adj. at the back.
● n. a female deer.

hinder v. delay or obstruct.
▷ SYNONYMS: **hamper**, impede, inhibit, thwart, foil, delay, interfere with, slow down, hold back, hold up,

h

restrict, handicap, hamstring.
ANTONYMS: facilitate.

Hindi n. a language of northern India.

hindmost adj. furthest back.

hindrance n. something that hinders.
▷ SYNONYMS: **impediment**, obstacle, barrier, obstruction, handicap, hurdle, restraint, restriction, encumbrance, complication, delay, drawback, setback, difficulty, inconvenience, hitch, stumbling block, fly in the ointment, hiccup; Brit. spanner in the works.
– ANTONYMS: aid, help.

hindsight n. understanding of something after it has happened.

Hindu n. (pl. **Hindus**) a follower of Hinduism.

Hinduism n. a major religion of the Indian subcontinent.

hinge n. a movable joint or mechanism by which a door, lid, etc. opens and closes.
• v. **1** attach with a hinge. **2** (**hinge on**) depend on.

hint n. **1** a slight or indirect suggestion. **2** a slight trace. **3** a piece of practical information.
▷ SYNONYMS: **1 clue**, inkling, suggestion, indication, sign, signal, intimation. **2 tip**, suggestion, pointer, guideline, recommendation. **3 trace**, touch, suspicion, suggestion, dash, soupçon; informal smidgen, tad.
• v. suggest indirectly.
▷ SYNONYMS: **imply**, insinuate, intimate, suggest, refer to, drive at, mean; informal get at.

hinterland n. the remote areas of a country away from the coast.

hip n. **1** the projection of the pelvis on each side of the body. **2** the fruit of a rose.

hip hop n. a style of pop music featuring rap with an electronic backing.

hippo n. (pl. **hippo** or **hippos**) a hippopotamus.

hippopotamus n. (pl. **hippopotamuses** or **hippopotami**) a large African river mammal with huge jaws.

hippy (or **hippie**) n. (pl. **hippies**) a person who rejects traditional values and dresses unconventionally.

hire v. **1** use or allow to be used temporarily in return for payment. **2** employ someone.
▷ SYNONYMS: **1 rent**, lease, charter. **2 employ**, engage, recruit, appoint, take on, sign up.
– ANTONYMS: dismiss.

• n. the act of hiring.
□ **hireling** someone willing to do any paid work. **hire purchase** Brit. a system of buying by payment in instalments.

hirsute /her-syoot/ adj. hairy.

his adj. & possess. pron. belonging to a male previously mentioned.

Hispanic adj. of Spain or a Spanish-speaking country.

hiss v. **1** make a sharp sound as of the letter *s*, esp. in disapproval. **2** whisper urgently.
▷ SYNONYMS: **1 fizz**, whistle, wheeze. **2 jeer**, catcall, whistle, hoot.
– ANTONYMS: cheer.
• n. a hissing sound.
▷ SYNONYMS: **1 fizz**, whistle, wheeze. **2 jeer**, catcall, whistle, abuse, derision.
– ANTONYMS: cheer.

histamine n. a substance released by cells in response to an allergy or injury.

histology n. the study of animal or plant tissues.
■ **histologist** n.

historian n. an expert in history.

historic adj. important in history, or likely to be so in the future.
▷ SYNONYMS: **significant**, notable, important, momentous, memorable, groundbreaking; informal earth-shattering.

historical adj. **1** of history. **2** belonging to or set in the past.
▷ SYNONYMS: **1 documented**, recorded, chronicled, authentic, factual, actual. **2 past**, bygone, ancient, old, former.
■ **historically** adv.

history n. (pl. **histories**) **1** the study of past events. **2** the past. **3** the past events connected with someone or something. **4** a record of past events.
▷ SYNONYMS: **1 the past**, former times, the olden days, yesterday, antiquity. **2 chronicle**, archive, record, report, narrative, account, study. **3 background**, past, life story, experiences, record.

histrionic adj. excessively dramatic.
• n. (**histrionics**) exaggerated behaviour.

hit v. (**hitting**, **hit**) **1** bring the hand or an object into sudden forceful contact with. **2** come into sudden forceful contact with. **3** cause harm or distress to. **4** reach a place, target, or level.
▷ SYNONYMS: **1 strike**, smack, slap, beat, punch, thump, thrash, batter, club, pummel, cuff, swat; informal whack, wallop, bash, clout, belt, clobber;

Brit. informal **slosh**, **stick one on**; N. Amer. informal **slug**; literary informal **smite**.
2 crash into, run into, smash into, knock into, bump into, plough into, collide with, meet head-on. **3** devastate, affect badly, upset, shatter, crush, traumatize; informal knock sideways; Brit. informal knock for six.
• n. **1** an instance of hitting or being hit. **2** a success. **3** an instance of accessing a website.
▷ SYNONYMS: **1** blow, slap, smack, thump, punch, knock, bang; informal whack, wallop, bash, clout, belt; N. Amer. informal slug. **2** success, sell-out, winner, triumph, sensation, best-seller; informal smash hit, chart-topper, crowd-puller.
□ **hit it off** informal like one another. **hit man** a person paid to kill someone.

hitch v. **1** move with a jerk. **2** informal travel by hitchhiking. **3** fasten with a rope.
▷ SYNONYMS: **1** pull, lift, raise; informal yank. **2** harness, yoke, couple, fasten, connect, attach.
• n. a temporary difficulty.
▷ SYNONYMS: **problem**, difficulty, snag, setback, obstacle, complication; informal glitch, hiccup.
□ **get hitched** informal get married.
hitchhike travel by getting free lifts in passing vehicles.

hither adv. to or towards this place.

hitherto adv. until this time.

HIV abbrev. human immunodeficiency virus (causing Aids).

hive n. **1** a beehive. **2** (**hives**) an allergic rash.
• v. (**hive off**) transfer part of a business to new ownership.

HM abbrev. Her (or His) Majesty or Majesty's.

HMS abbrev. Her (or His) Majesty's Ship.

HND abbrev. Higher National Diploma.

hoard n. a secret store of something valued.
▷ SYNONYMS: **cache**, stockpile, store, collection, supply, reserve; informal stash.
• v. build up a store of.
▷ SYNONYMS: **stockpile**, store up, put aside, put by, lay by, set aside, cache, save, squirrel away; informal salt away.
– ANTONYMS: squander.
■ **hoarder** n.

> USAGE Don't confuse **hoard** with **horde**, which means 'a large group or crowd'.

hoarding n. Brit. a large board for displaying advertisements.

hoar frost n. a feathery frost.

hoarse adj. (of a voice) rough and harsh.
▷ SYNONYMS: **rough**, harsh, croaky, throaty, gruff, husky, grating, rasping.
■ **hoarsely** adv. **hoarseness** n.

hoary adj. **1** having grey hair. **2** old and unoriginal.

hoax n. a deception or trick, esp. an unpleasant one.
▷ SYNONYMS: **practical joke**, prank, trick, deception, fraud; informal con, spoof, wind-up, scam.
• v. deceive with a hoax.
■ **hoaxer** n.

hob n. Brit. the flat top of a cooker, with hotplates or burners.

hobble v. **1** walk with difficulty or painfully. **2** strap together the legs of a horse to limit its movement.
▷ SYNONYMS: **limp**, shamble, totter, dodder, stagger, stumble.

hobby n. (pl. **hobbies**) a leisure activity done regularly for pleasure.
▷ SYNONYMS: **pastime**, leisure activity, sideline, diversion, relaxation, recreation, amusement.
□ **hobby horse 1** a person's favourite topic. **2** a toy consisting of a stick with a model of a horse's head.

hobgoblin n. a mischievous imp.

hobnail n. a heavy-headed nail for the soles of boots.
■ **hobnailed** adj.

hobnob v. (**hobnobbing**, **hobnobbed**) informal socialize with important people.

Hobson's choice n. a choice of taking what is offered or nothing at all.

hock n. **1** the middle joint in the back leg of a four-legged animal. **2** Brit. a dry white German wine.

hockey n. a game played with curved sticks and a small hard ball.

hocus-pocus n. meaningless talk used to deceive.

hod n. **1** a V-shaped trough on a pole for carrying mortar or bricks. **2** a container for coal.

hodgepodge US = HOTCHPOTCH.

hoe n. a gardening tool with a thin metal blade.
• v. use a hoe to cut through earth or weeds.

hog n. a castrated male pig reared for its meat.
• v. (**hogging**, **hogged**) informal take or hoard selfishly.

Hogmanay n. (in Scotland) New Year's Eve.

h

hoick v. Brit. informal lift or pull with a jerk.

hoi polloi /hoy puh-**loy**/ pl. n. the ordinary people.

hoist v. haul or lift up.
▷ SYNONYMS: **raise**, lift, haul up, heave up, winch up, pull up, elevate.
• n. a piece of equipment for hoisting.
▷ SYNONYMS: **crane**, winch, pulley, windlass.

hoity-toity adj. snobbish.

hokum n. informal **1** nonsense. **2** overused or sentimental material in a film etc.

hold v. (holding, held) **1** grasp, carry, or support. **2** contain or be able to contain. **3** have, own, or occupy. **4** keep or detain. **5** stay or keep at a certain level. **6** arrange and take part in. **7** regard in a specified way.
▷ SYNONYMS: **1 clasp**, clutch, grasp, grip, clench, cling to, hold on to, embrace, hug, squeeze. **2 take**, contain, accommodate, fit, have room for. **3** *he still holds a UK passport*: **have**, own, possess, bear. **4 detain**, imprison, lock up, keep behind bars, confine, intern, incarcerate. **5 maintain**, consider, take the view, believe, think, feel, deem, be of the opinion, rule, decide; informal reckon. **6 convene**, call, summon, conduct, organize, run.
– ANTONYMS: release.
• n. **1** a grip. **2** a place to grip while climbing. **3** a degree of control. **4** a storage space in a ship or aircraft.
▷ SYNONYMS: **1 grip**, grasp, clasp, clutch. **2 influence**, power, control, grip, dominance, authority, sway.
□ **holdall** Brit. a large, soft bag. **hold on 1** wait. **2** keep going in difficult circumstances. **hold out 1** resist difficult circumstances. **2** continue to be sufficient. **hold up 1** delay. **2** rob with a gun. **no holds barred** without restrictions.

holder n. **1** a device for holding something. **2** a person who holds or possesses something.
▷ SYNONYMS: **container**, receptacle, case, cover, housing, sheath.

holding n. **1** land held by lease. **2** (holdings) stocks and property owned by someone.

hold-up n. **1** a delay. **2** an armed robbery.
▷ SYNONYMS: **1 delay**, setback, hitch, snag, difficulty, problem, glitch, hiccup; traffic jam, tailback; informal snarl-up. **2 robbery**, raid, armed robbery, mugging; informal stick-up; N. Amer. informal heist.

hole n. **1** a hollow space or opening in an object or surface. **2** informal an awkward or unpleasant place or situation.
▷ SYNONYMS: **1 opening**, aperture, orifice, gap, space, interstice, fissure, vent, chink, breach, crack, rupture, puncture. **2 pit**, crater, depression, hollow, cavern, cave, chamber. **3 burrow**, lair, den, earth, sett.
• v. **1** make a hole in. **2** Golf hit the ball into a hole.
■ **holey** adj.

Holi /**hoh**-li/ n. a Hindu spring festival.

holiday n. **1** Brit. a period spent away from home for enjoyment. **2** a day when most organizations are closed.
▷ SYNONYMS: **break**, rest, recess, time off, leave, day off, festival, feast day; N. Amer. vacation.
• v. spend a holiday.
■ **holidaymaker** n.

holistic adj. treating the whole person rather than just the symptoms of a disease.
■ **holism** n.

hollow adj. **1** having empty space inside. **2** curving inwards. **3** worthless.
▷ SYNONYMS: **1 empty**, hollowed out, void. **2 sunken**, deep-set, concave, depressed, recessed. **3 worthless**, meaningless, empty, profitless, fruitless, pointless, pyrrhic. **4 insincere**, false, deceitful, hypocritical, sham, untrue.
– ANTONYMS: solid, convex.
• n. **1** a hole or sunken place. **2** a small valley.
▷ SYNONYMS: **1 hole**, pit, cavity, crater, trough, depression, indentation, dip. **2 valley**, vale, dale, dell.
• v. form by making a hole.
▷ SYNONYMS: **gouge**, scoop, dig, cut, excavate, channel.

holly n. an evergreen shrub with prickly leaves and red berries.

hollyhock n. a tall plant with large showy flowers.

holmium n. a soft metallic element.

holocaust n. destruction or killing on a mass scale.

hologram n. a three-dimensional photographic image.
■ **holographic** adj.

holster n. a holder for a handgun.

holy adj. (holier, holiest) **1** dedicated to God or a religious purpose. **2** morally and spiritually good.
▷ SYNONYMS: **1 saintly**, godly, pious, religious, devout, God-fearing, spiritual. **2 sacred**, consecrated,

hallowed, sanctified, venerated, revered.
– ANTONYMS: sinful, irreligious.
■ **holiness** n.

homage n. a public act of respect shown to someone.
▷ SYNONYMS: **respect**, honour, reverence, worship, admiration, esteem, adulation, tribute.
– ANTONYMS: contempt.

home n. **1** the place where someone lives. **2** an institution for people needing special care.
▷ SYNONYMS: **1 residence**, house, accommodation, property, quarters, lodgings, address, place; informal pad; formal abode, dwelling. **2 homeland**, native land, home town, birthplace, roots, fatherland, mother country, motherland. **3 institution**, hospice, shelter, refuge, retreat, asylum, hostel.
• adj. **1** of a person's home or country. **2** (of a match) played on a team's own ground.
▷ SYNONYMS: **domestic**, internal, local, national.
– ANTONYMS: foreign, international.
• adv. **1** to or at a person's home. **2** to the intended position.
• v. (of an animal) return by instinct to its territory.
□ **home in on** move or be aimed towards. **homeland** a person's native land. **home page** the main page of an Internet site. **homesick** missing your home during a time away from it. **home truth** an unpleasant fact about yourself. **homework** school work to be done at home.
■ **homeward** adj. & adv. **homewards** adv.

homeless adj. having nowhere to live.
▷ SYNONYMS: **of no fixed abode**, without a roof over your head, on the streets, vagrant, sleeping rough, destitute.

homely adj. **1** Brit. simple but comfortable. **2** Brit. unsophisticated. **3** N. Amer. unattractive.
▷ SYNONYMS: **1 cosy**, comfortable, snug, welcoming, friendly; informal comfy. **2 unattractive**, plain, unprepossessing, ugly; Brit. informal no oil painting.

homeopathy (or **homoeopathy**) n. a system of treating diseases by tiny doses of substances that would normally produce symptoms of the disease.
■ **homeopath** n. **homeopathic** adj.

homicide n. the killing of another person.
▷ SYNONYMS: **murder**, manslaughter,

killing, assassination, slaughter, butchery.
■ **homicidal** adj.

homily n. (pl. **homilies**) a talk on a moral or religious issue.

hominid n. a member of a family of primates including humans and their prehistoric ancestors.

homogeneous /hom-uh-**jee**-ni-uhss/ adj. **1** alike. **2** made up of parts of the same kind.
■ **homogeneity** n.

homogenize (or **-ise**) v. **1** treat milk so that the cream does not separate. **2** make alike.

homograph n. a word with the same spelling as another but a different meaning.

homonym n. a word having the same spelling and pronunciation as another but a different meaning.

homophobia n. hatred or fear of homosexuality and homosexuals.
■ **homophobe** n. **homophobic** adj.

homophone n. a word with the same pronunciation as another.

Homo sapiens n. the species to which modern humans belong.

homosexual adj. sexually attracted to people of your own sex.
• n. a homosexual person.
■ **homosexuality** n.

hone v. **1** make better. **2** sharpen.

honest adj. **1** truthful and sincere. **2** fairly earned.
▷ SYNONYMS: **1** an honest man: **upright**, honourable, principled, virtuous, good, decent, law-abiding, trustworthy, scrupulous, ethical, upstanding, right-minded. **2** I haven't been honest with you: **truthful**, sincere, candid, frank, open, forthright, straight; informal upfront.
– ANTONYMS: dishonest, insincere.

honestly adv. **1** in an honest way. **2** really.
▷ SYNONYMS: **1 fairly**, lawfully, legally, legitimately, honourably, decently, ethically; informal on the level. **2 sincerely**, genuinely, truthfully, truly, wholeheartedly, to be honest, to be frank, in all honesty, in all sincerity.

honesty n. the quality of being honest.
▷ SYNONYMS: **1 integrity**, uprightness, honour, righteousness, virtue, goodness, probity, trustworthiness. **2 sincerity**, candour, frankness, directness, truthfulness, truth, openness, straightforwardness.
– ANTONYMS: dishonesty, insincerity.

honey n. (pl. **honeys**) a sweet, sticky

fluid made by bees from nectar.
◻ **honeybee** the common bee.
honeycomb n. a structure of six-sided wax compartments made by bees to store honey and eggs. **honeydew** a type of melon with sweet green flesh. **honeymoon 1** a holiday taken by a newly married couple. **2** an initial period of goodwill. **honeysuckle** a climbing shrub with scented flowers.

honk n. **1** the cry of a goose. **2** the sound of a car horn.
● v. make a honk.

honorarium n. (pl. **honorariums** or **honoraria**) a voluntary payment for services offered without charge.

honorary adj. **1** given as an honour. **2** Brit. (of a position or its holder) unpaid.
▷ SYNONYMS: **1** titular, nominal, in name only, unofficial, token. **2** unpaid, unsalaried, voluntary, volunteer.

honour (US **honor**) n. **1** great respect. **2** a clear sense of what is morally right. **3** a privilege. **4** an award for achievement. **5** (**honours**) a university course of a higher level than an ordinary one.
▷ SYNONYMS: **1** integrity, honesty, uprightness, morality, probity, principles, high-mindedness, decency, scrupulousness, fairness, justness. **2** distinction, privilege, glory, kudos, cachet, prestige. **3** reputation, good name, character, repute, image, standing, status. **4** privilege, pleasure, compliment.
– ANTONYMS: shame.
● v. **1** regard or treat with great respect. **2** keep an agreement.
▷ SYNONYMS: **1** respect, esteem, admire, look up to, value, cherish, revere, venerate. **2** applaud, acclaim, praise, salute, recognize, celebrate, pay tribute to. **3** fulfil, observe, keep, obey, heed, follow, carry out, keep to, abide by, adhere to, comply with, conform to, be true to.
– ANTONYMS: disobey, break.

honourable (US **honorable**) adj. deserving or bringing honour.
▷ SYNONYMS: **1** honest, moral, principled, righteous, decent, respectable, virtuous, good, upstanding, upright, noble, fair, trustworthy, law-abiding. **2** illustrious, distinguished, eminent, great, glorious, prestigious.
– ANTONYMS: dishonourable.
■ **honourably** adv.

hood n. **1** a covering for the head and neck. **2** Brit. a folding waterproof cover of a vehicle or pram. **3** US a car bonnet.

4 informal a gangster or gunman.
■ **hooded** adj.

hoodlum n. a gangster or violent criminal.

hoodoo n. a run or cause of bad luck.

hoodwink v. deceive or trick.

hoody (or **hoodie**) n. (pl. **hoodies**) **1** a hooded top. **2** informal a youth wearing a hooded top.

hoof n. (pl. **hoofs** or **hooves**) the horny part of the foot of a horse, cow, etc.
■ **hoofed** adj.

hook n. **1** a curved object for catching hold of things or hanging things on. **2** a short punch made with the elbow bent.
▷ SYNONYMS: **peg**, nail; fastener, clasp, hasp, clip.
● v. **1** catch or fasten with a hook. **2** (**hook up**) link to electronic equipment. **3** (**hook up**) meet or join another person or group of people.
▷ SYNONYMS: attach, hitch, fasten, fix, secure, hang, clasp.
◻ **hookworm** an intestinal worm with hook-like mouthparts.

hookah n. an oriental tobacco pipe with a long tube to draw the smoke through water.

hooked adj. **1** having or resembling a hook. **2** informal addicted or very interested.
▷ SYNONYMS: **1** curved, hook-shaped, aquiline, angular, bent. **2** *he's hooked on science fiction:* addicted to, enthusiastic about, keen on, obsessed with, fanatical about; informal mad about, crazy about, wild about.

hooligan n. a violent young troublemaker.
▷ SYNONYMS: lout, thug, tearaway, vandal, delinquent, ruffian, troublemaker; Austral. larrikin; informal tough, bruiser; Brit. informal yob, yobbo, lager lout; Scottish informal ned.
■ **hooliganism** n.

hoop n. **1** a rigid circular band. **2** a large ring used as a toy.
▷ SYNONYMS: ring, band, circle, wheel, circlet, loop.
■ **hooped** adj.

hoopla n. Brit. a game in which rings are thrown over a prize.

hoopoe n. a crested bird.

hooray exclam. hurrah.

hoot n. **1** a low sound made by owls or a hooter. **2** a short laugh or mocking shout. **3** informal an amusing person or thing.
● v. make a hoot.

hooter n. a siren, steam whistle, or horn.

Hoover Brit. n. trademark a vacuum cleaner.
• v. (**hoover**) clean with a vacuum cleaner.

hooves pl. of HOOF.

hop v. (**hopping**, **hopped**) **1** jump along on one foot. **2** (of an animal) jump along. **3** informal move or go quickly.
▷ SYNONYMS: **jump**, bound, spring, bounce, skip, leap, prance, caper.
• n. **1** a hopping movement. **2** a short journey. **3** a plant used to flavour beer.
□ **hopscotch** a children's game of hopping into and over marked squares. **on the hop** Brit. informal unprepared.

hope n. **1** a feeling that something wanted may happen. **2** a cause for hope. **3** something wished for.
▷ SYNONYMS: **1** optimism, expectation, confidence, faith, belief. **2** aspiration, desire, wish, expectation, ambition, aim, plan, dream.
– ANTONYMS: pessimism.
• v. expect and want to happen.
▷ SYNONYMS: **1** expect, anticipate, look for, be hopeful of, dream of. **2** aim, intend, have in mind, plan.

hopeful adj. feeling or inspiring hope.
▷ SYNONYMS: **1** optimistic, full of hope, confident, sanguine, positive, buoyant, bullish, upbeat. **2** promising, encouraging, heartening, reassuring, favourable, optimistic.
– ANTONYMS: pessimistic, discouraging.

hopefully adv. **1** in a hopeful way. **2** it is to be hoped that.
▷ SYNONYMS: **1** optimistically, full of hope, confidently, buoyantly, expectantly. **2** all being well, if all goes well, God willing, with luck, touch wood, fingers crossed.

hopeless adj. **1** feeling or causing despair. **2** very bad or unskilful.
▷ SYNONYMS: **1** forlorn, beyond hope, lost, irreparable, irreversible, incurable, impossible, futile. **2** bad, poor, awful, terrible, dreadful, appalling, atrocious, incompetent; informal pathetic, useless, lousy, rotten; Brit. informal rubbish.
– ANTONYMS: competent.
■ **hopelessly** adv.

hopper n. a tapering container that empties its contents at the bottom.

horde n. a large group or crowd.
▷ SYNONYMS: **crowd**, mob, pack, gang, troop, army, swarm, mass, throng.

> **USAGE** Don't confuse **horde** with **hoard**, which means 'a store of something valued'.

horizon n. **1** the line at which the earth's surface and the sky appear to meet. **2** the limit of a person's understanding or interests.

horizontal adj. parallel to the horizon.
▷ SYNONYMS: **level**, flat, parallel.
– ANTONYMS: vertical.
■ **horizontally** adv.

hormone n. a substance produced in the body that controls the action of cells or tissues.
■ **hormonal** adj.

horn n. **1** a hard bony growth on the heads of cattle, sheep, etc. **2** the substance of a horn. **3** a wind instrument shaped like a cone or wound into a spiral. **4** an instrument sounding a warning.
□ **hornpipe** a lively solo dance traditionally performed by sailors.
■ **horned** adj.

hornblende n. a dark brown, black, or green mineral.

hornet n. a large wasp.

horny adj. (**hornier**, **horniest**) **1** of or like horn. **2** informal sexually aroused.

horology n. **1** the study and measurement of time. **2** the making of clocks and watches.

horoscope n. a forecast of events based on the positions of stars.

horrendous adj. very unpleasant or horrifying.
■ **horrendously** adv.

horrible adj. **1** causing horror. **2** very unpleasant.
▷ SYNONYMS: **1** dreadful, awful, terrible, shocking, appalling, horrifying, horrific, horrendous, grisly, ghastly, gruesome, harrowing, unspeakable, abhorrent. **2** nasty, horrid, disagreeable, obnoxious, disgusting, hateful, odious, objectionable, insufferable.
– ANTONYMS: pleasant.
■ **horribly** adv.

horrid adj. horrible.

horrific adj. causing horror.
▷ SYNONYMS: **dreadful**, horrendous, horrible, terrible, atrocious, horrifying, shocking, appalling, harrowing, hideous, grisly, ghastly, sickening.
■ **horrifically** adv.

horrify v. (**horrifying**, **horrified**) fill with horror.
▷ SYNONYMS: **shock**, appal, outrage, scandalize, offend, disgust, revolt, nauseate, sicken.

horror n. **1** great fear, shock, disgust, or dismay. **2** a cause of this.
▷ SYNONYMS: **1** terror, fear, fright, alarm,

h

panic. **2 dismay**, consternation, alarm, distress, disgust, shock.
– ANTONYMS: delight, satisfaction.

hors d'oeuvre /or derv/ n. a small savoury first course of a meal.

horse n. a four-legged mammal used for riding and for pulling heavy loads.
▷ SYNONYMS: **mount**, charger, cob, nag, hack, colt, stallion, mare, filly; N. Amer. **bronco**; Austral./NZ **moke**; informal gee-gee.
• v. (**horse around/about**) informal fool about.
□ **horsebox** Brit. a vehicle for transporting horses. **horse chestnut** a large tree producing nuts (conkers). **horsefly** a large biting fly. **horseman** (or **horsewoman**) a rider on horseback. **horseplay** boisterous play. **horsepower** a unit measuring the power of an engine. **horseradish** a hot-tasting root used to make a sauce. **horseshoe** a U-shaped iron band attached to the base of a horse's hoof. **on horseback** mounted on a horse.

WORD LINKS
equine relating to horses
equestrian relating to horse riding

horsey (or **horsy**) adj. **1** of or like a horse. **2** very keen on horses.

horticulture n. the cultivation of gardens.
■ **horticultural** adj. **horticulturist** n.

hose n. **1** a flexible tube for conveying water. **2** hosiery.
• v. wash with a hose.

hosiery n. stockings, socks, and tights.

hospice n. a home for the care of the terminally ill.

hospitable adj. friendly and welcoming.
▷ SYNONYMS: **welcoming**, friendly, sociable, cordial, gracious, accommodating, warm.
■ **hospitably** adv.

hospital n. an institution for the treatment and care of sick or injured people.
▷ SYNONYMS: **infirmary**, clinic, sanatorium, hospice; Brit. cottage hospital; Military field hospital.

hospitality n. friendly and generous treatment of guests or visitors.
▷ SYNONYMS: **friendliness**, neighbourliness, sociability, welcome, warmth, kindness, cordiality, generosity.

hospitalize (or **-ise**) v. admit to hospital for treatment.
■ **hospitalization** n.

host n. **1** a person who receives or entertains guests. **2** the presenter

of a television or radio programme. **3** a place holding an event to which others are invited. **4** an animal or plant on or in which a parasite lives. **5** a large number of people or things.
▷ SYNONYMS: **presenter**, compère, anchor, anchorman, anchorwoman, announcer.
– ANTONYMS: guest.
• v. act as host at or for.
▷ SYNONYMS: **present**, introduce, compère, front, anchor.

hostage n. a person held captive in an attempt to ensure that a demand is met.
▷ SYNONYMS: **captive**, prisoner, detainee, internee.

hostel n. a place providing cheap food and lodging for a particular group.

hostelry n. (pl. **hostelries**) old use an inn or pub.

hostess n. a female host.

hostile adj. **1** showing dislike or opposition. **2** of a military enemy.
▷ SYNONYMS: **1 unfriendly**, unkind, unsympathetic, antagonistic, aggressive, confrontational, belligerent. **2 unfavourable**, adverse, bad, harsh, grim, inhospitable, forbidding. **3** they are hostile to the idea: **opposed**, averse, antagonistic, ill-disposed, unsympathetic, antipathetic, against; informal anti.
– ANTONYMS: friendly, favourable.

hostility n. **1** hostile behaviour. **2** (**hostilities**) acts of warfare.
▷ SYNONYMS: **1 antagonism**, unfriendliness, malevolence, venom, hatred, aggression, belligerence. **2 opposition**, antagonism, animosity, antipathy. **3** a cessation of hostilities: **fighting**, armed conflict, combat, warfare, war, bloodshed, violence.

hot adj. (**hotter**, **hottest**) **1** having a high temperature. **2** feeling or producing an uncomfortable sensation of heat. **3** currently popular or interesting. **4** showing strong emotion.
▷ SYNONYMS: **1** hot food: **heated**, sizzling, boiling, piping hot, red-hot. **2** a hot day: **very warm**, balmy, summery, tropical, scorching, searing, blistering, roasting, scalding, sweltering, torrid, sultry; informal boiling, baking, roasting. **3** a hot chilli sauce: **spicy**, peppery, fiery, strong, piquant, powerful. **4 popular**, successful, in demand, sought after, all the rage; informal big, hip, cool. **5** she's hot on local history: **knowledgeable**, well informed, au fait, well

up, well versed; informal clued up.
6 *a hot debate:* **heated**, passionate, impassioned, fiery; fierce, vehement, angry, furious.

– ANTONYMS: cold, mild.

• v. (**hotting**, **hotted**) (**hot up**) Brit. informal become more exciting or intense.

◻ **hotbed** a place where an activity happens or flourishes. **hot-blooded** passionate. **hot dog** a hot sausage served in a bread roll. **hotfoot** in eager haste. **hothead** a rash or quick-tempered person. **hothouse 1** a heated greenhouse. **2** an environment encouraging rapid development. **hotline** a direct phone line set up for a purpose. **hotplate** a flat heated surface on an electric cooker.

■ **hotly** adv.

hotchpotch (US **hodgepodge**) n. a confused mixture.

hotel n. a place providing rooms and meals for guests.

hotelier n. a hotel owner or manager.

houmous var. of HUMMUS.

hound n. a hunting dog.

• v. harass.

▷ SYNONYMS: **pursue**, chase, stalk, harry, harass, pester, badger, torment.

hour n. **1** a period of 60 minutes, one of the 24 parts of a day. **2** a point in time. **3** a time set aside for a purpose or activity.

◻ **hourglass** a device with two connected glass bulbs containing sand that takes an hour to fall from the upper to the lower bulb.

■ **hourly** adj. & adv.

houri /hoor-i/ n. (in Islamic belief) a beautiful virgin in paradise.

house n. **1** a building for people to live in, or for a specific purpose. **2** a business. **3** a dynasty. **4** a law-making assembly. **5** a group of pupils living together at boarding school. **6** a style of fast popular dance music.

▷ SYNONYMS: **1 residence**, home; informal pad; Brit. informal gaff; formal dwelling, abode, habitation, domicile. **2 firm**, business, company, corporation, enterprise, establishment, institution, concern, organization, operation; informal outfit. **3 family**, clan, tribe, dynasty, line, bloodline, lineage. **4 assembly**, legislative body, chamber, council, parliament, congress, senate.

• v. **1** provide accommodation or space for. **2** enclose.

▷ SYNONYMS: **1 accommodate**, give someone a roof over their head,

lodge, quarter, board, billet, take in, sleep, put up. **2 contain**, hold, store, cover, protect, enclose.

◻ **house arrest** detention in a person's own house. **houseboat** a boat that people can live in. **housebound** unable to leave your house because of illness or old age. **housebreaking** breaking into a building to commit a crime. **housecoat** a woman's dressing gown. **housekeeper** a person employed to manage a household. **housemaster** (or **housemistress**) a teacher in charge of a house at a boarding school. **house-proud** very concerned with the appearance of your home. **house-train** train a pet to urinate and defecate outdoors. **house-warming** a party celebrating a move to a new home. **housewife** a woman whose main occupation is looking after her family and the home. **housework** cleaning, cooking, etc. done in running a home. **on the house** at the management's expense.

household n. a house and its occupants.

▷ SYNONYMS: **family**, house, occupants, clan, tribe; informal brood.

householder n. a person who owns or rents a house.

housing n. **1** houses and flats. **2** a rigid case for a piece of equipment.

▷ SYNONYMS: **1 accommodation**, houses, homes, living quarters; formal dwellings. **2 casing**, covering, case, cover, holder, fairing, sleeve.

hove Nautical past of HEAVE.

hovel n. a small dirty or run-down house.

▷ SYNONYMS: **shack**, slum, shanty, hut; informal dump, hole.

hover v. **1** remain in one place in the air. **2** wait about uncertainly. **3** remain at or near a particular level.

▷ SYNONYMS: **1 hang**, be poised, be suspended, float, fly, drift. **2 wait**, linger, loiter.

◻ **hovercraft** a vehicle that travels over land or water on a cushion of air.

how adv. **1** in what way or by what means. **2** in what condition. **3** to what extent or degree. **4** the way in which.

howdah n. a seat on an elephant's back.

however adv. **1** nevertheless; despite this. **2** in whatever way or to whatever extent.

▷ SYNONYMS: **nevertheless**, nonetheless, even so, but, for all that, despite that, in spite of that.

howitzer n. a short gun firing shells

at a high angle.

howl n. a long wailing cry or sound.
▷ SYNONYMS: **1 baying**, cry, bark, yelp, yowl. **2 wail**, cry, yell, yelp, bellow, roar, shout, shriek, scream, screech.
• v. make a howl.
▷ SYNONYMS: **1 bay**, cry, bark, yelp, yowl. **2 wail**, cry, yell, bawl, bellow, shriek, scream, screech, caterwaul, ululate; informal holler.

howler n. informal a stupid mistake.

hoyden n. dated a high-spirited or wild girl.

h.p. (or HP) abbrev. **1** Brit. hire purchase. **2** horsepower.

HQ abbrev. headquarters.

HRH abbrev. Brit. Her (or His) Royal Highness.

HRT abbrev. hormone replacement therapy.

HTML n. Hypertext Markup Language.

hub n. **1** the central part of a wheel. **2** the centre of an activity.
▷ SYNONYMS: **centre**, core, heart, focus, focal point, nucleus, kernel, nerve centre.
– ANTONYMS: periphery.
□ **hubcap** a cover for the hub of a wheel.

hubbub n. a confused noise of a crowd.

hubris /hyoo-briss/ n. excessive pride or self-confidence.

huddle v. crowd together.
▷ SYNONYMS: **1 crowd**, cluster, gather, bunch, throng, flock, collect, group, congregate. **2 curl up**, snuggle, nestle, hunch up.
– ANTONYMS: disperse.
• n. a close group of people or things.
▷ SYNONYMS: **group**, cluster, bunch, collection; informal gaggle.

hue n. a colour or shade.
▷ SYNONYMS: **colour**, shade, tone, tint, tinge.

hue and cry n. a strong public outcry.

huff n. a fit of annoyance.
• v. (huff and puff) **1** breathe out noisily. **2** show annoyance.
■ **huffy** adj. **huffily** adv.

hug v. (hugging, hugged) **1** hold tightly in your arms. **2** keep close to.
▷ SYNONYMS: **embrace**, cuddle, squeeze, clasp, clutch, hold tight.
• n. an embrace.
▷ SYNONYMS: **embrace**, cuddle, squeeze, bear hug.

huge adj. very large.
▷ SYNONYMS: **enormous**, vast, immense, massive, colossal, prodigious, gigantic, gargantuan, mammoth,

monumental, giant, towering, mountainous; informal mega, monster, astronomical; Brit. informal ginormous.
– ANTONYMS: tiny.
■ **hugely** adv.

hula hoop n. trademark a large hoop spun round the body.

hulk n. **1** a large or clumsy person or thing. **2** an old ship stripped of its fittings.

hulking adj. very large or clumsy.

hull n. **1** the main body of a ship. **2** the outer covering of a fruit or seed. **3** the cluster of leaves on a strawberry.
▷ SYNONYMS: **framework**, body, shell, frame, skeleton, structure.

hullabaloo n. informal an uproar.

hullo var. of HELLO.

hum v. (humming, hummed) **1** make a low continuous sound. **2** sing with closed lips. **3** informal be very busy.
▷ SYNONYMS: **1 purr**, drone, murmur, buzz, whirr, throb. **2 be busy**, be active, be lively, buzz, bustle, be a hive of activity, throb.
• n. a low continuous sound.
▷ SYNONYMS: **murmur**, drone, purr, buzz.

human adj. **1** of people. **2** showing kindness, emotion, etc.
▷ SYNONYMS: **1 mortal**, flesh and blood, fallible, weak, frail, imperfect, vulnerable, physical, bodily, fleshly. **2 compassionate**, humane, kind, considerate, understanding, sympathetic.
• n. (or **human being**) a person.
▷ SYNONYMS: **person**, human being, Homo sapiens, man, woman, individual, mortal, living soul, earthling; (**humans**) the human race, humanity, humankind, mankind, people.
□ **humankind** people as a whole. **human resources** the section of an organization dealing with recruitment etc. **human rights** basic rights to which all people are entitled.
■ **humanly** adv.

> **WORD LINKS**
> **anthropology** the study of humankind

humane adj. kind and considerate.
▷ SYNONYMS: **compassionate**, kind, considerate, understanding, sympathetic, tolerant, forbearing, forgiving, merciful, humanitarian, charitable.
– ANTONYMS: cruel.
■ **humanely** adv.

humanism n. the belief that people are able to live by reason rather than relying on religious faith.

■ **humanist** n. & adj.

humanitarian adj. concerned with human welfare.
▷ SYNONYMS: **1 compassionate**, humane, unselfish, altruistic, generous. **2 charitable**, philanthropic, public-spirited, socially concerned.
■ **humanitarianism** n.

humanity n. (pl. **humanities**) **1** people as a whole. **2** the condition of being human. **3** sympathy and kindness. **4** (**humanities**) studies concerned with culture.
▷ SYNONYMS: **1 humankind**, mankind, man, people, the human race, Homo sapiens. **2 compassion**, brotherly love, fellow feeling, humaneness, kindness, consideration, understanding, sympathy, tolerance.

humanize (or **-ise**) v. make more pleasant or suitable for people.

humble adj. **1** having a low opinion of your importance. **2** of low rank. **3** not large or elaborate.
▷ SYNONYMS: **1 meek**, deferential, respectful, submissive, self-effacing, unassertive, modest, unassuming, self-deprecating. **2 lowly**, poor, undistinguished, mean, common, ordinary, simple, modest.
– ANTONYMS: proud, arrogant.
• v. cause to seem less important.
▷ SYNONYMS: **humiliate**, demean, lower, degrade, debase, mortify, shame.
■ **humbly** adv.

humbug n. **1** misleading or foolish talk. **2** a peppermint sweet.

humdrum adj. dull or ordinary.
▷ SYNONYMS: **mundane**, dull, dreary, boring, tedious, monotonous, prosaic, routine, ordinary, everyday, run-of-the-mill, workaday, pedestrian.

humerus n. (pl. **humeri**) the bone in the upper arm.

humid adj. (of the air) damp and warm.
▷ SYNONYMS: **muggy**, close, sultry, sticky, steamy, clammy, heavy.
– ANTONYMS: dry, fresh.
■ **humidity** n.

humidifier n. a device for regulating moisture in the air of a room.

humiliate v. cause to feel ashamed or stupid.
▷ SYNONYMS: **embarrass**, mortify, shame, humble, disgrace, chasten, deflate, crush, squash, demean, take down a peg or two; informal show up, put down, cut down to size; N. Amer. informal make someone eat crow.
– ANTONYMS: dignify.

humiliating adj. making you feel ashamed or stupid.

▷ SYNONYMS: **embarrassing**, mortifying, ignominious, inglorious, undignified, shaming, chastening, demeaning, degrading, humbling.

humiliation n. the state of being humiliated.
▷ SYNONYMS: **embarrassment**, mortification, shame, indignity, ignominy, disgrace, dishonour, degradation, discredit, loss of face, blow to your pride.

humility n. the quality of being humble.
▷ SYNONYMS: **modesty**, humbleness, meekness, respect, deference, diffidence.
– ANTONYMS: pride.

hummingbird n. a small tropical bird able to hover by beating its wings very fast.

hummock n. a small hill or mound.

hummus (or **houmous**) n. a dip made from puréed chickpeas.

humorist n. a writer or speaker noted for being amusing.

humorous adj. **1** causing amusement. **2** showing a sense of humour.
▷ SYNONYMS: **amusing**, funny, comic, comical, entertaining, diverting, witty, jocular, light-hearted, hilarious.
– ANTONYMS: serious.
■ **humorously** adv.

USAGE -or- not -our-: humorous.

humour (US **humor**) n. **1** the quality of being amusing. **2** a state of mind.
▷ SYNONYMS: **1 comedy**, funny side, hilarity, absurdity, ludicrousness, satire, irony. **2 jokes**, jests, quips, witticisms, funny remarks, wit, comedy; informal gags, wisecracks. **3 mood**, temper, disposition, spirits.
– ANTONYMS: seriousness.
• v. agree with someone to keep them happy.
▷ SYNONYMS: **indulge**, accommodate, pander to, cater to, give in to, go along with, flatter, mollify, placate.
■ **humourless** adj.

hump n. **1** a rounded lump or mound. **2** a rounded part projecting from the back of a camel or as an abnormality on a person's back.
• v. informal carry with difficulty.
■ **humped** adj.

humus /hyoo-muhss/ n. a substance found in soil, formed from dead plant material.

hunch v. raise the shoulders and bend the top of the body forward.
• n. an idea or feeling that is not based on evidence.

h

▷ SYNONYMS: **feeling**, guess, suspicion, impression, inkling, idea, notion, fancy, intuition; informal gut feeling.
□ **hunchback** offens. a person with a hump on their back.

hundred adj. & n. ten more than ninety; 100.
□ **hundredweight 1** Brit. a unit of weight equal to 112 lb (about 50.8 kg). **2** US a unit of weight equal to 100 lb (about 45.4 kg).
■ **hundredth** adj. & n.

hung past & past part. of **HANG**.
• adj. **1** having no political party with an overall majority. **2** (of a jury) unable to agree on a verdict.
□ **hungover** suffering from a hangover.

hunger n. **1** a feeling of discomfort caused by lack of food. **2** a strong desire.
▷ SYNONYMS: **1 lack of food**, starvation, malnutrition, undernourishment. **2 desire**, craving, longing, yearning, hankering, appetite, thirst; informal itch.
• v. (**hunger after/for**) have a strong desire for.
□ **hunger strike** refusal to eat as a means of protest.

hungry adj. (**hungrier**, **hungriest**) feeling hunger.
▷ SYNONYMS: **1 ravenous**, famished, starving, starved, malnourished, undernourished, underfed; informal peckish. **2** they are hungry for success: **eager**, keen, avid, longing, yearning, aching, greedy, craving, desirous of, hankering after; informal itching, dying, gagging.
– ANTONYMS: full.
■ **hungrily** adv.

hunk n. **1** a large piece cut or broken off. **2** informal a strong, attractive man.
▷ SYNONYMS: **chunk**, wedge, block, slab, lump, square, gobbet; Brit. informal wodge.

hunt v. **1** chase and kill a wild animal for sport or food. **2** search. **3** (**hunt down**) chase and capture.
▷ SYNONYMS: **1 chase**, stalk, pursue, course, track, trail. **2 search**, seek, look high and low, scour the area.
• n. **1** an act of hunting. **2** a group who hunt animals as a sport.
▷ SYNONYMS: **1 chase**, pursuit. **2 search**, quest.
■ **hunter** n.

hurdle n. **1** an upright frame to be jumped over in a race. **2** an obstacle or difficulty.
▷ SYNONYMS: **obstacle**, difficulty, problem, barrier, bar, snag, stumbling

block, impediment, obstruction, complication, hindrance.
• v. jump over while running.
■ **hurdler** n.

hurl v. throw forcefully.
▷ SYNONYMS: **throw**, toss, fling, launch, pitch, cast, lob; informal chuck, sling, bung.

hurly-burly n. noisy activity.

hurrah (or **hooray**, **hurray**) exclam. used to express joy or approval.

hurricane n. a severe storm with a strong wind.
▷ SYNONYMS: **cyclone**, typhoon, tornado, storm, windstorm, whirlwind, gale, tempest; Austral. willy-willy; N. Amer. informal twister.

hurried adj. done quickly or too quickly.
▷ SYNONYMS: **1 quick**, fast, swift, rapid, speedy, brisk, cursory, perfunctory, brief, short, fleeting. **2 hasty**, rushed, precipitate, spur-of-the-moment.
– ANTONYMS: slow.

hurry v. (**hurrying**, **hurried**) **1** move or act quickly. **2** do too quickly.
▷ SYNONYMS: **1 be quick**, hurry up, hasten, speed up, run, dash, rush, race, scurry, scramble, scuttle, sprint; informal get a move on, step on it, get a wiggle on, hightail it, hotfoot it; Brit. informal get your skates on. **2 hustle**, hasten, push, urge.
– ANTONYMS: dawdle, delay.
• n. great haste.
▷ SYNONYMS: **rush**, haste, speed, urgency, hustle and bustle.
■ **hurriedly** adv.

hurt v. (**hurting**, **hurt**) **1** cause pain or harm to. **2** feel pain. **3** make upset.
▷ SYNONYMS: **1 injure**, wound, damage, bruise, cut, gash, graze, scrape, scratch. **2 be painful**, ache, be sore, be tender, smart, sting, burn, throb. **3 distress**, pain, wound, sting, upset, sadden, devastate, grieve, mortify.
• n. injury or pain.
▷ SYNONYMS: **distress**, pain, agony, suffering, grief, misery, anguish, upset, sadness, sorrow.

hurtful adj. causing mental pain or distress.
▷ SYNONYMS: **upsetting**, distressing, wounding, unkind, cruel, nasty, mean, malicious, spiteful.

hurtle v. move very fast.

husband n. a married man in relation to his wife.
▷ SYNONYMS: **spouse**, partner, mate, consort,; informal better half; Brit. informal other half.
• v. use resources carefully.

h

husbandry n. **1** farming. **2** careful use of resources.

hush v. **1** make or become quiet. **2** (**hush up**) prevent from becoming known.
▷ SYNONYMS: **silence**, quieten, shush, gag, muzzle; informal shut up.
• n. a silence.
▷ SYNONYMS: **silence**, quiet, stillness, peace, calm, tranquillity.
− ANTONYMS: noise.

husk n. the dry outer covering of some fruits or seeds.

husky adj. (**huskier**, **huskiest**) **1** (of a voice) deep and rough. **2** big and strong.
• n. (pl. **huskies**) a dog used for pulling sledges.
■ **huskily** adv. **huskiness** n.

hussy n. (pl. **hussies**) a cheeky or immoral girl or woman.

hustings n. the political meetings and speeches before an election.

hustle v. push or move roughly.
• n. busy activity.

hut n. a small simple house or shelter.
▷ SYNONYMS: **shack**, shanty, cabin, shelter, shed, lean-to, hovel; Scottish bothy; N. Amer. cabana.

hutch n. a box with a wire mesh front, for keeping rabbits etc.

hyacinth n. a plant with scented flowers.

hyaena var. of HYENA.

hybrid n. **1** the offspring of two plants or animals of different species or varieties. **2** something made by combining two different things.
▷ SYNONYMS: **cross**, cross-breed, mixture, blend, combination, composite, fusion, amalgam.

hydrangea /hy-**drayn**-juh/ n. a shrub with white, blue, or pink flowers.

hydrant n. a water pipe with a nozzle for attaching a fire hose.

hydrate v. cause to absorb or combine with water.
• n. a chemical compound of water and another substance.
■ **hydration** n.

hydraulic adj. operated by a liquid moving under pressure.
• n. (**hydraulics**) the study of the use of liquids moving under pressure to provide mechanical force.
■ **hydraulically** adv.

hydrocarbon n. a compound of hydrogen and carbon.

hydrochloric acid n. an acid containing hydrogen and chlorine.

hydroelectric adj. using flowing water to generate electricity.

hydrofoil n. a boat designed to rise above the water when travelling at speed.

hydrogen n. a highly flammable gas which is the lightest chemical element.
□ **hydrogen bomb** a nuclear bomb whose power comes from the fusion of hydrogen nuclei.

hydrolysis n. the chemical breakdown of a compound due to reaction with water.

hydrophobia n. **1** extreme fear of water, esp. as a symptom of rabies. **2** rabies.

hydroplane n. a light, fast motor boat designed to skim over the water.

hydroponics n. the growing of plants in sand or liquid rather than soil.

hydrotherapy n. therapeutic exercises in water.

hydrous adj. containing water.

hyena (or **hyaena**) n. a doglike African mammal.

hygiene n. the practice of keeping yourself and your surroundings clean to prevent disease.
▷ SYNONYMS: **cleanliness**, sanitation, sterility, purity, disinfection.
■ **hygienist** n..

hygienic adj. free of the organisms which spread disease.
▷ SYNONYMS: **sanitary**, clean, germ-free, disinfected, sterilized, sterile, anti-septic, aseptic.
− ANTONYMS: unhygienic, insanitary.
■ **hygienically** adv.

hymen n. the membrane partially closing the opening of the vagina, usu. broken when a woman or girl first has sex.

hymn n. a religious song of praise.

hype informal n. excessive publicity.
• v. publicize in an excessive way.

hyper- prefix **1** over; above. **2** excessively.

hyperactive adj. excessively active.

hyperbola /hy-**per**-buh-luh/ n. (pl. **hyperbolas**) a symmetrical curve formed when a cone is cut by a plane nearly parallel to the cone's axis.

hyperbole /hy-**per**-buh-li/ n. statements that are deliberately exaggerated for effect.

hyperlink n. a link from a hypertext document to another location.

hypermarket n. Brit. a very large supermarket.

hypersonic adj. of speeds more than five times that of sound.

hypertension n. abnormally high blood pressure.

hypertext n. software enabling quick movement between documents or sections of data.

hyperventilate v. breathe at an abnormally rapid rate.
■ **hyperventilation** n.

hyphen n. the sign (-) used to join words together or to split a word at the end of a line.
■ **hyphenate** v. **hyphenation** n.

hypnosis n. the practice of causing a person to enter a state in which they respond very readily to suggestions or commands.
■ **hypnotic** adj. **hypnotically** adv.

hypnotism n. hypnosis.
■ **hypnotist** n. **hypnotize** (or **-ise**) v.

hypo- prefix **1** under. **2** below normal.

hypoallergenic adj. unlikely to cause an allergic reaction.

hypochondria n. excessive anxiety about your health.
■ **hypochondriac** n.

hypocrisy n. behaviour in which a person pretends to have higher standards than is really the case.

hypocrite n. a person guilty of hypocrisy.

hypocritical adj. pretending to have higher standards than is really the case.
▷ SYNONYMS: **sanctimonious**, pious, self-righteous, holier-than-thou, superior, insincere, two-faced.
■ **hypocritically** adv.

hypodermic adj. used to inject a drug etc. beneath the skin.
• n. a hypodermic syringe.

hypotension n. abnormally low blood pressure.

hypotenuse /hy-**pot**-uh-nyooz/ n. the longest side of a right-angled triangle.

hypothermia n. the condition of having an abnormally low body temperature.

hypothesis n. (pl. **hypotheses**) an idea or explanation that has not yet been proved to be true or correct.
■ **hypothesize** (or **-ise**) v.

hypothetical adj. based on a possible situation rather than fact.
■ **hypothetically** adv.

hysterectomy n. (pl. **hysterectomies**) an operation to remove all or part of the womb.

hysteria n. extreme or uncontrollable emotion.
▷ SYNONYMS: **frenzy**, feverishness, hysterics, agitation, mania, panic, alarm, distress.
− ANTONYMS: calm.

hysterical adj. **1** in a state of extreme or controllable emotion. **2** informal very funny.
▷ SYNONYMS: **1 overwrought**, over-emotional, out of control, frenzied, frantic, wild, beside yourself, manic, delirious; informal in a state. **2 very funny**, hilarious, uproarious, rib-tickling; informal side-splitting, price-less, a scream, a hoot.
− ANTONYMS: calm.
■ **hysterically** adv.

hysterics pl. n. **1** wildly emotional behaviour. **2** informal uncontrollable laughter.

Hz abbrev. hertz.

I pron. used by a speaker to refer to himself or herself.
• n. (or i) the Roman numeral for one.

iambic /I-am-bik/ adj. (of verse) having one short syllable followed by one long syllable.

ibex n. (pl. **ibexes**) a wild mountain goat.

ibid. adv. in the book just mentioned.

ice n. **1** frozen water. **2** an ice cream.
▷ SYNONYMS: **1** icicles, black ice, frost, permafrost, hoar frost; literary rime. **2** ice cream, water ice, sorbet; N. Amer. sherbet.
• v. **1** decorate with icing. **2** become covered with ice.
□ **break the ice** start a conversation on first meeting. **ice age** a period when ice covered much of the earth's surface. **iceberg** a large mass of ice floating in the sea. **icebox** Brit. a freezing compartment in a fridge. **ice cream** a frozen dessert made with milk fat. **ice skate** a boot with a blade on the sole, for skating on ice.

> WORD LINKS
> **glacial** relating to ice

ichthyology /ik-thi-ol-uh-ji/ n. the study of fish.
■ **ichthyologist** n.

icicle n. a hanging, tapering piece of ice.

icing n. a mixture of sugar with liquid or fat, used to coat cakes.

icon n. **1** a famous person who symbolizes something. **2** a symbol on a computer screen representing a program. **3** (or **ikon**) a sacred painting of a holy person.
■ **iconic** adj.

iconoclast n. a person who attacks established customs and values.
■ **iconoclastic** adj.

icy adj. (**icier**, **iciest**) **1** covered with ice. **2** very cold. **3** very unfriendly.
▷ SYNONYMS: **1** iced over, frozen, frosty, slippery, treacherous; literary rimy. **2** freezing, chill, biting, bitter, raw, arctic. **3** unfriendly, hostile, forbidding, cold, chilly, frosty, stern.

■ **icily** adv. **iciness** n.

ID abbrev. identification or identity.

Id n. var. of EID.

id n. the part of the unconscious mind consisting of basic inherited instincts and feelings.

idea n. **1** a thought or suggestion about a possible course of action. **2** a mental impression. **3** a belief.
▷ SYNONYMS: **1 concept**, notion, conception, thought. **2 plan**, scheme, design, proposal, proposition, suggestion, aim, intention, objective, goal. **3 thought**, theory, view, opinion, feeling, belief. **4 sense**, feeling, suspicion, fancy, inkling, hunch, notion. **5 estimate**, approximation, guess, conjecture; informal guesstimate.

ideal adj. most suitable; perfect.
▷ SYNONYMS: **perfect**, faultless, exemplary, classic, archetypal, quintessential, model, ultimate, utopian, fairy-tale.
• n. **1** a principle or standard that is worth aiming for. **2** a person or thing regarded as perfect.
▷ SYNONYMS: **1** *an ideal to aim at:* **model**, pattern, archetype, exemplar, example, perfection, epitome, last word. **2** *liberal ideals:* **principle**, standard, value, belief, conviction, ethos.
■ **ideally** adv.

idealism n. the belief that ideals can be achieved.
■ **idealist** n. utopian

idealistic adj. believing or reflecting a belief that ideals can be achieved.
▷ SYNONYMS: **utopian**, visionary, romantic, quixotic, unrealistic, impractical.

idealize (or **-ise**) v. represent as better than in reality.

identical adj. **1** exactly alike. **2** the same.
▷ SYNONYMS: **exactly the same**, indistinguishable, twin, duplicate, interchangeable, alike, matching.
– ANTONYMS: different.

■ **identically** adv.
identification n. **1** the action of identifying or the fact of being identified. **2** an official document or other proof of your identity.
▷ SYNONYMS: **1 recognition**, singling out, pinpointing, naming. **2 determination**, establishing, ascertainment, discovery, diagnosis. **3 ID**, papers, documents, credentials, card, pass.
identify v. (**identifying**, **identified**) **1** prove or recognize as being a specified person or thing.
2 understand or share the feelings of. **3** consider to be the same.
▷ SYNONYMS: **1 recognize**, pick out, spot, point out, pinpoint, put your finger on, name. **2 determine**, establish, ascertain, make out, discern, distinguish. **3** *he identified with the team captain:* **empathize**, sympathize, understand, relate to, feel for. **4** *we identify sport with glamour:* **associate**, link, connect, relate.
■ **identifiable** adj.
identikit n. trademark a picture of a wanted person, put together from typical facial features.
identity n. (pl. **identities**) **1** the fact of being who or what a person or thing is. **2** a close similarity.
▷ SYNONYMS: **individuality**, self, personality, character, originality, distinctiveness, uniqueness.
ideology n. (pl. **ideologies**) a system of ideas forming the basis of an economic or political theory.
▷ SYNONYMS: **belief**; doctrine, creed, theory.
■ **ideological** adj.
idiocy n. (pl. **idiocies**) very stupid behaviour.
idiom n. a phrase whose meaning is different from the meanings of the individual words.
idiomatic adj. using expressions natural to a native speaker.
▷ SYNONYMS: **colloquial**, everyday, conversational, vernacular, natural.
idiosyncrasy n. (pl. **idiosyncrasies**) a person's particular way of behaving or thinking.
▷ SYNONYMS: **peculiarity**, oddity, eccentricity, mannerism, quirk, characteristic.
■ **idiosyncratic** adj.

USAGE The ending is -*asy*, not -*acy*: idiosyncrasy.

idiot n. a stupid person.
▷ SYNONYMS: **fool**, ass, halfwit, blockhead, dunce, simpleton; informal

nincompoop, clod, dimwit, dummy, fathead, numbskull; Brit. informal nitwit, twit, clot, berk, prat, pillock, wally, dork, twerp, charlie, moron; N. Amer. informal schmuck; Austral./NZ informal drongo.
– ANTONYMS: genius.
■ **idiotic** adj. **idiotically** adv.
idle adj. **1** avoiding work; lazy. **2** not working or in use. **3** having no purpose or effect.
▷ SYNONYMS: **1 lazy**, indolent, slothful, shiftless, work-shy. **2 unemployed**, jobless, out of work, redundant, unoccupied; Brit. informal on the dole. **3 unoccupied**, spare, empty, unfilled. **4 frivolous**, trivial, trifling, minor, insignificant, unimportant, empty, meaningless, vain.
– ANTONYMS: industrious, busy.
● v. **1** spend time doing nothing. **2** (of an engine) run slowly while out of gear.
■ **idleness** n. **idler** n. **idly** adv.
idol n. **1** a greatly admired person. **2** a statue or picture of a god that is worshipped.
▷ SYNONYMS: **1 icon**, effigy, statue, figurine, totem. **2 hero**, heroine, star, superstar, icon, celebrity, darling; informal pin-up, heart-throb.
idolatry n. worship of idols.
■ **idolatrous** adj.
idolize (or -**ise**) v. admire or love greatly.
▷ SYNONYMS: **hero-worship**, worship, revere, venerate, look up to, exalt; informal put on a pedestal.
idyll /i-dil/ n. **1** a very happy or peaceful situation. **2** a short poem describing a peaceful country scene.
■ **idyllic** adj. **idyllically** adv.
i.e. abbrev. that is.
if conj. **1** on the condition or in the event that. **2** whether.
▷ SYNONYMS: **provided**, providing, on condition that, presuming, supposing, assuming, as long as, in the event that.
iffy adj. informal uncertain or in poor condition.
igloo n. a dome-shaped Eskimo house built from blocks of snow.
igneous adj. (of rock) formed from solidified molten rock.
ignite v. catch or set on fire.
▷ SYNONYMS: **1 catch fire**, burst into flames, explode. **2 light**, set fire to, set alight, kindle.
– ANTONYMS: extinguish.
ignition n. **1** the act of igniting. **2** the mechanism igniting the fuel in an engine.

ignoble adj. dishonourable.
ignominy n. public disgrace.
  ■ **ignominious** adj. **ignominiously** adv.
ignoramus n. (pl. **ignoramuses**) an ignorant person.
ignorance n. lack of knowledge or awareness.
▷ SYNONYMS: **1 lack of knowledge**, lack of education, unenlightenment. **2 unfamiliarity**, incomprehension, inexperience, innocence.
– ANTONYMS: education, knowledge.
ignorant adj. **1** lacking knowledge or awareness. **2** informal not polite.
▷ SYNONYMS: **1 uneducated**, unschooled, illiterate, uninformed, unenlightened, inexperienced, unsophisticated. **2 unaware**, unconscious, unfamiliar, unacquainted, uninformed; informal in the dark.
– ANTONYMS: educated, knowledgeable.
ignore v. **1** deliberately take no notice of. **2** fail to consider.
▷ SYNONYMS: **1 snub**, look right through, cold-shoulder, take no notice of, pay no attention to, cut; informal blank. **2 disregard**, take no account of, fail to observe, disobey, defy, overlook, brush aside, turn a blind eye to.
– ANTONYMS: acknowledge, obey.
iguana n. a large tropical lizard.
ikon var. of ICON (sense 3).
ilk n. a type.
ill adj. **1** not in good health. **2** bad or harmful.
▷ SYNONYMS: **1 unwell**, sick, poorly, peaky, indisposed, nauseous, queasy; informal rough, under the weather; Brit. informal grotty; Austral./NZ informal crook. **2** *ill effects*: **harmful**, damaging, detrimental, deleterious, adverse, injurious, destructive, dangerous.
– ANTONYMS: well, beneficial.
  • adv. **1** badly or wrongly. **2** only with difficulty.
▷ SYNONYMS: **1 barely**, scarcely, hardly, only just. **2 inadequately**, insufficiently, poorly, badly.
  • n. **1** a problem or misfortune. **2** harm.
▷ SYNONYMS: **problem**, trouble, difficulty, misfortune, trial, tribulation; informal headache, hassle.
  □ **ill-advised** unwise. **ill at ease** uncomfortable or embarrassed. **ill-gotten** obtained illegally or unfairly. **ill-starred** unlucky. **ill-treat** treat cruelly. **ill will** hostility.
illegal adj. against the law.
▷ SYNONYMS: **unlawful**, illicit, illegitimate, criminal, fraudulent, corrupt, dishonest, outlawed, banned, forbidden, prohibited, proscribed, unlicensed, unauthorized; informal crooked, shady; Brit. informal bent, dodgy.
– ANTONYMS: legal.
  ■ **illegality** n. **illegally** adv.
illegible adj. not clear enough to be read.
▷ SYNONYMS: **unreadable**, indecipherable, unintelligible.
  ■ **illegibility** n.
illegitimate adj. **1** not allowed by law or rules. **2** born of parents not married to each other.
▷ SYNONYMS: **illegal**, unlawful, illicit, criminal, felonious, fraudulent, corrupt, dishonest; informal crooked, shady; Brit. informal bent, dodgy.
– ANTONYMS: legal, legitimate.
  ■ **illegitimacy** n.
illicit adj. forbidden by law, rules, or standards.
▷ SYNONYMS: **illegal**, unlawful, criminal, outlawed, banned, forbidden, prohibited, proscribed, unlicensed, unauthorized, improper, disapproved of.
– ANTONYMS: legal.
  ■ **illicitly** adv.
illiterate adj. **1** unable to read or write. **2** not knowledgeable about a subject.
  ■ **illiteracy** n.
illness n. a disease or period of being ill.
▷ SYNONYMS: **sickness**, poor health, disease, ailment, disorder, complaint, indisposition, malady, affliction, infection; informal bug, virus.
– ANTONYMS: health.
illogical adj. not sensible or based on sound reasoning.
▷ SYNONYMS: **irrational**, unreasonable, erroneous, invalid, spurious, fallacious, specious.
  ■ **illogicality** n. **illogically** adv.
illuminate v. **1** light up. **2** help to explain.
illuminating adj. making something easier to understand.
▷ SYNONYMS: **informative**, enlightening, revealing, explanatory, instructive, helpful, educational.
– ANTONYMS: confusing.
illumination n. **1** light. **2** understanding or enlightenment.
▷ SYNONYMS: **light**, lighting, radiance, gleam, glow, glare.
illumine v. illuminate.
illusion n. **1** a false idea or belief. **2** a thing that seems to be something it is not.

i

▷ SYNONYMS: **1 delusion**, misapprehension, misconception, false impression, mistaken impression, fantasy, dream, fancy. **2 appearance**, impression, semblance. **3 mirage**, hallucination, apparition, figment of the imagination, trick of the light.

illusionist n. a magician.

illusory (or **illusive**) adj. not real.
▷ SYNONYMS: **false**, imagined, imaginary, fanciful, unreal, sham, fallacious.
– ANTONYMS: genuine.

illustrate v. **1** provide a book etc. with pictures. **2** make clear by using examples etc. **3** act as an example of.
▷ SYNONYMS: **1 decorate**, ornament, accompany, support. **2 explain**, elucidate, clarify, demonstrate, show, point up; informal get across/over.
■ **illustrative** adj. **illustrator** n.

illustration n. **1** a picture in a book etc. **2** the act of illustrating. **3** an explanatory example.
▷ SYNONYMS: **1 picture**, drawing, sketch, figure, plate, image, print. **2 example**, sample, case, instance, exemplification, demonstration.

illustrious adj. famous and greatly admired.

image n. **1** a picture or statue. **2** a picture seen on a screen, through a lens, or in a mirror. **3** a picture in the mind. **4** an impression presented to the public.
▷ SYNONYMS: **1 likeness**, depiction, portrayal, representation, painting, picture, portrait, drawing, photograph. **2 conception**, impression, perception, notion, idea. **3 persona**, profile, face, impression.

> **WORD LINKS**
> **iconography** the study of images

imagery n. language producing images in the mind.

imaginary adj. existing only in the imagination.
▷ SYNONYMS: **unreal**, non-existent, fictional, make-believe, invented, made-up, illusory; informal pretend.
– ANTONYMS: real.

imagination n. **1** the part of the mind that imagines things. **2** the ability to be creative or solve problems.
▷ SYNONYMS: **1 mind's eye**, fancy. **2 creativity**, vision, inventiveness, resourcefulness, ingenuity, originality.

imaginative adj. having or showing creativity.
▷ SYNONYMS: **creative**, visionary, inventive, resourceful, ingenious,

original, innovative.
■ **imaginatively** adv.

imagine v. **1** form a mental picture of. **2** suppose; assume. **3** believe something unreal to exist.
▷ SYNONYMS: **1 visualize**, envisage, picture, see in your mind's eye, dream up, think up/of, conceive. **2 assume**, presume, expect, take it, suppose.
■ **imaginable** adj.

imam n. the person who leads prayers in a mosque.

imbalance n. a lack of balance.

imbecile n. informal a stupid person.
■ **imbecilic** adj. **imbecility** n.

imbed var. of EMBED.

imbibe v. **1** drink alcohol. **2** absorb ideas.

imbroglio /im-broh-li-oh/ n. (pl. **imbroglios**) a confused or complicated situation.

imbue v. fill with a feeling or quality.
▷ SYNONYMS: **permeate**, saturate, suffuse, inject, inculcate, fill.

IMF abbrev. International Monetary Fund.

imitate v. **1** follow as a model. **2** copy or mimic.
▷ SYNONYMS: **1 copy**, emulate, follow, echo; informal rip off. **2 mimic**, do an impression of, impersonate, parody, caricature, ape; informal take off, send up.
■ **imitative** adj. **imitator** n.

imitation n. **1** a copy. **2** the action of imitating.
▷ SYNONYMS: **1 copy**, reproduction, replica, simulation, forgery. **2 emulation**, copying. **3 impersonation**, impression, parody, caricature; informal take-off, send-up, spoof.
● adj. not real or genuine.
▷ SYNONYMS: **artificial**, synthetic, mock, fake, simulated, man-made, manufactured, substitute, ersatz.
– ANTONYMS: real.

immaculate adj. **1** completely clean or tidy. **2** free from flaws or mistakes.
▷ SYNONYMS: **1 clean**, spotless, shining, shiny, gleaming, perfect, pristine, mint, flawless, faultless, unblemished; informal tip-top, A1. **2** his immaculate record: **impeccable**, unsullied, spotless, unblemished, untarnished; informal squeaky clean.
– ANTONYMS: dirty, damaged.
■ **immaculately** adv.

immanent adj. present throughout; inherent.
■ **immanence** n.

immaterial adj. not important or relevant.

immature adj. **1** not fully developed. **2** childish.
▷ SYNONYMS: **childish**, babyish, infantile, juvenile, puerile, callow.
■ **immaturity** n.

immeasurable adj. too large or extreme to measure.
■ **immeasurably** adv.

immediate adj. **1** occurring or done at once. **2** nearest in time, space, or relationship. **3** most urgent; current.
▷ SYNONYMS: **1 instant**, instantaneous, prompt, swift, speedy, rapid, quick. **2 nearest**, close, next-door, adjacent, adjoining. **3 current**, present, urgent, pressing.
– ANTONYMS: delayed.
■ **immediacy** n.

immediately adv. **1** at once. **2** without any intervening time or space.
▷ SYNONYMS: **1 straight away**, at once, right away, instantly, now, directly, forthwith, there and then; informal pronto. **2 directly**, right, exactly, precisely, squarely, just, dead; informal slap bang; N. Amer. informal smack dab.
– ANTONYMS: later.

immemorial adj. existing for longer than can be remembered.

immense adj. very large or great.
▷ SYNONYMS: **huge**, massive, vast, enormous, gigantic, colossal, monumental, towering, giant, mammoth; informal monster, whopping; Brit. informal ginormous.
– ANTONYMS: tiny.
■ **immensely** adv. **immensity** n.

immerse v. **1** dip or cover completely in a liquid. **2** involve deeply in an activity.
▷ SYNONYMS: **1 dip**, submerge, dunk, duck, sink. **2 absorb**, engross, occupy, engage, involve, bury, preoccupy; informal lose.
■ **immersion** n.

immersion heater n. an electric heating device in a water tank.

immigrant n. a person who comes to live permanently in a foreign country.
▷ SYNONYMS: **newcomer**, settler, incomer, migrant, non-native; foreigner, alien, expatriate.
– ANTONYMS: native.

immigration n. the act of coming to live permanently in a foreign country.
■ **immigrate** v.

imminent adj. about to happen.
▷ SYNONYMS: **near**, close at hand, impending, approaching, coming, forthcoming, on the way, expected, looming.
– ANTONYMS: distant.

■ **imminence** n. **imminently** adv.

immobile adj. not moving or able to move.
▷ SYNONYMS: **motionless**, still, stock-still, static, stationary, rooted to the spot, rigid, frozen, transfixed.
■ **immobility** n. **immobilize** (or **-ise**) v.

immoderate adj. excessive.

immodest adj. **1** tending to be boastful. **2** tending to show off your body.
▷ SYNONYMS: **indecorous**, improper, indecent, indelicate, immoral, forward, bold, brazen, shameless.

immolate v. kill or sacrifice by burning.

immoral adj. not following accepted moral standards.
▷ SYNONYMS: **wicked**, bad, wrong, unethical, unprincipled, unscrupulous, dishonest, corrupt, sinful, impure.
– ANTONYMS: moral, ethical.
■ **immorality** n.

immortal adj. **1** living forever. **2** deserving to be remembered forever.
▷ SYNONYMS: **1 undying**, deathless, eternal, everlasting, imperishable, indestructible. **2 timeless**, perennial, classic, time-honoured, enduring, evergreen.
– ANTONYMS: mortal, ephemeral.
■ **immortality** n. **immortalize** (or **-ise**) v.

immovable adj. **1** unable to be moved. **2** unable to be changed.
▷ SYNONYMS: **1 fixed**, secure, set firm, set fast, stuck, jammed, stiff. **2 motionless**, unmoving, stationary, still, stock-still, rooted to the spot, transfixed, paralysed, frozen.
– ANTONYMS: mobile.
■ **immovably** adv.

immune adj. **1** naturally resistant to an infection. **2** not affected. **3** exempt or protected.
▷ SYNONYMS: **resistant**, not subject, not liable, not vulnerable, protected from, safe from, secure against.
– ANTONYMS: susceptible, liable.

immunity n. **1** the ability to resist a particular infection. **2** exemption; protection.
▷ SYNONYMS: **1 resistance**, protection, defence. **2 exemption**, exception, freedom, indemnity, privilege, prerogative, licence, impunity, protection .
– ANTONYMS: susceptibility, liability.

immunize (or **-ise**) v. make a person or animal resistant to an infection.

i

▷ SYNONYMS: **vaccinate**, inoculate, inject.
■ **immunization** n.

immunodeficiency n. failure of the body's ability to resist infection.

immunology n. the study of resistance to infection.
■ **immunological** adj. **immunologist** n.

immure v. confine or imprison.

immutable adj. unchanging or unchangeable.

imp n. **1** a small devil. **2** a mischievous child.
■ **impish** adj.

impact n. **1** an act of one object hitting another. **2** a noticeable effect.
▷ SYNONYMS: **1 collision**, crash, smash, bump, knock. **2 effect**, influence, consequences, repercussions, ramifications.
• v. **1** hit another object. **2** have a strong effect.
▷ SYNONYMS: **1 crash into**, smash into, collide with, hit, strike, smack into, bang into. **2** *interest rates impacted on spending:* **affect**, influence, hit, have an effect, make an impression.

impair v. weaken or damage.
▷ SYNONYMS: **weaken**, damage, harm, undermine, diminish, reduce, lessen, decrease.
– ANTONYMS: improve, enhance.
■ **impairment** n.

impala n. (pl. **impala**) an African antelope with lyre-shaped horns.

impale v. pierce with a sharp object.

impalpable adj. **1** unable to be felt by touch. **2** not easily understood.

impart v. **1** communicate information. **2** give a quality to.
▷ SYNONYMS: **communicate**, pass on, convey, transmit, relay, relate, tell, make known, report, announce.

impartial adj. not favouring one more than another.
▷ SYNONYMS: **unbiased**, unprejudiced, neutral, non-partisan, disinterested, detached, dispassionate, objective.
– ANTONYMS: biased, partisan.
■ **impartiality** n. **impartially** adv.

impassable adj. impossible to travel along or over.

impasse /am-pahss/ n. a deadlock.
▷ SYNONYMS: **deadlock**, dead end, stalemate, stand-off, standstill.

impassioned adj. filled with or showing great emotion.

impassive adj. not feeling or showing emotion.

impatient adj. **1** lacking patience or tolerance. **2** restlessly eager.
▷ SYNONYMS: **1 restless**, agitated,

nervous, anxious. **2 anxious**, eager, keen; informal itching, dying. **3 irritated**, annoyed, angry, tetchy, snappy, cross, curt, brusque.
– ANTONYMS: patient.
■ **impatience** n. **impatiently** adv.

impeach v. charge a public official with serious misconduct.
■ **impeachment** n.

impeccable adj. faultless.
▷ SYNONYMS: **flawless**, faultless, unblemished, spotless, stainless, perfect, exemplary, irreproachable; informal squeaky clean.
– ANTONYMS: imperfect.
■ **impeccably** adv.

impecunious adj. having little or no money.

impedance n. the total resistance of an electric circuit to the flow of alternating current.

impede v. delay or block the progress of.
▷ SYNONYMS: **hinder**, obstruct, hamper, hold back/up, delay, interfere with, disrupt, retard, slow.
– ANTONYMS: facilitate.

impediment n. **1** a hindrance. **2** a defect in a person's speech.
▷ SYNONYMS: **1 hindrance**, obstruction, obstacle, barrier, bar, block, check, curb, restriction. **2 defect**, impairment, stammer, stutter, lisp.

impel v. (**impelling**, **impelled**) drive or urge to do something.

impending adj. imminent.
▷ SYNONYMS: **imminent**, close at hand, near, approaching, coming, brewing, looming, threatening.

impenetrable adj. impossible to get through or into or to understand.
▷ SYNONYMS: **1 unbreakable**, indestructible, solid, thick, unyielding. **2 impassable**, dense, thick, overgrown. **3 incomprehensible**, unfathomable, unintelligible, baffling, bewildering, confusing, opaque.

imperative adj. **1** essential or vital. **2** giving or expressing a command.
▷ SYNONYMS: **vital**, crucial, critical, essential, pressing, urgent.
• n. an essential thing.

imperceptible adj. too slight to be seen or felt.
▷ SYNONYMS: **unnoticeable**, undetectable, indiscernible, invisible, inaudible, impalpable, slight, small, subtle, faint.
■ **imperceptibly** adv.

imperfect adj. **1** faulty or incomplete. **2** (of a tense) referring to a past action not yet completed.

▷ SYNONYMS: **faulty**, flawed, defective, inferior, second-rate, shoddy, substandard, damaged, blemished, torn, broken, cracked, scratched; Brit. informal duff.
■ **imperfection** n. **imperfectly** adv.

imperial adj. **1** of an empire or an emperor. **2** (of measures) in a non-metric system formerly used in the UK.

imperialism n. a policy of extending a country's power and influence by military force etc.
■ **imperialist** n. & adj.

imperil v. (imperilling, imperilled; US imperiling, imperiled) endanger.

imperious adj. expecting unquestioning obedience.
▷ SYNONYMS: **peremptory**, high-handed, overbearing, domineering, authoritarian, dictatorial, authoritative, bossy, arrogant; informal pushy, high and mighty.
■ **imperiously** adv.

impermeable adj. not allowing fluid to pass through.

impersonal adj. **1** not influenced by personal feelings. **2** distant, unemotional, etc.
▷ SYNONYMS: **aloof**, distant, remote, detached, unemotional, unsentimental, cold, cool, indifferent, unconcerned, formal, stiff, businesslike, matter-of-fact; informal starchy, stand-offish.
■ **impersonally** adv.

impersonate v. pretend to be another person.
▷ SYNONYMS: **imitate**, mimic, do an impression of, ape, parody, caricature, satirize, lampoon, masquerade as, pose as, pass yourself off as; informal take off, send up.
■ **impersonation** n. **impersonator** n.

impertinent adj. not showing proper respect.
▷ SYNONYMS: **rude**, insolent, impolite, ill-mannered, disrespectful, impudent, cheeky, presumptuous, forward.
– ANTONYMS: polite, respectful.
■ **impertinence** n. **impertinently** adv.

imperturbable adj. unable to be upset.

impervious adj. **1** impermeable. **2** (impervious to) unaffected by.

impetigo /im-pi-ty-goh/ n. a contagious skin infection.

impetuous adj. acting or done quickly and without thought.
▷ SYNONYMS: **impulsive**, rash, hasty, reckless, foolhardy, imprudent, ill-considered, spontaneous, impromptu, spur-of-the-moment.
■ **impetuously** adv.

impetus n. **1** the force or energy with which something moves. **2** a driving force.
▷ SYNONYMS: **1 momentum**, drive, thrust, energy, force, power, push. **2 motivation**, stimulus, incentive, inspiration, driving force.

impinge v. have an effect or impact.

impious adj. irreverent.

implacable adj. **1** unwilling to be reconciled. **2** (of negative feelings) unable to be changed.
■ **implacably** adv.

implant v. **1** insert tissue or a device surgically into the body. **2** establish in the mind.
▷ SYNONYMS: **1 insert**, embed, bury, inject, transplant, graft. **2 instil**, inculcate, introduce, plant, sow.
• n. something implanted.
■ **implantation** n.

implausible adj. not probable or convincing.
▷ SYNONYMS: **unlikely**, improbable, questionable, doubtful, debatable, unconvincing, far-fetched.
– ANTONYMS: convincing.
■ **implausibly** adv.

implement n. a tool.
▷ SYNONYMS: **tool**, utensil, instrument, device, apparatus, gadget, contraption, appliance; informal gizmo.
• v. put into effect.
▷ SYNONYMS: **execute**, apply, put into effect, put into practice, carry out/through, perform, enact, fulfil.
– ANTONYMS: abolish, cancel.
■ **implementation** n.

implicate v. **1** show to be involved in a crime. **2** (be implicated in) be partly responsible for.
▷ SYNONYMS: **incriminate**, involve, connect, embroil, enmesh.

implication n. **1** a conclusion implied by something. **2** a possible effect. **3** involvement in something.
▷ SYNONYMS: **1 suggestion**, inference, insinuation, innuendo, intimation, imputation. **2 consequence**, result, ramification, repercussion, reverberation, effect. **3 incrimination**, involvement, connection, entanglement, association.

implicit adj. **1** suggested but not stated directly. **2** with no doubt or question.
▷ SYNONYMS: **1 implied**, inferred, understood, hinted at, suggested, unspoken, unstated, tacit, taken for granted. **2 inherent**, latent, underlying, inbuilt, incorporated. **3 absolute**,

i

complete, total, wholehearted, utter, unqualified, unconditional, unshakeable, unquestioning, firm.
– ANTONYMS: explicit.
■ **implicitly** adv.

implode v. collapse violently inwards.
■ **implosion** n.

implore v. beg earnestly.
▷ SYNONYMS: **plead with**, beg, entreat, appeal to, ask, request, call on, exhort, urge.

imply v. (**implying**, **implied**) **1** suggest rather than state directly. **2** suggest as a possible effect.
▷ SYNONYMS: **1 insinuate**, suggest, infer, hint, intimate, give someone to understand, make out. **2 involve**, entail, mean, point to, signify, indicate, presuppose.

> USAGE Don't confuse **imply** and **infer**. If you **imply** something, you are suggesting it though not saying it directly. If you **infer** something from a statement, you come to the conclusion that this is what was meant.

impolite adj. not having good manners.
▷ SYNONYMS: **rude**, bad-mannered, ill-mannered, discourteous, uncivil, disrespectful, insolent, impudent, impertinent, cheeky; informal lippy.

impolitic adj. unwise.

imponderable adj. difficult or impossible to assess.

import v. bring goods into a country from abroad.
▷ SYNONYMS: **bring in**, buy in, ship in.
– ANTONYMS: export.
•n. **1** an imported item. **2** the act of importing. **3** implied meaning. **4** importance.
▷ SYNONYMS: **1 importance**, significance, consequence, momentousness, magnitude, substance, weight, note, gravity, seriousness. **2 meaning**, sense, essence, gist, drift, message, thrust, substance, implication.
– ANTONYMS: insignificance.
■ **importation** n. **importer** n.

importance n. the quality of being important.
▷ SYNONYMS: **1 significance**, momentousness, moment, import, consequence, note, weight, seriousness, gravity. **2 status**, eminence, prestige, worth, influence, power, authority.
– ANTONYMS: insignificance.

important adj. **1** of great value or significance. **2** having great authority or influence.
▷ SYNONYMS: **1 significant**, consequen-

tial, momentous, of great import, major, valuable, necessary, crucial, vital, essential, pivotal, decisive, far-reaching, historic. **2 powerful**, influential, well connected, high-ranking, prominent, eminent, notable, distinguished, esteemed, respected, great, prestigious.
– ANTONYMS: unimportant, insignificant.
■ **importantly** adv.

importunate adj. very persistent.

importune v. bother with persistent requests.

impose v. **1** force something to be done or accepted. **2** (**impose on**) take unfair advantage of.
▷ SYNONYMS: **1** *he imposed his ideas on everyone*: **foist**, force, inflict, press, saddle someone with. **2** *new taxes were imposed*: **levy**, charge, apply, enforce, set, establish, institute, introduce, bring into effect.
– ANTONYMS: abolish.
■ **imposition** n.

imposing adj. impressive.
▷ SYNONYMS: **impressive**, spectacular, striking, dramatic, commanding, arresting, awesome, formidable, splendid, grand, majestic.
– ANTONYMS: modest.

impossible adj. **1** not able to occur, exist, or be done. **2** very difficult to deal with.
▷ SYNONYMS: **1 out of the question**, impracticable, non-viable, unworkable. **2 unattainable**, unachievable, unobtainable, hopeless, impracticable, unworkable. **3 unbearable**, intolerable, unendurable. **4 unreasonable**, difficult, awkward, intolerable, unbearable, exasperating, maddening, infuriating.
– ANTONYMS: possible.
■ **impossibility** n. **impossibly** adv.

impostor (or **imposter**) n. a person who pretends to be someone else so as to deceive.
▷ SYNONYMS: **impersonator**, deceiver, hoaxer, fraudster, fake, fraud; informal phoney.

impotent adj. **1** helpless or powerless. **2** (of a man) unable to achieve an erection.
■ **impotence** n.

impound v. **1** seize and take legal possession of. **2** shut up animals in an enclosure.
▷ SYNONYMS: **confiscate**, appropriate, take possession of, seize, commandeer, expropriate, requisition, take over.

impoverish v. **1** make poor. **2** make worse in quality.

impracticable adj. unable to be done.
▷ SYNONYMS: **unworkable**, unfeasible, non-viable, unachievable, unattainable, impractical.
– ANTONYMS: practicable.

impractical adj. not sensible or realistic.
▷ SYNONYMS: **unrealistic**, unworkable, unfeasible, non-viable, ill-thought-out, absurd, idealistic, fanciful, romantic, starry-eyed, pie-in-the-sky; informal cockeyed, crackpot, crazy.
– ANTONYMS: realistic, practical.

imprecation n. a spoken curse.

imprecise adj. not exact.
▷ SYNONYMS: **1 vague**, loose, indistinct, inaccurate, non-specific, sweeping, broad, general, hazy, fuzzy, woolly, nebulous, ambiguous, equivocal, uncertain. **2 inexact**, approximate, rough; N. Amer. informal ballpark.
– ANTONYMS: exact.

impregnable adj. unable to be captured or broken into.

impregnate v. **1** saturate with a substance. **2** make pregnant.
■ impregnation n.

impresario n. (pl. **impresarios**) an organizer of plays, operas, etc.

impress v. **1** cause to feel admiration. **2** (impress on) cause to realize the importance of. **3** make a mark with a stamp etc.
▷ SYNONYMS: **make an impression on**, have an impact on, influence, affect, move, stir, rouse, excite, inspire, dazzle, awe.
– ANTONYMS: disappoint.

impression n. **1** an idea, feeling, or opinion. **2** an effect produced on someone. **3** an imitation of a person, done to entertain. **4** a mark made by pressing.
▷ SYNONYMS: **1 feeling**, sense, fancy, sneaking suspicion, inkling, intuition, hunch, notion, idea. **2 opinion**, view, image, picture, perception, reaction, judgement, verdict, estimation. **3 impact**, effect, influence. **4 impersonation**, imitation, caricature; informal take-off. **5 indentation**, dent, mark, outline, imprint.

impressionable adj. easily influenced.
▷ SYNONYMS: **easily influenced**, suggestible, susceptible, persuadable, pliable, malleable, pliant, ingenuous, trusting, naive, gullible.

Impressionism n. a style of art depicting the visual impression of a moment.
■ **Impressionist** n. & adj.

impressionist n. an entertainer who impersonates famous people.

impressionistic adj. based on personal impressions.

impressive adj. of admirable size, quality, or skill.
▷ SYNONYMS: **magnificent**, majestic, imposing, splendid, spectacular, grand, awe-inspiring, stunning, breathtaking.
■ impressively adv. impressiveness n.

imprint v. make a mark on by pressure.
▷ SYNONYMS: **stamp**, print, impress, mark, emboss.
• n. **1** a mark made by pressure. **2** a publisher's name etc. in a book.
▷ SYNONYMS: **impression**, print, mark, stamp, indentation.

imprison v. put or keep in prison.
▷ SYNONYMS: **incarcerate**, send to prison, jail, lock up, put away, intern, detain, hold prisoner, hold captive; informal send down; Brit. informal bang up.

imprisonment n. the state of being imprisoned.
▷ SYNONYMS: **custody**, incarceration, internment, confinement, detention, captivity; informal time; Brit. informal porridge.

improbable adj. not likely to be true or to happen.
▷ SYNONYMS: **1 unlikely**, doubtful, dubious, debatable, questionable, uncertain. **2 unconvincing**, unbelievable, implausible, unlikely.
■ improbability n. improbably adv.

impromptu adj. & adv. done without being planned or rehearsed.
▷ SYNONYMS: **unrehearsed**, unprepared, unscripted, extempore, extemporized, improvised, spontaneous, unplanned; informal off-the-cuff.

improper adj. **1** not conforming to rules or standards. **2** not modest or decent.
▷ SYNONYMS: **1 unacceptable**, unprofessional, irregular, unethical, dishonest. **2 unseemly**, unfitting, unbecoming, unladylike, ungentlemanly, inappropriate, indelicate, indecent, immodest, indecorous, immoral. **3 indecent**, risqué, suggestive, naughty, dirty, filthy, vulgar, crude, rude, obscene, lewd; informal blue, raunchy, steamy.
– ANTONYMS: proper, seemly.
■ improperly adv. impropriety n.

improve v. make or become better.
▷ SYNONYMS: **1 make better**, ameliorate,

upgrade, refine, enhance, boost, build on, raise. **2 get better**, advance, progress, develop, make headway, make progress, pick up, look up, move forward. **3 recover**, get better, recuperate, rally, revive, be on the mend.

– ANTONYMS: worsen, deteriorate.

improvement n. **1** the act of improving. **2** a thing that improves or is better than something.

▷ SYNONYMS: **advance**, development, upgrade, refinement, enhancement, betterment, amelioration, boost, augmentation, rally, recovery, upswing.

improvident adj. not providing for future needs.

improvise v. **1** invent and perform drama, music, etc. without preparation. **2** make from whatever is available.

▷ SYNONYMS: **1 extemporize**, ad-lib; informal speak off the cuff, play it by ear, busk it, wing it. **2 contrive**, devise, throw together, cobble together, rig up; informal whip up, rustle up; Brit. informal knock up.

■ **improvisation** n.

imprudent adj. not careful; rash.

impudent adj. not showing proper respect.

■ **impudence** n. **impudently** adv.

impugn /im-pyoon/ v. express doubts about the truth or honesty of.

impulse n. **1** a sudden urge to do something. **2** a driving force.

▷ SYNONYMS: **1 urge**, instinct, drive, compulsion, itch, whim, desire, fancy, notion. **2 spontaneity**, impetuosity, recklessness, rashness.

■ **impulsion** n.

impulsive adj. acting without thinking ahead.

▷ SYNONYMS: **1 hasty**, sudden, quick, precipitate, impetuous, impromptu, spontaneous, snap, unplanned, unpremeditated, thoughtless, rash, reckless. **2 impetuous**, instinctive, passionate, intuitive, emotional, devil-may-care.

– ANTONYMS: cautious, premeditated.

■ **impulsively** adv.

impunity n. freedom from punishment or harm.

impure adj. **1** mixed with unwanted substances. **2** morally wrong.

■ **impurity** n.

impute v. (**impute to**) believe to have been done or caused by.

■ **imputation** n.

in prep. **1** enclosed, surrounded, or inside. **2** during or within a period of time. **3** expressing a state or quality. **4** included or involved. **5** indicating the language or medium used.

• adv. **1** so as to be enclosed, surrounded, or inside. **2** present at your home or office. **3** expressing arrival.

• adj. informal fashionable.

□ **in-house** within an organization. **in-law** a relative by marriage. **the ins and outs** informal all the details.

in. abbrev. inches.

inability n. the state of being unable to do something.

in absentia adv. while not present.

inaccessible adj. **1** unable to be reached. **2** difficult to understand.

inaccurate adj. not accurate.

▷ SYNONYMS: **inexact**, imprecise, incorrect, wrong, erroneous, faulty, imperfect, defective, unreliable, false, mistaken, untrue; Brit. informal adrift.

■ **inaccuracy** n. **inaccurately** adv.

inaction n. lack of action.

inactive adj. not active or working.

▷ SYNONYMS: **1 idle**, indolent, lazy, slothful, lethargic, inert, sluggish, list-less, torpid. **2 inoperative**, idle, out of service, out of commission.

inactivity n. lack of activity.

▷ SYNONYMS: **inaction**, inertia, idleness, non-intervention, negligence, apathy, indolence, laziness, slothfulness.

inadequate adj. **1** not enough or not good enough. **2** unable to deal with a situation.

▷ SYNONYMS: **1 insufficient**, deficient, poor, scant, scarce, sparse, in short supply, paltry, meagre. **2 incapable**, incompetent, ineffective, inefficient, inept, unfit; informal not up to scratch.

■ **inadequacy** n. **inadequately** adv.

inadmissible adj. (of evidence in court) not accepted as valid.

inadvertent adj. not deliberate.

▷ SYNONYMS: **accidental**, unintentional, unwitting, unintended, unplanned.

USAGE -ent, not -ant: inadvertent.

■ **inadvertently** adv.

inalienable adj. unable to be taken or given away.

inane adj. silly.

■ **inanely** adv. **inanity** n.

inanimate adj. not alive.

inapplicable adj. not relevant or appropriate.

inappropriate adj. unsuitable.

▷ SYNONYMS: **unsuitable**, unfitting, unseemly, unbecoming, improper, out of place/keeping, inapposite; informal

out of order.
■ **inappropriately** adv.
inarticulate adj. **1** unable to express yourself clearly. **2** not expressed in words.
inasmuch adv. (**inasmuch as**) **1** to the extent that. **2** considering that.
inattentive adj. not paying attention.
inaudible adj. unable to be heard.
▷ SYNONYMS: **unclear**, indistinct, faint, muted, soft, low, muffled, whispered, muttered, murmured, mumbled.
■ **inaudibly** adv.
inaugurate v. **1** begin or introduce a system etc. **2** establish someone in office or mark the opening of a building etc. with a ceremony.
▷ SYNONYMS: **1 initiate**, begin, start, institute, launch, get going, get under way, establish, bring in, usher in; informal kick off. **2 install**, instate, swear in, invest, ordain, crown.
■ **inaugural** adj. **inauguration** n.
inborn adj. existing from birth.
inbred adj. **1** produced by inbreeding. **2** inborn.
inbreeding n. breeding from closely related people or animals.
incalculable adj. too great to be calculated or estimated.
incandescent adj. glowing with heat.
■ **incandescence** n.
incantation n. words said as a magic spell.
incapable adj. **1** not able to do something. **2** not able to care for yourself.
▷ SYNONYMS: **incompetent**, inept, inadequate, ineffective, ineffectual, unfit, unqualified; informal not up to it.
– ANTONYMS: competent.
incapacitate v. prevent from functioning.
incapacity n. inability to do something.
incarcerate v. imprison.
■ **incarceration** n.
incarnate adj. in human or physical form.
incarnation n. **1** a god, spirit, or quality in human form. **2** (**the Incarnation**) (in Christian belief) God as Jesus Christ.
incendiary adj. **1** (of a bomb) designed to cause fire. **2** stirring up conflict.
• n. (pl. **incendiaries**) an incendiary bomb.
incense¹ n. a substance burnt to produce a sweet smell.
incense² v. make very angry.

▷ SYNONYMS: **enrage**, infuriate, anger, madden, outrage, exasperate, antagonize, provoke; (**incensed**) furious, irate, raging, incandescent, fuming, seething, beside yourself, outraged; informal mad, hopping mad, wild, livid.
– ANTONYMS: placate.
incentive n. something that encourages action or effort.
▷ SYNONYMS: **inducement**, motivation, motive, reason, stimulus, spur, impetus, encouragement, carrot; informal sweetener.
– ANTONYMS: deterrent.
inception n. the beginning of something.
incessant adj. never stopping.
■ **incessantly** adv.
incest n. sex between very closely related people.
■ **incestuous** adj.
inch n. a unit of length equal to one twelfth of a foot (2.54 cm).
• v. move slowly and carefully.
inchoate adj. not fully formed or developed.
incidence n. **1** the rate of occurrence of something. **2** Physics the meeting of a line or ray with a surface.
incident n. an event, esp. a distinctive or unpleasant one.
▷ SYNONYMS: **1 event**, occurrence, episode, happening, affair, business, adventure, exploit, escapade. **2 disturbance**, commotion, clash, confrontation, scene, accident, fracas, contretemps; Brit. row. **3** the journey was not without incident: **excitement**, adventure, drama, crisis, danger.
incidental adj. **1** minor or unimportant. **2** occurring as a result of something else.
▷ SYNONYMS: **1 secondary**, subsidiary, minor, peripheral, background, by-the-by, unimportant, insignificant, tangential. **2 chance**, accidental, random, fortuitous, serendipitous, coincidental, unlooked-for.
– ANTONYMS: essential.
□ **incidental music** background music in a film.
■ **incidentally** adv.
incinerate v. destroy by burning.
■ **incineration** n. **incinerator** n.
incipient adj. beginning to happen or develop.
incise v. make a cut in a surface.
■ **incision** n.
incisive adj. **1** showing clear thought and understanding. **2** quick and direct.

incisor n. a narrow-edged front tooth.

incite v. urge to act violently or unlawfully.
▷ SYNONYMS: **1 stir up**, whip up, encourage, stoke up, fuel, kindle, inflame, instigate, provoke, excite, trigger, spark off. **2 provoke**, encourage, urge, goad, spur on, egg on, drive, prod, prompt; informal put up to.
– ANTONYMS: discourage, deter.
■ **incitement** n.

incivility n. rudeness.

inclement adj. (of the weather) unpleasantly cold or wet.

inclination n. **1** a tendency to act in a particular way. **2** an interest or liking. **3** a slope or slant.
▷ SYNONYMS: **tendency**, propensity, leaning, predisposition, predilection, impulse, bent, liking, taste, penchant, preference.
– ANTONYMS: aversion.

incline v. **1** make someone disposed to do something. **2** feel favourably disposed towards. **3** lean or bend.
▷ SYNONYMS: **1** *his prejudice inclines him to overlook obvious facts:* **predispose**, lead, make, dispose, prompt, induce. **2** *I incline to the opposite view:* **tend**, lean, swing, veer, gravitate, be drawn, prefer, favour, go for. **3 bend**, bow, nod, bob, lower, dip.
• n. a slope.
▷ SYNONYMS: **slope**, gradient, pitch, ramp, bank, ascent, rise, hill, dip, descent; N. Amer. grade.

inclined adj. **1** favourably disposed towards or willing to do something. **2** having a tendency to do something.
▷ SYNONYMS: **1** *I'm inclined to believe her:* **disposed**, minded, of a mind, given, in the habit of, liable, apt. **2 prone**, liable, apt.

include v. **1** have as part of a whole. **2** make or treat as part of a whole.
▷ SYNONYMS: **1 incorporate**, comprise, encompass, cover, embrace, take in, number, contain. **2 allow for**, count, take into account, take into consideration. **3 add**, insert, put in, append, enter.
– ANTONYMS: exclude, leave out.

inclusion n. **1** the act of including. **2** a person or thing that is included.

inclusive adj. **1** including everything expected or required. **2** including the specified limits.
▷ SYNONYMS: **all-in**, comprehensive, overall, full, all-round, umbrella, catch-all, all-encompassing.
– ANTONYMS: exclusive, limited.

incognito /in-kog-nee-toh/ adj. & adv. with your true identity concealed.

incoherent adj. **1** hard to understand. **2** not logical or well-organized.
■ **incoherence** n. **incoherently** adv.

income n. money received for work or from investments.
▷ SYNONYMS: **earnings**, salary, wages, pay, remuneration, revenue, receipts, takings, profits, proceeds, yield, dividend; N. Amer. take.
– ANTONYMS: expenditure, outgoings.

incoming adj. coming in.
▷ SYNONYMS: **1 arriving**, approaching, inbound, inward, returning, homeward. **2 new**, next, future, elect, designate.
– ANTONYMS: outward, outgoing.

incommunicado adj. & adv. not able to communicate with other people.

incomparable adj. so good that nothing can be compared to it.
■ **incomparably** adv.

incompatible adj. not able to exist, be used, or to live or work together.
▷ SYNONYMS: **mismatched**, unsuited, poles apart, irreconcilable, inconsistent, conflicting, opposed, opposite, contradictory, at odds, at variance.
– ANTONYMS: harmonious, consistent.
■ **incompatibility** n.

incompetent adj. lacking the skill to do something.
▷ SYNONYMS: **inept**, unskilled, inexpert, amateurish, unprofessional, bungling, blundering, clumsy; informal useless, not up to it.
■ **incompetence** n.

incomplete adj. not complete.
▷ SYNONYMS: **1 unfinished**, uncompleted, partial, half-finished. **2 deficient**, insufficient, partial, sketchy, fragmentary, scrappy, bitty.
– ANTONYMS: completed, full.

incomprehensible adj. unable to be understood.
▷ SYNONYMS: **unintelligible**, impenetrable, unclear, indecipherable, unfathomable, abstruse, difficult, involved; Brit. informal double Dutch.
– ANTONYMS: intelligible, clear.

inconceivable adj. unable to be believed.
■ **inconceivably** adv.

inconclusive adj. not leading to a firm conclusion.

incongruous adj. out of place.
■ **incongruity** n. **incongruously** adv.

inconsequential adj. not important.

inconsiderable adj. small in size, amount, etc.

inconsiderate adj. not thinking of

others' feelings.

inconsistent adj. not consistent.
▷ SYNONYMS: **1 erratic**, changeable, unpredictable, variable, unstable, fickle, unreliable, volatile; informal up and down. **2 incompatible**, conflicting, at odds, at variance, irreconcilable, out of keeping, contrary.
■ **inconsistency** n.

inconsolable adj. unable to be comforted.
■ **inconsolably** adv.

inconspicuous adj. not noticeable.

inconstant adj. frequently changing.

incontestable adj. unable to be disputed.

incontinent adj. unable to control your bladder or bowels.
■ **incontinence** n.

incontrovertible adj. unable to be denied or disputed.
■ **incontrovertibly** adv.

inconvenience n. slight trouble or difficulty.
▷ SYNONYMS: **trouble**, nuisance, bother, problem, disruption, difficulty, disturbance; informal aggravation, hassle, headache, pain, pain in the neck.
• v. cause inconvenience to.
▷ SYNONYMS: **trouble**, bother, put out, put to any trouble, disturb, impose on.

inconvenient adj. causing slight trouble or difficulty.
▷ SYNONYMS: **awkward**, difficult, inopportune, badly timed, unsuitable, inappropriate, unfortunate.

incorporate v. **1** include as part of a whole. **2** form a company into a corporation.
▷ SYNONYMS: **1 absorb**, include, subsume, assimilate, integrate, swallow up. **2 include**, contain, embrace, build in, offer, boast. **3 blend**, mix, combine, fold in, stir in.
■ **incorporation** n.

incorrect adj. not true or accurate.
▷ SYNONYMS: **1 wrong**, erroneous, mistaken, untrue, false, fallacious, flawed; informal wide of the mark. **2 inappropriate**, unsuitable, unacceptable, improper, unseemly; informal out of order.
■ **incorrectly** adv.

incorrigible adj. having bad habits that cannot be changed.

incorruptible adj. too honest to take bribes.

increase v. make or become greater in size, amount, or intensity.
▷ SYNONYMS: **1 grow**, get bigger, get larger, enlarge, expand, swell, rise, climb, mount, intensify, strengthen, extend, spread, widen. **2 add to**, make larger, make bigger, augment, supplement, top up, build up, extend, raise, swell, inflate, intensify, heighten; informal up, bump up.
• n. a rise in amount, size, or intensity.
▷ SYNONYMS: **growth**, rise, enlargement, expansion, extension, increment, gain, addition, augmentation, surge; informal hike.
– ANTONYMS: decrease.
■ **increasingly** adv.

incredible adj. impossible or hard to believe.
▷ SYNONYMS: **1 unbelievable**, unconvincing, far-fetched, implausible, improbable, inconceivable, unimaginable. **2 wonderful**, marvellous, spectacular, remarkable, phenomenal, prodigious, breathtaking; informal fantastic, terrific.
■ **incredibly** adv.

incredulous adj. unwilling or unable to believe something.
■ **incredulity** n. **incredulously** adv.

increment n. an increase in a number or amount.
■ **incremental** adj.

incriminate v. cause to appear guilty of a crime.

incubate v. **1** hatch eggs by keeping them warm. **2** (of an infectious disease) develop slowly without obvious signs.
■ **incubation** n. **incubator** n.

inculcate v. fix an idea in the mind by repetition.

incumbent adj. **1** necessary as a duty. **2** currently holding office.
• n. the holder of an office.

incur v. (**incurring**, **incurred**) bring something unwelcome on yourself.
▷ SYNONYMS: **bring on yourself**, expose yourself to, lay yourself open to, run up, earn, sustain, experience.

incurable adj. unable to be cured.
■ **incurably** adv.

incursion n. a sudden invasion or attack.

indebted adj. **1** grateful. **2** owing money.

indecent adj. not following accepted standards, esp. in relation to sex.
▷ SYNONYMS: **1 obscene**, dirty, filthy, rude, naughty, vulgar, smutty, pornographic; informal blue; euphemistic adult. **2 unseemly**, improper, unbecoming, inappropriate.
□ **indecent assault** sexual assault that does not involve rape. **indecent**

i

exposure the crime of showing the genitals in public.
■ **indecency** n. **indecently** adv.

indecipherable adj. unable to be read or understood.

indecisive adj. not decisive.
■ **indecision** n.

indeed adv. used to emphasize a statement.

indefatigable adj. never tiring.

indefensible adj. unable to be justified.

indefinable adj. unable to be defined exactly.

indefinite adj. **1** not clearly defined; vague. **2** lasting for an unknown period.
□ **indefinite article** the word *a* or *an*. ■ **indefinitely** adv.

indelible adj. **1** (of ink or a mark) unable to be removed. **2** unable to be forgotten.
■ **indelibly** adv.

indelicate adj. tactless or rude.

indemnity n. (pl. **indemnities**)
1 insurance against legal responsibility for your actions.
2 compensation for damage or loss.
■ **indemnify** v.

indent v. **1** form hollows or notches in. **2** begin a line of writing further from the margin than the other lines.
■ **indentation** n.

indenture n. a formal contract, esp. of apprenticeship.

independence n. the fact or state of being independent.
▷ SYNONYMS: **1 self-government**, self-rule, home rule, self-determination, sovereignty, autonomy.
2 impartiality, neutrality, disinterestedness, detachment, objectivity.

independent adj. **1** free from outside control or influence. **2** self-governing. **3** having enough money to support yourself. **4** not supported by public funds. **5** not connected; separate.
▷ SYNONYMS: **1** *an independent country*: **self-governing**, self-ruling, self-determining, sovereign, autonomous, non-aligned, free. **2** *you should take independent advice*: **impartial**, unbiased, unprejudiced, neutral, disinterested, uninvolved, detached, dispassionate, objective, non-partisan. **3** *an independent school*: **private**, private-sector, fee-paying, privatized, deregulated, denationalized. **4 separate**, different, unconnected, unrelated, discrete.
– ANTONYMS: related, biased.
■ **independently** adv.

USAGE *-ent*, not *-ant*: independ*ent*.

indescribable adj. too extreme or unusual to be described.
■ **indescribably** adv.

indestructible adj. unable to be destroyed.

indeterminate adj. not exactly known.

index n. (pl. **indexes** or **indices**)
1 an alphabetical list of names or subjects referred to in a book.
2 an alphabetical list of books or documents. **3** a sign or measure of something. **4** a number indicating the relative level of prices or wages compared with a previous level.
▷ SYNONYMS: **list**, listing, inventory, catalogue, register, directory, database.
● v. record in or provide with an index.
□ **index finger** the forefinger.

Indian n. **1** a person from India. **2** an American Indian.
● adj. of India.
□ **Indian ink** deep black ink used in drawing. **Indian summer** dry, warm weather in autumn.

indicate v. **1** point out. **2** be a sign of. **3** state briefly.
▷ SYNONYMS: **1 point to**, be a sign of, be evidence of, demonstrate, show, testify to, be symptomatic of, denote, mark, signal, reflect, signify, suggest, imply. **2 state**, declare, make known, communicate, announce, put on record.
■ **indicative** adj.

indication n. a sign, remark, etc. that indicates something.
▷ SYNONYMS: **sign**, signal, indicator, symptom, mark, demonstration, pointer, guide, hint, clue, omen, warning.

indicator n. **1** a thing that indicates a state or level. **2** Brit. a flashing light on a vehicle showing that it is about to pull out or turn.
▷ SYNONYMS: **measure**, gauge, meter, barometer, guide, index, mark, sign, signal.

indict /in-**dyt**/ v. formally accuse of or charge with a serious crime.
▷ SYNONYMS: **charge**, accuse, arraign; summons, prefer charges against; N. Amer. impeach.
■ **indictable** adj. **indictment** n.

indifference n. lack of interest or concern.
▷ SYNONYMS: **detachment**, disinterest, nonchalance, boredom, unresponsiveness, impassivity, coolness.
– ANTONYMS: concern.

indifferent adj. **1** having no interest or sympathy. **2** not very good.
▷ SYNONYMS: **1 detached**, unconcerned, uninterested, uncaring, casual, nonchalant, offhand, unenthusiastic, unimpressed, unmoved, impassive, cool. **2 mediocre**, ordinary, average, middle-of-the-road, uninspired, undistinguished, unexceptional, pedestrian, forgettable, amateurish; informal no great shakes.
– ANTONYMS: enthusiastic, brilliant.
■ **indifferently** adv.

indigenous adj. native.

indigent adj. very poor.

indigestible adj. difficult to digest.

indigestion n. discomfort caused by difficulty in digesting food.

indignant adj. feeling or showing indignation.
▷ SYNONYMS: **aggrieved**, affronted, displeased, resentful, angry, annoyed, offended, exasperated; informal peeved, irked, put out; Brit. informal narked; N. Amer. informal sore.
■ **indignantly** adv.

indignation n. annoyance caused by unfair treatment.

indignity n. (pl. **indignities**) humiliating treatment.

indigo n. a dark blue colour or dye.

indirect adj. **1** not direct. **2** (of tax) charged on goods etc. rather than income or profits.
▷ SYNONYMS: **1 incidental**, secondary, subordinate, ancillary, collateral, concomitant, contingent. **2 round-about**, circuitous, meandering, winding, tortuous. **3 oblique**, implicit, implied.
□ **indirect object** a person or thing that is affected by the action of a transitive verb but is not the main object.
■ **indirectly** adv.

indiscreet adj. revealing things that should remain private.
■ **indiscretion** n. **indiscreetly** adv.

indiscriminate adj. done or acting without careful judgement.
■ **indiscriminately** adv.

indispensable adj. essential.

USAGE -able, not -ible: indispensable.

indisposed adj. **1** slightly unwell. **2** unwilling.
■ **indisposition** n.

indisputable adj. undeniable.
■ **indisputably** adv.

indistinct adj. not clear or sharp.
■ **indistinctly** adv.

indistinguishable adj. not identifiable as different.

indium n. a soft metallic element.

individual adj. **1** single; separate. **2** of or for one person. **3** striking or unusual.
▷ SYNONYMS: **1 single**, separate, discrete, independent, lone. **2 unique**, characteristic, distinctive, distinct, particular, idiosyncratic, peculiar, personal, special. **3 original**, exclusive, different, unusual, novel, unorthodox, out of the ordinary.
– ANTONYMS: multiple, shared, ordinary.
• n. a single person or item.
▷ SYNONYMS: **person**, human being, soul, creature, character; informal type, sort, customer.
■ **individuality** n. **individually** adv.

individualism n. the quality of being independent in thought and action.
■ **individualist** n.

indivisible adj. unable to be divided.

indoctrinate v. force to accept a set of beliefs.
■ **indoctrination** n.

indolent adj. lazy.
■ **indolence** n.

indomitable adj. impossible to defeat or subdue.

indoor adj. situated, done, or used inside a building.
• adv. (**indoors**) into or inside a building.

indubitable adj. impossible to doubt.
■ **indubitably** adv.

induce v. **1** persuade. **2** bring about. **3** bring on labour in childbirth by drugs etc.
▷ SYNONYMS: **1 persuade**, convince, prevail on, get, make, prompt, encourage, cajole into, talk into. **2 bring about**, cause, produce, create, give rise to, generate, engender.
– ANTONYMS: dissuade.

inducement n. a thing that persuades someone to do something.

induct v. introduce formally to a post or organization.

inductance n. a process by which a change in the current of an electric circuit produces an electromotive force.

induction n. **1** the act of inducting. **2** reasoning in which a general rule is drawn from particular examples. **3** the passing of electricity or magnetism from one object to another without them touching.
■ **inductive** adj. **inductor** n.

indulge v. **1** (**indulge in**) allow yourself something enjoyable. **2** satisfy a desire. **3** allow someone to

i

do or have what they want.
▷ SYNONYMS: **1 satisfy**, gratify, fulfil, feed, yield to, give in to, go along with. **2 pamper**, spoil, overindulge, coddle, mollycoddle, cosset, pander to, wait on hand and foot.

indulgence n. **1** the action of indulging in something. **2** a thing that is indulged in; a luxury. **3** a willingness to tolerate someone's faults. **4** esp. historical (in the RC Church) the setting aside or cancellation by the Pope of the punishment still due for sins after absolution.
▷ SYNONYMS: **1 satisfaction**, gratification, fulfilment; self-gratification, self-indulgence, overindulgence, intemperance, excess, extravagance, hedonism. **2 extravagance**, luxury, treat, non-essential, extra, frill. **3 tolerance**, forbearance, understanding, compassion, sympathy, leniency.
– ANTONYMS: asceticism, intolerance.

indulgent adj. allowing someone to do what they want or overlooking their faults.
▷ SYNONYMS: **generous**, permissive, easy-going, liberal, tolerant, forgiving, forbearing, lenient, kind, kindly, soft-hearted.
– ANTONYMS: strict.
■ **indulgently** adv.

industrial adj. of industry.
□ **industrial action** Brit. a strike or similar protest by workers. **industrial estate** an area of land developed for factories. **industrial relations** relations between management and workers.
■ **industrially** adv.

industrialism n. a system in which industry is the basis of the economy.

industrialist n. a person who owns or controls a manufacturing business.
▷ SYNONYMS: **manufacturer**, factory owner, captain of industry, magnate, tycoon.

industrialize (or **-ise**) v. develop industries in a country or region on a wide scale.
■ **industrialization** n.

industrious adj. hard-working.
■ **industriously** adv.

industry n. (pl. **industries**) **1** the manufacture of goods in factories. **2** a branch of economic activity. **3** hard work.
▷ SYNONYMS: **1 manufacturing**, production, construction, trade, commerce. **2 business**, trade,

field, line of business, profession. **3 activity**, energy, effort, endeavour, hard work, industriousness, diligence, application.

inebriated adj. drunk.
■ **inebriation** n.

inedible adj. not fit for eating.

ineffable adj. too great to be described.

ineffective adj. not producing any or the desired effect.
▷ SYNONYMS: **1 unsuccessful**, unproductive, unprofitable, ineffectual, unavailing, to no avail, fruitless, futile. **2 ineffectual**, inefficient, inadequate, incompetent, incapable, unfit, inept; informal useless, hopeless.
– ANTONYMS: effective.
■ **ineffectively** adv.

ineffectual adj. **1** ineffective. **2** not forceful enough to do something.
■ **ineffectually** adv.

inefficient adj. not making the best use of time or resources.
▷ SYNONYMS: **1 ineffective**, ineffectual, incompetent, inept, disorganized. **2 uneconomical**, wasteful, unproductive, time-wasting, slow, unsystematic.
■ **inefficiency** n. **inefficiently** adv.

inelegant adj. not elegant or graceful.

ineligible adj. not eligible.

ineluctable adj. unable to be avoided.

inept adj. lacking skill.
■ **ineptitude** n.

inequality n. (pl. **inequalities**) lack of equality.
▷ SYNONYMS: **imbalance**, inequity, inconsistency, disparity, discrepancy, dissimilarity, difference, bias, prejudice, discrimination, unfairness.

inequitable adj. unfair; unjust.
■ **inequity** n.

inert adj. **1** lacking the power to move or act. **2** without active chemical properties.

inertia /i-**ner**-shuh/ n. **1** a tendency to do nothing or to remain unchanged. **2** a property by which matter remains still or continues moving unless acted on by an external force.

inescapable adj. unavoidable.

inessential adj. not essential.

inestimable adj. too great to be measured.

inevitable adj. certain to happen.
▷ SYNONYMS: **unavoidable**, inescapable, inexorable, assured, certain, sure.
– ANTONYMS: avoidable.
■ **inevitability** n. **inevitably** adv.

inexact adj. not exact.

inexcusable adj. too bad to be justified or tolerated.
inexhaustible adj. available in unlimited quantities.
inexorable adj. impossible to stop or prevent.
  ■ **inexorably** adv.
inexpensive adj. cheap.
▷ SYNONYMS: **cheap**, affordable, low-cost, economical, competitive, reasonable, budget, economy, bargain, cut-price, reduced.
inexperience n. lack of experience.
inexperienced adj. lacking experience.
▷ SYNONYMS: **inexpert**, untrained, unqualified, unskilled, unseasoned, naive, new, callow, immature; informal wet behind the ears, wide-eyed.
inexpert adj. lacking skill or knowledge.
inexplicable adj. unable to be explained.
  ■ **inexplicably** adv.
in extremis adv. **1** in a very difficult situation. **2** at the point of death.
inextricable adj. impossible to separate.
  ■ **inextricably** adv.
infallible adj. incapable of being wrong.
  ■ **infallibility** n. **infallibly** adv.
infamous adj. well known for something bad.
▷ SYNONYMS: **notorious**, disreputable, scandalous.
– ANTONYMS: reputable.
  ■ **infamy** n.
infancy n. **1** early childhood or babyhood. **2** an early stage of development.
▷ SYNONYMS: **beginnings**, early days, early stages, emergence, dawn, outset, birth, inception.
– ANTONYMS: end.
infant n. a very young child or baby.
▷ SYNONYMS: **baby**, newborn, young child, tiny tot; Medicine neonate; Scottish & N. English bairn, wean; informal tiny, sprog.
infanticide n. the killing of an infant.
infantile adj. **1** of infants. **2** childish.
infantry n. soldiers who fight on foot.
infatuated adj. feeling an intense passion for someone.
  ■ **infatuation** n.
infect v. **1** affect with an organism that causes disease. **2** contaminate.
▷ SYNONYMS: **contaminate**, pollute, taint, foul, poison, blight.
infection n. **1** the process of infecting.

2 an infectious disease.
▷ SYNONYMS: **1 disease**, virus, illness, ailment, disorder, sickness; informal bug. **2 contamination**, poison, bacteria, germs; Medicine sepsis.
infectious adj. **1** (of a disease) able to be transmitted through the environment. **2** likely to spread infection. **3** likely to spread to others.
▷ SYNONYMS: **communicable**, contagious, catching, transmittable, transmissible, transferable.
infer v. (**inferring**, **inferred**) work out from suggestions or evidence.
  ■ **inference** n.

  USAGE On the difference between **imply** and **infer**, see **IMPLY**.

inferior adj. lower in status or quality.
▷ SYNONYMS: **1 second-class**, lower-ranking, subordinate, junior, minor, lowly, humble, menial, beneath someone. **2 second-rate**, mediocre, substandard, low-grade, unsatisfactory, shoddy, poor; informal crummy, lousy.
– ANTONYMS: superior.
  • n. an inferior person.
▷ SYNONYMS: **subordinate**, junior, underling, minion.
  ■ **inferiority** n.
infernal adj. **1** of hell. **2** informal very annoying.
inferno n. (pl. **infernos**) a large uncontrollable fire.
infertile adj. **1** unable to bear young. **2** (of land) unable to produce crops.
▷ SYNONYMS: **barren**, sterile; childless.
  ■ **infertility** n.
infest v. be present in large numbers, so as to cause damage or disease.
▷ SYNONYMS: (**be infested with**) **be overrun by**, be swarming with, be teeming with, be crawling with, be alive with, be plagued by.
  ■ **infestation** n.
infidel n. old use a person who does not believe in a religion.
infidelity n. (pl. **infidelities**) unfaithfulness to your sexual partner.
infighting n. conflict within a group.
infiltrate v. secretly and gradually gain access to a group etc.
▷ SYNONYMS: **penetrate**, insinuate yourself into, worm your way into, sneak into, slip into, creep into, invade.
  ■ **infiltration** n.
infiltrator n. a person who infiltrates a group etc.
▷ SYNONYMS: **spy**, secret agent, plant, intruder, interloper, subversive, informer, mole, fifth columnist;

N. Amer. informal **spook**.

infinite adj. **1** limitless. **2** very great or very many.
▷ SYNONYMS: **boundless**, unbounded, unlimited, limitless, never-ending, incalculable, untold, countless, uncountable, innumerable, number-less, immeasurable.
– ANTONYMS: limited.
■ **infinitely** adv.

infinitesimal adj. very small.
■ **infinitesimally** adv.

infinitive n. the basic form of a verb, occurring in English with the word *to*.

infinity n. (pl. **infinities**) **1** the state of being infinite. **2** a very great number or amount.

infirm adj. physically weak.
■ **infirmity** n.

infirmary n. (pl. **infirmaries**) a hospital.

inflame v. **1** make something bad worse. **2** arouse strong feelings.
▷ SYNONYMS: **1 aggravate**, exacerbate, intensify, worsen, compound. **2 enrage**, incense, anger, madden, infuriate, exasperate, provoke, antagonize; informal make someone see red.

inflamed adj. (of a part of the body) red, swollen, and hot.
▷ SYNONYMS: **swollen**, red, hot, burning, itchy, sore, painful, tender, infected.

inflammable adj. easily set on fire.

inflammation n. redness, swelling, heat, and pain in a part of the body.

inflammatory adj. arousing strong feeling.

inflatable adj. able to be inflated.
• n. an object that is inflated before use.

inflate v. **1** expand by filling with air or gas. **2** increase a cost or price significantly.
▷ SYNONYMS: **1 blow up**, pump up, fill, puff up/out, dilate, distend, swell, bloat. **2 increase**, raise, boost, escalate, put up; informal hike up, jack up.
– ANTONYMS: deflate, lower.

inflated adj. **1** (of a cost or price) too high. **2** exaggerated.
▷ SYNONYMS: **1 high**, sky-high, excessive, unreasonable, outrageous, exorbitant, extortionate; Brit. over the odds; informal steep. **2 exaggerated**, immoderate, overblown, overstated.
– ANTONYMS: low, modest.

inflation n. **1** the act of inflating. **2** a general increase in prices.
■ **inflationary** adj.

inflect v. **1** (of a word) change in form

to show its grammatical function, number, etc. **2** vary the tone or pitch of the voice.
■ **inflection** n.

inflexible adj. **1** unable to be altered. **2** unwilling to change or compromise. **3** unable to be bent.

inflict v. cause to experience something painful or unpleasant.
▷ SYNONYMS: **1 give**, administer, deal out, mete out, exact, wreak. **2 impose**, force, thrust, foist.
■ **infliction** n.

inflorescence n. the complete flower head of a plant.

influence n. **1** the power or ability to affect beliefs or actions. **2** a person or thing with such ability or power.
▷ SYNONYMS: **1 effect**, impact, control, spell, hold. **2 power**, authority, sway, leverage, weight, pull; informal clout. **3** *he's a good influence on her:* **example to**, role model for, inspiration to.
• v. have an influence on.
▷ SYNONYMS: **1 affect**, have an impact on, determine, guide, control, shape, govern, decide, change, alter. **2 sway**, bias, prejudice, manipulate, persuade, induce.

influential adj. having great influence.
▷ SYNONYMS: **powerful**, controlling, important, authoritative, leading, significant, instrumental.

influenza n. a viral infection causing fever, aches, and catarrh.

influx n. an arrival of large numbers of people or things.

inform v. **1** give information to. **2** (**inform on**) reveal someone's criminal activity to the police.
▷ SYNONYMS: **1 tell**, notify, apprise, advise, impart to, communicate to, let someone know, brief, enlighten, send word to. **2** *he informed on two colleagues:* **betray**, give away, denounce, incriminate, report; informal rat, squeal, split, snitch, tell, blow the whistle; Brit. informal grass, shop; N. Amer. informal finger; Austral./NZ informal dob in.
■ **informant** n. **informer** n.

informal adj. **1** relaxed or unofficial. **2** (of clothes) casual.
▷ SYNONYMS: **1 unofficial**, casual, relaxed, easy-going, low-key. **2 colloquial**, vernacular, idiomatic, popular, familiar, everyday; informal slangy, chatty. **3 casual**, relaxed, comfortable, everyday; informal comfy.
– ANTONYMS: formal.
■ **informality** n. **informally** adv.

information n. facts or knowledge provided or learned.
▷ SYNONYMS: **facts**, particulars, details, figures, statistics, data, knowledge, intelligence; informal info, gen.
□ **information technology** the use of computers and telecommunications for storing and sending information.

informative adj. providing useful information.
▷ SYNONYMS: **instructive**, illuminating, enlightening, revealing, explanatory, factual, educational, edifying.

informed adj. showing knowledge or understanding.
▷ SYNONYMS: **knowledgeable**, enlightened, educated, briefed, up to date, up to speed, in the picture, in the know, au fait; informal clued up.
– ANTONYMS: ignorant.

infraction n. a breaking of a law or agreement.

infrared adj. (of electromagnetic radiation) having a wavelength just greater than that of red light.

infrastructure n. the basic structures and facilities (e.g. roads or power) needed for the operation of a society or organization.

infrequent adj. not happening often.
■ **infrequently** adv.

infringe v. **1** break a law or agreement. **2** limit a right or privilege.
■ **infringement** n.

infuriate v. make angry.
▷ SYNONYMS: **enrage**, incense, provoke, anger, madden, exasperate; informal make someone see red; Brit. informal wind up.
– ANTONYMS: please.

infuse v. **1** spread throughout. **2** soak tea or herbs to extract the flavour.
■ **infuser** n. **infusion** n.

ingenious adj. clever and inventive.
▷ SYNONYMS: **inventive**, creative, imaginative, original, innovative, pioneering, resourceful, enterprising, inspired, clever.
– ANTONYMS: unimaginative.
■ **ingeniously** adv. **ingenuity** n.

ingenuous adj. innocent and unsuspecting.
■ **ingenuously** adv.

ingest v. take food or drink into the body.
■ **ingestion** n.

inglenook n. a space on either side of a large fireplace.

inglorious adj. causing shame.

ingot n. a rectangular block of metal.

ingrained adj. **1** (of a habit or belief) firmly established. **2** (of dirt) deeply embedded.

ingratiate v. (**ingratiate yourself**) gain favour by flattery or trying to please.

ingratitude n. a lack of gratitude.

ingredient n. any of the substances combined to make a dish.
▷ SYNONYMS: **constituent**, component, element, item, part, strand, unit, feature, aspect, attribute.

ingress n. **1** the act of entering. **2** a place or means of access.

ingrown (or **ingrowing**) adj. (of a toenail) having grown into the flesh.

inhabit v. live in or occupy.
▷ SYNONYMS: **live in**, occupy, settle, people, populate, colonize.
■ **inhabitable** adj.

inhabitant n. a person or animal that lives in or occupies a place.
▷ SYNONYMS: **resident**, occupant, occupier, settler, local, native; (**inhabitants**) population, populace, people, public, community, citizenry, townsfolk, townspeople.

inhalant n. a medicine that is inhaled.

inhale v. breathe in air, smoke, etc.
▷ SYNONYMS: **breathe in**, draw in, suck in, sniff in, drink in, gasp.
– ANTONYMS: exhale.
■ **inhalation** n.

inhaler n. a device for inhaling a drug.

inherent adj. existing in something as a permanent or essential quality.
■ **inherently** adv.

inherit v. (**inheriting, inherited**) **1** receive property or a title from someone when they die. **2** have a characteristic passed on from parents or ancestors.
▷ SYNONYMS: **be bequeathed**, be left, be willed, come into, succeed to, assume, take over.

inheritance n. property or a title inherited from the previous owner.
▷ SYNONYMS: **legacy**, bequest, endowment, birthright, heritage, patrimony.

> **WORD LINKS**
> **hereditary** relating to inheritance

inhibit v. **1** hinder or prevent. **2** cause to feel inhibitions.
▷ SYNONYMS: **impede**, hinder, hamper, hold back, discourage, interfere with, obstruct, slow down, retard.
– ANTONYMS: assist, allow.

inhibited adj. unable to act naturally or express your feelings.
▷ SYNONYMS: **reserved**, reticent, guarded, self-conscious, insecure,

i

withdrawn, repressed, undemonstrative, shy, diffident, bashful; informal uptight.

inhibition n. a feeling preventing you from acting naturally.

inhospitable adj. (of a place) harsh and difficult to live in.

inhuman adj. cruel and barbaric.
■ **inhumanity** n.

inimical adj. harmful; hostile.

inimitable adj. impossible to imitate.
■ **inimitably** adv.

iniquity n. (pl. **iniquities**) great injustice.
■ **iniquitous** adj.

initial adj. at the beginning; first.
▷ SYNONYMS: **beginning**, opening, commencing, starting, first, earliest, primary, preliminary, preparatory, introductory, inaugural.
– ANTONYMS: final.
• n. the first letter of a name or word.
• v. (**initialling**, **initialled**; US **initialing**, **initialed**) mark with your initials.

initially adv. at first.
▷ SYNONYMS: **at first**, at the start, at the outset, in/at the beginning, to begin with, to start with, originally.

initiate v. **1** cause a process etc. to begin. **2** admit to a group with a formal ceremony. **3** introduce to a new activity.
▷ SYNONYMS: **1 begin**, start, commence, institute, inaugurate, launch, instigate, establish, set up. **2** *he was initiated into a religious cult:* **introduce**, admit, induct, install, swear in, ordain, invest.
– ANTONYMS: end, expel.
■ **initiation** n.

initiative n. **1** the ability to act independently. **2** the opportunity to act before others do. **3** a new approach to a problem.
▷ SYNONYMS: **1 enterprise**, resourcefulness, inventiveness, imagination, ingenuity, originality, creativity. **2 advantage**, upper hand, edge, lead, start. **3 scheme**, plan, strategy, measure, proposal, step, action.

inject v. **1** put a drug etc. into the body with a syringe. **2** introduce a different quality.
▷ SYNONYMS: **1 administer**, take; informal shoot up, mainline, fix. **2 inoculate**, vaccinate. **3 introduce**, instil, infuse, imbue, breathe.

injection n. **1** an act of injecting. **2** a substance that is injected.
▷ SYNONYMS: **inoculation**, vaccination, immunization, booster, dose, infusion; informal jab, shot.

injudicious adj. unwise.

injunction n. a court order stating that someone must or must not do something.
▷ SYNONYMS: **order**, ruling, direction, directive, command, instruction, mandate.

injure v. **1** do physical harm to. **2** damage.
▷ SYNONYMS: **1 hurt**, wound, damage, harm, bruise, break, fracture; Medicine traumatize. **2** *the incident injured her reputation:* **damage**, mar, spoil, weaken, ruin, blight, blemish, tarnish, blacken.

injured adj. **1** physically harmed. **2** offended or upset.
▷ SYNONYMS: **1 hurt**, wounded, damaged, sore, bruised, broken, fractured; Medicine traumatized; Brit. informal gammy. **2 upset**, hurt, wounded, offended, reproachful, pained, aggrieved.

injurious adj. harmful.

injury n. (pl. **injuries**) **1** an instance of harm to the body. **2** damage or harm.
▷ SYNONYMS: **1 wound**, bruise, cut, gash, scratch, graze; Medicine trauma, lesion. **2 harm**, hurt, damage, pain, suffering. **3 offence**, abuse, injustice, disservice, affront, insult.

injustice n. **1** lack of justice. **2** an unjust act.
▷ SYNONYMS: **1 unfairness**, one-sidedness, inequity, bias, prejudice, discrimination, intolerance, exploitation, corruption. **2 wrong**, offence, crime, sin, outrage, scandal, disgrace, affront.

ink n. coloured liquid for writing, drawing, or printing.
• v. apply ink to.
■ **inky** adj.

inkling n. a slight suspicion.

inland adj. & adv. in or into the interior of a country.
▷ SYNONYMS: **interior**, inshore, internal, upcountry.
– ANTONYMS: coastal.

inlay v. (**inlaying**, **inlaid**) decorate by embedding pieces of a different material in a surface.

inlet n. **1** a narrow inland extension of the sea etc. **2** a way in.
▷ SYNONYMS: **1 cove**, bay, bight, creek, estuary, fjord, sound; Scottish firth. **2 vent**, flue, shaft, duct, channel, pipe.

in loco parentis adv. & adj. in the place of a parent.

inmate n. a person living in a prison or other institution.
▷ SYNONYMS: **1 patient**, inpatient, resident, occupant. **2 prisoner**, convict,

captive, detainee, internee.
inmost adj. innermost.
inn n. a pub.
innards pl. n. informal internal organs or parts.
innate adj. inborn; natural.
■ **innately** adv.
inner adj. **1** inside; close to the centre. **2** mental or spiritual. **3** private.
▷ SYNONYMS: **1 central**, innermost; N. Amer. downtown. **2 internal**, interior, inside, innermost. **3 hidden**, secret, deep, underlying, veiled.
– ANTONYMS: outer.
□ **inner city** an area in or near the centre of a city.
innermost adj. **1** furthest in. **2** most private.
innings n. (pl. **innings**) (in cricket) a batsman's or side's turn at batting.
innocence n. the state or quality of being innocent.
▷ SYNONYMS: **1 guiltlessness**, blamelessness. **2 naivety**, credulity, inexperience, gullibility, ingenuousness.
innocent adj. **1** not guilty of a crime etc. **2** having little experience of life. **3** not intended to offend.
▷ SYNONYMS: **1 guiltless**, blameless, clean, irreproachable, above reproach, honest, upright, law-abiding. **2 naive**, ingenuous, trusting, credulous, impressionable, easily led, inexperienced, unsophisticated, artless. **3 harmless**, innocuous, safe, inoffensive, unobjectionable.
– ANTONYMS: guilty.
• n. an innocent person.
■ **innocently** adv.
innocuous adj. harmless.
■ **innocuously** adv.
innovate v. introduce something new.
■ **innovator** n.
innovation n. **1** a new method, product, etc. **2** the act of introducing something new.
▷ SYNONYMS: **change**, alteration, upheaval, reorganization, restructuring, novelty, departure.
innovative adj. introducing or using new methods, products, etc.
▷ SYNONYMS: **original**, new, novel, fresh, unusual, experimental, inventive, ingenious, pioneering, groundbreaking, revolutionary, radical, cutting-edge.
innuendo n. (pl. **innuendoes** or **innuendos**) a remark indirectly referring to something.
innumerable adj. too many to be counted.
innumerate adj. without a basic

knowledge of mathematics.
inoculate v. vaccinate.
■ **inoculation** n.

USAGE One *n*, one *c*: *inoculate*.

inoperable adj. unable to be cured by a medical operation.
inoperative adj. not working or taking effect.
inopportune adj. occurring at an inconvenient time.
inordinate adj. unusually large; excessive.
■ **inordinately** adv.
inorganic adj. **1** not consisting of or coming from living matter. **2** not containing carbon.
inpatient n. a hospital patient staying day and night during treatment.
input n. **1** something put in or contributed. **2** the act of inputting computer data.
• v. (**inputting**, **input**) put data into a computer.
inquest n. an official inquiry, esp. by a coroner into the cause of a death.
▷ SYNONYMS: **enquiry**, investigation, probe, examination, review, hearing.
inquire v. enquire.
■ **inquiry** n.
inquisition n. a long period of intensive questioning.
■ **inquisitor** n.
inquisitive adj. eager to find things out.
■ **inquisitively** adv.
inroad n. a gradual entry into or effect on a situation.
insalubrious adj. seedy; unwholesome.
insane adj. **1** seriously mentally ill. **2** very foolish.
▷ SYNONYMS: **1 mad**, of unsound mind, certifiable, psychotic, schizophrenic, unhinged; informal crazy, raving mad, bonkers, loony, round the bend; Brit. informal crackers, off your trolley; N. Amer. informal nutso. **2 stupid**, idiotic, nonsensical, absurd, ridiculous, ludicrous, preposterous; informal crazy, mad; Brit. informal daft, barmy.
– ANTONYMS: sane.
■ **insanely** adv. **insanity** n.
insanitary adj. dirty and unhygienic.
insatiable adj. impossible to satisfy.
■ **insatiably** adv.
inscribe v. **1** write or carve words on a surface. **2** write a dedication in a book.
inscription n. words inscribed.
inscrutable adj. impossible to interpret.
■ **inscrutably** adv.

insect n. a small invertebrate animal with six legs and a segmented body.
▷ SYNONYMS: **bug**; informal creepy-crawly; Brit. informal minibeast.

> **WORD LINKS**
> **entomology** the study of insects

insecticide n. a substance for killing insects.

insectivore n. an animal that eats insects.
■ insectivorous adj.

insecure adj. **1** not confident. **2** not firmly fixed.
▷ SYNONYMS: **1 unconfident**, uncertain, unsure, doubtful, diffident, hesitant, self-conscious, anxious, fearful. **2 unstable**, rickety, wobbly, shaky, unsteady, precarious. **3 unprotected**, unguarded, vulnerable, unsecured.
– ANTONYMS: confident, stable, secure.

insecurity n. (pl. **insecurities**) the quality or state of being insecure.
▷ SYNONYMS: **lack of confidence**, uncertainty, self-doubt, diffidence, hesitancy, nervousness, self-consciousness, anxiety, worry, unease.

inseminate v. introduce semen into.
■ insemination n.

insensible adj. unconscious.

insensitive adj. not sensitive.
■ insensitively adv. insensitivity n.

inseparable adj. unable to be separated or treated separately.
■ inseparably adv.

insert v. place, fit, or add into.
▷ SYNONYMS: **put**, place, push, thrust, slide, slip, load, fit, slot, install; informal pop, stick, bung.
– ANTONYMS: extract, remove.
• n. a loose page or section in a magazine.
■ insertion n.

inset n. a thing inserted.
• v. (**insetting**, **inset**) insert.

inshore adj. & adv. at sea but close or towards the shore.

inside n. **1** an inner side, part, or surface. **2** (**insides**) informal the stomach and bowels.
▷ SYNONYMS: **1 interior**, centre, core, middle, heart. **2** (**insides**) **stomach**, gut, bowels, intestines; informal tummy, belly, guts.
• adj. on or in the inside.
▷ SYNONYMS: **1 inner**, interior, internal, innermost. **2 confidential**, classified, restricted, privileged, private, secret, exclusive; informal hush-hush.
– ANTONYMS: outside.
• prep. & adv. **1** situated or moving within. **2** informal in prison. **3** within a

specified time.
□ **inside out** with the inner surface turned outwards.

insider n. a person in an organization who has information not known to those outside it.

insidious adj. developing in a gradual and harmful way.
■ insidiously adv.

insight n. understanding of the truth about people or situations.
▷ SYNONYMS: **intuition**, perception, understanding, comprehension, appreciation, judgement, discernment, vision, imagination, wisdom; informal nous.

insignia n. (pl. **insignia**) a badge or symbol indicating rank or office.

insignificant adj. of little or no importance or value.
▷ SYNONYMS: **unimportant**, trivial, trifling, negligible, inconsequential, of no account, paltry, petty, insubstantial; informal piddling.
■ insignificance n.

insincere adj. saying things that you do not mean.
▷ SYNONYMS: **false**, fake, hollow, artificial, feigned, pretended, put-on, disingenuous, hypocritical, cynical; informal phoney, pretend.
■ insincerely adv. insincerity n.

insinuate v. **1** suggest something bad indirectly. **2** move yourself gradually into a favourable position.
■ insinuation n.

insipid adj. **1** lacking flavour. **2** dull.

insist v. **1** demand or state forcefully. **2** (**insist on**) persist in doing.
▷ SYNONYMS: **1 stand firm**, stand your ground, be resolute, be determined, hold out, persist, be emphatic, lay down the law, not take no for an answer; informal stick to your guns, put your foot down. **2 demand**, command, order, require. **3 maintain**, assert, protest, swear, declare, repeat.

insistent adj. **1** insisting. **2** sustained and demanding attention.
▷ SYNONYMS: **persistent**, determined, tenacious, unyielding, dogged, unrelenting, importunate, relentless, inexorable.
■ insistence n. insistently adv.

in situ adv. & adj. in the original position.

insolent adj. rude and disrespectful.
■ insolence n. insolently adv.

insoluble adj. **1** impossible to solve. **2** unable to be dissolved.

insolvent adj. unable to pay your debts.

■ **insolvency** n.

insomnia n. inability to sleep.
■ **insomniac** n.

insouciant adj. unconcerned.
■ **insouciance** n.

inspect v. **1** look at closely. **2** visit officially to check on standards.
▷ SYNONYMS: **examine**, check, scrutinize, investigate, vet, test, monitor, survey, study, look over; informal check out, give something a once-over.

inspection n. the act of inspecting.
▷ SYNONYMS: **examination**, check-up, survey, scrutiny, exploration, investigation; informal once-over, going-over.

inspector n. **1** an official who inspects. **2** a police officer ranking below a chief inspector.
▷ SYNONYMS: **examiner**, scrutineer, investigator, surveyor, assessor, supervisor, monitor, watchdog, ombudsman, auditor.

inspiration n. **1** the process of being inspired. **2** an inspiring person or thing. **3** a sudden clever idea.
▷ SYNONYMS: **1 stimulus**, motivation, encouragement, influence, spur, fillip; informal shot in the arm. **2 creativity**, invention, innovation, ingenuity, imagination, originality, insight, vision. **3 bright idea**, revelation; informal brainwave; N. Amer. informal brainstorm.
■ **inspirational** adj.

inspire v. **1** fill with the urge to do something. **2** create a feeling in a person.
▷ SYNONYMS: **1 stimulate**, motivate, encourage, influence, move, spur, energize, galvanize. **2 give rise to**, lead to, bring about, engender, arouse, awaken, prompt, induce, ignite, trigger, kindle, produce, bring out.

inspired adj. displaying creativity or excellence.
▷ SYNONYMS: *he gave an inspired performance:* **outstanding**, wonderful, marvellous, excellent, magnificent, exceptional, first-class, virtuoso, superlative; informal tremendous, superb, awesome, out of this world; Brit. informal brilliant.

inspiring adj. arousing enthusiasm or confidence.
▷ SYNONYMS: **inspirational**, encouraging, heartening, uplifting, stirring, rousing, electrifying, moving.

instability n. lack of stability.
▷ SYNONYMS: **unreliability**, uncertainty, unpredictability, insecurity, volatility, capriciousness, changeability, variability, inconsistency, mutability.
– ANTONYMS: stability.

install v. **1** place in position ready for use. **2** establish in a new place or role.
▷ SYNONYMS: **1 put**, place, station, site, insert. **2 swear in**, induct, inaugurate, invest, appoint, ordain, consecrate, anoint, enthrone, crown. **3** *the cat installed herself in my lap:* **ensconce**, position, settle, seat, plant, sit; informal plonk, park.
– ANTONYMS: remove.
■ **installation** n.

instalment (US **installment**) n. **1** each of several payments made over a period of time. **2** each of the parts of a serial.
▷ SYNONYMS: **1 payment**, repayment, tranche, portion. **2 part**, episode, chapter, issue, programme, section, segment, volume.

instance n. a particular example or occurrence.
▷ SYNONYMS: **example**, occasion, occurrence, case, illustration, sample.
• v. give as an example.

instant adj. **1** immediate. **2** (of food) processed to allow quick preparation.
▷ SYNONYMS: **1 immediate**, instantaneous, on-the-spot, prompt, swift, speedy, rapid, quick; informal snappy. **2 prepared**, pre-cooked, microwaveable.
– ANTONYMS: delayed.
• n. **1** a precise moment of time. **2** a very short time.
▷ SYNONYMS: **moment**, minute, second, split second, trice, twinkling of an eye, flash; informal jiffy.

instantaneous adj. instant.
■ **instantaneously** adv.

instantly adv. straight away.
▷ SYNONYMS: **immediately**, at once, straight away, right away, instantaneously, forthwith, there and then, here and now, this/that minute, this/that second.

instead adv. as an alternative.
▷ SYNONYMS: **as an alternative**, in lieu, alternatively, rather, on second thoughts; N. Amer. alternately.

instep n. the middle part of the foot.

instigate v. cause to happen or begin.
■ **instigation** n. **instigator** n.

instil (US **instill**) v. (**instilling**, **instilled**) gradually establish in the mind.

instinct n. an inborn tendency or ability.
▷ SYNONYMS: **1 inclination**, urge, drive, compulsion, intuition, feeling, sixth sense, nose. **2 talent**, gift, ability, aptitude, skill, flair, feel, knack.

i

instinctive adj. based on instinct rather than thought or training.
▷ SYNONYMS: **intuitive**, natural, instinctual, innate, inborn, inherent, unconscious, subconscious, automatic, reflex, knee-jerk; informal gut.
■ **instinctively** adv.

institute n. an organization for the promotion of science, education, etc.
▷ SYNONYMS: **organization**, establishment, institution, foundation, centre, academy, school, college, university, society, association, federation, body.
• v. begin or establish.
▷ SYNONYMS: **set up**, inaugurate, found, establish, organize, initiate, set in motion, get under way, get off the ground, start, launch.
– ANTONYMS: abolish, end.

institution n. **1** an important organization or public body. **2** a home providing care for people with special needs. **3** an established law or custom.
▷ SYNONYMS: **1 establishment**, organization, institute, foundation, centre, academy, school, college, university, society, association, body. **2 home**, hospital; asylum; prison. **3** *the institution of marriage*: **practice**, custom, convention, tradition.

institutional adj. relating to or typical of an institution.
▷ SYNONYMS: **organized**, established, bureaucratic, conventional, procedural, formal, formalized, systematic, systematized, structured, regulated.

institutionalize (or **-ise**) v.
1 establish as an accepted part of an organization etc. **2** place in a residential institution.

instruct v. **1** direct or order. **2** teach.
▷ SYNONYMS: **1 order**, direct, command, tell, mandate; old use bid. **2 teach**, coach, train, educate, tutor, guide, school, show.

instruction n. **1** a direction or order. **2** teaching or education.
▷ SYNONYMS: **1 order**, command, directive, direction, decree, injunction, mandate, commandment; old use bidding. **2** *read the instructions*: **directions**, handbook, manual, guide, advice, guidance. **3 tuition**, teaching, coaching, schooling, lessons, classes, lectures, training, drill, guidance.
■ **instructional** adj.

instructive adj. useful and informative.

instructor n. a teacher or coach.
▷ SYNONYMS: **trainer**, coach, teacher, tutor, adviser, counsellor, guide.

instrument n. **1** a tool or implement for precise work. **2** a measuring device. **3** a device for producing musical sounds.
▷ SYNONYMS: **1 implement**, tool, utensil, device, apparatus, gadget. **2 gauge**, meter, indicator, dial, display. **3 agent**, cause, agency, channel, medium, means, vehicle.

instrumental adj. **1** important in achieving something. **2** performed on musical instruments.
■ **instrumentalist** n.

insubordinate adj. disobedient.
■ **insubordination** n.

insubstantial adj. not strong or solid.

insufferable adj. intolerable.
■ **insufferably** adv.

insufficient adj. not enough.
▷ SYNONYMS: **inadequate**, deficient, poor, scant, scanty, not enough, too little, too few.
■ **insufficiency** n. **insufficiently** adv.

insular adj. **1** narrow-minded. **2** of an island.
■ **insularity** n.

insulate v. **1** cover or line with material to prevent heat, electricity, etc. being conducted. **2** protect from something unpleasant.
▷ SYNONYMS: **1 wrap**, sheathe, cover, encase, enclose, lag, soundproof. **2 protect**, save, shield, shelter, screen, cushion, cocoon.
■ **insulation** n. **insulator** n.

insulin n. a hormone regulating glucose levels in the blood.

insult v. speak to or treat in a way that offends.
▷ SYNONYMS: **abuse**, be rude to, call someone names, slight, disparage, discredit, malign, defame, denigrate, offend, hurt, humiliate; informal bad-mouth; Brit. informal slag off.
– ANTONYMS: compliment.
• n. an insulting remark or act.
▷ SYNONYMS: **jibe**, affront, slight, slur, barb, indignity, abuse, aspersions; informal dig, put-down.

insulting adj. abusive or disrespectful.
▷ SYNONYMS: **abusive**, rude, offensive, disparaging, belittling, derogatory, deprecating, disrespectful, uncomplimentary; informal bitchy, catty.

insuperable adj. impossible to overcome.

insupportable adj. intolerable.

insurance n. **1** an arrangement by which payments are made to a company who in return pay compensation in the event of loss,

damage, death, etc. **2** money paid by or to an insurance company. **3** a safeguard.
▷ SYNONYMS: **indemnity**, assurance, protection, security, cover, safeguard, warranty.

insure v. **1** pay money to receive compensation in the event of damage, loss, death, etc. **2** ensure.
▷ SYNONYMS: **cover**, indemnify, protect, underwrite, warrant; Brit. assure.
■ **insurer** n.

insurgent n. a rebel.

insurmountable adj. too great to be overcome.

insurrection n. a violent revolt.

intact adj. not damaged.
▷ SYNONYMS: **whole**, entire, complete, unbroken, undamaged, unscathed, unblemished, unmarked, in one piece.
− ANTONYMS: damaged.

intake n. **1** an amount or number taken in. **2** an act of taking in.

intangible adj. **1** not solid or real. **2** vague and abstract.

integer n. a whole number.

integral adj. necessary to make a whole complete.
▷ SYNONYMS: **1 essential**, fundamental, component, basic, intrinsic, inherent, vital, necessary. **2 built-in**, inbuilt, integrated, inboard, fitted. **3 unified**, integrated, comprehensive, holistic, joined-up, all-embracing.
− ANTONYMS: peripheral, supplementary.

integrate v. **1** combine to form a whole. **2** make accepted within a social group.
▷ SYNONYMS: **combine**, amalgamate, merge, unite, fuse, blend, consolidate, meld, mix, incorporate, assimilate, homogenize, desegregate.
− ANTONYMS: separate.
■ **integration** n.

integrity n. **1** the quality of being morally good. **2** wholeness or unity.
▷ SYNONYMS: **1 honesty**, probity, rectitude, uprightness, fairness, honour, sincerity, truthfulness, trustworthiness. **2 unity**, coherence, cohesion, solidity. **3 soundness**, strength, sturdiness, solidity, durability, stability, rigidity.
− ANTONYMS: dishonesty.

intellect n. the ability to think logically and understand things.
▷ SYNONYMS: **mind**, brains, intelligence, reason, judgement, grey matter, brain cells.

intellectual adj. **1** of the intellect. **2** having a highly developed intellect.

▷ SYNONYMS: **1 mental**, cerebral, rational, conceptual, theoretical, analytical, logical, cognitive. **2 learned**, academic, erudite, bookish, highbrow, scholarly, donnish.
• n. an intellectual person.
■ **intellectually** adv.

intellectualize (or **-ise**) v. talk or write in an intellectual way.

intelligence n. **1** the ability to gain and apply knowledge and skills. **2** secret information obtained about an opponent.
▷ SYNONYMS: **1 intellect**, cleverness, brainpower, judgement, reasoning, acumen, wit, insight, perception. **2 information**, facts, details, particulars, data, knowledge.

intelligent adj. good at learning and understanding.
▷ SYNONYMS: **clever**, bright, quick-witted, smart, astute, sharp, insightful, perceptive, penetrating, educated, knowledgeable, enlightened; informal brainy.
■ **intelligently** adv.

intelligentsia n. intellectual or highly educated people.

intelligible adj. able to be understood.
▷ SYNONYMS: **comprehensible**, understandable, accessible, digestible, user-friendly, clear, coherent, plain, unambiguous.
■ **intelligibility** n. **intelligibly** adv.

intend v. **1** have as an aim or plan. **2** plan a particular role, use, or meaning for.
▷ SYNONYMS: **plan**, mean, have in mind, aim, propose, hope, expect, envisage.

intense adj. **1** great in force, strength, or degree. **2** very earnest.
▷ SYNONYMS: **1 extreme**, great, acute, fierce, severe, high, exceptional, extraordinary, harsh, strong, powerful, violent; informal serious. **2 passionate**, impassioned, zealous, vehement, fervent, earnest, eager, committed.
− ANTONYMS: mild, apathetic.

intensify v. (intensifying, intensified) increase in force, strength, or degree.
▷ SYNONYMS: **escalate**, increase, step up, raise, strengthen, reinforce, pick up, build up, heighten, deepen, extend, expand, amplify, magnify, aggravate, exacerbate, worsen, inflame, compound.
− ANTONYMS: reduce.
■ **intensification** n.

intensity n. the state or quality of being intense.

▷ SYNONYMS: **1 strength**, power, force, severity, ferocity, fierceness, harshness, violence. **2 passion**, ardour, fervour, vehemence, fire, emotion, eagerness.

intensive adj. **1** involving much effort over a short time. **2** (of farming) aiming to achieve maximum yields.
▷ SYNONYMS: **thorough**, thoroughgoing, in-depth, rigorous, exhaustive, vigorous, detailed, minute, meticulous, painstaking, methodical, extensive.
– ANTONYMS: cursory.
□ **intensive care** special medical treatment of a dangerously ill patient.
■ **intensively** adv.

intent n. an aim, plan, or purpose.
▷ SYNONYMS: **aim**, intention, purpose, objective, goal.
● adj. **1** (**intent on**) determined to do. **2** showing concentrated attention.
▷ SYNONYMS: **1** *he was intent on proving his point:* **bent**, set, determined, insistent, resolved, hell-bent, keen, committed to, determined to. **2 attentive**, absorbed, engrossed, fascinated, enthralled, rapt, focused, concentrating.
– ANTONYMS: distracted.
■ **intently** adv.

intention n. an aim or plan.
▷ SYNONYMS: **aim**, purpose, intent, objective, goal.

intentional adj. deliberate.
▷ SYNONYMS: **deliberate**, done on purpose, wilful, calculated, conscious, intended, planned, meant, knowing.
■ **intentionally** adv.

inter v. (**interring**, **interred**) bury a dead body.
▷ SYNONYMS: **bury**, lay to rest, consign to the grave, entomb.
– ANTONYMS: exhume.

interact v. act so as to affect each other.
■ **interaction** n. **interactive** adj.

interbreed v. (**interbreeding**, **interbred**) breed with an animal of a different species.

intercede v. intervene on behalf of another.

intercept v. stop and prevent from continuing.
▷ SYNONYMS: **stop**, head off, cut off, catch, seize, block, interrupt.
■ **interception** n. **interceptor** n.

intercession n. the act of interceding.

interchange v. **1** (of two people) exchange things. **2** put each of two things in the other's place.

● n. **1** the act of interchanging. **2** a road junction on several levels.
■ **interchangeable** adj.

intercom n. an electrical device allowing one-way or two-way communication.

interconnect v. connect with each other.

intercontinental adj. between continents.

intercourse n. **1** dealings between people. **2** sexual intercourse.
▷ SYNONYMS: **1 dealings**, relations, relationships, contact, interchange, communication, networking. **2 sexual intercourse**, sex, sexual relations, mating, copulation, fornication; technical coitus.

interdependent adj. dependent on each other.

interdict n. an order forbidding something.
▷ SYNONYMS: **prohibition**, ban, bar, veto, embargo, moratorium, injunction.

interdisciplinary adj. involving more than one branch of knowledge.

interest n. **1** eagerness to know about something or someone. **2** the quality of arousing such a feeling. **3** a subject arousing enthusiasm or concern. **4** money paid for the use of money lent. **5** a person's advantage. **6** a share in a business.
▷ SYNONYMS: **1** *we listened with interest:* **attentiveness**, attention, regard, notice, curiosity, enjoyment, delight. **2** *this will be of interest to shareholders:* **concern**, consequence, importance, import, significance, note, relevance, value. **3 hobby**, pastime, leisure pursuit, amusement, recreation, diversion, passion. **4 stake**, share, claim, investment, involvement, concern.
– ANTONYMS: boredom.
● v. **1** arouse the curiosity or attention of. **2** (**interested**) not impartial: *the interested parties will be notified.*
▷ SYNONYMS: **1 appeal to**, be of interest to, attract, intrigue, amuse, divert, entertain, arouse someone's curiosity, whet someone's appetite; informal tickle someone's fancy. **2** (**interested**) **concerned**, involved, affected.

interesting adj. arousing curiosity or interest.
▷ SYNONYMS: **absorbing**, engrossing, fascinating, riveting, gripping, compelling, captivating, engaging, enthralling, appealing, entertaining, stimulating, diverting, intriguing.

interface n. **1** a point where two

things interact. **2** a device or program enabling a user to communicate with a computer, or for connecting two items of hardware or software.

interfere v. **1** prevent from continuing or operating. **2** become involved in something without being asked. **3** (**interfere with**) handle without permission.

▷ SYNONYMS: **butt in**, barge in, intrude, meddle, tamper, encroach; informal poke your nose in, stick your oar in.

interference n. **1** the act of interfering. **2** disturbance to radio signals.

▷ SYNONYMS: **1 intrusion**, intervention, involvement, meddling, prying. **2 disruption**, disturbance, static, noise.

interferon n. a protein preventing a virus from reproducing.

intergalactic adj. moving or situated between galaxies.

interim n. the time between two events.
  • adj. temporary.

interior adj. inner.

▷ SYNONYMS: **1 inside**, inner, internal, inland, upcountry, central. **2 internal**, home, domestic, national, state, civil, local. **3 inner**, mental, spiritual, psychological, private, personal, secret.
  • n. **1** the inner part. **2** the internal affairs of a country.

▷ SYNONYMS: **1 inside**, depths, recesses, bowels, belly, heart. **2 centre**, heartland.

– ANTONYMS: exterior.

interject v. say suddenly as an interruption.
  ■ **interjection** n.

interlace v. weave together.

interlink v. link together.

interlock v. (of two parts) fit together.

interlocutor n. a participant in a conversation.

interloper n. an intruder.

interlude n. **1** a period of time that contrasts with what goes before or after. **2** an interval.

intermarry v. (**intermarrying, intermarried**) (of people of different races, religions, etc.) marry each other.
  ■ **intermarriage** n.

intermediary n. (pl. **intermediaries**) a person who tries to settle a dispute.

▷ SYNONYMS: **mediator**, go-between, negotiator, arbitrator, peacemaker, middleman, broker.

intermediate adj. **1** coming between two things in time, place, etc.

2 having more than basic knowledge or skills.

▷ SYNONYMS: **halfway**, in-between, middle, mid, midway, intervening, transitional.

interment n. burial.

intermezzo /in-ter-**met**-zoh/ n. (pl. **intermezzi** or **intermezzos**) a short piece of music between parts of an opera etc.

interminable adj. seemingly endless.
  ■ **interminably** adv.

intermission n. a pause or interval.

intermittent adj. happening at irregular intervals.

▷ SYNONYMS: **sporadic**, irregular, fitful, spasmodic, discontinuous, isolated, random, patchy, scattered, occasional, periodic.

– ANTONYMS: continuous.
  ■ **intermittently** adv.

intern v. confine as a prisoner.
  • n. US a junior doctor receiving training in a hospital.
  ■ **internee** n. **internment** n.

internal adj. **1** of the inside. **2** inside the body. **3** of affairs within a country. **4** used within an organization.

▷ SYNONYMS: **1 inner**, interior, inside, central. **2 domestic**, home, interior, civil, local, national, state.

– ANTONYMS: external, foreign.
  □ **internal-combustion engine** an engine generating power by the explosion of fuel and air inside the engine.
  ■ **internally** adv.

internalize (or -**ise**) v. make part of your behaviour or thinking.

international adj. **1** between nations. **2** agreed on or used by all or many nations.

▷ SYNONYMS: **global**, worldwide, world, intercontinental, universal, cosmopolitan, multiracial, multinational.

– ANTONYMS: national, local.
  • n. Brit. a match between teams from different countries.
  ■ **internationally** adv.

internecine /in-ter-**nee**-syn/ adj. (of conflict) happening between members of a group.

Internet n. a huge global computer network.

interplay n. interaction.

interpolate /in-ter-**puh**-layt/ v. **1** insert. **2** interject a remark.
  ■ **interpolation** n.

interpose v. **1** place between one thing and another. **2** interject a remark.

i

interpret v. **1** explain the meaning of. **2** translate aloud the words of a person speaking a different language. **3** understand as meaning.
▷ SYNONYMS: **1 explain**, elucidate, expound, clarify, analyse. **2 translate**; decode, decipher. **3 understand**, construe, take, see, regard.
■ **interpretable** adj. **interpretation** n. **interpreter** n.

interracial adj. involving different races.

interregnum n. a period between regimes when normal government is suspended.

interrelate v. relate or connect to one other.
■ **interrelation** n.

interrogate v. question closely or aggressively.
■ **interrogation** n. **interrogator** n.

interrogative adj. in the form of a question or used in questions.

interrupt v. **1** break the progress or continuity of. **2** stop a speaker by saying or doing something.
▷ SYNONYMS: **1 suspend**, discontinue, adjourn, break off, stop, halt; informal put on ice. **2 cut in**, break in, barge in, intrude, intervene; informal butt in, chime in; Brit. informal chip in.

interruption n. **1** an act, period, etc. that stops the progress of something. **2** the action of interrupting.
▷ SYNONYMS: **1 suspension**, breaking off, discontinuation, discontinuance, stopping. **2 intrusion**, interference, intervention, disturbance.

intersect v. divide or cross by passing or lying across.
■ **intersection** n.

intersperse v. scatter or place among or between things.

interstate adj. between states.

interstice /in-ter-stiss/ n. a crack or small space.

interval n. **1** a period or pause between two events. **2** a pause between parts of a play etc. **3** a difference in musical pitch.
▷ SYNONYMS: **intermission**, interlude, break, recess, time out.

intervene v. **1** become involved in a situation to improve or control it. **2** occur between events.
▷ SYNONYMS: **intercede**, involve yourself, get involved, step in, interfere, intrude.
■ **intervention** n.

interview n. **1** an occasion when a journalist questions someone. **2** a formal meeting to assess a job applicant etc.
▷ SYNONYMS: **meeting**, discussion, interrogation, cross-examination, debriefing, audience, talk, chat; informal grilling.
• v. hold an interview with.
▷ SYNONYMS: **talk to**, question, quiz, interrogate, cross-examine, debrief, poll, canvass, sound out; informal grill, pump.
■ **interviewee** n. **interviewer** n.

interweave v. (**interweaving**, **interwove**; past part. **interwoven**) weave together.

intestate adj. (of a dead person) not having made a will.

intestine n. the long tubular organ leading from the stomach to the anus.
■ **intestinal** adj.

intimacy n. close familiarity or friendship.
▷ SYNONYMS: **closeness**, togetherness, rapport, attachment, familiarity, friendliness, affection, warmth.
– ANTONYMS: formality.

intimate¹ /in-ti-muht/ adj. **1** close and friendly. **2** private and personal. **3** having a sexual relationship. **4** (of knowledge) detailed.
▷ SYNONYMS: **1 close**, bosom, dear, cherished, fast, firm. **2 friendly**, warm, welcoming, hospitable, relaxed, informal, cosy, comfortable. **3 personal**, private, confidential, secret, inward. **4 detailed**, thorough, exhaustive, deep, in-depth, profound.
– ANTONYMS: distant, formal, cold.
• n. a close friend.
■ **intimately** adv.

intimate² /in-ti-mayt/ v. state indirectly.
▷ SYNONYMS: **imply**, suggest, hint at, indicate, insinuate; disclose, reveal, divulge, let it be known.
■ **intimation** n.

intimidate v. frighten into doing something.
▷ SYNONYMS: **frighten**, menace, scare, terrorize, threaten, browbeat, bully, harass, hound; informal lean on.
■ **intimidation** n.

into prep. **1** to a point on or within. **2** expressing a change or result. **3** in the direction of. **4** concerning. **5** expressing division.

intolerable adj. unable to be endured.
■ **intolerably** adv.

intolerant adj. unwilling to accept ideas or behaviour different to your own.
■ **intolerance** n.

intonation n. the rise and fall of the voice in speaking.

intone v. say with little intonation.

intoxicate v. **1** (of alcohol or a drug) cause to lose control. **2** excite.
■ **intoxication** n.

intractable adj. **1** hard to deal with. **2** stubborn.

intranet n. a computer network within an organization.

intransigent adj. stubborn.
■ **intransigence** n.

intransitive adj. (of a verb) not taking a direct object.

intrauterine adj. within the womb.

intravenous adj. within or into a vein.

intrepid adj. fearless.

intricate adj. very complicated.
▷ SYNONYMS: **complex**, complicated, convoluted, tangled, elaborate, ornate, detailed.
– ANTONYMS: simple.
■ **intricacy** n. **intricately** adv.

intrigue v. **1** arouse the curiosity of. **2** plot secretly.
▷ SYNONYMS: **interest**, fascinate, arouse someone's curiosity, attract, engage.
•n. **1** the action of making secret plots. **2** a secret love affair.
▷ SYNONYMS: **plotting**, conniving, scheming, machination, double-dealing, subterfuge.
■ **intriguing** adj.

intrinsic adj. forming part of the basic nature of something.
■ **intrinsically** adv.

introduce v. **1** bring into use. **2** present someone by name. **3** bring to someone's attention for the first time. **4** insert. **5** occur at the start of.
▷ SYNONYMS: **1 institute**, initiate, launch, inaugurate, establish, found, bring in, set in motion, start, begin, get going. **2 present**, make known, acquaint with. **3 insert**, inject, put, force, shoot, feed. **4 instil**, infuse, inject, add.
– ANTONYMS: end, remove.

introduction n. **1** the act of introducing. **2** a thing introducing another. **3** a thing newly brought in.
▷ SYNONYMS: **1 institution**, establishment, initiation, launch, inauguration, foundation. **2 foreword**, preface, preamble, prologue, prelude; informal intro.
– ANTONYMS: ending, epilogue.

introductory adj. serving as an introduction.
▷ SYNONYMS: **1 opening**, initial, starting, initiatory, first, preliminary.

2 elementary, basic, rudimentary, entry-level.
– ANTONYMS: final, advanced.

introspection n. examination of your thoughts or feelings.
■ **introspective** adj.

introvert n. a shy, introspective person.
■ **introverted** adj.

intrude v. enter a place or situation where you are unwelcome or uninvited.
▷ SYNONYMS: **encroach**, impinge, trespass, infringe, invade, violate, disturb, disrupt.
■ **intrusion** n.

intruder n. a person who intrudes.
▷ SYNONYMS: **trespasser**, interloper, invader, infiltrator, burglar, house-breaker; informal gatecrasher.

intrusive adj. disturbing or unwelcome.

intuition n. the ability to understand or know something without conscious reasoning.
▷ SYNONYMS: **instinct**, feeling, sixth sense, hunch, feeling in your bones, inkling, sneaking suspicion, premonition; informal gut feeling.

intuitive adj. based on what you feel to be true; instinctive.
▷ SYNONYMS: **instinctive**, innate, inborn, inherent, natural, unconscious, subconscious; informal gut.

Inuit /in-yuu-it/ n. (pl. **Inuit** or **Inuits**) a member of a people of northern Canada and parts of Greenland and Alaska.

USAGE For an explanation of **Inuit** and Eskimo, see **ESKIMO**.

inundate v. **1** flood. **2** overwhelm.

inure v. accustom to something unpleasant.

invade v. **1** enter a country so as to conquer or occupy it. **2** enter in large numbers. **3** intrude on.
▷ SYNONYMS: **1 occupy**, conquer, capture, seize, take, annex, overrun, storm. **2 intrude on**, violate, encroach on, infringe on, trespass on, disturb, disrupt.
– ANTONYMS: leave, liberate.

invader n. a person who invades.
▷ SYNONYMS: **attacker**, conqueror, raider, marauder, occupier, intruder, trespasser.

invalid¹ n. a person made weak or disabled by illness or injury.
•v. (**be invalided**) be removed from service in the armed forces because of injury or illness.

invalid² adj. **1** not legally or officially recognized. **2** incorrect.
▷ SYNONYMS: **1 void**, null and void, not binding, illegitimate, inapplicable. **2 false**, fallacious, spurious, incorrect, wrong, untenable.
invalidate v. make invalid.
invalidity n. **1** Brit. the condition of being an invalid. **2** the fact of being invalid.
invaluable adj. very useful.
▷ SYNONYMS: **indispensable**, irreplaceable, all-important, crucial, vital, worth its weight in gold.
– ANTONYMS: dispensable.
invariable adj. never changing.
▷ SYNONYMS: **unvarying**, unchanging, unvaried; constant, stable, set, steady; unchangeable, unalterable.
invariably adv. in every case or on every occasion.
▷ SYNONYMS: **always**, at all times, without fail, without exception, consistently, habitually, unfailingly.
invasion n. an act of invading.
▷ SYNONYMS: **occupation**, conquering, capture, seizure, annexation, take-over. **2 violation**, infringement, interruption, encroachment, disturbance, disruption, breach.
– ANTONYMS: withdrawal.
invasive adj. **1** tending to invade. **2** (of medical procedures) involving the introduction of instruments into the body.
invective n. abusive language.
inveigh /in-vay/ v. (**inveigh against**) speak or write about with great hostility.
inveigle /in-vay-g'l/ v. persuade by trickery or flattery.
invent v. **1** create or design something new. **2** make up a false story, name, etc.
▷ SYNONYMS: **1 originate**, create, design, devise, develop. **2 make up**, fabricate, concoct, hatch, contrive, dream up; informal cook up.
invention n. **1** the act of inventing. **2** something invented. **3** creative ability.
▷ SYNONYMS: **1 origination**, creation, development, design, discovery. **2 innovation**, contraption, contrivance, device, gadget. **3 fabrication**, concoction, piece of fiction, story, tale, lie, untruth, falsehood, fib.
inventive adj. having or showing creativity or original thought.
▷ SYNONYMS: **creative**, original, innovative, imaginative, resourceful, unusual, fresh, novel, new,

groundbreaking, unorthodox, unconventional.
– ANTONYMS: unimaginative.
inventor n. a person who invents something.
▷ SYNONYMS: **originator**, creator, designer, deviser, developer, author, architect, father.
inventory n. (pl. **inventories**) **1** a complete list of items. **2** a quantity of goods in stock.
▷ SYNONYMS: **list**, listing, catalogue, record, register, checklist, log, archive.
inverse adj. opposite.
invert v. put upside down or in the opposite position or order.
  □ **inverted comma** a quotation mark.
  ■ **inversion** n.
invertebrate n. an animal without a backbone.
invest v. **1** use money or spend time so as to make a profit or achieve a result. **2** provide with a quality. **3** formally give a rank or office to.
▷ SYNONYMS: **put in**, plough in, put up, advance, expend, spend; informal lay out.
  ■ **investor** n.
investigate v. **1** carry out a systematic inquiry into. **2** research.
▷ SYNONYMS: **enquire into**, look into, go into, probe, explore, scrutinize, analyse, study, examine; informal check out, suss out.
  ■ **investigative** adj. **investigator** n.
investigation n. a formal inquiry or systematic study.
▷ SYNONYMS: **examination**, enquiry, study, inspection, exploration, analysis, research, scrutiny, probe, review.
investiture n. the act or ceremony of investing a person with an office etc.
investment n. **1** the act of investing. **2** something worth buying because it will be useful.
▷ SYNONYMS: **1 investing**, speculation, outlay, funding, backing, financing, underwriting. **2 stake**, payment, outlay, venture, proposition.
inveterate adj. having a firmly established habit.
invidious adj. likely to cause resentment.
▷ SYNONYMS: **1 unpleasant**, awkward, difficult, undesirable, unenviable. **2 unfair**, unjust, unwarranted.
invigilate v. Brit. supervise exam candidates.
  ■ **invigilator** n.
invigorate v. give strength or energy to.

▷ SYNONYMS: **revitalize**, energize, refresh, revive, enliven, liven up, perk up, wake up, animate, galvanize, fortify, rouse, exhilarate; informal buck up, pep up.
– ANTONYMS: tire.

invincible adj. too powerful to be defeated.
▷ SYNONYMS: **invulnerable**, indestructible, unconquerable, unbeatable, indomitable, unassailable, impregnable.
– ANTONYMS: vulnerable.
■ invincibility n.

inviolable adj. never to be attacked or dishonoured.

inviolate adj. free from injury or violation.

invisible adj. unable to be seen.
▷ SYNONYMS: **unseen**, imperceptible, undetectable, inconspicuous, unnoticed, unobserved, hidden, out of sight.
– ANTONYMS: visible.
■ invisibility n. invisibly adv.

invitation n. **1** a request that someone should join you in going somewhere or doing something. **2** the act of inviting.
▷ SYNONYMS: **request**, call, summons; informal invite.

invite v. **1** ask someone to come somewhere or do something. **2** ask for. **3** risk provoking.
▷ SYNONYMS: **1 ask**, summon. **2 ask for**, request, call for, appeal for, solicit, seek. **3 cause**, induce, provoke, ask for, encourage, lead to, bring on yourself, arouse.

inviting adj. tempting or attractive.
▷ SYNONYMS: **tempting**, enticing, alluring, attractive, appealing, appetizing, mouth-watering, intriguing, seductive.
– ANTONYMS: repellent.

in vitro adj. & adv. in a test tube or elsewhere outside a living organism.

invocation n. the act of invoking.

invoice n. a bill for goods or services.
● v. send an invoice to.

invoke v. **1** appeal to as an authority. **2** call on a god or spirit.
▷ SYNONYMS: **1 cite**, refer to, resort to, have recourse to, turn to. **2 pray to**, call on, appeal to. **3 bring forth**, bring out, elicit, conjure up, generate.

involuntary adj. **1** done without conscious control. **2** done against someone's will.
▷ SYNONYMS: **1 reflex**, automatic, instinctive, unintentional, uncontrollable. **2 compulsory**, obliga-

tory, mandatory, forced, prescribed.
– ANTONYMS: deliberate, optional.
■ involuntarily adv.

involve v. **1** have as a necessary part or result. **2** cause to participate.
▷ SYNONYMS: **entail**, require, necessitate, demand, call for.
– ANTONYMS: preclude, exclude.

involved adj. **1** participating in or connected with something. **2** occupied in something. **3** having a close personal relationship. **4** complicated.
▷ SYNONYMS: **1** social workers involved in the case: **associated**, connected, concerned; caught up, mixed up. **2 engrossed**, absorbed, immersed, occupied, preoccupied, intent. **3 complicated**, intricate, complex, elaborate, convoluted, confusing.

involvement n. the fact or condition of being involved.
▷ SYNONYMS: **1 participation**, collaboration, collusion, complicity, association, connection, entanglement. **2 attachment**, friendship, intimacy, commitment.

invulnerable adj. impossible to harm.

inward adj. **1** towards the inside. **2** mental or spiritual.
● adv. (or **inwards**) towards the inside.
▷ SYNONYMS: **inside**, towards the inside, into the interior, within.
■ inwardly adv.

iodine n. a chemical element used in solution as an antiseptic.

ion n. an electrically charged atom that has lost or gained an electron.
■ ionic adj.

ionize (or **-ise**) v. convert into an ion or ions.

ionosphere n. a layer of the atmosphere containing a high concentration of ions.

iota n. a very small amount.
▷ SYNONYMS: **bit**, mite, speck, scrap, shred, ounce, jot.

IOU n. a signed document acknowledging a debt.

ipso facto adv. by that very fact.

IQ abbrev. intelligence quotient.

IRA abbrev. Irish Republican Army.

Iranian n. a person from Iran.
● adj. of Iran.

Iraqi n. (pl. **Iraqis**) a person from Iraq.
● adj. of Iraq.

irascible adj. bad-tempered.

irate adj. very angry.

ire n. anger.

iridescent adj. shimmering with many colours.

■ **iridescence** n.

iridium n. a hard metallic element.

iris n. **1** the coloured part of the eyeball, with the pupil in the centre. **2** a plant with large bright flowers.

Irish n. the language of Ireland.
• adj. of Ireland.

irk v. annoy.
■ **irksome** adj.

iron n. **1** a strong magnetic metallic element. **2** an implement with a flat base heated for smoothing clothes. **3** (**irons**) fetters or handcuffs.
• v. **1** smooth clothes with an iron. **2** (**iron out**) solve a problem.
□ **ironmonger** Brit. a person selling tools and other hardware.

ironic adj. **1** expressing an idea with words that normally mean the opposite so as to amuse or make a point. **2** happening in the opposite way to what is expected.
▷ SYNONYMS: **1 sarcastic**, sardonic, satirical, dry, wry, double-edged; mocking, derisive, scornful; Brit. informal sarky. **2 paradoxical**, funny, strange.
■ **ironical** adj. **ironically** adv.

irony n. (pl. **ironies**) **1** the use of words that say the opposite of what you mean so as to amuse or to make a point. **2** aspects of a situation that are opposite to what are expected.
▷ SYNONYMS: **1 sarcasm**; mockery, ridicule, derision, scorn; Brit. informal sarkiness. **2 paradox**.

irradiate v. **1** expose to radiation. **2** illuminate.
■ **irradiation** n.

irrational adj. not logical or reasonable.
▷ SYNONYMS: **unreasonable**, illogical, groundless, baseless, unfounded, unjustifiable.
– ANTONYMS: rational, logical.
■ **irrationally** adv.

irreconcilable adj. **1** incompatible. **2** unable to be resolved.

irredeemable adj. unable to be saved or put right.

irrefutable adj. impossible to disprove.
▷ SYNONYMS: **indisputable**, undeniable, unquestionable, incontrovertible, incontestable, beyond question, beyond doubt, conclusive, definite, definitive, decisive.

irregular adj. **1** not regular in shape, arrangement, or occurrence. **2** not according to a rule or standard.
▷ SYNONYMS: **1 uneven**, crooked, misshapen, lopsided, asymmetrical, twisted. **2 inconsistent**, unsteady,

uneven, fitful, patchy, variable, varying, changeable, inconstant, erratic, unstable, spasmodic, intermittent. **3** irregular financial dealings: **improper**, illegitimate, unethical, unprofessional; informal shady, dodgy. **4** an irregular army: **guerrilla**, underground, paramilitary, partisan, mercenary, terrorist.
■ **irregularity** n.

irrelevant adj. not relevant.
▷ SYNONYMS: **beside the point**, immaterial, unconnected, unrelated, peripheral, extraneous.
■ **irrelevance** n. **irrelevantly** adv.

USAGE -*ant*, not -*ent*: irrelev*ant*.

irreparable adj. impossible to put right or repair.
▷ SYNONYMS: **irreversible**, irrevocable, irrecoverable, unrepairable, beyond repair.
■ **irreparably** adv.

irreplaceable adj. impossible to replace.

irrepressible adj. unable to be restrained.
▷ SYNONYMS: **ebullient**, exuberant, buoyant, breezy, jaunty, high-spirited, vivacious, animated, full of life, lively; informal bubbly, bouncy, peppy, chipper, chirpy, full of beans.

irreproachable adj. very good and unable to be criticized.

irresistible adj. too tempting or powerful to be resisted.
▷ SYNONYMS: **1 captivating**, enticing, alluring, enchanting, fascinating, seductive. **2 uncontrollable**, overwhelming, overpowering, ungovernable, compelling.
■ **irresistibly** adv.

USAGE -*ible*, not -*able*: irresist*ible*.

irresolute adj. uncertain.

irrespective adj. (**irrespective of**) regardless of.

irresponsible adj. not showing a proper sense of responsibility.
▷ SYNONYMS: **reckless**, rash, careless, unwise, imprudent, ill-advised, injudicious, hasty, impetuous, foolhardy, foolish, unreliable, undependable, untrustworthy.
■ **irresponsibly** adv.

irretrievable adj. unable to be retrieved or set right.

irreverent adj. disrespectful.
▷ SYNONYMS: **disrespectful**, impertinent, cheeky, flippant, rude, discourteous.
– ANTONYMS: respectful.
■ **irreverence** n. **irreverently** adv.

irreversible adj. impossible to alter or undo.
 ■ **irreversibly** adv.
irrevocable adj. unable to be changed or reversed.
 ▷ SYNONYMS: **irreversible**, unalterable, unchangeable, immutable, final, binding, permanent, set in stone.
 ■ **irrevocably** adv.
irrigate v. supply water to land or crops by means of channels.
 ■ **irrigation** n.
irritable adj. easily annoyed or angered.
 ▷ SYNONYMS: **bad-tempered**, short-tempered, irascible, tetchy, testy, grumpy, grouchy, crotchety, cantankerous, fractious, curmudgeonly.
 – ANTONYMS: good-humoured.
 ■ **irritability** n. **irritably** adv.
irritate v. **1** make annoyed. **2** cause inflammation in a part of the body.
 ▷ SYNONYMS: **1 annoy**, bother, vex, make cross, exasperate, infuriate, anger, madden; Brit. rub up the wrong way; informal aggravate, peeve, rile, needle, bug, hack off; Brit. informal nark, get on someone's wick; N. Amer. informal tee off, tick off. **2 inflame**, hurt, chafe, scratch, scrape, rub.
 – ANTONYMS: delight, soothe.
 ■ **irritant** n.
irritation n. annoyance.
 ▷ SYNONYMS: **annoyance**, exasperation, vexation, indignation, anger, displeasure, chagrin.
 – ANTONYMS: delight.
is see BE.
Islam n. the Muslim religion.
 ■ **Islamic** adj.
island n. a piece of land surrounded by water.
 ▷ SYNONYMS: **isle**, islet, atoll; Brit. holm; (**islands**) archipelago.
 ■ **islander** n.

> **WORD LINKS**
> **insular** relating to an island

isle n. an island.
islet n. a small island.
isn't contr. is not.
isobar n. a line on a map connecting points with the same atmospheric pressure.
isolate v. **1** place apart or alone. **2** extract a substance in a pure form.
 ▷ SYNONYMS: **separate**, segregate, detach, cut off, shut away, alienate, distance, cloister, seclude, cordon off, seal off, close off, fence off.
 – ANTONYMS: integrate.

 ■ **isolation** n.
isolated adj. **1** remote. **2** single; exceptional.
 ▷ SYNONYMS: **1 remote**, out of the way, outlying, off the beaten track, in the back of beyond, godforsaken, inaccessible, cut-off; informal in the middle of nowhere, in the sticks; N. Amer. informal jerkwater. **2 solitary**, lonely, secluded, reclusive, hermit-like; N. Amer. lonesome. **3 unique**, lone, solitary, unusual, exceptional, untypical, freak; informal one-off.
 – ANTONYMS: accessible.
isolationism n. a policy of remaining apart from the political affairs of other countries.
 ■ **isolationist** n. & adj.
isomer n. each of two or more compounds with the same formula but a different arrangement of atoms.
isosceles /I-soss-i-leez/ adj. (of a triangle) having two sides of equal length.
isotope n. each of two or more forms of the same element that contain equal numbers of protons but different numbers of neutrons.
ISP abbrev. Internet service provider.
Israeli n. (pl. **Israelis**) a person from Israel.
 • adj. of Israel.
Israelite /iz-ruh-lyt/ n. a member of the people of ancient Israel.
issue n. **1** an important topic to be discussed or resolved. **2** the act of issuing. **3** each of a regular series of publications.
 ▷ SYNONYMS: **1 matter**, question, point at issue, affair, case, subject, topic, problem, situation. **2 edition**, number, instalment, copy, impression. **3 issuing**, release, publication, distribution.
 • v. **1** supply or give out. **2** formally send out or make known. **3** come or flow out.
 ▷ SYNONYMS: **1 release**, put out, deliver, publish, broadcast, circulate, distribute. **2 supply**, provide, furnish, arm, equip, fit out, rig out, kit out; informal fix up.
isthmus /iss-muhss/ n. (pl. **isthmuses**) a narrow strip of land linking two larger areas.
IT abbrev. information technology.
it pron. **1** a thing previously mentioned or easily identified. **2** an animal or child of unspecified sex. **3** used as a subject in statements about time, distance, or weather: *it is raining.*
Italian n. **1** a person from Italy. **2** the

language of Italy.
• **adj.** of Italy.

italic adj. (of a typeface) sloping.
• n. (or **italics**) an italic typeface.
■ **italicize** v.

itch n. an uncomfortable sensation that causes a desire to scratch.
▷ SYNONYMS: **1 tingling**, irritation, itchiness, prickle. **2 longing**, yearning, craving, ache, hunger, thirst, urge, hankering; informal yen.
• v. **1** have an itch. **2** informal impatiently desire to do.
▷ SYNONYMS: **1 tingle**, be irritated, be itchy, sting, hurt, be sore. **2 long**, yearn, ache, burn, crave, hanker for/ after, hunger, thirst, be eager, be desperate; informal be dying.
■ **itchy** adj.

item n. an individual article or unit.
▷ SYNONYMS: **1 thing**, article, object, piece, element, constituent, component, ingredient. **2 issue**, matter, affair, case, subject, topic, question, point. **3 report**, story, article, piece, write-up, bulletin, feature, review.

itemize (or **-ise**) v. present as a list of items.

iterate v. do or say repeatedly.
■ **iteration** n.

itinerant adj. travelling.

itinerary n. (pl. **itineraries**) a planned route or journey.
▷ SYNONYMS: **route**, plan, schedule, timetable, programme.

its adj. belonging to it.

> **USAGE** Don't confuse **its** (as in *turn the camera on its side*) with the form **it's** (short for either **it is** or **it has**, as in *it's my fault* or *it's been raining*).

it's contr. **1** it is. **2** it has.

itself pron. **1** used when a thing which performs an action is also affected by it. **2** used to emphasize a particular thing mentioned.

ITV abbrev. Independent Television.

IUD abbrev. intrauterine device, a contraceptive fitted inside the womb.

IVF abbrev. in vitro fertilization.

ivory n. (pl. **ivories**) **1** a hard creamywhite substance forming the tusks of an elephant. **2** a creamy-white colour.
□ **ivory tower** a privileged position remote from normal difficulties.

ivy n. an evergreen climbing plant.

Jj

J abbrev. joules.

jab v. (jabbing, jabbed) poke with something pointed.
▷ SYNONYMS: **poke**, prod, dig, elbow, nudge, thrust, stab, push.
• n. **1** a sharp poke or blow. **2** Brit. informal an injection.

jabber v. talk quickly but unintelligibly.

jacaranda n. a tropical tree with scented wood.

jack n. **1** a device for lifting a vehicle off the ground. **2** a playing card next below a queen. **3** a connection between two pieces of electrical equipment. **4** a small ball aimed at in bowls.
• v. (**jack up**) raise with a jack.

jackal n. a wild dog of Africa and Asia.

jackass n. **1** a stupid person. **2** a male ass.

jackboot n. a military boot reaching to the knee.

jackdaw n. a small grey-headed crow.

jacket n. **1** a short coat. **2** an outer covering. **3** Brit. the skin of a potato.
▷ SYNONYMS: **wrapping**, wrapper, sleeve, cover, covering, sheath.

jackknife n. a large folding knife.
• v. (of an articulated lorry) bend into a V-shape in a skid.

jackpot n. a large cash prize in a game or lottery.

Jacobean adj. of the reign of James I of England (1603–1625).

Jacobite n. a supporter of the deposed James II and his descendants.

jacquard n. a fabric with a woven pattern.

jacuzzi /juh-koo-zi/ n. (pl. **jacuzzis**) trademark a large bath with jets of water.

jade n. a green precious stone.

jaded adj. tired and bored.

jagged adj. with rough, sharp projections.
▷ SYNONYMS: **spiky**, barbed, ragged, rough, uneven, irregular, serrated.
– ANTONYMS: smooth.

jaguar n. a large cat of Central and South America.

jail (Brit. also **gaol**) n. prison.
▷ SYNONYMS: **prison**, lock-up, detention centre; N. Amer. penitentiary, jailhouse; informal clink, cooler, the slammer, inside; Brit. informal nick; N. Amer. informal can, pen, slam, pokey.
• v. put in jail.
▷ SYNONYMS: **imprison**, incarcerate, lock up, put away, detain; informal send down, put behind bars, put inside; Brit. informal bang up.
– ANTONYMS: acquit, release.
■ **jailer** n.

jalopy /juh-lop-i/ n. (pl. **jalopies**) informal an old car.

jam v. (jamming, jammed) **1** pack tightly into a space. **2** block through crowding. **3** become stuck. **4** block a radio transmission.
▷ SYNONYMS: **1 stuff**, shove, force, ram, thrust, press, push, wedge, stick, cram. **2 crowd**, pack, pile, press, squeeze, sandwich, cram, throng, mob, fill, block, clog, congest. **3 stick**, become stuck, catch, seize up.
• n. **1** a spread made from fruit and sugar. **2** an instance of being blocked. **3** informal a difficult situation.
▷ SYNONYMS: **tailback**, hold-up, queue, congestion, bottleneck; N. Amer. grid-lock; informal snarl-up.

jamb n. a side post of a door or window.

jamboree n. a lavish or noisy party.

jangle v. **1** make a ringing metallic sound. **2** feel upset or on edge.
• n. a jangling sound.

janitor n. a caretaker.

January n. the first month.

Japanese n. (pl. **Japanese**) **1** a person from Japan. **2** the language of Japan.
• adj. of Japan.

japanned adj. coated with a black glossy varnish.

jape n. a practical joke.

japonica n. a shrub with bright red flowers.

j

jar n. a cylindrical glass or pottery container.
▷ SYNONYMS: **pot**, container, crock.
• v. (**jarring**, **jarred**) **1** hit with a painful jolt. **2** have an unpleasant effect.
▷ SYNONYMS: **1 jolt**, jerk, shake, vibrate. **2 grate**, set someone's teeth on edge, irritate, annoy, get on someone's nerves. **3 clash**, conflict, contrast, be incompatible, be at variance, be at odds.

jargon n. words used by a particular group and hard for others to understand.
▷ SYNONYMS: **slang**, idiom, cant, argot, gobbledegook; informal lingo, -speak, -ese.

jasmine n. a shrub with scented flowers.

jasper n. a reddish-brown quartz.

jaundice n. **1** yellowing of the skin due to a liver disorder. **2** bitterness or resentment.
■ **jaundiced** adj.

jaunt n. a short trip for pleasure.
▷ SYNONYMS: **trip**, outing, excursion, tour, drive, ride, run; informal spin, junket.

jaunty adj. lively and self-confident.
■ **jauntily** adv.

javelin n. a long spear thrown in a sport.

jaw n. **1** the bony structures forming the framework of the mouth. **2** (**jaws**) the gripping parts of a tool.
▷ SYNONYMS: **mouth**, maw, muzzle, mandibles; informal chops.
• v. informal talk at length.

jay n. a bird of the crow family.

jaywalk v. cross a road without regard for the traffic.
■ **jaywalker** n.

jazz n. a type of music characterized by improvisation.
• v. (**jazz up**) make more lively.

jazzy adj. (**jazzier**, **jazziest**) **1** in the style of jazz. **2** colourful and showy.

jealous adj. **1** envious of someone's success. **2** resentful of someone seen as a sexual rival. **3** very protective of your possessions.
▷ SYNONYMS: **1 envious**, covetous, resentful, grudging, green with envy. **2 suspicious**, distrustful, possessive, proprietorial, overprotective. **3 protective**, vigilant, watchful, mindful, careful.
– ANTONYMS: trusting.

jealousy n. (pl. **jealousies**) the feeling of being jealous.
▷ SYNONYMS: **envy**, resentment, bitter-

ness; humorous the green-eyed monster.

jeans pl. n. denim trousers.

jeep n. trademark a sturdy four-wheel drive vehicle.

jeer v. make rude mocking remarks at.
▷ SYNONYMS: **taunt**, mock, ridicule, deride, insult, abuse, heckle, catcall, boo, whistle at, scoff at, sneer at; Brit. barrack.
– ANTONYMS: applaud, cheer.
• n. a rude mocking remark.
▷ SYNONYMS: **taunt**, sneer, insult, shout, jibe, boo, catcall, derision, teasing, scoffing, abuse, scorn, heckling, catcalling; Brit. barracking.
– ANTONYMS: applause, cheer.

Jehovah n. the name of God in some translations of the Bible.

jejune adj. **1** simplistic. **2** dull.

jell v. = GEL.

jelly n. (pl. **jellies**) **1** a dessert made of a flavoured liquid set with gelatin. **2** a semi-solid substance.
□ **jellyfish** a sea animal with a soft body and stinging tentacles.

jemmy n. (pl. **jemmies**) a short crowbar.

jenny n. (pl. **jennies**) a female donkey.

jeopardize (or **-ise**) v. put at risk of harm or loss.
▷ SYNONYMS: **threaten**, endanger, imperil, risk, compromise, prejudice.
– ANTONYMS: safeguard.

jeopardy n. danger of harm or loss.
▷ SYNONYMS: **danger**, peril, risk.

jerk n. a sharp, sudden movement.
• v. move with a jerk.
▷ SYNONYMS: **1 yank**, tug, pull, wrench, wrest, drag, snatch. **2 jolt**, lurch, bump, judder, bounce, jounce, shake.

jerkin n. a sleeveless jacket.

jerky adj. (**jerkier**, **jerkiest**) making sudden stops and starts.
▷ SYNONYMS: **convulsive**, spasmodic, fitful, twitchy, shaky.
– ANTONYMS: smooth.
■ **jerkily** adv.

jerry-built adj. badly or hastily built.

jerrycan n. a large flat-sided can for liquids.

jersey n. (pl. **jerseys**) **1** a knitted top with sleeves. **2** a soft knitted fabric.

Jerusalem artichoke n. a knobbly root vegetable.

jest n. a joke.
• v. speak in a joking way.

jester n. a comic entertainer at a medieval court.

Jesuit n. a member of a Roman Catholic order of priests.

jet n. **1** a stream of liquid or gas forced

out of a small opening. **2** an aircraft powered by jet engines. **3** a hard black mineral. **4** (or **jet black**) a glossy black colour.

▷ SYNONYMS: **1 stream**, spurt, spray, fountain, rush, spout, gush, surge, burst. **2 nozzle**, head, spout.

• v. (**jetting**, **jetted**) travel by jet aircraft.

□ **jet engine** an aircraft engine providing propulsion by ejecting a high-speed jet of gas from burning fuel. **jet lag** extreme tiredness felt after a long flight. **jet ski** trademark a small vehicle which skims across the water.

jetsam n. unwanted material thrown from a ship and washed ashore.

jettison v. throw or drop from an aircraft or ship.

▷ SYNONYMS: **dump**, drop, ditch, throw out, get rid of, discard, dispose of, scrap.

jetty n. (pl. **jetties**) a landing stage or small pier.

▷ SYNONYMS: **pier**, landing stage, quay, wharf, dock, breakwater, groyne, mole; N. Amer. levee.

Jew n. a person whose religion is Judaism and who is of ancient Hebrew descent.

■ **Jewish** adj.

jewel n. **1** a precious stone cut or set as an ornament. **2** a highly valued person or thing.

▷ SYNONYMS: **1 gem**, gemstone, precious stone; informal sparkler, rock. **2 showpiece**, pride and joy, cream, crème de la crème, jewel in the crown, prize, pick.

■ **jewelled** (US **jeweled**) adj.

jewellery (US **jewelry**) n. personal ornaments such as necklaces or rings.

■ **jeweller** n.

Jewry n. Jews as a group.

jib n. **1** a triangular sail in front of a mast. **2** the arm of a crane.

• v. (**jibbing**, **jibbed**) (**jib at**) be unwilling to do or accept.

jibe (or **gibe**) n. **1** an insulting remark. **2** US = GYBE.

▷ SYNONYMS: **taunt**, sneer, jeer, insult, barb; informal dig, put-down.

• v. **1** make jibes. **2** US = GYBE.

jiffy n. informal a moment.

jig n. **1** a lively dance. **2** a device that holds something and guides the tools working on it.

• v. (**jigging**, **jigged**) move up and down jerkily.

jiggery-pokery n. informal suspicious behaviour.

jiggle v. rock or shake lightly.

jigsaw n. **1** a picture cut into interlocking shapes that have to be fitted together. **2** a machine saw for cutting curved lines in a material.

jihad n. (in Islam) a war or struggle against non-Muslims.

jilt v. break off a relationship with a lover.

▷ SYNONYMS: **leave**, walk out on, throw over, finish with, break up with, stand up, leave at the altar; informal chuck, ditch, dump, drop, run out on, give someone the push/elbow, give someone the big E.

jingle n. **1** a light ringing sound. **2** a short memorable slogan etc.

▷ SYNONYMS: **clink**, chink, tinkle, jangle, ring.

• v. make a jingle.

jingoism n. excessive pride in your country.

■ **jingoistic** adj.

jinx n. a person or thing that brings bad luck.

▷ SYNONYMS: **curse**, spell, the evil eye, black magic, voodoo, bad luck; N. Amer. hex.

■ **jinxed** adj.

jitters pl. n. informal nervousness.

■ **jittery** adj.

jive n. a lively dance to swing music.

• v. dance the jive.

job n. **1** a paid position of employment. **2** a task.

▷ SYNONYMS: **1 position**, post, situation, appointment, occupation, profession, trade, career, work, vocation, calling, métier. **2 task**, piece of work, assignment, mission, project, undertaking, operation, duty, chore, errand, responsibility, charge, role, function; informal department.

• v. (**jobbing**, **jobbed**) do casual work.

□ **jobcentre** (in the UK) a government office providing information about available jobs. **job lot** a batch of articles sold or bought at one time.

jobless adj. without a paid job.

▷ SYNONYMS: **unemployed**, out of work, unwaged, redundant, laid off; Brit. informal on the dole; Canad. informal on pogey; Austral./NZ informal on the wallaby track.

– ANTONYMS: employed.

jockey n. (pl. **jockeys**) a professional rider in horse races.

• v. struggle to gain or achieve.

jockstrap n. a support or protection for a man's genitals.

jocose adj. humorous.

jocular adj. humorous.

j

■ **jocularity** n.

jocund adj. cheerful.

jodhpurs pl. n. trousers worn for horse riding that fit closely below the knee.

jog v. (**jogging**, **jogged**) **1** run at a steady, gentle pace. **2** knock slightly.
▷ SYNONYMS: **1 run**, trot, lope. **2 nudge**, prod, poke, push, bump, jar.
● n. **1** a period of jogging. **2** a slight knock.
□ **jog someone's memory** make someone remember something.
■ **jogger** n.

joggle v. shake slightly.

joie de vivre /zhwah duh **vee**-vruh/ n. lively enjoyment of life.

join v. **1** link or become linked. **2** unite to form a whole. **3** become a member or employee of. **4** (also **join in**) take part in. **5** meet or go with someone. **6** (**join up**) enlist in the armed forces.
▷ SYNONYMS: **1** *the two parts are joined with clay:* **connect**, unite, couple, fix, affix, attach, fasten, stick, glue, fuse, weld, amalgamate, bond, link, yoke, merge, secure, make fast, tie, bind. **2** *the path joins a major road:* **meet**, touch, reach. **3** *he joined the search party:* **help in**, participate in, get involved in, contribute to, enlist in, join up, sign up, band together, get together, team up.
– ANTONYMS: separate, leave.
● n. a place where things join.

joiner n. a person who makes the wooden parts of a building.
■ **joinery** n.

joint n. **1** a join. **2** a structure in the body joining two bones. **3** Brit. a large piece of meat. **4** informal a place of a specified kind. **5** informal a cannabis cigarette.
▷ SYNONYMS: **join**, junction, intersection, link, connection, weld, seam, coupling.
● adj. shared, held, or made by two or more people.
▷ SYNONYMS: **common**, shared, communal, collective, mutual, cooperative, collaborative, concerted, combined, united, allied.
– ANTONYMS: separate.
● v. cut meat into joints.
■ **jointed** adj.

jointly adv. with or by two or more people.
▷ SYNONYMS: **together**, in partnership, in cooperation, cooperatively, in conjunction, in combination, mutually, in league.

joist n. a beam supporting the floor or ceiling of a building.

jojoba /hoh-**hoh**-buh/ n. an oil from the seeds of a shrub, used in cosmetics.

joke n. **1** something said or done to cause laughter. **2** informal a ridiculously inadequate person or thing.
▷ SYNONYMS: **1 witticism**, jest, quip, pun; informal gag, wisecrack, crack, funny, one-liner. **2 trick**, prank, stunt, hoax, jape; informal leg-pull, spoof, wind-up. **3 laughing stock**, figure of fun, Aunt Sally. **4 farce**, travesty.
● v. make jokes.
▷ SYNONYMS: **tell jokes**, jest, banter, quip; informal wisecrack, josh.
■ **jokey** adj.

joker n. **1** a person who jokes. **2** a playing card used as a wild card.
▷ SYNONYMS: **comedian**, comedienne, comic, humorist, wit, jester, prankster, practical joker, clown.

jollification n. time spent having fun.

jollity n. **1** lively and cheerful activity. **2** cheerfulness.

jolly adj. (**jollier**, **jolliest**) **1** happy and cheerful. **2** lively and entertaining.
▷ SYNONYMS: **cheerful**, happy, cheery, good-humoured, jovial, merry, sunny, joyful, light-hearted, in high spirits, buoyant, bubbly, genial; informal chipper, chirpy, perky; literary blithe.
– ANTONYMS: miserable.
● v. (**jollying**, **jollied**) informal encourage in a friendly way.
● adv. Brit. informal very.

jolt v. **1** push or shake abruptly. **2** shock into action.
▷ SYNONYMS: **1 push**, jar, bump, knock, bang, shake, jog. **2 bump**, bounce, jerk, rattle, lurch, shudder, judder, jounce. **3 startle**, surprise, shock, stun, shake; informal rock, knock sideways.
● n. **1** an act of jolting. **2** a shock.
▷ SYNONYMS: **bump**, bounce, shake, jerk, lurch, jounce.

josh v. informal tease playfully.

joss stick n. a thin stick of incense.

jostle v. push roughly.
▷ SYNONYMS: **1 push**, shove, elbow, barge into, bang into, bump against, knock against. **2** *photographers jostled for position:* **struggle**, vie, jockey, scramble, fight.

jot v. (**jotting**, **jotted**) write quickly.
● n. a very small amount.

jotter n. Brit. a small notebook.

joule n. a unit of energy.

journal n. **1** a newspaper or magazine. **2** a diary.
▷ SYNONYMS: **1 periodical**, magazine, gazette, review, newsletter, news-

sheet, bulletin, newspaper, paper, daily, weekly, monthly, quarterly. **2** diary, log, logbook, weblog, blog, chronicle, history, yearbook; N. Amer. daybook.

journalese n. informal a clichéd style of writing.

journalist n. a person who writes for a newspaper etc. or prepares reports to be broadcast.
▷ SYNONYMS: **reporter**, correspondent, columnist; Brit. pressman; informal news hound, hack, hackette, stringer, journo.
■ journalism n.

journey n. (pl. **journeys**) an act of travelling from one place to another.
▷ SYNONYMS: **trip**, expedition, tour, trek, travels, voyage, cruise, ride, drive, crossing, passage, flight, odyssey, pilgrimage, safari, globetrotting; old use peregrinations.
• v. travel.
▷ SYNONYMS: **travel**, go, voyage, sail, cruise, fly, hike, trek, ride, drive, make your way.

journeyman n. a skilled worker employed by another.

joust v. (of medieval knights) fight on horseback with lances.

jovial adj. cheerful.
▷ SYNONYMS: **cheerful**, jolly, happy, cheery, jocular, good-humoured, convivial, genial, good-natured, affable, outgoing, smiling, merry, sunny; literary blithe.
– ANTONYMS: miserable.
■ joviality n. jovially adv.

jowl n. the lower part of the cheek.

joy n. **1** great happiness. **2** a cause of joy.
▷ SYNONYMS: **delight**, pleasure, jubilation, triumph, exultation, rejoicing, happiness, elation, euphoria, bliss, ecstasy, rapture.
– ANTONYMS: misery.
■ joyless adj.

joyful adj. feeling or causing great happiness.
▷ SYNONYMS: **1 cheerful**, happy, jolly, merry, sunny, joyous, cheery, smiling, jovial, mirthful, gleeful, pleased, delighted, thrilled, jubilant, elated, ecstatic; informal over the moon, on cloud nine. **2** joyful news: **pleasing**, happy, good, cheering, gladdening, welcome, gratifying, heart-warming.
– ANTONYMS: sad.
■ joyfully adv.

joyous adj. very happy.
■ joyously adv.

joyriding n. informal the crime of

stealing a vehicle and driving it very fast.
■ joyride n. joyrider n.

joystick n. **1** the control column of an aircraft. **2** a lever controlling the movement of an image on a screen.

JP abbrev. Justice of the Peace.

jubilant adj. happy and triumphant.
▷ SYNONYMS: **overjoyed**, exultant, triumphant, joyful, cock-a-hoop, elated, thrilled, gleeful, euphoric, ecstatic; informal over the moon, on cloud nine.
– ANTONYMS: despondent.
■ jubilation n.

jubilee n. a special anniversary.
▷ SYNONYMS: **anniversary**, commemoration, celebration, festival.

Judaism n. the religion of the Jews.
■ Judaic adj.

judder v. shake noisily or violently.

judge n. **1** a public official who decides cases in a law court. **2** a person who decides who has won a competition. **3** a person able to give an opinion.
▷ SYNONYMS: **1 justice**, magistrate, recorder, sheriff; N. Amer. jurist; Brit. informal beak. **2 adjudicator**, referee, umpire, arbiter, assessor, examiner, moderator, scrutineer.
• v. **1** form an opinion about. **2** decide a case in a law court. **3** decide the winner of.
▷ SYNONYMS: **1 conclude**, decide, consider, believe, think, deduce, infer, gauge, estimate, guess, surmise, conjecture, regard as, rate as, class as; informal reckon, figure. **2** she was judged innocent: **pronounce**, decree, rule, find. **3 adjudicate**, arbitrate, moderate, referee, umpire. **4 assess**, evaluate, appraise, examine, review.

judgement (or judgment) n. **1** the ability to make sound decisions. **2** an opinion or conclusion. **3** a decision of a law court or judge.
▷ SYNONYMS: **1 sense**, discernment, perception, discrimination, understanding, powers of reasoning, reason, logic. **2 opinion**, view, estimate, appraisal, conclusion, diagnosis, assessment, impression, conviction, perception, thinking. **3** a court judgement: **verdict**, decision, adjudication, ruling, pronouncement, decree, finding, sentence.

judgemental (or judgmental) adj. **1** of judgement. **2** excessively critical of others.
▷ SYNONYMS: **critical**, censorious, disapproving, disparaging, deprecating, negative, overcritical.

judicial adj. of a law court or judge.
■ **judicially** adv.

judiciary n. judges as a group.

judicious adj. having or done with good judgement.
▷ SYNONYMS: **wise**, sensible, prudent, shrewd, astute, canny, discerning, sagacious, strategic, politic, expedient.
− ANTONYMS: ill-advised.
■ **judiciously** adv.

judo n. a sport of unarmed combat.

jug n. Brit. a container with a handle and a lip, for holding and pouring liquids.
▷ SYNONYMS: **pitcher**, ewer, crock, jar, urn, carafe, flask, flagon, decanter; N. Amer. creamer.

juggernaut n. Brit. a large heavy vehicle.

juggle v. **1** continuously toss and catch several objects, keeping one or more in the air at any time. **2** do several things at the same time.
■ **juggler** n.

jugular n. any of several large veins in the neck.

juice n. **1** the liquid in fruit, vegetables, or meat. **2** (**juices**) fluid produced by the stomach.
▷ SYNONYMS: **liquid**, fluid, sap, extract, concentrate, essence.
• v. extract the juice from.

juicy adj. (**juicier**, **juiciest**) **1** full of juice. **2** informal (of gossip) very interesting.
▷ SYNONYMS: **1 succulent**, tender, moist, ripe. **2 sensational**, fascinating, intriguing, exciting, graphic, lurid.
− ANTONYMS: dry.

ju-jitsu n. a Japanese sport of unarmed combat.

jukebox n. a coin-operated machine playing musical recordings.

julep n. a sweet drink made from sugar syrup.

julienne n. a portion of vegetables cut into thin strips.

July n. the seventh month.

jumble n. an untidy collection.
▷ SYNONYMS: **heap**, muddle, mess, tangle, confusion, disarray, chaos, hotchpotch; N. Amer. hodgepodge; informal shambles.
• v. mix up in a confused way.
▷ SYNONYMS: **mix up**, muddle up, disorganize, disorder, tangle, confuse.
□ **jumble sale** Brit. a sale of second-hand goods.

jumbo informal adj. very large.
• n. (pl. **jumbos**) (or **jumbo jet**) a very large airliner.

jump v. **1** push yourself off the ground with your legs and feet. **2** leap across. **3** move suddenly from surprise.
4 (**jump at**) accept eagerly. **5** pass abruptly from one thing to another.
▷ SYNONYMS: **1 leap**, spring, bound, vault, hop, skip, caper, dance, prance. **2** pre-tax profits jumped: **rise**, go up, shoot up, soar, surge, climb, increase; informal skyrocket. **3** the noise made her jump: **start**, jolt, flinch, recoil, shudder.
• n. **1** an act of jumping. **2** a large or sudden increase. **3** an obstacle to be jumped.
▷ SYNONYMS: **1 leap**, spring, bound, hop, skip. **2 rise**, leap, increase, upsurge, upswing; informal hike. **3 start**, jerk, spasm, shudder.
□ **jump leads** Brit. a pair of cables for recharging a battery in a vehicle by connecting it to the battery in another. **jumpsuit** a one-piece garment of trousers and a top. **jump the queue** move ahead of your proper place in a queue.

jumper n. **1** Brit. a pullover. **2** a person or animal that jumps.
▷ SYNONYMS: **sweater**, pullover, jersey; informal woolly.

jumpy adj. (**jumpier**, **jumpiest**) informal anxious and uneasy.
▷ SYNONYMS: **nervous**, on edge, edgy, tense, anxious, restless, fidgety, keyed up, overwrought; informal jittery, uptight, het up; N. Amer. informal antsy.
− ANTONYMS: calm.

junction n. **1** a point where things meet or join. **2** a place where roads or railway lines meet.
▷ SYNONYMS: **crossroads**, intersection, interchange, T-junction, turn, turn-off, exit; Brit. roundabout; N. Amer. turnout, cloverleaf.

juncture n. **1** a point in time. **2** a join.

June n. the sixth month.

jungle n. **1** an area of thick tropical forest and tangled vegetation. **2** a bewildering or difficult situation.

junior adj. **1** of younger people.
2 Brit. of schoolchildren aged 7–11.
3 younger. **4** low or lower in status.
▷ SYNONYMS: **younger**, minor, subordinate, lower, lesser, low-ranking, inferior, secondary.
− ANTONYMS: senior, older.
• n. a junior person.

juniper n. an evergreen shrub.

junk n. **1** informal useless or worthless articles. **2** a flat-bottomed sailing boat used in China.

▷ SYNONYMS: **rubbish**, clutter, odds and ends, bric-a-brac, refuse, litter, scrap, waste, debris; N. Amer. trash.
□ **junk food** unhealthy food. **junk mail** unwanted advertising material sent by post.

junket n. **1** informal an official trip paid for using public funds. **2** a dish of sweetened curds of milk.

junkie n. informal a drug addict.

junta n. a group ruling a country after taking power by force.

jurisdiction n. **1** the official power to make legal decisions. **2** the extent of this.

jurisprudence n. the theory of law.

jurist n. an expert in law.

juror n. a member of a jury.

jury n. (pl. **juries**) a group of people required to attend a legal case and give a verdict based on the evidence presented.

just adj. **1** right and fair. **2** deserved.
▷ SYNONYMS: **1** *a just society:* **fair**, fair-minded, equitable, even-handed, impartial, unbiased, objective, neutral, disinterested, unprejudiced, honourable, upright, decent, principled. **2** *a just reward:* **deserved**, well deserved, well earned, merited, rightful, due, proper, fitting, appropriate, defensible, justified, justifiable.
– ANTONYMS: unfair.
• adv. **1** exactly. **2** at the same moment. **3** very recently. **4** by a small amount. **5** only.
▷ SYNONYMS: **1 exactly**, precisely, absolutely, completely, totally, entirely, perfectly, utterly, thoroughly; informal dead. **2 narrowly**, only just, by a hair's breadth, by the skin of your teeth, barely, scarcely, hardly; informal by a whisker.
■ **justly** adv.

justice n. **1** just behaviour or treatment. **2** the administration of law. **3** a judge or magistrate.
▷ SYNONYMS: **1 fairness**, justness, fair play, fair-mindedness, equity, right,

even-handedness, honesty, morality. **2** *the justice of his case:* **validity**, justification, soundness, well-foundedness, legitimacy. **3 judge**, magistrate, recorder, sheriff; N. Amer. jurist.
□ **Justice of the Peace** a non-professional magistrate.

> **WORD LINKS**
> **judicial** relating to a system of justice

justifiable adj. able to be shown to be right or reasonable.
▷ SYNONYMS: **valid**, legitimate, warranted, well founded, justified, just, reasonable, tenable, defensible, sound, warrantable.
– ANTONYMS: unjustifiable, unwarranted.
■ **justifiably** adv.

justification n. a good reason why something exists or has been done.
▷ SYNONYMS: **grounds**, reason, basis, rationale, premise, vindication, explanation, defence, argument, case.

justify v. (**justifying**, **justified**) **1** show to be right or reasonable. **2** be a good reason for. **3** adjust lines of type to form straight edges at both sides.
▷ SYNONYMS: **1 give grounds for**, give reasons for, explain, account for, defend, vindicate, excuse, exonerate. **2 warrant**, be good reason for.

jut v. (**jutting**, **jutted**) extend out beyond.
▷ SYNONYMS: **stick out**, project, protrude, bulge out, overhang, beetle.

jute n. rough fibre from the stems of a tropical plant.

juvenile adj. **1** of young people or animals. **2** childish.
▷ SYNONYMS: **1 young**, teenage, adolescent, junior. **2 childish**, immature, puerile, infantile, babyish.
– ANTONYMS: adult, mature.
• n. a young person or animal.
▷ SYNONYMS: **child**, youngster, teenager, adolescent, minor, junior; informal kid.
– ANTONYMS: adult.
□ **juvenile deliquent** a young person who regularly commits crimes.

juxtapose v. place close together.
■ **juxtaposition** n.

j

Kk

K abbrev. **1** kilobytes. **2** informal thousand.

kaftan (or **caftan**) n. a long, loose dress or tunic.

kaiser n. hist. the German or Austrian Emperor.

kale n. a type of cabbage.

kaleidoscope /kuh-**ly**-duh-skohp/ n. a tube containing mirrors and coloured fragments whose reflections produce changing patterns when the tube is turned.
  ■ **kaleidoscopic** adj.

kamikaze /ka-mi-**kah**-zi/ n. (in the Second World War) a Japanese aircraft loaded with explosives and deliberately crashed on its target.
  • adj. reckless or suicidal.

kangaroo n. a large Australian marsupial with strong hind legs for leaping.
  □ **kangaroo court** a court set up unofficially and intended to find someone guilty.

kaolin n. a fine white clay, used for making china and in medicine.

kapok n. a fluffy fibre used as padding.

kaput /kuh-**put**/ adj. informal broken.

karaoke /ka-ri-**oh**-ki/ n. an entertainment in which people sing popular songs to pre-recorded backing tracks.

karate /kuh-**rah**-ti/ n. a Japanese system of unarmed combat.

karma n. (in Hinduism and Buddhism) a person's actions in this and previous lives, seen as affecting their future fate.

kasbah (or **casbah**) n. (in North Africa) an old fortress in a city and the narrow streets surrounding it.

kayak /**ky**-ak/ n. a light covered canoe.

kebab n. pieces of meat etc. cooked on a skewer.

kedgeree n. Brit. a dish of smoked fish, rice, and hard-boiled eggs.

keel n. a structure running along the base of a ship.
  • v. (**keel over**) **1** (of a boat) turn over on its side. **2** fall over.
  ▷ SYNONYMS: **1** capsize, turn turtle, turn upside down, founder, overturn, turn over, tip over. **2** collapse, faint, pass out, black out; literary swoon.

keen adj. **1** eager and enthusiastic. **2** sharp. **3** quick to understand. **4** highly developed.
  ▷ SYNONYMS: **1** I'm keen to help: **eager**, anxious, intent, impatient, determined; informal raring, itching, dying. **2** a keen birdwatcher: **enthusiastic**, avid, ardent, fervent, conscientious, committed, dedicated. **3** a girl he was keen on: **attracted to**, interested in, fond of, taken with, smitten with, enamoured of; informal struck on. **4** a keen mind: **acute**, penetrating, astute, incisive, sharp, perceptive, piercing, razor-sharp, shrewd, discerning, clever, intelligent, brilliant, bright, smart, wise, insightful. **5** a keen sense of duty: **intense**, acute, fierce, passionate, burning, fervent, strong, powerful.
  – ANTONYMS: reluctant, unenthusiastic.
  ■ **keenly** adv. **keenness** n.

keep v. (**keeping**, **kept**) **1** continue to have. **2** continue in a specified condition, position, or activity. **3** save for future use. **4** store in a regular place. **5** do something agreed. **6** cause to be late. **7** support financially.
  ▷ SYNONYMS: **1** I kept all the photos: **retain**, hold on to, save, store, put by/aside, set aside; informal hang on to. **2** try to keep calm: **remain**, stay. **3** he keeps going on about it: **persist in**, keep on, carry on, continue, insist on. **4** keep the rules: **comply with**, obey, observe, conform to, abide by, adhere to, stick to, heed, follow, carry out, act on, make good, honour, keep to, stand by. **5** keeping the old traditions: **preserve**, keep alive/up, carry on, perpetuate, maintain, uphold. **6** he stole to keep his family: **provide for**, support, feed, maintain, sustain, take

care of, look after. **7** *she keeps rabbits:* breed, rear, raise, tend, farm, own.
• **n. 1** food and other essentials for living. **2** the strongest or central tower of a castle.
▷ SYNONYMS: **maintenance**, upkeep, sustenance, board and lodging, food, livelihood.
□ **keep on** continue. **keepsake** a small item kept in memory of the person who gave it. **keep up 1** move at the same rate as another. **2** continue.

keeper n. **1** a person who manages or looks after something or someone. **2** a goalkeeper or wicketkeeper.
▷ SYNONYMS: **curator**, custodian, guardian, conservator, administrator, overseer, steward, caretaker, attendant, concierge.

keeping n. **(in** (or **out of**) **keeping with)** in (or not in) harmony or agreement with.
▷ SYNONYMS: **care**, custody, charge, guardianship, possession, trust, protection.

keg n. a small barrel.

kelp n. a type of seaweed.

kelvin n. a unit of temperature.

ken n. (**your ken**) your range of knowledge or experience.

kennel n. **1** a shelter for a dog. **2** (**kennels**) a boarding or breeding establishment for dogs.

kept past & past part. of KEEP.

keratin n. a protein forming the basis of hair, nails, horns, etc.

kerb (US **curb**) n. a stone edging to a pavement.

kerchief n. a piece of fabric worn over the head.

kerfuffle n. Brit. informal a commotion or fuss.

kernel n. **1** the softer part inside the shell of a nut, seed, or fruit stone. **2** the seed and husk of a cereal. **3** a central part.

kerosene n. US paraffin.

kestrel n. a small falcon.

ketch n. a two-masted sailing boat.

ketchup n. a thick tomato sauce.

kettle n. a container with a lid, spout, and handle, for boiling water.
□ **kettledrum** a large bowl-shaped drum.

key n. **1** a piece of shaped metal for opening or closing a lock or turning a screw etc. **2** a lever pressed down by the finger on a piano etc. **3** a button on a panel for operating a typewriter or computer. **4** a thing providing access or understanding. **5** an

explanatory list of the symbols in a map etc. **6** a group of related notes forming a musical scale.
▷ SYNONYMS: **1** *the key to the mystery:* answer, clue, solution, explanation, basis, foundation. **2** *the key to success:* means, way, route, path, passport, secret, formula.
• **adj.** of central importance.
▷ SYNONYMS: **crucial**, central, essential, indispensable, pivotal, critical, vital, principal, prime, major, leading, main, important.
• **v. 1** enter data using a computer keyboard. **2** (**be keyed up**) be tense or excited.
□ **keynote 1** a central theme. **2** the note on which a musical key is based. **keypad** a set of buttons for operating an electronic device or phone. **key ring** a metal ring for holding keys. **keystone 1** the central part of a policy or system. **2** the central stone at the top of an arch, locking the whole together. **keyword 1** a significant word mentioned in an index. **2** a word used in a computer system to indicate a document's content.

keyboard n. **1** a set of keys on a computer, typewriter, piano, etc. **2** an electronic musical instrument with keys arranged as on a piano.
• **v.** key data.
■ **keyboarder** n.

keyhole n. a hole in a lock for a key.
□ **keyhole surgery** surgery carried out through a very small incision.

kg abbrev. kilograms.

KGB abbrev. the secret police of the former Soviet Union.

khaki n. a dull greenish- or yellowish-brown.

kHz abbrev. kilohertz.

kibbutz n. (pl. **kibbutzim**) (in Israel) a communal farming settlement.

kibosh n. (**put the kibosh on**) informal firmly put an end to.

kick v. **1** hit or propel forcibly with the foot. **2** informal give up a habit. **3** (of a gun) spring back when fired.
▷ SYNONYMS: **boot**, punt.
• **n. 1** an act of kicking. **2** informal a thrill. **3** informal the strong effect of alcohol.
▷ SYNONYMS: *I get a kick out of driving:* thrill, excitement, stimulation, tingle, frisson; informal buzz, high; N. Amer. informal charge.
□ **kick in** come into effect. **kick-off** the start of a football match. **kick out** informal force to leave. **kick-start 1** start a motorcycle engine with a downward

k

thrust of a pedal. **2** cause to develop more quickly.

kid n. **1** informal a child or young person. **2** a young goat.
▷ SYNONYMS: **child**, youngster, baby, toddler, tot, infant, boy, girl, minor, juvenile, adolescent, teenager, youth, stripling; Scottish bairn; informal kiddie, nipper, kiddiewink; Brit. informal sprog; N. Amer. informal rug rat; Austral./NZ ankle-biter; derogatory brat.
• v. (**kidding**, **kidded**) informal fool into believing.

kidnap v. (**kidnapping**, **kidnapped**; US **kidnaping**, **kidnaped**) take by force and hold captive for a ransom.
▷ SYNONYMS: **abduct**, carry off, capture, seize, snatch, take hostage.
• n. an act of kidnapping.
■ **kidnapper** n.

kidney n. (pl. **kidneys**) each of a pair of organs that remove waste products from the blood and produce urine.

> **WORD LINKS**
> **renal** relating to the kidneys

kilim /ki-leem/ n. a carpet woven without a pile, made in Turkey etc.

kill v. **1** cause the death of. **2** put an end to. **3** pass time.
▷ SYNONYMS: **murder**, assassinate, eliminate, terminate, dispatch, execute, slaughter, exterminate, butcher, massacre; informal bump off, do away with, do in, top, take out, blow away; N. Amer. informal rub out, waste; literary slay.
• n. **1** an act of killing. **2** an animal or animals killed by a hunter.
□ **killjoy** a person who spoils the enjoyment of others.

killer n. **1** a person or thing that kills. **2** informal a very impressive or difficult thing.
▷ SYNONYMS: **murderer**, assassin, butcher, gunman, terminator, executioner; informal hit man.

killing n. an act of causing death.
▷ SYNONYMS: **murder**, assassination, homicide, manslaughter, execution, slaughter, massacre, butchery, bloodshed, carnage, extermination, genocide.
□ **make a killing** make a great deal of money out of something.

kiln n. a furnace for baking or drying pottery etc.

kilo n. (pl. **kilos**) a kilogram.

kilobyte n. Computing 1,024 bytes.

kilocalorie n. 1,000 calories.

kilogram n. 1,000 grams.

kilohertz n. 1,000 hertz.

kilojoule n. 1,000 joules.

kilometre (US **kilometer**) n. 1,000 metres.

kilovolt n. 1,000 volts.

kilowatt n. 1,000 watts.

kilt n. a pleated tartan skirt, traditionally worn by men as part of Scottish Highland dress.

kilter n. (**out of kilter**) out of balance.

kimono n. (pl. **kimonos**) a loose Japanese robe worn with a sash.

kin (or **kinsfolk**) pl. n. your relations.
▷ SYNONYMS: **relatives**, relations, family, kith and kin, kindred, kinsfolk, kinsmen, kinswomen, people; informal folks.
□ **kinship 1** blood relationship. **2** relationship based on similar characteristics.
■ **kinsman** n. **kinswoman** n.

kind n. a class of similar people or things.
▷ SYNONYMS: **sort**, type, variety, style, form, class, category, genre, genus, species.
• adj. considerate and generous.
▷ SYNONYMS: **considerate**, obliging, good-natured, kind-hearted, kindly, warm-hearted, caring, affectionate, loving, warm, compassionate, sympathetic, understanding, benevolent, benign, altruistic, unselfish, generous, charitable, philanthropic, helpful, thoughtful, humane; Brit. informal decent.
– ANTONYMS: unkind.
□ **in kind 1** in the same way. **2** (of payment) in goods or services instead of money.

kindergarten n. a nursery school.

kindle v. **1** light a flame. **2** arouse an emotion.
▷ SYNONYMS: **1 light**, ignite, set light to, set fire to; informal torch. **2 rouse**, arouse, wake, awaken, stimulate, inspire, stir up, excite, fire, trigger, activate, spark off.
– ANTONYMS: extinguish.

kindling n. small sticks used for lighting fires.

kindly adv. **1** in a kind way. **2** please (used in a polite request).
• adj. kind.
▷ SYNONYMS: **benevolent**, kind, kind-hearted, warm-hearted, generous, good-natured, gentle, warm, compassionate, caring, loving, benign, well meaning, considerate.
– ANTONYMS: unkind, cruel.
■ **kindliness** n.

kindness n. **1** the quality of being kind. **2** a kind act.

▷ SYNONYMS: **consideration**, kindliness, affection, warmth, gentleness, concern, care, altruism, unselfishness, compassion, sympathy, benevolence, generosity.
– ANTONYMS: unkindness.
kindred pl. n. your relatives.
• adj. similar in kind.
kinetic adj. of or resulting from motion.
■ **kinetically** adv.
king n. **1** the male ruler of a country. **2** the best or most important person or thing. **3** a playing card ranking next below an ace. **4** the most important chess piece.
▷ SYNONYMS: **ruler**, sovereign, monarch, Crown, His Majesty, emperor, prince, potentate.
□ **kingpin** an important person or thing. **king-size** (or **king-sized**) extra large.
kingdom n. **1** a country ruled by a king or queen. **2** each of the three divisions in which natural objects are classified.
▷ SYNONYMS: **realm**, domain, dominion, country, empire, land, territory, nation, state, sovereign state.
kingfisher n. a colourful diving bird.
kink n. **1** a bend or twist in something straight. **2** a flaw. **3** a peculiar characteristic.
kinky adj. (**kinkier**, **kinkiest**) **1** informal of or liking unusual sexual activities. **2** having kinks.
kiosk /kee-ossk/ n. a booth from which newspapers, tickets, etc. are sold, or (Brit.) containing a public phone.
kip n. Brit. informal a sleep.
kipper n. a smoked herring.
kirk n. Scottish a church.
kismet n. fate.
kiss v. touch with the lips.
▷ SYNONYMS: informal peck, smooch, canoodle, neck, pet; Brit. informal snog; N. Amer. informal buss; formal osculate.
• n. a touch with the lips.
▷ SYNONYMS: informal peck, smack, smacker, smooch; Brit. informal snog; N. Amer. informal buss.
□ **kiss of life** mouth-to-mouth resuscitation.
kit n. a set of equipment or clothes for a specific purpose.
▷ SYNONYMS: **1 equipment**, tools, implements, instruments, gadgets, utensils, appliances, gear, tackle, hardware, paraphernalia; informal things, stuff; Military accoutrements. **2 clothes**, clothing, garments, outfit, dress, costume, attire, garb, strip; informal

gear, get-up, rig-out. **3** a tool kit: set, selection, collection, pack.
• v. (**kitting**, **kitted**) (**kit out**) provide with appropriate clothing or equipment.
kitchen n. a room where food is prepared and cooked.
□ **kitchenette** a small kitchen. **kitchen garden** a garden for vegetables, fruit, and herbs.
kite n. **1** a light frame with fabric stretched over it, flown in the wind at the end of a long string. **2** a bird of prey.
□ **Kitemark** trademark an official mark on goods approved by the British Standards Institution.
kith n. (**kith and kin**) your family and relations.
kitsch n. art, objects, or design regarded as tasteless or too sentimental.
kitten n. a young cat.
kittiwake n. a type of small gull.
kitty n. (pl. **kitties**) a fund of money for use by a number of people.
kiwi n. (pl. **kiwis**) a flightless New Zealand bird.
□ **kiwi fruit** a fruit with hairy skin and green flesh.
kJ abbrev. kilojoules.
klaxon n. trademark a vehicle horn or a hooter.
kleptomania n. a recurring urge to steal.
■ **kleptomaniac** n. & adj.
km abbrev. kilometres.
knack n. a skill at performing a task.
▷ SYNONYMS: **1 gift**, talent, flair, instinct, genius, ability, capability, capacity, aptitude, bent, facility, trick; informal the hang of something. **2 tendency**, habit, liability, propensity.
knacker v. Brit. informal **1** damage. **2** (**knackered**) very tired.
knapsack n. a small rucksack.
knave n. **1** old use a dishonest man. **2** (in cards) a jack.
knead v. **1** work dough or clay with the hands. **2** massage as if kneading.
knee n. **1** the joint between the thigh and the lower leg. **2** the upper surface of a sitting person's thigh.
• v. (**kneeing**, **kneed**) hit with the knee.
□ **kneecap 1** the bone in front of the knee joint. **2** shoot in the knee as a punishment. **knee-jerk** automatic and unthinking. **knees-up** Brit. informal a lively party.
kneel v. (**kneeling**, **knelt** or US **kneeled**)

k

fall or rest on the knees.

knell n. the sound of a bell rung solemnly.

knew past of KNOW.

knickerbockers pl. n. loose-fitting trousers or knickers gathered at the knee or calf.

knickers pl. n. Brit. women's or girls' underpants.

knick-knack n. a cheap ornament.

knife n. (pl. **knives**) a cutting instrument with a blade fixed in a handle.
• v. stab with a knife.
▷ SYNONYMS: **stab**, hack, gash, slash, lacerate, cut, bayonet, wound.
□ **knife-edge** a very tense or dangerous situation.

knight n. **1** (in the Middle Ages) a man of noble rank with a duty to fight for his king. **2** a man awarded a title and entitled to use 'Sir' in front of his name. **3** a chess piece shaped like a horse's head.
• v. give the title of knight to.
■ **knighthood** n.

knit v. (**knitting**, **knitted** or **knit**) **1** make a garment by looping yarn together with long blunt needles or a machine. **2** join together. **3** tighten the eyebrows in a frown.
▷ SYNONYMS: **unite**, unify, bond, fuse, coalesce, merge, meld, blend, join, link.
■ **knitter** n. **knitting** n.

knob n. **1** a rounded lump. **2** a ball-shaped handle. **3** a round button on a machine.
▷ SYNONYMS: **lump**, bump, protrusion, protuberance, bulge, swelling, knot, nodule, boss.
■ **knobbly** adj.

knock v. **1** hit a surface noisily to attract attention. **2** collide with. **3** cause to move or fall by hitting. **4** make a hole etc. by hitting. **5** informal criticize.
▷ SYNONYMS: **1** bang, tap, rap, thump, pound, hammer, beat, strike, hit; informal bash. **2** **collide with**, bump into, run into, crash into, smash into, plough into; N. Amer. impact.
• n. **1** a short sound made by a blow. **2** a blow. **3** a setback.
▷ SYNONYMS: **tap**, rap, rat-tat, knocking, bang, banging, pounding, hammering, thump, thud.
□ **knock-down** informal (of a price) very low. **knock-kneed** having legs that curve inwards at the knee. **knock off** informal **1** stop work. **2** produce work quickly. **knock-on effect** a

secondary or indirect result of an action. **knockout 1** an act of knocking someone out. **2** Brit. a tournament in which the loser in each round is eliminated. **3** informal a very impressive person or thing. **knock out 1** make unconscious. **2** eliminate from a competition.

knocker n. a hinged object for knocking on a door.

knoll n. a small hill.

knot n. **1** a fastening made by tying a piece of string, rope, etc. **2** a tangled mass of strands. **3** a hard mass in wood at the point where a branch joins the trunk. **4** a small group of people. **5** a unit of speed of ships, aircraft, or winds.
▷ SYNONYMS: *a knot of people:* **cluster**, group, band, huddle, bunch, circle, ring.
• v. (**knotting**, **knotted**) **1** fasten with a knot. **2** tangle.
▷ SYNONYMS: **1** tie, fasten, secure, bind, do up. **2** (**knotted**) tangled, matted, snarled, unkempt, tousled; informal mussed up.

knotty adj. (**knottier**, **knottiest**) **1** full of knots. **2** very complex.

know v. (**knowing**, **knew**; past part. **known**) **1** be aware of as a result of observing, asking, or being told. **2** be certain. **3** be familiar with. **4** have a good grasp of a language etc. **5** (**known as**) called or referred to as.
▷ SYNONYMS: **1** *she doesn't know I'm here:* **be aware**, realize, be conscious, be cognizant. **2** *I know the rules:* **be familiar with**, be conversant with, be acquainted with, be versed in, have a grasp of, understand, comprehend; informal be clued up on. **3** *do you know her?:* **be acquainted with**, have met, be familiar with; Scottish ken.
□ **be in the know** informal have information known only to a few people.

know-how n. practical knowledge or skill.
▷ SYNONYMS: **expertise**, skill, proficiency, knowledge, understanding, mastery, technique; informal savvy.

knowing adj. suggesting that you have secret knowledge.
▷ SYNONYMS: **significant**, meaningful, expressive, suggestive, eloquent, superior.
■ **knowingly** adv.

knowledge n. **1** information or awareness gained through experience or education. **2** the total of what is known.

▷ SYNONYMS: **1 understanding**, comprehension, grasp, command, mastery, familiarity, acquaintance; informal know-how. **2 awareness**, consciousness, realization, cognition, apprehension, perception, appreciation, cognizance. **3 learning**, erudition, education, scholarship, schooling, wisdom.
– ANTONYMS: ignorance.

> **USAGE** Remember the *d*: knowle*d*ge.

> **WORD LINKS**
> **gnostic** relating to knowledge

knowledgeable (or **knowledgable**) adj. intelligent and well informed.
▷ SYNONYMS: **1 well informed**, learned, well read, well educated, erudite, scholarly, cultured, cultivated, enlightened. **2** *he's knowledgeable about art:* **conversant with**, familiar with, well acquainted with, au fait with, up on, up to date with, abreast of; informal clued up on.
– ANTONYMS: ignorant.
■ **knowledgeably** adv.

known adj. publicly acknowledged to be: *a known womanizer.*
▷ SYNONYMS: **recognized**, well known, widely known, noted, notorious, acknowledged; famous, celebrated.

knuckle n. **1** a finger joint. **2** a joint of an animal's leg as meat. □ **knuckle down** apply yourself seriously to a task. **knuckleduster** a metal device worn over the knuckles in fighting. **knuckle under** submit to authority.

koala n. a bear-like tree-dwelling Australian marsupial.

kohl n. a black powder used as eye make-up.

koi /koy/ n. (pl. **koi**) a large Japanese carp.

kookaburra n. a large, noisy, Australasian kingfisher.

kopek (or **kopeck**) n. a unit of money of Russia and some other countries.

Koran n. the sacred book of Islam.

kosher /koh-sher/ adj. **1** (of food) prepared according to Jewish law. **2** informal genuine and legitimate.

kowtow v. be excessively meek and obedient.

kph abbrev. kilometres per hour.

kraal n. S. Afr. **1** a traditional African village. **2** an enclosure for sheep and cattle.

krill pl. n. small shrimp-like crustaceans that are eaten by whales etc.

krona n. **1** (pl. **kronor**) the basic unit of money of Sweden. **2** (pl. **kronur**) the basic unit of money of Iceland.

krone n. (pl. **kroner**) the basic unit of money of Denmark and Norway.

krypton n. an inert gaseous chemical element.

kudos n. praise and honour.
▷ SYNONYMS: **prestige**, cachet, glory, honour, status, standing, distinction, admiration, respect, esteem.

kumquat n. a small orange-like fruit.

kung fu n. a Chinese martial art.

Kurd n. a member of a people of SW Asia.
■ **Kurdish** adj.

kV abbrev. kilovolts.

kW abbrev. kilowatts.

k

LI

L (or **l**) n. the Roman numeral for 50.
• **abbrev. 1** Brit. learner driver. **2** (**l**) litres.

lab n. informal a laboratory.

label n. **1** a small piece of paper etc. attached to an object and giving information about it. **2** the name or trademark of a fashion company. **3** a classifying name.
▷ SYNONYMS: **1 tag**, ticket, tab, sticker, marker, docket. **2 description**, designation, name, epithet, nickname, sobriquet, title.
• v. (**labelling**, **labelled**; US **labeling**, **labeled**) **1** attach a label to. **2** put in a category.
▷ SYNONYMS: **1 tag**, ticket, mark, stamp. **2 categorize**, classify, class, describe, designate, identify, mark, stamp, brand, call, name, term, dub.

labia pl. n. the inner and outer folds of the vulva.
■ **labial** adj.

laboratory n. (pl. **laboratories**) a room or building equipped for scientific work.

laborious adj. requiring or showing much effort.
▷ SYNONYMS: **1 arduous**, hard, heavy, difficult, strenuous, gruelling, punishing, exacting, tough, onerous, challenging, painstaking, time-consuming. **2 laboured**, strained, forced, stiff, stilted, unnatural, artificial, ponderous.
– ANTONYMS: easy, effortless.
■ **laboriously** adv.

labour (US **labor**) n. **1** work. **2** workers as a group. **3** (**Labour** or **the Labour Party**) a left-wing political party. **4** the process of childbirth.
▷ SYNONYMS: **1 work**, toil, exertion, effort, industry, drudgery; informal slog, grind; old use travail. **2 workers**, employees, labourers, workforce, staff. **3 childbirth**, birth, delivery; technical parturition.
• v. **1** do hard physical work. **2** move or do with difficulty. **3** (**labour under**)

have a mistaken belief.
▷ SYNONYMS: **work**, toil, slave, struggle, strive, exert yourself, endeavour, try hard; informal slog away, plug away.
□ **labour the point** explain at excessive length.

laboured (US **labored**) adj. **1** done with great difficulty. **2** not natural or spontaneous.
▷ SYNONYMS: **1** laboured breathing: **strained**, difficult, forced, laborious. **2** a rather laboured joke: **contrived**, forced, unconvincing, unnatural, artificial, overdone.
– ANTONYMS: natural, easy.

labourer (US **laborer**) n. an unskilled manual worker.
▷ SYNONYMS: **workman**, worker, manual worker, blue-collar worker, hand, roustabout, drudge, menial; Austral./NZ rouseabout; dated navvy.

Labrador n. a large breed of dog.

laburnum n. a tree with hanging clusters of yellow flowers.

labyrinth n. **1** a complicated network of passages. **2** an intricate and confusing arrangement.

labyrinthine adj. **1** like a labyrinth. **2** intricate and confusing.
▷ SYNONYMS: **1 maze-like**, winding, twisting, serpentine, meandering. **2** the labyrinthine plot: **complicated**, intricate, complex, involved, tortuous, convoluted, elaborate, confusing, puzzling, mystifying, bewildering, baffling.

lace n. **1** a fine open fabric made by looping thread in patterns. **2** a cord used to fasten a shoe or garment.
• v. **1** fasten with a lace or laces. **2** entwine. **3** add alcohol to a drink or dish.
▷ SYNONYMS: **1 fasten**, do up, tie up, secure, knot. **2 flavour**, mix, blend, fortify, strengthen, season, spice, liven up, doctor, adulterate; informal spike.

lacerate v. tear the flesh or skin.

laceration n. a cut or wound.
▷ SYNONYMS: **gash**, cut, wound, injury, tear, slash, scratch, scrape, abrasion, graze.

lachrymose /lak-ri-mohss/ adj. tearful.

lack n. the state of being without or not having enough of something.
▷ SYNONYMS: **absence**, want, need, deficiency, dearth, shortage, shortfall, scarcity, paucity.
– ANTONYMS: abundance.
• v. be without or without enough of.
▷ SYNONYMS: **be without**, be in need of, be short of, be deficient in, be low on, be pressed for, need; informal be strapped for.

lackadaisical adj. unenthusiastic or careless.

lackey n. (pl. **lackeys**) **1** a servant. **2** a servile person.

lacklustre (US **lackluster**) adj.
1 lacking energy or inspiration. **2** (of the hair or eyes) dull.
▷ SYNONYMS: **uninspired**, uninspiring, unimaginative, dull, humdrum, colourless, bland, insipid, flat, dry, lifeless, tame, prosaic, dreary, tedious.
– ANTONYMS: inspired.

laconic adj. using few words.
■ **laconically** adv.

lacquer n. **1** a hard glossy varnish. **2** a substance sprayed on hair to keep it in place.
• v. coat with lacquer.

lacrosse n. a team game in which a ball is thrown, carried, and caught using a stick with a net at one end.

lactate v. (of a female mammal) produce milk.
■ **lactation** n.

lactic acid n. an acid present in sour milk and produced in the muscles during exercise.

lactose n. a sugar present in milk.

lacuna /luh-kyoo-nuh/ n. (pl. **lacunae** or **lacunas**) a gap or missing part.

lacy adj. (**lacier**, **laciest**) of or like lace.

lad n. informal a boy or young man.
▷ SYNONYMS: **1 boy**, schoolboy, youth, youngster, juvenile, stripling; informal kid, nipper; Scottish informal laddie; derogatory brat. **2 young man**, fellow; informal guy, geezer; Brit. informal chap, bloke; N. Amer. informal dude, hombre.

ladder n. **1** a set of bars or steps between two uprights, used for climbing up. **2** a series of stages by which progress can be made. **3** Brit. a strip of unravelled fabric in tights or stockings.
• v. Brit. make a ladder in tights or stockings.

laden adj. heavily loaded.
▷ SYNONYMS: **loaded**, burdened, weighed down, overloaded, piled high, full, packed, stuffed, crammed; informal chock-full, chock-a-block.

ladle n. a long-handled spoon with a cup-shaped bowl.
• v. serve with a ladle.

lady n. (pl. **ladies**) **1** a woman. **2** a woman of good social position. **3** (**Lady**) a title used by peeresses and the wives and widows of knights. **4** a well-mannered woman.
▷ SYNONYMS: **1 woman**, female, girl; Scottish & N. English lass, lassie; N. Amer. informal dame, broad; Austral. informal sheila. **2 noblewoman**, aristocrat, duchess, countess, peeress, viscountess, baroness.
□ **lady-in-waiting** a woman who accompanies and looks after a queen or princess. **Your/Her Ladyship** a respectful way of referring to or addressing a Lady.

ladybird n. a small flying beetle, usu. red with black spots.

ladylike adj. appropriate for a well-mannered woman or girl.
▷ SYNONYMS: **refined**, well bred, well mannered, polite, cultivated, polished, decorous, proper, respectable, genteel; cultured, sophisticated, elegant; Brit. informal posh.

lag v. (**lagging**, **lagged**) **1** fall behind. **2** cover a water tank etc. with insulating material.
▷ SYNONYMS: **fall behind**, trail, bring up the rear, dawdle, hang back, delay, loiter, linger, dally, straggle.
• n. (or **time lag**) a period between two events.

lager n. a light fizzy beer.

laggard n. a person who lags behind others.

lagging n. insulating material for a water tank etc.

lagoon n. an area of salt water separated from the sea by a sandbank or reef.

laid past & past part. of LAY¹.

laid-back adj. informal relaxed and easy-going.
▷ SYNONYMS: **relaxed**, easy-going, free and easy, casual, nonchalant, blasé, cool, calm, unconcerned, leisurely, unhurried; informal unflappable.
– ANTONYMS: uptight.

lain past part. of LIE¹.

lair n. a wild animal's resting place.

laird n. (in Scotland) an owner of a

large estate.

laissez-faire /less-ay-**fair**/ n. a policy of not interfering in the course of things.

laity n. people who do not belong to the clergy.

lake n. a large area of water surrounded by land.

▷ SYNONYMS: **pool**, pond, tarn, reservoir, lagoon, waterhole; Scottish **loch**; Anglo-Irish **lough**; N. Amer. **bayou**.

lama n. a Tibetan or Mongolian Buddhist monk.

lamb n. **1** a young sheep. **2** an innocent or gentle person.
• v. give birth to a lamb.

lambaste (or **lambast**) v. criticize harshly.

lambent adj. softly glowing or flickering.

lame adj. **1** walking with difficulty because of an injured leg or foot. **2** unconvincing and feeble.

▷ SYNONYMS: *a lame excuse:* **feeble**, weak, thin, flimsy, poor, unconvincing, implausible, unlikely.
• v. make lame.
□ **lame duck** an unsuccessful person or thing.
■ **lamely** adv. **lameness** n.

lamé /**lah**-may/ n. fabric with interwoven gold or silver threads.

lament n. **1** an emotional expression of grief. **2** a song or poem expressing grief.
• v. feel or express grief or regret for.

▷ SYNONYMS: **1 mourn**, grieve, sorrow, weep, cry, wail, keen. **2 complain about**, bewail, bemoan, deplore.
– ANTONYMS: celebrate, welcome.
■ **lamentation** n.

lamentable adj. very bad or regrettable.

▷ SYNONYMS: **deplorable**, regrettable, terrible, awful, wretched, woeful, dire, disastrous, desperate, grave, appalling, dreadful, pitiful, shameful, unfortunate; formal **egregious**.
– ANTONYMS: wonderful.
■ **lamentably** adv.

laminate v. **1** cover with a protective layer. **2** make by sticking layers together.
• n. laminated material.

lamp n. a device for giving light.

lampoon v. publicly mock or ridicule.
• n. a mocking attack.

lamprey n. (pl. **lampreys**) an eel-like fish with a sucking mouth.

lance n. a weapon with a long shaft and pointed steel head.
• v. prick or cut open a boil etc.

□ **lance corporal** an army rank below corporal.

lancet n. a pointed two-edged knife used in surgery.

land n. **1** the part of the earth's surface not covered by water. **2** an area of ground. **3** ground or soil used for farming. **4** a country or state.

▷ SYNONYMS: **1 dry land**, terra firma, coast, coastline, shore. **2 grounds**, fields, property, acres, acreage, estate, real estate. **3 country**, nation, state, realm, kingdom, province, region, territory, area, domain.
• v. **1** put or go ashore. **2** come or bring down to the ground. **3** informal succeed in obtaining or achieving. **4** informal put or end up in a difficult situation. **5** informal inflict a blow.

▷ SYNONYMS: **1 disembark**, go ashore, debark, alight, get off, berth, dock, moor, anchor, tie up, put in, touch down, come to rest. **2 get**, obtain, acquire, secure, gain, net, win, achieve, attain, bag, carry off.
– ANTONYMS: embark, take off.
□ **landfall** arrival on land after a sea journey. **landfill 1** the disposal of waste by burying it. **2** buried waste. **landlocked** surrounded by land. **landlubber** informal a person unfamiliar with the sea or sailing. **landmine** an explosive mine laid on or just under the surface of the ground. **landslide 1** (or **landslip**) a fall of earth or rock from a mountain or cliff. **2** an overwhelming majority of votes.
■ **landward** adv. & adj. **landwards** adv.

> **WORD LINKS**
> **terrestrial** relating to land

landed adj. owning much land.

landing n. **1** a level area at the top of a staircase. **2** a place where people and goods can be landed from a boat.
□ **landing stage** a platform for coming ashore from a boat.

landlord (or **landlady**) n. **1** a person who rents out property or land. **2** Brit. a person who runs a pub.

▷ SYNONYMS: **1 owner**, proprietor, lessor, householder, landowner. **2 licensee**, innkeeper, hotelier; Brit. **publican**; humorous **mine host**.
– ANTONYMS: tenant.

landmark n. **1** an object or feature easily seen from a distance. **2** an event marking an important stage.

▷ SYNONYMS: **1 feature**, sight, monument, building. **2** *a landmark in Indian history:* **turning point**, milestone, watershed.

landscape n. **1** all the visible features of an area of land. **2** a picture of a country area.
▷ SYNONYMS: **scenery**, country, countryside, topography, terrain, view, panorama.
• v. improve the appearance of a piece of land.

lane n. **1** a narrow road. **2** a division of a road for a single line of traffic. **3** a strip of track or water for each of the competitors in a race. **4** a route followed by ships or aircraft.
▷ SYNONYMS: **road**, street, track, trail, alley, alleyway, passage, path.

language n. **1** human communication through the structured use of words. **2** a particular system or style of this. **3** a system of symbols and rules for writing computer programs.
▷ SYNONYMS: **1 speech**, speaking, talk, discourse, communication, words, vocabulary. **2 tongue**, mother tongue, native tongue, dialect, patois; informal lingo. **3 wording**, phrasing, phraseology, style, vocabulary, terminology, expressions, turn of phrase, parlance.

WORD LINKS
linguistic relating to language

languid adj. relaxed or lacking energy.
■ **languidly** adv.
languish v. **1** become weak or feeble. **2** be forced to remain in an unpleasant place.
▷ SYNONYMS: **1 deteriorate**, decline, go downhill, wither, droop, wilt, fade. **2 waste away**, rot, be abandoned, be neglected, be forgotten, suffer.
– ANTONYMS: thrive.
languor n. tiredness or lack of energy.
■ **languorous** adj.
lank adj. (of hair) long, limp, and straight.
lanky adj. tall, thin, and awkward.
lanolin n. a fatty substance from sheep's wool, used in skin cream.
lantern n. a lamp enclosed in a metal frame with transparent panels.
lanthanum n. a metallic element.
lanyard n. **1** a rope used on a ship for securing sails etc. **2** a cord for hanging a whistle etc. round the neck or shoulder.
lap n. **1** the flat area between the waist and knees of a seated person. **2** one circuit of a racetrack. **3** a part of a journey.
▷ SYNONYMS: **circuit**, leg, circle, round, stretch.
• v. (**lapping**, **lapped**) **1** take up liquid with the tongue. **2** (**lap up**) accept

with obvious pleasure. **3** (of water) move against something with a gentle sound. **4** overtake a competitor in a race to become one lap ahead.
▷ SYNONYMS: **1 drink**, lick up, sup, swallow, slurp, gulp. **2 splash**, wash, swish, slosh, break, plash; literary purl.
□ **lapdog** a small pampered pet dog.
laptop a portable computer.
laparoscopy n. a surgical operation in which a fibre-optic instrument is inserted through the abdomen to view the internal organs.
lapel n. a flap folded back on each side of a coat etc. below the collar.
lapidary adj. of the cutting or polishing of stones and gems.
lapis lazuli n. a blue semi-precious stone.
Lapp n. a member of a people of the extreme north of Scandinavia.

USAGE The people themselves prefer to be called **Sami**.

lapse n. **1** a brief failure of concentration, memory, etc. **2** a decline in standards. **3** an interval of time.
▷ SYNONYMS: **1 failure**, slip, error, mistake, blunder, fault, omission; informal slip-up. **2 decline**, fall, deterioration, degeneration, backsliding, regression. **3 interval**, gap, pause, interlude, lull, hiatus, break.
• v. **1** (of a right or agreement) become invalid because not used or renewed. **2** cease to follow the rules of a religion. **3** pass gradually into a different state.
▷ SYNONYMS: **1 expire**, run out, end, come to an end, cease, stop, terminate. **2 revert**, relapse, drift, slide, slip, sink.
lapwing n. a dark green and white bird with a crest on the head.
larceny n. esp. US theft of personal property.
larch n. a deciduous coniferous tree.
lard n. fat from a pig, used in cooking.
• v. **1** insert strips of bacon in meat before cooking. **2** add technical or obscure expressions to talk or writing.
larder n. a room or large cupboard for storing food.
large adj. of great size or extent.
▷ SYNONYMS: **big**, great, sizeable, substantial, considerable, huge, extensive, voluminous, vast, prodigious, massive, immense, enormous, colossal, king-size, heavy, mammoth, gigantic, giant, fat, stout, strapping,

bulky, burly; informal jumbo, mega, whopping.
– ANTONYMS: small.
□ **at large 1** escaped or not yet captured. **2** as a whole.

largely adv. on the whole; mostly.
▷ SYNONYMS: **mostly**, mainly, to a large/ great extent, chiefly, predominantly, primarily, principally, for the most part, in the main, on the whole.

largesse (or **largess**) /lar-**zhess**/ n. **1** generosity. **2** money or gifts given generously.

lariat n. a lasso.

lark n. **1** a brown bird that sings in flight. **2** something done for fun or as a joke.
● v. Brit. behave playfully.

larva n. (pl. **larvae**) a form taken by certain insects before metamorphosing into an adult.
■ **larval** adj.

laryngitis n. inflammation of the larynx.

larynx n. (pl. **larynges**) the part of the throat containing the vocal cords.

lasagne /luh-**zan**-yuh/ n. a dish of strips of pasta layered with meat and a cheese sauce.

lascivious /luh-**siv**-i-uhss/ adj. feeling or showing open or offensive sexual desire.
■ **lasciviousness** n.

laser n. a device producing an intense narrow beam of light.

lash v. **1** beat with a whip or stick. **2** beat against. **3** (**lash out**) attack verbally or physically. **4** (of an animal) move its tail quickly to and fro. **5** fasten securely with a rope.
▷ SYNONYMS: **1 beat against**, dash against, pound, batter, hammer against, strike, hit, drum. **2 fasten**, bind, tie, tether, hitch, knot, rope.
● n. **1** an eyelash. **2** a blow with a whip or stick. **3** the flexible part of a whip.

lashings pl. n. Brit. informal a large amount.

lass (or **lassie**) n. Scottish & N. English a girl or young woman.

lassitude n. weariness or lack of energy.

lasso /luh-**soo**/ n. (pl. **lassos**) a rope with a noose for catching cattle.
● v. (**lassoing**, **lassoed**) catch with a lasso.

last adj. **1** coming after all others in time or order. **2** most recent. **3** lowest in importance. **4** only remaining.
▷ SYNONYMS: **1 final**, closing, concluding, end, ultimate, terminal, later, latter. **2 rearmost**, hindmost, endmost,

furthest back. **3 previous**, preceding, prior, former, latest, most recent.
– ANTONYMS: first, next.
● v. **1** continue or be enough for a specified time. **2** remain operating or usable.
▷ SYNONYMS: **1** *the hearing lasted for six days*: **continue**, go on, carry on, keep on/going, take. **2** *he won't last long as manager*: **survive**, endure, hold on/ out, keep going, persevere, persist, stay, remain; informal stick it out, hang on, go the distance.
– ANTONYMS: end.
● adv. on the last occasion before the present.
● n. **1** the last person or thing. **2** the only remaining part. **3** a foot-shaped block used in making or repairing a shoe.
□ **at last** eventually. **last post** a military bugle call sounded at sunset and at military funerals. **the last straw** the final thing making a situation unbearable. **last word 1** a final statement. **2** the ultimate or most modern example.
■ **lastly** adv.

lasting adj. enduring for a long time.
▷ SYNONYMS: **enduring**, long-lasting, long-lived, abiding, continuing, long-term, permanent, durable, stable, secure, long-standing, eternal, undying, everlasting, unending, never-ending.
– ANTONYMS: passing, ephemeral.

latch n. **1** a bar with a catch and lever for fastening a door or gate. **2** a door lock which can only be opened from the outside with a key.
● v. **1** fasten with a latch. **2** (**latch on to**) become very interested in.

late adj. **1** arriving or happening after the proper or usual time. **2** far on in the day or night or a period. **3** (of a person) dead. **4** (**latest**) most recent.
▷ SYNONYMS: **1 behind schedule**, tardy, overdue, delayed, belated, behind-hand. **2 recent**, fresh, new, up to date, latter-day, current. **3** (*later*) *more detail will be given in later chapters*: **subsequent**, following, succeeding, future, upcoming, to come, ensuing, next. **4** *her late husband*: **dead**, departed, lamented, behind; formal deceased. **5** (*latest*) **most recent**, newest, up to the minute, current, state-of-the-art, cutting-edge; informal in, with it, trendy, hip, hot, happening, cool.
– ANTONYMS: punctual, early.
● adv. **1** after the proper or usual time. **2** far on in the day or night or

a period. **3** (**later**) in the near future: *later, the film rights were sold.*

▷ SYNONYMS: (**later**) **subsequently**, eventually, then, next, later on, afterwards, at a later date, in the future, in due course, by and by, in a while, in time; formal thereafter.

□ **of late** recently.

■ **lateness** n.

lately adv. recently.

▷ SYNONYMS: **recently**, not long ago, of late, latterly, in recent times.

latent adj. existing but not yet developed, apparent, or active.

▷ SYNONYMS: **dormant**, untapped, undiscovered, hidden, concealed, undeveloped, unrealized, unfulfilled, potential.

■ **latency** n.

lateral adj. of, at, to, or from the side or sides.

■ **laterally** adv.

latex n. **1** a milky fluid in some plants, esp. the rubber tree. **2** a similar synthetic product used to make coatings etc.

lath n. a thin, flat strip of wood.

lathe n. a machine for shaping pieces of wood or metal by turning them against a cutting tool.

lather n. **1** froth from soap and water. **2** heavy frothy sweat on a horse's coat.
• v. form or cover with a lather.

Latin n. the language of the ancient Romans.
• adj. of Latin.
□ **Latin America** the parts of the American continent where Spanish or Portuguese is spoken.

latitude n. **1** the distance of a place north or south of the equator. **2** freedom of action or thought.

▷ SYNONYMS: **freedom**, scope, leeway, breathing space, flexibility, liberty, independence, free rein, licence.

– ANTONYMS: restriction.

latrine n. a communal toilet in a camp or barracks.

latte /lat-tay/ n. a drink of frothy hot milk with an added shot of espresso coffee.

latter adj. **1** nearer to the end than to the beginning. **2** recent. **3** (**the latter**) the second-mentioned of two people or things.

▷ SYNONYMS: **1** later, closing, end, concluding, final. **2** last-mentioned, second, last, final.

– ANTONYMS: earlier, former.

□ **latter-day** modern or contemporary.

■ **latterly** adv.

lattice n. a structure of strips crossing each other.

laud /lawd/ v. praise highly.

laudable adj. deserving praise.

▷ SYNONYMS: **praiseworthy**, commendable, admirable, worthy, deserving, creditable, estimable, exemplary.

– ANTONYMS: shameful.

laudanum n. a solution of opium formerly used as a sedative.

laudatory adj. expressing praise.

laugh v. **1** make sounds that express amusement. **2** (**laugh at**) make fun of.

▷ SYNONYMS: **chuckle**, chortle, guffaw, giggle, titter, snigger, roar, split your sides; informal be in stitches, be rolling in the aisles, crease up, fall about, crack up; Brit. informal kill yourself.
• n. **1** an act of laughing. **2** (**a laugh**) informal a cause of laughter.

▷ SYNONYMS: **1 chuckle**, chortle, guffaw, giggle, titter, snigger, roar, shriek. **2** joke, prank, jest; informal lark, hoot, scream.

□ **laughing stock** a person ridiculed by everyone.

laughable adj. ridiculous.

laughter n. the act or sound of laughing.

▷ SYNONYMS: **1 laughing**, chuckling, chortling, guffawing, giggling, tittering, sniggering. **2 amusement**, entertainment, humour, mirth, merriment, gaiety, hilarity, jollity, fun.

launch v. **1** move a boat into the water. **2** send a rocket etc. into the air. **3** start an enterprise or introduce a new product.

▷ SYNONYMS: **1 propel**, fire, shoot, throw, hurl, fling, pitch, lob, let fly; informal chuck, heave, sling. **2 start**, begin, initiate, put in place, set up, inaugurate, introduce; informal kick off.
• n. **1** an act of launching. **2** a large motorboat.

launder v. **1** wash and iron clothes etc. **2** informal pass illegally obtained money through a bank or business to conceal its origin.

launderette n. Brit. a place with coin-operated washing machines and dryers for public use.

laundry n. (pl. **laundries**) **1** clothes etc. for washing. **2** a place where clothes etc. are laundered.

laurel n. **1** an evergreen shrub. **2** (**laurels**) honour or praise.

lava n. flowing or hardened molten rock from a volcano.

lavatory n. (pl. **lavatories**) a toilet.

▷ SYNONYMS: **toilet**, WC, convenience, privy, latrine; Brit. cloakroom; N. Amer.

washroom, bathroom, rest room, men's/ladies' room, comfort station; Brit. informal loo, bog, the Ladies, the Gents, khazi; N. Amer. informal can, john; Austral./NZ informal dunny.

lavender n. **1** a shrub with scented purple flowers. **2** a light purple colour.

lavish adj. **1** very rich, elaborate, or luxurious. **2** generous.
▷ SYNONYMS: **1 sumptuous**, luxurious, gorgeous, costly, expensive, opulent, grand, splendid, rich, fancy; informal posh, bling-bling. **2 generous**, liberal, bountiful, unstinting, unsparing, free, munificent, extravagant, abundant, copious, plentiful, prolific, excessive, wasteful, prodigal; literary plenteous.
– ANTONYMS: meagre, frugal.
• v. give in large quantities.
▷ SYNONYMS: **shower**, heap, pour, deluge, throw at, squander, dissipate.
– ANTONYMS: begrudge, stint.
■ **lavishly** adv.

law n. **1** a rule or system of rules established by authority. **2** a statement that a particular phenomenon always occurs if certain conditions are present.
▷ SYNONYMS: **1 regulation**, statute, act, bill, decree, edict, rule, ruling, dictum, command, order, directive, dictate, diktat, fiat, by-law; (**laws**) legislation, constitution, code; N. Amer. formal ordinance. **2 principle**, rule, precept, commandment, belief, creed, credo, maxim, tenet, doctrine, canon.
□ **law court** a place where legal cases or trials are heard. **lawsuit** a claim brought to a law court to be decided.

WORD LINKS
legal, **legislative** relating to laws

lawful adj. allowed by or obeying the law or rules.
▷ SYNONYMS: **legitimate**, legal, licit, permissible, permitted, allowable, allowed, rightful, sanctioned, authorized, warranted; informal legit.
– ANTONYMS: illegal.
■ **lawfully** adv.

lawless adj. not obeying the law.
■ **lawlessness** n.

lawn n. **1** an area of mown grass in a garden or park. **2** a fine linen or cotton fabric.
□ **lawnmower** a machine for cutting grass.

lawrencium n. a radioactive metallic element.

lawyer n. a person who practises law.

▷ SYNONYMS: solicitor, barrister, advocate, counsel, Queen's Counsel, QC; N. Amer. attorney, counselor-at-law; informal brief, legal eagle.

lax adj. not strict, severe, or careful.
▷ SYNONYMS: **slack**, slipshod, negligent, remiss, careless, sloppy, slapdash, offhand, casual.
– ANTONYMS: strict.
■ **laxity** n.

laxative n. a medicine causing the bowels to empty.

lay¹ v. (**laying**, **laid**) **1** put down carefully. **2** put down in position for use. **3** assign or place. **4** (of a female bird etc.) produce an egg.
▷ SYNONYMS: **1 put**, place, set, deposit, rest, position; informal stick, dump, park, plonk; Brit. informal bung. **2** *we laid plans for the voyage*: **devise**, arrange, prepare, work out, hatch, design, plan, scheme, plot, conceive, put together, draw up, produce, develop, formulate; informal cook up. **3** *I'd lay money on it*: **bet**, wager, gamble, stake.
□ **layabout** an idle person. **lay-by** Brit. a roadside area where vehicles may stop. **lay off 1** dismiss a worker because of a shortage of work. **2** informal stop doing something. **lay on** Brit. provide. **lay out** arrange according to a plan. **lay up** put out of action through illness or injury.

USAGE Don't confuse **lay**, 'put something down' and **lie**, 'recline on a flat surface'. The past tense and past participle of **lay** is **laid** (*they laid the carpet*); the past tense of **lie** is **lay** (*he lay on the floor*) and the past participle is **lain** (*she had lain awake for hours*).

lay² adj. **1** not belonging to the clergy. **2** non-professional or non-specialist: *layman*.
▷ SYNONYMS: **1** *a lay preacher*: **nonordained**, non-clerical. **2** *science books for a lay audience*: **non-expert**, non-professional, non-specialist, non-technical, amateur, unqualified, untrained.

lay³ past of LIE¹.

layer n. **1** a sheet or thickness of material covering a surface. **2** a person or thing that lays something.
▷ SYNONYMS: **sheet**, stratum, level, tier, seam, coat, coating, film, covering, blanket, skin.
• v. arrange or cut in a layer or layers.

layette n. a set of clothing etc. for a newborn child.

layout n. the way in which something

is laid out.
▷ SYNONYMS: **arrangement**, design, plan, formation, format, configuration, composition, organization, geography, structure.

laze v. spend time idly.
▷ SYNONYMS: **relax**, unwind, loaf around/about, lounge around/about, loll around/about, lie around/about, take it easy, idle; informal hang around, chill.

lazy adj. (**lazier, laziest**) **1** unwilling to work or use energy. **2** showing a lack of effort or care.
▷ SYNONYMS: **1 idle**, indolent, slothful, bone idle, work-shy, shiftless. **2 slow**, slow-moving, languid, leisurely, lethargic, sluggish, torpid.
– ANTONYMS: industrious.
■ lazily adv. laziness n.

lb abbrev. pounds (in weight).

lbw abbrev. Cricket leg before wicket.

lea n. literary an area of grassy land.

leach v. (of chemicals or minerals) be removed from soil by water passing through it.

lead¹ v. (**leading, led**) **1** cause to go with you. **2** be a route or means of access. **3** (**lead to**) result in. **4** influence. **5** be in charge of. **6** be ahead of or superior to a competitor. **7** have a particular way of life. **8** (**lead up to**) come before or result in. **9** (**lead on**) deceive into believing.
▷ SYNONYMS: **1 guide**, conduct, show, usher, escort, steer, shepherd, accompany, see, take. **2** this could lead to job losses: **result in**, cause, bring on/about, give rise to, create, produce, effect, generate, contribute to, promote, provoke, stir up, spark off. **3** what led you to believe him?: **cause**, induce, prompt, move, persuade, drive, make. **4 control**, preside over, head, command, govern, run, manage, rule, be in charge of; informal head up. **5 be ahead**, be winning, be in front, be in the lead, be first, outrun, outstrip, outpace, leave behind, outdo, outclass, beat. **6** I want to lead a normal life: **live**, have, spend, follow, pass, enjoy.
– ANTONYMS: follow.
• n. **1** an example for others to follow. **2** a position of advantage. **3** the chief part in a play or film. **4** a clue. **5** Brit. a strap or cord for leading a dog. **6** Brit. a wire conveying electric current.
▷ SYNONYMS: **1 example**, model, pattern, standard, guidance, direction, role model. **2 first place**, winning position, vanguard. **3** a 3–0 lead: **margin**, advantage, gap, edge.

4 leading role, starring role, title role, principal role. **5 clue**, pointer, hint, tip, tip-off, suggestion, indication. **6 leash**, tether, rope, chain.
□ **leading question** a question worded to prompt the answer wanted.

lead² n. **1** a heavy grey metallic element. **2** the part of a pencil that makes a mark.
■ leaded adj.

leaden adj. **1** heavy or slow. **2** dull grey.

leader n. **1** a person or thing that leads. **2** Brit. a newspaper article giving the editor's opinion.
▷ SYNONYMS: **chief**, head, principal, commander, captain, controller, superior, chairman, chair, director, manager, superintendent, supervisor, overseer, master, mistress, prime minister, president, premier, governor, ruler, monarch, sovereign; informal boss, skipper, gaffer, guv'nor, number one.
– ANTONYMS: follower, supporter.

leadership n. the action of leading a group of people, or the position of being a leader.
▷ SYNONYMS: **control**, rule, command, dominion, headship, directorship, premiership, chairmanship, governorship, captaincy; guidance, direction, authority, management, supervision, government.

leading adj. most important or in first place.
▷ SYNONYMS: **main**, chief, top, front, major, prime, principal, foremost, key, central, dominant, greatest, pre-eminent, star.
– ANTONYMS: subordinate, minor.

leaf n. (pl. **leaves**) **1** a flat green part growing from the stem of a plant. **2** a single sheet of paper. **3** very thin gold or silver foil. **4** a hinged or detachable part of a table.
▷ SYNONYMS: **1** (**leaves**) **foliage**, greenery. **2 page**, sheet, folio.
• v. (**leaf through**) turn over pages, reading them casually.
▷ SYNONYMS: I leafed through a magazine: **flick**, flip, thumb, skim, browse, glance, riffle, scan, run your eye over, peruse.
■ leafy adj.

leaflet n. **1** a printed sheet of paper giving information. **2** a small leaf.
▷ SYNONYMS: **pamphlet**, booklet, brochure, handbill, circular, flyer, handout; N. Amer. folder, dodger.
• v. (**leafleted, leafleting**) distribute leaflets to.

league n. 1 a group of people or countries united for a purpose. 2 a group of sports clubs which play each other over a period for a championship. 3 a class of quality.
▷ SYNONYMS: **1 alliance**, confederation, confederacy, federation, union, association, coalition, consortium, affiliation, cooperative, partnership, fellowship, syndicate. **2 class**, group, category, level, standard.
□ **in league** (of people) making secret plans.

leak v. 1 accidentally allow contents to pass through a gap. 2 (of liquid, gas, etc.) pass accidentally through a gap. 3 deliberately reveal secret information.
▷ SYNONYMS: **1 seep**, escape, ooze, drip, dribble, drain, run. **2 disclose**, divulge, reveal, make public, tell, expose, release, let slip.
• n. 1 a gap through which contents leak. 2 an instance of leaking.
▷ SYNONYMS: **1 hole**, opening, puncture, perforation, gash, slit, break, crack, chink, fissure, rupture, tear. **2 escape**, leakage, discharge, seepage. **3 disclosure**, revelation, exposé.
■ **leakage** n. **leaky** adj.

lean v. (**leaning**, **leaned** or **leant**) 1 be in or put into a sloping position. 2 (**lean against/on**) rest against. 3 (**lean on**) rely on for support.
▷ SYNONYMS: **1 rest**, recline, be propped. **2 slant**, incline, bend, tilt, slope, tip, list. **3** (**lean towards**) **tend towards**, incline towards, gravitate towards, favour, prefer, have a preference for, have an affinity with. **4** (**lean on**) **depend on**, rely on, count on, bank on, trust in, have faith in.
• adj. 1 (of a person) thin. 2 (of meat) with little fat. 3 (of a period) unproductive.
▷ SYNONYMS: **1 thin**, slim, slender, skinny, spare, angular, spindly, wiry, lanky. **2 meagre**, sparse, poor, mean, inadequate, insufficient, paltry.
– ANTONYMS: fat, abundant.
□ **lean-to** a small building sharing a wall with a larger one.

leaning n. a tendency or preference.
▷ SYNONYMS: **inclination**, tendency, bent, propensity, penchant, preference, predisposition, predilection, proclivity.

leap v. (**leaping**, **leaped** or **leapt**) 1 jump high, suddenly, or a long way. 2 (**leap at**) accept eagerly.
▷ SYNONYMS: **1 jump**, vault, spring, bound, hop, clear. **2 rise**, soar, rocket, skyrocket, shoot up, escalate.
• n. an act of leaping.
▷ SYNONYMS: **rise**, surge, upsurge, escalation, upswing, upturn.
□ **leap year** a year with 366 days, occurring once every four years.

leapfrog n. a game in which players vault over others who are bending down.
• v. (**leapfrogging**, **leapfrogged**) 1 perform such a vault. 2 overtake others to reach a leading position.

learn v. (**learning**, **learned** or **learnt**) 1 gain knowledge of or skill in. 2 become aware of. 3 memorize.
▷ SYNONYMS: **1 master**, grasp, take in, absorb, assimilate, digest, familiarize yourself with; informal get the hang of. **2 memorize**, learn by heart, learn parrot-fashion, get off pat. **3 discover**, find out, become aware, be informed, hear, understand, gather; informal get wind of.

learned adj. having gained much knowledge by study.
▷ SYNONYMS: **scholarly**, erudite, knowledgeable, widely read, cultured, intellectual, academic, literary, bookish, highbrow; informal brainy.
– ANTONYMS: ignorant.

learner n. a person learning a subject or skill.
▷ SYNONYMS: **beginner**, novice, starter, trainee, apprentice, pupil, student, fledgling, neophyte, tyro; informal rookie; N. Amer. informal greenhorn, tenderfoot.
– ANTONYMS: expert, veteran.

learning n. knowledge gained through study.
▷ SYNONYMS: **study**, knowledge, education, schooling, tuition, teaching, scholarship, erudition, understanding, wisdom.
– ANTONYMS: ignorance.

lease n. a contract by which one party lets land, property, etc. to another for a specified time.
• v. let or rent on lease.
▷ SYNONYMS: **rent**, hire, charter, let, sublet.
□ **leasehold** the holding of property by a lease.

leash n. a dog's lead.

least adj. & pron. smallest in amount, extent, or significance.
• adv. to the smallest extent or degree.
□ **at least 1** not less than. **2** if nothing else. **3** anyway.

leather n. a material made from the skin of an animal by tanning or a similar process.

leathery adj. tough and hard in texture.

leave v. (**leaving**, **left**) **1** go away from. **2** stop living at or working for. **3** go away without taking. **4** (**be left**) remain to be used or dealt with. **5** allow to do without interfering. **6** deposit something to be collected or dealt with. **7** give in a will.

▷ SYNONYMS: **1 go away**, depart, withdraw, retire, take your leave, pull out, quit, decamp, flee, escape, abandon, desert, vacate; set off, get going; informal vamoose, push off, shove off, clear out/off, split, make tracks, do a bunk. **2 abandon**, desert, jilt, leave in the lurch, leave high and dry, throw over; informal dump, ditch, walk/run out on. **3 resign**, retire, step down, give up, drop out; informal quit, jack in. **4 leave behind**, forget, lose, mislay. **5 entrust**, hand over, pass on, refer, delegate. **6 bequeath**, will, endow, hand down.
− ANTONYMS: arrive.

• n. **1** time when you are permitted to be absent from work or duty. **2** permission.

▷ SYNONYMS: **1 holiday**, break, furlough, sabbatical, leave of absence; N. Amer. vacation; informal vac. **2 permission**, consent, authorization, sanction, dispensation, approval, clearance, blessing, agreement, assent; informal the go-ahead, the green light.
◻ **leave out** fail to include.

leaven /lev-uhn/ n. a substance added to dough to make it ferment and rise.
• v. **1** (**leavened**) fermented by adding leaven. **2** make less serious or dull.

leaves pl. of LEAF.

lecher n. a lecherous man.
■ **lechery** n.

lecherous adj. showing sexual desire in an offensive way.

▷ SYNONYMS: **lustful**, licentious, lascivious, libidinous, lewd, salacious, prurient; informal randy; formal concupiscent.

lectern n. a stand with a sloping top from which a speaker can read while standing.

lecture n. **1** an educational talk. **2** a lengthy reprimand.

▷ SYNONYMS: **1 speech**, talk, address, discourse, presentation, oration. **2 reprimand**, scolding, rebuke, reproach; informal dressing-down, telling-off, talking-to, tongue-lashing.
• v. **1** give a lecture or lectures. **2** reprimand.

▷ SYNONYMS: **1 talk**, speak, discourse, hold forth, teach; informal spout, sound off. **2 reprimand**, scold, rebuke, reproach, take to task, berate, upbraid, remonstrate with, castigate; informal tell off, bawl out; Brit. informal tick off, carpet.
■ **lecturer** n.

led past & past part. of LEAD[1].

ledge n. a narrow horizontal projection or shelf.

ledger n. a book of financial accounts.

lee n. the side of something providing shelter from wind or weather.
■ **leeward** adj. & adv.

leech n. a small bloodsucking worm.

leek n. a long vegetable related to the onion.

leer v. look in a lustful or unpleasant way.
• n. a lustful or unpleasant look.

lees pl. n. sediment in wine.

leeway n. the available amount of freedom to move or act.

▷ SYNONYMS: **freedom**, scope, latitude, space, room, liberty, flexibility, licence, free hand, free rein.

left[1] adj. & adv. of, on, or towards the side which is to the west when facing north.

▷ SYNONYMS: **left-hand**, sinistral; Nautical port; Heraldry sinister.
− ANTONYMS: right, starboard.
• n. **1** (**the left**) the left-hand side or direction. **2** (**the Left**) a left-wing group or party.
◻ **left-handed** using or done with the left hand.

left[2] past & past part. of LEAVE.
◻ **leftovers** food remaining after the rest has been used.

left-wing adj. radical, reforming, or socialist.

▷ SYNONYMS: **socialist**, communist, leftist; informal Commie, lefty, red, pinko.
− ANTONYMS: right-wing, conservative.

leg n. **1** each of the limbs on which a person or animal moves and stands. **2** a part that supports a chair, table, etc. **3** a section of a journey, race, etc.

▷ SYNONYMS: **1 limb**, member, shank; informal pin, peg. **2 part**, stage, section, phase, stretch, lap.
◻ **leg it** Brit. informal run away.

legacy n. (pl. **legacies**) **1** money etc. left to someone in a will. **2** something handed down by a predecessor.

▷ SYNONYMS: **bequest**, inheritance, endowment, gift, birthright, estate, heirloom.

legal adj. of or permitted by law.

▷ SYNONYMS: **1 lawful**, legitimate, legalized, valid, permissible, permitted, sanctioned, authorized, licensed, allowed, allowable, above board, acceptable, constitutional; informal legit. **2** *the legal system:* **judicial**, juridical, forensic.
– ANTONYMS: illegal.
□ **legal aid** payment from public funds towards the cost of legal action.
legal tender accepted methods of payment such as coins or banknotes.
■ **legality** n. **legalize** (or **-ise**) v. **legally** adv.

legate n. a representative of the Pope.
legation n. **1** a diplomatic minister and staff. **2** the official residence of a diplomat.
legato adv. & adj. *Music* in a smooth, flowing way.
legend n. **1** a traditional story from the past which may or may not be true. **2** a very famous person. **3** a caption or explanatory key.
▷ SYNONYMS: **1 myth**, saga, epic, folk tale, folk story, fable; **(legends)** lore, folklore, mythology. **2 celebrity**, star, superstar, icon, phenomenon, luminary, giant, hero; informal celeb, megastar. **3 caption**, inscription, dedication, slogan, heading, title.
legendary adj. **1** described in legends. **2** famous.
▷ SYNONYMS: **1 fabled**, mythical, traditional, fairy-tale, storybook, mythological, fictional, fictitious. **2 famous**, celebrated, famed, renowned, acclaimed, illustrious, esteemed, honoured, exalted, venerable, eminent, distinguished, great.
legerdemain /lej-er-di-**mayn**/ n. **1** skilful use of the hands when doing conjuring tricks. **2** trickery.
leggings pl. n. tight-fitting stretchy trousers.
legible adj. clear enough to read.
■ **legibility** n. **legibly** adv.
legion n. **1** a division of the ancient Roman army. **2** a great number.
▷ SYNONYMS: **horde**, throng, multitude, crowd, mass, mob, gang, swarm, flock, herd, army.
• adj. great in number.
legionnaire n. a member of the Foreign Legion, or of an association of former members of the armed forces.
□ **legionnaires' disease** a form of pneumonia.
legislate v. make laws.
■ **legislative** adj. **legislator** n.
legislation n. laws as a whole.

▷ SYNONYMS: **law**, rules, rulings, regulations, acts, bills, statutes; N. Amer. formal ordinances.
legislature n. the law-making body of a state.
▷ SYNONYMS: **parliament**, senate, congress, council, chamber, house.
legitimate adj. **1** allowed by the law or rules. **2** justifiable. **3** (of a child) born of parents married to each other.
▷ SYNONYMS: **1** *the legitimate use of such weapons:* **legal**, lawful, authorized, permitted, sanctioned, approved, licensed; informal legit. **2** *the legitimate heir:* **rightful**, lawful, genuine, authentic, real, true, proper; informal kosher. **3** *a legitimate excuse:* **valid**, sound, admissible, acceptable, well founded, justifiable, reasonable, sensible, just, fair, bona fide.
– ANTONYMS: illegal, invalid.
■ **legitimacy** n. **legitimately** adv. **legitimize** (or **-ise**) v.
legume n. a plant bearing seeds in pods.
■ **leguminous** adj.
leisure n. time free for relaxation or enjoyment.
▷ SYNONYMS: **free time**, spare time, time off, rest, recreation, relaxation, R & R.
– ANTONYMS: work.
□ **at leisure 1** not busy; free. **2** in an unhurried way.
■ **leisured** adj.
leisurely adj. unhurried.
▷ SYNONYMS: **unhurried**, relaxed, easy, gentle, sedate, comfortable, restful, undemanding, slow.
– ANTONYMS: hurried.
leitmotif (or **leitmotiv**) /**lyt**-moh-teef/ n. a frequently repeated theme in a musical or literary composition.
lemming n. a small Arctic rodent, noted for its periodic mass migrations.
lemon n. **1** a pale yellow citrus fruit with acidic juice. **2** a pale yellow colour.
lemonade n. a lemon-flavoured drink.
lemur n. a primate with a pointed snout, found in Madagascar.
lend v. (**lending**, **lent**) **1** allow someone to use something providing that they will return it. **2** give someone money under an agreement to pay it back later. **3** add a quality to. **4** (**lend itself to**) be suitable for.
▷ SYNONYMS: **1 loan**, advance; Brit. informal sub. **2 add**, impart, give, bestow, confer, provide, supply, furnish, contribute.
– ANTONYMS: borrow.

■ **lender** n.

length n. **1** measurement or extent from end to end. **2** the amount of time occupied by something. **3** the quality of being long. **4** a stretch or piece. **5** a degree of effort: *go to great lengths.*
▷ SYNONYMS: **1 extent**, distance, span, reach, area, expanse, range. **2 period**, duration, stretch, span, term. **3** *a length of silk:* **piece**, strip, section, swatch.
□ **lengthways** (or **lengthwise**) in a direction parallel with a thing's length.

lengthen v. make or become longer.
▷ SYNONYMS: **extend**, elongate, increase, prolong, draw out, protract, spin out.
− ANTONYMS: shorten.

lengthy adj. (**lengthier, lengthiest**) very long.
▷ SYNONYMS: **long**, long-lasting, protracted, extended, long-drawn-out, prolonged, interminable, time-consuming, long-winded.
− ANTONYMS: short.
■ **lengthily** adv.

lenient adj. not strict; merciful.
▷ SYNONYMS: **merciful**, forgiving, forbearing, tolerant, charitable, humane, indulgent, magnanimous, clement.
− ANTONYMS: severe.
■ **leniency** n. **leniently** adv.

lens n. **1** a piece of transparent curved material that concentrates or disperses light rays, used in cameras, glasses, etc. **2** the transparent part of the eye that focuses light on to the retina.

Lent n. (in the Christian Church) the period immediately before Easter.

lent past & past part. of **LEND**.

lentil n. a pulse (edible seed).

leonine adj. of or like a lion.

leopard n. a large spotted cat, found in Africa and Asia.

leotard n. a stretchy garment worn by dancers, gymnasts, etc.

leper n. **1** a person with leprosy. **2** a person shunned by others.

leprechaun n. (in Irish folklore) a mischievous elf.

leprosy n. a contagious disease which affects the skin and can cause deformities.
■ **leprous** adj.

lesbian n. a homosexual woman.
• adj. of lesbians.
■ **lesbianism** n.

lesion n. a damaged area of the skin or a body part.

less adj. & pron. **1** a smaller amount of. **2** fewer in number.
• adv. to a smaller extent.
• prep. minus.

| USAGE For the difference between **less** and **fewer**, see **FEW**. |

lessee n. a person who holds the lease of a property.

lessen v. make or become less.
▷ SYNONYMS: **1** *aspirin will lessen the pain:* **reduce**, decrease, minimize, moderate, diminish, allay, assuage, alleviate, dull, deaden, take the edge off. **2** *the rain had lessened:* **subside**, decline, decrease, slacken, abate, fade, die down, let up, ease off, tail off, dwindle, ebb, wane, recede.
− ANTONYMS: increase.

lesser adj. not so great or important as the other or the rest.
▷ SYNONYMS: **1 less important**, minor, secondary, subsidiary, peripheral. **2 subordinate**, inferior, second-class, subservient, lowly, humble.
− ANTONYMS: greater, superior.

lesson n. **1** a period of learning or teaching. **2** a thing learned. **3** a thing acting as a warning or encouragement. **4** a passage from the Bible read aloud.
▷ SYNONYMS: **1 class**, session, seminar, tutorial, lecture, period. **2 warning**, deterrent, caution, example, message, moral.

lessor n. a person who leases a property to another.

lest conj. to avoid the risk of.

let v. (**letting, let**) **1** allow. **2** used to express an intention, suggestion, or order: *let's try.* **3** Brit. allow someone to use a room or property in return for payment.
▷ SYNONYMS: **1 allow**, permit, give permission to, give leave to, authorize, license, empower, enable, entitle; informal give the go-ahead to, OK. **2 rent**, lease, hire out, sublet.
− ANTONYMS: prevent, prohibit.
• n. **1** Brit. a period during which a room or property is rented. **2** (in tennis etc.) a situation in which a point is not counted and is played for again.
□ **let alone** not to mention. **let down** fail to support or help. **let go** allow to go free. **let off 1** cause a gun, firework, etc. to fire or explode. **2** choose not to punish. **3** excuse. **let up** informal become less intense.

let-down n. a disappointment.
▷ SYNONYMS: **disappointment**, anti-climax, comedown, non-event, fiasco;

informal **washout**, damp squib.
lethal adj. able to cause death.
▷ SYNONYMS: **fatal**, deadly, mortal, terminal, life-threatening, murderous, poisonous, toxic, noxious, venomous, dangerous.
– ANTONYMS: harmless, safe.
lethargic adj. having no energy or enthusiasm.
▷ SYNONYMS: **sluggish**, slow, languid, listless, apathetic, weary, tired, fatigued, enervated, inert, inactive, lifeless.
– ANTONYMS: energetic.
■ **lethargically** adv.
lethargy n. lack of energy and enthusiasm.
letter n. **1** a symbol representing a speech sound. **2** a written communication sent by post or messenger. **3** (**letters**) literature.
▷ SYNONYMS: **1 character**, sign, symbol, figure. **2 message**, note, line, missive, dispatch, communication; formal epistle; (**letters**) correspondence, post, mail.
• v. write letters on.
□ **letter box** Brit. a slot in a door through which post is delivered. **letterhead** a printed heading on stationery. **the letter of the law** the precise terms of a law.

WORD LINKS
epistolary relating to letter-writing

lettuce n. a vegetable eaten in salads.
leucocyte /loo-koh-syt/ n. a white blood cell.
leukaemia /loo-kee-mi-uh/ (US **leukemia**) n. a disease in which too many white blood cells are produced.
levee /lev-i/ n. an embankment built against flooding.
level n. **1** a position on a scale of amount, quality, etc. **2** a horizontal line or surface. **3** a height from the ground or another base. **4** an instrument to test a horizontal line.
▷ SYNONYMS: **1 rank**, position, degree, grade, stage, standard, class, group, set, classification. **2** *a high level of employment:* **quantity**, amount, extent, measure, degree, volume.
• adj. **1** having a flat, horizontal surface. **2** having the same relative height or position as another.
▷ SYNONYMS: **1** *a level surface:* **flat**, smooth, even, uniform, plane, flush, horizontal. **2** *a level voice:* **steady**, even, uniform, regular, constant, unchanging. **3** *the scores were level:* **equal**, even, drawn, tied, all square, neck and neck, level pegging, on a

par, evenly matched; informal even-stevens, nip and tuck.
– ANTONYMS: uneven, unequal.
• v. (**levelling, levelled;** US **leveling, leveled**) **1** make or become level. **2** aim a gun, criticism, etc.
▷ SYNONYMS: **1 even off**, even out, flatten, smooth. **2** *Carter levelled the score:* **equalize**, equal, even up. **3** aim, point, direct, train, focus, turn.
□ **level crossing** Brit. a place where a railway and road cross at the same level. **level-headed** sensible. **on the level** honest.
■ **leveller** n. **levelly** adv.
lever n. **1** a bar on a pivot, used to move a load with one end when pressure is applied to the other. **2** a handle for operating a mechanism.
▷ SYNONYMS: **handle**, arm, switch, crowbar, bar, jemmy.
• v. lift or move with a lever.
▷ SYNONYMS: **prise**, force, wrench; N. Amer. pry; informal jemmy.
leverage n. **1** the exertion of force with a lever. **2** the power to influence.
▷ SYNONYMS: **1 force**, purchase, grip, hold, anchorage. **2** *more leverage in negotiations:* **influence**, power, authority, weight, sway, pull, control, say, advantage, pressure; informal clout, muscle, teeth.
leveret n. a young hare.
leviathan /li-vy-uh-thuhn/ n. a very large or powerful thing.
levitate v. rise and hover in the air.
■ **levitation** n.
levity n. humorous treatment of a serious matter.
levy v. (**levying, levied**) impose a tax or fine.
▷ SYNONYMS: **impose**, charge, exact, raise, collect.
• n. (pl. **levies**) a sum of money paid as a tax.
▷ SYNONYMS: **tax**, tariff, toll, excise, duty.
lewd adj. crude and offensive in a sexual way.
lexical adj. of words.
lexicography n. the writing of dictionaries.
■ **lexicographer** n.
lexicon n. **1** a vocabulary. **2** a dictionary.
liability n. (pl. **liabilities**) **1** the state of being liable. **2** a debt. **3** a cause of difficulty.
▷ SYNONYMS: **1 responsibility**, accountability. **2** (**liabilities**) **obligations**, debts, arrears, dues, commitments. **3** *he became a liability on and off the field:* **hindrance**, handicap, nuisance,

inconvenience, embarrassment, impediment, disadvantage, millstone, encumbrance, burden.
– ANTONYMS: asset.

liable adj. **1** responsible by law. **2** (**liable to**) subject by law to. **3** (**liable to do**) likely to do.
▷ SYNONYMS: **1 responsible**, accountable, answerable, blameworthy, at fault. **2 likely**, inclined, tending, apt, prone, given, subject, susceptible, vulnerable, exposed, in danger of, at risk of.

liaise v. **1** cooperate on a matter. **2** act as a link.
▷ SYNONYMS: **cooperate**, collaborate, communicate, network, interface, link up; informal hook up.

liaison n. **1** communication and cooperation. **2** a sexual relationship.
▷ SYNONYMS: **1 cooperation**, contact, association, connection, collaboration, communication, alliance, partnership. **2 love affair**, relationship, romance, attachment, fling.

> USAGE Remember the second *i*: li*ai*son.

liana n. a tropical climbing plant.

liar n. a person who tells lies.
▷ SYNONYMS: **fibber**, deceiver, perjurer, dissembler, faker, hoaxer, impostor.

libation n. a drink poured as an offering to a god.

libel n. the crime of publishing a false statement that harms a person's reputation.
▷ SYNONYMS: **defamation of character**, character assassination, calumny, misrepresentation, scandalmongering, slur, smear; informal mud-slinging.
• v. (**libelling**, **libelled**; US **libeling**, **libeled**) publish something false about.
▷ SYNONYMS: **defame**, malign, blacken someone's name, sully someone's reputation, smear, cast aspersions on, drag someone's name through the mud/mire, denigrate, traduce; N. Amer. slur.

libellous adj. constituting libel.
▷ SYNONYMS: **defamatory**, denigratory, disparaging, derogatory, false, untrue, insulting, scurrilous.

liberal adj. **1** willing to accept behaviour or opinions different from your own. **2** (in politics) supporting individual liberty and moderate reform. **3** (**Liberal**) of the Liberal or Liberal Democrat Party. **4** generous.
▷ SYNONYMS: **1 tolerant**, unprejudiced, broad-minded, open-minded, enlightened, permissive, free and easy, easy-going, libertarian, indulgent, lenient. **2** a liberal social agenda: **progressive**, advanced, modern, forward-looking, forward-thinking, enlightened, reformist, radical; informal go-ahead. **3** a liberal interpretation of the law: **flexible**, broad, loose, rough, free, non-literal. **4 abundant**, copious, ample, plentiful, lavish, generous, open-handed, unsparing, unstinting, free, munificent.
– ANTONYMS: reactionary, strict.
• n. a person with liberal views.
■ **liberally** adv.

liberalize (or **-ise**) v. make less strict.
■ **liberalization** n.

liberate v. **1** set free. **2** (**liberated**) free from social conventions.
▷ SYNONYMS: **set free**, free, release, let out, let go, set loose, save, rescue, emancipate; historical enfranchise.
– ANTONYMS: imprison, enslave.
■ **liberation** n. **liberator** n.

libertarian n. a person believing in very limited state intervention in people's lives.
■ **libertarianism** n.

libertine n. a man who leads an immoral life.

liberty n. (pl. **liberties**) **1** freedom. **2** a right or privilege.
▷ SYNONYMS: **freedom**, independence, immunity, self-determination, autonomy, emancipation, sovereignty, self-government, self-rule, self determination, civil liberties, human rights.
– ANTONYMS: slavery.
□ **take liberties with** treat with undue freedom or familiarity.

libidinous adj. having a strong sex drive.

libido n. (pl. **libidos**) sexual desire.

librarian n. a person who works in a library.

library n. (pl. **libraries**) **1** a building or room containing a collection of books etc. for consulting or borrowing. **2** a private collection of books.

libretto n. (pl. **libretti** or **librettos**) the words of an opera.

lice pl. of LOUSE.

licence (US **license**) n. **1** an official permit to own, use, or do something. **2** freedom to do what you want.
▷ SYNONYMS: **1 permit**, certificate, document, documentation, authorization, warrant, credentials, pass, papers. **2 franchise**, consent, sanction, warrant, charter, concession. **3 freedom**, liberty, free rein, latitude, independence, scope, carte blanche;

informal **a blank cheque.**

> **USAGE** licence is the spelling for the noun, license for the verb; in US English the -se spelling is used for both.

license v. grant a licence to or for.
▷ SYNONYMS: **permit**, allow, authorize, give permission to, certify, accredit, empower, entitle, enable, sanction.
– ANTONYMS: ban.

licensee n. the holder of a licence.

licentiate /ly-sen-shi-uht/ n. the holder of a certificate permitting them to practise a particular profession.

licentious adj. sexually immoral.

lichen /ly-kuhn/ n. a plant resembling moss which grows on rocks, walls, and trees.

lick v. **1** pass the tongue over. **2** move lightly and quickly.
• n. **1** an act of licking. **2** informal a quick application of something.

licorice US = LIQUORICE.

lid n. **1** a removable or hinged cover for a container. **2** an eyelid.
▷ SYNONYMS: **cover**, top, cap, covering, stopper.

lie¹ v. (**lying, lay**; past part. **lain**) **1** be in a horizontal position on a supporting surface. **2** be in a particular state. **3** be found or situated.
▷ SYNONYMS: **1** he was lying on the bed: **recline**, lie down, be recumbent, be prostrate, be supine, be prone, be stretched out, sprawl, rest, repose, lounge, loll. **2** her bag lay on the chair: **be**, be situated, be positioned, be located, be placed, be found, be sited, be arranged, rest.
– ANTONYMS: stand.
□ **lie-in** Brit. a prolonged stay in bed in the morning. **lie low** avoid attention. **the lie of the land** the features of an area.

> **USAGE** Don't confuse lay and lie: see LAY¹.

lie² n. a deliberately false statement.
▷ SYNONYMS: **untruth**, falsehood, fib, fabrication, deception, invention, piece of fiction, falsification, white lie; informal tall story, whopper; humorous terminological inexactitude.
– ANTONYMS: truth.
• v. (**lying, lied**) tell a lie or lies.
▷ SYNONYMS: **1 tell a lie**, fib, dissemble, perjure yourself. **2** (**lying**) he accused her of lying: **dishonesty**, fabrication, fibbing, perjury, untruthfulness, mendacity, misrepresentation, deceit, duplicity.

liege /leej/ n. hist. **1** a feudal lord. **2** a person who served a feudal lord.

lieu /loo/ n. (**in lieu**) instead.

lieutenant /lef-ten-uhnt/ n. **1** a deputy or substitute acting for a superior. **2** a rank of officer in the army and navy.

life n. (pl. **lives**) **1** the condition of being able to function and grow. **2** the existence of an individual. **3** a particular type or aspect of existence. **4** living things and their activity. **5** vitality or energy.
▷ SYNONYMS: **1 existence**, being, living, animation, sentience, creation, viability. **2 way of life**, lifestyle, situation, fate, lot. **3 lifetime**, lifespan, days, time on earth. **4 living creatures**, fauna, flora, the ecosystem, the biosphere, the ecosphere. **5** she's full of life: **vitality**, animation, liveliness, vivacity, verve, high spirits, exuberance, zest, enthusiasm, energy, vigour, dynamism, elan, gusto, bounce, spirit, fire.
– ANTONYMS: death.
□ **lifebelt** a ring of buoyant material to keep a person afloat. **lifeboat 1** a boat for rescuing people at sea. **2** a small boat on a ship for emergency use. **life cycle** the series of changes in the life of an organism. **lifeguard** a person employed to rescue swimmers in difficulty. **life jacket** an inflatable jacket for keeping a person afloat. **lifeline 1** a thing on which someone depends. **2** a rope thrown to rescue someone in difficulty in water. **lifelong** lasting throughout a person's life. **life-support** (of medical equipment) keeping the body functioning after serious illness or injury.

lifeless adj. **1** dead or apparently dead. **2** without living things. **3** lacking energy.
▷ SYNONYMS: **1 dead**, stiff, cold, inert, inanimate; formal deceased. **2 barren**, sterile, bare, desolate, stark, bleak, arid, infertile, uninhabited. **3 lacklustre**, apathetic, lethargic, uninspired, dull, colourless, characterless, wooden.
– ANTONYMS: alive, lively.

lifelike adj. exactly like a real person or thing.
▷ SYNONYMS: **realistic**, true to

life, faithful, detailed, vivid, graphic, natural, naturalistic, representational.

lifestyle n. the way in which a person lives.

▷ SYNONYMS: **way of life**, life, situation, conduct, behaviour, ways, habits, mores.

lifetime n. the length of time that a person lives or a thing lasts.

▷ SYNONYMS: **lifespan**, life, days, time on earth, existence, career.

lift v. **1** raise or be raised. **2** pick up and move to a different position. **3** formally end a restriction.

▷ SYNONYMS: **1 raise**, hoist, heave, haul up, heft, elevate, hold high, pick up, grab, take up, winch up, jack up; informal hump. **2** *the fog had lifted:* **clear**, rise, disperse, dissipate, disappear, vanish, dissolve. **3** *the ban has been lifted:* **cancel**, remove, withdraw, revoke, rescind, end, stop, terminate.
  • n. **1** Brit. a device for moving people or things between levels of a building. **2** an act of lifting. **3** a free ride in another person's vehicle. **4** a feeling of increased cheerfulness.

▷ SYNONYMS: *the goal will give his confidence a lift:* **boost**, fillip, impetus, encouragement, spur, push; informal shot in the arm.
  □ **lift-off** the vertical take-off of a spacecraft or rocket.

ligament n. a band of tissue connecting bones or cartilages.

ligature n. a cord for tying up a bleeding artery.

light n. **1** the natural form of energy that makes things visible. **2** a lamp or other device that gives light. **3** a match or cigarette lighter. **4** understanding or enlightenment.

▷ SYNONYMS: **1 illumination**, brightness, shining, gleam, brilliance, radiance, luminosity, luminescence, incandescence, blaze, glare, glow, lustre; literary refulgence, effulgence. **2 lamp**, lantern, torch, beacon, candle, bulb.
– ANTONYMS: darkness.
  • v. (**lighting**, **lit**; past part. **lit** or **lighted**) **1** provide with light. **2** cause to start burning. **3** (**light up**) become lively or happy. **4** (**light on**) discover by chance.

▷ SYNONYMS: **1 illuminate**, irradiate, floodlight; literary illumine. **2 set fire to**, ignite, kindle.
  • adj. **1** having a lot of light. **2** (of a colour) pale. **3** of little weight. **4** not heavily built. **5** relatively low in

density or amount. **6** not serious or profound.

▷ SYNONYMS: **1 bright**, well lit, sunny. **2 pale**, pastel, delicate, subtle, faded, bleached. **3 lightweight**, portable; flimsy, thin, lightweight, floaty, gauzy, diaphanous, filmy. **4** *a light touch:* **gentle**, delicate, dainty, soft, faint, careful, sensitive, subtle. **5** *light entertainment:* **undemanding**, middle-of-the-road, mainstream, lightweight, lowbrow, mass-market, superficial, frivolous, trivial.
– ANTONYMS: dark, heavy.
  □ **bring** (or **come**) **to light** make (or become) widely known. **in the light of** taking something into consideration. **light-fingered** informal prone to steal. **light-headed** dizzy and slightly faint. **lighthouse** a tower with a powerful light to guide ships at sea. **light industry** industry producing small articles. **light year** the distance light travels in one year, nearly 6 million million miles. **make light of** treat as unimportant.
  ■ **lightness** n.

> **WORD LINKS**
> **optics** the study of the behaviour of light

lighten[1] v. make or become brighter.

▷ SYNONYMS: **1 brighten**, light up, illuminate, irradiate; literary illumine. **2 bleach**, whiten, blanch.
– ANTONYMS: darken.

lighten[2] v. **1** make or become lighter in weight. **2** make or become less serious.

▷ SYNONYMS: **1 reduce**, lessen, decrease, diminish, ease, alleviate, relieve. **2 cheer up**, brighten, gladden, lift, boost, buoy up, revive, restore, revitalize.
– ANTONYMS: increase.

lighter n. **1** a device for lighting cigarettes. **2** a barge used to transfer goods to and from ships in harbour.

light-hearted adj. **1** amusing and entertaining. **2** cheerful and carefree.

▷ SYNONYMS: **1 entertaining**, amusing, diverting; informal upbeat, fun. **2 carefree**, cheerful, cheery, happy, merry, glad, playful, blithe, bright; dated gay, sportive.
– ANTONYMS: serious, miserable.

lighting n. **1** equipment for producing light. **2** the effect of lights.

lightning n. the discharge of electricity between a cloud and the ground or within a cloud, accompanied by a bright flash.
  • adj. very quick.

USAGE The spelling is **lightning**, not -*tening*.

lights pl. n. the lungs of certain animals used as food.

lightweight n. **1** a weight in boxing between featherweight and welterweight. **2** informal an unimportant or weak person.
• adj. **1** of thin material or build. **2** lacking seriousness or value.
▷ SYNONYMS: **1 thin**, light, filmy, flimsy, insubstantial, summery. **2 trivial**, insubstantial, superficial, shallow, undemanding, frivolous.
– ANTONYMS: heavy, serious.

lignite n. soft brown coal.

like prep. **1** similar to. **2** in a way similar or appropriate to. **3** such as.
▷ SYNONYMS: **1 similar to**, the same as, identical to, akin to, resembling. **2 in the manner of**, in the same way/ manner as, in a similar way to. **3 such as**, for example, for instance, namely, in particular, viz. **4 characteristic of**, typical of, in character with.
– ANTONYMS: unlike.
• v. **1** find pleasant or satisfactory. **2** wish for.
▷ SYNONYMS: **1 be fond of**, have a soft spot for, care about, think well/highly of, admire, respect; be attracted to, fancy, be keen on, be taken with; informal rate. **2 enjoy**, have a taste for, care for, be partial to, take pleasure in, be keen on, appreciate, love, adore, relish; informal have a thing about, be into, be mad about, be hooked on. **3** *feel free to say what you like*: **choose**, please, wish, want, see/ think fit, care to, will.
– ANTONYMS: hate.
• conj. informal **1** in the same way that. **2** as if.
• n. **1** (**the like**) things of the same kind. **2** (**likes**) things that you like.
• adj. similar.

likeable (or **likable**) adj. pleasant.
▷ SYNONYMS: **pleasant**, friendly, agreeable, affable, amiable, genial, personable, nice, good-natured, engaging, appealing, endearing, convivial, congenial.
– ANTONYMS: unpleasant.

likelihood n. probability.
▷ SYNONYMS: **probability**, chance, prospect, possibility, odds, risk, threat, danger, hope, promise.

likely adj. (**likelier**, **likeliest**) **1** probable. **2** promising.
▷ SYNONYMS: **1 probable**, possible, odds-on, expected, anticipated; informal on the cards. **2 plausible**, reasonable, feasible, acceptable, believable, credible, tenable. **3 suitable**, promising, appropriate.
– ANTONYMS: unlikely, implausible.
• adv. probably.

liken v. (**liken to**) point out the resemblance to.
▷ SYNONYMS: **compare**, equate, set beside.
– ANTONYMS: contrast.

likeness n. **1** resemblance. **2** a portrait or representation.
▷ SYNONYMS: **1 resemblance**, similarity, similitude, correspondence. **2 representation**, image, depiction, portrayal, picture, drawing, sketch, painting, portrait, photograph, study.
– ANTONYMS: dissimilarity.

likewise adv. **1** also. **2** similarly.
▷ SYNONYMS: **1 also**, equally, in addition, too, as well, to boot, besides, moreover, furthermore. **2 the same**, similarly, correspondingly.

liking n. **1** a fondness. **2** (**your liking**) your taste.
▷ SYNONYMS: **fondness**, love, affection, penchant, soft spot, attachment, taste, passion, preference, partiality, predilection, weakness.
– ANTONYMS: dislike.

lilac n. **1** a shrub with scented purple or white blossom. **2** a pale purple colour.

lilt n. **1** a rise and fall of the voice when speaking. **2** a gentle rhythm in a tune.
■ **lilting** adj.

lily n. (pl. **lilies**) a tall plant with large flowers.

limb n. **1** an arm, leg, or wing. **2** a large branch of a tree.
▷ SYNONYMS: **1 arm**, leg, wing, appendage; old use member. **2 branch**, bough.

limber v. (**limber up**) warm up before exercise.
• adj. supple.

limbo n. **1** an uncertain period of waiting. **2** (pl. **limbos**) a West Indian dance in which the dancer bends back to pass under a bar.

lime n. **1** a white alkaline substance used as a building material or fertilizer. **2** a round green citrus fruit. **3** a bright green colour. **4** a tree with heart-shaped leaves.
□ **limestone** a rock composed mainly of calcium carbonate.

limelight n. the focus of public attention.
▷ SYNONYMS: **attention**, interest, scrutiny, the public eye, publicity, promin-

ence, the spotlight, fame, celebrity.
– ANTONYMS: obscurity.
limerick n. a humorous five-line poem.
limit n. **1** a point beyond which something does not or may not pass. **2** a restriction on size or amount.
▷ SYNONYMS: **1 boundary**, border, frontier, bound, edge, perimeter, margin. **2 maximum**, ceiling, cap, cut-off point.
• v. put a limit on.
▷ SYNONYMS: **restrict**, curb, cap, hold in check, restrain, circumscribe, regulate, control, govern, ration.
□ **limited company** a company whose owners have a limited responsibility for its debts. **off limits** out of bounds.
■ **limitless** adj.
limitation n. **1** a restriction. **2** a fault.
▷ SYNONYMS: **1 restriction**, curb, restraint, control, check. **2 imperfection**, flaw, defect, failing, shortcoming, weak point, deficiency, frailty, weakness.
– ANTONYMS: strength.
limited adj. restricted in size, amount, extent, etc.
▷ SYNONYMS: **restricted**, circumscribed, finite, small, tight, slight, in short supply, short, meagre, scanty, sparse, inadequate, insufficient, paltry, poor, minimal.
– ANTONYMS: limitless, ample.
limousine n. a large, luxurious car.
limp v. walk with difficulty because of an injured leg or foot.
▷ SYNONYMS: **hobble**, hop, lurch, stagger, shuffle, totter, shamble.
• n. a limping walk.
• adj. not stiff or firm.
▷ SYNONYMS: **soft**, flaccid, loose, slack, lax, floppy, drooping, droopy, sagging.
– ANTONYMS: firm.
■ **limply** adv.
limpet n. a shellfish that clings tightly to rocks.
limpid adj. (of a liquid or the eyes) clear.
linchpin n. **1** a very important person or thing. **2** a pin through the end of an axle keeping a wheel in position.
linctus n. Brit. thick liquid cough medicine.
line n. **1** a long, narrow mark. **2** a row or series. **3** a course or channel. **4** a length of cord, wire, etc. **5** a phone connection. **6** a railway track or route. **7** a wrinkle. **8** a series of military defences. **9** an area of activity. **10** (**lines**) the words of an actor's part.
▷ SYNONYMS: **1 stroke**, dash, score,

underline, underscore, slash, stripe, strip, band, belt; Brit. oblique. **2** *a line of vehicles:* **file**, column, string, train, procession, row, queue; Brit. informal crocodile. **3** *the county line:* **boundary**, limit, border, frontier, touchline, margin, perimeter. **4** *the Bentley's classic lines:* **contour**, outline, configuration, shape, design, profile, silhouette. **5 cord**, rope, cable, wire, thread, string. **6 wrinkle**, furrow, crease, crinkle, crow's foot.
• v. **1** be positioned along. **2** (**line up**) arrange in a row. **3** (**lined**) marked with lines. **4** cover the inner surface of.
▷ SYNONYMS: **1 border**, edge, fringe, bound. **2** (**lined**) **wrinkled**, wrinkly, furrowed, wizened.
□ **line dancing** country and western dancing in which a line of dancers follow set steps. **linesman** (in sport) an official who assists the referee or umpire. **line-up** a group assembled for a purpose.
lineage /lin-i-ij/ n. ancestry.
▷ SYNONYMS: **ancestry**, family, parentage, birth, descent, extraction, genealogy, roots, origins.
lineal adj. in a line of descent.
linear adj. **1** arranged in or extending along a straight line. **2** consisting of lines. **3** progressing in stages.
linen n. **1** cloth woven from flax. **2** sheets, pillowcases, etc.
liner n. **1** a large passenger ship. **2** a lining.
ling n. **1** an edible sea fish. **2** heather.
linger v. **1** be slow or reluctant to leave. **2** (**linger over**) spend a long time over.
▷ SYNONYMS: **1 wait**, stand around, remain, loiter; informal stick around, hang around. **2 persist**, continue, remain, stay, endure, carry on, last.
lingerie /lan-zhuh-ri/ n. women's underwear.
lingo n. (pl. **lingos**) informal a language.
lingua franca n. (pl. **lingua francas**) a common language used among speakers whose native languages are different.
linguist n. **1** a person skilled in foreign languages. **2** a person who studies linguistics.
linguistic adj. of language.
• n. (**linguistics**) the study of language.
■ **linguistically** adv.
liniment n. an ointment to relieve pain or bruising.
lining n. a layer of material covering the inside of something.

▷ SYNONYMS: **backing**, facing, padding, insulation.

link n. **1** a connection. **2** a means of communication. **3** a loop in a chain.
▷ SYNONYMS: **connection**, relationship, association, linkage, tie-up, tie, bond, attachment, affiliation.
• v. connect or join.
▷ SYNONYMS: **1 join**, connect, fasten, attach, bind, secure, fix, tie, couple, yoke. **2** *the evidence linking him with the body*: **associate**, connect, relate, bracket.
– ANTONYMS: separate.
■ **linkage** n.

linnet n. a type of finch.

lino n. informal linoleum.

linoleum n. a smooth covering for floors.

linseed n. the seeds of the flax plant, used to make oil.

lint n. **1** fluff from cloth or yarn. **2** a fabric for dressing wounds.

lintel n. a horizontal support across the top of a door or window.

lion n. a large cat of Africa and NW India.

> WORD LINKS
> **leonine** relating to lions

lionize (or **-ise**) v. treat as a celebrity.

lip n. **1** either of the two fleshy parts forming the edges of the mouth opening. **2** the edge of a container or opening. **3** informal cheeky talk.
▷ SYNONYMS: **edge**, rim, brim, border, verge, brink.
□ **lip-read** understand speech from watching a speaker's lips. **lipstick** a cosmetic for colouring the lips.

liposuction n. cosmetic surgery in which fat is removed from under the skin by suction.

liquefy v. (**liquefying**, **liquefied**) make or become liquid.
■ **liquefaction** n.

> USAGE liquefy, not -ify.

liqueur /li-**kyoor**/ n. a strong, sweet alcoholic spirit.

liquid n. a substance such as water or oil that flows freely.
▷ SYNONYMS: **fluid**, moisture, solution, liquor, juice, sap.
• adj. **1** of or like liquid. **2** (of assets) held in or easily converted into cash.
▷ SYNONYMS: **fluid**, liquefied, melted, molten, thawed, dissolved, runny.
– ANTONYMS: solid.

liquidate v. **1** close a company and sell its assets to pay its debts. **2** convert assets into cash.

■ **liquidation** n.

liquidity n. the availability of liquid assets to a market or company.

liquidize (or **-ise**) v. Brit. convert solid food to a liquid.
■ **liquidizer** n.

liquor n. **1** alcoholic drink. **2** liquid produced in cooking.
▷ SYNONYMS: **1 alcohol**, spirits, drink; informal booze, the hard stuff, hooch, moonshine. **2 stock**, broth, bouillon, juice, liquid.

liquorice (US **licorice**) n. a black substance used as a sweet.

lira n. (pl. **lire**) the basic unit of money of Turkey and formerly of Italy.

lisp n. a speech defect in which s is pronounced like th.
• v. speak with a lisp.

lissom adj. slim and supple.

list n. a number of connected items or names written as a series.
▷ SYNONYMS: **catalogue**, inventory, record, register, roll, file, index, directory, checklist.
• v. **1** make a list of. **2** include in a list. **3** (of a ship) lean to one side.
▷ SYNONYMS: **1 record**, register, enter, itemize, enumerate, catalogue, file, log, minute, categorize, inventory, classify, group, sort, rank, index. **2 lean**, tilt, tip, heel, pitch, incline, slant, slope, bank, careen, cant.

listen v. **1** pay attention to a sound. **2** take notice of advice or a request. **3** (**listen in**) listen to a private conversation.
▷ SYNONYMS: **1 pay attention**, be attentive, attend, concentrate, keep your ears open, prick up your ears; informal be all ears. **2 heed**, take heed of, take notice/note of, bear in mind, take into consideration/account.
■ **listener** n.

listeria n. a type of bacterium causing food poisoning.

listing n. **1** a list. **2** an item in a list.

listless adj. lacking energy or enthusiasm.
▷ SYNONYMS: **lethargic**, lifeless, enervated, languid, inactive, inert, sluggish, apathetic, passive, supine, indifferent, uninterested, impassive.
– ANTONYMS: energetic.
■ **listlessly** adv.

lit past & past part. of LIGHT.

litany n. (pl. **litanies**) **1** a series of prayers. **2** a long, boring list of complaints etc.

liter US = LITRE.

literal adj. using or interpreting words in their usual or most basic sense.

▷ SYNONYMS: **1 strict**, technical, original, true. **2 word for word**, verbatim, exact, accurate, faithful.
– ANTONYMS: figurative.
■ **literally** adv.

literary adj. of literature.
▷ SYNONYMS: **1 artistic**, poetic, dramatic. **2 scholarly**, intellectual, academic, bookish, erudite, well read, cultured.

literate adj. **1** able to read and write. **2** knowledgeable about a particular subject: *computer-literate*.
■ **literacy** n.

literati pl. n. educated people interested in literature.

literature n. **1** books, plays, etc. valued as works of art. **2** books and printed information on a particular subject.
▷ SYNONYMS: **1 writing**, poetry, drama, plays, prose. **2 publications**, reports, studies, material, documentation, leaflets, pamphlets, brochures, handouts, publicity, advertising; informal bumf.

lithe /lyth/ adj. slim and supple.
▷ SYNONYMS: **agile**, graceful, supple, flexible, lissom, loose-limbed, nimble.
– ANTONYMS: clumsy.

lithium n. a metallic element.

lithography n. printing from a flat metal surface treated so that ink sticks only where required.
■ **lithograph** n.

litigant n. a person involved in a lawsuit.

litigate v. take a dispute to a law court.

litigation n. the process of making or defending a claim in a law court.
▷ SYNONYMS: **legal proceedings**, legal action, case, lawsuit, suit, prosecution, indictment.

litigious adj. tending to take legal action to settle disputes.

litmus n. a dye turned red by acids and blue by alkalis.

litre (US **liter**) n. a metric unit of capacity equal to 1,000 cubic centimetres (1.76 pints).

litter n. **1** rubbish left in a public place. **2** a number of young born to an animal at one time. **3** material to absorb a cat's excrement. **4** straw used as animal bedding. **5** hist. an enclosed bed or seat carried by men or animals.
▷ SYNONYMS: **rubbish**, refuse, junk, waste, debris, detritus; N. Amer. trash, garbage.
• v. make untidy with scattered articles.

▷ SYNONYMS: **cover**, clutter up, mess up, be scattered/strewn around.

little adj. **1** small in size, amount, or degree. **2** young or younger.
▷ SYNONYMS: **1 small**, compact, miniature, tiny, minute, minuscule, toy, baby, undersized, dwarf, midget; Scottish wee; informal teeny-weeny; Brit. informal titchy, dinky; N. Amer. informal vest-pocket. **2 short**, small, slight, petite, diminutive, tiny, elfin; Scottish wee; informal pint-sized. **3** *a few little problems:* **minor**, unimportant, insignificant, trivial, trifling, petty, paltry, inconsequential, negligible.
– ANTONYMS: big, large, major.
• n. & pron. not much.
▷ SYNONYMS: *he has little political influence:* **hardly any**, barely any, scarcely any, not much.
• adv. **1** (**a little**) to a small extent. **2** hardly or not at all.
▷ SYNONYMS: **rarely**, seldom, infrequently, hardly ever, scarcely ever, not much.
– ANTONYMS: often.

littoral adj. of a seashore.

liturgy n. (pl. **liturgies**) a set form of public Christian worship.
■ **liturgical** adj.

live v. **1** be or remain alive. **2** spend your life in a particular way. **3** have your home in a place. **4** obtain the things necessary for staying alive. **5** (**live down**) succeed in making others forget something embarrassing.
▷ SYNONYMS: **1 exist**, be alive, be, have life, breathe, draw breath, walk the earth. **2 reside**, have your home, lodge, inhabit, occupy; Scottish stay; formal dwell; old use abide, bide. **3** *she had lived a difficult life:* **experience**, spend, pass, lead, have, go through, undergo. **4** *he lived by scavenging:* **survive**, make a living, eke out a living, subsist, support yourself, sustain yourself, make ends meet, keep body and soul together.
– ANTONYMS: die.
• adj. **1** living. **2** (of a broadcast) transmitted while it is happening. **3** (of music) played in front of an audience. **4** connected to an electric current. **5** able to explode.
▷ SYNONYMS: **1 living**, alive, conscious, animate, vital. **2** *a live rail:* **electrified**, charged, powered up, active, switched on. **3** *a live grenade:* **unexploded**, explosive, active, primed. **4** *a live issue:* **topical**, current, controversial, hot, burning, pressing, important,

relevant.

– ANTONYMS: dead, inanimate.

livelihood n. a way of earning enough money to live on.

▷ SYNONYMS: **source of income**, income, living, subsistence, bread and butter, job, work, employment, occupation.

lively adj. (**livelier**, **liveliest**) full of energy or activity.

▷ SYNONYMS: **1 energetic**, active, animated, dynamic, full of life, outgoing, spirited, sprightly, high-spirited, vivacious, enthusiastic, vibrant, buoyant, exuberant, boisterous, effervescent, cheerful; informal chirpy, full of beans. **2 busy**, crowded, bustling, hectic, buzzing, vibrant, colourful. **3** a lively debate: **stimulating**, interesting, vigorous, animated, spirited, heated.

– ANTONYMS: quiet, dull.

▪ **liveliness** n.

liven v. (**liven up**) make or become lively.

liver n. a large organ in the abdomen producing bile.

> WORD LINKS
> **hepatic** relating to the liver

livery n. (pl. **liveries**) **1** a special uniform. **2** a distinctive design and colour scheme used on a company's vehicles or products.

▪ **liveried** adj.

lives pl. of LIFE.

livestock n. farm animals.

livid adj. **1** informal very angry. **2** dark blue-grey in colour.

▷ SYNONYMS: **furious**, enraged, very angry, infuriated, irate, incensed, fuming, ranting, raving, seething, beside yourself, outraged; informal hopping mad, wild.

living n. **1** a way or style of life. **2** an income, or the means of earning it.

▷ SYNONYMS: **1 way of life**, lifestyle, life, conduct, behaviour, activities, habits. **2 livelihood**, income, source of income, subsistence, keep, daily bread, bread and butter, job, work, employment, occupation.

• adj. alive.

▷ SYNONYMS: **1 alive**, live, animate, sentient, breathing, existing. **2** a living language: **current**, contemporary.

– ANTONYMS: dead, extinct.

▫ **living room** a room for everyday use.

lizard n. a four-legged reptile with a long tail.

llama /lah-muh/ n. a South American animal related to the camel.

load n. **1** a thing or quantity carried. **2** a weight or source of pressure. **3** (**a load/loads of**) informal a lot of. **4** the amount of work to be done.

▷ SYNONYMS: **1 cargo**, freight, consignment, delivery, shipment, goods, pack, bundle, parcel. **2** a heavy teaching load: **commitment**, responsibility, duty, obligation, burden, onus.

• v. **1** put a load on or in. **2** put something into a device so that it will operate. **3** put ammunition into a gun. **4** (**loaded**) biased towards a particular outcome.

▷ SYNONYMS: **1 fill**, pack, stock, stack, stow, store, bundle, place, put, deposit, pile, stuff, cram; old use lade. **2 burden**, weigh down, saddle, oppress, charge, overburden, overwhelm, encumber, tax, strain, trouble, worry. **3** he loaded the gun: **prime**, charge, set up, prepare. **4** load the cassette into the camcorder: **insert**, put, place, slot, slide.

loaf n. (pl. **loaves**) a piece of shaped and baked bread.

• v. spend time idly.

▷ SYNONYMS: **laze**, lounge, loll, idle; informal hang around; Brit. informal hang about, mooch about/around; N. Amer. informal bum around.

▪ **loafer** n.

loam n. a fertile soil.

loan n. **1** a sum of money lent. **2** the act of lending.

▷ SYNONYMS: **credit**, advance, mortgage, overdraft, Brit. informal sub.

• v. lend.

▷ SYNONYMS: **lend**, advance.

▫ **loan shark** informal a moneylender charging very high rates of interest.

loath adj. unwilling.

▷ SYNONYMS: **reluctant**, unwilling, disinclined, averse, opposed, resistant.

– ANTONYMS: eager, willing.

loathe v. feel hatred or disgust for.

▷ SYNONYMS: **hate**, detest, abhor, despise, abominate, not be able to bear/stand, execrate.

– ANTONYMS: love.

loathing n. intense dislike or disgust.

▷ SYNONYMS: **hatred**, hate, detestation, abhorrence, abomination, antipathy, aversion, dislike, disgust, repugnance.

loathsome adj. arousing hatred or disgust.

▷ SYNONYMS: **hateful**, detestable, abhorrent, repulsive, odious, repugnant, repellent, disgusting, revolting, sickening, nauseating, abominable, despicable, contemptible, reprehensible, vile, horrible, nasty, obnoxious, gross, foul, execrable; informal horrid; literary noisome.

lob v. (**lobbing**, **lobbed**) throw or hit in a high arc.
• n. a lobbed ball.

lobby n. (pl. **lobbies**) **1** an open area inside the entrance of a public building. **2** a group trying to influence politicians on an issue.
▷ SYNONYMS: **1 entrance**, hallway, hall, vestibule, foyer, reception. **2** the anti-hunt lobby: **pressure group**, interest group, movement, campaign, crusade, faction, camp, ginger group.
• v. (**lobbying**, **lobbied**) try to influence a politician on an issue.
▷ SYNONYMS: **1 approach**, contact, petition, appeal to, pressurize, importune. **2 campaign**, crusade, press, push, ask, call, demand, promote, advocate, champion.
■ **lobbyist** n.

lobe n. a roundish part or projection.

lobelia n. a garden plant with blue or scarlet flowers.

lobotomy n. (pl. **lobotomies**) an operation involving cutting into part of the brain.

lobster n. a shellfish with large pincers.

local adj. of a particular place or part.
▷ SYNONYMS: **1** the local council: **district**, regional, town, municipal, provincial, parish. **2** a local restaurant: **neighbourhood**, nearby, near, at hand, close by, handy, convenient. **3** a local infection: **confined**, restricted, contained, localized.
– ANTONYMS: national, widespread.
• n. **1** a person who lives in a particular place. **2** Brit. informal a pub near a person's home.
▷ SYNONYMS: **resident**, native, inhabitant, parishioner.
– ANTONYMS: outsider.
□ **local anaesthetic** an anaesthetic affecting a particular part of the body.
■ **locally** adv.

locale /loh-**kahl**/ n. a place where something happens.

locality n. (pl. **localities**) **1** an area or neighbourhood. **2** the position of something.

localize (or **-ise**) v. restrict to a particular place.
■ **localization** n.

locate v. **1** discover the exact place of. **2** (**be located**) be situated.
▷ SYNONYMS: **1 find**, pinpoint, track down, unearth, sniff out, smoke out, search out, uncover, run to earth. **2**

situate, site, position, place, base, put, build, establish, station.

location n. **1** a place where something is located. **2** the act of locating. **3** a place outside a studio where a film etc. is made.
▷ SYNONYMS: **position**, place, situation, site, locality, locale, spot, whereabouts, scene, setting, area, environment, venue, address; technical locus.

loch n. (in Scotland) a lake or inlet of the sea.

loci pl. of LOCUS.

lock n. **1** a device for keeping something fastened or for preventing something from functioning, operated by a key. **2** a section of a canal with gates at each end allowing the water level to be changed. **3** a wrestling hold. **4** a coil or hanging piece of hair.
▷ SYNONYMS: **1 bolt**, catch, fastener, clasp, hasp, latch. **2** a lock of hair: **strand**, tress, curl, ringlet, hank, tuft, wisp, coil, tendril.
• v. **1** fasten with a lock. **2** shut in by locking a door. **3** make or become fixed.
▷ SYNONYMS: **1 bolt**, fasten, secure, padlock, latch, chain. **2 become stuck**, stick, jam, seize.
– ANTONYMS: unlock, open.
□ **lockjaw** tetanus. **lockout** the exclusion of employees from their workplace during a dispute. **locksmith** a person who makes and repairs locks. **lock-up 1** a makeshift jail. **2** Brit. a garage or small shop separate from other premises.
■ **lockable** adj.

locker n. a small lockable cupboard.
▷ SYNONYMS: **cupboard**, cabinet, chest, safe, box, case, coffer, storeroom.

locket n. a small ornamental case worn on a chain round the neck.

locomotion n. movement from one place to another.

locomotive n. a powered railway vehicle for pulling trains.
• adj. of locomotion.

locum n. Brit. a doctor or priest standing in for another who is temporarily away.

locus n. (pl. **loci**) a particular position or place.

locust n. a large destructive tropical grasshopper.

locution n. **1** a word or phrase. **2** a person's way of speaking.

lode n. a vein of metal ore.
□ **lodestone** a piece of magnetic iron ore used as a magnet.

lodge n. **1** a small house at the gates of a large house with grounds. **2** a porter's room at the entrance of a building. **3** a small house where people stay while hunting or shooting. **4** a branch of certain organizations. **5** a beaver's den.

▷ SYNONYMS: **1 gatehouse**, cottage, house, cabin, hut. **2** a Masonic lodge: **section**, branch, wing, group; N. Amer. chapter.

• v. **1** present a complaint, appeal, etc. **2** fix in a place. **3** live as a lodger.

▷ SYNONYMS: **1 submit**, register, enter, put forward, advance, lay, present, tender, proffer, put on record, record, table, file. **2** the bullet lodged in his back: **become embedded**, get stuck, stick, catch, get caught, wedge. **3** reside, board, stay, live, stop; N. Amer. room; literary sojourn. **4 deposit**, put, bank, stash, store, stow, put away.

lodger n. a person who pays rent to live in a property with the owner.

lodging n. **1** temporary accommodation. **2** (**lodgings**) a rented room or rooms in the same house as the owner.

▷ SYNONYMS: **accommodation**, rooms, chambers, living quarters, a roof over your head, housing, shelter; informal digs; N. Amer. informal crib; formal residence, dwelling, abode.

loft n. **1** a room or space under a roof. **2** a large, open flat in a converted building. **3** a gallery in a church or hall.

• v. hit or throw a ball high into the air.

lofty adj. (**loftier**, **loftiest**) **1** very tall. **2** morally good. **3** haughty and aloof.

▷ SYNONYMS: **1 tall**, high, towering. **2** lofty ideals: **noble**, exalted, high, high-minded, worthy, grand, fine, elevated. **3** lofty disdain: **haughty**, arrogant, disdainful, supercilious, condescending, patronizing, scornful, contemptuous, self-important, conceited, snobbish; informal stuck-up, snooty; Brit. informal toffee-nosed.

– ANTONYMS: low, short.

■ **loftily** adv.

log n. **1** a piece cut from the trunk or a branch of a tree. **2** an official record of a ship's or aircraft's journey.

▷ SYNONYMS: **1 register**, record, logbook, journal, diary, minutes, ledger, account, tally.

• v. (**logging**, **logged**) **1** enter facts in a log. **2** (**log in/on** or **out/off**) begin (or finish) using a computer system. **3** cut down trees for commercial use.

▷ SYNONYMS: **1 register**, record, note, write down, put in writing, enter, file. **2** the pilot had logged 95 hours: **attain**, achieve, chalk up, make, do, go, cover, clock up.

□ **logbook 1** a log of a ship or aircraft. **2** Brit. a document recording details of a vehicle and its owner.

loganberry n. a red soft fruit, similar to a raspberry.

logarithm n. each of a series of numbers set out in tables, used to simplify calculations.

loggerheads pl. n. (**at loggerheads**) in strong disagreement.

logic n. **1** the science of reasoning. **2** good reasoning.

▷ SYNONYMS: **1 reason**, judgement, rationality, wisdom, sense, good sense, common sense, sanity. **2** the logic of their argument: **reasoning**, rationale, argument.

■ **logician** n.

logical adj. **1** based on logic; using sound reasoning. **2** expected or reasonable.

▷ SYNONYMS: **1 reasoned**, rational, sound, cogent, valid, coherent, clear, systematic, orderly, methodical, analytical, consistent. **2** the logical outcome: **natural**, reasonable, sensible, understandable, predictable, unsurprising, likely.

– ANTONYMS: illogical

■ **logically** adv.

logistics n. the detailed organization of a large and complex exercise.

■ **logistical** adj.

logo n. (pl. **logos**) a design or symbol used to identify an organization.

▷ SYNONYMS: **design**, symbol, emblem, trademark, motif, monogram.

loin n. the part of the body between the ribs and the hip bones.

□ **loincloth** a cloth worn round the hips.

loiter v. stand around idly.

▷ SYNONYMS: **linger**, wait, skulk, loaf, lounge, idle; informal hang about/around; Brit. informal mooch about/around.

■ **loiterer** n.

loll v. **1** sit, lie, or stand in a relaxed way. **2** hang loosely.

lollipop n. a large boiled sweet on a stick.

lollop v. (**lolloped**, **lolloping**) move with clumsy bounding steps.

lolly n. (pl. **lollies**) Brit. informal **1** a lollipop. **2** money.

lone adj. solitary.

▷ SYNONYMS: **1 solitary**, single, solo, unaccompanied, sole, isolated. **2** a *lone parent*: **single**, unmarried, separated, divorced, widowed.

lonely adj. (**lonelier**, **loneliest**) **1** sad because of having no friends or company. **2** (of time) spent alone. **3** remote.
▷ SYNONYMS: **1 isolated**, alone, friendless, with no one to turn to, abandoned, rejected, unloved, unwanted; N. Amer. lonesome. **2** *a lonely cottage on the moors*: **remote**, isolated, out of the way, off the beaten track, secluded, in the back of beyond, godforsaken; **deserted**, uninhabited, solitary; informal in the middle of nowhere.
■ **loneliness** n.

loner n. a person who prefers to be alone.

lonesome adj. US lonely.

long adj. **1** of great or a particular length. **2** (of odds) reflecting a low probability.
▷ SYNONYMS: **lengthy**, extended, prolonged, protracted, long-lasting, drawn-out, endless, lingering, interminable.
– ANTONYMS: short, brief.
• adv. **1** for a long time. **2** throughout a specific period.
• v. have a strong wish.
▷ SYNONYMS: *I longed for the holidays*: **yearn**, pine, ache, hanker for/after, hunger, thirst, itch, be eager, be desperate, crave, dream of; informal be dying.
□ **as** (or **so**) **long as** provided that. **longhand** ordinary handwriting as opposed to shorthand etc. **long-haul** involving transport over a long distance. **long johns** informal close-fitting underpants with long legs. **long-range 1** able to travel long distances. **2** of a period far in the future. **long shot** a scheme or guess very unlikely to succeed. **long-sighted** Brit. unable to see close things clearly. **long-term** of or for a long time. **long wave** a radio wave of a wavelength above a kilometre and a frequency below 300 kHz. **longways** lengthways.

longevity /lon-jev-i-ti/ n. long life.

longing n. a strong wish.
▷ SYNONYMS: **yearning**, craving, ache, burning, hunger, thirst, hankering, desire, wish, hope, aspiration; informal yen, itch.
■ **longingly** adv.

longitude n. the distance east or west of the Greenwich meridian, measured in degrees.

■ **longitudinal** adj.

long-standing adj. having existed for a long time.
▷ SYNONYMS: **well established**, time-honoured, traditional, abiding, enduring.
– ANTONYMS: new, recent.

long-suffering adj. bearing problems or annoyance patiently.
▷ SYNONYMS: **patient**, forbearing, tolerant, uncomplaining, philo-sophical, stoical, forgiving.

long-winded adj. long and boring.
▷ SYNONYMS: **verbose**, wordy, lengthy, long, prolix, interminable, rambling, tortuous, meandering, repetitious, repetitive; Brit. informal waffly.
– ANTONYMS: concise, succinct.

loo n. Brit. informal a toilet.

loofah n. the dried inner parts of a tropical fruit, used as a bath sponge.

look v. **1** direct your eyes. **2** appear; seem. **3** face towards.
▷ SYNONYMS: **1 glance**, gaze, stare, gape, peer, peep, peek, watch, observe, view, regard, examine, inspect, eye, scan, scrutinize, survey, study, contemplate, take in, ogle, leer at; informal take a gander, rubberneck, get a load of; Brit. informal gawp; N. Amer. informal eyeball. **2 seem**, appear, come across/over as.
• n. **1** an act of looking. **2** appearance. **3** (**looks**) a person's facial appearance.
▷ SYNONYMS: **1 glance**, examination, study, inspection, scrutiny, peep, peek, glimpse; informal eyeful, once-over, squint; Brit. informal dekko, butcher's, shufti. **2 appearance**, air, style, effect, ambience, impression, aspect, manner, demeanour. **3 expression**, mien, countenance.
□ **look after** take care of. **look down on** think that you are better than. **look for** try to find. **look into** investigate. **look on** watch without getting involved. **look out** be vigilant. **lookout 1** a place from which to keep watch. **2** a person keeping watch. **look up 1** improve. **2** search for information. **3** informal visit or contact. **look up to** admire and respect.

lookalike n. a person who looks very similar to another.
▷ SYNONYMS: **double**, twin, clone, living image, doppelgänger, replica; informal spitting image, dead ringer.

loom n. a machine for weaving cloth.
• v. **1** appear as a vague and threatening shape. **2** seem ominously close.
▷ SYNONYMS: **1 emerge**, appear,

materialize, take shape. **2 be imminent**, be on the horizon, impend, threaten, brew, be just around the corner.

loony n. (pl. **loonies**) informal a mad person.

loop n. **1** a curve that bends round and crosses itself. **2** an endless strip of tape or film.

▷ SYNONYMS: **coil**, ring, circle, noose, spiral, curl, bend, curve, arc, twirl, whorl, twist, helix.

• v. form into a loop.

▷ SYNONYMS: **1 coil**, wind, twist, snake, spiral, curve, bend, turn. **2 fasten**, tie, join, connect, knot, bind.

□ **loophole** a way of avoiding something stipulated by a law or contract. **loop the loop** fly an aircraft in a vertical circle.

loose adj. **1** not firmly fixed in place. **2** not tied up or shut in. **3** (of a garment) not fitting tightly. **4** not fastened or packaged together. **5** not exact.

▷ SYNONYMS: **1 not secure**, unsecured, unattached, untied, detached, wobbly, unsteady, dangling, free. **2 free**, at large, at liberty, on the loose. **3 baggy**, roomy, oversized, voluminous, shapeless, sloppy. **4** *a loose interpretation:* **vague**, imprecise, approximate, broad, general, rough, liberal.

– ANTONYMS: secure, tight.

• v. unfasten or set free.

▷ SYNONYMS: **1 free**, let loose, release, untie, unchain, unfasten, unleash; undo, detach, disconnect. **2 relax**, slacken, loosen, weaken.

– ANTONYMS: confine, tighten.

□ **at a loose end** with nothing to do. **loose box** Brit. a stall for a horse. **loose-leaf** with each page removable. **on the loose** having escaped from being imprisoned or tied up.

■ **loosely** adv. **loosen** v. **looseness** n.

loot n. goods stolen by a thief, or during a war or riot.

▷ SYNONYMS: **booty**, spoils, plunder, haul, informal swag, boodle.

• v. steal goods from a place during a war or riot.

▷ SYNONYMS: **plunder**, pillage, ransack, sack, rifle, rob, strip, gut.

■ **looter** n.

lop v. (**lopping**, **lopped**) cut off a branch from a tree.

lope v. run with a long bounding stride.

lop-eared adj. with drooping ears.

lopsided adj. with one side lower or smaller than the other.

▷ SYNONYMS: **crooked**, askew, awry, off-centre, uneven, out of true, asymmetrical, tilted, at an angle, slanting; Scottish **agley**; informal **cockeyed**; Brit. informal **skew-whiff**, wonky.

– ANTONYMS: even, level.

loquacious adj. talkative.

■ **loquacity** n.

lord n. **1** a nobleman. **2** (**Lord**) a title given to certain British peers or high officials. **3** a master or ruler. **4** (**Lord**) a name for God or Jesus.

▷ SYNONYMS: **1 noble**, nobleman, peer, aristocrat. **2 master**, ruler, leader, chief, superior, monarch, sovereign, king, emperor, prince, governor, commander.

□ **lord it over** act in an arrogant and bullying way towards. **Your/His Lordship** a form of address to a judge, bishop, or nobleman.

lordly adj. proud or superior.

lore n. traditional knowledge.

lorgnette /lor-nyet/ n. a pair of glasses held by a long handle.

lorry n. (pl. **lorries**) Brit. a large vehicle for transporting goods.

▷ SYNONYMS: **truck**, wagon, van, juggernaut, trailer, HGV; dated pantechnicon.

lose v. (**losing**, **lost**) **1** have taken away; no longer have. **2** become unable to find. **3** fail to win. **4** waste time or an opportunity. **5** (**lose yourself in**) become deeply involved in.

▷ SYNONYMS: **1 mislay**, misplace, lose track of. **2** *he managed to lose his pursuers:* **escape from**, evade, elude, dodge, avoid, give someone the slip, shake off, throw off, leave behind, outdistance, outrun. **3 be defeated**, be beaten; informal come a cropper, go down. **4 waste**, squander, let pass, miss; informal pass up, blow.

– ANTONYMS: find, win.

□ **lose out** not get a fair chance or advantage.

loser n. **1** a person or thing that loses a contest. **2** informal an unsuccessful person.

▷ SYNONYMS: **failure**, underachiever, dead loss, write-off, has-been, informal also-ran, non-starter, no-hoper.

loss n. **1** the act of losing. **2** a person or thing lost. **3** sadness after losing a valued person or thing.

▷ SYNONYMS: **1 mislaying**, deprivation, forfeiture, erosion, reduction, depletion. **2 casualty**, fatality, victim, death. **3 deficit**, debit, debt.

– ANTONYMS: recovery, profit.

□ **at a loss** uncertain or puzzled. **loss-leader** a product sold at a loss to attract customers.

lost past and past participle of LOSE.
adj. **1** unable to find your way.
2 unable to be found or recovered.
▷ SYNONYMS: **1 off course**, going round in circles, adrift, at sea; stray. **2 missing**, mislaid, misplaced, gone astray. **3** *lost traditions:* **bygone**, past, former, old, vanished, forgotten, dead. **4** *lost species and habitats:* **extinct**, died out, defunct, vanished, gone, destroyed, wiped out, exterminated. **5** *he was lost in thought:* **engrossed**, absorbed, rapt, immersed, deep, intent, engaged, wrapped up.

lot pron. & adv. (**a lot/lots**) informal a large number or amount.
▷ SYNONYMS: **a large amount**, a good/ great deal, an abundance, a wealth, a profusion, plenty, many, a great many, a large number, a cornucopia; informal hundreds, loads, masses, heaps, piles, stacks, tons, oodles; Brit. informal lashings.
• n. **1** an item for sale at an auction. **2** informal a group of people. **3** (**the lot**) informal the whole number or quantity. **4** a piece of paper chosen at random from a number of marked pieces as a method of deciding something. **5** a person's situation in life. **6** a plot of land.
▷ SYNONYMS: **1 item**, article, batch, group, bundle, parcel. **2 group**, crowd, circle, crew; informal bunch, gang, mob. **3** *his lot in life:* **fate**, destiny, fortune, situation, circumstances, plight, predicament.

lotion n. a medicinal or cosmetic liquid put on the skin.
▷ SYNONYMS: **ointment**, cream, balm, rub, moisturizer, lubricant, embrocation, liniment, salve, unguent.

lottery n. (pl. **lotteries**) **1** a means of raising money by selling numbered tickets and giving prizes to the holders of numbers drawn at random. **2** something whose success is controlled by luck.
▷ SYNONYMS: **raffle**, draw, sweepstake, sweep, tombola, lotto, pools.

lotus n. a large water lily.

louche /loosh/ adj. having a bad reputation but still attractive.

loud adj. **1** making a lot of noise. **2** expressed forcefully. **3** garish.
▷ SYNONYMS: **1 noisy**, blaring, booming, roaring, thunderous, resounding, sonorous, powerful, stentorian, deafening, ear-splitting, piercing, shrill, raucous; Music forte, fortissimo.

2 vociferous, clamorous, insistent, vehement, emphatic. **3 garish**, gaudy, lurid, showy, flamboyant, ostentatious, vulgar, tasteless; informal flashy.
– ANTONYMS: quiet.
□ **loudhailer** Brit. an electronic megaphone. **loudspeaker** a device that converts electrical impulses into sound.
■ **loudly** adv. **loudness** n.

lough /lok/ n. (in Ireland) a loch.

lounge v. lie, sit, or stand in a relaxed way.
▷ SYNONYMS: **laze**, lie, loll, recline, relax, rest, take it easy, sprawl, slump, slouch, loaf, idle.
• n. **1** Brit. a sitting room. **2** a waiting room at an airport etc.
▷ SYNONYMS: **living room**, sitting room, front room, drawing room; dated parlour.
□ **lounge suit** Brit. a man's ordinary suit.

lour (or **lower**) v. (of the sky) look dark and threatening.

louse n. **1** (pl. **lice**) a small parasitic insect. **2** (pl. **louses**) informal an unpleasant person.

lousy adj. (**lousier**, **lousiest**) **1** informal very bad. **2** infested with lice.

lout n. a rude or aggressive man or boy.
▷ SYNONYMS: **hooligan**, ruffian, thug, boor, oaf, rowdy; informal tough, bruiser; Brit. informal yob, yobbo.
■ **loutish** adj.

louvre /loo-ver/ (US **louver**) n. each of a set of slanting slats fixed at intervals to allow air or light through.

lovable (or **loveable**) adj. inspiring love or affection.
▷ SYNONYMS: **adorable**, dear, sweet, cute, charming, lovely, likeable, engaging, endearing, winning, winsome.
– ANTONYMS: hateful, loathsome.

love n. **1** very strong affection. **2** very strong affection and sexual attraction. **3** great liking. **4** a person or thing that you love. **5** (in tennis etc.) a score of zero.
▷ SYNONYMS: **1 adoration**, devotion, affection, fondness, tenderness, attachment, warmth, passion, desire, lust, yearning, infatuation, besottedness. **2 liking**, taste, zeal, zest, enthusiasm, keenness, fondness, weakness, partiality, predilection, penchant. **3 compassion**, care, regard, concern, altruism, unselfishness, philanthropy, benevolence, humanity.
– ANTONYMS: hatred.

• v. **1** feel love for. **2** like very much.
▷ SYNONYMS: **1 be in love with**, adore, be devoted to, be infatuated with, be smitten with, be besotted with, idolize, worship, think the world of, dote on, care for, hold dear, cherish; informal be mad/crazy about, carry a torch for. **2 like**, delight in, relish, enjoy, have a soft spot for, have a weakness for, be addicted to, be taken with; informal have a thing about, be hooked on, get a kick out of.
– ANTONYMS: hate.
□ **lovelorn** unhappy because you love someone who does not love you. **make love** have sex.
■ **loveless** adj. **lovingly** adv.

> **WORD LINKS**
> **amatory** relating to love

love affair n. a romantic or sexual relationship between two people who are not married to each other.
▷ SYNONYMS: **relationship**, romance, liaison, fling, amour, entanglement, involvement, intrigue, affaire; Brit. informal carry-on.

lovely adj. (**lovelier**, **loveliest**) very beautiful or pleasant.
▷ SYNONYMS: **1 beautiful**, pretty, attractive, good-looking, handsome, adorable, charming, engaging, enchanting, gorgeous, alluring, ravishing, glamorous; Scottish & N. English bonny; informal tasty, stunning, drop-dead gorgeous; Brit. informal fit; N. Amer. informal cute, foxy; old use comely. **2 delightful**, marvellous, magnificent, stunning, splendid, wonderful, superb, pleasant, enjoyable; informal terrific, fabulous, heavenly, divine, amazing, glorious.
– ANTONYMS: ugly, horrible.
■ **loveliness** n.

lover n. **1** a partner in a sexual or romantic relationship outside marriage. **2** a person who likes or enjoys something.
▷ SYNONYMS: **1 boyfriend**, girlfriend, beloved, sweetheart, inamorato/a, mistress, partner, gigolo; informal bit on the side, fancy man/woman; dated beau; literary swain; old use paramour. **2** an opera lover: **devotee**, admirer, fan, enthusiast, aficionado; informal buff, nut.

loving adj. showing great love or care.
▷ SYNONYMS: **affectionate**, fond, devoted, adoring, doting, caring, tender, warm, close, amorous, passionate.
– ANTONYMS: cold, cruel.

low adj. **1** not high or tall or far above the ground. **2** below average in amount or strength. **3** not good or important. **4** (of a sound) deep or quiet. **5** depressed. **6** not moral.
▷ SYNONYMS: **1 short**, small, little, squat, stubby, stunted. **2** low prices: **cheap**, economical, moderate, reasonable, affordable, modest, bargain, bargain-basement, rock-bottom. **3** fuel supplies are running low: **scarce**, scant, meagre, sparse, few, little, reduced, depleted, diminished. **4 inferior**, substandard, poor, low-grade, unsatisfactory, inadequate, second-rate. **5** a low voice: **quiet**, soft, faint, gentle, muted, subdued, muffled, hushed; bass, deep, sonorous. **6 depressed**, dejected, despondent, downhearted, downcast, down, miserable, dispirited, gloomy, glum, flat; informal fed up, down in the dumps, blue.
– ANTONYMS: high, expensive, loud.
• n. **1** a low point. **2** an area of low atmospheric pressure.
• adv. at or into a low point.
• v. (of a cow) moo.
□ **lowbrow** not intellectual or cultured. **the low-down** the important facts. **lowland** (or **lowlands**) low-lying country. **low season** Brit. the least popular time for a holiday. **low tide** the time when the sea is furthest out.

lower¹ adj. less high.
▷ SYNONYMS: **1 subordinate**, inferior, lesser, junior, minor, secondary, subsidiary, subservient. **2** her lower lip: **bottom**, nether, bottommost, under.
– ANTONYMS: upper.
• v. **1** make or become lower. **2** move downwards.
▷ SYNONYMS: **1 let down**, take down, drop, let fall. **2** she lowered her voice: **soften**, modulate, quieten, hush, tone down, muffle, turn down, mute. **3** they lowered the prices: **reduce**, decrease, lessen, bring down, cut, slash.
– ANTONYMS: raise, increase.
□ **lower case** small letters as opposed to capitals.

lower² var. of LOUR.

low-key adj. not elaborate or showy.
▷ SYNONYMS: **restrained**, modest, understated, muted, subtle, quiet, low-profile, inconspicuous, unobtrusive, discreet.
– ANTONYMS: ostentatious, obtrusive.

lowly adj. (**lowlier**, **lowliest**) low in status or importance.
▷ SYNONYMS: **humble**, low, low-ranking,

common, ordinary, plain, modest, simple, obscure.
– ANTONYMS: aristocratic, exalted.

loyal adj. firm and faithful in your support.
▷ SYNONYMS: **faithful**, true, true-blue, devoted, constant, steadfast, staunch, dependable, reliable, trustworthy, trusty, patriotic, unswerving.
– ANTONYMS: disloyal, treacherous.
■ **loyally** adv.

loyalist n. a person who remains loyal to the established ruler or government.

loyalty n. (pl. **loyalties**) the state of being loyal.
▷ SYNONYMS: **allegiance**, faithfulness, fidelity, obedience, adherence, devotion, steadfastness, staunchness, dedication, commitment, patriotism; old use fealty.
– ANTONYMS: disloyalty, treachery.

lozenge n. 1 a tablet sucked to soothe a sore throat. 2 a diamond-shaped figure.

LP abbrev. long-playing record.

LSD n. a powerful hallucinogenic drug.

Ltd abbrev. Brit. (after a company name) Limited.

lubricant n. a lubricating substance.

lubricate v. oil or grease machinery so that it moves easily.
■ **lubrication** n.

lubricious adj. lewd.

lucerne n. alfalfa.

lucid adj. 1 easy to understand. 2 able to think clearly.
▷ SYNONYMS: **1 clear**, crystal clear, intelligible, comprehensible, cogent, coherent, articulate. **2 rational**, sane, in possession of your faculties, compos mentis, clear-headed, sober; informal all there.
– ANTONYMS: confused.
■ **lucidity** n. **lucidly** adv.

luck n. 1 good or bad things that happen by chance. 2 good fortune.
▷ SYNONYMS: **1 good fortune**, good luck, stroke of luck, fluke; informal lucky break. **2 fortune**, fate, serendipity, chance, accident, a twist of fate.
– ANTONYMS: bad luck, misfortune.
■ **luckless** adj.

lucky adj. (**luckier**, **luckiest**) having, bringing, or resulting from good luck.
▷ SYNONYMS: **1 fortunate**, in luck, favoured, leading a charmed life, successful; Brit. informal jammy.
2 providential, fortunate, timely, opportune, serendipitous, chance, fortuitous, accidental.
– ANTONYMS: unlucky.

□ **lucky dip** Brit. a game in which small prizes are hidden in a container for people to pick out at random.
■ **luckily** adv.

lucrative adj. making a large profit.
▷ SYNONYMS: **profitable**, gainful, remunerative, moneymaking, well paid, rewarding, worthwhile.
– ANTONYMS: unprofitable.

lucre /loo-ker/ n. money.

Luddite n. a person opposed to new technology.

ludicrous adj. ridiculous.
▷ SYNONYMS: **absurd**, ridiculous, farcical, laughable, risible, preposterous, mad, insane, idiotic, stupid, asinine, nonsensical; informal crazy.
– ANTONYMS: sensible.
■ **ludicrously** adv.

lug v. (**lugging**, **lugged**) carry or drag with great effort.
• n. 1 Brit. informal an ear. 2 a projection on an object for carrying it or fixing it in place.

luggage n. suitcases etc. for a traveller's belongings.
▷ SYNONYMS: **baggage**, bags, suitcases, cases.

lugubrious adj. sad; gloomy.

lukewarm adj. 1 only slightly warm. 2 unenthusiastic.
▷ SYNONYMS: *a lukewarm response:* **indifferent**, cool, half-hearted, apathetic, tepid, unenthusiastic, uninterested, non-committal.
– ANTONYMS: warm.

lull v. 1 calm or send to sleep. 2 cause to feel deceptively safe or confident.
▷ SYNONYMS: **soothe**, calm, quiet, still, assuage, allay, ease, quell.
• n. a period of quiet or inactivity.
▷ SYNONYMS: **1 pause**, respite, interval, break, suspension, breathing space, hiatus; informal let-up, breather. **2** *the lull before the storm:* **calm**, stillness, quiet, tranquillity, peace, silence, hush.

lullaby n. (pl. **lullabies**) a soothing song to send a child to sleep.

lumbago n. lower back pain.

lumbar adj. of the lower back.

lumber n. 1 Brit. disused articles of furniture. 2 US timber sawn into planks.
• v. 1 Brit. informal give an unwanted responsibility to. 2 move slowly and awkwardly.
▷ SYNONYMS: **1 burden**, saddle, encumber, land. **2 trundle**, stump, clump, plod, stumble, shamble, shuffle, trudge.
□ **lumberjack** a person who fells and

cuts up trees.

lumbering adj. moving slowly and awkwardly.

▷ SYNONYMS: **clumsy**, awkward, slow, blundering, bumbling, ponderous, ungainly; informal clodhopping.

– ANTONYMS: nimble, agile.

luminary n. (pl. **luminaries**) an important or influential person.

luminescence n. light given off by a substance that has not been heated.
■ **luminescent** adj.

luminous adj. giving off light, esp. in the dark.

▷ SYNONYMS: **shining**, bright, brilliant, radiant, dazzling, glowing, luminescent, phosphorescent, fluorescent, incandescent.

– ANTONYMS: dark.
■ **luminosity** n.

lump n. **1** an irregular hard or solid mass. **2** a swelling under the skin.

▷ SYNONYMS: **1 chunk**, hunk, piece, block, wedge, slab, ball, knob, pat, clod, clump, nugget, gobbet. **2 swelling**, bump, bulge, protuberance, protrusion, growth, nodule, tumour.

• v. treat as alike, without regard for differences.

▷ SYNONYMS: **combine**, put, group, bunch, throw.

□ **lump sum** a single payment as opposed to several smaller payments.
■ **lumpy** adj.

lumpectomy n. (pl. **lumpectomies**) an operation to remove a lump from the breast.

lunacy n. **1** insanity. **2** great stupidity.

lunar adj. of the moon.

lunatic n. **1** a mentally ill person (not in technical use). **2** a very foolish person.

▷ SYNONYMS: *he drives like a lunatic:* **maniac**, madman, madwoman, idiot; informal loony, nutcase, headcase, psycho; Brit. informal nutter; N. Amer. informal screwball.

lunch n. a midday meal.
• v. eat lunch.

luncheon n. lunch.

lung n. either of the pair of organs in the chest into which air is drawn in breathing.

WORD LINKS
pulmonary relating to the lungs

---

lunge n. a sudden forward movement of the body.

▷ SYNONYMS: *Darren made a lunge at his attacker:* **thrust**, dive, rush, charge, grab.

• v. make a lunge.

▷ SYNONYMS: *he lunged at her with a knife:* **thrust**, dive, spring, launch yourself, rush.

lupin n. a plant with spikes of tall flowers.

lupine adj. of or like a wolf.

lurch n. a sudden unsteady movement.
• v. make a lurch.

▷ SYNONYMS: **1 stagger**, stumble, sway, reel, roll, totter. **2 swing**, list, roll, pitch, veer, swerve.

□ **leave in the lurch** leave in a difficult situation.

lure v. tempt into doing.

▷ SYNONYMS: **tempt**, entice, attract, induce, coax, persuade, inveigle, seduce, beguile, draw.

– ANTONYMS: deter, put off.

• n. **1** the tempting aspects of something. **2** a bait used in fishing or hunting.

▷ SYNONYMS: **temptation**, attraction, pull, draw, appeal, inducement, allure, fascination, interest, glamour.

lurid adj. **1** unpleasantly bright in colour. **2** vividly shocking.

▷ SYNONYMS: **1 bright**, vivid, glaring, fluorescent, gaudy, loud. **2** *lurid details:* **sensational**, colourful, salacious, graphic, explicit, prurient, shocking, gruesome, gory, grisly; informal juicy.
■ **luridly** adv.

lurk v. wait in hiding to attack someone.

▷ SYNONYMS: **skulk**, loiter, lie in wait, hide.

luscious adj. **1** rich and sweet in taste. **2** sexually attractive.

lush adj. **1** growing thickly and strongly. **2** luxurious.

▷ SYNONYMS: **1 profuse**, abundant, luxuriant, flourishing, rich, riotous, vigorous, dense, thick, rampant. **2 luxurious**, sumptuous, palatial, opulent, lavish, elaborate, extravagant, fancy; informal plush, posh, swanky, bling-bling; Brit. informal swish; N. Amer. informal swank.

– ANTONYMS: sparse, austere.
■ **lushly** adv. **lushness** n.

lust n. **1** strong sexual desire. **2** a strong desire.

▷ SYNONYMS: **1 desire**, longing, passion, libido, sex drive, sexuality, lecherousness, lasciviousness; Brit. informal randiness. **2 greed**, desire, craving, eagerness, longing, yearning, hunger, thirst, appetite, hankering.

• v. feel lust.
■ **lustful** adj.

lustre (US **luster**) n. **1** a soft glow or shine. **2** prestige.
■ **lustrous** adj.

lusty adj. (**lustier**, **lustiest**) healthy and strong.
■ **lustily** adv.

lute n. a guitar-like instrument with a rounded body.
■ **lutenist** n.

luxuriant adj. growing thickly and strongly.
■ **luxuriance** n. **luxuriantly** adv.

luxuriate v. take pleasure in something enjoyable.

luxurious adj. very comfortable or elegant and expensive.
▷ SYNONYMS: **opulent**, sumptuous, grand, palatial, magnificent, extravagant, fancy, deluxe, expensive; Brit. upmarket; informal plush, posh, classy, swanky, bling-bling; Brit. informal swish; N. Amer. informal swank.
– ANTONYMS: plain, basic.
■ **luxuriously** adv.

luxury n. (pl. **luxuries**) **1** comfortable and expensive living or surroundings. **2** something enjoyable but not essential.
▷ SYNONYMS: **1** opulence, sumptuousness, grandeur, magnificence, splendour, luxuriousness, affluence. **2** indulgence, extravagance, treat, extra, frill.
– ANTONYMS: simplicity, necessity.

lychee n. a fruit with sweet white flesh and rough skin.

lychgate n. a roofed gateway to a churchyard.

Lycra n. trademark an elastic fibre or fabric.

lye n. an alkaline solution used for cleaning.

lying pres. part. of LIE¹, LIE².

lymph n. a colourless fluid containing white blood cells.
□ **lymph gland** each of a number of small swellings where lymph is filtered.
■ **lymphatic** adj.

lymphoma n. cancer of the lymph glands.

lynch v. (of a mob) kill someone for an alleged crime without a legal trial.

lynx n. a wild cat with tufted ears.

lyre n. an ancient stringed instrument like a small harp.

lyric n. (or **lyrics**) the words of a song.
• adj. (of poetry) expressing the writer's emotions.

lyrical adj. (of literature or music) expressing the writer's emotions imaginatively.
▷ SYNONYMS: **1** expressive, emotional, deeply felt, personal. **2** enthusiastic, effusive, rapturous, ecstatic, euphoric, passionate, impassioned.
– ANTONYMS: unenthusiastic.
■ **lyrically** adv.

lyricism n. the imaginative expression of emotion in writing or music.

lyricist n. a person who writes lyrics.

Wordfinder

Contents

Wordfinder

Vocabulary lists

Animals

Birds

albatross
auk
avocet
barnacle goose
barn owl
bird of paradise
bittern
blackbird
blackcap
bluebird
blue tit
booby
bowerbird
brambling
budgerigar
bullfinch
bunting
bustard
butcher-bird
buzzard
Canada goose
canary
capercaillie
caracara
cassowary
chaffinch
chicken
chiffchaff
chough
coal tit
cockatiel
cockatoo
condor
coot
cormorant
corncrake
crane
crossbill

crow
cuckoo
curlew
dabchick
dodo
dotterel
dove
duck
dunlin
dunnock
eagle
egret
eider duck
emu
falcon
fantail
fieldfare
finch
flamingo
flycatcher
fulmar
gannet
goldcrest
golden eagle
goldfinch
goose
goshawk
great tit
grebe
greenfinch
grouse
guillemot
guineafowl
gull
gyrfalcon
harrier
hawfinch
hawk

hen
heron
hobby
hoopoe
hornbill
house martin
hummingbird
ibis
jackdaw
jay
kestrel
kingfisher
kite
kittiwake
kiwi
kookaburra
lammergeier
lapwing
lark
linnet
lovebird
lyrebird
macaw
magpie
mallard
martin
merlin
mistle thrush
moa
mockingbird
moorhen
mynah bird
nightingale
nightjar
nuthatch
ortolan
osprey
ostrich

ouzel
owl
oystercatcher
parakeet
parrot
partridge
peacock
peewit
pelican
penguin
peregrine
 falcon
petrel
pheasant
pigeon
pintail
pipit
plover
ptarmigan
puffin
quail
rail
raven
red kite
redpoll
redstart
redwing
rhea
ringdove
roadrunner
robin
rook
sandpiper
seagull
shag
shearwater
shelduck
shrike

siskin
skua
skylark
snipe
song thrush
sparrow
sparrowhawk
spoonbill
starling
stonechat
stork
sunbird
swallow
swan
swift
tawny owl
tern
thrush
tit
toucan
treecreeper
turkey
turtle dove
vulture
wagtail
warbler
waxwing
weaver bird
wigeon
whinchat
whippoorwill
woodcock
woodlark
woodpecker
wren
yellowhammer

Dinosaurs

allosaurus
ankylosaur
apatosaurus
brachiosaurus
brontosaurus
carnosaur

coelurosaur
deinonychus
diplodocus
dromaeosaur
duck-billed
 dinosaur

hadrosaur
iguanodon
megalosaurus
pliosaur
protoceratops
pteranodon

pterodactyl
raptor
saurischian
sauropod
seismosaurus
stegosaurus

theropod
triceratops
tyrannosaurus
velociraptor

Fish

anchovy
angelfish
anglerfish
archerfish
barbel
barracouta
barracuda
bass
beluga
blenny
bluefin
bonito
boxfish
bream
brill
brisling
bullhead
carp
catfish
charr
chub
clownfish
cod
coelacanth
coley
conger eel
dab
dace
damselfish

dogfish
dorado
dory
Dover sole
eel
filefish
flatfish
flathead
flounder
flying fish
garfish
goby
goldfish
gourami
grayling
great white
  shark
grouper
gudgeon
guppy
gurnard
haddock
hake
halfbeak
halibut
hammerhead
herring
hoki
huss

John Dory
koi
lamprey
lanternfish
lemon sole
ling
loach
lumpsucker
lungfish
mackerel
mako
manta
marlin
megamouth
minnow
monkfish
moray eel
mudskipper
mullet
needlefish
nurse shark
oarfish
orfe
parrotfish
perch
pike
pilchard
pilotfish
pipefish

piranha
plaice
pollack
porbeagle
puffer fish
rabbitfish
rainbow trout
ray
remora
roach
sailfish
saithe
salmon
sardine
sawfish
scorpionfish
sea horse
shad
shark
skate
skipjack
skipper
smelt
snapper
sockeye
sole
sprat
stargazer
stickleback

stingray
stonefish
sturgeon
sunfish
surgeonfish
swordfish
swordtail
tarpon
tench
tetra
thresher
tope
triggerfish
trout
tuna
turbot
weever
whaler shark
whitebait
whitefish
whiting
wobbegong
wrasse
yellowfin
zander

Insects and arachnids

ant
aphid
bedbug
bee
beetle
blackfly
black widow
blowfly
bluebottle
bombardier
  beetle
borer
botfly
bumblebee
butterfly
cabbage white
caddis fly
caterpillar
chafer

chigger
cicada
cockchafer
cockroach
crane fly
cricket
daddy-long-
  legs
damselfly
death-watch
  beetle
dragonfly
earwig
firefly
flea
fly
fritillary
froghopper
gadfly

glow-worm
gnat
grasshopper
greenfly
harvestman
hawkmoth
honeybee
hornet
horsefly
housefly
hoverfly
ichneumon
lacewing
ladybird
leafcutter ant
leafhopper
leatherjacket
locust
louse

mantis
May bug
mayfly
mealy bug
midge
mite
mosquito
moth
pond skater
praying mantis
red admiral
sandfly
sawfly
scarab
scorpion
silverfish
spider
springtail
stag beetle

stick insect
swallowtail
tarantula
termite
thrips
thunderbug
thunderfly
tick
tortoiseshell
tsetse fly
warble fly
wasp
water boatman
weevil
whirligig
whitefly
witchetty grub

Mammals

aardvark
alpaca
angora
anteater

antelope
ape
armadillo
ass

aurochs
baboon
badger
bandicoot

bat
bear
beaver
beluga

bison
blue whale
boar
bobcat

bottlenose dolphin
buffalo
bushbaby
camel
capuchin monkey
capybara
caribou
cat
chamois
cheetah
chimpanzee
chinchilla
chipmunk
civet
coati
colobus
cougar
cow
coyote
coypu
deer
dingo
dog
dolphin
donkey
dormouse
dromedary
duck-billed platypus
dugong
duiker
echidna
eland
elephant

elk
ermine
fallow deer
fennec
ferret
flying fox
fox
gazelle
gemsbok
gerbil
gibbon
giraffe
gnu
goat
gopher
gorilla
grampus
grizzly bear
groundhog
guinea pig
hamster
hare
hartebeest
hedgehog
hippopotamus
hog
horse
howler monkey
humpback whale
hyena
hyrax
ibex
impala
jackal
jaguar

jerboa
kangaroo
killer whale
kinkajou
koala
kudu
langur
lemming
lemur
leopard
lion
llama
loris
lynx
macaque
manatee
mandrill
margay
marmot
marmoset
marten
meerkat
mink
minke whale
mole
mongoose
monkey
moose
mouse
mule
muntjac
musk ox
narwhal
ocelot
okapi
onager

opossum
orang-utan
orca
oryx
otter
ox
panda
pangolin
panther
peccary
phalanger
pig
pine marten
pipistrelle
platypus
polar bear
polecat
porcupine
porpoise
possum
potto
prairie dog
proboscis monkey
puma
rabbit
raccoon
rat
reindeer
rhesus monkey
rhinoceros
roe deer
rorqual
sea cow
seal
sea lion

serval
sheep
shrew
skunk
sloth
sperm whale
spider monkey
springbok
squirrel
stoat
tamarin
tapir
tarsier
Tasmanian devil
tiger
vampire bat
vervet monkey
vole
wallaby
walrus
wapiti
warthog
waterbuck
water buffalo
weasel
whale
wildcat
wildebeest
wolf
wolverine
wombat
woodchuck
yak
zebra

Reptiles and amphibians

adder
alligator
anaconda
asp
axolotl
basilisk
boa constrictor
bullfrog
caiman
cane toad

chameleon
cobra
constrictor
crocodile
frog
galliwasp
gecko
gharial
Gila monster
grass snake

iguana
Komodo dragon
leatherback
lizard
loggerhead turtle
mamba
moloch
monitor lizard

natterjack toad
newt
puff adder
python
rattlesnake
rinkhals
salamander
sidewinder
skink
slow-worm

snake
taipan
terrapin
toad
tortoise
turtle
viper

Shellfish and other crustaceans and molluscs

abalone
argonaut
auger shell
barnacle
clam
cockle
conch

cowrie
crab
crawfish
crayfish
cuttlefish
hermit crab
krill

langoustine
limpet
lobster
mitre
murex
mussel
nautilus

nerite
octopus
ormer
oyster
paua
periwinkle
piddock

prawn
quahog
razor shell
sandhopper
scallop
sea slug
slug

shrimp	spider crab	teredo	wentletrap	winkle
snail	squid	triton	whelk	woodlouse

Male and female animals

antelope: *buck, doe*
badger: *boar, sow*
bear: *boar, sow*
bird: *cock, hen*
buffalo: *bull, cow*
cat: *tom, queen*
cattle: *bull, cow*
chicken: *cock, hen*
deer: *stag, doe*
dog: *dog, bitch*
donkey: *jackass, jenny*
duck: *drake, duck*

elephant: *bull, cow*
ferret: *hob, gill*
fish: *cock, hen*
fox: *dog, vixen*
goat: *billy goat, nanny goat*
goose: *gander, goose*
hare: *buck, doe*
horse: *stallion, mare*
kangaroo: *buck, doe*
leopard: *leopard, leopardess*

lion: *lion, lioness*
otter: *dog, bitch*
pheasant: *cock, hen*
pig: *boar, sow*
rabbit: *buck, doe*
seal: *bull, cow*
sheep: *ram, ewe*
swan: *cob, pen*
tiger: *tiger, tigress*
whale: *bull, cow*
wolf: *dog, bitch*
zebra: *stallion, mare*

Young animals

calf (*antelope, buffalo, camel, cattle, elephant, elk, giraffe, rhinoceros, seal, whale*)
chick (*chicken, hawk, pheasant*)
colt (*male horse*)
cub (*badger, bear, fox, leopard, lion, tiger, walrus, wolf*)
cygnet (*swan*)
duckling (*duck*)
eaglet (*eagle*)

elver (*eel*)
eyas (*hawk*)
fawn (*caribou, deer*)
filly (*female horse*)
foal (*horse, zebra*)
fry (*fish*)
gosling (*goose*)
joey (*kangaroo, wallaby, possum*)
kid (*goat, roe deer*)
kit (*beaver, ferret, fox, mink, weasel*)

kitten (*cat, cougar, rabbit, skunk*)
lamb (*sheep*)
leveret (*hare*)
owlet (*owl*)
parr (*salmon*)
piglet (*pig*)
pup (*dog, rat, seal, wolf*)
puppy (*coyote, dog*)
smolt (*salmon*)
squab (*pigeon*)
tadpole (*frog, toad*)
whelp (*dog, wolf*)

Collective names for animals

shrewdness of **apes**
herd/pace of **asses**
troop of **baboons**
cete of **badgers**
sloth of **bears**
swarm/drift/hive/erst of **bees**
flock/flight/pod of **birds**
herd/gang/obstinacy of **buffalo**
bellowing of **bullfinches**
drove of **bullocks**
army of **caterpillars**
clowder/glaring of **cats**
herd/drove of **cattle**
brood/clutch/peep of **chickens**
chattering of **choughs**
rag/rake of **colts**
covert of **coots**
herd of **cranes**
bask of **crocodiles**
murder of **crows**
litter of **cubs**

herd of **curlew**
herd/mob of **deer**
pack/kennel of **dogs**
school of **dolphins**
trip of **dotterel** (type of plover)
flight/dole/piteousness of **doves**
paddling of **ducks** (on water)
safe of **ducks** (on land)
fling of **dunlins**
herd/parade of **elephants**
herd/gang of **elk**
busyness of **ferrets**
charm of **finches**
shoal/run of **fish**
swarm/cloud of **flies**
skulk of **foxes**
gaggle of **geese** (on land)
skein/team/wedge of **geese** (in flight)
herd of **giraffes**
cloud of **gnats**
flock/herd/trip of **goats**

band of **gorillas**
pack/covey of **grouse**
down/mute/husk of **hares**
cast of **hawks**
siege of **herons**
bloat of **hippopotami**
drove/string/stud/team of **horses**
pack/cry/kennel of **hounds**
flight/swarm of **insects**
fluther/smack of **jellyfish**
mob/troop of **kangaroos**
kindle/litter of **kittens**
desert of **lapwings**
bevy/exaltation of **larks**
leap/lepe of **leopards**
pride/sawt of **lions**
tiding of **magpies**
sord/suit of **mallard**
stud of **mares**
richesse of **martens**
labour of **moles**
troop of **monkeys**

Wordfinder

span/barren of **mules**
watch of **nightingales**
parliament/stare of **owls**
yoke of **oxen**
pandemonium of **parrots**
covey of **partridges**
muster of **peacocks**
muster/parcel/rookery of **penguins**
bevy/head of **pheasants**
kit of **pigeons** (in flight)
litter/herd of **pigs**
congregation/stand/wing of **plovers**
rush/flight of **pochards**
pod/school/herd/turmoil of **porpoises**
covey of **ptarmigan**
litter of **pups**
bevy/drift of **quail**
bury of **rabbits**

string of **racehorses**
unkindness of **ravens**
crash of **rhinoceros**
bevy of **roe deer**
parliament/building/rookery of **rooks**
pod/herd/rookery of **seals**
flock/herd/trip/mob of **sheep**
dopping of **sheldrake**
wisp/walk of **snipe**
host of **sparrows**
murmuration of **starlings**
flight of **swallows**
game/herd of **swans** (on land)
wedge of **swans** (in flight)
drift/herd/sounder of **swine**
spring of **teal**

knot of **toads**
hover of **trout**
rafter of **turkeys**
bale/turn of **turtles**
bunch/knob of **waterfowl**
school/herd/pod/gam of **whales**
company/trip of **wigeon**
sounder of **wild boar**
dout/destruction of **wild cats**
team of **wild ducks** (in flight)
bunch/trip/plump/knob of **wildfowl**
pack/rout of **wolves**
fall of **woodcock**
descent of **woodpeckers**
herd of **wrens**
zeal of **zebras**

Many of these are fanciful or humorous terms which probably never had any real currency but have been popularized in books such as *Sports and Pastimes of England* (1801) by Joseph Strutt.

Plants

Flowering plants

acacia
acanthus
aconite
African violet
agapanthus
aloe
alstroemeria
alyssum
amaranth
amaryllis
anemone
aquilegia
arrowgrass
arum lily
asphodel
aspidistra
aster
astilbe
aubretia
avens
azalea
balsam
banksia
bedstraw
begonia
belladonna

bellflower
bergamot
betony
bilberry
bindweed
bird's-foot trefoil
blackthorn
bluebell
boneset
borage
bougainvillea
bramble
broom
bryony
buddleia
bugloss
bulrush
burdock
burnet
busy Lizzie
buttercup
cactus
calceolaria
calendula
camellia

camomile
campanula
campion
candytuft
Canterbury bell
carnation
catmint
ceanothus
celandine
chickweed
chicory
Chinese lantern
chives
choisya
chokeberry
Christmas cactus
Christmas rose
chrysanthemum
cicely
cinquefoil
clematis
clove pink
clover

cockscomb
coltsfoot
columbine
comfrey
convolvulus
coreopsis
cornflower
corydalis
cotoneaster
cottonweed
cow parsley
cowslip
cranesbill
crocus
cuckoo pint
cyclamen
daffodil
dahlia
daisy
damask rose
dandelion
daphne
deadly nightshade
delphinium
dianthus

dill
dittany
dock
dog rose
duckweed
echinacea
edelweiss
eglantine
elder
evening primrose
eyebright
feverfew
figwort
firethorn
flax
forget-me-not
forsythia
foxglove
frangipani
freesia
fritillary
fuchsia
furze
gardenia
gentian

geranium
gerbera
gladiolus
gloxinia
golden rod
gorse
grape hyacinth
groundsel
guelder rose
gypsophila
harebell
hawkweed
hawthorn
heartsease
heather
hebe
helianthemum
helianthus
heliotrope
hellebore
hemlock
heuchera
hibiscus
hogweed
holly
hollyhock
honesty
honeysuckle
hosta
hyacinth
hydrangea
iris
jacaranda
japonica
jasmine
jonquil
kingcup
knapweed
knotgrass

laburnum
lady's mantle
lady's tresses
larkspur
lavatera
lavender
lemon balm
lilac
lily
lily of the valley
lobelia
London pride
loosestrife
lords and ladies
lotus
lovage
love-in-a-mist
love-lies-
  bleeding
lungwort
lupin
madonna lily
magnolia
mahonia
mallow
mandrake
marguerite
marigold
marshwort
may
mayflower
meadow rue
meadow
  saffron
meadowsweet
Michaelmas
  daisy
milfoil
mimosa

mint
mistletoe
mock orange
montbretia
morning glory
musk rose
myrtle
narcissus
nasturtium
nettle
nicotiana
nigella
night-scented
  stock
nightshade
old man's
  beard
oleander
orchid
ox-eye daisy
oxlip
pansy
Parma violet
parsley
pasque flower
passion flower
pelargonium
pennyroyal
penstemon
peony
peppermint
periwinkle
petunia
phlox
pimpernel
pink
pitcher plant
plantain
plumbago

poinsettia
polyanthus
poppy
potentilla
prickly pear
primrose
primula
privet
pulsatilla
pyracantha
pyrethrum
ragwort
ramsons
red-hot poker
rhododendron
rock rose
rose
rosebay
  willowherb
rose of Sharon
safflower
St John's wort
salvia
samphire
saxifrage
scabious
scarlet
  pimpernel
scilla
sedum
shamrock
skimmia
snapdragon
snowdrop
soapwort
sorrel
speedwell
spikenard
spiraea

spurge
spurrey
squill
starwort
stock
stonecrop
streptocarpus
sunflower
sweet pea
sweet william
tansy
teasel
thistle
thrift
toadflax
tradescantia
trefoil
tulip
valerian
Venus flytrap
verbena
veronica
vervain
vetch
viburnum
violet
viper's bugloss
wallflower
water lily
willowherb
wintergreen
wisteria
witch hazel
wolfsbane
woodruff
wormwood
yarrow
yucca
zinnia

Trees and shrubs

acacia
acer
alder
almond
apple
apricot
araucaria
ash
aspen
azalea
balsa
bamboo
banksia
banyan
baobab
basswood
bay tree
beech

beefwood
bergamot
birch
blackthorn
bottlebrush
bottle tree
bo tree
box
box elder
bristlecone
  pine
broom
buckeye
buckthorn
butternut
cacao
calabash
camellia

candleberry
candlenut
carambola
carob
cassava
cassia
casuarina
cedar
cherimoya
cherry
chestnut
cinnamon
citron
coco de mer
coconut palm
cola
coolibah
copper beech

cork oak
coromandel
cottonwood
crab apple
cypress
dogwood
dragon tree
ebony
elder
elm
eucalyptus
euonymus
ficus
fig
filbert
fir
firethorn
flame tree

frangipani
gean
ginkgo
gorse
grapefruit
greengage
guava
gum tree
hawthorn
hazel
hickory
holly
holm oak
honeysuckle
hornbeam
horse chestnut
hydrangea
ilex

iroko
ironbark
ironwood
jacaranda
jackfruit
jack pine
japonica
jasmine
juniper
kalmia
kapok
kermes oak
laburnum
larch
laurel
lemon
Leyland cypress
leylandii
lilac
lime
linden
lodgepole pine
logwood

macadamia
magnolia
mahogany
maidenhair
  tree
mango
mangosteen
mangrove
maple
mastic
may
mimosa
mirabelle
monkey puzzle
mountain ash
mulberry
mulga
myrtle
nutmeg
nux vomica
oak
oleaster
olive

osier
pagoda tree
palm
papaya
paperbark
pawpaw
pear
persimmon
pine
pistachio
pitch pine
plane
plum
pomegranate
pomelo
poplar
privet
pussy willow
quassia
quince
rambutan
red cedar
redwood

rhododendron
robinia
rosewood
rowan
rubber plant
rubber tree
sallow
sandalwood
sapele
sapodilla
sassafras
satinwood
senna
sequoia
service tree
silver birch
Sitka cypress
slippery elm
smoke tree
soapberry
spindle
spruce
star anise

stinkwood
storax
sumac
sycamore
tamarind
tamarisk
tea
teak
tea tree
thuja
tulip tree
tulipwood
umbrella tree
viburnum
walnut
weeping
  willow
wellingtonia
whitebeam
willow
witch hazel
wych elm
yew

Food and drink

Bread

bagel
baguette
bannock
bap
bloomer
bridge roll
brioche
bun

chapatti
ciabatta
cob
cornbread
cottage loaf
crumpet
farl
flatbread

focaccia
French stick
fruit loaf
granary bread
  (trademark)
hoagie
malt loaf
matzo

muffin
nan/naan
paratha
pikelet
pitta
pone
poppadom
pumpernickel

puri
rye
soda bread
sourdough

Cakes, biscuits, and desserts

angel cake
apfelstrudel
baba
baked Alaska
Bakewell tart
baklava
banana split
banoffi/
  banoffee pie
Bath bun
Battenberg
beignet
biscotti
Black Forest
  gateau
blancmange
bombe

bourbon
brack
brandy snap
bread pudding
bread-and-
  butter
  pudding
Brown Betty
brownie
bun
butterfly cake
cabinet
  pudding
cassata
charlotte
charlotte russe
cheesecake

clafoutis
cobbler
compote
cookie
cream cracker
cream puff
crème brûlée
crème caramel
crêpe
crêpe Suzette
crispbread
crumble
crumpet
cupcake
custard cream
custard pie
custard tart

Danish pastry
devil's food
  cake
digestive
doughnut
drop scone
dumpling
Dundee cake
Eccles cake
eclair
egg custard
Eve's pudding
fairy cake
fancy
flapjack
Florentine
flummery

fool
fortune cookie
frangipane
garibaldi
gateau
Genoa cake
gingerbread
ginger nut
ginger snap
granita
halwa
hot cross bun
ice cream
jelly
junket
Knickerbocker
  Glory

kulfi
lady's finger
langue de chat
lardy cake
macaroon
Madeira cake
madeleine
marble cake
meringue
milk pudding
millefeuille
mince pie
Mississippi
 mud pie
mousse
muffin
oatcake

pancake
panettone
panforte
panna cotta
parfait
parkin
pavlova
peach Melba
petit four
plum duff
plum pudding
popover
pound cake
profiterole
queen of
 puddings
ratafia

rice pudding
rock cake
roly-poly
rusk
Sachertorte
sago pudding
Sally Lunn
sandwich
savarin
scone
seed cake
shortbread
shortcake
simnel cake
sorbet
soufflé
sponge

spotted dick
stollen
strudel
summer
 pudding
sundae
Swiss roll
syllabub
tart
tarte Tatin
tartlet
tartufo
tipsy cake
tiramisu
torte
treacle tart
trifle

turnover
tutti-frutti
upside-down
 cake
Victoria sponge
waffle
water biscuit
water ice
whip
yogurt
yule log
zabaglione

Cheeses

asiago
Bel Paese
 (trademark)
blue vinny
Boursin
 (trademark)
Brie
Caerphilly
Camembert
Chaumes
Cheddar
Cheshire

chèvre
cottage cheese
cream cheese
Danish blue
Derby
Dolcelatte
 (trademark)
Double
 Gloucester
Edam
Emmental
feta

fontina
Gloucester
Gorgonzola
Gouda
Gruyère
halloumi
havarti
Jarlsberg
 (trademark)
Lancashire
Leicester
Limburger

Manchego
mascarpone
Monterey Jack
mozzarella
paneer/panir
Parmesan
Parmigiano
 Reggiano
pecorino
Port Salut
provolone
Red Leicester

ricotta
Romano
Roquefort
 (trademark)
sage Derby
scamorza
Stilton
 (trademark)
taleggio
Tilsit
Wensleydale

Fruit and nuts

almond
apple
apricot
avocado
banana
betel nut
bilberry
blackberry
blackcurrant
blueberry
boysenberry
Brazil nut
breadfruit
butternut
cantaloupe
Cape
 gooseberry
carambola
cashew
cherimoya
cherry
chestnut

Chinese
 gooseberry
citron
clementine
cloudberry
cobnut
coconut
cola nut
cowberry
crab apple
cranberry
currant
damson
date
elderberry
fig
filbert
galia melon
gooseberry
gourd
grape
grapefruit

greengage
groundnut
guava
hazelnut
honeydew
 melon
huckleberry
jackfruit
jujube
kiwi fruit
kumquat
lemon
lime
loganberry
loquat
lychee
macadamia
mandarin
mango
medlar
melon
monkey nut

mulberry
nectarine
olive
orange
ortanique
papaya
passion fruit
pawpaw
peach
peanut
pear
pecan
persimmon
pineapple
pine nut
pistachio
plum
pomegranate
pomelo
prickly pear
pumpkin
quince

rambutan
raspberry
redcurrant
salmonberry
sapodilla
satsuma
serviceberry
sharon fruit
sloe
star anise
starfruit
strawberry
tamarillo
tangerine
tayberry
tiger nut
Ugli fruit
 (trademark)
walnut
watermelon
whortleberry

Meat

bacon	gammon	mince	pâté	sweetbreads
beef	goose	mutton	pork	tripe
brawn	ham	offal	prosciutto	turkey
chicken	haslet	oxtail	rabbit	veal
duck	lamb	ox tongue	sausage	venison
game	luncheon meat	Parma ham	steak	

Pasta

agnolotti	farfalle	noodles	ravioli	tortelli
angel hair	fettuccine	orecchiette	rigatoni	tortellini
cannelloni	fusilli	orzo	spaghetti	tortelloni
capellini	lasagne	pappardelle	spaghettini	vermicelli
conchiglie	linguine	penne	tagliatelle	ziti
ditalini	macaroni	radiatori	tagliolini	

Vegetables

aduki/adzuki bean	cannellini bean	garlic	mushroom	soybean
alfalfa	capsicum	gherkin	okra	spinach
artichoke	carrot	globe artichoke	onion	spring greens
asparagus	cassava	gourd	pak choi	spring onion
aubergine	cauliflower	haricot bean	parsnip	squash
bamboo shoots	celeriac	iceberg lettuce	pea	string bean
bean	celery	Jerusalem artichoke	pepper	sugar pea
beet	chard	kale	petits pois	sugar snap pea
beetroot	chervil	kidney bean	pimiento	swede
black bean	chickpea	kohlrabi	pinto bean	sweetcorn
black-eyed bean	chicory	lamb's lettuce	plantain	sweet pepper
borlotti bean	Chinese leaves	leek	potato	sweet potato
breadfruit	corn on the cob	lentil	pumpkin	tomato
broad bean	cos lettuce	lettuce	radicchio	turnip
broccoli	courgette	lima bean	radish	vegetable spaghetti
Brussels sprout	cress	lollo rosso	rocket	water chestnut
butter bean	cucumber	mache	romaine	watercress
butternut squash	eggplant	mangetout	runner bean	waxpod
cabbage	endive	marrow	salsify	yam
calabrese	fennel	marrowfat pea	samphire	zucchini
	flageolet	mooli	savoy cabbage	
	French bean	mung bean	shallot	
			snow pea	

Alcoholic drinks

absinthe	burgundy	fino	Madeira	ouzo
advocaat	Calvados	genever	malmsey	pale ale
alcopop	cassis	gin	malt whisky	perry
ale	cava	ginger wine	manzanilla	Pils
amaretto	champagne	grappa	maraschino	Pilsner/Pilsener
amontillado	chartreuse	hock	Marsala	port
aquavit	cherry brandy	ice beer	mead	porter
Armagnac	cider	Irish coffee	mescal	poteen
barley wine	claret	Irish whiskey	mild	raki
beer	cocktail	kirsch	milk stout	ratafia
bitter	cognac	kümmel	moscato	retsina
bock	crème de menthe	kvass	muscat	rum
bourbon		lager	muscatel	rye
brandy	curaçao	liqueur	oloroso	sack

sake	scrumpy	slivovitz	tequila	whiskey/
sambuca	Sekt	sloe gin	triple sec	whisky
sangria	shandy	spritzer	vermouth	wine
schnapps	sherry	spumante	vinho verde	
Scotch whisky	single malt	stout	vodka	

Non-alcoholic drinks

barley water	cola	latte	root beer
bitter lemon	cordial	lemonade	sarsaparilla
buttermilk	cream soda	limeade	seltzer
cafè au lait	dandelion and	malted milk	sherbet
caffè latte	burdock	maté	smoothie
caffè macchiato	espresso	milkshake	soda water
camomile tea	filter coffee	mineral water	squash
cappuccino	ginger ale	mint tea	St Clements
cherryade	ginger beer	mocha	tea
citron pressé	green tea	mochaccino	tisane
club soda (trademark)	horchata	orangeade	tonic water
cocoa	hot chocolate	prairie oyster	yerba maté
coffee	lassi	pressé	

Clothing

Clothes

anorak	burnous	djellaba	jerkin	muff
apron	bustier	dolman	jersey	muffler
ballgown	cagoule	donkey jacket	jilbab	muumuu
bandanna	camisole	doublet	jodhpurs	neckerchief
bandeau	camiknickers	drainpipes	jumper	nightdress
basque	cape	dress	jumpsuit	nightshirt
bell-bottoms	capri pants	dressing gown	kaftan	oilskins
belt	cardigan	dress shirt	kagoul	overalls
Bermuda	cargo pants	duffel coat	kameez	overcoat
shorts	carpenter	dungarees	kilt	Oxford bags
bib	trousers	fichu	kimono	palazzo pants
bikini	catsuit	flares	knickers	pantaloons
blazer	chador	fleece	knickerbockers	panties
bloomers	chemise	flying jacket	lederhosen	pants
blouse	cheongsam	foulard	leggings	pantyhose
blouson	chinos	frock coat	leg warmers	parka
boa	churidars	gilet	leotard	pashmina
bodice	coat	glove	loincloth	pedal pushers
body	combat	gown	lumberjacket	peignoir
body stocking	trousers	greatcoat	mac	pencil skirt
bolero	corset	guernsey	mackintosh/	peplum
bolo tie	cravat	gymslip	macintosh	petticoat
bomber jacket	crew neck	hipsters	maillot	pinafore
bow tie	crinoline	hoody/hoodie	mantilla	pinafore dress
boxer shorts	crop top	hose	mantle	plus fours
bra	culottes	hot pants	maxi	polo neck
braces	cummerbund	housecoat	mini	polo shirt
breeches	dhoti	hula skirt	miniskirt	poncho
burka/burkha/	dinner jacket	jacket	mitten	pullover
burqa	dirndl	jeans	morning coat	pyjamas

raincoat
redingote
reefer jacket
robe
ruff
safari jacket
sailor suit
salopettes
sari
sarong
sash
scarf
serape/sarape
shalwar
shawl

sheepskin
shell suit
shift
shirt
shirtwaister
shorts
shrug
skinny-rib
ski pants
skirt
slacks
slip
smock
smoking jacket
sock

stirrup pants
stock
stocking
stole
suit
sundress
suspenders
sweater
sweatpants
sweatshirt
swimsuit
T-shirt
tabard
tailcoat
tails

tank top
tee
thong
tie
tights
tippet
toga
top
topcoat
tracksuit
trench coat
trews
trousers
trouser suit
trunks

tunic
turtleneck
tutu
tux/tuxedo
twinset
ulster
underpants
underskirt
veil
vest
V-neck
waistcoat
windcheater
wrap
yashmak

Footwear

beetle-crusher
boot
bootee
brogue
Chelsea boot
clog
court shoe
cowboy boot
Cuban heel
deck shoe

desert boot
Dr Martens
   (trademark)
espadrille
flip-flop
galosh
gumboot
high top
hobnail boot
jackboot

jelly shoe
kitten heel
lace-up
loafer
moccasin
moon boot
mukluk
mule
overshoe
Oxford

patten
peep-toe
platform
plimsoll
pump
sabot
sandal
shoe
slingback
slip-on

slipper
sneaker
stiletto
trainer
wader
wedge
wellington
   boot
winkle-picker

Headgear

balaclava
balmoral
bandeau
baseball cap
beanie
bearskin
beret
biretta
boater
bonnet
bowler
busby
cap
chaplet

circlet
cloche
coif
coronet
cowl
crown
deerstalker
derby
diadem
Dolly Varden
fedora
fez
garland
glengarry

headband
headscarf
helmet
hijab
homburg
hood
Juliet cap
keffiyeh
kepi
mantilla
mitre
mob cap
mortar board
panama

pillbox hat
pork-pie hat
skullcap
slouch hat
snood
sola topi
sombrero
sou'wester
Stetson
   (trademark)
stovepipe hat
tam-o'-shanter
tarboosh
ten-gallon hat

tiara
top hat
topi
topper
toque
tricorne
trilby
turban
veil
wimple

Useful words for games and puzzles

In many word games, it's handy to know some very short words or words with unusual spellings, especially those which are not in everyday use. Proper names and abbreviations which are not pronounced as they are spelled (such as *Dr* or *Mr*) are not included, as most word games don't allow them.

Two-letter words

aa rough cindery lava

ab an abdominal muscle

ad an advertisement

ag S. African expressing various emotions, e.g. irritation, grief, or pleasure

ah expressing surprise, sympathy, pleasure, etc.

ai the three-toed sloth

am the present tense of be

an a form of the indefinite article

as used to convey relative extent or degree

at expressing location or time

aw expressing mild protest, entreaty, etc.

ax dialect form of ask

ay variant spelling of aye

ba (in Egyptian mythology) the soul

be to exist

bi bisexual

bo a kind of fig tree

by beside

da a person's father

DJ a disc jockey

do to perform an action

dy a type of sediment

ee dialect form of oh

eh seeking explanation or agreement

El an elevated railway or section of railway

em a measuring unit in printing

en a measuring unit in printing

er expressing doubt or hesitation

ex a former spouse or partner

fa a musical note

Ga a member of a people living in Ghana

GI a soldier in the US army

go to move or travel

ha expressing surprise, triumph, etc.

he a male person or animal previously mentioned

hi used as a greeting

ho expressing surprise, triumph, etc.

id a part of the mind

if introducing a conditional clause

in within

io a North American moth

is the present tense of be

it a thing previously mentioned

ja (S. African) yes

jo (Scottish, old use): a sweetheart

Ju a kind of Chinese pottery

ka (in Egyptian mythology) the spirit

ki a plant of the lily family

KO a knockout in boxing match

la a musical note

li a Chinese unit of distance

lo (old use) used to draw attention to something

ma a person's mother

MD (Brit.) a managing director

me the objective case of I

mi a musical note

mo a moment

MP a Member of Parliament

mu the 12th letter of the Greek alphabet

my belonging to me

no not any

nu the 13th letter of the Greek alphabet

ob a type of gene

od a power once thought to pervade the natural world

of belonging to

og (Australian, old use) a shilling

oh expressing surprise, anger, disappointment, etc.

oi used to attract attention

OJ orange juice

OK used to express assent, agreement, etc.

om a mystic syllable which constitutes a sacred mantra

on supported by or covering

op an operation

or used to link alternatives

os a bone

ou a Hawaiian bird

ow expressing pain

ox a cow or bull

oy = oi

Oz Australia

pa a person's father

pi the 16th letter of the Greek alphabet

po a chamber pot

qi (in Chinese philosophy) the life force

ra (in Norway and Sweden) a moraine

re a musical note

ri a Japanese unit of length

se a Chinese musical instrument

si = te

so therefore

ta thank you

te a musical note

ti = te

TV television

uh expressing hesitation

um expressing

hesitation

up towards a higher position

us the objective case of we

Wa a member of a people living on the borders of China and Burma

we oneself and other people

Wu a dialect of Chinese

xi the 14th letter of Greek alphabet

xu a Vietnamese unit of money

ye (old use) the plural form of **thou**

Yi a people living in parts of China

yo used as a greeting

yu an ancient Chinese wine container

Three-letter words containing x or z

axe a tool for chopping wood etc.

biz business

box a container

coz (old use) a cousin

cox the person who steers a rowing boat

dux (Scottish) the top pupil in a school or class

dzo a crossbreed of a cow and a yak

fax an electronic copy of a document

fez a type of hat

fix to attach something

fox an animal with a bushy tail

hex (N. Amer.) to cast a spell on someone

lax not strict or careful enough

lox (N. Amer.) smoked salmon

lux a unit for measuring illumination

max maximum

Mex Mexican

mix to blend or combine

nix nothing

pax a call for a truce

pix pictures

pox a disease

pyx the container which holds the consecrated bread used in Holy Communion

Rex the reigning king

sax a saxophone

saz a musical instrument

sex being male or female

six one more than five

tax money paid to the government

tux a tuxedo

Uzi a type of sub-machine gun

vex to annoy

vox vocals; voice

wax substance used to make candles etc.

wiz = whizz

zag a sharp change of direction

zap to destroy

zed the letter Z

zee (N. Amer.) the letter Z

Zen a type of Buddhism

zig a sharp change of direction

zip a fastener

zit a spot

zol (S. African) a hand-rolled cigarette

zoo a place where wild animals are kept

Words with a q not followed by a u

burqa = burka, a garment worn by Muslim women

fiqh the theory or philosophy of Islamic law

Iraqi a person from Iraq; relating to Iraq

niqab a Muslim woman's veil

qadi a Muslim judge

qanat an irrigation tunnel

qasida an Arabic or Persian poem

qawwal a qawwali singer

Wordfinder

qawwali Muslim devotional music

qi (in Chinese philosophy) the life force

qibla the direction towards Mecca

qigong a Chinese system of physical exercises

qin a Chinese musical instrument

qintar a monetary unit of Albania

qiviut wool from the musk ox

qwerty the standard layout of typewriters and keyboards

tariqa the Sufi method of spiritual learning

Words beginning with x

xanthan a polysaccharide

xanthate a chemical compound

xanthene a chemical compound

xanthic yellowish

xanthin a yellow colouring matter

xanthine a biochemical compound

xanthoma a yellow patch on the skin

xebec a sailing ship

xeme a fork-tailed gull

xenia gifts to a guest or guests

xenial relating to hospitality

xenon a gaseous chemical element

xeric very dry

xeroma abnormal dryness of a body part

xerophyte a plant needing very little water

xerox to photocopy

Xhosa a South African people or their language

xi the 14th letter of the Greek alphabet

Xiang a dialect of Chinese

xiphoid sword-shaped

Xmas Christmas

xoanon a wooden image of a god

xography a photographic process

xu a Vietnamese unit of money

xylan a compound found in wood

xylary of or relating to xylem

xylem plant tissue

xylene a liquid hydrocarbon

xylite a volatile liquid

xylitol a chemical substance

xylol = xylene

xylose a plant sugar

xyrid a sedge-like herb

xyster a surgical instrument

xyston an ancient Greek spear

xystus an ancient Greek portico

Wordfinder

Countries of the world

Country	Capital	Currency unit
Afghanistan	Kabul	afghani = 100 puls
Albania	Tirana	lek = 100 quintars
Algeria	Algiers	dinar = 100 centimes
Andorra	Andorra la Vella	euro = 100 cents
Angola	Luanda	kwanza = 100 lwei
Antigua and Barbuda	St John's	dollar = 100 cents
Argentina	Buenos Aires	peso = 100 centavos
Armenia	Yerevan	dram = 100 luma
Australia	Canberra	dollar = 100 cents
Austria	Vienna	euro = 100 cents
Azerbaijan	Baku	manat = 100 gopik
Bahamas	Nassau	dollar = 100 cents
Bahrain	Manama	dinar = 1,000 fils
Bangladesh	Dhaka	taka = 100 poisha
Barbados	Bridgetown	dollar = 100 cents
Belarus	Minsk	Belarusian rouble
Belgium	Brussels	euro = 100 cents
Belize	Belmopan	dollar = 100 cents
Benin	Porto Novo	franc = 100 centimes
Bhutan	Thimphu	ngultrum = 100 chetrum, Indian rupee
Bolivia	La Paz	boliviano = 100 centavos
Bosnia-Herzegovina	Sarajevo	dinar = 100 paras
Botswana	Gaborone	pula = 100 thebe
Brazil	Brasilia	real = 100 centavos
Brunei	Bandar Seri Begawan	dollar = 100 sen
Bulgaria	Sofia	lev = 100 stotinki
Burkina Faso	Ouagadougou	franc = 100 centimes
Burma (Myanmar)	Pyinmana	kyat = 100 pyas
Burundi	Bujumbura	franc = 100 centimes
Cambodia	Phnom Penh	riel = 100 sen
Cameroon	Yaoundé	franc = 100 centimes
Canada	Ottawa	dollar = 100 cents
Cape Verde Islands	Praia	escudo = 100 centavos
Central African Republic	Bangui	franc = 100 centimes
Chad	N'Djamena	franc = 100 centimes
Chile	Santiago	peso = 100 centavos
China	Beijing	yuan = 10 jiao or 100 fen
Colombia	Bogotá	peso = 100 centavos
Comoros	Moroni	franc = 100 centimes
Congo	Brazzaville	franc = 100 centimes
Congo, Democratic Republic of (Zaire)	Kinshasa	franc = 100 centimes
Costa Rica	San José	colón = 100 centimos
Croatia	Zagreb	kuna = 100 lipa
Cuba	Havana	peso = 100 centavos
Cyprus	Nicosia	pound = 100 cents
Czech Republic	Prague	koruna = 100 halers

Country	Capital	Currency unit
Denmark	Copenhagen	krone = 100 øre
Djibouti	Djibouti	franc = 100 centimes
Dominica	Roseau	dollar = 100 cents
Dominican Republic	Santo Domingo	peso = 100 centavos
Ecuador	Quito	sucre = 100 centavos
Egypt	Cairo	pound = 100 piastres or 1,000 milliemes
El Salvador	San Salvador	colón = 100 centavos
Equatorial Guinea	Malabo	franc = 100 centimes
Eritrea	Asmara	nakfa; Ethiopian birr
Estonia	Tallinn	kroon = 100 sents
Ethiopia	Addis Ababa	birr = 100 cents
Fiji	Suva	dollar = 100 cents
Finland	Helsinki	euro = 100 cents
France	Paris	euro = 100 cents
Gabon	Libreville	franc = 100 centimes
Gambia	Banjul	dalasi = 100 butut
Georgia	Tbilisi	lari = 100 tetri
Germany	Berlin	euro = 100 cents
Ghana	Accra	cedi = 100 pesewas
Greece	Athens	euro = 100 cents
Grenada	St George's	dollar = 100 cents
Guatemala	Guatemala City	quetzal = 100 centavos
Guinea	Conakry	franc = 100 centimes
Guinea-Bissau	Bissau	peso = 100 centavos
Guyana	Georgetown	dollar = 100 cents
Haiti	Port-au-Prince	gourde = 100 centimes
Holland (see Netherlands)		
Honduras	Tegucigalpa	lempira = 100 centavos
Hungary	Budapest	forint = 100 filler
Iceland	Reykjavik	krona = 100 aurar
India	New Delhi	rupee = 100 paisa
Indonesia	Djakarta	rupiah = 100 sen
Iran	Tehran	rial = 100 dinars
Iraq	Baghdad	dinar = 1,000 fils
Ireland, Republic of	Dublin	euro = 100 cents
Israel	Jerusalem	shekel = 100 agora
Italy	Rome	euro = 100 cents
Ivory Coast	Yamoussoukro	franc = 100 centimes
Jamaica	Kingston	dollar = 100 cents
Japan	Tokyo	yen = 100 sen
Jordan	Amman	dinar = 1,000 fils
Kazakhstan	Astana	tenge = 100 teins
Kenya	Nairobi	shilling = 100 cents
Kiribati	Bairiki	Australian dollar
Kuwait	Kuwait City	dinar = 1,000 fils
Kyrgyzstan	Bishkek	som = 100 tiyin
Laos	Vientiane	kip = 100 ats
Latvia	Riga	lat = 100 santims
Lebanon	Beirut	pound = 100 piastres
Lesotho	Maseru	loti = 100 lisente
Liberia	Monrovia	dollar = 100 cents

Wordfinder

Country	Capital	Currency unit
Libya	Tripoli	dinar = 1,000 dirhams
Liechtenstein	Vaduz	franc = 100 centimes
Lithuania	Vilnius	litas = 100 centas
Luxembourg	Luxembourg	euro = 100 cents
Macedonia	Skopje	denar = 100 deni
Madagascar	Antananarivo	franc = 100 centimes
Malawi	Lilongwe	kwacha = 100 tambala
Malaysia	Kuala Lumpur	ringgit = 100 sen
Maldives	Male	rufiyaa = 100 laris
Mali	Bamako	franc = 100 centimes
Malta	Valletta	lira = 100 cents
Marshall Islands	Majuro	US dollar
Mauritania	Nouakchott	ouguiya = 5 khoums
Mauritius	Port Louis	rupee = 100 cents
Mexico	Mexico City	peso = 100 centavos
Micronesia	Kolonia	US dollar
Moldova	Chisinau	leu = 100 bani
Monaco	–	euro = 100 cents
Mongolia	Ulan Bator	tugrik = 100 mongos
Montenegro	Podgorica	euro = 100 cents
Morocco	Rabat	dirham = 100 centimes
Mozambique	Maputo	metical = 100 centavos
Myanmar (see Burma)		
Namibia	Windhoek	dollar = 100 cents
Nauru	–	Australian dollar
Nepal	Kathmandu	rupee = 100 paisa
Netherlands	Amsterdam	euro = 100 cents
New Zealand	Wellington	dollar = 100 cents
Nicaragua	Managua	cordoba = 100 centavos
Niger	Niamey	franc = 100 centimes
Nigeria	Abuja	naira = 100 kobo
North Korea	Pyongyang	won = 100 jun
Norway	Oslo	krone = 100 øre
Oman	Muscat	rial = 1,000 baiza
Pakistan	Islamabad	rupee = 100 paisa
Panama	Panama City	balboa = 100 centésimos
Papua New Guinea	Port Moresby	kina = 100 toea
Paraguay	Asunción	guarani = 100 centimos
Peru	Lima	sol = 100 cents
Philippines	Manila	peso = 100 centavos
Poland	Warsaw	zloty = 100 groszy
Portugal	Lisbon	euro = 100 cents
Qatar	Doha	riyal = 100 dirhams
Romania	Bucharest	leu = 100 bani
Russia	Moscow	rouble = 100 copecks
Rwanda	Kigali	franc = 100 centimes
St Kitts and Nevis	Basseterre	dollar = 100 cents
St Lucia	Castries	dollar = 100 cents
St Vincent and the Grenadines	Kingstown	dollar = 100 cents
Samoa	Apia	tala = 100 sene
San Marino	San Marino	euro = 100 cents

Wordfinder

Country	Capital	Currency unit
São Tomé and Principe	São Tomé	dobra = 100 centavos
Saudi Arabia	Riyadh	riyal = 20 qursh or 100 halalas
Senegal	Dakar	franc = 100 centimes
Serbia	Belgrade	dinar = 100 paras
Seychelles	Victoria	rupee = 100 cents
Sierra Leone	Freetown	leone = 100 cents
Singapore	Singapore City	dollar = 100 cents
Slovakia	Bratislava	koruna = 100 haliers
Slovenia	Ljubljana	tolar = 100 stotins
Solomon Islands	Honiara	dollar = 100 cents
Somalia	Mogadishu	shilling = 100 cents
South Africa	Pretoria	rand = 100 cents
South Korea	Seoul	won = 100 jeon
Spain	Madrid	euro = 100 cents
Sri Lanka	Colombo	rupee = 100 cents
Sudan	Khartoum	dinar = 10 pounds
Suriname	Paramaribo	guilder = 100 cents
Swaziland	Mbabane	lilangeni = 100 cents
Sweden	Stockholm	krona = 100 öre
Switzerland	Berne	franc = 100 centimes
Syria	Damascus	pound = 100 piastres
Taiwan	Taipei	New Taiwan dollar = 100 cents
Tajikistan	Dushanbe	somoni = 100 dirams
Tanzania	Dodoma	shilling = 100 cents
Thailand	Bangkok	baht = 100 satangs
Togo	Lomé	franc = 100 centimes
Tonga	Nuku'alofa	pa'anga = 100 seniti
Trinidad and Tobago	Port-of-Spain	dollar = 100 cents
Tunisia	Tunis	dinar = 1,000 milliemes
Turkey	Ankara	lira = 100 kurus
Turkmenistan	Ashgabat	manat = 100 tenesi
Tuvalu	Funafuti	dollar = 100 cents
Uganda	Kampala	shilling = 100 cents
Ukraine	Kiev	hryvna = 100 kopiykas
United Arab Emirates	Abu Dhabi	dirham = 100 fils
United Kingdom	London	pound = 100 pence
United States	Washington DC	dollar = 100 cents
Uruguay	Montevideo	peso = 100 centésimos
Uzbekistan	Tashkent	som = 100 tiyin
Vanuatu	Vila	vatu = 100 centimes
Vatican City	–	euro = 100 cents
Venezuela	Caracas	bolivar = 100 centimos
Vietnam	Hanoi	dong = 100 xu
Yemen	Sana'a	riyal = 100 fils
Zambia	Lusaka	kwacha = 100 ngwee
Zimbabwe	Harare	dollar = 100 cents

Wordfinder

Chemical elements and symbols

actinium	Ac	gold	Au	praseodymium	Pr
aluminium	Al	hafnium	Hf	promethium	Pm
americium	Am	hassium	Hs	protactinium	Pa
antimony	Sb	helium	He	radium	Ra
argon	Ar	holmium	Ho	radon	Rn
arsenic	As	hydrogen	H	rhenium	Re
astatine	At	indium	In	rhodium	Rh
barium	Ba	iodine	I	roentgenium	Rg
berkelium	Bk	iridium	Ir	rubidium	Rb
beryllium	Be	iron	Fe	ruthenium	Ru
bismuth	Bi	krypton	Kr	rutherfordium	Rf
bohrium	Bh	lanthanum	La	samarium	Sm
boron	B	lawrencium	Lr	scandium	Sc
bromine	Br	lead	Pb	seaborgium	Sg
cadmium	Cd	lithium	Li	selenium	Se
caesium	Cs	lutetium	Lu	silicon	Si
calcium	Ca	magnesium	Mg	silver	Ag
californium	Cf	manganese	Mn	sodium	Na
carbon	C	meitnerium	Mt	strontium	Sr
cerium	Ce	mendelevium	Md	sulphur	S
chlorine	Cl	mercury	Hg	tantalum	Ta
chromium	Cr	molybdenum	Mo	technetium	Tc
cobalt	Co	neodymium	Nd	tellurium	Te
copper	Cu	neon	Ne	terbium	Tb
curium	Cm	neptunium	Np	thallium	Tl
darmstadtium	Ds	nickel	Ni	thorium	Th
dubnium	Db	niobium	Nb	thulium	Tm
dysprosium	Dy	nitrogen	N	tin	Sn
einsteinium	Es	nobelium	Nb	titanium	Ti
erbium	Er	osmium	Os	tungsten	W
europium	Eu	oxygen	O	uranium	U
fermium	Fm	palladium	Pd	vanadium	V
fluorine	F	phosphorus	P	xenon	Xe
francium	Fr	platinum	Pt	ytterbium	Yb
gadolinium	Gd	plutonium	Pu	yttrium	Y
gallium	Ga	polonium	Po	zinc	Zn
germanium	Ge	potassium	K	zirconium	Zr

Mm

M (or **m**) n. the Roman numeral for 1,000.
• abbrev. **1** (**m**) metres. **2** (**m**) miles. **3** (**m**) millions. **4** motorway.
MA abbrev. Master of Arts.
ma'am n. madam.
mac n. Brit. informal a mackintosh.
macabre adj. disturbing because concerned with death or injury.
macadam n. broken stone used in surfacing roads.
macadamia n. the nut of an Australian tree.
macaroni n. narrow tubes of pasta.
macaroon n. a biscuit made with almonds.
macaw n. a parrot of Central and South America.
mace n. **1** a ceremonial staff carried by a mayor etc. **2** a spice made from nutmeg husks.
macerate v. soften food by soaking.
■ **maceration** n.
Mach /mak/ n. (Mach 1, Mach 2, etc.) the speed of sound, twice the speed of sound, etc.
machete /muh-**shet**-i/ n. a broad, heavy knife.
Machiavellian /ma-ki-uh-**vel**-i-uhn/ adj. cunning and underhand.
machinations pl. n. plots and scheming.
machine n. **1** a mechanical device for performing a particular task. **2** an efficient group of influential people.
▷ SYNONYMS: **1** device, appliance, apparatus, engine, gadget, mechanism, tool, instrument, contraption. **2** *an efficient publicity machine:* organization, system, structure, machinery; informal set-up.
• v. make or work on with a machine.
□ **machine gun** an automatic gun firing bullets in rapid succession.
machine-readable in a form that a computer can process.
machinery n. **1** machines, or the parts of a machine. **2** a system or structure.

▷ SYNONYMS: **1** equipment, apparatus, plant, hardware, gear, gadgetry, technology. **2** *the machinery of local government:* workings, organization, system, structure; informal set-up.
machinist n. a person who operates a machine.
machismo /muh-**kiz**-moh/ n. aggressive male pride.
macho /**ma**-choh/ adj. aggressively masculine.
▷ SYNONYMS: manly, male, masculine, virile, red-blooded; informal butch, laddish.
mackerel n. (pl. mackerel) an edible sea fish.
mackintosh (or macintosh) n. Brit. a waterproof coat.
macramé /muh-**krah**-may/ n. the craft of knotting cord in patterns.
macrobiotic adj. (of diet) consisting of organic unprocessed foods.
macrocosm n. the whole of a complex structure.
mad adj. (madder, maddest) **1** insane. **2** very foolish. **3** frantic. **4** informal very enthusiastic. **5** informal angry.
▷ SYNONYMS: **1** insane, crazy, out of your mind, deranged, demented, crazed, lunatic, unbalanced, unhinged, psychotic, non compos mentis; informal mental, off your head, round the bend, nuts, nutty, off your rocker, bonkers, loony, loopy, batty, cuckoo; Brit. informal barmy, crackers, barking, potty, round the twist. **2** *a mad scheme:* foolish, insane, stupid, lunatic, idiotic, foolhardy, absurd, ludicrous, silly, asinine, wild, crack-brained, senseless, preposterous; informal crazy, crackpot; Brit. informal daft. **3** *a mad dash to get ready:* frenzied, frantic, frenetic, feverish, hysterical, wild, hectic, manic. **4** *he's mad about jazz:* passionate, fanatical, ardent, fervent, devoted; infatuated; informal crazy, dotty, nuts, wild, hooked; Brit. informal potty. **5** angry,

furious, infuriated, enraged, fuming, incensed, beside yourself; informal livid, spare; N. Amer. informal sore.
– ANTONYMS: sane, sensible.
□ **mad cow disease** BSE.
■ **madly** adv.

madam n. a polite form of address for a woman.

Madame /muh-**dam**/ n. (pl. **Mesdames**) a title for a French woman.

madcap adj. reckless.

madden v. make very angry.
▷ SYNONYMS: **infuriate**, exasperate, irritate, incense, anger, enrage, provoke, inflame, antagonize; informal aggravate, make someone see red, make someone's blood boil.
– ANTONYMS: calm.

madder n. a red dye.

made past & past part. of **MAKE**.

Madeira n. a strong sweet wine from Madeira.
□ **Madeira cake** Brit. a rich sponge cake.

Mademoiselle /ma-duh-mwah-**zel**/ n. (pl. **Mesdemoiselles**) a title for an unmarried French woman.

madman (or **madwoman**) n. (pl. **madmen** or **madwomen**) **1** a person who is mentally ill. **2** a foolish or reckless person.
▷ SYNONYMS: **lunatic**, maniac, psychopath; informal loony, nut, nutcase, head case, psycho; Brit. informal nutter; N. Amer. informal screwball.

madness n. **1** insanity. **2** very foolish behaviour. **3** a state of chaotic activity.
▷ SYNONYMS: **1 insanity**, mental illness, dementia, derangement, lunacy, mania, psychosis. **2 folly**, foolishness, idiocy, stupidity, foolhardiness. **3 bedlam**, mayhem, chaos, pandemonium, uproar, turmoil.
– ANTONYMS: sanity.

Madonna n. (**the Madonna**) the Virgin Mary.

madrigal n. a song for several unaccompanied voices.

maelstrom /**mayl**-struhm/ n. **1** a confused situation. **2** a powerful whirlpool.

maestro /**my**-stroh/ n. (pl. **maestros**) a famous and talented man, esp. a classical musician.

Mafia n. **1** an international criminal organization originating in Sicily. **2** (**mafia**) a powerful, secretly influential group.

magazine n. **1** a periodical containing articles and pictures. **2** a chamber holding cartridges in a gun. **3** a store for arms or ammunition.
▷ SYNONYMS: **journal**, periodical, supplement, fanzine; informal glossy, mag.

magenta n. a purplish crimson.

maggot n. a larva of a fly or other insect.

Magi /**may**-jI/ pl. n. the three wise men from the East who brought gifts to the infant Jesus.

magic n. **1** the supposed use of mysterious or supernatural powers to influence events. **2** conjuring tricks. **3** a mysterious or wonderful quality.
▷ SYNONYMS: **1 sorcery**, witchcraft, wizardry, necromancy, enchantment, the supernatural, occultism, the occult, black magic, the black arts, voodoo, hoodoo. **2 conjuring tricks**, sleight of hand, legerdemain, illusion; formal prestidigitation. **3 allure**, excitement, fascination, charm, glamour.
• adj. having supernatural powers.

magical adj. **1** relating to magic. **2** very pleasant or enjoyable.
▷ SYNONYMS: **1 supernatural**, magic, mystical, other-worldly. **2 enchanting**, entrancing, spellbinding, bewitching, fascinating, captivating, alluring, enthralling, charming, lovely, delightful, beautiful, amazing; informal heavenly, gorgeous.
■ **magically** adv.

magician n. **1** a person with magic powers. **2** a conjuror.
▷ SYNONYMS: **1 sorcerer**, sorceress, witch, wizard, warlock, enchanter, enchantress, necromancer; formal thaumaturge. **2 conjuror**, illusionist; formal prestidigitator.

magisterial adj. **1** authoritative. **2** of a magistrate.

magistrate n. an official authorized to judge minor cases and hold preliminary hearings.
■ **magistracy** n.

magma n. molten rock under the earth's crust.

magnanimous adj. generous or forgiving.
▷ SYNONYMS: **generous**, charitable, benevolent, beneficent, big-hearted, open-handed, munificent, philanthropic, noble, unselfish, altruistic.
– ANTONYMS: mean.
■ **magnanimity** n.

magnate n. a wealthy and influential businessman or businesswoman.

magnesium n. a metallic element which burns with a bright white flame.

magnet n. **1** a piece of iron that attracts objects containing iron and points north and south when suspended. **2** a powerful attraction.
■ **magnetize** (or **-ise**) v.

magnetic adj. **1** having the property of a magnet. **2** very attractive.
▷ SYNONYMS: **attractive**, irresistible, seductive, charismatic, hypnotic, alluring, fascinating, captivating.
□ **magnetic pole** each of the points near the geographical North and South Poles, which the needle of a compass points to. **magnetic tape** tape used in recording sound, pictures, or computer data.
■ **magnetically** adv.

magnetism n. **1** the property displayed by magnets of attracting or repelling metal objects. **2** the ability to attract and charm people.

magneto /mag-nee-toh/ n. (pl. **magnetos**) a small electric generator using a magnet.

magnificent adj. **1** very attractive and impressive. **2** very good.
▷ SYNONYMS: **1 splendid**, spectacular, impressive, striking, glorious, superb, majestic, awe-inspiring, breathtaking, sublime, resplendent, sumptuous, grand, imposing, monumental, palatial, opulent, luxurious, lavish, rich, dazzling, beautiful. **2 excellent**, outstanding, marvellous, brilliant, wonderful, virtuoso, fine, superb.
– ANTONYMS: uninspiring, ordinary.
■ **magnificence** n. **magnificently** adv.

magnify v. (**magnifying**, **magnified**) **1** make something appear larger than it is with a lens or microscope. **2** make larger or stronger. **3** old use praise.
▷ SYNONYMS: **enlarge**, increase, augment, extend, expand, boost, enhance, maximize, amplify, intensify; informal blow up.
– ANTONYMS: reduce, minimize.
■ **magnification** n.

magnitude n. **1** great size or importance. **2** size.
▷ SYNONYMS: **1 size**, extent, immensity, vastness, hugeness, enormity. **2 importance**, import, significance, consequence.

magnolia n. a tree with large white or pink flowers.

magnum n. (pl. **magnums**) a wine bottle of twice the standard size.

magnum opus /mag-nuhm oh-puhss/ n. the most important work of art etc. that a person has produced.

magpie n. a black and white bird with a long tail.

maharaja (or **maharajah**) n. hist. an Indian prince.

mah-jong (or **mah-jongg**) n. a Chinese game played with small rectangular tiles.

mahogany n. hard reddish-brown wood.

mahout /muh-howt/ n. (in South and SE Asia) an elephant driver or keeper.

maid n. **1** a female servant. **2** old use a girl or young woman.

maiden n. old use a girl or young woman, esp. a virgin.
• adj. **1** first of its kind. **2** (of an older woman) unmarried.
□ **maiden name** the surname of a married woman before her marriage. **maiden over** an over in cricket in which no runs are scored.

mail n. **1** letters etc. sent by post. **2** email. **3** hist. armour made of linked metal rings.
▷ SYNONYMS: **post**, letters, correspondence, email.
• v. send by post or email.
▷ SYNONYMS: **send**, post, dispatch, forward, ship, email.
□ **mail order** the buying or selling of goods by post. **mailshot** Brit. a piece of advertising material sent to many people.

maim v. inflict a permanent injury on.
▷ SYNONYMS: **injure**, wound, incapacitate, mutilate, disfigure, mangle.

main adj. greatest or most important.
▷ SYNONYMS: **principal**, chief, head, leading, foremost, most important, major, dominant, central, focal, key, prime, primary, first, fundamental, predominant, pre-eminent, paramount.
– ANTONYMS: subsidiary, minor.
• n. a chief water or gas pipe or electricity cable.
□ **in the main** on the whole.
mainframe a large computer. **mainland** the main area of land of a country, not including islands. **mainspring** the most important part. **mainstay** a thing on which something depends or is based. **mainstream** the ideas, attitudes, etc. shared by most people.

mainly adv. mostly; chiefly.
▷ SYNONYMS: **mostly**, for the most part, in the main, on the whole, largely, by and large, to a large extent, predominantly, chiefly, principally, primarily.

maintain v. **1** cause to continue in the same state. **2** regularly check and repair. **3** support financially. **4** assert.
▷ SYNONYMS: **1 preserve**, conserve,

m

keep, retain, keep going, prolong, perpetuate, sustain, carry on, continue. **2 look after**, service, care for, take care of, support, provide for, keep. **3 insist**, declare, assert, protest, affirm, profess, avow, claim, contend, argue; formal aver.
– ANTONYMS: discontinue.

maintenance n. **1** the action of maintaining. **2** Brit. financial support given to a former husband or wife after divorce.
▷ SYNONYMS: **1 preservation**, conservation, prolongation, continuation. **2 servicing**, service, repair, running repairs, care. **3 support**, upkeep, alimony, allowance.

maisonette n. a flat on two storeys of a larger building.

maître d'hôtel /may-truh doh-**tel**/ n. (pl. **maîtres d'hôtel**) a head waiter.

maize n. Brit. a cereal plant whose large grains are eaten as a vegetable.

majestic adj. impressively grand or beautiful.
▷ SYNONYMS: **stately**, dignified, distinguished, magnificent, grand, splendid, glorious, impressive, regal, noble, awe-inspiring, monumental, palatial, imposing.
– ANTONYMS: modest.
■ **majestically** adv.

majesty n. (pl. **majesties**) **1** impressive beauty or grandeur. **2** (**His**, **Your**, etc. **Majesty**) a title given to a king or queen or their wife or widow.
▷ SYNONYMS: **stateliness**, dignity, magnificence, pomp, grandeur, splendour, glory, impressiveness, nobility.

major adj. **1** important or serious. **2** main. **3** Music (of a scale) having intervals of a semitone between the 3rd and 4th, and 7th and 8th notes.
▷ SYNONYMS: **1 greatest**, best, finest, most important, chief, main, prime, principal, leading, foremost, outstanding, pre-eminent. **2 crucial**, vital, important, big, significant, considerable, weighty, serious, key, utmost, great, paramount, prime.
– ANTONYMS: minor, trivial.
• n. the army rank above captain.
• v. (**major in**) US specialize in a subject at college.
□ **major general** the army rank above brigadier.

majority n. (pl. **majorities**) **1** the greater number. **2** Brit. the number of votes by which one party or candidate in an election defeats the opposition. **3** the age when a person is legally an adult.

▷ SYNONYMS: **1 most**, bulk, mass, best part, lion's share, main body, preponderance, predominance. **2 coming of age**, age of consent, adulthood, seniority.
– ANTONYMS: minority.

make v. (**making**, **made**) **1** form by combining parts. **2** cause. **3** force to do. **4** add up to. **5** be suitable as. **6** estimate as or decide on. **7** earn money. **8** arrive at or achieve.
▷ SYNONYMS: **1 construct**, build, erect, assemble, put together, manufacture, produce, fabricate, create, form, forge, fashion, model, improvise. **2 cause**, create, bring about, produce, generate, give rise to, effect. **3 force**, compel, coerce, press, drive, dragoon, pressurize, oblige, require; informal railroad, steamroller. **4** they made him chairman: **appoint**, designate, name, nominate, select, elect, vote in. **5** he's made a lot of money: **acquire**, obtain, gain, get, secure, win, earn. **6** he made the tea: **prepare**, concoct, cook, whip up, brew; informal fix.
– ANTONYMS: destroy.
• n. a brand of goods.
▷ SYNONYMS: **brand**, marque, label, type, sort, kind, variety.
□ **make do** manage with something unsatisfactory. **make for** move towards. **make it** be successful. **make off** leave hurriedly. **make off with** steal. **make out 1** manage to see, hear, or understand. **2** claim or pretend. **makeover** an improvement of the appearance of a person, house, etc. **make up 1** put together from parts or ingredients. **2** invent. **3** be reconciled after a quarrel. **4** apply cosmetics to. **make up for** compensate.
■ **maker** n.

make-believe n. a state of fantasy or pretence.
▷ SYNONYMS: **fantasy**, pretence, daydreaming, invention, fabrication, charade, play-acting, masquerade.
• adj. pretend.
▷ SYNONYMS: **imaginary**, imagined, made-up, fanciful, fictitious; informal pretend.
– ANTONYMS: real, actual.

makeshift adj. temporary and improvised.
▷ SYNONYMS: **temporary**, provisional, stopgap, standby, rough and ready, improvised, ad hoc.

make-up n. **1** cosmetics. **2** the composition of something.
▷ SYNONYMS: **1 cosmetics**, greasepaint; informal warpaint, slap. **2 composition**,

m

constitution, structure, configuration, arrangement. **3** *jealousy isn't part of his make-up*: **character**, nature, temperament, personality, mentality, persona.

malachite n. a green mineral.

maladjusted adj. unable to cope with normal social situations.

▷ SYNONYMS: **disturbed**, unstable, neurotic, dysfunctional; informal mixed up, screwed up.

maladministration n. bad or corrupt management of an organization.

maladroit adj. clumsy.

malady n. (pl. **maladies**) an illness.

malaise n. a feeling of unease, illness, or low spirits.

malapropism n. the mistaken use of a word in place of a similar-sounding one.

malaria n. a disease which causes recurrent fever, transmitted by some mosquitoes.
■ malarial adj.

Malay n. **1** a member of a people inhabiting Malaysia and Indonesia. **2** the language of the Malays.

malcontent n. a dissatisfied and rebellious person.

male adj. **1** of the sex that can fertilize or inseminate the female. **2** (of a plant or flower) having stamens but not a pistil. **3** (of a fitting) for insertion into a corresponding part.

▷ SYNONYMS: **masculine**, manly, virile, macho.

– ANTONYMS: female.
• n. a male person, animal, or plant.

malediction n. a curse.

malefactor n. a wrongdoer.

malevolent /muh-lev-uh-luhnt/ adj. wishing harm to others.
■ malevolence n.

malformation n. the state of being abnormally shaped.
■ malformed adj.

malfunction v. fail to function normally.

▷ SYNONYMS: **break down**, fail, stop working, crash, go down; informal conk out, go kaput; Brit. informal play up, pack up.
• n. such a failure.

malice n. the desire to harm someone.

▷ SYNONYMS: **spite**, malevolence, ill will, vindictiveness, vengefulness, malignity, animus, enmity, rancour.

– ANTONYMS: benevolence.

malicious adj. meaning or meant to cause harm or distress.

▷ SYNONYMS: **spiteful**, malevolent, vindictive, vengeful, malign, nasty, hurtful, cruel, catty, venomous, poisonous, barbed; informal bitchy.

– ANTONYMS: benevolent.
■ maliciously adv.

malign /muh-lyn/ adj. harmful or evil.
• v. say unpleasant things about.

malignant adj. **1** (of a tumour) cancerous. **2** harmful; malevolent.
■ malignancy n.

malinger v. pretend to be ill to avoid work.
■ malingerer n.

mall /mawl/ n. **1** a large enclosed shopping area. **2** a sheltered walk.

mallard n. a kind of wild duck.

malleable adj. **1** able to be hammered or pressed into shape. **2** easily influenced.
■ malleability n.

mallet n. **1** a hammer with a large wooden head. **2** a wooden stick with a head, used in croquet or polo.

mallow n. a plant with pink or purple flowers.

malnutrition n. poor health caused by not having enough food, or not enough of the right food.
■ malnourished adj.

malodorous adj. smelling very unpleasant.

malpractice n. illegal or corrupt professional behaviour.

malt n. **1** barley or other grain soaked in water then dried. **2** whisky made with malt.

maltreat v. treat cruelly.

▷ SYNONYMS: **ill-treat**, mistreat, abuse, ill-use, mishandle, misuse, persecute, harm, hurt, injure.
■ maltreatment n.

mamba n. a poisonous African snake.

mammal n. a warm-blooded animal that produces milk and bears live young.
■ mammalian adj.

mammary adj. of the breasts.

mammography n. the use of X-rays to detect tumours in the breasts.

Mammon n. wealth regarded as being worshipped like a god.

mammoth n. a large extinct elephant.
• adj. huge.

man n. (pl. **men**) **1** an adult human male. **2** a person. **3** human beings.

▷ SYNONYMS: **1 male**, gentleman, fellow, youth; informal guy, gent, geezer; Brit. informal bloke, chap, lad; N. Amer. informal dude, hombre. **2 human being**, human, person, mortal, individual,

m

soul. **3 the human race,** Homo sapiens, humankind, humanity, human beings, humans, people, mankind.

• v. (**manning, manned**) provide a place etc. with people to work in or defend it.

▷ SYNONYMS: **1 staff,** crew, occupy. **2** operate, work, use.

□ **manhandle** move forcibly or roughly. **manhole** a covered opening giving access to a sewer etc. **manhood 1** the state or period of being a man. **2** strength, courage, etc. **mankind** human beings as a whole. **manpower** the number of people available for work. **manservant** a male servant. **manslaughter** the crime of killing a person without meaning to do so.

■ **mannish** adj.

WORD LINKS
male, masculine, virile relating to men

---

manacle n. a shackle for the wrists or ankles.

• v. restrict with manacles.

manage v. **1** be in charge of. **2** succeed in doing. **3** be able to cope. **4** control the use of money or resources.

▷ SYNONYMS: **1 be in charge of,** run, head, direct, control, preside over, lead, govern, rule, command, supervise, oversee, administer; informal head up. **2 accomplish,** achieve, carry out, perform, undertake, deal with, cope with, get through. **3 cope,** get along/on, make do, survive, get by, muddle through/along, make ends meet; informal make out, hack it.

manageable adj. able to be managed without difficulty.

▷ SYNONYMS: **1** a manageable task: **achievable,** doable, practicable, feasible, reasonable, attainable, viable. **2** a manageable child: **compliant,** tractable, pliant, biddable, docile, amenable, accommodating, acquiescent.

management n. **1** the act of managing. **2** the managers of an organization.

▷ SYNONYMS: **1 administration,** running, managing, organization, direction, leadership, control, governance, rule, command, supervision, guidance, operation. **2 managers,** employers, directors, board, directorate, executive, administration; informal bosses, top brass.

– ANTONYMS: employees.

manager n. (fem. **manageress**) a person who manages staff, an organization, etc.

▷ SYNONYMS: **executive,** head, supervisor, principal, director, superintendent, foreman, forewoman, overseer, organizer, administrator; informal boss, chief, governor; Brit. informal gaffer, guv'nor, honcho.

■ **managerial** adj.

manatee n. a large sea mammal.

mandarin n. **1** a small citrus fruit. **2** (**Mandarin**) the official form of the Chinese language. **3** a powerful official.

mandate n. an official order or authority to do something.

▷ SYNONYMS: **1 authority,** approval, ratification, endorsement, sanction, authorization. **2 instruction,** directive, decree, command, order, injunction.

• v. give authority to do something.

mandatory adj. compulsory.

▷ SYNONYMS: **obligatory,** compulsory, binding, required, requisite, necessary.

– ANTONYMS: optional.

mandible n. a jaw or jaw-like part.

mandolin n. a musical instrument like a lute.

mandrake n. a plant with a forked fleshy root.

mandrel n. a shaft holding work in a lathe.

mane n. a growth of long hair on the neck of a horse or lion.

maneuver US = MANOEUVRE.

manful adj. brave or determined.

■ **manfully** adv.

manganese n. a hard metallic element.

mange n. a skin disease in some animals.

■ **mangy** adj.

manger n. a long trough from which horses etc. feed.

mangetout /monzh-too/ n. Brit. a variety of pea eaten with the pod.

mangle v. destroy or severely damage.

• n. Brit. a machine with rollers for wringing out wet laundry.

mango n. (pl. **mangoes** or **mangos**) a tropical fruit.

mangrove n. a tropical tree growing in swamps.

mania n. **1** mental illness involving periods of wild excitement. **2** an extreme enthusiasm.

▷ SYNONYMS: **obsession,** compulsion, fixation, fetish, fascination, preoccupation, passion, enthusiasm, desire, urge, craving, craze, fad, rage; informal thing.

maniac n. **1** a person who behaves

very wildly or violently. **2** informal a person with an extreme enthusiasm.
▷ SYNONYMS: **lunatic**, madman, madwoman, psychopath; informal loony, nutcase, nut, head case, headbanger, psycho; Brit. informal nutter; N. Amer. informal screwball.
■ **maniacal** adj.

manic adj. **1** of or affected by mania. **2** showing wild excitement or energy.
■ **manically** adv.

manicure n. a cosmetic treatment of the hands and nails.
• v. give a manicure to.
■ **manicurist** n.

manifest adj. clear and obvious.
▷ SYNONYMS: **obvious**, clear, plain, apparent, evident, patent, distinct, definite, blatant, overt, glaring, transparent, conspicuous, undisguised.
• v. **1** show or display. **2** become noticeable.
▷ SYNONYMS: **display**, show, exhibit, demonstrate, betray, present, reveal; formal evince.
– ANTONYMS: hide.
• n. a list of the cargo, crew, or passengers of a ship or aircraft.
■ **manifestly** adv.

manifestation n. evidence or a sign of something.
▷ SYNONYMS: **sign**, indication, evidence, symptom, testimony, proof, mark, reflection, demonstration, example, instance.

manifesto n. (pl. **manifestos**) a public declaration of policy.

manifold adj. many and various.
• n. a pipe with several openings, esp. in an engine.

manikin n. a very small person.

Manila n. strong brown paper.

manipulate v. **1** handle skilfully. **2** control or influence in a clever or underhand way.
▷ SYNONYMS: **1 operate**, work, handle, turn, pull, push, twist, slide. **2 control**, influence, use to your advantage, exploit, twist.
■ **manipulation** n. **manipulative** adj. **manipulator** n.

manly adj. (**manlier**, **manliest**) **1** brave or strong. **2** suitable for a man.
▷ SYNONYMS: **virile**, masculine, strong, all-male, red-blooded, muscular, muscly, strapping, well built, rugged, tough, powerful, brawny; informal hunky.
– ANTONYMS: effeminate.
■ **manliness** n.

man-made adj. made or caused by human beings.

▷ SYNONYMS: **artificial**, synthetic, manufactured, imitation, ersatz, simulated, mock, fake, faux.
– ANTONYMS: natural, real.

manna n. something unexpected and welcome.

mannequin n. a dummy used to display clothes in a shop.

manner n. **1** a way in which something is done or happens. **2** a person's behaviour towards others. **3** (**manners**) polite behaviour. **4** a kind or sort.
▷ SYNONYMS: **1 way**, fashion, mode, means, method, methodology, system, style, approach, technique, procedure, process. **2** her unfriendly manner: **behaviour**, attitude, demeanour, air, aspect, mien, bearing, conduct. **3** (**manners**) social graces, politeness, Ps and Qs, etiquette, protocol, decorum, propriety, civility.

mannered adj. **1** behaving in a specified way. **2** artificial and affected.

mannerism n. a distinctive gesture or way of speaking.
▷ SYNONYMS: **idiosyncrasy**, quirk, oddity, foible, trait, peculiarity, habit, characteristic.

manoeuvre /muh-**noo**-ver/ (US **maneuver**) n. **1** a skilful or careful movement. **2** a well-planned scheme. **3** (**manoeuvres**) a large-scale military exercise.
▷ SYNONYMS: **1 operation**, exercise, move, movement, action. **2 stratagem**, tactic, gambit, ploy, trick, dodge, ruse, scheme, device, plot, machination, artifice, subterfuge, intrigue.
• v. **1** move with skill or care. **2** cleverly manipulate to achieve an aim.
▷ SYNONYMS: **1 steer**, guide, drive, negotiate, jockey, navigate, pilot, direct, move, work. **2 manipulate**, contrive, manage, engineer, fix, organize, arrange, orchestrate, choreograph, stage-manage; informal wangle, pull strings.
■ **manoeuvrable** adj.

manor n. a large country house with lands.
■ **manorial** adj.

manqué /mong-**kay**/ adj. having never become what you might have been: an actor manqué.

manse n. a house provided for a minister of certain Christian Churches.

mansion n. a large, impressive house.

m

▷ SYNONYMS: **country house**, stately home, hall, manor house; informal pile.
– ANTONYMS: hovel.

mantelpiece (or **mantelshelf**) n. the shelf above a fireplace.

mantilla n. a lace scarf worn by Spanish women over the hair and shoulders.

mantis n. (pl. **mantis** or **mantises**) a large insect that waits motionless for its prey.

mantle n. **1** a loose cloak. **2** a cover or covering. **3** a role passed on to another person. **4** the region of very hot, dense rock between the earth's crust and its core.

mantra n. a word or sound repeated to aid concentration when meditating.

manual adj. **1** operated by the hands. **2** working with the hands.
▷ SYNONYMS: **physical**, labouring, blue-collar.
• n. a book giving instructions.
▷ SYNONYMS: **handbook**, instructions, guide, companion, ABC, guidebook, vade mecum; informal bible.
■ **manually** adv.

manufacture v. **1** make on a large scale with machinery. **2** invent a story.
▷ SYNONYMS: **1 make**, produce, mass-produce, build, construct, assemble, put together, turn out, process.
2 make up, invent, fabricate, concoct, hatch, dream up, think up, contrive; informal cook up.
• n. the process of manufacturing.
▷ SYNONYMS: **production**, making, manufacturing, mass production, construction, building, assembly.
■ **manufacturer** n.

manure n. animal dung used as fertilizer.

manuscript n. **1** a handwritten book etc. **2** an author's written or typed work before printing.

Manx adj. of the Isle of Man.

many pron. & adj. a large number of.
▷ SYNONYMS: *she received many gifts:*
numerous, a lot of, plenty of, count-less, innumerable, scores of, untold, copious, abundant; informal lots of, umpteen, loads of, masses of, stacks of, heaps of, oodles of, a slew of; literary myriad.
– ANTONYMS: few.
• n. the majority of people.

Maori /mow-ri/ n. (pl. **Maori** or **Maoris**) a member of the aboriginal people of New Zealand.

map n. a diagram of an area showing physical features, cities, roads, etc.

▷ SYNONYMS: **plan**, chart, A to Z, atlas.
• v. (**mapping, mapped**) **1** make a map of. **2** (**map out**) plan in detail.
▷ SYNONYMS: **chart**, plot, draw, record.

> **WORD LINKS**
> **cartography** map-drawing

maple n. a tree with five-pointed leaves.

mar v. (**marring, marred**) spoil the appearance or quality of.
▷ SYNONYMS: **spoil**, impair, detract from, disfigure, blemish, scar, deface, ruin, damage, wreck, taint, tarnish.
– ANTONYMS: enhance.

maraca n. a container filled with small beans etc., shaken as a musical instrument.

marathon n. **1** a long-distance running race. **2** a long, difficult task.

maraud v. go around stealing things or attacking people.
■ **marauder** n.

marble n. **1** a hard stone, usu. white with coloured streaks, which is polished and used in sculpture and building. **2** a small ball of coloured glass used as a toy.
■ **marbled** adj.

March n. the third month.

march v. **1** walk in time and with regular paces. **2** walk or force to walk quickly. **3** walk in an organized procession to make a protest.
▷ SYNONYMS: **1 stride**, walk, troop, step, pace, tread, slog, tramp, hike, trudge, parade, file. **2 stalk**, strut, flounce, storm, stomp, sweep.
• n. **1** an act of marching. **2** a piece of music written to accompany marching. **3** (**Marches**) border regions.
▷ SYNONYMS: **1 walk**, trek, slog, route march, hike. **2 parade**, procession, cortège, demonstration; informal demo.
■ **marcher** n.

marchioness /mar-shuh-ness/ n.
1 the wife or widow of a marquess.
2 a woman with the rank of marquess.

mare n. the female of a horse or related animal.

margarine n. a butter substitute made from vegetable oils or animal fats.

margin n. **1** an edge or border. **2** the blank border on each side of the print on a page. **3** an amount by which something is won.
▷ SYNONYMS: **1 edge**, side, verge, border, perimeter, brink, brim, rim, fringe, boundary, periphery, extremity.
2 leeway, latitude, scope, room,

space, allowance.

marginal adj. **1** in a margin. **2** of minor importance.
▷ SYNONYMS: **slight**, small, tiny, minute, insignificant, minimal, negligible.
– ANTONYMS: considerable.
■ **marginally** adv.

marginalize (or **-ise**) v. treat as unimportant.

marguerite n. a large daisy.

marigold n. a plant with yellow or orange flowers.

marijuana /ma-ri-**hwah**-nuh/ n. cannabis.

marina n. a harbour for yachts and small boats.

marinade n. a flavoured liquid in which food is soaked before cooking.
• v. marinate.

marinate v. soak in a marinade.

marine adj. of the sea or shipping.
▷ SYNONYMS: **1 seawater**, sea, saltwater, aquatic. **2 maritime**, nautical, naval, seafaring, seagoing, ocean-going.
• n. a soldier trained to serve on land or sea.

mariner n. a sailor.
▷ SYNONYMS: **sailor**, seaman, seafarer; informal matelot, sea dog, old salt; dated tar.

marionette n. a puppet worked by strings.

marital adj. of marriage.
▷ SYNONYMS: **matrimonial**, conjugal, married, wedded, nuptial.

maritime adj. **1** of shipping or other activity taking place at sea. **2** living or found in or near the sea.
▷ SYNONYMS: **naval**, marine, nautical, seafaring, seagoing, sea, ocean-going, oceanic, coastal.

marjoram n. a herb used in cooking.

mark n. **1** a small area on a surface different in colour from the rest. **2** something indicating position. **3** a sign or symbol. **4** a characteristic feature. **5** a point awarded for a correct answer or a piece of work. **6** a particular model of a vehicle or machine. **7** a Deutschmark.
▷ SYNONYMS: **1 blemish**, streak, spot, fleck, blot, stain, smear, speck, smudge, blotch, bruise, scratch, scar, dent, chip, nick; informal splodge. **2 sign**, token, symbol, emblem, badge, indication, characteristic, feature, trait, attribute, quality, hallmark, indicator, symptom, proof. **3 grade**, grading, rating, score, percentage.
• v. **1** make a mark on. **2** write a word or symbol on an object to identify it. **3** indicate the position of. **4** (**mark out**) distinguish. **5** acknowledge an event. **6** give a mark to a piece of work. **7** pay attention to. **8** (in team games) stay close to an opponent to prevent them getting or passing the ball.
▷ SYNONYMS: **1 discolour**, stain, smear, smudge, streak, dirty, scratch, scar, dent; informal splodge. **2 label**, identify, flag, tag, initial, highlight, name, brand. **3 celebrate**, observe, recognize, acknowledge, keep, honour, commemorate, remember, solemnize. **4 represent**, signify, indicate, herald. **5 characterize**, distinguish, identify, typify. **6 assess**, evaluate, appraise, correct; N. Amer. grade.
□ **mark time** fill in time with routine activities. **markup** an amount added to the cost price of goods to cover overheads and profit. **quick off the mark** fast in responding.

marked adj. clearly noticeable.
▷ SYNONYMS: **noticeable**, pronounced, decided, distinct, striking, clear, unmistakable, obvious, conspicuous, notable.
– ANTONYMS: imperceptible.
■ **markedly** adv.

marker n. **1** an object used to indicate a position or route. **2** a broad felt-tip pen.

market n. **1** a place or gathering for the sale of food, livestock, etc. **2** demand for a particular product or service.
▷ SYNONYMS: **shopping centre**, marketplace, bazaar, souk, fair; N. Amer. mart.
• v. (**marketing**, **marketed**) advertise or promote.
▷ SYNONYMS: **sell**, retail, merchandise, trade, advertise, promote.
□ **market garden** a place where produce is grown for sale. **marketplace** the world of commercial activity. **on the market** offered for sale.
■ **marketable** adj.

marking n. **1** an identifying mark. **2** a pattern of marks on an animal.

marksman n. a person skilled in shooting.
■ **marksmanship** n.

marl n. soil consisting of clay and lime.

marlin n. a large fish of warm seas.

marmalade n. a jam made from oranges.

marmoset n. a small tropical American monkey.

maroon n. a dark brownish-red colour.
• v. (**be marooned**) be abandoned

m

alone in a remote place.
▷ SYNONYMS: **strand**, cast away, cast ashore, abandon, desert, leave behind, leave.

marquee n. a large tent for special events.

marquess n. a nobleman ranking above an earl.

marquetry n. inlaid work made from pieces of coloured wood.

marquis n. (in some European countries) a nobleman ranking above a count.

marram grass n. a coarse grass growing on sand.

marriage n. **1** the formal union of a man and a woman as husband and wife. **2** a combination.
▷ SYNONYMS: **1 matrimony**, wedlock, wedding, nuptials, union, match. **2** *a marriage of jazz, pop, and gospel*: **union**, fusion, mixture, mix, blend, amalgamation, combination, hybrid.
– ANTONYMS: divorce, separation.
■ **marriageable** adj.

> **WORD LINKS**
> **marital**, **matrimonial**, **nuptial**, **conjugal** relating to marriage

marrow n. **1** Brit. a long vegetable. **2** a soft fatty substance in the cavities of bones.

marry v. (**marrying**, **married**) **1** become the husband or wife of. **2** join in marriage. **3** join together.
▷ SYNONYMS: **1 get married**, wed, become man and wife; informal tie the knot, walk down the aisle, get spliced, get hitched. **2** *the show marries poetry with art*: **join**, unite, combine, fuse, mix, blend, merge, amalgamate.
– ANTONYMS: divorce, separate.

marsh n. an area of low-lying water-logged land.
▷ SYNONYMS: **swamp**, marshland, bog, morass, mire, quagmire, slough, fen.
■ **marshy** adj.

marshal n. **1** an officer of the highest rank in some armed forces. **2** an official supervising public events. **3** (in the US) a law-enforcement officer.
• v. (**marshalling**, **marshalled**; US **marshaling**, **marshaled**) assemble in an organized way.
▷ SYNONYMS: **assemble**, gather together, collect, muster, call together, draw up, line up, array, organize, group, arrange, deploy, position, summon, round up.

marshmallow n. a spongy sweet made from sugar, egg white, etc.

marsupial n. a mammal whose young are carried and suckled in a pouch.

mart n. a market.

marten n. a weasel-like forest animal.

martial adj. of war.
▷ SYNONYMS: **military**, soldierly, warlike, fighting, militaristic; informal gung-ho.
□ **martial arts** sports which originated as forms of self-defence or attack. **martial law** government by the military forces of a country.

martin n. a small short-tailed swallow.

martinet n. a person who enforces strict discipline.

martyr n. **1** a person who is killed because of their beliefs. **2** a person who exaggerates their difficulties to gain sympathy.
• v. make a martyr of.
■ **martyrdom** n.

marvel v. (**marvelling**, **marvelled**; US **marveling**, **marveled**) feel wonder.
▷ SYNONYMS: **be amazed**, be astonished, be in awe, stand in awe, wonder; informal be gobsmacked.
• n. a cause of wonder.
▷ SYNONYMS: **wonder**, miracle, sensation, spectacle, phenomenon, prodigy.

marvellous (US **marvelous**) adj. very good; wonderful.
▷ SYNONYMS: **excellent**, splendid, wonderful, magnificent, superb, sensational, glorious, sublime, lovely, delightful; informal super, great, amazing, fantastic, terrific, tremen-dous, fabulous, cracking, awesome, divine, ace, wicked; Brit. informal smashing, brilliant.
– ANTONYMS: commonplace, awful.
■ **marvellously** adv.

Marxism n. the political and economic theories of Karl Marx.
■ **Marxist** n. & adj.

marzipan n. a sweet paste made with ground almonds.

mascara n. a cosmetic for darkening the eyelashes.

mascot n. a person or thing supposed to bring good luck.

masculine adj. **1** having qualities associated with men. **2** of men.
▷ SYNONYMS: **1 virile**, macho, manly, male, muscular, muscly, strong, strapping, well built, rugged, robust, brawny, powerful, red-blooded, vigorous; informal hunky, laddish. **2 mannish**, unfeminine, unladylike; informal butch.
– ANTONYMS: feminine, effeminate.
■ **masculinity** n.

mash v. crush or beat to a soft mass.

▷ SYNONYMS: **pulp**, crush, purée, cream, pound, beat.
• n. a soft mass made by mashing.

mask n. a covering worn over the face as a disguise or protection.

▷ SYNONYMS: **pretence**, semblance, veil, screen, front, facade, veneer, disguise, cover, cloak, camouflage.
• v. **1** cover with a mask. **2** conceal or disguise.

▷ SYNONYMS: **hide**, conceal, disguise, cover up, obscure, screen, cloak, camouflage.

masochism n. the enjoyment of your own pain or humiliation.
■ **masochist** n. **masochistic** adj.

mason n. a person who works with stone.

masonry n. the stone parts of a building.

masque /mahsk/ n. hist. a dramatic entertainment with masked actors.

masquerade n. a pretence.
• v. pretend.

mass n. **1** an amount of matter with no definite shape. **2** a large group. **3** (**the masses**) ordinary people. **4** (**masses**) a large amount. **5** the quantity of matter which a body contains. **6** (**Mass**) a Christian service of the Eucharist.

▷ SYNONYMS: **1** *a mass of fallen leaves:* **pile**, heap, accumulation, aggregation, mat, tangle. **2** *a mass of cyclists:* **crowd**, horde, throng, host, troop, army, herd, flock, swarm, mob, pack, flood, multitude. **3** *the mass of the population:* **majority**, most, preponderance, greater part, best/better part, bulk, body.
• adj. done by or affecting large numbers of people or things.

▷ SYNONYMS: *the mass killing of civilians:* **widespread**, general, extensive, large-scale, wholesale, universal, indiscriminate.
• v. gather into a mass.

▷ SYNONYMS: **assemble**, gather together, collect, rally.
□ **mass-produced** produced in large quantities using machinery.

massacre n. a brutal slaughter of many people.

▷ SYNONYMS: **slaughter**, mass murder, mass execution, ethnic cleansing, genocide, holocaust, annihilation, liquidation, extermination, carnage, butchery, bloodbath, bloodletting.
• v. brutally kill many people.

▷ SYNONYMS: **slaughter**, butcher, murder, kill, annihilate, exterminate, execute, liquidate, eliminate, mow down.

massage n. rubbing and kneading of the body to relieve tension or pain.

▷ SYNONYMS: **rub**, rub-down, kneading.
• v. **1** give a massage to. **2** manipulate figures to give a better result.

▷ SYNONYMS: **1 rub**, knead, manipulate, pummel, work. **2 alter**, tamper with, manipulate, doctor, falsify, juggle, fiddle with, tinker with, distort, rig; informal cook, fiddle.

masseur n. (fem. **masseuse**) a person who provides massage professionally.

massif n. a compact group of mountains.

massive adj. large and heavy or solid.

▷ SYNONYMS: **huge**, enormous, vast, immense, mighty, great, colossal, tremendous, gigantic, mammoth, monumental, giant, mountainous; informal monster, whopping, astronomical, mega; Brit. informal whacking, ginormous.
– ANTONYMS: tiny.
■ **massively** adv.

mast n. a tall upright post, esp. one carrying a boat's sail or sails.

mastectomy n. (pl. **mastectomies**) an operation to remove a breast.

master n. **1** a man in a position of authority, control, or ownership. **2** a person skilled in a particular activity. **3** Brit. a male schoolteacher. **4** a holder of a second or further degree. **5** an original recording etc. from which copies are made.

▷ SYNONYMS: **1 lord**, liege, ruler, sovereign, monarch. **2 expert**, genius, maestro, virtuoso, authority; informal ace, wizard, whizz, hotshot, pro; Brit. informal dab hand; N. Amer. informal maven, crackerjack. **3 teacher**, schoolteacher, schoolmaster, tutor, instructor. **4 guru**, teacher, leader, guide, mentor.
• adj. **1** highly skilled. **2** main.

▷ SYNONYMS: **expert**, adept, proficient, skilled, skilful, deft, dexterous, adroit, practised, experienced, masterly, accomplished; informal crack, ace; N. Amer. informal crackerjack.
– ANTONYMS: amateur.
• v. **1** gain complete knowledge or skill in. **2** gain control of.

▷ SYNONYMS: **1** *he'd mastered the technique:* **learn**, become proficient in, pick up, grasp, understand; informal get the hang of. **2 overcome**, conquer, beat, quell, suppress, control, triumph over, subdue, vanquish, subjugate, curb, check, defeat, get the better of; informal lick.
□ **master key** a key that opens several

m

different locks.

masterful adj. **1** powerful and able to control others. **2** very skilful.

▷ SYNONYMS: **commanding**, powerful, imposing, magisterial, authoritative.

− ANTONYMS: weak.

■ **masterfully** adv.

masterly adj. performed or performing very well.

▷ SYNONYMS: **expert**, adept, skilful, skilled, adroit, proficient, deft, dexterous, accomplished, polished, consummate.

− ANTONYMS: inept.

mastermind n. a person who plans and directs a complex scheme.

▷ SYNONYMS: **genius**, intellect; informal brains.

● v. be the mastermind of.

▷ SYNONYMS: **plan**, control, direct, be in charge of, run, conduct, organize, arrange, preside over, orchestrate, stage-manage, engineer, manage, coordinate.

masterpiece n. a work of outstanding skill.

▷ SYNONYMS: **magnum opus**, chef-d'œuvre, masterwork, pièce de résistance, tour de force, classic.

mastery n. **1** complete knowledge or command of a subject or skill. **2** control or superiority.

▷ SYNONYMS: **1 proficiency**, ability, capability, knowledge, under-standing, comprehension, com-mand, grasp. **2 control**, domination, command, supremacy, superiority, power, authority, jurisdiction, dominion, sovereignty.

mastic n. **1** gum from a Mediterranean tree. **2** a putty-like substance used in building.

masticate v. chew.

mastiff n. a dog of a large, strong breed.

mastitis n. inflammation of the breast or udder.

mastoid n. a projecting part of the bone behind the ear.

masturbate v. stimulate the genitals with the hand.

■ **masturbation** n.

mat n. **1** a piece of decorative or protective material placed on the floor. **2** a piece of protective material placed on a table etc.

▷ SYNONYMS: **rug**, carpet, doormat, runner.

matador n. a bullfighter.

match n. **1** a contest in a game or sport. **2** a person or thing equal to another in quality etc. **3** an exact or near equivalent to another. **4** a potential marriage partner. **5** a short stick with a tip that ignites when rubbed on a rough surface.

▷ SYNONYMS: **1 contest**, competition, game, tournament, tie, fixture, meet, friendly, derby, bout, fight. **2** an exact match: **lookalike**, double, twin, dupli-cate, mate, companion, counterpart, pair, replica, copy, doppelgänger; informal spitting image, dead ringer.

● v. **1** correspond; combine together well. **2** be equal to.

▷ SYNONYMS: **1 go with**, coordinate with, complement, suit, set off. **2** their statements do not match the evidence: **correspond with**, tally with, agree with, coincide with. **3 equal**, compare with, be in the same league as, touch, rival, compete with; informal hold a candle to.

□ **matchmaker** a person who arranges marriages or relationships between others.

mate n. **1** Brit. informal a friend. **2** a fellow member or occupant: flatmate. **3** an animal's sexual partner. **4** an officer on a merchant ship.

▷ SYNONYMS: **1 friend**, companion, schoolmate, classmate, workmate; informal pal, chum; N. Amer. informal buddy, amigo, compadre. **2 partner**, husband, wife, spouse, consort, lover; informal better half, other half. **3** a plumber's mate: **assistant**, helper, apprentice.

● v. (of animals) have sex.

▷ SYNONYMS: **breed**, couple, copulate, pair.

material n. **1** the matter from which something is or can be made. **2** items needed for creating something. **3** cloth.

▷ SYNONYMS: **1 matter**, substance, stuff, constituents. **2 fabric**, cloth, textiles. **3 information**, data, facts, facts and figures, statistics, evidence, details, particulars, background; informal info.

● adj. **1** of physical things. **2** essential or relevant.

▷ SYNONYMS: **1 physical**, corporeal, fleshly, bodily, tangible, mundane, worldly, earthly, secular, temporal, concrete, real. **2** information material to the enquiry: **relevant**, pertinent, applicable, germane, vital, essential, key.

− ANTONYMS: spiritual.

■ **materially** adv.

materialism n. a strong interest in material possessions rather than spiritual values.

m

■ **materialist** n. **materialistic** adj.
materialize (or **-ise**) v. **1** happen.
2 appear suddenly.
▷ SYNONYMS: **1 happen**, occur, come about, take place, transpire; informal come off; literary come to pass.
2 appear, turn up, arrive, emerge, surface, pop up; informal show up, fetch up.
maternal adj. **1** of or like a mother.
2 related through a person's mother.
▷ SYNONYMS: **motherly**, protective, caring, nurturing, maternalistic.
■ **maternally** adv.
maternity n. motherhood.
mathematics n. the study of numbers, quantities, and space.
■ **mathematical** adj. **mathematically** adv. **mathematician** n.
maths (US **math**) n. mathematics.
matinee /ma-ti-nay/ n. an afternoon performance in a theatre or cinema.
matins n. a service of morning prayer.
matriarch n. a female head of a family or tribe.
■ **matriarchal** adj. **matriarchy** n.
matricide n. **1** the killing of a mother by her child. **2** a person who kills their mother.
matriculate v. enrol at a college or university.
■ **matriculation** n.
matrimonial adj. relating to marriage.
▷ SYNONYMS: **marital**, conjugal, married, wedded, nuptial; literary connubial.
matrimony n. marriage.
matrix n. (pl. **matrices** or **matrixes**)
1 an environment in which something develops. **2** a mould in which something is cast. **3** a grid-like array of elements.
matron n. **1** a woman in charge of medical and living arrangements at a school. **2** an older married woman.
3 Brit. dated a woman in charge of nursing in a hospital.
■ **matronly** adj.
matt (or **matte**) adj. not shiny.
matted adj. (of hair or fur) in a thick tangled mass.
▷ SYNONYMS: **tangled**, knotted, tousled, dishevelled, uncombed, unkempt, ratty.
matter n. **1** physical substance or material. **2** a situation to be dealt with. **3** (**the matter**) the reason for a problem.
▷ SYNONYMS: **1 material**, stuff, substance. **2 affair**, business, situation, concern, incident, episode, subject,

topic, issue, question, point at issue, case.
• v. be important.
▷ SYNONYMS: **be important**, be of consequence, be relevant, count, signify.
matter-of-fact adj. unemotional and practical.
▷ SYNONYMS: **unemotional**, practical, down-to-earth, sensible, realistic, unsentimental, pragmatic, business-like, commonsensical, level-headed, hard-headed, no-nonsense, straightforward.
mattress n. a fabric case filled with soft, firm, or springy material for sleeping on.
mature adj. **1** fully grown. **2** like a sensible adult. **3** full-flavoured.
▷ SYNONYMS: **1 adult**, of age, grown-up, fully grown, in your prime.
2 sensible, responsible, level-headed, reliable, dependable. **3 ripe**, ripened, mellow, seasoned, ready.
– ANTONYMS: immature.
• v. **1** become mature. **2** (of an insurance policy) reach the end of its term and so become payable.
▷ SYNONYMS: **grow up**, come of age; develop, grow, bloom, blossom.
■ **maturation** n. **maturely** adv. **maturity** n.
maudlin adj. sentimental and full of self pity.
maul v. **1** wound by scratching and tearing. **2** treat roughly.
▷ SYNONYMS: **savage**, attack, claw, scratch, lacerate, mangle, tear.
maunder v. talk in a rambling way.
mausoleum n. a building housing a tomb or tombs.
mauve n. a pale purple colour.
maverick n. an unconventional, independent-minded person.
▷ SYNONYMS: **individualist**, free spirit, nonconformist, original, eccentric, rebel, dissenter, dissident.
– ANTONYMS: conformist.
maw n. the jaws or throat.
mawkish adj. sentimental in a sickly way.
maxim n. a sentence expressing a general truth or rule of behaviour.
▷ SYNONYMS: **saying**, adage, aphorism, proverb, motto, saw, axiom, dictum, precept, epigram.
maximize (or **-ise**) v. make as great as possible.
maximum n. (pl. **maxima** or **maximums**) the greatest amount or size possible.
▷ SYNONYMS: **upper limit**, limit, utmost,

m

greatest, most, peak, pinnacle, height, ceiling, top.
– ANTONYMS: minimum.
• adj. greatest in amount or size.
▷ SYNONYMS: **greatest**, highest, biggest, largest, top, most, utmost, supreme.
■ **maximal** adj.

May n. **1** the fifth month. **2** (**may**) the hawthorn or its blossom.
□ **mayfly** a short-lived insect living near water. **maypole** a decorated pole for dancing round on the first day of May.

may aux. v. (past **might**) expressing possibility, permission, or a wish.

maybe adv. perhaps.
▷ SYNONYMS: **perhaps**, possibly, for all you know; N. English happen; literary perchance.

Mayday n. an international radio distress signal used by ships and aircraft.

mayhem n. violent disorder.
▷ SYNONYMS: **chaos**, havoc, bedlam, pandemonium, uproar, turmoil, a riot, anarchy; informal a madhouse.

mayonnaise n. a dressing made from egg yolks, oil, and vinegar.

mayor n. the elected head of a city or borough council.
■ **mayoral** adj. **mayoralty** n.

mayoress n. **1** the wife of a mayor. **2** a woman elected as mayor.

maze n. a network of paths and walls or hedges through which you have to find a way.
▷ SYNONYMS: **labyrinth**, network, warren, web, tangle, confusion, jungle.

MB (or **Mb**) abbrev. megabytes.

MBA abbrev. Master of Business Administration.

MBE abbrev. Member of the Order of the British Empire.

MC abbrev. Master of Ceremonies.

MD abbrev. **1** Doctor of Medicine. **2** Brit. Managing Director.

ME abbrev. myalgic encephalomyelitis, a medical condition causing aches and prolonged tiredness.

me pron. the form of 'I' used when the speaker or writer is the object of a verb or preposition.

USAGE It's wrong to use *me* as the subject of a verb, as in *John and me went to the shops*; in this case use *I* instead.

mead n. an alcoholic drink made from honey and water.

meadow n. a field of grass.
▷ SYNONYMS: **field**, paddock, pasture;

literary lea, mead.

meagre (US **meager**) adj. small in quantity.
▷ SYNONYMS: **inadequate**, scant, paltry, limited, restricted, sparse, negligible, skimpy, slender, pitiful, miserly, niggardly; informal measly, stingy.
– ANTONYMS: abundant.
■ **meagreness** n.

meal n. **1** a regular occasion when food is eaten. **2** the food eaten on such an occasion. **3** coarsely ground grain.
▷ SYNONYMS: **snack**, feast, banquet; informal spread, blowout; Brit. informal nosh-up; formal repast.

WORD LINKS
prandial relating to meals

mealy adj. of or like meal.
□ **mealy-mouthed** unwilling to speak frankly.

mean v. (**meaning**, **meant**) **1** intend. **2** (of a word) have as its explanation in the same language or its equivalent in another. **3** have as a result. **4** be of specified importance.
▷ SYNONYMS: **1** signify, denote, indicate, convey, designate, show, express, spell out, stand for, represent, symbolize, imply, suggest, intimate, portend. **2** intend, aim, plan, have in mind, set out, want. **3** *this will mean war*: entail, involve, necessitate, lead to, result in, give rise to, bring about, cause, engender, produce.
• adj. **1** unwilling to give or share. **2** unkind. **3** US aggressive. **4** poor in quality or appearance. **5** calculated as a mean. **6** in the middle of two extremes.
▷ SYNONYMS: **1** miserly, niggardly, parsimonious, penny-pinching, cheese-paring; informal tight-fisted, stingy, tight; N. Amer. informal cheap. **2** unkind, nasty, unpleasant, spiteful, malicious, unfair, shabby, horrible, despicable, contemptible, obnoxious, vile, loathsome, base, low; informal rotten.
– ANTONYMS: generous, kind.
• n. **1** the average value of a set of quantities. **2** something in the middle of two extremes.
■ **meanly** adv. **meanness** n.

meander v. **1** follow a winding course. **2** wander aimlessly.
• n. a winding bend of a river.

meaning n. **1** what is meant. **2** a sense of purpose.
▷ SYNONYMS: **significance**, sense, signification, import, gist, thrust, drift, implication, message; definition, explanation, denotation, interpretation, connotation.

m

WORD LINKS
semantic relating to meaning

meaningful adj. **1** having meaning.
2 important or worthwhile.
3 intended to express something.
▷ SYNONYMS: **1** *a meaningful experience:*
significant, important, serious;
worthwhile, rewarding, valuable,
constructive. **2** *a meaningful glance:*
expressive, eloquent, pointed,
revealing, telling, suggestive.
■ **meaningfully** adv.

meaningless adj. having no meaning
or significance.
▷ SYNONYMS: *a meaningless existence:*
futile, pointless, hollow, vain,
purposeless, valueless, useless,
worthless, senseless, unimportant,
insignificant.

means pl. n. **1** a thing or method
for achieving a result. **2** financial
resources.
▷ SYNONYMS: **1 method**, way, manner,
course, agency, channel, avenue,
procedure, process, methodology,
expedient. **2 money**, resources,
capital, income, finance, funds, cash,
the wherewithal, assets, wealth,
riches, affluence, fortune.
□ **by all means** of course. **by no
means** certainly not. **means test** an
official investigation of a person's
finances to find out their eligibility
for welfare benefits.

meantime adv. (**in the meantime**)
meanwhile.

meanwhile adv. **1** in the period of
time between two events. **2** at the
same time.
▷ SYNONYMS: **1 for now**, for the moment,
for the present, for the time being,
in the meanwhile, in the meantime,
in the interim. **2 at the same time**,
simultaneously, concurrently.

measles n. an infectious disease
causing fever and a red rash.

measly adj. informal meagre.

measure v. **1** find the size, amount,
etc. of something in standard units.
2 be of a specified size. **3** (**measure
out**) take an exact quantity of.
4 (**measure up**) reach the required
standard.
▷ SYNONYMS: **quantify**, gauge, size,
count, weigh, evaluate, assess, determine, calculate, compute.
● n. **1** a course of action. **2** a proposal
for a law. **3** a standard unit used in
measuring. **4** a measuring device
marked with such units. **5** (**a measure
of**) a certain amount of.

▷ SYNONYMS: **1 action**, act, course
of action, deed, procedure, step,
expedient, initiative, programme.
2 statute, act, bill, law. **3 ruler**,
tape measure, gauge, meter, scale.
4 *sales are a measure of their success:*
yardstick, test, standard, barometer,
touchstone, benchmark.
■ **measurable** adj. **measurably** adv.

measured adj. **1** slow and regular in
rhythm. **2** carefully considered.
▷ SYNONYMS: **1 regular**, steady, even,
rhythmic, unfaltering, slow,
dignified, stately, sedate, leisurely,
unhurried. **2 careful**, thoughtful,
considered, reasoned, calculated.

measurement n. **1** the act of
measuring. **2** a size etc. found by
measuring.
▷ SYNONYMS: **1 quantification**, evaluation, assessment, calculation,
computation, mensuration. **2 size**,
dimension, proportions, value,
amount, quantity.

meat n. animal flesh as food.

WORD LINKS
carnivorous meat-eating

meaty adj. (**meatier**, **meatiest**) **1** like
or full of meat. **2** substantial or
satisfying.

mechanic n. a skilled worker who
repairs and maintains machinery.

mechanical adj. **1** of or operated by
machinery. **2** done without conscious
thought.
▷ SYNONYMS: **1 mechanized**, machine-
driven, automated, automatic.
2 automatic, knee-jerk, unthinking,
instinctive, habitual, routine,
unemotional, unfeeling.
– ANTONYMS: manual.
■ **mechanically** adv.

mechanics n. **1** the study of
the forces producing motion.
2 mechanical parts.

mechanism n. **1** a piece of machinery.
2 the way something works or
happens.
▷ SYNONYMS: **1 apparatus**, machine,
machinery, appliance, device,
instrument, tool, contraption,
gadget; informal gizmo. **2** *a complaints
mechanism:* **procedure**, process,
system, method, means, medium,
channel.

mechanize (or **-ise**) v. equip with
machinery.
■ **mechanization** n.

medal n. an inscribed metal disc
awarded for achievement or to mark
an event.

m

medallion n. a pendant shaped like a medal.

medallist (US **medalist**) n. a person awarded a medal.

meddle v. interfere in something that is not your business.
▷ SYNONYMS: **1 interfere**, intrude, intervene, pry; informal poke your nose in. **2 fiddle**, interfere, tamper, mess about; Brit. informal muck about.
■ **meddler** n. **meddlesome** adj.

media n. **1** television, radio, and newspapers as the means of mass communication. **2** pl. of **MEDIUM**.

mediaeval var. of **MEDIEVAL**.

medial adj. situated in the middle.
■ **medially** adv.

median adj. situated in the middle.

mediate v. try to settle a dispute between two other parties.
▷ SYNONYMS: **arbitrate**, conciliate, moderate, make peace, intervene, intercede, act as an intermediary, negotiate, liaise, referee.

mediation n. the process of mediating.
▷ SYNONYMS: **arbitration**, conciliation, negotiation, intervention, intercession, shuttle diplomacy.

mediator n. a person or organization that mediates between two other parties.
▷ SYNONYMS: **arbitrator**, arbiter, negotiator, conciliator, peacemaker, go-between, middleman, intermediary, moderator, honest broker.

medic n. informal a doctor or medical student.

medical adj. of the science of medicine.
• n. an examination to assess a person's physical health.
■ **medically** adv.

medicament n. a medicine.

medicate v. **1** give medicine to. **2** (**medicated**) containing a medicinal substance.

medication n. **1** a medicine. **2** treatment with medicines.

medicinal adj. having healing properties.
▷ SYNONYMS: **curative**, healing, remedial, therapeutic, restorative, health-giving.
■ **medicinally** adv.

medicine n. **1** the science or practice of treating and preventing disease. **2** a substance taken to treat or prevent disease.
▷ SYNONYMS: **medication**, drug, prescription, treatment, remedy, cure, nostrum, panacea, cure-all.

> **WORD LINKS**
> **pharmaceutical** relating to medicines

medieval (or **mediaeval**) adj. of the Middle Ages.

mediocre adj. of average or fairly low quality.
▷ SYNONYMS: **average**, ordinary, undistinguished, uninspired, indifferent, unexceptional, unexciting, unremarkable, run-of-the-mill, pedestrian, prosaic, lacklustre, forgettable, amateurish; informal so-so.
– ANTONYMS: excellent.
■ **mediocrity** n.

meditate v. **1** focus the mind for spiritual purposes or relaxation. **2** think carefully.
▷ SYNONYMS: **contemplate**, think, consider, ponder, muse, reflect, deliberate, ruminate, brood, mull over.
■ **meditation** n. **meditative** adj. **meditatively** adv.

Mediterranean adj. of the Mediterranean Sea.

medium n. (pl. **media** or **mediums**) **1** a means of doing or communicating something. **2** a substance through which something acts or is conveyed. **3** (pl. **mediums**) a person claiming to communicate between the dead and the living. **4** the middle state between two extremes.
▷ SYNONYMS: *a medium of expression:* **means**, method, avenue, channel, vehicle, organ, instrument, mechanism.
• adj. between two extremes.
▷ SYNONYMS: **average**, middling, medium-sized, middle-sized, moderate, normal, standard.
□ **medium wave** a radio wave of a frequency between 300 kHz and 3 MHz.

medlar n. a small brown apple-like fruit.

medley n. (pl. **medleys**) **1** a varied mixture. **2** various musical excerpts performed as a continuous piece.

medulla n. a separate inner region of an organ or tissue.

meek adj. quiet, gentle, and obedient.
▷ SYNONYMS: **submissive**, obedient, compliant, tame, biddable, acquiescent, timid, quiet, mild, gentle, docile, shy, diffident, unassuming, self-effacing.
– ANTONYMS: assertive.
■ **meekly** adv. **meekness** n.

meerschaum /meer-shawm/ n. a

tobacco pipe with a white clay bowl.

meet v. (**meeting**, **met**) **1** come together with someone at the same place and time. **2** be introduced to or encounter for the first time. **3** touch or join. **4** experience. **5** (**meet with**) receive a reaction. **6** satisfy a requirement.
▷ SYNONYMS: **1 encounter**, come face to face with, run into, run across, come across/upon, chance on, happen on, stumble across; informal bump into. **2 get to know**, be introduced to, make the acquaintance of. **3 assemble**, gather, congregate, convene; formal foregather. **4 converge**, connect, touch, link up, intersect, cross, join.
• n. a meeting.
• adj. old use suitable or proper.

meeting n. **1** an organized gathering for a discussion etc. **2** a situation in which people meet.
▷ SYNONYMS: **1 gathering**, assembly, conference, congregation, convention, forum, summit, rally, consultation, audience, interview, conclave; informal get-together. **2 encounter**, contact, appointment, assignation, rendezvous; literary tryst. **3** the meeting of land and sea: **convergence**, confluence, conjunction, union, intersection, crossing. **4** an athletics meeting: **event**, tournament, meet, rally, competition, match, game, contest.

mega adj. informal **1** huge. **2** excellent.

megabyte n. a unit of information equal to 1,048,576 bytes.

megahertz n. (pl. **megahertz**) a unit of frequency equal to one million hertz.

megalith n. a large stone forming a prehistoric monument or part of one.
■ **megalithic** adj.

megalomania n. **1** the false belief that you are very powerful and important. **2** strong desire for power.
■ **megalomaniac** n. & adj.

megaphone n. a cone-shaped device for amplifying the voice.

megapixel n. a unit for measuring the resolution of a digital image, equal to 1,048,576 pixels.

megawatt n. a unit of power equal to one million watts.

melamine n. a hard plastic used for laminated coatings.

melancholia n. great sadness or depression.

melancholy n. deep and long-lasting sadness.
▷ SYNONYMS: **sadness**, sorrow, unhappiness, depression, despondency, dejection, gloom, misery; informal the blues.
– ANTONYMS: happiness.
• adj. sad.
▷ SYNONYMS: **sad**, sorrowful, unhappy, gloomy, despondent, dejected, disconsolate, downcast, downhearted, woebegone, glum, miserable, morose, depressed, dispirited, mournful, doleful, lugubrious; informal down in the dumps, blue.
– ANTONYMS: cheerful.

melange /may-**lonzh**/ n. a varied mixture.

melanin n. a dark pigment in the hair and skin.

melanoma n. a form of skin cancer.

meld v. blend.

melee /**mel**-ay/ n. **1** a confused fight. **2** a disorderly crowd.

mellifluous adj. sweet-sounding.

mellow adj. **1** pleasantly smooth or soft in sound, taste, or colour. **2** relaxed and good-humoured.
▷ SYNONYMS: **1 sweet-sounding**, dulcet, melodious, mellifluous, soft, smooth, rich. **2 genial**, affable, amiable, good-humoured, good-natured, pleasant, relaxed, easy-going.
– ANTONYMS: harsh, rough.
• v. make or become mellow.

melodeon n. a small accordion or organ.

melodic adj. **1** of melody. **2** pleasant-sounding.
■ **melodically** adv.

melodious adj. tuneful.
▷ SYNONYMS: **tuneful**, melodic, musical, mellifluous, dulcet, sweet-sounding, harmonious, euphonious, lyrical.
– ANTONYMS: discordant.

melodrama n. **1** a play with exciting events and exaggerated characters. **2** exaggerated behaviour.

melodramatic adj. too dramatic or exaggerated.
▷ SYNONYMS: **exaggerated**, histrionic, extravagant, overdramatic, overdone, sensationalized, overemotional, stagy, theatrical; informal hammy.
■ **melodramatically** adv.

melody n. (pl. **melodies**) **1** a tune. **2** the main part in harmonized music.
▷ SYNONYMS: **tune**, air, strain, theme, song, refrain.

melon n. a large round fruit.

melt v. **1** make or become liquid by heating. **2** gradually disappear.
▷ SYNONYMS: **1 liquefy**, thaw, defrost, soften, dissolve; technical deliquesce.

m

2 vanish, disappear, fade, evaporate.
– ANTONYMS: freeze, solidify.
□ **meltdown** an accident in a nuclear reactor in which the fuel overheats and melts the core.
member n. **1** a person belonging to a group or society. **2** a part of a structure.
▷ SYNONYMS: **subscriber**, associate, fellow, representative.
■ **membership** n.
membrane n. a thin flexible skin-like tissue.
■ **membranous** adj.
memento n. (pl. **mementos** or **mementoes**) an object kept as a reminder.
▷ SYNONYMS: **souvenir**, keepsake, reminder, remembrance, token, memorial.
memo n. (pl. **memos**) a note sent within an organization.
memoir /mem-war/ n. a written account of events etc. from personal knowledge.
▷ SYNONYMS: **1 account**, history, record, chronicle, narrative, story, portrayal, depiction, portrait, profile. **2** (**memoirs**) **autobiography**, life story, journal, diary.
memorabilia pl. n. objects collected because of their links with people or events.
memorable adj. worth remembering or easy to remember.
▷ SYNONYMS: **unforgettable**, momentous, significant, historic, remarkable, notable, noteworthy, important, outstanding, arresting, indelible, catchy, haunting.
■ **memorably** adv.
memorandum n. (pl. **memoranda** or **memorandums**) **1** a memo. **2** a formal record or report.
memorial n. an object that commemorates a person or event.
▷ SYNONYMS: **1 monument**, cenotaph, mausoleum, statue, plaque, cairn, shrine, tombstone. **2 tribute**, testimonial, remembrance, memento.
• adj. in memory of someone.
memorize (or **-ise**) v. learn and remember exactly.
▷ SYNONYMS: **commit to memory**, remember, learn by heart, become word-perfect in, get/have off pat.
memory n. (pl. **memories**) **1** the ability to remember things. **2** a thing remembered. **3** a computer's equipment or capacity for storing data.
▷ SYNONYMS: **1 recollection**, recall,

remembrance, reminiscence. **2** *the club is devoted to the memory of her grandfather:* **commemoration**, remembrance, honour, tribute, recognition, respect.
□ **in memory of** so as to commemorate. **Memory Stick** Computing trademark a small device for storing or transferring data from a computer, digital camera, etc.

WORD LINKS
mnemonic helping the memory

men pl. of MAN.
menace n. **1** a dangerous or troublesome person or thing. **2** a threatening quality.
▷ SYNONYMS: **1 danger**, peril, risk, hazard, threat. **2 nuisance**, pest, troublemaker, mischief-maker. **3** *an atmosphere full of menace:* **threat**, intimidation, malevolence, oppression.
• v. be a threat or possible danger to.
▷ SYNONYMS: **threaten**, endanger, put at risk, jeopardize, imperil.
menacing adj. seeming likely to cause harm or danger.
▷ SYNONYMS: **threatening**, ominous, intimidating, frightening, forbidding, hostile, sinister, baleful.
ménage /may-nahj/ n. the members of a household.
menagerie n. a small zoo.
mend v. **1** restore to the correct or working condition. **2** improve a bad situation.
▷ SYNONYMS: **repair**, fix, restore, renovate; sew up, darn, patch, renew; informal patch up.
– ANTONYMS: break.
mendacious adj. untruthful.
■ **mendacity** n.
mendicant adj. living by begging.
• n. a beggar.
menhir /men-heer/ n. a tall stone set up in prehistoric times.
menial adj. (of work) unskilled and lacking status.
▷ SYNONYMS: **unskilled**, lowly, humble, low-grade, low-status, humdrum, routine, boring, dull.
• n. a person with a menial job.
meningitis n. inflammation of the membranes enclosing the brain and spinal cord.
meniscus n. (pl. **menisci**) **1** the curved surface of a liquid in a tube. **2** a lens convex on one side and concave on the other.
menopause n. the period in a woman's life when menstruation

gradually stops.

■ **menopausal** adj.

menorah n. a large branched candlestick used in Jewish worship.

menstruate v. discharge blood from the lining of the womb each month.

■ **menstrual** adj. **menstruation** n.

mensuration n. measurement, esp. in geometry.

mental adj. **1** of the mind. **2** informal mad.

▷ SYNONYMS: **intellectual**, cerebral, cognitive, psychological, rational.

– ANTONYMS: physical.

◻ **mental age** a person's mental ability expressed as the age at which an average person reaches that ability.

■ **mentally** adv.

mentality n. (pl. **mentalities**) a typical way of thinking.

▷ SYNONYMS: **way of thinking**, mind set, mind, psychology, attitude, outlook, make-up, disposition, character.

menthol n. a substance in peppermint oil used in decongestants etc.

■ **mentholated** adj.

mention v. refer to briefly.

▷ SYNONYMS: **1 allude to**, refer to, touch on, bring up, raise, broach. **2 state**, say, observe, remark, indicate, disclose, divulge, reveal.

• n. a reference to someone or something.

▷ SYNONYMS: **reference**, allusion, comment, citation; informal namecheck, plug.

mentor n. an experienced person acting as an adviser.

▷ SYNONYMS: **adviser**, counsellor, guide, guru, consultant, confidant/ confidante, trainer, teacher, tutor, instructor.

menu n. **1** a list of dishes available. **2** a list of options on a computer screen.

▷ SYNONYMS: **bill of fare**, tariff, carte du jour, set menu, table d'hôte.

meow var. of MIAOW.

MEP abbrev. Member of the European Parliament.

mercantile adj. of trade.

mercenary adj. motivated by the desire to make money.

▷ SYNONYMS: **grasping**, greedy, acquisitive, avaricious, materialistic, venal; informal money-grubbing.

• n. (pl. **mercenaries**) a professional soldier hired by a foreign army.

merchandise n. goods for sale.

▷ SYNONYMS: **goods**, wares, stock, commodities, produce, products.

• v. promote the sale of.

merchant n. a trader who sells goods in large quantities.

▷ SYNONYMS: **trader**, tradesman, dealer, wholesaler, broker, agent, seller, retailer, supplier, buyer, vendor, distributor.

◻ **merchant bank** Brit. a bank whose customers are large businesses. **merchantman** a ship carrying merchandise. **merchant navy** a country's commercial shipping.

merchantable adj. suitable for sale.

merciful adj. **1** showing mercy. **2** giving relief from suffering.

▷ SYNONYMS: **forgiving**, compassionate, pitying, forbearing, lenient, humane, mild, kind, soft-hearted, tender-hearted, sympathetic, humanitarian, liberal, generous, magnanimous.

– ANTONYMS: cruel.

■ **mercifully** adv.

merciless adj. showing no mercy.

▷ SYNONYMS: **ruthless**, remorseless, pitiless, unforgiving, implacable, inexorable, relentless, inhumane, inhuman, unfeeling, severe, cold-blooded, hard-hearted, stony-hearted, heartless, harsh, callous, cruel, brutal.

– ANTONYMS: compassionate.

■ **mercilessly** adv.

mercurial adj. **1** tending to change mood suddenly. **2** of mercury.

mercury n. a heavy liquid metallic element.

mercy n. (pl. **mercies**) **1** pity or forgiveness shown towards someone in your power. **2** something to be grateful for.

▷ SYNONYMS: **pity**, compassion, leniency, clemency, charity, forgiveness, forbearance, kindness, sympathy, indulgence, tolerance, generosity, magnanimity.

– ANTONYMS: ruthlessness, cruelty.

◻ **at the mercy of** in the power of.

mere adj. **1** no more than what is specified. **2** (**the merest**) the slightest.

• n. literary a lake.

merely adv. just.

▷ SYNONYMS: the interview is merely a formality: **only**, just, purely, simply, solely.

meretricious adj. superficially attractive but having no real value.

merge v. **1** combine into a whole. **2** blend gradually.

▷ SYNONYMS: **1** they merged with a European firm: **join**, join forces, unite, affiliate, team up. **2** the two companies were merged: **amalgamate**, bring together, join, consolidate, conflate, unite, unify, combine, incorporate, integrate. **3 mingle**, blend, fuse, mix,

m

intermix, intermingle, coalesce.
– ANTONYMS: separate.
merger n. a merging of two organizations into one.
▷ SYNONYMS: **amalgamation**, combination, union, fusion, coalition, affiliation, unification, incorporation, consolidation, link-up, alliance.
– ANTONYMS: split.
meridian n. a circle passing at the same longitude through a given place on the earth's surface and the poles.
meringue /muh-rang/ n. beaten egg whites and sugar baked until crisp.
merino n. (pl. **merinos**) a soft woollen material.
merit n. **1** excellence. **2** a good point or quality.
▷ SYNONYMS: **1 excellence**, quality, calibre, worth, value, distinction, eminence. **2 good point**, strong point, advantage, benefit, value, asset, plus.
– ANTONYMS: fault, disadvantage.
 • v. (**meriting**, **merited**) deserve.
▷ SYNONYMS: **deserve**, warrant, justify, earn, rate, be worthy of, be entitled to, have a right to, have a claim to.
meritocracy n. (pl. **meritocracies**) a society in which power is held by those with the greatest ability.
meritorious adj. deserving reward or praise.
merlin n. a small falcon.
mermaid n. a mythical sea creature with a woman's head and body and a fish's tail.
merry adj. (**merrier**, **merriest**) **1** cheerful and lively. **2** informal slightly drunk.
▷ SYNONYMS: **cheerful**, cheery, in high spirits, sunny, smiling, light-hearted, lively, carefree, joyful, joyous, jolly, convivial, festive, gleeful, happy, laughing; informal chirpy.
– ANTONYMS: miserable.
 □ **merry-go-round** a funfair ride consisting of a revolving platform with model horses or cars.
 merrymaking lively celebration and fun.
 ■ **merrily** adv. **merriment** n.
mescaline n. a hallucinogenic drug.
Mesdames pl. of MADAME.
Mesdemoiselles pl. of MADEMOISELLE.
mesh n. **1** material made of a network of wire or thread. **2** the spacing of the strands of a net.
▷ SYNONYMS: **netting**, net, grille, screen, lattice, gauze.
 • v. **1** be in harmony. **2** become entangled. **3** (of a gearwheel) lock

together with another.
▷ SYNONYMS: **1 engage**, connect, lock, interlock. **2 harmonize**, fit together, match, dovetail, connect, interconnect.
mesmeric /mez-me-rik/ adj. hypnotic.
mesmerize (or **-ise**) v. completely capture the attention of.
mess n. **1** a dirty or untidy state. **2** a state of confusion or difficulty. **3** a place where members of the armed forces eat and relax.
▷ SYNONYMS: **1 untidiness**, disorder, disarray, clutter, muddle, jumble, chaos; informal shambles; Brit. informal tip. **2 plight**, predicament, tight spot, tight corner, difficulty, trouble, quandary, dilemma, problem, muddle, mix-up; informal jam, fix, pickle, hole.
 • v. **1** make untidy or dirty. **2** (**mess about/around**) behave in a silly or playful way.
message n. **1** a spoken, written, or electronic communication. **2** a significant point or central theme.
▷ SYNONYMS: **1 communication**, news, note, memo, email, letter, missive, report, bulletin, communiqué, dispatch. **2** the message of his teaching: meaning, sense, import, idea, point, thrust, moral, gist, essence, implication.
 • v. send a message to.
messenger n. a person who carries a message.
▷ SYNONYMS: **courier**, postman, runner, dispatch rider, envoy, emissary, agent, go-between.
Messiah n. **1** (in Judaism) the person who will be sent by God as the saviour of the Jewish people. **2** Jesus regarded by Christians as this saviour.
 ■ **messianic** adj.
Messieurs pl. of MONSIEUR.
Messrs pl. of MR.
messy adj. (**messier**, **messiest**) **1** untidy or dirty. **2** confused and difficult.
▷ SYNONYMS: **1 dirty**, filthy, grubby, soiled, grimy, mucky, muddy, stained, smeared, smudged, dishevelled, scruffy, unkempt, rumpled, matted, tousled. **2 untidy**, disordered, in a muddle, chaotic, confused, disorganized, in disarray, cluttered, in a jumble; informal higgledy-piggledy; Brit. informal shambolic. **3** a messy legal battle: complex, tangled, confused, convoluted, unpleasant, nasty, bitter, acrimonious.
– ANTONYMS: clean, tidy.

■ **messily** adv. **messiness** n.

met past & past part. of MEET.

metabolism n. the process by which food is used for growth or energy.
■ **metabolic** adj.

metabolize (or **-ise**) v. process by metabolism.

metacarpus n. (pl. **metacarpi**) the set of bones between the wrist and fingers.

metal n. **1** a hard, shiny, solid material which conducts electricity and heat. **2** broken stone used in making roads.
■ **metallic** adj.

metalled adj. Brit. (of a road) having a hard surface.

metallurgy n. the study of metals.
■ **metallurgist** n.

metamorphic adj. (of rock) changed by heat, pressure, etc.

metamorphosis n. (pl. **meta-morphoses**) a change in form or nature.
■ **metamorphose** v.

metaphor n. a word or phrase used to represent or stand for something else (e.g. *food for thought*).
▷ SYNONYMS: **figure of speech**, image, trope, analogy, comparison, symbol.
■ **metaphorical** (or **metaphoric**) adj. **metaphorically** adv.

metaphysics n. philosophy concerning the nature of existence, truth, and knowledge.
■ **metaphysical** adj.

metatarsus n. (pl. **metatarsi**) the set of bones between the ankle and the toes.

mete v. (**mete out**) deal out justice, punishment, etc.

meteor n. a small body of matter from outer space appearing as a streak of light.

meteoric adj. **1** of meteors or meteorites. **2** (of progress) very rapid.

meteorite n. a meteor that has fallen to earth.

meteorology n. the study of atmospheric conditions for weather forecasting.
■ **meteorological** adj. **meteorologist** n.

meter n. **1** a device that measures and records the quantity, degree, or rate of something. **2** US = METRE.
• v. measure with a meter.

methadone n. a powerful painkilling drug.

methane n. a flammable gas.

methanol n. a poisonous flammable alcohol, used to make methylated spirit.

method n. **1** a way of doing something. **2** the quality of being well organized.
▷ SYNONYMS: **1 procedure**, technique, system, practice, routine, modus operandi, process, strategy, tactic, approach, way, manner, mode.
2 *there's no method in his approach:* **order**, organization, structure, form, system, logic, planning, design, consistency.
– ANTONYMS: disorder.

methodical adj. well organized and systematic.
▷ SYNONYMS: **orderly**, well ordered, well organized, well planned, efficient, businesslike, systematic, structured, logical, disciplined, consistent, scientific.
■ **methodically** adv.

Methodist n. a member of a Protestant group originating in the 18th century.
• adj. of Methodists.
■ **Methodism** n.

methodology n. (pl. **methodologies**) a system of methods used in a particular field.

meths n. Brit. informal methylated spirit.

methyl n. a chemical unit derived from methane.

methylated spirit n. a form of alcohol used as a solvent or fuel.

meticulous adj. careful and precise.
▷ SYNONYMS: **careful**, conscientious, diligent, scrupulous, punctilious, painstaking, thorough, studious, rigorous, detailed, perfectionist, fastidious.
– ANTONYMS: careless.
■ **meticulously** adv. **meticulousness** n.

métier /may-ti-ay/ n. a person's trade, profession, or special ability.

metre (US **meter**) n. **1** a metric unit of length equal to 100 cm (approx. 39.37 inches). **2** rhythm in poetry.

metric adj. of or using the metric system.
□ **metric system** the decimal measuring system based on the metre, litre, and gram. **metric ton** a unit of weight equal to 1,000 kg (2,205 lb).

metrical adj. of poetic metre.

metricate v. convert to a metric system.
■ **metrication** n.

metro n. (pl. **metros**) an underground railway.

metronome n. a device for indicating tempo while practising music.

metropolis n. the main city of a country or region.

m

■ **metropolitan** adj.

mettle n. spirit and strength of character.

mew v. (of a cat or gull) make a high-pitched cry.
• n. a mewing cry.

mews n. (pl. **mews**) Brit. a row of houses converted from stables.

mezzanine n. a partial floor of a building, between two full floors.

mezzo /met-soh/ (or **mezzo-soprano**) n. (pl. **mezzos**) a female singer with a voice pitched between soprano and contralto.

mg abbrev. milligrams.

MHz abbrev. megahertz.

miaow (or **meow**) n. the cry of a cat.
• v. make a miaow.

miasma n. an unpleasant or unhealthy atmosphere.

mica /my-kuh/ n. a mineral found as tiny shiny scales in rocks.

mice pl. of MOUSE.

microbe n. a microorganism, esp. one that causes disease.
■ **microbial** adj.

microbiology n. the study of microorganisms.

microchip n. a miniature electronic circuit made from a tiny wafer of silicon.

microclimate n. the climate of a very small area.

microcosm n. a thing representing something much larger.

microfiche (or **microfilm**) n. a piece of film containing greatly reduced photos of the pages of a book etc.

microlight n. a very small, light aircraft for one or two people.

micrometer n. an instrument for measuring small distances or thicknesses.

micron n. one millionth of a metre.

microorganism n. a microscopic organism.

microphone n. an instrument for changing sound waves into electrical energy which is then amplified or transmitted.

microprocessor n. an integrated circuit which can function as the main part of a computer.

microscope n. an instrument for magnifying small objects.

microscopic adj. **1** so small as to be visible only with a microscope. **2** of a microscope.
■ **microscopically** adv.

microsurgery n. surgery performed using very small instruments and a microscope.

microwave n. **1** an electromagnetic wave with a wavelength in the range 0.001–0.3 m. **2** an oven that uses microwaves to cook or heat food.

mid adj. in the middle.

midday n. 12 o'clock in the day.
▷ SYNONYMS: **noon**, twelve noon, high noon, noonday.
– ANTONYMS: midnight.

midden n. a heap of dung or rubbish.

middle adj. **1** at an equal distance from the edges or ends of something. **2** medium in rank, quality, etc.
▷ SYNONYMS: **central**, mid, mean, medium, median, midway, halfway, equidistant.
• n. a middle point or position.
▷ SYNONYMS: **1** centre, midpoint, halfway point, dead centre, hub, eye, heart, core, kernel. **2** midriff, waist, belly, stomach; informal tummy.
– ANTONYMS: edge.
□ **middle-aged** in the period of life between about 45 and 60. **Middle Ages** the period of European history from about 1000 to 1450. **middle class** the social class between the upper and working classes. **Middle East** an area of SW Asia and northern Africa, stretching from the Mediterranean to Pakistan. **middleman** a person who buys goods from producers and sells them to consumers. **middle-of-the-road** (of music) popular but rather unadventurous. **middleweight** a weight in boxing etc. above welter-weight.

middling adj. average in size, amount, or rank.

midfield n. the central part of a sports field.
■ **midfielder** n.

midge n. a small biting fly.

midget n. a very small person.

Midlands pl. n. the inland counties of central England.

midnight n. 12 o'clock at night.

midriff n. the front of the body between the chest and the waist.

midshipman n. a low-ranking officer in the Royal Navy.

midst n. the middle.

midway adv. halfway.

midwife n. a nurse trained to assist at childbirth.

mien /meen/ n. a person's look or manner.

might aux. v. **1** used to express possibility. **2** used in polite questions

and requests.
• n. great power or strength.

mighty adj. (**mightier**, **mightiest**)
powerful or strong.
▷ SYNONYMS: **powerful**, forceful, strong,
hard, heavy, violent, vigorous, hefty.
− ANTONYMS: feeble.
• adv. informal very.
■ **mightily** adv.

migraine n. a very severe headache.

migrant n. **1** a worker who travels to
find work. **2** a migrating animal.
▷ SYNONYMS: **immigrant**, **emigrant**,
nomad, itinerant, traveller, transient,
wanderer, drifter.
• adj. migrating or having migrated.
▷ SYNONYMS: **travelling**, wandering,
drifting, nomadic, itinerant, transient.

migrate v. **1** (of an animal) move
from one area to another according to
the seasons. **2** move to a new area to
find work.
■ **migration** n. **migratory** adj.

mike n. informal a microphone.

mild adj. **1** not severe, harsh, or
extreme. **2** (of weather) fairly warm.
3 not strong in flavour. **4** gentle.
▷ SYNONYMS: **1** gentle, tender, soft,
sympathetic, peaceable, good-
natured, quiet, placid, docile, meek.
2 a mild punishment: lenient, light.
3 warm, balmy, temperate, clement.
4 bland, tasteless, insipid.
− ANTONYMS: harsh, strong, severe.
■ **mildly** adv. **mildness** n.

mildew n. a coating of tiny fungi on
plants or damp material.
■ **mildewed** adj.

mile n. a unit of length equal to 1,760
yds (approx. 1.609 km).
□ **mileage** a number of miles covered.
milestone 1 a stone showing the
distance to a particular place. **2** a
significant event or stage.

milieu /mee-lyer/ n. (pl. **milieux**
or **milieus**) a person's social
environment.

militant adj. prepared to take
aggressive action in support of a
cause.
▷ SYNONYMS: **hard-line**, extreme,
extremist, committed, zealous,
fanatical, radical.
• n. a militant person.
▷ SYNONYMS: **activist**, extremist,
partisan, radical, zealot.
■ **militancy** n.

militarism n. belief in the value of
military strength.
■ **militaristic** adj.

military adj. of soldiers or the armed
forces.
• n. (**the military**) the armed forces.
▷ SYNONYMS: **armed forces**, armed
services, militia, army, navy, air force,
marines.
■ **militarily** adv.

militate v. (**militate against**) be a
powerful factor in preventing.

> USAGE Don't confuse **militate** with
> **mitigate**, which means 'make less
> severe'.

militia n. a military force made up of
trained civilians.

milk n. **1** a white fluid produced by
female mammals to feed their young.
2 cows' milk as a drink for humans.
• v. **1** draw milk from. **2** exploit a
person or situation.
▷ SYNONYMS: **exploit**, take advantage
of, suck dry; informal bleed, squeeze,
fleece.
□ **milk float** Brit. an electric van for
delivering milk to houses. **milkman**
a man who delivers milk to houses.
milkshake a cold drink made from
milk whisked with a flavouring.
milksop a timid person. **milk tooth** a
temporary tooth in a child or young
mammal.
■ **milky** adj.

> WORD LINKS
> **lactic** relating to milk

mill n. **1** a building with machinery for
grinding grain into flour. **2** a device
for grinding a specified substance. **3** a
building containing machinery for
manufacturing.
▷ SYNONYMS: **factory**, plant, works, workshop, shop, foundry.
• v. **1** grind in a mill. **2** (**milled**) (of a
coin) having ribbed markings on the
edge. **3** (**mill about/around**) move
around in a confused mass.
▷ SYNONYMS: **grind**, pulverize, powder,
granulate, pound, crush, press.
□ **millstone 1** each of a pair of circular
stones for grinding grain. **2** a burden
of responsibility.

millennium n. (pl. **millennia** or
millenniums) a period of a thousand
years.
■ **millennial** adj.

> USAGE Two *l*s, two *n*s: mille*nn*ium.

miller n. a person who owns or works
in a grain mill.

millet n. a cereal plant used to make
flour etc.

millibar n. a unit for measuring
atmospheric pressure.

m

milligram (or **milligramme**) n. one thousandth of a gram.

millilitre (US **milliliter**) n. one thousandth of a litre.

millimetre (US **millimeter**) n. one thousandth of a metre.

milliner n. a person who makes or sells women's hats.
■ **millinery** n.

million n. **1** one thousand thousand; 1,000,000. **2** (**millions**) informal very many.
■ **millionth** adj. & n.

millionaire n. a person who has more than one million pounds or dollars.

millipede n. a small invertebrate animal with many legs.

millisecond n. one thousandth of a second.

milometer n. Brit. an instrument on a vehicle recording the number of miles travelled.

mime n. the use of gestures and expressions only to tell a story or convey feelings.
•v. use mime to act out.

mimic v. (**mimicking**, **mimicked**) imitate the voice or behaviour of.
▷ SYNONYMS: **imitate**, copy, impersonate, do an impression of, ape, caricature, parody; informal send up, take off.
•n. a person skilled in mimicking.
▷ SYNONYMS: **impersonator**, impressionist; informal copycat.
■ **mimicry** n.

mimosa n. an acacia tree with yellow flowers.

minaret n. a slender tower on or by a mosque.

mince v. **1** cut meat into very small pieces. **2** walk in an affected way with short, quick steps.
▷ SYNONYMS: **grind**, chop up, cut up, dice, crumble; N. Amer. hash.
•n. Brit. minced meat.
□ **mincemeat** a mixture of dried fruit, sugar, etc. **mince pie** a small pie containing mincemeat. **not mince (your) words** speak plainly.
■ **mincer** n.

mind n. **1** the faculty of consciousness and thought. **2** a person's intellect or memory. **3** a person's attention or will.
▷ SYNONYMS: **1 sanity**, mental faculties, senses, wits, reason, reasoning, judgement. **2 brain**, intelligence, intellect, brains, brainpower, wits, understanding, reasoning, judgement, sense, head; informal grey matter; N. Amer. informal smarts. **3 attention**, thoughts, concentration. **4** one of

the great minds of his day: **intellect**, thinker, brain, scholar, genius.
•v. **1** be distressed or annoyed by. **2** remember to do. **3** watch out for. **4** take care of temporarily. **5** (**minded**) inclined to think in a particular way: *liberal-minded*.
▷ SYNONYMS: **1 object**, care, be bothered, be annoyed, be upset, take offence, disapprove, look askance; informal give/care a damn. **2 watch out for**, look out for, beware of. **3 look after**, take care of, keep an eye on, watch, attend to, care for.
■ **minder** n.

> **WORD LINKS**
> **cognitive**, **mental** relating to the mind

mindful adj. conscious or aware of something.

mindless adj. **1** acting or done without thought. **2** simple and repetitive.
▷ SYNONYMS: **1 stupid**, idiotic, brainless, asinine, witless, empty-headed; informal dumb, dopey, dim, half-witted, fat-headed, boneheaded. **2 unthinking**, thoughtless, senseless, gratuitous, wanton, indiscriminate. **3 mechanical**, routine, tedious, boring, monotonous, mind-numbing.
■ **mindlessly** adv.

mine[1] possess. pron. belonging to or associated with me.

mine[2] n. **1** a hole or passage dug in the earth for extracting coal etc. **2** an abundant source. **3** a bomb placed on or in the ground or water, which explodes on contact.
▷ SYNONYMS: **1 pit**, colliery, excavation, quarry. **2** *a mine of information*: **store**, storehouse, reservoir, repository, gold mine, treasure house, treasury.
•v. **1** obtain from a mine. **2** lay explosive mines on or in.
▷ SYNONYMS: **quarry**, excavate, dig, extract.
□ **minefield 1** an area planted with explosive mines. **2** a situation presenting hidden dangers. **minesweeper** a warship equipped for detecting and removing explosive mines.

miner n. a person who works in a mine.

mineral n. an inorganic natural substance, e.g. copper.
□ **mineral water** water containing dissolved mineral salts.

mineralogy n. the scientific study of minerals.
■ **mineralogical** adj. **mineralogist** n.

minestrone /mi-ni-stroh-ni/ n. an

m

Italian soup containing vegetables and pasta.

mingle v. **1** mix together. **2** move around and chat at a party.

▷ SYNONYMS: **1 mix**, blend, intermingle, intermix, interweave, interlace, combine, merge, fuse, unite, join, amalgamate. **2 socialize**, circulate, associate, fraternize, get together; informal hobnob.

– ANTONYMS: separate.

mini adj. very small of its kind.
• n. (pl. **minis**) a miniskirt.

miniature adj. much smaller than normal.

▷ SYNONYMS: **small**, mini, little, small-scale, baby, toy, pocket, diminutive; informal pint-sized; Scottish wee; N. Amer. vest-pocket.

– ANTONYMS: giant.
• n. a miniature thing.
■ **miniaturize** (or **-ise**) v.

minibus n. a small bus for about twelve people.

minicab n. Brit. an ordinary car that is used as a taxi but which must be ordered in advance.

minidisc n. a disc similar to a small CD, used for recording and playing back sound or data.

minim n. Brit. a musical note lasting as long as two crotchets.

minimal adj. of a minimum amount, quantity, or degree.

▷ SYNONYMS: **very little**, very small, minimum, the least possible, nominal, token, negligible.

– ANTONYMS: maximum.
■ **minimally** adv.

minimalist adj. **1** (of art) using simple forms and structures. **2** deliberately simple or basic in design.
• n. an artist who uses simple forms and structures.
■ **minimalism** n.

minimize (or **-ise**) v. **1** reduce to a minimum. **2** represent as less important than in reality.

▷ SYNONYMS: **1 keep down**, keep to a minimum, reduce, decrease, cut, lessen, curtail, prune; informal slash. **2 belittle**, make light of, play down, underrate, downplay, undervalue.

– ANTONYMS: maximize, exaggerate.

minimum n. (pl. **minima** or **minimums**) the smallest amount or extent possible.

▷ SYNONYMS: **lowest level**, lower limit, rock bottom, least, lowest.
• adj. smallest in amount or extent.

▷ SYNONYMS: **minimal**, least, smallest, least possible, slightest, lowest.

– ANTONYMS: maximum.

minion n. a lowly worker or assistant.

miniskirt n. a very short skirt.

minister n. **1** a head of a government department. **2** a senior diplomatic representative. **3** a member of the clergy.

▷ SYNONYMS: **1 member of the government**, member of the cabinet, Secretary of State. **2 clergyman**, clergywoman, cleric, pastor, vicar, rector, priest, parson, curate; informal reverend, padre.
• v. (**minister to**) attend to the needs of.

▷ SYNONYMS: *doctors ministered to the injured*: **tend**, care for, take care of, look after, nurse, treat, see to, help.
■ **ministerial** adj.

ministrations pl. n. the providing of help or care.

ministry n. (pl. **ministries**) **1** a government department headed by a minister. **2** a period of government under one Prime Minister. **3** the work of a minister of religion.

▷ SYNONYMS: **1 department**, bureau, agency, office. **2 the priesthood**, holy orders, the church.

mink n. a small stoat-like animal farmed for its fur.

minnow n. a small fish.

minor adj. **1** not important or serious. **2** Music (of a scale) having intervals of a semitone between the 2nd and 3rd, 5th and 6th, and 7th and 8th notes.

▷ SYNONYMS: **1 slight**, small, unimportant, insignificant, inconsequential, negligible, trivial, trifling, paltry, petty; N. Amer. nickel-and-dime; informal piffling. **2** *a minor poet*: **little known**, unknown, lesser, unimportant, obscure; N. Amer. minor-league; informal small-time; N. Amer. informal two-bit.

– ANTONYMS: major, important.
• n. a person under the age of full legal responsibility.

▷ SYNONYMS: **child**, infant, youth, adolescent, teenager, boy, girl; informal kid.

– ANTONYMS: adult.

minority n. (pl. **minorities**) **1** the smaller number or part. **2** a small group differing from the majority in race, religion, etc.

minster n. Brit. a large church.

minstrel n. a medieval singer or musician.

mint n. **1** a herb used in cookery. **2** the

m

flavour of mint. **3** a mint sweet. **4** a place where money is made.
• v. make coins.
▷ SYNONYMS: **coin**, stamp, strike, cast, make, manufacture.
□ **in mint condition** as good as new.
■ **minty** adj.

minuet n. a slow ballroom dance.

minus prep. **1** with the subtraction of. **2** falling below zero by a specific number of degrees. **3** informal lacking.
• adj. **1** (before a number) below zero. **2** (after a grade) slightly below.
• n. the symbol –.

minuscule adj. very tiny.

> USAGE -*u*-, not -*i*- in the middle: min*u*scule.

minute[1] /min-it/ n. **1** one sixtieth of an hour or degree. **2** informal a very short time. **3** (**minutes**) a written summary of the points discussed at a meeting.
▷ SYNONYMS: **1 moment**, short time, little while, second, instant; informal sec, jiffy; Brit. informal tick, mo, two ticks. **2** (**minutes**) **record**, proceedings, log, notes, transcript, summary.
• v. record in the minutes of a meeting.

minute[2] /my-**nyoot**/ adj. **1** very small. **2** precise and careful.
▷ SYNONYMS: **1 tiny**, minuscule, microscopic, miniature; Scottish wee; informal teeny, teeny-weeny; Brit. informal titchy, tiddly. **2** minute detail: **exhaustive**, painstaking, meticulous, rigorous, thorough, careful, precise.
– ANTONYMS: huge.
■ **minutely** adv.

minutiae /mi-**nyoo**-shi-ee/ pl. n. small or precise details.

minx n. a cheeky girl or young woman.

miracle n. **1** a welcome event so extraordinary that it is believed to be the work of God or a saint. **2** a remarkable event or thing.
▷ SYNONYMS: **wonder**, marvel, sensation, phenomenon.

miraculous adj. very surprising and welcome.
▷ SYNONYMS: **amazing**, astounding, remarkable, extraordinary, incredible, unbelievable, sensational, phenomenal, inexplicable.
■ **miraculously** adv.

mirage n. an effect caused by hot air, in which a sheet of water seems to appear in a desert or on a hot road.

mire n. a boggy area.

mirror n. a surface which reflects a clear image.
▷ SYNONYMS: **looking glass**; Brit. glass.
• v. reflect.
▷ SYNONYMS: **reflect**, match, reproduce, imitate, copy, mimic, echo, parallel.

mirth n. laughter.
■ **mirthful** adj. **mirthless** adj.

misadventure n. a mishap.
□ **death by misadventure** death caused by accident and not involving crime.

misanthrope n. a person who dislikes other people.
■ **misanthropic** adj. **misanthropy** n.

misapprehension n. a mistaken belief.

misappropriate v. dishonestly take for your own use.
■ **misappropriation** n.

misbehave v. behave badly; be disobedient.

miscalculate v. calculate wrongly.
■ **miscalculation** n.

miscarriage n. the birth of a fetus before it can survive independently.
□ **miscarriage of justice** a failure of a court of law to achieve justice.

miscarry v. (**miscarrying**, **miscarried**) **1** have a miscarriage. **2** (of a plan) fail.

miscellaneous adj. consisting of many different kinds.
▷ SYNONYMS: **various**, varied, different, assorted, mixed, sundry, diverse, disparate, heterogeneous.

miscellany n. (pl. **miscellanies**) a collection of different things.

mischance n. bad luck.

mischief n. **1** playful bad behaviour. **2** harm or trouble.
▷ SYNONYMS: **naughtiness**, bad behaviour, misbehaviour, misconduct, disobedience, wrongdoing; informal monkey business, shenanigans.

mischievous adj. **1** full of mischief. **2** intended to cause trouble.
▷ SYNONYMS: **1 naughty**, bad, badly behaved, troublesome, disobedient, rascally. **2 playful**, wicked, impish, roguish.
– ANTONYMS: well behaved.
■ **mischievously** adv.

> USAGE The ending is -*ous*, not -*ious*: mischiev*ous*.

misconceived adj. badly judged or planned.

misconception n. a mistaken idea or belief.

misconduct n. bad behaviour.
▷ SYNONYMS: **1 wrongdoing**, criminality, unprofessionalism, malpractice,

negligence, impropriety; *formal* maladministration. **2** misbehaviour, bad behaviour, mischief, misdeeds, naughtiness.

misconstrue v. interpret wrongly.
■ misconstruction n.

miscreant n. a wrongdoer.

misdeed n. a wrongful act.

misdemeanour (US **misdemeanor**) n. a minor wrongdoing.

miser n. a person who hoards money and spends as little as possible.
▷ SYNONYMS: **penny-pincher**, Scrooge; *informal* skinflint, cheapskate; N. Amer. *informal* tightwad.
– ANTONYMS: spendthrift.

miserable adj. **1** very unhappy. **2** causing unhappiness.
▷ SYNONYMS: **1 unhappy**, sad, sorrowful, melancholy, dejected, depressed, downhearted, downcast, despondent, disconsolate, wretched, glum, gloomy, forlorn, woebegone, mournful; *informal* blue, down in the dumps. **2** *their miserable surroundings*: **dreary**, dismal, gloomy, drab, wretched, depressing, grim, cheerless, bleak, desolate.
– ANTONYMS: cheerful, lovely.
■ miserably adv.

miserly adj. **1** unwilling to spend money. **2** (of a quantity) too small.
▷ SYNONYMS: **mean**, parsimonious, close-fisted, penny-pinching, cheese-paring, grasping; *informal* stingy, tight, tight-fisted; N. Amer. *informal* cheap.
– ANTONYMS: generous.
■ miserliness n.

misery n. (pl. **miseries**) **1** great unhappiness. **2** a cause of this. **3** Brit. *informal* a constantly miserable person.
▷ SYNONYMS: **unhappiness**, distress, wretchedness, suffering, angst, anguish, anxiety, torment, pain, grief, heartache, heartbreak, despair, despondency, dejection, depression, gloom, sorrow; *informal* the blues.
– ANTONYMS: contentment, pleasure.

misfire v. **1** fail to produce the intended result. **2** (of an engine) fail to ignite the fuel correctly. **3** (of a gun) fail to fire properly.

misfit n. a person whose behaviour or views set them apart from others.

misfortune n. **1** bad luck. **2** an unfortunate event.
▷ SYNONYMS: **problem**, difficulty, setback, trouble, adversity, bad luck, misadventure, mishap, blow, failure, accident, disaster, trial, tribulation.

misgivings pl. n. feelings of doubt or worry.

misguided adj. showing bad judgement.
▷ SYNONYMS: **unwise**, foolish, ill-advised, ill-judged, ill-considered, injudicious, imprudent, unsound, mistaken, misplaced.
– ANTONYMS: wise.

mishandle v. handle badly or wrongly.

mishap n. an unlucky accident.

mishmash n. a confused mixture.

misinform v. give wrong information to.
■ misinformation n.

misinterpret v. interpret wrongly.
■ misinterpretation n.

misjudge v. **1** form a wrong opinion of. **2** estimate wrongly.

mislay v. (**mislaying**, **mislaid**) lose temporarily.
▷ SYNONYMS: **lose**, misplace, be unable to find.
– ANTONYMS: find.

mislead v. (**misleading**, **misled**) give a wrong impression or wrong information to.
▷ SYNONYMS: **deceive**, delude, take in, lie to, fool, hoodwink, misinform; *informal* lead up the garden path, take for a ride; N. Amer. *informal* give someone a bum steer.

misleading adj. giving the wrong idea or information.
▷ SYNONYMS: **deceptive**, confusing, deceiving, equivocal, false.
– ANTONYMS: clear, straightforward.

mismanage v. manage badly or wrongly.
■ mismanagement n.

mismatch n. a combination of people or things that do not match.
• v. match unsuitably or incorrectly.

misnomer n. a wrongly applied name or description.

misogynist /mi-soj-uh-nist/ n. a man who hates women.
■ misogyny n.

misplace v. **1** put something in the wrong place. **2** (**misplaced**) unwise or inappropriate.

misprint n. a mistake in printed text.

misquote v. quote inaccurately.

misread v. (**misreading**, **misread**) read or interpret wrongly.

misrepresent v. give a misleading account of.
■ misrepresentation n.

misrule n. **1** bad government. **2** disorder.

Miss n. a title for an unmarried woman or girl.

miss v. **1** fail to hit or reach. **2** be too late for. **3** fail to see or hear. **4** fail to be present at. **5** avoid. **6** (**miss out**) Brit. omit. **7** feel the loss or absence of.
▷ SYNONYMS: **1 go wide of**, fall short of, pass, overshoot. **2 avoid**, evade, escape, dodge, sidestep, elude, circumvent, bypass. **3 pine for**, yearn for, ache for, long for. **4 fail to attend**, be absent from, play truant from, cut, skip, omit; Brit. informal skive off.
− ANTONYMS: hit, catch.
• n. a failure to hit or reach something.

misshapen adj. not having the normal shape.

missile n. an object thrown or fired at a target.

missing adj. lost or absent.
▷ SYNONYMS: **1 lost**, mislaid, misplaced, absent, gone astray, unaccounted for. **2 absent**, lacking, wanting.
− ANTONYMS: present.

mission n. **1** an important assignment. **2** an organization involved in a long-term assignment abroad. **3** a strongly felt aim or calling. **4** the work of teaching people about Christianity.
▷ SYNONYMS: **1 assignment**, commission, expedition, journey, trip, undertaking, operation, project. **2** *her mission in life:* **vocation**, calling, goal, aim, quest, purpose, function, task, job, labour, work, duty.

missionary n. (pl. **missionaries**) a person sent to teach others about Christianity.
▷ SYNONYMS: **evangelist**, apostle, proselytizer, preacher.

missive n. a letter.

misspell v. (**misspelling**, **misspelled** or **misspelt**) spell wrongly.

mist n. tiny water droplets in the air or on a surface.
▷ SYNONYMS: **haze**, fog, smog, murk, cloud, vapour, steam, spray, condensation.
• v. cover or become covered with mist.

mistaken adj. **1** based on a misunderstanding or faulty judgement. **2** wrong in your opinion or judgement.
▷ SYNONYMS: **wrong**, inaccurate, erroneous, incorrect, off beam, false, fallacious, unfounded, misguided, misinformed.
− ANTONYMS: correct.

mister var. of MR.

mistletoe n. a plant with white berries, growing on trees as a parasite.

mistral n. a strong north-westerly wind in southern France.

mistreat v. treat badly or unfairly.
▷ SYNONYMS: **ill-treat**, maltreat, abuse, knock about/around, hit, beat, injure, harm, hurt, misuse.
■ **mistreatment** n.

mistress n. **1** a woman in a position of authority. **2** a woman having a sexual relationship with a man married to someone else. **3** Brit. a female schoolteacher.

mistrial n. a trial made invalid through a mistake in proceedings.

mistrust v. have no trust in.
▷ SYNONYMS: **be suspicious of**, be sceptical of, be wary of, be chary of, distrust, have doubts about, have misgivings about, have reservations about, suspect.
• n. lack of trust.

misty adj. (**mistier**, **mistiest**) **1** covered with mist. **2** indistinct.
▷ SYNONYMS: **hazy**, foggy, cloudy, blurred, vague, indistinct.
− ANTONYMS: clear.

misunderstand v. (**misunderstanding**, **misunderstood**) fail to understand correctly.
▷ SYNONYMS: **misapprehend**, misinterpret, misconstrue, misconceive, mistake, misread, be mistaken, get the wrong idea; informal get the wrong end of the stick.

misunderstanding n. **1** a failure to understand correctly. **2** a minor disagreement.
▷ SYNONYMS: **1 misinterpretation**, misreading, misapprehension, misconception, false impression. **2 disagreement**, difference of opinion, dispute, falling-out, quarrel, argument, clash.

misuse v. **1** use wrongly. **2** treat badly.
▷ SYNONYMS: **misapply**, misemploy, abuse, squander, waste, dissipate; misappropriate, embezzle.
• n. wrong use.

mite n. **1** a tiny animal like a spider. **2** a small child or animal. **3** a very small amount.

mitigate v. make less severe or serious.
■ **mitigation** n.

> **USAGE** Don't confuse **mitigate** with **militate**: **militate against** means 'be a powerful factor in preventing'.

mitre (US **miter**) n. **1** a bishop's pointed headdress. **2** a joint between two pieces of wood cut to form a right angle.

mitt n. a mitten.

mitten n. a glove with a single section for all four fingers.

mix v. **1** combine or be combined. **2** make by mixing ingredients. **3** (**mix up**) confuse or spoil the arrangement of. **4** meet people socially.
▷ SYNONYMS: **1 blend**, mingle, combine, fuse, unite, join, amalgamate, incorporate, meld, homogenize; technical admix; literary commingle. **2 associate**, socialize, keep company, consort, mingle, circulate; Brit. rub shoulders; N. Amer. rub elbows; informal hang out/around, hobnob.
– ANTONYMS: separate.
• n. a mixture.
▷ SYNONYMS: **mixture**, blend, combination, compound, fusion, union, amalgamation, medley, selection, assortment, variety, jumble, mishmash, ragbag, hotchpotch; N. Amer. hodgepodge.
■ **mixer** n.

mixed adj. consisting of different qualities, elements, etc.
▷ SYNONYMS: **1** *a mixed collection:* **assorted**, varied, variegated, miscellaneous, disparate, diverse, diversified, motley, sundry, jumbled, heterogeneous. **2** *mixed reactions:* **ambivalent**, equivocal, contradictory, conflicting, confused, muddled.
– ANTONYMS: homogeneous.

mixture n. **1** a substance made by mixing. **2** (**a mixture of**) a combination of different but distinct things.
▷ SYNONYMS: **1 blend**, mix, brew, combination, concoction, composition, compound, alloy, amalgam. **2 assortment**, miscellany, medley, blend, variety, mixed bag, mix, diversity, collection, selection, hotchpotch, ragbag, mishmash; N. Amer. hodgepodge.

mizzen (or **mizzenmast**) n. the mast behind a ship's main mast.

ml abbrev. millilitres.

mm abbrev. millimetres.

MMR abbrev. measles, mumps, and rubella (a vaccination given to children).

mnemonic /ni-mon-ik/ n. a pattern of words or letters used to aid the memory.

moan n. **1** a low mournful sound. **2** a grumble.
• v. **1** make a moan. **2** grumble.
▷ SYNONYMS: **1 groan**, wail, whimper, sob, cry. **2 complain**, grouse, grumble, whine, carp; informal gripe, grouch, bellyache, bitch, beef, whinge.

moat n. a wide water-filled ditch round a castle or town.

mob n. **1** a disorderly crowd. **2** Brit. informal a group.
▷ SYNONYMS: **crowd**, horde, multitude, rabble, mass, throng, gathering, assembly.
• v. (**mobbing**, **mobbed**) crowd round in an unruly way.
▷ SYNONYMS: **surround**, crowd round, besiege, jostle.

mobile adj. able to move or be moved easily.
▷ SYNONYMS: **1 able to move**, able to walk, walking; informal up and about. **2** *a mobile library:* **travelling**, transportable, portable, movable, itinerant, peripatetic.
– ANTONYMS: immobile.
• n. **1** a decorative structure hung so as to turn freely in the air. **2** (or **mobile phone**) a portable phone.
■ **mobility** n.

mobilize (or **-ise**) v. organize troops for active service.
▷ SYNONYMS: **1** *mobilize the troops:* **marshal**, deploy, muster, rally, call up, assemble, mass, organize, prepare. **2** *mobilizing support for the party:* **generate**, arouse, awaken, excite, stimulate, stir up, encourage, inspire, whip up.
■ **mobilization** n.

moccasin n. a soft flat shoe.

mocha /mok-uh/ n. a drink of coffee and chocolate.

mock v. tease or imitate in an unkind way.
▷ SYNONYMS: **ridicule**, jeer at, sneer at, deride, make fun of, laugh at, scoff at, tease, taunt; informal take the mickey out of; N. Amer. informal goof on, rag on.
• adj. not genuine or real.
▷ SYNONYMS: **imitation**, artificial, manmade, simulated, synthetic, ersatz, fake, reproduction, pseudo, false, faux, spurious; informal pretend.
– ANTONYMS: genuine.
□ **mock-up** a model for testing or study.

mockery n. (pl. **mockeries**) **1** ridicule. **2** an absurd or worthless version of something.

mocking adj. contemptuous or scornful.
▷ SYNONYMS: **sneering**, derisive, contemptuous, scornful, sardonic, ironic, sarcastic, satirical.

mode n. **1** a way of doing something. **2** a style in clothes, art, etc.
▷ SYNONYMS: **1 manner**, way, means,

m

method, system, style, approach.
2 *the camera is in manual mode:*
function, position, operation, setting,
option.

model n. **1** a three-dimensional copy
of a person or thing. **2** something
used as an example. **3** an excellent
or perfect example of a quality. **4** a
person employed to pose for an artist
or to wear and display clothes. **5** a
particular version of a product.
▷ SYNONYMS: **1 replica**, copy, representation, mock-up, dummy, imitation,
duplicate, reproduction, facsimile.
2 prototype, archetype, type, paradigm, version, mould, template,
framework, pattern, design, blueprint. **3 ideal**, paragon, nonpareil,
exemplar. **4** supermodel, mannequin;
informal clothes horse.
• v. (**modelling**, **modelled**; US
modeling, modeled) **1** make a model
of. **2** (**model on**) use as an example
for. **3** work as a model.

modem n. a device connecting a
computer to a phone line.

moderate adj. **1** average in amount,
intensity, etc. **2** not politically
extreme.
▷ SYNONYMS: **1 average**, modest,
medium, middling, reasonable, acceptable, adequate, fair, tolerable, passable; informal OK, so-so, bog-standard,
fair-to-middling. **2** *moderate views:*
middle-of-the-road, non-extremist,
liberal, pragmatic.
– ANTONYMS: immoderate, extreme.
• n. a person with moderate views.
• v. make or become moderate.
▷ SYNONYMS: **1 die down**, abate, let
up, calm down, lessen, decrease,
diminish, recede, weaken, subside.
2 curb, control, check, temper,
restrain, subdue, tame, lessen,
decrease, lower, reduce, diminish,
alleviate, allay, appease, ease, soothe,
calm, tone down.
– ANTONYMS: increase.
■ **moderately** adv. **moderation** n.

moderator n. a person who helps to
solve a dispute.

modern adj. **1** of the present or
recent times. **2** involving up-to-date
techniques or equipment.
▷ SYNONYMS: **1 present-day**,
contemporary, present, current,
twenty-first-century, latter-day,
recent. **2 fashionable**, up to date,
trendsetting, stylish, chic, à la mode,
the latest, new, newest, advanced,
newfangled; informal trendy, cool, funky.
– ANTONYMS: past, old-fashioned.

■ **modernity** n.
modernism n. modern ideas,
methods, or styles.
■ **modernist** n. & adj.

modernize (or **-ise**) v. bring up
to date with modern equipment,
techniques, etc.
▷ SYNONYMS: **update**, bring up to date,
streamline, rationalize, overhaul,
renovate, remodel, refashion, revamp.
■ **modernization** n.

modest adj. **1** not boasting about
yourself. **2** relatively moderate or
small. **3** not showing off the body.
▷ SYNONYMS: **1 self-deprecating**,
humble, self-effacing, unassuming,
shy, diffident, reserved, bashful.
2 *modest success:* **moderate**,
fair, limited, tolerable, passable,
adequate, satisfactory, acceptable,
unexceptional. **3** *a modest house:*
small, ordinary, simple, plain,
humble, inexpensive, unostentatious,
unpretentious. **4** *her modest dress:*
demure, decent, seemly, decorous,
proper.
– ANTONYMS: conceited, grand,
immodest.
■ **modestly** adv. **modesty** n.

modicum n. a small amount.

modify v. (**modifying**, **modified**) make
small changes to.
▷ SYNONYMS: **1 change**, alter, adjust,
adapt, amend, revise, refine; informal
tweak. **2** *he's modified his views since
then:* **moderate**, temper, soften, tone
down, qualify.
■ **modification** n.

modish adj. fashionable.

modulate v. **1** regulate. **2** vary in tone
or pitch.
■ **modulation** n.

module n. **1** each of a set of parts
or units that can be used to create
a more complex structure. **2** a unit
forming part of a course of study.
■ **modular** adj.

modus operandi n. a way of doing
something.

mogul n. an important or powerful
person.

mohair n. a yarn made from the hair
of the angora goat.

moiety /moy-it-ee/ n. (pl. **moieties**)
a half.

moist adj. slightly wet; damp.
▷ SYNONYMS: **damp**, wet, steamy, humid,
muggy, sweaty, sticky; clammy, dank.
– ANTONYMS: dry.
■ **moisten** v.

moisture n. tiny drops of water
making something damp.

▷ SYNONYMS: **wetness**, wet, water, liquid, condensation, steam, vapour, dampness, damp, humidity.

moisturize (or **-ise**) v. make the skin less dry.
■ **moisturizer** n.

molar n. a grinding tooth at the back of the mouth.

molasses n. a thick brown liquid obtained from raw sugar.

mold etc. US = **MOULD** etc.

mole n. **1** a small furry burrowing mammal. **2** a spy within an organization. **3** a small dark patch on the skin. **4** a pier or breakwater.
□ **molehill** a small mound of earth thrown up by a mole.

molecule n. a group of atoms forming the smallest unit that can take part in a chemical reaction.
■ **molecular** adj.

molest v. **1** assault sexually. **2** dated harass.
■ **molestation** n. **molester** n.

mollify v. (**mollifying**, **mollified**) cause to feel less angry.

mollusc (US **mollusk**) n. an animal with a soft body and often an external shell.

mollycoddle v. pamper.

Molotov cocktail n. a bomb made of a bottle of flammable liquid.

molt US = **MOULT**.

molten adj. made liquid by heat.

molybdenum /muh-**lib**-duh-nuhm/ n. a brittle metallic element.

moment n. **1** an exact point or brief period of time. **2** importance.
▷ SYNONYMS: **1** *please wait a moment:* **minute**, second; informal sec, jiffy; Brit. informal tick, mo, two ticks. **3** *at that moment the phone rang:* **point**, stage, juncture, instant, time, second, minute.

momentary adj. very brief or short-lived.
▷ SYNONYMS: **brief**, short, short-lived, fleeting, passing, transitory, transient, ephemeral.
– ANTONYMS: lengthy.
■ **momentarily** adv.

momentous adj. very important.
▷ SYNONYMS: **important**, significant, historic, critical, crucial, pivotal, consequential, far-reaching; informal earth-shattering.
– ANTONYMS: insignificant.

momentum n. **1** the force gained by a moving object. **2** the force caused by the development of something.
▷ SYNONYMS: **impetus**, energy, force, driving force, power, strength, thrust,

speed, velocity.

monarch n. a king or queen.
▷ SYNONYMS: **sovereign**, ruler, Crown, crowned head, potentate, king, queen, emperor, empress, prince, princess.
■ **monarchical** adj.

monarchist n. a supporter of monarchy.

monarchy n. (pl. **monarchies**) **1** government by a monarch. **2** a state ruled by a monarch.

monastery n. (pl. **monasteries**) a community of monks living under religious vows.
▷ SYNONYMS: friary, abbey, priory, cloister.

monastic adj. of monks or nuns or their communities.

Monday n. the day before Tuesday.

monetarism n. the theory that inflation is best controlled by limiting the supply of money.
■ **monetarist** n. & adj.

monetary adj. of money.
▷ SYNONYMS: **financial**, fiscal, pecuniary, economic, budgetary.

money n. **1** coins and banknotes. **2** wealth. **3** payment or profit. **4** (**moneys** or **monies**) sums of money.
▷ SYNONYMS: **cash**, hard cash, means, wherewithal, funds, capital, finances, lucre, notes, coins, change, currency, specie; informal dough, bread, loot, readies; Brit. informal dosh, brass, lolly, spondulicks, the readies; N. Amer. informal dinero.

moneyed adj. wealthy.

Mongol n. **1** a person from Mongolia. **2** (**mongol**) offens. a person with Down's syndrome.

mongoose n. (pl. **mongooses**) a small carnivorous mammal of Africa and Asia.

mongrel n. a dog of no particular breed.

moniker n. informal a name.

monitor n. **1** a person or device that monitors something. **2** a television used to view a picture from a camera or a display from a computer. **3** a school pupil with special duties.
▷ SYNONYMS: **1** detector, scanner, recorder, sensor, security camera, CCTV. **2** *UN monitors:* observer, watchdog, overseer, supervisor, scrutineer. **3** *a computer monitor:* screen, display, VDU.
• v. keep under observation.
▷ SYNONYMS: **observe**, watch, track, keep an eye on, keep under surveillance, record, note, oversee; informal keep

m

tabs on.

monk n. a man belonging to a religious community.

monkey n. (pl. **monkeys**) **1** a small primate, usu. with a long tail and living in trees. **2** a mischievous child.

▷ SYNONYMS: **simian**, primate, ape.

• v. (**monkeying**, **monkeyed**) **1** (**monkey about/around**) behave in a silly way. **2** (**monkey with**) tamper with.

□ **monkey wrench** a spanner with large adjustable jaws.

mono n. monophonic sound.

monochrome adj. produced in black and white or in tones of one colour.

monocle n. a single lens worn at one eye.

monoculture n. the cultivation of only one crop in an area.

monogamy n. the practice of having only one husband or wife at a time.

■ **monogamous** adj.

monogram n. a design of interwoven letters, usu. a person's initials.

■ **monogrammed** adj.

monograph n. a scholarly written study about a single subject.

monolingual adj. speaking or expressed in one language.

monolith n. a large single upright block of stone.

■ **monolithic** adj.

monologue n. a long speech.

monomania n. an obsession with one thing.

■ **monomaniac** n.

monophonic adj. (of sound reproduction) using only one transmission channel.

monoplane n. an aircraft with one pair of wings.

monopolize (or **-ise**) v. dominate or take control of.

monopoly n. (pl. **monopolies**) the control of the supply of a product or service by one person or organization.

monorail n. a railway in which the track consists of a single rail.

monosodium glutamate n. a compound used to add flavour to food.

monosyllable n. a word of one syllable.

■ **monosyllabic** adj.

monotheism n. the belief that there is only one god.

■ **monotheist** n. **monotheistic** adj.

monotone n. a level unchanging tone of voice.

monotonous adj. dull because

lacking in change or variety.

▷ SYNONYMS: **tedious**, boring, uninteresting, unexciting, dull, repetitive, repetitious, unvarying, unchanging, mechanical, mind-numbing, soul-destroying; informal deadly.

– ANTONYMS: interesting.

■ **monotonously** adv. **monotony** n.

monoxide n. an oxide with one atom of oxygen.

Monsieur /muh-**syer**/ n. (pl. **Messieurs**) a form of address for a French man.

monsoon n. **1** a seasonal wind in the Indian subcontinent and SE Asia. **2** the rainy season accompanying this.

monster n. **1** a large, frightening imaginary creature. **2** a very cruel person.

▷ SYNONYMS: **1 giant**, mammoth, demon, dragon, colossus, leviathan. **2 fiend**, animal, beast, devil, demon, barbarian, savage, brute; informal swine.

• adj. informal very large.

monstrosity n. (pl. **monstrosities**) **1** a very large and ugly object. **2** an evil act.

monstrous adj. **1** very large and ugly or frightening. **2** very evil or wrong.

▷ SYNONYMS: **1 grotesque**, hideous, ugly, ghastly, gruesome, horrible, horrific, horrifying, grisly, disgusting, repulsive, dreadful, frightening, terrible, terrifying. **2 appalling**, wicked, abominable, terrible, horrible, dreadful, vile, outrageous, unspeakable, despicable, vicious, savage, barbaric, inhuman.

– ANTONYMS: beautiful, humane.

■ **monstrously** adv.

montage /mon-**tahzh**/ n. a picture or film made by putting together pieces from other pictures or films.

month n. **1** each of the twelve periods into which a year is divided. **2** a period of 28 days.

■ **monthly** adj. & adv.

monument n. **1** a statue or structure built to commemorate a person or event. **2** a structure or site of historical importance.

▷ SYNONYMS: **memorial**, statue, pillar, cairn, column, obelisk, cross, ceno-taph, tomb, mausoleum, shrine.

monumental adj. **1** very large or impressive. **2** acting as a monument.

▷ SYNONYMS: **1 huge**, enormous, gigantic, massive, colossal, mammoth, immense, tremendous, mighty, stupendous. **2 significant**, important,

majestic, memorable, remarkable, noteworthy, momentous, grand, awe-inspiring, heroic, epic.
– ANTONYMS: tiny.

moo v. (of a cow) make a long, deep sound.

mooch v. Brit. informal pass time aimlessly.

mood n. **1** a temporary state of mind. **2** a fit of bad temper.
▷ SYNONYMS: **1 frame of mind**, state of mind, humour, temper. **2 bad mood**, temper, bad temper, sulk, low spirits, the doldrums, the blues; Brit. informal paddy. **3 atmosphere**, feeling, spirit, ambience, aura, character, flavour, feel, tone.

moody adj. (**moodier**, **moodiest**) **1** having sudden changes of mood. **2** gloomy or sulky.
▷ SYNONYMS: **temperamental**, emotional, volatile, capricious, erratic, bad-tempered, petulant, sulky, sullen, morose.
– ANTONYMS: cheerful.
■ **moodily** adv.

moon n. **1** the natural satellite of the earth. **2** a natural satellite of any planet.
• v. behave in a dreamy way.
□ **moonscape** a rocky landscape like that of the moon. **moonshine** **1** foolish ideas. **2** US illegally made alcoholic drink. **moonstone** a white semi-precious stone.

WORD LINKS
lunar relating to the moon

moonlight n. the light of the moon.
• v. (**moonlighting**, **moonlighted**) informal do a second job without declaring it for tax purposes.
■ **moonlit** adj.

Moor n. a member of a NW African Muslim people.
■ **Moorish** adj.

moor n. an area of high, open uncultivated land.
▷ SYNONYMS: **upland**, heath, moorland; Brit. fell, wold.
• v. fasten a boat to the shore or to an anchor.
▷ SYNONYMS: **tie up**, secure, fasten, make fast, berth, dock.
□ **moorhen** a small black waterbird. **mooring** (or **moorings**) **1** a place where a boat is moored. **2** the ropes for mooring a boat.

moose (pl. **moose**) = ELK.

moot adj. uncertain or undecided: a moot point.

mop n. **1** a bundle of thick strings or

a sponge on a stick, used for wiping floors. **2** a thick mass of hair.
▷ SYNONYMS: a tousled mop of hair: **shock**, mane, tangle, mass.
• v. (**mopping**, **mopped**) clean or soak up by wiping.

mope v. be listless and unhappy.

moped n. a light motorcycle.

moraine n. rocks and stones deposited by a glacier.

moral adj. **1** concerned with the principles of right and wrong behaviour. **2** following accepted standards of behaviour.
▷ SYNONYMS: **1 ethical**, good, virtuous, righteous, upright, upstanding, high-minded, principled, honourable, honest, just, noble. **2** moral support: **psychological**, emotional, mental.
– ANTONYMS: immoral, unethical.
• n. **1** a moral lesson learned from a story or experience. **2** (**morals**) standards of good behaviour.
▷ SYNONYMS: **1 lesson**, message, meaning, significance, import, point, teaching. **2** he's got no morals: **moral code**, code of ethics, values, principles, standards, morality, scruples.
□ **moral victory** a defeat that can be interpreted as a victory because you have done the right thing.
■ **morally** adv.

morale n. a feeling of confidence and satisfaction.
▷ SYNONYMS: **confidence**, self-confidence, self-esteem, spirit, team spirit, esprit de corps, motivation.

moralist n. a person promoting strict moral views.

morality n. (pl. **moralities**) **1** moral principles or behaviour. **2** the extent to which an action is right or wrong.
▷ SYNONYMS: **1 ethics**, rights and wrongs, whys and wherefores. **2 virtue**, good behaviour, righteousness, upright-ness, morals, standards, principles, honesty, integrity, propriety, honour, decency.

moralize (or **-ise**) v. comment on moral matters in a disapproving way.

morass n. **1** a boggy area of ground. **2** a complicated situation.

moratorium n. (pl. **moratoriums** or **moratoria**) a temporary ban on an activity.

morbid adj. **1** having a strong interest in death and disease. **2** of disease.
▷ SYNONYMS: **ghoulish**, macabre, unhealthy, gruesome, unwholesome; informal sick.
– ANTONYMS: wholesome.

m

■ **morbidity** n. **morbidly** adv.

mordant adj. (of wit) sharply sarcastic.
• n. a substance combining with a dye to fix it.

more adj. & pron. a greater or additional amount or degree.
▷ SYNONYMS: **extra**, further, added, additional, supplementary, increased, new.
– ANTONYMS: less, fewer.
• adv. **1** to a greater extent. **2** again.

moreover adv. besides.
▷ SYNONYMS: **besides**, furthermore, in addition, also, as well, too, to boot, additionally, on top of that, into the bargain.

mores /mor-ayz/ pl. n. the customs and conventions of a community.

morgue n. a mortuary.

moribund adj. at the point of death.

Mormon n. a member of the Church of Jesus Christ of Latter-Day Saints.

morning n. the part of the day before noon.
▷ SYNONYMS: **1** a.m.; literary morn; Nautical & N. Amer. forenoon. **2** dawn, daybreak, sunrise, first light; N. Amer. sunup.
□ **morning sickness** nausea occurring during early pregnancy.

moron n. informal a stupid person.
■ **moronic** adj.

morose adj. sullen and bad-tempered.
■ **morosely** adv.

morphine n. a painkilling drug obtained from opium.

morphology n. the study of forms, esp. of words.
■ **morphological** adj.

morris dancing n. traditional English folk dancing.

Morse code n. a code in which letters are represented by long and short sounds or flashes of light.

morsel n. a small piece of food.

mortal adj. **1** having to die at some time. **2** causing death.
▷ SYNONYMS: **1** all men are mortal: **perishable**, physical, bodily, corporeal, human, fleshly, earthly, impermanent, transient, ephemeral. **2** a mortal blow: **fatal**, lethal, deadly, death-dealing, murderous, terminal. **3** mortal enemies: **deadly**, sworn, irreconcilable, bitter, implacable, unrelenting, remorseless.
– ANTONYMS: eternal.
• n. a human being.
■ **mortally** adv.

mortality n. **1** the state of being

mortal. **2** death. **3** the number of deaths in a particular place or period.

mortar n. **1** a mixture of lime, cement, sand, and water for holding bricks or stones together. **2** a bowl in which substances are crushed with a pestle. **3** a short cannon.
□ **mortar board** an academic cap with a flat square top.

mortgage n. **1** a legal agreement by which a person takes out a loan using their house as security. **2** the amount of money lent in a mortgage.
• v. transfer a property to a creditor as security for a loan.

mortgagee n. the lender in a mortgage.

mortgagor n. the borrower in a mortgage.

mortician n. US an undertaker.

mortify v. (mortifying, mortified) embarrass or humiliate.
■ **mortification** n.

mortise (or **mortice**) n. a slot cut in a piece of wood so as to hold the end of another piece of wood.
□ **mortise lock** a lock set into the framework of a door.

mortuary n. (pl. mortuaries) a place where corpses are kept until burial or cremation.
▷ SYNONYMS: **morgue**, funeral parlour; Brit. chapel of rest.

mosaic n. a picture or pattern made with small coloured pieces of stone, tile, or glass.

Moslem var. of MUSLIM.

mosque n. a Muslim place of worship.

mosquito n. (pl. mosquitoes) a small bloodsucking fly.

moss n. a small green spreading plant growing in damp places.
■ **mossy** adj.

most n. & pron. **1** greatest in amount or degree. **2** the majority of.
• adv. **1** to the greatest extent. **2** very.

mostly adv. on the whole; mainly.
▷ SYNONYMS: **1** mainly, for the most part, on the whole, in the main, largely, chiefly, predominantly, principally, primarily. **2** usually, generally, in general, as a rule, ordinarily, normally, customarily, typically, most of the time, almost always.

MOT n. a compulsory annual safety test of vehicles of more than a specified age.

motel n. a roadside hotel for motorists.

motet n. a short religious choral work.

moth n. an insect like a butterfly, usu.

active at night.

□ **mothball** a small ball of camphor for keeping moths away from stored clothes.

mother n. **1** a female parent. **2** (**Mother**) the title of the head of a convent.

▷ SYNONYMS: matriarch, materfamilias; informal ma; Brit. informal mum, mummy; N. Amer. informal mom, mommy; Brit. informal, dated mater.

• v. SYNONYMS: **look after**, care for, take care of, nurse, protect, tend, raise, rear; pamper, coddle, cosset, fuss over.

□ **motherboard** a printed circuit board containing the main components of a computer. **mother-in-law** (pl. **mothers-in-law**) the mother of a person's husband or wife. **motherland** a person's native country. **mother-of-pearl** a pearly substance lining the shells of oysters. **mother tongue** a person's native language. ■ **motherhood** n. **motherless** adj.

> **WORD LINKS**
> **maternal** relating to a mother
> **matricide** the killing of a mother by her child

motherly adj. kind and protective.

▷ SYNONYMS: **maternal**, maternalistic, protective, kind, caring, loving, affectionate, warm, nurturing.

motif n. **1** a single or repeated image forming a design. **2** a recurring theme in an artistic work.

▷ SYNONYMS: **1 design**, pattern, decoration, figure, shape, device, emblem. **2 theme**, idea, concept, subject, topic, leitmotif.

motion n. **1** an act of moving. **2** a formal proposal put to a meeting. **3** Brit. an emptying of the bowels.

▷ SYNONYMS: **1 movement**, locomotion, progress, passage, transit, course, travel, orbit. **2 gesture**, movement, signal, sign, indication, wave, nod, gesticulation. **3 proposal**, proposition, recommendation.

• v. direct with a gesture.

▷ SYNONYMS: **gesture**, signal, direct, indicate, wave, beckon, nod.

□ **motion picture** a cinema film. ■ **motionless** adj.

> **WORD LINKS**
> **kinetic** relating to motion

motivate v. **1** provide with a motive. **2** stimulate the interest of.

▷ SYNONYMS: **prompt**, drive, move, inspire, stimulate, influence, activate, impel, propel, push, spur, encourage,

incentivize.

motivation n. **1** the reason for a person's actions or behaviour. **2** enthusiasm.

▷ SYNONYMS: **motive**, motivating force, incentive, stimulus, stimulation, inspiration, inducement, incitement, spur.

motive n. a person's reason for doing something.

▷ SYNONYMS: **reason**, motivation, motivating force, rationale, grounds, cause, basis.

• adj. producing motion.

motley adj. varied or assorted.

motocross n. cross-country racing on motorcycles.

motor n. **1** a machine supplying power to drive a device. **2** Brit. informal a car.

• adj. giving or producing motion.

• v. travel by car.

□ **motorbike** a motorcycle. **motorboat** a boat powered by a motor. **motorcade** a procession of vehicles. **motor vehicle** a road vehicle powered by an engine. **motorway** Brit. a road for fast long-distance traffic. ■ **motorized** (or **-ised**) adj.

motorcycle n. a two-wheeled vehicle powered by a motor. ■ **motorcyclist** n.

motorist n. a car driver.

mottled adj. marked with patches of a different colour.

motto n. (pl. **mottoes** or **mottos**) a short sentence or phrase expressing a belief or aim.

▷ SYNONYMS: **slogan**, maxim, saying, proverb, aphorism, adage, saw, axiom, formula, catchphrase.

mould (US **mold**) n. **1** a container into which a liquid is poured to set in a desired shape. **2** a distinctive style or character. **3** a furry growth of tiny fungi on a damp surface.

▷ SYNONYMS: **1 cast**, die, matrix, form, shape, template, pattern, frame. **2** an actress in the Hollywood mould: **pattern**, form, type, style, tradition, school.

• v. **1** shape an object out of a soft substance. **2** influence the formation or development of.

▷ SYNONYMS: **1 shape**, form, fashion, model, work, construct, make, create, sculpt, cast. **2 determine**, direct, control, guide, influence, shape, form, fashion, make. ■ **mouldy** adj.

moulder (US **molder**) v. decay.

moulding (US **molding**) n. a decorative strip of wood, stone, or

m

plaster.

moult (US **molt**) v. shed feathers, hair, or skin before new growth.

mound n. **1** a raised mass of earth. **2** a heap.

▷ SYNONYMS: **1 heap**, pile, stack, mountain. **2 hillock**, hill, knoll, rise, hummock, hump; Scottish brae.

mount v. **1** climb up or on to. **2** get up on an animal or bicycle to ride it. **3** increase in number or intensity. **4** organize a course of action. **5** put or fix in place.

▷ SYNONYMS: **1 go up**, ascend, climb, scale. **2 increase**, grow, rise, escalate, soar, spiral, shoot up, rocket, climb, accumulate, build up, multiply. **3** *mount an exhibition*: **put on**, present, install, organize, stage, set up, prepare, launch, set in motion.
– ANTONYMS: descend, fall.

• v. n. **1** a support or setting. **2** a horse for riding. **3** (in names) a mountain.

▷ SYNONYMS: **setting**, backing, support, mounting, frame, stand.

mountain n. **1** a very high, steep hill. **2** a large pile or quantity.

▷ SYNONYMS: **1 peak**, summit; (**mountains**) range, massif, sierra; Scottish ben. **2 lot**; informal heap, pile, stack, slew, lots, loads, tons, masses. □ **mountain bike** a sturdy bicycle with broad deep-treaded tyres.

mountaineering n. the sport or activity of climbing mountains.
■ **mountaineer** n.

mountainous adj. **1** having many mountains. **2** huge.

mourn v. feel deep sorrow about the death or loss of.

▷ SYNONYMS: **1 grieve for**, sorrow over, lament for, weep for. **2 deplore**, bewail, bemoan, rue, regret.
■ **mourner** n.

mournful adj. very sad or depressing.
■ **mournfully** adv.

mourning n. **1** the expression of deep sorrow for someone who has died. **2** black clothes worn in a period of mourning.

▷ SYNONYMS: **grief**, grieving, sorrowing, lamentation.

mouse n. (pl. **mice**) **1** a small rodent with a long tail. **2** a quiet, timid person. **3** (pl. also **mouses**) a small hand-held device controlling the cursor on a computer screen.

moussaka n. a Greek dish of minced lamb and aubergines.

mousse n. **1** a dish made with whipped cream or egg white. **2** a light substance for styling hair.

moustache (US **mustache**) n. a strip of hair on a man's upper lip.

mousy adj. **1** (of hair) light brown. **2** timid.

mouth n. **1** the opening in the body through which food is taken and sounds are made. **2** an opening or entrance. **3** the place where a river enters the sea.

▷ SYNONYMS: **1 lips**, jaws, muzzle; informal **trap**, **chops**, **kisser**; Brit. informal gob; N. Amer. informal puss. **2 entrance**, opening. **3 estuary**, delta, firth, outlet, outfall.

• v. **1** move the lips as if to form words. **2** say insincerely. □ **mouth organ** a small instrument played by blowing and sucking. **mouthpiece** a part of a musical instrument etc. put in or against the mouth. **mouthwash** an antiseptic liquid for rinsing the mouth.
■ **mouthful** n.

WORD LINKS
oral relating to the mouth

move v. **1** go or cause to go in a specified direction or way. **2** change in position, state, etc. **3** change the place where you live. **4** take action. **5** make progress. **6** provoke emotion in.

▷ SYNONYMS: **1 go**, walk, step, proceed, progress, advance, budge, stir, shift. **2 carry**, transfer, shift, push, pull, lift, slide. **3 relocate**, move house, move away/out, go away, decamp. **4 progress**, advance, develop, evolve, change, happen. **5 affect**, touch, impress, shake, upset, disturb. **6 inspire**, prompt, stimulate, motivate, provoke, influence, rouse, induce, incite. **7 propose**, submit, suggest, advocate, recommend, urge.

• n. **1** an act of moving. **2** a purposeful action. **3** a player's turn in a board game.

▷ SYNONYMS: **1 movement**, motion, action, gesture. **2 initiative**, step, action, measure, manoeuvre, tactic, stratagem. **3 turn**, go.
■ **movable** (or **moveable**) adj.

movement n. **1** an act of moving. **2** a group with a shared cause. **3** (**movements**) a person's activities during a particular period. **4** a main division of a musical work.

▷ SYNONYMS: **1 motion**, move, gesture, sign, signal, action. **2 transportation**, shifting, conveyance, moving, transfer. **3 group**, party, faction, wing, lobby, camp. **4 campaign**, crusade, drive, push, initiative.

movie n. US a cinema film.
▷ SYNONYMS: **film**, picture, motion picture, feature film; informal flick.

moving adj. arousing sadness or sympathy.
▷ SYNONYMS: **1 in motion**, operating, operational, working, on the move, active, movable, mobile. **2 touching**, poignant, heart-warming, heart-rending, affecting, emotional, inspiring, inspirational, stimulating, stirring.
– ANTONYMS: stationary, fixed.
■ **movingly** adv.

mow v. (**mowing**, **mowed**; past part. **mowed** or **mown**) **1** cut down or trim grass or hay. **2** (**mow down**) kill by gunfire or by knocking down with a vehicle.
▷ SYNONYMS: **cut**, trim, crop, clip, shear.
■ **mower** n.

mozzarella /mot-suh-**rel**-luh/ n. a firm white Italian cheese.

MP abbrev. Member of Parliament.

mpg abbrev. miles per gallon.

mph abbrev. miles per hour.

Mr n. a title used before a man's name.

Mrs n. a title used before a married woman's name.

MRSA n. a strain of bacteria resistant to antibiotics.

MS abbrev. **1** manuscript. **2** multiple sclerosis.

Ms n. a title used before a married or unmarried woman's name.

MSc abbrev. Master of Science.

Mt abbrev. Mount.

much det. & pron. a large amount.
▷ SYNONYMS: **a lot**, a great/good deal, plenty; informal lots, loads, heaps, masses, tons.
– ANTONYMS: little.
• adv. **1** to a great extent. **2** often.
▷ SYNONYMS: **1 greatly**, a great deal, a lot, considerably, appreciably. **2 often**, frequently, many times, regularly, habitually, routinely, usually, normally, commonly.

mucilage /**myoo**-si-lij/ n. a sticky solution taken from plants, used in adhesives.

muck n. **1** dirt or rubbish. **2** manure.
▷ SYNONYMS: **1 dirt**, grime, filth, mud, mess; Brit. informal gunge. **2 dung**, manure, excrement, droppings, ordure.
• v. **1** (**muck up**) informal spoil. **2** (**muck about/around**) Brit. informal behave in a silly way. **3** (**muck out**) clean a stable.

□ **muckraking** the searching out and publicizing of scandal.
■ **mucky** adj.

mucous adj. of mucus.

mucus n. a slimy substance coating the lining of many body cavities and organs.

mud n. wet, soft earth.
▷ SYNONYMS: **dirt**, sludge, ooze, silt, clay, mire, soil.
□ **mudguard** a curved cover above a wheel to protect against spray from the road.

muddle v. **1** bring into a disordered state. **2** confuse. **3** (**muddle through** or Brit. **along**) cope more or less satisfactorily.
▷ SYNONYMS: **1 confuse**, mix up, jumble, disarrange, disorganize, disorder, mess up. **2 bewilder**, confuse, bemuse, perplex, puzzle, baffle, mystify.
• n. a muddled state.
▷ SYNONYMS: **mess**, confusion, jumble, tangle, chaos, disorder, disarray, disorganization.

muddy adj. (**muddier**, **muddiest**) **1** covered in or full of mud. **2** not bright or clear.
▷ SYNONYMS: **1** muddy ground: **water-logged**, boggy, marshy, squelchy, squishy, mucky, wet, soft. **2** muddy boots: **dirty**, filthy, mucky, grimy, soiled. **3** muddy water: **murky**, cloudy, turbid.
– ANTONYMS: clean, clear.

muesli /**myooz**-li/ n. a breakfast cereal consisting of oats, dried fruit, and nuts.

muezzin /moo-**ez**-zin/ n. a man who calls Muslims to prayer.

muff n. a tube-shaped furry covering for the hands.

muffin n. **1** a flat bread roll eaten toasted with butter. **2** a small cake.

muffle v. **1** wrap or cover for warmth. **2** make a sound quieter.
▷ SYNONYMS: **1 wrap**, swathe, enfold, envelop, cloak. **2 deaden**, dull, dampen, mute, soften, quieten, mask, stifle, smother.

muffler n. a scarf.

mufti n. civilian clothes when worn by military or police staff.

mug n. **1** a large cylindrical cup with a handle. **2** informal the face. **3** Brit. informal a stupid or gullible person.
▷ SYNONYMS: **beaker**, cup, tankard, glass, stein.
• v. (**mugging**, **mugged**) **1** attack and rob in a public place. **2** (**mug up**) Brit. informal learn a subject intensively.

m

▷ SYNONYMS: **assault**, attack, set upon, beat up, rob; informal **jump**.
■ **mugger** n.

muggy adj. (of the weather) unpleasantly warm and humid.
▷ SYNONYMS: **humid**, close, sultry, sticky, oppressive, airless, stifling, suffocating, stuffy.
− ANTONYMS: fresh.

mulberry n. a dark red or white fruit similar to a loganberry.

mulch n. leaves, bark, etc. spread around a plant for protection or to enrich the soil.
• v. cover with mulch.

mule n. **1** the offspring of a male donkey and a female horse. **2** a light backless shoe.

mulish adj. stubborn.

mull v. **1** (**mull over**) think about at length. **2** heat wine with sugar and spices.
▷ SYNONYMS: **ponder**, consider, think over/about, reflect on, contemplate, chew over; formal **cogitate on**.

mullah n. a Muslim learned in Islamic theology and law.

mullet n. (pl. **mullet**) an edible sea fish.

mulligatawny n. a spicy meat soup.

mullion n. a vertical bar between the panes in a window.

multi- comb. form many.

multicoloured (US **multicolored**) adj. having many different colours.
▷ SYNONYMS: **kaleidoscopic**, psychedelic, colourful, many-hued, jazzy, variegated.
− ANTONYMS: monochrome.

multicultural adj. of or involving several cultural or ethnic groups.

multifarious adj. very varied.

multilateral adj. involving three or more participants.

multimedia n. a computer system providing video and audio material as well as text.

multinational adj. involving several countries.
• n. a company operating in several countries.

multiple adj. having or involving several parts.
▷ SYNONYMS: **numerous**, many, various, different, diverse, several, manifold.
− ANTONYMS: single.
• n. a number divisible by another a certain number of times without a remainder.
□ **multiple sclerosis** a serious disease of the nervous system that can cause paralysis.

multiplex n. a cinema with several separate screens.

multiplicity n. (pl. **multiplicities**) a large number or variety.

multiply v. (**multiplying**, **multiplied**) **1** add a number to itself a specified number of times. **2** increase in number or quantity.
▷ SYNONYMS: **increase**, grow, accumulate, proliferate, mount up, mushroom, snowball.
− ANTONYMS: decrease.
■ **multiplication** n. **multiplier** n.

multiracial adj. of or involving people of many races.

multitask v. (of a computer) **1** operate more than one program at the same time. **2** do several things at once.

multitude n. a large number of people or things.

multitudinous adj. very numerous.

mum n. Brit. informal a person's mother.
□ **keep mum** say nothing so as not to reveal a secret.

mumble v. say indistinctly.
▷ SYNONYMS: **mutter**, murmur, talk under your breath.
• n. indistinct speech.

mumbo-jumbo n. informal complicated but meaningless language.

mummify v. (**mummifying**, **mummified**) preserve a body as a mummy.
■ **mummification** n.

mummy n. (pl. **mummies**) **1** Brit. informal a person's mother. **2** (in ancient Egypt) a body preserved for burial by embalming and wrapping in bandages.

mumps pl. n. a disease causing swelling of the glands at the sides of the face.

munch v. eat steadily and noisily.

mundane adj. dull or routine.
▷ SYNONYMS: **humdrum**, dull, boring, tedious, monotonous, tiresome, unexciting, uninteresting, uneventful, unremarkable, routine, ordinary.
− ANTONYMS: extraordinary.

municipal adj. relating to a town or city or its governing council.
■ **municipally** adv.

municipality n. (pl. **municipalities**) a town or district with its own local government.

munificent adj. very generous.
■ **munificence** n.

munitions pl. n. military weapons, ammunition, etc.

mural n. a painting done directly on a wall.

murder n. the illegal deliberate killing of one person by another.
▷ SYNONYMS: **killing**, assassination, execution, slaughter, butchery, massacre, extermination; homicide, manslaughter; literary slaying.
• v. kill illegally and deliberately.
▷ SYNONYMS: **kill**, put to death, assassinate, execute, butcher, slaughter, massacre, wipe out; informal bump off; N. Amer. informal ice, waste; literary slay.

murderer n. a person who commits murder.
▷ SYNONYMS: **killer**, assassin, serial killer, butcher; informal hit man, hired gun.

murderous adj. capable of or involving murder or extreme violence.
▷ SYNONYMS: **homicidal**, brutal, violent, savage, ferocious, fierce, vicious, bloodthirsty, barbarous, barbaric, fatal, lethal, deadly.

murk n. darkness or fog.

murky adj. **1** dark or dirty. **2** dishonest and secret.
▷ SYNONYMS: **1 dark**, gloomy, grey, leaden, dull, dim, overcast, cloudy, clouded, sunless, dismal, dreary, bleak. **2 dirty**, muddy, cloudy, turbid.
– ANTONYMS: bright, clear.

murmur v. **1** say quietly. **2** make a low continuous sound.
▷ SYNONYMS: **mutter**, mumble, whisper, talk under your breath, talk sotto voce.
• n. **1** something said quietly. **2** a low continuous sound.
▷ SYNONYMS: **1 whisper**, mutter, mumble, undertone. **2 hum**, buzz, drone.

muscle n. **1** a band of bodily tissue that can contract to move a body part. **2** power or strength.
▷ SYNONYMS: **1 strength**, power, brawn; informal beef, beefiness. **2** financial muscle: **influence**, power, strength, might, force, forcefulness, weight; informal clout.
• v. (**muscle in**) informal interfere in another's affairs.

Muscovite n. a person from Moscow.

muscular adj. **1** of the muscles. **2** having well-developed muscles.
▷ SYNONYMS: **strong**, brawny, muscly, well built, burly, strapping, sturdy, powerful, athletic; informal hunky, beefy.
□ **muscular dystrophy** a condition

in which the muscles gradually get weaker.
■ **muscularity** n.

muse n. a woman who is a creative artist's inspiration.
• v. be deep in thought.
▷ SYNONYMS: **ponder**, consider, think over/about, mull over, reflect on, contemplate, turn over in your mind, chew over.

museum n. a building in which objects of interest or importance are stored and displayed.

mush n. **1** a soft, wet mass. **2** excessive sentimentality.
■ **mushy** adj.

mushroom n. an edible fungus with a domed head on a stalk.
• v. increase or develop rapidly.

music n. **1** vocal or instrumental sounds combined in a pleasing way. **2** the art of writing or playing music. **3** the written signs representing music.

musical adj. **1** of or accompanied by music. **2** fond of or skilled in music. **3** pleasant-sounding.
▷ SYNONYMS: **tuneful**, melodic, melodious, harmonious, sweet-sounding, dulcet, euphonious, mellifluous.
– ANTONYMS: discordant.
• n. a play or film with singing and dancing.
■ **musically** adv.

musician n. a person who plays a musical instrument or writes music.

musicology n. the study of the history and theory of music.

musk n. a strong-smelling substance produced by a type of male deer, used in perfumes.
■ **musky** adj.

musket n. hist. a light gun with a long barrel.

Muslim (or **Moslem**) n. a follower of Islam.
• adj. of Muslims or Islam.

muslin n. thin cotton cloth.

mussel n. a small shellfish with a dark shell.

must aux. v. expressing obligation, insistence, or certainty.
▷ SYNONYMS: **ought to**, should, have to, need to, be obliged to, be required to, be compelled to.

mustache US = MOUSTACHE.

mustang n. a small wild horse of the south-western US.

mustard n. a hot-tasting paste eaten with meat etc.

muster v. **1** summon up a feeling.

m

2 bring troops together.

▷ SYNONYMS: **1** *she mustered her courage:* summon up, screw up, call up, rally. **2 assemble**, mobilize, rally, raise, summon, gather, call up, call to arms, recruit, conscript; US draft.

□ **pass muster** be satisfactory.

musty adj. smelling stale or mouldy.
■ **mustiness** n.

mutable adj. liable to change.
■ **mutability** n.

mutant adj. resulting from or showing the effect of mutation.
• n. a mutant form.

mutate v. change in form or nature.

mutation n. **1** the process of mutating. **2** a change in genetic structure resulting in a variant form. **3** a mutant.

▷ SYNONYMS: **1 alteration**, change, transformation, metamorphosis, transmutation. **2 mutant**, freak, monstrosity, monster.

mute adj. **1** not speaking. **2** unable to speak.

▷ SYNONYMS: **1 silent**, speechless, dumb, unspeaking, tight-lipped, taciturn; informal mum. **2** *a mute appeal for help:* wordless, silent, unspoken.
– ANTONYMS: voluble, spoken.
• n. **1** dated a person who is unable to speak. **2** a device used to muffle a musical instrument.
• v. **1** muffle the sound of. **2** reduce the intensity of.
■ **mutely** adv.

muted adj. **1** not as loud as usual. **2** not bright.

▷ SYNONYMS: **1 muffled**, faint, indistinct, quiet, soft, low, distant, faraway. **2 subdued**, pastel, delicate, subtle, understated, restrained.

mutilate v. severely injure or damage.

▷ SYNONYMS: **1 disfigure**, maim, mangle, dismember, slash, hack up. **2 vandalize**, damage, slash, deface, violate, desecrate.
■ **mutilation** n.

mutinous adj. rebellious.

▷ SYNONYMS: **rebellious**, insubordinate, subversive, seditious, insurgent, insurrectionary, disobedient, restive.

mutiny n. (pl. **mutinies**) an open rebellion against authority, esp. by soldiers or sailors.

▷ SYNONYMS: **insurrection**, rebellion, revolt, riot, uprising, insurgence, insubordination.
• v. (**mutinying**, **mutinied**) rebel against authority.

▷ SYNONYMS: **rise up**, rebel, revolt, riot, strike.

■ **mutineer** n.

mutter v. **1** say quietly and indistinctly. **2** talk or grumble in private.

▷ SYNONYMS: **1 murmur**, talk under your breath, talk sotto voce, mumble, whisper. **2 grumble**, complain, grouse, carp, whine; informal moan, whinge.
• n. something muttered.

mutton n. the flesh of mature sheep as food.

mutual adj. **1** felt or done by two or more people equally. **2** shared by two or more people.

▷ SYNONYMS: **reciprocal**, reciprocated, requited, returned, common, joint, shared.
■ **mutuality** n. **mutually** adv.

muzzle n. **1** the nose and mouth of an animal. **2** a guard fitted over an animal's muzzle to stop it biting. **3** the open end of the barrel of a gun.
• v. **1** put a muzzle on. **2** prevent from expressing opinions freely.

muzzy adj. **1** dazed or confused. **2** blurred.

MW abbrev. **1** medium wave. **2** megawatts.

my adj. belonging to me.

myalgia n. muscle pain.

mycology n. the study of fungi.

mynah n. an Asian or Australasian bird, some kinds of which can mimic speech.

myopia n. short-sightedness.
■ **myopic** adj.

myriad n. (or **myriads**) a very great number.
• adj. countless.

myrrh /mer/ n. a scented resin used in perfumes and incense.

myrtle n. an evergreen shrub with purple berries.

myself pron. **1** used when the speaker is also the person affected by an action. **2** I or me personally.

mysterious adj. difficult or impossible to understand or explain.

▷ SYNONYMS: **1 puzzling**, strange, peculiar, curious, funny, odd, weird, queer, bizarre, mystifying, inexplicable, baffling, perplexing, arcane, esoteric, cryptic, obscure. **2 secretive**, inscrutable, impenetrable, enigmatic, reticent, evasive.
■ **mysteriously** adv.

mystery n. (pl. **mysteries**) **1** something that remains unexplained. **2** secrecy. **3** a story dealing with a puzzling crime.

▷ SYNONYMS: **1 puzzle**, enigma, conundrum, riddle, secret, paradox, question mark, closed book. **2 secrecy**, obscurity, uncertainty.

mystic n. a person who seeks to know God through contemplation and prayer.
• adj. mystical.
▷ SYNONYMS: **spiritual**, religious, transcendental, paranormal, other-worldly, supernatural, occult, metaphysical.
■ mysticism n.

mystical adj. **1** having a spiritual significance beyond human understanding. **2** inspiring a sense of mystery and awe.

mystify v. (mystifying, mystified) utterly bewilder.
▷ SYNONYMS: **bewilder**, puzzle, perplex, baffle, confuse, confound, bemuse, throw; informal flummox, stump, bamboozle.
■ mystification n.

mystique n. an impressive quality of mystery, glamour, or power.

myth n. **1** a traditional story of early history or explaining a natural event. **2** a widely held but false belief.
▷ SYNONYMS: **1 folk tale**, folk story, legend, fable, saga, lore, folklore. **2 misconception**, fallacy, old wives' tale, fairy story, fiction; informal cock and bull story.
■ mythical adj.

mythology n. a collection of myths.
■ mythological adj.

myxomatosis n. a highly infectious and usu. fatal disease of rabbits.

m

Nn

N abbrev. North or Northern.

naan var. of NAN².

nab v. (**nabbing**, **nabbed**) informal
1 catch a wrongdoer. 2 take suddenly.

nacho /na-choh/ n. (pl. **nachos**) a small
piece of tortilla topped with melted
cheese etc.

nadir n. the lowest point.
▷ SYNONYMS: **low point**, all-time low,
bottom, rock bottom; informal the pits.
– ANTONYMS: zenith.

naevus /nee-vuhss/ (US **nevus**) n. (pl.
naevi) a birthmark.

naff adj. Brit. informal lacking taste or
style.

nag v. (**nagging**, **nagged**) 1 harass
constantly to do something. 2 be
constantly worrying or painful to.
▷ SYNONYMS: 1 harass, keep on at, go
on at, badger, chivvy, hound, plague,
criticize, find fault with, moan at,
grumble at, henpeck; informal hassle;
N. Amer. informal ride. 2 **trouble**, worry,
bother, torment, niggle, prey on your
mind; informal bug.
• n. informal a horse.

naiad /ny-ad/ n. (in Greek mythology)
a water nymph.

nail n. 1 a small metal spike with a
flat head, used to join pieces of wood
together. 2 a thin hard layer over the
tip of a finger or toe.
▷ SYNONYMS: **tack**, pin, brad, hobnail,
spike, staple, rivet.
• v. 1 fasten with a nail or nails.
2 informal catch or arrest.
▷ SYNONYMS: **fasten**, fix, attach, secure,
affix, pin, tack, hammer.

naive /ny-eev/ adj. lacking experience
or judgement.
▷ SYNONYMS: **innocent**, unsophisticated,
artless, inexperienced, unworldly,
trusting, gullible, credulous, immature, callow, raw, green; informal wet
behind the ears.
– ANTONYMS: worldly.
■ **naively** adv. **naivety** n.

naked adj. 1 without clothes.

2 without coverings. 3 not hidden;
open.
▷ SYNONYMS: **nude**, bare, in the nude,
stark naked, stripped, unclothed,
undressed; informal without a stitch on,
in your birthday suit, in the raw/buff,
in the altogether; Brit. informal starkers;
N. Amer. informal buck naked.
– ANTONYMS: dressed.
□ **the naked eye** the normal power of
the eyes, without using a microscope
etc.
■ **nakedness** n.

namby-pamby adj. feeble or
cowardly.

name n. 1 a word or words by which
someone or something is known. 2 a
famous person. 3 a reputation.
▷ SYNONYMS: **title**, designation, tag,
nickname, sobriquet, epithet, label,
honorific; informal moniker, handle;
formal appellation, denomination,
cognomen.
• v. 1 give a name to. 2 identify by
name. 3 specify a time etc.
▷ SYNONYMS: 1 **call**, dub, label, style,
term, title, baptize, christen.
2 **nominate**, designate, select, pick,
decide on, choose.
□ **namesake** a person or thing with
the same name as another.

> **WORD LINKS**
> **onomastic** relating to names

namely adv. that is to say.
▷ SYNONYMS: **that is**, to be specific,
specifically, viz., to wit, in other
words.

nan¹ n. Brit. informal a person's
grandmother.

nan² /nahn/ (or **naan**) n. a soft flat
Indian bread.

nanny n. (pl. **nannies**) a woman
employed to look after a child in its
own home.

nanosecond n. one thousand
millionth of a second.

nanotechnology n. technology on
an atomic or molecular scale.

nap n. **1** a short sleep during the day. **2** short raised fibres on the surface of some fabrics.
▷ SYNONYMS: **sleep**, catnap, siesta, doze, lie-down, rest; informal snooze, forty winks, shut-eye; Brit. informal kip, zizz.
• v. (**napping, napped**) have a short sleep.

napalm /nay-pahm/ n. a jelly-like form of petrol used in firebombs.

nape n. the back of the neck.

naphtha /naf-thuh/ n. a flammable oil.

naphthalene n. a strong-smelling substance used in mothballs.

napkin n. a piece of cloth or paper used at meals to protect clothes or wipe the lips.

nappy n. (pl. **nappies**) Brit. a piece of material worn by a baby to absorb urine and faeces.

narcissism n. excessive interest in yourself and your appearance.
■ **narcissistic** adj.

narcissus n. (pl. **narcissi** or **narcissuses**) a daffodil with pale outer petals.

narcotic n. **1** an addictive drug affecting mood or behaviour. **2** a drug causing drowsiness or unconsciousness.
▷ SYNONYMS: **drug**, sedative, opiate, painkiller, analgesic, palliative.
• adj. of narcotics.
▷ SYNONYMS: **soporific**, sedative, calming, painkilling, pain-relieving, analgesic, anodyne.

narrate v. **1** tell a story. **2** provide a commentary for.
▷ SYNONYMS: **tell**, relate, recount, recite, describe, chronicle, report, present.
■ **narration** n. **narrator** n.

narrative n. a story.
▷ SYNONYMS: **account**, chronicle, history, description, record, report, story, tale.
• adj. of stories or the telling of stories.

narrow adj. **1** of small width in comparison to length. **2** limited in extent, amount, or scope. **3** only just achieved.
▷ SYNONYMS: **1 slender**, slim, small, slight, attenuated, tapering, thin, tiny. **2 confined**, cramped, tight, restricted, limited, constricted, small, tiny, inadequate, insufficient.
– ANTONYMS: wide, broad.
• v. become or make narrower.
▷ SYNONYMS: **reduce**, restrict, limit, decrease, diminish, taper, contract, shrink, constrict.
– ANTONYMS: widen.
• n. (**narrows**) a narrow channel connecting two areas of water.
□ **narrowboat** Brit. a canal boat less

than 7 ft (2.1 metres) wide.

narrowly adv. only by a small amount.
▷ SYNONYMS: *the car narrowly missed a cyclist*: **just**, barely, scarcely, hardly, by a hair's breadth; informal by a whisker.

narrow-minded adj. intolerant.
▷ SYNONYMS: **intolerant**, illiberal, reactionary, conservative, parochial, provincial, insular, small-minded, petty, blinkered, inward-looking, hidebound, prejudiced, bigoted.
– ANTONYMS: tolerant.

narwhal n. an Arctic whale with a spiral tusk.

NASA abbrev. (in the US) National Aeronautics and Space Administration.

nasal adj. of the nose.
■ **nasally** adv.

nascent adj. just coming into existence.

nasturtium n. a garden plant with orange, yellow, or red flowers.

nasty adj. (**nastier, nastiest**) **1** unpleasant. **2** spiteful.
▷ SYNONYMS: **1 unpleasant**, disagreeable, disgusting, vile, foul, abominable, revolting, repulsive, repellent, horrible, obnoxious, unsavoury, loathsome, noxious, foul-smelling, smelly, stinking, rank, fetid, malodorous; informal ghastly, horrid, gross; N. Amer. informal lousy; literary noisome. **2 unkind**, unpleasant, unfriendly, disagreeable, rude, spiteful, malicious, mean, vicious, malevolent, hurtful. **3** *a nasty accident*: **serious**, dangerous, bad, awful, dreadful, terrible, severe, painful.
– ANTONYMS: nice, pleasant.
■ **nastily** adv. **nastiness** n.

natal adj. of the place or time of a person's birth.

nation n. a large group sharing the same culture, language, or history, and inhabiting a particular state or area.
▷ SYNONYMS: **country**, state, land, realm, kingdom, republic, people, race, tribe.

national adj. **1** of a nation. **2** owned or supported by the state.
▷ SYNONYMS: **1** *national politics*: **state**, public, federal, governmental. **2** *a national strike*: **nationwide**, country-wide, general, widespread.
– ANTONYMS: local, international.
• n. a citizen of a particular country.
▷ SYNONYMS: **citizen**, subject, native, resident, inhabitant, voter, passport holder.
■ **nationally** adv.

nationalism n. **1** patriotic feeling.

n

2 belief in independence for a particular country.
▷ SYNONYMS: **patriotism**, allegiance; xenophobia, chauvinism, jingoism, flag-waving.
■ **nationalist** n. & adj. **nationalistic** adj.

nationality n. (pl. **nationalities**) **1** the status of belonging to a particular nation. **2** an ethnic group.

nationalize (or **-ise**) v. transfer from private to state ownership.
■ **nationalization** n.

nationwide adj. & adv. throughout the whole of a country or nation.
▷ SYNONYMS: **national**, countrywide, state, general, widespread, extensive.
– ANTONYMS: local.

native n. **1** a person born in a specified place. **2** a local inhabitant. **3** an animal or plant that lives or grows naturally in a particular area.
▷ SYNONYMS: **inhabitant**, resident, local, citizen, national, countryman.
– ANTONYMS: foreigner.
• adj. **1** associated with a person's place of birth. **2** (of a plant or animal) occurring naturally in a place. **3** in a person's character.
▷ SYNONYMS: **1** *the country's native species:* **indigenous**, original, local, domestic. **2** *native wit:* **innate**, inborn, natural, inherent, intrinsic.

Nativity n. (**the Nativity**) the birth of Jesus.

NATO abbrev. North Atlantic Treaty Organization.

natter v. & n. informal chat.

natty adj. informal smart and fashionable.
■ **nattily** adv.

natural adj. **1** of or produced by nature; not made or caused by humans. **2** born with a particular skill or quality. **3** relaxed and unaffected.
▷ SYNONYMS: **1 unprocessed**, organic, pure, unrefined, additive-free, green, GM-free. **2** *a natural occurrence:* **normal**, ordinary, everyday, usual, regular, common, commonplace, typical, routine, standard, logical, understandable, to be expected, predictable. **3** *a natural leader:* **born**, instinctive; congenital, pathological. **4** *his natural instincts:* **innate**, inherent, native, inherited, hereditary. **5** *she seemed very natural:* **unaffected**, spontaneous, uninhibited, relaxed, unselfconscious, genuine, open, artless, guileless, unpretentious, unstudied.
– ANTONYMS: unnatural, artificial, affected.

• n. a person with a natural skill or talent.
□ **natural gas** gas found underground, used as fuel. **natural history** the study of animals and plants. **natural selection** the evolutionary process by which organisms better adapted to their environment tend to survive and produce more offspring.
■ **naturally** adv.

naturalism n. realism in art or literature.
■ **naturalistic** adj.

naturalist n. an expert in natural history.

naturalize (or **-ise**) v. **1** make a foreigner a citizen of a country. **2** introduce a plant or animal into a region where it is not native.
■ **naturalization** n.

nature n. **1** the physical world, including plants, animals, and all things not made by people. **2** the typical qualities or characteristics of a person or thing. **3** a kind or sort.
▷ SYNONYMS: **1 the natural world**, the environment, Mother Earth, the universe, the cosmos, wildlife, the countryside, the land. **2 character**, personality, disposition, temperament, make-up, psyche. **3 kind**, sort, type, variety, category, class, genre, order, quality, complexion; N. Amer. stripe.

naturism n. nudism.
■ **naturist** n.

naught pron. old use nothing.

naughty adj. (**naughtier**, **naughtiest**) **1** disobedient; badly behaved. **2** informal mildly indecent.
▷ SYNONYMS: **1 badly behaved**, disobedient, bad, wayward, defiant, unruly, insubordinate, wilful, delinquent, undisciplined, refractory, disruptive, mischievous, impish. **2 indecent**, risqué, rude, racy, vulgar, dirty, filthy, smutty, crude, coarse.
– ANTONYMS: well behaved.
■ **naughtily** adv. **naughtiness** n.

nausea /naw-zi-uh/ n. a feeling of sickness.
▷ SYNONYMS: **sickness**, biliousness, queasiness, vomiting, retching.

nauseate v. cause to feel sick or disgusted.

nauseous adj. affected with or causing nausea.

nautical adj. of sailors or navigation.
▷ SYNONYMS: **maritime**, marine, naval, seafaring, seagoing, sailing.
□ **nautical mile** a unit of 1,852 m (approx. 2,025 yds).

nautilus n. (pl. **nautiluses**) a swimming mollusc with a spiral shell.

naval adj. of a navy.

nave n. the central part of a church.

navel n. the small hollow in a person's stomach where the umbilical cord was cut at birth.

navigable adj. able to be used by boats and ships.

navigate v. **1** plan and direct the route of a ship, aircraft, etc. **2** sail or travel over.
▷ SYNONYMS: **1 steer**, pilot, guide, direct, captain; informal skipper.
■ **navigation** n. **navigator** n.

navvy n. (pl. **navvies**) Brit. dated a labourer employed in building a road etc.

navy n. (pl. **navies**) **1** the branch of a country's armed services which fights at sea. **2** a dark blue colour.
▷ SYNONYMS: **fleet**, flotilla, armada.

nay adv. old use or dialect no.

Nazi /naht-si/ n. (pl. **Nazis**) hist. a member of the far-right National Socialist German Workers' Party.

NB abbrev. note well.

NE abbrev. north-east or north-eastern.

Neanderthal /ni-an-der-tahl/ n. an extinct human living in Europe between about 120,000 and 35,000 years ago.

neap tide n. a tide when there is least difference between high and low water.

near adv. **1** at or to a short distance in space or time. **2** almost.
• prep. **1** a short distance from. **2** on the verge of.
• adj. **1** at a short distance away. **2** close to being: a near disaster.
▷ SYNONYMS: **1 close**, nearby, at hand, a stone's throw away, neighbouring, within reach, accessible, handy, convenient; informal within spitting distance. **2 imminent**, in the offing, on its way, coming, impending, looming.
– ANTONYMS: far, distant.
• v. approach.
■ **nearness** n.

nearby adj. & adv. not far away.
▷ SYNONYMS: **not far away**, not far off, close at hand, close by, near, within reach, neighbouring, local, accessible, convenient, handy.
– ANTONYMS: distant.

nearly adv. very close to; almost.
▷ SYNONYMS: **almost**, just about, more or less, practically, virtually, all but, as good as, not far off, to all intents

and purposes, not quite; informal pretty well.

neat adj. **1** tidy or carefully arranged. **2** clever but simple. **3** not diluted.
▷ SYNONYMS: **1 tidy**, orderly, well ordered, in order, spick and span, uncluttered, shipshape, straight, trim. **2 smart**, spruce, dapper, trim, well groomed, well turned out; informal natty. **3** his neat footwork: **skilful**, deft, dexterous, adroit, adept, expert, nimble, elegant, graceful, accurate; informal nifty. **4** a neat solution: **clever**, ingenious, inventive, imaginative. **5** neat gin: **undiluted**, straight, pure.
– ANTONYMS: untidy.
■ **neaten** v. **neatly** adv. **neatness** n.

nebula n. (pl. **nebulae** or **nebulas**) a cloud of gas or dust in space.

nebulous adj. not clearly defined; vague.

necessarily adv. as a necessary result; unavoidably.
▷ SYNONYMS: **as a consequence**, as a result, automatically, as a matter of course, certainly, incontrovertibly, inevitably, unavoidably, inescapably, of necessity.

necessary adj. needing to be done or present; essential.
▷ SYNONYMS: **1 obligatory**, required, requisite, compulsory, mandatory, imperative, needed, essential, vital, indispensable, de rigueur; formal needful. **2** a necessary consequence: **inevitable**, unavoidable, inescapable, inexorable.
• n. (**necessaries**) basic requirements.

USAGE One c, two s's: necessary.

necessitate v. make necessary.

necessity n. (pl. **necessities**) **1** the fact of being necessary. **2** something essential.
▷ SYNONYMS: **1 essential**, prerequisite, requisite, sine qua non; informal must-have. **2** political necessity forced him to resign: **force of circumstance**, obligation, need, exigency.

neck n. **1** the part connecting the head to the rest of the body. **2** a narrow connecting or end part.
□ **neck and neck** level in a race.

necklace n. a piece of jewellery worn round the neck. **neckline** the edge of a dress or top at or below the neck.

necromancy n. **1** attempted communication with dead people to predict the future. **2** witchcraft or black magic.
■ **necromancer** n.

necrophilia n. sexual activity with or

interest in dead bodies.
■ **necrophiliac** n.

necrosis n. the death of cells in the body.

nectar n. a sweet fluid produced by flowers and made into honey by bees.

nectarine n. a kind of peach with a smooth skin.

née /nay/ adj. born (used in giving a married woman's maiden name).

need v. **1** want something because it is essential. **2** be obliged or required to.
▷ SYNONYMS: **1** require, be in need of, want, be crying out for, lack, be without, be short of; demand, call for, necessitate, entail, involve. **2** (needed) *basic IT skills are needed:* necessary, required, called for, wanted, desired; lacking.
• n. **1** a situation in which something is necessary or must be done. **2** something needed. **3** great poverty.
▷ SYNONYMS: **1** *there's no need for air conditioning:* necessity, requirement, call, demand. **2** *basic human needs:* requirement, necessity, want, requisite, prerequisite, desideratum. **3** *my hour of need:* difficulty, trouble, distress, crisis, emergency, urgency, extremity.

needful adj. necessary.

needle n. **1** a very thin pointed piece of metal used in sewing. **2** a long thin rod used in knitting. **3** the end of a hypodermic syringe. **4** a stylus for playing records. **5** a thin pointer on a dial, compass, etc. **6** the thin, stiff leaf of a fir or pine tree.
• v. informal deliberately annoy.
□ **needlework** sewing or embroidery.

needless adj. unnecessary.
▷ SYNONYMS: unnecessary, unneeded, uncalled for, gratuitous, pointless, superfluous, redundant, excessive.
– ANTONYMS: necessary.
■ **needlessly** adv.

needy adj. (needier, neediest) very poor.
▷ SYNONYMS: poor, deprived, disadvantaged, underprivileged, in need, hard up, poverty-stricken, impoverished, destitute, penniless; informal broke, strapped for cash; Brit. informal skint; dated needful.
– ANTONYMS: wealthy.

ne'er-do-well n. a lazy or useless person.

nefarious adj. wicked or criminal.

negate v. **1** stop or undo the effect of. **2** deny the existence of.
■ **negation** n.

negative adj. **1** showing the absence rather than the presence of something. **2** expressing denial, disagreement, or refusal. **3** not hopeful or favourable. **4** (of a quantity) less than zero. **5** of the kind of electric charge carried by electrons.
▷ SYNONYMS: **1** pessimistic, defeatist, gloomy, critical, cynical, fatalistic, dismissive, unenthusiastic, apathetic, unresponsive. **2** harmful, bad, adverse, damaging, detrimental, unfavourable, disadvantageous.
– ANTONYMS: positive, optimistic, favourable.
• n. **1** a negative word or statement. **2** a photo showing light and shade or colours reversed from those of the original, from which positive prints may be made.
■ **negatively** adv. **negativity** n.

neglect v. **1** fail to give proper care or attention to. **2** fail to do.
▷ SYNONYMS: **1** fail to look after, abandon, ignore, pay no attention to, let slide, be remiss about, be lax about, shirk. **2** fail, omit, forget.
– ANTONYMS: cherish, remember.
• n. the act of neglecting or the state of being neglected.
▷ SYNONYMS: **1** *the place had an air of neglect:* disrepair, dilapidation, shabbiness, abandonment, disuse. **2** negligence, dereliction of duty, carelessness, laxity, slackness, irresponsibility.
– ANTONYMS: care.
■ **neglectful** adj.

neglected adj. not receiving proper care or attention.
▷ SYNONYMS: **1** *a neglected cottage:* derelict, dilapidated, tumble-down, ramshackle, untended, abandoned. **2** *a neglected masterpiece:* disregarded, forgotten, overlooked, ignored, unrecognized, unnoticed, unsung, underrated.

negligee /neg-li-zhay/ n. a woman's light, flimsy dressing gown.

negligence n. lack of proper care and attention.

negligent adj. showing a lack of proper care and attention.
▷ SYNONYMS: neglectful, remiss, careless, lax, irresponsible, inattentive, thoughtless, uncaring, unmindful, forgetful, slack, sloppy; N. Amer. derelict.
– ANTONYMS: dutiful.

negligible adj. so small or unimportant as to be not worth considering.

▷ SYNONYMS: **trivial**, trifling, insignificant, unimportant, of no account, minor, inconsequential, minimal, small, slight, infinitesimal, minuscule.
– ANTONYMS: significant.

negotiate v. **1** try to reach an agreement by discussion. **2** bring about by discussion. **3** find a way over or through.
▷ SYNONYMS: **1 discuss terms**, talk, consult, confer, debate, compromise, bargain, haggle. **2 arrange**, broker, work out, thrash out, complete, close, conclude, agree on. **3 get round**, get past, get over, clear, cross, surmount, overcome, deal with, cope with.
■ **negotiable** adj.

negotiation (or **negotiations**) n. discussion aimed at reaching an agreement or compromise.
▷ SYNONYMS: **discussions**, talks, conference, debate, dialogue, consultation.

negotiator n. a person taking part in negotiations.
▷ SYNONYMS: **mediator**, arbitrator, moderator, go-between, middleman, intermediary, representative, spokesperson, broker.

Negro n. (pl. **Negroes**) a black person.

> USAGE The term **Negro** is now regarded as old-fashioned and offensive.

neigh n. a high-pitched cry made by a horse.
• v. make this cry.

neighbour (US **neighbor**) n. a person living next or very near to another.
• v. be next or very near to.

neighbourhood (US **neighborhood**) n. **1** a district within a town or city. **2** the area surrounding a place, person, etc.
▷ SYNONYMS: **1 district**, area, locality, locale, quarter, community; informal neck of the woods; N. Amer. informal hood. **2 vicinity**, environs.

neighbouring adj. near or next to a place or person.
▷ SYNONYMS: **adjacent**, adjoining, bordering, connecting, next-door, nearby, in the vicinity.
– ANTONYMS: remote.

neighbourly adj. friendly and helpful.
▷ SYNONYMS: **obliging**, helpful, friendly, kind, considerate, amicable, sociable, hospitable, companionable, civil, cordial.
– ANTONYMS: unfriendly.

neither adj. & pron. not either.
• adv. **1** not either. **2** not also.

nemesis /nem-i-siss/ n. (pl. **nemeses**) a means of deserved and unavoidable downfall.

neoclassical adj. of the revival of a classical style in the arts.

Neolithic adj. of the later part of the Stone Age.

neologism n. a new word.

neon n. an inert gas used in fluorescent lighting.

neonatal adj. of newborn children.

neophyte n. a novice.

nephew n. a son of a person's brother or sister.

nephritis n. inflammation of the kidneys.

nepotism n. favouritism shown to relatives or friends, esp. by giving them jobs.

neptunium n. a radioactive metallic element.

nerd n. informal an unfashionable person obsessed with a particular interest.

nerve n. **1** a fibre transmitting impulses of sensation between the brain or spinal cord and other parts of the body. **2** steadiness and courage. **3** (**nerves**) nervousness. **4** informal cheeky boldness.
▷ SYNONYMS: **1 confidence**, assurance, courage, bravery, determination, will power, spirit, grit; informal guts; Brit. informal bottle; N. Amer. informal moxie. **2** (**nerves**) **anxiety**, tension, nervousness, stress, worry, cold feet, apprehension; informal butterflies, collywobbles, jitters, the heebie-jeebies. **3 audacity**, cheek, effrontery, gall, temerity, presumption, impudence, impertinence, arrogance; informal face, front, brass neck, chutzpah.
• v. (**nerve yourself**) brace yourself for a demanding situation.
□ **get on someone's nerves** informal irritate someone. **nerve-racking** (or **nerve-wracking**) frightening or stressful.

> WORD LINKS
> **neural** relating to nerves in the body

nervous adj. **1** easily frightened or worried. **2** anxious. **3** of the nerves.
▷ SYNONYMS: **anxious**, worried, apprehensive, on edge, edgy, tense, stressed, agitated, uneasy, restless, worked up, keyed up, overwrought, jumpy, on tenterhooks, highly strung, nervy, excitable, neurotic; informal jittery, twitchy, in a state, uptight, wired, trepidatious; N. Amer. informal squirrelly.
– ANTONYMS: relaxed, calm.
□ **nervous breakdown** a period of

mental illness resulting from severe depression or stress.

■ **nervously** adv. **nervousness** n.

nervy adj. (**nervier**, **nerviest**) Brit. nervous or tense.

nest n. **1** a structure made by a bird for laying eggs and sheltering its young. **2** a place where an animal or insect breeds or shelters. **3** a set of similar objects designed to fit inside each other.
• v. **1** use or build a nest. **2** fit an object inside a larger one.
□ **nest egg** a sum of money saved for the future.

nestle v. **1** settle comfortably within or against something. **2** (of a place) lie in a sheltered position.
▷ SYNONYMS: **snuggle**, cuddle, huddle, nuzzle, settle, burrow.

nestling n. a bird too young to leave the nest.

net n. **1** a material made of twine or cord woven or tied together to form small open squares. **2** a piece or structure of net for catching fish, surrounding a goal, etc. **3** (**the Net**) the Internet.
▷ SYNONYMS: **netting**, mesh, tulle, fishnet, lace, openwork.
• v. (**netting**, **netted**) **1** catch in a net. **2** gain as net profit.
▷ SYNONYMS: **1 catch**, capture, trap, snare; informal bag. **2 earn**, make, clear, take home, bring in, pocket, realize.
• adj. (Brit. also **nett**) **1** remaining after tax or expenses have been deducted. **2** (of a weight) not including packaging.
▷ SYNONYMS: **after tax**, take-home, final.
– ANTONYMS: gross.
□ **netball** a team game in which a ball has to be thrown into a high net.

nether adj. lower.

netting n. material made of net.

nettle n. a plant covered with stinging hairs.
• v. annoy.

network n. **1** a system of crossing or connecting railways, lines, etc. **2** a group of interconnected broadcasting stations, computers, etc. **3** a group of people who keep in contact to exchange information.
▷ SYNONYMS: **web**, lattice, net, matrix, mesh, criss-cross, grid, maze, labyrinth, warren, tangle.
• v. keep in contact with others to exchange information.

neural adj. of nerves.

neuralgia n. intense pain along a nerve.

■ **neuralgic** adj.

neurology n. the study of the nervous system.
■ **neurological** adj. **neurologist** n.

neurosis n. (pl. **neuroses**) a mental illness involving depression, anxiety, or obsessive behaviour.

neurotic adj. **1** of neurosis. **2** informal excessively sensitive, anxious, or obsessive.
▷ SYNONYMS: **highly strung**, oversensitive, nervous, tense, paranoid, obsessive, fixated, hysterical, overwrought, irrational.
– ANTONYMS: stable, calm.

neuter adj. **1** (of a noun) not masculine or feminine. **2** having no sexual or reproductive organs.
• v. castrate or spay an animal.

neutral adj. **1** not supporting either side in a dispute or war. **2** lacking noticeable or strong qualities. **3** neither acid nor alkaline.
▷ SYNONYMS: **1 impartial**, unbiased, unprejudiced, objective, open-minded, non-partisan, even-handed, disinterested, dispassionate, detached, non-aligned, unaffiliated, uninvolved. **2 inoffensive**, bland, unobjectionable, unexceptional, anodyne, uncontroversial, safe, harmless, innocuous. **3 pale**, light, colourless, indeterminate, drab, insipid, nondescript, dull.
– ANTONYMS: biased, provocative.
• n. **1** a neutral state or person. **2** a position of a gear mechanism in which the engine is disconnected from the driven parts.
■ **neutrality** n. **neutrally** adv.

neutralize (or **-ise**) v. prevent from having an effect.
▷ SYNONYMS: **counteract**, offset, counterbalance, balance, cancel out, nullify, negate.
■ **neutralization** n.

neutrino n. (pl. **neutrinos**) a subatomic particle with a mass close to zero and no electric charge.

neutron n. a subatomic particle of about the same mass as a proton but without an electric charge.
□ **neutron bomb** a nuclear bomb that kills people but does little harm to property.

never adv. **1** not ever. **2** not at all.

never-ending adj. seeming to last for ever.
▷ SYNONYMS: **incessant**, continuous, ceaseless, constant, continual, perpetual, uninterrupted, unbroken, steady, unremitting, relentless,

persistent, interminable, non-stop, endless, unending.
nevermore adv. never again.
nevertheless adv. in spite of that.
▷ SYNONYMS: **nonetheless**, even so, however, still, yet, in spite of that, despite that, be that as it may, notwithstanding.
nevus US = NAEVUS.
new adj. **1** made, introduced, discovered, or experienced recently. **2** not previously used or owned. **3** (**new to/at**) not used to or experienced at. **4** replacing a former one of the same kind.
▷ SYNONYMS: **1** recent, up to date, the latest, current, state-of-the-art, contemporary, advanced, cutting-edge, modern, avant-garde.
2 unused, brand new, pristine, fresh. **3** different, another, alternative, additional, extra, supplementary, further, unfamiliar, unknown, strange. **4** *he's new to this kind of work*: **unfamiliar with**, unused to, inexperienced in, unaccustomed to, a stranger to.
– ANTONYMS: old, second-hand.
• adv. newly.
□ **New Age** a movement concerned with alternative approaches to spirituality, medicine, etc. **newfangled** derogatory newly developed and unfamiliar. **new moon** the moon when it appears as a thin crescent. **New Testament** the second part of the Christian Bible. **new year** the first days of January.
■ newness n.
newcomer n. a person who has recently arrived or is new to an activity.
▷ SYNONYMS: **1** incomer, immigrant, settler, stranger, outsider, foreigner, alien; informal new kid on the block. **2** beginner, novice, learner, trainee, apprentice, probationer; informal rookie, newbie; N. Amer. informal tender-foot.
newel n. the top or bottom post of a stair rail.
newly adv. **1** recently. **2** again.
▷ SYNONYMS: **recently**, only just, lately, freshly, not long ago.
□ **newly-wed** a recently married person.
news n. **1** new information about recent events. **2** (**the news**) a broadcast or published news report.
▷ SYNONYMS: **report**, story, account, announcement, press release, communication, communiqué,

bulletin, intelligence, information, word, revelation, disclosure, exposé; Brit. stop press; informal scoop; literary tidings.
□ **newsagent** Brit. a shopkeeper who sells newspapers, magazines, etc. **newsflash** a brief item of important news, interrupting other radio or television programmes. **newsgroup** a group of Internet users who exchange information about a subject online. **newsletter** a bulletin issued periodically to the members of a society etc. **newsprint** cheap, low-quality paper used for newspapers. **newsreader** Brit. a person who reads the news on radio or television. **newsworthy** important enough to report as news.
newspaper n. a daily or weekly publication containing news and articles.
▷ SYNONYMS: **paper**, journal, gazette, news-sheet, tabloid, broadsheet, periodical; Brit. red top; informal rag.
newt n. a small lizard-like animal that can live in water or on land.
newton n. a unit of force.
next adj. nearest in position or time.
▷ SYNONYMS: **1** following, succeeding, subsequent, ensuing, upcoming, to come. **2** neighbouring, adjacent, adjoining, next-door, bordering, connected, closest, nearest; formal contiguous, proximate.
– ANTONYMS: previous.
• adv. **1** immediately afterwards. **2** following in the specified order.
▷ SYNONYMS: **afterwards**, after, then, later, subsequently; formal thereafter.
□ **next door** in or to the next house or room. **next of kin** a person's closest living relative or relatives.
nexus n. (pl. **nexus** or **nexuses**) a connection or series of connections.
NHS abbrev. National Health Service.
NI abbrev. **1** National Insurance. **2** Northern Ireland.
niacin = NICOTINIC ACID.
nib n. the pointed end part of a pen.
nibble v. take small quick or gentle bites at.
• n. a small bite of food.
nice adj. **1** enjoyable or attractive; pleasant. **2** kind. **3** involving a very small detail or difference.
▷ SYNONYMS: **1** *have a nice time*: **enjoy-able**, pleasant, agreeable, good, pleasurable, satisfying, entertaining, amusing; informal lovely, great; N. Amer. informal neat. **2** *nice people*: **pleasant**, likeable, agreeable, personable,

n

good-natured, congenial, amiable, affable, genial, friendly, charming, delightful, engaging, sympathetic, polite, courteous, well mannered, civil, kind, obliging, helpful. **3** *nice weather:* **fine**, dry, sunny, warm, mild, clement. **4** *a nice distinction:* **subtle**, fine, slight, delicate, precise.
– ANTONYMS: unpleasant, nasty.
■ **nicely** adv. **niceness** n.

nicety n. (pl. **niceties**) **1** a very small detail. **2** accuracy.

niche n. **1** a shallow recess in a wall. **2** (**your niche**) a job or role that suits you.
▷ SYNONYMS: **1** recess, alcove, nook, cranny, hollow, bay, cavity, pigeon-hole. **2** position, slot, place, vocation, calling, métier, station, job, level.

nick n. **1** a small cut. **2** (**the nick**) Brit. informal prison or a police station. **3** Brit. informal condition: *in good nick.*
▷ SYNONYMS: **cut**, scratch, incision, notch, chip, dent, indentation.
• v. **1** make a nick in. **2** Brit. informal steal. **3** Brit. informal arrest.
▷ SYNONYMS: **cut**, scratch, graze, chip, dent.
□ **in the nick of time** only just in time.

nickel n. **1** a metallic element used in alloys. **2** US a five-cent coin.

nickname n. an alternative, usu. amusing name for a person or thing.
▷ SYNONYMS: **pet name**, diminutive, endearment, tag, label, sobriquet, epithet; informal handle, moniker.
• v. give a nickname to.

nicotine n. a poisonous oily liquid found in tobacco.

nicotinic acid n. a vitamin of the B complex.

niece n. a daughter of a person's brother or sister.

niggardly adj. not generous; mean.

nigger n. offens. a black person.

niggle v. worry or annoy slightly.
• n. a minor worry or criticism.
■ **niggly** adj.

nigh adv., prep., & adj. old use near.

night n. **1** the time from sunset to sunrise. **2** an evening until bedtime.
▷ SYNONYMS: **night-time**, the hours of darkness, dark.
– ANTONYMS: day.
□ **nightcap** a hot or alcoholic drink taken at bedtime. **nightclub** a club open at night, with a bar and music. **nightdress** (or **nightgown**) a loose garment worn by a woman or girl in bed. **nightjar** a nocturnal bird with a harsh cry. **nightlife** entertainment available at night. **nightshirt** a long

shirt worn in bed. **nightspot** informal a nightclub.
■ **nightly** adj. & adv.

> **WORD LINKS**
> **nocturnal** occurring or active at night

nightfall n. dusk.
▷ SYNONYMS: **sunset**, sundown, dusk, twilight, evening, dark; literary eventide, gloaming.
– ANTONYMS: dawn.

nightingale n. a small thrush with a tuneful song.

nightmare n. **1** a frightening dream. **2** a very unpleasant experience.
▷ SYNONYMS: **ordeal**, trial, hell, misery, agony, torture, murder, purgatory, disaster; informal the pits.
■ **nightmarish** adj.

nihilism n. the belief that nothing has any value.
■ **nihilist** n. **nihilistic** adj.

nil n. nothing; zero.
▷ SYNONYMS: **nothing**, none, nought, zero; Tennis love; Cricket a duck.

nimble adj. quick and agile.
▷ SYNONYMS: **1** agile, light, quick, lithe, skilful, deft, dexterous, adroit, sprightly, spry; informal nippy. **2** *a nimble mind:* **quick**, alert, lively, astute, perceptive, penetrating, discerning, shrewd, sharp, intelligent, bright, smart, clever, brilliant; informal quick on the uptake.
– ANTONYMS: clumsy.
■ **nimbly** adv.

nimbus n. (pl. **nimbi** or **nimbuses**) a rain cloud.

nincompoop n. a stupid person.

nine adj. & n. one less than ten; 9.
■ **ninth** adj. & n.

nineteen adj. & n. one more than eighteen; 19.
■ **nineteenth** adj. & n.

ninety adj. & n. ten less than one hundred; 90.
■ **ninetieth** adj. & n.

ninny n. (pl. **ninnies**) informal a foolish person.

niobium n. a metallic element.

nip v. (**nipping**, **nipped**) **1** pinch or bite sharply. **2** Brit. informal go quickly.
▷ SYNONYMS: **bite**, nibble, peck, pinch, tweak.
• n. **1** an act of nipping. **2** a sharp coldness. **3** a small drink of spirits.

nipple n. a small projection in the centre of each breast.

nippy adj. (**nippier**, **nippiest**) informal **1** Brit. quick; nimble. **2** chilly.

nirvana n. (in Buddhism) a state of perfect happiness.

nit n. informal **1** the egg of a human head louse. **2** Brit. a stupid person.
□ **nit-picking** petty criticism.

nitrate n. a substance formed from nitric acid.

nitric acid n. a very corrosive acid.

nitrogen n. a gas forming about 78 per cent of the earth's atmosphere.

nitroglycerine (or **nitroglycerin**) n. a powerful explosive.

nitrous oxide n. a gas used as an anaesthetic.

nitty-gritty n. informal the most important details.

nitwit n. informal a foolish person.

no adj. not any.
• exclam. used to refuse or disagree.
• adv. not at all.
▷ SYNONYMS: **absolutely not**, of course not, under no circumstances, not at all, never; informal nope, no way, not a chance, not on your life; Brit. informal no fear; old use nay.
– ANTONYMS: yes.
□ **no-man's-land** an area between two opposing armies that is not controlled by either. **no one** no person.

no. abbrev. number.

nobble v. Brit. informal try to influence by underhand methods.

nobelium n. a radioactive metallic element.

nobility n. **1** the quality of being noble. **2** the aristocracy.

noble adj. **1** belonging to the aristocracy. **2** having fine personal qualities. **3** magnificent; impressive.
▷ SYNONYMS: **1 aristocratic**, blue-blooded, patrician, high-born, titled. **2 worthy**, righteous, good, honourable, virtuous, upright. **3 magnificent**, splendid, grand, impressive, stately, imposing, dignified, proud, striking, majestic.
– ANTONYMS: humble, lowly.
• n. a nobleman or noblewoman.
▷ SYNONYMS: **aristocrat**, nobleman, noblewoman, lord, lady, peer, peeress, patrician; informal aristo.
– ANTONYMS: commoner.
□ **nobleman** (or **noblewoman**) a member of the aristocracy.
■ **nobly** adv.

nobody pron. no person.
• n. (pl. **nobodies**) an unimportant person.

nocturnal adj. done or active at night.
■ **nocturnally** adj.

nocturne n. a short romantic piece of music.

nod v. (**nodding**, **nodded**) **1** lower and raise the head briefly to show agreement or as a greeting or signal. **2** let the head fall forward when drowsy or asleep. **3** (**nod off**) informal fall asleep.
▷ SYNONYMS: **1 incline**, bob, bow, dip. **2 signal**, gesture, gesticulate, motion, sign, indicate.
• n. an act of nodding.

node n. **1** a point in a network where lines cross or branch. **2** the part of a plant stem from which a leaf grows. **3** a small mass of tissue in the body.
■ **nodal** adj.

nodule n. a small swelling or lump.
■ **nodular** adj.

noggin n. informal a small quantity of alcoholic drink.

noise n. **1** a sound or series of sounds, esp. a loud or unpleasant one. **2** disturbances that accompany and interfere with an electrical signal.
▷ SYNONYMS: **sound**, din, hubbub, clamour, racket, uproar, tumult, commotion, pandemonium; Brit. row; informal hullabaloo.
– ANTONYMS: silence.
■ **noiseless** adj.

noisome adj. having a very unpleasant smell.

noisy adj. (**noisier**, **noisiest**) full of or making a lot of noise.
▷ SYNONYMS: **1 raucous**, rowdy, strident, clamorous, vociferous, boisterous. **2 loud**, blaring, booming, deafening, thunderous, ear-splitting, piercing, cacophonous, tumultuous.
– ANTONYMS: quiet, soft.
■ **noisily** adv.

nomad n. a member of a people that travels from place to place to find fresh pasture for its animals.
■ **nomadic** adj.

nom de plume n. (pl. **noms de plume**) a writer's pen name.

nomenclature n. a system of names used in a particular subject.

nominal adj. **1** in name but not in reality. **2** (of a fee) very small.
▷ SYNONYMS: **1 in name only**, titular, formal, official, theoretical, supposed, ostensible, so-called, self-styled. **2 token**, symbolic, minimal; Brit. peppercorn.
– ANTONYMS: real, considerable.
■ **nominally** adv.

nominate v. **1** put forward as a candidate for a job, award, etc. **2** formally specify something.
▷ SYNONYMS: **1 propose**, put forward, put up, submit, present, recommend, suggest. **2 appoint**, choose, decide on,

select, designate, assign.

■ **nomination** n. **nominee** n.

nominative n. the grammatical case used for the subject of a verb.

non- prefix not.

nonagenarian n. a person between 90 and 99 years old.

non-aligned adj. not allied with a major world power.

nonchalant adj. calm and relaxed.

▷ SYNONYMS: **calm**, composed, unconcerned, cool, imperturbable, casual, blasé, offhand, insouciant; informal laid-back.

– ANTONYMS: anxious.

■ **nonchalance** n. **nonchalantly** adv.

non-commissioned adj. (of a military officer) appointed from the lower ranks.

non-committal adj. not showing what you think or which side you are on.

▷ SYNONYMS: **evasive**, equivocal, guarded, circumspect, reserved; informal cagey.

■ **non-committally** adv.

nonconformist n. **1** a person who does not follow accepted ideas or behaviour. **2** (**Nonconformist**) a member of a Protestant Church which does not follow the beliefs of the established Church of England.

▷ SYNONYMS: **dissenter**, protester, rebel, freethinker, individualist, free spirit, maverick, renegade, schismatic, apostate, heretic.

non-contributory adj. (of a pension) funded by regular payments by the employer, not the employee.

nondescript adj. lacking special or interesting features.

▷ SYNONYMS: **undistinguished**, featureless, unremarkable, unmemorable, ordinary, average, run-of-the-mill, mundane, uninteresting, uninspiring, colourless, bland.

– ANTONYMS: distinctive.

none pron. **1** not any. **2** no one.
• adv. not at all: *none the wiser.*
□ **nonetheless** nevertheless.

nonentity n. (pl. **nonentities**) an unimportant person or thing.

non-event n. a very disappointing or uninteresting event.

non-existent adj. not real or present.

▷ SYNONYMS: **imaginary**, imagined, unreal, fictional, fictitious, made up, invented, fanciful, mythical, illusory.

– ANTONYMS: real.

nonplussed adj. surprised and confused.

nonsense n. **1** words that make no

sense. **2** foolish ideas or behaviour.

▷ SYNONYMS: **1 rubbish**, gibberish, claptrap, balderdash, garbage; informal baloney, bosh, tripe, drivel, gobbledegook, mumbo-jumbo, poppycock, twaddle, guff, tosh, bilge, hogwash, piffle; Brit. informal cobblers, codswallop, double Dutch, rot. **2 mischief**, misbehaviour; informal tomfoolery, monkey business, shenanigans, malarkey; Brit. informal monkey tricks, jiggery-pokery.

– ANTONYMS: sense.

■ **nonsensical** adj.

non sequitur /non sek-wi-ter/ n. a statement that does not follow logically from the previous one.

non-starter n. informal something that has no chance of succeeding.

non-stop adj. & adv. **1** without stopping. **2** having no stops on the way to a destination.

▷ SYNONYMS: **continuous**, constant, continual, incessant, ceaseless, uninterrupted, unbroken, neverending, perpetual, round-the-clock, persistent, steady, unremitting, relentless, interminable.

– ANTONYMS: intermittent, occasional.

noodles pl. n. long, thin strips of pasta.

nook n. a sheltered or hidden place.

noon n. 12 o'clock in the day.

▷ SYNONYMS: **midday**, twelve o'clock, twelve hundred hours, high noon, noonday.

noose n. a loop with a knot which tightens as the rope or wire is pulled.

nor conj. & adv. and not; and not either.

Nordic adj. of Scandinavia, Finland, and Iceland.

norm n. **1** (**the norm**) the usual or standard thing. **2** a required or acceptable standard.

▷ SYNONYMS: **standard**, convention, criterion, yardstick, benchmark, touchstone, rule, formula, pattern.

normal adj. usual, typical, or expected.

▷ SYNONYMS: **1 usual**, standard, ordinary, customary, conventional, habitual, accustomed, typical, common, regular, routine, traditional, commonplace, everyday, average, run-of-the-mill, middle-of-the-road, conventional, mainstream; N. Amer. garden-variety; Brit. informal common or garden, bog-standard. **2 sane**, in your right mind, right in the head, of sound mind, compos mentis; informal all there.

– ANTONYMS: abnormal, unusual.
• n. the normal state or condition.

■ **normality** n..

normalize (or **-ise**) v. make or become normal.

■ **normalization** n.

normally adv. **1** in a normal way. **2** under normal conditions.

▷ SYNONYMS: **usually**, ordinarily, as a rule, generally, in general, mostly, on the whole, typically, habitually.

normative adj. relating to or setting a norm.

north n. **1** the direction on the left-hand side of a person facing east. **2** the northern part of a place. • adj. **1** lying towards or facing the north. **2** (of a wind) from the north. • adv. towards the north.

■ **northerly** adj. & adv. **northward** adj. & adv. **northwards** adv.

north-east n. the direction or region halfway between north and east. • adj. & adv. **1** towards or facing the north-east. **2** (of a wind) from the north-east.

■ **north-easterly** adj. & adv. **north-eastern** adj.

northern adj. situated in or facing the north.

□ **Northern Lights** the aurora borealis.

northerner n. a person from the north of a region.

north-west n. the direction or region halfway between north and west. • adj. & adv. **1** towards or facing the north-west. **2** (of a wind) from the north-west.

■ **north-westerly** adj. & adv. **north-western** adj.

Norwegian n. **1** a person from Norway. **2** the language spoken in Norway. • adj. of Norway.

nose n. **1** the part of the face containing the nostrils, used in breathing and smelling. **2** the front end of an aircraft etc. **3** the sense of smell. **4** a talent for finding something.

▷ SYNONYMS: **snout**, muzzle, proboscis, trunk; informal beak, conk, schnozzle, hooter. • v. **1** move forward slowly. **2** look around or pry. **3** thrust the nose against something.

▷ SYNONYMS: **1 ease**, inch, edge, move, manoeuvre, steer, guide. **2 pry**, enquire, poke about/around, interfere, meddle, stick/poke your nose in; informal snoop; Austral./NZ informal stickybeak.

□ **nosebag** Brit. a bag of fodder hung from a horse's head. **nosedive** a steep downward plunge by an aircraft. **nosegay** a posy of flowers.

> **WORD LINKS**
> **nasal** relating to the nose

nosh n. Brit. informal food.

nostalgia n. longing for a happier or better time in the past.

nostalgic adj. feeling or characterized by nostalgia.

▷ SYNONYMS: **wistful**, romantic, sentimental, emotional, homesick; regretful, dewy-eyed, maudlin.

■ **nostalgically** adv.

nostril n. either of the two external openings in the nose.

nostrum n. **1** a favourite method for improving something. **2** an ineffective medicine.

nosy adj. (**nosier**, **nosiest**) informal too inquisitive.

▷ SYNONYMS: **prying**, inquisitive, curious, spying, eavesdropping, intrusive; informal snooping.

not adv. used to express a negative.

notable adj. worthy of notice.

▷ SYNONYMS: **1 noteworthy**, remarkable, outstanding, important, significant, memorable, marked, striking, impressive, momentous, uncommon. **2 prominent**, well known, famous, famed, noted, of note. – ANTONYMS: unremarkable, unknown. • n. a famous or important person.

▷ SYNONYMS: **celebrity**, VIP, dignitary, luminary, star, big name, personage; informal celeb, bigwig.

notably adv. especially; remarkably.

▷ SYNONYMS: **1** other countries, notably the USA: **in particular**, particularly, especially, primarily, principally, chiefly. **2** a notably successful example: **remarkably**, especially, exceptionally, singularly, particularly, distinctly, significantly, unusually, uncommonly, conspicuously.

notary n. (pl. **notaries**) a lawyer authorized to draw up and witness the signing of contracts etc.

notation n. a system of symbols used in music, mathematics, etc.

notch n. **1** a V-shaped cut or indentation. **2** a point on a scale.

▷ SYNONYMS: **nick**, cut, incision, score, scratch, slit, snick, slot, groove. • v. **1** make notches in. **2** (**notch up**) score or achieve.

note n. **1** a brief written record. **2** a short written message. **3** Brit. a banknote. **4** a single musical sound of a particular pitch and length, or a symbol representing this. **5** a

n

particular quality: *a note of scorn.*
▷ SYNONYMS: **1 record**, entry, reminder, comment, jotting. **2 message**, letter, line, missive; informal memo; formal memorandum, epistle. **3 annotation**, footnote, marginalia. **4 banknote**; N. Amer. bill; US informal greenback. **5** *the note of hopelessness in her voice:* tone, hint, indication, sign, element, suggestion, sense.
• v. **1** pay attention to or notice.
2 write down.
▷ SYNONYMS: **1 bear in mind**, be mindful of, consider, take notice of, register, be aware, take in, notice, observe, see, perceive. **2 write down**, put down, jot down, take down, scribble, enter, mark, record, register, pencil in.
☐ **notepaper** paper for writing letters on. **take note** pay attention.

notebook n. a small book for writing notes in.
▷ SYNONYMS: **notepad**, exercise book, logbook, log, diary, journal, record, register; Brit. jotter, pocketbook; N. Amer. scratch pad; trademark Filofax.

noted adj. well known.
▷ SYNONYMS: **famous**, famed, well known, renowned, prominent, notable, important, eminent, great, acclaimed, celebrated, distinguished.
– ANTONYMS: unknown.

noteworthy adj. interesting or important.
▷ SYNONYMS: **notable**, interesting, significant, important, remarkable, striking, memorable, unique, special, unusual.
– ANTONYMS: unexceptional.

nothing pron. **1** not anything. **2** something unimportant or uninteresting. **3** nought.
▷ SYNONYMS: **1 not a thing**, zero; N. English nowt; informal zilch, sweet FA, not a dicky bird; N. Amer. informal zip, nada, diddly-squat. **2 zero**, nought, nil; Tennis love; Cricket a duck.
• adv. not at all.

notice n. **1** the fact of being aware or paying attention. **2** warning that something is going to happen. **3** a formal statement that someone is going to leave a job or end an agreement. **4** a sheet or placard displaying information. **5** a short published review.
▷ SYNONYMS: **1 sign**, announcement, advertisement, poster, placard, bill, handbill, flyer. **2 attention**, observation, awareness, consciousness, perception, regard, consideration, scrutiny; formal cognizance. **3** *advance notice of the price increase:* notifi-

cation, warning, information, news, word.
• v. become aware of.
▷ SYNONYMS: **observe**, note, see, discern, detect, spot, perceive, make out; Brit. informal clock.
– ANTONYMS: overlook.
☐ **take notice (of)** pay attention (to).

noticeable adj. easily seen or noticed.
▷ SYNONYMS: **obvious**, evident, apparent, manifest, plain, clear, conspicuous, perceptible, discernible, detectable, observable, visible, appreciable, unmistakable, patent.
– ANTONYMS: imperceptible.
■ **noticeably** adv.

notifiable adj. (of a disease) that must be reported to the health authorities.

notify v. (**notifying**, **notified**) inform formally about something.
▷ SYNONYMS: **inform**, tell, let someone know, advise, apprise, alert, warn.
■ **notification** n.

notion n. **1** an idea or belief. **2** an understanding.
▷ SYNONYMS: **idea**, impression, belief, opinion, view, concept, conception, understanding, feeling, suspicion, intuition, inkling.

notional adj. hypothetical.
■ **notionally** adv.

notorious adj. famous for something bad.
▷ SYNONYMS: **infamous**, scandalous, disreputable, of ill repute.
■ **notoriety** n. **notoriously** adv.

notwithstanding prep. in spite of.
• adv. nevertheless.

nougat /noo-gah/ n. a sweet made from sugar or honey, nuts, and egg white.

nought n. Brit. the figure 0.
▷ SYNONYMS: **nil**, zero, nothing; Tennis love; Cricket a duck; informal zilch; N. Amer. informal zip, nada.
• pron. nothing.

noun n. a word referring to a person, place, or thing.

nourish v. provide with the food etc. necessary for growth and health.
▷ SYNONYMS: **feed**, sustain, provide for, care for, nurture.

nourishing adj. full of nutrients; nutritious.
▷ SYNONYMS: **nutritious**, wholesome, good for you, nutritive, healthy, health-giving, beneficial.
– ANTONYMS: unhealthy.

nourishment n. the food and other substances necessary for life, growth, and good health.

▷ SYNONYMS: **food**, nutriment, nutrients, nutrition, sustenance.

nous /nowss/ n. Brit. informal common sense.

nouveau riche /noo-voh **reesh**/ n. people who have recently become rich and display their wealth in a tasteless way.

nova n. (pl. **novae** or **novas**) a star that suddenly becomes brighter for a short time.

novel n. a fictitious story of book length.

▷ SYNONYMS: **story**, tale, narrative, romance, novella.
• adj. new and unusual.
▷ SYNONYMS: **new**, original, unusual, unconventional, unorthodox, different, fresh, imaginative, innovative, unfamiliar, surprising.
– ANTONYMS: traditional.

novelist n. a person who writes novels.

novelty n. (pl. **novelties**) **1** the quality of being new and unusual. **2** a small toy or ornament.
▷ SYNONYMS: **1 originality**, newness, freshness, unconventionality, innovation, unfamiliarity. **2 knick-knack**, trinket, bauble, toy, trifle, ornament; N. Amer. kickshaw.

November n. the eleventh month.

novice n. **1** a person new to and lacking experience in a job or situation. **2** a person who has entered a religious order but has not yet taken their vows.
▷ SYNONYMS: **beginner**, learner, trainee, newcomer, fledgling, probationer, student, pupil, apprentice, tyro, neophyte; informal rookie, newbie; N. Amer. informal tenderfoot, greenhorn.
– ANTONYMS: expert, veteran.

now adv. **1** at the present time. **2** immediately.
▷ SYNONYMS: **1 at the moment**, at present, presently, at this moment in time, currently, nowadays, these days, today, in this day and age. **2 at once**, straight away, right away, this minute, this instant, immediately, instantly, directly; informal pronto, asap.
• conj. as a result of the fact.
□ **nowadays** at the present time, in contrast with the past. **now and again** (or **then**) from time to time.

nowhere adv. not anywhere.
• pron. no place.

noxious adj. harmful or very unpleasant.
▷ SYNONYMS: **poisonous**, toxic, deadly,

harmful, dangerous, unhealthy, unpleasant.
– ANTONYMS: innocuous.

nozzle n. a spout controlling a stream of liquid or gas.

nuance /nyoo-ahnss/ n. a slight difference in meaning or expression.
▷ SYNONYMS: **distinction**, shade, gradation, refinement, degree, subtlety, nicety.

nub n. **1** the central point of a matter. **2** a small lump.

nubile adj. (of a young woman) sexually attractive.

nuclear adj. **1** of a nucleus. **2** using energy released in the fission or fusion of atomic nuclei.
□ **nuclear family** a couple and their children.

nucleic acid n. either of two complex organic substances, DNA and RNA, present in all living cells.

nucleus n. (pl. **nuclei**) **1** the central and most important part of something. **2** the positively charged central core of an atom. **3** a structure in a cell containing the genetic material.
▷ SYNONYMS: **core**, centre, heart, kernel, nub, hub, middle, focus.

nude adj. wearing no clothes.
▷ SYNONYMS: **naked**, stark naked, bare, unclothed, undressed, stripped; informal without a stitch on, in your birthday suit, in the raw/buff, in the altogether; Brit. informal starkers; N. Amer. informal buck naked.
– ANTONYMS: dressed.
• n. a painting or sculpture of a naked person.
■ **nudity** n.

nudge v. **1** prod with the elbow to attract attention. **2** touch or push gently.
▷ SYNONYMS: **prod**, elbow, dig, poke, jab, jog, push, touch.
• n. a light prod or push.
▷ SYNONYMS: **prod**, dig in the ribs, poke, jab, push.

nudist n. a person who goes naked wherever possible.
■ **nudism** n.

nugatory /nyoo-guh-tuh-ri/ adj. lacking purpose or value.

nugget n. a small lump of precious metal found in the earth.

nuisance n. an annoying person or thing.
▷ SYNONYMS: **annoyance**, inconvenience, bore, bother, irritation, trial, burden, pest; informal pain, hassle, bind, drag, headache.

nuke v. informal attack with nuclear

weapons.

null adj. having the value zero.
□ **null and void** having no legal force.
■ **nullity** n.

nullify v. (**nullifying**, **nullified**) **1** make legally invalid. **2** cancel out the effect of.
▷ SYNONYMS: **annul**, render null and void, invalidate, repeal, reverse, rescind, revoke, cancel, neutralize, negate, counteract.
■ **nullification** n.

numb adj. **1** (of a body part) having no sensation. **2** lacking the power to feel, think, or react.
▷ SYNONYMS: **1 without feeling**, without sensation, dead, numbed, desensitized, frozen, anaesthetized, insensible, insensate. **2 dazed**, stunned, stupefied, paralysed, immobilized.
• v. make numb.
▷ SYNONYMS: **1 deaden**, desensitize, anaesthetize, immobilize, freeze. **2 daze**, stun, stupefy, paralyse, immobilize.
■ **numbly** adv. **numbness** n.

number n. **1** a quantity or value expressed by a word or symbol. **2** a quantity. **3** (**a number of**) several. **4** a single issue of a magazine. **5** a song, dance, or other musical item.
▷ SYNONYMS: **1 numeral**, integer, figure, digit, character. **2 quantity**, total, aggregate, tally, quota. **3 song**, piece, tune, track, dance.
• v. **1** amount to. **2** give a number to. **3** count.
▷ SYNONYMS: **1 add up to**, amount to, total, come to. **2 include**, count, reckon, deem.
□ **number plate** Brit. a sign on the front and rear of a vehicle showing its registration number.
■ **numberless** adj.

> **WORD LINKS**
> **numerical** relating to numbers

numeral n. a symbol or word that represents a number.

numerate adj. having a good basic knowledge of arithmetic.
■ **numeracy** n.

numerator n. the number above the line in a fraction.

numerical adj. of a number or numbers.
■ **numerically** adv.

numerous adj. many.
▷ SYNONYMS: **many**, a number of, a lot of/lots of, several, plenty of, countless, copious, an abundance of,

frequent; informal **umpteen**.
– ANTONYMS: few.

numinous adj. having a religious or spiritual quality.

numismatics n. the study of coins and medals.
■ **numismatist** n.

nun n. a woman belonging to a female religious community.

nuncio n. (pl. **nuncios**) a diplomatic representative of the pope.

nunnery n. (pl. **nunneries**) a convent.

nuptial adj. of marriage or weddings.
• n. (**nuptials**) a wedding.

nurse n. **1** a person trained to care for sick or injured people. **2** dated a person employed to look after young children.
• v. **1** act as nurse to. **2** hold carefully. **3** harbour a belief or feeling. **4** feed a baby at the breast.
▷ SYNONYMS: **1 care for**, take care of, look after, tend, minister to. **2** *they nursed old grievances:* **harbour**, foster, bear, have, hold, retain.
□ **nursing home** a place providing accommodation and health care for old people.

nursery n. (pl. **nurseries**) **1** a room for children. **2** a nursery school. **3** a place where plants are grown for sale.
□ **nurseryman** a worker in or owner of a plant nursery. **nursery rhyme** a traditional song or poem for children. **nursery school** a school for children between three and five.

nurture v. **1** care for and encourage the growth or development of. **2** have a hope or belief for a long time.
▷ SYNONYMS: **1 bring up**, care for, take care of, look after, tend, rear, raise. **2** *he nurtured my love of art:* **encourage**, promote, stimulate, develop, foster, cultivate, boost, strengthen, fuel.
– ANTONYMS: neglect.
• n. the act of nurturing.

nut n. **1** a fruit consisting of a hard shell around an edible kernel. **2** the kernel of such a fruit. **3** a small flat metal ring for screwing on to a bolt. **4** (or **nutcase**) informal a mad person. **5** informal the head.
▷ SYNONYMS: **1 maniac**, lunatic, madman, madwoman; informal loony, nutcase, head case; Brit. informal nutter; N. Amer. informal screwball. **2 enthusiast**, fan, devotee, aficionado; informal freak, fanatic, addict, buff.
• adj. (**nuts**) informal mad.
□ **in a nutshell** in the fewest possible words.

n

■ **nutty** adj.

nutmeg n. a spice made from the seed of a tropical tree.

nutrient n. a substance essential for life and growth.

nutriment n. nourishment.

nutrition n. **1** the process of eating or taking nourishment. **2** the study of this.

■ **nutritional** adj. **nutritionist** n.

nutritious adj. full of nutrients.

▷ SYNONYMS: **nourishing**, nutritive, wholesome, good for you, healthy, health-giving, beneficial.

nutritive adj. **1** of nutrition.

2 nutritious.

nuzzle v. rub or push against gently with the nose.

NVQ abbrev. National Vocational Qualification.

NW abbrev. north-west or north-western.

nylon n. a strong, light, synthetic fibre.

nymph n. **1** a mythological spirit in the form of a beautiful young woman. **2** an immature form of an insect.

nymphomania n. uncontrollable sexual desire in a woman.

■ **nymphomaniac** n.

NZ abbrev. New Zealand.

n

Oo

oaf n. a stupid or clumsy man.
- ■ **oafish** adj.

oak n. a large tree producing acorns and a hard wood.
- ■ **oaken** adj.

OAP abbrev. Brit. old-age pensioner.

oar n. a pole with a flat blade used to row a boat.

oasis n. (pl. **oases**) **1** a fertile place in a desert where water rises to ground level. **2** a pleasant area or period in the midst of a difficult situation.

oast house n. a building with a kiln for drying hops.

oat n. **1** a hardy cereal plant. **2** (**oats**) the edible grain of this.
- □ **oatcake** an oatmeal biscuit. **oatmeal** ground oats.

oath n. (pl. **oaths**) **1** a solemn promise, esp. that something is true. **2** a swear word.
- ▷ SYNONYMS: **1 vow**, pledge, promise, affirmation, word of honour, guarantee. **2 swear word**, expletive, profanity, four-letter word, dirty word, obscenity, curse; formal imprecation.

obdurate adj. stubborn.
- ■ **obduracy** n.

OBE abbrev. Officer of the Order of the British Empire.

obedient adj. willing to do what you are told.
- ▷ SYNONYMS: **compliant**, biddable, good, acquiescent, law-abiding, deferential, governable, docile, submissive.
- – ANTONYMS: rebellious.
- ■ **obedience** n. **obediently** adv.

obeisance n. **1** humble respect. **2** a bow or curtsy.

obelisk n. a stone pillar tapering to a point, set up as a monument.

obese adj. very fat.
- ■ **obesity** n.

obey v. **1** carry out the orders of. **2** behave in accordance with a law etc.
- ▷ SYNONYMS: **1 do as you are told**, defer to, submit to, bow to. **2** *he refused to*

obey the order: **carry out**, perform, act on, execute, discharge, implement. **3** *rules have to be obeyed:* **comply with**, adhere to, observe, abide by, act in accordance with, conform to, respect, follow, keep to, stick to.
- – ANTONYMS: defy, ignore.

obfuscate v. make unclear or hard to understand.
- ■ **obfuscation** n.

obituary n. (pl. **obituaries**) a short biography of someone published in a newspaper when they die.

object n. **1** a physical thing that can be seen and touched. **2** a person or thing to which an action or feeling is directed. **3** a purpose. **4** a noun acted on by a transitive verb or by a preposition.
- ▷ SYNONYMS: **1 thing**, article, item, entity, device, gadget. **2 target**, butt, focus, recipient, victim. **3 objective**, aim, goal, target, purpose, end, plan, point, ambition, intention, idea.
- • v. express disapproval or opposition.
- ▷ SYNONYMS: *they objected to the scheme:* **protest about**, oppose, take exception to, take issue with, take a stand against, argue against, quarrel with, condemn, draw the line at, demur at, mind, complain about.
- – ANTONYMS: approve of, accept.
- ■ **objector** n.

objection n. an expression of disapproval or opposition.
- ▷ SYNONYMS: **protest**, protestation, complaint, opposition, demurral, counter-argument, disagreement, disapproval, dissent.

objectionable adj. unpleasant or offensive.

objective adj. **1** not influenced by personal feelings or opinions. **2** having actual existence outside the mind. **3** of a case of nouns and pronouns used for the object of a transitive verb or a preposition.
- ▷ SYNONYMS: **1 impartial**, unbiased,

unprejudiced, non-partisan, disinterested, neutral, uninvolved, even-handed, fair, dispassionate, detached. **2 factual**, actual, real, empirical, verifiable.
– ANTONYMS: subjective, emotional.
•n. a goal or aim.
▷ SYNONYMS: **aim**, intention, purpose, target, goal, object, end, idea, plan, ambition.
□ **object lesson** a clear practical example of a principle or ideal.
■ **objectively** adv. **objectivity** n.

objet d'art /ob-zhay dar/ n. (pl. **objets d'art**) a small decorative or artistic object.

oblation n. an offering made to a god.

obligated adj. obliged or compelled.

obligation n. **1** something that must be done because of a law, agreement, etc. **2** the state of being obliged to do something.
▷ SYNONYMS: **1 commitment**, duty, responsibility, function, task, job, charge, onus, liability, requirement, debt. **2** *a sense of obligation*: **duty**, compulsion, indebtedness, necessity, pressure, constraint.

obligatory adj. compulsory.
▷ SYNONYMS: **compulsory**, mandatory, prescribed, required, statutory, enforced, binding, requisite, necessary, imperative, de rigueur.
– ANTONYMS: optional.

oblige v. **1** make someone do something by law, necessity, or because it is their duty. **2** perform a service or favour for. **3** (**be obliged**) be grateful.
▷ SYNONYMS: **1 compel**, force, require, make, bind, constrain. **2 do someone a favour**, accommodate, help, assist, indulge, humour. **3** (**obliged**) *I'm much obliged for your help*: **thankful**, grateful, appreciative, beholden, indebted, in someone's debt.

obliging adj. willing to help.
▷ SYNONYMS: **helpful**, accommodating, cooperative, agreeable, amenable, generous, kind; Brit. informal decent.
■ **obligingly** adv.

oblique /uh-**bleek**/ adj. **1** at an angle; slanting. **2** not explicit or direct.
■ **obliquely** adv.

obliterate v. destroy or cover completely.
▷ SYNONYMS: **1 destroy**, wipe out, annihilate, demolish; informal zap. **2 hide**, obscure, blot out, block, cover, screen.
■ **obliteration** n.

oblivion n. **1** the state of being unaware. **2** the state of being

forgotten or destroyed.

oblivious adj. unaware.
▷ SYNONYMS: **unaware**, unconscious, heedless, unmindful, insensible, ignorant, blind, deaf, impervious.
– ANTONYMS: conscious.

oblong adj. rectangular in shape.
•n. an oblong shape.

obloquy /ob-luh-kwi/ n. **1** strong public criticism. **2** disgrace.

obnoxious adj. very unpleasant.

oboe n. a woodwind instrument of treble pitch with a double reed.
■ **oboist** n.

obscene adj. **1** dealing with sexual matters in an offensive or disgusting way. **2** (of an amount) unacceptably large.
▷ SYNONYMS: **1 pornographic**, indecent, smutty, dirty, filthy, X-rated, explicit, lewd, rude, vulgar, coarse, scatological; informal blue; euphemistic adult. **2 scandalous**, shocking, outrageous, immoral.
■ **obscenely** adv. **obscenity** n.

obscure adj. **1** hard to understand or see. **2** not known about or well known.
▷ SYNONYMS: **1 unclear**, uncertain, unknown, mysterious, hazy, vague, indeterminate. **2 abstruse**, oblique, opaque, cryptic, arcane, enigmatic, puzzling, perplexing, baffling, incomprehensible, impenetrable, elliptical. **3 little known**, unknown, unheard of, unsung, minor, unrecognized, forgotten.
– ANTONYMS: clear, plain, famous.
•v. hide or make unclear.
▷ SYNONYMS: **1 hide**, conceal, cover, veil, shroud, screen, mask, cloak, block, obliterate, eclipse. **2 confuse**, complicate, obfuscate, cloud, blur, muddy.
– ANTONYMS: reveal, clarify.
■ **obscurely** adv. **obscurity** n.

obsequies /ob-si-kwiz/ pl. n. funeral rites.

obsequious adj. excessively obedient or respectful.
■ **obsequiously** adv. **obsequiousness** n.

observance n. behaving in accordance with a law, rule, or ritual.

observant adj. quick to notice things.
▷ SYNONYMS: **alert**, sharp-eyed, eagle-eyed, attentive, watchful; informal beady-eyed, on the ball.
– ANTONYMS: inattentive.

observation n. **1** the close watching of someone or something. **2** the ability to notice important details. **3** a remark.
▷ SYNONYMS: **1 monitoring**, watching, scrutiny, survey, surveillance,

o

attention, study. **2 remark**, comment, opinion, impression, thought, reflection.
■ **observational** adj.

observatory n. (pl. **observatories**) a building equipped for observing the stars and planets.

observe v. **1** notice. **2** watch carefully. **3** make a remark. **4** obey a law or rule. **5** celebrate a festival.
▷ SYNONYMS: **1 notice**, see, note, perceive, discern, spot. **2 watch**, look at, contemplate, view, survey, regard, keep an eye on, scrutinize, keep under surveillance, monitor; informal keep tabs on. **3 remark**, comment, say, mention, declare, announce, state; formal opine. **4 comply with**, abide by, keep, obey, adhere to, heed, honour, fulfil, respect, follow, consent to, accept.
■ **observable** adj.

observer n. a person who observes.
▷ SYNONYMS: **spectator**, onlooker, watcher, fly on the wall, viewer, witness.

obsess v. preoccupy to a disturbing extent.
▷ SYNONYMS: **preoccupy**, prey on someone's mind, possess, haunt, consume, eat up; be fixated, be infatuated, be besotted.

obsession n. **1** the state of being obsessed. **2** a persistent thought.
▷ SYNONYMS: **fixation**, passion, mania, compulsion, fetish, preoccupation, infatuation, hobby horse, phobia, complex, neurosis; informal bee in your bonnet, hang-up, thing.
■ **obsessional** adj.

obsessive adj. **1** thinking continually about a person or thing. **2** preoccupying a person's mind to a disturbing extent.
▷ SYNONYMS: *his obsessive jealousy:* **all-consuming**, consuming, compulsive, controlling, fanatical, neurotic, excessive; informal pathological.
■ **obsessively** adv.

obsolescent adj. becoming obsolete.
■ **obsolescence** n.

obsolete adj. no longer produced or used; out of date.
▷ SYNONYMS: **out of date**, outdated, outmoded, old-fashioned, passé, antiquated, antediluvian, anachronistic, superannuated, archaic, ancient, fossilized, extinct, defunct; informal out of the ark; Brit. informal past its sell-by date.
– ANTONYMS: current, modern.

obstacle n. a thing that obstructs progress.
▷ SYNONYMS: **barrier**, hurdle, stumbling block, obstruction, bar, block, impediment, hindrance, snag, catch, drawback, hitch, fly in the ointment, handicap, difficulty, problem, disadvantage; Brit. spanner in the works.
– ANTONYMS: advantage, aid.

obstetrics n. the branch of medicine concerned with childbirth.
■ **obstetric** adj. **obstetrician** n.

obstinate adj. **1** stubbornly refusing to change your mind. **2** (of a problem) hard to deal with.
▷ SYNONYMS: **stubborn**, pig-headed, mulish, self-willed, unyielding, inflexible, unbending, intransigent, intractable; old use contumacious.
– ANTONYMS: compliant.
■ **obstinacy** n. **obstinately** adv.

obstreperous adj. noisy and unruly.

obstruct v. **1** be in the way of. **2** stop or hinder progress.
▷ SYNONYMS: **1 block**, cut off, clog, bung up, choke, dam up; technical occlude. **2 impede**, hinder, interfere with, hamper, block, interrupt, hold up, stand in the way of, frustrate, slow down, delay, bring to a standstill, stop, halt.
– ANTONYMS: clear, facilitate.
■ **obstructive** adj.

obstruction n. **1** an obstacle or blockage. **2** the action of obstructing.
▷ SYNONYMS: **obstacle**, barrier, stumbling block, impediment, hindrance, difficulty, check, restriction, blockage, stoppage, congestion, bottleneck, hold-up.

obtain v. **1** come into possession of; get. **2** be established or usual.
▷ SYNONYMS: **get**, acquire, come by, secure, procure, pick up, gain, earn, achieve, attain; informal get hold of, lay your hands on, land.

obtainable adj. able to be obtained.
▷ SYNONYMS: **available**, to be had, in circulation, on the market, on offer, in season, at your disposal, accessible; informal up for grabs, on tap.

obtrude v. become noticeable in an unwelcome way.

obtrusive adj. noticeable in an unwelcome way.

obtuse adj. **1** annoyingly slow to understand. **2** (of an angle) more than 90° and less than 180°. **3** blunt.

obverse n. **1** the side of a coin or medal bearing the head or main design. **2** the opposite.

obviate v. remove a need or difficulty.
obvious adj. **1** easily seen or understood; clear. **2** predictable.
▷ SYNONYMS: **clear**, plain, evident,
apparent, patent, manifest,
conspicuous, pronounced, prominent,
distinct, noticeable, unmistakable,
perceptible, visible, palpable; informal
sticking out a mile.
– ANTONYMS: imperceptible.
■ **obviously** adv.
ocarina n. an egg-shaped wind
instrument.
occasion n. **1** a particular event, or
the time at which it happens. **2** a
special event. **3** a suitable time.
4 reason or cause.
▷ SYNONYMS: **1 time**, instance, juncture,
point, moment, experience, case.
2 event, affair, function, celebration,
party, get-together, gathering; informal
do, bash.
• v. cause.
▷ SYNONYMS: **cause**, give rise to, bring
about, result in, lead to, prompt,
create, engender.

> USAGE Two c's and one s: occasion.

occasional adj. happening or done
from time to time.
▷ SYNONYMS: **infrequent**, intermittent,
irregular, periodic, sporadic, odd;
N. Amer. sometime.
– ANTONYMS: regular, frequent.
occasionally adv. from time to time.
▷ SYNONYMS: **sometimes**, from time to
time, every now and then, every now
and again, at times, every so often,
every once in a while, on occasion,
periodically.
– ANTONYMS: often.
occidental adj. of the countries of
the West.
occlude v. close up or block.
□ **occluded front** a weather front
produced when a cold front catches
up with a warm front, so that the
warm air in between rises.
■ **occlusion** n.
occult n. (**the occult**) supernatural
beliefs, practices, or events.
• adj. of the occult.
▷ SYNONYMS: **supernatural**, magic,
magical, satanic, mystical, unearthly,
esoteric, psychic.
occupant n. a person occupying a
place or job.
▷ SYNONYMS: **resident**, inhabitant,
owner, householder, tenant,
leaseholder, lessee; Brit. occupier,
owner-occupier.
■ **occupancy** n.

occupation n. **1** a job or profession.
2 the act of occupying or state of
being occupied. **3** a way of spending
time.
▷ SYNONYMS: **1 job**, profession, work,
line of work, trade, employment,
business, career, métier, calling.
2 pastime, activity, hobby, pursuit,
interest, entertainment, recreation.
3 conquest, capture, invasion,
seizure, annexation, colonization,
subjugation.
occupational adj. of a job or
profession.
□ **occupational therapy** the use of
particular activities as an aid to
recovery from illness.
occupied adj. **1** busy. **2** being used.
▷ SYNONYMS: **1 busy**, working, at work,
active; informal tied up, hard at it, on
the go. **2 in use**, full, engaged, taken.
occupy v. (**occupying**, **occupied**) **1** live
or work in. **2** enter and take control
of a place. **3** fill a space, time, or
position. **4** keep busy.
▷ SYNONYMS: **1 live in**, inhabit, lodge in,
tenant, move into, people, populate,
settle; Scottish stay in. **2** *the region was
occupied by Japan:* **capture**, seize,
conquer, invade, colonize, annex,
subjugate. **3 engage**, busy, distract,
absorb, hold, interest, involve,
involve, entertain.
■ **occupier** n.
occur v. (**occurring**, **occurred**)
1 happen. **2** be found or present.
3 (**occur to**) come into the mind of.
▷ SYNONYMS: **1 happen**, take place, come
about, transpire; N. Amer. informal go
down. **2 be found**, be present, exist,
appear, develop, manifest itself.
occurrence n. **1** an incident or event.
2 the fact of something occurring.
▷ SYNONYMS: **1 event**, incident,
happening, phenomenon, circumstance, episode. **2 existence**, instance,
appearance, frequency, incidence,
prevalence, rate; Statistics distribution.
ocean n. a very large expanse of sea.
■ **oceanic** adj.
oceanography n. the study of the
sea.
■ **oceanographer** n.
ocelot n. a wild cat found in South and
Central America.
ochre /oh-ker/ (US **ocher**) n. a light
yellowish brown.
o'clock adv. used to specify the hour
when telling the time.
octagon n. a plane figure with eight
sides.
■ **octagonal** adj.

o

octane n. a hydrocarbon present in petrol.

octave n. **1** a series of eight musical notes occupying the interval between (and including) two notes. **2** the interval between two such notes.

octavo n. (pl. **octavos**) a size of book page formed by folding each printed sheet into eight leaves.

octet n. **1** a group of eight voices or musicians. **2** a piece of music for an octet.

October n. the tenth month.

octogenarian n. a person between 80 and 89 years old.

octopus n. (pl. **octopuses**) a sea animal with eight tentacles.

ocular adj. of, for, or by the eyes.

OD v. (**OD'ing**, **OD'd**) informal take an overdose of a drug.

odd adj. **1** unusual or unexpected; strange. **2** (of a number) having a remainder of one when divided by two. **3** occasional. **4** separated from a pair or set.

▷ SYNONYMS: **1 strange**, peculiar, queer, funny, bizarre, eccentric, unconventional, outlandish, unusual, weird, curious, abnormal, puzzling, mystifying, baffling, unaccountable; informal wacky. **2** odd jobs: **occasional**, casual, irregular, isolated, sporadic, periodic, miscellaneous, various, varied, sundry. **3** an odd shoe: **mismatched**, unmatched, unpaired, single, lone, solitary, extra, leftover, spare.

– ANTONYMS: normal, ordinary, regular.
□ **oddment** an item or piece left over from a larger piece or set.
■ **oddly** adv. **oddness** n.

oddity n. (pl. **oddities**) **1** the quality of being strange. **2** a strange person or thing.

odds pl. n. **1** the ratio between the amount placed as a bet and the money which would be received if the bet was won. **2** the chances of something happening.

▷ SYNONYMS: **likelihood**, probability, chances.
□ **at odds** in conflict or disagreement. **odds and ends** various articles or remnants. **odds-on** very likely to win, succeed, or happen.

ode n. a poem addressed to a person or thing or celebrating an event.

odious adj. very unpleasant.

odium n. widespread hatred or disgust.

odometer n. a milometer.

odoriferous adj. smelly.

odour (US **odor**) n. a smell.

▷ SYNONYMS: **smell**, stench, stink, reek; aroma, bouquet, scent, perfume, fragrance; Brit. informal pong, whiff, niff; N. Amer. informal funk; literary redolence.
■ **odorous** adj.

odyssey n. (pl. **odysseys**) a long eventful journey.

▷ SYNONYMS: **journey**, voyage, trip, trek, travels, quest, crusade, pilgrimage.

oedema /i-**dee**-muh/ (US **edema**) n. excess fluid in the tissues of the body.

oesophagus /ee-**sof**-fuh-guhss/ (US **esophagus**) n. (pl. **oesophagi** or **oesophaguses**) the tube connecting the throat to the stomach.

oestrogen /ee-struh-juhn/ (US **estrogen**) n. a hormone which produces female physical and sexual characteristics.

of prep. **1** helping to form; made up from. **2** belonging to; involving. **3** indicating measurement, value, or age.

off adv. **1** away from a place. **2** so as to be separated. **3** so as to finish or be discontinued. **4** not working or connected.
• prep. **1** away from. **2** so as to be separated from. **3** informal having a temporary dislike of.
• adj. (of food) no longer fresh.

▷ SYNONYMS: **rotten**, bad, stale, mouldy, sour, rancid, turned, spoiled.
□ **offbeat** informal unconventional. **off colour** Brit. slightly unwell. **offcut** Brit. a piece of wood, fabric, etc. left after cutting a larger piece. **off-licence** Brit. a shop selling alcoholic drink to be drunk elsewhere. **offline** not connected to a computer. **offload** unload. **off-putting** unpleasant or unsettling. **offshoot** a thing that develops from something else. **offside** (in football etc.) in a position on the field where playing the ball is not allowed. **off-white** a white colour with a grey or yellow tinge.

offal n. the internal organs of an animal used as food.

offence (US **offense**) n. **1** an illegal act. **2** a feeling of hurt or annoyance.

▷ SYNONYMS: **1 crime**, illegal act, misdemeanour, felony, infringement, violation, wrongdoing, sin. **2 annoy-ance**, resentment, indignation, displeasure, bad feeling, animosity.

offend v. **1** cause to feel hurt or annoyed. **2** do something illegal.

▷ SYNONYMS: **1 upset**, give offence to, affront, hurt someone's feelings, insult, hurt, wound, slight. **2 break the law**, commit a crime, do wrong.

offender n. a person who commits a crime or does something wrong.

▷ SYNONYMS: **wrongdoer**, criminal, lawbreaker, crook, villain, miscreant, felon, delinquent, malefactor, culprit, guilty party.

offensive adj. **1** causing offence. **2** used in attack.

▷ SYNONYMS: **1 insulting**, rude, derogatory, disrespectful, personal, hurtful, upsetting, wounding, abusive. **2 unpleasant**, disagreeable, nasty, distasteful, objectionable, off-putting, dreadful, frightful, obnoxious, abominable, disgusting, repulsive, repellent, vile, foul, horrible, sickening, nauseating; informal ghastly, horrid, gross; Brit. informal beastly. **3 hostile**, attacking, aggressive, invading, combative, threatening, martial, warlike, belligerent, bellicose.

– ANTONYMS: complimentary, pleasant, defensive.

• n. a campaign to attack or achieve something.

▷ SYNONYMS: **attack**, assault, onslaught, invasion, push, thrust, charge, raid, incursion, blitz, campaign.

■ **offensively** adv.

offer v. **1** present for acceptance, rejection, or consideration. **2** express willingness to do something for someone.

▷ SYNONYMS: **1 put forward**, proffer, give, present, come up with, suggest, propose, advance, submit, tender. **2 volunteer**, step forward, show willing.

– ANTONYMS: withdraw, refuse.

• n. **1** an expression of willingness to do or give something. **2** an amount of money offered. **3** a specially reduced price.

▷ SYNONYMS: **1 proposal**, proposition, suggestion, submission, approach, overture. **2 bid**, tender, bidding price.

offering n. a gift or contribution.

▷ SYNONYMS: **contribution**, donation, gift, present, sacrifice, tribute.

offertory n. (pl. **offertories**) **1** the offering of the bread and wine at Holy Communion. **2** a collection of money at a Christian church service.

offhand adj. rudely casual or abrupt.

▷ SYNONYMS: **casual**, careless, uninterested, indifferent, cool, nonchalant, blasé, insouciant, cavalier, glib, perfunctory, cursory, dismissive, abrupt.

• adv. without previous thought.

office n. **1** a room or building used for business or clerical work. **2** a position of authority. **3** the holding of an official position.

▷ SYNONYMS: **1 place of work**, workplace, workroom. **2** the company's Paris office: **branch**, division, section, bureau, department. **3** the office of President: **post**, position, appointment, job, occupation, role, situation, function.

officer n. a person holding a position of authority, esp. in the armed services.

▷ SYNONYMS: **official**, functionary, executive.

official adj. of or authorized by an authority or public organization.

▷ SYNONYMS: **1 authorized**, approved, validated, authenticated, certified, accredited, endorsed, sanctioned, licensed, recognized, legitimate, legal, lawful, valid, bona fide, proper; informal kosher. **2 ceremonial**, formal, solemn, bureaucratic.

– ANTONYMS: unauthorized, unofficial.

• n. a person having official duties.

▷ SYNONYMS: **officer**, executive, functionary, administrator, bureaucrat, mandarin, representative, agent; derogatory apparatchik.

■ **officially** adv.

officiate v. **1** act as an official in charge of something. **2** perform a religious ceremony.

officious adj. asserting authority in an overbearing way.

▷ SYNONYMS: **self-important**, bumptious, self-assertive, overbearing, interfering, intrusive, meddlesome, meddling; informal bossy.

■ **officiously** adv.

offset v. (**offsetting**, **offset**) counteract by having an equal and opposite force or effect.

▷ SYNONYMS: **counteract**, balance out, even out/up, counterbalance, compensate for, make up for, neutralize, cancel out.

offspring n. (pl. **offspring**) a person's child or children, or the young of an animal.

▷ SYNONYMS: **children**, family, progeny, young, brood, descendants, heirs, successors; informal kids; Brit. informal sprogs, brats.

often adv. **1** frequently. **2** in many cases.

▷ SYNONYMS: **frequently**, many times, a lot, repeatedly, again and again, time after time, regularly, commonly,

o

generally, ordinarily; N. Amer. oftentimes.
– ANTONYMS: seldom.

ogle v. stare at in a lecherous way.

ogre n. **1** (in folklore) a man-eating
giant. **2** a terrifying person.

oh exclam. expressing surprise, joy,
disappointment, etc.

ohm /ohm/ n. a unit of electrical
resistance.

oil n. **1** a thick, sticky liquid obtained
from petroleum. **2** a thick liquid
which does not dissolve in water.
3 oil paint.
• v. treat or coat with oil.
▫ **oilfield** an area where oil is found
beneath the ground or the seabed. **oil
paint** paint made from pigment mixed
with oil. **oil rig** a structure providing
a stable base above water for drilling
for and extracting oil. **oilskin 1** heavy
cotton cloth waterproofed with oil.
2 (**oilskins**) clothing made of oilskin.

oily adj. (**oilier**, **oiliest**) **1** containing,
covered with, or resembling oil.
2 insincerely polite or flattering.
▷ SYNONYMS: **greasy**, fatty, buttery, rich,
oleaginous.

ointment n. a cream rubbed on the
skin for medicinal purposes.
▷ SYNONYMS: **lotion**, cream, salve, liniment, embrocation, rub, gel, balm,
emollient, unguent.

OK (or **okay**) informal adj. **1** satisfactory.
2 permissible; allowed.
▷ SYNONYMS: **1 satisfactory**, all
right, acceptable, competent,
adequate, tolerable, passable,
reasonable, decent, fair, average,
middling, moderate, unremarkable, unexceptional; informal so-so,
fair-to-middling. **2 permissible**,
allowable, acceptable, all right, in
order, permitted, fitting, suitable,
appropriate.
– ANTONYMS: unsatisfactory.
• adv. in a satisfactory way.

okapi /oh-kah-pi/ n. (pl. **okapi** or
okapis) a large African mammal of
the giraffe family.

okra n. the long seed pods of a tropical
plant, eaten as a vegetable.

old adj. **1** having lived or existed for a
long time. **2** former. **3** showing signs
of age. **4** of a specified age.
▷ SYNONYMS: **1** a very old man: **elderly**,
aged, older, senior, venerable, in
your dotage, past your prime, long
in the tooth, grizzled, ancient,
decrepit, doddery, senescent, senile;
informal getting on, past it, over the
hill. **2** the old days: **bygone**, olden,

past, prehistoric, primitive. **3** an
old girlfriend: **former**, previous,
earlier, past, ex-, one-time, sometime,
erstwhile; formal quondam. **4** old
clothes: **worn**, shabby, threadbare,
frayed, patched, tattered, moth-
eaten, ragged; informal tatty. **5** old cars:
antique, veteran, vintage, classic.
– ANTONYMS: young, new, current,
modern.
▫ **old age** the later part of normal
life. **Old Testament** the first part of
the Christian Bible. **old wives' tale** a
traditional belief now thought to be
incorrect.

> **WORD LINKS**
> **geriatric** relating to old people

old-fashioned adj. no longer current
or modern.
▷ SYNONYMS: **out of date**, outdated,
dated, out of fashion, outmoded,
unfashionable, passé, outworn,
behind the times, antiquated, antediluvian, archaic, obsolescent, obsolete, superannuated; informal out of the
ark, old hat, clunky.
– ANTONYMS: modern.

oleaginous /oh-li-aj-i-nuhss/ adj.
1 oily. **2** excessively flattering.

oleander /oh-li-an-der/ n. a flowering
evergreen shrub of warm countries.

olfactory adj. of the sense of smell.

oligarchy n. (pl. **oligarchies**) **1** a small
group governing a state. **2** a state
governed by such a group.
■ **oligarch** n. **oligarchic** adj.

olive n. **1** a small oval fruit with bitter
flesh which yields **olive oil**, or the
tree producing this fruit. **2** a greyish-
green colour.
• adj. **1** greyish-green. **2** (of skin)
yellowish brown.
▫ **olive branch** an offer to restore
friendly relations.

Olympic adj. of the Olympic Games.
• n. (**the Olympics**) the Olympic
Games.

ombudsman n. an official appointed
to investigate complaints against
public organizations.

omelette n. a dish of beaten eggs
cooked in a frying pan.

omen n. an event seen as a sign of
future good or bad luck.
▷ SYNONYMS: **portent**, sign, signal, token,
forewarning, warning, harbinger,
presage, indication; literary foretoken.

ominous adj. suggesting that
something bad is going to happen.
▷ SYNONYMS: **threatening**, menacing,
baleful, forbidding, foreboding,

fateful, sinister, black, dark, gloomy.
– ANTONYMS: promising.
■ **ominously** adv.

omission n. **1** the action or fact of omitting. **2** a thing that has been omitted.
▷ SYNONYMS: **negligence**, neglect, dereliction, oversight, lapse, failure.

omit v. (**omitting**, **omitted**) **1** leave out or exclude. **2** fail to do.
▷ SYNONYMS: **1 leave out**, exclude, miss out, miss, cut, drop, skip. **2 forget**, neglect, overlook, fail.
– ANTONYMS: include, remember.

omnibus n. **1** a book or programme containing several works or programmes previously published or broadcast separately. **2** dated a bus.

omnipotent adj. having unlimited or very great power.
■ **omnipotence** n.

omnipresent adj. present everywhere.
■ **omnipresence** n.

omniscient /om-**ni**-si-uhnt/ adj. knowing everything.
■ **omniscience** n.

omnivorous adj. eating both plants and meat.

on prep. **1** (or **on to**) into contact with, or aboard. **2** about; concerning. **3** as a member of. **4** stored in or broadcast by. **5** in the course of. **6** at a point in time.
• adv. **1** in contact with or covering something. **2** with continued movement or action. **3** taking place or being presented. **4** functioning.
□ **oncoming** approaching. **ongoing** still in progress. **online** controlled by or connected to a computer.
■ **onward** adv. & adj. **onwards** adv.

once adv. **1** on one occasion only. **2** formerly.
▷ SYNONYMS: **formerly**, previously, in the past, once upon a time, in days/times gone by, in the old days, long ago.
• conj. as soon as.
□ **at once 1** immediately. **2** at the same time. **once upon a time** at some time in the past. **once-over** informal a rapid inspection or search.

oncogene n. a gene that transforms a gene into a cancer cell.

oncology n. the study and treatment of tumours.

one n. & adj. **1** the lowest cardinal number; 1. **2** single, or a single person or thing. **3** a certain. **4** the same.
• pron. **1** used to refer to a person or thing previously mentioned. **2** used

to refer to the speaker or to represent people in general.
□ **one-upmanship** informal the technique of gaining an advantage over someone else. **one-way** allowing movement in one direction only.

onerous /**oh**-nuh-ruhss/ adj. involving much effort and difficulty.

oneself pron. **1** used when 'one' is the subject of the verb and is also affected by it. **2** used to emphasize 'one'.

one-sided adj. **1** unfairly biased. **2** very unequal.
▷ SYNONYMS: **1 biased**, prejudiced, partisan, partial, slanted, distorted, unfair. **2 unequal**, uneven, unbalanced.
– ANTONYMS: impartial, equal.

onion n. a vegetable with a bulb having a strong taste and smell.

onlooker n. a spectator.
▷ SYNONYMS: **eyewitness**, witness, observer, spectator, bystander; informal rubberneck.

only adv. **1** and no one or nothing more besides. **2** no longer ago than.
▷ SYNONYMS: **1 at most**, at best, just, no more than, hardly, barely, scarcely. **2 exclusively**, solely, purely.
• adj. **1** single or solitary. **2** alone deserving consideration.
▷ SYNONYMS: **sole**, single, one and only, solitary, lone, unique, exclusive.
• conj. informal except that.

onomatopoeia /on-uh-mat-uh-**pee**-uh/ n. the formation of a word from the sound of the thing described.
■ **onomatopoeic** adj.

onset n. a beginning.
▷ SYNONYMS: **start**, beginning, commencement, arrival, appearance, inception, day one, outbreak; informal kick-off.
– ANTONYMS: end.

onslaught n. a fierce attack.
▷ SYNONYMS: **attack**, assault, offensive, advance, charge, blitz, bombardment, barrage.

onto var. of **on to** (see **ON**).

ontology n. philosophy dealing with the nature of being.
■ **ontological** adj.

onus /**oh**-nuhss/ n. a responsibility.
▷ SYNONYMS: **burden**, responsibility, obligation, duty, weight, load.

onyx n. a semi-precious stone with layers of different colours.

oodles pl. n. informal a very great quantity.

ooze v. **1** slowly seep out. **2** exude.
▷ SYNONYMS: **seep**, discharge, flow,

o

exude, trickle, drip, dribble, drain, leak.
• n. wet mud or slime.

opal n. an iridescent gem.

opalescent adj. iridescent like an opal.

opaque adj. **1** impossible to see through. **2** difficult to understand.
▷ SYNONYMS: **1 non-transparent**, cloudy, filmy, blurred, smeared, misty.
2 obscure, unclear, unfathomable, incomprehensible, unintelligible, impenetrable; informal as clear as mud.
– ANTONYMS: transparent, clear.
■ **opacity** n.

op. cit. adv. in the work already mentioned.

open adj. **1** not closed, fastened, or restricted. **2** not covered or protected. **3** (**open to**) likely to be affected by. **4** expanded or unfolded. **5** undisguised. **6** not concealing thoughts or feelings. **7** not finally settled.
▷ SYNONYMS: **1 unlocked**, unlatched, off the latch, ajar, gaping, yawning. **2** open countryside | open spaces: **unenclosed**, rolling, sweeping, wide open, exposed, spacious, uncrowded, uncluttered, undeveloped. **3** the position is still open: **available**, free, vacant, unfilled; informal up for grabs. **4** the system is open to abuse: **vulnerable**, subject, susceptible, liable, exposed, an easy target for. **5** she was very open: **frank**, candid, honest, forthcoming, communicative, forthright, direct, unreserved, plain-spoken, outspoken, blunt; informal upfront. **6** open hostility: **overt**, manifest, conspicuous, plain, undisguised, unconcealed, clear, naked, blatant, flagrant, barefaced, brazen.
– ANTONYMS: shut, closed.
• v. **1** make or become open. **2** formally begin or establish.
▷ SYNONYMS: **1 unfasten**, unlock, unbolt, throw wide. **2 unwrap**, undo, untie. **3 spread out**, unfold, unfurl, unroll, straighten out. **4 begin**, start, commence, initiate, set in motion, get going, get under way, get off the ground; informal kick off.
– ANTONYMS: close, shut.
• n. (**the open**) fresh air or open countryside.
□ **in the open** not secret. **opencast** (of mining) near the surface, rather than from shafts. **open-ended** with no limit decided in advance. **open-handed** generous. **open house** a situation in which all visitors

are welcome. **open letter** a letter addressed to a particular person but published in a newspaper. **open-plan** having few or no dividing walls. **open prison** a prison with the minimum of restrictions on prisoners' movements. **open verdict** a verdict that a person's death is suspicious but that the cause is unknown.
■ **opener** n. **openly** adv. **openness** n.

> WORD LINKS
> **agoraphobia** fear of open spaces

open-air adj. located or happening out of doors.
▷ SYNONYMS: **outdoor**, outside, alfresco.

opening n. **1** a gap. **2** a beginning, or a ceremony marking this. **3** an opportunity.
▷ SYNONYMS: **1 hole**, gap, aperture, space, orifice, vent, crack, slit, chink, fissure, cleft, crevice, interstice. **2 beginning**, start, commencement, outset; informal kick-off. **3 vacancy**, position, post, job, opportunity.
• adj. coming at the beginning.
▷ SYNONYMS: **first**, initial, introductory, preliminary, maiden, inaugural.
– ANTONYMS: final, closing.

open-minded adj. willing to consider new ideas.
▷ SYNONYMS: **unbiased**, unprejudiced, neutral, objective, disinterested, tolerant, liberal, permissive, broad-minded.
– ANTONYMS: prejudiced, narrow-minded.

opera n. **1** a play set to music for singers and musicians. **2** pl. of OPUS.
□ **opera glasses** small binoculars for use at a theatre.
■ **operatic** adj.

operable adj. **1** able to be operated. **2** able to be treated by surgery.

operate v. **1** function. **2** control the functioning of a machine or the activities of an organization. **3** perform a surgical operation.
▷ SYNONYMS: **1 work**, run, use, handle, control, manage, drive, steer, manoeuvre, function, go, perform. **2 direct**, control, manage, run, handle, be in control/charge of.
□ **operating system** the software supporting a computer's basic functions.

operation n. **1** the act of operating. **2** an act of surgery performed on a patient. **3** an organized action involving a number of people.
▷ SYNONYMS: **1 functioning**, working, running, performance, action. **2** a

military operation: **action**, exercise, undertaking, enterprise, manoeuvre, campaign. **3 business**, enterprise, company, firm.

operational adj. **1** in or ready for use. **2** of the functioning of an organization.
▷ SYNONYMS: **running**, up and running, working, functioning, operative, in operation, in use, in action, in working order, serviceable, functional.

operative adj. **1** functioning. **2** of surgery.
▷ SYNONYMS: **running**, up and running, working, functioning, operational, in operation, in use, in action, in effect.
• n. **1** a worker. **2** a secret agent.
▷ SYNONYMS: **1 machinist**, operator, mechanic, engineer, worker, workman, hand. **2 agent**, secret/undercover agent, spy, mole, plant; N. Amer. informal **spook**.

operator n. **1** a person who operates equipment or a machine. **2** a person who works at the switchboard of a phone exchange.

operetta n. a short opera on a light theme.

ophthalmic adj. of the eye and its diseases.
□ **ophthalmic optician** an optician qualified to prescribe and supply glasses etc. and to detect eye diseases.

ophthalmology /off-thal-**mol**-uh-ji/ n. the study of disorders and diseases of the eye.
■ **ophthalmologist** n.

opiate n. a drug containing opium.

opine v. state as your opinion.

opinion n. **1** a personal view not necessarily based on fact or knowledge. **2** a formal statement of advice by an expert.
▷ SYNONYMS: **belief**, thought, idea, way of thinking, feeling, mind, view, point of view, viewpoint, standpoint, assessment, estimation, judgement, conviction.

opinionated adj. tending to put your views forward forcefully.

opium n. an addictive drug made from the juice of a poppy.

opossum n. a small tree-dwelling marsupial.

opponent n. **1** a person who competes with or fights another. **2** a person who disagrees with something.
▷ SYNONYMS: **1 rival**, adversary, competitor, enemy, antagonist, combatant, contender, challenger;

literary **foe**. **2 critic**, objector, dissenter.
– ANTONYMS: ally, supporter.

opportune adj. occurring at an especially appropriate time.

opportunist n. a person who exploits opportunities as and when they arise, esp. unscrupulously.
■ **opportunism** n. **opportunistic** adj.

opportunity n. (pl. **opportunities**) a favourable time or situation for doing something.
▷ SYNONYMS: **chance**, time, occasion, moment, opening, option, window, possibility, scope, freedom; informal **shot**, break, look-in.

oppose v. **1** disagree with and try to prevent or resist. **2** compete with or fight. **3** (**opposed**) (of two or more things) contrasting or conflicting. **4** (**opposing**) opposite.
▷ SYNONYMS: **be against**, object to, be hostile to, disagree with, be averse to, disapprove of, resist, take a stand against, put up a fight against, fight, counter, challenge, take issue with.
– ANTONYMS: support.

opposite adj. **1** facing. **2** completely different. **3** being the other of a contrasted pair.
▷ SYNONYMS: **1 conflicting**, contrasting, incompatible, irreconcilable, contra-dictory, at variance, at odds, differing. **2 rival**, opposing, competing, enemy.
• n. an opposite person or thing.
▷ SYNONYMS: **reverse**, converse, antith-esis, contrary.
– ANTONYMS: same.
• adv. & prep. in an opposite position to something.

opposition n. **1** resistance or disagree-ment. **2** a group of opponents. **3** (**the Opposition**) Brit. the main party in parliament opposing the one in power. **4** a contrast or opposite.
▷ SYNONYMS: **1 resistance**, hostility, antagonism, antipathy, objection, dissent, disapproval. **2 opponents**, opposing side, competition, rivals, adversaries.
– ANTONYMS: agreement.

oppress v. **1** treat harshly and unfairly. **2** distress or make anxious.
▷ SYNONYMS: **persecute**, tyrannize, crush, repress, subjugate, subdue, keep down, rule with a rod of iron.
■ **oppressor** n.

oppression n. the action of oppressing or the condition of being oppressed.
▷ SYNONYMS: **persecution**, abuse, ill-treatment, tyranny, repression,

o

suppression, subjugation, cruelty, brutality, injustice.
– ANTONYMS: freedom.

oppressive adj. **1** harsh and unfair. **2** causing distress or anxiety. **3** (of weather) close and sultry.
▷ SYNONYMS: **1 harsh**, cruel, brutal, repressive, tyrannical, despotic, draconian, ruthless, merciless, pitiless. **2 muggy**, close, heavy, hot, humid, sticky, airless, stuffy, stifling, sultry.
– ANTONYMS: lenient, fresh.

opprobrious adj. highly critical.

opprobrium n. **1** harsh criticism. **2** public disgrace as a result of bad behaviour.

opt v. make a choice.
▷ SYNONYMS: **choose**, select, pick, decide, elect; (**opt for**) go for, settle on, plump for.
□ **opt out 1** choose not to participate. **2** Brit. (of a school or hospital) withdraw from local authority control.

optic adj. of the eye or vision.

optical adj. of vision, light, or optics.
□ **optical fibre** a thin glass fibre through which light can be transmitted.
■ **optically** adv.

optician n. Brit. a person qualified to prescribe and supply glasses etc. and to detect eye diseases.

optics n. the study of vision and the behaviour of light.

optimal adj. best or most favourable.
■ **optimally** adv.

optimism n. hopefulness and confidence about the future or success of something.
■ **optimist** n.

optimistic adj. hopeful and confident.
▷ SYNONYMS: **1 positive**, confident, hopeful, sanguine, bullish, buoyant, upbeat. **2** *an optimistic forecast:* **encouraging**, promising, reassuring, favourable.
– ANTONYMS: pessimistic.
■ **optimistically** adv.

optimize (or **-ise**) v. make the best use of.

optimum adj. most likely to lead to a favourable outcome.
▷ SYNONYMS: **best**, most favourable, most advantageous, ideal, perfect, prime, optimal.
• n. (pl. **optima** or **optimums**) the most favourable conditions for growth or success.

option n. **1** a thing that is or may be chosen. **2** the freedom or right to choose. **3** a right to buy or sell something at a specified price within

a set time.
▷ SYNONYMS: **choice**, preference, alternative, selection, possibility.

optional adj. not compulsory.
▷ SYNONYMS: **voluntary**, noncompulsory, elective, discretionary.
– ANTONYMS: compulsory.
■ **optionally** adv.

optometry n. the occupation of measuring eyesight, prescribing lenses, and detecting eye disease.
■ **optometrist** n.

opulent adj. ostentatiously luxurious.
▷ SYNONYMS: **luxurious**, sumptuous, palatial, lavishly appointed, rich, splendid, magnificent, grand, fancy; informal **plush**; Brit. informal **swish**; N. Amer. informal **swank**.
– ANTONYMS: spartan.
■ **opulence** n. **opulently** adv.

opus n. (pl. **opuses** or **opera**) a separate musical composition or set of compositions.

or conj. **1** used to link alternatives. **2** otherwise.

oracle n. **1** (in ancient Greece or Rome) a priest or priestess who acted as a channel for prophecy from the gods. **2** an authority which is always correct.

oracular adj. **1** of an oracle. **2** hard to interpret.

oral adj. **1** spoken rather than written. **2** of or done by the mouth.
▷ SYNONYMS: **spoken**, verbal, unwritten, vocal, uttered.
– ANTONYMS: written.
• n. a spoken exam.
■ **orally** adv.

orange n. **1** a large round citrus fruit with reddish-yellow rind. **2** a bright reddish-yellow colour.

orang-utan (or **orang-utang**) n. a large ape with reddish hair.

oration n. a formal speech.

orator n. a skilful public speaker.

oratorio n. (pl. **oratorios**) a musical work on a religious theme for orchestra and voices.

oratory n. formal public speaking, esp. when inspiring.
■ **oratorical** adj.

orb n. **1** a sphere. **2** a golden globe with a cross on top, carried by a monarch.

orbit n. **1** the regularly repeated course of a planet, spacecraft, etc. around a star or planet. **2** an area of activity or influence.
▷ SYNONYMS: **circuit**, course, path, track, trajectory, rotation, revolution.
• v. (**orbiting**, **orbited**) move in orbit round.

▷ SYNONYMS: **circle**, go round, revolve round, travel round, circumnavigate.

orbital adj. **1** of an orbit or orbits. **2** Brit. (of a road) passing round the outside of a town.

orchard n. a piece of land planted with fruit trees.

orchestra n. a large group of musicians with string, woodwind, brass, and percussion sections.

▷ SYNONYMS: **ensemble**, group; informal band, combo.

■ **orchestral** adj.

orchestrate v. **1** arrange music for performance by an orchestra. **2** direct a situation to produce a desired effect.

▷ SYNONYMS: **organize**, arrange, plan, set up, mobilize, mount, stage, mastermind, coordinate, direct.

■ **orchestration** n.

orchid n. a plant with unusually shaped flowers.

ordain v. **1** make someone a priest or minister. **2** order officially.

▷ SYNONYMS: **1 confer holy orders on**, admit to the priesthood, appoint, anoint, consecrate. **2 determine**, predestine, preordain, predetermine, prescribe, designate.

ordeal n. a prolonged painful or horrific experience.

▷ SYNONYMS: **trial**, hardship, suffering, nightmare, trauma, hell, torture, torment, agony.

order n. **1** the arrangement of people or things according to a particular sequence or method. **2** a state in which everything is in its correct place. **3** a state in which the laws regulating public behaviour are followed. **4** a command. **5** a request for something to be supplied. **6** the set procedure followed in a court, religious service, etc. **7** a rank, kind, or quality. **8** a religious community living according to particular rules. **9** a classifying category of plants and animals.

▷ SYNONYMS: **1** *alphabetical order:* **sequence**, arrangement, organization, codification, classification, system, series, succession. **2** *some semblance of order:* **tidiness**, neatness, orderliness, method, symmetry, uniformity, regularity, routine. **3** *the police managed to keep order:* **peace**, control, law and order, calm. **4** *in good order:* **condition**, state, repair, shape, situation; Brit. informal nick. **5** *I had to obey orders:* **command**, instruction, directive, direction, decree, edict,

injunction, dictate. **6** *the lower orders of society:* **class**, level, rank, grade, caste. **7** *a religious order:* **community**, brotherhood, sisterhood. **8** *the Orange Order:* **organization**, association, society, fellowship, fraternity, lodge, guild, league, union, club.

– ANTONYMS: chaos.

• v. **1** give a command. **2** request that something be supplied. **3** arrange methodically.

▷ SYNONYMS: **1 instruct**, tell, command, direct, charge, require, enjoin, ordain, decree, rule. **2 request**, apply for, book, reserve, requisition. **3 organize**, arrange, sort out, lay out, classify, group, categorize, catalogue.

□ **in order 1** in the correct condition for use. **2** suitable in the circumstances. **out of order** not functioning.

orderly adj. **1** neatly arranged. **2** well behaved.

▷ SYNONYMS: **1 neat**, tidy, well ordered, in order, trim, in apple-pie order, shipshape. **2 organized**, efficient, methodical, systematic, coherent, structured, logical. **3 well behaved**, law-abiding, disciplined, peaceful, peaceable.

– ANTONYMS: untidy, unruly, disorderly.

• n. (pl. **orderlies**) **1** a hospital attendant. **2** a soldier assisting an officer.

■ **orderliness** n.

ordinal number n. a number expressing order (1st, 2nd, 3rd, etc.), rather than quantity (1, 2, 3, etc.).

ordinance n. an official order.

ordinand n. a candidate for ordination.

ordinary adj. normal or usual.

▷ SYNONYMS: **1 usual**, normal, standard, typical, common, customary, habitual, everyday, regular, routine, day-to-day, quotidian. **2 average**, run-of-the-mill, typical, middle-of-the-road, conventional, humdrum, unremarkable, unexceptional, pedestrian, prosaic, workday; informal bog-standard; Brit. informal common or garden; N. Amer. informal garden-variety.

– ANTONYMS: unusual.

■ **ordinarily** adv.

ordination n. the ordaining of someone as a priest or minister.

ordnance n. **1** large guns mounted on wheels. **2** military equipment and stores.

ordure n. dung.

ore n. naturally occurring material from which a metal or mineral can be extracted.

oregano /o-ri-**gah**-noh/ n. a herb.

organ n. **1** a body part with a particular function. **2** a keyboard instrument with rows of pipes supplied with air from bellows, or one producing similar sounds electronically. **3** a newspaper which puts forward particular views.
▷ SYNONYMS: **newspaper**, paper, journal, periodical, magazine, voice, mouthpiece.
■ **organist** n.

organic adj. **1** of or derived from living matter. **2** produced without artificial chemicals such as fertilizers. **3** of a bodily organ or organs. **4** (of development or change) continuous or natural.
▷ SYNONYMS: **1** *organic matter:* **living**, live, animate, biological. **2** *organic vegetables:* **natural**, chemical-free, pesticide-free, bio-. **3** *an organic whole:* **structured**, organized, coherent, integrated, coordinated, ordered, harmonious.
■ **organically** adv.

organism n. an individual animal, plant, or life form.
▷ SYNONYMS: **living thing**, being, creature, animal, plant, life form.

organization (or **-isation**) n. **1** the act of organizing. **2** a systematic arrangement or approach. **3** an organized group with a particular purpose, e.g. a business.
▷ SYNONYMS: **1 planning**, arrangement, coordination, organizing, running, management. **2 structure**, arrangement, plan, pattern, order, form, format, framework, composition. **3 institution**, body, group, company, concern, firm, business, corporation, conglomerate, consortium, syndicate, agency, association, society; informal outfit.
■ **organizational** adj.

organize (or **-ise**) v. **1** arrange in an orderly way. **2** make arrangements for.
▷ SYNONYMS: **1 order**, arrange, sort, assemble, marshal, put straight, group, classify, collate, categorize, catalogue, codify. **2 arrange**, coordinate, sort out, put together, fix up, set up, lay on, orchestrate, see to, mobilize.
■ **organizer** n.

orgasm n. a climax of sexual excitement.

orgy n. (pl. **orgies**) **1** a wild party with indiscriminate sexual activity. **2** excessive indulgence in a specified activity.

■ **orgiastic** adj.

orient n. (**the Orient**) the countries of the East.
● v. (or **orientate**) **1** position in relation to the points of a compass. **2** (**orient yourself**) find your position in relation to unfamiliar surroundings. **3** tailor to meet particular needs.
▷ SYNONYMS: **1** *you need time to orient yourself:* **acclimatize**, familiarize, adjust, accustom, find your feet, get your bearings. **2 aim**, direct, pitch, design, intend. **3 align**, place, position, arrange.
■ **oriental** adj. **orientation** n.

orienteering n. the sport of finding your way across country with a map and compass.

orifice n. an opening in the body.

origami /o-ri-**gah**-mi/ n. the Japanese art of folding paper into decorative shapes.

origin n. **1** the point where something begins. **2** a person's social background or ancestry.
▷ SYNONYMS: **1 beginning**, start, genesis, birth, dawning, dawn, emergence, creation, source, basis, cause, root, derivation, provenance. **2 descent**, ancestry, parentage, pedigree, lineage, line, heritage, birth, extraction, family, roots.

original adj. **1** existing from the beginning. **2** produced by an artist, author, etc. rather than copied. **3** inventive or novel.
▷ SYNONYMS: **1** *the original plan:* **first**, initial, earliest. **2** *the country's original inhabitants:* **indigenous**, aboriginal, native. **3** *an original Rembrandt:* **authentic**, genuine, actual, true, bona fide. **4** *his highly original style:* **innovative**, creative, imaginative, inventive, new, novel, fresh, unusual, unconventional, unorthodox, groundbreaking, pioneering, unique, distinctive.
● n. the earliest form of something, from which copies can be made.
▷ SYNONYMS: **prototype**, source, master.
■ **originality** n. **originally** adv.

originate v. bring or come into being.
▷ SYNONYMS: **1 arise**, have its origin, begin, start, stem, spring, emerge, emanate. **2 invent**, create, devise, think up, dream up, conceive, formulate, form, develop, produce, mastermind, pioneer.
■ **origination** n. **originator** n.

ormolu n. a gold-coloured alloy of copper, zinc, and tin.

ornament n. **1** an object designed to add beauty to something. **2** decorative items as a whole.
▷ SYNONYMS: **1 knick-knack**, trinket, bauble, gewgaw; N. Amer. informal kickshaw. **2 decoration**, adornment, embellishment, ornamentation, trimming, accessories, frills.
■ ornamentation n.

ornamental adj. intended as decoration.
▷ SYNONYMS: **decorative**, fancy, ornate, ornamented, attractive, pretty.

ornate adj. highly decorated.
▷ SYNONYMS: **elaborate**, decorated, embellished, adorned, ornamented, rococo, fancy, fussy, ostentatious, showy; informal flashy.
– ANTONYMS: plain.

ornithology n. the study of birds.
■ ornithological adj. ornithologist n.

orphan n. a child whose parents are dead.
• v. (**be orphaned**) (of a child) be made an orphan.

orphanage n. a home which cares for orphans.

orthodontics n. the treatment of irregularities in the teeth.
■ orthodontic adj. orthodontist n.

orthodox adj. **1** of or holding traditional or generally accepted beliefs. **2** conventional.
▷ SYNONYMS: **1 conventional**, mainstream, conformist, established, traditional, traditionalist, prevalent, popular, conservative, received. **2** an orthodox Muslim: observant, devout, strict.
– ANTONYMS: unconventional.
□ **Orthodox Church** the Christian Church in Greece and eastern Europe.
■ orthodoxy n.

orthography n. the conventional spelling system of a language.
■ orthographic adj.

orthopaedics (US **orthopedics**) n. the branch of medicine concerned with bones or muscles.
■ orthopaedic adj.

oscillate v. move or swing back and forth.
▷ SYNONYMS: **1 swing to and fro**, swing back and forth, sway. **2 waver**, swing, fluctuate, alternate, see-saw, yo-yo, vacillate.
■ oscillation n.

osier /**oh**-zi-er/ n. a willow with long flexible shoots.

osmium n. a hard metallic element.

osmosis n. a process by which molecules pass through a membrane from a less concentrated solution into a more concentrated one.
■ osmotic adj.

osprey n. (pl. **ospreys**) a large fish-eating bird of prey.

osseous adj. consisting of or turned into bone.

ossify v. (**ossifying, ossified**) **1** turn into bone. **2** stop developing.
■ ossification n.

ostensible adj. apparently true, but not necessarily so.
■ ostensibly adv.

ostentation n. showy display intended to impress.

ostentatious adj. expensive or showy in a way intended to impress other people.
▷ SYNONYMS: **showy**, conspicuous, flamboyant, gaudy, brash, vulgar, loud, extravagant, fancy, ornate, rococo; informal flash, flashy, bling, over the top, OTT, glitzy.
– ANTONYMS: restrained.
■ ostentatiously adv.

osteopathy n. a system of complementary medicine involving manipulation of bones and muscles.
■ osteopath n.

ostracize (or **-ise**) v. exclude from a society or group.
▷ SYNONYMS: **exclude**, shun, spurn, cold-shoulder, reject, ignore, snub, cut dead, blackball, blacklist; Brit. send to Coventry; informal freeze out; Brit. informal blank.
■ ostracism n.

ostrich n. a large flightless African bird.

other adj. & pron. **1** used to refer to a person or thing different from one already mentioned or known. **2** alternative of two. **3** additional. **4** those not already mentioned.
▷ SYNONYMS: **1 alternative**, different, distinct, separate, various. **2 more**, further, additional, extra, fresh, new, added, supplementary.
□ **otherwise 1** in different circumstances. **2** in other respects. **3** in a different way.

otiose adj. serving no practical purpose.

otter n. a fish-eating water mammal.

ottoman n. (pl. **ottomans**) a low padded seat without a back or arms.

ought aux. v. **1** expressing duty, advisability, or a desired state. **2** expressing probability.

Ouija board /**wee**-juh/ n. trademark a board marked with letters and signs, to which a pointer moves, supposedly

o

in answer to questions at a seance.

ounce n. **1** a unit of weight equal to one sixteenth of a pound (approx. 28 g). **2** a very small amount.

our adj. of or belonging to us.

ours possess. pron. belonging to us.

ourselves pron. **1** the form of 'we' used when you and another person or people are the subject of the verb and are also affected by it. **2** we or us personally.

oust v. force from a position of power.
▷ SYNONYMS: **expel**, drive out, force out, eject, get rid of, depose, topple, unseat, overthrow, bring down, overturn, dismiss, dislodge.

out adv. **1** moving away from a place. **2** away from your home or place of work. **3** outdoors. **4** so as to be revealed, heard, or known. **5** at or to an end. **6** so as to be extinguished. **7** away from the land.
• adj. **1** not possible. **2** unconscious. **3** (of the ball in tennis etc.) not in the playing area.
• v. informal reveal the homosexuality of.
□ **out-and-out** complete.

outback n. the remote, sparsely populated part of Australia.

outboard adj. (of a motor) attached to the outside of a boat.

outbreak n. a sudden or violent occurrence of war, disease, etc.
▷ SYNONYMS: **1 eruption**, flare-up, upsurge, rash, wave, spate, burst, flurry. **2 start**, beginning, commencement, onset.

outbuilding n. a smaller building in the grounds of a main building.

outburst n. a sudden release of emotion.
▷ SYNONYMS: **eruption**, explosion, flare-up, storm, outpouring, burst, surge, fit, paroxysm, spasm.

outcast n. a person rejected by their society or social group.

outclass v. be far better than.

outcome n. a consequence.
▷ SYNONYMS: **result**, end result, net result, consequence, upshot, conclusion, outcome, end product; informal pay-off.

outcrop n. a part of a rock formation visible on the surface.

outcry n. (pl. **outcries**) a strong expression of public disapproval.
▷ SYNONYMS: **protest**, protestation, complaints, objections, furore, hue and cry, fuss, uproar, opposition, dissent; informal hullabaloo, ructions, stink.

outdated adj. no longer used or fashionable.
▷ SYNONYMS: **old-fashioned**, out of date, outmoded, out of fashion, unfashionable, dated, passé, old, behind the times, antiquated; informal out, old hat, square, clunky.
– ANTONYMS: modern.

outdistance v. leave a pursuer far behind.

outdo v. (**outdoes, outdoing, outdid;** past part. **outdone**) do better than.
▷ SYNONYMS: **surpass**, outshine, overshadow, eclipse, outclass, outmanoeuvre, put in the shade, upstage, exceed, transcend, top, cap, beat, better; informal be a cut above.

outdoor adj. done, situated, or used in the open air.
▷ SYNONYMS: **open-air**, out-of-doors, outside, alfresco.
– ANTONYMS: indoor.
■ **outdoors** adv.

outer adj. **1** outside. **2** further from the centre or the inside.
▷ SYNONYMS: **1 outside**, outermost, outward, exterior, external, surface. **2 outlying**, distant, remote, faraway, far-flung, furthest.
– ANTONYMS: inner.
■ **outermost** adj.

outface v. defeat someone by confronting them boldly.

outfit n. **1** a set of clothes worn together. **2** informal a business or team of people.
▷ SYNONYMS: **1 costume**, suit, uniform, ensemble, clothes, clothing, dress, garb; informal get-up, gear; Brit. informal kit. **2 organization**, enterprise, company, firm, business, group, body, team; informal set-up.

outflank v. **1** move round the side of an enemy. **2** outwit.

outgoing adj. **1** friendly and confident. **2** leaving a job or position.
▷ SYNONYMS: **1 extrovert**, uninhibited, unreserved, demonstrative, affectionate, warm, sociable, gregarious, convivial, lively, expansive. **2 departing**, retiring, leaving.
– ANTONYMS: introverted, incoming.
• n. (**outgoings**) Brit. regular expenditure.
▷ SYNONYMS: **expenses**, expenditure, spending, outlay, payments, costs, overheads.

outgrow v. (**outgrowing, outgrew;** past part. **outgrown**) **1** grow too big for. **2** leave behind or cease to be interested in as you mature.

outhouse n. a smaller building attached or close to a house.

outing n. a short trip taken for pleasure.
▷ SYNONYMS: **trip**, excursion, jaunt, expedition, day out, tour, drive, ride, run; informal spin, junket.

outlandish adj. strange or unfamiliar.

outlast v. last longer than.

outlaw n. a person who has broken the law and remains at large.
▷ SYNONYMS: **fugitive**, bandit, robber.
• v. make illegal.
▷ SYNONYMS: **ban**, bar, prohibit, forbid, proscribe.
– ANTONYMS: permit.

outlay n. an amount of money spent.

outlet n. **1** a pipe or hole for water or gas to escape. **2** a point from which goods are sold. **3** a means of expressing your energy, emotions, etc.
▷ SYNONYMS: **1 vent**, way out, outfall, opening, channel, conduit, duct. **2 market**, shop, store.

outline n. **1** a sketch or diagram showing the shape of an object. **2** the outer edges of an object. **3** a summary.
▷ SYNONYMS: **1 silhouette**, profile, shape, contours, form, lines. **2 rough idea**, thumbnail sketch, rundown, summary, synopsis, résumé, precis, gist, bare bones.
• v. **1** draw the outer edge or shape of. **2** summarize.
▷ SYNONYMS: **rough out**, sketch out, draft, summarize, precis.

outlook n. **1** a person's attitude to life. **2** a view. **3** what is likely to happen in the future.
▷ SYNONYMS: **1 point of view**, viewpoint, way of thinking, perspective, attitude, standpoint, stance, frame of mind. **2 view**, vista, prospect, panorama. **3 prospects**, future, expectations, prognosis.

outlying adj. situated far from a centre.

outmoded adj. old-fashioned.

outnumber v. be more numerous than.

out of date adj. no longer current, valid, or fashionable.
▷ SYNONYMS: **1 old-fashioned**, outmoded, outdated, dated, old, passé, behind the times, obsolete, antiquated, anachronistic, antediluvian; informal old hat, clunky. **2 expired**, lapsed, invalid, void.
– ANTONYMS: fashionable, up to date.

outpace v. go faster than.

outpatient n. a patient attending a hospital for treatment without staying overnight.

outpost n. **1** a small military camp at a distance from the main army. **2** a remote settlement.

output n. the amount of power, energy, work, etc. produced.
▷ SYNONYMS: **production**, yield, product, productivity, work, result.
• v. (**outputting**, **output** or **outputted**) (of a computer) produce data.

outrage n. **1** extreme shock and anger. **2** a very cruel, wicked, or shocking act.
▷ SYNONYMS: **1 indignation**, fury, anger, rage, wrath, annoyance; literary ire. **2 scandal**, offence, insult, affront, disgrace, atrocity.
• v. cause to feel outrage.
▷ SYNONYMS: **enrage**, infuriate, incense, anger, scandalize, offend, affront, shock.

outrageous adj. **1** shockingly bad or excessive. **2** very bold and unusual.
▷ SYNONYMS: **1 shocking**, disgraceful, scandalous, atrocious, appalling, dreadful, insufferable, intolerable. **2 exaggerated**, improbable, preposterous, ridiculous, unwarranted.
■ **outrageously** adv.

outré /oo-tray/ adj. unusual and rather shocking.

outrider n. a person in a vehicle or on horseback escorting another vehicle.

outrigger n. a float fixed parallel to a canoe or small ship to aid stability.

outright adv. **1** totally. **2** openly. **3** immediately.
▷ SYNONYMS: **1 completely**, entirely, wholly, totally, categorically, absolutely, utterly, flatly, unreservedly, out of hand. **2 explicitly**, directly, frankly, candidly, bluntly, plainly, to someone's face; Brit. informal straight up. **3 instantly**, instantaneously, immediately, at once, straight away, then and there, on the spot.
• adj. **1** open and direct. **2** complete.
▷ SYNONYMS: **1 complete**, absolute, out-and-out, downright, utter, sheer, categorical. **2 definite**, unequivocal, unmistakable, clear.

outrun v. (**outrunning**, **outran**; past part. **outrun**) run faster or further than.

outset n. the beginning.
▷ SYNONYMS: **start**, starting point, beginning, inception; informal the word go.
– ANTONYMS: end.

outside n. the external side, part, or surface.
▷ SYNONYMS: **exterior**, case, skin, shell, covering, facade.

o

• **adj. 1** on or near the outside. **2** not of or from a particular group.

▷ SYNONYMS: **exterior**, external, outer, outdoor, out-of-doors, alfresco.

• **prep. & adv. 1** situated or moving beyond the boundaries of. **2** not being a member of.

□ **an outside chance** a remote possibility.

outsider n. **1** a person who does not belong to a particular group. **2** a competitor thought to have little chance of success.

▷ SYNONYMS: **stranger**, visitor, foreigner, alien, interloper, immigrant, incomer, newcomer.

outsize adj. very large.

outskirts pl. n. the outer parts of a town or city.

▷ SYNONYMS: **edges**, fringes, margins, suburbs, suburbia, environs, borders, periphery.

outsource v. arrange for work to be done outside a company.

outspoken adj. very frank.

▷ SYNONYMS: **forthright**, direct, candid, frank, straightforward, open, straight from the shoulder, plain-spoken, blunt.

outstanding adj. **1** very good. **2** clearly noticeable. **3** not yet dealt with or paid.

▷ SYNONYMS: **1 excellent**, marvellous, fine, magnificent, superb, wonderful, superlative, exceptional, pre-eminent, renowned, celebrated; informal great, terrific, tremendous, super; Brit. informal brilliant; N. Amer. informal neat. **2 to be done**, undone, unfinished, incomplete, remaining, pending. **3 unpaid**, unsettled, owing, owed, to be paid, payable, due, overdue; N. Amer. delinquent.

■ **outstandingly** adv.

outstrip v. (**outstripping, outstripped**) **1** move faster than and overtake. **2** surpass.

outvote v. defeat by gaining more votes.

outward adj. & adv. **1** on or from the outside. **2** out or away from a place.

■ **outwardly** adv. **outwards** adv.

outweigh v. be greater or more important than.

▷ SYNONYMS: **be greater than**, exceed, be superior to, prevail over, over-ride, supersede, offset, cancel out, outbalance, compensate for.

outwit v. (**outwitting, outwitted**) defeat by cunning or ingenuity.

▷ SYNONYMS: **outsmart**, outmanoeuvre, steal a march on, trick, get the better

of; informal pull a fast one on, put one over on.

ova pl. of **ovum**.

oval adj. having a rounded and slightly elongated outline.

• n. an oval object or shape.

ovary n. (pl. **ovaries**) **1** a female reproductive organ in which eggs are produced. **2** the base of the reproductive organ of a flower.

■ **ovarian** adj.

ovate adj. oval.

ovation n. a long, enthusiastic round of applause.

▷ SYNONYMS: **applause**, round of applause, cheers, bravos, acclaim, standing ovation; informal big hand.

oven n. an enclosed compartment in which things are cooked or heated.

over prep. **1** extending upwards from or above. **2** above so as to cover or protect. **3** expressing movement across. **4** beyond and falling or hanging from. **5** expressing length of time. **6** higher or more than. **7** expressing authority or control.

▷ SYNONYMS: **1 above**, on top of, atop, covering. **2 more than**, above, in excess of, upwards of.

– ANTONYMS: under.

• adv. **1** expressing movement across an area. **2** beyond and falling or hanging from a point. **3** finished. **4** repeatedly.

▷ SYNONYMS: **1 overhead**, past, by. **2 at an end**, finished, ended, no more, a thing of the past; informal finito.

• n. Cricket a sequence of six balls bowled from one end of the pitch.

over- prefix **1** excessively. **2** over; above.

overall adj. & adv. including everything; taken as a whole.

▷ SYNONYMS: **1** the overall cost: **total**, all-inclusive, gross, final, inclusive, complete, entire. **2** overall, things have improved: **generally**, in general, altogether, all in all, on balance, on average, for the most part, in the main, on the whole, by and large.

• n. (or **overalls**) Brit. a loose protective garment worn over ordinary clothes.

overarm adj. & adv. (of an arm action) made with the hand brought forward and down from above shoulder level.

overawe v. impress someone so much that they are silent or nervous.

overbalance v. fall due to loss of balance.

overbearing adj. unpleasantly overpowering.

▷ SYNONYMS: **domineering**, dominating,

autocratic, tyrannical, despotic, high-handed; informal bossy.

overblown adj. pretentious.

overboard adv. from a ship into the water.

□ **go overboard** be very or too enthusiastic.

overcast adj. cloudy.

▷ SYNONYMS: **cloudy**, sunless, dark, grey, black, leaden, heavy, dull, murky.

– ANTONYMS: bright.

overcharge v. charge too high a price.

overcoat n. a long, warm coat.

overcome v. (**overcoming, overcame**; past part. **overcome**) **1** succeed in dealing with a problem. **2** defeat. **3** (**be overcome**) be overwhelmed by an emotion.

▷ SYNONYMS: **1 conquer**, defeat, beat, prevail over, control, get/bring under control, master, get the better of; informal lick, best. **2** *she was overcome with excitement:* **overwhelmed**, speechless, helpless; moved, affected.

overdo v. (**overdoes, overdoing, overdid**; past part. **overdone**) **1** do excessively or in an exaggerated way. **2** use too much of. **3** cook for too long.

overdose n. a dangerously large dose of a drug.

• v. take an overdose.

overdraft n. an arrangement with a bank allowing someone to take out more money than their account holds.

overdrawn adj. (of a bank account) having had more money taken out of it than it holds.

overdrive n. **1** a mechanism providing an extra gear above top gear. **2** a state of great activity.

overdue adj. not having arrived, happened, or been done by the expected or required time.

▷ SYNONYMS: **1 late**, behind schedule, behind time, delayed, tardy. **2 unpaid**, unsettled, owing, owed, payable, due, outstanding, undischarged; N. Amer. delinquent.

– ANTONYMS: early, punctual.

overestimate v. form too high an estimate of.

• n. an estimate which is too high.

overflow v. **1** flow over the edge of a container. **2** be too full or crowded.

▷ SYNONYMS: **spill over**, flow over, brim over, well over, flood.

• n. **1** an excess or surplus. **2** an outlet for excess water.

▷ SYNONYMS: **surplus**, excess, extra, remainder, overspill.

overgrown adj. **1** covered with weeds. **2** grown too large.

overhaul v. **1** examine and repair. **2** Brit. overtake.

▷ SYNONYMS: **service**, maintain, repair, mend, fix up, rebuild, renovate, recondition, refit, refurbish.

• n. an act of examining and repairing.

overhead adv. & adj. above the head.

• n. (**overheads**) expenses incurred in running a business etc.

overhear v. (**overhearing, overheard**) hear accidentally.

overjoyed adj. very happy.

overkill n. too much of something.

overland adj. & adv. by land.

overlap v. (**overlapping, overlapped**) **1** extend over so as to partly cover. **2** partly coincide in time.

• n. an overlapping part or amount.

overleaf adv. on the other side of the page.

overload v. **1** load too heavily. **2** put too great a demand on.

• n. an excessive amount.

overlook v. **1** fail to notice. **2** ignore a fault. **3** have a view of from above.

▷ SYNONYMS: **1 fail to notice**, fail to spot, miss. **2 disregard**, neglect, ignore, pass over, forget, take no notice of, make allowances for, turn a blind eye to, excuse, pardon, forgive. **3 have a view of**, look over/across, look on to, look out on.

overly adv. excessively.

overnight adv. & adj. during or for a night.

overpass n. a bridge by which a road crosses another.

overpower v. **1** defeat with greater strength. **2** overwhelm.

▷ SYNONYMS: **overwhelm**, get the better of, overthrow, subdue, suppress, subjugate, repress, bring someone to their knees.

overpowering adj. very strong or powerful.

▷ SYNONYMS: **overwhelming**, profound, oppressive, unbearable, unendurable, intolerable.

overrate v. rate more highly than is deserved.

overreach v. (**overreach yourself**) fail through being too ambitious.

overreact v. react more strongly than is justified.

■ **overreaction** n.

override v. (**overriding, overrode**; past part. **overridden**) **1** overrule. **2** interrupt the action of an automatic device. **3** be more important than.

▷ SYNONYMS: **1 disallow**, overrule, countermand, veto, quash, overturn,

o

overthrow, cancel, reverse, rescind, revoke, repeal. **2 outweigh**, supersede, take precedence over, take priority over, cancel out, outbalance.

overriding adj. more important than anything else: *safety was our overriding concern.*
▷ SYNONYMS: **most important**, top, first, predominant, principal, primary, paramount, chief, main, major, foremost, central, key.

overrule v. reject or disallow by using your higher authority.
▷ SYNONYMS: **countermand**, cancel, reverse, rescind, repeal, revoke, disallow, override, veto, quash, overturn, overthrow.

overrun v. (**overrunning**, **overran**; past part. **overrun**) **1** spread over or occupy in large numbers. **2** exceed a limit.
▷ SYNONYMS: **invade**, storm, occupy, swarm into, surge into, inundate, overwhelm.

overseas adv. & adj. in or to a foreign country.

oversee v. (**overseeing**, **oversaw**; past part. **overseen**) supervise.
■ **overseer** n.

overshadow v. **1** cast a shadow over. **2** appear more important or successful than.
▷ SYNONYMS: **outshine**, eclipse, surpass, exceed, outclass, outstrip, outdo, upstage; informal be head and shoulders above.

overshoot v. (**overshooting**, **overshot**) go past an intended place or limit.

oversight n. an unintentional failure to notice or do something.

overspill n. Brit. people who move from an overcrowded area to live elsewhere.

oversteer v. (of a car) tend to turn more sharply than intended.

overstep v. (**overstepping**, **overstepped**) go beyond a limit.

overt adj. done or shown openly.
▷ SYNONYMS: **undisguised**, unconcealed, plain, clear, conspicuous, obvious, noticeable, manifest, patent, open, blatant.
– ANTONYMS: covert.
■ **overtly** adv.

overtake v. (**overtaking**, **overtook**; past part. **overtaken**) **1** catch up with and pass while travelling in the same direction. **2** suddenly affect.
▷ SYNONYMS: **1 pass**, go past, pull ahead of; Brit. overhaul. **2 outstrip**, surpass, overshadow, eclipse, outshine, outclass, exceed, top, cap. **3 befall**,

happen to, come upon, hit, strike, overwhelm, overcome.

overthrow v. (**overthrowing**, **overthrew**; past part. **overthrown**) remove from power by force.
▷ SYNONYMS: **oust**, remove, bring down, topple, depose, displace, unseat, defeat, conquer.
• n. a removal from power.
▷ SYNONYMS: **removal**, ousting, defeat, fall, collapse, demise.

overtime n. time worked in addition to normal working hours.

overtone n. a subtle or additional quality or implication.

overture n. **1** an orchestral piece at the beginning of a musical work. **2** an approach towards opening negotiations or establishing a relationship.
▷ SYNONYMS: **1 preliminary**, prelude, introduction, lead-in, precursor, start, beginning. **2 opening move**, approach, advances, feeler, signal.

overturn v. **1** turn over and come to rest upside down, or cause to do this. **2** abolish or reverse a decision, system, etc.
▷ SYNONYMS: **1 capsize**, turn turtle, keel over, tip over, topple over, upset, turn over, knock over, upend. **2 cancel**, reverse, rescind, repeal, revoke, countermand, disallow, override, overrule, veto, quash, overthrow.

overview n. a general review.

overweening adj. showing too much confidence or pride.

overweight adj. too heavy or fat.
▷ SYNONYMS: **fat**, obese, stout, plump, portly, chubby, pot-bellied, flabby; informal tubby; Brit. informal podgy.

overwhelm v. **1** bury beneath a huge mass. **2** overpower. **3** have a strong emotional effect on.
▷ SYNONYMS: **1 trounce**, rout, beat hollow, conquer, crush; informal thrash, lick, wipe the floor with. **2 overcome**, move, stir, affect, touch, strike, dumbfound, shake, leave speechless; informal bowl over, knock sideways; Brit. informal knock/hit for six.

overwhelming adj. very great or strong.
▷ SYNONYMS: **1** *an overwhelming majority*: very large, enormous, immense, massive, huge, inordinate. **2** *an overwhelming desire to laugh*: very strong, powerful, uncontrollable, irrepressible, irresistible, overpowering, compelling.

overwrought adj. very worried or nervously excited.

o

oviduct n. the tube through which an ovum passes from an ovary.

oviparous adj. egg-laying.

ovoid adj. egg-shaped.

ovulate v. discharge ova from the ovary.
■ ovulation n.

ovule n. the part of the ovary of a plant that after fertilization becomes the seed.

ovum n. (pl. **ova**) a female reproductive cell, which can develop into an embryo if fertilized by a male cell.

owe v. (**owing**, **owed**) **1** be required to pay or repay money etc. in return for something received. **2** have something because of: *I owe him my life.*
▷ SYNONYMS: **be in debt**, be in arrears; be indebted, be under an obligation.

owing adj. yet to be paid.
▷ SYNONYMS: **unpaid**, payable, due, overdue, undischarged, owed, outstanding, in arrears; N. Amer. delinquent.
□ owing to because of.

owl n. a bird of prey with large eyes, active at night.
■ owlish adj.

own adj. & pron. belonging to or done by the person specified.
▷ SYNONYMS: **personal**, individual, particular, private, personalized, unique.
• v. **1** possess. **2** admit to be the case. **3** (**own up**) confess to a wrongdoing.
▷ SYNONYMS: **1** possess, keep, hold, have to your name. **2** confess, admit, acknowledge; informal come clean.

owner n. a person who owns something.
▷ SYNONYMS: **possessor**, holder, proprietor, homeowner, freeholder, landlord, landlady.

ownership n. the fact or right of owning something.
▷ SYNONYMS: **possession**, freehold, proprietorship, title.

ox n. (pl. **oxen**) **1** a cow or bull. **2** a castrated bull, used for pulling heavy loads.

oxide n. a compound of oxygen and another element.

oxidize (or -**ise**) v. combine with oxygen.
■ oxidation n. oxidization n.

oxyacetylene adj. (of welding or cutting) using a very hot flame produced by mixing acetylene and oxygen.

oxygen n. a gas forming about 20 per cent of the earth's atmosphere.

oxygenate v. supply or treat with oxygen.

oxymoron n. a figure of speech in which apparently contradictory terms appear together (e.g. *a deafening silence*).

oyster n. an edible shellfish.

oz abbrev. ounces.

ozone n. a strong-smelling, poisonous form of oxygen.
□ ozone hole an area of the ozone layer where the ozone is greatly reduced. ozone layer a layer in the earth's stratosphere containing much ozone, absorbing ultraviolet radiation.

o

Pp

p abbrev. **1** page. **2** Brit. penny or pence.
PA abbrev. **1** Brit. personal assistant.
2 public address.
p.a. abbrev. per annum.
pace n. **1** a single step when walking
or running. **2** rate of movement or
change.
▷ SYNONYMS: **1 step**, stride. **2 gait**, walk,
march, tread. **3 speed**, rate, velocity,
tempo.
• v. **1** walk steadily or to and fro.
2 measure a distance by pacing.
3 (**pace yourself**) do something at a
steady rate.
▷ SYNONYMS: **walk**, step, stride, march,
pound.
□ **pacemaker 1** an artificial device
for regulating the heart muscle. **2** a
runner who sets the pace for other
competitors.
pachyderm /pak-i-derm/ n. a large
thick-skinned mammal, e.g. an
elephant.
pacific adj. **1** peaceful. **2** (**Pacific**) of
the Pacific Ocean.
pacifism n. the belief that disputes
should be settled without the use of
war and violence.
■ **pacifist** n. & adj.
pacify v. (**pacifying**, **pacified**) **1** make
less angry or upset. **2** establish peace
in a country.
▷ SYNONYMS: **placate**, appease, calm
down, conciliate, propitiate, assuage,
mollify, soothe.
− ANTONYMS: enrage.
■ **pacification** n.
pack n. **1** a cardboard or paper
container and the items in it. **2** Brit. a
set of playing cards. **3** a group of dogs
or wolves. **4** a group of similar things
or people.
▷ SYNONYMS: **1 packet**, container,
package, box, carton, parcel. **2 group**,
herd, troop, crowd, mob, band, party,
set, gang, rabble, horde, throng,
huddle, mass, assembly, gathering,
host; informal crew, bunch.
• v. **1** fill a bag with items needed

for travel. **2** put or cram items in a
container. **3** cover or surround with
something crammed tightly.
▷ SYNONYMS: **1 fill**, load, stow, store,
bundle, stuff, cram. **2** glasses packed in
straw: **wrap**, package, parcel, swathe,
swaddle, encase, envelop, bundle up.
3 shoppers packed the stores: **throng**,
crowd, fill, cram, jam, squash into,
squeeze into.
□ **pack in** informal stop doing. **pack off**
informal send away.
■ **packer** n.
package n. **1** something wrapped
in paper or packed in a box. **2** a set
of proposals offered or agreed as a
whole.
▷ SYNONYMS: **1 parcel**, packet, box,
carton. **2 collection**, bundle, combination, range, complement, raft,
platform.
• v. **1** put into a box or wrapping.
2 present in an attractive way.
▷ SYNONYMS: **wrap**, gift-wrap, pack, box,
seal.
□ **package holiday** a holiday
whose price covers transport and
accommodation.
packed adj. very crowded.
▷ SYNONYMS: **crowded**, full, filled to
capacity, crammed, jammed, teeming,
seething, swarming; informal jam-
packed, chock-full, chock-a-block,
full to the gunwales, bursting at the
seams; Brit. informal rammed.
packet n. **1** a small container or plastic
bag in which goods are packed. **2** (**a
packet**) informal a large sum of money.
▷ SYNONYMS: **pack**, carton, container,
case, package.
pact n. a formal agreement.
▷ SYNONYMS: **agreement**, treaty, entente,
protocol, deal, settlement, armistice,
truce.
pad n. **1** a piece of soft or absorbent
material. **2** the fleshy underpart of an
animal's foot. **3** a number of sheets of
blank paper fastened together at one
edge. **4** a flat surface for helicopter

take-off and landing or for rocket-launching.

▷ SYNONYMS: **1 dressing**, pack, wad. **2 notebook**, notepad, writing pad, jotter; N. Amer. scratch pad.

• v. (**padding, padded**) **1** fill or cover with a pad. **2** lengthen a speech etc. with unnecessary material. **3** walk with soft, steady steps.

▷ SYNONYMS: **creep**, sneak, steal, tiptoe, pussyfoot.

padding n. soft material used to pad or stuff something.

▷ SYNONYMS: **1 wadding**, cushioning, stuffing, packing, filling, lining. **2 verbiage**, wordiness; Brit. informal waffle.

paddle n. a short oar with a broad blade.

• v. **1** propel with a paddle. **2** walk with bare feet in shallow water.

paddock n. a small field or enclosure for horses.

padlock n. a detachable lock hanging by a hinged hook through a ring on the object fastened.

• v. secure with a padlock.

padre /pah-dray/ n. a chaplain in the armed services.

paean /pee-uhn/ n. a song of praise or triumph.

paediatrics /pee-di-at-riks/ (US **pediatrics**) n. the branch of medicine concerned with children and their diseases.

■ **paediatric** adj. **paediatrician** n.

paedophile /pee-duh-fyl/ (US **pedophile**) n. a person who is sexually attracted to children.

■ **paedophilia** n.

paella /py-el-uh/ n. a Spanish dish of rice, seafood, etc.

pagan n. a person holding religious beliefs other than those of established religions.

▷ SYNONYMS: **heathen**, infidel, unbeliever.

• adj. of pagans or their beliefs.

■ **paganism** n.

page n. **1** a leaf of a book etc. **2** one side of this. **3** a young male attendant in a hotel. **4** (also **pageboy**) a young boy attending a bride. **5** hist. a boy in training for knighthood.

▷ SYNONYMS: **1 folio**, sheet, side, leaf. **2 errand boy**, messenger boy; N. Amer. bellboy, bellhop

• v. **1** (**page through**) leaf through. **2** summon over a public address system or by a pager.

pageant /paj-uhnt/ n. a public entertainment performed by people in elaborate or historical costumes.

▷ SYNONYMS: **parade**, procession, cavalcade, tableau, spectacle, extravaganza, show.

pageantry n. elaborate display or ceremony.

▷ SYNONYMS: **spectacle**, display, ceremony, magnificence, pomp, splendour, grandeur, show; informal razzle-dazzle, razzmatazz.

pager n. a radio device that bleeps or vibrates to summon the wearer.

pagoda n. a Hindu or Buddhist temple or other sacred building.

paid past & past part. of PAY.

pail n. a bucket.

pain n. **1** strong physical discomfort caused by illness or injury. **2** mental suffering. **3** (**pains**) great care or trouble.

▷ SYNONYMS: **1 suffering**, agony, torture, torment; ache, aching, soreness, throbbing, sting, twinge, stab, pang, discomfort. **2 sorrow**, grief, heartache, heartbreak, sadness, unhappiness, distress, misery, despair, agony, torment, torture. **3** he took pains to hide his feelings: **care**, effort, bother, trouble.

• v. cause pain to.

▷ SYNONYMS: **sadden**, grieve, distress, upset, trouble.

□ **painkiller** a medicine for relieving pain.

■ **painlessly** adv..

> **WORD LINKS**
> **analgesic** a drug for reducing pain
> **anaesthetic** a drug that makes someone unable to feel pain

painful adj. suffering or causing pain.

▷ SYNONYMS: **1** a painful finger: **sore**, hurting, tender, aching, throbbing. **2** a painful experience: **unpleasant**, nasty, distressing, upsetting, sad, traumatic, miserable, heartbreaking, agonizing, harrowing.

■ **painfully** adv.

painless adj. **1** not causing pain. **2** involving little effort or stress.

■ **painlessly** adv.

painstaking adj. very careful and thorough.

▷ SYNONYMS: **careful**, meticulous, thorough, assiduous, attentive, conscientious, punctilious, scrupulous, rigorous.

– ANTONYMS: slapdash.

paint n. a coloured substance spread over a surface to give a decorative or protective coating.

▷ SYNONYMS: **colouring**, colour, tint, dye, stain, pigment, emulsion, gloss.

p

• v. **1** apply paint to. **2** apply a liquid to a surface with a brush. **3** produce a picture with paint. **4** describe.
▷ SYNONYMS: **1 colour**, decorate, whitewash, airbrush, daub, smear. **2** portray, picture, depict, represent.
painter n. **1** a person who paints as an artist or decorator. **2** a rope attached to a boat's bow for tying it up.
painting n. **1** the action of painting. **2** a painted picture.
▷ SYNONYMS: **picture**, illustration, portrayal, depiction, representation, image, artwork, canvas, oil, watercolour.
pair n. **1** a set of two things or people. **2** an article consisting of two parts: *a pair of scissors*.
▷ SYNONYMS: **set**, brace, couple, duo, two.
• v. **1** connect to form a pair. **2** (**pair off/up**) form a couple.
▷ SYNONYMS: **match**, put together, couple, combine.
paisley n. an intricate pattern of curved shapes like feathers.
pajamas US = **PYJAMAS**.
pal n. informal a friend.
palace n. an official residence of a monarch, archbishop, etc.
▷ SYNONYMS: **castle**, chateau, mansion, stately home, schloss.
palaeography /pa-li-**og**-ruh-fi/ (US **paleography**) n. the study of ancient writing and manuscripts.
Palaeolithic /pa-li-uh-**li**-thik/ (US **Paleolithic**) adj. of the early phase of the Stone Age.
palaeontology /pa-li-on-**tol**-uh-ji/ (US **paleontology**) n. the study of fossil animals and plants.
■ **palaeontologist** n.
palatable adj. **1** pleasant to taste. **2** acceptable.
▷ SYNONYMS: **1 edible**, tasty, appetizing, delicious, mouth-watering, toothsome, succulent; informal scrumptious, yummy, scrummy, moreish. **2** pleasant, acceptable, agreeable, to your liking.
– ANTONYMS: disagreeable.
palate n. **1** the roof of the mouth. **2** the sense of taste.
palatial /puh-**lay**-sh'l/ adj. like a palace; very luxurious or grand.
▷ SYNONYMS: **luxurious**, magnificent, sumptuous, splendid, grand, opulent, lavish, stately, fancy; Brit. upmarket; informal plush, swanky, posh, ritzy; Brit. informal swish.
– ANTONYMS: modest.
palaver n. informal a lengthy, boring fuss.

pale adj. **1** light in colour. **2** (of the face) having less colour than normal.
▷ SYNONYMS: **1 white**, pallid, pasty, wan, colourless, anaemic, washed out, peaky, ashen, sickly; informal like death warmed up. **2 light**, pastel, muted, subtle, soft, faded, bleached, washed out. **3 dim**, faint, weak, feeble.
– ANTONYMS: ruddy, dark.
• v. **1** become pale. **2** seem less important.
▷ SYNONYMS: **turn white**, turn pale, blanch, lose colour.
□ **beyond the pale** outside the bounds of acceptable behaviour.
Palestinian n. a member of the native Arab population of Palestine.
• adj. of Palestine.
palette n. **1** a board on which an artist mixes paints. **2** a range of colours used.
□ **palette knife** a knife with a blunt, flexible blade for applying paint or smoothing soft substances.
palindrome n. a word or phrase that reads the same backwards as forwards.
paling n. **1** a fence made from stakes. **2** a stake.
palisade n. a fence of stakes or iron railings.
pall /pawl/ n. **1** a cloth spread over a coffin. **2** a dark cloud of smoke, dust, etc.
• v. become less appealing through familiarity.
□ **pall-bearer** a person helping to carry or escorting a coffin at a funeral.
palladium n. a rare silvery-white metallic element.
pallet n. **1** a straw mattress or makeshift bed. **2** a portable platform on which goods can be moved or stacked.
palliate v. **1** make the symptoms of a disease less severe. **2** make something bad less serious.
■ **palliative** adj.
pallid adj. pale, esp. from illness.
■ **pallor** n.
pally adj. informal friendly.
palm n. **1** an evergreen tree of warm regions, with a crown of long leaves. **2** the inner surface of the hand.
• v. **1** hide in the hand. **2** (**palm off**) informal persuade someone to accept something by deception.
□ **palmtop** a computer small enough to be held in one hand.
palmistry n. the prediction of a person's future by examining their hand.

p

■ **palmist** n.

palomino n. (pl. **palominos**) a pale golden horse with a white mane and tail.

palpable adj. able to be touched or felt.
▷ SYNONYMS: **1 tangible**, touchable. **2 perceptible**, visible, noticeable, discernible, detectable, observable, unmistakable, transparent, obvious, clear, plain, evident, apparent, manifest, staring you in the face, written all over someone.
– ANTONYMS: imperceptible.
■ **palpably** adv.

palpate v. medically examine by touch.

palpitate v. **1** (of the heart) beat rapidly. **2** shake; tremble.
■ **palpitations** pl. n.

palsy n. (pl. **palsies**) dated paralysis.
■ **palsied** adj.

paltry adj. **1** (of an amount) very small. **2** trivial.
▷ SYNONYMS: **small**, meagre, trifling, insignificant, negligible, inadequate, insufficient, derisory, pitiful, pathetic, miserable, niggardly, beggarly; informal measly, piddling, poxy.
– ANTONYMS: considerable.

pampas n. vast treeless plains in South America.

pamper v. treat very indulgently.
▷ SYNONYMS: **spoil**, indulge, overindulge, cosset, mollycoddle, coddle, baby, wait on someone hand and foot.

pamphlet n. a small booklet or leaflet.
▷ SYNONYMS: **brochure**, leaflet, booklet, circular; N. Amer. mailer, folder.

pamphleteer n. a writer of pamphlets.

pan n. **1** a metal container for cooking food in. **2** Brit. the bowl of a toilet.
▷ SYNONYMS: **saucepan**, pot, bowl, frying pan, skillet.
• v. (**panning**, **panned**) **1** informal criticize severely. **2** swing a film camera to give a panoramic effect or follow a subject. **3** wash gravel in a bowl to separate out gold.

pan- comb. form all or whole.

panacea /pan-uh-see-uh/ n. a solution or remedy for all difficulties or diseases.

panache /puh-nash/ n. a confident stylish manner.
▷ SYNONYMS: **flamboyance**, confidence, self-assurance, style, flair, elan, dash, verve, zest, spirit, brio, vivacity, gusto, liveliness, vitality, energy; informal pizzazz, oomph, zip, zing.

panama n. a straw hat.

pancake n. a thin, flat cake of fried batter.

pancreas n. a gland behind the stomach producing insulin.
■ **pancreatic** adj.

panda n. a large black and white bear-like mammal.

pandemic adj. (of a disease) occurring over a whole country or a wide area.

pandemonium n. uproar.

pander v. (**pander to**) indulge an immoral or distasteful desire or habit.

p. & p. abbrev. Brit. postage and packing.

pane n. a single sheet of glass in a window or door.

panegyric /pa-ni-ji-rik/ n. a speech or text in praise of someone or something.

panel n. **1** a section of a door, vehicle, garment, etc. **2** a small group assembled to investigate or decide on a matter.
▷ SYNONYMS: **1 console**, dashboard, instruments, controls, dials. **2 group**, team, body, committee, board.
■ **panelled** (US **paneled**) adj. **panellist** (US **panelist**) n.

panelling (US **paneling**) n. wooden panels as a wall covering.

pang n. a sudden sharp pain or painful emotion.

panic n. **1** sudden uncontrollable fear. **2** a frenzied hurry to do something.
▷ SYNONYMS: **alarm**, anxiety, fear, fright, trepidation, dread, terror, hysteria, apprehension; informal flap, fluster, cold sweat.
– ANTONYMS: calm.
• v. (**panicking**, **panicked**) feel panic.
▷ SYNONYMS: **1 be alarmed**, be scared, be afraid, take fright, be hysterical, lose your nerve, get worked up. **2 frighten**, alarm, scare, unnerve; Brit. informal put the wind up.
■ **panic-stricken** adj. **panicky** adj.

panjandrum n. a self-important official.

pannier n. **1** a bag fitted on the back of a bicycle or motorcycle. **2** a basket carried by a donkey etc.

panoply n. an impressive display.

panorama n. a view of a wide area or sequence of events.
▷ SYNONYMS: **view**, vista, prospect, scenery, landscape, seascape, cityscape, skyline.

panoramic adj. wide in range.
▷ SYNONYMS: **sweeping**, wide, extensive,

p

scenic, commanding.

pan pipes pl. n. a musical instrument made from a row of short pipes.

pansy n. **1** a plant with brightly coloured flowers. **2** offens. an effeminate or homosexual man.

pant v. breathe with short, quick breaths.
▷ SYNONYMS: **breathe heavily**, breathe hard, puff and blow, huff and puff, gasp, heave, wheeze.

pantaloons pl. n. baggy trousers gathered at the ankles.

pantechnicon n. Brit. a large van for transporting furniture.

pantheism n. the belief that God is present in all things.
■ **pantheist** n. **pantheistic** adj.

pantheon n. **1** all the gods of a people or religion. **2** an ancient temple dedicated to all the gods.

panther n. a black leopard.

panties pl. n. informal women's underpants.

pantile n. a curved roof tile.

pantograph n. a device for copying a plan etc. on any scale.

pantomime n. Brit. a theatrical entertainment based on a fairy tale.

pantry n. (pl. **pantries**) a small room or cupboard for storing food, crockery, etc.

pants pl. n. **1** Brit. underpants or knickers. **2** US trousers.
▷ SYNONYMS: **1 underpants**, briefs, boxer shorts, boxers, knickers; N. Amer. shorts, undershorts; informal panties; dated drawers, bloomers. **2 trousers**, slacks; Brit. informal trews, strides, kecks; Austral. informal daks.

pap n. **1** bland soft food suitable for babies or invalids. **2** undemanding reading matter or entertainment.

papacy n. (pl. **papacies**) the position or period of office of the pope.

papal adj. of the pope or papacy.

paparazzo /pa-puh-**rat**-zoh/ n. (pl. **paparazzi**) a freelance photographer who pursues celebrities to get photos of them.

papaya /puh-**py**-uh/ n. a tropical fruit with orange flesh.

paper n. **1** material manufactured in thin sheets from wood pulp, used for writing on, wrapping, etc. **2** a document. **3** a newspaper. **4** an essay. **5** Brit. a set of exam questions.
▷ SYNONYMS: **1 document**, certificate, letter, file, deed, record, archive; (**papers**) paperwork, documentation. **2** they asked us for our papers: identifi-

cation, identity card, ID, credentials. **3 newspaper**, journal, gazette, periodical, tabloid, broadsheet, daily, weekly; informal rag. **4 essay**, article, monograph, thesis, work, dissertation, treatise, study, report, analysis; N. Amer. theme. **5 exam**, examination, test.
• v. cover with wallpaper.
□ **paperback** a book bound in flexible card. **paperweight** a small, heavy object for keeping loose papers in place. **paperwork** routine work involving written documents.

papier mâché /pa-pi-ay **mash**-ay/ n. a mixture of paper and glue that becomes hard when dry.

paprika n. a powdered spice made from red peppers.

papyrus n. (pl. **papyri** or **papyruses**) a material made in ancient Egypt from the stem of a water plant, used for writing or painting on.

par n. Golf the number of strokes required by a first-class player for a hole or course.
□ **above** (or **below** or **under**) **par** above (or below) the usual or expected level. **on a par with** equal to.

parable n. a story told to illustrate a moral.
▷ SYNONYMS: **allegory**, moral tale, fable.

parabola n. a curve resembling the path of an object that is thrown into the air and falls back down.
■ **parabolic** adj.

paracetamol n. Brit. a drug used to reduce pain and fever.

parachute n. a cloth canopy used to slow the descent of a person or object dropping from a great height.
• v. drop by parachute.
■ **parachutist** n.

parade n. **1** a public procession. **2** a formal assembly of troops. **3** Brit. a public square, promenade, or row of shops. **4** an ostentatious display.
▷ SYNONYMS: **1 procession**, march, cavalcade, motorcade, spectacle, display, pageant, review, tattoo; Brit. march past. **2 promenade**, walkway, esplanade, mall; N. Amer. boardwalk; Brit. informal prom.
• v. **1** march in a parade. **2** display ostentatiously.
▷ SYNONYMS: **1 march**, process, file, troop. **2 strut**, swagger, stride; informal sashay. **3 display**, exhibit, make a show of, flaunt, show off; informal flash.

paradigm /**pa**-ruh-dym/ n. a typical example or model.

paradise n. **1** heaven. **2** a very

pleasant or beautiful place or state.
▷ SYNONYMS: **1 heaven**, the promised land, the Elysian Fields. **2 Utopia**, Shangri-La, Eden, nirvana, idyll. **3 bliss**, heaven on earth, ecstasy, delight, joy, happiness.
– ANTONYMS: hell.

paradox n. a statement that seems to contradict itself, but may in fact be true.
▷ SYNONYMS: **contradiction**, self-contradiction, inconsistency, incongruity, conflict, enigma, puzzle, conundrum.
  ■ **paradoxical** adj. **paradoxically** adv.

paraffin n. a flammable substance obtained from petroleum or shale, used as fuel.

paragliding n. a sport in which a person glides with a wide parachute after jumping from or being hauled to a height.

paragon n. a model of excellence or of a particular quality.

paragraph n. a distinct section of a piece of writing, begun on a new line.
▷ SYNONYMS: **section**, division, part, portion, segment, passage, clause.

parakeet n. a small parrot.

parallax n. an apparent difference in an object's position when viewed from different points.

parallel adj. **1** (of lines or planes) side by side and having the same distance continuously between them. **2** existing at the same time or in a similar way.
▷ SYNONYMS: **1 aligned**, side by side, equidistant. **2 similar**, analogous, comparable, corresponding, like, equivalent, matching.
– ANTONYMS: divergent, different.
  • n. **1** a person or thing similar to another. **2** a comparison. **3** a line of latitude.
▷ SYNONYMS: **1 counterpart**, analogue, equivalent, match, twin, duplicate, mirror. **2 similarity**, likeness, resemblance, analogy, correspondence, comparison, equivalence, symmetry.
– ANTONYMS: divergence, difference.
  • v. (**paralleling**, **paralleled**) **1** be parallel to. **2** be similar to.

parallelogram n. a plane figure with four straight sides and opposite sides parallel.

paralyse (US **paralyze**) v. affect with paralysis.

paralysis n. (pl. **paralyses**) **1** the loss of the power of movement. **2** inability to act or function.
▷ SYNONYMS: **1 immobility**, powerlessness, incapacity; Medicine paraplegia, quadriplegia. **2 shutdown**, immobilization, stoppage, gridlock, standstill, blockage.
  ■ **paralytic** adj.

paramedic n. a person who is trained to do medical work but is not a fully qualified doctor.

parameter n. a limit defining the scope of a process or activity.
▷ SYNONYMS: **framework**, variable, limit, boundary, limitation, restriction, criterion, guideline.

paramilitary adj. organized like a military force.

paramount adj. more important than anything else.
▷ SYNONYMS: **most important**, supreme, chief, overriding, predominant, foremost, prime, primary, principal, main, key, central; informal number-one.

paramour n. old use a lover.

paranoia n. **1** a mental condition in which a person has delusions of persecution or grandeur. **2** unjustified mistrust of others.

paranoid adj. relating to or suffering from paranoia.
▷ SYNONYMS: **suspicious**, mistrustful, anxious, fearful, insecure, obsessive.

paranormal adj. beyond the scope of scientific knowledge.

parapet n. a low wall along the edge of a bridge, balcony, etc.

paraphernalia n. miscellaneous equipment.

paraphrase v. express using different words.
▷ SYNONYMS: **reword**, rephrase, express differently, rewrite, gloss.
  • n. a rewording of a passage.

paraplegia /pa-ruh-**plee**-juh/ n. paralysis of the legs and lower body.
  ■ **paraplegic** adj. & n.

parapsychology n. the study of mental phenomena such as telepathy or hypnosis.

paraquat n. a poisonous weedkiller.

parasite n. **1** an organism living in or on another. **2** a person living off others.
▷ SYNONYMS: **hanger-on**, cadger, leech, passenger; informal freeloader, sponger, scrounger; N. Amer. informal mooch; Austral./NZ informal bludger.
  ■ **parasitic** adj.

parasol n. a light umbrella used to give shade from the sun.

paratroops pl. n. troops trained to parachute into an attack.
  ■ **paratrooper** n.

p

parboil v. partly cook by boiling.

parcel n. something wrapped in paper so as to be carried or posted.
▷ SYNONYMS: **package**, packet, pack, bundle, box, case, bale.
• v. (**parcelling**, **parcelled**; US **parceling**, **parceled**) **1** wrap as a parcel. **2** divide into portions.
▷ SYNONYMS: **pack**, package, wrap, gift-wrap, tie up, bundle.

parched adj. **1** dried out through heat. **2** informal very thirsty.
▷ SYNONYMS: **1 dry**, bone dry, dried up/out, arid, desiccated, dehydrated, baked, burned, scorched, withered, shrivelled. **2 dehydrated**, dry; informal gasping.

parchment n. **1** hist. writing material made from animal skin. **2** paper treated to resemble this.

pardon n. **1** forgiveness. **2** a cancellation of the punishment for an offence.
▷ SYNONYMS: **1 forgiveness**, absolution. **2 reprieve**, amnesty, exoneration, release, acquittal, discharge.
• v. (**pardoning**, **pardoned**) **1** forgive. **2** give an offender a pardon.
▷ SYNONYMS: **1 forgive**, absolve. **2 exonerate**, acquit, reprieve; informal let off.
− ANTONYMS: blame, punish.
■ **pardonable** adj.

pare v. **1** trim the edges of. **2** gradually reduce.

parent n. **1** a father or mother. **2** an organization owning or controlling subsidiary ones.
■ **parental** adj. **parenthood** n. **parenting** n.

parentage n. the identity and origins of a person's parents.
▷ SYNONYMS: **origins**, extraction, birth, family, ancestry, lineage, heritage, pedigree, descent, blood, stock, roots.

parenthesis /puh-ren-thi-siss/ n. (pl. **parentheses**) **1** a word or phrase added as an explanation or aside. **2** (**parentheses**) a pair of round brackets ().
■ **parenthetic** adj. **parenthetical** adj.

pariah n. an outcast.

parietal bone n. either of two bones forming part of the skull.

parings pl. n. thin strips pared off something.

parish n. **1** a district with its own church and clergy. **2** Brit. the smallest unit of local government in rural areas.
▷ SYNONYMS: *the new vicar scandalized the parish*: **parishioners**, churchgoers, congregation, fold, flock; district, community.
■ **parishioner** n.

WORD LINKS
parochial relating to a parish

parity n. equality.

park n. **1** a large public garden in a town. **2** the enclosed land of a country house. **3** an area devoted to a specified purpose. **4** an area for parking vehicles.
▷ SYNONYMS: **1 public garden**, recreation ground, playground. **2 parkland**, grassland, woodland, garden, lawns, grounds, estate.
• v. stop and leave a vehicle temporarily.

parka n. a windproof hooded jacket.

Parkinson's disease n. a disease causing trembling and muscular rigidity.

parky adj. Brit. informal chilly.

parlance n. a particular way of using words.

parley n. (pl. **parleys**) a meeting between enemies to settle a dispute.
• v. (**parleying**, **parleyed**) hold a parley.

parliament n. an assembly making the laws in a country.
▷ SYNONYMS: **legislature**, assembly, chamber, house, congress, senate, diet.
■ **parliamentarian** n. **parliamentary** adj.

parlour (US **parlor**) n. **1** dated a sitting room. **2** a shop providing particular goods or services.

parlous adj. precarious.

Parmesan n. a hard Italian cheese.

parochial adj. **1** of a parish. **2** having a narrow outlook.
▷ SYNONYMS: **narrow-minded**, small-minded, provincial, small-town, conservative; N. Amer. informal jerkwater.
− ANTONYMS: broad-minded.
■ **parochialism** n.

parody n. (pl. **parodies**) a piece of writing etc. that imitates the style of another so as to be amusing.
▷ SYNONYMS: **1 satire**, burlesque, lampoon, pastiche, caricature, imitation; informal spoof, take-off, send-up. **2 distortion**, travesty, misrepresentation, perversion, corruption.
• v. (**parodying**, **parodied**) produce a parody of.

parole n. the release of a prisoner before the end of their sentence, on the condition of good behaviour.
• v. release on parole.

paroxysm n. a sudden attack or outburst.

parquet /par-kay/ n. flooring composed of wooden blocks arranged in a geometric pattern.

parricide n. the killing of someone's own parent.

parrot n. a tropical bird with a hooked bill, some kinds of which can copy human speech.
• v. (**parroting, parroted**) repeat mechanically.

parry v. (**parrying, parried**) **1** ward off a weapon or blow. **2** evade a question.
▷ SYNONYMS: **1** *he parried the blow:* **ward off,** fend off, deflect, block. **2** *I parried her questions:* **evade,** sidestep, avoid, dodge, field.

parse v. analyse a sentence in terms of grammar.

parsimony n. extreme reluctance to spend money.
■ **parsimonious** adj.

parsley n. a herb with crinkly or flat leaves.

parsnip n. a long tapering cream-coloured root vegetable.

parson n. an Anglican parish priest.
▷ SYNONYMS: **priest,** minister, clergyman, vicar, rector, cleric, chaplain, pastor, curate; informal reverend, padre.

parsonage n. a parson's house.

part n. **1** a piece combining with others to make up a whole. **2** some but not all of something. **3** an acting role. **4** a person's contribution to a situation.
▷ SYNONYMS: **1 piece,** amount, portion, proportion, percentage, fraction; informal slice, chunk. **2 component,** bit, constituent, element, module, unit. **3 section,** division, volume, chapter, act, scene, instalment. **4 district,** neighbourhood, quarter, section, area, region. **5 role,** character. **6 involvement,** role, function, hand, responsibility, capacity, participation, contribution; informal bit.
– ANTONYMS: whole.
• v. **1** separate or be separated. **2** (**part with**) give up possession of.
▷ SYNONYMS: **1 separate,** divide, split, move apart. **2 part company,** say goodbye/farewell, go your separate ways, take your leave.
– ANTONYMS: join, meet.
• adv. partly.
□ **in good part** without taking offence. **part of speech** a category in which a word is placed according to its grammatical function, e.g. noun, verb, etc. **part-time** for only part of

the usual working day or week. **take part** join in.

partake v. (**partaking, partook;** past part. **partaken**) **1** (**partake in**) participate in. **2** (**partake of**) eat or drink.

partial adj. **1** not complete or whole. **2** favouring one side in a dispute. **3** (**partial to**) having a liking for.
▷ SYNONYMS: **1 incomplete,** limited, qualified, imperfect, fragmentary, unfinished. **2 biased,** prejudiced, partisan, one-sided, slanted, skewed, coloured, unbalanced.
– ANTONYMS: complete, unbiased.
■ **partiality** n. **partially** adv.

participant n. a person who takes part in something.
▷ SYNONYMS: **participator,** contributor, party, member, entrant, competitor, player, contestant, candidate.

participate v. take part.
▷ SYNONYMS: **take part,** join, engage, get involved, share, play a part, play a role, contribute, partake, have a hand in.
■ **participation** n.

participle n. a word formed from a verb (e.g. *burning, burnt*) and used in compound tenses or as an adjective or noun.
■ **participial** adj.

particle n. a tiny portion of matter.
▷ SYNONYMS: **speck,** fragment, grain, spot, sliver, splinter.

particular adj. **1** of an individual member of a group or class. **2** more than is usual. **3** very careful or concerned about something.
▷ SYNONYMS: **1 specific,** individual, certain, distinct, separate, definite, precise. **2 special,** exceptional, unusual, uncommon, notable, note-worthy, outstanding, remarkable, unique. **3 fussy,** fastidious, finicky, discriminating, selective; informal pernickety, choosy, picky; Brit. informal faddy.
– ANTONYMS: general, indiscriminate.
• n. a detail.
▷ SYNONYMS: **detail,** item, point, element, fact, circumstance, feature.
□ **in particular** especially.
■ **particularly** adv.

parting n. **1** an act of leaving someone. **2** Brit. a line of scalp visible when the hair is combed in different directions.
▷ SYNONYMS: **farewell,** leave-taking, goodbye, adieu, departure.

partisan n. **1** a strong supporter. **2** a guerrilla.

p

▷ SYNONYMS: **guerrilla**, freedom fighter, resistance fighter, underground fighter, irregular.

• **adj.** prejudiced.

▷ SYNONYMS: **biased**, prejudiced, one-sided, discriminatory, partial, sectarian, factional.

– ANTONYMS: neutral.

partition n. **1** a structure dividing a space or room. **2** division into parts.

▷ SYNONYMS: **1 division**, partitioning, separation, break-up. **2 screen**, divider, dividing wall, barrier, panel.

• **v.** divide into parts or with a partition.

▷ SYNONYMS: **divide**, separate, split up; subdivide, section off, screen off.

partly adv. to some extent.

▷ SYNONYMS: **in part**, partially, somewhat, a little, up to a point, in some measure, slightly, to some extent.

partner n. **1** each of two or more people who are involved in an undertaking. **2** either of two people doing something as a pair. **3** either member of a couple having a sexual or romantic relationship.

▷ SYNONYMS: **1 colleague**, associate, co-worker, fellow worker, collaborator, comrade, teammate. **2 accomplice**, confederate, accessory, collaborator, fellow conspirator, helper; informal sidekick. **3 spouse**, husband, wife, lover, girlfriend, boyfriend, fiancé, fiancée, significant other, live-in lover, mate; Brit. informal other half.

• **v.** be the partner of.

partnership n. **1** the state of being a partner or partners. **2** an association of two or more people as partners.

▷ SYNONYMS: **1 cooperation**, association, collaboration, coalition, alliance, union, affiliation, connection. **2 company**, association, consortium, syndicate, firm, business, organization.

partook past of PARTAKE.

partridge n. a short-tailed game bird.

parturition n. the act of giving birth.

party n. (pl. **parties**) **1** a social gathering. **2** an organized political group. **3** a group taking part in an activity or trip. **4** one side in an agreement or dispute.

▷ SYNONYMS: **1 social gathering**, function, get-together, celebration, reunion, festivity, reception, soirée, social; informal bash, do. **2 group**, company, body, gang, band, crowd, pack, contingent; informal bunch, crew, load. **3 faction**, group, bloc, camp,

caucus, alliance.

□ **party line** a policy officially adopted by a political party. **party wall** a wall shared by two adjoining buildings or rooms.

parvenu n. derogatory a person who has recently become wealthy or famous.

pascal n. a unit of pressure.

paschal /pass-kuhl/ adj. **1** of Easter. **2** of Passover.

pass v. **1** move or go onward, past, through, or across. **2** change from one state to another. **3** transfer. **4** kick, hit, or throw the ball to a teammate. **5** (of time) go by. **6** spend time. **7** be successful in an exam. **8** declare to be satisfactory. **9** approve a proposal etc. by voting.

▷ SYNONYMS: **1 go**, proceed, move, progress, make your way, travel. **2 overtake**, go past/by, pull ahead of, leave behind. **3** *her estate passed to her grandson:* **be transferred**, go, be left, be bequeathed, be handed down/on; Law devolve. **4** *he passed the time reading:* **occupy**, spend, fill, use, employ, while away. **5 elapse**, go by, advance, wear on, roll by, tick by. **6 be successful in**, succeed in, get through; informal sail through, scrape through. **7 approve**, vote for, accept, ratify, adopt, agree to, authorize, endorse, legalize, enact; informal OK.

– ANTONYMS: fail, reject.

• **n. 1** an act of passing. **2** a success in an exam. **3** a permit to enter a place. **4** a route over or through mountains. **5** informal a sexual advance.

▷ SYNONYMS: **permit**, warrant, authorization, licence.

□ **pass away** die. **pass off as** pretend that something is something else. **pass out** become unconscious. **pass up** refrain from taking an opportunity. **password** a secret word or phrase used to gain admission.

passable adj. **1** just satisfactory. **2** able to be travelled along or on.

▷ SYNONYMS: **1 adequate**, all right, acceptable, satisfactory, average, tolerable, fair, mediocre, middling, ordinary, indifferent, unremarkable, unexceptional; informal OK, so-so. **2 navigable**, traversable, negotiable, open, clear.

■ **passably** adv.

passage n. **1** the act of passing. **2** a way through something. **3** a journey by sea. **4** the right to pass through. **5** a short section from a text etc.

▷ SYNONYMS: **1 journey**, voyage, crossing, transit, trip. **2 passing**, progress, advance, course, march, flow. **3 corridor**, hall, hallway. **4 alley**, alleyway, passageway, lane, path, footpath, track, thoroughfare; N. Amer. areaway. **5 extract**, excerpt, quotation, quote.

□ **passageway** a corridor or walled access between buildings or rooms.

passé /pass-ay/ adj. old-fashioned.

passenger n. a person travelling in a vehicle, ship, or aircraft, other than the driver, pilot, or crew.

▷ SYNONYMS: **traveller**, commuter, fare-payer, rider, fare.

passer-by n. (pl. passers-by) a person who happens to be walking past something or someone.

passim adv. at various places throughout a text.

passing adj. done or carried out quickly and casually.

▷ SYNONYMS: **1 fleeting**, transient, transitory, ephemeral, brief, short-lived, temporary, momentary. **2 quick**, hurried, hasty, cursory, superficial, casual, perfunctory, desultory.

passion n. **1** very strong emotion. **2** intense sexual love. **3** great enthusiasm. **4** (**the Passion**) the suffering and death of Jesus on the cross.

▷ SYNONYMS: **1 intensity**, enthusiasm, fervour, eagerness, zeal, vigour, fire, energy, spirit, fanaticism. **2 love**, desire, ardour, lust, lustfulness. **3 fascination**, love, mania, obsession, preoccupation, fanaticism, fixation, compulsion, appetite, addiction; informal thing.

– ANTONYMS: apathy.

passionate adj. showing or caused by passion.

▷ SYNONYMS: **1** a passionate plea for help: **intense**, impassioned, ardent, fervent, vehement, heated, emotional, heartfelt, excited. **2** a passionate embrace: **amorous**, ardent, sexy, sensual, erotic, lustful; informal steamy, hot, turned on.

– ANTONYMS: apathetic, cool.

■ **passionately** adv.

passive adj. **1** accepting what happens without resistance. **2** (of a verb) in which the subject undergoes the action of the verb.

▷ SYNONYMS: **1 inactive**, non-active, non-participative, uninvolved. **2 submissive**, acquiescent, unresisting, compliant, docile.

– ANTONYMS: active, resistant.

■ **passively** adv. **passivity** n.

Passover n. a Jewish spring festival

commemorating the liberation of the Israelites from slavery in Egypt.

passport n. an official document certifying the holder's identity and citizenship and entitling them to travel abroad.

past adj. **1** gone by in time and no longer existing. **2** (of time) that has gone by.

▷ SYNONYMS: **1 gone by**, bygone, former, previous, old, of old, olden, long-ago. **2 last**, recent, preceding. **3 previous**, former, foregoing, erstwhile, one-time, sometime, ex-.

– ANTONYMS: present, future.

• n. **1** a past period or the events in it. **2** a person's previous experiences.

▷ SYNONYMS: **history**, background, past life, life story.

• prep. **1** beyond in time or space. **2** in front of or from one side to the other of. **3** beyond the scope or power of.

• adv. going past or beyond.

□ **past master** an expert.

pasta n. dough formed into various shapes and cooked in boiling water.

paste n. **1** a soft, moist substance. **2** a glue. **3** a hard substance used in making imitation gems.

▷ SYNONYMS: **1 purée**, pulp, mush, spread, pâté. **2 adhesive**, glue, gum; N. Amer. mucilage.

• v. coat or stick with paste.

▷ SYNONYMS: **stick**, glue, gum, fix, affix.

□ **pasteboard** cardboard.

pastel n. **1** a crayon made of powdered pigments. **2** a picture drawn with pastels. **3** a pale shade of a colour.

pasteurize (or -**ise**) v. sterilize by heating.

■ **pasteurization** n.

pastiche /pa-**steesh**/ n. a work in the style of another artist.

pastille n. a small sweet or lozenge.

pastime n. an activity done regularly for enjoyment.

▷ SYNONYMS: **hobby**, leisure activity, leisure pursuit, recreation, game, amusement, diversion, entertainment, interest.

pastor n. a minister in charge of a church or congregation.

▷ SYNONYMS: **priest**, minister, parson, clergyman, cleric, chaplain, vicar, rector, curate; informal reverend, padre.

pastoral adj. **1** of or used for the keeping of sheep or cattle. **2** of country life. **3** of spiritual and moral guidance.

▷ SYNONYMS: **1 rural**, country, rustic, agricultural, bucolic; literary Arcadian. **2 priestly**, clerical, ecclesiastical,

p

ministerial.
– ANTONYMS: urban, lay.

pastrami /pass-trah-mi/ n. highly seasoned smoked beef.

pastry n. (pl. **pastries**) **1** a dough of flour, fat, and water, used for making pies etc. **2** a cake of sweet pastry with a filling.

pasture n. grassy land suitable for grazing cattle or sheep.
▷ SYNONYMS: **grassland**, grass, grazing, meadow, field; literary lea.
• v. put animals to graze in a pasture.
■ **pasturer** n.

pasty¹ /pass-ti/ n. (pl. **pasties**) Brit. a folded pastry case filled with meat and vegetables.

pasty² /pay-sti/ adj. unhealthily pale.

pat v. (**patted**, **patting**) tap quickly and gently with the flat of the hand.
▷ SYNONYMS: **tap**, touch, stroke, pet.
• n. **1** an act of patting. **2** a mass of a soft substance.
• adj. too quick or easy and not convincing.
□ **off pat** perfectly memorized.

patch n. **1** a piece of material used to mend a hole or strengthen a weak point. **2** a small area differing from its surroundings. **3** a small plot of land. **4** Brit. informal a period of time. **5** a cover worn over an injured eye.
▷ SYNONYMS: **1 blotch**, mark, spot, smudge, smear, stain, streak, blemish; informal splodge. **2 plot**, area, piece, strip, tract, parcel, bed; Brit. allotment; N. Amer. lot. **3 period**, time, spell, phase, stretch.
• v. mend with a patch.
▷ SYNONYMS: **mend**, repair, sew up, stitch up, cover, reinforce.
□ **patch up** informal **1** repair quickly or temporarily. **2** settle a dispute.
patchwork needlework in which small pieces of cloth are joined to make a pattern.

patchy adj. **1** existing in small, isolated areas. **2** uneven in quality.

pâté /pa-tay/ n. a rich savoury paste of meat etc.

patella n. (pl. **patellae**) the kneecap.

patent n. a licence giving someone the sole right to make, use, or sell their invention.
• adj. **1** obvious. **2** patented.
▷ SYNONYMS: **1 obvious**, clear, plain, evident, manifest, conspicuous, blatant, barefaced, flagrant. **2 proprietary**, patented, licensed, branded.
• v. obtain a patent for.
□ **patent leather** glossy varnished leather.

■ **patently** adv.

paternal adj. **1** of or like a father.
2 related through a person's father.
■ **paternally** adv.

paternalism n. the policy of protecting the people you have control over, but also of restricting their freedom.
■ **paternalistic** adj.

paternity n. the state or fact of being a father.

path n. **1** a way laid down for or made by walking. **2** the course along which a person or thing moves. **3** a course of action.
▷ SYNONYMS: **1 footpath**, pathway, track, trail, bridle path, lane, towpath.
2 route, way, course, direction, orbit, trajectory. **3 course of action**, route, road, avenue, line, approach, tack.

pathetic adj. **1** arousing pity. **2** informal completely inadequate.
▷ SYNONYMS: **1 pitiful**, piteous, moving, touching, poignant, plaintive, wretched, heart-rending, sad.
2 feeble, woeful, sorry, poor, weak, pitiful, lamentable, deplorable, contemptible.
■ **pathetically** adv.

pathological adj. **1** of or caused by a disease. **2** informal compulsive.
▷ SYNONYMS: **1 morbid**, diseased.
2 compulsive, obsessive, inveterate, habitual, persistent, chronic, hardened, confirmed.
■ **pathologically** adv.

pathology n. the study of diseases.
■ **pathologist** n.

pathos n. a quality arousing pity or sadness.

patience n. **1** the ability to accept delay or trouble calmly. **2** Brit. a card game for one player.
▷ SYNONYMS: **1 forbearance**, tolerance, restraint, equanimity, understanding, indulgence. **2 perseverance**, persistence, endurance, tenacity, application, doggedness, staying power.

patient adj. showing patience.
▷ SYNONYMS: **1 forbearing**, uncomplaining, long-suffering, resigned, stoical, calm, imperturbable, tolerant, accommodating, indulgent. **2 persevering**, persistent, tenacious, dogged, determined.
• n. a person receiving medical treatment.
■ **patiently** adv.

patina n. **1** a green film on bronze. **2** a sheen on a surface produced by age and polishing.

patio n. (pl. **patios**) a paved outdoor

area next to a house.

patisserie n. a shop where cakes etc. are sold.

patois /pat-wah/ n. (pl. **patois**) a dialect.

patriarch n. **1** the male head of a family or tribe. **2** a high-ranking bishop in certain Churches.
■ **patriarchal** adj. **patriarchy** n.

patricide n. **1** the killing of a father by his child. **2** a person who kills their father.

patrimony n. (pl. **patrimonies**) property inherited from a person's father or male ancestor.

patriot n. a person who strongly supports their country.
■ **patriotism** n.

patriotic adj. vigorously supporting your own country.
▷ SYNONYMS: **nationalistic**, loyalist, loyal; chauvinistic, jingoistic, flag-waving.

patrol v. (**patrolling**, **patrolled**) keep watch over an area by regularly walking or travelling around it.
▷ SYNONYMS: **guard**, keep watch on, police, make the rounds of, stand guard over, defend, safeguard.
•n. **1** a person or group sent to patrol an area. **2** the act of patrolling an area.
▷ SYNONYMS: **1 squad**, detachment, party, force. **2** *ships on patrol in the straits:* guard, watch, vigil.

patron n. **1** a person giving financial or other support to a cause. **2** a regular customer of a hotel etc.
▷ SYNONYMS: **1 sponsor**, backer, benefactor, contributor, subscriber, donor, philanthropist, promoter, friend, supporter; informal angel. **2 customer**, client, consumer, user, visitor, guest; informal regular.
□ **patron saint** a saint believed to protect a particular place or group.

patronage n. **1** the support given by a patron. **2** the regular custom attracted by a hotel etc.
▷ SYNONYMS: **1 sponsorship**, backing, funding, financing, assistance, support. **2 custom**, trade, business.

patronize (or **-ise**) v. **1** treat someone in a way that suggests they are inferior. **2** be a regular customer of.
▷ SYNONYMS: **1 talk down to**, look down on, condescend to, treat like a child. **2 use**, buy from, shop at, deal with, frequent, support.

patronizing (or **-ising**) adj. showing that you think you are superior to others.

▷ SYNONYMS: **condescending**, super-cilious, superior, imperious, scornful; informal high and mighty.

patronymic n. a name derived from that of a father or ancestor.

patter v. make a repeated light tapping sound.
•n. **1** a pattering sound. **2** fast continuous talk.

pattern n. **1** a repeated decorative design. **2** a regular sequence of actions or events. **3** a model, design, or set of instructions for making something. **4** an example to follow. **5** a sample of cloth etc.
▷ SYNONYMS: **1 design**, decoration, motif, device, marking. **2 system**, order, arrangement, form, method, structure, scheme, plan, format. **3 model**, example, blueprint, criterion, standard, norm, yardstick, touchstone, benchmark.
■ **patterned** adj.

patty n. (pl. **patties**) a small pie or pasty.

paucity n. scarcity or lack of something.

paunch n. a protruding stomach.

pauper n. a very poor person.

pause n. a temporary stop.
▷ SYNONYMS: **break**, interruption, lull, respite, breathing space, gap, interlude, adjournment, rest, wait, hesitation; informal let-up, breather.
•v. stop temporarily.
▷ SYNONYMS: **stop**, break off, take a break, adjourn, rest, wait, hesitate; informal take a breather.

pave v. cover a piece of ground with flat stones or bricks.
▷ SYNONYMS: **surface**, floor, cover, tile, flag.
■ **paving** n.

pavement n. Brit. a raised path at the side of a road.
▷ SYNONYMS: **footpath**, walkway; N. Amer. sidewalk.

pavilion n. **1** Brit. a building at a sports ground for changing and taking refreshments. **2** a summer house in a park etc.

paw n. an animal's foot having claws and pads.
•v. feel or scrape with a paw or hoof.

pawn n. **1** a chess piece of the smallest size and value. **2** a person used by others for their own purposes.
•v. leave an item with a pawnbroker as security for money lent.
□ **pawnbroker** a person licensed to lend money in exchange for an item left with them. **pawnshop** a

p

pawnbroker's shop.

pawpaw n. a papaya.

pay v. (**paying**, **paid**) **1** give someone money for goods or goods. **2** give a sum of money owed. **3** result in a profit or advantage. **4** suffer as a result of an action. **5** give attention etc. to.

▷ SYNONYMS: **1 reward**, reimburse, recompense, remunerate. **2 spend**, pay out; informal lay out, shell out, fork out, cough up; N. Amer. informal ante up, pony up. **3** *I've paid my debts:* **discharge**, settle, pay off, clear. **4 be advantageous to**, benefit, profit, be of advantage to, be beneficial to. **5** *he must pay for his mistakes:* **suffer**, be punished, atone, pay the penalty.

• n. money paid for work.

▷ SYNONYMS: **salary**, wages, payment, earnings, remuneration, fee, reimbursement, income, revenue, stipend, emolument.

□ **payload** an explosive warhead carried by an aircraft or missile. **pay-off** informal a payment made as a bribe or on leaving a job. **pay off 1** dismiss with a final payment. **2** informal yield good results. **payroll** a list of a company's employees and their wages.

■ **payable** adj.

PAYE abbrev. pay as you earn, a system whereby tax is deducted from wages before payment.

payee n. a person to whom money is paid.

payment n. **1** an amount that is paid. **2** the act of paying.

▷ SYNONYMS: **1 remittance**, settlement, discharge, clearance. **2 instalment**, premium. **3 salary**, wages, pay, earnings, fees, remuneration, reimbursement, income, stipend, emolument.

payola n. US bribery in return for the unofficial promotion of a product in the media.

PC abbrev. **1** personal computer. **2** Brit. police constable. **3** politically correct; political correctness.

PCT abbrev. primary care trust.

PDF n. an electronic file which can be sent by any system and displayed on any computer.

PE abbrev. physical education.

pea n. a round green seed in a pod, eaten as a vegetable.

peace n. **1** freedom from noise or anxiety. **2** freedom from war.

▷ SYNONYMS: **1 quiet**, silence, peace and quiet, hush, stillness, still. **2 serenity**, peacefulness, tranquillity, calm, calm-ness, composure, ease, contentment, rest, repose. **3 treaty**, truce, ceasefire, armistice.

– ANTONYMS: noise, war.

peaceable adj. **1** avoiding conflict. **2** peaceful.

■ **peaceably** adv.

peaceful adj. **1** free from noise or anxiety. **2** not involving war or violence.

▷ SYNONYMS: **1 tranquil**, calm, restful, quiet, still, relaxing, serene, composed, placid, at ease, untroubled, unworried. **2 harmonious**, on good terms, amicable, friendly, cordial, non-violent.

– ANTONYMS: noisy.

■ **peacefully** adv. **peacefulness** n.

peacemaker n. a person who tries to bring about peace.

▷ SYNONYMS: **arbitrator**, arbiter, mediator, negotiator, conciliator, go-between, intermediary.

peach n. **1** a round juicy fruit with a rough stone inside. **2** a pinkish-orange colour.

peacock n. a colourful bird with long tail feathers that can be fanned out in display.

peahen n. the female of the peacock.

peak n. **1** the pointed top of a mountain. **2** the point of highest activity, achievement, etc. **3** Brit. a stiff brim at the front of a cap.

▷ SYNONYMS: **1 summit**, top, crest, pinnacle, cap. **2 mountain**, hill, height. **3 height**, high point, pinnacle, summit, top, climax, culmination, apex, zenith, acme.

• v. reach a highest point.

▷ SYNONYMS: **reach its height**, climax, culminate.

• adj. maximum.

▷ SYNONYMS: **maximum**, greatest, busiest, highest.

■ **peaked** adj.

peaky adj. Brit. pale from illness or tiredness.

peal n. **1** the loud ringing sound of a bell or bells. **2** a loud sound of thunder or laughter. **3** a set of bells.

• v. ring or sound loudly.

peanut n. **1** the oval edible seed of a South American plant. **2** (**peanuts**) informal a very small sum of money.

pear n. a rounded fruit tapering towards the stalk.

pearl n. a small, hard, shiny white gem formed within the shell of an oyster.

■ **pearly** adj.

peasant n. a poor smallholder or farm labourer.

■ **peasantry** n.

peat n. decomposed vegetable matter formed in boggy ground, used in gardening or as fuel.
■ **peaty** adj.

pebble n. a small, smooth, round stone.
■ **pebbly** adj.

pecan n. a smooth pinkish-brown nut.

peccadillo n. (pl. **peccadilloes** or **peccadillos**) a minor fault.

peccary n. (pl. **peccaries**) a small piglike mammal.

peck v. **1** hit or bite with the beak. **2** kiss lightly and quickly.
• n. an act of pecking.

peckish adj. informal hungry.

pectin n. a substance present in fruits, used to set jam.

pectoral adj. of, in, or on the breast or chest.
• n. a pectoral fin or muscle.

peculiar adj. **1** strange or odd. **2** (**peculiar to**) belonging only to.
▷ SYNONYMS: **1 strange**, unusual, odd, funny, curious, bizarre, weird, eccentric, queer, abnormal, unconventional, outlandish, anomalous, out of the ordinary, unexpected, offbeat. **2** *customs peculiar to the area:* **distinctive**, exclusive, unique, characteristic, distinct, individual, typical, special.
– ANTONYMS: ordinary.
■ **peculiarity** n. **peculiarly** adv.

pecuniary adj. of or in money.

pedagogue n. a teacher.
■ **pedagogy** n.

pedal n. a lever operated by the foot.
• v. (**pedalling**, **pedalled**; US **pedaling**, **pedaled**) move a bicycle by working the pedals.

> USAGE Don't confuse **pedal** with **peddle**, which means 'sell goods'.

pedalo n. (pl. **pedalos** or **pedaloes**) Brit. a small pedal-operated pleasure boat.

pedantic adj. excessively concerned with minor details or rules.
▷ SYNONYMS: **finicky**, fussy, fastidious, dogmatic, purist, hair-splitting, quibbling; informal nit-picking, pernickety.
■ **pedant** n. **pedantry** n.

peddle v. **1** sell goods by going from place to place. **2** sell an illegal drug.
▷ SYNONYMS: **sell**, hawk, tout, trade, deal in, traffic in.

> USAGE Don't confuse **peddle** with **pedal**.

peddler var. of PEDLAR.

pedestal n. the base supporting a statue or column etc.
▷ SYNONYMS: **plinth**, base, support, mount, stand, pillar, column.

pedestrian n. a person walking rather than travelling in a vehicle.
▷ SYNONYMS: **walker**, person on foot.
• adj. dull.
▷ SYNONYMS: **dull**, boring, tedious, monotonous, unremarkable, uninspired, unimaginative, unexciting, routine, commonplace, ordinary, everyday, run-of-the-mill, mundane, humdrum; informal bog-standard.
– ANTONYMS: exciting.

pediatrics etc. US = PAEDIATRICS etc.

pedicure n. a cosmetic treatment of the feet and toenails.

pedigree n. **1** an animal's record of descent, showing that all the animals from which it is descended are of the same breed. **2** a person's ancestry.
▷ SYNONYMS: **ancestry**, lineage, line, descent, genealogy, extraction, parentage, bloodline, family tree.

pediment n. the triangular part above the entrance of a classical building.

pedlar (or **peddler**) n. **1** a travelling trader who sells small goods. **2** a person who sells illegal drugs.

pedometer n. an instrument for estimating the distance travelled on foot.

peek v. look quickly.
▷ SYNONYMS: **peep**, look; informal take a gander, have a squint; Brit. informal have a dekko, take a butcher's, take a shufti.
• n. a quick look.
▷ SYNONYMS: **look**, peep, glance, glimpse.

peel v. **1** remove the skin from a fruit or vegetable. **2** remove a thin covering or layer from. **3** (of a surface) come off in small pieces.
▷ SYNONYMS: **1 pare**, skin, hull, shell. **2 flake off**, come off, fall off, strip off.
• n. the outer skin of a fruit or vegetable.
▷ SYNONYMS: **rind**, skin, covering, zest.
■ **peeler** n. **peelings** pl. n.

peep v. **1** look quickly or secretly. **2** (**peep out**) be just visible.
▷ SYNONYMS: **peek**, look, sneak a look, glance; informal squint.
• n. **1** a quick or secret look. **2** a glimpse.
▷ SYNONYMS: **peek**, look, glance; informal squint, dekko.
□ **peephole** a small hole in a door through which callers can be seen. **peeping Tom** a furtive voyeur.

peer v. look with difficulty or

p

concentration.
▷ SYNONYMS: **look closely**, squint, gaze.
• n. **1** a member of the nobility in
Britain or Ireland. **2** a person of the
same age, status, etc. as another.
▷ SYNONYMS: **1 aristocrat**, lord, lady,
noble, nobleman, noblewoman.
2 equal, fellow, contemporary.
peerage n. **1** the rank of peer or
peeress. **2** peers as a whole.
peeress n. **1** a woman holding the
rank of a peer. **2** a peer's wife or
widow.
peerless adj. better than all others.
peeved adj. informal irritated.
▷ SYNONYMS: **irritated**, annoyed, cross,
vexed, piqued, put out, disgruntled,
indignant, nettled; informal miffed,
aggravated, riled, hacked off; Brit.
informal narked; N. Amer. informal teed off,
ticked off.
peevish adj. irritable.
  ■ **peevishly** adv.
peg n. **1** a pin or bolt used for hanging
things on or fastening something. **2** a
clip for holding clothes on a line.
▷ SYNONYMS: **pin**, nail, dowel.
• v. (**pegging, pegged**) **1** fix, attach, or
mark with a peg or pegs. **2** fix a price
etc. at a particular level.
▷ SYNONYMS: **1 fix**, pin, attach, fasten,
secure. **2 set**, hold, fix, limit, freeze,
keep down, hold down.
  □ **off the peg** Brit. (of clothes) ready-
made.
pejorative adj. expressing contempt
or disapproval.
Pekinese n. (pl. **Pekinese**) a small dog
with long hair, short legs, and a snub
nose.
pelican n. a waterbird with a long bill
and a throat pouch.
  □ **pelican crossing** a pedestrian
crossing with traffic lights operated
by pedestrians.
pellagra n. a disease involving
inflamed skin, diarrhoea, etc., caused
by an inadequate diet.
pellet n. **1** a small compressed mass of
a substance. **2** a piece of small shot.
pell-mell adj. & adv. in a confused or
rushed way.
pellucid adj. very clear.
pelmet n. a strip of wood or fabric
fitted above a window to conceal
curtain fittings.
pelt v. **1** hurl missiles at. **2** (**pelt down**)
fall very heavily.
• n. an animal skin with the fur or
wool still on it.
  □ (**at**) **full pelt** as fast as possible.
pelvis n. the bony frame at the base

of the spine to which the legs are
attached.
  ■ **pelvic** adj.
pen n. **1** an instrument for writing or
drawing with ink. **2** a small enclosure
for farm animals. **3** a female swan.
▷ SYNONYMS: **enclosure**, fold, pound,
compound, stockade, sty, coop; N. Amer.
corral.
• v. (**penning, penned**) **1** write or
compose. **2** put or keep in a pen or
restricted space.
▷ SYNONYMS: **1 write**, compose, draft,
dash off, scribble. **2 confine**, coop,
cage, shut, box, lock, trap, imprison,
incarcerate.
  □ **penfriend** a person with whom
someone forms a friendship by
exchanging letters. **pen name** a name
used by a writer instead of their real
name.
penal adj. of the use of punishment as
part of the legal system.
penalize (or **-ise**) v. **1** give a penalty
or punishment to. **2** put in an
unfavourable position.
▷ SYNONYMS: **1 punish**, discipline.
2 handicap, disadvantage,
discriminate against.
− ANTONYMS: reward.
penalty n. (pl. **penalties**) a punishment
for breaking a law, rule, or contract.
▷ SYNONYMS: **punishment**, sanction,
fine, forfeit, sentence.
− ANTONYMS: reward.
penance n. an act done as a
punishment for or acknowledgement
of wrongdoing.
▷ SYNONYMS: **atonement**, expiation,
amends, punishment, penalty.
pence Brit. pl. of **PENNY**.
penchant /pon-shon/ n. a strong
liking.
▷ SYNONYMS: **liking**, fondness, preference, taste, appetite, partiality,
love, passion, weakness, inclination, bent, proclivity, predilection,
predisposition.
pencil n. an instrument for writing or
drawing, consisting of a stick of wood
with a graphite core.
• v. (**pencilling, pencilled**; US **penciling,
penciled**) write, draw, or mark with
a pencil.
pendant n. a piece of jewellery hung
from a chain around the neck.
pendent (or **pendant**) adj. hanging
down.
pending adj. waiting to be decided or
settled.
▷ SYNONYMS: **1 unresolved**, undecided,
unsettled, up in the air, ongoing,

p

outstanding; *informal* on the back
burner. **2 imminent**, impending,
about to happen, forthcoming, on the
way, coming, approaching, looming,
near, on the horizon, in the offing.
• **prep.** until.

pendulous adj. hanging loosely.

pendulum n. a weight hung from a
fixed point so that it can swing freely,
used to regulate a clock's mechanism.

penetrate v. **1** force a way into or
through. **2** understand or gain insight
into. **3** be fully understood.
▷ SYNONYMS: **1 pierce**, puncture, enter,
perforate, stab, gore. **2** *the sunlight
penetrates every room:* **permeate**,
pervade, fill, suffuse, saturate.
3 register, sink in, become clear, fall
into place; *informal* click.
■ **penetration** n.

penetrating adj. **1** (of a sound)
clearly heard above other sounds.
2 having or showing great insight.
▷ SYNONYMS: **1 shrill**, strident, piercing,
ear-splitting; loud, carrying. **2** *her
penetrating gaze:* **intent**, searching,
piercing, probing, sharp, keen. **3** *a
penetrating analysis:* **perceptive**,
insightful, keen, sharp, intelligent,
clever, smart, incisive, trenchant,
astute.

penguin n. a flightless seabird of the
southern hemisphere.

penicillin n. an antibiotic.

peninsula n. a long piece of land
projecting into the sea.
■ **peninsular** adj.

penis n. the male organ used for
urinating and having sex.

penitent adj. feeling regret for having
done wrong.
• **n.** a penitent person.
■ **penitence** n. **penitential** adj.

penitentiary n. (pl. **penitentiaries**) US
a prison.

pennant n. a long, tapering flag.

penniless adj. without money.

pennon n. a pennant.

penny n. (pl. **pennies**; **pence**) **1** a
British bronze coin worth one
hundredth of a pound. **2** a former
coin worth one twelfth of a shilling.
□ **penny-farthing** Brit. an early type of
bicycle with a large front wheel and
small rear wheel. **penny-pinching**
miserly.

pension¹ n. a regular payment made
to retired people, widows, etc., either
by the state or from an investment
fund.
• **v.** (**pension off**) dismiss with a
pension.

■ **pensionable** adj. **pensioner** n.

pension² /pon-syon/ n. a small hotel
in Europe.

pensive adj. deep in thought.
■ **pensively** adv.

pentagon n. a plane figure with five
sides.

pentagram n. a five-pointed star.

Pentateuch /pen-tuh-tyook/ n. the
first five books of the Old Testament
and Hebrew Scriptures.

pentathlon n. an athletic contest
involving five events.

Pentecost n. a Christian festival
celebrating the descent of the Holy
Spirit on the disciples of Jesus.

penthouse n. a flat on the top floor of
a tall building.

pent-up adj. not expressed or
released.

penultimate adj. last but one.

penumbra n. (pl. **penumbrae** or
penumbras) the partially shaded
outer part of a shadow.

penury n. extreme poverty.
■ **penurious** adj.

peony n. (pl. **peonies**) a plant grown
for its showy flowers.

people pl. n. **1** human beings. **2** the
ordinary citizens of a country. **3** (pl.
peoples) the members of a particular
nation, community, or ethnic group.
▷ SYNONYMS: **1 human beings**, persons,
individuals, humans, mortals, living
souls, personages, {men, women,
and children}; *informal* folk. **2 citizens**,
subjects, electors, voters, taxpayers,
residents, inhabitants, public, citizenry, nation, population, populace;
the common people, the proletariat,
the masses, the rank and file; *derogatory*
the hoi polloi; *informal, derogatory* the
proles, the plebs. **3** (dated) **family**,
parents, relatives, relations, folk,
kinsfolk, flesh and blood, nearest and
dearest; *informal* folks. **4 ethnic group**,
race, tribe.
• **v.** fill with people.
▷ SYNONYMS: **populate**, settle in,
colonize, inhabit, live in, occupy.

> **WORD LINKS**
> **anthropology** the study of people
> and human origins
> **ethnic** relating to a people with a
> common national or cultural tradition

pep *informal* n. liveliness.
• **v.** (**pepping**, **pepped**) (**pep up**) make
more lively.
□ **pep talk** a talk intended to make
someone feel braver or more
enthusiastic.

p

pepper n. **1** a hot-tasting seasoning made from peppercorns. **2** the fruit of a tropical American plant.
• v. **1** sprinkle with pepper. **2** (**pepper with**) scatter in large amounts over or through. **3** hit repeatedly with small missiles or gunshot.
▷ SYNONYMS: **1** sprinkle, fleck, dot, spot, stipple. **2** bombard, pelt, shower, rain down on, strafe, rake, blitz.
■ **peppery** adj.

peppercorn n. the dried berry of a plant, ground to make pepper.
□ **peppercorn rent** Brit. a very low or nominal rent.

peppermint n. **1** a plant producing an aromatic oil. **2** a sweet flavoured with peppermint oil.

pepperoni n. beef and pork sausage seasoned with pepper.

pepsin n. the chief digestive enzyme in the stomach.

peptic adj. of digestion.

per prep. **1** for each. **2** (**as per**) in accordance with.
□ **per annum** for each year. **per capita** for each person. **per cent** in or for every hundred. **per se** by or in itself.

perambulate v. walk or travel from place to place.
■ **perambulation** n.

perambulator n. a pram.

perceive v. **1** become aware of through the senses. **2** regard as.
▷ SYNONYMS: **1** see, discern, detect, catch sight of, spot, observe, notice; literary espy. **2** regard, look on, view, consider, think of, judge, deem.

percentage n. **1** a rate or amount in each hundred. **2** a proportion or share, esp. of profits.

perceptible adj. able to be perceived.
■ **perceptibly** adv.

perception n. the ability to perceive, or the act of perceiving.
▷ SYNONYMS: **1** impression, idea, conception, notion, thought, belief. **2** insight, perceptiveness, understanding, intelligence, intuition, incisiveness.

perceptive adj. having or showing insight.
▷ SYNONYMS: insightful, discerning, sensitive, intuitive, observant, penetrating, intelligent, clever, canny, keen, sharp, astute, shrewd, quick, smart, acute; informal on the ball; N. Amer. informal heads-up.
− ANTONYMS: obtuse.
■ **perceptively** adv.

perch n. **1** a branch, bar, etc. on which a bird rests or roosts. **2** a high or narrow seat. **3** (pl. **perch**) an edible freshwater fish.
• v. **1** sit or rest somewhere. **2** place or balance somewhere.
▷ SYNONYMS: **1** sit, rest, alight, settle, land, roost. **2** put, place, set, rest, balance.

percipient adj. perceptive.
■ **percipience** n.

percolate v. **1** filter, esp. through small holes. **2** prepare coffee in a percolator.
■ **percolation** n.

percolator n. a device for making coffee, consisting of a pot in which boiling water is circulated through ground coffee held in a small chamber.

percussion n. musical instruments that are played by being struck or shaken.

perdition n. eternal damnation.

peregrinations pl. n. old use travels.

peregrine n. a falcon.

peremptory adj. insisting on immediate attention or obedience.
■ **peremptorily** adv.

perennial adj. **1** lasting for a long time or forever. **2** (of a plant) living for several years. **3** constantly recurring.
▷ SYNONYMS: **lasting**, enduring, abiding, long-lasting, long-lived, perpetual, continuing, continual, recurring.
− ANTONYMS: ephemeral.
• n. a perennial plant.
■ **perennially** adv.

perestroika /pe-ri-**stroy**-kuh/ n. (in the former USSR) the economic and political reforms introduced during the 1980s.

perfect adj. **1** without any faults or defects. **2** complete; total: *it made perfect sense.*
▷ SYNONYMS: **1** *a perfect example:* **ideal**, model, faultless, flawless, consummate, exemplary, best, ultimate, copybook. **2** *the car's in perfect condition:* **flawless**, mint, as good as new, pristine, immaculate, optimum, prime, peak; informal tip-top, A1. **3** *a perfect copy:* **exact**, precise, accurate, faithful, true. **4** *I felt a perfect idiot:* **absolute**, complete, total, real, out-and-out, thorough, downright, utter; Brit. informal right; Austral./NZ informal fair.
• v. make perfect.
▷ SYNONYMS: **improve**, polish up, hone, refine, brush up, fine-tune.
■ **perfection** n. **perfectly** adv.

perfectionism n. refusal to accept any standard short of perfection.

■ **perfectionist** n.

perfidious adj. deceitful and disloyal.
■ **perfidy** n.

perforate v. pierce and make a hole or holes in.
■ **perforation** n.

perforce adv. necessarily; unavoidably.

perform v. **1** carry out or complete an action. **2** work, function, etc. to a certain standard. **3** present entertainment to an audience.
▷ SYNONYMS: **1 carry out**, do, execute, discharge, complete, conduct, implement; informal pull off. **2 function**, work, operate, run, go, respond, behave, act. **3 stage**, put on, present, mount, act, produce.

performance n. **1** an act of performing a play, piece of music, etc. **2** the process of performing. **3** informal a fuss.
▷ SYNONYMS: **1 show**, production, showing, presentation, staging, concert, recital, rendition; informal gig. **2 carrying out**, execution, discharge, completion, fulfilment.

performer n. a person who performs for an audience.
▷ SYNONYMS: **actor**, **actress**, artiste, artist, entertainer, trouper, player, musician, singer, dancer, comic, comedian, comedienne.

perfume n. **1** a scented liquid for applying to the body. **2** a pleasant smell.
▷ SYNONYMS: **1 scent**, fragrance, eau de toilette, toilet water, cologne, eau de cologne. **2 smell**, scent, fragrance, aroma, bouquet, nose.
 • v. give a pleasant smell to.
■ **perfumery** n.

perfunctory adj. done with a minimum of effort or thought.
■ **perfunctorily** adv.

pergola n. an arched framework for climbing plants.

perhaps adv. possibly; maybe.
▷ SYNONYMS: **maybe**, for all you know, it could be, it may be, it's possible, possibly, conceivably; N. English happen.

pericardium n. (pl. **pericardia**) the membrane enclosing the heart.

perigee n. the point in the moon's orbit when it is nearest to the earth.

peril n. serious danger.
▷ SYNONYMS: **danger**, jeopardy, risk, hazard, menace, threat.
– ANTONYMS: safety.
■ **perilous** adj. **perilously** adv.

perimeter n. the outer edge or boundary of something.

▷ SYNONYMS: **boundary**, border, limits, bounds, edge, margin, fringes, periphery.
– ANTONYMS: centre.

perinatal adj. of the time immediately before and after birth.

period n. **1** a length or portion of time. **2** a lesson in a school. **3** a flow of blood each month from the lining of a woman's womb. **4** a full stop.
▷ SYNONYMS: **1 time**, spell, interval, stretch, term, span, phase, bout; Brit. informal patch. **2 era**, age, epoch, aeon, time, days, years.
 • adj. belonging to a past historical time.

periodic adj. occurring at intervals.
▷ SYNONYMS: **regular**, recurrent, recurring, repeated, cyclical, seasonal, occasional, intermittent, sporadic, odd.
□ **periodic table** a table of all the chemical elements.

periodical adj. periodic.
 • n. a magazine etc. published at regular intervals.
▷ SYNONYMS: **journal**, magazine, newspaper, paper, review, newsletter, digest, gazette, organ; informal mag, glossy.
■ **periodically** adv.

peripatetic adj. travelling from place to place.

peripheral adj. **1** relating to the outer limits of something. **2** of secondary importance. **3** (of a device) able to be attached to and used with a computer.
▷ SYNONYMS: **secondary**, subsidiary, incidental, tangential, marginal, minor, unimportant, ancillary.
– ANTONYMS: central.

periphery n. (pl. **peripheries**) **1** the outer limits of an area or object. **2** the less important part of a subject or group.

periphrasis n. (pl. **periphrases**) indirect language.

periscope n. a tube attached to a set of mirrors, by which things can be seen that are above or behind something else.

perish v. **1** die. **2** be destroyed. **3** rot.
▷ SYNONYMS: **1 die**, lose your life, be killed, fall, be lost; informal buy it. **2 go bad**, spoil, rot, decay, decompose.

perishable adj. (of food) likely to rot quickly.

peritoneum /pe-ri-tuh-**nee**-uhm/ n. (pl. **peritoneums** or **peritonea**) the membrane lining the abdominal cavity.

peritonitis n. inflammation of the peritoneum.

p

periwinkle n. a plant with flat five-petalled flowers.

perjure v. (**perjure yourself**) commit perjury.

perjury n. the offence of deliberately telling a lie in court when under oath.

perk v. (**perk up**) make or become more cheerful or lively.
•n. informal a benefit to which an employee is entitled.
▷ SYNONYMS: **fringe benefit**, advantage, bonus, extra, plus; informal freebie.

perky adj. (**perkier, perkiest**) cheerful and lively.
■ **perkily** adv.

perm n. a chemical treatment giving hair a long-lasting curly style.
•v. treat hair with a perm.

permafrost n. a layer of soil beneath the surface that remains frozen throughout the year.

permanent adj. lasting for a long time or forever.
▷ SYNONYMS: **lasting**, enduring, indefinite, continuing, constant, perpetual, indelible, irreparable, irreversible, lifelong, perennial, established, standing, long-term, stable, secure.
– ANTONYMS: temporary.
■ **permanence** n. **permanently** adv.

permeable adj. allowing liquids or gases to pass through.
■ **permeability** n.

permeate v. spread throughout.

permissible adj. allowable.

permission n. the act of allowing someone to do something.
▷ SYNONYMS: **authorization**, consent, leave, authority, sanction, licence, dispensation, assent, agreement, approval, blessing, clearance; informal the go-ahead, the green light, say-so.
– ANTONYMS: ban.

permissive adj. allowing freedom of behaviour, esp. in sexual matters.
■ **permissiveness** n.

permit v. (**permitting, permitted**) **1** give permission to or for. **2** make possible.
▷ SYNONYMS: **allow**, let, authorize, give permission, sanction, grant, license, consent to, assent to, agree to; informal give the go-ahead to, give the green light to.
– ANTONYMS: forbid.
•n. an official document giving permission to do something.
▷ SYNONYMS: **authorization**, licence, pass, ticket, warrant, passport, visa.

permutation n. each of several possible ways of ordering or arranging a number of things.

pernicious adj. harmful.

pernickety adj. Brit. informal fussy.

peroration n. the concluding part of a speech.

peroxide n. a chemical used to bleach hair.

perpendicular adj. at an angle of 90° to a line or surface.
•n. a perpendicular line.

perpetrate v. carry out a bad or illegal action.
■ **perpetration** n. **perpetrator** n.

perpetual adj. **1** never ending or changing. **2** very frequent.
▷ SYNONYMS: **1 constant**, permanent, uninterrupted, continuous, unremitting, unending, ever-lasting, eternal, unceasing, without end, persistent, lasting, abiding. **2 interminable**, incessant, ceaseless, endless, relentless, unrelenting, persistent, continual, continuous, non-stop, never-ending, repeated, unremitting, round-the-clock, unabating; informal eternal.
– ANTONYMS: temporary, intermittent.
■ **perpetually** adv.

perpetuate v. cause to continue for a long time.
▷ SYNONYMS: **keep alive**, keep going, preserve, conserve, sustain, maintain, continue, extend.
■ **perpetuation** n.

perpetuity n. the state of lasting forever.

perplex v. puzzle greatly.
▷ SYNONYMS: **puzzle**, baffle, mystify, bemuse, bewilder, confound, confuse, nonplus, disconcert; informal flummox.
■ **perplexity** n.

perquisite n. a special right or privilege resulting from a person's position.

perry n. an alcoholic drink made from fermented pears.

persecute v. **1** treat badly over a long period. **2** persistently harass.
▷ SYNONYMS: **1 oppress**, abuse, victimize, ill-treat, mistreat, maltreat, torment, torture. **2 harass**, hound, plague, badger, harry, intimidate, pick on, pester; informal hassle.
■ **persecution** n. **persecutor** n.

persevere v. continue in spite of difficulty or lack of success.
▷ SYNONYMS: **persist**, continue, carry on, go on, keep on, keep going, struggle on, hammer away, be persistent, keep at it, not take no for an answer, be tenacious, plod on, plough on; informal soldier on, hang on, plug away, stick

to your guns, stick it out, hang in there.
– ANTONYMS: give up.
  ■ **perseverance** n.

persimmon n. a tropical fruit.

persist v. **1** continue doing something in spite of difficulty or opposition. **2** continue to exist.
▷ SYNONYMS: **1** *he persisted with his questioning:* **persevere**, continue, carry on, go on, keep on, keep going, hammer away, keep at it; informal soldier on, plug away. **2** *the dry weather persists:* **continue**, hold, carry on, last, keep on, remain, linger, stay, endure.
– ANTONYMS: give up, stop.
  ■ **persistently** adv..

persistent adj. **1** continuing to do something in spite of difficulty or opposition. **2** continuing or recurring over a long period.
▷ SYNONYMS: **1 tenacious**, determined, resolute, dogged, tireless, indefatigable, persevering, insistent, unrelenting; formal pertinacious. **2 constant**, continuous, continuing, continual, non-stop, never-ending, steady, uninterrupted, unbroken, interminable, incessant, endless, unending, unrelenting. **3** *a persistent cough:* **chronic**, nagging, frequent, repeated, habitual.
– ANTONYMS: irresolute, intermittent.
  ■ **persistence** n.

person n. (pl. **people** or **persons**) **1** an individual human being. **2** an individual's body. **3** Grammar a category used in classifying pronouns or verb forms according to whether they indicate the speaker (**first person**), the person spoken to (**second person**), or a third party (**third person**).
▷ SYNONYMS: **human being**, individual, man, woman, human, being, living soul, mortal, creature; informal type, sort, beggar, cookie.
□ **in person** actually present.

persona n. (pl. **personas** or **personae**) the aspect of a person's character that is presented to others.

personable adj. having a pleasant appearance and manner.

personage n. an important or famous person.

personal adj. **1** belonging to or affecting a particular person. **2** done by a particular person rather than someone else. **3** concerning a person's private life. **4** of a person's body.
▷ SYNONYMS: **1 distinctive**, characteristic, unique, individual, idio-

syncratic. **2 in person**, in the flesh, actual, live, physical. **3 private**, intimate. **4 derogatory**, disparaging, belittling, insulting, rude, disrespectful, offensive, pejorative.
□ **personal organizer** a loose-leaf notebook with a diary and address section. **personal pronoun** each of the pronouns (*I*, *you*, *he*, *she*, etc.) that show person, gender, number, and case.

personality n. (pl. **personalities**) **1** the qualities that form a person's character. **2** qualities that make someone interesting or popular. **3** a celebrity.
▷ SYNONYMS: **1 character**, nature, disposition, temperament, make-up, psyche. **2 charisma**, magnetism, character, charm, presence. **3 celebrity**, VIP, star, superstar, big name, somebody, leading light, luminary, notable; informal celeb.

personalize (or **-ise**) v. **1** design to suit or identify as belonging to a particular person. **2** cause an issue to be concerned with personalities or feelings.

personally adv. **1** in person. **2** from your own viewpoint.

personification n. **1** a good or perfect example of a quality. **2** the representation of a non-human thing in human form.
▷ SYNONYMS: *she was the personification of elegance:* **embodiment**, incarnation, epitome, quintessence, essence, type, symbol, soul, model, exemplification, exemplar, image, representation.

personify v. (**personifying**, **personified**) **1** represent in human form or as having human characteristics. **2** be an example of a quality.

personnel pl. n. employees; staff.
▷ SYNONYMS: **staff**, employees, workforce, workers, labour force, manpower, human resources.

perspective n. **1** the art of drawing things so as to give an effect of solidity and relative distance. **2** a way of seeing something. **3** understanding of the relative importance of things.
▷ SYNONYMS: **outlook**, view, viewpoint, point of view, standpoint, position, stand, stance, angle, slant, attitude.

perspex n. trademark a tough, light transparent plastic.

perspicacious adj. quickly gaining insight into things.
  ■ **perspicacity** n.

p

perspicuous adj. expressing things clearly.
■ **perspicuity** n.

perspire v. sweat.
■ **perspiration** n.

persuade v. cause to do or believe something by reasoning.
▷ SYNONYMS: **1 prevail on**, talk into, coax, convince, get, induce, win over, bring round, influence, sway; informal sweet-talk. **2 cause**, lead, move, dispose, incline.
– ANTONYMS: dissuade, deter.

persuasion n. **1** the act or a means of persuading. **2** a belief or set of beliefs.
▷ SYNONYMS: **1 coaxing**, urging, inducement, encouragement; informal sweet-talking. **2 group**, grouping, sect, denomination, party, camp, side, faction, school of thought, belief, creed, faith.

persuasive adj. **1** good at persuading. **2** providing sound reasoning.
▷ SYNONYMS: **convincing**, compelling, effective, telling, forceful, powerful, eloquent, impressive, sound, cogent, valid, strong, plausible, credible.
– ANTONYMS: unconvincing.
■ **persuasively** adv.

pert adj. attractively lively or cheeky.

pertain v. be related or relevant.
▷ SYNONYMS: **1** developments pertaining to the economy: **concern**, relate to, be connected with, be relevant to, apply to, refer to, have a bearing on, affect, involve, touch on. **2 exist**, be the case, prevail.

pertinacious adj. persistent.
■ **pertinacity** n.

pertinent adj. relevant.
▷ SYNONYMS: **relevant**, to the point, apposite, appropriate, suitable, applicable, material, germane.
– ANTONYMS: irrelevant.
■ **pertinence** n. **pertinently** adv.

perturb v. make anxious.
▷ SYNONYMS: **worry**, upset, disturb, unsettle, concern, trouble, disquiet, disconcert, discomfit, unnerve, alarm, bother; informal rattle.
– ANTONYMS: reassure.
■ **perturbation** n.

peruse v. read carefully.
■ **perusal** n.

pervade v. spread or be present throughout.
▷ SYNONYMS: **permeate**, spread through, fill, suffuse, imbue, penetrate, filter through, infuse, inform.

pervasive adj. spreading widely or present everywhere.

▷ SYNONYMS: **prevalent**, pervading, extensive, ubiquitous, omnipresent, universal, widespread, general.

perverse adj. **1** deliberately choosing to behave in an unacceptable way. **2** contrary to what is accepted or expected.
▷ SYNONYMS: **1 awkward**, contrary, difficult, unreasonable, uncooperative, unhelpful, obstructive, stubborn, obstinate; Brit. informal bloody-minded, bolshie. **2 illogical**, irrational, wrong-headed.
■ **perversely** adv. **perversity** n.

pervert v. **1** divert from the correct or intended meaning or course. **2** lead into abnormal or unacceptable sexual behaviour.
▷ SYNONYMS: **distort**, warp, corrupt, subvert, twist, bend, abuse, divert.
• n. a person whose sexual behaviour is abnormal or unacceptable.
■ **perversion** n.

perverted adj. sexually abnormal or unacceptable.
▷ SYNONYMS: **unnatural**, deviant, warped, twisted, abnormal, unhealthy, depraved, aberrant, debased, degenerate; informal sick, kinky.

pervious adj. allowing water to pass through.

peseta n. a former currency unit of Spain.

peso n. a currency unit of several South American countries.

pessary n. (pl. **pessaries**) a small soluble block inserted into the vagina to treat infection.

pessimist n. a pessimistic person.
▷ SYNONYMS: **defeatist**, fatalist, prophet of doom, alarmist, cynic, sceptic, misery, killjoy, Cassandra; informal doom and gloom merchant, wet blanket.
– ANTONYMS: optimist.

pessimistic adj. having or showing a lack of hope or confidence in the future.
▷ SYNONYMS: **gloomy**, negative, cynical, defeatist, downbeat, bleak, fatalistic, depressed.
– ANTONYMS: optimistic.
■ **pessimism** n. **pessimistically** adv.

pest n. a destructive insect or other animal that attacks plants, crops, etc.
▷ SYNONYMS: **nuisance**, annoyance, irritant, thorn in your flesh/side, trial, menace, trouble, problem, worry, bother; informal pain in the neck, headache.

pester v. trouble with persistent

requests or interruptions.

▷ SYNONYMS: **badger**, hound, harass, plague, annoy, bother, harry, worry; informal hassle, bug.

pesticide n. a substance for destroying insects or other pests.

pestilence n. old use a deadly epidemic disease.

■ **pestilential** adj.

pestle n. a heavy tool with a rounded end for crushing things in a mortar.

pesto n. a sauce of basil, pine nuts, Parmesan cheese, and olive oil, served with pasta.

pet n. **1** a tame animal kept for company and pleasure. **2** a person treated with special favour.
• adj. **1** of or kept as a pet. **2** favourite or particular.

▷ SYNONYMS: **1 tame**, domesticated, companion; Brit. house-trained; N. Amer. housebroken. **2 favourite**, favoured, cherished, particular, special, personal.
• v. (**petting, petted**) **1** stroke or pat an animal. **2** caress sexually.

▷ SYNONYMS: **1 stroke**, caress, fondle, pat, tickle. **2 cuddle**, embrace, caress, kiss; informal canoodle, neck, smooch; Brit. informal snog; N. Amer. informal make out.

petal n. each of the segments forming the outer part of a flower.

peter v. (**peter out**) come to an end gradually.

▷ SYNONYMS: **fizzle out**, fade away, die away/out, dwindle, diminish, taper off, tail off, wane, ebb, melt away, evaporate, disappear.

petite adj. small and dainty.

petition n. **1** an appeal or request, esp. a written one signed by many people. **2** an application to a law court for a writ etc.

▷ SYNONYMS: **appeal**, round robin, letter, request, entreaty, application, plea.
• v. present a petition to.

▷ SYNONYMS: **appeal to**, request, ask, call on, entreat, beg, implore, plead with, apply to, press, urge.

petrel n. a seabird.

petrify v. (**petrifying, petrified**) **1** paralyse with fear. **2** change organic matter into stone.

▷ SYNONYMS: **1 terrify**, horrify, scare someone to death; paralyse, transfix. **2 ossify**, fossilize, calcify.

■ **petrifaction** n.

petrochemical n. a chemical obtained from petroleum and natural gas.

petrol n. Brit. refined petroleum used as fuel in vehicles.

petroleum n. an oil found in layers of rock and refined to produce fuels.

petticoat n. a woman's undergarment in the form of a skirt.

pettifogging adj. petty; trivial.

pettish adj. childishly sulky.

petty adj. (**pettier, pettiest**) **1** unimportant; trivial. **2** small-minded. **3** minor.

▷ SYNONYMS: **1 trivial**, trifling, minor, insignificant, paltry, unimportant, inconsequential, footling, negligible; informal piffling. **2 small-minded**, mean, shabby, spiteful.

– ANTONYMS: important, magnanimous.

□ **petty cash** money kept in an office for small payments.

■ **pettiness** n.

petulant adj. childishly sulky or bad-tempered.

▷ SYNONYMS: **peevish**, bad-tempered, querulous, pettish, fretful, irritable, sulky, tetchy, crotchety, testy, fractious; informal grouchy; Brit. informal ratty; N. English informal mardy; N. Amer. informal cranky.

– ANTONYMS: good-humoured.

■ **petulance** n. **petulantly** adv.

petunia n. a plant with white, purple, or red funnel-shaped flowers.

pew n. a long bench with a back in a church.

pewter n. a grey alloy of tin with copper and antimony.

pfennig n. a former currency unit of Germany.

PG abbrev. (in film classification) parental guidance.

pH n. a measure of the acidity or alkalinity of a substance.

phalanx n. (pl. **phalanxes**) a group of people or things, esp. a body of troops or police officers.

phallus n. (pl. **phalli** or **phalluses**) a penis.

■ **phallic** adj.

phantom n. a ghost.

▷ SYNONYMS: **ghost**, apparition, spirit, spectre, wraith; informal spook.

pharaoh /fair-oh/ n. a ruler in ancient Egypt.

> **USAGE** Remember, -aoh not -oah: pharaoh.

pharmaceutical adj. of medicinal drugs.

pharmacist n. a person qualified to prepare and dispense medicinal drugs.

pharmacology n. the study of the uses and effects of drugs.

■ **pharmacological** adj. **pharmacologist** n.

pharmacopoeia /far-muh-kuh-pee-uh/ n. an official list of medicinal drugs with their effects.

pharmacy n. (pl. **pharmacies**) **1** a place where medicinal drugs are prepared or sold. **2** the preparation and dispensing of medicinal drugs.

pharynx n. (pl. **pharynges** /fa-rin-jeez/) the cavity behind the nose and mouth.

phase n. a distinct stage in a process of change or development.
▷ SYNONYMS: **stage**, period, chapter, episode, part, step.
• v. **1** carry out in gradual stages. **2** (**phase in/out**) gradually introduce or withdraw.

PhD abbrev. Doctor of Philosophy.

pheasant n. a long-tailed game bird.

phenomenal adj. excellent.
▷ SYNONYMS: **remarkable**, exceptional, extraordinary, marvellous, miraculous, wonderful, outstanding, unprecedented; informal fantastic, terrific, tremendous, stupendous.
■ **phenomenally** adv.

phenomenon n. (pl. **phenomena**) **1** a fact or situation observed to exist or happen. **2** a remarkable person or thing.
▷ SYNONYMS: **1 occurrence**, event, happening, fact, situation, circumstance, experience, case, incident, episode. **2 marvel**, sensation, wonder, prodigy.

USAGE The plural of **phenomenon** is **phenomena**. Don't use **phenomena** as a singular form.

pheromone n. a chemical released by an animal and causing a response in others of its species.

phial n. a small bottle.

philanderer n. a man who has numerous sexual relationships with women.
▷ SYNONYMS: **womanizer**, Casanova, Don Juan, Lothario, flirt, ladies' man, playboy; informal stud, ladykiller.
■ **philandering** n. & adj.

philanthropic adj. seeking to help people in need.
▷ SYNONYMS: **charitable**, generous, benevolent, humanitarian, public-spirited, altruistic, magnanimous, unselfish, kind.
– ANTONYMS: selfish, mean.

philanthropy n. the practice of helping people in need.
■ **philanthropist** n.

philately n. stamp collecting.
■ **philatelist** n.

philistine n. a person who is not interested in culture.
• adj. having or showing no interest in culture.
▷ SYNONYMS: **uncultured**, lowbrow, uncultivated, uncivilized, uneducated, unenlightened, materialist, bourgeois.

philology n. the study of languages.
■ **philological** adj. **philologist** n.

philosophical adj. **1** of philosophy. **2** calm in difficult circumstances.
▷ SYNONYMS: **1 theoretical**, metaphysical. **2 thoughtful**, reflective, pensive, meditative, contemplative, introspective. **3 stoical**, self-possessed, serene, dispassionate, phlegmatic, long-suffering, resigned.
■ **philosophically** adv.

philosophize (or **-ise**) v. theorize.

philosophy n. (pl. **philosophies**) **1** the study of the fundamental nature of knowledge, reality, and existence. **2** a set or system of beliefs.
▷ SYNONYMS: **beliefs**, credo, ideology, ideas, thinking, thought, theories, doctrine, principles, views.
■ **philosopher** n.

philtre (US **philter**) n. a love potion.

phlegm /flem/ n. mucus in the nose and throat.

phlegmatic /fleg-mat-ik/ adj. calm and unemotional.

phlox n. a flowering garden plant.

phobia n. an extreme or irrational fear.
▷ SYNONYMS: **fear**, dread, horror, terror, aversion, antipathy, revulsion; informal hang-up.
■ **phobic** adj. & n.

phoenix /fee-niks/ n. a mythological bird said to burn itself and be born again from its ashes.

phone n. a telephone.
▷ SYNONYMS: **telephone**, mobile; N. Amer. cellphone, cell; Brit. informal blower.
• v. telephone.
▷ SYNONYMS: **call**, telephone; Brit. ring, give someone a ring; informal give someone a buzz; Brit. informal give someone a bell.
□ **phonecard** a prepaid card allowing calls to be made on a public phone. **phone-in** a broadcast during which listeners or viewers join in by phone.

phonetic adj. **1** of or representing speech sounds. **2** (of spelling) closely matching the sounds represented.
• n. (**phonetics**) the study of speech sounds.
■ **phonetically** adv.

phoney (or **phony**) informal adj.

(**phonier**, **phoniest**) not genuine.
▷ SYNONYMS: **bogus**, false, fake, fraudulent, counterfeit, forged, imitation, affected, insincere; informal pretend; Brit. informal cod.
− ANTONYMS: authentic.
• n. (pl. **phoneys** or **phonies**) a phoney person or thing.
▷ SYNONYMS: **1 impostor**, sham, fake, fraud, charlatan; informal con artist. **2 fake**, imitation, counterfeit, forgery.

phonograph n. US a record player.

phosphate n. a compound of phosphorus.

phosphorescent adj. luminous.
■ phosphorescence n.

phosphorus n. a yellowish waxy element which glows in the dark and ignites in air.

photo n. (pl. **photos**) a photograph.
□ **photo finish** a finish of a race so close that the winner has to be decided from a photo. **photofit** Brit. a picture of a person made up of separate photos of facial features. **photogenic** looking attractive in photos.

photocopy n. (pl. **photocopies**) a photographic copy of a document etc.
▷ SYNONYMS: **copy**, duplicate, reproduction, facsimile; trademark Xerox, photostat.
• v. (**photocopying**, **photocopied**) make a photocopy of.
▷ SYNONYMS: **copy**, duplicate, xerox, photostat, reproduce.
■ photocopier n.

photoelectric cell n. a device generating an electric current when light falls on it.

photograph n. a picture made with a camera.
▷ SYNONYMS: **picture**, photo, snap, snapshot, shot, print, still, transparency.
• v. take a photo of.
■ photographer n. photographic adj. photography n.

photon n. an indivisible unit of electromagnetic radiation.

photosensitive adj. responding to light.

photostat n. trademark **1** a type of photocopier. **2** a copy made by a photostat.

photosynthesis n. the process by which green plants use sunlight to form nutrients from carbon dioxide and water.
■ photosynthesize (or -ise) v.

phrase n. **1** a small group of words forming a unit. **2** a group of musical notes forming a distinct unit.
▷ SYNONYMS: **expression**, construction, term, turn of phrase, idiom, saying.
• v. put into a particular form of words.
▷ SYNONYMS: **express**, put into words, put, word, formulate, couch, frame.
■ phrasal adj.

phraseology n. (pl. **phraseologies**) a particular form or use of words.

phrenology n. the study of the shape of a person's skull as a supposed indication of their character.

phylum n. (pl. **phyla**) a category used in classifying animals.

physical adj. **1** of the body. **2** of things that can be seen, heard, or touched. **3** of physics or the operation of natural forces.
▷ SYNONYMS: **1 bodily**, corporeal, corporal, carnal, fleshly, non-spiritual. **2 manual**, labouring, blue-collar. **3 material**, concrete, tangible, palpable, solid, substantial, real, actual, visible.
− ANTONYMS: mental, spiritual.
□ **physical education** instruction in physical exercise and games. **physical geography** the study of the earth's natural features. **physical sciences** the sciences studying inanimate natural objects.
■ physically adv.

physician n. a person qualified to practise medicine.
▷ SYNONYMS: **doctor**, medical practitioner, general practitioner, GP, clinician, specialist, consultant; informal doc, medic, quack.

physics n. the study of the nature and properties of matter and energy.
■ physicist n.

physiognomy n. (pl. **physiognomies**) a person's face.

physiology n. the study of the way in which living organisms function.
■ physiological adj. physiologist n.

physiotherapy n. the treatment of an injury etc. by massage and exercise.
■ physiotherapist n.

physique n. the shape and size of a person's body.

pi n. the ratio of a circle's circumference to its diameter (about 3.14).

pianissimo adv. & adj. Music very softly.

piano n. (pl. **pianos**) a musical instrument with strings struck by hammers when keys are pressed.
• adv. & adj. Music softly.
■ pianist n.

pianoforte n. formal a piano.

p

piazza /pi-at-zuh/ n. a public square or marketplace.

picador n. a bullfighter on horseback.

picaresque adj. of fiction dealing with the adventures of a dishonest but appealing hero.

piccalilli n. a pickle of chopped vegetables and hot spices.

piccolo n. (pl. **piccolos**) a small flute.

pick v. **1** take hold of and lift or remove from its place. **2** select.
▷ SYNONYMS: **1** *she picked up her books:* lift, take up, scoop up, gather up. **2** choose, select, single out, opt for, plump for, elect, decide on, settle on, fix on, name, nominate, identify. **3** *pick a fight:* **provoke**, start, cause, incite, instigate, prompt.
• n. **1** an act of selecting. **2** the best of a group. **3** (or **pickaxe**) a tool with a pointed iron bar at right angles to its handle, for breaking up hard ground.
▷ SYNONYMS: **best**, finest, choice, choicest, cream, flower, crème de la crème, elite.
□ **pick holes in** criticize. **pick a lock** open a lock with something other than a key. **pick on** single out for unfair treatment. **pickpocket** a person who steals from people's pockets. **pickup 1** a small truck with low sides. **2** an act of picking up. **3** a device converting sound vibrations into electrical signals for amplification. **pick up 1** go to collect. **2** improve or increase. **3** casually get to know someone as a sexual approach.
■ **picker** n.

picket n. **1** a person or group standing outside a workplace to dissuade others from entering during a strike. **2** a pointed wooden stake driven into the ground.
▷ SYNONYMS: **1 demonstrator**, striker, protester. **2 demonstration**, picket line, blockade, boycott, strike.
• v. (**picketing**, **picketed**) act as a picket outside a workplace.

pickings pl. n. profits or gains.

pickle n. **1** vegetables or fruit preserved in vinegar or brine. **2** (a **pickle**) informal a difficult situation.
• v. preserve in vinegar or brine.

picnic n. an informal meal eaten outdoors.
• v. (**picnicking**, **picnicked**) have a picnic.
■ **picnicker** n.

pictograph n. a picture representing a word or phrase.

pictorial adj. of or using pictures.
■ **pictorially** adv.

picture n. **1** a painting, drawing, or photo. **2** an image. **3** (**the pictures**) the cinema.
▷ SYNONYMS: **1 painting**, **drawing**, sketch, watercolour, print, canvas, portrait, illustration, depiction, likeness, representation, image. **2 photograph**, photo, snap, snapshot, shot, frame, exposure, still, print. **3 concept**, idea, impression, image, vision, visualization, notion. **4 personification**, embodiment, epitome, essence, quintessence, soul, model.
• v. **1** show in a picture. **2** imagine.
▷ SYNONYMS: **1 depict**, portray, show, represent, draw, sketch, photograph, paint. **2 visualize**, see in your mind's eye, imagine, remember.

picturesque adj. attractive in a quaint or charming way.
▷ SYNONYMS: **attractive**, pretty, beautiful, lovely, scenic, charming, quaint, pleasing, delightful.
– ANTONYMS: ugly.

pidgin n. a simple form of a language with elements taken from local languages.

pie n. a baked dish of ingredients topped with pastry.
□ **pie chart** a diagram representing quantities as sections of a circle.

piebald adj. (of a horse) having irregular patches of two colours.

piece n. **1** a portion or part. **2** an item forming part of a set. **3** a musical, literary, or artistic work. **4** a small object used in a board game.
▷ SYNONYMS: **1** *a piece of cheese:* **portion**, bit, slice, chunk, segment, section, lump, hunk, wedge, slab, block, cake, bar, stick, length. **2** *the pieces of a jigsaw:* **component**, part, bit, constituent, element, section, unit. **3** *a piece of the profit:* **share**, portion, slice, quota, part, percentage, amount, quantity, ration, fraction; Brit. informal whack. **4 work of art**, artwork, artefact, composition, opus. **5 article**, item, story, report, essay, feature, review, column.
• v. (**piece together**) assemble from individual parts.
□ **piecemeal** done in a gradual and inconsistent way. **piecework** work paid for according to the amount produced.

pièce de résistance /pyess duh ray-ziss-tonss/ n. the most impressive feature.

pied adj. having two or more different colours.

pied-à-terre /pyay-dah-**tair**/ n. (pl. **pieds-à-terre**) a small flat or house for occasional use.

pier n. a structure built out into the sea, used as a landing stage or promenade.

▷ SYNONYMS: **jetty**, quay, wharf, dock, landing stage.

pierce v. **1** make a hole in or through with a sharp object. **2** force a way through.

▷ SYNONYMS: **penetrate**, puncture, perforate, prick, spike, stab, drill, bore.

piercing adj. **1** very loud or high-pitched. **2** very astute or intelligent.

▷ SYNONYMS: **1 shrill**, ear-splitting, high-pitched, penetrating, strident, loud, deafening. **2 searching**, probing, penetrating, sharp, keen, shrewd, astute.

piety n. (pl. **pieties**) the quality of being deeply religious.

piffle n. informal nonsense.

pig n. **1** a domestic or wild mammal with a flat snout. **2** informal a greedy or dirty person.

▷ SYNONYMS: **hog**, boar, sow, porker, swine, piglet.

  □ **pig-headed** stubborn. **pig iron** oblong blocks of crude iron from a smelting furnace. **pigsty** an enclosure for pigs. **pigtail** a length of hair worn in a plait at the back or on each side of the head.

  ■ **piglet** n.

WORD LINKS
porcine relating to pigs

---

pigeon n. a plump bird with a cooing voice.

pigeonhole n. each of a set of small compartments where letters etc. may be left.

  • v. place in a particular category.

piggery n. (pl. **piggeries**) a farm or enclosure where pigs are kept.

piggy adj. like a pig.

  □ **piggyback** a ride on someone's back and shoulders. **piggy bank** a money box shaped like a pig.

pigment n. **1** natural colouring. **2** a colouring matter.

▷ SYNONYMS: **colouring**, colour, tint, dye, stain.

  ■ **pigmentation** n.

pigmy var. of PYGMY.

pike n. **1** (pl. **pike**) a large predatory freshwater fish. **2** a spear with a long wooden shaft.

pilaf (or **pilau**) n. a dish of rice with spices, meat, etc.

pilaster n. a rectangular column projecting from a wall.

pilchard n. a small edible fish.

pile n. **1** a number of things lying one on top of another. **2** informal a large amount. **3** a heavy post driven into the ground to support foundations. **4** the surface of a carpet or fabric, consisting of many small projecting threads. **5** (**piles**) haemorrhoids.

▷ SYNONYMS: **1 heap**, stack, mound, pyramid, mass, collection, accumulation, assemblage, stockpile, hoard. **2 lot**, mountain, abundance; informal load, heap, mass, slew, stack, ton, oodles. **3 nap**, fibres, threads.

  • v. **1** place in a pile. **2** (**pile up**) accumulate.

▷ SYNONYMS: **1 heap**, stack, load, fill, charge. **2 accumulate**, grow, mount up, escalate, soar, spiral, increase, accrue, build up, multiply.

pile-up n. informal a crash involving several vehicles.

▷ SYNONYMS: **crash**, collision, smash, accident; Brit. RTA; N. Amer. wreck; Brit. informal shunt.

pilfer v. steal items of little value.

pilgrim n. a person who travels to a holy place for religious reasons.

pilgrimage n. **1** a pilgrim's journey to a holy place. **2** a journey to a place of interest or importance.

▷ SYNONYMS: **journey**, expedition, mission, visit, trek, trip, odyssey.

pill n. **1** a small piece of solid medicine for swallowing whole. **2** (**the Pill**) a contraceptive pill.

▷ SYNONYMS: **tablet**, capsule, pellet, lozenge, pastille.

  □ **pillbox 1** a small round hat with a flat top. **2** a small concrete fort.

pillage v. & n. plunder.

pillar n. an upright structure used as a support for a building.

▷ SYNONYMS: **1 column**, post, support, upright, pier, pile, prop, stanchion, obelisk. **2 stalwart**, mainstay, bastion, leading light, worthy, backbone, supporter, upholder, champion.

  □ **pillar box** a red cylindrical postbox.

pillion n. a seat for a passenger behind a motorcyclist.

pillory n. (pl. **pillories**) a wooden frame with holes for the head and hands, in which offenders were formerly locked and exposed to public abuse.

  • v. (**pillorying**, **pilloried**) ridicule publicly.

pillow n. a cushion to support the head when lying down.

  • v. rest the head as if on a pillow.

  □ **pillowcase** a cloth cover for a pillow.

p

pilot n. **1** a person who operates an aircraft's flying controls. **2** a person qualified to steer ships into or out of a harbour. **3** something done as a test before being introduced more widely.

▷ SYNONYMS: **1 airman**, **airwoman**, flyer, captain; informal skipper; dated aviator. **2 navigator**, helmsman, steersman, coxswain. **3 trial**, test, sample, experiment.

• v. (**piloting**, **piloted**) **1** act as a pilot of an aircraft or ship. **2** test a project before introducing it more widely.

▷ SYNONYMS: **navigate**, guide, manoeuvre, steer, control, direct, captain, fly, drive, sail; informal skipper.

□ **pilot light** a small gas burner kept alight permanently to light a larger burner.

pimiento n. (pl. **pimientos**) a red sweet pepper.

pimp n. a man who controls prostitutes and takes a percentage of their earnings.

• v. act as a pimp.

pimple n. a small inflamed spot on the skin.

■ **pimply** adj.

PIN (or **PIN number**) abbrev. personal identification number.

pin n. **1** a thin pointed piece of metal with a round head, used as a fastener. **2** a short metal rod or peg.

• v. (**pinning**, **pinned**) **1** attach or fasten with a pin or pins. **2** hold someone firmly so they are unable to move. **3** (**pin down**) force someone to be specific. **4** (**pin on**) fix blame on.

▷ SYNONYMS: **1 attach**, fasten, affix, fix, join, secure, clip, staple, nail. **2 hold**, press, pinion.

□ **pinball** a game in which small balls are propelled across a sloping board to hit targets. **pin money** a small sum of money for everyday items. **pins and needles** a tingling sensation. **pinstripe** a very narrow pale stripe in dark cloth. **pin-up** a poster of an attractive person.

pinafore n. **1** a collarless sleeveless dress worn over a blouse or jumper. **2** Brit. an apron.

pince-nez /panss-**nay**/ n. a pair of glasses with a nose clip instead of earpieces.

pincer n. **1** (**pincers**) a metal tool with blunt jaws for gripping and pulling things. **2** a front claw of a lobster or similar crustacean.

pinch v. **1** grip flesh tightly between the finger and thumb. **2** hurt by being too tight. **3** informal steal.

▷ SYNONYMS: **nip**, tweak, squeeze, grasp, compress.

• n. **1** an act of pinching. **2** a very small amount.

▷ SYNONYMS: **1 nip**, tweak, squeeze. **2 bit**, touch, dash, spot, trace, soupçon, speck, taste; informal smidgen, tad.

□ **at a pinch** if absolutely necessary. **feel the pinch** experience financial hardship.

pine v. **1** become weak because of grief etc. **2** (**pine for**) miss someone intensely.

▷ SYNONYMS: **fade**, waste away, weaken, decline, languish, wilt, sicken.

• n. an evergreen coniferous tree with needle-shaped leaves.

□ **pine marten** a dark brown weasel-like mammal.

pineapple n. a large tropical fruit.

ping n. a short high-pitched ringing sound.

• v. make a pinging sound.

□ **ping-pong** informal table tennis.

pinion v. tie or hold the arms or legs of.

• n. **1** the outer part of a bird's wing. **2** a small cogwheel.

pink adj. pale red.

▷ SYNONYMS: **rose**, rosy, rosé, pale red, salmon, coral, flushed, blushing.

• n. **1** pink colour. **2** (**the pink**) informal the best condition. **3** a plant with scented flowers.

• v. **1** cut a zigzag edge on. **2** Brit. (of an engine) make rattling sounds when running imperfectly.

pinnacle n. **1** a high pointed rock. **2** a small turret. **3** the most successful point.

▷ SYNONYMS: **1 peak**, needle, crag, tor. **2 height**, peak, high point, top, apex, zenith, acme.

– ANTONYMS: nadir.

pinpoint v. locate exactly.

▷ SYNONYMS: **identify**, determine, distinguish, discover, find, locate, detect, track down, spot, diagnose, recognize, pin down, home in on.

pint n. a liquid measure equal to one eighth of a gallon (0.568 litre).

pioneer n. **1** a person who explores or settles in a new region. **2** a person who develops a new idea or technique.

▷ SYNONYMS: **1 settler**, colonist, colonizer, frontiersman, explorer. **2 developer**, innovator, trailblazer, groundbreaker, founding father, architect, creator.

• v. be a pioneer of.

p

▷ SYNONYMS: **introduce**, develop, launch, instigate, initiate, spearhead, institute, establish, found.

pious adj. **1** deeply religious. **2** pretending to be good or religious.
▷ SYNONYMS: **religious**, devout, God-fearing, churchgoing, holy, godly, saintly, reverent, righteous.
– ANTONYMS: irreligious.
■ **piously** adv.

pip n. **1** a small seed in a fruit. **2** a short high-pitched sound. **3** Brit. a star on an army officer's uniform, showing rank.
• v. (**be pipped**) Brit. informal be only just defeated.

pipe n. **1** a tube through which water, gas, oil, etc. can flow. **2** a narrow tube with a bowl at one end for smoking tobacco. **3** a wind instrument.
4 (**pipes**) bagpipes.
▷ SYNONYMS: **tube**, conduit, hose, main, duct, line, channel, pipeline, drain.
• v. **1** send through a pipe. **2** play a tune on a pipe. **3** say in a high voice.
▷ SYNONYMS: **feed**, siphon, channel, run, convey.
□ **pipe down** informal be quiet. **pipe dream** an unrealistic hope or scheme. **piping hot** very hot.
■ **piper** n.

pipeline n. a long pipe for carrying oil, gas, etc. over a distance.
□ **in the pipeline** being developed.

pipette n. a thin tube for transferring or measuring small quantities of liquid.

piquant adj. having a pleasantly sharp or spicy taste.
▷ SYNONYMS: **1** *a piquant sauce:* spicy, tangy, peppery, hot, tasty, flavour-some, savoury, pungent, sharp, tart, zesty, strong, salty. **2** *a piquant story:* intriguing, stimulating, interesting, fascinating, colourful, exciting, lively, spicy, provocative, racy; informal juicy.
– ANTONYMS: bland, dull.
■ **piquancy** n.

pique /peek/ n. resentment arising from hurt pride.
• v. **1** stimulate someone's interest. **2** (**be piqued**) feel resentful.

piquet /pee-kay/ n. a card game for two players.

piranha /pi-rah-nuh/ n. a freshwater fish with very sharp teeth.

pirate n. a person who attacks and robs ships at sea.
▷ SYNONYMS: **raider**, hijacker, free-booter, marauder; historical privateer, buccaneer; old use corsair.
• adj. (of a film etc.) pirated.
• v. reproduce a film, recording, etc.

for profit without permission.
▷ SYNONYMS: **steal**, copy, plagiarize, poach, appropriate, bootleg; informal crib, lift, rip off.
■ **piracy** n. **piratical** adj.

pirouette n. (in ballet) an act of spinning on one foot.
• v. perform a pirouette.

pistachio /pi-sta-shi-oh/ n. (pl. **pistachios**) a nut with a green kernel.

piste /peest/ n. a ski run.

pistil n. the female organs of a flower.

pistol n. a small gun.

piston n. a sliding disc or cylinder inside a tube, esp. as part of an engine or pump.

pit n. **1** a large hole in the ground. **2** a coal mine. **3** a sunken area. **4** an area at the side of a track where racing cars are refuelled etc. **5** (**the pits**) informal a very bad place or situation.
▷ SYNONYMS: **1** hole, trough, hollow, excavation, cavity, crater, pothole. **2** coal mine, colliery, quarry, shaft.
• v. (**pitting**, **pitted**) **1** (**pit against**) set in competition with. **2** make a hollow in the surface of.
▷ SYNONYMS: **mark**, pockmark, pock, scar, dent, indent.

pitch n. **1** Brit. an area of ground for outdoor team games. **2** the extent to which a sound is high or low. **3** a level of intensity. **4** a form of words used to persuade. **5** Brit. a place where a street seller or performer is stationed. **6** the steepness of a roof. **7** a sticky black substance.
▷ SYNONYMS: **1** playing field, ground, sports field, stadium; Brit. park. **2** tone, key, modulation, frequency. **3** level, intensity, point, degree, height, extent. **4** patter, talk; informal spiel, line. **5** gradient, slope, slant, angle, tilt, incline.
• v. **1** throw roughly. **2** set at a particular musical pitch. **3** aim at a particular level, target, etc. **4** set up a tent. **5** (**pitch in**) informal join in enthusiastically. **6** (of a ship etc.) rock up and down. **7** (**pitched**) (of a roof) sloping.
▷ SYNONYMS: **1** throw, toss, fling, hurl, cast, lob, flip; informal chuck, sling, heave, bung. **2** fall, tumble, topple, plunge, plummet. **3** put up, set up, erect, raise. **4** lurch, toss, plunge, roll, reel, sway, rock, list.
□ **pitch-black** (or **pitch-dark**) completely dark. **pitched battle** a fierce fight involving many people. **pitchfork** a long-handled fork for lifting hay.

p

pitchblende n. a mineral containing radium.

pitcher n. a large jug.

piteous adj. deserving or arousing pity. ■ **piteously** adv.

pitfall n. a hidden danger or difficulty.
▷ SYNONYMS: **hazard**, danger, risk, peril, difficulty, catch, snag, stumbling block, drawback.

pith n. spongy white tissue in stems or fruits.

pithy adj. **1** full of pith. **2** (of language or style) concise and expressive.

pitiful adj. **1** deserving or arousing pity. **2** very small or poor.
▷ SYNONYMS: **1 distressing**, sad, piteous, pitiable, pathetic, heart-rending, moving, touching, tear-jerking, plaintive, poignant, forlorn, poor, sorry, wretched, miserable. **2 paltry**, miserable, meagre, trifling, negligible, pitiable, derisory; informal pathetic, measly; Brit. informal poxy. **3 dreadful**, awful, terrible, appalling, lamentable, hopeless, feeble, pitiable, woeful, inadequate, deplorable, laughable; informal pathetic, useless, lousy, abysmal, dire.
■ **pitifully** adv.

pitiless adj. showing no pity.
▷ SYNONYMS: **merciless**, unmerciful, ruthless, cruel, heartless, remorseless, hard-hearted, cold-hearted, harsh, callous, severe, unsparing, unforgiving, unfeeling, uncaring, unsympathetic, uncharitable.
– ANTONYMS: merciful.

piton /pee-ton/ n. a peg used in rock climbing.

pitta n. a type of flat bread, hollow inside.

pittance n. a very small amount of money.

pituitary gland n. a gland at the base of the brain controlling growth and development.

pity n. (pl. **pities**) **1** a feeling of sorrow for another's suffering. **2** a cause for regret.
▷ SYNONYMS: **1 compassion**, commiseration, condolence, sympathy, fellow feeling, understanding. **2** it's a pity you can't go: **shame**, misfortune.
– ANTONYMS: indifference.
• v. (**pitying, pitied**) feel pity for.
▷ SYNONYMS: **feel sorry for**, feel for, sympathize with, empathize with, commiserate with, take pity on, be moved by, bleed for.

pivot n. a central point or shaft on which a mechanism turns or is balanced.

▷ SYNONYMS: **fulcrum**, axis, axle, swivel, pin, shaft, hub, spindle, hinge, kingpin.
• v. (**pivoting, pivoted**) turn on a pivot.
▷ SYNONYMS: **1 rotate**, turn, swivel, revolve, spin. **2** it all pivoted on his response: **depend**, hinge, turn, centre, hang, rely, rest, revolve around.

pivotal adj. **1** of a pivot. **2** of central importance.

pixel n. any of the tiny areas of light on a display screen making up an image.

pixelate v. divide an image into pixels.

pixie (or **pixy**) n. (pl. **pixies**) (in fairy tales etc.) a tiny being with pointed ears.

pizza n. a flat base of dough baked with a savoury topping.

pizzeria n. a pizza restaurant.

pizzicato adv. & adj. plucking the strings of a violin etc. instead of using the bow.

placard n. a sign or notice.

placate v. make less angry.
▷ SYNONYMS: **pacify**, calm, appease, mollify, soothe, win over, conciliate, propitiate, make peace with, humour.
– ANTONYMS: provoke.
■ **placatory** adj.

place n. **1** a particular position or area. **2** a portion of space occupied by or set aside for someone or something. **3** a position in a sequence. **4** a person's status, or a right arising from this.
▷ SYNONYMS: **1** an ideal place for a picnic: **location**, site, spot, setting, position, situation, area, region, locale, venue. **2** a place of your own: **home**, house, flat, apartment, pied-à-terre, accommodation, property, rooms, quarters; informal pad; formal residence, abode, dwelling. **3** he's saved you a place: **seat**, chair, space. **4** he was offered a place in the cabinet: **job**, position, post, appointment, situation, employment. **5** I know my place: **status**, position, standing, rank. **6** it's not my place to give advice: **responsibility**, duty, job, task, role, function, concern, affair, charge.
• v. **1** put in a particular position or situation. **2** give a specified position in a sequence. **3** make an order for goods etc.
▷ SYNONYMS: **1 put**, set, lay, deposit, position, plant, rest, stand, station, situate, leave; informal stick, dump, bung, park, plonk, pop; N. Amer. informal plunk. **2 rank**, order, grade, class,

classify, put. **3 identify**, recognize, remember, put a name to, pin down, locate, pinpoint.

□ **out of place** inappropriate or incongruous. **take place** occur.

placebo /pluh-see-boh/ n. (pl. **placebos**) a medicine prescribed for the mental benefit of the patient rather than for any physical effect.

placement n. **1** the act of placing. **2** Brit. a temporary job undertaken for work experience.

placenta n. (pl. **placentae** or **placentas**) an organ in the womb of a pregnant mammal supplying nourishment to the fetus through the umbilical cord.

placid adj. not easily upset or excited.
▷ SYNONYMS: **1 even-tempered**, calm, tranquil, equable, unexcitable, serene, mild, composed, self-possessed, poised, easy-going, level-headed, steady, unruffled, unperturbed, phlegmatic; informal unflappable. **2 quiet**, calm, tranquil, still, peaceful, undisturbed, restful, sleepy.
– ANTONYMS: excitable.
■ **placidity** n. **placidly** adv.

placket n. an opening in a garment, covering fastenings or for access to a pocket.

plagiarize (or **-ise**) v. take someone else's work etc. and pretend it is your own.
▷ SYNONYMS: **copy**, pirate, steal, poach, appropriate; informal rip off, crib; Brit. informal pinch, nick.
■ **plagiarism** n. **plagiarist** n.

plague n. **1** a very serious infectious disease. **2** an infestation of destructive insects or animals.
▷ SYNONYMS: **1 pandemic**, epidemic, disease, sickness; dated contagion; old use pestilence. **2 infestation**, invasion, swarm.
• v. **1** cause continual trouble to. **2** pester continually.
▷ SYNONYMS: **1 afflict**, trouble, torment, beset, dog, curse, bedevil. **2 pester**, harass, badger, bother, torment, harry, hound, trouble, nag; informal hassle, bug.

plaice n. (pl. **plaice**) an edible flatfish.

plaid /plad/ n. tartan fabric.

plain adj. **1** simple or ordinary. **2** without a pattern. **3** easy to see or understand. **4** (of language) direct. **5** not attractive.
▷ SYNONYMS: **1 obvious**, clear, evident, apparent, manifest, unmistakable. **2 intelligible**, comprehensible, understandable, clear, lucid, simple,

straightforward, user-friendly. **3 candid**, frank, outspoken, forthright, direct, honest, truthful, blunt, bald, unequivocal; informal upfront. **4 simple**, ordinary, unadorned, homely, basic, modest, unsophisticated, unprepossessing, ugly, ordinary; N. Amer. homely; Brit. informal no oil painting. **5 unattractive**, pure, downright, out-and-out.
– ANTONYMS: obscure, fancy, attractive.
• adv. informal used for emphasis: plain stupid.
• n. a large area of flat land with few trees.
▷ SYNONYMS: **grassland**, flatland, prairie, savannah, steppe, tundra, pampas, veld, plateau.
□ **plain clothes** ordinary clothes rather than uniform. **plain sailing** easy progress. **plainsong** unaccompanied medieval church music for several voices.
■ **plainly** adv. **plainness** n.

plaintiff n. a person bringing a case against another in a court of law.

plaintive adj. sounding sad.
▷ SYNONYMS: **mournful**, sad, pathetic, pitiful, melancholy, sorrowful, unhappy, wretched, woeful, forlorn.
■ **plaintively** adv.

plait n. Brit. a single length of hair or rope made up of three or more intertwined strands.
• v. form into a plait or plaits.

plan n. **1** a proposal for doing or achieving something. **2** an intention. **3** a map or diagram.
▷ SYNONYMS: **1 scheme**, idea, proposal, proposition, project, programme, system, method, strategy, stratagem, formula, recipe. **2 intention**, aim, idea, objective, object, goal, target, ambition. **3 map**, diagram, chart, blueprint, drawing, sketch, impression; N. Amer. plat.
• v. (**planning**, **planned**) **1** decide on and arrange in advance. **2** intend. **3** draw a plan of a proposed building etc.
▷ SYNONYMS: **1 organize**, arrange, work out, outline, map out, prepare, formulate, frame, develop, devise. **2 intend**, aim, propose, mean, hope. **3 design**, sketch out, map out; N. Amer. plat.
■ **planner** n.

plane n. **1** a completely flat surface. **2** a level of existence or thought. **3** an aeroplane. **4** a tool for smoothing wood by cutting shavings from it. **5** a tall tree with a peeling bark.

▷ SYNONYMS: **1** *a higher plane of consciousness:* **level**, degree, standard, stratum, dimension. **2 aircraft**, airliner, jet, flying machine; Brit. aeroplane; N. Amer. airplane.
• adj. completely flat.
• v. smooth with a plane.

planet n. a large round mass in space orbiting round a star.
■ **planetary** adj.

planetarium n. (pl. **planetariums** or **planetaria**) a building in which images of stars and planets are projected on to a domed ceiling.

plangent adj. loud and mournful.

plank n. a long, flat piece of timber.

plankton n. tiny organisms living in the sea or fresh water.

plant n. **1** a living thing that absorbs substances through its roots and makes nutrients in its leaves by photosynthesis. **2** a factory. **3** machinery used in manufacturing. **4** a person sent to a group as a spy. **5** a thing put among someone's belongings to incriminate them.
▷ SYNONYMS: **1 flower**, vegetable, herb, shrub, bush, weed; (**plants**) vegetation, greenery, flora. **2 factory**, works, facility, refinery, mill. **3 machinery**, machines, equipment, apparatus, appliances, gear. **4 spy**, informant, informer, secret agent, mole, infiltrator, operative; N. Amer. informal spook.
• v. **1** place a seed, bulb, etc. in the ground to grow. **2** place in a specified position. **3** send or place as a plant.
▷ SYNONYMS: **1 sow**, scatter. **2 place**, put, set, position, situate, settle, fix; informal plonk.
■ **planter** n.

> **WORD LINKS**
> **botany** the scientific study of plants
> **herbivorous** plant-eating

plantain n. **1** a low-growing plant. **2** a type of banana.

plantation n. **1** an estate on which coffee, tobacco, etc. is grown. **2** an area in which trees have been planted.

plaque n. **1** a commemorative plate fixed to a wall. **2** a sticky deposit on teeth, encouraging the growth of bacteria.

plasma n. **1** the colourless fluid part of blood. **2** a type of gas.

plaster n. **1** a mixture of lime, sand, water, etc. used for coating walls. **2** Brit. a sticky strip of material for covering wounds. **3** (or **plaster of Paris**) a white paste of gypsum and water that hardens when dry, used for making moulds and casts.
• v. **1** apply plaster to. **2** coat thickly.
▷ SYNONYMS: **1 spread**, smother, smear, cake, coat, bedaub. **2 flatten**, smooth down, slick down.
□ **plasterboard** board made of plaster set between two sheets of paper, used to line interior walls and ceilings.
■ **plasterer** n.

plastic n. a chemically produced material that can be moulded to a permanent shape.
• adj. **1** made of plastic. **2** easily shaped.
▷ SYNONYMS: **1 soft**, pliable, pliant, flexible, malleable, workable, mouldable; informal bendy. **2 artificial**, false, fake, bogus, insincere; informal phoney, pretend.
□ **plastic surgery** surgery performed to repair or reconstruct parts of the body.
■ **plasticity** n.

plasticine n. trademark a soft modelling material.

plate n. **1** a flat dish for holding food. **2** bowls, cups, etc. made of gold or silver. **3** a thin, flat piece of metal, glass, etc. **4** a printed photo or illustration in a book.
▷ SYNONYMS: **1 dish**, platter, salver; historical trencher; old use charger. **2 plateful**, helping, portion, serving. **3 panel**, sheet, slab. **4 plaque**, sign, tablet. **5 picture**, print, illustration, photograph, photo.
• v. coat a metal object with a different metal.
▷ SYNONYMS: **cover**, coat, overlay, laminate, gild.
□ **plate glass** thick glass for windows and doors.

plateau /plat-oh/ n. (pl. **plateaux** or **plateaus**) **1** an area of level high ground. **2** a state of little change following a period of progress.
▷ SYNONYMS: **upland**, mesa, highland, tableland.

platelet n. a disc-shaped cell fragment in blood, involved in clotting.

platen n. the roller in a typewriter against which the paper is held.

platform n. **1** a raised level area on which people or things can stand. **2** the stated policy of a political party.
▷ SYNONYMS: **1 stage**, dais, rostrum, podium, stand. **2 programme**, manifesto, policies, principles, party line.

platinum n. a precious silvery-white metallic element.

platitude n. a remark used too often to be interesting.
▷ SYNONYMS: **cliché**, truism, commonplace, old chestnut, banality.
■ **platitudinous** adj.

platonic adj. friendly and affectionate but not sexual.

platoon n. a subdivision of a company of soldiers.

platter n. a large flat serving dish.
▷ SYNONYMS: **plate**, dish, salver, tray; old use charger.

platypus n. (pl. **platypuses**) an egg-laying Australian mammal with a duck-like bill.

plaudits pl. n. praise.

plausible adj. seeming reasonable or probable.
▷ SYNONYMS: **credible**, believable, reasonable, likely, possible, conceivable, imaginable, convincing, persuasive.
– ANTONYMS: unlikely.
■ **plausibility** n. **plausibly** adv.

play v. **1** take part in games for enjoyment. **2** compete against in a sport or contest. **3** act the role of. **4** perform a piece of music on an instrument. **5** move a piece or display a playing card in a game. **6** make a CD, tape, etc. produce sounds. **7** move or flicker over a surface.
▷ SYNONYMS: **1 amuse yourself**, entertain yourself, enjoy yourself, have fun; frolic, romp, cavort. **2 take part in**, participate in, be involved in, compete in, do. **3 compete against**, take on, meet. **4 perform**, portray, appear as.
• n. **1** a piece of writing performed by actors. **2** games taken part in for enjoyment. **3** the performing of a sports match. **4** action or operation. **5** freedom of movement.
▷ SYNONYMS: **1 drama**, theatrical work, piece, comedy, tragedy, production, performance. **2 amusement**, relaxation, recreation, diversion, leisure, enjoyment, pleasure, fun.
□ **playboy** a wealthy man who spends his time seeking pleasure. **play down** disguise the importance of. **playgroup** Brit. a regular play session for preschool children. **playhouse** a theatre. **playing card** each of a set of pieces of card used in various games. **playmate** a friend with whom a child plays. **play on** exploit a weakness. **playpen** a portable enclosure for a young child to play in. **play up** Brit. informal cause problems. **playwright** a person who writes plays.
■ **player** n.

playful adj. **1** fond of games and amusement. **2** for amusement; not serious.
▷ SYNONYMS: **1 frisky**, lively, full of fun, frolicsome, high-spirited, exuberant, mischievous, impish; informal full of beans. **2 light-hearted**, jokey, teasing, humorous, jocular, facetious, frivolous, flippant.
– ANTONYMS: serious.
■ **playfully** adv. **playfulness** n.

plaza n. a public square.

plc (or **PLC**) abbrev. Brit. public limited company.

plea n. **1** an emotional request. **2** a formal statement by or on behalf of a defendant or prisoner.
▷ SYNONYMS: **appeal**, entreaty, supplication, petition, request, call.

plead v. (**pleading**, **pleaded** or US or Scottish **pled**) **1** make an emotional request. **2** argue in support of. **3** state formally in court whether you are guilty or not guilty of an offence. **4** present as an excuse.
▷ SYNONYMS: **beg**, implore, entreat, appeal to, ask, importune, supplicate; literary beseech.

pleasant adj. **1** satisfactory and enjoyable. **2** likeable.
▷ SYNONYMS: **1 enjoyable**, pleasurable, nice, agreeable, entertaining, amusing, delightful, charming; informal lovely, great. **2 friendly**, charming, agreeable, amiable, nice, delightful, sweet, genial, cordial, good-natured, personable, hospitable, polite.
■ **pleasantly** adv. **pleasantness** n.

pleasantry n. (pl. **pleasantries**) a friendly or humorous remark.

please v. **1** cause to feel happy and satisfied. **2** wish: *do as you please*. **3** (**please yourself**) consider only your own wishes.
▷ SYNONYMS: **1 delight**, charm, amuse, entertain, divert, satisfy, gratify; humour. **2 like**, want, wish, desire, see fit, think fit, choose, will, prefer.
– ANTONYMS: annoy.
• adv. used in polite requests.

pleased adj. feeling or showing pleasure and satisfaction.
▷ SYNONYMS: **happy**, glad, delighted, gratified, grateful, thankful, content, contented, satisfied, thrilled; informal over the moon, on cloud nine; Brit. informal chuffed; N. English informal made up; Austral. informal wrapped.
– ANTONYMS: unhappy.

pleasing adj. pleasant or satisfying.
▷ SYNONYMS: **1** *a pleasing result*: **good**, satisfying, gratifying, welcome. **2** *her*

p

pleasing manner: **friendly**, amiable, pleasant, agreeable, affable, nice, genial, likeable, charming, engaging, delightful; informal lovely.

pleasurable adj. enjoyable.
■ **pleasurably** adv.

pleasure n. **1** a feeling of satisfaction and enjoyment. **2** a source of this.
▷ SYNONYMS: **happiness**, delight, joy, gladness, glee, satisfaction, gratification, contentment, enjoyment, amusement, fun, entertainment, relaxation, recreation, diversion.

pleat n. a fold in fabric, held by stitching at the top or side.
• v. form into pleats.

pleb n. informal, derogatory a member of the lower social classes.

plebeian /pli-bee-uhn/ adj. lower-class or unsophisticated.

plebiscite /pleb-i-syt/ n. a referendum.

plectrum n. (pl. **plectrums** or **plectra**) a small piece of plastic etc. for plucking the strings of a musical instrument.

pled US or Sc. past part. of PLEAD.

pledge n. **1** a solemn promise. **2** a valuable item given as a guarantee that a debt will be paid etc. **3** a token of love or loyalty.
▷ SYNONYMS: **promise**, vow, undertaking, word, commitment, assurance, oath, guarantee.
• v. **1** make a solemn promise. **2** give as a pledge.
▷ SYNONYMS: **promise**, vow, undertake, swear, commit yourself, declare, affirm.

plenary adj. (of a meeting at a conference etc.) attended by all participants.

plenipotentiary n. (pl. **plenipotentiaries**) a person given full power by a government to act on its behalf.

plenitude n. an abundance.

plentiful adj. existing in large amounts.
▷ SYNONYMS: **abundant**, copious, ample, profuse, rich, lavish, generous, bountiful, bumper, prolific; informal galore.
– ANTONYMS: scarce.
■ **plentifully** adv.

plenty pron. a large or sufficient amount or quantity.
▷ SYNONYMS: **a lot of**, many, a great deal of, a plethora of, enough and to spare, a wealth of; informal loads of, heaps of, stacks of, masses of, oodles of.
■ **plenteous** adj.

plethora n. an excessive amount.
▷ SYNONYMS: **excess**, abundance, super-abundance, surplus, glut, surfeit, profusion, enough and to spare.
– ANTONYMS: dearth.

pleurisy n. inflammation of the membrane round the lungs.

pliable adj. **1** easily bent. **2** easily influenced.
▷ SYNONYMS: **1 flexible**, pliant, bendable, supple, workable, plastic; informal bendy. **2 malleable**, impressionable, flexible, adaptable, biddable, pliant, tractable, suggestible, persuadable.
– ANTONYMS: rigid.
■ **pliability** n.

pliant adj. pliable.
■ **pliancy** n.

pliers pl. n. pincers with flat surfaces for gripping small objects.

plight n. a dangerous or difficult situation.
▷ SYNONYMS: **predicament**, difficult situation, dire straits, trouble, difficulty, bind; informal tight corner, tight spot, hole, pickle, jam, fix.
• v. (**plight your troth**) make a solemn promise to marry.

plimsoll n. Brit. a light rubber-soled canvas shoe.

Plimsoll line n. a mark on a ship's side showing the legal water level when loaded.

plinth n. a slab forming the base of a column, statue, etc.

plod v. (**plodding**, **plodded**) **1** walk with heavy slow steps. **2** work slowly and steadily.
▷ SYNONYMS: **trudge**, walk heavily, clump, stomp, tramp, lumber, slog.

plonk informal v. set down heavily or carelessly.
• n. Brit. cheap wine.

plop n. a sound like that of a small object dropping into water.
• v. (**plopping**, **plopped**) fall with a plop.

plot n. **1** a secret plan to do something illegal or harmful. **2** the story in a play, novel, or film. **3** a small piece of land.
▷ SYNONYMS: **1 conspiracy**, intrigue, stratagem, plan, machinations. **2 storyline**, story, scenario, action, thread, narrative. **3 piece of ground**, patch, area, tract, acreage; Brit. allotment; N. Amer. lot, plat.
• v. (**plotting**, **plotted**) **1** secretly plan an illegal or harmful act. **2** mark a route or position on a map or graph.
▷ SYNONYMS: **1 plan**, scheme, arrange, organize, contrive. **2 conspire**, scheme, intrigue, connive. **3 mark**, chart, map.

■ **plotter** n.

plough (US **plow**) n. a large implement for turning over and cutting furrows in soil.
• v. **1** turn soil with a plough. **2** progress with difficulty.
▷ SYNONYMS: **1** till, furrow, harrow, cultivate, work. **2** crash, smash, career, plunge, bulldoze, hurtle, cannon.

ploy n. a cunning act.
▷ SYNONYMS: **ruse**, tactic, move, device, stratagem, scheme, trick, gambit, plan, manoeuvre, dodge, subterfuge; Brit. informal wheeze.

pluck v. **1** take hold of and quickly remove from its place. **2** pull out or at. **3** pull the feathers from a bird's carcass.
▷ SYNONYMS: **1** remove, pick, pull, extract. **2** pull, tug, clutch, snatch, grab, catch, tweak, jerk; informal yank. **3** strum, pick, thrum, twang.
• n. courage.
▷ SYNONYMS: **courage**, bravery, nerve, daring, spirit, grit; informal guts; Brit. informal bottle; N. Amer. informal moxie.

plucky adj. (**pluckier**, **pluckiest**) determined and brave.
■ **pluckily** adv.

plug n. **1** a piece of solid material tightly blocking a hole. **2** a device with metal pins that fit into holes in a socket to make an electrical connection.
▷ SYNONYMS: **1** stopper, bung, cork; N. Amer. stopple. **2** advertisement, promotion, commercial, recommendation, mention, good word; informal hype, push, puff.
• v. (**plugging**, **plugged**) **1** block a hole. **2** (**plug in**) connect an electrical appliance to the mains by means of a socket. **3** informal promote something by mentioning it publicly. **4** (**plug away**) informal work steadily.
▷ SYNONYMS: **1** stop, seal, close, block, fill. **2** publicize, promote, advertise, mention, bang the drum for, draw attention to; informal hype, push.

plum n. **1** an oval, usu. reddish-purple fruit. **2** a reddish-purple colour.
• adj. informal highly desirable.

plumage n. a bird's feathers.

plumb v. **1** measure or test with a plumb line. **2** explore or experience fully. **3** Brit. connect an appliance etc. to water and drainage pipes.
▷ SYNONYMS: **explore**, probe, delve into, search, examine, investigate, fathom, penetrate, understand.
• n. a weight attached to a plumb line.
• adv. informal exactly.

▷ SYNONYMS: **right**, exactly, precisely, directly, dead, straight; informal slap bang.
□ **plumb line** a cord with a weight attached to it, used to find the depth of water or test whether an upright surface is vertical.

plumber n. a person who fits and repairs plumbing.

plumbing n. the system of pipes, tanks, and fittings for the water supply, heating, and sanitation in a building.

plume n. **1** a long, soft feather. **2** a long cloud of smoke.
■ **plumed** adj.

plummet v. (**plummeting**, **plummeted**) fall steeply or rapidly.
▷ SYNONYMS: **plunge**, dive, drop, fall, hurtle, nosedive, tumble.
– ANTONYMS: soar.

plump adj. **1** full and rounded in shape. **2** rather fat.
▷ SYNONYMS: **fat**, chubby, rotund, ample, round, stout, portly, overweight; informal tubby, roly-poly, pudgy; Brit. informal podgy; N. Amer. informal zaftig, corn-fed.
– ANTONYMS: thin.
• v. **1** (**plump up**) make or become plump. **2** sit or set down heavily. **3** (**plump for**) decide on.
■ **plumpness** n.

plunder v. enter a place by force and steal goods from it.
▷ SYNONYMS: **1** pillage, loot, rob, raid, ransack, rifle, strip, sack. **2** steal, seize, thieve, pilfer, embezzle.
• n. **1** the act of plundering. **2** goods obtained by plundering.
▷ SYNONYMS: **booty**, loot, stolen goods, spoils, ill-gotten gains; informal swag.

plunge v. **1** fall suddenly. **2** jump or dive quickly. **3** push or thrust quickly.
▷ SYNONYMS: **1** dive, jump, throw yourself, immerse yourself. **2** plummet, nosedive, drop, fall, tumble, descend. **3** charge, hurtle, career, plough, tear; N. Amer. informal barrel. **4** thrust, stab, sink, stick, ram, drive, push, shove, force.
• n. an act of plunging.

plunger n. a device that works with a plunging movement.

pluperfect adj. (of a tense) referring to an action completed earlier than some past point of time.

plural adj. **1** more than one in number. **2** (of a word or form) referring to more than one.
• n. a plural word or form.
■ **plurality** n.

p

plus prep. with the addition of.
▷ SYNONYMS: **as well as**, together with, along with, in addition to, and, added to, not to mention.
– ANTONYMS: minus.
• adj. **1** more than the amount indicated. **2** above zero.
• n. **1** the symbol +. **2** informal an advantage.
▷ SYNONYMS: **advantage**, good point, asset, pro, benefit, bonus, attraction; informal perk.
– ANTONYMS: disadvantage.
• conj. also.

plush n. fabric with a long, soft nap.
• adj. informal expensively luxurious.
▷ SYNONYMS: **luxurious**, luxury, deluxe, sumptuous, opulent, magnificent, rich, expensive, fancy; Brit. upmarket; informal posh, classy; Brit. informal swish; N. Amer. informal swank.
– ANTONYMS: austere.

plutocracy n. (pl. plutocracies) government by the wealthy.
■ plutocrat n.

plutonium n. a radioactive metallic element.

ply n. (pl. plies) a layer or strand of a material.
• v. (plying, plied) **1** work steadily with a tool or at a job. **2** (of a ship etc.) travel regularly over a route. **3** (ply with) keep presenting with food etc.
▷ SYNONYMS: **1** engage in, carry on, pursue, conduct, practise. **2** travel, shuttle, go back and forth. **3** she plied me with scones: **provide**, supply, shower. **4** he plied her with questions: **bombard**, assail, pester, plague, harass; informal hassle.
□ plywood board made of layers of wood glued together.

PM abbrev. Prime Minister.

p.m. abbrev. after noon.

PMT abbrev. premenstrual tension.

pneumatic /nyoo-**mat**-ik/ adj. containing or operated by air or gas under pressure.

pneumonia /nyoo-**moh**-ni-uh/ n. inflammation of one or both lungs.

PO abbrev. Post Office.

poach v. **1** simmer in a small amount of liquid. **2** take game or fish illegally. **3** unfairly entice customers, workers, etc. away from someone else.
■ poacher n.

pocket n. **1** a small bag or pouch sewn into or on clothing for carrying things. **2** an isolated group or area. **3** an opening at the corner or side of a billiard table.
• v. (pocketing, pocketed) **1** put into your pocket. **2** take dishonestly.
□ **out of pocket** having made a loss.

pocket money Brit. a small regular allowance given to children by their parents.

pockmarked adj. (of the skin) marked by hollow scars.

pod n. a long narrow seed case.
▷ SYNONYMS: **shell**, husk, hull, case; N. Amer. shuck.

podcast n. a digital recording of a radio broadcast, made available on the Internet for downloading to a personal audio player.
■ podcasting n.

podgy adj. Brit. informal rather fat.

podium n. (pl. podiums or podia) a small platform.
▷ SYNONYMS: **platform**, stage, dais, rostrum, stand.

poem n. a piece of imaginative writing in verse.
▷ SYNONYMS: **verse**, rhyme, lyric, piece of poetry.

poet n. a person who writes poems.
□ **Poet Laureate** a poet appointed by the British monarch to write poems for important occasions.

poetic (or **poetical**) adj. of or like poetry.
▷ SYNONYMS: **expressive**, figurative, symbolic, flowery, artistic, imaginative, creative.
■ poetically adv.

poetry n. **1** poems as a whole or as a form of literature. **2** a quality of beauty or emotional power.
▷ SYNONYMS: **poems**, verse, versification, rhyme.

po-faced adj. informal serious and disapproving.

pogrom n. an organized massacre of an ethnic group.

poignant adj. arousing a sense of sadness or regret.
▷ SYNONYMS: **touching**, moving, sad, affecting, pitiful, pathetic, plaintive.
■ poignancy n. poignantly adv.

poinsettia n. a plant with large scarlet bracts.

point n. **1** a tapered, sharp end. **2** a particular place or moment. **3** an item, detail, or idea. **4** the advantage or purpose of something. **5** a feature or quality. **6** a unit of scoring, value, or measurement. **7** a dot. **8** a promontory. **9** (points) Brit. a movable pair of rails at a junction of two railway lines. **10** Brit. an electrical socket.
▷ SYNONYMS: **1** tip, end, extremity,

prong, spike, tine, nib, barb. **2 place**, position, location, site, spot, locus. **3 time**, stage, juncture, period, phase. **4 detail**, item, fact, argument, consideration, factor, element, subject, issue, topic, question, matter. **5 attribute**, characteristic, feature, trait, quality, property, aspect, side. **6 purpose**, aim, object, objective, goal, intention, use, sense, value, advantage. **7 pinpoint**, dot, spot, speck. **8 level**, degree, stage, pitch, extent.

• v. **1** direct someone's attention by extending the finger. **2** aim or face in a particular direction. **3** (**point out**) make someone aware of. **4** fill the joints of brickwork with mortar.

▷ SYNONYMS: **aim**, direct, level, train, focus.

□ **beside the point** irrelevant. **point-blank 1** at very close range. **2** in a blunt and very direct way. **point of view** an attitude or opinion. **to the point** relevant.

pointed adj. **1** tapering to a point. **2** (of a remark or look) expressing a clear message.

▷ SYNONYMS: **1 sharp**, spiky, spiked, tapering, barbed. **2 cutting**, biting, incisive, trenchant, acerbic, caustic, scathing, venomous, sarcastic.

■ **pointedly** adv.

pointer n. **1** a thing that points to something. **2** a dog that on scenting game stands rigid looking towards it.

▷ SYNONYMS: **1 indicator**, needle, arrow, hand. **2 indication**, indicator, clue, hint, sign, signal, evidence. **3 tip**, hint, suggestion, guideline, recommendation.

pointing n. mortar used to fill the joints of brickwork.

pointless adj. having little or no purpose.

▷ SYNONYMS: **senseless**, futile, useless, hopeless, unavailing, unproductive, aimless, idle, worthless, valueless.

− ANTONYMS: valuable.

■ **pointlessly** adv.

poise n. **1** a graceful way of holding the body. **2** a calm and confident manner.

▷ SYNONYMS: **1 grace**, gracefulness, elegance, balance, control. **2 composure**, equanimity, self-possession, aplomb, self-assurance, self-control, sangfroid, dignity, presence of mind; informal cool.

• v. be or cause to be balanced.

poised adj. **1** calm and self-assured. **2** prepared to do something.

▷ SYNONYMS: **1 calm**, cool, self-possessed, self-assured, self-controlled, composed, collected, serene, tranquil, relaxed; informal unflappable, together. **2 prepared**, ready, braced, geared up, all set, standing by.

poison n. a substance that causes death or injury when swallowed or absorbed.

▷ SYNONYMS: **toxin**, venom.

• v. **1** harm or kill with poison. **2** put poison on or in. **3** have a harmful effect on.

▷ SYNONYMS: **pollute**, contaminate, infect, taint, spoil.

■ **poisoner** n.

> **WORD LINKS**
> **toxicology** the branch of science concerned with poisons

poisonous adj. **1** causing death or injury when swallowed or absorbed. **2** very unpleasant or spiteful.

▷ SYNONYMS: **1 toxic**, noxious, deadly, fatal, lethal, mortal; venomous. **2 malicious**, malevolent, hostile, spiteful, bitter, venomous, malign.

− ANTONYMS: harmless.

poke v. **1** push a finger or pointed object into. **2** search or pry. **3** push or stick out.

▷ SYNONYMS: **1 prod**, jab, dig, elbow, nudge, shove, jolt, stab, stick. **2** *leave the cable poking out*: **stick out**, jut out, protrude, project, extend.

• n. an act of poking.

▷ SYNONYMS: **prod**, jab, dig, elbow, nudge.

poker n. **1** a metal rod for prodding an open fire. **2** a gambling card game.

□ **poker face** a blank expression.

poky adj. (**pokier**, **pokiest**) small and cramped.

▷ SYNONYMS: **small**, little, tiny, cramped, confined, restricted, boxy.

− ANTONYMS: spacious.

polar adj. **1** of or near the North or South Pole. **2** having an electrical or magnetic field. **3** completely opposite.

□ **polar bear** a large white Arctic bear.

■ **polarity** n.

polarize (or **-ise**) v. **1** divide into two groups with completely opposite views. **2** restrict the vibrations of a light wave to one direction. **3** give magnetic or electric polarity to.

■ **polarization** n.

Polaroid n. trademark **1** a material that polarizes light passing through it, used in sunglasses. **2** a camera that produces a finished print rapidly after each exposure.

p

Pole n. a person from Poland.

pole n. **1** a long, thin rod or post.
2 either of the two points (**North Pole**
or **South Pole**) at opposite ends of
the earth's axis. **3** either of the two
opposite points of a magnet. **4** the
positive or negative terminal of an
electric cell or battery.

▷ SYNONYMS: **post**, pillar, stanchion,
stake, support, prop, stick, paling,
staff.

• v. push a boat along with a pole.
□ **poles apart** having nothing in
common. **pole position** the most
favourable starting position in a motor
race. **Pole Star** a star located in the
part of the sky above the North Pole.

polecat n. **1** a dark brown weasel-like
animal. **2** US a skunk.

polemic n. a strong verbal or written
attack.
■ **polemical** adj.

polenta n. maize flour or a dough
made from this.

police n. an official body of people
employed by a state to prevent crime
and keep public order.

▷ SYNONYMS: **police force**, police
officers, policemen, policewomen;
Brit. constabulary; informal the cops,
the fuzz, the law, the boys in blue;
Brit. informal the Old Bill; N. Amer. informal
the heat.

• v. keep law and order in an area.

▷ SYNONYMS: **1 guard**, watch over,
protect, defend, patrol. **2 enforce**,
regulate, oversee, supervise, monitor,
observe, check.
□ **police state** a country in which
political police secretly watch and
control citizens' activities.
■ **policeman** n. **policewoman** n.

policy n. (pl. **policies**) **1** a course of
action adopted or proposed. **2** a
contract of insurance.

▷ SYNONYMS: **plans**, approach, code,
system, guidelines, theory, line,
position, stance.

polio (or **poliomyelitis**) n. an
infectious disease causing temporary
or permanent paralysis.

Polish n. the language of Poland.
• adj. of Poland.

polish v. **1** make smooth and shiny
by rubbing. **2** refine or improve.
3 (**polish off**) finish quickly.

▷ SYNONYMS: **1 shine**, wax, buff, rub,
gloss, burnish. **2** polish up your essay:
perfect, refine, improve, hone,
enhance, brush up, revise, edit,
correct, rewrite, go over, touch up.
3 (**polished**) a polished performance:

expert, accomplished, masterly,
skilful, adept, adroit, dexterous,
consummate, superlative, superb.
• n. **1** a substance used to polish
something. **2** an act of polishing.
3 shiny appearance. **4** refinement or
elegance.

▷ SYNONYMS: **sophistication**, refinement,
urbanity, suaveness, elegance, style,
grace, finesse; informal class.
■ **polisher** n.

polite adj. **1** respectful and
considerate. **2** civilized or well bred.

▷ SYNONYMS: **1 well mannered**, civil,
courteous, respectful, well behaved,
well bred, gentlemanly, ladylike,
genteel, gracious, tactful, diplomatic. **2 civilized**, refined, cultured,
sophisticated, urbane.
– ANTONYMS: rude.
■ **politely** adv. **politeness** n.

politic adj. sensible and wise in the
circumstances.

▷ SYNONYMS: **wise**, prudent, sensible,
shrewd, astute, judicious, expedient,
advantageous, beneficial, profitable.
– ANTONYMS: unwise.

political adj. **1** of the government
or public affairs of a country. **2** of
politics.

▷ SYNONYMS: **governmental**, government, constitutional, ministerial,
parliamentary, diplomatic, legislative,
administrative.
□ **political correctness** the conscious
avoidance of language or behaviour
that could offend certain groups.
■ **politically** adv.

politician n. an elected political
representative.

▷ SYNONYMS: **legislator**, Member of
Parliament, MP, representative,
minister, statesman, stateswoman,
senator, congressman, congress-
woman; informal politico.

politics n. **1** the activities concerned
with governing a country or area. **2** a
set of political beliefs.

polity n. (pl. **polities**) **1** a form of
government. **2** a society.

polka n. a lively dance for couples.

poll n. **1** the process of voting in an
election. **2** a record of the number of
votes cast.

▷ SYNONYMS: **1 vote**, ballot, show of
hands, referendum, plebiscite, election. **2 survey**, opinion poll, market
research, census.

• v. **1** record the opinion or vote of.
2 receive a specified number of votes.

▷ SYNONYMS: **1 canvass**, survey, ask, question, interview, ballot. **2 get**, gain,

p

register, record, return.

□ **poll tax** a tax paid at the same rate by every adult.

pollard v. cut off the top and branches of a tree to encourage new growth.

pollen n. a powder produced by the male part of a flower, containing the fertilizing agent.

□ **pollen count** a measure of the amount of pollen in the air.

pollinate v. fertilize with pollen.
■ **pollination** n.

pollster n. a person who carries out opinion polls.

pollute v. make dirty with harmful or poisonous substances.

▷ SYNONYMS: **contaminate**, taint, poison, foul, dirty, soil, infect.
– ANTONYMS: purify.
■ **pollutant** n. **pollution** n.

polo n. a game like hockey, played on horseback.

□ **polo neck** Brit. a high turned-over collar on a sweater.

polonium n. a radioactive metallic element.

poltergeist n. a ghost said to throw objects about.

polyandry n. the practice of having more than one husband at the same time.

polychromatic (or **polychrome**) adj. multicoloured.

polyester n. a synthetic fibre or resin.

polyethylene n. polythene.

polygamy n. the practice of having more than one wife or husband at the same time.
■ **polygamist** n. **polygamous** adj.

polyglot adj. knowing or using several languages.

polygon n. a figure with three or more straight sides.
■ **polygonal** adj.

polygraph n. a lie detector.

polyhedron n. (pl. **polyhedra** or **polyhedrons**) a solid with many sides.
■ **polyhedral** adj.

polymath n. a person with knowledge of many subjects.

polymer n. a substance with a molecular structure formed from many identical small molecules bonded together.

polymerize (or **-ise**) v. combine to form a polymer.

polyp n. **1** a simple sea animal which remains fixed in the same place, such as coral. **2** a small lump projecting from a mucous membrane.

polyphony n. the combination of a

number of harmonizing melodies.
■ **polyphonic** adj.

polystyrene n. a light synthetic material, used esp. as packaging.

polytechnic n. hist. a college offering courses up to degree level (now called a 'university').

polytheism n. the belief in more than one god.
■ **polytheistic** adj.

polythene n. Brit. a tough, light, flexible plastic.

polyunsaturated adj. (of a fat) not associated with the formation of cholesterol in the blood.

polyurethane n. a synthetic resin used in paints and varnishes.

Pom n. Austral./NZ informal a British person.
■ **Pommy** adj. & n.

pomander n. a ball of scented substances.

pomegranate n. a round tropical fruit with many seeds in red flesh.

pommel /pum-m'l/ n. **1** the upward projecting front part of a saddle. **2** a knob on the hilt of a sword.

pomp n. splendid display and ceremony.

▷ SYNONYMS: **ceremony**, solemnity, ritual, display, spectacle, pageantry, show, ostentation, splendour, grandeur, magnificence, majesty, stateliness, glory; informal razzmatazz.

pompom n. a small woollen ball sewn on a garment for decoration.

pompous adj. ostentatiously or foolishly self-important.

▷ SYNONYMS: **self-important**, overbearing, sententious, grandiose, affected, pretentious, puffed up, haughty, proud, conceited, super-cilious, condescending, patronizing.
■ **pomposity** n. **pompously** adv.

poncho n. (pl. **ponchos**) a garment made of a thick piece of cloth with a slit for the head.

pond n. a small area of still water.

ponder v. consider carefully.

▷ SYNONYMS: **think about**, contemplate, consider, review, reflect on, mull over, meditate on, muse on, dwell on.

ponderous adj. moving slowly and heavily.
■ **ponderously** adv.

pong Brit. informal n. a strong, unpleasant smell.
• v. smell strongly and unpleasantly.

pontiff n. the Pope.

pontificate v. speak pompously and at length.

▷ SYNONYMS: **hold forth**, expound,

declaim, preach, lay down the law, sound off, lecture; informal **mouth off**.

pontoon n. **1** Brit. a card game. **2** a flat-bottomed boat supporting a temporary bridge. **3** a bridge supported by pontoons.

pony n. (pl. **ponies**) a horse of a small breed.
□ **ponytail** a hairstyle in which the hair is drawn back and tied at the back of the head.

poodle n. a dog with a curly coat.

pool n. **1** a small area of still water. **2** (or **swimming pool**) an artificial pool for swimming in. **3** a shallow patch of liquid on a surface. **4** a shared fund or supply. **5** a game resembling snooker. **6** (**the pools**) a form of gambling on the results of football matches.
▷ SYNONYMS: **1** pond, lake; puddle literary mere. **2** supply, reserve, fund, store, bank, stock, cache; kitty, pot.
• v. put into a common fund; share.
▷ SYNONYMS: **combine**, share, group, join, unite, merge.

poop n. a raised deck at the back of a ship.

poor adj. **1** having little money. **2** of a low standard or quality. **3** deserving sympathy.
▷ SYNONYMS: **1 poverty-stricken**, penniless, impoverished, impecunious, needy, destitute; Brit. on the breadline; informal hard up, strapped, on your uppers; formal penurious. **2 substandard**, bad, deficient, defective, faulty, imperfect, inferior, unsatisfactory, shoddy, crude, inadequate, unacceptable; informal crummy, rotten; Brit. informal duff. **3 meagre**, scanty, scant, paltry, reduced, modest, sparse, spare, deficient, insubstantial, skimpy, lean; informal measly, stingy. **4 unfortunate**, unlucky, unhappy, hapless, wretched, luckless, ill-fated, ill-starred.
– ANTONYMS: rich.

poorly adv. badly.
▷ SYNONYMS: **badly**, imperfectly, incompetently, crudely, shoddily, inadequately.
• adj. unwell.
▷ SYNONYMS: **ill**, unwell, ailing, indisposed, out of sorts, under par, peaky; sick, nauseous, queasy; Brit. off colour; informal under the weather, rough; Brit. informal ropy; Scottish informal wabbit; Austral./NZ informal crook.

pop v. (**popping**, **popped**) **1** make a sudden short explosive sound. **2** go or put somewhere quickly.

▷ SYNONYMS: **1 go bang**, go off, crack, snap, burst, explode. **2 go**; informal tootle, whip; Brit. informal nip. **3 put**, place, slip, throw, slide, stick, set, lay, position.
• n. **1** a sudden short explosive sound. **2** informal a soft fizzy drink. **3** (or **pop music**) modern popular music with a strong melody and beat.
▷ SYNONYMS: **bang**, crack, snap, explosion, report.
• adj. **1** of pop music. **2** made intellectually accessible to the general public.
□ **popcorn** maize kernels heated until they burst open.

pope n. the head of the Roman Catholic Church.

poplar n. a tall, slender tree.

poplin n. a cotton fabric.

poppadom n. a thin circular piece of Indian bread fried until crisp.

popper n. Brit. informal a press stud.

poppy n. a plant with large bright flowers.

poppycock n. informal nonsense.

populace n. the general public.
▷ SYNONYMS: **population**, inhabitants, residents, community, country, general public, people, nation, common people, masses, multitude, rank and file; Brit. informal Joe Public; derogatory hoi polloi, common herd, rabble, riff-raff.

popular adj. **1** liked by many people. **2** of or for the general public.
▷ SYNONYMS: **1 well liked**, sought-after, in demand, commercial, marketable, fashionable, in vogue, all the rage, hot; informal in, cool, big. **2 non-specialist**, non-technical, amateur, lay person's, general, middle-of-the-road, accessible, simplified, understandable, mass-market. **3 widespread**, general, common, current, prevailing, standard, ordinary, conventional.
■ **popularity** n. **popularly** adv.

popularize (or **-ise**) v. **1** make popular. **2** make accessible or interesting to the general public.

populate v. form the population of.
▷ SYNONYMS: **inhabit**, occupy, people, settle, colonize.

population n. the inhabitants of a place.
▷ SYNONYMS: **inhabitants**, residents, people, citizens, public, community, populace, society, occupants.

> **WORD LINKS**
> **demography** the statistical study of populations

populous adj. densely populated.

porcelain n. fine china.

porch n. a covered shelter over the entrance of a building.

porcine adj. of or like a pig.

porcupine n. an animal covered with long protective spines.

pore n. a tiny opening in the skin or another surface.
• v. (**pore over**) study closely.

pork n. the flesh of a pig as food.

porn n. informal pornography.

pornography n. pictures, writing, or films intended to arouse sexual excitement.
■ **pornographer** n. **pornographic** adj.

porous adj. having tiny spaces through which liquid or air may pass.
▷ SYNONYMS: **permeable**, penetrable, absorbent, spongy.
– ANTONYMS: impermeable.
■ **porosity** n.

porpoise n. a small whale.

porridge n. a dish of oats or oatmeal boiled with water or milk.

port n. **1** a town or city with a harbour. **2** a harbour. **3** an opening for boarding or loading a ship or for firing a gun from a tank etc. **4** a socket in a computer network into which a device can be plugged. **5** a strong, sweet dark red wine. **6** the left-hand side of a ship or aircraft.
▷ SYNONYMS: **harbour**, docks, marina, haven, seaport.
□ **porthole** a small window in the side of a ship or aircraft.

portable adj. able to be carried.
▷ SYNONYMS: **transportable**, movable, mobile, wireless, lightweight, compact, handy, convenient.
■ **portability** n.

portal n. a large impressive doorway or gate.

portcullis n. a strong grating lowered to block a castle's gateway.

portend v. be a portent of.
▷ SYNONYMS: **presage**, augur, foreshadow, foretell, prophesy, be a sign, warn, be an omen, indicate, herald, signal, bode, promise, threaten, signify, spell, denote.

portent n. a sign or warning of a future event.
■ **portentous** adj.

porter n. **1** a person employed to carry luggage or goods or move hospital equipment or patients. **2** Brit. a doorkeeper of a large building.
▷ SYNONYMS: **doorman**, doorkeeper, commissionaire, concierge.

portfolio n. (pl. **portfolios**) **1** a thin, flat case for drawings, maps, etc. **2** a set of investments. **3** a government minister's area of responsibility.

portico n. (pl. **porticoes** or **porticos**) a roof supported by columns forming a porch.

portion n. **1** a part or share. **2** an amount of food for one person.
▷ SYNONYMS: **1 part**, piece, bit, section, segment. **2 share**, quota, ration, allocation, tranche; Brit. informal whack. **3 helping**, serving, plateful, slice, piece.
• v. divide into portions and share out.

portly adj. rather fat.

portmanteau /port-man-toh/ n. (pl. **portmanteaus** or **portmanteaux**) a large travelling bag.

portrait n. **1** a picture of a person. **2** a description.
▷ SYNONYMS: **1 picture**, likeness, painting, drawing, photograph, image. **2 description**, portrayal, representation, depiction, impression, account, profile.
■ **portraiture** n.

portray v. show or describe in a work of art or literature.
▷ SYNONYMS: **1 describe**, depict, characterize, represent, delineate, render, show, illustrate, picture, paint, draw, sketch, picture. **2** in his next film, he portrays a spy: **play**, act the part of, take the role of, represent, appear as.

portrayal n. the act of portraying.
▷ SYNONYMS: **description**, representation, characterization, depiction, delineation.

Portuguese n. (pl. **Portuguese**) **1** a person from Portugal. **2** the language of Portugal and Brazil.
• adj. of Portugal.
□ **Portuguese man-of-war** a sea animal like a jellyfish.

pose v. **1** present or be a problem, question, etc. **2** sit or stand in a particular position to be photographed, painted, etc. **3** (**pose as**) pretend to be.
▷ SYNONYMS: **1 constitute**, present, offer. **2 raise**, ask, put, submit, advance, propose. **3 posture**, attitudinize, put on airs; informal show off, ponce about.
• n. **1** a position adopted to be photographed, painted, etc. **2** a way of behaving intended to impress or mislead.
▷ SYNONYMS: **1 posture**, position, stance, attitude. **2 act**, affectation, show, display, front, airs.

p

poser n. **1** a poseur. **2** a puzzling question.
▷ SYNONYMS: **1 exhibitionist**, poseur; informal show-off, pseud. **2 difficult question**, problem, puzzle, mystery, riddle, conundrum; informal dilemma.

poseur n. a person who behaves in a way intended to impress.

posh adj. informal **1** very elegant or luxurious. **2** upper-class.
▷ SYNONYMS: **1 smart**, stylish, fancy, high-class, fashionable, chic, luxurious, luxury, exclusive; Brit. upmarket; informal classy, plush, flash; Brit. informal swish; N. Amer. informal swank, tony. **2 upper-class**, aristocratic.

posit v. (**positing**, **posited**) put forward as a basis for argument.

position n. **1** a place where someone or something is or should be. **2** a way in which someone or something is placed or arranged. **3** a situation. **4** a job. **5** a person's status. **6** a point of view.
▷ SYNONYMS: **1 location**, place, situation, spot, site, locality, setting, area, whereabouts, bearings. **2 posture**, stance, attitude, pose. **3 situation**, state, condition, circumstances, predicament, plight. **4 status**, place, level, rank, standing, stature, prestige, reputation. **5 job**, post, situation, appointment, opening, vacancy, placement. **6 viewpoint**, opinion, outlook, attitude, stand, standpoint, stance, perspective, thinking, policy, feelings.
• v. place or arrange.
▷ SYNONYMS: **put**, place, locate, situate, set, site, stand, station, plant, stick; informal plonk, park.
■ **positional** adj.

positive adj. **1** expressing agreement or permission. **2** hopeful or favourable. **3** not allowing doubt; certain. **4** (of a test) showing the presence of something. **5** (of a quantity) greater than zero. **6** of the kind of electric charge opposite to that carried by electrons.
▷ SYNONYMS: **1 affirmative**, good, enthusiastic, supportive, constructive, useful, helpful. **2 optimistic**, hopeful, confident, cheerful, sanguine, buoyant; informal upbeat. **3** positive economic signs: **good**, promising, favourable, encouraging, heartening, propitious, auspicious. **4 definite**, certain, reliable, concrete, tangible, clear-cut, explicit, firm, decisive, real, actual. **5 convinced**, sure, confident, satisfied.
− ANTONYMS: negative, pessimistic.

• n. a positive quality.
□ **positive discrimination** Brit. the policy of employing members of groups which suffer discrimination.
■ **positively** adv. **positivity** n.

positron n. a particle with the same mass as an electron but a positive charge.

posse /poss-i/ n. **1** US hist. a body of men summoned by a sheriff to enforce the law. **2** informal a group or gang.

possess v. **1** have or own. **2** dominate or have complete power over.
▷ SYNONYMS: **1 own**, have to your name, be in possession of. **2 have**, be blessed with, be endowed with, enjoy, boast. **3 take control of**, take over, bewitch, enchant, enslave.
■ **possessor** n.

possession n. **1** the state of possessing something. **2** a thing owned.
▷ SYNONYMS: **1 ownership**, control, hands, keeping, care, custody, charge. **2** she packed her possessions: **belongings**, things, property, worldly goods, goods and chattels, personal effects, stuff, bits and pieces; informal gear, junk; Brit. informal clobber.

possessive adj. **1** demanding someone's total attention and love. **2** unwilling to share your possessions. **3** Grammar expressing possession.
▷ SYNONYMS: **proprietorial**, overprotective, controlling, dominating, jealous, clingy.
□ **possessive pronoun** a pronoun showing possession (e.g. *mine*).
■ **possessively** adv.

possibility n. (pl. **possibilities**) **1** a thing that is possible. **2** the state of being possible. **3** a thing that may be chosen or done.
▷ SYNONYMS: **1** there's no possibility of a full recovery: **chance**, likelihood, probability, potentiality, hope; risk, hazard, danger, fear. **2** leaving early is one possibility: **option**, alternative, choice, course of action, solution. **3** he has possibilities as a gymnast: **potential**, promise, prospects.

possible adj. capable of existing, happening, or being done.
▷ SYNONYMS: **1** it's not possible to check the figures: **feasible**, practicable, viable, attainable, achievable, workable, within reach; informal doable. **2** a possible reason for his disappearance: **likely**, plausible, imaginable, believable, potential, probable, credible.
− ANTONYMS: impossible, unlikely.

possibly adv. **1** perhaps. **2** in accordance with what is possible.
▷ SYNONYMS: **1 perhaps**, maybe, it is possible, for all you know. **2 conceivably**, under any circumstances, by any means.

possum n. an opossum.

post n. **1** the official service or system for delivering letters and parcels. **2** letters and parcels sent or delivered. **3** an upright piece of timber or metal used as a support or marker. **4** a place where someone is on duty or where an activity is carried out. **5** a job.
▷ SYNONYMS: **1 letters**, correspondence, mail. **2 pole**, stake, upright, shaft, prop, support, picket, strut, pillar, stanchion, baluster. **3 job**, position, appointment, situation, place, vacancy, opening.
• v. **1** send via the postal system. **2** put up a notice. **3** send to a place to take up a job or duty.
▷ SYNONYMS: **1 affix**, attach, fasten, display, pin up, put up, stick up. **2 send**, assign, dispatch, consign. □ **keep posted** keep informed. **postbox** a large public box into which letters are put for sending by post. **postcard** a card for sending a message by post without an envelope. **postcode** Brit. a group of letters and numbers in a postal address to assist the sorting of mail. **postman** (or **postwoman**) Brit. a person employed to deliver or collect post. **postmark** an official mark stamped on a letter or parcel, giving the date of posting. **post office** a building where postal business is carried on.

post- prefix after.

postage n. the charge for sending something by post.

postal adj. of or sent by post.

post-date v. **1** put a date later than the actual one on a cheque etc. **2** occur later than.

poster n. a large picture or notice used for decoration or advertisement.
▷ SYNONYMS: **notice**, placard, bill, sign, advertisement, playbill.

poste restante /pohst ress-tuhnt/ n. Brit. a post office department where letters are kept until collected by the addressee.

posterior adj. at or nearer the back.
• n. a person's bottom.

posterity n. future generations.

postern n. a back or side entrance.

postgraduate n. a person studying for a higher degree.

post-haste adv. with great speed.

posthumous adj. happening, awarded, or published after the person involved has died.
■ **posthumously** adv.

post-mortem n. **1** an examination of a dead body to find out the cause of death. **2** an analysis of an event after it has occurred.

post-natal adj. after childbirth.

postpone v. arrange for something to take place later than originally planned.
▷ SYNONYMS: **put off**, put back, delay, defer, hold over, reschedule, adjourn, shelve; informal put on ice, put on the back burner.
■ **postponement** n.

postprandial adj. after a meal.

postscript n. a remark added at the end of a letter.

postulant n. a candidate wishing to enter a religious order.

postulate v. assume to be true, as a basis for a theory or discussion.
■ **postulation** n.

posture n. the way in which a person holds their body.
▷ SYNONYMS: **1 position**, pose, attitude, stance, carriage, bearing, comportment; Brit. deportment. **2 attitude**, standpoint, point of view, viewpoint, opinion, position, stance.
• v. behave in a way intended to impress or mislead.
▷ SYNONYMS: **pose**, strike an attitude, attitudinize, strut; informal show off.
■ **postural** adj.

posy n. (pl. **posies**) a small bunch of flowers.

pot n. **1** a rounded container for storage or cooking. **2** informal cannabis.
• v. (**potting**, **potted**) **1** plant in a pot. **2** preserve food in a pot. **3** (**potted**) in a short, understandable form. **4** hit a billiard ball into a pocket.
□ **pot belly** a large protruding stomach. **pot luck** a situation of taking a chance that whatever is available will be acceptable. **potsherd** a broken piece of earthenware. **potshot** a shot aimed at random.

potable adj. drinkable.

potash n. a compound of potassium.

potassium n. a soft silvery-white metallic element.

potato n. (pl. **potatoes**) a vegetable with starchy white flesh that grows underground as a tuber.

poteen n. illegally distilled whisky.

potent adj. **1** having great power,

p

influence, or effect. **2** (of a man) able to achieve an erection.
▷ SYNONYMS: **1 powerful**, strong, mighty, formidable, influential, dominant. **2 forceful**, convincing, cogent, compelling, persuasive, powerful, strong.
– ANTONYMS: weak.
■ **potency** n.

potentate n. a monarch or ruler.

potential adj. capable of becoming or developing into something.
▷ SYNONYMS: **possible**, likely, prospective, future, probable.
• n. qualities that may be developed.
▷ SYNONYMS: **possibilities**, potentiality, prospects, promise, capability, capacity.
■ **potentiality** n. **potentially** adv.

pothole n. **1** a deep underground cave. **2** a hole in a road surface.
□ **potholing** Brit. exploring potholes as a sport.

potion n. a drink with healing, magical, or poisonous powers.
▷ SYNONYMS: **concoction**, mixture, brew, elixir, drink, medicine, tonic, philtre.

potpourri /poh-poor-i/ n. (pl. **potpourris**) **1** a scented mixture of dried petals and spices. **2** a mixture.

pottage n. old use soup or stew.

potter v. do minor pleasant tasks in a relaxed way.
▷ SYNONYMS: **amble**, wander, meander, stroll, saunter; informal mosey, tootle, toddle; N. Amer. informal putter.
• n. a person who makes pottery.

pottery n. (pl. **potteries**) **1** articles made of baked clay. **2** the craft of making pottery.
▷ SYNONYMS: **ceramics**, crockery, earthen-ware, terracotta, stoneware, china, porcelain.

potty adj. informal foolish; mad.
• n. (pl. **potties**) a bowl for a child to use as a toilet.

pouch n. **1** a small flexible bag. **2** a pocket of skin in which certain animals carry their young.
▷ SYNONYMS: **bag**, purse, sack, sac, pocket; Scottish sporran.

pouffe n. a large firm cushion used as a seat.

poult n. a young chicken or game bird.

poulterer n. Brit. a person who sells poultry.

poultice n. a moist mass put on the skin to reduce inflammation.

poultry n. chickens, turkeys, ducks, and geese.

pounce v. move suddenly so as to seize or attack.

▷ SYNONYMS: **jump**, spring, leap, dive, lunge, swoop, attack.
• n. an act of pouncing.

pound n. **1** a unit of weight equal to 16 oz avoirdupois (0.454 kg), or 12 oz troy (0.373 kg). **2** the basic unit of money of the UK. **3** a place where stray dogs or illegally parked vehicles are kept until claimed.
▷ SYNONYMS: **enclosure**, compound, pen, yard, corral.
• v. **1** hit heavily again and again. **2** run with heavy steps. **3** beat or throb with a strong regular rhythm. **4** crush to a powder or paste.
▷ SYNONYMS: **1 beat**, strike, hit, batter, thump, pummel, punch, rain blows on, belabour, hammer; informal bash, clobber, wallop. **2 beat against**, crash against, batter, dash against, lash, buffet. **3 bombard**, bomb, shell. **4 crush**, grind, pulverize, mash, pulp. **5 stomp**, stamp, clomp, clump, tramp, lumber. **6 throb**, thump, thud, hammer, pulse, race.

poundage n. Brit. a charge made per pound in weight or value.

pour v. **1** flow or cause to flow. **2** rain heavily. **3** come or go in large numbers.
▷ SYNONYMS: **1 stream**, flow, run, gush, course, jet, spurt, surge, spill. **2 tip**, splash, spill, decant; informal slosh, slop. **3 rain hard**, teem down, pelt down, tip down, rain cats and dogs; informal be chucking it down; Brit. informal bucket down; N. Amer. informal rain pitchforks. **4 crowd**, throng, swarm, stream, flood.

pout v. push out the lips.
• n. a pouting expression.

poverty n. **1** the state of being very poor. **2** lack or scarcity of a quality etc.
▷ SYNONYMS: **1 pennilessness**, desti-tution, penury, impoverishment, neediness, hardship, impecunious-ness, indigence. **2 scarcity**, deficiency, dearth, shortage, paucity, absence, lack, inadequacy.
– ANTONYMS: wealth, abundance.

POW abbrev. prisoner of war.

powder n. **1** a mass of fine dry particles. **2** a cosmetic in this form.
• v. sprinkle or cover with powder.
□ **powder room** a women's toilet.

powdery adj. like or covered with powder.
▷ SYNONYMS: **fine**, dry, fine-grained, dusty, chalky, floury, sandy, crumbly, friable.

power n. **1** the ability to do

something. **2** influence or control.
3 right or authority. **4** a country of international influence and military strength. **5** strength or force.
6 energy produced by mechanical, electrical, or other means. **7** the product of a number multiplied by itself a certain number of times.
▷ SYNONYMS: **1 ability**, capacity, capability, potential, potentiality, faculty. **2 control**, command, authority, dominance, supremacy, ascendancy, mastery, influence, sway, leverage; informal clout, teeth.
3 authority, right, authorization.
4 state, country, nation. **5 strength**, might, force, forcefulness, vigour, energy; Brit. informal welly.
– ANTONYMS: impotence, weakness.
• v. supply with power.
□ **power of attorney** the authority to act for another person in legal or financial matters. **power station** a building where electricity is generated.

> **WORD LINKS**
> **megalomania** an obsession with power

powerful adj. having power.
▷ SYNONYMS: **1 strong**, muscular, muscly, sturdy, strapping, robust, brawny, burly, athletic, manly, well built, solid; informal beefy. **2 intoxicating**, hard, strong, stiff, potent. **3 violent**, forceful, hard, mighty. **4 intense**, keen, fierce, strong, irresistible, overpowering, overwhelming.
5 influential, strong, important, dominant, commanding, formidable.
6 cogent, compelling, convincing, persuasive, forceful, potent.
– ANTONYMS: weak, gentle.
■ **powerfully** adv.

powerless adj. without ability, influence, or power.
▷ SYNONYMS: **impotent**, helpless, ineffectual, ineffective, useless, defenceless, vulnerable.

pp abbrev. **1** (**pp.**) pages. **2** per procurationem (used when signing a letter on someone else's behalf).

PR abbrev. **1** proportional representation. **2** public relations.

practicable adj. able to be done.
▷ SYNONYMS: **realistic**, feasible, possible, viable, reasonable, sensible, workable, achievable; informal doable.
■ **practicability** n.

practical adj. **1** involving the actual doing or use of something rather than theory. **2** likely to be successful or useful. **3** skilled at making or doing

things. **4** almost complete; virtual.
▷ SYNONYMS: **1 empirical**, hands-on, actual. **2 feasible**, practicable, realistic, viable, workable, possible, reasonable, sensible; informal doable.
3 *a practical car, ideal for city use:* **useful**, **functional**, utilitarian, sensible, suitable. **4** *I'm just being practical—we can't afford it:* **realistic**, sensible, down-to-earth, matter-of-fact, businesslike, commonsensical, hard-headed, no-nonsense; informal hard-nosed.
– ANTONYMS: theoretical, impractical.
□ **practical joke** a humorous trick played on someone.
■ **practicality** n.

practically adv. **1** virtually. **2** in a practical way.
▷ SYNONYMS: **almost**, very nearly, virtually, just about, all but, more or less, as good as, to all intents and purposes.

practice n. **1** the action rather than the theory of doing something.
2 the usual way of doing something.
3 the business of a doctor, dentist, or lawyer. **4** the doing of something repeatedly to improve your skill.
▷ SYNONYMS: **1 application**, exercise, use, operation, implementation, execution. **2 custom**, procedure, policy, convention, tradition.
3 training, rehearsal, repetition, preparation, dummy run, run-through; informal dry run. **4 profession**, career, business, work. **5 business**, firm, office, company; informal outfit.

> **USAGE practice** is the spelling for the noun, and in America for the verb as well; **practise** is the British spelling for the verb.

practise (US **practice**) v. **1** do something repeatedly to improve your skill. **2** do regularly. **3** be working in a particular profession.
▷ SYNONYMS: **1 rehearse**, train; run through, go through, work on/at, polish, perfect, refine. **2** *they still practise these rituals today:* **carry out**, perform, observe, follow.

practised (US **practiced**) adj. expert or experienced: *a practised performer.*
▷ SYNONYMS: **expert**, experienced, seasoned, skilled, skilful, accomplished, proficient, talented, able, adept.

practitioner n. a person who practises a profession.

pragmatic adj. dealing with things in a practical and sensible way.

p

▷ SYNONYMS: **practical**, matter-of-fact, sensible, down-to-earth, common-sensical, businesslike, hard-headed, no-nonsense; informal hard-nosed.
– ANTONYMS: impractical.
■ **pragmatically** adv. **pragmatism** n. **pragmatist** n.

prairie n. a large open area of grassland, esp. in North America.
□ **prairie dog** a North American rodent that lives in burrows.

praise v. **1** express approval of or admiration for. **2** express thanks to or respect for God.
▷ SYNONYMS: **commend**, applaud, pay tribute to, speak highly of, compliment, congratulate, sing the praises of, eulogize; informal rave about.
– ANTONYMS: criticize.
• n. the expression of approval or admiration.
▷ SYNONYMS: **approval**, acclaim, admiration, approbation, plaudits, congratulations, commendation, accolade, compliment, a pat on the back, eulogy.
– ANTONYMS: criticism.

praiseworthy adj. deserving praise.
▷ SYNONYMS: **commendable**, admirable, laudable, worthy, meritorious, estimable, excellent, exemplary.

praline n. a sweet substance made from nuts boiled in sugar.

pram n. Brit. a wheeled vehicle for a baby, pushed by a person on foot.

prance v. move with high steps.
▷ SYNONYMS: **cavort**, dance, jig, trip, caper, jump, leap, spring, bound, skip, hop, frisk, romp, frolic.

prang v. Brit. informal crash a vehicle.

prank n. a mischievous act.
▷ SYNONYMS: **practical joke**, trick, escapade, stunt, caper, jape, game, hoax; informal lark, leg-pull.

prankster n. a person fond of playing pranks.

prat n. Brit. informal a stupid person.

prattle v. chatter in a foolish or trivial way.
• n. foolish or trivial talk.

prawn n. an edible shellfish like a large shrimp.

pray v. **1** say a prayer. **2** wish or hope strongly for something.

prayer n. **1** a request for help or expression of thanks made to God or a god. **2** an earnest hope or wish.

pre- prefix before.

preach v. **1** give a religious talk to a group. **2** recommend a course of action. **3** give moral advice in an annoying or self-righteous way.

▷ SYNONYMS: **1** *he preached the gospel of Jesus:* **proclaim**, teach, spread, propagate, expound. **2** *they preach toleration:* **advocate**, recommend, advise, urge, teach, counsel.
■ **preacher** n.

> **WORD LINKS**
> **homiletics** the art of preaching or writing sermons

preamble n. an introduction or opening statement.

prearrange v. arrange beforehand.

precarious adj. **1** likely to tip or fall. **2** unsafe or uncertain.
▷ SYNONYMS: **insecure**, uncertain, unpredictable, risky, hazardous, dangerous, parlous, unsafe, unstable, unsteady, shaky; informal dicey, iffy; Brit. informal dodgy.
– ANTONYMS: safe.
■ **precariously** adv.

precaution n. something done in advance to avoid problems or danger.
▷ SYNONYMS: **safeguard**, preventive measure, safety measure, insurance; informal backstop.
■ **precautionary** adj.

precede v. come, go, or happen before in time or order.
▷ SYNONYMS: **1 go before**, come before, lead up to, pave the way for, herald, introduce, usher in. **2 go ahead of**, go in front of, lead the way.
– ANTONYMS: follow.

precedence n. the state of coming before others in order or importance.
▷ SYNONYMS: **seniority**, superiority, ascendancy, supremacy.

precedent n. a previous case taken as an example to be followed in a similar situation.
▷ SYNONYMS: **model**, exemplar, example, pattern, paradigm, criterion, yardstick, standard.

precept n. a general rule of behaviour.

precinct n. **1** Brit. an area closed to traffic in a town. **2** the area around a place or building, often enclosed by a wall. **3** US each of the electoral or policing districts of a city or town.
▷ SYNONYMS: **district**, zone, sector, quarter, area.

precious adj. **1** having great value. **2** greatly loved or valued. **3** affectedly refined.
▷ SYNONYMS: **1 valuable**, costly, expensive, invaluable, priceless. **2 valued**, cherished, treasured, prized, favourite, dear, beloved, special. **3 affected**, pretentious; informal la-di-da; Brit. informal poncey.

p

precipice n. a very steep rock face or cliff.

precipitate v. **1** cause to happen suddenly or too soon. **2** cause to move suddenly and with force. **3** cause a substance to be deposited in solid form from a solution. **4** cause vapour to condense and fall as rain, snow, etc.
▷ SYNONYMS: **bring about**, bring on, cause, lead to, give rise to, instigate, trigger, spark off, touch off, provoke, hasten, speed up, accelerate.
• adj. rash or hasty.
▷ SYNONYMS: **hasty**, overhasty, rash, hurried, rushed, impetuous, impulsive, precipitous, incautious, imprudent, injudicious, ill-advised, reckless.
• n. a substance precipitated from a solution.

precipitation n. **1** rain, snow, sleet, or hail. **2** the act of precipitating.

precipitous adj. very steep.
▷ SYNONYMS: **1 steep**, sheer, perpendicular, abrupt, sharp, vertical. **2 sudden**, rapid, swift, abrupt, head-long, speedy, quick, fast.

precis /**pray**-si/ n. (pl. **precis**) a summary.
• v. make a precis of.

precise adj. **1** clear and detailed. **2** careful about details and accuracy. **3** particular.
▷ SYNONYMS: **1** *precise instructions:* **exact**, accurate, correct, specific, detailed, explicit. **2** *precise attention to detail:* **meticulous**, scrupulous, punctilious, careful, strict, rigorous **3** *at that precise moment:* **exact**, particular, actual, specific, distinct.
– ANTONYMS: imprecise, inaccurate.
■ **precisely** adv.

precision n. the quality of being precise.
▷ SYNONYMS: **exactness**, accuracy, exactitude, correctness, care, meticulousness, scrupulousness, punctiliousness, rigour.

preclude v. prevent something from happening.
▷ SYNONYMS: **prevent**, rule out, stop, prohibit, debar, bar, hinder, impede, inhibit, exclude.

precocious adj. having developed certain abilities etc. earlier than usual.
■ **precocity** n.

precognition n. foreknowledge by paranormal means.

preconceived adj. (of an idea) formed before having full knowledge or evidence.

preconception n. a preconceived idea.
▷ SYNONYMS: **assumption**, presupposition, presumption, prejudgement, prejudice.

precondition n. a condition that must be fulfilled beforehand.

precursor n. a forerunner.

pre-date v. exist or occur at a date earlier than.

predator n. a predatory animal.

predatory adj. (of an animal) killing others for food.
▷ SYNONYMS: **1 predacious**, carnivorous, hunting. **2 exploitative**, wolfish, rapacious, manipulative.

predecease v. die before another person.

predecessor n. a person who held a job etc. before the current holder.
▷ SYNONYMS: **1 forerunner**, precursor, antecedent. **2 ancestor**, forefather, forebear, antecedent.
– ANTONYMS: successor, descendant.

predestination n. the belief that everything has been decided in advance by God or fate.

predicament n. a difficult situation.
▷ SYNONYMS: **difficulty**, mess, plight, quandary, muddle, dilemma; informal hole, fix, jam, pickle.

predicate n. the part of a sentence or clause containing a verb and stating something about the subject (e.g. *went home* in *we went home*).
■ **predicative** adj.

predict v. state that an event will happen in the future.
▷ SYNONYMS: **forecast**, foretell, foresee, prophesy; project; old use augur.
■ **predictive** adj. **predictor** n.

predictable adj. able to be predicted.
▷ SYNONYMS: **foreseeable**, to be expected, anticipated, likely, fore-seen, unsurprising, reliable; informal inevitable.
■ **predictably** adv.

prediction n. **1** a forecast. **2** the action of predicting.
▷ SYNONYMS: **forecast**, prophecy, prognosis, prognostication; projection.

predilection n. a special liking.

predispose v. make likely to be, do, or think something.

predisposition n. a liability or tendency.
▷ SYNONYMS: **1** *a predisposition to heart disease:* **susceptibility**, proneness, tendency, liability, inclination, vulnerability. **2** *their political predispositions:* **preference**, predilection, inclination,

p

leaning, bent.

predominant adj. **1** present as the main part. **2** having the greatest power.
▷ SYNONYMS: **main**, chief, principal, biggest, primary, prime, central, leading, foremost, key, paramount; informal number-one.
■ **predominance** n. **predominantly** adv. **predominate** v.

pre-eminent adj. better than all others; outstanding.
■ **pre-eminence** n.

pre-empt v. **1** take action to prevent something happening. **2** prevent from saying something by speaking first.
■ **pre-emption** n. **pre-emptive** adj.

preen v. **1** (of a bird) tidy and clean its feathers with its beak. **2** attend to and admire your appearance. **3** (**preen yourself**) feel very self-satisfied.

prefabricated adj. (of a building) made in sections for easy assembly on site.

preface n. an introduction to a book.
▷ SYNONYMS: **introduction**, foreword, preamble, prologue, prelude, front matter; informal intro.
• v. say or do something to introduce a book, speech, etc.
▷ SYNONYMS: **precede**, introduce, begin, open, start.

prefect n. **1** a senior pupil in a school who has some authority over other pupils. **2** an administrative official in certain countries.
■ **prefecture** n.

p

prefer v. (**preferring**, **preferred**) **1** like better than another or others. **2** put forward a formal accusation.
▷ SYNONYMS: **like better**, would rather, would sooner, favour, be more partial to, choose, select, pick, opt for, go for, plump for.

preferable adj. more desirable.
▷ SYNONYMS: **better**, best, more desirable, more suitable, more advantageous, superior, preferred, recommended.
■ **preferably** adv.

preference n. **1** a greater liking for one alternative over another or others. **2** a thing preferred. **3** favour shown to one person over others.
▷ SYNONYMS: **1 liking**, partiality, fondness, taste, inclination, leaning, bent, penchant, predisposition. **2 priority**, favour, precedence, preferential treatment.

preferential adj. favouring a particular person or group.
■ **preferentially** adv.

preferment n. promotion.

prefix n. a letter or group of letters placed at the beginning of a word to alter its meaning.
• v. add a prefix to.

pregnant adj. **1** having a child or young developing in the womb. **2** full of meaning.
▷ SYNONYMS: **1 expecting**, expectant, carrying a child, with child; informal in the family way. **2 meaningful**, significant, suggestive, expressive, charged.
■ **pregnancy** n.

prehensile adj. (of an animal's limb or tail) able to grasp things.

prehistoric adj. of the period before written records.

prejudge v. form a judgement before knowing all the facts.

prejudice n. **1** an opinion not based on reason or experience. **2** dislike or unfair behaviour based on such opinions.
▷ SYNONYMS: **bigotry**, bias, partiality, intolerance, discrimination, unfairness, inequality.
• v. **1** give rise to prejudice in. **2** cause harm to.
▷ SYNONYMS: **1 bias**, influence, sway, predispose, colour. **2 damage**, be detrimental to, be prejudicial to, injure, harm, hurt, spoil, impair, undermine, compromise.

prejudiced adj. having or showing a prejudice.
▷ SYNONYMS: **biased**, bigoted, discriminatory, partisan, intolerant, narrow-minded, unfair, unjust, inequitable.
– ANTONYMS: impartial.

prejudicial adj. harmful to rights etc.

prelate n. a high-ranking member of the clergy.

preliminary adj. happening before or preparing for a main action or event.
▷ SYNONYMS: **preparatory**, introductory, initial, opening, early, exploratory.
– ANTONYMS: final.
• n. (pl. **preliminaries**) a preliminary action or event.
▷ SYNONYMS: **introduction**, preamble, preface, opening remarks, formalities.

prelude n. **1** an action or event acting as an introduction to something more important. **2** an introductory piece of music.
▷ SYNONYMS: **preliminary**, overture, opening, preparation, introduction, lead-in, precursor.

premarital adj. before marriage.

premature adj. occurring or done before the usual or proper time.

▷ SYNONYMS: **1 untimely**, too early, before time, unseasonable. **2 rash**, overhasty, hasty, precipitate, impulsive, impetuous; informal previous.
– ANTONYMS: overdue.
■ **prematurely** adv.

premeditated adj. planned in advance.
■ **premeditation** n.

premenstrual adj. occurring before menstruation.

premier adj. first in importance, order, or position.
▷ SYNONYMS: **leading**, foremost, chief, principal, head, top-ranking, top, prime, primary, first, highest, pre-eminent, senior, outstanding; N. Amer. ranking.
•n. a Prime Minister or other head of government.
▷ SYNONYMS: **head of government**, prime minister, PM, president, chancellor.
■ **premiership** n.

premiere n. the first performance of a play, film, etc.
▷ SYNONYMS: **first performance**, first night, opening night, debut.

premise (also Brit. **premiss**) n. a statement or idea forming the basis for a theory or argument.
▷ SYNONYMS: **proposition**, assumption, hypothesis, thesis, presupposition, supposition, presumption, assertion.

premises pl. n. the building and land occupied by a business.
▷ SYNONYMS: **building**, property, site, office, establishment.

premium n. (pl. **premiums**) **1** an amount paid for an insurance policy. **2** a sum added to a usual price or charge.
▷ SYNONYMS: **1 payment**, instalment. **2 surcharge**, additional payment, extra.
□ **at a premium 1** scarce and in demand. **2** above the usual price.

premonition n. a feeling that something is about to happen.
■ **premonitory** adj.

preoccupied adj. deep in thought and so not paying attention.
▷ SYNONYMS: **lost in thought**, oblivious, pensive, distracted, absorbed, immersed, engrossed, involved.

preoccupy v. (**preoccupying**, **preoccupied**) fill the mind of completely.
▷ SYNONYMS: **engross**, obsess, absorb, distract, prey on someone's mind, haunt.
■ **preoccupation** n.

preparation n. **1** the act of preparing. **2** something done to prepare for an event or undertaking. **3** a substance prepared for use.
▷ SYNONYMS: **1** preparations for the party: **arrangements**, planning, plans, groundwork, spadework, provision. **2 devising**, drawing up, construction, composition, development. **3 mixture**, compound, concoction, solution, medicine, potion.

preparatory adj. done so as to prepare for something.
□ **preparatory school** Brit. a private school for pupils aged 7 to 13.

prepare v. **1** make ready for use. **2** make or get ready to do or deal with something.
▷ SYNONYMS: **1 get ready**, put together, draw up, produce, arrange, assemble, construct, compose, formulate. **2** I'll go and prepare some lunch: **cook**, make, get, concoct; informal fix, rustle up; Brit. informal knock up. **3** prepare yourself for a shock: **brace**, ready, tense, steel, steady.

prepared adj. **1** ready. **2** willing.
▷ SYNONYMS: **1 ready**, all set, equipped, primed, poised. **2 willing**, ready, disposed, inclined, of a mind, minded.

preponderance n. the state of being greater in number.
■ **preponderant** adj. **preponderate** v.

preposition n. a word used with a noun or pronoun to show place, position, time, or method.
■ **prepositional** adj.

prepossessing adj. attractive.

preposterous adj. completely ridiculous or outrageous.
■ **preposterously** adv.

prepuce /pree-pyooss/ n. the foreskin.

prerequisite n. something that must exist or happen before something else can exist or happen.

prerogative n. a right or privilege.

presage v. be an omen of.
•n. an omen.

Presbyterian adj. of a Protestant Church governed by elders of equal rank.
•n. a member of a Presbyterian Church.
■ **Presbyterianism** n.

presbytery n. (pl. **presbyteries**) **1** an administrative body in a Presbyterian Church. **2** the house of a Roman Catholic priest.

prescient /press-i-uhnt/ adj. having knowledge of events before they happen.
■ **prescience** n.

p

prescribe v. **1** recommend and permit the use of a medicine etc. **2** state officially that something should be done.

▷ SYNONYMS: **1 advise**, recommend, advocate, suggest. **2 stipulate**, lay down, dictate, order, direct, specify, determine.

USAGE Don't confuse **prescribe** with **proscribe**, which means 'forbid'.

prescription n. a doctor's written instruction stating that a patient may be issued with a medicine.

prescriptive adj. stating what should be done.

presence n. **1** the state of being present. **2** an impressive manner or appearance. **3** a person or thing that seems to be present but is not seen.

▷ SYNONYMS: **1 existence**, being. **2 attendance**, appearance. **3 aura**, charisma, personality, magnetism.

– ANTONYMS: absence.
□ **presence of mind** the ability to act quickly and sensibly in a crisis.

present[1] /pre-z'nt/ adj. **1** being or occurring in a particular place. **2** existing or occurring now.

▷ SYNONYMS: **1 in attendance**, here, there, near, nearby, at hand, available. **2 in existence**, detectable, occurring, existing, extant, current.

– ANTONYMS: absent.
• n. the present time.

▷ SYNONYMS: **now**, today, the present time, the here and now, modern times.

– ANTONYMS: past, future.

present[2] v. /pri-zent/ **1** give formally at a ceremony. **2** offer for consideration. **3** introduce and appear in a broadcast. **4** be the cause of a problem. **5** give a particular impression.

▷ SYNONYMS: **1 hand over**, give, confer, bestow, award, grant, accord. **2 submit**, set forth, put forward, offer, tender, table. **3 host**, introduce, compère; N. Amer. informal emcee. **4** they presented him as a criminal: **represent**, describe, portray, depict.
• n. /pre-z'nt/ a gift.

▷ SYNONYMS: **gift**, donation, offering, contribution, gratuity, tip.
■ **presenter** n..

presentable adj. clean or smart enough to be seen in public.

presentation n. the action of presenting something or the way in which it is presented.

▷ SYNONYMS: **1** the presentation of your product is important: **appearance**, arrangement, packaging, layout. **2** he gave a 10-minute presentation: **demonstration**, talk, lecture, address, speech, show, exhibition, display, introduction, launch.

presentiment n. a feeling that something unpleasant is going to happen.

presently adv. **1** soon. **2** now.

▷ SYNONYMS: **1 soon**, shortly, in a little while, at any moment, before long; N. Amer. momentarily. **2 at present**, currently, at the/this moment.

preservative n. a substance used to prevent food or wood from decaying.

preserve v. **1** keep in its original or existing state. **2** keep safe from harm. **3** treat food to prevent it from decaying.

▷ SYNONYMS: **1** records of the past are carefully preserved: **conserve**, protect, maintain, care for, look after. **2** a fight to preserve democracy: **retain**, keep, uphold, sustain, perpetuate, prolong. **3** the aim is to preserve endangered species: **save**, conserve, keep safe, safeguard; defend, shelter, shield.

– ANTONYMS: attack, abandon.
• n. **1** jam. **2** something seen as reserved for a particular person or group.

▷ SYNONYMS: **1** jobs which are no longer the preserve of men: **domain**, area, field, sphere, orbit, realm, province, territory; informal turf, bailiwick. **2** a game preserve: **sanctuary**, reserve, reservation.
■ **preservation** n. **preserver** n.

preside v. be in charge of a meeting, court, etc.

▷ SYNONYMS: **head**, be responsible for, manage, administer, control, direct, chair, conduct, officiate at, lead, govern, rule, command, supervise, oversee.

president n. **1** the elected head of a republic. **2** the head of an organization.
■ **presidency** n. **presidential** adj.

press v. **1** move into contact with something by using steady force. **2** push something to operate a device. **3** apply pressure to something to flatten or shape it. **4** move along by pushing. **5** (**press on/ahead**) continue with something. **6** forcefully put forward an opinion. **7** try hard to persuade. **8** (**be pressed for**) have too little of.

▷ SYNONYMS: **1 push**, depress, hold down, force, thrust, squeeze,

p

compress, flatten. **2** *the crowd pressed in on him:* **cluster**, gather, converge, congregate, flock, swarm, crowd. **3** *they pressed for a ban:* **call**, ask, clamour, push, campaign, demand. **4** *he pressed us to agree:* **urge**, put pressure on, pressurize, force, push, coerce, dragoon, steamroller, brow-beat; informal lean on, put the screws on, twist someone's arm, railroad, bulldoze. **5** *they pressed their case for extra funding:* **put forward**, advance, present, submit, plead.
• n. **1** a device for flattening or shaping something. **2** a printing press. **3** newspapers or journalists as a whole.
▷ SYNONYMS: **the media**, newspapers, journalism, reporters, the fourth estate; Brit. dated Fleet Street.
□ **press conference** a meeting with a number of journalists. **press-gang** force into doing something. **press into service** put to a particular use as a makeshift measure. **press stud** Brit. a small fastener with two parts that fit together when pressed. **press-up** Brit. an exercise in which a person lies on the floor and raises their body by pressing down on their hands.

pressing adj. urgent.
▷ SYNONYMS: **1 urgent**, critical, crucial, acute, desperate, serious, grave, life-and-death. **2 important**, high-priority, critical, crucial, unavoidable.

pressure n. **1** steady force applied to an object. **2** the use of persuasion or threats. **3** stress. **4** the force per unit area applied by a fluid against a surface.
▷ SYNONYMS: **1 force**, load, stress, thrust, compression, weight. **2 persuasion**, intimidation, coercion, compulsion, duress, harassment, nagging, badgering. **3 strain**, stress, tension, trouble, difficulty, burden; informal hassle.
• v. pressurize.
▷ SYNONYMS: **coerce**, push, persuade, force, bulldoze, hound, nag, badger, browbeat, bully, intimidate, dragoon, twist someone's arm; informal railroad, lean on; N. Amer. informal hustle.
□ **pressure cooker** an airtight pot for cooking food quickly under steam pressure. **pressure group** a group that tries to influence public policy in the interest of a particular cause.

pressurize (or **-ise**) v. **1** persuade or force into doing something. **2** keep the air pressure in an aircraft cabin the same as it is at ground level.

▷ SYNONYMS: **coerce**, pressure, push, persuade, force, bulldoze, hound, nag, badger, browbeat, bully, bludgeon, intimidate, dragoon, twist someone's arm; informal railroad, lean on; N. Amer. informal hustle.

prestige n. respect and admiration resulting from achievements, high quality, etc.
▷ SYNONYMS: **status**, standing, kudos, cachet, stature, reputation, repute, renown, honour, esteem, importance, prominence, distinction.

prestigious adj. having or bringing prestige.
▷ SYNONYMS: **reputable**, distinguished, respected, high-status, esteemed, eminent, highly regarded, renowned, influential.
– ANTONYMS: disreputable, obscure.

presto adv. & adj. Music quickly.

prestressed adj. (of concrete) strengthened by rods or wires inside it.

presumably adv. as may be presumed.

presume v. **1** suppose to be true. **2** be bold enough to do something that you should not do. **3** (**presume on**) take advantage of someone's kindness, friendship, etc.
▷ SYNONYMS: **1 assume**, suppose, surmise, imagine, take it, expect. **2 dare**, venture, have the effrontery, be so bold as, go so far as, take the liberty of.
■ presumption n.

presumptuous adj. behaving too confidently.
■ presumptuously adv.

presuppose v. **1** require as a precondition. **2** assume to be the case.
■ presupposition n.

pretence (US **pretense**) n. **1** an act of pretending. **2** a claim to have or be something.
▷ SYNONYMS: **1 make-believe**, acting, faking, play-acting, posturing, deception, trickery. **2 show**, semblance, affectation, appearance, outward appearance, impression, guise, facade.
– ANTONYMS: honesty.

pretend v. **1** make it seem that something is the case when in fact it is not. **2** (**pretend to**) claim to have.
▷ SYNONYMS: **put on an act**, act, play-act, put it on, dissemble, sham, feign, fake, dissimulate, make believe, put on a false front, posture, go through the motions, make as if.
• adj. informal imaginary.

p

▷ SYNONYMS: **imaginary**, non-existent, fictional, make-believe, invented, made-up, illusory.
■ **pretender** n.

pretension n. **1** a claim to have or be something. **2** pretentiousness.

pretentious adj. trying to appear more important or better than you actually are.
■ **pretentiousness** n.

preternatural adj. beyond what is normal or natural.
■ **preternaturally** adv.

pretext n. a false reason used to justify an action.

prettify v. (**prettifying**, **prettified**) make something seem pretty.

pretty adj. (**prettier**, **prettiest**) attractive in a delicate way.
▷ SYNONYMS: **attractive**, good-looking, nice-looking, personable, fetching, prepossessing, appealing, charming, delightful, cute; Scottish & N. English bonny; old use fair, comely.
− ANTONYMS: plain, ugly.
• adv. informal to a certain extent.
▷ SYNONYMS: **quite**, rather, somewhat, fairly.
■ **prettily** adv. **prettiness** n.

pretzel n. a knot-shaped salted biscuit.

prevail v. **1** be more powerful than. **2** (**prevail on**) persuade. **3** be widespread or current.
▷ SYNONYMS: **1 win**, triumph, be victorious, carry the day, come out on top, succeed, rule, reign. **2 exist**, be present, be the case, occur, be prevalent, be in force.

prevailing adj. current or widespread.
▷ SYNONYMS: **current**, existing, prevalent, usual, common, general, widespread.

prevalent adj. widespread.
▷ SYNONYMS: **widespread**, frequent, usual, common, current, popular, general.
− ANTONYMS: rare.
■ **prevalence** n.

prevaricate v. avoid giving a direct answer.
■ **prevarication** n.

prevent v. stop something from happening or someone from doing something.
▷ SYNONYMS: **stop**, avert, nip in the bud, foil, inhibit, thwart, prohibit, forbid.
− ANTONYMS: allow.
■ **preventable** adj. **prevention** n.

preventive (or **preventative**) adj. designed to prevent something.

preview n. a viewing or showing of something before it becomes widely available.

previous adj. coming before in time or order.
▷ SYNONYMS: **1** *the previous five years*: **preceding**, foregoing, prior, past, last. **2** *her previous boyfriend*: **former**, preceding, old, earlier, ex-, last, sometime, one-time, erstwhile; formal quondam.
− ANTONYMS: next.
■ **previously** adv.

prey n. **1** an animal hunted and killed by another for food. **2** a victim.
▷ SYNONYMS: **1 quarry**, kill. **2 victim**, target, dupe; informal sucker; Brit. informal mug.
− ANTONYMS: predator.
• v. (**prey on**) **1** hunt and kill for food. **2** take advantage of or cause distress to.

price n. **1** the amount of money for which something is bought or sold. **2** something unwelcome that must be done to achieve something.
▷ SYNONYMS: **1 cost**, charge, fee, fare, amount, sum; informal damage. **2 consequence**, result, cost, penalty, toll, sacrifice, downside, drawback, disadvantage, minus.
• v. decide the price of.

priceless adj. **1** very valuable. **2** informal very amusing.
▷ SYNONYMS: **invaluable**, beyond price, irreplaceable, expensive, costly.
− ANTONYMS: worthless, cheap.

prick v. **1** pierce slightly. **2** cause to have a slight prickling feeling.
▷ SYNONYMS: **pierce**, puncture, stab, perforate, spike, penetrate, jab.
• n. a mark, hole, or pain caused by pricking.
▷ SYNONYMS: **jab**, sting, pinprick, stab, pinhole, wound.
☐ **prick up your ears 1** (of an animal) make the ears stand erect. **2** begin to pay attention.

prickle n. **1** a small thorn or a pointed spine. **2** a tingling feeling.
• v. have a tingling feeling.

prickly adj. **1** having prickles. **2** easily offended or annoyed.
▷ SYNONYMS: **spiky**, spiked, thorny, barbed, spiny, bristly.

pride n. **1** pleasure or satisfaction gained from achievements, qualities, or possessions. **2** a source of this. **3** self-respect. **4** a group of lions.
▷ SYNONYMS: **1 self-esteem**, dignity, honour, self-respect. **2 pleasure**, joy, delight, gratification, fulfilment, satisfaction, sense of achievement. **3 arrogance**, vanity, self-importance,

563 | priest | principal

hubris, conceitedness, egotism, snobbery.

– ANTONYMS: shame, humility.

• v. (**pride yourself on**) be proud of.

□ **pride of place** the most noticeable or important position.

priest n. **1** a member of the clergy. **2** (fem. **priestess**) a person who performs ceremonies in a non-Christian religion.

▷ SYNONYMS: **clergyman**, clergywoman, minister, cleric, pastor, vicar, rector, parson, churchman, churchwoman, father, curate; N. Amer. dominie; informal reverend, padre.

■ **priesthood** n. **priestly** adj.

> **WORD LINKS**
> **clerical**, **hieratic**, **sacerdotal**
> relating to priests

prig n. a self-righteous person.

■ **priggish** adj.

prim adj. showing prudish disapproval of anything improper.

■ **primly** adv.

prima ballerina n. the chief female dancer in a ballet company.

primacy n. the fact of being most important.

prima donna n. **1** the chief female singer in an opera. **2** a temperamental self-important person.

prima facie /pry-muh fay-shi-ee/ adj. & adv. Law accepted as correct until proved otherwise.

primal adj. primitive; primeval.

primarily adv. mainly; chiefly.

▷ SYNONYMS: **mainly**, in the main, chiefly, for the most part, mostly, on the whole, largely, principally, predominantly; first and foremost, firstly, essentially, in essence, fundamentally.

primary adj. **1** most important. **2** earliest in time or order. **3** of education for children below the age of 11.

▷ SYNONYMS: **main**, chief, key, prime, central, principal, foremost, first, most important, predominant, paramount; informal number-one.

– ANTONYMS: secondary.

• n. (pl. **primaries**) (in the US) a preliminary election to select delegates or candidates.

□ **primary colour** each of the colours blue, red, and yellow, from which all other colours can be obtained by mixing.

primate n. **1** a mammal of an order including monkeys, apes, and humans. **2** an archbishop.

prime adj. **1** most important. **2** excellent. **3** (of a number) that can be divided only by itself and one.

▷ SYNONYMS: **1 main**, chief, key, primary, central, principal, foremost, first, most important, paramount, major; informal number-one. **2 top-quality**, top, best, first-class, superior, choice, select, finest; informal tip-top, A1.

– ANTONYMS: secondary, inferior.

• n. a time of greatest strength, success, etc.

▷ SYNONYMS: **heyday**, peak, pinnacle, high point/spot, zenith, flower, bloom, flush.

• v. **1** make ready for use or action. **2** provide with information in preparation for something.

▷ SYNONYMS: **brief**, fill in, prepare, advise, instruct, coach, drill, train.

□ **prime minister** the head of a government.

primer n. **1** a substance painted on a surface as a base coat. **2** a book giving a basic introduction to a subject.

primeval adj. of the earliest times in history.

primitive adj. **1** of the earliest times in history or stages in development. **2** simple or crude.

▷ SYNONYMS: **1 ancient**, earliest, first, prehistoric, primordial, primeval. **2 crude**, simple, rough, rough and ready, basic, rudimentary, makeshift.

– ANTONYMS: modern, sophisticated.

primogeniture n. a system by which an eldest son inherits all his parents' property.

primordial adj. primeval.

primrose n. a pale yellow spring flower.

primula n. a kind of primrose.

prince n. a son or other close male relative of a monarch.

▷ SYNONYMS: **ruler**, sovereign, monarch, crowned head.

princely adj. **1** of or suitable for a prince. **2** (of a sum of money) generous.

princess n. **1** a daughter or other close female relative of a monarch. **2** a prince's wife or widow.

principal adj. most important; main.

▷ SYNONYMS: **main**, chief, primary, leading, foremost, first, most important, predominant, dominant, pre-eminent, highest, top; informal number-one.

– ANTONYMS: minor.

• n. **1** the most important person in an organization or group. **2** the head of a school or college. **3** a sum of money

p

lent or invested, on which interest is paid.

▷ SYNONYMS: **head teacher**, headmaster, headmistress, head, dean, rector, master, mistress, chancellor, vice chancellor, president, provost, warden.
■ **principally** adv.

USAGE Don't confuse **principal** and **principle**, a noun meaning 'a truth or general law'.

principality n. (pl. **principalities**) a state ruled by a prince.

principle n. **1** a truth or general law used as a basis for a theory or system of belief. **2** (**principles**) beliefs governing someone's behaviour. **3** a general scientific law.
▷ SYNONYMS: **1 truth**, concept, idea, theory, fundamental, essential, precept, rule, law. **2 doctrine**, belief, creed, credo, code, ethic. **3 morals**, morality, ethics, ideals, standards, integrity, virtue, probity, honour, decency, conscience, scruples.
▢ **in principle** in theory. **on principle** because of your moral beliefs.

print v. **1** produce a book etc. by a process involving the transfer of words or pictures to paper. **2** produce a photographic print from a negative. **3** write words clearly without joining the letters. **4** mark with a coloured design.
▷ SYNONYMS: **1 publish**, issue, release, circulate, run off, copy, reproduce. **2 imprint**, impress, stamp, mark.
● n. **1** printed words. **2** a mark where something has pressed or touched a surface. **3** a printed picture, design, or fabric. **4** a photo printed on paper from a negative or transparency.
▷ SYNONYMS: **1 type**, printing, letters, lettering, characters, typeface, font. **2 impression**, handprint, fingerprint, footprint. **3 picture**, engraving, etching, lithograph, woodcut. **4 photograph**, photo, snap, snapshot, picture, still, enlargement, reproduction, copy.
▢ **printed circuit** an electronic circuit with thin strips of conducting material on an insulating board. **printing press** a machine for printing from type or plates. **printout** a page of printed material from a computer's printer.
■ **printer** n.

prior adj. coming before in time, order, or importance.
▷ SYNONYMS: **earlier**, previous, preceding, advance, pre-existing.
– ANTONYMS: subsequent.

● n. (fem. **prioress**) **1** the person next in rank below an abbot (or abbess). **2** the head of a priory.

prioritize (or **-ise**) v. **1** treat as most important. **2** decide the order of importance of tasks.

priority n. (pl. **priorities**) **1** the state of being more important. **2** a thing seen as more important than others. **3** Brit. the right to go before other traffic.
▷ SYNONYMS: **precedence**, preference, pre-eminence, predominance, primacy.

priory n. (pl. **priories**) a monastery or nunnery governed by a prior or prioress.

prise (US **prize**) v. force open or apart.

prism n. **1** a transparent object with triangular ends, used to separate white light into colours. **2** a solid geometric figure whose ends are parallel and of the same size and shape.
■ **prismatic** adj.

prison n. a building used to confine criminals or people awaiting trial.
▷ SYNONYMS: **jail**, penal institution; N. Amer. jailhouse, penitentiary, correctional facility; informal clink, slammer; Brit. informal nick; N. Amer. informal can, pen.

prisoner n. **1** a person kept in prison. **2** a person captured and kept confined.
▷ SYNONYMS: **1 convict**, detainee, inmate; informal jailbird, con; Brit. informal lag; N. Amer. informal yardbird. **2 prisoner of war**, POW, internee, captive, hostage.

prissy adj. prim.

pristine adj. in its original and unspoilt condition.
▷ SYNONYMS: **immaculate**, perfect, in mint condition, as new, spotless, unspoilt.
– ANTONYMS: dirty, spoilt.

privacy n. a state in which you are not watched or disturbed by others.
▷ SYNONYMS: **seclusion**, solitude, isolation.

private adj. **1** for or belonging to a particular person or group only. **2** not to be made known. **3** not provided or owned by the state. **4** not connected with a person's work. **5** where you will not be disturbed; secluded.
▷ SYNONYMS: **1 personal**, own, special, exclusive. **2 confidential**, secret, classified, privileged, unofficial, off the record; informal hush-hush. **3 intimate**, personal, secret, innermost, undisclosed, unspoken,

p

unvoiced. **4 reserved**, introverted, self-contained, reticent, retiring, unsociable, withdrawn, solitary, reclusive, secretive. **5 secluded**, undisturbed, out of the way, remote, isolated. **6 independent**, non-state, privatized, commercial, private-enterprise.
– ANTONYMS: public, open, official.
• n. a soldier of the lowest rank.
▷ SYNONYMS: **private soldier**, trooper; Brit. sapper, gunner; US GI; Brit. informal Tommy, squaddie.
■ **privately** adv.

privation n. lack of food and other essentials.

privatize (or **-ise**) v. transfer from state to private ownership.
■ **privatization** n.

privet n. a shrub with small dark green leaves.

privilege n. a special right or advantage for a particular person or group.
▷ SYNONYMS: **advantage**, benefit, prerogative, entitlement, right, concession, freedom, liberty.

> USAGE There's no d: privilege.

privileged adj. **1** having a privilege or privileges. **2** (of information) legally protected from being made public.
▷ SYNONYMS: **1** a privileged background: **wealthy**, rich, affluent, prosperous, elite, advantaged. **2 confidential**, private, secret, restricted, classified, not for publication, off the record, inside; informal hush-hush.
– ANTONYMS: underprivileged, disadvantaged.

privy adj. (**privy to**) sharing in the knowledge of a secret.
• n. (pl. **privies**) an outside toilet.

prize n. a thing given to a winner or to mark an outstanding achievement.
▷ SYNONYMS: **award**, reward, trophy, medal, cup, winnings, purse, honour.
• adj. **1** having been awarded a prize. **2** excellent.
▷ SYNONYMS: **1** a prize bull: **champion**, award-winning, top, best. **2** a prize idiot: **utter**, complete, total, absolute, real, perfect; Brit. informal right.
• v. **1** value highly. **2** US = PRISE.

pro n. (pl. **pros**) **1** informal a professional. **2** (**pros and cons**) arguments for and against something.

pro- prefix in favour of.

proactive adj. creating or controlling a situation rather than just responding to it.
■ **proactively** adv.

probability n. (pl. **probabilities**) **1** the extent to which something is probable. **2** a probable event.
▷ SYNONYMS: **likelihood**, prospect, expectation, chances, odds, possibility.

probable adj. likely to happen or be the case.
▷ SYNONYMS: **likely**, odds-on, expected, anticipated, predictable; informal on the cards, a safe bet.
– ANTONYMS: improbable, unlikely.
■ **probably** adv.

probate n. the official process of proving that a will is valid.

probation n. **1** a system whereby an offender is not sent to prison subject to a period of good behaviour under supervision. **2** a period of training and testing a new employee.
▷ SYNONYMS: **trial**, trial period, apprenticeship, training.
■ **probationary** adj. **probationer** n.

probe n. **1** a blunt surgical instrument for exploring a wound etc. **2** an investigation. **3** an unmanned exploratory spacecraft.
▷ SYNONYMS: **investigation**, enquiry, examination, inquest, study.
• v. **1** examine with a probe. **2** investigate closely.
▷ SYNONYMS: **1 prod**, poke, dig into, delve into, explore, feel around in, examine. **2 investigate**, enquire into, look into, go into, study, examine, explore.

probity /proh-bi-ti/ n. honesty.

problem n. something difficult to deal with or understand.
▷ SYNONYMS: **1 difficulty**, worry, complication, snag, hitch, drawback, stumbling block, obstacle, hiccup, setback, catch, dilemma, quandary; informal headache, fly in the ointment. **2 nuisance**, bother; informal drag, pain, hassle. **3 puzzle**, question, poser, riddle, conundrum; informal brain-teaser.

problematic (or **problematical**) adj. causing or presenting a problem.
▷ SYNONYMS: **difficult**, troublesome, tricky, awkward, controversial, ticklish, complicated, complex, knotty.
– ANTONYMS: easy, straightforward.

proboscis /pruh-**boss**-iss/ n. (pl. **proboscs** or **proboscises**) **1** a long, flexible nose. **2** an insect's elongated sucking mouthpart.

procedure n. **1** an established or official way of doing something. **2** a series of actions done in a certain way.
▷ SYNONYMS: **course of action**, method,

p

system, strategy, way, approach, formula, mechanism, technique, routine, drill, practice.
■ **procedural** adj.

proceed v. **1** begin a course of action. **2** go on to do. **3** continue. **4** move forward.
▷ SYNONYMS: **1 begin**, make a start, get going, move. **2 go**, make your way, advance, move, progress, carry on, continue, press on, push on.
– ANTONYMS: stop.

proceedings pl. n. **1** a series of activities. **2** a lawsuit.
▷ SYNONYMS: **1 events**, activities, action, happenings, goings-on. **2 legal action**, litigation, suit, lawsuit, case, prosecution. **3 report**, transactions, minutes, account, story, records.

proceeds pl. n. money obtained from an event or activity.
▷ SYNONYMS: **profits**, earnings, receipts, returns, takings, income, revenue, profit, yield; Sport gate; N. Amer. take.

process n. **1** a series of actions to achieve an end. **2** a natural series of changes.
▷ SYNONYMS: **1 procedure**, operation, action, activity, exercise, business, job, task, undertaking. **2** *a new manufacturing process*: **method**, system, technique, means.
• v. **1** perform a series of actions to change or preserve something. **2** deal with using an established procedure.
▷ SYNONYMS: **deal with**, attend to, see to, sort out, handle, take care of.
■ **processor** n.

procession n. a number of people, vehicles, etc. moving forward in an orderly line.
▷ SYNONYMS: **parade**, march, march past, cavalcade, motorcade, cortège, column, file; Brit. informal crocodile.

proclaim v. announce publicly.
▷ SYNONYMS: **declare**, announce, pronounce, state, make known, give out, advertise, publish, broadcast, trumpet.
■ **proclamation** n.

proclivity n. (pl. **proclivities**) a tendency or inclination.

procrastinate v. postpone action.
■ **procrastination** n.

procreate v. produce young.
■ **procreation** n.

procurator fiscal n. (in Scotland) a local coroner and public prosecutor.

procure v. obtain.
■ **procurement** n.

procurer n. a person who obtains a prostitute for another person.

prod v. (**prodding, prodded**) **1** poke. **2** prompt or remind to do something.
▷ SYNONYMS: **1 poke**, jab, stab, dig, nudge, elbow. **2 spur**, stimulate, prompt, push, galvanize, persuade, urge, chivvy, remind.
• n. **1** a poke. **2** a prompt or reminder. **3** a pointed implement.

prodigal adj. wasteful or extravagant.
▷ SYNONYMS: **wasteful**, extravagant, spendthrift.
– ANTONYMS: thrifty.

prodigious adj. impressively large.
■ **prodigiously** adv.

prodigy n. (pl. **prodigies**) **1** a young person with exceptional abilities. **2** an amazing or unusual thing.
▷ SYNONYMS: **genius**, mastermind, virtuoso, wunderkind; informal whizz-kid, whizz.

produce v. **1** make, manufacture, or create. **2** cause to happen or exist. **3** show or provide for consideration. **4** administer the financing of a film or the staging of a play. **5** supervise the making of a recording.
▷ SYNONYMS: **1 manufacture**, make, construct, build, fabricate, put together, assemble, turn out, create, mass-produce. **2 cause**, bring about, give rise to, occasion, generate, lead to, result in, provoke, precipitate, spark off, trigger. **3** *the fields produced a good harvest*: **yield**, grow, give, supply, provide, furnish, bear. **4 pull out**, extract, fish out, present, offer, proffer, show. **5 stage**, put on, mount, present.
• n. things that have been produced or grown.
▷ SYNONYMS: **food**, foodstuffs, products, crops, harvest.

producer n. a person, company, etc. that produces something.
▷ SYNONYMS: **1 manufacturer**, maker, builder, constructor. **2 impresario**, manager, administrator, promoter, director.

product n. **1** a thing produced. **2** a number obtained by multiplying.
▷ SYNONYMS: **1 artefact**, commodity; (**products**) goods, wares, merchandise, produce. **2 result**, consequence, outcome, effect, upshot.

production n. **1** the action of producing something. **2** the amount of something produced. **3** a film, record, or play regarded in terms of the way it has been made or staged.
▷ SYNONYMS: **1 manufacture**, making, construction, building, fabrication, assembly, creation, mass production.

2 output, yield, productivity.
productive adj. producing or achieving a great deal.
▷ SYNONYMS: **1 prolific**, inventive, creative. **2 useful**, constructive, profitable, fruitful, valuable, effective, worthwhile, helpful. **3 fertile**, fruitful, rich, fecund.
productivity n. the efficiency with which things are produced.
▷ SYNONYMS: **efficiency**, work rate, output, yield, production.
profane adj. **1** not holy or religious. **2** not reverent.
• v. treat irreverently.
■ **profanity** n.
profess v. **1** claim to have, feel, or be. **2** declare your faith in a religion.
▷ SYNONYMS: **1** *he professed his love for her:* **declare**, announce, proclaim, assert, state, affirm, maintain, protest. **2** *she professed to loathe publicity:* **claim**, pretend, purport, affect, make out.
professed adj. **1** (of a quality or feeling) claimed openly but often falsely. **2** openly declared to be.
▷ SYNONYMS: **1** *their professed liberalism:* **claimed**, supposed, ostensible, self-styled, apparent, pretended, purported. **2** *a professed womanizer:* **declared**, sworn, confirmed, self-confessed.
profession n. **1** a job requiring special training and a formal qualification. **2** a body of people engaged in this. **3** a declaration.
▷ SYNONYMS: **career**, occupation, calling, vocation, métier, line of work, job, business, trade, craft.
professional adj. **1** of or belonging to a profession. **2** doing something as a job rather than as a hobby. **3** competent.
▷ SYNONYMS: **1 white-collar**, non-manual, graduate, qualified, chartered. **2 paid**, salaried. **3 expert**, accomplished, skilful, masterly, fine, polished, skilled, proficient, competent, able, businesslike, deft. **4** *he always behaved in a professional way:* **appropriate**, fitting, proper, honourable, ethical.
– ANTONYMS: amateur, amateurish.
• n. a professional person.
▷ SYNONYMS: **expert**, virtuoso, old hand, master, maestro, past master; informal pro, ace.
■ **professionalism** n. **professionally** adv.
professor n. a university academic of the highest rank.
■ **professorial** adj.

proffer v. offer.
proficient adj. competent; skilled.
■ **proficiency** n.
profile n. **1** an outline of a person's face seen from the side. **2** a short descriptive article about someone. **3** the extent to which a person or organization attracts notice.
▷ SYNONYMS: **1 outline**, silhouette, side view, contour, shape, form, lines. **2 description**, account, study, portrait, rundown, sketch, outline.
profit n. **1** a financial gain. **2** advantage; benefit.
▷ SYNONYMS: **1 financial gain**, returns, yield, proceeds, earnings, winnings, surplus; informal pay dirt, bottom line. **2 advantage**, benefit, value, use, good; informal mileage.
– ANTONYMS: loss, disadvantage.
• v. (**profiting**, **profited**) benefit, esp. financially.
▷ SYNONYMS: **1 make money**, earn; informal rake it in, clean up, make a killing; N. Amer. informal make a fast buck. **2 benefit**, be advantageous to, be of use to, do someone good, help, be of service to, serve.
– ANTONYMS: lose.
profitable adj. **1** making a profit. **2** useful.
▷ SYNONYMS: **1 moneymaking**, profit-making, paying, lucrative, commercial, successful, money-spinning, gainful. **2 beneficial**, useful, advantageous, valuable, productive, worthwhile, rewarding, fruitful, illuminating, informative, well spent.
■ **profitability** n. **profitably** adv.
profiteering n. the making of a large profit in an unfair way.
profligate adj. **1** extravagant or wasteful. **2** dissolute.
• n. a profligate person.
■ **profligacy** n.
profound adj. **1** very great. **2** showing or needing great knowledge or understanding.
▷ SYNONYMS: **1 heartfelt**, intense, keen, extreme, acute, severe, sincere, earnest, deep, deep-seated, overpowering, overwhelming. **2 far-reaching**, radical, extensive, sweeping, exhaustive, thoroughgoing. **3 wise**, learned, intelligent, scholarly, discerning, penetrating, perceptive, astute, thoughtful, insightful.
– ANTONYMS: superficial.
■ **profoundly** adv. **profundity** n.
profuse adj. plentiful.
■ **profusely** adv. **profusion** n.

p

progenitor n. an ancestor.

progeny n. offspring.

progesterone n. a hormone that stimulates the womb to prepare for pregnancy.

prognosis n. (pl. **prognoses**) a forecast, esp. of the likely course of an illness.
■ **prognostic** adj.

prognosticate v. forecast.
■ **prognostication** n.

programme (US **program**) n. **1** a planned series of events. **2** a radio or television broadcast. **3** a set of related measures with a long-term aim. **4** a sheet or booklet giving details about a play, concert, etc. **5** (**program**) a series of software instructions to control the operation of a computer.
▷ SYNONYMS: **1 schedule**, agenda, calendar, timetable, order of the day, line-up. **2 broadcast**, production, show, presentation, transmission, performance. **3 scheme**, plan, package, strategy, initiative, proposal. **4 course**, syllabus, curriculum.
• v. **1** (**program**) (**programming**, **programmed**; US **programing**, **programed**) provide a computer with a program. **2** arrange according to a plan.
▷ SYNONYMS: **arrange**, organize, schedule, plan, map out, timetable, line up; N. Amer. slate.
■ **programmer** n.

progress n. **1** forward movement. **2** development or improvement.
▷ SYNONYMS: **development**, movement, advance, advancement, headway, step forward, improvement, growth.
• v. move forward or develop.
▷ SYNONYMS: **1 go**, make your way, move, proceed, advance, continue, work your way. **2 develop**, make progress, advance, make headway, move on, get on, gain ground, improve, get better, come on, come along, make strides.
– ANTONYMS: regress.

progression n. **1** a gradual movement or development towards a destination or a more advanced state. **2** a number of things coming one after the other.
▷ SYNONYMS: **1 progress**, advancement, movement, passage, development, evolution, growth. **2 succession**, series, sequence, string, stream, chain, train, row, cycle.

progressive adj. **1** happening gradually. **2** favouring new ideas or social reform.
▷ SYNONYMS: **1 continuing**, continuous, ongoing, gradual, step-by-step, cumu-

lative. **2 modern**, liberal, advanced, forward-thinking, enlightened, pioneering, reforming, reformist, radical; informal go-ahead.
– ANTONYMS: conservative.
■ **progressively** adv.

prohibit v. (**prohibiting**, **prohibited**) **1** forbid. **2** make impossible; prevent.
▷ SYNONYMS: **1 forbid**, ban, bar, proscribe, make illegal, outlaw, disallow, veto. **2 prevent**, stop, rule out, preclude.
– ANTONYMS: allow.

prohibition n. **1** the action of forbidding something. **2** an order that forbids something.
▷ SYNONYMS: **ban**, bar, veto, embargo, boycott, injunction, moratorium, interdict.

prohibitive adj. **1** forbidding something. **2** (of a price) too high.

project n. **1** a piece of work planned to achieve a particular aim. **2** a piece of work involving research.
▷ SYNONYMS: **1 scheme**, plan, programme, enterprise, undertaking, venture, proposal, idea, concept. **2 assignment**, piece of work, task.
• v. **1** estimate. **2** plan. **3** stick out beyond something else. **4** make light or an image fall on a surface. **5** present an image of yourself to others.
▷ SYNONYMS: **1 forecast**, predict, expect, estimate, calculate, reckon. **2 stick out**, jut out, protrude, extend, stand out, bulge out. **3 cast**, throw, send, shed, shine.

projectile n. a missile.

projection n. **1** a forecast based on present trends. **2** the projecting of an image etc. **3** a thing that sticks out.
▷ SYNONYMS: **1 forecast**, prediction, prognosis, expectation, estimate. **2 outcrop**, outgrowth, overhang, ledge, shelf, prominence, protrusion, protuberance.
■ **projectionist** n.

projector n. a device for projecting slides or film on to a screen.

prolapse n. a condition in which an organ of the body has slipped from its normal position.

proletariat n. workers or working-class people.
■ **proletarian** adj. & n.

proliferate v. reproduce or grow rapidly.
▷ SYNONYMS: **increase**, grow, multiply, rocket, mushroom, snowball, burgeon, spread, expand, run riot.
– ANTONYMS: decrease, dwindle.

■ **proliferation** n.

prolific adj. producing things in abundance.
▷ SYNONYMS: **1 plentiful**, abundant, bountiful, profuse, copious, luxuriant, rich, lush, fruitful. **2 productive**, fertile, creative, inventive.
− ANTONYMS: meagre.
■ **prolifically** adv.

prolix adj. (of speech or writing) long and boring.
■ **prolixity** n.

prologue n. an introduction to a book, play, etc.

prolong v. cause to last longer.
▷ SYNONYMS: **lengthen**, extend, drag out, draw out, protract, spin out, carry on, continue, keep up, perpetuate.
− ANTONYMS: shorten.
■ **prolongation** n.

prom n. Brit. **1** a promenade by the sea. **2** a promenade concert.

promenade n. **1** a paved public walk along a seafront. **2** a leisurely walk, ride, or drive.
□ **promenade concert** Brit. a concert of classical music at which part of the audience stands.

prominence n. the state of being prominent.
▷ SYNONYMS: **fame**, celebrity, eminence, importance, distinction, greatness, prestige, stature, standing.

prominent adj. **1** important; famous. **2** sticking out. **3** conspicuous.
▷ SYNONYMS: **1 important**, well known, leading, eminent, distinguished, notable, noteworthy, noted, illustrious, celebrated, famous, renowned; N. Amer. major-league. **2 protruding**, jutting out, projecting, protuberant, standing out, sticking out, proud, bulging. **3 conspicuous**, noticeable, obvious, unmistakable, eye-catching, pronounced, salient, striking, dominant, obtrusive.
− ANTONYMS: unimportant, inconspicuous.
■ **prominently** adv.

promiscuous adj. having many sexual relationships.
■ **promiscuity** n.

promise n. **1** an assurance that you will do something or that something will happen. **2** potential excellence.
▷ SYNONYMS: **1 word**, word of honour, assurance, pledge, vow, guarantee, oath, bond, undertaking, agreement, commitment, contract. **2 potential**, ability, talent, aptitude, possibility.
• v. **1** make a promise. **2** give good

grounds for expecting.
▷ SYNONYMS: **1 give your word**, swear, pledge, vow, undertake, give an undertaking, guarantee, warrant, contract, give an assurance, commit yourself. **2 indicate**, lead someone to expect, point to, be a sign of, betoken, give hope of, augur, herald, portend, presage.

promising adj. showing signs of future success.
▷ SYNONYMS: **1 good**, encouraging, favourable, hopeful, auspicious, propitious, bright, rosy, heartening. **2 talented**, gifted, budding, up-and-coming, rising, coming, in the making.
− ANTONYMS: unfavourable.

promissory note n. a written signed promise to pay a stated sum.

promontory n. (pl. **promontories**) high land jutting out into the sea.

promote v. **1** aid the progress of a cause or aim. **2** publicize a product. **3** raise to a higher rank or office.
▷ SYNONYMS: **1 encourage**, further, advance, foster, develop, contribute to, boost, stimulate. **2 advertise**, publicize, beat/bang the drum for, market, merchandise; informal push, plug, hype. **3 upgrade**, elevate, advance, move up.
− ANTONYMS: obstruct, demote.
■ **promoter** n.

promotion n. **1** the action or activity of promoting something or someone. **2** movement to a higher position or rank.
▷ SYNONYMS: **1 encouragement**, furtherance, furthering, advancement, contribution to, fostering, boosting, stimulation. **2 advertising**, marketing, publicity, propaganda; informal hard sell, plug, hype, puff. **3 upgrading**, preferment, elevation, advancement, step up.

prompt v. **1** cause to happen or to do. **2** tell an actor a word they have forgotten.
▷ SYNONYMS: **1 give rise to**, bring about, cause, occasion, result in, lead to, elicit, produce, precipitate, trigger, spark off, provoke. **2 induce**, make, move, motivate, lead, dispose, persuade, incline, encourage, stimulate, prod, impel, spur on, inspire. **3 remind**, cue, feed, help out, jog someone's memory.
− ANTONYMS: deter.
• n. an act of prompting.
• adj. done or acting without delay.
▷ SYNONYMS: **quick**, swift, rapid, speedy, fast, expeditious, direct, immediate,

p

instant, early, punctual, in good time, on time.
– ANTONYMS: slow, late.
• adv. Brit. punctually.
▷ SYNONYMS: **exactly**, precisely, sharp, on the dot, dead, punctually; informal bang on; N. Amer. informal on the button, on the nose.
■ **prompter** n. **promptly** adv.
promulgate v. make widely known.
■ **promulgation** n.
prone adj. **1** likely to suffer from or do. **2** lying face downwards.
▷ SYNONYMS: **1 susceptible**, vulnerable, subject, open, liable, given, predisposed, likely, disposed, inclined, apt. **2 lying face down**, on your stomach/front, lying flat, lying down, horizontal, prostrate.
prong n. each of the projecting pointed parts of a fork.
pronoun n. a word used instead of a noun to indicate someone or something already mentioned or known, e.g. *I, this*.
pronounce v. **1** make the sound of a word or part of a word. **2** declare or announce.
▷ SYNONYMS: **1 say**, enunciate, articulate, utter, voice, sound, vocalize, get your tongue round. **2 declare**, proclaim, judge, rule, decree, ordain.
■ **pronouncement** n. **pronunciation** n.

> USAGE **pronunciation** has no o after the first n.

pronounced adj. noticeable.
▷ SYNONYMS: **noticeable**, marked, strong, conspicuous, striking, distinct, prominent, unmistakable, obvious.
– ANTONYMS: slight.
proof n. **1** evidence proving that something is true. **2** a copy of printed material used for making corrections before final printing.
▷ SYNONYMS: **evidence**, verification, corroboration, demonstration, authentication, confirmation, certification, documentation.
• adj. resistant to: *damp-proof*.
▷ SYNONYMS: **resistant**, immune, unaffected, impervious.
□ **proofread** read printed proofs and mark any errors.
prop n. **1** a pole or beam used as a temporary support. **2** a portable object used on the set of a play or film.
▷ SYNONYMS: **1 pole**, post, support, upright, brace, buttress, stay, strut. **2 mainstay**, pillar, anchor, support, cornerstone.

• v. (**propping, propped**) support with or as if with a prop.
▷ SYNONYMS: **lean**, rest, stand, balance.
propaganda n. false or exaggerated information used to promote a political cause etc.
▷ SYNONYMS: **information**, promotion, advertising, publicity, disinformation; informal hype.
propagate v. **1** produce a new plant from a parent plant. **2** promote an idea etc. widely.
■ **propagation** n. **propagator** n.
propane n. a gas present in natural gas, used as fuel.
propel v. (**propelling, propelled**) drive or push forwards.
▷ SYNONYMS: **1 move**, power, push, drive. **2 throw**, thrust, toss, fling, hurl, pitch, send, shoot.
■ **propellant** n.
propeller n. a revolving shaft with angled blades, for propelling a ship or aircraft.
propensity n. (pl. **propensities**) a tendency.
proper adj. **1** deserving the description; genuine. **2** appropriate or correct. **3** very respectable. **4** (**proper to**) belonging exclusively to.
▷ SYNONYMS: **1 real**, genuine, actual, true, bona fide; informal kosher. **2 right**, correct, accepted, conventional, established, official, regular, acceptable, appropriate, suitable, apt. **3 formal**, conventional, correct, orthodox, polite, respectable, seemly.
– ANTONYMS: wrong, improper.
□ **proper name** (or **proper noun**) a name for a person, place, or organization.
■ **properly** adv.
property n. (pl. **properties**) **1** a thing or things belonging to someone. **2** a building and the land belonging to it. **3** a quality or characteristic.
▷ SYNONYMS: **1 possessions**, belongings, things, effects, stuff, goods; informal gear. **2 building**, premises, house, land; N. Amer. real estate. **3 quality**, attribute, characteristic, feature, power, trait, hallmark.
prophecy n. (pl. **prophecies**) a prediction about what will happen.
▷ SYNONYMS: **prediction**, forecast, prognostication, prognosis, divination.
prophesy v. (**prophesying, prophesied**) predict.
▷ SYNONYMS: **predict**, foretell, forecast, foresee, prognosticate.
prophet n. **1** a person regarded as being sent by God to teach people. **2** a

p

person who predicts the future.

▷ SYNONYMS: **forecaster**, seer, sooth-sayer, fortune teller, clairvoyant, oracle.

prophetic adj. **1** accurately predicting the future. **2** of a prophet or prophecy.

prophylactic adj. intended to prevent disease.

• n. a preventive medicine.

propinquity n. nearness.

propitiate v. win or regain the favour of.

■ **propitiation** n. **propitiatory** adj.

propitious adj. favourable.

proponent n. a person proposing a theory or plan.

proportion n. **1** a part or share of a whole. **2** relative size or amount. **3** the correct relation between things. **4** (**proportions**) the size and shape of something.

▷ SYNONYMS: **1 part**, portion, amount, quantity, bit, piece, percentage, fraction, section, segment, share. **2 ratio**, distribution, relative amount/number, relationship. **3 balance**, symmetry, harmony, correspondence, correlation, agreement. **4** *men of huge proportions*: **size**, dimensions, magnitude, measurements, mass, volume, bulk, expanse, extent.

proportional (or **proportionate**) adj. corresponding in size or amount to something else.

▷ SYNONYMS: **corresponding**, comparable, in proportion, pro rata, commensurate, equivalent, consistent.

– ANTONYMS: disproportionate.

□ **proportional representation** an electoral system in which parties gain seats in proportion to the number of votes cast for them.

■ **proportionally** adv.

proposal n. **1** a plan or suggestion. **2** the act of proposing. **3** an offer of marriage.

▷ SYNONYMS: **scheme**, plan, idea, project, programme, motion, proposition, suggestion, submission.

propose v. **1** put forward an idea for consideration. **2** nominate for a post. **3** make an offer of marriage to someone.

▷ SYNONYMS: **1 put forward**, suggest, submit, advance, offer, present, move, come up with, nominate, recommend. **2 intend**, mean, plan, have in mind, aim.

proposition n. **1** a statement expressing an opinion. **2** a plan of action.

▷ SYNONYMS: **1 proposal**, scheme, plan, project, idea, programme. **2 task**, job, undertaking, venture, activity, affair.

• v. informal ask someone to have sex with you.

propound v. put forward an idea for consideration.

proprietary adj. **1** of an owner or ownership. **2** (of a product) marketed under a registered trade name.

proprietor n. the owner of a business.

▷ SYNONYMS: **owner**, possessor, holder, householder, master, mistress, landowner, landlord, landlady, shopkeeper.

■ **proprietorial** adj.

propriety n. (pl. **proprieties**) correctness of behaviour.

propulsion n. the act of propelling.

pro rata adj. proportional.

• adv. proportionally.

prorogue /pruh-**rohg**/ v. suspend a session of parliament without dissolving it.

prosaic adj. ordinary or unimaginative.

■ **prosaically** adv.

proscenium n. (pl. **prosceniums** or **proscenia**) the part of a stage in front of the curtain.

proscribe v. forbid.

> **USAGE** Don't confuse **proscribe** with **prescribe**.

prose n. ordinary written or spoken language.

prosecute v. **1** take legal proceedings against someone for a crime. **2** continue a course of action.

▷ SYNONYMS: **charge**, take to court, sue, try, bring to trial, put on trial, put in the dock, indict; N. Amer. impeach.

– ANTONYMS: defend.

■ **prosecution** n. **prosecutor** n.

proselyte /**pross**-i-lyt/ n. a convert from one religion to another.

■ **proselytize** (or **-ise**) v.

prospect n. **1** the possibility of something occurring. **2** (**prospects**) chances for success.

▷ SYNONYMS: **likelihood**, hope, expect-ation, chance, odds, probability, possi-bility, promise, outlook, lookout.

• v. search for mineral deposits.

▷ SYNONYMS: **search**, look, explore, survey, scout, hunt, dowse.

■ **prospector** n.

prospective adj. likely to happen or be in the future.

▷ SYNONYMS: **potential**, possible, prob-able, likely, future, eventual, -to-be, soon-to-be, in the making, intending,

p

aspiring, would-be.

prospectus n. (pl. **prospectuses**) a booklet giving details of a school etc. or a share offer.

▷ SYNONYMS: **brochure**, syllabus, curriculum, catalogue, programme, list, schedule.

prosper v. succeed or flourish.

▷ SYNONYMS: **flourish**, thrive, do well, bloom, blossom, burgeon, progress, get ahead, get on, be successful; informal go places.

− ANTONYMS: fail.

prosperity n. the state of being prosperous.

▷ SYNONYMS: **success**, affluence, wealth, ease, plenty.

− ANTONYMS: hardship.

prosperous adj. rich and successful.

▷ SYNONYMS: **thriving**, flourishing, successful, strong, vigorous, profitable, lucrative, expanding, booming, burgeoning, affluent, wealthy, rich, moneyed, well off, well-to-do; informal in the money.

− ANTONYMS: ailing, poor.

prostate n. a gland surrounding the neck of the bladder in male mammals.

prosthesis n. (pl. **prostheses**) an artificial body part.

■ **prosthetic** adj.

prostitute n. a person who has sex for payment.

▷ SYNONYMS: sex worker, call girl, courtesan; informal working girl; N. Amer. informal hooker, hustler; derogatory whore.

• v. **1** offer as a prostitute. **2** put your abilities to an unworthy use.

▷ SYNONYMS: **betray**, sacrifice, sell, sell out, debase, degrade, demean, devalue, cheapen, lower, shame, misuse.

■ **prostitution** n.

prostrate adj. **1** lying stretched with the face downwards. **2** overcome with distress or exhaustion.

• v. **1** (**prostrate yourself**) throw yourself flat on the ground. **2** (**be prostrated**) be overcome with distress or exhaustion.

■ **prostration** n.

protagonist n. **1** the leading character in a drama, novel, etc. **2** a supporter of a cause etc.

protean adj. able to change or adapt.

protect v. keep safe from harm or injury.

▷ SYNONYMS: **keep safe**, guard, defend, shield, save, safeguard, preserve, cushion, insulate, shelter, screen, keep, look after.

− ANTONYMS: expose, harm.

■ **protector** n.

protection n. **1** the action of protecting or the state of being protected. **2** a thing that protects.

▷ SYNONYMS: **1 defence**, security, safety, sanctuary, shelter, refuge, immunity, indemnity. **2 safe keeping**, care, charge, guardianship, support, aegis, patronage. **3 barrier**, buffer, shield, screen, safeguard, cushion, bulwark, armour, insulation.

protectionism n. the policy of shielding a country's industries from foreign competition by taxing imports.

■ **protectionist** n. & adj.

protective adj. serving or wishing to protect.

▷ SYNONYMS: **1 protecting**, covering, insulated, impermeable, -proof, -resistant. **2 solicitous**, careful, caring, defensive, paternal, maternal, overprotective, possessive.

■ **protectively** adv.

protectorate n. a state that is controlled and protected by another.

protégé /prot-i-zhay/ n. (fem. **protégée**) a person who is guided and supported by a more experienced person.

protein n. a substance which forms part of body tissues and is an important part of the diet.

> USAGE **protein** is an exception to the usual rule of *i* before *e* except after *c*.

pro tem adv. & adj. for the time being.

protest n. a statement or action expressing disapproval or objection.

▷ SYNONYMS: **1 objection**, complaint, challenge, dissent, demurral, remonstration, fuss, outcry. **2 demonstration**, rally, vigil, sit-in, occupation, work-to-rule, stoppage, strike, walkout, mutiny, picket, boycott; informal demo.

• v. **1** express an objection. **2** state strongly.

▷ SYNONYMS: **1 object**, express opposition, dissent, take issue, take a stand, put up a fight, take exception, complain, express disapproval, disagree, make a fuss, speak out; informal kick up a fuss. **2 insist on**, maintain, assert, affirm, announce, proclaim, declare, profess, avow.

■ **protestation** n. **protester** n.

Protestant n. a member of any of the Western Christian Churches that are separate from the Roman Catholic Church.

■ **Protestantism** n.

protocol n. **1** the system of rules governing formal occasions. **2** the accepted code of behaviour in a situation. **3** a draft of a treaty.
▷ SYNONYMS: **etiquette**, convention, formalities, custom, the rules, procedure, ritual, decorum, the done thing.

proton n. a subatomic particle with a positive electric charge.

protoplasm n. the material comprising the living part of a cell.

prototype n. a first or earlier form from which others are developed.
▷ SYNONYMS: **original**, master, template, pattern, sample.

protozoan n. a single-celled microscopic animal.

protracted adj. lasting longer than usual or expected.
▷ SYNONYMS: **prolonged**, extended, long-drawn-out, lengthy, long.
– ANTONYMS: short.

protractor n. an instrument for measuring angles.

protrude v. stick out from a surface.
■ **protrusion** n.

protuberance n. a protruding part.
■ **protuberant** adj.

proud adj. **1** feeling pride. **2** giving cause for pride. **3** slightly projecting from a surface.
▷ SYNONYMS: **1 pleased**, glad, happy, delighted, thrilled, satisfied, gratified. **2** *a proud moment*: **pleasing**, gratifying, satisfying, cheering, heart-warming, happy, glorious. **3 arrogant**, conceited, vain, self-important, full of yourself, overbearing, bumptious, presumptuous, overweening, haughty, high and mighty; informal big-headed, too big for your boots, stuck-up.
– ANTONYMS: ashamed, humble.
■ **proudly** adv.

prove v. (**proving**, **proved**; past part. **proved** or **proven**) **1** show by evidence or argument that something is true or exists. **2** show or be seen to be.
▷ SYNONYMS: **show**, demonstrate, substantiate, corroborate, verify, validate, authenticate, confirm.
– ANTONYMS: disprove.

provenance n. the place of origin of something.

provender n. animal fodder.

proverb n. a short saying stating a general truth or piece of advice.
▷ SYNONYMS: **saying**, adage, saw, maxim, axiom, motto, aphorism, epigram.

proverbial adj. **1** referred to in a proverb. **2** well known.

provide v. **1** make available for use; supply. **2** (**provide for**) make enough preparation for.
▷ SYNONYMS: **1 supply**, give, come up with, produce, deliver, donate, contribute; informal fork out, lay out. **2** *he was provided with tools*: **equip**, furnish, issue, supply, fit out, rig out, kit out, arm, provision; informal fix up. **3** *various products on the market may provide a solution*: **offer**, present, afford, give, bring, yield; impart, lend.
■ **provider** n.

provided (or **providing**) conj. on the condition that.
▷ SYNONYMS: **if**, on condition that, provided that, presuming that, assuming that, as long as, with/on the understanding that.

providence n. **1** the protective care of God or of nature. **2** the state of being provident.

provident adj. careful in planning for the future.

providential adj. happening at a favourable time.
■ **providentially** adv.

province n. **1** a main administrative division of a country. **2** (**the provinces**) the whole of a country outside the capital. **3** an area of knowledge or responsibility.
▷ SYNONYMS: **1 territory**, region, state, department, canton, area, district, sector, zone, division. **2** (**the provinces**) **the regions**, rural areas, the countryside; informal the sticks, the middle of nowhere; N. Amer. informal the boondocks. **3 domain**, area, department, responsibility, sphere, world, realm, field, discipline, territory; informal bailiwick.

provincial adj. **1** of a province or the provinces. **2** unsophisticated or narrow-minded.
▷ SYNONYMS: **1 local**, small-town, rural, country, outlying, backwoods; informal one-horse. **2 unsophisticated**, parochial, insular, narrow-minded, inward-looking, suburban, small-town; N. Amer. informal corn-fed.
– ANTONYMS: cosmopolitan, sophisticated.
• n. a person who lives in the provinces.

provision n. **1** the act of providing. **2** something provided. **3** (**provisions**) supplies of food and drink. **4** a condition in a legal document.
▷ SYNONYMS: **1** *there's only limited provision for young children*: **facilities**,

p

services, amenities, resources, arrangements. **2 (provisions)** supplies, food and drink, stores, groceries, foodstuffs, rations. **3 term**, requirement, specification, stipulation.

provisional adj. arranged temporarily.
▷ SYNONYMS: **interim**, temporary, transitional, changeover, stopgap, short-term, fill-in, acting, working.
− ANTONYMS: permanent, definite.
■ **provisionally** adv.

proviso /pruh-**vy**-zoh/ n. (pl. **provisos**) a condition attached to an agreement.

provocation n. the action of provoking someone or something.
▷ SYNONYMS: **goading**, harassment, incitement, pressure, teasing, taunting, torment; informal hassle, aggravation.

provocative adj. **1** deliberately causing annoyance or anger. **2** intended to arouse sexual desire.
▷ SYNONYMS: **annoying**, irritating, galling, insulting, offensive, inflammatory, incendiary, like a red rag to a bull; controversial, contentious; informal aggravating.

provoke v. **1** cause a strong reaction. **2** deliberately annoy or anger. **3** stir up to do something.
▷ SYNONYMS: **1 arouse**, produce, evoke, cause, give rise to, excite, spark off, touch off, kindle, generate, engender, instigate, result in, lead to, bring on, precipitate, prompt, trigger. **2** goad, spur, prick, sting, prod, incite, rouse, stimulate. **3** annoy, anger, enrage, irritate, madden, nettle; Brit. rub up the wrong way; informal aggravate, rile, needle, get/put someone's back up; Brit. informal wind up.
− ANTONYMS: allay, appease.

provost n. Brit. the head of certain colleges and schools.

prow n. the pointed front part of a ship.

prowess n. skill or expertise.
▷ SYNONYMS: **skill**, expertise, mastery, ability, capability, capacity, talent, aptitude, dexterity, proficiency, finesse; informal know-how.
− ANTONYMS: inability, ineptitude.

prowl v. move about in a stealthy or restless way.
▷ SYNONYMS: **steal**, slink, skulk, sneak, stalk, creep; informal snoop.
■ **prowler** n.

proximity n. nearness.
■ **proximate** adj.

proxy n. (pl. **proxies**) **1** the authority to represent someone else, esp. in

voting. **2** a person authorized to act on behalf of another.
▷ SYNONYMS: **deputy**, representative, substitute, delegate, agent, surrogate, stand-in, go-between.

prude n. a person who is easily shocked by sexual matters.
■ **prudery** n.

prudent adj. showing thought for the future.
▷ SYNONYMS: **1 wise**, well judged, sensible, politic, judicious, shrewd, sage, sagacious, far-sighted, canny. **2** cautious, careful, provident, circumspect, thrifty, economical.
− ANTONYMS: unwise, extravagant.
■ **prudence** n. **prudently** adv.

prudish adj. easily shocked by sexual matters.
▷ SYNONYMS: **puritanical**, priggish, prim, moralistic, censorious, strait-laced, Victorian, stuffy; informal goody-goody.
− ANTONYMS: permissive.

prune n. a dried plum.
● v. trim a shrub etc. by cutting away dead or unwanted parts.
▷ SYNONYMS: **1 cut back**, trim, clip, shear, shorten, thin, shape. **2** staff numbers have been pruned: **reduce**, cut, pare down, slim down, trim, downsize, axe, shrink; informal slash.
− ANTONYMS: increase.

prurient adj. showing excessive interest in sexual matters.
■ **prurience** n.

pry v. (**prying**, **pried**) enquire too intrusively into a person's private affairs.
▷ SYNONYMS: **be inquisitive**, poke about/around, ferret about/around, spy, be a busybody; informal stick/poke your nose in/into, be nosy, snoop; Austral./NZ informal stickybeak.

PS abbrev. postscript.

psalm /sahm/ n. a song or poem praising God.

psalter /**sawl**-ter/ n. a copy of the Book of Psalms in the Bible.

psephology /se-**fol**-uh-ji/ n. the study of trends in voting.

pseudo /**syoo**-doh/ adj. fake.

pseudonym /**syoo**-duh-nim/ n. a false name, esp. one used by an author.
▷ SYNONYMS: **pen name**, nom de plume, assumed name, alias, sobriquet, stage name, nom de guerre.
■ **pseudonymous** adj.

PSHE abbrev. personal, social, and health education (as a school subject)

psoriasis /suh-**ry**-uh-siss/ n. a skin condition causing itchy, scaly patches.

psyche /**sy**-ki/ n. the human soul,

mind, or spirit.

psychedelic /sy-kuh-**del**-ik/ adj. **1** (of a drug) producing hallucinations. **2** having bright colours or an abstract pattern.

psychiatry /sy-**ky**-uh-tri/ n. the study and treatment of mental illness.
■ **psychiatric** adj. **psychiatrist** n.

psychic /sy-kik/ adj. **1** of or possessing abilities that cannot be explained by science. **2** of the mind.
▷ SYNONYMS: **supernatural**, paranormal, other-worldly, metaphysical, extra-sensory, magic, mystical, occult; clairvoyant, telepathic.
• n. a person claiming to have psychic powers.
▷ SYNONYMS: **clairvoyant**, fortune teller, medium, spiritualist, telepath, mind-reader.
■ **psychically** adv.

psychoanalyse (US **-yze**) v. treat using psychoanalysis.

psychoanalysis n. a method of treating mental illnesses by investigating the unconscious elements of the mind.
■ **psychoanalyst** n.

psychological adj. **1** relating to the mind. **2** relating to psychology.
▷ SYNONYMS: **mental**, cognitive, emotional, subjective, subconscious, unconscious; psychosomatic.
− ANTONYMS: physical.
■ **psychologically** adv.

psychology n. **1** the study of the human mind and its functions. **2** a person's mental characteristics.
▷ SYNONYMS: **mind**, mindset, thought processes, way of thinking, mentality, psyche, attitudes, make-up, character, temperament.
■ **psychologist** n.

psychopath n. a person with a serious mental illness causing violent behaviour.
■ **psychopathic** adj.

psychosis n. (pl. **psychoses**) a severe mental illness in which a person loses contact with reality.
■ **psychotic** adj.

psychosomatic adj. (of a physical illness) caused or made worse by a mental factor such as stress.

psychotherapy n. the treatment of mental illness by psychological rather than medical means.
■ **psychotherapist** n.

PT abbrev. Brit. physical training.

Pt abbrev. **1** Part. **2** (**pt**) pint. **3** (**pt.**) point.

PTA abbrev. parent-teacher association.

ptarmigan /tar-mi-guhn/ n. a grouse of northern regions.

pterodactyl /te-ruh-**dak**-til/ n. an extinct reptile with wings.

PTO abbrev. Brit. please turn over.

pub n. Brit. a building licensed to serve alcoholic drinks.
▷ SYNONYMS: **bar**, inn, tavern, hostelry; Brit. public house; informal watering hole; Brit. informal local, boozer; N. Amer. historical saloon.

puberty n. the period during which adolescents reach sexual maturity.
▷ SYNONYMS: **adolescence**, pubescence, youth, teenage years, teens.

pubescence n. the time when puberty begins.
■ **pubescent** adj.

pubic adj. of the lower abdomen.

public adj. **1** of, for, or known to people in general. **2** provided by the state rather than an independent company.
▷ SYNONYMS: **1** public affairs: **state**, national, constitutional, civic, civil, official, social, municipal, nationalized. **2** public demand: **popular**, general, common, communal, collective, shared, joint, universal, widespread. **3** a public figure: **prominent**, well known, important, leading, eminent, distinguished, celebrated, household, famous; N. Amer. major-league.
− ANTONYMS: private, secret.
• n. (**the public**) **1** ordinary people in general. **2** a group with a particular interest.
▷ SYNONYMS: **1 people**, citizens, subjects, electors, electorate, voters, taxpayers, residents, inhabitants, citizenry, population, populace, community, society, country, nation. **2 audience**, spectators, followers, following, fans, devotees, admirers.
□ **public address system** a system of microphones and loudspeakers for amplifying speech or music. **public house** a pub. **public relations** the business of maintaining a good public image for an organization or famous person. **public school** (in the UK) a private fee-paying secondary school. **public servant** a person working for the state or for local government.
■ **publicly** adv.

┌─────────────────────────────
│ **WORD LINKS**
│ **agoraphobia** fear of public places
└─────────────────────────────

publican n. Brit. a person who owns or manages a pub.

publication n. **1** the act of

publishing. **2** a published book etc.
▷ SYNONYMS: **1 book**, volume, title, opus, tome, newspaper, paper, magazine, periodical, newsletter, bulletin, journal, report. **2 issuing**, publishing, printing, distribution.

publicity n. **1** attention given to someone or something by the media. **2** information used for advertising.
▷ SYNONYMS: **1 public attention**, media attention, exposure, glare, limelight, spotlight. **2 promotion**, advertising, propaganda, boost, push; informal hype, ballyhoo, puff, build-up, plug.

publicize (or **-ise**) v. **1** make widely known. **2** advertise.
▷ SYNONYMS: **1 make known**, make public, announce, broadcast, spread, promulgate, disseminate, circulate, air. **2 advertise**, promote, build up, talk up, push, beat the drum for, boost; informal hype, plug.
– ANTONYMS: conceal, suppress.
■ **publicist** n.

publish v. **1** produce a book etc. for public sale. **2** print in a book or newspaper.
▷ SYNONYMS: **1 issue**, bring out, produce, print. **2 make known**, make public, publicize, announce, broadcast, issue, put out, distribute, spread, promulgate, disseminate, circulate, air.
■ **publisher** n.

puce n. a purple-brown colour.

puck n. a hard rubber disc used in ice hockey.

pucker v. gather into wrinkles.
● n. a wrinkle.

pudding n. **1** a cooked dessert. **2** a savoury dish made with suet and flour. **3** Brit. a kind of sausage.
▷ SYNONYMS: **dessert**, sweet, last course; Brit. informal afters, pud.

puddle n. a small pool of rainwater or other liquid.

puerile /pyoor-yl/ adj. childishly silly.
▷ SYNONYMS: **childish**, immature, infantile, juvenile, babyish, silly, inane, fatuous, foolish.
– ANTONYMS: mature.

puerperal fever n. fever caused by infection of the womb after childbirth.

puff n. **1** a short amount of air or smoke blown out. **2** an act of drawing quickly on a cigarette etc. **3** a light pastry case.
▷ SYNONYMS: **1 gust**, blast, flurry, rush, draught, waft, breeze, breath. **2 pull**; informal drag, toke.
● v. **1** breathe in repeated short gasps. **2** move with short, noisy puffs of

air or steam. **3** smoke a cigarette etc. **4** (**puff out/up**) swell or cause to swell.
▷ SYNONYMS: **1 breathe heavily**, pant, blow, gasp. **2 smoke**, draw on, drag on, inhale.
□ **puffball** a ball-shaped fungus. **puff pastry** light flaky pastry.

puffin n. a seabird with a large brightly coloured bill.

puffy adj. (**puffier**, **puffiest**) swollen.
■ **puffiness** n.

pug n. a small dog with a flat nose and wrinkled face.

pugilist n. a boxer.
■ **pugilistic** adj.

pugnacious adj. quick to argue or fight.
▷ SYNONYMS: **combative**, aggressive, antagonistic, belligerent, quarrelsome, argumentative, hostile, truculent.
– ANTONYMS: peaceable.
■ **pugnaciously** adv. **pugnacity** n.

puke v. & n. informal vomit.

pukka adj. informal **1** genuine. **2** Brit. excellent.

pull v. **1** apply force to something so as to move it towards yourself. **2** move steadily or with effort. **3** strain a muscle etc. **4** inhale deeply while smoking.
▷ SYNONYMS: **1 tug**, haul, drag, draw, tow, heave, jerk, wrench; informal yank. **2 strain**, sprain, wrench, tear. **3 attract**, draw, bring in, pull in, lure, seduce, entice, tempt.
– ANTONYMS: push.
● n. **1** an act of pulling. **2** a deep drink of something or a deep breath of smoke from a cigarette etc. **3** a force or attraction.
▷ SYNONYMS: **1 tug**, jerk, heave; informal yank. **2 gulp**, draught, drink, swallow, mouthful, slug; informal swig. **3 puff**; informal drag, toke. **4 attraction**, draw, lure, magnetism, fascination, appeal, allure.
□ **pull back** retreat. **pull off** informal succeed in doing. **pull out** withdraw. **pull through** recover from a serious illness or injury. **pull up** (of a vehicle) stop.

pullet n. a young hen.

pulley n. (pl. **pulleys**) a wheel around which a rope etc. passes, used in lifting things.

pullover n. a knitted garment for the upper body.

pulmonary adj. of the lungs.

pulp n. **1** a soft, wet mass of crushed material. **2** the soft fleshy part of a fruit.

▷ SYNONYMS: **1 mush**, mash, paste, purée, slop, slush, mulch. **2 flesh**, marrow, meat.
• v. crush into a pulp.
▷ SYNONYMS: **mash**, purée, cream, crush, press, liquidize.
• adj. (of writing) popular and badly written.
■ **pulpy** adj.

pulpit n. a raised platform in a church from which a preacher speaks.

pulsar n. a star emitting regular pulses of radio waves.

pulsate v. expand and contract rhythmically.
■ **pulsation** n.

pulse n. **1** the regular throbbing of the arteries as blood is sent through them. **2** a single vibration or short burst of sound, light, etc. **3** the edible seeds of some plants of the pea family.
▷ SYNONYMS: **1 heartbeat**, heart rate. **2 rhythm**, beat, tempo, pounding, throb, throbbing, thudding, drumming.
• v. pulsate.
▷ SYNONYMS: **throb**, pulsate, vibrate, beat, pound, thud, thump, drum, reverberate, echo.

pulverize (or **-ise**) v. crush to fine particles.

puma n. a large American wild cat.

pumice /pum-iss/ n. solidified lava, used to remove hard skin.

pummel v. (**pummelling**, **pummelled**; US **pummeling**, **pummeled**) hit repeatedly with the fists.

pump n. **1** a device for moving liquid, gas, or air. **2** a plimsoll.
• v. **1** move with a pump. **2** fill with liquid, gas, etc. **3** move vigorously up and down.
▷ SYNONYMS: **1 force**, drive, push, inject, suck, draw. **2 inflate**, blow up, fill up, swell, enlarge, distend, expand, dilate, puff up. **3 spurt**, spout, squirt, jet, surge, spew, gush, stream, flow, pour, spill, well, cascade.

pumpkin n. a large round orange fruit.

pun n. a joke that uses a word or words with more than one meaning.
• v. (**punning**, **punned**) make a pun.

punch v. **1** hit with the fist. **2** press a key on a machine. **3** pierce a hole in a material.
▷ SYNONYMS: **1 hit**, strike, thump, jab; informal sock, slug, biff, bop, wallop, bash, clout, clobber; Brit. informal stick one on, slosh; N. Amer. informal boff, bust. **2 perforate**, puncture, pierce, prick, hole, spike, skewer.
• n. **1** a blow with the fist. **2** a device for cutting holes or impressing a

design. **3** a drink of wine or spirits mixed with fruit juices etc.
□ **punch-drunk** dazed by a series of punches. **punchline** the final part of a joke, providing the humour.

punctilious adj. showing great attention to detail or correct behaviour.

punctual adj. happening or doing something at the appointed time.
▷ SYNONYMS: **on time**, prompt, on schedule, in good time; informal on the dot.
– ANTONYMS: late.
■ **punctuality** n. **punctually** adv.

punctuate v. **1** interrupt at intervals. **2** put punctuation marks in.
▷ SYNONYMS: **break up**, interrupt, intersperse, pepper, sprinkle, scatter.

punctuation n. the marks, such as full stop and comma, used in writing to separate sentences and to make meaning clear.

puncture n. a small hole made by a sharp object.
▷ SYNONYMS: **1 hole**, perforation, rupture, cut, gash, slit, leak. **2 flat tyre**; informal flat.
• v. make a puncture in.
▷ SYNONYMS: **prick**, pierce, stab, rupture, perforate, cut, slit, deflate.

pundit n. an expert.

pungent adj. having a strong taste or smell.
▷ SYNONYMS: **strong**, powerful, pervasive, penetrating, sharp, acid, sour, biting, bitter, tart, vinegary, tangy, aromatic, spicy, piquant, peppery, hot, garlicky.
– ANTONYMS: bland, mild.
■ **pungency** n.

punish v. impose a penalty on someone for an offence.
▷ SYNONYMS: **discipline**, penalize, correct, sentence, teach someone a lesson; dated chastise.

punishing adj. very demanding or severe.
▷ SYNONYMS: **arduous**, demanding, taxing, strenuous, rigorous, stressful, trying, heavy, difficult, tough, exhausting, tiring, gruelling.
– ANTONYMS: easy.

punishment n. **1** a penalty imposed for an offence. **2** the action of punishing.
▷ SYNONYMS: **penalty**, sanction, penance, discipline, forfeit, sentence.

p

> **WORD LINKS**
> **penal**, **punitive** relating to punishment

punitive adj. intended as punishment.
▷ SYNONYMS: **penal**, disciplinary, corrective.

punk n. **1** a loud, fast form of rock music with aggressive lyrics and behaviour. **2** an admirer of punk music.

punnet n. Brit. a small container for fruit.

punt n. a long, narrow, flat-bottomed boat moved with a long pole.
• v. travel in a punt.

punter n. informal **1** a person who places a bet. **2** Brit. a customer.

puny adj. (**punier**, **puniest**) small and weak.
▷ SYNONYMS: **1 small**, weak, feeble, slight, undersized, stunted, under-developed; informal weedy. **2 pitiful**, pitiable, miserable, sorry, meagre, paltry; informal pathetic, measly.
– ANTONYMS: sturdy.

pup n. **1** a puppy. **2** a young wolf, seal, or rat.

pupa /pyoo-puh/ n. (pl. **pupae**) an insect in the form between larva and adult.

pupate v. become a pupa.

pupil n. **1** a person who is taught by another. **2** the dark opening in the centre of the iris of the eye.
▷ SYNONYMS: **1 student**, scholar, schoolchild, schoolboy, schoolgirl. **2 disciple**, follower, student, protégé, apprentice, trainee, novice.
– ANTONYMS: teacher.

puppet n. **1** a model of a person or animal moved either by strings or by a hand inside it. **2** a person under the control of another.
▷ SYNONYMS: **1 marionette**, glove puppet, finger puppet. **2 pawn**, tool, instrument, cat's paw, poodle, mouth-piece, stooge.
■ **puppetry** n.

puppy n. (pl. **puppies**) a young dog.

purchase v. buy.
▷ SYNONYMS: **buy**, acquire, obtain, pick up, procure, pay for, invest in; informal get hold of, score.
– ANTONYMS: sell.
• n. **1** the act of buying. **2** a thing bought. **3** firm contact or grip.
▷ SYNONYMS: **1 acquisition**, buy, invest-ment, order. **2 grip**, grasp, hold, foot-hold, toehold, anchorage, support, traction, leverage.
– ANTONYMS: sale.
■ **purchaser** n.

purdah n. the practice in certain Muslim and Hindu societies of screening women from men or strangers.

pure adj. **1** not mixed with any other substance. **2** innocent or good. **3** complete; nothing but. **4** theoretical rather than practical.
▷ SYNONYMS: **1** *pure gold:* **unadulterated**, undiluted, sterling, solid, unalloyed. **2** *the pure waters of the lake:* **clean**, clear, fresh, sparkling, unpolluted, uncontaminated, untainted. **3 virtuous**, moral, good, righteous, honourable, reputable, wholesome, clean, honest, upright, upstanding, exemplary, innocent, chaste, unsullied, undefiled; informal squeaky clean. **4 sheer**, utter, absolute, out-and-out, complete, total, perfect.
– ANTONYMS: impure, polluted.

purée /pyoor-ay/ n. pulped fruit or vegetables.
• v. make a purée of.

purely adv. completely; exclusively: *the fee is purely to cover our costs.*
▷ SYNONYMS: **entirely**, wholly, exclusively, solely, only, just, merely.

purgative adj. having a strongly laxative effect.
• n. a laxative.

purgatory n. (pl. **purgatories**) (in RC belief) a place of suffering inhabited by the souls of sinners making amends before going to heaven.

purge v. rid of undesirable people or things.
▷ SYNONYMS: **1 cleanse**, clear, purify, rid, empty, strip, scour. **2 remove**, get rid of, eliminate, clear out, sweep out, expel, eject, evict, dismiss, sack, oust, axe, depose, root out, weed out.
• n. an act of purging.
▷ SYNONYMS: **removal**, elimination, expulsion, ejection, exclusion, evic-tion, dismissal.

purify v. (**purifying**, **purified**) make pure.
▷ SYNONYMS: **clean**, cleanse, refine, decontaminate, filter, clear, freshen, deodorize, sanitize, disinfect, sterilize.
■ **purification** n. **purifier** n.

purist n. an adherent of traditional rules in language, style, etc.

puritan n. a person with strict moral beliefs who is critical of self-indulgent behaviour.

puritanical adj. having a very strict or critical attitude towards self-indulgent behaviour.
▷ SYNONYMS: **moralistic**, strait-laced, stuffy, prudish, prim, priggish, narrow-minded, censorious, austere, severe, ascetic, abstemious; informal

goody-goody, starchy.
– ANTONYMS: permissive.
purity n. the quality or state of being pure.
▷ SYNONYMS: **1 cleanness**, freshness,. **2 virtue**, morality, goodness, righteousness, piety, honour, honesty, integrity, innocence.
purl n. a knitting stitch.
purlieus /per-lyooz/ pl. n. the area surrounding a place.
purloin v. steal.
purple n. a colour between red and blue.
purport v. appear to be or do, esp. falsely.
• n. meaning.
■ **purportedly** adv.
purpose n. **1** the reason for an action or for existence. **2** strong determination.
▷ SYNONYMS: **1 motive**, motivation, grounds, occasion, reason, point, basis, justification. **2 intention**, aim, object, objective, goal, plan, ambition, aspiration. **3 function**, role, use. **4 determination**, resolution, resolve, steadfastness, single-mindedness, enthusiasm, ambition, motivation, commitment, conviction, dedication.
□ **on purpose** intentionally.
purposeful adj. having or showing determination.
▷ SYNONYMS: **determined**, resolute, steadfast, single-minded, committed.
– ANTONYMS: aimless.
■ **purposefully** adv.
purposely adv. on purpose.
▷ SYNONYMS: **deliberately**, intentionally, on purpose, wilfully, knowingly, consciously.
purr v. (of a cat) make a low continuous sound of contentment.
• n. a purring sound.
purse n. **1** a small pouch for carrying money. **2** US a handbag.
▷ SYNONYMS: **1 wallet**; N. Amer. change purse, billfold. **2 handbag**, shoulder bag, clutch bag; N. Amer. pocketbook.
• v. pucker the lips.
▷ SYNONYMS: **press together**, compress, tighten, pucker, pout.
purser n. a ship's officer who keeps the accounts.
pursuance n. the carrying out of a plan etc.
pursue v. **1** follow so as to catch or attack. **2** try to achieve a goal. **3** engage in an activity. **4** continue to investigate or discuss.
▷ SYNONYMS: **1 follow**, run after, chase, hunt, stalk, track, trail, hound.

2 strive for, work towards, seek, search for, aim at/for, aspire to.
3 engage in, practise, follow, conduct, ply, take up, undertake, carry on with, continue, proceed with, apply yourself to.
■ **pursuer** n.

USAGE pur-, not per-: pursue.

pursuit n. **1** the act of pursuing. **2** a leisure activity.
▷ SYNONYMS: *a range of leisure pursuits:* **activity**, hobby, pastime, diversion, recreation, amusement, occupation.
purulent adj. of or containing pus.
purvey v. supply food or drink as a business.
■ **purveyor** n.
pus n. a thick yellowish liquid produced in infected tissue.
push v. **1** apply force to something so as to move it away from yourself. **2** move forward by using force. **3** urge to greater effort. **4** informal sell an illegal drug.
▷ SYNONYMS: **1 shove**, thrust, propel, send, drive, force, prod, poke, nudge, elbow, shoulder, ram, squeeze, jostle. **2 press**, depress, hold down, squeeze, operate, activate. **3 urge**, press, pressure, pressurize, force, coerce, dragoon, browbeat; informal lean on, twist someone's arm.
– ANTONYMS: pull.
• n. **1** an act of pushing. **2** a great effort.
▷ SYNONYMS: **1 shove**, thrust, nudge, bump, jolt, prod, poke. **2** *the army's eastward push:* **advance**, drive, thrust, charge, attack, assault, onslaught, onrush, offensive.
□ **pushchair** Brit. a folding chair on wheels, in which a young child can be pushed along.
■ **pusher** n.
pushy adj. (**pushier**, **pushiest**) very self-assertive or ambitious.
▷ SYNONYMS: **assertive**, overbearing, domineering, aggressive, forceful, forward, thrusting, ambitious, over-confident, cocky; informal bossy.
pusillanimous adj. cowardly.
puss (or **pussy**) n. informal a cat.
□ **pussyfoot** act cautiously.
pustule n. a small pimple containing pus.
■ **pustular** adj.
put v. (**putting**, **put**) **1** move or bring into a particular position or state. **2** express or phrase. **3** throw a shot or weight as a sport.
▷ SYNONYMS: **1 place**, set, lay, deposit,

p

position, leave, plant, locate, situate, settle, install; informal stick, dump, park, plonk, pop; N. Amer. informal plunk. **2 express**, word, phrase, frame, formulate, render, convey, state.
□ **put down 1** suppress by force. **2** kill a sick animal. **put off 1** postpone. **2** discourage or cause to feel dislike. **put on 1** organize an event. **2** gain weight. **put out** inconvenience or annoy. **put up** accommodate for a short time. **put up with** tolerate.

putative adj. reputed.

putrefy v. (**putrefying**, **putrefied**) rot.
■ **putrefaction** n. **putrescent** adj.

putrid adj. rotting and foul-smelling.

putt v. hit a golf ball gently so that it rolls into or near a hole.
• n. a stroke of this kind.
■ **putter** n.

putty n. a soft paste that sets hard, used for sealing glass in window frames.

puzzle v. **1** confuse because hard to understand. **2** think hard about a problem.
▷ synonyms: **baffle**, perplex, bewilder, confuse, bemuse, mystify, nonplus; informal flummox, stump, beat.
• n. **1** a toy or problem designed to test mental skills. **2** a difficult question or problem.
▷ synonyms: **enigma**, mystery, paradox, conundrum, poser, riddle, problem.
■ **puzzlement** n.

puzzling adj. causing confusion or bafflement.

▷ synonyms: **baffling**, perplexing, bewildering, confusing, complicated, unclear, mysterious, enigmatic, cryptic, incomprehensible, obscure.

PVC abbrev. polyvinyl chloride, a type of plastic.

pygmy (or **pigmy**) n. (pl. **pygmies**) a member of an African people of very short stature.

pyjamas (US **pajamas**) pl. n. a jacket and loose trousers for sleeping in.

pylon n. a tall metal structure carrying electricity cables.

pyramid n. a structure with a square or triangular base and sloping sides that meet in a point at the top.
■ **pyramidal** adj.

pyre n. a large pile of wood for the ritual burning of a dead body.

pyretic adj. of or producing fever.

Pyrex n. trademark a hard heat-resistant glass.

pyrites /py-ry-teez/ n. a shiny mineral that is a compound of iron and sulphur.

pyromania n. a strong urge to set fire to things.
■ **pyromaniac** n.

pyrotechnics pl. n. a firework display, or the art of staging these.
■ **pyrotechnic** adj.

pyrrhic /pir-rik/ adj. (of a victory) won at too great a cost to have been worthwhile.

python n. a large snake that crushes its prey.

p

Qq

QC abbrev. Queen's Counsel.

QED abbrev. quod erat demonstrandum, used to say that something proves the truth of a claim.

qua /kway, kwah/ conj. in the capacity of.

quack n. **1** the harsh sound made by a duck. **2** a person who falsely claims to have medical knowledge.
• v. (of a duck) make a quack.

quad n. **1** a quadrangle. **2** a quadruplet.
□ **quad bike** a motorcycle with four large tyres, for off-road use.

quadrangle n. a square or rectangular courtyard enclosed by buildings.

quadrant n. **1** a quarter of a circle or of its circumference. **2** hist. an instrument for measuring altitude in astronomy and navigation.

quadraphonic adj. (of sound reproduction) using four channels.

quadratic adj. Math. involving the second and no higher power of an unknown quantity.

quadrilateral n. a four-sided figure.
• adj. having four straight sides.

quadrille n. a square dance.

quadriplegia n. paralysis of all four limbs.
■ **quadriplegic** adj. & n.

quadruped n. a four-footed animal.

quadruple adj. **1** having four parts or elements. **2** four times as much.
• v. multiply by four.

quadruplet n. each of four children born at one birth.

quaff /kwoff/ v. drink heartily.

quagmire n. a bog or marsh.

quail n. a small game bird.
• v. feel or show fear.

quaint adj. attractively unusual or old-fashioned.
▷ SYNONYMS: **1** picturesque, charming, sweet, attractive, old-fashioned, old-world; Brit. twee. **2** unusual, curious, eccentric, quirky, bizarre, whimsical,

unconventional; informal offbeat.
– ANTONYMS: ugly.
■ **quaintly** adv.

quake v. shake or tremble.
▷ SYNONYMS: shake, tremble, quiver, shudder, sway, rock, wobble, move, heave, convulse.

Quaker n. a member of the Religious Society of Friends, a Christian movement rejecting set forms of worship.

qualification n. **1** the act of qualifying. **2** a pass in an exam or the completion of a course. **3** a statement limiting the meaning of another statement.
▷ SYNONYMS: **1** certificate, diploma, degree, licence, document, warrant. **2** modification, limitation, reservation, stipulation, alteration, amendment, revision, moderation, mitigation, condition, proviso, caveat.

qualified adj. **1** officially recognized as able to do a particular job. **2** limited in some way: *his plan received qualified support.*
▷ SYNONYMS: **1** certified, certificated, chartered, licensed, professional. **2** limited, conditional, restricted, contingent, guarded, equivocal.
– ANTONYMS: wholehearted.

qualify v. (**qualifying, qualified**) **1** meet the necessary standard or conditions to be entitled to something. **2** become officially recognized as able to do a particular job. **3** limit the meaning of a statement.
▷ SYNONYMS: **1** be eligible, meet the requirements, be entitled, be permitted. **2** be certified, be licensed, pass, graduate, succeed. **3** authorize, empower, allow, permit, license. **4** modify, limit, restrict, make conditional, moderate, temper, modulate, mitigate.
■ **qualifier** n.

qualitative adj. of or measured by quality.

quality n. (pl. **qualities**) **1** the standard of something as measured against similar things. **2** excellence. **3** a distinctive feature.
▷ SYNONYMS: **1 standard**, grade, class, calibre, condition, character, nature, form, rank, value, level. **2 excellence**, superiority, merit, worth, value, virtue, calibre, distinction. **3 feature**, trait, attribute, characteristic, point, aspect, facet, side, property.

qualm /kwahm/ n. a feeling of doubt or unease.

quandary n. (pl. **quandaries**) a state of uncertainty.

quango n. (pl. **quangos**) Brit. a semi-public organization with senior appointments made by the government.

quantify v. (**quantifying**, **quantified**) express or measure the quantity of.
■ **quantifiable** adj.

quantitative adj. of or measured by quantity.

quantity n. (pl. **quantities**) **1** an amount or number. **2** a large number or amount.
▷ SYNONYMS: **amount**, total, aggregate, sum, quota, mass, weight, volume, bulk.
□ **quantity surveyor** Brit. a person who calculates the amount and cost of materials needed for building work.

quantum n. (pl. **quanta**) the minimum amount of energy that can take part in a physical process.
□ **quantum leap** a sudden large increase or advance.

quarantine n. a period of isolation for people or animals that have or may have a disease.
• v. put in quarantine.

quark n. any of a group of subatomic particles believed to form protons, neutrons, etc.

quarrel n. **1** an angry argument. **2** a reason for disagreement.
▷ SYNONYMS: **argument**, disagreement, squabble, fight, dispute, wrangle, clash, altercation, feud, vendetta; Brit. row; informal tiff, slanging match, run-in, spat; Brit. informal bust-up.
• v. (**quarrelling**, **quarrelled**; US **quarreling**, **quarreled**) have a quarrel.
▷ SYNONYMS: **argue**, fight, disagree, fall out, differ, be at odds, bicker, squabble, cross swords; Brit. row.
– ANTONYMS: agree.

quarrelsome adj. likely to quarrel.
▷ SYNONYMS: **argumentative**, disputatious, confrontational, captious, pugnacious, combative, antagonistic,

bellicose, belligerent, cantankerous, choleric; Brit. informal stroppy.
– ANTONYMS: peaceable.

quarry n. (pl. **quarries**) **1** a place where stone etc. is dug out of the earth. **2** a person or animal being chased or hunted.
▷ SYNONYMS: **prey**, victim, object, goal, target, kill, game, prize.
• v. (**quarrying**, **quarried**) take stone etc. from a quarry.

quart n. a quarter of a gallon, approx. 1.13 litres.

quarter n. **1** each of four equal parts of something. **2** three months. **3** fifteen minutes. **4** a particular part of a town or city. **5** a US or Canadian coin worth 25 cents. **6** (**quarters**) rooms or lodgings. **7** mercy shown to an opponent.
▷ SYNONYMS: **1 district**, area, region, part, side, neighbourhood, precinct, locality, sector, zone, ghetto, community, enclave. **2** *help came from an unexpected quarter*: **source**, direction, place, location. **3** *the servants' quarters*: **accommodation**, lodgings, rooms, chambers, home; informal pad, digs; formal abode, residence, domicile. **4** *riot squads gave no quarter*: **mercy**, leniency, clemency, compassion, pity, charity, sympathy, tolerance.
• v. **1** divide into quarters. **2** (**be quartered**) be lodged.
▷ SYNONYMS: **accommodate**, house, board, lodge, put up, take in, install, shelter; Military billet.
□ **quarterdeck** the part of a ship's upper deck near the stern. **quarterfinal** a match of a competition preceding the semi-final. **quartermaster** an army officer in charge of accommodation and supplies.

quarterly adj. & adv. produced or occurring once every three months.
• n. (pl. **quarterlies**) a quarterly publication.

quartet n. **1** a group of four playing music or singing together. **2** music for a quartet.

quarto n. (pl. **quartos**) a size of book page resulting from folding a sheet into four leaves.

quartz n. a hard mineral.

quasar /kway-zar/ n. a galaxy giving off enormous amounts of energy.

quash v. **1** officially declare a legal decision invalid. **2** put an end to.
▷ SYNONYMS: **1 cancel**, reverse, rescind, repeal, revoke, retract, countermand,

withdraw, overturn, overrule. **2 stop**, put an end to, stamp out, crush, put down, check, curb, nip in the bud, squash, suppress, stifle.

quasi- /kway-zy/ comb. form seemingly.

quatrain n. a verse of four lines.

quaver v. (of a voice) tremble.
• n. **1** a tremble in a voice. **2** a musical note with the value of half a crotchet.
■ **quavery** adj.

quay /kee/ n. a platform in a harbour for loading and unloading ships.
□ **quayside** a quay and the area around it.

queasy adj. (**queasier**, **queasiest**) feeling sick.
▷ SYNONYMS: **nauseous**, bilious, sick, ill, unwell, poorly, green about the gills; Brit. off colour.
■ **queasiness** n.

queen n. **1** the female ruler of a country. **2** a king's wife. **3** the best or most important woman or thing. **4** a playing card ranking next below a king. **5** the most powerful chess piece. **6** a reproductive bee, ant, etc. **7** informal a homosexual man who behaves like a woman.
▷ SYNONYMS: **monarch**, sovereign, ruler, head of state, Crown, Her Majesty.
□ **queen mother** the widow of a king and mother of the sovereign.
■ **queenly** adj.

queer adj. **1** strange; odd. **2** derogatory homosexual.
▷ SYNONYMS: **odd**, strange, unusual, funny, peculiar, curious, bizarre, weird, uncanny, freakish, eerie, unnatural, abnormal, anomalous; informal spooky.
– ANTONYMS: normal.
• n. derogatory a homosexual man.
□ **queer someone's pitch** Brit. informal spoil someone's chances.

quell v. suppress.
▷ SYNONYMS: **1 put an end to**, put a stop to, crush, put down, check, crack down on, curb, nip in the bud, squash, quash, subdue, suppress, overcome. **2 calm**, soothe, pacify, settle, quieten, silence, allay, assuage, mitigate, moderate.

quench v. **1** satisfy thirst. **2** put out a fire.

quern n. a hand mill for grinding grain.

querulous adj. complaining petulantly.
■ **querulously** adv.

query n. (pl. **queries**) a question, esp. one expressing doubt.
▷ SYNONYMS: **1 question**, enquiry.

2 doubt, uncertainty, question mark, reservation.
• v. (**querying**, **queried**) raise a query.
▷ SYNONYMS: **ask**, enquire, question; challenge, dispute.

quest n. a long search.
▷ SYNONYMS: **1 search**, hunt, pursuance. **2 expedition**, journey, voyage, trek, travels, odyssey, adventure, exploration, search, crusade, mission, pilgrimage.

question n. **1** a sentence requesting information. **2** a matter needing to be dealt with. **3** doubt, or the raising of doubt.
▷ SYNONYMS: **1 enquiry**, query, interrogation. **2 issue**, matter, topic, business, problem, concern, debate, argument, dispute, controversy. **3 doubt**, dispute, argument, debate, uncertainty, reservation.
– ANTONYMS: answer, certainty.
• v. **1** ask questions of. **2** express doubt about.
▷ SYNONYMS: **1 interrogate**, cross-examine, cross-question, quiz, interview, debrief, examine; informal grill, pump. **2 query**, challenge, dispute, cast aspersions on, doubt, suspect.
□ **in question** being discussed.
out of the question not possible.
question mark a punctuation mark (?) indicating a question.

WORD LINKS
interrogative expressing a question

questionable adj. open to doubt.
▷ SYNONYMS: **suspicious**, suspect, dubious, irregular, odd, strange, murky, dark, unsavoury, disreputable; informal funny, fishy, shady, iffy; Brit. informal dodgy.

questionnaire n. a set of printed questions for a survey.

queue n. a line of people or vehicles waiting their turn for something.
▷ SYNONYMS: **row**, column, file, chain, string, procession, waiting list; N. Amer. line, wait list.
• v. (**queuing** or **queueing**, **queued**) wait in a queue.

quibble n. a minor objection.
• v. raise a minor objection.

quiche /keesh/ n. a baked flan with a savoury filling.

quick adj. **1** moving fast. **2** taking a short time. **3** intelligent or alert.
▷ SYNONYMS: **1 fast**, swift, rapid, speedy, brisk, smart, lightning, whirlwind, whistle-stop, breakneck; informal nippy, zippy; literary fleet. **2 hasty**, hurried, cursory, perfunctory, desultory,

q

superficial, brief. **3 sudden,**
instantaneous, instant, immediate,
abrupt, precipitate. **4 intelligent,**
bright, clever, gifted, able, astute,
sharp-witted, smart, alert, sharp,
perceptive; informal brainy, on the ball.
– ANTONYMS: slow, long.
• n. the tender flesh below a fingernail
or toenail.
□ **quicklime** = LIME (sense 1).
quicksand loose wet sand that sucks
in anything resting on it. **quicksilver**
mercury. **quickstep** a fast foxtrot.
quick-tempered easily angered.
■ **quickness** n.
quicken v. make or become quicker.
▷ SYNONYMS: **speed up**, accelerate, step
up, hasten, hurry.
quickly adv. with speed or haste.
▷ SYNONYMS: **1 fast**, swiftly, briskly,
rapidly, speedily, at full tilt, at the
double, post-haste, hotfoot; informal
like lightning, hell for leather, like
the wind; Brit. informal like the clappers;
N. Amer. informal lickety-split. **2 immediately**, directly, at once, straight away,
right away, instantly, forthwith;
N. Amer. momentarily; informal like a
shot, asap, p.d.q., pronto. **3 briefly**,
fleetingly, briskly, hastily, hurriedly,
cursorily, perfunctorily.
quid n. (pl. **quid**) Brit. informal one pound
in money.
quid pro quo n. (pl. **quid pro quos**) a
favour given in return for another.
quiescent adj. not active.
■ **quiescence** n.
quiet adj. **1** making little or no noise.
2 calm and tranquil. **3** discreet.
▷ SYNONYMS: **1 silent**, still, hushed, noiseless, soundless, mute, dumb, speechless. **2 soft**, low, muted, muffled,
faint, hushed, whispered, sotto voce.
3 peaceful, sleepy, tranquil, calm,
still, restful.
– ANTONYMS: loud, busy.
• n. absence of noise or disturbance.
▷ SYNONYMS: **silence**, still, hush, rest-
fulness, calm, tranquillity, serenity,
peace.
□ **on the quiet** informal secretly.
■ **quieten** v. **quietly** adv. **quietness** n.
quietude n. calmness and quiet.
quiff n. Brit. a piece of hair brushed up
and back from the forehead.
quill n. **1** a large feather. **2** a pen made
from this. **3** a spine of a porcupine or
hedgehog.
quilt n. a padded bed covering.
▷ SYNONYMS: **duvet**, cover; Brit. eiderdown; N. Amer. comforter; Austral.
trademark Doona.

quilted adj. made of two layers of
fabric filled with padding.
quin n. Brit. informal a quintuplet.
quince n. a hard yellowish fruit.
quinine n. a drug formerly used to
treat malaria.
quintessence n. the perfect or most
typical example.
■ **quintessential** adj. **quintessentially**
adv.
quintet n. **1** a group of five playing
music or singing together. **2** music for
a quintet.
quintuple adj. **1** having five parts or
elements. **2** five times as much.
quintuplet n. each of five children
born at one birth.
quip n. a witty remark.
• v. (**quipping**, **quipped**) make a quip.
quire n. 25 sheets of paper.
quirk n. **1** a peculiar habit. **2** a strange
thing happening by chance.
▷ SYNONYMS: **1 idiosyncrasy**, peculiarity,
oddity, eccentricity, foible, whim,
vagary, habit, characteristic, trait, fad.
2 chance, fluke, freak, anomaly, twist.
quirky adj. (**quirkier**, **quirkiest**) having
peculiar or unexpected habits or
qualities.
▷ SYNONYMS: **eccentric**, idiosyncratic,
unconventional, unorthodox,
unusual, strange, bizarre, peculiar,
zany; informal wacky, way-out, offbeat.
– ANTONYMS: conventional.
quisling n. a traitor collaborating with
an occupying force.
quit v. (**quitting**, **quitted** or **quit**)
1 leave a place. **2** resign from a job.
3 informal stop doing something.
▷ SYNONYMS: **1 leave**, vacate, exit, depart
from. **2 resign from**, leave, give up,
hand in your notice; informal chuck,
pack in. **3 give up**, stop, discontinue,
drop, abandon, abstain from; informal
pack in, leave off.
quite adv. **1** to a certain extent.
2 completely.
▷ SYNONYMS: **1 completely**, entirely,
totally, wholly, absolutely, utterly,
thoroughly, altogether. **2 fairly**,
rather, somewhat, relatively, comparatively, moderately, reasonably; informal
pretty.
quits adj. on equal terms because a
debt or score has been settled.
quiver v. shake or vibrate slightly.
• n. **1** a quivering movement. **2** a case
for carrying arrows.
quixotic adj. idealistic and
impractical.
quiz n. (pl. **quizzes**) a competition

involving a set of questions as a test of knowledge.

▷ SYNONYMS: **competition**, test of knowledge.

• v. (**quizzing**, **quizzed**) question.

▷ SYNONYMS: **question**, interrogate, cross-examine, cross-question, interview; informal grill, pump.

quizzical adj. showing mild or amused puzzlement.

■ **quizzically** adv.

quoit /koyt/ n. a ring thrown to land over a peg in the game of **quoits**.

quondam /kwon-dam/ adj. former.

quorate /kwor-uht/ adj. Brit. (of a meeting) having a quorum.

quorum /kwor-uhm/ n. a minimum number of people that must be present at a meeting to make it valid.

quota n. **1** a limited quantity allowed. **2** a share that is expected or needed.

▷ SYNONYMS: **share**, allocation, allowance, ration, portion, slice, percentage; Brit. informal whack.

quotation n. **1** a passage repeated by someone other than the originator. **2** a formal estimate of the cost of a job.

▷ SYNONYMS: **1 extract**, quote, citation, excerpt, passage; N. Amer. cite. **2 estimate**, quote, price, tender, bid, costing.

□ **quotation mark** each of a set of punctuation marks, (' ' or " "), enclosing quoted words.

quote v. **1** repeat something spoken or written by another person. **2** give an estimated price.

▷ SYNONYMS: **1 recite**, repeat, reproduce, retell, echo. **2 mention**, cite, refer to, name, instance, allude to, point out.

• n. a quotation.

■ **quotable** adj.

quoth v. old use said.

quotidian /kwuh-tid-i-uhn/ adj. daily.

quotient /kwoh-shuhnt/ n. a result obtained by dividing one quantity by another.

q.v. abbrev. used to direct a reader to another part of a book for further information.

q

Rr

R abbrev. **1** Regina or Rex. **2** (**R.**) River.

rabbi n. (pl. **rabbis**) a Jewish religious leader.
■ **rabbinical** adj.

rabbit n. a burrowing mammal with long ears and a short tail.
• v. (**rabbiting, rabbited**) Brit. informal chatter.

rabble n. a disorderly crowd.

rabid adj. **1** fanatical. **2** affected with rabies.

rabies n. a dangerous disease of dogs etc. that can be transmitted through saliva to humans.

raccoon (or **racoon**) n. an American mammal with a black face and striped tail.

race n. **1** a competition to determine the fastest over a set course. **2** each of the major divisions of humankind. **3** a group with a common feature. **4** a subdivision of a species.
▷ SYNONYMS: **contest**, competition, event, fixture, heat, trial, meeting.
• v. **1** compete in a race against. **2** move or operate at full or excessive speed.
▷ SYNONYMS: **1 compete**, contend, run, be pitted against. **2 hurry**, dash, rush, run, sprint, bolt, charge, career, shoot, hurtle, hare, fly, speed, zoom; informal tear, belt.
□ **racecourse** a ground or track for horse or dog racing. **racehorse** a horse bred and trained for racing. **racetrack 1** a racecourse. **2** a track for motor racing.
■ **racer** n.

raceme n. a flower cluster with separate flowers along a central stem.

racial adj. of or based on race.
▷ SYNONYMS: **ethnic**, ethnological, race-related, cultural, national, tribal, genetic.
■ **racially** adv.

racialism n. racism.
■ **racialist** n. & adj.

racism n. **1** the belief that certain races are better than others. **2** discrimination against or hostility towards other races.
■ **racist** n. & adj.

rack n. **1** a framework for holding or storing things. **2** hist. a frame on which a person was tortured by being stretched.
▷ SYNONYMS: **frame**, framework, stand, holder, trestle, support, shelf.
• v. (or **wrack**) cause great pain to.
▷ SYNONYMS: **torment**, afflict, torture, agonize, harrow, plague, persecute, trouble, worry.
□ **go to rack and ruin** fall into a bad condition. **rack up** achieve or accumulate. **rack your brains** think very hard.

racket n. **1** (or **racquet**) a bat with a stringed frame, used in tennis etc. **2** a loud unpleasant noise. **3** informal a dishonest scheme for making money.
▷ SYNONYMS: **1 noise**, din, hubbub, clamour, uproar, tumult, commotion, rumpus, pandemonium; Brit. row; informal hullabaloo. **2 fraud**, swindle, sharp practice; informal scam, rip-off.

racketeer n. a person who makes money through dishonest activities.
■ **racketeering** n.

raconteur /ra-kon-ter/ n. a person who tells stories in an entertaining way.

racoon var. of RACCOON.

racy adj. (**racier, raciest**) lively and exciting, esp. in a sexual way.

radar n. a system for detecting aircraft, ships, etc. by means of reflected radio waves.

radial adj. **1** arranged in lines coming out from a central point to the edge of a circle. **2** (of a tyre) in which fabric layers run at right angles to the tyre's circumference.
■ **radially** adv.

radiant adj. **1** shining or glowing brightly. **2** showing joy or health. **3** (of heat) transmitted by radiation.

▷ SYNONYMS: **1 shining**, bright, illuminated, brilliant, gleaming, glowing, ablaze, luminous, lustrous, incandescent, dazzling, shimmering. **2 joyful**, elated, thrilled, over-joyed, jubilant, rapturous, ecstatic, euphoric, in seventh heaven, on cloud nine, delighted, very happy; informal on top of the world, over the moon.
– ANTONYMS: dark, gloomy.
■ **radiance** n. **radiantly** adv.

radiate v. **1** (of energy) be sent out in rays or waves. **2** spread out from a central point.
▷ SYNONYMS: **1 emit**, give off, discharge, diffuse, scatter, shed, cast. **2 shine**, beam, emanate, pour. **3 fan out**, spread out, branch out/off, extend, issue.

radiation n. energy sent out as electromagnetic waves or subatomic particles.

radiator n. **1** a metal device that radiates heat, esp. one filled with hot water pumped in through pipes. **2** a cooling device in a vehicle.

radical adj. **1** of the basic nature of something; fundamental. **2** supporting complete political or social reform. **3** Math. relating to the root of a number or quantity.
▷ SYNONYMS: **1 thorough**, complete, total, comprehensive, exhaustive, sweeping, far-reaching, wide-ranging, extensive, profound, major. **2 fundamental**, basic, deep-seated, essential, structural. **3 revolutionary**, progressive, reformist, revisionist, progressivist, extreme, fanatical, militant.
– ANTONYMS: superficial, minor, conservative.
• n. a person holding radical views.
■ **radically** adv.

radicchio /ra-dee-ki-oh/ n. (pl. **radicchios**) a dark red variety of chicory.

radicle n. an embryonic plant root.

radii pl. of RADIUS.

radio n. (pl. **radios**) **1** the sending and receiving of electromagnetic waves carrying sound messages. **2** broadcasting in sound. **3** a device for receiving radio broadcasts, or for sending and receiving radio messages.
• v. (**radioing**, **radioed**) send by radio.

radioactive adj. giving out harmful radiation or particles.
■ **radioactivity** n.

radiocarbon n. a radioactive form of carbon used in carbon dating.

radiography n. the production of images by X-rays or other radiation.
■ **radiographer** n.

radiology n. the study and use of X-rays and similar radiation in medicine.
■ **radiologist** n.

radiotherapy n. the treatment of disease using X-rays or similar radiation.
■ **radiotherapist** n.

radish n. a plant with a crisp, hot-tasting root eaten raw.

radium n. a radioactive metallic element.

radius n. (pl. **radii** or **radiuses**) **1** a straight line from the centre to the circumference of a circle. **2** a specified distance from a centre in all directions. **3** the thicker of the two bones in the forearm.

radon n. a radioactive gas.

RAF abbrev. Royal Air Force.

raffia n. fibre from the leaves of a palm tree, used for hats etc.

raffish adj. slightly disreputable.

raffle n. a lottery with goods as prizes.
▷ SYNONYMS: **lottery**, draw, sweepstake, sweep, tombola; N. Amer. lotto.
• v. offer as a prize in a raffle.

raft n. **1** a flat floating structure used as a boat. **2** a large amount.

rafter n. a beam forming part of the internal framework of a roof.

rag n. **1** a piece of old cloth. **2** (**rags**) old torn clothes. **3** informal a low-quality newspaper. **4** Brit. a programme of entertainments by students in aid of charity.
• v. (**ragging**, **ragged**) make fun of.

ragamuffin n. a person in ragged, dirty clothes.

rage n. violent anger.
▷ SYNONYMS: **1 fury**, anger, wrath, outrage, indignation, temper, spleen; formal ire. **2 craze**, passion, fashion, taste, trend, vogue, fad, mania; informal thing.
• v. **1** feel or express rage. **2** continue with great force.
▷ SYNONYMS: **be angry**, be furious, be enraged, be incensed, seethe, be beside yourself, rave, storm, fume, spit; informal be livid, be wild, be steamed up.
□ **all the rage** very popular or fashionable.

ragged adj. **1** (of clothes) old and torn. **2** rough or irregular.
▷ SYNONYMS: **1 tattered**, torn, ripped, frayed, worn, threadbare, scruffy,

r

shabby; informal tatty. **2** jagged, craggy, rugged, uneven, rough, irregular, indented.

raglan adj. (of a sleeve) continuing in one piece up to the neck.

ragout /ra-goo/ n. a stew of meat and vegetables.

ragtime n. an early form of jazz, played esp. on the piano.

raid n. **1** a sudden attack on an enemy or a building. **2** a surprise visit by police to arrest suspects or seize illegal goods.
▷ SYNONYMS: **1 attack**, assault, descent, blitz, incursion, sortie, onslaught. **2 robbery**, burglary, hold-up, break-in, ram raid; informal smash-and-grab, stick-up; N. Amer. informal heist.
• v. make a raid on.
▷ SYNONYMS: **1 attack**, assault, set upon, descend on, swoop on, storm, rush. **2 rob**, hold up, break into, plunder, steal from, pillage, loot, ransack; informal stick up.
■ **raider** n.

rail n. **1** a fixed horizontal bar. **2** each of the two metal bars forming a railway track. **3** railways as a means of transport.
• v. **1** provide or enclose with a rail or rails. **2** (**rail against/at**) complain strongly about.
□ **railroad 1** US a railway. **2** informal force into doing something. **railway 1** a track made of rails along which trains run. **2** a transport system using trains and tracks.

railing n. a fence made of rails.
▷ SYNONYMS: **fence**, fencing, rails, palisade, balustrade, banister.

raiment n. old use clothing.

rain n. **1** condensed moisture from the atmosphere falling in separate drops. **2** (**rains**) falls of rain.
▷ SYNONYMS: **rainfall**, precipitation, raindrops, drizzle, mizzle, shower, rainstorm, cloudburst, torrent, downpour, deluge, storm.
• v. **1** fall as rain. **2** fall in large quantities.
▷ SYNONYMS: **1 pour**, pelt down, tip down, teem down, beat down, lash down, drizzle, spit; informal be chucking it down; Brit. informal bucket down. **2** bombs rained on the city: **fall**, hail, drop, shower.
□ **rainbow** an arch of colours in the sky, caused by the sun shining through water droplets in the atmosphere. **raincoat** a coat made from water-resistant fabric. **rainfall** the amount of rain falling.

rainforest a dense tropical forest with consistently heavy rainfall.

> **WORD LINKS**
> **pluvial** relating to rain

rainy adj. (**rainier**, **rainiest**) having a great deal of rain.
▷ SYNONYMS: **wet**, showery, drizzly, damp, inclement.
– ANTONYMS: dry, fine.

raise v. **1** lift or move upwards or into an upright position. **2** increase the amount or level of. **3** cause to be heard, felt, or considered. **4** collect money. **5** bring up a child. **6** (**raise to**) multiply a quantity to a specified power.
▷ SYNONYMS: **1 lift**, hold up, elevate, uplift, hoist, haul up, hitch up; Brit. informal hoick up. **2 increase**, put up, push up, up, mark up, inflate; informal hike up, jack up, bump up. **3 amplify**, louden, magnify, intensify, boost, lift, increase. **4** you've raised a good point: **bring up**, air, present, table, propose, submit, advance, suggest, put forward. **5** the disaster raised doubts about safety: **give rise to**, occasion, cause, produce, engender, elicit, create, result in, lead to, prompt. **6 get**, obtain, acquire, accumulate, amass, collect, fetch, net, make. **7 bring up**, rear, nurture, educate.
– ANTONYMS: lower, reduce.
• n. US an increase in salary.

raisin n. a partially dried grape.

raison d'être /ray-zon de-truh/ n. (pl. **raisons d'être**) the most important reason for someone or something's existence.

Raj n. the period of British rule in India.

raja (or **rajah**) n. hist. an Indian king or prince.

rake n. **1** a pole with prongs at the end for collecting fallen leaves, smoothing soil, etc. **2** a fashionable, wealthy, but immoral man.
• v. **1** collect or smooth with a rake. **2** scratch with a sweeping movement. **3** sweep with gunfire etc. **4** search through. **5** (**rake up**) bring up something best forgotten. **6** set at a sloping angle.
▷ SYNONYMS: **1 scrape**, collect, gather. **2 smooth**, level, even out, flatten, comb. **3 rummage**, search, hunt, sift, rifle.

rakish adj. dashing but slightly disreputable in appearance.

rally n. (pl. **rallies**) **1** a mass meeting

held as a protest or in support of a cause. **2** a long-distance driving competition over roads or rough country. **3** a recovery. **4** a long exchange of strokes in tennis etc.
▷ SYNONYMS: **1 meeting**, gathering, assembly, demonstration, march; informal demo. **2 recovery**, upturn, improvement, comeback, resurgence.
• v. (**rallying**, **rallied**) **1** bring or come together again for united action. **2** recover in health or strength.
▷ SYNONYMS: **1 regroup**, reassemble, re-form, reunite, convene, mobilize. **2 recover**, improve, get better, pick up, revive, bounce back, perk up, look up, turn a corner.

RAM abbrev. Computing random-access memory.

ram n. **1** an adult male sheep. **2** a striking or plunging device in a machine.
• v. (**ramming**, **rammed**) hit or push with force.
▷ SYNONYMS: **1 force**, thrust, plunge, stab, push, sink, dig, stick, cram, jam, stuff. **2 hit**, strike, crash into, collide with, impact, smash into, butt.
□ **ram raid** Brit. a robbery in which a shop window is rammed with a vehicle. **ramrod** a rod formerly used to ram down the charge of a firearm.

Ramadan n. the ninth month of the Muslim year, during which Muslims fast from dawn to sunset.

ramble v. **1** walk for pleasure in the countryside. **2** talk in a confused way and at length.
▷ SYNONYMS: **1 walk**, hike, tramp, trek, backpack. **2 chatter**, babble, prattle, blather, gabble, jabber, twitter, rattle; Brit. informal witter, chunter, rabbit.
• n. a country walk for pleasure.
■ **rambler** n.

rambling adj. **1** (of talk or writing) lengthy and unfocused. **2** spreading or winding in various directions.
▷ SYNONYMS: **1 long-winded**, verbose, wordy, prolix, unfocused, disjointed, disconnected. **2 sprawling**, spreading, labyrinthine, maze-like.
– ANTONYMS: concise, compact.

ramekin /ra-mi-kin/ n. a small individual baking dish.

ramifications pl. n. complex results of an action or event.
▷ SYNONYMS: **consequences**, results, aftermath, outcome, effect, upshot, implications.

ramify v. (**ramifying**, **ramified**) branch out.

ramp n. a slope joining two levels.

▷ SYNONYMS: **slope**, bank, incline, gradient, rise, drop.

rampage v. rush around in a wild, violent way.
▷ SYNONYMS: **riot**, run amok, go berserk, storm, charge, tear.
• n. a period of wild, violent behaviour.

rampant adj. **1** flourishing or spreading uncontrollably. **2** (of an animal in heraldry) standing on its left hind leg with its front legs in the air.
▷ SYNONYMS: **uncontrolled**, unbridled, unrestrained, unchecked, out of control, out of hand, widespread, rife, spreading.
– ANTONYMS: controlled.

rampart n. a defensive wall having a broad top with a walkway.

ramshackle adj. in a very bad condition.

ran past of RUN.

ranch n. a large cattle farm in America.
■ **rancher** n.

rancid adj. smelling or tasting of stale fat.

rancour (US **rancor**) n. bitter feeling or resentment.
■ **rancorous** adj.

rand n. the basic unit of money of South Africa.

R & B abbrev. rhythm and blues.

random adj. done or happening without order, purpose, or planning.
▷ SYNONYMS: **unsystematic**, unmethodical, arbitrary, unplanned, chance, casual, indiscriminate, non-specific, haphazard, stray, erratic, hit-or-miss.
– ANTONYMS: systematic.
■ **randomly** adv. **randomness** n.

randy adj. (**randier**, **randiest**) informal sexually excited.

rang past of RING.

range n. **1** the limits between which something varies. **2** a set of things of the same general type. **3** the distance over which a sound, missile, etc. can travel. **4** a line of mountains or hills. **5** a large open area for grazing or hunting. **6** an area for testing military equipment or for shooting practice.
▷ SYNONYMS: **1 extent**, limit, reach, span, scope, compass, sweep, area, field, orbit, ambit, horizon, latitude. **2 row**, chain, sierra, ridge, massif. **3 assortment**, variety, diversity, mixture, collection, array, selection, choice.
• v. **1** vary between particular limits. **2** arrange in order. **3** travel over or

r

cover a wide area.

▷ SYNONYMS: **1 vary**, fluctuate, differ, extend, stretch, reach, go, run, cover. **2 roam**, wander, travel, journey, rove, traverse, walk, hike, trek.

ranger n. a keeper of a park, forest, or area of countryside.

rangy adj. tall and slim.

rank n. **1** a position within the armed forces or an organization. **2** a row of people or things. **3** high social position. **4** (**the ranks**) ordinary soldiers rather than officers.

▷ SYNONYMS: **1 position**, level, grade, echelon, class, status, standing. **2 high standing**, blue blood, high birth, nobility, aristocracy. **3 row**, line, file, column, string, train, procession.

• v. **1** give a rank to. **2** hold a specified rank. **3** arrange in a row or rows.

▷ SYNONYMS: **1 classify**, class, categorize, rate, grade, bracket, group, designate, list. **2 line up**, align, order, arrange, dispose, set out, array, range.

• adj. **1** foul-smelling. **2** complete: *a rank amateur*. **3** growing too thickly.

▷ SYNONYMS: **1 offensive**, nasty, revolting, sickening, obnoxious, foul, fetid, rancid, putrid. **2 abundant**, lush, luxuriant, dense, profuse, vigorous, overgrown; informal jungly. **3** *rank stupidity*: **downright**, utter, out-and-out, absolute, complete, sheer, blatant, arrant, thorough, unqualified.

□ **rank and file** the ordinary members of an organization.

rankle v. cause continuing resentment.

▷ SYNONYMS: **annoy**, upset, anger, irritate, offend, affront, displease, provoke, irk, vex, pique, nettle, gall; informal rile, miff, peeve, aggravate, hack off; Brit. informal nark; N. Amer. informal tick off.

ransack v. go hurriedly through a place stealing or searching for things.

▷ SYNONYMS: **1 plunder**, pillage, raid, rob, loot, sack, strip, despoil, ravage, devastate. **2 scour**, rifle through, comb, search, turn upside down

ransom n. a sum of money demanded or paid for the release of a captive.

▷ SYNONYMS: **pay-off**, payment, sum, price.

• v. demand or pay a ransom for.

rant v. speak in a loud, forceful way.

▷ SYNONYMS: **shout**, sound off, hold forth, go on, fulminate, spout, bluster; informal mouth off.

rap v. (**rapping**, **rapped**) **1** hit sharply. **2** informal criticize sharply.

▷ SYNONYMS: **hit**, knock, strike, smack, bang; informal whack, thwack, bash, wallop.

• n. **1** a quick, sharp knock or blow. **2** informal criticism. **3** a type of pop music in which words are spoken rhythmically over an instrumental backing.

■ **rapper** n.

rapacious adj. very greedy.

■ **rapacity** n.

rape v. (of a man) force someone to have sex with him against their will.

• n. **1** an act of raping. **2** a plant with oil-rich seeds.

rapid adj. quick.

▷ SYNONYMS: **quick**, fast, swift, speedy, express, expeditious, brisk, lightning, meteoric, whirlwind, sudden, instantaneous, instant, immediate.

– ANTONYMS: slow.

• pl. n. (**rapids**) a fast-flowing stretch of a river.

■ **rapidity** n. **rapidly** adv.

rapier n. a thin, light sword.

rapist n. a man who commits rape.

rapport /rap-por/ n. a close and harmonious relationship.

▷ SYNONYMS: **affinity**, close relationship, mutual understanding, bond, empathy, sympathy, accord.

rapprochement /ra-prosh-mon/ n. a renewal of friendly relations.

rapt adj. fascinated or totally absorbed.

rapture n. great joy.

■ **rapturous** adj.

rare adj. **1** not occurring or found very often. **2** unusually good. **3** (of meat) lightly cooked, so that the inside is still red.

▷ SYNONYMS: **1 infrequent**, scarce, sparse, few and far between, occasional, limited, isolated, odd, unaccustomed. **2 unusual**, recherché, uncommon, thin on the ground, like gold dust, unfamiliar, atypical. **3 exceptional**, outstanding, unparalleled, peerless, matchless, unique, unrivalled, beyond compare.

– ANTONYMS: common, commonplace.

rarebit (or **Welsh rarebit**) n. a dish of melted cheese on toast.

rarefied adj. **1** (of air) of lower pressure than usual. **2** understood by only a limited group.

USAGE -ref-, not -rif-: rarefied.

rarely adv. not often.

▷ SYNONYMS: **seldom**, infrequently, hardly ever, scarcely ever; informal once in a blue moon.

– ANTONYMS: often.

raring adj. informal very eager: *raring to go.*

▷ SYNONYMS: **eager**, keen, enthusiastic, impatient, longing, desperate; informal dying, itching.

rarity n. (pl. **rarities**) **1** a rare or unusual thing. **2** the state of being rare.

▷ SYNONYMS: **1 curiosity**, oddity, collector's item, rare bird, wonder, nonpareil, one of a kind; Brit. informal one-off. **2 infrequency**, scarcity.

rascal n. **1** a mischievous person. **2** a dishonest man.
  ■ **rascally** adj.

rash adj. acting or done without considering the possible results.

▷ SYNONYMS: **reckless**, impulsive, impetuous, hot-headed, daredevil, madcap, hasty, foolhardy, incautious, precipitate, careless, heedless, thoughtless, unthinking, imprudent, foolish.

– ANTONYMS: prudent.
  • n. an area of red spots or patches on the skin.

▷ SYNONYMS: **1 spots**, eruption, nettle-rash, hives. **2** *a rash of articles in the press:* **series**, succession, spate, wave, flood, deluge, torrent, outbreak, epidemic, flurry.
  ■ **rashly** adv.

rasher n. a slice of bacon.

rasp n. **1** a harsh, grating noise. **2** a coarse file.
  • v. **1** (of a rough surface) scrape. **2** make a rasping noise.

raspberry n. **1** an edible red soft fruit. **2** informal a rude sound made with the tongue and lips.

Rastafarian n. a member of a Jamaican religious movement which worships Haile Selassie, the former Emperor of Ethiopia.
  ■ **Rastafarianism** n.

rat n. **1** a rodent like a large mouse. **2** informal an unpleasant person.
  • v. (**ratting**, **ratted**) (**rat on**) informal inform on.
  □ **the rat race** informal a fiercely competitive way of life.

ratatouille /ra-tuh-**too**-i/ n. a dish of stewed courgettes, peppers, tomatoes, etc.

ratchet n. a bar or wheel with a set of angled teeth in which a cog etc. fits, allowing movement in one direction only.

rate n. **1** a measure, quantity, or frequency measured against another. **2** the speed of something. **3** a fixed price or charge. **4** (**rates**) a local tax on land and buildings paid by a business.

▷ SYNONYMS: **1 percentage**, ratio, proportion, scale, standard. **2 charge**, price, cost, tariff, fare, fee, remuneration, payment. **3 speed**, pace, tempo, velocity.
  • v. **1** give something a standard or value according to a particular scale. **2** judge to be of a certain quality. **3** be worthy of.

▷ SYNONYMS: **1 assess**, evaluate, appraise, judge, weigh up, estimate, gauge. **2 merit**, deserve, warrant, be worthy of.
  □ **at any rate** whatever happens.
  ■ **rateable** (or **ratable**) adj.

rather adv. **1** (**would rather**) would prefer. **2** to some extent. **3** on the contrary or more precisely.

▷ SYNONYMS: **1 sooner**, by preference, by choice, more readily. **2 quite**, a bit, a little, fairly, slightly, somewhat, relatively, comparatively; informal pretty.

ratify v. (**ratifying**, **ratified**) confirm an agreement etc. formally.

▷ SYNONYMS: **confirm**, approve, sanction, endorse, agree to, accept, uphold, authorize, formalize, sign.
  ■ **ratification** n.

rating n. **1** a classification based on quality or standard. **2** (**ratings**) the estimated audience of a broadcast. **3** Brit. a sailor in the navy who does not hold a commission.

▷ SYNONYMS: **grade**, classification, ranking, position, category, assessment, evaluation, mark, score.

ratio n. (pl. **ratios**) the relationship between two amounts, showing the number of times one value contains the other.

▷ SYNONYMS: **proportion**, relationship, rate, percentage, fraction, correlation.

ratiocination n. logical reasoning.

ration n. a fixed allowance of food, fuel, etc.

▷ SYNONYMS: **1 allowance**, allocation, quota, share, portion, helping. **2** *the garrison ran out of rations:* **supplies**, provisions, food, stores.
  • v. limit the supply of food, fuel, etc.

▷ SYNONYMS: **control**, limit, restrict, conserve.

rational adj. **1** based on reason or logic. **2** able to think sensibly or logically.

▷ SYNONYMS: **logical**, reasoned, sensible, reasonable, realistic, cogent, intelligent, shrewd, common-sense, sane, sound.
  ■ **rationality** n. **rationally** adv.

r

rationale /ra-shuh-**nahl**/ n. the reason for a course of action or a belief.
▷ SYNONYMS: **reason**, thinking, logic, grounds, sense.

rationalism n. the belief that opinions and actions should be based on reason rather than on religious belief or emotions.
■ **rationalist** n.

rationalize (or **-ise**) v. **1** try to find a logical reason for. **2** Brit. reorganize so as to become more efficient.
▷ SYNONYMS: **1 justify**, explain, account for, defend, vindicate, excuse. **2 streamline**, reorganize, modernize, update, trim, hone, simplify, downsize, prune.
■ **rationalization** n.

rattan n. the thin, pliable stems of a palm, used to make furniture.

rattle v. **1** make a rapid series of short, sharp sounds. **2** informal make nervous or irritated. **3** (**rattle off**) say or do quickly.
▷ SYNONYMS: **1 clatter**, clank, knock, clunk, clink, jangle, tinkle. **2 unnerve**, disconcert, disturb, fluster, shake, perturb, throw, discomfit; informal faze.
• n. **1** a rattling sound. **2** a device or toy that makes this.
□ **rattlesnake** an American viper with horny rings on the tail that make a rattling sound.

raucous adj. sounding loud and harsh.
▷ SYNONYMS: **1 harsh**, strident, screeching, piercing, shrill, grating, discordant, dissonant, noisy, loud, cacophonous. **2 rowdy**, noisy, boisterous, roisterous, wild.
– ANTONYMS: soft, quiet.
■ **raucously** adv.

raunchy adj. (**raunchier**, **raunchiest**) informal sexually exciting or direct.

ravage v. do great damage to.
▷ SYNONYMS: **lay waste**, devastate, ruin, destroy, wreak havoc on.
• n. (**ravages**) damage.

rave v. **1** talk angrily or incoherently. **2** speak or write about enthusiastically.
▷ SYNONYMS: **1 rant**, rage, lose your temper, storm, fume, shout; informal fly off the handle, hit the roof; Brit. informal go spare; N. Amer. informal flip your wig. **2 enthuse**, go into raptures, wax lyrical, rhapsodize, sing the praises of, acclaim, eulogize, extol; N. Amer. informal ballyhoo.
– ANTONYMS: criticize.
• n. a very large event with dancing to fast electronic music.

raven n. a large black crow.

• adj. (of hair) glossy black.

ravenous adj. very hungry.
■ **ravenously** adv.

ravine n. a deep, narrow gorge.

ravioli pl. n. small pasta cases with a savoury filling.

ravish v. **1** dated rape. **2** (**ravishing**) very beautiful.

raw adj. **1** not cooked. **2** not yet processed. **3** (of the skin) red and painful from being rubbed. **4** new and inexperienced. **5** (of the weather) cold and damp.
▷ SYNONYMS: **1 uncooked**, fresh, natural. **2 unprocessed**, untreated, unrefined, crude, natural. **3 inexperienced**, new, untrained, untried, untested, callow, green; informal wet behind the ears. **4 sore**, red, painful, tender, chafed.
– ANTONYMS: cooked, processed.
□ **raw deal** unfair treatment. **rawhide** untanned leather.
■ **rawness** n.

ray n. **1** a line of light or other radiation. **2** a large flat fish.
▷ SYNONYMS: **beam**, shaft, stream, streak, flash, glimmer, flicker, spark.

rayon n. a synthetic fibre or fabric made from viscose.

raze v. completely destroy a building etc.
▷ SYNONYMS: **destroy**, demolish, tear down, pull down, knock down, level, flatten, bulldoze, wipe out, lay waste.

razor n. an instrument with a sharp blade for shaving.

razzmatazz n. informal noisy, showy, and exciting activity or display.

RC abbrev. Roman Catholic.

RE abbrev. religious education.

re prep. with regard to.

reach v. **1** stretch out an arm to touch or grasp something. **2** be able to touch. **3** arrive at; get as far as. **4** achieve. **5** make contact with.
▷ SYNONYMS: **1 extend**, stretch, outstretch, thrust, stick, hold. **2 arrive at**, get to, come to, end up at. **3** *the temperature reached 75°*: **attain**, get to, rise to, fall to, sink to, drop to; informal hit. **4** *ministers reached an agreement*: **achieve**, work out, draw up, put together, negotiate, thrash out, hammer out. **5 contact**, get in touch with, get through to, get, speak to; informal get hold of.
• n. **1** the distance over which someone or something can reach. **2** a stretch of river between two bends.
▷ SYNONYMS: **1 grasp**, range, stretch, capabilities, capacity. **2 jurisdiction**, authority, influence, power, scope,

range, compass, ambit.

react v. **1** respond in a particular way. **2** interact and undergo a chemical or physical change.

▷ SYNONYMS: **respond**, act in response, reply, answer, behave.

■ **reactive** adj.

reaction n. **1** something done or experienced as a result of an event. **2** a bad response by the body to a drug etc. **3** a process in which substances interact causing chemical or physical change.

▷ SYNONYMS: **1 response**, answer, reply, rejoinder, retort, riposte; informal comeback. **2 backlash**, counteraction.

reactionary adj. opposing political or social progress or reform.

▷ SYNONYMS: **right-wing**, conservative, traditionalist, conventional, diehard.

– ANTONYMS: radical, progressive.

• n. (pl. **reactionaries**) a reactionary person.

reactor n. a piece of equipment for producing nuclear energy.

read v. (**reading**, **read**) **1** understand the meaning of written or printed words or symbols. **2** speak written or printed words aloud. **3** interpret in a particular way. **4** (**read into**) think that something has a meaning that it may not possess. **5** (of an instrument) show a measurement.

▷ SYNONYMS: **1 peruse**, study, scrutinize, pore over; cast an eye over, leaf through, scan. **2 understand**, make out, make sense of, decipher, interpret, construe. **3 register**, record, display, show, indicate.

• n. informal a book that is interesting to read.

■ **readable** adj. **reader** n.

> **WORD LINKS**
> **legible** readable
> **illegible** unreadable
> **literacy** the ability to read
> **illiteracy** the inability to read

readership n. the readers of a publication as a group.

readily adv. **1** without hesitation or reluctance. **2** without difficulty; easily.

▷ SYNONYMS: **willingly**, unhesitatingly, ungrudgingly, gladly, happily, eagerly.

readjust v. **1** adjust again. **2** adapt to a changed situation.

■ **readjustment** n.

ready adj. (**readier**, **readiest**) **1** prepared. **2** available for immediate use. **3** easily obtained. **4** willing. **5** quick.

▷ SYNONYMS: **1 prepared**, equipped, all set, organized, primed; informal fit, psyched up, geared up. **2 completed**, finished, prepared, organized, done, arranged, fixed. **3** a ready supply of food: **available**, accessible, handy, close at hand, to/on hand, convenient, within reach, near, at your fingertips; informal on tap. **4** he's always ready to help: **willing**, prepared, pleased, inclined, disposed, eager, keen, happy, glad; informal game. **5** a ready answer: **prompt**, quick, swift, speedy, fast, immediate, unhesitating.

• v. (**readying**, **readied**) prepare.

▷ SYNONYMS: **prepare**, organize, gear up; informal psych up.

• n. (**readies** or **the ready**) Brit. informal cash.

■ **readiness** n.

reagent /ri-ay-juhnt/ n. a substance that produces a chemical reaction, used in tests.

real adj. **1** actually existing or occurring. **2** not artificial; genuine.

▷ SYNONYMS: **1 actual**, true, factual, non-fictional, historical, material, physical, tangible, concrete. **2 genuine**, authentic, bona fide, proper, true; informal pukka, kosher. **3 sincere**, genuine, true, unfeigned, heartfelt. **4 complete**, utter, thorough, absolute, total, prize, perfect; Brit. informal right, proper.

– ANTONYMS: imaginary, false.

□ **real estate** US buildings or land.

realign v. change to a different position or state.

■ **realignment** n.

realism n. **1** the acceptance of a situation as it is. **2** the accurate and true representation of things.

▷ SYNONYMS: **1 pragmatism**, practicality, common sense, level-headedness. **2 authenticity**, accuracy, fidelity, truthfulness, verisimilitude.

■ **realist** n.

realistic adj. **1** sensible and practical. **2** (of representation) true to life.

▷ SYNONYMS: **1 practical**, pragmatic, matter-of-fact, down-to-earth, sensible, commonsensical, rational, level-headed; informal no-nonsense. **2 achievable**, attainable, feasible, practicable, reasonable, sensible, workable; informal doable. **3 authentic**, accurate, true to life, lifelike, truthful, faithful, natural, naturalistic.

– ANTONYMS: unrealistic.

■ **realistically** adv.

reality n. (pl. **realities**) **1** the state of

r

things as they actually exist. **2** a thing that is experienced or seen.

▷ SYNONYMS: **1 the real world**, real life, actuality, corporeality. **2 fact**, actuality, truth. **3 authenticity**, verisimilitude, fidelity, truthfulness, accuracy.

− ANTONYMS: fantasy.

realization (or **-isation**) n. the action or an act of realizing.

▷ SYNONYMS: **1 awareness**, understanding, comprehension, consciousness, appreciation, recognition, discernment. **2 fulfilment**, achievement, accomplishment, attainment.

realize (or **-ise**) v. **1** become aware of as a fact. **2** achieve a wish or plan. **3** convert property etc. into money by selling it.

▷ SYNONYMS: **1 register**, perceive, understand, grasp, comprehend, see, recognize, take in; informal tumble to; Brit. informal twig. **2 fulfil**, achieve, accomplish, make happen, bring to fruition, bring about/off, actualize. **3 make**, clear, gain, earn, return, produce.

really adv. **1** in fact. **2** very.

▷ SYNONYMS: **1 in fact**, actually, in reality, in truth. **2 genuinely**, truly, certainly, honestly, undoubtedly, unquestionably.
• exclam. expressing interest, surprise, doubt, etc.

realm n. **1** a kingdom. **2** a field of activity or interest.

▷ SYNONYMS: **1 kingdom**, country, land, state, nation, territory, dominion, empire, monarchy, principality. **2** the realm of academia: **domain**, sphere, area, field, world, province.

ream n. **1** 500 sheets of paper. **2** (**reams**) a large quantity.

reap v. **1** cut a crop as harvest. **2** receive as a result of your actions.

▷ SYNONYMS: **1 harvest**, cut, pick, gather, garner. **2 receive**, obtain, get, derive, acquire, secure, realize.
■ **reaper** n.

reappear v. appear again.
■ **reappearance** n.

rear n. the back part.

▷ SYNONYMS: **back**, hind part, end, tail; Nautical stern.
• adj. at the back.

▷ SYNONYMS: **back**, end, rearmost, hind, last; technical posterior.

− ANTONYMS: front.
• v. **1** bring up children. **2** breed or cultivate animals or plants. **3** (of an animal) raise itself upright on its hind legs. **4** extend to a great height.

▷ SYNONYMS: **1 bring up**, care for, look after, nurture, parent; N. Amer. raise. **2 breed**, raise, keep, grow, cultivate. **3** houses reared up on either side: **rise**, tower, soar, loom.
□ **rear admiral** a naval rank below vice admiral. **rearguard** a group of troops protecting the rear of the main force.
■ **rearward** adj. & adv. **rearwards** adv.

rearm v. arm again.
■ **rearmament** n.

rearrange v. arrange in a different way.
■ **rearrangement** n.

reason n. **1** a cause or explanation. **2** the power to think logically and draw conclusions. **3** (**your reason**) your sanity. **4** what is right or practical.

▷ SYNONYMS: **1 cause**, grounds, basis, rationale, motive, explanation, justification, defence, vindication, excuse, apologia. **2 rationality**, logic, cognition, reasoning, intellect, thought, understanding; formal ratiocination. **3 sanity**, mind, mental faculties, senses, wits; informal marbles.
• v. **1** think logically and draw conclusions. **2** (**reason with**) persuade by giving reasons.

▷ SYNONYMS: **conclude**, calculate, reckon, think, judge, deduce, infer, surmise; informal figure.

> **WORD LINKS**
> **rational** relating to reason

reasonable adj. **1** fair and sensible. **2** appropriate. **3** fairly good. **4** not too expensive.

▷ SYNONYMS: **1 sensible**, rational, logical, fair, just, equitable, intelligent, wise, level-headed, practical, realistic, sound, valid, commonsensical, tenable, plausible, credible, believable. **2 practicable**, sensible, appropriate, suitable. **3 fairly good**, acceptable, satisfactory, average, adequate, fair, tolerable, passable; informal OK. **4 inexpensive**, affordable, moderate, low, cheap, within your means.
■ **reasonably** adv.

reassess v. reconsider.
■ **reassessment** n.

reassure v. cause to feel less worried or afraid.

▷ SYNONYMS: **put someone's mind at rest**, encourage, hearten, buoy up, cheer up, comfort, soothe.

− ANTONYMS: alarm.
■ **reassurance** n.

rebate n. a partial refund.

▷ SYNONYMS: **partial refund**, partial repayment, discount, deduction, reduction.

rebel v. (**rebelling**, **rebelled**) **1** fight against an established government or ruler. **2** oppose authority or accepted behaviour.

▷ SYNONYMS: **revolt**, mutiny, riot, rise up, take up arms.
•n. a person who rebels.

▷ SYNONYMS: **1 revolutionary**, insurgent, insurrectionist, mutineer, guerrilla, terrorist, freedom fighter. **2 nonconformist**, dissenter, dissident, maverick.
– ANTONYMS: loyalist, conformist.
•adj. rebelling or having a tendency to rebel: *rebel MPs voted against the ban.*

▷ SYNONYMS: **defiant**, disobedient, insubordinate, subversive, rebellious, nonconformist, maverick.

rebellion n. **1** an act of rebelling. **2** defiance of authority.

▷ SYNONYMS: **1 revolt**, uprising, insurrection, mutiny, revolution, insurgence. **2 defiance**, disobedience, insubordination, subversion, resistance.
– ANTONYMS: compliance.

rebellious adj. rebelling or showing a desire to rebel.

▷ SYNONYMS: **1 rebel**, insurgent, mutinous, revolutionary. **2 defiant**, disobedient, insubordinate, unruly, mutinous, obstreperous, recalcitrant, intractable; Brit. informal bolshie.
– ANTONYMS: loyal, obedient.

rebirth n. a return to life or activity.

rebound v. **1** bounce back after impact. **2** (**rebound on**) have an unexpected and unpleasant effect on.

▷ SYNONYMS: **1 bounce back**, spring back, ricochet, boomerang. **2 backfire**, misfire, come back to.
•n. a ball or shot that rebounds.
□ **on the rebound** while still upset after the end of a romantic relationship.

rebuff v. reject in an abrupt or unkind way.

▷ SYNONYMS: **reject**, turn down, spurn, refuse, decline, snub, slight, dismiss, brush off.
– ANTONYMS: accept.
•n. an act of rebuffing.

▷ SYNONYMS: **rejection**, snub, slight, refusal, spurning; informal brush-off, kick in the teeth, slap in the face.

rebuild v. (**rebuilding**, **rebuilt**) build again.

rebuke v. reprimand.

▷ SYNONYMS: **reprimand**, reproach,

scold, admonish, reprove, chastise, upbraid, berate, take to task; informal tell off; Brit. informal tick off; N. Amer. informal chew out; formal castigate.
•n. a reprimand.

▷ SYNONYMS: **reprimand**, reproach, scolding, admonition; informal telling-off, dressing-down; Brit. informal ticking-off.
– ANTONYMS: praise.

rebut v. (**rebutting**, **rebutted**) claim or prove to be false.
■ **rebuttal** n.

recalcitrant adj. unwilling to cooperate.

▷ SYNONYMS: **uncooperative**, intractable, insubordinate, defiant, rebellious, wilful, wayward, headstrong, self-willed, contrary, perverse, difficult, awkward; Brit. informal bloody-minded, bolshie, stroppy; formal refractory.
– ANTONYMS: amenable.
■ **recalcitrance** n.

recall v. **1** remember. **2** make someone think of. **3** order someone to return.

▷ SYNONYMS: **1 remember**, recollect, call to mind, think back on/to, reminisce about. **2 remind someone of**, bring to mind, call up, conjure up, evoke. **3 call back**, order home, withdraw.
– ANTONYMS: forget.
•n. the act of recalling.

▷ SYNONYMS: **recollection**, remembrance, memory.

recant v. withdraw a former opinion or belief.

recap v. (**recapping**, **recapped**) give a summary of.

recapitulate v. give a summary of.
■ **recapitulation** n.

recapture v. **1** capture again. **2** experience a past time etc. again.

recce /rek-ki/ n. Brit. a reconnaissance.

recede v. **1** move back or further away. **2** diminish. **3** (**receding**) (of the chin) sloping backwards.

▷ SYNONYMS: **1 retreat**, go back/down/away, withdraw, ebb, subside. **2 diminish**, lessen, dwindle, fade, abate, subside.
– ANTONYMS: advance, grow.

receipt n. **1** a note confirming that something has been paid for or received. **2** the act of receiving.

receive v. **1** be given or paid. **2** accept or take in. **3** experience or meet with. **4** greet or welcome. **5** detect or pick up broadcast signals.

▷ SYNONYMS: **1 be given**, be presented with, be awarded, be sent, be in receipt of, get, obtain, gain, acquire, be paid. **2 hear**, listen to, respond

r

to, react to. **3 experience**, sustain, undergo, meet with, suffer, bear.
– ANTONYMS: give, send.

receiver n. **1** a device that converts broadcast signals into sound or images. **2** the part of a phone that converts electrical signals into sounds. **3** a person appointed to manage the financial affairs of a bankrupt business.
■ **receivership** n.

recent adj. having happened or been done shortly before the present.
▷ SYNONYMS: **new**, the latest, current, fresh, modern, late, contemporary, up to date, up to the minute.
– ANTONYMS: old.
■ **recently** adv.

receptacle n. a container.

reception n. **1** the act of receiving. **2** a reaction to something. **3** a formal social occasion. **4** the area in a hotel, office, etc. where visitors are greeted. **5** the quality of broadcast signals received.
▷ SYNONYMS: **1 response**, reaction, treatment. **2 party**, function, social occasion, celebration, get-together, gathering, soirée; N. Amer. levee; informal do.

receptionist n. a person who greets and deals with visitors to an office, hotel, etc.

receptive adj. willing to consider new ideas.
▷ SYNONYMS: **open-minded**, responsive, amenable, well disposed, flexible, approachable, accessible.
– ANTONYMS: unresponsive.
■ **receptivity** n.

receptor n. a nerve ending that responds to a stimulus and transmits a signal to a nerve.

recess n. **1** a small space set back in a wall or into a surface. **2** a break between sessions of a parliament, law court, etc.
▷ SYNONYMS: **1 alcove**, bay, niche, nook, corner. **2 break**, adjournment, interlude, interval, rest, holiday; N. Amer. vacation.
• v. set back into a wall etc.

recession n. a temporary decline in economic activity.
▷ SYNONYMS: **downturn**, depression, slump, slowdown.
– ANTONYMS: boom.

recessive adj. (of a gene) appearing in offspring only if a contrary gene is not also inherited.

recharge v. charge a battery etc. again.

■ **rechargeable** adj.

recherché /ruh-**shair**-shay/ adj. unusual and not easily understood.

recidivist n. a person who constantly commits crimes.
■ **recidivism** n.

recipe n. **1** a list of ingredients and instructions for preparing a dish. **2** something likely to lead to a particular outcome.
▷ SYNONYMS: *a recipe for success*: **formula**, prescription, blueprint.

recipient n. a person who receives something.

reciprocal adj. **1** given or done in return. **2** affecting two parties equally.
▷ SYNONYMS: **mutual**, common, shared, give-and-take, joint, corresponding, complementary.
■ **reciprocally** adv. **reciprocity** n.

reciprocate v. respond to an action with a similar one.
▷ SYNONYMS: **requite**, return, give back.

recital n. **1** a musical performance. **2** a listing of facts etc.
▷ SYNONYMS: **1 performance**, concert, recitation, reading. **2 report**, account, listing, catalogue, litany.

recitative /re-si-tuh-**teev**/ n. a passage in an opera sung in a rhythm like that of ordinary speech.

recite v. **1** repeat aloud from memory. **2** state facts in order.
▷ SYNONYMS: **1 quote**, say, speak, read aloud, declaim, deliver, render. **2 recount**, list, detail, reel off, relate, enumerate.
■ **recitation** n.

reckless adj. without thought or care for the results of an action.
▷ SYNONYMS: **rash**, careless, thoughtless, heedless, precipitate, impetuous, impulsive, irresponsible, foolhardy, devil-may-care.
– ANTONYMS: cautious.
■ **recklessly** adv. **recklessness** n.

reckon v. **1** have as an opinion. **2** (**reckon on**) expect. **3** calculate. **4** (**reckon with** or **without**) take (or fail to take) into account.
▷ SYNONYMS: **1 think**, believe, be of the opinion, suppose, assume. **2** *they had reckoned on sales of £300 million*: **expect**, anticipate, hope for; count on, rely on, depend on, bank on; N. Amer. informal figure on. **3 calculate**, compute, work out, figure, count, add up, total, tally; Brit. tot up.

reclaim v. **1** recover possession of. **2** make waste land usable.
▷ SYNONYMS: **1 get back**, claim back,

recover, retrieve, recoup. **2** save, rescue, redeem, salvage.
■ **reclamation** n.

recline v. lean or lie back in a relaxed position.
▷ SYNONYMS: **lie**, lie down/back, lean back, relax, loll, lounge, sprawl, stretch out.

recluse n. a person who avoids other people.
▷ SYNONYMS: **hermit**, ascetic, eremite, loner, lone wolf; historical anchorite.
■ **reclusive** adj.

recognition n. **1** the act of recognizing. **2** appreciation or acknowledgement.
▷ SYNONYMS: **1 identification**, recollection, remembrance. **2 acknowledgement**, acceptance, admission, confession. **3 appreciation**, gratitude, thanks, congratulations, credit, commendation, acclaim, acknowledgement.

recognize (or **-ise**) v. **1** know from having encountered before. **2** accept as genuine, legal, or valid. **3** show official appreciation of.
▷ SYNONYMS: **1 identify**, place, know, put a name to, remember, recall, recollect; Scottish & N. English ken. **2 acknowledge**, accept, admit, concede, confess, realize. **3 pay tribute to**, appreciate, be grateful for, acclaim, commend.
■ **recognizable** adj.

recoil v. **1** suddenly move back in fear, disgust, etc. **2** (of a gun) suddenly move back after firing. **3** (**recoil on**) have an unpleasant effect on.
▷ SYNONYMS: **draw back**, jump back, pull back, flinch, shy away, shrink, blench.
• n. the act of recoiling.

recollect v. remember.
▷ SYNONYMS: **remember**, recall, call to mind, think of, think back to, reminisce about.
– ANTONYMS: forget.

recollection n. **1** the action of remembering or the ability to remember. **2** a memory.
▷ SYNONYMS: **memory**, recall, remembrance, impression, reminiscence.

recommend v. **1** suggest as suitable for a purpose or role. **2** make appealing or desirable.
▷ SYNONYMS: **1 advocate**, endorse, commend, suggest, put forward, propose, nominate, put up, speak favourably of, put in a good word for, vouch for; informal plug. **2 advise**, counsel, urge, exhort, enjoin, prescribe, argue for, back, support.

recommendation n. **1** a proposal as

to the best course of action. **2** the act of recommending.
▷ SYNONYMS: **1 advice**, counsel, guidance, suggestion, proposal. **2 commendation**, endorsement, good word, testimonial, tip; informal plug.

recompense v. **1** compensate. **2** pay for work.
• n. compensation or reward.

reconcile v. **1** restore friendly relations between. **2** find a satisfactory way of dealing with opposing facts, ideas, etc. **3** (**reconcile to**) cause to accept an unwelcome situation.
▷ SYNONYMS: **1 reunite**, bring back together, pacify, appease, placate, mollify; formal conciliate. **2** *reconciling his religious beliefs with his career:* **make compatible**, harmonize, square, make congruent, balance. **3 settle**, resolve, sort out, smooth over, iron out, mend, remedy, heal, rectify; informal patch up. **4** *they had to reconcile themselves to drastic losses:* **accept**, resign yourself to, come to terms with, learn to live with, get used to, make the best of.
■ **reconciliation** n.

recondite adj. obscure and little known.

recondition v. Brit. renovate.

reconnaissance /ri-kon-ni-suhnss/ n. military observation of an area to gain information.

reconnoitre /rek-uh-noy-ter/ (US **reconnoiter**) v. make a reconnaissance of.
▷ SYNONYMS: **survey**, explore, scout out, find out the lie of the land, investigate, examine, scrutinize, inspect, observe, take a look at, patrol; informal recce, check out.

reconsider v. consider again, with a view to changing a decision.
▷ SYNONYMS: **rethink**, review, revise, re-evaluate, reassess, have second thoughts, change your mind.
■ **reconsideration** n.

reconstitute v. **1** change the form of an organization. **2** restore dried food to its original state by adding water.
■ **reconstitution** n.

reconstruct v. **1** construct again. **2** act out a past event.
▷ SYNONYMS: **rebuild**, remake, recreate, restore, reassemble, remodel, revamp, renovate.
■ **reconstruction** n.

record n. **1** a permanent account kept for evidence or information. **2** previous behaviour or performance.

r

3 a list of an offender's past convictions. **4** the best officially recognized performance of its kind. **5** a disc carrying recorded sound in grooves.

▷ SYNONYMS: **1 account**, document, data, file, dossier, evidence, report, annals, archive, chronicle, minutes, transactions, proceedings, transcript, certificate, deed, register, log. **2 disc**, recording, album, LP, single.

• v. **1** make a record of. **2** convert sound etc. into permanent form so as to be reproduced later.

▷ SYNONYMS: **1 write down**, take down, note, jot down, put down on paper, document, enter, log, minute, register. **2 indicate**, register, show, display. **3 film**, photograph, tape, tape-record, video-record, videotape. □ **off the record** not made as an official statement.

recorder n. **1** a person or thing that records. **2** a barrister serving as a part-time judge. **3** a simple woodwind instrument.

recount¹ v. tell in detail.

▷ SYNONYMS: **tell**, relate, narrate, describe, report, relay, convey, communicate, impart.

recount² v. count again.
• n. an act of recounting.

recoup v. recover money spent or lost.

recourse n. (**have recourse to**) be able to use as a source of help.

recover v. **1** return to health. **2** regain possession or control of.

▷ SYNONYMS: **1 get better**, improve, rally, recuperate, convalesce, revive, be on the mend, get back on your feet, pick up, heal, bounce back, pull through. **2 retrieve**, regain, get back, recoup, reclaim, repossess, recapture. **3 salvage**, save, rescue, retrieve.

– ANTONYMS: deteriorate.

recovery n. (pl. **recoveries**) the act or process of recovering.

▷ SYNONYMS: **1 improvement**, recuperation, convalescence, rally, revival. **2 retrieval**, repossession, reclamation, recapture.

– ANTONYMS: relapse.

recreate v. make or do again.

recreation n. enjoyable leisure activity.

▷ SYNONYMS: **1 pleasure**, leisure, relaxation, fun, enjoyment, entertainment, amusement, diversion. **2 pastime**, hobby, leisure activity.

– ANTONYMS: work.

■ **recreational** adj.

recrimination n. an accusation in response to another.

recruit v. take on someone to serve in the armed forces or work for an organization.

▷ SYNONYMS: **1 enlist**, call up, conscript; US draft. **2 muster**, form, raise, mobilize. **3 hire**, employ, take on, enrol, sign up, engage.

– ANTONYMS: demobilize.

• n. a newly recruited person.

▷ SYNONYMS: **1 conscript**; US draftee; N. Amer. informal yardbird. **2 newcomer**, trainee, initiate, joiner, beginner, novice.

■ **recruitment** n.

rectangle n. a plane figure with four straight sides and four right angles, and with unequal adjacent sides.

■ **rectangular** adj.

rectify v. (**rectifying**, **rectified**) **1** put right. **2** convert alternating current to direct current.

▷ SYNONYMS: **correct**, put right, right, sort out, deal with, amend, remedy, repair, fix, make good, resolve, settle; informal patch up.

■ **rectification** n.

rectilinear adj. within or moving in a straight line or lines.

rectitude n. correct behaviour.

recto n. (pl. **rectos**) a right-hand page of an open book.

rector n. **1** a priest in charge of a parish. **2** the head of certain universities, colleges, and schools.

rectory n. (pl. **rectories**) the house of a rector.

rectum n. (pl. **rectums** or **recta**) the final section of the large intestine, ending at the anus.

■ **rectal** adj.

recumbent adj. lying down.

recuperate v. **1** recover from illness. **2** regain.

■ **recuperation** n. **recuperative** adj.

recur v. (**recurring**, **recurred**) happen again or repeatedly.

▷ SYNONYMS: **happen again**, reoccur, repeat itself, come back, return, reappear.

■ **recurrence** n. **recurrent** adj.

recycle v. convert waste into a reusable form.

▷ SYNONYMS: **reuse**, reprocess, reclaim, recover, salvage.

■ **recyclable** adj.

red adj. (**redder**, **reddest**) **1** of the colour of blood or fire. **2** (of hair) reddish-brown. **3** informal communist.

▷ SYNONYMS: **1 scarlet**, vermilion, ruby, cherry, cerise, cardinal, carmine, crimson, maroon, magenta, burgundy,

claret. **2** flushed, blushing, pink, rosy, florid, ruddy. **3** auburn, Titian, chestnut, carroty, ginger.
• n. **1** red colour or material. **2** informal a communist.
▫ **in the red** overdrawn. **redcurrant** a small edible red berry. **red-handed** in the act of doing something wrong. **redhead** a person with red hair. **red herring** a thing drawing attention away from something important. **red-hot 1** so hot as to glow red. **2** very exciting. **red-letter day** an important or memorable day. **red-light district** an area with many brothels, strip clubs, etc. **red tape** complicated official rules which hinder progress. **redwood** a giant coniferous tree with reddish wood. **see red** informal become very angry.
■ **red** v. **reddish** adj. **redness** n.

redeem v. **1** make up for the faults of. **2** save from sin. **3** pay a debt. **4** exchange a coupon for goods or money. **5** fulfil a promise.
▷ SYNONYMS: **1** save, deliver from sin, absolve. **2** repay, pay, pay off, clear, discharge. **3** exchange, convert, trade in, cash in.
■ **redemption** n.

redeploy v. assign to a new place or task.
■ **redeployment** n.

redolent adj. (**redolent of/with**) **1** strongly suggestive of. **2** smelling of.
▷ SYNONYMS: **evocative**, suggestive, reminiscent.
■ **redolence** n.

redouble v. increase or intensify.

redoubtable adj. formidable.

redound v. (**redound to**) be to a person's credit.

redress v. set right.
▷ SYNONYMS: **rectify**, correct, right, compensate for, make amends for, remedy, make good.
• n. reparation or amends.
▷ SYNONYMS: **compensation**, reparation, restitution, recompense, repayment, amends.

reduce v. **1** make or become less. **2** (**reduce to**) change to a simpler form. **3** (**reduce to**) bring to a particular state or condition.
▷ SYNONYMS: **1** lessen, make smaller, lower, decrease, diminish, minimize, shrink, narrow, cut, curtail, contract, shorten, downsize; informal chop. **2** bring down, make cheaper, lower, mark down, slash, discount. **3** he reduced her to tears: **bring to**, bring to

the point of, drive to.
– ANTONYMS: increase.
■ **reducible** adj.

reduction n. **1** the act of reducing. **2** the amount by which something is reduced.
▷ SYNONYMS: **1** lessening, lowering, decrease, diminution, cut, cutback, downsizing. **2** discount, deduction, cut.

reductive adj. presenting something in an oversimplified form.

redundant adj. **1** Brit. unemployed because your job is no longer needed. **2** no longer needed or useful.
▷ SYNONYMS: **1** unemployed, jobless, out of work. **2** unnecessary, not required, unneeded, surplus, superfluous.
■ **redundancy** n.

reed n. **1** a water or marsh plant with hollow stems. **2** a piece of thin cane or metal in certain wind instruments which vibrates to produce the sound.

reedy adj. (of a voice) high and thin in tone.

reef n. **1** a ridge of rock or coral near the surface of the sea. **2** a strip in a sail that can be drawn in to reduce the area exposed to the wind.
• v. take in a reef or reefs of a sail.
▫ **reef knot** a secure double knot.

reefer n. informal a cannabis cigarette.

reefer jacket n. a thick double-breasted jacket.

reek v. have an unpleasant smell.
• n. a strong unpleasant smell.

reel n. **1** a cylinder on which something is wound. **2** a lively Scottish or Irish folk dance.
• v. **1** (**reel in**) bring towards you by turning a reel. **2** (**reel off**) say rapidly and with ease. **3** stagger.
▷ SYNONYMS: **stagger**, lurch, sway, rock, stumble, totter, wobble, teeter.

refectory n. (pl. **refectories**) a room for meals in a college or religious institution.

refer v. (**referring, referred**) (**refer to**) **1** mention. **2** turn to for information. **3** pass to an authority or specialist for a decision.
▷ SYNONYMS: **pass**, direct, hand on/over, send on, transfer, entrust, assign.
■ **referral** n.

referee n. **1** an official who supervises a game to ensure that players keep to the rules. **2** Brit. a person who gives a reference for a job applicant.
▷ SYNONYMS: **umpire**, judge, adjudicator, arbitrator; informal ref.
• v. (**refereeing, refereed**) be a referee of.

r

reference n. **1** the act of referring. **2** a mention of a source of information in a book etc. **3** a letter testifying to someone's suitability for a job.

▷ SYNONYMS: **1 mention**, allusion, quotation, comment, remark. **2 source**, citation, authority, credit. **3 testimonial**, recommendation, character reference, credentials.

□ **with** (or **in**) **reference to** in relation to.

referendum n. (pl. **referendums** or **referenda**) a vote by a country's electorate on a single political issue.

▷ SYNONYMS: **vote**, ballot, poll, plebiscite.

refill v. fill again.
• n. an act of refilling.

refine v. **1** remove unwanted substances from. **2** improve by making minor changes.

▷ SYNONYMS: **1 purify**, filter, distil, process, treat. **2 improve**, perfect, polish up, hone, fine-tune.
■ **refinement** n.

refined adj. well educated and elegant.

▷ SYNONYMS: **1** *a refined woman:* **cultivated**, cultured, polished, elegant, sophisticated, urbane, polite, gracious, well bred, well educated. **2** *her refined taste:* **discriminating**, discerning, fastidious, exquisite, impeccable, fine.

– ANTONYMS: crude, coarse.

refinery n. (pl. **refineries**) a factory where a substance is refined.

refit v. (**refitting**, **refitted**) replace or repair fittings in a ship, building, etc.
• n. an act of refitting.

reflect v. **1** throw back heat, light, or sound from a surface. **2** (of a mirror) show an image of. **3** show the nature of. **4** think seriously. **5** (**reflect well/badly on**) give a good or bad impression of.

▷ SYNONYMS: **1 mirror**, send back, throw back, echo. **2 indicate**, show, display, demonstrate, be evidence of, evince, reveal, betray. **3 think**, consider, review, mull over, ponder, contemplate, deliberate, ruminate, meditate, muse, brood; formal cogitate.
■ **reflector** n.

reflection n. **1** the act of reflecting. **2** a reflected image. **3** a sign. **4** a source of shame or blame.

▷ SYNONYMS: **1 image**, likeness. **2 indication**, display, demonstration, manifestation, expression, evidence. **3 thought**, consideration, contemplation, deliberation, pondering, rumination, meditation, musing; formal cogitation.

reflective adj. **1** providing a reflection. **2** thoughtful.
■ **reflectively** adv.

reflex n. an action done without conscious thought as a response to something.
• adj. **1** done as a reflex. **2** (of an angle) more than 180°.

reflexive adj. Grammar referring back to the subject of a clause or verb, e.g. *myself* in *I hurt myself*.

reflexology n. a system of massage of points on the feet used to relieve tension and treat illness.
■ **reflexologist** n.

reform v. **1** improve by making changes. **2** cause to improve behaviour.

▷ SYNONYMS: **1 improve**, better, ameliorate, correct, rectify, restore, revise, refine, adapt, revamp, redesign, reconstruct, reorganize. **2 mend your ways**, change for the better, turn over a new leaf.
• n. the act of reforming.

▷ SYNONYMS: **improvement**, amelioration, refinement, rectification, restoration, adaptation, revision, redesign, revamp, reconstruction, reorganization.
■ **reformation** n. **reformer** n. **reformist** adj. & n.

refract v. (of water, air, or glass) make a ray of light change direction when it enters at an angle.
■ **refraction** n. **refractive** adj. **refractor** n.

refractory adj. **1** stubborn or difficult to control. **2** (of a disease) not responding to treatment.

refrain v. (**refrain from**) stop yourself from doing something.

▷ SYNONYMS: **abstain**, desist, hold back, stop yourself, forbear, avoid; informal swear off.
• n. the part of a song that is repeated at the end of each verse.

refresh v. **1** give new energy to. **2** prompt someone's memory.

▷ SYNONYMS: **1 reinvigorate**, revitalize, revive, rejuvenate, restore, energize, enliven, perk up, brace, freshen, wake up, breathe new life into; informal buck up. **2** *let me refresh your memory:* **jog**, stimulate, prompt, prod.
■ **refreshingly** adv.

refreshing adj. **1** giving new energy or strength. **2** pleasantly new or different.

▷ SYNONYMS: **1 invigorating**, revitalizing, reviving, bracing, fortifying,

enlivening, stimulating, exhilarating, energizing. **2** *a refreshing change of direction:* **welcome**, stimulating, fresh, new, imaginative, innovative.
■ **refreshingly** adv.

refreshment n. **1** a snack or drink. **2** the giving of new energy.
▷ SYNONYMS: **food and drink**, snacks, titbits; informal nibbles.

refrigerate v. chill food or drink to keep it fresh.
■ **refrigeration** n.

refrigerator n. a fridge.

USAGE No *d* in the middle: refrigerator, not -ridg-.

refuge n. a place or state of safety from danger or trouble.
▷ SYNONYMS: **1** shelter, protection, safety, security, asylum, sanctuary. **2** place of safety, shelter, haven, sanctuary, sanctum, retreat, bolt-hole, hiding place.

refugee n. a person forced to leave their country because of war or persecution.
▷ SYNONYMS: **asylum seeker**, fugitive, displaced person, exile, émigré.

refulgent adj. literary shining.

refund v. pay back.
▷ SYNONYMS: **repay**, give back, return, pay back, reimburse, compensate, recompense.
• n. a repayment of a sum of money.
▷ SYNONYMS: **repayment**, reimbursement, compensation, rebate.

refurbish v. redecorate and improve a building or room.
▷ SYNONYMS: **renovate**, recondition, rehabilitate, revamp, overhaul, restore, redecorate, upgrade, refit; informal do up.
■ **refurbishment** n.

refuse[1] /ri-fyooz/ v. state that you are unwilling to do, accept, or grant something.
▷ SYNONYMS: **1** decline, turn down, say no to, reject, spurn, rebuff; informal pass up, knock back. **2** withhold, deny.
– ANTONYMS: accept.
■ **refusal** n.

refuse[2] /ref-yooss/ n. waste material; rubbish.
▷ SYNONYMS: **rubbish**, waste, litter, detritus, flotsam and jetsam; N. Amer. garbage, trash; informal dreck, junk.

refute v. prove wrong.
▷ SYNONYMS: **disprove**, prove wrong, rebut, explode, debunk, discredit, invalidate; informal shoot full of holes.

■ **refutation** n.

regain v. **1** get back after loss. **2** get back to a place.
▷ SYNONYMS: **recover**, get back, win back, recoup, retrieve, repossess, take back, retake, recapture, reconquer.

regal adj. of or like a monarch.
▷ SYNONYMS: **royal**, kingly, queenly, princely, majestic.
■ **regality** n. **regally** adv.

regale v. **1** entertain with stories. **2** supply generously with food or drink.

regalia n. the distinctive clothing and objects of royalty or other rank or office, used at formal occasions.

regard v. **1** think of in a particular way. **2** look steadily at.
▷ SYNONYMS: **1** consider, look on, view, see, think of, judge, deem, estimate, assess, reckon, rate. **2** look at, contemplate, eye, gaze at, stare at, observe, view, study, scrutinize.
• n. **1** concern or care. **2** high opinion; respect. **3** a steady gaze. **4** (**regards**) best wishes.
▷ SYNONYMS: **1** consideration, care, concern, thought, notice, heed, attention. **2** *doctors are held in high regard:* esteem, respect, admiration, approval, honour, estimation. **3** gaze, stare, observation, contemplation, study, scrutiny. **4** *he sends his regards:* best wishes, greetings, respects, compliments.
□ **as regards** concerning. **with** (or **in**) **regard to** concerning.

regarding prep. concerning.
▷ SYNONYMS: **concerning**, as regards, with/in regard to, with respect to, with reference to, relating to, respecting, re, about, apropos, on the subject of, in connection with, vis-à-vis.

regardless adv. **1** (**regardless of**) without concern for. **2** despite what is happening.
▷ SYNONYMS: **anyway**, anyhow, in any case, nevertheless, nonetheless, despite everything, even so, all the same, in any event, come what may.

regatta n. a series of boat or yacht races.

regency n. (pl. **regencies**) a period of rule by a regent.

regenerate v. **1** bring new life or strength to. **2** grow new tissue.
■ **regeneration** n. **regenerative** adj.

regent n. a person appointed to rule while the monarch is too young or unfit to rule, or is absent.

r

reggae /reg-gay/ n. a style of pop music originating in Jamaica.

regicide n. **1** the killing of a king. **2** a person who kills a king.

regime /ray-**zheem**/ n. **1** a government. **2** a system of doing something.

▷ SYNONYMS: **1 government**, administration, leadership, rule, authority, control, command. **2 system**, arrangement, scheme, policy, method, course, plan, programme.

regimen n. a course of medical treatment, diet, or exercise.

regiment n. a permanent unit of an army.
• v. organize according to a strict system.
■ **regimental** adj. **regimentation** n.

Regina n. the reigning queen (used in referring to lawsuits).

region n. **1** an area of a country or the world. **2** an administrative district. **3** a part of the body.

▷ SYNONYMS: **area**, district, province, territory, division, section, sector, zone, belt, quarter, locality.
□ **in the region of** approximately.
■ **regional** adj.

register n. **1** an official list. **2** a part of the range of a voice or musical instrument. **3** the level and style of writing or speech (e.g. formal, informal).

▷ SYNONYMS: **1 list**, roll, roster, index, directory, catalogue, inventory. **2 record**, chronicle, log, ledger, archive, annals, files.
• v. **1** enter in a register. **2** express an opinion or emotion. **3** become aware of. **4** (of a measuring instrument) show a reading.

▷ SYNONYMS: **1 record**, enter, file, lodge, write down, submit, report, note, minute, log. **2 enrol**, put your name down, enlist, sign on/up, apply. **3 indicate**, read, record, show. **4 display**, show, express, exhibit, betray, reveal.
□ **register office** a local government building where civil marriages are performed and births, marriages, and deaths are recorded.
■ **registration** n.

registrar n. **1** an official responsible for keeping official records. **2** Brit. a hospital doctor who is training to be a specialist.

registry n. (pl. **registries**) a place where official records are kept.
□ **registry office** a register office.

regress v. return to an earlier or less advanced state.

■ **regression** n. **regressive** adj.

regret n. a feeling of sorrow or disappointment about something you have done or should have done.

▷ SYNONYMS: **1 remorse**, contrition, repentance, compunction, ruefulness, self-reproach, pangs of conscience. **2 sadness**, sorrow, disappointment, unhappiness, grief.
• v. (**regretting**, **regretted**) feel regret about.

▷ SYNONYMS: **1 be sorry about**, feel contrite about, feel remorse for, rue, repent of. **2 mourn**, grieve for/over, weep over, sigh over, lament, bemoan.
– ANTONYMS: welcome.
■ **regretful** adj. **regretfully** adv.

regrettable adj. giving rise to regret.

▷ SYNONYMS: **unfortunate**, unwelcome, sorry, woeful, disappointing, reprehensible, deplorable, disgraceful.
■ **regrettably** adv.

regular adj. **1** following or arranged in an evenly spaced pattern or sequence. **2** done, happening, or doing something frequently. **3** following an accepted standard. **4** belonging to a country's permanent armed forces. **5** (of a geometrical figure) having all sides and all angles equal.

▷ SYNONYMS: **1 uniform**, even, consistent, constant, unchanging, unvarying, fixed. **2 frequent**, repeated, continual, recurrent, periodic, constant, perpetual, numerous. **3 usual**, normal, customary, habitual, routine, typical, accustomed, established.
– ANTONYMS: erratic, occasional, unusual.
• n. a regular customer, soldier, etc.
■ **regularity** n. **regularly** adv.

regularize (or **-ise**) v. **1** make regular. **2** make a temporary situation legal or official.

regulate v. **1** control the rate or speed of a machine or process. **2** control by rules.

▷ SYNONYMS: **1 control**, adjust, balance, set, synchronize. **2 police**, supervise, monitor, be responsible for, control, manage, direct, govern.
■ **regulator** n. **regulatory** adj.

regulation n. **1** a rule. **2** the act of regulating.

▷ SYNONYMS: **1 rule**, order, directive, act, law, by-law, statute, dictate, decree. **2 control**, policing, supervision, superintendence, monitoring, governance, management, administration, responsibility.

regurgitate v. **1** bring swallowed food up again to the mouth. **2** repeat facts without understanding them.
■ regurgitation n.

rehabilitate v. help back to normal life after imprisonment or illness.
▷ SYNONYMS: **1 reintegrate**, readapt; N. Amer. informal rehab. **2 reinstate**, restore, bring back, pardon, absolve, exonerate, forgive; formal exculpate. **3 recondition**, restore, renovate, refurbish, revamp, overhaul, redevelop, rebuild, reconstruct.
■ rehabilitation n.

rehash v. reuse old ideas or material.
• n. an act of rehashing.

rehearsal n. a trial performance of a play or other work for later public performance.
▷ SYNONYMS: **practice**, trial performance, read-through, run-through, drill, training, coaching; informal dry run.

rehearse v. **1** practise a play, music, etc. for later public performance. **2** state points made many times before.
▷ SYNONYMS: **1 prepare**, practise, read through, run through/over, go over. **2 train**, drill, prepare, coach. **3 list**, enumerate, itemize, detail, spell out, catalogue, recite, repeat, go over, run through, recap.

reign v. **1** rule as monarch. **2** be the main quality or aspect.
▷ SYNONYMS: **1 be king/queen**, sit on the throne, wear the crown, be supreme, rule. **2** chaos reigned: **prevail**, exist, be present, be the case, occur, be rife, be rampant, be the order of the day.
• n. a monarch's period of rule.
▷ SYNONYMS: **rule**, sovereignty, monarchy, dominion, control.

reimburse v. repay money to.
■ reimbursement n.

rein n. (reins) **1** long, narrow straps attached to a bridle, used to control a horse. **2** the power to direct and control.
• v. **1** control with reins. **2** (**rein in/back**) restrain.
▷ SYNONYMS: **restrain**, check, curb, constrain, hold back/in, keep under control, regulate, restrict, control, curtail, limit.
□ **free rein** freedom of action.

> USAGE Remember: free *rein*, not *reign*.

reincarnate v. (**be reincarnated**) be born again in another body.
■ reincarnation n.

reindeer n. (pl. **reindeer** or **reindeers**) a deer with large antlers, found in cold northern regions.

reinforce v. **1** make stronger. **2** strengthen a military force with additional personnel.
▷ SYNONYMS: **1 strengthen**, fortify, bolster up, shore up, buttress, prop up, underpin, brace, support, boost. **2 augment**, increase, add to, supplement, boost, top up.

reinforcement n. **1** extra personnel sent to strengthen an army etc. **2** the action of reinforcing.
▷ SYNONYMS: **1** send in some reinforcements: **additional troops**, auxiliaries, reserves, support, backup, help. **2 strengthening**, fortification, bolstering, shoring up, buttressing.

reinstate v. restore to a former position.
▷ SYNONYMS: **restore**, put back, bring back, reinstitute, reinstall, re-establish.
■ reinstatement n.

reiterate v. say again or repeatedly.
▷ SYNONYMS: **repeat**, restate, recapitulate, recap, go over, rehearse.
■ reiteration n.

reject v. refuse to accept or agree to.
▷ SYNONYMS: **1 turn down**, refuse, decline, say no to, spurn; informal pass up, give the thumbs down to. **2 rebuff**, spurn, shun, snub, cast off/aside, discard, abandon, desert, turn your back on, cold-shoulder; informal give someone the brush-off.
– ANTONYMS: accept, welcome.
• n. a rejected person or thing.
▷ SYNONYMS: **second**, discard, misshape, faulty item, cast-off.
■ rejection n.

rejig v. (**rejigging**, **rejigged**) Brit. rearrange.

rejoice v. feel or show great joy.
▷ SYNONYMS: **be happy**, be glad, be delighted, celebrate, make merry; informal be over the moon.
– ANTONYMS: mourn.

rejoin v. **1** join again. **2** say in reply.
▷ SYNONYMS: **return to**, be reunited with, join again, reach again, regain.

rejoinder n. a quick reply.

rejuvenate v. make more lively or youthful.
▷ SYNONYMS: **revive**, revitalize, regenerate, breathe new life into, revivify, reanimate, resuscitate, refresh, reawaken; informal give a shot in the arm to, pep up, buck up.
■ rejuvenation n.

relapse v. **1** become ill again after a period of improvement. **2** revert to a worse state.

r

▷ SYNONYMS: **deteriorate**, degenerate, lapse, slip back, slide back, regress, revert, retrogress.
– ANTONYMS: improve.
• n. an instance of relapsing.

relate v. **1** make or show a connection between. **2** (**relate to**) have to do with. **3** (**be related**) be connected by blood or marriage. **4** (**relate to**) feel sympathy with. **5** give an account of.
▷ SYNONYMS: **1** *the charges relate to offences committed in August:* **apply**, be relevant, concern, pertain to, be pertinent to, have a bearing on, appertain to, involve. **2** *I can't relate to him:* **empathize with**, identify with, understand, sympathize with, feel for. **3** **tell**, recount, narrate, report, describe, recite, rehearse.

related adj. having a connection.
▷ SYNONYMS: **connected**, interconnected, associated, linked, allied, corresponding, analogous, parallel, comparable, equivalent.

relation n. **1** a connection between people or things. **2** (**relations**) people's feelings and behaviour towards each other. **3** a relative. **4** (**relations**) sex.
▷ SYNONYMS: **1 connection**, relationship, association, link, tie-in, correlation, correspondence, parallel. **2** relative, family member, kinsman, kinswoman; (**relations**) family, kin, kith and kin, kindred. **3** *our relations with Europe:* **dealings**, communication, relationship, connections, contact, interaction.

relationship n. **1** the way in which people or things are connected. **2** the way in which people behave towards each other. **3** a loving and sexual association between two people.
▷ SYNONYMS: **1 connection**, relation, association, link, correlation, correspondence, parallel. **2 family ties**, kinship, affinity, common ancestry. **3 romance**, affair, love affair, liaison, amour, fling.

relative adj. **1** considered in relation to something else. **2** existing only in comparison to something else. **3** Grammar referring to an earlier noun or clause.
▷ SYNONYMS: **1 comparative**, respective, comparable. **2 proportionate**, in proportion, commensurate, corresponding.
– ANTONYMS: disproportionate.
• n. a person connected by blood or marriage.
▷ SYNONYMS: **relation**, member of

the family, kinsman, kinswoman; (**relatives**) family, kin, kith and kin, kindred.
■ **relatively** adv.

relativity n. **1** the state of being relative. **2** Physics a description of matter, energy, space, and time according to Einstein's theories.

relax v. **1** become less tense or rigid. **2** rest from work; do something recreational. **3** make a rule less strict.
▷ SYNONYMS: **1** *relax your grip:* **loosen**, slacken, unclench, weaken. **2** **rest**, loosen up, ease up/off, slow down, de-stress, unbend, unwind, put your feet up, take it easy; informal chill out; N. Amer. informal hang loose, decompress. **3** *they relaxed the restrictions:* **moderate**, ease, lighten, dilute, weaken, reduce, decrease; informal let up on.
– ANTONYMS: tense, tighten.

relaxation n. the action of relaxing or the state of being relaxed.
▷ SYNONYMS: **recreation**, enjoyment, amusement, entertainment, fun, pleasure, leisure; informal R & R.

relay n. **1** a group engaged in a task for a time and then replaced by a similar group. **2** a race between teams, each team member in turn covering part of the total distance. **3** an electrical device activating a circuit. **4** a device to receive and transmit a signal.
▷ SYNONYMS: **broadcast**, transmission, showing, feed.
• v. receive and pass on or transmit again.
▷ SYNONYMS: **pass on**, hand on, transfer, repeat, communicate, send, transmit, circulate.

release v. **1** set free. **2** allow to move freely. **3** make information, a film, or a recording available to the public.
▷ SYNONYMS: **1 free**, set free, turn loose, let go/out, liberate, discharge. **2 untie**, undo, unfasten, loose, let go, unleash. **3 make public**, make known, issue, put out, publish, broadcast, circulate, launch, distribute.
– ANTONYMS: imprison.
• n. **1** the act of releasing. **2** a film or recording released to the public.

relegate v. place in a lower rank or position.
▷ SYNONYMS: **downgrade**, demote, lower, put down, move down.
– ANTONYMS: upgrade, promote.
■ **relegation** n.

relent v. **1** finally agree to something after refusing it. **2** become less intense.

▷ SYNONYMS: **1 change your mind**, do a U-turn, back-pedal, back down, give way/in, capitulate; Brit. do an about-turn. **2 ease**, slacken, let up, abate, drop, die down, lessen, decrease, subside, weaken, tail off.

relentless adj. **1** never stopping or weakening. **2** harsh or inflexible.
▷ SYNONYMS: **1 persistent**, unfaltering, unremitting, unflagging, untiring, unwavering, dogged, single-minded, tireless, indefatigable. **2 harsh**, cruel, remorseless, unrelenting, merciless, pitiless, implacable, inexorable, unforgiving, unbending, unyielding.
■ **relentlessly** adv.

relevant adj. connected or appropriate to the current matter.
▷ SYNONYMS: **pertinent**, applicable, apposite, material, apropos, to the point, germane.
■ **relevance** n.

reliable adj. able to be relied on.
▷ SYNONYMS: **dependable**, trustworthy, good, safe, authentic, faithful, genuine, sound, true, loyal, unfailing; humorous trusty.
– ANTONYMS: unreliable.
■ **reliability** n. **reliably** adv.

reliance n. dependence on or trust in someone or something.
▷ SYNONYMS: **1 dependence**, need. **2 trust**, confidence, faith, belief, conviction.
■ **reliant** adj.

relic n. **1** something surviving from an earlier time. **2** a part of a holy person's body or belongings kept after their death.
▷ SYNONYMS: **artefact**, historical object, antiquity, remnant, vestige, remains.

relief n. **1** a feeling of relaxation after anxiety. **2** the act of relieving. **3** a break in a tense or boring situation. **4** help given to people in need. **5** a person or group replacing another on duty. **6** a carving in which the design stands out from the surface.
▷ SYNONYMS: **1 respite**, remission, interruption, variation, diversion; informal let-up. **2 alleviation**, relieving, palliation, soothing, easing, lessening, mitigation. **3 help**, aid, assistance, charity, succour. **4 replacement**, substitute, deputy, reserve, cover, stand-in, supply, locum, understudy. □ **relief map** a map showing hills and valleys by shading.

relieve v. **1** lessen or remove pain, difficulty, or anxiety. **2** replace someone on duty. **3** (**relieve of**) take a responsibility from. **4** bring military support for a place under siege. **5** (**relieve yourself**) urinate or defecate.
▷ SYNONYMS: **1 alleviate**, mitigate, ease, counteract, dull, reduce. **2 replace**, take over from, stand in for, fill in for, substitute for, deputize for, cover for. **3 free**, release, exempt, excuse, absolve, let off.
– ANTONYMS: aggravate.

relieved adj. happy that pain, difficulty, or anxiety, etc. has been reduced or removed.
▷ SYNONYMS: **glad**, thankful, grateful, pleased, happy, easy in your mind, reassured.
– ANTONYMS: worried.

religion n. **1** the belief in and worship of a God or gods. **2** a particular system of faith and worship.
▷ SYNONYMS: **faith**, belief, worship, creed, church, denomination, sect; cult.

WORD LINKS
theology, **divinity** the study of religious belief

religious adj. **1** of or believing in a religion. **2** very careful or regular.
▷ SYNONYMS: **1 devout**, pious, reverent, godly, God-fearing, churchgoing. **2 spiritual**, theological, scriptural, doctrinal, ecclesiastical, church, holy, divine, sacred. **3 scrupulous**, conscientious, meticulous, punctilious, strict, rigorous.
– ANTONYMS: atheistic, secular.
■ **religiously** adv.

relinquish v. give up.
▷ SYNONYMS: **1 renounce**, resign, give up/away, hand over, let go of. **2 leave**, resign from, stand down from, bow out of, give up; informal quit, chuck.
– ANTONYMS: retain.
■ **relinquishment** n.

reliquary n. (pl. **reliquaries**) a container for holy relics.

relish v. enjoy or look forward to.
▷ SYNONYMS: **enjoy**, delight in, love, adore, take great pleasure in, rejoice in, appreciate, savour, revel in, luxuriate in, glory in.
– ANTONYMS: dislike.
● n. **1** great enjoyment. **2** a spicy sauce or pickle.
▷ SYNONYMS: **1 enjoyment**, gusto, delight, pleasure, glee, appreciation, enthusiasm. **2 condiment**, sauce, dressing.
– ANTONYMS: distaste.

relocate v. move to a different place.
■ **relocation** n.

r

reluctance n. unwillingness to do something.
▷ SYNONYMS: **unwillingness**, disinclination, hesitation, wavering, vacillation, doubts, second thoughts, misgivings.

reluctant adj. unwilling and hesitant.
▷ SYNONYMS: **unwilling**, disinclined, unenthusiastic, resistant, opposed, hesitant, loath.
– ANTONYMS: willing, eager.
■ **reluctantly** adv.

rely v. (relying, relied) (rely on) **1** be dependent on. **2** trust or have faith in.
▷ SYNONYMS: **depend on**, count on, bank on, be confident of, be sure of, have faith in, trust in; informal swear by; N. Amer. informal figure on.

remain v. **1** still be in the same place or condition. **2** continue to be. **3** be left over.
▷ SYNONYMS: **1 continue**, endure, last, abide, carry on, persist, stay around, survive, live on. **2 stay**, stay behind, stay put, wait behind, be left, hang on; informal hang around/round. **3** he remained calm: **continue to be**, stay, keep.

remainder n. **1** a remaining part, number, or amount. **2** the number left over when one quantity does not exactly divide into another.
▷ SYNONYMS: **rest**, balance, residue, remnant, leftovers, surplus, extra, excess.

remains pl. n. **1** things remaining. **2** archaeological relics. **3** a dead body.
▷ SYNONYMS: **1 remainder**, residue, rest, remnant, leftovers, scraps, debris, detritus. **2 antiquities**, relics, artefacts. **3 corpse**, body, carcass, bones; Medicine cadaver.

remand v. send a defendant to await trial, either on bail or in jail.
□ **on remand** in jail awaiting trial.

remark v. **1** say as a comment. **2** notice.
▷ SYNONYMS: **comment**, say, observe, mention, reflect; formal opine.
• n. a comment.
▷ SYNONYMS: **comment**, statement, utterance, observation, reflection.

remarkable adj. extraordinary or striking.
▷ SYNONYMS: **extraordinary**, exceptional, outstanding, notable, striking, memorable, unusual, conspicuous, momentous.
– ANTONYMS: ordinary.
■ **remarkably** adv.

remedial adj. **1** intended as a remedy. **2** for children with learning difficulties.

remedy n. (pl. remedies) **1** a medicine or treatment for a disease or injury. **2** a means of putting a matter right.
▷ SYNONYMS: **1 treatment**, cure, medicine, medication, medicament, drug. **2 solution**, answer, cure, fix, antidote, panacea.
• v. (remedying, remedied) put right.
▷ SYNONYMS: **put right**, set right, rectify, solve, sort out, straighten out, resolve, correct, repair, mend, fix.

remember v. **1** have in or bring to the mind someone or something from the past. **2** keep something to be done in mind.
▷ SYNONYMS: **1 recall**, call to mind, recollect, think of, reminisce about, look back on. **2 memorize**, retain, learn off by heart, get off pat. **3** a service to remember those who died: **commemorate**, pay tribute to, honour, salute, pay homage to.
– ANTONYMS: forget.
■ **remembrance** n.

remind v. cause to remember.
▷ SYNONYMS: **jog someone's memory**, prompt.
■ **reminder** n.

reminisce v. think or talk about the past.

reminiscence n. **1** an account of something remembered. **2** the enjoyable remembering of past events.

reminiscent adj. tending to remind you of something.
▷ SYNONYMS: **similar to**, comparable with, evocative of, suggestive of, redolent of.

remiss adj. negligent.
▷ SYNONYMS: **negligent**, neglectful, irresponsible, careless, thoughtless, heedless, lax, slack, slipshod, lackadaisical; N. Amer. derelict; informal sloppy.
– ANTONYMS: careful.

remission n. **1** a temporary period during which an illness becomes less severe. **2** Brit. the reduction of a prison sentence for good behaviour.

remit n. the area of responsibility officially assigned to someone.
▷ SYNONYMS: **area of responsibility**, sphere, orbit, scope, ambit, province, brief, instructions, orders; informal bailiwick.
• v. (remitting, remitted) **1** send payment. **2** cancel a debt or punishment. **3** refer a matter for decision to an authority.
▷ SYNONYMS: **1 send**, dispatch, forward,

hand over, pay. **2 pardon**, forgive, excuse.

remittance n. a sum of money sent in payment.

remnant n. a small remaining quantity.
▷ SYNONYMS: **remains**, remainder, leftovers, offcut, residue, rest.

remonstrate v. make a protest.
▷ SYNONYMS: **protest**, complain, object, take issue, argue, expostulate.
■ **remonstration** n.

remorse n. deep regret or guilt for something wrong that you have done.
▷ SYNONYMS: **regret**, guilt, contrition, repentance, shame.

remorseful adj. filled with remorse.
▷ SYNONYMS: **sorry**, regretful, contrite, repentant, penitent, guilt-ridden, conscience-stricken, chastened, self-reproachful.
– ANTONYMS: unrepentant.
■ **remorsefully** adv..

remorseless adj. **1** never ending. **2** without remorse.
■ **remorselessly** adv.

remote adj. **1** far away in space or time. **2** not closely connected. **3** (of a possibility) slight. **4** unfriendly and aloof. **5** operating or operated by means of radio or infrared signals.
▷ SYNONYMS: **1** isolated, far-off, faraway, distant, out of the way, off the beaten track, secluded, lonely, inaccessible; N. Amer. in the backwoods; informal in the middle of nowhere.
2 a remote possibility: **unlikely**, improbable, doubtful, dubious, faint, slight, slim, small, slender. **3** aloof, distant, detached, withdrawn, unforthcoming, unapproachable, unresponsive, unfriendly, unsociable, introspective, introverted; informal stand-offish.
– ANTONYMS: close.
■ **remotely** adv. **remoteness** n.

removal n. **1** the act of removing. **2** Brit. the transfer of furniture etc. when moving house.
▷ SYNONYMS: **1** taking away, withdrawal, abolition. **2** dismissal, ejection, expulsion, ousting, deposition; informal sacking, firing. **3** move, transfer, relocation.

remove v. **1** take off or away. **2** get rid of. **3** dismiss from a post.
▷ SYNONYMS: **1** take off, take away, move, take out, pull out, withdraw, detach, undo, unfasten, disconnect. **2** dismiss, discharge, get rid of, eject, expel, oust, depose, unseat; informal sack, fire, kick out. **3** abolish, with-

draw, eliminate, get rid of, do away with, stop, cut; informal axe.
– ANTONYMS: attach, insert.
● n. the extent to which things are separated.
■ **removable** adj. **remover** n.

remunerate v. pay for work.
■ **remuneration** n. **remunerative** adj.

Renaissance n. **1** the revival of classical styles in art and literature in the 14th–16th centuries.
2 (**renaissance**) a revival of interest in something.
▷ SYNONYMS: **revival**, renewal, resurrection, reawakening, re-emergence, rebirth, reappearance, resurgence.

renal adj. of the kidneys.

rend v. (**rending**, **rent**) tear to pieces.

render v. **1** provide a service, help, etc. **2** present for inspection, payment, etc. **3** cause to become. **4** perform music or drama. **5** melt down fat.
▷ SYNONYMS: **1** give, provide, supply, furnish, contribute. **2** her fury rendered her speechless: **make**, leave, turn. **3** act, perform, play, depict, portray, interpret, represent, draw, paint, execute.

rendezvous /ˈron-day-voo/ n. (pl. **rendezvous**) an arranged meeting or meeting place.
▷ SYNONYMS: **meeting**, appointment, assignation; informal date; literary tryst.
● v. meet at an agreed time and place.
▷ SYNONYMS: **meet**, come together, gather, assemble.

rendition n. a performance of a dramatic or musical work.

renegade n. a person who deserts and betrays a group, cause, etc.
▷ SYNONYMS: **traitor**, defector, deserter, turncoat, rebel, mutineer.
● adj. having treacherously changed allegiance.
▷ SYNONYMS: renegade troops: **treacherous**, traitorous, disloyal, treasonous, rebel, mutinous.
– ANTONYMS: loyal.

renege /ri-nayg/ v. fail to keep a promise or agreement.
▷ SYNONYMS: **default on**, fail to honour, go back on, break, back out of, withdraw from, retreat from, backtrack on, break your word/promise.
– ANTONYMS: honour.

renew v. **1** begin again after an interruption. **2** give fresh life or strength to. **3** extend the period of validity of a licence etc. **4** replace something broken or worn out.
▷ SYNONYMS: **1** resume, return to, take up again, come back to,

r

begin again, restart, recommence, continue, carry on. **2** reaffirm, repeat, reiterate, restate. **3** revive, regenerate, revitalize, reinvigorate, restore, resuscitate. **4** renovate, restore, refurbish, revamp, remodel, modernize; informal **do up**; N. Amer. informal **rehab**.
■ **renewable** adj. **renewal** n.

rennet n. a substance that curdles milk, used in making cheese.

renounce v. formally give up.
▷ SYNONYMS: **1 give up**, relinquish, abandon, surrender, waive, forego, desist from, keep off; informal **say goodbye to**. **2 reject**, repudiate, deny, abandon, wash your hands of, turn your back on, disown, spurn, shun.

renovate v. restore to a good state of repair.
▷ SYNONYMS: **modernize**, restore, refurbish, revamp, recondition, rehabilitate, update, upgrade, refit; informal **do up**; N. Amer. informal **rehab**.
■ **renovation** n.

renown n. fame.
▷ SYNONYMS: **fame**, distinction, eminence, illustriousness, prominence, repute, reputation, prestige, acclaim, celebrity, notability.

renowned adj. famous and respected.
▷ SYNONYMS: **famous**, well known, celebrated, famed, eminent, distinguished, acclaimed, illustrious, prominent, great, esteemed, respected.
− ANTONYMS: unknown.

rent[1] n. a regular payment for the use of property or land.
▷ SYNONYMS: **hire charge**, rental, payment.
• v. pay or receive rent for.
▷ SYNONYMS: **let**, lease, hire, charter.

rent[2] past & past part. of REND.
• n. a large tear in a piece of fabric.

rental n. **1** an amount paid as rent. **2** the act of renting.

renunciation n. the act of renouncing something.

reoccur v. (**reoccurring**, **reoccurred**) occur again or repeatedly.
■ **reoccurrence** n.

reorganize (or **-ise**) v. change the organization of.
■ **reorganization** n.

reorient v. **1** change the focus of. **2** (**reorient yourself**) find your bearings again.

rep n. informal a representative.

repair v. **1** restore to a good condition. **2** (**repair to**) go to a place.
▷ SYNONYMS: **1 mend**, fix, put/set right,

restore to working order, overhaul, renovate; informal **patch up**. **2** I cannot repair the wrongs I have done: **rectify**, make good, put right, correct, make up for, make amends for, compensate for, redress.
• n. **1** the act of repairing. **2** the condition of something.
▷ SYNONYMS: **1 restoration**, mending, overhaul, renovation. **2** the bike's in good repair: **condition**, working order, state, shape, fettle; Brit. informal **nick**.
■ **repairer** n.

reparation n. **1** the making of amends for a wrong. **2** (**reparations**) compensation for war damage paid by a defeated state.

repartee n. quick, witty comments or replies.

repast n. a meal.

repatriate v. send someone back to their own country.
■ **repatriation** n.

repay v. (**repaying**, **repaid**) **1** pay back. **2** Brit. be worth spending time on.
▷ SYNONYMS: **1 reimburse**, refund, pay back, recompense, compensate, remunerate, settle up with. **2** he repaid her kindness: **reciprocate**, return, requite, reward.
■ **repayable** n. **repayment** n.

repeal v. officially cancel a law.
▷ SYNONYMS: **cancel**, abolish, reverse, rescind, revoke, annul, quash.
− ANTONYMS: enact.
• n. the act of repealing.
▷ SYNONYMS: **cancellation**, abolition, reversal, rescinding, annulment.

repeat v. **1** say or do again. **2** (**repeat itself**) occur again in the same way.
▷ SYNONYMS: **1 restate**, reiterate, recapitulate, recap; redo, replicate, duplicate. **2 recite**, quote, parrot, regurgitate, echo; informal **trot out**.
• n. a repeated broadcast.
▷ SYNONYMS: **repetition**, replication, duplicate.

repeated adj. done or happening frequently.
▷ SYNONYMS: **recurrent**, frequent, persistent, continual, incessant, constant, regular, periodic, numerous, many.
− ANTONYMS: occasional.
■ **repeatedly** adv.

repel v. (**repelling**, **repelled**) **1** force back or away. **2** disgust. **3** (of a substance) be able to keep something out.
▷ SYNONYMS: **1 fight off**, repulse, drive back, force back, beat back, hold off,

ward off, fend off, keep at bay; Brit. see off. **2** revolt, disgust, repulse, sicken, nauseate, turn someone's stomach; informal **turn off**; N. Amer. informal **gross out**.

– ANTONYMS: attract.

repellent adj. **1** causing disgust. **2** able to repel a particular thing.
▷ SYNONYMS: **1 revolting**, repulsive, disgusting, repugnant, sickening, nauseating, stomach-turning, vile, nasty, foul, awful, horrible, dreadful, terrible, obnoxious, loathsome, offensive, objectionable, abhor- rent, despicable, reprehensible, contemptible, odious, hateful; N. Amer. vomitous; informal ghastly, horrid, gross; literary noisome. **2 impermeable**, impervious, resistant, -proof.
• n. a substance that repels insects etc.

repent v. feel or express remorse.
▷ SYNONYMS: **feel remorse**, regret, be sorry, rue, reproach yourself, be ashamed, feel contrite, be penitent, be remorseful.
■ **repentance** n.

repentant adj. feeling or expressing remorse.
▷ SYNONYMS: **penitent**, contrite, regretful, rueful, remorseful, apologetic, chastened, ashamed, shamefaced.
– ANTONYMS: impenitent, unrepentant.

repercussions pl. n. the consequences of an event or action.
▷ SYNONYMS: **consequences**, results, effects, outcome, reverberations, backlash, aftermath, fallout.

repertoire /rep-er-twar/ n. the works known or regularly performed by a performer or company.
▷ SYNONYMS: **collection**, range, reper- tory, list, store, stock, repository, supply.

repertory n. (pl. **repertories**) **1** the performance by a company of various plays, operas, etc. at regular intervals. **2** a repertoire.

repetition n. **1** the act of repeating. **2** a thing that repeats another.
▷ SYNONYMS: **1 reiteration**, restate- ment, retelling. **2 repetitiousness**, repetitiveness, tautology.

repetitious adj. repetitive.

repetitive adj. repeated many times or too much.
▷ SYNONYMS: **recurring**, recurrent, repeated, unvaried, unchanging, routine, mechanical, automatic, monotonous, boring; informal samey.
– ANTONYMS: varied.
■ **repetitively** adv.

repine v. literary be unhappy.

replace v. **1** provide or be a substitute for. **2** put back in place.
▷ SYNONYMS: **1 take the place of**, succeed, take over from, supersede, stand in for, substitute for, deputize for; informal step into someone's shoes/boots. **2 substitute**, exchange, change, swap. **3 put back**, return, restore.

replacement n. **1** the action of replacing someone or something. **2** a person or thing that replaces another.
▷ SYNONYMS: **substitute**, stand-in, fill-in, locum, understudy, relief, cover, proxy, surrogate.

replay v. **1** play back a recording. **2** play a match again.
• n. **1** a replayed match. **2** an act of replaying.

replenish v. fill up a supply again after some has been used.
▷ SYNONYMS: **1 refill**, top up, fill up, recharge; N. Amer. freshen. **2 stock up**, restock, restore, replace.
– ANTONYMS: empty.
■ **replenishment** n.

replete adj. **1** well supplied. **2** very full with food.

replica n. an exact copy.
▷ SYNONYMS: **copy**, model, duplicate, reproduction, dummy, imitation, facsimile.

replicate v. make a replica of.
■ **replication** n. **replicator** n.

reply v. (**replying**, **replied**) answer or respond.
▷ SYNONYMS: **respond**, answer, write back, rejoin, retort, riposte, counter, come back.
• n. (pl. **replies**) an answer.
▷ SYNONYMS: **answer**, response, rejoinder, retort, riposte; informal comeback.

report v. **1** give an account of. **2** make a formal complaint about. **3** present yourself on arrival. **4** (**report to**) be responsible to a manager.
▷ SYNONYMS: **1 communicate**, announce, divulge, disclose, reveal, relay, describe, narrate, delineate, detail, document, give an account of, make public, publish, broadcast, proclaim, publicize. **2 inform on**; informal shop, tell on, squeal on, rat on; Brit. informal grass on. **3** I reported for duty: **present yourself**, arrive, turn up, clock in; informal show up.
• n. **1** a spoken or written account. **2** Brit. a teacher's written assessment of a pupil's progress. **3** the sound of an explosion or gunfire.

r

▷ SYNONYMS: **1 account**, record, minutes, proceedings, transcript. **2 news**, information, word, intelligence. **3 story**, account, article, piece, item, column, feature, bulletin, dispatch, communiqué. **4 rumour**, whisper; informal buzz. **5 bang**, crack, explosion, boom.

reportage /rep-or-**tahzh**/ n. the reporting of news.

reporter n. a person who reports news for a newspaper or broadcasting company.

▷ SYNONYMS: **journalist**, correspondent, newsman, newswoman, columnist; Brit. pressman; informal hack, stringer, journo.

repose n. a state of calm or peace.
• v. rest; lie.

repository n. (pl. **repositories**) a place or container for storage.

repossess v. take back goods etc. when the required payments are not made.
■ repossession n.

reprehensible adj. deserving condemnation.

▷ SYNONYMS: **deplorable**, disgraceful, discreditable, despicable, blame-worthy, culpable, wrong, bad, shameful, dishonourable, inexcus-able, unforgivable, indefensible, unjustifiable.
− ANTONYMS: praiseworthy.

represent v. **1** act and speak on behalf of. **2** be an example of. **3** amount to. **4** describe in a particular way. **5** depict in a work of art. **6** be a symbol of.

▷ SYNONYMS: **1 stand for**, symbolize, personify, epitomize, typify, embody, illustrate, exemplify. **2 depict**, portray, render, picture, delineate, show, illustrate. **3 appear for**, act for, speak on behalf of.

representation n. **1** the act of representing. **2** an image, model, etc. **3** (**representations**) an appeal or protest.

▷ SYNONYMS: **1 portrayal**, depiction, delineation, presentation, rendition. **2 likeness**, painting, drawing, picture, illustration, sketch, image, model, figure, statue.

representative adj. **1** typical of a class or group. **2** consisting of people chosen to represent a wider group.

▷ SYNONYMS: **1 typical**, archetypal, characteristic, illustrative, indicative. **2 symbolic**, emblematic.
− ANTONYMS: atypical.
• n. **1** a person chosen to represent

others. **2** a person who visits potential clients to sell their company's products.

▷ SYNONYMS: **1 spokesperson**, spokesman, spokeswoman, agent, official, mouthpiece. **2 salesman**, commercial traveller, agent, negoti-ator; informal rep. **3 deputy**, substitute, stand-in, proxy, delegate, ambassador, emissary.

repress v. **1** bring under control by force. **2** restrain or suppress a thought or feeling. **3** (**repressed**) tending to keep your feelings or desires hidden.

▷ SYNONYMS: **1 suppress**, quell, quash, subdue, put down, crush, extinguish, stamp out, defeat, contain. **2 oppress**, subjugate, keep down, tyrannize. **3 restrain**, hold back/in, suppress, keep in check, control, curb, stifle, bottle up; informal button up, keep the lid on.
− ANTONYMS: express.
■ repression n.

repressive adj. severely restricting personal freedom.

▷ SYNONYMS: **oppressive**, authoritarian, despotic, tyrannical, dictatorial, fascist, autocratic, totalitarian, undemocratic.
− ANTONYMS: liberal.

reprieve v. cancel the punishment of.

▷ SYNONYMS: **pardon**, spare, amnesty; informal let off.
• n. **1** an act of reprieving. **2** a brief delay before an undesirable event.

▷ SYNONYMS: **pardon**, stay of execution, amnesty.

reprimand v. express strong disapproval to.

▷ SYNONYMS: **rebuke**, reproach, scold, admonish, reprove, chastise, upbraid, berate, take to task, castigate; informal tell off; Brit. informal tick off; N. Amer. informal chew out.
• n. an act of reprimanding.

▷ SYNONYMS: **rebuke**, reproach, scolding, admonition; informal telling-off, dressing-down, carpeting; Brit. informal ticking-off.

reprint v. print again.
• n. a copy of a book that has been reprinted.

reprisal n. an act of retaliation.

▷ SYNONYMS: **retaliation**, counter-attack, comeback, revenge, vengeance, retri-bution, requital; informal a taste of your own medicine.

reproach v. express disapproval of or disappointment with.
• n. an act of reproaching.

reproachful adj. expressing reproach; disapproving.
▷ SYNONYMS: **disapproving**, reproving, critical, censorious, disparaging, withering, accusatory, admonitory.
– ANTONYMS: approving.
■ **reproachfully** adv.

reprobate n. an immoral person.

reproduce v. **1** produce a copy of. **2** produce again in a different situation. **3** produce offspring.
▷ SYNONYMS: **1 copy**, duplicate, replicate, photocopy, xerox, photostat, print. **2 repeat**, replicate, recreate, redo, simulate, imitate, emulate, mimic. **3 breed**, procreate, propagate, multiply, proliferate.

reproduction n. **1** the act of reproducing. **2** a copy of a work of art.
▷ SYNONYMS: **1 print**, copy, reprint, duplicate, facsimile, photocopy; trademark Xerox. **2 breeding**, procreation, propagation, proliferation.
■ **reproductive** adj.

reproof n. a reprimand.

reprove v. reprimand.

reptile n. a cold-blooded animal of a group that includes snakes.
■ **reptilian** adj.

republic n. a state in which power is held by the people's representatives, with a president rather than a monarch.

republican adj. **1** of or supporting the principles of a republic. **2** (**Republican**) (in the US) of the Republican Party.
• n. **1** a person in favour of republican government. **2** (**Republican**) (in the US) a member of the Republican Party.

repudiate v. **1** refuse to accept or be associated with. **2** deny the truth of.
▷ SYNONYMS: **1 reject**, renounce, disown, abandon, give up, turn your back on, cast off, lay aside, wash your hands of; formal forswear; literary forsake. **2 deny**, refute, contradict, controvert, rebut, dispute, dismiss, brush aside; formal gainsay.
– ANTONYMS: embrace.
■ **repudiation** n.

repugnant adj. disgusting or very unpleasant.
▷ SYNONYMS: **abhorrent**, revolting, repulsive, repellent, disgusting, offensive, objectionable, vile, foul, nasty, loathsome, sickening, nauseating, hateful, detestable, execrable, abominable, monstrous, appalling, unsavoury, unpalatable.
– ANTONYMS: pleasant.

■ **repugnance** n.

repulse v. **1** force back an attacking enemy. **2** reject or rebuff.

repulsion n. **1** a feeling of intense disgust. **2** a force by which objects tend to move away from each other.

repulsive adj. highly disgusting.
▷ SYNONYMS: **disgusting**, revolting, foul, nasty, obnoxious, sickening, nauseating, stomach-churning, vile; informal ghastly, gross, horrible; literary noisome.
– ANTONYMS: attractive.
■ **repulsively** adv.

reputable adj. having a good reputation.
▷ SYNONYMS: **well thought of**, highly regarded, respected, respectable, of good repute, prestigious, established, reliable, dependable, trustworthy.
– ANTONYMS: untrustworthy.

reputation n. the opinion generally held about someone or something.
▷ SYNONYMS: **name**, good name, character, repute, standing, stature, position, renown, esteem, prestige.

repute n. reputation, esp. when good.
• v. (**be reputed**) be said or thought to be.
■ **reputedly** adv.

request n. **1** a formal or polite act of asking. **2** a thing asked for.
▷ SYNONYMS: **1 appeal**, entreaty, plea, petition, application, demand, call, solicitation. **2 requirement**, wish, desire, choice.
• v. ask formally or politely.
▷ SYNONYMS: **ask for**, appeal for, call for, seek, solicit, plead for, beg for, apply for, put in for, demand, petition for, sue for, implore, entreat; literary beseech.

requiem n. a musical work based on a Mass for the souls of the dead.

require v. **1** need for a purpose. **2** order or expect to do.
▷ SYNONYMS: **1 need**, have need of, be short of, want, desire, lack, miss. **2 necessitate**, demand, call for, involve, entail, take. **3 demand**, insist on, call for, ask for, expect. **4 order**, instruct, command, enjoin, oblige, compel, force.

requirement n. something needed or compulsory.
▷ SYNONYMS: **need**, necessity, prerequisite, stipulation, demand, want, essential.

requisite adj. necessary because of circumstances or rules.
• n. something needed.

requisition n. an official order

r

allowing property or materials to be taken and used.

▷ SYNONYMS: **1 order**, request, call, application, claim, demand; Brit. indent. **2 appropriation**, commandeering, seizure, confiscation, expropriation.
• v. officially take or use, esp. during a war.

▷ SYNONYMS: **1 commandeer**, appropriate, take over, take possession of, occupy, seize, confiscate, expropriate. **2 request**, order, call for, demand.

rescind v. cancel a law, order, etc.

rescue v. save from danger or distress.

▷ SYNONYMS: **1 save**, free, set free, release, liberate, deliver. **2 retrieve**, recover, salvage.
• n. an act of rescuing.

▷ SYNONYMS: **saving**, rescuing, release, freeing, liberation, deliverance.
■ **rescuer** n.

research n. the study of materials and sources to discover facts.

▷ SYNONYMS: **investigation**, experimentation, testing, analysis, fact-finding, examination, scrutiny.
• v. carry out research into a subject or for a book etc.

▷ SYNONYMS: **investigate**, study, enquire into, look into, probe, explore, analyse, examine, scrutinize.
■ **researcher** n.

resemblance n. **1** the fact of resembling. **2** a way in which things resemble each other.

▷ SYNONYMS: **similarity**, likeness, similitude, correspondence, congruence, conformity, comparability, parallel.
– ANTONYMS: dissimilarity.

resemble v. look like or be similar to.

▷ SYNONYMS: **look like**, be similar to, remind someone of, take after, approximate to, smack of, correspond to, echo, mirror, parallel.
– ANTONYMS: differ from.

resent v. feel bitter or angry about.

▷ SYNONYMS: **begrudge**, feel aggrieved about, grudge, be resentful of, take exception to, object to, take amiss, take offence at.
– ANTONYMS: welcome.

resentful adj. filled with resentment.

▷ SYNONYMS: **aggrieved**, bitter, disgruntled, discontented, grudging, jaundiced, jealous, envious, dissatisfied, indignant, irritated, offended, piqued, put out, in high dudgeon; informal miffed, peeved; Brit. informal narked; N. Amer. informal sore.
■ **resentfully** adv.

resentment n. bitterness or anger at being treated unfairly.

▷ SYNONYMS: **bitterness**, indignation, irritation, pique, dissatisfaction, disgruntlement, discontentment, acrimony, rancour.

reservation n. **1** the act of reserving. **2** an arrangement for something to be reserved. **3** an expression of doubt. **4** an area of land set aside for native people.

▷ SYNONYMS: **1 doubt**, qualm, scruple; (**reservations**) misgivings, scepticism, unease, hesitation, objection. **2 reserve**, enclave, sanctuary, territory, homeland.

reserve v. **1** keep for future use. **2** arrange for a room, seat, etc. to be kept for a particular person. **3** have or keep a right etc.

▷ SYNONYMS: **1 put aside**, set aside, keep, save, hold back, keep in reserve, earmark, retain. **2 book**, order, arrange for, secure, engage, hire.
• n. **1** a supply kept available for use if required. **2** a military force kept to reinforce others or for use in an emergency. **3** an extra player in a team, serving as a possible substitute. **4** a lack of warmth or openness. **5** an area set aside for wildlife.

▷ SYNONYMS: **1 stock**, store, supply, stockpile, pool, hoard, cache, fund. **2 reinforcements**, extras, auxiliaries. **3 shyness**, diffidence, timidity, taciturnity, inhibition, reticence, detachment, aloofness, distance, remoteness. **4 substitute**, stand-in, replacement, fallback, extra. **5 national park**, sanctuary, preserve, reservation.

reserved adj. slow to reveal emotion or opinions.

▷ SYNONYMS: **1 uncommunicative**, reticent, unforthcoming, aloof, cool, undemonstrative, unsociable, unfriendly, quiet, silent, taciturn, withdrawn, secretive, shy, retiring, diffident, timid, introverted; informal stand-offish. **2 booked**, taken, spoken for, prearranged.
– ANTONYMS: outgoing.

reservist n. a member of a military reserve force.

reservoir n. **1** a lake used as a source of water supply. **2** a container for a supply of fluid.

▷ SYNONYMS: **1 lake**, pool, pond, basin. **2 receptacle**, container, holder, tank. **3 stock**, store, stockpile, reserves, supply, bank, pool.

reshuffle v. change the roles or positions of government ministers.
• n. an act of reshuffling.

reside v. **1** live in a particular place.
2 (**reside in/with**) (of a right or
power) belong to a person or group.
3 (**reside in**) be present in.
▷ SYNONYMS: **1 live**, lodge, stay, occupy,
inhabit; formal dwell, be domiciled.
2 *power resides with the president:*
be vested in, be bestowed on, be
conferred on, be in the hands of.
residence n. **1** the fact of residing. **2** a
person's home.
▷ SYNONYMS: **home**, house, address,
quarters, lodgings; informal pad; formal
dwelling, abode, domicile.
resident n. **1** a person living
somewhere on a long-term basis.
2 Brit. a guest in a hotel.
▷ SYNONYMS: **inhabitant**, local, citizen,
native, householder, homeowner,
occupier, tenant; humorous denizen.
• adj. living somewhere on a long-term
basis.
residential adj. **1** suitable for living
in. **2** providing accommodation.
residue n. an amount remaining after
the greater part has gone or been
taken.
▷ SYNONYMS: **remainder**, rest, remnant,
surplus, extra, excess, remains,
leftovers.
■ **residual** adj.
resign v. **1** voluntarily leave a job or
post. **2** (**resign yourself**) accept that
something unpleasant cannot be
avoided.
▷ SYNONYMS: **leave**, give notice, stand
down, step down; informal quit, pack in.
resignation n. **1** an act of resigning.
2 a letter stating an intention to
resign. **3** acceptance of something bad
but inevitable.
▷ SYNONYMS: *he accepted his fate with
resignation:* **patience**, forbearance, stoicism, fortitude, fatalism,
acceptance.
resigned adj. able to accept that
something unpleasant cannot be
avoided.
▷ SYNONYMS: **patient**, long-suffering,
uncomplaining, forbearing, stoical,
philosophical, fatalistic.
resilient adj. **1** able to spring back
into shape after bending, stretching,
etc. **2** able to recover quickly from
difficulty.
▷ SYNONYMS: **1 flexible**, pliable, supple,
durable, hard-wearing, stout, strong,
sturdy, tough. **2 strong**, tough,
hardy, quick to recover, buoyant,
irrepressible.
■ **resilience** n.
resin n. **1** a sticky substance produced

by some trees. **2** a synthetic substance
used in plastics, adhesives, etc.
■ **resinous** adj.
resist v. **1** withstand the action or
effect of. **2** try to prevent or oppose.
3 refrain from something tempting.
▷ SYNONYMS: **1 withstand**, be proof
against, combat, weather, endure, be
resistant to, keep out. **2 oppose**, fight
against, object to, defy, kick against,
obstruct. **3 refrain from**, abstain
from, forbear from, desist from,
restrain yourself from.
resistance n. **1** the act of resisting
or the ability to resist. **2** a secret
organization that fights against an
occupying enemy. **3** the degree to
which a material or device opposes
the passage of an electric current.
▷ SYNONYMS: **1 opposition**, hostility,
struggle, fight, battle, stand, defiance.
2 immunity, defences.
■ **resistor** n..
resistant adj. **1** able to resist
something. **2** not willing to do or
accept something.
▷ SYNONYMS: **1 impervious**, immune,
invulnerable, proof, unaffected.
2 *they are resistant to change:*
opposed, averse, hostile, inimical,
against; informal anti.
− ANTONYMS: vulnerable.
resolute adj. determined.
▷ SYNONYMS: **determined**, purposeful,
resolved, adamant, single-minded,
firm, unswerving, unwavering, steadfast, staunch, stalwart, unfaltering,
indefatigable, tenacious, strong-
willed, unshakeable.
− ANTONYMS: half-hearted.
■ **resolutely** adv.
resolution n. **1** a firm decision. **2** a
formal expression of opinion by a
law-making body. **3** determination.
4 the solving of a problem etc. **5** the
degree to which detail is visible in
an image.
▷ SYNONYMS: **1 intention**, decision,
intent, aim, plan, commitment,
pledge, promise. **2 motion**, proposal,
proposition. **3 determination**,
purpose, purposefulness, resolve,
single-mindedness, firmness,
will power, strength of character.
4 solution, answer, end, settlement,
conclusion.
resolve v. **1** find a solution to.
2 firmly decide to do. **3** separate into
constituent parts.
▷ SYNONYMS: **1 settle**, sort out, solve, fix,
straighten out, deal with, put right,
rectify; informal hammer out, thrash

r

out. **2 determine**, decide, make up your mind. **3 vote**, rule, decide formally, agree.

• n. determination.

▷ SYNONYMS: **determination**, purpose, resolution, single-mindedness; informal guts.

resonant adj. **1** deep, clear, and ringing. **2** suggesting images, a quality, etc.

■ **resonance** n.

resonate v. make a deep, clear, ringing sound.

resort n. **1** a place visited for holidays. **2** a course of action.

▷ SYNONYMS: **option**, alternative, choice, possibility, hope, measure, step, recourse, expedient.

• v. (**resort to**) adopt a strategy to solve a problem.

resound v. be filled with a ringing or echoing sound.

▷ SYNONYMS: **echo**, reverberate, ring, boom, thunder, rumble, resonate.

resounding adj. **1** loud enough to reverberate. **2** definite; emphatic.

▷ SYNONYMS: **1 reverberating**, resonating, echoing, ringing, sonorous, deep, rich. **2** *a resounding success:* **enormous**, huge, very great, tremendous, terrific, colossal, emphatic, outstanding, remarkable, phenomenal.

resource n. **1** (**resources**) a stock or supply of materials or assets. **2** a source of help or information. **3** (**resources**) personal qualities for dealing with difficult situations.

▷ SYNONYMS: **1 facility**, amenity, aid, help, support. **2 initiative**, resourcefulness, enterprise, ingenuity, inventiveness. **3** *we lack resources:* **assets**, funds, wealth, money, capital, supplies, materials, stores, stocks, reserves.

resourceful adj. quick and clever at overcoming difficulties.

▷ SYNONYMS: **ingenious**, enterprising, inventive, creative, clever, talented, able, capable.

■ **resourcefully** adv. **resourcefulness** n.

respect n. **1** admiration for someone because of their qualities or achievements. **2** consideration for the feelings or rights of others. **3** a particular aspect or point.

▷ SYNONYMS: **1 esteem**, regard, high opinion, admiration, reverence, deference, honour. **2** *the report was accurate in every respect:* **aspect**, regard, feature, way, sense, particular, point, detail. **3** (**respects**) **regards**,

compliments, greetings, best/good wishes.

– ANTONYMS: contempt.

• v. **1** have respect for. **2** agree to observe a law etc.

▷ SYNONYMS: **1 esteem**, admire, think highly of, have a high opinion of, look up to, revere, honour. **2 show consideration for**, have regard for, observe, be mindful of, be heedful of. **3 abide by**, comply with, follow, adhere to, conform to, act in accordance with, obey, observe, keep.

– ANTONYMS: despise, disobey.

■ **respectfully** adv..

respectable adj. **1** regarded by society as proper or correct. **2** adequate or acceptable.

▷ SYNONYMS: **1 reputable**, upright, honest, honourable, trustworthy, decent, good, well bred, clean-living. **2 fairly good**, decent, fair-sized, reasonable, moderately good, large, sizeable, considerable.

– ANTONYMS: disreputable.

■ **respectability** n. **respectably** adv.

respectful adj. feeling or showing respect.

▷ SYNONYMS: **deferential**, reverent, dutiful, polite, well mannered, civil, courteous, gracious.

– ANTONYMS: rude.

■ **respectfully** adv.

respective adj. belonging to each as an individual.

▷ SYNONYMS: **separate**, personal, own, particular, individual, specific, special.

respectively adv. separately and in the order mentioned.

respiration n. the act of breathing.

respirator n. **1** a device worn over the face to prevent the breathing in of smoke etc. **2** a device enabling someone to breathe when they are unable to do so naturally.

respiratory adj. of breathing.

respire v. breathe.

respite n. rest or relief from something difficult or unpleasant.

▷ SYNONYMS: **rest**, break, breathing space, interval, lull, pause, time out, relief; informal breather, let-up.

resplendent adj. impressively colourful or attractive.

respond v. say or do in reply or as a reaction.

▷ SYNONYMS: **1 answer**, reply, write back, come back, rejoin, retort, riposte, counter. **2 react**, reciprocate, retaliate.

respondent n. a person against whom

a legal petition is filed, esp. one in a divorce case.

response n. an answer or reaction.
▷ SYNONYMS: **1 answer**, reply, rejoinder, retort, riposte; informal comeback.
2 reaction, reply, retaliation; informal comeback.
– ANTONYMS: question.

responsibility n. (pl. **responsibilities**)
1 the state of being responsible. **2** a thing required as part of a job or legal obligation.
▷ SYNONYMS: **1** *he denied responsibility for the error:* **blame**, fault, guilt, culpability, liability, accountability, answerability. **2 trustworthiness**, common sense, maturity, reliability, dependability. **3 duty**, task, function, job, role, onus; Brit. informal pigeon.

responsible adj. **1** obliged to do something or care for someone. **2** being the cause of something and so deserving blame or credit for it. **3** able to be trusted. **4** involving important duties. **5** having to report to a senior person.
▷ SYNONYMS: **1 in charge of**, in control of, at the helm of, accountable for, liable for. **2 accountable**, answerable, to blame, guilty, culpable, blameworthy, at fault, in the wrong. **3 trustworthy**, sensible, mature, reliable, dependable, level-headed, stable.
– ANTONYMS: irresponsible.
■ **responsibly** adv.

responsive adj. responding readily.
▷ SYNONYMS: **reactive**, receptive, open to suggestions, amenable, flexible, forthcoming.

rest v. **1** stop work or movement so as to relax or recover your strength. **2** place in a specified position. **3** remain or be left in a specified state: *rest assured.* **4** (**rest on**) depend or be based on. **5** (**rest with**) (of power etc.) belong to.
▷ SYNONYMS: **1 relax**, ease up/off, let up, slow down, take a break, unbend, unwind, take it easy, put your feet up; informal take five, take a breather, chill out. **2** *rest the ladder up against the wall:* **support**, prop, lean, lay, set, stand, position, place, put.
● n. **1** a period of resting. **2** a motionless state. **3** an object used to hold or support something. **4** the remaining part, people, or things.
▷ SYNONYMS: **1 relaxation**, repose, leisure, time off; informal lie-down.
2 break, breathing space, interval, interlude, intermission, time off/out, respite, lull, pause; informal breather.

3 stand, base, holder, support, rack, frame, shelf. **4 remainder**, residue, balance, remnant, surplus, excess.

restaurant n. a place where people pay to eat meals cooked on the premises.

restaurateur /ress-tuh-ruh-**ter**/ n. the owner or manager of a restaurant.

USAGE There is no n: restaura*teur*.

restful adj. relaxing.
▷ SYNONYMS: **relaxing**, quiet, calm, tranquil, soothing, peaceful, leisurely, undisturbed, untroubled.
– ANTONYMS: exciting.

restitution n. **1** the restoration of something lost or stolen to its owner. **2** payment for injury or loss.

restive adj. restless; impatient.

restless adj. unable to rest or relax.
▷ SYNONYMS: **1 uneasy**, ill at ease, fidgety, edgy, tense, worked up, nervous, nervy, agitated, anxious; informal jumpy, jittery, twitchy, uptight. **2** *a restless night:* **sleepless**, wakeful, fitful, broken, disturbed, troubled, unsettled.
■ **restlessly** adv. **restlessness** n.

restorative adj. able to restore health or strength.

restore v. **1** bring back a previous practice, situation, etc. **2** return to a previous condition, place, or owner. **3** repair or renovate.
▷ SYNONYMS: **1** *they aimed to restore democracy:* **reinstate**, bring back, reinstitute, reimpose, reinstall, re-establish. **2** *a good night's sleep will restore you:* **reinvigorate**, revitalize, revive, refresh, energize, freshen. **3 repair**, fix, mend, refurbish, recondition, rehabilitate, renovate, revamp, rebuild; informal do up; N. Amer. informal rehab.
■ **restoration** n. **restorer** n.

restrain v. **1** keep under control. **2** stop from moving or acting freely.
▷ SYNONYMS: **control**, check, hold in check, curb, suppress, repress, contain, rein back/in, smother, stifle, bottle up; informal keep the lid on.

restrained adj. **1** unemotional. **2** not bright or conspicuous.
▷ SYNONYMS: **1 self-controlled**, sober, steady, unemotional, undemonstrative, reserved. **2 muted**, soft, discreet, subtle, quiet, unobtrusive, unostentatious, understated, tasteful.

restraint n. **1** the act of restraining. **2** something that restrains. **3** self-controlled behaviour.
▷ SYNONYMS: **1 constraint**, check,

r

control, restriction, limitation, curtailment, rein, brake, deterrent. **2 self-control**, self-discipline, control, moderation, judiciousness. **3 subtlety**, taste, discretion, discrimination.

restrict v. **1** put a limit on. **2** stop from moving or acting freely.
▷ SYNONYMS: **1 limit**, keep within bounds, regulate, control, moderate, cut down, curtail, curb. **2 hinder**, interfere with, impede, hamper, obstruct, block, check.
■ **restrictive** adj.

restriction n. **1** a limiting condition or measure. **2** the act of restricting.
▷ SYNONYMS: **limitation**, constraint, control, regulation, check, curb, reduction, diminution, curtailment.

result n. **1** a thing caused or produced by something else. **2** information obtained by experiment or calculation. **3** a final score or mark in a contest or exam.
▷ SYNONYMS: **consequence**, outcome, upshot, sequel, effect, reaction, repercussion.
– ANTONYMS: cause.
• v. **1** occur as a result. **2** (**result in**) have as a result.
▷ SYNONYMS: *anger may result from an argument:* **follow**, ensue, develop, stem, spring, arise, derive, proceed; be caused by, be brought about by, be produced by, originate in.

resultant adj. occurring as a result.

resume v. begin again or continue after a pause.
▷ SYNONYMS: **restart**, recommence, begin again, start again, reopen, renew, return to, continue with, carry on with.
– ANTONYMS: suspend, abandon.

résumé /rez-yuu-may/ n. **1** a summary. **2** US a curriculum vitae.
▷ SYNONYMS: **summary**, precis, synopsis, abstract, outline, abridgement, overview.

resumption n. an act of resuming something.

resurgence n. an increase in or revival of activity, popularity, etc.
▷ SYNONYMS: **renewal**, revival, renaissance, recovery, comeback, reawakening, resurrection, reappearance, re-emergence.

resurgent adj. becoming stronger or more popular again.

resurrect v. **1** restore to life. **2** revive a practice etc.
▷ SYNONYMS: **revive**, restore, regenerate, revitalize, breathe new life into,

reinvigorate, resuscitate, rejuvenate, re-establish, relaunch.
■ **resurrection** n.

resuscitate v. revive from unconsciousness.
■ **resuscitation** n.

retail n. the sale of goods to the general public.
• v. sell or be sold to the public.
■ **retailer** n.

retain v. **1** keep possession of. **2** absorb and hold. **3** keep in place. **4** secure the services of.
▷ SYNONYMS: **keep**, keep hold of, hang on to, maintain, preserve, conserve.

retainer n. **1** a fee paid in advance to a barrister to secure their services. **2** a servant who has worked for a family for a long time.

retaliate v. attack in return for a similar attack.
▷ SYNONYMS: **fight back**, hit back, respond, react, reply, reciprocate, counter-attack, get back at someone, pay someone back; informal get your own back.
■ **retaliatory** adj.

retaliation n. the action of retaliating.
▷ SYNONYMS: **revenge**, vengeance, reprisal, retribution, repayment, response, reaction, reply, counter-attack.

retard v. prevent from developing or progressing.
▷ SYNONYMS: **delay**, slow down/up, hold back/up, postpone, detain, decelerate, hinder, impede, check.
– ANTONYMS: accelerate.
■ **retardation** n.

retarded adj. offens. less developed mentally than is usual at a particular age.

retch v. make the sound and movement of vomiting.

retention n. the act of retaining.

retentive adj. able to retain facts easily.

rethink v. (**rethinking**, **rethought**) consider again.

reticent adj. not revealing your thoughts or feelings.
▷ SYNONYMS: **uncommunicative**, unforthcoming, unresponsive, tight-lipped, quiet, taciturn, silent, reserved.
– ANTONYMS: expansive.
■ **reticence** n.

retina n. (pl. **retinas** or **retinae**) a layer at the back of the eyeball that is sensitive to light.

retinue n. a group of assistants

accompanying an important person.

retire v. **1** stop working because you have reached a particular age. **2** withdraw from a competition. **3** go to bed.
▷ SYNONYMS: **1 give up work**, stop work, be pensioned off; informal be put out to grass. **2 withdraw**, go away, exit, leave, take yourself off, absent yourself. **3 go to bed**, call it a day; informal turn in, hit the hay/sack.
■ **retirement** n.

retiring adj. shy.
▷ SYNONYMS: **1 departing**, outgoing. **2 shy**, diffident, self-effacing, unassuming, unassertive, reserved, reticent, quiet, timid, modest.
– ANTONYMS: incoming, outgoing.

retort v. make a sharp or witty reply.
▷ SYNONYMS: **answer**, reply, respond, return, counter, riposte, retaliate.
• n. **1** a sharp or witty reply. **2** a glass container with a long neck, used in distilling.
▷ SYNONYMS: **answer**, reply, response, counter, rejoinder, riposte, retaliation; informal comeback.

retouch v. improve a painting or photo with slight alterations.

retrace v. go back over or follow a route.

retract v. **1** draw or be drawn back. **2** withdraw an accusation etc.
▷ SYNONYMS: **1 pull in**, pull back, draw in. **2 take back**, withdraw, recant, disavow, disclaim, repudiate, renounce, reverse, revoke, rescind, go back on, backtrack on; formal abjure.
■ **retractable** adj. **retraction** n.

retractile adj. able to be retracted.

retreat v. **1** (of an army) withdraw from attacking enemy forces. **2** move back from a difficult situation.
▷ SYNONYMS: **withdraw**, retire, draw back, pull back/out, fall back, give way, give ground.
– ANTONYMS: advance.
• n. **1** an act of retreating. **2** a quiet or secluded place.
▷ SYNONYMS: **1 withdrawal**, retirement, pullback, flight. **2 refuge**, haven, sanctuary, hideaway, hideout, hiding place; informal hidey-hole.

retrench v. reduce costs or spending.
■ **retrenchment** n.

retrial n. a second or further trial.

retribution n. severe punishment inflicted as revenge.
▷ SYNONYMS: **punishment**, penalty, your just deserts, revenge, reprisal, requital, retaliation, vengeance, an eye for an eye (and a tooth for a tooth), tit for tat, nemesis.

retrieve v. **1** get or bring back. **2** extract information from a computer. **3** improve a bad situation.
▷ SYNONYMS: **get back**, bring back, recover, recapture, regain, recoup, salvage, rescue.
■ **retrieval** n.

retriever n. a dog of a breed used to retrieve game.

retro adj. imitative of a style from the recent past.

retroactive adj. taking effect from a date in the past.

retrograde adj. moving backwards or to a worse state.
▷ SYNONYMS: **for the worse**, regressive, retrogressive, negative, downhill, backward, backwards, unwelcome.

retrogressive adj. returning to an earlier and worse state.
■ **retrogression** n.

retrospect n. (**in retrospect**) when looking back on a past event.

retrospective adj. **1** looking back on or dealing with past events. **2** retroactive.
■ **retrospectively** adv.

retroussé /ruh-**troo**-say/ adj. (of a nose) turned up at the tip.

retsina n. a Greek wine flavoured with resin.

return v. **1** come or go back. **2** give, send, or put back. **3** feel, say, or do the same thing in response. **4** give a verdict. **5** yield a profit. **6** elect to office.
▷ SYNONYMS: **1 go back**, come back, arrive back, come home. **2** *the symptoms returned*: **recur**, reoccur, repeat itself, reappear. **3 give back**, hand back, pay back, repay, restore, put back, replace, reinstall, reinstate.
– ANTONYMS: leave.
• n. **1** an act of returning. **2** a profit. **3** Brit. a ticket allowing travel to a place and back again.
▷ SYNONYMS: **1 recurrence**, reoccurrence, repeat, reappearance. **2 replacement**, restoration, reinstatement, restitution. **3 yield**, profit, gain, revenue, interest, dividend.

reunion n. a social gathering of people who have not seen each other for some time.

reunite v. bring or come together again.

reuse v. use again.
■ **reusable** adj.

Rev. (or **Rev**) abbrev. Reverend.

rev informal v. (**revving**, **revved**) increase the running speed of an engine.

r

• **n.** a revolution of an engine.

revamp v. alter so as to improve.

▷ SYNONYMS: **renovate**, redecorate, refurbish, remodel, refashion, redesign, restyle; informal do up, give something a facelift, give something a makeover, vamp up; Brit. informal tart up.

reveal v. **1** make known. **2** allow something hidden to be seen.

▷ SYNONYMS: **1 disclose**, make known, make public, broadcast, publicize, circulate, divulge, tell, let slip/drop, give away/out, blurt out, release, leak, bring to light, lay bare, unveil; informal let on. **2 show**, display, exhibit, unveil, uncover.

– ANTONYMS: conceal, hide.

reveille /ri-**val**-li/ n. a signal sounded to wake up soldiers.

revel v. (**revelling, revelled**; US **reveling, reveled**) **1** (**revel in**) gain great pleasure from. **2** enjoy yourself in a lively way.

▷ SYNONYMS: **1** *he revelled in the applause*: **enjoy**, delight in, love, like, adore, take great pleasure in, appreciate, relish, lap up, savour; informal get a kick out of. **2 celebrate**, make merry, roister; informal party, live it up, paint the town red.

• **n.** (**revels**) lively celebrations.

▷ SYNONYMS: **celebrations**, festivity, jollification, merrymaking, carousal, roistering; informal partying.

■ **reveller** n. **revelry** n.

revelation n. **1** the act of revealing. **2** a surprising thing.

▷ SYNONYMS: **disclosure**, announcement, report, admission, confession, divulging, giving away/out, leak, betrayal, publicizing.

revelatory adj. revealing something previously unknown.

revenge n. something harmful done in return for an injury or wrong.

▷ SYNONYMS: **retaliation**, retribution, vengeance, reprisal, recrimination, an eye for an eye (and a tooth for a tooth), redress.

– ANTONYMS: forgiveness.

• **v.** (**be revenged**) take revenge.

▷ SYNONYMS: **avenge yourself**, exact retribution, take reprisals, make someone pay; informal get your own back.

revenue n. the income received by an organization, or by a state from taxes.

▷ SYNONYMS: **income**, takings, receipts, proceeds, earnings, profit, gain, yield.

– ANTONYMS: expenditure.

reverberate v. **1** be repeated as an echo. **2** have continuing effects.

▷ SYNONYMS: **resound**, echo, resonate, ring, boom, rumble.

■ **reverberation** n.

revere v. respect or admire deeply.

▷ SYNONYMS: **respect**, admire, think highly of, esteem, venerate, look up to, be in awe of.

– ANTONYMS: despise.

reverence n. deep respect.

▷ SYNONYMS: **high esteem**, high regard, great respect, honour, veneration, homage, admiration, appreciation, deference.

– ANTONYMS: scorn.

reverend adj. a title given to Christian ministers.

reverent adj. showing deep respect.

▷ SYNONYMS: **respectful**, admiring, devoted, devout, awed, deferential; pious.

■ **reverential** adj.

reverie n. a daydream.

reversal n. a change to an opposite direction, course of action, etc.

▷ SYNONYMS: **1 turnaround**, turnabout, about-face, volte-face, change of heart, U-turn, backtracking; Brit. about-turn. **2 swap**, exchange, change, interchange, switch. **3 alteration**, overturning, overthrow, disallowing, overriding, overruling, veto, revocation. **4 setback**, upset, failure, misfortune, mishap, disaster, blow, disappointment, adversity, hardship, affliction, vicissitude, defeat.

reverse v. **1** move backwards. **2** make something the opposite of what it was. **3** turn the other way round. **4** cancel a judgement.

▷ SYNONYMS: **1 back**, move back/backwards. **2 turn upside down**, turn over, upend, invert, turn back to front. **3 swap**, change round, exchange, switch, transpose. **4 alter**, change, overturn, overthrow, disallow, override, overrule, veto, revoke.

• **adj.** opposite in direction, order, etc.

▷ SYNONYMS: **backward**, backwards, inverted, transposed, opposite.

• **n. 1** a change of direction or action. **2** the opposite. **3** a setback.

▷ SYNONYMS: **1 opposite**, contrary, converse, inverse, antithesis. **2 setback**, reversal, upset, failure, misfortune, mishap, disaster, blow, disappointment, adversity, hardship, affliction, vicissitude, defeat. **3 other side**, back, underside, flip side.

– ANTONYMS: front.

■ **reversible** adj.

revert v. return to a previous state,

practice, etc.
▷ SYNONYMS: **return**, go back, change back, default, relapse.
■ **reversion** n.

review n. **1** a formal examination so as to make changes if necessary. **2** a critical assessment of a book etc. **3** a report of events. **4** a ceremonial inspection of military forces.
▷ SYNONYMS: **1 analysis**, evaluation, assessment, appraisal, examination, investigation, enquiry, probe, inspection, study; reconsideration, reassessment, re-evaluation, reappraisal. **2 criticism**, critique, write-up, assessment, commentary.
• v. carry out or write a review of.
▷ SYNONYMS: **survey**, study, consider, analyse, examine, scrutinize, explore, look into, probe, investigate, inspect, assess, evaluate, appraise; reconsider, re-examine, reassess, re-evaluate, reappraise, rethink, revisit.
■ **reviewer** n.

revile v. criticize in a scornful way.

revise v. **1** examine and alter. **2** Brit. study previous work to prepare for an exam.
▷ SYNONYMS: **1 reconsider**, review, re-examine, reassess, re-evaluate, reappraise, rethink, revisit; change, alter, modify, amend, correct, edit, rewrite, redraft, rephrase, rework. **2 reread**, memorize, cram; informal bone up on; Brit. informal swot up on, mug up on.
■ **revision** n.

revitalize (or **-ise**) v. give new life or vitality to.
▷ SYNONYMS: **reinvigorate**, re-energize, boost, regenerate, revive, revivify, rejuvenate, reanimate, resuscitate, refresh, stimulate, breathe new life into; informal give a shot in the arm to, pep up, buck up.

revival n. **1** an improvement in condition, strength, or popularity. **2** a new production of an old play.
▷ SYNONYMS: **improvement**, rally, upturn, upswing, resurgence; comeback, reappearance, resurrection, rebirth.
– ANTONYMS: downturn.

revivalism n. the promotion of a revival of religious faith.
■ **revivalist** n. & adj.

revive v. **1** restore to consciousness, health, or strength. **2** start doing or using again.
▷ SYNONYMS: **1 resuscitate**, bring round; informal give the kiss of life to. **2 reinvigorate**, revitalize, refresh,

energize, reanimate. **3** *reviving old traditions*: **reintroduce**, re-establish, restore, resurrect, bring back.

revivify v. (**revivifying**, **revivified**) revive.

revoke v. make a decree, law, etc. no longer valid.
▷ SYNONYMS: **cancel**, repeal, rescind, reverse, annul, nullify, void, invalidate, countermand, retract, withdraw, overrule, override; formal abrogate.
■ **revocation** n.

revolt v. **1** rebel against an authority. **2** disgust.
▷ SYNONYMS: **1 rebel**, rise up, take to the streets, riot, mutiny. **2 disgust**, sicken, nauseate, turn someone's stomach, put off, offend; informal turn off; N. Amer. informal gross out.
• n. an act of rebellion.
▷ SYNONYMS: **rebellion**, revolution, insurrection, mutiny, uprising, riot, insurgence, coup, coup d'état.

revolting adj. very unpleasant.
▷ SYNONYMS: **disgusting**, sickening, nauseating, stomach-turning, repulsive, repugnant, hideous, nasty, foul, offensive, vile; N. Amer. vomitous; informal ghastly, horrid, gross.
– ANTONYMS: lovely, pleasant.

revolution n. **1** the overthrow of a government by force, in favour of a new system. **2** a great and influential change. **3** a single movement around a central point.
▷ SYNONYMS: **1 rebellion**, revolt, insurrection, mutiny, uprising, rising, riot, insurgence, coup, coup d'état. **2 dramatic change**, sea change, metamorphosis, transformation, innovation, reorganization, restructuring; informal shake-up; N. Amer. informal shakedown. **3 turn**, rotation, circle, spin, orbit, circuit, lap.

revolutionary adj. **1** involving great change. **2** of or engaged in political revolution.
▷ SYNONYMS: **1 rebellious**, rebel, insurgent, rioting, mutinous, renegade. **2 new**, novel, original, unusual, unconventional, unorthodox, newfangled, innovatory, modern, state-of-the-art, futuristic, pioneering.
• n. (pl. **revolutionaries**) a person who starts or supports a political revolution.
▷ SYNONYMS: **rebel**, insurgent, mutineer, insurrectionist, agitator.

revolutionize (or **-ise**) v. change completely.
▷ SYNONYMS: **transform**, shake up, turn

r

upside down, restructure, reorganize, transmute, metamorphose; humorous transmogrify.

revolve v. **1** move in a circle around a central point. **2 (revolve around)** treat as the most important aspect.
▷ SYNONYMS: **1 go round**, turn round, rotate, spin. **2 circle**, travel, orbit.

revolver n. a type of pistol.

revue n. a theatrical show with short sketches, songs, etc.

revulsion n. strong disgust.
▷ SYNONYMS: **disgust**, repulsion, abhorrence, repugnance, nausea, horror, aversion, abomination, distaste.
– ANTONYMS: delight.

reward n. a thing given in recognition of service, effort, or achievement.
▷ SYNONYMS: **award**, honour, decoration, bonus, premium, bounty, present, gift, payment, recompense, prize; informal pay-off.
• v. give a reward to or for.
▷ SYNONYMS: **recompense**, pay, remunerate.
– ANTONYMS: punish.

rewarding adj. providing satisfaction.
▷ SYNONYMS: **satisfying**, gratifying, pleasing, fulfilling, enriching, illuminating, worthwhile, productive, fruitful.

rhapsodize (or **-ise**) v. express great enthusiasm.

rhapsody n. (pl. **rhapsodies**) **1** an expression of great enthusiasm. **2** a piece of music in one extended movement.
■ **rhapsodic** adj.

rhenium n. a metallic element.

rheostat n. a device for varying the resistance in an electrical circuit.

rhesus factor n. a substance in red blood cells which can cause disease in a newborn baby.

rhesus monkey n. a small southern Asian monkey.

rhetoric n. **1** effective or persuasive public speaking. **2** persuasive but insincere language.
▷ SYNONYMS: **1 oratory**, eloquence, command of language, way with words. **2** verbosity, grandiloquence, bombast, pomposity, purple prose; informal hot air.

rhetorical adj. **1** intended to impress. **2** (of a question) asked to make a statement rather than to obtain an answer.
▷ SYNONYMS: **1** a rhetorical device: **stylistic**, oratorical, linguistic, verbal. **2 extravagant**, grandiloquent, high-flown, bombastic, grandiose,

pompous, pretentious, overblown, turgid, flowery; informal highfalutin.
■ **rhetorically** adv.

rheumatism n. a disease causing inflammation and pain in the joints and muscles.
■ **rheumatic** adj.

rheumatoid adj. of or resembling rheumatism.

rhinestone n. an imitation diamond.

rhino n. (pl. **rhino** or **rhinos**) informal a rhinoceros.

rhinoceros n. (pl. **rhinoceros** or **rhinoceroses**) a large thick-skinned mammal with one or two horns on the nose.

rhizome n. an underground stem bearing both roots and shoots.

rhodium n. a metallic element.

rhododendron n. a shrub with large clusters of flowers.

rhombus n. (pl. **rhombuses** or **rhombi**) a quadrilateral whose sides are of equal length.
■ **rhomboid** adj. & n.

rhubarb n. a plant with thick red stems cooked and eaten as a fruit.

rhyme n. **1** a word that has or ends with the same sound as another. **2** similarity of sound between words or the endings of words. **3** a short poem with rhyming lines.
▷ SYNONYMS: **poem**, verse, ode; (**rhymes**) poetry, doggerel.
• v. have or end with the same sound.

> USAGE Remember the first h, following the r, in rhyme and rhythm.

rhythm n. **1** a strong, regular repeated pattern of sound or movement. **2** a regularly recurring sequence of events.
▷ SYNONYMS: **1 beat**, cadence, tempo, time, pulse. **2 metre**, measure, pattern.
□ **rhythm and blues** a type of music that is a combination of blues and jazz.
■ **rhythmic** adj. **rhythmical** adj. **rhythmically** adv.

rib n. **1** each of a series of bones curving round the chest. **2** a curved structure forming part of a boat's framework.
• v. (**ribbing**, **ribbed**) **1** (**ribbed**) having a pattern of raised bands. **2** informal tease.

ribald adj. humorous in a coarse way.
■ **ribaldry** n.

riband n. old use a ribbon.

ribbon n. **1** a long, narrow strip of fabric, for tying or decoration. **2** a long, narrow strip.

riboflavin n. vitamin B₂.

rice n. the edible grains of a cereal plant grown on wet land in warm countries.

rich adj. **1** having a great deal of money or assets. **2** plentiful. **3** having something in large amounts. **4** (of a colour, sound, or smell) pleasantly deep and strong. **5** (of soil) fertile.
▷ SYNONYMS: **1 wealthy**, affluent, moneyed, well off, well-to-do, prosperous; informal loaded, well heeled, made of money. **2** *rich furnishings:* **sumptuous**, opulent, luxurious, lavish, gorgeous, splendid, magnificent, costly, expensive, fancy, palatial; informal plush; Brit. informal swish; N. Amer. informal swank. **3** *a rich supply:* **plentiful**, abundant, copious, ample, profuse, lavish, liberal, generous. **4** *a garden rich in flowers:* **well stocked**, well provided, abounding, crammed, packed, teeming, bursting. **5** *rich colours:* **strong**, deep, full, intense, vivid, brilliant. **6 fertile**, productive, fruitful, fecund.
– ANTONYMS: poor, plain.
• pl. n. (**riches**) wealth.
▷ SYNONYMS: **money**, wealth, funds, cash, means, assets, capital, resources; informal bread, loot; Brit. informal dosh, brass, lolly; N. Amer. informal bucks.
■ **richness** n.

richly adv. **1** in a rich way. **2** fully.
▷ SYNONYMS: **1 sumptuously**, opulently, luxuriously, lavishly, gorgeously, splendidly, magnificently. **2** *the reward she richly deserves:* **fully**, amply, well, thoroughly, completely, wholly, totally, entirely, absolutely, utterly.

Richter scale /rik-ter/ n. a scale for measuring the severity of an earthquake.

rick n. **1** a stack of hay etc. **2** Brit. a slight sprain or strain.
• v. Brit. strain slightly.

rickets n. a bone disease of children caused by lack of vitamin D.

rickety adj. likely to collapse.

rickshaw n. a light two-wheeled vehicle pulled by a person walking or riding a bicycle.

ricochet /ri-kuh-shay/ v. (**ricocheting**, **ricocheted**) rebound off a surface.
• n. a shot or hit that ricochets.

ricotta n. a soft white Italian cheese.

rictus n. a fixed grimace or grin.

rid v. (**ridding**, **rid**) **1** (**rid of**) free of something unwanted. **2** (**be/get rid of**) be or make yourself free of.
▷ SYNONYMS: **clear**, free, purge, empty, strip.

riddance n. (**good riddance**) expressing relief at being rid of someone or something.

riddle n. **1** a cleverly worded question asked as a game. **2** a puzzling person or thing. **3** a large coarse sieve.
▷ SYNONYMS: **puzzle**, conundrum, brain-teaser, problem, question, poser, enigma, mystery.
• v. (**be riddled**) **1** have many holes. **2** be filled with something undesirable.

ride v. (**riding**, **rode**; past part. **ridden**) **1** sit on and control the movement of a horse, bicycle, etc. **2** travel in a vehicle. **3** be carried or supported by.
▷ SYNONYMS: **1 sit on**, mount, control, manage, handle. **2 travel**, move, proceed, drive, cycle, trot, canter, gallop.
• n. **1** an act of riding. **2** a roundabout etc. ridden at a fair or amusement park.
▷ SYNONYMS: **trip**, journey, drive, run, excursion, outing, jaunt, lift; informal spin.
□ **ride on** depend on. **ride up** (of clothing) move upwards.

rider n. **1** a person who rides a horse etc. **2** an additional condition.

ridge n. **1** a long narrow hilltop. **2** a narrow raised band. **3** a long region of high pressure. **4** the edge formed where the two slopes of a roof meet at the top.
■ **ridged** adj.

ridicule n. mockery or derision.
▷ SYNONYMS: **mockery**, derision, laughter, scorn, scoffing, jeering.
– ANTONYMS: respect.
• v. make fun of.
▷ SYNONYMS: **mock**, deride, laugh at, pour scorn on, jeer at, make fun of, scoff at, satirize, caricature, parody.

ridiculous adj. very silly or unreasonable.
▷ SYNONYMS: **laughable**, absurd, ludicrous, risible, comical, funny, hilarious, amusing, farcical, silly, stupid, idiotic, preposterous.
– ANTONYMS: sensible.
■ **ridiculously** adv.

rife adj. **1** widespread. **2** (**rife with**) full of.
▷ SYNONYMS: **widespread**, general, common, universal, extensive, ubiquitous, endemic, inescapable.

riff n. a short repeated phrase in jazz etc.

r

riffle v. turn over pages quickly and casually.

riff-raff n. people considered to be socially unacceptable.

rifle n. a gun with a long barrel.
• v. search through hurriedly.
▷ SYNONYMS: **1 rummage**, search, hunt, forage. **2 burgle**, rob, steal from, loot, raid, plunder, ransack.

rift n. **1** a crack, split, or break. **2** a serious break in friendly relations.
▷ SYNONYMS: **1 crack**, split, breach, fissure, fracture, cleft, crevice, opening. **2 disagreement**, estrangement, breach, split, schism, quarrel, falling-out, conflict, feud; Brit. row; Brit. informal bust-up.
□ **rift valley** a steep-sided valley formed by subsidence of the earth's surface.

rig v. (**rigging**, **rigged**) **1** arrange dishonestly to gain an advantage. **2** set up a device or structure. **3** fit sails and rigging on a boat.
▷ SYNONYMS: **1 manipulate**, engineer, distort, misrepresent, pervert, tamper with, falsify, fake; informal fix; Brit. informal fiddle. **2 set up**, erect, assemble, put together, improvise, contrive; Brit. informal knock up.
• n. **1** a piece of equipment for a particular purpose. **2** an oil rig.

rigging n. the system of ropes etc. supporting a ship's masts.

right adj. **1** of, on, or towards the side which is to the east when facing north. **2** morally good or justified. **3** factually correct. **4** most appropriate. **5** satisfactory, sound, or normal. **6** Brit. informal complete: *a right idiot.*
▷ SYNONYMS: **1 just**, fair, equitable, proper, good, upright, righteous, virtuous, moral, ethical, principled, honourable, honest, lawful, legal. **2 correct**, unerring, accurate, exact, precise, valid; Brit. informal spot on. **3 suitable**, appropriate, fitting, apposite, apt, correct, proper, desirable, preferable, ideal. **4 opportune**, advantageous, favourable, convenient, good, lucky, fortunate. **5 right-hand**; Nautical starboard; Heraldry dexter.
– ANTONYMS: wrong, left.
• adv. **1** on or to the right side. **2** completely. **3** exactly; directly. **4** correctly.
▷ SYNONYMS: **1 completely**, fully, totally, absolutely, utterly, thoroughly, quite. **2 exactly**, precisely, directly, immediately, just, squarely, dead; informal slap bang, smack, plumb. **3 correctly**,

accurately, perfectly.
– ANTONYMS: wrong, badly.
• n. **1** what is morally right. **2** an entitlement to have or do something. **3** (**the right**) the right-hand side or direction. **4** (**the Right**) a right-wing group or party.
▷ SYNONYMS: **1 goodness**, righteousness, virtue, integrity, propriety, probity, morality, truth, honesty, honour, justice, fairness, equity. **2 entitlement**, prerogative, privilege, liberty, authority, power, licence, permission, dispensation, leave, due.
– ANTONYMS: wrong.
• v. **1** restore to a normal or upright position. **2** correct or make amends for.
▷ SYNONYMS: **remedy**, rectify, retrieve, fix, resolve, sort out, settle, square, straighten out, correct, repair, mend, redress.
□ **by rights** if things were fair or correct. **in your own right** as a result of your own qualifications or efforts. **right angle** an angle of 90°. **right away** immediately. **right-handed** using or done with the right hand. **right-hand man** an indispensable assistant. **right of way 1** the legal right to go through another's property. **2** a public path through another's property. **3** the right to proceed before another vehicle.
■ **rightly** adv.

righteous adj. morally right.
▷ SYNONYMS: **good**, virtuous, upright, upstanding, decent, ethical, principled, moral, honest, honourable, blameless.
– ANTONYMS: wicked.
■ **righteousness** n.

rightful adj. **1** having a right to something. **2** just; fitting.
▷ SYNONYMS: **1 legal**, lawful, real, true, proper, correct, recognized, genuine, authentic, acknowledged, approved, valid, bona fide; informal legit, kosher. **2 deserved**, merited, due, just, right, fair, proper, fitting, appropriate, suitable.
– ANTONYMS: wrongful.
■ **rightfully** adv.

right-wing adj. conservative or reactionary.
▷ SYNONYMS: **conservative**, rightist, reactionary, traditionalist, conventional.
– ANTONYMS: left-wing.

rigid adj. **1** unable to bend. **2** strict or inflexible.
▷ SYNONYMS: **1 stiff**, hard, taut, firm,

inflexible, unbendable, unyielding, inelastic. **2** *a rigid routine:* **fixed**, set, firm, inflexible, invariable, hard and fast, cast-iron, strict, stringent, rigorous, uncompromising, intransigent.
– ANTONYMS: flexible.
■ **rigidity** n. **rigidly** adv.

rigmarole n. a long, complicated procedure.

rigor mortis n. stiffening of the body after death.

rigorous adj. **1** very thorough or accurate. **2** (of a rule etc.) strictly applied or followed. **3** harsh or severe.
▷ SYNONYMS: **1 meticulous**, conscientious, punctilious, careful, scrupulous, painstaking, exact, precise, accurate, particular, strict. **2 strict**, stringent, rigid, inflexible, draconian, intransigent, uncompromising. **3** *rigorous conditions:* **harsh**, severe, bleak, extreme, demanding.
– ANTONYMS: slapdash, lax.
■ **rigorously** adv.

rigour (US **rigor**) n. **1** the quality of being rigorous. **2** (**rigours**) demanding conditions.

rile v. informal annoy.

rill n. a small stream.

rim n. an edge or border, esp. of something circular.
▷ SYNONYMS: **edge**, brim, lip, border, side, margin, brink, boundary, perimeter, circumference, limits, periphery.
• v. (**rimming**, **rimmed**) provide with a rim.

rime n. literary frost.

rind n. a tough outer layer on fruit, cheese, or bacon.
▷ SYNONYMS: **skin**, peel, zest, integument.

ring¹ n. **1** a small circular band worn on a finger. **2** a circular band, object, or mark. **3** an enclosed space in which a sport or show takes place. **4** a group working together illegally or secretly.
▷ SYNONYMS: **1 circle**, band, halo, disc. **2 arena**, enclosure, amphitheatre, bowl. **3 gang**, syndicate, cartel, mob, band, circle, organization, association, society, alliance, league.
• v. **1** surround. **2** draw a circle round.
▷ SYNONYMS: **surround**, circle, encircle, enclose, hem in, confine, seal off.
□ **ringleader** a person who leads others in crime or causing trouble. **ringlet** a corkscrew-shaped curl of hair. **ringworm** a skin disease causing small circular itchy patches.

WORD LINKS
annular ring-shaped

ring² v. (**ringing**, **rang**; past part. **rung**) **1** make a clear resonating sound. **2** (**ring with**) echo with a sound. **3** Brit. call by phone. **4** Brit. (**ring off**) end a phone call. **5** call for attention by sounding a bell.
▷ SYNONYMS: **1 chime**, sound, peal, toll, clang, bong; literary knell. **2 resound**, reverberate, resonate, echo. **3 telephone**, phone, call; informal give someone a buzz; Brit. informal give someone a bell.
• n. **1** an act of ringing. **2** a loud clear sound or tone. **3** Brit. informal a phone call. **4** a quality conveyed by words: *a ring of truth.*
□ **ringtone** a sound made by a mobile phone when an incoming call is received.

rink n. an enclosed area of ice for skating etc.

rinse v. wash with clean water to remove soap or dirt.
▷ SYNONYMS: **wash**, clean, cleanse, bathe, dip, drench, splash, swill, sluice.
• n. **1** an act of rinsing. **2** a mouthwash. **3** a liquid for conditioning or colouring the hair.

riot n. **1** a violent disturbance by a crowd. **2** a confused combination or display. **3** informal a very amusing person or thing.
▷ SYNONYMS: **uproar**, commotion, upheaval, disturbance, furore, tumult, melee, fracas, free-for-all; disorder, violence, fighting, lawlessness.
• v. take part in a riot.
▷ SYNONYMS: **rampage**, go on the rampage, run wild, run amok, run riot, go berserk; informal raise hell.
□ **run riot** behave in an uncontrolled way.
■ **rioter** n.

riotous adj. **1** involving wild and uncontrolled behaviour. **2** involving public disorder.
▷ SYNONYMS: **1** *a riotous party:* **wild**, lively, loud, noisy, unrestrained, uninhibited, uproarious; Brit. informal rumbustious. **2** *a riotous demonstration:* **unruly**, rowdy, disorderly, uncontrollable, unmanageable, undisciplined, tumultuous, violent, wild, lawless, anarchic.
– ANTONYMS: peaceful.

RIP abbrev. rest in peace (used on graves).

rip v. (**ripping**, **ripped**) **1** tear or become torn. **2** pull forcibly away.

▷ SYNONYMS: **tear**, pull, wrench, snatch, drag, pluck; informal yank.
• n. a long tear.
□ **let rip** informal act or speak without restraint. **ripcord** a cord pulled to open a parachute. **rip-off** informal a very overpriced article. **rip off** informal **1** cheat someone. **2** steal.

ripe adj. **1** ready for harvesting and eating. **2** (of a cheese) fully matured. **3** (**ripe for**) ready for. **4** (of age) advanced.
▷ SYNONYMS: **1 mature**, full grown, fully developed. **2** *land ripe for development*: **ready**, fit, suitable, right. **3** *the ripe old age of ninety*: **advanced**, hoary, venerable.
■ **ripen** v. **ripeness** n.

riposte n. a quick reply.
▷ SYNONYMS: **retort**, counter, rejoinder, sally, return, answer, reply, response; informal comeback.

ripple n. **1** a small wave or waves. **2** a feeling or effect that spreads through someone or something.
• v. **1** form ripples. **2** (of a feeling etc.) spread through.

rise v. (**rising**, **rose**; past part. **risen**) **1** come up or go up. **2** get up from lying, sitting, or kneeling. **3** increase. **4** (of land) slope upwards. **5** (of the sun etc.) appear above the horizon. **6** reach a higher rank or position. **7** rebel. **8** (of a river) have its source.
▷ SYNONYMS: **1 climb**, come up, arise, ascend, mount, soar. **2 stand up**, get to your feet, get up, jump up, leap up, stir, bestir yourself. **3 go up**, increase, soar, shoot up, surge, leap, jump, rocket, escalate, spiral. **4 get higher**, grow, increase, become louder, swell, intensify. **5 loom**, tower, soar.
– ANTONYMS: fall, descend, drop.
• n. **1** an act of rising. **2** an upward slope. **3** Brit. a pay increase.
▷ SYNONYMS: **1 increase**, hike, leap, upsurge, upswing, climb. **2 slope**, incline, hill, elevation, acclivity. **3 raise**, increase, increment.

risible adj. causing laughter.
■ **risibly** adv.

rising n. a revolt.

risk n. **1** the possibility of something bad happening. **2** a person or thing causing this.
▷ SYNONYMS: **1 chance**, uncertainty, unpredictability, instability, insecurity. **2 possibility**, chance, probability, likelihood, danger, peril, threat, menace, prospect.
• v. **1** expose to danger or loss. **2** act in such a way that something bad could

happen.
▷ SYNONYMS: **endanger**, jeopardize, imperil, hazard, gamble with, chance, put at risk, put on the line.

risky adj. (**riskier**, **riskiest**) involving risk.
▷ SYNONYMS: **dangerous**, hazardous, perilous, unsafe, insecure, precarious, touch-and-go, treacherous, uncertain, unpredictable; informal dicey.
■ **riskily** adv. **riskiness** n.

risotto n. (pl. **risottos**) a dish of rice with meat, seafood, etc.

risqué /riss-kay/ adj. slightly indecent.

rissole n. Brit. a small cake of minced meat, coated in breadcrumbs and fried.

rite n. a ritual.
▷ SYNONYMS: **ceremony**, ritual, ceremonial, custom, service, observance, liturgy, worship, office.

ritual n. a religious or solemn ceremony involving a set series of actions.
▷ SYNONYMS: **ceremony**, rite, act, practice, custom, tradition, convention, formality, protocol.
• adj. of or done as a ritual.
▷ SYNONYMS: **ceremonial**, prescribed, set, conventional, traditional, formal.
■ **ritualistic** adj. **ritually** adv.

rival n. a person or thing competing with or equal to another.
▷ SYNONYMS: **opponent**, opposition, challenger, competitor, contender, adversary, antagonist, enemy; literary foe.
– ANTONYMS: ally.
• v. (**rivalling**, **rivalled**; US **rivaling**, **rivaled**) be comparable to.
▷ SYNONYMS: **match**, compare with, compete with, vie with, equal, emulate, measure up to, touch; informal hold a candle to.

rivalry n. (pl **rivalries**) a situation in which two people are competing for the same thing.
▷ SYNONYMS: **competition**, contention, opposition, conflict, feuding; informal keeping up with the Joneses.

riven adj. torn apart.

river n. a large natural flow of water along a channel.
▷ SYNONYMS: **1 stream**, brook, watercourse, rivulet, tributary; Scottish & N. English burn; N. English beck; S. English bourn; N. Amer. & Austral./NZ creek. **2** *a river of molten lava*: **stream**, torrent, flood, deluge, cascade.

> **WORD LINKS**
> **fluvial** relating to or found in rivers

rivet n. a short bolt for holding

together two metal plates.

• v. (**riveting**, **riveted**) 1 fasten with a rivet or rivets. 2 (**be riveted**) be completely engrossed.

riveting adj. extremely interesting.

▷ SYNONYMS: **fascinating**, gripping, engrossing, intriguing, absorbing, captivating, enthralling, compelling, spellbinding, mesmerizing; informal unputdownable.

– ANTONYMS: boring.

rivulet n. a small stream.

RN abbrev. Royal Navy.

RNA n. ribonucleic acid, a substance in living cells which carries instructions from DNA.

roach n. (pl. **roach**) a freshwater fish of the carp family.

road n. 1 a wide track with a hard surface for vehicles to travel on. 2 a way leading to a particular outcome.

▷ SYNONYMS: 1 **street**, thoroughfare, roadway, highway, lane; Brit. motorway. 2 *the road to recovery*: **way**, path, route, course.

□ **road rage** violent anger caused by conflict with another driver. **roadway** 1 a road. 2 the part of a road intended for vehicles. **roadworks** Brit. repairs to roads or to pipes under roads. **roadworthy** (of a vehicle) fit to be used on the road.

roadie n. informal a person who sets up equipment for a rock group.

roadster n. an open-top sports car.

roam v. wander.

▷ SYNONYMS: **wander**, rove, ramble, drift, walk, traipse, range, travel, tramp, trek; informal cruise.

roan adj. (of a horse) having a dark coat interspersed with white hairs.

roar n. 1 a long, deep sound made by a lion, engine, etc. 2 a loud sound expressing anger, amusement, etc.

• v. 1 make a roar. 2 laugh loudly. 3 move very fast.

▷ SYNONYMS: **bellow**, yell, shout, thunder, bawl, howl, scream, cry, bay; informal holler.

roaring adj. informal complete: *a roaring success*.

▷ SYNONYMS: **blazing**, burning, flaming.

roast v. 1 cook food in an oven or over a fire. 2 make or become very warm.

• adj. (of food) having been roasted.

• n. a roast joint of meat.

rob v. (**robbing**, **robbed**) 1 steal from by force or threat of force. 2 deprive of something valued.

▷ SYNONYMS: 1 **burgle**, steal from, hold up, break into, raid, loot, plunder, pillage; informal **mug**; N. Amer. burglarize.

2 **cheat**, swindle, defraud; informal do out of, con out of.

■ **robber** n.

robbery n. (pl. **robberies**) the action or an act of robbing a person or place.

▷ SYNONYMS: **burglary**, theft, stealing, housebreaking, shoplifting, embezzlement, fraud, hold-up, raid; informal mugging, smash-and-grab, stick-up; N. Amer. informal heist.

robe n. a long loose outer garment for formal or ceremonial occasions.

▷ SYNONYMS: 1 **cloak**, kaftan, djellaba, wrap, mantle, cape; N. Amer. wrapper. 2 *ceremonial robes*: **garb**, vestments, regalia, finery.

• v. dress in a robe.

robin n. a red-breasted songbird.

robot n. a machine able to carry out a complex series of actions automatically.

▷ SYNONYMS: **machine**, automaton, android; informal bot, droid.

■ **robotic** adj.

robotics n. the study of the design, construction, and use of robots.

robust adj. 1 sturdy. 2 healthy. 3 forceful.

▷ SYNONYMS: 1 **strong**, vigorous, sturdy, tough, powerful, solid, rugged, hardy, strapping, healthy, fit, fighting fit, hale and hearty. 2 **durable**, resilient, tough, hard-wearing, long-lasting, sturdy, strong.

– ANTONYMS: frail, fragile.

rock n. 1 the hard material of the earth's crust. 2 a piece or mass of rock. 3 Brit. a hard sweet in the form of a cylindrical stick. 4 a type of loud pop music with a strong beat.

▷ SYNONYMS: **boulder**, stone, pebble.

• v. 1 move to and fro or from side to side. 2 shock or distress greatly.

▷ SYNONYMS: 1 **move to and fro**, sway, see-saw, roll, pitch, plunge, toss, lurch. 2 **stun**, shock, stagger, astonish, startle, surprise, shake, take aback, throw, stagger, disconcert.

□ **on the rocks** informal 1 in difficulties and likely to fail. 2 (of a drink) served with ice cubes. **rock and roll** a type of popular dance music with simple melodies. **rock bottom** the lowest possible level.

rocker n. 1 a person who performs or likes rock music. 2 a curved piece of wood on which something may rock.

rockery n. (pl. **rockeries**) an arrangement of rocks in a garden with plants growing between them.

rocket n. 1 a cylindrical missile or spacecraft propelled by a stream

r

of burning gases. **2** a firework that shoots into the air and explodes. **3** Brit. informal a severe reprimand. **4** Brit. a plant eaten in salads.
• v. (**rocketing, rocketed**) move or increase very rapidly.

rocky adj. (**rockier, rockiest**) **1** of rock. **2** full of rocks. **3** unsteady or unstable.
▷ SYNONYMS: **1 stony**, pebbly, shingly, rough, bumpy, craggy, mountainous. **2 unsteady**, shaky, unstable, wobbly, tottery, rickety.
– ANTONYMS: steady, stable.

rococo adj. of an ornate style of furniture or architecture of the 18th century.

rod n. **1** a thin straight bar of wood, metal, etc. **2** (or **fishing rod**) a long stick with a line and hook attached, for catching fish.
▷ SYNONYMS: **bar**, stick, pole, baton, staff, shaft, strut, rail, spoke.

rode past of RIDE.

rodent n. a mammal of a group with large front teeth.

rodeo n. (pl. **rodeos**) a contest or entertainment in which cowboys show their skills.

roe n. **1** the eggs of a fish, eaten as food. **2** (pl. **roe** or **roes**) a small deer.

roentgen /**runt**-yuhn/ n. a unit of ionizing radiation.

rogue n. **1** a dishonest man. **2** an elephant living apart from the herd.
▷ SYNONYMS: **scoundrel**, rascal, good-for-nothing, wretch, villain, criminal, lawbreaker; informal crook.

roguish adj. playfully mischievous.

roister v. enjoy yourself in a lively, noisy way.

role n. **1** an actor's part. **2** a person's or thing's function.
▷ SYNONYMS: **1 part**, character. **2 capacity**, position, function, job, post, office, duty, responsibility.

roll v. **1** move by turning over and over. **2** move on wheels or with a smooth motion. **3** (of a ship, aircraft, etc.) sway from side to side. **4** turn something flexible over and over on itself. **5** flatten with a roller. **6** (of a deep sound) reverberate.
▷ SYNONYMS: **1 turn over and over**, spin, rotate, revolve, wheel, trundle, bowl. **2 flow**, run, course, stream, pour, trickle. **3 wind**, coil, fold, curl, twist. **4 rock**, sway, reel, list, pitch, plunge, lurch, toss.
• n. **1** a cylinder formed by rolling material. **2** a rolling movement. **3** a very small loaf of bread. **4** a

reverberating sound. **5** an official list of names.
▷ SYNONYMS: **1 cylinder**, tube, scroll, reel, spool, bobbin. **2 turn**, rotation, revolution, spin, whirl. **3 list**, register, directory, record, file, index, catalogue, inventory. **4** a roll of thunder: **rumble**, reverberation, echo, boom, clap, crack.
□ **roll call** the reading aloud of a list of names to check who is present. **rolled gold** a thin coating of gold on another metal. **rolling pin** a cylinder for rolling out dough. **rolling stock** locomotives, carriages, and other railway vehicles. **roll out** launch a new product.

roller n. **1** a rotating cylinder used to move, flatten, or spread something. **2** a small cylinder on which hair is wound to produce curls. **3** a long swelling wave.
□ **roller coaster** a railway at a fairground with a steep, twisting track. **roller skate** a boot with wheels, for gliding across a hard surface.

rollicking adj. very lively and amusing.

roly-poly adj. informal plump.

ROM abbrev. Computing read-only memory.

Roman adj. of Rome or its ancient empire.
• n. **1** an inhabitant of Rome. **2** (**roman**) plain upright type.
□ **Roman Catholic** a member of the part of the Christian Church which has the Pope as its head. **Roman numeral** each of the letters used as numbers in the ancient Roman system.

romance n. **1** a love affair. **2** a feeling of excitement associated with love. **3** a book or film about a love affair. **4** a feeling of mystery and excitement: the romance of the past. **5** (**Romance**) French, Italian, and other languages descended from Latin.
▷ SYNONYMS: **1 love affair**, relationship, liaison, courtship, attachment, amour. **2 story**, tale, legend, fairy tale. **3 mystery**, glamour, excitement, exoticism, mystique, appeal, allure, charm.
• v. try to gain the love of.

Romanesque adj. of a style of architecture common in Europe c.900–1200.

romantic adj. **1** of love or romance. **2** showing or regarding life in an unrealistic and idealized way.

3 (**Romantic**) of Romanticism.
▷ SYNONYMS: **1 loving**, amorous, passionate, tender, affectionate; informal lovey-dovey. **2 sentimental**, hearts-and-flowers; informal slushy, schmaltzy; Brit. informal soppy. **3 idyllic**, picturesque, fairy-tale, beautiful, lovely, charming, pretty. **4 idealistic**, unrealistic, fanciful, impractical, head-in-the-clouds, starry-eyed, utopian, rose-tinted.
– ANTONYMS: unsentimental, realistic.
• **n. 1** a romantic person. **2** (**Romantic**) a writer or artist of the Romantic movement.
▷ SYNONYMS: **idealist**, sentimentalist, dreamer, fantasist.
– ANTONYMS: realist.
■ **romantically** adv.
Romanticism n. a literary and artistic movement which emphasized creative inspiration and emotion.
romanticize (or **-ise**) v. cause to seem more attractive than in reality.
Romany n. (pl. **Romanies**) **1** the language of the Gypsies. **2** a Gypsy.
romp v. **1** play about roughly and energetically. **2** informal achieve something easily.
▷ SYNONYMS: **play**, frolic, frisk, gambol, skip, prance, caper, cavort.
rondo n. (pl. **rondos**) a piece of music with a recurring theme.
rood screen n. a screen separating the nave from the chancel of a church.
roof n. (pl. **roofs**) the upper covering of a building, vehicle, etc.
• v. cover with a roof.
■ **roofer** n.
rook n. **1** a bird of the crow family. **2** a chess piece that can move in any direction.
rookery n. (pl. **rookeries**) a colony of rooks.
rookie n. informal a new recruit.
room n. **1** a part of a building enclosed by walls, a floor, and a ceiling. **2** space for holding things or moving in. **3** opportunity or scope.
▷ SYNONYMS: **1 space**, headroom, legroom, area, expanse, extent. **2** *there's very little room for manoeuvre*: **scope**, opportunity, capacity, leeway, latitude, freedom.
roomy adj. (**roomier**, **roomiest**) having plenty of space.
▷ SYNONYMS: **spacious**, capacious, sizeable, generous, big, large, extensive, voluminous, ample; formal commodious.
– ANTONYMS: cramped.

roost n. a place where birds regularly settle to rest.
• v. (of a bird) settle for rest.
rooster n. a male domestic fowl.
root n. **1** the part of a plant below ground, which collects water and nourishment. **2** the embedded part of a hair, tooth, etc. **3** the basic cause or origin. **4** (**roots**) family, ethnic, or cultural origins. **5** a number that when multiplied by itself one or more times gives a specified number.
▷ SYNONYMS: **1 source**, origin, cause, reason, basis, foundation, bottom, seat. **2** *his Irish roots*: **origins**, beginnings, family, birth, heritage.
• v. **1** (**be rooted**) be firmly established. **2** (of a plant) grow roots. **3** rummage. **4** (of an animal) turn up the ground with its snout in search of food.
▷ SYNONYMS: **rummage**, hunt, search, rifle, delve, forage, dig, poke.
□ **root for** informal support enthusiastically. **root out** find and get rid of. **take root** become established.
■ **rootless** adj.
rope n. **1** strong thick cord. **2** (**the ropes**) informal the established procedure.
▷ SYNONYMS: **cord**, cable, line, hawser, string.
• v. **1** catch or tie with rope. **2** (**rope in**) persuade to take part in.
□ **on the ropes** in a state of near collapse.
ropy (or **ropey**) adj. Brit. informal poor in quality or health.
rosary n. (pl. **rosaries**) **1** (in the RC Church) a set series of prayers. **2** a string of beads for keeping count of prayers said.
rose[1] n. **1** a scented flower growing on a prickly bush. **2** a warm pink colour.
□ **rosewood** the dark wood of a tropical tree, used for making furniture.
rose[2] past of RISE.
rosé /roh-zay/ n. light pink wine.
rosemary n. an evergreen shrub with leaves used as a herb.
rosette n. a round badge made of ribbon.
Rosh Hashana /rosh huh-shah-nuh/ (or **Rosh Hashanah**) n. the Jewish New Year festival.
rosin n. a resin rubbed on the bows of stringed instruments.
roster n. a list of people's names and their turns of duty etc.
▷ SYNONYMS: **schedule**, list, register, agenda, calendar; Brit. rota.

r

rostrum n. (pl. **rostra** or **rostrums**) a platform for standing on to make a speech, conduct an orchestra, etc.

rosy adj. (**rosier**, **rosiest**) **1** pink. **2** promising.
▷ SYNONYMS: **1 pink**, roseate, reddish, glowing, healthy, fresh, radiant, blooming, blushing, flushed, ruddy. **2 promising**, optimistic, auspicious, hopeful, encouraging, favourable, bright, golden.
– ANTONYMS: pale, bleak.

rot v. (**rotting**, **rotted**) decay as a result of bacterial action.
▷ SYNONYMS: **1 decay**, decompose, disintegrate, crumble, perish. **2 go bad**, go off, spoil, moulder, putrefy, fester. **3 deteriorate**, degenerate, decline, decay, go to seed, go downhill; informal go to pot, go to the dogs.
•n. **1** the process of rotting. **2** informal nonsense.
▷ SYNONYMS: **decay**, decomposition, mould, mildew, blight, canker.

rota n. Brit. a list showing when each of a number of people has to do a particular job.

rotary adj. **1** revolving around a central point. **2** having a rotating part or parts.

rotate v. **1** move in a circle round a central point. **2** (of a job) pass on a regular basis to each of a group in turn. **3** grow different crops one after the other on a piece of land.
▷ SYNONYMS: **1 revolve**, go round, turn, spin, gyrate, whirl, twirl, swivel, circle, pivot. **2 alternate**, take turns, change, switch, interchange, exchange, swap.
■ **rotation** n. **rotatory** adj.

rote n. regular repetition of something to be learned.

rotisserie n. a rotating spit for roasting meat.

rotor n. the rotating part of a machine.

rotten adj. **1** decayed. **2** corrupt. **3** informal very bad.
▷ SYNONYMS: **1 decaying**, mouldy, bad, off, decomposing, spoiled, putrid, rancid, festering, fetid. **2 corrupt**, unprincipled, dishonest, dishonourable, unscrupulous, untrustworthy, immoral; informal crooked; Brit. informal bent.
– ANTONYMS: fresh.

Rottweiler n. a large powerful breed of dog.

rotund adj. rounded and plump.
■ **rotundity** n.

rotunda n. a round building or room.

rouble (or **ruble**) n. the basic unit of money of Russia.

roué /roo-ay/ n. a man who leads an immoral life.

rouge n. a cosmetic for colouring the cheeks.

rough adj. **1** not smooth or level. **2** not gentle. **3** (of weather or the sea) wild and stormy. **4** plain and basic. **5** not detailed; approximate. **6** harsh in sound or taste. **7** informal difficult and unpleasant.
▷ SYNONYMS: **1 uneven**, irregular, bumpy, stony, rocky, rugged, rutted, pitted. **2 coarse**, bristly, scratchy, prickly, shaggy, hairy, bushy. **3 dry**, leathery, weather-beaten, chapped, calloused, scaly. **4 gruff**, hoarse, harsh, rasping, husky, throaty, gravelly. **5 violent**, aggressive, belligerent, pugnacious, boisterous, rowdy, disorderly, unruly, riotous. **6 boorish**, loutish, oafish, brutish, coarse, crude, uncouth, vulgar, unrefined, unladylike, ungentlemanly, uncultured. **7 turbulent**, stormy, squally, tempestuous, violent, heavy, choppy. **8 preliminary**, hasty, quick, sketchy, cursory, basic, crude, rudimentary, raw, unpolished, incomplete, unfinished. **9 approximate**, inexact, imprecise, vague, estimated; N. Amer. informal ballpark.
– ANTONYMS: smooth, gentle, calm, exact.
•n. **1** a basic version. **2** long grass at the edge of a golf course.
▷ SYNONYMS: **sketch**, draft, outline, mock-up.
•v. **1** (**rough out**) make a first version of. **2** (**rough it**) informal live with only very basic necessities. **3** (**rough up**) informal beat up.
□ **rough and ready** basic but effective. **rough and tumble** a competitive situation without rules. **rough diamond** Brit. a person of good character but lacking manners or education.
■ **roughen** v. **roughly** adv. **roughness** n.

roughage n. indigestible material in cereals, vegetables, and fruit.

roughshod adj. (**ride roughshod over**) fail to consider the wishes or feelings of.

roulette n. a gambling game in which a ball is dropped on to a revolving wheel with numbered compartments.

round adj. **1** curved, circular, cylindrical, or spherical. **2** (of a number) expressed in convenient units rather than exactly.
▷ SYNONYMS: **circular**, spherical, globular, cylindrical.

•**n. 1** a circular shape or piece. **2** a route by which a number of people or places are visited in turn. **3** a regular sequence of activities. **4** each of a sequence of stages in a sports contest. **5** a song for several voices, each singing the same theme but starting one after another. **6** the amount of ammunition needed to fire one shot. **7** a set of drinks bought for all the members of a group.

▷ SYNONYMS: **1 ball**, sphere, globe, orb, circle, disc, ring, hoop. **2** *a policeman on his rounds:* **circuit**, beat, route, tour. **3 stage**, level, heat, game, bout, contest. **4 succession**, sequence, series, cycle.

•**adv. 1** in a circle or curve. **2** so as to include a whole area or group. **3** so as to face in the opposite direction. **4** so as to surround.

•**prep. 1** on every side of. **2** so as to encircle.

•**v. 1** pass and go round. **2** make or become round in shape.

▷ SYNONYMS: **go round**, travel round, skirt, circumnavigate, orbit.
☐ **round off** complete. **round robin** a tournament in which each competitor plays in turn against every other. **round trip** a journey to a place and back again. **round-up** a summary. **round up** collect into one place. **round up/down** make a figure less exact but more convenient. **roundworm** a parasitic worm with a rounded body.
■ **roundness** n.

roundabout n. Brit. **1** a road junction with a circular island round which traffic has to move in one direction. **2** a large revolving device in a playground. **3** a merry-go-round.
•**adj.** indirect.

▷ SYNONYMS: **circuitous**, indirect, meandering, serpentine, tortuous, oblique, circumlocutory.
– ANTONYMS: direct.

roundel n. a small disc or circular design.

rounders n. a ball game in which players run round a circuit after hitting the ball with a bat.

Roundhead n. hist. a supporter of Parliament in the English Civil War.

roundly adv. in a firm or thorough way.

▷ SYNONYMS: **1 vehemently**, emphatically, fiercely, forcefully, severely, plainly, frankly, candidly. **2 utterly**, completely, thoroughly, decisively, conclusively, heavily, soundly.

rouse v. **1** wake. **2** stir up; arouse.

▷ SYNONYMS: **1 wake**, wake up, awake, awaken, rise, bestir yourself. **2 stir up**, arouse, inspire, excite, galvanize, electrify, stimulate, move, inflame, agitate, goad, provoke, prompt.

rousing adj. exciting; stirring: *a rousing speech.*

▷ SYNONYMS: **stirring**, inspiring, exciting, stimulating, moving, electrifying, invigorating, energizing, exhilarating.

rout n. **1** a disorderly retreat. **2** a decisive defeat.

▷ SYNONYMS: **defeat**, beating, retreat, flight; informal licking, hammering, thrashing, pasting, drubbing.
– ANTONYMS: victory.
•**v.** defeat decisively.

▷ SYNONYMS: **defeat**, beat, conquer, vanquish, crush, put to flight, drive off, scatter; informal lick, hammer, clobber, thrash.

route n. a way taken in getting from a starting point to a destination.

▷ SYNONYMS: **way**, course, road, path, direction.
•**v.** (**routeing** or **routing**, **routed**) send along a route.

routine n. **1** a regular procedure. **2** a set sequence in a performance.

▷ SYNONYMS: **1 procedure**, practice, pattern, drill, regime, programme, schedule, plan. **2 act**, performance, number, turn, piece; informal spiel, patter.
•**adj.** performed as part of a regular procedure.

▷ SYNONYMS: **1 standard**, regular, customary, normal, usual, ordinary, typical, everyday. **2 boring**, tedious, monotonous, humdrum, run-of-the-mill, pedestrian, predictable, hackneyed, unimaginative, unoriginal, banal, trite.
– ANTONYMS: unusual.
■ **routinely** adv.

roux /roo/ n. (pl. **roux**) a mixture of butter and flour used in making sauces.

rove v. wander.
■ **rover** n.

row[1] /roh/ n. **1** a number of people or things in a line. **2** a period of rowing.

▷ SYNONYMS: **1 line**, column, file, queue, procession, chain, string, succession; informal crocodile. **2 tier**, line, rank, bank.
•**v.** propel a boat with oars.

row[2] /row/ n. **1** an angry quarrel. **2** a loud noise.

▷ SYNONYMS: **1 argument**, quarrel, squabble, fight, dispute, altercation,

r

falling-out; informal tiff, run-in, slanging match, spat; Brit. informal bust-up. **2 din**, noise, racket, uproar, hubbub, rumpus; informal hullabaloo.
• v. quarrel angrily.
▷ SYNONYMS: **argue**, quarrel, squabble, bicker, fight, fall out, disagree, have words; informal scrap.

rowan n. a small tree with red berries.

rowdy adj. (**rowdier, rowdiest**) noisy and disorderly.
▷ SYNONYMS: **unruly**, disorderly, riotous, undisciplined, uncontrollable, ungovernable, disruptive, obstreperous, out of control, rough, wild, boisterous, uproarious, noisy, loud; Brit. informal rumbustious.
– ANTONYMS: peaceful.
• n. (pl. **rowdies**) a rowdy person.
■ **rowdily** adv. **rowdiness** n.

rowlock /rol-luhk/ n. Brit. a fitting on the side of a boat for holding an oar.

royal adj. **1** of or having the status of a king or queen or a member of their family. **2** impressive in quality or size.
▷ SYNONYMS: **regal**, kingly, queenly, princely, sovereign.
• n. informal a member of a royal family.
□ **royal blue** a deep, vivid blue.
■ **royally** adv.

royalist n. a person supporting the principle of having a king or queen.

royalty n. (pl. **royalties**) **1** people of royal status. **2** the status of a king or queen. **3** a sum paid to the author of a book for each copy sold or to a composer for each performance of a work.

rpm abbrev. revolutions per minute.

RSI abbrev. repetitive strain injury.

RSPCA abbrev. Royal Society for the Prevention of Cruelty to Animals.

RSVP abbrev. répondez s'il vous plaît; please reply.

rub v. (**rubbing, rubbed**) **1** move the hand, a cloth, etc. back and forth over a surface while pressing against it. **2** dry, smooth, or make sore by rubbing. **3** (**rub out**) remove pencil marks with a rubber.
▷ SYNONYMS: **1 massage**, knead, stroke, pat. **2 apply**, smear, spread, work in. **3 chafe**, scrape, pinch.
• n. **1** an act of rubbing. **2** an ointment for rubbing on the skin.

rubber n. **1** a tough elastic substance made from a tropical plant or from chemicals. **2** Brit. a piece of this for erasing pencil marks. **3** a unit of play in the card game bridge.
□ **rubber-stamp** approve automatically without proper consideration.
■ **rubbery** adj.

rubberneck v. informal turn to stare at something as you pass.

rubbish n. **1** waste material. **2** nonsense.
▷ SYNONYMS: **1 refuse**, waste, litter, scrap, detritus, debris, dross; N. Amer. garbage, trash; informal dreck, junk. **2 nonsense**, gibberish, claptrap, garbage; informal baloney, tripe, drivel, bilge, bunk, piffle, twaddle, poppycock, gobbledegook; Brit. informal codswallop, cobblers, tosh.
• v. Brit. informal criticize harshly.

rubble n. rough fragments of stone, brick, etc.

rubella n. a viral disease with symptoms like mild measles.

rubidium n. a soft silvery metallic element.

ruble var. of ROUBLE.

rubric n. **1** a document heading. **2** a set of instructions.

ruby n. (pl. **rubies**) **1** a deep red precious stone. **2** a deep red colour.
□ **ruby wedding** Brit. the 40th anniversary of a wedding.

ruche /roosh/ n. a frill or pleat.
■ **ruched** adj.

ruck n. **1** Rugby a loose scrum. **2** a tightly packed crowd.
• v. (**ruck up**) make or form creases.

rucksack n. a bag carried on the back.

ruckus n. a row or commotion.

ructions pl. n. Brit. informal angry protests or trouble.

rudder n. a hinged upright piece of wood or metal at the back of a boat or aircraft, used for steering.

ruddy adj. (**ruddier, ruddiest**) of a reddish colour.

rude adj. **1** impolite or bad-mannered. **2** referring to sex in an offensive way. **3** sudden or abrupt.
▷ SYNONYMS: **1 ill-mannered**, bad-mannered, impolite, discourteous, uncivil, impertinent, insolent, impudent, disparaging, abusive, curt, brusque, offhand. **2 vulgar**, coarse, smutty, dirty, filthy, crude, lewd, obscene, risqué; informal blue; Brit. informal near the knuckle.
– ANTONYMS: polite.
□ **in rude health** very healthy.
■ **rudely** adv. **rudeness** n.

rudiment n. **1** (**rudiments**) the basic facts of a subject. **2** an undeveloped part.
▷ SYNONYMS: *the rudiments of algebra:* **basics**, fundamentals, essentials, first

principles, foundations; informal nuts and bolts, ABC.

rudimentary adj. **1** basic or elementary. **2** not highly developed.
▷ SYNONYMS: **1 basic**, elementary, fundamental, essential. **2 primitive**, crude, simple, unsophisticated, rough, rough and ready, makeshift. **3 vestigial**, undeveloped, incomplete.

rue v. bitterly regret.

rueful adj. expressing regret.
▷ SYNONYMS: **regretful**, apologetic, sorry, remorseful, shamefaced, sheepish, hangdog, contrite, repentant, penitent, conscience-stricken, self-reproachful, sorrowful, sad.
■ **ruefully** adv.

ruff n. **1** a starched frill worn round the neck. **2** a ring of feathers or hair round the neck of a bird or mammal.

ruffian n. a violent person.

ruffle v. **1** disturb the smooth surface of. **2** upset or worry.
▷ SYNONYMS: **1 disarrange**, tousle, dishevel, rumple, mess up; N. Amer. informal muss up. **2 disconcert**, unnerve, fluster, agitate, upset, disturb, discomfit, put off, perturb, unsettle; informal faze, throw, get to.
– ANTONYMS: smooth.
• n. a gathered frill.

rug n. **1** a small carpet. **2** Brit. a thick blanket.

rugby n. a team game played with an oval ball that may be kicked or carried.

rugged adj. **1** rocky or uneven. **2** (of a man) having strong, attractive features.
▷ SYNONYMS: **1 rough**, uneven, bumpy, rocky, stony, pitted. **2 robust**, durable, sturdy, strong, tough, resilient. **3 well built**, burly, strong, muscular, muscly, brawny, strapping, tough, hardy, robust, sturdy, solid; informal hunky. **4** his rugged features: **strong**, craggy, rough-hewn, manly, masculine.
– ANTONYMS: smooth, delicate.
■ **ruggedly** adv.

rugger n. Brit. informal rugby.

ruin n. **1** the state of being destroyed or severely damaged. **2** (or **ruins**) a badly damaged building. **3** the loss of everything a person owns.
▷ SYNONYMS: **1 disintegration**, decay, disrepair, dilapidation, destruction, demolition, devastation. **2** the ruins of a church: **remains**, remnants, fragments, rubble, debris, wreckage. **3 downfall**, collapse, defeat, undoing, failure. **4 bankruptcy**, insolvency, penury, destitution, poverty.
• v. **1** destroy or severely damage. **2** make bankrupt or very poor.
▷ SYNONYMS: **1 spoil**, wreck, blight, shatter, dash, scotch, mess up, sabotage; informal screw up; Brit. informal scupper. **2 bankrupt**, make insolvent, impoverish, pauperize, wipe out, break, cripple, bring someone to their knees. **3 destroy**, devastate, lay waste, ravage, raze, demolish, wreck, wipe out, flatten.
■ **ruination** n.

ruined adj. in a state of ruin.
▷ SYNONYMS: **derelict**, dilapidated, tumbledown, ramshackle, decrepit, falling to pieces, crumbling, decaying, disintegrating, in ruins.

ruinous adj. **1** disastrous or destructive. **2** in ruins.
▷ SYNONYMS: **1 disastrous**, devastating, catastrophic, calamitous, crippling, crushing, damaging, destructive, harmful, costly. **2 extortionate**, exorbitant, excessive, sky-high, outrageous, inflated; Brit. over the odds; informal steep.

rule n. **1** a statement of what must be done or not done. **2** control over a people or country. **3** a ruler for measuring etc.
▷ SYNONYMS: **1 regulation**, ruling, directive, order, law, statute, ordinance. **2 procedure**, practice, protocol, convention, norm, routine, custom, habit. **3 principle**, precept, standard, axiom, truth, maxim. **4 government**, jurisdiction, command, power, dominion, control, administration, sovereignty, leadership.
• v. **1** have control over. **2** state with legal authority. **3** make lines on paper.
▷ SYNONYMS: **1 govern**, preside over, control, lead, dominate, run, head, administer. **2 reign**, be on the throne, be in power, govern. **3 decree**, order, pronounce, judge, adjudge, ordain, decide, determine, find.
□ **as a rule** usually. **rule of thumb** a rough guide. **rule out** exclude. **the rule** the normal state of things.

ruler n. **1** a person who rules. **2** a strip of plastic, wood, etc. for drawing straight lines or measuring distances.
▷ SYNONYMS: **leader**, sovereign, monarch, potentate, king, queen, emperor, empress, prince, princess, crowned head, head of state, president, premier, governor.
– ANTONYMS: subject.

ruling n. an authoritative decision or statement.
▷ SYNONYMS: **judgement**, decision,

r

rum n. an alcoholic spirit made from sugar cane.
●adj. Brit. informal, dated peculiar.

rumba n. a ballroom dance.

rumble v. 1 make a low continuous sound. 2 Brit. informal find out the truth about.
●n. a rumbling sound.

rumbustious adj. informal boisterous or difficult to control.

ruminant n. a mammal that chews the cud.

ruminate v. 1 think deeply. 2 chew the cud.
■ **rumination** n. **ruminative** adj.

rummage v. search in a disorderly way.
▷ SYNONYMS: **search**, hunt, root about/around, ferret about/around, fish about/around, dig, delve, go through, explore, sift through, rifle through.
●n. an act of rummaging.

rummy n. a card game.

rumour (US **rumor**) n. a story spread among a number of people which is not confirmed or may be false.
▷ SYNONYMS: **gossip**, hearsay, talk, tittle-tattle, speculation, word, report, story, whisper; informal the grapevine, the word on the street, the buzz.
●v. (**be rumoured**) be spread as a rumour.

rump n. the hind part of the body of a mammal or the lower back of a bird.

rumple v. make untidy.

rumpus n. (pl. **rumpuses**) a noisy disturbance.

run v. (**running**, **ran**; past part. **run**)
1 move at a speed faster than walking. 2 be in charge of. 3 continue or proceed. 4 function or cause to function. 5 be at or in a particular level or state. 6 (of a liquid) flow or spread. 7 stand as a candidate in an election. 8 (of a bus, train, etc.) travel on a particular route. 9 publish in a newspaper etc.
▷ SYNONYMS: **1 sprint**, race, dart, rush, dash, hasten, hurry, scurry, scamper, gallop, jog, trot. **2 flee**, take flight, make off, take off, take to your heels, bolt, make your getaway, escape; informal beat it, clear off/out, scram, leg it; Brit. informal scarper. **3 extend**, stretch, reach, continue. **4 flow**, pour, stream, gush, flood, cascade, roll, course, glide, spill, trickle, drip, dribble, leak. **5 be in charge of**, manage, direct, control, head, govern,

supervise, superintend, oversee, organize, coordinate. **6** it's expensive to run a car: **maintain**, keep, own, possess, have, use, operate. **7** I left the engine running: **operate**, function, work, go.
●n. **1** an act or spell of running. **2** a journey or route. **3** a continuous period or sequence. **4** an enclosed area in which animals or birds may run freely. **5** (**the run of**) unrestricted use of or access to a place. **6** a point scored in cricket or baseball. **7** a ladder in tights etc.
▷ SYNONYMS: **1 jog**, sprint, dash, gallop, trot. **2 route**, journey, circuit, round, beat. **3 drive**, ride, turn, trip, excursion, outing, jaunt; informal spin, tootle. **4 series**, succession, sequence, string, streak, spate. **5 enclosure**, pen, coop. **6** a ski run: **slope**, track, piste; N. Amer. trail.
□ **in** (or **out of**) **the running** in (or no longer in) with a chance of success. **on the run** escaping. **run down 1** criticize. **2** reduce in size or resources. **run into** meet by chance. **run off** produce a copy on a machine. **run-of-the-mill** ordinary. **run out** use up or be used up. **run over** knock down with a vehicle. **run up** allow a bill to build up. **run-up** the period before an important event. **runway** a strip of hard ground where aircraft take off and land.

runaway n. a person who has run away from home or an institution.
▷ SYNONYMS: **fugitive**, refugee, truant, absconder, deserter.

rundown n. a brief analysis or summary.
▷ SYNONYMS: **summary**, synopsis, precis, run-through, recap, review, overview, briefing, sketch, outline; informal low-down.
●adj. (**run-down**) **1** in a neglected state. **2** tired and rather unwell.
▷ SYNONYMS: **1 dilapidated**, tumble-down, ramshackle, derelict, crumbling, neglected, uncared-for. **2 unwell**, ill, poorly, unhealthy, peaky, tired, drained, exhausted, worn out, below par, washed out; Brit. off colour; informal under the weather; Austral./NZ informal crook.

rune n. a letter of an ancient Germanic alphabet.
■ **runic** adj.

rung¹ n. a horizontal bar on a ladder.

rung² past part. of RING².

runnel n. a stream.

runner n. **1** a person or animal that

runs. **2** a messenger. **3** a rod, groove, or roller on which something slides. **4** a creeping shoot of a plant which can take root. **5** a long, narrow rug.

▷ SYNONYMS: **1** athlete, sprinter, hurdler, racer, jogger. **2** messenger, courier, errand boy; informal gofer.

□ **runner-up** (pl. **runners-up**) a competitor who comes second.

running adj. **1** (of water) flowing naturally or supplied through pipes and taps. **2** in succession: *the third week running*.

▷ SYNONYMS: **in succession**, in a row, in sequence, consecutively, straight, together; informal on the trot.

runny adj. (**runnier**, **runniest**) **1** more liquid than is usual. **2** (of the nose) producing mucus.

▷ SYNONYMS: liquid, liquefied, fluid, melted, molten, watery, thin.
– ANTONYMS: solid, thick.

runt n. the smallest animal in a litter.

rupee n. the basic unit of money of India, Pakistan, etc.

rupture v. **1** break or burst suddenly. **2** suffer an abdominal hernia.
• n. **1** an instance of rupturing. **2** an abdominal hernia.

▷ SYNONYMS: break, fracture, crack, burst, split, fissure, breach.

rural adj. of the countryside.

▷ SYNONYMS: country, rustic, bucolic, pastoral, agricultural, agrarian.
– ANTONYMS: urban.

ruse n. a trick or deception.

▷ SYNONYMS: ploy, stratagem, tactic, scheme, trick, gambit, dodge, subterfuge, machination, wile; Brit. informal wheeze.

rush v. **1** move or act very quickly or too quickly. **2** produce, deal with, or transport very quickly. **3** dash towards in a sudden attack.

▷ SYNONYMS: **1** hurry, dash, run, race, sprint, bolt, dart, gallop, career, charge, shoot, hurtle, hare, fly, speed, zoom, scurry, scuttle, scamper, hasten; informal tear, belt, pelt, scoot, zip, whip, hotfoot it; Brit. informal bomb. **2** gush, pour, surge, stream, course, cascade. **3** attack, charge, storm.
• n. **1** a sudden quick movement. **2** a very busy spell of activity. **3** a sudden strong feeling. **4** a water plant used in making baskets etc.

▷ SYNONYMS: **1** dash, run, sprint, dart,

bolt, charge, scramble. **2** hustle and bustle, commotion, hubbub, hurly-burly, stir. **3** charge, onslaught, attack, assault.

□ **rush hour** a time at the start and end of the working day when traffic is heaviest.

rusk n. a biscuit for babies.

russet n. a reddish-brown colour.

Russian n. **1** a person from Russia. **2** the language of Russia.
• adj. of Russia.

rust n. a reddish-brown flaky coating formed on iron exposed to moisture.
• v. be affected with rust.

▷ SYNONYMS: corrode, oxidize, tarnish.

rustic adj. **1** of life in the country. **2** simple and charming.

▷ SYNONYMS: **1** rural, country, pastoral, bucolic, agricultural, agrarian; literary Arcadian. **2** plain, simple, homely, unsophisticated, rough, crude.
– ANTONYMS: urban.

rustle v. **1** make a soft crackling sound. **2** steal cattle, horses, or sheep. **3** (**rustle up**) informal produce food or a drink quickly.

▷ SYNONYMS: **1** swish, whoosh, whisper, sigh. **2** steal, thieve, take, abduct, kidnap.
• n. a rustling sound.
■ **rustler** n.

rusty adj. **1** affected by rust. **2** (of knowledge or a skill) weakened by lack of recent practice.

rut n. **1** a deep track made by wheels. **2** a dull pattern of behaviour that is hard to change. **3** an annual period of sexual activity in deer etc., when males fight for access to the females.

▷ SYNONYMS: **1** furrow, groove, trough, ditch, hollow, pothole, crater. **2** boring routine, humdrum existence, groove, dead end.
• v. (**rutting**, **rutted**) (of male deer etc.) be in rut.

ruthless adj. having no pity; hard and determined.

▷ SYNONYMS: merciless, pitiless, cruel, heartless, hard-hearted, cold-hearted, cold-blooded, harsh, callous.
– ANTONYMS: merciful.
■ **ruthlessly** adv. **ruthlessness** n.

rye n. **1** a cereal plant. **2** whisky made from rye.

□ **ryegrass** a grass used for fodder.

r

Ss

S abbrev. **1** South or Southern. **2** (s) seconds.

SA abbrev. **1** South Africa. **2** South Australia.

sabbath n. a day for rest and religious worship.

sabbatical n. a period of paid leave for study or travel.

sable n. a dark brown marten native to Japan and Siberia.

sabotage /sab-uh-tahzh/ v. deliberately destroy or damage.
▷ SYNONYMS: **vandalize**, wreck, damage, destroy, incapacitate, obstruct, disrupt, spoil, ruin, undermine; Brit. informal throw a spanner in the works.
• n. the act of sabotaging.
▷ SYNONYMS: **vandalism**, wrecking, destruction, damage, obstruction, disruption; Brit. informal a spanner in the works.
■ **saboteur** n.

sabre (US **saber**) n. a curved sword.

sac n. a hollow, flexible bag-like structure.

saccharin n. a synthetic sugar substitute.

saccharine adj. excessively sweet or sentimental.

sacerdotal adj. of priests.

sachet /sa-shay/ n. Brit. a small sealed packet.

sack n. **1** a large strong bag for storing or carrying goods. **2** (**the sack**) informal dismissal from employment.
▷ SYNONYMS: **bag**, pouch, pocket, pack.
• v. **1** informal dismiss from employment. **2** (in the past) attack, steal from, and destroy a place.
▷ SYNONYMS: **dismiss**, discharge, lay off, make redundant, let go, throw out; informal fire, give someone the sack; Brit. informal give someone their cards.
□ **sackcloth** a rough fabric woven from flax or hemp.

sacrament n. (in the Christian Church) a symbolic religious ceremony.

■ **sacramental** adj.

sacred adj. **1** connected with God or a god or goddess, and treated as holy. **2** religious.
▷ SYNONYMS: **1 holy**, hallowed, blessed, consecrated, sanctified. **2 religious**, spiritual, devotional, church, ecclesiastical.
– ANTONYMS: secular, profane.
□ **sacred cow** an established idea, custom, etc. regarded as above criticism.

sacrifice n. **1** the killing of an animal or person or giving up of a possession as an offering to a god or goddess. **2** an animal, person, etc. offered in this way. **3** an act of giving up something valued for the sake of something else.
▷ SYNONYMS: **1 offering**, gift, oblation. **2 surrender**, giving up, abandon-ment, renunciation, forfeiture.
• v. give as a sacrifice.
▷ SYNONYMS: **1 offer up**, immolate. **2 give up**, forgo, abandon, renounce, relinquish, cede, surrender, forfeit.
■ **sacrificial** adj.

sacrilege n. disrespect to something sacred or highly valued.
▷ SYNONYMS: **desecration**, profanity, blas-phemy, irreverence, disrespect.
■ **sacrilegious** adj.

sacristan n. a person in charge of a sacristy.

sacristy n. (pl. **sacristies**) a room in a church where sacred objects are kept.

sacrosanct adj. too important or valuable to be changed.

sacrum n. (pl. **sacra** or **sacrums**) a triangular bone between the two hip bones.
■ **sacral** adj.

sad adj. (**sadder**, **saddest**) feeling or causing sorrow: *a sad story.*
▷ SYNONYMS: **1 unhappy**, sorrowful, depressed, downcast, miserable, down, despondent, wretched, glum, gloomy, doleful, melancholy, mournful, woebegone, forlorn,

heartbroken; informal blue, down in the mouth, down in the dumps. **2 tragic**, unhappy, miserable, wretched, sorry, pitiful, pathetic, heartbreaking, heart-rending. **3** *a sad state of affairs:* unfortunate, regrettable, sorry, deplorable, lamentable, pitiful, shameful, disgraceful.

– ANTONYMS: happy, cheerful.

■ **sadly** adv.

sadden v. make sad.

▷ SYNONYMS: **depress**, dispirit, dishearten, disappoint; grieve, upset, pain, break someone's heart.

saddle n. **1** a seat on a bicycle or motorcycle or fastened on the back of a horse. **2** a joint of meat consisting of the two loins.

• v. **1** put a saddle on a horse. **2** burden with a task.

▷ SYNONYMS: **burden**, encumber, lumber, land, impose something on.

saddler n. a person who makes, repairs, or deals in equipment for horses.

sadism n. pleasure felt from hurting or humiliating other people.

■ **sadist** n. **sadistic** adj.

sadness n. the feeling of being sad.

▷ SYNONYMS: **unhappiness**, sorrow, depression, misery, despondency, wretchedness, heartache, grief; gloom, gloominess, dejection, melancholy.

safari n. (pl. **safaris**) a trip to observe or hunt animals in their natural environment.

□ **safari park** an area where animals are kept in the open and may be observed by visitors.

safe adj. **1** protected from danger or risk. **2** not leading to harm. **3** giving security.

▷ SYNONYMS: **1 secure**, protected, sheltered, guarded, out of harm's way. **2 unharmed**, unhurt, uninjured, unscathed, all right, fine, well, in one piece, out of danger, safe and sound. **3 cautious**, circumspect, prudent, careful, unadventurous, conservative. **4 harmless**, innocuous, non-toxic, non-poisonous.

– ANTONYMS: dangerous, harmful.

• n. a strong cabinet with a complex lock, for storing valuables.

□ **safe conduct** protection from arrest or harm.

■ **safely** adv.

safeguard n. a measure taken to protect or prevent something.

▷ SYNONYMS: **protection**, defence, buffer, provision, security, cover, insurance.

• v. protect.

▷ SYNONYMS: **protect**, preserve, conserve, save, secure, shield, guard, keep safe.

– ANTONYMS: jeopardize.

safety n. the condition of being safe.

▷ SYNONYMS: **1 welfare**, well-being, protection, security. **2 shelter**, sanctuary, refuge.

□ **safety belt** a seat belt. **safety pin** a pin with a point bent back to the head and held in a guard when closed. **safety valve** a valve that opens automatically to relieve excessive pressure.

saffron n. a yellow spice.

sag v. (**sagging**, **sagged**) sink or droop gradually.

▷ SYNONYMS: **1 sink**, slump, loll, flop, crumple. **2 dip**, droop, bulge, bag.

■ **saggy** adj.

saga n. a long story.

▷ SYNONYMS: **epic**, tale, story, narrative, legend, myth; yarn.

sagacious adj. wise.

■ **sagacity** n.

sage n. **1** a herb. **2** a very wise man.

▷ SYNONYMS: **wise man/woman**, philosopher, scholar, guru, prophet, mystic.

• adj. wise.

■ **sagely** adv.

sago n. a pudding made with starchy granules from a palm tree, cooked with milk.

said past & past part. of SAY.

sail n. **1** a piece of fabric spread on a mast to catch the wind and propel a boat or ship. **2** a trip in a sailing boat. **3** a flat board attached to the arm of a windmill.

• v. **1** travel in a ship or boat. **2** begin a voyage. **3** control a boat. **4** move smoothly. **5** (**sail through**) informal succeed easily at.

▷ SYNONYMS: **1 voyage**, travel, navigate, cruise. **2 set sail**, put to sea, leave, weigh anchor. **3 steer**, pilot, captain; informal skipper. **4 glide**, drift, float, flow, sweep, skim, coast, flit, scud.

□ **sailboard** a board with a mast and a sail, used in windsurfing. **sailcloth** strong fabric for sails. **sailing boat** (or **sailboat**) a boat with sails.

sailor n. a member of a ship's crew.

▷ SYNONYMS: **seaman**, seafarer, mariner, boatman, yachtsman, yachtswoman, hand; informal old salt, matelot, Jack tar.

saint n. **1** a very good person who is declared to be a saint by the Church after death. **2** a very good or kind person.

- **sainthood** n.

saintly adj. very holy or virtuous.
▷ SYNONYMS: **holy**, godly, pious, religious, devout, spiritual, virtuous, righteous, good, pure.
– ANTONYMS: ungodly.
- **saintliness** n.

sake¹ n. (**for the sake of**) **1** so as to get or keep. **2** out of consideration for.
▷ SYNONYMS: **1** *for the sake of clarity:* **purpose**, reason. **2** *for her son's sake:* **benefit**, advantage, good, well-being, welfare.

sake² /**sah**-ki/ n. a Japanese alcoholic drink made from rice.

salaam /suh-**lahm**/ n. a low bow with the hand touching the forehead, used as a gesture of respect by Muslims.

salacious adj. containing too much sexual detail.

salad n. a cold dish of raw vegetables.

salamander n. an animal resembling a newt.

salami n. (pl. **salami** or **salamis**) a type of spicy preserved sausage.

salary n. (pl. **salaries**) a fixed regular payment made by an employer to an employee.
▷ SYNONYMS: **pay**, wages, earnings, payment, remuneration, fees, stipend, income.
- **salaried** adj.

sale n. **1** the exchange of something for money. **2** (**sales**) the activity or profession of selling. **3** a period in which goods are sold at reduced prices. **4** a public event at which goods are sold.
▷ SYNONYMS: **1 selling**, dealing, trading. **2 deal**, transaction, bargain.
– ANTONYMS: purchase.
□ **salesman** (or **saleswoman** or **salesperson**) a person whose job is to sell goods.
- **saleable** (or **salable**) adj.

salient adj. most noticeable or important.

saline adj. containing salt.
- **salinity** n.

saliva n. a watery liquid produced in the mouth.
- **salivary** adj.

salivate v. produce saliva.
- **salivation** n.

sallow adj. (of the complexion) yellowish in colour.

sally n. (pl. **sallies**) **1** a sudden charge out of a place surrounded by an enemy. **2** a witty reply.
• v. (**sallying**, **sallied**) (**sally forth**) set out.

salmon n. (pl. **salmon**) a large edible fish with pink flesh.

salmonella n. a bacterium causing food poisoning.

salon n. **1** a place where a hairdresser, beautician, etc. works. **2** a reception room in a large house.

saloon n. **1** Brit. a car with a separate boot. **2** a public lounge on a ship.

salsa n. **1** a Latin American dance performed to music combining jazz and rock. **2** a spicy sauce.

salt n. **1** a white crystalline substance (sodium chloride), used for flavouring and preserving food. **2** a chemical compound of an acid and a metal.
• v. flavour or preserve with salt.
□ **salt cellar** a container for salt.
saltpetre (US **saltpeter**) potassium nitrate. **the salt of the earth** a very kind, reliable, or honest person. **take with a pinch** (or **grain**) **of salt** recognize as untrue or exaggerated. **worth your salt** competent.

salty adj. (**saltier**, **saltiest**) tasting of or containing salt.
▷ SYNONYMS: **saline**, briny, brackish; savoury.
- **saltiness** n.

salubrious adj. good for the health.
▷ SYNONYMS: **pleasant**, agreeable, nice, select, high-class; Brit. upmarket; informal posh, classy; Brit. informal swish.

salutary adj. (esp. of something unpleasant) producing a good effect.

salutation n. a greeting.

salute n. **1** a gesture of respect or acknowledgement. **2** a raising of a hand to the head, made as a formal military gesture of respect.
▷ SYNONYMS: **tribute**, testimonial, homage, honour, celebration, acknowledgement.
• v. **1** make a salute to. **2** express admiration for.
▷ SYNONYMS: **pay tribute to**, pay homage to, honour, celebrate, acknowledge, take your hat off to.

salvage v. **1** save from being lost or destroyed. **2** rescue a ship or its cargo from loss at sea.
▷ SYNONYMS: **rescue**, save, recover, retrieve, reclaim.
• n. **1** the act of salvaging. **2** salvaged cargo.

salvation n. the saving of someone from harm or (in Christian belief) from the consequences of sin.
▷ SYNONYMS: **1 redemption**, deliverance. **2 lifeline**, means of escape, saviour.
– ANTONYMS: damnation, ruin.

S

salve n. **1** a soothing ointment.
2 something that reduces guilty
feelings.
● v. reduce guilty feelings.

salver n. a tray.

salvia n. a garden plant with scarlet
flowers.

salvo n. (pl. **salvos** or **salvoes**)
1 a simultaneous firing of guns.
2 a sudden series of aggressive
statements or acts.

Samaritan (or **good Samaritan**) n. a
kind or helpful person.

samba n. a Brazilian dance.

same adj. **1** exactly alike. **2** referring to
a person or thing already mentioned.
▷ SYNONYMS: **1 identical**, selfsame, very
same. **2 matching**, identical, alike,
carbon-copy, twin, indistinguishable,
interchangeable, corresponding,
equivalent, parallel, like, comparable,
similar, homogeneous.
– ANTONYMS: another, different.
● pron. the person or thing already
mentioned.
● adv. in the same way.
■ sameness n.

Sami pl. n. the Lapps of northern
Scandinavia.

samosa n. a triangular fried Indian
pastry containing spiced vegetables
or meat.

samovar n. a Russian tea urn.

sampan n. a small boat used in the
Far East.

sample n. **1** a small part or quantity
intended to show what the whole is
like. **2** a specimen.
▷ SYNONYMS: **specimen**, example,
snippet, swatch, taste, taster,
selection.
● v. **1** take a sample or samples of.
2 try out. **3** take an extract from one
musical recording and use it as part
of another.
▷ SYNONYMS: **try**, taste, test, put to the
test, appraise, evaluate; informal check
out.

sampler n. **1** a piece of embroidery
showing various stitches. **2** a device
for sampling music.

samurai /sam-uh-ry/ n. (pl. **samurai**)
hist. a member of a powerful Japanese
military class.

sanatorium n. (pl. **sanatoriums** or
sanatoria) **1** a place for the care
of people with a long-term illness
or convalescents. **2** Brit. a place in a
boarding school for sick pupils.

sanctify v. (**sanctifying**, **sanctified**)
make or declare holy.
■ sanctification n.

sanctimonious adj. making a show
of being morally superior.
▷ SYNONYMS: **self-righteous**, holier-
than-thou, pious, moralizing, smug,
superior, priggish, hypocritical,
insincere; informal goody-goody.

sanction n. **1** (**sanctions**) measures
taken by a state to force another
into doing something. **2** a penalty
for disobeying a law. **3** official
permission.
▷ SYNONYMS: **1 penalty**, punishment,
deterrent, restriction, embargo, ban,
prohibition, boycott. **2 authorization**,
consent, leave, permission, authority,
dispensation, assent, acquiescence,
agreement, approval, endorsement,
blessing; informal the thumbs up, the
OK, the green light.
– ANTONYMS: prohibition.
● v. give permission for.
▷ SYNONYMS: **authorize**, permit, allow,
endorse, approve, accept, back,
support; informal OK.
– ANTONYMS: prohibit.

sanctity n. (pl. **sanctities**) **1** holiness.
2 supreme importance.

sanctuary n. (pl. **sanctuaries**) **1** a place
of safety. **2** a nature reserve. **3** a holy
place.
▷ SYNONYMS: **1 refuge**, haven, oasis,
shelter, retreat, bolt-hole, hideaway. **2 safety**, protection, shelter,
immunity, asylum. **3 reserve**, wildlife
reserve, park.

sanctum n. (pl. **sanctums**) a sacred or
private place.

sand n. **1** very fine particles of crushed
rock. **2** (**sands**) a wide area of sand.
● v. smooth with sandpaper or a
sander.
□ **sandbag** a bag of sand, used to
protect against floods etc. **sandbank**
a raised bank of sand in the sea
or a river. **sandblast** roughen or
clean with a jet of sand. **sandcastle**
a model castle built out of sand.
sandpaper paper with a coating of
sand or another rough substance,
for smoothing surfaces. **sandstone**
rock formed from compressed sand.
sandstorm a strong desert wind
carrying clouds of sand.

sandal n. a shoe with a partly open
upper part or straps.

sandalwood n. the scented wood of
an Asian tree.

sander n. a power tool used for
smoothing a surface.

sandwich n. two pieces of bread with
a filling between them.
● v. insert between two people or

S

things.
□ **sandwich course** a course of study which includes periods working in business or industry.

sandy adj. (**sandier, sandiest**)
1 covered in or consisting of sand.
2 light yellowish brown.

sane adj. **1** not mad. **2** sensible.
▷ SYNONYMS: **1 of sound mind**, in your right mind, compos mentis, lucid, rational, balanced, normal; informal all there. **2 sensible**, practical, realistic, prudent, reasonable, rational, level-headed, commonsensical.
– ANTONYMS: mad, foolish.

sang past of SING.

sangfroid /song-frwah/ n. calmness in difficult situations.

sangria n. a Spanish drink of red wine, lemonade, and fruit.

sanguinary adj. old use involving much bloodshed.

sanguine adj. optimistic.
▷ SYNONYMS: **optimistic**, hopeful, buoyant, positive, confident, cheerful, bullish; informal upbeat.
– ANTONYMS: gloomy.

sanitarium n. US a sanatorium.

sanitary adj. **1** of sanitation.
2 hygienic.
□ **sanitary towel** a pad worn to absorb menstrual blood.

sanitation n. arrangements to protect public health, esp. the provision of clean drinking water and the disposal of sewage.

sanitize (or **-ise**) v. **1** make hygienic.
2 make something unpleasant seem more acceptable.

sanity n. the condition of being sane.
▷ SYNONYMS: **1 mental health**, reason, rationality, stability, lucidity, sense, wits, mind. **2 sense**, good sense, common sense, wisdom, prudence, rationality.

sank past of SINK.

Sanskrit n. an ancient language of India.

sap n. the liquid in plants, carrying food to all parts.
▷ SYNONYMS: **juice**, secretion, fluid, liquid.
• v. (**sapping, sapped**) gradually weaken.
▷ SYNONYMS: **erode**, wear away/down, deplete, reduce, lessen, undermine, drain, bleed.

sapling n. a young tree.

sapper n. a military engineer who lays or finds and defuses mines.

sapphire n. **1** a blue precious stone.

2 a bright blue colour.

saprophyte n. a plant or fungus living on decaying matter.

sarcasm n. the use of irony to mock or convey contempt.
▷ SYNONYMS: **irony**, derision, mockery, ridicule, scorn.

sarcastic adj. showing or expressing sarcasm.
▷ SYNONYMS: **ironic**, sardonic, derisive, scornful, contemptuous, mocking, caustic, scathing, trenchant, acerbic.
■ **sarcastically** adv.

sarcoma n. a cancerous tumour found esp. in connective tissue.

sarcophagus n. (pl. **sarcophagi**) a stone coffin.

sardine n. a young pilchard or similar small fish.

sardonic adj. mocking.
▷ SYNONYMS: **mocking**, cynical, scornful, derisive, sneering, scathing, caustic, trenchant, cutting, acerbic.
■ **sardonically** adv.

sari n. (pl. **saris**) a length of fabric draped round the body, worn by women from the Indian subcontinent.

sarong n. a length of fabric wrapped round the body and tucked at the waist or armpits.

sartorial adj. of a person's style of dress.

SAS abbrev. Special Air Service.

sash n. **1** a strip of cloth worn over one shoulder or round the waist. **2** a frame holding the glass in a window.
□ **sash window** a window with two sashes which can be slid up and down to open it.

sashay v. informal swing the hips from side to side when walking.

Sassenach n. Sc. & Ir. derogatory an English person.

sassy adj. (**sassier, sassiest**) informal confident or cheeky.

SAT abbrev. standard assessment task.

sat past & past part. of SIT.

Satan n. the Devil.

satanic adj. of Satan or the worship of Satan.
▷ SYNONYMS: **diabolical**, fiendish, devilish, demonic, ungodly, hellish, infernal, wicked, evil, sinful.
– ANTONYMS: godly.

satanism n. the worship of Satan.
■ **satanist** n. & adj.

satchel n. a bag with a long strap, worn over one shoulder.

sated adj. fully satisfied.

satellite n. **1** an artificial object placed

in orbit round a planet to collect information or for communication. **2** a natural object orbiting a planet.
• **adj.** (of a country etc.) dependent on another.
□ **satellite dish** a bowl-shaped aerial for receiving satellite television.
satellite television television in which the signals are broadcast via satellite.

satiate /say-shi-ayt/ **v.** satisfy fully.
■ **satiation** n. **satiety** n.

satin n. a smooth, glossy fabric.
■ **satiny** adj.

satire n. **1** the use of humour, irony, etc. to criticize or ridicule. **2** a play, novel, etc. using satire.
▷ SYNONYMS: **parody**, burlesque, caricature, lampoon, skit; informal spoof, take-off, send-up.
■ **satirist** n.

satirical adj. using satire to criticize or ridicule.
▷ SYNONYMS: **mocking**, ironic, sardonic, critical, disparaging, disrespectful, irreverent.
■ **satirically** adv.

satirize (or **-ise**) **v.** criticize using satire.
▷ SYNONYMS: **mock**, ridicule, deride, make fun of, parody, lampoon, caricature, take off, criticize; informal send up, take the mickey out of.

satisfaction n. **1** pleasure arising from having what you want or need. **2** a satisfactory way of dealing with an injustice, complaint, etc.
▷ SYNONYMS: **contentment**, content, pleasure, gratification, fulfilment, enjoyment, happiness, pride.

satisfactory adj. acceptable.
▷ SYNONYMS: **adequate**, all right, acceptable, good enough, sufficient, reasonable, competent, fair, decent, average, passable, fine, in order, up to scratch, up to the mark.
■ **satisfactorily** adv.

satisfy v. (**satisfying**, **satisfied**)
1 please someone by doing what they want or giving them what they need. **2** meet a demand, desire, or need.
▷ SYNONYMS: **1 fulfil**, gratify, meet, fill, indulge, appease, assuage, quench, slake, satiate. **2 convince**, assure, reassure, put someone's mind at rest. **3 comply with**, meet, fulfil, answer, conform to, measure up to, come up to.
– ANTONYMS: frustrate.
■ **satisfaction** n.

satsuma n. a variety of tangerine.

saturate v. **1** soak thoroughly.
2 supply a market beyond the point at

which there is demand for a product.
▷ SYNONYMS: **1 soak**, drench, wet through. **2 flood**, glut, oversupply, overfill, overload.
■ **saturation** n.

saturated adj. **1** completely wet; soaked. **2** Chem. (of fats) having only single bonds between carbon atoms in their molecules and therefore being less easily processed by the body.
▷ SYNONYMS: **1 soaked**, soaking, wet through, sopping, sodden, dripping, wringing wet, drenched. **2 waterlogged**, flooded, boggy, awash.
– ANTONYMS: dry.

Saturday n. the day before Sunday.

saturnine adj. gloomy or brooding.

satyr /sat-er/ n. a woodland god in classical mythology, with a goat's ears, legs, and tail.

sauce n. **1** a thick liquid served with food to add moistness and flavour.
2 informal impudence.
▷ SYNONYMS: **relish**, condiment, ketchup, dip, dressing, jus, coulis, gravy.
□ **saucepan** a deep cooking pan with a long handle.

saucer n. a shallow dish on which a cup stands.

saucy adj. (**saucier**, **sauciest**) informal **1** cheeky. **2** sexually suggestive.
■ **saucily** adv.

sauerkraut /sow-er-krowt/ n. chopped pickled cabbage.

sauna /saw-nuh/ n. a small room used as a hot-air or steam bath.

saunter v. stroll.
▷ SYNONYMS: **stroll**, amble, wander, meander, walk; informal mosey, tootle; formal promenade.
• n. a stroll.

sausage n. a short tube of minced meat encased in a skin.

sauté /soh-tay/ v. (**sautéing**, **sautéed** or **sautéd**) fry quickly in shallow fat.

savage adj. **1** fierce and violent.
2 cruel and vicious. **3** uncivilized or primitive.
▷ SYNONYMS: **1 vicious**, brutal, cruel, sadistic, ferocious, fierce, violent, barbaric, bloodthirsty, merciless, pitiless. **2 untamed**, wild, feral, undomesticated. **3** a savage attack on the government: **fierce**, blistering, scathing, searing, stinging, devastating, withering, virulent, vitriolic.
– ANTONYMS: mild, tame.
• n. a primitive and uncivilized person.
▷ SYNONYMS: **brute**, beast, monster, barbarian, sadist, animal.
• v. attack fiercely and maul.

S

▷ SYNONYMS: **maul**, attack, lacerate, claw, bite, tear to pieces.
■ **savagely** adv. **savagery** n.

savannah n. a grassy plain in tropical regions.

save v. **1** rescue or protect from harm or danger. **2** store or keep for future use. **3** avoid or guard against. **4** prevent the scoring of a goal.
▷ SYNONYMS: **1 rescue**, set free, free, liberate, deliver, redeem. **2 preserve**, keep, protect, safeguard, salvage, retrieve, reclaim, rescue. **3 put aside**, set aside, put by, keep, conserve, retain, store, hoard, stockpile; informal squirrel away. **4 prevent**, avoid, forestall, spare, stop, obviate, avert.
• n. an act of preventing a goal.
■ **saver** n.

saveloy n. Brit. a smoked pork sausage.

savings pl. n. money saved.
▷ SYNONYMS: **nest egg**, capital, assets, funds, resources, reserves.

saviour (US **savior**) n. a person who saves someone from danger or harm.
▷ SYNONYMS: **rescuer**, liberator, deliverer, champion, protector, redeemer.

savoir faire /sav-war **fair**/ n. the ability to act appropriately in social situations.

savour (US **savor**) v. **1** enjoy the taste of food or drink. **2** enjoy or appreciate fully.
▷ SYNONYMS: **relish**, enjoy, appreciate, delight in, revel in, luxuriate in.
• n. a flavour or smell.
▷ SYNONYMS: **smell**, aroma, fragrance, scent, perfume, bouquet, taste, flavour, tang, smack.

savoury (US **savory**) adj. **1** (of food) salty or spicy. **2** morally acceptable.
▷ SYNONYMS: **salty**, spicy, tangy, piquant.
– ANTONYMS: sweet.
• n. (pl. **savouries**) a savoury snack.
▷ SYNONYMS: **canapé**, hors d'oeuvre, appetizer, titbit.

saw¹ n. **1** a cutting tool with a jagged blade. **2** a proverb or wise saying.
• v. (**sawing**, **sawed**; past part. **sawn** or US **sawed**) cut with a saw.

saw² past of SEE.

sax n. informal a saxophone.

saxophone n. a metal wind instrument.
■ **saxophonist** n.

say v. (**saying**, **said**) **1** speak words. **2** convey or express information. **3** (**be said**) be reported. **4** suggest as an example or theory.
▷ SYNONYMS: **1 speak**, utter, voice, pronounce. **2 declare**, state,

announce, remark, observe, mention, comment, note, add. **3 recite**, repeat, utter, deliver, perform. **4 indicate**, show, read.
• n. an opportunity to state your opinion.
▷ SYNONYMS: **influence**, sway, weight, voice, input.

saying n. a well-known phrase or proverb.
▷ SYNONYMS: **proverb**, maxim, aphorism, axiom, expression, phrase, formula, slogan, catchphrase.

scab n. **1** a crust forming over a wound. **2** informal, derogatory a person who refuses to take part in a strike.
■ **scabby** adj.

scabbard n. a cover for a sword or dagger.

scabies n. a skin disease causing itching.

scabrous adj. **1** indecent or sordid. **2** covered with scabs.

scaffold n. **1** a platform used formerly for public executions. **2** a structure of scaffolding.

scaffolding n. a structure of planks and metal poles, used while working on a building.

scald v. burn with very hot liquid or steam.
• n. a burn caused by scalding.

scale n. **1** relative size or extent. **2** an ordered range of values for measuring or grading something. **3** (**scales**) an instrument for weighing. **4** a fixed series of notes in a system of music. **5** each of the overlapping plates protecting the skin of fish and reptiles. **6** a white deposit formed in a kettle etc. by hard water. **7** tartar on teeth.
▷ SYNONYMS: **1 extent**, size, scope, magnitude, dimensions, range, breadth, degree; ratio, proportion. **2 hierarchy**, ladder, ranking, pecking order, order, spectrum.
• v. **1** climb. **2** represent in proportion to the size of the original. **3** remove scale or scales from.
▷ SYNONYMS: **climb**, ascend, clamber up, scramble up, shin up, mount; N. Amer. shinny up.

scalene adj. (of a triangle) having unequal sides.

scallop n. **1** an edible shellfish with two hinged fan-shaped shells. **2** each of a series of small curves as a decorative edging.
■ **scalloped** adj.

scallywag n. informal a mischievous person.

S

scalp n. the skin covering the top and back of the head.
• v. cut the scalp from.

scalpel n. a surgeon's knife with a small blade.

scaly adj. 1 covered in scales. 2 (of skin) dry and flaking.
▷ SYNONYMS: **dry**, flaky, scurfy, rough, scabrous.

scam n. informal a dishonest scheme.

scamp n. informal a mischievous person.

scamper v. run with quick light steps.

scampi pl. n. the tails of large prawns, coated in breadcrumbs and fried.

scan v. (**scanning**, **scanned**) 1 look over quickly to find relevant features. 2 move a detector or beam across. 3 convert a document etc. into digital form for storing or processing on a computer. 4 analyse the metre of a line of verse. 5 (of verse) follow metrical rules.
▷ SYNONYMS: 1 **study**, examine, scrutinize, inspect, survey, search, scour, sweep, watch. 2 **glance through**, look through, have a look at, run your eye over, cast your eye over, flick through, browse through, leaf through, thumb through.
• n. an act of scanning.
■ **scanner** n.

scandal n. 1 an action or event causing general outrage. 2 outrage or gossip arising from this.
▷ SYNONYMS: 1 **gossip**, rumours, slander, libel, muckraking; informal dirt. 2 *it's a scandal that the hospital has closed:* **disgrace**, outrage, sin, crying shame.

scandalize (or **-ise**) v. shock or outrage.

scandalous adj. causing general outrage by being wrong, illegal, or shockingly bad.
▷ SYNONYMS: **disgraceful**, shocking, outrageous, monstrous, wicked, shameful, appalling, deplorable, inexcusable, intolerable, unforgivable, unpardonable, unacceptable, discreditable, unseemly.
■ **scandalously** adv.

Scandinavian adj. of the countries of Scandinavia, esp. Norway, Sweden, and Denmark.

scandium n. a soft silvery-white metallic element.

scansion n. the rhythm of a line of verse.

scant adj. barely enough.
▷ SYNONYMS: **little**, little or no, minimal, limited, negligible, meagre, insufficient, inadequate.
– ANTONYMS: abundant, ample.

scanty adj. (**scantier**, **scantiest**) too little in quantity or amount.
▷ SYNONYMS: 1 **meagre**, scant, minimal, limited, modest, restricted, sparse, tiny, small, paltry, negligible, scarce, in short supply, thin on the ground, few and far between; informal measly, piddling, mingy, pathetic. 2 **skimpy**, revealing, short, brief, low-cut.
– ANTONYMS: ample, plentiful.
■ **scantily** adv.

scapegoat n. a person blamed for the wrongdoings of others.
▷ SYNONYMS: **whipping boy**, Aunt Sally; informal **fall guy**; N. Amer. informal **patsy**.

scapula n. (pl. **scapulae** or **scapulas**) the shoulder blade.
■ **scapular** adj.

scar n. 1 a mark left where a wound has healed. 2 a lasting effect of an unpleasant experience.
▷ SYNONYMS: 1 **mark**, blemish, disfigurement, discoloration, pockmark, pit, lesion, cicatrix. 2 *psychological scars:* **trauma**, damage, injury.
• v. (**scarring**, **scarred**) mark or be marked with a scar.
▷ SYNONYMS: **disfigure**, mark, blemish, discolour, mar, spoil.

scarab n. a beetle treated as sacred in ancient Egypt.

scarce adj. 1 available in quantities that are too small to meet demand. 2 rare.
▷ SYNONYMS: **in short supply**, scant, scanty, inadequate, lacking, meagre, sparse, hard to come by, at a premium, few and far between, thin on the ground, rare.
– ANTONYMS: plentiful.

scarcely adv. 1 only just. 2 surely or probably not.
▷ SYNONYMS: 1 **hardly**, barely, only just. 2 **rarely**, seldom, infrequently, not often, hardly ever; informal once in a blue moon.

scarcity n. (pl. **scarcities**) a shortage of something needed.
▷ SYNONYMS: **shortage**, dearth, lack, undersupply, insufficiency, paucity, poverty, deficiency, inadequacy, unavailability, absence.

scare v. frighten or be frightened.
▷ SYNONYMS: **frighten**, startle, alarm, terrify, unnerve, worry, intimidate, terrorize, cow; informal **freak out**; Brit. informal **put the wind up**; N. Amer. informal **spook**.
• n. 1 a fright. 2 a period of general alarm.
▷ SYNONYMS: **fright**, shock, start, turn, jump.

S

□ **scarecrow** a figure set up to scare birds away from crops.
scaremongering the spreading of alarming rumours.

scared adj. afraid.
▷ SYNONYMS: **frightened**, afraid, fearful, nervous, panicky, terrified; informal in a cold sweat; N. Amer. informal spooked.

scarf n. (pl. **scarves** or **scarfs**) a length or square of fabric worn around the neck or head.

scarlet n. a bright red colour.
□ **scarlet fever** an infectious disease causing fever and a scarlet rash.

scarp n. a steep slope.

scary adj. (**scarier**, **scariest**) informal frightening.
▷ SYNONYMS: **frightening**, terrifying, hair-raising, spine-chilling, blood-curdling, eerie, sinister; informal creepy, spine-tingling, spooky.
■ **scarily** adv.

scathing adj. harshly critical.
▷ SYNONYMS: **withering**, blistering, searing, devastating, fierce, ferocious, savage, severe, stinging, biting, cutting, virulent, vitriolic, scornful, bitter, harsh.
– ANTONYMS: mild.

scatological adj. obsessed with excrement.
■ **scatology** n.

scatter v. **1** throw in various random directions. **2** separate and move off in different directions.
▷ SYNONYMS: **1 spread**, sprinkle, distribute, strew, disseminate, sow, throw, toss, fling. **2 disperse**, break up, disband, separate, dissolve.
– ANTONYMS: gather, assemble.
□ **scatterbrained** (or **scatty**) disorganized and forgetful.

scavenge v. **1** search for and collect anything usable from waste. **2** (of an animal) search for dead animals as food.
▷ SYNONYMS: **search**, hunt, look, forage, rummage, root about/around, grub about/around.
■ **scavenger** n.

scenario n. (pl. **scenarios**) **1** a possible sequence of future events. **2** a written outline of a film, play, etc.
▷ SYNONYMS: **1 plot**, outline, storyline, framework, screenplay, script. **2 situation**, chain of events, course of events.

scene n. **1** the place where an incident occurs. **2** a view of a place. **3** an incident. **4** a sequence of continuous action in a play, film, etc. **5** a display of emotion or anger. **6** an area of activity or interest.
▷ SYNONYMS: **1 location**, site, place, position, spot, locale. **2 background**, setting, context, milieu, backdrop. **3 incident**, event, episode, happening, proceeding. **4 view**, vista, outlook, panorama, landscape, scenery. **5** she made a scene: fuss, exhibition of yourself, performance, tantrum, commotion, disturbance, row; informal to-do; Brit. informal carry-on. **6** the political scene: arena, stage, sphere, world, milieu, realm. **7 clip**, section, segment, part, sequence, extract.
□ **behind the scenes** out of public view.

scenery n. **1** the features of a landscape. **2** the background used to represent a place on a stage or film set.
▷ SYNONYMS: **1 landscape**, countryside, country, terrain, setting, surroundings, environment. **2 set**, setting, backdrop.

scenic adj. picturesque.
▷ SYNONYMS: **picturesque**, pretty, attractive, beautiful, charming, impressive, striking, spectacular, breathtaking, panoramic.

scent n. **1** a pleasant smell. **2** perfume. **3** a trail left by an animal, indicated by its smell.
▷ SYNONYMS: **1 smell**, fragrance, aroma, perfume, savour, odour. **2 perfume**, fragrance, eau de toilette, toilet water, eau de cologne. **3 spoor**, trail, track.
• v. **1** give a pleasant smell to. **2** detect by smell. **3** sense the imminence of.
▷ SYNONYMS: **smell**, nose out, detect, pick up, sense.

sceptic /skep-tik/ (US **skeptic**) n. a sceptical person.
▷ SYNONYMS: **cynic**, doubter, unbeliever, doubting Thomas.
■ **scepticism** n.

sceptical adj. not easily convinced; having doubts.
▷ SYNONYMS: **dubious**, doubtful, doubting, cynical, distrustful, suspicious, disbelieving, unconvinced.
– ANTONYMS: certain, convinced.
■ **sceptically** adv.

sceptre /sep-ter/ (US **scepter**) n. a staff carried by a monarch on ceremonial occasions.

schedule n. a programme or timetable of intended events.
▷ SYNONYMS: **plan**, programme, timetable, scheme, agenda, diary,

S

calendar, itinerary.
• v. **1** plan for a particular time.
2 (**scheduled**) (of a flight) forming part of a regular service rather than specially chartered.
▷ SYNONYMS: **arrange**, organize, plan, programme, timetable, set up, line up; N. Amer. slate.
schema n. (pl. **schemata** or **schemas**) an outline of a plan or theory.
schematic adj. (of a diagram) outlining the main features; simplified.
■ **schematically** adv. **schematize** (or **-ise**) v.
scheme n. **1** a systematic plan for achieving something. **2** a plot. **3** a system or pattern.
▷ SYNONYMS: **1** plan, project, programme, strategy, stratagem, tactic; Brit. informal wheeze. **2** plot, intrigue, conspiracy, ruse, ploy, stratagem, manoeuvre, subterfuge, machinations; informal racket, scam.
• v. plot.
▷ SYNONYMS: **plot**, conspire, intrigue, connive, manoeuvre, plan.
scheming adj. devious or cunning.
▷ SYNONYMS: **cunning**, crafty, calculating, devious, Machiavellian, conniving, wily, sly, tricky, artful.
− ANTONYMS: ingenuous, honest.
scherzo /skair-tsoh/ n. (pl. **scherzos** or **scherzi**) a lively piece of music.
schism /ski-z'm/ n. a strong disagreement within an organization, causing it to split into groups.
▷ SYNONYMS: **division**, split, rift, breach, rupture, break, separation, severance, chasm, gulf, disagreement.
■ **schismatic** adj.
schist /shist/ n. a rock consisting of different layers of minerals.
schizoid /skit-soyd/ adj. having a mental condition similar to schizophrenia.
schizophrenia n. a mental disorder whose symptoms include withdrawal from reality into fantasy.
■ **schizophrenic** adj. & n.
schmaltz n. informal excessive sentimentality.
■ **schmaltzy** adj.
schnapps n. a strong alcoholic drink.
scholar n. **1** a person studying at an advanced level. **2** the holder of a scholarship.
▷ SYNONYMS: **academic**, intellectual, learned person, man/woman of letters, authority, expert; informal egghead; N. Amer. informal pointy-head.
scholarly adj. relating to academic

study, or devoted to academic pursuits.
▷ SYNONYMS: **learned**, educated, erudite, academic, well read, intellectual, literary, highbrow.
− ANTONYMS: uneducated, illiterate.
scholarship n. **1** academic study. **2** a grant made to support a student's education.
▷ SYNONYMS: **1** learning, knowledge, erudition, education, academic study. **2** grant, award, endowment; Brit. bursary.
scholastic adj. of schools or education.
school n. **1** an educational institution. **2** a group of artists, philosophers, etc. sharing similar ideas. **3** a large group of fish or sea mammals.
▷ SYNONYMS: **1** college, academy, seminary; alma mater. **2** the university's School of English: department, faculty, division.
• v. educate or train.
▷ SYNONYMS: **train**, teach, educate, tutor, coach, instruct, drill.

> **WORD LINKS**
> **scholastic** relating to schools and education

schooner n. **1** a sailing ship. **2** Brit. a large sherry glass.
sciatica /sy-at-ik-uh/ n. pain in the back, hip, and thigh.
science n. the study or knowledge of the physical world, based on observation and experiment.
scientific adj. **1** relating to or based on science. **2** systematic; methodical.
▷ SYNONYMS: we need to take a more scientific approach: **systematic**, methodical, organized, ordered, rigorous, exact, precise, accurate, mathematical.
■ **scientifically** adv.
scientist n. a person who studies or is an expert in science.
scimitar /sim-i-ter/ n. a short curved sword.
scintilla n. a trace.
scintillating adj. very impressive or skilful.
▷ SYNONYMS: **brilliant**, dazzling, exciting, exhilarating, stimulating, sparkling, lively, vivacious, vibrant, animated, effervescent, witty, clever.
− ANTONYMS: dull, boring.
scion /sy-uhn/ n. **1** a plant shoot cut off for grafting. **2** a descendant of a family.
scissors pl. n. a cutting tool with two crossing pivoted blades.

S

sclerosis n. abnormal hardening of body tissue.

scoff v. **1** speak about scornfully. **2** informal eat greedily.
▷ SYNONYMS: **sneer**, jeer, laugh; (**scoff at**) mock, deride, ridicule, dismiss, belittle; informal pooh-pooh.

scold v. angrily rebuke.

sconce n. a candle holder attached to a wall.

scone n. a small plain cake.

scoop n. **1** a utensil resembling a spoon, with a short handle and a deep bowl. **2** informal a news item printed by one newspaper before its rivals.
▷ SYNONYMS: **spoon**, ladle, dipper.
• v. **1** pick up or hollow out with a scoop. **2** pick up in a quick, smooth movement.

scooter n. **1** a light motorcycle. **2** a child's toy with two wheels and a long steering handle, moved by pushing a foot against the ground.

scope n. **1** opportunity for doing something. **2** the range of a subject, activity, etc.
▷ SYNONYMS: **1 extent**, range, breadth, reach, sweep, span, area, sphere, realm, compass, orbit, ambit, terms of reference, remit. **2 opportunity**, freedom, latitude, leeway, capacity, room to manoeuvre.

scorch v. burn on the surface.
▷ SYNONYMS: **1 burn**, sear, singe, char, blacken, discolour. **2 dry up**, parch, wither, shrivel, desiccate.

scorching adj. very hot.
▷ SYNONYMS: **hot**, red-hot, blazing, flaming, fiery, burning, blistering, searing; informal boiling, baking, sizzling.
– ANTONYMS: freezing, mild.

score n. **1** the number of points, goals, etc. achieved in a game. **2** (pl. **score**) a set of twenty. **3** the written music for a composition.
▷ SYNONYMS: **1 result**, outcome, total, tally, count. **2 rating**, grade, mark, percentage.
• v. **1** gain a point, goal, etc. in a game. **2** record the score during a game. **3** cut a mark on a surface. **4** (**score out**) cross out a word or words. **5** arrange a piece of music.
▷ SYNONYMS: **1 get**, gain, chalk up, achieve, make, record, rack up, notch up; informal bag, knock up. **2 arrange**, set, adapt, orchestrate, write, compose. **3 scratch**, cut, notch, incise, scrape, nick, gouge.
■ **scorer** n.

scorn n. open contempt.
▷ SYNONYMS: **contempt**, derision, disdain, mockery, sneering.
– ANTONYMS: admiration, respect.
• v. **1** express scorn for. **2** reject with scorn.
▷ SYNONYMS: **1 deride**, dismiss, pour scorn on, mock, scoff at, sneer at, jeer at, laugh at. **2 spurn**, rebuff, reject, ignore, shun, snub.
– ANTONYMS: admire, respect.

scornful adj. showing or expressing open contempt.
▷ SYNONYMS: **contemptuous**, mocking, derisive, withering, sneering, jeering, scathing, snide, disparaging, super-cilious, disdainful.
– ANTONYMS: admiring.
■ **scornfully** adv.

scorpion n. a small six-legged creature with a poisonous sting at the end of its tail.

Scot n. a person from Scotland.

Scotch n. whisky made in Scotland.
• adj. dated Scottish.

USAGE Use **Scotch** only to refer to things: people are **Scots** or **Scottish**.

scotch v. put an end to a rumour.

scot-free adv. without punishment or injury.

Scots adj. Scottish.
• n. the form of English used in Scotland.

Scottish adj. of Scotland or its people.

scoundrel n. a dishonest person.

scour v. **1** clean by rubbing with something rough. **2** search thoroughly.
▷ SYNONYMS: **1 scrub**, rub, clean, polish, buff, shine, burnish, grind, abrade. **2 search**, comb, hunt through, rummage through, look high and low in, ransack, turn upside-down, go through with a fine-tooth comb.

scourge n. **1** a cause of great suffering. **2** hist. a whip.
▷ SYNONYMS: **affliction**, bane, curse, plague, menace, evil, misfortune, burden, blight, cancer, canker.
• v. **1** cause suffering to. **2** hist. whip.

scout n. **1** a person sent ahead to gather information about an enemy. **2** (or **talent scout**) a person whose job is searching for talented performers.
▷ SYNONYMS: **1 lookout**, outrider, spy. **2 reconnaissance**, reconnoitre, survey, exploration, search; informal recce; Brit. informal shufti.
• v. **1** search. **2** act as a scout.
▷ SYNONYMS: **1** *I scouted around for some logs*: **search**, look, hunt, ferret around, root around. **2** *a patrol was*

sent to scout out the area: **reconnoitre**, explore, inspect, investigate, spy out, survey, scan, study; informal check out, case.

scowl n. a bad-tempered expression.
• v. make a scowl.
▷ SYNONYMS: **glower**, frown, glare, grimace, lour, look daggers.
– ANTONYMS: smile.

scrabble v. grope around with the fingers to find or hold on to something.

scraggy adj. thin and bony.

scram v. (**scramming, scrammed**) informal go away quickly.

scramble v. **1** move quickly and awkwardly, using hands as well as feet. **2** muddle. **3** put a transmission into a form intelligible only with a decoding device. **4** stir and cook beaten eggs. **5** (of fighter aircraft) take off immediately in an emergency.
▷ SYNONYMS: **1 clamber**, climb, crawl, claw your way, scrabble, struggle; N. Amer. shinny. **2 muddle**, confuse, mix up, jumble, disarrange, disorganize, disorder, disturb, mess up.
• n. **1** an act of scrambling. **2** Brit. a motorcycle race over rough ground.
▷ SYNONYMS: *the scramble for a seat:* **struggle**, jostle, scrimmage, scuffle, tussle, free-for-all, jockeying, competition, race.
■ **scrambler** n.

scrap n. **1** a small piece. **2** (**scraps**) uneaten food left after a meal. **3** waste metal that can be used again. **4** informal a short fight or quarrel.
▷ SYNONYMS: **1 fragment**, piece, bit, snippet, oddment, remnant, morsel, sliver. **2** *not a scrap of evidence:* **bit**, shred, speck, iota, particle, ounce, jot. **3 waste**, rubbish, refuse, debris; N. Amer. garbage, trash; informal junk.
• v. (**scrapping, scrapped**) **1** abolish or remove from use. **2** informal have a short fight or quarrel.
▷ SYNONYMS: **1 throw away**, throw out, dispose of, get rid of, discard, dispense with, bin, decommission, break up, demolish; informal chuck away/out, ditch, dump, junk; Brit. informal get shot of; N. Amer. informal trash. **2 abandon**, drop, abolish, withdraw, do away with, put an end to, cancel, axe; informal ditch, dump, junk.
– ANTONYMS: keep.
□ **scrapbook** a book for sticking cuttings etc. in.

scrape v. **1** drag a hard or sharp implement across a surface. **2** rub

against a rough surface. **3** just manage to achieve.
▷ SYNONYMS: **1 rub**, scratch, scour, grind, sand, sandpaper, abrade, file. **2 grate**, creak, rasp, scratch. **3 graze**, scratch, scuff, rasp, skin, cut, lacerate, bark, chafe.
• n. **1** an act of scraping. **2** an injury or mark caused by scraping. **3** informal an embarrassing or difficult situation.
▷ SYNONYMS: **1 grating**, creaking, rasp, scratch. **2 graze**, scratch, abrasion, cut, laceration, wound.

scrappy adj. disorganized or incomplete.

scratch v. **1** mark or wound with something sharp. **2** rub part of the body with the fingernails to relieve itching. **3** abandon a plan or withdraw from a competition.
▷ SYNONYMS: **scrape**, abrade, graze, score, scuff, skin, cut, lacerate, bark, chafe.
• n. a mark or wound made by scratching.
▷ SYNONYMS: **abrasion**, graze, scrape, cut, laceration, wound, mark, line.
• adj. assembled from whatever is available.
□ **from scratch** from the very beginning. **scratch card** a card with sections which may be scraped to reveal whether a prize has been won. **up to scratch** up to the required standard.
■ **scratchy** adj.

scrawl v. write in a hurried, careless way.
• n. scrawled handwriting.

scrawny adj. (**scrawnier, scrawniest**) thin and bony.

scream v. make a loud, piercing cry.
▷ SYNONYMS: **shriek**, screech, yell, howl, bawl, yelp, squeal, wail, squawk.
• n. **1** a loud, piercing cry or sound. **2** informal a very funny person or thing.

scree n. a mass of small loose stones on a mountain slope.

screech n. a loud, harsh cry or sound.
• v. make a screech.

screed n. a long speech or piece of writing.

screen n. **1** the flat front surface of a television or computer monitor, on which images and data are displayed. **2** an upright partition used to divide a room or hide something. **3** a thing that conceals or protects. **4** a blank surface on to which films are projected.
▷ SYNONYMS: **1 partition**, divider, windbreak. **2 display**, monitor, visual

S

display unit. **3 mesh**, net, netting.
4 buffer, protection, shield, shelter,
guard.
• v. **1** conceal or protect. **2** show
or broadcast a film or television
programme. **3** test for the presence or
absence of a disease.
▷ SYNONYMS: **1 partition**, divide,
separate, curtain. **2 conceal**, hide,
veil, shield, shelter, shade, protect.
3 *all blood is screened for the virus:*
check, test, examine, investigate, vet;
informal check out. **4 show**, broadcast,
transmit, televise, put out, air.
□ **screenplay** the script of a film.
screen saver a computer program
which replaces an unchanging screen
display with a moving image.

screw n. **1** a metal pin with a spiral
thread, turned and pressed into a
surface to join things together. **2** a
propeller. **3** informal a prison warder.
▷ SYNONYMS: **1 bolt**, fastener.
2 propeller, rotor.
• v. **1** fasten or tighten with a screw
or screws. **2** rotate so as to attach or
remove. **3** informal swindle.
▷ SYNONYMS: **1 tighten**, turn, twist,
wind. **2 fasten**, secure, fix, attach.
3 extort, force, extract, wrest, wring,
squeeze; informal bleed.
□ **screwdriver** a tool for turning
screws. **screw up 1** crush into a tight
mass. **2** informal cause to go wrong.
3 informal make emotionally disturbed.

scribble v. write or draw carelessly or
hurriedly.
▷ SYNONYMS: **scrawl**, scratch, dash off,
jot down, doodle, sketch.
• n. something scribbled.
▷ SYNONYMS: **scrawl**, squiggle, jottings,
doodle, doodlings.

scribe n. (in the past) a person who
copied out documents.

scrimmage n. a confused struggle.

scrimp v. economize; save.

script n. **1** the written text of a play,
film, or broadcast. **2** handwriting as
distinct from print.
▷ SYNONYMS: **1 text**, screenplay, libretto,
score, lines, dialogue, words. **2 handwriting**, writing, hand.
• v. write a script for.

scripture (or **scriptures**) n. the sacred
writings of Christianity or another
religion.
■ **scriptural** adj.

scroll n. a roll of parchment or paper.
• v. move displayed data up or down
on a computer screen.

Scrooge n. a person who is mean with
money.

scrotum n. (pl. **scrota** or **scrotums**) the
pouch of skin containing the testicles.

scrounge v. informal try to get
something without paying or working
for it.
▷ SYNONYMS: **beg**, borrow; informal cadge,
sponge, bum, touch someone for
something, freeload; N. Amer. informal
mooch; Austral./NZ informal bludge.
■ **scrounger** n.

scrub v. (**scrubbing**, **scrubbed**) **1** rub
hard to clean. **2** informal cancel.
▷ SYNONYMS: **1 brush**, scour, rub, clean,
cleanse, wash. **2 abandon**, scrap,
drop, cancel, call off, axe; informal ditch,
dump, junk.
• n. **1** an act of scrubbing. **2** land
covered mainly with bushes and
small trees.

scruff n. the back of the neck.

scruffy adj. (**scruffier**, **scruffiest**)
shabby and untidy.
▷ SYNONYMS: **shabby**, worn, down at
heel, ragged, tattered, mangy, dirty,
untidy, unkempt, bedraggled, messy,
dishevelled, ill-groomed; informal tatty.
– ANTONYMS: smart.
■ **scruffily** adv.

scrum n. **1** (or **scrummage**) Rugby a
formation in which players push
against each other with heads down
and the ball is thrown in. **2** Brit. informal
a disorderly crowd.

scrumptious adj. informal delicious.

scrumpy n. Brit. strong cider made in
the west of England.

scrunch v. crush or squeeze into a
tight mass.

scruple n. a feeling of doubt as to
whether an action is morally right.
▷ SYNONYMS: *he had no scruples
about working illegally:* **qualms**,
compunction, hesitation,
reservations, second thoughts,
doubts, misgivings, uneasiness,
reluctance.
• v. (**not scruple to do**) not hesitate
to do something, even if it may be
wrong.

scrupulous adj. very careful and
thorough.
▷ SYNONYMS: **careful**, meticulous,
painstaking, thorough, assiduous,
sedulous, attentive, conscientious,
punctilious, searching, close,
rigorous, strict.
– ANTONYMS: careless.
■ **scrupulously** adv.

scrutinize (or **-ise**) v. examine
carefully.
▷ SYNONYMS: **examine**, inspect, survey,
study, look at, peruse, investigate,

explore, probe, enquire into, go into, check.

scrutiny n. (pl. **scrutinies**) careful examination.

scuba-diving n. swimming underwater using an aqualung.

scud v. (**scudding**, **scudded**) move quickly, driven by the wind.

scuff v. mark a shoe etc. by scraping it against something.

scuffle n. a short, confused fight or struggle.
• v. take part in a scuffle.

scull n. 1 each of a pair of small oars used by a single rower. 2 a light boat for a single rower.
• v. row with sculls.

scullery n. (pl. **sculleries**) a room for washing dishes and other household work.

sculpt v. carve or shape.

sculpture n. 1 the art of making figures and shapes by carving or shaping stone, metal, etc. 2 a work made in this way.
▷ SYNONYMS: **carving**, statue, statuette, figure, figurine, effigy, bust, head, model.
• v. make by sculpture.
■ **sculptor** (fem. **sculptress**) n. **sculptural** adj.

scum n. 1 a layer of dirt or froth on the surface of a liquid. 2 informal a worthless person.
▷ SYNONYMS: **film**, layer, covering, froth, filth, dross, dirt.

scupper v. 1 informal stop from working or succeeding. 2 sink a ship deliberately.
▷ SYNONYMS: **ruin**, wreck, destroy, sabotage, torpedo, spoil.

scurf n. flakes of skin.

scurrilous adj. insulting and abusive; slanderous.
▷ SYNONYMS: **defamatory**, slanderous, libellous, scandalous, insulting, offensive, abusive, malicious; informal bitchy.

scurry v. (**scurrying**, **scurried**) move hurriedly with short steps.

scurvy n. a disease caused by a lack of vitamin C.

scut n. the short tail of a hare, rabbit, or deer.

scuttle n. a metal container used to store coal for a fire.
• v. 1 scurry. 2 cause a plan to fail. 3 sink a ship deliberately.

scythe n. a tool with a long curved blade, for cutting long grass.

SE abbrev. south-east or south-eastern.

sea n. 1 the salt water surrounding the land masses of the earth. 2 a particular area of sea. 3 a vast expanse.
▷ SYNONYMS: 1 **ocean**, waves; informal the drink; Brit. informal the briny; literary the deep. 2 a sea of roofs: **expanse**, stretch, area, tract, sweep, mass.
□ **at sea** confused. **sea anemone** a sea creature with stinging tentacles. **seabird** a bird that lives near the sea. **seaboard** the coast. **sea change** a great or remarkable change. **seafaring** travelling by sea. **seafood** shellfish and sea fish as food. **seagoing** of or for sea voyages. **seagull** a gull. **sea horse** a small sea fish that swims upright and has a horse-like head. **sea lion** a large seal. **seaman** a sailor. **seaplane** an aircraft designed to land on and take off from water. **seascape** a view or picture of the sea. **seasick** feeling nausea caused by the motion of a ship. **seaside** a beach area or holiday resort. **sea urchin** a sea animal with a round spiny shell. **seaweed** large algae growing in the sea. **seaworthy** (of a boat) in good enough condition to sail on the sea.
■ **seaward** adj. & adv. **seawards** adv.

> **WORD LINKS**
> **marine**, **maritime** relating to the sea

seal n. 1 a device or substance used to join things or prevent fluid passing through. 2 a piece of wax with a design stamped into it, attached to a document. 3 a confirmation or guarantee. 4 a sea mammal with flippers and a streamlined body.
▷ SYNONYMS: 1 **sealant**, adhesive, mastic. 2 **emblem**, symbol, insignia, badge, crest.
• v. 1 fasten or close securely. 2 coat so as to prevent fluid passing through. 3 make definite.
▷ SYNONYMS: 1 **stop up**, seal up, cork, stopper, plug, make watertight. 2 **clinch**, secure, settle, conclude, complete, finalize, confirm.

sealant n. material used to make something airtight or watertight.

seam n. 1 a line where two pieces of fabric are sewn together. 2 an underground layer of coal etc.
▷ SYNONYMS: 1 **join**, stitching, joint. 2 **layer**, stratum, vein, lode.
■ **seamed** adj.

seamless adj. smooth and without obvious joins.
■ **seamlessly** adv.

seamstress n. a woman who sews, esp. as a job.

seamy adj. (**seamier**, **seamiest**)

immoral or sordid.

seance /say-onss/ n. a meeting at which people try to contact the dead.

sear v. burn or scorch.
▷ SYNONYMS: **1 scorch**, burn, singe, char, dry up, wither. **2 flash-fry**, seal, brown.

search v. **1** try to find. **2** examine thoroughly so as to find.
▷ SYNONYMS: **1 hunt**, look, seek, forage, look high and low, ferret about, root about, rummage. **2** *police searched the building*: **look through**, scour, comb, go through with a fine-tooth comb, turn upside down, ransack, rifle through; frisk; Austral./NZ informal fossick through.
• n. an act of searching.
▷ SYNONYMS: **hunt**, look, quest.
□ **search engine** a computer program that searches the Internet for web pages containing a specified item.
searchlight a powerful outdoor light with a movable beam.
■ **searcher** n.

searching adj. trying to find out the truth: *a searching look*.
▷ SYNONYMS: **penetrating**, piercing, probing, keen, shrewd, sharp, intent.

season n. **1** each of the four divisions of the year (spring, summer, autumn, and winter). **2** a part of the year with particular weather, or when a particular activity takes place: *the rainy season*.
▷ SYNONYMS: **period**, time, time of year, spell, term.
• v. **1** add salt etc. to food. **2** dry wood for use as timber.
▷ SYNONYMS: *roast turkey seasoned with coriander*: **flavour**, spice.
□ **in season 1** (of fresh food) plentiful and ready to eat. **2** (of a female mammal) ready to mate. **season ticket** a ticket allowing travel or admission within a particular period.

seasonable adj. usual for a particular season.

seasonal adj. **1** of a particular season. **2** changing according to the season.
■ **seasonally** adv.

seasoned adj. experienced.
▷ SYNONYMS: **experienced**, practised, well versed, knowledgeable, established, veteran, hardened.
– ANTONYMS: inexperienced.

seasoning n. salt or spices added to food to improve the flavour.
▷ SYNONYMS: **flavouring**, salt and pepper, herbs, spices, condiments.

seat n. **1** a thing made or used for sitting on. **2** a site or location. **3** Brit. a large country house. **4** a place in an elected parliament or council. **5** Brit. a parliamentary constituency. **6** the buttocks.
▷ SYNONYMS: **1 chair**, bench, stool; (seats) seating. **2 headquarters**, base, centre, nerve centre, hub, heart, location, site. **3 residence**, ancestral home, mansion.
• v. **1** cause to sit. **2** have enough seats for.
▷ SYNONYMS: **1 position**, put, place, ensconce, install, settle. **2 have room for**, contain, take, sit, hold, accommodate.
□ **seat belt** a belt used to secure a seated person in a vehicle or aircraft.

sebaceous /si-bay-shuhss/ adj. producing oil or fat.

secateurs pl. n. Brit. pruning clippers.

secede v. withdraw from an alliance or federation.
■ **secession** n.

secluded adj. (of a place) sheltered and private.
▷ SYNONYMS: **sheltered**, private, concealed, hidden, unfrequented, sequestered, tucked away, remote, isolated, off the beaten track.

seclusion n. the state of being private and apart from others.

second¹ adj. & n. **1** that is number two in a sequence. **2** lower in position, rank, or importance. **3** (**seconds**) imperfect goods. **4** an attendant at a duel or boxing match.
▷ SYNONYMS: **1 next**, following, subsequent. **2 additional**, extra, alternative, another, spare, backup; N. Amer. alternate. **3 secondary**, subordinate, subsidiary, lesser, inferior.
– ANTONYMS: first.
• v. formally support a proposal etc.
▷ SYNONYMS: **support**, vote for, back, approve, endorse.
□ **second class** of a lower standard or quality than first class. **second-degree** (of burns) causing blistering but not permanent scars. **second nature** a habit that has become instinctive. **second-rate** of poor quality. **second sight** the supposed ability to foresee the future. **second thoughts** a change of opinion after reconsideration. **second wind** fresh energy for an activity.
■ **secondly** adv.

second² n. one-sixtieth of a minute.
▷ SYNONYMS: **moment**, bit, little while, instant, flash; informal sec, jiffy; Brit. informal mo, tick.

second³ /si-kond/ v. Brit. temporarily

move a worker to another job or role.
■ **secondment** n.

secondary adj. **1** coming after or less important than something primary. **2** (of education) for pupils aged 11 to 16 or 18.
▷ SYNONYMS: **1 less important**, subordinate, lesser, minor, peripheral, incidental, subsidiary, ancillary. **2 accompanying**, attendant, concomitant, consequential, resulting, resultant.
– ANTONYMS: primary, main.
■ **secondarily** adv.

second-hand adj. & adv. **1** having had a previous owner. **2** learned from other people.
▷ SYNONYMS: as adj. **used**, old, worn, pre-owned, nearly new, handed-down, hand-me-down, cast-off.
– ANTONYMS: new, direct.

secret adj. kept from or not known by others.
▷ SYNONYMS: **1** *secret information:* **confidential**, top secret, classified, undisclosed, unknown, private, under wraps; informal hush-hush. **2** *a secret affair:* **clandestine**, covert, undercover, underground, surreptitious, stealthy, cloak-and-dagger, furtive, conspiratorial. **3** *a secret door:* **hidden**, concealed, camouflaged.
– ANTONYMS: public, open.
● n. **1** something secret. **2** an effective method of achieving something.
■ **secrecy** n. **secretly** adv.

secretariat n. a government office or department.

secretary n. (pl. **secretaries**) **1** a person employed to type letters, keep records, etc. **2** an official of a society or other organization.
□ **Secretary of State** (in the UK) the head of a major government department.
■ **secretarial** adj.

secrete v. **1** (of a cell, gland, etc.) produce and discharge a substance. **2** hide.
■ **secretion** n. **secretory** adj.

secretive adj. inclined to hide your feelings or withhold information.
▷ SYNONYMS: **uncommunicative**, secret, unforthcoming, playing your cards close to your chest, reticent, tight-lipped.
– ANTONYMS: open, communicative.
■ **secretively** adv.

sect n. a group with different religious beliefs from those of a larger group to which they belong.
▷ SYNONYMS: **group**, cult, denomination,

order, splinter group, faction, camp.

sectarian adj. of a sect or sects.
▷ SYNONYMS: **factional**, separatist, partisan, doctrinaire, dogmatic, illiberal, intolerant, bigoted, narrow-minded.
■ **sectarianism** n.

section n. **1** any of the parts into which something is divided. **2** a distinct group within a larger one. **3** a cross section.
▷ SYNONYMS: **1 part**, bit, portion, segment, compartment, module, element, unit. **2 passage**, subsection, chapter, subdivision, clause. **3 department**, area, division.
● v. divide into sections.
■ **sectional** adj.

sector n. **1** a distinct area or part. **2** a part of a circle between two lines drawn from its centre to its circumference.
▷ SYNONYMS: **1 part**, branch, arm, division, area, department, field, sphere. **2 district**, quarter, section, zone, region, area, belt.

secular adj. not religious or spiritual.
▷ SYNONYMS: **non-religious**, lay, temporal, civil, worldly, earthly, profane.
– ANTONYMS: sacred, religious.

secure adj. **1** certain to remain safe. **2** fixed or fastened so as not to give way or become loose. **3** free from fear or anxiety.
▷ SYNONYMS: **1 fastened**, fixed, secured, done up, closed, shut, locked. **2 safe**, protected, safe and sound, out of harm's way, in safe hands, invulnerable, undamaged, unharmed. **3** *his position as leader was secure:* **certain**, assured, settled, stable, not at risk. **4 unworried**, at ease, relaxed, happy, confident.
– ANTONYMS: loose, insecure.
● v. **1** make secure. **2** succeed in obtaining.
▷ SYNONYMS: **1 fasten**, close, shut, lock, bolt, chain, seal. **2 obtain**, acquire, gain, get, get hold of, come by; informal land.
■ **securely** adv.

security n. (pl. **securities**) **1** the state of being secure. **2** the safety of a state or organization. **3** a valuable item given as a guarantee that you will repay a loan.
▷ SYNONYMS: **1 safety**, protection. **2 safety measures**, safeguards, surveillance, defence, policing. **3 guarantee**, collateral, surety, pledge, bond.

S

sedan n. **1** hist. an enclosed chair carried between two horizontal poles. **2** US a car for four or more people.

sedate adj. calm and unhurried.
▷ SYNONYMS: **1 slow**, steady, dignified, unhurried, relaxed, measured, leisurely, slow-moving, easy, gentle. **2 calm**, placid, tranquil, quiet, uneventful, staid, boring, dull.
− ANTONYMS: fast, exciting.
• v. give a sedative to.
■ **sedately** adv. **sedation** n.

sedative n. a drug that makes someone calm or sleepy.

sedentary adj. involving or taking little exercise.

sedge n. a grass-like marsh plant.

sediment n. **1** matter that settles to the bottom of a liquid. **2** material carried and deposited by water or wind.
▷ SYNONYMS: **dregs**, grounds, lees, residue, deposit, silt.
■ **sedimentary** adj.

sedition n. actions or speech inciting rebellion.
■ **seditious** adj.

seduce v. **1** persuade someone to have sex with you. **2** persuade to do something unwise.
▷ SYNONYMS: **attract**, allure, lure, tempt, entice, beguile, inveigle, manipulate.
■ **seducer** n. **seduction** n.

seductive adj. attractive or tempting.
▷ SYNONYMS: **tempting**, inviting, enticing, alluring, beguiling, attractive, appealing.

sedulous adj. dedicated and careful.

see v. (**seeing**, **saw**; past part. **seen**) **1** perceive with the eyes. **2** experience. **3** realize or deduce. **4** think of in a particular way. **5** meet. **6** meet regularly as a boyfriend or girlfriend. **7** guide or lead to a place.
▷ SYNONYMS: **1 discern**, detect, perceive, spot, notice, catch sight of, glimpse, make out, pick out, distinguish, spy; watch, look at; informal clap eyes on, clock; literary behold, espy, descry. **2 inspect**, view, look round, tour, survey, examine, scrutinize. **3 understand**, grasp, comprehend, follow, fathom, realize, appreciate, recognize, work out, deduce; informal get, latch on to, tumble to, figure out; Brit. informal twig, suss. **4** go and see what he's up to: **find out**, discover, learn, ascertain, determine, establish. **5** I see trouble ahead: **foresee**, predict, forecast, prophesy, anticipate, envisage. **6** you need to see a solicitor: **consult**, confer with, talk to, have recourse to, call on,

turn to. **7 go out with**, date, take out, be involved with; informal go steady with; dated court.
• n. the district or position of a bishop or archbishop.
□ **see off** escort to the point of departure. **see to 1** deal with. **2** ensure that.

seed n. **1** a small object produced by a plant, from which a new plant may grow. **2** the beginning of a feeling, process, etc. **3** any of the stronger competitors in a sports tournament who are kept from playing each other in the early rounds. **4** old use semen.
▷ SYNONYMS: **pip**, stone, kernel.
• v. **1** sow with seeds. **2** remove the seeds from. **3** make a competitor a seed in a tournament.

seedling n. a young plant raised from seed.

seedy adj. (**seedier**, **seediest**) sordid or disreputable.
■ **seediness** n.

seek v. (**seeking**, **sought**) **1** try to find or obtain. **2** try or want to do.
▷ SYNONYMS: **1 search for**, try to find, look for, be after, hunt for. **2 ask for**, request, solicit, call for, appeal for, apply for. **3 try**, attempt, endeavour, strive, work, do your best.

seem v. give the impression of being.
▷ SYNONYMS: **appear to be**, have the appearance/air of being, give the impression of being, look, sound, come across as, strike someone as.

seeming adj. appearing to be real or true.
■ **seemingly** adv.

seemly adj. socially appropriate.

seen past part. of SEE.

seep v. flow or leak slowly through a substance.
▷ SYNONYMS: **ooze**, trickle, exude, drip, dribble, flow, leak, drain, bleed, filter, percolate, soak.
■ **seepage** n.

seer n. a person supposedly able to foresee the future.

seersucker n. a fabric with a puckered surface.

see-saw n. a long plank balanced on a fixed support, on which children sit at each end and move up and down.
• v. repeatedly change between two states or positions.

seethe v. **1** be filled with great but unexpressed anger. **2** boil or churn.
▷ SYNONYMS: **1 teem**, swarm, boil, swirl, churn, surge, bubble, heave. **2 be angry**, be furious, be enraged, rage, be incensed, be beside yourself, boil,

rant, fume; informal be livid, foam at the mouth.

segment n. each of the parts into which something is divided.
▷ SYNONYMS: **piece**, bit, section, part, portion, division, slice, wedge.
• v. divide into segments.

segregate v. keep separate from others.
▷ SYNONYMS: **separate**, set apart, keep apart, isolate, quarantine, partition, divide, discriminate against.
– ANTONYMS: integrate.
■ **segregation** n.

seine /sayn/ n. a fishing net which hangs vertically from floats.

seismic /syz-mik/ adj. of earthquakes.

seismograph n. an instrument for measuring and recording earthquakes.

seismology n. the study of earthquakes.
■ **seismologist** n.

seize v. **1** take hold of suddenly and forcibly. **2** take possession of by force or by right. **3** (**seize on**) take eager advantage of. **4** (**seize up**) become jammed.
▷ SYNONYMS: **1 grab**, grasp, snatch, take hold of, clutch, grip. **2 capture**, take, overrun, occupy, conquer, take over. **3 confiscate**, impound, commandeer, requisition, appropriate, expropriate, sequestrate. **4 kidnap**, abduct, take captive, take prisoner, take hostage, hijack; informal snatch.
– ANTONYMS: release.

> USAGE **seize** is an exception to the usual rule of i before e except after c.

seizure n. **1** the act of seizing. **2** a stroke or an epileptic fit.
▷ SYNONYMS: **1 capture**, takeover, annexation, invasion, occupation. **2 confiscation**, appropriation, expropriation, sequestration. **3 kidnap**, abduction, hijack. **4 convulsion**, fit, spasm, paroxysm.

seldom adv. not often.
▷ SYNONYMS: **rarely**, infrequently, hardly ever, scarcely ever; informal once in a blue moon.
– ANTONYMS: often.

select v. carefully choose from a group.
▷ SYNONYMS: **choose**, pick, single out, opt for, decide on, settle on, sort out, take, adopt.
• adj. **1** carefully chosen. **2** used by or made up of wealthy people.
▷ SYNONYMS: **1 choice**, prime, hand-picked, top-quality, first-class; informal top-flight. **2 exclusive**, elite,

privileged, wealthy; informal posh.
– ANTONYMS: inferior.
■ **selector** n.

selection n. **1** the act of selecting. **2** things selected. **3** a range from which to choose.
▷ SYNONYMS: **1 choice**, pick, option, preference. **2 range**, array, diversity, variety, assortment, mixture. **3 anthology**, assortment, collection, assemblage, miscellany, medley.

selective adj. **1** of selection. **2** choosing carefully. **3** affecting some things and not others.
▷ SYNONYMS: **discerning**, discriminating, exacting, demanding, particular; informal choosy, picky.
– ANTONYMS: indiscriminate.
■ **selectively** adv. **selectivity** n.

selenium n. a crystalline chemical element.

self n. (pl. **selves**) **1** a person's essential being that distinguishes them from others. **2** a person's particular nature.

self- comb. form of or to yourself or itself.

self-assurance n. confidence.
■ **self-assured** adj.

self-centred adj. obsessed with yourself.
▷ SYNONYMS: **egocentric**, egotistic, self-absorbed, self-obsessed, self-seeking, self-serving, narcissistic, vain, inconsiderate, thoughtless; informal looking after number one.

self-confidence n. trust in your abilities and qualities.
▷ SYNONYMS: **self-assurance**, assurance, confidence, composure, aplomb, poise, sangfroid.
■ **self-confident** adj.

self-conscious adj. nervous or awkward because worried about what others think of you.
▷ SYNONYMS: **embarrassed**, uncomfortable, uneasy, ill at ease, nervous, awkward, shy, diffident, timid.
– ANTONYMS: confident.

self-contained adj. **1** (of accommodation) having its own facilities and entrance. **2** independent.

self-control n. the ability to control your emotions and behaviour.
■ **self-controlled** adj.

self-denial n. not allowing yourself to have things that you like.

self-determination n. the right of a country to run its own affairs.

self-evident adj. obvious.

self-importance n. an exaggerated sense of your own importance.

S

■ **self-important** adj.

self-interest n. your own interest or advantage.

selfish adj. concerned mainly with your own needs or wishes.
▷ SYNONYMS: **egocentric**, egotistic, self-centred, self-absorbed, self-obsessed, self-seeking, wrapped up in yourself, mean, greedy; informal looking after number one.
– ANTONYMS: unselfish, altruistic.
■ **selfishly** adv. **selfishness** n.

selfless adj. concerned more with the needs and wishes of others than with your own.
▷ SYNONYMS: **unselfish**, altruistic, considerate, compassionate, kind, noble, generous, magnanimous, ungrudging.
– ANTONYMS: selfish, inconsiderate.

self-made adj. having become successful by your own efforts.

self-possessed adj. confident and in control of your feelings.
■ **self-possession** n.

self-raising adj. Brit. (of flour) having baking powder already added.

self-respect n. pride and confidence in yourself.

self-righteous adj. certain that you are correct or morally superior.
▷ SYNONYMS: **sanctimonious**, holier-than-thou, pious, self-satisfied, smug, priggish, complacent, moralizing, superior, hypocritical; informal goody-goody.
– ANTONYMS: humble.

selfsame adj. (**the selfsame**) the very same.

self-satisfied adj. smugly pleased with yourself.
■ **self-satisfaction** n.

self-seeking adj. concerned only with your own interests.

self-service adj. (of a shop etc.) in which customers select goods and pay at a checkout.

self-styled adj. using a description or title that you have given yourself.

self-sufficient adj. able to do or produce what you need without outside help.
■ **self-sufficiency** n.

sell v. (**selling**, **sold**) **1** exchange or offer something in return for money. **2** (of goods) be bought in specified amounts. **3** persuade someone of the merits of.
▷ SYNONYMS: **put up for sale**, put on the market, auction, trade in, deal in, retail, market; traffic in, peddle, hawk.
– ANTONYMS: buy.

□ **sell out 1** sell all of your stock. **2** abandon your principles. **sell up** sell all your property etc.

seller n. **1** a person who sells something. **2** a product that sells in a particular way: *the book was one of our biggest sellers.*
▷ SYNONYMS: **vendor**, dealer, retailer, trader, merchant, agent, purveyor, supplier, stockist; hawker, pedlar.
– ANTONYMS: buyer, vendor.

Sellotape n. Brit. trademark transparent adhesive tape.

selvedge n. an edge on woven fabric that prevents it from unravelling.

selves pl. of SELF.

semantic adj. of meaning.
• n. (**semantics**) the study of the meaning of words.
■ **semantically** adv.

semaphore n. a system of signalling with the arms.

semblance n. the way something looks or seems.
▷ SYNONYMS: **appearance**, air, show, facade, front, veneer, guise, pretence.

semen n. the liquid containing sperm that is produced by males.

semester n. a half-year term in a school or university.

semi- prefix **1** half. **2** partly.

semibreve n. Brit. a musical note equal to four crotchets.

semicircle n. a half of a circle.
■ **semicircular** adj.

semicolon n. a punctuation mark (;).

semiconductor n. a solid that conducts electricity in certain conditions.

semi-detached adj. Brit. (of a house) joined to another house by a shared wall.

semi-final n. (in sport) a match or round preceding the final.
■ **semi-finalist** n.

seminal adj. **1** strongly influencing later developments. **2** of semen.

seminar n. **1** a meeting for discussion or training. **2** a small university class meeting to discuss topics with a teacher.
▷ SYNONYMS: **1 conference**, symposium, meeting, convention, forum, summit. **2 study group**, workshop, tutorial, class.

seminary n. (pl. **seminaries**) a training college for priests or rabbis.

semiotics n. the study of signs and symbols.
■ **semiotic** adj.

semi-precious adj. (of minerals)

S

used as gems but less valuable than precious stones.

semiquaver n. Brit. a musical note equal to half a quaver.

Semitic adj. of the group of peoples that includes Jews and Arabs.

semitone n. Brit. half a tone in music.

semolina n. the hard grains left after flour is milled, used in puddings and pasta.

senate n. **1** the smaller but higher law-making body in the US and some other countries. **2** the governing body of a university or college.

senator n. a member of a senate.

send v. (**sending**, **sent**) **1** cause to go or be taken to a destination. **2** cause to move sharply or quickly. **3** put in a specified state.

▷ SYNONYMS: **1 dispatch**, post, mail, email, consign, forward, transmit, convey, communicate, broadcast, radio. **2** *the volcano sent clouds of ash into the air:* **propel**, project, eject, discharge, spout, fire, shoot, release, throw, fling, cast, hurl. **3** *you're sending me crazy:* **make**, drive, turn.

– ANTONYMS: receive.

□ **send for** order to come or be brought. **send-off** a gathering of people to wish good luck to someone who is leaving. **send up** informal ridicule by imitation.

senile adj. having a loss of mental abilities because of old age.

■ **senility** n.

senior adj. **1** of older people. **2** high or higher in status. **3** Brit. of schoolchildren above the age of about 11. **4** older.

▷ SYNONYMS: **1 older**, elder. **2 superior**, higher-ranking, more important; N. Amer. ranking.

– ANTONYMS: junior, subordinate.

• n. a senior person.

□ **senior citizen** an elderly person.

■ **seniority** n.

senna n. a laxative made from the dried pods of a tropical tree.

sensation n. **1** a feeling resulting from something that happens to or touches the body. **2** a vague awareness. **3** a widespread reaction of excited interest, or a cause of this.

▷ SYNONYMS: **1 feeling**, sense, perception, impression. **2 commotion**, stir, uproar, furore, scandal, impact; informal splash, to-do.

sensational adj. causing or trying to cause great public interest and excitement.

▷ SYNONYMS: **1 shocking**, scandalous, fascinating, exciting, thrilling, interesting, dramatic, momentous, historic, newsworthy. **2 overdramatized**, melodramatic, exaggerated, sensationalist, graphic, explicit, lurid; informal shock-horror, juicy. **3 gorgeous**, stunning, wonderful, superb, excellent, first-class; informal great, terrific, tremendous, fantastic, fabulous, out of this world; Brit. informal smashing.

– ANTONYMS: dull, unremarkable.

■ **sensationalism** n. **sensationalist** adj. **sensationally** adv.

sensationalize (or **-ise**) v. present information in an exaggerated way to make it seem more interesting.

sense n. **1** any of the powers of sight, smell, taste, and touch, by which the body perceives things. **2** a feeling that something is the case. **3** awareness or sensitivity. **4** a sensible and practical attitude. **5** a meaning.

▷ SYNONYMS: **1 feeling**, faculty, awareness, sensation, recognition, perception. **2 appreciation**, awareness, understanding, sensitivity. **3 wisdom**, common sense, wit, reason, intelligence, judgement, brains, sagacity; informal gumption, nous, horse sense, savvy; Brit. informal loaf; N. Amer. informal smarts. **4 purpose**, point, use, value, advantage, benefit. **5 meaning**, definition, denotation, nuance, drift, gist, thrust, tenor, message.

– ANTONYMS: stupidity.

• v. **1** perceive by a sense. **2** be vaguely aware of.

▷ SYNONYMS: **detect**, feel, observe, notice, recognize, pick up, be aware of, distinguish, make out, perceive, discern, divine, intuit; informal catch on to.

□ **make sense** be understandable or sensible.

senseless adj. **1** lacking meaning, purpose, or common sense. **2** unconscious.

▷ SYNONYMS: **pointless**, futile, useless, needless, meaningless, absurd, foolish, insane, stupid, idiotic, mindless, illogical.

– ANTONYMS: wise.

sensibility n. (pl. **sensibilities**) the ability to understand emotion or art.

sensible adj. having or showing common sense.

▷ SYNONYMS: **practical**, realistic, responsible, reasonable, commonsensical, rational, logical, sound, no-nonsense,

S

level-headed, down-to-earth, wise.
– ANTONYMS: foolish.
■ sensibly adv.

sensitive adj. **1** quick to detect
or be affected by slight changes.
2 appreciating the feelings of others.
3 easily offended or upset. **4** secret or
controversial.
▷ SYNONYMS: **1** *she's sensitive to changes
in temperature*: **responsive to**,
reactive to, sensitized to, aware of,
conscious of, susceptible to, affected
by, vulnerable to. **2 tactful**, careful,
thoughtful, diplomatic, delicate,
subtle, kid-glove. **3 touchy**, oversensitive, hypersensitive, easily offended,
thin-skinned, defensive, paranoid,
neurotic. **4** *a sensitive issue*: **difficult**,
delicate, tricky, awkward, problem-
atic, ticklish, controversial, emotive.
– ANTONYMS: insensitive, resilient.
■ sensitively adv. sensitivity n.

sensitize (or **-ise**) v. make sensitive
or aware.

sensor n. a device for detecting or
measuring heat, light, etc.

sensory adj. of sensation or the
senses.

sensual adj. of the senses as a source
of pleasure.
▷ SYNONYMS: **1 physical**, carnal, bodily,
fleshly, animal. **2 passionate**, sexual,
physical, tactile, hedonistic.
– ANTONYMS: spiritual.
■ sensuality n. sensually adv.

sensuous adj. **1** of the senses rather
than the intellect. **2** physically
attractive or pleasing.
▷ SYNONYMS: **1 rich**, sumptuous,
luxurious. **2 voluptuous**, sexy, seductive, luscious, lush, ripe.
■ sensuously adv.

sent past & past part. of SEND.

sentence n. **1** a set of words that
is complete in itself, conveying
a statement, question, etc. **2** a
punishment given to someone found
guilty by a court.
▷ SYNONYMS: **1 judgement**, ruling,
decision, verdict. **2** *a long sentence*:
punishment, prison term; informal
time, stretch.
• v. state in a court that an offender is
to receive a particular punishment.
▷ SYNONYMS: **condemn**, doom, punish,
convict.

sententious adj. making pompous
comments on moral issues.

sentient adj. able to perceive or feel
things.
■ sentience n.

sentiment n. **1** an opinion or feeling.

2 exaggerated tenderness, sadness, or
nostalgia.
▷ SYNONYMS: **1 view**, feeling, attitude,
thought, opinion, belief. **2 sentimentality**, emotion, tenderness,
softness; informal **schmaltz**; Brit. informal
soppiness.

sentimental adj. showing or having
excessive tenderness, sadness, or
nostalgia.
▷ SYNONYMS: **1 nostalgic**, emotional,
affectionate, loving, tender.
2 mawkish, overemotional, romantic,
hearts-and-flowers; Brit. twee; informal
schmaltzy, corny; Brit. informal **soppy**;
N. Amer. informal **sappy**.
■ sentimentality n. sentimentally adv.

sentinel n. a sentry.

sentry n. (pl. **sentries**) a soldier
stationed to keep guard or control
access to a place.

sepal n. each of the leaf-like parts of a
flower surrounding the petals.

separate adj. forming or viewed as a
unit or by itself.
▷ SYNONYMS: **1** *this raises two separate
issues*: **unconnected**, unrelated,
different, distinct, discrete, detached,
divorced, disconnected, independent.
2 *the kitchen is in a separate
building*: **detached**, free-standing,
self-contained.
• v. **1** move, come, or keep apart.
2 stop living together as a couple.
3 divide into parts.
▷ SYNONYMS: **1 disconnect**, detach,
disengage, uncouple, split, sunder,
sever. **2** *a wall separates the two
communities*: **partition**, divide, stand
between, come between, keep apart,
isolate, section off. **3 split up**, break
up, part, part company, become
estranged; divorce; informal bust up.
– ANTONYMS: unite, join.
■ separable adj. separation n.

USAGE The middle is *-par-*, not *-per-*:
separate.

separately adv. as a separate person
or thing; not together.
▷ SYNONYMS: **individually**, one by one,
one at a time, singly, severally, apart,
independently, alone, by yourself, on
your own.

separatist n. a member of a group
seeking independence from a larger
group.
■ separatism n.

sepia n. a reddish-brown colour.

sepsis n. the presence in tissues of
harmful bacteria.

September n. the ninth month.

S

septet n. a group of seven musicians.

septic adj. infected with bacteria.
▷ SYNONYMS: **infected**, festering, suppurating, putrid, putrefying, poisoned; Medicine purulent.
◻ **septic tank** an underground tank in which sewage decomposes before draining into the soil.

septicaemia (US **septicemia**) n. blood poisoning caused by bacteria.

septuagenarian n. a person between 70 and 79 years old.

sepulchral adj. gloomy.

sepulchre /sep-uhl-ker/ (US **sepulcher**) n. a stone tomb.

sequel n. **1** a book, film, etc. continuing the story of an earlier one. **2** something taking place after or as a result of an earlier event.
▷ SYNONYMS: **continuation**, further episode, follow-up.

sequence n. **1** an order in which related things follow each other. **2** a set of things following each other in a particular order.
▷ SYNONYMS: **1 succession**, order, course, series, chain, train, progression, chronology, pattern, flow. **2 excerpt**, clip, extract, section.

sequential adj. following in a logical sequence.
■ **sequentially** adv.

sequester v. **1** isolate. **2** sequestrate.

sequestrate v. take legal possession of assets until a debt has been paid.
■ **sequestration** n.

sequin n. a small, shiny disc for decorating clothes.
■ **sequinned** adj.

sequoia n. a redwood tree.

seraglio /si-**rah**-li-oh/ n. (pl. **seraglios**) the women's quarters in a Muslim household.

seraph n. (pl. **seraphim** or **seraphs**) a type of angel.
■ **seraphic** adj.

serenade n. a piece of music sung or played by a man to his lover, outdoors and at night.
• v. perform a serenade for.

serendipity n. the fortunate occurrence of events by chance.
■ **serendipitous** adj.

serene adj. calm and peaceful.
▷ SYNONYMS: **calm**, composed, tranquil, peaceful, placid, untroubled, relaxed, at ease, unperturbed, unruffled, unworried; N. Amer. centered; informal together, unflappable.
– ANTONYMS: agitated.
■ **serenely** adv. **serenity** n.

serf n. (in the feudal system) an agricultural labourer tied to working on a particular estate.

serge n. a hard-wearing fabric.

sergeant n. **1** a non-commissioned officer in the army or air force above corporal. **2** Brit. a police officer ranking below an inspector.
◻ **sergeant major** an army officer who helps with administrative duties.

serial adj. **1** arranged in a series. **2** repeatedly committing the same offence.
• n. a story published or broadcast in regular instalments.
◻ **serial number** an identification number given to a manufactured item.
■ **serially** adv.

serialize (or **-ise**) v. publish or broadcast as a serial.
■ **serialization** n.

series n. (pl. **series**) **1** a number of similar things coming one after another. **2** a sequence of related television or radio programmes.
▷ SYNONYMS: **succession**, sequence, string, chain, run, round, spate, wave, rash, course, cycle, row.

serious adj. **1** dangerous or severe. **2** needing careful consideration or action. **3** solemn or thoughtful. **4** sincere and in earnest.
▷ SYNONYMS: **1 solemn**, earnest, grave, sombre, unsmiling, stern, grim, humourless, stony, dour, poker-faced, long-faced. **2 important**, significant, momentous, weighty, far-reaching, consequential. **3 intellectual**, high-brow, heavyweight, deep, profound, literary, learned, scholarly; informal heavy. **4** a serious injury: severe, grave, bad, critical, acute, terrible, dire, dangerous, grievous. **5 sincere**, earnest, genuine, wholehearted, committed, resolute, determined.
– ANTONYMS: light-hearted, trivial, minor.
■ **seriously** adv. **seriousness** n.

sermon n. a talk on a religious or moral subject, esp. during a church service.
▷ SYNONYMS: **address**, homily, talk, speech, lecture.

sermonize (or **-ise**) v. give moral advice.

serpent n. a large snake.

serpentine adj. winding or twisting.

serrated adj. having a jagged edge.
■ **serration** n.

serried adj. (of rows of people or things) standing close together.

S

serum n. (pl. **sera** or **serums**) the thin liquid which separates out when blood clots.

servant n. a person employed to do domestic work in a household or for a person.

▷ SYNONYMS: **attendant**, domestic, maid, housemaid, retainer, flunkey, minion, slave, lackey, drudge; informal skivvy.

serve v. **1** perform duties or services for. **2** be a member of the armed forces. **3** spend a period in a job or in prison. **4** present food or drink to. **5** attend to a customer. **6** fulfil a purpose. **7** hit the ball in tennis etc. to begin play for each point of a game.

▷ SYNONYMS: **1 work for**, obey, do the bidding of. **2** *this job serves the community:* **benefit**, help, assist, aid, make a contribution to. **3** *he served a six-month apprenticeship:* **carry out**, perform, do, fulfil, complete, discharge, spend. **4 present**, give out, distribute, dish up, provide, supply. **5 attend to**, deal with, see to, assist, help, look after. **6** *a saucer serving as an ashtray:* **act as**, function as, do duty.

• n. an act of serving in tennis etc.

server n. **1** a person or thing that serves. **2** a computer or program that controls or supplies information to a network.

service n. **1** the act of serving. **2** a period of employment with an organization. **3** help or advice. **4** a religious ceremony. **5** a system supplying a public need. **6** a department run by the state. **7** (**the services**) the armed forces. **8** a routine inspection and maintenance of a vehicle etc. **9** a set of matching crockery. **10** a serve in tennis etc.

▷ SYNONYMS: **1 work**, employment, labour. **2** *he has done us a service:* **favour**, kindness, good turn, helping hand. **3 ceremony**, ritual, rite, sacrament. **4** *a range of local services:* **amenity**, facility, resource, utility. **5 armed forces**, military, army, navy, air force. **6 overhaul**, check, maintenance, servicing, repair.

• v. **1** perform maintenance on. **2** provide services for. **3** pay interest on a debt.

▷ SYNONYMS: **overhaul**, check, go over, maintain, repair.

□ **service area** (or **services**) Brit. a roadside area with a service station, cafe, etc. for motorists. **serviceman** (or **servicewoman**) a member of the armed forces. **service provider**

a company which provides access to the Internet. **service road** a road parallel to a main road, giving access to houses, shops, etc. **service station** a garage selling petrol etc.

serviceable adj. **1** in working order. **2** useful and hard-wearing.

▷ SYNONYMS: **1 in working order**, working, functioning, operational, usable, workable, viable. **2 functional**, utilitarian, sensible, practical, hard-wearing, durable, tough, robust.

serviette n. Brit. a table napkin.

servile adj. excessively willing to serve or please others.

■ **servility** n.

serving n. a quantity of food for one person.

servitude n. the state of being a slave or of being controlled by someone more powerful.

sesame n. a tropical plant grown for its oil-rich seeds.

session n. **1** a period devoted to a particular activity. **2** a meeting of a council, court, etc. to conduct its business.

▷ SYNONYMS: **1 meeting**, sitting, assembly, conclave; N. Amer. & NZ caucus. **2 period**, time, term.

set v. (**setting**, **set**) **1** put in a specified place, position, or state. **2** give a task to. **3** decide on or fix a time, value, etc. **4** establish as an example or record. **5** adjust a device as required. **6** prepare a table for a meal. **7** harden into a solid, semi-solid, or fixed state. **8** (of the sun etc.) appear to move towards and below the earth's horizon.

▷ SYNONYMS: **1 put**, place, lay, deposit, position, settle, leave, stand, plant; informal stick, dump, park, plonk, pop. **2** *the fence is set in concrete:* **fix**, embed, insert, mount. **3** *he set us some work:* **assign**, allocate, give, allot. **4** *we need to set a date for the meeting:* **arrange**, schedule, fix, decide on, settle on, choose, agree on, determine, designate, appoint, name, specify, stipulate. **5** *set your watches:* **adjust**, regulate, synchronize, calibrate, put right, correct. **6** *I set the table:* **lay**, prepare, arrange. **7 solidify**, harden, stiffen, thicken, gel, cake, congeal, coagulate, clot.

• n. **1** a number of things or people grouped together. **2** the way something is set. **3** a radio or television receiver. **4** a group of games counting as a unit towards a match in tennis etc. **5** a collection of scenery

etc. used for a scene in a play or film.
▷ SYNONYMS: **1 series**, collection, group, batch, arrangement, array, assortment, selection. **2 group**, circle, crowd, crew, band, fraternity, company, ring, camp, school, clique, faction; informal gang, bunch.
• adj. **1** fixed or established beforehand. **2** (**set on**) determined to do. **3** ready or likely to do something.
▷ SYNONYMS: **1 fixed**, established, scheduled, specified, appointed, arranged, settled, decided, agreed, predetermined, hard and fast, unvarying, unchanging, invariable, rigid, inflexible. **2** *he's set on going with her*: **determined**, resolved, bent, hell-bent, intent. **3 ready**, prepared, organized, equipped, primed; informal geared up, psyched up.
– ANTONYMS: variable, unprepared.
□ **set about** start doing. **set aside** temporarily stop using land for growing crops. **set off 1** begin a journey. **2** make a bomb or alarm go off. **set out 1** begin a journey. **2** intend. **set square** a right-angled triangular drawing instrument. **set up** establish a business.
setback n. a problem that delays progress.
▷ SYNONYMS: **problem**, difficulty, hitch, complication, upset, blow; informal glitch, hiccup.
– ANTONYMS: breakthrough.
sett n. a badger's burrow.
settee n. Brit. a sofa.
setter n. a breed of dog trained to stand rigid on scenting game.
setting n. **1** the way or place in which something is set. **2** a set of crockery and cutlery laid for one person.
▷ SYNONYMS: **surroundings**, position, situation, environment, background, backdrop, spot, place, location, locale, site, scene.
settle v. **1** resolve a dispute or problem. **2** decide or arrange finally. **3** make your home in a new place. **4** adopt a more steady lifestyle. **5** become or make calmer. **6** begin to feel at ease in a new situation. **7** sit or rest comfortably or securely. **8** pay a debt. **9** (**settle for**) accept something less than satisfactory.
▷ SYNONYMS: **1 resolve**, sort out, clear up, end, fix, work out, iron out, set right, reconcile; informal patch up. **2 put in order**, sort out, tidy up, arrange, organize, order, clear up, straighten out. **3 decide on**, set, fix, agree on, name, establish, arrange,

choose, pick. **4 set up home**, take up residence, put down roots, establish yourself, move to. **5** *a drink will settle your nerves*: **calm**, quieten, quiet, soothe, relax. **6 land**, come to rest, alight, perch. **7** *I've settled the bill*: **pay**, square, clear.
• n. a wooden bench with a high back and arms.
settlement n. **1** the act of settling. **2** a place where people establish a community. **3** an agreement intended to settle a dispute.
▷ SYNONYMS: **1 agreement**, deal, arrangement, conclusion, resolution, understanding, pact. **2 community**, colony, outpost, encampment, post, village.
settler n. a person who establishes a community in a new area.
▷ SYNONYMS: **colonist**, frontiersman, pioneer; immigrant, newcomer, incomer.
seven adj. & n. one more than six; 7.
■ **seventh** adj. & n.
seventeen adj. & n. one more than sixteen; 17.
■ **seventeenth** adj. & n.
seventy adj. & n. (pl. **seventies**) ten less than eighty; 70.
■ **seventieth** adj. & n.
sever v. **1** cut off. **2** put an end to.
▷ SYNONYMS: **1 cut**, cut off, chop off, detach, separate, amputate. **2 break off**, discontinue, suspend, end, cease, dissolve.
– ANTONYMS: join.
■ **severance** n.
several adj. & pron. more than two but not many.
▷ SYNONYMS: **some**, a number of, a few, various, assorted.
• adj. separate or respective.
■ **severally** adv.
severe adj. **1** (of something bad) very great. **2** strict or harsh. **3** very plain in style or appearance.
▷ SYNONYMS: **1 acute**, very bad, serious, grave, critical, dire, dangerous, life-threatening. **2** *severe storms*: **fierce**, violent, strong, powerful, intense, forceful. **3 cold**, freezing, icy, arctic, harsh, bitter. **4** *severe criticism*: **harsh**, scathing, sharp, strong, fierce, savage, devastating, withering. **5** *a severe expression*: **stern**, dour, grim, forbidding, disapproving, unsmiling, unfriendly, sombre, stony, cold, frosty. **6 plain**, simple, austere, spartan, unadorned, stark, clinical, uncluttered, minimalist, functional.
– ANTONYMS: minor, gentle, mild.

S

■ **severely** adv. **severity** n.

sew v. (**sewing, sewed**; past part. **sewn** or **sewed**) join or repair by stitching with a needle and thread.

▷ SYNONYMS: **stitch**, tack, seam, hem, embroider.

sewage /soo-ij/ n. waste water and excrement conveyed in sewers.

sewer /soo-er/ n. an underground pipe for sewage.

■ **sewerage** n.

sex n. **1** either of the two main categories (male and female) into which living things are divided. **2** the fact of being male or female. **3** sexual intercourse.

▷ SYNONYMS: **1 gender. 2 sexual intercourse**, lovemaking, making love, copulation; formal fornication, coitus.

> WORD LINKS
> **carnal** relating to sexual urges and activities

sexagenarian n. a person between 60 and 69 years old.

sexism n. prejudice or discrimination on the basis of sex.

■ **sexist** adj. & n.

sexless adj. **1** not sexually attractive or active. **2** neither male nor female.

sextant n. an instrument for measuring angles and distances, used in navigation and surveying.

sextet n. **1** a group of six musicians. **2** music for a sextet.

sexton n. a person who looks after a church and churchyard.

sextuplet n. each of six children born at one birth.

sexual adj. **1** of sex or physical attraction or contact. **2** of the sexes. **3** (of reproduction) involving the fusion of male and female cells.
□ **sexual intercourse** sexual contact in which a man puts his erect penis into a woman's vagina.

■ **sexually** adv.

sexuality n. (pl. **sexualities**) **1** capacity for sexual feelings. **2** a person's sexual preference.

▷ SYNONYMS: **1 sensuality**, sexiness, seductiveness, eroticism, physicality, sexual appetite, passion, desire, lust. **2 sexual orientation**, sexual preference, leaning, persuasion.

sexy adj. (**sexier, sexiest**) **1** sexually attractive or exciting. **2** sexually aroused. **3** informal exciting or interesting.

▷ SYNONYMS: **1 sexually attractive**, seductive, desirable, alluring; informal fanciable; Brit. informal fit; N. Amer. informal

foxy. **2 erotic**, sexually explicit, titillating, naughty, X-rated, rude, pornographic, crude; informal raunchy, steamy; euphemistic adult.

■ **sexily** adv. **sexiness** n.

shabby adj. (**shabbier, shabbiest**) **1** worn out or scruffy. **2** mean and unfair.

▷ SYNONYMS: **1 run down**, scruffy, dilapidated, in disrepair, ramshackle, tumbledown, dingy; Brit. informal grotty. **2 scruffy**, old, worn out, threadbare, ragged, frayed, tattered, battered, faded, moth-eaten, the worse for wear; informal tatty; N. Amer. informal raggedy. **3 mean**, unkind, unfair, shameful, shoddy, unworthy, contemptible, despicable, discreditable, ignoble; informal rotten.

– ANTONYMS: smart.

■ **shabbily** adv. **shabbiness** n.

shack n. a roughly built hut.

▷ SYNONYMS: **hut**, cabin, shanty, lean-to, shed, hovel; Scottish bothy.

shackle n. (**shackles**) a pair of rings connected by a chain, used to fasten a prisoner's wrists or ankles.
• v. **1** put shackles on. **2** restrain; limit.

▷ SYNONYMS: **1 chain**, fetter, manacle, secure, tie, bind, tether, hobble, put in chains, clap in irons, handcuff. **2 restrain**, restrict, limit, constrain, handicap, hamstring, hamper, hinder, impede, obstruct, inhibit.

shade n. **1** darkness and coolness caused by shelter from direct sunlight. **2** a colour, esp. with regard to how light or dark it is. **3** a variety. **4** a slight amount. **5** a lampshade. **6** (**shades**) informal sunglasses. **7** literary a ghost.

▷ SYNONYMS: **1 shadow**, shadiness, shelter, cover. **2 colour**, hue, tone, tint, tinge. **3 nuance**, gradation, degree, difference, variation, variety, nicety, subtlety, undertone, overtone. **4 little**, bit, trace, touch, modicum, tinge; informal tad, smidgen. **5 blind**, curtain, screen, cover, covering, awning, canopy.

– ANTONYMS: light.
• v. **1** screen from direct light. **2** cover or reduce the light of. **3** darken parts of a drawing etc.

▷ SYNONYMS: **cast a shadow over**, shadow, shelter, cover, screen.

shadow n. **1** a dark area produced by an object coming between light rays and a surface. **2** partial or complete darkness. **3** sadness or gloom. **4** a slight trace. **5** a person who constantly accompanies or secretly

follows another.
▷ SYNONYMS: **1 silhouette**, outline, shape, contour, profile. **2 shade**, darkness, twilight, gloom.
• v. **1** follow and observe secretly. **2** cast a shadow over.
▷ SYNONYMS: **follow**, trail, track, stalk, pursue; informal tail, keep tabs on.
□ **shadow-boxing** boxing against an imaginary opponent as a form of training. **Shadow Cabinet** Brit. members of the main opposition party in Parliament holding posts corresponding to those of the government Cabinet.
■ **shadowy** adj.

shady adj. (**shadier, shadiest**) **1** giving or situated in shade. **2** informal seeming to be dishonest or illegal.
▷ SYNONYMS: **1 shaded**, shadowy, dim, dark, sheltered, leafy. **2 suspicious**, suspect, questionable, dubious, irregular, underhand; informal fishy, murky; Brit. informal dodgy; Austral./NZ informal shonky.
− ANTONYMS: bright, honest.

shaft n. **1** the long, narrow handle of a tool or body of an arrow etc. **2** a ray of light. **3** a narrow vertical passage. **4** each of the two poles between which a horse is harnessed to a vehicle. **5** a rotating rod transmitting mechanical power in a machine.
▷ SYNONYMS: **1 pole**, stick, rod, staff, shank, handle, stem. *2 a shaft of light:* **ray**, beam, gleam, streak, pencil. **3 tunnel**, passage, hole, bore, duct, well, flue, vent.

shag n. **1** coarse tobacco. **2** a cormorant.
• adj. (of pile on a carpet) long and rough.

shaggy adj. (**shaggier, shaggiest**) (of hair or fur) long, thick, and untidy.

shah n. a title of the former king of Iran.

shake v. (**shaking, shook**; past part. **shaken**) **1** move quickly and jerkily up and down or to and fro. **2** tremble. **3** shock or disturb.
▷ SYNONYMS: **1 vibrate**, tremble, quiver, quake, shiver, shudder, judder, wobble, rock, sway, convulse. **2 jiggle**, joggle, jerk, agitate; informal wiggle, waggle. **3 brandish**, wave, flourish, swing, wield. **4 upset**, distress, disturb, unsettle, disconcert, discompose, unnerve, throw off balance, agitate, fluster, shock, alarm, scare, worry; informal rattle.
• n. an act of shaking.
▷ SYNONYMS: **judder**, trembling,

quivering, quake, tremor, shiver, shudder, wobble.
□ **shake hands** clasp right hands on meeting, parting, or as a sign of agreement. **shake off** get rid of. **shake up** make major changes to.
■ **shaker** n.

shaky adj. (**shakier, shakiest**) **1** shaking; unsteady. **2** not safe or certain.
▷ SYNONYMS: **1 unsteady**, unstable, rickety, wobbly; Brit. informal wonky. **2 faint**, dizzy, light-headed, giddy, weak, wobbly, in shock. **3 unreliable**, untrustworthy, questionable, dubious, doubtful, tenuous, suspect, flimsy, weak; informal iffy; Brit. informal dodgy.
− ANTONYMS: steady, stable.
■ **shakily** adv.

shale n. soft rock that splits easily.

shall aux. v. **1** used with *I* and *we* to express the future tense. **2** expressing determination or an order.

shallot n. a small onion.

shallow adj. **1** not deep. **2** not thinking or thought out seriously.
▷ SYNONYMS: **superficial**, trivial, facile, insubstantial, lightweight, empty, trifling, surface, skin-deep, frivolous, foolish, silly.
− ANTONYMS: profound.
• n. (**shallows**) a shallow area of water.
■ **shallowness** n.

sham n. a thing that is not as good or genuine as it seems to be.
▷ SYNONYMS: **pretence**, fake, act, simulation, fraud, lie, counterfeit, humbug.
• adj. not genuine; false.
▷ SYNONYMS: **fake**, pretended, feigned, simulated, false, artificial, bogus, insincere, affected, make-believe; informal pretend, put-on, phoney.
− ANTONYMS: genuine.
• v. (**shamming, shammed**) pretend.
▷ SYNONYMS: **pretend**, fake, malinger; informal put it on; Brit. informal swing the lead.

shaman /shay-muhn/ n. (in some societies) a person believed to be able to contact good and evil spirits.

shamble v. walk in a slow, shuffling way.

shambles n. informal a state of complete disorder.
▷ SYNONYMS: **chaos**, muddle, mess, jumble, confusion, disorder, havoc.

shame n. **1** embarrassment or distress arising from awareness that you have done something wrong or foolish. **2** loss of respect. **3** a cause of shame.

S

4 a cause for regret.

▷ SYNONYMS: **1 guilt**, remorse, contrition. **2 humiliation**, embarrassment, indignity, loss of face, mortification, disgrace, dishonour, discredit, ignominy, disrepute, infamy, scandal. **3** *it's a shame she never married:* **pity**, bad luck; informal crime, sin.

– ANTONYMS: pride, honour.

• v. cause to feel ashamed.

▷ SYNONYMS: **1 disgrace**, dishonour, discredit, blacken, drag through the mud. **2 humiliate**, embarrass, humble, take down a peg or two, cut down to size; informal show up.

– ANTONYMS: honour.

shamefaced adj. showing shame.

▷ SYNONYMS: **ashamed**, abashed, sheepish, guilty, contrite, sorry, remorseful, repentant, penitent, regretful, rueful, apologetic; informal with your tail between your legs.

– ANTONYMS: unrepentant.

shameful adj. that causes or ought to cause shame.

▷ SYNONYMS: **1 disgraceful**, deplorable, despicable, contemptible, discreditable, unworthy, reprehensible, shabby, shocking, scandalous, outrageous, abominable, atrocious, appalling, inexcusable, unforgivable. **2 embarrassing**, mortifying, humiliating, ignominious.

– ANTONYMS: admirable.

■ **shamefully** adv.

shameless adj. showing a lack of shame.

▷ SYNONYMS: **flagrant**, blatant, barefaced, overt, brazen, undisguised, unconcealed, unabashed, unashamed, unblushing, unrepentant.

shampoo n. **1** a liquid soap for washing the hair. **2** a similar substance for cleaning a carpet etc. **3** an act of shampooing.

• v. (**shampooing, shampooed**) wash or clean with shampoo.

shamrock n. a clover-like plant.

shandy n. (pl. **shandies**) beer mixed with lemonade or ginger beer.

shank n. **1** the lower part of the leg. **2** the shaft of a tool.

shan't contr. shall not.

shantung n. a silk fabric with a rough surface.

shanty n. (pl. **shanties**) **1** a small roughly built hut. **2** a sailors' traditional song.

□ **shanty town** a settlement in or near a town where people live in shanties.

shape n. **1** the form of something produced by its outline. **2** a particular

condition: *in poor shape*. **3** welldefined structure or arrangement.

▷ SYNONYMS: **1 form**, appearance, configuration, structure, contours, lines, outline, silhouette, profile. **2 condition**, health, trim, fettle, order; Brit. informal nick. **3** *a spirit in the shape of a fox:* **guise**, likeness, semblance, form, appearance, image.

• v. **1** give a shape to. **2** influence greatly. **3** (**shape up**) develop in a particular way.

▷ SYNONYMS: **1 form**, fashion, make, mould, model. **2** *events which shaped the course of her life:* **determine**, form, influence, affect.

shapeless adj. lacking a definite or attractive shape.

▷ SYNONYMS: **1 formless**, amorphous, unformed, indefinite. **2 baggy**, saggy, ill-fitting, oversized, unstructured, badly cut.

shapely adj. having an attractive shape.

▷ SYNONYMS: **well proportioned**, curvaceous, voluptuous, full-figured, attractive, sexy; informal curvy.

shard n. a piece of broken pottery, glass, etc.

share n. **1** a part of a larger amount which is divided among or contributed by a number of people. **2** any of the equal parts into which a company's wealth is divided, entitling the holder to a proportion of the profits.

▷ SYNONYMS: **portion**, part, division, quota, allowance, ration, allocation; informal cut, slice; Brit. informal whack.

• v. **1** have or give a share of. **2** have or use jointly.

▷ SYNONYMS: **1 split**, divide, go halves on; informal go fifty-fifty on. **2 apportion**, divide up, allocate, portion out, measure out, carve up; Brit. informal divvy up. **3 participate**, take part, play a part, be involved, have a hand. □ **shareholder** an owner of shares in a company.

■ **sharer** n.

shark n. **1** a large sea fish with a triangular fin on the back. **2** informal a person who exploits or swindles others.

sharp adj. **1** having a cutting or piercing edge or point. **2** tapering to a point or edge. **3** sudden and noticeable. **4** clear and definite. **5** producing a sudden, piercing feeling. **6** quick to understand, notice, or respond. **7** (of a taste or smell) strong and slightly bitter. **8** cricitcal or hurtful. **9** above true or normal pitch in music.

▷ SYNONYMS: **1 keen**, razor-edged, sharpened, well honed. **2** *a sharp increase:* **sudden**, abrupt, unexpected, rapid, steep. **3** *a sharp pain:* **intense**, acute, severe, agonizing, excruciating, stabbing, shooting, searing. **4 astute**, intelligent, bright, incisive, keen, quick-witted, shrewd, canny, perceptive, smart, quick; informal on the ball, quick on the uptake; N. Amer. informal heads-up. **5** *a sharp taste:* **tangy**, piquant, acidic, acid, sour, tart, pungent, vinegary. **6** *sharp words:* **harsh**, bitter, cutting, caustic, scathing, barbed, spiteful, hurtful, unkind, cruel, malicious.

– ANTONYMS: blunt, mild.

• adv. **1** precisely. **2** suddenly or abruptly.

▷ SYNONYMS: **precisely**, exactly, prompt, promptly, punctually; informal on the dot; N. Amer. informal on the button.

• n. a musical note raised by a semitone, or the sign showing this. □ **sharp practice** dishonest business dealings. **sharpshooter** a person skilled in shooting.

■ **sharpener** n. **sharply** adv. **sharpness** n.

sharpen v. make sharp or sharper.

▷ SYNONYMS: **hone**, whet, strop, grind, file.

shatter v. **1** break violently into pieces. **2** destroy. **3** upset greatly.

▷ SYNONYMS: **1 smash**, break, splinter, crack, fracture, fragment, disintegrate. **2 destroy**, wreck, ruin, dash, crush, devastate, demolish, torpedo, scotch; informal do for, put paid to; Brit. informal scupper.

shave v. **1** remove hair by cutting it off close to the skin with a razor. **2** cut a thin slice from something. **3** pass very close to.

▷ SYNONYMS: **1 cut off**, crop, trim, barber. **2 plane**, pare, whittle, scrape, shear.

• n. an act of shaving.

■ **shaver** n.

shaven adj. shaved.

shaving n. a thin strip cut off a surface.

shawl n. a large piece of fabric worn over the shoulders or wrapped round a baby.

she pron. the female previously mentioned.

sheaf n. (pl. **sheaves**) **1** a bundle of papers. **2** a bundle of grain stalks.

shear v. (**shearing**, **sheared**; past part. **shorn** or **sheared**) **1** cut off or trim with shears. **2** break off because

of strain. **3** (**be shorn of**) have something taken away from you.

• pl. n. (**shears**) a cutting implement like very large scissors.

■ **shearer** n.

sheath n. (pl. **sheaths**) **1** a cover for the blade of a knife or sword. **2** a condom.

▷ SYNONYMS: **covering**, cover, case, casing, sleeve, scabbard.

sheathe v. **1** put a sword etc. into a sheath. **2** encase in a close-fitting cover.

shed n. a simple building used for storage or to shelter animals.

▷ SYNONYMS: **hut**, lean-to, outhouse, outbuilding, cabin, shack.

• v. (**shedding**, **shed**) **1** have leaves, hair, etc. fall off naturally. **2** get rid of. **3** give off light. **4** Brit. accidentally drop or spill.

▷ SYNONYMS: **1 throw off**, cast off, discard, slough off, moult. **2 take off**, remove, discard, climb out of, slip out of; Brit. informal peel off. **3** *the moon shed a faint light:* **cast**, radiate, emit, give out. **4 drop**, scatter, spill.

sheen n. a soft shine on a surface.

▷ SYNONYMS: **shine**, lustre, gloss, patina, burnish, polish, shimmer.

sheep n. (pl. **sheep**) a mammal with a woolly coat, kept for its wool or meat. □ **sheepdog** a dog trained to guard and herd sheep. **sheepskin** a sheep's skin with the wool on.

sheepish adj. embarrassed or shy.

■ **sheepishly** adv.

sheer adj. **1** nothing but; absolute. **2** vertical or almost vertical. **3** (of a fabric) very thin.

▷ SYNONYMS: **1 utter**, complete, absolute, total, thorough, pure, downright, out-and-out, unqualified, unmitigated, unalloyed. **2 steep**, abrupt, sharp, precipitous, vertical. **3 thin**, fine, gauzy, diaphanous, transparent, see-through, flimsy, filmy, translucent.

• v. change course quickly.

sheet n. **1** a large piece of cotton or other fabric, used to cover a bed. **2** a broad thin piece of metal, glass, paper, etc. **3** an expanse of water, flame, etc. **4** a rope attached to the lower corner of a sail.

▷ SYNONYMS: **1 layer**, covering, blanket, coat, film, veneer, crust, skin, surface, stratum. **2 pane**, panel, slab, plate, piece. **3 page**, leaf, folio. **4** *a sheet of water:* **expanse**, area, stretch, sweep.

sheikh (or **sheik**) /shayk/ n. a Muslim or Arab leader.

■ **sheikhdom** n.

S

shekel n. the basic unit of money of Israel.

shelf n. (pl. **shelves**) **1** a flat length of wood etc. fixed horizontally for displaying or storing things. **2** a ledge of rock.
□ **shelf life** the time for which an item to be sold remains fresh or usable.

shell n. **1** the hard outer covering of an egg, nut kernel, or an animal. **2** a metal case filled with explosive, fired from a large gun. **3** a hollow case or outer structure.
▷ SYNONYMS: **1** pod, hull, husk. **2** body, case, casing, framework, hull, fuselage, hulk.
• v. **1** fire explosive shells at. **2** remove the shell or pod from. **3** (**shell out**) informal pay a sum of money.
▷ SYNONYMS: **1** pod, hull, husk; N. Amer. shuck. **2** bombard, fire on, attack, bomb, blitz.
□ **shellfish** an edible water animal that has a shell. **shell shock** a mental condition that can affect soldiers after prolonged combat.

shellac n. a resin used in varnish.

shelter n. **1** a place giving protection from bad weather or danger. **2** protection.
▷ SYNONYMS: **1** protection, cover, shade, safety, security, refuge. **2** sanctuary, refuge, home, haven, safe house.
– ANTONYMS: exposure.
• v. **1** provide with shelter. **2** find or take shelter.
▷ SYNONYMS: **1** protect, shield, screen, cover, shade, defend, cushion, guard, insulate, cocoon. **2 take shelter**, take refuge, take cover; informal hole up.
– ANTONYMS: expose.

sheltered adj. **1** providing shelter or protection. **2** protected from the unpleasant aspects of life.
▷ SYNONYMS: **1** shady, shaded, protected, still, tranquil. **2** a sheltered life: protected, cloistered, isolated, secluded, cocooned, insulated, secure, safe, quiet.

shelve v. **1** put on a shelf. **2** postpone or cancel. **3** slope downwards.
▷ SYNONYMS: **postpone**, put off, delay, defer, put back, reschedule, hold over/off, put to one side, suspend, stay, mothball; N. Amer. put over, table; informal put on ice, put on the back burner.

shenanigans pl. n. informal high-spirited or underhand behaviour.

shepherd n. a person who looks after sheep.
• v. guide.

▷ SYNONYMS: **usher**, steer, herd, lead, take, escort, guide, conduct, marshal, walk.
□ **shepherd's pie** Brit. a dish of minced meat topped with mashed potato.
■ **shepherdess** n.

sherbet n. Brit. a sweet fizzing powder eaten alone or made into a drink.

sheriff n. **1** (in England and Wales) the chief executive officer of the Crown in a county. **2** (in Scotland) a judge. **3** US an elected officer in a county, responsible for keeping law and order.

Sherpa n. (pl. **Sherpa** or **Sherpas**) a member of a Himalayan people of Nepal and Tibet.

sherry n. (pl. **sherries**) a strong wine from southern Spain.

Shia /shi-uh/ n. (pl. **Shia** or **Shias**) **1** one of the two main branches of Islam. **2** (or **Shiite**) a Muslim who follows the Shia branch of Islam.

shiatsu /shi-at-soo/ n. a Japanese therapy in which pressure is applied with the hands to points on the body.

shibboleth n. a long-standing belief or principle, regarded by many as outdated.

shied past & past part. of SHY.

shield n. **1** a broad piece of armour held for protection against blows or missiles. **2** a person or thing acting as a barrier or screen. **3** a sporting trophy in the form of a metal plate mounted on a piece of wood.
▷ SYNONYMS: **protection**, guard, defence, cover, screen, shelter.
• v. protect or hide.
▷ SYNONYMS: **protect**, guard, defend, cover, screen, shade, shelter.
– ANTONYMS: expose.

shift v. **1** move or change from one position to another. **2** transfer blame etc. **3** Brit. informal move quickly.
▷ SYNONYMS: **1** move, transfer, transport, switch, relocate, reposition, rearrange. **2** the wind shifted: veer, alter, change, turn.
• n. **1** a slight change in position or direction. **2** a period of time worked by a group of workers who start work as another group finishes. **3** a straight dress without a waist.
▷ SYNONYMS: **1** change, alteration, adjustment, variation, modification, revision, reversal, U-turn. **2** stint, stretch, spell.

shiftless adj. lazy and lacking ambition.

shifty adj. informal dishonest or untrustworthy.

Shiite /shee-yt/ n. = **SHIA** (sense 2).

shilling n. a former British coin worth 12 old pence.

shilly-shally v. (**shilly-shallying, shilly-shallied**) be indecisive.

shimmer v. shine with a soft wavering light.
▷ SYNONYMS: **glint**, glisten, twinkle, sparkle, flash, gleam, glow, glimmer, wink.
• n. a soft wavering light or shine.
▷ SYNONYMS: **glint**, twinkle, sparkle, flash, gleam, glow, glimmer, lustre, glitter.

shimmy v. (**shimmying, shimmied**) move swiftly and smoothly.

shin n. the front of the leg below the knee.
• v. (**shinning, shinned**) climb quickly up or down by gripping with the arms and legs.

shindig n. informal a lively party.

shine v. (**shining, shone** or **shined**) **1** give out or reflect light. **2** direct a torch etc. somewhere. **3** be very good at something. **4** (past & past part. **shined**) polish.
▷ SYNONYMS: **1** beam, gleam, radiate, glow, glint, glimmer, sparkle, twinkle, glitter, glisten, shimmer, flash. **2** excel, stand out. **3** polish, burnish, buff, rub up, brush, clean.
• n. brightness.
▷ SYNONYMS: **polish**, gleam, gloss, lustre, sheen, patina.
□ **take a shine to** informal develop a liking for.

shingle n. **1** a mass of small rounded pebbles, esp. on a beach. **2** a wooden roof tile. **3** (**shingles**) a disease with a rash of painful blisters forming along a nerve path.

Shinto n. a Japanese religion involving the worship of ancestors and nature spirits.

shiny adj. (**shinier, shiniest**) (of something clean, smooth, or polished) reflecting light.
▷ SYNONYMS: **glossy**, bright, glassy, polished, gleaming, satiny, lustrous.
– ANTONYMS: matt.

ship n. a large boat for transporting people or goods by sea.
▷ SYNONYMS: **boat**, vessel, craft.
• v. (**shipping, shipped**) transport on a ship or by other means.
▷ SYNONYMS: **deliver**, send, dispatch, transport, carry, distribute.
□ **shipment 1** the act of transporting goods. **2** an amount of goods shipped.
shipping ships as a whole. **shipshape** orderly and neat. **shipwreck** the

sinking or breaking up of a ship at sea. **shipwrecked** having suffered a shipwreck. **shipyard** a place where ships are built and repaired.
■ **shipper** n.

WORD LINKS
marine, maritime, nautical, naval relating to ships or sailing

shire n. Brit. a county.
□ **shire horse** a heavy powerful horse.

shirk v. avoid work or a duty.
▷ SYNONYMS: **evade**, dodge, avoid, get out of, sidestep, shrink from, shun, skip, neglect; informal duck out of, cop out of; Brit. informal skive off; N. Amer. informal cut.
■ **shirker** n.

shirt n. a garment for the upper body, with sleeves and buttons down the front.

shirty adj. Brit. informal angry or annoyed.

shiver v. shake slightly, esp. from fear or cold.
▷ SYNONYMS: **tremble**, quiver, shake, shudder, quake.
• n. a shivering movement.
▷ SYNONYMS: **shudder**, twitch, start.
■ **shivery** adj.

shoal n. **1** a large number of fish swimming together. **2** an area of shallow water. **3** a submerged sandbank.

shock n. **1** a sudden upsetting or surprising experience. **2** sudden surprise and distress. **3** a serious medical condition caused by loss of blood, severe injury, etc. **4** a violent shaking movement caused by an impact, earthquake, etc. **5** a sudden discharge of electricity through the body. **6** a thick mass of hair.
▷ SYNONYMS: **1** blow, upset, surprise, revelation, bolt from the blue, rude awakening, eye-opener. **2** fright, scare, start; informal turn. **3** trauma, collapse, breakdown. **4** vibration, reverberation, shake, jolt, impact, blow.
• v. **1** surprise and upset. **2** outrage or disgust.
▷ SYNONYMS: **appal**, horrify, outrage, scandalize, disgust, traumatize, distress, upset, disturb, stun, rock, shake.
– ANTONYMS: delight.
■ **shocker** n.

shocking adj. **1** causing outrage or disgust. **2** Brit. informal very bad.
▷ SYNONYMS: **appalling**, horrifying, horrific, dreadful, awful, terrible, scandalous, outrageous, disgraceful,

S

abominable, atrocious, disgusting, distressing, upsetting, disturbing, startling.
■ **shockingly** adv.

shoddy adj. **1** badly made or done. **2** dishonest or unfair.
▷ SYNONYMS: **poor-quality**, inferior, second-rate, tawdry, jerry-built, cheap-jack, gimcrack; informal tatty.
■ **shoddily** adv.

shoe n. **1** a covering for the foot with a stiff sole. **2** a horseshoe.
• v. (**shoeing, shod**) fit with a shoe or shoes.
□ **on a shoestring** with only a very small amount of money. **shoehorn** a curved implement for easing the heel into a shoe. **shoe tree** a shaped block for keeping a shoe in shape.

shone past & past part. of SHINE.

shoo exclam. a word said to drive away animals.
• v. drive away.

shook past of SHAKE.

shoot v. (**shooting, shot**) **1** kill or wound with a bullet or arrow. **2** fire a gun. **3** move suddenly and rapidly. **4** (in sport) kick, hit, or throw the ball etc. in an attempt to score. **5** film or photograph. **6** (of a plant) send out shoots.
▷ SYNONYMS: **1 gun down**, mow down, pick off, hit, wound, injure, kill. **2 fire**, open fire, snipe, let fly, bombard, shell, discharge, launch. **3 race**, speed, flash, dash, rush, hurtle, streak, whizz, zoom, career, fly; informal belt, tear, zip, whip; Brit. informal bomb; N. Amer. informal hightail it, barrel. **4 film**, photograph, record.
• n. **1** a new part growing from a plant. **2** an act of shooting.
▷ SYNONYMS: **sprout**, bud, runner, tendril, offshoot, cutting.
□ **shooting star** a small, rapidly moving meteor. **shooting stick** a walking stick with a handle that unfolds to form a seat.
■ **shooter** n.

shop n. **1** a building where goods or services are sold. **2** a workshop.
▷ SYNONYMS: **store**, retail outlet, boutique, emporium, department store, supermarket, hypermarket, superstore, chain store; N. Amer. mart.
• v. (**shopping, shopped**) **1** go to a shop or shops to buy goods. **2** (**shop around**) look for the best available price. **3** Brit. informal inform on.
□ **shop floor** Brit. the part of a factory where production is carried out.
shopkeeper the owner or manager of

a shop. **shoplifter** a person who steals goods from a shop. **shop-soiled** dirty or damaged from being displayed in a shop. **shop steward** a trade union official elected by workers as their representative. **talk shop** discuss work in a social setting.
■ **shopper** n. **shopping** n.

shore n. the land along the edge of a sea, lake, etc.
▷ SYNONYMS: **seashore**, beach, sands, shoreline, coast; literary littoral.
• v. (**shore up**) **1** support or strengthen. **2** hold up with a beam.

shorn past part. of SHEAR.

short adj. **1** of a small length in space or time. **2** small in height. **3** (**short of/on**) not having enough of. **4** rude and abrupt. **5** (of odds in betting) reflecting a high probability. **6** (of pastry) crumbly.
▷ SYNONYMS: **1 concise**, brief, succinct, to the point, compact, pithy, abridged, abbreviated, condensed. **2 brief**, fleeting, short-lived, momentary, passing, lightning, quick, rapid, cursory. **3 small**, little, petite, tiny, diminutive, elfin; Scottish wee; informal pint-sized, knee-high to a grass-hopper. **4 scarce**, scant, meagre, sparse, insufficient, deficient, inadequate, lacking. **5 curt**, sharp, abrupt, blunt, brusque, terse, offhand, rude.
– ANTONYMS: tall, long, plentiful.
• adv. not as far as expected or required.
• n. **1** Brit. a small drink of spirits. **2** (**shorts**) short trousers reaching to the knees or thighs.
• v. have a short-circuit.
□ **shortbread** (Brit. also **shortcake**) a rich, crumbly biscuit. **short-change** cheat, esp. by giving insufficient change. **short circuit** a fault in an electrical circuit when the current flows along a shorter route than it should do. **short-circuit** cause a short circuit in. **shortcrust pastry** Brit. crumbly pastry, esp. for making pies. **short cut** a quicker route or method. **shortfall** an amount by which something is less than what is required. **shorthand** a method of rapid writing using abbreviations and symbols. **short-handed** without enough staff. **shortlist** a list of selected candidates from which a final choice is made. **short shrift** abrupt or unsympathetic treatment. **short-sighted** Brit. **1** unable to see things clearly unless they are close

to the eyes. **2** lacking foresight.
short-tempered losing your temper
quickly. **short-term** of or for a short
time. **short wave** a radio wave of a
frequency of about 3 to 30 megahertz.
■ **shortness** n.

shortage n. a lack of something
needed.
▷ SYNONYMS: **scarcity**, dearth, poverty,
insufficiency, deficiency, inadequacy,
famine, lack, deficit, shortfall.
− ANTONYMS: abundance.

shortcoming n. a fault or defect.
▷ SYNONYMS: **fault**, defect, flaw, imperfection, deficiency, limitation, failing,
drawback, weakness, weak point.
− ANTONYMS: strength.

shorten v. make or become shorter.
▷ SYNONYMS: **abbreviate**, abridge, cut,
condense, contract, compress, reduce,
shrink, diminish, trim, pare down,
prune, curtail, truncate.
− ANTONYMS: lengthen.

shortening n. fat used to make pastry.

shortly adv. **1** soon. **2** abruptly or
sharply.
▷ SYNONYMS: **soon**, presently, in a little
while, at any moment, in a minute, in
next to no time, before long, by and
by; N. Amer. momentarily; informal anon,
in a jiffy.

shot past & past part. of SHOOT.
• n. **1** the firing of a gun etc. **2** (in
sport) a hit, stroke, or kick of the ball
as an attempt to score. **3** informal an
attempt. **4** a photo. **5** informal a small
drink of spirits. **6** informal an injection.
7 tiny lead pellets used in a shotgun.
8 a heavy ball thrown in the sport of
shot put.
▷ SYNONYMS: **1 report**, crack, bang, blast;
(shots) gunfire, firing. **2** the winning
shot: **stroke**, hit, strike, kick, throw.
3 marksman, markswoman, shooter.
4 photograph, photo, snap, snapshot,
picture, print, slide, still.
• adj. woven with different colours to
give a contrasting effect.
▢ **like a shot** informal without
hesitation. **shotgun** a gun for firing
small shot at short range. **shot
put** an athletic contest in which a
heavy round ball is thrown as far as
possible. **shot through with** filled
with.

should aux. v. **1** expressing duty or
obligation, or a possible or probable
future event. **2** expressing a polite
request, opinion, or hope.

shoulder n. the joint between the
upper arm and the main part of the
body.

• v. **1** take on a responsibility. **2** push
aside with the shoulder.
▷ SYNONYMS: **1 take on**, undertake,
accept, assume, bear, carry. **2 push**,
shove, thrust, jostle, force, bulldoze,
bundle.
▢ **shoulder blade** either of the flat
triangular bones at the top of the
back.

shout v. **1** speak or call out very
loudly. **2** (**shout down**) prevent from
speaking or being heard by shouting.
▷ SYNONYMS: **yell**, cry out, call out, roar,
howl, bellow, bawl, raise your voice;
informal holler.
− ANTONYMS: whisper.
• n. a loud cry or call.
▷ SYNONYMS: **yell**, cry, call, roar, howl,
bellow, bawl; informal holler.

shove v. **1** push roughly. **2** place
carelessly or roughly. **3** (**shove off**)
informal go away.
▷ SYNONYMS: **push**, thrust, propel, drive,
force, ram, knock, elbow, shoulder,
jostle.
• n. a strong push.

shovel n. a tool resembling a spade for
moving earth, snow, etc.
• v. (**shovelling, shovelled**; US
shoveling, shoveled) move with a
shovel.

show v. (**showing, showed**; past part.
shown or **showed**) **1** be or make
visible. **2** offer for inspection or
viewing. **3** present an image of. **4** lead
or guide. **5** treat in a particular way.
6 demonstrate or prove.
▷ SYNONYMS: **1** she was showing signs of
mental instability: **display**, exhibit,
manifest, reveal, convey, communicate, express, evince, betray. **2** she
showed them to their seats: **escort**,
accompany, take, conduct, lead,
usher, guide, direct. **3** I'll show you
how to do it: **demonstrate**, explain,
describe, illustrate, teach, instruct.
4 this shows that his conclusions were
correct: **prove**, demonstrate, confirm,
substantiate, corroborate, verify,
bear out.
− ANTONYMS: conceal.
• n. **1** a theatrical performance or
light entertainment programme. **2** a
competition involving the public
display of animals, plants, etc.
3 an impressive or pleasing sight.
4 an outward display, esp. when
misleading.
▷ SYNONYMS: **1 programme**, broadcast,
presentation, production. **2 exhibition**, display, fair, exposition,
festival, parade; N. Amer. exhibit.

S

3 display, array, sight, spectacle.
4 appearance, outward appearance, image, pretence, front, guise, pose, affectation, semblance.
□ **show business** theatre, films, television, etc. as a profession or industry. **showjumping** the sport of riding horses over a course of obstacles in an arena. **showman** the manager or presenter of a circus, fair, etc. **show off 1** try to impress by boasting about your abilities etc. **2** display. **showpiece** an outstanding example. **showroom** a room where goods for sale are displayed. **show up 1** reveal as bad or faulty. **2** informal humiliate.

showcase n. **1** an occasion for presenting something favourably. **2** a glass display case.
• v. put on display.

showdown n. a final confrontation intended to settle a dispute.

shower n. **1** a brief fall of rain or snow. **2** a large number of things that fall or arrive together. **3** a device producing a spray of water under which someone stands to wash. **4** a wash in a shower.
▷ SYNONYMS: **1 fall**, drizzle, sprinkling, flurry. **2 volley**, hail, salvo, barrage.
• v. **1** fall or throw in a shower. **2** (**shower with**) give a great number of things to. **3** wash in a shower.
▷ SYNONYMS: **1 rain**, fall, hail. **2 deluge**, flood, inundate, swamp, overwhelm, snow under.
■ **showery** adj.

show-off n. a person who shows off.
▷ SYNONYMS: **exhibitionist**, poser, poseur, self-publicist, extrovert.

showy adj. very bright or colourful and noticeable.
▷ SYNONYMS: **ostentatious**, flamboyant, gaudy, garish, brash, vulgar, loud, fancy, ornate; informal flash, flashy.
– ANTONYMS: restrained.
■ **showily** adv.

shrank past of SHRINK.

shrapnel n. small metal fragments from an exploding shell or bomb.

shred n. **1** a strip of material torn or cut from something. **2** a very small amount.
▷ SYNONYMS: **1 strip**, ribbon, rag, fragment, sliver, snippet, remnant. **2 scrap**, bit, speck, particle, ounce, jot, crumb, fragment, grain, drop, trace.
• v. (**shredding**, **shredded**) tear or cut into shreds.
▷ SYNONYMS: **grate**, cut up, tear up.

■ **shredder** n.

shrew n. a small mouse-like mammal with a pointed snout.

shrewd adj. having or showing good judgement.
▷ SYNONYMS: **astute**, sharp, smart, intelligent, clever, canny, perceptive; informal on the ball.
– ANTONYMS: stupid.
■ **shrewdly** adv. **shrewdness** n.

shrewish adj. (of a woman) bad-tempered.

shriek v. make a piercing cry.
▷ SYNONYMS: **scream**, screech, squeal, squawk, roar, howl, shout, yelp; informal holler.
• n. a piercing cry.

shrill adj. high-pitched and piercing.
▷ SYNONYMS: **high-pitched**, piercing, high, sharp, ear-piercing, ear-splitting, penetrating.
■ **shrillness** n. **shrilly** adv.

shrimp n. (pl. **shrimp** or **shrimps**) a small edible shellfish.

shrine n. a place connected with a holy person or event, where people go to pray.

shrink v. (**shrinking**, **shrank**; past part. **shrunk** or (esp. as adj.) **shrunken**) **1** become or make smaller. **2** move back or away in fear or disgust.
▷ SYNONYMS: **1 get smaller**, contract, diminish, lessen, reduce, decrease, dwindle, decline, fall off. **2 recoil**, shy away, flinch, be averse, be afraid, hesitate.
– ANTONYMS: expand, increase.
• n. informal a psychiatrist.
■ **shrinkage** n.

shrivel v. (**shrivelling**, **shrivelled**; US **shriveling**, **shriveled**) wrinkle and shrink through loss of moisture.
▷ SYNONYMS: **wither**, shrink, wilt, dry up, dehydrate, parch, frazzle.

shroud n. **1** a length of cloth in which a dead person is wrapped for burial. **2** a thing covering or hiding something.
▷ SYNONYMS: **covering**, cover, cloak, mantle, blanket, layer, cloud, veil, winding sheet.
• v. cover or hide.
▷ SYNONYMS: **cover**, envelop, veil, cloak, blanket, screen, conceal, hide, mask, obscure.

shrub n. a woody plant smaller than a tree.
■ **shrubby** adj.

shrubbery n. (pl. **shrubberies**) an area planted with shrubs.

shrug v. (**shrugging**, **shrugged**) **1** raise the shoulders briefly as a sign of

indifference or ignorance. **2** (**shrug off**) treat as unimportant.
•n. an act of shrugging.

shrunk (or **shrunken**) past part. of **SHRINK**.

shudder v. tremble or shake violently.
▷ SYNONYMS: **shake**, shiver, tremble, quiver, judder.
•n. an act of shuddering.
▷ SYNONYMS: **shake**, shiver, tremor, trembling, quivering, judder, vibration.

shuffle v. **1** walk without lifting the feet clear of the ground. **2** reorder a pack of cards. **3** rearrange.
▷ SYNONYMS: **1 shamble**, hobble, limp, drag your feet. **2 mix up**, rearrange, jumble up, reorganize.
•n. an act of shuffling.

shun v. (**shunning, shunned**) avoid or reject.
▷ SYNONYMS: **avoid**, steer clear of, give a wide berth to, have nothing to do with; informal freeze out; Brit. informal send to Coventry.
– ANTONYMS: welcome.

shunt v. push or pull a train from one set of tracks to another.

shut v. (**shutting, shut**) **1** move into position to block an opening. **2** (**shut in/out**) keep in or out by closing a door etc. **3** prevent access to. **4** (referring to a shop etc.) stop operating for business. **5** close a book, curtains, etc.
▷ SYNONYMS: **close**, pull to, push to, slam, fasten, put the lid on, lock, secure.
– ANTONYMS: open.
□ **shut down** cease business or operation. **shut up** informal stop talking.

shutter n. **1** a pair of hinged panels that can be closed over a window. **2** a device that opens and closes to expose the film in a camera.
■ **shuttered** adj.

shuttle n. **1** a form of transport travelling regularly between two places. **2** a bobbin carrying the weft thread in weaving.
•v. **1** travel regularly between places. **2** transport in a shuttle.
▷ SYNONYMS: **commute**, run, ply, go/travel back and forth, ferry.
□ **shuttlecock** a light cone-shaped object, struck with rackets in badminton.

shy adj. nervous or timid in the company of others.
▷ SYNONYMS: **bashful**, diffident, timid, reserved, introverted, retiring, self-effacing, withdrawn.
– ANTONYMS: confident.
•v. (**shying, shied**) **1** (of a horse) turn aside in fright. **2** (**shy away from**) avoid through lack of confidence. **3** throw.
■ **shyly** adv. **shyness** n.

SI abbrev. Système International, the international system of units of measurement.

Siamese adj. of Siam (the former name for Thailand).
□ **Siamese cat** a breed of cat with pale fur and darker face, paws, and tail. **Siamese twins** twins whose bodies are joined at birth.

sibilant adj. making a hissing sound.

sibling n. a brother or sister.

sibyl n. (in ancient Greece and Rome) a woman believed to pass on prophecies from a god.

sic adv. written exactly as it stands in the original.

sick adj. **1** ill. **2** wanting to vomit. **3** (**sick of**) bored by or annoyed with. **4** informal (of humour) dealing with unpleasant subjects in an offensive way.
▷ SYNONYMS: **1 ill**, unwell, poorly, ailing, indisposed, out of sorts; informal under the weather, laid up; Austral./NZ informal crook. **2 nauseous**, queasy, bilious, green about the gills. **3** *I'm sick of this music:* fed up, bored, tired, weary, jaded. **4 macabre**, tasteless, ghoulish, morbid, black, gruesome, perverted, cruel.
– ANTONYMS: well.

sicken v. **1** disgust or shock. **2** (**be sickening for**) start to develop an illness.
▷ SYNONYMS: **1 nauseate**, make sick, turn someone's stomach, disgust, revolt, repel, appal; N. Amer. informal gross out. **2 fall ill**, become infected, be stricken.

sickening adj. disgusting.
▷ SYNONYMS: **nauseating**, repulsive, revolting, repellent, repugnant, disgusting, offensive, off-putting, distasteful, obscene, gruesome, grisly, vile; N. Amer. vomitous; informal gross, ghastly.

sickle n. a short-handled cutting tool with a curved blade.

sickly adj. (**sicklier, sickliest**) **1** often ill. **2** looking unhealthy. **3** so bright or sweet as to cause sickness.
▷ SYNONYMS: **1 unhealthy**, in poor health, delicate, frail, weak. **2 pale**, wan, pasty, sallow, pallid, ashen, anaemic. **3 sentimental**, mawkish, cloying, sugary, syrupy, saccharine; informal slushy, schmaltzy, cheesy,

S

corny; Brit. informal soppy.
– ANTONYMS: healthy.

sickness n. **1** the state of being ill. **2** an illness or disease. **3** nausea or vomiting.

▷ SYNONYMS: **1 illness**, disease, ailment, infection, malady, infirmity; informal bug, virus; Brit. informal lurgy. **2 nausea**, biliousness, queasiness, vomiting, retching; informal throwing up, puking.

side n. **1** a position to the left or right of an object, place, or central point. **2** either of the halves into which something is divided. **3** a surface of an object, esp. one that is not the top, bottom, front, or back. **4** a part near the edge of something. **5** a person or group opposing another in a dispute or contest. **6** a particular aspect. **7** each of the lines forming the boundary of a plane figure.

▷ SYNONYMS: **1 edge**, border, verge, boundary, margin, rim, fringe, flank, bank, perimeter, extremity, periphery, limits. **2 district**, quarter, area, region, part, neighbourhood, sector, zone. **3 surface**, face. **4 faction**, camp, bloc, party, wing. **5 team**, squad, line-up. **6 point of view**, viewpoint, perspective, opinion, standpoint, position, outlook, slant, angle, aspect, facet.
– ANTONYMS: centre, end.
• v. (**side with/against**) support or oppose in a conflict or dispute.
• adj. additional or less important.
▷ SYNONYMS: **subordinate**, secondary, minor, peripheral, incidental, subsidiary.
– ANTONYMS: main, central.
▫ **sideboard** a piece of furniture with cupboards and drawers for crockery, glasses, etc. **sideboards** Brit. (or **sideburns**) a strip of hair growing down each side of a man's face. **sidecar** a small passenger vehicle attached to one side of a motorcycle. **side effect** a secondary, usu. bad effect of a drug. **sidelong** to or from one side; sideways. **side-saddle** (of a rider) sitting with both feet on the same side of the horse. **sideshow** a small show or stall at a fair etc. **sidestep 1** avoid by stepping sideways. **2** avoid dealing with or discussing. **sidetrack** distract. **sidewalk** US a pavement. **sideways** to, towards, or from the side.

> **WORD LINKS**
> **lateral** relating to the side or sides of something

sideline n. **1** an activity done in addition to someone's main job. **2** either of the two lines along the longer sides of a sports field or court.
• v. remove from an influential position.
▫ **on/from the sidelines** watching something but not involved in it.

sidereal /sy-deer-i-uhl/ adj. of the stars or their apparent positions in the sky.

siding n. a short track beside a railway, where trains are left.

sidle v. walk in a stealthy or timid way.

siege n. a military operation in which forces surround a town and cut off its supplies.

sienna n. a brownish earth used as a pigment.

sierra n. a long jagged mountain chain.

siesta n. an afternoon rest or nap.

sieve n. a piece of mesh held in a frame, used for straining solids from liquids or separating coarser from finer particles.
• v. put through a sieve.

sift v. **1** sieve. **2** examine to select what is important.
▷ SYNONYMS: **1 sieve**, strain, screen, filter. **2** we sift out unsuitable applications: **separate out**, filter out, sort out, weed out, get rid of, remove. **3** sifting through the data: **search**, look, examine, inspect, scrutinize.

sigh v. let out a long, deep, breath expressing sadness, relief, etc.
▷ SYNONYMS: **1 breathe out**, exhale, groan, moan. **2 rustle**, whisper, murmur.
• n. an act of sighing.

sight n. **1** the ability to see. **2** the act of seeing. **3** the distance within which someone can see. **4** a thing seen or worth seeing. **5** informal a person or thing that looks ridiculous or unattractive. **6** a device looked through to aim a gun or see with a telescope.
▷ SYNONYMS: **1 eyesight**, vision, eyes. **2 view**, glimpse, glance, look. **3 landmark**, place of interest, monument, spectacle, marvel, wonder.
• v. see or glimpse.
▷ SYNONYMS: **glimpse**, catch sight of, see, spot, spy, make out, pick out, notice, observe.
▫ **sight-read** perform music without previous study of the score.
■ **sighted** adj. **sightless** adj.

> **WORD LINKS**
> **optical**, **visual** relating to sight or vision

sightseeing n. visiting places of interest.
  ■ **sightseer** n.
sign n. **1** an indication that something exists, is occurring, or may occur. **2** a signal, gesture, or notice giving information or an instruction. **3** a symbol or word representing something in algebra, music, etc. **4** each of the twelve divisions of the zodiac.
  ▷ SYNONYMS: **1 indication**, signal, symptom, pointer, suggestion, intimation, mark, manifestation, demonstration, token. **2 warning**, omen, portent, threat, promise. **3 notice**, board, placard, signpost. **4 symbol**, figure, emblem, device, logo, character.
  • v. **1** write your name on something to authorize it. **2** recruit or be recruited by signing a contract. **3** use gestures to give instructions.
  ▷ SYNONYMS: **1 autograph**, initial, countersign. **2 endorse**, validate, agree to, approve, ratify.
  □ **sign on 1** commit yourself to a job. **2** Brit. register as unemployed.
signpost a sign on a post, giving the direction and distance to a place.
sign up commit yourself to a course, job, etc.
signal n. **1** a gesture, action, or sound giving information or an instruction. **2** a device that indicates whether a road or railway is clear. **3** an electrical impulse or radio wave sent or received.
  ▷ SYNONYMS: **1 gesture**, gesticulation, sign, wave, cue, indication, warning, prompt, reminder. **2 indication**, sign, symptom, hint, pointer, clue, demonstration, evidence, proof.
  • v. (**signalling**, **signalled**; US **signaling**, **signaled**) **1** give a signal. **2** show by means of a signal.
  ▷ SYNONYMS: **1 gesture**, gesticulate, sign, indicate, motion, wave, beckon, nod. **2** *his death signals the end of an era:* **mark**, signify, mean, indicate, be a sign of, be evidence of.
  • adj. noteworthy.
  □ **signal box** Brit. a building beside a railway track from which signals and points are controlled.
signatory n. (pl. **signatories**) a person who has signed an agreement.
signature n. a person's name written in a distinctive way, used in signing something.
  □ **signature tune** a tune announcing a particular television or radio programme.
signet ring n. a ring with an engraved design.
significance n. **1** importance. **2** meaning.
  ▷ SYNONYMS: **importance**, import, consequence, seriousness, gravity, weight, magnitude.
significant adj. **1** important or large enough to have an effect. **2** having a particular or secret meaning.
  ▷ SYNONYMS: **1 notable**, noteworthy, remarkable, important, of consequence, momentous. **2 large**, considerable, sizeable, appreciable, conspicuous, obvious, sudden. **3 meaningful**, expressive, eloquent, suggestive, knowing, telling.
  ■ **significantly** adv.
signify v. (**signifying**, **signified**) **1** be a sign of; mean. **2** make known.
  ▷ SYNONYMS: **mean**, denote, designate, represent, symbolize, stand for.
  ■ **signification** n.
Sikh /seek/ n. a follower of a religion that developed from Hinduism.
  ■ **Sikhism** n.
silage /sy-lij/ n. grass or green crops stored in a silo without being dried, used as animal feed.
silence n. complete lack of sound or speech.
  ▷ SYNONYMS: **1 quietness**, quiet, still, stillness, hush, tranquillity, peace, peacefulness. **2 failure to speak**, dumbness, muteness, reticence, taciturnity.
  – ANTONYMS: noise, loquacity.
  • v. make silent.
  ▷ SYNONYMS: **1 quieten**, quiet, hush, still, muffle. **2 gag**, muzzle, censor.
silencer n. a device for reducing the noise made by a gun or (Brit.) exhaust system.
silent adj. **1** without sound. **2** not speaking or not spoken aloud.
  ▷ SYNONYMS: **1 quiet**, still, hushed, noiseless, soundless, inaudible. **2 speechless**, quiet, unspeaking, dumb, mute, taciturn, uncommunicative, tight-lipped. **3 unspoken**, wordless, tacit, unvoiced, unexpressed, implied, implicit, understood.
  – ANTONYMS: audible, loquacious.
  ■ **silently** adv.
silhouette n. a dark shadow or outline seen against a lighter background.
  ▷ SYNONYMS: **outline**, contour, profile, form, shape.
  • v. show as a silhouette.
  ▷ SYNONYMS: **outline**, define.

s

silica n. a compound of silicon occurring as quartz and found in sandstone.

silicon n. a non-metallic element, used to make electronic circuits.
□ **silicon chip** a microchip.

silicone n. a substance made from silicon, used in implants etc.

silk n. a fine, soft shiny fibre produced by silkworms, made into thread or fabric.
□ **silkworm** a caterpillar that spins a silk cocoon.
■ **silken** adj. **silky** adj.

sill n. a shelf or ledge at the foot of a window or doorway.

silly adj. (**sillier**, **silliest**) lacking common sense or judgement.
▷ SYNONYMS: **1 foolish**, stupid, inane, feather-brained, birdbrained, frivolous, immature, childish, empty-headed, scatterbrained; informal dotty, scatty. **2 unwise**, imprudent, thoughtless, foolish, stupid, unintelligent, rash, reckless, foolhardy, irresponsible, hare-brained; informal crazy, barmy; Brit. informal daft. **3** *he brooded about silly things*: trivial, trifling, petty, small, insignificant, unimportant.
– ANTONYMS: sensible.
■ **silliness** n.

silo n. (pl. **silos**) **1** a tower for storing grain. **2** a pit or airtight structure for storing silage. **3** an underground chamber in which a guided missile is kept ready for firing.

silt n. fine sand or clay deposited by running water.
• v. (**silt up**) fill or block with silt.

silvan var. of SYLVAN.

silver n. **1** a shiny greyish-white precious metal. **2** a shiny grey-white colour. **3** coins or articles made of silver or of a metal resembling silver.
□ **silverfish** a small wingless insect. **silver jubilee** the 25th anniversary of an important event. **silverside** Brit. a joint of beef from the outside of the leg. **silver wedding** Brit. the 25th anniversary of a wedding.
■ **silvery** adj.

SIM card n. an electronic card in a mobile phone that stores personal data etc.

simian adj. of or like apes or monkeys.

similar adj. alike but not identical.
▷ SYNONYMS: **alike**, like, much the same, comparable, corresponding, equivalent, parallel, analogous, kindred; informal much of a muchness.
– ANTONYMS: different, dissimilar.

■ **similarly** adv.

similarity n. (pl. **similarities**) the state of being similar, or a similar feature or aspect.
▷ SYNONYMS: **resemblance**, likeness, comparability, correspondence, parallel, equivalence, uniformity.

simile /sim-i-li/ n. a phrase that compares one thing to another, using *as* or *like*.

simmer v. **1** stay or keep just below boiling point. **2** be full of barely suppressed anger or excitement. **3** (**simmer down**) become calmer.
▷ SYNONYMS: **1 boil gently**, cook gently, bubble, stew, poach. **2 seethe**, fume, smoulder.

simper v. smile coyly.
• n. a coy smile.

simple adj. **1** easily understood or done. **2** plain and basic. **3** composed of a single element. **4** of very low intelligence.
▷ SYNONYMS: **1 straightforward**, easy, uncomplicated, uninvolved, undemanding, elementary; informal child's play, a cinch, a piece of cake, like falling off a log. **2 clear**, plain, lucid, unambiguous, understandable, comprehensible, accessible; informal user-friendly. **3 plain**, unadorned, basic, unsophisticated, no-frills, classic, understated, uncluttered, restrained; unpretentious, unsophisticated.
– ANTONYMS: difficult, complex, ornate.
■ **simplicity** n.

simpleton n. a foolish or unintelligent person.

simplify v. (**simplifying**, **simplified**) make easier to do or understand.
▷ SYNONYMS: **make simpler**, clarify, put into words of one syllable, streamline; informal dumb down.
– ANTONYMS: complicate.
■ **simplification** n.

simplistic adj. treating complex issues as more simple than they really are.
■ **simplistically** adv.

simply adv. **1** in a simple way. **2** merely; just. **3** absolutely; completely.
▷ SYNONYMS: **1** *they stay together simply because there's no alternative*: merely, just, purely, solely, only. **2** *she was simply delighted*: utterly, absolutely, completely, positively, just; informal plain.

simulate v. **1** imitate. **2** produce a computer model of. **3** pretend to feel.
▷ SYNONYMS: **1 feign**, pretend, fake, affect, put on. **2 replicate**, reproduce,

imitate, mimic.
■ **simulation** n. **simulator** n.
simultaneous adj. occurring or done at the same time.
▷ SYNONYMS: **concurrent**, happening at the same time, contemporaneous, coinciding, coincident, synchronized.
– ANTONYMS: separate.
■ **simultaneity** n.
simultaneously adv. at the same time.
▷ SYNONYMS: **at the same time**, at one and the same time, at once, concurrently, together, in unison, in concert, in chorus.
sin n. an act that breaks a religious or moral law.
▷ SYNONYMS: **1 wrong**, transgression, crime, offence, misdeed; old use trespass. **2 wickedness**, wrongdoing, evil, immorality, iniquity, vice, crime.
– ANTONYMS: virtue.
• v. (**sinning, sinned**) commit a sin.
▷ SYNONYMS: **transgress**, do wrong, err, go astray; old use trespass.
■ **sinner** n.
since prep. in the period between a time in the past until the present.
• conj. **1** from the time that. **2** because.
• adv. from the time mentioned until the present.
sincere adj. not pretending to be or feel; genuine and honest.
▷ SYNONYMS: **1 heartfelt**, wholehearted, profound, deep, true, honest, earnest, fervent. **2 honest**, genuine, truthful, direct, frank, candid; informal straight, on the level, upfront; N. Amer. informal on the up and up.
■ **sincerely** adv.
sincerity n. the quality of being sincere.
▷ SYNONYMS: **genuineness**, honesty, truthfulness, integrity, directness, openness, candour.
sine n. (in a right-angled triangle) the ratio of the side opposite a particular acute angle to the hypotenuse.
sinecure /sin-i-kyoor/ n. a paid job requiring little or no work.
sine qua non /see-nay kwah nohn/ n. a thing that is absolutely necessary.
sinew n. a band of strong tissue joining muscle to bone.
■ **sinewy** adj.
sinful adj. wicked.
▷ SYNONYMS: **immoral**, wicked, wrong, evil, bad, iniquitous, ungodly, irreligious, sacrilegious.
– ANTONYMS: virtuous.
■ **sinfully** adv. **sinfulness** n.
sing v. (**singing, sang**; past part. **sung**)

1 make musical sounds with the voice in the form of a song. **2** make a whistling sound.
▷ SYNONYMS: **1 chant**, intone, croon, chorus. **2 trill**, warble, chirp, chirrup, cheep.
□ **sing-song 1** a rising and falling rhythm in a person's voice. **2** Brit. informal an informal gathering for singing.
singe v. burn slightly.
▷ SYNONYMS: **scorch**, burn, sear, char.
• n. a slight burn.
singer n. a person who sings.
▷ SYNONYMS: **vocalist**, songster, songstress, soloist, chorister, cantor.
single adj. **1** one only. **2** designed for one person. **3** consisting of one part. **4** individual and distinct. **5** not involved in a romantic or sexual relationship. **6** Brit. (of a ticket) for an outward journey only.
▷ SYNONYMS: **1 sole**, one, lone, solitary, unaccompanied, alone. **2 individual**, separate, particular, distinct. **3 unmarried**, unwed, unattached, free.
– ANTONYMS: double, multiple.
• n. **1** a single person or thing. **2** a short record or CD. **3** (**singles**) a game or contest for individual players.
• v. (**single out**) choose from a group.
□ **single-breasted** (of a coat) having one row of buttons at the centre of the front. **single-handed** done without help. **single market** an association of countries trading with few or no restrictions. **single parent** a person bringing up a child or children without a partner.
■ **singly** adv.
single-minded adj. concentrating on one particular aim.
▷ SYNONYMS: **determined**, committed, unswerving, unwavering, resolute, purposeful, devoted, dedicated, uncompromising, tireless, tenacious, persistent, dogged.
– ANTONYMS: half-hearted.
singlet n. a sleeveless vest.
singleton n. a single person or thing.
singular adj. **1** (of a word or form) referring to just one person or thing. **2** very good; remarkable.
• n. the singular form of a word.
■ **singularity** n. **singularly** adv.
sinister adj. seeming evil or dangerous.
▷ SYNONYMS: **1 menacing**, threatening, forbidding, baleful, frightening, alarming, disturbing, ominous. **2 evil**, wicked, criminal, nefarious,

S

villainous; informal **shady**.
– ANTONYMS: innocent.
sink v. (**sinking**, **sank**; past part. **sunk**)
1 go down below the surface of
liquid. **2** go or send to the bottom of
the sea. **3** move slowly downwards.
4 decrease in amount or strength.
5 force something sharp through a
surface. **6** (**sink in**) be understood.
7 invest money.
▷ SYNONYMS: **1 submerge**, founder,
capsize, go down, be engulfed.
2 scuttle; Brit. scupper. **3 fall**, drop,
descend, plunge, plummet, slump.
4 embed, insert, drive, plant.
– ANTONYMS: float, rise.
  • n. a fixed basin with taps and a
drainage pipe.
sinker n. a weight used to keep a
fishing line beneath the water.
sinuous adj. **1** curving. **2** gracefully
swaying.
sinus /sy-nuhss/ n. a hollow space in
the bones of the face that connects
with the nostrils.
sinusitis n. inflammation of a sinus.
sip v. (**sipping**, **sipped**) drink in small
mouthfuls.
▷ SYNONYMS: **drink**, taste, sample, nip.
  • n. a small mouthful of liquid.
▷ SYNONYMS: **mouthful**, swallow, drink,
drop, dram, nip; informal swig.
siphon n. a tube for transferring
liquid from one container to another,
using air pressure so as to maintain
the flow.
  • v. **1** draw off by means of a siphon.
2 (**siphon off**) take small amounts of
money over time.
sir n. **1** a polite form of address to a
man. **2** used as the title of a knight or
baronet.
sire n. **1** an animal's male parent. **2** old
use a respectful form of address to
a king.
  • v. be the male parent of.
siren n. **1** a device that makes a long
loud warning sound. **2** an attractive
but dangerous woman.
sirloin n. the best part of a loin of
beef.
sirocco n. (pl. **siroccos**) a hot wind
blowing from Africa to southern
Europe.
sisal n. fibre made from a tropical
plant, used for ropes or matting.
sissy n. (pl. **sissies**) informal an
effeminate or weak person.
sister n. **1** a woman or girl in relation
to other children of her parents. **2** a
female friend or colleague. **3** a nun.
4 Brit. a senior female nurse.

□ **sisterhood 1** friendship and
understanding between women.
2 a group of women with a shared
interest. **sister-in-law** (pl. **sisters-in-
law**) the sister of a person's wife or
husband, or the wife of a person's
brother.
■ **sisterly** adj.
sit v. (**sitting**, **sat**) **1** rest your weight on
your buttocks with your back upright.
2 be in a particular position or state.
3 be a member of a committee etc.
4 (of a parliament, law court, etc.) be
carrying on its business. **5** pose for a
portrait. **6** Brit. take an exam.
▷ SYNONYMS: **1 take a seat**, sit down, be
seated, perch, ensconce yourself, flop;
informal take the load off your feet;
Brit. informal take a pew. **2 be placed**,
be positioned, be situated, be set,
rest, stand, perch. **3** she sits on the
tribunal: **serve on**, have a seat on, be a
member of. **4 be in session**, meet, be
convened.
– ANTONYMS: stand.

USAGE Use **sitting** rather than **sat** with
the verb 'to be': we were sitting there
for hours not we were sat there for
hours.

sitar n. a long-necked Indian lute.
sitcom n. informal a situation comedy.
site n. **1** a place where something is,
was, or will be located. **2** a website.
▷ SYNONYMS: **location**, place, position,
situation, locality, whereabouts.
  • v. establish or build in a particular
place.
▷ SYNONYMS: **place**, put, position,
situate, locate.
sitter n. **1** a person who sits for an
artist. **2** a babysitter.
sitting n. **1** a period of time when a
group are served a meal. **2** a period of
time when a law court etc. is carrying
on its business. **3** a period of posing
for a portrait.
□ **sitting room** a room for relaxing in.
sitting tenant Brit. a tenant who has
the legal right to remain living in a
property.
situate v. put in a particular place.
situation n. **1** a set of circumstances.
2 the location and surroundings of a
place. **3** a job.
▷ SYNONYMS: **1 circumstances**, state
of affairs, affairs, state, condition,
case, predicament, plight. **2 location**,
position, spot, site, setting,
environment. **3 post**, position, job,
employment.
□ **situation comedy** a comedy series

in which the same characters are involved in amusing situations.
■ **situational** adj.

six adj. & n. one more than five; 6.
■ **sixth** adj. & n.

sixteen adj. & n. one more than fifteen; 16.
■ **sixteenth** adj. & n.

sixty adj. & n. (pl. **sixties**) ten more than fifty; 60.
■ **sixtieth** adj. & n.

size n. **1** the overall measurements or extent of something. **2** each of the series of standard measurements in which articles are made. **3** a sticky solution used to glaze paper, stiffen textiles, etc.
▷ SYNONYMS: **dimensions**, measurements, proportions, magnitude, largeness, area, expanse, breadth, width, length, height, depth.
• v. (**size up**) assess.

sizeable (or **sizable**) adj. fairly large.
▷ SYNONYMS: **large**, substantial, considerable, respectable, significant, goodly.
– ANTONYMS: small.

sizzle v. (of food) hiss when being fried.
▷ SYNONYMS: **crackle**, fizzle, sputter, hiss, spit.

skate n. **1** an ice skate or roller skate. **2** an edible flatfish.
• v. **1** move on skates. **2** (**skate over**) refer only briefly to.
▫ **skateboard** a narrow board with wheels fixed to the bottom, for riding on while standing.
■ **skater** n.

skedaddle v. informal leave quickly.

skein /skayn/ n. a loosely coiled bundle of yarn.

skeletal adj. **1** of the skeleton. **2** very thin.

skeleton n. **1** a framework of bone or cartilage supporting or containing an animal's body. **2** a supporting structure.
• adj. comprising an essential or minimum number: *a skeleton staff.*
▫ **skeleton key** a key designed to fit many locks.

skeptic US = SCEPTIC.

sketch n. **1** a rough drawing. **2** a short humorous scene in a comedy show. **3** a brief account.
▷ SYNONYMS: **drawing**, outline, draft, diagram, design, plan; informal rough.
• v. make a sketch of.
▷ SYNONYMS: **draw**, make a drawing of, pencil, rough out, outline.

sketchy adj. not thorough or detailed.
▷ SYNONYMS: **incomplete**, patchy, fragmentary, scrappy, cursory, perfunctory, scanty, vague, inadequate, insufficient.
– ANTONYMS: detailed.
■ **sketchily** adv.

skew v. **1** suddenly change direction or move at an angle. **2** make biased or distorted.
▫ **skewbald** (of a horse) having patches of white and brown.

skewer n. a thin length of wood or metal for holding pieces of food during cooking.
• v. hold or pierce with a skewer.

ski n. (pl. **skis**) each of a pair of long, narrow pieces of plastic etc. attached to boots for travelling over snow.
• v. (**skiing**, **skied**) travel on skis.
■ **skier** n.

skid v. (**skidding**, **skidded**) slide sideways in an uncontrolled way.
• n. an act of skidding.

skiff n. a light rowing boat.

skilful (US **skillful**) adj. having or showing skill.
▷ SYNONYMS: **expert**, accomplished, skilled, masterly, talented, deft, dexterous, handy; informal mean, crack, ace; N. Amer. informal crackerjack.
– ANTONYMS: incompetent.
■ **skilfully** adv.

> **USAGE** There is only one *l* in the middle in British English: *skilful.*

skill n. **1** the ability to do something well. **2** a particular ability.
▷ SYNONYMS: **expertise**, accomplishment, skilfulness, mastery, talent, deftness, dexterity, prowess, competence, artistry.
– ANTONYMS: incompetence.
■ **skilled** adj.

skillet n. US a frying pan.

skim v. (**skimming**, **skimmed**) **1** remove a substance from the surface of a liquid. **2** glide. **3** read quickly. **4** (**skim over**) deal with briefly.
▷ SYNONYMS: **1** *skim off the fat:* **remove**, scoop off, separate. **2** **glide**, move lightly, slide, sail, skate. **3** *she skimmed through the paper:* **glance**, flick, flip, leaf, thumb, scan, run your eye over.
▫ **skimmed milk** milk from which the cream has been removed.

skimp v. spend less money, time, etc. than is really needed.

skimpy adj. (**skimpier**, **skimpiest**) **1** meagre. **2** (of clothes) short and revealing.

skin n. **1** the thin layer of tissue

S

forming the outer covering of the body. **2** the skin of a dead animal used for clothing etc. **3** an outer layer.
▷ SYNONYMS: **1 hide**, pelt, fleece. **2 peel**, rind. **3 film**, layer, membrane, crust, covering, coating.

• v. (**skinning**, **skinned**) remove the skin from.
▷ SYNONYMS: **1 peel**, pare. **2 graze**, scrape, abrade, bark, rub raw, chafe.
□ **skin-diving** swimming under water without a diving suit, using an aqualung and flippers. **skinflint** informal a miser. **skinhead** a young person of a group with very short shaved hair.

> **WORD LINKS**
> **cutaneous** relating to the skin
> **dermatology** the branch of medicine concerned with skin disorders

skinny adj. (**skinnier**, **skinniest**) very thin.
▷ SYNONYMS: **thin**, underweight, scrawny, bony, gaunt, emaciated, skeletal, wasted, pinched, spindly, gangly; informal anorexic.

skint adj. Brit. informal having little or no money.

skip v. (**skipping**, **skipped**) **1** move lightly, jumping from one foot to the other. **2** omit or miss. **3** Brit. jump repeatedly over a rope turned over the head and under the feet.
▷ SYNONYMS: **1 caper**, prance, trip, dance, bound, bounce, gambol. **2 omit**, leave out, miss out, dispense with, pass over, skim over, disregard; informal give something a miss.
• n. **1** a skipping movement. **2** Brit. a large open container for bulky refuse.

skipper n. informal a captain.

skirmish n. a short spell of fighting.
• v. take part in a skirmish.

skirt n. a woman's garment hanging from the waist, or this part of a coat or dress.
• v. **1** go round or past the edge of. **2** avoid dealing with.
▷ SYNONYMS: **1 go round**, walk round, circle. **2 border**, edge, flank, line. **3** *he skirted round the subject:* avoid, evade, sidestep, dodge, pass over, gloss over; informal duck.
□ **skirting board** Brit. a wooden board along the base of the wall of a room.

skit n. a short comedy sketch.

skittish adj. nervous, lively, or unpredictable.

skittle n. **1** (**skittles**) a game played with wooden pins set up to be bowled down with a ball. **2** a pin used in skittles.

skive v. Brit. informal avoid work or a duty by staying away or leaving early.
■ **skiver** n.

skivvy n. (pl. **skivvies**) Brit. informal a female domestic servant.

skulduggery n. underhand behaviour.

skulk v. loiter stealthily.

skull n. the bony framework surrounding the brain.
▷ SYNONYMS: cranium.
□ **skullcap** a small cap without a peak.

skunk n. a black-and-white striped mammal able to spray foul-smelling liquid.

sky n. (pl. **skies**) the upper atmosphere seen from the earth.
▷ SYNONYMS: literary the heavens, the firmament, the ether, the wide blue yonder.
□ **skydiving** the sport of parachuting from an aircraft and performing acrobatic movements in the air. **skylark** a lark that sings while in flight. **skylight** a window set in a roof. **skyscraper** a very tall building.

> **WORD LINKS**
> **celestial** relating to the sky

slab n. a broad, flat piece of something solid.
▷ SYNONYMS: **piece**, block, hunk, chunk, lump, cake, tablet, brick, panel, plate, sheet.

slack adj. **1** not taut or tight. **2** not busy. **3** careless or lazy.
▷ SYNONYMS: **1 limp**, loose; sagging, flabby, flaccid, saggy. **2 sluggish**, slow, quiet, slow-moving, flat, depressed, stagnant. **3 lax**, negligent, careless, slapdash, slipshod; informal sloppy.
– ANTONYMS: taut, firm.
• n. **1** a slack part of a rope. **2** (**slacks**) casual trousers.
• v. **1** Brit. informal work slowly. **2** decrease in intensity or speed.
▷ SYNONYMS: **idle**, shirk, be lazy, be indolent, waste time, lounge about; Brit. informal skive; N. Amer. informal goof off.
■ **slacken** v. **slacker** n. **slackness** n.

slag n. **1** stony waste left when metal has been smelted. **2** Brit. informal, derogatory a promiscuous woman.
• v. (**slagging**, **slagged**) (**slag off**) Brit. informal criticize rudely.

slain past part. of SLAY.

slake v. satisfy a thirst.

slalom n. a skiing or canoeing race following a winding course.

slam v. (**slamming**, **slammed**) **1** shut forcefully and loudly. **2** put or hit with great force. **3** informal criticize

severely.
▷ SYNONYMS: **bang**, thump, crash, smash, plough, run, bump, collide with, hit, strike, ram; N. Amer. impact.
• n. a noise of slamming.

slander n. the crime of making false statements that damage a person's reputation.
• v. make false and harmful statements about.

slanderous adj. featuring or constituting slander.
▷ SYNONYMS: **defamatory**, denigratory, disparaging, libellous, pejorative, false, misrepresentative, scurrilous, scandalous, malicious.

slang n. very informal language used esp. in speech and by a particular group.

slant v. **1** slope. **2** present information from a particular point of view.
▷ SYNONYMS: **1 slope**, tilt, incline, tip, lean, dip, pitch, shelve, list, bank. **2 bias**, distort, twist, skew, weight.
• n. **1** a slope. **2** a point of view.
▷ SYNONYMS: **1 slope**, incline, tilt, gradient, pitch, angle, camber. **2 point of view**, viewpoint, standpoint, stance, angle, perspective, approach, view, attitude, position, bias, spin.
■ **slantwise** adv.

slap v. (**slapping**, **slapped**) **1** hit with the palm of the hand or a flat object. **2** place quickly or carelessly.
▷ SYNONYMS: **smack**, strike, hit, cuff, clip, spank; informal whack.
• n. an act of slapping.
▷ SYNONYMS: **smack**, blow, cuff, clip, spank; informal whack.
• adv. informal suddenly and forcefully.
□ **slapdash** hurried and careless.
slapstick comedy based on deliberately clumsy actions.

slash v. **1** cut with a sweeping stroke. **2** informal reduce greatly.
▷ SYNONYMS: **1 cut**, gash, slit, lacerate, knife. **2 reduce**, cut, lower, bring down, mark down.
• n. **1** a cut made with a sweeping stroke. **2** a slanting line (/) used between alternatives.
▷ SYNONYMS: **cut**, gash, slit, laceration, incision, wound.

slat n. a thin, narrow piece of wood etc.

slate n. a greyish rock that splits into smooth, flat plates, used for roofs and formerly for writing on.
• v. **1** Brit. informal criticize severely. **2** plan; schedule.

slattern n. old use a dirty, untidy woman.
■ **slatternly** adj.

slaughter n. **1** the killing of farm animals for food. **2** the killing of many people in a brutal way.
▷ SYNONYMS: **massacre**, murder, killing, execution, extermination, carnage, bloodshed, bloodletting, bloodbath; literary slaying.
• v. kill in this way.
▷ SYNONYMS: **1 kill**, butcher, cull, put down. **2 massacre**, murder, butcher, kill, exterminate, wipe out, put to death, execute; literary slay.
□ **slaughterhouse** a place where animals are killed for food.

Slav n. a member of a group of peoples in central and eastern Europe.
■ **Slavic** adj.

slave n. **1** hist. a person owned by another and forced to obey them. **2** a person strongly influenced or controlled by something.
▷ SYNONYMS: **servant**, lackey, drudge; Brit. informal skivvy, dogsbody; historical serf, vassal.
– ANTONYMS: master.
• v. work very hard.
▷ SYNONYMS: **toil**, labour, sweat, work like a Trojan/dog, work your fingers to the bone; informal sweat blood, slog away; Brit. informal graft.
□ **slave-driver** informal a person who makes others work very hard.

> **WORD LINKS**
> **servile** relating to or like a slave

slaver v. let saliva run from the mouth.

slavery n. **1** the state of being a slave. **2** the practice of owning slaves.
▷ SYNONYMS: **enslavement**, servitude, serfdom, bondage, captivity.
– ANTONYMS: freedom.

slavish adj. showing no originality.
■ **slavishly** adv.

slay v. (**slaying**, **slew**; past part. **slain**) old use kill.
■ **slayer** n.

sleaze n. informal immoral or dishonest behaviour.

sleazy adj. (**sleazier**, **sleaziest**) **1** immoral or dishonest. **2** dirty and seedy.
▷ SYNONYMS: **1 corrupt**, immoral, ignoble, dishonourable. **2 squalid**, seedy, seamy, sordid, insalubrious.
■ **sleaziness** n.

sled n. US a sledge.

sledge n. a vehicle on runners for travelling over snow.
• v. ride on a sledge.

sledgehammer n. a large, heavy hammer.

S

sleek adj. **1** smooth and glossy.
2 looking wealthy and smart.
▷ SYNONYMS: **1 smooth**, glossy, shiny,
shining, lustrous, silken, silky.
2 streamlined, elegant, graceful.
– ANTONYMS: scruffy.

sleep n. a state of rest in which
the eyes are closed and the mind
unconscious.
▷ SYNONYMS: **nap**, doze, siesta, catnap;
informal snooze, forty winks, shut-eye;
Brit. informal kip; literary slumber.
• v. (**sleeping, slept**) **1** be asleep.
2 (**sleep in**) remain asleep later
than usual. **3** have sleeping
accommodation for.
▷ SYNONYMS: **be asleep**, doze, take a
siesta, take a nap, catnap; informal
snooze, get some shut-eye; Brit. informal
kip; literary slumber.
– ANTONYMS: wake up.
□ **sleeping bag** a padded bag to sleep
in. **sleeping partner** Brit. a partner
who invests in a business but is not
involved in running it. **sleepover** a
night spent by children at another
person's house. **sleepwalk** walk
around while asleep.
■ **sleepless** adj.

> **WORD LINKS**
> **sedative, soporific** causing
> drowsiness or sleep

sleeper n. **1** Brit. a beam on which a
railway track rests. **2** a ring or bar
worn in a pierced ear to keep the hole
from closing. **3** a train with carriages
having sleeping accommodation.
sleepy adj. (**sleepier, sleepiest**)
1 needing or ready for sleep.
2 without much activity.
▷ SYNONYMS: **1 drowsy**, tired, somnolent, heavy-eyed; informal dopey.
2 quiet, peaceful, tranquil, placid,
slow-moving, dull, boring.
– ANTONYMS: awake, alert.
■ **sleepily** adv. **sleepiness** n.
sleet n. rain containing snow.
• v. fall as sleet.
sleeve n. **1** the part of a garment
covering the arm. **2** a protective
cover.
□ **up your sleeve** secret but ready
for use.
■ **sleeveless** adj.
sleigh n. a sledge pulled by horses or
reindeer.
sleight /slyt/ n. (**sleight of hand**)
skilful use of the hands when
performing conjuring tricks.
slender adj. **1** gracefully thin. **2** barely
enough.

▷ SYNONYMS: **1 slim**, lean, willowy,
svelte, lissom, graceful, slight, thin,
skinny. **2 faint**, remote, tenuous,
fragile, slim, small, slight.
– ANTONYMS: plump, strong.
slept past & past part. of SLEEP.
sleuth /slooth/ n. informal a detective.
slew¹ v. turn or slide uncontrollably.
slew² past of SLAY.
slice n. **1** a thin, broad piece of food
cut from a larger portion. **2** a share.
3 a utensil for lifting food.
▷ SYNONYMS: **1 piece**, portion, slab,
wedge, rasher, sliver, wafer. **2 share**,
part, portion, tranche, percentage,
proportion, allocation; informal cut,
whack.
• v. **1** cut into slices. **2** (in sport) hit a
ball so that it spins and curves as it
travels.
▷ SYNONYMS: **cut**, carve, divide.
slick adj. **1** smooth and efficient. **2** self-
confident but insincere. **3** smooth and
glossy or slippery.
▷ SYNONYMS: **1 efficient**, smooth,
smooth-running, polished, well
organized, well run, streamlined.
2 glib, polished, assured, self-assured,
smooth-talking, plausible; informal
smarmy.
• n. a patch of oil.
• v. make hair smooth and glossy.
▷ SYNONYMS: **smooth**, plaster, sleek,
grease, oil, gel.
■ **slickly** adv. **slickness** n.
slide v. (**sliding, slid**) **1** move along a
smooth surface while remaining in
contact with it. **2** move smoothly or
without being noticed.
▷ SYNONYMS: **glide**, slip, slither, skim,
skate, skid, slew.
• n. **1** a structure with a smooth
sloping surface for sliding down.
2 a piece of glass on which an
object is placed for viewing under a
microscope. **3** a piece of photographic
film for viewing with a projector.
□ **sliding scale** a scale of fees,
wages, etc., that varies according to
particular conditions.
slight adj. **1** small in degree. **2** not
sturdy. **3** superficial or trivial.
▷ SYNONYMS: **1 small**, tiny, minute,
negligible, insignificant, minimal,
remote, slim, faint. **2 slim**, slender,
delicate, dainty, fragile.
– ANTONYMS: large, plump.
• v. treat disrespectfully.
▷ SYNONYMS: **insult**, snub, rebuff, spurn,
give someone the cold shoulder, cut
dead, take no notice of, scorn, ignore.
• n. an insult.

▷ SYNONYMS: **insult**, affront, snub, rebuff; informal put-down, slap in the face.
■ **slightly** adv.

slim adj. (**slimmer**, **slimmest**) **1** gracefully thin. **2** small in width. **3** very small.
▷ SYNONYMS: **1 slender**, lean, thin, willowy, sylphlike, svelte, lissom, slight, trim. **2** *a slim chance:* **slight**, small, slender, faint, remote.
− ANTONYMS: fat.
• v. (**slimming**, **slimmed**) Brit. become thinner.
□ **slimline** slender in design.
■ **slimmer** n.

slime n. an unpleasantly moist, slippery substance.

slimy adj. (**slimier**, **slimiest**) **1** like or covered by slime. **2** informal insincerely flattering.
▷ SYNONYMS: **slippery**, slithery, greasy, sticky, viscous; informal slippy.

sling n. **1** a loop of fabric used to support or lift something. **2** a strap or loop for hurling small missiles.
• v. (**slinging**, **slung**) **1** hang or carry loosely. **2** Brit. informal throw.
▷ SYNONYMS: **1 hang**, suspend, string, swing. **2 throw**, toss, fling, hurl, cast, pitch, lob, flip; informal chuck, heave, bung.

slink v. (**slinking**, **slunk**) move stealthily.

slinky adj. (of a garment) close-fitting and sexy.

slip v. (**slipping**, **slipped**) **1** lose your balance and slide. **2** slide out of position or from someone's grasp. **3** gradually worsen. **4** (**slip up**) make a careless error. **5** move or place quietly, quickly, or secretly. **6** get free from.
▷ SYNONYMS: **1 slide**, skid, slither, fall over, lose your balance, lose your footing, tumble. **2 creep**, steal, sneak, slide, sidle, slope, slink, tiptoe.
• n. **1** an act of slipping. **2** a minor mistake. **3** a petticoat. **4** a small piece of paper.
▷ SYNONYMS: **1 false step**, slide, skid, fall, tumble. **2 mistake**, error, blunder, gaffe, oversight, miscalculation, omission, lapse; informal slip-up, boo-boo, howler; Brit. informal boob, clanger, bloomer; N. Amer. informal goof, blooper.
□ **give someone the slip** informal escape from someone. **slipped disc** a displaced disc between vertebrae in the spine. **slip road** Brit. a road entering or leaving a motorway.

slipshod careless or disorganized. **slipstream** a current of air or water driven back by a propeller or jet engine. **slipway** a slope leading into water, for launching or landing boats.

slipper n. a light indoor shoe.

slippery adj. **1** difficult to hold or stand on because smooth or wet. **2** not trustworthy.
▷ SYNONYMS: **1 slithery**, greasy, oily, icy, glassy, smooth, slimy, wet; informal slippy. **2 sneaky**, sly, devious, crafty, cunning, tricky, evasive, scheming, unreliable, untrustworthy; informal shady, shifty; Brit. informal dodgy; Austral./NZ informal shonky.
■ **slipperiness** n.

slit n. a long, narrow cut or opening.
▷ SYNONYMS: **1 cut**, incision, split, slash, gash. **2 opening**, gap, chink, crack, aperture, slot.
• v. (**slitting**, **slit**) make a slit in.
▷ SYNONYMS: **cut**, slash, split open, slice open.

slither v. slide unsteadily.
▷ SYNONYMS: **slide**, slip, glide, wriggle, crawl, skid.

sliver n. a small, sharp piece.
▷ SYNONYMS: **splinter**, shard, chip, flake, shred, scrap, shaving, paring, piece, fragment.

slob n. Brit. informal a lazy, untidy person.

slobber v. slaver or dribble.
▷ SYNONYMS: **drool**, slaver, dribble, salivate.

sloe n. a small sour bluish-black fruit.

slog informal v. (**slogging**, **slogged**) **1** work hard. **2** move with effort. **3** hit hard.
• n. a period of hard work or travelling.

slogan n. a short, memorable phrase used in advertising or politics.
▷ SYNONYMS: **catchphrase**, catchline, motto, jingle; N. Amer. informal tag line.

sloop n. a sailing boat with one mast.

slop v. (**slopping**, **slopped**) spill or overflow.
• pl. n. (**slops**) **1** unappetizing semi-liquid food. **2** waste liquid.

slope n. a surface with one end higher than another.
▷ SYNONYMS: **tilt**, pitch, slant, angle, gradient, incline, inclination, fall, camber.
• v. **1** form a slope. **2** (**slope off**) informal leave without being noticed.
▷ SYNONYMS: **tilt**, slant, incline, lean, drop/fall away, descend, shelve, be cambered, rise, ascend, climb.

sloppy adj. (**sloppier**, **sloppiest**) **1** careless or disorganized.

2 containing too much liquid.
▷ SYNONYMS: **1 runny**, watery, liquid, mushy; informal gloopy. **2 careless**, slapdash, slipshod, disorganized, untidy, slack, slovenly; informal slap-happy.
■ **sloppily** adv. **sloppiness** n.

slosh v. move with a splashing sound.

slot n. **1** a long, narrow opening into which something may be inserted. **2** a place in an arrangement etc.
▷ SYNONYMS: **1 aperture**, slit, crack, hole, opening. **2 time**, spot, period, niche, space; informal window.
• v. (**slotting**, **slotted**) fit into a slot.
▷ SYNONYMS: **insert**, slide, fit, put, place.
□ **slot machine** a fruit machine or (Brit.) vending machine.

sloth /slohth/ n. **1** laziness. **2** a slow-moving tropical American mammal.
■ **slothful** adj.

slouch v. stand, move, or sit in a lazy, drooping way.
• n. a lazy, drooping posture.

slough[1] /slow/ n. a swamp.

slough[2] /sluf/ v. (of an animal) shed an old skin.

slovenly adj. **1** untidy. **2** careless.
▷ SYNONYMS: **1 scruffy**, untidy, messy, unkempt, ill-groomed, dishevelled, bedraggled, rumpled, frowzy. **2 careless**, slapdash, slipshod, haphazard, hit-or-miss, untidy, messy, negligent, lax, lackadaisical, slack; informal sloppy, slap-happy.
– ANTONYMS: tidy, careful.
■ **slovenliness** n.

slow adj. **1** not moving or able to move quickly. **2** taking a long time. **3** (of a clock etc.) showing a time earlier than the correct time. **4** not quick to understand or learn.
▷ SYNONYMS: **1 unhurried**, leisurely, steady, sedate, measured, ponderous, sluggish, plodding; gradual, step-by-step. **2 lengthy**, time-consuming, long-drawn-out, protracted, prolonged, gradual. **3 stupid**, unintelligent, obtuse; informal dense, dim, thick, slow on the uptake, dumb, dopey; Brit. informal dozy.
– ANTONYMS: fast, quick.
• v. reduce speed.
▷ SYNONYMS: **1 reduce speed**, go slower, decelerate, brake. **2 hold back**, hold up, delay, retard, set back, check, curb.
– ANTONYMS: accelerate.
□ **slow-worm** a small lizard without legs.
■ **slowly** adv. **slowness** n.

sludge n. thick, soft mud.

slug n. **1** a small creature like a snail without a shell. **2** a small amount of

an alcoholic drink. **3** a bullet.
• v. (**slugging**, **slugged**) informal hit hard.

sluggard n. a lazy person.

sluggish adj. **1** slow-moving. **2** not lively.
▷ SYNONYMS: **lethargic**, listless, lacking in energy, lifeless, inactive, slow, torpid, enervated.
– ANTONYMS: vigorous.
■ **sluggishly** adv. **sluggishness** n.

sluice /slooss/ n. **1** a sliding gate controlling a flow of water. **2** a channel for surplus water.
• v. rinse with water.

slum n. a run-down city area inhabited by very poor people.
▷ SYNONYMS: **hovel**; (**slums**) ghetto, shanty town.

slumber v. sleep.
• n. a sleep.

slump v. **1** sit or lean heavily and limply. **2** decline greatly.
▷ SYNONYMS: **1 sit heavily**, flop, collapse, sink; informal plonk yourself. **2 fall**, plummet, tumble, collapse, drop; informal crash, nosedive.
• n. a sudden fall in prices or demand.
▷ SYNONYMS: **1 fall**, drop, tumble, downturn, downswing, slide, decline, decrease; informal nosedive. **2 recession**, decline, depression, slowdown.
– ANTONYMS: rise, boom.

slung past & past part. of SLING.

slunk past & past part. of SLINK.

slur v. (**slurring**, **slurred**) **1** speak in an unclear way. **2** perform a group of musical notes in a flowing way.
▷ SYNONYMS: **mumble**, speak unclearly, garble.
• n. **1** an insult or accusation. **2** a curved line indicating that notes are to be slurred.
▷ SYNONYMS: **insult**, slight, slander, smear, allegation, imputation.

slurp v. eat or drink with a loud sucking sound.

slurry n. a semi-liquid mixture of water and manure, cement, or coal.

slush n. **1** partially melted snow or ice. **2** informal sentimental talk or writing.
□ **slush fund** a reserve of money for illegal purposes.
■ **slushy** adj.

slut n. a slovenly or promiscuous woman.
■ **sluttish** adj.

sly adj. **1** cunning and deceitful. **2** (of a remark etc.) suggesting secret knowledge.
▷ SYNONYMS: **1 cunning**, crafty, clever,

wily, artful, tricky, scheming, devious, underhand, sneaky. **2 roguish**, mischievous, impish, playful, wicked, arch, knowing. **3 surreptitious**, furtive, stealthy, covert.
– ANTONYMS: open, straightforward.
□ **on the sly** secretly.
■ **slyly** adv. **slyness** n.

smack n. **1** a slap. **2** a loud, sharp sound. **3** a loud kiss. **4** informal heroin. **5** a sailing boat with one mast.
▷ SYNONYMS: **slap**, blow, cuff, clip, spank; informal whack, wallop, clout.
• v. **1** slap. **2** part the lips noisily.
▷ SYNONYMS: **slap**, strike, hit, cuff, clip, spank; informal whack, wallop, clout.
□ **smack of 1** suggest the presence of. **2** taste of.

small adj. **1** of less than normal size. **2** not great in amount, power, or importance. **3** young.
▷ SYNONYMS: **1 little**, tiny, short, petite, diminutive, elfin, miniature, mini, minute, toy, baby, undersized, poky, cramped; Scottish wee; informal teeny, tiddly, pint-sized; Brit. informal titchy. **2 slight**, minor, unimportant, trifling, trivial, insignificant, inconsequential, negligible, inappreciable; informal piffling.
– ANTONYMS: big, large.
□ **smallholding** Brit. a small area of leased agricultural land. **small hours** the early hours of the morning after midnight. **smallpox** a viral disease with blisters that leave permanent scars. **small talk** polite conversation about unimportant matters.
■ **smallness** n.

smarmy adj. Brit. informal excessively and insincerely friendly.
▷ SYNONYMS: **unctuous**, ingratiating, slick, oily, greasy, obsequious, sycophantic, fawning; informal slimy.

smart adj. **1** neat and stylish. **2** fashionable and upmarket. **3** intelligent. **4** quick.
▷ SYNONYMS: **1 well dressed**, well turned out, stylish, chic, fashionable, modish, elegant, dapper; N. Amer. trig; informal natty, snappy. **2** a smart restaurant: **fashionable**, stylish, high-class, exclusive, chic, fancy; Brit. upmarket; N. Amer. high-toned; informal trendy, classy, swanky; Brit. informal swish; N. Amer. informal swank. **3 clever**, bright, intelligent, quick-witted, shrewd, astute, perceptive; informal brainy, quick on the uptake. **4** a smart pace: **brisk**, quick, fast, rapid, lively, energetic, vigorous; informal cracking.
– ANTONYMS: scruffy, stupid.
• v. **1** give a sharp, stinging pain. **2** feel annoyed or upset.
▷ SYNONYMS: **1 sting**, burn, tingle, prickle, hurt. **2** she smarted at the accusation: **feel hurt**, feel upset, take offence, feel aggrieved, feel indignant, be put out.
□ **smart card** a plastic card on which electronic information is stored.
■ **smarten** v. **smartly** adv. **smartness** n.

smash v. **1** break violently into pieces. **2** hit or collide forcefully. **3** destroy or ruin.
▷ SYNONYMS: **1 break**, shatter, splinter, crack; informal bust. **2** he smashed into a wall: **crash**, smack, slam, plough, run, bump, hit, strike, ram, collide with; N. Amer. impact.
• n. **1** an act of smashing. **2** informal a very successful song, film, etc.
▷ SYNONYMS: **crash**, collision, accident; N. Amer. wreck; informal pile-up; Brit. informal shunt.

smashing adj. Brit. informal excellent.

smattering n. **1** a small amount. **2** a slight knowledge.
▷ SYNONYMS: **bit**, little, modicum, touch, soupçon, rudiments, basics; informal smidgen, smidge, tad.

smear v. **1** coat or mark with a greasy or sticky substance. **2** damage the reputation of.
▷ SYNONYMS: **1 spread**, rub, daub, slap, cover, coat, smother, plaster. **2 smudge**, streak, mark. **3 sully**, tarnish, blacken, drag through the mud, damage, defame, malign, slander, libel; N. Amer. slur.
• n. **1** a greasy or sticky mark. **2** a false accusation.
▷ SYNONYMS: **1 streak**, smudge, daub, dab, spot, patch, blotch, mark; informal splodge. **2 accusation**, lie, untruth, slur, slander, libel, defamation.
□ **smear test** Brit. a test to detect signs of cervical cancer.

smell n. **1** the ability to sense things with the nose. **2** something sensed by the nose. **3** an act of smelling.
▷ SYNONYMS: **1 odour**, aroma, fragrance, scent, perfume, bouquet, nose. **2 stink**, stench, reek; Brit. informal pong, whiff.
• v. (**smelling**, **smelt** or **smelled**) **1** sense the smell of. **2** give off a smell.
▷ SYNONYMS: **1 scent**, sniff, get a whiff of, detect. **2 stink**, reek; Brit. informal pong, hum.

WORD LINKS
olfactory relating to the sense of smell

---

smelly adj. (**smellier**, **smelliest**) having

S

an unpleasant smell.
▷ SYNONYMS: **foul-smelling**, stinking, reeking, rank, fetid, malodorous, pungent; literary noisome.

smelt v. heat and melt ore to extract metal.

smidgen (or **smidgin**) n. informal a tiny amount.

smile v. turn up the corners of the mouth to show pleasure, amusement, or friendliness.
▷ SYNONYMS: **beam**, grin, smirk, simper, leer.
– ANTONYMS: frown.
• n. an act of smiling.

smirk v. smile smugly.
▷ SYNONYMS: **sneer**, simper, snigger, leer, grin.
• n. a smug smile.

smite v. (**smiting**, **smote**; past part. **smitten**) old use hit hard.

smith n. **1** a worker in metal. **2** a blacksmith.

smithereens pl. n. informal small pieces.

smithy n. (pl. **smithies**) a blacksmith's workshop.

smitten adj. **1** strongly attracted to someone. **2** severely affected by a disease.
▷ SYNONYMS: **1 infatuated**, besotted, in love, obsessed, head over heels, enamoured, captivated, enchanted, under someone's spell; informal bowled over, swept off your feet. **2 struck down**, laid low, suffering, affected, afflicted.

smock n. a loose dress, shirt, or overall.

smog n. fog or haze made worse by atmospheric pollution.

smoke n. **1** a visible vapour produced by a burning substance. **2** an act of smoking tobacco.
▷ SYNONYMS: **fumes**, exhaust, gas, vapour, smog.
• v. **1** give out smoke. **2** breathe smoke from a cigarette etc. in and out. **3** preserve meat or fish by exposure to smoke.
▷ SYNONYMS: **1 smoulder**; old use reek. **2 puff on**, draw on, pull on, inhale; informal drag on.
□ **smokescreen** something intended to disguise your real motives etc.
■ **smokeless** adj. **smoker** n. **smoky** adj.

smolder US = SMOULDER.

smooch v. informal kiss and cuddle.

smooth adj. **1** having an even and regular surface. **2** moving without jerks. **3** without difficulties. **4** charming but possibly insincere. **5** not harsh or bitter.

▷ SYNONYMS: **1 even**, level, flat, plane, unwrinkled, glassy, glossy, silky, polished. **2** the smooth waters of the lake: **calm**, still, tranquil, undisturbed, unruffled, even, flat, like a millpond. **3 steady**, regular, uninterrupted, unbroken, easy, effortless, trouble-free. **4 suave**, urbane, sophisticated, polished, debonair, courteous, gracious, persuasive, glib, slick, smooth-tongued; informal smarmy.
– ANTONYMS: uneven, rough.
• v. make smooth.
▷ SYNONYMS: **1 flatten**, level out/off, even out/off, press, roll, iron, plane. **2 ease**, facilitate, expedite, help, assist, aid, pave the way for.
– ANTONYMS: roughen, hinder.
■ **smoothly** adv. **smoothness** n.

smoothie n. **1** a drink made of fruit puréed with milk or ice cream. **2** informal a charming and confident man.

smorgasbord n. a meal consisting of a range of savoury items.

smote past of SMITE.

smother v. **1** suffocate. **2** cover completely. **3** prevent from happening.
▷ SYNONYMS: **1 suffocate**, asphyxiate, stifle, choke. **2 extinguish**, put out, snuff out, douse, stamp out. **3 smear**, daub, spread, cover, plaster. **4** she smothered a giggle: **stifle**, muffle, strangle, suppress, hold back, fight back, swallow, conceal.

smoulder (US **smolder**) v. **1** burn slowly with smoke but no flame. **2** feel strong and barely hidden anger etc.

SMS abbrev. Short Message Service, used to send and receive text messages.
• n. a message sent or received using SMS.

smudge v. make or become blurred or smeared.
▷ SYNONYMS: **streak**, mark, dirty, soil, blotch, blacken, smear, blot, daub, stain; informal splotch, splodge.
• n. a smudged mark.
▷ SYNONYMS: **streak**, smear, mark, stain, blotch, blob, dab; informal splotch, splodge.
■ **smudgy** adj.

smug adj. (**smugger**, **smuggest**) irritatingly pleased with yourself.
▷ SYNONYMS: **self-satisfied**, conceited, complacent, superior, pleased with yourself.
■ **smugly** adv. **smugness** n.

smuggle v. **1** move goods illegally into or out of a country. **2** convey secretly.
■ **smuggler** n.

smut n. **1** a small flake of soot or dirt. **2** indecent writing, pictures, etc.
■ **smutty** adj.

snack n. a small or casual meal.
▷ SYNONYMS: **light meal**, sandwich, refreshments, nibbles, titbit; informal bite to eat.

snaffle v. Brit. informal take quickly or secretly.
• n. a simple bit on a bridle.

snag n. **1** an unexpected difficulty. **2** a jagged projection. **3** a small tear.
▷ SYNONYMS: **complication**, difficulty, catch, hitch, obstacle, pitfall, problem, setback, disadvantage, drawback.
• v. (**snagging**, **snagged**) catch or tear on a snag.
▷ SYNONYMS: **catch**, hook, tear.

snail n. a mollusc with a spiral shell.

snake n. a reptile with no legs and a long slender body.
▷ SYNONYMS: serpent.
• v. move with a twisting motion.
▷ SYNONYMS: *the road snakes inland:* **twist**, wind, meander, zigzag, curve.
■ **snaky** adj.

snap v. (**snapping**, **snapped**) **1** break with a sharp crack. **2** say quickly and irritably. **3** open or close with a brisk movement or sharp sound. **4** (**snap up**) quickly buy. **5** take a snapshot of.
▷ SYNONYMS: **1 break**, fracture, splinter, split, crack; informal bust. **2 bark**, snarl, growl, retort; informal jump down someone's throat.
• n. **1** an act of snapping. **2** a snapshot.
▷ SYNONYMS: **photograph**, picture, photo, shot, snapshot, print, slide.
• adj. done on the spur of the moment.
□ **snapdragon** a plant with brightly coloured flowers that have a mouth-like opening. **snapshot** an informal photo.

snapper n. an edible sea fish.

snappy adj. (**snappier**, **snappiest**) informal **1** short and clever: *snappy slogans.* **2** neat and stylish. **3** irritable.

snare n. a trap with a loop of wire that pulls tight.
▷ SYNONYMS: **trap**, gin, wire, net, noose.
• v. catch or trap.
▷ SYNONYMS: **trap**, catch, net, bag, ensnare, hook.

snarl v. **1** growl with bared teeth. **2** say aggressively. **3** (**snarl up**) entangle.
• n. an act of snarling.
□ **snarl-up** Brit. informal a traffic jam.

snatch v. seize quickly or eagerly.
▷ SYNONYMS: **1 grab**, seize, take hold of, take, pluck, grasp at, clutch at. **2 steal**, take, thieve, make off with; informal swipe, nab, lift; Brit. informal nick, pinch, whip. **3 kidnap**, abduct, take as hostage.
• n. **1** an act of snatching. **2** a fragment of music or talk.

snazzy adj. (**snazzier**, **snazziest**) informal stylish.

sneak v. **1** go, do, or obtain furtively. **2** Brit. informal report another's wrongdoings. **3** (**sneaking**) (of a feeling) persisting.
▷ SYNONYMS: **1 creep**, slink, steal, slip, slide, sidle, tiptoe, pad. **2** (**sneaking**) *a sneaking suspicion:* **niggling**, nagging, lingering, persistent.
• n. Brit. informal a telltale.

sneaker n. a soft shoe worn for sports or casual occasions.

sneaky adj. (**sneakier**, **sneakiest**) secretive or sly.
▷ SYNONYMS: **sly**, crafty, cunning, wily, scheming, devious, deceitful, under-hand; furtive, secret, stealthy, surreptitious. secretive.
■ **sneakily** adv.

sneer n. a scornful smile or remark.
▷ SYNONYMS: **1 smirk**, snigger. **2 jeer**, jibe, insult; informal dig.
• v. smile or speak scornfully.
▷ SYNONYMS: **1 smirk**, snigger, curl your lip. **2 scoff**, laugh, scorn, disdain, be contemptuous, mock, ridicule, deride, jeer, jibe.

sneeze v. suddenly expel air from the nose and mouth.
• n. an act of sneezing.

snicker v. & n. = SNIGGER.

snide adj. disrespectful or mocking in an indirect way.

sniff v. **1** draw in air audibly through the nose. **2** (**sniff around**) informal investigate secretly. **3** (**sniff out**) informal discover.
▷ SYNONYMS: **1 inhale**, snuffle. **2 smell**, scent, get a whiff of.
• n. an act of sniffing.
▷ SYNONYMS: **1 snuffle**, snort. **2 smell**, scent, whiff, lungful.
■ **sniffer** n.

sniffle v. sniff slightly or repeatedly.
• n. an act of sniffling.

snifter n. Brit. informal a small quantity of an alcoholic drink.

snigger n. a half-suppressed laugh.
• v. give a snigger.
▷ SYNONYMS: **giggle**, titter, snicker, chortle, laugh, sneer, smirk.

snip v. (**snipping**, **snipped**) cut with

S

small, quick strokes.

• **n. 1** an act of snipping. **2** Brit. informal a bargain.

snipe v. **1** fire shots from a hiding place at long range. **2** criticize in a sly way.

• **n.** (pl. **snipe** or **snipes**) a wading bird with a long bill.

■ **sniper** n.

snippet n. a small piece.

▷ SYNONYMS: **piece**, bit, scrap, fragment, particle, shred, excerpt, extract.

snivel v. (**snivelling, snivelled**; US **sniveling, sniveled**) **1** cry. **2** complain in a whining way.

▷ SYNONYMS: **sniffle**, snuffle, whimper, whine, weep, cry; Scottish greet; informal blubber; Brit. informal grizzle.

snob n. a person who greatly respects high social status or wealth and who looks down on lower-class people.

■ **snobbery** n. **snobby** adj.

snobbish adj. relating to or typical of a snob.

▷ SYNONYMS: **elitist**, superior, supercilious, arrogant, condescending, pretentious, affected; informal snooty, high and mighty, la-di-da, stuck-up; Brit. informal toffee-nosed.

snog Brit. informal v. (**snogging, snogged**) kiss.

• **n.** a kiss.

snood n. a hairnet worn at the back of a woman's head.

snooker n. a game played with cues on a billiard table.

snoop v. informal investigate secretly.

▷ SYNONYMS: **pry**, spy, be a busybody, poke your nose into, root about, ferret about; informal be nosy; Austral. informal stickybeak.

■ **snooper** n.

snooty adj. (**snootier, snootiest**) informal superior towards others.

■ **snootily** adv.

snooze informal n. a nap.

• **v.** have a nap.

snore n. a snorting sound made whilst asleep.

• **v.** make such sounds.

snorkel n. a tube for a swimmer to breathe through while under water.

• **v.** (**snorkelling, snorkelled**; US **snorkeling, snorkeled**) swim with a snorkel.

snort n. an explosive sound made by forcing breath through the nose.

• **v. 1** make a snort. **2** informal inhale cocaine.

snot n. informal mucus in the nose.

snout n. an animal's projecting nose and mouth.

snow n. frozen water vapour in the atmosphere that falls in light white flakes.

• **v. 1** fall as snow. **2** (**be snowed under**) be overwhelmed with work etc.

□ **snowboarding** the sport of sliding downhill over snow on a single short, broad ski. **snowdrift** a bank of deep snow heaped up by the wind. **snowdrop** a plant bearing drooping white flowers in late winter. **snowman** a human figure made of compressed snow. **snowplough** (US **snowplow**) a device or vehicle for clearing roads of snow.

■ **snowy** adj.

snowball n. a ball of packed snow.

• **v.** increase rapidly in size or importance.

snub v. (**snubbing, snubbed**) ignore or reject scornfully.

▷ SYNONYMS: **rebuff**, spurn, coldshoulder, cut, ignore, insult, slight; informal freeze out; N. Amer. informal stiff.

• **n.** an act of snubbing.

▷ SYNONYMS: **rebuff**, slap in the face; informal brush-off, put-down.

• **adj.** (of the nose) short and turned up at the end.

snuff v. **1** put out a candle. **2** (**snuff it**) Brit. informal die.

• **n.** powdered tobacco for sniffing up the nostril.

snuffle v. breathe with noisy sniffs.

• **n.** a snuffling sound.

snug adj. (**snugger, snuggest**) **1** cosy. **2** close-fitting.

▷ SYNONYMS: **1 cosy**, comfortable, warm, sheltered, secure; informal comfy. **2 tight**, skintight, close-fitting, figure-hugging.

– ANTONYMS: loose.

• **n.** Brit. a small, cosy bar in a pub.

■ **snugly** adv.

snuggle v. settle into a warm, comfortable position.

▷ SYNONYMS: **nestle**, curl up, cuddle up, nuzzle, huddle up, settle; N. Amer. snug down.

so adv. **1** to such a great extent. **2** to the same extent. **3** similarly. **4** thus.

• **conj. 1** therefore. **2** (**so that**) with the result or aim that.

□ **so-and-so** informal **1** a person whose name you do not know. **2** a disliked person.

soak v. **1** keep immersed in liquid until thoroughly wet. **2** (of a liquid) spread throughout. **3** (**soak up**) absorb.

▷ SYNONYMS: **1 dip**, immerse, steep, submerge, douse, marinate, souse.

2 drench, wet through, saturate.
3 *water soaked through the carpet*: **permeate**, penetrate, impregnate, percolate, seep, spread. **4 absorb**, suck up, blot, mop up.

soaking adj. completely wet.
▷ SYNONYMS: **drenched**, wet through, soaked, sodden, soggy, waterlogged, saturated, sopping, dripping, wringing.

soap n. **1** a substance used with water for washing. **2** *informal* a soap opera.
• v. wash with soap.
□ **soap opera** a television or radio serial dealing with the lives of a group of characters.
■ **soapy** adj.

soar v. **1** rise high into the air.
2 increase rapidly.
▷ SYNONYMS: **1 rise**, ascend, climb.
2 glide, plane, float, hover.
3 increase, escalate, shoot up, spiral, rocket; *informal* go through the roof, skyrocket.
– ANTONYMS: plummet.

sob v. (**sobbing**, **sobbed**) cry with loud gasps.
▷ SYNONYMS: **weep**, cry, snivel, whimper; Scottish greet; *informal* blubber; Brit. *informal* grizzle.
• n. an act of sobbing.

sober adj. **1** not drunk. **2** serious. **3** (of a colour) not bright.
▷ SYNONYMS: **1 clear-headed**, teetotal, abstinent, dry; *informal* on the wagon.
2 serious, solemn, sensible, staid, sedate, quiet, dignified, grave, level-headed, down-to-earth. **3 sombre**, subdued, restrained, austere, severe, drab, plain, dark.
– ANTONYMS: drunk.
• v. make or become sober.
■ **soberly** adv. **sobriety** n.

sobriquet (or **soubriquet**) /soh-bri-kay/ n. a nickname.

so-called adj. wrongly called by the name or term specified: *I was immune to his so-called charm*.
▷ SYNONYMS: **supposed**, alleged, presumed, ostensible, reputed, self-styled.

soccer n. a form of football played with a round ball.

sociable adj. **1** enjoying the company of others. **2** friendly and welcoming.
▷ SYNONYMS: **friendly**, amicable, affable, companionable, gregarious, cordial, warm, genial.
– ANTONYMS: unfriendly.
■ **sociability** n. **sociably** adv.

social adj. **1** of society. **2** needing the company of others. **3** (of an activity)

in which people meet for pleasure.
4 (of animals) living in organized communities.
▷ SYNONYMS: **1 communal**, community, collective, general, popular, civil, public, civic. **2 recreational**, leisure, entertainment.
• n. a social gathering.
▷ SYNONYMS: **party**, gathering, function, get-together; *informal* do.
□ **social security** money provided by the state for people with little or no income. **social services** services provided by the state such as medical care. **social worker** a person whose job is to help people with family or financial problems.
■ **socially** adv.

socialism n. a political theory that a country's transport, resources, and industries should be owned or controlled by the state.
■ **socialist** n. & adj.

socialite n. a person who mixes in fashionable society.

socialize (or **-ise**) v. mix socially with others.
▷ SYNONYMS: **interact**, converse, be sociable, mix, mingle, get together, meet, fraternize, consort; *informal* hobnob, hang out.

society n. (pl. **societies**) **1** people living together in an ordered community.
2 a particular community of people.
3 fashionable and wealthy people.
4 an organization or club. **5** the company of other people.
▷ SYNONYMS: **1 the community**, the general public, the people, the population, civilization, humankind, mankind, the world at large. **2** *an industrial society*: **culture**, community, civilization, nation. **3 high society**, polite society, the upper classes, the gentry, the elite, the smart set, the beau monde; *informal* the upper crust.
4 club, association, group, circle, institute, guild, lodge, league, union, alliance. **5 company**, companionship, fellowship, friendship.

> **WORD LINKS**
> **sociology** the study of human society

sociology n. the study of human society.
■ **sociological** adj. **sociologist** n.

sock n. **1** a knitted garment for the foot and lower leg. **2** *informal* a hard blow.
• v. *informal* hit hard.

socket n. a hollow or device into which something fits.

S

sod n. grass-covered ground, or a piece of this.

soda n. **1** fizzy water. **2** a compound of sodium.

sodden adj. soaked through.

sodium n. a soft silver-white metallic element.
□ **sodium chloride** the chemical name for salt.

sodomy n. anal intercourse.
■ **sodomite** n.

sofa n. a long padded seat with a back and arms.
▷ SYNONYMS: **settee**, couch, divan, chaise longue, chesterfield.

soft adj. **1** easy to mould, cut, compress, or fold. **2** not rough in texture. **3** quiet and gentle. **4** (of light or colour) not harsh. **5** not strict. **6** (of a drink) not alcoholic. **7** (of a drug) not likely to cause addiction. **8** (of water) free from mineral salts.
▷ SYNONYMS: **1 mushy**, squashy, pulpy, squishy, doughy, spongy, springy, elastic, pliable, pliant; informal gooey; Brit. informal squidgy. **2 swampy**, marshy, boggy, muddy, squelchy. **3 smooth**, velvety, fleecy, downy, furry, silky, silken. **4 dim**, low, faint, subdued, muted, subtle. **5 quiet**, low, gentle, faint, muted, subdued, muffled, hushed, whispered. **6 lenient**, easy-going, tolerant, forgiving, forbearing, indulgent, liberal, lax.
– ANTONYMS: hard, firm, harsh.
□ **softball** a form of baseball played with a larger, softer ball. **soft fruit** Brit. a small fruit without a stone. **soft-hearted** kind and compassionate. **software** computer programs. **softwood** wood from coniferous trees.
■ **softly** adv. **softness** n.

soften v. make or become soft or softer.
▷ SYNONYMS: *the compensation should soften the blow:* **ease**, alleviate, relieve, soothe, take the edge off, cushion, lessen, diminish, blunt, deaden.
■ **softener** n.

soggy adj. (**soggier**, **soggiest**) very wet and soft.
▷ SYNONYMS: **mushy**, squashy, pulpy, slushy, squelchy, swampy, marshy, boggy, soaking, wet, saturated, drenched; Brit. informal squidgy.

soigné /swun-yay/ adj. elegant and well groomed.

soil n. **1** the upper layer of the earth. **2** a nation's territory.
▷ SYNONYMS: **1 earth**, dirt, clay, ground, loam. **2 territory**, land, region, country, domain, dominion.
• v. make dirty.
▷ SYNONYMS: **dirty**, stain, smear, smudge, spoil, foul.

soirée /swah-ray/ n. an evening social gathering.

sojourn /so-juhn/ n. a temporary stay.
• v. stay temporarily.

solace n. comfort in time of distress.
• v. give solace to.

solar adj. of the sun or its rays.
□ **solar plexus** a network of nerves at the pit of the stomach. **solar system** the sun with the planets etc. in orbit around it.

solarium n. (pl. **solariums** or **solaria**) a room equipped with sunbeds.

sold past & past part. of SELL.

solder n. a soft alloy for joining metals.
• v. join with solder.
□ **soldering iron** a tool for melting and applying solder.

soldier n. a person serving in an army.
▷ SYNONYMS: **fighter**, trooper, serviceman/woman, warrior; US GI; Brit. informal squaddie.
• v. **1** serve as a soldier. **2** (**soldier on**) informal keep trying.

> **WORD LINKS**
> **military** relating to soldiers or the armed forces

sole n. **1** the underside of the foot. **2** the underside of a piece of footwear. **3** (pl. **sole**) an edible flatfish.
• adj. **1** one and only. **2** belonging or restricted to one person or group.
▷ SYNONYMS: **only**, one, single, solitary, lone, unique, exclusive.
• v. put a sole on a shoe.

solecism /sol-i-si-z'm/ n. **1** a grammatical mistake. **2** an instance of incorrect behaviour.

solely adv. not involving anyone or anything else.
▷ SYNONYMS: *he was appointed solely on the basis of merit:* **only**, simply, purely, just, merely, uniquely, exclusively, entirely, wholly, alone.

solemn adj. **1** formal and dignified. **2** serious.
▷ SYNONYMS: **1 dignified**, ceremonial, stately, formal, majestic, imposing, splendid, magnificent, grand. **2 serious**, grave, sober, sombre, unsmiling, stern, grim, dour, humourless. **3 sincere**, earnest, honest, genuine, firm, heartfelt, whole-hearted, sworn.
– ANTONYMS: frivolous, light-hearted.

S

■ **solemnity** n. **solemnly** adv.

solemnize (or **-ise**) v. perform or mark with a ceremony.

solenoid n. a coil of wire which becomes magnetic when an electric current is passed through it.

solicit v. (**soliciting**, **solicited**) **1** try to obtain. **2** (of a prostitute) approach someone and offer sex for money.

▷ SYNONYMS: **1 ask for**, request, seek, apply for, put in for, call for, beg for, plead for. **2 ask**, approach, appeal to, lobby, petition, importune, call on, press.

■ **solicitation** n.

solicitor n. Brit. a lawyer who advises clients and instructs barristers.

solicitous adj. concerned about a person's well-being.

■ **solicitously** adv. **solicitude** n.

solid adj. **1** firm and stable in shape. **2** strongly built. **3** not hollow or having spaces. **4** consisting of the same substance throughout. **5** (of time) uninterrupted. **6** reliable. **7** three-dimensional.

▷ SYNONYMS: **1 hard**, rock-hard, rigid, firm, solidified, set, frozen, compact, compressed, dense. **2** *solid gold*: **pure**, unadulterated, genuine. **3 well built**, sound, substantial, strong, sturdy, durable, stout. **4 well founded**, valid, sound, logical, authoritative, convincing, cogent. **5** *solid support*: **unanimous**, united, consistent, undivided.

– ANTONYMS: liquid, flimsy, untenable.
• n. a solid substance, object, or food.
■ **solidity** n. **solidly** adv.

solidarity n. agreement and support resulting from shared interests, feelings, etc.

▷ SYNONYMS: **unanimity**, unity, agreement, team spirit, accord, harmony, consensus; formal concord.

solidify v. (**solidifying**, **solidified**) make or become solid.

▷ SYNONYMS: **harden**, set, thicken, stiffen, congeal, cake, freeze, ossify, fossilize, petrify.

– ANTONYMS: liquefy.
■ **solidification** n.

soliloquy n. (pl. **soliloquies**) a speech in a play made by a character while alone.

solipsism n. the view that the self is all that can be known to exist.

solitaire n. **1** Brit. a game for one person played on a board with pegs. **2** a single gem in a piece of jewellery.

solitary adj. **1** alone. **2** isolated. **3** single.

▷ SYNONYMS: **1 lonely**, unaccompanied, by yourself, on your own, alone, friendless, unsociable, withdrawn, reclusive; N. Amer. lonesome. **2 isolated**, remote, lonely, out of the way, in the back of beyond, outlying, off the beaten track, secluded; N. Amer. in the backwoods. **3 single**, lone, sole, only, one, individual.

– ANTONYMS: sociable.

solitude n. the state of being alone.

▷ SYNONYMS: **loneliness**, solitariness, isolation, seclusion, privacy, peace.

solo n. (pl. **solos**) a song, dance, or piece of music for or by one performer.

• adj. & adv. for or done by one person.
■ **soloist** n.

solstice n. either of the two times in the year, midsummer and midwinter, when the sun reaches its highest or lowest point in the sky at noon.

soluble adj. **1** able to be dissolved. **2** able to be solved.

■ **solubility** n.

solution n. **1** a way of solving a problem. **2** the correct answer to a puzzle. **3** a mixture formed when a substance is dissolved in a liquid.

▷ SYNONYMS: **1 answer**, result, resolution, key, explanation. **2 mixture**, blend, emulsion, compound.

solve v. find the answer to a problem or mystery.

▷ SYNONYMS: **answer**, resolve, work out, puzzle out, fathom, decipher, decode, clear up, straighten out, get to the bottom of, unravel, explain; informal figure out, crack; Brit. informal suss out.

solvent adj. **1** having more money than you owe. **2** able to dissolve other substances.

• n. a liquid used to dissolve other substances.
■ **solvency** n.

somatic adj. of the body rather than the mind.

sombre (US **somber**) adj. dark and gloomy.

▷ SYNONYMS: **1 dark**, drab, dull, dingy, restrained, sober, funereal. **2 solemn**, earnest, serious, grave, sober, unsmiling, gloomy, sad, mournful, melancholy, lugubrious, cheerless.

– ANTONYMS: bright, cheerful.

sombrero n. (pl. **sombreros**) a broad-brimmed hat.

some adj. **1** an unspecified amount or number of. **2** unknown or unspecified. **3** approximately. **4** considerable. **5** expressing admiration.

S

• **pron.** a certain amount or number of people or things.

somebody **pron.** someone.

somehow adv. **1** by one way or another. **2** for an unknown reason.

someone **pron.** **1** an unknown or unspecified person. **2** an important person.

somersault n. a movement in which a person turns head over heels and finishes on their feet.
• **v.** perform a somersault.

something **pron.** an unspecified or unknown thing.

sometime adv. at an unspecified or unknown time.

sometimes adv. occasionally.
▷ SYNONYMS: **occasionally**, from time to time, now and then, every so often, once in a while, on occasion, at times, off and on.

somewhat adv. to some extent.

somewhere adv. in or to an unspecified or unknown place.

somnambulism n. sleepwalking.
■ **somnambulist** n.

somnolent adj. sleepy.
■ **somnolence** n.

son n. a boy or man in relation to his parents.
□ **son-in-law** (pl. **sons-in-law**) the husband of a person's daughter.

sonar n. a system for detecting objects under water by giving out sound pulses.

sonata n. a piece of music for a solo instrument, often with a piano accompaniment.

son et lumière /son ay loo-mi-air/ n. a night-time entertainment dramatizing a historical event with lighting and sound effects.

song n. **1** a set of words set to music. **2** singing.
▷ SYNONYMS: **air**, strain, ditty, chant, number, track, melody, tune.
□ **songbird** a bird with a musical song. **songster** (fem. **songstress**) a singer.

sonic adj. of or using sound waves.
□ **sonic boom** a loud noise caused by the shock wave from an object travelling faster than the speed of sound.
■ **sonically** adv.

sonnet n. a poem of 14 lines.

sonorous adj. (of a sound) deep and full.
▷ SYNONYMS: **resonant**, rich, full, round, booming, deep, clear, mellow, strong, resounding, reverberant.
■ **sonority** n. **sonorously** adv.

soon adv. **1** in or after a short time. **2** (**would sooner**) would rather.
▷ SYNONYMS: **shortly**, presently, in the near future, before long, in a little while, in a minute, in a moment; Brit. informal in a tick.
□ **sooner or later** eventually.

soot n. a black powdery substance produced when coal, wood, etc. is burnt.
■ **sooty** adj.

soothe v. **1** calm a person or their fears. **2** relieve pain or discomfort.
▷ SYNONYMS: **1 calm**, pacify, comfort, hush, quiet, settle, appease, mollify; Brit. quieten. **2 ease**, alleviate, relieve, take the edge off, allay, lessen, reduce.
– ANTONYMS: agitate, aggravate.

soothing adj. reducing anxiety, discomfort, etc.
▷ SYNONYMS: **relaxing**, restful, calm, calming, comforting, tranquil, peaceful.

soothsayer n. a prophet.

sop n. a thing given or done to pacify someone.
• **v.** (**sopping**, **sopped**) (**sop up**) soak up liquid.

sophist n. a person who uses clever but false arguments.
■ **sophism** n. **sophistry** n.

sophisticate n. a sophisticated person.

sophisticated adj. **1** having experience and taste in matters of culture or fashion. **2** highly developed and complex.
▷ SYNONYMS: **1 worldly**, worldly-wise, experienced, cosmopolitan, urbane, cultured, cultivated, polished, refined. **2 advanced**, state-of-the-art, the latest, up-to-the-minute, cutting-edge, complex.
– ANTONYMS: naive, crude.

sophistication n. the quality of being sophisticated.
▷ SYNONYMS: **worldliness**, experience, urbanity, culture, polish, refinement, elegance, style, poise, finesse, savoir faire.

sophomore n. US a second-year university or high-school student.

soporific adj. causing drowsiness or sleep.

sopping adj. wet through.

soppy adj. (**soppier**, **soppiest**) Brit. informal too sentimental.
■ **soppily** adv.

soprano n. (pl. **sopranos**) the highest singing voice.

sorbet /sor-bay/ n. a water ice.

sorcerer n. (fem. **sorceress**) a person who practises magic.
■ **sorcery** n.

sordid adj. **1** dishonest or immoral. **2** very dirty and unpleasant.
▷ SYNONYMS: **1 sleazy**, seedy, seamy, unsavoury, tawdry, cheap, disreputable, discreditable, ignominious, shameful, wretched, despicable. **2 squalid**, slummy, dirty, filthy, shabby, scummy; informal scuzzy; Brit. informal grotty.
– ANTONYMS: respectable.
■ **sordidly** adv. **sordidness** n.

sore adj. **1** painful or aching. **2** N. Amer. informal upset and angry.
▷ SYNONYMS: **1 painful**, hurting, aching, throbbing, smarting, stinging, inflamed, sensitive, tender, raw, wounded, injured. **2 upset**, angry, annoyed, cross, disgruntled, dissatisfied, irritated; informal aggravated, miffed, peeved; Brit. informal narked; N. Amer. informal ticked off.
• n. a sore place on the body.
□ **sore point** a cause of distress or annoyance.
■ **soreness** n.

sorely adv. very; badly.

sorghum n. a cereal grown for grain and animal feed.

sorrel n. **1** a sharp-tasting herb. **2** a light reddish-brown colour.

sorrow n. **1** deep distress caused by loss or disappointment. **2** a cause of this.
▷ SYNONYMS: **1 sadness**, unhappiness, misery, despondency, regret, despair, desolation, heartache, grief. **2** the sorrows of life: **trouble**, difficulty, problem, woe, affliction, trial, tribulation, misfortune.
– ANTONYMS: joy.
■ **sorrowful** adj. **sorrowfully** adv.

sorry adj. (**sorrier**, **sorriest**) **1** feeling sympathy for another's misfortune. **2** feeling regret. **3** in a bad or pitiful state.
▷ SYNONYMS: **1 regretful**, apologetic, remorseful, contrite, repentant, rueful, penitent, guilty, shamefaced, ashamed. **2** he felt sorry for her: **full of pity**, sympathetic, compassionate, moved, concerned. **3** I was sorry to hear about the accident: **sad**, sorrowful, distressed.
– ANTONYMS: glad, unrepentant.

sort n. **1** a kind or category. **2** informal a person with a specified nature.
▷ SYNONYMS: **type**, kind, variety, class, category, style, form, genre, species, breed, make, model, brand.

• v. **1** arrange in groups. **2** separate from a mixed group. **3** (**sort out**) solve a problem.
▷ SYNONYMS: **1 classify**, class, group, organize, arrange, order, grade, catalogue. **2** the problem was soon sorted out: **resolve**, settle, solve, fix, work out, straighten out, deal with, put right, set right, rectify, iron out.

sortie n. **1** an attack by troops from a defended position. **2** a flight by an aircraft on a military operation.

SOS n. **1** an international distress signal. **2** an urgent appeal for help.

sot n. a habitual drunkard.

sotto voce /sot-toh voh-chay/ adv. & adj. in a quiet voice.

soubriquet var. of SOBRIQUET.

soufflé n. a light, spongy dish made with beaten egg whites.

sough /sow, suf/ v. make a moaning or whistling sound.

sought past & past part. of SEEK.

souk /sook/ n. an Arab market.

soul n. **1** the spiritual or immortal element of a person. **2** a person's inner nature. **3** emotional energy or power. **4** a perfect example of a quality: the soul of discretion. **5** a person. **6** a kind of music with elements of gospel and rhythm and blues.
▷ SYNONYMS: **1 spirit**, psyche, inner self. **2 feeling**, emotion, passion, animation, intensity, warmth, energy, vitality, spirit.
□ **soulmate** a person ideally suited to another.

soulful adj. expressing deep emotion.
■ **soulfully** adv.

soulless adj. lacking character, interest, or emotion.

sound n. **1** vibrations travelling through the air and sensed by the ear. **2** a thing that can be heard. **3** an impression. **4** a narrow stretch of water.
▷ SYNONYMS: **1 noise**, din, racket, resonance, reverberation; Brit. row. **2 utterance**, cry, word, noise, peep.
– ANTONYMS: silence.
• v. **1** make a sound. **2** make a sound to show or warn. **3** give a specified impression. **4** (**sound off**) express opinions forcefully. **5** (**sound out**) ask someone what they think. **6** find out the depth of water using sound echoes etc.
▷ SYNONYMS: **1 reverberate**, resonate, resound; ring, chime, ping, peal. **2** sound the horn: **blow**, blast, toot, ring, use, operate, activate, set off.

S

3 appear, look, seem, give every indication of being, strike someone as.
•**adj. 1** in good condition. **2** based on good judgement. **3** (of sleep) deep.
▷ SYNONYMS: **1 healthy**, in good condition/shape, fit, hale and hearty, in fine fettle, strong, sturdy; undamaged, unimpaired, intact.
2 well founded, valid, reasonable, logical, weighty, authoritative, reliable. **3** *a sound judge of character:* **reliable**, dependable, trustworthy, good. **4 deep**, undisturbed, uninterrupted, untroubled, peaceful.
– ANTONYMS: unhealthy.
□ **sound barrier** the point at which an aircraft reaches the speed of sound. **sound bite** a short memorable extract from a speech. **soundproof** preventing sound getting in or out. **soundtrack** the sound accompaniment to a film.
■ **soundly** adv.

> **WORD LINKS**
> **acoustic**, **sonic** relating to sound or sound waves

sounding n. **1** a measurement of the depth of water. **2** (**soundings**) information found out before taking action.
□ **sounding board** a person used to test new ideas.
soup n. a liquid dish of meat, fish, or vegetables.
•v. (**soup up**) informal make more powerful.
□ **soup kitchen** a place where free food is served to very poor people.
soupçon /soop-son/ n. a very small quantity.
sour adj. **1** having a sharp taste. **2** unpleasantly stale. **3** resentful or angry.
▷ SYNONYMS: **1 acid**, acidic, tart, bitter, sharp, vinegary, pungent. **2 bad**, off, turned, curdled, rancid, high, fetid. **3 embittered**, resentful, jaundiced, bitter, cross, crabby, crotchety, cantankerous, bad-tempered, disagreeable, unpleasant; informal grouchy.
– ANTONYMS: sweet, fresh.
•v. make or become sour.
▷ SYNONYMS: **spoil**, mar, damage, harm, impair, upset, poison, blight.
■ **sourly** adv. **sourness** n.
source n. **1** a place, person, or thing from which something originates. **2** a place where a river begins. **3** a person, book, etc. providing information.
▷ SYNONYMS: **1 spring**, wellspring, wellhead, origin. **2 origin**, derivation,

starting point, start, beginning, fountainhead, root, author, originator.
souse v. **1** soak. **2** (**soused**) pickled.
south n. **1** the direction on the right-hand side of a person facing east. **2** the southern part of a place.
•adj. **1** lying towards or facing the south. **2** (of a wind) from the south.
•adv. towards the south.
■ **southerly** adj. & adv. **southward** adj. & adv. **southwards** adv.
south-east n. the direction or region halfway between south and east.
•adj. & adv. **1** towards or facing the south-east. **2** (of a wind) from the south-east.
■ **south-easterly** adj. & adv. **south-eastern** adj.
southern adj. situated in or facing the south.
southerner n. a person from the south of a region.
south-west n. the direction or region halfway between south and west.
•adj. & adv. **1** towards or facing the south-west. **2** (of a wind) from the south-west.
■ **south-westerly** adj. & adv. **south-western** adj.
souvenir n. a thing kept as a reminder of a person, place, or event.
▷ SYNONYMS: **memento**, keepsake, reminder, memorial, trophy.
sou'wester n. a waterproof hat with a broad flap at the back.
sovereign n. **1** a king or queen who is the supreme ruler of a country. **2** a former British gold coin worth one pound sterling.
▷ SYNONYMS: **ruler**, monarch, potentate, overlord, king, queen, emperor, empress, prince, princess.
•adj. **1** having supreme power. **2** (of a state) independent.
▷ SYNONYMS: **autonomous**, independent, self-governing, self-determining, non-aligned, free.
sovereignty n. **1** supreme power or authority. **2** a self-governing state.
▷ SYNONYMS: **1 power**, rule, supremacy, dominion, jurisdiction, ascendancy, domination, authority, control.
2 autonomy, independence, self-rule, self-government, home rule, self-determination, freedom.
Soviet n. a citizen of the former Soviet Union.
•adj. of the former Soviet Union.
sow[1] /soh/ v. (**sowing**, **sowed**; past part. **sown** or **sowed**) **1** plant seed by scattering it on or in the earth. **2** spread something unwelcome.

▷ SYNONYMS: **plant**, scatter, disperse, strew, broadcast, seed.
sow² /sow/ n. an adult female pig.
soya bean n. an edible bean that is high in protein.
soy sauce n. a sauce made with fermented soya beans.
sozzled adj. informal very drunk.
spa n. a place with a mineral spring believed to have health-giving properties.
space n. **1** an unoccupied expanse or area. **2** a blank between written words or characters. **3** the universe beyond the earth's atmosphere. **4** the whole expanse in which all things exist and move. **5** an interval of time.
▷ SYNONYMS: **1 room**, capacity, latitude, margin, leeway, play, elbow room, clearance. **2 area**, expanse, stretch, sweep, tract. **3 gap**, interval, opening, aperture, cavity, niche, interstice. **4 blank**, gap, box. **5 period**, span, time, duration, stretch, course, interval, gap. **6 outer space**, deep space, the universe, the galaxy, the solar system.
• v. **1** position items at a distance from one another. **2** (**spaced out**) informal dazed.
▷ SYNONYMS: **position**, arrange, range, array, spread, lay out, set.
□ **spacecraft** a vehicle for travelling in space. **spaceship** a manned spacecraft.
spacious adj. having plenty of space.
▷ SYNONYMS: **roomy**, capacious, commodious, voluminous, sizeable, generous.
− ANTONYMS: cramped.
■ **spaciousness** n.
spade n. **1** a tool for digging, with a broad metal blade on a long handle. **2** (**spades**) one of the four suits in a pack of playing cards.
□ **spadework** hard preparatory work.
spaghetti pl. n. pasta in long strands.
spam n. unwanted email sent to many Internet users.
• v. (**spamming**, **spammed**) send unwanted email to many people.
span n. **1** extent from side to side. **2** duration. **3** a part of a bridge between the uprights supporting it.
▷ SYNONYMS: **1 extent**, length, width, reach, stretch, spread, distance, range. **2 period**, space, time, duration, course, interval.
• v. (**spanning**, **spanned**) extend across or over.
▷ SYNONYMS: **1 bridge**, cross, traverse, pass over. **2 last**, cover, extend, spread over.

spangle n. a small piece of decorative glittering material.
■ **spangled** adj.
Spaniard n. a person from Spain.
spaniel n. a dog with a long silky coat and drooping ears.
Spanish n. the main language of Spain and of much of Central and South America.
• adj. of Spain.
spank v. slap on the buttocks.
spanking adj. **1** brisk. **2** informal impressive.
spanner n. a tool for gripping and turning a nut or bolt.
spar v. (**sparring**, **sparred**) **1** make the motions of boxing but without force, as a form of training. **2** argue without hostility.
• n. a strong pole used to support a ship's sails.
spare adj. **1** additional to what is required. **2** not currently in use or occupied. **3** thin.
▷ SYNONYMS: **1 extra**, supplementary, additional, second, other, alternative, emergency, reserve, backup, relief, substitute; N. Amer. alternate. **2 surplus**, superfluous, excess, leftover, redundant, unnecessary, unwanted; informal going begging. **3** your spare time: **free**, leisure, unoccupied. **4 slender**, lean, willowy, svelte, lissom, thin, skinny, gaunt, lanky, spindly.
• n. an item kept in case another is lost, broken, etc.
• v. **1** give someone something that you have enough of. **2** refrain from killing or harming.
▷ SYNONYMS: **1 afford**, manage, part with, give, provide, do without. **2 pardon**, let off, forgive, have mercy on, reprieve, release, free.
□ **to spare** left over.
sparing adj. not wasteful; economical.
▷ SYNONYMS: **thrifty**, economical, frugal, careful, prudent, cautious.
− ANTONYMS: lavish, extravagant.
■ **sparingly** adv.
spark n. **1** a fiery particle. **2** a flash of light produced by an electrical discharge. **3** a small amount of a quality or feeling.
▷ SYNONYMS: **flash**, glint, twinkle, flicker, flare.
• v. **1** produce sparks. **2** cause.
▷ SYNONYMS: the arrest sparked off riots: **cause**, give rise to, occasion, bring about, start, precipitate, prompt, trigger, provoke, stimulate, stir up.
□ **spark plug** a device which ignites

S

the fuel in an internal-combustion engine.

sparkle v. **1** shine with flashes of light. **2** be lively and witty. **3** (**sparkling**) (of drink) fizzy.
▷ SYNONYMS: **1 glitter**, glint, glisten, twinkle, flicker, flash, shimmer. **2** (**sparkling**) *a sparkling conversation*: **scintillating**, exciting, exhilarating, stimulating, invigorating, vivacious, lively, vibrant. **3** (**sparkling**) *a glass of sparkling water*: **effervescent**, fizzy, carbonated, aerated.
• n. a sparkling light.
■ **sparkly** adj.

sparkler n. a hand-held firework that gives out sparks.

sparrow n. a small brown and grey bird.

sparse adj. thinly scattered.
▷ SYNONYMS: **scant**, scanty, scattered, scarce, infrequent, few and far between, meagre, paltry, limited, in short supply.
− ANTONYMS: abundant.
■ **sparsely** adv. **sparsity** n.

spartan adj. not comfortable or luxurious.
▷ SYNONYMS: **austere**, harsh, hard, frugal, rigorous, strict, severe, ascetic, self-denying, abstemious, bleak, bare, plain.
− ANTONYMS: luxurious.

spasm n. **1** a sudden involuntary contraction of a muscle. **2** a sudden spell of an activity etc.

spasmodic adj. occurring or done in brief, irregular bursts.
■ **spasmodically** adv.

spastic adj. **1** of muscle spasm. **2** offens. of cerebral palsy.
• n. offens. a person with cerebral palsy.
■ **spasticity** n.

> USAGE Say *person with cerebral palsy* rather than *spastic*, which many people find offensive.

spat¹ past & past part. of **SPIT**.

spat² n. **1** informal a petty quarrel. **2** a cloth covering formerly worn over the ankles and shoes.

spate n. **1** a large number of similar things coming one after another. **2** a sudden flood.
▷ SYNONYMS: **series**, succession, run, cluster, string, rash, epidemic, outbreak, wave, flurry.

spatial adj. of space.
■ **spatially** adv.

spatter v. spray or splash with drops or spots.

spatula n. an implement with a

broad, flat, blunt blade for mixing or spreading.

spawn v. **1** (of a fish, frog, etc.) release or deposit eggs. **2** give rise to.
• n. the eggs of fish, frogs, etc.

spay v. sterilize a female animal by removing the ovaries.

speak v. (**speaking, spoke**; past part. **spoken**) **1** say something. **2** communicate or be able to communicate in a specified language. **3** (**speak for**) express the views of. **4** be evidence of.
▷ SYNONYMS: **1 talk**, converse, communicate, chat, have a word, gossip, commune, say something; informal chew the fat. **2 say**, utter, state, declare, voice, express, pronounce, articulate, enunciate, verbalize. **3 give a speech**, talk, lecture, hold forth; informal spout, sound off.

speaker n. **1** a person who speaks. **2** (**Speaker**) the person in charge of proceedings in a parliament. **3** a loudspeaker.
▷ SYNONYMS: **speech-maker**, lecturer, talker, orator, spokesperson, spokesman/woman, reader, commentator, broadcaster, narrator.

spear n. **1** a weapon with a pointed tip and a long shaft. **2** a stem of asparagus or broccoli.
• v. pierce with a pointed object.
▫ **spearhead 1** a person leading a campaign or attack. **2** lead a campaign or attack.

spearmint n. a type of mint used in cooking.

spec n. (**on spec**) informal without any preparation or plan.

special adj. **1** better than or different from what is usual. **2** for a particular purpose or person.
▷ SYNONYMS: **1 exceptional**, unusual, remarkable, out of the ordinary, outstanding, unique. **2 distinctive**, distinct, individual, particular, specific, peculiar. **3 momentous**, significant, memorable, important, historic, red-letter.
− ANTONYMS: ordinary, general.
▫ **special effects** illusions created for films and television by computer graphics etc.
■ **specially** adv.

specialist n. an expert in a particular field.
▷ SYNONYMS: **expert**, authority, pundit, professional, connoisseur, master, maestro; informal buff.
■ **specialism** n.

speciality n. (pl. **specialities**) a subject

or skill in which someone is an expert.

▷ SYNONYMS: **strength**, strong point, forte, métier, strong suit, party piece, pièce de résistance, claim to fame.

specialize (or **-ise**) v. **1** be a specialist. **2** (**be specialized**) be adapted for a special function.

■ **specialization** n.

species n. (pl. **species**) a group of animals or plants able to breed with each other.

▷ SYNONYMS: **type**, kind, sort, breed, strain, variety, class, classification, category.

specific adj. **1** clearly defined or identified. **2** precise and clear.

▷ SYNONYMS: **1 particular**, specified, fixed, set, determined, distinct, definite. **2 detailed**, explicit, express, clear-cut, unequivocal, precise, exact.

– ANTONYMS: general, vague.

• n. (**specifics**) precise details.

■ **specifically** adv.

specification n. **1** the act of specifying. **2** a detailed description of the design and materials used to make something.

▷ SYNONYMS: *a shelter built to their specifications:* **instruction**, guideline, parameter, stipulation, requirement, condition, order, detail.

specify v. (**specifying**, **specified**) state or identify clearly and definitely.

▷ SYNONYMS: **state**, name, identify, define, set out, itemize, detail, list, enumerate, spell out, stipulate, lay down.

specimen n. **1** an individual animal, plant, etc. used as an example for study or display. **2** a sample for medical testing.

▷ SYNONYMS: **sample**, example, model, instance, illustration, demonstration.

specious adj. seeming reasonable, but actually wrong.

speck n. a tiny spot or particle.

speckle n. a small spot or patch of colour.

■ **speckled** adj.

specs pl. n. informal spectacles.

spectacle n. **1** a visually striking performance or display. **2** (**spectacles**) Brit. a pair of glasses.

▷ SYNONYMS: **1 display**, show, pageantry, performance, exhibition, pomp and circumstance, extravaganza, spectacular. **2 sight**, vision, scene, prospect, picture.

spectacular adj. very impressive or dramatic.

▷ SYNONYMS: **impressive**, magnificent, splendid, dazzling, sensational, stunning, dramatic, outstanding, memorable, unforgettable, striking, picturesque, eye-catching, breath-taking, glorious; informal out of this world.

– ANTONYMS: dull, unimpressive.

• n. a spectacular performance or event.

■ **spectacularly** adv.

spectator n. a person who watches a game or event.

▷ SYNONYMS: **watcher**, viewer, observer, onlooker, bystander, witness.

spectral adj. **1** of or like a ghost. **2** of the spectrum.

spectre (US **specter**) n. **1** a ghost. **2** a possible unwelcome occurrence.

▷ SYNONYMS: **ghost**, phantom, apparition, spirit, wraith, presence; informal spook.

spectrum n. (pl. **spectra**) **1** a band of colours produced by separating light into parts with different wavelengths. **2** a range of sound waves or other types of wave. **3** a range of beliefs, qualities, etc.

speculate v. **1** form a theory without firm evidence. **2** invest in stocks, property, etc. in the hope of making a profit.

▷ SYNONYMS: **1 conjecture**, theorize, hypothesize, guess, surmise, wonder, muse. **2 gamble**, venture, wager, invest, play the market.

■ **speculation** n. **speculator** n.

speculative adj. involving speculation.

▷ SYNONYMS: **1 conjectural**, suppositional, theoretical, hypothetical, tentative, unproven, unfounded, groundless, unsubstantiated. **2 risky**, hazardous, unsafe, uncertain, unpredictable; informal chancy.

speculum n. (pl. **specula**) a medical instrument for widening openings in the body to allow inspection.

speech n. **1** the expression of thoughts and feelings using spoken language. **2** a formal talk given to an audience. **3** a sequence of lines for one character in a play.

▷ SYNONYMS: **1 speaking**, talking, verbal communication, conversation, dialogue, discussion. **2** *her speech was slurred:* **diction**, elocution, articulation, enunciation, pronunciation, delivery. **3** *the everyday speech of ordinary people:* **language**, words, parlance, idiom, dialect, vernacular. **4 talk**, address, lecture, discourse, oration, presentation, sermon.

S

WORD LINKS
oral, **phonetic**, **phonic** relating to speech or speech sounds
verbal spoken rather than written

speechless adj. unable to speak due to shock or emotion.
▷ SYNONYMS: **lost for words**, dumb-struck, struck dumb, tongue-tied, inarticulate, mute, dumb, voiceless, silent.
speed n. **1** rate of movement or operation. **2** rapidity of movement or action. **3** each of the possible gear ratios of a bicycle. **4** informal an amphetamine drug.
▷ SYNONYMS: **1** rate, pace, tempo, momentum, velocity; informal lick. **2 rapidity**, swiftness, promptness, alacrity, briskness, haste, hurry; old use celerity.
– ANTONYMS: slowness.
 • v. (**speeding**, **speeded** or **sped**) **1** move quickly. **2** (**speed up**) move or work more quickly. **3** break the legal speed limit.
▷ SYNONYMS: **1 hurry**, rush, dash, race, sprint, career, shoot, hurtle, hare, fly, zoom, hasten; informal tear, belt, pelt; Brit. informal bomb. **2** *a holiday will speed his recovery:* **hasten**, accelerate, advance, further, promote, boost, stimulate, aid, assist, facilitate.
– ANTONYMS: slow, hinder.
 □ **speedboat** a fast motorboat. **speedometer** a device indicating a vehicle's speed. **speedway** Brit. motorcycle racing on a dirt track.
speedy adj. (**speedier**, **speediest**) rapid.
▷ SYNONYMS: **fast**, swift, quick, rapid, expeditious, prompt, immediate, brisk, hasty, hurried, precipitate, rushed.
– ANTONYMS: slow.
 ■ **speedily** adv.
speleology /spee-li-**ol**-uh-ji/ n. the study or exploration of caves.
spell v. (**spelling**, **spelled** or **spelt**) **1** write or say the letters forming a word in correct order. **2** mean or have as a result. **3** (**spell out**) state explicitly.
▷ SYNONYMS: *the plans spell disaster for the economy:* **signify**, signal, mean, amount to, add up to, constitute.
 • n. **1** a short period of time. **2** words spoken to make a piece of magic work. **3** a very attractive or fascinating quality.
▷ SYNONYMS: **1** *a spell of wet and windy weather:* **period**, time, bout, interval, season, stretch, run; Brit. informal patch.

2 charm, incantation, magic formula, curse; N. Amer. hex; (**spells**) magic, sorcery, witchcraft. **3** *she surrendered to his spell:* **influence**, charm, magnetism, charisma, magic.
 □ **spellchecker** a computer program which checks spelling in an electronic document.
 ■ **spelling** n.
spellbound adj. completely fascinated.
▷ SYNONYMS: **enthralled**, fascinated, rapt, riveted, transfixed, gripped, captivated, entranced, bewitched, enchanted, mesmerized, hypnotized.
spend v. (**spending**, **spent**) **1** pay money to buy or hire goods or services. **2** pass time. **3** use or use up.
▷ SYNONYMS: **1 pay out**, expend, disburse; informal lay out, blow, splurge. **2 pass**, occupy, fill, take up, while away.
 □ **spendthrift** a person who spends money irresponsibly.
 ■ **spender** n.
sperm n. (pl. **sperm** or **sperms**) **1** semen. **2** a spermatozoon.
spermatozoon /sper-muh-tuh-**zoh**-on/ n. (pl. **spermatozoa**) the male sex cell of an animal, that fertilizes the egg.
spermicide n. a contraceptive substance that kills sperm.
spew v. **1** pour out in large quantities. **2** informal vomit.
sphere n. **1** a perfectly round solid figure. **2** an area of activity or interest.
▷ SYNONYMS: **1 globe**, ball, orb, bubble. **2** *his sphere of influence:* **area**, field, compass, orbit, range, scope, extent. **3 domain**, realm, province, field, area, territory, arena, department.
 ■ **spherical** adj. **spherically** adv.
sphincter n. a ring of muscle surrounding an opening in the body.
sphinx n. an ancient Egyptian stone figure with a lion's body and a human or animal head.
spice n. **1** a strong-tasting vegetable substance for flavouring food. **2** interest and excitement.
▷ SYNONYMS: **1 seasoning**, flavouring, condiment. **2 excitement**, interest, colour, piquancy, zest, an edge.
 • v. **1** flavour with spice. **2** (**spice up**) make more interesting.
spick and span adj. neat and clean.
spicy adj. (**spicier**, **spiciest**) strongly flavoured.
▷ SYNONYMS: **hot**, tangy, peppery, piquant, spiced, pungent.
– ANTONYMS: bland.

S

■ **spiciness** n.

spider n. an eight-legged insect-like animal.
▷ SYNONYMS: arachnid.
■ **spidery** adj.

> **WORD LINKS**
> **arachnophobia** fear of spiders

spiel /shpeel, speel/ n. informal an elaborate and insincere persuasive speech.

spigot n. a small peg or plug.

spike n. a thin, pointed piece of metal, wood, etc.
▷ SYNONYMS: **prong**, pin, barb, point, skewer, stake, spit.
• v. **1** pierce with a pointed object. **2** put an end to. **3** informal secretly add alcohol or a drug to drink or food.
■ **spiked** adj. **spiky** adj.

spill v. (**spilling, spilt** or **spilled**) **1** flow or cause to flow over the edge of a container. **2** move or empty out from a place.
▷ SYNONYMS: **1 knock over**, tip over, upset, overturn. **2 overflow**, brim over, run over, pour, slop, slosh, splash, leak.
• n. **1** an amount spilt. **2** a fall from a horse or bicycle. **3** a thin strip of wood or paper for lighting a fire.
■ **spillage** n.

spin v. (**spinning, spun**) **1** turn round quickly. **2** draw out and twist fibres to make yarn. **3** (**spin out**) prolong.
▷ SYNONYMS: **1 revolve**, rotate, turn, go round, whirl, twirl, gyrate. **2** she spun round to face him: **whirl**, wheel, turn, swing, twist, swivel, pivot.
• n. **1** a spinning motion. **2** informal a short drive for pleasure. **3** a favourable slant given to a news story.
▷ SYNONYMS: **1 rotation**, revolution, turn, whirl, twirl, gyration. **2 slant**, angle, twist, bias. **3 trip**, jaunt, outing, excursion, journey, drive, ride, run, turn; informal tootle.
□ **spin doctor** informal a person employed by a political party to give a favourable interpretation of events to the media. **spin-off** a product or benefit produced after the main activity.
■ **spinner** n.

spina bifida n. a condition in which part of the spinal cord is exposed, often causing paralysis.

spinach n. a vegetable with large green leaves.

spinal adj. of the spine.
□ **spinal cord** the nerve fibres in the spine connecting all parts of the body to the brain.

spindle n. **1** a rod with tapered ends, used in spinning wool etc. by hand. **2** a rod around which something revolves.

spindly adj. long or tall and thin.

spindrift n. sea spray.

spine n. **1** the row of bones extending from the skull to the small of the back. **2** the part of a book enclosing the inner edges of the pages. **3** a hard pointed projection on certain plants and animals.
▷ SYNONYMS: **1 backbone**, vertebrae, spinal column, back. **2 needle**, quill, bristle, barb, spike, prickle, thorn.
■ **spiny** adj.

spineless adj. **1** not brave or determined. **2** having no spine.

spinet n. a small harpsichord.

spinnaker n. a large extra sail on a racing yacht.

spinney n. (pl. **spinneys**) Brit. a small wooded area.

spinster n. an unmarried woman.

spiral adj. forming a continuous curve around a central point or axis.
▷ SYNONYMS: **coiled**, helical, curling, winding, twisting.
• n. **1** a spiral curve or shape. **2** a progressive rise or fall of prices, wages, etc.
▷ SYNONYMS: **coil**, curl, twist, whorl, scroll, helix, corkscrew.
• v. (**spiralling, spiralled**; US **spiraling, spiraled**) **1** follow a spiral course. **2** increase or decrease rapidly.
▷ SYNONYMS: smoke spiralled up: **coil**, wind, swirl, twist, snake.
■ **spirally** adv.

spire n. a tall pointed structure on the top of a church tower.

spirit n. **1** a person's character and feelings, often believed to survive after the body is dead. **2** a supernatural being. **3** typical character, quality, or mood. **4** (**spirits**) a person's mood. **5** courage and determination. **6** the intended meaning of a law etc. **7** strong distilled alcoholic drink.
▷ SYNONYMS: **1 soul**, psyche, inner self, mind. **2 ghost**, phantom, spectre, apparition, presence. **3 mood**, frame/state of mind, humour, temper, morale, esprit de corps. **4 ethos**, essence, atmosphere, mood, feeling, climate. **5 enthusiasm**, energy, verve, vigour, dynamism, dash, sparkle, exuberance, gusto, fervour, zeal, fire, passion; informal get-up-and-go.
– ANTONYMS: body, flesh.

S

• v. (**spiriting**, **spirited**) take away rapidly and secretly.
□ **spirit level** a sealed glass tube containing a bubble in liquid whose position shows whether a surface is level.

spirited adj. energetic and determined.
▷ SYNONYMS: **lively**, energetic, enthusiastic, vigorous, dynamic, passionate; informal **feisty**, **gutsy**; N. Amer. informal **peppy**.
– ANTONYMS: apathetic, lifeless.
■ **spiritedly** adv.

spiritual adj. **1** of the human spirit. **2** of religion or religious belief.
▷ SYNONYMS: **1 inner**, mental, psychological, incorporeal, non-material. **2 religious**, sacred, divine, holy, devotional.
– ANTONYMS: physical, secular.
• n. a kind of religious song associated with black American Christians.
■ **spirituality** n. **spiritually** adv.

spiritualism n. the belief that it is possible to communicate with the spirits of the dead.
■ **spiritualist** n.

spirituous adj. old use strongly alcoholic.

spit v. (**spitting**, **spat** or **spit**) **1** forcibly eject saliva, food, or liquid from the mouth. **2** say in a hostile way. **3** Brit. rain lightly.
▷ SYNONYMS: **expectorate**, hawk; Brit. informal **gob**.
• n. **1** saliva. **2** a metal rod for holding and turning roasting meat. **3** a narrow point of land projecting into the sea.
▷ SYNONYMS: **spittle**, saliva, sputum, slobber, dribble.
□ **spitfire** a hot-tempered person.

spite n. a desire to annoy or upset.
▷ SYNONYMS: **malice**, malevolence, ill will, vindictiveness, meanness, nastiness; informal **bitchiness**, **cattiness**.
• v. deliberately annoy or upset.
▷ SYNONYMS: **upset**, hurt, wound.
– ANTONYMS: please.
□ **in spite of** without being affected by.

spiteful adj. deliberately hurtful.
▷ SYNONYMS: **malicious**, malevolent, vindictive, vengeful, mean, nasty, hurtful, mischievous, cruel, unkind; informal **bitchy**, **catty**.
– ANTONYMS: benevolent.
■ **spitefully** adv.

spittle n. saliva.

spittoon n. a container for spitting into.

splash v. **1** (of a liquid) fall in scattered drops. **2** wet with scattered drops. **3** move around in water, causing it to fly about. **4** display a story etc. prominently in a newspaper. **5** (**splash out**) Brit. informal spend money freely.
▷ SYNONYMS: **1 sprinkle**, spatter, splatter, spray, shower, wash, squirt, slosh, slop. **2 wash**, break, lap, pound. **3 paddle**, wade, wallow.
• n. **1** an act of splashing. **2** a patch of colour.

splatter v. spatter.

splay v. spread wide apart.

spleen n. **1** an abdominal organ involved in producing and removing blood cells. **2** bad temper.

splendid adj. **1** very impressive. **2** excellent.
▷ SYNONYMS: **1 magnificent**, sumptuous, grand, imposing, superb, spectacular, resplendent, rich, lavish, ornate, gorgeous, glorious, dazzling, handsome, beautiful; informal **plush**; Brit. informal **swish**. **2 excellent**, wonderful, marvellous, superb, glorious, lovely, delightful, first-class; informal **super**, great, amazing, fantastic, terrific, tremendous; Brit. informal **smashing**, brilliant.
– ANTONYMS: simple, modest, inferior.
■ **splendidly** adv.

splendour (US **splendor**) n. magnificent and impressive appearance.
▷ SYNONYMS: **magnificence**, sumptuousness, grandeur, resplendence, richness, glory, majesty.
– ANTONYMS: simplicity.

splenetic adj. bad-tempered.

splice v. join by interweaving or overlapping the ends.

splint n. a rigid support for a broken bone.

splinter n. a small, thin, sharp fragment of wood etc.
▷ SYNONYMS: **sliver**, chip, shard, fragment, shred; Scottish **skelf**.
• v. break into splinters.
▷ SYNONYMS: **shatter**, smash, smash into smithereens, fracture, split, crack, disintegrate.
□ **splinter group** a small organization that has broken away from a larger one.

split v. (**splitting**, **split**) **1** break into parts by force. **2** divide into parts or groups. **3** (often **split up**) end a relationship.
▷ SYNONYMS: **1 break**, cut, burst, snap, crack, splinter, fracture, rupture, come apart. **2 tear**, rip, slash, slit.

3 share, divide up, distribute, dole out, parcel out, carve up, slice up, apportion. **4 fork**, divide, branch, diverge. **5** *the band split up last year:* **break up**, separate, part, part company, go their separate ways.
– ANTONYMS: join, unite, converge.
•n. **1** a tear or crack. **2** an act of splitting. **3** (**the splits**) a leap or seated position with the legs straight and at right angles to the body.
▷ SYNONYMS: **1 crack**, fissure, cleft, crevice, break, fracture, breach. **2 rip**, tear, cut, rent, slash, slit. **3 division**, rift, breach, schism, rupture, separation, estrangement. **4 break-up**, split-up, separation, parting, estrangement, rift.
– ANTONYMS: merger.
□ **split infinitive** an infinitive with a word placed between *to* and the verb.
split second a very brief moment.
splodge n. Brit. informal a spot or smear.
splurge informal v. spend extravagantly.
•n. a burst of extravagance.
splutter v. **1** make a series of short spitting sounds. **2** say incoherently.
spoil v. (**spoiling**, **spoilt** or **spoiled**) **1** make less good or enjoyable. **2** harm a child's character by being too indulgent. **3** (of food) become unfit for eating. **4** (**be spoiling for**) be very eager for.
▷ SYNONYMS: **1 damage**, ruin, impair, blemish, disfigure, blight, deface, harm, destroy, wreck. **2** *rain spoiled my plans:* **upset**, mess up, ruin, wreck, undo, sabotage, scotch, torpedo; informal muck up, screw up, do for; Brit. informal scupper. **3 overindulge**, pamper, indulge, mollycoddle, cosset, wait on someone hand and foot. **4 go bad**, go off, go rancid, turn, go sour, rot, decompose, decay, perish.
– ANTONYMS: improve, enhance.
•n. (**spoils**) stolen goods.
spoiler n. **1** a flap on an aircraft wing raised to create drag and so reduce speed. **2** a similar device on a vehicle to improve roadholding at speed.
spoilsport n. a person who spoils others' enjoyment.
▷ SYNONYMS: **killjoy**, dog in the manger, misery; informal wet blanket, party-pooper.
spoke¹ n. each of the rods connecting the centre of a wheel to its rim.
spoke² past of SPEAK.
spoken past part. of SPEAK.
•adj. said rather than written: *spoken communication.*
▷ SYNONYMS: **verbal**, oral, vocal,

unwritten, word-of-mouth.
spokesman (or **spokeswoman** or **spokesperson**) n. a person who makes statements on behalf of a group.
sponge n. **1** an invertebrate sea creature with a soft porous body. **2** a piece of a light, absorbent substance for washing, padding, etc. **3** Brit. a very light cake.
•v. (**sponging** or **spongeing**, **sponged**) **1** clean with a wet sponge. **2** informal live at the expense of others.
■ **sponger** n. **spongy** adj.
spongiform adj. with a porous sponge-like texture.
sponsor n. **1** a person or organization that contributes to the costs of an event in return for advertising. **2** a person who promises to give money to a charity after another person has taken part in a stated activity. **3** a person who proposes a new law.
▷ SYNONYMS: **backer**, patron, promoter, benefactor, supporter, contributor.
•v. be a sponsor for.
▷ SYNONYMS: **finance**, fund, subsidize, back, promote, support, contribute to; N. Amer. informal bankroll.
■ **sponsorship** n.

USAGE -*or*, not -*er*: sponsor.

spontaneous adj. **1** done or occurring as a result of an impulse or without apparent external cause. **2** natural and relaxed.
▷ SYNONYMS: **1 unplanned**, unpremeditated, impulsive, impromptu, spur-of-the-moment, unprompted; informal off-the-cuff. **2 natural**, uninhibited, relaxed, unselfconscious, unaffected.
■ **spontaneity** n. **spontaneously** adv.
spoof n. informal a parody.
spook n. informal a ghost.
■ **spookily** adv. **spooky** adj.
spool n. a reel on which thread, film, etc. is wound.
•v. wind on to a spool.
spoon n. an eating and cooking utensil with a small, shallow bowl on a handle.
•v. transfer with a spoon.
□ **spoon-feed** give excessive help to.
■ **spoonful** n.
spoonerism n. the accidental swapping round of the initial sounds or letters of two or more words, as in *you hissed the mystery lectures.*
spoor n. the track or scent of an animal.
sporadic adj. occurring irregularly or only in a few places.

S

▷ SYNONYMS: **occasional**, infrequent, irregular, periodic, scattered, patchy, isolated, odd, intermittent, spasmodic, fitful, desultory, erratic, unpredictable.

– ANTONYMS: frequent, continuous.

■ **sporadically** adv.

spore n. a tiny reproductive cell produced by ferns, fungi, etc.

sporran n. a pouch worn in front of a kilt.

sport n. **1** a competitive activity involving physical effort and skill. **2** informal a person who behaves well when teased or defeated.
• v. **1** wear a distinctive item. **2** play.

▷ SYNONYMS: **wear**, have on, dress in, show off, parade, flaunt.
□ **sports car** a low-built fast car. **sports jacket** a man's informal jacket. **sportsman** (or **sportswoman**) **1** a person who takes part in a sport. **2** a fair and generous person.

■ **sporty**

sporting adj. **1** connected with or interested in sport. **2** fair and generous.

▷ SYNONYMS: **sportsmanlike**, generous, considerate, fair; Brit. informal decent.
□ **sporting chance** a reasonable chance of success.

sportive adj. playful.

sporty adj. (**sportier**, **sportiest**) informal **1** good at sport. **2** (of clothing) suitable for sport or casual wear. **3** (of a car) compact and with fast acceleration.

▷ SYNONYMS: **athletic**, fit, active, energetic.

spot n. **1** a small round mark. **2** a pimple. **3** a place or position.

▷ SYNONYMS: **1 mark**, patch, dot, fleck, smudge, smear, stain, blotch, splash; informal splotch, splodge. **2 pimple**, pustule, blackhead, boil, blemish; informal zit; Scottish informal plook; (**spots**) acne, rash. **3 place**, site, position, situation, setting, location, venue.
• v. (**spotting**, **spotted**) **1** notice or perceive. **2** mark with spots.

▷ SYNONYMS: **see**, notice, observe, catch sight of, detect, make out, discern, recognize, identify, locate; Brit. informal clock; literary espy, descry.
□ **on the spot 1** immediately. **2** at the scene of an event. **spot check** a random check.

■ **spotter** n. **spotty** adj.

spotless adj. absolutely clean or pure.

▷ SYNONYMS: **clean**, pristine, immaculate, shining, shiny, gleaming, spick

and span.

– ANTONYMS: filthy.

■ **spotlessly** adv.

spotlight n. **1** a lamp projecting a strong beam of light on a small area. **2** intense public attention.

▷ SYNONYMS: **attention**, glare of publicity, limelight, public eye.

spouse n. a husband or wife.

▷ SYNONYMS: **partner**, husband, wife, mate, consort; informal better half; Brit. informal other half.

spout n. **1** a projecting tube or lip through or over which liquid can be poured. **2** a stream of liquid.
• v. **1** send out or flow in a stream. **2** express in a lengthy or emphatic way.

sprain v. injure a joint by wrenching it violently.
• n. such an injury.

sprang past of SPRING.

sprat n. a small edible sea fish.

sprawl v. **1** sit, lie, or fall with the arms and legs spread out awkwardly. **2** spread out in a disorganized way.

▷ SYNONYMS: **stretch out**, lounge, loll, slump, flop, slouch.
• n. the disorganized expansion of a city.

spray n. **1** liquid sent through the air in tiny drops. **2** a liquid or device for spraying. **3** a stem or branch with flowers and leaves. **4** a bunch of cut flowers.

▷ SYNONYMS: **1 shower**, sprinkle, jet, squirt, mist, spume, foam, froth, spindrift. **2 aerosol**, vaporizer, atomizer, sprinkler.
• v. **1** apply a spray of liquid to. **2** scatter over an area.

▷ SYNONYMS: **1 sprinkle**, dribble, drizzle, water, soak, douse, drench. **2 spout**, jet, gush, spurt, shoot, squirt.
□ **spray gun** a device for spraying paint etc.

spread v. (**spreading**, **spread**) **1** open out so as to be wider, longer, etc. **2** extend over a wide area or period. **3** reach or cause to reach more and more people. **4** apply in an even layer.

▷ SYNONYMS: **1 lay out**, open out, unfurl, unroll, roll out, straighten out, fan out, stretch out, extend. **2** *the landscape spread out below:* **extend**, stretch, sprawl. **3 scatter**, strew, disperse, distribute. **4 circulate**, broadcast, put about, publicize, propagate, repeat. **5 travel**, move, be borne, sweep, diffuse, reproduce, be passed on, be transmitted. **6 smear**, daub, plaster, apply, rub.

S

•n. **1** the act of spreading. **2** extent or range. **3** a paste for spreading on bread. **4** an article covering several pages of a newspaper. **5** informal a lavish meal.
▷ SYNONYMS: **1 expansion**, proliferation, dissemination, diffusion, transmission, propagation. **2 span**, width, extent, stretch, reach.
□ **spreadeagled** with the arms and legs extended. **spreadsheet** a computer program in which figures in a grid are used in calculations.

spree n. a period of unrestrained activity.
▷ SYNONYMS: **bout**, orgy; informal binge, splurge.

sprig n. a small stem with leaves or flowers.

sprightly adj. (**sprightlier**, **sprightliest**) lively or energetic.
■ **sprightliness** n.

spring v. (**springing**, **sprang**; past part. **sprung**) **1** jump. **2** move or do suddenly. **3** (**spring from**) come or appear from. **4** (**spring up**) suddenly develop or appear. **5** (**sprung**) having springs.
▷ SYNONYMS: **1 leap**, jump, bound, vault, hop. **2** (**spring from**) **originate from**, derive from, arise in, stem from, emanate from, evolve from
•n. **1** the season between winter and summer. **2** a spiral coil that returns to its former shape after being pressed or pulled. **3** a jump. **4** a place where water flows from an underground source. **5** elasticity.
▷ SYNONYMS: **springiness**, bounce, resilience, elasticity, flexibility, stretch, stretchiness, give.
□ **springboard** a flexible board from which a diver or gymnast jumps to gain more power. **spring-clean** Brit. clean thoroughly. **spring tide** a tide when there is the greatest difference between high and low water.
■ **springy** adj.

> **WORD LINKS**
> **vernal** relating to the season of spring

springbok n. a southern African gazelle.

sprinkle v. scatter small drops or particles over a surface.
▷ SYNONYMS: **splash**, trickle, drizzle, spray, shower, drip, scatter, strew, dredge, dust.

sprinkler n. a device for watering lawns or putting out fires.

sprinkling n. a small, thinly distributed amount.

sprint v. run at full speed.
▷ SYNONYMS: **run**, race, rush, dash, bolt, fly, charge, shoot, speed; informal hotfoot it, leg it.
− ANTONYMS: stroll.
•n. **1** a fast run. **2** a short, fast race.
■ **sprinter** n.

sprite n. an elf or fairy.

spritzer n. a drink of white wine and soda water.

sprocket n. a projection on a wheel, engaging with links on a chain etc.

sprout v. **1** produce shoots, hair, etc. **2** appear or develop suddenly.
▷ SYNONYMS: **1 germinate**, put/send out shoots, bud. **2 spring**, come up, grow, develop, appear.
•n. **1** a shoot of a plant. **2** a Brussels sprout.

spruce n. a coniferous tree.
•adj. neat and smart.
▷ SYNONYMS: **neat**, well groomed, well turned out, well dressed, smart, trim, dapper; informal natty, snazzy.
− ANTONYMS: dishevelled.
•v. (**spruce up**) make smarter.

sprung past part. of **SPRING**.

spry adj. lively.

spud n. informal a potato.

spume n. froth.

spun past & past part. of **SPIN**.

spunk n. informal courage and spirit.

spur n. **1** a spiked device worn on a rider's heel for urging a horse on. **2** an encouragement. **3** an area projecting from a mountain.
▷ SYNONYMS: **stimulus**, incentive, encouragement, inducement, impetus, motivation.
− ANTONYMS: disincentive.
•v. (**spurring**, **spurred**) **1** encourage. **2** urge a horse on with spurs.
▷ SYNONYMS: **stimulate**, encourage, prompt, prod, impel, motivate, move, galvanize, inspire, drive.
− ANTONYMS: discourage.
□ **on the spur of the moment** on impulse.

spurious adj. false or fake.
▷ SYNONYMS: **bogus**, fake, false, fraudulent, sham, artificial, imitation, simulated, feigned; informal phoney.
− ANTONYMS: genuine.
■ **spuriously** adv.

spurn v. reject with contempt.
▷ SYNONYMS: **reject**, rebuff, scorn, turn down, treat with contempt, disdain, look down your nose at; informal turn your nose up at.
− ANTONYMS: welcome, accept.

spurt v. **1** gush out in a stream. **2** move with a sudden burst of speed.

S

▷ SYNONYMS: **squirt**, shoot, jet, erupt, gush, pour, stream, pump, surge, spew, course, well, spring, burst, spout.
• n. **1** a gushing stream. **2** a sudden burst of activity or speed.
▷ SYNONYMS: **squirt**, jet, gush, stream, rush, surge, flood, cascade, torrent.

sputter v. splutter.

sputum n. saliva and mucus that is coughed up.

spy n. (pl. **spies**) a person who secretly collects information on an enemy or competitor.
▷ SYNONYMS: **agent**, mole, plant; N. Amer. informal spook.
• v. (**spying**, **spied**) **1** be a spy. **2** watch secretly. **3** see.
▷ SYNONYMS: **notice**, observe, see, spot, sight, catch sight of, glimpse, make out, discern, detect.

spying n. the activity of a spy.
▷ SYNONYMS: **espionage**, intelligence gathering, surveillance, infiltration.

sq. abbrev. square.

squabble n. a noisy quarrel about a trivial matter.
▷ SYNONYMS: **quarrel**, disagreement, row, argument, dispute, wrangle, clash, altercation; informal tiff, set-to, run-in, scrap, dust-up; Brit. informal barney, ding-dong.
• v. have a squabble.
▷ SYNONYMS: **quarrel**, row, argue, bicker, disagree; informal scrap.

squad n. **1** a division of a police force. **2** a group of sports players from which a team is chosen. **3** a small group of soldiers.
▷ SYNONYMS: **1 team**, crew, gang, force. **2 detachment**, detail, unit, platoon, battery, troop, patrol, squadron, commando.

squadron n. **1** a unit of an air force. **2** a division of an armoured regiment. **3** a group of warships.

squalid adj. **1** dirty and unpleasant. **2** immoral or dishonest.
▷ SYNONYMS: **1 dirty**, filthy, dingy, grubby, grimy, wretched, miserable, mean, seedy, shabby, sordid, insalubrious; Brit. informal grotty. **2 improper**, sordid, unseemly, unsavoury, sleazy, cheap, base, low, corrupt, dishonest, dishonourable, disreputable, discreditable, contemptible, shameful.
– ANTONYMS: clean.
■ **squalor** n.

squall n. a sudden storm or wind.
■ **squally** adj.

squander v. waste money, time, etc.

▷ SYNONYMS: **waste**, throw away, misuse, misspend, fritter away, spend like water; informal blow, run through, splurge, pour down the drain.
– ANTONYMS: save.

square n. **1** a plane figure with four equal straight sides and four right angles. **2** an open area surrounded by buildings. **3** the product of a number multiplied by itself. **4** an instrument for testing right angles.
▷ SYNONYMS: **piazza**, plaza, quadrangle.
• adj. **1** having the shape of a square. **2** right-angled. **3** equal to the area of a square whose side is of the unit specified. **4** level or parallel. **5** informal old-fashioned or conventional.
▷ SYNONYMS: **level**, even, drawn, equal, tied, level pegging; informal even-stevens.
• adv. directly; straight.
• v. **1** make square. **2** (**squared**) marked out in squares. **3** multiply a number by itself. **4** make or be compatible. **5** settle a bill.
□ **square dance** a dance in which four couples face one another in a square. **square meal** a large meal. **square root** a number which produces a specified quantity when multiplied by itself. **square up** take up the position of a person about to fight.
■ **squarely** adv.

squash v. **1** crush or squeeze so as to become flat or out of shape. **2** force into a restricted space. **3** suppress or reject.
▷ SYNONYMS: **1 crush**, squeeze, mash, pulp, flatten, compress, distort, pound, trample. **2 force**, ram, thrust, push, cram, jam, stuff, pack, squeeze, wedge.
• n. **1** a state of being squashed. **2** Brit. a concentrated fruit-flavoured liquid, diluted to make a drink. **3** a game played with rackets and a small ball in a closed court. **4** a vegetable like a marrow.
■ **squashy** adj.

squat v. (**squatting**, **squatted**) **1** crouch or sit on the heels. **2** unlawfully occupy an uninhabited building.
• adj. short and wide.
• n. **1** a squatting position. **2** a building occupied unlawfully.
■ **squatter** n.

squawk v. make a loud, harsh noise.
• n. a squawking sound.

squeak n. a short, high-pitched sound.
▷ SYNONYMS: **peep**, cheep, squeal, tweet, yelp, whimper.

• v. make a squeak.
■ **squeaky** adj.

squeal n. a long, high-pitched sound.
• v. **1** make a squeal. **2** (**squeal on**) informal inform on.

squeamish adj. easily disgusted or made to feel sick.

squeeze v. **1** firmly press from opposite or all sides. **2** crush to extract liquid. **3** manage to get into or through a restricted space.
▷ SYNONYMS: **1 compress**, press, crush, squash, pinch, nip, grasp, grip, clutch. **2 extract**, press, force, express. **3 force**, thrust, cram, ram, jam, stuff, pack, wedge, press, push, squash, crush, crowd, force your way.
• n. **1** an act of squeezing. **2** a hug. **3** a small amount of liquid produced by squeezing. **4** a strong financial demand or pressure.
▷ SYNONYMS: **1 press**, pinch, nip, grasp, grip, clutch, hug. **2 crush**, jam, squash, congestion.

squelch v. make a soft sucking sound, e.g. by treading in mud.
• n. a squelching sound.
■ **squelchy** adj.

squib n. a small firework.

squid n. a sea animal with a long body and tentacles.

squiggle n. a short curly line.
■ **squiggly** adj.

squint v. **1** look at with partly closed eyes. **2** have a squint affecting one eye.
• n. a condition in which one eye looks in a different direction from the other.

squire n. a country gentleman.

squirm v. **1** wriggle. **2** be embarrassed.
▷ SYNONYMS: **1 wriggle**, wiggle, writhe, twist, slither, fidget, twitch, toss and turn. **2 wince**, shudder.

squirrel n. a bushy-tailed rodent that lives in trees.

squirt v. **1** force liquid out in a thin jet from a small opening. **2** wet with a jet of liquid.
▷ SYNONYMS: **1 spurt**, shoot, spray, jet, erupt, gush, rush, pump, surge, stream, spew, well, issue, emanate. **2 splash**, spray, shower, sprinkle.
• n. **1** a thin jet of liquid. **2** informal an insignificant person.

squish v. make a soft squelching sound.
■ **squishy** adj.

SS abbrev. **1** Saints. **2** steamship.
• n. the Nazi special police force.

St abbrev. **1** Saint. **2** Street. **3** (**st**) stone (in weight).

stab v. (**stabbing**, **stabbed**) pierce, wound, or kill with a knife or other pointed object.
▷ SYNONYMS: **knife**, run through, skewer, spear, gore, spike, impale.
• n. **1** an act of stabbing. **2** a sudden sharp feeling or pain. **3** informal an attempt.
▷ SYNONYMS: **1** *a stab of pain:* **twinge**, pang, throb, spasm, cramp, prick. **2 attempt**, try, endeavour, effort; informal go, shot, crack, bash.

stabilize (or **-ise**) v. make or become stable.
■ **stabilization** n. **stabilizer** n.

stable adj. **1** firmly fixed. **2** emotionally well-balanced. **3** not likely to change or fail.
▷ SYNONYMS: **1 firm**, solid, steady, secure. **2 well balanced**, well adjusted, of sound mind, compos mentis, sane, normal, rational, reasonable, sensible. **3** *a stable relationship:* **secure**, solid, strong, steady, firm, sure, steadfast, established, enduring, lasting, durable.
– ANTONYMS: unstable.
• n. **1** a building for housing horses. **2** an establishment where racehorses are kept and trained.
• v. put or keep in a stable.
■ **stability** n. **stably** adv.

staccato adv. & adj. Music with each sound sharply distinct.

stack n. **1** a neat pile or heap. **2** informal a large quantity. **3** a chimney.
▷ SYNONYMS: **heap**, pile, mound, mountain, pyramid, tower.
• v. **1** arrange in a stack. **2** arrange a pack of cards dishonestly.
▷ SYNONYMS: **heap up**, pile up, assemble, put together, collect.

stadium n. (pl. **stadiums** or **stadia**) a sports ground with tiers of seats for spectators.

staff n. **1** the employees of an organization. **2** a long stick used as a support or sign of authority. **3** a stave in music.
▷ SYNONYMS: **1 employees**, workers, workforce, personnel, human resources, manpower, labour. **2 stick**, stave, pole, rod.
• v. provide with staff.
▷ SYNONYMS: **man**, people, crew, work, operate.

stag n. a fully adult male deer.
□ **stag night** an all-male celebration for a man about to be married.

stage n. **1** a point or step in a process. **2** a raised platform on which actors, entertainers, etc. perform. **3** the

S

acting profession.

▷ SYNONYMS: **1 phase**, period, juncture, step, point, level. **2 part**, section, portion, leg, lap, circuit. **3 platform**, dais, stand, rostrum, podium.

• v. **1** present a performance of a play etc. **2** organize an event.

☐ **stagecoach** a horse-drawn vehicle formerly used to carry passengers along a regular route. **stage-manage** arrange carefully to create a specific effect. **stage manager** the person responsible for a play's technical arrangements. **stage whisper** a whisper intended to be overheard.

stagger v. **1** walk or move unsteadily. **2** astonish. **3** spread over a period.

▷ SYNONYMS: **1 lurch**, reel, sway, teeter, totter, stumble. **2 amaze**, astound, astonish, surprise, stun, confound, daze, take aback; informal flabbergast; Brit. informal knock for six.

• n. an act of staggering.

stagnant adj. **1** not flowing and having an unpleasant smell. **2** showing little activity.

▷ SYNONYMS: **1 still**, motionless, standing, stale, dirty, brackish. **2 inactive**, sluggish, slow-moving, static, flat, depressed, moribund, dead, dormant.

– ANTONYMS: flowing.

stagnate v. become stagnant.

■ **stagnation** n.

staid adj. respectable and unadventurous.

▷ SYNONYMS: **sedate**, respectable, serious, steady, conventional, trad-itional, unadventurous, set in your ways, sober, formal, stuffy, stiff; informal starchy, stick-in-the-mud.

– ANTONYMS: frivolous.

stain v. **1** mark or discolour with something that is hard to remove. **2** dye.

▷ SYNONYMS: **1 discolour**, soil, mark, spot, spatter, splatter, smear, splash, smudge, begrime. **2 colour**, tint, dye, paint.

• n. **1** a discoloured patch or mark. **2** a thing that damages a person's reputation. **3** a dye.

▷ SYNONYMS: **1 mark**, spot, blotch, smudge, smear. **2 blemish**, taint, blot, smear, slur, stigma.

☐ **stainless steel** a form of steel resistant to tarnishing and rust.

stair n. **1** each of a set of fixed steps. **2** (**stairs**) a set of such steps.

☐ **staircase** (or **stairway**) a set of stairs and its surrounding structure.

stairwell a shaft in which a staircase is built.

stake n. **1** a pointed post driven into the ground as a support, part of a fence, etc. **2** a sum of money gambled. **3** a share or interest in a business etc.

▷ SYNONYMS: **1 post**, pole, stick, spike, upright, support, cane. **2 bet**, wager, ante. **3 share**, interest, investment, involvement, concern.

• v. **1** support with a stake. **2** gamble.

▷ SYNONYMS: **bet**, wager, lay, put on, gamble, risk.

☐ **at stake** at risk. **stake out 1** keep under secret observation. **2** state a claim or opinion forcefully.

stalactite n. a deposit of calcium salts hanging from the roof of a cave.

stalagmite n. a deposit of calcium salts rising from the floor of a cave.

stale adj. **1** not fresh. **2** no longer new and interesting. **3** no longer interested or motivated.

▷ SYNONYMS: **1 old**, past its best, off, dry, hard, musty, mouldy, rancid. **2 stuffy**, musty, fusty, stagnant. **3 overused**, hackneyed, tired, worn out, overworked, threadbare, banal, clichéd, trite, unimaginative, uninspired, flat; informal old hat; N. Amer. played out.

– ANTONYMS: fresh.

■ **staleness** n.

stalemate n. **1** a situation in which progress seems impossible. **2** a position counting as a draw in chess.

▷ SYNONYMS: **deadlock**, impasse, stand-off; standstill.

stalk n. a stem or other supporting part of a plant.

• v. **1** follow stealthily. **2** harass with unwanted and obsessive attention. **3** walk stiffly or proudly.

▷ SYNONYMS: **1 trail**, follow, shadow, track, go after, hunt; informal tail. **2 strut**, stride, march, flounce, storm, stomp, sweep.

☐ **stalking horse** a person or thing used to disguise a real purpose.

■ **stalker** n.

stall n. **1** a stand or booth for the sale of goods in a market. **2** a compartment in a stable, toilet, etc. **3** (**stalls**) Brit. the ground-floor seats in a theatre. **4** a seat in the choir or chancel of a church.

▷ SYNONYMS: **1 stand**, table, counter, booth, kiosk. **2 pen**, coop, sty, corral, enclosure, compartment.

• v. **1** (of an engine) stop running. **2** stop making progress. **3** be vague so as to gain more time. **4** (of an aircraft) be moving too slowly to be controlled effectively.

▷ SYNONYMS: **1 delay**, play for time, procrastinate, hedge, drag your feet, filibuster, stonewall. **2 hold off**, stave off, keep at bay, evade, avoid.

stallion n. an uncastrated adult male horse.

stalwart adj. loyal and hard-working.

▷ SYNONYMS: **staunch**, loyal, faithful, committed, devoted, dedicated, dependable, reliable.

− ANTONYMS: disloyal.

• n. a stalwart supporter.

stamen n. a male fertilizing organ of a flower.

stamina n. the ability to sustain effort over a long period.

▷ SYNONYMS: **endurance**, staying power, energy, toughness, determination, tenacity, perseverance, grit.

stammer v. speak with difficulty, making sudden pauses and repeating the first letters of words.

▷ SYNONYMS: **stutter**, stumble over your words, hesitate, falter, pause, splutter.

• n. a tendency to stammer.

stamp v. **1** bring down the foot heavily. **2** (**stamp out**) put an end to decisively. **3** impress a pattern or mark on a surface.

▷ SYNONYMS: **1 trample**, step, tread, tramp, stomp, stump, clump, crush, squash, flatten. **2 imprint**, print, impress, punch, inscribe, emboss.

• n. **1** a small piece of paper stuck to a posted item to show that postage has been paid. **2** an instrument for stamping a pattern or mark. **3** a mark made by this. **4** a distinctive quality. **5** an act of stamping the foot.

▷ SYNONYMS: **mark**, hallmark, sign, seal, sure sign, smack, savour, air.

□ **stamping ground** a place where someone regularly spends time.

stampede n. a sudden rush of animals or people.

• v. take part in or cause a stampede.

stance n. **1** the way in which someone stands. **2** a standpoint.

▷ SYNONYMS: **1 posture**, body position, pose, attitude. **2 attitude**, opinion, standpoint, position, approach, policy, line.

stanch US = STAUNCH.

stanchion n. an upright bar or post.

stand v. (**standing, stood**) **1** be or become upright, supported by the feet. **2** place or be situated in a particular position. **3** remain valid or unchanged. **4** be in a specified condition. **5** tolerate. **6** Brit. be a candidate in an election.

▷ SYNONYMS: **1 rise**, get to your feet, get up, pick yourself up. **2 be situated**, be located, be positioned, be sited. **3 put**, set, erect, place, position, prop, install, arrange; informal park. **4 remain in force**, remain in operation, hold, hold good, apply, be the case, exist, prevail. **5 withstand**, endure, bear, put up with, take, cope with, handle, sustain, resist, stand up to. **6 put up with**, endure, tolerate, accept, take, abide, stand for, support, countenance; formal brook.

− ANTONYMS: sit, lie down.

• n. **1** an attitude towards an issue. **2** a determined effort to resist attack etc. **3** a structure for holding or displaying something. **4** a large structure for spectators. **5** a platform. **6** a stall or booth.

▷ SYNONYMS: **1 attitude**, stance, opinion, standpoint, position, approach, policy, line. **2 opposition**, resistance. **3 base**, support, platform, stage, dais, rest, plinth, tripod, rack, trivet. **4 stall**, counter, booth, kiosk.

□ **standby 1** readiness for action. **2** a person or thing ready to be used in an emergency. **3** (of tickets) sold only at the last minute. **stand by 1** look on without interfering. **2** remain loyal to or abide by. **3** be ready for action. **stand down** resign or withdraw. **stand for 1** be an abbreviation of or symbol for. **2** tolerate. **stand-in** a substitute. **stand in** deputize. **stand-off** a deadlock between two opponents. **stand-offish** informal distant and cold. **stand out** be noticeable. **standpipe** a vertical pipe extending from a water supply. **standpoint** an attitude towards a particular issue. **standstill** a situation without movement or activity. **stand up** informal fail to keep a date with someone. **stand up for** speak or act in support of.

standard n. **1** a level of quality or achievement. **2** a measure or model used to make comparisons. **3** (**standards**) principles of good behaviour. **4** a flag.

▷ SYNONYMS: **1 quality**, level, calibre, merit, excellence. **2 guideline**, norm, yardstick, benchmark, gauge, measure, criterion, guide, touchstone, model, pattern. **3** (**standards**) **principles**, ideals; morals, code of behaviour, ethics. **4 flag**, banner, ensign, colours.

• adj. used or accepted as normal or

S

average.

▷ SYNONYMS: **1 normal**, usual, average, typical, stock, common, ordinary, customary, conventional, established. **2 definitive**, classic, recognized, accepted, approved, authoritative.

– ANTONYMS: unusual, special.

□ **standard lamp** a tall lamp placed on the floor.

standardize (or **-ise**) v. cause to meet a standard.

■ **standardization** n.

standing n. **1** status or reputation. **2** duration.

▷ SYNONYMS: **1 status**, ranking, position, reputation, stature. **2 prestige**, rank, eminence, seniority, repute, stature, esteem, importance, account.

□ **standing order** Brit. an instruction to a bank to make regular fixed payments to someone.

stank past of STINK.

stanza n. a verse of poetry.

staphylococcus n. (pl. **staphylococci**) a bacterium causing pus to be formed.

staple n. **1** a small piece of bent wire used to fasten papers together. **2** a main item of trade or production. **3** a main or important element.

• adj. main or important.

▷ SYNONYMS: **main**, principal, chief, major, primary, leading, foremost, first, most important, predominant, dominant, basic, prime; informal number-one.

• v. secure with a staple or staples.

■ **stapler** n.

star n. **1** a huge mass of burning gas visible as a glowing point in the night sky. **2** a shape representing a star, often used as a mark of excellence. **3** a famous entertainer or sports player.

▷ SYNONYMS: **1 heavenly body**, celestial body. **2 celebrity**, superstar, famous name, household name, leading light, VIP, personality, luminary; informal celeb, big shot, megastar.

• v. (**starring**, **starred**) **1** have as a leading performer. **2** have a leading role in a film etc. **3** mark with a star.

□ **starfish** a star-shaped sea animal.

star sign a sign of the zodiac.

■ **stardom** n.

> **WORD LINKS**
> **astral**, **stellar**, **sidereal** relating to stars
> **astronomy** the science of stars, planets, and the universe

starboard n. the right-hand side of a ship or aircraft.

starch n. **1** a carbohydrate obtained from cereals and potatoes. **2** powder or spray used to stiffen fabric.

• v. stiffen with starch.

■ **starchy** adj.

stare v. look at with great concentration.

▷ SYNONYMS: **gaze**, gape, goggle, glare, ogle, peer; informal gawk; Brit. informal gawp.

• n. an act of staring.

stark adj. **1** desolate or bare. **2** sharply clear. **3** complete; sheer.

▷ SYNONYMS: **1 desolate**, bare, barren, empty, bleak, dreary, depressing, grim. **2 sharp**, sharply defined, crisp, distinct, clear, clear-cut.

– ANTONYMS: indistinct, ornate.

• adv. completely.

▷ SYNONYMS: *stark naked:* **completely**, totally, utterly, absolutely, entirely, wholly, fully, quite, altogether, thoroughly.

starlet n. informal a promising young female film star etc.

starling n. a bird with dark shiny plumage.

starry adj. (**starrier**, **starriest**) full of or lit by stars.

□ **starry-eyed** full of unrealistic hopes.

start v. **1** begin to do, be, happen, or operate. **2** cause to happen or operate. **3** begin to move or travel. **4** jerk from surprise.

▷ SYNONYMS: **1 begin**, commence, get under way, get going, go ahead, make a start; informal kick off, get the ball rolling, get the show on the road. **2 come into being**, begin, arise, originate, develop. **3 establish**, set up, found, create, bring into being, institute, initiate, inaugurate, introduce, open, launch. **4 activate**, switch/turn on, start up, fire up, boot up. **5 flinch**, jerk, jump, twitch, wince.

– ANTONYMS: end, finish, stop.

• n. **1** a beginning, or the point at which something begins. **2** an advantage given at the beginning of a race. **3** a jerk of surprise.

▷ SYNONYMS: **1 beginning**, commencement, inception, onset, inauguration, dawn, birth, emergence; informal kick-off. **2 lead**, head start, advantage. **3 jerk**, twitch, spasm, jump.

– ANTONYMS: end.

■ **starter** n.

startle v. shock or surprise.

▷ SYNONYMS: **surprise**, frighten, scare, alarm, shock, give someone a fright, make someone jump.

starve v. **1** suffer or die from hunger. **2** cause to starve. **3** informal feel very hungry. **4** (**be starved of**) be deprived of.
■ **starvation** n.

starving adj. suffering from hunger.
▷ SYNONYMS: **hungry**, undernourished, malnourished, starved; ravenous, famished.

stash informal v. store secretly.
• n. a secret store.

stasis /stay-sis/ n. a period or state when there is no activity or change.

state n. **1** the condition of someone or something at a particular time. **2** a country considered as an organized political unit. **3** an area forming part of a federal republic. **4** the government of a country. **5** ceremony associated with monarchy or government. **6** informal an agitated condition.
▷ SYNONYMS: **1 condition**, shape, position, situation, circumstances, state of affairs, predicament, plight. **2 country**, nation, land, kingdom, realm, power, republic. **3 government**, parliament, administration, regime. **4 state of anxiety**, panic, fluster; informal flap, tizzy.
• v. express in words.
▷ SYNONYMS: **express**, voice, utter, put into words, declare, announce, make known, put across/over, communicate, air.
□ **stateroom** a private cabin on a ship. **statesman** (or **stateswoman**) an experienced and respected political leader.

stateless adj. not recognized as a citizen of any country.

stately adj. (**statelier**, **stateliest**) dignified or grand.
▷ SYNONYMS: **dignified**, majestic, ceremonious, courtly, imposing, solemn, regal, grand.
– ANTONYMS: undignified.

statement n. **1** a clear expression of something in words. **2** a formal account of facts or events. **3** a document listing amounts paid into and out of a bank account.
▷ SYNONYMS: **declaration**, expression, affirmation, assertion, announcement, utterance, communication, bulletin, communiqué.

static adj. not moving, active, or changing.
▷ SYNONYMS: **1 unchanged**, fixed, stable, steady, unchanging, unvarying, constant. **2 stationary**, motionless, immobile, unmoving, still, at a

standstill.
– ANTONYMS: variable, dynamic.
• n. **1** (or **static electricity**) an electric charge acquired by an object that is not a conductor of electricity. **2** crackling on a phone, radio, etc.
■ **statically** adv.

station n. **1** a place where trains stop on a railway line. **2** a place where an activity or service is based. **3** a broadcasting company. **4** the place where someone or something stands. **5** a person's social rank.
▷ SYNONYMS: **1 establishment**, base, camp, post, depot, mission, site, facility, installation. **2 office**, depot, base, headquarters. **3 channel**, wavelength.
• v. assign to a station.
▷ SYNONYMS: **base**, post, establish, deploy, garrison.
□ **station wagon** US & Austral./NZ an estate car.

stationary adj. not moving or changing.
▷ SYNONYMS: **static**, parked, motionless, immobile, still, stock-still, at a standstill, at rest.
– ANTONYMS: moving.

> **USAGE** Don't confuse **stationary** with **stationery**, which means 'paper and other writing materials'.

stationer n. a seller of stationery.

stationery n. paper and other writing materials.

statistic n. **1** a fact or piece of information obtained by studying numerical data. **2** (**statistics**) the collection and analysis of numerical data.
■ **statistical** adj. **statistically** adv. **statistician** n.

statuary n. statues.

statue n. a carved or cast figure of a person or animal.

statuesque adj. tall and graceful.

statuette n. a small statue.

stature n. **1** a person's height. **2** importance or reputation.
▷ SYNONYMS: **1 height**, size, build. **2 reputation**, repute, standing, status, position, prestige, distinction, eminence, prominence, importance.

status n. **1** a person's social or professional position. **2** high rank or social standing. **3** the situation at a particular time.
▷ SYNONYMS: **1 standing**, rank, position, level, place. **2 prestige**, kudos, cachet, standing, stature, esteem, image, importance, authority, fame.

S

□ **status quo** the existing situation.
statute n. a written law.
statutory adj. required or permitted by law.
staunch adj. loyal and committed.
▷ SYNONYMS: **stalwart**, loyal, faithful, committed, devoted, dedicated, reliable.
– ANTONYMS: disloyal, unfaithful.
• v. (US **stanch**) stop the flow of blood from a wound.
▷ SYNONYMS: **stem**, stop, halt, check, curb; N. Amer. stanch.
■ **staunchly** adv.
stave n. **1** any of the strips of wood forming the side of a barrel etc. **2** a strong post. **3** a set of five horizontal lines on which musical notes are written.
• v. (**staving, staved** or **stove**) **1** (stave in) dent or break a hole in. **2** (past & past part. **staved**) (**stave off**) stop or delay.
stay v. **1** remain in the same place or in a specified state. **2** live temporarily. **3** stop or delay.
▷ SYNONYMS: **1 remain**, continue, keep; wait, linger, hold on, hang on; informal hang around, stick around; Brit. informal hang about; old use tarry. **2** *I'm going to stay with a friend:* **visit**, stop over, holiday, lodge; N. Amer. vacation.
– ANTONYMS: leave.
• n. **1** a period of staying somewhere. **2** a brace or support.
▷ SYNONYMS: **visit**, stop, stopover, break, holiday; N. Amer. vacation; literary sojourn.
□ **stay of execution** a delay in carrying out the orders of a law court.
stead n. (**in someone's** or **something's stead**) instead of someone or something.
□ **stand in good stead** be useful to in the future.
steadfast adj. not changing in your attitudes or aims.
■ **steadfastly** adv.
steady adj. (**steadier, steadiest**) **1** firmly fixed or supported. **2** not wavering. **3** sensible and reliable. **4** regular and continuous.
▷ SYNONYMS: **1 stable**, firm, fixed, secure. **2 still**, motionless, static, stationary, unmoving. **3** *a steady gaze:* **fixed**, intent, unwavering, unfaltering. **4** *steady breathing:* **constant**, consistent, regular, even, rhythmic. **5 continuous**, continual, unceasing, ceaseless, perpetual, unremitting, endless. **6 regular**, settled, firm,

committed, long-term.
– ANTONYMS: unstable, shaky, fluctuating.
• v. (**steadying, steadied**) make or become steady.
▷ SYNONYMS: **1 stabilize**, hold steady, brace, support, balance, rest. **2 calm**, soothe, quieten, compose, settle, subdue, quell.
■ **steadily** adv. **steadiness** n.
steak n. a thick slice of meat (esp. beef) or fish.
steal v. (**stealing, stole**; past part. **stolen**) **1** take something without permission and without intending to return it. **2** move stealthily.
▷ SYNONYMS: **1 take**, thieve, help yourself to, pilfer, embezzle; informal rip off, swipe, lift, filch; Brit. informal nick, pinch, knock off; N. Amer. informal heist. **2 plagiarize**, copy, pirate; informal crib. **3 creep**, sneak, slink, slip, glide, tiptoe, slope.
□ **steal the show** attract the most attention and praise.

> **WORD LINKS**
> **kleptomania** a recurrent urge to steal things

stealth n. cautious and secretive action or movement.
▷ SYNONYMS: **furtiveness**, secretiveness, secrecy, surreptitiousness.
stealthy adj. cautious and surreptitious.
▷ SYNONYMS: **furtive**, secretive, secret, surreptitious, cautious; sneaky, sly.
– ANTONYMS: open.
■ **stealthily** adv.
steam n. **1** the hot vapour into which water is converted when heated. **2** power derived from this. **3** momentum.
• v. **1** give off steam. **2** (steam up) mist over with steam. **3** cook with steam. **4** move under steam power. **5** informal move quickly.
□ **steamroller** a heavy, slow vehicle with a roller, used in road construction.
■ **steamer** n. **steamy** adj.
steed n. literary a horse.
steel n. **1** a hard, strong alloy of iron with carbon. **2** strength and determination.
• v. mentally prepare yourself to do something difficult.
■ **steely** adj.
steep adj. **1** rising or falling sharply. **2** informal (of a price) excessive.
▷ SYNONYMS: **1 sheer**, precipitous, abrupt, sharp, perpendicular, vertical.

2 *a steep increase:* **sharp**, sudden, dramatic, precipitate.
– ANTONYMS: gentle, gradual.
• v. **1** soak in liquid. **2** (**steeped in**) full of a particular quality.
▷ SYNONYMS: (**steeped in**) **imbued with**, filled with, permeated with, suffused with, soaked in, pervaded by.
■ **steeply** adv. **steepness** n.
steeple n. a church tower and spire.
□ **steeplejack** a person who repairs tall structures such as chimneys.
steeplechase n. **1** a horse race with ditches and hedges as jumps. **2** a running race with hurdles and water jumps.
■ **steeplechaser** n.
steer v. **1** direct the course of a vehicle, ship, etc. **2** guide.
▷ SYNONYMS: **guide**, direct, manoeuvre, drive, pilot, navigate.
• n. a bullock.
□ **steer clear of** take care to avoid.
stellar adj. of a star or stars.
stem n. **1** the supporting part of a plant. **2** a long, thin supporting part of a wine glass etc. **3** the main part of a word, to which other elements are added.
▷ SYNONYMS: **stalk**, shoot, trunk.
• v. (**stemming, stemmed**) **1** (**stem from**) be caused by. **2** stop the flow of.
▷ SYNONYMS: **stop**, staunch, halt, check, curb; N. Amer. stanch.
stench n. a foul smell.
▷ SYNONYMS: **stink**, reek; Brit. informal niff, pong, whiff; N. Amer. informal funk; literary miasma.
stencil n. a sheet of card etc. with a cut-out design, painted over to produce a design on the surface below.
• v. (**stencilling, stencilled;** US **stenciling, stenciled**) decorate with a stencil.
stenographer n. US a shorthand typist.
stentorian adj. (of a voice) very loud.
step n. **1** an act of lifting and putting down the foot or feet in walking. **2** the distance covered by this. **3** a flat surface on which to step in moving from one level to another. **4** a position or grade in a scale. **5** a measure taken to achieve something.
▷ SYNONYMS: **1 pace**, stride, footstep, footfall, tread, tramp. **2 stair**, tread; (**steps**) stairs, staircase, flight of stairs. **3 action**, act, course of action, measure, move, operation, procedure. **4 stage**, level, grade, rank, degree, phase. **5 advance**, development, move, movement, breakthrough.

• v. (**stepping, stepped**) lift and put down your foot or feet.
▷ SYNONYMS: **walk**, move, tread, pace, stride.
□ **step down** resign. **step in** intervene. **stepladder** a short freestanding folding ladder. **stepping stone 1** a raised stone on which to step when crossing a stream. **2** a stage in progress towards a goal. **step up** increase.
step- comb. form referring to a relationship resulting from a remarriage: *stepmother, stepsister.*
steppe n. a large grassy treeless plain in SE Europe or Siberia.
stereo n. (pl. **stereos**) **1** stereophonic sound. **2** a stereo CD player, record player, etc.
• adj. stereophonic.
stereophonic adj. (of sound reproduction) using two or more channels so that the sound seems to come from more than one source.
stereoscopic adj. (of a photo) taken with a special device to give a three-dimensional effect.
stereotype n. an oversimplified idea of the typical characteristics of a person or thing.
▷ SYNONYMS: **conventional idea**, standard image, cliché, formula.
• v. view as a stereotype.
▷ SYNONYMS: **typecast**, pigeonhole, conventionalize, categorize, label, tag.
■ **stereotypical** adj.
sterile adj. **1** not able to produce children, young, or fruit. **2** free from bacteria etc.
▷ SYNONYMS: **1 infertile**, unfruitful, barren, unproductive. **2 hygienic**, clean, pure, uncontaminated, sterilized, disinfected, germ-free, antiseptic.
– ANTONYMS: fertile, contaminated.
■ **sterility** n.
sterilize (or **-ise**) v. make sterile.
▷ SYNONYMS: **1 disinfect**, fumigate, decontaminate, sanitize, clean, cleanse, purify. **2 neuter**, castrate, spay, geld; N. Amer. & Austral. alter; Brit. informal doctor.
– ANTONYMS: contaminate.
■ **sterilization** n.
sterling n. British money.
• adj. excellent.
stern adj. severe or strict.
▷ SYNONYMS: **1 unsmiling**, frowning, serious, severe, forbidding, grim, unfriendly, austere, dour. **2 strict**, severe, stringent, harsh, drastic, hard,

S

tough, extreme, draconian.
– ANTONYMS: genial, lax.
• n. the rear of a ship or aircraft.
■ **sternly** adv. **sternness** n.
sternum n. (pl. **sternums** or **sterna**)
the breastbone.
steroid n. any of a class of organic
compounds including certain
hormones.
stertorous adj. (of breathing) noisy
and laboured.
stethoscope n. a medical instrument
for listening to a person's heart or
breathing.
stevedore n. a docker.
stew n. a dish of meat and vegetables
cooked slowly in a closed dish.
• v. **1** cook slowly in a closed dish. **2** be
anxious.
steward n. **1** (fem. **stewardess**) an
attendant on a ship or aircraft. **2** an
official who helps to organize a
public event. **3** a person employed
to manage an estate. **4** a person
responsible for supplies of food to a
college, club, etc.
stick n. **1** a thin piece of wood. **2** a
long, thin object or piece. **3** an
implement used to hit the ball in
hockey etc. **4** Brit. informal criticism.
▷ SYNONYMS: **1 branch**, twig, switch.
2 walking stick, cane, staff, crutch.
3 post, pole, cane, stake, rod.
• v. (**sticking, stuck**) **1** push a pointed
object into or through something.
2 adhere or cause to adhere. **3** (**be
stuck**) be fixed or unable to move or
to make progress. **4** informal put quickly
or carelessly.
▷ SYNONYMS: **1 thrust**, push, insert, jab,
poke, dig, plunge. **2 pierce**, penetrate,
puncture, prick, stab. **3 adhere**, cling.
4 stick the stamp there: **attach**, fasten,
affix, fix, paste, glue, gum, tape.
5 jam, get jammed, catch, get caught,
get trapped. **6 tolerate**, put up with,
take, stand, stomach, endure, bear,
abide.
□ **stick out 1** protrude or extend. **2** be
conspicuous. **stick to** continue doing
or using. **stick up for** support.
sticker n. a sticky label or notice.
stickleback n. a small fish with spines
along its back.
stickler n. a person who insists on a
certain type of behaviour.
sticky adj. (**stickier, stickiest**) **1** tending
or designed to stick. **2** humid.
▷ SYNONYMS: **1 adhesive**, self-adhesive,
gummed. **2 tacky**, gluey, gummy,
treacly, glutinous, viscous; informal
gooey. **3 humid**, muggy, close, sultry,

steamy, sweaty, sweltering, oppressive. **4 awkward**, difficult, tricky, ticklish, delicate, embarrassing, sensitive;
informal hairy.
– ANTONYMS: dry, fresh, cool.
stiff adj. **1** not easily bent. **2** unable to
move easily. **3** not relaxed or friendly.
4 severe or strong.
▷ SYNONYMS: **1 rigid**, hard, firm,
inelastic, unyielding, brittle. **2 thick**,
firm, viscous, semi-solid. **3 aching**,
achy, painful, arthritic; informal creaky.
4 formal, reserved, wooden, forced,
strained, stilted; informal starchy,
uptight. **5** stiff penalties: **harsh**,
severe, heavy, stringent, drastic, draconian; Brit. swingeing. **6** they put up a
stiff resistance: **vigorous**, determined,
strong, spirited, resolute, tenacious,
dogged, stubborn. **7 difficult**, hard,
arduous, tough, strenuous, laborious,
exacting, tiring, demanding. **8 strong**,
potent, alcoholic.
– ANTONYMS: flexible, soft, limp.
□ **stiff-necked** obstinate.
■ **stiffen** v. **stiffly** adv. **stiffness** n.
stifle v. **1** prevent from breathing
freely. **2** restrain or prevent.
▷ SYNONYMS: **1 smother**, check, restrain,
keep back, hold back, hold in, withhold, choke back, muffle, suppress,
curb. **2 suppress**, quash, quell, put an
end to, put down, stop, extinguish,
stamp out, crush, subdue, repress.
3 suffocate, smother, asphyxiate,
choke.
stigma n. **1** a mark of disgrace. **2** a
part of a flower pistil that receives
the pollen.
▷ SYNONYMS: **shame**, disgrace,
dishonour, ignominy, humiliation,
stain, taint.
– ANTONYMS: honour,.
stigmata pl. n. marks on a person's
body corresponding to the
Crucifixion marks on Christ's body.
stigmatize (or **-ise**) v. regard or treat
as shameful.
stile n. a set of steps in a fence or wall
allowing people to climb over.
stiletto n. (pl. **stilettos**) **1** a thin, high
heel. **2** a short, narrow dagger.
still adj. **1** not moving. **2** Brit. (of a
drink) not fizzy.
▷ SYNONYMS: **1 motionless**, unmoving,
stock-still, immobile, rooted to the
spot, transfixed, static, stationary.
2 quiet, silent, calm, peaceful, serene,
windless, noiseless, undisturbed, flat,
smooth, like a millpond.
– ANTONYMS: moving, noisy.
• n. **1** deep, quiet calm. **2** a photo or

a single shot from a cinema film. **3** a device for distilling alcohol.

• adv. **1** even now or at a particular time. **2** nevertheless. **3** even: *better still.*

▷ SYNONYMS: **1 even now**, yet. **2 nevertheless**, nonetheless, all the same, even so, but, however, despite that, in spite of that.

• v. make or become still.

▷ SYNONYMS: **quieten**, quiet, silence, hush, calm, settle, pacify, subdue. □ **stillborn** born dead. **still life** a painting or drawing of inanimate objects.

■ **stillness** n.

stilt n. **1** either of a pair of upright poles enabling the user to walk above the ground. **2** each of a set of posts supporting a building.

stilted adj. (of speech or writing) stiff and unnatural.

stimulant n. something that stimulates.

stimulate v. **1** make more active, interested, or excited. **2** raise levels of physiological or nervous activity in the body.

▷ SYNONYMS: **encourage**, prompt, motivate, trigger, spark, spur on, galvanize, fire, inspire, excite; N. Amer. light a fire under.

– ANTONYMS: discourage.

■ **stimulation** n.

stimulating adj. arousing interest or enthusiasm.

▷ SYNONYMS: **1** *a stimulating debate:* **thought-provoking**, interesting, inspiring, inspirational, lively, exciting, stirring, provocative. **2** *a stimulating peppermint shower gel:* **invigorating**, refreshing, energizing, revitalizing.

– ANTONYMS: uninspiring, boring.

stimulus n. (pl. **stimuli**) something that stimulates.

▷ SYNONYMS: **motivation**, encouragement, impetus, prompt, spur, inducement, incentive, inspiration, fillip; informal shot in the arm.

– ANTONYMS: deterrent.

sting n. **1** a sharp part of an insect able to wound by injecting poison. **2** a wound from this. **3** a sharp tingling sensation.

▷ SYNONYMS: **1 prick**, wound, injury. **2 pain**, pricking, smarting, soreness, hurt, irritation.

• v. (**stinging**, **stung**) **1** wound with a sting. **2** produce a stinging sensation. **3** upset.

▷ SYNONYMS: **1 prick**, wound. **2 smart**,

burn, hurt, be irritated, be sore. **3** *the criticism stung her:* **upset**, wound, hurt, distress, pain, mortify.

stingy adj. (**stingier**, **stingiest**) informal mean.

stink v. (**stinking**, **stank** or **stunk**; past part. **stunk**) **1** have a foul smell. **2** informal be corrupt or bad.

▷ SYNONYMS: **reek**, smell.

• n. **1** a foul smell. **2** informal a row or fuss.

▷ SYNONYMS: **stench**, reek; Brit. informal pong; N. Amer. informal funk.

stint n. a period of work.

▷ SYNONYMS: **spell**, stretch, turn, session, term, time, shift, tour of duty.

• v. (**stint on**) provide or use in a very economical or mean way.

stipend /**sty**-pend/ n. a salary paid to a priest etc.

stipendiary adj. receiving a stipend.

stipple v. mark with many small dots.

stipulate v. demand or specify as part of an agreement.

▷ SYNONYMS: **specify**, set out, lay down, demand, require, insist on.

■ **stipulation** n.

stir v. (**stirring**, **stirred**) **1** move an implement round in a liquid etc. to mix it. **2** move slightly or begin to be active. **3** wake or get up. **4** arouse a strong feeling.

▷ SYNONYMS: **1 mix**, blend, beat, whip, whisk, fold in; N. Amer. muddle. **2 move**, get up, rise, rouse yourself, bestir yourself. **3 disturb**, rustle, shake, move, agitate. **4** *the war stirred him to action:* **spur**, drive, rouse, prompt, propel, motivate, encourage, urge, impel, provoke, goad.

• n. **1** an act of stirring. **2** a commotion.

▷ SYNONYMS: **commotion**, disturbance, fuss, excitement, sensation; informal to-do, hoo-ha.

stirrup n. each of a pair of loops attached to a horse's saddle to support the rider's foot.

stitch n. **1** a loop of thread or yarn resulting from a single pass of the needle in sewing, knitting, etc. **2** a method of sewing etc. that produces a particular pattern. **3** a sudden pain in the side.

• v. make or mend with stitches. □ **in stitches** informal laughing uncontrollably.

stoat n. a small brown mammal of the weasel family.

stock n. **1** a supply of goods or materials available for sale or use. **2** livestock. **3** money raised by selling shares in a company. **4** (**stocks**) shares

S

in a company. **5** water in which bones, meat, etc. have been simmered. **6** ancestry. **7** the trunk or stem of a tree or shrub. **8** (**the stocks**) hist. a wooden structure with holes in which a criminal's feet and hands were locked as punishment.

▷ SYNONYMS: **1 merchandise**, goods, wares. **2 store**, supply, stockpile, reserve, hoard, cache, bank. **3 animals**, livestock, beasts, flocks, herds. **4 descent**, ancestry, origins, lineage, birth, extraction, family, blood, pedigree.

• adj. common or conventional.

▷ SYNONYMS: **usual**, routine, predictable, set, standard, staple, customary, familiar, conventional, traditional, stereotyped, clichéd, hackneyed, unoriginal, formulaic.

– ANTONYMS: unusual, original.

• v. **1** keep a stock of. **2** provide with a supply.

▷ SYNONYMS: **sell**, carry, keep in stock, offer, supply, provide, furnish.

□ **stockbroker** a broker who buys and sells shares for clients. **stock car** a car used in a type of racing in which cars collide with each other. **stock exchange** (or **stock market**) a market in which shares are bought and sold. **stock-in-trade** the typical thing a person or company uses or deals in. **stock-still** completely still. **stocktaking** the recording of the amount of stock held by a business.

stockade n. an enclosure of wooden posts.

stocking n. a close-fitting covering for the foot and leg.

stockist n. Brit. a retailer stocking goods of a particular type.

stockpile n. a large stock of goods.

▷ SYNONYMS: **stock**, store, supply, collection, reserve, hoard, cache; informal stash.

• v. gather together a large stock of goods.

▷ SYNONYMS: **store up**, amass, accumulate, stock up on, hoard, collect, lay in, put away, put/set aside, put by, stow away, save; informal salt away, stash away.

stocky adj. (**stockier, stockiest**) short and sturdy.

▷ SYNONYMS: **thickset**, sturdy, heavily built, chunky, burly, strapping, brawny, solid, heavy, hefty, beefy.

– ANTONYMS: slender.

stodge n. Brit. informal heavy, filling food.

■ **stodgy** adj.

stoic n. a stoical person.

• adj. stoical.

■ **stoicism** n.

stoical adj. enduring pain and hardship without complaint.

■ **stoically** adv.

stoke v. **1** add coal to a fire etc. **2** increase a strong emotion.

■ **stoker** n.

stole[1] n. a woman's wide scarf or shawl.

stole[2] past of STEAL.

stolen past part. of STEAL.

stolid adj. calm and dependable.

■ **stolidly** adv.

stomach n. **1** the internal organ in which the first part of digestion occurs. **2** the belly. **3** appetite or desire.

▷ SYNONYMS: **1 abdomen**, middle, belly, gut, paunch; informal tummy, insides, pot, spare tyre. **2 appetite**, taste, inclination, desire, wish.

• v. tolerate.

▷ SYNONYMS: **tolerate**, put up with, take, stand, endure, bear; informal hack, abide; Brit. informal stick.

> **WORD LINKS**
> **gastric** relating to the stomach

stomp v. tread heavily.

stone n. **1** the hard material of which rock is made. **2** a piece of stone. **3** a gem. **4** a hard seed in certain fruits. **5** (pl. **stone**) Brit. a unit of weight equal to 14 lb (6.35 kg).

▷ SYNONYMS: **1 rock**, pebble, boulder. **2 gem**, gemstone, jewel; informal rock, sparkler. **3 kernel**, seed, pip, pit.

• v. **1** throw stones at. **2** remove the stone from a fruit.

□ **Stone Age** the prehistoric period when tools were made of stone. **stonewall** delay or block by giving evasive replies. **stonewashed** washed with small stones to give a faded appearance.

> **WORD LINKS**
> **lapidary** relating to the cutting or polishing of stones and gems

stony adj. (**stonier, stoniest**) **1** full of stones. **2** cold and unfeeling.

■ **stonily** adv.

stood past & past part. of STAND.

stooge n. **1** a person doing routine or unpleasant work for another. **2** a performer who is the butt of a comedian's jokes.

stool n. **1** a seat without a back or arms. **2** a piece of faeces.

□ **stool pigeon** informal a police

informer.

stoop v. **1** bend forwards and down. **2** lower your standards to do something wrong.
▷ SYNONYMS: **bend**, lean, crouch, bow, duck.
• n. a stooping posture.

stop v. (**stopping**, **stopped**) **1** come or bring to an end. **2** prevent from happening or from doing something. **3** cease moving. **4** block a hole.
▷ SYNONYMS: **1 end**, halt, finish, terminate, wind up, bring to a stop/halt, discontinue, cut short, interrupt, nip in the bud, shut down. **2** *he stopped smoking:* **cease**, refrain from, discontinue, desist from, break off, give up, abandon, cut out; informal quit, pack in; Brit. informal jack in. **3 pull up**, draw up, come to a stop/halt, come to rest, pull in/over. **4** *the music stopped:* **come to an end**, draw to a close, end, cease, halt, finish, be over, conclude. **5 prevent**, obstruct, impede, block, bar, preclude, dissuade from.
– ANTONYMS: start, begin, continue.
• n. **1** an act of stopping. **2** a place where a bus stops regularly. **3** a thing preventing movement. **4** a set of organ pipes.
▷ SYNONYMS: **1 halt**, end, finish, cessation, close, conclusion, termination, standstill. **2 break**, stopover, stop-off, stay, visit; literary sojourn. **3 stopping place**, station, halt.
□ **stopcock** a valve regulating the flow in a pipe. **stopgap** a temporary substitute. **stop press** Brit. late news added to a newspaper. **stopwatch** a watch that can be started and stopped, used to time races.
■ **stoppage** n.

stopper n. a plug for a bottle etc.

storage n. **1** the act of storing. **2** space for storing.
□ **storage heater** Brit. an electric heater that stores up heat during the night.

store n. **1** a supply kept for use as needed. **2** a place to keep things for future use. **3** a large shop.
▷ SYNONYMS: **1 stock**, supply, stockpile, hoard, cache, reserve, bank, pool; informal stash. **2 storeroom**, storehouse, repository, stockroom, depot, depository, warehouse. **3** *ship's stores:* **supplies**, provisions, stocks, food, rations, materials, equipment. **4 shop**, emporium, retail outlet, boutique, department store, supermarket, hypermarket, superstore, megastore; N. Amer. mart.
• v. keep for future use.
▷ SYNONYMS: **keep**, stockpile, stock up with, lay in, set aside, put aside, put away/by, save, collect, accumulate, amass, hoard; informal squirrel away, salt away, stash.
– ANTONYMS: use, discard.
□ **in store** about to happen. **set store by** consider important.

storehouse n. a building used for storing goods.
▷ SYNONYMS: **warehouse**, depository, repository, store, storeroom, depot.

storey (US **story**) n. (pl. **storeys** or **stories**) a particular level of a building.

stork n. a tall long-legged bird with a long bill.

storm n. **1** a disturbance of the atmosphere with strong winds and rain or snow. **2** an uproar or outburst.
▷ SYNONYMS: **1 tempest**, squall, gale, hurricane, tornado, cyclone, typhoon, thunderstorm, monsoon, hailstorm, snowstorm, blizzard. **2 uproar**, outcry, fuss, furore, rumpus, trouble; informal to-do, hoo-ha, ructions, stink; Brit. informal row.
• v. **1** move angrily and forcefully. **2** suddenly attack and capture.
▷ SYNONYMS: **1 stride**, march, stomp, stamp, stalk, flounce, fling. **2 attack**, charge, rush, swoop on.

stormy adj. (**stormier**, **stormiest**) **1** affected by a storm. **2** full of angry or violent outbursts of feeling.
▷ SYNONYMS: **1 blustery**, squally, windy, gusty, blowy, thundery, wild, violent, rough, foul. **2 angry**, heated, fierce, furious, passionate, acrimonious.
– ANTONYMS: calm, peaceful.

story n. (pl. **stories**) an account of imaginary or real events.
▷ SYNONYMS: **1 tale**, narrative, account, history, anecdote, saga; informal yarn. **2 plot**, storyline, scenario. **3 news**, report, item, article, feature, piece. **4 rumour**, whisper, allegation, speculation, gossip.

stout adj. **1** rather fat. **2** sturdy and thick. **3** brave and determined.
▷ SYNONYMS: **1 fat**, big, plump, portly, rotund, dumpy, corpulent, thickset, burly, bulky; informal tubby; Brit. informal podgy; N. Amer. informal zaftig, corn-fed. **2 strong**, sturdy, solid, robust, tough, durable, hard-wearing. **3 determined**, vigorous, forceful, spirited, committed, brave, fearless, valiant, gallant, bold, plucky; informal gutsy.
– ANTONYMS: thin, flimsy.
• n. strong, dark beer.

S

■ **stoutly** adv.

stove[1] n. a device for cooking or heating.

stove[2] past & past part. of STAVE.

stow v. **1** store tidily. **2** (**stow away**) hide on a ship, aircraft, etc. so as to travel without paying.
□ **stowaway** a person who stows away.

straddle v. **1** sit or stand with one leg on either side of. **2** extend across.

strafe v. attack with gunfire from the air.

straggle v. **1** lag behind. **2** grow or spread untidily.
■ **straggler** n. **straggly** adj.

straight adj. **1** extending in one direction only; without a curve or bend. **2** level or symmetrical. **3** tidy or ordered. **4** honest and direct. **5** in continuous succession. **6** (of an alcoholic drink) undiluted. **7** informal heterosexual.
▷ SYNONYMS: **1 direct**, linear, unswerving, undeviating. **2 level**, even, in line, aligned, square, vertical, upright, perpendicular, horizontal. **3 in order**, tidy, neat, shipshape, spick and span, orderly, organized, arranged, sorted out, straightened out. **4 honest**, direct, frank, candid, truthful, sincere, forthright, straightforward, plain-spoken, blunt, unambiguous; informal upfront. **5 undiluted**, neat, pure; N. Amer. informal straight up.
– ANTONYMS: winding, crooked.
• adv. **1** in a straight line or a straight way. **2** without delay. **3** clearly and logically.
▷ SYNONYMS: *she looked at him straight in the eye*: **right**, directly, squarely, full.
• n. the straight part of something.
□ **straight away** immediately.
straight-faced having a serious expression.

straighten v. **1** make or become straight. **2** make tidy or put in order.
▷ SYNONYMS: **1 put straight**, adjust, put in order, arrange, rearrange, tidy, neaten. **2** *we must straighten things out with him*: **put right**, sort out, clear up, settle, resolve, rectify, remedy; informal patch up.

straightforward adj. **1** easy to do or understand. **2** honest and open.
▷ SYNONYMS: **1 uncomplicated**, easy, simple, plain sailing, elementary, undemanding. **2 honest**, frank, candid, open, truthful, sincere, on the level, forthright, plain-speaking, direct; informal upfront; N. Amer. informal on the up and up.
– ANTONYMS: complicated, devious.

strain v. **1** make an unusually great effort. **2** injure by overexertion. **3** make great or excessive demands on. **4** pour a liquid through a sieve to separate out any solid matter.
▷ SYNONYMS: **1 overtax**, overwork, over-extend, overreach, overdo it, exhaust, wear out; informal knacker, knock yourself out. **2 injure**, damage, pull, wrench, twist, sprain. **3 sieve**, sift, filter, screen.
• n. **1** a force pulling or stretching something. **2** an injury caused by straining. **3** a severe demand on strength or resources. **4** the sound of a piece of music. **5** a breed or variety of an animal or plant. **6** a tendency in a person's character.
▷ SYNONYMS: **1 tension**, tightness, tautness. **2 injury**, sprain, wrench, twist. **3** *these families cannot cope with the strain*: **pressure**, demands, burdens, stress; tension, exhaustion, fatigue; informal hassle. **4 variety**, kind, type, sort, breed, genus.
■ **strainer** n.

strained adj. **1** not relaxed. **2** not spontaneous.
▷ SYNONYMS: **1 awkward**, tense, uneasy, uncomfortable, edgy, difficult, troubled. **2 forced**, unnatural, artificial, insincere, false, affected, put-on.

strait n. **1** (or **straits**) a narrow stretch of water connecting two seas. **2** (**straits**) a difficult situation.
▷ SYNONYMS: **1 channel**, sound, narrows, stretch of water. **2** (**straits**) **difficulty**, trouble, crisis, mess, predicament, plight; informal hot water, jam, hole, fix, scrape.

straitened adj. without enough money; poor.

straitjacket (or **straightjacket**) n. a strong garment with long sleeves for confining the arms of a violent person.

strait-laced (or **straight-laced**) adj. strictly moral and conventional.

strand v. **1** run aground. **2** leave without the means to move from a place.
▷ SYNONYMS: **1** *their boat was stranded on a sandbank*: **beached**, grounded, aground, cast away. **2** *she was left stranded in the middle of nowhere*: **marooned**, abandoned, left high and dry, left in the lurch, helpless.
• n. **1** a single length of thread etc. **2** an element in a complex whole.

S

3 literary a beach or shore.
▷ SYNONYMS: **thread**, filament, fibre, length.

strange adj. **1** unusual or odd. **2** not seen or met before.
▷ SYNONYMS: **1 unusual**, odd, curious, peculiar, funny, queer, bizarre, weird, uncanny, surprising, unexpected, anomalous, atypical; informal fishy. **2 unfamiliar**, unknown, new, novel.
– ANTONYMS: ordinary, familiar.
■ **strangely** adv. **strangeness** n.

stranger n. **1** a person that you do not know. **2** a person who does not know a particular place.
▷ SYNONYMS: **newcomer**, new arrival, visitor, guest, outsider, foreigner.

strangle v. **1** kill or injure by squeezing the neck. **2** suppress or hinder.
▷ SYNONYMS: **throttle**, choke, garrotte, asphyxiate.
□ **stranglehold 1** a strangling grip. **2** complete control.
■ **strangler** n.

strangulation n. the act of strangling.

strap n. a strip of flexible material used for fastening, carrying, or holding on to.
▷ SYNONYMS: **belt**, tie, band, thong.
• v. (**strapping**, **strapped**) fasten with a strap.
▷ SYNONYMS: **tie**, lash, secure, fasten, bind, make fast, truss.

strapping adj. big and strong.
▷ SYNONYMS: **big**, strong, well built, brawny, burly, muscular; informal beefy.

strata pl. of **STRATUM**.

stratagem n. a plan intended to outwit an opponent.

strategic adj. **1** of strategy. **2** (of weapons) for use against enemy territory rather than in battle.
▷ SYNONYMS: **planned**, calculated, deliberate, tactical, judicious, prudent, shrewd.
■ **strategically** adv.

strategy n. (pl. **strategies**) **1** a plan designed to achieve a long-term aim. **2** the planning and directing of military activity in a war or battle.
▷ SYNONYMS: **plan**, grand design, game plan, policy, programme, scheme.
■ **strategist** n.

stratify v. (**stratifying**, **stratified**) form or arrange into strata.
■ **stratification** n.

stratosphere n. the layer of the atmosphere about 10–50 km above the earth's surface.

stratum n. (pl. **strata**) a layer or level

in a series.

straw n. **1** dried stalks of corn etc. **2** a single dried stalk. **3** a thin hollow tube for sucking up a drink.
□ **straw poll** an unofficial test of opinion.

strawberry n. a sweet red fruit.

stray v. move away aimlessly from a group or from the right course or place.
▷ SYNONYMS: **1 wander off**, go astray, get separated, get lost, drift away. **2 digress**, deviate, wander, get sidetracked, go off at a tangent, get off the subject.
• adj. **1** not in the right place. **2** (of a domestic animal) having no home.
▷ SYNONYMS: **1 homeless**, lost, abandoned, feral. **2** a stray bullet: **random**, chance, freak, unexpected, isolated.
• n. a stray animal.

streak n. **1** a long, thin mark. **2** an element in someone's character. **3** a period of specified success or luck.
▷ SYNONYMS: **1 band**, line, strip, stripe, vein, slash, ray, smear. **2 element**, vein, strain, touch. **3 period**, spell, stretch, run; Brit. informal patch.
• v. **1** mark with streaks. **2** move very fast. **3** informal run naked in a public place.
▷ SYNONYMS: **1 stripe**, band, fleck, smear, mark. **2 race**, speed, flash, shoot, dash, rush, hurtle, whizz, zoom, career, fly; informal belt, tear, zip, whip; Brit. informal bomb; N. Amer. informal barrel.
■ **streaker** n. **streaky** adj.

stream n. **1** a small, narrow river. **2** a continuous flow of liquid, air, people, etc. **3** Brit. a group in which schoolchildren of the same age and ability are taught.
▷ SYNONYMS: **1 brook**, rivulet, tributary; Scottish & N. English burn; N. English beck; S. English bourn; N. Amer. & Austral./NZ creek. **2 jet**, flow, rush, gush, surge, torrent, flood, cascade. **3 succession**, series, string.
• v. **1** move in a continuous flow. **2** run with tears, sweat, etc. **3** float out in the wind. **4** Brit. put schoolchildren in streams.
▷ SYNONYMS: **flow**, pour, course, run, gush, surge, flood, cascade, spill.
□ **on stream** in or into operation.

streamer n. a long, narrow strip of decorative material.

streamline adj. **1** design with a shape presenting little resistance to a flow of air or water. **2** make more efficient.
▷ SYNONYMS: **1** the streamlined contours

S

of the chassis: **aerodynamic**, smooth, sleek. **2** *a streamlined organization:* **efficient**, smooth-running, well run, well oiled, slick.

street n. a public road in a city, town, etc.
▷ SYNONYMS: **road**, thoroughfare, avenue, drive, boulevard, lane; N. Amer. highway.
□ **streetcar** US a tram.

strength n. **1** the quality of being strong. **2** a good or useful quality. **3** the number of people making up a group.
▷ SYNONYMS: **1 power**, muscle, might, brawn, muscularity, robustness, sturdiness, vigour, stamina. **2 fortitude**, resilience, spirit, backbone, courage, bravery, pluck, grit; informal guts. **3** *strength of feeling:* **intensity**, vehemence, force, depth. **4** *the strength of their argument:* **force**, weight, power, persuasiveness, soundness, cogency, validity. **5 strong point**, advantage, asset, forte, aptitude, talent, skill, speciality.
– ANTONYMS: weakness.
□ **on the strength of** on the basis of.
■ **strengthen** v.

strenuous adj. requiring or using great effort.
▷ SYNONYMS: **1 difficult**, arduous, hard, tough, taxing, demanding, exacting, exhausting, tiring, gruelling, backbreaking; Brit. informal knackering. **2 vigorous**, energetic, forceful, strong, spirited, intense, determined, resolute, dogged.
– ANTONYMS: easy, half-hearted.
■ **strenuously** adv.

streptococcus n. (pl. **streptococci**) a bacterium causing serious infections.

stress n. **1** pressure or tension on an object. **2** mental or emotional tension or strain. **3** emphasis. **4** emphasis given to a syllable or word in speech.
▷ SYNONYMS: **1 strain**, pressure, tension, worry, anxiety, trouble, difficulty; informal hassle. **2 emphasis**, importance, weight, accent, accentuation.
• v. **1** emphasize. **2** subject to pressure, tension, or strain.
▷ SYNONYMS: **1 emphasize**, draw attention to, underline, underscore, point up, highlight, accentuate. **2 overstretch**, overtax, pressurize, pressure, push to the limit, worry, harass; informal hassle.
– ANTONYMS: play down.

stressful adj. causing mental or emotional stress.
▷ SYNONYMS: **demanding**, trying, taxing,

difficult, hard, tough, fraught, traumatic, tense, frustrating.
– ANTONYMS: relaxing.

stretch v. **1** be able to be lengthened or widened without tearing or breaking. **2** pull tightly from one point to another. **3** extend a part of the body to its full length. **4** extend over an area or period. **5** make demands on.
▷ SYNONYMS: **1 pull**, draw out, extend, lengthen, elongate, expand. **2** *she stretched out her arm:* **reach out**, hold out, extend, straighten. **3** *I stretched out on the sofa:* **lie down**, recline, lean back, sprawl, lounge, loll. **4** *the desert stretches for miles:* **extend**, spread, continue, go on.
– ANTONYMS: shorten, contract.
• n. **1** an act of stretching. **2** the capacity to stretch. **3** a continuous area or period.
▷ SYNONYMS: **1 expanse**, area, tract, belt, sweep, extent. **2 period**, time, spell, run, stint, session, shift.

stretcher n. a framework covered with canvas, for carrying injured or dead people.

stretchy adj. able to stretch or be stretched easily.
▷ SYNONYMS: **elastic**, elasticated, tensile, springy, flexible, pliant, pliable, supple.

strew v. (**strewing**, **strewed**; past part. **strewn** or **strewed**) **1** scatter over a surface or area. **2** cover with scattered things.

striation n. each of a series of ridges or grooves.

stricken adj. affected by something unpleasant.

strict adj. **1** demanding that rules are obeyed. **2** (of a rule) rigidly enforced. **3** following rules or beliefs exactly.
▷ SYNONYMS: **1 precise**, exact, literal, faithful, accurate, careful, scrupulous, meticulous, punctilious. **2 stringent**, rigorous, severe, harsh, hard, stern, rigid, tough, uncompromising, authoritarian, firm. **3** *in strict confidence:* **absolute**, utter, complete, total.
– ANTONYMS: loose, liberal.
■ **strictly** adv. **strictness** n.

stricture n. **1** a restriction. **2** a critical remark.

stride v. (**striding**, **strode**) walk with long steps.
▷ SYNONYMS: **step**, pace, march, stalk.
• n. a long step.
□ **get into your stride** start making good progress. **take in your stride**

deal calmly with.

strident adj. **1** loud and harsh.
2 excessively forceful.
■ **stridency** n. **stridently** adv.

strife n. bitter disagreement.
▷ SYNONYMS: **conflict**, friction, discord, disagreement, dissension, dispute, argument, quarrelling.
− ANTONYMS: peace.

strike v. (**striking**, **struck**) **1** hit with force. **2** occur or attack suddenly. **3** refuse to work as a form of organized protest. **4** suddenly come into the mind of. **5** light a match by rubbing it against a rough surface. **6** find oil, gold, etc. **7** reach an agreement. **8** (of a clock) show the time by chiming.
▷ SYNONYMS: **1** hit, slap, smack, thump, punch, beat, cuff; informal clout, wallop, belt, whack, thwack, bash, clobber, bop, biff, swipe; literary smite. **2 crash into**, collide with, hit, run into, bump into, smash into, bang into; N. Amer. impact. **3** take industrial action, go on strike, down tools, walk out. **4** a thought struck her: **occur to**, come to mind, dawn on someone, hit, spring to mind, enter your head.
• n. **1** an act of striking by employees. **2** a sudden attack.
▷ SYNONYMS: **1** industrial action, walkout. **2** attack, assault, bombing.
□ **strike off** officially expel from a professional group. **strike up 1** begin to play a piece of music. **2** begin a friendship or conversation.

striker n. **1** an employee on strike. **2** a forward in football.

striking adj. **1** noticeable. **2** very good-looking.
▷ SYNONYMS: **1** noticeable, obvious, conspicuous, visible, distinct, marked, unmistakable, strong, remarkable. **2** impressive, imposing, magnificent, spectacular, breathtaking, marvellous, wonderful, stunning, sensational, dramatic.
− ANTONYMS: unremarkable.
■ **strikingly** adv.

string n. **1** material consisting of threads twisted together to form a thin length. **2** a length of catgut or wire on a musical instrument, producing a note by vibration. **3** (**strings**) stringed instruments. **4** a set of things strung together. **5** a series. **6** (**strings**) informal conditions or restrictions.
▷ SYNONYMS: **1** twine, cord, yarn, thread. **2** series, succession, chain, sequence, run, streak. **3** queue, procession, line,

file, column, convoy, train, cavalcade. **4** (**strings**) **conditions**, qualifications, provisions, provisos, caveats, stipulations, riders, limitations, restrictions; informal catches.
• v. (**stringing**, **strung**) **1** arrange on a string. **2** (**be strung out**) be spread out in a long line. **3** fit strings on a musical instrument etc. **4** (**string up**) kill by hanging.
▷ SYNONYMS: **hang**, suspend, sling, stretch, run, thread, loop, festoon.

stringent adj. strict and precise.
▷ SYNONYMS: **strict**, firm, rigid, rigorous, severe, harsh, tough, tight, exacting, demanding.
− ANTONYMS: lax.
■ **stringency** n. **stringently** adv.

stringy adj. (**stringier**, **stringiest**) **1** like string. **2** (of food) tough and fibrous.

strip v. (**stripping**, **stripped**) **1** remove covers or clothes from. **2** deprive of rank or property. **3** remove all the contents of a room, vehicle, etc.
▷ SYNONYMS: **1** undress, strip off, take your clothes off, disrobe. **2** dismantle, disassemble, take to pieces, take apart. **3** empty, clear, clean out, plunder, rob, burgle, loot, pillage, ransack, sack.
• n. **1** a long, narrow piece or area. **2** an act of undressing. **3** Brit. the identifying outfit of a sports team.
▷ SYNONYMS: **piece**, band, belt, ribbon, slip, shred, stretch.
□ **strip light** Brit. a tubular fluorescent lamp. **striptease** an entertainment in which a performer gradually undresses.

stripe n. **1** a long narrow band differing in colour or texture from its surroundings. **2** a V-shaped stripe on a uniform showing rank.
■ **striped** adj. **stripy** adj.

stripling n. old use a young man.

stripper n. **1** a device or substance for removing paint etc. **2** a striptease performer.

strive v. (**striving**, **strove** or **strived**; past part. **striven** or **strived**) make great efforts.
▷ SYNONYMS: **try**, attempt, endeavour, aim, make an effort, exert yourself, struggle, do your best, do all you can, do your utmost, labour, work, toil, strain; informal go all out, give it your best shot.

strobe n. a bright light which flashes at rapid intervals.

strode past of STRIDE.

stroke n. **1** an act of hitting. **2** a

S

sound of a striking clock. **3** an act of stroking. **4** a mark made by drawing a pen, paintbrush, etc. across a surface. **5** a style of swimming. **6** a sudden disabling attack caused by an interruption in the flow of blood to the brain.

▷ SYNONYMS: **1 blow**, hit, slap, smack, thump, punch. **2 movement**, action, motion. **3 mark**, line. **4 thrombosis**, embolism, seizure; dated apoplexy.
• v. gently move the hand over.

▷ SYNONYMS: **caress**, fondle, pat, pet, touch, rub, massage, soothe.

stroll v. walk in a leisurely way.

▷ SYNONYMS: **walk**, amble, wander, meander, ramble, promenade, saunter; informal mosey.
• n. a leisurely walk.

strong adj. **1** physically powerful. **2** done with or exerting great force. **3** able to withstand pressure. **4** secure or stable. **5** great in power or ability. **6** intense. **7** full-flavoured. **8** containing much alcohol. **9** indicating the size of a group: *fifty strong*.

▷ SYNONYMS: **1 powerful**, sturdy, robust, athletic, fit, tough, rugged, strapping, well built, muscular, brawny, lusty, healthy. **2 forceful**, determined, spirited, assertive, self-assertive, tough, formidable, strong-minded, redoubtable; informal gutsy, feisty. **3 secure**, solid, well built, durable, hard-wearing, heavy-duty, tough, sturdy, well made, long-lasting. **4** *a strong supporter:* **keen**, passionate, fervent, zealous, enthusiastic, eager, dedicated, loyal. **5** *strong feelings:* **intense**, vehement, passionate, ardent, fervent, deep-seated. **6 forceful**, compelling, powerful, convincing, persuasive, sound, valid, cogent, well founded. **7 intense**, bright, brilliant, vivid, vibrant, dazzling, glaring. **8 concentrated**, undiluted; alcoholic, intoxicating, hard, stiff.
– ANTONYMS: weak, gentle, mild.
□ **strong language** swearing. **strongroom** a room designed for the safe storage of valuable items.
■ **strongly** adv.

stronghold n. **1** a place of strong support for a cause or political party. **2** a place strengthened against attack.

▷ SYNONYMS: **1** *a Tory stronghold:* **bastion**, centre; hotbed. **2 fortress**, fort, castle, citadel, garrison.

strontium n. a soft silvery-white metallic element.

strop n. a leather strip used for sharpening razors.

stroppy adj. Brit. informal bad-tempered.

strove past of STRIVE.

struck past & past part. of STRIKE.

structural adj. of or forming part of a structure.
■ **structurally** adv.

structure n. **1** the way a thing is constructed or organized. **2** a building or other constructed object.

▷ SYNONYMS: **1 building**, edifice, construction, erection. **2 construction**, organization, system, arrangement, framework, form, formation, shape, composition, anatomy, make-up.
• v. give structure to.

▷ SYNONYMS: **arrange**, organize, design, shape, construct, build.

strudel n. a baked roll of flaky pastry with a fruit filling.

struggle v. **1** make great efforts to get free. **2** make your way or try to do with difficulty.

▷ SYNONYMS: **1 strive**, try hard, endeavour, make every effort, exert yourself, do your best, do your utmost. **2 fight**, battle, grapple, wrestle, scuffle.
• n. **1** an act of struggling. **2** a difficult task.

▷ SYNONYMS: **1 striving**, endeavour, effort, exertion, campaign, battle, drive, push. **2 fight**, scuffle, brawl, tussle, fracas; informal bust-up, set-to. **3** *a power struggle:* **contest**, competition, fight, clash, rivalry, friction, feuding, conflict.

strum v. (**strumming**, **strummed**) play a guitar etc. by sweeping the thumb across the strings.

strumpet n. old use a promiscuous woman.

strung past & past part. of STRING.

strut n. **1** a bar supporting a structure. **2** a strutting walk.
• v. (**strutting**, **strutted**) walk in a stiff, proud way.

▷ SYNONYMS: **swagger**, prance, parade, stride, sweep, flounce; N. Amer. informal sashay.

strychnine /strik-neen/ n. a bitter, highly poisonous substance.

Stuart adj. of the royal family ruling Scotland 1371–1714, and Britain 1603–1649 and 1660–1714.

stub n. **1** the part of a pencil, cigarette, etc. remaining after use. **2** the counterfoil of a cheque, ticket, etc.
• v. (**stubbing**, **stubbed**) **1** hit your toe against something. **2** extinguish

a cigarette by pressing it against something.
■ **stubby** adj.

stubble n. **1** short, stiff hairs growing after shaving. **2** the cut stalks of cereal plants left in the ground after harvesting.
■ **stubbly** adj.

stubborn adj. determined not to change your mind.
▷ SYNONYMS: **1 obstinate**, headstrong, wilful, strong-willed, pig-headed, mulish, inflexible, uncompromising, unbending, unyielding, obdurate, intractable, recalcitrant; informal stiff-necked. **2** *a stubborn stain:* **indelible**, permanent, persistent, tenacious, resistant.
■ **stubbornly** adv. **stubbornness** n.

stucco n. plaster used for coating walls or moulding into decorations.
■ **stuccoed** adj.

stuck past part. of **stick**. adj. **1** unable to move or be moved. **2** unable to progress with a task.
▷ SYNONYMS: **1 fixed**, jammed, wedged, trapped, immovable, seized up. **2 baffled**, beaten, at a loss; informal stumped, up against a brick wall.
□ **stuck-up** informal arrogantly snobbish.

stud n. **1** a piece of metal with a large head projecting from a surface. **2** a fastener for clothes. **3** a small piece of jewellery for a pierced ear etc. **4** an establishment where horses are kept for breeding. **5** a stallion.
•v. (**studding, studded**) decorate with studs or other small objects.

student n. a person studying at a university, college, or school.
▷ SYNONYMS: **1 undergraduate**, scholar, pupil, schoolchild, schoolboy, schoolgirl. **2 trainee**, apprentice, probationer, novice, learner.

studio n. (pl. **studios**) **1** a room where an artist works or where dancers practise. **2** a room from which programmes are broadcast or recordings are made.
▷ SYNONYMS: **workshop**, workroom, atelier.
□ **studio flat** Brit. a flat containing one main room.

studious adj. **1** spending a lot of time studying. **2** deliberate and careful.
▷ SYNONYMS: **scholarly**, academic, bookish, intellectual, erudite, learned, donnish; informal brainy.
■ **studiously** adv.

study n. (pl. **studies**) **1** time and effort spent in reading etc. to gain knowledge. **2** a detailed analysis of

a subject or situation. **3** a room for reading and writing. **4** a piece of art, esp. one done in preparation for a larger picture.
▷ SYNONYMS: **1 learning**, education, schooling, scholarship, tuition, research. **2 investigation**, enquiry, research, examination, analysis, review, survey. **3 office**, workroom, studio.
•v. (**studying, studied**) **1** learn about or investigate. **2** look at closely. **3** (**studied**) done with careful effort.
▷ SYNONYMS: **1 work**, revise; informal swot, cram, mug up. **2 learn**, read up on, be taught. **3 investigate**, research, inquire into, look into, examine, analyse, survey. **4 scrutinize**, examine, inspect, consider, regard, look at, observe, watch, survey.

stuff n. **1** material, objects, etc. of a particular or unspecified kind. **2** basic characteristics.
▷ SYNONYMS: **1 material**, substance, fabric, matter. **2 items**, articles, objects, goods, belongings, possessions, effects, paraphernalia; informal gear, kit, bits and pieces, odds and ends; Brit. informal clobber.
•v. **1** fill a container or space tightly or hastily. **2** fill out the skin of a dead animal to restore its original appearance.
▷ SYNONYMS: **1 fill**, pack, pad, upholster. **2 shove**, thrust, push, ram, cram, squeeze, force, jam, pack, pile.

stuffing n. **1** a mixture put inside poultry before cooking. **2** padding used to stuff cushions etc.
▷ SYNONYMS: **padding**, wadding, filling, packing.

stuffy adj. (**stuffier, stuffiest**) **1** lacking fresh air or ventilation. **2** narrow-minded.
▷ SYNONYMS: **1 airless**, close, musty, stale, unventilated. **2 staid**, sedate, sober, priggish, strait-laced, conformist, conservative, old-fashioned; informal straight, starchy, fuddy-duddy.
– ANTONYMS: airy.

stultify v. (**stultifying, stultified**) cause to feel bored or drained of energy.

stumble v. **1** trip and lose your balance. **2** walk unsteadily. **3** make a mistake in speaking. **4** (**stumble across/on**) find by chance.
▷ SYNONYMS: **1 trip**, lose your balance, lose your footing, slip. **2 stagger**, totter, blunder, hobble.

S

• **n.** an act of stumbling.
□ **stumbling block** an obstacle.

stump n. **1** the part of a tree trunk left in the ground after the rest has fallen or been cut down. **2** a remaining piece. **3** each of the uprights of a wicket in cricket.
• **v. 1** baffle. **2** (**stump up**) informal pay a sum of money.
▷ SYNONYMS: **baffle**, perplex, puzzle, confound, defeat; informal flummox, fox, throw, floor.
■ **stumpy** adj.

stun v. (**stunning**, **stunned**) **1** knock unconscious. **2** astonish.
▷ SYNONYMS: **1 daze**, stupefy, knock out, lay out. **2 astound**, amaze, astonish, dumbfound, stupefy, stagger, shock, take aback; informal flabbergast, knock sideways.

stung past & past part. of STING.

stunk past & past part. of STINK.

stunner n. informal a strikingly attractive or impressive person or thing.

stunning adj. very attractive or impressive.
▷ SYNONYMS: **beautiful**, lovely, glorious, wonderful, marvellous, magnificent, superb, sublime, spectacular, fine, delightful; informal fantastic, terrific, tremendous, sensational, heavenly, divine, gorgeous, fabulous, awesome.
– ANTONYMS: ordinary.
■ **stunningly** adv.

stunt[1] v. hinder the growth or development of.

stunt[2] n. **1** an action displaying skill and daring. **2** something done to attract attention.
▷ SYNONYMS: **feat**, exploit, act, deed; trick.

stupefy v. (**stupefying**, **stupefied**) make unable to think.
■ **stupefaction** n.

stupendous adj. very impressive.

stupid adj. **1** lacking intelligence. **2** dazed.
▷ SYNONYMS: **1 unintelligent**, dense, obtuse, foolish, idiotic, slow, simple-minded, brainless, mindless; informal thick, dim, dumb, dopey, dozy, moronic, cretinous; Brit. informal daft. **2 foolish**, silly, senseless, idiotic, ill-advised, ill-considered, unwise, nonsensical, ludicrous, ridiculous, laughable, fatuous, asinine, lunatic; informal crazy, half-baked, cockeyed, hare-brained, crackbrained; Brit. informal potty.
– ANTONYMS: intelligent, sensible.
■ **stupidity** n. **stupidly** adv.

stupor n. a state of being nearly unconscious.

sturdy adj. (**sturdier**, **sturdiest**) strongly built.
▷ SYNONYMS: **1 strapping**, well built, muscular, strong, hefty, brawny, powerful, solid, burly; informal beefy. **2 robust**, strong, well built, solid, stout, tough, durable, long-lasting, hard-wearing.
– ANTONYMS: feeble.
■ **sturdily** adv. **sturdiness** n.

sturgeon n. (pl. **sturgeon**) a large edible fish.

stutter v. stammer, esp. by repeating the first sound of a word.
▷ SYNONYMS: **stammer**, stumble, falter, hesitate.
• **n.** a tendency to stutter.

sty n. (pl. **sties**) **1** a pigsty. **2** (or **stye**) an inflamed swelling on the edge of an eyelid.

Stygian /ˈsti-ji-uhn/ adj. literary very dark.

style n. **1** a way of doing something. **2** a particular design or arrangement. **3** elegance.
▷ SYNONYMS: **1 manner**, way, technique, method, methodology, approach, system, mode. **2 flair**, elegance, stylishness, chic, taste, grace, poise, polish, sophistication, suavity, urbanity; informal class. **3 kind**, type, variety, sort, design, pattern, genre. **4 fashion**, trend, vogue, mode.
• **v.** design or arrange in a particular form.
▷ SYNONYMS: **design**, fashion, tailor, cut.

stylish adj. fashionably elegant.
▷ SYNONYMS: **fashionable**, modern, up to date, modish, smart, sophisticated, elegant, chic, dapper, dashing; informal trendy, natty; N. Amer. informal kicky, tony.
– ANTONYMS: unfashionable.
■ **stylishly** adv. **stylishness** n.

stylist n. a person who designs fashionable clothes or cuts hair.

stylistic adj. of literary or artistic style.
■ **stylistically** adv.

stylized (or **-ised**) adj. represented in an artificial style.

stylus n. (pl. **styli**) **1** a hard point following a groove in a record. **2** a pointed implement for scratching letters or engraving.

stymie v. (**stymying** or **stymieing**, **stymied**) informal obstruct or thwart.

styptic adj. able to make bleeding stop.

suave /swahv/ adj. charming,

confident, and elegant.
■ **suavely** adv. **suavity** n.

sub informal n. **1** a submarine. **2** a substitute.

sub- prefix **1** under. **2** subordinate.

subaltern n. the army rank below captain.

subatomic adj. smaller than or occurring within an atom.

subconscious adj. of the part of the mind of which a person is not fully aware.
• n. this part of the mind.
■ **subconsciously** adv.

subcontinent n. a large part of a continent considered as a particular area.

subcontract v. employ a firm or person outside your company to do work.
■ **subcontractor** n.

subculture n. a distinct group in a society having beliefs or interests different from those of the majority.

subcutaneous adj. under the skin.

subdivide v. divide into smaller parts.
■ **subdivision** n.

subdue v. **1** overcome, quieten, or make less intense. **2** bring under control.
▷ SYNONYMS: **conquer**, defeat, vanquish, overcome, overwhelm, crush, beat, subjugate, suppress.

subdued adj. **1** quiet and seeming depressed. **2** soft; muted.
▷ SYNONYMS: **1** *a subdued mood:* **sombre**, downcast, sad, dejected, depressed, gloomy, despondent. **2** *subdued voices:* **hushed**, muted, quiet, low, soft, faint, muffled, subtle, indistinct, dim, unobtrusive.
− ANTONYMS: cheerful, loud, bright.

subedit v. check and correct text before printing.
■ **subeditor** n.

subhuman adj. not behaving like a human being.

subject n. **1** a person or thing that is being discussed or dealt with. **2** a branch of knowledge studied or taught. **3** the word in a sentence naming who or what performs the action of the verb. **4** a member of a state ruled by a monarch.
▷ SYNONYMS: **1 theme**, subject matter, topic, issue, thesis, question, concern. **2 branch of study**, discipline, field. **3 citizen**, national, resident, taxpayer, voter.
• adj. (**subject to**) **1** able to be affected by. **2** dependent on. **3** under the authority of.

• v. (**subject to**) cause to undergo.
▷ SYNONYMS: **expose to**, submit to, treat with, put through.
■ **subjection** n.

subjective adj. based on or influenced by personal opinions.
▷ SYNONYMS: **personal**, individual, emotional, biased, intuitive.
− ANTONYMS: objective.
■ **subjectively** adv. **subjectivity** n.

sub judice /sub joo-di-si/ adj. being considered by a law court and so forbidden to be discussed elsewhere.

subjugate v. forcibly bring under control.
■ **subjugation** n.

subjunctive adj. (of a form of a verb) expressing what is imagined, wished, or possible.

sublet v. (**subletting**, **sublet**) let a property that you are already renting to another person.

sublimate v. transform into a purer or idealized form.
■ **sublimation** n.

sublime adj. **1** of great excellence. **2** very great; extreme.
■ **sublimely** adv.

subliminal adj. affecting someone's mind without their being aware of it.
■ **subliminally** adv.

sub-machine gun n. a lightweight machine gun.

submarine n. a streamlined warship operating under the sea.
• adj. existing or done under the sea's surface.
■ **submariner** n.

submerge v. **1** push or go under water. **2** cover or hide.
▷ SYNONYMS: **1 sink**, dive, plunge, plummet. **2 immerse**, dip, push, duck, dunk. **3** *the farmland was submerged:* **flood**, deluge, swamp, overwhelm, inundate.

submerse v. submerge.
■ **submersion** n.

submersible adj. designed to operate under water.

submission n. **1** the act of submitting. **2** a proposal submitted for consideration.
▷ SYNONYMS: **1 yielding**, capitulation, surrender, resignation, acceptance, consent, compliance, acquiescence, obedience, subjection, subservience, servility. **2 proposal**, suggestion, proposition, tender, presentation. **3 argument**, assertion, contention, statement, claim, allegation.
− ANTONYMS: defiance.

submissive adj. very obedient or

S

passive.
▷ SYNONYMS: **compliant**, yielding, acquiescent, passive, obedient, dutiful,
docile, pliant, tractable, biddable,
malleable, meek, unassertive; informal
under someone's thumb.
■ **submissively** adv.
submit v. (**submitting, submitted**)
1 give in to authority or greater
power. **2** present for consideration.
▷ SYNONYMS: **1 yield**, give in/way, back
down, cave in, capitulate, surrender,
acquiesce. **2** *he refused to submit to
their authority:* **be governed by**, abide
by, comply with, accept, be subject
to, agree to, consent to, conform to.
3 put forward, present, offer, tender,
propose, suggest, enter, put in, send
in. **4 contend**, assert, argue, state,
claim, allege.
– ANTONYMS: resist.
subordinate adj. **1** lower in rank.
2 less important.
▷ SYNONYMS: **inferior**, junior, lower-
ranking, lower, supporting.
• n. a subordinate person.
▷ SYNONYMS: **junior**, assistant, second in
command, number two, deputy, aide,
underling, minion.
– ANTONYMS: superior, senior.
• v. treat as less important.
■ **subordination** n.
suborn v. pay or persuade to commit
an unlawful act.
subpoena /suh-pee-nuh/ n. a writ
ordering a person to attend a court.
• v. (**subpoenaing, subpoenaed**)
summon with a subpoena.
subscribe v. **1** arrange to receive
something regularly by paying in
advance. **2** contribute to a cause.
3 apply to take part in. **4** (**subscribe
to**) agree with.
▷ SYNONYMS: **contribute**, donate, give,
pay.
■ **subscriber** n.
subscript adj. (of a letter, figure, etc.)
written below the line.
subscription n. **1** a payment to
subscribe to something. **2** the act of
subscribing.
▷ SYNONYMS: **membership fee**, dues,
annual payment, charge.
subsequent adj. coming after.
▷ SYNONYMS: **following**, ensuing,
succeeding, later, future, coming, to
come, next, eventual.
– ANTONYMS: previous.
■ **subsequently** adv.
subservient adj. **1** too willing to obey
others. **2** less important.
■ **subservience** n.

subset n. Math. a set of which all the
elements are contained in another set.
subside v. **1** become less intense.
2 sink to a lower or the normal level.
▷ SYNONYMS: **1 abate**, let up, quieten
down, calm down, slacken off, ease
up, relent, die down, diminish,
decline. **2 recede**, ebb, fall, go down,
sink.
– ANTONYMS: intensify, rise.
■ **subsidence** n.
subsidiary adj. **1** related but
less important. **2** (of a company)
controlled by another.
▷ SYNONYMS: **subordinate**, secondary,
subservient, supplementary,
peripheral, auxiliary.
– ANTONYMS: principal.
• n. (pl. **subsidiaries**) a subsidiary
company.
▷ SYNONYMS: **branch**, division,
subdivision, derivative, offshoot.
subsidize (or **-ise**) v. **1** pay part of
the cost of producing something.
2 support financially.
▷ SYNONYMS: **finance**, fund, support,
contribute to, give money to, underwrite, sponsor; informal shell out for;
N. Amer. informal bankroll.
subsidy n. (pl. **subsidies**) a sum of
money given to help keep the price of
something low.
▷ SYNONYMS: **finance**, funding, backing,
support, grant, sponsorship, allowance, contribution, handout.
subsist v. maintain or support
yourself at a basic level.
■ **subsistence** n.
subsoil n. the soil lying under the
surface soil.
subsonic adj. of or flying at speeds
less than that of sound.
substance n. **1** a type of solid, liquid,
or gas that has particular qualities.
2 the physical matter of which a
thing consists. **3** solid basis in reality.
4 importance. **5** the most important
or essential part or meaning. **6** an
intoxicating or narcotic drug.
▷ SYNONYMS: **1 material**, compound,
matter, stuff. **2 significance**, importance, import, validity, foundation.
3 content, subject matter, theme,
message, essence. **4 wealth**, fortune,
riches, affluence, prosperity, money,
means.
substantial adj. **1** of considerable
importance or size. **2** strongly built.
▷ SYNONYMS: **1 considerable**, real,
significant, important, major,
valuable, useful, sizeable, appreciable. **2 sturdy**, solid, stout, strong,

well built, durable, long-lasting, hard-wearing.
– ANTONYMS: insubstantial.
■ **substantially** adv.

substantiate v. support with evidence.
■ **substantiation** n.

substantive adj. real and meaningful.

substitute n. a person or thing acting or used in place of another.
▷ SYNONYMS: **replacement**, deputy, relief, proxy, reserve, surrogate, cover, stand-in, understudy; informal sub.
• v. use or act as a substitute.
▷ SYNONYMS: **1 exchange**, swap, use instead of, use as an alternative to, use in place of, replace with. **2** *I found someone to substitute for me:* **deputize for**, stand in for, cover for, fill in for, take over from.
■ **substitution** n.

subsume v. include in something else.

subterfuge n. a secret or dishonest act used to achieve a goal.

subterranean adj. underground.

subtext n. an underlying theme.

subtitle n. **1** (subtitles) captions at the bottom of a cinema or television screen that translate dialogue. **2** a secondary title.
• v. provide with subtitles.

subtle adj. **1** so delicate or precise as to be difficult to analyse or describe. **2** able to make fine distinctions. **3** using clever and indirect methods.
▷ SYNONYMS: **1 understated**, muted, subdued, delicate, soft, low-key, toned-down. **2 gentle**, slight, gradual. **3** *a subtle distinction:* **fine**, fine-drawn, nice, tenuous.
– ANTONYMS: gaudy, crude.
■ **subtlety** n. **subtly** adv.

subtotal n. the total of part of a group of figures.

subtract v. take away a number or amount from another.
■ **subtraction** n.

subtropical adj. of regions bordering on the tropics.

suburb n. an outlying residential part of a city.

suburban adj. **1** relating to or like a suburb. **2** boringly conventional.
▷ SYNONYMS: **1 residential**, commuter-belt. **2 dull**, boring, uninteresting, conventional, ordinary, unsophisticated, provincial, parochial, bourgeois, middle-class.

suburbia n. suburbs and suburban life.

subversive adj. trying to undermine an established system or institution.

▷ SYNONYMS: **disruptive**, troublemaking, insurrectionary, seditious, dissident.
• n. a subversive person.
▷ SYNONYMS: **troublemaker**, dissident, agitator, renegade.
■ **subversively** adv.

subvert v. damage or weaken the power of.
■ **subversion** n.

subway n. **1** Brit. a tunnel under a road for pedestrians. **2** US an underground railway.

succeed v. **1** achieve an aim. **2** take over a role, title, etc., from someone. **3** come after and take the place of.
▷ SYNONYMS: **1 triumph**, be successful, do well, flourish, thrive; informal make it, make the grade. **2 be successful**, turn out well, work, be effective; informal come off, pay off. **3 replace**, take over from, follow, supersede.
– ANTONYMS: fail, precede.

success n. **1** the achievement of an aim. **2** the gaining of wealth or status. **3** a successful person or thing.
▷ SYNONYMS: **1 victory**, triumph. **2 prosperity**, affluence, wealth, riches, opulence. **3 best-seller**, sell-out, winner, triumph; informal hit, smash, sensation.
– ANTONYMS: failure.

successful adj. **1** having achieved an aim. **2** having achieved wealth or status.
▷ SYNONYMS: **1 prosperous**, affluent, wealthy, rich, famous, eminent, top, respected. **2 flourishing**, thriving, booming, buoyant, profitable, money-making, lucrative.
■ **successfully** adv.

succession n. **1** a number of people or things following one after the other. **2** the act or right of inheriting a position, title, etc.
▷ SYNONYMS: **sequence**, series, progression, chain, string, train, line, run.
◻ **in succession** following one another.
■ **successor** n.

successive adj. following one another or others.
▷ SYNONYMS: **consecutive**, in a row, sequential, in succession, running; informal on the trot.
■ **successively** adv.

succinct adj. concise and clear.
▷ SYNONYMS: **concise**, short, short and sweet, brief, compact, condensed, crisp, laconic, terse, to the point, pithy.
– ANTONYMS: verbose.

S

■ **succinctly** adv.
succour (US **succor**) n. help.
succulent adj. **1** juicy. **2** having thick fleshy leaves.
▷ SYNONYMS: **juicy**, moist, luscious, soft, tender, choice, mouth-watering, appetizing, flavoursome, tasty, delicious; informal scrumptious, scrummy.
– ANTONYMS: dry.
● n. a succulent plant.
■ **succulence** n.
succumb v. give in to pressure, temptation, etc.
▷ SYNONYMS: **yield**, give in/way, submit, surrender, capitulate, cave in, fall victim.
– ANTONYMS: resist.
such adj. & pron. **1** of the type previously mentioned or about to be mentioned. **2** to so high a degree. □ **such as 1** for example. **2** of a kind that. **suchlike** things of the type mentioned.
suck v. **1** draw into the mouth by tightening the lips and breathing in. **2** hold in the mouth and pull at with the mouth muscles. **3** pull in a specified direction. **4** (**suck up to**) informal try to please to gain advantage.
▷ SYNONYMS: **sip**, sup, slurp, drink, siphon.
● n. an act of sucking.
sucker n. **1** an organ or device that can stick to a surface by suction. **2** informal a person who is easily fooled. **3** a shoot springing from the base of a plant.
suckle v. feed from the breast or teat.
suckling n. a young child or animal that has not been weaned.
sucrose n. sugar.
suction n. the force produced when a partial vacuum is created by the removal of air.
sudden adj. occurring or done quickly and unexpectedly.
▷ SYNONYMS: **unexpected**, unforeseen, immediate, instantaneous, instant, precipitous, abrupt, rapid, swift, quick.
■ **suddenness** n.
suddenly adv. quickly and unexpectedly.
▷ SYNONYMS: **all of a sudden**, all at once, abruptly, swiftly, unexpectedly, without warning, out of the blue.
– ANTONYMS: gradually.
sudoku /soo-**doh**-koo, soo-**doo**-koo/ n. a type of number puzzle.
suds pl. n. froth from soap and water.
sue v. take legal action against.
▷ SYNONYMS: **take legal action**, go to

court, take to court, litigate.
suede n. leather with a velvety nap on one side.
suet n. the hard white fat from round an animal's kidneys, used in cooking.
suffer v. **1** experience something bad. **2** be affected by a disease etc. **3** become worse. **4** old use tolerate.
▷ SYNONYMS: **1** the team suffered a humiliating defeat: **undergo**, experience, be subjected to, receive, sustain, endure, face, meet with. **2** he suffers from asthma: **be afflicted by**, be affected by, be troubled with, be a martyr to.
■ **sufferer** n.
sufferance n. toleration rather than actual approval.
suffering n. physical or mental pain or distress.
▷ SYNONYMS: **hardship**, distress, misery, adversity, pain, agony, anguish, trauma, torment, torture, hurt, affliction.
– ANTONYMS: pleasure, joy.
suffice v. be enough.
sufficient adj. enough.
▷ SYNONYMS: **enough**, adequate, plenty of, ample.
– ANTONYMS: insufficient.
■ **sufficiency** n. **sufficiently** adv.
suffix n. a part added at the end of a word to form another word.
suffocate v. die or kill from lack of air.
■ **suffocation** n.
suffrage n. the right to vote in political elections.
suffragette n. hist. a woman who campaigned for female suffrage.
suffuse v. spread through or over.
■ **suffusion** n.
sugar n. a sweet substance obtained from various plants.
● v. sweeten or coat with sugar. □ **sugar beet** beet from which sugar is extracted. **sugar cane** a tropical grass from which sugar is extracted.
■ **sugary** adj.
suggest v. **1** put forward for consideration. **2** make you think of. **3** express indirectly.
▷ SYNONYMS: **1 propose**, put forward, recommend, advocate, advise. **2 indicate**, lead someone to the belief, give the impression, demonstrate, show. **3 hint**, insinuate, imply, intimate.
suggestible adj. easily influenced.
suggestion n. **1** something suggested. **2** the act of suggesting. **3** a slight trace.
▷ SYNONYMS: **1 proposal**, proposition,

S

recommendation, advice, counsel, hint, tip, clue, idea. **2 hint**, trace, touch, suspicion, ghost, semblance, shadow, glimmer. **3 insinuation**, hint, implication.

suggestive adj. **1** making you think of something. **2** hinting at sexual matters.
▷ SYNONYMS: **1 redolent**, evocative, reminiscent, characteristic, indicative, typical. **2 provocative**, titillating, sexual, sexy, risqué, **indecent**, indelicate, improper, unseemly, smutty, dirty.
■ **suggestively** adv.

suicide n. **1** the act of killing yourself deliberately. **2** a person who does this. **3** an act which is damaging to your own interests.
■ **suicidal** adj. **suicidally** adv.

suit n. **1** a jacket and trousers or a jacket and skirt of the same fabric. **2** a set of clothes for a particular activity. **3** any of the sets into which a pack of playing cards is divided. **4** a lawsuit.
▷ SYNONYMS: **1 outfit**, ensemble. **2 legal action**, lawsuit, court case, action, legal proceedings, litigation.
• v. **1** be convenient for or acceptable to. **2** (of clothes etc.) be right for the features or figure of.
▷ SYNONYMS: **1 be convenient**, be suitable, meet someone's needs, serve someone's purpose; fit/fill the bill, do. **2 look attractive on**, look good on, become, flatter.
□ **suitcase** a case with a handle and a hinged lid for carrying clothes.

suitable adj. right for the purpose or occasion.
▷ SYNONYMS: **1 acceptable**, satisfactory, convenient. **2 appropriate**, apposite, apt, fitting, fit, suited, tailor-made, in keeping, ideal; informal right up someone's street. **3 proper**, right, seemly, decent, appropriate, fitting, correct, due.
– ANTONYMS: unsuitable.
■ **suitability** n. **suitably** adv.

suite /sweet/ n. **1** a set of rooms or furniture. **2** a set of musical pieces.
▷ SYNONYMS: **apartment**, flat, rooms.

suitor n. a man seeking to marry a particular woman.

sulk v. be silently bad-tempered or resentful.
• n. a period of sulking.
■ **sulkily** adv. **sulky** adj.

sullen adj. silently bad-tempered.
▷ SYNONYMS: **surly**, sulky, morose, resentful, moody, grumpy, bad-tempered, unsociable, uncommuni-cative, unresponsive.
– ANTONYMS: cheerful.
■ **sullenly** adv. **sullenness** n.

sully v. (**sullying, sullied**) spoil the purity or cleanness of.

sulphate (US **sulfate**) n. a salt of sulphuric acid.

sulphide (US **sulfide**) n. a compound of sulphur with another element.

sulphur (US **sulfur**) n. a yellow non-metallic element.
□ **sulphuric acid** a strong corrosive acid.
■ **sulphurous** adj.

sultan n. a Muslim ruler.
■ **sultanate** n.

sultana n. **1** Brit. a seedless raisin. **2** the wife of a sultan.

sultry adj. **1** (of the weather) hot and humid. **2** suggesting sexual passion.

sum n. **1** an amount of money. **2** a total. **3** an arithmetical calculation.
▷ SYNONYMS: **1 amount**, quantity, price, charge, fee, cost. **2 total**, sum total, grand total, tally, aggregate. **3 entirety**, totality, total, whole, beginning and end. **4 calculation**, problem; (**sums**) arithmetic, mathematics; Brit. informal **maths**; N. Amer. informal **math**.
• v. (**summing, summed**) (**sum up**) describe concisely or summarize.

summarize (or **-ise**) v. give a brief account of.
▷ SYNONYMS: **sum up**, abridge, condense, outline, put in a nutshell, precis.

summary n. (pl. **summaries**) a brief statement of the main points of something.
▷ SYNONYMS: **synopsis**, precis, résumé, abstract, outline, rundown, summing-up, overview.
• adj. **1** brief and without unnecessary detail. **2** without the usual legal procedures.
■ **summarily** adv.

summation n. **1** the act of adding up. **2** a summary.

summer n. the season between spring and autumn.
■ **summery** adj.

summit n. **1** the top of a mountain. **2** the highest level of achievement. **3** a meeting between heads of government.
▷ SYNONYMS: **1 top**, peak, crest, crown, apex, tip, cap, hilltop. **2 meeting**, conference, talks.
– ANTONYMS: base.

summon v. **1** instruct to be present. **2** send for help. **3** arrange a meeting. **4** make an effort to produce a quality

S

or reaction.
▷ SYNONYMS: **1 send for**, call for, request the presence of, ask, invite. **2 convene**, call, assemble, rally, muster, gather together. **3 summons**, subpoena.

summons n. (pl. **summonses**) **1** an order to appear in a law court. **2** an act of summoning.
• v. order to appear in a law court.

sumo n. Japanese wrestling.

sump n. a reservoir of oil in a petrol engine.

sumptuous adj. splendid; lavish.
▷ SYNONYMS: **lavish**, luxurious, opulent, magnificent, resplendent, gorgeous, splendid; informal **plush**; Brit. informal swish.
– ANTONYMS: plain.
■ **sumptuously** adv.

sun n. **1** the star round which the earth orbits. **2** any similar star. **3** the light or warmth from the sun.
▷ SYNONYMS: **sunshine**, sunlight, daylight, light, warmth.
• v. (**sunning**, **sunned**) (**sun yourself**) sit or lie in the sun.
□ **sunbathe** sit or lie in the sun to get a suntan. **sunbed** Brit. a device with ultraviolet lamps for acquiring an artificial suntan. **sunburn** inflammation of the skin caused by too much exposure to the sun. **sunburnt** (or **sunburned**) suffering from sunburn. **sundial** a device showing the time by the shadow cast by a pointer. **sundown** sunset. **sunflower** a tall plant with large yellow flowers. **sunglasses** glasses tinted to protect the eyes from sunlight. **sunlight** light from the sun. **sunshine** sunlight unbroken by cloud. **sunspot** a dark patch on the sun's surface. **sunstroke** illness caused by excessive exposure to the sun. **suntan** a golden-brown skin colouring caused by exposure to the sun.

> **WORD LINKS**
> **solar** relating to the sun

sundae n. a dish of ice cream with fruit and syrup.

Sunday n. the day following Saturday.
□ **Sunday school** a class held on Sundays to teach children about Christianity or Judaism.

sunder v. literary split apart.

sundry adj. of various kinds.
▷ SYNONYMS: **various**, varied, miscellaneous, assorted, mixed, diverse, diversified, several, numerous, many, manifold, multifarious, multi-

tudinous; literary divers.
• n. (**sundries**) various small items.

sung past part. of SING.

sunk past part. of SINK.

sunken adj. **1** having sunk. **2** lower than the surrounding area.

Sunni n. (pl. **Sunni** or **Sunnis**) a follower of one of the two main branches of Islam.

sunny adj. (**sunnier**, **sunniest**) **1** bright with or receiving much sunlight. **2** cheerful.
▷ SYNONYMS: **1 bright**, sunlit, clear, fine, cloudless. **2 cheerful**, cheery, happy, bright, merry, bubbly, jolly, good-natured, good-tempered, optimistic, upbeat.
– ANTONYMS: dull, cloudy.

sunrise n. the time when the sun rises.
▷ SYNONYMS: **dawn**, crack of dawn, daybreak, break of day, first light; N. Amer. sunup.

sunset n. **1** the time when the sun sets. **2** the colours in the sky at sunset.
▷ SYNONYMS: **nightfall**, twilight, dusk, evening; N. Amer. sundown.

super adj. informal excellent.

superannuation n. regular payment made by an employee towards a pension.

superb adj. **1** excellent. **2** magnificent.
▷ SYNONYMS: **excellent**, first-class, outstanding, marvellous, wonderful, splendid, admirable, fine, exceptional, glorious; informal great, fantastic, fabulous, terrific, super, awesome, ace; Brit. informal brilliant, smashing.
– ANTONYMS: poor, unimpressive.
■ **superbly** adv.

supercharger n. a device improving the efficiency of an engine by forcing more air or fuel into it.
■ **supercharged** adj.

supercilious adj. haughty and superior.
▷ SYNONYMS: **arrogant**, haughty, conceited, disdainful, overbearing, pompous, condescending, superior, patronizing, imperious, proud, snobbish, smug, scornful, sneering; informal high and mighty, snooty, stuck-up.
■ **superciliously** adv.

supercomputer n. a very powerful computer.

superficial adj. **1** of or on the surface. **2** apparent rather than real. **3** not thorough or deep.
▷ SYNONYMS: **1 surface**, exterior, external, outer, slight. **2 cursory**,

perfunctory, casual, sketchy, desultory, token, slapdash, offhand, rushed, hasty, hurried. **3 apparent**, seeming, outward, ostensible, cosmetic, slight. **4 facile**, shallow, flippant, empty-headed, trivial, frivolous, silly, inane.
− ANTONYMS: deep, thorough.
■ **superficiality** n. **superficially** adv.

superfluous adj. more than is needed.
▷ SYNONYMS: **surplus**, redundant, unneeded, unnecessary, excess, extra, spare, remaining, unused, left over, waste.
− ANTONYMS: necessary.
■ **superfluity** n.

superhuman adj. having exceptional ability or powers.
▷ SYNONYMS: **extraordinary**, phenomenal, prodigious, stupendous, exceptional, immense, heroic, Herculean.

superimpose v. place one thing over another.

superintend v. supervise.

superintendent n. **1** a supervisor. **2** a senior police officer.

superior adj. **1** higher in status, quality, or power. **2** thinking that you are better than others.
▷ SYNONYMS: **1 senior**, higher-ranking, higher. **2 better**, finer, higher quality, top-quality, choice, select, prime, excellent. **3 condescending**, supercilious, patronizing, haughty, disdainful, lordly, snobbish; informal high and mighty, snooty, toffee-nosed.
− ANTONYMS: junior, inferior.
• n. a person of superior rank.
▷ SYNONYMS: **manager**, chief, supervisor, senior, controller, foreman; informal boss.
− ANTONYMS: subordinate.

superiority n. the state of being superior.
▷ SYNONYMS: **supremacy**, advantage, lead, dominance, primacy, ascendancy, eminence.

superlative adj. **1** of the highest quality. **2** (of an adjective or adverb) expressing the highest degree of a quality.

supermarket n. a large self-service shop selling food and household goods.

supernatural adj. not able to be explained by the laws of nature.
▷ SYNONYMS: **1 paranormal**, psychic, magic, magical, occult, mystic, mystical. **2 ghostly**, phantom, spec-

tral, other-worldly, unearthly.
■ **supernaturally** adv.

supernova n. (pl. **supernovae** or **supernovas**) a star that suddenly becomes much brighter because of an explosion.

supernumerary adj. extra.

superpower n. a very powerful nation.

superscript adj. (of a letter, figure, etc.) written above the line.

supersede v. take the place of.
▷ SYNONYMS: **replace**, take the place of, take over from, succeed, supplant.

USAGE -sede, not -cede.

supersonic adj. of or flying at a speed greater than that of sound.

superstition n. a belief in supernatural influences, or a practice based on this.
■ **superstitious** adj.

superstore n. a very large supermarket.

superstructure n. **1** a structure built on top of something else. **2** the upper part of a building or ship.

supervene v. occur as an interruption or change.
■ **supervention** n.

supervise v. watch and direct the performance of a task or the work of a person.
▷ SYNONYMS: **oversee**, be in charge of, superintend, preside over, direct, manage, run, look after, be responsible for, govern, keep an eye on, observe, monitor, mind.
■ **supervision** n.

supervisor n. a person who supervises someone or something.
▷ SYNONYMS: **manager**, director, overseer, controller, superintendent, governor, chief, head, foreman; informal boss; Brit. informal gaffer.
■ **supervisory** adj.

supine adj. **1** lying face upwards. **2** passive or lazy.

supper n. a light or informal evening meal.

supplant v. take the place of.

supple adj. bending easily.
▷ SYNONYMS: **1 lithe**, lissom, willowy, flexible, agile, acrobatic, nimble. **2 pliable**, flexible, soft, bendy, workable, stretchy, springy.
− ANTONYMS: stiff, rigid.
■ **suppleness** n.

supplement n. **1** a thing added to improve or complete something. **2** a separate additional section of a newspaper. **3** an additional charge for

an extra facility.
▷ SYNONYMS: **1 extra**, add-on, accessory, adjunct. **2 surcharge**, addition, increase, increment. **3 appendix**, addendum, postscript, addition, coda. **4 pull-out**, insert.
• v. provide a supplement for.
▷ SYNONYMS: **add to**, augment, increase, boost, swell, amplify, enlarge, top up.
■ **supplemental** adj.

supplementary adj. completing or improving something.
▷ SYNONYMS: **additional**, supplemental, extra, more, further, add-on, subsidiary, auxiliary, ancillary.

suppliant n. a person making a humble request.

supplicate v. humbly ask for something.
■ **supplicant** n. **supplication** n.

supply v. (**supplying**, **supplied**) make available to; provide.
▷ SYNONYMS: **1 provide**, give, furnish, equip, contribute, donate, grant, confer, dispense. **2 satisfy**, meet, fulfil, cater for.
• n. (pl. **supplies**) **1** a stock of something available. **2** the act of supplying. **3** (**supplies**) necessary provisions and equipment.
▷ SYNONYMS: **1 stock**, store, reserve, reservoir, stockpile, hoard, cache, fund, bank. **2** *we're running out of supplies*: **provisions**, stores, rations, food, necessities.
■ **supplier** n.

support v. **1** bear the weight of. **2** help, encourage, or approve of. **3** provide with the necessities of life. **4** confirm.
▷ SYNONYMS: **1 hold up**, bear, carry, prop up, keep up, brace, shore up, underpin, buttress, reinforce. **2 help**, aid, assist, contribute to, back, subsidize, fund, finance; N. Amer. informal bankroll. **3 back**, champion, favour, be in favour of, advocate, encourage, promote, endorse, espouse. **4 stand by**, defend, back, stand/stick up for, take someone's side, side with. **5 provide for**, maintain, sustain, keep, take care of, look after. **6 back up**, substantiate, bear out, corroborate, confirm, verify.
– ANTONYMS: contradict, oppose.
• n. **1** a person or thing that supports. **2** the act of supporting.
▷ SYNONYMS: **1 pillar**, post, prop, upright, brace, buttress, foundation, underpinning. **2 encouragement**, friendship, backing, endorsement, help, assistance, comfort. **3 contributions**,

donations, money, subsidy, funding, funds, finance, capital.

supporter n. a person who supports a team, political party, policy, etc.
▷ SYNONYMS: **1 advocate**, backer, adherent, champion, defender, upholder, campaigner. **2 fan**, follower, enthusiast, devotee, admirer. **3 contributor**, donor, benefactor, sponsor, backer, patron, subscriber, well-wisher.

supportive adj. providing encouragement or emotional help.
▷ SYNONYMS: **encouraging**, caring, sympathetic, reassuring, understanding, concerned, helpful.

suppose v. **1** think to be true or likely. **2** require as a necessary condition. **3** (**be supposed to do**) be required or expected to do.
▷ SYNONYMS: **1 assume**, presume, surmise, expect, imagine, dare say, take it, take as read, suspect, guess, conjecture. **2 hypothesize**, postulate, posit.
■ **supposedly** adv.

supposed adj. alleged or assumed to be the case: *his supposed athletic prowess.*
▷ SYNONYMS: **alleged**, reputed, rumoured, claimed, purported.

supposition n. a belief not based on proof or certainty.
▷ SYNONYMS: **belief**, conjecture, speculation, assumption, presumption, inference, theory, hypothesis, feeling, idea, notion, guesswork.

suppository n. (pl. **suppositories**) a solid medical preparation designed to dissolve after being inserted in the rectum or vagina.

suppress v. **1** forcibly put an end to. **2** prevent from developing. **3** prevent from being stated or published.
▷ SYNONYMS: **1 subdue**, crush, quell, quash, squash, stamp out, crack down on, clamp down on, put an end to. **2 restrain**, repress, hold back, control, stifle, smother, check, keep in check, curb, contain, bottle up. **3 censor**, keep secret, conceal, hide, hush up, gag, withhold, cover up, stifle.
– ANTONYMS: encourage, reveal.
■ **suppressant** n. **suppression** n.

suppurate v. form pus.
■ **suppuration** n.

supremacy n. the state of being superior to all others.
▷ SYNONYMS: **control**, power, rule, sovereignty, dominance, superiority, predominance, primacy, dominion,

authority, mastery, ascendancy.

supreme adj. **1** highest in authority or rank. **2** very great or greatest.

▷ SYNONYMS: **1 highest**, chief, head, top, foremost, principal, superior, premier, first, prime. **2 extraordinary**, remarkable, phenomenal, exceptional, outstanding, incomparable, unparalleled. **3** *the supreme sacrifice:* **ultimate**, greatest, highest, extreme, final, last.

– ANTONYMS: subordinate.

■ **supremely** adv.

supremo n. (pl. **supremos**) Brit. informal a person in overall charge.

surcharge n. an extra charge.

sure adj. **1** confident that you are right. **2** (**sure of/to do**) certain to get or do. **3** undoubtedly true. **4** steady and confident.

▷ SYNONYMS: **1 certain**, positive, convinced, confident, definite, satisfied, persuaded, assured, free from doubt. **2 guaranteed**, unfailing, infallible, unerring, foolproof, certain, reliable, dependable, trustworthy, trusty; informal sure-fire.

– ANTONYMS: uncertain, unlikely.

• adv. informal certainly.

■ **sureness** n.

surely adv. **1** it must be true that. **2** certainly.

surety n. (pl. **sureties**) **1** a person who guarantees that someone will do something. **2** money given as a guarantee.

surf n. waves that break and form foam on a shore or reef.

• v. **1** stand on a surfboard and ride on the crest of a wave. **2** move from site to site on the Internet.

□ **surfboard** a long, narrow board used in surfing.

■ **surfer** n.

surface n. **1** the outside or uppermost layer of something. **2** outward appearance.

▷ SYNONYMS: **1 outside**, exterior, top, side, finish. **2 outward appearance**, facade, veneer.

– ANTONYMS: inside, interior.

• v. **1** come up to the surface. **2** become apparent. **3** provide with a surface.

▷ SYNONYMS: **emerge**, arise, appear, come to light, crop up, materialize, spring up.

surfeit n. an excess.

surge n. **1** a sudden powerful forward or upward movement. **2** a sudden increase.

▷ SYNONYMS: **1 gush**, rush, outpouring, stream, flow. **2** *a surge in demand:*

increase, rise, growth, upswing, upsurge, escalation, leap.

• v. **1** move in a surge. **2** increase suddenly.

▷ SYNONYMS: **1 gush**, rush, stream, flow, burst, pour, cascade, spill, sweep, roll. **2 increase**, rise, grow, leap.

surgeon n. a doctor qualified to practise surgery.

surgery n. (pl. **surgeries**) **1** medical treatment involving cutting open the body and removing or repairing parts. **2** Brit. a place where a doctor or nurse sees patients. **3** Brit. a time when an MP is available for consultation.

■ **surgical** adj. **surgically** adv.

surly adj. (**surlier**, **surliest**) bad-tempered and unfriendly.

▷ SYNONYMS: **sullen**, sulky, moody, morose, unfriendly, unpleasant, scowling, unsmiling, bad-tempered, grumpy, gruff, churlish, ill-humoured.

– ANTONYMS: friendly.

■ **surliness** n.

surmise v. suppose or guess.

▷ SYNONYMS: **guess**, conjecture, suspect, deduce, infer, conclude, theorize, speculate, assume, presume, suppose, understand, gather.

• n. a guess.

surmount v. **1** overcome a difficulty. **2** be on top of.

▷ SYNONYMS: **overcome**, prevail over, triumph over, beat, vanquish, conquer, get the better of.

surname n. a family name.

surpass v. be greater or better than.

▷ SYNONYMS: **excel**, exceed, transcend, outdo, outshine, outstrip, outclass, eclipse, improve on, top, trump, cap, beat, better, outperform.

surplice n. a white robe worn over a cassock by Christian clergy and choristers.

surplus n. an amount left over after what is needed has been used.

▷ SYNONYMS: **excess**, surfeit, superfluity, oversupply, glut, remainder, residue, remains, leftovers.

– ANTONYMS: dearth.

• adj. more than is needed or used; extra.

▷ SYNONYMS: **excess**, leftover, unused, remaining, extra, additional, spare, superfluous, redundant, unwanted, unneeded, dispensable.

– ANTONYMS: insufficient.

surprise n. **1** a feeling caused by something sudden or unexpected. **2** an unexpected or astonishing thing.

▷ SYNONYMS: **1 astonishment**,

S

amazement, wonder, bewilderment, disbelief. **2 shock**, bolt from the blue, bombshell, revelation, rude awakening, eye-opener.
• v. **1** cause to feel surprise. **2** attack or find suddenly and unexpectedly.
▷ SYNONYMS: **1 astonish**, amaze, startle, astound, stun, stagger, shock, dumbfound, leave speechless; nonplus, take aback; informal bowl over, floor, flabbergast; Brit. informal knock for six. **2 take by surprise**, catch unawares, catch off guard, catch red-handed.

> USAGE Don't forget the first r.

surprising adj. causing surprise.
▷ SYNONYMS: **unexpected**, unforeseen, astonishing, amazing, startling, astounding, staggering, incredible, extraordinary.
surreal adj. strange and dreamlike.
■ **surreally** adv.
surrealism n. an artistic movement combining normally unrelated images in a strange way.
■ **surrealist** n. **surrealistic** adj.
surrender v. **1** give in to an opponent. **2** give up a right or possession.
▷ SYNONYMS: **1 give up**, give yourself up, give in, cave in, capitulate, concede defeat, submit, lay down your arms/ weapons. **2 give up**, relinquish, renounce, cede, abdicate, forfeit, sacrifice, hand over, turn over, yield.
– ANTONYMS: resist.
• n. an act of surrendering.
▷ SYNONYMS: **1 capitulation**, submission, yielding. **2 renunciation**, abdication, resignation.
surreptitious adj. done secretly.
▷ SYNONYMS: **secret**, secretive, stealthy, clandestine, sneaky, sly, furtive, covert.
– ANTONYMS: blatant.
■ **surreptitiously** adv.
surrogate n. a deputy.
□ **surrogate mother** a woman who bears a child on behalf of another.
■ **surrogacy** n.
surround v. be or place all round.
▷ SYNONYMS: **encircle**, enclose, encompass, ring, hem in, confine, cut off, besiege, trap.
• n. a border.
surroundings pl. n. the conditions or area around a person or thing.
▷ SYNONYMS: **environment**, setting, background, backdrop, vicinity, locality, habitat.
surtax n. an extra tax.
surveillance n. close observation.
▷ SYNONYMS: **observation**, scrutiny,

watch, view, inspection, supervision, spying, espionage.
survey v. **1** look carefully at. **2** question a group to find out their opinions. **3** record the features of an area to produce a map. **4** Brit. examine and report on the condition of a building.
▷ SYNONYMS: **1 look at**, look over, view, contemplate, regard, gaze at, stare at, eye, scrutinize, examine, inspect, scan, study, assess, appraise, take stock of; informal size up. **2 interview**, question, canvass, poll, investigate, research.
• n. **1** an act of surveying. **2** a general examination or description. **3** a map or report obtained by surveying.
▷ SYNONYMS: **1 study**, review, overview, examination, inspection, assessment, appraisal. **2 poll**, investigation, enquiry, study, probe, questionnaire, census, research.
■ **surveyor** n.
survival n. **1** the state of surviving. **2** something that has survived from an earlier time.
survive v. **1** continue to live or exist, esp. despite an accident or ordeal. **2** remain alive after the death of; outlive.
▷ SYNONYMS: **1 remain alive**, live, sustain yourself, pull through, hold out, make it. **2 continue**, remain, persist, endure, live on, persevere, abide, go on, carry on.
■ **survivor** n.
susceptible adj. easily influenced or harmed by a particular thing.
▷ SYNONYMS: **impressionable**, credulous, gullible, innocent, ingenuous, naive, easily led, defenceless, vulnerable.
– ANTONYMS: immune, resistant.
■ **susceptibility** n.
sushi n. a Japanese dish of balls of cold rice served esp. with raw seafood.
suspect v. **1** believe to be likely or possible. **2** believe to be guilty without certain proof. **3** doubt the genuineness of.
▷ SYNONYMS: **1 have a suspicion**, have a feeling, feel, be inclined to think, fancy, reckon, guess, conjecture, surmise, have a hunch, fear. **2 doubt**, distrust, mistrust, have misgivings about, have qualms about, be suspicious of, be sceptical about.
• n. a person suspected of a crime.
• adj. possibly dangerous or false.
▷ SYNONYMS: **suspicious**, dubious, doubtful, untrustworthy; informal fishy, funny; Brit. informal dodgy.

suspend v. **1** halt temporarily.
2 temporarily bar from a job or from attending school. **3** (**suspended**) (of a sentence) not enforced as long as no further offence is committed.
4 hang up.
▷ SYNONYMS: **1 adjourn**, interrupt, break off, cut short, discontinue; N. Amer. table. **2 exclude**, debar, remove, expel, eject, rusticate. **3 hang**, sling, string, swing, dangle.

suspender n. **1** Brit. an elastic strap attached to a belt and fastened to the top of a stocking to hold it up.
2 (**suspenders**) US braces for trousers.

suspense n. excited or anxious uncertainty about what may happen.
▷ SYNONYMS: **tension**, uncertainty, doubt, anticipation, excitement, anxiety, strain.

suspension n. **1** the act of suspending. **2** the mechanism by which a vehicle is supported on its wheels. **3** a mixture in which particles are spread throughout a fluid.
□ **suspension bridge** a bridge suspended from cables running between towers.

suspicion n. **1** a feeling that something is possible or that someone is guilty. **2** distrust. **3** a slight trace.
▷ SYNONYMS: **1 intuition**, feeling, impression, inkling, hunch, fancy, notion, idea, theory, premonition; informal gut feeling. **2 misgiving**, doubt, qualm, reservation, hesitation, scepticism.
– ANTONYMS: trust.

suspicious adj. **1** feeling suspicion.
2 apparently dishonest or dangerous.
▷ SYNONYMS: **1 doubtful**, unsure, dubious, wary, chary, sceptical, mistrustful. **2 suspect**, dubious, unsavoury, disreputable; informal shifty, shady; Brit. informal dodgy.
3 suspicious circumstances: **strange**, odd, questionable, irregular, funny, doubtful, mysterious; informal fishy.
– ANTONYMS: trusting, innocent.
■ **suspiciously** adv.

suss v. Brit. informal realize the true nature of.

sustain v. **1** support mentally or physically. **2** keep going over time or continuously. **3** experience something unpleasant. **4** uphold the validity of.
▷ SYNONYMS: **1** her memories sustained her: **comfort**, help, assist, encourage, support, buoy up, nurture. **2** they were unable to sustain the momentum: **continue**, maintain, carry on, keep

up, keep alive, preserve. **3 suffer**, experience, undergo, receive.
4 confirm, corroborate, substantiate, bear out, prove, authenticate, back up, uphold.

sustainable adj. (of industry etc.) avoiding using up natural resources.
■ **sustainability** n.

sustained adj. continuous: two days of sustained bombing.
▷ SYNONYMS: **continuous**, ongoing, steady, continual, constant, prolonged, persistent, non-stop, relentless.
– ANTONYMS: sporadic.

sustenance n. food and drink as needed to stay alive.
▷ SYNONYMS: **nourishment**, food, nutrition, provisions, rations; informal grub, chow; Brit. informal scoff; literary viands; dated victuals.

suture n. a stitch holding together the edges of a wound.
• v. stitch with a suture.

suzerainty /soo-zuh-rayn-ty/ n. the right of one country to rule over another country that is not fully independent.

svelte adj. slender and elegant.

SW abbrev. south-west or south-western.

swab n. **1** a pad for cleaning wounds or taking specimens from the body.
2 a specimen taken with a swab.
• v. (**swabbing**, **swabbed**) clean with a swab.

swaddle v. wrap in garments or cloth.

swag n. **1** a drooping ornamental arrangement of flowers, fabric, etc.
2 informal items stolen by a burglar.

swagger v. walk or behave in a very confident way.
▷ SYNONYMS: **strut**, parade, stride, prance; informal sashay.
• n. a swaggering walk.

Swahili n. a Bantu language widely used in East Africa.

swain n. old use a young male lover.

swallow v. **1** cause to pass down the throat. **2** take in or cover completely.
3 accept or believe.
▷ SYNONYMS: **eat**, drink, gulp down, consume, devour, put away, quaff, slug; informal swig, swill, down; Brit. informal scoff.
• n. **1** an act of swallowing. **2** a swift-flying bird with a forked tail.

swam past of **swim**.

swamp n. a marsh.
▷ SYNONYMS: **marsh**, bog, fen, quagmire, morass.
• v. **1** flood with water. **2** overwhelm

S

with too much of something.

▷ SYNONYMS: **1 flood**, inundate, deluge, fill. **2** *fans swamped her website with messages:* **overwhelm**, engulf, snow under, overload, inundate, deluge.

■ **swampy** adj.

swan n. a large white waterbird with a long neck.

□ **swansong** the final performance or activity of a person's career.

swank v. informal show off.

swanky adj. (**swankier, swankiest**) informal luxurious and expensive.

swap (or **swop**) v. (**swapping, swapped**) exchange.

▷ SYNONYMS: **exchange**, trade, barter, switch, change, replace.

• n. an act of exchanging.

sward n. an area of short grass.

swarm n. a large of group of flying insects, people, etc.

▷ SYNONYMS: **1 hive**, flock. **2 crowd**, horde, mob, throng, mass, army, herd, pack.

• v. **1** move in a swarm. **2** be crowded. **3** (**swarm up**) climb by gripping with the hands and feet.

▷ SYNONYMS: **flock**, crowd, throng, surge, stream.

swarthy adj. (**swarthier, swarthiest**) dark-skinned.

swashbuckling adj. having daring and romantic adventures.

■ **swashbuckler** n.

swastika n. a symbol in the form of a cross with each arm bent at a right angle.

swat v. (**swatting, swatted**) hit hard with a flat object.

swatch n. a sample of fabric.

swathe n. (US **swath**) **1** a broad strip. **2** a row of grass etc. as it falls when cut down.

• v. wrap in layers of fabric.

▷ SYNONYMS: **wrap**, envelop, bandage, cover, shroud, drape, wind, enfold.

sway v. **1** move gently to and fro. **2** make someone change their opinion.

▷ SYNONYMS: **1 swing**, shake, undulate, move to and fro. **2 stagger**, wobble, rock, lurch, reel, roll. **3 influence**, affect, manipulate, bend, mould.

• n. **1** a swaying movement. **2** power or influence.

▷ SYNONYMS: **1 swing**, roll, shake, undulation. **2 power**, rule, government, sovereignty, dominion, control, jurisdiction, authority.

swear v. (**swearing, swore**; past part. **sworn**) **1** promise solemnly or on oath. **2** use offensive or obscene

language.

▷ SYNONYMS: **1 promise**, vow, pledge, give your word, undertake, guarantee. **2 insist**, declare, proclaim, assert, maintain, emphasize, stress. **3 curse**, blaspheme, use bad language; informal cuss, eff and blind.

□ **swear by** have great confidence in.

swear word an offensive or obscene word.

swearing n. offensive or obscene language.

▷ SYNONYMS: **bad language**, cursing, blaspheming, obscenities, expletives, swear words; informal effing and blinding, four-letter words.

sweat n. moisture given out through the pores of the skin.

• v. **1** produce sweat. **2** make a great effort. **3** be very anxious.

▷ SYNONYMS: **1 perspire**. **2 work**, labour, toil, slog, slave, work your fingers to the bone.

□ **sweatshirt** a loose cotton sweater.

sweatshop a place employing workers for long hours in poor conditions.

■ **sweaty** adj.

> **WORD LINKS**
> **sudorific** relating to or causing sweating

sweater n. a pullover with long sleeves.

Swede n. a person from Sweden.

■ **Swedish** adj. & n.

swede n. Brit. a yellow root vegetable.

sweep v. (**sweeping, swept**) **1** clean by brushing away dirt or litter. **2** move or affect quickly or forcefully. **3** extend in a long curve.

• n. **1** an act of sweeping. **2** a long curving movement. **3** a long curved stretch of road etc. **4** a person who cleans soot from chimneys.

□ **sweepstake** a form of gambling in which the winner receives all the money bet by the other players.

■ **sweeper** n.

sweeping adj. **1** wide in range or effect. **2** (of a statement) too general.

▷ SYNONYMS: **1 extensive**, wide-ranging, broad, comprehensive, far-reaching, thorough, radical. **2 wholesale**, blanket, general, unqualified, indiscriminate, oversimplified.

– ANTONYMS: limited.

sweet adj. **1** having the pleasant taste of sugar. **2** having a pleasant smell. **3** pleasant and kind. **4** charming.

▷ SYNONYMS: **1 sugary**, sweetened, sugared, honeyed, syrupy, sickly, cloying. **2 fragrant**, aromatic,

perfumed. **3 likeable**, appealing, engaging, amiable, pleasant, agreeable, kind, nice, thoughtful, considerate, delightful, lovely. **4 cute**, lovable, adorable, endearing, charming, winsome. **5 musical**, melodious, dulcet, tuneful, soft, harmonious, silvery, mellifluous.
– ANTONYMS: sour, savoury, disagreeable.
• n. Brit. **1** a small piece of confectionery made with sugar. **2** a sweet dish forming a course of a meal.
▷ SYNONYMS: **1 confectionery**, bonbon; N. Amer. candy; old use sweetmeat. **2 dessert**, pudding; Brit. informal afters, pud.
□ **sweetbread** an animal's pancreas, eaten as food. **sweetcorn** a variety of maize with sweet kernels eaten as a vegetable. **sweetheart** a lover. **sweet-talk** informal persuade by using charm or flattery. **sweet tooth** a liking for sweet foods.
■ **sweeten** v. **sweetly** adv. **sweetness** n.
sweetener n. **1** a sweetening substance. **2** informal a bribe.
swell v. (**swelling**, **swelled**, past part. **swollen** or **swelled**) **1** become larger or more rounded. **2** increase in strength or amount.
▷ SYNONYMS: **1 expand**, bulge, distend, inflate, dilate, bloat, blow up, puff up, balloon, fatten, fill out. **2 grow**, enlarge, increase, expand, rise, escalate, multiply, proliferate, snowball, mushroom.
– ANTONYMS: shrink, decrease.
• n. **1** a full or rounded form. **2** a gradual increase in strength or amount. **3** a slow, regular movement of the sea.
swelling n. a swollen place on the body.
▷ SYNONYMS: **bump**, lump, bulge, protuberance, protrusion, distension.
swelter v. be uncomfortably hot.
swept past & past part. of **sweep**.
swerve v. abruptly go off from a straight course.
▷ SYNONYMS: **veer**, deviate, diverge, weave, zigzag, change direction; Sailing tack.
• n. an abrupt change of course.
swift adj. quick; fast.
▷ SYNONYMS: **fast**, rapid, quick, speedy, expeditious, prompt, brisk, immediate, instant, hasty, hurried, sudden, abrupt.
– ANTONYMS: slow, leisurely.
• n. a fast-flying bird with slender wings.

■ **swiftly** adv. **swiftness** n.
swig v. (**swigging**, **swigged**) informal drink quickly.
swill v. Brit. rinse out.
• n. waste food mixed with water for feeding to pigs.
swim v. (**swimming**, **swam**; past part. **swum**) **1** move through water using your arms and legs. **2** be covered with liquid. **3** experience a dizzy feeling.
• n. a period of swimming.
■ **swimmer** n.
swimmingly adv. informal smoothly and satisfactorily.
swindle v. cheat someone of money etc.
▷ SYNONYMS: **defraud**, cheat, trick, dupe, deceive, fool, hoax, hoodwink, bamboozle; informal fleece, do, con, diddle, rip off, take for a ride, pull a fast one on, put one over on; N. Amer. informal stiff.
• n. a dishonest scheme to obtain money.
▷ SYNONYMS: **fraud**, trick, deception, cheat, racket, sharp practice; informal con, fiddle, diddle, rip-off.
■ **swindler** n.
swine n. **1** (pl. **swine**) a pig. **2** (pl. **swine** or **swines**) informal an unpleasant person.
swing v. (**swinging**, **swung**) **1** move back and forth or from side to side while suspended. **2** move by grasping a support and leaping. **3** move in a smooth, curving line. **4** change from one opinion, mood, or situation to another. **5** have a decisive influence on.
▷ SYNONYMS: **1 sway**, move back and forth, oscillate, wave, rock, swivel, pivot, turn, rotate. **2 brandish**, wave, flourish, wield. **3 curve**, bend, veer, turn, bear, wind, twist, deviate, slew. **4 change**, fluctuate, waver, see-saw.
• n. **1** a hanging seat on which to sit and swing. **2** an act of swinging. **3** a change in public opinion. **4** a style of jazz with a flowing rhythm.
▷ SYNONYMS: **1 oscillation**, sway, wave. **2 change**, move, turnaround, turnabout, reversal, fluctuation, variation.
□ **in full swing** at the height of activity.
swingeing adj. Brit. severe or extreme.
swipe informal v. **1** hit with a swinging blow. **2** steal. **3** pass a swipe card through an electronic reader.
• n. a swinging blow.
□ **swipe card** a plastic card carrying coded information which is read when the card is slid through an

S

electronic device.

swirl v. move in a twisting pattern.
▷ SYNONYMS: **whirl**, eddy, billow, spiral, twist, twirl, circulate, revolve, spin.
• n. a swirling movement or pattern.

swish v. move with a soft hissing sound.
• n. a swishing sound.

Swiss adj. of Switzerland.
□ **Swiss roll** Brit. a thin sponge cake spread with jam etc. and rolled up.

switch n. **1** a device operated to turn electric current on or off. **2** a change or exchange. **3** a flexible shoot cut from a tree.
▷ SYNONYMS: **1 button**, lever, control. **2 change**, move, shift, transition, transformation, reversal, turn-around, U-turn, changeover, transfer, conversion.
• v. **1** change in position or direction. **2** exchange. **3** (**switch off/on**) turn an electrical device off (or on).
▷ SYNONYMS: **1 change**, shift; informal chop and change. **2 exchange**, swap, inter-change, change round, rotate.
□ **switchback** Brit. a road with alternate sharp ascents and descents. **switchboard** a device for routing phone calls within an organization.

swivel v. (**swivelling**, **swivelled**; US **swiveling**, **swiveled**) turn around a central point.
• n. a link or pivot enabling one part to revolve without turning the other.

swollen past part. of SWELL. adj. larger or rounder in size than normal.
▷ SYNONYMS: **distended**, bulging, inflated, dilated, bloated, puffed up, puffy, tumescent, inflamed.

swoon v. literary faint.

swoop v. **1** move rapidly downwards through the air. **2** carry out a sudden raid.
▷ SYNONYMS: **dive**, descend, pounce, sweep down, plunge, drop down.
• n. an act of swooping.

swop var. of SWAP.

sword n. a weapon with a long metal blade.
□ **swordfish** an edible sea fish with a sword-like snout.

swore past of SWEAR.

sworn past part. of SWEAR.
• adj. determined to remain the specified thing: *sworn enemies.*

swot Brit. informal v. (**swotting**, **swotted**) study hard.
• n. a person who studies hard.

swum past part. of SWIM.

swung past & past part. of SWING.

sybarite n. a person fond of luxury

and pleasure.
■ **sybaritic** adj.

sycamore n. a large tree of the maple family.

sycophant n. a person who tries to win favour by flattery.
▷ SYNONYMS: **toady**, creep, flatterer; informal bootlicker, yes-man.
■ **sycophancy** n.

sycophantic adj. excessively complimentary or flattering.
▷ SYNONYMS: **obsequious**, ingratiating, unctuous, servile, subservient, grovelling, toadying, fawning; informal smarmy, bootlicking.

syllable n. a unit of pronunciation in a word.
■ **syllabic** adj.

syllabub n. a dish of flavoured whipped cream.

syllabus n. (pl. **syllabuses** or **syllabi**) the topics in a course of study or teaching.

syllogism n. a form of reasoning in which a conclusion is drawn from two propositions.

sylph n. **1** a slender woman or girl. **2** an imaginary spirit of the air.

sylvan (or **silvan**) adj. literary of woods; wooded.

symbiosis n. (pl. **symbioses**) a situation in which two different organisms live with and are dependent on each other, to the advantage of both.
■ **symbiotic** adj.

symbol n. **1** a thing representing something else. **2** a mark or character used as a standard representation of something.
▷ SYNONYMS: **1 representation**, token, sign, emblem, figure, image, meta-phor, allegory. **2 sign**, character, mark, letter. **3 logo**, emblem, badge, stamp, trademark, crest, insignia, coat of arms, seal, device, monogram, hallmark, motif.

symbolic adj. **1** acting as a symbol. **2** involving the use of symbols.
▷ SYNONYMS: **1 emblematic**, represen-tative; characteristic, typical. **2 figura-tive**, metaphorical, allegorical.
– ANTONYMS: literal.
■ **symbolically** adv.

symbolism n. the use of symbols to represent ideas or qualities.
■ **symbolist** n.

symbolize (or **-ise**) v. **1** be a symbol of. **2** represent by symbols.
▷ SYNONYMS: **represent**, stand for, be a sign of, denote, signify, mean, indicate, convey, express, embody,

epitomize, encapsulate, personify.

symmetrical adj. showing symmetry.
▷ SYNONYMS: **regular**, uniform, consistent, even, equal, balanced, proportional.
■ **symmetrically** adv.

symmetry n. (pl. **symmetries**) **1** the state of having exactly matching parts facing each other or round an axis. **2** the quality of being similar or equal.

sympathetic adj. **1** feeling or showing sympathy. **2** showing or inspiring approval.
▷ SYNONYMS: **1 compassionate**, caring, concerned, understanding, sensitive, supportive, empathetic, kind-hearted, warm-hearted. **2 likeable**, pleasant, agreeable, congenial, companionable.
– ANTONYMS: unsympathetic.
■ **sympathetically** adv.

sympathize (or **-ise**) v. feel or express sympathy.
▷ SYNONYMS: **commiserate**, show concern, offer condolences; (**sympathize with**) pity, feel sorry for, feel for, identify with, understand, relate to.
■ **sympathizer** n.

sympathy n. (pl. **sympathies**) **1** the feeling of being sorry for someone. **2** understanding between people. **3** support or approval.
▷ SYNONYMS: **compassion**, care, concern, commiseration, pity, condolence.
– ANTONYMS: indifference.

symphony n. (pl. **symphonies**) an elaborate musical composition for a full orchestra.
■ **symphonic** adj.

symposium n. (pl. **symposia** or **symposiums**) a conference to discuss a particular academic subject.

symptom n. **1** a change in the body or mind which is the sign of a disease. **2** a sign of an undesirable situation.
▷ SYNONYMS: **indication**, indicator, manifestation, sign, mark, feature, trait, clue, hint, warning, evidence, proof.

symptomatic adj. acting as a symptom or sign.
▷ SYNONYMS: **indicative**, characteristic, suggestive, typical, representative.

synagogue n. a building where Jews meet for religious worship and teaching.

synapse n. a connection between two nerve cells.

sync (also **synch**) n. (**in** or **out of sync**) informal working well (or badly) together.

synchronize (or **-ise**) v. cause to happen or operate at the same time or rate.

synchronous adj. existing or occurring at the same time.

syncopate v. alter the accents in music so that strong beats become weak and vice versa.
■ **syncopation** n.

syndicate n. a group of people or firms combining to achieve a common interest.
• v. **1** manage by a syndicate. **2** publish or broadcast in different media at the same time.
■ **syndication** n.

syndrome n. a group of symptoms consistently occurring together.

synergy n. cooperation of two or more things to produce a combined effect greater than the sum of their separate effects.

synod n. an official meeting of Church ministers and members.

synonym n. a word or phrase meaning the same as another in the same language.
■ **synonymous** adj.

synopsis n. (pl. **synopses**) a brief summary.

syntax n. the arrangement of words and phrases to form sentences.
■ **syntactic** adj.

synthesis n. (pl. **syntheses**) **1** the combination of parts to form a connected whole. **2** the production of chemical compounds by reaction from simpler materials.
▷ SYNONYMS: **combination**, union, amalgam, blend, mixture, compound, fusion, composite, alloy.

synthesize (or **-ise**) v. make by synthesis.

synthesizer n. an electronic musical instrument.

synthetic adj. **1** made by chemical synthesis, esp. to imitate a natural product. **2** not genuine.
▷ SYNONYMS: **artificial**, fake, imitation, mock, simulated, man-made, manufactured; informal pretend.
– ANTONYMS: natural.
■ **synthetically** adv.

syphilis n. a serious sexually transmitted disease.
■ **syphilitic** adj.

syringe n. a tube with a nozzle and piston for sucking in and forcing out liquid.
• v. clean with liquid sprayed from a syringe.

S

syrup (US **sirup**) n. a thick sweet liquid.
■ **syrupy** adj.

system n. **1** a set of things that are connected or that work together.
2 an organized scheme or method.
3 (**the system**) the laws and rules that govern society.
▷ SYNONYMS: **1 structure**, organization, arrangement, order, network; informal set-up. **2 method**, methodology, modus operandi, technique, procedure, means, way, scheme, plan, policy, programme, formula, routine. **3** (**the system**) **the establishment**, the administration, the authorities, the powers that be, bureaucracy, officialdom.
■ **systematize** (or **-ise**) v.

systematic adj. done according to a system.
▷ SYNONYMS: **structured**, methodical, organized, orderly, planned, regular, routine, standardized, standard, logical, coherent, consistent.
– ANTONYMS: disorganized.
■ **systematically** adv.

systemic adj. affecting the whole of a system.

S

Tt

T n. (**to a T**) informal to perfection.
□ **T-bone** a piece of steak containing a T-shaped bone. **T-shirt** a short-sleeved casual top. **T-square** a T-shaped instrument for drawing or testing right angles.

ta exclam. Brit. informal thank you.

tab n. a small projecting flap or strip.
□ **keep tabs on** informal monitor.

tabard n. a short sleeveless tunic.

tabby n. (pl. **tabbies**) a grey or brown cat with dark stripes.

tabernacle n. **1** a place of worship for some religions. **2** (in the RC church) a container for the Eucharist.

table n. **1** a piece of furniture with a flat top supported by legs. **2** a set of facts or figures displayed in rows or columns.
▷ SYNONYMS: **chart**, diagram, figure, graphic, graph, plan, list.
• v. Brit. present formally for discussion at a meeting.
□ **tableland** a plateau. **tablespoon** a large spoon for serving food. **table tennis** a game played with bats and a light hollow ball on a table.

tableau /tab-loh/ n. (pl. **tableaux**) a group of models or motionless figures representing a scene.

table d'hôte /tah-bluh **doht**/ n. a restaurant meal at a fixed price and with limited choices.

tablet n. **1** a pill. **2** a slab on which an inscription is written.
▷ SYNONYMS: **1 slab**, stone, panel, plaque, plate, sign. **2 pill**, capsule, lozenge, pastille, drop. **3 bar**, cake, slab, brick, block.

tabloid n. a small-sized newspaper written in a popular style.

taboo n. (pl. **taboos**) a ban or restriction made by social custom.
▷ SYNONYMS: **prohibition**, proscription, veto, ban, interdict.
• adj. banned or restricted by social custom.
▷ SYNONYMS: **forbidden**, prohibited,

vetoed, banned, proscribed, outlawed, off limits, beyond the pale, unmentionable, unspeakable; informal no go.
– ANTONYMS: acceptable.

tabular adj. arranged in columns or tables.

tabulate v. arrange in columns or tables.
■ **tabulation** n.

tachograph n. an instrument used in commercial road vehicles to provide a record of speed and distance travelled.

tachometer /ta-**kom**-i-ter/ n. an instrument measuring the speed of an engine.

tachycardia /ta-ki-**kar**-di-uh/ n. an abnormally rapid heart rate.

tacit adj. understood or meant without being stated.
▷ SYNONYMS: **implicit**, understood, implied, inferred, hinted, suggested, unspoken, unstated, unsaid, unexpressed, unvoiced, taken for granted, taken as read.
– ANTONYMS: explicit.
■ **tacitly** adv.

taciturn adj. saying little.
■ **taciturnity** n.

tack n. **1** a small broad-headed nail. **2** a long stitch used to fasten fabrics together temporarily. **3** a course of action. **4** an act of tacking in sailing. **5** equipment used in horse riding.
▷ SYNONYMS: **pin**, nail, staple, rivet.
• v. **1** fasten with tacks. **2** (**tack on**) add as an extra. **3** change course by turning a sailing boat into the wind.
▷ SYNONYMS: **pin**, nail, staple, fix, fasten, attach, secure.

tackle v. **1** try to deal with a difficult task. **2** confront someone about a difficulty. **3** (in football, rugby, etc.) try to take the ball from or prevent the movement of an opponent.
▷ SYNONYMS: **1 deal with**, take care of, attend to, see to, handle, manage, get

t

to grips with, address. **2 confront**, face up to, take on, challenge, attack, grab, struggle with, intercept, block, stop, bring down, floor, fell; informal have a go at.

• **n. 1** the equipment needed for a task or sport. **2** a set of ropes and pulleys for lifting heavy objects. **3** an act of tackling in sport.

▷ SYNONYMS: **1 equipment**, apparatus, kit, implements, paraphernalia; informal gear, clobber. **2 interception**, challenge, block, attack.

tacky adj. (**tackier, tackiest**) **1** (of glue etc.) not fully dry. **2** informal lacking in taste and quality.

▷ SYNONYMS: **1 sticky**, wet, gluey, viscous, gummy; informal gooey. **2 tawdry**, tasteless, kitsch, vulgar, crude, garish, gaudy, trashy, cheap; informal cheesy; Brit. informal naff.

– ANTONYMS: tasteful.

taco n. (pl. **tacos**) a folded tortilla filled with spicy meat or beans.

tact n. sensitivity and skill in dealing with others.

tactful adj. having or showing tact.

▷ SYNONYMS: **diplomatic**, discreet, considerate, sensitive, understanding, thoughtful, delicate, judicious, subtle.

■ **tactfully** adv.

tactic n. **1** an action intended to achieve something. **2** (**tactics**) the directing and organizing of armed forces and equipment during a war.

▷ SYNONYMS: **1 scheme**, plan, manoeuvre, method, trick, ploy. **2** (**tactics**) **strategy**, policy, campaign, game plan, planning, manoeuvres, logistics.

■ **tactician** n.

tactical adj. **1** planned to achieve a particular end. **2** (of weapons) for use in direct support of military operations. **3** Brit. (of voting) done to prevent the leading candidate from winning by supporting whoever is next strongest.

▷ SYNONYMS: **calculated**, planned, strategic, prudent, politic, diplomatic, judicious, shrewd.

■ **tactically** adv.

tactile adj. **1** of the sense of touch. **2** liking to touch others.

tactless adj. thoughtless or insensitive.

▷ SYNONYMS: **insensitive**, inconsiderate, thoughtless, indelicate, undiplomatic, indiscreet, unsubtle, inept, gauche, blunt.

■ **tactlessly** adv.

tadpole n. the larva of a frog or toad, at the stage when it has gills and a tail.

tae kwon do /ty kwon doh/ n. a Korean martial art.

taffeta n. a crisp shiny fabric.

tag n. **1** a label. **2** a description by which a person or thing is widely known. **3** an electronic device attached to someone to monitor their movements. **4** a much repeated saying etc.

▷ SYNONYMS: **label**, ticket, badge, mark, tab, sticker, docket.

• v. (**tagging, tagged**) **1** attach a tag to. **2** (**tag on**) add at the end. **3** (**tag along**) accompany someone without being invited.

▷ SYNONYMS: **label**, mark, ticket, identify, flag, indicate.

tagliatelle /tal-yuh-tel-li/ pl. n. pasta in narrow ribbons.

t'ai chi /ty chee/ n. a Chinese martial art and system of exercises.

tail n. **1** the part sticking out at the rear of an animal. **2** the rear part of an aircraft. **3** the final, more distant, or weaker part. **4** (**tails**) the side of a coin without the image of a head. **5** (**tails**) informal a tailcoat.

▷ SYNONYMS: **rear**, end, back, extremity, bottom.

– ANTONYMS: head, front.

• v. **1** secretly follow and observe. **2** (**tail off**) become smaller or weaker.

▷ SYNONYMS: **follow**, shadow, stalk, trail, track, keep under surveillance.

□ **tailback** Brit. a long queue of traffic. **tailcoat** Brit. a man's formal coat with a long divided flap at the back. **tailgate 1** the door at the back of an estate or hatchback car. **2** a hinged flap at the back of a truck. **tailplane** Brit. a small wing at the tail of an aircraft. **tailspin** a spinning dive by an aircraft. **tailwind** a wind blowing from behind.

tailor n. a person who makes men's clothing for individual customers.

• v. **1** make clothes to fit individual customers. **2** make or adapt for a particular purpose.

▷ SYNONYMS: **customize**, adapt, adjust, modify, change, convert, alter, mould, gear, fit, shape, tune.

□ **tailor-made** made for a particular purpose.

taint v. spoil the purity or quality of; contaminate.

▷ SYNONYMS: **1 contaminate**, pollute, adulterate, infect, blight, spoil, soil, ruin. **2 tarnish**, sully, blacken, stain, blot, damage.

• n. a trace of an undesirable quality.
take v. (**taking**, **took**; past part. **taken**)
1 reach for and hold. **2** occupy a place or position. **3** gain possession of by force. **4** carry or bring with you. **5** remove. **6** use. **7** accept. **8** require. **9** regard or react to. **10** experience or endure. **11** perform an action etc.
▷ SYNONYMS: **1** *she took his hand:* grasp, get hold of, grip, clasp, clutch, grab. **2** *he took an envelope from his pocket:* remove, pull, draw, withdraw, extract, fish. **3** capture, seize, catch, arrest, apprehend, take into custody, carry off, abduct. **4** steal, remove, appropriate, make off with, pilfer, purloin; informal filch, swipe, snaffle; Brit. informal pinch, nick. **5** escort, accompany, help, assist, show, lead, guide, see, usher, convey. **6** bring, carry, bear, transport, convey, move, transfer, shift, ferry; informal cart, tote. **7** *this seat's taken, I'm afraid:* occupy, use, utilize, fill, hold, reserve, engage; informal bag. **8** *take four from the total:* subtract, deduct, remove, discount; informal knock off, minus. **9** *I'll take the minutes:* write, note down, jot down, scribble, scrawl, record, register, document, minute. **10** *I can't take much more:* endure, bear, tolerate, stand, put up with, abide, stomach, accept, allow, countenance, support, shoulder; formal brook.
– ANTONYMS: give, add.
• n. **1** a sequence of sound or film recorded at one time. **2** an amount gained.
☐ **take after** resemble a parent.
takeaway Brit. **1** a restaurant or shop selling cooked food to be eaten elsewhere. **2** a meal of such food.
take in 1 deceive. **2** make a garment tighter. **3** understand. **take off 1** become airborne. **2** mimic. **3** leave hastily. **take-off** an act of taking off. **take on 1** employ. **2** undertake. **take over** assume control. **take to 1** fall into the habit of. **2** develop a liking or ability for. **3** go to a place to escape danger. **take up 1** adopt a pursuit. **2** occupy time or space. **3** pursue a matter. **4** accept an offer.
takeover n. an act of assuming control of something, especially a business.
▷ SYNONYMS: **buyout**, purchase, acquisition, amalgamation, merger.
takings pl. n. money received for goods sold.
▷ SYNONYMS: **proceeds**, returns, receipts, earnings, winnings, pickings, spoils, profit, gain, income, revenue.

talc n. **1** talcum powder. **2** a soft mineral.
talcum powder n. a powder used to make the skin feel smooth and dry.
tale n. a story.
▷ SYNONYMS: **story**, narrative, anecdote, account, history, legend, fable, myth, saga; informal yarn.
talent n. natural ability or skill.
▷ SYNONYMS: **flair**, aptitude, facility, gift, knack, technique, bent, ability, forte, genius, brilliance.
talented adj. having a natural ability or skill.
▷ SYNONYMS: **gifted**, skilful, accomplished, brilliant, adroit, adept, expert, consummate, able, proficient; informal ace.
– ANTONYMS: inept.
talisman n. (pl. **talismans**) an object believed to bring good luck.
talk v. **1** speak so as to give information or express ideas or feelings. **2** be able to speak.
▷ SYNONYMS: **speak**, converse, communicate; confer, consult, negotiate, parley; chat, chatter, gossip, jabber, prattle; informal yak; Brit. informal natter, rabbit.
• n. **1** conversation. **2** a speech or lecture. **3** (**talks**) formal discussions.
▷ SYNONYMS: **1** conversation, chat, discussion, tête-à-tête, heart-to-heart, dialogue; informal confab, gossip. **2** lecture, speech, address, discourse, oration, presentation, report, sermon. **3** (**talks**) negotiations, discussions, conference, summit, meeting, consultation, dialogue.
☐ **talk back** reply disrespectfully.
talking-to informal a reprimand.
talkative adj. fond of talking.
▷ SYNONYMS: **chatty**, garrulous, loquacious, voluble, communicative; informal mouthy.
– ANTONYMS: taciturn.
tall adj. of great or specified height.
▷ SYNONYMS: **1** *a tall man:* big, large, huge, giant, lanky, gangling. **2** *tall buildings:* high, big, lofty, towering, sky-high, gigantic, colossal.
– ANTONYMS: short, low.
☐ **a tall order** a difficult task. **a tall story** an implausible account.
tallow n. animal fat used to make candles and soap.
tally n. (pl. **tallies**) a current score or amount.
▷ SYNONYMS: **running total**, count, record, reckoning, register, account, roll.
• v. (**tallying**, **tallied**) **1** agree or

t

correspond. **2** calculate the total of.

▷ SYNONYMS: **correspond**, agree, accord, concur, coincide, match, fit, be consistent, conform, equate, parallel; informal square.

– ANTONYMS: disagree.

Talmud n. the ancient writings on Jewish law and legend.

■ **Talmudic** adj.

talon n. a claw of a bird of prey.

tamarind n. a tropical fruit with sticky pulp used in Asian cookery.

tambourine n. a shallow drum with metal discs around the edge.

tame adj. **1** (of an animal) not dangerous or frightened of people. **2** unexciting.

▷ SYNONYMS: **1 domesticated**, docile, trained, gentle, mild, pet. **2 unexciting**, uninteresting, uninspiring, uninspired, dull, bland, flat, pedestrian, humdrum, boring.

– ANTONYMS: wild.

• v. make tame or easier to control.

▷ SYNONYMS: **1 domesticate**, break in, train. **2** she learned to tame her emotions: **subdue**, curb, control, calm, master, moderate, discipline, overcome.

■ **tamely** adv.

Tamil n. **1** a member of a people of South India and Sri Lanka. **2** their language.

tamp v. pack down firmly.

tamper v. (**tamper with**) interfere with.

▷ SYNONYMS: **interfere**, meddle, monkey around, tinker, fiddle; informal mess about; Brit. informal muck about.

tampon n. a plug of soft material inserted into the vagina to absorb menstrual blood.

tan n. **1** a suntan. **2** a yellowish-brown colour.

• v. (**tanning, tanned**) **1** develop a suntan. **2** convert animal skin into leather.

tandem n. a bicycle for two riders, one behind the other.

□ **in tandem** together or at the same time.

tandoori adj. (of Indian food) cooked in a clay oven.

tang n. a strong taste or smell.

■ **tangy** adj.

tangent n. **1** a straight line that touches a curve but does not cross it. **2** (in a right-angled triangle) the ratio of the sides opposite and adjacent to a particular angle. **3** a completely different line of thought or action.

■ **tangential** adj.

tangerine n. a small orange citrus fruit.

tangible adj. **1** able to be perceived by touch. **2** definite or real.

▷ SYNONYMS: **real**, actual, physical, solid, palpable, material, substantial, concrete, visible, definite, perceptible, discernible.

– ANTONYMS: abstract, theoretical.

■ **tangibility** n. **tangibly** adv.

tangle v. **1** twist into a confused mass. **2** informal come into conflict.

▷ SYNONYMS: **entangle**, snarl, catch, entwine, twist, knot, mat.

• n. a confused mass or muddle.

▷ SYNONYMS: **1 snarl**, mass, knot, mesh. **2 muddle**, jumble, mix-up, confusion, shambles.

tango n. (pl. **tangos**) a Latin American ballroom dance.

tank n. **1** a large container for liquid or gas. **2** a heavy armoured fighting vehicle moving on a continuous metal track.

▷ SYNONYMS: **container**, receptacle, vat, cistern, repository, reservoir, basin.

tankard n. a tall beer mug.

tanker n. a ship, vehicle, or aircraft for carrying liquid in bulk.

tannery n. (pl. **tanneries**) a place where animal skins are tanned.

tannin (or **tannic acid**) n. a bitter substance present in tea, grapes, etc.

tannoy n. Brit. trademark a public address system.

tantalize (or -ise) v. tease with the sight or promise of something unobtainable.

▷ SYNONYMS: **tease**, torment, torture, tempt, entice, lure, beguile, excite, fascinate, titillate, intrigue.

tantalum n. a hard silver-grey metallic element.

tantamount adj. (**tantamount to**) equivalent in seriousness to.

tantra n. a Hindu or Buddhist text on mystical practices.

■ **tantric** adj.

tantrum n. an uncontrolled outburst of anger and frustration.

▷ SYNONYMS: **fit of temper**, fit of rage, outburst, pet, paroxysm, frenzy; informal paddy, wobbly; N. Amer. informal hissy fit.

tap n. **1** a device for controlling a flow of liquid or gas from a pipe or container. **2** a light blow. **3** a device for listening secretly to phone conversations.

▷ SYNONYMS: **valve**, stopcock; N. Amer. faucet, spigot.

• v. (**tapping, tapped**) **1** knock gently.

2 take some of a supply. **3** draw liquid from a barrel etc. **4** connect a device to a phone to listen secretly to conversations.

▷ SYNONYMS: **1 knock**, rap, strike, beat, pat, drum. **2 draw on**, exploit, milk, mine, use, utilize, turn to account. **3 bug**, wiretap, monitor, eavesdrop on.

□ **on tap** informal readily available. **tap dancing** a style of dancing performed in shoes fitted with metal pieces on the toes and heels. **taproot** a plant's main root.

tapas pl. n. small Spanish savoury dishes.

tape n. **1** light, flexible material in a narrow strip, used to hold, fasten, or mark off something. **2** magnetic tape, used for recording. **3** a cassette or reel of magnetic tape.

▷ SYNONYMS: **1 binding**, ribbon, string, braid, band. **2 cassette**, recording, video.

• v. **1** record on magnetic tape. **2** fasten or mark off with tape.

▷ SYNONYMS: **1 bind**, stick, fix, fasten, secure, attach. **2 record**, tape-record, video.

□ **tape measure** a strip of tape marked for measuring length. **tape recorder** a device for recording and reproducing sounds on magnetic tape. **tapeworm** a long worm living as a parasite in the intestines.

taper v. **1** reduce in thickness towards one end. **2** (**taper off**) gradually lessen.

▷ SYNONYMS: **narrow**, thin, come to a point, become attenuated.

– ANTONYMS: thicken.

• n. a thin candle.

tapestry n. (pl. **tapestries**) a piece of thick fabric with a design woven or embroidered on it.

tapioca n. starchy grains used for puddings etc.

tapir /tay-peer/ n. a piglike animal with a flexible snout.

tappet n. a moving part in a machine which transmits motion from one part to another.

tar n. **1** a dark, thick liquid distilled from wood or coal. **2** a similar substance formed by burning tobacco.

• v. (**tarring**, **tarred**) coat with tar.

taramasalata n. a creamy dip made from fish roe.

tarantula n. a large hairy spider.

tardy adj. (**tardier**, **tardiest**) **1** late. **2** slow to act or respond.

■ **tardily** adv. **tardiness** n.

tare n. **1** the weight of a vehicle without its fuel or load. **2** a weed.

target n. **1** a person or thing that is the aim of an attack. **2** a result that you aim to achieve.

▷ SYNONYMS: **1 objective**, goal, aim, mark, end, plan, intention, aspiration, ambition. **2 victim**, butt, recipient, focus, object, subject.

• v. (**targeting**, **targeted**) **1** select as an object of attack. **2** aim or direct.

▷ SYNONYMS: **1 pick out**, single out, earmark, fix on, attack, aim at, fire at. **2** *a product targeted at women:* **aim**, direct, level, intend, focus.

tariff n. **1** a tax paid on some imports or exports. **2** a list of charges in a hotel etc.

▷ SYNONYMS: **1 tax**, duty, toll, excise, levy, charge, rate, fee. **2 price list**, menu.

tarmac n. **1** trademark broken stone mixed with tar for surfacing roads etc. **2** a tarmacked area.

• v. (**tarmacking**, **tarmacked**) surface with tarmac.

tarn n. a small mountain lake.

tarnish v. **1** cause metal to lose its shine. **2** damage or spoil.

▷ SYNONYMS: **1 discolour**, rust, oxidize, corrode, stain, dull, blacken. **2 sully**, blacken, stain, blemish, ruin, disgrace, mar, damage, harm, drag through the mud.

• n. a film or stain on metal.

▷ SYNONYMS: **discoloration**, oxidation, rust, verdigris.

tarot /ta-roh/ n. a set of cards for fortune-telling.

tarpaulin n. a sheet of heavy waterproof cloth.

tarragon n. a herb.

tarsus n. (pl. **tarsi**) the set of small bones in the ankle and upper foot.

tart n. **1** an open pastry case with a filling. **2** informal a prostitute.

▷ SYNONYMS: **pastry**, flan, quiche, tartlet, vol-au-vent, pie.

• v. (**tart up**) informal improve the appearance of.

▷ SYNONYMS: **1 dress up**, smarten up; informal doll yourself up, titivate yourself. **2 decorate**, renovate, refurbish, redecorate, smarten up; informal do up, fix up.

• adj. **1** sour. **2** (of a remark etc.) unkind.

▷ SYNONYMS: **1 sour**, sharp, acidic, zesty, tangy, piquant. **2 scathing**, sharp, biting, cutting, sarcastic, hurtful, spiteful.

– ANTONYMS: sweet, kind.

t

■ **tartly** adv. **tartness** n.

tartan n. woollen cloth woven in a pattern of coloured checks and lines.

tartar n. **1** a hard deposit forming on teeth. **2** a deposit formed during the fermentation of wine.

tartare sauce n. mayonnaise mixed with gherkins and capers.

tartrazine n. a yellow dye used to colour food.

task n. a piece of work to be done.
▷ SYNONYMS: **job**, duty, chore, charge, assignment, detail, mission, engagement, occupation, undertaking, exercise.
□ **take to task** reprimand. **task force** a group organized for a special task. **taskmaster** a person who makes others work hard.

tassel n. a decorative tuft of threads knotted at one end.
■ **tasselled** adj.

taste n. **1** the sensation of flavour perceived in the mouth on contact with a substance. **2** the sense by which taste is perceived. **3** a small sample of food or drink. **4** a brief experience. **5** a liking. **6** the ability to judge what is good quality or appropriate behaviour.
▷ SYNONYMS: **1 flavour**, savour, relish, tang, smack. **2 mouthful**, morsel, drop, bit, sip, nip, touch, soupçon, dash. **3** *his first taste of opera:* **experience**, impression, exposure to, contact with, involvement with. **4** *a taste for adventure:* **liking**, love, fondness, fancy, desire, penchant, partiality, inclination, appetite, stomach, palate, thirst, hunger. **5 judgement**, discrimination, discernment, refinement, elegance, grace, style. **6 sensitivity**, decorum, propriety, etiquette, nicety, discretion.
• v. **1** perceive or test the flavour of. **2** have a particular flavour. **3** experience briefly.
▷ SYNONYMS: **1** *I tasted the wine:* **sample**, test, try, savour. **2** *he could taste blood:* **perceive**, discern, make out, distinguish.
■ **taster** n.

> **WORD LINKS**
> **gustatory** relating to the sense of taste

tasteful adj. showing good judgement as to quality etc.
▷ SYNONYMS: **stylish**, refined, cultured, elegant, smart, chic, exquisite.
– ANTONYMS: tasteless.
■ **tastefully** adv.

tasteless adj. **1** lacking flavour. **2** showing poor judgement as to quality etc.
▷ SYNONYMS: **1 flavourless**, bland, insipid, unappetizing, watery, weak, thin. **2 vulgar**, crude, tawdry, garish, gaudy, loud, trashy, showy, ostentatious, cheap; informal flash, tacky, kitsch; Brit. informal naff. **3 crude**, indelicate, uncouth, crass, tactless, undiplomatic, indiscreet, inappropriate, offensive.
– ANTONYMS: tasty, tasteful.
■ **tastelessly** adv.

tasty adj. (**tastier**, **tastiest**) having a pleasant flavour.
▷ SYNONYMS: **delicious**, palatable, luscious, mouth-watering, delectable, appetizing, tempting; informal yummy, scrumptious, moreish.
– ANTONYMS: bland.

tat n. Brit. informal tasteless or badly made articles.

tattered adj. old and torn.

tatters pl. n. torn pieces.

tattle n. & v. gossip.

tattoo n. (pl. **tattoos**) **1** a permanent design made on the skin with a needle and ink. **2** Brit. a military display with music and marching. **3** a rhythmic tapping.
• v. mark with a tattoo.
■ **tattooist** n.

tatty adj. (**tattier**, **tattiest**) informal worn and shabby.

taught past & past part. of TEACH.

taunt n. a jeering or mocking remark.
▷ SYNONYMS: **jeer**, jibe, sneer, insult, barb; informal dig, put-down; (**taunts**) teasing, provocation, goading, derision, mockery.
• v. anger or upset with taunts.
▷ SYNONYMS: **jeer at**, sneer at, scoff at, poke fun at, make fun of, get at, insult, tease, torment, ridicule, deride, mock; N. Amer. ride; informal rib, needle.

taupe /tohp/ n. a greyish brown.

taut adj. stretched tight.
▷ SYNONYMS: **tight**, stretched, rigid, flexed, tensed.
– ANTONYMS: slack.
■ **tauten** v. **tautly** adv.

tautology n. (pl. **tautologies**) the saying of the same thing over again in different words.
■ **tautological** adj. **tautologous** adj.

tavern n. old use an inn or pub.

taverna n. a Greek restaurant.

tawdry adj. (**tawdrier**, **tawdriest**) showy but cheap and of poor quality.
▷ SYNONYMS: **gaudy**, flashy, showy,

garish, loud, tasteless, vulgar, trashy, cheapjack, shoddy, shabby, gimcrack; informal rubbishy, tacky, kitsch.
– ANTONYMS: tasteful.
■ **tawdriness** n.

tawny adj. of an orange-brown or yellowish-brown colour.

tax n. money that must be paid to the state.
▷ SYNONYMS: **duty**, excise, customs, dues, levy, tariff, toll, tithe, charge.
• v. **1** impose a tax on. **2** make heavy demands on.
▷ SYNONYMS: **strain**, stretch, overburden, overload, overwhelm, try, wear out, exhaust, sap, drain, weary, weaken.
□ **tax return** a form on which a person states their income, used for tax assessment.
■ **taxable** adj. **taxation** n.

> **WORD LINKS**
> **fiscal** relating to government revenue raised through taxes

taxi n. (or **taxicab**) (pl. **taxis**) a car licensed to transport passengers in return for payment of a fare.
• v. (**taxiing**, **taxied**) (of an aircraft) move slowly along the ground before take-off or after landing.

taxidermy n. the art of preparing and stuffing the skins of dead animals to make them look lifelike.
■ **taxidermist** n.

taxonomy n. the scientific classification of organisms.
■ **taxonomic** adj.

TB abbrev. tuberculosis.

tbsp (or **tbs**) abbrev. tablespoonful.

tea n. **1** a drink made by soaking the dried leaves of an Asian shrub in boiling water. **2** these leaves. **3** Brit. an afternoon or evening meal.
□ **tea bag** a sachet of tea leaves. **teacake** Brit. a currant bun. **teapot** a pot with a handle, spout, and lid, in which tea is made. **tea towel** (or **tea cloth**) a cloth for drying washed crockery etc. **teaspoon** a small spoon for stirring hot drinks.

teach v. (**teaching**, **taught**) **1** give lessons in a subject to a class or pupil. **2** show how to do something.
▷ SYNONYMS: **educate**, instruct, school, tutor, inform, coach, train, drill.

> **WORD LINKS**
> **didactic** intended to teach

teacher n. a person who teaches.
▷ SYNONYMS: **tutor**, instructor, schoolteacher, schoolmaster, schoolmistress, governess, coach, trainer, lecturer, professor, don, guide,

mentor, guru.

teak n. hard wood from a SE Asian tree.

team n. **1** a group of players forming one side in a game or sport. **2** two or more people or animals working together.
▷ SYNONYMS: **group**, squad, company, party, crew, troupe, band, side, line-up; informal bunch, gang.
• v. **1** (**team up**) work together. **2** (**team with**) match with.
▷ SYNONYMS: ankle boots teamed with jeans: **match**, coordinate, complement, pair up.
□ **teamwork** organized effort as a group.

tear¹ v. (**tearing**, **tore**; past part. **torn**) **1** rip a hole in. **2** pull apart or to pieces. **3** informal move very quickly. **4** (**be torn**) be unsure about which option to choose.
▷ SYNONYMS: **1 rip**, split, slit, pull apart, pull to pieces, shred, rupture, sever. **2 lacerate**, cut open, gash, slash, scratch, hack, pierce, stab. **3 rush**, dash, run, race, sprint, bolt, dart, gallop, career, charge, shoot, hurry, hurtle, hare, fly, speed, zoom, scurry, scuttle, scamper, hasten; informal belt, pelt, scoot, zip, whip, hotfoot it; Brit. informal bomb.
• n. a hole or split caused by tearing.
▷ SYNONYMS: **rip**, hole, split, slash, slit, ladder, snag.
□ **tearaway** Brit. a wild or reckless person.

tear² n. a drop of clear salty liquid forming in and falling from a person's eye.
□ **in tears** crying. **teardrop** a single tear. **tear gas** gas causing severe irritation to the eye.

tearful adj. **1** crying or about to cry. **2** causing tears: a tearful farewell.
▷ SYNONYMS: **1 upset**, emotional, distressed, sad, unhappy, in tears, crying, weeping, sobbing, snivelling; informal weepy, blubbing; formal lachrymose. **2 emotional**, upsetting, distressing, sad, heartbreaking, poignant, moving, touching, tear-jerking.
– ANTONYMS: cheerful.
■ **tearfully** adv.

tease v. **1** playfully make fun of or attempt to provoke. **2** gently pull into separate strands.
▷ SYNONYMS: **make fun of**, laugh at, deride, mock, ridicule, guy, taunt, bait, goad, pick on; informal take the mickey out of, rag, have on, pull someone's leg; Brit. informal wind up.

t

• **n.** informal a person who teases.
■ **teaser** n.

teasel n. a plant with spiny flower heads.

teat n. **1** Brit. a plastic device through which milk can be sucked from a bottle. **2** a nipple or similar body part.

technetium n. a radioactive metallic element.

technical adj. **1** of a particular subject, craft, etc. **2** of the practical use of machinery and methods in science and industry. **3** needing specialized knowledge. **4** according to the law or rules when applied strictly.
▷ SYNONYMS: **1 practical**, scientific, technological, high-tech. **2 specialist**, specialized, scientific, complex, complicated, esoteric.
■ **technically** adv.

technicality n. (pl. **technicalities**) a small technical detail in a set of rules.

technician n. **1** a person employed to look after technical equipment. **2** an expert in the technique of a subject, craft, etc.

Technicolor n. trademark a process of producing cinema films in colour.

technique n. **1** a special way of doing something. **2** a person's level of practical skill.
▷ SYNONYMS: **1 method**, approach, procedure, system, way, manner, means, strategy. **2 skill**, ability, proficiency, expertise, artistry, craftsmanship, adroitness, deftness, dexterity.

technocracy n. (pl. **technocracies**) a social or political system in which technical experts have great power.
■ **technocrat** n.

technology n. (pl. **technologies**) **1** the application of scientific knowledge for practical purposes. **2** machinery developed from this.
■ **technological** adj. **technologically** adv. **technologist** n.

tectonic adj. of the earth's crust.

teddy (or **teddy bear**) n. (pl. **teddies**) a soft toy bear.

tedious adj. too long or dull.
▷ SYNONYMS: **boring**, dull, monotonous, repetitive, unrelieved, unvaried, uneventful, lifeless, uninteresting, unexciting, uninspiring, lacklustre, dreary, soul-destroying; informal deadly; N. Amer. informal dullsville.
− ANTONYMS: exciting.
■ **tediously** adv.

tedium n. the state of being tedious.

tee n. **1** a place from which a golf ball is struck at the start of each hole. **2** a small peg for supporting a golf ball on a tee.
• **v.** (**teeing, teed**) **1** (**tee up**) place the ball on a tee. **2** (**tee off**) begin a round or hole in golf.

teem v. **1** (**teem with**) be swarming with. **2** (of rain) fall heavily.

teen informal adj. of teenagers.
• **n.** **1** a teenager. **2** (**teens**) the years of age from 13 to 19.

teenager n. a person aged between 13 and 19 years.
▷ SYNONYMS: **adolescent**, youth, young person, minor, juvenile; informal teen.
■ **teenage** (or **teenaged**) adj.

teeny adj. (**teenier, teeniest**) informal tiny.

teepee n. var. of TEPEE.

tee shirt n. a T-shirt.

teeter v. move or sway unsteadily.

teeth pl. of TOOTH.

teethe v. (of a baby) develop its first teeth.
□ **teething troubles** problems occurring in the early stages of a project.

teetotal adj. choosing not to drink alcohol.
▷ SYNONYMS: **abstinent**, abstemious, sober, dry; informal on the wagon.
■ **teetotaller** n.

TEFL abbrev. teaching of English as a foreign language.

Teflon n. trademark a non-stick coating for saucepans etc.

telecommunications n. the technology concerned with long-distance communication by cable, telephone, broadcasting, satellite, etc.

telegram n. a message sent by telegraph.

telegraph n. a system or device for sending messages from a distance along a wire.
■ **telegraphic** adj. **telegraphy** n.

telekinesis n. the supposed ability to move objects by mental power.

telepathy n. supposed communication by means other than the senses.
■ **telepathic** adj.

telephone n. a device for transmitting speech over a distance using wire or radio.
▷ SYNONYMS: **phone**, handset, receiver; Brit. informal blower.
• **v.** contact by telephone.
▷ SYNONYMS: **phone**, call, dial; Brit. ring; informal give someone a buzz; Brit. informal give someone a bell.
■ **telephonic** adj. **telephonically** adv. **telephony** n.

telephonist n. Brit. an operator of a phone switchboard.

telephoto lens n. a lens that produces a magnified image of a distant object.

teleprinter n. Brit. a device for transmitting telegraph messages as they are keyed.

telesales n. the selling of goods or services by phone.

telescope n. an optical instrument for making distant objects appear nearer. • v. **1** (of an object made up of several tubes) slide into itself so as to become smaller. **2** condense into less space or time.
■ **telescopic** adj.

teletext n. an information service transmitted to televisions.

televise v. show on television.

television n. **1** a system for transmitting visual images with sound and displaying them electronically on a screen. **2** a device with a screen for receiving television signals. **3** the activity or medium of broadcasting on television.
▷ SYNONYMS: TV; informal the small screen; Brit. informal telly, the box; N. Amer. informal the tube.
■ **televisual** adj.

telex n. **1** an international system in which printed messages are transmitted and received by teleprinters. **2** a message sent by telex.

tell v. (**telling**, **told**) **1** communicate information to. **2** order or advise. **3** express in words. **4** (**tell off**) informal reprimand. **5** determine or establish. **6** distinguish. **7** have a noticeable effect. **8** (**tell on**) informal inform about a person's wrongdoings.
▷ SYNONYMS: **1** *why didn't you tell me?*: **inform**, notify, let know, make aware, acquaint with, advise, put in the picture, brief, fill in, alert, warn; informal clue in/up. **2** *she told the story slowly*: **relate**, recount, narrate, report, recite, describe, sketch. **3** **instruct**, order, command, direct, charge, enjoin, call on, require. **4** *it was hard to tell what he meant*: **ascertain**, determine, work out, make out, deduce, discern, perceive, see, identify, recognize, understand, comprehend; informal figure out; Brit. informal suss out. **5** *he couldn't tell one from the other*: **distinguish**, differentiate, discriminate. **6** *the strain began to tell on him*: **take its toll**, leave its mark, affect.

teller n. **1** esp. US a bank cashier. **2** a person who counts votes. **3** a narrator.

telling adj. having a striking or revealing effect.
▷ SYNONYMS: **revealing**, significant, weighty, important, meaningful, influential, striking, potent, powerful, compelling.
− ANTONYMS: insignificant.
■ **tellingly** adv.

telltale adj. revealing something. • n. Brit. a person who reports others' wrongdoings.

tellurium n. a crystalline element.

telly n. (pl. **tellies**) Brit. informal a television.

temerity n. very confident behaviour, likely to be regarded as disrespectful.

temp informal n. a temporary employee. • v. work as a temp.

temper n. **1** a state of mind. **2** a tendency to become angry easily. **3** an angry mood.
▷ SYNONYMS: **1** *he walked out in a temper*: **rage**, fury, fit of pique, tantrum, bad mood, pet, sulk, huff; Brit. informal strop, paddy; N. Amer. informal hissy fit. **2** *a display of temper*: **anger**, fury, rage, annoyance, irritation, pique, petulance; Brit. informal stroppiness. **3** *she struggled to keep her temper*: **composure**, self-control, self-possession, calm, good humour; informal cool.
• v. **1** make less extreme; moderate. **2** harden a metal by reheating and then cooling it.
▷ SYNONYMS: *their idealism is tempered with realism*: **moderate**, modify, modulate, mitigate, alleviate, reduce, weaken, lighten, soften.

tempera n. a method of painting using colours mixed with egg.

temperament n. a person's nature in terms of the effect it has on their behaviour.
▷ SYNONYMS: **character**, nature, disposition, personality, make-up, constitution, temper.

temperamental adj. **1** tending to change mood in an unreasonable way. **2** of or caused by temperament.
▷ SYNONYMS: **volatile**, excitable, emotional, unpredictable, hot-headed, quick-tempered, impatient, touchy, moody, sensitive, highly strung.
− ANTONYMS: placid.
■ **temperamentally** adv.

temperance n. complete avoidance of alcohol.

temperate adj. **1** (of a climate)

t

having mild temperatures. **2** self-controlled.

temperature n. **1** the degree of heat or cold. **2** a body temperature above normal.

tempest n. a violent storm.

tempestuous adj. **1** stormy. **2** full of strong and changeable emotion.
▷ SYNONYMS: **turbulent**, wild, stormy, violent, emotional, passionate, impassioned, fiery, intense, uncontrolled, unrestrained.
– ANTONYMS: calm.

template n. a shaped piece of rigid material used as a pattern for cutting out etc.

temple n. **1** a building for the worship of a god or gods. **2** the flat part between the forehead and the ear.
▷ SYNONYMS: **place of worship**, shrine, sanctuary, church, cathedral, mosque, synagogue, mandir, gurdwara.

tempo n. (pl. **tempos** or **tempi**) **1** the speed of a piece of music. **2** the pace of an activity or process.

temporal adj. **1** of time. **2** of worldly affairs. **3** of or situated in the temples of the head.
■ **temporally** adv.

temporary adj. lasting for a limited time.
▷ SYNONYMS: **1** *a temporary solution:* **interim**, short-term, provisional, makeshift, stopgap, pro tem; acting, fill-in, stand-in, caretaker. **2** *a temporary loss of self-control:* **brief**, short-lived, momentary, fleeting, passing, ephemeral.
– ANTONYMS: permanent, lasting.
■ **temporarily** adv.

temporize (or **-ise**) v. delay making a decision.

tempt v. entice someone to do something against their better judgement.
▷ SYNONYMS: **entice**, persuade, convince, inveigle, induce, cajole, coax, lure, attract, appeal to, tantalize, whet the appetite of, seduce; informal sweet-talk.
– ANTONYMS: discourage, deter.
■ **tempter** n. **temptress** n..

temptation n. **1** the desire to do something which is against your better judgement. **2** a thing that attracts or tempts.
▷ SYNONYMS: **1 desire**, urge, itch, impulse, inclination. **2 lure**, allure, enticement, attraction, draw, pull.

tempting adj. appealing or attractive.
▷ SYNONYMS: **enticing**, alluring, attractive, appealing, inviting, seductive, beguiling, fascinating,

mouth-watering.
– ANTONYMS: uninviting.

ten adj. & n. one more than nine; 10.
■ **tenfold** adj. & adv.

tenable adj. able to be defended or upheld.
▷ SYNONYMS: **defensible**, justifiable, supportable, sustainable, arguable, reasonable, rational, sound, viable, plausible, credible, believable, conceivable.
– ANTONYMS: untenable.

tenacious adj. holding firmly to something.
▷ SYNONYMS: **persevering**, persistent, determined, dogged, strong-willed, indefatigable, tireless, resolute, patient, purposeful, unflagging, staunch, steadfast, untiring, unwavering, unswerving, unshakeable; formal pertinacious.
■ **tenaciously** adv. **tenacity** n.

tenancy n. (pl. **tenancies**) use of land or property as a tenant.

tenant n. a person who rents land or property from a landlord.
▷ SYNONYMS: **occupant**, resident, inhabitant, leaseholder, lessee, lodger; Brit. occupier.

tend v. **1** frequently behave in a particular way or have a certain characteristic. **2** take care of.
▷ SYNONYMS: **1 be inclined**, be apt, be disposed, be prone, be liable, be likely, have a tendency. **2 look after**, take care of, minister to, attend to, see to, watch over, keep an eye on, mind, protect, guard.
– ANTONYMS: neglect.

tendency n. (pl. **tendencies**) an inclination to behave in a particular way.
▷ SYNONYMS: **inclination**, propensity, proclivity, proneness, aptness, likeli-hood, bent, leaning, liability.

tendentious adj. promoting a particular point of view.

tender adj. **1** gentle and kind. **2** easy to cut or chew. **3** painful to the touch. **4** easily damaged.
▷ SYNONYMS: **1** *a gentle, tender man:* **caring**, kind, kind-hearted, soft-hearted, compassionate, sympathetic, warm, gentle, mild, benevolent. **2** *a tender kiss:* **affectionate**, fond, loving, romantic, emotional; informal lovey-dovey. **3 soft**, succulent, juicy, melt-in-the-mouth. **4 sore**, sensitive, inflamed, raw, painful, hurting, aching, throbbing. **5** *the tender age of fifteen:* **young**, youthful, impression-able, inexperienced; informal wet

behind the ears.
– ANTONYMS: hard-hearted, callous, tough.
• v. **1** offer formally. **2** make a formal written offer to carry out work, supply goods, etc. for a stated fixed price.
▷ SYNONYMS: **offer**, proffer, put forward, present, propose, suggest, advance, submit, hand in.
• n. **1** a tendered offer. **2** a vehicle used by a fire service for carrying equipment. **3** a wagon attached to a steam locomotive to carry fuel and water.
▷ SYNONYMS: **bid**, offer, quotation, quote, estimate, price.
■ **tenderly** adv. **tenderness** n.

tendon n. a strong band of tissue attaching a muscle to a bone.

tendril n. **1** a thread-like part by which a climbing plant clings. **2** a slender curl of hair.

tenement n. a large house divided into flats.

tenet n. a central principle or belief.

tenner n. Brit. informal a ten-pound note.

tennis n. a game in which players use rackets to hit a ball over a net stretched across an open court.

tenon n. a projecting piece of wood shaped to fit into a mortise.

tenor n. **1** the highest ordinary adult male singing voice. **2** the general meaning or nature of something.

tense adj. **1** stretched tight. **2** anxious or nervous.
▷ SYNONYMS: **1 taut**, tight, rigid, stretched, strained, stiff. **2 anxious**, nervous, on edge, edgy, strained, stressed, ill at ease, uneasy, restless, worked up, keyed up, overwrought, jumpy, nervy; informal a bundle of nerves, jittery, twitchy, uptight. **3 nerve-racking**, stressful, anxious, worrying, fraught, charged, strained, nail-biting.
– ANTONYMS: relaxed, calm.
• v. make or become tense.
▷ SYNONYMS: **tighten**, tauten, flex, contract, brace, stiffen.
– ANTONYMS: relax.
• n. a set of forms of a verb indicating the time of the action.
■ **tensely** adv.

tensile adj. **1** of tension. **2** able to be stretched.

tension n. **1** the state of being stretched tight. **2** mental or emotional strain. **3** a strained political or social state. **4** voltage of specified magnitude.

▷ SYNONYMS: **1 tightness**, tautness, rigidity, pull. **2 strain**, stress, anxiety, pressure, worry, nervousness, jumpiness, edginess, restlessness, suspense, uncertainty. **3 strained relations**, strain, ill feeling, friction, antagonism, antipathy, hostility.

tent n. a portable fabric shelter supported by poles.

tentacle n. a long, thin, flexible part of certain animals, used for feeling or grasping.

tentative adj. **1** hesitant. **2** not certain.
▷ SYNONYMS: **1** a few tentative steps: **hesitant**, uncertain, cautious, timid, hesitating, faltering, shaky, unsteady, halting. **2** a tentative arrangement: **provisional**, unconfirmed, preliminary, exploratory, experimental.
– ANTONYMS: confident, definite.
■ **tentatively** adv.

tenterhook n. (**on tenterhooks**) in a state of nervous suspense.

tenth adj. & n. next after ninth; 10th.

tenuous adj. very slight or weak.
▷ SYNONYMS: **slight**, insubstantial, flimsy, weak, doubtful, dubious, questionable, suspect, vague, nebulous, hazy.
– ANTONYMS: convincing.
■ **tenuously** adv.

tenure n. the holding of a job, or of land or buildings.

tepee (or **teepee**) n. a conical tent used by American Indians.

tepid adj. lukewarm.
▷ SYNONYMS: **1 lukewarm**, warmish. **2 unenthusiastic**, apathetic, half-hearted, indifferent, cool, lukewarm, uninterested.

tequila n. a Mexican alcoholic spirit.

tercentenary n. (pl. **tercentenaries**) a 300th anniversary.

tergiversation n. evasive or ambiguous language.

term n. **1** a word or phrase. **2** (**terms**) conditions laid down or agreed. **3** (**terms**) relations: on good terms. **4** a period for which something lasts. **5** each period in the year during which teaching is given in a school or college. **6** each quantity in a mathematical ratio, series, etc.
▷ SYNONYMS: **1 word**, expression, phrase, name, title, designation, label, description. **2** the terms of the contract: **condition**, stipulation, specification, provision, proviso, restriction, qualification. **3 period**, length of time, spell, stint, duration, stretch, run, session.

t

• v. call by a specified term.
▷ SYNONYMS: **call**, name, entitle, title, style, designate, describe as, dub, label, tag.
□ **come to terms with** become able to accept or deal with.
■ **termly** adj. & adv.

termagant n. a bad-tempered or overbearing woman.

terminal adj. **1** of or situated at the end. **2** (of a disease) predicted to lead to death.
▷ SYNONYMS: **1 incurable**, untreatable, inoperable, fatal, lethal, mortal, deadly. **2 final**, last, concluding, closing, end.
• n. **1** the station at the end of a railway or bus route. **2** an airport building for passengers arriving and departing. **3** a point of connection in an electric circuit. **4** a keyboard and screen connected to a central computer system.
▷ SYNONYMS: **1 station**, last stop, end of the line, depot; Brit. **terminus**. **2 workstation**, VDU, visual display unit.
■ **terminally** adv.

terminate v. come or bring to an end.
▷ SYNONYMS: **bring to an end**, end, bring to a close, close, conclude, finish, stop, wind up, discontinue, cease, cut short, abort, axe; informal **pull the plug on**.
– ANTONYMS: begin.
■ **termination** n.

terminology n. (pl. **terminologies**) the set of terms used in a subject.
▷ SYNONYMS: **phraseology**, terms, expressions, words, language, parlance, vocabulary, nomenclature, usage, idiom, jargon; informal **lingo**.
■ **terminological** adj.

terminus n. (pl. **termini** or **terminuses**) a railway or bus terminal.

termite n. a small insect which eats wood.

tern n. a seabird.

ternary adj. composed of three parts.

terrace n. **1** a raised flat area, esp. forming part of a tier. **2** a patio. **3** Brit. a row of houses built in one block.
■ **terraced** adj.

terracotta n. **1** unglazed, brownish-red pottery. **2** a brownish-red colour.

terra firma n. dry land.

terrain n. land with regard to its physical features.
▷ SYNONYMS: **land**, ground, territory, topography, landscape, countryside, country.

terrapin n. a freshwater turtle.

terrarium /ter-**rair**-i-uhm/ n. (pl.

terrariums or **terraria**) an enclosed container in which small reptiles or amphibians are kept or plants are grown.

terrestrial adj. **1** of the earth. **2** living on or in the ground. **3** (of television broadcasting) not using a satellite.
▷ SYNONYMS: **earthly**, worldly, mundane, earthbound.

terrible adj. very bad, serious, or unpleasant.
▷ SYNONYMS: **1** a terrible crime: **dreadful**, awful, appalling, horrific, horrible, horrendous, atrocious, monstrous, sickening, heinous, vile, gruesome, unspeakable. **2** terrible pain: **severe**, extreme, intense, excruciating, agonizing, unbearable. **3** a terrible film: **very bad**, dreadful, awful, frightful, atrocious, execrable; informal **pathetic**, pitiful, useless, lousy, appalling; Brit. informal **chronic**.
– ANTONYMS: minor, slight, excellent.
■ **terribly** adv.

terrier n. a small dog.

terrific adj. **1** very great or intense. **2** informal excellent.
▷ SYNONYMS: **1 tremendous**, huge, massive, gigantic, colossal, mighty, considerable; informal **mega**, whopping; Brit. informal **ginormous**. **2 marvellous**, wonderful, sensational, outstanding, superb, excellent, first-rate, dazzling, out of this world, breathtaking; informal **great**, fantastic, fabulous, super, ace, wicked, awesome; Brit. informal **brilliant**.
■ **terrifically** adv.

terrify v. (**terrifying**, **terrified**) cause to feel terror.
▷ SYNONYMS: **frighten**, horrify, petrify, scare, strike terror into, paralyse, transfix.

terrine n. a mixture of chopped meat, fish, etc. pressed into a container and served cold.

territorial adj. of, having, or defending a territory.
■ **territorially** adv.

Territorial Army n. a voluntary military reserve force.

territory n. (pl. **territories**) **1** an area under the control of a ruler or state. **2** an area defended by an animal against others. **3** an area in which someone has rights, responsibilities, or knowledge.
▷ SYNONYMS: **1 region**, area, enclave, country, state, land, dependency, colony, dominion. **2** mountainous territory: **terrain**, land, ground, countryside.

terror n. **1** extreme fear. **2** a cause of this. **3** informal a very annoying person.
▷ SYNONYMS: **fear**, dread, horror, fright, alarm, panic, shock.

terrorism n. the unofficial use of violence and intimidation in the attempt to achieve political aims.
■ **terrorist** n.

terrorize (or **-ise**) v. threaten and frighten over a period of time.
▷ SYNONYMS: **persecute**, victimize, torment, tyrannize, intimidate, menace, threaten, bully, browbeat, scare, frighten, terrify, petrify; Brit. informal put the frighteners on.

terry n. a towelling fabric.

terse adj. using few words.
▷ SYNONYMS: **brief**, short, to the point, concise, succinct, crisp, pithy, incisive, laconic, elliptical, brusque, abrupt, curt, clipped, blunt.
– ANTONYMS: long-winded, polite.
■ **tersely** adv. **terseness** n.

tertiary /ter-shuh-ri/ adj. third in order or level.

tessellated adj. decorated with mosaics.
■ **tessellation** n.

test n. **1** a procedure to establish the quality, performance, presence, etc. of something. **2** a short examination of skill or knowledge. **3** (or **Test match**) an international cricket or rugby match.
▷ SYNONYMS: **1 trial**, experiment, check, examination, assessment, evaluation, appraisal, investigation. **2 exam**, examination; N. Amer. quiz.
• v. subject to a test.
▷ SYNONYMS: **try out**, trial, put through its paces, experiment with, check, examine, assess, evaluate, appraise, investigate, sample.
□ **test tube** a thin glass tube closed at one end, used to hold material in laboratory tests. **test-tube baby** informal a baby conceived by in vitro fertilization.
■ **tester** n.

testament n. **1** a will. **2** evidence or proof. **3** (**Testament**) each of the two divisions of the Bible.

testate adj. having made a valid will before dying.

testator n. (fem. **testatrix**) a person who has made a will.

testicle n. either of the two organs producing sperm in male mammals.
■ **testicular** adj.

testify v. (**testifying**, **testified**) **1** give evidence in a law court. **2** serve as evidence or proof.
▷ SYNONYMS: **swear**, attest, give evidence, state on oath, declare, assert, affirm.

testimonial n. **1** a formal statement of a person's good character and qualifications. **2** a public tribute to someone.
▷ SYNONYMS: **reference**, letter of recommendation, commendation.

testimony n. (pl. **testimonies**) **1** a formal statement, esp. one given in a law court. **2** evidence or proof.
▷ SYNONYMS: **evidence**, sworn statement, attestation, affidavit, statement, declaration, assertion.

testing adj. difficult; challenging: *a testing time.*
▷ SYNONYMS: **difficult**, challenging, tough, hard, demanding, taxing, stressful.
– ANTONYMS: easy.

testis n. (pl. **testes**) a testicle.

testosterone n. a male sex hormone.

testy adj. irritable.
■ **testily** adv.

tetanus n. a disease causing muscular spasms and rigidity.

tetchy adj. bad-tempered and irritable.
■ **tetchily** adv.

tête-à-tête /tet-ah-tet/ n. a private conversation between two people.

tether v. fasten an animal to a post etc.
• n. a rope or chain used to tether an animal.

tetrahedron n. (pl. **tetrahedra** or **tetrahedrons**) a solid with four triangular faces.

Teutonic adj. German.

text n. **1** a written or printed work. **2** the main body of a book as distinct from illustrations etc. **3** (or **text message**) an electronic message sent and received via mobile phone. **4** a passage from the Bible as the subject of a sermon.
▷ SYNONYMS: **1 book**, work, textbook. **2** *the pictures relate well to the text:* **words**, content, body, wording, script, copy.
• v. send a text message to.
□ **textbook** a book used for the study of a subject.
■ **textual** adj.

textile n. a woven or knitted fabric.

texture n. the feel or consistency of a substance.
▷ SYNONYMS: **feel**, touch, appearance, finish, surface, grain, consistency.
• v. give a rough texture to.
■ **textural** adj.

thalidomide n. a sedative drug which was found to cause malformation

t

of the fetus when taken during pregnancy.

thallium n. a highly toxic metallic element.

than conj. & prep. used to introduce the second part of a comparison.

thank v. express gratitude to.
• n. (**thanks**) 1 an expression of gratitude. 2 thank you.
▷ SYNONYMS: **gratitude**, appreciation, acknowledgement, recognition, credit.
□ **thanksgiving** the expression of gratitude to God. **Thanksgiving** a national holiday held in the autumn in North America. **thank you** a polite expression of gratitude.

thankful adj. pleased and relieved.
▷ SYNONYMS: **grateful**, relieved, pleased, glad.
■ **thankfulness** n.

thankfully adv. 1 in a thankful way. 2 fortunately.

thankless adj. unpleasant and unlikely to be appreciated by others.
▷ SYNONYMS: **unenviable**, difficult, unpleasant, unrewarding, unappreciated, unrecognized, unacknowledged.
– ANTONYMS: rewarding.

that pron. & adj. (pl. **those**) referring to a person or thing seen or heard or already mentioned or known, or to the more distant of two things.
• pron. introducing a clause defining or identifying something.
• adv. to such a degree.
• conj. introducing a statement or suggestion.

thatch n. a roof covering of straw, reeds, etc.
• v. cover with thatch.
■ **thatcher** n.

thaw v. 1 make or become unfrozen. 2 make or become friendlier.
▷ SYNONYMS: **melt**, unfreeze, defrost, soften, liquefy.
– ANTONYMS: freeze.
• n. 1 a period of warmer weather that thaws ice and snow. 2 an increase in friendliness.

the adj. used to refer to one or more people or things already mentioned or understood; the definite article.

theatre (US **theater**) n. 1 a building in which plays etc. are performed. 2 the writing and production of plays. 3 a room for lectures with seats in tiers. 4 Brit. a room where surgical operations are performed.
▷ SYNONYMS: 1 **playhouse**, auditorium, amphitheatre. 2 **acting**, the stage,

drama, dramaturgy, show business; informal **showbiz**. 3 *a lecture theatre:* **hall**, room, auditorium.

theatrical adj. 1 of acting, actors, or the theatre. 2 exaggerated for effect.
▷ SYNONYMS: 1 **stage**, dramatic, thespian, show-business; informal **showbiz**. 2 **exaggerated**, ostentatious, stagy, melodramatic, showy, affected, over-done; informal **hammy**.
• n. (**theatricals**) theatrical performances.
■ **theatricality** n. **theatrically** adv.

thee pron. old use you (as the singular object of a verb or preposition).

theft n. stealing.
▷ SYNONYMS: **robbery**, stealing, larceny, shoplifting, burglary, embezzlement, raid, hold-up; informal **smash-and-grab**; N. Amer. informal **heist**.

> **WORD LINKS**
> **kleptomania** compulsive theft

their adj. of or belonging to them.

> **USAGE** Don't confuse **their** with **there**, which means 'in, at, or to that place or position'.

theirs possess. pron. belonging to them.

> **USAGE** No apostrophe: theirs.

them pron. used as the object of a verb or preposition to refer to two or more people or things previously mentioned, or to a person of unspecified sex.

theme n. 1 a subject being discussed. 2 a prominent or frequently recurring melody in a musical piece.
▷ SYNONYMS: 1 **subject**, topic, argument, idea, thrust, thread, motif, keynote. 2 **melody**, tune, air, motif, leitmotif.
□ **theme park** an amusement park based around a particular idea.
■ **thematic** adj. **thematically** adv.

themselves pron. 1 used when a group of people or things or a person of unspecified sex performing an action are also affected by it. 2 they or them personally.

then adv. 1 at that time. 2 after that. 3 in that case.

thence adv. formal from that place or source.
□ **thenceforth** from that time onward.

theocracy n. (pl. **theocracies**) a system of government by priests.
■ **theocratic** adj.

theodolite n. a surveying instrument for measuring angles.

theology n. (pl. **theologies**) 1 the study of God and religious belief. 2 a

system of religious beliefs.
■ **theologian** n. **theological** adj. **theologist** n.

theorem n. a scientific or mathematical proposition that can be proved by reasoning.

theoretical adj. concerning or based on theory rather than practice.
▷ SYNONYMS: **hypothetical**, speculative, academic, conjectural, suppositional, notional, unproven.
– ANTONYMS: actual.
■ **theoretically** adv.

theorize (or **-ise**) v. form a theory or theories about something.
■ **theorist** n.

theory n. (pl. **theories**) **1** a set of ideas intended to explain something. **2** a set of principles on which an activity is based.
▷ SYNONYMS: **1 hypothesis**, thesis, conjecture, supposition, speculation, postulation, proposition, premise, opinion, view, belief, contention. **2** *modern economic theory:* **ideas**, concepts, philosophy, ideology, thinking, principles.

theosophy n. a philosophy believing that knowledge of God is achievable through intuition and meditation.
■ **theosophical** adj.

therapeutic adj. **1** of the curing of disease. **2** having a good effect on the body or mind.
▷ SYNONYMS: **healing**, curative, remedial, medicinal, restorative, health-giving.
■ **therapeutically** adv.

therapy n. (pl. **therapies**) treatment for a physical or mental disorder.
▷ SYNONYMS: **psychotherapy**, psycho-analysis, analysis; counselling.
■ **therapist** n.

there adv. **1** in, at, or to that place or position. **2** on that issue.

USAGE Don't confuse **there** with **their**, which means 'belonging to them'.

thereabouts adv. near that place, time, or figure.

thereafter adv. after that time.

thereby adv. by that means.

therefore adv. for that reason.
▷ SYNONYMS: **consequently**, that being the case, so, as a result, hence, accordingly, ergo, thus.

therein adv. formal in that place, document, or respect.

thereof adv. formal of that.

thereupon adv. formal immediately after that.

thermal adj. **1** of heat. **2** (of a garment) made of a fabric providing good insulation.
• n. an upward current of warm air.

thermodynamics n. the study of the relations between heat and other forms of energy.

thermometer n. an instrument for measuring temperature.

thermonuclear adj. of or using nuclear reactions occurring at very high temperatures.

thermoplastic adj. (of a substance) becoming soft when heated and hardening when cooled.

Thermos n. trademark a vacuum flask.

thermosetting adj. (of a substance) setting permanently when heated.

thermostat n. a device that regulates temperature automatically.
■ **thermostatic** adj. **thermostatically** adv.

thesaurus n. (pl. **thesauri** or **thesauruses**) a book containing lists of synonyms.

these pl. of THIS.

thesis n. (pl. **theses**) **1** a theory put forward to be supported or proved. **2** a long essay written as part of a university degree.
▷ SYNONYMS: **1 theory**, contention, argument, proposal, proposition, premise, assumption, supposition, hypothesis. **2 dissertation**, essay, paper, treatise, composition, study; N. Amer. theme.

thespian adj. of the theatre.
• n. an actor or actress.

they pron. **1** the people or things or person of unspecified sex previously mentioned. **2** people in general.

thiamine (or **thiamin**) n. vitamin B_1, found in unrefined cereals, beans, and liver.

thick adj. **1** with opposite sides or surfaces relatively far apart. **2** made up of a large number of things close together. **3** dense or difficult to see through. **4** relatively firm in consistency. **5** informal stupid. **6** informal very friendly.
▷ SYNONYMS: **1 broad**, wide, deep, stout, bulky, hefty, chunky, solid, plump. **2** *thick vegetation:* **plentiful**, abundant, profuse, luxuriant, bushy, rich, riotous, exuberant, rank, rampant, dense; informal jungly. **3** *the station was thick with people:* **crowded**, full, packed, teeming, seething, swarming, crawling, crammed, thronged, bursting at the seams, solid, overflowing; informal jam-packed, chock-a-block, stuffed; Austral./NZ informal chocker. **4** *thick fog:* **dense**, heavy, opaque, impenetrable, soupy,

t

murky. **5** *a thick paste*: **semi-solid**, firm, stiff, heavy, viscous, gelatinous.
– ANTONYMS: thin, slender, sparse.
• n. (**the thick**) the busiest or most intense part.
□ **thickset** heavily or solidly built. **thick-skinned** not sensitive to criticism etc.
■ **thickly** adv. **thickness** n.

thicken v. make or become thick or thicker.
▷ SYNONYMS: **stiffen**, condense, solidify, set, gel, congeal, clot, coagulate.

thicket n. a dense group of bushes or trees.

thief n. (pl. **thieves**) a person who steals.
▷ SYNONYMS: **robber**, burglar, house-breaker, shoplifter, pickpocket, mugger, kleptomaniac; informal crook.

thieve v. steal.
▷ SYNONYMS: **steal**, take, purloin, help yourself to, snatch, pilfer, embezzle, misappropriate; informal rob, swipe, nab, lift; Brit. informal nick, pinch, knock off; N. Amer. informal heist.
■ **thievery** n.

thigh n. the part of the leg between the hip and the knee.

thimble n. a hard cap worn to protect the end of the finger in sewing.

thin adj. (**thinner**, **thinnest**) **1** not thick. **2** having little fat on the body. **3** (of a sound) faint and high-pitched. **4** weak and inadequate.
▷ SYNONYMS: **1 narrow**, fine, attenuated. **2 lightweight**, light, fine, delicate, flimsy, diaphanous, gauzy, gossamer, sheer, filmy, transparent, see-through. **3 slim**, lean, slender, willowy, svelte, sylphlike, spare, slight, skinny, underweight, scrawny, scraggy, bony, gaunt, emaciated, skeletal, lanky, spindly, gangly; informal anorexic. **4 watery**, weak, runny, sloppy.
– ANTONYMS: thick, broad, fat.
• v. (**thinning**, **thinned**) make or become thinner.
▷ SYNONYMS: **1 dilute**, water down, weaken. **2** *the crowds thinned out*: **disperse**, dissipate, scatter.
– ANTONYMS: thicken.
■ **thinly** adv. **thinness** n.

thine possess. pron. & adj. old use your or yours.

thing n. **1** an inanimate object. **2** an unspecified object, action, activity, thought, etc. **3** (**things**) belongings. **4** (**the thing**) informal what is needed, acceptable, or fashionable.
▷ SYNONYMS: **1 object**, article, item,

artefact, commodity; informal doodah, whatsit; Brit. informal gubbins. **2** (**things**) **belongings**, possessions, stuff, property, worldly goods, goods and chattels, effects, paraphernalia, bits and pieces, luggage, baggage; informal gear, junk; Brit. informal clobber. **3** (**things**) **equipment**, apparatus, gear, kit, tackle, stuff, implements, tools, utensils, impedimenta, accoutrements.

think v. (**thinking**, **thought**) **1** have a particular opinion or belief. **2** use or direct the mind. **3** (**think of/about**) take into account or consideration. **4** (**think up**) informal devise.
▷ SYNONYMS: **1 believe**, consider, be of the opinion, hold, judge, deem, be of the view, be under the impression, expect, presume, imagine, anticipate, suppose, guess, estimate; informal reckon, figure. **2 ponder**, reflect, deliberate, consider, meditate, contemplate, muse, ruminate, brood; formal cogitate. **3** *she thought of all the visits she had made*: **recall**, remember, recollect, call to mind, imagine, picture, visualize, envisage.
• n. an act of thinking.
□ **think better of** reconsider and decide not to do. **think tank** a body of experts providing advice and ideas.

thinker n. a person who thinks deeply and seriously.
▷ SYNONYMS: **intellectual**, philosopher, scholar, sage, ideologist, theorist, intellect, mind; informal brain.

thinking n. ideas or opinions: *what was the thinking behind this campaign?*
▷ SYNONYMS: **reasoning**, ideas, theory, thoughts, philosophy, beliefs, opinions, views.

thinner n. a solvent used to thin paint etc.

third adj. & n. **1** next after second. **2** each of three equal parts.
□ **third-degree** (of burns) affecting tissue below the skin. **the third degree** long and harsh questioning. **third party 1** a person or group besides the two main ones involved in a situation. **2** Brit. (of insurance) covering damage or injury suffered by a person other than the insured. **third-rate** of very poor quality. **Third World** the developing countries of Asia, Africa, and Latin America.
■ **thirdly** adv.

thirst n. **1** a feeling of needing or wanting to drink. **2** a strong desire.
▷ SYNONYMS: *his thirst for knowledge*: **craving**, desire, longing, yearning,

thirsty | thrash

hunger, hankering, eagerness, lust, appetite; informal yen, itch.
• v. (**thirst for/after**) have a strong desire for.

thirsty adj. (**thirstier, thirstiest**)
1 feeling or causing thirst. **2** having a strong desire for something.
▷ SYNONYMS: **1 dehydrated**, dry; informal parched, gasping. **2** *he was thirsty for more knowledge:* **eager**, longing, yearning, burning, desirous; informal itching, dying.
■ **thirstily** adv.

thirteen adj. & n. one more than twelve; 13.
■ **thirteenth** adj. & n.

thirty adj. & n. (pl. **thirties**) ten less than forty; 30.
■ **thirtieth** adj. & n.

this pron. & adj. (pl. **these**) referring to the person or thing near, mentioned, or indicated.
• adv. to the degree or extent indicated.

thistle n. a prickly plant.
□ **thistledown** the light fluff on thistle seeds.

thither adv. old use to or towards that place.

thong n. **1** a narrow strip of leather etc. used as a fastening or as the lash of a whip. **2** a G-string.

thorax n. (pl. **thoraces** or **thoraxes**) the part of the body between the neck and the abdomen.
■ **thoracic** adj.

thorn n. **1** a stiff, sharp woody projection on a plant. **2** a thorny bush or tree.
▷ SYNONYMS: **prickle**, spike, barb, spine.

thorny adj. (**thornier, thorniest**)
1 having many thorns. **2** causing difficulty or trouble: *a thorny issue*.
▷ SYNONYMS: **1 prickly**, spiky, barbed, spiny, sharp. **2 problematic**, tricky, ticklish, delicate, controversial, awkward, difficult, knotty, tough, complicated, complex, involved, intricate, vexed; informal sticky.

thorough adj. **1** complete with regard to every detail. **2** very careful and detailed.
▷ SYNONYMS: **1** *a thorough investigation:* **rigorous**, in-depth, exhaustive, minute, detailed, close, meticulous, methodical, careful, complete, comprehensive. **2** *he's slow but thorough:* **meticulous**, scrupulous, assiduous, conscientious, painstaking, punctilious, methodical, careful. **3 utter**, downright, absolute, complete, total, out-and-out, real,

perfect, proper; Brit. informal right; Austral./NZ informal fair.
– ANTONYMS: superficial, cursory.
□ **thoroughbred** an animal of pure breed. **thoroughfare** a road or path between two places.
■ **thoroughly** adv. **thoroughness** n.

those pl. of THAT.

thou pron. old use singular form of 'you'.

though conj. despite the fact that.
• adv. however.

thought past & past part. of THINK.
• n. **1** an idea. **2** the process of thinking. **3** careful consideration.
▷ SYNONYMS: **1 idea**, notion, opinion, view, impression, feeling, theory.
2 thinking, contemplation, musing, pondering, consideration, reflection, rumination, deliberation, meditation; formal cogitation. **3** *have you no thought for others?:* **consideration**, understanding, regard, sensitivity, care, concern, compassion, sympathy.

thoughtful adj. **1** deep in thought. **2** thought out carefully. **3** considerate.
▷ SYNONYMS: **1 pensive**, reflective, contemplative, musing, meditative, ruminative, introspective, philosophical, preoccupied, in a brown study. **2 considerate**, caring, attentive, understanding, sympathetic, solicitous, concerned, helpful, obliging, accommodating, kind, compassionate.
– ANTONYMS: thoughtless.
■ **thoughtfully** adv.

thoughtless adj. **1** inconsiderate. **2** without thinking of the consequences.
▷ SYNONYMS: **1 inconsiderate**, uncaring, insensitive, uncharitable, unkind, tactless, undiplomatic, indiscreet, careless. **2 unthinking**, heedless, careless, unmindful, absent-minded, injudicious, ill-advised, ill-considered, imprudent, unwise, foolish, silly, stupid, reckless, rash, precipitate, negligent, neglectful, remiss.
– ANTONYMS: thoughtful.
■ **thoughtlessly** adv.

thousand adj. & n. ten hundred; 1,000 or M.
■ **thousandth** adj. & n.

thrall n. the state of being in another's power.

thrash v. **1** beat repeatedly and violently. **2** move in a violent or uncontrolled way. **3** informal defeat heavily. **4** (**thrash out**) discuss thoroughly.
▷ SYNONYMS: **1 hit**, beat, strike, batter,

t

thump, hammer, pound; informal belt.
2 *he was thrashing around in pain:*
flail, writhe, thresh, jerk, toss, twist,
twitch.

thread n. **1** a long, thin strand of
cotton, nylon, etc. **2** the spiral ridge
of a screw etc. **3** a theme running
through a situation or piece of
writing.
▷ SYNONYMS: **cotton**, yarn, fibre,
filament.
• v. **1** pass a thread through. **2** move or
weave in and out of obstacles.
▷ SYNONYMS: *she threaded her way
through the tables:* **weave**, inch,
squeeze, navigate, negotiate.

threadbare adj. worn and tattered
with age.
▷ SYNONYMS: **worn**, old, holey, moth-
eaten, mangy, ragged, frayed,
tattered, decrepit, shabby, scruffy;
informal **tatty**, the worse for wear.

threat n. **1** a stated intention to harm
someone. **2** a person or thing likely to
cause harm or danger.
▷ SYNONYMS: **1 threatening remark**,
warning, ultimatum. **2** *a possible
threat to aircraft:* **danger**, peril,
hazard, menace, risk. **3** *the company
faces the threat of liquidation:* **possibility**, chance, probability, likelihood,
risk.

threaten v. **1** make a threat to or to
do. **2** put at risk.
▷ SYNONYMS: **1 menace**, intimidate, browbeat, bully, terrorize. **2 endanger**,
jeopardize, imperil, put at risk.
3 herald, bode, warn of, presage,
foreshadow, indicate, point to, be a
sign of, signal.

three adj. & n. one more than two; 3.
□ **three-dimensional** having or
appearing to have length, breadth,
and depth. **threesome** a group of
three people.
■ **threefold** adj. & adv.

thresh v. **1** separate grain from the
husks of corn etc. **2** move about
wildly.

threshold n. **1** a strip of wood or
stone forming the bottom of a
doorway. **2** a level or point marking
the start of something.
▷ SYNONYMS: **1 doorstep**, entrance,
entry, gate, portal. **2 start**, beginning,
commencement, brink, verge, dawn,
inception, day one, opening, debut.

USAGE There is only one *h* in the
middle: thres*h*old.

---

threw past of **THROW**.

thrice adv. old use three times.

thrift n. economy in the use of money
or other resources.

thrifty adj. (**thriftier**, **thriftiest**) careful
with money; economical.
▷ SYNONYMS: **frugal**, economical,
sparing, careful, provident,
prudent, abstemious, parsimonious,
penny-pinching.
− ANTONYMS: extravagant.

thrill n. **1** a sudden feeling of
excitement. **2** an exciting experience.
3 a wave of emotion.
▷ SYNONYMS: **excitement**, stimulation,
pleasure, tingle; informal **buzz**, kick;
N. Amer. informal **charge**.
− ANTONYMS: boredom.
• v. have or cause to have a thrill.
▷ SYNONYMS: **excite**, stimulate, arouse,
rouse, inspire, delight, exhilarate,
intoxicate, stir, electrify, move; informal
give someone a buzz/kick; N. Amer.
informal give someone a charge.
− ANTONYMS: bore.

thriller n. an exciting novel, play, or
film, esp. involving crime.

thrilling adj. very exciting and
enjoyable.
▷ SYNONYMS: **exciting**, stimulating,
stirring, action-packed, rip-roaring,
gripping, electrifying, riveting, fascinating, dramatic, hair-raising.
− ANTONYMS: boring.

thrive v. (**thriving**, **thrived** or **throve**;
past part. **thrived** or **thriven**) **1** grow or
develop well. **2** prosper.
▷ SYNONYMS: **flourish**, prosper, burgeon,
bloom, blossom, do well, advance,
succeed, boom.
− ANTONYMS: decline, wither.

thriving adj. growing or developing
well.
▷ SYNONYMS: **flourishing**, growing,
developing, blooming, healthy,
successful, booming, profitable;
informal going strong.
− ANTONYMS: declining.

throat n. **1** the passage from the back
of the mouth to the oesophagus and
lungs. **2** the front of the neck.

throaty adj. (of a voice) deep and
husky.
■ **throatily** adv.

throb v. (**throbbing**, **throbbed**) **1** beat
or sound with a strong rhythm. **2** feel
regular bursts of pain.
▷ SYNONYMS: **pulsate**, beat, pulse,
palpitate, pound, thud, thump, drum,
judder, vibrate, quiver.
• n. a strong, regular beat or sound.
▷ SYNONYMS: **pulsation**, beat, pulse,
palpitation, pounding, thudding,
thumping, drumming, juddering,

vibration, quivering.

throes pl. n. severe or violent pains. □ **in the throes of** struggling in the midst of.

thrombosis n. (pl. **thromboses**) the formation of a blood clot in a blood vessel or the heart.

throne n. **1** a ceremonial chair for a monarch or bishop. **2** the power or rank of a monarch.

throng n. a densely packed crowd.
▷ SYNONYMS: **crowd**, horde, mass, army, herd, flock, drove, swarm, sea, troupe, pack; informal bunch, gaggle, gang.
• v. gather in large numbers in a place.
▷ SYNONYMS: **1** *pavements thronged with tourists:* **fill**, crowd, pack, cram, jam. **2** *visitors thronged round him:* **flock**, crowd, cluster, mill, swarm, congregate, gather.

throttle n. a device controlling the flow of fuel or power to an engine.
• v. strangle.
▷ SYNONYMS: **choke**, strangle, garrotte.

through prep. & adv. **1** from end to end or side to side of. **2** from start to finish. **3** by means of.
▷ SYNONYMS: **1** **throughout**, for the duration of, all. **2** **by means of**, by way of, by dint of, via, using, thanks to, by virtue of, as a result of, as a consequence of, on account of, owing to.
• adj. **1** (of public transport) continuing to the final destination. **2** passing straight through a place. **3** having passed to the next stage of a competition.

throughout prep. all the way through.

throughput n. the amount of material processed.

throve past of THRIVE.

throw v. (**throwing**, **threw**; past part. **thrown**) **1** send through the air from the hand. **2** move or place hurriedly or roughly. **3** direct or cast light, a look, etc. somewhere. **4** send suddenly into a particular state. **5** confuse; put off. **6** form pottery on a wheel.
▷ SYNONYMS: **1** **hurl**, toss, fling, pitch, cast, lob, launch, bowl; informal chuck, heave, sling, bung. **2** *he threw the door open:* **push**, thrust, fling, bang. **3** **cast**, send, give off, emit, radiate, project. **4** **disconcert**, unnerve, fluster, ruffle, put off, throw off balance, unsettle, confuse; informal rattle, faze.
• n. **1** an act of throwing, or the distance thrown. **2** a light cover for

furniture.
▷ SYNONYMS: **lob**, toss, pitch, bowl. □ **throw away** discard as useless. **throwback** a return to an earlier ancestral type or characteristic. **throw up** vomit.

thrum v. (**thrumming**, **thrummed**) make a rhythmic humming sound.

thrush n. **1** a brown songbird with spotted breast. **2** a fungal infection of the mouth and throat or the genitals.

thrust v. (**thrusting**, **thrust**) **1** push suddenly or violently. **2** make your way forcibly.
▷ SYNONYMS: **1** **shove**, push, force, plunge, stick, drive, ram, lunge. **2** *fame had been thrust on him:* **force**, foist, impose, inflict.
• n. **1** a thrusting force or movement. **2** the main point of an argument.
▷ SYNONYMS: **1** **shove**, push, lunge, poke. **2** **advance**, push, drive, attack, assault, onslaught, offensive. **3** **force**, propulsion, power, impetus. **4** **gist**, substance, drift, message, import, tenor.

thud n. a dull, heavy sound.
• v. (**thudding**, **thudded**) move or fall with a thud.

thug n. a violent man.
▷ SYNONYMS: **ruffian**, hooligan, bully boy, hoodlum, gangster, villain; informal tough, bruiser, heavy; Brit. informal rough, bovver boy; N. Amer. informal hood, goon.
■ **thuggery** n. **thuggish** adj.

thumb n. the short, thick first digit of the hand.
• v. **1** turn over pages with the thumb. **2** request a lift in a passing vehicle by signalling with the thumb.
□ **under someone's thumb** completely under someone's control. **thumbnail** brief or concise. **thumbscrew** an instrument of torture that crushes the thumbs.

thump v. **1** hit heavily. **2** (of the heart) beat rapidly.
▷ SYNONYMS: **1** **hit**, beat, punch, strike, smack, batter, pummel; informal whack, wallop, bash, biff, clobber, clout; Brit. informal slosh; N. Amer. informal slug. **2** **throb**, pound, beat, thud, hammer.
• n. a heavy blow or noise.

thunder n. **1** a loud rumbling or crashing noise heard after lightning. **2** a loud, deep noise.
▷ SYNONYMS: **rumble**, boom, roar, pounding, crash, reverberation.
• v. **1** make the sound of thunder. **2** move noisily and forcefully. **3** speak loudly and angrily.

▷ SYNONYMS: **1 rumble**, boom, roar, pound, crash, resound, reverberate. **2** *'Answer me!' he thundered:* **shout**, roar, bellow, bark, bawl.
□ **thunderbolt** a flash of lightning with a crash of thunder. **thunderclap** a crash of thunder. **thunderstorm** a storm with thunder and lightning. **thunderstruck** very surprised.
■ **thunderous** adj. **thundery** adj.

Thursday n. the day before Friday.

thus adv. formal **1** as a result of this. **2** in this way.

thwack v. hit forcefully.
• n. a heavy blow.

thwart v. prevent from accomplishing something.
▷ SYNONYMS: **foil**, frustrate, forestall, stop, check, block, prevent, defeat, impede, obstruct, derail, snooker; informal put paid to, do for, stymie; Brit. informal scupper.
– ANTONYMS: help.

thy adj. old use your.

thyme /tym/ n. a herb used in cookery.

thymus n. (pl. **thymi**) a gland in the neck producing white blood cells.

thyroid n. a gland in the neck producing growth hormones.

thyself pron. old use yourself.

tiara n. a woman's jewelled semicircular headdress.

tibia n. (pl. **tibiae**) the inner of the two bones between the knee and the ankle.

tic n. a recurring spasm in the muscles of the face.

tick n. **1** Brit. a mark (✓) used to show that something is correct or has been chosen or checked. **2** a regular clicking sound, as made by a clock etc. **3** a bloodsucking insect-like animal. **4** Brit. informal a moment.
• v. **1** mark with a tick. **2** make regular ticking sounds. **3** (**tick over**) (of an engine) run slowly in neutral. **4** (**tick off**) Brit. informal reprimand.
□ **on tick** on credit.

ticket n. **1** a piece of paper or card entitling the holder to enter a place or to travel on public transport. **2** an official notice of a traffic offence. **3** a label showing the price, size, etc. of an item for sale.
▷ SYNONYMS: **1 pass**, authorization, permit, token, coupon, voucher. **2 label**, tag, sticker, tab, slip, docket.
• v. (**ticketing**, **ticketed**) give a ticket to.

ticking n. a strong fabric used to cover mattresses.

tickle v. **1** lightly touch in a way that causes itching or twitching and often laughter. **2** appeal to or amuse.
▷ SYNONYMS: **1 stroke**, pet. **2 stimulate**, interest, appeal to, amuse, entertain, divert, please, delight.
• n. an act of tickling or feeling of being tickled.
■ **tickly** adj.

ticklish adj. **1** sensitive to being tickled. **2** requiring care and tact.

tidal adj. of or affected by tides.
□ **tidal wave** a very large ocean wave.

tiddler n. Brit. informal a small fish.

tiddly adj. Brit. informal **1** slightly drunk. **2** tiny.
□ **tiddlywinks** a game involving flicking small counters into a cup.

tide n. **1** the regular alternate rise and fall of the sea. **2** a powerful surge of feeling or trend of events.
▷ SYNONYMS: **1 current**, flow, stream, ebb. **2** *the tide of history:* **course**, movement, direction, trend, current, drift, run.
• v. (**tide over**) help through a difficult period.

tidings pl. n. literary news.

tidy adj. (**tidier**, **tidiest**) neat and orderly.
▷ SYNONYMS: **1** *a tidy room:* **neat**, orderly, in good order, well kept, in apple-pie order, shipshape, spick and span, spruce, uncluttered, straight. **2** *a tidy person:* **organized**, neat, methodical, meticulous, systematic.
– ANTONYMS: untidy.
• v. (**tidying**, **tidied**) make tidy.
▷ SYNONYMS: **put in order**, clear up, sort out, straighten up, clean up, spruce up, smarten up.
■ **tidily** adv. **tidiness** n.

tie v. (**tying**, **tied**) **1** attach or fasten with string etc. **2** form into a knot or bow. **3** restrict. **4** connect. **5** achieve the same score as another competitor.
▷ SYNONYMS: **1 bind**, tie up, tether, hitch, strap, truss, fetter, rope, make fast, moor, lash. **2 do up**, lace, knot. **3** restrict, restrain, limit, tie down, constrain, cramp, hamper, handicap, hamstring, encumber, shackle. **4 link**, connect, couple, relate, join, marry. **5** draw, be equal, be even.
• n. (pl. **ties**) **1** a thing that ties. **2** a strip of material worn beneath a collar and knotted at the front. **3** an equal score in a game or match. **4** Brit. a sports match in which the winners proceed to the next round.
▷ SYNONYMS: **1 lace**, string, cord, fastening. **2 bond**, connection, link, relationship, attachment, affiliation.

3 restriction, constraint, curb, limitation, restraint, hindrance, encumbrance, handicap, obligation, commitment. **4 draw**, dead heat. □ **tiebreak** a means of deciding a winner when competitors have tied. **tie in** link or agree. **tie-up** a link. **tie up 1** bind someone's arms and legs. **2** conclude. **3** informal occupy fully.

tied adj. Brit. **1** (of a house) for occupation only by someone working for its owner. **2** (of a pub) owned and controlled by a brewery.

tier n. any of a series of rows or levels placed one above and behind the other.
▷ SYNONYMS: **1 row**, rank, bank, line, layer, level. **2 grade**, gradation, echelon, rung on the ladder.
■ **tiered** adj.

tiff n. informal a trivial quarrel.

tiger n. a large striped member of the cat family.

tight adj. **1** closed or fastened firmly. **2** close-fitting. **3** stretched so as to leave no slack. **4** allowing little room for movement. **5** strictly imposed. **6** (of money or time) limited.
▷ SYNONYMS: **1 firm**, secure, fast. **2 close-fitting**, narrow, figure-hugging, skintight; informal sprayed on. **3** *the rope was pulled tight*: **taut**, rigid, stiff, tense, stretched, strained. **4** *a tight mass of fibres*: **compact**, compressed, dense, solid. **5** *a tight space*: **small**, tiny, narrow, limited, restricted, confined, cramped, constricted. **6** *tight security*: **strict**, rigorous, stringent, tough.
– ANTONYMS: slack, loose.
● pl. n. (**tights**) a close-fitting stretchy garment covering the legs, hips, and bottom.
□ **tightrope** a rope or wire stretched high above the ground, on which acrobats balance.
■ **tightly** adv. **tightness** n.

tighten v. become or make tight or tighter.
▷ SYNONYMS: **stretch**, tauten, strain, stiffen, tense.
– ANTONYMS: loosen, slacken.

tigress n. a female tiger.

tilde /til-duh/ n. an accent (~) placed over a letter to mark a change in pronunciation.

tile n. a thin piece of baked clay etc. for covering roofs, floors, or walls.
● v. cover with tiles.
■ **tiling** n.

till prep. & conj. until.
● n. a cash register or drawer for money in a shop etc.
● v. prepare land for crops.

tiller n. a horizontal bar fitted to a boat's rudder, used for steering.

tilt v. move into a sloping position.
▷ SYNONYMS: **slope**, tip, lean, list, bank, slant, incline, pitch, cant, angle.
● n. a sloping position.
▷ SYNONYMS: **slope**, list, camber, gradient, bank, slant, incline, pitch, cant, bevel, angle.
□ (**at**) **full tilt** with maximum speed or force.

timber n. wood prepared for use in building and carpentry.
▷ SYNONYMS: **1 wood**; N. Amer. lumber. **2 beam**, spar, plank, batten, lath, board, joist, rafter.
■ **timbered** adj.

timbre /**tam**-ber/ n. the quality of a voice or musical sound.

time n. **1** the continuing progress of existence and events in the past, present, and future. **2** a period of time. **3** a point of time measured in hours and minutes. **4** an instance of something happening or being done. **5** (**times**) expressing multiplication. **6** rhythm in music.
▷ SYNONYMS: **1 moment**, point, occasion, instant, juncture, stage. **2** *he worked there for a time*: **while**, spell, stretch, stint, interval, period, length of time, duration, phase. **3 era**, age, epoch, aeon, period.
● v. **1** arrange a time for. **2** do at a certain time. **3** measure the time taken by.
▷ SYNONYMS: **schedule**, arrange, set, organize, fix, book, line up, timetable, plan; N. Amer. slate.
□ **time bomb** a bomb designed to explode at a set time. **time-honoured** (of a custom) respected because of its long existence. **timepiece** a clock or watch. **timeshare** an arrangement in which joint owners use a property as a holiday home at different times.
■ **timer** n. **timing** n.

> **WORD LINKS**
> **chronological**, **temporal** relating to time

timeless adj. not affected by the passage of time.
▷ SYNONYMS: **lasting**, enduring, classic, ageless, permanent, perennial, abiding, unchanging, unvarying, never-changing, eternal, everlasting.
– ANTONYMS: ephemeral.

timely adj. done or occurring at a good time.

t

▷ SYNONYMS: **opportune**, well timed, convenient, appropriate, expedient, seasonable, propitious.
– ANTONYMS: ill-timed.

timetable n. a list of times at which events are scheduled to take place.
▷ SYNONYMS: **schedule**, programme, agenda, calendar, diary.
• v. schedule to take place at a certain time.
▷ SYNONYMS: **schedule**, arrange, programme, organize, fix, time, line up; Brit. diarize; N. Amer. slate.

timid adj. lacking courage or confidence.
▷ SYNONYMS: **fearful**, afraid, faint-hearted, timorous, nervous, scared, frightened, shy, diffident.
– ANTONYMS: bold.
■ **timidity** n. **timidly** adv.

timorous adj. timid.

timpani (or **tympani**) pl. n. kettledrums.
■ **timpanist** n.

tin n. **1** a silvery-white metallic element. **2** a metal container. **3** Brit. a sealed metal container for preserving food.
• v. (**tinning**, **tinned**) **1** coat with tin. **2** (**tinned**) Brit. preserved in a tin.
□ **tinpot** informal of poor quality.

tincture n. a medicine made by dissolving a drug in alcohol.

tinder n. dry material which burns easily.

tine n. a prong or point, esp. of a fork.

tinge n. a slight trace of a colour or quality.
▷ SYNONYMS: **1 tint**, colour, shade, tone, hue. **2 trace**, note, touch, suggestion, hint, flavour, element, streak, suspicion, soupçon.
• v. (**tinging** or **tingeing**, **tinged**) give a tinge to.
▷ SYNONYMS: **tint**, colour, stain, shade, wash.

tingle n. a slight prickling or stinging sensation.
▷ SYNONYMS: **prickle**, pricking, tingling, sting, itch, pins and needles.
• v. have or cause a tingle.
▷ SYNONYMS: **prickle**, prick, sting, itch, tickle.

tinker v. casually try to repair or improve.
▷ SYNONYMS: **fiddle**, play about, mess about, adjust, try to mend; Brit. informal muck about.
• n. a travelling mender of pots, kettles, etc.

tinkle v. make a light, clear ringing sound.

• n. a tinkling sound.

tinnitus n. ringing or buzzing in the ears.

tinny adj. **1** having a thin, metallic sound. **2** made of thin or poor-quality metal.

tinsel n. a decoration made of thin strips of shiny metal foil.

tint n. **1** a shade of colour. **2** a dye for colouring the hair.
▷ SYNONYMS: **1 shade**, colour, tone, hue, tinge, cast, flush, blush. **2 dye**, colourant, colouring, wash.
• v. colour slightly.
▷ SYNONYMS: **dye**, colour, tinge.

tiny adj. (**tinier**, **tiniest**) very small.
▷ SYNONYMS: **minute**, minuscule, microscopic, very small, mini, diminutive, miniature, baby, toy, dwarf; Scottish wee; informal teeny, tiddly; Brit. informal titchy.
– ANTONYMS: huge.

tip n. **1** the end of something thin or tapering. **2** a small sum of money given for good service in a restaurant, taxi, etc. **3** a piece of advice. Brit. **4** a place where rubbish is left. **5** a prediction as to the likely winner of a race etc.
▷ SYNONYMS: **1 point**, end, extremity, head, spike, prong, nib. **2 gratuity**, baksheesh, present, gift, reward. **3 suggestion**, word of advice, pointer, hint; informal wrinkle.
• v. (**tipping**, **tipped**) **1** overbalance so as to fall over. **2** empty out the contents of a container by holding it at an angle. **3** cover the end of something thin or tapering with a material. **4** give a tip to someone for good service. **5** predict as likely to win or achieve something. **6** (**tip off**) informal give someone secret information.
▷ SYNONYMS: **1 overturn**, overbalance, topple, fall over, keel over. **2 pour**, empty, drain, dump, discharge, decant.
□ **tip-off** informal a piece of secret information.

tipple v. drink alcohol regularly.
• n. an alcoholic drink.
■ **tippler** n.

tipster n. a person who gives tips as to the likely winner of a race etc.

tipsy adj. slightly drunk.
■ **tipsily** adv.

tiptoe v. (**tiptoeing**, **tiptoed**) walk quietly and carefully with the heels raised.

tirade n. a long angry speech.
▷ SYNONYMS: **diatribe**, harangue, rant,

attack, polemic, broadside, fulmin-ation, tongue-lashing; informal blast.

tire v. **1** make or become tired. **2** (**tire of**) become impatient or bored with.
▷ SYNONYMS: **1 get tired**, weaken, flag, droop. **2 fatigue**, tire out, exhaust, wear out, drain, weary, enervate; informal take it out of; Brit. informal knacker.
• n. US = **TYRE**.

tired adj. **1** in need of sleep or rest. **2** (**tired of**) impatient or bored with.
▷ SYNONYMS: **1 exhausted**, worn out, weary, fatigued, ready to drop, drained, enervated; informal all in, dead beat, shattered, done in; Brit. informal knackered, whacked; N. Amer. informal pooped, tuckered out; Austral./NZ informal stonkered. **2** *I'm tired of him*: fed up with, weary of, bored with/by, sick of. **3** *tired expressions and clichés*: hackneyed, overused, stale, clichéd, predictable, unimaginative, unoriginal, dull, boring; informal corny.
– ANTONYMS: energetic, fresh.
■ tiredness n.

tireless adj. having or showing great energy.
■ tirelessly adv.

tiresome adj. annoying or tedious.
▷ SYNONYMS: **1 wearisome**, laborious, wearing, tedious, boring, monotonous, dull, uninteresting, unexciting, humdrum, routine. **2 troublesome**, irksome, vexatious, irritating, annoying, exasperating, trying; informal aggravating, pesky.
– ANTONYMS: interesting, pleasant.

tiring adj. causing tiredness.
▷ SYNONYMS: **exhausting**, wearying, taxing, draining, hard, arduous, strenuous, onerous, gruelling; informal killing; Brit. informal knackering.

tissue n. **1** any of the substances of which animals or plants are made. **2** a disposable paper handkerchief.
□ tissue paper very thin, soft paper.

tit n. a small songbird.

titanic adj. of very great size or power.

titanium n. a silver-grey metallic element.

titbit n. **1** a small piece of tasty food. **2** an item of interesting information.

tit for tat n. a situation in which someone takes retaliation for an insult or injury.

tithe n. one tenth of annual income or produce, formerly paid to the Church.

titillate v. interest or excite, esp. sexually.
■ titillation n.

USAGE Don't confuse **titillate** with **titivate**.

titivate v. informal make smarter or more attractive.
■ titivation n.

title n. **1** the name of a book, piece of music, etc. **2** a word describing a position or job, or used in speaking to someone with a particular rank or job. **3** the position of champion in a sports contest. **4** the legal right to ownership of property.
▷ SYNONYMS: **1 heading**, label, inscription, caption, subheading, legend. **2 name**, designation, form of address, rank, office, position; informal moniker, handle. **3** *an Olympic title*: championship, crown, first place.
□ title role the part in a play or film from which the title is taken.

titled adj. having a title indicating nobility or rank.

titter n. a short, quiet laugh.
• v. give a titter.

tittle-tattle n. & v. gossip.

titular adj. holding a formal position or title but no real authority.

tizzy n. (pl. tizzies) informal a state of nervous excitement or worry.

TNT abbrev. trinitrotoluene, a high explosive.

to prep. **1** in the direction of. **2** so as to reach a state. **3** indicating the person or thing affected. **4** indicating that a verb is in the infinitive.
• adv. so as to be closed or nearly closed.
□ to and fro backwards and forwards or from side to side. **to-do** informal a commotion or fuss.

toad n. a short, stout, tailless amphibian.

toadstool n. a fungus with a rounded cap on a stalk.

toady n. (pl. toadies) an ingratiating person.
• v. act in an ingratiating way.

toast n. **1** sliced bread heated until brown and crisp. **2** an act of raising glasses and drinking together in honour of a person or thing. **3** a respected or admired person.
• v. **1** make bread brown and crisp by heating it. **2** drink a toast to.
▷ SYNONYMS: **drink to the health of**, raise your glass to, salute, honour, pay tribute to; old use pledge.

toaster n. an electrical device for making toast.

tobacco n. (pl. tobaccos) the dried leaves of an American plant which can be smoked or chewed.

t

tobacconist n. a shopkeeper selling cigarettes etc.

toboggan n. a small sledge for sliding downhill.

■ **tobogganing** n.

today adv. **1** on this present day. **2** at the present time.

• n. **1** this present day. **2** the present time.

toddle v. (of a young child) move with short unsteady steps.

▷ SYNONYMS: **totter**, teeter, wobble, falter, waddle, stumble.

toddler n. a young child who is just beginning to walk.

toddy n. (pl. **toddies**) a hot drink of spirits, water, and sugar.

toe n. any of the digits at the end of the foot.

• v. push or touch with the toes.

□ **toe the line** obey authority. **toehold** a small foothold.

toff n. Brit. informal a rich, upper-class person.

toffee n. a sweet made by boiling together sugar and butter.

tofu n. a soft food made from mashed soya beans.

tog n. **1** (**togs**) informal clothes. **2** Brit. a unit for measuring the insulating properties of duvets.

• v. (**be togged out/up**) informal be dressed.

toga n. a loose outer garment worn by men in ancient Rome.

together adv. **1** in company. **2** so as to touch or combine. **3** regarded as a whole. **4** at the same time.

• adj. informal sensible and well balanced.

▷ SYNONYMS: **level-headed**, well adjusted, well balanced, sensible, practical, realistic, mature, stable, full of common sense, well organized, efficient, methodical, self-confident, self-assured; informal **unflappable**.

toggle n. **1** a narrow piece of wood etc. pushed through a loop to fasten a garment. **2** a switch or key turning a function on and off alternately.

toil v. work or move laboriously.

▷ SYNONYMS: **1 work**, labour, slave, strive; informal **slog**, beaver; Brit. informal **graft**. **2 struggle**, drag yourself, trudge, slog, plod; N. Amer. informal **schlep**.

• n. laborious work.

▷ SYNONYMS: **hard work**, labour, exertion, slaving, drudgery, effort, {blood, sweat, and tears}; informal **slog**, elbow grease; Brit. informal **graft**; old use **travail**.

■ **toilsome** adj.

toilet n. **1** a large bowl for urinating or defecating into. **2** old use the process of washing and dressing yourself.

▷ SYNONYMS: **lavatory**, WC, public convenience, cloakroom, powder room, latrine, privy, urinal; N. Amer. bathroom, washroom, rest room, comfort station; Brit. informal **loo**, bog; N. Amer. informal **can**, john; Austral./NZ informal **dunny**.

□ **toilet water** a light perfume.

toiletries pl. n. articles used in washing and grooming.

token n. **1** a thing representing a fact, quality, or feeling. **2** a voucher that can be exchanged for goods. **3** a disc used to operate a machine.

▷ SYNONYMS: **1 symbol**, sign, emblem, badge, representation, indication, mark, expression, demonstration. **2 memento**, souvenir, keepsake, reminder. **3 voucher**, coupon, note.

• adj. done just for the sake of appearances.

▷ SYNONYMS: token resistance: **symbolic**, nominal, perfunctory, slight, minimal, superficial.

told past & past part. of **TELL**.

tolerable adj. **1** able to be tolerated. **2** fairly good.

▷ SYNONYMS: **1 bearable**, endurable, supportable, acceptable. **2 fairly good**, fair, passable, adequate, all right, acceptable, satisfactory, average, run-of-the-mill, mediocre, middling, ordinary, unexceptional; informal **OK**, so-so, no great shakes.

– ANTONYMS: intolerable.

■ **tolerably** adv.

tolerance n. **1** the ability to tolerate something. **2** an allowable variation in the size of a machine part.

▷ SYNONYMS: **1 toleration**, acceptance, open-mindedness, broad-mindedness, forbearance, patience, charity, understanding, lenience. **2** the plant's tolerance to pests and herbicides: resilience to, resistance to, immunity from.

tolerant adj. **1** able to accept things you dislike or disagree with. **2** able to endure particular conditions or treatment.

▷ SYNONYMS: **open-minded**, forbearing, broad-minded, liberal, unprejudiced, unbiased, patient, long-suffering, understanding, charitable, lenient, easy-going, indulgent, permissive.

tolerate v. **1** allow something you dislike or disagree with to exist or continue. **2** endure patiently. **3** be able to be exposed to a drug, toxin, etc. without a bad reaction.

▷ SYNONYMS: **1 allow**, permit, condone, accept, swallow, countenance; formal

brook. **2** *he couldn't tolerate her moods any longer:* **endure**, put up with, bear, take, stand, support, stomach, abide; Brit. informal stick.
■ **toleration** n.

toll n. **1** a charge payable for the use of certain bridges or roads. **2** the number of casualties arising from a disaster etc. **3** a single ring of a bell.
▷ SYNONYMS: **1 charge**, fee, payment, levy, tariff, tax. **2 number**, count, tally, total, sum. **3** *the toll on the environment has been high:* **harm**, damage, injury, detriment, adverse effect, cost, price, loss.
• v. (of a bell) sound with slow strokes, esp. to mark a death.
▷ SYNONYMS: **ring**, sound, clang, chime, strike, peal.

tom (or **tomcat**) n. a male cat.

tomahawk n. a light axe formerly used by American Indians.

tomato n. (pl. **tomatoes**) a red fruit eaten as a vegetable.

> USAGE No e at the end in the singular: *tomato*.

tomb n. a stone structure forming a burial place.
▷ SYNONYMS: **burial chamber**, vault, crypt, catacomb, sepulchre, mausoleum, grave.
□ **tombstone** a flat inscribed stone marking a grave.

> WORD LINKS
> **sepulchral** relating to a tomb

tombola n. Brit. a lottery in which tickets are drawn from a revolving drum.

tomboy n. a girl who enjoys rough, noisy activities.

tome n. a large book.

tomfoolery n. silly behaviour.

tomography n. a technique for displaying a cross section through the body using X-rays or ultrasound.

tomorrow adv. **1** on the day after today. **2** in the near future.
• n. **1** the day after today. **2** the near future.

tom-tom n. a drum beaten with the hands.

ton n. **1** a unit of weight equal to 2,240 lb or 1016.05 kg (**long ton**) or (especially in the US) 2,000 lb or 907.19 kg (**short ton**). **2** (or **tonne**) a metric ton. **3** a unit of measurement of a ship's weight equal to 2,240 lb or 35 cu. ft (0.99 cu. m). **4** informal a great weight or large number.

tone n. **1** the quality of a musical sound. **2** the feeling or mood expressed in a person's voice. **3** general character. **4** a basic interval in music, equal to two semitones. **5** a shade of colour. **6** firmness in a resting muscle.
▷ SYNONYMS: **1 sound**, timbre, voice, colour, tonality, intonation, inflection, modulation. **2 mood**, air, feel, flavour, note, attitude, character, spirit, vein. **3 shade**, colour, hue, tint, tinge.
• v. **1** give firmness to the body or a muscle. **2** (**tone down**) make less harsh or extreme. **3** harmonize with.
▷ SYNONYMS: **harmonize**, go, blend, coordinate, team, match, suit, complement.
□ **tone-deaf** unable to perceive differences of musical pitch.
■ **tonal** adj. **tonality** n. **tonally** adv. **toneless** adj.

toner n. **1** a liquid applied to the skin to reduce oiliness. **2** a powder used in photocopiers.

tongs pl. n. an implement with two joined arms for picking up and holding things.

tongue n. **1** the muscular organ in the mouth, used in tasting and speech. **2** a language. **3** a strip of leather or fabric under a shoe's laces.
□ **tongue in cheek** not seriously meaning what you are saying.
tongue-tied too nervous to speak.

tonic n. **1** a medicinal drink taken to give a feeling of energy or well-being. **2** (also **tonic water**) a carbonated soft drink with a bitter flavour.
▷ SYNONYMS: **stimulant**, boost, restorative, refresher, fillip; informal shot in the arm, pick-me-up, bracer.

tonight adv. on the present evening or night.
• n. the evening or night of the present day.

tonnage n. **1** weight in tons. **2** a ship's carrying capacity measured in tons.

tonne n. a metric ton.

tonsil n. either of two small masses of tissue in the throat.

tonsillitis n. inflammation of the tonsils.

tonsure n. a circular area on a monk's or priest's head where the hair is shaved off.
■ **tonsured** adj.

too adv. **1** more than is desirable or possible. **2** also.
▷ SYNONYMS: **1 excessively**, overly, unduly, immoderately, inordinately, unreasonably, extremely, very. **2 also**,

as well, in addition, into the bargain, besides, furthermore, moreover.

took past of TAKE.

tool n. **1** a device or implement used for a particular task. **2** a person used by another.
▷ SYNONYMS: **implement**, utensil, instrument, device, apparatus, gadget, appliance, machine, contrivance, contraption; informal gizmo.
• v. **1** impress a design on leather. **2** equip with tools.
□ **toolbar** Computing a strip of icons used to perform certain functions.

toot n. a short, sharp sound made by a horn, trumpet, etc.
• v. make a toot.

tooth n. (pl. **teeth**) **1** each of a set of hard white structures in the jaws, used for biting and chewing. **2** a cog on a gearwheel or a point on a saw or comb.
▷ SYNONYMS: **fang**, tusk; informal gnasher.
□ **toothpaste** a paste for cleaning the teeth. **toothpick** a thin, pointed piece of wood etc. for removing food stuck between the teeth.
■ **toothed** adj. **toothless** adj.

> **WORD LINKS**
> **dental** relating to teeth

toothy adj. having or showing large teeth.

top n. **1** the highest or uppermost point, part, or surface. **2** a thing placed on or covering the upper part of something. **3** the utmost degree. **4** a garment for the upper part of the body. **5** a toy with a pointed base, that can be made to spin.
▷ SYNONYMS: **1 summit**, peak, pinnacle, crest, crown, brow, head, tip, apex, apogee. **2 lid**, cap, cover, stopper, cork. **3** he was at the top of his career: **height**, peak, pinnacle, zenith, culmination, climax, prime.
− ANTONYMS: bottom, base.
• adj. highest in position, rank, or degree.
▷ SYNONYMS: **1 highest**, topmost, uppermost. **2 foremost**, chief, leading, principal, pre-eminent, greatest, best, finest, elite, premier, prime, superior, select, five-star, grade A. **3 maximum**, greatest, utmost.
− ANTONYMS: lowest, minimum.
• v. (**topping**, **topped**) **1** be more or better than. **2** be at the highest place or rank in. **3** reach the top of. **4** put a top or topping on. **5** (**top up**) fill up a partly full container.
▷ SYNONYMS: **1 exceed**, surpass, go beyond, better, beat, outstrip, outdo,

outshine, eclipse, transcend. **2** mousse topped with cream: **cover**, cap, coat, finish, garnish.
□ **topcoat 1** an overcoat. **2** an outer coat of paint. **top-dress** apply fertilizer on the top of soil. **top hat** a man's formal black hat with a high crown. **top-heavy** unstable because too heavy at the top. **topknot** a knot of hair arranged on the top of the head. **topsoil** the top layer of soil. **topspin** a fast forward spin given to a moving ball.
■ **topmost** adj.

topaz n. a colourless, yellow, or blue precious stone.

topiary n. the art of clipping shrubs or trees into attractive shapes.

topic n. a subject of a text, speech, etc.
▷ SYNONYMS: **subject**, theme, issue, matter, point, question, concern, argument, thesis.

topical adj. of or dealing with current affairs.
▷ SYNONYMS: **current**, up to date, up to the minute, contemporary, recent, relevant, in the news.
− ANTONYMS: out of date.
■ **topicality** n. **topically** adv.

topless adj. having the breasts uncovered.

topography n. the arrangement of the physical features of an area.
■ **topographical** adj.

topology n. the study of geometrical properties unaffected by changes in shape or size.

topping n. a layer of food poured or spread over another food.

topple v. overbalance or cause to overbalance and fall.
▷ SYNONYMS: **1 fall**, tumble, tip, overbalance, overturn, keel over, lose your balance. **2 knock over**, upset, push over, tip over, upend. **3 overthrow**, oust, unseat, overturn, bring down, defeat, get rid of, dislodge, eject.

topsy-turvy adj. & adv. **1** upside down. **2** in disorder.

tor n. a hill or rocky peak.

Torah n. (in Judaism) the law of God as revealed to Moses.

torch n. **1** Brit. a portable electric lamp. **2** a burning piece of wood etc. carried as a light.

tore past of TEAR¹.

toreador n. a bullfighter.

torment n. **1** great suffering. **2** a cause of this.
▷ SYNONYMS: **agony**, suffering, torture, pain, anguish, misery, distress, trauma.
• v. **1** cause to suffer greatly. **2** annoy

or tease unkindly.

▷ SYNONYMS: **1 torture**, afflict, rack, harrow, plague, haunt, agonize. **2 tease**, taunt, bait, provoke, harass, bother, persecute; informal needle.

■ **tormentor** n.

torn past part. of TEAR¹.

tornado n. (pl. **tornadoes** or **tornados**) a violent rotating wind storm.

▷ SYNONYMS: **whirlwind**, cyclone, typhoon, storm, hurricane; N. Amer. informal **twister**.

torpedo n. (pl. **torpedoes**) a self-propelled underwater missile.

• v. (**torpedoing**, **torpedoed**) attack or destroy with a torpedo.

torpid adj. sluggish and inactive.

■ **torpidity** n. **torpidly** adv. **torpor** n.

torque n. a force causing rotation.

torrent n. **1** a strong, fast-moving stream of liquid. **2** an outpouring.

▷ SYNONYMS: **1** *a torrent of water*: **flood**, deluge, spate, cascade, rush. **2** *a torrent of abuse*: **outburst**, outpouring, stream, flood, volley, barrage, tide.

– ANTONYMS: trickle.

■ **torrential** adj.

torrid adj. **1** very hot and dry. **2** passionate.

torsion n. the state of being twisted.

torso n. (pl. **torsos**) the trunk of the human body.

tort n. Law a wrongful act or a violation of a right for which damages may be claimed.

tortellini /tor-tuh-lee-ni/ n. stuffed pasta parcels rolled into small rings.

tortilla /tor-tee-yuh/ n. a thin, flat maize pancake.

tortoise n. a slow-moving reptile with a domed shell.

□ **tortoiseshell 1** the mottled brown and yellow shell of certain turtles, used to make ornaments. **2** a cat with markings that resemble tortoiseshell.

tortuous adj. **1** full of twists and turns. **2** lengthy and complex.

▷ SYNONYMS: **1 twisting**, winding, zigzag, sinuous, snaky, meandering, serpentine. **2 convoluted**, complicated, complex, labyrinthine, involved, Byzantine, lengthy.

– ANTONYMS: straight.

■ **tortuously** adv.

torture n. **1** the inflicting of severe pain as a punishment or means of coercion. **2** great suffering.

▷ SYNONYMS: **1 abuse**, ill-treatment, mistreatment, maltreatment, persecution, cruelty, atrocity.

2 torment, agony, suffering, pain, anguish, misery, distress, heartbreak, trauma.

• v. inflict torture on.

▷ SYNONYMS: **1 abuse**, ill-treat, mistreat, maltreat, persecute. **2 torment**, rack, afflict, harrow, plague, distress, trouble.

■ **torturer** n. **torturous** adj.

Tory n. (pl. **Tories**) a member or supporter of the British Conservative Party.

toss v. **1** throw lightly. **2** move from side to side. **3** throw a coin into the air to make a choice based on which side lands uppermost. **4** turn food in a liquid to coat it lightly.

▷ SYNONYMS: **1 throw**, hurl, fling, sling, pitch, lob, launch; informal heave, chuck, bung. **2** *he tossed a coin*: **flip**, flick, spin. **3 pitch**, lurch, rock, roll, plunge, reel, sway.

• n. an act of tossing.

tot n. **1** a very young child. **2** a small drink of spirits.

• v. (**totting**, **totted**) (**tot up**) add up.

total adj. **1** comprising the whole number or amount. **2** complete.

▷ SYNONYMS: **1 entire**, complete, whole, full, combined, aggregate, gross, overall. **2 utter**, complete, absolute, thorough, perfect, downright, out-and-out, outright, sheer, unmitigated, unqualified, unalloyed.

– ANTONYMS: partial.

• n. a total number or amount.

▷ SYNONYMS: **sum**, aggregate, whole, entirety, totality.

• v. (**totalling**, **totalled**; US **totaling**, **totaled**) **1** amount to. **2** find the total of.

▷ SYNONYMS: **1 add up to**, amount to, come to, run to, make. **2** *he totalled up his score*: **add**, count, reckon, tot up, compute, work out.

■ **totality** n.

totalitarian adj. (of government) consisting of only one leader or party and having complete control.

▷ SYNONYMS: **autocratic**, undemocratic, one-party, dictatorial, tyrannical, despotic, fascist, oppressive, authoritarian, absolutist.

– ANTONYMS: democratic.

■ **totalitarianism** n.

totalizator (or **totalisator**) n. a device showing the number and amount of bets staked on a race.

totally adv. completely.

▷ SYNONYMS: **completely**, entirely, wholly, thoroughly, fully, utterly, absolutely, perfectly, unreservedly,

t

unconditionally, downright.
– ANTONYMS: partly.
tote informal v. carry.
  • n. a system of betting using the totalizator.
totem n. a natural object or animal believed to have spiritual significance and adopted as an emblem.
  □ **totem pole** a pole decorated with totems.
totter v. walk or rock unsteadily.
toucan n. a tropical American bird with a massive bill.
touch v. **1** come into or be in physical contact with. **2** bring the hand or another part of the body into contact with. **3** harm or interfere with. **4** affect. **5** (**be touched**) feel gratitude or sympathy.
  ▷ SYNONYMS: **1 contact**, meet, brush, graze, come up against, be in contact with; border, abut. **2 feel**, pat, tap, stroke, fondle, caress, pet, handle. **3** *don't touch any of my stuff:* **interfere with**, meddle with, fiddle with, tamper with, disturb; informal mess about with. **4** *his story really touched me:* **affect**, move, stir, make an impression on. **5** *sales touched £20,000:* **reach**, attain, come to, make, rise to, soar to; informal hit. **6** *no one can touch him:* **compare with**, be on a par with, equal, match, rival, measure up to, better, beat; informal hold a candle to.
  • n. **1** an act or way of touching. **2** the ability to perceive something through physical contact. **3** a small amount. **4** a detail or feature. **5** a way of dealing with something.
  ▷ SYNONYMS: **1 tap**, pat, contact, stroke, caress. **2 trace**, bit, suggestion, suspicion, hint, scintilla, tinge, dash, taste, spot, drop, dab, soupçon. **3** *the gas lights are a nice touch:* **detail**, feature, point, element, addition. **4 skill**, expertise, dexterity, deftness, adroitness, adeptness, ability, talent, flair, facility, proficiency, knack.
  □ **in touch** in communication. **touch-and-go** (of an outcome) uncertain. **touch down** (of an aircraft) land. **touchline** the boundary line on each side of a rugby or football field. **touch on** deal briefly with. **touchstone** a standard by which something is judged. **touch up** make small improvements to.

WORD LINKS
tactile relating to the sense of touch

touché /too-**shay**/ exclam. used to acknowledge a good point made at your expense.
touching adj. arousing gratitude or sympathy; moving.
  ▷ SYNONYMS: **moving**, affecting, heart-warming, emotional, emotive, poignant, sad, tear-jerking.
touchy adj. (**touchier, touchiest**) quick to take offence.
  ▷ SYNONYMS: **1 sensitive**, oversensitive, hypersensitive, easily offended, thin-skinned, highly strung, tense, irritable, tetchy, testy, crotchety, peevish, querulous, bad-tempered, petulant; informal snappy, ratty; N. Amer. informal cranky. **2 delicate**, sensitive, tricky, ticklish, embarrassing, awkward, difficult, contentious, controversial.
tough adj. **1** strong enough to withstand wear and tear. **2** able to endure difficulty or pain. **3** strict. **4** involving difficulty or hardship. **5** (of a person) violent.
  ▷ SYNONYMS: **1 durable**, strong, resilient, sturdy, rugged, solid, stout, robust, hard-wearing, long-lasting, heavy-duty, well built, made to last. **2** *tough new laws on smoking:* **strict**, stringent, rigorous, stern, severe, hard, firm, hard-hitting, uncompromising. **3** *the training was pretty tough:* **difficult**, hard, strenuous, onerous, gruelling, exacting, arduous, demanding, taxing, tiring, exhausting, punishing. **4** *tough questions:* **difficult**, hard, knotty, thorny, tricky. **5** *the meat was dry and tough:* **chewy**, leathery, gristly, stringy, fibrous.
  – ANTONYMS: weak, lenient, easy.
  ■ **toughen** v. **toughness** n.
toupee /**too**-pay/ n. a small wig.
tour n. **1** a journey for pleasure in which several places are visited. **2** a series of performances or matches in several places.
  ▷ SYNONYMS: **1 trip**, excursion, journey, expedition, jaunt, outing, trek. **2** *a tour of the factory:* **visit**, inspection, walkabout.
  • v. make a tour of.
  ▷ SYNONYMS: **travel round**, visit, explore, holiday in, go round.
  □ **tour de force** something accomplished with great skill.
tourism n. the commercial organization of holidays and services for tourists.
tourist n. a person visiting a place for pleasure.
  ▷ SYNONYMS: **holidaymaker**, traveller, sightseer, visitor, backpacker, globe-trotter, tripper; N. Amer. vacationer.
  – ANTONYMS: local.

tourmaline n. a mineral used in jewellery and electrical devices.

tournament n. a sporting contest consisting of a number of matches.
▷ SYNONYMS: **competition**, contest, championship, meeting, event.

tourniquet /toor-ni-kay/ n. a bandage tied tightly round a limb to stop the flow of blood through an artery.

tousle v. make a person's hair untidy.

tout v. 1 try to sell. 2 Brit. resell a ticket for an event at a price higher than the official one.
• n. Brit. a person who buys up tickets for an event to resell them at a profit.

tow v. pull along behind.
▷ SYNONYMS: **pull**, haul, drag, draw, tug, lug.
• n. an act of towing.
□ **towpath** a path beside a river or canal, originally for horses towing barges.

towards (or toward) prep. 1 in the direction of. 2 in relation to. 3 contributing to the cost of.

towel n. a piece of absorbent cloth or paper used for drying.
• v. (**towelling, towelled**; US **toweling, toweled**) dry with a towel.

towelling (US **toweling**) n. absorbent cloth used for towels.

tower n. 1 a tall, narrow building or part of a building. 2 a tall structure.
• v. be very tall.
▷ SYNONYMS: **soar**, rise, rear, overshadow, overhang, hang over, dominate.
□ **tower block** Brit. a tall modern building with many storeys.

town n. 1 a settlement larger than a village. 2 the central business or shopping area of a town or city.
▷ SYNONYMS: **city**, metropolis, conurbation, municipality; Brit. borough; Scottish burgh.
– ANTONYMS: country.
□ **town hall** a building housing local government offices. **township** (in South Africa) a suburb or city mainly inhabited by black people.

> WORD LINKS
> **civic**, **municipal**, **urban** relating to a town

toxaemia (US **toxemia**) /tok-see-mi-uh/ n. blood poisoning.

toxic adj. 1 poisonous. 2 of or caused by poison.
▷ SYNONYMS: **poisonous**, dangerous, harmful, injurious, noxious, pernicious, deadly, lethal.
– ANTONYMS: harmless.

■ **toxicity** n.

toxicology n. the study of poisons.
■ **toxicologist** n.

toxin n. a poison produced by a living organism.

toy n. an object to play with.
▷ SYNONYMS: **plaything**, game.
• v. (**toy with**) 1 consider casually. 2 move or touch idly or nervously.
• adj. (of a breed of dog) very small.
▷ SYNONYMS: **model**, imitation, replica, miniature.

trace v. 1 find or follow by careful investigation. 2 copy a design etc. by drawing over it on transparent paper. 3 draw an outline.
▷ SYNONYMS: 1 **track down**, find, discover, detect, unearth, turn up, hunt down, ferret out, run to ground. 2 **draw**, outline, mark.
• n. 1 a mark or other sign of the existence or passing of something. 2 a very small amount. 3 a slight indication. 4 each of the two straps by which a horse pulls a vehicle.
▷ SYNONYMS: 1 **sign**, mark, indication, evidence, clue, vestige, remains, remnant. 2 **bit**, touch, hint, suggestion, suspicion, shadow, dash, tinge; informal smidgen, tad.
□ **trace element** a chemical element that is present or required only in tiny amounts.
■ **traceable** adj.

tracery n. (pl. **traceries**) a decorative pattern of interlacing lines, esp. in stone.

trachea /truh-kee-uh/ n. (pl. **tracheae** or **tracheas**) the windpipe.

tracheotomy n. (pl. **tracheotomies**) a surgical incision made in the windpipe.

tracing n. a copy of a drawing or map made by tracing.

track n. 1 a rough path or road. 2 a prepared course for racing. 3 a line of marks left by a person etc. in passing. 4 a railway line. 5 a section of a record, compact disc, etc. 6 a jointed metal band around the wheels of a heavy vehicle.
▷ SYNONYMS: 1 **path**, footpath, lane, trail, route, way. 2 **course**, racecourse, racetrack, velodrome; Brit. circuit. 3 the tracks of a fox: **traces**, marks, prints, footprints, trail, spoor. 4 the railway tracks: **rail**, line. 5 **song**, recording, number, piece.
• v. 1 follow the trail or course of. 2 (**track down**) find after a thorough search.
▷ SYNONYMS: **follow**, trail, pursue,

t

shadow, stalk; informal **tail**.
□ **track record** a person's past achievements. **tracksuit** an outfit consisting of a loose sweatshirt and trousers.
■ **tracker** n.

tract n. **1** a large area of land. **2** a major passage in the body. **3** a pamphlet on a religious or political subject.

tractable adj. easy to deal with or control.
■ **tractability** n.

traction n. **1** the act of pulling a thing along a surface. **2** the exertion of a sustained pull on a limb to keep a broken bone in position. **3** the grip of a tyre on a road.

tractor n. a powerful vehicle for pulling farm equipment.

trade n. **1** the buying and selling of goods and services. **2** a job requiring manual skills and training. **3** the people engaged in a particular business.
▷ SYNONYMS: **1 commerce**, business, buying and selling, dealing, traffic. **2 occupation**, work, craft, job, career, profession, business, métier.
• v. **1** buy and sell goods and services. **2** exchange. **3** give a used article as partial payment for a new one. **4** (**trade on**) take advantage of. **5** (**trade off**) exchange as a compromise.
▷ SYNONYMS: **1 deal**, do business, bargain, negotiate, buy and sell, merchandise; traffic. **2** *I traded the car for a newer model:* **swap**, exchange, barter, part-exchange.
□ **trademark** a symbol, word, or words chosen to represent a company or product. **tradesman** a person engaged in trading or a trade. **trade union** an organized association of workers formed to protect and promote their rights and interests. **trade wind** a wind blowing steadily towards the equator.

> **WORD LINKS**
> **mercantile** relating to trade

trader n. a person who trades goods, services, etc.
▷ SYNONYMS: **dealer**, merchant, buyer, seller, vendor, purveyor, supplier; trafficker.

tradition n. **1** the passing on of customs or beliefs from generation to generation. **2** a long-established custom.
▷ SYNONYMS: **custom**, practice, convention, ritual, observance, way, usage,

habit, institution, unwritten law; formal praxis.

traditional adj. relating to or following tradition.
▷ SYNONYMS: **customary**, long-established, time-honoured, classic, wonted, accustomed, standard, regular, normal, conventional, habitual, ritual, age-old.
■ **traditionally** adv.

traditionalism n. the upholding of tradition, esp. to resist change.
■ **traditionalist** n. & adj.

traduce v. slander.

traffic n. **1** vehicles, ships, or aircraft moving along a route. **2** the act of trading in something illegal.
• v. (**trafficking**, **trafficked**) trade in something illegal.
□ **traffic warden** Brit. an official who locates and reports on vehicles breaking parking regulations.
■ **trafficker** n.

tragedian n. **1** an actor who plays tragic roles. **2** a writer of tragedies.

tragedy n. (pl. **tragedies**) **1** an event causing great sadness or suffering. **2** a serious play with an unhappy ending.
▷ SYNONYMS: **disaster**, calamity, catastrophe, cataclysm, misfortune, adversity.

tragic adj. **1** very sad. **2** of dramatic tragedy.
▷ SYNONYMS: **1 disastrous**, calamitous, catastrophic, cataclysmic, devastating, terrible, dreadful, awful, appalling, horrendous, fatal. **2 sad**, unhappy, pathetic, moving, distressing, painful, harrowing, heart-rending, sorry.
– ANTONYMS: fortunate, happy.
■ **tragically** adv.

tragicomedy n. (pl. **tragicomedies**) a play or novel containing elements of both comedy and tragedy.
■ **tragicomic** adj.

trail n. **1** a series of signs left behind by a person etc. in passing. **2** a long thin part stretching behind or hanging down. **3** a line of people or things. **4** a path.
▷ SYNONYMS: **1** *a trail of clues:* **series**, string, chain, succession, sequence. **2 track**, spoor, path, scent, traces, marks, signs, prints, footprints. **3 path**, way, footpath, track, route.
• v. **1** draw or be drawn along behind. **2** follow the trail of. **3** walk or move slowly or wearily. **4** (**trail away/off**) (of the voice) fade gradually. **5** be losing to an opponent in a contest.

▷ SYNONYMS: **1 drag**, sweep, be drawn, dangle. **2** *roses trailed over the banks:* **hang**, droop, fall, spill, cascade. **3 follow**, pursue, track, shadow, stalk, hunt; informal **tail**. **4 lose**, be down, be behind, lag behind.

trailer n. **1** an unpowered vehicle pulled by another. **2** an extract from a film etc. used to advertise it.

train v. **1** teach a particular skill to. **2** learn a particular skill. **3** become physically fit through exercise. **4** (**train on**) point at. **5** make a plant grow in a particular direction or shape.
▷ SYNONYMS: **1 instruct**, teach, coach, tutor, school, educate, prime, drill, ground. **2 study**, learn, prepare, take instruction. **3 exercise**, work out, get into shape, practise. **4 aim**, point, direct, level, focus.
• n. **1** a series of railway carriages or wagons moved by a locomotive. **2** a line of vehicles or pack animals. **3** a series of connected events or thoughts. **4** a long piece of trailing material at the back of a dress.
▷ SYNONYMS: **chain**, string, series, set, sequence, succession, course.

trainee n. a person being trained.

trainer n. **1** a person who trains people or animals. **2** Brit. a soft shoe for sports or casual wear.
▷ SYNONYMS: **coach**, instructor, teacher, tutor, handler.

traipse v. walk or move wearily.

trait n. a characteristic.
▷ SYNONYMS: **characteristic**, attribute, feature, quality, habit, mannerism, idiosyncrasy, peculiarity.

traitor n. a person who betrays their country or a cause.
▷ SYNONYMS: **betrayer**, back-stabber, double-crosser, renegade, Judas, quisling, fifth columnist, turncoat, defector; informal **snake in the grass**.
■ **traitorous** adj.

trajectory n. (pl. **trajectories**) the path of an object moving through the air.

tram (or **tramcar**) n. Brit. a passenger vehicle powered by electricity and running on rails (**tramlines**) laid in a public road.

trammel v. (**trammelling**, **trammelled**; US **trammeling**, **trammeled**) hamper or restrict.

tramp v. **1** walk heavily or noisily. **2** walk wearily over a long distance.
▷ SYNONYMS: **trudge**, plod, stamp, trample, lumber, trek, walk, slog, hike; informal **traipse**; N. Amer. informal **schlep**.

• n. **1** a homeless person who travels around and lives by begging. **2** the sound of heavy steps. **3** a long walk. **4** a cargo vessel that does not sail a fixed route.
▷ SYNONYMS: **1 vagrant**, vagabond, homeless person, down-and-out, traveller, drifter; N. Amer. **hobo**; N. Amer. informal **bum**. **2 tread**, step, footstep, footfall. **3 trek**, walk, hike, slog, march, roam, ramble; N. Amer. informal **schlep**.

trample v. tread on and crush.
▷ SYNONYMS: **tread**, stamp, walk, squash, crush, flatten.

trampoline n. a strong fabric sheet connected by springs to a frame, used for performing acrobatic leaps.
■ **trampolining** n.

trance n. a half-conscious state.
▷ SYNONYMS: **daze**, stupor, hypnotic state, dream, reverie.

tranquil adj. free from disturbance; calm.
▷ SYNONYMS: **peaceful**, calm, restful, quiet, still, serene, relaxing, undisturbed.
– ANTONYMS: busy, excitable.
■ **tranquillity** n. **tranquilly** adv.

tranquillize (or **tranquillise**; US **tranquilize**) v. give a calming or sedative drug to.

tranquillizer (or **tranquilliser**; US **tranquilizer**) n. a drug used to reduce tension or anxiety.
▷ SYNONYMS: **sedative**, barbiturate, calmative, narcotic, opiate; informal **downer**.
– ANTONYMS: stimulant.

transact v. conduct or carry out business.

transaction n. an act of buying or selling, or the action of conducting business.
▷ SYNONYMS: **deal**, bargain, agreement, undertaking, arrangement, negotiation, settlement.

transatlantic adj. **1** crossing the Atlantic. **2** of or on the other side of the Atlantic.

transceiver n. a radio transmitter and receiver.

transcend v. **1** be or go beyond the range or limits of. **2** be better than.
▷ SYNONYMS: **go beyond**, rise above, exceed, surpass, excel, outstrip.
■ **transcendence** n. **transcendent** adj.

transcendental adj. of a spiritual or mystical realm.

transcontinental adj. crossing or extending across a continent.

transcribe v. **1** put into written form, or into a different written form.

t

2 arrange a piece of music for a different instrument.
■ **transcription** n.

transcript n. a written version of material that was originally spoken or in another form.

transducer n. a device that converts variations in a physical medium into an electrical signal, or vice versa.

transept n. a part lying at right angles to the nave in a church.

transfer v. (**transferring**, **transferred**) **1** move from one place etc. to another. **2** pass property etc. to another person.
▷ SYNONYMS: **move**, take, bring, shift, convey, remove, carry, transport, relocate.
• n. **1** an act of transferring. **2** Brit. a small picture which can be transferred to another surface by being pressed or heated.
■ **transferable** adj. **transference** n.

transfigure v. transform into something more beautiful or spiritual.
■ **transfiguration** n.

transfix v. **1** make motionless with fear or astonishment. **2** pierce with a sharp object.

transform v. **1** change or be changed in appearance or nature. **2** change the voltage of an electric current.
▷ SYNONYMS: **change**, alter, convert, metamorphose; revolutionize, overhaul, reconstruct, rebuild, reorganize, rearrange, rework; humorous transmogrify.

transformation n. a marked change in appearance or nature.
▷ SYNONYMS: **change**, sea change, alteration, conversion, metamorphosis, revolution, overhaul, reconstruction, rebuilding, reorganization, rearrangement, reworking; humorous transmogrification.

transformer n. a device for changing the voltage of an electric current.

transfuse v. **1** give a transfusion of blood to someone. **2** permeate or imbue.

transfusion n. a medical process in which blood is transferred from one person or animal to another.

transgress v. go beyond what is morally or legally acceptable.
■ **transgression** n. **transgressor** n.

transient adj. lasting only for a short time.
▷ SYNONYMS: **transitory**, temporary, short-lived, short-term, ephemeral, impermanent, brief, short,

momentary, fleeting, passing.
– ANTONYMS: permanent.
■ **transience** n.

transistor n. **1** a semiconductor device able to amplify or rectify an electric current. **2** a portable radio using circuits containing transistors.

transit n. **1** the carrying of people or things from one place to another. **2** an act of passing through a place.

transition n. the process of changing from one state or condition to another.
▷ SYNONYMS: **change**, passage, move, transformation, conversion, metamorphosis, alteration, changeover, shift, switch.

transitional adj. relating to a period of transition.
▷ SYNONYMS: **intermediate**, interim, temporary, provisional, pro tem; changing, fluid.

transitive adj. (of a verb) taking a direct object.
■ **transitivity** n.

transitory adj. short-lived.

translate v. express or be expressed in another language.
▷ SYNONYMS: **interpret**, convert, render, put, change, express, decipher, reword, decode, gloss, explain.
■ **translation** n. **translator** n.

transliterate v. write a letter or word using the letters of a different alphabet or language.
■ **transliteration** n.

translucent adj. allowing light to pass through partially.
■ **translucence** (or **translucency**) n.

transmigration n. the passing of the soul into another body after death.

transmission n. **1** the act of transmitting. **2** the mechanism transmitting power from an engine to the axle in a vehicle.
▷ SYNONYMS: **1 transfer**, communication, passing on, conveyance, dissemination, spread, circulation, relaying. **2 broadcasting**, televising, airing. **3 broadcast**, programme, show.

transmit v. (**transmitting**, **transmitted**) **1** cause to pass on from one place, person, or thing to another. **2** send out an electrical signal or a radio or television programme.
▷ SYNONYMS: **1 transfer**, communicate, pass on, hand on, convey, impart, channel, carry, relay, dispatch, disseminate, spread, circulate. **2 broadcast**, send out, air, televise.
■ **transmissible** adj. **transmittable** adj. **transmitter** n.

transmogrify v. (**transmogrifying**, **transmogrified**) transform in a surprising or magical way.

transmute v. change in form or substance.
■ **transmutation** n.

transom n. **1** the flat surface forming the stern of a boat. **2** a crossbar above a door or window.

transparency n. (pl. **transparencies**) **1** the condition of being transparent. **2** a photographic slide.

transparent adj. **1** able to be seen through. **2** obvious or evident.
▷ SYNONYMS: **1 clear**, translucent, limpid, crystal clear, crystalline, pellucid. **2 see-through**, sheer, filmy, gauzy, diaphanous. **3 obvious**, blatant, unambiguous, unequivocal, clear, plain, apparent, unmistakable, manifest, conspicuous, patent.
– ANTONYMS: opaque, obscure.
■ **transparently** adv.

transpire v. **1** become known. **2** happen. **3** (of a plant) give off water vapour from the leaves.
■ **transpiration** n.

transplant v. **1** transfer to another place or situation. **2** take living tissue and put it in another body or part of the body.
• n. **1** an operation in which living tissue is transplanted. **2** something transplanted.
■ **transplantation** n.

transport v. carry people or goods from one place to another.
▷ SYNONYMS: **convey**, carry, take, transfer, move, shift, send, deliver, bear, ship, ferry; informal cart.
• n. **1** a system, means, or the act of transporting. **2** (**transports**) strong emotions.
▷ SYNONYMS: **conveyance**, carriage, delivery, shipping, freight, shipment, haulage.
■ **transportation** n. **transporter** n.

transpose v. **1** cause two or more things to change places. **2** move to a different place or situation. **3** write or play music in a different key.
■ **transposition** n.

transsexual (or **transexual**) n. a person who emotionally and psychologically feels that they belong to the opposite sex.

transubstantiation n. the doctrine that the bread and wine of the Eucharist are converted by consecration into the body and blood of Christ.

transverse adj. placed or extending across something.

transvestite n. a person who derives pleasure from dressing in clothes worn by the opposite sex.
■ **transvestism** n.

trap n. **1** a device for catching and holding animals. **2** a scheme for tricking or catching someone. **3** a curve in a waste pipe that holds liquid to prevent gases from coming up. **4** a compartment from which a dog is released at the start of a race. **5** a two-wheeled horse-drawn carriage.
▷ SYNONYMS: **1 snare**, net, mesh, gin; N. Amer. deadfall. **2 trick**, ploy, ruse, deception, subterfuge; informal set-up.
• v. (**trapping**, **trapped**) catch or hold in a trap.
▷ SYNONYMS: **1 snare**, entrap, capture, catch, ambush. **2 confine**, cut off, corner, shut in, pen in, hem in, imprison. **3 trick**, dupe, deceive, fool, hoodwink.
□ **trapdoor** a hinged or removable panel in a floor, ceiling, or roof.

trapeze n. a hanging horizontal bar used by circus acrobats.

trapezium n. (pl. **trapezia** or **trapeziums**) Brit. a quadrilateral with one pair of sides parallel.

trapezoid n. Brit. a quadrilateral with no sides parallel.

trapper n. a person who traps wild animals.

trappings pl. n. the signs or objects associated with a particular status or role.

trash n. **1** US waste material. **2** poor-quality writing etc.
▷ SYNONYMS: **1 rubbish**, refuse, waste, litter, junk; N. Amer. garbage. **2 nonsense**, rubbish, trivia, pulp fiction, pap; informal drivel.
• v. informal wreck or destroy.
■ **trashy** adj.

trattoria n. an Italian restaurant.

trauma n. **1** a deeply distressing experience. **2** emotional shock following a stressful event. **3** physical injury.
▷ SYNONYMS: **1 shock**, upheaval, distress, stress, strain, pain, anguish, suffering, upset, ordeal. **2 injury**, damage, wound.
■ **traumatize** (or **-ise**) v.

traumatic adj. **1** deeply distressing. **2** relating to emotional or physical trauma.
▷ SYNONYMS: **disturbing**, shocking, distressing, upsetting, painful, agonizing, hurtful, stressful, devastating, harrowing.

t

travail n. old use labour.

travel v. (**travelling, travelled;** US **traveling, traveled**) **1** go from one place to another. **2** journey along or through.

▷ SYNONYMS: **journey**, tour, take a trip, voyage, go sightseeing, globetrot, backpack, trek.

•n. **1** the act of travelling. **2** (**travels**) journeys over a long distance.

▷ SYNONYMS: **travelling**, journeys, expeditions, trips, tours, excursions, voyages, treks, wanderings, jaunts.

traveller (US **traveler**) n. **1** a person who travels. **2** Brit. a Gypsy or other nomadic person.

▷ SYNONYMS: **tourist**, tripper, holiday-maker, sightseer, globetrotter, backpacker, passenger, commuter; N. Amer. vacationer.

□ **traveller's cheque** a cheque for a fixed amount that can be exchanged for cash in foreign countries.

travelogue n. a film, book, etc. about a person's travels.

traverse v. travel or extend across.

travesty n. (pl. **travesties**) an absurd or shocking misrepresentation.

trawl v. **1** catch fish with a trawl net. **2** search through thoroughly.

•n. **1** an act of trawling. **2** (or **trawl net**) a large wide-mouthed fishing net.

trawler n. a boat used for trawling.

tray n. a shallow container with a rim for carrying things.

treacherous adj. **1** guilty of or involving betrayal. **2** having hidden dangers.

▷ SYNONYMS: **1 traitorous**, disloyal, unfaithful, duplicitous, deceitful, false, back-stabbing, double-crossing, two-faced, untrustworthy, unreliable, apostate, renegade. **2 dangerous**, hazardous, perilous, unsafe, precarious, risky; informal dicey, hairy.

– ANTONYMS: loyal, faithful.

■ **treacherously** adv. **treachery** n.

treacle n. Brit. a thick sticky liquid produced when sugar is refined.

■ **treacly** adj.

tread v. (**treading, trod;** past part. **trodden** or **trod**) **1** walk in a specified way. **2** press down or crush with the feet. **3** walk on or along.

▷ SYNONYMS: **1 walk**, step, stride, pace, march, tramp, plod, stomp, trudge. **2 crush**, flatten, press down, squash, trample on, stamp on.

•n. **1** a way or the sound of walking. **2** the top surface of a step or stair. **3** the part of a vehicle tyre that grips the road.

▷ SYNONYMS: **step**, footstep, footfall, tramp.

□ **treadmill 1** a large wheel turned by the weight of people or animals treading on steps fitted into it, formerly used to drive machinery. **2** a tiring or boring job. **tread water** keep upright in deep water by making a walking movement.

treadle n. a lever worked by the foot to operate a machine.

treason n. the crime of betraying your country.

▷ SYNONYMS: **treachery**, disloyalty, betrayal, sedition, subversion, mutiny, rebellion.

■ **treasonable** adj.

treasure n. **1** a quantity of precious metals, gems, or other valuables. **2** a very valuable object. **3** informal a highly valued person.

▷ SYNONYMS: **1 riches**, valuables, jewels, gems, gold, silver, precious metals, money, cash, wealth, fortune. **2 masterpiece**, gem, pearl, jewel.

•v. **1** look after carefully. **2** value highly.

▷ SYNONYMS: **cherish**, hold dear, prize, set great store by, value greatly.

□ **treasure trove** valuables of unknown ownership, found hidden.

treasurer n. a person in charge of the finances of a society etc.

treasury n. (pl. **treasuries**) **1** the funds or revenue of a state, society, etc. **2** (**Treasury**) (in some countries) the government department responsible for the overall management of the economy.

▷ SYNONYMS: **storehouse**, repository, treasure house, exchequer, fund, mine, bank, coffers, purse.

treat v. **1** behave towards or deal with in a certain way. **2** give medical care or attention to. **3** apply a process or a substance to. **4** (**treat to**) provide with food, drink, etc. at your expense.

▷ SYNONYMS: **1** *police are treating the fires as arson*: **regard**, consider, view, look on, put down as. **2** *the issue is treated more fully in chapter five*: **deal with**, tackle, handle, discuss, explore, investigate. **3 tend**, nurse, attend to. **4** *he treated them to lunch*: **buy**, stand, pay for; informal foot the bill for. **5** *the crowd was treated to a superb display*: **entertain with**, regale with, fete with.

•n. a surprise gift, event, etc. that gives great pleasure.

▷ SYNONYMS: **1 celebration**, entertainment, amusement, surprise.

2 present, gift, titbit, delicacy, luxury, indulgence, extravagance; informal goody.

treatise n. a formal written work on a subject.

treatment n. **1** a way of treating someone or something. **2** medical care for an illness or injury.

▷ SYNONYMS: **1 behaviour**, conduct, handling, management, dealings. **2 discussion**, investigation, exploration, consideration, study, analysis. **3 care**, therapy, nursing, ministrations; medication, medicament, drugs.

treaty n. (pl. **treaties**) a formal agreement between states.

▷ SYNONYMS: **agreement**, settlement, pact, deal, entente, concordat, accord, protocol, compact, convention; formal concord.

treble adj. three times as much or as many.

• n. **1** an amount three times as large as usual. **2** a high-pitched voice, esp. a boy's singing voice.

• v. make or become treble.

tree n. a woody perennial plant with a single thick stem and branches that can grow to a great height.

> **WORD LINKS**
> **arboreal** relating to trees

trefoil n. **1** a plant with three-lobed leaves. **2** a design in the form of three rounded lobes.

trek n. a long difficult journey, esp. on foot.

▷ SYNONYMS: **journey**, trip, expedition, safari, hike, march, tramp, walk.
• v. (**trekking**, **trekked**) go on a trek.
■ **trekker** n.

trellis n. a framework of bars used to support climbing plants.

tremble v. **1** shake uncontrollably from fear, excitement, etc. **2** be very frightened.

▷ SYNONYMS: **shake**, quiver, shudder, judder, vibrate, wobble, rock, move, sway.
• n. a trembling movement.

tremendous adj. **1** very great. **2** informal very good or impressive.

▷ SYNONYMS: **1 huge**, enormous, immense, colossal, massive, prodigious, stupendous; informal whopping, astronomical; Brit. informal ginormous. **2 excellent**, first-class, outstanding, marvellous, wonderful, splendid, superb, admirable; informal great, fantastic, fabulous, terrific, super, awesome, ace; Brit. informal bril-

liant, smashing.
■ **tremendously** adv.

tremolo n. (pl. **tremolos**) a wavering effect in singing or music.

tremor n. **1** a trembling movement. **2** a slight earthquake. **3** a sudden feeling of fear or excitement.

tremulous adj. shaking slightly.

trench n. a deep ditch.

▷ SYNONYMS: **ditch**, channel, trough, excavation, furrow, rut, conduit.

trenchant adj. (of speech or writing) expressed strongly and clearly.
■ **trenchantly** adv.

trencher n. hist. a wooden platter.

trend n. **1** a general tendency. **2** a fashion.

▷ SYNONYMS: **1 tendency**, movement, drift, swing, shift, course, current, direction, inclination, leaning. **2 fashion**, vogue, style, mode, craze, mania, rage; informal fad, thing.
□ **trendsetter** a person leading the way in fashion or ideas.

trendy adj. (**trendier**, **trendiest**) informal fashionable.
■ **trendily** adv. **trendiness** n.

trepidation n. nervousness.

trespass v. enter land or property without permission.

▷ SYNONYMS: **intrude**, encroach, invade.
• n. the act of trespassing.
■ **trespasser** n.

tress n. a lock of hair.

trestle n. a framework of a horizontal bar on sloping legs, used in pairs to support a surface such as a table top.

trews pl. n. trousers.

triad n. a group or set of three.

trial n. **1** an examination of evidence in a law court to decide if a person is guilty of a crime. **2** a test of performance or quality. **3** something that tries a person's patience.

▷ SYNONYMS: **1 case**, lawsuit, hearing, tribunal, litigation, proceedings. **2 test**, experiment, pilot study, examination, check, assessment, audition, evaluation, appraisal; informal dry run. **3 trouble**, affliction, ordeal, tribulation, difficulty, problem, misfortune, mishap.
• v. (**trialling**, **trialled**; US **trialing**, **trialed**) test to assess performance etc.
□ **on trial 1** being tried in a law court. **2** undergoing tests.

triangle n. **1** a figure with three straight sides and three angles. **2** a triangular steel rod used as a percussion instrument.
■ **triangular** adj.

t

triangulation n. the division of an area into a series of triangles to determine distances and relative positions.

triathlon n. an athletic contest involving three different events.

tribe n. a social group in a traditional society consisting of linked families.
▷ SYNONYMS: **ethnic group**, people, family, clan, race, dynasty, house, nation.
■ **tribal** adj. **tribesman** n.

tribulation n. trouble or suffering.

tribunal n. Brit. a board of officials appointed to settle disputes.
▷ SYNONYMS: **court**, board, panel, committee.

tributary n. (pl. **tributaries**) a river flowing into a larger river or lake.

tribute n. **1** an act, statement, or gift intended to show gratitude or respect. **2** hist. a payment made by a state to a more powerful one.
▷ SYNONYMS: **accolade**, praise, commendation, salute, testimonial, homage, congratulations, compliments, plaudits.
– ANTONYMS: criticism.

trice n. (**in a trice**) in an instant.

triceps n. (pl. **triceps**) the large muscle at the back of the upper arm.

trichology /tri-kol-uh-ji/ n. the study of the hair and scalp and their diseases.
■ **trichologist** n.

trick n. **1** something done to deceive or outwit someone. **2** a skilful act performed for entertainment. **3** a mannerism.
▷ SYNONYMS: **1 stratagem**, ploy, ruse, scheme, device, manoeuvre, dodge, subterfuge, swindle, fraud; informal con, set-up, scam, sting. **2 practical joke**, hoax, prank; informal leg-pull, spoof, put-on. **3 knack**, skill, technique, secret, art.
• v. deceive or outwit.
▷ SYNONYMS: **deceive**, delude, hoodwink, mislead, take in, dupe, fool, gull, cheat, defraud, swindle; informal con, diddle, take for a ride, pull a fast one on; N. Amer. informal sucker.
■ **trickery** n.

trickle v. **1** flow in a small stream. **2** come or go gradually.
▷ SYNONYMS: **dribble**, drip, ooze, leak, seep, spill, exude, percolate.
– ANTONYMS: pour, gush.
• n. a trickling flow.
▷ SYNONYMS: **dribble**, drip, thin stream, rivulet.

tricky adj. (**trickier**, **trickiest**) **1** difficult or awkward. **2** deceitful.
▷ SYNONYMS: **1 difficult**, awkward, problematic, delicate, ticklish, sensitive; informal sticky. **2 cunning**, crafty, wily, devious, sly, scheming, calculating, deceitful.
– ANTONYMS: straightforward.

tricolour /tri-kuh-ler/ (US **tricolor**) n. a flag with three bands of different colours.

tricycle n. a vehicle similar to a bicycle but with three wheels.

trident n. a three-pronged spear.

tried past & past part. of TRY.

triennial adj. taking place every three years.

trier n. a person who tries hard.

trifle n. **1** a thing of little value or importance. **2** a small amount. **3** Brit. a cold dessert of sponge cake and fruit covered with custard and jelly.
▷ SYNONYMS: **triviality**, thing of no consequence, bagatelle, inessential, nothing, technicality; (**trifles**) trivia, minutiae.
• v. (**trifle with**) treat without seriousness or respect.

trifling adj. trivial.
▷ SYNONYMS: **trivial**, unimportant, insignificant, inconsequential, petty, minor, of no account, footling, incidental; informal piffling.
– ANTONYMS: important.

trigger n. **1** a lever for releasing a spring or catch, esp. to fire a gun. **2** an event that causes something to happen.
• v. **1** cause to function. **2** bring about.
▷ SYNONYMS: **start**, set off, initiate, spark off, activate, touch off, provoke, precipitate, prompt, stir up, cause, give rise to, lead to, set in motion, bring about.
□ **trigger-happy** tending to shoot on the slightest provocation.

trigonometry n. the study of the relationships between the sides and angles of triangles.

trilateral adj. **1** involving three parties. **2** on or with three sides.

trilby n. (pl. **trilbies**) a soft felt hat with an indented crown.

trill n. a high warbling sound.
• v. make a trilling sound.

trillion adj. & n. **1** a million million. **2** Brit. dated a million million million.

trilobite n. a fossil sea animal.

trilogy n. (pl. **trilogies**) a group of three related novels, plays, etc.

trim v. (**trimming**, **trimmed**) **1** cut away unwanted parts, esp. to neaten.

2 decorate along the edges. **3** adjust a sail.
▷ SYNONYMS: **1 cut**, crop, bob, shorten, clip, snip, shear, dock, lop off, prune, shave, pare. **2 decorate**, adorn, ornament, embellish, edge, border, fringe.
• n. **1** decoration along the edges. **2** an act of trimming. **3** good condition.
▷ SYNONYMS: **1 decoration**, ornamentation, adornment, embellishment, border, edging, piping, fringe, frill. **2 haircut**, cut, clip, snip.
• adj. (**trimmer**, **trimmest**) neat and smart.
▷ SYNONYMS: **1 neat**, tidy, orderly, uncluttered, well kept, well maintained, immaculate, spick and span, spruce, dapper. **2 slim**, slender, lean, sleek, willowy.
– ANTONYMS: untidy.

trimaran /try-muh-ran/ n. a yacht with three hulls side by side.

trimming n. **1** (**trimmings**) small pieces trimmed off. **2** decoration.
▷ SYNONYMS: **decoration**, ornamentation, adornment; (**trimmings**) accompaniments, extras, frills, accessories, trappings, paraphernalia.

trinity n. (pl. **trinities**) **1** (**the Trinity**) (in Christian belief) the three persons (Father, Son, and Holy Spirit) that together make up God. **2** a group of three.

trinket n. a small inexpensive ornament or item of jewellery.

trio n. (pl. **trios**) a set or group of three.
▷ SYNONYMS: **threesome**, three, triumvirate, triad, troika, trinity, trilogy.

trip v. (**tripping**, **tripped**) **1** catch the foot on something and stumble or fall. **2** (**trip up**) make a mistake. **3** move with quick light steps. **4** activate a mechanism.
▷ SYNONYMS: **1 stumble**, lose your footing, catch your foot, slip, fall, tumble. **2 skip**, dance, prance, bound, spring, scamper.
• n. **1** a journey or excursion. **2** an act of stumbling. **3** informal a hallucinatory experience caused by a drug. **4** a device that trips a mechanism.
▷ SYNONYMS: **1 excursion**, outing, jaunt, holiday, break, visit, tour, journey, expedition, voyage, drive, run; informal spin. **2 stumble**, slip, fall, misstep.

tripartite adj. **1** consisting of three parts. **2** involving three parties.

tripe n. **1** the stomach of a cow or sheep used as food. **2** informal nonsense.

triple adj. **1** having or involving three

parts, things, or people. **2** having three times as much or as many.
▷ SYNONYMS: **threefold**, tripartite, three-way, three times, treble.
• v. increase by three times the amount.

triplet n. **1** each of three children born at one birth. **2** a set of three.

triplicate adj. existing in three copies or examples.

tripod n. a three-legged stand for a camera etc.

triptych /trip-tik/ n. a picture or carving on three panels.

trite adj. unoriginal or overused.

tritium n. a radioactive isotope of hydrogen.

triumph n. **1** a great victory or achievement. **2** joy resulting from this.
▷ SYNONYMS: **1 victory**, win, conquest, success, achievement. **2 jubilation**, exultation, elation, delight, joy, happiness, glee, pride, satisfaction.
– ANTONYMS: defeat, disappointment.
• v. achieve a triumph.
▷ SYNONYMS: **win**, succeed, come first, be victorious, carry the day, prevail.
– ANTONYMS: lose.
■ **triumphal** adj.

triumphant adj. **1** having won a battle or contest. **2** joyful after a victory or achievement.
▷ SYNONYMS: **1 victorious**, successful, winning, conquering. **2 jubilant**, exultant, celebratory, elated, joyful, delighted, gleeful, proud, cock-a-hoop.
– ANTONYMS: defeated, despondent.
■ **triumphantly** adv.

triumvirate n. a group of three powerful people.

trivet n. a metal stand for a kettle or hot dish.

trivia pl. n. trivial details or pieces of information.

trivial adj. of little value or importance.
▷ SYNONYMS: **unimportant**, insignificant, inconsequential, minor, of no account, of no importance, petty, trifling, footling, negligible; informal piffling.
– ANTONYMS: important, significant.
■ **triviality** n. **trivialize** (or **-ise**) v. **trivially** adv.

trod past & past part. of TREAD.

trodden past part. of TREAD.

troglodyte n. a person who lives in a cave.

troika n. **1** a Russian vehicle pulled by a team of three horses. **2** a group of

t

three people working together.

troll n. (in folklore) an ugly giant or dwarf.

trolley n. (pl. **trolleys**) **1** Brit. a large metal basket on wheels, for transporting goods. **2** a small table on wheels.

trollop n. dated a promiscuous woman.

trombone n. a large brass wind instrument with a sliding tube.
■ **trombonist** n.

trompe l'œil /tromp **loy**/ n. a painting that creates the illusion of a three-dimensional object or space.

troop n. **1** (**troops**) soldiers or armed forces. **2** a group of people or animals.
▷ SYNONYMS: **1** (**troops**) **soldiers**, armed forces, soldiery, servicemen, service-women. **2 group**, party, band, gang, body, company, troupe, crowd, squad, unit.
• v. come or go as a group.
▷ SYNONYMS: **walk**, march, file, flock, crowd, throng, stream, swarm.

trooper n. **1** a private soldier in a cavalry or armoured unit. **2** US a state police officer.

trophy n. (pl. **trophies**) **1** an object awarded as a prize. **2** a souvenir of an achievement.
▷ SYNONYMS: **1 cup**, medal, prize, award. **2 souvenir**, memento, keepsake, spoils, booty.

tropic n. **1** a line of latitude 23°26′ north or south of the equator. **2** (**the tropics**) the region between these, with a hot climate.

tropical adj. **1** relating to the tropics. **2** very hot and humid.
▷ SYNONYMS: **hot**, sweltering, humid, sultry, steamy, sticky, oppressive, stifling.
– ANTONYMS: cold.

trot v. (**trotting**, **trotted**) **1** run at a moderate pace with short steps. **2** (of a horse) move at a pace faster than a walk. **3** (**trot out**) informal give an account that has been produced many times before.
▷ SYNONYMS: **run**, jog, scuttle, scurry, bustle, scamper.
• n. a trotting pace.
□ **on the trot** Brit. informal one after another.

trotter n. a pig's foot.

troubadour /troo-buh-dor/ n. a medieval travelling poet.

trouble n. **1** difficulty or inconvenience. **2** a cause of this. **3** a situation likely to bring punishment or blame. **4** public disorder.
▷ SYNONYMS: **1 difficulty**, problems,

bother, inconvenience, nuisance, worry, anxiety, distress, stress, agitation, harassment, unpleasant-ness; informal hassle. **2** she poured out all her troubles: **problem**, misfortune, difficulty, trial, tribulation, woe, grief, heartache, misery, affliction, suffering. **3** he has heart trouble: **disease**, illness, sickness, ailment, complaint, problem, disorder. **4** a match marred by crowd trouble: **disturbance**, disorder, unrest, fighting, scuffles, breach of the peace.
• v. **1** cause worry or inconvenience to. **2** make the effort to do something.
▷ SYNONYMS: **1 worry**, bother, concern, disturb, upset, agitate, distress, perturb, annoy, nag, prey on someone's mind; informal bug. **2** I'm sorry to trouble you: **inconvenience**, bother, impose on, disturb, put out, disoblige; informal hassle.
□ **troubleshooter** a person who investigates and solves problems in an organization.

troublesome adj. causing difficulty or annoyance.
▷ SYNONYMS: **1** a troublesome situation: **annoying**, irritating, exasperating, maddening, infuriating, bothersome, tiresome. **2** a troublesome child: **difficult**, awkward, uncooperative, rebellious, unmanageable, unruly, obstreperous, disruptive, disobedient, naughty, recalcitrant; N. Amer. informal pesky.

trough n. **1** a long, narrow open container for animals' food or drink. **2** a long region of low pressure.

trounce v. defeat heavily.

troupe n. a group of touring entertainers.

trouper n. **1** an entertainer with long experience. **2** a reliable person.

trousers pl. n. an outer garment for the body from the waist down, with a separate part for each leg.

trousseau /troo-soh/ n. (pl. **trousseaux** or **trousseaus**) the clothes etc. collected by a bride for her marriage.

trout n. (pl. **trout** or **trouts**) an edible fish of the salmon family.

trowel n. **1** a small hand-held tool for digging. **2** a similar tool for applying and spreading mortar or plaster.

troy (or **troy weight**) n. a system of weights used for precious metals and gems.

truant n. a pupil who stays away from school without permission.
▷ SYNONYMS: **absentee**; Brit. informal skiver;

Austral./NZ informal **wag**.
• v. (or **play truant**) stay away as a truant.
■ **truancy** n.

truce n. an agreement to stop fighting temporarily.
▷ SYNONYMS: **ceasefire**, armistice, cessation of hostilities, peace.

truck n. **1** a lorry. **2** Brit. an open railway wagon.

trucker n. a lorry driver.

truculent adj. quick to argue or fight.
■ **truculence** n. **truculently** adv.

trudge v. walk with slow, heavy steps.
• n. a long and tiring walk.

true adj. **1** in accordance with fact. **2** real or actual. **3** accurate. **4** loyal.
▷ SYNONYMS: **1 correct**, truthful, accurate, right, verifiable, the case; formal veracious. **2 genuine**, authentic, real, actual, bona fide, proper, legitimate; informal kosher. **3 sincere**, genuine, real, unfeigned, heartfelt. **4 loyal**, faithful, constant, devoted, trustworthy, reliable, dependable, staunch. **5** a true reflection: **accurate**, faithful, telling it like it is, realistic, factual, lifelike.
– ANTONYMS: false, untrue.
■ **truly** adv.

USAGE No e in **truly**.

truffle n. **1** an underground fungus eaten as a delicacy. **2** a soft chocolate sweet.

trug n. Brit. a shallow oblong wooden basket.

truism n. a statement that is obviously true and says nothing new.

trump n. (in card games) a card of a suit chosen to rank above the others.
• v. (**trump up**) invent a false accusation or excuse.

trumpet n. a brass musical instrument with a flared end.
• v. (**trumpeting, trumpeted**) **1** (of an elephant) make a loud sound through its trunk. **2** proclaim widely.
▷ SYNONYMS: **proclaim**, announce, declare, noise abroad, shout from the rooftops.
■ **trumpeter** n.

truncate v. shorten by cutting off the end.
■ **truncation** n.

truncheon n. a short thick stick carried as a weapon by a police officer.

trundle v. move or roll slowly.

trunk n. **1** the main woody stem of a tree. **2** the body apart from the limbs and head. **3** the long nose of an elephant. **4** a large box with a hinged lid for storing or transporting clothes etc. **5** US the boot of a car. **6** (**trunks**) men's shorts worn for swimming.
▷ SYNONYMS: **1 stem**, bole, stock, stalk. **2 torso**, body. **3 proboscis**, nose, snout. **4 chest**, box, crate, coffer, case, portmanteau.
□ **trunk call** a long-distance phone call. **trunk road** an important main road.

truss n. **1** a framework supporting a roof etc. **2** a padded belt worn to support a hernia.
• v. bind tightly.

trust n. **1** firm belief in the reliability, truth, or ability of someone or something. **2** responsibility for someone or something. **3** an arrangement whereby someone manages property for the benefit of another. **4** an organization managed by trustees.
▷ SYNONYMS: **confidence**, belief, faith, certainty, assurance, conviction, credence, reliance.
• v. **1** have trust in. **2** entrust. **3** hope.
▷ SYNONYMS: **1 have faith in**, have confidence in, believe in, pin your hopes on; rely on, depend on, bank on, count on, be sure of. **2 entrust**, consign, commit, give, hand over, turn over, assign. **3 hope**, expect, take it, assume, presume.
– ANTONYMS: distrust, mistrust.
■ **trustful** adj. **trustfully** adv.

trustee n. a person given legal powers to hold and manage property for the benefit of another.

trusting adj. tending to trust other people.
▷ SYNONYMS: **trustful**, unsuspecting, unquestioning, naive, innocent, child-like, ingenuous, wide-eyed, credulous, gullible, easily taken in.
– ANTONYMS: distrustful, suspicious.

trustworthy adj. able to be trusted or relied on.
▷ SYNONYMS: **reliable**, dependable, honest, honourable, upright, truthful, as good as your word, above suspicion, reputable; informal on the level.
– ANTONYMS: unreliable.
■ **trustworthiness** n.

trusty adj. old use reliable or faithful.

truth n. **1** the state of being true. **2** something which is true.
▷ SYNONYMS: **1 accuracy**, correctness, authenticity, veracity, verity, truthfulness. **2 fact**, reality, actuality.
– ANTONYMS: lie, fiction, falsehood.

t

truthful adj. **1** telling or expressing the truth. **2** realistic.

▷ SYNONYMS: **true**, accurate, correct, factual, faithful, reliable.

– ANTONYMS: deceitful, untrue.

■ **truthfully** adv. **truthfulness** n.

try v. (**trying**, **tried**) **1** attempt. **2** test by use. **3** (**try on**) put on a garment to see if it fits or suits you. **4** make severe demands on. **5** put on trial.

▷ SYNONYMS: **1 attempt**, endeavour, make an effort, exert yourself, strive, do your best, do your utmost, aim, seek; informal have a go/shot/crack/stab, go all out. **2 test**, put to the test, sample, taste, inspect, investigate, examine, appraise, evaluate, assess; informal check out. **3** *she tried his patience:* **tax**, strain, test, stretch, sap, drain, exhaust, wear out.

• n. (pl. **tries**) **1** an attempt. **2** an act of testing by use. **3** Rugby an act of touching the ball down behind the opposing goal line to score points.

▷ SYNONYMS: **attempt**, effort, endeavour; informal go, shot, crack, stab, bash.

trying adj. difficult or annoying.

▷ SYNONYMS: **1 stressful**, taxing, demanding, difficult, challenging, frustrating, fraught; informal hellish. **2 annoying**, irritating, exasperating, maddening, infuriating, tiresome, troublesome, irksome, vexatious.

tryst /trist/ n. a meeting between lovers.

tsar (or **czar**) /zar/ n. an emperor of Russia before 1917.

■ **tsarist** adj.

tsetse /tet-si/ n. an African bloodsucking fly which transmits diseases.

tsp abbrev. teaspoonful.

tsunami /tsoo-nah-mi/ n. a tidal wave caused by an earthquake.

tub n. **1** a wide, open container. **2** a small container for food.

tuba n. a large low-pitched brass wind instrument.

tubby adj. (**tubbier**, **tubbiest**) informal short and fat.

tube n. **1** a long, hollow cylinder. **2** a flexible container sealed at one end and having a cap at the other. **3** (**the Tube**) Brit. trademark the underground railway in London.

tuber n. a thick underground part of the stem or root of some plants from which new plants grow.

■ **tuberous** adj.

tubercle n. a small rounded swelling or protuberance.

tuberculosis n. a serious infectious disease in which small swellings appear, esp. in the lungs.

■ **tubercular** adj.

tubing n. tubular pieces of plastic etc.

tubular adj. tube-shaped.

TUC abbrev. Trades Union Congress.

tuck v. **1** push, fold, or turn under or between two surfaces. **2** store in a safe or secret place. **3** (**tuck in**) informal eat heartily.

▷ SYNONYMS: **push**, insert, slip, thrust, stuff, stick, cram; informal pop.

• n. **1** a flattened, stitched fold in a garment or material. **2** Brit. informal food eaten by schoolchildren as a snack.

Tudor adj. of the English royal dynasty which ruled 1485–1603.

Tuesday n. the day before Wednesday.

tufa n. a porous rock formed as a deposit from mineral springs.

tuft n. a bunch of threads, grass, or hair, held or growing together at the base.

■ **tufted** adj. **tufty** adj.

tug v. (**tugging**, **tugged**) pull hard or suddenly.

▷ SYNONYMS: **1** *he tugged at her sleeve:* **pull**, pluck, tweak, twitch, jerk, catch hold of; informal yank. **2 drag**, pull, lug, draw, haul, heave, tow, trail.

• n. **1** a hard or sudden pull. **2** a small, powerful boat for towing larger boats.

□ **tug of war** a contest of strength in which two teams pull at opposite ends of a rope.

tuition n. teaching or instruction.

▷ SYNONYMS: **instruction**, teaching, coaching, tutoring, tutelage, lessons, education, schooling, training.

tulip n. a plant with bright cup-shaped flowers.

tulle /tyool/ n. a soft, fine net fabric.

tumble v. **1** fall suddenly, clumsily, or headlong. **2** move in a headlong way.

▷ SYNONYMS: **1 fall over**, fall down, topple over, go head over heels, lose your balance, take a spill, trip, stumble. **2** *oil prices tumbled:* **plummet**, plunge, dive, nosedive, drop, slump, slide; informal crash.

– ANTONYMS: rise.

• n. **1** a fall. **2** an untidy or confused arrangement or state. **3** an acrobatic feat.

□ **tumbledown** dilapidated. **tumble dryer** Brit. a machine for drying washing in hot air inside a rotating drum.

tumbler n. **1** a drinking glass with no handle or stem. **2** an acrobat. **3** a part of a lock that holds the bolt until lifted by a key.

tumbril n. hist. an open cart used to take prisoners to the guillotine during the French Revolution.

tumescent adj. swollen.
■ **tumescence** n.

tummy n. (pl. **tummies**) informal the stomach or abdomen.

tumour (US **tumor**) n. a swelling of a part of the body caused by an abnormal growth of tissue.
▷ SYNONYMS: **cancer**, growth, lump, malignancy; Medicine carcinoma, sarcoma.

tumult n. **1** a loud, confused noise. **2** confusion or disorder.
■ **tumultuous** adj.

tun n. a large cask.

tuna n. (pl. **tuna** or **tunas**) a large edible sea fish.

tundra n. a vast, flat, treeless Arctic region with permanently frozen subsoil.

tune n. a pleasant-sounding sequence of musical notes.
▷ SYNONYMS: **melody**, air, strain, theme, song, jingle, ditty.
• v. **1** adjust a musical instrument to the correct pitch. **2** adjust a radio or television to the desired frequency. **3** adjust an engine to run smoothly.
▷ SYNONYMS: **attune**, adapt, adjust, regulate.
□ **in** (or **out of**) **tune** in (or not in) the correct musical pitch.
■ **tuneful** adj. **tunefully** adv. **tuneless** adj.

tuner n. **1** a person who tunes pianos etc. **2** a part of a stereo system that receives radio signals.

tungsten n. a hard grey metallic element.

tunic n. **1** a loose sleeveless garment reaching to the thighs or knees. **2** a close-fitting short coat worn as part of a uniform.

tunnel n. an underground passage.
▷ SYNONYMS: **underground passage**, underpass, subway, shaft, burrow, hole, warren, labyrinth.
• v. (**tunnelling**, **tunnelled**; US **tunneling**, **tunneled**) dig or force a passage underground or through something.
▷ SYNONYMS: **dig**, burrow, mine, bore, drill.

tunny n. (pl. **tunny** or **tunnies**) a tuna.

turban n. a long length of material wound round a cap or the head, worn by Muslim and Sikh men.

turbid adj. (of a liquid) cloudy or muddy.

turbine n. a machine in which a wheel or rotor is driven by a flow of water or gas.

turbocharger n. a supercharger driven by a turbine powered by the engine's exhaust gases.
■ **turbocharged** adj.

turbot n. (pl. **turbot** or **turbots**) a large edible flatfish.

turbulent adj. **1** involving much conflict, disorder, or confusion. **2** (of air or water) moving unsteadily or violently.
▷ SYNONYMS: **tempestuous**, stormy, unstable, unsettled, tumultuous, chaotic, anarchic, lawless.
– ANTONYMS: peaceful.
■ **turbulence** n. **turbulently** adv.

tureen n. a deep covered dish from which soup is served.

turf n. (pl. **turfs** or **turves**) **1** grass and the layer of soil just below it. **2** a piece of turf. **3** (**the turf**) horse racing and racecourses.
• v. **1** (**turf off/out**) informal force to leave. **2** cover with turf.
□ **turf accountant** Brit. formal a bookmaker.

turgid adj. **1** swollen or full. **2** (of language) pompous.
■ **turgidity** n.

Turk n. a person from Turkey.

turkey n. (pl. **turkeys**) a large bird bred for food.

Turkish n. the language of Turkey.
• adj. of Turkey.
□ **Turkish bath** a period of sitting in a room filled with very hot air or steam, followed by washing and massage. **Turkish delight** a sweet made of syrup and cornflour.

turmeric n. a bright yellow spice.

turmoil n. a state of great disturbance or confusion.
▷ SYNONYMS: **confusion**, upheaval, turbulence, tumult, disorder, disturbance, ferment, chaos, mayhem.
– ANTONYMS: peace, order.

turn v. **1** move around a central point. **2** move so as to face or go in a different direction. **3** make or become. **4** shape wood on a lathe. **5** twist or sprain an ankle.
▷ SYNONYMS: **1 go round**, revolve, rotate, spin, roll, circle, wheel, whirl, twirl, gyrate, swivel, pivot. **2 change direction**, change course, do a U-turn, wheel round. **3 bend**, curve, wind, twist, meander, snake, zigzag. **4** *he turned pale*: **become**, go, grow, get. **5** *the milk has turned*: **go sour**, go off, curdle, go bad, spoil.

t

• n. **1** an act of turning. **2** a bend or branch in a road, river, etc. **3** the time when a member of a group must or is allowed to do something. **4** a time when one period ends and another begins. **5** a change in circumstances. **6** a short walk. **7** a brief feeling of illness. **8** a short performance.

▷ SYNONYMS: **1 rotation**, revolution, spin, whirl, twirl, gyration, swivel. **2 bend**, corner, junction, twist, dog-leg; Brit. hairpin bend. **3 opportunity**, chance, say, stint, time, try; informal go, shot, stab, crack. **4** *she did me some good turns*: **service**, deed, act, favour, kindness.

□ **do someone a good turn** do something helpful for someone. **turn against** make or become hostile towards. **turncoat** a person who changes sides in a dispute etc. **turn down** reject. **turn in** hand over to the authorities. **turn off** switch off. **turn on 1** switch on. **2** suddenly attack. **3** informal excite sexually. **turnout** the number of people attending or taking part in an event. **turn out 1** switch off an electric light. **2** prove to be the case. **3** be present at an event. **4** (**be turned out**) be dressed in a particular way. **turnover 1** the amount of money taken by a business. **2** the rate at which employees leave or goods are sold and are replaced. **3** a small pie made of pastry folded over a filling. **turnpike** hist. & US a road on which a toll is collected. **turnstile** a revolving gate allowing only one person at a time to pass through. **turntable** a circular revolving platform. **turn up 1** increase the volume of. **2** be found. **3** appear. **turn-up** Brit. **1** the end of a trouser leg folded upwards on the outside. **2** informal an unexpected event.

turning n. a place where a road branches off another.

▷ SYNONYMS: **junction**, turn-off, side road, exit; N. Amer. turnout.

turning point n. a time when a decisive change in a situation occurs.

▷ SYNONYMS: **watershed**, critical moment, decisive moment, moment of truth, crossroads, crisis.

turnip n. a round root vegetable.

turnout n. the number of people attending or taking part in an event.

▷ SYNONYMS: **attendance**, audience, house, congregation, crowd, gate, gathering.

turnover n. **1** the amount of money taken by a business. **2** the rate at which employees leave or goods are

sold and are replaced.

▷ SYNONYMS: **revenue**, income, yield, sales, profits, business.

turpentine n. a liquid derived from certain trees, used to thin paint and clean brushes.

turpitude n. formal wickedness.

turps n. turpentine.

turquoise n. **1** a greenish-blue semi-precious stone. **2** a greenish-blue colour.

turret n. **1** a small tower. **2** an armoured tower for a gun on a ship, aircraft, or tank.

■ **turreted** adj.

turtle n. a sea reptile with a bony or leathery shell.

□ **turn turtle** capsize. **turtle dove** a small dove with a soft call. **turtleneck** Brit. a high, round, close-fitting neckline.

turves pl. of TURF.

tusk n. a long, pointed tooth protruding from the mouth of an elephant, walrus, etc.

tussle n. a struggle.

• v. engage in a tussle.

tussock n. a clump or tuft of grass.

tutelage /tyoo-ti-lij/ n. **1** protection or authority. **2** tuition.

tutor n. **1** a private teacher. **2** a university or college teacher.

▷ SYNONYMS: **teacher**, instructor, coach, educator, lecturer, trainer, mentor.

• v. act as a tutor to.

▷ SYNONYMS: **teach**, instruct, educate, school, coach, train, drill.

tutorial n. a period of tuition given by a university or college tutor.

• adj. of a tutor.

tutu n. a female ballet dancer's short, stiff skirt that projects from the waist.

tuxedo /tuk-see-doh/ n. (pl. **tuxedos** or **tuxedoes**) a man's dinner jacket.

TV abbrev. television.

twaddle n. informal nonsense.

twang n. **1** a strong ringing sound made by the plucked string of a musical instrument. **2** a nasal way of speaking.

• v. make a twang.

tweak v. **1** twist or pull sharply. **2** informal improve by making fine adjustments.

• n. an act of tweaking.

twee adj. Brit. affectedly quaint or sentimental.

tweed n. **1** a rough, flecked woollen cloth. **2** (**tweeds**) clothes made of tweed.

■ **tweedy** adj.

tweet v. give a chirp.
•n. a chirping sound.

tweeter n. a loudspeaker designed to reproduce high frequencies.

tweezers pl. n. a small pair of pincers for plucking out hairs and picking up small objects.

twelve adj. & n. two more than ten; 12.
■ **twelfth** adj. & n.

twenty adj. & n. (pl. **twenties**) ten less than thirty; 20.
■ **twentieth** adj. & n.

twerp n. informal a silly person.

twice adv. **1** two times. **2** double in degree or quantity.

twiddle v. play or fiddle with idly.
□ **twiddle your thumbs** have nothing to do.

twig n. a slender woody shoot growing from a branch or stem.
▷ SYNONYMS: **stick**, sprig, shoot, offshoot, stem, branchlet.
•v. (**twigging**, **twigged**) Brit. informal understand or realize.

twilight n. **1** the soft light from the sky when the sun is below the horizon. **2** the period of this.
▷ SYNONYMS: **dusk**, sunset, sundown, nightfall, evening, close of day; literary gloaming.

> **WORD LINKS**
> **crepuscular** resembling or relating to twilight

twill n. a woven fabric with a surface of diagonal parallel ridges.
■ **twilled** adj.

twin n. **1** one of two children born at one birth. **2** one of a pair that are exactly alike.
•v. (**twinning**, **twinned**) **1** link or combine as a pair. **2** Brit. link a town with another in a different country for the purposes of cultural exchange.
•adj. **1** forming or being one of a pair of twins. **2** forming a matching or closely connected pair.
▷ SYNONYMS: **matching**, related, linked, connected, parallel, complementary.

twine n. strong string.
•v. wind or coil.

twinge n. a brief, sharp pain or pang.
▷ SYNONYMS: **pain**, spasm, ache, throb, cramp, stitch, pang.

twinkle v. shine with a flickering light.
▷ SYNONYMS: & n. **glitter**, sparkle, shine, glimmer, shimmer, glint, gleam, glisten, flicker, flash, wink.
•n. a twinkling light.

twirl v. spin quickly and lightly round.
•n. **1** an act of twirling. **2** a spiral shape.

twist v. **1** bend or curl. **2** force out of the natural position. **3** have a winding course. **4** deliberately change the meaning of.
▷ SYNONYMS: **1** crumple, crush, buckle, mangle, warp, deform, distort, contort. **2** sprain, wrench, turn, rick, crick. **3** *she twisted her hair round her finger*: wind, twirl, coil, curl, wrap. **4** *the wires were twisted together*: intertwine, interlace, weave, plait, braid, coil, wind. **5** *the road twisted and turned*: wind, bend, curve, turn, meander, weave, zigzag, snake.
•n. **1** an act of twisting. **2** a spiral shape. **3** an unexpected development.
▷ SYNONYMS: **bend**, curve, turn, zigzag, dog-leg.

twit n. informal a silly person.

twitch v. make a short, sudden jerking movement.
▷ SYNONYMS: **jerk**, convulse, quiver, tremble, shiver, shudder.
•n. a twitching movement.
▷ SYNONYMS: **spasm**, convulsion, quiver, tremor, shiver, shudder, tic.

twitter v. **1** (of a bird) make a series of short high sounds. **2** talk rapidly in a nervous or trivial way.
•n. a twittering sound.

two adj. & n. one less than three; 2.
□ **two-dimensional** having or appearing to have length and breadth but no depth. **two-faced** insincere and deceitful. **twosome** a set of two people. **two-time** informal be unfaithful to a lover.
■ **twofold** adj. & adv.

tycoon n. a wealthy, powerful person in business or industry.
▷ SYNONYMS: **magnate**, mogul, businessman, captain of industry, industrialist, financier, entrepreneur; informal, derogatory fat cat.

tying pres. part. of TIE.

tyke n. informal a mischievous child.

tympani var. of TIMPANI.

tympanum n. (pl. **tympanums** or **tympana**) the eardrum.

type n. **1** a kind or category. **2** informal a person of a specified nature. **3** printed characters or letters.
▷ SYNONYMS: **1** kind, sort, variety, class, category, set, genre, species, order, breed, ilk. **2** print, typeface, characters, lettering, font; Brit. fount.
•v. write using a typewriter or computer.
□ **typecast** (of an actor) repeatedly cast in the same type of role. **typeface** a particular design of printed type. **typescript** a typed copy of a text.

typesetter a person or machine that arranges type for printing. **typewriter** a machine with keys for producing print-like characters.
■ **typist** n.

typhoid n. a serious infectious disease causing fever.

typhoon n. a tropical storm.

typhus n. an infectious disease causing a rash and fever.

typical adj. having the distinctive qualities of a particular type of person or thing.
▷ SYNONYMS: **1 representative**, characteristic, classic, quintessential, archetypal. **2 normal**, average, ordinary, standard, regular, routine, run-of-the-mill, conventional, unremarkable; informal bog-standard.
− ANTONYMS: unusual, exceptional.
■ **typically** adv.

typify v. (**typifying**, **typified**) be typical of.
▷ SYNONYMS: **epitomize**, exemplify, characterize, embody, be representative of, personify, symbolize.

typography n. the process or style of printing.
■ **typographer** n. **typographical** adj.

tyrannize (or **-ise**) v. dominate or treat cruelly.

tyrannosaurus rex n. a very large meat-eating dinosaur.

tyranny n. (pl. **tyrannies**) cruel and oppressive government or rule.
▷ SYNONYMS: **despotism**, absolute power, autocracy, dictatorship, totalitarianism, fascism, oppression, repression, subjugation, enslavement.
■ **tyrannical** adj. **tyrannically** adv. **tyrannous** adj.

tyrant n. a cruel and oppressive person, esp. a ruler.
▷ SYNONYMS: **dictator**, despot, autocrat, authoritarian, oppressor, slave-driver, martinet, bully.

tyre (US **tire**) n. a rubber covering, usu. inflated, that fits around a wheel.

tyro n. (pl. **tyros**) a beginner.

tzatziki /tsat-**see**-ki/ n. a Greek dip of yogurt, cucumber, mint, and garlic.

Uu

ubiquitous /yoo-bi-kwi-tuhss/ adj. appearing or found everywhere.
▷ SYNONYMS: **everywhere**, omnipresent, all over the place, all-pervasive, universal, worldwide, global.
− ANTONYMS: rare.
■ ubiquity n.

udder n. the bag-like milk-producing organ of female cattle, sheep, goats, etc.

UFO n. (pl. **UFOs**) a mysterious object seen in the sky, believed by some to carry beings from outer space (short for *unidentified flying object*).

ugly adj. (**uglier**, **ugliest**) **1** unpleasant or unattractive in appearance. **2** hostile or threatening.
▷ SYNONYMS: **1 unattractive**, unsightly, ill-favoured, hideous, plain, unprepossessing, horrible, ghastly, repellent, grotesque; N. Amer. homely; Brit. informal no oil painting. **2 unpleasant**, nasty, disagreeable, alarming, dangerous, perilous, threatening, menacing, hostile, ominous, sinister.
− ANTONYMS: beautiful.
■ ugliness n.

UHF abbrev. ultra-high frequency, a radio frequency in the range 300 to 3,000 MHz.

UHT abbrev. Brit. ultra heat treated (esp. of milk).

UK abbrev. United Kingdom.

ukulele /yoo-kuh-lay-li/ n. a small four-stringed guitar.

ulcer n. an open sore.
■ ulcerated adj. ulceration n.

ulna n. (pl. **ulnae** or **ulnas**) the thinner, longer bone of the human forearm.

ulterior adj. other than what is obvious or admitted.
▷ SYNONYMS: **underlying**, undisclosed, undivulged, concealed, hidden, covert, secret, unapparent.
− ANTONYMS: overt.

ultimate adj. **1** final. **2** best or most extreme. **3** fundamental.
▷ SYNONYMS: **1 eventual**, final, concluding, terminal, end. **2 best**, ideal, greatest, quintessential, supreme. **3 fundamental**, basic, primary, elementary, absolute, central, crucial, essential.
■ ultimately adv.

ultimatum n. (pl. **ultimatums** or **ultimata**) a final warning that action will be taken unless your demands are met.

ultra- prefix **1** beyond. **2** extremely.

ultramarine n. a brilliant deep blue.

ultrasonic adj. above the upper limit of human hearing.

ultrasound n. sound or other vibrations with an ultrasonic frequency, used in medical scans.

ultraviolet adj. of or using radiation with a wavelength just shorter than that of visible light rays.

ululate v. howl or wail.
■ ululation n.

umbel n. a broad flat flower cluster.

umber n. a brownish natural pigment.

umbilical adj. of the navel.
□ umbilical cord a flexible tube by which a fetus is nourished while in the womb.

umbra n. (pl. **umbras** or **umbrae**) the dark central part of the shadow cast by the earth or the moon in an eclipse.

umbrage n. (take umbrage) take offence; become annoyed.

umbrella n. a folding dome-shaped device used as protection against rain.

umlaut /uum-lowt/ n. a mark (¨) placed over a vowel in some languages to indicate a change in pronunciation.

umpire n. (in certain sports) an official who supervises a game to ensure that the rules are observed.
▷ SYNONYMS: **referee**, judge, line judge, linesman, adjudicator, arbitrator, moderator; informal ref.

u

• **v.** act as an umpire in.

umpteen adj. informal very many.
■ **umpteenth** adj.

UN abbrev. United Nations.

un- prefix **1** not. **2** reversing the action indicated by a verb.

unable adj. not having the skill, means, etc. to do something.
▷ SYNONYMS: **incapable**, powerless, impotent, inadequate, incompetent, unqualified, unfit.

unacceptable adj. not satisfactory or allowable.
▷ SYNONYMS: **unsatisfactory**, inadmissible, inappropriate, unsuitable, undesirable, unreasonable, insupportable, intolerable, objectionable, distasteful; informal out of order.
– ANTONYMS: satisfactory.

unaccountable adj. **1** unable to be explained. **2** not responsible for results or consequences.
■ **unaccountably** adv.

unadulterated adj. not mixed with any different or extra elements.

unalloyed adj. complete; total.

unanimous /yoo-nan-i-muhss/ adj.
1 fully in agreement. **2** agreed by everyone involved.
▷ SYNONYMS: **in agreement**, of one mind, in accord, united, undivided, with one voice.
– ANTONYMS: split.
■ **unanimity** n. **unanimously** adv.

unarmed adj. without weapons.
▷ SYNONYMS: **defenceless**, unprotected, unguarded.

unassailable adj. unable to be attacked or defeated.

unassuming adj. not pretentious or arrogant.
▷ SYNONYMS: **modest**, self-effacing, humble, meek, reserved, diffident, unobtrusive, unostentatious, unpretentious, unaffected, natural.

unattended adj. not being supervised or looked after.

unauthorized (or **-ised**) adj. not having official permission or approval.
▷ SYNONYMS: **unofficial**, unsanctioned, unaccredited, unlicensed, disallowed, prohibited, banned, forbidden, outlawed, illegal, illicit, proscribed.
– ANTONYMS: official.

unavoidable adj. unable to be avoided or prevented.
■ **unavoidably** adv.

unaware adj. not aware of something.
▷ SYNONYMS: **ignorant**, oblivious, unconscious, unwitting, unsuspecting, uninformed, unenlightened, innocent; informal in the dark.
– ANTONYMS: aware.
• adv. (**unawares**) so as to surprise; unexpectedly.

unbalanced adj. emotionally or mentally disturbed.

unbeknown (or **unbeknownst**) adj. (**unbeknown to**) without the knowledge of.

unbelievable adj. **1** unlikely to be true. **2** extraordinary.
▷ SYNONYMS: **incredible**, inconceivable, unthinkable, unimaginable, unconvincing, far-fetched, implausible, improbable; informal hard to swallow.
■ **unbelievably** adv.

unbend v. (**unbending**, **unbent**)
1 straighten. **2** become less formal or strict.

unbending adj. unwilling to change your mind.

unbiased adj. showing no prejudice.
▷ SYNONYMS: **impartial**, unprejudiced, neutral, non-partisan, disinterested, detached, dispassionate, objective, even-handed, fair.

unbidden adj. without having been invited.

unborn adj. not yet born.
▷ SYNONYMS: **expected**, embryonic, fetal, in utero.

unbounded adj. having no limits.

unbridled adj. uncontrolled.

unbroken adj. **1** not broken; intact.
2 not interrupted or disturbed. **3** (of a record) not beaten.
▷ SYNONYMS: **1 undamaged**, unharmed, unscathed, untouched, sound, intact, whole. **2 uninterrupted**, continuous, endless, constant, unremitting, ongoing. **3 unbeaten**, undefeated, unsurpassed, unrivalled, unmatched, supreme.

unburden v. (**unburden yourself**) confide in someone about a worry or problem.

uncalled adj. (**uncalled for**) undesirable and unnecessary.

uncanny adj. strange or mysterious.
▷ SYNONYMS: **1 eerie**, unnatural, unearthly, other-worldly, ghostly, strange, abnormal, weird; informal creepy, spooky. **2** an uncanny resemblance: **striking**, remarkable, extraordinary, exceptional, incredible.
■ **uncannily** adv.

unceremonious adj. impolite or abrupt.
■ **unceremoniously** adv.

uncertain adj. **1** not known, reliable,

or definite. **2** not completely sure.

▷ SYNONYMS: **1** *the effects are uncertain:* **unknown**, debatable, open to question, in doubt, in the balance, up in the air, unpredictable, unforeseeable, undetermined; informal **iffy**. **2** *he was uncertain about the decision:* **unsure**, doubtful, dubious, undecided, irresolute, hesitant, vacillating, vague, unclear, ambivalent, in two minds.

– ANTONYMS: certain, sure.

■ **uncertainly** adv. **uncertainty** n.

uncharitable adj. unkind or unsympathetic.

■ **uncharitably** adv.

uncharted adj. (of an area of land or sea) not mapped or surveyed.

uncle n. the brother of your father or mother or the husband of your aunt.

unclean adj. **1** dirty. **2** immoral. **3** (of food) forbidden by a religion.

unclear adj. **1** difficult to see, hear, or understand. **2** confused or uncertain.

▷ SYNONYMS: **1 ambiguous**, indefinite, vague, mysterious, obscure, hazy, nebulous. **2 uncertain**, unsure, confused, puzzled.

– ANTONYMS: clear, certain.

uncomfortable adj. **1** not comfortable. **2** uneasy or awkward.

▷ SYNONYMS: **1 painful**, awkward, lumpy, confining, cramped. **2 uneasy**, ill at ease, awkward, nervous, tense, edgy, restless, embarrassed, anxious; informal rattled, twitchy.

– ANTONYMS: comfortable, relaxed.

■ **uncomfortably** adv.

uncommon adj. unusual.

▷ SYNONYMS: **unusual**, abnormal, rare, atypical, exceptional, unconventional, unfamiliar, strange, extraordinary, peculiar, scarce, few and far between, isolated, infrequent.

■ **uncommonly** adv.

uncompromising adj. unwilling to compromise.

unconcern n. a lack of worry or interest.

■ **unconcerned** adj.

unconditional adj. not subject to any conditions.

▷ SYNONYMS: **unquestioning**, unqualified, unreserved, unlimited, unrestricted, wholehearted, complete, total, entire, full, absolute, unequivocal.

■ **unconditionally** adv.

unconscionable adj. not right or reasonable.

■ **unconscionably** adv.

unconscious adj. **1** not conscious. **2** done or existing without you

realizing. **3** unaware.

▷ SYNONYMS: **1 knocked out**, senseless, comatose, inert, stunned; informal **out cold**, out for the count. **2 subconscious**, instinctive, involuntary, uncontrolled, subliminal; informal **gut**. **3 unaware**, oblivious, ignorant, in ignorance, heedless.

– ANTONYMS: aware.

■ **unconsciously** adv. **unconsciousness** n.

uncouth adj. lacking good manners.

▷ SYNONYMS: **uncivilized**, uncultured, rough, coarse, crude, loutish, boorish, rude, discourteous, disrespectful, bad-mannered, ill-bred.

– ANTONYMS: civilized.

uncover v. **1** remove a cover from. **2** discover something secret or unknown.

▷ SYNONYMS: **1 expose**, reveal, lay bare, unwrap, unveil, strip. **2 discover**, detect, come across, stumble on, chance on, find, turn up, unearth, dig up.

unction n. **1** the smearing of someone with oil as a religious ceremony. **2** excessive politeness.

unctuous adj. excessively polite or flattering.

■ **unctuously** adv.

undeceive v. tell someone that an idea or belief is mistaken.

undecided adj. **1** not having made a decision. **2** not settled or resolved.

undeniable adj. undoubtedly true.

■ **undeniably** adv.

under prep. **1** extending or directly below. **2** at a lower level or grade than. **3** controlled by. **4** according to the rules of. **5** undergoing.

▷ SYNONYMS: **1 below**, beneath, underneath. **2 less than**, lower than, below. **3 subordinate to**, answerable to, responsible to, subject to, junior to, inferior to.

– ANTONYMS: above, over.

• adv. extending or directly below something.

□ **under way** making progress.

under- prefix **1** below; beneath. **2** insufficiently.

underarm adj. & adv. done with the arm or hand below shoulder level.

undercarriage n. **1** an aircraft's landing wheels and supporting structure. **2** the supporting framework of a vehicle.

underclass n. the lowest and poorest social class in a country.

undercoat n. a layer of paint applied before the topcoat.

u

undercover adj. & adv. involving secret investigative work.
▷ SYNONYMS: **secret**, covert, clandestine, underground, surreptitious, furtive, cloak-and-dagger, stealthy; informal hush-hush.
– ANTONYMS: overt.

undercurrent n. **1** a current of water flowing below the surface. **2** an underlying feeling or influence.

undercut v. (**undercutting, undercut**) **1** offer goods or services at a lower price than a competitor. **2** cut or wear away the part under. **3** weaken; undermine.

underdog n. a competitor thought to have little chance of winning.

underdone adj. not cooked enough.

underestimate v. **1** estimate to be smaller or less important than in reality. **2** regard as less capable than in reality.
▷ SYNONYMS: **underrate**, undervalue, miscalculate, misjudge, do an injustice to.
– ANTONYMS: overestimate.

underfoot adv. **1** on the ground. **2** getting in your way.

undergo v. (**undergoes, undergoing, underwent;** past part. **undergone**) experience something unpleasant or difficult.
▷ SYNONYMS: **experience**, go through, submit to, face, be subjected to, receive, endure, brave, bear, withstand, weather.

undergraduate n. a university student who has not yet taken a degree.

underground adj. & adv. **1** beneath the surface of the ground. **2** in secrecy or hiding.
▷ SYNONYMS: **1 subterranean**, buried, sunken. **2 secret**, clandestine, surreptitious, covert, undercover, closet, cloak-and-dagger, resistance, subversive.
• n. Brit. an underground railway.
▷ SYNONYMS: **metro**; N. Amer. **subway**; Brit. trademark **tube**.

undergrowth n. a dense growth of shrubs and other plants.

underhand adj. acting or done secretly or dishonestly.

underlay n. material laid under a carpet for support.

underlie v. (**underlying, underlay;** past part. **underlain**) be the cause or basis of.

underline v. **1** draw a line under. **2** emphasize.
▷ SYNONYMS: **1 underscore**, mark,

pick out, emphasize, highlight. **2 emphasize**, stress, highlight, accentuate, accent, focus on, spotlight.

underling n. a subordinate.

underlying adj. of basic importance but not always obvious or clearly stated: *the underlying causes of the problem.*
▷ SYNONYMS: **fundamental**, basic, primary, central, essential, key.

undermine v. **1** damage or weaken. **2** weaken the foundations of.
▷ SYNONYMS: **weaken**, diminish, reduce, impair, mar, spoil, ruin, damage, sap, shake, threaten, subvert, compromise, sabotage.
– ANTONYMS: strengthen.

underneath prep. & adv. **1** situated directly below. **2** so as to be hidden by.

underpants pl. n. an article of underwear covering the lower part of the body and having two holes for the legs.

underpass n. a road or tunnel passing under another road or a railway.

underpin v. (**underpinning, underpinned**) **1** strengthen from below. **2** form the basis for an argument or theory.

underprivileged adj. not enjoying the same rights or standard of living as the majority.

underrate v. underestimate.

underscore v. underline.

undersell v. sell something at a lower price than a competitor.

undershoot v. (**undershooting, undershot**) **1** fall short of a target. **2** land short of a runway.

underside n. the bottom or lower side or surface.

undersigned n. the person or people who have signed the document in question.

underskirt n. a petticoat.

understaffed adj. having too few members of staff.

understand v. (**understanding, understood**) **1** know or realize the intended meaning or cause of. **2** interpret or view in a particular way. **3** believe to be the case from information received.
▷ SYNONYMS: **1 comprehend**, grasp, take in, see, apprehend, follow, make sense of, fathom; informal work out, figure out, make head or tail of, get; Brit. informal twig, suss. **2 know**, realize, recognize, acknowledge, appreciate, be aware of, be conscious of.

3 believe, gather, take it, hear, notice, see, learn.

understandable adj. **1** able to be understood. **2** to be expected; normal or reasonable.

▷ SYNONYMS: **1 comprehensible**, intelligible, clear, plain, unambiguous, transparent, straightforward, explicit, coherent. **2 unsurprising**, expected, predictable, inevitable, reasonable, acceptable, logical, rational, normal, natural, justifiable, excusable, pardonable, forgivable.
– ANTONYMS: incomprehensible.
■ **understandably** adv.

understanding n. **1** the ability to understand. **2** sympathetic awareness or tolerance. **3** an agreement.

▷ SYNONYMS: **1 comprehension**, grasp, mastery, appreciation, knowledge, awareness, skill, expertise, proficiency; informal know-how. **2 intellect**, intelligence, brainpower, judgement, insight, intuition, acumen, sagacity, wisdom; informal nous. **3 belief**, perception, view, conviction, feeling, opinion, intuition, impression. **4 sympathy**, compassion, pity, feeling, concern, consideration, kindness, sensitivity, decency, goodwill. **5 agreement**, arrangement, deal, bargain, settlement, pledge, pact.
– ANTONYMS: ignorance.
• adj. sympathetically aware of others' feelings.
▷ SYNONYMS: **sympathetic**, compassionate, sensitive, considerate, kind, thoughtful, tolerant, patient, forbearing, lenient, forgiving.
■ **understandingly** adv.

understate v. represent as smaller or less important than in reality.
▷ SYNONYMS: **play down**, underrate, underplay, trivialize, minimize, diminish, downgrade, brush aside, gloss over.
– ANTONYMS: exaggerate.
■ **understatement** n.

understated adj. pleasingly subtle.

understudy n. (pl. **understudies**) an actor who learns another's role so as to take their place if needed.

undertake v. (**undertaking**, **undertook**; past part. **undertaken**) **1** begin an activity. **2** formally promise.
▷ SYNONYMS: **1 set about**, embark on, go about, engage in, take on, be responsible for, get down to, get to grips with, tackle, attempt; informal have a go at. **2 promise**, pledge, vow, give your word, swear, guarantee, contract, give

an assurance, commit yourself.

undertaker n. a person whose job is to prepare dead bodies for burial or cremation and to make arrangements for funerals.
▷ SYNONYMS: **funeral director**; N. Amer. mortician.

undertaking n. **1** a task. **2** a formal promise.
▷ SYNONYMS: **1 enterprise**, venture, project, campaign, scheme, plan, operation, endeavour, effort, task. **2 promise**, pledge, agreement, oath, covenant, vow, commitment, guarantee, assurance.

undertone n. **1** a low or subdued tone. **2** an underlying quality or feeling.

undertow n. an undercurrent moving in the opposite direction to the surface water.

underwater adj. & adv. situated or occurring beneath the surface of the water.
▷ SYNONYMS: **submerged**, sunken, undersea, submarine.

underwear n. clothing worn under other clothes next to the skin.
▷ SYNONYMS: **underclothes**, undergarments, underthings, lingerie; informal undies; Brit. informal smalls.

underwent past of UNDERGO.

underworld n. **1** the world of criminals or of organized crime. **2** (in myths and legends) the home of the dead, imagined as being under the earth.

underwrite v. (**underwriting**, **underwrote**; past part. **underwritten**) **1** accept legal responsibility for an insurance policy. **2** finance.
▷ SYNONYMS: **sponsor**, support, back, insure, indemnify, subsidize, pay for, finance, fund; N. Amer. informal bankroll.
■ **underwriter** n.

undesirable adj. harmful or unpleasant.
▷ SYNONYMS: **unpleasant**, disagreeable, nasty, unwelcome, unwanted, unfortunate.
– ANTONYMS: pleasant.

undies pl. n. informal articles of underwear.

undo v. (**undoes**, **undoing**, **undid**; past part. **undone**) **1** unfasten or loosen. **2** cancel the effect of. **3** cause the ruin or downfall of.
▷ SYNONYMS: **1 unfasten**, unbutton, unhook, untie, unlace, unlock, unbolt, loosen, detach, free, open. **2 cancel**, reverse, overrule, overturn, repeal,

u

rescind, countermand, revoke, annul, invalidate, negate. **3 ruin**, undermine, overturn, scotch, sabotage, spoil, impair, mar, destroy, wreck; informal blow; Brit. informal scupper.
– ANTONYMS: fasten.

undoing n. a person's ruin or downfall.

undone adj. **1** not tied or fastened. **2** not done or finished.

undoubted adj. not questioned or doubted.
▷ SYNONYMS: **undisputed**, unchallenged, unquestioned, indubitable, incontrovertible, irrefutable, incontestable, certain, unmistakable; definite, accepted, acknowledged, recognized.
■ **undoubtedly** adv.

undreamed (Brit. also **undreamt**) adj. (**undreamed of**) not previously thought to be possible.

undress v. take clothes off.
• n. the state of being naked or only partially clothed.

undue adj. excessive.
▷ SYNONYMS: **excessive**, immoderate, intemperate, inordinate, disproportionate, uncalled for, unnecessary, unwarranted, unjustified, unreasonable, inappropriate, unmerited, unsuitable, improper.
– ANTONYMS: appropriate.
■ **unduly** adv.

undulate v. **1** move with a smooth wave-like motion. **2** have a wavy form or outline.
■ **undulation** n.

undying adj. everlasting.

unearth v. **1** find in the ground by digging. **2** discover by searching.
▷ SYNONYMS: **1 dig up**, excavate, exhume, disinter, root out. **2** I unearthed an interesting fact: **discover**, find, come across, hit on, bring to light, expose, turn up.

unearthly adj. **1** supernatural or mysterious. **2** informal unreasonably early or inconvenient.

uneasy adj. (**uneasier**, **uneasiest**) troubled or uncomfortable.
▷ SYNONYMS: **1 worried**, anxious, troubled, disturbed, nervous, nervy, tense, edgy, on edge, apprehensive, fearful, uncomfortable, unsettled, ill at ease; informal jittery. **2** an uneasy peace: **tense**, awkward, strained, fraught, precarious, unstable, insecure.
– ANTONYMS: calm.
■ **unease** n. **uneasily** adv. **uneasiness** n.

uneatable adj. not fit to be eaten.

uneconomic adj. not profitable.

unemployable adj. not having enough skills or qualifications to get paid employment.

unemployed adj. **1** without a paid job. **2** not in use.
▷ SYNONYMS: **jobless**, out of work, unwaged, redundant, laid off, on benefit; Brit. signing on; N. Amer. on welfare; Brit. informal on the dole, resting.
■ **unemployment** n.

unending adj. seeming to last for ever.

unequalled (US **unequaled**) adj. better or greater than all others.

unequivocal /un-i-kwiv-uh-k'l/ adj. leaving no doubt.
■ **unequivocally** adv.

unerring adj. always right or accurate.
■ **unerringly** adv.

uneven adj. **1** not level or smooth. **2** not regular.
▷ SYNONYMS: **1 bumpy**, rough, lumpy, stony, rocky, rutted. **2 irregular**, crooked, lopsided, askew, asymmetrical. **3 inconsistent**, variable, fluctuating, irregular, erratic, patchy, fitful.
– ANTONYMS: flat, regular.
■ **unevenly** adv. **unevenness** n.

unexceptionable adj. not open to objection.

unexceptional adj. not out of the ordinary.

unexpected adj. not expected or thought likely to happen.
■ **unexpectedly** adv.

unfailing adj. reliable or constant.
■ **unfailingly** adv.

unfair adj. not based on or showing fairness.
▷ SYNONYMS: **1 unjust**, prejudiced, biased, discriminatory, one-sided, unequal, uneven, unbalanced, partisan. **2 undeserved**, unmerited, unreasonable, unjustified; Brit. informal out of order. **3 unsporting**, dirty, underhand, dishonourable, dishonest.
– ANTONYMS: just, justified.
■ **unfairly** adv. **unfairness** n.

unfaithful adj. **1** not faithful; disloyal. **2** having sex with a person other than your regular partner.
■ **unfaithfulness** n.

unfasten v. undo the fastening of.
▷ SYNONYMS: **undo**, open, untie, unbutton, unzip, loosen, free, unlock, unbolt.

unfeeling adj. unsympathetic, harsh, or cruel.

unfit adj. **1** unsuitable; inappropriate. **2** not in good physical condition.

unflappable adj. informal calm in a crisis.

unfold v. **1** open or spread out. **2** reveal or be revealed.
▷ SYNONYMS: **1 open out**, spread out, flatten, straighten out, unroll, unfurl. **2 develop**, evolve, happen, take place, occur.

unforeseen adj. not predicted.

unforgettable adj. highly memorable.
■ **unforgettably** adv.

unfortunate adj. **1** unlucky. **2** regrettable.
▷ SYNONYMS: **1 unlucky**, hapless, ill-starred, star-crossed, wretched, poor, pitiful; informal down on your luck. **2 unwelcome**, disadvantageous, unfavourable, unlucky, adverse, unpromising, inauspicious. **3 regrettable**, inappropriate, unsuitable, tactless, injudicious.
– ANTONYMS: lucky.
■ **unfortunately** adv.

unfounded adj. having no basis in fact.

unfriendly adj. (**unfriendlier**, **unfriendliest**) not friendly.
▷ SYNONYMS: **hostile**, disagreeable, antagonistic, aggressive, unpleasant, surly, uncongenial, inhospitable, unneighbourly, unwelcoming, unsociable, cool, cold, aloof, distant; informal stand-offish.

unfrock v. defrock.

unfurl v. spread out or unroll.

ungainly adj. clumsy; awkward.
▷ SYNONYMS: **awkward**, clumsy, grace-less, inelegant, gawky, gauche, uncoordinated.
– ANTONYMS: graceful.
■ **ungainliness** n.

ungodly adj. **1** sinful or immoral. **2** informal unreasonably early or late.

ungovernable adj. uncontrollable.

ungrateful adj. not feeling or showing gratitude.
■ **ungratefully** adv.

unguarded adj. **1** not guarded. **2** not well considered; careless.

unguent /ung-gwuhnt/ n. an ointment or lubricant.

ungulate n. a mammal with hoofs.

unhand v. old use let go of.

unhappy adj. (**unhappier**, **unhappiest**) **1** not happy; sad. **2** unfortunate.
▷ SYNONYMS: **1 sad**, miserable, sorrowful, dejected, despondent, disconsolate, morose, heartbroken, down, dispirited, downhearted, depressed, melancholy, mournful, gloomy, glum; informal down in the mouth, fed up, blue. **2** I was very unhappy with the service: **dissatisfied**, displeased, discontented, disappointed, disgruntled. **3 unfortunate**, unlucky, ill-starred, ill-fated, doomed; informal jinxed.
– ANTONYMS: happy, pleased.
■ **unhappily** adv. **unhappiness** n.

unhealthy adj. (**unhealthier**, **unhealthiest**) **1** in poor health. **2** not good for health.
▷ SYNONYMS: **1 harmful**, detrimental, destructive, injurious, damaging, noxious, poisonous. **2 sick**, poorly, ill, unwell, unfit, ailing, weak, frail, infirm, washed out, run down. **3 abnormal**, morbid, macabre, twisted, unwholesome, warped, depraved, unnatural; informal sick.
■ **unhealthily** adv.

unheard adj. (**unheard of**) previously unknown.

unhinged adj. mentally unbalanced.

unholy adj. **1** wicked. **2** informal dreadful.

unicorn n. a mythical animal like a horse with a single horn on its forehead.

uniform adj. not varying; the same in all cases and at all times.
▷ SYNONYMS: **1 constant**, consistent, steady, invariable, unchanging, stable, static, regular, fixed, even. **2 identical**, matching, similar, equal, same, like, consistent.
– ANTONYMS: variable.
• n. the distinctive clothing worn by members of the same organization or school.
▷ SYNONYMS: **costume**, outfit, suit, ensemble, livery, regalia; informal get-up, rig, gear.
■ **uniformed** adj. **uniformity** n. **uniformly** adv.

unify v. (**unifying**, **unified**) unite.
▷ SYNONYMS: **unite**, combine, bring together, join, merge, fuse, amalgamate, coalesce, consolidate.
– ANTONYMS: separate.
■ **unification** n.

unilateral adj. done by or affecting only one person, group, etc.
■ **unilaterally** adv.

unimpeachable adj. beyond doubt or criticism.

uninhabited adj. without inhabitants.

unintelligible adj. impossible to understand.

u

uninterested adj. not interested or concerned.

> USAGE Don't confuse **uninterested** with **disinterested**, which means 'impartial'.

uninteresting adj. not interesting; dull.
▷ SYNONYMS: **boring**, dull, unexciting, tiresome, tedious, dreary, lifeless, humdrum, colourless, bland, insipid, banal, dry.
– ANTONYMS: exciting.

uninviting adj. not attractive; unpleasant.

union n. **1** the act of uniting or the fact of being united. **2** a society or association, esp. a trade union. **3** (or **Union**) a political unit consisting of a number of states or provinces with the same central government.
▷ SYNONYMS: **1 unification**, joining, merger, fusion, amalgamation, coalition, combination, synthesis, blend. **2 association**, league, guild, confederation, federation.
– ANTONYMS: separation.
□ **Union Jack** the national flag of the UK.

unionist n. **1** a member of a trade union. **2** (**Unionist**) a person in favour of the union of Northern Ireland with Great Britain.

unionize (or **-ise**) v. make or become members of a trade union.

unique adj. **1** being the only one of its kind. **2** (**unique to**) belonging only to one person, group, or place. **3** very special or unusual.
▷ SYNONYMS: **1 distinctive**, individual, special, particular, specific, idiosyncratic, single, sole, lone, unrepeated, solitary, exclusive; informal one-off. **2 remarkable**, special, notable, unequalled, unparalleled, unmatched, unsurpassed, incomparable.
– ANTONYMS: common.
■ **uniquely** adv.

unisex adj. suitable for both sexes.

unison n. the fact of two or more things being said or happening at the same time.

unit n. **1** an individual thing, group, or person, esp. as part of a complex whole. **2** a device, item of furniture, or part of a building or organization with a specified function. **3** a fixed quantity that is used as a standard measurement.
▷ SYNONYMS: **1 component**, part, section, segment, element, module,

constituent, subdivision. **2 quantity**, measure, denomination. **3 group**, detachment, contingent, division, cell, faction, department, office, branch.
□ **unit trust** Brit. a company that invests money in a range of businesses on behalf of individuals, who can buy small units.

Unitarian n. a member of a Christian Church believing that God is one person and rejecting the idea of the Trinity.

unitary adj. **1** single. **2** of a unit or units.

unite v. come or bring together for a common purpose or to form a whole.
▷ SYNONYMS: **1 unify**, join, link, connect, combine, amalgamate, fuse, weld, bond, bring together. **2 join together**, join forces, combine, band together, ally, cooperate, collaborate, work together, team up. **3 merge**, mix, blend, mingle, combine.
– ANTONYMS: divide.

unity n. (pl. **unities**) **1** the state of being united. **2** a complex whole.
▷ SYNONYMS: **1 union**, unification, integration, amalgamation, coalition, federation, confederation. **2 harmony**, accord, cooperation, collaboration, agreement, consensus, solidarity. **3 oneness**, singleness, wholeness, uniformity, homogeneity.
– ANTONYMS: disunity.

universal adj. of, for, or done by all.
▷ SYNONYMS: **general**, common, widespread, ubiquitous, comprehensive, global, worldwide, international.

universally adv. by everyone; in every case.
▷ SYNONYMS: **always**, without exception, by everyone, in all cases, everywhere, worldwide, globally, internationally, commonly, generally.

universe n. all existing matter and space considered as a whole.
▷ SYNONYMS: **cosmos**, macrocosm, space, infinity, nature, all existence.

> WORD LINKS
> **cosmic** relating to the universe

university n. (pl. **universities**) an educational institution where students study for a degree and where academic research is done.

unkempt adj. having an untidy appearance.

unkind adj. not caring or kind.
▷ SYNONYMS: **unpleasant**, disagreeable, nasty, mean, cruel, vicious, spiteful, malicious, callous, unsympathetic,

uncharitable, harsh, hard-hearted, heartless, cold-hearted; informal bitchy, catty.

■ **unkindness** n.

unknown adj. not known.

▷ SYNONYMS: **1 undisclosed**, unrevealed, secret, undetermined, undecided. **2 unexplored**, uncharted, unmapped, undiscovered,untravelled.**3 unidentified**, unnamed, anonymous, nameless. **4 obscure**, unfamiliar, unheard of, unsung, minor, undistinguished.

– ANTONYMS: familiar.

•n. an unknown person, thing, or place.

unleaded adj. (of petrol) without added lead.

unleash v. release; set loose.

unleavened adj. (of bread) made without yeast or other raising agent.

unless conj. except when; if not.

unlike prep. **1** not like. **2** uncharacteristic of.

•adj. different.

unlikely adj. (unlikelier, unlikeliest) not likely to happen, be done, or be true.

▷ SYNONYMS: **improbable**, doubtful, dubious, questionable, unconvincing, implausible, far-fetched, unrealistic, incredible, unbelievable, inconceivable.

– ANTONYMS: probable, likely.

■ **unlikelihood** n.

unlimited adj. not limited; infinite.

unload v. **1** remove goods from a vehicle, ship, etc. **2** informal get rid of.

▷ SYNONYMS: **unpack**, empty, clear, remove, offload.

unlooked adj. (unlooked for) unexpected.

unlucky adj. (unluckier, unluckiest) having, bringing, or resulting from bad luck.

▷ SYNONYMS: **1 unfortunate**, hapless, luckless, unsuccessful, ill-fated, ill-starred, jinxed. **2 unfavourable**, inauspicious, unpropitious, ominous, ill-omened.

– ANTONYMS: lucky, fortunate.

■ **unluckily** adv.

unmanned adj. operated without a crew.

unmask v. reveal the true character of.

unmentionable adj. too shocking to be spoken about.

unmistakable (or unmistakeable) adj. unable to be mistaken for anything else.

■ **unmistakably** adv.

unmitigated adj. absolute.

unmoved adj. **1** not affected by emotion. **2** not changed in purpose.

unnatural adj. **1** different to what is found in nature. **2** different to what is normal or expected.

▷ SYNONYMS: **1 abnormal**, unusual, uncommon, extraordinary, strange, unorthodox, exceptional, irregular, untypical. **2 artificial**, man-made, synthetic. **3 affected**, stilted, forced, false, fake, insincere, contrived, mannered, self-conscious; informal put on, phoney.

– ANTONYMS: natural.

■ **unnaturally** adv.

unnecessary adj. not necessary, or more than is necessary.

▷ SYNONYMS: **unneeded**, inessential, not required, uncalled for, unwarranted, dispensable, optional, extraneous, expendable, redundant.

■ **unnecessarily** adv.

unnerve v. cause to feel nervous or frightened.

unnumbered adj. **1** not given a number. **2** countless.

unobtrusive adj. not conspicuous or attracting attention.

■ **unobtrusively** adv.

unorthodox adj. different from what is usual or accepted.

unpack v. open and remove the contents of a suitcase or container.

unparalleled adj. having no equal; exceptional.

unpick v. undo the stitching of.

unplaced adj. not placed as one of the first three in a race.

unpleasant adj. **1** not pleasant. **2** not friendly or kind.

▷ SYNONYMS: **1** an unpleasant situation: **disagreeable**, distressing, nasty, horrible, terrible, awful, dreadful, invidious, objectionable. **2** an unpleasant man: **unlikeable**, unlovable, disagreeable, bad-tempered, unfriendly, rude, impolite, obnoxious, nasty, spiteful, mean, objectionable, annoying, irritating. **3 unappetizing**, unpalatable, unsavoury, unappealing, disgusting, revolting, nauseating, sickening.

– ANTONYMS: pleasant, agreeable.

■ **unpleasantly** adv. **unpleasantness** n.

unpopular adj. not liked or popular.

▷ SYNONYMS: **disliked**, friendless, unloved, unwelcome, avoided, ignored, rejected, shunned, out of favour.

■ **unpopularity** n.

unprecedented adj. never done or known before.

u

unprepared adj. not ready or able to deal with something.

unpossessing adj. unattractive.

unprincipled adj. unscrupulous.

unprintable adj. too offensive to be published.

unprofessional adj. not in accordance with professional standards of behaviour.
■ **unprofessionally** adv.

unprompted adj. spontaneous.

unqualified adj. **1** not having the necessary qualifications or skills. **2** complete; absolute.

unquestionable adj. unable to be denied or doubted.
■ **unquestionably** adv.

unravel v. (**unravelling**, **unravelled**; US **unraveling**, **unraveled**) **1** undo twisted, knitted, or woven threads. **2** become undone. **3** solve a mystery.
▷ SYNONYMS: **1 untangle**, disentangle, separate out, unwind, untwist. **2 solve**, resolve, clear up, puzzle out, get to the bottom of, explain, clarify; informal figure out.
– ANTONYMS: entangle.

unreal adj. imaginary or illusory.
▷ SYNONYMS: **imaginary**, fictitious, make-believe, made-up, dreamed-up, false, illusory, fanciful; informal pretend.

unreasonable adj. **1** not based on good sense. **2** beyond what is acceptable or achievable.
■ **unreasonably** adv.

unrelenting adj. **1** not stopping or becoming less severe. **2** not giving in to requests.
■ **unrelentingly** adv.

unremitting adj. not stopping or slackening.

unrequited adj. (of love) not returned.

unreserved adj. without doubts or reservations; complete.
■ **unreservedly** adv.

unrest n. **1** rebellious discontent and disorder. **2** uneasiness.
▷ SYNONYMS: **disturbance**, trouble, turmoil, disruption, disorder, chaos, anarchy, dissatisfaction, dissent, strife, agitation, protest, rebellion, uprising, rioting.
– ANTONYMS: peace.

unrivalled (US **unrivaled**) adj. greater or better than all others.

unruly adj. (**unrulier**, **unruliest**) not easy to control.
■ **unruliness** n.

unsafe adj. not safe; dangerous.

▷ SYNONYMS: **dangerous**, risky, hazardous, high-risk, treacherous, insecure, unsound, harmful, injurious, toxic.

unsatisfactory adj. not satisfactory or acceptable.
▷ SYNONYMS: **disappointing**, inadequate, unacceptable, poor, bad, inferior, substandard, weak, mediocre, not up to par, defective, deficient.

unsaturated adj. Chem. (of fats) having double and triple bonds between carbon atoms in their molecules and therefore being more easily processed by the body.

unsavoury (US **unsavory**) adj. **1** unpleasant to taste, smell, or look at. **2** not respectable.

unscathed adj. without suffering any injury.

unscrupulous adj. without moral principles; dishonest.
▷ SYNONYMS: **dishonest**, deceitful, devious, underhand, unethical, immoral, shameless, exploitative, corrupt, unprincipled, dishonourable, disreputable; informal crooked, shady.
■ **unscrupulously** adv.

unseasonable adj. (of weather) unusual for the time of year.
■ **unseasonably** adv.

unseat v. **1** cause to fall from a saddle or seat. **2** remove from a position of power.

unselfish adj. putting other people's needs before your own.

unsettle v. make uneasy; disturb.
▷ SYNONYMS: **disturb**, disconcert, unnerve, upset, disquiet, perturb, alarm, dismay, trouble, bother, agitate, fluster, ruffle, shake, throw; informal rattle, faze.

unsettled adj. **1** changeable. **2** uneasy. **3** not yet resolved.

unshakeable (or **unshakable**) adj. (of a belief etc.) firm.

unsightly adj. unpleasant to look at.
▷ SYNONYMS: **unattractive**, ugly, unprepossessing, hideous, horrible, repulsive, revolting, offensive, grotesque.
– ANTONYMS: attractive.
■ **unsightliness** n.

unskilled adj. not having or needing special skill or training.

unsociable adj. not enjoying the company of others.
▷ SYNONYMS: **unfriendly**, uncongenial, unneighbourly, unapproachable, introverted, reserved, withdrawn, retiring, aloof, distant, remote, detached; informal stand-offish.

unsocial adj. **1** Brit. (of hours of work) falling outside the normal working day and so inconvenient. **2** antisocial.

unsolicited adj. not asked for.

unsound adj. **1** not safe or strong. **2** not based on reliable evidence or reasoning.

unsparing adj. **1** merciless; severe. **2** giving generously.

unspeakable adj. too bad or horrific to express in words.
  ▪ **unspeakably** adv.

unstable adj. **1** not stable. **2** prone to mental health problems or sudden mood changes.
  ▷ SYNONYMS: **1 unsteady**, rocky, wobbly, rickety, shaky, unsafe, insecure, precarious. **2 changeable**, volatile, variable, fluctuating, irregular, unpredictable, erratic. **3 unbalanced**, of unsound mind, mentally ill, deranged, demented, disturbed, unhinged.
  – ANTONYMS: steady, firm.

unstinting adj. given or giving freely or generously.

unstuck adj. (**come unstuck**) informal fail.

unstudied adj. natural and unaffected.

unsuccessful adj. not successful.
  ▷ SYNONYMS: **failed**, abortive, ineffective, fruitless, profitless, unproductive, vain, futile.
  ▪ **unsuccessfully** adv.

unsuitable adj. not right or appropriate.
  ▷ SYNONYMS: **inappropriate**, ill-suited, inapposite, inapt, infelicitous, unacceptable, unfitting, incompatible, out of place, not in keeping, incongruous, unseemly.
  – ANTONYMS: appropriate.
  ▪ **unsuitability** n. **unsuitably** adv.

unsung adj. not acknowledged or praised.

unsure adj. not feeling, showing, or done with confidence.
  ▷ SYNONYMS: **1 undecided**, uncertain, irresolute, dithering, in two minds, in a quandary, dubious, doubtful, sceptical, unconvinced. **2 unconfident**, insecure, hesitant, diffident, anxious, apprehensive.
  – ANTONYMS: sure, certain, confident.

unsuspecting adj. not aware of the presence of danger.

unswerving adj. not changing or becoming weaker.

untenable adj. unable to be defended against criticism or attack.

unthinkable adj. too unlikely or unpleasant to be considered a possibility.
  ▷ SYNONYMS: **unimaginable**, inconceivable, unbelievable, incredible, implausible, out of the question, impossible, unconscionable, unreasonable.

unthinking adj. without proper consideration.

untidy adj. (**untidier**, **untidiest**) **1** not arranged tidily. **2** not inclined to be neat.
  ▷ SYNONYMS: **1 disordered**, messy, disorganized, cluttered, in chaos, haywire, in disarray, disorderly, topsy-turvy, at sixes and sevens, jumbled; informal higgledy-piggledy. **2 scruffy**, dishevelled, unkempt, messy, rumpled, bedraggled.
  – ANTONYMS: neat, tidy.
  ▪ **untidily** adv. **untidiness** n.

untie v. (**untying**, **untied**) unfasten something tied.

until prep. & conj. up to the point in time or the event mentioned.

untimely adj. **1** happening or done at an unsuitable time. **2** (of a death or end) premature.
  ▪ **untimeliness** n.

unto prep. old use to.

untold adj. **1** too much or too many to be counted. **2** not told.

untouchable adj. **1** unable to be touched or affected. **2** unrivalled.
  • n. offens. a member of the lowest Hindu social class.

untoward adj. unexpected and unwanted.
  ▷ SYNONYMS: **unexpected**, unforeseen, surprising, unusual, inappropriate, inconvenient, unwelcome, unfavourable, adverse, unfortunate, infelicitous.

untried adj. not yet tested.

untrue adj. **1** false or incorrect. **2** not faithful or loyal.
  ▷ SYNONYMS: **false**, invented, made up, fabricated, concocted, trumped up, erroneous, wrong, incorrect, inaccurate.
  – ANTONYMS: true, correct.

untruth n. (pl. **untruths**) **1** a lie. **2** the quality of being false.
  ▪ **untruthful** adj. **untruthfully** adv.

unusual adj. **1** not often done or occurring. **2** exceptional.
  ▷ SYNONYMS: **1** an unusual sight: **uncommon**, abnormal, atypical, unexpected, surprising, unfamiliar, different, strange, odd, curious, extraordinary, unorthodox,

u

unconventional, peculiar, queer, unwonted; informal weird, offbeat. **2** *a man of unusual talent*: **remarkable**, extraordinary, exceptional, particular, outstanding, notable, noteworthy, distinctive, striking, significant, special, unique, unparalleled, prodigious.
– ANTONYMS: common.
■ **unusually** adv.

unutterable adj. too great or bad to describe.
■ **unutterably** adv.

unvarnished adj. **1** not varnished. **2** plain and straightforward.

unveil v. **1** remove a veil or covering from. **2** show or announce publicly for the first time.

unwarranted adj. not justified.
▷ SYNONYMS: **1 unjustified**, indefensible, inexcusable, unforgivable, unpardonable, uncalled for, unnecessary, unjust, groundless. **2 unauthorized**, unsanctioned, unapproved, uncertified, unlicensed, illegal, unlawful, illicit, illegitimate, criminal, actionable.
– ANTONYMS: justified.

unwell adj. ill.

unwieldy adj. hard to move or manage because of its size, shape, or weight.
▷ SYNONYMS: **awkward**, unmanageable, unmanoeuvrable, cumbersome, clumsy, massive, heavy, hefty, bulky.

unwilling adj. reluctant.
▷ SYNONYMS: **1 reluctant**, unenthusiastic, hesitant, resistant, grudging, involuntary, forced. **2** *he was unwilling to take sides*: **be disinclined**, be reluctant; be loath; baulk at, demur at, shy away from, flinch from, shrink from, have qualms about, have misgivings about, have reservations about.
– ANTONYMS: willing.
■ **unwillingly** adv. **unwillingness** n.

unwind v. (**unwinding**, **unwound**) **1** undo or become undone after winding. **2** relax after a period of work or tension.

unwise adj. foolish.
■ **unwisely** adv.

unwitting adj. **1** not aware of the full facts. **2** unintentional.
■ **unwittingly** adv.

unwonted adj. unaccustomed or unusual.

unworldly adj. having little awareness of the realities of life.
■ **unworldliness** n.

unworthy adj. not deserving attention, effort, or respect.
■ **unworthiness** n.

unwritten adj. (of a rule etc.) generally known about and accepted, although not made official.

up adv. **1** towards a higher place or position. **2** at or to a higher level or value. **3** into the desired condition or position. **4** out of bed.
● prep. from a lower to a higher point of.
● adj. **1** directed or moving towards a higher place or position. **2** at an end.
● v. (**upping**, **upped**) increase.
□ **uphill 1** going or sloping upwards. **2** difficult. **upstairs** on or to an upper floor. **upstream** in the direction opposite to that in which a stream or river flows. **upwind** into the wind.
■ **upward** adj. & adv. **upwards** adv.

upbeat adj. cheerful.
▷ SYNONYMS: **cheerful**, optimistic, cheery, positive, confident, hopeful, sanguine, bullish, buoyant.
– ANTONYMS: pessimistic.

upbraid v. scold.

upbringing n. the way a person is taught and looked after as a child.

upcoming adj. forthcoming.

update v. bring up to date.
▷ SYNONYMS: **1 modernize**, upgrade, improve, overhaul. **2 brief**, bring up to date, inform, fill in, tell, notify, keep posted; informal clue in, put in the picture, bring/keep up to speed.

upend v. set on its end or upside down.

upgrade v. raise to a higher standard or rank.
▷ SYNONYMS: **improve**, modernize, update, reform.
– ANTONYMS: downgrade.

upheaval n. a violent or sudden disruption.
▷ SYNONYMS: **disturbance**, disruption, trouble, turbulence, disorder, confusion, turmoil.

uphold v. (**upholding**, **upheld**) confirm or support.
▷ SYNONYMS: **1 confirm**, endorse, sustain, approve, support, back. **2 maintain**, sustain, continue, preserve, protect, keep, hold to, keep alive, keep going.
– ANTONYMS: oppose.

upholster v. put a soft, padded covering on furniture.

upholstery n. material used to upholster furniture.

upkeep n. the process or cost of supporting someone or keeping something in good condition.
▷ SYNONYMS: **maintenance**, repair,

u

servicing, care, conservation; support, keep, subsistence.

uplift v. make more hopeful or happy.
• n. **1** an act of uplifting. **2** hope or happiness.

uplifting adj. arousing hope or happiness.
▷ SYNONYMS: **inspiring**, stirring, inspirational, rousing, moving, touching, affecting, cheering, heartening, encouraging.

upload v. transfer data to a larger computer system.

upmarket adj. expensive and of high quality.

upon prep. formal on.

upper adj. higher in place, position, or status.
▷ SYNONYMS: **higher**, superior, senior, top.
− ANTONYMS: lower.
• n. the part of a boot or shoe above the sole.
□ **have the upper hand** have an advantage or control. **upper case** capital letters.
■ **uppermost** adj. & adv.

upper class n. the social group with the highest status.
• n. relating to the upper class.
▷ SYNONYMS: **aristocratic**, noble, patrician, titled, blue-blooded, highborn, elite; Brit. county; informal uppercrust, top-drawer; Brit. informal posh.

uppity adj. informal self-important.

upright adj. **1** vertical; erect. **2** strictly honest or respectable.
▷ SYNONYMS: **1 vertical**, perpendicular, plumb, straight, erect, on end.
2 honest, honourable, upstanding, respectable, high-minded, lawabiding, worthy, righteous, decent, good, virtuous, principled.
− ANTONYMS: flat, horizontal.
• n. a vertical part or support.

uprising n. a rebellion.
▷ SYNONYMS: **rebellion**, revolt, insurrection, mutiny, revolution, insurgence, rioting, coup.

uproar n. **1** a loud noise or disturbance. **2** a public expression of outrage.
▷ SYNONYMS: **1 commotion**, disturbance, rumpus, disorder, confusion, chaos, tumult, mayhem, pandemonium, bedlam, noise, din, clamour, hubbub, racket; Brit. row; informal hullabaloo.
2 outcry, furore, fuss, commotion, hue and cry, rumpus; Brit. row; informal hullabaloo, stink, ructions.
− ANTONYMS: calm.

uproarious adj. **1** very noisy. **2** very funny.
■ **uproariously** adv.

uproot v. **1** pull a plant, tree, etc. out of the ground. **2** move from home or a familiar location.

upset v. (**upsetting**, **upset**) **1** distress or worry. **2** knock over. **3** disrupt or disturb. **4** disturb the digestion of.
▷ SYNONYMS: **1 distress**, trouble, perturb, dismay, sadden, grieve, disturb, unsettle, disconcert, disquiet, worry, bother, agitate, fluster, throw, ruffle, unnerve, shake. **2 knock over**, overturn, upend, tip over, topple, spill.
3 disrupt, interfere with, disturb, throw into confusion, mess up.
− ANTONYMS: calm.
• adj. unhappy or worried.
▷ SYNONYMS: **1 distressed**, troubled, perturbed, dismayed, disturbed, unsettled, disconcerted, worried, bothered, anxious, agitated, flustered, ruffled, unnerved, shaken, saddened, grieved; informal cut up, choked; Brit. informal gutted. **2** an upset stomach: disturbed, unsettled, queasy, bad, poorly; informal gippy.
− ANTONYMS: calm.
• n. a state of distress or disruption.
▷ SYNONYMS: **1 distress**, trouble, dismay, disquiet, worry, bother, agitation, hurt, grief. **2** a stomach upset: disorder, complaint, ailment, illness, sickness; informal bug; Brit. informal lurgy.

upshot n. an outcome.

upside down adv. & adj. **1** with the upper part where the lower part should be. **2** in or into total disorder.
▷ SYNONYMS: **1 upturned**, upended, wrong side up, overturned, inverted, capsized. **2 in disarray**, in disorder, jumbled up, in a muddle, untidy, disorganized, in chaos, in confusion, topsy-turvy, at sixes and sevens; informal higgledy-piggledy.

upstage adv. & adj. at or towards the back of a stage.
• v. divert attention from.

upstanding adj. honest and respectable.

upstart n. a person who has suddenly become important and behaves arrogantly.

upsurge n. an increase.

upswing n. an upward trend.

uptake (quick/slow on the uptake) informal quick (or slow) to understand something.

uptight adj. informal nervously tense or angry.

up to date adj. using or aware of the latest developments and trends.
▷ SYNONYMS: **1 modern**, contemporary, the latest, state-of-the-art, new,

u

up-to-the-minute, advanced.
2 informed, up to speed, in the
picture, in touch, au fait, conversant,
familiar, knowledgeable, acquainted.
– ANTONYMS: out of date, old-fashioned.

upturn n. an improvement or upward
trend.

uranium n. a radioactive metallic
element.

urban adj. of a town or city.
▷ SYNONYMS: **town**, city, municipal,
metropolitan, built-up, inner-city,
suburban.
– ANTONYMS: rural.
■ **urbanize** (or **-ise**) v.

urbane adj. (of a man) sophisticated
and courteous.
■ **urbanity** n.

urchin n. a poor child.

Urdu n. a language related to Hindi.

ureter /yuu-ree-ter/ n. the duct from
the kidney to the bladder.

urethra /yuu-ree-thruh/ n. the duct
which carries urine out of the body.

urge v. **1** encourage or earnestly ask to
do something. **2** strongly recommend.
▷ SYNONYMS: **1 encourage**, exhort, press,
entreat, implore, call on, appeal to,
beg, plead with. **2 advise**, counsel,
advocate, recommend.
• n. a strong desire or impulse.
▷ SYNONYMS: *his urge to travel:* **desire**,
wish, need, compulsion, longing,
yearning, hankering, craving, hunger,
thirst; informal yen, itch.

urgent adj. requiring or calling for
immediate action or attention.
▷ SYNONYMS: **pressing**, acute, dire,
desperate, critical, serious, grave,
intense, crying, burning, compelling,
extreme, high-priority, life-and-death.
■ **urgency** n. **urgently** adv.

urinal n. a receptacle in a public toilet
into which men urinate.

urinate v. pass urine out of the body.
■ **urination** n.

urine n. a yellowish liquid containing
waste substances, stored in the
bladder before being passed out of
the body.
■ **urinary** adj.

URL abbrev. uniform (or universal)
resource locator, the address of a
World Wide Web page.

urn n. **1** a vase, esp. one for holding
a cremated person's ashes. **2** a large
metal container with a tap, for
keeping water or tea hot.

ursine adj. of bears.

US (or **USA**) abbrev. United States of
America.

us pron. the form of 'we' used when the
speaker or writer and another person
or people are the object of a verb or
preposition.

usable (or **useable**) adj. able to be
used.

usage n. the using of something.
▷ SYNONYMS: **1** *energy usage:*
consumption, use. **2** *the usage of
equipment:* **use**, utilization, operation,
manipulation, running, handling.
3 language, expression, phraseology,
parlance, idiom.

use v. **1** do something with an object
or adopt a method. **2** take or consume
an amount from a supply. **3** (**use
up**) consume the whole of. **4** exploit
unfairly. **5** (**used to**) did repeatedly or
existed in the past. **6** (**be/get used to**)
be or become familiar with through
experience.
▷ SYNONYMS: **1 utilize**, employ, avail
yourself of, work, operate, wield, ply,
apply, put into service. **2 exercise**,
employ, bring into play, practise. **3** *we
have used up our funds:* **consume**, get/
go through, exhaust, deplete, expend,
spend. **4 take advantage of**, exploit,
manipulate, take liberties with,
impose on, abuse, capitalize on, profit
from, trade on, milk; informal cash in
on, walk all over.
• n. **1** the act of using. **2** the ability to
use something. **3** a purpose. **4** value.
▷ SYNONYMS: **1 utilization**, application,
employment, operation, manipulation. **2 exploitation**, manipulation,
abuse. **3** *what is the use of that?:*
advantage, benefit, good, point,
object, purpose, sense, reason,
service, utility, help, gain, avail,
profit, value, worth.

used adj. second-hand.
▷ SYNONYMS: **second-hand**, pre-owned,
nearly new, old, worn, hand-me-down,
cast-off.

useful adj. able to be used for a
practical purpose.
▷ SYNONYMS: **1** *a useful tool:* **functional**,
practical, handy, convenient, utilitarian, serviceable, of service; informal
nifty. **2** *a useful experience:* **beneficial**,
advantageous, helpful, worthwhile,
profitable, rewarding, productive,
constructive, valuable, fruitful.
– ANTONYMS: useless.
■ **usefully** adv. **usefulness** n.

useless adj. **1** serving no purpose.
2 informal having little ability or skill.
▷ SYNONYMS: **1 futile**, pointless, to no
avail, vain, to no purpose, unavailing,
hopeless, ineffectual, fruitless,

u

unprofitable, unproductive, abortive.
2 incompetent, inept, ineffective,
incapable, inadequate, hopeless, bad;
informal a dead loss.
– ANTONYMS: useful, beneficial.
■ **uselessly** adv.
user n. a person who uses something.
□ **user-friendly** easy to use or
understand.
usher n. a person who shows people
to their seats in a cinema, theatre, or
church.
▷ SYNONYMS: **guide**, attendant, escort.
• v. lead or guide.
▷ SYNONYMS: **escort**, accompany, take,
show, see, lead, conduct, guide.
usherette n. a woman who shows
people to their seats in a cinema or
theatre.
USSR abbrev. hist. Union of Soviet
Socialist Republics.
usual adj. happening or done regularly
or often.
▷ SYNONYMS: **normal**, customary,
accustomed, wonted, habitual,
routine, regular, standard, typical,
established, set, stock, conventional,
traditional, expected, familiar.
– ANTONYMS: exceptional.
usually adv. under normal conditions;
most often.
▷ SYNONYMS: **normally**, generally,
habitually, customarily, routinely,
typically, ordinarily, commonly, as a
rule, in general, more often than not,
mainly, mostly.
usurp v. take a position of power
illegally or by force.
■ **usurpation** n. **usurper** n.
usury n. the lending of money at
unreasonably high rates of interest.
■ **usurer** n.
utensil n. a tool or container, esp. for
household use.
▷ SYNONYMS: **implement**, tool, instrument, device, apparatus, gadget,
appliance, contrivance, contraption;
informal gizmo.
uterus n. the womb.
■ **uterine** adj.
utilitarian adj. useful rather than
decorative.
utilitarianism n. the belief that the
right course of action is the one that

leads to the greatest happiness of the
majority.
utility n. (pl. **utilities**) **1** the state
of being useful or profitable. **2** a
company supplying water, electricity,
gas, etc. to the public.
▷ SYNONYMS: **usefulness**, use, benefit,
value, advantage, help, practicality,
effectiveness, service.
□ **utility room** a room in which a
washing machine and other domestic
equipment is kept.
utilize (or **-ise**) v. make use of.
▷ SYNONYMS: **use**, employ, avail yourself
of, press into service, bring into play,
deploy, draw on, exploit.
■ **utilization** n.
utmost adj. most extreme; greatest.
▷ SYNONYMS: **greatest**, highest,
maximum, most, extreme, supreme,
paramount.
• n. (**the utmost**) the greatest or most
extreme extent or amount.
Utopia n. an imagined perfect place.
■ **utopian** adj.
utter[1] adj. complete; absolute.
▷ SYNONYMS: **complete**, total, absolute,
thorough, perfect, downright,
out-and-out, outright, sheer, arrant,
positive, prize, pure, unmitigated,
unadulterated, unqualified,
unalloyed.
■ **utterly** adv.
utter[2] v. make a sound or say
something.
▷ SYNONYMS: **say**, speak, voice, mouth,
express, articulate, pronounce,
enunciate, emit, let out, give,
produce.
utterance n. **1** a word, statement, etc.
uttered. **2** the action of uttering.
▷ SYNONYMS: **remark**, comment, statement, observation, declaration,
pronouncement.
uttermost adj. & n. utmost.
U-turn n. **1** the turning of a vehicle in
a U-shaped course so as to face the
opposite way. **2** a reversal of policy.
UV abbrev. ultraviolet.
uvula /yoo-vyuu-luh/ n. (pl. **uvulae**)
the fleshy projection hanging at the
back of the throat.
uxorious adj. very or excessively fond
of your wife.

Vv

V (or **v**) n. the Roman numeral for five.
• **abbrev. 1** volts. **2** versus. **3** very.
□ **V-neck** a V-shaped neckline. **V-sign**
a gesture of abuse made with the first
two fingers pointing up and the back
of the hand facing outwards.

vacancy n. (pl. **vacancies**) **1** an
unoccupied position, job, or hotel
room. **2** empty space.
▷ SYNONYMS: **opening**, position, post,
job, opportunity.

vacant adj. **1** not occupied or filled.
2 showing no intelligence or interest.
▷ SYNONYMS: **1 empty**, unoccupied,
not in use, free, available, unfilled,
uninhabited, untenanted; informal
up for grabs. **2 blank**, expressionless, unresponsive, emotionless,
impassive, vacuous, empty, glazed.
– ANTONYMS: full, occupied.
■ **vacantly** adv.

vacate v. cease to occupy.
▷ SYNONYMS: **1 leave**, move out of,
evacuate, quit, depart from. **2 resign
from**, leave, stand down from, give
up, bow out of, relinquish, retire
from; informal quit.
– ANTONYMS: occupy.

vacation n. **1** a holiday period
between terms in universities etc.
2 US a holiday. **3** the act of vacating.
▷ SYNONYMS: **holiday**, trip, tour, break,
leave, time off, recess.

vaccinate v. inject with a vaccine.
■ **vaccination** n.

vaccine /vak-seen/ n. a substance
that causes the body to produce
antibodies, so providing immunity
against a disease.

vacillate /va-si-layt/ v. keep changing
your mind.
■ **vacillation** n.

vacuous adj. showing a lack of
thought or intelligence.
■ **vacuity** n.

vacuum n. (pl. **vacuums** or **vacua**) **1** a
completely empty space in which
there is no air or other matter. **2** a
gap left by the loss of someone or
something important.
• v. clean with a vacuum cleaner.
□ **vacuum cleaner** an electrical device
that collects dust by suction. **vacuum
flask** a container to keep liquids hot
or cold. **vacuum-packed** sealed in a
pack with the air removed.

vagabond n. a vagrant.

vagary n. (pl. **vagaries**) an
unpredictable change.

vagina /vuh-jy-nuh/ n. the passage
leading from a woman's external
genitals to the womb.
■ **vaginal** adj.

vagrant n. a person without a settled
home or job.
▷ SYNONYMS: **tramp**, drifter, down-and-
out, beggar, itinerant, wanderer;
N. Amer. **hobo**; N. Amer. informal **bum**.
■ **vagrancy** n.

vague adj. **1** not certain or definite.
2 not thinking or expressing yourself
clearly.
▷ SYNONYMS: **1 indistinct**, indefinite,
indeterminate, unclear, ill-defined,
hazy, fuzzy, misty, blurry, out of
focus, shadowy, obscure. **2 imprecise**,
rough, approximate, inexact, non-
specific, ambiguous, hazy, uncertain.
3 absent-minded, forgetful, dreamy,
abstracted; informal with your head in
the clouds, scatty.
– ANTONYMS: clear, definite.
■ **vaguely** adv. **vagueness** n.

vain adj. **1** having a very high opinion
of yourself. **2** useless or futile.
▷ SYNONYMS: **1 conceited**, narcissistic,
proud, arrogant, boastful, cocky,
egotistical, immodest; informal big-
headed. **2 futile**, useless, pointless,
ineffective, unavailing, fruitless,
unproductive, unsuccessful, failed,
abortive.
– ANTONYMS: modest, successful.
□ **in vain** without success.
■ **vainly** adv.

vainglorious adj. literary boastful or
vain.

valance n. a length of fabric around the base of a bed.

vale n. literary a valley.

valediction n. a farewell.
■ **valedictory** adj.

valency (or **valence**) n. (pl. **valencies**) the combining power of an element, as measured by the number of hydrogen atoms it can displace or combine with.

valentine n. 1 a card sent to a person you love on St Valentine's Day (14 February). 2 a person to whom you send such a card.

valet /va·lay/ n. a man's personal male attendant.
• v. (**valeting**, **valeted**) clean a car as a professional service.

valetudinarian /va-li-tyoo-di-**nair**-i-uhn/ n. a person in poor health or unduly anxious about their health.

valiant adj. brave.
▷ SYNONYMS: **brave**, courageous, plucky, intrepid, heroic, gallant, bold, fearless, daring, unflinching, unafraid, undaunted, doughty, indomitable, stout-hearted; informal game, gutsy.
− ANTONYMS: cowardly.
■ **valiantly** adv.

valid adj. 1 (of a reason etc.) sound or logical. 2 legally or officially acceptable.
▷ SYNONYMS: 1 **well founded**, sound, reasonable, rational, logical, justifiable, defensible, cogent, credible, forceful. 2 **legally binding**, lawful, official, in force, in effect.
■ **validity** n.

validate v. prove or declare to be valid.
▷ SYNONYMS: **ratify**, endorse, approve, agree to, accept, authorize, legalize, legitimize, warrant, license, certify, recognize.
■ **validation** n.

valise /vuh-**leez**/ n. a small suitcase.

valley n. (pl. **valleys**) a low area between hills.
▷ SYNONYMS: **dale**, vale, hollow, gully, gorge, ravine, canyon, rift; Brit. combe; Scottish glen.

valour (US **valor**) n. great bravery.
■ **valorous** adj.

valuable adj. 1 worth a great deal of money. 2 very useful or important.
▷ SYNONYMS: 1 **precious**, costly, high-priced, expensive, dear, priceless. 2 **useful**, helpful, beneficial, advantageous, invaluable, productive, worthwhile, worthy, important.
− ANTONYMS: worthless.
• n. (**valuables**) valuable items.

valuation n. an estimate of the worth of something.

value n. 1 importance or usefulness. 2 the amount of money that something is worth. 3 (**values**) standards of behaviour.
▷ SYNONYMS: 1 **worth**, importance, usefulness, advantage, benefit, gain, profit, good, help. 2 **price**, cost, worth, market price. 3 (**values**) **principles**, ethics, morals, standards, code of behaviour.
• v. 1 estimate the value of. 2 consider important or beneficial.
▷ SYNONYMS: 1 **evaluate**, assess, estimate, appraise, price. 2 **think highly of**, have a high opinion of, rate highly, esteem, set great store by, respect.
− ANTONYMS: despise.
□ **value added tax** a tax on the amount by which goods rise in value at each stage of production.
■ **valuer** n.

valve n. 1 a device controlling flow through a pipe. 2 a structure allowing blood to flow in one direction only.

vamp n. informal a woman who uses her sexuality to control men.
• v. (**vamp up**) improve by adding something interesting.

vampire n. a corpse supposed to leave its grave at night to drink the blood of the living.
□ **vampire bat** a bloodsucking tropical bat.

van n. 1 a motor vehicle for moving goods or people. 2 Brit. a railway carriage for luggage, mail, etc. 3 the leading part of an advancing group.

vanadium n. a hard grey metallic element.

vandal n. a person who deliberately damages property.
■ **vandalism** n.

vandalize (or -**ise**) v. deliberately damage.

vane n. a broad blade forming part of a windmill, propeller, etc.

vanguard n. 1 a group leading the way in new ideas. 2 the leading part of an advancing army.

vanilla n. a flavouring obtained from the pods of a tropical plant.

vanish v. disappear suddenly.
▷ SYNONYMS: **disappear**, be lost to sight, become invisible, recede from view, fade, evaporate, melt away, end, cease to exist.
− ANTONYMS: appear.

vanity n. (pl. **vanities**) 1 excessive pride in yourself. 2 futility.
▷ SYNONYMS: **conceit**, narcissism,

V

self-love, self-admiration, egotism, pride, arrogance, boastfulness, cockiness; informal big-headedness.
– ANTONYMS: modesty.

vanquish v. literary defeat thoroughly.

vantage (or **vantage point**) n. a position giving a good view.

vapid adj. not interesting or original.
■ vapidity n.

vaporize (or **-ise**) v. convert into vapour.
■ vaporization n.

vapour (US **vapor**) n. moisture suspended in the air.

variable adj. **1** often changing; not consistent. **2** able to be changed.
▷ SYNONYMS: **changeable**, shifting, fluctuating, irregular, inconstant, inconsistent, fluid, unstable; informal up and down.
– ANTONYMS: constant.
• n. a variable situation, feature, etc.
■ variability n. variably adv.

variance n. (**at variance**) disagreeing.

variant n. a form differing from other forms of the same thing.
▷ SYNONYMS: **variation**, version, form, alternative, adaptation, alteration, modification.

variation n. **1** a change or slight difference. **2** a variant. **3** a new but still recognizable version of a musical theme.
▷ SYNONYMS: **1** regional variations: **difference**, dissimilarity, disparity, contrast, discrepancy, imbalance. **2** there was little variation from the pattern: **deviation**, variance, divergence, departure, fluctuation, change, alteration, modification.

varicose adj. (of a vein) swollen and twisted.

varied adj. involving a number of different types or elements.
▷ SYNONYMS: **diverse**, assorted, miscellaneous, mixed, sundry, wide-ranging, disparate, heterogeneous, motley.

variegated adj. having irregular patches of a different colour.
■ variegation n.

variety n. (pl. **varieties**) **1** the quality of being varied. **2** a range of things of the same type that are distinct in character. **3** a sort or kind. **4** entertainment involving singing, dancing, and comedy.
▷ SYNONYMS: **1 diversity**, variation, diversification, change, difference. **2 assortment**, miscellany, range, array, collection, selection, mixture, medley. **3 sort**, kind, type, class, category, style, form, make, model,

brand, strain, breed.
– ANTONYMS: uniformity.

various adj. **1** of different kinds. **2** several.
▷ SYNONYMS: **diverse**, different, differing, varied, assorted, mixed, sundry, miscellaneous, disparate, heterogeneous, motley.
■ variously adv.

varlet n. old use a dishonest man.

varnish n. a liquid applied to wood etc., forming a hard, shiny surface when dry.
▷ SYNONYMS: **lacquer**, shellac, japan, enamel, glaze, polish.
• v. coat with varnish.

vary v. (**varying**, **varied**) make, be, or become different.
▷ SYNONYMS: **1 differ**, be dissimilar, disagree, be at variance. **2 fluctuate**, rise and fall, go up and down, change, alter, shift, swing.

vascular adj. of or containing veins.

vase n. a container for cut flowers.

vasectomy n. (pl. **vasectomies**) the surgical cutting and sealing of part of the ducts carrying semen as a means of sterilization.

vassal n. (in the feudal system) a man given land by a king or lord in return for military service.

vast adj. huge.
▷ SYNONYMS: **huge**, extensive, broad, wide, boundless, enormous, immense, great, massive, colossal, gigantic, mammoth, giant, mountainous; informal mega, whopping.
– ANTONYMS: tiny.
■ vastly adv. vastness n.

VAT abbrev. value added tax.

vat n. a large tank for liquids.

vaudeville n. entertainment featuring a mixture of musical and comedy acts.

vault n. **1** a large storage room, esp. in a bank. **2** a burial chamber. **3** a roof in the form of an arch. **4** an act of vaulting.
▷ SYNONYMS: **1 cellar**, basement, crypt, undercroft, catacomb, burial chamber. **2 strongroom**, safe deposit.
• v. jump using the hands or a pole to push yourself.
▷ SYNONYMS: **jump**, leap, spring, bound, clear.
■ vaulted adj.

vaunted adj. praised or boasted about.

VC abbrev. Victoria Cross.

VCR abbrev. video cassette recorder.

VDU abbrev. Brit. visual display unit.

veal n. meat from a young calf.

vector n. **1** a quantity having direction as well as magnitude. **2** the carrier of a disease or infection.

Veda /**vay**-duh, **vee**-duh/ n. the most ancient Hindu scriptures.

veer v. change direction.
▷ SYNONYMS: **turn**, swerve, swing, weave, wheel, change direction, change course, deviate.

vegan n. a person who does not eat or use any animal products.

vegetable n. a plant used as food.

vegetarian n. a person who does not eat meat or fish.
 • adj. eating or including no meat or fish.
 ■ **vegetarianism** n.

vegetate v. spend time in a dull, inactive way.

vegetation n. plants.

vegetative adj. **1** of vegetation. **2** alive but showing no sign of brain activity.

vehement adj. showing strong feeling.
▷ SYNONYMS: **passionate**, forceful, ardent, impassioned, heated, spirited, urgent, fervent, fierce, strong, forcible, powerful, emphatic, vigorous, intense, earnest, keen, enthusiastic, zealous.
– ANTONYMS: mild.
 ■ **vehemence** n. **vehemently** adv.

vehicle n. **1** a car, lorry, bus, etc. for transporting people or goods on land. **2** a means of expressing something.
▷ SYNONYMS: **1 means of transport**, transportation, conveyance. **2 channel**, medium, means, agent, instrument, mechanism, organ, apparatus.
 ■ **vehicular** adj.

> **WORD LINKS**
> **automotive** relating to vehicles

veil n. **1** a piece of fine fabric worn to protect or hide the face. **2** a thing that hides or disguises.
▷ SYNONYMS: **covering**, screen, curtain, mantle, cloak, mask, blanket, shroud, canopy, cloud, pall.
 • v. **1** cover with a veil. **2** (**veiled**) partially hidden or disguised.
▷ SYNONYMS: **cover**, surround, swathe, enfold, envelop, conceal, hide, obscure, screen, shield, cloak, blanket, shroud.

vein n. **1** any of the tubes by which blood is carried towards the heart. **2** (in plants) a structure carrying sap in a leaf. **3** a streak of a different colour. **4** a narrow deposit of a mineral or ore.
▷ SYNONYMS: **1 blood vessel**, capillary. **2 layer**, seam, lode, stratum, deposit.
 ■ **veined** adj.

> **WORD LINKS**
> **vascular**, **venous** relating to veins

Velcro n. trademark a fastener made of two strips of fabric which cling together when pressed.

veld (or **veldt**) n. open grassland in southern Africa.

vellum n. fine parchment made from animal skin.

velocity n. (pl. **velocities**) speed.
▷ SYNONYMS: **speed**, pace, rate, tempo, rapidity.

velour n. a fabric resembling velvet.

velvet n. a fabric with a soft, short pile on one side.
 ■ **velvety** adj.

venal adj. open to bribery.
 ■ **venality** n.

vend v. sell.
 ☐ **vending machine** a machine from which drinks, snacks, etc. can be bought by inserting coins.

vendetta n. a prolonged feud.

vendor n. a person selling something.

veneer n. **1** a thin covering of fine wood. **2** an outward appearance that hides someone's or something's true nature.
▷ SYNONYMS: **1 surface**, lamination, layer, overlay, facing, covering, finish, exterior. **2 facade**, front, show, outward display, appearance, impression, semblance, guise, mask, pretence, cover, camouflage.
 ■ **veneered** adj.

venerable adj. greatly respected because of wisdom, age, etc.

venerate v. respect greatly.
 ■ **veneration** n.

venereal disease n. a disease caught by having sex with an infected person.

Venetian adj. of Venice.
 ☐ **venetian blind** a window blind consisting of adjustable horizontal slats.

vengeance n. the act of harming or punishing someone in return for what they have done to you.
▷ SYNONYMS: **revenge**, retribution, retaliation, requital, reprisal, an eye for an eye.
– ANTONYMS: forgiveness.
 ☐ **with a vengeance** with great intensity.

vengeful adj. wanting revenge.

venial adj. (of a fault or offence) slight

V

and pardonable.

venison n. meat from a deer.

Venn diagram n. a diagram using overlapping circles to show relationships between mathematical sets.

venom n. **1** poisonous fluid produced by snakes, scorpions, etc. **2** hatred or bitterness.

venomous adj. **1** producing venom. **2** full of hatred or bitterness.
▷ SYNONYMS: **1 poisonous**, toxic, dangerous, deadly, lethal, fatal. **2 vicious**, spiteful, rancorous, malevolent, vitriolic, vindictive, malicious, poisonous, virulent, cruel; informal bitchy.
– ANTONYMS: harmless.

venous /vee-nuhss/ adj. of veins.

vent n. **1** an opening allowing air, gas, or liquid to pass through. **2** a slit in a garment.
▷ SYNONYMS: **outlet**, inlet, opening, aperture, hole, gap, orifice, space, duct, flue, shaft, well, passage, airway.
• v. express a strong emotion freely.
▷ SYNONYMS: **let out**, release, pour out, utter, express, air, voice.

ventilate v. cause air to enter and circulate freely in.
▷ SYNONYMS: **air**, aerate, oxygenate, freshen, cool.
■ ventilation n.

ventilator n. **1** a machine or opening for ventilating a room etc. **2** a machine that pumps air in and out of the lungs to assist breathing.

ventral adj. of the abdomen.

ventricle n. each of the two larger and lower cavities of the heart.

ventriloquist n. an entertainer who can make their voice seem to come from a puppet.
■ ventriloquism n.

venture n. a business project or other activity involving risk.
▷ SYNONYMS: **enterprise**, undertaking, project, scheme, operation, endeavour, speculation.
• v. dare to do or say.
▷ SYNONYMS: **1 put forward**, advance, proffer, offer, air, suggest, volunteer, submit, propose. **2 dare**, be so bold as, presume, have the audacity, have the nerve, take the liberty of.
■ venturesome adj.

venue n. the place where an event or meeting is held.

veracious adj. truthful.
■ veracity n.

veranda (or **verandah**) n. a roofed platform along the outside of a house.

verb n. a word describing an action, state, or occurrence.

verbal adj. **1** of or in the form of words. **2** spoken. **3** of a verb.
▷ SYNONYMS: **oral**, spoken, word-of-mouth, stated, said, unwritten.
■ verbally adv.

verbalize (or **-ise**) v. express in words.

verbatim /ver-bay-tim/ adv. & adj. in exactly the same words.

verbena n. a garden plant with showy flowers.

verbiage n. excessively long speech or writing.

verbose adj. using more words than are needed.
▷ SYNONYMS: **wordy**, loquacious, garrulous, talkative, voluble, long-winded, lengthy, prolix, circumlocutory, rambling.
– ANTONYMS: succinct.
■ verbosity n.

verdant adj. green with grass etc.

verdict n. **1** a formal decision made by a jury as to a person's innocence or guilt. **2** an opinion made after testing something.
▷ SYNONYMS: **judgement**, adjudication, decision, finding, ruling, sentence.

verdigris /ver-di-gree/ n. a green substance formed on copper or brass by oxidation.

verdure n. green vegetation.

verge n. **1** Brit. a grass edging by the side of a road or path. **2** an edge or border. **3** a limit beyond which something will happen.
▷ SYNONYMS: **1 edge**, border, margin, side, brink, rim, lip, fringe, boundary, perimeter. **2** I was on the verge of tears: **brink**, threshold, edge, point.
• v. (**verge on**) be very close or similar to.

verger n. a church caretaker.

verify v. (**verifying**, **verified**) check the truth or correctness of.
▷ SYNONYMS: **confirm**, prove, substantiate, corroborate, back up, bear out, justify, support, uphold, testify to, validate, authenticate.
– ANTONYMS: refute.
■ verifiable adj. verification n.

verily adv. old use truly; certainly.

verisimilitude n. the appearance of being true or real.

veritable adj. rightly so called.

verity n. (pl. **verities**) a true principle or belief.

vermicelli /ver-mi-chel-li/ pl. n. pasta made in long thin threads.

vermilion n. a brilliant red colour.

vermin n. wild animals and birds which carry disease or harm crops etc.
■ **verminous** adj.

vermouth /ver-**muhth**/ n. a red or white wine flavoured with herbs.

vernacular n. the language spoken by the ordinary people of a country or region.

vernal adj. of the season of spring.

verruca /vuh-**roo**-kuh/ n. a contagious wart on the sole of the foot.

versatile adj. able to do or be used for many different things.
▷ SYNONYMS: **1** *a versatile player:* **adaptable**, flexible, all-round, multi-talented, resourceful. **2** *a versatile device:* **adjustable**, adaptable, multi-purpose, all-purpose.
■ **versatility** n.

verse n. **1** writing arranged with a regular rhythm. **2** a group of lines forming a unit in a poem or song. **3** a numbered division of a chapter of the Bible.
▷ SYNONYMS: **1 poetry**, lyrics. **2 poem**, lyric, rhyme, ditty, limerick. **3 stanza**, canto.

versed adj. (**versed in**) experienced or skilled in.

versify v. (**versifying**, **versified**) write verse or express in verse.
■ **versification** n.

version n. **1** a form of something differing from other forms of the same type. **2** an account told from a particular person's point of view.
▷ SYNONYMS: **1 type**, sort, kind, form, equivalent, variety, variant, design, model, style. **2 account**, report, statement, description, record, story, rendering, interpretation, explanation, understanding, reading, impression, side. **3 edition**, translation, impression.

verso n. (pl. **versos**) a left-hand page of an open book.

versus prep. against.

vertebra n. (pl. **vertebrae**) each of the small bones forming the backbone.
■ **vertebral** adj.

vertebrate n. an animal having a backbone.

vertex n. (pl. **vertices** or **vertexes**) **1** the highest point. **2** a meeting point of two lines that form an angle.

vertical adj. at right angles to a horizontal line or surface.
▷ SYNONYMS: **upright**, erect, perpendicular, plumb, on end, standing.
− ANTONYMS: flat, horizontal.
■ **vertically** adv.

vertiginous /ver-**tij**-i-nuhss/ adj. very high or steep.

vertigo n. giddiness caused by looking down from a great height.

verve n. energy, spirit, and style.

very adv. in a high degree.
▷ SYNONYMS: **extremely**, exceedingly, exceptionally, extraordinarily, tremendously, immensely, acutely, singularly, decidedly, highly, remarkably, really; informal awfully, terribly, seriously, mega, ultra; Brit. informal well, dead, jolly; N. Amer. informal real, mighty.
− ANTONYMS: slightly.
• adj. **1** actual; precise. **2** mere.

vesicle n. a small fluid-filled sac.

vespers n. a Christian service of evening prayer.

vessel n. **1** a ship or large boat. **2** a tube or duct carrying fluid in an animal or plant. **3** a container for liquids.
▷ SYNONYMS: **1 boat**, ship, craft. **2 container**, receptacle, basin, bowl, pan, pot, jug.

vest n. **1** Brit. a sleeveless undergarment worn on the upper part of the body. **2** US & Austral. a waistcoat.
• v. (**vest in**) give someone the legal right or power to do or own.
□ **vested interest** a personal reason for wanting something to happen.

vestibule n. a small entrance hall.

vestige n. **1** a last remaining trace. **2** the smallest amount.
▷ SYNONYMS: **remnant**, fragment, relic, echo, trace, mark, legacy, reminder.
■ **vestigial** adj.

vestment n. a robe worn by the clergy or members of a choir during services.

vestry n. (pl. **vestries**) a room in a church, used as an office and for changing into robes.

vet n. esp. Brit. a veterinary surgeon.
• v. (**vetting**, **vetted**) check very carefully, esp. to decide on a candidate's suitability for a job.
▷ SYNONYMS: **check up on**, screen, investigate, examine, scrutinize, inspect, look over, assess, evaluate, appraise; informal check out.

veteran n. a person with long experience, esp. in the armed forces.
• adj. having long experience: *a veteran campaigner.*
▷ SYNONYMS: **long-serving**, seasoned, old, hardened, practised, experienced; informal battle-scarred.
− ANTONYMS: novice.

veterinarian n. US a veterinary surgeon.

v

veterinary /vet-uhn-ri, vet-ri-nuh-ri/ adj. of the treatment of injuries and diseases in animals.
□ **veterinary surgeon** Brit. a person qualified to treat sick or injured animals.

veto n. (pl. **vetoes**) **1** a right to reject a decision or proposal made by others. **2** a refusal to allow something.
▷ SYNONYMS: **rejection**, dismissal, prohibition, proscription, embargo, ban, interdict.
• v. (**vetoing**, **vetoed**) use a veto to prevent; refuse to allow.
▷ SYNONYMS: **reject**, turn down, throw out, dismiss, prohibit, forbid, proscribe, disallow, embargo, ban, rule out; informal kill, give the thumbs down to.
– ANTONYMS: approve.

vex v. annoy or worry.
□ **vexed question** a complex and widely discussed issue.
■ **vexation** n. **vexatious** adj.

VHF abbrev. very high frequency.

via prep. by way of; through.

viable adj. capable of working or surviving successfully.
▷ SYNONYMS: **feasible**, workable, practicable, practical, realistic, achievable, attainable; informal doable.
– ANTONYMS: impracticable.
■ **viability** n.

viaduct n. a long bridge carrying a road or railway across a valley.

vial n. a small medicine bottle.

viands pl. n. old use food.

vibe (or **vibes**) n. informal the atmosphere of a place or a mood passing among people.

vibrant adj. **1** full of energy and enthusiasm. **2** (of sound) resonant. **3** (of colour) bright.
▷ SYNONYMS: **1 spirited**, lively, energetic, vigorous, dynamic, passionate, fiery; informal feisty. **2 vivid**, bright, striking, brilliant, glowing, strong, rich.
– ANTONYMS: lifeless, pale.
■ **vibrancy** n. **vibrantly** adv.

vibraphone n. an electrical percussion instrument giving a vibrato effect.

vibrate v. **1** move with rapid small movements to and fro. **2** (of a sound) resonate.
▷ SYNONYMS: **shake**, tremble, shiver, quiver, shudder, throb, pulsate.
■ **vibration** n.

vibrato n. (in music) a rapid, slight variation in pitch.

vibrator n. a vibrating device used for massage or sexual stimulation.

vicar n. (in the Church of England) a minister in charge of a parish.

vicarage n. the house of a vicar.

vicarious adj. experienced in the imagination rather than directly.
■ **vicariously** adv.

vice n. **1** immoral or wicked behaviour. **2** criminal activities involving prostitution, pornography, or drugs. **3** a bad habit or characteristic. **4** a tool with movable jaws for holding an object firmly.
▷ SYNONYMS: **1 immorality**, wrongdoing, wickedness, evil, iniquity, villainy, corruption, misconduct, sin, depravity. **2 fault**, failing, flaw, defect, shortcoming, weakness, deficiency, foible, frailty.
– ANTONYMS: virtue.

vice- comb. form next in rank to; deputy.

viceroy n. a person sent by a monarch to govern a colony.
■ **viceregal** adj.

vice versa adv. reversing the order of the items just mentioned.

vicinity n. (pl. **vicinities**) the surrounding area.

vicious adj. **1** cruel or violent. **2** wild and dangerous.
▷ SYNONYMS: **1 brutal**, ferocious, savage, violent, ruthless, merciless, heartless, callous, cruel, cold-blooded, inhuman, barbaric, bloodthirsty. **2 malicious**, spiteful, vindictive, venomous, cruel, bitter, acrimonious, hostile, nasty; informal catty.
– ANTONYMS: gentle.
□ **vicious circle** a situation in which one problem leads to another, which then makes the first one worse.
■ **viciously** adv. **viciousness** n.

vicissitudes /vi-siss-i-tyoodz/ pl. n. changes of circumstance or fortune.

victim n. a person harmed or killed.
▷ SYNONYMS: **sufferer**, injured party, casualty, fatality, loss, survivor.

victimize (or **-ise**) v. single out for cruel or unfair treatment.
▷ SYNONYMS: **persecute**, pick on, bully, abuse, discriminate against, exploit, take advantage of; informal have it in for.
■ **victimization** n.

victor n. a person who defeats an opponent.

Victorian adj. of the reign of Queen Victoria (1837–1901).

victorious adj. having won a victory.
▷ SYNONYMS: **triumphant**, conquering, vanquishing, winning, champion, successful.
– ANTONYMS: unsuccessful.

V

■ **victoriously** adv.

victory n. (pl. **victories**) an act of defeating an opponent.
▷ SYNONYMS: **success**, triumph, conquest, win, coup; informal walkover.
– ANTONYMS: defeat, loss.

victualler /vit-ler/ n. Brit. a person licensed to sell alcoholic drinks.

victuals /vi-t'lz/ n. dated food or provisions.

video n. (pl. **videos**) **1** a system of recording and reproducing moving images on magnetic tape. **2** a film on magnetic tape.
• v. (**videoing**, **videoed**) make a video recording of.
□ **video recorder** a machine for recording television programmes and playing videos. **videotape 1** magnetic tape for recording images and sound. **2** a cassette of this.

vie v. (**vying**, **vied**) compete eagerly with others.
▷ SYNONYMS: **compete**, contend, struggle, fight, battle, jockey.

view n. **1** the ability to see something or to be seen from a particular position. **2** something seen from a particular position, esp. natural scenery. **3** an attitude or opinion.
▷ SYNONYMS: **1** *the church came into view:* sight, perspective, vision, visibility. **2** outlook, prospect, panorama, vista, scene, scenery, landscape. **3** opinion, viewpoint, belief, judgement, thinking, notion, idea, conviction, persuasion, attitude, feeling, sentiment.
• v. **1** look at or inspect. **2** regard as. **3** watch on television.
▷ SYNONYMS: **1** look at, observe, eye, gaze at, contemplate, regard, scan, survey, inspect, scrutinize; informal check out; N. Amer. informal eyeball. **2** *they viewed her as a troublemaker:* consider, regard, look on, see, perceive, judge, deem, reckon.
□ **in view of** because or as a result of. **viewfinder** a device on a camera showing what will appear in the picture. **viewpoint** an opinion. **with a view to** with the intention of.
■ **viewer** n.

vigil n. a period of staying awake to keep watch or pray.

vigilant adj. alert to possible danger or problems.
▷ SYNONYMS: **watchful**, observant, attentive, alert, eagle-eyed, on the lookout, on your guard; informal beady-eyed.
– ANTONYMS: inattentive.

■ **vigilance** n. **vigilantly** adv.

vigilante /vi-ji-lan-ti/ n. a member of a group undertaking crime prevention and punishment without legal authority.

vignette /vee-nyet/ n. a brief vivid description.

vigorous adj. **1** strong, healthy, and full of energy. **2** involving physical strength, effort, or energy.
▷ SYNONYMS: **1** robust, healthy, hale and hearty, strong, sturdy, fit, hardy, tough, energetic, lively, active. **2** strenuous, powerful, forceful, spirited, determined, aggressive, passionate; informal punchy, feisty.
– ANTONYMS: weak, feeble.
■ **vigorously** adv.

vigour (US **vigor**) n. **1** physical strength and good health. **2** energy and enthusiasm.
▷ SYNONYMS: **health**, strength, robustness, energy, life, vitality, spirit, passion, determination, dynamism, drive; informal oomph, get-up-and-go.
– ANTONYMS: lethargy.

Viking n. an ancient Scandinavian trader, pirate, and settler.

vile adj. very unpleasant or wicked.
▷ SYNONYMS: **foul**, nasty, unpleasant, bad, horrid, repulsive, disgusting, hateful, nauseating; informal gross.
– ANTONYMS: pleasant.
■ **vilely** adv.

vilify v. (**vilifying**, **vilified**) speak or write about in abusive terms.
■ **vilification** n.

villa n. **1** Brit. a rented holiday home abroad. **2** a large country house.

village n. a small settlement in a country area.
■ **villager** n.

villain n. a bad or wicked person.
▷ SYNONYMS: **criminal**, lawbreaker, offender, felon, miscreant, wrongdoer, rogue, scoundrel, reprobate; informal crook, baddy.
■ **villainous** adj. **villainy** n.

villein n. hist. a poor man who had to work for a lord in return for a small plot of land.

vim n. informal vigour.

vinaigrette n. salad dressing of oil and vinegar.

vindicate v. **1** clear of blame or suspicion. **2** show to be justified.
▷ SYNONYMS: **1** acquit, clear, absolve, exonerate; informal let off. **2** justify, warrant, substantiate, confirm, corroborate, prove, defend, support, back, endorse.
– ANTONYMS: incriminate.

V

■ **vindication** n.

vindictive adj. having a strong or excessive desire for revenge.

■ **vindictively** adv. **vindictiveness** n.

vine n. a climbing plant producing grapes.

□ **vineyard** a plantation of vines producing grapes for making wine.

vinegar n. a sour liquid made from wine, beer, or cider.

■ **vinegary** adj.

vintage n. **1** the year in which a wine was produced. **2** a wine of high quality from a particular district and year. **3** the time that something was produced.

• adj. (of something from the past) of high quality.

▷ SYNONYMS: **high-quality**, quality, choice, select, superior; classic, ageless, timeless, old, antique, historic.

vintner n. a wine merchant.

vinyl /vy-n'l/ n. a type of plastic.

viola[1] /vi-oh-luh/ n. an instrument like a violin but of lower pitch.

viola[2] /vy-uh-luh/ n. a plant of a group including pansies and violets.

violate v. **1** break a rule or agreement. **2** treat with disrespect. **3** dated rape.

▷ SYNONYMS: **1 contravene**, breach, infringe, break, transgress, disobey, defy, flout, disregard, ignore. **2 desecrate**, profane, defile, degrade, debase, damage, vandalize, deface, destroy.

– ANTONYMS: respect.

■ **violator** n..

violation n. the action of violation.

▷ SYNONYMS: **1 contravention**, breach, infringement, transgression, defiance, flouting, disregard. **2 desecration**, defilement, damage, vandalism, destruction.

violence n. **1** actions using physical force intended to hurt, damage, or kill. **2** great force or intensity.

▷ SYNONYMS: **1 brutality**, savagery, cruelty, barbarity. **2 force**, power, strength, might, ferocity, intensity, vehemence.

violent adj. **1** using or involving violence. **2** very intense.

▷ SYNONYMS: **1 brutal**, vicious, savage, rough, aggressive, threatening, fierce, ferocious, bloodthirsty. **2 powerful**, forceful, hard, sharp, smart, strong, vigorous, mighty, hefty. **3 intense**, extreme, strong, powerful, fierce, unbridled, uncontrollable, ungovernable, consuming, passionate.

– ANTONYMS: gentle, mild.

■ **violently** adv.

violet n. **1** a small plant with purple or blue flowers. **2** a bluish-purple colour.

violin n. a musical instrument with four strings, played with a bow.

■ **violinist** n.

violoncello n. a cello.

VIP abbrev. very important person.

viper n. a type of poisonous snake.

virago n. (pl. **viragos** or **viragoes**) a domineering or bad-tempered woman.

viral adj. of a virus or viruses.

virgin n. **1** a person who has never had sex. **2** (**the Virgin**) Mary, the mother of Jesus.

• adj. **1** not yet used or spoilt. **2** having had no sexual experience.

■ **virginal** adj. **virginity** n.

virile adj. (of a man) strong, vigorous, and having a strong sex drive.

■ **virility** n.

virology n. the study of viruses.

■ **virologist** n.

virtual adj. **1** almost as described, but not completely. **2** of or using virtual reality.

▷ SYNONYMS: they have a virtual monopoly in the market: **effective**, near, essential, practical, to all intents and purposes, in all but name, implied, unacknowledged.

□ **virtual reality** a system in which images that look like real objects are created by computer.

virtually adv. nearly; almost.

▷ SYNONYMS: **nearly**, practically, almost, more or less, close to, verging on, just about, as good as, effectively, essentially, to all intents and purposes.

virtue n. **1** behaviour showing high moral standards. **2** a good or desirable quality. **3** old use virginity or chastity.

▷ SYNONYMS: **1 goodness**, righteousness, morality, integrity, dignity, rectitude, honour, probity. **2 good point**, good quality, strong point, asset, forte, attribute, strength, merit, advantage, benefit; informal plus.

– ANTONYMS: vice.

□ **by virtue of** as a result of.

virtuoso n. (pl. **virtuosi** or **virtuosos**) a person highly skilled in music or another art.

■ **virtuosity** n.

virtuous adj. having high moral standards.

■ **virtuously** adv.

virulent adj. **1** (of a disease or poison) very harmful. **2** bitterly hostile.

■ **virulence** n. **virulently** adv.

virus n. **1** a minute organism which can cause disease. **2** a destructive code introduced secretly into a computer system.

visa n. a permit on a passport allowing someone to enter, leave, or stay in a country.

visage n. literary a person's face.

vis-à-vis /veez-ah-vee/ prep. in relation to.

viscera /viss-uh-ruh/ pl. n. the internal organs of the body.
■ **visceral** adj.

viscid /viss-id/ adj. sticky.

viscose n. a synthetic fabric made from cellulose.

viscount /vy-kownt/ n. a nobleman ranking between earl and baron.

viscountess n. **1** the wife or widow of a viscount. **2** a woman holding the rank of viscount.

viscous adj. thick and sticky.
■ **viscosity** n.

visibility n. **1** the state of being able to see or be seen. **2** the distance a person can see, depending on light and weather conditions.

visible adj. able to be seen or noticed.
▷ SYNONYMS: **observable**, perceptible, noticeable, detectable, discernible, in sight, in view, on display, evident, apparent, manifest, plain.
■ **visibly** adv.

vision n. **1** the ability to see. **2** the ability to think about the future with imagination or wisdom. **3** a mental image. **4** the images on a television screen.
▷ SYNONYMS: **1 eyesight**, sight, observation, eyes, view, perspective. **2** *a man of vision and conviction:* **imagination**, creativity, inventiveness, inspiration, intuition, perception, insight. **3 apparition**, spectre, phantom, ghost, wraith, manifestation, hallucination, illusion, mirage.

> **WORD LINKS**
> **visual**, **optical** relating to vision

visionary adj. thinking about the future with imagination or wisdom.
• n. (pl. **visionaries**) a visionary person.

visit v. **1** go to spend time with a person or in a place. **2** view a website or web page. **3** (**visit on**) cause something unpleasant to affect.
▷ SYNONYMS: **call on**, go to see, look in on, stay with, holiday with, stop by, drop by; informal pop/drop in on, look up.
• n. an act of visiting.
▷ SYNONYMS: **social call**, stay, stopover,

trip, holiday; N. Amer. vacation; literary sojourn.

visitation n. **1** an official or formal visit. **2** a disaster or difficulty seen as a divine punishment.

visitor n. a person visiting someone or somewhere.
▷ SYNONYMS: **1 guest**, caller, company. **2 tourist**, traveller, holidaymaker, tripper, sightseer; N. Amer. vacationer.

visor (or **vizor**) n. **1** a movable part of a helmet for covering the face. **2** a screen for shielding the eyes from light.

vista n. a pleasing view.
▷ SYNONYMS: **view**, scene, prospect, panorama, sight, scenery, landscape.

visual adj. of seeing or sight.
▷ SYNONYMS: **1 optical**, ocular. **2 visible**, observable, perceptible, discernible.
□ **visual display unit** Brit. a device displaying information from a computer on a screen.
■ **visually** adv.

visualize (or **-ise**) v. form a mental image of.
▷ SYNONYMS: **envisage**, conjure up, picture, call to mind, see, imagine, dream up.
■ **visualization** n.

vital adj. **1** absolutely necessary. **2** essential for life. **3** full of energy.
▷ SYNONYMS: **1 essential**, critical, crucial, indispensable, all-important, imperative, mandatory, high-priority, key, life-and-death. **2 lively**, energetic, active, sprightly, spirited, vivacious, exuberant, dynamic, vigorous; informal full of beans.
– ANTONYMS: unimportant.
• n. (**vitals**) the body's important internal organs.
□ **vital statistics** informal the measurements of a woman's bust, waist, and hips.
■ **vitally** adv..

vitality n. the state of being strong and active.
▷ SYNONYMS: **life**, energy, spirit, vivacity, exuberance, dynamism, vigour, passion, drive; informal get-up-and-go.

vitalize (or **-ise**) v. give strength and energy to.

vitamin n. an organic compound present in food and essential for normal nutrition.

vitiate /vi-shee-ayt/ v. make less good or effective.

viticulture n. the cultivation of grapevines.

vitreous adj. like or containing glass.

vitrify v. (**vitrifying**, **vitrified**) convert

V

into glass or a glass-like substance by exposure to heat.

vitriol n. **1** great bitterness or malice. **2** old use sulphuric acid.
■ **vitriolic** adj.

vituperation n. bitter and abusive language.
■ **vituperative** adj.

viva¹ /vee-vuh/ exclam. long live!

viva² /vy-vuh/ (or **viva voce** /vy-vuh voh-chi/) n. Brit. an oral university exam.

vivacious adj. attractively lively.
■ **vivaciously** adv. **vivacity** n.

vivarium n. (pl. **vivaria**) a place for keeping animals in natural conditions.

vivid adj. **1** producing strong, clear images in the mind. **2** (of colour) very deep or bright.
▷ SYNONYMS: **1 bright**, colourful, brilliant, radiant, vibrant, strong, bold, deep, intense, rich, warm. **2 graphic**, realistic, lifelike, faithful, authentic, striking, evocative, arresting, colourful, dramatic, memorable, powerful, stirring, moving, haunting.
– ANTONYMS: dull, vague.
■ **vividly** adv. **vividness** n.

vivify v. (**vivifying**, **vivified**) make more lively.

viviparous /vi-vip-uh-ruhss/ adj. giving birth to live young.

vivisection n. the performing of operations on live animals for scientific research.

vixen n. a female fox.

viz. adv. namely; in other words.

vizor var. of VISOR.

vocabulary n. (pl. **vocabularies**) **1** the words used in a particular language or activity or known to a person. **2** a list of words and their meanings.

vocal adj. **1** of or for the voice. **2** expressing opinions freely.
▷ SYNONYMS: **1 spoken**, said, voiced, uttered, articulated, oral. **2 vociferous**, outspoken, forthright, plain-spoken, blunt, frank, candid, passionate, vehement, vigorous.
• n. (or **vocals**) a piece of sung music.
□ **vocal cords** membranes in the throat that vibrate to produce the voice.
■ **vocally** adv.

vocalist n. a singer.

vocalize (or **-ise**) v. utter sounds or words.

vocation n. **1** a strong feeling that you ought to pursue a particular career. **2** a career.

▷ SYNONYMS: **calling**, life's work, mission, purpose, profession, occupation, career, job, employment, trade, craft, line of work.
■ **vocational** adj.

vociferous adj. expressing opinions forcefully and loudly.
■ **vociferously** adv.

vodka n. an alcoholic spirit made from rye, wheat, or potatoes.

vogue n. the current fashion or style.
▷ SYNONYMS: **fashion**, trend, fad, fancy, craze, rage, enthusiasm, passion.

voice n. **1** the sound produced in the larynx and uttered through the mouth, as speech or song. **2** an opinion or the right to express an opinion.
▷ SYNONYMS: **opinion**, view, feeling, wish, desire, vote.
• v. express in words.
▷ SYNONYMS: **express**, communicate, declare, state, vent, utter, say, speak, articulate, air; informal come out with.
□ **voicemail** an electronic system for storing messages from phone callers.
voice-over spoken information in a film provided by a person who does not appear on the screen.

> **WORD LINKS**
> **vocal** relating to the human voice

void adj. **1** not valid. **2** empty.
▷ SYNONYMS: **1 invalid**, null and void, ineffective, worthless. **2 empty**, vacant, blank, bare, clear, free.
– ANTONYMS: valid, full.
• n. an empty space.
▷ SYNONYMS: **vacuum**, emptiness, nothingness, blankness, space, gap, cavity, chasm, gulf.
• v. **1** discharge waste from the bowels or bladder. **2** declare to be no longer valid.

voile /voyl, vwahl/ n. a thin, semi-transparent fabric.

volatile adj. **1** liable to change unpredictably. **2** easily evaporated.
▷ SYNONYMS: **1 unpredictable**, temperamental, capricious, fickle, impulsive, emotional, excitable, turbulent, erratic, unstable. **2** a volatile situation: **tense**, strained, fraught, uneasy, uncomfortable, charged, explosive, inflammatory, turbulent.
– ANTONYMS: stable.
■ **volatility** n.

vol-au-vent /vol-oh-von/ n. a small round case of puff pastry with a savoury filling.

volcano n. (pl. **volcanoes** or **volcanos**) a mountain with an opening through

which lava, gas, etc. is forced out.
■ **volcanic** adj.

vole n. a small mouse-like rodent.

volition n. the power of choosing and deciding for yourself.

volley n. (pl. **volleys**) **1** a number of bullets, missiles, etc. fired at one time. **2** a series of questions, insults, etc. **3** (in sport) a hit of the ball made before it touches the ground.
▷ SYNONYMS: **barrage**, cannonade, battery, bombardment, salvo, burst, storm, hail, shower, deluge, torrent.
• v. hit the ball before it touches the ground.
☐ **volleyball** a team game in which a ball is hit by hand over a net.

volt n. a basic unit of electromotive force.

voltage n. electromotive force expressed in volts.

volte-face /volt-fass/ n. an abrupt and complete reversal of attitude or policy.

voluble adj. speaking fluently and at length.
■ **volubility** n. **volubly** adv.

volume n. **1** the amount of space occupied by something or enclosed within a container. **2** an amount or quantity. **3** degree of loudness. **4** a book.
▷ SYNONYMS: **1 book**, publication, tome, work, title. **2 capacity**, mass, bulk, extent, size, dimensions. **3 quantity**, amount, mass, bulk, measure. **4 loudness**, sound, amplification.

voluminous adj. (of clothing) loose and full.

voluntarily adv. of your own free will.
▷ SYNONYMS: **willingly**, of your own free will, of your own volition, by choice, by preference, spontaneously, readily, freely.

voluntary adj. **1** done or acting of your own free will. **2** working or done without payment.
▷ SYNONYMS: **1 optional**, discretionary, at your discretion, elective, non-compulsory. **2 unpaid**, unsalaried, for free, honorary.
– ANTONYMS: compulsory.

volunteer n. **1** a person who offers to do something. **2** a person who works for no pay. **3** a person who freely joins the armed forces.
• v. **1** freely offer to do. **2** say without being asked.
▷ SYNONYMS: **1 offer**, tender, proffer, put forward, put up, venture. **2 offer your services**, present yourself, make

yourself available, come forward.

voluptuary n. (pl. **voluptuaries**) a person who loves luxury and pleasure.

voluptuous adj. **1** (of a woman) curvaceous and sexually attractive. **2** giving sensual pleasure.
■ **voluptuously** adv.

vomit v. (**vomiting**, **vomited**) bring up food from the stomach through the mouth.
▷ SYNONYMS: **be sick**, spew, heave, retch, gag; informal throw up, puke; N. Amer. informal barf.
• n. vomited food.

voodoo n. a religious cult practised esp. in the Caribbean and involving sorcery and possession by spirits.

voracious adj. **1** wanting or eating great quantities of food. **2** very eager and enthusiastic.
■ **voraciously** adv. **voracity** n.

vortex n. (pl. **vortexes** or **vortices**) a whirling mass of water or air.

votary n. (pl. **votaries**) **1** a person who has dedicated themselves to God. **2** a devoted follower.

vote n. **1** a formal choice made between two or more candidates or options. **2** (**the vote**) the right to participate in an election.
▷ SYNONYMS: **1 ballot**, poll, election, referendum, plebiscite, show of hands. **2** (**the vote**) **suffrage**, franchise, voting rights.
• v. give or register a vote.
■ **voter** n.

WORD LINKS
psephology the study of elections and voting

votive adj. offered to a god as a sign of thanks.

vouch v. (**vouch for**) confirm the truth, accuracy, or honesty of.

voucher n. a piece of paper that may be exchanged for goods or services.
▷ SYNONYMS: **coupon**, token, ticket, pass, chit, slip, stub, docket; Brit. informal chitty.

vouchsafe v. give or grant.

vow n. a solemn promise.
▷ SYNONYMS: **promise**, pledge, oath, bond, covenant, commitment, word, word of honour.
• v. solemnly promise.
▷ SYNONYMS: **promise**, pledge, swear, undertake, make a commitment, give your word, guarantee.

vowel n. a letter of the alphabet representing a speech sound in which the mouth is open and the tongue not touching the top of the mouth, the teeth, or the lips (e.g. *a* or *e*).

vox pop n. Brit. informal popular opinion represented by informal comments from the public.

voyage n. a long journey by sea or in space.

▷ SYNONYMS: **journey**, trip, cruise, passage, sail, crossing, expedition, odyssey.

• v. go on a voyage.

■ voyager n.

voyeur /vwa-**yer**/ n. a person who gets sexual pleasure from watching others when they are naked or having sex.

vs abbrev. versus.

vulcanize (or **-ise**) v. harden rubber by treating it with sulphur at a high temperature.

vulgar adj. **1** lacking sophistication or good taste. **2** referring to sex or bodily functions in a rude way.

▷ SYNONYMS: **1 tasteless**, crass, tawdry, ostentatious, flamboyant, showy, gaudy, garish; informal flash, tacky. **2 impolite**, ill-mannered, boorish,

uncouth, unsophisticated, unrefined. **3 rude**, crude, dirty, filthy, smutty, naughty, indecent, obscene, coarse, risqué; informal blue.

– ANTONYMS: tasteful.

◻ **vulgar fraction** Brit. a fraction shown by numbers above and below a line, not decimally.

■ vulgarity n. vulgarly adv.

vulgarian n. a person lacking in sophistication and taste.

vulnerable adj. exposed to being attacked or harmed.

▷ SYNONYMS: **1 in danger**, in peril, in jeopardy, at risk, unprotected, undefended, unguarded, open to attack, exposed, defenceless, an easy target. **2 helpless**, weak, sensitive, thin-skinned.

– ANTONYMS: invulnerable.

■ vulnerability n.

vulpine adj. of or like a fox.

vulture n. a large bird of prey that feeds on dead animals.

vulva n. the female external genitals.

vying pres. part. of VIE.

Ww

W abbrev. **1** watts. **2** West or Western.

wacky adj. (**wackier, wackiest**) informal odd but funny.

wad n. **1** a pad of soft material. **2** a bundle of papers or banknotes.
• v. (**wadding, wadded**) press into a wad.

waddle v. walk with short steps and a swaying motion.
▷ SYNONYMS: **toddle**, totter, wobble, shuffle.
• n. a waddling walk.

wade v. **1** walk through water or mud. **2** (**wade through**) read something very long or boring.

wader n. **1** a long-legged waterbird. **2** (**waders**) high waterproof boots.

wadi n. (pl. **wadis**) a valley or channel that is dry except in the rainy season.

wafer n. **1** a thin, light biscuit. **2** a very thin slice.

waffle v. Brit. informal speak or write at length in a vague or trivial way.
• n. **1** Brit. informal lengthy but vague or trivial talk or writing. **2** a small crisp batter cake, eaten hot.

waft v. move easily or gently through the air.
• n. a scent carried in the air.

wag v. (**wagging, wagged**) move rapidly to and fro.
▷ SYNONYMS: **1 swing**, swish, switch, sway, shake; informal waggle. **2 shake**, wave, wiggle, flourish, brandish.
• n. **1** a wagging movement. **2** informal a person fond of making jokes.

wage n. (also **wages**) a fixed regular payment for work.
▷ SYNONYMS: **pay**, salary, stipend, fee, remuneration, income, earnings.
• v. carry on a war or campaign.
▷ SYNONYMS: **engage in**, carry on, conduct, execute, pursue, prosecute, proceed with.

wager n. & v. = BET.

waggle v. move rapidly from side to side or up and down.

wagon (Brit. also **waggon**) n. **1** a vehicle, esp. a horse-drawn one, for transporting goods in bulk. **2** Brit. a railway vehicle for carrying goods in bulk.

wagtail n. a small bird with a long tail that it wags up and down.

waif n. **1** a homeless child. **2** a person who is thin and pale.

wail n. a long, high-pitched cry of pain or grief.
▷ SYNONYMS: **howl**, cry, bawl, moan, groan, yowl, whine, lament.
• v. make a wail.

wainscot (or **wainscoting**) n. wooden panelling on the lower part of the walls of a room.

waist n. **1** the part of the body between the ribs and hips. **2** a narrow middle part.
□ **waistcoat** Brit. a waist-length garment with no sleeves or collar.
waistline the measurement around a person's waist.

wait v. **1** stay in a place or delay action until a particular time or event. **2** be delayed or deferred. **3** (**wait on**) act as an attendant to. **4** act as a waiter or waitress.
▷ SYNONYMS: **1** *we waited in the airport:* **stay**, stay put, remain, rest, stop, linger, loiter; informal stick around; old use tarry. **2** *she had to wait until her bags arrived:* **stand by**, hold back, bide your time, mark time, kill time, waste time, kick your heels, twiddle your thumbs; informal hold on, hang around, sit tight.
• n. a period of waiting.
▷ SYNONYMS: **delay**, hold-up, interval, interlude, pause, break, suspension, stoppage, halt, interruption, lull, gap.

waiter (or **waitress**) n. a person whose job is to serve customers in a restaurant.
▷ SYNONYMS: **server**, steward, stewardess, attendant, butler, servant; N. Amer. waitperson.

waive v. choose not to insist on a right or claim.
▷ SYNONYMS: **1 give up**, abandon,

w

renounce, relinquish, surrender, sacrifice, turn down. **2 disregard**, ignore, overlook, set aside, forgo.
■ **waiver** n.

wake v. (**waking**, **woke**; past part. **woken**) **1** stop sleeping. **2** stir; rouse.
▷SYNONYMS: **awake**, waken, wake up, stir, come to, come round, rouse.
•n. **1** a party held after a funeral. **2** a watch kept beside the body of a dead person. **3** a trail of disturbed water left by a ship.
▷SYNONYMS: **backwash**, slipstream, trail, path, track.
□ **in the wake of** coming after.

wakeful adj. unable to sleep.
■ **wakefulness** n.

waken v. wake.

walk v. **1** move fairly slowly using the legs. **2** travel over on foot. **3** accompany on foot.
▷SYNONYMS: **1 stroll**, saunter, amble, trudge, plod, hike, tramp, trek, march, stride, troop, wander, ramble, promenade, traipse; informal mosey, hoof it. **2 accompany**, escort, guide, show, see, take, usher.
•n. **1** a journey on foot. **2** a way of walking. **3** a path for walking.
▷SYNONYMS: **1 ramble**, hike, tramp, march, stroll, promenade, constitutional, turn. **2 gait**, step, stride, tread. **3 path**, pathway, footpath, track, walkway, promenade, footway, pavement, trail, towpath.
□ **walking stick** a stick used for support when walking. **walk of life** social rank. **walkout** a sudden angry departure as a protest or strike. **walkover** an easy victory.
■ **walker** n.

walkie-talkie n. a portable two-way radio.

wall n. **1** a continuous upright structure forming a side of a building or room, or enclosing or dividing an area of land. **2** a barrier. **3** the outer layer or lining of a body organ or cavity.
▷SYNONYMS: **fortification**, rampart, barricade, bulwark, partition.
•v. enclose or block with a wall.
□ **wallflower 1** a garden plant. **2** informal a girl who has no one to dance with at a party. **wallpaper** decorative paper for covering the walls of a room.

wallaby n. (pl. **wallabies**) a marsupial like a small kangaroo.

wallet n. a small, flat, folding holder for money etc.
▷SYNONYMS: **purse**, case, pouch, holder;

N. Amer. billfold, pocketbook.

wallop informal v. (**walloping**, **walloped**) hit hard.
•n. a heavy blow.

wallow v. **1** roll in mud or water. **2** (**wallow in**) indulge in.
▷SYNONYMS: **1 roll**, loll about, lie around, splash about. **2 luxuriate**, bask, take great pleasure, take great satisfaction, indulge yourself, delight, revel, glory.

wally n. (pl. **wallies**) informal a silly person.

walnut n. a wrinkled edible nut.

walrus n. a large sea mammal with long tusks.

waltz n. a ballroom dance in triple time.
•v. **1** dance a waltz. **2** move or act casually.

wan /won/ adj. pale and appearing ill.
▷SYNONYMS: **pale**, ashen, white, grey, anaemic, colourless, waxen, pasty, peaky, sickly, washed out, ghostly.
■ **wanly** adv.

wand n. a slender rod, esp. one used in performing magic.

wander v. **1** walk or move in a leisurely or aimless way. **2** move slowly away from a fixed point.
▷SYNONYMS: **1 stroll**, amble, saunter, walk, potter, ramble, meander, roam, range, drift; informal traipse, mosey. **2 stray**, depart, diverge, deviate, digress, drift, get sidetracked.
•n. an act of wandering.
□ **wanderlust** a strong desire to travel.
■ **wanderer** n.

wane v. **1** (of the moon) gradually appear to decrease in size. **2** become weaker.
▷SYNONYMS: **decline**, diminish, decrease, dwindle, shrink, tail off, ebb, fade, lessen, peter out, fall off, recede, slump, weaken, wither, evaporate, die out.
– ANTONYMS: grow.
□ **on the wane** waning.

wangle v. informal obtain by trickery or persuasion.

want v. **1** desire to have or do. **2** (**wanted**) (of a suspected criminal) sought by the police. **3** lack or be short of.
▷SYNONYMS: **desire**, wish for, hope for, fancy, care for, like, long for, yearn for, crave, hanker after, hunger for, thirst for, cry out for, covet; informal have a yen for, be dying for.
•n. **1** lack or shortage. **2** a desire.

▷ SYNONYMS: **1 lack**, absence, non-existence, dearth, deficiency, inadequacy, insufficiency, paucity, shortage, scarcity. **2 need**, austerity, privation, deprivation, poverty, destitution. **3** *her wants would be taken care of:* **wish**, desire, demand, longing, fancy, craving, need, requirement; informal yen.

wanting adj. **1** lacking something required. **2** not good enough.
▷ SYNONYMS: **deficient**, inadequate, lacking, insufficient, imperfect, flawed, unsound, substandard, inferior, second-rate.

wanton adj. **1** deliberate and unprovoked. **2** having many sexual partners.
▷ SYNONYMS: **deliberate**, wilful, malicious, gratuitous, unprovoked, motiveless, arbitrary, unjustifiable, senseless.
■ **wantonly** adv.

WAP abbrev. Wireless Application Protocol, a means of enabling mobile phones to access the Internet.

war n. a state of armed conflict between different nations or groups.
▷ SYNONYMS: **1 conflict**, warfare, combat, fighting, action, bloodshed, fight, campaign, hostilities. **2 campaign**, crusade, battle, fight, struggle.
– ANTONYMS: peace.
• v. (**warring**, **warred**) take part in a war.
▷ SYNONYMS: **fight**, battle, combat, wage war, take up arms, feud, quarrel, struggle, contend, wrangle, cross swords.
□ **warfare** the activity of fighting a war. **warhead** the explosive head of a missile. **warlike** hostile. **warmonger** a person who tries to bring about war. **warship** an armed ship designed for warfare at sea.

> **WORD LINKS**
> **martial** relating to war
> **belligerent** engaged in a war

warble v. sing with constantly changing notes.

ward n. **1** a room in a hospital for a patient or patients. **2** a division of a city or borough represented by a councillor. **3** a young person looked after by a guardian appointed by their parents or a court.
▷ SYNONYMS: **1 room**, department, unit, area. **2 district**, constituency, division, quarter, zone, parish. **3 dependant**, charge, protégé.
• v. (**ward off**) prevent from doing harm.

warden n. a person supervising a place or procedure.
▷ SYNONYMS: **1 superintendent**, caretaker, porter, steward, custodian, watchman, concierge, doorman, commissionaire. **2 prison officer**, guard, jailer, warder, keeper; informal screw.

warder n. a prison guard.

wardrobe n. **1** a large, tall cupboard for hanging clothes in. **2** a collection of clothes.

ware n. **1** manufactured articles of a specified type. **2** (**wares**) articles offered for sale.
▷ SYNONYMS: **goods**, merchandise, products, produce, stock, commodities.

warehouse n. a large building for storing goods.
▷ SYNONYMS: **storeroom**, depot, depository, stockroom; informal lock-up.

warlock n. a man who practises witchcraft.

warm adj. **1** moderately hot. **2** helping the body to retain heat. **3** enthusiastic, affectionate, or kind.
▷ SYNONYMS: **1** *a warm kitchen:* **hot**, cosy, snug. **2** *a warm day:* **balmy**, summery, sultry, hot, mild, temperate. **3** *warm water:* **tepid**, lukewarm, heated. **4** *a warm sweater:* **thick**, chunky, thermal, woolly. **5** *a warm welcome:* **friendly**, cordial, amiable, genial, kind, pleasant, fond, welcoming, hospitable, hearty.
– ANTONYMS: cold, chilly.
• v. **1** make or become warm. **2** (**warm to**) become more interested in or enthusiastic about.
□ **warm-blooded** (of animals) maintaining a constant body temperature. **warm up** prepare for exercise by doing gentle stretches.
■ **warmly** adv. **warmness** n.

warmth n. **1** the quality of being warm. **2** enthusiasm, affection, or kindness.
▷ SYNONYMS: **1 heat**, cosiness, snugness. **2 friendliness**, amiability, geniality, cordiality, kindness, tenderness, fondness.

warn v. **1** inform of a possible danger or problem. **2** advise not to do. **3** (**warn off**) order to keep away.
▷ SYNONYMS: **1 inform**, notify, tell, alert, apprise, make someone aware, remind; informal tip off. **2 advise**, exhort, urge, counsel, caution.

warning n. **1** something indicating a possible danger or problem. **2** advice against wrong or foolish actions.

W

3 advance notice.
▷ SYNONYMS: **1** *there was no warning of things to come:* **advance notice**, signal, sign; alarm bells; informal a tip-off. **2** *a word of warning—don't park illegally:* **caution**, information, advice. **3** *his sentence serves as a warning to other drunk drivers:* **example**, deterrent, lesson, message, moral.

warp v. **1** bend or twist out of shape. **2** make abnormal or strange.
▷ SYNONYMS: **1 buckle**, twist, bend, distort, deform, curve, bow, contort. **2 corrupt**, twist, pervert, deprave.
• n. **1** a distortion. **2** the lengthwise threads on a loom.

warrant n. **1** an official authorization allowing the police to make an arrest, search premises, etc. **2** justification.
▷ SYNONYMS: **1 authorization**, order, writ, mandate, licence, permit, summons. **2 voucher**, chit, slip, ticket, coupon, pass.
• v. **1** justify. **2** guarantee.
▷ SYNONYMS: **1 justify**, deserve, vindicate, call for, sanction, permit, authorize, excuse, account for, legitimatize, support, license, merit, qualify for, rate. **2 guarantee**, promise, affirm, swear, vouch, vow, pledge, undertake, declare, testify.

warranty n. (pl. **warranties**) a written guarantee promising to repair or replace a purchased article if necessary.
▷ SYNONYMS: **guarantee**, assurance, promise, commitment, undertaking, pledge, agreement, covenant.

warren n. a network of interconnecting rabbit burrows.

warrior n. a brave or experienced fighter.
▷ SYNONYMS: **fighter**, soldier, serviceman, combatant.

wart n. a small, hard growth on the skin.
□ **warthog** an African wild pig with warty lumps on its face.
■ **warty** adj.

wary adj. (**warier**, **wariest**) cautious.
▷ SYNONYMS: **1 cautious**, careful, circumspect, on your guard, chary, alert, on the lookout, attentive, heedful, watchful, vigilant, observant. **2** *we are wary of strangers:* **suspicious**, chary, leery, careful, distrustful.
− ANTONYMS: inattentive, trustful.
■ **warily** adv. **wariness** n.

was see BE.

wash v. **1** clean with water and usu. soap or detergent. **2** (of flowing water) carry or move in a particular direction. **3** (**wash over**) occur without greatly affecting. **4** informal seem convincing or genuine.
▷ SYNONYMS: **1 clean**, cleanse, scrub, wipe, sponge, rinse, sluice, shower, swill, douse, swab, bathe; shampoo, launder, lather. **2 splash**, lap, dash, break, beat, surge, ripple, roll.
• n. **1** an act of washing. **2** clothes etc. to be washed. **3** the water or air disturbed by a moving boat or aircraft. **4** a cleansing solution. **5** a thin coating of paint.
▷ SYNONYMS: **1 laundry**, washing. **2 backwash**, wake, trail, path.
□ **washbasin** a basin for washing the hands and face. **washed out** pale and tired. **washout** informal a disappointing failure. **wash up** clean dirty crockery and cutlery. **wash your hands of** take no further responsibility for.
■ **washable** adj.

washer n. a small flat ring fixed between a nut and bolt.

washing n. clothes etc. to be washed or that have just been washed.
□ **washing-up** crockery, cutlery, etc. to be washed.

wasp n. a stinging winged insect with a black and yellow striped body.

waspish adj. sharply irritable.
■ **waspishly** adv.

wassail old use n. lively festivities involving the drinking of much alcohol.
• v. **1** celebrate in this way. **2** go carol-singing.

wastage n. **1** the act of wasting. **2** an amount wasted. **3** Brit. the reduction of a workforce by resignations or retirements.

waste v. **1** use more of something than is necessary. **2** fail to make use of. **3** become weaker and thinner.
▷ SYNONYMS: **1 squander**, misspend, misuse, fritter away, throw away, lavish, dissipate; informal blow, splurge. **2** *she is wasting away:* **grow weak**, grow thin, wilt, fade, deteriorate.
− ANTONYMS: conserve.
• adj. **1** discarded because no longer required. **2** (of land) not used, cultivated, or built on.
▷ SYNONYMS: **1 unwanted**, excess, superfluous, left over, scrap, unusable, unprofitable. **2 uncultivated**, barren, desert, arid, bare, desolate.
• n. **1** an act of wasting. **2** waste material. **3** a large area of barren, uninhabited land.
▷ SYNONYMS: **1 misuse**, misapplication,

abuse; extravagance. **2 rubbish**, refuse, litter, debris, junk, sewage, effluent; N. Amer. garbage, trash.
3 (**wastes**) **desert**, wasteland, wilderness, emptiness, wilds.
□ **lay waste to** completely destroy.
■ **waster** n.

wasteful adj. using more of something than is necessary.
▷ SYNONYMS: **prodigal**, profligate, uneconomical, extravagant, lavish, excessive, imprudent, improvident, spendthrift.
– ANTONYMS: frugal.
■ **wastefully** adv.

watch v. **1** look at attentively. **2** keep under careful observation. **3** be careful about. **4** (**watch out**) be careful.
▷ SYNONYMS: **1 observe**, view, look at, eye, gaze at, peer at, contemplate, inspect, scrutinize, scan; informal check out, get a load of, recce, eyeball.
2 spy on, keep in sight, keep under surveillance, track, monitor, tail; informal keep tabs on, stake out.
3 guard, mind, protect, look after, keep an eye on, take care of, shield, defend.
– ANTONYMS: ignore.
• n. **1** a small timepiece usu. worn on the wrist. **2** an act of watching. **3** a shift worked by sailors, firefighters, or police officers.
▷ SYNONYMS: **1 wristwatch**, timepiece, chronometer. **2 guard**, vigil, lookout, observation, surveillance.
□ **watchman** a man employed to guard an empty building. **watchtower** a tower built as a high observation point. **watchword** a word or phrase expressing a central aim or belief.
■ **watchable** adj. **watcher** n.

watchdog n. **1** a dog kept to guard property. **2** a group monitoring the practices of companies.
▷ SYNONYMS: **ombudsman**, monitor, scrutineer, inspector, supervisor.

watchful adj. alert to possible difficulty or danger.
▷ SYNONYMS: **observant**, alert, vigilant, attentive, aware, sharp-eyed, eagle-eyed, on the lookout, wary, cautious, careful.
■ **watchfully** adv.

water n. **1** the liquid forming the seas, lakes, rivers, and rain. **2** (**waters**) an area of sea under a particular country's authority.
• v. **1** pour water over. **2** give a drink of water to. **3** produce tears or saliva. **4** dilute with water. **5** (**water down**)

make less forceful.
▷ SYNONYMS: **sprinkle**, moisten, dampen, wet, spray, splash, hose, douse.
□ **waterbed** a bed with a water-filled mattress. **water cannon** a device that ejects a powerful jet of water to disperse a crowd. **water chestnut** the crisp edible tuber of a tropical plant. **watercolour 1** artists' paint mixed with water. **2** a picture painted with watercolours. **watercourse** a stream or artificial water channel. **watercress** a cress which grows in running water. **waterfront** a part of a town alongside an area of water. **water ice** a frozen dessert of fruit juice in sugar syrup. **water lily** a plant that grows in water, with broad floating leaves. **waterline** the level normally reached by the water on the side of a ship. **waterlogged** saturated with water. **watermark** a faint design made in some paper, visible when held against the light. **water meadow** a meadow periodically flooded by a stream. **watermelon** a melon with watery red pulp. **watermill** a mill worked by a waterwheel. **waterproof** unable to be penetrated by water. **watershed 1** an area of land separating two river systems. **2** a turning point in a situation. **waterskiing** the sport of skimming over water on skis while towed by a motorboat. **waterspout** a column of water formed by a whirlwind over the sea. **water table** the level below which the ground is saturated with water. **waterway** a river or other route for travel by water. **waterwheel** a wheel driven by flowing water to work machinery.

> **WORD LINKS**
> **aquatic**, **aqueous** relating to or containing water

waterfall n. a stream of water falling from a height.
▷ SYNONYMS: **falls**, cascade, cataract, rapids.

watertight adj. **1** not allowing water to pass through. **2** unable to be questioned.
▷ SYNONYMS: **1 impermeable**, impervious, hermetically sealed, waterproof. **2 indisputable**, unquestionable, incontrovertible, irrefutable, unassailable, foolproof, sound, flawless, conclusive.
– ANTONYMS: leaky.

watery adj. **1** of or like water. **2** containing too much water. **3** weak or pale.

watt n. a basic unit of electric power.

W

wattage n. an amount of electrical power expressed in watts.

wattle n. **1** interwoven sticks used to make fences etc. **2** a fleshy part hanging from the head or neck of a turkey etc.

wave v. **1** move your hand to and fro as a greeting or signal. **2** move to and fro.
▷ SYNONYMS: **1 flap**, wag, shake, swish, swing, brandish, flourish, wield; gesture, signal, beckon, motion. **2 ripple**, flutter, undulate, stir, flap, sway, shake, quiver.
• n. **1** a moving ridge of water. **2** a sudden increase in an emotion or activity. **3** an act of waving. **4** a slightly curling lock of hair. **5** a regular to-and-fro motion of particles of matter involved in transmitting sound, light, heat, etc.
▷ SYNONYMS: **1 breaker**, roller, comber, boomer, ripple; (**waves**) swell, surf. **2** *the act sparked a wave of protests:* **spate**, surge, flow, flood, stream, torrent, rush, tide. **3 signal**, sign, motion, gesture.
□ **waveband** a range of wavelengths. **wavelength 1** the distance between successive crests of a wave of sound, light, etc. **2** a person's way of thinking.

waver v. **1** flicker. **2** begin to weaken. **3** be indecisive.
▷ SYNONYMS: **1** *the candlelight wavered:* **flicker**, quiver. **2** *his voice wavered:* **falter**, wobble, tremble, quaver. **3 hesitate**, dither, be irresolute, be undecided, vacillate, blow hot and cold; Brit. haver, hum and haw; informal shilly-shally, sit on the fence.

wavy adj. (**wavier**, **waviest**) having a series of wave-like curves.

wax n. a soft solid substance used for making candles or polishes.
• v. **1** polish or treat with wax. **2** remove hair from the body by applying then peeling off wax. **3** (of the moon) gradually appear to increase in size. **4** literary speak or write in a specified way.
□ **waxwork** a lifelike dummy made of wax.
■ **waxen** adj. **waxy** adj.

way n. **1** a method or manner of doing something. **2** a road or path. **3** a route or means taken to reach, enter, or leave a place. **4** a direction. **5** a distance. **6** a condition.
▷ SYNONYMS: **1 method**, process, procedure, technique, system, plan, strategy, scheme, means, mechanism,

approach. **2 manner**, style, fashion, mode. **3** *I've changed my ways:* **practice**, wont, habit, custom, convention, routine, trait, attribute, peculiarity, idiosyncrasy, conduct, behaviour. **4 route**, course, direction, track, path, access, gate, exit, entrance, door. **5 distance**, length, stretch, journey. **6** *April is a long way away:* **time**, stretch, term, span, duration. **7 direction**, bearing, course, orientation, line, tack. **8** *in some ways, he may be better off:* **respect**, regard, aspect, facet, sense, detail, point, particular. **9** *the country is in a bad way:* **state**, condition, situation, circumstances, position, predicament, plight; informal shape.
• adv. informal by a great deal.
□ **by the way** used to introduce an incidental remark. **in the way** obstructing progress. **wayfarer** literary a traveller. **wayside** the edge of a road.

waylay v. (**waylaying**, **waylaid**) intercept someone so as to attack or question them.
▷ SYNONYMS: **1 ambush**, hold up, attack, pounce on; informal mug. **2 accost**, detain, intercept; informal buttonhole.

wayward adj. unpredictable and hard to control.
▷ SYNONYMS: **wilful**, headstrong, stubborn, obstinate, perverse, contrary, disobedient, undisciplined, rebellious, defiant, recalcitrant, unruly, wild; formal refractory.
■ **waywardness** n.

WC abbrev. Brit. water closet (a toilet).

we pron. **1** used by a speaker to refer to himself or herself and one or more other people. **2** people in general.

weak adj. **1** lacking strength and energy. **2** likely to break or give way. **3** not secure or stable. **4** lacking power, influence, or ability. **5** heavily diluted.
▷ SYNONYMS: **1 feeble**, frail, delicate, fragile, infirm, ailing, debilitated, decrepit, exhausted, enervated; informal weedy. **2** *a weak bridge:* **flimsy**, fragile, rickety, insubstantial, wobbly, unstable, ramshackle, jerry-built, shoddy. **3** *a weak excuse:* **unconvincing**, tenuous, implausible, unsatisfactory, poor, inadequate, lame, feeble, flimsy, hollow; informal pathetic. **4** *a weak character:* **spineless**, craven, cowardly, timid, irresolute, indecisive, ineffectual, meek, tame, soft, faint-hearted; informal gutless. **5** *a weak voice:* **indistinct**, muffled, muted, hushed, faint, low.

6 *weak coffee:* **watery**, dilute, diluted, watered down, thin, tasteless.
– ANTONYMS: strong.
■ **weakly** adv.

weaken v. make or become weak.
▷ SYNONYMS: **1 enfeeble**, debilitate, incapacitate, sap, tire, exhaust. **2** *the storm was beginning to weaken:* **dwindle**, diminish, ebb, subside, peter out, fizzle out, tail off, decline. **3** *the move weakened her authority:* **decrease**, impair, undermine, compromise, lessen.
– ANTONYMS: strengthen, bolster.

weakling n. a weak person or animal.

weakness n. **1** the state of being weak. **2** a fault. **3** a self-indulgent liking.
▷ SYNONYMS: **1 frailty**, feebleness, fragility, delicacy, debility, incapacity, decrepitude; informal weediness. **2 fault**, flaw, defect, deficiency, failing, shortcoming, imperfection, Achilles heel. **3** *a weakness for champagne:* **fondness**, liking, partiality, love, penchant, predilection, inclination, taste. **4 timidity**, cravenness, cowardliness, indecision, irresolution, ineffectuality, ineffectiveness, impotence.

weal n. a red, swollen mark left on flesh by a blow or pressure.

wealth n. **1** a large amount of money and valuable possessions. **2** the state of being rich. **3** a large amount.
▷ SYNONYMS: **1 affluence**, prosperity, riches, means, fortune, money, cash, capital, treasure, finance; informal wherewithal, dough, bread. **2 abundance**, profusion, plethora, mine, store; informal lot, load, mountain, stack, ton.
– ANTONYMS: poverty, dearth.

wealthy adj. (**wealthier, wealthiest**) rich.
▷ SYNONYMS: **rich**, affluent, moneyed, well off, well-to-do, prosperous; informal well heeled, rolling in it, made of money, loaded, flush.
– ANTONYMS: poor.

wean v. **1** make a young mammal eat food other than its mother's milk. **2** cause to give up a habit etc. gradually.

weapon n. **1** a thing used to cause harm or damage. **2** a means of gaining an advantage or defending yourself.
■ **weaponry** n.

wear v. (**wearing, wore**; past part. **worn**) **1** have on the body as clothing, decoration, or protection. **2** damage by friction or use. **3** withstand

continued use. **4** (**wear off**) lose effectiveness or strength. **5** (**wear down**) overcome by persistence. **6** (**wear out**) exhaust. **7** (**wear on**) (of time) pass slowly.
▷ SYNONYMS: **1 be dressed in**, be clothed in, sport. **2** *his face wore a pained expression:* **bear**, show, display, exhibit, adopt, assume. **3** *the sea has worn away the limestone:* **erode**, abrade, rub away, wash away, crumble away, eat away. **4** last, endure, hold up, bear up.
• n. **1** clothing of a particular type. **2** damage from friction or use.
▷ SYNONYMS: **1 clothes**, garments, dress, attire, garb, wardrobe; informal get-up, gear, togs; Brit. informal kit, clobber. **2 damage**, friction, abrasion, erosion. **3 use**, service, value; informal mileage.
■ **wearable** adj. **wearer** n.

wearisome adj. causing weariness.

weary adj. (**wearier, weariest**) **1** tired. **2** tiring.
▷ SYNONYMS: **1 tired**, worn out, exhausted, fatigued, sapped, spent, drained; informal done in, ready to drop, shattered, bushed; Brit. informal knackered, whacked; N. Amer. informal pooped. **2 tiring**, exhausting, fatiguing, enervating, draining, sapping, demanding, taxing, arduous, gruelling.
– ANTONYMS: energetic.
• v. (**wearying, wearied**) make or become weary.
■ **wearily** adv. **weariness** n.

weasel n. a small, slender reddish-brown mammal.

weather n. the state of the atmosphere in terms of temperature, wind, rain, etc.
▷ SYNONYMS: **conditions**, climate, elements, forecast, outlook.
• v. **1** wear away through the action of the weather. **2** come safely through.
▷ SYNONYMS: **survive**, come through, ride out, pull through, withstand, endure, rise above; informal stick out.
□ **under the weather** informal slightly unwell. **weather-beaten** damaged or tanned by exposure to the weather. **weathercock** a weathervane in the form of a cockerel. **weathervane** a revolving pointer to show the direction of the wind.

weave v. (**weaving, wove**; past part. **woven** or **wove**) **1** make fabric or baskets by passing crosswise threads or strips under and over lengthwise ones. **2** form a story from different elements. **3** (past & past part **weaved**)

W

move from side to side to avoid things.

▷ SYNONYMS: **1 entwine**, lace, twist, knit, braid, plait. **2 invent**, make up, fabricate, construct, create, spin. **3** *he wove his way through the crowds:* **thread**, wind, wend, dodge, zigzag.
• n. a way in which fabric is woven.
■ **weaver** n.

web n. **1** a network of fine threads made by a spider. **2** a complex network of elements. **3** (**the Web**) the World Wide Web. **4** the skin between the toes of a duck, frog, etc.

▷ SYNONYMS: **1 mesh**, net, lattice, lace-work, gauze, gossamer. **2 network**, nexus, complex, tangle, chain.
□ **webcam** (trademark in the US) a video camera connected to a computer, allowing images to be viewed on the Internet. **weblog** a personal website on which someone regularly records their opinions or experiences. **web page** a document that can be accessed via the Internet. **website** a location on the Internet having one or more web pages.
■ **webbed** adj.

webbing n. strong fabric used for straps and belts.

weblink n. **1** = HYPERLINK. **2** a printed address of a website in a book, magazine, etc.

wed v. (**wedding, wedded** or **wed**) **1** formal marry. **2** combine two desirable elements. **3** (**be wedded to**) be completely devoted to.
□ **wedlock** the state of being married.

wedding n. a marriage ceremony.

▷ SYNONYMS: **marriage**, nuptials, union.

wedge n. a piece of wood, metal, etc. with a thick end that tapers to a thin edge.

▷ SYNONYMS: **triangle**, segment, slice, section, chunk, lump, slab, hunk, block, piece.
• v. **1** fix in position with a wedge. **2** force into a narrow space.

▷ SYNONYMS: **squeeze**, cram, jam, ram, force, push, shove; informal stuff, bung.

Wednesday n. the day before Thursday.

wee adj. Scottish little.

weed n. **1** a wild plant growing where it is not wanted. **2** Brit. informal a weak or thin person.
• v. **1** remove weeds from. **2** (**weed out**) remove as unwanted.
■ **weedy** adj.

week n. **1** a period of seven days. **2** the five days from Monday to Friday, when many people work.

□ **weekday** a day of the week other than Sunday or Saturday. **weekend** Saturday and Sunday.
■ **weekly** adj. & adv.

weeny adj. (**weenier, weeniest**) informal tiny.

weep v. (**weeping, wept**) **1** shed tears. **2** (of a wound) discharge liquid.

▷ SYNONYMS: **cry**, shed tears, sob, snivel, whimper, wail, bawl, keen; Scottish greet; informal boohoo, blub.
• n. a period of weeping.

weepy adj. (**weepier, weepiest**) informal **1** tearful. **2** sentimental.

weevil n. a small beetle that eats crops or stored food.

weft n. the crosswise threads in weaving.

weigh v. **1** find out the weight of. **2** have a specified weight. **3** (**weigh down**) be troublesome to. **4** (often **weigh up**) assess the nature or importance of. **5** (**weigh on**) be worrying to. **6** influence a decision or action.

▷ SYNONYMS: **1** *he weighed up the possibilities:* **consider**, contemplate, think about, mull over, chew over, reflect on, ruminate about, muse on, assess, examine, review, explore, take stock of. **2** *they need to weigh benefit against risk:* **balance**, evaluate, compare, juxtapose, contrast.
□ **weigh anchor** take up the anchor when ready to sail. **weighbridge** a machine on to which vehicles are driven to be weighed.

weight n. **1** the heaviness of a person or thing. **2** a unit or system for expressing this. **3** a piece of metal of known weight, used in weighing. **4** a heavy object. **5** ability to influence decisions. **6** importance.

▷ SYNONYMS: **1 mass**, heaviness, load, burden. **2 influence**, force, leverage, sway, pull, power, authority; informal clout. **3 burden**, load, millstone, trouble, worry. **4** *the weight of the evidence is against him:* **most**, bulk, majority, preponderance, body, lion's share.
• v. **1** make heavier or keep in place with a weight. **2** attach comparative importance or value to.
■ **weightless** adj.

weighting n. Brit. additional wages paid to allow for a higher cost of living in a particular area.

weightlifting n. the sport of lifting heavy weights.
■ **weightlifter** n.

weighty adj. (**weightier, weightiest**)

1 heavy. **2** serious and important. **3** influential.

weir n. a low dam built to regulate the flow of a river.

weird adj. strange; bizarre.
▷ SYNONYMS: **1 uncanny**, eerie, unnatural, supernatural, unearthly, other-worldly, ghostly, mysterious, strange, abnormal, unusual; informal creepy, spooky, freaky. **2 bizarre**, odd, curious, strange, quirky, outlandish, eccentric, unconventional, unorthodox, idiosyncratic, surreal, crazy, absurd, grotesque, peculiar; informal wacky, freaky; N. Amer. informal wacko.
− ANTONYMS: normal, conventional.
■ **weirdly** adv. **weirdness** n.

> USAGE **weird** is an exception to the usual rule of *i* before *e* except after *c*.

welch var. of **WELSH**.

welcome n. **1** an instance or way of greeting someone. **2** an approving reaction.
▷ SYNONYMS: **greeting**, salutation, reception, hospitality, the red carpet.
• v. **1** greet in a polite or friendly way. **2** be glad to receive or hear of.
▷ SYNONYMS: **1 greet**, salute, receive, meet, usher in. **2 be pleased by**, be glad about, approve of, applaud, appreciate, embrace.
− ANTONYMS: resent.
• adj. **1** much needed or desired. **2** gladly received. **3** allowed or invited to do something.
▷ SYNONYMS: **pleasing**, good, agreeable, encouraging, gratifying, heartening, promising, favourable, pleasant.

weld v. **1** join metal parts by heating and pressing them together. **2** combine to form a whole.
▷ SYNONYMS: **fuse**, bond, stick, join, attach, seal, splice, melt, solder.
• n. a welded joint.
■ **welder** n.

welfare n. **1** the health, happiness, and safety of a person or group. **2** organized help given to people in need.
▷ SYNONYMS: **1 well-being**, health, comfort, security, safety, protection, success, interest, good. **2 social security**, benefit, public assistance, pension, credit, support, sick pay, unemployment benefit; Brit. informal the dole.
□ **welfare state** a system under which the state provides pensions, health care, etc.

well¹ adv. (**better**, **best**) **1** in a good

or appropriate way. **2** thoroughly. **3** to a great extent or degree. **4** very probably. **5** without difficulty. **6** with good reason.
▷ SYNONYMS: **1 satisfactorily**, correctly, properly, fittingly, suitably, appropriately, nicely. **2 skilfully**, ably, competently, proficiently, adeptly, deftly, expertly, excellently. **3** *they speak well of him:* **admiringly**, highly, approvingly, favourably, appreciatively, warmly, enthusiastically, in glowing terms.
− ANTONYMS: badly.
• adj. (**better**, **best**) **1** in good health. **2** satisfactory.
▷ SYNONYMS: **1 healthy**, fine, fit, robust, strong, vigorous, blooming, thriving, in fine fettle; informal in the pink. **2 satisfactory**, all right, fine, in order, acceptable; informal OK, hunky-dory.
− ANTONYMS: unwell, unsatisfactory.
• exclam. expressing surprise, anger, etc.
□ **as well 1** in addition. **2** with equal reason or an equally good result. **well advised** sensible. **well appointed** well equipped or furnished. **well-being** comfort, good health, and happiness. **well disposed** sympathetic or friendly. **well heeled** informal wealthy. **well-nigh** almost. **well off 1** wealthy. **2** in a good situation. **well read** having read many literary works. **well spoken** having an educated and refined voice. **well-to-do** wealthy.

well² n. **1** a shaft sunk into the ground to obtain water, oil, or gas. **2** an enclosed space in a building for stairs, a lift, etc.
▷ SYNONYMS: **borehole**, spring, waterhole, shaft.
• v. **1** (of a liquid) rise up to the surface. **2** (of an emotion) arise and intensify.
▷ SYNONYMS: **flow**, spill, stream, gush, roll, cascade, flood, spout, burst, issue.

well built adj. strong and sturdy.
▷ SYNONYMS: **sturdy**, strapping, brawny, burly, hefty, muscular, strong, rugged; informal hunky, beefy.
− ANTONYMS: puny.

wellington n. Brit. a knee-length waterproof rubber or plastic boot.

well known adj. known widely or thoroughly.
▷ SYNONYMS: **1 familiar**, popular, common, everyday, established, proverbial. **2 famous**, famed, prominent, notable, renowned, distinguished, eminent, illustrious,

W

acclaimed; notorious, infamous.
– ANTONYMS: unknown.
Welsh n. the language of Wales.
  • adj. of Wales.
  □ **Welsh rarebit** (or **Welsh rabbit**) melted cheese on toast.
welsh (or **welch**) v. (**welsh on**) fail to honour a debt or obligation.
welt n. 1 a leather rim to which the sole of a shoe is attached. 2 a border on a knitted garment. 3 a weal.
welter n. a large and disorganized number of items.
welterweight n. a weight in boxing etc. between lightweight and middleweight.
wench n. old use a girl or young woman.
wend v. (**wend your way**) go slowly or by an indirect route.
went past of GO.
wept past & past part. of WEEP.
were see BE.
werewolf n. (pl. **werewolves**) (in folklore) a person who periodically changes into a wolf.
west n. 1 the direction in which the sun sets. 2 the western part of a place. 3 (**the West**) Europe and North America.
  • adj. & adv. 1 towards or facing the west. 2 (of a wind) from the west.
  ■ **westerly** adj. & adv. **westward** adj. & adv. **westwards** adv.
western adj. situated in or facing the west.
  • n. a film or novel about cowboys in the western US.
westerner n. a person from the west of a region.
westernize (or **-ise**) v. bring under the influence of Europe and North America.
wet adj. (**wetter, wettest**) 1 covered or saturated with liquid. 2 rainy. 3 (of paint etc.) not yet dry. 4 Brit. informal feeble.
  ▷ SYNONYMS: 1 **damp**, moist, soaked, drenched, saturated, sopping, dripping, soggy, waterlogged, squelchy. 2 **rainy**, pouring, teeming, showery, drizzly. 3 **sticky**, tacky.
  • v. (**wetting, wet** or **wetted**) make wet.
  ▷ SYNONYMS: **dampen**, moisten, sprinkle, spray, splash, soak, saturate, flood, douse, drench.
  – ANTONYMS: dry.
  • n. 1 rainy weather. 2 liquid causing dampness.
  □ **wet blanket** informal a person who spoils others' enjoyment by being unenthusiastic. **wet nurse** a woman

employed to breastfeed another woman's child. **wetsuit** a rubber garment worn for warmth in water sports.
  ■ **wetly** adv. **wetness** n.
wether n. a castrated ram.
whack informal v. 1 hit forcefully.
  2 (**whacked**) Brit. exhausted.
  • n. 1 a sharp blow. 2 Brit. a share or contribution.
whale n. (pl. **whale** or **whales**) a very large sea mammal.
  □ **a whale of a time** informal a very enjoyable time. **whalebone** a horny substance from the upper jaw of whales, formerly used to stiffen corsets etc.
whaler n. 1 a whaling ship. 2 a seaman engaged in whaling.
whaling n. the hunting and killing of whales.
wharf /worf/ n. (pl. **wharves** or **wharfs**) a level area where ships are moored to load and unload.
  ▷ SYNONYMS: quay, pier, dock, berth, landing, jetty, harbour, dockyard.
what pron. & adj. 1 asking for information. 2 whatever.
  3 emphasizing a surprising or remarkable thing.
  • pron. the thing or things that.
  • adv. to what extent?
  □ **whatever** 1 everything or anything that. 2 at all; of any kind. **whatnot** informal an unspecified item or items. **whatsoever** whatever.
wheat n. a cereal crop whose grain is ground to make flour.
  □ **wheatmeal** flour made from wheat from which some of the bran has been removed.
wheaten adj. made of wheat.
wheedle v. use insincere praise etc. so as to persuade.
wheel n. 1 a revolving circular object fixed below a vehicle to enable it to move along, or forming part of a machine. 2 a turn or rotation.
  • v. 1 push or pull a vehicle with wheels. 2 move in a wide circle or curve. 3 turn round quickly.
  ▷ SYNONYMS: 1 **push**, trundle, roll. 2 *gulls wheeled overhead:* **turn**, go round, circle, orbit.
  □ **wheel and deal** take part in commercial or political scheming. **wheelbarrow** a small cart with a single wheel at the front and two handles at the rear. **wheelbase** the distance between a vehicle's front and rear axles. **wheelchair** a chair on wheels for an ill or disabled person.

wheeze v. breathe with a whistling or rattling sound in the chest.
▷ SYNONYMS: **gasp**, whistle, hiss, rasp, croak, pant, cough.
•n. **1** a sound of wheezing. **2** Brit. informal a clever scheme.
■ **wheezy** adj.

whelk n. a shellfish with a spiral shell.

whelp n. a puppy.
•v. give birth to a puppy.

when adv. **1** at what time? **2** at which time or in which situation.
•conj. **1** at or during the time that. **2** whenever. **3** and just then. **4** although.
□ **whenever 1** at whatever time. **2** every time that.

whence adv. formal from which or from where.

where adv. **1** in or to what place? **2** in what direction or respect? **3** at, in, or to which. **4** in or to a place or situation in which.

whereabouts adv. where or approximately where?
•n. the place where someone or something is.
▷ SYNONYMS: **location**, position, site, situation, spot, point, home, address, neighbourhood.

whereas conj. in contrast with the fact that.

whereby adv. by which.

whereupon conj. immediately after which.

wherever adv. in or to whatever place.
•conj. in every case when.

wherewithal n. the money etc. needed for something.

wherry n. (pl. **wherries**) a light barge or rowing boat.

whet v. (**whetting**, **whetted**) **1** sharpen a blade. **2** stimulate someone's interest or appetite.
□ **whetstone** a stone for sharpening blades.

whether conj. **1** expressing a choice between alternatives. **2** expressing an enquiry or investigation.

whey n. the watery part of milk remaining after curds have formed.

which pron. & adj. **1** asking for information specifying one or more members of a set. **2** introducing a clause giving further information about something previously mentioned.
□ **whichever 1** any which; that or those which. **2** regardless of which.

whiff n. **1** a smell, esp. one smelt only briefly. **2** a trace.

Whig n. hist. a member of a British political party that was succeeded by the Liberals.

while n. **1** (**a while**) a period of time. **2** (**the while**) meanwhile.
▷ SYNONYMS: *we chatted for a while:* **time**, spell, stretch, stint, span, interval, period; Brit. informal patch.
•conj. **1** at the same time as. **2** whereas. **3** although.
•v. (**while away**) pass time in a leisurely way.
▷ SYNONYMS: *tennis helped to while away the time:* **pass**, spend, occupy, use up, kill.
□ **worth** (**your**) **while** worth the time or effort spent.

whilst conj. while.

whim n. a sudden desire or change of mind.
▷ SYNONYMS: **impulse**, urge, notion, fancy, inclination, caprice, vagary.

whimper v. make low, feeble sounds.
▷ SYNONYMS: **whine**, cry, sob, moan, snivel, wail, groan; Brit. informal grizzle.
•n. a whimpering sound.

whimsical adj. **1** quaint or fanciful. **2** showing sudden changes of mood.
▷ SYNONYMS: **fanciful**, playful, mischievous, waggish, quaint, curious, droll, eccentric, quirky, idiosyncratic, unconventional.
■ **whimsically** adv.

whimsy n. playfully unusual behaviour or humour.

whine n. **1** a long, high-pitched complaining cry. **2** a long, shrill sound.
•v. **1** give or make a whine. **2** complain in a sulky way.
▷ SYNONYMS: **1 wail**, whimper, cry, mewl, moan, howl, yowl; informal grizzle. **2 complain**, grouse, grouch, grumble, moan, carp; informal gripe, bellyache, whinge.
■ **whiny** adj.

whinge v. (**whingeing**, **whinged**) Brit. informal complain persistently.

whinny n. (pl. **whinnies**) a gentle neigh.
•v. (**whinnying**, **whinnied**) neigh gently.

whip n. **1** a length of leather or cord on a handle, used to beat a person or urge on an animal. **2** a dessert made with whipped cream etc. **3** an official maintaining discipline in a political party. **4** Brit. a written notice from a party whip requesting attendance for voting.
▷ SYNONYMS: **lash**, scourge, strap, belt.
•v. (**whipping**, **whipped**) **1** beat with

W

a whip. **2** move or take out fast. **3** beat into a froth. **4** (**whip up**) deliberately excite or provoke.

▷ SYNONYMS: **1 flog**, lash, flagellate, cane, belt, thrash, beat; informal tan someone's hide. **2 whisk**, beat. **3 rouse**, stir up, excite, galvanize, electrify, stimulate, inspire, fire up, inflame, provoke.

□ **whiplash** injury caused by a severe jerk to the head. **whipping boy** a scapegoat. **whip-round** Brit. informal a collection of money from a group.

whippersnapper n. informal a young and inexperienced but overconfident person.

whippet n. a small dog resembling a greyhound.

whirl v. **1** move rapidly round and round. **2** (of the head etc.) seem to spin round.

▷ SYNONYMS: **rotate**, circle, wheel, turn, revolve, orbit, spin, twirl, pirouette, gyrate.

• n. **1** a whirling movement. **2** frantic activity. **3** a state of confusion.

whirlpool n. a current of water whirling in a circle.

▷ SYNONYMS: **eddy**, vortex, maelstrom.

whirlwind n. a column of air moving rapidly round and round.

▷ SYNONYMS: **tornado**, hurricane, typhoon, cyclone, vortex; N. Amer. informal twister.

• adj. very quick and unexpected: *a whirlwind romance*.

▷ SYNONYMS: **rapid**, lightning, headlong, impulsive, breakneck, meteoric, sudden, swift, fast, quick, speedy.

whirr v. make a low, continuous, regular sound.

• n. a whirring sound.

whisk v. **1** move or take suddenly, quickly, and lightly. **2** beat eggs etc. with a light, rapid movement.

▷ SYNONYMS: **1 speed**, hurry, rush, sweep, hurtle, shoot. **2 pull**, snatch, pluck, tug, jerk; informal whip, yank. **3 whip**, beat, mix.

• n. a utensil for whisking eggs etc.

whisker n. **1** each of the long hairs or bristles growing from the face of an animal. **2** (**whiskers**) the hair growing on a man's face.

whisky (Irish & US **whiskey**) n. (pl. **whiskies**) a spirit distilled from malted grain.

whisper v. speak very softly.

▷ SYNONYMS: **murmur**, mutter, mumble, speak softly, breathe, say sotto voce.

• n. **1** a whispered remark. **2** a very soft voice.

▷ SYNONYMS: **1 murmur**, mutter, mumble, low voice, undertone. **2 rumour**, story, report, gossip, speculation, suggestion, hint; informal buzz.

– ANTONYMS: shout.

whist n. a card game in which points are scored according to the number of tricks won.

whistle n. **1** a clear, high-pitched sound made by forcing breath between the lips or teeth. **2** any similar sound. **3** a device producing a whistling sound.

• v. **1** produce a whistle. **2** blow a whistle.

□ **whistle-blower** informal a person who exposes dishonest or illicit activity. **whistle-stop** very fast and with only brief pauses.

Whit n. a Christian festival held on the seventh Sunday after Easter.

whit n. a very small part or amount.

white adj. **1** of the colour of fresh snow. **2** very pale. **3** of people with light-coloured skin. **4** Brit. (of coffee or tea) with milk.

▷ SYNONYMS: **pale**, pallid, wan, ashen, chalky, pasty, peaky, washed out, ghostly, deathly.

• n. **1** white colour. **2** the pale part of the eyeball around the iris. **3** the outer part around the yolk of an egg. **4** a white person.

□ **whitebait** the young of herrings, sprats, etc. used as food. **white-collar** of work done in an office or other professional environment. **white elephant** a useless or unwanted possession. **white flag** a white flag waved as a symbol of surrender. **white-hot** so hot as to glow white. **white lie** a lie told to avoid hurting someone's feelings. **white noise** noise containing many frequencies with equal intensities. **White Paper** a government report giving information or proposals. **white spirit** Brit. a colourless liquid used as a solvent.

■ **whiten** v. **whiteness** n.

whitewash n. **1** a solution of lime or chalk and water, used for painting walls white. **2** a deliberate concealment of mistakes.

• v. **1** paint with whitewash. **2** conceal mistakes.

whither adv. old use to what place or state?

whiting n. (pl. **whiting**) a small edible sea fish.

Whitsun (or **Whitsuntide**) n. the weekend or week including Whit

Sunday.

Whit Sunday n. a Christian festival held on the seventh Sunday after Easter.

whittle v. **1** carve wood by cutting small slices from it. **2** (**whittle away/down**) gradually reduce.

whizz (or **whiz**) v. **1** move quickly through the air. **2** move or go fast.
• n. a whizzing sound.
□ **whizz-kid** informal a very successful or skilful young person.

who pron. **1** what or which person or people? **2** introducing a clause giving further information about a person or people previously mentioned.
□ **whodunnit** (US **whodunit**) informal a detective story or play. **whoever 1** any person who. **2** regardless of who. **whosoever** formal whoever.

whoa exclam. a command to a horse to stop or slow down.

whole adj. **1** complete; entire. **2** in one piece.
▷ SYNONYMS: **1 entire**, complete, full, unabridged, uncut. **2 intact**, in one piece, unbroken, undamaged, flawless, unmarked, perfect.
– ANTONYMS: incomplete.
• n. **1** a thing that is complete in itself. **2** all of something.
▷ SYNONYMS: **1 entity**, unit, body, ensemble. **2** *the whole of the year:* **all**, every part, the lot, the sum.
□ **on the whole** taking everything into account. **wholefood** Brit. food that has been processed as little as possible. **wholehearted** completely sincere and committed. **wholemeal** Brit. made from the whole grain of wheat. **whole number** a number without fractions.

wholehearted adj. completely sincere and committed.
▷ SYNONYMS: **unqualified**, unreserved, unconditional, complete, full, total, absolute; ardent, fervent, heartfelt, sincere, earnest.
– ANTONYMS: half-hearted.

wholesale n. the selling of goods in large quantities to be sold to the public by others.
• adv. & adj. **1** being sold in such a way. **2** on a large scale.
▷ SYNONYMS: *the wholesale destruction of livestock and crops:* **extensive**, widespread, large-scale, wide-ranging, comprehensive, total, mass, indiscriminate, sweeping.
■ **wholesaler** n.

wholesome adj. **1** good for health or well-being. **2** morally good.

▷ SYNONYMS: **1 healthy**, health-giving, good, nutritious, natural, organic. **2 moral**, ethical, good, clean, virtuous, pure, innocent, chaste, uplifting, edifying.

wholly adv. entirely; fully.
▷ SYNONYMS: **completely**, totally, absolutely, entirely, fully, thoroughly, utterly, downright, in every respect; informal one hundred per cent.

whom pron. used instead of 'who' as the object of a verb or preposition.

whoop n. a loud cry of joy or excitement.
• v. give a whoop.
□ **whooping cough** a disease characterized by coughs followed by a rasping breath.

whopper n. informal **1** something very large. **2** a blatant lie.

whore n. a prostitute.

whorl /worl/ n. **1** each of the turns in a spiral or coil. **2** a ring of leaves or petals. **3** a circle in a fingerprint.

who's contr. **1** who is. **2** who has.

> **USAGE** Don't confuse **who's** with **whose**. **Who's** is short for **who is** or **who has**, as in *who's there* or *who's taken it?*; **whose** means 'belonging to which person' or 'of whom or which', as in *whose is this?* or *a man whose opinion I respect.*

whose adj. & pron. **1** belonging to which person. **2** of whom or which.

why adv. **1** for what reason or purpose? **2** on account of which; the reason that.

wick n. a length of cord in a candle, lamp, etc. which carries liquid fuel to the flame.

wicked adj. **1** evil. **2** playfully mischievous. **3** informal excellent.
▷ SYNONYMS: **1 evil**, sinful, immoral, wrong, bad, iniquitous, corrupt, base, vile, villainous, criminal, nefarious; informal crooked. **2 mischievous**, playful, naughty, impish, roguish, puckish, cheeky.
– ANTONYMS: virtuous.
■ **wickedly** adv. **wickedness** n.

wicker n. thin canes woven to make furniture, baskets, etc.
■ **wickerwork** n.

wicket n. (in cricket) either of the two sets of three stumps with two bails across the top that are defended by a batsman.
□ **wicketkeeper** a fielder positioned close behind a batsman's wicket.

wide adj. **1** of great or specified width. **2** including a great variety of people

W

or things. **3** at a distance from a point or mark.
▷ SYNONYMS: **1 broad**, extensive, spacious, vast. **2 comprehensive**, ample, broad, extensive, wide-ranging, large, exhaustive, all-inclusive, expansive, all-embracing, encyclopedic, catholic. **3 off target**, off the mark, inaccurate.
– ANTONYMS: narrow.
• adv. **1** to the full extent. **2** far from a point or target.
□ **wide awake** fully awake.
■ **widely** adv.

widen v. make or become wider.
▷ SYNONYMS: **broaden**, open up/out, expand, extend, spread out, enlarge.

widespread adj. spread among a large number or over a large area.
▷ SYNONYMS: **general**, extensive, universal, common, global, world-wide, omnipresent, ubiquitous, whole-sale, across the board, pervasive, prevalent, rife, rampant.
– ANTONYMS: limited.

widow n. a woman whose husband has died and who has not remarried.
• v. (**be widowed**) become a widow or widower.

widower n. a man whose wife has died and who has not remarried.

width n. **1** the measurement or extent of something from side to side. **2** a piece of something at its full extent from side to side.
▷ SYNONYMS: **breadth**, thickness, span, diameter, girth.

wield v. **1** hold and use a weapon or tool. **2** have and use power.
▷ SYNONYMS: **1 brandish**, flourish, wave, swing, use, employ, handle. **2** *he wields enormous power*: **exercise**, exert, hold, maintain, command, control.

wife n. (pl. **wives**) a married woman in relation to her husband.
▷ SYNONYMS: **spouse**, partner, mate, consort, bride; informal **better half**, missus; Brit. informal **other half**.
■ **wifely** adj.

> **WORD LINKS**
> **uxorious** very fond of your wife

wig n. a covering of hair worn on the head.

wiggle v. move with short movements from side to side.
• n. a wiggling movement.
■ **wiggly** adj.

wigwam n. a conical tent formerly lived in by some North American Indian peoples.

wiki n. a website or database developed by a group of users, allowing any user to add to or edit the content.

wild adj. **1** living or growing in the natural environment. **2** (of a place) not inhabited or changed by people. **3** uncontrolled. **4** not based on reason or evidence. **5** informal very enthusiastic or excited. **6** informal very angry.
▷ SYNONYMS: **1 untamed**, undomesticated, feral, fierce, ferocious, savage. **2 uncultivated**, native, indigenous. **3 uninhabited**, unpopulated, uncultivated, rugged, rough, inhospitable, desolate, barren. **4 stormy**, squally, tempestuous, turbulent, blustery. **5 uncontrolled**, unrestrained, undisciplined, unruly, rowdy, disorderly, riotous, out of control, unbridled. **6** *a wild scheme*: **foolish**, ridiculous, ludicrous, stupid, foolhardy, idiotic, madcap, absurd, silly, impractical, impracticable, unworkable; informal **crazy**, crackpot. **7** *a wild guess*: **random**, arbitrary, haphazard, uninformed.
– ANTONYMS: tame, cultivated, calm, disciplined.
• n. **1** (**the wild**) a natural environment. **2** (**the wilds**) a remote area.
□ **spread like wildfire** spread very fast. **wild card** a playing card that can have any value, suit, etc. that the player holding it requires. **wildcat** (of a strike) sudden and unofficial. **wildfowl** game birds. **wild goose chase** a hopeless search. **wildlife** the native animals of a region.
■ **wildly** adv. **wildness** n.

wildebeest n. a gnu.

wilderness n. an uncultivated and uninhabited area.
▷ SYNONYMS: **wilds**, wastes, desert, wasteland.

wiles pl. n. cunning methods used to achieve something.
▷ SYNONYMS: **tricks**, ruses, ploys, schemes, dodges, manoeuvres, subterfuges, guile, artfulness, cunning.

wilful (US **willful**) adj. **1** deliberate. **2** stubborn and determined.
▷ SYNONYMS: **1 deliberate**, intentional, premeditated, planned, conscious, calculated. **2 headstrong**, strong-willed, obstinate, stubborn, pig-headed, recalcitrant; Brit. informal **bloody-minded**, bolshie.
– ANTONYMS: accidental.

■ **wilfully** adv. **wilfulness** n.

will[1] aux. v. (past **would**) **1** expressing the future tense. **2** expressing intention, ability, or a request.

will[2] n. **1** a person's power to decide on something and take action. **2** (or **willpower**) a person's ability to control their actions. **3** a desire or intention. **4** a legal document with instructions for the disposal of someone's money and property after their death.

▷ SYNONYMS: **1 determination**, strength of character, resolve, single-mindedness, drive, commitment, dedication, doggedness, tenacity, staying power. **2** *they stayed against their will:* **desire**, wish, preference, inclination, intention. **3** *it was God's will:* **wish**, desire, decision, choice, decree, command.

• v. **1** intend or desire. **2** achieve by mental powers. **3** leave to someone in a will.

▷ SYNONYMS: **1** *do what you will:* **want**, desire, wish, please, see fit, think fit/best, like, choose, prefer. **2** *God willed it:* **decree**, order, ordain, command.

□ **at will** whenever you like.

willing adj. **1** ready or eager to do something. **2** given or done readily.

▷ SYNONYMS: **ready**, prepared, disposed, inclined, minded, happy, glad, pleased, agreeable, amenable; *informal* game.

– ANTONYMS: reluctant.

■ **willingness** n.

willingly adv. readily.

▷ SYNONYMS: **voluntarily**, of your own free will, of your own accord, readily, ungrudgingly, cheerfully, happily, gladly, with pleasure.

– ANTONYMS: reluctantly.

will-o'-the-wisp n. **1** something impossible to obtain. **2** a dim, flickering light seen over marshy ground.

willow n. a tree with narrow leaves and catkins.

willowy adj. tall and slim.

willy-nilly adv. whether you like it or not.

wilt v. **1** (of a plant) become limp through lack of water. **2** feel tired and weak.

▷ SYNONYMS: **1 droop**, sag, become limp, flop. **2 languish**, flag, droop, become listless, fade.

– ANTONYMS: flourish.

wily adj. clever in a cunning way.

▷ SYNONYMS: **shrewd**, clever, sharp, astute, canny, smart, crafty, cunning, artful, sly, scheming, calculating, devious; *informal* foxy.

– ANTONYMS: naive.

■ **wiliness** n.

wimp n. *informal* a weak or timid person.

wimple n. a cloth headdress covering the head, neck, and sides of the face, worn esp. by some nuns.

win v. (**winning**, **won**) **1** be the most successful in a contest etc. **2** gain as a result of success in a contest etc. **3** gain the attention, love, etc. of. **4** (also **win over**) gain the support of.

▷ SYNONYMS: **1 come first**, be victorious, carry the day, come out on top, succeed, triumph, prevail. **2 earn**, gain, secure, collect, pick up, walk away/off with, carry off; *informal* land, net, bag, scoop.

– ANTONYMS: lose.

• n. a victory in a game or contest.

▷ SYNONYMS: **victory**, triumph, conquest.

– ANTONYMS: defeat.

wince v. grimace or flinch from pain or distress.

▷ SYNONYMS: **grimace**, pull a face, flinch, blench, start.

winch n. a hauling or lifting device consisting of a cable winding round a horizontal rotating drum.

• v. hoist or pull with a winch.

wind[1] n. **1** a natural movement of the air. **2** breath needed to do exercise or play an instrument. **3** Brit. gas in the stomach and intestines. **4** wind instruments as a section of an orchestra.

▷ SYNONYMS: **breeze**, current of air, gale, hurricane, gust, draught; *informal* blow; *literary* zephyr.

• v. make breathless.

□ **get wind of** *informal* hear a rumour of. **windbag** *informal* a person who talks at unnecessary length. **windbreak** a screen providing shelter from the wind. **wind instrument** a musical instrument sounded by the player blowing into it. **windmill** a building with sails or vanes that turn in the wind and generate power to grind corn etc. **windpipe** the tube carrying air down the throat to the lungs. **windscreen** (US **windshield**) Brit. the glass screen at the front of a vehicle. **windsock** a light, flexible cone mounted on a mast to show the direction and strength of the wind. **windsurfing** the sport of riding on water on a sailboard. **windswept** exposed to strong winds. **wind tunnel** a tunnel-like structure in which a strong current of air is created to test the effect of wind on vehicles.

W

■ **windward** adj. & adv.

wind² v. (**winding, wound**) **1** move in or take a twisting or spiral course. **2** pass or twist around a thing or person or itself. **3** make a clockwork device work by turning a key or handle.

▷ SYNONYMS: **1 twist and turn**, bend, curve, loop, zigzag, weave, snake. **2 wrap**, furl, entwine, lace; coil, roll, twist, twine.

□ **wind down 1** draw or bring to a close. **2** informal relax. **wind up 1** bring or come to an end. **2** Brit. informal irritate.

windfall n. **1** a piece of unexpected good fortune. **2** fruit blown off a tree by the wind.

▷ SYNONYMS: **bonanza**, jackpot, pennies from heaven, godsend.

windlass n. a winch on a ship or in a harbour.

window n. **1** an opening in a wall, fitted with glass to let in light and allow people to see out. **2** a framed area on a computer screen for viewing information.

□ **window dressing 1** the arrangement of a display in a shop window. **2** the presentation of something to give a misleadingly good impression. **window-shopping** looking at goods displayed in shop windows without intending to buy.

windy adj. (**windier, windiest**) marked by or exposed to strong winds.

▷ SYNONYMS: **breezy**, blowy, fresh, blustery, gusty, wild, stormy, squally.

– ANTONYMS: still.

wine n. an alcoholic drink made esp. from fermented grape juice.

> **WORD LINKS**
> **vinous** relating to wine

winery n. (pl. **wineries**) a place where wine is made.

wing n. **1** a projecting part enabling a bird, insect, or bat to fly. **2** a structure projecting from both sides of an aircraft and supporting it in the air. **3** a part of a large building. **4** a group within an organization. **5** (**the wings**) the sides of a stage out of view of the audience. **6** the part of a football or rugby field close to the sidelines. **7** an attacking player near the sidelines. **8** Brit. the bodywork of a vehicle above the wheel.

▷ SYNONYMS: **1 part**, section, side, annexe, extension. **2 faction**, camp, caucus, arm, branch, group, section, set.

• v. **1** fly, or move quickly as if flying. **2** wound in the wing or arm.

▷ SYNONYMS: **1 fly**, glide, soar. **2 wound**, graze, hit.

□ **under your wing** in or into your protective care. **wingspan** the measurement from tip to tip of the wings of a bird etc.

■ **winged** adj.

winger n. an attacking player on the wing in football etc.

wink v. **1** close and open one eye quickly as a signal. **2** shine or flash on and off.

▷ SYNONYMS: **1 blink**, flutter, bat. **2 sparkle**, twinkle, flash, glitter, gleam, shine, scintillate.

• n. an act of winking.

winkle n. a small edible shellfish.

• v. (**winkle out**) take out or obtain with difficulty.

winner n. **1** a person or thing that wins. **2** informal a successful thing.

▷ SYNONYMS: **victor**, champion, conqueror, medallist; informal champ, top dog.

– ANTONYMS: loser.

winning adj. attractive.

▷ SYNONYMS: **engaging**, charming, appealing, endearing, sweet, cute, winsome, attractive, prepossessing, fetching, disarming, captivating.

• n. (**winnings**) money won by gambling.

▷ SYNONYMS: **prize money**, gains, booty, spoils, proceeds, profits, takings, purse.

■ **winningly** adv.

winnow v. **1** remove members from a group until only the best are left. **2** blow air through grain to remove the chaff.

winsome adj. charming.

winter n. the cold season between autumn and spring.

• v. spend the winter in a particular place.

wintry adj. feeling or looking cold or bleak.

▷ SYNONYMS: **bleak**, cold, chilly, frosty, freezing, icy, snowy, arctic, glacial, bitter, raw; informal nippy; Brit. informal parky.

– ANTONYMS: warm.

wipe v. **1** clean or dry by rubbing with a cloth or the hand. **2** erase data from a computer, video, etc.

▷ SYNONYMS: **1 rub**, mop, sponge, swab, clean, dry, polish. **2** he wiped off the marks: **rub off**, clean off, remove, erase, efface.

• n. **1** an act of wiping. **2** a disposable

W

cleaning cloth.
□ **wipe out** completely destroy or eliminate.
■ **wiper** n.

wire n. **1** a thin, flexible strand of metal. **2** a length of wire used for fencing, to carry an electric current, etc.
• v. **1** install electric wires in. **2** fasten or reinforce with wire.
□ **wiretapping** the secret tapping of phone lines.

wireless adj. using radio, microwaves, etc. (as opposed to wires) to transmit signals.
• n. dated **1** a radio. **2** broadcasting using radio signals.

wiring n. a system of electric wires in a device or building.

wiry adj. (**wirier**, **wiriest**) **1** like wire. **2** lean and strong.

wisdom n. **1** the quality of being wise. **2** a body of knowledge and experience.
▷ SYNONYMS: **1 understanding**, intelligence, sagacity, sense, common sense, shrewdness, astuteness, judgement, prudence, circumspection, logic, rationale, soundness, advisability.
2 knowledge, learning, erudition, scholarship, philosophy, lore.
– ANTONYMS: folly.
□ **wisdom tooth** each of the four molars at the back of the mouth, usu. appearing around the age of 20.

wise adj. **1** having or showing experience, knowledge, and good judgement. **2** (**wise to**) informal aware of.
▷ SYNONYMS: **sage**, sagacious, intelligent, clever, learned, knowledgeable, enlightened, astute, smart, shrewd, sharp-witted, canny, knowing, sensible, prudent, discerning, perceptive.
– ANTONYMS: foolish.
• v. (**wise up**) informal become aware.
□ **wisecrack** informal a joke or witty remark.
■ **wisely** adv.

wish v. **1** desire something that is unlikely or impossible. **2** want to do. **3** express a hope that someone has happiness or success.
▷ SYNONYMS: **want**, desire, feel inclined, feel like, care, choose, please, think fit.
• n. **1** a desire or hope. **2** (**wishes**) an expression of friendly feeling. **3** a thing wished for.
▷ SYNONYMS: **1 desire**, longing, yearning, whim, craving, hunger, hope, aspiration, aim, ambition, dream; informal

hankering, yen. **2** her parents' wishes: **request**, requirement, bidding, instruction, direction, demand, order, command, want, desire, will.
□ **wishbone** a forked bone between the neck and breast of a bird.

wishful adj. based on impractical wishes rather than facts: wishful thinking.

wishy-washy adj. feeble.

wisp n. a small thin bunch or strand of something.
■ **wispy** adj.

wisteria n. a climbing shrub with bluish-lilac flowers.

wistful adj. having or showing vague or regretful longing.
▷ SYNONYMS: **nostalgic**, yearning, longing, forlorn, melancholy, sad, mournful, pensive, reflective, contemplative.
■ **wistfully** adv.

wit n. **1** (or **wits**) the ability to think quickly and make good decisions. **2** a natural talent for using words and ideas in a quick amusing way. **3** a witty person.
▷ SYNONYMS: **1** he needed all his wits to escape: **intelligence**, shrewdness, astuteness, cleverness, canniness, sense, judgement, acumen, insight, brains, mind; informal nous. **2 wittiness**, humour, drollery, repartee, badinage, banter, wordplay, jokes, witticisms, quips, puns. **3 comedian**, humorist, comic, joker; informal wag.

witch n. a woman believed to have evil magic powers.
▷ SYNONYMS: **sorceress**, enchantress, hex.
□ **witch doctor** a person believed to have magic powers of healing etc. **witch hazel** an astringent lotion made from a plant. **witch-hunt** a campaign against a person with unpopular views.

witchcraft n. the practice of magic.
▷ SYNONYMS: **sorcery**, magic, black magic, wizardry, spells, incantations, necromancy; Wicca.

with prep. **1** accompanied by. **2** in the same direction as. **3** having. **4** using. **5** in opposition to or competition with. **6** indicating manner or attitude. **7** in relation to.
□ **with it** informal **1** fashionable. **2** alert.

withdraw v. (**withdrawing**, **withdrew**; past part. **withdrawn**) **1** remove or take away. **2** leave or cause to leave a place. **3** stop taking part in an activity. **4** retract a statement. **5** take money out of an

W

account. **6** stop taking an addictive drug.
▷ SYNONYMS: **1 remove**, extract, pull out, take out, take back. **2** *troops withdrew from the city*: **leave**, retreat from, depart from, pull out of, evacuate, quit, exit, decamp. **3 retract**, take back, go back on, recant, repudiate, renounce, back down, climb down, backtrack, back-pedal, do a U-turn, eat your words.
– ANTONYMS: insert, enter.
■ **withdrawal** n.

withdrawn adj. very shy or reserved.
▷ SYNONYMS: **introverted**, unsociable, inhibited, uncommunicative, unforthcoming, quiet, reticent, reserved, retiring, private, reclusive, distant, shy, timid.
– ANTONYMS: outgoing.

wither v. **1** become shrivelled and dry. **2** become weaker.
▷ SYNONYMS: **1 shrivel**, dry up, wilt, droop, fade, perish. **2** *the muscles in his legs withered*: **waste away**, shrink, atrophy. **3** *public support withered away*: **diminish**, dwindle, shrink, lessen, wane, evaporate, disappear.
– ANTONYMS: thrive.

withering adj. scornful.
▷ SYNONYMS: **scornful**, contemptuous, scathing, bitter, stinging, searing, blistering, fierce, savage.

withers pl. n. the highest part of a horse's back, at the base of the neck.

withhold v. (**withholding**, **withheld**) **1** refuse to give. **2** suppress a reaction etc.
▷ SYNONYMS: **1 hold back**, keep back, refuse to give, retain, hold on to, hide, conceal, keep secret; informal sit on. **2 suppress**, repress, hold back, fight back, choke back, control, check, restrain, contain.
– ANTONYMS: release.

within prep. **1** inside. **2** inside the range or limits of. **3** in a time no longer than.
• adv. inside.

without prep. **1** not accompanied by or having. **2** not doing the action specified.

withstand v. (**withstanding**, **withstood**) remain undamaged or unaffected by.
▷ SYNONYMS: **resist**, weather, survive, endure, cope with, stand, tolerate, bear, defy, brave, hold out against.

witless adj. stupid.

witness n. **1** a person who sees an event take place. **2** a person giving evidence in a law court. **3** a person

who is present at the signing of a document and signs to confirm this.
▷ SYNONYMS: **observer**, onlooker, eyewitness, spectator, viewer, watcher, bystander, passer-by.
• v. be a witness to.
▷ SYNONYMS: **1 see**, observe, watch, view, notice, spot, be present at, attend. **2 countersign**, sign, endorse, validate.

witter v. Brit. informal speak trivially and at length.

witticism n. a witty remark.

witty adj. (**wittier**, **wittiest**) quick, inventive, and amusing with words.
▷ SYNONYMS: **humorous**, amusing, droll, funny, comic, jocular, sparkling, scintillating, entertaining, clever, quick-witted.
■ **wittily** adv. **wittiness** n.

wives pl. of **WIFE**.

wizard n. **1** a man with magical powers. **2** a person who is very skilled in something.
▷ SYNONYMS: **1 sorcerer**, warlock, magus, magician, enchanter. **2 genius**, expert, master, virtuoso, maestro, marvel; informal hotshot, whizz-kid; Brit. informal dab hand; N. Amer. informal **maven**.
■ **wizardry** n.

wizened adj. shrivelled or wrinkled with age.

woad n. a blue dye obtained from a plant.

wobble v. **1** move unsteadily from side to side. **2** (of the voice) tremble.
▷ SYNONYMS: **1 rock**, sway, see-saw, teeter, jiggle, shake; totter, stagger, lurch, waddle. **2** *her voice wobbled*: **tremble**, shake, quiver, quaver, waver.
• n. a wobbling movement or sound.

wobbly adj. unsteady.
▷ SYNONYMS: **unsteady**, unstable, shaky, rocky, rickety, unsafe, precarious; informal wonky.
– ANTONYMS: stable.

wodge n. Brit. informal a large piece or amount.

woe n. **1** sorrow or distress. **2** (**woes**) troubles.
▷ SYNONYMS: **1 misery**, sorrow, distress, sadness, unhappiness, heartache, heartbreak, despair, adversity, misfortune, disaster, suffering, hardship. **2** *financial woes*: **trouble**, difficulty, problem, trial, tribulation, misfortune, setback, reverse.
– ANTONYMS: joy.
▫ **woebegone** sad or miserable.

woeful adj. **1** very sad. **2** very bad.
▷ SYNONYMS: **1 sad**, unhappy, sorrowful, miserable, gloomy, doleful, plaintive,

w

           wok | wood

wretched. **2 dreadful**, awful, terrible, atrocious, disgraceful, deplorable, hopeless, lamentable; informal rotten, appalling, pathetic, pitiful, lousy, abysmal, dire; Brit. informal duff, chronic.
– ANTONYMS: cheerful, excellent.
■ **woefully** adv.

wok n. a bowl-shaped frying pan used in Chinese cookery.

woke past of WAKE.

woken past part. of WAKE.

wold n. an area of high, open land.

wolf n. (pl. **wolves**) a wild animal of the dog family.
• v. eat greedily.
□ **cry wolf** raise false alarms. **wolf whistle** a whistle with a rising and falling pitch, expressing sexual admiration.
■ **wolfish** adj.

> **WORD LINKS**
> **lupine** relating or like a wolf

wolfram n. tungsten or its ore.

wolverine n. a mammal with a long brown coat, found in cold northern regions.

woman n. (pl. **women**) an adult human female.
▷ SYNONYMS: **lady**, female; Scottish & N. English lass; Irish colleen; informal chick; N. Amer. informal sister, dame, broad; Austral./NZ informal sheila; literary damsel.
□ **womankind** women as a group.
■ **womanhood** n..

> **WORD LINKS**
> **female**, **feminine** relating to women
> **gynaecology** the branch of medicine concerning women
> **misogyny** hatred of women

womanize (or **-ise**) v. (of a man) have many casual affairs with women.
■ **womanizer** n.

womanly adj. relating to or like a woman or women.
▷ SYNONYMS: **1 feminine**, female. **2** her womanly figure: **voluptuous**, curvaceous, shapely, ample, buxom, full-figured; informal curvy.
– ANTONYMS: manly, boyish.

womb n. the organ in a woman or female mammal in which offspring develop before birth.

wombat n. a burrowing Australian marsupial resembling a small bear.

won past & past part. of WIN.

wonder v. **1** want to know something. **2** feel amazement and admiration.
▷ SYNONYMS: **1 ponder**, think about, meditate on, reflect on, muse on, speculate about, conjecture,

be curious about. **2 marvel**, be amazed, be astonished, stand in awe, be dumbfounded; informal be flabbergasted.
• n. **1** amazement and admiration. **2** a cause of this.
▷ SYNONYMS: **1 awe**, admiration, fascination, surprise, astonishment, amazement. **2** the wonders of nature: **marvel**, miracle, phenomenon, sensation, spectacle, beauty, curiosity.
□ **wonderland** a place full of wonderful things.
■ **wonderment** n.

wonderful adj. very good or remarkable.
▷ SYNONYMS: **marvellous**, magnificent, superb, glorious, sublime, lovely, delightful; informal super, great, fantastic, terrific, tremendous, sensational, fabulous, awesome, magic, wicked; Brit. informal smashing, brilliant; N. Amer. informal peachy, dandy, neat; Austral./NZ informal beaut, bonzer.
■ **wonderfully** adv.

wondrous adj. inspiring wonder.

wonky adj. (**wonkier**, **wonkiest**) informal **1** crooked. **2** unsteady or faulty.

wont /wohnt/ formal n. (**your wont**) your normal behaviour.
• adj. (**wont to**) accustomed to.

woo v. **1** try to gain a woman's love. **2** seek the support or custom of.
▷ SYNONYMS: **1 pay court to**, pursue, chase; dated court, romance, seek the hand of. **2 seek**, pursue, curry favour with, try to win, try to attract, try to cultivate. **3 entice**, tempt, coax, persuade, wheedle, seduce; informal sweet-talk.

wood n. **1** the hard material forming the trunk and branches of a tree. **2** (or **woods**) a small forest.
▷ SYNONYMS: **1 timber**, planks, logs; N. Amer. lumber. **2 forest**, woodland, trees, copse, coppice, grove; Brit. spinney.
□ **woodcut** a print made from a design cut in a block of wood. **woodland** land covered with trees. **woodlouse** a small insect-like animal with a segmented body. **woodpecker** a bird with a strong bill that pecks at tree trunks to find insects. **woodwind** wind instruments other than brass instruments. **woodwork 1** the wooden parts of a room. **2** Brit. the activity of making things from wood. **woodworm** the larva of a kind of beetle, that bores into wood.
■ **woody** adj.

w

WORD LINKS
ligneous consisting of or like wood

wooded adj. covered with trees.
▷ SYNONYMS: **forested**, afforested, tree-covered; literary sylvan.

wooden adj. **1** made of wood. **2** stiff and awkward.
▷ SYNONYMS: **1 wood**, timber. **2 stilted**, stiff, unnatural, awkward, flat, clumsy, graceless, inelegant.
3 expressionless, impassive, poker-faced, emotionless, blank, vacant, unresponsive, lifeless.
■ **woodenly** adv.

woof n. the bark of a dog.
• v. bark.

woofer n. a loudspeaker for reproducing low frequencies.

wool n. the soft hair forming the coat of a sheep, made into yarn or fabric.
▷ SYNONYMS: **fleece**, hair, coat.

woollen (US **woolen**) adj. made of wool.
• n. (**woollens**) woollen clothing.

woolly adj. **1** made of or like wool.
2 confused or unclear.
▷ SYNONYMS: **1 woollen**, wool. **2 fleecy**, shaggy, hairy, fluffy. **3 vague**, ill-defined, hazy, unclear, fuzzy, indefinite, confused, muddled.

woozy adj. informal dizzy or dazed.
■ **woozily** adv.

word n. **1** a single meaningful unit of language, used with others to form sentences. **2** a remark or statement.
3 (**words**) angry talk. **4** a command.
5 (**your word**) a promise. **6** news.
▷ SYNONYMS: **1 term**, name, expression, designation. **2 remark**, comment, observation, statement, utterance.
3 talk, conversation, chat, tête-à-tête, heart-to-heart, one-to-one, discussion; informal confab. **4** *I give you my word:* **promise**, assurance, guarantee, undertaking, pledge, vow, oath, bond. **5** *there's no word from the hospital:* **news**, information, communication, intelligence, message, report, communiqué, dispatch, bulletin; literary tidings.
• v. express in particular words.
▷ SYNONYMS: **phrase**, express, put, couch, frame, formulate, style.
▫ **word of mouth** spoken communication. **word processor** a computer or program for creating and printing a piece of writing.

WORD LINKS
verbal, **lexical** relating to words

wording n. the way something is worded.

▷ SYNONYMS: **phrasing**, phraseology, language, words, expression, terminology.

wordy adj. using too many words.
▷ SYNONYMS: **long-winded**, verbose, lengthy, rambling, garrulous, voluble; informal **windy**; Brit. informal **waffly**.
– ANTONYMS: succinct.

wore past of WEAR.

work n. **1** activity involving mental or physical effort. **2** such activity as a means of earning money. **3** a task to be done. **4** a thing or things done or made. **5** (**works**) a factory. **6** (**works**) the mechanism of a machine.
▷ SYNONYMS: **1 labour**, toil, slog, drudgery, exertion, effort, industry; informal **grind**, sweat; Brit. informal **graft**; old use travail. **2 employment**, job, post, position, situation, occupation, profession, career, vocation, calling.
3 tasks, jobs, duties, assignments, projects, chores. **4 composition**, piece, creation, opus; (**works**) oeuvre, canon.
– ANTONYMS: leisure.
• v. **1** do work as a job. **2** (of a machine etc.) function properly. **3** have the desired result. **4** bring into a desired state. **5** produce or create. **6** move gradually or with difficulty into another position.
▷ SYNONYMS: **1** *we worked late into the night:* **labour**, toil, exert yourself, slave away; informal slog away, beaver away; Brit. informal graft. **2 function**, go, run, operate, handle. **3 succeed**, turn out well, go as planned, get results, be effective; informal come off, pay off, do the trick. **4** *I can't work miracles:* **achieve**, accomplish, bring about, produce, perform.
– ANTONYMS: rest, fail.
▫ **get worked up** become stressed or angry. **workforce** the people working or available for work in an area, organization, etc. **workhouse** hist. a place where poor people were housed and fed in return for work. **workout** a session of vigorous exercise. **work out 1** solve. **2** develop in the required way. **3** plan in detail.
4 do vigorous exercise. **workstation** a desktop computer that is part of a network. **worktop** Brit. a flat surface for working on in a kitchen. **work-to-rule** a form of industrial action in which workers refuse to do overtime or extra work.

workable adj. capable of producing the desired result.

workaday adj. ordinary.

worker n. **1** a person who works. **2** a neuter bee, wasp, ant, etc. that does the basic work of a colony.
▷ SYNONYMS: **employee**, member of staff, workman, labourer, hand, operator, operative, agent, wage-earner, bread-winner, proletarian.

working n. **1** a mine or part of a mine. **2** (**workings**) the way in which a system etc. operates.
• adj. used as the basis for work or discussion and likely to be changed later.
□ **working class** the social group consisting largely of people who do manual or industrial work. **working party** Brit. a group set up to study and report on an issue and make recommendations.

workman n. a man employed to do manual work.
□ **workmanlike** showing efficient skill. **workmanship** the skill with which something is made or done.

workshop n. **1** a room or building in which goods are made or repaired. **2** a meeting for discussion and activity on a particular subject or project.
▷ SYNONYMS: **1 workroom**, studio, factory, works, plant, industrial unit. **2 study group**, seminar, forum, class.

world n. **1** the earth with all its countries and peoples. **2** all that belongs to a region, period, or area of activity.
▷ SYNONYMS: **1 earth**, globe, planet, sphere. **2 sphere**, society, circle, arena, milieu, province, domain, preserve, realm, field. **3** (**the world**) **humankind**, mankind, people, humanity; the public, all and sundry.
□ **World Wide Web** an information system on the Internet allowing documents to be connected to each other by hypertext links.

worldly adj. **1** of material rather than spiritual things. **2** experienced and sophisticated.
▷ SYNONYMS: **1 earthly**, terrestrial, temporal, mundane, mortal, human, material, physical. **2 sophisticated**, experienced, worldly-wise, knowledgeable, knowing, enlightened, mature, seasoned, cosmopolitan, urbane, cultured.
– ANTONYMS: spiritual, naive.

worldwide adj. throughout the world.
▷ SYNONYMS: **global**, international, inter-continental, universal, ubiquitous.
– ANTONYMS: local.

worm n. **1** an animal with a long,

soft body and no backbone or limbs. **2** (**worms**) intestinal parasites.
• v. **1** move by crawling or wriggling. **2** (**worm your way into**) gradually move into a situation. **3** (**worm out of**) obtain information from someone reluctant to give it.
□ **worm cast** a spiral mass of soil etc. thrown up by a burrowing worm.
wormwood a bitter-tasting plant, used in vermouth etc.

worn past part. of WEAR.
• adj. damaged by wear.
▷ SYNONYMS: **shabby**, worn out, thread-bare, in tatters, falling to pieces, ragged, frayed, moth-eaten, scruffy, having seen better days.
– ANTONYMS: new, smart.
□ **worn out 1** exhausted. **2** damaged by wear and no longer usable.

worried adj. feeling or showing worry.
▷ SYNONYMS: **anxious**, troubled, bothered, concerned, uneasy, fretful, agitated, nervous, edgy, tense, appre-hensive, fearful, afraid, frightened; Brit. informal in a stew, in a flap.
– ANTONYMS: carefree.
■ **worriedly** adv.

worrisome adj. causing anxiety or concern.

worry v. (**worrying, worried**) **1** feel or cause to feel concern or anxiety. **2** annoy or disturb. **3** (of a dog) tear at with the teeth. **4** (of a dog) chase and attack sheep etc.
▷ SYNONYMS: **1 fret**, brood, be anxious, be concerned, agonize, panic, lose sleep. **2 trouble**, bother, disturb, distress, upset, concern, unsettle, perturb, scare, prey on someone's mind; informal bug, get to.
• n. (pl. **worries**) **1** anxiety or concern. **2** a source of this.
▷ SYNONYMS: **1 anxiety**, distress, concern, unease, disquiet, nerves, agitation, edginess, tension, appre-hension, fear, misgiving. **2 problem**, cause for concern, nuisance, pest, trial, trouble, bane, bugbear; informal pain, headache, hassle.
■ **worrier** n.

worse adj. **1** less good or pleasing. **2** more serious or severe. **3** more ill or unhappy.
• adv. **1** less well. **2** more seriously or severely.
• n. something worse.

worsen v. make or become worse.
▷ SYNONYMS: **1** going on strike may worsen the situation: **aggravate**, add to, intensify, increase, compound, magnify, heighten, inflame,

w

exacerbate. **2** *his condition worsened:* **deteriorate**, degenerate, decline; informal go downhill.

– ANTONYMS: improve.

worship n. **1** deep respect paid to God or a god or goddess. **2** great admiration and respect.

▷ SYNONYMS: **reverence**, veneration, adoration, glorification, exaltation, devotion, praise, thanksgiving, homage, honour, observance.

• v. (**worshipping**, **worshipped**; US **worshiping**, **worshiped**) **1** take part in an act of worship. **2** greatly admire and respect.

▷ SYNONYMS: **1 revere**, pray to, pay homage to, honour, adore, venerate, praise, glorify, exalt. **2 love**, cherish, treasure, hold dear, esteem, adulate, idolize, deify, hero-worship, lionize; informal put on a pedestal.

■ **worshipper** n.

worst adj. most bad, severe, or serious.
• adv. **1** most severely or seriously. **2** least well.
• n. the worst event etc.
• v. defeat.

worsted /wuus-tid/ n. a smooth, fine woollen fabric.

worth adj. **1** having a specified value. **2** deserving a particular treatment.
• n. **1** value or merit. **2** an amount of something equivalent to a particular sum of money.

▷ SYNONYMS: **1 value**, price, cost, valuation, estimate. **2 benefit**, good, advantage, use, value, virtue, desirability, sense.

worthless adj. **1** having no real value or use. **2** having no good qualities.

▷ SYNONYMS: **1 valueless**, of no value; informal trashy. **2 useless**, pointless, meaningless, senseless, inconsequential, ineffective, ineffectual, fruitless, unproductive, unavailing, valueless. **3 good-for-nothing**, ne'er-do-well, useless, despicable, contemptible, degenerate; informal no-good, lousy.

– ANTONYMS: valuable, useful.

worthwhile adj. worth the time or effort spent.

▷ SYNONYMS: **valuable**, useful, of service, beneficial, rewarding, advantageous, positive, helpful, profitable, gainful, fruitful, productive, constructive, effective.

worthy adj. (**worthier**, **worthiest**) **1** deserving effort, attention, or respect. **2** (**worthy of**) deserving.

▷ SYNONYMS: **good**, righteous, virtuous, moral, ethical, upright, respectable,

upstanding, high-minded, principled, reputable, decent.

– ANTONYMS: disreputable.

• n. (pl. **worthies**) an important person.

▷ SYNONYMS: **dignitary**, grandee, VIP, notable, pillar of society, luminary, leading light; informal bigwig.

■ **worthily** adv. **worthiness** n.

would aux. v. **1** past of WILL¹. **2** expressing possible consequence. **3** expressing a desire, polite request, or opinion.

would-be adj. wishing to be a particular type of person.

▷ SYNONYMS: **aspiring**, hopeful, keen, eager, ambitious, prospective, potential, budding, promising; informal wannabe.

wound¹ n. **1** an injury caused by a cut, blow, or other impact. **2** an injury to a person's feelings.

▷ SYNONYMS: **1 injury**, cut, gash, laceration, graze, scratch, abrasion, puncture, lesion; Medicine trauma. **2 insult**, blow, slight, offence, affront, hurt, damage, injury.

• v. injure or hurt.

▷ SYNONYMS: **1 injure**, hurt, harm, lacerate, cut, graze, gash, stab, slash. **2** *her words wounded him:* **hurt**, offend, affront, distress, grieve, pain.

wound² past & past part. of WIND².

wove past of WEAVE.

woven past part. of WEAVE.

wow informal exclam. expressing astonishment or admiration.

• v. impress greatly.

WPC abbrev. woman police constable.

wrack n. a seaweed.
• v. var. of RACK.

wraith n. a ghost.

wrangle n. a long dispute.
• v. engage in a wrangle.

wrap v. (**wrapping**, **wrapped**) **1** enclose in paper or soft material. **2** encircle or wind round.

▷ SYNONYMS: **1 enclose**, enfold, envelop, encase, cover, fold, wind, swathe, bundle, swaddle. **2 pack**, package, parcel up, bundle up, gift-wrap.

• n. a shawl.

▷ SYNONYMS: **shawl**, stole, pashmina, cloak, cape, mantle, scarf.

□ **under wraps** kept secret. **wrap up 1** dress in warm clothes. **2** complete a meeting or deal. **3** (**wrapped up**) totally engrossed.

■ **wrapper** n. **wrapping** n.

wrasse /rass/ n. a colourful sea fish.

wrath /roth/ n. extreme anger.

▷ SYNONYMS: **anger**, rage, temper, fury,

outrage, spleen, indignation; literary ire.
– ANTONYMS: happiness.
■ **wrathful** adj.

wreak v. **1** cause damage. **2** take revenge.

wreath n. a decorative ring of flowers and leaves.
▷ SYNONYMS: **garland**, circlet, chaplet, crown, festoon, lei, ring, loop, circle.

wreathe v. **1** encircle. **2** move with a curling motion.
▷ SYNONYMS: **1 festoon**, garland, drape, cover, deck, decorate, ornament, adorn. **2 spiral**, coil, loop, wind, curl, twist, snake.

wreck n. **1** the destruction of a ship at sea. **2** a ship destroyed at sea. **3** a badly damaged building, vehicle, etc. **4** a person in a very bad state.
▷ SYNONYMS: **1 shipwreck**, sunken ship, hull. **2 wreckage**, debris, ruins, remains, burnt-out shell.
• v. **1** destroy or badly damage. **2** cause a ship to sink or break up.
▷ SYNONYMS: **1 destroy**, break, demolish, crash, smash up, write off; N. Amer. informal trash, total. **2 ruin**, spoil, disrupt, undo, put a stop to, frustrate, blight, crush, dash, destroy, scotch, shatter, devastate, sabotage; informal mess up, screw up, put paid to, stymie; Brit. informal scupper.

wreckage n. the remains of something that has been wrecked.

wren n. **1** a very small bird. **2** a member of the former Women's Royal Naval Service.

wrench v. **1** pull or twist violently. **2** twist and injure a part of the body.
▷ SYNONYMS: **1 tug**, pull, jerk, wrest, heave, twist, force, prise; N. Amer. pry; informal yank. **2 sprain**, twist, turn, strain, rick, crick.
• n. **1** a sudden violent twist or pull. **2** distress caused by parting. **3** an adjustable tool like a spanner.

wrest v. **1** forcibly pull from a person's grasp. **2** take power after a struggle.

wrestle v. **1** take part in a fight or contest involving close grappling with an opponent. **2** struggle with a task or problem.
▷ SYNONYMS: **grapple**, fight, struggle, scuffle, tussle, brawl; informal scrap.
■ **wrestler** n.

wretch n. **1** an unfortunate person. **2** informal an unpleasant person.

wretched adj. **1** very unhappy or unfortunate. **2** very bad or annoying.
▷ SYNONYMS: **1 miserable**, unhappy, sad, heartbroken, grief-stricken,

distressed, desolate, devastated, disconsolate, downcast, dejected, depressed, melancholy, forlorn. **2 harsh**, hard, grim, difficult, poor, pitiful, piteous, pathetic, tragic, miserable, bleak, cheerless, hopeless, sorry, sordid; informal crummy.
– ANTONYMS: cheerful, comfortable.
■ **wretchedly** adv.

wriggle v. **1** move with quick twisting movements. **2** (**wriggle out of**) use excuses to avoid doing.
▷ SYNONYMS: **squirm**, writhe, wiggle, thresh, flounder, flail, twitch, twist and turn, snake, worm.
• n. a wriggling movement.

wring v. (**wringing**, **wrung**) **1** squeeze and twist, esp. to remove liquid. **2** squeeze someone's hand tightly. **3** (**wring from/out of**) obtain with difficulty.

wrinkle n. a slight line or fold in fabric or the skin.
▷ SYNONYMS: **crease**, fold, pucker, line, crinkle, furrow, ridge, groove; informal crow's feet.
• v. form or cause to form wrinkles.
▷ SYNONYMS: **crease**, pucker, gather, crinkle, crumple, rumple, ruck up, scrunch up.
■ **wrinkly** adj.

wrist n. the joint connecting the hand and forearm.

writ n. an official written order issued by a court or other legal authority.

write v. (**writing**, **wrote**; past part. **written**) **1** mark letters, words, or other symbols on a surface with a pen, pencil, etc. **2** write and send a letter. **3** compose a written or musical work. **4** fill out a cheque.
▷ SYNONYMS: **1 put in writing**, put down, jot down, note down, take down, record, inscribe, sign, scribble, scrawl. **2 correspond**, communicate, get in touch, keep in contact; informal drop someone a line. **3 compose**, draft, think up, formulate, compile, pen, dash off, produce.
□ **write off 1** dismiss as insignificant. **2** decide not to pursue a plan. **write-off** Brit. a vehicle too badly damaged to be repaired. **write-up** a newspaper review of a recent performance etc.

writer n. a person who has written something, or who writes as an occupation.
▷ SYNONYMS: **author**, wordsmith; informal scribbler, scribe, pen-pusher, hack.

writhe v. twist or squirm in pain or embarrassment.
▷ SYNONYMS: **squirm**, wriggle, thrash,

w

flail, toss, twist.

writing n. **1** a sequence of letters or symbols forming words. **2** (**writings**) books or other written works.

▷ SYNONYMS: **1 handwriting**, hand, script, calligraphy, lettering, print, printing; informal scribble, scrawl. **2 written work**, compositions, books, publications, papers, articles, essays, oeuvre.

> **WORD LINKS**
> **graphology** the study of handwriting

wrong adj. **1** not correct or true; mistaken. **2** unjust, dishonest, or immoral. **3** in a bad or abnormal condition.

▷ SYNONYMS: **1 incorrect**, mistaken, erroneous, inaccurate, wide of the mark, inexact, imprecise; informal off beam, out. **2 inappropriate**, unsuitable, ill-advised, ill-considered, ill-judged, unwise, infelicitous; informal out of order. **3 bad**, dishonest, illegal, unlawful, illicit, criminal, corrupt, unethical, immoral, wicked, sinful, iniquitous, nefarious, reprehensible; informal crooked. **4 amiss**, awry, out of order, not right, defective, faulty.

– ANTONYMS: right, correct.
• adv. **1** mistakenly. **2** with an incorrect result.

▷ SYNONYMS: **incorrectly**, wrongly, inaccurately, erroneously, mistakenly.
• n. an unjust or immoral action.

▷ SYNONYMS: **1 immorality**, sin, wickedness, evil, illegality, unlawfulness, crime, corruption, villainy, dishonesty, injustice, misconduct, transgression. **2 misdeed**, offence,

injury, crime, transgression, sin, injustice, outrage, atrocity.

– ANTONYMS: right.
• v. treat unjustly.

▷ SYNONYMS: **mistreat**, ill-use, ill-treat, do an injustice to, abuse, harm, hurt, injure.
□ **in the wrong** responsible for a mistake or offence.
■ **wrongly** adv.

wrongdoer n. a person who commits illegal or dishonest acts.

▷ SYNONYMS: **offender**, lawbreaker, criminal, felon, delinquent, villain, culprit, evildoer, sinner, transgressor, malefactor, miscreant, rogue, scoundrel; informal crook.

wrongdoing n. illegal or dishonest behaviour.

▷ SYNONYMS: **crime**, lawbreaking, lawlessness, criminality, villainy, misconduct, misbehaviour, malpractice, corruption, immorality, wickedness, vice; offence, felony, misdeed, misdemeanour, fault, peccadillo, transgression, sin.

wrongful adj. not fair, just, or legal.
■ **wrongfully** adv.

wrote past of WRITE.

wrought adj. (of metals) shaped by hammering.
□ **wrought iron** a tough form of iron suitable for forging or rolling.

wrung past & past part. of WRING.

wry adj. (**wryer**, **wryest** or **wrier**, **wriest**) **1** using dry, mocking humour. **2** (of the face) expressing disappointment or annoyance.
■ **wryly** adv.

WWW abbrev. World Wide Web.

Xx

X (or **x**) n. the Roman numeral for ten.

X chromosome n. a sex chromosome, two of which are normally present in female cells and one in male cells.

xenon /zen-on/ n. an inert gas.

xenophobia /zen-uh-**foh**-bi-uh/ n. dislike or fear of people from other countries.
 ■ **xenophobic** adj.

Xerox /**zeer**-oks/ n. trademark **1** a photocopying machine. **2** a photocopy.
 •v. (**xerox**) photocopy.

Xmas n. informal Christmas.

X-ray n. **1** an electromagnetic wave able to pass through solids. **2** an image of an object's internal structure produced by passing X-rays through it.

xylophone /**zy**-loh-fohn/ n. a musical instrument played by hitting a row of wooden bars with small hammers.

Yy

yacht /yot/ n. **1** a medium-sized sailing boat. **2** a powered boat equipped for cruising.
■ **yachting** n. **yachtsman** (or **yachtswoman**) n.

yak n. a large Asian ox with shaggy hair.

yam n. the tuber of a tropical plant, eaten as a vegetable.

yang n. (in Chinese philosophy) the active male force in the universe.

Yank n. informal an American.

yank informal v. pull sharply.
▷ SYNONYMS: **jerk**, pull, tug, wrench.
• n. a sharp pull.

yap v. (**yapping**, **yapped**) bark shrilly.
• n. a shrill bark.

yard n. **1** a unit of length equal to 3 ft (0.9144 m). **2** Brit. a piece of enclosed ground next to a building. **3** a pole slung across a ship's mast for a sail to hang from.
■ **yardage** n.

yardstick n. a standard for comparison.
▷ SYNONYMS: **standard**, measure, gauge, scale, guide, guideline, indicator, test, touchstone, barometer, criterion, benchmark.

yarmulke (or **yarmulka**) /yar-muul-kuh/ n. a skullcap worn by Jewish men.

yarn n. **1** spun thread. **2** informal a story.
▷ SYNONYMS: **thread**, cotton, wool, fibre, filament.

yashmak n. a veil concealing all of the face except the eyes, worn by some Muslim women.

yaw v. (of a ship or aircraft) turn unsteadily from side to side.

yawn v. **1** open the mouth wide and breathe in deeply due to tiredness or boredom. **2** (**yawning**) wide open.
▷ SYNONYMS: (**yawning**) **gaping**, wide, cavernous, deep, huge.
• n. an act of yawning.

Y chromosome n. a sex chromosome normally present only in male cells.

yd abbrev. yard.

year n. **1** (or **calendar year**) the period of 365 days (or 366 days in leap years) starting from January 1. **2** the time taken by the earth to go once around the sun.
□ **yearbook** an annual publication listing events or aspects of the previous year. **yearling** an animal between one and two years old.

yearly adv. & adj. happening or produced once a year or every year.
▷ SYNONYMS: as adv. **annually**, per annum, once a year, each/every year.

yearn v. feel great longing.
▷ SYNONYMS: **long**, pine, crave, desire, want, wish, hanker, covet, hunger, thirst, ache; informal itch.

yeast n. a fungus, or substance made from this, used to ferment beer and wine and to make dough rise.
■ **yeasty** adv.

yell n. a loud, sharp cry or call.
• v. utter a yell.
▷ SYNONYMS: **shout**, cry out, howl, wail, scream, shriek, screech, yelp, squeal, roar, bawl; informal holler.

yellow adj. **1** of the colour of ripe lemons. **2** informal cowardly.
▷ SYNONYMS: **golden**, gold, blonde, fair, flaxen, lemon, primrose, mustard.
• n. yellow colour.
• v. turn yellow with age.
■ **yellowish** adj.

yelp n. a short, sharp cry.
• v. utter a yelp.

yen n. (pl. **yen**) **1** the basic unit of money of Japan. **2** informal a longing.

yeoman /yoh-muhn/ n. hist. a man owning a house and a small area of farmland.

yes exclam. **1** expressing agreement or consent. **2** used as a reply to a summons.
□ **yes-man** informal a person who always agrees with their superiors.

yesterday adv. on the day before today.

• n. **1** the day before today. **2** the recent past.

yet adv. **1** up until now or then. **2** this soon. **3** from now into the future. **4** still; even.
• conj. nevertheless.

yeti n. a large hairy manlike animal said to live in the Himalayas.

yew n. an evergreen tree with poisonous red berries.

Y-fronts pl. n. Brit. trademark men's or boys' underpants with a seam at the front in the shape of an inverted Y.

Yiddish n. a language used by Jews from central and eastern Europe.

yield v. **1** produce or provide a natural or industrial product. **2** produce a result. **3** give way to demands or pressure. **4** give up possession of.
▷ SYNONYMS: **1 produce**, bear, give, provide, afford, return, bring in, earn, realize, generate, deliver, pay out. **2 surrender**, capitulate, submit, admit defeat, back down, give in, cave in, raise the white flag, throw in the towel, give up the struggle.
− ANTONYMS: withhold, resist.
• n. an amount yielded.
▷ SYNONYMS: **profit**, gain, return, dividend, earnings.

yin n. (in Chinese philosophy) the passive female presence in the universe.

yob (or **yobbo**) n. Brit. informal a rude and aggressive young man.
▷ SYNONYMS: **lout**, thug, hooligan, tearaway, vandal, ruffian, troublemaker; Austral. larrikin; informal tough, bruiser, yahoo; Brit. informal lager lout; Scottish informal ned.
■ **yobbish** adj.

yodel v. (**yodelling**, **yodelled**; US **yodeling**, **yodeled**) sing in a style that alternates rapidly between a normal voice and a high-pitched voice.
• n. a yodelling song or call.
■ **yodeller** n.

yoga n. a system involving breathing exercises and the holding of particular body positions, based on Hindu philosophy.
■ **yogic** adj.

yogi n. (pl. **yogis**) a person skilled in yoga.

yogurt (or **yoghurt**) n. a thick liquid food made from milk with bacteria added.

yoke n. **1** a piece of wood fastened over the necks of two animals pulling a plough etc. **2** a part of a garment fitting over the shoulders. **3** a burden or oppressive restriction. **4** a frame fitting over the shoulders, used to carry buckets.
• v. join with a yoke.

yokel n. an unsophisticated country person.
▷ SYNONYMS: **rustic**, bumpkin, peasant, provincial; N. Amer. informal hayseed, hillbilly, hick.

yolk n. the yellow inner part of a bird's egg.

Yom Kippur n. an important day in the Jewish year, on which people pray and fast.

yonder adj. & adv. old use or dialect over there.

yonks pl. n. Brit. informal a very long time.

yore n. (**of yore**) literary long ago.

Yorkshire pudding n. a baked batter pudding traditionally eaten with roast beef.

you pron. **1** the person or people being addressed. **2** any person in general.

young adj. **1** having lived or existed for only a short time. **2** of or typical of young people.
▷ SYNONYMS: **1 youthful**, juvenile, junior, adolescent, teenage, in your salad days. **2** a young industry: **new**, fledgling, developing, budding, in its infancy, emerging, in the making. **3 immature**, childish, inexperienced, naive, green, wet behind the ears.
− ANTONYMS: old, mature.
• pl. n. young children or animals; offspring.
▷ SYNONYMS: **offspring**, progeny, family, babies, litter, brood.

youngster n. a young person.
▷ SYNONYMS: **child**, teenager, adolescent, youth, juvenile, minor, junior, boy, girl; Scottish & N. English lass, lassie; informal lad, kid, whippersnapper, teen.

your adj. of or belonging to you.

> USAGE Don't confuse **your** meaning 'belonging to you' (as in your daughter) with the form **you're**, short for **you are** (as in you're a good cook).

you're contr. you are.

yours possess. pron. belonging to you.

yourself pron. (pl. **yourselves**) **1** used when the person or people being addressed are affected by an action. **2** you personally.

youth n. (pl. **youths**) **1** the period between childhood and adult age. **2** the qualities associated with being young. **3** young people. **4** a young man.
▷ SYNONYMS: **1 early years**, teens, adolescence, boyhood, girlhood,

y

childhood, minority. **2 young man**, boy, juvenile, teenager, adolescent, junior, minor; informal lad, kid.
□ **youth club** a club providing leisure activities for young people. **youth hostel** a place providing cheap overnight accommodation, esp. for young people on holiday.

youthful adj. **1** young or seeming young. **2** characteristic of young people.
▷ SYNONYMS: **young**, boyish, girlish, fresh-faced, young-looking, spry, sprightly, vigorous, active.
– ANTONYMS: elderly.
■ **youthfully** adv. **youthfulness** n.

yowl n. a loud wailing cry.
• v. make a yowl.

yo-yo n. (pl. **yo-yos**) trademark a toy made of a pair of joined discs with a groove between them on which a string is wound, which can be spun down and up as the string unwinds and rewinds.
• v. (**yo-yoing, yo-yoed**) move up and down repeatedly.

yuan n. (pl. **yuan**) the basic unit of money of China.

yucca n. a plant with large spikes of white flowers.

yuck (or **yuk**) exclam. informal used to express disgust.
■ **yucky** adj.

Yule (or **Yuletide**) n. old use Christmas.

yummy adj. (**yummier, yummiest**) informal delicious.

yuppie (or **yuppy**) n. (pl. **yuppies**) informal a young middle-class professional person.

Zz

zany adj. (**zanier**, **zaniest**) amusingly unconventional.
▷ SYNONYMS: **eccentric**, odd, unconventional, bizarre, weird, mad, crazy, comic, madcap, quirky, idiosyncratic; informal wacky, oddball, off the wall; Brit. informal **daft**; N. Amer. informal kooky.
– ANTONYMS: conventional.

zap v. (**zapping**, **zapped**) informal **1** destroy. **2** move rapidly.

zeal n. great enthusiasm for a cause or aim.
▷ SYNONYMS: **enthusiasm**, passion, ardour, fervour, fervency, fire, devotion, gusto, vigour, energy, vehemence, intensity, eagerness, fanaticism.
– ANTONYMS: apathy.

zealot n. a fanatical follower of a religion, cause, etc.
▷ SYNONYMS: **fanatic**, enthusiast, extremist, radical, diehard, activist, militant.
■ **zealotry** n.

zealous adj. showing great enthusiasm for a cause or aim.
▷ SYNONYMS: **ardent**, fervent, passionate, impassioned, enthusiastic, devoted, committed, dedicated, eager, keen, avid, vehement, intense, fierce, fanatical.
– ANTONYMS: apathetic.
■ **zealously** adv.

zebra n. an African wild horse with black and white stripes.
□ **zebra crossing** Brit. a pedestrian crossing marked with broad white stripes.

zeitgeist /zyt-gysst/ n. the characteristic spirit or mood of a particular period.

Zen n. a form of Buddhism.

zenith n. **1** the point of greatest power or success. **2** the point in the sky directly overhead.
▷ SYNONYMS: **high point**, crowning point, height, top, acme, peak, pinnacle, apex, apogee, crown, crest, summit, culmination, climax.
– ANTONYMS: nadir.

zephyr n. literary a gentle wind.

zero adj. & n. (pl. **zeros**) **1** the figure 0; nought. **2** a temperature of 0°C (32°F).
▷ SYNONYMS: **nought**, nothing, nil, 0; informal zilch; old use naught.
• v. (**zeroing**, **zeroed**) (**zero in on**) take aim at or focus attention on.
□ **zero hour** the time at which an important event is set to begin.

zest n. **1** great enthusiasm and energy. **2** the outer coloured part of the peel of citrus fruit.
▷ SYNONYMS: **enthusiasm**, gusto, relish, appetite, eagerness, keenness, zeal, passion, energy, liveliness.

zigzag n. a line or course having sharp alternate right and left turns.
• v. (**zigzagging**, **zigzagged**) move in a zigzag.
▷ SYNONYMS: **twist**, meander, snake, wind, weave, swerve.

zilch n. informal nothing.

zinc n. a white metallic element.

zing n. informal energy or enthusiasm.

Zionism n. a movement for the development of a Jewish nation in Israel.
■ **Zionist** n. & adj.

zip n. **1** (N. Amer. **zipper**) Brit. a fastener consisting of two flexible interlocking metal or plastic strips, closed or opened by pulling a slide along them. **2** informal energy.
• v. (**zipping**, **zipped**) **1** fasten with a zip. **2** informal move quickly.
□ **zip code** US a postcode.
■ **zippy** adj.

zircon n. a brown or semi-transparent mineral.

zirconium n. a metallic element.

zit n. informal a spot on the skin.

zither n. a stringed instrument played with the fingers.

zloty n. (pl. **zloty** or **zlotys**) the basic

unit of money in Poland.

zodiac n. an area of the sky in which the sun, moon, and planets appear to lie, divided by astrologers into twelve equal parts or signs.
■ **zodiacal** adj.

zombie n. **1** a person who seems only partly alive or conscious. **2** a corpse supposedly brought back to life by witchcraft.

zone n. an area with particular characteristics or a particular use.
▷ SYNONYMS: **area**, sector, section, belt, stretch, region, territory, district, quarter, neighbourhood.
● v. divide into zones.
■ **zonal** adj.

zoo n. a place where wild animals are kept for study, conservation, or display to the public.

zoology n. the study of animals.
■ **zoological** adj. **zoologist** n.

zoom v. **1** move very quickly. **2** (of a camera) change smoothly from a long shot to a close-up or vice versa.
▷ SYNONYMS: **hurry**, rush, dash, race, speed, sprint, career, shoot, hurtle, hare, fly; informal tear, belt, whizz; Brit. informal bomb.

zucchini /zuu-kee-ni/ n. (pl. **zucchini** or **zucchinis**) US a courgette.

Zulu n. **1** a member of a South African people. **2** the language of the Zulus.

zygote n. a cell resulting from the joining of two gametes.